GEORGE GORDON, LORD BYRON
Born, London 22 *January* 1788
Died, Missolonghi, Greece 19 *April* 1824

BYRON
POETICAL WORKS

EDITED BY FREDERICK PAGE
A NEW EDITION REVISED BY JOHN JUMP

Oxford New York
OXFORD UNIVERSITY PRESS

Oxford University Press, Walton Street, Oxford OX2 6DP

Oxford New York
Athens Auckland Bangkok Bogota Bombay
Buenos Aires Calcutta Cape Town Dar es Salaam
Delhi Florence Hong Kong Istanbul Karachi
Kuala Lumpur Madras Madrid Melbourne
Mexico City Nairobi Paris Singapore
Taipei Tokyo Toronto

and associated companies in
Berlin Ibadan

Oxford is a trade mark of Oxford University Press

British Library Cataloguing in Publication Data
Data available

Library of Congress Cataloging in Publication Data
Data available

ISBN 0-19-281068-5

13 15 17 19 20 18 16 14

Printed in Hong Kong

CONTENTS

v

CONTENTS

CONTENTS

vii

CONTENTS

CONTENTS

A NOTE ON THE OXFORD PAPERBACKS EDITION

In revising the text of the Oxford Standard Authors *Byron* for reprinting and publication in the present format, I have respected the previous editor's preferences with regard to such accidental features as spelling, punctuation, italicization, and the use of initial capitals. He italicizes and capitalizes, and occasionally punctuates, rather more lightly than does E. H. Coleridge in what is still the standard edition (*The Works of Lord Byron: Poetry*, 7 vols., London, 1898-1904); and he adopts a small number of more modern spellings, such as 'control' for 'controul'. Many of these minor differences merely reflect divergent editorial tastes on matters to which the poet himself was relatively indifferent.

My chief aim in the time available to me as reviser has been to remove substantive errors by reference to the edition of *Don Juan* by T. G. Steffan and W. W. Pratt (4 vols., Austin, Texas, and Edinburgh, 1957) and to the texts of the other poems as edited by E. H. Coleridge. In addition, I have corrected a few minor misprints and have taken the opportunity of adding to the present text of *Don Juan* the fragment of a seventeenth canto which was evidently not available to my predecessor. But it has not been practicable to insert in *Cain* the three-and-a-half lines following I.i.163 in which Lucifer foretells the Atonement:

> perhaps he'll make
> One day a Son unto himself—as he
> Gave you a father—and if he so doth,
> Mark me! that Son will be a sacrifice!

All the early editions omitted these, but E. H. Coleridge restored them to the text from the manuscript.

Coleridge also prints some shorter pieces—mostly juvenile verses and *jeux d'esprit*—which do not appear in the Oxford Standard Authors *Byron*, and he provides fuller versions of a few of the *jeux d'esprit* which do appear there. None of this material is of major importance, and it has not been added in the present edition.

University of Manchester, 1969 JOHN D. JUMP

HOURS OF IDLENESS

A SERIES OF POEMS ORIGINAL AND TRANSLATED

[First published in 1807]

' Virginibus puerisque canto.'—HORACE, lib. iii, Ode 1.
' Μήτ' ἄρ με μάλ' αἴνεε, μήτε τι νείκει.'—HOMER, *Iliad*, x. 249.
' He whistled as he went, for want of thought.'—DRYDEN.

PREFACE TO THE FIRST EDITION

IN submitting to the public eye the following collection, I have not only to combat the difficulties that writers of verse generally encounter, but may incur the charge of presumption for obtruding myself on the world, when, without doubt, I might be, at my age, more usefully employed.

These productions are the fruits of the lighter hours of a young man who has lately completed his nineteenth year. As they bear the internal evidence of a boyish mind, this is, perhaps, unnecessary information. Some few were written during the disadvantages of illness and depression of spirits: under the former influence, 'CHILDISH RECOLLECTIONS,' in particular, were composed. This consideration, though it cannot excite the voice of praise, may at least arrest the arm of censure. A considerable portion of these poems has been privately printed, at the request and for the perusal of my friends. I am sensible that the partial and frequently injudicious admiration of a social circle is not the criterion by which poetical genius is to be estimated, yet 'to do greatly' we must 'dare greatly'; and I have hazarded my reputation and feelings in publishing this volume. I have 'passed the Rubicon,' and must stand or fall by the 'cast of the die.' In the latter event I shall submit without a murmur; for, though not without solicitude for the fate of these effusions, my expectations are by no means sanguine. It is probable that I may have dared much and done little; for, in the words of Cowper, 'it is one thing to write what may please our friends, who, because they are such, are apt to be a little biassed in our favour, and another to write what may please everybody; because they who have no connexion, or even knowledge of the author, will be sure to find fault if they can.' To the truth of this, however, I do not wholly subscribe; on the contrary, I feel convinced that these trifles will not be treated with injustice. Their merit, if they possess any, will be liberally allowed; their numerous faults, on the other hand, cannot expect that favour which has been denied to others of maturer years, decided character, and far greater ability.

I have not aimed at exclusive originality, still less have I studied any particular model for imitation; some translations are given, of which many are paraphrastic. In the original pieces there may appear a casual coincidence with authors whose works I have been accustomed to read; but I have not been guilty of intentional plagiarism. To produce anything entirely new, in an age so fertile in rhyme, would be a Herculean task, as every subject has already been treated to its utmost extent. Poetry, however, is not my primary vocation; to divert the dull moments of indisposition, or the monotony of a vacant hour, urged me 'to this sin': little can be expected from so unpromising a muse. My wreath, scanty as it must be, is all I shall derive from these productions; and I shall never attempt to replace its fading leaves, or pluck a single additional sprig from groves where I am, at best, an intruder. Though accustomed, in my younger days, to rove a careless mountaineer on the Highlands of Scotland, I have not, of late years, had the benefit of such pure air, or so elevated a residence, as might enable me to enter the lists with genuine bards, who have enjoyed both these advantages. But they derive considerable fame, and a few not less profit, from their productions; while I shall expiate my rashness as an interloper, certainly without the latter, and in all probability with a very slight share of the former. I leave to others 'virûm volitare per ora.' I look to the few who will hear with patience, 'dulce est desipere in loco.' To the former worthies I resign, without repining, the hope of immortality, and content myself with the not very magnificent prospect of ranking amongst 'the mob of gentlemen who write';—my readers must determine whether I dare say 'with ease,' or the honour of a posthumous page in 'The Catalogue of Royal and Noble Authors,'—a work to which the Peerage is under infinite obligations, inasmuch as many names of considerable length, sound, and antiquity, are thereby rescued from the obscurity which unluckily overshadows several voluminous productions of their illustrious bearers.

With slight hopes, and some fears, I publish this first and last attempt. To the dictates of young ambition may be ascribed many actions more criminal and equally absurd. To a few of my own age the contents may afford amusement; I trust they will, at least, be found harmless. It is highly

1

improbable, from my situation and pursuits hereafter, that I should ever obtrude myself a second time on the public; nor even, in the very doubtful event of present indulgence, shall I be tempted to commit a future trespass of the same nature. The opinion of Dr. Johnson on the poems of a noble relation of mine*, 'That when a man of rank appeared in the character of an author, he deserved to have his merit handsomely allowed,' can have little weight with verbal, and still less with periodical, censors; but were it otherwise, I should be loth to avail myself of the privilege, and would rather incur the bitterest censure of anonymous criticism, than triumph in honours granted solely to a title.

* The Earl of Carlisle, whose works have long received the meed of public applause, to which, by their intrinsic worth, they were well entitled.

TO

THE RIGHT HONOURABLE FREDERICK, EARL OF CARLISLE,

KNIGHT OF THE GARTER, ETC., ETC.,

THE SECOND EDITION OF THESE POEMS IS INSCRIBED,

BY HIS OBLIGED WARD AND AFFECTIONATE KINSMAN,

THE AUTHOR.

ON THE DEATH OF A YOUNG LADY

Cousin to the Author, and very dear to him.

HUSH'D are the winds, and still the even-
 ing gloom,
 Not e'en a zephyr wanders through the
 grove,
Whilst I return, to view my Margaret's
 tomb,
 And scatter flowers on the dust I love.

Within this narrow cell reclines her clay,
 That clay, where once such animation
 beam'd; 6
The King of Terrors seized her as his
 prey,
 Not worth nor beauty have her life re-
 deem'd.

Oh! could that King of Terrors pity feel,
 Or Heaven reverse the dread decree of
 fate, 10
Not here the mourner would his grief re-
 veal,
 Not here the muse her virtues would
 relate.

But wherefore weep? Her matchless
 spirit soars
 Beyond where splendid shines the orb
 of day;
And weeping angels lead her to those
 bowers 15
 Where endless pleasures virtuous deeds
 repay.

And shall presumptuous mortals Heaven
 arraign,
 And, madly, godlike Providence ac-
 cuse?
Ah! no, far fly from me attempts so
 vain;—
 I'll ne'er submission to my God
 refuse. 20

Yet is remembrance of those virtues dear,
 Yet fresh the memory of that beauteous
 face;
Still they call forth my warm affection's
 tear,
 Still in my heart retain their wonted
 place.
 1802.

TO E—

LET Folly smile, to view the names
 Of thee and me in friendship twined;
Yet Virtue will have greater claims
 To love, than rank with vice combined.

And though unequal is thy fate, 5
 Since title deck'd my higher birth!
Yet envy not this gaudy state;
 Thine is the pride of modest worth.

Our souls at least congenial meet,
 Nor can thy lot my rank disgrace; 10
Our intercourse is not less sweet,
 Since worth of rank supplies the
 place.
 November 1802.

TO D—

IN thee I fondly hoped to clasp
 A friend whom death alone could sever;
Till envy, with malignant grasp,
 Detach'd thee from my breast for ever.

True, she has forced thee from my
 breast, 5
 Yet in my heart thou keep'st thy seat;
There, there thine image still must rest,
 Until that heart shall cease to beat.

And when the grave restores her dead,
 When life again to dust is given, 10
On thy dear breast I'll lay my head—
 Without thee where would be my
 heaven?
 February 1803.

2

EPITAPH ON A BELOVED FRIEND

'Αστὴρ πρὶν μὲν ἔλαμπες ἐνὶ ζωοῖσιν ἑῷος.
LAERT.

OH, Friend! for ever loved, for ever dear!
What fruitless tears have bathed thy
honour'd bier!
What sighs re-echo'd to thy parting breath,
Whilst thou wast struggling in the pangs
of death!
Could tears retard the tyrant in his
course; 5
Could sighs avert his dart's relentless
force;
Could youth and virtue claim a short
delay,
Or beauty charm the spectre from his
prey;
Thou still hadst lived to bless my aching
sight,
Thy comrade's honour and thy friend's
delight. 10
If yet thy gentle spirit hover nigh
The spot where now thy mouldering
ashes lie,
Here wilt thou read, recorded on my
heart,
A grief too deep to trust the sculptor's art.
No marble marks thy couch of lowly
sleep, 15
But living statues there are seen to weep;
Affliction's semblance bends not o'er thy
tomb,
Affliction's self deplores thy youthful
doom.
What though thy sire lament his failing
line,
A father's sorrows cannot equal mine!
Though none, like thee, his dying hour
will cheer, 21
Yet other offspring soothe his anguish
here:
But who with me shall hold thy former
place?
Thine image what new friendship can
efface?
Ah, none!—a father's tears will cease to
flow, 25
Time will assuage an infant brother's woe;
To all, save one, is consolation known,
While solitary friendship sighs alone.
1803.

A FRAGMENT

WHEN, to their airy hall, my fathers' voice
Shall call my spirit, joyful in their choice;
When, poised upon the gale, my form
shall ride,
Or, dark in mist, descend the mountain's
side;
Oh! may my shade behold no sculptured
urns, 5
To mark the spot where earth to earth
returns!

No lengthen'd scroll, no praise-encum-
ber'd stone;
My epitaph shall be my name alone:
If *that* with honour fail to crown my clay,
Oh! may no other fame my deeds repay!
That, only *that*, shall single out the spot;
By that remember'd, or with that forgot.
1803.

ON LEAVING NEWSTEAD ABBEY

'Why dost thou build the hall, son of the winged
days? Thou lookest from thy tower to-day: yet
a few years, and the blast of the desert comes, it
howls in thy empty court.'—OSSIAN.

THROUGH thy battlements, Newstead,
the hollow winds whistle;
Thou, the hall of my fathers, art gone
to decay;
In thy once smiling garden, the hemlock
and thistle
Have choked up the rose which late
bloom'd in the way.

Of the mail-cover'd Barons, who proudly
to battle 5
Led their vassals from Europe to
Palestine's plain,
The escutcheon and shield, which with
every blast rattle,
Are the only sad vestiges now that remain.

No more doth old Robert, with harp-
stringing numbers,
Raise a flame in the breast for the war-
laurell'd wreath; 10
Near Askalon's towers, John of Horistan
slumbers,
Unnerved is the hand of his minstrel by
death.

Paul and Hubert, too, sleep in the valley
of Cressy;
For the safety of Edward and England
they fell:
My fathers! the tears of your country re-
dress ye; 15
How you fought, how you died, still her
annals can tell.

On Marston, with Rupert, 'gainst traitors
contending,
Four brothers enrich'd with their blood
the bleak field;
For the rights of a monarch their country
defending,
Till death their attachment to royalty
seal'd. 20

Shades of heroes, farewell! your descen-
dant, departing
From the seat of his ancestors, bids you
adieu!

3

Abroad, or at home, your remembrance
 imparting
 New courage, he'll think upon glory
 and you.

Though a tear dim his eye at this sad
 separation, 25
 'Tis nature, not fear, that excites his
 regret;
Far distant he goes, with the same emula-
 tion,
 The fame of his fathers he ne'er can
 forget.

That fame, and that memory, still will he
 cherish;
 He vows that he ne'er will disgrace
 your renown: 30
Like you will he live, or like you will he
 perish;
 When decay'd, may he mingle his dust
 with your own!
 1803.

LINES

WRITTEN IN 'LETTERS OF AN ITALIAN NUN
AND AN ENGLISH GENTLEMAN: BY J. J.
ROUSSEAU: FOUNDED ON FACTS.'

'AWAY, away, your flattering arts
May now betray some simpler hearts;
And you will smile at their believing,
And they shall weep at your deceiving.'

ANSWER TO THE FOREGOING, ADDRESSED TO
 MISS ——.

Dear, simple girl, those flattering arts,
From which thou'dst guard frail female
 hearts,
Exist but in imagination,—
Mere phantoms of thine own creation;
For he who views that witching grace, 5
That perfect form, that lovely face,
With eyes admiring, oh! believe me,
He never wishes to deceive thee:
Once in thy polish'd mirror glance,
Thou'lt there descry that elegance 10
Which from our sex demands such praises,
But envy in the other raises:
Then he who tells thee of thy beauty,
Believe me, only does his duty:
Ah! fly not from the candid youth; 15
It is not flattery,—'tis truth.
 July 1804.

ADRIAN'S ADDRESS TO HIS
SOUL WHEN DYING

[ANIMULA! vagula, blandula,
Hospes comesque corporis,
Quæ nunc abibis in loca—
Pallidula, rigida, nudula,
Nec, ut soles, dabis jocos?]

AH! gentle, fleeting, wav'ring sprite,
Friend and associate of this clay!
 To what unknown region borne,

Wilt thou now wing thy distant flight?
No more with wonted humour gay, 5
 But pallid, cheerless, and forlorn.

TRANSLATION FROM
CATULLUS

AD LESBIAM

EQUAL to Jove that youth must be—
Greater than Jove he seems to me—
Who, free from Jealousy's alarms,
Securely views thy matchless charms.
That cheek, which ever dimpling glows, 5
That mouth, from whence such music
 flows,
To him, alike, are always known,
Reserved for him, and him alone.
Ah! Lesbia! though 'tis death to me,
I cannot choose but look on thee; 10
But, at the sight, my senses fly;
I needs must gaze, but, gazing, die;
Whilst trembling with a thousand fears,
Parch'd to the throat my tongue adheres,
My pulse beats quick, my breath heaves
 short, 15
My limbs deny their slight support,
Cold dews my pallid face o'erspread,
With deadly languor droops my head,
My ears with tingling echoes ring,
And life itself is on the wing; 20
My eyes refuse the cheering light,
Their orbs are veil'd in starless night:
Such pangs my nature sinks beneath,
And feels a temporary death.

TRANSLATION OF THE EPITAPH
ON VIRGIL AND TIBULLUS

BY DOMITIUS MARSUS

HE who sublime in epic numbers roll'd,
 And he who struck the softer lyre of
 love,
By Death's unequal hand alike controll'd,
 Fit comrades in Elysian regions move!

IMITATION OF TIBULLUS

'Sulpicia ad Cerinthum.'—Lib. iv.

CRUEL Cerinthus! does the fell disease
Which racks my breast your fickle bosom
 please?
Alas! I wish'd but to o'ercome the pain,
That I might live for love and you again;
But now I scarcely shall bewail my fate:
By death alone I can avoid your hate.

TRANSLATION FROM
CATULLUS

[Lugete, Veneres, Cupidinesque, &c.]

YE Cupids, droop each little head,
Nor let your wings with joy be spread;
My Lesbia's favourite bird is dead,
 Whom dearer than her eyes she loved:

4

For he was gentle, and so true, 5
Obedient to her call he flew,
No fear, no wild alarm he knew,
 But lightly o'er her bosom moved:

And softly fluttering here and there,
He never sought to cleave the air, 10
But chirrup'd oft, and, free from care,
 Tuned to her ear his grateful strain.
Now having pass'd the gloomy bourne
From whence he never can return,
His death and Lesbia's grief I mourn, 15
 Who sighs, alas! but sighs in vain.

Oh! curst be thou, devouring grave!
Whose jaws eternal victims crave,
From whom no earthly power can save,
 For thou hast ta'en the bird away: 20
From thee my Lesbia's eyes o'erflow,
Her swollen cheeks with weeping glow;
Thou art the cause of all her woe,
 Receptacle of life's decay.

IMITATED FROM CATULLUS

TO ELLEN

Oh! might I kiss those eyes of fire,
A million scarce would quench desire:
Still would I steep my lips in bliss,
And dwell an age on every kiss:
Nor then my soul should sated be; 5
Still would I kiss and cling to thee:
Nought should my kiss from thine dis-
 sever:
Still would we kiss and kiss for ever;
E'en though the numbers did exceed
The yellow harvest's countless seed. 10
To part would be a vain endeavour:
Could I desist?—ah! never—never!

TRANSLATION FROM HORACE

[Justum et tenacem propositi virum, &c.]

The man of firm and noble soul
No factious clamours can control;
No threat'ning tyrant's darkling brow
 Can swerve him from his just intent:
Gales the warring waves which plough,
 By Auster on the billows spent, 6
To curb the Adriatic main,
Would awe his fix'd, determined mind in
 vain.

Ay, and the red right arm of Jove,
Hurtling his lightnings from above, 10
With all his terrors there unfurl'd,
 He would unmoved, unawed, behold.
The flames of an expiring world,
 Again in crashing chaos roll'd,
In vast promiscuous ruin hurl'd, 15
Might light his glorious funeral pile:
Still dauntless 'midst the wreck of earth
 he'd smile.

FROM ANACREON

[Θέλω λέγειν 'Ατρείδας, κ. τ. λ.]

I wish to tune my quivering lyre
To deeds of fame and notes of fire;
To echo, from its rising swell,
How heroes fought and nations fell,
When Atreus' sons advanced to war,
Or Tyrian Cadmus roved afar; 6
But still, to martial strains unknown,
My lyre recurs to love alone.
Fired with the hope of future fame,
I seek some nobler hero's name; 10
The dying chords are strung anew,
To war, to war, my harp is due:
With glowing strings, the epic strain
To Jove's great son I raise again;
Alcides and his glorious deeds, 15
Beneath whose arm the Hydra bleeds.
All, all in vain; my wayward lyre
Wakes silver notes of soft desire.
Adieu, ye chiefs renown'd in arms!
Adieu the clang of war's alarms! 20
To other deeds my soul is strung,
And sweeter notes shall now be sung;
My harp shall all its powers reveal,
To tell the tale my heart must feel;
Love, love alone, my lyre shall claim,
In songs of bliss and sighs of flame. 26

FROM ANACREON

[Μεσονυκτίοις ποθ' ὥραις, κ. τ. λ.]

'Twas now the hour when Night had
 driven
Her car half round yon sable heaven;
Boötes, only, seem'd to roll
His arctic charge around the pole;
While mortals, lost in gentle sleep, 5
Forgot to smile, or ceased to weep:
At this lone hour the Paphian boy,
Descending from the realms of joy,
Quick to my gate directs his course,
And knocks with all his little force. 10
My visions fled, alarm'd I rose,—
'What stranger breaks my blest repose?'
'Alas!' replies the wily child,
In faltering accents sweetly mild,
'A hapless infant here I roam, 15
Far from my dear maternal home.
Oh! shield me from the wintry blast!
The nightly storm is pouring fast.
No prowling robber lingers here.
A wandering baby who can fear?' 20
I heard his seeming artless tale,
I heard his sighs upon the gale:
My breast was never pity's foe,
But felt for all the baby's woe.
I drew the bar, and by the light 25
Young Love, the infant, met my sight;
His bow across his shoulders flung,
And thence his fatal quiver hung
(Ah! little did I think the dart
Would rankle soon within my heart). 30

5

With care I tend my weary guest,
His little fingers chill my breast;
His glossy curls, his azure wing,
Which droop with nightly showers,
 I wring; 34
His shivering limbs the embers warm;
And now reviving from the storm,
Scarce had he felt his wonted glow,
Than swift he seized his slender bow:—
'I fain would know, my gentle host,'
He cried, 'if this its strength has lost; 40
I fear, relax'd with midnight dews,
The strings their former aid refuse.'
With poison tipt, his arrow flies,
Deep in my tortured heart it lies: 44
Then loud the joyous urchin laugh'd:—
'My bow can still impel the shaft:
'Tis firmly fix'd, thy sighs reveal it;
Say, courteous host, canst thou not feel
 it?'

FROM THE PROMETHEUS VINCTUS OF ÆSCHYLUS

[Μηδάμ' ὁ πάντα νέμων, κ. τ. λ.]

GREAT Jove, to whose almighty throne
 Both gods and mortals homage pay,
Ne'er may my soul thy power disown,
 Thy dread behests ne'er disobey.
Oft shall the sacred victim fall 5
In sea-girt Ocean's mossy hall;
My voice shall raise no impious strain
'Gainst him who rules the sky and azure
 main.

How different now thy joyless fate,
 Since first Hesione thy bride, 10
When placed aloft in godlike state,
 The blushing beauty by thy side,
Thou sat'st, while reverend Ocean
 smiled,
And mirthful strains the hours beguiled;
The Nymphs and Tritons danced
 around, 15
Nor yet thy doom was fix'd, nor Jove
 relentless frown'd.

HARROW, *Dec.* 1, 1804.

TO EMMA

SINCE now the hour is come at last,
 When you must quit your anxious
 lover;
Since now our dream of bliss is past,
 One pang, my girl, and all is over.

Alas! that pang will be severe, 5
 Which bids us part to meet no more;
Which tears me far from one so dear,
 Departing for a distant shore.

Well! we have pass'd some happy hours,
 And joy will mingle with our tears; 10
When thinking on these ancient towers,
 The shelter of our infant years;

Where from this Gothic casement's
 height,
 We view'd the lake, the park, the dell,
And still, though tears obstruct our sight,
 We lingering look a last farewell, 16

O'er fields through which we used to run,
 And spend the hours in childish play;
O'er shades where, when our race was
 done,
 Reposing on my breast you lay; 20

Whilst I, admiring, too remiss,
 Forgot to scare the hovering flies,
Yet envied every fly the kiss
 It dared to give your slumbering eyes:

See still the little painted bark, 25
 In which I row'd you o'er the lake;
See there, high waving o'er the park,
 The elm I clamber'd for your sake.

These times are past—our joys are gone,
 You leave me, leave this happy vale;
These scenes I must retrace alone: 31
 Without thee what will they avail?

Who can conceive, who has not proved,
 The anguish of a last embrace?
When, torn from all you fondly loved,
 You bid a long adieu to peace. 36

This is the deepest of our woes,
 For this these tears our cheeks bedew;
This is of love the final close,
 Oh, God! the fondest, last adieu! 40

TO M. S. G.

WHENE'ER I view those lips of thine,
 Their hue invites my fervent kiss;
Yet I forego that bliss divine,
 Alas! it were unhallow'd bliss.

Whene'er I dream of that pure breast, 5
 How could I dwell upon its snows!
Yet is the daring wish represt,
 For that—would banish its repose.

A glance from thy soul-searching eye
 Can raise with hope, depress with fear;
Yet I conceal my love,—and why? 11
 I would not force a painful tear.

I ne'er have told my love, yet thou
 Hast seen my ardent flame too well;
And shall I plead my passion now, 15
 To make thy bosom's heaven a hell?

No! for thou never canst be mine,
 United by the priest's decree:
By any ties but those divine,
 Mine, my beloved, thou ne'er shalt be.

Then let the secret fire consume, 21
 Let it consume, thou shalt not know:
With joy I court a certain doom,
 Rather than spread its guilty glow.

6

I will not ease my tortured heart 25
 By driving dove-eyed peace from thine;
Rather than such a sting impart,
 Each thought presumptuous I resign.

Yes! yield those lips, for which I'd brave
 More than I here shall dare to tell; 30
Thy innocence and mine to save,—
 I bid thee now a last farewell.

Yes! yield that breast, to seek despair,
 And hope no more thy soft embrace;
Which to obtain my soul would dare 35
 All, all reproach, but thy disgrace.

At least from guilt shalt thou be free,
 No matron shall thy shame reprove;
Though cureless pangs may prey on me,
 No martyr shalt thou be to love. 40

TO CAROLINE

THINK'ST thou I saw thy beauteous eyes,
 Suffused in tears, implore to stay;
And heard unmoved thy plenteous sighs,
 Which said far more than words can say?

Though keen the grief thy tears exprest, 5
 When love and hope lay both o'er-
 thrown,
Yet still, my girl, this bleeding breast
 Throbb'd with deep sorrow as thine
 own.

But when our cheeks with anguish glow'd,
 When thy sweet lips were join'd to mine,
The tears that from my eyelids flow'd 11
 Were lost in those which fell from thine.

Thou couldst not feel my burning cheek,
 Thy gushing tears had quench'd its
 flame;
And as thy tongue essay'd to speak, 15
 In signs alone it breathed my name.

And yet, my girl, we weep in vain,
 In vain our fate in sighs deplore;
Remembrance only can remain,—
 But that will make us weep the more.

Again, thou best beloved, adieu! 21
 Ah! if thou canst, o'ercome regret;
Nor let thy mind past joys review,—
 Our only hope is to forget!

TO CAROLINE

WHEN I hear you express an affection so
 warm,
Ne'er think, my beloved, that I do not
 believe;
For your lip would the soul of suspicion
 disarm,
 And your eye beams a ray which can
 never deceive.

Yet still this fond bosom regrets, while
 adoring, 5
 That love, like the leaf, must fall into
 the sere;
That age will come on, when remem-
 brance, deploring,
 Contemplates the scenes of her youth
 with a tear;

That the time must arrive, when, no
 longer retaining
 Their auburn, those locks must wave
 thin to the breeze, 10
When a few silver hairs of those tresses
 remaining,
 Prove nature a prey to decay and
 disease.

'Tis this, my beloved, which spreads
 gloom o'er my features,
 Though I ne'er shall presume to
 arraign the decree
Which God has proclaim'd as the fate of
 his creatures, 15
 In the death which one day will deprive
 you of me.

Mistake not, sweet sceptic, the cause of
 emotion,
 No doubt can the mind of your lover
 invade;
He worships each look with such faithful
 devotion,
 A smile can enchant, or a tear can dis-
 suade. 20

But as death, my beloved, soon or late
 shall o'ertake us,
 And our breasts, which alive with such
 sympathy glow,
Will sleep in the grave till the blast shall
 awake us,
 When calling the dead, in earth's
 bosom laid low,—

Oh! then let us drain, while we may,
 draughts of pleasure, 25
 Which from passion like ours must un-
 ceasingly flow;
Let us pass round the cup of love's bliss
 in full measure,
 And quaff the contents as our nectar
 below.
 1805.

TO CAROLINE

OH! when shall the grave hide for ever my
 sorrow?
 Oh! when shall my soul wing her flight
 from this clay?
The present is hell, and the coming to-
 morrow
 But brings, with new torture, the curse
 of to-day.

From my eye flows no tear, from my lips
 flow no curses, 5
I blast not the fiends who have hurl'd
 me from bliss;
For poor is the soul which bewailing re-
 hearses
 Its querulous grief, when in anguish
 like this.

Was my eye, 'stead of tears, with red fury
 flakes bright'ning,
 Would my lips breathe a flame which
 no stream could assuage, 10
On our foes should my glance launch in
 vengeance its lightning,
 With transport my tongue give a loose
 to its rage.

But now tears and curses, alike unavailing,
 Would add to the souls of our tyrants
 delight;
Could they view us our sad separation be-
 wailing, 15
 Their merciless hearts would rejoice at
 the sight.

Yet still, though we bend with a feign'd
 resignation,
 Life beams not for us with one ray that
 can cheer;
Love and hope upon earth bring no more
 consolation;
 In the grave is our hope, for in life is
 our fear. 20

Oh! when, my adored, in the tomb will
 they place me,
 Since, in life, love and friendship for
 ever are fled?
If again in the mansion of death I
 embrace thee,
 Perhaps they will leave unmolested the
 dead.

 1805.

STANZAS TO A LADY, WITH THE POEMS OF CAMOËNS

This votive pledge of fond esteem,
 Perhaps, dear girl! for me thou'lt prize;
It sings of Love's enchanting dream,
 A theme we never can despise.

Who blames it but the envious fool, 5
 The old and disappointed maid;
Or pupil of the prudish school,
 In single sorrow doom'd to fade?

Then read, dear girl! with feeling read,
 For thou wilt ne'er be one of those;
To thee in vain I shall not plead 11
 In pity for the poet's woes.

He was in sooth a genuine bard;
 His was no faint, fictitious flame.
Like his, may love be thy reward, 15
 But not thy hapless fate the same.

THE FIRST KISS OF LOVE

'Α βάρβιτος δὲ χορδαῖς
'Ερωτα μοῦνον ἠχεῖ.—ANACREON.

Away with your fictions of flimsy
 romance;
 Those tissues of falsehood which folly
 has wove!
Give me the mild beam of the soul-
 breathing glance,
 Or the rapture which dwells on the
 first kiss of love.

Ye rhymers, whose bosoms with phantasy
 glow, 5
 Whose pastoral passions are made for
 the grove;
From what blest inspiration your sonnets
 would flow,
 Could you ever have tasted the first kiss
 of love!

If Apollo should e'er his assistance re-
 fuse,
 Or the Nine be disposed from your
 service to rove, 10
Invoke them no more, bid adieu to the
 muse,
 And try the effect of the first kiss of
 love.

I hate you, ye cold compositions of art!
 Though prudes may condemn me, and
 bigots reprove,
I court the effusions that spring from the
 heart, 15
 Which throbs with delight to the first
 kiss of love.

Your shepherds, your flocks, those fan-
 tastical themes,
 Perhaps may amuse, yet they never can
 move:
Arcadia displays but a region of dreams:
 What are visions like these to the first
 kiss of love? 20

Oh! cease to affirm that man, since his
 birth,
 From Adam till now, has with wretched-
 ness strove,
Some portion of paradise still is on earth,
 And Eden revives in the first kiss of
 love.

When age chills the blood, when our plea-
 sures are past— 25
 For years fleet away with the wings of
 the dove—
The dearest remembrance will still be the
 last,
 Our sweetest memorial the first kiss of
 love.

ON A CHANGE OF MASTERS AT A GREAT PUBLIC SCHOOL

WHERE are those honours, Ida! once your
 own,
When Probus fill'd your magisterial
 throne?
As ancient Rome, fast falling to disgrace,
Hail'd a barbarian in her Cæsar's place,
So you, degenerate, share as hard a fate,
And seat Pomposus where your Probus
 sate. 6
Of narrow brain, yet of a narrower soul,
Pomposus holds you in his harsh control;
Pomposus, by no social virtue sway'd,
With florid jargon, and with vain parade;
With noisy nonsense, and new-fangled
 rules, 11
Such as were ne'er before enforced in
 schools.
Mistaking pedantry for learning's laws,
He governs, sanction'd but by self-applause;
With him the same dire fate attending
 Rome, 15
Ill-fated Ida! soon must stamp your doom;
Like her o'erthrown, for ever lost to fame,
No trace of science left you, but the name.

July 1805.

TO THE DUKE OF DORSET

DORSET! whose early steps with mine
 have stray'd,
Exploring every path of Ida's glade;
Whom still affection taught me to defend,
And made me less a tyrant than a friend,
Though the harsh custom of our youth-
 ful band 5
Bade *thee* obey, and gave *me* to command;
Thee, on whose head a few short years
 will shower
The gift of riches and the pride of power;
E'en now a name illustrious is thine own,
Renown'd in rank, nor far beneath the
 throne. 10
Yet, Dorset, let not this seduce thy soul
To shun fair science, or evade control,
Though passive tutors, fearful to dispraise
The titled child, whose future breath may
 raise, 14
View ducal errors with indulgent eyes,
And wink at faults they tremble to
 chastise.
 When youthful parasites, who bend the
 knee
To wealth, their golden idol, not to thee,—
And even in simple boyhood's opening dawn
Some slaves are found to flatter and to
 fawn,— 20
When these declare, 'that pomp alone
 should wait
On one by birth predestined to be great;
That books were only meant for drudging
 fools,

That gallant spirits scorn the common
 rules;'
Believe them not;—they point the path to
 shame, 25
And seek to blast the honours of thy
 name.
Turn to the few in Ida's early throng,
Whose souls disdain not to condemn the
 wrong;
Or if, amidst the comrades of thy youth,
None dare to raise the sterner voice of
 truth, 30
Ask thine own heart; 'twill bid thee, boy,
 forbear;
For *well* I know that virtue lingers there.
 Yes! I have mark'd thee many a passing
 day,
But now new scenes invite me far away;
Yes! I have mark'd within that generous
 mind 35
A soul, if well matured, to bless mankind.
Ah! though myself by nature haughty,
 wild,
Whom Indiscretion hail'd her favourite
 child;
Though every error stamps me for her
 own,
And dooms my fall, I fain would fall
 alone; 40
Though my proud heart no precept now
 can tame,
I love the virtues which I cannot claim.
 'Tis not enough, with other sons of
 power,
To gleam the lambent meteor of an hour;
To swell some peerage page in feeble
 pride, 45
With long-drawn names that grace no
 page beside;
Then share with titled crowds the com-
 mon lot—
In life just gazed at, in the grave forgot;
While nought divides thee from the vulgar
 dead,
Except the dull cold stone that hides thy
 head, 50
The mouldering 'scutcheon, or the
 herald's roll,
That well-emblazon'd but neglected scroll,
Where lords, unhonour'd, in the tomb
 may find
One spot, to leave a worthless name
 behind.
There sleep, unnoticed as the gloomy
 vaults 55
That veil their dust, their follies, and their
 faults,
A race, with old armorial lists o'erspread,
In records destined never to be read.
Fain would I view thee, with prophetic
 eyes,
Exalted more among the good and wise,
A glorious and a long career pursue, 61
As first in rank, the first in talent too:

9

Spurn every vice, each little meanness
 shun;
Not Fortune's minion, but her noblest son.
 Turn to the annals of a former day; 65
Bright are the deeds thine earlier sires dis-
 play.
One, though a courtier, lived a man of
 worth,
And call'd, proud boast! the British
 drama forth.
Another view, not less renown'd for wit;
Alike for courts, and camps, or senates
 fit; 70
Bold in the field, and favour'd by the
 Nine;
In every splendid part ordain'd to shine;
Far, far distinguish'd from the glittering
 throng,
The pride of princes, and the boast of song.
Such were thy fathers; thus preserve their
 name; 75
Not heir to titles only, but to fame.
The hour draws nigh, a few brief days will
 close,
To me, this little scene of joys and woes;
Each knell of Time now warns me to re-
 sign
Shades where Hope, Peace, and Friend-
 ship all were mine: 80
Hope, that could vary like the rainbow's
 hue,
And gild their pinions as the moments flew;
Peace, that reflection never frown'd away,
By dreams of ill to cloud some future day;
Friendship, whose truth let childhood only
 tell; 85
Alas! they love not long, who love so well.
To these adieu! nor let me linger o'er
Scenes hail'd, as exiles hail their native
 shore,
Receding slowly through the dark-blue
 deep,
Beheld by eyes that mourn, yet cannot
 weep. 90
 Dorset, farewell! I will not ask one part
Of sad remembrance in so young a heart;
The coming morrow from thy youthful
 mind
Will sweep my name, nor leave a trace be-
 hind.
And yet, perhaps, in some maturer year,
Since chance has thrown us in the self-
 same sphere, 96
Since the same senate, nay, the same
 debate,
May one day claim our suffrage for the
 state,
We hence may meet, and pass each other
 by,
With faint regard, or cold and distant
 eye. 100
For me, in future, neither friend nor foe,
A stranger to thyself, thy weal or woe,
With thee no more again I hope to trace

The recollection of our early race;
No more, as once, in social hours rejoice,
Or hear, unless in crowds, thy well-known
 voice: 106
Still, if the wishes of a heart untaught
To veil those feelings which perchance
 it ought,
If these—but let me cease the lengthen'd
 strain,—
Oh! if these wishes are not breathed in
 vain, 110
The guardian seraph who directs thy fate
Will leave thee glorious, as he found thee
 great.
 1805.

FRAGMENT

WRITTEN SHORTLY AFTER THE
MARRIAGE OF MISS CHAWORTH

Hills of Annesley, bleak and barren,
 Where my thoughtless childhood stray'd,
How the northern tempests, warring,
 Howl above thy tufted shade!

Now no more, the hours beguiling, 5
 Former favourite haunts I see;
Now no more my Mary smiling
 Makes ye seem a heaven to me.
 1805.

GRANTA

A MEDLEY

Ἀργυρέαις λόγχαισι μάχου καὶ πάντα κρατήσεις.

Oh! could Le Sage's demon's gift
 Be realized at my desire,
This night my trembling form he'd lift
 To place it on St. Mary's spire.

Then would, unroof'd, old Granta's halls
 Pedantic inmates full display; 6
Fellows who dream on lawn or stalls,
 The price of venal votes to pay.

Then would I view each rival wight,
 Petty and Palmerston survey; 10
Who canvass there with all their might,
 Against the next elective day.

Lo! candidates and voters lie
 All lull'd in sleep, a goodly number;
A race renown'd for piety, 15
 Whose conscience won't disturb their
 slumber.

Lord H——, indeed, may not demur:
 Fellows are sage, reflecting men:
They know preferment can occur
 But very seldom,—now and then. 20

They know the Chancellor has got
 Some pretty livings in disposal:
Each hopes that one may be his lot,
 And therefore smiles on his proposal.

Now from the soporific scene 25
 I'll turn mine eye, as night grows later,
To view, unheeded and unseen,
 The studious sons of Alma Mater.

There, in apartments small and damp,
 The candidate for college prizes 30
Sits poring by the midnight lamp;
 Goes late to bed, yet early rises.

He surely well deserves to gain them,
 With all the honours of his college,
Who, striving hardly to obtain them, 35
 Thus seeks unprofitable knowledge:

Who sacrifices hours of rest
 To scan precisely metres Attic;
Or agitates his anxious breast
 In solving problems mathematic: 40

Who reads false quantities in Seale,
 Or puzzles o'er the deep triangle;
Deprived of many a wholesome meal;
 In barbarous Latin doom'd to wrangle:

Renouncing every pleasing page 45
 From authors of historic use;
Preferring to the letter'd sage
 The square of the hypothenuse.

Still, harmless are these occupations,
 That hurt none but the hapless student,
Compared with other recreations, 51
 Which bring together the imprudent;

Whose daring revels shock the sight,
 When vice and infamy combine,
When drunkenness and dice invite, 55
 As every sense is steep'd in wine.

Not so the methodistic crew,
 Who plans of reformation lay:
In humble attitude they sue,
 And for the sins of others pray: 60

Forgetting that their pride of spirit,
 Their exultation in their trial,
Detracts most largely from the merit
 Of all their boasted self-denial. 64

'Tis morn:—from these I turn my sight.
 What scene is this which meets the eye?
A numerous crowd, array'd in white,
 Across the green in numbers fly.

Loud rings in air the chapel bell;
 'Tis hush'd:—what sounds are these I
 hear? 70
The organ's soft celestial swell
 Rolls deeply on the list'ning ear.

To this is join'd the sacred song,
 The royal minstrel's hallow'd strain;
Though he who hears the music long 75
 Will never wish to hear again.

Our choir would scarcely be excused,
 Even as a band of raw beginners;
All mercy now must be refused
 To such a set of croaking sinners. 80

If David, when his toils were ended,
 Had heard these blockheads sing
 before him,
To us his psalms had ne'er descended,—
 In furious mood he would have tore 'em.

The luckless Israelites, when taken 85
 By some inhuman tyrant's order,
Were ask'd to sing, by joy forsaken,
 On Babylonian river's border.

Oh! had they sung in notes like these,
 Inspired by stratagem or fear, 90
They might have set their hearts at ease,
 The devil a soul had stay'd to hear.

But if I scribble longer now,
 The deuce a soul will stay to read;
My pen is blunt, my ink is low; 95
 'Tis almost time to stop, indeed.

Therefore, farewell, old Granta's spires!
 No more, like Cleofas, I fly;
No more thy theme my muse inspires;
 The reader's tired, and so am I. 100
 1806.

ON A DISTANT VIEW OF THE VILLAGE AND SCHOOL OF HARROW ON THE HILL

Oh! mihi præteritos referat si Jupiter annos.—
 VIRGIL.

YE scenes of my childhood, whose loved
 recollection
 Embitters the present, compared with
 the past;
Where science first dawn'd on the powers
 of reflection,
 And friendships were form'd, too
 romantic to last;

Where fancy yet joys to retrace the resem-
 blance 5
 Of comrades, in friendship and mischief
 allied;
How welcome to me your ne'er fading re-
 membrance,
 Which rests in the bosom, though
 hope is denied!

Again I revisit the hills where we sported,
 The streams where we swam, and the
 fields where we fought; 10
The school where, loud warn'd by the
 bell, we resorted,
 To pore o'er the precepts by pedagogues
 taught.

11

Again I behold where for hours I have
 ponder'd,
 As reclining, at eve, on yon tombstone
 I lay;
Or round the steep brow of the church-
 yard I wander'd, 15
 To catch the last gleam of the sun's
 setting ray.

I once more view the room, with spec-
 tators surrounded,
 Where, as Zanga, I trod on Alonzo
 o'erthrown;
While, to swell my young pride, such ap-
 plauses resounded,
 I fancied that Mossop himself was out-
 shone: 20

Or, as Lear, I pour'd forth the deep impre-
 cation,
 By my daughters of kingdom and
 reason deprived;
Till, fired by loud plaudits and self-adula-
 tion,
 I regarded myself as a Garrick revived.

Ye dreams of my boyhood, how much I
 regret you! 25
 Unfaded your memory dwells in my
 breast;
Though sad and deserted, I ne'er can
 forget you:
 Your pleasures may still be in fancy
 possest.

To Ida full oft may remembrance restore
 me,
 While fate shall the shades of the future
 unroll! 30
Since darkness o'ershadows the prospect
 before me,
 More dear is the beam of the past to my
 soul!

But if, through the course of the years
 which await me,
 Some new scene of pleasure should
 open to view,
I will say, while with rapture the thought
 shall elate me, 35
 'Oh! such were the days which my
 infancy knew.'
 1806.

TO M—

OH! did those eyes, instead of fire,
 With bright but mild affection shine,
Though they might kindle less desire,
 Love, more than mortal, would be thine.

For thou art form'd so heavenly fair, 5
 Howe'er those orbs may wildly beam,
We must admire, but still despair;
 That fatal glance forbids esteem.

When Nature stamp'd thy beauteous birth,
 So much perfection in thee shone, 10
She fear'd that, too divine for earth,
 The skies might claim thee for their own.

Therefore, to guard her dearest work,
 Lest angels might dispute the prize,
She bade a secret lightning lurk 15
 Within those once celestial eyes.

These might the boldest sylph appal,
 When gleaming with meridian blaze;
Thy beauty must enrapture all;
 But who can dare thine ardent gaze? 20

'Tis said that Berenice's hair
 In stars adorns the vault of heaven;
But they would ne'er permit thee there,
 Thou wouldst so far outshine the seven.

For did those eyes as planets roll, 25
 Thy sister-lights would scarce appear:
E'en suns, which systems now control,
 Would twinkle dimly through their
 sphere.
 1806.

TO WOMAN

WOMAN! experience might have told me
That all must love thee who behold thee:
Surely experience might have taught
Thy firmest promises are nought;
But, placed in all thy charms before me,
All I forget, but to adore thee. 6
Oh memory! thou choicest blessing
When join'd with hope, when still possess-
 ing;
But how much cursed by every lover
When hope is fled and passion's over. 10
Woman, that fair and fond deceiver,
How prompt are striplings to believe her!
How throbs the pulse when first we view
The eye that rolls in glossy blue,
Or sparkles black, or mildly throws 15
A beam from under hazel brows!
How quick we credit every oath,
And hear her plight the willing troth!
Fondly we hope 'twill last for aye,
When, lo! she changes in a day. 20
This record will for ever stand,
'Woman, thy vows are traced in sand.'

TO M. S. G.

WHEN I dream that you love me, you'll
 surely forgive;
 Extend not your anger to sleep;
For in visions alone your affection can
 live,—
 I rise, and it leaves me to weep.

Then, Morpheus! envelope my faculties
 fast, 5
 Shed o'er me your languor benign;
Should the dream of to-night but re-
 semble the last,
 What rapture celestial is mine!

12

They tell us that slumber, the sister of
 death,
 Mortality's emblem is given; 10
To fate how I long to resign my frail breath
 If this be a foretaste of heaven!

Ah! frown not, sweet lady, unbend your
 soft brow,
 Nor deem me too happy in this; 14
If I sin in my dream, I atone for it now,
 Thus doom'd but to gaze upon bliss.

Though in visions, sweet lady, perhaps
 you may smile,
 Oh! think not my penance deficient!
When dreams of your presence my
 slumbers beguile,
 To awake will be torture sufficient. 20

TO MARY

ON RECEIVING HER PICTURE

THIS faint resemblance of thy charms,
 Though strong as mortal art could give,
My constant heart of fear disarms,
 Revives my hopes, and bids me live.

Here I can trace the locks of gold 5
 Which round thy snowy forehead wave,
The cheeks which sprung from beauty's
 mould,
 The lips which made me beauty's slave.

Here I can trace—ah, no! that eye,
 Whose azure floats in liquid fire, 10
Must all the painter's art defy,
 And bid him from the task retire.

Here I behold its beauteous hue;
 But where's the beam so sweetly stray-
 ing,
Which gave a lustre to its blue, 15
 Like Luna o'er the ocean playing?

Sweet copy! far more dear to me,
 Lifeless, unfeeling as thou art,
Than all the living forms could be,
 Save her who placed thee next my heart.

She placed it, sad, with needless fear, 21
 Lest time might shake my wavering
 soul,
Unconscious that her image there
 Held every sense in fast control.

Through hours, through years, through
 time, 'twill cheer; 25
 My hope, in gloomy moments, raise;
In life's last conflict 'twill appear,
 And meet my fond expiring gaze.

TO LESBIA

LESBIA! since far from you I've ranged,
 Our souls with fond affection glow not;
You say 'tis I, not you, have changed.
 I'd tell you why,—but yet I know not.

Your polish'd brow no cares have crost;
 And, Lesbia! we are not much older
Since, trembling, first my heart I lost,
 Or told my love, with hope grown
 bolder.

Sixteen was then our utmost age,
 Two years have lingering pass'd away,
 love! 10
And now new thoughts our minds engage,
 At least I feel disposed to stray, love!

'Tis I that am alone to blame,
 I, that am guilty of love's treason;
Since your sweet breast is still the same, 15
 Caprice must be my only reason.

I do not, love! suspect your truth,
 With jealous doubt my bosom heaves
 not;
Warm was the passion of my youth,
 One trace of dark deceit it leaves not.

No, no, my flame was not pretended; 21
 For, oh! I loved you most sincerely;
And—though our dream at last is
 ended—
 My bosom still esteems you dearly.

No more we meet in yonder bowers; 25
 Absence has made me prone to roving;
But older, firmer hearts than ours,
 Have found monotony in loving.

Your cheek's soft bloom is unimpair'd,
 New beauties still are daily bright'ning,
Your eye for conquest beams prepared,
 The forge of love's resistless lightning.

Arm'd thus, to make their bosoms bleed,
 Many will throng to sigh like me, love!
More constant they may prove, indeed;
 Fonder, alas! they ne'er can be, love!

LINES ADDRESSED TO A
YOUNG LADY

[As the author was discharging his pistols in
a garden, two ladies passing near the spot were
alarmed by the sound of a bullet hissing near
them; to one of whom the following stanzas were
addressed the next morning.]

DOUBTLESS, sweet girl! the hissing lead,
 Wafting destruction o'er thy charms,
And hurtling o'er thy lovely head,
 Has fill'd that breast with fond alarms.

Surely some envious demon's force, 5
 Vex'd to behold such beauty here,
Impell'd the bullet's viewless course,
 Diverted from its first career.

Yes! in that nearly fatal hour 9
 The ball obey'd some hell-born guide;
But Heaven, with interposing power,
 In pity turn'd the death aside.

Yet, as perchance one trembling tear
 Upon that thrilling bosom fell;
Which I, th' unconscious cause of fear, 15
 Extracted from its glistening cell:

Say, what dire penance can atone
 For such an outrage done to thee?
Arraign'd before thy beauty's throne,
 What punishment wilt thou decree?

Might I perform the judge's part, 21
 The sentence I should scarce deplore;
It only would restore a heart
 Which but belong'd to thee before.

The least atonement I can make 25
 Is to become no longer free;
Henceforth I breathe but for thy sake,
 Thou shalt be all in all to me.

But thou, perhaps, may'st now reject
 Such expiation of my guilt; 30
Come then, some other mode elect;
 Let it be death, or what thou wilt.

Choose then, relentless! and I swear
 Nought shall thy dread decree prevent;
Yet hold—one little word forbear! 35
 Let it be aught but banishment.

LOVE'S LAST ADIEU

'Aεὶ δ' ἀεί με φεύγει.—ANACREON.

THE roses of love glad the garden of life,
 Though nurtured 'mid weeds dropping pestilent dew,
Till time crops the leaves with unmerciful knife,
 Or prunes them for ever, in love's last adieu!

In vain with endearments we soothe the sad heart, 5
 In vain do we vow for an age to be true;
The chance of an hour may command us to part,
 Or death disunite us in love's last adieu!

Still Hope, breathing peace through the grief-swollen breast,
 Will whisper, 'Our meeting we yet may renew: 10
With this dream of deceit half our sorrow's represt,
 Nor taste we the poison of love's last adieu!

Oh! mark you yon pair: in the sunshine of youth
 Love twined round their childhood his flowers as they grew; 14
They flourish awhile in the season of truth,
 Till chill'd by the winter of love's last adieu!

Sweet lady! why thus doth a tear steal its way
 Down a cheek which outrivals thy bosom in hue?
Yet why do I ask?—to distraction a prey,
 Thy reason has perish'd with love's last adieu! 20

Oh! who is yon misanthrope, shunning mankind?
 From cities to caves of the forest he flew:
There, raving, he howls his complaint to the wind,
 The mountains reverberate love's last adieu!

Now hate rules a heart which in love's easy chains 25
 Once passion's tumultuous blandishments knew;
Despair now inflames the dark tide of his veins,
 He ponders in frenzy on love's last adieu!

How he envies the wretch with a soul wrapt in steel!
 His pleasures are scarce, yet his troubles are few, 30
Who laughs at the pang that he never can feel,
 And dreads not the anguish of love's last adieu!

Youth flies, life decays, even hope is o'ercast;
 No more with love's former devotion we sue:
He spreads his young wing, he retires with the blast; 35
 The shroud of affection is love's last adieu!

In this life of probation for rapture divine,
 Astrea declares that some penance is due;
From him who has worshipp'd at love's gentle shrine,
 The atonement is ample in love's last adieu! 40

Who kneels to the god, on his altar of light
 Must myrtle and cypress alternately strew:
His myrtle, an emblem of purest delight;
 His cypress, the garland of love's last adieu!

DAMÆTAS

IN law an infant, and in years a boy,
In mind a slave to every vicious joy;
From every sense of shame and virtue wean'd;
In lies an adept, in deceit a fiend;

Versed in hypocrisy, while yet a child; 5
Fickle as wind, of inclinations wild;
Woman his dupe, his heedless friend a
 tool;
Old in the world, though scarcely broke
 from school;
Damætas ran through all the maze of sin,
And found the goal when others just
 begin: 10
Even still conflicting passions shake his
 soul,
And bid him drain the dregs of pleasure's
 bowl;
But, pall'd with vice, he breaks his former
 chain,
And what was once his bliss appears his
 bane.

TO MARION

MARION! why that pensive brow?
What disgust to life hast thou?
Change that discontented air;
Frowns become not one so fair.
'Tis not love disturbs thy rest, 5
Love's a stranger to thy breast;
He in dimpling smiles appears,
Or mourns in sweetly timid tears,
Or bends the languid eyelid down,
But shuns the cold forbidding frown. 10
Then resume thy former fire,
Some will love, and all admire;
While that icy aspect chills us,
Nought but cool indifference thrills us.
Wouldst thou wandering hearts beguile,
Smile at least, or seem to smile. 16
Eyes like thine were never meant
To hide their orbs in dark restraint.
Spite of all thou fain wouldst say,
Still in truant beams they play. 20
Thy lips—but here my modest Muse
Her impulse chaste must needs refuse:
She blushes, curt'sies, frowns,—in short
 she
Dreads lest the subject should transport
 me;
And flying off in search of reason, 25
Brings prudence back in proper season.
All I shall therefore say (whate'er
I think, is neither here nor there)
Is, that such lips, of looks endearing,
Were form'd for better things than sneer-
 ing: 30
Of soothing compliments divested,
Advice at least 's disinterested;
Such is my artless song to thee,
From all the flow of flattery free;
Counsel like mine is as a brother's, 35
My heart is given to some others;
That is to say, unskill'd to cozen,
It shares itself among a dozen.

Marion, adieu! oh, pr'ythee slight not
This warning, though it may delight not;

And, lest my precepts be displeasing 41
To those who think remonstrance teasing:
At once I'll tell thee our opinion
Concerning woman's soft dominion:
Howe'er we gaze with admiration 45
On eyes of blue or lips carnation,
Howe'er the flowing locks attract us,
Howe'er those beauties may distract us,
Still fickle, we are prone to rove,
These cannot fix our souls to love; 50
It is not too severe a stricture
To say they form a pretty picture;
But wouldst thou see the secret chain
Which binds us in your humble train,
To hail you queens of all creation, 55
Know, in a word, 'tis ANIMATION.

TO A LADY

WHO PRESENTED TO THE AUTHOR A LOCK
OF HAIR BRAIDED WITH HIS OWN, AND
APPOINTED A NIGHT IN DECEMBER TO
MEET HIM IN THE GARDEN

THESE locks, which fondly thus entwine,
In firmer chains our hearts confine,
Than all th' unmeaning protestations,
Which swell with nonsense love orations.
Our love is fix'd, I think we've proved it;
Nor time, nor place, nor art have moved it;
Then wherefore should we sigh and whine,
With groundless jealousy repine,
With silly whims and fancies frantic,
Merely to make our love romantic? 10
Why should you weep like Lydia Lan-
 guish,
And fret with self-created anguish,
Or doom the lover you have chosen,
On winter nights to sigh half frozen;
In leafless shades to sue for pardon, 15
Only because the scene's a garden?
For gardens seem, by one consent,
Since Shakspeare set the precedent,
Since Juliet first declared her passion,
To form the place of assignation. 20
Oh! would some modern muse inspire,
And seat her by a sea-coal fire;
Or had the bard at Christmas written,
And laid the scene of love in Britain,
He surely, in commiseration, 25
Had changed the place of declaration.
In Italy I've no objection;
Warm nights are proper for reflection;
But here our climate is so rigid,
That love itself is rather frigid: 30
Think on our chilly situation,
And curb this rage for imitation;
Then let us meet, as oft we've done,
Beneath the influence of the sun;
Or, if at midnight I must meet you, 35
Within your mansion let me greet you:
There we can love for hours together,
Much better, in such snowy weather,
Than placed in all th' Arcadian groves
That ever witness'd rural loves; 40

15

Then, if my passion fail to please,
 Next night I'll be content to freeze;
No more I'll give a loose to laughter
 But curse my fate for ever after.

OSCAR OF ALVA

A TALE

How sweetly shines through azure skies,
 The lamp of heaven on Lora's shore;
Where Alva's hoary turrets rise,
 And hear the din of arms no more!

But often has yon rolling moon 5
 On Alva's casques of silver play'd;
And view'd, at midnight's silent noon,
 Her chiefs in gleaming mail array'd:

And on the crimson'd rocks beneath,
 Which scowl o'er ocean's sullen flow,
Pale in the scatter'd ranks of death, 11
 She saw the gasping warrior low;

While many an eye which ne'er again
 Could mark the rising orb of day,
Turn'd feebly from the gory plain, 15
 Beheld in death her fading ray.

Once to those eyes the lamp of Love,
 They blest her dear propitious light;
But now she glimmer'd from above,
 A sad, funereal torch of night. 20

Faded is Alva's noble race,
 And gray her towers are seen afar;
No more her heroes urge the chase,
 Or roll the crimson tide of war.

But who was last of Alva's clan? 25
 Why grows the moss on Alva's stone?
Her towers resound no steps of man,
 They echo to the gale alone.

And when that gale is fierce and high,
 A sound is heard in yonder hall; 30
It rises hoarsely through the sky,
 And vibrates o'er the mould'ring wall.

Yes, when the eddying tempest sighs,
 It shakes the shield of Oscar brave;
But there no more his banners rise, 35
 No more his plumes of sable wave.

Fair shone the sun on Oscar's birth,
 When Angus hail'd his eldest born;
The vassals round their chieftain's hearth
 Crowd to applaud the happy morn. 40

They feast upon the mountain deer,
 The pibroch raised its piercing note;
To gladden more their highland cheer,
 The strains in martial numbers float:

And they who heard the war-notes wild
 Hoped that one day the pibroch's strain
Should play before the hero's child
 While he should lead the tartan train.

Another year is quickly past,
 And Angus hails another son; 50
His natal day is like the last,
 Nor soon the jocund feast was done.

Taught by their sire to bend the bow,
 On Alva's dusky hills of wind, 54
The boys in childhood chased the roe,
 And left their hounds in speed behind.

But ere their years of youth are o'er,
 They mingle in the ranks of war;
They lightly wheel the bright claymore,
 And send the whistling arrow far. 60

Dark was the flow of Oscar's hair,
 Wildly it stream'd along the gale;
But Allan's locks were bright and fair,
 And pensive seem'd his cheek, and pale.

But Oscar own'd a hero's soul, 65
 His dark eye shone through beams of truth;
Allan had early learn'd control,
 And smooth his words had been from youth.

Both, both were brave; the Saxon spear
 Was shiver'd oft beneath their steel; 70
And Oscar's bosom scorn'd to fear,
 But Oscar's bosom knew to feel;

While Allan's soul belied his form,
 Unworthy with such charms to dwell:
Keen as the lightning of the storm, 75
 On foes his deadly vengeance fell.

From high Southannon's distant tower
 Arrived a young and noble dame;
With Kenneth's lands to form her dower,
 Glenalvon's blue-eyed daughter came;

And Oscar claim'd the beauteous bride,
 And Angus on his Oscar smiled: 82
It soothed the father's feudal pride
 Thus to obtain Glenalvon's child.

Hark to the pibroch's pleasing note! 85
 Hark to the swelling nuptial song!
In joyous strains the voices float,
 And still the choral peal prolong.

See how the heroes' blood-red plumes
 Assembled wave in Alva's hall; 90
Each youth his varied plaid assumes,
 Attending on their chieftain's call.

It is not war their aid demands,
 The pibroch plays the song of peace;
To Oscar's nuptials throng the bands, 95
 Nor yet the sounds of pleasure cease.

But where is Oscar? sure 'tis late:
 Is this a bridegroom's ardent flame?
While thronging guests and ladies wait,
 Nor Oscar nor his brother came. 100

At length young Allan join'd the bride;
 'Why comes not Oscar?' Angus said:
'Is he not here?' the youth replied;
 'With me he roved not o'er the glade:

'Perchance, forgetful of the day, 105
 'Tis his to chase the bounding roe;
Or ocean's waves prolong his stay;
 Yet Oscar's bark is seldom slow.'

'Oh, no!' the anguish'd sire rejoin'd,
 'Nor chase, nor wave, my boy delay;
Would he to Mora seem unkind? 111
 Would aught to her impede his way?

'Oh, search, ye chiefs! oh, search around!
 Allan, with these through Alva fly;
Till Oscar, till my son is found, 115
 Haste, haste, nor dare attempt reply.'

All is confusion—through the vale
 The name of Oscar hoarsely rings,
It rises on the murmuring gale,
 Till night expands her dusky wings;

It breaks the stillness of the night, 121
 But echoes through her shades in vain:
It sounds through morning's misty light,
 But Oscar comes not o'er the plain.

Three days, three sleepless nights, the
 Chief 125
For Oscar search'd each mountain cave:
Then hope is lost; in boundless grief,
 His locks in gray-torn ringlets wave.

'Oscar! my son!—thou God of heaven,
 Restore the prop of sinking age! 130
Or if that hope no more is given,
 Yield his assassin to my rage.

'Yes, on some desert rocky shore
 My Oscar's whiten'd bones must lie;
Then grant, thou God! I ask no more,
 With him his frantic sire may die! 136

'Yet he may live,—away, despair!
 Be calm, my soul! he yet may live;
T' arraign my fate, my voice forbear!
 O God! my impious prayer forgive.

'What, if he live for me no more, 141
 I sink forgotten in the dust,
The hope of Alva's age is o'er:
 Alas! can pangs like these be just?'

Thus did the hapless parent mourn, 145
 Till Time, which soothes severest woe,
Had bade serenity return
 And made the tear-drop cease to flow.

For still some latent hope survived 149
 That Oscar might once more appear;
His hope now droop'd and now revived,
 Till Time had told a tedious year.

Days roll'd along, the orb of light
 Again had run his destined race;
No Oscar bless'd his father's sight, 155
 And sorrow left a fainter trace.

For youthful Allan still remain'd,
 And now his father's only joy:
And Mora's heart was quickly gain'd,
 For beauty crown'd the fair-hair'd boy.

She thought that Oscar low was laid,
 And Allan's face was wondrous fair;
If Oscar lived, some other maid
 Had claim'd his faithless bosom's care.

And Angus said, if one year more 165
 In fruitless hope was pass'd away,
His fondest scruples should be o'er,
 And he would name their nuptial day.

Slow roll'd the moons, but blest at last
 Arrived the dearly destined morn: 170
The year of anxious trembling past,
 What smiles the lovers' cheeks adorn!

Hark to the pibroch's pleasing note!
 Hark to the swelling nuptial song!
In joyous strains the voices float, 175
 And still the choral peal prolong.

Again the clan, in festive crowd,
 Throng through the gate of Alva's hall;
The sounds of mirth re-echo loud,
 And all their former joy recall. 180

But who is he, whose darken'd brow
 Glooms in the midst of general mirth?
Before his eyes' far fiercer glow
 The blue flames curdle o'er the hearth.

Dark is the robe which wraps his form,
 And tall his plume of gory red; 186
His voice is like the rising storm,
 But light and trackless is his tread.

'Tis noon of night, the pledge goes round,
 The bridegroom's health is deeply
 quaff'd; 190
With shouts the vaulted roofs resound,
 And all combine to hail the draught.

Sudden the stranger-chief arose,
 And all the clamorous crowd are
 hush'd; 194
And Angus' cheek with wonder glows,
 And Mora's tender bosom blush'd.

'Old man!' he cried, 'this pledge is done;
 Thou saw'st 'twas duly drank by me;
It hail'd the nuptials of thy son:
 Now will I claim a pledge from thee.

'While all around is mirth and joy, 201
 To bless thy Allan's happy lot,
Say, hadst thou ne'er another boy?
 Say, why should Oscar be forgot?'

17

'Alas!' the hapless sire replied, 205
 The big tear starting as he spoke,
'When Oscar left my hall, or died,
 This aged heart was almost broke.

'Thrice has the earth revolved her course
 Since Oscar's form has bless'd my
 sight; 210
And Allan is my last resource,
 Since martial Oscar's death or flight.'

''Tis well,' replied the stranger stern,
 And fiercely flash'd his rolling eye;
'Thy Oscar's fate I fain would learn; 215
 Perhaps the hero did not die.

'Perchance, if those whom most he
 loved
 Would call, thy Oscar might return;
Perchance the chief has only roved;
 For him thy beltane yet may burn. 220

'Fill high the bowl the table round,
 We will not claim the pledge by stealth;
With wine let every cup be crown'd;
 Pledge me departed Oscar's health.'

'With all my soul,' old Angus said, 225
 And fill'd his goblet to the brim:
'Here's to my boy! alive or dead,
 I ne'er shall find a son like him.'

'Bravely, old man, this health has sped;
 But why does Allan trembling stand?
Come, drink remembrance of the dead,
 And raise thy cup with firmer hand.'

The crimson glow of Allan's face
 Was turn'd at once to ghastly hue;
The drops of death each other chase 235
 Adown in agonizing dew.

Thrice did he raise the goblet high,
 And thrice his lips refused to taste;
For thrice he caught the stranger's eye
 On his with deadly fury placed. 240

'And is it thus a brother hails
 A brother's fond remembrance here?
If thus affection's strength prevails,
 What might we not expect from fear?'

Roused by the sneer, he raised the bowl,
 'Would Oscar now could share our
 mirth!' 246
Internal fear appall'd his soul;
 He said, and dash'd the cup to earth.

''Tis he! I hear my murderer's voice!'
 Loud shrieks a darkly gleaming form.
'A murderer's voice!' the roof replies,
 And deeply swells the bursting storm.

The tapers wink, the chieftains shrink,
 The stranger's gone,—amidst the crew,
A form was seen in tartan green, 255
 And tall the shade terrific grew.

His waist was bound with a broad belt
 round,
 His plume of sable stream'd on high;
But his breast was bare, with the red
 wounds there, 259
 And fix'd was the glare of his glassy eye.

And thrice he smiled, with his eye so wild,
 On Angus bending low the knee;
And thrice he frown'd on a chief on the
 ground, 263
 Whom shivering crowds with horror see.

The bolts loud roll from pole to pole,
 The thunders through the welkin ring,
And the gleaming form, through the mist
 of the storm,
 Was borne on high by the whirlwind's
 wing.

Cold was the feast, the revel ceased.
 Who lies upon the stony floor? 270
Oblivion press'd old Angus' breast,
 At length his life-pulse throbs once
 more.

'Away, away! let the leech essay
 To pour the light on Allan's eyes:'
His sand is done,—his race is run,— 275
 Oh! never more shall Allan rise!

But Oscar's breast is cold as clay,
 His locks are lifted by the gale;
And Allan's barbed arrow lay 279
 With him in dark Glentanar's vale.

And whence the dreadful stranger came,
 Or who, no mortal wight can tell; 282
But no one doubts the form of flame,
 For Alva's sons knew Oscar well.

Ambition nerved young Allan's hand,
 Exulting demons wing'd his dart;
While Envy waved her burning brand,
 And pour'd her venom round his heart.

Swift is the shaft from Allan's bow;
 Whose streaming life-blood stains his
 side? 290
Dark Oscar's sable crest is low,
 The dart has drunk his vital tide.

And Mora's eye could Allan move,
 She bade his wounded pride rebel;
Alas! that eyes which beam'd with love
 Should urge the soul to deeds of hell.

Lo! seest thou not a lonely tomb 297
 Which rises o'er a warrior dead?
It glimmers through the twilight gloom;
 Oh! that is Allan's nuptial bed. 300

Far, distant far, the noble grave
 Which held his clan's great ashes stood;
And o'er his corse no banners wave,
 For they were stain'd with kindred blood.

18

What minstrel gray, what hoary bard,
 Shall Allan's deeds on harp-strings
 raise?
The song is glory's chief reward,
 But who can strike a murderer's praise?

Unstrung, untouch'd, the harp must
 stand, 309
 No minstrel dare the theme awake;
Guilt would benumb his palsied hand,
 His harp in shuddering chords would
 break.

No lyre of fame, no hallow'd verse,
 Shall sound his glories high in air:
A dying father's bitter curse, 315
 A brother's death-groan echoes there.

THE EPISODE OF NISUS AND
EURYALUS

A PARAPHRASE FROM THE ÆNEID, LIB. IX

NISUS, the guardian of the portal, stood,
Eager to gild his arms with hostile blood;
Well skill'd in fight the quivering lance
 to wield,
Or pour his arrows through th' embattled
 field:
From Ida torn, he left his sylvan cave, 5
And sought a foreign home, a distant
 grave.
To watch the movements of the Daunian
 host,
With him Euryalus sustains the post;
No lovelier mien adorn'd the ranks of
 Troy,
And beardless bloom yet graced the gal-
 lant boy; 10
Though few the seasons of his youthful
 life,
As yet a novice in the martial strife,
'Twas his, with beauty, valour's gifts to
 share—
A soul heroic, as his form was fair:
These burn with one pure flame of gene-
 rous love; 15
In peace, in war, united still they move;
Friendship and glory form their joint
 reward;
And now combined they hold their
 nightly guard.

'What god,' exclaim'd the first, 'instils this fire?
Or, in itself a god, what great desire? 20
My labouring soul, with anxious thought
 oppress'd,
Abhors this station of inglorious rest;
The love of fame with this can ill accord,
Be 't mine to seek for glory with my sword.
Seest thou yon camp, with torches twink-
 ling dim, 25
Where drunken slumbers wrap each lazy
 limb?

Where confidence and ease the watch dis-
 dain,
And drowsy Silence holds her sable reign?
Then hear my thought:—In deep and
 sullen grief
Our troops and leaders mourn their
 absent chief: 30
Now could the gifts and promised prize
 be thine
(The deed, the danger, and the fame be
 mine),
Were this decreed, beneath yon rising
 mound,
Methinks, an easy path perchance were
 found;
Which past, I speed my way to Pallas'
 walls, 35
And lead Æneas from Evander's halls.'

With equal ardour fired, and warlike joy,
His glowing friend address'd the Dardan
 boy:—
'These deeds, my Nisus, shalt thou dare
 alone?
Must all the fame, the peril, be thine
 own? 40
Am I by thee despised, and left afar,
As one unfit to share the toils of war?
Not thus his son the great Opheltes
 taught;
Not thus my sire in Argive combats
 fought;
Not thus, when Ilion fell by heavenly hate,
I track'd Æneas through the walks of
 fate: 46
Thou know'st my deeds, my breast devoid
 of fear,
And hostile life-drops dim my gory spear.
Here is a soul with hope immortal burns,
And life, ignoble life, for *glory* spurns.
Fame, fame is cheaply earn'd by fleeting
 breath: 51
The price of honour is the sleep of
 death.'

Then Nisus:—'Calm thy bosom's
 fond alarms:
Thy heart beats fiercely to the din of arms.
More dear thy worth and valour than my
 own, 55
I swear by him who fills Olympus' throne!
So may I triumph, as I speak the truth,
And clasp again the comrade of my youth!
But should I fall,—and he who dares
 advance
Through hostile legions must abide by
 chance,— 60
If some Rutulian arm, with adverse blow,
Should lay the friend, who ever loved thee,
 low,
Live thou, such beauties I would fain pre-
 serve,
Thy budding years a lengthen'd term
 deserve.

19

When humbled in the dust, let some one
 be, 65
Whose gentle eyes will shed one tear for
 me;
Whose manly arm may snatch me back
 by force,
Or wealth redeem from foes my captive corse;
Or, if my destiny these last deny,
If in the spoiler's power my ashes lie, 70
Thy pious care may raise a simple tomb,
To mark thy love, and signalize my doom.
Why should thy doting wretched mother
 weep
Her only boy, reclined in endless sleep?
Who, for thy sake, the tempest's fury
 dared, 75
Who, for thy sake, war's deadly peril shared;
Who braved what woman never braved
 before,
And left her native for the Latian shore.'

'In vain you damp the ardour of my
 soul,'
Replied Euryalus; 'it scorns control! 80
Hence, let us haste!'—their brother
 guards arose,
Roused by their call, nor court again
 repose;
The pair, buoy'd up on Hope's exulting
 wing,
Their stations leave, and speed to seek the
 king.

Now o'er the earth a solemn stillness ran,
And lull'd alike the cares of brute and
 man; 86
Save where the Dardan leaders nightly
 hold
Alternate converse, and their plans un-
 fold.
On one great point the council are agreed,
An instant message to their prince de-
 creed; 90
Each lean'd upon the lance he well could
 wield,
And poised with easy arm his ancient
 shield;
When Nisus and his friend their leave
 request
To offer something to their high behest.
With anxious tremors, yet unawed by
 fear, 95
The faithful pair before the throne appear:
Iulus greets them; at his kind command,
The elder first address'd the hoary band.

 'With patience' (thus Hyrtacides began)
'Attend, nor judge from youth our humble
 plan. 100
Where yonder beacons half expiring beam,
Our slumbering foes of future conquest
 dream,
Nor heed that we a secret path have
 traced,
Between the ocean and the portal placed.

Beneath the covert of the blackening
 smoke, 105
Whose shade securely our design will
 cloak!
If you, ye chiefs, and fortune will allow,
We'll bend our course to yonder moun-
 tain's brow,
Where Pallas' walls at distance meet the
 sight,
Seen o'er the glade, when not obscured by
 night: 110
Then shall Æneas in his pride return,
When hostile matrons raise their off-
 spring's urn;
And Latian spoils and purpled heaps of
 dead
Shall mark the havoc of our hero's tread.
Such is our purpose, not unknown the
 way; 115
Where yonder torrent's devious waters
 stray,
Oft have we seen, when hunting by the
 stream,
The distant spires above the valleys
 gleam.'

 Mature in years, for sober wisdom
 famed,
Moved by the speech, Alethes here ex-
 claim'd,— 120
'Ye parent gods! who rule the fate of
 Troy,
Still dwells the Dardan spirit in the boy;
When minds like these in striplings thus ye
 raise,
Yours is the godlike act, be yours the
 praise;
In gallant youth, my fainting hopes
 revive, 125
And Ilion's wonted glories still survive.'
Then in his warm embrace the boys he
 press'd,
And, quivering, strain'd them to his aged
 breast;
With tears the burning cheek of each be-
 dew'd,
And, sobbing, thus his first discourse re-
 new'd: 130
'What gift, my countrymen, what martial
 prize,
Can we bestow, which you may not de-
 spise?
Our deities the first best boon have
 given—
Internal virtues are the gift of Heaven.
What poor rewards can bless your deeds
 on earth, 135
Doubtless await such young, exalted
 worth.
Æneas and Ascanius shall combine
To yield applause far, far surpassing mine.

 Iulus then:—'By all the powers above
By those Penates who my country love

By hoary Vesta's sacred fane, I swear, 141
My hopes are all in you, ye generous pair!
Restore my father to my grateful sight,
And all my sorrows yield to one delight.
Nisus! two silver goblets are thine own,
Saved from Arisba's stately domes o'er-
 thrown! 146
My sire secured them on that fatal day,
Nor left such bowls an Argive robber's
 prey:
Two massy tripods, also, shall be thine;
Two talents polish'd from the glittering
 mine; 150
An ancient cup, which Tyrian Dido gave,
While yet our vessels press'd the Punic
 wave:
But when the hostile chiefs at length bow
 down,
When great Æneas wears Hesperia's
 crown,
The casque, the buckler, and the fiery steed
Which Turnus guides with more than
 mortal speed, 156
Are thine; no envious lot shall then be
 cast,
I pledge my word, irrevocably past:
Nay more, twelve slaves, and twice six
 captive dames,
To soothe thy softer hours with amorous
 flames, 160
And all the realms which now the Latins
 sway,
The labours of to-night shall well repay.
But thou, my generous youth, whose
 tender years
Are near my own, whose worth my heart
 reveres,
Henceforth affection, sweetly thus begun,
Shall join our bosoms and our souls in
 one; 166
Without thy aid, no glory shall be mine;
Without thy dear advice, no great design;
Alike through life esteem'd, thou godlike
 boy,
In war my bulwark, and in peace my joy.'

To him Euryalus:—'No day shall
 shame 171
The rising glories which from this I claim.
Fortune may favour, or the skies may
 frown,
But valour, spite of fate, obtains renown.
Yet, ere from hence our eager steps de-
 part, 175
One boon I beg, the nearest to my heart:
My mother, sprung from Priam's royal
 line,
Like thine ennobled, hardly less divine,
Nor Troy nor king Acestes' realms re-
 strain 179
Her feeble age from dangers of the main:
Alone she came, all selfish fears above,
A bright example of maternal love.
Unknown the secret enterprise I brave,

Lest grief should bend my parent to the
 grave;
From this alone no fond adieus I seek,
No fainting mother's lips have press'd my
 cheek; 186
By gloomy night and thy right hand I vow
Her parting tears would shake my pur-
 pose now:
Do thou, my prince, her failing age sustain,
In thee her much-loved child may live
 again; 190
Her dying hours with pious conduct bless,
Assist her wants, relieve her fond distress:
So dear a hope must all my soul inflame,
To rise in glory, or to fall in fame.'
Struck with a filial care so deeply felt, 195
In tears at once the Trojan warriors melt;
Faster than all, Iulus' eyes o'erflow!
Such love was his, and such had been his
 woe.
'All thou hast ask'd, receive,' the prince
 replied;
'Nor this alone, but many a gift beside.
To cheer thy mother's years shall be my
 aim, 201
Creusa's style but wanting to the dame.
Fortune an adverse wayward course may
 run,
But bless'd thy mother in so dear a son.
Now, by my life!—my sire's most sacred
 oath— 205
To thee I pledge my full, my firmest troth,
All the rewards which once to thee were
 vow'd,
If thou shouldst fall, on her shall be be-
 stow'd.'
Thus spoke the weeping prince, then forth
 to view
A gleaming falchion from the sheath he
 drew; 210
Lycaon's utmost skill had graced the steel,
For friends to envy and for foes to feel:
A tawny hide, the Moorish lion's spoil,
Slain 'midst the forest, in the hunter's toil,
Mnestheus to guard the elder youth be-
 stows, 215
And old Alethes' casque defends his
 brows.
Arm'd, thence they go, while all th' as-
 sembled train,
To aid their cause, implore the gods in vain.
More than a boy, in wisdom and in grace,
Iulus holds amidst the chiefs his place:
His prayer he sends; but what can prayers
 avail, 221
Lost in the murmurs of the sighing gale?

The trench is pass'd, and, favour'd by
 the night,
Through sleeping foes they wheel their
 wary flight.
When shall the sleep of many a foe be o'er?
Alas! some slumber who shall wake no
 more! 226

Chariots and bridles, mix'd with arms, are
 seen;
And flowing flasks, and scatter'd troops
 between:
Bacchus and Mars to rule the camp com-
 bine;
A mingled chaos this of war and wine.
'Now,' cries the first, 'for deeds of blood
 prepare, 231
With me the conquest and the labour share:
Here lies our path; lest any hand arise,
Watch thou, while many a dreaming
 chieftain dies:
I'll carve our passage through the heed-
 less foe, 235
And clear thy road with many a deadly
 blow.'
His whispering accents then the youth re-
 press'd,
And pierced proud Rhamnes through his
 panting breast:
Stretch'd at his ease, th' incautious king
 reposed;
Debauch, and not fatigue, his eyes had
 closed: 240
To Turnus dear, a prophet and a prince,
His omens more than augur's skill evince;
But he, who thus foretold the fate of all,
Could not avert his own untimely fall.
Next Remus' armour-bearer, hapless, fell,
And three unhappy slaves the carnage
 swell; 246
The charioteer along his courser's sides
Expires, the steel his sever'd neck divides;
And, last, his lord is number'd with the
 dead:
Bounding convulsive, flies the gasping
 head; 250
From the swoll'n veins the blackening tor-
 rents pour;
Stain'd is the couch and earth with clot-
 ting gore.
Young Lamyrus and Lamus next expire,
And gay Serranus, fill'd with youthful fire;
Half the long night in childish games was
 pass'd; 255
Lull'd by the potent grape, he slept at last:
Ah! happier far had he the morn survey'd,
And till Aurora's dawn his skill display'd.

In slaughter'd folds, the keepers lost in
 sleep,
His hungry fangs a lion thus may steep;
'Mid the sad flock, at dead of night he
 prowls, 261
With murder glutted, and in carnage
 rolls:
Insatiate still, through teeming herds he
 roams;
In seas of gore the lordly tyrant foams.

Nor less the other's deadly vengeance
 came, 265
But falls on feeble crowds without a name;

His wound unconscious Fadus scarce can
 feel,
Yet wakeful Rhæsus sees the threatening
 steel;
His coward breast behind a jar he hides,
And vainly in the weak defence confides;
Full in his heart, the falchion search'd his
 veins, 271
The reeking weapon bears alternate stains;
Through wine and blood, commingling as
 they flow,
One feeble spirit seeks the shades below.
Now where Messapus dwelt they bend
 their way, 275
Whose fires emit a faint and trembling
 ray;
There, unconfined, behold each grazing
 steed,
Unwatch'd, unheeded, on the herbage
 feed:
Brave Nisus here arrests his comrade's
 arm,
Too flush'd with carnage, and with
 conquest warm: 280
'Hence let us haste, the dangerous path
 is pass'd;
Full foes enough to-night have breathed
 their last:
Soon will the day those eastern clouds
 adorn;
Now let us speed, nor tempt the rising
 morn.'

What silver arms, with various art em-
 boss'd, 285
What bowls and mantles in confusion
 toss'd,
They leave regardless! yet one glittering
 prize
Attracts the younger hero's wandering
 eyes;
The gilded harness Rhamnes' coursers
 felt,
The gems which stud the monarch's
 golden belt: 290
This from the pallid corse was quickly
 torn,
Once by a line of former chieftains worn,
Th' exulting boy the studded girdle wears
Messapus' helm his head in triumph
 bears;
Then from the tents their cautious steps
 they bend, 295
To seek the vale where safer paths extend

Just at this hour, a band of Latian
 horse
To Turnus' camp pursue their destined
 course:
While the slow foot their tardy march de-
 lay,
The knights, impatient, spur along the
 way; 300

22

Three hundred mail-clad men, by Volscens
 led,
To Turnus with their master's promise
 sped:
Now they approach the trench, and view
 the walls,
When, on the left, a light reflection falls;
The plunder'd helmet, through the
 waning night, 305
Sheds forth a silver radiance, glancing
 bright.
Volscens with question loud the pair
 alarms:—
'Stand, stragglers! stand! why early thus
 in arms?
From whence! to whom?'—He meets
 with no reply;
Trusting the covert of the night, they fly:
The thicket's depth with hurried pace
 they tread, 311
While round the wood the hostile squad-
 ron spread.

With brakes entangled, scarce a path
 between,
Dreary and dark appears the sylvan
 scene:
Euryalus his heavy spoils impede, 315
The boughs and winding turns his steps
 mislead;
But Nisus scours along the forest's maze
To where Latinus' steeds in safety graze,
Then backward o'er the plain his eyes
 extend, 319
On every side they seek his absent friend.
'O God! my boy,' he cries, 'of me bereft,
In what impending perils art thou left!'
Listening he runs—above the waving trees,
Tumultuous voices swell the passing
 breeze;
The war-cry rises, thundering hoofs
 around 325
Wake the dark echoes of the trembling
 ground.
Again he turns, of footsteps hears the
 noise;
The sound elates, the sight his hope de-
 stroys:
The hapless boy a ruffian train surround,
While lengthening shades his weary way
 confound; 330
Him with loud shouts the furious knights
 pursue,
Struggling in vain, a captive to the crew.
What can his friend 'gainst thronging
 numbers dare?
Ah! must he rush his comrade's fate to
 share?
What force, what aid, what stratagem
 essay, 335
Back to redeem the Latian spoiler's prey?
His life a votive ransom nobly give,
Or die with him for whom he wish'd to
 live?

Poising with strength his lifted lance on
 high,
On Luna's orb he cast his frenzied eye:—
'Goddess serene, transcending every star!
Queen of the sky, whose beams are seen
 afar! 342
By night heaven owns thy sway, by day
 the grove,
When, as chaste Dian, here thou deign'st
 to rove;
If e'er myself, or sire, have sought to
 grace 345
Thine altars with the produce of the chase,
Speed, speed my dart to pierce yon vaunt-
 ing crowd,
To free my friend, and scatter far the
 proud.'
Thus having said, the hissing dart he
 flung;
Through parted shades the hurtling
 weapon sung; 350
The thirsty point in Sulmo's entrails lay,
Transfix'd his heart, and stretch'd him on
 the clay:
He sobs, he dies,—the troop in wild
 amaze,
Unconscious whence the death, with
 horror gaze.
While pale they stare, through Tagus'
 temples riven, 355
A second shaft with equal force is driven:
Fierce Volscens rolls around his lowering
 eyes;
Veil'd by the night, secure the Trojan
 lies.
Burning with wrath, he view'd his soldiers
 fall.
'Thou youth accurst, thy life shall pay for
 all!' 360
Quick from the sheath his flaming glaive
 he drew,
And, raging, on the boy defenceless flew.
Nisus no more the blackening shade con-
 ceals,
Forth, forth he starts, and all his love
 reveals;
Aghast, confused, his fears to madness
 rise, 365
And pour these accents, shrieking as he
 flies:
'Me, me,—your vengeance hurl on me
 alone;
Here sheathe the steel, my blood is all
 your own,
Ye starry spheres! thou conscious Heaven!
 attest!
He could not—durst not—lo! the guile
 confest! 370
All, all was mine,—his early fate suspend;
He only loved too well his hapless friend:
Spare, spare, ye chiefs! from him your
 rage remove;
His fault was friendship, all his crime was
 love.'

He pray'd in vain; the dark assassin's
 sword 375
Pierced the fair side, the snowy bosom
 gored;
Lowly to earth inclines his plume-clad
 crest,
And sanguine torrents mantle o'er his
 breast:
As some young rose, whose blossom
 scents the air,
Languid in death, expires beneath the
 share; 380
Or crimson poppy, sinking with the shower,
Declining gently, falls a fading flower;
Thus, sweetly drooping, bends his lovely
 head,
And lingering beauty hovers round the
 dead.

But fiery Nisus stems the battle's tide,
Revenge his leader, and despair his guide;
Volscens he seeks amidst the gathering
 host, 387
Volscens must soon appease his comrade's
 ghost;
Steel, flashing, pours on steel, foe crowds
 on foe;
Rage nerves his arm, fate gleams in every
 blow; 390
In vain beneath unnumber'd wounds he
 bleeds,
Nor wounds, nor death, distracted Nisus
 heeds;
In viewless circles wheel'd, his falchion flies,
Nor quits the hero's grasp till Volscens
 dies;
Deep in his throat its end the weapon found,
The tyrant's soul fled groaning through
 the wound. 396
Thus Nisus all his fond affection proved—
Dying, revenged the fate of him he loved;
Then on his bosom sought his wonted
 place,
And death was heavenly in his friend's
 embrace! 400

Celestial pair! if aught my verse can
 claim,
Wafted on Time's broad pinion, yours is
 fame!
Ages on ages shall your fate admire,
No future day shall see your names
 expire,
While stands the Capitol, immortal dome!
And vanquish'd millions hail their em-
 press, Rome! 406

TRANSLATION FROM THE
MEDEA OF EURIPIDES

['Ερωτες ύπερ μὲν ἄγαν, κ. τ. λ.]

WHEN fierce conflicting passions urge
 The breast where love is wont to glow,
What mind can stem the stormy surge
 Which rolls the tide of human woe?

The hope of praise, the dread of shame,
 Can rouse the tortured breast no more;
The wild desire, the guilty flame,
 Absorbs each wish it felt before.

But if affection gently thrills
 The soul by purer dreams possest, 10
The pleasing balm of mortal ills
 In love can soothe the aching breast:
If thus thou comest in disguise,
 Fair Venus! from thy native heaven,
What heart unfeeling would despise 15
 The sweetest boon the gods have given

But never from thy golden bow
 May I beneath the shaft expire!
Whose creeping venom, sure and slow,
 Awakes an all-consuming fire: 20
Ye racking doubts! ye jealous fears!
 With others wage internal war;
Repentance, source of future tears,
 From me be ever distant far!

May no distracting thoughts destroy 25
 The holy calm of sacred love!
May all the hours be wing'd with joy,
 Which hover faithful hearts above!
Fair Venus! on thy myrtle shrine
 May I with some fond lover sigh, 30
Whose heart may mingle pure with mine—
 With me to live, with me to die!

My native soil! beloved before,
 Now dearer as my peaceful home,
Ne'er may I quit thy rocky shore, 35
 A hapless banish'd wretch to roam!
This very day, this very hour,
 May I resign this fleeting breath!
Nor quit my silent humble bower; 39
 A doom to me far worse than death.

Have I not heard the exile's sigh,
 And seen the exile's silent tear,
Through distant climes condemn'd to fly,
 A pensive weary wanderer here?
Ah! hapless dame! no sire bewails, 45
 No friend thy wretched fate deplores,
No kindred voice with rapture hails
 Thy steps within a stranger's doors.

Perish the fiend whose iron heart,
 To fair affection's truth unknown, 50
Bids her he fondly loved depart,
 Unpitied, helpless, and alone;
Who ne'er unlocks with silver key
 The milder treasures of his soul,—
May such a friend be far from me, 55
 And ocean's storms between us roll!

THOUGHTS SUGGESTED BY
A COLLEGE EXAMINATION

HIGH in the midst, surrounded by h[is]
 peers,
MAGNUS his ample front sublime up[-]
 rears:

24

Placed on his chair of state, he seems a god,
While Sophs and Freshmen tremble at
 his nod.
As all around sit wrapt in speechless gloom,
His voice in thunder shakes the sounding
 dome; 6
Denouncing dire reproach to luckless
 fools,
Unskill'd to plod in mathematic rules.

Happy the youth in Euclid's axioms
 tried,
Though little versed in any art beside; 10
Who, scarcely skill'd an English line to
 pen,
Scans Attic metres with a critic's ken.
What, though he knows not how his
 fathers bled,
When civil discord piled the fields with
 dead,
When Edward bade his conquering bands
 advance, 15
Or Henry trampled on the crest of France,
Though marvelling at the name of
 Magna Charta,
Yet well he recollects the laws of Sparta;
Can tell what edicts sage Lycurgus made,
While Blackstone's on the shelf neglected
 laid; 20
Of Grecian dramas vaunts the deathless
 fame,
Of Avon's bard remembering scarce the
 name.

Such is the youth whose scientific pate
Class-honours, medals, fellowships, await;
Or even, perhaps, the declamation prize,
If to such glorious height he lifts his
 eyes. 26
But lo! no common orator can hope
The envied silver cup within his scope.
Not that our heads much eloquence
 require,
Th' ATHENIAN's glowing style, or Tully's
 fire. 30
A manner clear or warm is useless, since
We do not try by speaking to convince.
Be other orators of pleasing proud,—
We speak to please ourselves, not move
 the crowd:
Our gravity prefers the muttering tone,
A proper mixture of the squeak and
 groan: 36
No borrow'd grace of action must be seen;
The slightest motion would displease the
 Dean;
Whilst every staring graduate would
 prate
Against what he could never imitate. 40

The man who hopes t' obtain the pro-
 mised cup
Must in one posture stand, and ne'er look
 up;

Nor stop, but rattle over every word—
No matter what, so it can *not* be heard.
Thus let him hurry on, nor think to rest:
Who speaks the fastest 's sure to speak the
 best; 46
Who utters most within the shortest space
May safely hope to win the wordy race.

The sons of science these, who, thus
 repaid,
Linger in ease in Granta's sluggish shade;
Where on Cam's sedgy banks supine they
 lie, 51
Unknown, unhonour'd live, unwept-for
 die:
Dull as the pictures which adorn their
 halls,
They think all learning fix'd within their
 walls:
In manners rude, in foolish forms pre-
 cise, 55
All modern arts affecting to despise;
Yet prizing Bentley's, Brunck's, or Por-
 son's note,
More than the verse on which the critic
 wrote:
Vain as their honours, heavy as their
 ale,
Sad as their wit, and tedious as their
 tale; 60
To friendship dead, though not untaught
 to feel
When Self and Church demand a bigot
 zeal.
With eager haste they court the lord of
 power,
Whether 'tis Pitt or Petty rules the hour;
To him, with suppliant smiles, they bend
 the head, 65
While distant mitres to their eyes are
 spread.
But should a storm o'erwhelm him with
 disgrace,
They'd fly to seek the next who fill'd his
 place.
Such are the men who learning's treasures
 guard!
Such is their practice, such is their reward!
This much, at least, we may presume to
 say— 71
The premium can't exceed the price they
 pay.

 1806.

TO A BEAUTIFUL QUAKER

SWEET girl! though only once we met,
That meeting I shall ne'er forget;
And though we ne'er may meet again,
Remembrance will thy form retain.
I would not say, 'I love,' but still 5
My senses struggle with my will:
In vain, to drive thee from my breast,
My thoughts are more and more represt;

HOURS OF IDLENESS

In vain I check the rising sighs,
 Another to the last replies: 10
Perhaps this is not love, but yet
 Our meeting I can ne'er forget.

What though we never silence broke,
 Our eyes a sweeter language spoke;
The tongue in flattering falsehood deals,
 And tells a tale it never feels: 16
Deceit the guilty lips impart,
 And hush the mandates of the heart;
But soul's interpreters, the eyes,
 Spurn such restraint, and scorn disguise.
As thus our glances oft conversed, 21
 And all our bosoms felt rehearsed,
No spirit, from within, reproved us,
 Say rather, ''twas the spirit moved us.'
Though what they utter'd I repress, 25
 Yet I conceive thou'lt partly guess;
For as on thee my memory ponders,
 Perchance to me thine also wanders.
This for myself, at least, I'll say,
 Thy form appears through night, through
 day; 30
Awake, with it my fancy teems;
 In sleep, it smiles in fleeting dreams;
The vision charms the hours away,
 And bids me curse Aurora's ray
For breaking slumbers of delight 35
 Which make me wish for endless night.
Since, oh! whate'er my future fate,
 Shall joy or woe my steps await,
Tempted by love, by storms beset,
 Thine image I can ne'er forget. 40

Alas! again no more we meet,
 No more our former looks repeat;
Then let me breathe this parting prayer,
 The dictate of my bosom's care:
'May Heaven so guard my lovely quaker,
 That anguish never can o'ertake her; 46
That peace and virtue ne'er forsake her,
 But bliss be aye her heart's partaker!
Oh! may the happy mortal, fated
 To be, by dearest ties, related, 50
For her each hour new joys discover,
 And lose the husband in the lover!
May that fair bosom never know
 What 'tis to feel the restless woe
Which stings the soul, with vain regret, 55
 Of him who never can forget!'

THE CORNELIAN

No specious splendour of this stone
 Endears it to my memory ever;
With lustre only once it shone,
 And blushes modest as the giver. 4

Some, who can sneer at friendship's ties,
 Have, for my weakness, oft reproved
 me;
Yet still the simple gift I prize,
 For I am sure the giver loved me.

He offer'd it with downcast look,
 As fearful that I might refuse it; 10
I told him, when the gift I took,
 My only fear should be to lose it.

This pledge attentively I view'd,
 And sparkling as I held it near,
Methought one drop the stone bedew'd,
 And ever since I've loved a tear. 16

Still, to adorn his humble youth,
 Nor wealth nor birth their treasures
 yield;
But he who seeks the flowers of truth
 Must quit the garden for the field. 20

'Tis not the plant uprear'd in sloth,
 Which beauty shows, and sheds per-
 fume;
The flowers which yield the most of both
 In Nature's wild luxuriance bloom.

Had Fortune aided Nature's care, 25
 For once forgetting to be blind,
His would have been an ample share,
 If well proportion'd to his mind.

But had the goddess clearly seen, 29
 His form had fix'd her fickle breast;
Her countless hoards would his have been,
 And none remain'd to give the rest.

AN OCCASIONAL PROLOGUE

DELIVERED PREVIOUS TO THE PERFOR-
MANCE OF 'THE WHEEL OF FORTUNE' AT
A PRIVATE THEATRE

SINCE the refinement of this polish'd age
Has swept immoral raillery from the stage;
Since taste has now expunged licentious
 wit,
Which stamp'd disgrace on all an author
 writ;
Since now to please with purer scenes we
 seek, 5
Nor dare to call the blush from Beauty's
 cheek;
Oh! let the modest Muse some pity claim,
And meet indulgence, though she find not
 fame.
Still, not for her alone we wish respect,
Others appear more conscious of defect;
To-night no veteran Roscii you behold,
In all the arts of scenic action old; 12
No Cooke, no Kemble, can salute you
 here,
No Siddons draw the sympathetic tear;
To-night you throng to witness the *début*
Of embryo actors, to the Drama new:
Here, then, our almost unfledged wings we
 try, 17
Clip not our pinions ere the birds can fly:
Failing in this our first attempt to soar,
Drooping, alas! we fall to rise no more.

Not one poor trembler only fear betrays
Who hopes, yet almost dreads, to meet
 your praise,
But all our dramatis personæ wait
In fond suspense this crisis of their fate.
No venal views our progress can retard, 25
Your generous plaudits are our sole re-
 ward.
For these, each Hero all his power displays,
Each timid Heroine shrinks before your
 gaze.
Surely the last will some protection find;
None to the softer sex can prove unkind:
While Youth and Beauty form the female
 shield, 31
The sternest censor to the fair must yield.
Yet, should our feeble efforts nought avail,
Should, after all, our best endeavours fail,
Still let some mercy in your bosoms live,
And, if you can't applaud, at least forgive.

ON THE DEATH OF MR. FOX

THE FOLLOWING ILLIBERAL IMPROMPTU
APPEARED IN A MORNING PAPER

'OUR nation's foes lament on Fox's death,
But bless the hour when PITT resign'd his
 breath:
These feelings wide, let sense and truth
 unclue,
We give the palm where Justice points its
 due.'

TO WHICH THE AUTHOR OF THESE PIECES
SENT THE FOLLOWING REPLY

OH factious viper! whose envenom'd
 tooth
Would mangle still the dead, perverting
 truth;
What though our 'nation's foes' lament
 the fate,
With generous feeling, of the good and great,
Shall dastard tongues essay to blast the
 name 5
Of him whose meed exists in endless fame?
When PITT expired in plenitude of power,
Though ill success obscured his dying hour,
Pity her dewy wings before him spread,
For noble spirits 'war not with the dead:'
His friends, in tears, a last sad requiem
 gave, 11
As all his errors slumber'd in the grave;
He sunk, an Atlas bending 'neath the
 weight
Of cares o'erwhelming our conflicting
 state:
When, lo! a Hercules in Fox appear'd, 15
Who for a time the ruin'd fabric rear'd:
He, too, is fall'n, who Britain's loss
 supplied,
With him our fast reviving hopes have
 died;
Not one great people only raise his urn,
All Europe's far-extended regions mourn.

'These feelings wide, let sense and truth
 unclue, 21
To give the palm where Justice points its
 due;'
Yet let not canker'd Calumny assail,
Or round our statesman wind her gloomy
 veil.
Fox! o'er whose corse a mourning world
 must weep, 25
Whose dear remains in honour'd marble
 sleep;
For whom, at last, e'en hostile nations
 groan,
While friends and foes alike his talents own;
Fox shall in Britain's future annals shine,
Nor e'en to PITT the patriot's palm resign;
Which Envy, wearing Candour's sacred
 mask, 31
For PITT, and PITT alone, has dared to
 ask.

THE TEAR

'O lachrymarum fons, tenero sacros
Ducentium ortus ex animo; quater
 Felix! in imo qui scatentem
 Pectore te, pia Nympha, sensit.'—GRAY.

WHEN Friendship or Love our sympathies
 move,
When Truth in a glance should appear,
The lips may beguile with a dimple or
 smile,
But the test of affection 's a Tear.

Too oft is a smile but the hypocrite's wile,
To mask detestation or fear; 6
Give me the soft sigh, whilst the soul-
 telling eye
Is dimm'd for a time with a Tear.

Mild Charity's glow, to us mortals below,
Shows the soul from barbarity clear; 10
Compassion will melt where this virtue is
 felt,
And its dew is diffused in a Tear.

The man doom'd to sail with the blast of
 the gale,
Through billows Atlantic to steer,
As he bends o'er the wave which may
 soon be his grave, 15
The green sparkles bright with a Tear.

The soldier braves death for a fanciful
 wreath
In Glory's romantic career;
But he raises the foe when in battle laid
 low,
And bathes every wound with a Tear.

If with high-bounding pride he return to
 his bride, 21
Renouncing the gore-crimson'd spear,
All his toils are repaid when, embracing
 the maid,
From her eyelid he kisses the Tear.

27

Sweet scene of my youth! seat of Friend-
 ship and Truth, 25
Where love chased each fast-fleeting
 year,
Loth to leave thee, I mourn'd, for a last
 look I turn'd,
But thy spire was scarce seen through a
 Tear.

Though my vows I can pour to my Mary
 no more,
My Mary to Love once so dear, 30
In the shade of her bower I remember the
 hour
She rewarded those vows with a Tear.

By another possest, may she live ever blest!
 Her name still my heart must revere:
With a sigh I resign what I once thought
 was mine, 35
And forgive her deceit with a Tear.

Ye friends of my heart, ere from you I de-
 part,
This hope to my breast is most near:
If again we shall meet in this rural retreat,
May we meet, as we part, with a Tear.

When my soul wings her flight to the
 regions of night, 41
And my corse shall recline on its bier,
As ye pass by the tomb where my ashes
 consume,
Oh! moisten their dust with a Tear.

May no marble bestow the splendour of
 woe 45
Which the children of vanity rear;
No fiction of fame shall blazon my name.
All I ask—all I wish—is a Tear.
 October 26, 1806.

REPLY TO SOME VERSES OF J. M. B.
PIGOT, ESQ., ON THE CRUELTY
OF HIS MISTRESS

WHY, Pigot, complain of this damsel's dis-
 dain,
Why thus in despair do you fret?
For months you may try, yet, believe me,
 a sigh
Will never obtain a coquette.

Would you teach her to love? for a time
 seem to rove; 5
At first she may frown in a pet;
But leave her awhile, she shortly will
 smile,
And then you may kiss your coquette.

For such are the airs of these fanciful
 fairs,
They think all our homage a debt: 10
Yet a partial neglect soon takes an effect,
And humbles the proudest coquette.

Dissemble your pain, and lengthen your
 chain,
And seem her hauteur to regret;
If again you shall sigh, she no more will
 deny, 15
That yours is the rosy coquette.

If still, from false pride, your pangs she
 deride,
This whimsical virgin forget;
Some other admire, who will melt with
 your fire,
And laugh at the little coquette. 20

For me, I adore some twenty or more,
 And love them most dearly; but yet,
Though my heart they enthral, I'd aban-
 don them all,
Did they act like your blooming
 coquette.

No longer repine, adopt this design, 25
 And break through her slight-woven
 net;
Away with despair, no longer forbear
To fly from the captious coquette.

Then quit her, my friend! your bosom defend,
 Ere quite with her snares you're beset;
Lest your deep-wounded heart, when in-
 censed by the smart, 31
Should lead you to curse the coquette.
 October 27, 1806.

TO THE SIGHING STREPHON

YOUR pardon, my friend, if my rhymes
 did offend;
Your pardon, a thousand times o'er:
From friendship I strove your pangs to
 remove,
But, I swear, I will do so no more.

Since your beautiful maid your flame has
 repaid, 5
No more I your folly regret;
She's now most divine, and I bow at the
 shrine
Of this quickly reformed coquette.

Yet still, I must own, I should never have
 known
From your verses what else she de-
 served; 10
Your pain seem'd so great, I pitied your
 fate,
As your fair was so devilish reserved.

Since the balm-breathing kiss of this
 magical miss
Can such wonderful transports produce;
Since the 'world you forget, when your
 lips once have met,' 15
My counsel will get but abuse.

You say, 'When I rove, I know nothing
 of love;'
'Tis true, I am given to range;
If I rightly remember, I've loved a good
 number,
 Yet there's pleasure, at least, in a change.

I will not advance, by the rules of ro-
 mance, 21
 To humour a whimsical fair;
Though a smile may delight, yet a frown
 won't affright,
 Or drive me to dreadful despair.

While my blood is thus warm I ne'er shall
 reform, 25
 To mix in the Platonists' school;
Of this I am sure, was my passion so pure,
 Thy mistress would think me a fool.

And if I should shun every woman for one,
 Whose image must fill my whole
 breast— 30
Whom I must prefer, and sigh but for
 her—
 What an insult 'twould be to the rest!

Now, Strephon, good bye, I cannot deny
 Your passion appears most absurd;
Such love as you plead is pure love in-
 deed, 35
 For it only consists in the word.

TO ELIZA

ELIZA, what fools are the Mussulman sect,
 Who to woman deny the soul's future
 existence!
Could they see thee, Eliza, they'd own
 their defect,
 And this doctrine would meet with a
 general resistance.

Had their prophet possess'd half an atom
 of sense, 5
He ne'er would have woman from para-
 dise driven;
Instead of his houris, a flimsy pretence,
 With woman alone he had peopled his
 heaven.

Yet still, to increase your calamities more,
 Not content with depriving your bodies
 of spirit, 10
He allots one poor husband to share
 amongst four!—
 With souls you'd dispense; but this
 last, who could bear it?

His religion to please neither party is
 made;
 On husbands 'tis hard, to the wives
 most uncivil;
Still I can't contradict, what so oft has
 been said, 15
 'Though women are angels, yet wed-
 lock's the devil.'

LACHIN Y GAIR

AWAY, ye gay landscapes, ye gardens of
 roses!
In you let the minions of luxury rove;
Restore me the rocks, where the snow-
 flake reposes,
 Though still they are sacred to freedom
 and love:
Yet, Caledonia, beloved are thy moun-
 tains, 5
 Round their white summits though
 elements war;
Though cataracts foam 'stead of smooth-
 flowing fountains,
I sigh for the valley of dark Loch na Garr.

Ah! there my young footsteps in infancy
 wander'd;
 My cap was the bonnet, my cloak was
 the plaid; 10
On chieftains long perish'd my memory
 ponder'd,
 As daily I strode through the pine-
 cover'd glade;
I sought not my home till the day's dying
 glory
 Gave place to the rays of the bright
 polar star;
For fancy was cheer'd by traditional
 story, 15
 Disclosed by the natives of dark Loch
 na Garr.

'Shades of the dead! have I not heard
 your voices
 Rise on the night-rolling breath of the
 gale?'
Surely the soul of the hero rejoices,
 And rides on the wind, o'er his own
 Highland vale. 20
Round Loch na Garr while the stormy
 mist gathers,
 Winter presides in his cold icy car:
Clouds there encircle the forms of my
 fathers;
 They dwell in the tempests of dark
 Loch na Garr.

'Ill-starr'd, though brave, did no visions
 foreboding 25
 Tell you that fate had forsaken your
 cause?'
Ah! were you destined to die at Cullo-
 den,
 Victory crown'd not your fall with ap-
 plause:
Still were you happy in death's earthy
 slumber,
 You rest with your clan in the caves of
 Braemar; 30
The pibroch resounds, to the piper's loud
 number,
 Your deeds on the echoes of dark Loch
 na Garr.

HOURS OF IDLENESS

Years have roll'd on, Loch na Garr,
 since I left you,
Years must elapse ere I tread you again:
Nature of verdure and flow'rs has bereft
 you, 35
Yet still are you dearer than Albion's
 plain.
England! thy beauties are tame and
 domestic
 To one who has roved o'er the mountains
 afar:
Oh for the crags that are wild and
 majestic!
The steep frowning glories of dark
 Loch na Garr. 40

TO ROMANCE

PARENT of golden dreams, Romance!
 Auspicious queen of childish joys,
Who lead'st along, in airy dance,
 Thy votive train of girls and boys;
At length, in spells no longer bound, 5
 I break the fetters of my youth;
No more I tread thy mystic round,
 But leave thy realms for those of Truth.

And yet 'tis hard to quit the dreams
 Which haunt the unsuspicious soul, 10
Where every nymph a goddess seems,
 Whose eyes through rays immortal roll;
While Fancy holds her boundless reign,
 And all assume a varied hue;
When virgins seem no longer vain, 15
 And even woman's smiles are true.

And must we own thee but a name,
 And from thy hall of clouds descend?
Nor find a sylph in every dame,
 A Pylades in every friend? 20
But leave at once thy realms of air
 To mingling bands of fairy elves;
Confess that woman's false as fair,
 And friends have feeling for—them-
 selves!

With shame I own I've felt thy sway; 25
 Repentant, now thy reign is o'er,
No more thy precepts I obey,
 No more on fancied pinions soar.
Fond fool! to love a sparkling eye,
 And think that eye to truth was dear;
To trust a passing wanton's sigh, 31
 And melt beneath a wanton's tear!

Romance! disgusted with deceit,
 Far from thy motley court I fly,
Where Affectation holds her seat, 35
 And sickly Sensibility;
Whose silly tears can never flow
 For any pangs excepting thine;
Who turns aside from real woe,
 To steep in dew thy gaudy shrine. 40

Now join with sable Sympathy,
 With cypress crown'd, array'd in weeds,
Who heaves with thee her simple sigh,
 Whose breast for every bosom bleeds;
And call thy sylvan female choir, 45
 To mourn a swain for ever gone,
Who once could glow with equal fire,
 But bends not now before thy throne.

Ye genial nymphs, whose ready tears
 On all occasions swiftly flow; 50
Whose bosoms heave with fancied fears,
 With fancied flames and phrensy glow;
Say, will you mourn my absent name,
 Apostate from your gentle train?
An infant bard at least may claim 55
 From you a sympathetic strain.

Adieu, fond race! a long adieu!
 The hour of fate is hovering nigh,
E'en now the gulf appears in view,
 Where unlamented you must lie: 60
Oblivion's blackening lake is seen,
 Convulsed by gales you cannot weather;
Where you, and eke your gentle queen,
 Alas! must perish altogether.

ANSWER TO SOME ELEGANT VERSES SENT BY A FRIEND TO THE AUTHOR, COMPLAINING THAT ONE OF HIS DESCRIPTIONS WAS RATHER TOO WARMLY DRAWN

'But if any old lady, knight, priest, or physician,
Should condemn me for printing a second edi-
 tion;
If good Madam Squintum my work should abuse,
May I venture to give her a smack of my muse?'
 New Bath Guide.

CANDOUR compels me, BECHER! to com-
 mend
The verse which blends the censor with
 the friend.
Your strong yet just reproof extorts ap-
 plause
From me, the heedless and imprudent
 cause.
For this wild error which pervades my
 strain, 5
I sue for pardon,—must I sue in vain?
The wise sometimes from Wisdom's ways
 depart:
Can youth then hush the dictates of the
 heart?
Precepts of prudence curb, but can't
 control,
The fierce emotions of the flowing soul. 10
When Love's delirium haunts the glowing
 mind,
Limping Decorum lingers far behind:
Vainly the dotard mends her prudish pace,
Outstript and vanquish'd in the mental
 chase.

The young, the old, have worn the chains
 of love; 15
Let those they ne'er confined my lay re-
 prove:
Let those whose souls contemn the pleas-
 ing power
Their censures on the hapless victim
 shower.
Oh! how I hate the nerveless, frigid song,
The ceaseless echo of the rhyming throng,
Whose labour'd lines in chilling numbers
 flow, 21
To paint a pang the author ne'er can
 know!
The artless Helicon I boast is youth;—
My lyre, the heart; my muse, the simple
 truth.
Far be 't from me the 'virgin's mind' to
 'taint': 25
Seduction's dread is here no slight re-
 straint.
The maid whose virgin breast is void of
 guile,
Whose wishes dimple in a modest smile,
Whose downcast eye disdains the wanton
 leer,
Firm in her virtue's strength, yet not
 severe— 30
She whom a conscious grace shall thus
 refine
Will ne'er be 'tainted' by a strain of
 mine.
But for the nymph whose premature
 desires
Torment her bosom with unholy fires,
No net to snare her willing heart is
 spread; 35
She would have fallen, though she ne'er
 had read.
For me, I fain would please the chosen
 few,
Whose souls, to feeling and to nature true,
Will spare the childish verse, and not de-
 stroy
The light effusions of a heedless boy. 40
I seek not glory from the senseless crowd;
Of fancied laurels I shall ne'er be proud;
Their warmest plaudits I would scarcely
 prize,
Their sneers or censures I alike despise.
 November 26, 1806.

ELEGY ON NEWSTEAD ABBEY

'It is the voice of years that are gone! they roll
before me with all their deeds.'—OSSIAN.

NEWSTEAD! fast-falling, once-resplendent
 dome!
 Religion's shrine! repentant HENRY's
 pride!
Of warriors, monks, and dames the clois-
 ter'd tomb,
 Whose pensive shades around thy
 ruins glide,

Hail to thy pile! more honour'd in thy
 fall 5
 Than modern mansions in their pillar'd
 state:
Proudly majestic frowns thy vaulted hall,
 Scowling defiance on the blasts of fate.

No mail-clad serfs, obedient to their lord,
 In grim array the crimson cross de-
 mand; 10
Or gay assemble round the festive board
 Their chief's retainers, an immortal
 band:

Else might inspiring Fancy's magic eye
 Retrace their progress through the
 lapse of time,
Marking each ardent youth, ordain'd to
 die, 15
 A votive pilgrim in Judea's clime.

But not from thee, dark pile! departs the
 chief;
 His feudal realm in other regions lay:
In thee the wounded conscience courts
 relief,
 Retiring from the garish blaze of day.

Yes! in thy gloomy cells and shades pro-
 found 21
 The monk abjured a world he ne'er
 could view;
Or blood-stain'd guilt repenting solace
 found,
 Or innocence from stern oppression flew.

A monarch bade thee from that wild
 arise, 25
 Where Sherwood's outlaws once were
 wont to prowl;
And Superstition's crimes, of various
 dyes,
 Sought shelter in the priest's protecting
 cowl.

Where now the grass exhales a murky
 dew,
 The humid pall of life-extinguish'd
 clay, 30
In sainted fame the sacred fathers grew,
 Nor raised their pious voices but to pray.

Where now the bats their wavering wings
 extend
 Soon as the gloaming spreads her
 waning shade,
The choir did oft their mingling vespers
 blend, 35
 Or matin orisons to Mary paid.

Years roll on years; to ages, ages yield;
 Abbots to abbots, in a line, succeed;
Religion's charter their protecting shield,
 Till royal sacrilege their doom decreed.

One holy HENRY rear'd the Gothic walls,
 And bade the pious inmates rest in
 peace; 42
Another HENRY the kind gift recalls,
 And bids devotion's hallow'd echoes
 cease.

Vain is each threat or supplicating prayer;
 He drives them exiles from their blest
 abode, 46
To roam a dreary world in deep despair—
 No friend, no home, no refuge, but
 their God.

Hark how the hall, resounding to the
 strain,
 Shakes with the martial music's novel
 din! 50
The heralds of a warrior's haughty reign,
 High crested banners wave thy walls
 within.

Of changing sentinels the distant hum,
 The mirth of feasts, the clang of
 burnish'd arms,
The braying trumpet and the hoarser
 drum, 55
 Unite in concert with increased alarms.

* An abbey once, a regal fortress now,
 Encircled by insulting rebel powers,
War's dread machines o'erhang thy
 threat'ning brow,
 And dart destruction in sulphureous
 showers. 60

Ah vain defence! the hostile traitor's siege,
 Though oft repulsed, by guile o'er-
 comes the brave;
His thronging foes oppress the faithful
 liege,
 Rebellion's reeking standards o'er him
 wave. 64

Not unavenged the raging baron yields;
 The blood of traitors smears the purple
 plain;
Unconquer'd still, his falchion there he
 wields,
 And days of glory yet for him remain.

Still in that hour the warrior wish'd to
 strew
 Self-gather'd laurels on a self-sought
 grave; 70
But Charles' protecting genius hither flew,
 The monarch's friend, the monarch's
 hope, to save.

Trembling, she snatch'd him from th'
 unequal strife,
 In other fields the torrent to repel;
For nobler combats, here, reserved his life,
 To lead the band where godlike FALK-
 LAND fell. 76

From thee, poor pile! to lawless plunder
 given,
 While dying groans their painful re-
 quiem sound,
Far different incense now ascends to
 heaven,
 Such victims wallow on the gory
 ground. 80

There many a pale and ruthless robber's
 corse,
 Noisome and ghast, defiles thy sacred
 sod;
O'er mingling man, and horse commix'd
 with horse,
 Corruption's heap, the savage spoilers
 trod.

Graves, long with rank and sighing weeds
 o'erspread, 85
 Ransack'd, resign perforce their mortal
 mould:
From ruffian fangs escape not e'en the
 dead,
 Raked from repose in search of buried
 gold.

Hush'd is the harp, unstrung the warlike
 lyre,
 The minstrel's palsied hand reclines in
 death; 90
No more he strikes the quivering chords
 with fire,
 Or sings the glories of the martial
 wreath.

At length the sated murderers, gorged
 with prey,
 Retire: the clamour of the fight is o'er;
Silence again resumes her awful sway, 95
 And sable Horror guards the massy
 door.

Here Desolation holds her dreary court:
 What satellites declare her dismal reign!
Shrieking their dirge, ill-omen'd birds
 resort, 99
 To flit their vigils in the hoary fane.

Soon a new morn's restoring beams dispel
 The clouds of anarchy from Britain's
 skies;
The fierce usurper seeks his native hell,
 And Nature triumphs as the tyrant dies.

With storms she welcomes his expiring
 groans, 105
 Whirlwinds, responsive, greet his
 labouring breath;
Earth shudders as her caves receive his
 bones,
 Loathing the offering of so dark a
 death.

The legal ruler now resumes the helm,
 He guides through gentle seas the prow
 of state; 110
Hope cheers, with wonted smiles, the
 peaceful realm,
 And heals the bleeding wounds of
 wearied hate.

The gloomy tenants, Newstead! of thy
 cells,
 Howling, resign their violated nest;
Again the master on his tenure dwells,
 Enjoy'd, from absence, with enraptured
 zest. 116

Vassals, within thy hospitable pale,
 Loudly carousing, bless their lord's
 return;
Culture again adorns the gladdening vale,
 And matrons, once lamenting, cease to
 mourn. 120

A thousand songs on tuneful echo float,
 Unwonted foliage mantles o'er the
 trees;
And hark! the horns proclaim a mellow
 note,
 The hunters' cry hangs lengthening on
 the breeze.

Beneath their coursers' hoofs the valleys
 shake: 125
 What fears, what anxious hopes, attend
 the chase!
The dying stag seeks refuge in the lake;
 Exulting shouts announce the finish'd
 race.

Ah happy days! too happy to endure!
 Such simple sports our plain forefathers
 knew: 130
No splendid vices glitter'd to allure;
 Their joys were many, as their cares
 were few.

From these descending, sons to sires
 succeed;
 Time steals along, and Death uprears
 his dart;
Another chief impels the foaming steed,
 Another crowd pursue the panting
 hart. 136

Newstead! what saddening change of
 scene is thine!
 Thy yawning arch betokens slow decay;
The last and youngest of a noble line
 Now holds thy mouldering turrets in
 his sway. 140

Deserted now, he scans thy gray worn
 towers;
 Thy vaults, where dead of feudal ages
 sleep;

Thy cloisters, pervious to the wintry
 showers;
 These, these he views, and views them
 but to weep.

Yet are his tears no emblem of regret:
 Cherish'd affection only bids them
 flow. 146
Pride, hope, and love forbid him to forget,
 But warm his bosom with impassion'd
 glow.

Yet he prefers thee to the gilded domes
 Or gewgaw grottos of the vainly great,
Yet lingers 'mid thy damp and mossy
 tombs, 151
 Nor breathes a murmur 'gainst the will
 of fate.

Haply thy sun, emerging, yet may shine,
 Thee to irradiate with meridian ray;
Hours splendid as the past may still be
 thine, 155
 And bless thy future as thy former day.

CHILDISH RECOLLECTIONS

'I cannot but remember such things were,
And were most dear to me.'

WHEN slow Disease, with all her host of
 pains,
Chills the warm tide which flows along
 the veins;
When Health, affrighted, spreads her rosy
 wing,
And flies with every changing gale of
 spring; 4
Not to the aching frame alone confined,
Unyielding pangs assail the drooping
 mind:
What grisly forms, the spectre-train of woe,
Bid shuddering Nature shrink beneath
 the blow,
With Resignation wage relentless strife,
While Hope retires appall'd, and clings to
 life! 10
Yet less the pang when, through the
 tedious hour,
Remembrance sheds around her genial
 power,
Calls back the vanish'd days to rapture
 given,
When love was bliss, and Beauty form'd
 our heaven;
Or, dear to youth, portrays each childish
 scene, 15
Those fairy bowers, where all in turn have
 been.
As when through clouds that pour the
 summer storm
The orb of day unveils his distant form,
Gilds with faint beams the crystal dews of
 rain,
And dimly twinkles o'er the watery plain;

Thus, while the future dark and cheerless
gleams, 21
The sun of memory, glowing through my
dreams,
Though sunk the radiance of his former
blaze,
To scenes far distant points his paler rays;
Still rules my senses with unbounded sway,
The past confounding with the present day.

Oft does my heart indulge the rising
thought, 27
Which still recurs, unlook'd for and un-
sought;
My soul to Fancy's fond suggestion yields,
And roams romantic o'er her airy fields.
Scenes of my youth, developed, crowd to
view, 31
To which I long have bade a last adieu!
Seats of delight, inspiring youthful themes;
Friends lost to me for aye, except in
dreams; 34
Some who in marble prematurely sleep,
Whose forms I now remember but to weep;
Some who yet urge the same scholastic
course
Of early science, future fame the source;
Who, still contending in the studious race,
In quick rotation fill the senior place. 40
These with a thousand visions now unite,
To dazzle, though they please, my aching
sight.
IDA! blest spot, where Science holds her
reign,
How joyous once I join'd thy youthful
train!
Bright in idea gleams thy lofty spire, 45
Again I mingle with thy playful quire;
Our tricks of mischief, every childish game,
Unchanged by time or distance, seem the
same;
Through winding paths along the glade, I
trace
The social smile of every welcome face; 50
My wonted haunts, my scenes of joy and
woe,
Each early boyish friend, or youthful foe,
Our feuds dissolved, but not my friendship
past,
I bless the former, and forgive the last.
Hours of my youth! when, nurtured in my
breast, 55
To love a stranger, friendship made me
blest,—
Friendship, the dear peculiar bond of
youth,
When every artless bosom throbs with
truth;
Untaught by worldly wisdom how to feign,
And check each impulse with prudential
rein; 60
When all we feel, our honest souls dis-
close—
In love to friends, in open hate to foes;

No varnish'd tales the lips of youth repeat,
No dear-bought knowledge purchased by
deceit,
Hypocrisy, the gift of lengthen'd years, 65
Matured by age, the garb of prudence
wears.
When now the boy is ripen'd into man,
His careful sire chalks forth some wary
plan;
Instructs his son from candour's path to
shrink,
Smoothly to speak, and cautiously to think;
Still to assent, and never to deny— 71
A patron's praise can well reward the lie:
And who, when Fortune's warning voice is
heard,
Would lose his opening prospects for a word,
Although against that word his heart rebel,
And truth indignant all his bosom swell.

Away with themes like this! not mine
the task 77
From flattering friends to tear the hateful
mask;
Let keener bards delight in satire's sting;
My fancy soars not on Detraction's wing:
Once, and but once, she aim'd a deadly
blow, 81
To hurl defiance on a secret foe;
But when that foe, from feeling or from
shame,
The cause unknown, yet still to me the
same,
Warn'd by some friendly hint, perchance,
retired, 85
With this submission all her rage expired.
From dreaded pangs that feeble foe to save,
She hush'd her young resentment, and for-
gave;
Or, if my muse a pedant's portrait drew,
POMPOSUS' virtues are but known to few:
I never fear'd the young usurper's nod,
And he who wields must sometimes feel the
rod. 92
If since on Granta's failings, known to all
Who share the converse of a college hall,
She sometimes trifled in a lighter strain,
'Tis past, and thus she will not sin again;
Soon must her early song for ever cease,
And all may rail when I shall rest in peace.

Here first remember'd be the joyous
band,
Who hail'd me chief, obedient to com-
mand; 100
Who join'd with me in every boyish
sport—
Their first adviser, and their last resort;
Nor shrunk beneath the upstart pedant's
frown,
Or all the sable glories of his gown;
Who, thus transplanted from his father's
school— 105
Unfit to govern, ignorant of rule—

Succeeded him, whom all unite to praise,
The dear preceptor of my early days!
PROBUS, the pride of science, and the boast, 110
To IDA now, alas! for ever lost,
With him, for years, we search'd the classic page,
And fear'd the master, though we loved the sage:
Retired at last, his small yet peaceful seat
From learning's labour is the blest retreat.
POMPOSUS fills his magisterial chair; 115
POMPOSUS governs,—but, my muse, forbear:
Contempt, in silence, be the pedant's lot;
His name and precepts be alike forgot;
No more his mention shall my verse degrade,—
To him my tribute is already paid. 120

High through those elms, with hoary branches crown'd,
Fair IDA's bower adorns the landscape round;
There Science, from her favour'd seat, surveys
The vale where rural Nature claims her praise;
To her awhile resigns her youthful train,
Who move in joy, and dance along the plain; 126
In scatter'd groups each favour'd haunt pursue,
Repeat old pastimes, and discover new;
Flush'd with his rays, beneath the noon-tide sun,
In rival bands, between the wickets run,
Drive o'er the sward the ball with active force, 131
Or chase with nimble feet its rapid course.
But these with slower steps direct their way,
Where Brent's cool waves in limpid currents stray;
While yonder few search out some green retreat 135
And arbours shade them from the summer heat:
Others, again, a pert and lively crew,
Some rough and thoughtless stranger placed in view,
With frolic quaint their antic jests expose,
And tease the grumbling rustic as he goes;
Nor rest with this, but many a passing fray
Tradition treasures for a future day: 142
''Twas here the gather'd swains for vengeance fought,
And here we earn'd the conquest dearly bought;
Here have we fled before superior might,
And here renew'd the wild tumultuous fight.' 146
While thus our souls with early passions swell,
In lingering tones resounds the distant bell,

Th' allotted hour of daily sport is o'er,
And Learning beckons from her temple's door. 150
No splendid tablets grace her simple hall,
But ruder records fill the dusky wall;
There, deeply carved, behold! each tyro's name
Secures its owner's academic fame;
Here mingling view the names of sire and son— 155
The one long graved, the other just begun:
These shall survive alike when son and sire
Beneath one common stroke of fate expire;
Perhaps their last memorial these alone,
Denied in death a monumental stone, 160
Whilst o'er the gale in mournful cadence wave
The sighing weeds that hide their nameless grave.
And here my name, and many an early friend's,
Along the wall in lengthen'd line extends.
Though still our deeds amuse the youthful race, 165
Who tread our steps, and fill our former place,
Who young obey'd their lords in silent awe,
Whose nod commanded, and whose voice was law;
And now, in turn, possess the reins of power,
To rule, the little tyrants of an hour; 170
Though sometimes, with the tales of ancient day,
They pass the dreary winter's eve away—
'And thus our former rulers stemm'd the tide,
And thus they dealt the combat side by side;
Just in this place the mouldering walls they scaled, 175
Nor bolts nor bars against their strength avail'd;
Here PROBUS came, the rising fray to quell,
And here he falter'd forth his last farewell;
And here one night abroad they dared to roam,
While bold POMPOSUS bravely stay'd at home;' 180
While thus they speak, the hour must soon arrive,
When names of these, like ours, alone survive:
Yet a few years, one general wreck will whelm
The faint remembrance of our fairy realm.

Dear honest race! though now we meet no more, 185
One last long look on what we were before—

35

Our first kind greetings, and our last
 adieu—
Drew tears from eyes unused to weep with
 you.
Through splendid circles, fashion's gaudy
 world,
Where folly's glaring standard waves un-
 furl'd, 190
I plunged to drown in noise my fond regret,
And all I sought or hoped was to forget.
Vain wish! if chance some well-remember'd
 face,
Some old companion of my early race,
Advanced to claim his friend with honest
 joy, 195
My eyes, my heart, proclaim'd me still a
 boy;
The glittering scene, the fluttering groups
 around,
Were quite forgotten when my friend was
 found;
The smiles of beauty—(for, alas! I've
 known
What 'tis to bend before Love's mighty
 throne)— 200
The smiles of beauty, though those smiles
 were dear,
Could hardly charm me, when that friend
 was near;
My thoughts bewilder'd in the fond sur-
 prise,
The woods of IDA danced before my eyes;
I saw the sprightly wand'rers pour along,
I saw and join'd again the joyous throng;
Panting, again I traced her lofty grove,
And friendship's feelings triumph'd over
 love. 208

 Yet why should I alone with such de-
 light
Retrace the circuit of my former flight?
Is there no cause beyond the common claim
Endear'd to all in childhood's very name?
Ah! sure some stronger impulse vibrates
 here,
Which whispers friendship will be doubly
 dear
To one who thus for kindred hearts must
 roam, 215
And seek abroad the love denied at home.
Those hearts, dear IDA, have I found in
 thee—
A home, a world, a paradise to me.
Stern Death forbade my orphan youth to
 share 219
The tender guidance of a father's care.
Can rank, or e'en a guardian's name supply
The love which glistens in a father's eye?
For this can wealth or title's sound atone,
Made, by a parent's early loss, my own?
What brother springs a brother's love to
 seek? 225
What sister's gentle kiss has prest my
 cheek?

For me how dull the vacant moments rise,
To no fond bosom link'd by kindred ties!
Oft in the progress of some fleeting dream
Fraternal smiles collected round me seem;
While still the visions to my heart are
 prest, 231
The voice of love will murmur in my rest:
I hear—I wake—and in the sound rejoice;
I hear again,—but, ah! no brother's voice.
A hermit, 'midst of crowds, I fain must
 stray 235
Alone, though thousand pilgrims fill the
 way;
While these a thousand kindred wreaths
 entwine,
I cannot call one single blossom mine:
What then remains? in solitude to groan,
To mix in friendship, or to sigh alone.
Thus must I cling to some endearing hand,
And none more dear than IDA's social
 band.

 Alonzo! best and dearest of my friends,
Thy name ennobles him who thus com-
 mends;
From this fond tribute thou canst gain no
 praise; 245
The praise is his who now that tribute pays.
Oh! in the promise of thy early youth,
If hope anticipate the words of truth,
Some loftier bard shall sing thy glorious
 name, 249
To build his own upon thy deathless fame.
Friend of my heart, and foremost of the list
Of those with whom I lived supremely
 blest,
Oft have we drain'd the font of ancient
 lore;
Though drinking deeply, thirsting still the
 more.
Yet, when confinement's lingering hour
 was done, 255
Our sports, our studies, and our souls were
 one;
Together we impell'd the flying ball;
Together waited in our tutor's hall;
Together join'd in cricket's manly toil,
Or shared the produce of the river's spoil;
Or, plunging from the green declining
 shore, 261
Our pliant limbs the buoyant billows bore;
In every element, unchanged, the same,
All, all that brothers should be, but the
 name.

 Nor yet are you forgot, my jocund boy!
DAVUS, the harbinger of childish joy;
For ever foremost in the ranks of fun,
The laughing herald of the harmless pun;
Yet with a breast of such materials made—
Anxious to please, of pleasing half afraid;
Candid and liberal, with a heart of steel
In danger's path, though not untaught to
 feel.

Still I remember, in the factious strife,
The rustic's musket aim'd against my life:
High pois'd in air the massy weapon
 hung, 275
A cry of horror burst from every tongue;
Whilst I, in combat with another foe,
Fought on, unconscious of th' impending
 blow;
Your arm, brave boy, arrested his career—
Forward you sprung, insensible to fear;
Disarm'd and baffled by your conquering
 hand, 281
The grovelling savage roll'd upon the sand:
An act like this, can simple thanks repay?
Or all the labours of a grateful lay? 284
Oh no! whene'er my breast forgets the deed,
That instant, DAVUS, it deserves to bleed.

 LYCUS! on me thy claims are justly great:
Thy milder virtues could my muse relate,
To thee alone, unrivall'd, would belong
The feeble efforts of my lengthen'd song.
Well canst thou boast, to lead in senates
 fit, 291
A Spartan firmness with Athenian wit:
Though yet in embryo these perfections
 shine,
LYCUS! thy father's fame will soon be
 thine.
Where learning nurtures the superior
 mind, 295
What may we hope from genius thus re-
 fined!
When time at length matures thy growing
 years,
How wilt thou tower above thy fellow
 peers!
Prudence and sense, a spirit bold and free,
With honour's soul, united beam in thee.

 Shall fair EURYALUS pass by unsung?
From ancient lineage, not unworthy
 sprung:
What though one sad dissension bade us
 part?
That name is yet embalm'd within my heart,
Yet at the mention does that heart re-
 bound, 305
And palpitate, responsive to the sound.
Envy dissolved our ties, and not our will:
We once were friends,—I'll think we are
 so still.
A form unmatch'd in nature's partial
 mould,
A heart untainted, we in thee behold:
Yet not the senate's thunder thou shalt
 wield, 311
Nor seek for glory in the tented field;
To minds of ruder texture these be given—
Thy soul shall nearer soar its native
 heaven.
Haply, in polish'd courts might be thy seat,
But that thy tongue could never forge
 deceit: 316

The courtier's supple bow and sneering
 smile,
The flow of compliment, the slippery
 wile,
Would make that breast with indignation
 burn,
And all the glittering snares to tempt thee
 spurn. 320
Domestic happiness will stamp thy fate;
Sacred to love, unclouded e'er by hate;
The world admire thee, and thy friends
 adore;
Ambition's slave alone would toil for
 more. 324

 Now last, but nearest of the social band,
See honest, open, generous CLEON stand;
With scarce one speck to cloud the pleas-
 ing scene,
No vice degrades that purest soul serene.
On the same day our studious race begun,
On the same day our studious race was
 run; 330
Thus side by side we pass'd our first career,
Thus side by side we strove for many a
 year;
At last concluded our scholastic life,
We neither conquer'd in the classic strife:
As speakers each supports an equal name,
And crowds allow to both a partial fame:
To soothe a youthful rival's early pride,
Though Cleon's candour would the palm
 divide,
Yet candour's self compels me now to own
Justice awards it to my friend alone. 340

 Oh! friends regretted, scenes for ever
 dear,
Remembrance hails you with her warmest
 tear!
Drooping, she bends o'er pensive Fancy's
 urn,
To trace the hours which never can return;
Yet with the retrospection loves to dwell,
And soothe the sorrows of her last fare-
 well! 346
Yet greets the triumph of my boyish mind,
As infant laurels round my head were
 twined,
When PROBUS' praise repaid my lyric song,
Or placed me higher in the studious
 throng; 350
Or when my first harangue received
 applause,
His sage instruction the primeval cause,
What gratitude to him my soul possest,
While hope of dawning honours fill'd my
 breast!
For all my humble fame, to him alone
The praise is due, who made that fame my
 own. 356
Oh! could I soar above these feeble lays,
These young effusions of my early days,

37

To him my muse her noblest strain would
give:
The song might perish, but the theme
might live. 360
Yet why for him the needless verse essay?
His honour'd name requires no vain dis-
play:
By every son of grateful IDA blest,
It finds an echo in each youthful breast;
A fame beyond the glories of the proud,
Or all the plaudits of the venal crowd.

IDA! not yet exhausted is the theme,
Nor closed the progress of my youthful
dream.
How many a friend deserves the grateful
strain!
What scenes of childhood still unsung re-
main! 370
Yet let me hush this echo of the past,
This parting song, the dearest and the last;
And brood in secret o'er those hours of
joy,
To me a silent and a sweet employ, 374
While future hope and fear alike unknown,
I think with pleasure on the past alone;
Yes, to the past alone my heart confine,
And chase the phantom of what once was
mine.

IDA! still o'er thy hills in joy preside,
And proudly steer through time's eventful
tide; 380
Still may thy blooming sons thy name
revere,
Smile in thy bower, but quit thee with a
tear,—
That tear, perhaps, the fondest which will
flow,
O'er their last scene of happiness be-
low. 384
Tell me, ye hoary few, who glide along,
The feeble veterans of some former throng,
Whose friends, like autumn leaves by tem-
pests whirl'd,
Are swept for ever from this busy world;
Revolve the fleeting moments of your
youth,
While Care has yet withheld her venom'd
tooth; 390
Say if remembrance days like these endears
Beyond the rapture of succeeding years?
Say, can ambition's fever'd dream bestow
So sweet a balm to soothe your hours of
woe?
Can treasures, hoarded for some thankless
son, 395
Can royal smiles, or wreaths by slaughter
won,
Can stars or ermine, man's maturer toys
(For glittering baubles are not left to boys),
Recall one scene so much beloved to view,
As those where Youth her garland twined
for you? 400

Ah, no! amidst the gloomy calm of age
You turn with faltering hand life's varied
page;
Peruse the record of your days on earth,
Unsullied only where it marks your birth;
Still lingering pause above each chequer'd
leaf, 405
And blot with tears the sable lines of grief,
Where Passion o'er the theme her mantle
threw,
Or weeping Virtue sigh'd a faint adieu;
But bless the scroll which fairer words
adorn,
Traced by the rosy finger of the morn;
When Friendship bow'd before the shrine
of Truth, 411
And Love, without his pinion, smiled on
Youth.

ANSWER TO A BEAUTIFUL POEM

ENTITLED 'THE COMMON LOT'

MONTGOMERY! true, the common lot
Of mortals lies in Lethe's wave;
Yet some shall never be forgot,
Some shall exist beyond the grave.

'Unknown the region of his birth,' 5
The hero rolls the tide of war;
Yet not unknown his martial worth,
Which glares a meteor from afar.

His joy or grief, his weal or woe,
Perchance may 'scape the page of fame;
Yet nations now unborn will know 11
The record of his deathless name.

The patriot's and the poet's frame
Must share the common tomb of all:
Their glory will not sleep the same; 15
That will arise, though empires fall.

The lustre of a beauty's eye
Assumes the ghastly stare of death;
The fair, the brave, the good must die,
And sink the yawning grave beneath.

Once more the speaking eye revives, 21
Still beaming through the lover's strain;
For Petrarch's Laura still survives:
She died, but ne'er will die again.

The rolling seasons pass away, 25
And Time, untiring, waves his wing;
Whilst honour's laurels ne'er decay,
But bloom in fresh, unfading spring.

All, all must sleep in grim repose,
Collected in the silent tomb; 30
The old and young, with friends and foes,
Fest'ring alike in shrouds, consume.

The mouldering marble lasts its day,
Yet falls at length an useless fane;
To ruin's ruthless fangs a prey, 35
The wrecks of pillar'd pride remain.

What, though the sculpture be destroy'd,
From dark oblivion meant to guard;
A bright renown shall be enjoy'd
By those whose virtues claim reward.

Then do not say the common lot 41
Of all lies deep in Lethe's wave;
Some few who ne'er will be forgot
Shall burst the bondage of the grave.
1806.

TO A LADY

WHO PRESENTED THE AUTHOR WITH THE
VELVET BAND WHICH BOUND HER TRESSES

THIS Band, which bound thy yellow hair,
Is mine, sweet girl! thy pledge of love;
It claims my warmest, dearest care,
Like relics left of saints above.

Oh! I will wear it next my heart; 5
'Twill bind my soul in bonds to thee:
From me again 'twill ne'er depart,
But mingle in the grave with me.

The dew I gather from thy lip
Is not so dear to me as this; 10
That I but for a moment sip,
And banquet on a transient bliss:

This will recall each youthful scene,
E'en when our lives are on the wane;
The leaves of Love will still be green 15
When Memory bids them bud again.

Oh! little lock of golden hue,
In gently waving ringlet curl'd,
By the dear head on which you grew,
I would not lose you for a world. 20

Not though a thousand more adorn
The polish'd brow where once you shone,
Like rays which gild a cloudless morn,
Beneath Columbia's fervid zone.

1806. [First published, 1832, as
a single poem, though the last two
stanzas are apparently indepen-
dent of the first four.]

LINES

ADDRESSED TO THE REV. J. T. BECHER, ON
HIS ADVISING THE AUTHOR TO MIX MORE
WITH SOCIETY

DEAR Becher, you tell me to mix with man-
kind;
I cannot deny such a precept is wise;
But retirement accords with the tone of my
mind:
I will not descend to a world I despise.

Did the senate or camp my exertions re-
quire, 5
Ambition might prompt me, at once, to
go forth;
When infancy's years of probation expire,
Perchance I may strive to distinguish
my birth.

The fire in the cavern of Etna conceal'd
Still mantles unseen in its secret recess;
At length, in a volume terrific reveal'd,
No torrent can quench it, no bounds
can repress. 12

Oh! thus, the desire in my bosom for fame
Bids me live but to hope for posterity's
praise.
Could I soar with the phœnix on pinions
of flame, 15
With him I would wish to expire in the
blaze.

For the life of a Fox, of a Chatham the
death,
What censure, what danger, what woe
would I brave!
Their lives did not end when they yielded
their breath;
Their glory illumines the gloom of
their grave. 20

Yet why should I mingle in Fashion's full
herd?
Why crouch to her leaders, or cringe to
her rules?
Why bend to the proud, or applaud the
absurd?
Why search for delight in the friendship
of fools?

I have tasted the sweets and the bitters of
love; 25
In friendship I early was taught to
believe;
My passion the matrons of prudence reprove;
I have found that a friend may profess,
yet deceive.

To me what is wealth?—it may pass in an
hour,
If tyrants prevail, or if Fortune should
frown: 30
To me what is title?—the phantom of
power;
To me what is fashion?—I seek but re-
nown.

Deceit is a stranger as yet to my soul:
I still am unpractised to varnish the
truth:
Then why should I live in a hateful con-
trol? 35
Why waste upon folly the days of my
youth?
1806.

REMEMBRANCE

'TIS done!—I saw it in my dreams;
No more with Hope the future beams;
My days of happiness are few:
Chill'd by misfortune's wintry blast,
My dawn of life is overcast; 5
Love, Hope, and Joy, alike adieu!
Would I could add Remembrance too!
1806. [First published, 1832.]

THE DEATH OF
CALMAR AND ORLA

AN IMITATION OF MACPHERSON'S OSSIAN

DEAR are the days of youth! Age dwells on their remembrance through the mist of time. In the twilight he recalls the sunny hours of morn. He lifts his spear with trembling hand. 'Not thus feebly did I raise the steel before my fathers!' Past is the race of heroes. But their fame rises on the harp; their souls ride on the wings of the wind; they hear the sound through the sighs of the storm, and rejoice in their hall of clouds! Such is Calmar. The gray stone marks his narrow house. He looks down from eddying tempests: he rolls his form in the whirlwind, and hovers on the blast of the mountain.

In Morven dwelt the chief; a beam of war to Fingal. His steps in the field were marked in blood. Lochlin's sons had fled before his angry spear; but mild was the eye of Calmar; soft was the flow of his yellow locks: they streamed like the meteor of the night. No maid was the sigh of his soul: his thoughts were given to friendship,—to dark-haired Orla, destroyer of heroes! Equal were their swords in battle; but fierce was the pride of Orla:—gentle alone to Calmar. Together they dwelt in the cave of Oithona.

From Lochlin, Swaran bounded o'er the blue waves. Erin's sons fell beneath his might. Fingal roused his chiefs to combat. Their ships cover the ocean. Their hosts throng on the green hills. They come to the aid of Erin.

Night rose in clouds. Darkness veils the armies: but the blazing oaks gleam through the valley. The sons of Lochlin slept: their dreams were of blood. They lift the spear in thought, and Fingal flies. Not so the host of Morven. To watch was the post of Orla. Calmar stood by his side. Their spears were in their hands. Fingal called his chiefs: they stood around. The king was in the midst. Gray were his locks, but strong was the arm of the king. Age withered not his powers. 'Sons of Morven,' said the hero, 'to-morrow we meet the foe. But where is Cuthullin, the shield of Erin? He rests in the halls of Tura; he knows not of our coming. Who will speed through Lochlin to the hero, and call the chief to arms? The path is by the swords of foes; but many are my heroes. They are thunderbolts of war. Speak, ye chiefs! Who will arise?'

'Son of Trenmor! mine be the deed,' said dark-haired Orla, 'and mine alone. What is death to me? I love the sleep of the mighty, but little is the danger. The sons of Lochlin dream. I will seek car-borne Cuthullin. If I fall, raise the song of bards; and lay me by the stream of Lubar.' —'And shalt thou fall alone?' said fair-haired Calmar. 'Wilt thou leave thy friend afar? Chief of Oithona! not feeble is my arm in fight. Could I see thee die, and not lift the spear? No, Orla! ours has been the chase of the roebuck, and the feast of shells; ours be the path of danger: ours has been the cave of Oithona; ours be the narrow dwelling on the banks of Lubar.' 'Calmar,' said the chief of Oithona, 'why should thy yellow locks be darkened in the dust of Erin? Let me fall alone. My father dwells in his hall of air: he will rejoice in his boy; but the blue-eyed Mora spreads the feast for her son in Morven. She listens to the steps of the hunter on the heath, and thinks it is the tread of Calmar. Let her not say, "Calmar has fallen by the steel of Lochlin: he died with gloomy Orla, the chief of the dark brow." Why should tears dim the azure eye of Mora? Why should her voice curse Orla, the destroyer of Calmar? Live, Calmar! Live to raise my stone of moss; live to revenge me in the blood of Lochlin. Join the song of bards above my grave. Sweet will be the song of death to Orla, from the voice of Calmar. My ghost shall smile on the notes of praise.' 'Orla,' said the son of Mora, 'could I raise the song of death to my friend? Could I give his fame to the winds? No, my heart would speak in sighs: faint and broken are the sounds of sorrow. Orla! our souls shall hear the song together. One cloud shall be ours on high: the bards will mingle the names of Orla and Calmar.'

They quit the circle of the chiefs. Their steps are to the host of Lochlin. The dying blaze of oak dim twinkles through the night. The northern star points the path to Tura. Swaran, the king, rests on his lonely hill. Here the troops are mixed: they frown in sleep; their shields beneath their heads. Their swords gleam at distance in heaps. The fires are faint; their embers fail in smoke. All is hushed; but the gale sighs on the rocks above. Lightly wheel the heroes through the slumbering band. Half the journey is past, when Mathon, resting on his shield, meets the eye of Orla. It rolls in flame, and glistens through the shade. His spear is raised on high. 'Why dost thou bend thy brow, chief of Oithona?' said fair-haired Calmar: 'we are in the midst of foes. Is this a time for delay?' 'It is a time for vengeance,' said Orla of the gloomy brow. 'Mathon of Lochlin sleeps: seest thou his spear? Its point is dim with the gore of my father. The blood of Mathon shall reek on mine; but shall I slay him sleeping, son of Mora?

No! he shall feel his wound: my fame shall not soar on the blood of slumber. Rise, Mathon, rise! The son of Conna calls; thy life is his; rise to combat.' Mathon starts from sleep; but did he rise alone? No: the gathering chiefs bound on the plain. 'Fly! Calmar, fly!' said dark-haired Orla. 'Mathon is mine. I shall die in joy: but Lochlin crowds around. Fly through the shade of night.' Orla turns. The helm of Mathon is cleft; his shield falls from his arm: he shudders in his blood. He rolls by the side of the blazing oak. Strumon sees him fall: his wrath rises: his weapon glitters on the head of Orla: but a spear pierced his eye. His brain gushes through the wound, and foams on the spear of Calmar. As roll the waves of the Ocean on two mighty barks of the north, so pour the men of Lochlin on the chiefs. As, breaking the surge in foam, proudly steer the barks of the north, so rise the chiefs of Morven on the scattered crests of Lochlin. The din of arms came to the ear of Fingal. He strikes his shield; his sons throng around; the people pour along the heath. Ryno bounds in joy. Ossian stalks in his arms. Oscar shakes the spear. The eagle wing of Fillan floats on the wind. Dreadful is the clang of death! many are the widows of Lochlin! Morven prevails in its strength.

Morn glimmers on the hills: no living foe is seen; but the sleepers are many; grim they lie on Erin. The breeze of ocean lifts their locks; yet they do not awake. The hawks scream above their prey.

Whose yellow locks wave o'er the breast of a chief? Bright as the gold of the stranger, they mingle with the dark hair of his friend. 'Tis Calmar: he lies on the bosom of Orla. Theirs is one stream of blood. Fierce is the look of the gloomy Orla. He breathes not; but his eye is still a flame. It glares in death unclosed. His hand is grasped in Calmar's; but Calmar lives! he lives, though low. 'Rise,' said the king, 'rise, son of Mora: 'tis mine to heal the wounds of heroes. Calmar may yet bound on the hills of Morven.'

'Never more shall Calmar chase the deer of Morven with Orla,' said the hero. 'What were the chase to me alone? Who should share the spoils of battle with Calmar? Orla is at rest! Rough was thy soul, Orla! yet soft to me as the dew of morn. It glared on others in lightning: to me a silver beam of night. Bear my sword to blue-eyed Mora; let it hang in my empty hall. It is not pure from blood: but it could not save Orla. Lay me with my friend. Raise the song when I am dark!'

They are laid by the stream of Lubar. Four gray stones mark the dwelling of Orla and Calmar. When Swaran was bound, our sails rose on the blue waves. The winds gave our barks to Morven:—the bards raised the song.

'What form rises on the roar of clouds? Whose dark ghost gleams on the red streams of tempests? His voice rolls on the thunder. 'Tis Orla, the brown chief of Oithona. He was unmatched in war. Peace to thy soul, Orla! thy fame will not perish. Nor thine, Calmar! Lovely wast thou, son of blue-eyed Mora; but not harmless was thy sword. It hangs in thy cave. The ghosts of Lochlin shriek around its steel. Hear thy praise, Calmar! It dwells on the voice of the mighty. Thy name shakes on the echoes of Morven. Then raise thy fair locks, son of Mora. Spread them on the arch of the rainbow; and smile through the tears of the storm.'

L'AMITIÉ EST L'AMOUR SANS AILES

Why should my anxious breast repine,
 Because my youth is fled?
Days of delight may still be mine;
 Affection is not dead.
In tracing back the years of youth, 5
One firm record, one lasting truth,
 Celestial consolation brings;
Bear it, ye breezes, to the seat,
Where first my heart responsive beat,—
 'Friendship is Love without his wings!'

Through few, but deeply chequer'd years,
 What moments have been mine! 12
Now half obscured by clouds of tears,
 Now bright in rays divine;
Howe'er my future doom be cast, 15
My soul, enraptured with the past,
 To one idea fondly clings;
Friendship! that thought is all thine own,
Worth worlds of bliss, that thought alone—
 'Friendship is Love without his wings!'

Where yonder yew-trees lightly wave 21
 Their branches on the gale,
Unheeded heaves a simple grave,
 Which tells the common tale;
Round this unconscious schoolboys stray,
Till the dull knell of childish play 26
 From yonder studious mansion rings;
But here whene'er my footsteps move,
My silent tears too plainly prove
 'Friendship is Love without his wings!'

Oh, Love! before thy glowing shrine 31
 My early vows were paid;
My hopes, my dreams, my heart was thine,
 But these are now decay'd;
For thine are pinions like the wind, 35
No trace of thee remains behind,

Except, alas! thy jealous stings.
Away, away! delusive power,
Thou shalt not haunt my coming hour;
 Unless, indeed, without thy wings. 40

Seat of my youth! thy distant spire
 Recalls each scene of joy;
My bosom glows with former fire,—
 In mind again a boy.
Thy grove of elms, thy verdant hill, 45
Thy every path delights me still,
 Each flower a double fragrance flings;
Again, as once, in converse gay,
Each dear associate seems to say,
 'Friendship is Love without his wings!'

My Lycus! wherefore dost thou weep?
 Thy falling tears restrain; 52
Affection for a time may sleep,
 But, oh, 'twill wake again.
Think, think, my friend, when next we
 meet, 55
Our long-wish'd interview, how sweet!
 From this my hope of rapture springs;
While youthful hearts thus fondly swell,
Absence, my friend, can only tell,
 'Friendship is Love without his wings!'

In one, and one alone deceived, 61
 Did I my error mourn?
No—from oppressive bonds relieved,
 I left the wretch to scorn.
I turn'd to those my childhood knew,
With feelings warm, with bosoms true,
 Twined with my heart's according
 strings;
And till those vital chords shall break,
For none but these my breast shall wake
 Friendship, the power deprived of
 wings! 70

Ye few! my soul, my life is yours,
 My memory and my hope;
Your worth a lasting love insures,
 Unfetter'd in its scope; 74
From smooth deceit and terror sprung
With aspect fair and honey'd tongue,
 Let Adulation wait on kings;
With joy elate, by snares beset,
We, we, my friends, can ne'er forget
 'Friendship is Love without his wings!'

Fictions and dreams inspire the bard 81
 Who rolls the epic song;
Friendship and truth be my reward—
 To me no bays belong;
If laurell'd Fame but dwells with lies, 85
Me the enchantress ever flies,
 Whose heart and not whose fancy sings;
Simple and young, I dare not feign;
Mine be the rude yet heartfelt strain, 89
 'Friendship is Love without his wings!'

 December 1806.
 [First published, 1832.]

THE PRAYER OF NATURE

FATHER of Light! great God of Heaven!
 Hear'st thou the accents of despair?
Can guilt like man's be e'er forgiven?
 Can vice atone for crimes by prayer?

Father of Light, on thee I call! 5
 Thou seest my soul is dark within;
Thou who canst mark the sparrow's fall,
 Avert from me the death of sin.

No shrine I seek, to sects unknown;
 Oh, point to me the path of truth! 10
Thy dread omnipotence I own;
 Spare, yet amend, the faults of youth.

Let bigots rear a gloomy fane,
 Let superstition hail the pile, 14
Let priests, to spread their sable reign,
 With tales of mystic rites beguile.

Shall man confine his Maker's sway
 To Gothic domes of mouldering stone?
Thy temple is the face of day;
 Earth, ocean, heaven, thy boundless
 throne. 20

Shall man condemn his race to hell,
 Unless they bend in pompous form?
Tell us that all, for one who fell,
 Must perish in the mingling storm?

Shall each pretend to reach the skies, 25
 Yet doom his brother to expire,
Whose soul a different hope supplies,
 Or doctrines less severe inspire?

Shall these, by creeds they can't expound,
 Prepare a fancied bliss or woe? 30
Shall reptiles, grovelling on the ground,
 Their great Creator's purpose know?

Shall those, who live for self alone,
 Whose years float on in daily crime—
Shall they by Faith for guilt atone, 35
 And live beyond the bounds of Time?

Father! no prophet's laws I seek,—
 Thy laws in Nature's works appear;—
I own myself corrupt and weak,
 Yet will I pray, for thou wilt hear! 40

Thou, who canst guide the wandering star
 Through trackless realms of æther's
 space;
Who calm'st the elemental war,
 Whose hand from pole to pole I trace:

Thou, who in wisdom placed me here,
 Who, when thou wilt, canst take me
 hence, 46
Ah! whilst I tread this earthly sphere,
 Extend to me thy wide defence.

42

To Thee, my God, to thee I call!
 Whatever weal or woe betide, 50
By thy command I rise or fall,
 In thy protection I confide.

If, when this dust to dust's restored,
 My soul shall float on airy wing,
How shall thy glorious name adored 55
 Inspire her feeble voice to sing!

But, if this fleeting spirit share
 With clay the grave's eternal bed,
While life yet throbs I raise my prayer,
 Though doom'd no more to quit the 60
 dead.

To Thee I breathe my humble strain,
 Grateful for all thy mercies past,
And hope, my God, to thee again
 This erring life may fly at last.
December 29, 1806.
[First published, 1830.]

TO EDWARD NOEL LONG, ESQ.

'Nil ego contulerim jucundo sanus amico.'—HOR.

DEAR LONG, in this sequester'd scene,
 While all around in slumber lie,
The joyous days which ours have been
 Come rolling fresh on Fancy's eye;
Thus if amidst the gathering storm, 5
 While clouds the darken'd noon deform,
Yon heaven assumes a varied glow,
I hail the sky's celestial bow,
Which spreads the sign of future peace,
And bids the war of tempests cease. 10
Ah! though the present brings but pain
I think those days may come again;
Or if, in melancholy mood,
 Some lurking envious fear intrude,
To check my bosom's fondest thought,
 And interrupt the golden dream, 16
I crush the fiend with malice fraught,
 And still indulge my wonted theme.
Although we ne'er again can trace,
 In Granta's vale, the pedant's lore; 20
Nor through the groves of Ida chase
 Our raptured visions as before,
Though Youth has flown on rosy pinion,
And Manhood claims his stern dominion,
Age will not every hope destroy, 25
But yield some hours of sober joy.

Yes, I will hope that Time's broad wing
Will shed around some dews of spring:
But if his scythe must sweep the flowers
Which bloom among the fairy bowers,
Where smiling youth delights to dwell,
And hearts with early rapture swell;
If frowning Age, with cold control,
Confines the current of the soul,
Congeals the tear of Pity's eye, 35
Or checks the sympathetic sigh,
Or hears unmoved misfortune's groan,
And bids me feel for self alone;

Oh! may my bosom never learn
 To soothe its wonted heedless flow, 40
Still, still despise the censor stern,
 But ne'er forget another's woe.
Yes, as you knew me in the days
O'er which Remembrance yet delays,
Still may I rove, untutor'd, wild, 45
And even in age at heart a child.

Though now on airy visions borne,
 To you my soul is still the same.
Oft has it been my fate to mourn,
 And all my former joys are tame. 50
But, hence! ye hours of sable hue!
 Your frowns are gone, my sorrows o'er:
By every bliss my childhood knew,
 I'll think upon your shade no more.
Thus, when the whirlwind's rage is past,
 And caves their sullen roar enclose,
We heed no more the wintry blast,
 When lull'd by zephyr to repose.

Full often has my infant Muse
 Attuned to love her languid lyre; 60
But now, without a theme to choose,
 The strains in stolen sighs expire.
My youthful nymphs, alas! are flown;
 E—— is a wife, and C—— a mother,
And Carolina sighs alone, 65
 And Mary's given to another;
And Cora's eye, which roll'd on me,
 Can now no more my love recall:
In truth, dear LONG, 'twas time to flee;
 For Cora's eye will shine on all. 70
And though the sun, with genial rays,
His beams alike to all displays,
And every lady's eye's a *sun*,
These last should be confined to one. 74
The soul's meridian don't become her,
Whose sun displays a general *summer*!
Thus faint is every former flame,
And passion's self is now a name.
As, when ebbing flames are low,
 The aid which once improved their
 light, 80
And bade them burn with fiercer glow,
 Now quenches all their sparks in night;
Thus has it been with passion's fires,
 As many a boy and girl remembers,
While all the force of love expires, 85
 Extinguish'd with the dying embers.

But now, dear LONG, 'tis midnight's
 noon,
And clouds obscure the watery moon,
Whose beauties I shall not rehearse,
Described in every stripling's verse; 90
For why should I the path go o'er,
Which every bard has trod before?
Yet ere yon silver lamp of night
 Has thrice perform'd her stated round,
Has thrice retraced her path of light, 95
 And chased away the gloom profound,

43

HOURS OF IDLENESS

I trust that we, my gentle friend,
Shall see her rolling orbit wend
Above the dear-loved peaceful seat,
Which once contain'd our youth's re- 100
treat;
And then with those our childhood knew
We'll mingle in the festive crew;
While many a tale of former day
Shall wing the laughing hours away;
And all the flow of souls shall pour 105
The sacred intellectual shower,
Nor cease till Luna's waning horn
Scarce glimmers through the mist of
morn.

TO A LADY

OH! had my fate been join'd with thine,
As once this pledge appear'd a token,
These follies had not then been mine,
For then my peace had not been broken.

To thee these early faults I owe, 5
To thee, the wise and old reproving:
They know my sins, but do not know
'Twas thine to break the bonds of
loving.

For once my soul, like thine, was pure,
And all its rising fires could smother;
But now thy vows no more endure, 11
Bestow'd by thee upon another;

Perhaps his peace I could destroy,
And spoil the blisses that await him;
Yet let my rival smile in joy, 15
For thy dear sake I cannot hate him.

Ah! since thy angel form is gone,
My heart no more can rest with any;
But what it sought in thee alone,
Attempts, alas! to find in many. 20

Then fare thee well, deceitful maid!
'Twere vain and fruitless to regret thee;
Nor hope nor memory yield their aid,
But pride may teach me to forget thee.

Yet all this giddy waste of years, 25
This tiresome round of palling pleasures;
These varied loves, these matrons' fears,
These thoughtless strains to passion's
measures—

If thou wert mine, had all been hush'd:—
This cheek, now pale from early riot,
With passion's hectic ne'er had flushed,
But bloom'd in calm domestic quiet.

Yes, once the rural scene was sweet, 33
For Nature seem'd to smile before thee;
And once my breast abhorr'd deceit,—
For then it beat but to adore thee.

But now I seek for other joys: 37
To think would drive my soul to mad-
ness;
In thoughtless throngs and empty noise
I conquer half my bosom's sadness.

Yet, even in these a thought will steal
In spite of every vain endeavour,—
And fiends might pity what I feel,—
To know that thou art lost for ever.

I WOULD I WERE A CARELESS CHILD

I WOULD I were a careless child,
Still dwelling in my Highland cave,
Or roaming through the dusky wild,
Or bounding o'er the dark blue wave;
The cumbrous pomp of Saxon pride 5
Accords not with the freeborn soul,
Which loves the mountain's craggy side,
And seeks the rocks where billows
roll.

Fortune! take back these cultured lands,
Take back this name of splendid sound!
I hate the touch of servile hands, 11
I hate the slaves that cringe around.
Place me among the rocks I love,
Which sound to Ocean's wildest roar;
I ask but this—again to rove 15
Through scenes my youth hath known
before.

Few are my years, and yet I feel
The world was ne'er design'd for me:
Ah! why do dark'ning shades conceal
The hour when man must cease to be?
Once I beheld a splendid dream, 21
A visionary scene of bliss:
Truth!—wherefore did thy hated beam
Awake me to a world like this?

I loved—but those I loved are gone; 25
Had friends—my early friends are fled:
How cheerless feels the heart alone,
When all its former hopes are dead!
Though gay companions o'er the bowl
Dispel awhile the sense of ill; 30
Though pleasure stirs the maddening soul,
The heart—the heart—is lonely still.

How dull! to hear the voice of those
Whom rank or chance, whom wealth or
power,
Have made, though neither friends nor
foes, 35
Associates of the festive hour.
Give me again a faithful few,
In years and feelings still the same,
And I will fly the midnight crew, 39
Where boist'rous joy is but a name.

And woman, lovely woman! thou,
 My hope, my comforter, my all!
How cold must be my bosom now,
 When e'en thy smiles begin to pall!
Without a sigh would I resign 45
 This busy scene of splendid woe,
To make that calm contentment mine,
 Which virtue knows, or seems to
 know.

Fain would I fly the haunts of men—
 I seek to shun, not hate mankind; 50
My breast requires the sullen glen,
 Whose gloom may suit a darken'd
 mind.
Oh! that to me the wings were given
 Which bear the turtle to her nest!
Then would I cleave the vault of
 heaven, 55
 To flee away, and be at rest.

WHEN I ROVED A YOUNG HIGHLANDER

WHEN I roved a young Highlander o'er
 the dark heath,
And climb'd thy steep summit, oh
 Morven of snow!
To gaze on the torrent that thunder'd
 beneath,
Or the mist of the tempest that gather'd
 below, 4
Untutor'd by science, a stranger to fear,
 And rude as the rocks where my in-
 fancy grew,
No feeling, save one, to my bosom was
 dear;
Need I say, my sweet Mary, 'twas
 centred in you?

Yet it could not be love, for I knew not
 the name,—
What passion can dwell in the heart of
 a child? 10
But still I perceive an emotion the same
 As I felt, when a boy, on the crag-
 cover'd wild:
One image alone on my bosom impress'd,
 I loved my bleak regions, nor panted
 for new;
And few were my wants, for my wishes
 were bless'd; 15
And pure were my thoughts, for my
 soul was with you.

I arose with the dawn; with my dog as my
 guide,
From mountain to mountain I bounded
 along;
I breasted the billows of Dee's rushing
 tide,
And heard at a distance the High-
 lander's song: 20

At eve, on my heath-cover'd couch of re-
 pose,
 No dreams, save of Mary, were spread
 to my view;
And warm to the skies my devotions arose,
 For the first of my prayers was a bless-
 ing on you.

I left my bleak home, and my visions are
 gone; 25
 The mountains are vanish'd, my youth
 is no more;
As the last of my race, I must wither alone,
 And delight but in days I have wit-
 ness'd before:
Ah! splendour has raised but embitter'd
 my lot;
 More dear were the scenes which my
 infancy knew: 30
Though my hopes may have fail'd, yet
 they are not forgot;
 Though cold is my heart, still it lingers
 with you.

When I see some dark hill point its crest
 to the sky,
 I think of the rocks that o'ershadow
 Colbleen;
When I see the soft blue of a love-speaking
 eye, 35
 I think of those eyes that endear'd the
 rude scene;
When, haply, some light-waving locks I
 behold,
 That faintly resemble my Mary's in hue,
I think on the long, flowing ringlets of
 gold,
 The locks that were sacred to beauty,
 and you. 40

Yet the day may arrive when the moun-
 tains once more
 Shall rise to my sight in their mantles of
 snow:
But while these soar above me, unchanged
 as before,
 Will Mary be there to receive me?—ah,
 no!
Adieu, then, ye hills, where my childhood
 was bred! 45
 Thou sweet flowing Dee, to thy waters
 adieu!
No home in the forest shall shelter my
 head,—
 Ah! Mary, what home could be mine but
 with you?

TO GEORGE, EARL DELAWARR

OH! yes, I will own we were dear to each
 other;
 The friendships of childhood, though
 fleeting, are true;
The love which you felt was the love of a
 brother,
 Nor less the affection I cherish'd for you.

45

But Friendship can vary her gentle do-
minion; 5
The attachment of years in a moment
expires:
Like Love, too, she moves on a swift-
waving pinion,
But glows not, like Love, with un-
quenchable fires.

Full oft have we wander'd through Ida
together,
And blest were the scenes of our youth,
I allow: 10
In the spring of our life, how serene is the
weather!
But winter's rude tempests are gathering
now.

No more with affection shall memory
blending,
The wonted delights of our childhood
retrace:
When pride steels the bosom, the heart is
unbending, 15
And what would be justice appears a
disgrace.

However, dear George, for I still must
esteem you;
The few whom I love I can never up-
braid:
The chance which has lost may in future
redeem you,
Repentance will cancel the vow you
have made. 20

I will not complain, and though chill'd is
affection,
With me no corroding resentment shall
live:
My bosom is calm'd by the simple reflec-
tion,
That both may be wrong, and that both
should forgive.

You knew that my soul, that my heart, my
existence, 25
If danger demanded, were wholly your
own;
You knew me unalter'd by years or by dis-
tance,
Devoted to love and to friendship alone.

You knew,—but away with the vain retro-
spection!
The bond of affection no longer endures;
Too late you may droop o'er the fond
recollection, 31
And sigh for the friend who was for-
merly yours.

For the present, we part,—I will hope not
for ever;
For time and regret will restore you at
last:

To forget our dissension we both should
endeavour, 35
I ask no atonement, but days like the
past.

TO THE EARL OF CLARE

'Tu semper amoris
Sis memor, et cari comitis ne abscedat imago.'
VAL FLAC.

FRIEND of my youth! when young we
roved,
Like striplings, mutually beloved,
With friendship's purest glow,
The bliss which wing'd those rosy hours
Was such as pleasure seldom showers 5
On mortals here below.

The recollection seems alone
Dearer than all the joys I've known,
When distant far from you: 9
Though pain, 'tis still a pleasing pain,
To trace those days and hours again,
And sigh again, adieu!

My pensive memory lingers o'er
Those scenes to be enjoy'd no more,
Those scenes regretted ever; 15
The measure of our youth is full,
Life's evening dream is dark and dull,
And we may meet—ah! never!

As when one parent spring supplies
Two streams which from one fountain
rise, 20
Together join'd in vain;
How soon, diverging from their source,
Each, murmuring, seeks another course,
Till mingled in the main!

Our vital streams of weal or woe, 25
Though near, alas! distinctly flow,
Nor mingle as before:
Now swift or slow, now black or clear,
Till death's unfathom'd gulf appear,
And both shall quit the shore. 30

Our souls, my friend! which once supplied
One wish, nor breathed a thought beside,
Now flow in different channels:
Disdaining humbler rural sports,
'Tis yours to mix in polish'd courts, 35
And shine in fashion's annals;

'Tis mine to waste on love my time,
Or vent my reveries in rhyme,
Without the aid of reason;
For sense and reason (critics know it) 40
Have quitted every amorous poet,
Nor left a thought to seize on.

Poor LITTLE! sweet, melodious bard!
Of late esteem'd it monstrous hard
That he, who sang before all,— 45
He who the lore of love expanded,—
By dire reviewers should be branded
As void of wit and moral.

46

nd yet, while Beauty's praise is thine,
Harmonious favourite of the Nine! 50
 Repine not at thy lot.
hy soothing lays may still be read,
When Persecution's arm is dead,
 And critics are forgot.

till I must yield those worthies merit, 55
Who chasten, with unsparing spirit,
 Bad rhymes, and those who write them;
And though myself may be the next
By criticism to be vext,
 I really will not fight them. 60

erhaps they would do quite as well
To break the rudely sounding shell
 Of such a young beginner:
He who offends at pert nineteen,
Ere thirty may become, I ween, 65
 A very harden'd sinner.

Now, Clare, I must return to you;
And, sure, apologies are due:
 Accept, then, my concession.
In truth, dear Clare, in fancy's flight 70
I soar along from left to right;
 My muse admires digression.

I think I said 'twould be your fate
To add one star to royal state;—
 May regal smiles attend you! 75
And should a noble monarch reign,
You will not seek his smiles in vain,
 If worth can recommend you.

Yet since in danger courts abound,
Where specious rivals glitter round, 80
 From snares may saints preserve you;
And grant your love or friendship ne'er
From any claim a kindred care,
 But those who best deserve you!

Not for a moment may you stray 85
From truth's secure, unerring way!
 May no delights decoy!
O'er roses may your footsteps move,
Your smiles be ever smiles of love,
 Your tears be tears of joy! 90

Oh! if you wish that happiness
Your coming days and years may bless,
 And virtues crown your brow;
Be still as you were wont to be,
Spotless as you've been known to me,—
 Be still as you are now. 96

And though some trifling share of praise,
To cheer my last declining days,
 To me were doubly dear;
Whilst blessing your beloved name 100
I'd waive at once a *poet's* fame,
 To prove a *prophet* here.

LINES WRITTEN BENEATH AN ELM IN THE CHURCHYARD OF HARROW

SPOT of my youth! whose hoary branches
 sigh,
Swept by the breeze that fans thy cloud-
 less sky;
Where now alone I muse, who oft have trod,
With those I loved, thy soft and verdant sod;
With those who, scatter'd far, perchance
 deplore, 5
Like me, the happy scenes they knew be-
 fore:
Oh! as I trace again thy winding hill,
Mine eyes admire, my heart adores thee
 still,
Thou drooping Elm! beneath whose
 boughs I lay,
And frequent mused the twilight hours
 away; 10
Where, as they once were wont, my limbs
 recline,
But, ah! without the thoughts which then
 were mine:
How do thy branches, moaning to the blast,
Invite the bosom to recall the past,
And seem to whisper, as they gently swell,
'Take, while thou canst, a lingering, last
 farewell!' 16

When fate shall chill, at length, this
 fever'd breast,
And calm its cares and passions into rest,
Oft have I thought, 'twould soothe my
 dying hour,—
If aught may soothe when life resigns her
 power,— 20
To know some humble grave, some nar-
 row cell,
Would hide my bosom where it loved to
 dwell;
With this fond dream, methinks 'twere
 sweet to die—
And here it linger'd, here my heart might
 lie;
Here might I sleep where all my hopes
 arose, 25
Scene of my youth, and couch of my re-
 pose;
For ever stretch'd beneath this mantling
 shade,
Press'd by the turf where once my child-
 hood play'd;
Wrapt by the soil that veils the spot I loved,
Mix'd with the earth o'er which my foot-
 steps moved, 30
Blest by the tongues that charm'd my
 youthful ear,
Mourn'd by the few my soul acknow-
 ledged here;
Deplored by those in early days allied,
And unremember'd by the world beside.
 September 2, 1807.

47

OCCASIONAL PIECES

1807—1824

THE ADIEU

WRITTEN UNDER THE IMPRESSION THAT THE
AUTHOR WOULD SOON DIE

ADIEU, thou Hill! where early joy
　Spread roses o'er my brow;
Where Science seeks each loitering boy
　With knowledge to endow.
Adieu, my youthful friends or foes,　5
Partners of former bliss or woes;
　No more through Ida's paths we stray;
Soon must I share the gloomy cell,
Whose ever-slumbering inmates dwell
　Unconscious of the day.　10

Adieu, ye hoary Regal Fanes,
　Ye spires of Granta's vale,
Where Learning robed in sable reigns,
　And Melancholy pale.
Ye comrades of the jovial hour,　15
Ye tenants of the classic bower,
　On Cama's verdant margin placed,
Adieu! while memory still is mine,
For, offerings on Oblivion's shrine,
　These scenes must be effaced.　20

Adieu, ye mountains of the clime
　Where grew my youthful years;
Where Loch na Garr in snows sublime
　His giant summit rears.
Why did my childhood wander forth　25
From you, ye regions of the North,
　With sons of pride to roam?
Why did I quit my Highland cave,
Mar's dusky heath, and Dee's clear wave,
　To seek a Sotheron home!　30

Hall of my Sires! a long farewell—
　Yet why to thee adieu?
Thy vaults will echo back my knell,
　Thy towers my tomb will view:
The faltering tongue which sung thy fall,
And former glories of thy Hall,　36
　Forgets its wonted simple note—
But yet the Lyre retains the strings,
And sometimes, on Æolian wings,
　In dying strains may float.　40

Fields, which surround yon rustic cot,
　While yet I linger here,
Adieu! you are not now forgot,
　To retrospection dear.　44
Streamlet! along whose rippling surge
My youthful limbs were wont to urge,
　At noontide heat. their pliant course;
Plunging with ardour from the shore,
Thy springs will lave these limbs no more,
　Deprived of active force.　50

And shall I here forget the scene,
　Still nearest to my breast?
Rocks rise and rivers roll between
　The spot which passion blest;
Yet, Mary, all thy beauties seem　5
Fresh as in Love's bewitching dream,
　To me in smiles display'd;
Till slow disease resigns his prey
To Death, the parent of decay,
　Thine image cannot fade.　6

And thou, my Friend! whose gentle love
　Yet thrills my bosom's chords,
How much thy friendship was above
　Description's power of words!
Still near my breast thy gift I wear　6
Which sparkled once with Feeling's tear,
　Of Love the pure, the sacred gem;
Our souls were equal, and our lot
In that dear moment quite forgot;
　Let Pride alone condemn!　7

All, all is dark and cheerless now!
　No smile of Love's deceit
Can warm my veins with wonted glow,
　Can bid Life's pulses beat:
Not e'en the hope of future fame　7
Can wake my faint, exhausted frame,
　Or crown with fancied wreaths my
　　head.
Mine is a short inglorious race,—
To humble in the dust my face,
　And mingle with the dead.　8

Oh Fame! thou goddess of my heart;
　On him who gains thy praise,
Pointless must fall the Spectre's dart,
　Consumed in Glory's blaze;
But me she beckons from the earth,　8
My name obscure, unmark'd my birth,
　My life a short and vulgar dream:
Lost in the dull, ignoble crowd,
　My hopes recline within a shroud,
　My fate is Lethe's stream.　9

When I repose beneath the sod,
　Unheeded in the clay,
Where once my playful footsteps trod,
　Where now my head must lay,
The meed of Pity will be shed　9
In dew-drops o'er my narrow bed,
　By nightly skies, and storms alone;
No mortal eye will deign to steep
With tears the dark sepulchral deep
　Which hides a name unknown.　10

OCCASIONAL PIECES

Forget this world, my restless sprite,
 Turn, turn thy thoughts to Heaven:
There must thou soon direct thy flight,
 If errors be forgiven.
To bigots and to sects unknown, 105
Bow down beneath the Almighty's Throne;
To Him address thy trembling prayer:
He, who is merciful and just,
Will not reject a child of dust,
 Although his meanest care. 110

Father of Light! to Thee I call;
 My soul is dark within:
Thou who canst mark the sparrow's fall,
 Avert the death of sin.
Thou, who canst guide the wandering star,
Who calm'st the elemental war, 116
 Whose mantle is yon boundless sky,
My thoughts, my words, my crimes for-
 give:
And, since I soon must cease to live,
 Instruct me how to die. 120

 1807. [First published, 1832.]

TO A VAIN LADY

AH! heedless girl! why thus disclose
 What ne'er was meant for other ears:
Why thus destroy thine own repose
 And dig the source of future tears?

Oh, thou wilt weep, imprudent maid, 5
 While lurking envious foes will smile,
For all the follies thou hast said
 Of those who spoke but to beguile.

Vain girl! thy ling'ring woes are nigh,
 If thou believ'st what striplings say:
Oh, from the deep temptation fly, 11
 Nor fall the specious spoiler's prey.

Dost thou repeat, in childish boast,
 The words man utters to deceive?
Thy peace, thy hope, thy all is lost, 15
 If thou canst venture to believe.

While now amongst thy female peers
 Thou tell'st again the soothing tale,
Canst thou not mark the rising sneers
 Duplicity in vain would veil? 20

These tales in secret silence hush,
 Nor make thyself the public gaze:
What modest maid without a blush
 Recounts a flattering coxcomb's praise?

Will not the laughing boy despise 25
 Her who relates each fond conceit—
Who, thinking Heaven is in her eyes,
 Yet cannot see the slight deceit?

For she who takes a soft delight
 These amorous nothings in revealing,
Must credit all we say or write, 31
 While vanity prevents concealing.

Cease, if you prize your beauty's reign!
 No jealousy bids me reprove:
One, who is thus from nature vain, 35
 I pity, but I cannot love.

 January 15, 1807.
 [First published, 1832.]

TO ANNE

OH, Anne, your offences to me have been
 grievous:
 I thought from my wrath no atonement
 could save you:
But woman is made to command and de-
 ceive us—
 I look'd in your face, and I almost for-
 gave you.

I vow'd I could ne'er for a moment re-
 spect you, 5
 Yet thought that a day's separation was
 long;
When we met, I determined again to sus-
 pect you—
 Your smile soon convinced me suspi-
 cion was wrong.

I swore, in a transport of young indigna-
 tion,
 With fervent contempt evermore to dis-
 dain you: 10
I saw you—my anger became admiration;
 And now, all my wish, all my hope's to
 regain you.

With beauty like yours, oh, how vain the
 contention!
 Thus lowly I sue for forgiveness before
 you;
At once to conclude such a fruitless dis-
 sension, 15
 Be false, my sweet Anne, when I cease
 to adore you!

 January 16, 1807.
 [First published, 1832.]

TO THE SAME

OH, say not, sweet Anne, that the Fates
 have decreed
 The heart which adores you should
 wish to dissever;
Such Fates were to me most unkind ones
 indeed,—
 To bear me from love and from beauty
 for ever.

Your frowns, lovely girl, are the Fates
 which alone 5
 Could bid me from fond admiration
 refrain;
By these, every hope, every wish were
 o'erthrown,
 Till smiles should restore me to rapture
 again.

49

OCCASIONAL PIECES

As the ivy and oak, in the forest entwined,
　The rage of the tempest united must
　　weather;　　　　　　　　　　　　10
My love and my life were by nature de-
　　sign'd
　To flourish alike, or to perish together.

Then say not, sweet Anne, that the Fates
　have decreed
　Your lover should bid you a lasting
　adieu;
Till Fate can ordain that his bosom shall
　bleed,　　　　　　　　　　　　　15
　His soul, his existence, are centred in
　you.

　　　　　　1807. [First published, 1832.]

TO THE AUTHOR OF A SONNET

BEGINNING ' "SAD IS MY VERSE," YOU SAY,
　　"AND YET NO TEAR" '

THY verse is 'sad' enough, no doubt:
　A devilish deal more sad than witty!
Why we should weep I can't find out,
　Unless for *thee* we weep in pity.

Yet there is one I pity more;　　　　5
　And much, alas! I think he needs it;
For he, I'm sure, will suffer sore,
　Who, to his own misfortune, reads it.

Thy rhymes, without the aid of magic,
　May *once* be read—but never after:
Yet their effect's by no means tragic, 11
　Although by far too dull for laughter.

But would you make our bosoms bleed,
　And of no common pang complain—
If you would make us weep indeed,　15
　Tell us, you'll read them o'er again.
　　　　　　　　　　　　March 8, 1807.
　　　　　　　　　　[First published, 1832.]

ON FINDING A FAN

IN one who felt as once he felt,
　This might, perhaps, have fann'd the
　flame;
But now his heart no more will melt,
　Because that heart is not the same.

As when the ebbing flames are low,　5
　The aid which once improved their
　light,
And bade them burn with fiercer glow,
　Now quenches all their blaze in night.

Thus has it been with passion's fires—
　As many a boy and girl remembers—
While every hope of love expires,　11
　Extinguish'd with the dying embers.

The *first*, though not a spark survive,
　Some careful hand may teach to burn;
The *last*, alas! can ne'er survive;　15
　No touch can bid its warmth return.

Or, if it chance to wake again,
　Not always doom'd its heat to smother,
It sheds (so wayward fates ordain)
　Its former warmth around another. 20
　　　　　　1807. [First published, 1832.]

FAREWELL TO THE MUSE

THOU Power! who hast ruled me through
　infancy's days,
　Young offspring of fancy, 'tis time we
　should part;
Then rise on the gale this the last of my
　lays,
　The coldest effusion which springs from
　my heart.

This bosom, responsive to rapture no
　more,　　　　　　　　　　　　5
　Shall hush thy wild notes, nor implore
　thee to sing;
The feelings of childhood, which taught
　thee to soar,
　Are wafted far distant on Apathy's
　wing.

Though simple the themes of my rude
　flowing Lyre,
　Yet even these themes are departed for
　ever;　　　　　　　　　　　　10
No more beam the eyes which my dream
　could inspire,
　My visions are flown, to return,—alas!
　never.

When drain'd is the nectar which gladdens
　the bowl,
　How vain is the effort delight to pro-
　long!
When cold is the beauty which dwelt in
　my soul,　　　　　　　　　　　15
　What magic of Fancy can lengthen my
　song?

Can the lips sing of Love in the desert
　alone,
　Of kisses and smiles which they now
　must resign?
Or dwell with delight on the hours that
　are flown?
　Ah, no! for those hours can no longer
　be mine.　　　　　　　　　　　20

Can they speak of the friends that I lived
　but to love?
　Ah, surely affection ennobles the strain!
But how can my numbers in sympathy
　move,
　When I scarcely can hope to behold
　them again?

Can I sing of the deeds which my Fathers
　have done,　　　　　　　　　　25
　And raise my loud harp to the fame of
　my Sires?

For glories, like theirs, oh, how faint is my
 tone!
 For Heroes' exploits how unequal my
 fires!

Untouch'd, then, my Lyre shall reply to
 the blast—
 'Tis hush'd; and my feeble endeavours
 are o'er; 30
And those who have heard it will pardon
 the past,
 When they know that its murmurs shall
 vibrate no more.

And soon shall its wild erring notes be
 forgot,
 Since early affection and love is o'er-
 cast:
Oh! blest had my fate been, and happy
 my lot, 35
 Had the first strain of love been the
 dearest, the last.

Farewell, my young Muse! since we now
 can ne'er meet;
 If our songs have been languid, they
 surely are few;
Let us hope that the present at least will
 be sweet—
 The present—which seals our eternal
 Adieu. 40
 1807. [First published, 1832.]

TO AN OAK AT NEWSTEAD

Young Oak! when I planted thee deep in
 the ground,
 I hoped that thy days would be longer
 than mine;
That thy dark-waving branches would
 flourish around,
 And ivy thy trunk with its mantle en-
 twine.

Such, such was my hope, when in infancy's
 years, 5
 On the land of my fathers I rear'd thee
 with pride;
They are past, and I water thy stem with
 my tears,—
 Thy decay not the weeds that surround
 thee can hide.

I left thee, my Oak, and, since that fatal
 hour,
 A stranger has dwelt in the hall of my
 sire; 10
Till manhood shall crown me, not mine is
 the power,
 But his, whose neglect may have bade
 thee expire.

Oh! hardy thou wert—even now little care
 Might revive thy young head, and thy
 wounds gently heal:

But thou wert not fated affection to
 share— 15
 For who could suppose that a stranger
 would feel!

Ah, droop not, my Oak! lift thy head for
 a while;
 Ere twice round yon Glory this planet
 shall run,
The hand of thy Master will teach thee to
 smile,
 When Infancy's years of probation are
 done. 20

Oh, live then, my Oak! tow'r aloft from
 the weeds,
 That clog thy young growth, and assist
 thy decay,
For still in thy bosom are life's early seeds,
 And still may thy branches their beauty
 display.

Oh! yet, if maturity's years may be thine,
 Though I shall lie low in the cavern of
 death, 26
On thy leaves yet the day-beam of ages
 may shine,
 Uninjured by time, or the rude winter's
 breath.

For centuries still may thy boughs lightly
 wave
 O'er the corse of thy lord in thy canopy
 laid; 30
While the branches thus gratefully shelter
 his grave,
 The chief who survives may recline in
 thy shade.

And as he, with his boys, shall revisit this
 spot,
 He will tell them in whispers more softly
 to tread.
Oh! surely, by these I shall ne'er be for-
 got; 35
 Remembrance still hallows the dust of
 the dead.

And here, will they say, when in life's
 glowing prime,
 Perhaps he has pour'd forth his young
 simple lay,
And here must he sleep, till the moments
 of time
 Are lost in the hours of Eternity's day.
 1807. [First published, 1832.]

ON REVISITING HARROW

Here once engaged the stranger's view
 Young Friendship's record simply
 traced;
Few were her words,—but yet, though
 few,
 Resentment's hand the line defaced.

51

Deeply she cut—but not erased, 5
 The characters were still so plain,
That Friendship once return'd, and
 gazed,—
 Till Memory hail'd the words again.

Repentance placed them as before; 9
 Forgiveness join'd her gentle name;
So fair the inscription seem'd once more,
 That Friendship thought it still the
 same.

Thus might the Record now have been;
 But, ah, in spite of Hope's endeavour,
Or Friendship's tears, Pride rush'd be-
 tween, 15
 And blotted out the line for ever.
September 1807.

EPITAPH ON JOHN ADAMS, OF SOUTHWELL

A CARRIER, WHO DIED OF DRUNKENNESS

JOHN ADAMS lies here, of the parish of
 Southwell,
A *Carrier* who *carried* his can to his mouth
 well:
He *carried* so much, and he *carried* so fast,
He could *carry* no more—so was *carried*
 at last;
For, the liquor he drank, being too much
 for one, 5
He could not *carry* off,—so he's now
 carri-on.
September 1807.

TO MY SON

THOSE flaxen locks, those eyes of blue,
Bright as thy mother's in their hue;
Those rosy lips, whose dimples play
And smile to steal the heart away,
Recall a scene of former joy, 5
And touch thy father's heart, my Boy!

And thou canst lisp a father's name—
Ah, William, were thine own the same,—
No self-reproach—but, let me cease—
My care for thee shall purchase peace; 10
Thy mother's shade shall smile in joy,
And pardon all the past, my Boy!

Her lowly grave the turf has prest,
And thou hast known a stranger's breast;
Derision sneers upon thy birth, 15
And yields thee scarce a name on earth;
Yet shall not these one hope destroy,—
A Father's heart is thine, my Boy!

Why, let the world unfeeling frown,
Must I fond Nature's claim disown? 20
Ah, no—though moralists reprove,
I hail thee, dearest child of love,
Fair cherub, pledge of youth and joy—
A Father guards thy birth, my Boy!

Oh, 'twill be sweet in thee to trace, 25
Ere age has wrinkled o'er my face,
Ere half my glass of life is run,
At once a brother and a son;
And all my wane of years employ
In justice done to thee, my Boy! 30

Although so young thy heedless sire,
Youth will not damp parental fire;
And, wert thou still less dear to me,
While Helen's form revives in thee,
The breast which beat to former joy, 35
Will ne'er desert its pledge, my Boy!
1807. [First published, 1830.]

FAREWELL! IF EVER FONDEST PRAYER

FAREWELL! if ever fondest prayer
 For other's weal avail'd on high,
Mine will not all be lost in air,
 But waft thy name beyond the sky. 4
'Twere vain to speak, to weep, to sigh:
 Oh! more than tears of blood can tell,
When wrung from guilt's expiring eye,
 Are in that word—Farewell!—Fare-
 well!

These lips are mute, these eyes are dry;
 But in my breast and in my brain, 10
Awake the pangs that pass not by,
 The thought that ne'er shall sleep again.
My soul nor deigns nor dares complain,
 Though grief and passion there rebel;
I only know we loved in vain— 15
 I only feel—Farewell!—Farewell!
1808.

BRIGHT BE THE PLACE OF THY SOUL

BRIGHT be the place of thy soul!
 No lovelier spirit than thine
E'er burst from its mortal control
 In the orbs of the blessed to shine.

On earth thou wert all but divine, 5
 As thy soul shall immortally be;
And our sorrow may cease to repine,
 When we know that thy God is with
 thee.

Light be the turf of thy tomb!
 May its verdure like emeralds be: 10
There should not be the shadow of gloom
 In aught that reminds us of thee.

Young flowers and an evergreen tree
 May spring from the spot of thy rest:
But nor cypress nor yew let us see; 15
 For why should we mourn for the blest?
1808

52

WHEN WE TWO PARTED

WHEN we two parted
 In silence and tears,
Half broken-hearted
 To sever for years,
Pale grew thy cheek and cold, 5
 Colder thy kiss;
Truly that hour foretold
 Sorrow to this.

The dew of the morning
 Sunk chill on my brow— 10
It felt like the warning
 Of what I feel now.
Thy vows are all broken,
 And light is thy fame:
I hear thy name spoken, 15
 And share in its shame.

They name thee before me,
 A knell to mine ear;
A shudder comes o'er me—
 Why wert thou so dear? 20
They know not I knew thee,
 Who knew thee too well:—
Long, long shall I rue thee,
 Too deeply to tell.

In secret we met— 25
 In silence I grieve,
That thy heart could forget,
 Thy spirit deceive.
If I should meet thee
 After long years, 30
How should I greet thee?
 With silence and tears.

 1808.

TO A YOUTHFUL FRIEND

FEW years have pass'd since thou and I
 Were firmest friends, at least in name,
And childhood's gay sincerity
 Preserved our feelings long the same.

But now, like me, too well thou know'st
 What trifles oft the heart recall; 6
And those who once have loved the most
 Too soon forget they loved at all.

And such the change the heart displays,
 So frail is early friendship's reign, 10
A month's brief lapse, perhaps a day's,
 Will view thy mind estranged again.

If so, it never shall be mine
 To mourn the loss of such a heart; 14
The fault was Nature's fault, not thine,
 Which made thee fickle as thou art.

As rolls the ocean's changing tide,
 So human feelings ebb and flow;
And who would in a breast confide
 Where stormy passions ever glow? 20

It boots not that, together bred,
 Our childish days were days of joy:
My spring of life has quickly fled;
 Thou, too, hast ceased to be a boy.

And when we bid adieu to youth, 25
 Slaves to the specious world's control,
We sigh a long farewell to truth;
 That world corrupts the noblest soul.

Ah, joyous season! when the mind
 Dares all things boldly but to lie; 30
When thought ere spoke is unconfined,
 And sparkles in the placid eye.

Not so in Man's maturer years,
 When Man himself is but a tool; 34
When interest sways our hopes and fears,
 And all must love and hate by rule.

With fools in kindred vice the same,
 We learn at length our faults to blend;
And those, and those alone, may claim
 The prostituted name of friend. 40

Such is the common lot of man:
 Can we then 'scape from folly free?
Can we reverse the general plan,
 Nor be what all in turn must be?

No; for myself, so dark my fate 45
 Through every turn of life hath been;
Man and the world so much I hate,
 I care not when I quit the scene.

But thou, with spirit frail and light,
 Wilt shine awhile, and pass away; 50
As glow-worms sparkle through the night,
 But dare not stand the test of day.

Alas! whenever folly calls
 Where parasites and princes meet
(For cherish'd first in royal halls, 55
 The welcome vices kindly greet),

Ev'n now thou'rt nightly seen to add
 One insect to the fluttering crowd;
And still thy trifling heart is glad 59
 To join the vain and court the proud.

There dost thou glide from fair to fair,
 Still simpering on with eager haste,
As flies along the gay parterre
 That taint the flowers they scarcely taste.

But say, what nymph will prize the flame
 Which seems, as marshy vapours move,
To flit along from dame to dame, 67
 An ignis-fatuus gleam of love?

What friend for thee, howe'er inclined,
 Will deign to own a kindred care? 70
Who will debase his manly mind,
 For friendship every fool may share?

In time forbear; amidst the throng
 No more so base a thing be seen;
No more so idly pass along; 75
 Be something, anything, but—mean.
 1808.

LINES INSCRIBED UPON A CUP FORMED FROM A SKULL

START not—nor deem my spirit fled;
 In me behold the only skull,
From which, unlike a living head,
 Whatever flows is never dull.

I lived, I loved, I quaff'd, like thee: 5
 I died: let earth my bones resign;
Fill up—thou canst not injure me;
 The worm hath fouler lips than thine.

Better to hold the sparkling grape,
 Than nurse the earth-worm's slimy
 brood; 10
And circle in the goblet's shape
 The drink of gods, than reptile's food.

Where once my wit, perchance, hath shone,
 In aid of others' let me shine;
And when, alas! our brains are gone, 15
 What nobler substitute than wine?

Quaff while thou canst: another race,
 When thou and thine, like me, are sped,
May rescue thee from earth's embrace,
 And rhyme and revel with the dead.

Why not? since through life's little day
 Our heads such sad effects produce;
Redeem'd from worms and wasting clay,
 This chance is theirs, to be of use.
 Newstead Abbey, 1808.

WELL! THOU ART HAPPY

WELL! thou art happy, and I feel
 That I should thus be happy too;
For still my heart regards thy weal
 Warmly, as it was wont to do. 4

Thy husband's blest—and 'twill impart
 Some pangs to view his happier lot:
But let them pass—Oh! how my heart
 Would hate him if he loved thee not!

When late I saw thy favourite child, 9
 I thought my jealous heart would break;
But when the unconscious infant smiled,
 I kiss'd it for its mother's sake. 12

I kiss'd it,—and repress'd my sighs
 Its father in its face to see;
But then it had its mother's eyes, 15
 And they were all to love and me.

Mary, adieu! I must away:
 While thou art blest I'll not repine;
But near thee I can never stay; 19
 My heart would soon again be thine.

I deem'd that time, I deem'd that pride
 Had quench'd at length my boyish
 flame;
Nor knew, till seated by thy side,
 My heart in all,—save hope,—the same

Yet was I calm: I knew the time 25
 My breast would thrill before thy look
But now to tremble were a crime—
 We met,—and not a nerve was shook

I saw thee gaze upon my face,
 Yet meet with no confusion there: 30
One only feeling could'st thou trace;
 The sullen calmness of despair.

Away! away! my early dream
 Remembrance never must awake:
Oh! where is Lethe's fabled stream? 35
 My foolish heart, be still, or break.
 November 2, 1808

INSCRIPTION ON THE MONUMENT OF A NEWFOUNDLAND DOG

WHEN some proud son of man returns to
 earth,
Unknown to glory, but upheld by birth,
The sculptor's art exhausts the pomp of
 woe,
And storied urns record who rest below
When all is done, upon the tomb is seen,
Not what he was, but what he should
 have been:
But the poor dog, in life the firmest friend
The first to welcome, foremost to defend
Whose honest heart is still his master's
 own,
Who labours, fights, lives, breathes for
 him alone, 10
Unhonour'd falls, unnoticed all his worth
Denied in heaven the soul he held on earth
While man, vain insect! hopes to be for
 given,
And claims himself a sole exclusive heaven
Oh man! thou feeble tenant of an hour,
Debased by slavery, or corrupt by power
Who knows thee well must quit thee with
 disgust, 17
Degraded mass of animated dust!
Thy love is lust, thy friendship all a cheat
Thy smiles hypocrisy, thy words deceit!
By nature vile, ennobled but by name,
Each kindred brute might bid thee blush
 for shame.
Ye! who perchance behold this simple urn,
Pass on—it honours none you wish to
 mourn:
To mark a friend's remains these stones
 arise; 25
I never knew but one,—and here he lies.
 Newstead Abbey, *November* 30, 1808.

TO A LADY

ON BEING ASKED MY REASON FOR QUITTING
ENGLAND IN THE SPRING

WHEN Man, expell'd from Eden's bowers,
 A moment linger'd near the gate,
Each scene recall'd the vanish'd hours,
 And bade him curse his future fate.

But, wandering on through distant climes,
 He learnt to bear his load of grief; 6
Just gave a sigh to other times,
 And found in busier scenes relief.

Thus, lady! will it be with me,
 And I must view thy charms no more;
For, while I linger near to thee, 11
 I sigh for all I knew before.

In flight I shall be surely wise,
 Escaping from temptation's snare;
cannot view my paradise 15
 Without the wish of dwelling there.
 December 2, 1808.

REMIND ME NOT, REMIND ME NOT

REMIND me not, remind me not,
 Of those beloved, those vanish'd hours,
 When all my soul was given to thee;
Hours that may never be forgot,
 Till time unnerves our vital powers, 5
 And thou and I shall cease to be.

Can I forget—canst thou forget,
 When playing with thy golden hair,
 How quick thy fluttering heart did
 move?
Oh! by my soul, I see thee yet, 10
 With eyes so languid, breast so fair,
 And lips, though silent, breathing
 love.

When thus reclining on my breast,
 Those eyes threw back a glance so sweet,
 As half reproach'd yet raised desire,
And still we near and nearer prest, 16
 And still our glowing lips would meet,
 As if in kisses to expire.

And then those pensive eyes would close,
 And bid their lids each other seek, 20
 Veiling the azure orbs below;
While their long lashes' darken'd gloss
 Seem'd stealing o'er thy brilliant cheek,
 Like raven's plumage smooth'd on
 snow.

dreamt last night our love return'd, 25
 And, sooth to say, that very dream
 Was sweeter in its phantasy,
Than if for other hearts I burn'd,
 For eyes that ne'er like thine could
 beam
 In rapture's wild reality. 30

Then tell me not, remind me not,
 Of hours which, though for ever gone,
 Can still a pleasing dream restore,
Till thou and I shall be forgot, 34
 And senseless, as the mouldering stone
 Which tells that we shall be no more.

THERE WAS A TIME, I NEED NOT NAME

THERE was a time, I need not name,
 Since it will ne'er forgotten be,
When all our feelings were the same
 As still my soul hath been to thee.

And from that hour when first thy tongue
 Confess'd a love which equall'd mine,
Though many a grief my heart hath
 wrung, 7
 Unknown, and thus unfelt, by thine,

None, none hath sunk so deep as this—
 To think how all that love hath flown;
Transient as every faithless kiss, 11
 But transient in thy breast alone.

And yet my heart some solace knew,
 When late I heard thy lips declare,
In accents once imagined true, 15
 Remembrance of the days that were.

Yes! my adored, yet most unkind!
 Though thou wilt never love again,
To me 'tis doubly sweet to find
 Remembrance of that love remain. 20

Yes! 'tis a glorious thought to me,
 Nor longer shall my soul repine,
Whate'er thou art or e'er shalt be,
 Thou hast been dearly, solely mine.

AND WILT THOU WEEP WHEN I AM LOW?

AND wilt thou weep when I am low?
 Sweet lady! speak those words again:
Yet if they grieve thee, say not so—
 I would not give that bosom pain.

My heart is sad, my hopes are gone, 5
 My blood runs coldly through my
 breast;
And when I perish, thou alone
 Wilt sigh above my place of rest.

And yet, methinks, a gleam of peace
 Doth through my cloud of anguish
 shine: 10
And for a while my sorrows cease,
 To know thy heart hath felt for mine.

Oh lady! blessed be that tear—
 It falls for one who cannot weep;
Such precious drops are doubly dear 15
 To those whose eyes no tear may steep.

Sweet lady! once my heart was warm
 With every feeling soft as thine;
But beauty's self hath ceased to charm
 A wretch created to repine. 20

Yet wilt thou weep when I am low?
 Sweet lady! speak those words again:
Yet if they grieve thee, say not so—
 I would not give that bosom pain.

FILL THE GOBLET AGAIN

A SONG

FILL the goblet again! for I never before
Felt the glow which now gladdens my heart to its core;
Let us drink!—who would not?—since, through life's varied round,
In the goblet alone no deception is found.

I have tried in its turn all that life can supply; 5
I have bask'd in the beam of a dark rolling eye;
I have loved!—who has not?—but what heart can declare
That pleasure existed while passion was there?

In the days of my youth, when the heart's in its spring,
And dreams that affection can never take wing, 10
I had friends!—who has not?— but what tongue will avow,
That friends, rosy wine! are so faithful as thou?

The heart of a mistress some boy may estrange,
Friendship shifts with the sunbeam—thou never canst change;
Thou grow'st old—who does not?— but on earth what appears, 15
Whose virtues, like thine, still increase with its years?

Yet if blest to the utmost that love can bestow,
Should a rival bow down to our idol below,
We are jealous!—who's not?—thou hast no such alloy;
For the more that enjoy thee, the more we enjoy. 20

Then the season of youth and its vanities past,
For refuge we fly to the goblet at last;
There we find—do we not?—in the flow of the soul,
That truth, as of yore, is confined to the bowl.

When the box of Pandora was opened on earth, 2
And Misery's triumph commenced over Mirth,
Hope was left,—was she not?—but the goblet we kiss,
And care not for Hope, who are certain of bliss.

Long life to the grape! for when summer is flown,
The age of our nectar shall gladden our own! 3
We must die—who shall not?—May our sins be forgiven,
And Hebe shall never be idle in heaven.

STANZAS TO A LADY, ON LEAVING ENGLAND

'TIS done—and shivering in the gale
The bark unfurls her snowy sail;
And whistling o'er the bending mast,
Loud sings on high the fresh'ning blast;
And I must from this land be gone,
Because I cannot love but one.

But could I be what I have been,
And could I see what I have seen—
Could I repose upon the breast
Which once my warmest wishes blest—
I should not seek another zone 1
Because I cannot love but one.

'Tis long since I beheld that eye
Which gave me bliss or misery;
And I have striven, but in vain, 1
Never to think of it again:
For though I fly from Albion,
I still can only love but one.

As some lone bird, without a mate,
My weary heart is desolate; 2
I look around, and cannot trace
One friendly smile or welcome face,
And ev'n in crowds am still alone,
Because I cannot love but one.

And I will cross the whitening foam, 2
And I will seek a foreign home;
Till I forget a false fair face,
I ne'er shall find a resting-place;
My own dark thoughts I cannot shun,
But ever love, and love but one. 3

The poorest, veriest wretch on earth
Still finds some hospitable hearth,
Where friendship's or love's softer glow
May smile in joy or soothe in woe;
But friend or leman I have none, 3
Because I cannot love but one.

go—but wheresoe'er I flee
There's not an eye will weep for me;
There's not a kind congenial heart,
Where I can claim the meanest part;　40
Nor thou, who hast my hopes undone,
Wilt sigh, although I love but one.

To think of every early scene,
Of what we are, and what we've been,
Would whelm some softer hearts with
　　woe—　45
But mine, alas! has stood the blow;
Yet still beats on as it begun,
And never truly loves but one.

And who that dear loved one may be,
Is not for vulgar eyes to see;　50
And why that early love was cross'd,
Thou know'st the best, I feel the most;
But few that dwell beneath the sun
Have loved so long, and loved but one.

I've tried another's fetters too,　55
With charms perchance as fair to view;
And I would fain have loved as well,
But some unconquerable spell
Forbade my bleeding breast to own
A kindred care for aught but one.　60

Twould soothe to take one lingering view,
And bless thee in my last adieu;
Yet wish I not those eyes to weep
For him that wanders o'er the deep;　64
His home, his hope, his youth are gone,
Yet still he loves, and loves but one.

　　　　　　　　　　　　　　1809.

LINES TO MR. HODGSON

WRITTEN ON BOARD THE LISBON PACKET

HUZZA! Hodgson, we are going,
　Our embargo's off at last;
Favourable breezes blowing
　Bend the canvas o'er the mast.
From aloft the signal's streaming,　5
　Hark! the farewell gun is fired;
Women screeching, tars blaspheming,
　Tell us that our time's expired.
　　Here's a rascal
　　Come to task all,　10
Prying from the custom-house,
　　Trunks unpacking,
　　Cases cracking,
Not a corner for a mouse
Scapes unsearch'd amid the racket,　15
Ere we sail on board the Packet.

Now our boatmen quit their mooring,
　And all hands must ply the oar;
Baggage from the quay is lowering,
　We're impatient, push from shore.　20
'Have a care! that case holds liquor—
Stop the boat—I'm sick—oh Lord!'

'Sick, ma'am, damme, you'll be sicker
Ere you've been an hour on board.'
　　Thus are screaming　25
　　Men and women,
　Gemmen, ladies, servants, Jacks;
　　Here entangling,
　　All are wrangling,
Stuck together close as wax.—　30
Such the general noise and racket,
Ere we reach the Lisbon Packet.

Now we've reach'd her, lo! the captain,
　Gallant Kidd, commands the crew;
Passengers their berths are clapt in,　35
　Some to grumble, some to spew.
'Heyday! call you that a cabin?
　Why 'tis hardly three feet square:
Not enough to stow Queen Mab in—
　Who the deuce can harbour there?'　40
　　'Who, sir? plenty—
　　Nobles twenty
Did at once my vessel fill.'—
　　'Did they? Jesus,
　　How you squeeze us!　45
Would to God they did so still:
Then I'd scape the heat and racket
Of the good ship, Lisbon Packet.'

Fletcher! Murray! Bob! where are you?
　Stretch'd along the deck like logs—
Bear a hand, you jolly tar, you!　51
　Here's a rope's end for the dogs.
Hobhouse muttering fearful curses,
　As the hatchway down he rolls,
Now his breakfast, now his verses,　55
　Vomits forth—and damns our souls.
　　'Here's a stanza
　　On Braganza—
Help!'—'A couplet?'—'No, a cup
　　Of warm water—'　60
　　'What's the matter?'
'Zounds! my liver's coming up:
I shall not survive the racket
Of this brutal Lisbon Packet.'

Now at length we're off for Turkey,　65
　Lord knows when we shall come back!
Breezes foul and tempests murky
　May unship us in a crack.
But, since life at most a jest is,
　As philosophers allow,　70
Still to laugh by far the best is,
　Then laugh on—as I do now.
　　Laugh at all things,
　　Great and small things,
Sick or well, at sea or shore;　75
　　While we're quaffing,
　　Let's have laughing—
Who the devil cares for more?—
Some good wine! and who would lack it,
Ev'n on board the Lisbon Packet?　80

　　　　　　Falmouth Roads, *June* 30, 1809.
　　　　　　[First published, 1830.]

57

OCCASIONAL PIECES

TO FLORENCE

OH Lady! when I left the shore,
 The distant shore which gave me birth,
I hardly thought to grieve once more
 To quit another spot on earth:

Yet here, amidst this barren isle, 5
 Where panting Nature droops the head,
Where only thou art seen to smile,
 I view my parting hour with dread.

Though far from Albin's craggy shore,
 Divided by the dark-blue main; 10
A few, brief, rolling seasons o'er,
 Perchance I view her cliffs again:

But wheresoe'er I now may roam,
 Through scorching clime, and varied
 sea, 14
Though Time restore me to my home,
 I ne'er shall bend mine eyes on thee:

On thee, in whom at once conspire
 All charms which heedless hearts can
 move,
Whom but to see is to admire, 19
 And, oh! forgive the word—to love.

Forgive the word, in one who ne'er
 With such a word can more offend;
And since thy heart I cannot share,
 Believe me, what I am, thy friend.

And who so cold as look on thee, 25
 Thou lovely wand'rer, and be less?
Nor be, what man should ever be,
 The friend of Beauty in distress?

Ah! who would think that form had past
 Through Danger's most destructive
 path, 30
Had braved the death-wing'd tempest's
 blast,
 And 'scaped a tyrant's fiercer wrath?

Lady! when I shall view the walls
 Where free Byzantium once arose,
And Stamboul's Oriental halls 35
 The Turkish tyrants now enclose;

Though mightiest in the lists of fame,
 That glorious city still shall be;
On me 'twill hold a dearer claim,
 As spot of thy nativity: 40

And though I bid thee now farewell,
 When I behold that wondrous scene,
Since where thou art I may not dwell,
 'Twill soothe to be where thou hast
 been.
 September 1809.

LINES WRITTEN IN AN ALBUM AT MALTA

As o'er the cold sepulchral stone
 Some name arrests the passer-by;
Thus, when thou view'st this page alone
 May mine attract thy pensive eye!

And when by thee that name is read,
 Perchance in some succeeding year,
Reflect on me as on the dead,
 And think my heart is buried here.
 September 14, 1809

STANZAS COMPOSED DURING A THUNDER-STORM

CHILL and mirk is the nightly blast,
 Where Pindus' mountains rise,
And angry clouds are pouring fast
 The vengeance of the skies.

Our guides are gone, our hope is lost,
 And lightnings, as they play,
But show where rocks our path have crost
 Or gild the torrent's spray.

Is yon a cot I saw, though low?
 When lightning broke the gloom— 10
How welcome were its shade!—ah, no!
 'Tis but a Turkish tomb.

Through sounds of foaming waterfalls,
 I hear a voice exclaim—
My way-worn countryman, who calls 15
 On distant England's name.

A shot is fired—by foe or friend?
 Another—'tis to tell
The mountain-peasants to descend,
 And lead us where they dwell. 20

Oh! who in such a night will dare
 To tempt the wilderness?
And who 'mid thunder-peals can hear
 Our signal of distress?

And who that heard our shouts would
 rise 25
 To try the dubious road?
Nor rather deem from nightly cries
 That outlaws were abroad.

Clouds burst, skies flash, oh, dreadful
 hour!
 More fiercely pours the storm! 30
Yet here one thought has still the power
 To keep my bosom warm.

While wandering through each broken
 path,
 O'er brake and craggy brow;
While elements exhaust their wrath, 35
 Sweet Florence, where art thou?

58

Not on the sea, not on the sea,
 Thy bark hath long been gone:
Oh, may the storm that pours on me
 Bow down my head alone! 40

Full swiftly blew the swift Siroc,
 When last I press'd thy lip;
And long ere now, with foaming shock
 Impell'd thy gallant ship.

Now thou art safe; nay, long ere now
 Hast trod the shore of Spain; 46
'Twere hard if aught so fair as thou
 Should linger on the main.

And since I now remember thee
 In darkness and in dread, 50
As in those hours of revelry
 Which mirth and music sped;

Do thou, amid the fair white walls,
 If Cadiz yet be free,
At times from out her latticed halls 55
 Look o'er the dark blue sea;

Then think upon Calypso's isles,
 Endear'd by days gone by;
To others give a thousand smiles,
 To me a single sigh. 60

And when the admiring circle mark
 The paleness of thy face,
A half-form'd tear, a transient spark
 Of melancholy grace,

Again thou'lt smile, and blushing shun
 Some coxcomb's raillery; 66
Nor own for once thou thought'st on one,
 Who ever thinks on thee.

Though smile and sigh alike are vain,
 When sever'd hearts repine, 70
My spirit flies o'er mount and main,
 And mourns in search of thine.

STANZAS WRITTEN IN PASSING THE AMBRACIAN GULF

Through cloudless skies, in silvery sheen,
 Full beams the moon on Actium's
 coast:
And on these waves, for Egypt's queen,
 The ancient world was won and lost.

And now upon the scene I look, 5
 The azure grave of many a Roman;
Where stern Ambition once forsook
 His wavering crown to follow woman.

Florence! whom I will love as well
 As ever yet was said or sung 10
(Since Orpheus sang his spouse from hell),
 Whilst thou art fair and I am young;

Sweet Florence! those were pleasant times,
 When worlds were staked for ladies'
 eyes: 14
Had bards as many realms as rhymes,
 Thy charms might raise new Antonies.

Though Fate forbids such things to be,
 Yet, by thine eyes and ringlets curl'd!
I cannot lose a world for thee,
 But would not lose thee for a world.
 Nov. 14, 1809.

THE SPELL IS BROKE, THE CHARM IS FLOWN!

WRITTEN AT ATHENS, JANUARY 16, 1810

The spell is broke, the charm is flown!
 Thus is it with life's fitful fever:
We madly smile when we should groan:
 Delirium is our best deceiver.

Each lucid interval of thought 5
 Recalls the woes of Nature's charter;
And he that acts as wise men ought,
 But lives, as saints have died, a martyr.

WRITTEN AFTER SWIMMING FROM SESTOS TO ABYDOS

If, in the month of dark December,
 Leander, who was nightly wont
(What maid will not the tale remember?)
 To cross thy stream, broad Hellespont!

If, when the wintry tempest roar'd, 5
 He sped to Hero, nothing loth,
And thus of old thy current pour'd,
 Fair Venus! how I pity both!

For *me*, degenerate modern wretch,
 Though in the genial month of May,
My dripping limbs I faintly stretch, 11
 And think I've done a feat to-day.

But since he cross'd the rapid tide,
 According to the doubtful story,
To woo,—and—Lord knows what be-
 side, 15
 And swam for Love, as I for Glory;

'Twere hard to say who fared the best:
 Sad mortals! thus the gods still plague
 you!
He lost his labour, I my jest; 19
 For he was drown'd, and I've the ague.
 May 9, 1810.

LINES IN THE TRAVELLERS' BOOK AT ORCHOMENUS

IN THIS BOOK A TRAVELLER HAD WRITTEN:—

'Fair Albion, smiling, sees her son depart
To trace the birth and nursery of art:
Noble his object, glorious is his aim;
He comes to Athens, and he writes his
 name.'

OCCASIONAL PIECES

THE modest bard, like many a bard un-
 known,
Rhymes on our names, but wisely hides
 his own;
But yet, whoe'er he be, to say no worse,
His name would bring more credit than
 his verse.

1810.

MAID OF ATHENS, ERE WE PART

Ζωή μου, σᾶς ἀγαπῶ.

MAID of Athens, ere we part,
Give, oh give me back my heart!
Or, since that has left my breast,
Keep it now, and take the rest!
Hear my vow before I go, 5
Ζωή μου, σᾶς ἀγαπῶ.

By those tresses unconfined,
Woo'd by each Ægean wind;
By those lids whose jetty fringe
Kiss thy soft cheeks' blooming tinge;
By those wild eyes like the roe, 11
Ζωή μου, σᾶς ἀγαπῶ.

By that lip I long to taste;
By that zone-encircled waist;
By all the token-flowers that tell 15
What words can never speak so well;
By love's alternate joy and woe,
Ζωή μου, σᾶς ἀγαπῶ.

Maid of Athens! I am gone:
Think of me, sweet! when alone. 20
Though I fly to Istambol,
Athens holds my heart and soul:
Can I cease to love thee? No!
Ζωή μου, σᾶς ἀγαπῶ.

Athens, 1810.

TRANSLATION OF THE NURSE'S DOLE IN THE MEDEA OF EURI-PIDES

OH how I wish that an embargo
Had kept in port the good ship Argo!
Who, still unlaunch'd from Grecian docks,
Had never pass'd the Azure rocks;
But now I fear her trip will be a 5
Damn'd business for my Miss Medea,
&c. &c.

June 1810.

MY EPITAPH

YOUTH, Nature, and relenting Jove,
To keep my lamp *in* strongly strove;
But Romanelli was so stout,
He beat all three—and *blew* it *out*.

Oct. 1810.

SUBSTITUTE FOR AN EPITAPH

KIND Reader! take your choice to cry or
 laugh;
Here HAROLD lies—but where's his Epi-
 taph?
If such you seek, try Westminster, and
 view
Ten thousand just as fit for him as you.

Athens

LINES WRITTEN BENEATH A PICTURE

DEAR object of defeated care!
 Though now of Love and thee bereft,
To reconcile me with despair,
 Thine image and my tears are left.

'Tis said with Sorrow Time can cope;
 But this I feel can ne'er be true:
For by the death-blow of my Hope
 My Memory immortal grew.

Athens, *January* 1811

TRANSLATION OF THE FAMOUS GREEK WAR SONG

Δεῦτε παῖδες τῶν Ἑλλήνων.

SONS of the Greeks, arise!
 The glorious hour's gone forth,
And, worthy of such ties,
 Display who gave us birth.

CHORUS.

Sons of Greeks! let us go
In arms against the foe,
Till their hated blood shall flow
In a river past our feet.

Then manfully despising
 The Turkish tyrant's yoke, 10
Let your country see you rising,
 And all her chains are broke.
Brave shades of chiefs and sages,
 Behold the coming strife!
Hellénes of past ages, 15
 Oh, start again to life!
At the sound of my trumpet, breaking
 Your sleep, oh, join with me!
And the seven-hill'd city seeking,
 Fight, conquer, till we're free. 20

Sons of Greeks, &c

Sparta, Sparta, why in slumbers
 Lethargic dost thou lie?
Awake, and join thy numbers
 With Athens, old ally!
Leonidas recalling, 25
 That chief of ancient song,
Who saved ye once from falling,
 The terrible! the strong!

Who made that bold diversion
In old Thermopylæ, 30
And warring with the Persian
To keep his country free;
With his three hundred waging
The battle, long he stood,
And like a lion raging, 35
Expired in seas of blood.

Sons of Greeks, &c.

TRANSLATION OF THE ROMAIC SONG

"Μπένω μες' τὸ περιβόλι
'Ωραιοτάτη Χαηδή," κ.τ.λ.

I ENTER thy garden of roses,
Beloved and fair Haidée,
Each morning where Flora reposes,
For surely I see her in thee.
Oh, Lovely! thus low I implore thee, 5
Receive this fond truth from my
tongue,
Which utters its song to adore thee,
Yet trembles for what it has sung;
As the branch, at the bidding of Nature,
Adds fragrance and fruit to the tree,
Through her eyes, through her every
feature, 11
Shines the soul of the young Haidée.

But the loveliest garden grows hateful
When Love has abandon'd the bowers;
Bring me hemlock—since mine is un-
grateful, 15
That herb is more fragrant than flowers.
The poison, when pour'd from the chalice,
Will deeply embitter the bowl;
But when drunk to escape from thy malice,
The draught shall be sweet to my soul.
Too cruel! in vain I implore thee 21
My heart from these horrors to save:
Will nought to my bosom restore thee?
Then open the gates of the grave.

As the chief who to combat advances 25
Secure of his conquest before,
Thus thou, with those eyes for thy lances,
Hast pierced through my heart to its
core.
Ah, tell me, my soul! must I perish
By pangs which a smile would dispel?
Would the hope, which thou once bad'st
me cherish, 31
For torture repay me too well?
Now sad is the garden of roses,
Beloved but false Haidée!
There Flora all wither'd reposes, 35
And mourns o'er thine absence with me.
 1811.

ON PARTING

THE kiss, dear maid! thy lip has left
Shall never part from mine,
Till happier hours restore the gift
Untainted back to thine.

Thy parting glance, which fondly beams,
An equal love may see: 6
The tear that from thine eyelid streams
Can weep no change in me.

I ask no pledge to make me blest
In gazing when alone; 10
Nor one memorial for a breast,
Whose thoughts are all thine own.

Nor need I write—to tell the tale
My pen were doubly weak:
Oh! what can idle words avail, 15
Unless the heart could speak?

By day or night, in weal or woe,
That heart, no longer free,
Must bear the love it cannot show,
And silent ache for thee. 20
 March 1811.

EPITAPH FOR JOSEPH BLACKETT, LATE POET AND SHOEMAKER

STRANGER! behold, interr'd together,
The *souls* of learning and of leather.
Poor Joe is gone, but left his *all:*
You'll find his relics in a *stall.*
His works were neat, and often found 5
Well stitch'd, and with *morocco* bound.
Tread lightly—where the bard is laid
He cannot mend the shoe he made;
Yet is he happy in his hole,
With verse immortal as his *sole.* 10
But still to business he held fast,
And stuck to Phœbus to the last.
Then who shall say so good a fellow
Was only 'leather and prunella?'
For character—he did not lack it; 15
And if he did, 'twere shame to 'Black it.'
 Malta, *May* 16, 1811.

FAREWELL TO MALTA

ADIEU, ye joys of La Valette!
Adieu, sirocco, sun, and sweat!
Adieu, thou palace rarely enter'd!
Adieu, ye mansions where—I've ventured!
Adieu, ye cursed streets of stairs! 5
(How surely he who mounts you swears!)
Adieu, ye merchants often failing!
Adieu, thou mob for ever railing!
Adieu, ye packets—without letters!
Adieu, ye fools—who ape your betters!
Adieu, thou damned'st quarantine, 11
That gave me fever, and the spleen!
Adieu, that stage which makes us yawn,
Sirs,
Adieu, his Excellency's dancers!
Adieu to Peter—whom no fault's in, 15
But could not teach a colonel waltzing;
Adieu, ye females fraught with graces!
Adieu, red coats, and redder faces!
Adieu, the supercilious air
Of all that strut 'en militaire'! 20

61

OCCASIONAL PIECES

I go—but God knows when, or why,
To smoky towns and cloudy sky,
To things (the honest truth to say)
As bad—but in a different way.

Farewell to these, but not adieu, 25
Triumphant sons of truest blue!
While either Adriatic shore,
And fallen chiefs, and fleets no more,
And nightly smiles, and daily dinners,
Proclaim you war and woman's winners.
Pardon my Muse, who apt to prate is,
And take my rhyme—because 'tis 'gratis.'

And now I've got to Mrs. Fraser,
Perhaps you think I mean to praise her—
And were I vain enough to think 35
My praise was worth this drop of ink,
A line—or two—were no hard matter,
As here, indeed, I need not flatter:
But she must be content to shine
In better praises than in mine, 40
With lively air, and open heart,
And fashion's ease, without its art;
Her hours can gaily glide along,
Nor ask the aid of idle song.

And now, O Malta! since thou'st got us,
Thou little military hothouse! 46
I'll not offend with words uncivil,
And wish thee rudely at the Devil,
But only stare from out my casement,
And ask, for what is such a place meant?
Then, in my solitary nook, 51
Return to scribbling, or a book,
Or take my physic while I'm able
(Two spoonfuls hourly by the label),
Prefer my nightcap to my beaver, 55
And bless the gods I've got a fever.

May 26, 1811.
[First published, 1816.]

TO DIVES

A FRAGMENT

UNHAPPY DIVES! in an evil hour
'Gainst Nature's voice seduced to deeds
 accurst!
Once Fortune's minion, now thou feel'st
 her power;
Wrath's vial on thy lofty head hath
 burst. 4
In Wit, in Genius, as in Wealth the first,
How wondrous bright thy blooming morn
 arose!
But thou wert smitten with th' unhallow'd
 thirst
Of crime un-named, and thy sad noon
 must close
In scorn, and solitude unsought, the worst
 of woes.

1811. [First published, 1832.]

ON MOORE'S LAST OPERATIC FARCE, OR FARCICAL OPERA

GOOD plays are scarce,
So Moore writes farce:
The poet's fame grows brittle—
 We knew before
 That *Little*'s Moore,
But now 'tis *Moore* that's *little*.

September 14, 1811.
[First published, 1830.]

EPISTLE TO A FRIEND

IN ANSWER TO SOME LINES EXHORTING THE
AUTHOR TO BE CHEERFUL, AND TO 'BAN-
ISH CARE'

'OH! banish care'—such ever be
The motto of *thy* revelry!
Perchance of *mine*, when wassail nights
Renew those riotous delights,
Wherewith the children of Despair 5
Lull the lone heart, and 'banish care.'
But not in morn's reflecting hour,
When present, past, and future lower,
When all I loved is changed or gone, 9
Mock with such taunts the woes of one,
Whose every thought—but let them pass—
Thou know'st I am not what I was.
But, above all, if thou wouldst hold
Place in a heart that ne'er was cold,
By all the powers that men revere, 15
By all unto thy bosom dear,
Thy joys below, thy hopes above,
Speak—speak of anything but love.

'Twere long to tell, and vain to hear,
The tale of one who scorns a tear; 20
And there is little in that tale
Which better bosoms would bewail.
But mine has suffer'd more than well
'Twould suit philosophy to tell.
I've seen my bride another's bride,— 25
Have seen her seated by his side,—
Have seen the infant, which she bore,
Wear the sweet smile the mother wore,
When she and I in youth have smiled,
As fond and faultless as her child; 30
Have seen her eyes, in cold disdain,
Ask if I felt no secret pain;
And *I* have acted well my part,
And made my cheek belie my heart,
Return'd the freezing glance she gave,
Yet felt the while *that* woman's slave;—
Have kiss'd, as if without design,
The babe which ought to have been mine,
And show'd, alas! in each caress
Time had not made me love the less. 40

But let this pass—I'll whine no more,
Nor seek again an eastern shore;
The world befits a busy brain,—
I'll hie me to its haunts again.

62

But if, in some succeeding year, 45
 When Britain's 'May is in the sere,'
Thou hear'st of one whose deepening crimes
 Suit with the sablest of the times,
Of one, whom love nor pity sways,
 Nor hope of fame, nor good men's praise;
One, who in stern ambition's pride, 51
 Perchance not blood shall turn aside;
One rank'd in some recording page
 With the worst anarchs of the age,
Him wilt thou *know*—and *knowing* pause,
 Nor with the *effect* forget the cause. 56

 Newstead Abbey, *Oct.* 11, 1811.
 [First published, 1830.]

TO THYRZA

WITHOUT a stone to mark the spot,
 And say, what Truth might well have said,
By all, save one, perchance forgot,
 Ah! wherefore art thou lowly laid?

By many a shore and many a sea 5
 Divided, yet beloved in vain;
The past, the future fled to thee,
 To bid us meet—no—ne'er again!

Could this have been—a word, a look,
 That softly said, 'We part in peace,'
Had taught my bosom how to brook, 11
 With fainter sighs, thy soul's release.

And didst thou not, since Death for thee
 Prepared a light and pangless dart,
Once long for him thou ne'er shalt see,
 Who held, and holds thee in his heart?

Oh! who like him had watch'd thee here?
 Or sadly mark'd thy glazing eye,
In that dread hour ere death appear,
 When silent sorrow fears to sigh, 20

Till all was past? But when no more
 'Twas thine to reck of human woe,
Affection's heart-drops, gushing o'er,
 Had flow'd as fast—as now they flow.

Shall they not flow, when many a day
 In these, to me, deserted towers, 26
Ere call'd but for a time away,
 Affection's mingling tears were ours?

Ours too the glance none saw beside;
 The smile none else might understand;
The whisper'd thought of hearts allied,
 The pressure of the thrilling hand; 32

The kiss, so guiltless and refined,
 That Love each warmer wish forbore;
Those eyes proclaim'd so pure a mind,
 Even Passion blush'd to plead for more.

The tone, that taught me to rejoice,
 When prone, unlike thee, to repine;
The song, celestial from thy voice,
 But sweet to me from none but thine;

The pledge we wore—I wear it still, 41
 But where is thine?—Ah! where art thou?
Oft have I borne the weight of ill,
 But never bent beneath till now!

Well hast thou left in life's best bloom
 The cup of woe for me to drain. 46
If rest alone be in the tomb,
 I would not wish thee here again.

But if in worlds more blest than this
 Thy virtues seek a fitter sphere, 50
Impart some portion of thy bliss,
 To wean me from mine anguish here.

Teach me—too early taught by thee!
 To bear, forgiving and forgiven:
On earth thy love was such to me; 55
 It fain would form my hope in heaven!

 October 11, 1811.

AWAY, AWAY, YE NOTES OF WOE!

AWAY, away, ye notes of woe!
 Be silent, thou once soothing strain,
Or I must flee from hence—for, oh!
 I dare not trust those sounds again.
To me they speak of brighter days— 5
 But lull the chords, for now, alas!
I must not think, I may not gaze,
 On what I am—on what I was.

The voice that made those sounds more sweet
 Is hush'd, and all their charms are fled
And now their softest notes repeat 11
 A dirge, an anthem o'er the dead!
Yes, Thyrza! yes, they breathe of thee,
 Beloved dust! since dust thou art;
And all that once was harmony 15
 Is worse than discord to my heart!

'Tis silent all!—but on my ear
 The well remember'd echoes thrill;
I hear a voice I would not hear, 19
 A voice that now might well be still:
Yet oft my doubting soul 'twill shake;
 Even slumber owns its gentle tone,
Till consciousness will vainly wake
 To listen, though the dream be flown.

Sweet Thyrza! waking as in sleep, 25
 Thou art but now a lovely dream;
A star that trembled o'er the deep,
 Then turn'd from earth its tender beam.
But he who through life's dreary way
 Must pass, when heaven is veil'd in wrath, 30
Will long lament the vanish'd ray
 That scatter'd gladness o'er his path.

 December 6, 1811.

ONE STRUGGLE MORE, AND I AM FREE

ONE struggle more, and I am free
From pangs that rend my heart in twain;
One last long sigh to love and thee,
Then back to busy life again.
It suits me well to mingle now 5
With things that never pleased before!
Though every joy is fled below,
What future grief can touch me more?

Then bring me wine, the banquet bring;
Man was not form'd to live alone: 10
I'll be that light, unmeaning thing
That smiles with all, and weeps with
none.
It was not thus in days more dear,
It never would have been, but thou
Hast fled, and left me lonely here; 15
Thou'rt nothing—all are nothing now.

In vain my lyre would lightly breathe!
The smile that sorrow fain would wear
But mocks the woe that lurks beneath,
Like roses o'er a sepulchre. 20
Though gay companions o'er the bowl
Dispel awhile the sense of ill:
Though pleasure fires the maddening soul,
The heart,—the heart is lonely still!

On many a lone and lovely night 25
It sooth'd to gaze upon the sky;
For then I deem'd the heavenly light
Shone sweetly on thy pensive eye:
And oft I thought at Cynthia's noon,
When sailing o'er the Ægean wave,
'Now Thyrza gazes on that moon'—
Alas, it gleam'd upon her grave! 32

When stretch'd on fever's sleepless bed,
And sickness shrunk my throbbing
veins,
'Tis comfort still,' I faintly said, 35
'That Thyrza cannot know my pains:'
Like freedom to the time-worn slave,
A boon 'tis idle then to give,
Relenting Nature vainly gave
My life, when Thyrza ceased to live!

My Thyrza's pledge in better days, 41
When love and life alike were new!
How different now thou meet'st my gaze!
How tinged by time with sorrow's hue!
The heart that gave itself with thee 45
Is silent—ah, were mine as still!
Though cold as e'en the dead can be,
It feels, it sickens with the chill.

Thou bitter pledge! thou mournful token!
Though painful, welcome to my breast!
Still, still preserve that love unbroken,
Or break the heart to which thou'rt
press'd.

Time tempers love, but not removes,
More hallow'd when its hope is fled:
Oh! what are thousand living loves 55
To that which cannot quit the dead?

EUTHANASIA

WHEN Time, or soon or late, shall bring
The dreamless sleep that lulls the dead,
Oblivion! may thy languid wing
Wave gently o'er my dying bed!

No band of friends or heirs be there, 5
To weep, or wish, the coming blow:
No maiden, with dishevelled hair,
To feel, or feign, decorous woe.

But silent let me sink to earth,
With no officious mourners near: 10
I would not mar one hour of mirth,
Nor startle friendship with a tear.

Yet Love, if Love in such an hour
Could nobly check its useless sighs,
Might then exert its latest power 15
In her who lives, and him who dies.

'Twere sweet, my Psyche! to the last
Thy features still serene to see:
Forgetful of its struggles past,
E'en Pain itself should smile on thee.

But vain the wish—for Beauty still 21
Will shrink, as shrinks the ebbing
breath;
And women's tears, produced at will,
Deceive in life, unman in death.

Then lonely be my latest hour, 25
Without regret, without a groan;
For thousands Death hath ceas'd to lower,
And pain been transient or unknown.

'Ay, but to die, and go,' alas!
Where all have gone, and all must go!
To be the nothing that I was 31
Ere born to life and living woe!

Count o'er the joys thine hours have seen,
Count o'er thy days from anguish free,
And know, whatever thou hast been, 35
'Tis something better not to be.

AND THOU ART DEAD, AS YOUNG AND FAIR

'Heu, quanto minus est cum reliquis versari
quam tui meminisse!'

AND thou art dead, as young and fair
As aught of mortal birth;
And form so soft, and charms so rare,
Too soon return'd to Earth!

Though Earth received them in her bed 5
And o'er the spot the crowd may tread
 In carelessness or mirth,
There is an eye which could not brook
A moment on that grave to look.

I will not ask where thou liest low, 10
 Nor gaze upon the spot;
There flowers or weeds at will may grow,
 So I behold them not:
It is enough for me to prove
That what I loved, and long must love,
 Like common earth can rot; 16
To me there needs no stone to tell,
Tis Nothing that I loved so well.

Yet did I love thee to the last
 As fervently as thou, 20
Who didst not change through all the past,
 And canst not alter now.
The love where Death has set his seal,
Nor age can chill, nor rival steal,
 Nor falsehood disavow: 25
And, what were worse, thou canst not see
Or wrong, or change, or fault in me.

The better days of life were ours;
 The worst can be but mine:
The sun that cheers, the storm that lowers,
 Shall never more be thine. 31
The silence of that dreamless sleep
I envy now too much to weep;
 Nor need I to repine,
That all those charms have pass'd away
I might have watch'd through long decay.

The flower in ripen'd bloom unmatch'd
 Must fall the earliest prey;
Though by no hand untimely snatch'd,
 The leaves must drop away: 40
And yet it were a greater grief
To watch it withering, leaf by leaf,
 Than see it pluck'd to-day;
Since earthly eye but ill can bear
To trace the change to foul from fair.

I know not if I could have borne 46
 To see thy beauties fade;
The night that follow'd such a morn
 Had worn a deeper shade:
Thy day without a cloud hath pass'd, 50
And thou wert lovely to the last;
 Extinguish'd, not decay'd;
As stars that shoot along the sky
Shine brightest as they fall from high.

As once I wept, if I could weep, 55
 My tears might well be shed,
To think I was not near to keep
 One vigil o'er thy bed;
To gaze, how fondly! on thy face,
To fold thee in a faint embrace, 60
 Uphold thy drooping head;
And show that love, however vain,
Nor thou nor I can feel again.

Yet how much less it were to gain,
 Though thou hast left me free, 65
The loveliest things that still remain,
 Than thus remember thee!
The all of thine that cannot die
Through dark and dread Eternity
 Returns again to me, 70
And more thy buried love endears
Than aught except its living years.
 February 1812.

IF SOMETIMES IN THE HAUNTS OF MEN

IF sometimes in the haunts of men
 Thine image from my breast may fade,
The lonely hour presents again
 The semblance of thy gentle shade:
And now that sad and silent hour 5
 Thus much of thee can still restore,
And sorrow unobserved may pour
 The plaint she dare not speak before.

Oh, pardon that in crowds awhile
 I waste one thought I owe to thee, 10
And self-condemn'd, appear to smile,
 Unfaithful to thy memory:
Nor deem that memory less dear,
 That then I seem not to repine;
I would not fools should overhear 15
 One sigh that should be wholly *thine*.

If not the goblet pass unquaff'd,
 It is not drain'd to banish care;
The cup must hold a deadlier draught,
 That brings a Lethe for despair. 20
And could Oblivion set my soul
 From all her troubled visions free,
I'd dash to earth the sweetest bowl
 That drown'd a single thought of thee.

For wert thou vanish'd from my mind, 25
 Where could my vacant bosom turn?
And who would then remain behind
 To honour thine abandon'd Urn?
No, no—it is my sorrow's pride
 That last dear duty to fulfil: 30
Though all the world forget beside,
 'Tis meet that I remember still.

For well I know, that such had been
 Thy gentle care for him, who now 34
Unmourn'd shall quit this mortal scene,
 Where none regarded him, but thou:
And, oh! I feel in *that* was given
 A blessing never meant for me;
Thou wert too like a dream of Heaven
 For earthly Love to merit thee. 40
 March 14, 1812.

FROM THE FRENCH

ÆGLE, beauty and poet, has two little
 crimes;
She makes her own face, and does not
 make her rhymes.

OCCASIONAL PIECES

ON A CORNELIAN HEART WHICH WAS BROKEN

ILL-FATED Heart! and can it be,
 That thou should'st thus be rent in
 twain?
Have years of care for thine and thee
 Alike been all employ'd in vain?

Yet precious seems each shatter'd part,
 And every fragment dearer grown, 6
Since he who wears thee feels thou art
 A fitter emblem of *his* own.

March 16, 1812.

LINES TO A LADY WEEPING

WEEP, daughter of a royal line,
 A Sire's disgrace, a realm's decay;
Ah! happy if each tear of thine
 Could wash a father's fault away!

Weep—for thy tears are Virtue's tears—
 Auspicious to these suffering isles; 6
And be each drop in future years
 Repaid thee by thy people's smiles!

March 1812.

THE CHAIN I GAVE

FROM THE TURKISH

THE chain I gave was fair to view,
 The lute I added sweet in sound;
The heart that offer'd both was true,
 And ill deserved the fate it found.

These gifts were charm'd by secret spell,
 Thy truth in absence to divine; 6
And they have done their duty well,—
 Alas! they could not teach thee thine.

That chain was firm in every link,
 But not to bear a stranger's touch; 10
That lute was sweet—till thou could'st
 think
 In other hands its notes were such.

Let him who from thy neck unbound
 The chain which shiver'd in his grasp,
Who saw that lute refuse to sound, 15
 Restring the chords, renew the clasp.

When thou wert changed, they alter'd too;
 The chain is broke, the music mute:
'Tis past—to them and thee adieu—
 False heart, frail chain, and silent lute.

LINES WRITTEN ON A BLANK LEAF OF 'THE PLEASURES OF MEMORY'

ABSENT or present, still to thee,
 My friend, what magic spells belong!
As all can tell, who share, like me,
 In turn thy converse and thy song. 4

But when the dreaded hour shall come
 By Friendship ever deem'd too nigh,
And 'MEMORY' o'er her Druid's tomb
 Shall weep that aught of thee can die,

How fondly will she then repay
 Thy homage offer'd at her shrine, 10
And blend, while ages roll away,
 Her name immortally with *thine!*

April 19, 1812.

ADDRESS, SPOKEN AT THE OPENING OF DRURY-LANE THEATRE

SATURDAY, OCTOBER 10, 1812

IN one dread night our city saw, and sigh'd
Bow'd to the dust, the Drama's tower of
 pride;
In one short hour beheld the blazing fane,
Apollo sink, and Shakspeare cease to
 reign.

Ye who beheld, (oh! sight admired and
 mourn'd,
Whose radiance mock'd the ruin it
 adorn'd!)
Through clouds of fire the massy fragments riven,
Like Israel's pillar, chase the night from
 heaven;
Saw the long column of revolving flame
Shake its red shadow o'er the startled
 Thames, 10
While thousands, throng'd around the
 burning dome,
Shrank back appall'd, and trembled for
 their home,
As glared the volumed blaze, and ghastly
 shone
The skies, with lightnings awful as their
 own, 15
Till blackening ashes and the lonely wall
Usurp'd the Muse's realm, and mark'd
 her fall;
Say—shall this new, nor less aspiring pile,
Rear'd where once rose the mightiest in
 our isle,
Know the same favour which the former
 knew, 20
A shrine for Shakspeare—worthy him
 and *you?*

Yes—it shall be—the magic of that
 name
Defies the scythe of time, the torch of
 flame;
On the same spot still consecrates the
 scene,
And bids the Drama *be* where she hath
 been: 25
This fabric's birth attests the potent
 spell—
Indulge our honest pride, and say, *How
 well!*

66

As soars this fane to emulate the last,
Oh! might we draw our omens from the
past,
Some hour propitious to our prayers may
boast
Names such as hallow still the dome we
lost. 30
On Drury first your Siddons' thrilling art
O'erwhelm'd the gentlest, storm'd the
sternest heart.
On Drury, Garrick's latest laurels grew;
Here your last tears retiring Roscius drew,
Sigh'd his last thanks, and wept his last
adieu: 35
But still for living wit the wreaths may
bloom,
That only waste their odours o'er the
tomb.
Such Drury claim'd and claims—nor you
refuse
One tribute to revive his slumbering
muse;
With garlands deck your own Menander's
head, 40
Nor hoard your honours idly for the dead.
Dear are the days which made our annals
bright,
Ere Garrick fled, or Brinsley ceased to
write.
Heirs to their labours, like all high-born
heirs,
Vain of *our* ancestry as they of *theirs*;
While thus Remembrance borrows Ban-
quo's glass 46
To claim the sceptred shadows as they
pass,
And we the mirror hold, where imaged
shine
Immortal names, emblazon'd on our line,
Pause—ere their feebler offspring you
condemn, 50
Reflect how hard the task to rival them!

Friends of the stage! to whom both
Players and Plays
Must sue alike for pardon or for praise,
Whose judging voice and eye alone direct
The boundless power to cherish or reject;
If e'er frivolity has led to fame, 56
And made us blush that you forbore to
blame;
If e'er the sinking stage could condescend
To soothe the sickly taste it dare not mend,
All past reproach may present scenes re-
fute, 60
And censure, wisely loud, be justly mute!
Oh! since your fiat stamps the Drama's
laws,
Forbear to mock us with misplaced ap-
plause;
So pride shall doubly nerve the actor's
powers,
And reason's voice be echo'd back by
ours! 65

This greeting o'er, the ancient rule
obey'd,
The Drama's homage by her herald paid,
Receive *our* welcome too, whose every
tone
Springs from our hearts, and fain would
win your own.
The curtain rises—may our stage unfold
Scenes not unworthy Drury's days of old!
Britons our judges, Nature for our guide,
Still may *we* please—long, long may *you*
preside. 73

PARENTHETICAL ADDRESS

BY DR. PLAGIARY

Half stolen, with acknowledgments, to be spoken
in an inarticulate voice by Master P. at the open-
ing of the next new theatre. Stolen parts marked
with the inverted commas of quotation—thus
'——'.

'WHEN energising objects men pursue,'
Then Lord knows what is writ by Lord
knows who.
'A modest monologue you here survey,'
Hiss'd from the theatre the 'other day,'
As if Sir Fretful wrote 'the slumberous'
verse, 5
And gave his son 'the rubbish' to re-
hearse.
'Yet at the thing you'd never be amazed,'
Knew you the rumpus which the author
raised,
'Nor even here your smiles would be re-
prest,'
Knew you these lines—the badness of the
best, 10
'Flame! fire! and flame!' (words borrowed
from Lucretius,)
'Dread metaphors which open wounds'
like issues!
'And sleeping pangs awake—and—but
away'
(Confound me if I know what next to say).
'Lo Hope reviving re-expands her wings,'
And Master G—— recites what Dr. Busby
sings! 16
'If mighty things with small we may com-
pare,'
(Translated from the grammar for the
fair!)
Dramatic 'spirit drives a conquering car,'
And burn'd poor Moscow like a tub of
'tar.' 20
'This spirit Wellington has shown in
Spain,'
To furnish melodrames for Drury Lane.
'Another Marlborough points to Blen-
heim's story,'
And George and I will dramatise it for ye.

'In arts and sciences our isle hath
shone' 25
(This deep discovery is mine alone).

'Oh British poesy, whose powers inspire'
My verse—or I'm a fool—and Fame's a
 liar,
'Thee we invoke, your sister arts implore'
With 'smiles,' and 'lyres,' and 'pencils,'
 and much more. 30
These, if we win the Graces, too, we gain
Disgraces, too! 'inseparable train!'
'Three who have stolen their witching
 airs from Cupid'
(You all know what I mean, unless you're
 stupid):
'Harmonious throng' that I have kept *in
 petto* 35
Now to produce in a '*divine sestetto*'!!
'While Poesy,' with these delightful doxies,
'Sustains her part' in all the 'upper'
 boxes!
'Thus lifted gloriously, you'll soar along,'
Borne in the vast balloon of Busby's
 song; 40
'Shine in your farce, masque, scenery,
 and play'
(For this last line George had a holiday).
'Old Drury never, never soar'd so high,'
So says the manager, and so say I.
'But hold, you say, this self-complacent
 boast;' 45
Is this the poem which the public lost?
'True—true—that lowers at once our
 mounting pride;'
But lo:—the papers print what you
 deride.
''Tis ours to look on you—you hold the
 prize,'
'Tis *twenty guineas*, as they advertise! 50
'A double blessing your rewards impart'—
I wish I had them, then, with all my heart.
'Our *twofold* feeling *owns* its twofold
 cause,'
Why son and I both beg for your applause.
'When in your fostering beams you bid
 us live,' 55
My next subscription list shall say how
 much you give!
 October 1812.

VERSES FOUND IN A SUMMER-HOUSE AT HALES-OWEN

WHEN Dryden's fool, 'unknowing what
 he sought,'
His hours in whistling spent, 'for want of
 thought,'
This guiltless oaf his vacancy of sense
Supplied, and amply too, by innocence:
Did modern swains, possess'd of Cymon's
 powers, 5
In Cymon's manner waste their leisure
 hours,
Th' offended guests would not, with blush-
 ing, see
These fair green walks disgraced by in-
 famy.

Severe the fate of modern fools, alas!
When vice and folly mark them as they
 pass. 10
Like noxious reptiles o'er the whiten'd
 wall,
The filth they leave still points out where
 they crawl.

REMEMBER THEE! REMEMBER THEE!

REMEMBER thee! remember thee!
 Till Lethe quench life's burning stream
Remorse and shame shall cling to thee,
 And haunt thee like a feverish dream!

Remember thee! Ay, doubt it not.
 Thy husband too shall think of thee!
By neither shalt thou be forgot,
 Thou *false* to him, thou *fiend* to me!

TO TIME

TIME! on whose arbitrary wing
 The varying hours must flag or fly,
Whose tardy winter, fleeting spring,
 But drag or drive us on to die—

Hail thou! who on my birth bestow'd
 Those boons to all that know thee
 known;
Yet better I sustain thy load,
 For now I bear the weight alone.

I would not one fond heart should share
 The bitter moments thou hast given;
And pardon thee, since thou could'st
 spare
 All that I loved, to peace or heaven.

To them be joy or rest, on me
 Thy future ills shall press in vain;
I nothing owe but years to thee,
 A debt already paid in pain.

Yet even that pain was some relief,
 It felt, but still forgot thy power:
The active agony of grief
 Retards, but never counts the hour.

In joy I've sigh'd to think thy flight
 Would soon subside from swift to
 slow;
Thy cloud could overcast the light,
 But could not add a night to woe;

For then, however drear and dark,
 My soul was suited to thy sky;
One star alone shot forth a spark
 To prove thee—not Eternity.

That beam hath sunk, and now thou art
 A blank; a thing to count and curse,
Through each dull tedious trifling part,
 Which all regret, yet all rehearse. 3

One scene even thou canst not deform;
 The limit of thy sloth or speed
When future wanderers bear the storm
 Which we shall sleep too sound to
 heed: 36

And I can smile to think how weak
 Thine efforts shortly shall be shown,
When all the vengeance thou canst wreak
 Must fall upon—a nameless stone.

TRANSLATION OF A ROMAIC LOVE SONG

AH! Love was never yet without
 The pang, the agony, the doubt,
Which rends my heart with ceaseless sigh,
While day and night roll darkling by.

Without one friend to hear my woe, 5
 I faint, I die beneath the blow.
That Love had arrows well I knew;
 Alas! I find them poison'd too.

Birds, yet in freedom, shun the net
 Which Love around your haunts hath set;
Or, circled by his fatal fire, 11
 Your hearts shall burn, your hopes expire.

A bird of free and careless wing
 Was I through many a smiling spring;
But caught within the subtle snare, 15
 I burn, and feebly flutter there.

Who ne'er have loved, and loved in vain,
 Can neither feel nor pity pain,
The cold repulse, the look askance,
 The lightning of Love's angry glance. 20

In flattering dreams I deem'd thee mine;
 Now hope, and he who hoped, decline;
Like melting wax, or withering flower,
 I feel my passion, and thy power.

My light of life! ah, tell me why 25
 That pouting lip, and alter'd eye?
My bird of love! my beauteous mate!
 And art thou changed, and canst thou hate?

Mine eyes like wintry streams o'erflow:
 What wretch with me would barter woe?
My bird! relent: one note could give
 A charm to bid thy lover live. 32

My curdling blood, my madd'ning brain,
 In silent anguish I sustain;
And still thy heart, without partaking
 One pang, exults—while mine is breaking.

Pour me the poison; fear not thou!
 Thou canst not murder more than now:
I've lived to curse my natal day,
 And Love, that thus can lingering slay.

My wounded soul, my bleeding breast,
 Can patience preach thee into rest? 42
Alas! too late, I dearly know
 That joy is harbinger of woe.

THOU ART NOT FALSE, BUT THOU ART FICKLE

THOU art not false, but thou art fickle,
 To those thyself so fondly sought;
The tears that thou hast forced to trickle
 Are doubly bitter from that thought:
'Tis this which breaks the heart thou
 grievest, 5
Too well thou lov'st—too soon thou
 leavest.

The wholly false the heart despises,
 And spurns deceiver and deceit;
But she who not a thought disguises,
 Whose love is as sincere as sweet,—
When she can change who loved so truly,
 It feels what mine has felt so newly. 12

To dream of joy and wake to sorrow
 Is doom'd to all who love or live;
And if, when conscious on the morrow,
 We scarce our fancy can forgive, 16
That cheated us in slumber only,
To leave the waking soul more lonely,

What must they feel whom no false vision,
 But truest, tenderest passion warm'd?
Sincere, but swift in sad transition; 21
 As if a dream alone had charm'd?
Ah! sure such grief is fancy's scheming,
And all thy change can be but dreaming!

ON BEING ASKED WHAT WAS THE 'ORIGIN OF LOVE'

THE 'Origin of Love!'—Ah, why
 That cruel question ask of me,
When thou may'st read in many an eye
 He starts to life on seeing thee?

And should'st thou seek his *end* to
 know: 5
 My heart forebodes, my fears foresee,
He'll linger long in silent woe;
 But live—until I cease to be.

REMEMBER HIM WHOM PASSION'S POWER

REMEMBER him whom passion's power
 Severely, deeply, vainly proved;
Remember thou that dangerous hour,
 When neither fell, though both were
 loved. 4

That yielding breast, that melting eye,
 Too much invited to be bless'd:
That gentle prayer, that pleading sigh,
 The wilder wish reproved, repress'd.

Oh! let me feel that all I lost
 But saved thee all that conscience
 fears; 10
And blush for every pang it cost
 To spare the vain remorse of years.

OCCASIONAL PIECES

Yet think of this when many a tongue,
Whose busy accents whisper blame,
Would do the heart that loved thee wrong, 15
And brand a nearly blighted name.

Think that, whate'er to others, thou
Hast seen each selfish thought subdued:
I bless thy purer soul even now,
Even now, in midnight solitude. 20

Oh, God! that we had met in time,
Our hearts as fond, thy hand more free;
When thou hadst loved without a crime,
And I been less unworthy thee!

Far may thy days, as heretofore, 25
From this our gaudy world be past!
And that too bitter moment o'er,
Oh! may such trial be thy last.

This heart, alas! perverted long, 29
Itself destroy'd might there destroy;
To meet thee in the glittering throng,
Would wake Presumption's hope of joy.

Then to the things whose bliss or woe,
Like mine, is wild and worthless all,
That world resign—such scenes forego,
Where those who feel must surely fall.

Thy youth, thy charms, thy tenderness,
Thy soul from long seclusion pure;
From what even here hath pass'd, may guess
What there thy bosom must endure.

Oh! pardon that imploring tear, 41
Since not by Virtue shed in vain,
My frenzy drew from eyes so dear;
For me they shall not weep again.

Though long and mournful must it be,
The thought that we no more may meet; 46
Yet I deserve the stern decree,
And almost deem the sentence sweet.

Still, had I loved thee less, my heart
Had then less sacrificed to thine; 50
It felt not half so much to part
As if its guilt had made thee mine.
1813.

ON LORD THURLOW'S POEMS

WHEN Thurlow this damn'd nonsense sent
(I hope I am not violent),
Nor men nor gods knew what he meant.

And since not even our Rogers' praise
To common sense his thoughts could raise— 5
Why *would* they let him print his lays?
.
.

To me, divine Apollo, grant—O!
Hermilda's first and second canto,
I'm fitting up a new portmanteau;

And thus to furnish decent lining, 10
My own and others' bays I'm twining,—
So, gentle Thurlow, throw me thine in.

TO LORD THURLOW

'I lay my branch of laurel down,
Then thus to form Apollo's crown,
Let every other bring his own.'
Lord Thurlow's lines to Mr. Rogers

'*I lay my branch of laurel down.*'

THOU 'lay thy branch of *laurel* down!'
Why, what thou'st stole is not enow;
And, were it lawfully thine own,
Does Rogers want it most, or thou?
Keep to thyself thy wither'd bough, 5
Or send it back to Doctor Donne:
Were justice done to both, I trow,
He'd have but little, and thou—none.

'*Then thus to form Apollo's crown.*'

A crown! why, twist it how you will,
Thy chaplet must be foolscap still. 10
When next you visit Delphi's town,
Inquire amongst your fellow-lodgers,
They'll tell you Phœbus gave his crown,
Some years before your birth, to Rogers.

'*Let every other bring his own.*'

When coals to Newcastle are carried,
And owls sent to Athens, as wonders,
From his spouse when the Regent's unmarried, 17
Or Liverpool weeps o'er his blunders;
When Tories and Whigs cease to quarrel,
When Castlereagh's wife has an heir,
Then Rogers shall ask us for laurel,
And thou shalt have plenty to spare.

TO THOMAS MOORE

WRITTEN THE EVENING BEFORE HIS VISIT TO MR. LEIGH HUNT IN HORSEMONGER LANE GAOL, MAY 19, 1813

OH you, who in all names can tickle the town,
Anacreon, Tom Little, Tom Moore, or Tom Brown,
For hang me if I know of which you may most brag,
Your Quarto two-pounds, or your Two-penny Post Bag;
.
But now to my letter—to *yours* 'tis an answer— 5
To-morrow be with me, as soon as you can, sir,
All ready and dress'd for proceeding to spunge on
(According to compact) the wit in the dungeon—

Pray Phœbus at length our political ma-
lice
May not get us lodgings within the same
palace! 10
I suppose that to-night you're engaged
with some codgers,
And for Sotheby's Blues have deserted
Sam Rogers;
And I, though with cold I have nearly
my death got,
Must put on my breeches, and wait on
the Heathcote;
But to-morrow, at four, we will both
play the *Scurra*, 15
And you'll be Catullus, the Regent
Mamurra.

[First published in 1830.]

IMPROMPTU, IN REPLY TO A FRIEND

WHEN, from the heart where Sorrow sits,
Her dusky shadow mounts too high,
And o'er the changing aspect flits,
 And clouds the brow, or fills the eye;
Heed not that gloom, which soon shall
sink: 5
 My thoughts their dungeon know too
well;
Back to my breast the wanderers shrink,
 And droop within their silent cell.

September 1813.

SONNET, TO GENEVRA

THINE eyes' blue tenderness, thy long
fair hair,
 And the wan lustre of thy features—
caught
From contemplation—where serenely
wrought,
Seems Sorrow's softness charm'd from
its despair—
Have thrown such speaking sadness in
thine air, 5
 That—but I know thy blessed bosom
fraught
With mines of unalloy'd and stainless
thought—
I should have deem'd thee doom'd to
earthly care.
With such an aspect, by his colours blent,
 When from his beauty-breathing pen-
cil born 10
(Except that *thou* hast nothing to repent),
 The Magdalen of Guido saw the
morn—
Such seem'st thou—but how much more
excellent!
 With nought Remorse can claim—nor
Virtue scorn.

December 17, 1813.

SONNET, TO THE SAME

THY cheek is pale with thought, but not
from woe,
 And yet so lovely, that if Mirth could
flush
 Its rose of whiteness with the brightest
blush,
My heart would wish away that ruder
glow:
And dazzle not thy deep-blue eyes—but,
oh! 5
 While gazing on them sterner eyes will
gush,
 And into mine my mother's weakness
rush,
Soft as the last drops round heaven's
airy bow.
For, through thy long dark lashes low
depending,
 The soul of melancholy Gentleness
Gleams like a seraph from the sky de-
scending, 11
 Above all pain, yet pitying all distress;
At once such majesty with sweetness
blending,
 I worship more, but cannot love thee
less.

December 17, 1813.

FROM THE PORTUGUESE

'TU MI CHAMAS'

IN moments to delight devoted,
 'My life!' with tenderest tone, you cry;
Dear words! on which my heart had doted,
 If youth could neither fade nor die.

To death even hours like these must roll,
 Ah! then repeat those accents never;
Or change 'my life!' into 'my soul!'
 Which, like my love, exists for ever.

ANOTHER VERSION

YOU call me still your *life*.—Oh! change
the word—
Life is as transient as the inconstant
sigh:
Say rather I'm your soul; more just that
name,
For, like the soul, my love can never die.

THE DEVIL'S DRIVE

AN UNFINISHED RHAPSODY

THE Devil return'd to hell by two,
 And he stay'd at home till five;
When he dined on some homicides done
in *ragoût*,
 And a rebel or so in an *Irish* stew,
And sausages made of a self-slain Jew—
And bethought himself what next to do,
 'And,' quoth he, 'I'll take a drive. 7
I walk'd in the morning, I'll ride to-night;
In darkness my children take most delight,
 And I'll see how my favourites thrive,

71

'And what shall I ride in?' quoth Lucifer
 then—
 'If I follow'd my taste, indeed,
I should mount in a waggon of wounded
 men,
 And smile to see them bleed.
But these will be furnish'd again and
 again, 15
 And at present my purpose is speed;
To see my manor as much as I may,
 And watch that no souls shall be poach'd
 away.

'I have a state-coach at Carlton House,
 A chariot in Seymour Place; 20
But they're lent to two friends, who
 make me amends,
 By driving my favourite pace:
And they handle their reins with such
 a grace,
 I have something for both at the end of
 their race.

'So now for the earth to take my chance:'
 Then up to the earth sprung he; 26
And making a jump from Moscow to
 France,
 He stepp'd across the sea,
And rested his hoof on a turnpike road,
 No very great way from a bishop's
 abode. 30

But first as he flew, I forgot to say
That he hover'd a moment upon his way,
 To look upon Leipsic plain;
And so sweet to his eye was its sulphury
 glare,
And so soft to his ear was the cry of
 despair, 35
 That he perch'd on a mountain of
 slain:
And he gazed with delight from its grow-
 ing height,
 Nor often on earth had he seen such a
 sight,
 Nor his work done half as well:
For the field ran so red with the blood of
 the dead, 40
 That it blush'd like the waves of hell!
Then loudly, and wildly, and long laugh'd
 he:
 'Methinks they have here little need of
 me!' 43

But the softest note that soothed his ear
 Was the sound of a widow sighing;
And the sweetest sight was the icy tear,
 Which horror froze in the blue eye clear
Of a maid by her lover lying—
 As round her fell her long fair hair;
And she look'd to heaven with that
 frenzied air, 50
 Which seem'd to ask if a God were there!
And, stretch'd by the wall of a ruin'd hut,

With its hollow cheek, and eyes half shut,
 A child of famine dying:
And the carnage begun, when resistance
 is done, 55
 And the fall of the vainly flying!

But the Devil has reach'd our cliffs so
 white,
 And what did he there, I pray?
If his eyes were good, he but saw by
 night
 What we see every day: 60
But he coachman a tour, and kept a journal
Of all the wondrous sights nocturnal,
 And he sold it in shares to the *Men* of
 the *Row*,
 Who bid pretty well—but they *cheated*
 him, though!

The Devil first saw, as he thought, the
 Mail, 65
 Its coachman and his coat;
So instead of a pistol he cock'd his tail,
 And seized him by the throat:
'Aha!' quoth he, 'what have we here?
'Tis a new barouche, and an ancient
 peer!' 70

So he sat him on his box again,
 And bade him have no fear,
But be true to his club, and stanch to
 his rein,
 His brothel, and his beer;
'Next to seeing a lord at the council
 board, 75
 I would rather see him here.'

The Devil gat next to Westminster,
 And he turn'd to 'the room' of the
 Commons;
But he heard, as he purposed to enter in
 there,
 That 'the Lords' had received a sum-
 mons; 80
And he thought, as a '*quondam* aristocrat,'
 He might peep at the peers, though to
 hear them were flat;
And he walk'd up the house so like one
 of our own,
 That they say that he stood pretty near
 the throne.

He saw the Lord Liverpool seemingly
 wise, 85
 The Lord Westmoreland certainly
 silly,
And Johnny of Norfolk—a man of some
 size—
 And Chatham, so like his friend Billy;
And he saw the tears in Lord Eldon's
 eyes,
 Because the Catholics would *not* rise,
In spite of his prayers and his prophe-
 cies; 91

72

And he heard—which set Satan himself
 a staring—
A certain Chief Justice say something
 like *swearing*.
And the Devil was shock'd—and quoth
 he, 'I must go,
For I find we have much better manners
 below: 95
If thus he harangues when he passes my
 border,
I shall hint to friend Moloch to call him
 to order.'

WINDSOR POETICS

Lines composed on the occasion of His Royal
Highness the Prince Regent being seen standing
between the coffins of Henry VIII and Charles I,
in the royal vault at Windsor.

FAMED for contemptuous breach of sac-
 red ties,
By headless Charles see heartless Henry
 lies;
Between them stands another sceptred
 thing—
It moves, it reigns—in all but name, a
 king: 4

Charles to his people, Henry to his wife,
—In him the double tyrant starts to life:
Justice and death have mix'd their dust
 in vain,
Each royal vampire wakes to life again.
Ah, what can tombs avail!—since these
 disgorge
The blood and dust of both—to mould
 a George. 10

ODE TO NAPOLEON
BUONAPARTE

'Expende Annibalem:—quot libras in duce
 summo
Invenies?'—JUVENAL, *Sat.* x.

'The Emperor Nepos was acknowledged by the
Senate, by the Italians, and by the Provincials of
Gaul; his moral virtues, and military talents,
were loudly celebrated; and those who derived
any private benefit from his government an-
nounced in prophetic strains the restoration of
public felicity.... By this shameful abdication,
he protracted his life a few years, in a very am-
biguous state, between an Emperor and an
Exile, till ———.'—GIBBON'S *Decline and Fall*,
vol. vi, p. 220.

I

'TIS done—but yesterday a King!
 And arm'd with Kings to strive—
And now thou art a nameless thing:
 So abject—yet alive!
Is this the man of thousand thrones,
Who strew'd our earth with hostile bones,
 And can he thus survive?
Since he, miscall'd the Morning Star,
Nor man nor fiend hath fallen so far.

II

Ill-minded man! why scourge thy kind
 Who bow'd so low the knee?
By gazing on thyself grown blind,
 Thou taught'st the rest to see.
With might unquestion'd,—power to
 save,—
Thine only gift hath been the grave
 To those that worshipp'd thee;
Nor till thy fall could mortals guess
Ambition's less than littleness!

III

Thanks for that lesson—It will teach
 To after-warriors more
Than high Philosophy can preach,
 And vainly preach'd before.
That spell upon the minds of men
Breaks never to unite again,
 That led them to adore
Those Pagod things of sabre sway
With fronts of brass, and feet of clay.

IV

The triumph and the vanity,
 The rapture of the strife—
The earthquake voice of Victory,
 To thee the breath of life;
The sword, the sceptre, and that sway
Which man seem'd made but to obey,
 Wherewith renown was rife—
All quell'd!—Dark Spirit! what must be
The madness of thy memory!

V

The Desolator desolate!
 The Victor overthrown!
The Arbiter of others' fate
 A Suppliant for his own!
Is it some yet imperial hope
That with such change can calmly cope?
 Or dread of death alone?
To die a prince—or live a slave—
Thy choice is most ignobly brave!

VI

He who of old would rend the oak,
 Dream'd not of the rebound:
Chain'd by the trunk he vainly broke—
 Alone—how look'd he round?
Thou, in the sternness of thy strength,
An equal deed hast done at length,
 And darker fate hast found:
He fell, the forest prowlers' prey;
But thou must eat thy heart away!

VII

The Roman, when his burning heart
 Was slaked with blood of Rome,
Threw down the dagger—dared depart,
 In savage grandeur, home—

He dared depart in utter scorn
Of men that such a yoke had borne,
 Yet left him such a doom!
His only glory was that hour
Of self-upheld abandon'd power.

VIII

The Spaniard, when the lust of sway
 Had lost its quickening spell,
Cast crowns for rosaries away,
 An empire for a cell;
A strict accountant of his beads,
A subtle disputant on creeds,
 His dotage trifled well:
Yet better had he neither known
A bigot's shrine, nor despot's throne.

IX

But thou—from thy reluctant hand
 The thunderbolt is wrung—
Too late thou leav'st the high command
 To which thy weakness clung;
All Evil Spirit as thou art,
It is enough to grieve the heart
 To see thine own unstrung;
To think that God's fair world hath been
The footstool of a thing so mean;

X

And Earth hath spilt her blood for him,
 Who thus can hoard his own!
And Monarchs bow'd the trembling limb,
 And thank'd him for a throne!
Fair Freedom! we may hold thee dear,
When thus thy mightiest foes their fear
 In humblest guise have shown.
Oh! ne'er may tyrant leave behind
A brighter name to lure mankind!

XI

Thine evil deeds are writ in gore,
 Nor written thus in vain—
Thy triumphs tell of fame no more,
 Or deepen every stain:
If thou hadst died as honour dies,
Some new Napoleon might arise,
 To shame the world again—
But who would soar the solar height,
To set in such a starless night?

XII

Weigh'd in the balance, hero dust
 Is vile as vulgar clay;
Thy scales, Mortality! are just
 To all that pass away:
But yet methought the living great
Some higher sparks should animate,
 To dazzle and dismay:
Nor deem'd Contempt could thus make
 mirth
Of these, the Conquerors of the earth.

XIII

And she, proud Austria's mournful
 flower,
 Thy still imperial bride;
How bears her breast the torturing hour?
 Still clings she to thy side?
Must she too bend, must she too share
Thy late repentance, long despair,
 Thou throneless Homicide?
If still she loves thee, hoard that gem,—
'Tis worth thy vanish'd diadem!

XIV

Then haste thee to thy sullen Isle,
 And gaze upon the sea;
That element may meet thy smile—
 It ne'er was ruled by thee!
Or trace with thine all idle hand
In loitering mood upon the sand
 That Earth is now as free!
That Corinth's pedagogue hath now
Transferr'd his by-word to thy brow.

XV

Thou Timour! in his captive's cage
 What thoughts will there be thine,
While brooding in thy prison'd rage!
 But one—'The world was mine!'
Unless, like he of Babylon,
All sense is with thy sceptre gone,
 Life will not long confine
That spirit pour'd so widely forth—
So long obey'd—so little worth!

XVI

Or, like the thief of fire from heaven,
 Wilt thou withstand the shock?
And share with him, the unforgiven,
 His vulture and his rock!
Foredoom'd by God—by man accurst,
And that last act, though not thy worst,
 The very Fiend's arch mock;
He in his fall preserved his pride,
And, if a mortal, had as proudly died!

XVII

There was a day—there was an hour,
 While earth was Gaul's—Gaul thine—
When that immeasurable power
 Unsated to resign
Had been an act of purer fame
Than gathers round Marengo's name,
 And gilded thy decline,
Through the long twilight of all time,
Despite some passing clouds of crime.

XVIII

But thou forsooth must be a king,
 And don the purple vest,
As if that foolish robe could wring
 Remembrance from thy breast.

Where is that faded garment? where
The gewgaws thou wert fond to wear,
 The star, the string, the crest?
Vain froward child of empire! say,
Are all thy playthings snatched away?

XIX

Where may the wearied eye repose
 When gazing on the Great;
Where neither guilty glory glows,
 Nor despicable state?
Yes—one—the first—the last—the best—
The Cincinnatus of the West,
 Whom envy dared not hate,
Bequeath'd the name of Washington,
To make man blush there was but one!

STANZAS FOR MUSIC

I speak not, I trace not, I breathe not
 thy name,
There is grief in the sound, there is guilt
 in the fame:
But the tear which now burns on my
 cheek may impart
The deep thoughts that dwell in that
 silence of heart.

Too brief for our passion, too long for
 our peace, 5
Were those hours—can their joy or their
 bitterness cease?
We repent, we abjure, we will break from
 our chain,—
We will part, we will fly to—unite it
 again!

Oh! thine be the gladness, and mine be
 the guilt!
Forgive me, adored one!—forsake, if
 thou wilt;— 10
But the heart which is thine shall expire
 undebased,
And *man* shall not break it—whatever
 thou mayst.

And stern to the haughty, but humble to
 thee,
This soul, in its bitterest blackness, shall
 be;
And our days seem as swift, and our
 moments more sweet, 15
With thee by my side, than with worlds
 at our feet.

One sigh of thy sorrow, one look of thy
 love,
Shall turn me or fix, shall reward or re-
 prove;
And the heartless may wonder at all I
 resign—
Thy lip shall reply, not to them, but to
 mine. 20

May 1814.

ADDRESS INTENDED TO BE RE-CITED AT THE CALEDONIAN MEETING

Who hath not glow'd above the page
 where fame
Hath fix'd high Caledon's unconquer'd
 name;
The mountain-land which spurn'd the
 Roman chain,
And baffled back the fiery-crested Dane,
Whose bright claymore and hardihood
 of hand 5
No foe could tame—no tyrant could
 command?
That race is gone—but still their children
 breathe,
And glory crowns them with redoubled
 wreath:
O'er Gael and Saxon mingling banners
 shine,
And, England! add their stubborn
 strength to thine. 10
The blood which flow'd with Wallace
 flows as free,
But now 'tis only shed for fame and thee!
Oh! pass not by the northern veteran's
 claim,
But give support—the world hath given
 him fame!

The humbler ranks, the lowly brave, who
 bled 15
While cheerly following where the mighty
 led—
Who sleep beneath the undistinguish'd sod
Where happier comrades in their tri-
 umph trod,
To us bequeath—'tis all their fate allows—
The sireless offspring and the lonely
 spouse: 20
She on high Albyn's dusky hills may raise
The tearful eye in melancholy gaze,
Or view, while shadowy auguries disclose
The Highland Seer's anticipated woes,
The bleeding phantom of each martial
 form 25
Dim in the cloud, or darkling in the
 storm;
While sad, she chants the solitary song,
The soft lament for him who tarries
 long—
For him, whose distant relics vainly crave
The Coronach's wild requiem to the
 brave! 30

'Tis Heaven—not man—must charm
 away the woe,
Which bursts when Nature's feelings
 newly flow;
Yet tenderness and time may rob the tear
Of half its bitterness for one so dear;
A nation's gratitude perchance may
 spread 35
A thornless pillow for the widow'd head;

May lighten well her heart's maternal
 care,
And wean from penury the soldier's
 heir.

May 1814.

FRAGMENT OF AN EPISTLE TO THOMAS MOORE

'WHAT say *I?*'—not a syllable further in
 prose;
I'm your man 'of all measures,' dear
 Tom,—so here goes!
Here goes, for a swim on the stream of
 old Time,
On those buoyant supporters, the blad-
 ders of rhyme.
If our weight breaks them down, and we
 sink in the flood, 5
We are smother'd, at least, in respectable
 mud,
Where the Divers of Bathos lie drown'd
 in a heap,
And Southey's last Pæan has pillow'd his
 sleep;—
That 'Felo de se,' who, half drunk with
 his malmsey,
Walk'd out of his depth and was lost in
 a calm sea, 10
Singing 'Glory to God' in a spick and
 span stanza,
The like (since Tom Sternhold was
 choked) never man saw.

The papers have told you, no doubt,
 of the fusses,
The fêtes, and the gapings to get at these
 Russes,—
Of his Majesty's suite, up from coach-
 man to Hetman, 15
And what dignity decks the flat face of
 the great man.
I saw him, last week, at two balls and a
 party,—
For a prince, his demeanour was rather
 too hearty.
You know *we* are used to quite different
 graces,

.

The Czar's look, I own, was much
 brighter and brisker, 20
But then he is sadly deficient in whisker;
And wore but a starless blue coat, and in
 kersey-
-mere breeches whisk'd round, in a waltz
 with the Jersey,
Who lovely as ever, seem'd just as de-
 lighted
With Majesty's presence as those she
 invited. 25

.
• • • • •

June 1814.

CONDOLATORY ADDRESS TO SARAH, COUNTESS OF JERSEY

ON THE PRINCE REGENT'S RETURNING HER
 PICTURE TO MRS. MEE

WHEN the vain triumph of the imperial
 lord,
Whom servile Rome obey'd, and yet
 abhorr'd,
Gave to the vulgar gaze each glorious
 bust,
That left a likeness of the brave or
 just; 4
What most admired each scrutinising eye
Of all that deck'd that passing pageantry?
What spread from face to face that
 wondering air?
The thought of Brutus—for his was not
 there!
That absence proved his worth,—that
 absence fix'd
His memory on the longing mind, un-
 mix'd; 10
And more decreed his glory to endure,
Than all a gold Colossus could secure.
 If thus, fair Jersey, our desiring gaze
Search for thy form, in vain and mute
 amaze,
Amidst those pictured charms, whose
 loveliness, 15
Bright though they be, thine own had
 render'd less:
If he, that vain old man, whom truth
 admits
Heir of his father's crown, and of his wits,
If his corrupted eye, and wither'd heart,
Could with thy gentle image bear to part;
That tasteless shame be *his*, and ours the
 grief, 21
To gaze on Beauty's band without its
 chief:
Yet comfort still one selfish thought
 imparts,
We lose the portrait, but preserve our
 hearts.
 What can his vaulted gallery now
 disclose? 25
A garden with all flowers—except the
 rose;—
A fount that only wants its living stream;
A night, with every star, save Dian's
 beam.
Lost to our eyes the present forms shall
 be,
That turn from tracing them to dream of
 thee; 30
And more on that recall'd resemblance
 pause,
Than all he *shall* not force on our
 applause.
 Long may thy yet meridian lustre
 shine,
With all that Virtue asks of Homage
 thine:

The symmetry of youth, the grace of
 mien, 35
The eye that gladdens, and the brow
 serene;
The glossy darkness of that clustering
 hair,
Which shades, yet shows that forehead
 more than fair!
Each glance that wins us, and the life that
 throws
A spell which will not let our looks re-
 pose, 40
But turn to gaze again, and find anew
Some charm that well rewards another
 view.
These are not lessen'd, these are still as
 bright,
Albeit too dazzling for a dotard's sight;
And those must wait till ev'ry charm is
 gone, 45
To please the paltry heart that pleases
 none;—
That dull cold sensualist, whose sickly eye
In envious dimness pass'd thy portrait by;
Who rack'd his little spirit to combine
Its hate of *Freedom's* loveliness, and
 thine. 50
 August 1814.

ELEGIAC STANZAS ON THE DEATH OF SIR PETER PARKER, BART.

There is a tear for all that die,
 A mourner o'er the humblest grave;
But nations swell the funeral cry,
 And Triumph weeps above the brave.

For them is Sorrow's purest sigh 5
 O'er Ocean's heaving bosom sent:
In vain their bones unburied lie,
 All earth becomes their monument!

A tomb is theirs on every page,
 An epitaph on every tongue: 10
The present hours, the future age,
 For them bewail, to them belong.

For them the voice of festal mirth
 Grows hush'd, *their name* the only
 sound;
While deep Remembrance pours to
 Worth 15
 The goblet's tributary round.

A theme to crowds that knew them not,
 Lamented by admiring foes,
Who would not share their glorious lot?
 Who would not die the death they
 chose? 20

And, gallant Parker! thus enshrined
 Thy life, thy fall, thy fame shall be;
And early valour, glowing, find
 A model in thy memory.

But there are breasts that bleed with
 thee 25
 In woe, that glory cannot quell;
And shuddering hear of victory,
 Where one so dear, so dauntless, fell.

Where shall they turn to mourn thee less?
 When cease to hear thy cherish'd name?
Time cannot teach forgetfulness, 31
 While Grief's full heart is fed by Fame.

Alas! for them, though not for thee,
 They cannot choose but weep the more;
Deep for the dead the grief must be, 35
 Who ne'er gave cause to mourn before.
 October 1814.

TO BELSHAZZAR

Belshazzar! from the banquet turn,
 Nor in thy sensual fulness fall;
Behold! while yet before thee burn
 The graven words, the glowing wall,
Many a despot men miscall 5
 Crown'd and anointed from on high;
But thou, the weakest, worst of all—
 Is it not written, thou must die?

Go! dash the roses from thy brow—
 Grey hairs but poorly wreathe with
 them; 10
Youth's garlands misbecome thee now,
 More than thy very diadem,
Where thou hast tarnish'd every gem:—
 Then throw the worthless bauble by,
Which, worn by thee, ev'n slaves con-
 temn; 15
 And learn like better men to die!

Oh! early in the balance weigh'd,
 And ever light of word and worth,
Whose soul expired ere youth decay'd,
 And left thee but a mass of earth. 20
To see thee moves the scorner's mirth:
 But tears in Hope's averted eye
Lament that even thou hadst birth—
 Unfit to govern, live, or die.

HEBREW MELODIES

ADVERTISEMENT

The subsequent poems were written at the re-
quest of my friend, the Hon. Douglas Kinnaird,
for a Selection of Hebrew Melodies, and have been
published, with the music, arranged by Mr. Bra-
ham and Mr. Nathan.
January, 1815.

SHE WALKS IN BEAUTY

I

She walks in beauty, like the night
 Of cloudless climes and starry skies;
And all that's best of dark and bright
 Meet in her aspect and her eyes:
Thus mellow'd to that tender light
 Which heaven to gaudy day denies.

II

One shade the more, one ray the less,
 Had half impair'd the nameless grace
Which waves in every raven tress,
 Or softly lightens o'er her face;
Where thoughts serenely sweet express
 How pure, how dear their dwelling-
 place.

III

And on that cheek, and o'er that brow,
 So soft, so calm, yet eloquent,
The smiles that win, the tints that glow,
 But tell of days in goodness spent,
A mind at peace with all below,
 A heart whose love is innocent!

THE HARP THE MONARCH MINSTREL SWEPT

I

THE harp the monarch minstrel swept,
 The King of men, the loved of Heaven,
Which Music hallow'd while she wept
 O'er tones her heart of hearts had given,
 Redoubled be her tears, its chords are
 riven!
It soften'd men of iron mould,
 It gave them virtues not their own;
No ear so dull, no soul so cold,
 That felt not, fired not to the tone,
 Till David's lyre grew mightier than his
 throne!

II

It told the triumphs of our King,
 It wafted glory to our God;
It made our gladden'd valleys ring,
 The cedars bow, the mountains nod;
 Its sound aspired to heaven and there
 abode!
Since then, though heard on earth no
 more,
 Devotion and her daughter Love
Still bid the bursting spirit soar
 To sounds that seem as from above,
 In dreams that day's broad light can
 not remove.

IF THAT HIGH WORLD

I

IF that high world, which lies beyond
 Our own, surviving Love endears;
If there the cherish'd heart be fond,
 The eye the same, except in tears—
How welcome those untrodden spheres!
 How sweet this very hour to die!
To soar from earth and find all fears
 Lost in thy light—Eternity!

II

It must be so: 'tis not for self
 That we so tremble on the brink;
And striving to o'erleap the gulf,
 Yet cling to Being's severing link.
Oh! in that future let us think
 To hold each heart the heart that shares;
With them the immortal waters drink,
 And soul in soul grow deathless theirs!

THE WILD GAZELLE

I

THE wild gazelle on Judah's hills
 Exulting yet may bound,
And drink from all the living rills
 That gush on holy ground:
Its airy step and glorious eye
May glance in tameless transport by:—

II

A step as fleet, an eye more bright,
 Hath Judah witness'd there;
And o'er her scenes of lost delight
 Inhabitants more fair.
The cedars wave on Lebanon,
But Judah's statelier maids are gone!

III

More blest each palm that shades those
 plains
 Than Israel's scatter'd race;
For, taking root, it there remains
 In solitary grace:
It cannot quit its place of birth,
It will not live in other earth.

IV

But we must wander witheringly,
 In other lands to die;
And where our fathers' ashes be,
 Our own may never lie:
Our temple hath not left a stone,
And Mockery sits on Salem's throne.

OH! WEEP FOR THOSE

I

OH! weep for those that wept by Babel's
 stream,
Whose shrines are desolate, whose land a
 dream;
Weep for the harp of Judah's broken
 shell;
Mourn—where their God hath dwelt the
 godless dwell!

II

And where shall Israel lave her bleeding
 feet?
And when shall Zion's songs again seem
 sweet?
And Judah's melody once more rejoice
The hearts that leap'd before its heavenly
 voice?

III

Tribes of the wandering foot and weary breast,
How shall ye flee away and be at rest!
The wild-dove hath her nest, the fox his cave,
Mankind their country—Israel but the grave!

ON JORDAN'S BANKS

I

On Jordan's banks the Arab's camels stray,
On Sion's hill the False One's votaries pray,
The Baal-adorer bows on Sinai's steep—
Yet there—even there—Oh God! thy thunders sleep:

II

There—where thy finger scorch'd the tablet stone!
There—where thy shadow to thy people shone!
Thy glory shrouded in its garb of fire:
Thyself—none living see and not expire!

III

Oh! in the lightning let thy glance appear;
Sweep from his shiver'd hand the oppressor's spear:
How long by tyrants shall thy land be trod?
How long thy temple worshipless, Oh God?

JEPHTHA'S DAUGHTER

I

SINCE our Country, our God—Oh, my Sire!
Demand that thy Daughter expire;
Since thy triumph was bought by thy vow—
Strike the bosom that's bared for thee now!

II

And the voice of my mourning is o'er,
And the mountains behold me no more:
If the hand that I love lay me low,
There cannot be pain in the blow!

III

And of this, oh, my Father! be sure—
That the blood of thy child is as pure
As the blessing I beg ere it flow,
And the last thought that soothes me below.

IV

Though the virgins of Salem lament,
Be the judge and the hero unbent!
I have won the great battle for thee,
And my Father and Country are free!

When this blood of thy giving hath gush'd,
When the voice that thou lovest is hush'd,
Let my memory still be thy pride,
And forget not I smiled as I died!

OH! SNATCH'D AWAY IN BEAUTY'S BLOOM

I

OH! snatch'd away in beauty's bloom,
On thee shall press no ponderous tomb;
But on thy turf shall roses rear
Their leaves, the earliest of the year;
And the wild cypress wave in tender gloom:

II

And oft by yon blue gushing stream
Shall Sorrow lean her drooping head,
And feed deep thought with many a dream,
And lingering pause and lightly tread;
Fond wretch! as if her step disturb'd the dead!

III

Away! we know that tears are vain,
That death nor heeds nor hears distress:
Will this unteach us to complain?
Or make one mourner weep the less?
And thou—who tell'st me to forget,
Thy looks are wan, thine eyes are wet.

MY SOUL IS DARK

I

MY soul is dark—Oh! quickly string
The harp I yet can brook to hear;
And let thy gentle fingers fling
Its melting murmurs o'er mine ear.
If in this heart a hope be dear,
That sound shall charm it forth again:
If in these eyes there lurk a tear,
'Twill flow, and cease to burn my brain.

II

But bid the strain be wild and deep,
Nor let thy notes of joy be first:
I tell thee, minstrel, I must weep,
Or else this heavy heart will burst;
For it hath been by sorrow nursed,
And ached in sleepless silence long;
And now 'tis doom'd to know the worst,
And break at once—or yield to song.

I SAW THEE WEEP

I

I SAW thee weep—the big bright tear
Came o'er that eye of blue;
And then methought it did appear
A violet dropping dew;

79

OCCASIONAL PIECES

I saw thee smile—the sapphire's blaze
　Beside thee ceased to shine;
It could not match the living rays
　That fill'd that glance of thine.

II

As clouds from yonder sun receive
　A deep and mellow dye,
Which scarce the shade of coming eve
　Can banish from the sky,
Those smiles unto the moodiest mind
　Their own pure joy impart;
Their sunshine leaves a glow behind
　That lightens o'er the heart.

THY DAYS ARE DONE

I

THY days are done, thy fame begun;
　Thy country's strains record
The triumphs of her chosen Son,
　The slaughters of his sword!
The deeds he did, the fields he won,
　The freedom he restored!

II

Though thou art fall'n, while we are free
　Thou shalt not taste of death!
The generous blood that flow'd from thee
　Disdain'd to sink beneath:
Within our veins its currents be,
　Thy spirit on our breath!

III

Thy name, our charging hosts along,
　Shall be the battle-word!
Thy fall, the theme of choral song
　From virgin voices pour'd!
To weep would do thy glory wrong:
　Thou shalt not be deplored.

SAUL

I

THOU whose spell can raise the dead,
　Bid the prophet's form appear.
'Samuel, raise thy buried head!
　King, behold the phantom seer!'
Earth yawn'd; he stood the centre of a
　cloud:　　　　　　　　　　　　5
Light changed its hue, retiring from his
　shroud.
Death stood all glassy in his fixed eye;
His hand was wither'd, and his veins were
　dry;
His foot, in bony whiteness, glitter'd there,
Shrunken and sinewless, and ghastly bare;
From lips that moved not and unbreath-
　ing frame,　　　　　　　　　　　11
Like cavern'd winds, the hollow accents
　came.
Saul saw, and fell to earth, as falls the oak,
At once, and blasted by the thunder-
　stroke.

II

'Why is my sleep disquieted?　　15
Who is he that calls the dead?
Is it thou, O King? Behold,
Bloodless are these limbs, and cold:
Such are mine; and such shall be
Thine to-morrow, when with me:
Ere the coming day is done,　　21
Such shalt thou be, such thy son.
Fare thee well, but for a day,
Then we mix our mouldering clay.
Thou, thy race, lie pale and low,　25
Pierced by shafts of many a bow;
And the falchion by thy side
To thy heart thy hand shall guide:
Crownless, breathless, headless fall,
Son and sire, the house of Saul!'　30

SONG OF SAUL BEFORE HIS LAST BATTLE

I

WARRIORS and chiefs! should the shaft or
　the sword
Pierce me in leading the host of the Lord,
Heed not the corse, though a king's, in
　your path:
Bury your steel in the bosoms of Gath!

II

Thou who art bearing my buckler and bow,
Should the soldiers of Saul look away from
　the foe,
Stretch me that moment in blood at thy feet!
Mine be the doom which they dared not
　to meet.

III

Farewell to others, but never we part,
Heir to my royalty, son of my heart!
Bright is the diadem, boundless the sway,
Or kingly the death, which awaits us to-day!

'ALL IS VANITY, SAITH THE PREACHER'

I

FAME, wisdom, love, and power were mine,
　And health and youth possess'd me;
My goblets blush'd from every vine,
　And lovely forms caress'd me;
I sunn'd my heart in beauty's eyes,
　And felt my soul grow tender;
All earth can give, or mortal prize,
　Was mine of regal splendour.

II

I strive to number o'er what days
　Remembrance can discover,
Which all that life or earth displays
　Would lure me to live over.
There rose no day, there roll'd no hour
　Of pleasure unembitter'd;
And not a trapping deck'd my power
　That gall'd not while it glitter'd.

III

The serpent of the field, by art
 And spells, is won from harming;
But that which coils around the heart,
 Oh! who hath power of charming?
It will not list to wisdom's lore,
 Nor music's voice can lure it;
But there it stings for evermore
 The soul that must endure it.

WHEN COLDNESS WRAPS THIS SUFFERING CLAY

I

WHEN coldness wraps this suffering clay,
Ah! whither strays the immortal mind?
It cannot die, it cannot stay,
 But leaves its darken'd dust behind.
Then, unembodied, doth it trace
 By steps each planet's heavenly way?
Or fill at once the realms of space,
 A thing of eyes, that all survey?

II

Eternal, boundless, undecay'd,
 A thought unseen, but seeing all,
All, all in earth or skies display'd,
 Shall it survey, shall it recall:
Each fainter trace that memory holds
 So darkly of departed years,
In one broad glance the soul beholds,
 And all, that was, at once appears.

III

Before Creation peopled earth,
 Its eye shall roll through chaos back;
And where the farthest heaven had birth,
 The spirit trace its rising track.
And where the future mars or makes,
 Its glance dilate o'er all to be,
While sun is quench'd or system breaks,
 Fix'd in its own eternity.

IV

Above or Love, Hope, Hate, or Fear,
 It lives all passionless and pure:
An age shall fleet like earthly year;
 Its years as moments shall endure.
Away, away, without a wing,
 O'er all, through all, its thought shall fly,
A nameless and eternal thing,
 Forgetting what it was to die.

VISION OF BELSHAZZAR

I

THE King was on his throne,
 The Satraps throng'd the hall:
A thousand bright lamps shone
 O'er that high festival.

A thousand cups of gold,
 In Judah deem'd divine—
Jehovah's vessels hold
 The godless Heathen's wine!

II

In that same hour and hall,
 The fingers of a hand
Came forth against the wall,
 And wrote as if on sand:
The fingers of a man;—
 A solitary hand
Along the letters ran,
 And traced them like a wand.

III

The monarch saw, and shook,
 And bade no more rejoice;
All bloodless wax'd his look,
 And tremulous his voice.
'Let the men of lore appear,
 The wisest of the earth,
And expound the words of fear,
 Which mar our royal mirth.'

IV

Chaldea's seers are good,
 But here they have no skill;
And the unknown letters stood
 Untold and awful still.
And Babel's men of age
 Are wise and deep in lore;
But now they were not sage,
 They saw—but knew no more.

V

A captive in the land,
 A stranger and a youth,
He heard the king's command,
 He saw that writing's truth.
The lamps around were bright.
 The prophecy in view;
He read it on that night,—
 The morrow proved it true.

VI

'Belshazzar's grave is made,
 His kingdom pass'd away,
He, in the balance weigh'd,
 Is light and worthless clay;
The shroud his robe of state,
 His canopy the stone;
The Mede is at his gate!
 The Persian on his throne!'

SUN OF THE SLEEPLESS!

SUN of the sleepless! melancholy star!
Whose tearful beam glows tremulously far,
That show'st the darkness thou canst not dispel,
How like art thou to joy remember'd well!

OCCASIONAL PIECES

So gleams the past, the light of other
 days, 5
Which shines, but warms not with its
 powerless rays;
A night-beam Sorrow watcheth to behold,
Distinct, but distant—clear—but, oh how
 cold!

WERE MY BOSOM AS FALSE AS THOU DEEM'ST IT TO BE

I

WERE my bosom as false as thou deem'st
 it to be,
I need not have wander'd from far Galilee;
It was but abjuring my creed to efface
The curse which, thou say'st, is the crime
 of my race.

II

If the bad never triumph, then God is with
 thee!
If the slave only sin, thou art spotless
 and free!
If the Exile on earth is an Outcast on high,
Live on in thy faith, but in mine I will die.

III

I have lost for that faith more than thou
 canst bestow,
As the God who permits thee to prosper
 doth know;
In his hand is my heart and my hope—
 and in thine
The land and the life which for him I
 resign.

HEROD'S LAMENT FOR MARIAMNE

I

OH, Mariamne! now for thee
 The heart for which thou bled'st is
 bleeding;
Revenge is lost in agony,
 And wild remorse to rage succeeding.
Oh, Mariamne! where art thou?
 Thou canst not hear my bitter pleading:
Ah! could'st thou—thou would'st pardon
 now,
 Though Heaven were to my prayer un-
 heeding.

II

And is she dead?—and did they dare
 Obey my frenzy's jealous raving?
My wrath but doom'd my own despair:
 The sword that smote her's o'er me
 waving.—
But thou art cold, my murder'd love!
 And this dark heart is vainly craving
For her who soars alone above,
 And leaves my soul unworthy saving.

III

She's gone, who shared my diadem;
 She sunk, with her my joys entombing;
I swept that flower from Judah's stem,
 Whose leaves for me alone were bloom-
 ing;
And mine's the guilt, and mine the hell,
 This bosom's desolation dooming;
And I have earn'd those tortures well,
 Which unconsumed are still consum-
 ing!

ON THE DAY OF THE DESTRUCTION OF JERUSALEM BY TITUS

I

FROM the last hill that looks on thy once
 holy dome,
I beheld thee, oh Sion! when render'd to
 Rome:
'Twas thy last sun went down, and the
 flames of thy fall
Flash'd back on the last glance I gave to
 thy wall.

II

I look'd for thy temple, I look'd for my
 home,
And forgot for a moment my bondage to
 come;
I beheld but the death-fire that fed on thy
 fane,
And the fast-fetter'd hands that made
 vengeance in vain.

III

On many an eve, the high spot whence I
 gazed
Had reflected the last beam of day as it
 blazed;
While I stood on the height, and beheld
 the decline
Of the rays from the mountain that shone
 on thy shrine.

IV

And now on that mountain I stood on
 that day,
But I mark'd not the twilight beam melt-
 ing away;
Oh! would that the lightning had glared
 in its stead,
And the thunderbolt burst on the con-
 queror's head!

V

But the gods of the Pagan shall never pro-
 fane
The shrine where Jehovah disdain'd not
 to reign;
And scatter'd and scorn'd as thy people
 may be,
Our worship, oh Father! is only for thee.

BY THE RIVERS OF BABYLON WE SAT DOWN AND WEPT

I

WE sat down and wept by the waters
 Of Babel, and thought of the day
When our foe, in the hue of his slaughters,
 Made Salem's high places his prey;
And ye, oh her desolate daughters!
 Were scatter'd all weeping away.

II

While sadly we gazed on the river
 Which roll'd on in freedom below,
They demanded the song: but, oh never
 That triumph the stranger shall know!
May this right hand be wither'd for ever,
 Ere it string our high harp for the foe!

III

On the willow that harp is suspended,
 Oh Salem! its sound should be free;
And the hour when thy glories were ended
 But left me that token of thee:
And ne'er shall its soft tones be blended
 With the voice of the spoiler by me!

THE DESTRUCTION OF SENNACHERIB

I

THE Assyrian came down like the wolf on
 the fold,
And his cohorts were gleaming in purple
 and gold;
And the sheen of their spears was like
 stars on the sea,
When the blue wave rolls nightly on deep
 Galilee.

II

Like the leaves of the forest when Summer
 is green,
That host with their banners at sunset
 were seen:
Like the leaves of the forest when Autumn
 hath blown,
That host on the morrow lay wither'd and
 strown.

III

For the Angel of Death spread his wings
 on the blast,
And breathed in the face of the foe as he
 pass'd;
And the eyes of the sleepers wax'd deadly
 and chill,
And their hearts but once heaved, and for
 ever grew still!

IV

And there lay the steed with his nostril
 all wide,
But through it there roll'd not the breath
 of his pride;

And the foam of his gasping lay white on
 the turf,
And cold as the spray of the rock-beating
 surf.

V

And there lay the rider distorted and pale,
With the dew on his brow, and the rust
 on his mail:
And the tents were all silent, the banners
 alone,
The lances unlifted, the trumpet unblown.

VI

And the widows of Ashur are loud in
 their wail,
And the idols are broke in the temple of
 Baal;
And the might of the Gentile, unsmote
 by the sword,
Hath melted like snow in the glance of the
 Lord!

A SPIRIT PASS'D BEFORE ME

FROM JOB

I

A SPIRIT pass'd before me: I beheld
The face of immortality unveil'd—
Deep sleep came down on every eye save
 mine—
And there it stood,—all formless—but
 divine:
Along my bones the creeping flesh did
 quake;
And as my damp hair stiffen'd, thus it
 spake:

II

'Is man more just than God? Is man more
 pure
Than he who deems even Seraphs in-
 secure?
Creatures of clay—vain dwellers in the
 dust!
The moth survives you, and are ye more
 just?
Things of a day! you wither ere the night,
Heedless and blind to Wisdom's wasted
 light!'

STANZAS FOR MUSIC

THERE be none of Beauty's daughters
 With a magic like thee;
And like music on the waters
 Is thy sweet voice to me:
When, as if its sound were causing 5
 The charmed ocean's pausing,
The waves lie still and gleaming
And the lull'd winds seem dreaming:

83

And the midnight moon is weaving
 Her bright chain o'er the deep; 10
Whose breast is gently heaving,
 As an infant's asleep:
So the spirit bows before thee,
To listen and adore thee;
With a full but soft emotion, 15
Like the swell of Summer's ocean.

STANZAS FOR MUSIC

'O Lachrymarum fons, tenero sacros
Ducentium ortus ex animo: quater
Felix! in imo qui scatentem
Pectore te, pia Nympha, sensit.'
 GRAY's *Poemata.*

THERE's not a joy the world can give like
 that it takes away,
When the glow of early thought declines
 in feeling's dull decay;
'Tis not on youth's smooth cheek the
 blush alone, which fades so fast,
But the tender bloom of heart is gone, ere
 youth itself be past.

Then the few whose spirits float above the
 wreck of happiness 5
Are driven o'er the shoals of guilt or
 ocean of excess:
The magnet of their course is gone, or
 only points in vain
The shore to which their shiver'd sail shall
 never stretch again.

Then the mortal coldness of the soul like
 death itself comes down;
It cannot feel for others' woes, it dare not
 dream its own; 10
That heavy chill has frozen o'er the foun-
 tain of our tears,
And though the eye may sparkle still, 'tis
 where the ice appears.

Though wit may flash from fluent lips,
 and mirth distract the breast,
Through midnight hours that yield no
 more their former hope of rest;
'Tis but as ivy-leaves around the ruin'd
 turret wreath, 15
All green and wildly fresh without, but
 worn and grey beneath.

Oh could I feel as I have felt,—or be what
 I have been,
Or weep as I could once have wept o'er
 many a vanish'd scene;
As springs in deserts found seem sweet,
 all brackish though they be,
So, midst the wither'd waste of life, those
 tears would flow to me. 20

March 1815.

ON NAPOLEON'S ESCAPE FROM ELBA

ONCE fairly set out on his party of pleasure
Taking towns at his liking, and crown
 at his leisure,
From Elba to Lyons and Paris he goes,
Making *balls for* the ladies, and *bows to*
 his foes.

March 27, 181?

ODE FROM THE FRENCH

I

WE do not curse thee, Waterloo!
Though Freedom's blood thy plain bedew
There 'twas shed, but is not sunk—
Rising from each gory trunk,
Like the water-spout from ocean,
With a strong and growing motion—
It soars, and mingles in the air,
With that of lost Labedoyère—
With that of him whose honour'd grave
Contains the 'bravest of the brave.' 1
A crimson cloud it spreads and glows,
But shall return to whence it rose;
When 'tis full 'twill burst asunder—
Never yet was heard such thunder
As then shall shake the world with won-
 der— 1
Never yet was seen such lightning
As o'er heaven shall then be bright'ning
Like the Wormwood Star foretold
By the sainted Seer of old,
Show'ring down a fiery flood, 2
Turning rivers into blood.

II

The Chief has fallen, but not by you,
Vanquishers of Waterloo!
When the soldier citizen
Sway'd not o'er his fellow-men— 2
Save in deeds that led them on
Where Glory smiled on Freedom's son—
Who, of all the despots banded,
 With that youthful chief competed?
 Who could boast o'er France defeated
Till lone Tyranny commanded? 3
Till, goaded by ambition's sting,
The Hero sunk into the King?
Then he fell:—so perish all,
Who would men by man enthral! 3

III

And thou, too, of the snow-white plume
Whose realm refused thee ev'n a tomb;
Better hadst thou still been leading
France o'er hosts of hirelings bleeding,
Than sold thyself to death and shame
For a meanly royal name; 4
Such as he of Naples wears,
Who thy blood-bought title bears.
Little didst thou deem, when dashing
 On thy war-horse through the ranks,
 Like a stream which burst its banks,
While helmets cleft, and sabres clashing

Shone and shiver'd fast around thee—
Of the fate at last which found thee:
Was that haughty plume laid low 50
By a slave's dishonest blow?
Once—as the moon sways o'er the tide,
It roll'd in air, the warrior's guide;
Through the smoke-created night
Of the black and sulphurous fight, 55
The soldier raised his seeking eye
To catch that crest's ascendancy,—
And, as it onward rolling rose,
So moved his heart upon our foes.
There, where death's brief pang was quickest, 60
And the battle's wreck lay thickest,
Strew'd beneath the advancing banner
Of the eagle's burning crest—
There with thunder-clouds to fan her,
Who could then her wing arrest— 65
Victory beaming from her breast?)
While the broken line enlarging
Fell, or fled along the plain;
There be sure was Murat charging!
There he ne'er shall charge again! 70

IV

O'er glories gone the invaders march,
Weeps Triumph o'er each levell'd arch—
But let Freedom rejoice,
With her heart in her voice;
But, her hand on her sword, 75
Doubly shall she be adored;
France hath twice too well been taught
The 'moral lesson' dearly bought—
Her safety sits not on a throne,
With Capet or Napoleon! 80
But in equal rights and laws,
Hearts and hands in one great cause—
Freedom, such as God hath given
Unto all beneath his heaven,
With their breath, and from their birth,
Though guilt would sweep it from the earth; 86
With a fierce and lavish hand
Scattering nations' wealth like sand;
Pouring nations' blood like water,
In imperial seas of slaughter! 90

V

But the heart and the mind,
And the voice of mankind,
Shall arise in communion—
And who shall resist that proud union?
The time is past when swords subdued—
Man may die—the soul's renew'd: 96
Even in this low world of care
Freedom ne'er shall want an heir;
Millions breathe but to inherit
Her for ever bounding spirit— 100
When once more her hosts assemble,
Tyrants shall believe and tremble—
Smile they at this idle threat?
Crimson tears will follow yet.

FROM THE FRENCH

I

MUST thou go, my glorious Chief,
 Sever'd from thy faithful few?
Who can tell thy warrior's grief,
 Maddening o'er that long adieu?
Woman's love, and friendship's zeal,
 Dear as both have been to me—
What are they to all I feel,
 With a soldier's faith for thee?

II

Idol of the soldier's soul!
 First in fight, but mightiest now;
Many could a world control;
 Thee alone no doom can bow.
By thy side for years I dared
 Death; and envied those who fell,
When their dying shout was heard,
 Blessing him they served so well.

III

Would that I were cold with those,
 Since this hour I live to see;
When the doubts of coward foes
 Scarce dare trust a man with thee,
Dreading each should set thee free!
 Oh! although in dungeons pent,
All their chains were light to me,
 Gazing on thy soul unbent.

IV

Would the sycophants of him
 Now so deaf to duty's prayer,
Were his borrow'd glories dim,
 In his native darkness share?
Were that world this hour his own,
 All thou calmly dost resign,
Could he purchase with that throne
 Hearts like those which still are thine?

V

My chief, my king, my friend, adieu!
 Never did I droop before;
Never to my sovereign sue,
 As his foes I now implore:
All I ask is to divide
 Every peril he must brave;
Sharing by the hero's side
 His fall, his exile, and his grave.

ON THE STAR OF 'THE LEGION OF HONOUR'

[FROM THE FRENCH]

STAR of the brave!—whose beam hath shed
Such glory o'er the quick and dead—
Thou radiant and adored deceit!
Which millions rush'd in arms to greet,
Wild meteor of immortal birth; 5
Why rise in Heaven to set on Earth?

Souls of slain heroes form'd thy rays;
Eternity flash'd through thy blaze;
The music of thy martial sphere
Was fame on high and honour here; 10
And thy light broke on human eyes,
Like a volcano of the skies.

Like lava roll'd thy stream of blood,
And swept down empires with its flood;
Earth rock'd beneath thee to her base,
As thou didst lighten through all space;
And the shorn Sun grew dim in air,
And set while thou wert dwelling there.

Before thee rose, and with thee grew,
A rainbow of the loveliest hue 20
Of three bright colours, each divine,
And fit for that celestial sign;
For Freedom's hand had blended them,
Like tints in an immortal gem.

One tint was of the sunbeam's dyes; 25
One, the blue depth of Seraph's eyes;
One, the pure Spirit's veil of white
Had robed in radiance of its light:
The three so mingled did beseem
The texture of a heavenly dream. 30

Star of the brave! thy ray is pale,
And darkness must again prevail!
But, oh thou Rainbow of the free!
Our tears and blood must flow for thee.
When thy bright promise fades away, 35
Our life is but a load of clay.

And Freedom hallows with her tread
The silent cities of the dead;
For beautiful in death are they
Who proudly fall in her array; 40
And soon, oh Goddess! may we be
For evermore with them or thee!

NAPOLEON'S FAREWELL

[FROM THE FRENCH]

I

FAREWELL to the Land where the gloom
 of my Glory
Arose and o'ershadow'd the earth with
 her name—
She abandons me now—but the page of
 her story,
The brightest or blackest, is fill'd with my
 fame.
I have warr'd with a world which van-
 quish'd me only
When the meteor of conquest allured me
 too far;
I have coped with the nations which dread
 me thus lonely,
The last single Captive to millions in war.

II

Farewell to thee, France! when thy dia
 dem crown'd me,
I made thee the gem and the wonder o
 earth,
But thy weakness decrees I should leav
 as I found thee,
Decay'd in thy glory, and sunk in th
 worth.
Oh! for the veteran hearts that wer
 wasted
In strife with the storm, when their battle
 were won—
Then the Eagle, whose gaze in that mo
 ment was blasted,
Had still soar'd with eyes fix'd on victory'
 sun!

III

Farewell to thee, France!—but whe
 Liberty rallies
Once more in thy regions, remember m
 then,—
The violet still grows in the depth of th
 valleys;
Though wither'd, thy tear will unfold i
 again—
Yet, yet, I may baffle the hosts that sur
 round us,
And yet may thy heart leap awake to m
 voice—
There are links which must break in th
 chain that has bound us,
Then turn thee and call on the Chief o
 thy choice!

DOMESTIC PIECES

1816

FARE THEE WELL

'Alas! they had been friends in youth:
But whispering tongues can poison truth;
And constancy lives in realms above;
And life is thorny; and youth is vain;
And to be wroth with one we love,
Doth work like madness in the brain;

.

But never either found another
To free the hollow heart from paining—
They stood aloof, the scars remaining,
Like cliffs which had been rent asunder;
A dreary sea now flows between,
But neither heat, nor frost, nor thunder,
Shall wholly do away, I ween,
The marks of that which once hath been.'
COLERIDGE'S *Christabel*.

FARE thee well! and if for ever,
 Still for ever, fare thee well:
Even though unforgiving, never
 'Gainst thee shall my heart rebel.

Would that breast were bared before the
 Where thy head so oft hath lain.
While that placid sleep came o'er thee
 Which thou ne'er canst know again;

Would that breast, by thee glanced over,
 Every inmost thought could show! 10
Then thou wouldst at last discover
 'Twas not well to spurn it so.

Though the world for this commend
 thee—
 Though it smile upon the blow,
Even its praises must offend thee, 15
 Founded on another's woe:

Though my many faults defaced me,
 Could no other arm be found,
Than the one which once embraced me,
 To inflict a cureless wound? 20

Yet, oh yet, thyself deceive not;
 Love may sink by slow decay,
But by sudden wrench, believe not
 Hearts can thus be torn away:

Still thine own its life retaineth, 25
 Still must mine, though bleeding, beat;
And the undying thought which paineth
 Is—that we no more may meet.

These are words of deeper sorrow
 Than the wail above the dead; 30
Both shall live, but every morrow
 Wake us from a widow'd bed.

And when thou wouldst solace gather,
 When our child's first accents flow,
Wilt thou teach her to say 'Father!' 35
 Though his care she must forego?

When her little hands shall press thee,
 When her lip to thine is press'd,
Think of him whose prayer shall bless
 thee,
 Think of him thy love had bless'd! 40

Should her lineaments resemble
 Those thou never more may'st see,
Then thy heart will softly tremble
 With a pulse yet true to me. 44

All my faults perchance thou knowest,
 All my madness none can know;
All my hopes, where'er thou goest,
 Wither, yet with *thee* they go.

Every feeling hath been shaken; 49
 Pride, which not a world could bow,
Bows to thee—by thee forsaken,
 Even my soul forsakes me now:

But 'tis done—all words are idle—
 Words from me are vainer still;
But the thoughts we cannot bridle 55
 Force their way without the will.

Fare thee well! thus disunited,
 Torn from every nearer tie,
Sear'd in heart, and lone, and blighted,
 More than this I scarce can die. 60
 March 17, 1816.

OCCASIONAL PIECES

A SKETCH

'Honest—honest Iago!
If that thou be'st a devil, I cannot kill thee.'
 SHAKSPEARE.

BORN in the garret, in the kitchen bred,
Promoted thence to deck her mistress' head;
Next—for some gracious service un-
 express'd,
And from its wages only to be guess'd—
Raised from the toilette to the table,— 5
 where
Her wondering betters wait behind her
 chair.
With eye unmoved, and forehead un-
 abash'd,
She dines from off the plate she lately
 wash'd.
Quick with the tale, and ready with the lie,
The genial confidante, and general spy,
Who could, ye gods! her next employ-
 ment guess— 11
An only infant's earliest governess!
She taught the child to read, and taught
 so well,
That she herself, by teaching, learn'd to
 spell.
An adept next in penmanship she grows,
As many a nameless slander deftly shows:
What she had made the pupil of her art,
None know—but that high Soul secured
 the heart,
And panted for the truth it could not hear,
With longing breast and undeluded ear.
Foil'd was perversion by that youthful
 mind, 21
Which Flattery fool'd not, Baseness could
 not blind,
Deceit infect not, near Contagion soil,
Indulgence weaken, nor Example spoil,
Nor master'd Science tempt her to look
 down 25
On humbler talents with a pitying frown,
Nor Genius swell, nor Beauty render vain,
Nor Envy ruffle to retaliate pain,
Nor Fortune change, Pride raise, nor
 Passion bow,
Nor virtue teach austerity—till now. 30
Serenely purest of her sex that live,
But wanting one sweet weakness—to for-
 give,
Too shock'd at faults her soul can never
 know,
She deems that all could be like her be-
 low:
Foe to all vice, yet hardly Virtue's friend,
For Virtue pardons those she would
 amend. 36

 But to the theme, now laid aside too
 long,
The baleful burthen of this honest song,
Though all her former functions are no
 more,
She rules the circle which she served before.

If mothers—none know why—before her
 quake; 41
If daughters dread her for the mothers'
 sake;
If early habits—those false links, which
 bind
At times the loftiest to the meanest
 mind—
Have given her power too deeply to instil
The angry essence of her deadly will; 46
If like a snake she steal within your
 walls,
Till the black slime betray her as she
 crawls,
If like a viper to the heart she wind,
And leave the venom there she did not
 find; 50
What marvel that this hag of hatred works
Eternal evil latent as she lurks,
To make a Pandemonium where she
 dwells,
And reign the Hecate of domestic hells?
Skill'd by a touch to deepen scandal's
 tints 55
With all the kind mendacity of hints,
While mingling truth with falsehood,
 sneers with smiles,
A thread of candour with a web of
 wiles:
A plain blunt show of briefly-spoken
 seeming,
To hide her bloodless heart's soul-
 harden'd scheming; 60
A lip of lies; a face form'd to conceal,
And, without feeling, mock at all who
 feel:
With a vile mask the Gorgon would dis-
 own,—
A cheek of parchment, and an eye of
 stone.
Mark, how the channels of her yellow
 blood 65
Ooze to her skin, and stagnate there to
 mud,
Cased like the centipede in saffron mail,
Or darker greenness of the scorpion's
 scale—
(For drawn from reptiles only may we
 trace
Congenial colours in that soul or face)—
Look on her features! and behold her
 mind 71
As in a mirror of itself defined:
Look on the picture! deem it not o'er-
 charged—
There is no trait which might not be en-
 larged:
Yet true to 'Nature's journeymen,' who
 made 75
This monster when their mistress left off
 trade—
This female dog-star of her little sky,
Where all beneath her influence droop or
 die.

Oh! wretch without a tear—without a
 thought,
Save joy above the ruin thou has
 wrought— 8
The time shall come, nor long remote
 when thou
Shalt feel far more than thou inflictes
 now;
Feel for thy vile self-loving self in vain,
And turn thee howling in unpitied pain.
May the strong curse of crush'd affection
 light 8
Back on thy bosom with reflected blight
And make thee in thy leprosy of mind
As loathsome to thyself as to mankind!
Till all thy self-thoughts curdle into hate
Black—as thy will for others would cre
 ate: 9
Till thy hard heart be calcined into dus
And thy soul welter in its hideous crust
Oh, may thy grave be sleepless as the bed
The widow'd couch of fire, that thou has
 spread!
Then, when thou fain wouldst wear
 Heaven with prayer, 9
Look on thine earthly victims—and des
 pair!
Down to the dust!—and, as thou rott's
 away,
Even worms shall perish on thy poisonou
 clay.
But for the love I bore, and still must bea
To her thy malice from all ties woul
 tear— 10
Thy name—thy human name—to every ey
The climax of all scorn should hang o
 high,
Exalted o'er thy less abhorr'd compeers—
And festering in the infamy of years.
 March 29, 1816

ENDORSEMENT TO THE DEED OF SEPARATION

IN THE APRIL OF 1816

A YEAR ago, you swore, fond she!
'To love, to honour,' and so forth:
Such was the vow you pledged to me,
 And here's exactly what 'tis worth.

STANZAS TO AUGUSTA

I

WHEN all around grew drear and dark,
 And reason half withheld her ray—
And hope but shed a dying spark
 Which more misled my lonely way;

II

In that deep midnight of the mind,
 And that internal strife of heart,
When dreading to be deem'd too kind,
 The weak despair—the cold depart;

III

When fortune changed—and love fled far,
 And hatred's shafts flew thick and fast,
Thou wert the solitary star
 Which rose and set not to the last.

IV

Oh! blest be thine unbroken light!
 That watch'd me as a seraph's eye,
And stood between me and the night,
 For ever shining sweetly nigh.

V

And when the cloud upon us came,
 Which strove to blacken o'er thy ray—
Then purer spread its gentle flame,
 And dash'd the darkness all away.

VI

Still may thy spirit dwell on mine,
 And teach it what to brave or brook—
There's more in one soft word of thine
 Than in the world's defied rebuke.

VII

Thou stood'st, as stands a lovely tree,
 That still unbroke, though gently bent,
Still waves with fond fidelity
 Its boughs above a monument.

VIII

The winds might rend—the skies might pour,
 But there thou wert—and still wouldst be
Devoted in the stormiest hour
 To shed thy weeping leaves o'er me.

IX

But thou and thine shall know no blight,
 Whatever fate on me may fall;
For heaven in sunshine will requite
 The kind—and thee the most of all.

X

Then let the ties of baffled love
 Be broken—thine will never break;
Thy heart can feel—but will not move,
 Thy soul, though soft, will never shake.

XI

And these, when all was lost beside,
 Were found and still are fix'd in thee;—
And bearing still a breast so tried,
 Earth is no desert—ev'n to me.

STANZAS TO AUGUSTA

I

THOUGH the day of my destiny's over,
 And the star of my fate hath declined,
Thy soft heart refused to discover
 The faults which so many could find;

Though thy soul with my grief was acquainted,
 It shrunk not to share it with me,
And the love which my spirit hath painted
 It never hath found but in *thee*.

II

Then when nature around me is smiling,
 The last smile which answers to mine,
I do not believe it beguiling,
 Because it reminds me of thine;
And when winds are at war with the ocean,
 As the breasts I believed in with me,
If their billows excite an emotion,
 It is that they bear me from *thee*.

III

Though the rock of my last hope is shiver'd,
 And its fragments are sunk in the wave,
Though I feel that my soul is deliver'd
 To pain—it shall not be its slave.
There is many a pang to pursue me:
 They may crush, but they shall not contemn;
They may torture, but shall not subdue me;
 'Tis of *thee* that I think—not of them.

IV

Though human, thou didst not deceive me,
 Though woman, thou didst not forsake,
Though loved, thou forborest to grieve me,
 Though slander'd, thou never couldst shake;
Though trusted, thou didst not disclaim me,
 Though parted, it was not to fly,
Though watchful, 'twas not to defame me,
 Nor, mute, that the world might belie.

V

Yet I blame not the world, nor despise it,
 Nor the war of the many with one;
If my soul was not fitted to prize it,
 'Twas folly not sooner to shun:
And if dearly that error hath cost me,
 And more than I once could foresee,
I have found that, whatever it lost me,
 It could not deprive me of *thee*.

VI

From the wreck of the past, which hath perish'd,
 Thus much I at least may recall,
It hath taught me that what I most cherish'd
 Deserved to be dearest of all:
In the desert a fountain is springing,
 In the wide waste there still is a tree,
And a bird in the solitude singing,
 Which speaks to my spirit of *thee*.
 July 24, 1816.

EPISTLE TO AUGUSTA

I

My sister! my sweet sister! if a name
Dearer and purer were, it should be
 thine;
Mountains and seas divide us, but I
 claim
No tears, but tenderness to answer
 mine:
Go where I will, to me thou art the
 same—
A loved regret which I would not re-
 sign,
There yet are two things in my des-
 tiny,—
A world to roam through, and a home
 with thee.

II

The first were nothing—had I still the
 last,
It were the haven of my happiness;
But other claims and other ties thou
 hast,
And mine is not the wish to make
 them less.
A strange doom is thy father's son's,
 and past
Recalling, as it lies beyond redress;
Reversed for him our grandsire's fate
 of yore,—
He had no rest at sea, nor I on shore.

III

If my inheritance of storms hath been
In other elements, and on the rocks
Of perils, overlook'd or unforeseen,
I have sustain'd my share of worldly
 shocks,
The fault was mine; nor do I seek to
 screen
My errors with defensive paradox;
I have been cunning in mine overthrow,
The careful pilot of my proper woe.

IV

Mine were my faults, and mine be their
 reward.
My whole life was a contest, since the
 day
That gave me being, gave me that which
 marr'd
The gift,—a fate, or will, that walk'd
 astray;
And I at times have found the struggle
 hard,
And thought of shaking off my bonds
 of clay:
But now I fain would for a time sur-
 vive,
If but to see what next can well arrive.

V

Kingdoms and empires in my little da
I have outlived, and yet I am not old
And when I look on this, the petty spra
Of my own years of trouble, which hav
 roll'd
Like a wild bay of breakers, melts away
Something—I know not what—doe
 still uphold
A spirit of slight patience;—not in vain
Even for its own sake, do we purchas
 pain.

VI

Perhaps the workings of defiance stir
Within me—or perhaps a cold despai
Brought on when ills habitually recur,—
Perhaps a kinder clime, or purer air,
(For even to this may change of sou
 refer,
And with light armour we may learn t
 bear,)
Have taught me a strange quiet, whicl
 was not
The chief companion of a calmer lot.

VII

I feel almost at times as I have felt
In happy childhood; trees, and flowers
 and brooks,
Which do remember me of where I dwel
Ere my young mind was sacrificed t
 books,
Come as of yore upon me, and can mel
My heart with recognition of thei
 looks;
And even at moments I could think I se
Some living thing to love—but none lik
 thee.

VIII

Here are the Alpine landscapes whicl
 create
A fund for contemplation;—to admir
Is a brief feeling of a trivial date;
But something worthier do such scene
 inspire:
Here to be lonely is not desolate,
For much I view which I could mos
 desire,
And, above all, a lake I can behold
Lovelier, not dearer, than our own of ol

IX

Oh that thou wert but with me!—bu
 I grow
The fool of my own wishes, and forge
The solitude which I have vaunted so
Has lost its praise in this but one regre
There may be others which I less ma
 show;—
I am not of the plaintive mood, and ye
I feel an ebb in my philosophy,
And the tide rising in my alter'd eye.

X

I did remind thee of our own dear Lake,
By the old Hall which may be mine no
more.
Leman's is fair; but think not I forsake
The sweet remembrance of a dearer
shore:
Sad havoc Time must with my memory
make,
Ere *that* or *thou* can fade these eyes
before;
Though, like all things which I have
loved, they are
Resign'd for ever, or divided far.

XI

The world is all before me; I but ask
Of Nature that with which she will
comply—
It is but in her summer's sun to bask,
To mingle with the quiet of her sky,
To see her gentle face without a mask,
And never gaze on it with apathy.
She was my early friend, and now shall
be
My sister—till I look again on thee.

XII

I can reduce all feelings but this one;
And that I would not;—for at length I
see
Such scenes as those wherein my life
begun.
The earliest—even the only paths for
me—
Had I but sooner learnt the crowd to
shun,
I had been better than I now can be;
The passions which have torn me would
have slept;
I had not suffer'd, and *thou* hadst not
wept.

XIII

With false Ambition what had I to do?
Little with Love, and least of all with
Fame;
And yet they came unsought, and with
me grew,
And made me all which they can make
—a name.
Yet this was not the end I did pursue;
Surely I once beheld a nobler aim.
But all is over—I am one the more
To baffled millions which have gone be-
fore.

XIV

And for the future, this world's future
may
From me demand but little of my care;
I have outlived myself by many a day;
Having survived so many things that
were;

My years have been no slumber, but
the prey
Of ceaseless vigils; for I had the share
Of life which might have fill'd a cen-
tury,
Before its fourth in time had pass'd me by.

XV

And for the remnant which may be to
come
I am content; and for the past I feel
Not thankless,—for within the crowded
sum
Of struggles, happiness at times would
steal,
And for the present, I would not be-
numb
My feelings further.—Nor shall I con-
ceal
That with all this I still can look around,
And worship Nature with a thought pro-
found.

XVI

For thee, my own sweet sister, in thy
heart
I know myself secure, as thou in mine;
We were and are—I am, even as thou
art—
Beings who ne'er each other can resign;
It is the same, together or apart,
From life's commencement to its slow
decline
We are entwined—let death come slow
or fast,
The tie which bound the first endures the
last!

THE DREAM

I

Our life is two-fold: Sleep hath its own
world,
A boundary between the things misnamed
Death and existence: Sleep hath its own
world,
And a wide realm of wild reality.
And dreams in their development have
breath, 5
And tears, and tortures, and the touch of
joy;
They leave a weight upon our waking
thoughts,
They take a weight from off our waking
toils,
They do divide our being; they become
A portion of ourselves as of our time,
And look like heralds of eternity; 11
They pass like spirits of the past,—they
speak
Like Sibyls of the future: they have
power—
The tyranny of pleasure and of pain;

91

They make us what we were not—what
 they will, 15
And shake us with the vision that's gone
 by,
The dread of vanish'd shadows—Are they
 so?
Is not the past all shadow?—What are
 they?
Creations of the mind?—The mind can
 make
Substance, and people planets of its own
With beings brighter than have been, and
 give 21
A breath to forms which can outlive all
 flesh.
I would recall a vision which I dream'd
Perchance in sleep—for in itself a thought,
A slumbering thought, is capable of years,
And curdles a long life into one hour.

II

I saw two beings in the hues of youth
Standing upon a hill, a gentle hill,
Green and of mild declivity, the last
As 'twere the cape of a long ridge of such,
Save that there was no sea to lave its base,
But a most living landscape, and the wave
Of woods and corn-fields, and the abodes
 of men 33
Scatter'd at intervals, and wreathing
 smoke
Arising from such rustic roofs;—the hill
Was crown'd with a peculiar diadem 36
Of trees, in circular array, so fix'd,
Not by the sport of nature, but of man:
These two, a maiden and a youth, were
 there 39
Gazing—the one on all that was beneath
Fair as herself—but the boy gazed on her;
And both were young, and one was beauti-
 ful:
And both were young—yet not alike in
 youth.
As the sweet moon on the horizon's verge,
The maid was on the eve of womanhood;
The boy had fewer summers, but his heart
Had far outgrown his years, and to his
 eye 47
There was but one beloved face on earth,
And that was shining on him: he had
 look'd
Upon it till it could not pass away; 50
He had no breath, no being, but in hers;
She was his voice; he did not speak to her,
But trembled on her words; she was his
 sight,
For his eye follow'd hers, and saw with
 hers,
Which colour'd all his objects:—he had
 ceased 55
To live within himself; she was his life,
The ocean to the river of his thoughts,
Which terminated all: upon a tone,

A touch of hers, his blood would ebb and
 flow,
And his cheek change tempestuously—
 his heart 60
Unknowing of its cause of agony.
But she in these fond feelings had no share
Her sighs were not for him; to her he was
Even as a brother—but no more; 'twas
 much,
For brotherless she was, save in the name
Her infant friendship had bestow'd on
 him; 66
Herself the solitary scion left
Of a time-honour'd race.—It was a name
Which pleased him, and yet pleased him
 not—and why?
Time taught him a deep answer—when
 she loved 70
Another; even *now* she loved another,
And on the summit of that hill she stood
Looking afar if yet her lover's steed
Kept pace with her expectancy, and flew

III

A change came o'er the spirit of my
 dream. 75
There was an ancient mansion, and be-
 fore
Its walls there was a steed caparison'd:
Within an antique Oratory stood
The Boy of whom I spake;—he was alone,
And pale, and pacing to and fro: anon
He sate him down, and seized a pen, and
 traced 81
Words which I could not guess of; then
 he lean'd
His bow'd head on his hands, and shook
 as 'twere
With a convulsion—then arose again,
And with his teeth and quivering hands
 did tear 85
What he had written, but he shed no tears
And he did calm himself, and fix his brow
Into a kind of quiet: as he paused,
The Lady of his love re-entered there;
She was serene and smiling then, and yet
She knew she was by him beloved,—she
 knew, 91
For quickly comes such knowledge, that
 his heart
Was darken'd with her shadow, and she
 saw
That he was wretched, but she saw not all
He rose, and with a cold and gentle grasp
He took her hand; a moment o'er his face
A tablet of unutterable thoughts 97
Was traced, and then it faded, as it came
He dropp'd the hand he held, and with
 slow steps
Retired, but not as bidding her adieu,
For they did part with mutual smiles; he
 pass'd 101
From out the massy gate of that old Hall

And mounting on his steed he went his
 way;
And ne'er repass'd that hoary threshold
 more.

IV

A change came o'er the spirit of my
 dream. 105
The Boy was sprung to manhood: in the
 wilds
Of fiery climes he made himself a home,
And his soul drank their sunbeams: he
 was girt
With strange and dusky aspects; he was
 not 109
Himself like what he had been; on the sea
And on the shore he was a wanderer.
There was a mass of many images
Crowded like waves upon me, but he was
A part of all; and in the last he lay
Reposing from the noontide sultriness,
Couch'd among fallen columns, in the
 shade 116
Of ruin'd walls that had survived the
 names
Of those who rear'd them; by his sleeping
 side
Stood camels grazing, and some goodly
 steeds 119
Were fasten'd near a fountain; and a man
Clad in a flowing garb did watch the while,
While many of his tribe slumber'd around:
And they were canopied by the blue sky,
So cloudless, clear, and purely beautiful,
That God alone was to be seen in heaven.

V

A change came o'er the spirit of my dream.
The Lady of his love was wed with One
Who did not love her better:—in her
 home,
A thousand leagues from his,—her native
 home, 129
She dwelt, begirt with growing Infancy,
Daughters and sons of Beauty,—but be-
 hold!
Upon her face there was the tint of grief,
The settled shadow of an inward strife,
And an unquiet drooping of the eye,
As if its lid were charged with unshed
 tears. 135
What could her grief be?—she had all she
 loved,
And he who had so loved her was not
 there
To trouble with bad hopes, or evil wish,
Or ill-repress'd affliction, her pure thoughts.
What could her grief be?—she had loved
 him not, 140
Nor given him cause to deem himself be-
 loved,
Nor could he be a part of that which
 prey'd
Upon her mind—a spectre of the past.

VI

A change came o'er the spirit of my
 dream.
The Wanderer was return'd.—I saw him
 stand 145
Before an Altar—with a gentle bride;
Her face was fair, but was not that which
 made
The Starlight of his Boyhood;—as he
 stood
Even at the altar, o'er his brow there came
The self-same aspect, and the quivering
 shock 150
That in the antique Oratory shook
His bosom in its solitude; and then—
As in that hour—a moment o'er his face
The tablet of unutterable thoughts
Was traced,—and then it faded as it
 came, 155
And he stood calm and quiet, and he
 spoke
The fitting vows, but heard not his own
 words,
And all things reel'd around him; he
 could see
Not that which was, nor that which should
 have been—
But the old mansion, and the accustom'd
 hall, 160
And the remember'd chambers, and the
 place,
The day, the hour, the sunshine, and the
 shade,
All things pertaining to that place and
 hour,
And her who was his destiny,—came back
And thrust themselves between him and
 the light: 165
What business had they there at such a
 time?

VII

A change came o'er the spirit of my
 dream.
The Lady of his love:—Oh! she was
 changed
As by the sickness of the soul; her mind
Had wander'd from its dwelling, and her
 eyes 170
They had not their own lustre, but the
 look
Which is not of the earth; she was become
The queen of a fantastic realm; her
 thoughts
Were combinations of disjointed things;
And forms impalpable and unperceived
Of others' sight familiar were to hers. 176
And this the world calls frenzy; but the
 wise
Have a far deeper madness, and the glance
Of melancholy is a fearful gift;
What is it but the telescope of truth? 180
Which strips the distance of its fantasies,

93

And brings life near in utter nakedness,
Making the cold reality too real!

VIII

A change came o'er the spirit of my
 dream.
The Wanderer was alone as heretofore,
The beings which surrounded him were
 gone, 186
Or were at war with him; he was a mark
For blight and desolation, compass'd
 round
With Hatred and Contention; Pain was
 mix'd 189
In all which was served up to him, until,
Like to the Pontic monarch of old days,
He fed on poisons, and they had no power,
But were a kind of nutriment; he lived
Through that which had been death to
 many men,
And made him friends of mountains:
 with the stars 195
And the quick Spirit of the Universe
He held his dialogues; and they did teach
To him the magic of their mysteries;
To him the book of Night was open'd
 wide,
And voices from the deep abyss reveal'd
A marvel and a secret—Be it so. 201

IX

My dream was past; it had no further
 change.
It was of a strange order, that the doom
Of these two creatures should be thus
 traced out
Almost like a reality—the one 205
To end in madness—both in misery.

July 1816.

LINES ON HEARING THAT LADY BYRON WAS ILL

AND thou wert sad—yet I was not with
 thee;
 And thou wert sick, and yet I was not
 near;
Methought that joy and health alone
 could be
 Where I was *not*—and pain and sorrow
 here!
And is it thus?—it is as I foretold, 5
 And shall be more so; for the mind
 recoils
Upon itself, and the wreck'd heart lies
 cold,
 While heaviness collects the shatter'd
 spoils.
It is not in the storm nor in the strife
 We feel benumb'd, and wish to be no
 more, 10
 But in the after-silence on the shore,
When all is lost, except a little life.

I am too well avenged!—but 'twas my right
 Whate'er my sins might be, *thou* were
 not sent
To be the Nemesis who should requite—
 Nor did Heaven choose so near an
 instrument. 16
Mercy is for the merciful!—if thou
Hast been of such, 'twill be accorded now.
Thy nights are banish'd from the realms
 of sleep!—
 Yes! they may flatter thee, but thou
 shalt feel 20
A hollow agony which will not heal,
For thou art pillow'd on a curse too deep;
Thou hast sown in my sorrow, and must
 reap
 The bitter harvest in a woe as real!
I have had many foes, but none like thee;
 For 'gainst the rest myself I could de-
 fend, 26
 And be avenged, or turn them into
 friend;
But thou in safe implacability
Hadst nought to dread—in thy own
 weakness shielded,
And in my love, which hath but too much
 yielded, 30
 And spared, for thy sake, some I should
 not spare;
And thus upon the world—trust in thy
 truth,
And the wild fame of my ungovern'd
 youth—
 On things that were not, and on things
 that are— 34
Even upon such a basis hast thou built
A monument, whose cement hath been
 guilt!
 The moral Clytemnestra of thy lord,
And hew'd down, with an unsuspected
 sword,
Fame, peace, and hope—and all the better
 life,
 Which, but for this cold treason of thy
 heart, 40
Might still have risen from out the grave
 of strife,
 And found a nobler duty than to part.
But of thy virtues didst thou make a vice,
 Trafficking with them in a purpose cold,
For present anger, and for future
 gold— 45
And buying others' grief at any price.
And thus once enter'd into crooked ways,
 The earthly truth, which was thy proper
 praise,
Did not still walk beside thee—but at
 times,
And with a breast unknowing its own
 crimes, 50
Deceit, averments incompatible,
 Equivocations, and the thoughts which
 dwell
 In Janus-spirits—the significant eye

Which learns to lie with silence—the pre-
 text 54
Of prudence, with advantages annex'd—
The acquiescence in all things which tend,
No matter how, to the desired end—
 All found a place in thy philosophy.
The means were worthy, and the end is
 won—
I would not do by thee as thou hast done!
 September 1816.

DARKNESS

I HAD a dream, which was not all a dream.
The bright sun was extinguish'd, and the
 stars
Did wander darkling in the eternal space,
Rayless, and pathless, and the icy earth
Swung blind and blackening in the moon-
 less air; 5
Morn came and went—and came, and
 brought no day,
And men forgot their passions in the dread
Of this their desolation; and all hearts
Were chill'd into a selfish prayer for light:
And they did live by watchfires—and the
 thrones, 10
The palaces of crowned kings—the huts,
The habitations of all things which dwell,
Were burnt for beacons; cities were con-
 sumed,
And men were gather'd round their blaz-
 ing homes
To look once more into each other's face;
Happy were those who dwelt within the
 eye 16
Of the volcanos, and their mountain-torch:
A fearful hope was all the world contain'd;
Forests were set on fire—but hour by hour
They fell and faded—and the crackling
 trunks 20
Extinguish'd with a crash—and all was
 black.
The brows of men by the despairing light
Wore an unearthly aspect, as by fits
The flashes fell upon them; some lay down
And hid their eyes and wept; and some
 did rest 25
Their chins upon their clenched hands,
 and smiled;
And others hurried to and fro, and fed
Their funeral piles with fuel, and look'd up
With mad disquietude on the dull sky, 29
The pall of a past world; and then again
With curses cast them down upon the dust,
And gnash'd their teeth and howl'd: the
 wild birds shriek'd
And, terrified, did flutter on the ground,
And flap their useless wings; the wildest
 brutes
Came tame and tremulous; and vipers
 crawl'd 35
And twined themselves among the multi-
 tude,

Hissing, but stingless—they were slain for
 food.
And War, which for a moment was no
 more,
Did glut himself again:—a meal was
 bought
With blood, and each sate sullenly apart
Gorging himself in gloom: no love was
 left; 41
All earth was but one thought—and that
 was death
Immediate and inglorious; and the pang
Of famine fed upon all entrails—men
Died, and their bones were tombless as
 their flesh; 45
The meagre by the meagre were devour'd,
Even dogs assail'd their masters, all save
 one,
And he was faithful to a corse, and kept
The birds and beasts and famish'd men
 at bay,
Till hunger clung them, or the dropping
 dead 50
Lured their lank jaws; himself sought out
 no food,
But with a piteous and perpetual moan,
And a quick desolate cry, licking the hand
Which answer'd not with a caress—he
 died.
The crowd was famish'd by degrees; but
 two 55
Of an enormous city did survive,
And they were enemies: they met beside
The dying embers of an altar-place
Where had been heap'd a mass of holy
 things
For an unholy usage; they raked up, 60
And shivering scraped with their cold
 skeleton hands
The feeble ashes, and their feeble breath
Blew for a little life, and made a flame
Which was a mockery; then they lifted up
Their eyes as it grew lighter, and beheld
Each other's aspects—saw, and shriek'd,
 and died— 66
Even of their mutual hideousness they
 died,
Unknowing who he was upon whose brow
Famine had written Fiend. The world
 was void,
The populous and the powerful was a
 lump, 70
Seasonless, herbless, treeless, manless,
 lifeless,
A lump of death—a chaos of hard clay.
The rivers, lakes, and ocean all stood still,
And nothing stirr'd within their silent
 depths;
Ships sailorless lay rotting on the sea, 75
And their masts fell down piecemeal: as
 they dropp'd
They slept on the abyss without a surge—
The waves were dead; the tides were in
 their grave,

OCCASIONAL PIECES

The moon, their mistress, had expired
before;
The winds were wither'd in the stagnant
air, 80
And the clouds perish'd; Darkness had
no need
Of aid from them—She was the Universe.

Diodati, *July* 1816.

MONODY ON THE DEATH

OF

THE RIGHT HON. R. B. SHERIDAN

SPOKEN AT DRURY-LANE THEATRE

WHEN the last sunshine of expiring day
In summer's twilight weeps itself away,
Who hath not felt the softness of the hour
Sink on the heart, as dew along the flower?
With a pure feeling which absorbs and
awes 5
While Nature makes that melancholy
pause,
Her breathing moment on the bridge
where Time
Of light and darkness forms an arch sub-
lime,
Who hath not shared that calm, so still
and deep,
The voiceless thought which would not
speak but weep, 10
A holy concord, and a bright regret,
A glorious sympathy with suns that set?
'Tis not harsh sorrow, but a tenderer woe,
Nameless, but dear to gentle hearts below,
Felt without bitterness, but full and clear,
A sweet dejection, a transparent tear, 16
Unmix'd with worldly grief or selfish stain,
Shed without shame, and secret without
pain.

Even as the tenderness that hour instils
When Summer's day declines along the
hills. 20
So feels the fulness of our heart and eyes
When all of Genius which can perish dies.
A mighty Spirit is eclipsed—a Power
Hath pass'd from day to darkness—to
whose hour
Of light no likeness is bequeath'd—no
name, 25
Focus at once of all the rays of Fame!
The flash of Wit, the bright Intelligence,
The beam of Song, the blaze of Eloquence,
Set with their Sun, but still have left be-
hind 29
The enduring produce of immortal Mind;
Fruits of a genial morn, and glorious noon,
A deathless part of him who died too soon.
But small that portion of the wondrous
whole,
These sparkling segments of that circling
soul,

Which all embraced, and lighten'd over
all, 35
To cheer, to pierce, to please, or to appal.
From the charm'd council to the festive
board,
Of human feelings the unbounded lord;
In whose acclaim the loftiest voices vied,
The praised, the proud, who made his
praise their pride. 40
When the loud cry of trampled Hindostan
Arose to Heaven in her appeal from man,
His was the thunder, his the avenging rod,
The wrath—the delegated voice of God!
Which shook the nations through his lips
and blazed 45
Till vanquish'd senates trembled as they
praised.

And here, oh! here, where yet all
young and warm,
The gay creations of his spirit charm,
The matchless dialogue, the deathless wit,
Which knew not what it was to intermit;
The glowing portraits, fresh from life, that
bring 51
Home to our hearts the truth from which
they spring;
These wondrous beings of his fancy,
wrought
To fulness by the fiat of his thought,
Here in their first abode you still may
meet, 55
Bright with the hues of his Promethean
heat;
A halo of the light of other days,
Which still the splendour of its orb be-
trays.

But should there be to whom the fatal
blight 59
Of failing Wisdom yields a base delight,
Men who exult when minds of heavenly
tone
Jar in the music which was born their own,
Still let them pause—ah! little do they
know
That what to them seem'd Vice might be
but Woe. 64
Hard is his fate on whom the public gaze
Is fix'd for ever to detract or praise;
Repose denies her requiem to his name,
And Folly loves the martyrdom of Fame.
The secret enemy whose sleepless eye
Stands sentinel, accuser, judge, and spy,
The foe, the fool, the jealous, and the vain,
The envious who but breathe in others'
pain, 72
Behold the host! delighting to deprave,
Who track the steps of Glory to the grave,
Watch every fault that daring Genius owes
Half to the ardour which its birth bestows,
Distort the truth, accumulate the lie,
And pile the pyramid of Calumny! 78

These are his portion—but if join'd to
 these
Gaunt Poverty should league with deep
 Disease, 80
If the high Spirit must forget to soar,
And stoop to strive with Misery at the
 door,
To soothe Indignity—and face to face
Meet sordid Rage, and wrestle with Dis-
 grace,
To find in Hope but the renew'd caress,
The serpent-fold of further Faithless-
 ness:— 86
If such may be the ills which men assail,
What marvel if at last the mightiest fail?
Breasts to whom all the strength of feeling
 given
Bear hearts electric—charged with fire
 from Heaven, 90
Black with the rude collision, inly torn,
By clouds surrounded, and on whirl-
 winds borne,
Driven o'er the lowering atmosphere that
 nurst
Thoughts which have turn'd to thunder—
 scorch, and burst.

 But far from us and from our mimic
 scene 95
Such things should be—if such have ever
 been;
Ours be the gentler wish, the kinder task,
To give the tribute Glory need not ask,
To mourn the vanish'd beam, and add
 our mite 99
Of praise in payment of a long delight.
Ye Orators! whom yet our councils yield,
Mourn for the veteran Hero of your field!
The worthy rival of the wondrous *Three*!
Whose words were sparks of Immortality!
Ye Bards! to whom the Drama's muse is
 dear, 105
He was your Master—emulate him *here*!
Ye men of wit and social eloquence!
He was your brother—bear his ashes
 hence!
While Powers of mind almost of bound-
 less range,
Complete in kind, as various in their
 change, 110
While Eloquence, Wit, Poesy, and Mirth,
That humbler Harmonist of care on
 Earth,
Survive within our souls—while lives our
 sense
Of pride in Merit's proud pre-eminence,
Long shall we seek his likeness, long in
 vain, 115
And turn to all of him which may remain,
Sighing that nature form'd but one such
 man,
And broke the die—in moulding Sheri-
 dan!

 Diodati, July 17, 1816.

CHURCHILL'S GRAVE

A FACT LITERALLY RENDERED

I STOOD beside the grave of him who
 blazed
The comet of a season, and I saw
The humblest of all sepulchres, and gazed
 With not the less of sorrow and of awe
On that neglected turf and quiet stone,
With name no clearer than the names un-
 known, 6
Which lay unread around it; and I ask'd
 The Gardener of that ground, why it
 might be
That for this plant strangers his memory
 task'd,
 Through the thick deaths of half a cen-
 tury? 10
And thus he answer'd—'Well, I do not
 know
Why frequent travellers turn to pilgrims
 so;
He died before my day of Sextonship,
 And I had not the digging of this grave.'
And is this all? I thought—and do we rip
 The veil of Immortality, and crave
I know not what of honour and of light
Through unborn ages, to endure this
 blight, 18
So soon, and so successless? As I said,
The Architect of all on which we tread,
For Earth is but a tombstone, did essay,
To extricate remembrance from the clay,
Whose minglings might confuse a New-
 ton's thought,
Were it not that all life must end in one,
Of which we are but dreamers;—as he
 caught, 25
As 'twere the twilight of a former Sun,
Thus spoke he,—'I believe the man of
 whom
You wot, who lies in this selected tomb,
Was a most famous writer in his day,
And therefore travellers step from out
 their way 30
To pay him honour,—and myself whate'er
 Your honour pleases:'—then most
 pleased I shook
From out my pocket's avaricious nook
Some certain coins of silver, which as
 'twere
Perforce I gave this man, though I could
 spare 35
So much but inconveniently:—Ye smile,
I see ye, ye profane ones! all the while,
Because my homely phrase the truth
 would tell.
You are the fools, not I—for I did dwell
With a deep thought, and with a soften'd
 eye, 40
On that Old Sexton's natural homily,
In which there was Obscurity and Fame—
The Glory and the Nothing of a Name.
 Diodati, 1816.

OCCASIONAL PIECES

PROMETHEUS

I

TITAN! to whose immortal eyes
 The sufferings of mortality,
 Seen in their sad reality,
Were not as things that gods despise;
What was thy pity's recompense? 5
A silent suffering, and intense;
The rock, the vulture, and the chain,
All that the proud can feel of pain,
The agony they do not show,
The suffocating sense of woe, 10
 Which speaks but in its loneliness,
And then is jealous lest the sky
Should have a listener, nor will sigh
 Until its voice is echoless.

II

Titan! to thee the strife was given 15
 Between the suffering and the will,
 Which torture where they cannot kill;
And the inexorable Heaven,
And the deaf tyranny of Fate,
The ruling principle of Hate, 20
Which for its pleasure doth create
The things it may annihilate,
Refused even the boon to die:
The wretched gift eternity 24
Was thine—and thou hast borne it well.
All that the Thunderer wrung from thee
Was but the menace which flung back
On him the torments of thy rack;
The fate thou didst so well foresee,
But would not to appease him tell; 30
And in thy Silence was his Sentence,
And in his Soul a vain repentance,
And evil dread so ill dissembled,
That in his hand the lightnings trembled.

III

Thy Godlike crime was to be kind, 35
 To render with thy precepts less
 The sum of human wretchedness,
And strengthen Man with his own mind;
But baffled as thou wert from high,
Still in thy patient energy, 40
In the endurance, and repulse
 Of thine impenetrable Spirit,
Which Earth and Heaven could not con-
 vulse,
 A mighty lesson we inherit:
Thou art a symbol and a sign 45
 To Mortals of their fate and force;
Like thee, Man is in part divine,
 A troubled stream from a pure source;
And Man in portions can foresee
His own funereal destiny; 50
His wretchedness, and his resistance,
And his sad unallied existence:
To which his Spirit may oppose
Itself—and equal to all woes,
 And a firm will, and a deep sense, 55

Which even in torture can descry
 Its own concenter'd recompense,
Triumphant where it dares defy,
And making Death a Victory.

Diodati, *July* 1816

A FRAGMENT

COULD I remount the river of my year
To the first fountain of our smiles and
 tears,
I would not trace again the stream of
 hours
Between their outworn banks of wither'd
 flowers,
But bid it flow as now—until it glides
Into the number of the nameless tides.

.

What is this Death?—a quiet of the heart
The whole of that of which we are a part
For life is but a vision—what I see
Of all which lives alone is life to me, 1
And being so—the absent are the dead,
Who haunt us from tranquillity, and
 spread
A dreary shroud around us, and invest
With sad remembrances our hours of rest
 The absent are the dead—for they are
 cold, 1
And ne'er can be what once we did behold
And they are changed, and cheerless,—
 or if yet
The unforgotten do not all forget,
Since thus divided—equal must it be
If the deep barrier be of earth, or sea; 2
It may be both—but one day end it must
In the dark union of insensate dust.
 The under-earth inhabitants—are they
But mingled millions decomposed to clay
The ashes of a thousand ages spread 2
Wherever man has trodden or shall tread
Or do they in their silent cities dwell
Each in his incommunicative cell?
Or have they their own language? and a
 sense
Of breathless being?—darken'd and in-
 tense 3
As midnight in her solitude?—Oh Earth
Where are the past?—and wherefore had
 they birth?
The dead are thy inheritors—and we
But bubbles on thy surface; and the
 key
Of thy profundity is in the grave, 3
The ebon portal of thy peopled cave,
Where I would walk in spirit, and behold
Our elements resolved to things untold,
And fathom hidden wonders, and ex-
 plore
The essence of great bosoms now no
 more. 4

.

Diodati, *July* 1816

98

SONNET TO LAKE LEMAN

ROUSSEAU—Voltaire—our Gibbon—and
De Staël—
 Leman! these names are worthy of thy
 shore,
 Thy shore of names like these! wert
 thou no more,
Their memory thy remembrance would
 recall: 4
To them thy banks were lovely as to all,
 But they have made them lovelier, for
 the lore
Of mighty minds doth hallow in the core
Of human hearts the ruin of a wall
 Where dwelt the wise and wondrous;
 but by *thee*
How much more, Lake of Beauty! do we
 feel, 10
 In sweetly gliding o'er thy crystal sea,
The wild glow of that not ungentle zeal,
 Which of the heirs of immortality
Is proud, and makes the breath of glory
 real!

 Diodati, *July* 1816.

STANZAS FOR MUSIC*

I

BRIGHT be the place of thy soul!
 No lovelier spirit than thine
E'er burst from its mortal control,
 In the orbs of the blessed to shine.
On earth thou wert all but divine,
 As thy soul shall immortally be;
And our sorrow may cease to repine
 When we know that thy God is with
 thee.

II

Light be the turf of thy tomb!
 May its verdure like emeralds be!
There should not be the shadow of gloom
 In aught that reminds us of thee.
Young flowers and an evergreen tree
 May spring from the spot of thy rest:
But not cypress nor yew let us see;
 For why should we mourn for the blest?

A VERY MOURNFUL BALLAD ON THE SIEGE AND CONQUEST OF ALHAMA

Which, in the Arabic language, is to the following purport

I

THE Moorish King rides up and down,
Through Granada's royal town;
From Elvira's gate to those
Of Bivarambla on he goes.
 Woe is me, Alhama!

* [See also p. 52.]

II

Letters to the monarch tell
How Alhama's city fell:
In the fire the scroll he threw,
And the messenger he slew.
 Woe is me, Alhama!

III

He quits his mule, and mounts his horse,
And through the street directs his course;
Through the street of Zacatin
To the Alhambra spurring in.
 Woe is me, Alhama!

IV

When the Alhambra walls he gain'd,
On the moment he ordain'd
That the trumpet straight should sound
With the silver clarion round.
 Woe is me, Alhama!

V

And when the hollow drums of war
Beat the loud alarm afar,
That the Moors of town and plain
Might answer to the martial strain.
 Woe is me, Alhama!

VI

Then the Moors, by this aware,
That bloody Mars recall'd them there,
One by one, and two by two,
To a mighty squadron grew.
 Woe is me, Alhama!

VII

Out then spake an aged Moor
In these words the king before,
'Wherefore call on us, oh King?
What may mean this gathering?'
 Woe is me, Alhama!

VIII

'Friends! ye have, alas! to know
Of a most disastrous blow;
That the Christians, stern and bold,
Have obtain'd Alhama's hold.'
 Woe is me, Alhama!

IX

Out then spake old Alfaqui,
With his beard so white to see,
'Good King! thou art justly served,
Good King! this thou hast deserved.
 Woe is me, Alhama!

OCCASIONAL PIECES

X

'By thee were slain, in evil hour,
The Abencerrage, Granada's flower;
And strangers were received by thee
Of Cordova the Chivalry.
 Woe is me, Alhama!

XI

'And for this, oh King! is sent
On thee a double chastisement:
Thee and thine, thy crown and realm,
One last wreck shall overwhelm.
 Woe is me, Alhama!

XII

'He who holds no laws in awe,
He must perish by the law;
And Granada must be won,
And thyself with her undone.'
 Woe is me, Alhama!

XIII

Fire flash'd from out the old Moor's eyes,
The Monarch's wrath began to rise,
Because he answer'd, and because
He spake exceeding well of laws.
 Woe is me, Alhama!

XIV

'There is no law to say such things
As may disgust the ear of kings:'—
Thus, snorting with his choler, said
The Moorish King, and doom'd him dead.
 Woe is me, Alhama!

XV

Moor Alfaqui! Moor Alfaqui!
Though thy beard so hoary be,
The King hath sent to have thee seized,
For Alhama's loss displeased.
 Woe is me, Alhama!

XVI

And to fix thy head upon
High Alhambra's loftiest stone;
That this for thee should be the law,
And others tremble when they saw.
 Woe is me, Alhama!

XVII

'Cavalier, and man of worth!
Let these words of mine go forth!
Let the Moorish Monarch know,
That to him I nothing owe.
 Woe is me, Alhama!

XVIII

'But on my soul Alhama weighs,
And on my inmost spirit preys;

And if the King his land hath lost,
Yet others may have lost the most.
 Woe is me, Alhama!

XIX

'Sires have lost their children, wives
Their lords, and valiant men their lives!
One what best his love might claim
Hath lost, another wealth, or fame.
 Woe is me, Alhama!

XX

'I lost a damsel in that hour,
Of all the land the loveliest flower;
Doubloons a hundred I would pay,
And think her ransom cheap that day.'
 Woe is me, Alhama!

XXI

And as these things the old Moor said,
They sever'd from the trunk his head;
And to the Alhambra's wall with speed
'Twas carried, as the King decreed.
 Woe is me, Alhama!

XXII

And men and infants therein weep
Their loss, so heavy and so deep;
Granada's ladies, all she rears
Within her walls, burst into tears.
 Woe is me, Alhama!

XXIII

And from the windows o'er the walls
The sable web of mourning falls;
The King weeps as a woman o'er
His loss, for it is much and sore.
 Woe is me, Alhama!

STANZAS FOR MUSIC

I

THEY say that Hope is happiness;
 But genuine Love must prize the past,
And Memory wakes the thoughts that
 bless:
 They rose the first—they set the last;

II

And all that Memory loves the most
 Was once our only Hope to be,
And all that Hope adored and lost
 Hath melted into Memory.

III

Alas! it is delusion all:
 The future cheats us from afar,
Nor can we be what we recall,
 Nor dare we think on what we are.

100

TRANSLATION FROM VITTORELLI

ON A NUN

Sonnet composed in the name of a father, whose daughter had recently died shortly after her marriage; and addressed to the father of her who had lately taken the veil.

OF two fair virgins, modest, though admired,
 Heaven made us happy; and now,
 wretched sires,
 Heaven for a nobler doom their worth
 desires,
And gazing upon *either*, *both* required.
Mine, while the torch of Hymen newly
 fired 5
 Becomes extinguish'd, soon—too soon
 —expires:
But thine, within the closing grate retired,
 Eternal captive, to her God aspires.
But *thou* at least from out the jealous door,
 Which shuts between your never-meet-
 ing eyes, 10
 May'st hear her sweet and pious voice
 once more:
I to the marble, where *my* daughter lies,
 Rush,—the swoln flood of bitterness
 I pour,
 And knock, and knock, and knock—
 but none replies.

ON THE BUST OF HELEN BY CANOVA

IN this beloved marble view,
 Above the works and thoughts of man,
What Nature *could*, but *would not*, do,
 And Beauty and Canova *can*!
Beyond imagination's power, 5
 Beyond the Bard's defeated art,
With immortality her dower,
 Behold the *Helen* of the *heart*!

November 1816.

SONG FOR THE LUDDITES

I

AS the Liberty lads o'er the sea
Bought their freedom, and cheaply, with
 blood,
 So we, boys, we
 Will *die* fighting, or *live* free,
And down with all kings but King Ludd!

II

When the web that we weave is complete,
And the shuttle exchanged for the sword,
 We will fling the winding sheet
 O'er the despot at our feet,
And dye it deep in the gore he has pour'd.

III

Though black as his heart its hue,
Since his veins are corrupted to mud,
 Yet this is the dew
 Which the tree shall renew
Of Liberty, planted by Ludd!

December 1816.

VERSICLES

I READ the 'Christabel';
 Very well:
I read the 'Missionary';
 Pretty—very
I tried at 'Ilderim'; 5
 Ahem!
I read a sheet of 'Marg'ret of *Anjou*';
 Can you?
I turn'd a page of Scott's 'Waterloo';
 Pooh! pooh! 10
I look'd at Wordsworth's milk-white
 'Rylstone Doe';
 Hillo!
 &c. &c. &c.

March 1817.

SO, WE'LL GO NO MORE A ROVING

I

SO, we'll go no more a roving
 So late into the night,
Though the heart be still as loving,
 And the moon be still as bright.

II

For the sword outwears its sheath,
 And the soul wears out the breast,
And the heart must pause to breathe,
 And love itself have rest.

III

Though the night was made for loving,
 And the day returns too soon,
Yet we'll go no more a roving
 By the light of the moon.

1817.

TO THOMAS MOORE

WHAT are you doing now,
 Oh Thomas Moore?
What are you doing now,
 Oh Thomas Moore?
Sighing or suing now, 5
Rhyming or wooing now,
Billing or cooing now,
 Which, Thomas Moore?

But the Carnival's coming,
 Oh Thomas Moore! 10
The Carnival's coming,
 Oh Thomas Moore!

Masking and humming,
Fifing and drumming,
Guitarring and strumming, 15
 Oh Thomas Moore!

TO MR. MURRAY

To hook the reader, you, John Murray,
Have publish'd 'Anjou's Margaret,'
Which won't be sold off in a hurry
 (At least, it has not been as yet);
And then, still further to bewilder 'em, 5
Without remorse, you set up 'Ilderim;'
 So mind you don't get into debt,
Because as how, if you should fail,
These books would be but baddish bail.

And mind you do *not* let escape 10
 These rhymes to Morning Post or Perry,
 Which would be *very* treacherous—
 very,
And get me into such a scrape!
 For, firstly, I should have to sally,
 All in my little boat, against a *Galley;*
And, should I chance to slay the Assyrian
 wight, 16
Have next to combat with the female
 knight.

March 25, 1817.

TO THOMAS MOORE

I

My boat is on the shore,
 And my bark is on the sea;
But, before I go, Tom Moore,
 Here's a double health to thee!

II

Here's a sigh to those who love me,
 And a smile to those who hate;
And, whatever sky's above me,
 Here's a heart for every fate.

III

Though the ocean roar around me,
 Yet it still shall bear me on;
Though a desert should surround me,
 It hath springs that may be won.

IV

Were't the last drop in the well,
 As I gasp'd upon the brink,
Ere my fainting spirit fell,
 'Tis to thee that I would drink.

V

With that water, as this wine,
 The libation I would pour
Should be—peace with thine and mine,
 And a health to thee, Tom Moore.

July 1817.

EPISTLE FROM MR. MURRAY
TO DR. POLIDORI

Dear Doctor, I have read your play,
Which is a good one in its way,—
Purges the eyes and moves the bowels,
And drenches handkerchiefs like towels
With tears, that, in a flux of grief, 5
Afford hysterical relief
To shatter'd nerves and quicken'd pulses,
Which your catastrophe convulses.

I like your moral and machinery;
Your plot, too, has such scope for scen-
 ery: 10
Your dialogue is apt and smart:
The play's concoction full of art;
Your hero raves, your heroine cries,
All stab, and everybody dies.
In short, your tragedy would be 15
The very thing to hear and see:
And for a piece of publication,
If I decline on this occasion,
It is not that I am not sensible
To merits in themselves ostensible, 20
But—and I grieve to speak it—plays
Are drugs—mere drugs, sir—now-a-days.
I had a heavy loss by 'Manuel,'—
Too lucky if it prove not annual,—
And Sotheby, with his 'Orestes,' 25
(Which, by the by, the author's best is,)
Has lain so very long on hand,
That I despair of all demand.
I've advertised, but see my books,
Or only watch my shopman's looks;—
Still Ivan, Ina, and such lumber, 31
My back-shop glut, my shelves encumber.

There's Byron too, who once did better,
Has sent me, folded in a letter,
A sort of—it's no more a drama 35
Than Darnley, Ivan, or Kehama:
So alter'd since last year his pen is,
I think he's lost his wits at Venice.
In short, sir, what with one and t'other,
I dare not venture on another. 40
I write in haste; excuse each blunder;
The coaches through the street so thun-
 der!
My room's so full—we've Gifford here
Reading MS., with Hookham Frere,
Pronouncing on the nouns and particles
Of some of our forthcoming Articles. 46

The Quarterly—Ah, sir, if you
Had but the genius to review!—
A smart critique upon St. Helena,
Or if you only would but tell in a 50
Short compass what——but to resume:
As I was saying, sir, the room—
The room's so full of wits and bards,
Crabbes, Campbells, Crokers, Freres, and
 Wards,

And others, neither bards nor wits:—
My humble tenement admits 56
All persons in the dress of gent,
From Mr. Hammond to Dog Dent.

A party dines with me to-day,
All clever men, who make their way;
Crabbe, Malcolm, Hamilton, and Chan-
trey, 61
Are all partakers of my pantry.
They're at this moment in discussion
On poor De Staël's late dissolution.
Her book, they say, was in advance—
Pray Heaven, she tell the truth of France!
Thus run our time and tongues away;—
But, to return, sir, to your play:
Sorry, sir, but I cannot deal,
Unless 'twere acted by O'Neill; 70
My hands so full, my head so busy,
I'm almost dead, and always dizzy;
And so, with endless truth and hurry,
Dear Doctor, I am yours,
 JOHN MURRAY.
 August 1817.

EPISTLE TO MR. MURRAY

My dear Mr. Murray,
You're in a damn'd hurry,
 To set up this ultimate Canto;
But (if they don't rob us)
You'll see Mr. Hobhouse 5
 Will bring it safe in his portmanteau.

For the Journal you hint of,
As ready to print off,
 No doubt you do right to commend it;
But as yet I have writ off 10
The devil a bit of
 Our 'Beppo:'—when copied, I'll send
 it.

Then you've Sotheby's Tour,—
No great things, to be sure,—
 You could hardly begin with a less
 work; 15
For the pompous rascallion,
Who don't speak Italian
 Nor French, must have scribbled by
 guess work.

You can make any loss up
With 'Spence' and his gossip, 20
 A work which must surely succeed;
Then Queen Mary's Epistle-craft,
With the new 'Fytte' of 'Whistlecraft,'
 Must make people purchase and read.

Then you've General Gordon, 25
Who girded his sword on,
 To serve with a Muscovite master
And help him to polish
A nation so owlish,
 They thought shaving their beards a
 disaster. 30

For the man, 'poor and shrewd,'
With whom you'd conclude
 A compact without more delay,
Perhaps some such pen is
Still extant in Venice; 35
 But please, sir, to mention *your pay*.
 Venice, *January* 8, 1818.

TO MR. MURRAY

STRAHAN, Tonson, Lintot of the times,
Patron and publisher of rhymes,
For thee the bard up Pindus climbs,
 My Murray.

To thee, with hope and terror dumb, 5
The unfledged MS. authors come;
Thou printest all—and sellest some—
 My Murray.

Upon thy table's baize so green
The last new Quarterly is seen,— 10
But where is thy new Magazine,
 My Murray?

Along thy sprucest bookshelves shine
The works thou deemest most divine—
The 'Art of Cookery,' and mine, 15
 My Murray.

Tours, Travels, Essays, too, I wist,
And Sermons, to thy mill bring grist;
And then thou hast the 'Navy List,'
 My Murray. 20

And Heaven forbid I should conclude
Without 'the Board of Longitude,'
Although this narrow paper would,
 My Murray.
 Venice, *March* 25, 1818.

ON THE BIRTH OF
JOHN WILLIAM RIZZO HOPPNER

HIS father's sense, his mother's grace,
 In him, I hope, will always fit so;
With—still to keep him in good case—
 The health and appetite of Rizzo.
 February 1818.

ODE ON VENICE

I

OH Venice! Venice! when thy marble walls
 Are level with the waters, there shall be
A cry of nations o'er thy sunken halls,
 A loud lament along the sweeping sea!
If I, a northern wanderer, weep for thee,
What should thy sons do?—anything but
 weep: 6
And yet they only murmur in their sleep.
In contrast with their fathers—as the
 slime,
The dull green ooze of the receding deep,
Is with the dashing of the spring-tide foam
That drives the sailor shipless to his home,

Are they to those that were; and thus they creep, 12
Crouching and crab-like, through their sapping streets.
Oh! agony—that centuries should reap
No mellower harvest! Thirteen hundred years 15
Of wealth and glory turn'd to dust and tears;
And every monument the stranger meets,
Church, palace, pillar, as a mourner greets;
And even the Lion all subdued appears,
And the harsh sound of the barbarian drum, 20
With dull and daily dissonance, repeats
The echo of thy tyrant's voice along
The soft waves, once all musical to song,
That heaved beneath the moonlight with the throng
Of gondolas—and to the busy hum 25
Of cheerful creatures, whose most sinful deeds
Were but the overbeating of the heart,
And flow of too much happiness, which needs
The aid of age to turn its course apart
From the luxuriant and voluptuous flood
Of sweet sensations, battling with the blood. 31
But these are better than the gloomy errors,
The weeds of nations in their last decay,
When Vice walks forth with her unsoften'd terrors,
And Mirth is madness, and but smiles to slay; 35
And Hope is nothing but a false delay,
The sick man's lightning half an hour ere death,
When Faintness, the last mortal birth of Pain,
And apathy of limb, the dull beginning
Of the cold staggering race which Death is winning, 40
Steals vein by vein and pulse by pulse away;
Yet so relieving the o'er-tortured clay,
To him appears renewal of his breath,
And freedom the mere numbness of his chain; 44
And then he talks of life, and how again
He feels his spirit soaring—albeit weak,
And of the fresher air, which he would seek:
And as he whispers knows not that he gasps,
That his thin finger feels not what it clasps,
And so the film comes o'er him, and the dizzy 50
Chamber swims round and round, and shadows busy,
At which he vainly catches, flit and gleam,
Till the last rattle chokes the strangled scream,

And all is ice and blackness,—and the earth
That which it was the moment ere our birth. 55

II

There is no hope for nations!—Search the page
Of many thousand years—the daily scene,
The flow and ebb of each recurring age,
The everlasting *to be* which *hath been*,
Hath taught us nought, or little: still we lean 60
On things that rot beneath our weight, and wear
Our strength away in wrestling with the air:
For 'tis our nature strikes us down: the beasts
Slaughter'd in hourly hecatombs for feasts
Are of as high an order—they must go
Even where their driver goads them, though to slaughter. 66
Ye men, who pour your blood for kings as water,
What have they given your children in return?
A heritage of servitude and woes,
A blindfold bondage, where your hire is blows. 70
What! do not yet the red-hot plough-shares burn,
O'er which you stumble in a false ordeal,
And deem this proof of loyalty the *real;*
Kissing the hand that guides you to your scars,
And glorying as you tread the glowing bars? 75
All that your sires have left you, all that Time
Bequeaths of free, and History of sublime,
Spring from a different theme! Ye see and read,
Admire and sigh, and then succumb and bleed!
Save the few spirits who, despite of all,
And worse than all, the sudden crimes engender'd 81
By the down-thundering of the prison-wall,
And thirst to swallow the sweet waters tender'd,
Gushing from Freedom's fountains, when the crowd,
Madden'd with centuries of drought, are loud, 85
And trample on each other to obtain
The cup which brings oblivion of a chain
Heavy and sore, in which long yoked they plough'd
The sand,—or if there sprung the yellow grain,

'Twas not for them, their necks were too
 much bow'd, 90
And their dead palates chew'd the cud of
 pain:
Yes! the few spirits, who, despite of deeds
Which they abhor, confound not with the
 cause
Those momentary starts from Nature's
 laws,
Which, like the pestilence and earthquake,
 smite 95
But for a term, then pass, and leave the
 earth
With all her seasons to repair the blight
With a few summers, and again put forth
Cities and generations—fair, when free—
For, Tyranny, there blooms no bud for
 thee! 100

III

Glory and Empire! once upon these
 towers
 With Freedom—godlike Triad! how ye
 sate!
The league of mightiest nations, in those
 hours
 When Venice was an envy, might abate,
 But did not quench her spirit; in her
 fate 105
All were enwrapp'd: the feasted monarchs
 knew
 And loved their hostess, nor could learn
 to hate,
Although they humbled—with the kingly
 few
The many felt, for from all days and climes
She was the voyager's worship; even her
 crimes 110
Were of the softer order—born of Love,
She drank no blood, nor fatten'd on the
 dead,
But gladden'd where her harmless con-
 quests spread;
For these restored the Cross, that from
 above
Hallow'd her sheltering banners, which
 incessant 115
Flew between earth and the unholy Cres-
 cent,
Which, if it waned and dwindled, Earth
 may thank
The city it has clothed in chains, which
 clank
Now, creaking in the ears of those who
 owe
The name of Freedom to her glorious
 struggles; 120
Yet she but shares with them a common
 woe,
And call'd the 'kingdom' of a conquering
 foe,
But knows what all—and, most of all, *we*
 know—
With what set gilded terms a tyrant juggles!

IV

The name of Commonwealth is past and
 gone 125
O'er the three fractions of the groaning
 globe;
Venice is crush'd, and Holland deigns to
 own
 A sceptre, and endures the purple robe;
If the free Switzer yet bestrides alone
His chainless mountains, 'tis but for a
 time, 130
For tyranny of late is cunning grown,
And in its own good season tramples down
The sparkles of our ashes. One great
 clime,
Whose vigorous offspring by dividing ocean
Are kept apart and nursed in the devotion
Of Freedom, which their fathers fought
 for, and 136
Bequeath'd—a heritage of heart and hand,
And proud distinction from each other
 land,
Whose sons must bow them at a monarch's
 motion,
As if his senseless sceptre were a wand
Full of the magic of exploded science—
Still one great clime, in full and free de-
 fiance, 142
Yet rears her crest, unconquer'd and sub-
 lime,
Above the far Atlantic!—She has taught
Her Esau-brethren that the haughty flag,
The floating fence of Albion's feebler crag,
May strike to those whose red right hands
 have bought 147
Rights cheaply earn'd with blood. Still,
 still, for ever,
Better, though each man's life-blood were
 a river,
That it should flow, and overflow, than
 creep 150
Through thousand lazy channels in our
 veins,
Damm'd like the dull canal with locks and
 chains,
And moving, as a sick man in his sleep,
Three paces, and then faltering: better be
Where the extinguish'd Spartans still are
 free, 155
In their proud charnel of Thermopylæ,
Than stagnate in our marsh,—or o'er the
 deep
Fly, and one current to the ocean add,
One spirit to the souls our fathers had,
One freeman more, America, to thee!

STANZAS TO THE PO

RIVER, that rollest by the ancient walls,
 Where dwells the lady of my love, when
 she
Walks by thy brink, and there perchance
 recalls
 A faint and fleeting memory of me;

What if thy deep and ample stream should
 be 5
 A mirror of my heart, where she may
 read
The thousand thoughts I now betray to thee,
 Wild as thy wave, and headlong as thy
 speed!

What do I say—a mirror of my heart?
 Are not thy waters sweeping, dark, and
 strong? 10
Such as my feelings were and are, thou art;
 And such as thou art were my passions
 long.

Time may have somewhat tamed them,—
 not for ever;
 Thou overflow'st thy banks, and not for
 aye 14
Thy bosom overboils, congenial river!
 Thy floods subside, and mine have sunk
 away:

But left long wrecks behind, and now again,
 Borne on our old unchanged career, we
 move:
Thou tendest wildly onwards to the main,
 And I—to loving *one* I should not love.

The current I behold will sweep beneath
 Her native walls, and murmur at her
 feet; 22
Her eyes will look on thee, when she shall
 breathe
 The twilight air, unharm'd by summer's
 heat.

She will look on thee,—I have look'd on
 thee, 25
 Full of that thought: and, from that
 moment, ne'er
Thy waters could I dream of, name, or see
 Without the inseparable sigh for her!

Her bright eyes will be imaged in thy
 stream,
 Yes! they will meet the wave I gaze on
 now: 30
Mine cannot witness, even in a dream,
 That happy wave repass me in its flow!

The wave that bears my tears returns no
 more:
 Will she return by whom that wave shall
 sweep?—
Both tread thy banks, both wander on
 thy shore, 35
 I by thy source, she by the dark-blue
 deep.

But that which keepeth us apart is not
 Distance, nor depth of wave, nor space
 of earth,
But the distraction of a various lot,
 As various as the climates of our birth.

A stranger loves the lady of the land, 41
 Born far beyond the mountains, but his
 blood
Is all meridian, as if never fann'd
 By the black wind that chills the polar
 flood.

My blood is all meridian; were it not, 45
 I had not left my clime, nor should I be,
In spite of tortures ne'er to be forgot,
 A slave again of love,—at least of thee.

'Tis vain to struggle—let me perish
 young— 49
 Live as I lived, and love as I have loved;
To dust if I return, from dust I sprung,
 And then, at least, my heart can ne'er
 be moved.
 April 1819.

SONNET TO GEORGE THE FOURTH

ON THE REPEAL OF LORD EDWARD FITZGERALD'S FORFEITURE

To be the father of the fatherless,
 To stretch the hand from the throne's
 height, and raise
 His offspring, who expired in other days
To make thy sire's sway by a kingdom
 less,—
This is to be a monarch, and repress 5
 Envy into unutterable praise.
Dismiss thy guard, and trust thee to such
 traits,
For who would lift a hand, except to bless?
 Were it not easy, sir, and is't not sweet
To make thyself beloved? and to be
Omnipotent by mercy's means? for thus
 Thy sovereignty would grow but more
 complete: 12
A despot thou, and yet thy people free,
 And by the heart, not hand, enslaving us.
 Bologna, August 12, 1819.

EPIGRAM

FROM THE FRENCH OF RULHIÈRES

If, for silver or for gold,
 You could melt ten thousand pimples
 Into half a dozen dimples,
Then your face we might behold, 4
 Looking, doubtless, much more snugly;
 Yet even *then* 'twould be damned ugly.
 August 12, 1819.

STANZAS

Could Love for ever
 Run like a river,
 And Time's endeavour
 Be tried in vain—
No other pleasure 5
 With this could measure;
 And like a treasure
 We'd hug the chain.

But since our sighing
Ends not in dying, 10
And, form'd for flying,
 Love plumes his wing;
Then for this reason
Let's love a season;
But let that season be only Spring. 15

When lovers parted
Feel broken-hearted,
And, all hopes thwarted,
 Expect to die;
A few years older, 20
Ah! how much colder
They might behold her
 For whom they sigh!
When link'd together,
In every weather, 25
They pluck Love's feather
 From out his wing—
He'll stay for ever,
But sadly shiver
Without his plumage, when past the Spring.

Like chiefs of Faction, 31
His life is action—
A formal paction
 That curbs his reign,
Obscures his glory, 35
Despot no more, he
Such territory
 Quits with disdain.
Still, still advancing,
With banners glancing, 40
His power enhancing,
 He must move on—
Repose but cloys him,
Retreat destroys him,
Love brooks not a degraded throne. 45

Wait not, fond lover!
Till years are over,
And then recover
 As from a dream.
While each bewailing 50
The other's failing,
With wrath and railing,
 All hideous seem—
While first decreasing,
Yet not quite ceasing, 55
Wait not till teasing
 All passion blight:
If once diminish'd,
Love's reign is finish'd—
Then part in friendship—and bid good-
night. 60

So shall Affection
To recollection
The dear connexion
 Bring back with joy:
You had not waited 65
Till, tired or hated,
Your passions sated
 Began to cloy.

Your last embraces
Leave no cold traces— 70
The same fond faces
 As through the past:
And eyes, the mirrors
Of your sweet errors,
Reflect but rapture—not least though last.

True, separations 76
Ask more than patience;
What desperations
 From such have risen!
But yet remaining, 80
What is't but chaining
Hearts which, once waning,
 Beat 'gainst their prison?
Time can but cloy love
And use destroy love: 85
The winged boy, Love,
 Is but for boys—
You'll find it torture,
Though sharper, shorter,
To wean, and not wear out your joys.
 1819

ON MY WEDDING-DAY

Here's a happy new year! but with reason
I beg you'll permit me to say—
Wish me *many* returns of the *season*,
But as *few* as you please of the day.
 January 2, 1820.

EPITAPH FOR WILLIAM PITT

With death doom'd to grapple,
 Beneath this cold slab, he
Who lied in the Chapel
 Now lies in the Abbey.
 January 1820.

EPIGRAM

In digging up your bones, Tom Paine,
 Will. Cobbett has done well:
You visit him on earth again,
 He'll visit you in hell.
 January 1820.

STANZAS

When a man hath no freedom to fight
 for at home,
 Let him combat for that of his neigh-
 bours;
Let him think of the glories of Greece and
 of Rome,
 And get knock'd on the head for his
 labours.
To do good to mankind is the chivalrous
 plan, 5
 And is always as nobly requited;
Then battle for freedom wherever you can,
 And, if not shot or hang'd, you'll get
 knighted.
 November 1820.

107

OCCASIONAL PIECES

EPIGRAM

THE world is a bundle of hay,
 Mankind are the asses who pull;
Each tugs it a different way,
 And the greatest of all is John Bull.

THE CHARITY BALL

WHAT matter the pangs of a husband and
 father,
If his sorrows in exile be great or be small,
So the Pharisee's glories around her she
 gather,
 And the saint patronizes her 'charity
 ball!'

What matters—a heart which, though
 faulty, was feeling, 5
 Be driven to excesses which once could
 appal—
That the sinner should suffer is only fair
 dealing,
 As the saint keeps her charity back for
 'the ball'!

EPIGRAM

ON THE BRAZIERS' COMPANY HAVING RE-
SOLVED TO PRESENT AN ADDRESS TO
QUEEN CAROLINE

THE braziers, it seems, are preparing to pass
An address, and present it themselves all
 in brass;—
A superfluous pageant—for, by the Lord
 Harry!
They'll find where they're going much
 more than they carry.

EPIGRAM ON MY WEDDING-DAY

TO PENELOPE

THIS day, of all our days, has done
 The worst for me and you:—
'Tis just *six* years since we were *one*,
 And *five* since we were *two*.
 January 2, 1821.

ON MY THIRTY-THIRD BIRTHDAY

JANUARY 22, 1821

THROUGH life's dull road, so dim and dirty,
I have dragg'd to three-and-thirty.
What have these years left to me?
Nothing—except thirty-three.

MARTIAL, LIB. I, EPIG. I

'Hic est, quem legis, ille, quem requiris,
 Tota notus in orbe Martialis,' &c.

HE unto whom thou art so partial,
Oh, reader! is the well-known Martial,
The Epigrammatist: while living,
Give him the fame thou wouldst be giving;
So shall he hear, and feel, and know it— 5
 Post obits rarely reach a poet.

BOWLES AND CAMPBELL

To the tune of 'Why, how now, saucy jade?'

WHY, how now, saucy Tom?
 If you thus must ramble,
I will publish some
 Remarks on Mister Campbell.

ANSWER

WHY, how now, Billy Bowles? 5
 Sure the priest is maudlin!
(*To the public*) How can you, d—n your
 souls!
Listen to his twaddling?
 February 22, 1821.

EPIGRAMS

OH, Castlereagh! thou art a patriot now;
Cato died for his country, so didst thou:
He perish'd rather than see Rome en-
 slaved,
Thou cutt'st thy throat that Britain may
 be saved!

So Castlereagh has cut his throat!—The
 worst
Of this is,—that his own was not the first.

So *He* has cut his throat at last!—He!
 Who?
The man who cut his country's long ago.

EPITAPH

POSTERITY will ne'er survey
 A nobler grave than this:
Here lie the bones of Castlereagh:
 Stop, traveller———

JOHN KEATS

WHO kill'd John Keats?
 'I,' says the Quarterly,
 So savage and Tartarly;
 ' 'Twas one of my feats.'

Who shot the arrow? 5
 'The poet-priest Milman
(So ready to kill man),
 Or Southey, or Barrow.'
 July 1821.

THE CONQUEST

[This fragment was found amongst Lord Byron's
papers after his departure from Genoa for
Greece.]

THE Son of Love and Lord of War I sing;
 Him who bade England bow to Nor-
 mandy,
And left the name of conqueror more
 than king
 To his unconquerable dynasty.

Not fann'd alone by Victory's fleeting
 wing, 5
He rear'd his bold and brilliant throne
 on high:
The Bastard kept, like lions, his prey fast,
And Britain's bravest victor was the
 last.

 March 8–9, 1823.

TO MR. MURRAY

For Orford and for Waldegrave
You give much more than me you gave;
Which is not fairly to behave,
 My Murray.

Because if a live dog, 'tis said, 5
Be worth a lion fairly sped,
A *live lord* must be worth *two* dead,
 My Murray.

And if, as the opinion goes, 9
Verse hath a better sale than prose,—
Certes, I should have more than those,
 My Murray.

But now this sheet is nearly cramm'd,
So, if *you will, I* shan't be shamm'd,
And if you *won't, you* may be damn'd,
 My Murray. 16

THE IRISH AVATAR

'And Ireland, like a bastinadoed elephant,
kneeling to receive the paltry rider.'—CURRAN.

Ere the daughter of Brunswick is cold in
 her grave,
And her ashes still float to their home
 o'er the tide,
Lo! George the triumphant speeds over
 the wave,
To the long-cherish'd isle which he
 loved like his—bride!

True, the great of her bright and brief era
 are gone, 5
The rainbow-like epoch where Freedom
 could pause
For the few little years, out of centuries
 won,
Which betray'd not, or crush'd not, or
 wept not her cause.

True, the chains of the Catholic clank o'er
 his rags,
The castle still stands, and the senate 's
 no more, 10
And the famine which dwelt on her free-
 domless crags
Is extending its steps to her desolate
 shore.

To her desolate shore—where the emi-
 grant stands
For a moment to gaze ere he flies from
 his hearth;

Tears fall on his chain, though it drops
 from his hands, 15
For the dungeon he quits is the place of
 his birth.

But he comes! the Messiah of royalty
 comes!
Like a goodly Leviathan roll'd from the
 waves;
Then receive him as best such an advent
 becomes,
With a legion of cooks, and an army of
 slaves! 20

He comes in the promise and bloom of
 threescore,
To perform in the pageant the sove-
 reign's part—
But long live the shamrock, which sha-
 dows him o'er!
Could the green in his *hat* be transferr'd
 to his *heart!*

Could that long-wither'd spot but be ver-
 dant again, 25
And a new spring of noble affections
 arise—
Then might freedom forgive thee this
 dance in thy chain,
And this shout of thy slavery which sad-
 dens the skies.

Is it madness or meanness which clings to
 thee now?
Were he God—as he is but the com-
 monest clay, 30
With scarce fewer wrinkles than sins on
 his brow—
Such servile devotion might shame him
 away.

Ay, roar in his train! let thine orators lash
 Their fanciful spirits to pamper his
 pride—
Not thus did thy Grattan indignantly flash
 His soul o'er the freedom implored and
 denied. 36

Ever glorious Grattan! the best of the
 good!
So simple in heart, so sublime in the rest!
With all which Demosthenes wanted en-
 dued,
And his rival or victor in all he possess'd.

Ere Tully arose in the zenith of Rome,
 Though unequall'd, preceded, the task
 was begun— 42
But Grattan sprung up like a god from the
 tomb
Of ages, the first, last, the saviour, the
 one!

109

OCCASIONAL PIECES

With the skill of an Orpheus to soften the
 brute; 45
 With the fire of Prometheus to kindle
 mankind;
Even Tyranny listening sate melted or
 mute,
 And Corruption shrunk scorch'd from
 the glance of his mind.

But back to our theme! Back to despots
 and slaves!
 Feasts furnish'd by Famine! rejoicings
 by Pain! 50
True freedom but *welcomes*, while slavery
 still *raves*,
 When a week's saturnalia hath loosen'd
 her chain.

Let the poor squalid splendour thy wreck
 can afford
 (As the bankrupt's profusion his ruin
 would hide),
Gild over the palace, Lo! Erin, thy lord!
 Kiss his foot with thy blessing, his bless-
 ings denied! 56

Or *if* freedom past hope be extorted at last,
 If the idol of brass find his feet are of
 clay,
Must what terror or policy wring forth be
 class'd
 With what monarchs ne'er give, but as
 wolves yield their prey? 60

Each brute hath its nature; a king's is to
 reign,—
To *reign!* in that word see, ye ages, com-
 prised
The cause of the curses all annals contain,
 From Cæsar the dreaded to George the
 despised!

Wear, Fingal, thy trapping! O'Connell,
 proclaim 65
 His accomplishments! *Hist!!!* and thy
 country convince
Half an age's contempt was an error of
 fame,
 And that 'Hal is the rascaliest, sweet-
 est *young* prince!'

Will thy yard of blue riband, poor Fingal,
 recall
 The fetters from millions of Catholic
 limbs? 70
Or, has it not bound thee the fastest of all
 The slaves, who now hail their betrayer
 with hymns?

Ay! 'Build him a dwelling!' let each give
 his mite!
 Till, like Babel, the new royal dome
 hath arisen!

Let thy beggars and helots their pittance
 unite— 7
 And a palace bestow for a poor-house
 and prison!

Spread—spread, for Vitellius, the roya
 repast,
 Till the gluttonous despot be stuff'd to
 the gorge!
And the roar of his drunkards proclaim
 him at last
 The fourth of the fools and oppressor
 call'd 'George!' 8

Let the tables be loaded with feasts till the
 groan!
 Till they *groan* like thy people, through
 ages of woe!
Let the wine flow around the old Bac
 chanal's throne,
 Like their blood which has flow'd, and
 which yet has to flow.

But let not *his* name be thine idol alone—
 On his right hand behold a Sejanu
 appears! 8
Thine own Castlereagh! let him still be
 thine own!
 A wretch never named but with curse
 and jeers!

Till now, when the isle which should blush
 for his birth,
 Deep, deep as the gore which he shed
 on her soil, 9
Seems proud of the reptile which crawl'd
 from her earth,
 And for murder repays him with shout
 and a smile.

Without one single ray of her genius, with
 out
 The fancy, the manhood, the fire of he
 race—
The miscreant who well might plunge Erin
 in doubt 9
 If *she* ever gave birth to a being so base

If she did—let her long-boasted provert
 be hush'd,
 Which proclaims that from Erin ne
 reptile can spring—
See the cold-blooded serpent, with venom
 full flush'd,
 Still warming its folds in the breast of a
 king! 10

Shout, drink, feast, and flatter! Oh! Erin
 how low
 Wert thou sunk by misfortune and
 tyranny, till
Thy welcome of tyrants hath plunged thee
 below
 The depth of thy deep in a deeper gulf
 still!

My voice, though but humble, was raised
 for thy right, 105
My vote, as a freeman's, still voted thee
 free,
This hand, though but feeble, would arm
 in thy fight,
And this heart, though outworn, had a
 throb still for *thee!*

Yes, I loved thee and thine, though thou
 art not my land,
I have known noble hearts and great
 souls in thy sons, 110
And I wept with the world, o'er the patriot
 band
Who are gone, but I weep them no
 longer as once.

For happy are they now reposing afar,—
Thy Grattan, thy Curran, thy Sheridan,
 all
Who, for years, were the chiefs in the
 eloquent war, 115
And redeem'd, if they have not retarded,
 thy fall.

Yes, happy are they in their cold English
 graves!
Their shades cannot start to thy shouts
 of to-day—
Nor the steps of enslavers and chain-kiss-
 ing slaves
Be stamp'd in the turf o'er their fetter-
 less clay. 120

Till now I had envied thy sons and their
 shore,
Though their virtues were hunted, their
 liberties fled;
There was something so warm and sublime
 in the core
Of an Irishman's heart, that I envy—
 thy *dead.*

Or, if aught in my bosom can quench for
 an hour 125
My contempt for a nation so servile,
 though sore,
Which though trod like the worm will not
 turn upon power,
'Tis the glory of Grattan, and genius of
 Moore!

 September 1821.

STANZAS WRITTEN ON THE ROAD BETWEEN FLORENCE AND PISA

Oh, talk not to me of a name great in
 story;
The days of our youth are the days of our
 glory;
And the myrtle and ivy of sweet two-and-
 twenty
Are worth all your laurels, though ever so
 plenty.

What are garlands and crowns to the brow
 that is wrinkled? 5
'Tis but as a dead flower with May-dew
 besprinkled.
Then away with all such from the head
 that is hoary!
What care I for the wreaths that can *only*
 give glory!

Oh FAME!—if I e'er took delight in thy
 praises,
'Twas less for the sake of thy high-sound-
 ing phrases, 10
Than to see the bright eyes of the dear one
 discover,
She thought that I was not unworthy to
 love her.

There chiefly I sought thee, *there* only I
 found thee;
Her glance was the best of the rays that
 surround thee;
When it sparkled o'er aught that was
 bright in my story, 15
I knew it was love, and I felt it was glory.
 November, 1821.

STANZAS TO A HINDOO AIR

OH! my lonely—lonely—lonely—Pil-
 low!
Where is my lover? where is my lover?
Is it his bark which my dreary dreams dis-
 cover?
Far—far away! and alone along the
 billow?

Oh! my lonely—lonely—lonely—Pil-
 low! 5
Why must my head ache where his gentle
 brow lay?
How the long night flags lovelessly and
 slowly,
And my head droops over thee like the
 willow!

Oh! thou, my sad and solitary Pillow!
Send me kind dreams to keep my heart
 from breaking, 10
In return for the tears I shed upon thee
 waking;
Let me not die till he comes back o'er
 the billow.

Then if thou wilt—no more my *lonely*
 Pillow,
In one embrace let these arms again enfold
 him,
And then expire of the joy—but to behold
 him! 15
Oh! my lone bosom!—oh! my lonely
 Pillow!

111

OCCASIONAL PIECES

IMPROMPTU

BENEATH Blessington's eyes
The reclaimed Paradise
Should be free as the former from evil;
But if the new Eve
For an Apple should grieve, 5
What mortal would not play the Devil?
 1823.

TO THE COUNTESS OF BLESSINGTON

YOU have ask'd for a verse:—the request
In a rhymer 'twere strange to deny;
But my Hippocrene was but my breast,
And my feelings (its fountain) are dry.

Were I now as I was, I had sung 5
What Lawrence has painted so well;
But the strain would expire on my tongue,
And the theme is too soft for my shell.

I am ashes where once I was fire,
And the bard in my bosom is dead;
What I loved I now merely admire, 11
And my heart is as grey as my head.

My life is not dated by years—
There are moments which act as a
 plough;
And there is not a furrow appears 15
But is deep in my soul as my brow.

Let the young and the brilliant aspire
To sing what I gaze on in vain;
For sorrow has torn from my lyre 19
The string which was worthy the strain.

ON THIS DAY I COMPLETE MY THIRTY-SIXTH YEAR

MISSOLONGHI, Jan. 22, 1824.

'Tis time this heart should be unmoved,
Since others it hath ceased to move:
Yet, though I cannot be beloved,
 Still let me love!

My days are in the yellow leaf; 5
The flowers and fruits of love are gone
The worm, the canker, and the grief
 Are mine alone!

The fire that on my bosom preys
Is lone as some volcanic isle; 10
No torch is kindled at its blaze—
 A funeral pile.

The hope, the fear, the jealous care,
The exalted portion of the pain
And power of love, I cannot share, 15
 But wear the chain.

But 'tis not *thus*—and 'tis not *here*—
Such thoughts should shake my soul
 nor *now*,
Where glory decks the hero's bier,
 Or binds his brow. 20

The sword, the banner, and the field,
Glory and Greece, around me see!
The Spartan, borne upon his shield,
 Was not more free.

Awake! (not Greece—she *is* awake!) 25
Awake, my spirit! Think through *whom*
Thy life-blood tracks its parent lake,
 And then strike home!

Tread those reviving passions down,
Unworthy manhood!—unto thee 30
Indifferent should the smile or frown
 Of beauty be.

If thou regrett'st thy youth, *why live?*
The land of honourable death
Is here:—up to the field, and give 35
 Away thy breath!

Seek out—less often sought than found—
A soldier's grave, for thee the best;
Then look around, and choose thy ground,
 And take thy rest. 40

112

SATIRES

ENGLISH BARDS AND SCOTCH REVIEWERS

A SATIRE

'I had rather be a kitten, and cry mew!
Than one of these same metre ballad-mongers.'
<div align="right">SHAKSPEARE.</div>

'Such shameless bards we have; and yet 'tis true,
There are as mad, abandon'd critics too.'—POPE.

PREFACE*

ALL my friends, learned and unlearned, have urged me not to publish this Satire with my name. If I were to be 'turned from the career of my humour by quibbles quick, and paper bullets of the brain,' I should have complied with their counsel. But I am not to be terrified by abuse, or bullied by reviewers, with or without arms. I can safely say that I have attacked none personally, who did not commence on the offensive. An author's works are public property: he who purchases may judge, and publish his opinion if he pleases; and the authors I have endeavoured to commemorate may do by me as I have done by them. I dare say they will succeed better in condemning my scribblings, than in mending their own. But my object is not to prove that I can write well, but, if possible, to make others write better.

As the poem has met with far more success than I expected, I have endeavoured in this edition to make some additions and alterations, to render it more worthy of public perusal.

In the first edition of this satire, published anonymously, fourteen lines on the subject of Bowles's Pope were written by, and inserted at the request of, an ingenious friend of mine†, who has now in the press a volume of poetry. In the present edition they are erased, and some of my own substituted in their stead; my only reason for this being that which I conceive would operate with any other person in the same manner,—a determination not to publish with my name any production which was not entirely and exclusively my own composition.

With‡ regard to the real talents of many of the poetical persons whose performances are mentioned or alluded to in the following pages, it is presumed by the author that there can be little difference of opinion in the public at large; though, like other sectaries, each has his separate tabernacle of proselytes, by whom his abilities are over-rated, his faults overlooked, and his metrical canons received without scruple and without consideration. But the unquestionable possession of considerable genius by several of the writers here censured renders their mental prostitution more to be regretted. Imbecility may be pitied, or, at worst, laughed at and forgotten: perverted powers demand the most decided reprehension. No one can wish more than the author that some known and able writer had undertaken their exposure; but Mr. Gifford has devoted himself to Massinger, and, in the absence of the regular physician, a country practitioner may, in cases of absolute necessity, be allowed to prescribe his nostrum to prevent the extension of so deplorable an epidemic, provided there be no quackery in his treatment of the malady. A caustic is here offered; as it is to be feared nothing short of actual cautery can recover the numerous patients afflicted with the present prevalent and distressing *rabies* for rhyming.—As to the Edinburgh Reviewers, it would indeed require an Hercules to crush the Hydra; but if the author succeeds in merely 'bruising one of the heads of the serpent,' though his own hand should suffer in the encounter, he will be amply satisfied.

STILL must I hear?—shall hoarse Fitz-
 gerald bawl
His creaking couplets in a tavern hall,
And I not sing, lest, haply, Scotch reviews
Should dub me scribbler, and denounce
 my muse?
Prepare for rhyme—I'll publish, right or
 wrong: 5
Fools are my theme, let satire be my song.

 Oh! nature's noblest gift—my grey
 goose-quill!
Slave of my thoughts, obedient to my will,
Torn from thy parent bird to form a pen,
That mighty instrument of little men!

The pen! foredoom'd to aid the mental
 throes 11
Of brains that labour, big with verse or
 prose,
Though nymphs forsake, and critics may
 deride,
The lover's solace, and the author's pride.
What wits, what poets dost thou daily
 raise! 15
How frequent is thy use, how small thy
 praise!
Condemn'd at length to be forgotten
 quite,
With all the pages which 'twas thine to
 write.

* This preface was written for the second edition, and printed with it. The noble author had left this country previous to the publication of that edition, and is not yet returned.—*Note to the fourth edition*, 1811.

† [Mr. Hobhouse.] ‡ [Here the preface to the first edition commenced.]

ENGLISH BARDS AND SCOTCH REVIEWERS

But thou, at least, mine own especial pen!
Once laid aside, but now assumed again,
Our task complete, like Hamet's shall be
 free; 21
Though spurn'd by others, yet beloved by
 me:
Then let us soar to-day; no common theme,
No eastern vision, no distemper'd dream
Inspires—our path, though full of thorns,
 is plain; 25
Smooth be the verse, and easy be the
 strain.

When Vice triumphant holds her sov'-
 reign sway,
Obey'd by all who nought beside obey;
When Folly, frequent harbinger of crime,
Bedecks her cap with bells of every clime;
When knaves and fools combined o'er all
 prevail, 31
And weigh their justice in a golden scale;
E'en then the boldest start from public
 sneers,
Afraid of shame, unknown to other fears,
More darkly sin, by satire kept in awe,
And shrink from ridicule, though not
 from law. 36

Such is the force of wit! but not belong
To me the arrows of satiric song;
The royal vices of our age demand
A keener weapon, and a mightier hand.
Still there are follies, e'en for me to chase,
And yield at least amusement in the race:
Laugh when I laugh, I seek no other fame;
The cry is up, and scribblers are my game.
Speed, Pegasus!—ye strains of great and
 small, 45
Ode, epic, elegy, have at you all!
I too can scrawl, and once upon a time
I pour'd along the town a flood of rhyme,
A schoolboy freak, unworthy praise or
 blame;
I printed—older children do the same. 50
'Tis pleasant, sure, to see one's name in
 print;
A book's a book, although there's nothing
 in't.
Not that a title's sounding charm can save
Or scrawl or scribbler from an equal
 grave:
This Lambe must own, since his patrician
 name 55
Fail'd to preserve the spurious farce from
 shame.
No matter, George continues still to write,
Though now the name is veil'd from pub-
 lic sight.
Moved by the great example, I pursue
The self-same road, but make my own
 review: 60
Not seek great Jeffrey's, yet, like him,
 will be
Self-constituted judge of poesy.

A man must serve his time to every trade
Save censure—critics all are ready made.
Take hackney'd jokes from Miller, got by
 rote, 65
With just enough of learning to misquote;
A mind well skill'd to find or forge a fault;
A turn for punning, call it Attic salt;
To Jeffrey go, be silent and discreet,
His pay is just ten sterling pounds per
 sheet: 70
Fear not to lie, 'twill seem a sharper hit;
Shrink not from blasphemy, 'twill pass for
 wit;
Care not for feeling—pass your proper
 jest,
And stand a critic, hated yet caress'd.

And shall we own such judgment? no
 —as soon 75
Seek roses in December—ice in June;
Hope constancy in wind, or corn in chaff;
Believe a woman or an epitaph,
Or any other thing that's false, before
You trust in critics, who themselves are
 sore; 80
Or yield one single thought to be misled
By Jeffrey's heart, or Lambe's Bœotian
 head.
To these young tyrants, by themselves
 misplaced,
Combined usurpers on the throne of taste;
To these, when authors bend in humble
 awe, 85
And nail their voice as truth, their word
 as law—
While these are censors, 'twould be sin to
 spare;
While such are critics, why should I for-
 bear?
But yet, so near all modern worthies run,
'Tis doubtful whom to seek, or whom to
 shun; 90
Nor know we when to spare, or where to
 strike,
Our bards and censors are so much alike.

Then should you ask me, why I venture
 o'er
The path which Pope and Gifford trod be-
 fore;
If not yet sicken'd, you can still proceed:
Go on; my rhyme will tell you as you read.
'But hold!' exclaims a friend, 'here's some
 neglect: 97
This—that—and t'other line seem in-
 correct.'
What then? the self-same blunder Pope
 has got,
And careless Dryden—'Ay, but Pye has
 not:'— 100
Indeed!—'tis granted, faith!—but what
 care I?
Better to err with Pope, than shine with
 Pye.

114

Time was, ere yet in these degenerate
 days
Ignoble themes obtain'd mistaken praise,
When sense and wit with poesy allied,
No fabled graces, flourish'd side by side;
From the same fount their inspiration
 drew, 107
And, rear'd by taste, bloom'd fairer as they
 grew.
Then, in this happy isle, a Pope's pure
 strain
Sought the rapt soul to charm, nor sought
 in vain; 110
A polish'd nation's praise aspired to claim,
And raised the people's, as the poet's
 fame.
Like him great Dryden pour'd the tide of
 song,
In stream less smooth, indeed, yet doubly
 strong.
Then Congreve's scenes could cheer, or
 Otway's melt— 115
For nature then an English audience felt.
But why these names, or greater still, re-
 trace,
When all to feebler bards resign their
 place?
Yet to such times our lingering looks are
 cast,
When taste and reason with those times
 are past. 120
Now look around, and turn each trifling
 page,
Survey the precious works that please the
 age;
This truth at least let satire's self allow,
No dearth of bards can be complain'd of
 now.
The loaded press beneath her labour
 groans, 125
And printers' devils shake their weary
 bones;
While Southey's epics cram the creaking
 shelves,
And Little's lyrics shine in hot-press'd
 twelves.
Thus saith the Preacher: 'Nought beneath
 the sun
Is new,' yet still from change to change
 we run: 130
What varied wonders tempt us as they
 pass!
The cow-pox, tractors, galvanism, and
 gas,
In turns appear, to make the vulgar stare,
Till the swoln bubble bursts—and all is
 air!
Nor less new schools of Poetry arise,
Where dull pretenders grapple for the
 prize: 136
O'er taste awhile these pseudo-bards pre-
 vail;
Each country book-club bows the knee to
 Baal,

And, hurling lawful genius from the
 throne,
Erects a shrine and idol of its own; 140
Some leaden calf—but whom it matters
 not,
From soaring Southey down to grovelling
 Stott.

Behold! in various throngs the scrib-
 bling crew,
For notice eager, pass in long review:
Each spurs his jaded Pegasus apace, 145
And rhyme and blank maintain an equal
 race;
Sonnets on sonnets crowd, and ode on
 ode;
And tales of terror jostle on the road;
Immeasurable measures move along;
For simpering folly loves a varied song,
To strange mysterious dulness still the
 friend, 151
Admires the strain she cannot compre-
 hend.
Thus Lays of Minstrels—may they be the
 last!—
On half-strung harps whine mournful to
 the blast.
While mountain spirits prate to river
 sprites, 155
That dames may listen to the sound at
 nights;
And goblin brats, of Gilpin Horner's brood,
Decoy young border-nobles through the
 wood,
And skip at every step, Lord knows how
 high,
And frighten foolish babes, the Lord
 knows why; 160
While high-born ladies in their magic cell,
Forbidding knights to read who cannot
 spell,
Despatch a courier to a wizard's grave,
And fight with honest men to shield a
 knave.

Next view in state, proud prancing on
 his roan, 165
The golden-crested haughty Marmion,
Now forging scrolls, now foremost in the
 fight,
Not quite a felon, yet but half a knight,
The gibbet or the field prepared to grace;
A mighty mixture of the great and base.
And think'st thou, Scott! by vain conceit
 perchance, 171
On public taste to foist thy stale romance,
Though Murray with his Miller may com-
 bine
To yield thy muse just half-a-crown per
 line?
No! when the sons of song descend to
 trade, 175
Their bays are sear, their former laurels
 fade.

115

Let such forego the poet's sacred name,
Who rack their brains for lucre, not for
	fame:
Still for stern Mammon may they toil in
	vain!
And sadly gaze on gold they cannot gain!
Such be their meed, such still the just re-
	ward							181
Of prostituted muse and hireling bard!
For this we spurn Apollo's venal son,
And bid a long 'good night to Marmion.'

These are the themes that claim our
	plaudits now;						185
These are the bards to whom the muse
	must bow;
While Milton, Dryden, Pope, alike forgot,
Resign their hallow'd bays to Walter Scott.

The time has been, when yet the muse
	was young,
When Homer swept the lyre, and Maro
	sung,							190
An epic scarce ten centuries could claim,
While awe-struck nations hail'd the magic
	name:
The work of each immortal bard appears
The single wonder of a thousand years.
Empires have moulder'd from the face of
	earth,							195
Tongues have expired with those who gave
	them birth,
Without the glory such a strain can give,
As even in ruin bids the language live.
Not so with us, though minor bards, content
On one great work a life of labour spent:
With eagle pinion soaring to the skies,
Behold the ballad-monger Southey rise!
To him let Camoëns, Milton, Tasso yield,
Whose annual strains, like armies, take
	the field.
First in the ranks see Joan of Arc advance,
The scourge of England and the boast of
	France!						206
Though burnt by wicked Bedford for a
	witch,
Behold her statue placed in glory's niche;
Her fetters burst, and just released from
	prison,							209
A virgin phœnix from her ashes risen.
Next see tremendous Thalaba come on,
Arabia's monstrous, wild, and wondrous son:
Domdaniel's dread destroyer, who o'er-
	threw
More mad magicians than the world e'er
	knew.							214
Immortal hero! all thy foes o'ercome,
For ever reign—the rival of Tom Thumb!
Since startled metre fled before thy face,
Well wert thou doom'd the last of all thy
	race!							218
Well might triumphant genii bear thee
	hence,
Illustrious conqueror of common sense!

Now, last and greatest, Madoc spread
	his sails,						220
Cacique in Mexico, and prince in Wales
Tells us strange tales, as other travellers
	do,
More old than Mandeville's, and not so
	true.
Oh! Southey! Southey! cease thy varied
	song!							224
A bard may chant too often and too long
As thou art strong in verse, in mercy
	spare!
A fourth, alas! were more than we could
	bear.
But if, in spite of all the world can say,
Thou still wilt verseward plod thy weary
	way;							230
If still in Berkley ballads most uncivil,
Thou wilt devote old women to the devil,
The babe unborn thy dread intent may
	rue:
'God help thee,' Southey, and thy readers
	too.

Next comes the dull disciple of thy
	school,							235
That mild apostate from poetic rule,
The simple Wordsworth, framer of a lay
As soft as evening in his favourite May,
Who warns his friend 'to shake off toil
	and trouble,
And quit his books, for fear of growing
	double;'						240
Who, both by precept and example, shows
That prose is verse, and verse is merely
	prose;
Convincing all, by demonstration plain,
Poetic souls delight in prose insane;
And Christmas stories tortured into
	rhyme							245
Contain the essence of the true sublime.
Thus, when he tells the tale of Betty Foy,
The idiot mother of 'an idiot boy';
A moon-struck, silly lad, who lost his way
And, like his bard, confounded night with
	day;							250
So close on each pathetic part he dwells
And each adventure so sublimely tells,
That all who view the 'idiot in his glory'
Conceive the bard the hero of the story.

Shall gentle Coleridge pass unnoticed
	here,							255
To turgid ode and tumid stanza dear?
Though themes of innocence amuse him
	best,
Yet still obscurity's a welcome guest.
If Inspiration should her aid refuse	259
To him who takes a pixy for a muse,
Yet none in lofty numbers can surpass
The bard who soars to elegise an ass.
So well the subject suits his noble mind,
He brays the laureat of the long-ear'd
	kind.

Oh! wonder-working Lewis! monk, or
 bard, 265
Who fain wouldst make Parnassus a
 churchyard!
Lo! wreaths of yew, not laurel, bind thy
 brow,
Thy muse a sprite, Apollo's sexton thou!
Whether on ancient tombs thou tak'st thy
 stand,
By gibb'ring spectres hail'd, thy kindred
 band; 270
Or tracest chaste descriptions on thy page,
To please the females of our modest age;
All hail, M. P.! from whose infernal brain
Thin-sheeted phantoms glide, a grisly
 train;
At whose command 'grim women' throng
 in crowds, 275
And kings of fire, of water, and of clouds,
With 'small gray men,' 'wild yagers,' and
 what not,
To crown with honour thee and Walter
 Scott;
Again all hail! if tales like thine may
 please,
St. Luke alone can vanquish the disease;
Even Satan's self with thee might dread to
 dwell, 281
And in thy skull discern a deeper hell.

Who in soft guise, surrounded by a choir
Of virgins melting, not to Vesta's fire,
With sparkling eyes, and cheek by passion
 flush'd, 285
Strikes his wild lyre, whilst listening dames
 are hush'd?
'Tis Little! young Catullus of his day,
As sweet, but as immoral, in his lay!
Grieved to condemn, the muse must still
 be just,
Nor spare melodious advocates of lust.
Pure is the flame which o'er her altar
 burns; 291
From grosser incense with disgust she
 turns:
Yet kind to youth, this expiation o'er,
She bids thee 'mend thy line and sin no
 more.'

For thee, translator of the tinsel song,
To whom such glittering ornaments be-
 long, 296
Hibernian Strangford! with thine eyes of
 blue,
And boasted locks of red or auburn hue,
Whose plaintive strain each love-sick miss
 admires,
And o'er harmonious fustian half expires,
Learn, if thou canst, to yield thine author's
 sense, 301
Nor vend thy sonnets on a false pretence.
Think'st thou to gain thy verse a higher
 place,
By dressing Camoëns in a suit of lace?

Mend, Strangford! mend thy morals and
 thy taste; 305
Be warm, but pure; be amorous, but be
 chaste:
Cease to deceive; thy pilfer'd harp restore,
Nor teach the Lusian bard to copy Moore.

Behold!—ye tarts!—one moment spare
 the text—
Hayley's last work, and worst—until his
 next; 310
Whether he spin poor couplets into plays,
Or damn the dead with purgatorial praise,
His style in youth or age is still the same,
For ever feeble and for ever tame.
Triumphant first see 'Temper's Triumphs'
 shine! 315
At least I'm sure they triumph'd over mine.
Of 'Music's Triumphs,' all who read may
 swear
That luckless music never triumph'd there.

Moravians, rise! bestow some meet re-
 ward
On dull devotion—Lo! the Sabbath bard,
Sepulchral Grahame, pours his notes sub-
 lime 321
In mangled prose, nor e'en aspires to
 rhyme;
Breaks into blank the Gospel of St. Luke,
And boldly pilfers from the Pentateuch;
And, undisturb'd by conscientious qualms,
Perverts the Prophets, and purloins the
 Psalms. 326

Hail, Sympathy! thy soft idea brings
A thousand visions of a thousand things,
And shows, still whimpering through three-
 score of years,
The maudlin prince of mournful sonnet-
 eers. 330
And art thou not their prince, harmonious
 Bowles!
Thou first, great oracle of tender souls?
Whether thou sing'st with equal ease, and
 grief,
The fall of empires, or a yellow leaf;
Whether thy muse most lamentably tells
What merry sounds proceed from Oxford
 bells, 336
Or, still in bells delighting, finds a friend
In every chime that jingled from Ostend;
Ah! how much juster were thy muse's hap,
If to thy bells thou wouldst but add a cap!
Delightful Bowles! still blessing and still
 blest, 341
All love thy strain, but children like it
 best.
'Tis thine, with gentle Little's moral song,
To soothe the mania of the amorous
 throng!
With thee our nursery damsels shed their
 tears, 345
Ere miss as yet completes her infant years:

But in her teens thy whining powers are
vain;
She quits poor Bowles for Little's purer
strain.
Now to soft themes thou scornest to con-
fine 349
The lofty numbers of a harp like thine;
'Awake a louder and a loftier strain,'
Such as none heard before, or will again!
Where all Discoveries jumbled from the
flood,
Since first the leaky ark reposed in mud,
By more or less, are sung in every book,
From Captain Noah down to Captain
Cook. 356
Nor this alone; but, pausing on the road,
The bard sighs forth a gentle episode;
And gravely tells—attend, each beauteous
miss!—
When first Madeira trembled to a kiss.
Bowles! in thy memory let this precept
dwell, 361
Stick to thy sonnets, man!—at least they
sell.
But if some new-born whim, or larger
bribe,
Prompt thy crude brain, and claim thee for
a scribe;
If chance some bard, though once by
dunces fear'd, 365
Now, prone in dust, can only be revered;
If Pope, whose fame and genius, from the
first,
Have foil'd the best of critics, needs the
worst,
Do thou essay: each fault, each failing
scan;
The first of poets was, alas! but man.
Rake from each ancient dunghill every
pearl, 371
Consult Lord Fanny, and confide in Curll;
Let all the scandals of a former age
Perch on thy pen, and flutter o'er thy page;
Affect a candour which thou canst not
feel, 375
Clothe envy in the garb of honest zeal;
Write, as if St. John's soul could still in-
spire,
And do from hate what Mallet did for hire.
Oh! hadst thou lived in that congenial
time,
To rave with Dennis, and with Ralph to
rhyme; 380
Throng'd with the rest around his living
head,
Not raised thy hoof against the lion dead,
A meet reward had crown'd thy glorious
gains,
And link'd thee to the Dunciad for thy
pains.

Another epic! Who inflicts again 385
More books of blank upon the sons of
men?

Bœotian Cottle, rich Bristowa's boast,
Imports old stories from the Cambria
coast,
And sends his goods to market—all alive
Lines forty thousand, cantos twenty-five
Fresh fish from Helicon! who'll buy? 39
who'll buy?
The precious bargain's cheap—in faith
not I.
Your turtle-feeder's verse must needs be
flat,
Though Bristol bloat him with the ver-
dant fat;
If Commerce fills the purse, she clogs the
brain, 39
And Amos Cottle strikes the lyre in vain
In him an author's luckless lot behold,
Condemn'd to make the books which once
he sold.
Oh, Amos Cottle!—Phœbus! what a name
To fill the speaking trump of future
fame!— 40
Oh, Amos Cottle! for a moment think
What meagre profits spring from pen and ink
When thus devoted to poetic dreams,
Who will peruse thy prostituted reams?
Oh! pen perverted! paper misapplied!
Had Cottle still adorn'd the counter's side
Bent o'er the desk, or, born to useful toil
Been taught to make the paper which h
soils, 40
Plough'd, delved, or plied the oar wit
lusty limb,
He had not sung of Wales, nor I of him.

As Sisyphus against the infernal steep
Rolls the huge rock whose motions ne'e
may sleep,
So up thy hill, ambrosial Richmond
heaves
Dull Maurice all his granite weight o
leaves: 41
Smooth, solid monuments of mental pain
The petrifactions of a plodding brain,
That, ere they reach the top, fall lumberin
back again.

With broken lyre, and cheek serenel
pale,
Lo! sad Alcæus wanders down the vale:
Though fair they rose, and might hav
bloom'd at last, 42
His hopes have perish'd by the norther
blast:
Nipp'd in the bud by Caledonian gales,
His blossoms wither as the blast prevails
O'er his lost works let *classic* Sheffiel
weep;
May no rude hand disturb their earl
sleep! 42

Yet say! why should the bard at onc
resign
His claim to favour from the sacred Nine

or ever startled by the mingled howl
f northern wolves, that still in darkness
 prowl;
 coward brood, which mangle as they
 prey, 430
y hellish instinct, all that cross their way;
ged or young, the living or the dead,
o mercy find—these harpies must be fed.
Vhy do the injured unresisting yield
he calm possession of their native field?
Vhy tamely thus before their fangs re-
 treat, 436
or hunt the blood-hounds back to Ar-
 thur's Seat?

Health to immortal Jeffrey! once, in
 name,
ngland could boast a judge almost the
 same;
n soul so like, so merciful, yet just, 440
ome think that Satan has resign'd his trust,
nd given the spirit to the world again,
o sentence letters, as he sentenced men.
Vith hand less mighty, but with heart as
 black,
vith voice as willing to decree the rack;
red in the courts betimes, though all that
 law 446
s yet hath taught him is to find a flaw;
ince well instructed in the patriot school
o rail at party, though a party tool,
Vho knows, if chance his patrons should
 restore 450
ack to the sway they forfeited before,
Iis scribbling toils some recompense may
 meet,
nd raise this Daniel to the judgment-seat?
et Jeffreys' shade indulge the pious hope,
nd greeting thus, present him with a
 rope: 455
Heir to my virtues! man of equal mind!
kill'd to condemn as to traduce mankind,
his cord receive, for thee reserved with
 care,
o wield in judgment, and at length to
 wear.'

Health to great Jeffrey! Heaven pre-
 serve his life, 460
o flourish on the fertile shores of Fife,
nd guard it sacred in its future wars,
ince authors sometimes seek the field of
 Mars!
an none remember that eventful day,
hat ever-glorious, almost fatal fray,
Vhen Little's leadless pistol met his eye,
nd Bow-street myrmidons stood laugh-
 ing by?
Oh, day disastrous! on her firm-set rock,
Junedin's castle felt a secret shock;
Jark roll'd the sympathetic waves of
 Forth, 470
ow groan'd the startled whirlwinds of
 the north;

Tweed ruffled half his waves to form a tear,
The other half pursued its calm career;
Arthur's steep summit nodded to its base,
The surly Tolbooth scarcely kept her
 place. 475
The Tolbooth felt—for marble sometimes
 can,
On such occasions, feel as much as man—
The Tolbooth felt defrauded of his charms,
If Jeffrey died, except within her arms:
Nay last, not least, on that portentous
 morn, 480
The sixteenth story, where himself was
 born,
His patrimonial garret, fell to ground,
And pale Edina shudder'd at the sound:
Strew'd were the streets around with milk-
 white reams,
Flow'd all the Canongate with inky
 streams; 485
This of his candour seem'd the sable dew,
That of his valour show'd the bloodless
 hue;
And all with justice deem'd the two com-
 bined
The mingled emblems of his mighty mind.
But Caledonia's goddess hover'd o'er
The field, and saved him from the wrath
 of Moore; 491
From either pistol snatch'd the vengeful
 lead,
And straight restored it to her favourite's
 head;
That head, with greater than magnetic
 power,
Caught it, as Danaë caught the golden
 shower, 495
And, though the thickening dross will
 scarce refine,
Augments its ore, and is itself a mine.
'My son,' she cried, 'ne'er thirst for gore
 again,
Resign the pistol and resume the pen;
O'er politics and poesy preside, 500
Boast of thy country, and Britannia's
 guide!
For long as Albion's heedless sons submit,
Or Scottish taste decides on English wit,
So long shall last thine unmolested reign,
Nor any dare to take thy name in vain.
Behold, a chosen band shall aid thy plan,
And own thee chieftain of the critic clan.
First in the oat-fed phalanx shall be seen
The travell'd thane, Athenian Aberdeen.
Herbert shall wield Thor's hammer, and
 sometimes, 510
In gratitude, thou'lt praise his rugged
 rhymes.
Smug Sidney too thy bitter page shall seek,
And classic Hallam, much renown'd for
 Greek;
Scott may perchance his name and in-
 fluence lend, 514
And paltry Pillans shall traduce his friend;

While gay Thalia's luckless votary, Lambe,
Damn'd like the devil, devil-like will
 damn.
Known be thy name, unbounded be thy
 sway!
Thy Holland's banquets shall each toil re-
 pay;
While grateful Britain yields the praise she
 owes 520
To Holland's hirelings and to learning's
 foes.
Yet mark one caution ere thy next Review
Spread its light wings of saffron and of
 blue,
Beware lest blundering Brougham destroy
 the sale,
Turn beef to bannocks, cauliflowers to
 kail.' 525
Thus having said, the kilted goddess kiss'd
Her son, and vanish'd in a Scottish mist.

Then prosper, Jeffrey! pertest of the train
Whom Scotland pampers with her fiery
 grain!
Whatever blessing waits a genuine Scot,
In double portion swells thy glorious lot;
For thee Edina culls her evening sweets,
And showers their odours on thy candid
 sheets,
Whose hue and fragrance to thy work
 adhere—
This scents its pages, and that gilds its rear.
Lo! blushing Itch, coy nymph, enamour'd
 grown, 536
Forsakes the rest, and cleaves to thee
 alone;
And, too unjust to other Pictish men,
Enjoys thy person, and inspires thy pen!

Illustrious Holland! hard would be his
 lot, 540
His hirelings mention'd, and himself for-
 got!
Holland, with Henry Petty at his back,
The whipper-in and huntsman of the pack.
Blest be the banquets spread at Holland
 House,
Where Scotchmen feed, and critics may
 carouse! 545
Long, long beneath that hospitable roof
Shall Grub-street dine, while duns are kept
 aloof.
See honest Hallam lay aside his fork,
Resume his pen, review his Lordship's
 work, 549
And, grateful for the dainties on his plate,
Declare his landlord can at least translate!
Dunedin! view thy children with delight,
They write for food—and feed because
 they write:
And lest, when heated with the unusual
 grape,
Some glowing thoughts should to the press
 escape, 555

And tinge with red the female reader'
 cheek,
My lady skims the cream of each critique
Breathes o'er the page her purity of soul
Reforms each error, and refines the whole

Now to the Drama turn—Oh! motle
 sight! 56
What precious scenes the wondering eye
 invite!
Puns, and a prince within a barrel pent
And Dibdin's nonsense yield complet
 content.
Though now, thank Heaven! the Roscio
 mania's o'er,
And full-grown actors are endured onc
 more; 56
Yet what avail their vain attempts t
 please,
While British critics suffer scenes lik
 these;
While Reynolds vents his 'dammes'
 'poohs!' and 'zounds!'
And common-place and common sens
 confounds?
While Kenney's 'World'—ah! where
 Kenney's wit?— 57
Tires the sad gallery, lulls the listless pi
And Beaumont's pilfer'd Caratach afford
A tragedy complete in all but words?
Who but must mourn, while these are a
 the rage,
The degradation of our vaunted stage!
Heavens! is all sense of shame and taler
 gone? 57
Have we no living bard of merit?—non
Awake, George Colman! Cumberlan
 awake!
Ring the alarum bell! let folly quake!
Oh, Sheridan! if aught can move th
 pen, 58
Let Comedy assume her throne again;
Abjure the mummery of German schools
Leave new Pizarros to translating fools;
Give, as thy last memorial to the age,
One classic drama, and reform the stage.
Gods! o'er those boards shall Folly rear he
 head, 58
Where Garrick trod, and Siddons lives t
 tread?
On those shall Farce display Buffoon'ry'
 mask,
And Hook conceal his heroes in a cask?
Shall sapient managers new scenes pro
 duce 59
From Cherry, Skeffington, and Mothe
 Goose?
While Shakspeare, Otway Massinger
 forgot,
On stalls must moulder, or in close
 rot?
Lo! with what pomp the daily prints pre
 claim
The rival candidates for Attic fame! 59

n grim array though Lewis' spectres rise,
till Skeffington and Goose divide the prize.
And sure *great* Skeffington must claim our praise,
For skirtless coats and skeletons of plays
Renown'd alike; whose genius ne'er confines — 600
Her flight to garnish Greenwood's gay designs;
For sleeps with 'Sleeping Beauties,' but anon
In five facetious acts comes thundering on,
While poor John Bull, bewilder'd with the scene
Stares, wondering what the devil it can mean; 605
But as some hands applaud, a venal few!
Rather than sleep, why John applauds it too.

Such are we now. Ah! wherefore should we turn
To what our fathers were, unless to mourn? 609
Degenerate Britons! are ye dead to shame,
Or, kind to dulness, do you fear to blame?
Well may the nobles of our present race
Watch each distortion of a Naldi's face;
Well may they smile on Italy's buffoons, 615
And worship Catalani's pantaloons,
Since their own drama yields no fairer trace
Of wit than puns, of humour than grimace.

Then let Ausonia, skill'd in every art
To soften manners, but corrupt the heart,
Pour her exotic follies o'er the town,
To sanction Vice, and hunt Decorum down: 621
Let wedded strumpets languish o'er Deshayes,
And bless the promise which his form displays;
While Gayton bounds before th' enraptured looks 624
Of hoary marquises and stripling dukes:
Let high-born lechers eye the lively Présle
Twirl her light limbs, that spurn the needless veil;
Let Angiolini bare her breast of snow,
Wave the white arm, and point the pliant toe;
Collini trill her love-inspiring song, 630
Strain her fair neck, and charm the listening throng!
Whet not your scythe, suppressors of our vice!
Reforming saints! too delicately nice!
By whose decrees, our sinful souls to save,
No Sunday tankards foam, no barbers shave; 635
And beer undrawn, and beards unmown, display
Your holy reverence for the Sabbath-day.

Or hail at once the patron and the pile
Of vice and folly, Greville and Argyle!
Where yon proud palace, Fashion's hallow'd fane, 640
Spreads wide her portals for the motley train,
Behold the new Petronius of the day,
Our arbiter of pleasure and of play!
There the hired eunuch, the Hesperian choir, 644
The melting lute, the soft lascivious lyre,
The song from Italy, the step from France,
The midnight orgy, and the mazy dance,
The smile of beauty, and the flush of wine,
For fops, fools, gamesters, knaves, and lords combine:
Each to his humour—Comus all allows;
Champaign, dice, music, or your neighbour's spouse. 651
Talk not to us, ye starving sons of trade!
Of piteous ruin, which ourselves have made;
In plenty's sunshine Fortune's minions bask,
Nor think of poverty, except 'en masque,'
When for the night some lately titled ass
Appears the beggar which his grandsire was. 657
The curtain dropp'd, the gay burletta o'er,
The audience take their turn upon the floor;
Now round the room the circling dow'gers sweep, 660
Now in loose waltz the thin-clad daughters leap;
The first in lengthen'd line majestic swim,
The last display the free unfetter'd limb!
Those for Hibernia's lusty sons repair
With art the charms which nature could not spare; 665
These after husbands wing their eager flight,
Nor leave much mystery for the nuptial night.

Oh! blest retreats of infamy and ease,
Where, all forgotten but the power to please,
Each maid may give a loose to genial thought, 670
Each swain may teach new systems, or be taught:
There the blithe youngster, just return'd from Spain,
Cuts the light pack, or calls the rattling main;
The jovial caster's set, and seven's the nick,
Or—done!—a thousand on the coming trick! 675
If, mad with loss, existence 'gins to tire,
And all your hope or wish is to expire,

Here's Powell's pistol ready for your
life,
And, kinder still, two Pagets for your
wife; 679
Fit consummation of an earthly race
Begun in folly, ended in disgrace;
While none but menials o'er the bed of
death,
Wash thy red wounds, or watch thy waver-
ing breath:
Traduced by liars, and forgot by all,
The mangled victim of a drunken brawl,
To live like Clodius, and like Falkland
fall. 686

Truth! rouse some genuine bard, and
guide his hand
To drive this pestilence from out the land.
E'en I—least thinking of a thoughtless
throng,
Just skill'd to know the right and choose
the wrong, 690
Freed at that age when reason's shield is
lost,
To fight my course through passion's
countless host,
Whom every path of pleasure's flowery
way
Has lured in turn, and all have led astray—
E'en I must raise my voice, e'en I must
feel 695
Such scenes, such men, destroy the public
weal:
Although some kind, censorious friend
will say,
'What art thou better, meddling fool, than
they?'
And every brother rake will smile to see
That miracle, a moralist in me. 700
No matter—when some bard in virtue
strong,
Gifford perchance, shall raise the chasten-
ing song,
Then sleep my pen for ever! and my voice
Be only heard to hail him, and rejoice;
Rejoice, and yield my feeble praise, though
I 705
May feel the lash that Virtue must apply.

As for the smaller fry, who swarm in
shoals,
From silly Hafiz up to simple Bowles,
Why should we call them from their dark
abode,
In broad St. Giles's or in Tottenham-
road? 710
Or (since some men of fashion nobly dare
To scrawl in verse) from Bond-street or the
Square?
If things of ton their harmless lays indite,
Most wisely doom'd to shun the public
sight, 714
What harm? in spite of every critic elf,
Sir T. may read his stanzas to himself;

Miles Andrews still his strength in coup-
lets try,
And live in prologues, though his drama
die:
Lords too are bards, such things at time
befall, 71
And 'tis some praise in peers to write at all
Yet, did or taste or reason sway the times
Ah! who would take their titles with their
rhymes?
Roscommon! Sheffield! with your spirit
fled,
No future laurels deck a noble head;
No muse will cheer, with renovating smile
The paralytic puling of Carlisle. 72
The puny schoolboy and his early lay
Men pardon, if his follies pass away;
But who forgives the senior's ceaseless
verse,
Whose hairs grow hoary as his rhyme
grow worse? 73
What heterogeneous honours deck the
peer!
Lord, rhymester, petit-maître, and pamph-
leteer!
So dull in youth, so drivelling in his
age,
His scenes alone had damn'd our sinking
stage;
But managers for once cried, 'Hold!
enough!' 73
Nor drugg'd their audience with the tragic
stuff.
Yet at their judgment let his lordship
laugh,
And case his volumes in congenial calf;
Yes! doff that covering, where morocco
shines,
And hang a calf-skin on those recreant
lines. 74

With you, ye Druids! rich in native lead
Who daily scribble for your daily bread
With you I war not: Gifford's heavy hand
Has crush'd, without remorse, your nu-
merous band. 74
On 'all the talents' vent your venal spleen
Want is your plea, let pity be your screen
Let monodies on Fox regale your crew,
And Melville's Mantle prove a blanket
too!
One common Lethe waits each hapless
bard,
And, peace be with you! 'tis your best re-
ward. 75
Such damning fame as Dunciads only giv
Could bid your lines beyond a morning
live;
But now at once your fleeting labour
close,
With names of greater note in blest re-
pose. 75
Far be't from me unkindly to upbraid
The lovely Rosa's prose in masquerade,

Whose strains, the faithful echoes of her
mind,
Leave wondering comprehension far be-
hind.
Though Crusca's bards no more our
journals fill,
Some stragglers skirmish round the col-
umns still; 760
Last of the howling host which once was
Bell's,
Matilda snivels yet, and Hafiz yells;
And Merry's metaphors appear anew,
Chain'd to the signature of O. P. Q.

When some brisk youth, the tenant of a
stall, 765
Employs a pen less pointed than his awl,
Leaves his snug shop, forsakes his store
of shoes,
St. Crispin quits, and cobbles for the
muse,
Heavens! how the vulgar stare! how
crowds applaud!
How ladies read, and literati laud! 770
If chance some wicked wag should pass
his jest,
'Tis sheer ill-nature—don't the world
know best?
Genius must guide when wits admire the
rhyme,
And Capel Lofft declares 'tis quite sub-
lime.
Hear, then, ye happy sons of needless
trade! 775
Swains! quit the plough, resign the useless
spade!
Lo! Burns and Bloomfield, nay, a greater
far,
Gifford was born beneath an adverse
star,
Forsook the labours of a servile state,
Stemm'd the rude storm, and triumph'd
over fate: 780
Then why no more? if Phœbus smiled on
you,
Bloomfield! why not on brother Nathan
too?
Him too the mania, not the muse, has
seized;
Not inspiration, but a mind diseased:
And now no boor can seek his last abode,
No common be enclosed without an ode.
Oh! since increased refinement deigns to
smile
On Britain's sons, and bless our genial
isle, 788
Let poesy go forth, pervade the whole,
Alike the rustic, and mechanic soul!
Ye tuneful cobblers! still your notes pro-
long,
Compose at once a slipper and a song;
So shall the fair your handywork peruse,
Your sonnets sure shall please—perhaps
your shoes.

May Moorland weavers boast Pindaric
skill, 795
And tailors' lays be longer than their
bill!
While punctual beaux reward the grateful
notes,
And pay for poems—when they pay for
coats.

To the famed throng now paid the trib-
ute due,
Neglected genius! let me turn to you.
Come forth, oh Campbell! give thy talents
scope; 801
Who dares aspire if thou must cease to
hope?
And thou, melodious Rogers! rise at
last,
Recall the pleasing memory of the
past;
Arise! let blest remembrance still in-
spire, 805
And strike to wonted tones thy hallow'd
lyre;
Restore Apollo to his vacant throne,
Assert thy country's honour and thine
own.
What! must deserted Poesy still weep
Where her last hopes with pious Cowper
sleep? 810
Unless, perchance, from his cold bier she
turns,
To deck the turf that wraps her minstrel,
Burns!
No! though contempt hath mark'd the
spurious brood,
The race who rhyme from folly, or for
food,
Yet still some genuine sons 'tis hers to
boast, 815
Who, least affecting, still affect the most:
Feel as they write, and write but as they
feel—
Bear witness Gifford, Sotheby, Macneil.

'Why slumbers Gifford?' once was
ask'd in vain; 819
Why slumbers Gifford? let us ask again.
Are there no follies for his pen to purge?
Are there no fools whose backs demand
the scourge?
Are there no sins for satire's bard to
greet?
Stalks not gigantic Vice in every street?
Shall peers or princes tread pollution's
path, 825
And 'scape alike the law's and muse's
wrath?
Nor blaze with guilty glare through future
time,
Eternal beacons of consummate crime?
Arouse thee, Gifford! be thy promise
claim'd, 829
Make bad men better, or at least ashamed.

Unhappy White! while life was in its
spring,
And thy young muse just waved her joy-
ous wing,
The spoiler swept that soaring lyre away,
Which else had sounded an immortal lay.
Oh! what a noble heart was here un-
done, 835
When Science' self destroy'd her favourite
son!
Yes, she too much indulged thy fond pur-
suit,
She sow'd the seeds, but death has reap'd
the fruit.
'Twas thine own genius gave the final
blow,
And help'd to plant the wound that laid
thee low: 840
So the struck eagle, stretch'd upon the
plain,
No more through rolling clouds to soar
again,
View'd his own feather on the fatal dart,
And wing'd the shaft that quiver'd in his
heart;
Keen were his pangs, but keener far to
feel 845
He nursed the pinion which impell'd the
steel;
While the same plumage that had warm'd
his nest
Drank the last life-drop of his bleeding
breast.

There be who say, in these enlighten'd
days, 849
That splendid lies are all the poet's praise;
That strain'd invention, ever on the wing,
Alone impels the modern bard to sing:
'Tis true, that all who rhyme—nay, all who
write,
Shrink from that fatal word to genius—
trite;
Yet Truth sometimes will lend her noblest
fires, 855
And decorate the verse herself inspires:
This fact in Virtue's name let Crabbe
attest;
Though nature's sternest painter, yet the
best.

And here let Shee and Genius find a
place,
Whose pen and pencil yield an equal
grace; 860
To guide whose hand the sister arts com-
bine,
And trace the poet's or the painter's line;
Whose magic touch can bid the canvas
glow,
Or pour the easy rhyme's harmonious
flow; 864
While honours, doubly merited, attend
The poet's rival, but the painter's friend.

Blest is the man who dares approach
the bower
Where dwelt the muses at their natal hour,
Whose steps have press'd, whose eye has
mark'd afar,
The clime that nursed the sons of song and
war, 870
The scenes which glory still must hover
o'er,
Her place of birth, her own Achaian shore.
But doubly blest is he whose heart ex-
pands
With hallow'd feelings for those classic
lands; 875
Who rends the veil of ages long gone by,
And views their remnants with a poet's eye!
Wright! 'twas thy happy lot at once to view
Those shores of glory, and to sing them
too;
And sure no common muse inspired thy
pen 875
To hail the land of gods and godlike men.

And you, associate bards! who snatch'd
to light
Those gems too long withheld from
modern sight;
Whose mingling taste combined to cull the
wreath
Where Attic flowers Aonion odours
breathe, 885
And all their renovated fragrance flung
To grace the beauties of your native
tongue;
Now let those minds, that nobly could
transfuse
The glorious spirit of the Grecian muse,
Though soft the echo, scorn a borrow'd
tone:
Resign Achaia's lyre, and strike your own.

Let these, or such as these, with just
applause, 890
Restore the muse's violated laws;
But not in flimsy Darwin's pompous
chime,
That mighty master of unmeaning rhyme,
Whose gilded cymbals, more adorn'd than
clear, 895
The eye delighted, but fatigued the ear;
In show the simple lyre could once sur-
pass,
But now, worn down, appear in native
brass;
While all his train of hovering sylphs
around
Evaporate in similes and sound: 900
Him let them shun, with him let tinsel
die:
False glare attracts, but more offends the
eye.

Yet let them not to vulgar Wordsworth
stoop,
The meanest object of the lowly group,

124

Whose verse, of all but childish prattle
void, 905
Seems blessed harmony to Lamb and
Lloyd:
Let them—but hold, my muse, nor dare to
teach
A strain far, far beyond thy humble reach:
The native genius with their being given
Will point the path, and peal their notes to
heaven. 910

And thou, too, Scott! resign to minstrels
rude
The wilder slogan of a border feud:
Let others spin their meagre lines for
hire;
Enough for genius, if itself inspire!
Let Southey sing, although his teeming
muse, 915
Prolific every spring, be too profuse;
Let simple Wordsworth chime his childish
verse,
And brother Coleridge lull the babe at
nurse;
Let spectre-mongering Lewis aim, at most,
To rouse the galleries, or to raise a ghost;
Let Moore still sigh; let Strangford steal
from Moore, 921
And swear that Camoëns sang such notes
of yore;
Let Hayley hobble on, Montgomery rave,
And godly Grahame chant a stupid
stave:
Let sonneteering Bowles his strains re-
fine, 925
And whine and whimper to the fourteenth
line;
Let Stott, Carlisle, Matilda, and the
rest
Of Grub Street, and of Grosvenor Place
the best,
Scrawl on, till death release us from the
strain,
Or Common Sense assert her rights
again. 930
But thou, with powers that mock the aid
of praise,
Shouldst leave to humbler bards ignoble
lays:
Thy country's voice, the voice of all the
nine,
Demand a hallow'd harp—that harp is
thine.
Say! will not Caledonia's annals yield
The glorious record of some nobler
field, 936
Than the wild foray of a plundering
clan,
Whose proudest deeds disgrace the name
of man?
Or Marmion's acts of darkness, fitter
food
For Sherwood's outlaw tales of Robin
Hood? 940

Scotland! still proudly claim thy native
bard,
And be thy praise his first, his best re-
ward!
Yet not with thee alone his name should
live,
But own the vast renown a world can
give:
Be known, perchance, when Albion is no
more, 945
And tell the tale of what she was before;
To future times her faded fame re-
call,
And save her glory, though his country
fall.

Yet what avails the sanguine poet's
hope,
To conquer ages, and with time to
cope? 950
New eras spread their wings, new nations
rise,
And other victors fill the applauding skies;
A few brief generations fleet along,
Whose sons forget the poet and his song:
E'en now, what once-loved minstrels
scarce may claim 955
The transient mention of a dubious name!
When fame's loud trump hath blown its
noblest blast,
Though long the sound, the echo sleeps
at last;
And glory, like the phœnix midst her
fires, 959
Exhales her odours, blazes, and expires.

Shall hoary Granta call her sable sons,
Expert in science, more expert at
puns?
Shall these approach the muse? ah, no!
she flies,
Even from the tempting ore of Seaton's
prize;
Though printers condescend the press to
soil 965
With rhyme by Hoare, and epic blank by
Hoyle:
Not him whose page, if still upheld by
whist,
Requires no sacred theme to bid us
list.
Ye! who in Granta's honours would sur-
pass,
Must mount her Pegasus, a full-grown
ass; 970
A foal well worthy of her ancient dam,
Whose Helicon is duller than her Cam.

There Clarke, still striving piteously 'to
please,'
Forgetting doggrel leads not to degrees,
A would-be satirist, a hired buffoon, 975
A monthly scribbler of some low lam-
poon,

125

Condemn'd to drudge, the meanest of the mean,
And furbish falsehoods for a magazine,
Devotes to scandal his congenial mind;
Himself a living libel on mankind. 980

Oh! dark asylum of a Vandal race!
At once the boast of learning, and disgrace!
So lost to Phœbus, that nor Hodgson's verse
Can make thee better, nor poor Hewson's worse.
But where fair Isis rolls her purer wave,
The partial muse delighted loves to lave; 986
On her green banks a greener wreath she wove,
To crown the bards that haunt her classic grove:
Where Richards wakes a genuine poet's fires,
And modern Britons glory in their sires.

For me, who, thus unask'd, have dared to tell 991
My country what her sons should know too well,
Zeal for her honour bade me here engage
The host of idiots that infest her age;
No just applause her honour'd name shall lose, 995
As first in freedom, dearest to the muse.
Oh! would thy bards but emulate thy fame,
And rise more worthy, Albion, of thy name!
What Athens was in science, Rome in power,
What Tyre appear'd in her meridian hour, 1000
'Tis thine at once, fair Albion! to have been—
Earth's chief dictatress, ocean's lovely queen:
But Rome decay'd, and Athens strew'd the plain,
And Tyre's proud piers lie shatter'd in the main;
Like these, thy strength may sink, in ruin hurl'd, 1005
And Britain fall, the bulwark of the world.
But let me cease, and dread Cassandra's fate,
With warning ever scoff'd at, till too late;
To themes less lofty still my lay confine,
And urge thy bards to gain a name like thine. 1010

Then, hapless Britain! be thy rulers blest,
The senate's oracles, the people's jest!

Still hear thy motley orators dispense
The flowers of rhetoric, though not o'
sense,
While Canning's colleagues hate him fo'
his wit, 101
And old dame Portland fills the place o'
Pitt.

Yet once again, adieu! ere this th'
sail
That wafts me hence is shivering in th'
gale;
And Afric's coast and Calpe's adverse
height,
And Stamboul's minarets must greet m'
sight: 102
Thence shall I stray through beauty'
native clime,
Where Kaff is clad in rocks, and crown'
with snows sublime.
But should I back return, no temptin'
press
Shall drag my journal from the desk's re'
cess;
Let coxcombs, printing as they come from
far, 102'
Snatch his own wreath of ridicule from
Carr;
Let Aberdeen and Elgin still pursue
The shade of fame through regions o'
virtù;
Waste useless thousands on their Phidia'
freaks,
Misshapen monuments and maim'd an'
tiques; 103'
And make their grand saloons a genera'
mart
For all the mutilated blocks of art:
Of Dardan tours let dilettanti tell,
I leave topography to rapid Gell;
And, quite content, no more shall interpose 103'
To stun the public ear—at least with'
prose.

Thus far I've held my undisturb'd career,
Prepared for rancour, steel'd 'gainst selfish
fear:
This thing of rhyme I ne'er disdain'd to
own—
Though not obtrusive, yet not quite unknown: 104'
My voice was heard again, though not so
loud,
My page, though nameless, never dis'
avow'd;
And now at once I tear the veil away:—
Cheer on the pack! the quarry stands at
bay,
Unscared by all the din of Melbourne
House, 104'
By Lambe's resentment, or by Holland's
spouse,

126

By Jeffrey's harmless pistol, Hallam's rage,
Edina's brawny sons and brimstone page.
Our men in buckram shall have blows enough,
And feel they too are 'penetrable stuff': 1050
And though I hope not hence unscathed to go,
Who conquers me shall find a stubborn foe.
The time hath been, when no harsh sound would fall
From lips that now may seem imbued with gall;
Nor fools nor follies tempt me to despise 1055
The meanest thing that crawl'd beneath my eyes:
But now, so callous grown, so changed since youth,
I've learn'd to think, and sternly speak the truth;
Learn'd to deride the critic's starch decree,
And break him on the wheel he meant for me; 1060
To spurn the rod a scribbler bids me kiss,
Nor care if courts and crowds applaud or hiss:
Nay more, though all my rival rhymesters frown,
I too can hunt a poetaster down;
And, arm'd in proof, the gauntlet cast at once 1065
To Scotch marauder, and to southern dunce.
Thus much I've dared; if my incondite lay
Hath wrong'd these righteous times, let others say;
This, let the world, which knows not how to spare, 1069
Yet rarely blames unjustly, now declare.

POSTSCRIPT TO THE SECOND EDITION

I HAVE been informed, since the present edition went to the press, that my trusty and well-beloved cousins, the Edinburgh Reviewers, are preparing a most vehement critique on my poor, gentle, *unresisting* Muse, whom they have already so belevilled with their ungodly ribaldry:

'Tantæne animis cœlestibus iræ!'

I suppose I must say of Jeffrey as Sir Andrew Aguecheek saith, 'An I had known he was so cunning of fence, I had seen him damned ere I had fought him.' What a pity it is that I shall be beyond the Bosphorus before the next number has passed the Tweed! But I yet hope to light my pipe with it in Persia.

My northern friends have accused me, with justice, of personality towards their great literary anthropophagus, Jeffrey; but what else was to be done with him and his dirty pack, who feed by 'lying and slandering,' and slake their thirst by 'evil speaking'? I have adduced facts already well known, and of Jeffrey's mind I have stated my free opinion, nor has he thence sustained any injury; —what scavenger was ever soiled by being pelted with mud? It may be said that I quit England because I have censured there 'persons of honour and wit about town'; but I am coming back again, and their vengeance will keep hot till my return. Those who know me can testify that my motives for leaving England are very different from fears, literary or personal: those who do not, may one day be convinced. Since the publication of this thing, my name has not been concealed; I have been mostly in London, ready to answer for my transgressions, and in daily expectation of sundry cartels; but, alas! 'the age of chivalry is over,' or, in the vulgar tongue, there is no spirit now-a-days.

There is a youth ycleped Hewson Clarke (subaudi *esquire*), a sizer of Emanuel College, and, I believe, a denizen of Berwick-upon-Tweed, whom I have introduced in these pages to much better company than he has been accustomed to meet; he is, notwithstanding, a very sad dog, and for no reason that I can discover, except a personal quarrel with a bear, kept by me at Cambridge to sit for a fellowship, and whom the jealousy of his Trinity contemporaries prevented from success, has been abusing me, and, what is worse, the defenceless innocent above mentioned, in 'The Satirist,' for one year and some months. I am utterly unconscious of having given him any provocation; indeed, I am guiltless of having heard his name, till coupled with 'The Satirist.' He has therefore no reason to complain, and I dare say that, like Sir Fretful Plagiary, he is rather *pleased* than otherwise. I have now mentioned all who have done me the honour to notice me and mine, that is, my bear and my book, except the editor of 'The Satirist,' who, it seems, is a gentleman—God wot! I wish he could impart a little of his gentility to his subordinate scribblers. I hear that Mr. Jerningham is about to take up the cudgels for his Mæcenas, Lord Carlisle. I hope not: he was one of the few, who, in the very short intercourse I had with him, treated me with kindness when a boy; and whatever he may say or do, 'pour on, I will endure.' I have nothing further to add, save a general note of thanksgiving to readers, purchasers, and publishers, and, in the words of Scott, I wish

'To all and each a fair good night,
And rosy dreams and slumbers light.'

HINTS FROM HORACE

BEING AN ALLUSION IN ENGLISH VERSE TO THE EPISTLE 'AD PISONES,
DE ARTE POETICA,' AND INTENDED AS A SEQUEL TO 'ENGLISH BARDS
AND SCOTCH REVIEWERS'

——'Ergo fungar vice cotis, acutum
Reddere quae ferrum valet, exsors ipsa secandi'
HOR. *De Arte Poet.*

'Rhymes are difficult things—they are stubborn things, sir.'
FIELDING'S *Amelia.*

ATHENS: CAPUCHIN CONVENT,
March 12, 1811.

WHO would not laugh, if Lawrence, hired
 to grace
His costly canvas with each flatter'd face,
Abused his art, till Nature, with a blush,
Saw cits grow centaurs underneath his
 brush?
Or, should some limner join, for show or
 sale, 5
A maid of honour to a mermaid's tail?
Or low Dubost—as once the world has
 seen—
Degrade God's creatures in his graphic
 spleen?
Not all that forced politeness, which de-
 fends
Fools in their faults, could gag his grin-
 ning friends. 10
Believe me, Moschus, like that picture
 seems
The book which, sillier than a sick man's
 dreams,
Displays a crowd of figures incomplete,
Poetic nightmares, without head or feet.

Poets and painters, as all artists know,
May shoot a little with a lengthen'd bow;
We claim this mutual mercy for our task,
And grant in turn the pardon which we
 ask;
But make not monsters spring from gen-
 tle dams—
Birds breed not vipers, tigers nurse not
 lambs. 20

Humano capiti cervicem pictor equinam
Iungere si velit, et varias inducere plumas,
Undique collatis membris, ut turpiter atrum
Desinat in piscem mulier formosa superne:
Spectatum admissi risum teneatis, amici? 5
Credite, Pisones, isti tabulae fore librum
Persimilem, cuius, velut aegri somnia, vanae
Fingentur species; ut nec pes nec caput uni
Reddatur formae. Pictoribus atque poëtis
Quidlibet audendi semper fuit aequa potestas.
Scimus, et hanc veniam petimusque damusque
 vicissim? 11
Sed non ut placidis coëant immitia; non ut
Serpentes avibus geminentur, tigribus agni.
 Incoeptis gravibus plerumque et magna pro-
 fessis,

A labour'd, long exordium, sometimes
 tends
(Like patriot speeches) but to paltry ends;
And nonsense in a lofty note goes down,
As pertness passes with a legal gown:
Thus many a bard describes in pompous
 strain 25
The clear brook babbling through the
 goodly plain:
The groves of Granta, and her Gothic
 halls,
King's Coll., Cam's stream, stain'd win-
 dows, and old walls:
Or, in advent'rous numbers, neatly aims
To paint a rainbow, or—the river Thames

You sketch a tree, and so perhaps may
 shine— 31
But daub a shipwreck like an alehouse
 sign;
You plan a *vase*—it dwindles to a *pot*;
Then glide down Grub-street—fasting and
 forgot;
Laugh'd into Lethe by some quaint Re-
 view, 35
Whose wit is never troublesome till—true.

In fine, to whatsoever you aspire,
Let it at least be simple and entire.

The greater portion of the rhyming
 tribe
(Give ear, my friend, for thou hast been a
 scribe) 40
Are led astray by some peculiar lure.
I labour to be brief—become obscure;

Purpureus, late qui splendeat, unus et alter 15
Assuitur pannus; cum lucus et ara Dianae,
Et properantis aquae per amoenos ambitus
 agros,
Aut flumen Rhenum, aut pluvius describitur
 arcus.
Sed nunc non erat his locus: et fortasse cupres-
 sum 19
Scis simulare: quid hoc, si fractis enatat exspes
Navibus, aere dato qui pingitur? amphora
 coepit
Institui; currente rota cur urceus exit?
Denique sit quod vis, simplex duntaxat et unum.
 Maxima pars vatum, pater et iuvenes patre
 digni,
Decipimur specie recti. Brevis esse laboro, 25

128

)ne falls while following elegance too fast;
nother soars, inflated with bombast;
'oo low a third crawls on, afraid to fly,
Ie spins his subject to satiety; 46
bsurdly varying, he at last engraves
'ish in the woods, and boars beneath the waves!

Unless your care's exact, your judgment nice,
he flight from folly leads but into vice;
Ione are complete, all wanting in some part, 51
ike certain tailors, limited in art.
'or galligaskins Slowshears is your man;
Sut coats must claim another artisan.
Iow this to me, I own, seems much the same 55
As Vulcan's feet to bear Apollo's frame;
)r, with a fair complexion, to expose
Slack eyes, black ringlets, but—a bottle nose!

Dear authors! suit your topics to your strength,
And ponder well your subject and its length; 60
Nor lift your load before you're quite aware
What weight your shoulders will, or will not, bear.
Sut lucid Order, and Wit's siren voice,
Await the poet, skilful in his choice;
With native eloquence he soars along,
Grace in his thoughts, and music in his song. 66

Let judgment teach them wisely to combine
With future parts the now omitted line:
This shall the author choose, or that reject, 69
recise in style, and cautious to select;

Nor slight applause will candid pens afford
To him who furnishes a wanting word.
Then fear not, if 'tis needful, to produce
Some term unknown, or obsolete in use,
(As Pitt has furnish'd us a word or two,
Which lexicographers declined to do;)
So you indeed, with care,—(but be content
To take this license rarely)—may invent.
New words find credit in these latter days,
If neatly grafted on a Gallic phrase. 80
What Chaucer, Spenser did, we scarce refuse
To Dryden's or to Pope's maturer muse.
If you can add a little, say why not,
As well as William Pitt, and Walter Scott?
Since they, by force of rhyme and force of lungs, 85
Enrich'd our island's ill-united tongues;
'Tis then—and shall be—lawful to present
Reform in writing, as in parliament.

As forests shed their foliage by degrees,
So fade expressions which in season please; 90
And we and ours, alas! are due to fate,
And works and words but dwindle to a date.
Though as a monarch nods, and commerce calls,
Impetuous rivers stagnate in canals;
Though swamps subdued, and marshes drain'd, sustain 95
The heavy ploughshare and the yellow grain,
And rising ports along the busy shore
Protect the vessel from old Ocean's roar,
All, all, must perish; but, surviving last,
The love of letters half preserves the past.
True, some decay, yet not a few revive;
Though those shall sink, which now appear to thrive, 102

Obscurus fio: sectantem levia, nervi
Deficiunt animique: professus grandia, turget:
Serpit humi, tutus nimium, timidusque procellae:
Qui variare cupit rem prodigialiter unam,
Delphinum sylvis appingit, fluctibus aprum. 30
In vitium ducit culpae fuga, si caret arte.
Aemilium circa ludum faber unus et ungues
Exprimet, et molles imitabitur aere capillos;
Infelix operis summa, quia ponere totum
Nesciet. Hunc ego me, si quid componere curem, 35
Non magis esse velim, quam pravo vivere naso,
Spectandum nigris oculis nigroque capillo.
Sumite materiam vestris, qui scribitis, aequam
Viribus; et versate diu quid ferre recusent 39
Quid valeant humeri. Cui lecta potenter erit res,
Nec facundia deseret hunc nec lucidus ordo.
Ordinis haec virtus erit et venus, aut ego fallor,
Ut iam nunc dicat, iam nunc debentia dici
Pleraque differat, et praesens in tempus omittat;
In verbis etiam tenuis cautusque serendis: 45
Hoc amet, hoc spernat promissi carminis auctor.
Dixeris egregie, notum si callida verbum

Reddiderit iunctura novum. Si forte necesse est
Indiciis monstrare recentibus abdita rerum,
Fingere cinctutis non exaudita Cethegis 50
Continget; dabiturque licentia sumpta pudenter;
Et nova fictaque nuper habebunt verba fidem, si
Graeco fonte cadant, parce detorta. Quid autem
Caecilio Plautoque dabit Romanus, ademptum
Virgilio Varioque? ego cur, acquirere pauca 55
Si possum, invideor; cum lingua Catonis et Enni
Sermonem patrium ditaverit, et nova rerum
Nomina protulerit? Licuit, semperque licebit,
Signatum praesente nota producere nomen. 59
Ut silvae foliis pronos mutantur in annos;
Prima cadunt: ita verborum vetus interit aetas,
Et iuvenum ritu florent modo nata, vigentque.
Debemur morti nos, nostraque: sive receptus
Terra Neptunus classes Aquilonibus arcet,
Regis opus; sterilisque diu palus, aptaque remis
Vicinas urbes alit, et grave sentit aratrum: 66
Seu cursum mutavit iniquum frugibus amnis,
Doctus iter melius; mortalia facta peribunt:
Nedum sermonum stet honos, et gratia vivax.
Multa renascentur, quae iam cecidere; cadentque, 70

HINTS FROM HORACE

As custom arbitrates, whose shifting sway
Our life and language must alike obey.

The immortal wars which gods and angels wage, 105
Are they not shown in Milton's sacred page?
His strain will teach what numbers best belong
To themes celestial told in epic song.

The slow, sad stanza will correctly paint
The lover's anguish, or the friend's complaint. 110
But which deserves the laurel—rhyme or blank?
Which holds on Helicon the higher rank?
Let squabbling critics by themselves dispute
This point, as puzzling as a Chancery suit.

Satiric rhyme first sprang from selfish spleen. 115
You doubt—see Dryden, Pope, St. Patrick's dean.

Blank verse is now, with one consent, allied
To Tragedy, and rarely quits her side.
Though mad Almanzor rhymed in Dryden's days, 119
No sing-song hero rants in modern plays;
While modest Comedy her verse foregoes
For jest and *pun* in very middling prose.
Not that our Bens or Beaumonts show the worse,
Or lose one point, because they wrote in verse.
But so Thalia pleases to appear, 125
Poor virgin! damn'd some twenty times a year!

Whate'er the scene, let this advice have weight:—
Adapt your language to your hero's state
At times Melpomene forgets to groan,
And brisk Thalia takes a serious tone;
Nor unregarded will the act pass by 13.
Where angry Townly lifts his voice or high.
Again our Shakspeare limits verse to kings,
When common prose will serve for common things;
And lively Hal resigns heroic ire, 13
To 'hollowing Hotspur' and the sceptred sire.

'Tis not enough, ye bards, with all your art,
To polish poems; they must touch the heart:
Where'er the scene be laid, whate'er the song,
Still let it bear the hearer's soul along;
Command your audience or to smile or weep, 14.
Whiche'er may please you—anything but sleep.
The poet claims our tears; but, by his leave,
Before I shed them, let me see him grieve.
If banish'd Romeo feign'd nor sigh nor tear, 14.
Lull'd by his languor, I should sleep or sneer.
Sad words, no doubt, become a serious face,
And men look angry in the proper place.
At double meanings folks seem wondrous sly,
And sentiment prescribes a pensive eye;
For nature form'd at first the inward man, 15
And actors copy nature—when they can

Quae nunc sunt in honore vocabula, si volet usus.
Quem penes arbitrium est, et ius, et norma loquendi.
Res gestae regumque ducumque et tristia bella,
Quo scribi possent numero, monstravit Homerus.
 Versibus impariter iunctis querimonia primum: 75
Post etiam inclusa est voti sententia compos.
Quis tamen exiguos elegos emiserit auctor,
Grammatici certant, et adhuc sub iudice lis est.
 Archilochum proprio rabies armavit iambo;
Hunc socci cepere pedem grandesque cothurni,
Alternis aptum sermonibus, et populares 81
Vincentem strepitus, et natum rebus agendis.
 Musa dedit fidibus divos, puerosque deorum,
Et pugilem victorem, et equum certamine primum,
Et iuvenum curas, et libera vina referre. 85
 Descriptas servare vices, operumque colores,
Cur ego, si nequeo ignoroque, poeta salutor?

Cur nescire, pudens prave, quam discere malo
 Versibus exponi tragicis res comica non vult
Indignatur item privatis, ac prope socco 90
Dignis carminibus narrari coena Thyestae.
Singula quaeque locum teneant sortita decenter.
Interdum tamen et vocem comoedia tollit,
Iratusque Chremes tumido delitigat ore:
Et tragicus plerumque dolet sermone pedestri.
Telephus et Peleus, cum pauper et exul, uterque
Proicit ampullas, et sesquipedalia verba, 97
Si curat cor spectantis tetigisse querela.
 Non satis est pulchra esse poemata; dulcia sunto,
Et quocunque volent, animum auditoris agunto.
Ut ridentibus arrident, ita flentibus adsunt 101
Humani vultus; si vis me flere dolendum est
Primum ipsi tibi; tunc tua me infortunia laedent,
Telephe, vel Peleu; male si mandata loqueris
Aut dormitabo, aut ridebo: tristia moestum
Vultum verba decent; iratum, plena minarum;
Ludentem, lasciva; severum, seria dictu. 107
Format enim natura prius nos intus ad omnem

She bids the beating heart with rapture
 bound,
Raised to the stars, or levell'd with the
 ground; 154
And for expression's aid, 'tis said, or sung,
She gave our mind's interpreter—the
 tongue,
Who, worn with use, of late would fain
 dispense
At least in theatres) with common sense;
O'erwhelm with sound the boxes, gallery,
 pit, 159
And raise a laugh with anything—but wit.

To skilful writers it will much import,
Whence spring their scenes, from common
 life or court;
Whether they seek applause by smile or
 tear,
To draw a 'Lying Valet,' or a 'Lear,'
A sage, or rakish youngster wild from
 school, 165
A wandering 'Peregrine,' or plain 'John
 Bull';
All persons please when nature's voice
 prevails,
Scottish or Irish, born in Wilts or Wales.

Or follow common fame, or forge a
 plot; 169
Who cares if mimic heroes lived or not?
One precept serves to regulate the scene:—
Make it appear as if it *might* have *been*.

If some Drawcansir you aspire to draw,
Present him raving, and above all law:
If female furies in your scheme are
 plann'd, 175
Macbeth's fierce dame is ready to your
 hand;
For tears and treachery, for good and evil,
Constance, King Richard, Hamlet, and
 the Devil!
But if a new design you dare essay, 179
And freely wander from the beaten way,

True to your characters, till all be past,
Preserve consistency from first to last.

'Tis hard to venture where our betters
 fail,
Or lend fresh interest to a twice-told tale;
And yet, perchance, 'tis wiser to prefer
A hackney'd plot, than choose a new, and
 err; 186
Yet copy not too closely, but record,
More justly, thought for thought than
 word for word;
Nor trace your prototype through narrow
 ways,
But only follow where he merits praise.

For you, young bard! whom luckless
 fate may lead 191
To tremble on the nod of all who read,
Ere your first score of cantos time unrolls,
Beware—for God's sake, don't begin like
 Bowles!
'Awake a louder and a loftier strain,'—
And pray, what follows from his boiling
 brain?— 196
He sinks to Southey's level in a trice,
Whose epic mountains never fail in mice!
Not so of yore awoke your mighty sire
The temper'd warblings of his master-
 lyre; 200
Soft as the gentle breathing of the lute,
'Of man's first disobedience and the fruit'
He speaks, but, as his subject swells along,
Earth, Heaven, and Hades echo with the
 song.
Still to the midst of things he hastens on,
As if we witness'd all already done; 206
Leaves on his path whatever seems too
 mean
To raise the subject, or adorn the scene;
Gives, as each page improves upon the
 sight,
Not smoke from brightness, but from
 darkness—light; 210

Fortunarum habitum; iuvat, aut impellit ad
 iram;
Aut ad humum moerore gravi deducit, et angit;
Post effert animi motus interprete lingua. 111
Si dicentis erunt fortunis absona dicta,
Romani tollent equites, peditesque cachinnum.
 Intererit multum, Davusne loquatur an heros;
Maturusne senex, an adhuc florente iuventa
Fervidus; an matrona potens, an sedula nutrix;
Mercatorne vagus, cultorne virentis agelli;
Colchus an Assyrius; Thebis nutritus, an Argis.
 Aut famam sequere, aut sibi convenientia
 finge, 119
Scriptor. Honoratum si forte reponis Achillem;
Impiger, iracundus, inexorabilis, acer,
Iura neget sibi nata, nihil non arroget armis.
Sit Medea ferox invictaque; flebilis Ino;
Perfidus Ixion; Io vaga; tristis Orestes. 124
Si quid inexpertum scenae committis, et audes
Personam formare novam: servetur ad imum
Qualis ab incepto processerit, et sibi constet.
 Difficile est proprie communia dicere: tuque
Rectius Iliacum carmen deducis in actus,

Quam si proferres ignota indictaque primus.
Publica materies privati iuris erit, si 131
Nec circa vilem patulumque moraberis orbem;
Nec verbum verbo curabis reddere fidus
Interpres, nec desilies imitator in arctum
Unde pedem proferre pudor vetet, aut operis lex.
Nec sic incipies, ut scriptor Cyclicus olim: 136
'Fortunam Priami cantabo, et nobile bellum.'
Quid dignum tanto feret hic promissor hiatu?
Parturiunt montes: nascetur ridiculus mus.
Quanto rectius hic, qui nil molitur inepte! 140
'Dic mihi, Musa, virum, captae post tempora
 Troiae,
Qui mores hominum multorum vidit, et urbes.'
Non fumum ex fulgore, sed ex fumo dare lucem
Cogitat, ut speciosa dehinc miracula promat,
Antiphaten, Scyllamque, et cum Cyclope Cha-
 rybdin. 145
Nec reditum Diomedis ab interitu Meleagri,
Nec gemino bellum Troianum orditur ab ovo.
Semper ad eventum festinat; et in medias res
Non secus ac notas, auditorem rapit, et quae
Desperat tractata nitescere posse, relinquit: 150

131

And truth and fiction with such art compounds,
We know not where to fix their several bounds.
If you would please the public, deign to hear
What soothes the many-headed monster's ear:
If your heart triumph when the hands of all 215
Applaud in thunder at the curtain's fall,
Deserve those plaudits—study nature's page,
And sketch the striking traits of every age;
While varying man and varying years unfold
Life's little tale, so oft, so vainly told; 220
Observe his simple childhood's dawning days,
His pranks, his prate, his playmates, and his plays;
Till time at length the mannish tyro weans,
And prurient vice outstrips his tardy teens!

Behold him Freshman! forced no more to groan 225
O'er Virgil's devilish verses and his own;
Prayers are too tedious, lectures too abstruse,
He flies from Tavell's frown to 'Fordham's Mews';
(Unlucky Tavell! doom'd to daily cares
By pugilistic pupils, and by bears,) 230
Fines, tutors, tasks, conventions threat in vain,
Before hounds, hunters, and Newmarket plain.
Rough with his elders, with his equals rash,
Civil to sharpers, prodigal of cash;
Constant to nought—save hazard and a whore, 235
Yet cursing both—for both have made him sore;
Unread (unless, since books beguile disease,
The p—x becomes his passage to degrees);
Fool'd, pillaged, dunn'd, he wastes his term away,
And unexpell'd, perhaps, retires M.A.;

Master of arts! as *hells* and *clubs* proclaim, 241
Where scarce a blackleg bears a brighter name!

Launch'd into life, extinct his early fire,
He apes the selfish prudence of his sire;
Marries for money, chooses friends for rank, 245
Buys land, and shrewdly trusts not to the Bank;
Sits in the Senate; gets a son and heir;
Sends him to Harrow, for himself was there.
Mute, though he votes, unless when call'd to cheer,
His son's so sharp—he'll see the dog a peer! 250

Manhood declines—age palsies every limb;
He quits the scene—or else the scene quits him;
Scrapes wealth, o'er each departing penny grieves,
And avarice seizes all ambition leaves;
Counts cent. per cent., and smiles, or vainly frets, 255
O'er hoards diminish'd by young Hopeful's debts;
Weighs well and wisely what to sell or buy,
Complete in all life's lessons—but to die;
Peevish and spiteful, doting, hard to please,
Commending every time, save times like these; 260
Crazed, querulous, forsaken, half forgot,
Expires unwept—is buried—let him rot!

But from the Drama let me not digress,
Nor spare my precepts, though they please you less.
Though woman weep, and hardest hearts are stirr'd, 265
When what is done is rather seen than heard,
Yet many deeds preserved in history's page
Are better told than acted on the stage;

Atque ita mentitur, sic veris falsa remiscet,
Primo ne medium, medio ne discrepet imum.
 Tu, quid ego et populus mecum desideret, audi.
Si plausoris eges aulaea manentis, et usque
Sessuri, donec cantor, Vos plaudite, dicat; 155
Aetatis cuiusque notandi sunt tibi mores,
Mobilibusque decor naturis dandus et annis.
Reddere qui voces iam scit puer, et pede certo
Signat humum: gestit paribus colludere, et iram
Colligit ac ponit temere, et mutatur in horas.
 Imberbus iuvenis, tandem custode remoto,
Gaudet equis canibusque, et aprici gramine campi;
Cereus in vitium flecti, monitoribus asper,
Utilium tardus provisor, prodigus aeris,

Sublimis, cupidusque, et amata relinquere pernix. 165
 Conversis studiis, aetas animusque virilis
Quaerit opes et amicitias, inservit honori;
Commisisse cavet quod mox mutare laboret.
 Multa senem circumveniunt incommoda; vel quod 169
Quaerit, et inventis miser abstinet, ac timet uti;
Vel quod res omnes timide gelideque ministrat,
Dilator, spe longus, iners, avidusque futuri,
Difficilis, querulus, laudator temporis acti
Se puero, castigator censorque minorum. 174
Multa ferunt anni venientes commoda secum,
Multa recedentes adimunt. Ne forte seniles
Mandentur iuveni partes, pueroque viriles,
Semper in adiunctis, aevoque morabimur aptis.

The ear sustains what shocks the timid eye,
And horror thus subsides to sympathy.
True Briton all beside, I here am French—
Bloodshed 'tis surely better to retrench;
The gladiatorial gore we teach to flow
In tragic scene disgusts, though but in
 show;
We hate the carnage while we see the
 trick, 275
And find small sympathy in being sick.
Not on the stage the regicide Macbeth
Appals an audience with a monarch's death;
To gaze when sable Hubert threats to sear
Young Arthur's eyes, can *ours* or *nature*
 bear? 280
A halter'd heroine Johnson sought to slay—
We saved Irene, but half damn'd the play,
And (Heaven be praised!) our tolerating
 times
Stint metamorphoses to pantomimes;
And Lewis' self, with all his sprites, would
 quake 285
To change Earl Osmond's negro to a snake!
Because, in scenes exciting joy or grief,
We loathe the action which exceeds belief:
And yet, God knows! what may not
 authors do,
Whose postscripts prate of dyeing
 'heroines blue?' 290

Above all things, *Dan* Poet, if you can,
Eke out your acts, I pray, with mortal man,
Nor call a ghost, unless some cursed scrape
Must open ten trap-doors for your escape.
Of all the monstrous things I'd fain for-
 bid, 295
I loathe an opera worse than Dennis did;
Where good and evil persons, right or
 wrong,
Rage, love, and aught but moralise, in
 song.
Hail, last memorial of our foreign friends,
Which Gaul allows, and still Hesperia
 lends! 300
Napoleon's edicts no embargo lay
On whores, spies, singers, wisely shipp'd
 away.
Our giant capital, whose squares are
 spread
Where rustics earn'd, and now may beg,
 their bread,
In all iniquity is grown so nice, 305
It scorns amusements which are not of
 price.

Hence the pert shopkeeper, whose throb-
 bing ear
Aches with orchestras which he pays to
 hear,
Whom shame, not sympathy, forbids to
 snore,
His anguish doubling by his own 'encore';
Squeezed in 'Fop's Alley,' jostled by the
 beaux, 311
Teased with his hat, and trembling for his
 toes;
Scarce wrestles through the night, nor
 tastes of ease,
Till the dropp'd curtain gives a glad release:
Why this, and more, he suffers—can ye
 guess?— 315
Because it costs him dear, and makes him
 dress!

So prosper eunuchs from Etruscan
 schools;
Give us but fiddlers, and they're sure of
 fools!
Ere scenes were play'd by many a reverend
 clerk,
(What harm, if David danced before the
 ark?) 320
In Christmas revels, simple country folks
Were pleased with morrice-mumm'ry and
 coarse jokes.
Improving years, with things no longer
 known,
Produced blithe Punch and merry Ma-
 dame Joan, 324
Who still frisk on with feats so lewdly low,
'Tis strange Benvolio suffers such a show;
Suppressing peer! to whom each vice gives
 place,
Oaths, boxing, begging,—all, save rout
 and race.

Farce follow'd Comedy, and reach'd
 her prime,
In ever-laughing Foote's fantastic time:
Mad wag! who pardon'd none, nor spared
 the best, 331
And turn'd some very serious things to jest.
Nor church nor state escaped his public
 sneers,
Arms nor the gown, priests, lawyers, vol-
 unteers:
'Alas, poor Yorick!' now for ever mute!
Whoever loves a laugh must sigh for
 Foote. 336

Aut agitur res in scenis, aut acta refertur.
Segnius irritant animos demissa per aurem 180
Quam quae sunt oculis subiecta fidelibus, et quae
Ipse sibi tradit spectator. Non tamen intus
Digna geri promes in scenam; multaque tolles
Ex oculis, quae mox narret facundia praesens.
Ne pueros coram populo Medea trucidet; 185
Aut humana palam coquat exta nefarius Atreus;
Aut in avem Progne vertatur, Cadmus in anguem.
Quodcumque ostendis mihi sic, incredulus odi.

Neve minor, neu sit quinto productior actu
Fabula, quae posci vult, et spectata reponi. 190
Nec deus intersit, nisi dignus vindice nodus
Inciderit,
 Ex noto fictum carmen sequar, ut sibi
 quivis 240
Speret idem: sudet multum frustraque laboret
Ausus idem: tantum series iuncturaque pollet;
Tantum de medio sumtis accedit honoris.
Silvis deducti caveant, me iudice, Fauni,

We smile, perforce, when histrionic scenes
Ape the swoln dialogue of kings and queens,
When 'Chrononhotonthologos must die,'
And Arthur struts in mimic majesty.

Moschus! with whom once more I hope to sit, 341
And smile at folly, if we can't at wit;
Yes, friend! for thee I'll quit my cynic cell,
And bear Swift's motto, 'Vive la baga-
 telle!'
Which charm'd our days in each Aegean clime, 345
As oft at home, with revelry and rhyme.
Then may Euphrosyne, who sped the past,
Soothe thy life's scenes, nor leave thee in the last;
But find in thine, like pagan Plato's bed,
Some merry manuscript of mimes, when dead. 350

Now to the Drama let us bend our eyes,
Where fetter'd by whig Walpole low she lies;
Corruption foil'd her, for she fear'd her glance;
Decorum left her for an opera dance!
Yet Chesterfield, whose polished pen in-
 veighs 355
'Gainst laughter, fought for freedom to our plays;
Uncheck'd by megrims of patrician brains,
And damning dulness of lord chamberlains.
Repeal that act! again let Humour roam
Wild o'er the stage—we've time for tears at home, 360
Let 'Archer' plant the horns on 'Sullen's' brows,
And 'Estifania' gull her 'Copper' spouse;
The moral's scant—but that may be ex-
 cused,
Men go not to be lectured, but amused.
He whom our plays dispose to good or ill
Must wear a head in want of Willis' skill;
Ay, but Macheath's example—psha!—no more! 367
It form'd no thieves—the thief was form'd before;
And, spite of puritans and Collier's curse,
Plays make mankind no better, and no worse. 370
Then spare our stage, ye methodistic men!
Nor burn damn'd Drury if it rise again.

But why to brain-scorch'd bigots thus appeal?
Can heavenly mercy dwell with earthly zeal? 374
For times of fire and faggot let them hope!
Times dear alike to puritan or pope.
As pious Calvin saw Servetus blaze,
So would new sects on newer victims gaze.
E'en now the songs of Solyma begin; 379
Faith cants, perplex'd apologist of sin!
While the Lord's servant chastens whom he loves,
And Simeon kicks, where Baxter only 'shoves.'

Whom nature guides, so writes, that every dunce,
Enraptured, thinks to do the same at once;
But after inky thumbs and bitten nails,
And twenty scatter'd quires, the coxcomb fails. 386

Let Pastoral be dumb; for who can hope
To match the youthful eclogues of our Pope?
Yet his and Phillips' faults, of different kind, 389
For art too rude, for nature too refined,
Instruct how hard the medium 'tis to hit
'Twixt too much polish and too coarse a wit.

A vulgar scribbler, certes, stands dis-
 graced
In this nice age, when all aspire to taste;
The dirty language, and the noisome jest,
Which pleased in Swift of yore, we now detest; 396
Proscribed not only in the world polite,
But even too nasty for a city knight!

Peace to Swift's faults! his wit hath made them pass,
Unmatch'd by all, save matchless Hudi-
 bras! 400
Whose author is perhaps the first we meet,
Who from our couplet lopp'd two final feet;
Nor less in merit than the longer line,
This measure moves a favourite of the Nine.
Though at first view eight feet may seem in vain 405
Form'd, save in ode, to bear a serious strain,

Ne, velut innati triviis, ac pene forenses, 245
Aut nimium teneris iuvenentur versibus un-
 quam,
Aut immunda crepent, ignominiosaque dicta.
Offenduntur enim, quibus est equus, et pater, et
 res:
Nec, si quid fricti ciceris probat et nucis emtor,
Aequis accipiunt animis, donantve corona.
 Syllaba longa brevi subiecta vocatur iambus,
Pes citus: unde etiam trimetris accrescere iussit

Nomen iambeis, cum senos redderet ictus,
Primus ad extremum similis sibi: non ita pridem,
Tardior ut paulo graviorque veniret ad aures,
Spondeos stabiles in iura paterna recepit 256
Commodus et patiens; non ut de sede secunda
Cederet aut quarta socialiter. Hic et in Acci
Nobilibus trimetris apparet rarus, et Enni.
In scenam missos magno cum pondere versus,
Aut operae celeris nimium, curaque carentis,
Aut ignoratae premit artis crimine turpi. 262

Yet Scott has shown our wondering isle of
late
This measure shrinks not from a theme of
weight,
And, varied skilfully, surpasses far 409
Heroic rhyme, but most in love and war,
Whose fluctuations, tender or sublime,
Are curb'd too much by long-recurring
rhyme.

But many a skilful judge abhors to see,
What few admire—irregularity.
This some vouchsafe to pardon; but 'tis
hard 415
When such a word contents a British bard.

And must the bard his glowing thoughts
confine,
Lest censure hover o'er some faulty line?
Remove whate'er a critic may suspect,
To gain the paltry suffrage of ' *correct* '?
Or prune the spirit of each daring phrase,
To fly from error, not to merit praise?

Ye, who seek finish'd models, never
cease,
By day and night, to read the works of
Greece.
But our good fathers never bent their
brains 425
To heathen Greek, content with native
strains.
The few who read a page, or used a pen,
Were satisfied with Chaucer and old Ben;
The jokes and numbers suited to their taste
Were quaint and careless, anything but
chaste; 430
Yet whether right or wrong the ancient
rules,
It will not do to call our fathers fools!
Though you and I, who eruditely know
To separate the elegant and low, 434
Can also, when a hobbling line appears,
Detect with fingers, in default of ears.

In sooth I do not know, or greatly care
To learn, who our first English strollers
were;

Or if, till roofs received the vagrant art,
Our Muse, like that of Thespis, kept a
cart; 440
But this is certain, since our Shakspeare's
days,
There's pomp enough, if little else, in
plays;
Nor will Melpomene ascend her throne
Without high heels, white plume, and
Bristol stone.

Old comedies still meet with much
applause, 445
Though too licentious for dramatic laws;
At least, we moderns, wisely, 'tis confest,
Curtail, or silence, the lascivious jest.

Whate'er their follies, and their faults
beside,
Our enterprising bards pass nought un-
tried; 450
Nor do they merit slight applause who
choose
An English subject for an English muse,
And leave to minds which never dare invent
French flippancy and German sentiment.
Where is that living language which could
claim 455
Poetic more, as philosophic, fame,
If all our bards, more patient of delay,
Would stop, like Pope, to polish by the
way?

Lords of the quill, whose critical assaults
O'erthrow whole quartos with their quires
of faults, 460
Who soon detect, and mark where'er we
fail,
And prove our marble with too nice a nail!
Democritus himself was not so bad;
He only *thought*, but *you* would make, us
mad!

But truth to say, most rhymers rarely
guard 465
Against that ridicule they deem so hard;
In person negligent, they wear, from sloth,
Beards of a week, and nails of annual
growth;

Non quivis videt immodulata poemata iudex;
Et data Romanis venia est indigna poetis.
Idcircone vager, scribamque licenter? an omnes
Visuros peccata putem mea; tutus, et intra
Spem veniae cautus? vitavi denique culpam,
Non laudem merui. Vos exemplaria Graeca
Nocturna versate manu, versate diurna.
At vestri proavi Plautinos et numeros et 270
Laudavere sales; nimium patienter utrumque,
Ne dicam stulte, mirati; si modo ego et vos
Scimus inurbanum lepido seponere dicto,
Legitimumque sonum digitis callemus et aure.
 Ignotum tragicae genus invenisse Camoena_
Dicitur, et plaustris vexisse poemata Thespis,
Quae canerent agerentque peruncti faecibus
ora. 277
Post hunc personae pallaeque repertor honestae

Aeschylus, et modicis instravit pulpita tignis,
Et docuit magnumque loqui, nitique cothurno.
 Successit vetus his comoedia, non sine multa
Laude; sed in vitium libertas excidit, et vim
Dignam lege regi; lex est accepta; chorusque
Turpiter obticuit, sublato iure nocendi.
 Nil intentatum nostri liquere poetae; 285
Nec minimum meruere decus, vestigia Graeca
Ausi deserere, et celebrare domestica facta;
Vel qui praetextas, vel qui docuere togatas.
Nec virtute foret clarisve potentius armis,
Quam lingua, Latium, si non offenderet unum-
quemque poetarum limae labor, et mora. Vos, o
Pompilius sanguis, carmen reprehendite, quod
non 292
Multa dies et multa litura coercuit, atque
Praesectum decies non castigavit ad unguem.

HINTS FROM HORACE

Reside in garrets, fly from those they
 meet,
And walk in alleys, rather than the street.

With little rhyme, less reason, if you
 please, 471
The name of poet may be got with ease,
So that not tuns of helleboric juice
Shall ever turn your head to any use;
Write but like Wordsworth, live beside a
 Lake, 475
And keep your bushy locks a year from
 Blake;
Then print your book, once more return
 to town,
And boys shall hunt your bardship up and
 down.

Am I not wise, if such some poets' plight,
To purge in spring—like Bayes—before
 I write? 480
If this precaution soften'd not my bile,
I know no scribbler with a madder style;
But since (perhaps my feelings are too
 nice)
I cannot purchase fame at such a price,
I'll labour gratis as a grinder's wheel,
And, blunt myself, give edge to others'
 steel, 486
Nor write at all, unless to teach the art
To those rehearsing for the poet's part;
From Horace show the pleasing paths of
 song,
And from my own example—what is
 wrong. 490

Though modern practice sometimes
 differs quite,
'Tis just as well to think before you write;
Let every book that suits your theme be
 read,
So shall you trace it to the fountain-head.

He who has learn'd the duty which he
 owes 495

To friends and country, and to pardon foes;
Who models his deportment as may best
Accord with brother, sire, or stranger guest;
Who takes our laws and worship as they are,
Nor roars reform for senate, church, and
 bar; 500
In practice, rather than loud precept, wise,
Bids not his tongue, but heart, philoso-
 phise:
Such is the man the poet should rehearse,
As joint exemplar of his life and verse.

Sometimes a sprightly wit, and tale well
 told, 505
Without much grace, or weight, or art,
 will hold
A longer empire o'er the public mind
Than sounding trifles, empty, though re-
 fined.

Unhappy Greece! thy sons of ancient
 days
The muse may celebrate with perfect
 praise, 510
Whose generous children narrow'd not
 their hearts
With commerce, given alone to arms and
 arts.
Our boys (save those whom public schools
 compel
To 'long and short' before they're taught
 to spell) 514
From frugal fathers soon imbibe by rote,
'A penny saved, my lad, 's a penny got.'
Babe of a city birth! from sixpence take
The third, how much will the remainder
 make?—
'A groat.'—'Ah, bravo! Dick hath done
 the sum!
He'll swell my fifty thousand to a plum.'

They whose young souls receive this
 rust betimes, 521
'Tis clear, are fit for anything but rhymes;

Ingenium misera quia fortunatius arte 295
Credit, et excludit sanos Helicone poetas
Democritus; bona pars non ungues ponere
 curat,
Non barbam; secreta petit loca, balnea vitat.
Nanciscetur enim pretium nomenque poetae,
Si tribus Anticyris caput insanabile nunquam
Tonsori Licino commiserit. O ego laevus, 301
Qui purgor bilem sub verni temporis horam!
Non alius faceret meliora poemata: verum
Nil tanti est: ergo fungar vice cotis, acutum
Reddere quae ferrum valet, exsors ipsa secandi:
Munus et officium, nil scribens ipse, docebo;
Unde parentur opes; quid alat formetque
 poetam;
Quid deceat, quid non; quo virtus, quo ferat
 error. 308
 Scribendi recte sapere est et principium et fons.
Rem tibi Socraticae poterunt ostendere chartae:
Verbaque provisam rem non invita sequentur:
Qui didicit patriae quid debeat,˙ et quid amicis;

Quo sic amore parens, quo frater amandus, et
 hospes;
Quod sit conscripti, quod iudicis officium; quae
Partes in bellum missi ducis; ille profecto 315
Reddere personae scit convenientia cuique.
Respicere exemplar vitae morumque iubebo
Doctum imitatorem, et vivas hinc ducere voces.
 Interdum speciosa locis morataque recte
Fabula, nullius veneris, sine pondere et arte,
Valdius oblectat populum, meliusque moratur,
Quam versus inopes rerum, nugaeque canorae.
 Graiis ingenium, Graiis dedit ore rotundo
Musa loqui, praeter laudem nullius avaris.
Romani pueri longis rationibus assem 325
Discunt in partes centum diducere: dicat
Filius Albini, Si de quincunce remota est
Uncia, quid superat? poteras dixisse—Triens. Eu!
Rem poteris servare tuam. Redit uncia: quid
 fit? 329
Semis. An haec animos aerugo et cura peculi
Cum semel imbuerit, speramus carmina fingi

And Locke will tell you, that the father's
 right
Who hides all verses from his children's
 sight; 524
For poets (says this sage, and many more,)
Make sad mechanics with their lyric lore;
And Delphi now, however rich of old,
Discovers little silver, and less gold,
Because Parnassus, though a mount di-
 vine,
Is poor as Irus, or an Irish mine. 530

Two objects always should the poet
 move,
Or one or both,—to please or to improve.
Whate'er you teach, be brief, if you design
For our remembrance your didactic line;
Redundance places memory on the rack,
For brains may be o'erloaded, like the
 back. 536

Fiction does best when taught to look
 like truth,
And fairy fables bubble none but youth:
Expect no credit for too wondrous tales,
Since Jonas only springs alive from
 whales! 540

Young men with aught but elegance
 dispense;
Maturer years require a little sense.
To end at once:—that bard for all is fit
Who mingles well instruction with his wit;
For him reviews shall smile, for him o'er-
 flow 545
The patronage of Paternoster-row;
His book, with Longman's liberal aid,
 shall pass
(Who ne'er despises books that bring him
 brass)
Through three long weeks the taste of
 London lead,
And cross St. George's Channel and the
 Tweed. 550

But everything has faults, nor is 't un-
 known
That harps and fiddles often lose their tone,
And wayward voices, at their owner's call,
With all his best endeavours, only squall;
Dogs blink their covey, flints withhold the
 spark, 555
And double-barrels (damn them!) miss
 their mark.

Where frequent beauties strike the
 reader's view,
We must not quarrel for a blot or two;
But pardon equally to books or men,
The slips of human nature, and the pen.

Yet if an author, spite of foe or friend,
Despises all advice too much to mend,
But ever twangs the same discordant string,
Give him no quarter, howsoe'er he sing.
Let Havard's fate o'ertake him, who, for
 once, 565
Produced a play too dashing for a dunce:
At first none deem'd it his; but when his
 name
Announced the fact—what then?—it lost
 its fame.
Though all deplore when Milton deigns to
 doze,
In a long work 'tis fair to steal repose.

As pictures, so shall poems be; some
 stand 571
The critic eye, and please when near at
 hand;
But others at a distance strike the sight;
This seeks the shade, but that demands
 the light,
Nor dreads the connoisseur's fastidious
 view, 575
But, ten times scrutinised, is ten times new.

Parnassian pilgrims! ye whom chance or
 choice
Hath led to listen to the Muse's voice,

Posse linenda cedro, et levi servanda cupresso?
 Aut prodesse volunt, aut delectare poetae;
Aut simul et iucunda et idonea dicere vitae. 334
Quidquid praecipies, esto brevis: ut cito dicta
Percipiant animi dociles, teneantque fideles.
Omne supervacuum pleno de pectore manat.
 Ficta voluptatis causa sint proxima veris:
Nec, quodcunque volet, poscat sibi fabula credi:
Neu pransae Lamiae vivum puerum extrahat
 alvo. 340
 Centuriae seniorum agitant expertia frugis:
Celsi praetereunt austera poemata Rhamnes.
Omne tulit punctum, qui miscuit utile dulci:
Lectorem delectando pariterque monendo. 344
Hic meret aera liber Sosiis; hic et mare transit,
Et longum noto scriptori prorogat aevum.
 Sunt delicta tamen, quibus ignovisse velimus:
Nam neque chorda sonum reddit quem vult
 manus et mens,
Poscentique gravem persaepe remittit acutum;
Nec semper feriet quodcunque minabitur arcus.

Verum ubi plura nitent in carmine, non ego
 paucis 351
Offendar maculis, quas aut incuria fudit,
Aut humana parum cavit natura. Quid ergo est?
Ut scriptor si peccat idem librarius usque,
Quamvis est monitus, venia caret; ut citharoedus
Ridetur, chorda qui semper oberrat eadem:
Sic mihi, qui multum cessat, fit Choerilus ille,
Quem bis terve bonum cum risu miror; et idem
Indignor, quandoque bonus dormitat Homerus.
Verum operi longo fas est obrepere somnum.
 Ut pictura, poesis: erit quae, si propius stes,
Te capiat magis; et quaedam, si longius abstes:
Haec amat obscurum; volet haec sub luce videri,
Iudicis argutum quae non formidat acumen:
Haec placuit semel; haec decies repetita placebit.
 O maior iuvenum, quamvis et voce paterna
Fingeris ad rectum, et per te sapis, hoc tibi
 dictum 367
Tolle memor: certis medium et tolerabile rebus
Recte concedi: consultus iuris, et actor

HINTS FROM HORACE

Receive this counsel, and be timely wise;
Few reach the summit which before you
 lies. 580
Our church and state, our courts and
 camps, concede
Reward to very moderate heads indeed!
In these plain common sense will travel
 far;
All are not Erskines who mislead the bar:
But poesy between the best and worst
No medium knows; you must be last or
 first; 586
For middling poets' miserable volumes
Are damn'd alike by gods, and men, and
 columns.

Again, my Jeffrey!—as that sound in-
 spires, 589
How wakes my bosom to its wonted fires!
Fires, such as gentle Caledonians feel
When Southrons writhe upon their critic
 wheel,
Or mild Eclectics, when some, worse than
 Turks,
Would rob poor Faith to decorate 'good
 works.'
Such are the genial feelings thou canst
 claim— 595
My falcon flies not at ignoble game.
Mightiest of all Dunedin's beasts of chase!
For thee my Pegasus would mend his pace.
Arise, my Jeffrey! or my inkless pen 599
Shall never blunt its edge on meaner men;
Till thee or thine mine evil eye discerns,
Alas! 'I cannot strike at wretched kernes.'
Inhuman Saxon! wilt thou then resign
A muse and heart by choice so wholly
 thine?
Dear d——d contemner of my schoolboy
 songs, 605
Hast thou no vengeance for my man-
 hood's wrongs?
If unprovoked thou once could bid me
 bleed,
Hast thou no weapon for my daring deed?
What! not a word!—and am I then so low?
Wilt thou forbear, who never spared a
 foe? 610
Hast thou no wrath, or wish to give it vent?
No wit for nobles, dunces by descent?
No jest on 'minors,' quibbles on a name,
Nor one facetious paragraph of blame?

Is it for this on Ilion I have stood, 615
And thought of Homer less than Holy-
 rood!
On shore of Euxine or Aegean sea,
My hate, untravell'd, fondly turn'd to thee:
Ah! let me cease: in vain my bosom burns
From Corydon unkind Alexis turns: 620
Thy rhymes are vain; thy Jeffrey then
 forego,
Nor woo that anger which he will not
 show.
What then?—Edina starves some lanker
 son,
To write an article thou canst not shun;
Some less fastidious Scotchman shall be
 found, 625
As bold in Billingsgate, though less re-
 nown'd.

As if at table some discordant dish
Should shock our optics, such as frogs for
 fish;
As oil in lieu of butter men decry, 629
And poppies please not in a modern pie;
If all such mixtures then be half a crime,
We must have excellence to relish rhyme.
Mere roast and boil'd no epicure invites;
Thus poetry disgusts, or else delights.

Who shoot not flying rarely touch a
 gun: 635
Will he who swims not to the river run?
And men unpractised in exchanging
 knocks
Must go to Jackson ere they dare to box.
Whate'er the weapon, cudgel, fist, or foil
None reach expertness without years of
 toil; 640
But fifty dunces can, with perfect ease,
Tag twenty thousand couplets, when they
 please.
Why not?—shall I, thus qualified to sit
For rotten boroughs, never show my wit?
Shall I, whose fathers with the quorum
 sate, 645
And lived in freedom on a fair estate;
Who left me heir, with stables, kennels,
 packs,
To *all* their income, and to—*twice* its tax;
Whose form and pedigree have scarce a
 fault,
Shall I, I say, suppress my Attic salt? 650

Causarum mediocris abest virtute diserti 370
Messalae, nec scit quantum Cascellius Aulus:
Sed tamen in pretio est: mediocribus esse poetis
Non homines, non di, non concessere columnae.
Ut gratas inter mensas symphonia discors,
Et crassum unguentum, et Sardo cum melle
 papaver 375
Offendunt, poterat duci quia coena sine istis;
Sic animis natum inventumque poema iuvandis,
Si paulum a summo decessit, vergit ad imum.
 Ludere qui nescit, campestribus abstinet
 armis,

Indoctusque pilae, discive, trochive, quiescit,
Ne spissae risum tollant impune coronae: 381
Qui nescit, versus tamen audet fingere!—Quid-
 ni?
Liber et ingenuus praesertim census equestrem
Summam nummorum, vitioque remotus ab
 omni.
Tu nihil invita dices faciesve Minerva: 385
Id tibi iudicium est, ea mens: si quid tamen olim
Scripseris, in Metii descendat iudicis aures,
Et patris, et nostras, nonumque prematur in
 annum,

138

Thus think 'the mob of gentlemen;' but
you, 651
Besides all this, must have some genius
too.
Be this your sober judgment, and a rule,
And print not piping hot from Southey's
school,
Who (ere another Thalaba appears) 655
I trust will spare us for at least nine
years.
And hark 'ye, Southey! pray—but don't be
vex'd—
Burn all your last three works—and half
the next.
But why this vain advice? once published,
books
Can never be recall'd—from pastry-
cooks! 660
Though 'Madoc,' with 'Pucelle,' instead
of punk,
May travel back to Quito—on a trunk!

Orpheus, we learn from Ovid and Lem-
priere,
Led all wild beasts but women by the
ear;
And had he fiddled at the present hour,
We'd seen the lions waltzing in the
Tower; 666
And old Amphion, such were minstrels
then,
Had built St. Paul's without the aid of
Wren.
Verse too was justice, and the bards of
Greece
Did more than constables to keep the
peace; 670
Abolish'd cuckoldom with much ap-
plause,
Call'd county meetings, and enforced the
laws,
Cut down crown influence with reforming
scythes,
And served the church—without demand-
ing tithes;
And hence, throughout all Hellas and the
East, 675
Each poet was a prophet and a priest,
Whose old-establish'd board of joint con-
trols
Included kingdoms in the cure of souls.

Next rose the martial Homer, Epic's
prince,
And fighting's been in fashion ever since;
And old Tyrtæus, when the Spartans
warr'd, 681
(A limping leader, but a lofty bard,)
Though wall'd Ithome had resisted long,
Reduced the fortress by the force of song.

When oracles prevail'd, in times of old,
In song alone Apollo's will was told.
Then if your verse is what all verse should
be,
And gods were not ashamed on't, why
should we?

The Muse, like mortal females, may be
woo'd; 689
In turns she'll seem a Paphian, or a prude;
Fierce as a bride when first she feels af-
fright,
Mild as the same upon the second night;
Wild as the wife of alderman or peer,
Now for his grace, and now a grenadier!
Her eyes beseem, her heart belies, her
zone, 695
Ice in a crowd, and lava when alone.

If verse be studied with some show of
art,
Kind Nature always will perform her part;
Though without genius, and a native vein
Of wit, we loathe an artificial strain, 700
Yet art and nature join'd will win the prize,
Unless they act like us and our allies.

The youth who trains to ride, or run a
race,
Must bear privations with unruffled face,
Be call'd to labour when he thinks to
dine, 705
And, harder still, leave wenching and his
wine.
Ladies who sing, at least who sing at sight,
Have follow'd music through her farthest
flight;
But rhymers tell you neither more nor less,
'I've got a pretty poem for the press';
And that's enough; then write and print so
fast;— 711
If Satan take the hindmost, who'd be last?

Membranis intus positis: delere licebit 389
Quod non edideris; nescit vox missa reverti.
 Sylvestres homines sacer interpresque deorum
Caedibus et victu foedo deterruit Orpheus:
Dictus ob hoc lenire tigres, rabidosque leones:
Dictus et Amphion, Thebanae conditor arcis,
Saxa movere sono testudinis, et prece blanda
Ducere quo vellet: fuit haec sapientia quondam,
Publica privatis secernere, sacra profanis:
Concubitu prohibere vago; dare iura maritis;
Oppida moliri; leges incidere ligno. 399
Sic honor et nomen divinis vatibus atque
Carminibus venit. Post hos insignis Homerus
Tyrtaeusque mares animos in Martia bella

Versibus exacuit; dictae per carmina sortes:
Et vitae monstrata via est: et gratia regum
Pieriis tentata modis: ludusque repertus, 405
Et longorum operum finis: ne forte pudori
Sit tibi Musa lyrae solers, et cantor Apollo.
 Natura fieret laudabile carmen, an arte,
Quaesitum est: ego nec studium sine divite vena,
Nec rude quid possit video ingenium: alterius sic
Altera poscit opem res, et coniura amice. 411
Qui studet optatam cursu contingere metam,
Multa tulit fecitque puer; sudavit et alsit;
Abstinuit Venere et vino; qui Pythia cantat
Tibicen, didicit prius, extimuitque magistrum.
Nunc satis est dixisse: ego mira poemata pango:

139

HINTS FROM HORACE

They storm the types, they publish, one
 and all,
They leap the counter, and they leave the
 stall.
Provincial maidens, men of high com-
 mand, 715
Yea, baronets have ink'd the bloody hand!
Cash cannot quell them; Pollio play'd this
 prank,
(Then Phoebus first found credit in a bank!)
Not all the living only, but the dead,
Fool on, as fluent as an Orpheus' head;
Damn'd all their days, they posthumously
 thrive, 721
Dug up from dust, though buried when
 alive!
Reviews record this epidemic crime,
Those Books of Martyrs to the rage for
 rhyme, 724
Alas! woe worth the scribbler! often seen
In Morning Post or Monthly Magazine.
There lurk his earlier lays; but soon, hot
 press'd,
Behold a quarto!—Tarts must tell the rest.
Then leave, ye wise, the lyre's precarious
 chords 729
To muse-mad baronets, or madder lords,
Or country Crispins, now grown some-
 what stale,
Twin Doric minstrels, drunk with Doric
 ale!
Hark to those notes, narcotically soft!
The cobbler-laureats sing to Capel Lofft!
Till, lo! that modern Midas, as he hears,
Adds an ell growth to his egregious ears!

There lives one druid, who prepares in
 time 737
'Gainst future feuds his poor revenge of
 rhyme;
Racks his dull memory, and his duller
 muse,
To publish faults which friendship should
 excuse. 740
If friendship's nothing, self-regard might
 teach
More polish'd usage of his parts of speech.
But what is shame, or what is aught to
 him?
He vents his spleen, or gratifies his whim.
Some fancied slight has roused his lurk-
 ing hate, 745
Some folly cross'd, some jest, or some
 debate;
Up to his den Sir Scribbler hies, and soon
The gather'd gall is voided in lampoon.

Perhaps at some pert speech you've dared
 to frown,
Perhaps your poem may have pleased the
 town: 750
If so, alas! 'tis nature in the man—
May Heaven forgive you, for he never can!
Then be it so; and may his withering bays
Bloom fresh in satire, though they fade in
 praise!
While his lost songs no more shall steep
 and stink, 755
The dullest, fattest weeds on Lethe's brink,
But springing upwards from the sluggish
 mould,
Be (what they never were before) be—sold!
Should some rich bard (but such a mon-
 ster now, 759
In modern physics, we can scarce allow),
Should some pretending scribbler of the
 court,
Some rhyming peer—there's plenty of the
 sort—
All but one poor dependent priest with-
 drawn,
(Ah! too regardless of his chaplain's
 yawn!) 764
Condemn the unlucky curate to recite
Their last dramatic work by candle-light,
How would the preacher turn each rueful
 leaf,
Dull as his sermons, but not half so brief!
Yet, since 'tis promised at the rector's
 death,
He'll risk no living for a little breath.
Then spouts and foams, and cries at every
 line, 771
(The Lord forgive him!) 'Bravo! grand!
 divine!'
Hoarse with those praises (which, by
 flatt'ry fed,
Dependence barters for her bitter bread),
He strides and stamps along with creaking
 boot; 775
Till the floor echoes his emphatic foot,
Then sits again, then rolls his pious eye,
As when the dying vicar will not die!
Nor feels, forsooth, emotion at his
 heart;— 779
But all dissemblers overact their part.

Ye, who aspire to 'build the lofty rhyme,'
Believe not all who laud your false 'sub-
 lime;'
But if some friend shall hear your work,
 and say,
'Expunge that stanza, lop that line away,'

Occupet extremum scabies; mihi turpe relinqui
 est, 407
Et, quod non didici, sane nescire fateri.

. — Si carmina condes, 436
Nunquam te fallant animi sub vulpe latentes.
Quintilio si quid recitares, Corrige, sodes,
Hoc (aiebat) et hoc: melius te posse negares,
Bis terque expertum frustra, delere iubebat,

Et male tornatos incudi reddere versus. 441
Si defendere delictum quam vertere malles,
Nullum ultra verbum, aut operam insumebat
 inanem,
Quin sine rivali teque et tua solus amares.
 Vir bonus et prudens versus reprehendet
 inertes; 445
Culpabit duros; incomptis allinet atrum
Transverso calamo signum; ambitiosa recidet

And, after fruitless efforts, you return
Without amendment, and he answers,
 'Burn!' 786
That instant throw your paper in the fire,
Ask not his thoughts, or follow his desire;
But if (true bard!) you scorn to con-
 descend,
And will not alter what you can't defend,
If you will breed this bastard of your
 brains, 791
We'll have no words—I've only lost my
 pains.

Yet, if you only prize your favourite
 thought,
As critics kindly do, and authors ought;
If your cool friend annoy you now and
 then, 795
And cross whole pages with his plaguy
 pen;
No matter, throw your ornaments aside,—
Better let him than all the world deride.
Give light to passages too much in shade,
Nor let a doubt obscure one verse you've
 made; 800
Your friend's a 'Johnson,' not to leave
 one word,
However trifling, which may seem absurd;
Such erring trifles lead to serious ills,
And furnish food for critics, or their quills.

As the Scotch fiddle, with its touching
 tune, 805
Or the sad influence of the angry moon,
All men avoid bad writers' ready tongues,
As yawning waiters fly Fitzscribble's
 lungs;
Yet on he mouths—ten minutes—tedious
 each 809
As prelate's homily, or placeman's speech;
Long as the last years of a lingering lease,
When riot pauses until rents increase.
While such a minstrel, muttering fustian,
 strays
O'er hedge and ditch, through unfre-
 quented ways,

If by some chance he walks into a well,
And shouts for succour with stentorian
 yell, 816
'A rope! help, Christians, as ye hope for
 grace!'
Nor woman, man, nor child will stir a
 pace;
For there his carcass he might freely fling,
From frenzy, or the humour of the thing.
Though this has happen'd to more bards
 than one; 821
I'll tell you Budgell's story,—and have
 done.

Budgell, a rogue and rhymester, for no
 good,
(Unless his case be much misunderstood,)
When teased with creditors' continual
 claims, 825
'To die like Cato,' leapt into the Thames!
And therefore be it lawful through the
 town
For any bard to poison, hang, or drown.
Who saves the intended suicide receives
Small thanks from him who loathes the
 life he leaves; 830
And, sooth to say, mad poets must not
 lose
The glory of that death they freely choose.

Nor is it certain that some sorts of verse
Prick not the poet's conscience as a curse;
Dosed with vile drams on Sunday he was
 found, 835
Or got a child on consecrated ground!
And hence is haunted with a rhyming
 rage—
Fear'd like a bear just bursting from his
 cage.
If free, all fly his versifying fit,
Fatal at once to simpleton or wit: 840
But him, unhappy! whom he seizes,—him
He flays with recitation limb by limb;
Probes to the quick where'er he makes his
 breach,
And gorges like a lawyer—or a leech.

Ornamenta; parum claris lucem dare coget;
Arguet ambigue dictum; mutanda notabit;
Fiet Aristarchus: nec dicet, Cur ego amicum
Offendam in nugis? hae nugae seria ducent
In mala derisum semel exceptumque sinistre.
 Ut mala quem scabies aut morbus regius
 urget,
Aut fanaticus error et iracunda Diana, 454
Vesanum tetigisse timent fugiuntque poetam,
Qui sapiunt; agitant pueri, incautique sequuntur.
Hic, dum sublimis versus ructatur, et errat,
Si veluti merulis intentus decidit auceps
In puteum, foveamve; licet, Succurrite, longum
Clamet, Io cives! non sit qui tollere curet. 460
Si quis curet opem ferre, et demittere funem,
Qui scis an prudens huc se deieccrit, atque

Servari nolit? dicam: Siculique poetae
Narrabo interitum. Deus immortalis haberi
Dum cupit Empedocles, ardentem frigidus Aet-
 nam 465
Insiluit. Sit ius liceatque perire poetis:
Invitum qui servat, idem facit occidenti.
Nec semel hoc fecit; nec, si retractus erit,
 iam
Fiet homo, et ponet famosae mortis amorem.
Nec satis apparet cur versus factitet; utrum
Minxerit in patrios cineres, an triste bidental
Moverit incestus: certe furit, ac velut ursus,
Obiectos caveae valuit si frangere clathros, 473
Indoctum doctumque fugat recitator acerbus.
Quem vero arripuit, tenet, occiditque legendo,
Non missura cutem, nisi plena cruoris, hirudo.

141

THE CURSE OF MINERVA

——'Pallas te hoc vulnere, Pallas
Immolat, et poenam scelerato ex sanguine sumit.'
Aeneid, lib. xii.

ATHENS: CAPUCHIN CONVENT,
March 17, 1811.

SLOW sinks, more lovely ere his race be
run,
Along Morea's hills the setting sun;
Not, as in northern climes, obscurely
bright,
But one unclouded blaze of living light;
O'er the hush'd deep the yellow beam he
throws, 5
Gilds the green wave that trembles as it
glows;
On old Aegina's rock and Hydra's isle
The god of gladness sheds his parting smile;
O'er his own regions lingering loves to
shine,
Though there his altars are no more di-
vine. 10
Descending fast, the mountain-shadows
kiss
Thy glorious gulf, unconquer'd Salamis!
Their azure arches through the long ex-
panse,
More deeply purpled, meet his mellowing
glance,
And tenderest tints, along their summits
driven, 15
Mark his gay course, and own the hues of
heaven;
Till, darkly shaded from the land and
deep,
Behind his Delphian rock he sinks to
sleep.

On such an eve his palest beam he cast
When, Athens! here thy wisest look'd his
last, 20
How watch'd thy better sons his farewell
ray,
That closed their murder'd sage's latest
day!
Not yet—not yet—Sol pauses on the hill,
The precious hour of parting lingers still;
But sad his light to agonising eyes, 25
And dark the mountain's once delightful
dyes;
Gloom o'er the lovely land he seem'd to
pour,
The land where Phoebus never frown'd
before,
But ere he sunk below Cithaeron's head,
The cup of woe was quaff'd—the spirit
fled; 30
The soul of him that scorn'd to fear or fly,
Who lived and died as none can live or die.

But, lo! from high Hymettus to the plain
The queen of night asserts her silent reign;
No murky vapour, herald of the storm,
Hides her fair face, or girds her glowing
form,
With cornice glimmering as the moon-
beams play, 36
There the white column greets her grateful
ray,
And bright around, with quivering beams
beset,
Her emblem sparkles o'er the minaret:
The groves of olive scatter'd dark and
wide, 41
Where meek Cephisus sheds his scanty
tide,
The cypress saddening by the sacred mos-
que,
The gleaming turret of the gay kiosk,
And sad and sombre 'mid the holy calm,
Near Theseus' fane, yon solitary palm; 46
All, tinged with varied hues, arrest the eye;
And dull were his that pass'd them heed-
less by.

Again the Aegean, heard no more afar,
Lulls his chafed breast from elemental
war: 50
Again his waves in milder tints unfold
Their long expanse of sapphire and of
gold,
Mix'd with the shades of many a distant isle
That frown, where gentler ocean deigns to
smile. 54

As thus, within the walls of Pallas' fane,
I mark'd the beauties of the land and main,
Alone, and friendless, on the magic shore,
Whose arts and arms but live in poets' lore;
Oft as the matchless dome I turn'd to scan,
Sacred to gods, but not secure from man,
The past return'd, the present seem'd to
cease, 61
And Glory knew no clime beyond her
Greece!

Hours roll'd along, and Dian's orb on
high
Had gain'd the centre of her softest sky;
And yet unwearied still my footsteps trod
O'er the vain shrine of many a vanish'd
god: 66
But chiefly, Pallas! thine, when Hecate's
glare,
Check'd by thy columns, fell more sadly fair

142

O'er the chill marble, where the startling tread
Thrills the lone heart like echoes from the dead. 70
Long had I mused, and treasured every trace
The wreck of Greece recorded of her race,
When, lo! a giant form before me strode,
And Pallas hail'd me in her own abode!

Yes, 'twas Minerva's self; but, ah! how changed, 75
Since o'er the Dardan field in arms she ranged!
Not such as erst, by her divine command,
Her form appear'd from Phidias' plastic hand:
Gone were the terrors of her awful brow,
Her idle aegis bore no Gorgon now; 80
Her helm was dinted, and the broken lance
Seem'd weak and shaftless e'en to mortal glance;
The olive branch, which still she deign'd to clasp,
Shrunk from her touch, and wither'd in her grasp;
And, ah! though still the brightest of the sky, 85
Celestial tears bedimm'd her large blue eye:
Round the rent casque her owlet circled slow,
And mourn'd his mistress with a shriek of woe!

'Mortal!'—'twas thus she spake—'that blush of shame 89
Proclaims thee Briton, once a noble name;
First of the mighty, foremost of the free,
Now honour'd *less* by all, and *least* by me:
Chief of thy foes shall Pallas still be found.
Seek'st thou the cause of loathing?—look around. 94
Lo! here, despite of war and wasting fire,
Saw successive tyrannies expire.
Scaped from the ravage of the Turk and Goth,
Thy country sends a spoiler worse than both.
Survey this vacant, violated fane; 99
Recount the relics torn that yet remain:
These Cecrops placed, *this* Pericles adorn'd,
That Adrian rear'd when drooping Science mourn'd.
What more I owe let gratitude attest—
Know, Alaric and Elgin did the rest.
That all may learn from whence the plunderer came, 105
The insulted wall sustains his hated name:
For Elgin's fame thus grateful Pallas pleads,
Below, his name—above, behold his deeds!

Be ever hail'd with equal honour here
The Gothic monarch and the Pictish peer:
Arms gave the first his right, the last had none, 111
But basely stole what less barbarians won.
So when the lion quits his fell repast,
Next prowls the wolf, the filthy jackal last:
Flesh, limbs, and blood the former make their own, 115
The last poor brute securely gnaws the bone.
Yet still the gods are just, and crimes are cross'd:
See here what Elgin won, and what he lost!
Another name with *his* pollutes my shrine:
Behold where Dian's beams disdain to shine! 120
Some retribution still might Pallas claim,
When Venus half avenged Minerva's shame.'

She ceased awhile, and thus I dared reply,
To soothe the vengeance kindling in her eye:
'Daughter of Jove! in Britain's injured name, 125
A true-born Briton may the deed disclaim.
Frown not on England; England owns him not:
Athena, no! thy plunderer was a Scot.
Ask'st thou the difference? From fair Phyle's towers
Survey Bœotia;—Caledonia's ours. 130
And well I know within that bastard land
Hath Wisdom's goddess never held command;
A barren soil, where Nature's germs, confined
To stern sterility, can stint the mind;
Whose thistle well betrays the niggard earth, 135
Emblem of all to whom the land gives birth;
Each genial influence nurtured to resist;
A land of meanness, sophistry, and mist.
Each breeze from foggy mount and marshy plain
Dilutes with drivel every drizzly brain,
Till, burst at length, each wat'ry head o'er-flows, 141
Foul as their soil, and frigid as their snows.
Then thousand schemes of petulance and pride
Despatch her scheming children far and wide:
Some east, some west, some everywhere but north, 145
In quest of lawless gain, they issue forth.
And thus—accursed be the day and year!
She sent a Pict to play the felon here.
Yet Caledonia claims some native worth,
As dull Bœotia gave a Pindar birth; 150

So may her few, the letter'd and the brave,
Bound to no clime, and victors of the grave,
Shake off the sordid dust of such a land,
And shine like children of a happier
 strand;
As once, of yore, in some obnoxious
 place, 155
Ten names (if found) had saved a wretched
 race.'

'Mortal!' the blue-eyed maid resumed,
 'once more
Bear back my mandate to thy native shore.
Though fallen, alas! this vengeance yet is
 mine,
To turn my counsels far from lands like
 thine. 160
Hear then in silence Pallas' stern behest;
Hear and believe, for time will tell the rest.

'First on the head of him who did this
 deed
My curse shall light,—on him and all his
 seed: 164
Without one spark of intellectual fire,
Be all the sons as senseless as the sire:
If one with wit the parent brood disgrace,
Believe him bastard of a brighter race:
Still with his hireling artists let him prate,
And Folly's praise repay for Wisdom's
 hate; 170
Long of their patron's gusto let them tell,
Whose noblest, *native* gusto is—to sell:
To sell, and make—may shame record the
 day!—
The state receiver of his pilfer'd prey.
Meantime, the flattering, feeble dotard,
 West, 175
Europe's worst dauber, and poor Britain's
 best,
With palsied hand shall turn each model
 o'er,
And own himself an infant of fourscore.
Be all the bruisers cull'd from all St. Giles',
That art and nature may compare their
 styles; 180
While brawny brutes in stupid wonder
 stare,
And marvel at his lordship's "stone shop"
 there.
Round the throng'd gate shall sauntering
 coxcombs creep,
To lounge and lucubrate, to prate and
 peep;
While many a languid maid, with longing
 sigh, 185
On giant statues casts the curious eye;
The room with transient glance appears to
 skim
Yet marks the mighty back and length of
 limb;
Mourns o'er the difference of *now* and *then;*
Exclaims, "These Greeks indeed were
 proper men!" 190

Draws slight comparisons of *these* with
 those,
And envies Laïs all her Attic beaux.
When shall a modern maid have swains
 like these!
Alas! Sir Harry is no Hercules! 194
And last of all, amidst the gaping crew,
Some calm spectator, as he takes his view,
In silent indignation mix'd with grief,
Admires the plunder, but abhors the thief
Oh, loath'd in life, nor pardon'd in the
 dust,
May hate pursue his sacrilegious lust!
Link'd with the fool that fired the Ephe-
 sian dome, 201
Shall vengeance follow far beyond the
 tomb,
And Eratostratus and Elgin shine
In many a branding page and burning line;
Alike reserved for aye to stand accursed.
Perchance the second blacker than the
 first. 206

'So let him stand, through ages yet un-
 born,
Fix'd statue on the pedestal of Scorn;
Though not for him alone revenge shall
 wait,
But fits thy country for her coming fate:
Hers were the deeds that taught her law-
 less son 211
To do what oft Britannia's self had done.
Look to the Baltic—blazing from afar,
Your old ally yet mourns perfidious war.
Not to such deeds did Pallas lend her aid,
Or break the compact which herself had
 made; 216
Far from such councils, from the faithless
 field
She fled—but left behind her Gorgon
 shield;
A fatal gift that turn'd your friends to
 stone,
And left lost Albion hated and alone.

'Look to the East, where Ganges'
 swarthy race 221
Shall shake your tyrant empire to its base;
Lo! there Rebellion rears her ghastly head,
And glares the Nemesis of native dead;
Till Indus rolls a deep purpureal flood
And claims his long arrear of northern
 blood. 226
So may ye perish! Pallas, when she gave
Your free-born rights, forbade ye to en-
 slave.

'Look on your Spain!—she clasps the
 hand she hates,
But boldly clasps, and thrusts you from
 her gates. 230
Bear witness, bright Barossa! thou canst tell
Whose were the sons that bravely fought
 and fell.

THE CURSE OF MINERVA

But Lusitania, kind and dear ally, 233
Can spare a few to fight, and sometimes fly.
Oh glorious field! by Famine fiercely won,
The Gaul retires for once, and all is done!
But when did Pallas teach, that one retreat
Retrieved three long olympiads of defeat?

'Look last at home—ye love not to look
there; 239
On the grim smile of comfortless despair:
Your city saddens: loud though Revel
howls,
Here Famine faints, and yonder Rapine
prowls.
See all alike of more or less bereft;
No misers tremble when there's nothing
left.
"Blest paper credit;" who shall dare to
sing? 245
It clogs like lead Corruption's weary wing.
Yet Pallas pluck'd each premier by the ear,
Who gods and men alike disdain'd to hear;
But one, repentant o'er a bankrupt state,
On Pallas calls,—but calls, alas! too late:
Then raves for * *; to that Mentor bends,
Though he and Pallas never yet were
friends. 252
Him senates hear, whom never yet they
heard,
Contemptuous once, and now no less absurd.
So, once of yore, each reasonable frog
Swore faith and fealty to his sovereign
"log". 256
Thus hail'd your rulers their patrician
clod,
As Egypt chose an onion for a god.

'Now fare ye well! enjoy your little hour;
Go, grasp the shadow of your vanish'd
power; 260
Gloss o'er the failure of each fondest
scheme;
Your strength a name, your bloated wealth
a dream.
Gone is that gold, the marvel of mankind,
And pirates barter all that's left behind.
No more the hirelings, purchased near and
far, 265
Crowd to the ranks of mercenary war.
The idle merchant on the useless quay
Droops o'er the bales no bark may bear
away;
Or, back returning, sees rejected stores
Rot piecemeal on his own encumber'd
shores: 270
The starved mechanic breaks his rusting
loom,
And desperate mans him 'gainst the coming doom.
Then in the senate of your sinking state
Show me the man whose counsels may
have weight.

Vain is each voice where tones could once
command; 275
E'en factions cease to charm a factious
land:
Yet jarring sects convulse a sister isle,
And light with maddening hands the mutual pile.

''Tis done, 'tis past, since Pallas warns
in vain;
The Furies seize her abdicated reign:
Wide o'er the realm they wave their kindling brands, 281
And wring her vitals with their fiery hands.
But one convulsive struggle still remains,
And Gaul shall weep ere Albion wear her
chains.
The banner'd pomp of war, the glittering
files, 285
O'er whose gay trappings stern Bellona
smiles;
The brazen trump, the spirit-stirring drum,
That bid the foe defiance ere they come;
The hero bounding at his country's call,
The glorious death that consecrates his
fall, 290
Swell the young heart with visionary
charms,
And bid it antedate the joys of arms.
But know, a lesson you may yet be taught,
With death alone are laurels cheaply
bought:
Not in the conflict Havoc seeks delight,
His day of mercy is the day of fight. 296
But when the field is fought, the battle
won,
Though drench'd with gore, his woes are
but begun:
His deeper deeds as yet ye know by name;
The slaughter'd peasant and the ravish'd
dame, 300
The rifled mansion and the foe-reap'd
field,
Ill suit with souls at home, untaught to
yield.
Say with what eye along the distant down
Would flying burghers mark the blazing
town?
How view the column of ascending flames
Shake his red shadow o'er the startled
Thames? 306
Nay, frown not, Albion! for the torch was
thine
That lit such pyres from Tagus to the
Rhine:
Now should they burst on thy devoted
coast,
Go, ask thy bosom who deserves them
most. 310
The law of heaven and earth is life for
life,
And she who raised, in vain regrets, the
strife.'

145

THE WALTZ

AN APOSTROPHIC HYMN

'Qualis in Eurotae ripis, aut per iuga Cynthi,
Exercet Diana choros.'—VIRGIL.

'Such on Eurota's banks, or Cynthia's height,
Diana seems: and so she charms the sight,
When in the dance the graceful goddess leads
The quire of nymphs, and overtops their heads.'
DRYDEN'S VIRGIL.

TO THE PUBLISHER

SIR,

I AM a country gentleman of a midland county. I might have been a parliament man for a certain borough; having had the offer of as many votes as General T. at the general election in 1812*. But I was all for domestic happiness; as, fifteen years ago, on a visit to London, I married a middle-age maid of honour. We lived happily at Hornem Hall till last season, when my wife and I were invited by the Countess of Waltzaway (a distant relation of my spouse) to pass the winter in town. Thinking no harm, and our girls being come to a marriageable (or, as they call it, *marketable*) age, and having, besides a Chancery suit inveterately entailed upon the family estate, we came up in our old chariot,—of which, by the by, my wife grew so much ashamed in less than a week, that I was obliged to buy a second-hand barouche, of which I might mount the box, Mrs. H. says, if I could drive, but never see the inside—that place being reserved for the Honourable Augustus Tiptoe, her partner-general and opera-knight. Hearing great praises of Mrs. H.'s dancing (she was famous for birthnight minuet in the latter end of the last century), I unbooted, and went to a ball at the Countess's, expecting to see a country dance, or at most, cotillons, reels, and all the old paces to the newest tunes. But, judge of my surprise, on arriving, to see poor dear Mrs. Hornem with her arms half round the loins of a huge hussar-looking gentleman I never set eyes on before; and his, to say truth, rather more than half round her waist, turning round and round to a d——d see-saw up-and-down sort of tune, that reminded me of the 'Black Joke,' only more '*affettuoso*,' till it made me quite giddy with wondering they were not so. By-and-by they stopped a bit, and I thought they would sit or fall down:—but no; with Mrs. H.'s hand on his shoulder, '*quam familiariter†*,' (as Terence said, when I was at school,) they walked about a minute, and then at it again, like two cock-chafers spitted on the same bodkin. I asked what all this meant, when, with a loud laugh, a child no older than our Wilhelmina (a name I never heard but in the Vicar of Wakefield, though her mother would call her after the Princess of Swappenbach,) said, 'Lord! Mr. Hornem, can't you see they're valtzing?' or waltzing (I forget which); and then up she got, and her mother and sister, and away they went, and round-abouted it till supper-time. Now that I know what it is, I like it of all things, and so does Mrs. H. (though I have broken my shins, and four times overturned Mrs. Hornem's maid, in practising the preliminary steps in a morning). Indeed, so much do I like it, that having a turn for rhyme, tastily displayed in some election ballads, and songs in honour of all the victories (but till lately I have had little practice in that way), I sat down and with the aid of William Fitzgerald, Esq., and a few hints from Dr. Busby, (whose recitations I attend, and am monstrous fond of Master Busby's manner of delivering his father's late successful 'Drury Lane Address,') I composed the following hymn, wherewithal to make my sentiments known to the public, whom, nevertheless, I heartily despise, as well as the critics.

I am, Sir, yours, &c. &c.,
HORACE HORNEM.

MUSE of the many-twinkling feet! whose charms
Are now extended up from legs to arms;
Terpsichore!—too long misdeem'd a maid—
Reproachful term—bestow'd but to upbraid—
Henceforth in all the bronze of brightness shine, 5
The least a vestal of the virgin Nine.
Far be from thee and thine the name of prude:
Mock'd, yet triumphant; sneer'd at, unsubdued;

Thy legs must move to conquer as they fly,
If but thy coats are reasonably high; 10
Thy breast—if bare enough—requires no shield;
Dance forth—*sans armour* thou shalt take the field,
And own—impregnable to *most* assaults,
Thy not too lawfully begotten 'Waltz.'

Hail, nimble nymph! to whom the young hussar, 15
The whisker'd votary of waltz and war,
His night devotes, despite of spur and boots,
A sight unmatch'd since Orpheus and his brutes:

* State of the poll (last day) 5.

† My Latin is all forgotten, if a man can be said to have forgotten what he never remembered; but bought my title-page motto of a Catholic priest for a three-shilling bank token, after much haggling for the even sixpence. I grudged the money to a Papist, being all for the memory of Perceval and 'No Popery,' and quite regretting the downfall of the pope, because we can't burn him any more.

ail, spirit-stirring Waltz!—beneath whose
banners
A modern hero fought for modish man-
ners; 20
In Hounslow's heath to rival Wellesley's
fame,
'ock'd, fired, and miss'd his man—but
gain'd his aim;
ail, moving muse! to whom the fair one's
breast
ives all it can, and bids us take the rest.
h! for the flow of Busby, or of Fitz, 25
he latter's loyalty, the former's wits,
o 'energise the object I pursue,'
nd give both Belial and his dance their
due!

Imperial Waltz! imported from the
Rhine
Famed for the growth of pedigrees and
wine), 30
ong be thine import from all duty free,
nd hock itself be less esteem'd than thee;
a some few qualities alike—for hock
nproves our cellar—*thou* our living
stock.
he head to hock belongs—thy subtler
art 35
ntoxicates alone the heedless heart:
hrough the full veins thy gentler poison
swims,
nd wakes to wantonness the willing
limbs.

Oh, Germany! how much to thee we
owe,
s heaven-born Pitt can testify below,
re cursed confederation made thee
France's, 41
nd only left us thy d—d debts and
dances!
f subsidies and Hanover bereft,
Ve bless thee still—for George the Third
is left!
f kings the best—and last, not least in
worth, 45
or graciously begetting George the
Fourth.
o Germany, and highnesses serene,
Vho owe us millions—don't we owe the
queen?
o Germany, what owe we not besides?
o oft bestowing Brunswickers and
brides;
Vho paid for vulgar, with her royal blood,
Drawn from the stem of each Teutonic
stud: 52
Vho sent us—so be pardon'd all her
faults—
dozen dukes, some kings, a queen—and
Waltz.

But peace to her—her emperor and diet,
hough now transferr'd to Buonaparte's
'fiat!' 56

Back to my theme—O Muse of motion!
say,
How first to Albion found thy Waltz her
way!

Borne on the breath of hyperborean
gales,
From Hamburg's port (while Hamburg
yet had *mails*), 60
Ere yet unlucky Fame—compell'd to creep
To snowy Gottenburg—was chill'd to
sleep;
Or, starting from her slumbers, deign'd
arise,
Heligoland! to stock thy mart with lies;
While unburnt Moscow yet had news to
send, 65
Nor owed her fiery exit to a friend,
She came—Waltz came—and with her
certain sets
Of true despatches, and as true gazettes:
Then flamed of Austerlitz the blest des-
patch,
Which 'Moniteur' nor 'Morning Post'
can match; 70
And—almost crush'd beneath the glorious
news—
Ten plays, and forty tales of Kotzebue's;
One envoy's letters, six composers' airs,
And loads from Frankfort and from
Leipsic fairs; 74
Meiner's four volumes upon womankind,
Like Lapland witches to insure a wind;
Brunck's heaviest tome for ballast, and,
to back it,
Of Heyné, such as should not sink the
packet.

Fraught with this cargo—and her fair-
est freight, 79
Delightful Waltz, on tiptoe for a mate,
The welcome vessel reach'd the genial
strand,
And round her flock'd the daughters of the
land.
Not decent David, when, before the ark,
His grand pas-seul excited some remark;
Not love-lorn Quixote, when his Sancho
thought 85
The knight's fandango friskier than it
ought;
Not soft Herodias, when, with winning
tread,
Her nimble feet danced off another's
head;
Not Cleopatra on her galley's deck,
Display'd so much of *leg*, or more of
neck, 90
Than thou, ambrosial Waltz, when first
the moon
Beheld thee twirling to a Saxon tune!

To you, ye husbands of ten years! whose
brows
Ache with the annual tributes of a spouse;

THE WALTZ

To you of nine years less, who only bear
The budding sprouts of those that you
 shall wear, 96
With added ornaments around them roll'd
Of native brass, or law-awarded gold;
To you, ye matrons, ever on the watch
To mar a son's, or make a daughter's
 match; 100
To you, ye children of—whom chance
 accords—
Always the ladies, and *sometimes* their
 lords;
To you, ye single gentlemen, who seek
Torments for life, or pleasures for a week;
As Love or Hymen your endeavours
 guide, 105
To gain your own, or snatch another's
 bride:—
To one and all the lovely stranger came,
And every ball-room echoes with her
 name.

 Endearing Waltz!—to thy more melting
 tune
Bow Irish jig and ancient rigadoon. 110
Scotch reels, avaunt! and country-dance,
 forego
Your future claims to each fantastic toe!
Waltz—Waltz alone—both legs and arms
 demands,
Liberal of feet, and lavish of her hands;
Hands which may freely range in public
 sight 115
Where ne'er before—but—pray 'put out
 the light.'
Methinks the glare of yonder chandelier
Shines much too far—or I am much too
 near;
And true, though strange—Waltz whis-
 pers this remark, 119
'My slippery steps are safest in the dark!'
But here the Muse with due decorum halts,
And lends her longest petticoat to Waltz.

 Observant travellers of every time! 123
Ye quartos publish'd upon every clime!
O say, shall dull Romaika's heavy round,
Fandango's wriggles, or Bolero's bound;
Can Egypt's Almas—tantalising group—
Columbia's caperers to the warlike
 whoop—
Can aught from cold Kamschatka to Cape
 Horn
With Waltz compare, or after Waltz be
 borne? 130
Ah, no! from Morier's pages down to
 Galt's,
Each tourist pens a paragraph for 'Waltz.'

 Shades of those belles whose reign be-
 gan of yore,
With George the Third's—and ended long
 before!—
Though in your daughters' daughters yet
 you thrive, 135

Burst from your lead, and be yourselves
 alive!
Back to the ball-room speed your spectre
 host,
Fool's Paradise is dull to that you lost.
No treacherous powder bids conjecture
 quake;
No stiff-starched stays make meddling
 fingers ache; 140
(Transferr'd to those ambiguous things
 that ape
Goats in their visage, women in their
 shape;)
No damsel faints when rather closely
 press'd,
But more caressing seems when most ca-
 ress'd;
Superfluous hartshorn, and reviving salts
Both banish'd by the sovereign cordial
 'Waltz.' 146

 Seductive Waltz!—though on thy native
 shore
Even Werter's self proclaim'd thee half a
 whore;
Werter—to decent vice though much in-
 clined,
Yet warm, not wanton; dazzled, but not
 blind— 150
Though gentle Genlis, in her strife with
 Staël,
Would even proscribe thee from a Paris
 ball;
The fashion hails—from countesses to
 queens,
And maids and valets waltz behind the
 scenes;
Wide and more wide thy witching circle
 spreads, 155
And turns—if nothing else—at least our
 heads;
With thee even clumsy cits attempt to
 bounce,
And cockneys practise what they can't
 pronounce.
Gods! how the glorious theme my strain
 exalts,
And rhyme finds partner rhyme in praise
 of 'Waltz!' 160

 Blest was the time Waltz chose for her
 début;
The court, the Regent, like herself were
 new;
New face for friends, for foes some new
 rewards;
New ornaments for black and royal
 guards;
New laws to hang the rogues that roar'd
 for bread; 165
New coins (most new) to follow those that
 fled;
New victories—nor can we prize them less,
Though Jenky wonders at his own success;
New wars, because the old succeed so well

That most survivors envy those who fell;
New mistresses—no, old—and yet 'tis
 true, 171
Though they be *old*, the *thing* is something
 new;
Each new, quite new—(except some
 ancient tricks),
New white-sticks, gold-sticks, broom-
 sticks, all new sticks!
With vests or ribands—deck'd alike in hue,
New troopers strut, new turncoats blush
 in blue:
So saith the muse: my——, what say you?
Such was the time when Waltz might best
 maintain
Her new preferments in this novel reign;
Such was the time, nor ever yet was such;
Hoops are *no more*, and petticoats *not*
 much; 181
Morals and minuets, virtue and her stays,
And tell-tale powder—all have had their
 days.
The ball begins—the honours of the house
First duly done by daughter or by spouse,
Some potentate—or royal or serene—
With Kent's gay grace, or sapient Glos-
 ter's mien,
Leads forth the ready dame, whose rising
 flush
Might once have been mistaken for a blush.
From where the garb just leaves the
 bosom free, 190
That spot where hearts were once sup-
 posed to be;
Round all the confines of the yielded waist,
The strangest hand may wander undis-
 placed;
The lady's in return may grasp as much
As princely paunches offer to her touch.
Pleased round the chalky floor how well
 they trip, 196
One hand reposing on the royal hip;
The other to the shoulder no less royal
Ascending with affection truly loyal!
Thus front to front the partners move or
 stand, 200
The foot may rest, but none withdraw the
 hand;
And all in turn may follow in their rank,
The Earl of—Asterisk—and Lady—
 Blank;
Sir—Such-a-one—with those of fashion's
 host,
Or whose blest surnames—vide 'Morn-
 ing Post.' 205
Or if for that impartial print too late,
Search Doctors' Commons six months
 from my date)—
Thus all and each, in movement swift or
 slow,
The genial contact gently undergo;
Till some might marvel, with the modest
 Turk, 210
'nothing follows all this palming work?'

True, honest Mirza!—you may trust my
 rhyme—
Something does follow at a fitter time;
The breast thus publicly resign'd to man,
In private may resist him—if it can. 215

O ye who loved our grandmothers of
 yore,
Fitzpatrick, Sheridan, and many more!
And thou, my prince! whose sovereign
 taste and will
It is to love the lovely beldames still!
Thou ghost of Queensberry! whose judg-
 ing sprite 220
Satan may spare to peep a single night,
Pronounce—if ever in your days of bliss
Asmodeus struck so bright a stroke as this;
To teach the young ideas how to rise,
Flush in the cheek, and languish in the
 eyes; 225
Rush to the heart, and lighten through
 the frame,
With half-told wish, and ill-dissembled
 flame,
For prurient nature still will storm the
 breast—
Who, tempted thus, can answer for the
 rest? 229

But ye—who never felt a single thought
For what our morals are to be, or ought;
Who wisely wish the charms you view to
 reap,
Say—would you make those beauties
 quite so cheap?
Hot from the hands promiscuously ap-
 plied,
Round the slight waist, or down the glow-
 ing side, 235
Where were the rapture then to clasp the
 form
From this lewd grasp and lawless contact
 warm?
At once love's most endearing thought
 resign,
To press the hand so press'd by none but
 thine; 239
To gaze upon that eye which never met
Another's ardent look without regret,
Approach the lip which all, without re-
 straint,
Come near enough—if not to touch—to
 taint;
If such thou lovest—love her then no
 more,
Or give—like her—caresses to a score;
Her mind with these is gone, and with it
 go 246
The little left behind it to bestow.

Voluptuous Waltz! and dare I thus
 blaspheme?
Thy bard forgot thy praises were his
 theme.

Terpsichore, forgive!—at every ball 250
My wife *now* waltzes—and my daughters
 shall;
My son—(or stop—'tis needless to in-
 quire—
These little accidents should ne'er tran-
 spire;

Some ages hence our genealogic tree
Will wear as green a bough for him a[nd]
 me)— 25[5]
Waltzing shall rear, to make our nam[e]
 amends,
Grandsons for me—in heirs to all h[is]
 friends.

THE BLUES

A LITERARY ECLOGUE

'Nimium ne crede colori.'—VIRGIL.

O trust not, ye beautiful creatures, to hue,
Though your *hair* were as *red* as your *stockings* are *blue*.

ECLOGUE THE FIRST

*London.—Before the Door of a Lecture
Room.*

Enter TRACY, *meeting* INKEL.

Ink. YOU'RE too late.
Tra. Is it over?
Ink. Nor will be this hour.
But the benches are cramm'd like a garden
 in flower,
With the pride of our belles, who have
 made it the fashion;
So, instead of 'beaux arts,' we may say 'la
 belle passion'
For learning, which lately has taken the
 lead in 5
The world, and set all the fine gentlemen
 reading.
Tra. I know it too well, and have worn
 out my patience
With studying to study your new publica-
 tions.
There's Vamp, Scamp, and Mouthy, and
 Wordswords and Co.
With their damnable——
Ink. Hold, my good friend, do you
 know 10
Whom you speak to?
Tra. Right well, boy, and so does
 'the Row:'
You're an author—a poet—
Ink. And think you that I
Can stand tamely in silence, to hear you
 decry
The Muses?
Tra. Excuse me: I meant no offence
To the Nine; though the number who
 make some pretence 15
To their favours is such——but the sub-
 ject to drop,
I am just piping hot from a publisher's
 shop,
(Next door to the pastry-cook's; so that
 when I

Cannot find the new volume I wanted t[o]
 buy
On the bibliopole's shelves, it is only tw[o]
 paces, 2[0]
As one finds every author in one of thos[e]
 places:)
Where I just had been skimming a charm[-]
 ing critique,
So studded with wit, and so sprinkled wit[h]
 Greek!
Where your friend—you know who—ha[s]
 just got such a thrashing,
That it is, as the phrase goes, extreme[ly]
 '*refreshing*.' 2[5]
What a beautiful word!
Ink. Very true; 'tis so so[ft]
And so cooling—they use it a little to[o]
 oft;
And the papers have got it at last—but n[o]
 matter.
So they've cut up our friend then?
Tra. Not left him a tatter[—]
Not a rag of his present or past reput[a-]
 tion, 3[0]
Which they call a disgrace to the age an[d]
 the nation.
Ink. I'm sorry to hear this! for frien[d]
 ship, you know——
Our poor friend!—but I thought it woul[d]
 terminate so.
Our friendship is such, I'll read nothin[g]
 to shock it.
You don't happen to have the Review i[n]
 your pocket? 3[5]
Tra. No; I left a round dozen of autho[rs]
 and others
(Very sorry, no doubt, since the cause [is]
 a brother's)
All scrambling and jostling, like so man[y]
 imps,
And on fire with impatience to get the ne[xt]
 glimpse.
Ink. Let us join them.
Tra. What, won't you retur[n]
 to the lecture?

150

Ink. Why the place is so cramm'd,
 there's no room for a spectre.
esides, our friend Scamp is to-day so
 absurd—
Tra. How can you know that till you
 hear him?
Ink. I heard
uite enough; and, to tell you the truth,
 my retreat
'as from his vile nonsense, no less than
 the heat. 45
Tra. I have had no great loss then?
Ink. Loss!—such a palaver!
d inoculate sooner my wife with the
 slaver
f a dog when gone rabid, than listen two
 hours
o the torrent of trash which around him
 he pours,
imp'd up with such effort, disgorged
 with such labour, 50
hat——come—do not make me speak
 ill of one's neighbour.
Tra. I make you!
Ink. Yes, you! I said nothing until
ou compell'd me, by speaking the
 truth——
Tra. *To speak ill!*
 that your deduction?
Ink. When speaking of Scamp ill,
certainly *follow, not set* an example. 55
he fellow's a fool, an impostor, a
 zany.
Tra. And the crowd of to-day shows
 that one fool makes many.
ut we two will be wise.
Ink. Pray, then, let us retire.
Tra. I would, but——
Ink. There must be attraction much
 higher
han Scamp, or the Jew's harp he nick-
 names his lyre, 60
o call *you* to this hotbed.
Tra. I own it—'tis true—
 fair lady——
Ink. A spinster?
Tra. Miss Lilac.
Ink. The Blue!
he heiress!
Tra. The angel!
Ink. The devil! why, man,
ay get out of this hobble as fast as you
 can.
ou wed with Miss Lilac! 'twould be
 your perdition: 65
e's a poet, a chymist, a mathematician.
Tra. I say she's an angel.
Ink. Say rather an *angle.*
you and she marry, you'll certainly
 wrangle.
say she's a Blue, man, as blue as the
 ether.
Tra. And is that any cause for not
 coming together? 70

Ink. Humph! I can't say I know any
 happy alliance
Which has lately sprung up from a wed-
 lock with science.
She's so learned in all things, and fond
 of concerning
Herself in all matters connected with
 learning,
That——
Tra. What?
Ink. I perhaps may as well hold my
 tongue; 75
But there's five hundred people can tell
 you you're wrong.
Tra. You forget Lady Lilac's as rich as
 a Jew.
Ink. Is it miss or the cash of mamma
 you pursue?
Tra. Why, Jack, I'll be frank with you
 —something of both.
The girl's a fine girl.
Ink. And you feel nothing loth
To her good lady-mother's reversion; and
 yet 81
Her life is as good as your own, I will bet.
Tra. Let her live, and as long as she
 likes; I demand
Nothing more than the heart of her
 daughter and hand.
Ink. Why that heart's in the ink-
 stand—that hand on the pen. 85
Tra. A propos—Will you write me a
 song now and then?
Ink. To what purpose?
Tra. You know, my dear friend,
 that in prose
My talent is decent, as far as it goes;
But in rhyme——
Ink. You're a terrible stick, to be sure.
Tra. I own it: and yet, in these times,
 there's no lure 90
For the heart of the fair like a stanza or
 two;
And so, as I can't, will you furnish a few?
Ink. In your name?
Tra. In my name. I will copy
 them out,
To slip into her hand at the very next rout.
Ink. Are you so far advanced as to
 hazard this?
Tra. Why,
Do you think me subdued by a Blue-
 stocking's eye, 96
So far as to tremble to tell her in rhyme
What I've told her in prose, at the least,
 as sublime?
Ink. As sublime ! If it be so, no need of
 my Muse.
Tra. But consider, dear Inkel, she's
 one of the 'Blues.' 100
Ink. As sublime!—Mr. Tracy—I've
 nothing to say.
Stick to prose—As sublime!!—but I wish
 you good day.

Tra. Nay, stay, my dear fellow—con-
sider—I'm wrong;
I own it; but, prithee, compose me the
song.
Ink. As sublime!!
Tra. I but used the expression in haste.
Ink. That may be, Mr. Tracy, but
shows damn'd bad taste. 106
Tra. I own it—I know it—acknow-
ledge it—what
Can I say to you more?
Ink. I see what you'd be at:
You disparage my parts with insidious
abuse,
Till you think you can turn them best to
your own use. 110
Tra. And is that not a sign I respect
them?
Ink. Why that
To be sure makes a difference.
Tra. I know what is what:
And you, who're a man of the gay world
no less
Than a poet of t'other, may easily guess
That I never could mean, by a word, to
offend 115
A genius like you, and moreover, my
friend.
Ink. No doubt; you by this time should
know what is due
To a man of——but come—let us shake
hands.
Tra. You knew,
And you *know*, my dear fellow, how
heartily I
Whatever you publish, am ready to buy.
Ink. That's my bookseller's business;
I care not for sale; 121
Indeed the best poems at first rather fail.
There were Renegade's epics, and
Botherby's plays,
And my own grand romance——
Tra. Had its full share of praise.
I myself saw it puff'd in the 'Old Girl's
Review.' 125
Ink. What Review?
Tra. 'Tis the English 'Journal
de Trevoux;'
A clerical work of our Jesuits at home.
Have you never yet seen it?
Ink. That pleasure's to come.
Tra. Make haste then.
Ink. Why so?
Tra. I have heard people say
That it threaten'd to give up the *ghost*
t'other day. 130
Ink. Well, that is a sign of some *spirit*.
Tra. No doubt.
Shall you be at the Countess of Fiddle-
come's rout?
Ink. I've a card, and shall go: but at
present, as soon
As friend Scamp shall be pleased to step
down from the moon

(Where he seems to be soaring in searc[h]
of his wits), 1[
And an interval grants from his lecturin[g]
fits,
I'm engaged to the Lady Bluebottle['s]
collation,
To partake of a luncheon and learn[ed]
conversation:
'Tis a sort of reunion for Scamp, on the da[y]
Of his lecture, to treat him with co[ld]
tongue and praise. 1[
And I own, for my own part, that 'tis n[ot]
unpleasant.
Will you go? There's Miss Lilac will al[so]
be present.
Tra. That 'metal's attractive.'
Ink. No doubt—to the pocke[t]
Tra. You should rather encourage n[o]
passion than shock it.
But let us proceed; for I think by th[e]
hum—— 1[
Ink. Very true; let us go, then, befo[re]
they can come,
Or else we'll be kept here an hour at the[ir]
levee,
On the rack of cross questions, by all th[e]
blue bevy.
Hark! Zounds, they'll be on us; I kno[w]
by the drone
Of old Botherby's spouting ex-cathed[ra]
tone. 1[
Ay! there he is at it. Poor Scamp! bett[er]
join
Your friends, or he'll pay you back
your own coin.
Tra. All fair; 'tis but lecture for lectur[e]
Ink. That's clea[r]
But for God's sake let's go, or the Bo[re]
will be here.
Come, come: nay, I'm off. [*Exit* INKE[L]
Tra. You are right, and I'll follo[w]
'Tis high time for a '*Sic me serva[vit]
Apollo.*' 1[
And yet we shall have the whole crew o[n]
our kibes,
Blues, dandies, and dowagers, and secon[d]
hand scribes,
All flocking to moisten their exquisi[te]
throttles
With a glass of Madeira at Lady Blu[e]
bottle's. [*Exit* TRAC[Y]

ECLOGUE THE SECOND

An Apartment in the House of LADY
BLUEBOTTLE.—*A Table prepared.*

SIR RICHARD BLUEBOTTLE *solus.*

WAS there ever a man who was married
sorry?
Like a fool, I must needs do the thing
a hurry.
My life is reversed, and my quiet de[s-]
troy'd;

152

ly days, which once pass'd in so gentle a
 void,
ust now, every hour of the twelve, be
 employ'd; 5
he twelve, do I say?—of the whole
 twenty-four,
s there one which I dare call my own any
 more?
Vhat with driving and visiting, dancing,
 and dining,
Vhat with learning, and teaching, and
 scribbling, and shining
n science and art, I'll be cursed if I
 know 10
Myself from my wife; for although we
 are two,
et she somehow contrives that all things
 shall be done
n a style which proclaims us eternally
 one.
ut the thing of all things which distresses
 me more
han the bills of the week (though they
 trouble me sore) 15
s the numerous, humorous, backbiting
 crew
Of scribblers, wits, lecturers, white, black,
 and blue,
Vho are brought to my house as an inn, to
 my cost—
'or the bill here, it seems, is defray'd by
 the host—
Io pleasure! no leisure! no thought for
 my pains, 20
ut to hear a vile jargon which addles my
 brains;
A smatter and chatter, glean'd out of re-
 views,
y the rag, tag, and bobtail, of those they
 call 'BLUES;'
A rabble who know not—But soft, here
 they come!
Vould to God I were deaf! as I'm not,
 I'll be dumb. 25

Enter LADY BLUEBOTTLE, MISS LILAC,
 LADY BLUEMOUNT, MR. BOTHERBY, IN-
 KEL, TRACY, *Miss* MAZARINE, *and
 others, with* SCAMP *the Lecturer, &c. &c.*

Lady Blueb. Ah! Sir Richard, good
 morning: I've brought you some
 friends.
Sir Rich. [*bows, and afterwards aside.*]
 If friends, they're the first.
Lady Blueb. But the luncheon attends.
pray ye be seated, '*sans cérémonie.*'
Mr. Scamp, you're fatigued; take your
 chair there next me. [*They all sit.*
Sir Rich. [*aside.*] If he does, his fatigue
 is to come.
Lady Blueb. Mr. Tracy— 30
Lady Bluemount—Miss Lilac—be
 pleased, pray, to place ye;

And you, Mr. Botherby—
Both. Oh, my dear Lady,
I obey.
Lady Blueb. Mr. Inkel, I ought to up-
 braid ye:
You were not at the lecture.
Ink. Excuse me, I was;
But the heat forced me out in the best
 part—alas! 35
And when——
Lady Blueb. To be sure it was broiling;
 but then
You have lost such a lecture!
Both. The best of the ten.
Tra. How can you know that? there are
 two more.
Both. Because
I defy him to beat this day's wondrous
 applause.
The very walls shook.
Ink. Oh, if that be the test,
I allow our friend Scamp has this day done
 his best. 41
Miss Lilac, permit me to help you;—a
 wing?
Miss Lil. No more, sir, I thank you.
 Who lectures next spring?
Both. Dick Dunder.
Ink. That is, if he lives.
Miss Lil. And why not?
Ink. No reason whatever, save that he's
 a sot. 45
Lady Bluemount! a glass of Madeira?
Lady Bluem. With pleasure.
Ink. How does your friend Words-
 words, that Windermere treasure?
Does he stick to his lakes, like the leeches
 he sings,
And their gatherers, as Homer sung war-
 riors and kings?
Lady Bluem. He has just got a place.
Ink. As a footman?
Lady Bluem. For shame!
Nor profane with your sneers so poetic a
 name. 51
Ink. Nay, I meant him no evil, but
 pitied his master;
For the poet of pedlars 'twere, sure, no
 disaster
To wear a new livery; the more, as 'tis
 not
The first time he has turn'd both his creed
 and his coat. 55
Lady Bluem. For shame! I repeat. If
 Sir George could but hear——
Lady Bluem. Never mind our friend
 Inkel; we all know, my dear,
'Tis his way.
Sir Rich. But this place——
Ink. Is perhaps like friend Scamp's,
A lecturer's.
Lady Bluem. Excuse me—'tis one in the
 'Stamps':
He is made a collector.

Tra. Collector!

Sir Rich. How?

Miss Lil. What?

Ink. I shall think of him oft when I buy a new hat: 61

There his works will appear——

Lady Bluem. Sir, they reach to the Ganges.

Ink. I shan't go so far—I can have them at Grange's.

Lady Bluem. Oh fie!

Miss Lil. And for shame!

Lady Bluem. You're too bad.

Both. Very good!

Lady Bluem. How good?

Lady Blueb. He means nought—'tis his phrase.

Lady Bluem. He grows rude.

Lady Blueb. He means nothing; nay, ask him. 66

Lady Bluem. Pray, Sir! did you mean What you say?

Ink. Never mind if he did: 'twill be seen That whatever he means won't alloy what he says.

Both. Sir?

Ink. Pray be content with your portion of praise; 69

'Twas in your defence.

Both. If you please, with submission, I can make out my own.

Ink. It would be your perdition. While you live, my dear Botherby, never defend Yourself or your works; but leave both to a friend.

A propos—Is your play then accepted at last?

Both. At last?

Ink. Why I thought—that's to say— there had pass'd 75

A few green-room whispers, which hinted, —you know That the taste of the actors at best is so so.

Both. Sir, the green-room's in rapture, and so's the Committee.

Ink. Ay—yours are the plays for exciting our 'pity And fear,' as the Greek says: for 'purging the mind,' 80

I doubt if you'll leave us an equal behind.

Both. I have written the prologue, and meant to have pray'd For a spice of your wit in an epilogue's aid.

Ink. Well, time enough yet, when the play's to be play'd. 84

Is it cast yet?

Both. The actors are fighting for parts, As is usual in that most litigious of arts.

Lady Blueb. We'll all make a party, and go the *first* night.

Tra. And you promised the epilogue Inkel.

Ink. Not quite

However, to save my friend Botherby trouble, I'll do what I can, though my pains must be double. 9

Tra. Why so?

Ink. To do justice to what goes before

Both. Sir, I'm happy to say, I've no fears on that score.

Your parts, Mr. Inkel, are——

Ink. Never mind *mine* Stick to those of your play, which is quite your own line.

Lady Bluem. You're a fugitive writer, I think, sir, of rhymes? 9

Ink. Yes, ma'am; and a fugitive reader sometimes.

On Wordswords, for instance, I seldom alight, Or on Mouthey, his friend, without taking to flight.

Lady Bluem. Sir, your taste is too common; but time and posterity Will right these great men, and this age' severity 10

Become its reproach.

Ink. I've no sort of objection So I'm not of the party to take the infection.

Lady Blueb. Perhaps you have doubt that they ever will *take?*

Ink. Not at all; on the contrary, those of the lake Have taken already, and still will continue 10

To take—what they can, from a groat to a guinea, Of pension or place;—but the subject's a bore.

Lady Bluem. Well, sir, the time' coming.

Ink. Scamp! don't you feel sore What say you to this?

Scamp. They have merit, I own Though their system's absurdity keeps it unknown. 11

Ink. Then why not unearth it in one of your lectures.

Scamp. It is only time past which comes under my strictures.

Lady Blueb. Come, a truce with all tartness;—the joy of my heart Is to see Nature's triumph o'er all that is art.

Wild Nature!—Grand Shakspeare!

Both. And down Aristotle! 11

Lady Bluem. Sir George thinks exactl with Lady Bluebottle: And my Lord Seventy-four, who protect our dear Bard, And who gave him his place, has the greatest regard

154

'or the poet, who, singing of pedlars and
asses,
Ias found out the way to dispense with
Parnassus. 120
Tra. And you, Scamp!—
Scamp. I needs must confess I'm
embarrass'd.
Ink. Don't call upon Scamp, who's
already so harass'd
With old *schools*, and new *schools*, and no
schools, and all *schools*.
Tra. Well, one thing is certain, that
some must be fools.
should like to know who.
Ink. And I should not be sorry 125
To know who are *not*:—it would save us
some worry.
Lady Blueb. A truce with remark, and
let nothing control
This 'feast of our reason, and flow of the
soul.'
Oh! my dear Mr. Botherby! sympathise!
—I
Now feel such a rapture, I'm ready to
fly, 130
feel so elastic—'*so buoyant—so buoy-
ant!*'
Ink. Tracy! open the window.
Tra. I wish her much joy on't.
Both. For God's sake, my Lady Blue-
bottle, check not
This gentle emotion, so seldom our lot
Upon earth. Give it way: 'tis an impulse
which lifts 135
Our spirits from earth; the sublimest of
gifts;
For which poor Prometheus was chain'd
to his mountain:
Tis the source of all sentiment—feeling's
true fountain;
Tis the Vision of Heaven upon Earth: 'tis
the gas
Of the soul: 'tis the seizing of shades as
they pass, 140
And making them substance: 'tis some-
thing divine:—
Ink. Shall I help you, my friend, to a
little more wine?

Both. I thank you; not any more, sir,
till I dine.
Ink. A propos—Do you dine with Sir
Humphry to-day?
Tra. I should think with *Duke* Humphry
was more in your way. 145
Ink. It might be of yore; but we authors
now look
To the Knight, as a landlord, much more
than the Duke.
The truth is, each writer now quite at his
ease is,
And (except with his publisher) dines
where he pleases.
But 'tis now nearly five, and I must to the
Park. 150
Tra. And I'll take a turn with you
there till 'tis dark.
And you, Scamp—
Scamp. Excuse me! I must to my notes,
For my lecture next week.
Ink. He must mind whom he quotes
Out of 'Elegant Extracts.'
Lady Blueb. Well, now we break
up;
But remember Miss Diddle invites us to
sup. 155
Ink. Then at two hours past midnight
we all meet again,
For the sciences, sandwiches, hock, and
champagne!
Tra. And the sweet lobster salad!
Both. I honour that meal;
For 'tis then that our feelings most
genuinely—feel.
Ink. True; feeling is truest *then*, far
beyond question: 160
I wish to the gods 'twas the same with
digestion!
Lady Blueb. Pshaw!—never mind that;
for one moment of feeling
Is worth—God knows what.
Ink. 'Tis at least worth concealing
For itself, or what follows——But here
comes your carriage.
Sir Rich. [*aside.*] I wish all these people
were d——d with *my* marriage! 165
[*Exeunt.*

THE VISION OF JUDGMENT

BY

QUEVEDO REDIVIVUS

SUGGESTED BY THE COMPOSITION SO ENTITLED BY THE AUTHOR OF 'WAT TYLER'

'A Daniel come to judgment! yea, a Daniel!
I thank thee, Jew, for teaching me that word.'

PREFACE

IT hath been wisely said, that 'One fool makes many;' and it hath been poetically observed—

'That fools rush in where angels fear to tread.'—POPE.

If Mr. Southey had not rushed in where he had no business, and where he never was before, and never will be again, the following poem would not have been written. It is not impossible that it may be as good as his own, seeing that it cannot, by any species of stupidity, natural or acquired, be worse. The gross flattery, the dull impudence, the renegado intolerance, and impious cant, of the poem by the author of 'Wat Tyler,' are something so stupendous as to form the sublime of himself—containing the quintessence of his own attributes.

So much for his poem—a word on his preface. In this preface it has pleased the magnanimous Laureate to draw the picture of a supposed 'Satanic School,' the which he doth recommend to the notice of the legislature; thereby adding to his other laurels the ambition of those of an informer. If there exists anywhere, except in his imagination, such a School, is he not sufficiently armed against it by his own intense vanity? The truth is, that there are certain writers whom Mr. S. imagines, like Scrub, to have 'talked of *him;* for they laughed consumedly.'

I think I know enough of most of the writers to whom he is supposed to allude, to assert, that they, in their individual capacities, have done more good, in the charities of life, to their fellow-creatures, in any one year, than Mr. Southey has done harm to himself by his absurdities in his whole life; and this is saying a great deal. But I have a few questions to ask.

1stly, Is Mr. Southey the author of 'Wat Tyler'?

2ndly, Was he not refused a remedy at law by the highest judge of his beloved England, because it was a blasphemous and seditious publication?

3rdly, Was he not entitled by William Smith, in full parliament, 'a rancorous renegado'?

4thly, Is he not poet laureate, with his own lines on Martin the regicide staring him in the face?

And, 5thly, Putting the four preceding items together, with what conscience dare *he* call the attention of the laws to the publications of others, be they what they may?

I say nothing of the cowardice of such a proceeding; its meanness speaks for itself; but I wish to touch upon the *motive,* which is neither more nor less than that Mr. S. has been laughed at a little in some recent publications, as he was of yore in the 'Anti-jacobin,' by his present patrons. Hence all this 'skimble-scamble stuff' about 'Satanic,' and so forth. However, it is worthy of him—'*quali ab incepto.*'

If there is anything obnoxious to the political opinions of a portion of the public in the following poem, they may thank Mr. Southey. He might have written hexameters, as he has written everything else, for aught that the writer cared—had they been upon another subject. But to attempt to canonise a monarch, who, whatever were his household virtues, was neither a successful nor a patriot king,—inasmuch as several years of his reign passed in war with America and Ireland, to say nothing of the aggression upon France,—like all other exaggeration, necessarily begets opposition. In whatever manner he may be spoken of in this new 'Vision,' his *public* career will not be more favourably transmitted by history. Of his private virtues (although a little expensive to the nation) there can be no doubt.

With regard to the supernatural personages treated of, I can only say that I know as much about them, and (as an honest man) have a better right to talk of them than Robert Southey. I have also treated them more tolerantly. The way in which that poor insane creature, the Laureate, deals about his judgments in the next world, is like his own judgment in this. If it was not completely ludicrous it would be something worse. I don't think that there is much more to say at present.

QUEVEDO REDIVIVUS.

P.S.—It is possible that some readers may object, in these objectionable times, to the freedom with which saints, angels, and spiritual persons discourse in this 'Vision.' But, for precedents upon such points, I must refer him to Fielding's 'Journey from this World to the next,' and to the Visions of myself, the said Quevedo, in Spanish or translated. The reader is also requested to observe, that no doctrinal tenets are insisted upon or discussed; that the person of the Deity is carefully withheld from sight, which is more than can be said for the Laureate, who hath thought proper to make him talk, not 'like a school-divine,' but like the unscholarlike Mr. Southey. The whole action passes on the outside of heaven; and Chaucer's 'Wife of Bath,' Pulci's 'Morgante Maggiore,' Swift's 'Tale of a Tub,'

156

nd the other works above referred to, are cases in point of the freedom with which saints, &c. may e permitted to converse in works not intended to be serious.

Q. R.

*** Mr. Southey being, as he says, a good Christian and vindictive, threatens, I understand, a reply o this our answer. It is to be hoped that his visionary faculties will in the mean time have acquired little more judgment, properly so called: otherwise he will get himself into new dilemmas. These postate jacobins furnish rich rejoinders. Let him take a specimen. Mr. Southey laudeth grievously one Mr. Landor,' who cultivates much private renown in the shape of Latin verses; and not long ago, ne poet laureate dedicated to him, it appeareth, one of his fugitive lyrics, upon the strength of a poem alled 'Gebir.' Who could suppose, that in this same Gebir the aforesaid Savage Landor (for such his grim cognomen) putteth into the infernal regions no less a person than the hero of his friend 1r. Southey's heaven,—yea, even George the Third! See also how personal Savage becometh, when e hath a mind. The following is his portrait of our late gracious sovereign:

(Prince Gebir having descended into the infernal re-
gions, the shades of his royal ancestors are, at his
request, called up to his view; and he exclaims to
his ghostly guide)—

'Aroar, what wretch that nearest us? what wretch
Is that with eyebrows white and slanting brow?
Listen! him yonder who, bound down supine,
Shrinks yelling from that sword there, engine-hung.
He too amongst my ancestors! I hate
The despot, but the dastard I despise.
Was he our countryman?'

'Alas, O king!
Iberia bore him, but the breed accurst
Inclement winds blew blighting from north-east.'
'He was a warrior then, nor fear'd the gods?'
'Gebir, he fear'd the demons, not the gods,
Though them indeed his daily face adored;
And was no warrior, yet the thousand lives
Squander'd, as stones to exercise a sling,
And the tame cruelty and cold caprice—
Oh madness of mankind! address'd, adored!'
Gebir, p. 28.

I omit noticing some edifying Ithyphallics of Savagius, wishing to keep the proper veil over them, his grave but somewhat indiscreet worshipper will suffer it; but certainly these teachers of 'great noral lessons' are apt to be found in strange company.

I

SAINT PETER sat by the celestial gate:
 His keys were rusty, and the lock was
 dull,
So little trouble had been given of late;
 Not that the place by any means was full,
But since the Gallic era 'eighty-eight'
 The devils had ta'en a longer, stronger
 pull,
And 'a pull altogether,' as they say
At sea—which drew most souls another
 way.

II

The angels all were singing out of tune,
 And hoarse with having little else to do,
Excepting to wind up the sun and moon,
 Or curb a runaway young star or two,
Or wild colt of a comet, which too soon
 Broke out of bounds o'er th' ethereal
 blue,
Splitting some planet with its playful tail,
As boats are sometimes by a wanton
 whale.

III

The guardian seraphs had retired on high,
 Finding their charges past all care
 below;

Terrestrial business fill'd nought in the sky
 Save the recording angel's black bureau;
Who found, indeed, the facts to multiply
 With such rapidity of vice and woe,
That he had stripp'd off both his wings in
 quills,
And yet was in arrear of human ills.

IV

His business so augmented of late years,
 That he was forced, against his will no
 doubt,
(Just like those cherubs, earthly ministers,)
 For some resource to turn himself
 about,
And claim the help of his celestial peers,
 To aid him ere he should be quite worn
 out
By the increased demand for his remarks:
Six angels and twelve saints were named
 his clerks.

V

This was a handsome board—at least for
 heaven;
 And yet they had even then enough to do,
So many conquerors' cars were daily
 driven,
 So many kingdoms fitted up anew;

157

THE VISION OF JUDGMENT

Each day too slew its thousands six or
 seven,
Till at the crowning carnage, Waterloo,
They threw their pens down in divine
 disgust—
The page was so besmear'd with blood and
 dust.

VI

This by the way; 'tis not mine to record
 What angels shrink from: even the very
 devil
On this occasion his own work abhorr'd,
 So surfeited with the infernal revel:
Though he himself had sharpen'd every
 sword,
 It almost quench'd his innate thirst of
 evil.
(Here Satan's sole good work deserves
 insertion—
'Tis, that he has both generals in rever-
 sion.)

VII

Let's skip a few short years of hollow
 peace,
 Which peopled earth no better, hell as
 wont,
And heaven none—they form the tyrant's
 lease,
 With nothing but new names subscribed
 upon't;
'Twill one day finish: meantime they in-
 crease,
 'With seven heads and ten horns,' and
 all in front,
Like Saint John's foretold beast; but ours
 are born
Less formidable in the head than horn.

VIII

In the first year of freedom's second dawn
 Died George the Third; although no
 tyrant, one
Who shielded tyrants, till each sense with-
 drawn
 Left him nor mental nor external sun:
A better farmer ne'er brush'd dew from
 lawn,
 A worse king never left a realm undone!
He died—but left his subjects still be-
 hind,
One half as mad—and t'other no less
 blind.

IX

He died! his death made no great stir on
 earth:
 His burial made some pomp; there was
 profusion
Of velvet, gilding, brass, and no great
 dearth
 Of aught but tears—save those shed by
 collusion.

For these things may be bought at thei
 true worth;
 Of elegy there was the due infusion—
Bought also; and the torches, cloaks, an
 banners,
Heralds, and relics of old Gothic manners

X

Form'd a sepulchral melodrame. Of all
 The fools who flock'd to swell or see th
 show,
Who cared about the corpse? The funera
 Made the attraction, and the black th
 woe.
There throbb'd not there a thought whicl
 pierced the pall;
 And when the gorgeous coffin was lai
 low,
It seem'd the mockery of hell to fold
The rottenness of eighty years in gold.

XI

So mix his body with the dust! It migh
 Return to what it *must* far sooner, wer
The natural compound left alone to figh
 Its way back into earth, and fire, an
 air;
But the unnatural balsams merely blight
 What nature made him at his birth, a
 bare
As the mere million's base unmummie
 clay—
Yet all his spices but prolong decay.

XII

He's dead—and upper earth with him ha
 done;
 He's buried; save the undertaker's bill
Or lapidary scrawl, the world is gone
 For him, unless he left a German will
But where's the proctor who will ask hi
 son?
 In whom his qualities are reigning still
Except that household virtue, most un
 common,
Of constancy to a bad, ugly woman.

XIII

'God save the king!' It is a large econom
 In God to save the like; but if he will
Be saving, all the better; for not one am
 Of those who think damnation bette
 still:
I hardly know too if not quite alone am
 In this small hope of bettering future i
By circumscribing, with some slight re
 striction,
The eternity of hell's hot jurisdiction.

XIV

I know this is unpopular; I know
 'Tis blasphemous; I know one may b
 damn'd
For hoping no one else may e'er be so;

I know my catechism; I know we're cramm'd
With the best doctrines till we quite o'er-flow;
I know that all save England's church have shamm'd,
And that the other twice two hundred churches
And synagogues have made a *damn'd* bad purchase.

XV

God help us all! God help me too! I am,
God knows, as helpless as the devil can wish,
And not a whit more difficult to damn,
Than is to bring to land a late-hook'd fish,
Or to the butcher to purvey the lamb;
Not that I'm fit for such a noble dish,
As one day will be that immortal fry
Of almost everybody born to die.

XVI

Saint Peter sat by the celestial gate,
And nodded o'er his keys; when, lo! there came
A wondrous noise he had not heard of late—
A rushing sound of wind, and stream, and flame;
In short, a roar of things extremely great,
Which would have made aught save a saint exclaim;
But he, with first a start and then a wink,
Said, 'There's another star gone out, I think!'

XVII

But ere he could return to his repose,
A cherub flapp'd his right wing o'er his eyes—
At which St. Peter yawn'd, and rubb'd his nose:
'Saint porter,' said the angel, 'prithee rise!'
Waving a goodly wing, which glow'd, as glows
An earthly peacock's tail, with heavenly dyes:
To which the saint replied, 'Well, what's the matter?
Is Lucifer come back with all this clatter?'

XVIII

'No,' quoth the cherub; 'George the Third is dead.'
'And who *is* George the Third?' replied the apostle:
What George? what Third?' 'The king of England,' said
The angel. 'Well! he won't find kings to jostle
Him on his way; but does he wear his head?
Because the last we saw here had a tustle,
And ne'er would have got into heaven's good graces,
Had he not flung his head in all our faces.

XIX

'He was, if I remember, king of France;
That head of his, which could not keep a crown
On earth, yet ventured in my face to advance
A claim to those of martyrs—like my own:
If I had had my sword, as I had once
When I cut ears off, I had cut him down;
But having but my *keys*, and not my brand,
I only knock'd his head from out his hand.

XX

'And then he set up such a headless howl,
That all the saints came out and took him in;
And there he sits by St. Paul, cheek by jowl;
That fellow Paul—the parvenù! The skin
Of St. Bartholomew, which makes his cowl
In heaven, and upon earth redeem'd his sin,
So as to make a martyr, never sped
Better than did this weak and wooden head.

XXI

'But had it come up here upon its shoulders,
There would have been a different tale to tell:
The fellow-feeling in the saint's beholders
Seems to have acted on them like a spell,
And so this very foolish head heaven solders
Back on its trunk: it may be very well,
And seems the custom here to overthrow
Whatever has been wisely done below.'

XXII

The angel answer'd, 'Peter! do not pout:
The king who comes has head and all entire,
And never knew much what it was about—
He did as doth the puppet—by its wire,
And will be judged like all the rest, no doubt:
My business and your own is not to inquire
Into such matters but to mind our cue—
Which is to act as we are bid to do.'

XXIII

While thus they spake, the angelic cara-
van,
Arriving like a rush of mighty wind,
Cleaving the fields of space, as doth the
swan
Some silver stream (say Ganges, Nile,
or Inde,
Or Thames, or Tweed), and 'midst them
an old man
With an old soul, and both extremely
blind,
Halted before the gate, and in his shroud
Seated their fellow traveller on a cloud.

XXIV

But bringing up the rear of this bright host
A Spirit of a different aspect waved
His wings, like thunder-clouds above some
coast
Whose barren beach with frequent
wrecks is paved;
His brow was like the deep when tempest-
toss'd;
Fierce and unfathomable thoughts en-
graved
Eternal wrath on his immortal face,
And *where* he gazed a gloom pervaded
space.

XXV

As he drew near, he gazed upon the gate
Ne'er to be enter'd more by him or Sin,
With such a glance of supernatural hate,
As made Saint Peter wish himself with-
in;
He potter'd with his keys at a great rate,
And sweated through his apostolic skin:
Of course his perspiration was but ichor,
Or some such other spiritual liquor.

XXVI

The very cherubs huddled all together,
Like birds when soars the falcon; and
they felt
A tingling to the tip of every feather,
And form'd a circle like Orion's belt
Around their poor old charge; who scarce
knew whither
His guards had led him, though they
gently dealt
With royal manes (for by many stories,
And true, we learn the angels' all are
Tories).

XXVII

As things were in this posture, the gate flew
Asunder, and the flashing of its hinges
Flung over space an universal hue
Of many-colour'd flame, until its tinges
Reach'd even our own speck of earth, and
made a new
Aurora borealis spread its fringes

O'er the North Pole; the same seen, when
ice-bound,
By Captain Parry's crew, in 'Melville'
Sound.'

XXVIII

And from the gate thrown open issue
beaming
A beautiful and mighty Thing of Light
Radiant with glory, like a banner stream
ing
Victorious from some world-o'erthrow
ing fight:
My poor comparisons must needs be
teeming
With earthly likenesses, for here th
night
Of clay obscures our best conceptions
saving
Johanna Southcote, or Bob Southe
raving.

XXIX

'Twas the archangel Michael; all me
know
The make of angels and archangels
since
There's scarce a scribbler has not one t
show,
From the fiends' leader to the angels
prince;
There also are some altar-pieces, thoug
I really can't say that they much evinc
One's inner notions of immortal spirits;
But let the connoisseurs explain the
merits.

XXX

Michael flew forth in glory and in good
A goodly work of him from whom a
glory
And good arise; the portal past—he stood
Before him the young cherubs an
saints hoary—
(I say *young*, begging to be understood
By looks, not years; and should be ver
sorry
To state, they were not older than S
Peter,
But merely that they seem'd a littl
sweeter).

XXXI

The cherubs and the saints bow'd dow
before
That arch-angelic hierarch, the first
Of essences angelical, who wore
The aspect of a god; but this ne'
nursed
Pride in his heavenly bosom, in whose co
No thought, save for his Master
service, durst
Intrude, however glorified and high;
He knew him but the viceroy of the sky

THE VISION OF JUDGMENT

XXXII

He and the sombre, silent Spirit met—
 They knew each other both for good
 and ill;
Such was their power, that neither could
 forget
 His former friend and future foe; but still
There was a high, immortal, proud regret
 In either's eye, as if 'twere less their will
Than destiny to make the eternal years
Their date of war, and their 'champ clos'
 the spheres.

XXXIII

But here they were in neutral space: we
 know
 From Job, that Satan hath the power to
 pay
A heavenly visit thrice a year or so;
 And that the 'sons of God', like those
 of clay,
Must keep him company; and we might
 show
 From the same book, in how polite a
 way
The dialogue is held between the Powers
Of Good and Evil—but 'twould take up
 hours.

XXXIV

And this is not a theologic tract,
 To prove with Hebrew and with Arabic,
If Job be allegory or a fact,
 But a true narrative; and thus I pick
From out the whole but such and such an
 act
 As sets aside the slightest thought of
 trick.
'Tis every tittle true, beyond suspicion,
And accurate as any other vision.

XXXV

The spirits were in neutral space, before
 The gate of heaven; like eastern thres-
 holds is
The place where Death's grand cause is
 argued o'er,
 And souls despatch'd to that world or
 to this;
And therefore Michael and the other wore
 A civil aspect: though they did not kiss,
Yet still between his Darkness and his
 Brightness
There pass'd a mutual glance of great
 politeness.

XXXVI

The Archangel bow'd, not like a modern
 beau,
 But with a graceful Oriental bend,
Pressing one radiant arm just where below
 The heart in good men is supposed to
 tend;
He turn'd as to an equal, not too low,

But kindly; Satan met his ancient friend
With more hauteur, as might an old
 Castilian
Poor noble meet a mushroom rich civilian.

XXXVII

He merely bent his diabolic brow
 An instant; and then raising it, he stood
In act to assert his right or wrong, and show
 Cause why King George by no means
 could or should
Make out a case to be exempt from woe
 Eternal, more than other kings, endued
With better sense and hearts, whom
 history mentions,
Who long have 'paved hell with their good
 intentions.'

XXXVIII

Michael began: 'What wouldst thou with
 this man,
 Now dead, and brought before the
 Lord? What ill
Hath he wrought since his mortal race began,
 That thou canst claim him? Speak! and
 do thy will,
If it be just: if in this earthly span
 He hath been greatly failing to fulfil
His duties as a king and mortal, say,
And he is thine; if not, let him have way.'

XXXIX

'Michael!' replied the Prince of Air, 'even
 here,
 Before the Gate of him thou servest,
 must
I claim my subject: and will make appear
 That as he was my worshipper in dust,
So shall he be in spirit, although dear
 To thee and thine, because nor wine nor
 lust
Were of his weaknesses; yet on the throne
He reign'd o'er millions to serve me alone.

XL

'Look to our earth, or rather mine; it was,
 Once, more thy master's: but I triumph
 not
In this poor planet's conquest; nor, alas!
 Need he thou servest envy me my lot:
With all the myriads of bright worlds
 which pass
 In worship round him, he may have
 forgot
Yon weak creation of such paltry things:
I think few worth damnation save their
 kings,—

XLI

'And these but as a kind of quit-rent, to
 Assert my right as lord: and even had
I such an inclination, 'twere (as you
 Well know) superfluous; they are grown
 so bad,

161

That hell has nothing better left to do
 Than leave them to themselves: so much
 more mad
And evil by their own internal curse,
Heaven cannot make them better, nor I
 worse.

XLII

'Look to the earth, I said, and say again:
 When this old, blind, mad, helpless,
 weak, poor worm
Began in youth's first bloom and flush to
 reign,
 The world and he both wore a different
 form,
And much of earth and all the watery plain
 Of ocean call'd him king: through many
 a storm
His isles had floated on the abyss of time;
For the rough virtues chose them for their
 clime.

XLIII

'He came to his sceptre young; he leaves
 it old:
 Look to the state in which he found his
 realm,
And left it; and his annals too behold,
 How to a minion first he gave the helm;
How grew upon his heart a thirst for gold,
 The beggar's vice, which can but over-
 whelm
The meanest hearts; and for the rest, but
 glance
Thine eye along America and France.

XLIV

''Tis true, he was a tool from first to last
 (I have the workmen safe); but as a tool
So let him be consumed. From out the
 past
 Of ages, since mankind have known the
 rule
Of monarchs—from the bloody rolls
 amass'd
 Of sin and slaughter—from the Cæsar's
 school,
Take the worst pupil; and produce a reign
More drench'd with gore, more cumber'd
 with the slain.

XLV

'He ever warr'd with freedom and the
 free:
 Nations as men, home subjects, foreign
 foes,
So that they utter'd the word "Liberty!"
 Found George the Third their first
 opponent. Whose
History was ever stain'd as his will be
 With national and individual woes?
I grant his household abstinence; I grant
His neutral virtues, which most monarchs
 want;

XLVI

'I know he was a constant consort
 own
 He was a decent sire, and middling
 lord.
All this is much, and most upon a throne
 As temperance, if at Apicius' board,
Is more than at an anchorite's suppe
 shown.
 I grant him all the kindest can accord
And this was well for him, but not fo
 those
Millions who found him what oppressio
 chose.

XLVII

'The New World shook him off; the Ol
 yet groans
 Beneath what he and his prepared, i
 not
Completed: he leaves heirs on man
 thrones
 To all his vices, without what begot
Compassion for him—his tame virtues
 drones
 Who sleep, or despots who have nov
 forgot
A lesson which shall be re-taught them
 wake
Upon the thrones of earth; but let then
 quake!

XLVIII

'Five millions of the primitive, who hol
 The faith which makes ye great or
 earth, implored
A *part* of that vast *all* they held of old,—
 Freedom to worship—not alone you
 Lord,
Michael, but you, and you, Saint Peter
 Cold
 Must be your souls, if you have no
 abhorr'd
The foe to Catholic participation
In all the license of a Christian nation.

XLIX

'True! he allow'd them to pray God; bu
 as
 A consequence of prayer, refused the
 law
Which would have placed them upon the
 same base
 With those who did not hold the saints
 in awe.'
But here Saint Peter started from his
 place,
 And cried, 'You may the prisoner with-
 draw:
Ere heaven shall ope her portals to this
 Guelph,
While I am guard, may I be damn'd my-
 self!

L

'Sooner will I with Cerberus exchange
My office (and *his* is no sinecure)
Than see this royal Bedlam bigot range
The azure fields of heaven, of that be
sure!'
'Saint!' replied Satan, 'you do well to
avenge
The wrongs he made your satellites
endure;
And if to this exchange you should be
given,
I'll try to coax *our* Cerberus up to heaven!'

LI

Here Michael interposed: 'Good saint!
and devil!
Pray, not so fast; you both outrun dis-
cretion.
Saint Peter! you were wont to be more
civil!
Satan! excuse this warmth of his ex-
pression,
And condescension to the vulgar's level:
Even saints sometimes forget them-
selves in session.
Have you got more to say?'—'No.'—'If
you please,
I'll trouble you to call your witnesses.'

LII

Then Satan turn'd and waved his swarthy
hand,
Which stirr'd with its electric qualities
Clouds farther off than we can understand,
Although we find him sometimes in our
skies;
Infernal thunder shook both sea and land
In all the planets, and hell's batteries
Let off the artillery, which Milton men-
tions
As one of Satan's most sublime inventions.

LIII

This was a signal unto such damn'd souls
As have the privilege of their damnation
Extended far beyond the mere controls
Of worlds past, present, or to come; no
station
Is theirs particularly in the rolls
Of hell assign'd; but where their inclina-
tion
Or business carries them in search of
game,
They may range freely—being damn'd the
same.

LIV

They're proud of this—as very well they
may,
It being a sort of knighthood, or gilt key
Stuck in their loins; or like to an 'entré'
Up the back stairs, or such free-
masonry.

I borrow my comparisons from clay,
Being clay myself. Let not those spirits
be
Offended with such base low likenesses;
We know their posts are nobler far than
these.

LV

When the great signal ran from heaven to
hell—
About ten million times the distance
reckon'd
From our sun to its earth, as we can tell
How much time it takes up, even to a
second,
For every ray that travels to dispel
The fogs of London, through which,
dimly beacon'd,
The weathercocks are gilt some thrice a
year,
If that the *summer* is not too severe:

LVI

I say that I can tell—'twas half a minute;
I know the solar beams take up more
time
Ere, pack'd up for their journey, they
begin it;
But then their telegraph is less sublime,
And if they ran a race, they would not win
it
'Gainst Satan's couriers bound for their
own clime.
The sun takes up some years for every ray
To reach its goal—the devil not half a
day.

LVII

Upon the verge of space, about the size
Of half-a-crown, a little speck appear'd
(I've seen a something like it in the skies
In the Ægean, ere a squall); it near'd,
And, growing bigger, took another guise;
Like an aërial ship it tack'd, and steer'd,
Or *was* steer'd (I am doubtful of the
grammar
Of the last phrase, which makes the stanza
stammer;—

LVIII

But take your choice): and then it grew a
cloud;
And so it was—a cloud of witnesses.
But such a cloud! No land e'er saw a
crowd
Of locusts numerous as the heavens saw
these;
They shadow'd with their myriads space;
their loud
And varied cries were like those of wild
geese
(If nations may be liken'd to a goose),
And realised the phrase of 'hell broke
loose.'

163

LIX

Here crash'd a sturdy oath of stout John
 Bull,
Who damn'd away his eyes as hereto-
 fore:
There Paddy brogued 'By Jasus!'—
 'What's your wull?'
The temperate Scot exclaim'd: the French
 ghost swore
In certain terms I shan't translate in full,
 As the first coachman will; and 'midst
 the roar,
The voice of Jonathan was heard to ex-
 press,
'Our president is going to war, I guess.'

LX

Besides there were the Spaniard, Dutch,
 and Dane;
 In short, an universal shoal of shades,
From Otaheite's isle to Salisbury Plain,
 Of all climes and professions, years and
 trades,
Ready to swear against the good king's
 reign,
 Bitter as clubs in cards are against
 spades:
All summon'd by this grand 'subpœna,'
 to
Try if kings mayn't be damn'd like me or
 you.

LXI

When Michael saw this host, he first grew
 pale,
 As angels can; next, like Italian twilight,
He turn'd all colours—as a peacock's tail,
 Or sunset streaming through a Gothic
 skylight
In some old abbey, or a trout not stale,
 Or distant lightning on the horizon by
 night,
Or a fresh rainbow, or a grand review
Of thirty regiments in red, green, and blue.

LXII

Then he address'd himself to Satan:
 'Why—
 My good old friend, for such I deem
 you, though
Our different parties make us fight so shy,
 I ne'er mistake you for a personal foe;
Our difference is political, and I
 Trust that, whatever may occur below,
You know my great respect for you: and
 this
Makes me regret whate'er you do amiss—

LXIII

'Why, my dear Lucifer, would you abuse
 My call for witnesses? I did not mean
That you should half of earth and hell
 produce;

'Tis even superfluous, since two honest,
 clean,
True testimonies are enough: we lose
 Our time, nay, our eternity, between
The accusation and defence: if we
Hear both, 'twill stretch our immortality.'

LXIV

Satan replied, 'To me the matter is
 Indifferent, in a personal point of view:
I can have fifty better souls than this
 With far less trouble than we have gone
 through
Already; and I merely argued his
 Late majesty of Britain's case with you
Upon a point of form: you may dispose
Of him; I've kings enough below, God
 knows!'

LXV

Thus spoke the Demon (late call'd 'multi-
 faced'
 By multo-scribbling Southey). 'Then
 we'll call
One or two persons of the myriads placed
 Around our congress, and dispense with
 all
The rest,' quoth Michael: 'Who may be so
 graced
 As to speak first? there's choice
 enough—who shall
It be?' Then Satan answer'd, 'There are
 many;
But you may choose Jack Wilkes as well
 as any.'

LXVI

A merry, cock-eyed, curious-looking
 sprite
 Upon the instant started from the
 throng,
Dress'd in a fashion now forgotten quite;
 For all the fashions of the flesh stick
 long
By people in the next world; where unite
 All the costumes since Adam's, right or
 wrong,
From Eve's fig-leaf down to the petticoat,
Almost as scanty, of days less remote.

LXVII

The spirit look'd around upon the crowds
 Assembled, and exclaim'd, 'My friends
 of all
The spheres, we shall catch cold amongst
 these clouds;
 So let's to business: why this general
 call?
If those are freeholders I see in shrouds,
 And 'tis for an election that they
 bawl,
Behold a candidate with unturn'd coat!
Saint Peter, may I count upon your
 vote?'

LXVIII

'Sir,' replied Michael, 'you mistake; these things
 Are of a former life, and what we do
Above is more august; to judge of kings
 Is the tribunal met: so now you know.'
'Then I presume those gentlemen with wings,'
 Said Wilkes, 'are cherubs; and that soul below
Looks much like George the Third, but to my mind
 A good deal older—Bless me! is he blind?'

LXIX

'He is what you behold him, and his doom
 Depends upon his deeds,' the Angel said;
'If you have aught to arraign in him, the tomb
 Gives licence to the humblest beggar's head
To lift itself against the loftiest.'—'Some,'
 Said Wilkes, 'don't wait to see them laid in lead,
For such a liberty—and I, for one,
Have told them what I thought beneath the sun.'

LXX

'*Above* the sun repeat, then, what thou hast
 To urge against him,' said the Archangel. 'Why,'
Replied the spirit, 'since old scores are past,
 Must I turn evidence? In faith, not I.
Besides, I beat him hollow at the last,
 With all his Lords and Commons: in the sky
I don't like ripping up old stories, since
His conduct was but natural in a prince.

LXXI

'Foolish, no doubt, and wicked, to oppress
 A poor unlucky devil without a shilling;
But then I blame the man himself much less
 Than Bute and Grafton, and shall be unwilling
To see him punish'd here for their excess,
 Since they were both damn'd long ago, and still in
Their place below: for me, I have forgiven,
And vote his "habeas corpus" into heaven.'

LXXII

'Wilkes,' said the Devil, 'I understand all this;
 You turn'd to half a courtier ere you died,
And seem to think it would not be amiss
 To grow a whole one on the other side

Of Charon's ferry; you forget that *his*
 Reign is concluded; whatsoe'er betide,
He won't be sovereign more: you've lost your labour,
For at the best he will but be your neighbour.

LXXIII

'However, I knew what to think of it,
 When I beheld you in your jesting way,
Flitting and whispering round about the spit
 Where Belial, upon duty for the day,
With Fox's lard was basting William Pitt,
 His pupil; I knew what to think, I say:
That fellow even in hell breeds farther ills;
I'll have him *gagg'd*—'twas one of his own bills.

LXXIV

'Call Junius!' From the crowd a shadow stalk'd,
 And at the name there was a general squeeze,
So that the very ghosts no longer walk'd
 In comfort, at their own aërial ease,
But were all ramm'd, and jamm'd (but to be balk'd,
 As we shall see), and jostled hands and knees,
Like wind compress'd and pent within a bladder,
Or like a human colic, which is sadder.

LXXV

The shadow came—a tall, thin, grey-hair'd figure,
 That look'd as it had been a shade on earth;
Quick in its motions, with an air of vigour,
 But nought to mark its breeding or its birth;
Now it wax'd little, then again grew bigger,
 With now an air of gloom, or savage mirth;
But as you gazed upon its features, they
Changed every instant—to *what*, none could say.

LXXVI

The more intently the ghosts gazed, the less
 Could they distinguish whose the features were;
The Devil himself seem'd puzzled even to guess,
 They varied like a dream—now here, now there;
And several people swore from out the press,
 They knew him perfectly; and one could swear
He was his father: upon which another
Was sure he was his mother's cousin's brother:

LXXVII

Another, that he was a duke, or knight,
 An orator, a lawyer, or a priest,
A nabob, a man-midwife; but the wight
 Mysterious changed his countenance at
 least
As oft as they their minds; though in full
 sight
 He stood, the puzzle only was increased;
The man was a phantasmagoria in
Himself—he was so volatile and thin.

LXXVIII

The moment that you had pronounced
 him one,
 Presto! his face changed, and he was
 another;
And when that change was hardly well put
 on,
 It varied, till I don't think his own
 mother
(If that he had a mother) would her son
 Have known, he shifted so from one to
 t'other;
Till guessing from a pleasure grew a task,
At this epistolary 'Iron Mask.'

LXXIX

For sometimes he like Cerberus would
 seem—
 'Three gentlemen at once' (as sagely
 says
Good Mrs. Malaprop); then you might
 deem
 That he was not even one; now many
 rays
Were flashing round him; and now a thick
 steam
 Hid him from sight—like fogs on Lon-
 don days:
Now Burke, now Tooke, he grew to
 people's fancies,
And certes often like Sir Philip Francis.

LXXX

I've an hypothesis—'tis quite my own;
 I never let it out till now, for fear
Of doing people harm about the throne,
 And injuring some minister or peer,
On whom the stigma might perhaps be
 blown;
 It is—my gentle public, lend thine ear!
'Tis, that what Junius we are wont to call
Was really, truly, nobody at all.

LXXXI

I don't see wherefore letters should not be
 Written without hands, since we daily
 view
Them written without heads; and books,
 we see,
 Are fill'd as well without the latter too:
And really till we fix on somebody
 For certain sure to claim them as his
 due,
Their author, like the Niger's mouth, will
 bother
The world to say if there be mouth or
 author.

LXXXII

'And who and what art thou?' the Arch-
 angel said.
 'For that you may consult my title-
 page,'
Replied this mighty shadow of a shade:
 'If I have kept my secret half an age,
I scarce shall tell it now.'—'Canst thou
 upbraid,'
 Continued Michael, 'George Rex, or
 allege
Aught further?' Junius answer'd, 'You
 had better
First ask him for his answer to my letter:

LXXXIII

'My charges upon record will outlast
 The brass of both his epitaph and tomb.'
'Repent'st thou not,' said Michael, 'of
 some past
 Exaggeration? something which may
 doom
Thyself if false, as him if true? Thou wast
 Too bitter—is it not so?—in thy gloom
Of passion?'—'Passion!' cried the phan-
 tom dim,
'I loved my country, and I hated him.

LXXXIV

'What I have written, I have written: let
 The rest be on his head or mine!' So
 spoke
Old 'Nominis Umbra'; and while speak-
 ing yet,
 Away he melted in celestial smoke.
Then Satan said to Michael, 'Don't forget
 To call George Washington, and John
 Horne Tooke,
And Franklin;'—but at this time there
 was heard
A cry for room, though not a phantom
 stirr'd.

LXXXV

At length with jostling, elbowing, and the
 aid
 Of cherubim appointed to that post,
The devil Asmodeus to the circle made
 His way, and look'd as if his journey
 cost
Some trouble. When his burden down he
 laid,
 'What's this?' cried Michael; 'why,
 'tis not a ghost?'
'I know it,' quoth the incubus; 'but he
Shall be one, if you leave the affair to
 me.

LXXXVI

'Confound the renegado! I have sprain'd
　My left wing, he's so heavy; one would
　　think
Some of his works about his neck were
　　chain'd.
　But to the point; while hovering o'er
　　the brink
Of Skiddaw (where as usual it still rain'd),
　I saw a taper, far below me, wink,
And stooping, caught this fellow at a
　　libel—
No less on history than the Holy Bible.

LXXXVII

'The former is the devil's scripture, and
　The latter yours, good Michael: so the
　　affair
Belongs to all of us, you understand.
　I snatch'd him up just as you see him
　　there,
And brought him off for sentence out of
　　hand:
　I've scarcely been ten minutes in the
　　air—
At least a quarter it can hardly be:
I dare say that his wife is still at tea.'

LXXXVIII

Here Satan said, 'I know this man of old,
　And have expected him for some time
　　here;
A sillier fellow you will scarce behold,
　Or more conceited in his petty sphere:
But surely it was not worth while to fold
　Such trash below your wing, Asmodeus
　　dear:
We had the poor wretch safe (without
　　being bored
With carriage) coming of his own accord.

LXXXIX

'But since he's here, let's see what he has
　　done.'
　'Done!' cried Asmodeus, 'he antici-
　　pates
The very business you are now upon,
　And scribbles as if head clerk to the
　　Fates.
Who knows to what his ribaldry may run,
　When such an ass as this, like Balaam's,
　　prates?'
'Let's hear,' quoth Michael, 'what he has
　　to say:
You know we're bound to that in every
　　way.'

XC

Now the bard, glad to get an audience,
　　which
　By no means often was his case below,
Began to cough, and hawk, and hem, and
　　pitch
　His voice into that awful note of woe
To all unhappy hearers within reach
　Of poets when the tide of rhyme's in
　　flow;
But stuck fast with his first hexameter,
Not one of all whose gouty feet would stir.

XCI

But ere the spavin'd dactyls could be
　　spurr'd
　Into recitative, in great dismay
Both cherubim and seraphim were heard
　To murmur loudly through their long
　　array;
And Michael rose ere he could get a word
　Of all his founder'd verses under way,
And cried, 'For God's sake stop, my
　　friend! 'twere best—
Non Di, non homines—you know the rest.'

XCII

A general bustle spread throughout the
　　throng,
　Which seem'd to hold all verse in detes-
　　tation;
The angels had of course enough of song
　When upon service; and the generation
Of ghosts had heard too much in life, not
　　long
　Before, to profit by a new occasion:
The monarch, mute till then, exclaim'd,
　　'What! what!
Pye come again? No more—no more of
　　that!'

XCIII

The tumult grew; an universal cough
　Convulsed the skies, as during a debate,
When Castlereagh has been up long
　　enough
　(Before he was first minister of state,
I mean—the *slaves hear now*); some cried
　　'Off, off!'
As at a farce; till, grown quite desperate,
The bard Saint Peter pray'd to interpose
(Himself an author) only for his prose.

XCIV

The varlet was not an ill-favour'd knave;
　A good deal like a vulture in the face,
With a hook nose and a hawk's eye, which
　　gave
　A smart and sharper-looking sort of
　　grace
To his whole aspect, which, though rather
　　grave,
　Was by no means so ugly as his case;
But that, indeed, was hopeless as can be,
Quite a poetic felony '*de se*.'

XCV

Then Michael blew his trump, and still'd
　　the noise
　With one still greater, as is yet the mode
On earth besides; except some grumbling
　　voice,

167

Which now and then will make a slight
inroad
Upon decorous silence, few will twice
 Lift up their lungs when fairly over-
 crow'd;
And now the bard could plead his own bad
cause,
 With all the attitudes of self-applause.

XCVI

He said—(I only give the heads)—he said,
 He meant no harm in scribbling; 'twas
 his way
Upon all topics; 'twas, besides, his bread,
 Of which he butter'd both sides; 'twould
 delay
Too long the assembly (he was pleased to
 dread),
 And take up rather more time than a
 day,
To name his works—he would but cite a
 few—
'Wat Tyler'—'Rhymes on Blenheim'—
 'Waterloo.'

XCVII

He had written praises of a regicide;
 He had written praises of all kings what-
 ever;
He had written for republics far and wide,
 And then against them bitterer than ever;
For pantisocracy he once had cried
 Aloud, a scheme less moral than 'twas
 clever;
Then grew a hearty anti-jacobin—
Had turn'd his coat—and would have
 turn'd his skin.

XCVIII

He had sung against all battles, and again
 In their high praise and glory; he had
 call'd
Reviewing 'the ungentle craft,' and then
 Become as base a critic as e'er crawl'd—
Fed, paid, and pamper'd by the very men
 By whom his muse and morals had been
 maul'd:
He had written much blank verse, and
 blanker prose,
And more of both than anybody knows.

XCIX

He had written Wesley's life:—here turn-
 ing round
To Satan, 'Sir, I'm ready to write yours,
In two octavo volumes, nicely bound,
 With notes and preface, all that most
 allures
The pious purchaser; and there's no
 ground
 For fear, for I can choose my own re-
 viewers:
So let me have the proper documents,
That I may add you to my other saints.'

C

Satan bow'd, and was silent. 'Well, if you,
 With amiable modesty, decline
My offer, what says Michael? There are
 few
 Whose memoirs could be render'd more
 divine.
Mine is a pen of all work; not so new
 As it was once, but I would make you
 shine
Like your own trumpet. By the way, my
 own
Has more of brass in it, and is as well
 blown.

CI

'But talking about trumpets, here's my
 Vision!
 Now you shall judge, all people; yes,
 you shall
Judge with my judgment, and by my de-
 cision
 Be guided who shall enter heaven or fall.
I settle all these things by intuition,
 Times present, past, to come, heaven,
 hell, and all,
Like King Alfonso. When I thus see
 double,
I save the Deity some worlds of trouble.'

CII

He ceased, and drew forth an MS.; and no
 Persuasion on the part of devils, saints,
Or angels, now could stop the torrent; so
 He read the first three lines of the con-
 tents;
But at the fourth, the whole spiritual show
 Had vanish'd, with variety of scents,
Ambrosial and sulphureous, as they
 sprang,
Like lightning, off from his 'melodious
 twang.'

CIII

Those grand heroics acted as a spell:
 The angels stopp'd their ears and plied
 their pinions;
The devils ran howling, deafen'd, down to
 hell;
 The ghosts fled, gibbering, for their own
 dominions—
(For 'tis not yet decided where they dwell,
 And I leave every man to his opinions);
Michael took refuge in his trump—but, lo!
His teeth were set on edge, he could not
 blow!

CIV

Saint Peter, who has hitherto been known
 For an impetuous saint, upraised his
 keys,
And at the fifth line knock'd the poet
 down;
 Who fell like Phaeton, but more at ease,

168

Into his lake, for there he did not drown;
 A different web being by the Destinies
Woven for the Laureate's final wreath,
 whene'er
Reform shall happen either here or there.

CV

He first sank to the bottom—like his
 works,
 But soon rose to the surface—like him-
 self;
For all corrupted things are buoy'd like
 corks,
 By their own rottenness, light as an elf,
Or wisp that flits o'er a morass: he lurks,
 It may be, still, like dull books on a shelf,

In his own den, to scrawl some 'Life' or
 'Vision,'
As Welborn says—'the devil turn'd pre-
 cisian.'

CVI

As for the rest, to come to the conclusion
 Of this true dream, the telescope is gone
Which kept my optics free from all de-
 lusion,
 And show'd me what I in my turn have
 shown;
All I saw farther, in the last confusion,
 Was, that King George slipp'd into
 heaven for one;
And when the tumult dwindled to a calm,
I left him practising the hundredth psalm.

THE AGE OF BRONZE

OR,

CARMEN SECULARE ET ANNUS HAUD MIRABILIS

'Impar *Congressus* Achilli.'

I

THE 'good old times'—all times when old
 are good—
Are gone; the present might be if they
 would;
Great things have been, and are, and
 greater still
Want little of mere mortals but their will:
A wider space, a greener field, is given
To those who play their 'tricks before high
 heaven.' 6
I know not if the angels weep, but men
Have wept enough—for what?—to weep
 again!

II

All is exploded—be it good or bad. 9
Reader! remember when thou wert a lad,
Then Pitt was all; or, if not all, so much,
His very rival almost deem'd him such.
We, we have seen the intellectual race
Of giants stand, like Titans, face to face—
Athos and Ida, with a dashing sea 15
Of eloquence between, which flow'd all free,
As the deep billows of the Ægean roar
Betwixt the Hellenic and the Phrygian
 shore.
But where are they—the rivals! a few feet
Of sullen earth divide each winding sheet.
How peaceful and how powerful is the
 grave, 21
Which hushes all! a calm, unstormy wave,
Which oversweeps the world. The theme
 is old
Of 'dust to dust;' but half its tale untold:

Time tempers not its terrors—still the
 worm 25
Winds its cold folds, the tomb preserves
 its form,
Varied above, but still alike below;
The urn may shine, the ashes will not glow,
Though Cleopatra's mummy cross the sea
O'er which from empire she lured An-
 thony; 30
Though Alexander's urn a show be grown
On shores he wept to conquer, though un-
 known—
How vain, how worse than vain, at length
 appear
The madman's wish, the Macedonian's
 tear!
He wept for worlds to conquer—half the
 earth 35
Knows not his name, or but his death, and
 birth,
And desolation; while his native Greece
Hath all of desolation, save its peace.
He 'wept for worlds to conquer'! he who
 ne'er
Conceived the globe, he panted not to
 spare! 40
With even the busy Northern Isle un-
 known,
Which holds his urn, and never knew his
 throne.

III

But where is he, the modern, mightier far,
Who, born no king, made monarchs draw
 his car;

169

THE AGE OF BRONZE

The new Sesostris, whose unharness'd
 kings, 45
Freed from the bit, believe themselves
 with wings,
And spurn the dust o'er which they crawl'd
 of late,
Chain'd to the chariot of the chieftain's
 state?
Yes! where is he, the champion and the
 child
Of all that's great or little, wise or wild;
Whose game was empires, and whose
 stakes were thrones; 51
Whose table earth—whose dice were
 human bones?
Behold the grand result in yon lone isle,
And, as thy nature urges, weep or smile.
Sigh to behold the eagle's lofty rage 55
Reduced to nibble at his narrow cage;
Smile to survey the queller of the nations
Now daily squabbling o'er disputed
 rations;
Weep to perceive him mourning, as he
 dines,
O'er curtail'd dishes and o'er stinted
 wines; 60
O'er petty quarrels upon petty things.
Is this the man who scourged or feasted
 kings?
Behold the scales in which his fortune
 hangs,
A surgeon's statement, and an earl's
 harangues! 64
A bust delayed, a book refused, can shake
The sleep of him who kept the world
 awake.
Is this indeed the tamer of the great,
Now slave of all could tease or irritate—
The paltry gaoler and the prying spy,
The staring stranger with his note-book
 nigh? 70
Plunged in a dungeon he had still been
 great;
How low, how little was this middle state,
Between a prison and a palace, where
How few could feel for what he had to
 bear!
Vain his complaint,—my lord presents his
 bill, 75
His food and wine were doled out duly still;
Vain was his sickness, never was a clime
So free from homicide—to doubt's a
 crime;
And the stiff surgeon, who maintain'd his
 cause,
Hath lost his place, and gain'd the world's
 applause. 80
But smile—though all the pangs of brain
 and heart
Disdain, defy, the tardy aid of art;
Though, save the few fond friends and
 imaged face
Of that fair boy his sire shall ne'er em-
 brace,

None stand by his low bed—though even
 the mind 85
Be wavering, which long awed and awes
 mankind:
Smile—for the fetter'd eagle breaks his
 chain,
And higher worlds than this are his again.

IV

How, if that soaring spirit still retain
A conscious twilight of his blazing reign,
How must he smile, on looking down, to
 see 91
The little that he was and sought to be!
What though his name a wider empire
 found
Than his ambition, though with scarce a
 bound; 94
Though first in glory, deepest in reverse,
He tasted empire's blessings and its curse;
Though kings, rejoicing in their late escape
From chains, would gladly be *their* tyrant's
 ape;
How must he smile, and turn to yon lone
 grave,
The proudest sea-mark that o'ertops the
 wave! 100
What though his gaoler, duteous to the
 last,
Scarce deem'd the coffin's lead could keep
 him fast,
Refusing one poor line along the lid,
To date the birth and death of all it hid;
That name shall hallow the ignoble shore,
A talisman to all save him who bore: 106
The fleets that sweep before the eastern
 blast
Shall hear their sea-boys hail it from the
 mast;
When Victory's Gallic column shall but
 rise, 109
Like Pompey's pillar, in a desert's skies,
The rocky isle that holds or held his dust,
Shall crown the Atlantic like the hero's
 bust,
And mighty nature o'er his obsequies
Do more than niggard envy still denies.
But what are these to him? Can glory's
 lust 115
Touch the freed spirit or the fetter'd dust?
Small care hath he of what his tomb con-
 sists;
Nought if he sleeps—nor more if he exists:
Alike the better-seeing shade will smile
On the rude cavern of the rocky isle, 120
As if his ashes found their latest home
In Rome's Pantheon or Gaul's mimic
 dome.
He wants not this; but France shall feel
 the want
Of this last consolation, though so scant:
Her honour, fame, and faith demand his
 bones, 125
To rear above a pyramid of thrones;

THE AGE OF BRONZE is the header — let me wrap it.

Or carried onward in the battle's van,
To form, like Guesclin's dust, her talis-
man.
But be it as it is—the time may come
His name shall beat the alarm, like Ziska's
drum. 130

V

Oh heaven! of which he was in power a
feature;
Oh earth! of which he was a noble
creature;
Thou isle! to be remember'd long and
well,
That saw'st the unfledged eaglet chip his
shell!
Ye Alps, which view'd him in his dawning
flights 135
Hover, the victor of a hundred fights!
Thou Rome, who saw'st thy Cæsar's
deeds outdone!
Alas! why pass'd he too the Rubicon—
The Rubicon of man's awaken'd rights,
To herd with vulgar kings and parasites?
Egypt! from whose all dateless tombs
arose 141
Forgotten Pharaohs from their long re-
pose,
And shook within their pyramids to hear
A new Cambyses thundering in their ear;
While the dark shades of forty ages stood
Like startled giants by Nile's famous
flood; 146
Or from the pyramid's tall pinnacle
Beheld the desert peopled, as from hell,
With clashing hosts, who strew'd the
barren sand,
To re-manure the uncultivated land!
Spain! which, a moment mindless of the
Cid, 151
Beheld his banner flouting thy Madrid!
Austria! which saw thy twice-ta'en
capital
Twice spared to be the traitress of his fall!
Ye race of Frederic!—Frederics but in
name 155
And falsehood—heirs to all except his
fame:
Who, crush'd at Jena, crouch'd at Berlin,
fell
First, and but rose to follow! Ye who
dwell
Where Kosciusko dwelt, remembering yet
The unpaid amount of Catherine's bloody
debt! 160
Poland! o'er which the avenging angel
pass'd,
But left thee as he found thee, still a waste,
Forgetting all thy still enduring claim,
Thy lotted people and extinguish'd name,
Thy sigh for freedom, thy long-flowing
tear, 165
That sound that crashes in the tyrant's
ear—

Kosciusko! On—on—on—the thirst of
war
Gasps for the gore of serfs and of their
Czar.
The half barbaric Moscow's minarets
Gleam in the sun, but 'tis a sun that sets!
Moscow! thou limit of his long career,
For which rude Charles had wept his
frozen tear 172
To see in vain—he saw thee—how? with
spire
And palace fuel to one common fire.
To this the soldier lent his kindling match,
To this the peasant gave his cottage
thatch, 176
To this the merchant flung his hoarded
store,
The prince his hall—and Moscow was no
more!
Sublimest of volcanos! Etna's flame
Pales before thine, and quenchless Hecla's
tame; 180
Vesuvius shows his blaze, an usual sight
For gaping tourists, from his hackney'd
height:
Thou stand'st alone unrivall'd, till the fire
To come, in which all empires shall expire!

Thou other element! as strong and stern,
To teach a lesson conquerors will not
learn!— 186
Whose icy wing flapp'd o'er the faltering foe,
Till fell a hero with each flake of snow;
How did thy numbing beak and silent fang
Pierce, till hosts perish'd with a single
pang! 190
In vain shall Seine look up along his banks
For the gay thousands of his dashing
ranks!
In vain shall France recall beneath her vines
Her youth—their blood flows faster than
her wines; 194
Or stagnant in their human ice remains
In frozen mummies on the Polar plains.
In vain will Italy's broad sun awaken
Her offspring chill'd; its beams are now
forsaken.
Of all the trophies gather'd from the war,
What shall return? the conqueror's broken
car! 200
The conqueror's yet unbroken heart!
Again
The horn of Roland sounds, and not in
vain.
Lutzen, where fell the Swede of victory,
Beholds him conquer, but, alas! not die:
Dresden surveys three despots fly once
more 205
Before their sovereign,—sovereign as be-
fore;
But there exhausted Fortune quits the
field,
And Leipsic's treason bids the unvan-
quish'd yield;

The Saxon jackal leaves the lion's side
To turn the bear's, and wolf's, and fox's
 guide; 210
And backward to the den of his despair
The forest monarch shrinks, but finds no
 lair!

Oh ye! and each, and all! Oh France!
 who found
Thy long fair fields plough'd up as hostile
 ground, 214
Disputed foot by foot, till treason, still
His only victor, from Montmartre's hill
Look'd down o'er trampled Paris! and
 thou Isle,
Which seest Etruria from thy ramparts
 smile,
Thou momentary shelter of his pride,
Till woo'd by danger, his yet weeping
 bride! 220
Oh, France! retaken by a single march,
Whose path was through one long tri-
 umphal arch!
Oh, bloody and most bootless Waterloo!
Which proves how fools may have their
 fortune too,
Won half by blunder, half by treachery:
Oh, dull Saint Helen! with thy gaoler
 nigh— 226
Hear! hear Prometheus from his rock
 appeal
To earth, air, ocean, all that felt or feel
His power and glory, all who yet shall hear
A name eternal as the rolling year; 230
He teaches them the lesson taught so long,
So oft, so vainly—learn to do no wrong!
A single step into the right had made
This man the Washington of worlds be-
 tray'd: 234
A single step into the wrong has given
His name a doubt to all the winds of
 heaven;
The reed of Fortune, and of thrones the
 rod,
Of Fame the Moloch or the demigod;
His country's Cæsar, Europe's Hannibal,
Without their decent dignity of fall. 240
Yet Vanity herself had better taught
A surer path even to the fame he sought,
By pointing out on history's fruitless page
Ten thousand conquerors for a single sage.
While Franklin's quiet memory climbs to
 heaven, 245
Calming the lightning which he thence hath
 riven,
Or drawing from the no less kindled earth
Freedom and peace to that which boasts
 his birth;
While Washington's a watchword, such
 as ne'er
Shall sink while there's an echo left to air:
While even the Spaniard's thirst of gold
 and war 251
Forgets Pizarro to shout Bolivar!

Alas! why must the same Atlantic wave
Which wafted freedom gird a tyrant's
 grave—
The king of kings, and yet of slaves the
 slave, 255
Who burst the chains of millions to re-
 new
The very fetters which his arm broke
 through,
And crush'd the rights of Europe and his
 own,
To flit between a dungeon and a throne?

VI

But 'twill not be—the spark's awaken'd—
 lo! 260
The swarthy Spaniard feels his former
 glow;
The same high spirit which beat back the
 Moor
Through eight long ages of alternate gore
Revives—and where? in that avenging
 clime
Where Spain was once synonymous with
 crime, 265
Where Cortes and Pizarro's banner flew,
The infant world redeems her name of
 'New.'
'Tis the old aspiration breathed afresh,
To kindle souls within degraded flesh,
Such as repulsed the Persian from the
 shore 270
Where Greece was—No! she still is Greece
 once more.
One common cause makes myriads of one
 breast,
Slaves of the East, or helots of the West:
On Andes' and on Athos' peaks un-
 furl'd,
The self-same standard streams o'er either
 world: 275
The Athenian wears again Harmodius'
 sword;
The Chili chief abjures his foreign lord;
The Spartan knows himself once more a
 Greek,
Young Freedom plumes the crest of each
 cacique;
Debating despots, hemm'd on either
 shore, 280
Shrink vainly from the roused Atlantic's
 roar;
Through Calpe's strait the rolling tides
 advance,
Sweep slightly by the half-tamed land of
 France,
Dash o'er the old Spaniard's cradle, and
 would fain
Unite Ausonia to the mighty main: 285
But driven from thence awhile, yet not for
 aye,
Break o'er th' Ægean, mindful of the day
Of Salamis!—there, there the waves arise,
Not to be lull'd by tyrant victories.

Lone, lost, abandon'd in their utmost
 need 290
By Christians, unto whom they gave their
 creed,
The desolated lands, the ravaged isle,
The foster'd feud encouraged to beguile,
The aid evaded, and the cold delay,
Prolong'd but in the hope to make a
 prey;— 295
These, these shall tell the tale, and Greece
 can show
The false friend worse than the infuriate
 foe.
But this is well: Greeks only should free
 Greece,
Not the barbarian, with his mask of peace.
How should the autocrat of bondage be
The king of serfs, and set the nations free?
Better still serve the haughty Mussulman,
Than swell the Cossaque's prowling
 caravan;
Better still toil for masters, than await,
The slave of slaves, before a Russian
 gate,— 305
Number'd by hordes, a human capital,
A live estate, existing but for thrall,
Lotted by thousands, as a meet reward
For the first courtier in the Czar's regard;
While their immediate owner never tastes
His sleep, *sans* dreaming of Siberia's
 wastes: 311
Better succumb even to their own despair,
And drive the camel than purvey the bear.

VII

But not alone within the hoariest clime
Where Freedom dates her birth with that
 of Time, 315
And not alone where, plunged in night, a
 crowd
Of Incas darken to a dubious cloud,
The dawn revives: renown'd, romantic
 Spain
Holds back the invader from her soil
 again.
Not now the Roman tribe nor Punic
 horde 320
Demand her fields as lists to prove the
 sword;
Not now the Vandal or the Visigoth
Pollute the plains, alike abhorring both;
Nor old Pelayo on his mountain rears
The warlike fathers of a thousand years.
That seed is sown and reap'd, as oft the
 Moor 326
Sighs to remember on his dusky shore.
Long in the peasant's song or poet's page
Has dwelt the memory of Abencerrage;
The Zegri, and the captive victors, flung
Back to the barbarous realm from whence
 they sprung. 331
But these are gone—their faith, their
 swords, their sway,
Yet left more anti-christian foes than they;

The bigot monarch, and the butcher priest,
The Inquisition, with her burning feast,
The faith's red 'auto,' fed with human
 fuel, 336
While sate the catholic Moloch, calmly
 cruel,
Enjoying, with inexorable eye,
That fiery festival of agony!
The stern or feeble sovereign, one or both
By turns; the haughtiness whose pride was
 sloth; 341
The long degenerate noble; the debased
Hidalgo, and the peasant less disgraced,
But more degraded; the unpeopled realm;
The once proud navy which forgot the
 helm; 345
The once impervious phalanx disarray'd;
The idle forge that form'd Toledo's blade;
The foreign wealth that flow'd on ev'ry
 shore,
Save hers who earn'd it with the natives'
 gore;
The very language which might vie with
 Rome's, 350
And once was known to nations like
 their homes,
Neglected or forgotten:—such was Spain;
But such she is not, nor shall be again.
These worst, these *home* invaders, felt and
 feel
The new Numantine soul of old Castile;
Up! up again! undaunted Tauridor! 356
The bull of Phalaris renews his roar;
Mount, chivalrous Hidalgo! not in vain
Revive the cry!—'Iago! and close Spain!'
Yes, close her with your armed bosoms
 round, 360
And form the barrier which Napoleon
 found,—
The exterminating war, the desert plain,
The streets without a tenant, save the slain;
The wild sierra, with its wilder troop
Of vulture-plumed guerrillas, on the stoop
For their incessant prey; the desperate
 wall 366
Of Saragossa, mightiest in her fall;
The man nerved to a spirit, and the maid
Waving her more than Amazonian blade;
The knife of Arragon, Toledo's steel; 370
The famous lance of chivalrous Castile;
The unerring rifle of the Catalan;
The Andalusian courser in the van;
The torch to make a Moscow of Madrid;
And in each heart the spirit of the Cid:—
Such have been, such shall be, such are.
 Advance, 376
And win—not Spain! but thine own free-
 dom, France!

VIII

But lo! a Congress! What! that hallow'd
 name
Which freed the Atlantic! May we hope
 the same

173

For outworn Europe? With the sound
arise, 380
Like Samuel's shade to Saul's monarchic
eyes,
The prophets of young Freedom, sum-
mon'd far
From climes of Washington and Bolivar;
Henry, the forest-born Demosthenes,
Whose thunder shook the Philip of the
seas; 385
And stoic Franklin's energetic shade,
Robed in the lightnings which his hand
allay'd;
And Washington, the tyrant-tamer, wake,
To bid us blush for these old chains, or
break.
But *who* compose this senate of the few
That should redeem the many? *Who*
renew 391
This consecrated name, till now assign'd
To councils held to benefit mankind?
Who now assemble at the holy call?
The blest Alliance, which says three are
all! 395
An earthly trinity! which wears the shape
Of heaven's, as man is mimick'd by the ape.
A pious unity! in purpose one—
To melt three fools to a Napoleon.
Why, Egypt's gods were rational to these;
Their dogs and oxen knew their own
degrees, 401
And, quiet in their kennel or their shed,
Cared little, so that they were duly fed;
But these, more hungry, must have some-
thing more—
The power to bark and bite, to toss and
gore. 405
Ah, how much happier were good Æsop's
frogs
Than we! for ours are animated logs,
With ponderous malice swaying to and fro,
And crushing nations with a stupid blow;
All duly anxious to leave little work 410
Unto the revolutionary stork.

IX

Thrice blest Verona! since the holy three
With their imperial presence shine on
thee!
Honour'd by them, thy treacherous site
forgets
The vaunted tomb of 'all the Capulets';
Thy Scaligers—for what was 'Dog the
Great,' 416
'Can Grande,' (which I venture to tran-
slate,)
To these sublimer pugs? Thy poet too,
Catullus, whose old laurels yield to new;
Thine amphitheatre, where Romans sate;
And Dante's exile shelter'd by thy gate;
Thy good old man, whose world was all
within
Thy wall, nor knew the country held him in;

Would that the royal guests it girds about
Were so far like, as never to get out! 425
Ay, shout! inscribe! rear monuments of
shame,
To tell Oppression that the world is tame!
Crowd to the theatre with loyal rage,
The comedy is not upon the stage;
The show is rich in ribandry and stars,
Then gaze upon it through thy dungeon
bars; 431
Clap thy permitted palms, kind Italy,
For thus much still thy fetter'd hands are
free!

X

Resplendent sight! Behold the coxcomb
Czar,
The autocrat of waltzes and of war! 435
As eager for a plaudit as a realm,
And just as fit for flirting as the helm;
A Calmuck beauty with a Cossack wit,
And generous spirit, when 'tis not frost-
bit;
Now half dissolving to a liberal thaw, 440
But harden'd back whene'er the morning's
raw;
With no objection to true liberty,
Except that it would make the nations
free.
How well the imperial dandy prates of
peace!
How fain, if Greeks would be his slaves,
free Greece! 445
How nobly gave he back the Poles their
Diet,
Then told pugnacious Poland to be quiet!
How kindly would he send the mild
Ukraine,
With all her pleasant Pulks, to lecture
Spain!
How royally show off in proud Madrid
His goodly person, from the South long
hid! 451
A blessing cheaply purchased, the world
knows,
By having Muscovites for friends or foes.
Proceed, thou namesake of great Philip's
son!
La Harpe, thine Aristotle, beckons on;
And that which Scythia was to him of
yore 456
Find with thy Scythians on Iberia's shore.
Yet think upon, thou somewhat aged
youth,
Thy predecessor on the banks of Pruth;
Thou hast to aid thee, should his lot be
thine, 460
Many an old woman, but no Catherine.
Spain, too, hath rocks, and rivers, and
defiles—
The bear may rush into the lion's toils.
Fatal to Goths are Xeres' sunny fields;
Think'st thou to thee Napoleon's victor
yields? 465

Better reclaim thy deserts, turn thy swords
To ploughshares, shave and wash thy
 Bashkir hordes,
Redeem thy realms from slavery and the
 knout,
Than follow headlong in the fatal route,
To infest the clime whose skies and laws
 are pure 470
With thy foul legions. Spain wants no
 manure:
Her soil is fertile, but she feeds no foe:
Her vultures, too, were gorged not long ago;
And wouldst thou furnish them with
 fresher prey? 474
Alas! thou wilt not conquer, but purvey.
I am Diogenes, though Russ and Hun
Stand between mine and many a myriad's
 sun;
But were I not Diogenes, I'd wander
Rather a worm than *such* an Alexander!
Be slaves who will, the cynic shall be
 free; 480
His tub hath tougher walls than Sinopè:
Still will he hold his lantern up to scan
The face of monarchs for an 'honest man.'

XI

And what doth Gaul, the all-prolific land
Of *ne plus ultra* ultras and their band
Of mercenaries? and her noisy chambers
And tribune, which each orator first
 clambers
Before he finds a voice, and when 'tis
 found,
Hears 'the lie' echo for his answer round?
Our British Commons sometimes deign to
 'hear!' 490
A Gallic senate hath more tongue than ear;
Even Constant, their sole master of debate,
Must fight next day his speech to vindicate.
But this costs little to true Franks, who'd
 rather 494
Combat than listen, were it to their father.
What is the simple standing of a shot,
To listening long, and interrupting not?
Though this was not the method of old
 Rome,
When Tully fulmined o'er each vocal
 dome,
Demosthenes has sanction'd the trans-
 action, 500
In saying eloquence meant 'Action,
 action!'

XII

But where's the monarch? hath he dined?
 or yet
Groans beneath indigestion's heavy debt?
Have revolutionary pâtés risen,
And turn'd the royal entrails to a prison?
Have discontented movements stirr'd the
 troops? 506
Or have *no* movements follow'd traitorous
 soups?

Have Carbonaro cooks not carbonadoed
Each course enough! or doctors dire dis-
 suaded 509
Repletion? Ah! in thy dejected looks
I read all France's treason in her cooks!
Good classic Louis! is it, canst thou say,
Desirable to be the 'Desiré'?
Why wouldst thou leave calm Hartwell's
 green abode,
Apician table, and Horatian ode, 515
To rule a people who will not be ruled,
And love much rather to be scourged than
 school'd?
Ah! thine was not the temper or the taste
For thrones; the table sees thee better
 placed:
A mild Epicurean, form'd, at best, 520
To be a kind host and as good a guest,
To talk of letters, and to know by heart
One *half* the poet's, *all* the gourmand's
 art:
A scholar always, now and then a wit,
And gentle when digestion may permit;—
But not to govern lands enslaved or free;
The gout was martyrdom enough for thee.

XIII

Shall noble Albion pass without a phrase
From a bold Briton in her wonted praise?
'Arts, arms, and George, and glory, and
 the isles, 530
And happy Britain, wealth, and Free-
 dom's smiles,
White cliffs, that held invasion far aloof,
Contented subjects, all alike tax-proof,
Proud Wellington, with eagle beak so
 curl'd,
That nose, the hook where he suspends
 the world! 535
And Waterloo, and trade, and——(hush!
 not yet
A syllable of imposts or of debt)——
And ne'er (enough) lamented Castlereagh,
Whose penknife slit a goose-quill t' other
 day——
And "pilots who have weather'd every
 storm"— 540
(But, no, not even for rhyme's sake, name
 Reform).'
These are the themes thus sung so oft
 before,
Methinks we need not sing them any more;
Found in so many volumes far and
 near,
There's no occasion you should find them
 here. 545
Yet something may remain perchance to
 chime
With reason, and what's stranger still,
 with rhyme.
Even this thy genius, Canning! may per-
 mit,
Who, bred a statesman, still wast born a
 wit,

175

And never, even in that dull House,
 couldst tame 550
To unleaven'd prose thine own poetic
 flame;
Our last, our best, our only orator,
Even I can praise thee—Tories do no
 more:
Nay, not so much;—they hate thee, man,
 because
Thy spirit less upholds them than it awes.
The hounds will gather to their huntsman's
 hollo, 556
And where he leads the duteous pack will
 follow;
But not for love mistake their yelling cry;
Their yelp for game is not an eulogy;
Less faithful far than the four-footed
 pack, 560
A dubious scent would lure the bipeds
 back,
Thy saddle-girths are not yet quite secure,
Nor royal stallion's feet extremely sure;
The unwieldy old white horse is apt at last
To stumble, kick, and now and then stick
 fast 565
With his great self and rider in the mud;
But what of that? the animal shows blood.

XIV

Alas, the country! how shall tongue or pen
Bewail her now *uncountry* gentlemen?
The last to bid the cry of warfare cease,
The first to make a malady of peace. 571
For what were all these country patriots
 born?
To hunt, and vote, and raise the price of
 corn?
But corn, like every mortal thing, must fall,
Kings, conquerors, and markets most of
 all. 575
And must ye fall with every ear of grain?
Why would you trouble Buonaparté's
 reign?
He was your great Triptolemus; his vices
Destroy'd but realms, and still maintain'd
 your prices; 579
He amplified to every lord's content
The grand agrarian alchymy, high *rent*.
Why did the tyrant stumble on the Tartars,
And lower wheat to such desponding
 quarters?
Why did you chain him on yon isle so lone?
The man was worth much more upon his
 throne. 585
True, blood and treasure boundlessly were
 spilt,
But what of that? the Gaul may bear the
 guilt;
But bread was high, the farmer paid his
 way,
And acres told upon the appointed day.
But where is now the goodly audit ale?
The purse-proud tenant, never known to
 fail? 591

The farm which never yet was left on
 hand?
The marsh reclaim'd to most improving
 land?
The impatient hope of the expiring lease
The doubling rental? What an evil's
 peace! 595
In vain the prize excites the ploughman's
 skill,
In vain the Commons pass their patriot
 bill;
The *landed interest*—(you may understand
The phrase much better leaving out the
 land)—
The land self-interest groans from shore to
 shore, 600
For fear that plenty should attain the poor
Up, up again, ye rents! exalt your notes,
Or else the ministry will lose their votes,
And patriotism, so delicately nice,
Her loaves will lower to the market price,
For ah! 'the loaves and fishes,' once so
 high, 606
Are gone—their oven closed, their ocean
 dry,
And nought remains of all the millions
 spent,
Excepting to grow moderate and content
They who are not so, *had* their turn—and
 turn 611
About still flows from Fortune's equal
 urn;
Now let their virtue be its own reward
And share the blessings which themselves
 prepared.
See these inglorious Cincinnati swarm,
Farmers of war, dictators of the farm;
Their ploughshare was the sword in hire-
 ling hands, 616
Their fields manured by gore of other
 lands;
Safe in their barns, these Sabine tillers sent
Their brethren out to battle—why? for
 rent!
Year after year they voted cent. per cent.
Blood, sweat, and tear-wrung millions—
 why? for rent! 621
They roar'd, they dined, they drank, they
 swore they meant
To die for England—why then live?—for
 rent!
The peace has made one general malcon-
 tent
Of these high-market patriots; war was
 rent! 625
Their love of country, millions all mis-
 spent,
How reconcile? by reconciling rent!
And will they not repay the treasures lent?
No: down with everything, and up with
 rent!
Their good, ill, health, wealth, joy, or dis-
 content, 630
Being, end, aim, religion—rent, rent, rent!

Thou sold'st thy birthright, Esau! for a mess;
Thou shouldst have gotten more, or eaten less;
Now thou hast swill'd thy pottage, thy demands
Are idle; Israel says the bargain stands.
Such, landlords! was your appetite for war, 636
And gorged with blood, you grumble at a scar!
What! would they spread their earthquake even o'er cash?
And when land crumbles, bid firm paper crash?
So rent may rise, bid bank and nation fall, 640
And found on 'Change a *Fundling* Hospital?
Lo, Mother Church, while all religion writhes,
Like Niobe, weeps o'er her offspring, Tithes;
The prelates go to—where the saints have gone, 644
And proud pluralities subside to one;
Church, state, and faction wrestle in the dark,
Toss'd by the deluge in their common ark.
Shorn of her bishops, banks, and dividends,
Another Babel soars—but Britain ends.
And why? to pamper the self-seeking wants, 650
And prop the hill of these agrarian ants.
'Go to these ants, thou sluggard, and be wise;'
Admire their patience through each sacrifice,
Till taught to feel the lesson of their pride,
The price of taxes and of homicide; 655
Admire their justice, which would fain deny
The debt of nations:—pray, *who made it high?*

XV

Or turn to sail between those shifting rocks,
The new Symplegades—the crushing Stocks,
Where Midas might again his wish behold 660
In real paper or imagined gold.
That magic palace of Alcina shows
More wealth than Britain ever had to lose,
Were all her atoms of unleaven'd ore,
And all her pebbles from Pactolus' shore.
There Fortune plays, while Rumour holds the stake, 666
And the world trembles to bid brokers break.
How rich is Britain! not indeed in mines,
Or peace or plenty, corn or oil, or wines;

No land of Canaan, full of milk and honey, 670
Nor (save in paper shekels) ready money:
But let us not to own the truth refuse,
Was ever Christian land so rich in Jews?
Those parted with their teeth to good King John,
And now, ye kings! they kindly draw your own; 675
All states, all things, all sovereigns they control,
And waft a loan 'from Indus to the pole.'
The banker, broker, baron, brethren, speed
To aid these bankrupt tyrants in their need.
Nor these alone; Columbia feels no less
Fresh speculations follow each success;
And philanthropic Israel deigns to drain
Her mild per-centage from exhausted Spain.
Not without Abraham's seed can Russia march;
'Tis gold, not steel, that rears the conqueror's arch. 685
Two Jews, a chosen people, can command
In every realm their scripture-promised land:—
Two Jews keep down the Romans, and uphold
The accursed Hun, more brutal than of old: 689
Two Jews—but not Samaritans—direct
The world, with all the spirit of their sect.
What is the happiness of earth to them?
A congress forms their 'New Jerusalem,'
Where baronies and orders both invite—
Oh, holy Abraham! dost thou see the sight? 695
Thy followers mingling with these royal swine,
Who spit not 'on their Jewish gaberdine,'
But honour them as portion of the show—
(Where now, oh Pope! is thy forsaken toe?
Could it not favour Judah with some kicks? 700
Or has it ceased to 'kick against the pricks?')
On Shylock's shore behold them stand afresh,
To cut from nations' hearts their 'pound of flesh.'

XVI

Strange sight this Congress! destined to unite 704
All that's incongruous, all that's opposite.
I speak not of the sovereigns—they're alike,
A common coin as ever mint could strike;
But those who sway the puppets, pull the strings,
Have more of motley than their heavy kings.

Jews, authors, generals, charlatans, com-
 bine, 710
While Europe wonders at the vast design:
There Metternich, power's foremost para-
 site,
Cajoles; there Wellington forgets to fight;
There Chateaubriand forms new books of
 martyrs;
And subtle Greeks intrigue for stupid
 Tartars; 715
There Montmorenci, the sworn foe to
 charters,
Turns a diplomatist of great éclat,
To furnish articles for the 'Débats;'
Of war so certain—yet not quite so sure
As his dismissal in the 'Moniteur.' 720
Alas! how could his cabinet thus err!
Can peace be worth an ultra-minister?
He falls indeed, perhaps to rise again,
'Almost as quickly as he conquer'd Spain.'

XVII

Enough of this—a sight more mournful
 woos 725
The averted eye of the reluctant muse.
The imperial daughter, the imperial bride,
The imperial victim—sacrifice to pride;
The mother of the hero's hope, the boy,
The young Astyanax of modern Troy; 730
The still pale shadow of the loftiest queen
That earth has yet to see, or e'er hath seen;
She flits amidst the phantoms of the hour,
The theme of pity, and the wreck of power.
Oh, cruel mockery! Could not Austria
 spare 735
A daughter? What did France's widow
 there?
Her fitter place was by St. Helen's wave,
Her only throne is in Napoleon's grave.
But, no—she still must hold a petty reign,
Flank'd by her formidable chamberlain;
The martial Argus, whose not hundred
 eyes 741
Must watch her through these paltry page-
 antries.
What though she share no more, and
 shared in vain,
A sway surpassing that of Charlemagne,
Which swept from Moscow to the south-
 ern seas! 745
Yet still she rules the pastoral realm of
 cheese,

Where Parma views the traveller resort,
To note the trappings of her mimic court
But she appears! Verona sees her shorn
Of all her beams—while nations gaze and
 mourn— 750
Ere yet her husband's ashes have had time
To chill in their inhospitable clime;
(If e'er those awful ashes can grow cold;—
But no,—their embers soon will burst the
 mould;)
She comes!—the Andromache (but no
 Racine's, 755
Nor Homer's,)—Lo! on Pyrrhus' arm she
 leans!
Yes! the right arm, yet red from Water
 loo,
Which cut her lord's half-shatter'd sceptre
 through,
Is offer'd and accepted? Could a slave
Do more? or less?—and he in his new
 grave! 760
Her eye, her cheek, betray no inward
 strife,
And the ex-empress grows as ex a wife!
So much for human ties in royal breasts
Why spare men's feelings, when their own
 are jests?

XVIII

But, tired of foreign follies, I turn home
And sketch the group—the picture's yet
 to come, 766
My muse 'gan weep, but, ere a tear was
 spilt,
She caught Sir William Curtis in a kilt!
While throng'd the chiefs of every High-
 land clan
To hail their brother, Vich Ian Alder
 man! 770
Guildhall grows Gael, and echoes with
 Erse roar,
While all the Common Council cry 'Clay
 more!'
To see proud Albyn's tartans as a belt
Gird the gross sirloin of a city Celt,
She burst into a laughter so extreme, 775
That I awoke—and lo! it was no dream!

Here, reader, will we pause:—if there's no
 harm in
This first—you'll have, perhaps, a second
 'Carmen.'

CHILDE HAROLD'S PILGRIMAGE

A ROMAUNT

L'UNIVERS est une espèce de livre, dont on n'a lu que la première page quand on n'a vu que son pays. J'en ai feuilleté un assez grand nombre, que j'ai trouvé également mauvaises. Cet examen ne m'a point été infructueux. Je haïssais ma patrie. Toutes les impertinences des peuples divers, parmi lesquels j'ai vécu, m'ont réconcilié avec elle. Quand je n'aurais tiré d'autre bénéfice de mes voyages que celui-là, je n'en regretterais ni les frais ni les fatigues.—LE COSMOPOLITE.

PREFACE TO THE FIRST AND SECOND CANTOS

THE following poem was written, for the most part, amidst the scenes which it attempts to describe. It was begun in Albania; and the parts relative to Spain and Portugal were composed from the author's observations in those countries. Thus much it may be necessary to state for the correctness of the descriptions. The scenes attempted to be sketched are in Spain, Portugal, Epirus, Acarnania, and Greece. There, for the present, the poem stops; its reception will determine whether the author may venture to conduct his readers to the capital of the East, through Ionia and Phrygia: these two cantos are merely experimental.

A fictitious character is introduced for the sake of giving some connexion to the piece; which, however, makes no pretension to regularity. It has been suggested to me by friends, on whose opinions I set a high value, that in this fictitious character, 'Childe Harold,' I may incur the suspicion of having intended some real personage: this I beg leave, once for all, to disclaim—Harold is the child of imagination, for the purpose I have stated. In some very trivial particulars, and those merely local, there might be grounds for such a notion; but in the main points, I should hope, none whatever.

It is almost superfluous to mention that the appellation 'Childe,' as 'Childe Waters,' 'Childe Childers,' &c., is used as more consonant with the old structure of versification which I have adopted. The 'Good Night,' in the beginning of the first canto, was suggested by 'Lord Maxwell's Good Night,' in the Border Minstrelsy, edited by Mr. Scott.

With the different poems which have been published on Spanish subjects, there may be found some slight coincidence in the first part, which treats of the Peninsula, but it can only be casual; as, with the exception of a few concluding stanzas, the whole of this poem was written in the Levant.

The stanza of Spenser, according to one of our most successful poets, admits of every variety. Dr. Beattie makes the following observation:—'Not long ago, I began a poem in the style and stanza of Spenser, in which I propose to give full scope to my inclination, and be either droll or pathetic, descriptive or sentimental, tender or satirical, as the humour strikes me; for, if I mistake not, the measure which I have adopted admits equally of all these kinds of composition'.*—Strengthened in my opinion by such authority, and by the example of some in the highest order of Italian poets, I shall make no apology for attempts at similar variations in the following composition; satisfied that if they are unsuccessful, their failure must be in the execution, rather than in the design, sanctioned by the practice of Ariosto, Thomson, and Beattie.

LONDON, *February*, 1812.

ADDITION TO THE PREFACE

I HAVE now waited till almost all our periodical journals have distributed their usual portion of criticism. To the justice of the generality of their criticisms I have nothing to object: it would ill become me to quarrel with their very slight degree of censure, when, perhaps, if they had been less kind they had been more candid. Returning, therefore, to all and each my best thanks for their liberality, on one point alone shall I venture an observation. Amongst the many objections justly urged to the very indifferent character of the 'vagrant Childe' (whom, notwithstanding many hints to the contrary, I still maintain to be a fictitious personage), it has been stated, that, besides the anachronism, he is very *unknightly*, as the times of the Knights were times of Love, Honour, and so forth. Now, it so happens that the good old times, when 'l'amour du bon vieux tems, l'amour antique,' flourished, were the most profligate of all possible centuries. Those who have any doubts on this subject may consult Sainte-Palaye, *passim*, and more particularly vol. ii. p. 69. The vows of chivalry were no better kept than any other vows whatsoever; and the songs of the Troubadours were not more decent, and certainly much less refined, than those of Ovid. The 'Cours d'amour, parlemens d'amour, ou de courtesie et de gentilesse' had much more of love than of courtesy or gentleness. See Rolland on the same subject with Sainte-Palaye. Whatever other objection may be urged to that most unamiable personage Childe Harold, he was so far perfectly knightly in his attributes—'No waiter, but a knight templar†.' By the by, I fear that Sir Tristrem and Sir Lancelot were no better than they should be, although very poetical personages and true knights 'sans peur,' though not 'sans reproche.' If the story of the institution of the 'Garter' be not a fable, the knights of that order have for several centuries borne the badge of a Countess of Salisbury, of indifferent memory. So much for chivalry. Burke need not have regretted that its days are over, though Marie-Antoinette was quite as chaste as most of those in whose honour lances were shivered, and knights unhorsed.

Before the days of Bayard, and down to those of Sir Joseph Banks (the most chaste and celebrated of ancient and modern times), few exceptions will be found to this statement; and I fear a little investigation will teach us not to regret these monstrous mummeries of the middle ages.

I now leave 'Childe Harold' to live his day, such as he is; it had been more agreeable, and certainly

* Beattie's Letters.　　　　　　　　　　† The Rovers, or the Double Arrangement.

179

more easy, to have drawn an amiable character. It had been easy to varnish over his faults, to make
him do more and express less, but he never was intended as an example, further than to show, that
early perversion of mind and morals leads to satiety of past pleasures and disappointment in new ones,
and that even the beauties of nature and the stimulus of travel (except ambition, the most powerful
of all excitements) are lost on a soul so constituted, or rather misdirected. Had I proceeded with the
poem, this character would have deepened as he drew to the close; for the outline which I once meant
to fill up for him was, with some exceptions, the sketch of a modern Timon, perhaps a poetical Zelucco

LONDON, 1813.

TO IANTHE

NOT in those climes where I have late
 been straying,
Though Beauty long hath there been
 matchless deem'd;
Not in those visions to the heart dis-
 playing
Forms which it sighs but to have only
 dream'd,
Hath aught like thee in truth or fancy
 seem'd: 5
Nor, having seen thee, shall I vainly seek
To paint those charms which varied as
 they beam'd—
To such as see thee not my words were
 weak;
To those who gaze on thee what language
 could they speak?

Ah! may'st thou ever be what now thou
 art, 10
Nor unbeseem the promise of thy spring,
As fair in form, as warm yet pure in
 heart,
Love's image upon earth without his
 wing,
And guileless beyond Hope's imagining!
And surely she who now so fondly rears
Thy youth, in thee, thus hourly bright-
 ening, 16
Beholds the rainbow of her future years,
Before whose heavenly hues all sorrow
 disappears.

Young Peri of the West!—'tis well for me
My years already doubly number thine;
My loveless eye unmoved may gaze on
 thee, 21
And safely view thy ripening beauties
 shine;

Happy, I ne'er shall see them in decline;
Happier, that while all younger hearts
 shall bleed,
Mine shall escape the doom thine eyes
 assign 2
To those whose admiration shall succeed,
But mix'd with pangs to Love's even love-
 liest hours decreed.

Oh! let that eye, which, wild as the
 Gazelle's,
Now brightly bold or beautifully shy,
Wins as it wanders, dazzles where it
 dwells, 3
Glance o'er this page, nor to my verse
 deny
That smile for which my breast might
 vainly sigh
Could I to thee be ever more than friend:
This much, dear maid, accord; nor
 question why
To one so young my strain I would
 commend, 3
But bid me with my wreath one matchless
 lily blend.

Such is thy name with this my verse
 entwined;
And long as kinder eyes a look shall cast
On Harold's page, Ianthe's here en-
 shrined
Shall thus be first beheld, forgotten last:
My days once number'd, should this
 homage past 4
Attract thy fairy fingers near the lyre
Of him who hail'd thee loveliest, as
 thou wast,
Such is the most my memory may de-
 sire;
Though more than Hope can claim, could
 Friendship less require? 4

CHILDE HAROLD'S PILGRIMAGE

CANTO THE FIRST

I

OH, thou! in Hellas deem'd of heavenly
 birth,
Muse! form'd or fabled at the minstrel's
 will!
Since shamed full oft by later lyres on
 earth,
Mine dares not call thee from thy sacred
 hill:

Yet there I've wander'd by thy vaunted
 rill;
Yes! sigh'd o'er Delphi's long deserted
 shrine,
Where, save that feeble fountain, all is
 still;
Nor mote my shell awake the weary
 Nine
To grace so plain a tale—this lowly lay of
 mine.

II

Whilome in Albion's isle there dwelt a
 youth,
Who ne in virtue's ways did take de-
 light;
But spent his days in riot most uncouth,
And vex'd with mirth the drowsy ear of
 Night.
Ah me! in sooth he was a shameless
 wight,
Sore given to revel and ungodly glee;
Few earthly things found favour in his
 sight
Save concubines and carnal companie,
And flaunting wassailers of high and low
 degree.

III

Childe Harold was he hight:—but
 whence his name
And lineage long, it suits me not to say;
Suffice it, that perchance they were of
 fame,
And had been glorious in another day:
But one sad losel soils a name for aye,
However mighty in the olden time;
Nor all that heralds rake from coffin'd
 clay,
Nor florid prose, nor honeyed lies of
 rhyme,
Can blazon evil deeds, or consecrate a
 crime.

IV

Childe Harold bask'd him in the noon-
 tide sun,
Disporting there like any other fly;
Nor deem'd before his little day was
 done
One blast might chill him into misery.
But long ere scarce a third of his pass'd
 by,
Worse than adversity the Childe befell;
He felt the fulness of satiety:
Then loathed he in his native land to
 dwell,
Which seem'd to him more lone than
 Eremite's sad cell.

V

For he through Sin's long labyrinth had
 run,
Nor made atonement when he did
 amiss,
Had sigh'd to many though he loved but
 one,
And that loved one, alas! could ne'er
 be his.
Ah, happy she! to 'scape from him
 whose kiss
Had been pollution unto aught so chaste;
Who soon had left her charms for
 vulgar bliss,
And spoil'd her goodly lands to gild his
 waste,
Nor calm domestic peace had ever deign'd
 to taste.

VI

And now Childe Harold was sore sick
 at heart,
And from his fellow bacchanals would
 flee;
'Tis said, at times the sullen tear would
 start,
But Pride congeal'd the drop within his ee:
Apart he stalk'd in joyless reverie,
And from his native land resolved to go,
And visit scorching climes beyond the
 sea;
With pleasure drugg'd, he almost long'd
 for woe,
And e'en for change of scene would seek
 the shades below.

VII

The Childe departed from his father's
 hall:
It was a vast and venerable pile;
So old, it seemèd only not to fall,
Yet strength was pillar'd in each massy
 aisle.
Monastic dome! condemn'd to uses vile!
Where Superstition once had made her
 den
Now Paphian girls were known to sing
 and smile;
And monks might deem their time was
 come agen,
If ancient tales say true, nor wrong these
 holy men.

VIII

Yet oft-times in his maddest mirthful
 mood
Strange pangs would flash along Childe
 Harold's brow
As if the memory of some deadly feud
Or disappointed passion lurk'd below:
But this none knew, nor haply cared to
 know;
For his was not that open, artless soul
That feels relief by bidding sorrow flow,
Nor sought he friend to counsel or
 condole,
Whate'er this grief mote be, which he
 could not control.

IX

And none did love him: though to hall
 and bower
He gather'd revellers from far and near,
He knew them flatt'rers of the festa
 hour;
The heartless parasites of present cheer.

Yea! none did love him—not his lemans
 dear—
But pomp and power alone are woman's
 care,
And where these are light Eros finds a
 feere;
Maidens, like moths, are ever caught by
 glare,
And Mammon wins his way where
 Seraphs might despair.

X

Childe Harold had a mother—not for-
 got,
Though parting from that mother he
 did shun;
A sister whom he loved, but saw her not
Before his weary pilgrimage begun:
If friends he had, he bade adieu to
 none.
Yet deem not thence his breast a breast
 of steel:
Ye, who have known what 'tis to dote
 upon
A few dear objects, will in sadness feel
Such partings break the heart they fondly
 hope to heal.

XI

His house, his home, his heritage, his
 lands,
The laughing dames in whom he did
 delight,
Whose large blue eyes, fair locks, and
 snowy hands,
Might shake the saintship of an an-
 chorite,
And long had fed his youthful appetite;
His goblets brimm'd with every costly
 wine,
And all that mote to luxury invite,
Without a sigh he left, to cross the
 brine,
And traverse Paynim shores, and pass
 Earth's central line.

XII

The sails were fill'd, and fair the light
 winds blew,
As glad to waft him from his native
 home;
And fast the white rocks faded from his
 view,
And soon were lost in circumambient
 foam:
And then, it may be, of his wish to roam
Repented he, but in his bosom slept
The silent thought, nor from his lips did
 come
One word of wail, whilst others sate and
 wept,
And to the reckless gales unmanly moan-
 ing kept.

XIII

But when the sun was sinking in the sea
He seized his harp, which he at times
 could string,
And strike, albeit with untaught melody,
When deem'd he no strange ear was
 listening:
And now his fingers o'er it he did fling
And tuned his farewell in the dim
 twilight.
While flew the vessel on her snowy wing,
And fleeting shores receded from his
 sight,
Thus to the elements he pour'd his last
 'Good Night.'

1

ADIEU, adieu! my native shore
 Fades o'er the waters blue;
The night-winds sigh, the breakers roar,
 And shrieks the wild sea-mew.
Yon sun that sets upon the sea
 We follow in his flight;
Farewell awhile to him and thee,
 My native Land—Good Night!

2

A few short hours and he will rise
 To give the morrow birth;
And I shall hail the main and skies,
 But not my mother earth.
Deserted is my own good hall,
 Its hearth is desolate;
Wild weeds are gathering on the wall,
 My dog howls at the gate.

3

'Come hither, hither, my little page!
 Why dost thou weep and wail?
Or dost thou dread the billows' rage,
 Or tremble at the gale?
But dash the tear-drop from thine eye
 Our ship is swift and strong;
Our fleetest falcon scarce can fly
 More merrily along.'

4

'Let winds be shrill, let waves roll high,
 I fear not wave nor wind:
Yet marvel not, Sir Childe, that I
 Am sorrowful in mind;
For I have from my father gone,
 A mother whom I love,
And have no friend, save these alone,
 But thee—and one above.

5

'My father bless'd me fervently,
 Yet did not much complain;
But sorely will my mother sigh
 Till I come back again.'—
'Enough, enough, my little lad!
 Such tears become thine eye;
If I thy guileless bosom had,
 Mine own would not be dry.

6

'Come hither, hither, my staunch yeoman,
 Why dost thou look so pale?
Or dost thou dread a French foeman?
 Or shiver at the gale?'—
'Deem'st thou I tremble for my life?
 Sir Childe, I'm not so weak;
But thinking on an absent wife
 Will blanch a faithful cheek.

7

'My spouse and boys dwell near thy hall,
 Along the bordering lake,
And when they on their father call,
 What answer shall she make?'—
'Enough, enough, my yeoman good,
 Thy grief let none gainsay;
But I, who am of lighter mood,
 Will laugh to flee away.'

8

'or who would trust the seeming sighs
 Of wife or paramour?
'resh feeres will dry the bright blue eyes
 We late saw streaming o'er.
'or pleasures past I do not grieve,
 Nor perils gathering near;
My greatest grief is that I leave
 No thing that claims a tear.

9

And now I'm in the world alone,
 Upon the wide, wide sea:
But why should I for others groan,
 When none will sigh for me?
'erchance my dog will whine in vain,
 Till fed by stranger hands;
But long ere I come back again
 He'd tear me where he stands.

10

With thee, my bark, I'll swiftly go
 Athwart the foaming brine;
Nor care what land thou bear'st me to,
 So not again to mine.
Welcome, welcome, ye dark-blue waves!
 And when you fail my sight,
Welcome, ye deserts and ye caves!
 My native Land—Good Night!

XIV

On, on the vessel flies, the land is gone,
And winds are rude in Biscay's sleepless
 bay.
Four days are sped, but with the fifth,
 anon,
New shores descried make every bosom
 gay;
And Cintra's mountain greets them on
 their way,
And Tagus dashing onward to the deep,
His fabled golden tribute bent to pay;

And soon on board the Lusian pilots
 leap,
And steer 'twixt fertile shores where yet
 few rustics reap.

XV

Oh, Christ! it is a goodly sight to see
What Heaven hath done for this de-
 licious land!
What fruits of fragrance blush on every
 tree!
What goodly prospects o'er the hills
 expand!
But man would mar them with an im-
 pious hand:
And when the Almighty lifts his fiercest
 scourge
'Gainst those who most transgress his
 high command,
With treble vengeance will his hot
 shafts urge
Gaul's locust host, and earth from fellest
 foemen purge.

XVI

What beauties doth Lisboa first unfold!
Her image floating on that noble tide,
Which poets vainly pave with sands of
 gold,
But now whereon a thousand keels did
 ride
Of mighty strength, since Albion was
 allied,
And to the Lusians did her aid afford:
A nation swoln with ignorance and
 pride,
Who lick yet loathe the hand that waves
 the sword
To save them from the wrath of Gaul's
 unsparing lord.

XVII

But whoso entereth within this town,
That, sheening far, celestial seems to be,
Disconsolate will wander up and down,
'Mid many things unsightly to strange
 ee;
For hut and palace show like filthily:
The dingy denizens are rear'd in dirt;
Ne personage of high or mean degree
Doth care for cleanness of surtout or
 shirt;
Though shent with Egypt's plague, un-
 kempt, unwash'd, unhurt.

XVIII

Poor, paltry slaves! yet born 'midst
 noblest scenes—
Why, Nature, waste thy wonders on
 such men?
Lo! Cintra's glorious Eden intervenes
In variegated maze of mount and glen.

Ah me! what hand can pencil guide, or
 pen,
To follow half on which the eye dilates
Through views more dazzling unto
 mortal ken
Than those whereof such things the bard
 relates,
Who to the awe-struck world unlock'd
 Elysium's gates?

XIX

The horrid crags, by toppling convent
 crown'd,
The cork-trees hoar that clothe the
 shaggy steep,
The mountain-moss by scorching skies
 imbrown'd,
The sunken glen, whose sunless shrubs
 must weep,
The tender azure of the unruffled deep,
The orange tints that gild the greenest
 bough,
The torrents that from cliff to valley leap,
The vine on high, the willow branch
 below,
Mix'd in one mighty scene, with varied
 beauty glow.

XX

Then slowly climb the many-winding
 way,
And frequent turn to linger as you go,
From loftier rocks new loveliness survey,
And rest ye at 'Our Lady's house of
 woe;'
Where frugal monks their little relics
 show,
And sundry legends to the stranger tell:
Here impious men have punish'd been,
 and lo!
Deep in yon cave Honorius long did
 dwell,
In hope to merit Heaven by making earth
 a Hell.

XXI

And here and there, as up the crags you
 spring,
Mark many rude-carved crosses near
 the path:
Yet deem not these devotion's offer-
 ing—
These are memorials frail of murderous
 wrath:
For wheresoe'er the shrieking victim
 hath
Pour'd forth his blood beneath the
 assassin's knife,
Some hand erects a cross of mouldering
 lath;
And grove and glen with thousand such
 are rife
Throughout this purple land, where law
 secures not life.

XXII

On sloping mounds, or in the vale be-
 neath,
Are domes where whilome kings did
 make repair;
But now the wild flowers round them
 only breathe;
Yet ruin'd splendour still is lingering
 there.
And yonder towers the Prince's palace
 fair:
There thou too, Vathek! England's
 wealthiest son,
Once form'd thy Paradise, as not aware
When wanton Wealth her mightiest
 deeds hath done,
Meek Peace voluptuous lures was ever
 wont to shun.

XXIII

Here didst thou dwell, here schemes of
 pleasure plan,
Beneath yon mountain's ever beauteous
 brow:
But now, as if a thing unblest by
 Man,
Thy fairy dwelling is as lone as thou!
Here giant weeds a passage scarce allow
To halls deserted, portals gaping wide:
Fresh lessons to the thinking bosom,
 how
Vain are the pleasaunces on earth sup-
 plied;
Swept into wrecks anon by Time's un-
 gentle tide!

XXIV

Behold the hall where chiefs were late
 convened!
Oh! dome displeasing unto British
 eye!
With diadem hight foolscap, lo! a fiend,
A little fiend that scoffs incessantly,
There sits in parchment robe array'd,
 and by
His side is hung a seal and sable scroll,
Where blazon'd glare names known to
 chivalry,
And sundry signatures adorn the roll,
Whereat the Urchin points and laughs
 with all his soul.

XXV

Convention is the dwarfish demon
 styled
That foil'd the knights in Marialva's
 dome:
Of brains (if brains they had) he them
 beguiled,
And turned a nation's shallow joy to
 gloom.
Here Folly dash'd to earth the victor's
 plume,

And Policy regain'd what arms had lost:
For chiefs like ours in vain may laurels
 bloom!
Woe to the conqu'ring, not the con-
 quer'd host,
Since baffled Triumph droops on Lusi-
 tania's coast!

XXVI

And ever since that martial synod met,
Britannia sickens, Cintra! at thy name;
And folks in office at the mention fret,
And fain would blush, if blush they
 could, for shame.
How will posterity the deed proclaim!
Will not our own and fellow nations sneer,
To view these champions cheated of
 their fame,
By foes in fight o'erthrown, yet victors
 here,
Where Scorn her finger points through
 many a coming year?

XXVII

So deem'd the Childe, as o'er the moun-
 tains he
Did take his way in solitary guise:
Sweet was the scene, yet soon he thought
 to flee,
More restless than the swallow in the
 skies:
Though here awhile he learn'd to mora-
 lize,
For Meditation fix'd at times on him;
And conscious Reason whisper'd to
 despise
His early youth, misspent in maddest
 whim;
But as he gazed on truth his aching eyes
 grew dim.

XXVIII

To horse! to horse! he quits, for ever
 quits
A scene of peace, though soothing to
 his soul:
Again he rouses from his moping fits,
But seeks not now the harlot and the
 bowl.
Onward he flies, nor fix'd as yet the goal
Where he shall rest him on his pilgrim-
 age;
And o'er him many changing scenes
 must roll
Ere toil his thirst for travel can assuage,
Or he shall calm his breast, or learn ex-
 perience sage.

XXIX

Yet Mafra shall one moment claim delay,
Where dwelt of yore the Lusians' luck-
 less queen;
And church and court did mingle their
 array,
And mass and revel were alternate seen;

Lordlings and freres—ill-sorted fry I
 ween!
But here the Babylonian whore hath
 built
A dome, where flaunts she in such
 glorious sheen,
That men forget the blood which she
 hath spilt,
And bow the knee to Pomp that loves to
 varnish guilt.

XXX

O'er vales that teem with fruits, roman-
 tic hills,
(Oh, that such hills upheld a free-born
 race!)
Whereon to gaze the eye with joyaunce
 fills,
Childe Harold wends through many a
 pleasant place.
Though sluggards deem it but a foolish
 chase,
And marvel men should quit their easy
 chair,
The toilsome way, and long, long
 league to trace,
Oh! there is sweetness in the mountain
 air,
And life, that bloated Ease can never hope
 to share.

XXXI

More bleak to view the hills at length
 recede,
And, less luxuriant, smoother vales ex-
 tend;
Immense horizon-bounded plains succeed!
Far as the eye discerns, withouten end,
Spain's realms appear whereon her
 shepherds tend
Flocks, whose rich fleece right well the
 trader knows—
Now must the pastor's arm his lambs
 defend:
For Spain is compass'd by unyielding
 foes,
And all must shield their all, or share Sub-
 jection's woes.

XXXII

Where Lusitania and her Sister meet,
Deem ye what bounds the rival realms
 divide?
Or ere the jealous queens of nations
 greet,
Doth Tayo interpose his mighty tide?
Or dark Sierras rise in craggy pride?
Or fence of art, like China's vasty
 wall?—
Ne barrier wall, ne river deep and wide,
Ne horrid crags, nor mountains dark
 and tall,
Rise like the rocks that part Hispania's
 land from Gaul:

XXXIII

But these between a silver streamlet
glides,
And scarce a name distinguisheth the
brook,
Though rival kingdoms press its verdant
sides.
Here leans the idle shepherd on his
crook,
And vacant on the rippling waves doth
look,
That peaceful still 'twixt bitterest foe-
men flow;
For proud each peasant as the noblest
duke:
Well doth the Spanish hind the differ-
ence know
'Twixt him and Lusian slave, the lowest of
the low.

XXXIV

But ere the mingling bounds have far
been pass'd,
Dark Guadiana rolls his power along
In sullen billows, murmuring and vast,
So noted ancient roundelays among.
Whilome upon his banks did legions
throng
Of Moor and Knight, in mailèd splen-
dour drest:
Here ceased the swift their race, here
sunk the strong;
The Paynim turban and the Christian crest
Mix'd on the bleeding stream, by floating
hosts oppress'd.

XXXV

Oh, lovely Spain! renown'd, romantic
land!
Where is that standard which Pelagio
bore,
When Cava's traitor-sire first call'd the
band
That dyed thy mountain streams with
Gothic gore?
Where are those bloody banners which
of yore
Waved o'er thy sons, victorious to the
gale,
And drove at last the spoilers to their
shore?
Red gleam'd the cross, and waned the
crescent pale,
While Afric's echoes thrill'd with Moorish
matrons' wail.

XXXVI

Teems not each ditty with the glorious
tale?
Ah! such, alas! the hero's amplest fate!
When granite moulders and when
records fail,
A peasant's plaint prolongs his dubious
date.

Pride! bend thine eye from heaven t
thine estate,
See how the Mighty shrink into a song
Can Volume, Pillar, Pile preserve the
great?
Or must thou trust Tradition's simpl
tongue,
When Flattery sleeps with thee, and Hi
tory does thee wrong?

XXXVII

Awake, ye sons of Spain! awake! ad
vance!
Lo! Chivalry, your ancient goddess
cries,
But wields not, as of old, her thirsty lanc
Nor shakes her crimson plumage in th
skies:
Now on the smoke of blazing bolts sh
flies,
And speaks in thunder through yon er
gine's roar:
In every peal she calls—'Awake! arise'
Say, is her voice more feeble than o
yore,
When her war-song was heard on Anda
lusia's shore?

XXXVIII

Hark! heard you not those hoofs o
dreadful note?
Sounds not the clang of conflict on th
heath?
Saw ye not whom the reeking sabr
smote,
Nor saved your brethren ere they san
beneath
Tyrants and tyrants' slaves? the fires o
death,
The bale-fires flash on high:—from roc
to rock
Each volley tells that thousands ceas
to breathe;
Death rides upon the sulphury Siroc,
Red Battle stamps his foot, and nation
feel the shock.

XXXIX

Lo! where the Giant on the mountai
stands,
His blood-red tresses deep'ning in th
sun,
With death-shot glowing in his fier
hands,
And eye that scorcheth all it glare
upon;
Restless it rolls, now fix'd, and now ano
Flashing afar,—and at his iron feet
Destruction cowers, to mark what deed
are done;
For on this morn three potent nation
meet,
To shed before his shrine the blood h
deems most sweet.

XL

By Heaven! it is a splendid sight to see
(For one who hath no friend, no brother
 there)
Their rival scarfs of mix'd embroidery,
Their various arms that glitter in the air!
What gallant war-hounds rouse them
 from their lair,
And gnash their fangs, loud yelling for
 the prey!
All join the chase, but few the triumph
 share;
The Grave shall bear the chiefest prize
 away,
And Havoc scarce for joy can number
 their array.

XLI

Three hosts combine to offer sacrifice;
Three tongues prefer strange orisons
 on high;
Three gaudy standards flout the pale
 blue skies;
The shouts are France, Spain, Albion,
 Victory!
The foe, the victim, and the fond ally
That fights for all, but ever fights in vain,
Are met—as if at home they could not
 die—
To feed the crow on Talavera's plain,
And fertilize the field that each pretends
 to gain.

XLII

There shall they rot—Ambition's hon-
 our'd fools!
Yes, Honour decks the turf that wraps
 their clay!
Vain Sophistry! in these behold the
 tools,
The broken tools, that tyrants cast away
By myriads, when they dare to pave their
 way
With human hearts—to what?—a
 dream alone.
Can despots compass aught that hails
 their sway?
Or call with truth one span of earth their
 own,
Save that wherein at last they crumble
 bone by bone?

XLIII

Oh, Albuera! glorious field of grief!
As o'er thy plain the Pilgrim prick'd his
 steed,
Who could foresee thee, in a space so
 brief,
A scene where mingling foes should
 boast and bleed!
Peace to the perish'd! may the warrior's
 meed
And tears of triumph their reward pro-
 long!

Till others fall where other chieftains
 lead
Thy name shall circle round the gaping
 throng,
And shine in worthless lays the theme of
 transient song.

XLIV

Enough of battle's minions! let them
 play
Their game of lives, and barter breath
 for fame:
Fame that will scarce reanimate their
 clay,
Though thousands fall to deck some
 single name.
In sooth 'twere sad to thwart their noble
 aim
Who strike, blest hirelings! for their
 country's good,
And die, that living might have proved
 her shame;
Perish'd, perchance, in some domestic
 feud,
Or in a narrower sphere wild Rapine's
 path pursued.

XLV

Full swiftly Harold wends his lonely
 way
Where proud Sevilla triumphs unsub-
 dued:
Yet is she free—the spoiler's wish'd-for
 prey!
Soon, soon shall Conquest's fiery foot
 intrude,
Blackening her lovely domes with traces
 rude.
Inevitable hour! 'Gainst fate to strive
Where Desolation plants her famish'd
 brood
Is vain, or Ilion, Tyre, might yet sur-
 vive,
And Virtue vanquish all, and murder
 cease to thrive.

XLVI

But all unconscious of the coming
 doom,
The feast, the song, the revel here a-
 bounds;
Strange modes of merriment the hours
 consume,
Nor bleed these patriots with their
 country's wounds;
Nor here War's clarion, but Love's re-
 beck sounds;
Here Folly still his votaries inthrals;
And young-eyed Lewdness walks her
 midnight rounds;
Girt with the silent crimes of Capitals,
Still to the last kind Vice clings to the
 tott'ring walls.

XLVII

Not so the rustic—with his trembling
 mate
He lurks, nor casts his heavy eye afar,
Lest he should view his vineyard desolate,
Blasted below the dun hot breath of war.
No more beneath soft Eve's consenting
 star
Fandango twirls his jocund castanet:
Ah, monarchs! could ye taste the mirth
 ye mar,
Not in the toils of Glory would ye fret;
The hoarse dull drum would sleep, and
 Man be happy yet!

XLVIII

How carols now the lusty muleteer?
Of love, romance, devotion is his lay,
As whilome he was wont the leagues to
 cheer,
His quick bells wildly jingling on the
 way?
No! as he speeds, he chants 'Vivā el
 Rey!'
And checks his song to execrate Godoy,
The royal wittol Charles, and curse the
 day
When first Spain's queen beheld the
 black-eyed boy,
And gore-faced Treason sprung from her
 adulterate joy.

XLIX

On yon long, level plain, at distance
 crown'd
With crags, whereon those Moorish
 turrets rest,
Wide scatter'd hoof-marks dint the
 wounded ground;
And, scathed by fire, the greensward's
 darken'd vest
Tells that the foe was Andalusia's guest:
Here was the camp, the watch-flame,
 and the host,
Here the bold peasant storm'd the
 dragon's nest;
Still does he mark it with triumphant
 boast;
And points to yonder cliffs, which oft
 were won and lost.

L

And whomsoe'er along the path you
 meet
Bears in his cap the badge of crimson
 hue,
Which tells you whom to shun and
 whom to greet:
Woe to the man that walks in public
 view
Without of loyalty this token true:
Sharp is the knife, and sudden is the
 stroke;

And sorely would the Gallic foeman rue
If subtle poniards, wrapt beneath th
 cloke,
Could blunt the sabre's edge, or clear th
 cannon's smoke.

LI

At every turn Morena's dusky height
Sustains aloft the battery's iron load;
And, far as mortal eye can compas
 sight,
The mountain-howitzer, the broke
 road,
The bristling palisade, the fosse o'er
 flow'd,
The station'd bands, the never-vacan
 watch,
The magazine in rocky durance stow'd
The holster'd steed beneath the shed c
 thatch,
The ball-piled pyramid, the ever-blazin
 match,

LII

Portend the deeds to come:—but h
 whose nod
Has tumbled feebler despots from thei
 sway,
A moment pauseth ere he lifts the rod
A little moment deigneth to delay:
Soon will his legions sweep throug
 these their way;
The West must own the Scourger of th
 world.
Ah! Spain! how sad will be thy reckon
 ing day,
When soars Gaul's Vulture, with hi
 wings unfurl'd,
And thou shalt view thy sons in crowds t
 Hades hurl'd.

LIII

And must they fall? the young, th
 proud, the brave,
To swell one bloated Chief's unwhole
 some reign?
No step between submission and a grave
The rise of rapine and the fall of Spain
And doth the Power that man adore
 ordain
Their doom, nor heed the suppliant'
 appeal?
Is all that desperate Valour acts in vain
And Counsel sage, and patriotic Zeal
The Veteran's skill, Youth's fire, an
 Manhood's heart of steel?

LIV

Is it for this the Spanish maid, aroused
Hangs on the willow her unstrung guitar
And, all unsex'd, the Anlace hat
 espoused,
Sung the loud song, and dared the dee
 of war?

And she, whom once the semblance of a scar
Appall'd, an owlet's 'larum chill'd with dread,
Now views the column-scattering bay'-net jar,
The falchion flash, and o'er the yet warm dead
talks with Minerva's step where Mars might quake to tread.

LV

Ye who shall marvel when you hear her tale,
Oh! had you known her in her softer hour,
Mark'd her black eye that mocks her coal-black veil,
Heard her light, lively tones in Lady's bower,
Seen her long locks that foil the painter's power,
Her fairy form, with more than female grace,
Scarce would you deem that Saragoza's tower
Beheld her smile in Danger's Gorgon face,
hin the closed ranks, and lead in Glory's fearful chase.

LVI

Her lover sinks—she sheds no ill-timed tear;
Her chief is slain—she fills his fatal post;
Her fellows flee—she checks their base career;
The foe retires—she heads the sallying host:
Who can appease like her a lover's ghost?
Who can avenge so well a leader's fall?
What maid retrieve when man's flush'd hope is lost?
Who hang so fiercely on the flying Gaul,
oil'd by a woman's hand, before a batter'd wall?

LVII

Yet are Spain's maids no race of Amazons,
But form'd for all the witching arts of love:
Though thus in arms they emulate her sons,
And in the horrid phalanx dare to move,
'Tis but the tender fierceness of the dove,
Pecking the hand that hovers o'er her mate:
In softness as in firmness far above
Remoter females, famed for sickening prate;
Ier mind is nobler sure, her charms perchance as great.

LVIII

The seal Love's dimpling finger hath impress'd
Denotes how soft that chin which bears his touch:
Her lips, whose kisses pout to leave their nest,
Bid man be valiant ere he merit such:
Her glance how wildly beautiful! how much
Hath Phœbus woo'd in vain to spoil her cheek,
Which glows yet smoother from his amorous clutch!
Who round the North for paler dames would seek?
How poor their forms appear! how languid, wan, and weak!

LIX

Match me, ye climes! which poets love to laud;
Match me, ye harems of the land! where now
I strike my strain, far distant, to applaud
Beauties that ev'n a cynic must avow;
Match me those Houries, whom ye scarce allow
To taste the gale lest Love should ride the wind,
With Spain's dark-glancing daughters—deign to know,
There your wise Prophet's paradise we find,
His black-eyed maids of Heaven, angelically kind.

LX

Oh, thou Parnassus! whom I now survey,
Not in the phrensy of a dreamer's eye,
Not in the fabled landscape of a lay,
But soaring snow-clad through thy native sky,
In the wild pomp of mountain majesty!
What marvel if I thus essay to sing?
The humblest of thy pilgrims passing by
Would gladly woo thine Echoes with his string,
Though from thy heights no more one Muse will wave her wing.

LXI

Oft have I dream'd of Thee! whose glorious name
Who knows not, knows not man's divinest lore:
And now I view thee, 'tis, alas! with shame
That I in feeblest accents must adore.
When I recount thy worshippers of yore

I tremble, and can only bend the knee;
Nor raise my voice, nor vainly dare to
soar,
But gaze beneath thy cloudy canopy
In silent joy to think at last I look on Thee!

LXII

Happier in this than mightiest bards
have been,
Whose fate to distant homes confined
their lot,
Shall I unmoved behold the hallow'd
scene,
Which others rave of, though they know
it not?
Though here no more Apollo haunts his
grot,
And thou, the Muses' seat, art now their
grave,
Some gentle spirit still pervades the spot,
Sighs in the gale, keeps silence in the cave,
And glides with glassy foot o'er yon melo-
dious wave.

LXIII

Of thee hereafter.—Ev'n amidst my
strain
I turn'd aside to pay my homage here;
Forgot the land, the sons, the maids of
Spain;
Her fate, to every freeborn bosom dear;
And hail'd thee, not perchance without
a tear.
Now to my theme—but from thy holy
haunt
Let me some remnant, some memorial
bear;
Yield me one leaf of Daphne's deathless
plant,
Nor let thy votary's hope be deem'd an
idle vaunt.

LXIV

But ne'er didst thou, fair Mount, when
Greece was young,
See round thy giant base a brighter choir,
Nor e'er did Delphi, when her priestess
sung
The Pythian hymn with more than mor-
tal fire,
Behold a train more fitting to inspire
The song of love, than Andalusia's
maids,
Nurst in the glowing lap of soft desire:
Ah! that to these were given such peace-
ful shades
As Greece can still bestow, though Glory
fly her glades.

LXV

Fair is proud Seville; let her country
boast
Her strength, her wealth, her site of
ancient days;

But Cadiz, rising on the distant coast
Calls forth a sweeter, though ignobl
praise.
Ah, Vice! how soft are thy voluptuou
ways!
While boyish blood is mantling, wh
can 'scape
The fascination of thy magic gaze?
A Cherub-hydra round us dost tho
gape,
And mould to every taste thy dear delusi
shape.

LXVI

When Paphos fell by Time—accurse
Time!
The Queen who conquers all must yie
to thee—
The Pleasures fled, but sought as war
a clime;
And Venus, constant to her native se
To nought else constant, hither deign'
to flee,
And fix'd her shrine within these wal
of white;
Though not to one dome circumscribe
she
Her worship, but, devoted to her rite
A thousand altars rise, for ever blazin
bright.

LXVII

From morn till night, from night ti
startled Morn
Peeps blushing on the revel's laughin
crew,
The song is heard, the rosy garlan
worn;
Devices quaint, and frolics ever new,
Tread on each other's kibes. A lon
adieu
He bids to sober joy that here sojourns
Nought interrupts the riot, though i
lieu
Of true devotion monkish incens
burns,
And love and prayer unite, or rule the hou
by turns.

LXVIII

The Sabbath comes, a day of blesse
rest:
What hallows it upon this Christia
shore?
Lo! it is sacred to a solemn feast:
Hark! heard you not the forest-mon
arch's roar?
Crashing the lance, he snuffs the spout
ing gore
Of man and steed, o'erthrown beneat
his horn;
The throng'd arena shakes with shout
for more;

Yells the mad crowd o'er entrails freshly
 torn,
Nor shrinks the female eye, nor ev'n affects
 to mourn.

LXIX

The seventh day this; the jubilee of man.
London! right well thou know'st the
 day of prayer:
Then thy spruce citizen, wash'd artisan,
And smug apprentice gulp their weekly
 air:
Thy coach of hackney, whiskey, one-
 horse chair,
And humblest gig through sundry sub-
 urbs whirl;
To Hampstead, Brentford, Harrow
 make repair;
Till the tired jade the wheel forgets to
 hurl,
Provoking envious gibe from each pedes-
 trian churl.

LXX

Some o'er thy Thamis row the ribbon'd
 fair,
Others along the safer turnpike fly;
Some Richmond-hill ascend, some scud
 to Ware,
And many to the steep of Highgate hie.
Ask ye, Bœotian shades! the reason
 why?
'Tis to the worship of the solemn Horn,
Grasp'd in the holy hand of Mystery,
In whose dread name both men and
 maids are sworn,
And consecrate the oath with draught, and
 dance till morn.

LXXI

All have their fooleries—not alike are
 thine,
Fair Cadiz, rising o'er the dark blue sea!
Soon as the matin bell proclaimeth nine,
Thy Saint-adorers count the rosary:
Much is the VIRGIN teased to shrive
 them free
(Well do I ween the only virgin there)
From crimes as numerous as her beads-
 men be;
Then to the crowded circus forth they
 fare:
Young, old, high, low, at once the same
 diversion share.

LXXII

The lists are oped, the spacious area
 clear'd,
Thousands on thousands piled are
 seated round;
Long ere the first loud trumpet's note is
 heard,
Ne vacant space for lated wight is
 found:

Here dons, grandees, but chiefly dames
 abound,
Skill'd in the ogle of a roguish eye,
Yet ever well inclined to heal the wound;
None through their cold disdain are
 doom'd to die,
As moon-struck bards complain, by
 Love's sad archery.

LXXIII

Hush'd is the din of tongues—on gallant
 steeds,
With milk-white crest, gold spur, and
 light-poised lance,
Four cavaliers prepare for venturous
 deeds,
And lowly bending to the lists advance;
Rich are their scarfs, their chargers
 featly prance:
If in the dangerous game they shine to-
 day,
The crowd's loud shout and ladies' lovely
 glance,
Best prize of better acts, they bear
 away,
And all that kings or chiefs e'er gain their
 toils repay.

LXXIV

In costly sheen and gaudy cloak array'd,
But all afoot, the light-limb'd Matadore
Stands in the centre, eager to invade
The lord of lowing herds; but not be-
 fore
The ground, with cautious tread, is tra-
 versed o'er,
Lest aught unseen should lurk to thwart
 his speed:
His arms a dart, he fights aloof, nor
 more
Can man achieve without the friendly
 steed—
Alas! too oft condemn'd for him to bear
 and bleed.

LXXV

Thrice sounds the clarion; lo! the signal
 falls,
The den expands, and Expectation mute
Gapes round the silent circle's peopled
 walls.
Bounds with one lashing spring the
 mighty brute,
And, wildly staring, spurns, with sound-
 ing foot,
The sand, nor blindly rushes on his
 foe:
Here, there, he points his threatening
 front, to suit
His first attack, wide waving to and fro
His angry tail; red rolls his eye's dilated
 glow.

LXXVI

Sudden he stops; his eye is fix'd: away,
Away, thou heedless boy! prepare the
 spear:
Now is thy time to perish, or display
The skill that yet may check his mad
 career.
With well-timed croupe the nimble
 coursers veer;
On foams the bull, but not unscathed
 he goes;
Streams from his flank the crimson tor-
 rent clear:
He flies, he wheels, distracted with his
 throes;
Dart follows dart; lance, lance; loud
 bellowings speak his woes.

LXXVII

Again he comes; nor dart nor lance
 avail,
Nor the wild plunging of the tortured
 horse;
Though man and man's avenging arms
 assail,
Vain are his weapons, vainer is his force.
One gallant steed is stretch'd a mangled
 corse;
Another, hideous sight! unseam'd ap-
 pears,
His gory chest unveils life's panting
 source;
Though death-struck, still his feeble
 frame he rears;
Staggering, but stemming all, his lord un-
 harm'd he bears.

LXXVIII

Foil'd, bleeding, breathless, furious to
 the last,
Full in the centre stands the bull at bay,
Mid wounds, and clinging darts, and
 lances brast,
And foes disabled in the brutal fray;
And now the Matadores around him
 play,
Shake the red cloak and poise the ready
 brand:
Once more through all he bursts his
 thundering way—
Vain rage! the mantle quits the conynge
 hand,
Wraps his fierce eye—'tis past—he sinks
 upon the sand!

LXXIX

Where his vast neck just mingles with
 the spine,
Sheathed in his form the deadly weapon
 lies.
He stops—he starts—disdaining to de-
 cline:
Slowly he falls, amidst triumphant cries,

Without a groan, without a struggl
 dies.
The decorated car appears—on high
The corse is piled—sweet sight for vu
 gar eyes—
Four steeds that spurn the rein, as swif
 as shy,
Hurl the dark bulk along, scarce seen i
 dashing by.

LXXX

Such the ungentle sport that oft invite
The Spanish maid, and cheers the Spar
 ish swain.
Nurtured in blood betimes, his hear
 delights
In vengeance, gloating on another'
 pain.
What private feuds the troubled villag
 stain!
Though now one phalanx'd host shoul
 meet the foe,
Enough, alas! in humble homes remair
To meditate 'gainst friends the secre
 blow,
For some slight cause of wrath whenc
 life's warm stream must flow.

LXXXI

But Jealousy has fled: his bars, his bolts
His wither'd centinel, Duenna sage!
And all whereat the generous soul re
 volts,
Which the stern dotard deem'd he coul
 encage,
Have pass'd to darkness with the van
 ish'd age.
Who late so free as Spanish girls wer
 seen
(Ere War uprose in his volcanic rage)
With braided tresses bounding o'er th
 green,
While on the gay dance shone Night'
 lover-loving Queen?

LXXXII

Oh! many a time and oft, had Harol
 loved,
Or dream'd he loved, since rapture is
 dream;
But now his wayward bosom was un
 moved,
For not yet had he drunk of Lethe'
 stream;
And lately had he learn'd with truth t
 deem
Love has no gift so grateful as his wings
How fair, how young, how soft soe'e
 he seem,
Full from the fount of Joy's deliciou
 springs
Some bitter o'er the flowers its bubblin
 venom flings.

LXXXIII

Yet to the beauteous form he was not
 blind,
Though now it moved him as it moves
 the wise:
Not that Philosophy on such a mind
E'er deign'd to bend her chastely-awful
 eyes:
But Passion raves herself to rest, or flies;
And Vice, that digs her own voluptuous
 tomb,
Had buried long his hopes, no more to
 rise:
Pleasure's pall'd victim! life-abhorring
 gloom
Wrote on his faded brow curst Cain's un-
 resting doom.

LXXXIV

Still he beheld, nor mingled with the
 throng;
But view'd them not with misanthropic
 hate:
Fain would he now have join'd the
 dance, the song;
But who may smile that sinks beneath
 his fate?
Nought that he saw his sadness could
 abate:
Yet once he struggled 'gainst the de-
 mon's sway,
And as in Beauty's bower he pensive
 sate,
Pour'd forth his unpremeditated lay,
To charms as fair as those that soothed
 his happier day.

TO INEZ

1

Nay, smile not at my sullen brow;
 Alas! I cannot smile again:
Yet Heaven avert that ever thou
 Shouldst weep, and haply weep in vain.

2

And dost thou ask what secret woe
 I bear, corroding joy and youth?
And wilt thou vainly seek to know
 A pang, ev'n thou must fail to soothe?

3

It is not love, it is not hate,
 Nor low Ambition's honours lost,
That bids me loathe my present state,
 And fly from all I prized the most:

4

It is that weariness which springs
 From all I meet, or hear, or see:
To me no pleasure Beauty brings;
 Thine eyes have scarce a charm for me.

5

It is that settled, ceaseless gloom
 The fabled Hebrew wanderer bore;
That will not look beyond the tomb,
 But cannot hope for rest before.

6

What Exile from himself can flee?
 To zones though more and more remote,
Still, still pursues, where'er I be,
 The blight of life—the demon Thought.

7

Yet others rapt in pleasure seem,
 And taste of all that I forsake;
Oh! may they still of transport dream,
 And ne'er, at least like me, awake!

8

Through many a clime 'tis mine to go,
 With many a retrospection curst;
And all my solace is to know,
 Whate'er betides, I've khown the worst.

9

What is that worst? Nay, do not ask—
 In pity from the search forbear:
Smile on—nor venture to unmask
 Man's heart, and view the Hell that's
 there.

LXXXV

Adieu, fair Cadiz! yea, a long adieu!
Who may forget how well thy walls have
 stood?
When all were changing, thou alone
 wert true,
First to be free, and last to be subdued:
And if amidst a scene, a shock so rude,
Some native blood was seen thy streets
 to dye
A traitor only fell beneath the feud:
Here all were noble, save Nobility!
None hugg'd a conqueror's chain, save
 fallen Chivalry!

LXXXVI

Such be the sons of Spain, and strange
 her fate!
They fight for freedom who were never
 free,
A Kingless people for a nerveless state;
Her vassals combat when their chief-
 tains flee,
True to the veriest slaves of Treachery:
Fond of a land which gave them nought
 but life,
Pride points the path that leads to
 Liberty;
Back to the struggle, baffled in the strife,
War, war is still the cry, 'War even to the
 knife!'

LXXXVII

Ye, who would more of Spain and Span-
 iards know,
Go, read whate'er is writ of bloodiest
 strife:
Whate'er keen Vengeance urged on
 foreign foe
Can act, is acting there against man's
 life:
From flashing scimitar to secret knife,
War mouldeth there each weapon to his
 need—
So may he guard the sister and the wife,
So may he make each curst oppressor
 bleed—
So may such foes deserve the most re-
 morseless deed!

LXXXVIII

Flows there a tear of pity for the dead?
Look o'er the ravage of the reeking
 plain;
Look on the hands with female slaughter
 red;
Then to the dogs resign the unburied
 slain,
Then to the vulture let each corse re-
 main,
Albeit unworthy of the prey-bird's
 maw;
Let their bleach'd bones, and blood's
 unbleaching stain,
Long mark the battle-field with hideous
 awe:
Thus only may our sons conceive the
 scenes we saw!

LXXXIX

Nor yet, alas! the dreadful work is done;
Fresh legions pour adown the Pyrenees:
It deepens still, the work is scarce begun,
Nor mortal eye the distant end foresees.
Fall'n nations gaze on Spain; if freed,
 she frees
More than her fell Pizarros once en-
 chain'd:
Strange retribution! now Columbia's
 ease
Repairs the wrongs that Quito's sons
 sustain'd,
While o'er the parent clime prowls Mur-
 der unrestrain'd.

XC

Not all the blood at Talavera shed,
Not all the marvels of Barossa's fight,
Not Albuera lavish of the dead,
Have won for Spain her well-asserted
 right.
When shall her Olive-Branch be free
 from blight?
When shall she breathe her from the
 blushing toil?

How many a doubtful day shall sink in
 night,
Ere the Frank robber turn him from his
 spoil,
And Freedom's stranger-tree grow native
 of the soil!

XCI

And thou, my friend!—since unavail-
 ing woe
Bursts from my heart, and mingles with
 the strain—
Had the sword laid thee with the mighty
 low,
Pride might forbid e'en Friendship to
 complain:
But thus unlaurel'd to descend in vain,
By all forgotten, save the lonely breast,
And mix unbleeding with the boasted
 slain,
While Glory crowns so many a meaner
 crest!
What hadst thou done to sink so peacefully
 to rest?

XCII

Oh, known the earliest, and esteem'd the
 most!
Dear to a heart where nought was left so
 dear!
Though to my hopeless days for ever
 lost,
In dreams deny me not to see thee here!
And Morn in secret shall renew the
 tear
Of Consciousness awaking to her
 woes,
And Fancy hover o'er thy bloodless
 bier,
Till my frail frame return to whence it
 rose,
And mourn'd and mourner lie united in
 repose.

XCIII

Here is one fytte of Harold's pilgrim-
 age:
Ye who of him may further seek to
 know,
Shall find some tidings in a future
 page,
If he that rhymeth now may scribble
 moe.
Is this too much? stern Critic! say not
 so:
Patience! and ye shall hear what he be-
 held
In other lands, where he was doom'd to
 go:
Lands that contain the monuments of
 Eld,
Ere Greece and Grecian arts by barbarous
 hands were quell'd.

CANTO THE SECOND

I

COME, blue-eyed maid of heaven!—but thou, alas!
Didst never yet one mortal song inspire—
Goddess of Wisdom! here thy temple was,
And is, despite of war and wasting fire,
And years, that bade thy worship to expire:
But worse than steel, and flame, and ages slow,
Is the dread sceptre and dominion dire
Of men who never felt the sacred glow
That thoughts of thee and thine on polish'd breasts bestow.

II

Ancient of days! august Athena! where,
Where are thy men of might? thy grand in soul?
Gone—glimmering through the dream of things that were:
First in the race that led to Glory's goal,
They won, and pass'd away—is this the whole?
A schoolboy's tale, the wonder of an hour!
The warrior's weapon and the sophist's stole
Are sought in vain, and o'er each mouldering tower,
Dim with the mist of years, gray flits the shade of power.

III

Son of the morning, rise! approach you here!
Come—but molest not yon defenceless urn:
Look on this spot—a nation's sepulchre!
Abode of gods, whose shrines no longer burn.
Even gods must yield—religions take their turn:
'Twas Jove's—'tis Mahomet's—and other creeds
Will rise with other years, till man shall learn
Vainly his incense soars, his victim bleeds
Poor child of Doubt and Death, whose hope is built on reeds.

IV

Bound to the earth, he lifts his eye to heaven—
Is 't not enough, unhappy thing! to know
Thou art? Is this a boon so kindly given,
That being, thou wouldst be again, and go,
Thou know'st not, reck'st not, to what region, so
On earth no more, but mingled with the skies?
Still wilt thou dream on future joy and woe?
Regard and weigh yon dust before it flies:
That little urn saith more than thousand homilies.

V

Or burst the vanish'd Hero's lofty mound;
Far on the solitary shore he sleeps:
He fell, and falling nations mourn'd around;
But now not one of saddening thousands weeps,
Nor warlike worshipper his vigil keeps
Where demi-gods appear'd, as records tell.
Remove yon skull from out the scatter'd heaps:
Is that a temple where a God may dwell?
Why ev'n the worm at last disdains her shatter'd cell!

VI

Look on its broken arch, its ruin'd wall,
Its chambers desolate, and portals foul:
Yes, this was once Ambition's airy hall,
The dome of Thought, the palace of the Soul:
Behold through each lack-lustre, eyeless hole,
The gay recess of Wisdom and of Wit,
And Passion's host, that never brook'd control:
Can all saint, sage, or sophist ever writ,
People this lonely tower, this tenement refit?

VII

Well didst thou speak, Athena's wisest son!
'All that we know is, nothing can be known.'
Why should we shrink from what we cannot shun?
Each hath his pang, but feeble sufferers groan
With brain-born dreams of evil all their own.
Pursue what Chance or Fate proclaimeth best;
Peace waits us on the shores of Acheron:
There no forced banquet claims the sated guest,
But Silence spreads the couch of ever welcome rest.

195

VIII

Yet if, as holiest men have deem'd, there be
A land of souls beyond that sable shore,
To shame the doctrine of the Sadducee
And sophists, madly vain of dubious lore;
How sweet it were in concert to adore
With those who made our mortal labours light!
To hear each voice we fear'd to hear no more!
Behold each mighty shade reveal'd to sight,
The Bactrian, Samian sage, and all who taught the right!

IX

There, thou!—whose love and life together fled,
Have left me here to love and live in vain—
Twined with my heart, and can I deem thee dead
When busy Memory flashes on my brain?
Well—I will dream that we may meet again,
And woo the vision to my vacant breast:
If aught of young Remembrance then remain,
Be as it may Futurity's behest,
For me 'twere bliss enough to know thy spirit blest!

X

Here let me sit upon this massy stone,
The marble column's yet unshaken base;
Here, son of Saturn! was thy fav'rite throne:
Mightiest of many such! Hence let me trace
The latent grandeur of thy dwelling-place.
It may not be: nor ev'n can Fancy's eye
Restore what Time hath labour'd to deface.
Yet these proud pillars claim no passing sigh;
Unmoved the Moslem sits, the light Greek carols by.

XI

But who, of all the plunderers of yon fane
On high, where Pallas linger'd, loth to flee
The latest relic of her ancient reign;
The last, the worst, dull spoiler, who was he?
Blush, Caledonia! such thy son could be!

XII

But most the modern Pict's ignoble boast,
To rive what Goth, and Turk, and Time hath spared:
Cold as the crags upon his native coast,
His mind as barren and his heart as hard,
Is he whose head conceived, whose hand prepared,
Aught to displace Athena's poor remains:
Her sons, too weak the sacred shrine to guard,
Yet felt some portion of their mother's pains,
And never knew, till then, the weight of Despot's chains.

XIII

What! shall it e'er be said by British tongue,
Albion was happy in Athena's tears?
Though in thy name the slaves her bosom wrung,
Tell not the deed to blushing Europe's ears;
The ocean queen, the free Britannia, bears
The last poor plunder from a bleeding land:
Yes, she, whose gen'rous aid her name endears,
Tore down those remnants with a harpy's hand,
Which envious Eld forbore, and tyrants left to stand.

XIV

Where was thine Ægis, Pallas! that appall'd
Stern Alaric and Havoc on their way?
Where Peleus' son? whom Hell in vain enthrall'd,
His shade from Hades upon that dread day
Bursting to light in terrible array!
What! could not Pluto spare the chief once more,
To scare a second robber from his prey?
Idly he wander'd on the Stygian shore,
Nor now preserved the walls he loved to shield before.

England! I joy no child he was of thine:
Thy free-born men should spare what once was free;
Yet they could violate each saddening shrine,
And bear these altars o'er the long-reluctant brine.

196

XV

Cold is the heart, fair Greece! that looks
on thee,
Nor feels as lovers o'er the dust they
loved;
Dull is the eye that will not weep to see
Thy walls defaced, thy mouldering
shrines removed
By British hands, which it had best be-
hoved
To guard those relics ne'er to be re-
stored.
Curst be the hour when from their isle
they roved,
And once again thy hapless bosom
gored,
And snatch'd thy shrinking Gods to
northern climes abhorr'd!

XVI

But where is Harold? shall I then forget
To urge the gloomy wanderer o'er the
wave?
Little reck'd he of all that men regret;
No loved-one now in feign'd lament
could rave;
No friend the parting hand extended
gave,
Ere the cold stranger pass'd to other
climes:
Hard is his heart whom charms may not
enslave;
But Harold felt not as in other times,
And left without a sigh the land of war and
crimes.

XVII

He that has sail'd upon the dark blue
sea
Has view'd at times, I ween, a full fair
sight;
When the fresh breeze is fair as breeze
may be,
The white sail set, the gallant frigate
tight;
Masts, spires, and strand retiring to the
right,
The glorious main expanding o'er the
bow,
The convoy spread like wild swans in
their flight,
The dullest sailer wearing bravely now,
So gaily curl the waves before each dash-
ing prow.

XVIII

And oh, the little warlike world within!
The well-reeved guns, the netted can-
opy,
The hoarse command, the busy hum-
ming din,
When, at a word, the tops are mann'd
on high:

Hark, to the Boatswain's call, the cheer-
ing cry!
While through the seaman's hand the
tackle glides;
Or schoolboy Midshipman that, stand-
ing by,
Strains his shrill pipe as good or ill be-
tides,
And well the docile crew that skilful
urchin guides.

XIX

White is the glassy deck, without a stain,
Where on the watch the staid Lieutenant
walks:
Look on that part which sacred doth re-
main
For the lone chieftain, who majestic
stalks,
Silent and fear'd by all—not oft he talks
With aught beneath him, if he would
preserve
That strict restraint, which broken, ever
balks
Conquest and fame: but Britons rarely
swerve
From law, however stern, which tends
their strength to nerve.

XX

Blow! swiftly blow, thou keel-compel-
ling gale!
Till the broad sun withdraws his lessen-
ing ray;
Then must the pennant-bearer slacken
sail,
That lagging barks may make their lazy
way.
Ah! grievance sore, and listless dull de-
lay,
To waste on sluggish hulks the sweetest
breeze!
What leagues are lost, before the dawn
of day,
Thus loitering pensive on the willing seas,
The flapping sail haul'd down to halt for
logs like these!

XXI

The moon is up; by Heaven, a lovely eve!
Long streams of light o'er dancing
waves expand;
Now lads on shore may sigh, and maids
believe:
Such be our fate when we return to land!
Meantime some rude Arion's restless
hand
Wakes the brisk harmony that sailors
love;
A circle there of merry listeners stand,
Or to some well-known measure featly
move,
Thoughtless, as if on shore they still were
free to rove.

XXII

Through Calpe's straits survey the steepy
 shore;
Europe and Afric on each other gaze!
Lands of the dark-eyed Maid and dusky
 Moor
Alike beheld beneath pale Hecate's blaze:
How softly on the Spanish shore she
 plays,
Disclosing rock, and slope, and forest
 brown,
Distinct, though darkening with her
 waning phase;
But Mauritania's giant shadows frown,
From mountain-cliff to coast descending
 sombre down.

XXIII

'Tis night, when Meditation bids us
 feel
We once have loved, though love is at an
 end:
The heart, lone mourner of its baffled
 zeal,
Though friendless now, will dream it
 had a friend.
Who with the weight of years would
 wish to bend,
When Youth itself survives young Love
 and Joy?
Alas! when mingling souls forget to
 blend,
Death hath but little left him to destroy!
Ah! happy years! once more who would
 not be a boy?

XXIV

Thus bending o'er the vessel's laving
 side,
To gaze on Dian's wave-reflected
 sphere,
The soul forgets her schemes of hope
 and pride,
And flies unconscious o'er each back-
 ward year.
None are so desolate but something
 dear,
Dearer than self, possesses or possess'd
A thought, and claims the homage of a
 tear;
A flashing pang! of which the weary
 breast
Would still, albeit in vain, the heavy heart
 divest.

XXV

To sit on rocks, to muse o'er flood and
 fell,
To slowly trace the forest's shady scene,
Where things that own not man's do-
 minion dwell,
And mortal foot hath ne'er or rarely
 been;

To climb the trackless mountain a
 unseen,
With the wild flock that never needs
 fold;
Alone o'er steeps and foaming falls t
 lean;
This is not solitude; 'tis but to hold
Converse with Nature's charms, and view
 her stores unroll'd.

XXVI

But midst the crowd, the hum, the shock
 of men,
To hear, to see, to feel, and to possess
And roam along, the world's tired deni
 zen,
With none who bless us, none whom w
 can bless;
Minions of splendour shrinking from
 distress!
None that, with kindred consciousness
 endued,
If we were not, would seem to smile th
 less,
Of all that flatter'd, follow'd, sought
 and sued;
This is to be alone; this, this is solitude

XXVII

More blest the life of godly eremite,
Such as on lonely Athos may be seen,
Watching at eve upon the giant height
Which looks o'er waves so blue, skies s
 serene,
That he who there at such an hour hath
 been
Will wistful linger on that hallow'd spot
Then slowly tear him from the 'witching
 scene,
Sigh forth one wish that such had been
 his lot,
Then turn to hate a world he had almost
 forgot.

XXVIII

Pass we the long, unvarying course, the
 track
Oft trod, that never leaves a trace be-
 hind;
Pass we the calm, the gale, the change,
 the tack,
And each well-known caprice of wave
 and wind;
Pass we the joys and sorrows sailors
 find,
Coop'd in their winged sea-girt citadel;
The foul, the fair, the contrary, the
 kind,
As breezes rise and fall and billows
 swell,
Till on some jocund morn—lo, land! and
 all is well.

XXIX

But not in silence pass Calypso's isles,
The sister tenants of the middle deep;
There for the weary still a haven smiles,
Though the fair goddess long hath
 ceased to weep,
And o'er her cliffs a fruitless watch to
 keep
For him who dared prefer a mortal
 bride:
Here, too, his boy essay'd the dreadful
 leap
Stern Mentor urged from high to yon-
 der tide;
While thus of both bereft, the nymph-
 queen doubly sigh'd.

XXX

Her reign is past, her gentle glories gone:
But trust not this: too easy youth, be-
 ware!
A mortal sovereign holds her dangerous
 throne,
And thou mayst find a new Calypso
 there.
Sweet Florence! could another ever
 share
This wayward, loveless heart, it would
 be thine:
But check'd by every tie, I may not dare
To cast a worthless offering at thy shrine,
Nor ask so dear a breast to feel one pang
 for mine.

XXXI

Thus Harold deem'd, as on that lady's
 eye
He look'd, and met its beam without a
 thought
Save admiration glancing harmless by:
Love kept aloof, albeit not far remote,
Who knew his votary often lost and
 caught,
But knew him as his worshipper no
 more,
And ne'er again the boy his bosom
 sought:
Since now he vainly urged him to adore,
Well deem'd the little God his ancient
 sway was o'er.

XXXII

Fair Florence found, in sooth with some
 amaze,
One who, 'twas said, still sigh'd to all
 he saw,
Withstand, unmoved, the lustre of her
 gaze,
Which others hail'd with real or mimic
 awe,
Their hope, their doom, their punish-
 ment, their law;
All that gay Beauty from her bondsmen
 claims:

And much she marvell'd that a youth so
 raw
Nor felt, nor feign'd at least, the oft-told
 flames,
Which, though sometimes they frown, yet
 rarely anger dames.

XXXIII

Little knew she that seeming marble
 heart,
Now mask'd in silence or withheld by
 pride,
Was not unskilful in the spoiler's art,
And spread its snares licentious far and
 wide;
Nor from the base pursuit had turn'd
 aside,
As long as aught was worthy to pursue:
But Harold on such arts no more relied;
And had he doted on those eyes so blue,
Yet never would he join the lover's
 whining crew.

XXXIV

Not much he kens, I ween, of woman's
 breast,
Who thinks that wanton thing is won by
 sighs;
What careth she for hearts when once
 possess'd?
Do proper homage to thine idol's eyes;
But not too humbly, or she will despise
Thee and thy suit, though told in
 moving tropes:
Disguise ev'n tenderness, if thou art
 wise;
Brisk Confidence still best with woman
 copes:
Pique her and soothe in turn, soon Passion
 crowns thy hopes.

XXXV

'Tis an old lesson; Time approves it
 true,
And those who know it best deplore it
 most;
When all is won that all desire to woo,
The paltry prize is hardly worth the
 cost:
Youth wasted, minds degraded, honour
 lost,
These are thy fruits, successful Passion!
 these!
If, kindly cruel, early hope is crost,
Still to the last it rankles, a disease,
Not to be cured when love itself forgets to
 please.

XXXVI

Away! nor let me loiter in my song,
For we have many a mountain-path to
 tread,
And many a varied shore to sail along,
By pensive Sadness, not by Fiction,
 led—

Climes, fair withal as ever mortal head
Imagined in its little schemes of thought;
Or e'er in new Utopias were ared,
To teach man what he might be, or he
 ought;
If that corrupted thing could ever such be
 taught.

XXXVII

Dear Nature is the kindest mother still,
Though always changing in her aspect
 mild;
From her bare bosom let me take my
 fill,
Her never-wean'd, though not her
 favour'd child.
Oh! she is fairest in her features wild,
Where nothing polish'd dares pollute
 her path:
To me by day or night she ever smiled,
Though I have mark'd her when none
 other hath,
And sought her more and more, and loved
 her best in wrath.

XXXVIII

Land of Albania! where Iskander rose,
Theme of the young, and beacon of the
 wise,
And he his namesake, whose oft-baffled
 foes
Shrunk from his deeds of chivalrous
 emprize:
Land of Albania! let me bend mine eyes
On thee, thou rugged nurse of savage
 men!
The cross descends, thy minarets arise,
And the pale crescent sparkles in the
 glen,
Through many a cypress grove within each
 city's ken.

XXXIX

Childe Harold sail'd, and pass'd the
 barren spot,
Where sad Penelope o'erlook'd the
 wave;
And onward view'd the mount, not yet
 forgot,
The lover's refuge, and the Lesbian's
 grave.
Dark Sappho! could not verse immortal
 save
That breast imbued with such immortal
 fire?
Could she not live who life eternal gave?
If life eternal may await the lyre,
That only Heaven to which Earth's child-
 ren may aspire.

XL

'Twas on a Grecian autumn's gentle eve
Childe Harold hail'd Leucadia's cape
 afar;

A spot he longed to see, nor cared to
 leave:
Oft did he mark the scenes of vanish'd
 war,
Actium, Lepanto, fatal Trafalgar;
Mark them unmoved, for he would no
 delight
(Born beneath some remote inglorious
 star)
In themes of bloody fray, or gallant
 fight,
But loathed the bravo's trade, and laughed
 at martial wight.

XLI

But when he saw the evening star above
Leucadia's far-projecting rock of woe,
And hail'd the last resort of fruitless
 love,
He felt, or deem'd he felt, no common
 glow:
And as the stately vessel glided slow
Beneath the shadow of that ancient
 mount,
He watch'd the billows' melancholy
 flow,
And, sunk albeit in thought as he was
 wont,
More placid seem'd his eye, and smooth
 his pallid front.

XLII

Morn dawns: and with it stern Albania's
 hills,
Dark Suli's rocks, and Pindus' inland
 peak,
Robed half in mist, bedew'd with snowy
 rills,
Array'd in many a dun and purple
 streak,
Arise; and, as the clouds along them
 break,
Disclose the dwelling of the moun-
 taineer:
Here roams the wolf, the eagle whets his
 beak,
Birds, beasts of prey, and wilder men
 appear,
And gathering storms around convulse the
 closing year.

XLIII

Now Harold felt himself at length
 alone,
And bade to Christian tongues a long
 adieu;
Now he adventured on a shore unknown,
Which all admire, but many dread to
 view:
His breast was arm'd 'gainst fate, his
 wants were few;

Peril he sought not, but ne'er shrank to
 meet:
The scene was savage, but the scene was
 new;
This made the ceaseless toil of travel
 sweet,
Beat back keen winter's blast, and wel-
 comed summer's heat.

XLIV

Here the red cross, for still the cross is
 here,
Though sadly scoff'd at by the circum-
 cised,
Forgets that pride to pamper'd priest-
 hood dear;
Churchman and votary alike de-
 spised.
Foul Superstition! howsoe'er disguised,
Idol, saint, virgin, prophet, crescent,
 cross,
For whatsoever symbol thou art prized,
Thou sacerdotal gain, but general loss!
Who from true worship's gold can
 separate thy dross?

XLV

Ambracia's gulf behold, where once was
 lost
A world for woman, lovely, harmless
 thing!
In yonder rippling bay, their naval
 host
Did many a Roman chief and Asian
 king
To doubtful conflict, certain slaughter
 bring:
Look where the second Cæsar's trophies
 rose:
Now, like the hands that rear'd them,
 withering:
Imperial anarchs, doubling human
 woes!
GOD! was thy globe ordain'd for such to
 win and lose?

XLVI

From the dark barriers of that rugged
 clime,
Ev'n to the centre of Illyria's vales,
Childe Harold pass'd o'er many a
 mount sublime,
Through lands scarce noticed in historic
 tales;
Yet in famed Attica such lovely dales
Are rarely seen; nor can fair Tempe
 boast
A charm they know not; loved Par-
 nassus fails,
Though classic ground and consecrated
 most,
To match some spots that lurk within this
 lowering coast.

XLVII

He pass'd bleak Pindus, Acherusia's
 lake,
And left the primal city of the land,
And onwards did his further journey
 take
To greet Albania's chief, whose dread
 command
Is lawless law; for with a bloody hand
He sways a nation, turbulent and bold;
Yet here and there some daring moun-
 tain-band
Disdain his power, and from their rocky
 hold
Hurl their defiance far, nor yield, unless to
 gold.

XLVIII

Monastic Zitza! from thy shady brow,
Thou small but favour'd spot of holy
 ground!
Where'er we gaze, around, above, be-
 low,
What rainbow tints, what magic charms
 are found!
Rock, river, forest, mountain, all
 abound,
And bluest skies that harmonise the
 whole:
Beneath, the distant torrent's rushing
 sound
Tells where the volumed cataract doth
 roll
Between those hanging rocks, that shock
 yet please the soul.

XLIX

Amidst the grove that crowns yon
 tufted hill,
Which, were it not for many a mountain
 nigh
Rising in lofty ranks, and loftier still,
Might well itself be deem'd of dignity,
The convent's white walls glisten fair on
 high:
Here dwells the caloyer, nor rude is
 he,
Nor niggard of his cheer; the passer
 by
Is welcome still; nor heedless will he
 flee
From hence, if he delight kind Nature's
 sheen to see.

L

Here in the sultriest season let him rest,
Fresh is the green beneath those aged
 trees;
Here winds of gentlest wing will fan his
 breast,
From heaven itself he may inhale the
 breeze:

The plain is far beneath—oh! let him seize
Pure pleasure while he can; the scorching ray
Here pierceth not, impregnate with disease:
Then let his length the loitering pilgrim lay,
And gaze, untired, the morn, the noon, the eve away.

LI

Dusky and huge, enlarging on the sight,
Nature's volcanic amphitheatre,
Chimæra's alps extend from left to right:
Beneath, a living valley seems to stir;
Flocks play, trees wave, streams flow, the mountain-fir
Nodding above; behold black Acheron!
Once consecrated to the sepulchre.
Pluto! if this be hell I look upon,
Close shamed Elysium's gates, my shade shall seek for none.

LII

Ne city's towers pollute the lovely view;
Unseen is Yanina, though not remote,
Veil'd by the screen of hills: here men are few,
Scanty the hamlet, rare the lonely cot:
But, peering down each precipice, the goat
Browseth; and, pensive o'er his scatter'd flock,
The little shepherd in his white capote
Doth lean his boyish form along the rock,
Or in his cave awaits the tempest's short-lived shock.

LIII

Oh! where, Dodona! is thine aged grove,
Prophetic fount, and oracle divine?
What valley echoed the response of Jove?
What trace remaineth of the Thunderer's shrine?
All, all forgotten—and shall man repine
That his frail bonds to fleeting life are broke?
Cease, fool! the fate of gods may well be thine:
Wouldst thou survive the marble or the oak?
When nations, tongues, and worlds must sink beneath the stroke!

LIV

Epirus' bounds recede, and mountains fail;
Tired of up-gazing still, the wearied eye
Reposes gladly on as smooth a vale

As ever Spring yclad in grassy dye:
Ev'n on a plain no humble beauties lie,
Where some bold river breaks the long expanse,
And woods along the banks are waving high,
Whose shadows in the glassy waters dance,
Or with the moonbeam sleep in midnight's solemn trance.

LV

The sun had sunk behind vast Tomerit,
And Laos wide and fierce came roaring by;
The shades of wonted night were gathering yet,
When, down the steep banks winding warily,
Childe Harold saw, like meteors in the sky,
The glittering minarets of Tepalen,
Whose walls o'erlook the stream; and drawing nigh,
He heard the busy hum of warrior-men
Swelling the breeze that sigh'd along the lengthening glen.

LVI

He pass'd the sacred Haram's silent tower,
And underneath the wide o'erarching gate
Survey'd the dwelling of this chief of power,
Where all around proclaim'd his high estate.
Amidst no common pomp the despot sate,
While busy preparation shook the court,
Slaves, eunuchs, soldiers, guests, and santons wait;
Within, a palace, and, without, a fort:
Here men of every clime appear to make resort.

LVII

Richly caparison'd, a ready row
Of armed horse, and many a warlike store,
Circled the wide-extending court below;
Above, strange groups adorn'd the corridore;
And oft-times through the area's echoing door,
Some high-capp'd Tartar spurr'd his steed away:
The Turk, the Greek, the Albanian, and the Moor,
Here mingled in their many-hued array,
While the deep war-drum's sound announced the close of day.

LVIII

The wild Albanian kirtled to his knee,
With shawl-girt head and ornamented
 gun,
And gold-embroider'd garments, fair to
 see;
The crimson-scarfèd men of Macedon;
The Delhi with his cap of terror on,
And crooked glaive; the lively, supple
 Greek;
And swarthy Nubia's mutilated son;
The bearded Turk, that rarely deigns to
 speak,
Master of all around, too potent to be
 meek,

LIX

Are mix'd conspicuous: some recline in
 groups,
Scanning the motley scene that varies
 round;
There some grave Moslem to devotion
 stoops,
And some that smoke, and some that
 play, are found;
Here the Albanian proudly treads the
 ground;
Half whispering there the Greek is
 heard to prate;
Hark! from the mosque the nightly
 solemn sound,
The Muezzin's call doth shake the
 minaret,
'There is no god but God!—to prayer—
 lo! God is great!'

LX

Just at this season Ramazani's fast
Through the long day its penance did
 maintain:
But when the lingering twilight hour
 was past,
Revel and feast assumed the rule again:
Now all was bustle, and the menial train
Prepared and spread the plenteous
 board within;
The vacant gallery now seem'd made in
 vain,
But from the chambers came the
 mingling din,
As page and slave anon were passing out
 and in.

LXI

Here woman's voice is never heard:
 apart,
And scarce permitted, guarded, veil'd,
 to move,
She yields to one her person and her
 heart,
Tamed to her cage, nor feels a wish to
 rove:
For, not unhappy in her master's love,
And joyful in a mother's gentlest cares,
Blest cares! all other feelings far above!
Herself more sweetly rears the babe she
 bears,
Who never quits the breast, no meaner
 passion shares.

LXII

In marble-paved pavilion, where a
 spring
Of living water from the centre rose,
Whose bubbling did a genial freshness
 fling,
And soft voluptuous couches breathed
 repose,
ALI reclined, a man of war and woes:
Yet in his lineaments ye cannot trace,
While Gentleness her milder radiance
 throws
Along that aged venerable face,
The deeds that lurk beneath, and stain him
 with disgrace.

LXIII

It is not that yon hoary lengthening
 beard
Ill suits the passions which belong to
 youth;
Love conquers age—so Hafiz hath
 averr'd,
So sings the Teian, and he sings in
 sooth—
But crimes that scorn the tender voice
 of ruth,
Beseeming all men ill, but most the man
In years, have mark'd him with a tiger's
 tooth;
Blood follows blood, and, through their
 mortal span,
In bloodier acts conclude those who with
 blood began.

LXIV

'Mid many things most new to ear and
 eye
The pilgrim rested here his weary feet,
And gazed around on Moslem luxury,
Till quickly wearied with that spacious
 seat
Of Wealth and Wantonness, the choice
 retreat
Of sated Grandeur from the city's noise:
And were it humbler, it in sooth were
 sweet;
But Peace abhorreth artificial joys,
And Pleasure, leagued with Pomp, the
 zest of both destroys.

LXV

Fierce are Albania's children, yet they
 lack
Not virtues, were those virtues more
 mature.

Where is the foe that ever saw their back?
Who can so well the toil of war endure?
Their native fastnesses not more secure
Than they in doubtful time of troublous
 need:
Their wrath how deadly! but their
 friendship sure,
When Gratitude or Valour bids them bleed
Unshaken rushing on where'er their chief
 may lead.

LXVI

Childe Harold saw them in their chief-
 tain's tower
Thronging to war in splendour and
 success;
And after view'd them, when, within
 their power,
Himself awhile the victim of distress;
That saddening hour when bad men
 hotlier press:
But these did shelter him beneath their
 roof,
When less barbarians would have
 cheer'd him less,
And fellow-countrymen have stood
 aloof—
In aught that tries the heart how few
 withstand the proof!

LXVII

It chanced that adverse winds once
 drove his bark
Full on the coast of Suli's shaggy shore,
When all around was desolate and dark;
To land was perilous, to sojourn more;
Yet for a while the mariners forbore,
Dubious to trust where treachery might
 lurk:
At length they ventured forth, though
 doubting sore
That those who loathe alike the Frank
 and Turk
Might once again renew their ancient
 butcher-work.

LXVIII

Vain fear! the Suliotes stretch'd the
 welcome hand,
Led them o'er rocks and past the dan-
 gerous swamp,
Kinder than polish'd slaves, though not
 so bland,
And piled the hearth, and wrung their
 garments damp,
And fill'd the bowl, and trimm'd the
 cheerful lamp,
And spread their fare; though homely,
 all they had:
Such conduct bears Philanthropy's rare
 stamp:
To rest the weary and to soothe the sad,
Doth lesson happier men, and shames at
 least the bad.

LXIX

It came to pass, that when he did address
Himself to quit at length this mountain-
 land,
Combined marauders half-way barr'd
 egress,
And wasted far and near with glaive and
 brand;
And therefore did he take a trusty band
To traverse Acarnania's forest wide,
In war well season'd, and with labours
 tann'd,
Till he did greet white Achelous' tide,
And from his further bank Ætolia's wolds
 espied.

LXX

Where lone Utraikey forms its circling
 cove,
And weary waves retire to gleam at
 rest,
How brown the foliage of the green hill's
 grove,
Nodding at midnight o'er the calm bay's
 breast,
As winds come lightly whispering from
 the west,
Kissing, not ruffling, the blue deep's
 serene:—
Here Harold was received a welcome
 guest;
Nor did he pass unmoved the gentle
 scene,
For many a joy could he from Night's soft
 presence glean.

LXXI

On the smooth shore the night-fires
 brightly blazed,
The feast was done, the red wine circling
 fast,
And he that unawares had there ygazed
With gaping wonderment had stared
 aghast;
For ere night's midmost, stillest hour
 was past,
The native revels of the troop began;
Each Palikar his sabre from him cast,
And bounding hand in hand, man link'd
 to man,
Yelling their uncouth dirge, long daunced
 the kirtled clan.

LXXII

Childe Harold at a little distance stood
And view'd, but not displeased, the
 revelrie,
Nor hated harmless mirth, however
 rude:
In sooth, it was no vulgar sight to
 see
Their barbarous, yet their not indecent,
 glee;

And, as the flames along their faces gleam'd,
Their gestures nimble, dark eyes flashing free,
The long wild locks that to their girdles stream'd,
While thus in concert they this lay half sang, half screamed:—

1

TAMBOURGI! Tambourgi! thy 'larum afar
Gives hope to the valiant, and promise of war;
All the sons of the mountains arise at the note,
Chimariot, Illyrian, and dark Suliote!

2

Oh! who is more brave than a dark Suliote,
In his snowy camese and his shaggy capote?
To the wolf and the vulture he leaves his wild flock,
And descends to the plain like the stream from the rock.

3

Shall the sons of Chimari, who never forgive
The fault of a friend, bid an enemy live?
Let those guns so unerring such vengeance forego?
What mark is so fair as the breast of a foe?

4

Macedonia sends forth her invincible race;
For a time they abandon the cave and the chase;
But those scarfs of blood-red shall be redder, before
The sabre is sheathed and the battle is o'er.

5

Then the pirates of Parga that dwell by the waves,
And teach the pale Franks what it is to be slaves,
Shall leave on the beach the long galley and oar,
And track to his covert the captive on shore.

6

I ask not the pleasures that riches supply,
My sabre shall win what the feeble must buy;
Shall win the young bride with her long flowing hair,
And many a maid from her mother shall tear.

7

I love the fair face of the maid in her youth,
Her caresses shall lull me, her music shall soothe;
Let her bring from the chamber her many-toned lyre,
And sing us a song on the fall of her sire.

8

Remember the moment when Previsa fell,
The shrieks of the conquer'd, the conqueror's yell;
The roofs that we fired, and the plunder we shared,
The wealthy we slaughter'd, the lovely we spared.

9

I talk not of mercy, I talk not of fear;
He neither must know who would serve the Vizier:
Since the days of our prophet the Crescent ne'er saw
A chief ever glorious like Ali Pashaw.

10

Dark Muchtar his son to the Danube is sped,
Let the yellow-hair'd Giaours view his horse-tail with dread;
When his Delhis come dashing in blood o'er the banks,
How few shall escape from the Muscovite ranks!

11

Selictar! unsheathe then our chief's scimitar;
Tambourgi! thy 'larum gives promise of war.
Ye mountains, that see us descend to the shore,
Shall view us as victors, or view us no more!

LXXIII

Fair Greece! sad relic of departed worth!
Immortal, though no more; though fallen, great!
Who now shall lead thy scatter'd children forth,
And long accustom'd bondage uncreate?
Not such thy sons who whilome did await,
The hopeless warriors of a willing doom,
In bleak Thermopylæ's sepulchral strait—
Oh! who that gallant spirit shall resume,
Leap from Eurotas' banks, and call thee from the tomb?

LXXIV

Spirit of freedom! when on Phyle's
 brow
Thou sat'st with Thrasybulus and his
 train,
Couldst thou forebode the dismal hour
 which now
Dims the green beauties of thine Attic
 plain?
Not thirty tyrants now enforce the
 chain,
But every carle can lord it o'er thy land;
Nor rise thy sons, but idly rail in vain,
Trembling beneath the scourge of Turk-
 ish hand;
From birth till death enslaved; in word, in
 deed, unmann'd.

LXXV

In all save form alone, how changed!
 and who
That marks the fire still sparkling in
 each eye,
Who would but deem their bosoms
 burn'd anew
With thy unquenchèd beam, lost
 Liberty!
And many dream withal the hour is nigh
That gives them back their fathers'
 heritage:
For foreign arms and aid they fondly
 sigh,
Nor solely dare encounter hostile rage,
Or tear their name defiled from Slavery's
 mournful page.

LXXVI

Hereditary bondsmen! know ye not
Who would be free themselves must
 strike the blow?
By their right arms the conquest must
 be wrought?
Will Gaul or Muscovite redress ye? no!
True, they may lay your proud despoil-
 ers low,
But not for you will Freedom's altars
 flame.
Shades of the Helots! triumph o'er your
 foe!
Greece! change thy lords, thy state is
 still the same;
Thy glorious day is o'er, but not thy years
 of shame.

LXXVII

The city won for Allah from the Giaour,
The Giaour from Othman's race again
 may wrest;
And the Serai's impenetrable tower
Receive the fiery Frank, her former
 guest;
Or Wahab's rebel brood, who dared
 divest

The prophet's tomb of all its pious spoil
May wind their path of blood along the
 West;
But ne'er will freedom seek this fated
 soil,
But slave succeed to slave through years
 of endless toil.

LXXVIII

Yet mark their mirth—ere lenten days
 begin,
That penance which their holy rites
 prepare
To shrive from man his weight of
 mortal sin,
By daily abstinence and nightly prayer
But ere his sackcloth garb Repentance
 wear,
Some days of joyaunce are decreed to
 all,
To take of pleasaunce each his secret
 share,
In motley robe to dance at masking ball,
And join the mimic train of merry Carni-
 val.

LXXIX

And whose more rife with merriment
 than thine,
Oh Stamboul! once the empress of their
 reign?
Though turbans now pollute Sophia's
 shrine,
And Greece her very altars eyes in vain:
(Alas! her woes will still pervade my
 strain!)
Gay were her minstrels once, for free
 her throng,
All felt the common joy they now must
 feign,
Nor oft I've seen such sight, nor heard
 such song,
As woo'd the eye, and thrill'd the Bos-
 phorus along.

LXXX

Loud was the lightsome tumult on the
 shore,
Oft Music changed, but never ceased her
 tone,
And timely echo'd back the measured
 oar,
And rippling waters made a pleasant
 moan:
The Queen of tides on high consenting
 shone,
And when a transient breeze swept o'er
 the wave,
'Twas, as if darting from her heavenly
 throne,
A brighter glance her form reflected
 gave,
Till sparkling billows seem'd to light the
 banks they lave.

LXXXI

Glanced many a light caique along the
 foam,
Danced on the shore the daughters of
 the land,
No thought had man or maid of rest or
 home,
While many a languid eye and thrilling
 hand
Exchanged the look few bosoms may
 withstand,
Or gently prest, return'd the pressure
 still:
Oh Love! young Love! bound in thy
 rosy band,
Let sage or cynic prattle as he will,
These hours, and only these, redeem Life's
 years of ill!

LXXXII

But, midst the throng in merry mas-
 querade,
Lurk there no hearts that throb with
 secret pain,
Even through the closest searment half
 betray'd?
To such the gentle murmurs of the main
Seem to re-echo all they mourn in vain;
To such the gladness of the gamesome
 crowd
Is source of wayward thought and stern
 disdain:
How do they loathe the laughter idly
 loud,
And long to change the robe of revel for
 the shroud!

LXXXIII

This must he feel, the true-born son of
 Greece,
If Greece one true-born patriot still can
 boast:
Not such as prate of war, but skulk in
 peace,
The bondsman's peace, who sighs for
 all he lost,
Yet with smooth smile his tyrant can
 accost,
And wield the slavish sickle, not the
 sword:
Ah! Greece! they love thee least who
 owe thee most—
Their birth, their blood, and that sub-
 lime record
Of hero sires, who shame thy now de-
 generate horde!

LXXXIV

When riseth Lacedemon's hardihood,
When Thebes Epaminondas rears again,
When Athens' children are with hearts
 endued,
When Grecian mothers shall give birth
 to men.

Then may'st thou be restored; but not
 till then.
A thousand years scarce serve to form
 a state;
An hour may lay it in the dust: and
 when
Can man its shatter'd splendour reno-
 vate,
Recall its virtues back, and vanquish Time
 and Fate?

LXXXV

And yet how lovely in thine age of woe,
Land of lost gods and godlike men, art
 thou!
Thy vales of evergreen, thy hills of snow,
Proclaim thee Nature's varied favourite
 now:
Thy fanes, thy temples to thy surface
 bow,
Commingling slowly with heroic earth,
Broke by the share of every rustic
 plough:
So perish monuments of mortal birth,
So perish all in turn, save well-recorded
 Worth;

LXXXVI

Save where some solitary column
 mourns
Above its prostrate brethren of the
 cave;
Save where Tritonia's airy shrine adorns
Colonna's cliff, and gleams along the
 wave;
Save o'er some warrior's half-forgotten
 grave,
Where the gray stones and unmolested
 grass
Ages, but not oblivion, feebly brave;
While strangers only not regardless
 pass,
Lingering like me, perchance, to gaze, and
 sigh 'Alas!'

LXXXVII

Yet are thy skies as blue, thy crags as
 wild;
Sweet are thy groves, and verdant are
 thy fields,
Thine olive ripe as when Minerva
 smiled,
And still his honey'd wealth Hymettus
 yields;
There the blithe bee his fragrant fortress
 builds,
The freeborn wanderer of thy moun-
 tain-air;
Apollo still thy long, long summer gilds,
Still in his beam Mendeli's marbles
 glare;
Art, Glory, Freedom fail, but Nature still
 is fair.

LXXXVIII

Where'er we tread 'tis haunted, holy
 ground;
No earth of thine is lost in vulgar mould,
But one vast realm of wonder spreads
 around,
And all the Muse's tales seem truly told,
Till the sense aches with gazing to be-
 hold
The scenes our earliest dreams have
 dwelt upon;
Each hill and dale, each deepening glen
 and wold
Defies the power which crush'd thy
 temples gone:
Age shakes Athena's tower, but spares
 gray Marathon.

LXXXIX

The sun, the soil, but not the slave, the
 same;
Unchanged in all except its foreign
 lord;
Preserves alike its bounds and bound-
 less fame
The Battle-field, where Persia's victim
 horde
First bow'd beneath the brunt of Hellas'
 sword,
As on the morn to distant Glory dear,
When Marathon became a magic word;
Which utter'd, to the hearer's eye
 appear
The camp, the host, the fight, the con-
 queror's career,

XC

The flying Mede, his shaftless broken
 bow;
The fiery Greek, his red pursuing spear;
Mountains above, Earth's, Ocean's
 plain below;
Death in the front, Destruction in the
 rear!
Such was the scene—what now remain-
 eth here?
What sacred trophy marks the hallow'd
 ground,
Recording Freedom's smile and Asia's
 tear?
The rifled urn, the violated mound,
The dust thy courser's hoof, rude stranger!
 spurns around.

XCI

Yet to the remnants of thy splendour
 past
Shall pilgrims, pensive, but unwearied,
 throng;
Long shall the voyager, with th' Ionian
 blast,
Hail the bright clime of battle and of
 song;

Long shall thine annals and immortal
 tongue
Fill with thy fame the youth of many a
 shore;
Boast of the aged! lesson of the young!
Which sages venerate and bards adore,
As Pallas and the Muse unveil their awful
 lore.

XCII

The parted bosom clings to wonted
 home,
If aught that's kindred cheer the wel-
 come hearth;
He that is lonely, hither let him roam,
And gaze complacent on congenial
 earth.
Greece is no lightsome land of social
 mirth:
But he whom Sadness sootheth may
 abide,
And scarce regret the region of his
 birth,
When wandering slow by Delphi's
 sacred side,
Or gazing o'er the plains where Greek and
 Persian died.

XCIII

Let such approach this consecrated
 land,
And pass in peace along the magic
 waste;
But spare its relics—let no busy hand
Deface the scenes, already how de-
 faced!
Not for such purpose were these altars
 placed:
Revere the remnants nations once
 revered:
So may our country's name be undis-
 graced,
So may'st thou prosper where thy youth
 was rear'd,
By every honest joy of love and life en-
 dear'd!

XCIV

For thee, who thus in too protracted
 song
Hast soothed thine idlesse with in-
 glorious lays,
Soon shall thy voice be lost amid the
 throng
Of louder minstrels in these later days:
To such resign the strife for fading
 bays—
Ill may such contest now the spirit move
Which heeds nor keen reproach nor
 partial praise,
Since cold each kinder heart that might
 approve,
And none are left to please when none are
 left to love.

XCV

Thou too art gone, thou loved and
 lovely one!
Whom youth and youth's affections
 bound to me;
Who did for me what none beside have
 done,
Nor shrank from one albeit unworthy
 thee.
What is my being? thou hast ceased to
 be!
Nor staid to welcome here thy wanderer
 home,
Who mourns o'er hours which we no
 more shall see—
Would they had never been, or were to
 come!
'ould he had ne'er return'd to find fresh
 cause to roam!

XCVI

Oh! ever loving, lovely, and beloved!
How selfish Sorrow ponders on the past,
And clings to thoughts now better far
 removed!
But Time shall tear thy shadow from
 me last.
All thou couldst have of mine, stern
 Death! thou hast;
The parent, friend, and now the more
 than friend;
Ne'er yet for one thine arrows flew so
 fast,
And grief with grief continuing still to
 blend,
ath snatch'd the little joy that life had
 yet to lend.

XCVII

Then must I plunge again into the
 crowd,
And follow all that Peace disdains to
 seek?
Where Revel calls, and Laughter, vainly
 loud,
False to the heart, distorts the hollow
 cheek,
To leave the flagging spirit doubly weak;
Still o'er the features, which perforce
 they cheer,
To feign the pleasure or conceal the
 pique:
Smiles form the channel of a future tear,
ᴦ raise the writhing lip with ill-dis-
 sembled sneer.

XCVIII

What is the worst of woes that wait on
 age?
What stamps the wrinkle deeper on the
 brow?
To view each loved one blotted from
 life's page,
And be alone on earth, as I am now.

Before the Chastener humbly let me
 bow,
O'er hearts divided and o'er hopes
 destroy'd:
Roll on, vain days! full reckless may ye
 flow,
Since Time hath reft whate'er my soul
 enjoy'd,
And with the ills of Eld mine earlier years
alloy'd.

CANTO THE THIRD

'Afin que cette application vous forçât à penser
à autre chose; il n'y a en vérité de remède que
celui-là et le temps.'—*Lettre du Roi de Prusse à
D'Alembert, Sept.* 7, 1776.

I

Is thy face like thy mother's, my fair
 child!
ADA! sole daughter of my house and
 heart?
When last I saw thy young blue eyes
 they smiled,
And then we parted,—not as now we
 part,
But with a hope.—
 Awaking with a start,
The waters heave around me; and on
 high
The winds lift up their voices: I depart,
Whither I know not; but the hour's
 gone by,
When Albion's lessening shores could
 grieve or glad mine eye.

II

Once more upon the waters! yet once
 more!
And the waves bound beneath me as a
 steed
That knows his rider. Welcome to their
 roar!
Swift be their guidance, wheresoe'er it
 lead!
Though the strain'd mast should quiver
 as a reed,
And the rent canvas fluttering strew the
 gale,
Still must I on; for I am as a weed,
Flung from the rock, on Ocean's foam
 to sail
Where'er the surge may sweep, the tem-
 pest's breath prevail.

III

In my youth's summer I did sing of One,
The wandering outlaw of his own dark
 mind;
Again I seize the theme, then but begun,
And bear it with me, as the rushing wind
Bears the cloud onwards: in that Tale
 I find

209

The furrows of long thought, and dried-
up tears,
Which, ebbing, leave a sterile track
behind,
O'er which all heavily the journeying
years
Plod the last sands of life,—where not a
flower appears.

IV

Since my young days of passion—joy,
or pain,
Perchance my heart and harp have lost
a string,
And both may jar: it may be, that in vain
I would essay as I have sung to sing.
Yet, though a dreary strain, to this I
cling;
So that it wean me from the weary dream
Of selfish grief or gladness—so it fling
Forgetfulness around me—it shall seem
To me, though to none else, a not un-
grateful theme.

V

He, who grown aged in this world of woe,
In deeds, not years, piercing the depths
of life,
So that no wonder waits him; nor below
Can love or sorrow, fame, ambition,
strife,
Cut to his heart again with the keen knife
Of silent, sharp endurance: he can tell
Why thought seeks refuge in lone caves,
yet rife
With airy images, and shapes which
dwell
Still unimpair'd, though old, in the soul's
haunted cell.

VI

'Tis to create, and in creating live
A being more intense, that we endow
With form our fancy, gaining as we
give
The life we image, even as I do now.
What am I? Nothing: but not so art
thou,
Soul of my thought! with whom I
traverse earth,
Invisible but gazing, as I glow
Mix'd with thy spirit, blended with thy
birth,
And feeling still with thee in my crush'd
feelings' dearth.

VII

Yet must I think less wildly:—I *have*
thought
Too long and darkly, till my brain
became,
In its own eddy boiling and o'er-
wrought,
A whirling gulf of phantasy and flame.

And thus, untaught in youth my hear
to tame,
My springs of life were poison'd. 'T
too late!
Yet am I changed; though still enoug
the same
In strength to bear what time canne
abate,
And feed on bitter fruits without accusir
Fate.

VIII

Something too much of this:—but no
'tis past,
And the spell closes with its silent sea
Long absent HAROLD re-appears at las
He of the breast which fain no mo
would feel,
Wrung with the wounds which kill no
but ne'er heal;
Yet Time, who changes all, had alter
him
In soul and aspect as in age: years ste
Fire from the mind as vigour from th
limb;
And life's enchanted cup but sparkles ne
the brim.

IX

His had been quaff'd too quickly, an
he found
The dregs were wormwood; but he fill
again,
And from a purer fount, on holi
ground,
And deem'd its spring perpetual; but
vain!
Still round him clung invisibly a cha
Which gall'd for ever, fettering thoug
unseen,
And heavy though it clank'd not; wo
with pain,
Which pined although it spoke not, an
grew keen,
Entering with every step he took throug
many a scene.

X

Secure in guarded coldness, he ha
mix'd
Again in fancied safety with his kind
And deem'd his spirit now so firmly fix'
And sheath'd with an invulnerab
mind,
That, if no joy, no sorrow lurk'd behine
And he, as one, might 'midst the man
stand
Unheeded, searching through the crow
to find
Fit speculation; such as in strange lan
He found in wonder-works of God an
Nature's hand.

XI

But who can view the ripen'd rose, nor
 seek
To wear it? who can curiously behold
The smoothness and the sheen of
 beauty's cheek,
Nor feel the heart can never all grow
 old?
Who can contemplate Fame through
 clouds unfold
The star which rises o'er her steep, nor
 climb?
Harold, once more within the vortex,
 roll'd
On with the giddy circle, chasing Time,
et with a nobler aim than in his youth's
 fond prime.

XII

But soon he knew himself the most
 unfit
Of men to herd with Man; with whom
 he held
Little in common; untaught to submit
His thoughts to others, though his soul
 was quell'd
In youth by his own thoughts; still un-
 compell'd,
He would not yield dominion of his mind
To spirits against whom his own rebell'd;
Proud though in desolation; which
 could find
 life within itself, to breathe without
 mankind.

XIII

Where rose the mountains, there to him
 were friends;
Where roll'd the ocean, thereon was his
 home;
Where a blue sky, and glowing clime,
 extends,
He had the passion and the power to
 roam;
The desert, forest, cavern, breaker's
 foam,
Were unto him companionship; they
 spake
A mutual language, clearer than the
 tome
Of his land's tongue, which he would
 oft forsake
r Nature's pages glass'd by sunbeams
 on the lake.

XIV

Like the Chaldean, he could watch the
 stars,
Till he had peopled them with beings
 bright
As their own beams; and earth, and
 earthborn jars,
And human frailties, were forgotten
 quite:

Could he have kept his spirit to that
 flight
He had been happy; but this clay will
 sink
Its spark immortal, envying it the light
To which it mounts, as if to break the
 link
That keeps us from yon heaven which
 woos us to its brink.

XV

But in Man's dwellings he became a
 thing
Restless and worn, and stern and weari-
 some,
Droop'd as a wild-born falcon with
 clipt wing,
To whom the boundless air alone were
 home:
Then came his fit again, which to o'er-
 come,
As eagerly the barr'd-up bird will beat
His breast and beak against his wiry
 dome
Till the blood tinge his plumage, so the
 heat
Of his impeded soul would through his
 bosom eat.

XVI

Self-exiled Harold wanders forth again,
With nought of hope left, but with less
 of gloom;
The very knowledge that he lived in vain,
That all was over on this side the tomb,
Had made Despair a smilingness assume,
Which, though 'twere wild,—as on the
 plunder'd wreck
When mariners would madly meet their
 doom
With draughts intemperate on the
 sinking deck,—
Did yet inspire a cheer, which he forbore
 to check.

XVII

Stop!—for thy tread is on an Empire's
 dust!
An Earthquake's spoil is sepulchred
 below!
Is the spot mark'd with no colossal
 bust?
Nor column trophied for triumphal
 show?
None; but the moral's truth tells simpler
 so,
As the ground was before, thus let it
 be;—
How that red rain hath made the harvest
 grow!
And is this all the world has gain'd by
 thee,
Thou first and last of fields! king-making
 Victory?

211

XVIII

And Harold stands upon this place of
 skulls,
The grave of France, the deadly
 Waterloo!
How in an hour the power which gave
 annuls
Its gifts, transferring fame as fleeting
 too!
In 'pride of place' here last the eagle
 flew,
Then tore with bloody talon the rent
 plain,
Pierced by the shaft of banded nations
 through;
Ambition's life and labours all were
 vain;
He wears the shatter'd links of the world's
 broken chain.

XIX

Fit retribution! Gaul may champ the
 bit
And foam in fetters;—but is Earth
 more free?
Did nations combat to make *One*
 submit;
Or league to teach all kings true sove-
 reignty?
What! shall reviving Thraldom again be
The patch'd-up idol of enlighten'd days?
Shall we, who struck the Lion down,
 shall we
Pay the Wolf homage? proffering
 lowly gaze
And servile knees to thrones? No; *prove*
 before ye praise!

XX

If not, o'er one fallen despot boast no
 more!
In vain fair cheeks were furrow'd with
 hot tears
For Europe's flowers long rooted up
 before
The trampler of her vineyards; in vain
 years
Of death, depopulation, bondage, fears,
Have all been borne, and broken by
 the accord
Of roused-up millions; all that most
 endears
Glory, is when the myrtle wreathes a
 sword
Such as Harmodius drew on Athens'
 tyrant lord.

XXI

There was a sound of revelry by night,
And Belgium's capital had gather'd then
Her Beauty and her Chivalry, and
 bright
The lamps shone o'er fair women and
 brave men;

A thousand hearts beat happily; a
 when
Music arose with its voluptuous swe
Soft eyes look'd love to eyes whi
 spake again,
And all went merry as a marriage be
But hush! hark! a deep sound strikes li
 a rising knell!

XXII

Did ye not hear it?—No; 'twas but t
 wind,
Or the car rattling o'er the stony stre
On with the dance! let joy be unco
 fined;
No sleep till morn, when Youth a
 Pleasure meet
To chase the glowing Hours with flyi
 feet—
But hark!—that heavy sound breaks
 once more,
As if the clouds its echo would repea
And nearer, clearer, deadlier th
 before!
Arm! Arm! it is—it is—the canno
 opening roar!

XXIII

Within a window'd niche of that high h
Sate Brunswick's fated chieftain; l
 did hear
That sound the first amidst the festiva
And caught its tone with Death's pr
 phetic ear;
And when they smiled because l
 deem'd it near,
His heart more truly knew that peal t
 well
Which stretch'd his father on a bloo
 bier,
And roused the vengeance blood alo
 could quell;
He rush'd into the field, and, foremo
 fighting, fell.

XXIV

Ah! then and there was hurrying to a
 fro,
And gathering tears, and tremblings
 distress,
And cheeks all pale, which but an ho
 ago
Blush'd at the praise of their own lov
 liness;
And there were sudden partings, su
 as press
The life from out young hearts, a
 choking sighs
Which ne'er might be repeated; wl
 could guess
If ever more should meet those mutu
 eyes,
Since upon night so sweet such awf
 morn could rise!

XXV

And there was mounting in hot haste:
 the steed,
The mustering squadron, and the clat-
 tering car,
Went pouring forward with impetuous
 speed,
And swiftly forming in the ranks of
 war:
And the deep thunder peal on peal
 afar;
And near, the beat of the alarming
 drum
Roused up the soldier ere the morning
 star;
While throng'd the citizens with terror
 dumb,
r whispering, with white lips—'The foe!
 they come! they come!'

XXVI

And wild and high the 'Cameron's
 gathering' rose!
The war-note of Lochiel, which Albyn's
 hills
Have heard, and heard, too, have her
 Saxon foes:—
How in the noon of night that pibroch
 thrills,
Savage and shrill! But with the breath
 which fills
Their mountain-pipe, so fill the moun-
 taineers
With the fierce native daring which
 instils
The stirring memory of a thousand
 years,
nd Evan's, Donald's fame rings in each
 clansman's ears!

XXVII

And Ardennes waves above them her
 green leaves,
Dewy with nature's tear-drops as they
 pass,
Grieving, if aught inanimate e'er grieves,
Over the unreturning brave,—alas!
Ere evening to be trodden like the grass
Which now beneath them, but above
 shall grow
In its next verdure, when this fiery mass
Of living valour, rolling on the foe
nd burning with high hope shall moulder
 cold and low.

XXVIII

Last noon beheld them full of lusty life,
Last eve in Beauty's circle proudly gay,
The midnight brought the signal-sound
 of strife,
The morn the marshalling in arms,—
 the day
Battle's magnificently stern array!

The thunder-clouds close o'er it, which
 when rent
The earth is cover'd thick with other
 clay,
Which her own clay shall cover, heap'd
 and pent,
Rider and horse,—friend, foe,—in one red
 burial blent!

XXIX

Their praise is hymn'd by loftier harps
 than mine:
Yet one I would select from that proud
 throng,
Partly because they blend me with his
 line,
And partly that I did his sire some
 wrong,
And partly that bright names will hal-
 low song;
And his was of the bravest, and when
 shower'd
The death-bolts deadliest the thinn'd
 files along,
Even where the thickest of war's tem-
 pest lower'd,
They reach'd no nobler breast than thine,
 young gallant Howard!

XXX

There have been tears and breaking
 hearts for thee,
And mine were nothing had I such to
 give;
But when I stood beneath the fresh
 green tree,
Which living waves where thou didst
 cease to live,
And saw around me the wide field revive
With fruits and fertile promise, and the
 Spring
Came forth her work of gladness to
 contrive,
With all her reckless birds upon the
 wing,
I turn'd from all she brought to those she
 could not bring.

XXXI

I turn'd to thee, to thousands, of whom
 each
And one as all a ghastly gap did make
In his own kind and kindred, whom to
 teach
Forgetfulness were mercy for their sake;
The Archangel's trump, not Glory's,
 must awake
Those whom they thirst for; though the
 sound of Fame
May for a moment soothe, it cannot
 slake
The fever of vain longing, and the name
So honour'd but assumes a stronger,
 bitterer claim.

XXXII

They mourn, but smile at length; and,
 smiling, mourn;
The tree will wither long before it fall;
The hull drives on, though mast and
 sail be torn;
The roof-tree sinks, but moulders on
 the hall
In massy hoariness; the ruin'd wall
Stands when its wind-worn battlements
 are gone;
The bars survive the captive they en-
 thral;
The day drags through, though storms
 keep out the sun;
And thus the heart will break, yet brokenly
 live on

XXXIII

Even as a broken mirror, which the
 glass
In every fragment multiplies; and makes
A thousand images of one that was,
The same, and still the more, the more
 it breaks;
And thus the heart will do which not
 forsakes,
Living in shatter'd guise; and still, and
 cold,
And bloodless, with its sleepless sorrow
 aches,
Yet withers on till all without is old,
Showing no visible sign, for such things
 are untold.

XXXIV

There is a very life in our despair,
Vitality of poison,—a quick root
Which feeds these deadly branches; for
 it were
As nothing did we die; but Life will
 suit
Itself to Sorrow's most detested fruit,
Like to the apples on the Dead Sea's
 shore,
All ashes to the taste: Did man com-
 pute
Existence by enjoyment, and count o'er
Such hours 'gainst years of life,—say,
 would he name threescore?

XXXV

The Psalmist number'd out the years of
 man:
They are enough: and if thy tale be *true*,
Thou, who didst grudge him even that
 fleeting span,
More than enough, thou fatal Water-
 loo!
Millions of tongues record thee, and
 anew
Their children's lips shall echo them,
 and say—

'Here, where the sword united nation
 drew,
Our countrymen were warring on tha
 day!'
And this is much, and all which will no
 pass away.

XXXVI

There sunk the greatest, nor the wors
 of men,
Whose spirit, antithetically mixt,
One moment of the mightiest, an
 again
On little objects with like firmness fixt
Extreme in all things! hadst thou bee
 betwixt,
Thy throne had still been thine, o
 never been;
For daring made thy rise as fall: tho
 seek'st
Even now to re-assume the imperia
 mien,
And shake again the world, the Thundere
 of the scene!

XXXVII

Conqueror and captive of the earth ar
 thou!
She trembles at thee still, and thy wil
 name
Was ne'er more bruited in men's mind
 than now
That thou art nothing, save the jest o
 Fame,
Who woo'd thee once, thy vassal, an
 became
The flatterer of thy fierceness, till tho
 wert
A god unto thyself; nor less the sam
To the astounded kingdoms all inert,
Who deem'd thee for a time whate'er tho
 didst assert.

XXXVIII

Oh, more or less than man—in high o
 low,
Battling with nations, flying from th
 field;
Now making monarchs' necks th
 footstool, now
More than thy meanest soldier taugh
 to yield;
An empire thou couldst crush, com
 mand, rebuild,
But govern not thy pettiest passion
 nor,
However deeply in men's spirits skill'd
Look through thine own, nor curb the
 lust of war,
Nor learn that tempted Fate will leave th
 loftiest star.

214

XXXIX

Yet well thy soul hath brook'd the
 turning tide
With that untaught innate philosophy,
Which, be it wisdom, coldness, or deep
 pride,
Is gall and wormwood to an enemy.
When the whole host of hatred stood
 hard by,
To watch and mock thee shrinking,
 thou hast smiled
With a sedate and all-enduring eye;—
When Fortune fled her spoil'd and
 favourite child,
He stood unbow'd beneath the ills upon
 him piled.

XL

Sager than in thy fortunes; for in them
Ambition steel'd thee on too far to
 show
That just habitual scorn, which could
 contemn
Men and their thoughts; 'twas wise to
 feel, not so
To wear it ever on thy lip and brow,
And spurn the instruments thou wert to
 use
Till they were turn'd unto thine over-
 throw:
'Tis but a worthless world to win or
 lose;
So hath it proved to thee, and all such lot
 who choose.

XLI

If, like a tower upon a headland rock,
Thou hadst been made to stand or fall
 alone,
Such scorn of man had help'd to brave
 the shock;
But men's thoughts were the steps which
 paved thy throne,
Their admiration thy best weapon
 shone;
The part of Philip's son was thine, not
 then
(Unless aside thy purple had been
 thrown)
Like stern Diogenes to mock at men;
For sceptred cynics earth were far too
 wide a den.

XLII

But quiet to quick bosoms is a hell,
And *there* hath been thy bane; there is
 a fire
And motion of the soul which will not
 dwell
In its own narrow being, but aspire
Beyond the fitting medium of desire;
And, but once kindled, quenchless ever-
 more,
Preys upon high adventure, nor can tire

Of aught but rest; a fever at the core,
Fatal to him who bears, to all who ever
 bore.

XLIII

This makes the madmen who have
 made men mad
By their contagion; Conquerors and
 Kings,
Founders of sects and systems, to whom
 add
Sophists, Bards, Statesmen, all un-
 quiet things
Which stir too strongly the soul's
 secret springs,
And are themselves the fools to those
 they fool;
Envied, yet how unenviable! what
 stings
Are theirs! One breast laid open were
 a school
Which would unteach mankind the lust
 to shine or rule:

XLIV

Their breath is agitation, and their life
A storm whereon they ride, to sink at
 last,
And yet so nursed and bigoted to strife,
That should their days, surviving perils
 past,
Melt to calm twilight, they feel overcast
With sorrow and supineness, and so die;
Even as a flame unfed, which runs to
 waste
With its own flickering, or a sword laid
 by,
Which eats into itself, and rusts inglori-
 ously.

XLV

He who ascends to mountain-tops,
 shall find
The loftiest peaks most wrapt in clouds
 and snow;
He who surpasses or subdues mankind,
Must look down on the hate of those
 below.
Though high *above* the sun of glory
 glow,
And far *beneath* the earth and ocean
 spread,
Round him are icy rocks, and loudly
 blow
Contending tempests on his naked head,
And thus reward the toils which to those
 summits led.

XLVI

Away with these! true Wisdom's world
 will be
Within its own creation, or in thine,
Maternal Nature! for who teems like
 thee,
Thus on the banks of thy majestic Rhine?

There Harold gazes on a work divine,
A blending of all beauties; streams and dells,
Fruit, foliage, crag, wood, cornfield, mountain, vine,
And chiefless castles breathing stern farewells
From gray but leafy walls, where Ruin greenly dwells.

XLVII

And there they stand, as stands a lofty mind,
Worn, but unstooping to the baser crowd,
All tenantless, save to the crannying wind,
Or holding dark communion with the cloud.
There was a day when they were young and proud,
Banners on high, and battles pass'd below;
But they who fought are in a bloody shroud,
And those which waved are shredless dust ere now,
And the bleak battlements shall bear no future blow.

XLVIII

Beneath these battlements, within those walls,
Power dwelt amidst her passions; in proud state
Each robber chief upheld his armed halls,
Doing his evil will, nor less elate
Than mightier heroes of a longer date.
What want these outlaws conquerors should have
But history's purchased page to call them great?
A wider space, an ornamented grave?
Their hopes were not less warm, their souls were full as brave.

XLIX

In their baronial feuds and single fields,
What deeds of prowess unrecorded died!
And Love, which lent a blazon to their shields,
With emblems well devised by amorous pride,
Through all the mail of iron hearts would glide;
But still their flame was fierceness, and drew on
Keen contest and destruction near allied,
And many a tower for some fair mischief won,
Saw the discolour'd Rhine beneath its ruin run.

L

But Thou, exulting and abounding river!
Making thy waves a blessing as they flow
Through banks whose beauty would endure for ever
Could man but leave thy bright creation so,
Nor its fair promise from the surface mow
With the sharp scythe of conflict,—then to see
Thy valley of sweet waters, were to know
Earth paved like Heaven; and to seem such to me,
Even now what wants thy stream?—that it should Lethe be.

LI

A thousand battles have assail'd thy banks,
But these and half their fame have pass'd away,
And Slaughter heap'd on high his weltering ranks;
Their very graves are gone, and what are they?
Thy tide wash'd down the blood of yesterday,
And all was stainless, and on thy clear stream
Glass'd, with its dancing light, the sunny ray;
But o'er the blacken'd memory's blighting dream
Thy waves would vainly roll, all sweeping as they seem.

LII

Thus Harold inly said, and pass'd along
Yet not insensible to all which here
Awoke the jocund birds to early song
In glens which might have made even exile dear:
Though on his brow were graven lines austere,
And tranquil sternness, which had ta'en the place
Of feelings fierier far but less severe,
Joy was not always absent from his face,
But o'er it in such scenes would steal with transient trace.

LIII

Nor was all love shut from him, though his days
Of passion had consumed themselves to dust.
It is in vain that we would coldly gaze
On such as smile upon us; the heart must
Leap kindly back to kindness, though disgust

Hath wean'd it from all worldlings:
 thus he felt,
For there was soft remembrance, and
 •sweet trust
In one fond breast, to which his own
 would melt,
nd in its tenderer hour on that his bosom
 dwelt.

LIV

And he had learn'd to love,—I know not
 why,
For this in such as him seems strange
 of mood,—
The helpless looks of blooming infancy,
Even in its earliest nurture; what sub-
 dued,
To change like this, a mind so far im-
 bued
With scorn of man, it little boots to
 know;
But thus it was; and though in solitude
Small power the nipp'd affections have
 to grow,
 him this glow'd when all beside had
 ceased to glow.

LV

And there was one soft breast, as hath
 been said,
Which unto his was bound by stronger
 ties
Than the church links withal; and,
 though unwed,
That love was pure, and, far above dis-
 guise,
Had stood the test of mortal enmities
Still undivided, and cemented more
By peril, dreaded most in female eyes;
But this was firm, and from a foreign
 shore
ell to that heart might his these absent
 greetings pour!

1

The castled crag of Drachenfels
Frowns o'er the wide and winding
 Rhine,
Whose breast of waters broadly swells
Between the banks which bear the vine,
And hills all rich with blossom'd trees,
And fields which promise corn and
 wine,
And scatter'd cities crowning these,
Whose far white walls along them
 shine,
Have strew'd a scene, which I should
 see
With double joy wert *thou* with me.

2

And peasant girls, with deep blue eyes,
And hands which offer early flowers,
Walk smiling o'er this paradise;
Above, the frequent feudal towers

Through green leaves lift their walls
 of gray;
And many a rock which steeply lowers,
And noble arch in proud decay,
Look o'er this vale of vintage-bowers;
But one thing want these banks of
 Rhine,—
Thy gentle hand to clasp in mine!

3

I send the lilies given to me;
Though long before thy hand they
 touch,
I know that they must wither'd be,
But yet reject them not as such;
For I have cherish'd them as dear,
Because they yet may meet thine eye,
And guide thy soul to mine even here,
When thou behold'st them drooping
 nigh,
And know'st them gather'd by the
 Rhine,
And offer'd from my heart to thine!

4

The river nobly foams and flows,
The charm of this enchanted ground,
And all its thousand turns disclose
Some fresher beauty varying round:
The haughtiest breast its wish might
 bound
Through life to dwell delighted here;
Nor could on earth a spot be found
To nature and to me so dear,
Could thy dear eyes in following mine
Still sweeten more these banks of
 Rhine!

LVI

By Coblentz, on a rise of gentle ground,
There is a small and simple pyramid,
Crowning the summit of the verdant
 mound;
Beneath its base are heroes' ashes hid,
Our enemy's—but let not that forbid
Honour to Marceau! o'er whose early
 tomb
Tears, big tears, gush'd from the rough
 soldier's lid,
Lamenting and yet envying such a doom,
Falling for France, whose rights he battled
 to resume.

LVII

Brief, brave, and glorious was his young
 career,—
His mourners were two hosts, his friends
 and foes;
And fitly may the stranger lingering here
Pray for his gallant spirit's bright re-
 pose;
For he was Freedom's champion, one of
 those,

The few in number, who had not o'er-
 stept
The charter to chastise which she be-
 stows
On such as wield her weapons; he had
 kept
The whiteness of his soul, and thus men
 o'er him wept.

LVIII

Here Ehrenbreitstein, with her shatter'd
 wall
Black with the miner's blast, upon her
 height
Yet shows of what she was, when shell
 and ball
Rebounding idly on her strength did
 light:
A tower of victory! from whence the
 flight
Of baffled foes was watch'd along the
 plain:
But Peace destroy'd what War could
 never blight,
And laid those proud roofs bare to Sum-
 mer's rain—
On which the iron shower for years had
 pour'd in vain.

LIX

Adieu to thee, fair Rhine! How long
 delighted
The stranger fain would linger on his
 way!
Thine is a scene alike where souls
 united
Or lonely Contemplation thus might
 stray;
And could the ceaseless vultures cease
 to prey
On self-condemning bosoms, it were
 here,
Where Nature, nor too sombre nor too
 gay,
Wild but not rude, awful yet not austere,
Is to the mellow Earth as Autumn to the
 year.

LX

Adieu to thee again! a vain adieu!
There can be no farewell to scene like
 thine;
The mind is colour'd by thy every hue;
And if reluctantly the eyes resign
Their cherish'd gaze upon thee, lovely
 Rhine!
'Tis with the thankful glance of parting
 praise;
More mighty spots may rise, more glar-
 ing shine,
But none unite in one attaching maze
The brilliant, fair, and soft,—the glories
 of old days.

LXI

The negligently grand, the fruitful bloo
Of coming ripeness, the white city
 sheen,
The rolling stream, the precipice
 gloom,
The forest's growth, and Gothic wa'
 between,
The wild rocks shaped as they h.
 turrets been,
In mockery of man's art; and the
 withal
A race of faces happy as the scene,
Whose fertile bounties here extend to a
Still springing o'er thy banks, though Er
 pires near them fall.

LXII

But these recede. Above me are t'
 Alps,
The palaces of Nature, whose vast wa
Have pinnacled in clouds their snov
 scalps,
And throned Eternity in icy halls
Of cold sublimity, where forms and fa
The avalanche—the thunderbolt
 snow!
All that expands the spirit, yet appa'
Gather around these summits, as
 show
How Earth may pierce to Heaven, y
 leave vain man below.

LXIII

But ere these matchless heights I dare
 scan,
There is a spot should not be pass'd
 vain,—
Morat! the proud, the patriot fiel
 where man
May gaze on ghastly trophies of t
 slain,
Nor blush for those who conquer'd e
 that plain;
Here Burgundy bequeath'd his tomble
 host,
A bony heap, through ages to remain
Themselves their monument;—the S
 gian coast
Unsepulchred they roam'd, and shriek
 each wandering ghost.

LXIV

While Waterloo with Cannæ's carna
 vies,
Morat and Marathon twin names sh.
 stand;
They were true Glory's stainless vi
 tories,
Won by the unambitious heart and ha
Of a proud, brotherly, and civic ban
All unbought champions in no prince
 cause

218

Of vice-entail'd Corruption; they no land
Doom'd to bewail the blasphemy of laws
Taking kings' rights divine, by some
 Draconic clause.

LXV

By a lone wall a lonelier column rears
A gray and grief-worn aspect of old
 days;
'Tis the last remnant of the wreck of
 years,
And looks as with the wild-bewilder'd
 gaze
Of one to stone converted by amaze,
Yet still with consciousness; and there
 it stands
Making a marvel that it not decays,
When the coeval pride of human hands,
Levell'd Adventicum, hath strew'd her
 subject lands.

LXVI

And there—oh! sweet and sacred be the
 name!—
Julia—the daughter, the devoted—gave
Her youth to Heaven; her heart, be-
 neath a claim
Nearest to Heaven's, broke o'er a
 father's grave.
Justice is sworn 'gainst tears, and hers
 would crave
The life she lived in; but the judge was
 just,
And then she died on him she could not
 save.
Their tomb was simple, and without a
 bust,
And held within their urn one mind, one
 heart, one dust.

LXVII

But these are deeds which should not
 pass away,
And names that must not wither, though
 the earth
Forgets her empires with a just decay,
The enslavers and the enslaved, their
 death and birth;
The high, the mountain-majesty of worth
Should be, and shall, survivor of its woe,
And from its immortality look forth
In the sun's face, like yonder Alpine
 snow,
Imperishably pure beyond all things
 below.

LXVIII

Lake Leman woos me with its crystal
 face,
The mirror where the stars and moun-
 tains view
The stillness of their aspect in each trace
Its clear depth yields of their far height
 and hue:

There is too much of man here, to look
 through
With a fit mind the might which I be-
 hold;
But soon in me shall Loneliness renew
Thoughts hid, but not less cherish'd
 than of old,
Ere mingling with the herd had penn'd me
 in their fold.

LXIX

To fly from, need not be to hate, mankind:
All are not fit with them to stir and toil,
Nor is it discontent to keep the mind
Deep in its fountain, lest it overboil
In the hot throng, where we become the
 spoil
Of our infection, till too late and long
We may deplore and struggle with the
 coil,
In wretched interchange of wrong for
 wrong
Midst a contentious world, striving where
 none are strong.

LXX

There, in a moment we may plunge our
 years
In fatal penitence, and in the blight
Of our own soul turn all our blood to tears,
And colour things to come with hues of
 Night;
The race of life becomes a hopeless flight
To those that walk in darkness: on the
 sea
The boldest steer but where their ports
 invite;
But there are wanderers o'er Eternity
Whose bark drives on and on, and an-
 chor'd ne'er shall be.

LXXI

Is it not better, then, to be alone,
And love Earth only for its earthly sake?
By the blue rushing of the arrowy
 Rhone,
Or the pure bosom of its nursing lake,
Which feeds it as a mother who doth
 make
A fair but froward infant her own care,
Kissing its cries away as these awake;—
Is it not better thus our lives to wear,
Than join the crushing crowd, doom'd to
 inflict or bear?

LXXII

I live not in myself, but I become
Portion of that around me; and to me
High mountains are a feeling, but the
 hum
Of human cities torture: I can see
Nothing to loathe in nature, save to be

A link reluctant in a fleshly chain,
Class'd among creatures, when the soul
 can flee,
And with the sky, the peak, the heaving
 plain
Of ocean, or the stars, mingle, and not in
 vain.

LXXIII

And thus I am absorb'd, and this is life:
I look upon the peopled desert past,
As on a place of agony and strife,
Where, for some sin, to sorrow I was
 cast,
To act and suffer, but remount at last
With a fresh pinion; which I feel to
 spring,
Though young, yet waxing vigorous as
 the blast
Which it would cope with, on delighted
 wing,
Spurning the clay-cold bonds which round
 our being cling.

LXXIV

And when, at length, the mind shall be
 all free
From what it hates in this degraded
 form,
Reft of its carnal life, save what shall be
Existent happier in the fly and worm,—
When elements to elements conform,
And dust is as it should be, shall I not
Feel all I see, less dazzling, but more
 warm?
The bodiless thought? the Spirit of each
 spot?
Of which, even now, I share at times the
 immortal lot?

LXXV

Are not the mountains, waves, and
 skies, a part
Of me and of my soul, as I of them?
Is not the love of these deep in my heart
With a pure passion? should I not con-
 temn
All objects, if compared with these? and
 stem
A tide of suffering, rather than forego
Such feelings for the hard and worldly
 phlegm
Of those whose eyes are only turn'd
 below,
Gazing upon the ground, with thoughts
 which dare not glow?

LXXVI

But this is not my theme; and I return
To that which is immediate, and require
Those who find contemplation in the
 urn,
To look on One, whose dust was once
 all fire,

A native of the land where I respire
The clear air for a while—a passing
 guest,
Where he became a being,—whose
 desire
Was to be glorious; 'twas a foolish
 quest,
The which to gain and keep, he sacrific
 all rest.

LXXVII

Here the self-torturing sophist, will
 Rousseau,
The apostle of affliction, he who threw
Enchantment over passion, and from
 woe
Wrung overwhelming eloquence, first
 drew
The breath which made him wretched
 yet he knew
How to make madness beautiful, an
 cast
O'er erring deeds and thoughts
 heavenly hue
Of words, like sunbeams, dazzling a
 they past
The eyes, which o'er them shed tears fee
 ingly and fast.

LXXVIII

His love was passion's essence:—as
 tree
On fire by lightning, with ethereal flam
Kindled he was, and blasted; for t
 be
Thus, and enamour'd, were in him th
 same.
But his was not the love of livin
 dame,
Nor of the dead who rise upon ou
 dreams,
But of ideal beauty, which became
In him existence, and o'erflowing teem
Along his burning page, distemper'
 though it seems.

LXXIX

This breathed itself to life in Julie, *thi*
Invested her with all that's wild an
 sweet;
This hallow'd, too, the memorable kis
Which every morn his fever'd lip woul
 greet,
From hers, who but with friendship hi
 would meet;
But to that gentle touch through brai
 and breast
Flash'd the thrill'd spirit's love-devour
 ing heat;
In that absorbing sigh perchance mor
 blest
Than vulgar minds may be with all they
 seek possest.

LXXX

His life was one long war with self-
 sought foes,
Or friends by him self-banish'd; for his
 mind
Had grown Suspicion's sanctuary, and
 chose,
For its own cruel sacrifice, the kind,
'Gainst whom he raged with fury
 strange and blind.
But he was phrensied,—wherefore, who
 may know?
Since cause might be which skill could
 never find;
But he was phrensied by disease or
 woe,
o that worst pitch of all, which wears a
 reasoning show.

LXXXI

For then he was inspired, and from him
 came,
As from the Pythian's mystic cave of
 yore,
Those oracles which set the world in
 flame,
Nor ceased to burn till kingdoms were
 no more:
Did he not this for France? which lay
 before
Bow'd to the inborn tyranny of years?
Broken and trembling to the yoke she
 bore,
Till by the voice of him and his compeers
oused up to too much wrath, which
 follows o'ergrown fears?

LXXXII

They made themselves a fearful monu-
 ment!
The wreck of old opinions—things
 which grew,
Breathed from the birth of time: the
 veil they rent,
And what behind it lay, all earth shall
 view.
But good with ill they also overthrew,
Leaving but ruins, wherewith to rebuild
Upon the same foundation, and renew
Dungeons and thrones, which the same
 hour refill'd
s heretofore, because ambition was self-
 will'd.

LXXXIII

But this will not endure, nor be endured!
Mankind have felt their strength, and
 made it felt.
They might have used it better, but,
 allured
By their new vigour, sternly have they
 dealt
On one another; pity ceased to melt

With her once natural charities. But
 they,
Who in oppression's darkness caved
 had dwelt,
They were not eagles, nourish'd with
 the day;
What marvel then, at times, if they mis-
 took their prey?

LXXXIV

What deep wounds ever closed without
 a scar?
The heart's bleed longest, and but heal
 to wear
That which disfigures it; and they who
 war
With their own hopes, and have been
 vanquish'd, bear
Silence, but not submission: in his lair
Fix'd Passion holds his breath, until the
 hour
Which shall atone for years; none need
 despair:
It came, it cometh, and will come,—the
 power
To punish or forgive—in *one* we shall be
 slower.

LXXXV

Clear, placid Leman! thy contrasted
 lake,
With the wild world I dwelt in, is a
 thing
Which warns me, with its stillness, to
 forsake
Earth's troubled waters for a purer
 spring.
This quiet sail is as a noiseless wing
To waft me from distraction; once I
 loved
Torn ocean's roar, but thy soft murmur-
 ing
Sounds sweet as if a Sister's voice re-
 proved,
That I with stern delights should e'er have
 been so moved.

LXXXVI

It is the hush of night, and all between
Thy margin and the mountains, dusk,
 yet clear,
Mellow'd and mingling, yet distinctly
 seen,
Save darken'd Jura, whose capt heights
 appear
Precipitously steep; and drawing near,
There breathes a living fragrance from
 the shore,
Of flowers yet fresh with childhood; on
 the ear
Drops the light drip of the suspended
 oar,
Or chirps the grasshopper one good-night
 carol more·

221

LXXXVII

He is an evening reveller, who makes
His life an infancy, and sings his fill;
At intervals, some bird from out the
 brakes
Starts into voice a moment, then is still.
There seems a floating whisper on the hill,
But that is fancy, for the starlight dews
All silently their tears of love instil,
Weeping themselves away, till they infuse
Deep into nature's breast the spirit of her
 hues.

LXXXVIII

Ye stars! which are the poetry of heaven!
If in your bright leaves we would read
 the fate
Of men and empires,—'tis to be for-
 given,
That in our aspirations to be great,
Our destinies o'erleap their mortal state,
And claim a kindred with you; for ye are
A beauty and a mystery, and create
In us such love and reverence from afar,
That fortune, fame, power, life, have
 named themselves a star.

LXXXIX

All heaven and earth are still—though
 not in sleep,
But breathless, as we grow when feeling
 most;
And silent, as we stand in thoughts too
 deep:—
All heaven and earth are still: From the
 high host
Of stars, to the lull'd lake and mountain-
 coast,
All is concenter'd in a life intense,
Where not a beam, nor air, nor leaf is lost,
But hath a part of being, and a sense
Of that which is of all Creator and defence.

XC

Then stirs the feeling infinite, so felt
In solitude, where we are *least* alone;
A truth, which through our being then
 doth melt,
And purifies from self: it is a tone,
The soul and source of music, which
 makes known
Eternal harmony, and sheds a charm
Like to the fabled Cytherea's zone,
Binding all things with beauty;—
 'twould disarm
The spectre Death, had he substantial
power to harm.

XCI

Not vainly did the early Persian make
His altar the high places, and the peak
Of earth-o'ergazing mountains, and
 thus take
A fit and unwall'd temple, there to seek

The Spirit, in whose honour shrines are
 weak,
Uprear'd of human hands. Come, and
 compare
Columns and idol-dwellings, Goth or
 Greek,
With Nature's realms of worship, earth
 and air,
Nor fix on fond abodes to circumscribe
 thy pray'r!

XCII

The sky is changed!—and such a change!
 Oh night,
And storm, and darkness, ye are won-
 drous strong,
Yet lovely in your strength, as is the light
Of a dark eye in woman! Far along,
From peak to peak, the rattling crags
 among
Leaps the live thunder! Not from one
 lone cloud,
But every mountain now hath found a
 tongue,
And Jura answers, through her misty
 shroud,
Back to the joyous Alps, who call to her
 aloud!

XCIII

And this is in the night:—Most glorious
 night!
Thou wert not sent for slumber! let me
 be
A sharer in thy fierce and far delight,—
A portion of the tempest and of thee!
How the lit lake shines, a phosphoric
 sea,
And the big rain comes dancing to the
 earth!
And now again 'tis black,—and now
 the glee
Of the loud hills shakes with its moun-
 tain-mirth,
As if they did rejoice o'er a young earth-
 quake's birth.

XCIV

Now, where the swift Rhone cleaves his
 way between
Heights which appear as lovers who
 have parted
In hate, whose mining depths so inter-
 vene,
That they can meet no more, though
 broken-hearted;
Though in their souls, which thus each
 other thwarted,
Love was the very root of the fond rage
Which blighted their life's bloom, and
 then departed:
Itself expired, but leaving them an age
Of years all winters,—war within them-
 selves to wage.

XCV

Now, where the quick Rhone thus hath
 cleft his way,
The mightiest of the storms hath ta'en
 his stand:
For here, not one, but many, make their
 play,
And fling their thunder-bolts from hand
 to hand,
Flashing and cast around; of all the
 band,
The brightest through these parted hills
 hath fork'd
His lightnings,—as if he did under-
 stand,
That in such gaps as desolation work'd,
here the hot shaft should blast whatever
 therein lurk'd.

XCVI

Sky, mountains, river, winds, lake,
 lightnings! ye!
With night, and clouds, and thunder,
 and a soul
To make these felt and feeling, well may
 be
Things that have made me watchful; the
 far roll
Of your departing voices, is the knoll
Of what in me is sleepless,—if I rest.
But where of ye, O tempests! is the
 goal?
Are ye like those within the human
 breast?
r do ye find, at length, like eagles, some
 high nest?

XCVII

Could I embody and unbosom now
That which is most within me,—could
 I wreak
My thoughts upon expression, and thus
 throw
Soul, heart, mind, passions, feelings,
 strong or weak,
All that I would have sought, and all I
 seek,
Bear, know, feel, and yet breathe—into
 one word,
And that one word were Lightning, I
 would speak;
But as it is, I live and die unheard,
ith a most voiceless thought, sheathing
 it as a sword.

XCVIII

The morn is up again, the dewy morn,
With breath all incense, and with cheek
 all bloom,
Laughing the clouds away with playful
 scorn,
And living as if earth contain'd no
 tomb,—

And glowing into day: we may resume
The march of our existence: and thus I,
Still on thy shores, fair Leman! may find
 room
And food for meditation, nor pass by
Much, that may give us pause, if ponder'd
 fittingly.

XCIX

Clarens! sweet Clarens, birthplace of
 deep Love!
Thine air is the young breath of passion-
 ate thought;
Thy trees take root in Love; the snows
 above,
The very Glaciers have his colours
 caught,
And sun-set into rose-hues sees them
 wrought
By rays which sleep there lovingly: the
 rocks,
The permanent crags, tell here of Love,
 who sought
In them a refuge from the worldly
 shocks,
Which stir and sting the soul with hope
 that woos, then mocks.

C

Clarens! by heavenly feet thy paths are
 trod,—
Undying Love's, who here ascends a
 throne
To which the steps are mountains; where
 the god
Is a pervading life and light,—so shown
Not on those summits solely, nor alone
In the still cave and forest; o'er the flower
His eye is sparkling, and his breath hath
 blown,
His soft and summer breath, whose
 tender power
Passes the strength of storms in their most
 desolate hour.

CI

All things are here of *him*; from the
 black pines,
Which are his shade on high, and the
 loud roar
Of torrents, where he listeneth, to the
 vines
Which slope his green path downward
 to the shore,
Where the bow'd waters meet him, and
 adore,
Kissing his feet with murmurs; and the
 wood,
The covert of old trees, with trunks all
 hoar,
But light leaves, young as joy, stands
 where it stood,
Offering to him, and his, a populous soli-
 tude.

CII

A populous solitude of bees and birds,
And fairy-form'd and many-colour'd
things,
Who worship him with notes more
sweet than words,
And innocently open their glad wings,
Fearless and full of life: the gush of
springs,
And fall of lofty fountains, and the bend
Of stirring branches, and the bud which
brings
The swiftest thought of beauty, here ex-
tend,
Mingling, and made by Love, unto one
mighty end.

CIII

He who hath loved not, here would learn
that lore,
And make his heart a spirit; he who
knows
That tender mystery, will love the more;
For this is Love's recess, where vain
men's woes,
And the world's waste, have driven him
far from those,
For 'tis his nature to advance or die;
He stands not still, but or decays, or
grows
Into a boundless blessing, which may vie
With the immortal lights, in its eternity!

CIV

'Twas not for fiction chose Rousseau
this spot,
Peopling it with affections; but he found
It was the scene which Passion must
allot
To the Mind's purified beings; 'twas the
ground
Where early Love his Psyche's zone
unbound,
And hallow'd it with loveliness: 'tis
lone,
And wonderful, and deep, and hath a
sound,
And sense, and sight of sweetness; here
the Rhone
Hath spread himself a couch, the Alps
have rear'd a throne.

CV

Lausanne! and Ferney! ye have been
the abodes
Of names which unto you bequeath'd a
name;
Mortals, who sought and found, by
dangerous roads,
A path to perpetuity of fame:
They were gigantic minds, and their
steep aim
Was, Titan-like, on daring doubts to pile

Thoughts which should call down thun
der, and the flame
Of Heaven again assail'd, if Heaven th
while
On man and man's research could deig
do more than smile.

CVI

The one was fire and fickleness, a chil
Most mutable in wishes, but in mind
A wit as various,—gay, grave, sage, o
wild,—
Historian, bard, philosopher, combine
He multiplied himself among mankin
The Proteus of their talents: But his ow
Breathed most in ridicule,—which, a
the wind,
Blew where it listed, laying all thing
prone,—
Now to o'erthrow a fool, and now to shak
a throne.

CVII

The other, deep and slow, exhaustin
thought,
And hiving wisdom with each studiou
year,
In meditation dwelt, with learnin
wrought,
And shaped his weapon with an edg
severe,
Sapping a solemn creed with solemn snee
The lord of irony,—that master-spell
Which stung his foes to wrath, whic
grew from fear,
And doom'd him to the zealot's read
Hell,
Which answers to all doubts so eloquentl
well.

CVIII

Yet, peace be with their ashes,—for b
them,
If merited, the penalty is paid;
It is not ours to judge,—far less con
demn;
The hour must come when such thing
shall be made
Known unto all, or hope and drea
allay'd
By slumber, on one pillow, in the dus
Which, thus much we are sure, must li
decay'd;
And when it shall revive, as is our trus
'Twill be to be forgiven, or suffer what i
just.

CIX

But let me quit man's works, again t
read
His Maker's, spread around me, an
suspend
This page, which from my reveries
feed,
Until it seems prolonging without end

The clouds above me to the white Alps
 tend,
And I must pierce them, and survey
 whate'er
May be permitted, as my steps I bend
To their most great and growing region,
 where
The earth to her embrace compels the
 powers of air.

CX

Italia! too, Italia! looking on thee,
Full flashes on the soul the light of ages,
Since the fierce Carthaginian almost
 won thee,
To the last halo of the chiefs and sages
Who glorify thy consecrated pages;
Thou wert the throne and grave of em-
 pires; still,
The fount at which the panting mind
 assuages
Her thirst of knowledge, quaffing there
 her fill,
Flows from the eternal source of Rome's
 imperial hill.

CXI

Thus far have I proceeded in a theme
Renew'd with no kind auspices:—to feel
We are not what we have been, and to
 deem
We are not what we should be, and to
 steel
The heart against itself; and to conceal,
With a proud caution, love, or hate, or
 aught,—
Passion or feeling, purpose, grief or
 zeal,—
Which is the tyrant spirit of our thought,
Is a stern task of soul:—No matter,—it is
 taught.

CXII

And for these words, thus woven into
 song,
It may be that they are a harmless wile,—
The colouring of the scenes which fleet
 along,
Which I would seize, in passing, to be-
 guile
My breast, or that of others, for a while.
Fame is the thirst of youth, but I am not
So young as to regard men's frown or
 smile,
As loss or guerdon of a glorious lot;
I stood and stand alone,—remember'd or
 forgot.

CXIII

I have not loved the world, nor the world
 me;
I have not flatter'd its rank breath, nor
 bow'd
To its idolatries a patient knee,

Nor coin'd my cheek to smiles, nor cried
 aloud
In worship of an echo; in the crowd
They could not deem me one of such; I
 stood
Among them, but not of them; in a
 shroud
Of thoughts which were not their
 thoughts, and still could,
Had I not filed my mind, which thus itself
 subdued.

CXIV

I have not loved the world, nor the world
 me,—
But let us part fair foes; I do believe,
Though I have found them not, that
 there may be
Words which are things, hopes which
 will not deceive,
And virtues which are merciful, nor
 weave
Snares for the failing; I would also deem
O'er others' griefs that some sincerely
 grieve;
That two, or one, are almost what they
 seem,
That goodness is no name, and happiness
 no dream.

CXV

My daughter! with thy name this song
 begun;
My daughter! with thy name thus much
 shall end;
I see thee not, I hear thee not, but none
Can be so wrapt in thee; thou art the
 friend
To whom the shadows of far years ex-
 tend:
Albeit my brow thou never shouldst be-
 hold,
My voice shall with thy future visions
 blend,
And reach into thy heart, when mine is
 cold,
A token and a tone, even from thy father's
 mould.

CXVI

To aid thy mind's development, to watch
Thy dawn of little joys, to sit and see
Almost thy very growth, to view thee
 catch
Knowledge of objects,—wonders yet to
 thee!
To hold thee lightly on a gentle knee,
And print on thy soft cheek a parent's
 kiss,—
This, it should seem, was not reserved
 for me;
Yet this was in my nature: as it is,
I know not what is there, yet something
 like to this.

225

CXVII

Yet, though dull Hate as duty should be
　taught,
I know that thou wilt love me; though
　my name
Should be shut from thee, as a spell still
　fraught
With desolation, and a broken claim:
Though the grave closed between us,—
　'twere the same,
I know that thou wilt love me; though
　to drain
My blood from out thy being were an
　aim,
And an attainment,—all would be in
　vain,—
Still thou wouldst love me, still that more
　than life retain.

CXVIII

The child of love, though born in bitter-
　ness,
And nurtured in convulsion. Of thy sire
These were the elements, and thine no
　less.
As yet such are around thee, but thy fire
Shall be more temper'd, and thy hope
　far higher.
Sweet be thy cradled slumbers! O'er the
　sea
And from the mountains where I now
　respire,
Fain would I waft such blessing upon
　thee,
As, with a sigh, I deem thou might'st have
　been to me.

CANTO THE FOURTH

'Visto ho Toscana, Lombardia, Romagna,
　Quel Monte che divide, e quel che serra
Italia, e un mare e l' altro, che la bagna.'
　　　　　　　　　Ariosto, Satira iii.

TO

JOHN HOBHOUSE, ESQ., A.M., F.R.S.,
　　　　&c. &c. &c.

VENICE, *January* 2, 1818.
MY DEAR HOBHOUSE,

　AFTER an interval of eight years between the composition of the first and last cantos of Childe Harold, the conclusion of the poem is about to be submitted to the public. In parting with so old a friend, it is not extraordinary that I should recur to one still older and better,—to one who has beheld the birth and death of the other, and to whom I am far more indebted for the social advantages of an enlightened friendship, than—though not ungrate-ful—I can, or could be, to Childe Harold, for any public favour reflected through the poem on the poet,—to one, whom I have known long and ac-companied far, whom I have found wakeful over my sickness and kind in my sorrow, glad in my prosperity and firm in my adversity, true in counsel and trusty in peril,—to a friend often tried and never found wanting;—to yourself.

In so doing, I recur from fiction to truth; and in dedicating to you in its complete, or at least con-cluded state, a poetical work which is the longest the most thoughtful and comprehensive of my compositions, I wish to do honour to myself by the record of many years' intimacy with a man of learning, of talent, of steadiness, and of honour It is not for minds like ours to give or to receive flattery; yet the praises of sincerity have ever been permitted to the voice of friendship; and it is no for you, nor even for others, but to relieve a hear which has not elsewhere, or lately, been so much accustomed to the encounter of good-will as to withstand the shock firmly, that I thus attempt to commemorate your good qualities, or rather the advantages which I have derived from their exer tion. Even the recurrence of the date of this letter the anniversary of the most unfortunate day of my past existence*, but which cannot poison my future while I retain the resource of your friendship, and of my own faculties, will henceforth have a more agreeable recollection for both, inasmuch as it wil remind us of this my attempt to thank you for an indefatigable regard, such as few men have experi enced, and no one could experience without think-ing better of his species and of himself.

It has been our fortune to traverse together, at various periods, the countries of chivalry, history, and fable—Spain, Greece, Asia Minor, and Italy; and what Athens and Constantinople were to us a few years ago, Venice and Rome have been more recently. The poem also, or the pilgrim, or both have accompanied me from first to last; and per-haps it may be a pardonable vanity which induces me to reflect with complacency on a composition which in some degree connects me with the spot where it was produced, and the objects it would fain describe; and however unworthy it may be deemed of those magical and memorable abodes, however short it may fall of our distant concep-tions and immediate impressions, yet as a mark of respect for what is venerable, and of feeling for what is glorious, it has been to me a source of pleasure in the production, and I part with it with a kind of regret, which I hardly suspected that events could have left me for imaginary objects.

With regard to the conduct of the last canto, there will be found less of the pilgrim than in any of the preceding, and that little slightly, if at all, separated from the author speaking in his own person. The fact is, that I had become weary of drawing a line which every one seemed determined not to perceive: like the Chinese in Goldsmith's 'Citizen of the World,' whom nobody would be-lieve to be a Chinese, it was in vain that I asserted, and imagined that I had drawn, a distinction between the author and the pilgrim; and the very anxiety to preserve this difference, and disappoint-ment at finding it unavailing, so far crushed my efforts in the composition, that I determined to abandon it altogether—and have done so. The opinions which have been, or may be, formed on that subject are *now* a matter of indifference; the work is to depend on itself, and not on the writer; and the author, who has no resources in his own mind beyond the reputation, transient or per-manent, which is to arise from his literary efforts, deserves the fate of authors.

In the course of the following canto it was my intention, either in the text or in the notes, to have touched upon the present state of Italian literature, and perhaps of manners. But the text, within the limits I proposed, I soon found hardly sufficient

* His marriage.

226

or the labyrinth of external objects, and the consequent reflections; and for the whole of the notes, excepting a few of the shortest, I am indebted to ourself, and these were necessarily limited to the lucidation of the text.

It is also a delicate, and no very grateful task, to dissert upon the literature and manners of a nation o dissimilar; and requires an attention and impartiality which would induce us—though perhaps no inattentive observers, nor ignorant of the language r customs of the people amongst whom we have recently abode—to distrust, or at least defer our udgment, and more narrowly examine our information. The state of literary, as well as political arty, appears to run, or to *have* run, so high, that or a stranger to steer impartially between them is ext to impossible. It may be enough, then, at least or my purpose, to quote from their own beautiful anguage—'Mi pare che in un paese tutto poetico, he vanta la lingua la più nobile ed insieme la più iolce, tutte tutte le vie diverse si possono tentare, che sinche la patria di Alfieri e di Monti non ha erduto l' antico valore, in tutte essa dovrebbe ssere la prima.' Italy has great names still—Canova, Monti, Ugo Foscolo, Pindemonte, Visonti, Morelli, Cicognara, Albrizzi, Mezzofanti, Mai, Mustoxidi, Aglietti, and Vacca, will secure o the present generation an honourable place in nost of the departments of Art, Science, and Belles Lettres; and in some the very highest—Europe—he World—has but one Canova.

It has been somewhere said by Alfieri, that 'La ianta uomo nasce più robusta in Italia che in qualunque altra terra—e che gli stessi atroci delitti he vi si commettono ne sono una prova.' Without ubscribing to the latter part of his proposition, a dangerous doctrine, the truth of which may be lisputed on better grounds, namely, that the Italians are in no respect more ferocious than their neighbours, that man must be wilfully blind, or gnorantly heedless, who is not struck with the extraordinary capacity of this people, or, if such a word be admissible, their *capabilities*, the facility of their acquisitions, the rapidity of their conceptions, the fire of their genius, their sense of beauty, ind, amidst all the disadvantages of repeated revoutions, the desolation of battles, and the despair of ages, their still unquenched 'longing after imnortality,'—the immortality of independence. And when we ourselves, in riding round the walls of Rome, heard the simple lament of the labourers' chorus, 'Roma! Roma! Roma! Roma non è più ome era prima!' it was difficult not to contrast his melancholy dirge with the bacchanal roar of he songs of exultation still yelled from the London averns, over the carnage of Mont St. Jean, and he betrayal of Genoa, of Italy, of France, and of the world, by men whose conduct you yourself rave exposed in a work worthy of the better days of our history. For me,—

'Non moverò mai corda
Ove la turba di sue ciance assorda.'

What Italy has gained by the late transfer of nations, it were useless for Englishmen to inquire, ill it becomes ascertained that England has acquired something more than a permanent army and a suspended Habeas Corpus; it is enough for them to look at home. For what they have done abroad, and especially in the South, 'Verily they will have their reward,' and at no very distant period.

Wishing you, my dear Hobhouse, a safe and agreeable return to that country whose real welfare can be dearer to none than to yourself, I dedicate to you this poem in its completed state; and repeat once more how truly I am ever

Your obliged and affectionate friend,

BYRON.

I

I STOOD in Venice, on the Bridge of Sighs;
A palace and a prison on each hand:
I saw from out the wave her structures rise
As from the stroke of the enchanter's wand:
A thousand years their cloudy wings expand
Around me, and a dying Glory smiles
O'er the far times, when many a subject land
Look'd to the winged Lion's marble piles,
Where Venice sate in state, throned on her hundred isles!

II

She looks a sea Cybele, fresh from ocean,
Rising with her tiara of proud towers
At airy distance, with majestic motion,
A ruler of the waters and their powers:
And such she was;—her daughters had their dowers
From spoils of nations, and the exhaustless East
Pour'd in her lap all gems in sparkling showers.
In purple was she robed, and of her feast
Monarchs partook, and deem'd their dignity increased.

III

In Venice Tasso's echoes are no more,
And silent rows the songless gondolier;
Her palaces are crumbling to the shore,
And music meets not always now the ear:
Those days are gone—but Beauty still is here.
States fall, arts fade—but Nature doth not die,
Nor yet forget how Venice once was dear,
The pleasant place of all festivity,
The revel of the earth, the masque of Italy!

IV

But unto us she hath a spell beyond
Her name in story, and her long array
Of mighty shadows, whose dim forms despond
Above the dogeless city's vanish'd sway;

Ours is a trophy which will not decay
With the Rialto; Shylock and the Moor,
And Pierre, cannot be swept or worn
away—
The keystones of the arch! though all
were o'er,
For us repeopled were the solitary shore.

V

The beings of the mind are not of clay;
Essentially immortal, they create
And multiply in us a brighter ray
And more beloved existence: that which
Fate
Prohibits to dull life, in this our state
Of mortal bondage, by these spirits
supplied,
First exiles, then replaces what we hate;
Watering the heart whose early flowers
have died,
And with a fresher growth replenishing
the void.

VI

Such is the refuge of our youth and age,
The first from Hope, the last from
Vacancy;
And this worn feeling peoples many a
page,
And, may be, that which grows beneath
mine eye:
Yet there are things whose strong reality
Outshines our fairy-land; in shape and
hues
More beautiful than our fantastic sky,
And the strange constellations which
the Muse
O'er her wild universe is skilful to diffuse:

VII

I saw or dream'd of such,—but let them
go,—
They came like truth, and disappear'd
like dreams;
And whatsoe'er they were—are now but
so:
I could replace them if I would; still
teems
My mind with many a form which aptly
seems
Such as I sought for, and at moments
found;
Let these too go—for waking Reason
deems
Such overweening phantasies unsound,
And other voices speak, and other sights
surround.

VIII

I've taught me other tongues, and in
strange eyes
Have made me not a stranger; to the
mind
Which is itself, no changes bring sur-
prise;

Nor is it harsh to make, nor hard to
find
A country with—ay, or without man-
kind;
Yet was I born where men are proud
be,—
Not without cause; and should I leave
behind
The inviolate island of the sage and
free,
And seek me out a home by a remoter
sea,

IX

Perhaps I loved it well: and should I
lay
My ashes in a soil which is not mine,
My spirit shall resume it—if we may
Unbodied choose a sanctuary. I twine
My hopes of being remember'd in my
line
With my land's language: if too fond
and far
These aspirations in their scope in-
cline,—
If my fame should be, as my fortunes
are,
Of hasty growth and blight, and dull
Oblivion bar

X

My name from out the temple where the
dead
Are honour'd by the nations—let it be—
And light the laurels on a loftier head!
And be the Spartan's epitaph on me—
'Sparta hath many a worthier son than
he.'
Meantime I seek no sympathies, nor
need;
The thorns which I have reap'd are of
the tree
I planted: they have torn me, and I
bleed:
I should have known what fruit would
spring from such a seed.

XI

The spouseless Adriatic mourns her
lord;
And, annual marriage now no more re-
new'd,
The Bucentaur lies rotting unrestored,
Neglected garment of her widowhood!
St. Mark yet sees his lion where he
stood
Stand, but in mockery of his wither'd
power,
Over the proud Place where an Emperor
sued,
And monarchs gazed and envied in the
hour
When Venice was a queen with an un-
equall'd dower.

XII

The Suabian sued, and now the Austrian
 reigns—
An Emperor tramples where an Emper-
 or knelt;
Kingdoms are shrunk to provinces, and
 chains
Clank over sceptred cities; nations melt
From power's high pinnacle, when they
 have felt
The sunshine for a while, and downward
 go
Like Lauwine loosen'd from the moun-
 tain's belt;
Oh for one hour of blind old Dandolo!
Th' octogenarian chief, Byzantium's con-
 quering foe.

XIII

Before St. Mark still glow his steeds of
 brass,
Their gilded collars glittering in the sun;
But is not Doria's menace come to pass?
Are they not bridled?—Venice, lost and
 won,
Her thirteen hundred years of freedom
 done,
Sinks, like a seaweed, unto whence she
 rose!
Better be whelm'd beneath the waves,
 and shun,
Even in destruction's depth, her foreign
 foes,
From whom submission wrings an in-
 famous repose.

XIV

In youth she was all glory,—a new Tyre;
Her very by-word sprung from victory,
The 'Planter of the Lion,' which
 through fire
And blood she bore o'er subject earth
 and sea;
Though making many slaves, herself
 still free,
And Europe's bulwark 'gainst the Otto-
 mite;
Witness Troy's rival, Candia! Vouch
 it, ye
Immortal waves that saw Lepanto's
 fight!
For ye are names no time nor tyranny can
 blight.

XV

Statues of glass—all shiver'd—the long
 file
Of her dead Doges are declined to dust;
But where they dwelt, the vast and
 sumptuous pile
Bespeaks the pageant of their splendid
 trust;
Their sceptre broken, and their sword
 in rust,

Have yielded to the stranger: empty
 halls,
Thin streets, and foreign aspects, such
 as must
Too oft remind her who and what en-
 thrals,
Have flung a desolate cloud o'er Venice'
 lovely walls.

XVI

When Athens' armies fell at Syracuse,
And fetter'd thousands bore the yoke
 of war,
Redemption rose up in the Attic Muse,
Her voice their only ransom from afar:
See! as they chant the tragic hymn, the
 car
Of the o'ermaster'd victor stops, the
 reins
Fall from his hands, his idle scimitar
Starts from its belt—he rends his cap-
 tive's chains,
And bids him thank the bard for freedom
 and his strains.

XVII

Thus, Venice, if no stronger claim were
 thine,
Were all thy proud historic deeds forgot,
Thy choral memory of the Bard divine,
Thy love of Tasso, should have cut the
 knot
Which ties thee to thy tyrants; and thy lot
Is shameful to the nations,—most of all,
Albion! to thee: the Ocean queen should
 not
Abandon Ocean's children; in the fall
Of Venice think of thine, despite thy
 watery wall.

XVIII

I loved her from my boyhood; she to me
Was as a fairy city of the heart,
Rising like water-columns from the sea,
Of joy the sojourn, and of wealth the
 mart;
And Otway, Radcliffe, Schiller, Shak-
 speare's art,
Had stamp'd her image in me, and even
 so,
Although I found her thus, we did not
 part;
Perchance even dearer in her day of woe,
Than when she was a boast, a marvel, and
 a show.

XIX

I can repeople with the past—and of
The present there is still for eye and
 thought,
And meditation chasten'd down,
 enough;
And more, it may be, than I hoped or
 sought;

And of the happiest moments which
 were wrought
Within the web of my existence, some
From thee, fair Venice! have their col-
 ours caught:
There are some feelings Time cannot be-
 numb,
Nor Torture shake, or mine would now be
 cold and dumb.

XX

But from their nature will the Tannen
 grow
Loftiest on loftiest and least shelter'd
 rocks,
Rooted in barrenness, where nought
 below
Of soil supports them 'gainst the Alpine
 shocks
Of eddying storms; yet springs the
 trunk, and mocks
The howling tempest, till its height and
 frame
Are worthy of the mountains from
 whose blocks
Of bleak, gray granite into life it came,
And grew a giant tree;—the mind may
 grow the same.

XXI

Existence may be borne, and the deep
 root
Of life and sufferance make its firm
 abode
The bare and desolated bosoms: mute
The camel labours with the heaviest
 load,
And the wolf dies in silence,—not be-
 stow'd
In vain should such example be; if they,
Things of ignoble or of savage mood,
Endure and shrink not, we of nobler
 clay
May temper it to bear,—it is but for a
 day.

XXII

All suffering doth destroy, or is de-
 stroy'd,
Even by the sufferer; and, in each event,
Ends:—Some, with hope replenish'd
 and rebuoy'd,
Return to whence they came—with like
 intent,
And weave their web again; some,
 bow'd and bent,
Wax gray and ghastly, withering ere
 their time,
And perish with the reed on which they
 leant;
Some seek devotion, toil, war, good or
 crime,
According as their souls were form'd to
 sink or climb.

XXIII

But ever and anon of griefs subdued
There comes a token like a scorpion's
 sting,
Scarce seen, but with fresh bitterness
 imbued;
And slight withal may be the things
 which bring
Back on the heart the weight which it
 would fling
Aside for ever: it may be a sound—
A tone of music—summer's eve—or
 spring—
A flower—the wind—the ocean—which
 shall wound,
Striking the electric chain wherewith we
 are darkly bound;

XXIV

And how and why we know not, nor can
 trace
Home to its cloud this lightning of the
 mind,
But feel the shock renew'd, nor can
 efface
The blight and blackening which it
 leaves behind,
Which out of things familiar, un-
 design'd,
When least we deem of such, calls up to
 view
The spectres whom no exorcism can
 bind,—
The cold, the changed, perchance the
 dead—anew,
The mourn'd, the loved, the lost—too
 many! yet how few!

XXV

But my soul wanders; I demand it
 back
To meditate amongst decay, and stand
A ruin amidst ruins; there to track
Fall'n states and buried greatness, o'er
 a land
Which *was* the mightiest in its old com-
 mand,
And *is* the loveliest, and must ever be
The master-mould of Nature's heavenly
 hand;
Wherein were cast the heroic and the
 free,
The beautiful, the brave, the lords of earth
 and sea,

XXVI

The commonwealth of kings, the men
 of Rome!
And even since, and now, fair Italy!
Thou art the garden of the world, the
 home
Of all Art yields, and Nature can
 decree;

Even in thy desert, what is like to thee?
Thy very weeds are beautiful, thy waste
More rich than other climes' fertility;
Thy wreck a glory, and thy ruin graced
With an immaculate charm which cannot
 be defaced.

XXVII

The moon is up, and yet it is not night;
Sunset divides the sky with her; a sea
Of glory streams along the Alpine
 height
Of blue Friuli's mountains; Heaven is
 free
From clouds, but of all colours seems
 to be,—
Melted to one vast Iris of the West,—
Where the Day joins the past Eternity,
While, on the other hand, meek Dian's
 crest
Floats through the azure air—an island of
 the blest!

XXVIII

A single star is at her side, and reigns
With her o'er half the lovely heaven; but
 still
Yon sunny sea heaves brightly, and re-
 mains
Roll'd o'er the peak of the far Rhætian
 hill,
As Day and Night contending were,
 until
Nature reclaim'd her order:—gently
 flows
The deep-dyed Brenta, where their hues
 instil
The odorous purple of a new-born rose,
Which streams upon her stream, and
 glass'd within it glows,

XXIX

Fill'd with the face of heaven, which,
 from afar,
Comes down upon the waters; all its
 hues,
From the rich sunset to the rising star,
Their magical variety diffuse:
And now they change; a paler shadow
 strews
Its mantle o'er the mountains; parting
 day
Dies like the dolphin, whom each pang
 imbues
With a new colour as it gasps away—
The last still loveliest,—till—'tis gone—
 and all is gray.

XXX

There is a tomb in Arqua;—rear'd in
 air,
Pillar'd in their sarcophagus, repose
The bones of Laura's lover: here repair
Many familiar with his well-sung woes,

The pilgrims of his genius. He arose
To raise a language, and his land reclaim
From the dull yoke of her barbaric foes:
Watering the tree which bears his lady's
 name
With his melodious tears, he gave himself
 to fame.

XXXI

They keep his dust in Arqua, where he
 died;
The mountain-village where his latter
 days
Went down the vale of years; and 'tis
 their pride—
An honest pride—and let it be their
 praise,
To offer to the passing stranger's gaze
His mansion and his sepulchre; both
 plain
And venerably simple, such as raise
A feeling more accordant with his strain
Than if a pyramid form'd his monumental
 fane.

XXXII

And the soft quiet hamlet where he dwelt
Is one of that complexion which seems
 made
For those who their mortality have felt,
And sought a refuge from their hopes
 decay'd
In the deep umbrage of a green hill's
 shade,
Which shows a distant prospect far away
Of busy cities, now in vain display'd,
For they can lure no further; and the ray
Of a bright sun can make sufficient
 holiday,

XXXIII

Developing the mountains, leaves, and
 flowers,
And shining in the brawling brook,
 whereby,
Clear as its current, glide the sauntering
 hours
With a calm languor, which, though to
 the eye
Idlesse it seem, hath its morality.
If from society we learn to live,
'Tis solitude should teach us how to die;
It hath no flatterers; vanity can give
No hollow aid; alone—man with his God
 must strive:

XXXIV

Or, it may be, with demons, who impair
The strength of better thoughts, and
 seek their prey
In melancholy bosoms, such as were
Of moody texture from their earliest
 day,

And loved to dwell in darkness and dis-
may,
Deeming themselves predestined to a
doom
Which is not of the pangs that pass
away;
Making the sun like blood, the earth a
tomb,
The tomb a hell, and hell itself a murkier
gloom.

XXXV

Ferrara! in thy wide and grass-grown
streets,
Whose symmetry was not for solitude,
There seems as 'twere a curse upon the
seats
Of former sovereigns, and the antique
brood
Of Este, which for many an age made
good
Its strength within thy walls, and was of
yore
Patron or tyrant, as the changing mood
Of petty power impell'd, of those who
wore
The wreath which Dante's brow alone had
worn before.

XXXVI

And Tasso is their glory and their
shame.
Hark to his strain! and then survey his
cell!
And see how dearly earn'd Torquato's
fame,
And where Alfonso bade his poet dwell:
The miserable despot could not quell
The insulted mind he sought to quench,
and blend
With the surrounding maniacs, in the
hell
Where he had plunged it. Glory with-
out end
Scatter'd the clouds away; and on that
name attend

XXXVII

The tears and praises of all time; while
thine
Would rot in its oblivion—in the sink
Of worthless dust, which from thy
boasted line
Is shaken into nothing—but the link
Thou formest in his fortunes bids us
think
Of thy poor malice, naming thee with
scorn:
Alfonso! how thy ducal pageants shrink
From thee! if in another station born,
Scarce fit to be the slave of him thou
madest to mourn:

XXXVIII

Thou! form'd to eat, and be despised
and die,
Even as the beasts that perish, save that
thou
Hadst a more splendid trough and wider
sty:
He! with a glory round his furrow'd
brow,
Which emanated then, and dazzles now,
In face of all his foes, the Cruscan quire,
And Boileau, whose rash envy could
allow
No strain which shamed his country's
creaking lyre,
That whetstone of the teeth—monotony
in wire!

XXXIX

Peace to Torquato's injured shade!
'twas his
In life and death to be the mark where
Wrong
Aim'd with her poison'd arrows,—but
to miss.
Oh, victor unsurpass'd in modern song!
Each year brings forth its millions; but
how long
The tide of generations shall roll on,
And not the whole combined and count-
less throng
Compose a mind like thine? though all
in one
Condensed their scatter'd rays, they would
not form a sun.

XL

Great as thou art, yet parallel'd by those,
Thy countrymen, before thee born to
shine,
The Bards of Hell and Chivalry: first rose
The Tuscan father's Comedy Divine;
Then, not unequal to the Florentine,
The southern Scott, the minstrel who
call'd forth
A new creation with his magic line,
And, like the Ariosto of the North,
Sang ladye-love and war, romance and
knightly worth.

XLI

The lightning rent from Ariosto's bust
The iron crown of laurel's mimick'd
leaves;
Nor was the ominous element unjust,
For the true laurel-wreath which Glory
weaves
Is of the tree no bolt of thunder cleaves,
And the false semblance but disgraced
his brow;
Yet still, if fondly Superstition grieves,
Know, that the lightning sanctifies below
Whate'er it strikes;—yon head is doubly
sacred now.

XLII

Italia! oh Italia! thou who hast
The fatal gift of beauty, which became
A funeral dower of present woes and
 past,
On thy sweet brow is sorrow plough'd
 by shame,
And annals graved in characters of
 flame.
Oh, God! that thou wert in thy naked-
 ness
Less lovely or more powerful, and
 couldst claim
Thy right, and awe the robbers back,
 who press
To shed thy blood, and drink the tears of
 thy distress;

XLIII

Then might'st thou more appal; or, less
 desired,
Be homely and be peaceful, undeplored
For thy destructive charms; then, still
 untired,
Would not be seen the armed torrents
 pour'd
Down the deep Alps; nor would the
 hostile horde
Of many-nation'd spoilers from the Po
Quaff blood and water; nor the stran-
 ger's sword
Be thy sad weapon of defence, and so,
Victor or vanquish'd, thou the slave of
 friend or foe.

XLIV

Wandering in youth, I traced the path
 of him,
The Roman friend of Rome's least-
 mortal mind,
The friend of Tully: as my bark did
 skim
The bright blue waters with a fanning
 wind,
Came Megara before me, and behind
Ægina lay, Piræus on the right,
And Corinth on the left; I lay re-
 clined
Along the prow, and saw all these unite
In ruin, even as he had seen the desolate
 sight;

XLV

For Time hath not rebuilt them, but
 uprear'd
Barbaric dwellings on their shatter'd
 site,
Which only make more mourn'd and
 more endear'd
The few last rays of their far-scatter'd
 light,
And the crush'd relics of their vanish'd
 might.

The Roman saw these tombs in his own
 age,
These sepulchres of cities, which excite
Sad wonder, and his yet surviving page
The moral lesson bears, drawn from such
 pilgrimage.

XLVI

That page is now before me, and on
 mine
His country's ruin added to the mass
Of perish'd states he mourn'd in their
 decline,
And I in desolation: all that *was*
Of then destruction *is*; and now, alas!
Rome—Rome imperial, bows her to the
 storm,
In the same dust and blackness, and we
 pass
The skeleton of her Titanic form,
Wrecks of another world, whose ashes still
 are warm.

XLVII

Yet, Italy! through every other land
Thy wrongs should ring, and shall, from
 side to side;
Mother of Arts! as once of arms; thy
 hand
Was then our guardian, and is still our
 guide;
Parent of our religion! whom the wide
Nations have knelt to for the keys of
 heaven!
Europe, repentant of her parricide,
Shall yet redeem thee, and, all backward
 driven,
Roll the barbarian tide, and sue to be for-
 given.

XLVIII

But Arno wins us to the fair white walls,
Where the Etrurian Athens claims and
 keeps
A softer feeling for her fairy halls.
Girt by her theatre of hills, she reaps
Her corn, and wine, and oil, and Plenty
 leaps
To laughing life, with her redundant
 horn.
Along the banks where smiling Arno
 sweeps
Was modern Luxury of Commerce
 born,
And buried Learning rose, redeem'd to a
 new morn.

XLIX

There, too, the Goddess loves in stone,
 and fills
The air around with beauty; we inhale
The ambrosial aspect, which, beheld,
 instils
Part of its immortality; the veil

233

Of heaven is half undrawn; within the
 pale
We stand, and in that form and face be-
 hold
What Mind can make, when Nature's
 self would fail;
And to the fond idolaters of old
Envy the innate flash which such a soul
 could mould:

L

We gaze and turn away, and know not
 where,
Dazzled and drunk with beauty, till the
 heart
Reels with its fulness; there—for ever
 there—
Chain'd to the chariot of triumphal Art,
We stand as captives, and would not
 depart.
Away!—there need no words nor terms
 precise,
The paltry jargon of the marble mart,
Where Pedantry gulls Folly—we have
 eyes:
Blood, pulse, and breast confirm the Dar-
 dan Shepherd's prize.

LI

Appear'dst thou not to Paris in this
 guise?
Or to more deeply blest Anchises? or,
In all thy perfect Goddess-ship, when lies
Before thee thy own vanquish'd Lord
 of War?
And gazing in thy face as toward a star,
Laid on thy lap, his eyes to thee upturn,
Feeding on thy sweet cheek! while thy
 lips are
With lava kisses melting while they burn,
Shower'd on his eyelids, brow, and mouth,
 as from an urn?

LII

Glowing, and circumfused in speech-
 less love
Their full divinity inadequate
That feeling to express, or to improve,
The gods become as mortals, and man's
 fate
Has moments like their brightest; but
 the weight
Of earth recoils upon us;—let it go!
We can recall such visions, and create,
From what has been, or might be, things
 which grow
Into thy statue's form, and look like gods
 below.

LIII

I leave to learned fingers and wise
 hands,
The artist and his ape, to teach and tell
How well his connoisseurship under-
 stands

The graceful bend, and the voluptuous
 swell:
Let these describe the undescribable:
I would not their vile breath should
 crisp the stream
Wherein that image shall for ever dwell;
The unruffled mirror of the loveliest
 dream
That ever left the sky on the deep soul to
 beam.

LIV

In Santa Croce's holy precincts lie
Ashes which make it holier, dust which is
Even in itself an immortality,
Though there were nothing save the
 past, and this,
The particle of those sublimities
Which have relapsed to chaos: here
 repose
Angelo's, Alfieri's bones, and his,
The starry Galileo, with his woes;
Here Machiavelli's earth return'd to
 whence it rose.

LV

These are four minds, which, like the
 elements,
Might furnish forth creation:—Italy!
Time, which hath wrong'd thee with ten
 thousand rents
Of thine imperial garment, shall deny,
And hath denied, to every other sky,
Spirits which soar from ruin: thy decay
Is still impregnate with divinity,
Which gilds it with revivifying ray;
Such as the great of yore, Canova is to-day.

LVI

But where repose the all Etruscan three—
Dante, and Petrarch, and, scarce less
 than they,
The Bard of Prose, creative spirit! he
Of the Hundred Tales of love—where
 did they lay
Their bones, distinguish'd from our
 common clay
In death as life? Are they resolved to
 dust,
And have their country's marbles nought
 to say?
Could not her quarries furnish forth one
 bust?
Did they not to her breast their filial earth
 entrust?

LVII

Ungrateful Florence! Dante sleeps afar,
Like Scipio, buried by the upbraiding
 shore;
Thy factions, in their worse than civil
 war,
Proscribed the bard whose name for
 evermore

Their children's children would in vain
 adore
With the remorse of ages; and the crown
Which Petrarch's laureate brow su-
 premely wore,
Upon a far and foreign soil had grown,
His life, his fame, his grave, though rifled—
 not thine own.

LVIII

Boccaccio to his parent earth be-
 queath'd
His dust,—and lies it not her great
 among,
With many a sweet and solemn requiem
 breathed
O'er him who form'd the Tuscan's siren
 tongue?
That music in itself, whose sounds are
 song,
The poetry of speech? No;—even his
 tomb
Uptorn, must bear the hyæna bigot's
 wrong,
No more amidst the meaner dead find
 room,
Nor claim a passing sigh, because it told
 for *whom*!

LIX

And Santa Croce wants their mighty
 dust;
Yet for this want more noted, as of
 yore
The Cæsar's pageant, shorn of Brutus'
 bust,
Did but of Rome's best Son remind her
 more:
Happier Ravenna! on thy hoary shore,
Fortress of falling empire! honour'd
 sleeps
The immortal exile;—Arqua, too, her
 store
Of tuneful relics proudly claims and
 keeps,
While Florence vainly begs her banish'd
 dead and weeps.

LX

What is her pyramid of precious stones?
Of porphyry, jasper, agate, and all hues
Of gem and marble, to encrust the bones
Of merchant-dukes? the momentary
 dews
Which, sparkling to the twilight stars,
 infuse
Freshness in the green turf that wraps
 the dead,
Whose names are mausoleums of the
 Muse,
Are gently prest with far more reverent
 tread
Than ever paced the slab which paves the
 princely head.

LXI

There be more things to greet the heart
 and eyes
In Arno's dome of Art's most princely
 shrine,
Where Sculpture with her rainbow sis-
 ter vies;
There be more marvels yet—but not for
 mine;
For I have been accustom'd to entwine
My thoughts with Nature rather in the
 fields,
Than Art in galleries; though a work
 divine
Calls for my spirit's homage, yet it yields
Less than it feels, because the weapon
 which it wields

LXII

Is of another temper, and I roam
By Thrasimene's lake, in the defiles
Fatal to Roman rashness, more at
 home;
For there the Carthaginian's warlike
 wiles
Come back before me, as his skill be-
 guiles
The host between the mountains and the
 shore,
Where Courage falls in her despairing
 files,
And torrents, swoll'n to rivers with their
 gore,
Reek through the sultry plain, with legions
 scatter'd o'er,

LXIII

Like to a forest fell'd by mountain winds;
And such the storm of battle on this
 day,
And such the frenzy, whose convulsion
 blinds
To all save carnage, that, beneath the
 fray,
An earthquake reel'd unheededly away!
None felt stern Nature rocking at his
 feet,
And yawning forth a grave for those
 who lay
Upon their bucklers for a winding-
 sheet;
Such is the absorbing hate when warring
 nations meet!

LXIV

The Earth to them was as a rolling bark
Which bore them to Eternity; they saw
The Ocean round, but had no time to
 mark
The motions of their vessel; Nature's
 law,
In them suspended, reck'd not of the
 awe

Which reigns when mountains tremble,
 and the birds
Plunge in the clouds for refuge, and
 withdraw
From their down-toppling nests; and
 bellowing herds
Stumble o'er heaving plains, and man's
 dread hath no words.

LXV

Far other scene is Thrasimene now;
Her lake a sheet of silver, and her plain
Rent by no ravage save the gentle
 plough;
Her aged trees rise thick as once the
 slain
Lay where their roots are; but a brook
 hath ta'en—
A little rill of scanty stream and bed—
A name of blood from that day's san-
 guine rain;
And Sanguinetto tells ye where the dead
Made the earth wet, and turn'd the un-
 willing waters red.

LXVI

But thou, Clitumnus! in thy sweetest
 wave
Of the most living crystal that was e'er
The haunt of river nymph, to gaze and
 lave
Her limbs where nothing hid them, thou
 dost rear
Thy grassy banks whereon the milk-
 white steer
Grazes; the purest god of gentle waters!
And most serene of aspect, and most
 clear;
Surely that stream was unprofaned by
 slaughters,
A mirror and a bath for Beauty's youngest
 daughters!

LXVII

And on thy happy shore a Temple still,
Of small and delicate proportion, keeps,
Upon a mild declivity of hill,
Its memory of thee; beneath it sweeps
Thy current's calmness; oft from out it
 leaps
The finny darter with the glittering
 scales,
Who dwells and revels in thy glassy
 deeps;
While, chance, some scatter'd water-
 lily sails
Down where the shallower wave still tells
 its bubbling tales.

LXVIII

Pass not unblest the Genius of the place!
If through the air a zephyr more serene
Win to the brow, 'tis his; and if ye trace
Along his margin a more eloquent green,

If on the heart the freshness of the scene
Sprinkle its coolness, and from the dry
 dust
Of weary life a moment lave it clean
With Nature's baptism,—'tis to him ye
 must
Pay orisons for this suspension of disgust.

LXIX

The roar of waters!—from the headlong
 height
Velino cleaves the wave-worn precipice;
The fall of waters! rapid as the light
The flashing mass foams shaking the
 abyss;
The hell of waters! where they howl and
 hiss,
And boil in endless torture; while the
 sweat
Of their great agony, wrung out from this
Their Phlegethon, curls round the rocks
 of jet
That guard the gulf around, in pitiless
 horror set,

LXX

And mounts in spray the skies, and
 thence again
Returns in an unceasing shower, which
 round,
With its unemptied cloud of gentle rain,
Is an eternal April to the ground,
Making it all one emerald:—how pro-
 found
The gulf! and how the giant element
From rock to rock leaps with delirious
 bound,
Crushing the cliffs, which, downward
 worn and rent
With his fierce footsteps, yield in chasms
 a fearful vent

LXXI

To the broad column which rolls on,
 and shows
More like the fountain of an infant sea
Torn from the womb of mountains by
 the throes
Of a new world, than only thus to be
Parent of rivers, which flow gushingly,
With many windings, through the
 vale:—Look back!
Lo! where it comes like an eternity,
As if to sweep down all things in its track,
Charming the eye with dread,—a match-
 less cataract,

LXXII

Horribly beautiful! but on the verge,
From side to side, beneath the glittering
 morn,
An Iris sits, amidst the infernal surge,
Like Hope upon a death-bed, and, un-
 worn

Its steady dyes, while all around is torn
By the distracted waters, bears serene
Its brilliant hues with all their beams
unshorn:
Resembling, 'mid the torture of the
scene,
Love watching Madness with unalterable
mien.

LXXIII

Once more upon the woody Apennine,
The infant Alps, which—had I not be-
fore
Gazed on their mightier parents, where
the pine
Sits on more shaggy summits, and where
roar
The thundering Lauwine—might be
worshipp'd more;
But I have seen the soaring Jungfrau rear
Her never-trodden snow, and seen the
hoar
Glaciers of bleak Mont Blanc both far
and near,
And in Chimari heard the thunder-hills of
fear,

LXXIV

Th' Acroceraunian mountains of old
name;
And on Parnassus seen the eagles fly
Like spirits of the spot, as 'twere for
fame,
For still they soared unutterably high:
I've look'd on Ida with a Trojan's eye;
Athos, Olympus, Ætna, Atlas, made
These hills seem things of lesser dignity,
All, save the lone Soracte's height, dis-
play'd
Not now in snow, which asks the lyric
Roman's aid

LXXV

For our remembrance, and from out the
plain
Heaves like a long-swept wave about to
break,
And on the curl hangs pausing: not in
vain
May he, who will, his recollections rake,
And quote in classic raptures, and awake
The hills with Latin echoes; I abhorr'd
Too much, to conquer for the poet's
sake,
The drill'd dull lesson, forced down
word by word
In my repugnant youth, with pleasure to
record

LXXVI

Aught that recalls the daily drug which
turn'd
My sickening memory; and, though
Time hath taught

My mind to meditate what then it
learn'd,
Yet such the fix'd inveteracy wrought
By the impatience of my early thought,
That, with the freshness wearing out
before
My mind could relish what it might have
sought,
If free to choose, I cannot now restore
Its health; but what it then detested, still
abhor.

LXXVII

Then farewell, Horace; whom I hated so,
Not for thy faults, but mine; it is a curse
To understand, not feel thy lyric flow,
To comprehend, but never love thy verse:
Although no deeper Moralist rehearse
Our little life, nor Bard prescribe his art,
Nor livelier Satirist the conscience
pierce,
Awakening without wounding the
touch'd heart,
Yet fare thee well—upon Soracte's ridge
we part.

LXXVIII

Oh Rome! my country! city of the soul!
The orphans of the heart must turn to
thee,
Lone mother of dead empires! and con-
trol
In their shut breasts their petty misery.
What are our woes and sufferance? Come
and see
The cypress, hear the owl, and plod your
way
O'er steps of broken thrones and tem-
ples, Ye!
Whose agonies are evils of a day—
A world is at our feet as fragile as our clay.

LXXIX

The Niobe of nations! there she stands,
Childless and crownless, in her voiceless
woe;
An empty urn within her wither'd hands,
Whose holy dust was scatter'd long ago;
The Scipios' tomb contains no ashes
now;
The very sepulchres lie tenantless
Of their heroic dwellers: dost thou flow,
Old Tiber! through a marble wilderness?
Rise, with thy yellow waves, and mantle
her distress.

LXXX

The Goth, the Christian, Time, War,
Flood, and Fire,
Have dealt upon the seven-hill'd city's
pride;
She saw her glories star by star expire,
And up the steep barbarian monarchs
ride,

237

Where the car climb'd the Capitol; far
and wide
Temple and tower went down, nor left a
site:
Chaos of ruins! who shall trace the
void,
O'er the dim fragments cast a lunar
light,
And say, 'here was, or is,' where all is
doubly night?

LXXXI

The double night of ages, and of her,
Night's daughter, Ignorance, hath wrapt
and wrap
All round us: we but feel our way to
err:
The ocean hath his chart, the stars their
map,
And Knowledge spreads them on her
ample lap;
But Rome is as the desert, where we
steer
Stumbling o'er recollections; now we
clap
Our hands, and cry 'Eureka!' it is
clear—
When but some false mirage of ruin rises
near.

LXXXII

Alas! the lofty city! and alas!
The trebly hundred triumphs! and the
day
When Brutus made the dagger's edge
surpass
The conqueror's sword in bearing fame
away!
Alas, for Tully's voice, and Virgil's lay,
And Livy's pictured page!—but these
shall be
Her resurrection; all beside—decay.
Alas, for Earth, for never shall we see
That brightness in her eye she bore when
Rome was free!

LXXXIII

Oh thou, whose chariot roll'd on For-
tune's wheel,
Triumphant Sylla! Thou, who didst sub-
due
Thy country's foes ere thou wouldst
pause to feel
The wrath of thy own wrongs, or reap
the due
Of hoarded vengeance till thine eagles
flew
O'er prostrate Asia;—thou, who with
thy frown
Annihilated senates—Roman, too,
With all thy vices, for thou didst lay
down
With an atoning smile a more than earthly
crown—

LXXXIV

The dictatorial wreath—couldst thou
divine
To what would one day dwindle that
which made
Thee more than mortal? and that so supine
By aught than Romans Rome should
thus be laid?
She who was named Eternal, and array'd
Her warriors but to conquer—she who
veil'd
Earth with her haughty shadow, and
display'd,
Until the o'er-canopied horizon fail'd,
Her rushing wings—Oh! she who was Al-
mighty hail'd!

LXXXV

Sylla was first of victors; but our own
The sagest of usurpers, Cromwell!—he
Too swept off senates while he hew'd the
throne
Down to a block—immortal rebel! See
What crimes it costs to be a moment free,
And famous through all ages! but be-
neath
His fate the moral lurks of destiny;
His day of double victory and death
Beheld him win two realms, and, happier,
yield his breath.

LXXXVI

The third of the same moon whose for-
mer course
Had all but crown'd him, on the self-
same day
Deposed him gently from his throne or
force,
And laid him with the earth's preceding
clay.
And show'd not Fortune thus how fame
and sway,
And all we deem delightful, and consume
Our souls to compass through each
arduous way,
Are in her eyes less happy than the
tomb?
Were they but so in man's, how different
were his doom!

LXXXVII

And thou, dread statue! yet existent in
The austerest form of naked majesty,
Thou who beheldest, 'mid the assassins'
din,
At thy bathed base the bloody Cæsar lie,
Folding his robe in dying dignity,
An offering to thine altar from the queen
Of gods and men, great Nemesis! did he
die,
And thou, too, perish, Pompey? have ye
been
Victors of countless kings, or puppets of
a scene?

LXXXVIII

And thou, the thunder-stricken nurse of
 Rome!
She-wolf! whose brazen-imaged dugs
 impart
The milk of conquest yet within the
 dome
Where, as a monument of antique art,
Thou standest:—Mother of the mighty
 heart,
Which the great founder suck'd from
 thy wild teat,
Scorch'd by the Roman Jove's ethereal
 dart,
And thy limbs black with lightning—
 dost thou yet
Guard thine immortal cubs, nor thy fond
 charge forget?

LXXXIX

Thou dost; but all thy foster-babes are
 dead—
The men of iron: and the world hath
 rear'd
Cities from out their sepulchres: men bled
In imitation of the things they fear'd,
And fought and conquer'd, and the
 same course steer'd,
At apish distance; but as yet none have,
Nor could, the same supremacy have
 near'd,
Save one vain man, who is not in the grave,
But, vanquish'd by himself, to his own
 slaves a slave—

XC

The fool of false dominion—and a kind
Of bastard Cæsar, following him of old
With steps unequal; for the Roman's
 mind
Was modell'd in a less terrestrial mould,
With passions fiercer, yet a judgment cold,
And an immortal instinct which re-
 deem'd
The frailties of a heart so soft, yet bold,
Alcides with the distaff now he seem'd
At Cleopatra's feet,—and now himself he
 beam'd,

XCI

And came—and saw—and conquer'd!
 But the man
Who would have tamed his eagles down
 to flee,
Like a train'd falcon, in the Gallic van,
Which he, in sooth, long led to victory,
With a deaf heart, which never seem'd
 to be
A listener to itself, was strangely framed;
With but one weakest weakness—
 vanity,
Coquettish in ambition, still he aim'd—
At what? can he avouch, or answer what
 he claim'd?

XCII

And would be all or nothing—nor could
 wait
For the sure grave to level him; few years
Had fix'd him with the Cæsars in his fate,
On whom we tread: For *this* the con-
 queror rears
The arch of triumph and for this the tears
And blood of earth flow on as they have
 flow'd,
An universal deluge, which appears
Without an ark for wretched man's abode,
And ebbs but to reflow! Renew thy rain-
 bow, God!

XCIII

What from this barren being do we reap?
Our senses narrow, and our reason frail,
Life short, and truth a gem which loves
 the deep,
And all things weigh'd in custom's fals-
 est scale;
Opinion an omnipotence,—whose veil
Mantles the earth with darkness, until
 right
And wrong are accidents, and men
 grow pale
Lest their own judgments should become
 too bright,
And their free thoughts be crimes, and
 earth have too much light.

XCIV

And thus they plod in sluggish misery,
Rotting from sire to son, and age to age,
Proud of their trampled nature, and so
 die,
Bequeathing their hereditary rage
To the new race of inborn slaves, who
 wage
War for their chains, and rather than
 be free,
Bleed gladiator-like, and still engage
Within the same arena where they see
Their fellows fall before, like leaves of the
 same tree.

XCV

I speak not of men's creeds—they rest
 between
Man and his Maker—but of things
 allow'd,
Averr'd, and known, and daily, hourly
 seen—
The yoke that is upon us doubly bow'd,
And the intent of tyranny avow'd,
The edict of Earth's rulers, who are
 grown
The apes of him who humbled once the
 proud,
And shook them from their slumbers
 on the throne:
Too glorious, were this all his mighty arm
 had done.

XCVI

Can tyrants but by tyrants conquer'd be,
And Freedom find no champion and no
child
Such as Columbia saw arise when she
Sprung forth a Pallas, arm'd and un-
defiled?
Or must such minds be nourish'd in the
wild,
Deep in the unpruned forest, 'midst the
roar
Of cataracts, where nursing Nature
smiled
On infant Washington? Has Earth no
more
Such seeds within her breast, or Europe
no such shore?

XCVII

But France got drunk with blood to
vomit crime,
And fatal have her Saturnalia been
To Freedom's cause, in every age and
clime;
Because the deadly days which we have
seen,
And vile Ambition, that built up be-
tween
Man and his hopes an adamantine wall,
And the base pageant last upon the
scene,
Are grown the pretext for the eternal
thrall
Which nips life's tree, and dooms man's
worst—his second fall.

XCVIII

Yet, Freedom! yet thy banner, torn, but
flying,
Streams like the thunder-storm *against*
the wind;
Thy trumpet voice, though broken now
and dying,
The loudest still the tempest leaves be-
hind;
Thy tree hath lost its blossoms, and the
rind,
Chopp'd by the axe, looks rough and
little worth,
But the sap lasts,—and still the seed
we find
Sown deep, even in the bosom of the
North;
So shall a better spring less bitter fruit
bring forth.

XCIX

There is a stern round tower of other
days,
Firm as a fortress, with its fence of stone,
Such as an army's baffled strength de-
lays,
Standing with half its battlements alone,

And with two thousand years of ivy
grown,
The garland of eternity, where wave
The green leaves over all by time o'er-
thrown;—
What was this tower of strength? within
its cave
What treasure lay so lock'd, so hid?—A
woman's grave.

C

But who was she, the lady of the
dead,
Tomb'd in a palace? Was she chaste
and fair?
Worthy a king's, or more—a Roman's
bed?
What race of chiefs and heroes did she
bear?
What daughter of her beauties was the
heir?
How lived, how loved, how died she?
Was she not
So honoured—and conspicuously there,
Where meaner relics must not dare to
rot,
Placed to commemorate a more than mor-
tal lot?

CI

Was she as those who love their lords, or
they
Who love the lords of others? such have
been
Even in the olden time, Rome's annals
say.
Was she a matron of Cornelia's mien,
Or the light air of Egypt's graceful
queen,
Profuse of joy—or 'gainst it did she war,
Inveterate in virtue? Did she lean
To the soft side of the heart, or wisely
bar
Love from amongst her griefs?—for such
the affections are.

CII

Perchance she died in youth: it may be,
bow'd
With woes far heavier than the ponder-
ous tomb
That weigh'd upon her gentle dust, a
cloud
Might gather o'er her beauty, and a
gloom
In her dark eye, prophetic of the doom
Heaven gives its favourites—early
death; yet shed
A sunset charm around her, and illume
With hectic light, the Hesperus of the
dead,
Of her consuming cheek the autumnal
leaf-like red.

CIII

Perchance she died in age—surviving all,
Charms, kindred, children—with the
 silver gray
On her long tresses, which might yet re-
 call,
It may be, still a something of the day
When they were braided, and her proud
 array
And lovely form were envied, praised,
 and eyed
By Rome—But whither would Conjec-
 ture stray?
Thus much alone we know—Metella
 died,
he wealthiest Roman's wife: Behold his
 love or pride!

CIV

I know not why—but standing thus by
 thee
It seems as if I had thine inmate known,
Thou Tomb! and other days come back
 on me
With recollected music, though the tone
Is changed and solemn, like the cloudy
 groan
Of dying thunder on the distant wind;
Yet could I seat me by this ivied stone
Till I had bodied, forth the heated mind,
orms from the floating wreck which Ruin
 leaves behind;

CV

And from the planks, far shatter'd o'er
 the rocks,
Built me a little bark of hope, once more
To battle with the ocean and the shocks
Of the loud breakers, and the ceaseless
 roar
Which rushes on the solitary shore
Where all lies founder'd that was ever
 dear:
But could I gather from the wave-worn
 store
Enough for my rude boat, where should
 I steer?
here woos no home, nor hope, nor life,
 save what is here.

CVI

Then let the winds howl on! their har-
 mony
Shall henceforth be my music, and the
 night
The sound shall temper with the owlets'
 cry,
As I now hear them, in the fading light
Dim o'er the bird of darkness' native
 site,
Answering each other on the Palatine,
With their large eyes, all glistening gray
 and bright,

And sailing pinions.—Upon such a
 shrine
What are our petty griefs?—let me not
 number mine.

CVII

Cypress and ivy, weed and wallflower
 grown,
Matted and mass'd together, hillocks
 heap'd
On what were chambers, arch crush'd,
 column strown
In fragments, choked up vaults, and
 frescos steep'd
In subterranean damps, where the owl
 peep'd,
Deeming it midnight:—Temples, baths,
 or halls?
Pronounce who can; for all that Learn-
 ing reap'd
From her research hath been, that these
 are walls—
Behold the Imperial Mount! 'tis thus the
 mighty falls.

CVIII

There is the moral of all human tales;
'Tis but the same rehearsal of the past,
First Freedom, and then Glory—when
 that fails,
Wealth, vice, corruption,—barbarism
 at last.
And History, with all her volumes vast,
Hath but *one* page,—'tis better writ-
 ten here
Where gorgeous Tyranny hath thus
 amass'd
All treasures, all delights, that eye or ear,
Heart, soul, could seek, tongue ask—
 Away with words! draw near,

CIX

Admire, exult, despise, laugh, weep,—
 for here
There is such matter for all feeling:—
 Man!
Thou pendulum betwixt a smile and tear,
Ages and realms are crowded in this span,
This mountain, whose obliterated plan
The pyramid of empires pinnacled,
Of Glory's gewgaws shining in the van
Till the sun's rays with added flame were
 fill'd!
Where are its golden roofs? where those
 who dared to build?

CX

Tully was not so eloquent as thou,
Thou nameless column with the buried
 base!
What are the laurels of the Cæsar's
 brow?
Crown me with ivy from his dwelling-
 place.

Whose arch or pillar meets me in the face,
Titus or Trajan's? No—'tis that of Time:
Triumph, arch, pillar, all he doth displace
Scoffing; and apostolic statues climb
To crush the imperial urn, whose ashes slept sublime,

CXI

Buried in air, the deep blue sky of Rome,
And looking to the stars: they had contain'd
A spirit which with these would find a home,
The last of those who o'er the whole earth reign'd,
The Roman globe, for after none sustain'd,
But yielded back his conquests:—he was more
Than a mere Alexander, and, unstain'd
With household blood and wine, serenely wore
His sovereign virtues—still we Trajan's name adore.

CXII

Where is the rock of Triumph, the high place
Where Rome embraced her heroes? where the steep
Tarpeian? fittest goal of Treason's race,
The promontory whence the Traitor's Leap
Cured all ambition. Did the conquerors heap
Their spoils here? Yes; and in yon field below,
A thousand years of silenced factions sleep—
The Forum, where the immortal accents glow,
And still the eloquent air breathes—burns with Cicero!

CXIII

The field of freedom, faction, fame, and blood:
Here a proud people's passions were exhaled,
From the first hour of empire in the bud
To that when further worlds to conquer fail'd;
But long before had Freedom's face been veil'd,
And Anarchy assumed her attributes;
Till every lawless soldier who assail'd
Trod on the trembling senate's slavish mutes,
Or raised the venal voice of baser prostitutes.

CXIV

Then turn we to her latest tribune's name
From her ten thousand tyrants turn to thee,
Redeemer of dark centuries of shame—
The friend of Petrarch—hope of Italy—
Rienzi! last of Romans! While the tre
Of freedom's wither'd trunk puts fort a leaf
Even for thy tomb a garland let it be—
The forum's champion, and the people chief—
Her new-born Numa thou—with reign alas! too brief.

CXV

Egeria! sweet creation of some heart
Which found no mortal resting-plac so fair
As thine ideal breast; whate'er thou a
Or wert,—a young Aurora of the air,
The nympholepsy of some fond despai
Or, it might be, a beauty of the earth
Who found a more than common votar there
Too much adoring; whatsoe'er thy birth
Thou wert a beautiful thought, and soft bodied forth.

CXVI

The mosses of thy fountain still a
sprinkled
With thine Elysian water-drops; the fac
Of thy cave-guarded spring with yea
unwrinkled,
Reflects the meek-eyed genius of th
place,
Whose green, wild margin now no mo
erase
Art's works; nor must the delica
waters sleep,
Prison'd in marble—bubbling from t
base
Of the cleft statue, with a gentle leap
The rill runs o'er—and round—fern, flower
and ivy creep,

CXVII

Fantastically tangled: the green hills
Are clothed with early blossom
through the grass
The quick-eyed lizard rustles, and t
bills
Of summer-birds sing welcome as
pass;
Flowers fresh in hue, and many in the
class,
Implore the pausing step, and with the
dyes,
Dance in the soft breeze in a fairy mas
The sweetness of the violet's deep blu
eyes,
Kiss'd by the breath of heaven, seen
colour'd by its skies.

CXVIII

Here didst thou dwell, in this enchanted
 cover,
Egeria! thy all heavenly bosom beating
For the far footsteps of thy mortal lover;
The purple Midnight veil'd that mystic
 meeting
With her most starry canopy, and seat-
 ing
Thyself by thine adorer, what befell?
This cave was surely shaped out for the
 greeting
Of an enamour'd Goddess, and the cell
Haunted by holy Love—the earliest oracle!

CXIX

And didst thou not, thy breast to his
 replying,
Blend a celestial with a human heart;
And Love, which dies as it was born, in
 sighing,
Share with immortal transports? could
 thine art
Make them indeed immortal, and impart
The purity of heaven to earthly joys,
Expel the venom and not blunt the
 dart—
The dull satiety which all destroys—
And root from out the soul the deadly
 weed which cloys?

CXX

Alas! our young affections run to waste,
Or water but the desert; whence arise
But weeds of dark luxuriance, tares of
 haste,
Rank at the core, though tempting to the
 eyes,
Flowers whose wild odours breathe but
 agonies,
And trees whose gums are poisons; such
 the plants
Which spring beneath her steps as
 Passion flies
O'er the world's wilderness, and vainly
 pants
For some celestial fruit forbidden to our
 wants.

CXXI

Oh. Love! no habitant of earth thou
 art—
An unseen seraph, we believe in thee,—
A faith whose martyrs are the broken
 heart,—
But never yet hath seen, nor e'er shall see
The naked eye, thy form, as it should be;
The mind hath made thee, as it peopled
 heaven,
Even with its own desiring phantasy,
And to a thought such shape and image
 given,
Which haunts the unquench'd soul—parch'd,
 wearied, wrung, and riven.

CXXII

Of its own beauty is the mind diseased,
And fevers into false creation:—where,
Where are the forms the sculptor's soul
 hath seiz'd?
In him alone. Can Nature show so fair?
Where are the charms and virtues which
 we dare
Conceive in boyhood and pursue as
 men,
The unreach'd Paradise of our despair,
Which o'er-informs the pencil and the
 pen,
And overpowers the page where it would
 bloom again?

CXXIII

Who loves, raves—'tis youth's frenzy
 —but the cure
Is bitterer still, as charm by charm un-
 winds
Which robed our idols, and we see too
 sure
Nor worth nor beauty dwells from out
 the mind's
Ideal shape of such; yet still it binds
The fatal spell, and still it draws us on,
Reaping the whirlwind from the oft-
 sown winds;
The stubborn heart, its alchemy begun,
Seems ever near the prize—wealthiest
 when most undone.

CXXIV

We wither from our youth, we gasp
 away—
Sick—sick; unfound the boon, unslaked
 the thirst,
Though to the last, in verge of our decay,
Some phantom lures, such as we sought
 at first—
But all too late,—so are we doubly curst.
Love, fame, ambition, avarice—'tis
 the same,
Each idle, and all ill, and none the
 worst—
For all are meteors with a different name,
And Death the sable smoke where van-
 ishes the flame.

CXXV

Few—none—find what they love or
 could have loved,
Though accident, blind contact, and the
 strong
Necessity of loving, have removed
Antipathies—but to recur, ere long,
Envenom'd with irrevocable wrong;
And Circumstance, that unspiritual god
And miscreator, makes and helps along
Our coming evils with a crutch-like rod,
Whose touch turns Hope to dust,—the
 dust we all have trod.

243

CXXVI

Our life is a false nature: 'tis not in
The harmony of things,—this hard de-
 cree,
This uneradicable taint of sin,
This boundless upas, this all-blasting
 tree,
Whose root is earth, whose leaves and
 branches be
The skies which rain their plagues on
 men like dew—
Disease, death, bondage—all the woes
 we see,
And worse, the woes we see not—which
 throb through
The immedicable soul, with heart-aches
 ever new.

CXXVII

Yet let us ponder boldly—'tis a base
Abandonment of reason to resign
Our right of thought—our last and only
 place
Of refuge; this, at least, shall still be
 mine:
Though from our birth the faculty
 divine
Is chain'd and tortured—cabin'd,
 cribb'd, confined,
And bred in darkness, lest the truth
 should shine
Too brightly on the unprepared mind,
The beam pours in, for time and skill will
 couch the blind.

CXXVIII

Arches on arches! as it were that Rome,
Collecting the chief trophies of her
 line,
Would build up all her triumphs in one
 dome,
Her Coliseum stands; the moonbeams
 shine
As 'twere its natural torches, for divine
Should be the light which streams here
 to illume
This long-explored but still exhaustless
 mine
Of contemplation; and the azure gloom
Of an Italian night, where the deep skies
 assume

CXXIX

Hues which have words, and speak to
 ye of heaven,
Floats o'er this vast and wondrous
 monument,
And shadows forth its glory. There is
 given
Unto the things of earth, which Time
 hath bent,
A spirit's feeling, and where he hath
 leant

His hand, but broke his scythe, there i
 a power
And magic in the ruin'd battlement,
For which the palace of the present hou
Must yield its pomp, and wait till ages ar
 its dower.

CXXX

Oh Time! the beautifier of the dead,
Adorner of the ruin, comforter
And only healer when the heart hath blee
Time! the corrector where our judg
 ments err,
The test of truth, love—sole philosophe
For all beside are sophists—from th
 thrift,
Which never loses though it doth defer—
Time, the avenger! unto thee I lift
My hands, and eyes, and heart, and crav
 of thee a gift:

CXXXI

Amidst this wreck, where thou ha
 made a shrine
And temple more divinely desolate,
Among thy mightier offerings here ar
 mine,
Ruins of years, though few, yet full c
 fate:
If thou hast ever seen me too elate,
Hear me not; but if calmly I have born
Good, and reserved my pride against th
 hate
Which shall not whelm me, let me ne
 have worn
This iron in my soul in vain—shall the
 not mourn?

CXXXII

And thou, who never yet of huma
 wrong
Left the unbalanced scale, great Neme
 sis!
Here, where the ancient paid thee hom
 age long—
Thou who didst call the Furies from th
 abyss,
And round Orestes bade them howl an
 hiss
For that unnatural retribution—just,
Had it but been from hands less near—
 in this
Thy former realm, I call thee from th
 dust!
Dost thou not hear my heart?—Awake
 thou shalt, and must.

CXXXIII

It is not that I may not have incurr
For my ancestral faults or mine th
 wound
I bleed withal, and, had it been con
 ferr'd
With a just weapon, it had flow'd u
 bound;

244

But now my blood shall not sink in the
ground;
To thee I do devote it—*thou* shalt take
The vengeance, which shall yet be
sought and found,
Which if *I* have not taken for the sake—
But let that pass—I sleep, but thou shalt
yet awake.

CXXXIV

And if my voice break forth, 'tis not that
now
I shrink from what is suffer'd: let him
speak
Who hath beheld decline upon my brow,
Or seen my mind's convulsion leave it
weak;
But in this page a record will I seek.
Not in the air shall these my words dis-
perse,
Though I be ashes; a far hour shall
wreak
The deep prophetic fulness of this verse,
And pile on human heads the mountain
of my curse!

CXXXV

That curse shall be Forgiveness.—Have
I not—
Hear me, my mother Earth! behold it,
Heaven!
Have I not had to wrestle with my lot?
Have I not suffer'd things to be forgiven?
Have I not had my brain sear'd, my
heart riven,
Hopes sapp'd, name blighted, Life's
life lied away?
And only not to desperation driven,
Because not altogether of such clay
As rots into the souls of those whom I
survey.

CXXXVI

From mighty wrongs to petty perfidy
Have I not seen what human things
could do?
From the loud roar of foaming calumny
To the small whisper of the as paltry few,
And subtler venom of the reptile crew,
The Janus glance of whose significant eye,
Learning to lie with silence, would *seem*
true,
And without utterance, save the shrug
or sigh,
Deal round to happy fools its speechless
obloquy.

CXXXVII

But I have lived, and have not lived in
vain:
My mind may lose its force, my blood its
fire,
And my frame perish even in conquer-
ing pain;

But there is that within me which shall tire
Torture and Time, and breathe when I
expire;
Something unearthly, which they deem
not of,
Like the remember'd tone of a mute lyre,
Shall on their soften'd spirits sink, and
move
In hearts all rocky now the late remorse of
love.

CXXXVIII

The seal is set.—Now welcome, thou
dread power!
Nameless, yet thus omnipotent, which
here
Walk'st in the shadow of the midnight
hour
With a deep awe, yet all distinct from
fear;
Thy haunts are ever where the dead
walls rear
Their ivy mantles, and the solemn scene
Derives from thee a sense so deep and
clear
That we become a part of what has been,
And grow unto the spot, all-seeing but
unseen.

CXXXIX

And here the buzz of eager nations ran,
In murmur'd pity, or loud-roar'd ap-
plause,
As man was slaughter'd by his fellow-
man.
And wherefore slaughter'd? wherefore,
but because
Such were the bloody Circus' genial
laws,
And the imperial pleasure.—Wherefore
not?
What matters where we fall to fill the
maws
Of worms—on battle-plains or listed
spot?
Both are but theatres—where the chief
actors rot.

CXL

I see before me the Gladiator lie:
He leans upon his hand—his manly
brow
Consents to death, but conquers agony,
And his droop'd head sinks gradually
low—
And through his side the last drops, ebb-
ing slow
From the red gash, fall heavy, one by
one,
Like the first of a thunder-shower; and
now
The arena swims around him—he is
gone,
Ere ceased the inhuman shout which hail'd
the wretch who won.

CXLI

He heard it, but he heeded not—his eyes
Were with his heart, and that was far
 away;
He reck'd not of the life he lost nor prize,
But where his rude hut by the Danube
 lay,
There were his young barbarians all at
 play,
There was their Dacian mother—he,
 their sire,
Butcher'd to make a Roman holiday—
All this rush'd with his blood—Shall he
 expire
And unavenged? Arise! ye Goths, and glut
 your ire!

CXLII

But here, where Murder breathed her
 bloody steam;
And here, where buzzing nations choked
 the ways,
And roar'd or murmur'd like a moun-
 tain stream
Dashing or winding as its torrent strays;
Here, where the Roman million's blame
 or praise
Was death or life, the playthings of a
 crowd,
My voice sounds much—and fall the
 stars' faint rays
On the arena void—seats crush'd—
 walls bow'd—
And galleries, where my steps seem echoes
 strangely loud.

CXLIII

A ruin—yet what ruin! from its mass
Walls, palaces, half-cities, have been
 rear'd;
Yet oft the enormous skeleton ye pass,
And marvel where the spoil could have
 appear'd.
Hath it indeed been plunder'd, or but
 clear'd?
Alas! developed, opens the decay,
When the colossal fabric's form is near'd:
It will not bear the brightness of the day,
Which streams too much on all—years—
 man—have reft away.

CXLIV

But when the rising moon begins to
 climb
Its topmost arch, and gently pauses
 there;
When the stars twinkle through the
 loops of time,
And the low night-breeze waves along
 the air
The garland-forest, which the gray walls
 wear,
Like laurels on the bald first Cæsar's
 head;

When the light shines serene but doth
 not glare,
Then in this magic circle raise the dead
Heroes have trod this spot—'tis on their
 dust ye tread.

CXLV

'While stands the Coliseum, Rome shall
 stand;
'When falls the Coliseum, Rome shall
 fall;
'And when Rome falls—the World.'
 From our own land
Thus spake the pilgrims o'er this mighty
 wall
In Saxon times, which we are wont to call
Ancient; and these three mortal things
 are still
On their foundations, and unalter'd all
Rome and her Ruin past Redemption's
 skill,
The World, the same wide den—of thieves
 or what ye will.

CXLVI

Simple, erect, severe, austere, sublime—
Shrine of all saints and temple of all
 gods,
From Jove to Jesus—spared and bless
 by time;
Looking tranquillity, while falls or nods
Arch, empire, each thing round thee
 and man plods
His way through thorns to ashes—
 glorious dome!
Shalt thou not last? Time's scythe and
 tyrants' rods
Shiver upon thee—sanctuary and home
Of art and piety—Pantheon!—pride of
 Rome!

CXLVII

Relic of nobler days, and noblest arts
Despoil'd yet perfect, with thy circle
 spreads
A holiness appealing to all hearts—
To art a model; and to him who treads
Rome for the sake of ages, Glory shed
Her light through thy sole aperture; to
 those
Who worship, here are altars for their
 beads;
And they who feel for genius may repose
Their eyes on honour'd forms, whose busts
 around them close.

CXLVIII

There is a dungeon, in whose dim drear
 light
What do I gaze on? Nothing: Look
 again!
Two forms are slowly shadow'd on my
 sight—
Two insulated phantoms of the brain:

It is not so; I see them full and plain—
An old man, and a female young and
 fair,
Fresh as a nursing mother, in whose
 vein
The blood is nectar:—but what doth
 she there,
With her unmantled neck, and bosom
 white and bare?

CXLIX

Full swells the deep pure fountain of
 young life,
Where *on* the heart and *from* the heart
 we took
Our first and sweetest nurture, when the
 wife,
Blest into mother, in the innocent look,
Or even the piping cry of lips that brook
No pain and small suspense, a joy per-
 ceives
Man knows not, when from out its
 cradled nook
She sees her little bud put forth its
 leaves—
What may the fruit be yet? I know not—
 Cain was Eve's.

CL

But here youth offers to old age the
 food,
The milk of his own gift: it is her
 sire
To whom she renders back the debt of
 blood
Born with her birth. No; he shall not
 expire
While in those warm and lovely veins
 the fire
Of health and holy feeling can pro-
 vide
Great Nature's Nile, whose deep stream
 rises higher
Than Egypt's river: from that gentle
 side
Drink, drink and live, old man! Heaven's
 realm holds no such tide.

CLI

The starry fable of the milky way
Has not thy story's purity; it is
A constellation of a sweeter ray,
And sacred Nature triumphs more in
 this
Reverse of her decree, than in the
 abyss
Where sparkle distant worlds:—Oh,
 holiest nurse!
No drop of that clear stream its way
 shall miss
To thy sire's heart, replenishing its
 source
With life, as our freed souls rejoin the
 universe.

CLII

Turn to the mole which Hadrian rear'd
 on high,
Imperial mimic of old Egypt's piles,
Colossal copyist of deformity
Whose travell'd phantasy from the far
 Nile's
Enormous model, doom'd the artist's
 toils
To build for giants, and for his vain
 earth,
His shrunken ashes, raise this dome:
 How smiles
The gazer's eye with philosophic mirth,
To view the huge design which sprung
 from such a birth!

CLIII

But lo! the dome—the vast and won-
 drous dome,
To which Diana's marvel was a cell—
Christ's mighty shrine above his mar-
 tyr's tomb!
I have beheld the Ephesian's miracle;—
Its columns strew the wilderness, and
 dwell
The hyæna and the jackal in their shade;
I have beheld Sophia's bright roofs
 swell
Their glittering mass i' the sun, and have
 survey'd
Its sanctuary the while the usurping Mos-
 lem pray'd;

CLIV

But thou, of temples old, or altars new,
Standest alone, with nothing like to
 thee—
Worthiest of God, the holy and the true.
Since Zion's desolation, when that He
Forsook his former city, what could be,
Of earthly structures, in his honour
 piled,
Of a sublimer aspect? Majesty,
Power, Glory, Strength, and Beauty all
 are aisled
In this eternal ark of worship undefiled.

CLV

Enter: its grandeur overwhelms thee
 not;
And why? It is not lessen'd; but thy
 mind,
Expanded by the genius of the spot,
Has grown colossal, and can only find
A fit abode wherein appear enshrined
Thy hopes of immortality; and thou
Shalt one day, if found worthy, so de-
 fined,
See thy God face to face, as thou dost
 now
His Holy of Holies, nor be blasted by his
 brow.

CLVI

Thou movest, but increasing with the
advance,
Like climbing some great Alp, which
still doth rise,
Deceived by its gigantic elegance;
Vastness which grows, but grows to
harmonise—
All musical in its immensities;
Rich marbles, richer painting—shrines
where flame
The lamps of gold—and haughty dome
which vies
In air with Earth's chief structures,
though their frame
Sits on the firm-set ground, and this the
clouds must claim.

CLVII

Thou seest not all; but piecemeal thou
must break,
To separate contemplation, the great
whole;
And as the ocean many bays will make
That ask the eye—so here condense thy
soul
To more immediate objects, and control
Thy thoughts until thy mind hath got by
heart
Its eloquent proportions, and unroll
In mighty graduations, part by part,
The glory which at once upon thee did not
dart,

CLVIII

Not by its fault—but thine: Our out-
ward sense
Is but of gradual grasp—and as it is
That what we have of feeling most in-
tense
Outstrips our faint expression; even so
this
Outshining and o'erwhelming edifice
Fools our fond gaze, and greatest of the
great
Defies at first our Nature's littleness,
Till, growing with its growth, we thus
dilate
Our spirits to the size of that they contem-
plate.

CLIX

Then pause, and be enlighten'd; there is
more
In such a survey than the sating gaze
Of wonder pleased, or awe which would
adore
The worship of the place, or the mere
praise
Of art and its great masters, who could
raise
What former time, nor skill, nor thought
could plan;
The fountain of sublimity displays
Its depth, and thence may draw the
mind of man
Its golden sands, and learn what great
conceptions can.

CLX

Or, turning to the Vatican, go see
Laocoön's torture dignifying pain—
A father's love and mortal's agony
With an immortal's patience blending
—Vain
The struggle; vain, against the coiling
strain
And gripe, and deepening of the dra-
gon's grasp,
The old man's clench; the long en-
venom'd chain
Rivets the living links,—the enormous
asp
Enforces pang on pang, and stifles gasp on
gasp.

CLXI

Or view the Lord of the unerring bow
The God of life, and poesy, and light—
The Sun in human limbs array'd, and
brow
All radiant from his triumph in the fight;
The shaft hath just been shot—the
arrow bright
With an immortal's vengeance; in his
eye
And nostril beautiful disdain, and might
And majesty, flash their full lightnings
by,
Developing in that one glance the Deity

CLXII

But in his delicate form—a dream of
Love,
Shaped by some solitary nymph, whose
breast
Long'd for a deathless lover from above,
And madden'd in that vision—are ex-
prest
All that ideal beauty ever bless'd
The mind with in its most unearthly
mood,
When each conception was a heavenly
guest—
A ray of immortality—and stood
Starlike, around, until they gather'd to a
god!

CLXIII

And if it be Prometheus stole from
Heaven
The fire which we endure, it was repaid
By him to whom the energy was given
Which this poetic marble hath array'd
With an eternal glory—which, if made
By human hands, is not of human
thought;

And Time himself hath hallow'd it, nor
laid
One ringlet in the dust—nor hath it
caught
tinge of years, but breathes the flame
with which 'twas wrought.

CLXIV

But where is he, the Pilgrim of my song,
The being who upheld it through the
past?
Methinks he cometh late and tarries
long.
He is no more—these breathings are his
last;
His wanderings done, his visions ebbing
fast,
And he himself as nothing:—if he was
Aught but a phantasy, and could be
class'd
With forms which live and suffer—let
that pass—
Is shadow fades away into Destruction's
mass,

CLXV

Which gathers shadow, substance, life,
and all
That we inherit in its mortal shroud,
And spreads the dim and universal pall
Through which all things grow phan-
toms; and the cloud
Between us sinks and all which ever
glow'd,
Till Glory's self is twilight, and displays
A melancholy halo scarce allow'd
To hover on the verge of darkness; rays
Adder than saddest night, for they dis-
tract the gaze.

CLXVI

And send us prying into the abyss,
To gather what we shall be when the
frame
Shall be resolved to something less than
this
Its wretched essence; and to dream of
fame,
And wipe the dust from off the idle
name
We never more shall hear,—but never
more,
Oh, happier thought! can we be made
the same:
It is enough in sooth that *once* we bore
These fardels of the heart—the heart
whose sweat was gore.

CLXVII

Hark! forth from the abyss a voice pro-
ceeds,
A long low distant murmur of dread
sound,
Such as arises when a nation bleeds

With some deep and immedicable
wound;
Through storm and darkness yawns the
rending ground,
The gulf is thick with phantoms, but the
chief
Seems royal still, though with her head
discrown'd,
And pale, but lovely, with maternal
grief
She clasps a babe, to whom her breast
yields no relief.

CLXVIII

Scion of chiefs and monarchs, where
art thou?
Fond hope of many nations, art thou
dead?
Could not the grave forget thee, and lay
low
Some less majestic, less beloved head?
In the sad midnight, while thy heart still
bled,
The mother of a moment, o'er thy boy,
Death hush'd that pang for ever: with
thee fled
The present happiness and promised joy
Which fill'd the imperial isles so full it
seem'd to cloy.

CLXIX

Peasants bring forth in safety.—Can it
be,
Oh thou that wert so happy, so adored!
Those who weep not for kings shall
weep for thee,
And Freedom's heart, grown heavy,
cease to hoard
Her many griefs for ONE; for she had
pour'd
Her orisons for thee, and o'er thy head
Beheld her Iris.—Thou, too, lonely lord,
And desolate consort—vainly wert thou
wed!
The husband of a year! the father of the
dead!

CLXX

Of sackcloth was thy wedding garment
made;
Thy bridal's fruit is ashes: in the dust
The fair-hair'd Daughter of the Isles is
laid,
The love of millions! How we did in-
trust
Futurity to her! and, though it must
Darken above our bones, yet fondly
deem'd
Our children should obey her child, and
bless'd
Her and her hoped-for seed, whose
promise seem'd
Like stars to shepherds' eyes:—'twas but
a meteor beam'd.

CLXXI

Woe unto us, not her; for she sleeps
 well:
The fickle reek of popular breath, the
 tongue
Of hollow counsel, the false oracle,
Which from the birth of monarchy hath
 rung
Its knell in princely ears, till the o'er-
 stung
Nations have arm'd in madness, the
 strange fate
Which tumbles mightiest sovereigns,
 and hath flung
Against their blind omnipotence a
 weight
Within the opposing scale, which crushes
 soon or late,—

CLXXII

These might have been her destiny; but
 no,
Our hearts deny it: and so young, so fair,
Good without effort, great without a
 foe;
But now a bride and mother—and now
 there!
How many ties did that stern moment
 tear!
From thy Sire's to his humblest subject's
 breast
Is link'd the electric chain of that de-
 spair,
Whose shock was as an earthquake's,
 and opprest
The land which loved thee so that none
 could love thee best.

CLXXIII

Lo, Nemi! navell'd in the woody hills
So far, that the uprooting wind which
 tears
The oak from his foundation, and which
 spills
The ocean o'er its boundary, and bears
Its foam against the skies, reluctant
 spares
The oval mirror of thy glassy lake;
And calm as cherish'd hate, its surface
 wears
A deep cold settled aspect nought can
 shake,
All coil'd into itself and round, as sleeps
 the snake.

CLXXIV

And near, Albano's scarce divided
 waves
Shine from a sister valley;—and afar
The Tiber winds, and the broad ocean
 laves
The Latian coast where sprung the Epic
 war,

'Arms and the man,' whose re-ascend
 ing star
Rose o'er an empire:—but beneath th
 right
Tully reposed from Rome;—and wher
 yon bar
Of girdling mountains intercepts th
 sight
The Sabine farm was till'd, the wear
 bard's delight.

CLXXV

But I forget.—My Pilgrim's shrine
 won,
And he and I must part,—so let it be,-
His task and mine alike are nearly don
Yet once more let us look upon the se
The midland ocean breaks on him an
 me,
And from the Alban Mount we no
 behold
Our friend of youth, that Ocean, whic
 when we
Beheld it last by Calpe's rock unfold
Those waves, we follow'd on till the da
 Euxine roll'd

CLXXVI

Upon the blue Symplegades: lor
 years—
Long, though not very many—sin
 have done
Their work on both; some suffering an
 some tears
Have left us nearly where we had begur
Yet not in vain our mortal race hat
 run;
We have had our reward, and it
 here,—
That we can yet feel gladden'd by th
 sun,
And reap from earth, sea, joy almost a
 dear
As if there were no man to trouble what
 clear.

CLXXVII

Oh! that the Desert were my dwellin
 place,
With one fair Spirit for my minister,
That I might all forget the human rac
And, hating no one, love but only he
Ye elements!—in whose ennobling st
I feel myself exalted—Can ye not
Accord me such a being? Do I err
In deeming such inhabit many a spot
Though with them to converse can rarel
 be our lot.

CLXXVIII

There is a pleasure in the pathless wood
There is a rapture on the lonely shor
There is society, where none intrude
By the deep Sea, and music in its roar

250

I love not Man the less, but Nature
more,
From these our interviews, in which I
steal
From all I may be, or have been before,
To mingle with the Universe, and feel
'hat I can ne'er express, yet cannot all
conceal.

CLXXIX

Roll on, thou deep and dark blue
Ocean—roll!
Ten thousand fleets sweep over thee in
vain;
Man marks the earth with ruin—his
control
Stops with the shore; upon the watery
plain
The wrecks are all thy deed, nor doth
remain
A shadow of man's ravage, save his own,
When, for a moment, like a drop of
rain,
He sinks into thy depths with bubbling
groan,
/ithout a grave, unknell'd, uncoffin'd,
and unknown.

CLXXX

His steps are not upon thy paths,—thy
fields
Are not a spoil for him,—thou dost
arise
And shake him from thee; the vile
strength he wields
For earth's destruction thou dost all de-
pise,
Spurning him from thy bosom to the
skies,
And send'st him, shivering in thy play-
ful spray
And howling, to his Gods, where haply
lies
His petty hope in some near port or
bay,
and dashest him again to earth:—there
let him lay.

CLXXXI

The armaments which thunderstrike
the walls
Of rock-built cities, bidding nations
quake,
And monarchs tremble in their capitals,
The oak leviathans, whose huge ribs
make
Their clay creator the vain title take
Of lord of thee, and arbiter of war—
These are thy toys, and, as the snowy
flake,
They melt into thy yeast of waves, which
mar
like the Armada's pride or spoils of
Trafalgar.

CLXXXII

Thy shores are empires, changed in all
save thee—
Assyria, Greece, Rome, Carthage, what
are they?
Thy waters wash'd them power while
they were free,
And many a tyrant since; their shores
obey
The stranger, slave, or savage; their
decay
Has dried up realms to deserts:—not so
thou;—
Unchangeable, save to thy wild waves'
play,
Time writes no wrinkle on thine azure
brow:
Such as creation's dawn beheld, thou
rollest now.

CLXXXIII

Thou glorious mirror, where the Al-
mighty's form
Glasses itself in tempests; in all time,—
Calm or convulsed, in breeze, or gale, or
storm,
Icing the pole, or in the torrid clime
Dark-heaving—boundless, endless, and
sublime,
The image of eternity, the throne
Of the Invisible; even from out thy
slime
The monsters of the deep are made;
each zone
Obeys thee; thou goest forth, dread,
fathomless, alone.

CLXXXIV

And I have loved thee, Ocean! and my
joy
Of youthful sports was on thy breast to
be
Borne, like thy bubbles, onward: from
a boy
I wanton'd with thy breakers—they to
me
Were a delight; and if the freshening
sea
Made them a terror—'twas a pleasing
fear,
For I was as it were a child of thee,
And trusted to thy billows far and near,
And laid my hand upon thy mane—as I do
here.

CLXXXV

My task is done, my song hath ceased,
my theme
Has died into an echo; it is fit
The spell should break of this protracted
dream.
The torch shall be extinguish'd which
hath lit

My midnight lamp—and what is writ,
 is writ;
Would it were worthier! but I am not
 now
That which I have been—and my visions
 flit
Less palpably before me—and the
 glow
Which in my spirit dwelt is fluttering,
 faint, and low.

CLXXXVI

Farewell! a word that must be, and hath
 been—

A sound which makes us linger;—yet—
 farewell!
Ye! who have traced the Pilgrim to th
 scene
Which is his last, if in your memorie
 dwell
A thought which once was his, if on y
 swell
A single recollection, not in vain
He wore his sandal-shoon and scallop
 shell;
Farewell! with *him* alone may rest th
 pain,
If such there were—with *you*, the moral
 his strain.

TALES

THE GIAOUR

A FRAGMENT OF A TURKISH TALE

'One fatal remembrance—one sorrow that throws
Its bleak shade alike o'er our joys and our woes—
To which Life nothing darker nor brighter can bring,
For which joy hath no balm—and affliction no sting.'—MOORE.

TO

SAMUEL ROGERS, ESQ.

AS A SLIGHT BUT MOST SINCERE TOKEN OF ADMIRATION FOR HIS GENIUS, RESPECT FOR
HIS CHARACTER, AND GRATITUDE FOR HIS FRIENDSHIP,

THIS PRODUCTION IS INSCRIBED,

BY HIS OBLIGED AND AFFECTIONATE SERVANT,

LONDON, *May*, 1813. BYRON.

ADVERTISEMENT

THE tale which these disjointed fragments present is founded upon circumstances now less commo
in the East than formerly; either because the ladies are more circumspect than in the 'olden time
or because the Christians have better fortune, or less enterprise.
 The story, when entire, contained the adventures of a female slave, who was thrown, in the Mussu'
man manner, into the sea for infidelity, and avenged by a young Venetian, her lover, at the time th
Seven Islands were possessed by the Republic of Venice, and soon after the Arnauts were beaten bac
from the Morea, which they had ravaged for some time subsequent to the Russian invasion. Th
desertion of the Mainotes, on being refused the plunder of Misitra, led to the abandonment of tha
enterprise, and to the desolation of the Morea; during which the cruelty exercised on all sides wa
unparalleled even in the annals of the faithful.

No breath of air to break the wave
That rolls below the Athenian's grave,
That tomb which, gleaming o'er the cliff,
First greets the homeward-veering skiff,
High o'er the land he saved in vain; 5
When shall such hero live again?

Fair clime! where every season smiles
Benignant o'er those blessed isles,

Which, seen from far Colonna's heigh
Make glad the heart that hails th
 sight,
And lend to loneliness delight.
There mildly dimpling, Ocean's cheek
Reflects the tints of many a peak
Caught by the laughing tides that lave
These Edens of the eastern wave:
And if at times a transient breeze
Break the blue crystal of the seas,

252

r sweep one blossom from the trees,
Low welcome is each gentle air
hat wakes and wafts the odours there!
or there the Rose, o'er crag or vale, 21
ultana of the Nightingale,
The maid for whom his melody,
His thousand songs are heard on high,
Blooms blushing to her lover's tale: 25
His queen, the garden queen, his Rose,
Unbent by winds, unchill'd by snows,
ar from the winters of the west,
By every breeze and season blest,
Returns the sweets by nature given 30
In softest incense back to heaven;
And grateful yields that smiling sky
Her fairest hue and fragrant sigh.
And many a summer flower is there,
And many a shade that love might share, 35
And many a grotto, meant for rest,
That holds the pirate for a guest;
Whose bark in sheltering cove below
Lurks for the passing peaceful prow,
Till the gay mariner's guitar 40
Is heard, and seen the evening star;
Then stealing with the muffled oar,
Far shaded by the rocky shore,
Rush the night-prowlers on the prey,
And turn to groans his roundelay. 45
Strange—that where Nature loved to trace,
As if for gods, a dwelling-place,
And every charm and grace hath mix'd
Within the paradise she fix'd,
There man, enamour'd of distress, 50
Should mar it into wilderness,
And trample, brute-like, o'er each flower
That tasks not one laborious hour;
Nor claims the culture of his hand
To bloom along the fairy land, 55
But springs as to preclude his care,
And sweetly woos him—but to spare!
Strange—that where all is peace beside,
There passion riots in her pride,
And lust and rapine wildly reign 60
To darken o'er the fair domain.
It is as though the fiends prevail'd
Against the seraphs they assail'd,
And, fix'd on heavenly thrones, should dwell
The freed inheritors of hell; 65
So soft the scene, so form'd for joy,
So curst the tyrants that destroy!

He who hath bent him o'er the dead
Ere the first day of death is fled,
The first dark day of nothingness, 70
The last of danger and distress,
Before Decay's effacing fingers
Have swept the lines where beauty lingers,)
And mark'd the mild angelic air,
The rapture of repose that's there, 75
The fix'd yet tender traits that streak
The languor of the placid cheek,

And—but for that sad shrouded eye,
That fires not, wins not, weeps not, now,
And but for that chill, changeless brow,
Where cold Obstruction's apathy 81
Appals the gazing mourner's heart,
As if to him it could impart
The doom he dreads, yet dwells upon;
Yes, but for these and these alone, 85
Some moments, ay, one treacherous hour,
He still might doubt the tyrant's power;
So fair, so calm, so softly seal'd,
The first, last look by death reveal'd!
Such is the aspect of this shore; 90
'Tis Greece, but living Greece no more!
So coldly sweet, so deadly fair,
We start, for soul is wanting there.
Hers is the loveliness in death,
That parts not quite with parting breath; 95
But beauty with that fearful bloom,
That hue which haunts it to the tomb,
Expression's last receding ray,
A gilded halo hovering round decay,
The farewell beam of Feeling pass'd away! 100
Spark of that flame, perchance of heavenly birth,
Which gleams, but warms no more its cherish'd earth!

Clime of the unforgotten brave!
Whose land from plain to mountain-cave
Was Freedom's home or Glory's grave!
Shrine of the mighty! can it be, 106
That this is all remains of thee?
Approach, thou craven crouching slave:
Say, is not this Thermopylæ?
These waters blue that round you lave,— 110
Oh servile offspring of the free,
Pronounce what sea, what shore is this?
The gulf, the rock of Salamis!
These scenes, their story not unknown,
Arise, and make again your own; 115
Snatch from the ashes of your sires
The embers of their former fires;
And he who in the strife expires
Will add to theirs a name of fear
That Tyranny shall quake to hear, 120
And leave his sons a hope, a fame,
They too will rather die than shame:
For Freedom's battle once begun,
Bequeath'd by bleeding Sire to Son,
Though baffled oft is ever won. 125
Bear witness, Greece, thy living page!
Attest it many a deathless age!
While kings, in dusty darkness hid,
Have left a nameless pyramid, 129
Thy heroes, though the general doom
Hath swept the column from their tomb,
A mightier monument command,
The mountains of their native land!

There points thy Muse to stranger's eye
The graves of those that cannot die!
'Twere long to tell, and sad to trace, 136
Each step from splendour to disgrace;
Enough—no foreign foe could quell
Thy soul, till from itself it fell;
Yes! Self-abasement paved the way 140
To villain-bonds and despot sway.

What can he tell who treads thy shore?
 No legend of thine olden time,
No theme on which the Muse might soar
High as thine own in days of yore, 145
 When man was worthy of thy clime.
The hearts within thy valleys bred,
The fiery souls that might have led
 Thy sons to deeds sublime,
Now crawl from cradle to the grave, 150
Slaves—nay, the bondsmen of a slave,
 And callous, save to crime;
Stain'd with each evil that pollutes
Mankind, where least above the brutes;
Without even savage virtue blest, 155
Without one free or valiant breast,
Still to the neighbouring ports they waft
Proverbial wiles and ancient craft;
In this the subtle Greek is found,
For this, and this alone, renown'd. 160
In vain might Liberty invoke
The spirit to its bondage broke,
Or raise the neck that courts the yoke:
No more her sorrows I bewail,
Yet this will be a mournful tale, 165
And they who listen may believe,
Who heard it first had cause to grieve.

 Far, dark, along the blue sea glancing,
The shadows of the rocks advancing
Start on the fisher's eye like boat 170
Of island-pirate or Mainote;
And fearful for his light caïque,
He shuns the near but doubtful creek:
Though worn and weary with his toil,
And cumber'd with his scaly spoil, 175
Slowly, yet strongly, plies the oar,
Till Port Leone's safer shore
Receives him by the lovely light
That best becomes an Eastern night.

· · · · · ·

Who thundering comes on blackest
 steed, 180
With slacken'd bit and hoof of speed?
Beneath the clattering iron's sound
The cavern'd echoes wake around
In lash for lash, and bound for bound;
The foam that streaks the courser's side
Seems gather'd from the ocean-tide: 186
Though weary waves are sunk to rest,
There's none within his rider's breast;
And though to-morrow's tempest lower,
'Tis calmer than thy heart, young Giaour!
I know thee not, I loathe thy race, 191
But in thy lineaments I trace
What Time shall strengthen, not efface:

Though young and pale, that sallow fron
Is scathed by fiery passion's brunt; 19
Though bent on earth thine evil eye,
As meteor-like thou glidest by,
Right well I view and deem thee one
Whom Othman's sons should slay or shun

 On—on he hasten'd, and he drew 20
My gaze of wonder as he flew:
Though like a demon of the night
He pass'd, and vanish'd from my sight,
His aspect and his air impress'd
A troubled memory on my breast, 20
And long upon my startled ear
Rung his dark courser's hoofs of fear.
He spurs his steed; he nears the steep,
That, jutting, shadows o'er the deep;
He winds around; he hurries by; 2»
The rock relieves him from mine eye;
For well I ween unwelcome he
Whose glance is fix'd on those that flee;
And not a star but shines too bright
On him who takes such timeless flight.
He wound along; but ere he pass'd, 2»
One glance he snatch'd, as if his last,
A moment check'd his wheeling steed,
A moment breathed him from his speed
A moment on his stirrup stood— 22
Why looks he o'er the olive wood?
The crescent glimmers on the hill,
The Mosque's high lamps are quivering
 still;
Though too remote for sound to wake
In echoes of the far tophaike, 22
The flashes of each joyous peal
Are seen to prove the Moslem's zeal.
To-night, set Rhamazani's sun;
To-night, the Bairam feast's begun;
To-night—but who and what art thou 23
Of foreign garb and fearful brow?
And what are these to thine or thee,
That thou shouldst either pause or flee?

He stood—some dread was on hi
 face,
Soon Hatred settled in its place: 23
It rose not with the reddening flush
Of transient Anger's hasty blush,
But pale as marble o'er the tomb,
Whose ghastly whiteness aids its gloom.
His brow|was bent, his eye was glazed; 24
He raised his arm, and fiercely raised,
And sternly shook his hand on high,
As doubting to return or fly;
Impatient of his flight delay'd,
Here loud his raven charger neigh'd—
Down glanced that hand, and grasp'd hi
 blade; 24
That sound had burst his waking dream
As Slumber starts at owlet's scream,
The spur hath lanced his courser's sides
Away, away, for life he rides: 25»
Swift as the hurl'd on high jerreed
Springs to the touch his startled steed:

he rock is doubled, and the shore
hakes with the clattering tramp no more; 255
he crag is won, no more is seen
Iis Christian crest and haughty mien.
Twas but an instant he restrain'd
hat fiery barb so sternly rein'd;
Twas but a moment that he stood,
hen sped as if by death pursued; 260
ut in that instant o'er his soul
Vinters of Memory seem'd to roll,
And gather in that drop of time
A life of pain, an age of crime.
O'er him who loves, or hates, or fears, 265
uch moment pours the grief of years:
Vhat felt *he* then, at once opprest
By all that most distracts the breast?
hat pause, which ponder'd o'er his fate,
Oh, who its dreary length shall date! 270
hough in Time's record nearly nought,
t was Eternity to Thought!
For infinite as boundless space
he thought that Conscience must embrace,
Vhich in itself can comprehend 275
Voe without name, or hope, or end.

The hour is past, the Giaour is gone;
And did he fly or fall alone?
Voe to that hour he came or went!
he curse for Hassan's sin was sent 280
To turn a palace to a tomb;
He came, he went, like the simoom,
hat harbinger of fate and gloom,
Beneath whose widely-wasting breath
he very cypress droops to death— 285
Dark tree, still sad when others' grief is fled,
he only constant mourner o'er the dead!

The steed is vanish'd from the stall;
No serf is seen in Hassan's hall;
he lonely spider's thin gray pall 290
Waves slowly widening o'er the wall;
he bat builds in his haram bower,
And in the fortress of his power
he owl usurps the beacon-tower;
he wild-dog howls o'er the fountain's brim, 295
Vith baffled thirst, and famine, grim;
For the stream has shrunk from its marble bed,
Vhere the weeds and the desolate dust are spread.
Twas sweet of yore to see it play
And chase the sultriness of day, 300
As springing high the silver dew
n whirls fantastically flew,
And flung luxurious coolness round
he air, and verdure o'er the ground.
Twas sweet, when cloudless stars were bright, 305
To view the wave of watery light,
And hear its melody by night.
And oft had Hassan's Childhood play'd
Around the verge of that cascade;

And oft upon his mother's breast 310
That sound had harmonized his rest;
And oft had Hassan's Youth along
Its bank been soothed by Beauty's song;
And softer seem'd each melting tone
Of Music mingled with its own. 315
But ne'er shall Hassan's Age repose
Along the brink at twilight's close:
The stream that fill'd that font is fled—
The blood that warm'd his heart is shed!
And here no more shall human voice
Be heard to rage, regret, rejoice. 321
The last sad note that swell'd the gale
Was woman's wildest funeral wail:
That quench'd in silence, all is still,
But the lattice that flaps when the wind is shrill: 325
Though raves the gust, and floods the rain,
No hand shall close its clasp again.
On desert sands 'twere joy to scan
The rudest steps of fellow man,
So here the very voice of Grief 330
Might wake an Echo like relief—
At least 'twould say, 'All are not gone:'
There lingers Life, though but in one'—
For many a gilded chamber's there,
Which Solitude might well forbear;
Within that dome as yet Decay 336
Hath slowly work'd her cankering way—
But gloom is gather'd o'er the gate,
Nor there the Fakir's self will wait;
Nor there will wandering Dervise stay.
For bounty cheers not his delay; 341
Nor there will weary stranger halt
To bless the sacred 'bread and salt.'
Alike must Wealth and Poverty
Pass heedless and unheeded by, 345
For Courtesy and Pity died
With Hassan on the mountain side.
His roof, that refuge unto men,
Is Desolation's hungry den.
The guest flies the hall, and the vassal from labour, 350
Since his turban was cleft by the infidel's sabre!

.

I hear the sound of coming feet,
But not a voice mine ear to greet;
More near—each turban I can scan,
And silver-sheathèd ataghan; 355
The foremost of the band is seen
An Emir by his garb of green:
'Ho! who art thou?'—'This low salam
Replies of Moslem faith I am.'
'The burthen ye so gently bear 360
Seems one that claims your utmost care,
And, doubtless, holds some precious freight—
My humble bark would gladly wait.'

THE GIAOUR

'Thou speakest sooth: thy skiff unmoor,
And waft us from the silent shore; 365
Nay, leave the sail still furl'd, and ply
The nearest oar that's scatter'd by,
And midway to those rocks where sleep
The channell'd waters dark and deep.
Rest from your task—so—bravely done,
Our course has been right swiftly run; 371
Yet 'tis the longest voyage, I trow,
That one of— '

Sullen it plunged, and slowly sank,
The calm wave rippled to the bank; 375
I watch'd it as it sank, methought
Some motion from the current caught
Bestirr'd it more,—'twas but the beam
That checker'd o'er the living stream:
I gaz'd, till vanishing from view, 380
Like lessening pebble it withdrew;
Still less and less, a speck of white
That gemm'd the tide, then mock'd the
 sight;
And all its hidden secrets sleep,
Known but to Genii of the deep, 385
Which, trembling in their coral caves,
They dare not whisper to the waves.

As rising on its purple wing
The insect queen of eastern spring,
O'er emerald meadows of Kashmeer 390
Invites the young pursuer near,
And leads him on from flower to flower
A weary chase and wasted hour,
Then leaves him as it soars on high,
With panting heart and tearful eye: 395
So Beauty lures the full-grown child,
With hue as bright, and wing as wild;
A chase of idle hopes and fears,
Begun in folly, closed in tears.
If won, to equal ills betray'd, 400
Woe waits the insect and the maid;
A life of pain, the loss of peace,
From infant's play, and man's caprice:
The lovely toy so fiercely sought
Hath lost its charm by being caught, 405
For every touch that woo'd its stay
Hath brush'd its brightest hues away,
Till charm, and hue, and beauty gone,
'Tis left to fly or fall alone.
With wounded wing, or bleeding breast,
Ah! where shall either victim rest? 411
Can this with faded pinion soar
From rose to tulip as before?
Or Beauty, blighted in an hour,
Find joy within her broken bower? 415
No: gayer insects fluttering by
Ne'er droop the wing o'er those that die,
And lovelier things have mercy shown
To every failing but their own,
And every woe a tear can claim 420
Except an erring sister's shame.

The Mind, that broods o'er guilty woe
Is like the Scorpion girt by fire;
In circle narrowing as it glows,
The flames around their captive close,
Till inly search'd by thousand throes, 42
And maddening in her ire,
One sad and sole relief she knows,
The sting she nourish'd for her foes,
Whose venom never yet was vain, 43
Gives but one pang and cures all pain,
And darts into her desperate brain:
So do the dark in soul expire,
Or live like Scorpion girt by fire;
So writhes the mind Remorse hath riven
Unfit for earth, undoom'd for heaven,
Darkness above, despair beneath, 43
Around it flame, within it death!

Black Hassan from the Haram flies,
Nor bends on woman's form his eyes;
The unwonted chase each hour employs,
Yet shares he not the hunter's joys.
Not thus was Hassan wont to fly
When Leila dwelt in his Serai.
Doth Leila there no longer dwell? 44
That tale can only Hassan tell:
Strange rumours in our city say
Upon that eve she fled away
When Rhamazan's last sun was set,
And flashing from each minaret 45
Millions of lamps proclaim'd the feast
Of Bairam through the boundless East.
'Twas then she went as to the bath,
Which Hassan vainly search'd in wrath;
For she was flown her master's rage 45
In likeness of a Georgian page,
And far beyond the Moslem's power
Had wrong'd him with the faithless Giaour
Somewhat of this had Hassan deem'd;
But still so fond, so fair she seem'd, 46
Too well he trusted to the slave
Whose treachery deserved a grave:
And on that eve had gone to mosque,
And thence to feast in his kiosk.
Such is the tale his Nubians tell, 46
Who did not watch their charge too well
But others say, that on that night,
By pale Phingari's trembling light,
The Giaour upon his jet-black steed
Was seen, but seen alone to speed 47
With bloody spur along the shore,
Nor maid nor page behind him bore.

Her eye's dark charm 'twere vain to tell
But gaze on that of the Gazelle,
It will assist thy fancy well; 47
As large, as languishingly dark,
But Soul beam'd forth in every spark
That darted from beneath the lid,
Bright as the jewel of Giamschid. 47
Yea, *Soul*, and should our prophet say
That form was nought but breathing clay

By Alla! I would answer nay;
Though on Al-Sirat's arch I stood,
Which totters o'er the fiery flood,
With Paradise within my view,⠀⠀⠀⠀485
And all his Houris beckoning through.
Oh! who young Leila's glance could read
And keep that portion of his creed
Which saith that woman is but dust,
A soulless toy for tyrant's lust?⠀⠀⠀490
On her might Muftis gaze, and own
That through her eye the Immortal shone;
On her fair cheek's unfading hue
The young pomegranate's blossoms strew
Their bloom in blushes ever new;⠀⠀⠀495
Her hair in hyacinthine flow,
When left to roll its folds below,
As midst her handmaids in the hall
She stood superior to them all,
Hath swept the marble where her feet⠀⠀500
Gleam'd whiter than the mountain sleet
Ere from the cloud that gave it birth
It fell, and caught one stain of earth.
The cygnet nobly walks the water;
So moved on earth Circassia's daughter,
The loveliest bird of Franguestan!⠀⠀506
As rears her crest the ruffled Swan,
⠀And spurns the waves with wings of pride,
When pass the steps of stranger man
⠀Along the banks that bound her tide;
⠀Thus rose fair Leila's whiter neck:—⠀511
Thus arm'd with beauty would she check
Intrusion's glance, till Folly's gaze
Shrunk from the charms it meant to praise.
Thus high and graceful was her gait;⠀515
Her heart as tender to her mate;
Her mate—stern Hassan, who was he?
Alas! that name was not for thee!

⠀⠀⠀⠀.⠀⠀⠀.⠀⠀⠀.⠀⠀⠀.⠀⠀⠀.

Stern Hassan hath a journey ta'en
With twenty vassals in his train,⠀⠀⠀520
Each arm'd, as best becomes a man,
With arquebuss and ataghan;
The chief before, as deck'd for war,
Bears in his belt the scimitar
Stain'd with the best of Arnaut blood,⠀525
When in the pass the rebels stood,
And few return'd to tell the tale
Of what befell in Parne's vale.
The pistols which his girdle bore
Were those that once a pasha wore,⠀530
Which still, though gemm'd and boss'd
⠀⠀with gold,
Even robbers tremble to behold.
'Tis said he goes to woo a bride
More true than her who left his side;
The faithless slave that broke her bower,
And, worse than faithless, for a Giaour!

⠀⠀⠀⠀.⠀⠀⠀.⠀⠀⠀.⠀⠀⠀.⠀⠀⠀.

The sun's last rays are on the hill,
And sparkle in the fountain rill,⠀⠀⠀538
Whose welcome waters, cool and clear,
Draw blessings from the mountaineer:

Here may the loitering merchant Greek
Find that repose 'twere vain to seek
In cities lodged too near his lord,
And trembling for his secret hoard—
Here may he rest where none can see,⠀545
In crowds a slave, in deserts free;
And with forbidden wine may stain
The bowl a Moslem must not drain.

The foremost Tartar's in the gap
Conspicuous by his yellow cap;⠀⠀⠀550
The rest in lengthening line the while
Wind slowly through the long defile:
Above, the mountain rears a peak,
Where vultures whet the thirsty beak,
And theirs may be a feast to-night,⠀555
Shall tempt them down ere morrow's
⠀⠀light;
Beneath, a river's wintry stream
Has shrunk before the summer beam,
And left a channel bleak and bare,
Save shrubs that spring to perish there;
Each side the midway path there lay⠀561
Small broken crags of granite gray,
By time, or mountain lightning, riven
From summits clad in mists of heaven;
For where is he that hath beheld⠀⠀565
The peak of Liakura unveil'd?

⠀⠀⠀.⠀⠀⠀.⠀⠀⠀.⠀⠀⠀.⠀⠀⠀.

They reach the grove of pine at last;
'Bismillah! now the peril's past;
For yonder view the opening plain,
And there we'll prick our steeds amain:'
The Chiaus spake, and as he said,⠀⠀571
A bullet whistles o'er his head;
The foremost Tartar bites the ground!
Scarce had they time to check the rein,
Swift from their steeds the riders bound;
⠀But three shall never mount again:⠀576
Unseen the foes that gave the wound,
⠀The dying ask revenge in vain.
With steel unsheath'd, and carbine bent,
Some o'er their courser's harness leant,
⠀Half shelter'd by the steed;⠀⠀⠀⠀581
Some fly behind the nearest rock,
And there await the coming shock,
⠀Nor tamely stand to bleed
Beneath the shaft of foes unseen,⠀⠀585
Who dare not quit their craggy screen.
Stern Hassan only from his horse
Disdains to light, and keeps his course,
Till fiery flashes in the van
Proclaim too sure the robber-clan⠀⠀590
Have well secured the only way
Could now avail the promised prey;
Then curl'd his very beard with ire,
And glared his eye with fiercer fire;
'Though far and near the bullets hiss,⠀595
I've scaped a bloodier hour than this.'
And now the foe their covert quit,
And call his vassals to submit;
But Hassan's frown and furious word
Are dreaded more than hostile sword,⠀600

257

THE GIAOUR

Nor of his little band a man
Resign'd carbine or ataghan,
Nor raised the craven cry, Amaun!
In fuller sight, more near and near,
The lately ambush'd foes appear, 605
And issuing from the grove, advance
Some who on battle-charger prance.
Who leads them on with foreign brand
Far flashing in his red right hand?
''Tis he! 'tis he! I know him now; 610
I know him by his pallid brow;
I know him by the evil eye
That aids his envious treachery;
I know him by his jet-black barb;
Though now array'd in Arnaut garb, 615
Apostate from his own vile faith,
It shall not save him from the death:
'Tis he! well met in any hour,
Lost Leila's love, accursed Giaour!'

As rolls the river into ocean, 620
In sable torrent wildly streaming;
As the sea-tide's opposing motion,
In azure column proudly gleaming,
Beats back the current many a rood,
In curling foam and mingling flood, 625
While eddying whirl, and breaking wave,
Roused by the blast of winter, rave;
Through sparkling spray, in thundering
 clash,
The lightnings of the waters flash
In awful whiteness o'er the shore, 630
That shines and shakes beneath the roar;
Thus—as the stream and ocean greet,
With waves that madden as they meet—
Thus join the bands, whom mutual wrong,
And fate, and fury, drive along. 635
The bickering sabres' shivering jar;
 And pealing wide or ringing near
Its echoes on the throbbing ear,
The deathshot hissing from afar;
The shock, the shout, the groan of war, 641
Reverberate along that vale,
 More suited to the shepherd's tale:
Though few the numbers—theirs the
 strife,
That neither spares nor speaks for life!
Ah! fondly youthful hearts can press, 645
To seize and share the dear caress;
But Love itself could never pant
For all that Beauty sighs to grant
With half the fervour Hate bestows
Upon the last embrace of foes, 650
When grappling in the fight they fold
Those arms that ne'er shall lose their hold:
Friends meet to part; Love laughs at faith:
True foes, once met, are join'd till death!

With sabre shiver'd to the hilt, 655
Yet dripping with the blood he spilt;
Yet strain'd within the sever'd hand
Which quivers round that faithless brand;

His turban far behind him roll'd,
And cleft in twain its firmest fold; 660
His flowing robe by falchion torn,
And crimson as those clouds of morn
That, streak'd with dusky red, portend
The day shall have a stormy end;
A stain on every bush that bore 665
A fragment of his palampore;
His breast with wounds unnumber'd riven,
His back to earth, his face to heaven,
Fall'n Hassan lies—his unclosed eye
Yet lowering on his enemy, 670
As if the hour that seal'd his fate
Surviving left his quenchless hate;
And o'er him bends that foe with brow
As dark as his that bled below.—

'Yes, Leila sleeps beneath the wave, 675
But his shall be a redder grave;
Her spirit pointed well the steel
Which taught that felon heart to feel.
He call'd the Prophet, but his power
Was vain against the vengeful Giaour:
He call'd on Alla, but the word 681
Arose unheeded or unheard.
Thou Paynim fool! could Leila's prayer
Be pass'd, and thine accorded there?
I watch'd my time, I leagued with these,
The traitor in his turn to seize; 686
My wrath is wreak'd, the deed is done,
And now I go—but go alone.'

The browsing camels' bells are tinkling:
His mother look'd from her lattice high—
 She saw the dews of eve besprinkling
The pasture green beneath her eye, 692
 She saw the planets faintly twinkling:
''Tis twilight—sure his train is nigh.'
She could not rest in the garden-bower,
But gazed through the grate of his steepest
 tower: 696
'Why comes he not? his steeds are fleet,
Nor shrink they from the summer heat;
Why sends not the Bridegroom his prom-
 ised gift?
Is his heart more cold, or his barb less
 swift? 700
Oh, false reproach! yon Tartar now
Has gain'd our nearest mountain's brow,
And warily the steep descends,
And now within the valley bends;
And he bears the gift at his saddle-bow—
How could I deem his courser slow? 706
Right well my largess shall repay
His welcome speed and weary way.'

The Tartar lighted at the gate,
But scarce upheld his fainting weight: 710
His swarthy visage spake distress,
But this might be from weariness;

His garb with sanguine spots was dyed,
But these might be from his courser's side;
He drew the token from his vest— 715
Angel of Death! 'tis Hassan's cloven crest!
His calpac rent—his caftan red—
'Lady, a fearful bride thy son hath wed:
Me, not from mercy, did they spare,
But this empurpled pledge to bear. 720
Peace to the brave! whose blood is spilt;
Woe to the Giaour! for his the guilt.'

A turban carved in coarsest stone,
A pillar with rank weeds o'ergrown,
Whereon can now be scarcely read 725
The Koran verse that mourns the dead,
Point out the spot where Hassan fell
A victim in that lonely dell.
There sleeps as true an Osmanlie
As e'er at Mecca bent the knee; 730
As ever scorn'd forbidden wine,
Or pray'd with face towards the shrine,
In orisons resumed anew
At solemn sound of 'Alla Hu!'
Yet died he by a stranger's hand, 735
And stranger in his native land;
Yet died he as in arms he stood,
And unavenged, at least in blood.
But him the maids of Paradise
Impatient to their halls invite, 740
And the dark heaven of Houris' eyes
On him shall glance for ever bright;
They come—their kerchiefs green they wave,
And welcome with a kiss the brave!
Who falls in battle 'gainst a Giaour 745
Is worthiest an immortal bower.

But thou, false Infidel! shalt writhe
Beneath avenging Monkir's scythe;
And from its torment 'scape alone
To wander round lost Eblis' throne; 750
And fire unquench'd, unquenchable,
Around, within, thy heart shall dwell;
Nor ear can hear nor tongue can tell
The tortures of that inward hell!
But first, on earth as Vampire sent, 755
Thy corse shall from its tomb be rent:
Then ghastly haunt thy native place,
And suck the blood of all thy race;
There from thy daughter, sister, wife,
At midnight drain the stream of life; 760
Yet loathe the banquet which perforce
Must feed thy livid living corse:
Thy victims ere they yet expire
Shall know the demon for their sire,
As cursing thee, thou cursing them, 765
Thy flowers are wither'd on the stem.
But one that for thy crime must fall,
The youngest, most beloved of all,
Shall bless thee with a *father's* name—
That word shall wrap thy heart in flame!
Yet must thou end thy task, and mark 771
Her cheek's last tinge, her eye's last spark,

And the last glassy glance must view
Which freezes o'er its lifeless blue;
Then with unhallow'd hand shalt tear 775
The tresses of her yellow hair,
Of which in life a lock when shorn,
Affection's fondest pledge was worn,
But now is borne away by thee,
Memorial of thine agony! 780
Wet with thine own best blood shall drip
Thy gnashing tooth and haggard lip;
Then stalking to thy sullen grave,
Go—and with Gouls and Afrits rave;
Till these in horror shrink away 785
From spectre more accursed than they!

'How name ye yon lone Caloyer?
His features I have scann'd before
In mine own land: 'tis many a year,
Since, dashing by the lonely shore, 790
I saw him urge as fleet a steed
As ever served a horseman's need.
But once I saw that face, yet then
It was so mark'd with inward pain,
I could not pass it by again; 795
It breathes the same dark spirit now,
As death were stamp'd upon his brow.

"'Tis twice three years at summer tide
Since first among our freres he came;
And here it soothes him to abide 800
For some dark deed he will not name.
But never at our vesper prayer,
Nor e'er before confession chair
Kneels he, nor recks he when arise
Incense or anthem to the skies, 805
But broods within his cell alone,
His faith and race alike unknown.
The sea from Paynim land he crost,
And here ascended from the coast;
Yet seems he not of Othman race, 810
But only Christian in his face:
I'd judge him some stray renegade,
Repentant of the change he made,
Save that he shuns our holy shrine, 814
Nor tastes the sacred bread and wine.
Great largess to these walls be brought,
And thus our abbot's favour bought;
But were I prior, not a day
Should brook such stranger's further stay
Or pent within our penance cell 820
Should doom him there for aye to dwell.
Much in his visions mutters he
Of maiden whelm'd beneath the sea;
Of sabres clashing, foemen flying,
Wrongs avenged, and Moslem dying. 825
On cliff he hath been known to stand,
And rave as to some bloody hand
Fresh sever'd from its parent limb,
Invisible to all but him,
Which beckons onward to his grave, 830
And lures to leap into the wave.'

THE GIAOUR

Dark and unearthly is the scowl
That glares beneath his dusky cowl.
The flash of that dilating eye
Reveals too much of times gone by; 835
Though varying, indistinct its hue,
Oft will his glance the gazer rue,
For in it lurks that nameless spell,
Which speaks, itself unspeakable,
A spirit yet unquell'd and high, 840
That claims and keeps ascendency;
And like the bird whose pinions quake,
But cannot fly the gazing snake,
Will others quail beneath his look,
Nor 'scape the glance they scarce can
brook. 845
From him the half-affrighted Friar
When met alone would fain retire,
As if that eye and bitter smile
Transferr'd to others fear and guile:
Not oft to smile descendeth he, 850
And when he doth 'tis sad to see
That he but mocks at Misery.
How that pale lip will curl and quiver!
Then fix once more as if for ever;
As if his sorrow or disdain 855
Forbade him e'er to smile again.
Well were it so—such ghastly mirth
From joyaunce ne'er derived its birth.
But sadder still it were to trace
What once were feelings in that face: 860
Time hath not yet the features fix'd,
But brighter traits with evil mix'd;
And there are hues not always faded,
Which speak a mind not all degraded
Even by the crimes through which it
waded: 865
The common crowd but see the gloom
Of wayward deeds, and fitting doom;
The close observer can espy
A noble soul, and lineage high:
Alas! though both bestow'd in vain, 870
Which Grief could change, and Guilt
could stain,
It was no vulgar tenement
To which such lofty gifts were lent,
And still with little less than dread
On such the sight is riveted. 875
The roofless cot, decay'd and rent,
 Will scarce delay the passer by;
The tower by war or tempest bent,
While yet may frown one battlement,
 Demands and daunts the stranger's
 eye; 880
Each ivied arch, and pillar lone,
Pleads haughtily for glories gone!

His floating robe around him folding,
 Slow sweeps he through the column'd
 aisle;
With dread beheld, with gloom behold-
 ing 885
 The rites that sanctify the pile.
But when the anthem shakes the choir,
And kneel the monks, his steps retire;

By yonder lone and wavering torch
His aspect glares within the porch; 890
There will he pause till all is done—
And hear the prayer, but utter none.
See—by the half-illumined wall
His hood be back, his dark hair fall,
That pale brow wildly wreathing round,
As if the Gorgon there had bound 896
The sablest of the serpent-braid
That o'er her fearful forehead stray'd:
For he declines the convent oath,
And leaves those locks unhallow'd growth
But wears our garb in all beside; 901
And, not from piety but pride,
Gives wealth to walls that never heard
Of his one holy vow nor word.
Lo!—mark ye, as the harmony 905
Peals louder praises to the sky,
That livid cheek, that stony air
Of mix'd defiance and despair!
Saint Francis, keep him from the shrine!
Else may we dread the wrath divine 910
Made manifest by awful sign.
If ever evil angel bore
The form of mortal, such he wore;
By all my hope of sins forgiven,
Such looks are not of earth nor heaven!'

To love the softest hearts are prone, 916
But such can ne'er be all his own;
Too timid in his woes to share,
Too meek to meet, or brave despair;
And sterner hearts alone may feel 920
The wound that time can never heal.
The rugged metal of the mine
Must burn before its surface shine,
But plunged within the furnace-flame,
It bends and melts—though still the
same; 925
Then temper'd to thy want, or will,
'Twill serve thee to defend or kill;
A breastplate for thine hour of need,
Or blade to bid thy foeman bleed;
But if a dagger's form it bear, 930
Let those who shape its edge beware!
Thus passion's fire, and woman's art,
Can turn and tame the sterner heart;
From these its form and tone are ta'en,
And what they make it, must remain, 935
But break—before it bend again.

.

If solitude succeed to grief,
Release from pain is slight relief;
The vacant bosom's wilderness 939
Might thank the pang that made it less.
We loathe what none are left to share:
Even bliss—'twere woe alone to bear;
The heart once thus left desolate
Must fly at last for ease—to hate.
It is as if the dead could feel 945
The icy worm around them steal,
And shudder, as the reptiles creep
To revel o'er their rotting sleep,

Without the power to scare away
The cold consumers of their clay! 950
It is as if the desert bird,
 Whose beak unlocks her bosom's
 stream
 To still her famish'd nestlings' scream,
Nor mourns a life to them transferr'd, 955
Should rend her rash devoted breast,
And find them flown her empty nest.
The keenest pangs the wretched find
 Are rapture to the dreary void,
The leafless desert of the mind,
 The waste of feelings unemploy'd. 960
Who would be doom'd to gaze upon
A sky without a cloud or sun?
Less hideous far the tempest's roar
Than ne'er to brave the billows more—
Thrown, when the war of winds is o'er,
A lonely wreck on fortune's shore, 966
Mid sullen calm, and silent bay,
Unseen to drop by dull decay;—
Better to sink beneath the shock
Than moulder piecemeal on the rock!

Father! thy days have pass'd in peace,
 'Mid counted beads, and countless
 prayer;
To bid the sins of others cease,
 Thyself without a crime or care,
Save transient ills that all must bear, 975
Has been thy lot from youth to age;
And thou wilt bless thee from the rage
Of passions fierce and uncontroll'd,
Such as thy penitents unfold,
Whose secret sins and sorrows rest 980
Within thy pure and pitying breast.
My days, though few, have pass'd below
In much of joy, but more of woe;
Yet still in hours of love or strife,
I've 'scaped the weariness of life: 985
Now leagued with friends, now girt by
 foes,
I loathed the languor of repose.
Now nothing left to love or hate,
No more with hope or pride elate,
I'd rather be the thing that crawls 990
Most noxious o'er a dungeon's walls,
Than pass my dull, unvarying days,
Condemn'd to meditate and gaze.
Yet, lurks a wish within my breast
For rest—but not to feel 'tis rest. 995
Soon shall my fate that wish fulfil;
 And I shall sleep without the dream
Of what I was, and would be still,
 Dark as to thee my deeds may seem:
My memory now is but the tomb 1000
Of joys long dead; my hope, their doom:
Though better to have died with those
Than bear a life of lingering woes.
My spirit shrunk not to sustain
The searching throes of ceaseless pain;
Nor sought the self-accorded grave 1006
Of ancient fool and modern knave:

Yet death I have not fear'd to meet;
And in the field it had been sweet,
Had danger woo'd me on to move 1010
The slave of glory, not of love.
I've braved it—not for honour's boast;
I smile at laurels won or lost;
To such let others carve their way,
For high renown, or hireling pay: 1015
But place again before my eyes
Aught that I deem a worthy prize—
The maid I love, the man I hate—
And I will hunt the steps of fate,
To save or slay, as these require, 1020
Through rending steel and rolling fire:
Nor need'st thou doubt this speech from
 one
Who would but do—what he *hath* done.
Death is but what the haughty brave,
The weak must bear, the wretch must
 crave; 1025
Then let life go to Him who gave:
I have not quail'd to danger's brow
When high and happy—need I *now*?

'I loved her, Friar! nay, adored—
 But these are words that all can use—
I proved it more in deed than word; 1031
There's blood upon that dinted sword,
 A stain its steel can never lose:
'Twas shed for her, who died for me,
 It warm'd the heart of one abhorr'd:
Nay, start not—no—nor bend thy knee,
 Nor midst my sins such act record;
Thou wilt absolve me from the deed,
For he was hostile to thy creed!
The very name of Nazarene 1040
Was wormwood to his Paynim spleen.
Ungrateful fool! since but for brands
Well wielded in some hardy hands,
And wounds by Galileans given,
The surest pass to Turkish heaven, 1045
For him his Houris still might wait
Impatient at the Prophet's gate.
I loved her—love will find its way
Through paths where wolves would fear
 to prey;
And if it dares enough, 'twere hard 1050
If passion met not some reward—
No matter how, or where, or why,
I did not vainly seek, nor sigh:
Yet sometimes, with remorse, in vain
I wish she had not loved again. 1055
She died—I dare not tell thee how;
But look—'tis written on my brow!
There read of Cain the curse and crime,
In characters unworn by time: 1059
Still, ere thou dost condemn me, pause;
Not mine the act, though I the cause.
Yet did he but what I had done
Had she been false to more than one,
Faithless to him, he gave the blow;
But true to me, I laid him low: 1065

261

Howe'er deserved her doom might be,
Her treachery was truth to me;
To me she gave her heart, that all
Which tyranny can ne'er enthral:
And I, alas! too late to save! 1070
Yet all I then could give, I gave,
'Twas some relief, our foe a grave.
His death sits lightly; but her fate
Has made me—what thou well may'st
 hate.
 His doom was seal'd—he knew it well,
Warn'd by the voice of stern Taheer, 1076
Deep in whose darkly boding ear
The deathshot peal'd of murder near
 As filed the troop to where they fell!
He died too in the battle broil, 1080
A time that heeds nor pain nor toil;
One cry to Mahomet for aid,
One prayer to Alla all he made:
He knew and cross'd me in the fray—
I gazed upon him where he lay, 1085
And watch'd his spirit ebb away;
Though pierced like pard by hunter's steel,
He felt not half that now I feel.
I search'd, but vainly search'd, to find
The workings of a wounded mind; 1090
Each feature of that sullen corse
Betray'd his rage, but no remorse.
Oh, what had Vengeance given to trace
Despair upon his dying face!
The late repentance of that hour, 1095
When Penitence hath lost her power
To tear one terror from the grave,
And will not soothe, and cannot save.

'The cold in clime are cold in blood,
 Their love can scarce deserve the name;
But mine was like the lava flood 1101
 That boils in Ætna's breast of flame.
I cannot prate in puling strain
Of ladye-love and beauty's chain: 1104
If changing cheek, and scorching vein,
Lips taught to writhe, but not complain,
If bursting heart, and madd'ning brain,
And daring deed, and vengeful steel,
And all that I have felt, and feel,
Betoken love—that love was mine, 1110
And shown by many a bitter sign.
'Tis true, I could not whine nor sigh,
I knew but to obtain or die.
I die—but first I have possess'd,
And come what may, I have been bless'd.
Shall I the doom I sought upbraid? 1116
No—reft of all, yet undismay'd
But for the thought of Leila slain,
Give me the pleasure with the pain,
So would I live and love again. 1120
I grieve, but not, my holy guide!
For him who dies, but her who died:
She sleeps beneath the wandering wave—
Ah! had she but an earthly grave, 1124
This breaking heart and throbbing head
Should seek and share her narrow bed.

She was a form of life and light,
That, seen, became a part of sight;
And rose, where'er I turn'd mine eye,
The Morning-star of Memory! 1130

'Yes, Love indeed is light from heaven;
 A spark of that immortal fire
With angels shared, by Alla given,
 To lift from earth our low desire.
Devotion wafts the mind above, 1135
But Heaven itself descends in love;
A feeling from the Godhead caught,
To wean from self each sordid thought;
A Ray of him who form'd the whole;
A Glory circling round the soul! 1140
I grant my love imperfect, all
That mortals by the name miscall;
Then deem it evil, what thou wilt;
But say, oh say, hers was not guilt!
She was my life's unerring light: 1145
That quench'd, what beam shall break my
 night?
Oh! would it shone to lead me still,
Although to death or deadliest ill!
Why marvel ye, if they who lose
 This present joy, this future hope, 1150
 No more with sorrow meekly cope;
In phrensy then their fate accuse;
In madness do those fearful deeds
 That seem to add but guilt to woe?
Alas! the breast that inly bleeds 1155
 Hath nought to dread from outward
 blow:
Who falls from all he knows of bliss,
Cares little into what abyss.
Fierce as the gloomy vulture's now
 To thee, old man, my deeds appear:
I read abhorrence on thy brow, 1161
 And this too was I born to bear!
'Tis true, that, like that bird of prey,
With havoc have I mark'd my way:
But this was taught me by the dove, 1165
To die—and know no second love.
This lesson yet hath man to learn,
Taught by the thing he dares to spurn:
The bird that sings within the brake,
The swan that swims upon the lake, 1170
One mate, and one alone, will take.
And let the fool still prone to range,
And sneer on all who cannot change,
Partake his jest with boasting boys;
I envy not his varied joys, 1175
But deem such feeble, heartless man
Less than yon solitary swan;
Far, far beneath the shallow maid
He left believing and betray'd. 1179
Such shame at least was never mine—
Leila! each thought was only thine!
My good, my guilt, my weal, my woe,
My hope on high—my all below.
Earth holds no other like to thee,
Or, if it doth, in vain for me: 1185
For worlds I dare not view the dame
Resembling thee, yet not the same.

The very crimes that mar my youth,
This bed of death—attest my truth!
'Tis all too late—thou wert, thou art
The cherish'd madness of my heart! 1191

And she was lost—and yet I breathed,
 But not the breath of human life:
A serpent round my heart was wreathed,
 And stung my every thought to strife.
Alike all time, abhorr'd all place, 1196
Shuddering I shrunk from Nature's face,
Where every hue that charm'd before
The blackness of my bosom wore.
The rest thou dost already know, 1200
And all my sins, and half my woe.
But talk no more of penitence;
Thou seest I soon shall part from hence;
And if thy holy tale were true, 1204
The deed that's done canst *thou* undo?
Think me not thankless—but this grief
Looks not to priesthood for relief.
My soul's estate in secret guess:
But wouldst thou pity more, say less.
When thou canst bid my Leila live, 1210
Then will I sue thee to forgive;
Then plead my cause in that high place
Where purchased masses proffer grace.
Go, when the hunter's hand hath wrung
From forest-cave her shrieking young,
And calm the lonely lioness: 1216
But soothe not—mock not *my* distress!

In earlier days, and calmer hours,
 When heart with heart delights to blend,
Where bloom my native valley's bowers,
 I had—Ah! have I now?—a friend!
To him this pledge I charge thee send,
 Memorial of a youthful vow; 1223
I would remind him of my end:
 Though souls absorb'd like mine allow
Brief thought to distant friendship's claim,
Yet dear to him my blighted name. 1227
'Tis strange—he prophesied my doom,
 And I have smiled—I then could smile—
When Prudence would his voice assume,
 And warn—I reck'd not what—the
 while: 1231
But now remembrance whispers o'er
Those accents scarcely mark'd before.
Say—that his bodings came to pass,
 And he will start to hear their truth,
 And wish his words had not been sooth:
Tell him, unheeding as I was, 1237
 Through many a busy bitter scene
 Of all our golden youth had been,
In pain, my faltering tongue had tried
To bless his memory ere I died; 1241
But Heaven in wrath would turn away
If Guilt should for the guiltless pray.
I do not ask him not to blame,
Too gentle he to wound my name; 1245
And what have I to do with fame?
I do not ask him not to mourn,
Such cold request might sound like scorn;

And what than friendship's manly tear
May better grace a brother's bier? 1250
But bear this ring, his own of old,
And tell him—what thou dost behold!
The wither'd frame, the ruin'd mind,
The wrack by passion left behind,
A shrivell'd scroll, a scatter'd leaf, 1255
Sear'd by the autumn blast of grief!

.

'Tell me no more of fancy's gleam,
No, father, no, 'twas not a dream;
Alas! the dreamer first must sleep,—
I only watch'd, and wish'd to weep, 1260
But could not, for my burning brow
Throbb'd to the very brain as now:
I wish'd but for a single tear,
As something welcome, new, and dear:
I wish'd it then, I wish it still; 1265
Despair is stronger than my will.
Waste not thine orison, despair
Is mightier than thy pious prayer:
I would not, if I might, be blest;
I want no paradise, but rest. 1270
'Twas then, I tell thee, father! then
I saw her; yes, she lived again;
And shining in her white symar,
As through yon pale gray cloud the
 star
Which now I gaze on, as on her, 1275
Who look'd and looks far lovelier;
Dimly I view its trembling spark;
To-morrow's night shall be more dark;
And I, before its rays appear,
That lifeless thing the living fear. 1280
I wander, father! for my soul
Is fleeting towards the final goal.
I saw her, friar! and I rose
Forgetful of our former woes; 1284
And rushing from my couch, I dart,
And clasp her to my desperate heart;
I clasp—what is it that I clasp?
No breathing form within my grasp,
No heart that beats reply to mine—
Yet, Leila! yet the form is thine! 1290
And art thou, dearest, changed so much
As meet my eye, yet mock my touch?
Ah! were thy beauties e'er so cold,
I care not so my arms enfold
The all they ever wish'd to hold. 1295
Alas! around a shadow prest
They shrink upon my lonely breast;
Yet still 'tis there! In silence stands,
And beckons with beseeching hands!
With braided hair, and bright-black eye—
I knew 'twas false—she could not die!
But he is dead! within the dell 1302
I saw him buried where he fell;
He comes not, for he cannot break
From earth; why then art thou awake?
They told me wild waves roll'd above
The face I view, the form I love; 1307
They told me—'twas a hideous tale!—
I'd tell it, but my tongue would fail:

263

If true, and from thine ocean-cave 1310
Thou com'st to claim a calmer grave,
Oh! pass thy dewy fingers o'er
This brow that then will burn no more;
Or place them on my hopeless heart:
But, shape or shade! whate'er thou art,
In mercy ne'er again depart! 1316
Or farther with thee bear my soul
Than winds can waft or waters roll!

.
.

'Such is my name, and such my tale.
Confessor! to thy secret ear 1320
I breathe the sorrows I bewail,
And thank thee for the generous tear
This glazing eye could never shed.
Then lay me with the humblest dead,
And, save the cross above my head, 132
Be neither name nor emblem spread,
By prying stranger to be read,
Or stay the passing pilgrim's tread.'

He pass'd—nor of his name and race
Hath left a token or a trace, 133
Save what the father must not say
Who shrived him on his dying day:
This broken tale was all we knew
Of her he loved, or him he slew.

THE BRIDE OF ABYDOS

A TURKISH TALE,

'Had we never loved so kindly,
Had we never loved so blindly,
Never met or never parted,
We had ne'er been broken-hearted.'—BURNS.

TO

THE RIGHT HON. LORD HOLLAND,

THIS TALE IS INSCRIBED,

WITH EVERY SENTIMENT OF REGARD AND RESPECT,
BY HIS GRATEFULLY OBLIGED AND SINCERE FRIEND,

BYRON.

CANTO THE FIRST

I

KNOW ye the land where the cypress and myrtle
Are emblems of deeds that are done in their clime?
Where the rage of the vulture, the love of the turtle,
Now melt into sorrow, now madden to crime!
Know ye the land of the cedar and vine,
Where the flowers ever blossom, the beams ever shine; 6
Where the light wings of Zephyr, oppress'd with perfume,
Wax faint o'er the gardens of Gúl in her bloom;
Where the citron and olive are fairest of fruit,
And the voice of the nightingale never is mute: 10
Where the tints of the earth, and the hues of the sky,
In colour though varied, in beauty may vie,
And the purple of ocean is deepest in dye;
Where the virgins are soft as the roses they twine, 1
And all, save the spirit of man, is divine
'Tis the clime of the East; 'tis the land o the Sun—
Can he smile on such deeds as his children have done?
Oh! wild as the accents of lovers' farewell
Are the hearts which they bear, and the tales which they tell.

II

Begirt with many a gallant slave, 20
Apparell'd as becomes the brave,
Awaiting each his lord's behest
To guide his steps, or guard his rest,
Old Giaffir sate in his Divan: 2
Deep thought was in his aged eye;
And though the face of Mussulman
Not oft betrays to standers by
The mind within, well skill'd to hide
All but unconquerable pride,
His pensive cheek and pondering brow
Did more than he was wont avow. 3

III

'Let the chamber be clear'd.'—The train
 disappear'd.—
'Now call me the chief of the Haram
 guard.'
With Giaffir is none but his only son,
And the Nubian awaiting the sire's
 award. 35
'Haroun—when all the crowd that
 wait
Are pass'd beneath the outer gate,
(Woe to the head whose eye beheld
My child Zuleika's face unveil'd!)
Hence, lead my daughter from her
 tower; 40
Her fate is fix'd this very hour:
Yet not to her repeat my thought;
By me alone be duty taught!'

'Pacha! to hear is to obey.' 44
No more must slave to despot say—
Then to the tower had ta'en his way,
But here young Selim silence brake,
First lowly rendering reverence meet;
And downcast look'd, and gently spake,
Still standing at the Pacha's feet:
For son of Moslem must expire, 51
Ere dare to sit before his sire!

'Father! for fear that thou shouldst
 chide
My sister, or her sable guide, 54
Know—for the fault, if fault there be,
Was mine, then fall thy frowns on me—
So lovelily the morning shone,
 That—let the old and weary sleep—
I could not; and to view alone 59
 The fairest scenes of land and deep,
With none to listen and reply
To thoughts with which my heart beat
 high
Were irksome—for whate'er my mood,
In sooth I love not solitude;
I on Zuleika's slumber broke, 65
 And, as thou knowest that for me
Soon turns the Haram's grating key,
Before the guardian slaves awoke
We to the cypress groves had flown,
And made earth, main, and heaven our
 own! 70
There linger'd we, beguiled too long
With Mejnoun's tale, or Sadi's song;
Till I, who heard the deep tambour
Beat thy Divan's approaching hour,
To thee, and to my duty true, 75
Warn'd by the sound, to greet thee flew:
But there Zuleika wanders yet—
Nay, Father, rage not—nor forget
That none can pierce that secret bower
But those who watch the women's
 tower.' 80

IV

'Son of a slave'—the Pacha said—
'From unbelieving mother bred,
Vain were a father's hope to see
Aught that beseems a man in thee.
Thou, when thine arm should bend the
 bow, 85
 And hurl the dart, and curb the steed,
 Thou, Greek in soul if not in creed,
Must pore where babbling waters flow,
And watch unfolding roses blow.
Would that yon orb, whose matin glow
Thy listless eyes so much admire, 91
Would lend thee something of his fire!
Thou, who wouldst see this battlement
By Christian cannon piecemeal rent;
Nay, tamely view old Stambol's wall
Before the dogs of Moscow fall, 96
Nor strike one stroke for life and death
Against the curs of Nazareth!
Go—let thy less than woman's hand
Assume the distaff—not the brand.
But, Haroun!—to my daughter speed;
And hark—of thine own head take
 heed— 102
If thus Zuleika oft takes wing—
Thou see'st yon bow—it hath a string!'

V

No sound from Selim's lip was heard,
 At least that met old Giaffir's ear,
But every frown and every word 107
Pierced keener than a Christian's sword.
 'Son of a slave!—reproach'd with fear!
 Those gibes had cost another dear.
Son of a slave!—and who my sire?'
 Thus held his thoughts their dark
 career;
And glances ev'n of more than ire
Flash forth, then faintly disappear.
Old Giaffir gazed upon his son 115
 And started; for within his eye
He read how much his wrath had done;
He saw rebellion there begun:
 'Come hither, boy—what, no reply?
I mark thee—and I know thee too; 120
But there be deeds thou dar'st not do:
But if thy beard had manlier length,
And if thy hand had skill and strength,
I'd joy to see thee break a lance,
Albeit against my own perchance.' 125

As sneeringly these accents fell,
On Selim's eye he fiercely gazed:
 That eye return'd him glance for
 glance,
And proudly to his sire's was raised,
 Till Giaffir's quail'd and shrunk
 askance— 130
And why—he felt, but durst not tell.
'Much I misdoubt this wayward boy
Will one day work me more annoy:
I never loved him from his birth,
And—but his arm is little worth, 135
And scarcely in the chase could cope
With timid fawn or antelope,
Far less would venture into strife

Where man contends for fame and
 life—
I would not trust that look or tone: 140
No—nor the blood so near my own.
That blood—he hath not heard—no
 more—
I'll watch him closer than before.
He is an Arab to my sight, 144
Or Christian crouching in the fight—
But hark!—I hear Zuleika's voice;
 Like Houris' hymn it meets mine ear:
She is the offspring of my choice;
 Oh! more than ev'n her mother dear,
With all to hope, and nought to fear—
My Peri! ever welcome here! 151
Sweet, as the desert fountain's wave
To lips just cool'd in time to save—
 Such to my longing sight art thou;
Nor can they waft to Mecca's shrine
More thanks for life, than I for thine,
 Who blest thy birth and bless thee
 now.'

VI

Fair, as the first that fell of womankind,
 When on that dread yet lovely serpent
 smiling,
Whose image then was stamp'd upon her
 mind— 160
 But once beguil'd—and ever more be-
 guiling;
Dazzling, as that, oh! too transcendent
 vision
 To Sorrow's phantom-peopled slumber
 given,
When heart meets heart again in dreams
 Elysian,
 And paints the lost on Earth revived in
 Heaven; 165
Soft, as the memory of buried love;
Pure, as the prayer which Childhood
 wafts above,
Was she—the daughter of that rude old
 Chief,
Who met the maid with tears—but not of
 grief.

Who hath not proved how feebly words
 essay 170
To fix one spark of Beauty's heavenly ray?
Who doth not feel, until his failing sight
Faints into dimness with its own delight,
His changing cheek, his sinking heart
 confess 174
The might, the majesty of Loveliness?
Such was Zuleika, such around her shone
The nameless charms unmark'd by her
 alone—
The light of love, the purity of grace,
The mind, the Music breathing from her
 face,
The heart whose softness harmonized the
 whole, 180
And oh! that eye was in itself a Soul!

Her graceful arms in meekness bending
 Across her gently-budding breast;
At one kind word those arms extending
 To clasp the neck of him who blest
His child caressing and carest, 186
Zuleika came—and Giaffir felt
His purpose half within him melt;
Not that against her fancied weal
His heart though stern could ever feel;
Affection chain'd her to that heart; 191
Ambition tore the links apart.

VII

'Zuleika! child of gentleness!
 How dear this very day must tell,
When I forget my own distress, 195
 In losing what I love so well,
To bid thee with another dwell:
Another! and a braver man
Was never seen in battle's van.
We Moslem reck not much of blood; 200
 But yet the line of Carasman
Unchanged, unchangeable hath stood
 First of the bold Timariot bands
That won and well can keep their lands.
Enough that he who comes to woo
Is kinsman of the Bey Oglou: 206
His years need scarce a thought employ;
I would not have thee wed a boy.
And thou shalt have a noble dower—
And his and my united power 210
Will laugh to scorn the death-firman,
Which others tremble but to scan,
And teach the messenger what fate
The bearer of such boon may wait.
And now thou know'st thy father's
 will: 215
 All that thy sex hath need to know:
'Twas mine to teach obedience still—
 The way to love, thy lord may show.'

VIII

In silence bow'd the virgin's head;
 And if her eye was fill'd with tears
That stifled feeling dare not shed, 221
And changed her cheek from pale to
 red,
 And red to pale, as through her ears
Those winged words like arrows sped,
 What could such be but maiden
 fears? 225
So bright the tear in Beauty's eye,
Love half regrets to kiss it dry;
So sweet the blush of Bashfulness,
Even Pity scarce can wish it less!

Whate'er it was the sire forgot; 230
Or if remember'd, mark'd it not;
Thrice clapp'd his hands, and call'd his
 steed,
 Resign'd his gem-adorn'd chibouque,
And mounting featly for the mead,

With Maugrabee and Mamaluke,
His way amid his Delis took, 236
To witness many an active deed
With sabre keen, or blunt jerreed.
The Kislar only and his Moors
Watch well the Haram's massy doors.

IX

His head was leant upon his hand, 241
His eye look'd o'er the dark blue
 water
That swiftly glides and gently swells
Between the winding Dardanelles;
But yet he saw nor sea nor strand, 245
Nor even his Pacha's turban'd band
Mix in the game of mimic slaughter,
Careering cleave the folded felt,
With sabre stroke right sharply dealt;
Nor mark'd the javelin-darting crowd
Nor heard their Ollahs wild and loud—
He thought but of old Giaffir's
 daughter! 252

X

No word from Selim's bosom broke;
One sigh Zuleika's thoughts bespoke:
Still gazed he through the lattice grate,
Pale, mute, and mournfully sedate. 256
To him Zuleika's eye was turn'd,
But little from his aspect learn'd:
Equal her grief, yet not the same;
Her heart confess'd a gentler flame: 260
But yet that heart, alarm'd or weak,
She knew not why, forbade to speak.
Yet speak she must—but when essay?
'How strange he thus should turn away!
Not thus we e'er before have met; 265
Nor thus shall be our parting yet.'
Thrice paced she slowly through the
 room,
And watch'd his eye—it still was fix'd:
She snatch'd the urn wherein was
 mix'd
The Persian Atar-gul's perfume, 270
And sprinkled all its odours o'er
The pictured roof and marble floor:
The drops, that through his glittering
 vest
The playful girl's appeal address'd,
Unheeded o'er his bosom flew, 275
As if that breast were marble too.
'What, sullen yet? it must not be—
Oh! gentle Selim, this from thee!'
She saw in curious order set
The fairest flowers of eastern land—
'He loved them once; may touch them
 yet, 281
If offer'd by Zuleika's hand.'
The childish thought was hardly
 breathed
Before the rose was pluck'd and
 wreathed;
The next fond moment saw her seat
Her fairy form at Selim's feet: 286

'This rose to calm my brother's cares
A message from the Bulbul bears;
It says to-night he will prolong
For Selim's ear his sweetest song; 290
And though his note is somewhat sad,
He'll try for once a strain more glad,
With some faint hope his alter'd lay
May sing these gloomy thoughts away.

XI

'What! not receive my foolish flower?
Nay then I am indeed unblest: 296
On me can thus thy forehead lower?
And know'st thou not who loves thee
 best?
Oh, Selim dear! oh, more than dearest!
Say, is it me thou hat'st or fearest?
Come, lay thy head upon my breast,
And I will kiss thee into rest,
Since words of mine, and songs must
 fail,
Ev'n from my fabled nightingale.
I knew our sire at times was stern, 305
But this from thee had yet to learn:
Too well I know he loves thee not;
But is Zuleika's love forgot?
Ah! deem I right? the Pacha's plan—
This kinsman Bey of Carasman 310
Perhaps may prove some foe of thine.
If so, I swear by Mecca's shrine,—
If shrines that ne'er approach allow
To woman's step admit her vow,—
Without thy free consent, command,
The Sultan should not have my hand!
Think'st thou that I could bear to part
With thee, and learn to halve my heart?
Ah! were I sever'd from thy side,
Where were thy friend—and who my
 guide? 320
Years have not seen, Time shall not see,
The hour that tears my soul from thee:
Ev'n Azrael, from his deadly quiver
When flies that shaft, and fly it must,
That parts all else, shall doom for ever
Our hearts to undivided dust!' 326

XII

He lived, he breathed, he moved, he
 felt;
He raised the maid from where she
 knelt;
His trance was gone, his keen eye shone
With thoughts that long in darkness
 dwelt; 330
With thoughts that burn—in rays that
 melt.
As the stream late conceal'd
By the fringe of its willows,
When it rushes reveal'd
In the light of its billows; 335
As the bolt bursts on high
From the black cloud that bound it,
Flash'd the soul of that eye
Through the long lashes round it.

267

A war-horse at the trumpet's sound,
A lion roused by heedless hound, 341
A tyrant waked to sudden strife
By graze of ill-directed knife,
Starts not to more convulsive life
Than he, who heard that vow, dis-
 play'd, 345
And all, before repress'd, betray'd:
'Now thou art mine, for ever mine,
With life to keep, and scarce with life
 resign;
Now thou art mine, that sacred oath,
Though sworn by one, hath bound us
 both. 350
Yes, fondly, wisely hast thou done;
That vow hath saved more heads than
 one:
But blench not thou—thy simplest tress
Claims more from me than tenderness;
I would not wrong the slenderest hair
That clusters round thy forehead fair,
For all the treasures buried far 357
Within the caves of Istakar.
This morning clouds upon me lower'd,
Reproaches on my head were shower'd,
And Giaffir almost call'd me coward!
Now I have motive to be brave; 362
The son of his neglected slave,
Nay, start not, 'twas the term he gave,
May show, though little apt to vaunt,
A heart his words nor deeds can
 daunt. 366
His son, indeed!—yet, thanks to thee,
Perchance I am, at least shall be;
But let our plighted secret vow
Be only known to us as now. 370
I know the wretch who dares demand
From Giaffir thy reluctant hand;
More ill-got wealth, a meaner soul
Holds in a Musselim's control:
Was he not bred in Egripo? 375
A viler race let Israel show!
But let that pass—to none be told
Our oath; the rest shall time unfold.
To me and mine leave Osman Bey;
I've partisans for peril's day; 380
Think not I am what I appear;
I've arms, and friends, and vengeance
 near.'

XIII

'Think not thou art what thou appear-
 est!
My Selim, thou art sadly changed:
This morn I saw thee gentlest, dearest;
But now thou'rt from thyself es-
 tranged. 386
My love thou surely knew'st before,
It ne'er was less, nor can be more.
To see thee, hear thee, near thee stay,
 And hate the night I know not why,
Save that we meet not but by day;
 With thee to live, with thee to die,
I dare not to my hope deny:

Thy cheek, thine eyes, thy lips to kiss,
Like this—and this—no more than
 this; 395
For, Allah! sure thy lips are flame:
 What fever in thy veins is flushing?
My own have nearly caught the same,
 At least I feel my cheek, too, blush-
 ing.
To soothe thy sickness, watch thy
 health, 400
Partake, but never waste thy wealth,
Or stand with smiles unmurmuring by,
And lighten half thy poverty;
Do all but close thy dying eye,
For that I could not live to try; 405
To these alone my thoughts aspire:
More can I do? or thou require?
But, Selim, thou must answer why
We need so much of mystery?
The cause I cannot dream nor tell, 410
But be it, since thou say'st 'tis well;
Yet what thou mean'st by "arms" and
 "friends,"
Beyond my weaker sense extends.
I meant that Giaffir should have heard
 The very vow I plighted thee; 415
His wrath would not revoke my word:
 But surely he would leave me free.
Can this fond wish seem strange in
 me,
To be what I have ever been?
What other hath Zuleika seen 420
From simple childhood's earliest hour?
 What other can she seek to see
Than thee, companion of her bower,
 The partner of her infancy?
These cherish'd thoughts with life
 begun, 425
 Say, why must I no more avow?
What change is wrought to make me
 shun
 The truth; my pride, and thine till
 now?
To meet the gaze of stranger's eyes
Our law, our creed, our God denies;
Nor shall one wandering thought of
 mine 431
At such, our Prophet's will, repine:
No! happier made by that decree,
He left me all in leaving thee.
Deep were my anguish, thus compell'd
To wed with one I ne'er beheld: 436
This wherefore should I not reveal?
Why wilt thou urge me to conceal?
I know the Pacha's haughty mood
To thee hath never boded good; 440
And he so often storms at nought,
Allah! forbid that e'er he ought!
And why I know not, but within
My heart concealment weighs like sin.
If then such secrecy be crime, 445
 And such it feels while lurking here;
Oh, Selim! tell me yet in time,
 Nor leave me thus to thoughts of fear.

'Ah! yonder see the Tchocadar,
My father leaves the mimic war; 450
I tremble now to meet his eye—
Say, Selim, canst thou tell me why?'

XIV

'Zuleika—to thy tower's retreat
Betake thee—Giaffir I can greet;
And now with him I fain must prate
Of firmans, imposts, levies, state. 456
There's fearful news from Danube's
 banks,
Our Vizier nobly thins his ranks,
For which the Giaour may give him
 thanks!
Our Sultan hath a shorter way 460
Such costly triumph to repay.
But, mark me, when the twilight drum
 Hath warn'd the troops to food and
 sleep,
Unto thy cell will Selim come: 464
 Then softly from the Haram creep
 Where we may wander by the deep:
 Our garden battlements are steep;
Nor these will rash intruder climb
To list our words, or stint our time;
And if he doth, I want not steel 470
Which some have felt, and more may
 feel.
Then shalt thou learn of Selim more
Than thou hast heard or thought be-
 fore:
Trust me, Zuleika—fear not me! 474
Thou know'st I hold a Haram key.'
'Fear thee, my Selim! ne'er till now
Did word like this——'
 'Delay not thou;
I keep the key—and Haroun's guard
Have some, and hope of more reward.
To-night, Zuleika, thou shalt hear 480
My tale, my purpose, and my fear:
I am not, love! what I appear.'

CANTO THE SECOND

I

The winds are high on Helle's wave,
 As on that night of stormy water
When Love, who sent, forgot to save
The young, the beautiful, the brave,
 The lonely hope of Sestos' daughter.
Oh! when alone along the sky 6
Her turret-torch was blazing high,
Though rising gale, and breaking foam,
And shrieking sea-birds warn'd him
 home;
And clouds aloft and tides below, 10
With signs and sounds, forbade to go,
He could not see, he would not hear,
Or sound or sign foreboding fear;
His eye but saw that light of love,
The only star it hail'd above, 15
His ear but rang with Hero's song,
Ye waves, divide not lovers long!'—

That tale is old, but love anew
May nerve young hearts to prove as
 true. 19

II

The winds are high, and Helle's tide
 Rolls darkly heaving to the main;
And Night's descending shadows hide
 That field with blood bedew'd in vain,
The desert of old Priam's pride; 24
 The tombs, sole relics of his reign,
All—save immortal dreams that could
 beguile
The blind old man of Scio's rocky isle!

III

Oh! yet—for there my steps have been;
 These feet have press'd the sacred
 shore,
These limbs that buoyant wave hath
 borne— 30
Minstrel! with thee to muse, to mourn,
 To trace again those fields of yore,
Believing every hillock green
 Contains no fabled hero's ashes,
And that around the undoubted scene
 Thine own 'broad Hellespont' still
 dashes, 36
Be long my lot! and cold were he
Who there could gaze denying thee!

IV

The night hath closed on Helle's
 stream,
 Nor yet hath risen on Ida's hill 40
That moon, which shone on his high
 theme:
No warrior chides her peaceful beam,
 But conscious shepherds bless it still.
Their flocks are grazing on the mound
 Of him who felt the Dardan's arrow:
That mighty heap of gather'd ground
 Which Ammon's son ran proudly round
By nations raised, by monarchs crown'd,
 Is now a lone and nameless barrow!
Within—thy dwelling-place how nar-
 row! 50
Without—can only strangers breathe
The name of him that was beneath:
Dust long outlasts the storied stone;
But Thou—thy very dust is gone!

V

Late, late to-night will Dian cheer 55
The swain, and chase the boatman's
 fear;
Till then—no beacon on the cliff
May shape the course of struggling
 skiff;
The scatter'd lights that skirt the bay,
All, one by one, have died away; 60
The only lamp of this lone hour
Is glimmering in Zuleika's tower.

Yes! there is light in that lone chamber,
 And o'er her silken ottoman
Are thrown the fragrant beads of
 amber, 65
O'er which her fairy fingers ran;
Near these, with emerald rays beset,
(How could she thus that gem forget?)
Her mother's sainted amulet,
Whereon engraved the Koorsee text,
Could smooth this life, and win the
 next; 71
And by her comboloio lies
A Koran of illumined dyes;
And many a bright emblazon'd rhyme
By Persian scribes redeem'd from time;
And o'er those scrolls, not oft so
 mute, 76
Reclines her now neglected lute;
And round her lamp of fretted gold
Bloom flowers in urns of China's
 mould;
The richest work of Iran's loom, 80
And Sheeraz' tribute of perfume;
All that can eye or sense delight
 Are gather'd in that gorgeous room:
 But yet it hath an air of gloom.
She, of this Peri cell the sprite, 85
What doth she hence, and on so rude
 a night?

VI

Wrapt in the darkest sable vest,
 Which none save noblest Moslem
 wear,
To guard from winds of heaven the
 breast
 As heaven itself to Selim dear, 90
With cautious steps the thicket thread-
 ing,
 And starting oft, as through the glade
The gust its hollow moanings made,
Till on the smoother pathway tread-
 ing,
More free her timid bosom beat, 95
 The maid pursued her silent guide;
And though her terror urged retreat,
 How could she quit her Selim's side?
 How teach her tender lips to chide?

VII

They reach'd at length a grotto, hewn
 By nature, but enlarged by art, 101
Where oft her lute she wont to tune,
 And oft her Koran conn'd apart;
And oft in youthful reverie 104
She dream'd what Paradise might be:
Where woman's parted soul shall go
Her Prophet had disdain'd to show;
But Selim's mansion was secure,
Nor deem'd she, could he long endure
His bower in other worlds of bliss 110
Without her, most beloved in this!
Oh! who so dear with him could dwell?
What Houri soothe him half so well?

VIII

Since last she visited the spot
Some change seem'd wrought within
 the grot: 11
It might be only that the night
Disguised things seen by better light:
That brazen lamp but dimly threw
A ray of no celestial hue;
But in a nook within the cell 12
Her eye on stranger objects fell.
There arms were piled, not such a
 wield
The turban'd Delis in the field;
But brands of foreign blade and hilt,
And one was red—perchance with
 guilt! 12
Ah! how without can blood be spilt?
A cup too on the board was set
That did not seem to hold sherbet.
What may this mean? she turn'd to see
Her Selim—'Oh! can this be he?' 13

IX

His robe of pride was thrown aside,
 His brow no high-crown'd turban
 bore,
But in its stead a shawl of red,
 Wreathed lightly round, his temple
 wore: 13
That dagger, on whose hilt the gem
Were worthy of a diadem,
No longer glitter'd at his waist,
Where pistols unadorn'd were braced
And from his belt a sabre swung, 13
And from his shoulder loosely hung
The cloak of white, the thin capote
That decks the wandering Candiote;
Beneath—his golden plated vest
Clung like a cuirass to his breast;
The greaves below his knee that wound
With silvery scales were sheathed and
 bound. 14
But were it not that high command
Spake in his eye, and tone, and hand,
All that a careless eye could see
In him was some young Galiongée.

X

'I said I was not what I seem'd; 15
 And now thou see'st my words were
 true:
I have a tale thou hast not dream'd,
 If sooth—its truth must others rue.
My story now 'twere vain to hide, 15
I must not see thee Osman's bride:
But had not thine own lips declared
How much of that young heart I shared
I could not, must not, yet have shown
The darker secret of my own. 16
In this I speak not now of love;
That, let time, truth, and peril prove:
But first—Oh! never wed another—
Zuleika! I am not thy brother!'

XI

'Oh! not my brother!—yet unsay—
 God! am I left alone on earth 166
To mourn—I dare not curse—the day
 That saw my solitary birth?
Oh! thou wilt love me now no more!
 My sinking heart foreboded ill; 170
But know *me* all I was before,
 Thy sister—friend—Zuleika still.
Thou led'st me here perchance to kill;
 If thou hast cause for vengeance, see!
My breast is offer'd—take thy fill! 175
 Far better with the dead to be
Than live thus nothing now to thee!
Perhaps far worse, for now I know
Why Giaffir always seem'd thy foe;
And I, alas! am Giaffir's child, 180
For whom thou wert contemn'd, reviled.
If not thy sister—wouldst thou save
My life, oh! bid me be thy slave!'

XII

'My slave, Zuleika!—nay, I'm thine:
 But, gentle love, this transport calm.
Thy lot shall yet be link'd with mine;
 I swear it by our Prophet's shrine,
 And be that thought thy sorrow's
 balm.
So may the Koran verse display'd
 Upon its steel direct my blade, 190
In danger's hour to guard us both,
 As I preserve that awful oath!
The name in which thy heart hath
 prided
 Must change; but, my Zuleika, know,
That tie is widen'd, not divided, 195
 Although thy Sire 's my deadliest foe.
My father was to Giaffir all
 That Selim late was deem'd to thee:
That brother wrought a brother's fall,
 But spared, at least, my infancy;
And lull'd me with a vain deceit 201
 That yet a like return may meet.
He rear'd me, not with tender help,
 But like the nephew of a Cain;
He watch'd me like a lion's whelp, 205
 That gnaws and yet may break his
 chain.
My father's blood in every vein
 Is boiling; but for thy dear sake
No present vengeance will I take;
 Though here I must no more remain.
But first, beloved Zuleika! hear 211
 How Giaffir wrought this deed of fear.

XIII

'How first their strife to rancour grew,
 If love or envy made them foes,
It matters little if I knew; 215
 In fiery spirits, slights, though few
 And thoughtless, will disturb repose.
In war Abdallah's arm was strong,
Remember'd yet in Bosniac song,

And Paswan's rebel hordes attest 220
How little they bore such guest:
His death is all I need relate,
The stern effect of Giaffir's hate;
And how my birth disclosed to me,
Whate'er beside it makes, hath made
 me free. 225

XIV

'When Paswan, after years of strife,
At last for power, but first for life,
In Widdin's walls too proudly sate,
Our Pachas rallied round the state;
Nor last nor least in high command,
Each brother led a separate band; 231
They gave their horse-tails to the
 wind,
 And mustering in Sophia's plain
Their tents were pitch'd, their post
 assign'd;
 To one, alas! assign'd in vain! 235
What need of words! the deadly bowl,
 By Giaffir's order drugged and given,
With venom subtle as his soul,
 Dismiss'd Abdallah's hence to heaven.
Reclined and feverish in the bath, 240
He, when the hunter's sport was up,
But little deem'd a brother's wrath
 To quench his thirst had such a
 cup:
The bowl a bribed attendant bore;
He drank one draught, nor needed
 more! 245
If thou my tale, Zuleika, doubt,
Call Haroun—he can tell it out.

XV

'The deed once done, and Paswan's
 feud
In part suppress'd, though ne'er sub-
 dued, 249
 Abdallah's Pachalick was gain'd:—
Thou know'st not what in our Divan
Can wealth procure for worse than
 man—
 Abdallah's honours were obtain'd
By him a brother's murder stain'd;
'Tis true, the purchase nearly drain'd
His ill-got treasure, soon replaced. 256
Wouldst question whence? Survey the
 waste,
And ask the squalid peasant how
His gains repay his broiling brow!—
Why me the stern usurper spared, 260
Why thus with me his palace shared,
I know not. Shame, regret, remorse,
And little fear from infant's force;
Besides, adoption as a son
By him whom Heaven accorded none,
Or some unknown cabal, caprice, 266
Preserved me thus:—but not in peace:
He cannot curb his haughty mood,
Nor I forgive a father's blood.

XVI

'Within thy father's house are foes;
 Not all who break his bread are
 true: 271
To these should I my birth disclose,
 His days, his very hours were few:
They only want a heart to lead,
A hand to point them to the deed. 275
But Haroun only knows, or knew,
 This tale, whose close is almost nigh:
He in Abdallah's palace grew,
 And held that post in his Serai
 Which holds he here—he saw him
 die: 280
But what could single slavery do?
Avenge his lord? alas! too late;
Or save his son from such a fate?
He chose the last, and when elate
 With foes subdued, or friends be-
 tray'd, 285
Proud Giaffir in high triumph sate,
He led me helpless to his gate,
 And not in vain it seems essay'd
To save the life for which he pray'd.
The knowledge of my birth secured
 From all and each, but most from
 me; 291
Thus Giaffir's safety was insured.
 Removed he too from Roumelie
To this our Asiatic side,
Far from our seats by Danube's tide,
 With none but Haroun, who retains
Such knowledge—and that Nubian feels
 A tyrant's secrets are but chains,
From which the captive gladly steals,
And this and more to me reveals: 300
Such still to guilt just Allah sends—
Slaves, tools, accomplices—no friends!

XVII

'All this, Zuleika, harshly sounds;
 But harsher still my tale must be:
Howe'er my tongue thy softness
 wounds, 305
 Yet I must prove all truth to thee.
I saw thee start this garb to see,
Yet is it one I oft have worn,
 And long must wear: this Galiongée,
To whom thy plighted vow is sworn, 311
 Is leader of those pirate hordes,
 Whose laws and lives are on their
 swords;
To hear whose desolating tale
Would make thy waning cheek more
 pale:
Those arms thou see'st my band have
 brought, 315
The hands that wield are not remote;
This cup too for the rugged knaves
 Is fill'd—once quaff'd, they ne'er
 repine:
Our Prophet might forgive the slaves:
 They're only infidels in wine. 320

XVIII

'What could I be? Proscribed at home,
And taunted to a wish to roam;
And listless left—for Giaffir's fear
Denied the courser and the spear—
Though oft—Oh, Mahomet! how oft!—
 In full Divan the despot scoff'd, 326
As if my weak unwilling hand
Refused the bridle or the brand:
He ever went to war alone, 329
And pent me here untried—unknown;
To Haroun's care with women left,
By hope unblest, of fame bereft,
While thou—whose softness long en-
 dear'd,
Though it unmann'd me, still had
 cheer'd—
To Brusa's walls for safety sent, 335
Awaited'st there the field's event.
Haroun, who saw my spirit pining
 Beneath inaction's sluggish yoke,
His captive, though with dread resign-
 ing,
 My thraldom for a season broke,
On promise to return before 341
The day when Giaffir's charge was o'er.
'Tis vain—my tongue cannot impart
My almost drunkenness of heart,
When first this liberated eye 345
Survey'd Earth, Ocean, Sun, and Sky,
As if my spirit pierced them through,
And all their inmost wonders knew!
One word alone can paint to thee
That more than feeling—I was Free!
E'en for thy presence ceased to pine;
The World—nay, Heaven itself was
 mine!

XIX

'The shallop of a trusty Moor
Convey'd me from this idle shore;
I long'd to see the isles that gem 355
Old Ocean's purple diadem:
I sought by turns, and saw them all;
 But when and where I join'd the crew,
With whom I'm pledged to rise or fall,
 When all that we design to do 360
Is done, 'twill then be time more meet
To tell thee, when the tale's complete.

XX

''Tis true, they are a lawless brood,
But rough in form, nor mild in mood;
And every creed, and every race, 365
With them hath found—may find a
 place;
But open speech, and ready hand,
Obedience to their chief's command:
A soul for every enterprise,
That never sees with terror's eyes; 370
Friendship for each, and faith to all,
And vengeance vow'd for those who
 fall,

Have made them fitting instruments
For more than ev'n my own intents.
And some—and I have studied all 375
 Distinguish'd from the vulgar rank,
But chiefly to my council call
 The wisdom of the cautious Frank—
And some to higher thoughts aspire,
 The last of Lambro's patriots there
 Anticipated freedom share; 381
And oft around the cavern fire
On visionary schemes debate,
To snatch the Rayahs from their fate.
So let them ease their hearts with prate
Of equal rights, which man ne'er knew;
I have a love for freedom too. 387
y! let me like the ocean-Patriarch roam,
r only know on land the Tartar's home!
ly tent on shore, my galley on the sea,
re more than cities and Serais to me:
orne by my steed, or wafted by my sail,
cross the desert, or before the gale,
ound where thou wilt, my barb! or glide,
 my prow!
ut be the star that guides the wanderer,
 Thou! 395
hou, my Zuleika, share and bless my
 bark;
he Dove of peace and promise to mine
 ark!
r, since that hope denied in worlds of
 strife,
e thou the rainbow to the storms of
 life!
he evening beam that smiles the clouds
 away, 400
nd tints to-morrow with prophetic ray!
lest—as the Muezzin's strain from
 Mecca's wall
o pilgrims pure and prostrate at his call;
oft—as the melody of youthful days,
hat steals the trembling tear of speech-
 less praise; 405
ear—as his native song to Exile's ears,
hall sound each tone thy long-loved
 voice endears.
or thee in those bright isles is built a
 bower
looming as Aden in its earliest hour.
thousand swords, with Selim's heart and
 hand, 410
ait—wave—defend—destroy—at thy
 command!
irt by my band, Zuleika at my side,
he spoil of nations shall bedeck my
 bride.
he Haram's languid years of listless ease
re well resign'd for cares—for joys like
 these: 415
ot blind to fate, I see, where'er I rove,
nnumber'd perils—but one only love!
et well my toils shall that fond breast
 repay,
hough fortune frown, or falser friends
 betray.

How dear the dream in darkest hours of
 ill, 420
Should all be changed, to find thee faithful
 still!
Be but thy soul, like Selim's, firmly shown;
To thee be Selim's tender as thine own;
To soothe each sorrow, share in each
 delight,
Blend every thought, do all—but disunite!
Once free, 'tis mine our horde again to
 guide; 426
Friends to each other, foes to aught be-
 side:
Yet there we follow but the bent assign'd
By fatal Nature to man's warring kind:
Mark! where his carnage and his con-
 quests cease! 430
He makes a solitude, and calls it—peace!
I, like the rest, must use my skill or
 strength,
But ask no land beyond my sabre's
 length:
Power sways but by division—her re-
 source 434
The blest alternative of fraud or force!
Ours be the last; in time deceit may come
When cities cage us in a social home:
There ev'n thy soul might err—how oft
 the heart
Corruption shakes which peril could not
 part!
And woman, more than man, when death
 or woe, 440
Or even Disgrace, would lay her lover low,
Sunk in the lap of Luxury will shame—
Away suspicion!—not Zuleika's name!
But life is hazard at the best; and here
No more remains to win, and much to
 fear: 445
Yes, fear! the doubt, the dread of losing
 thee,
By Osman's power, and Giaffir's stern
 decree.
That dread shall vanish with the favouring
 gale,
Which Love to-night hath promised to my
 sail:
No danger daunts the pair his smile hath
 blest, 450
Their steps still roving, but their hearts at
 rest.
With thee all toils are sweet, each clime
 hath charms;
Earth—sea alike—our world within our
 arms!
Ay—let the loud winds whistle o'er the
 deck,
So that those arms cling closer round my
 neck: 455
The deepest murmur of this lip shall be
No sigh for safety, but a prayer for thee!
The war of elements no fears impart
To Love, whose deadliest bane is human
 Art:

There lie the only rocks our course can
 check; 460
Here moments menace—*there* are years
 of wreck!
But hence ye thoughts that rise in Horror's
 shape!
This hour bestows, or ever bars escape.
Few words remain of mine my tale to
 close;
Of thine but *one* to waft us from our foes;
Yea—foes—to me will Giaffir's hate de-
 cline? 466
And is not Osman, who would part us,
 thine?

XXI

'His head and faith from doubt and
 death
Return'd in time my guard to save;
Few heard, none told, that o'er the
 wave 470
From isle to isle I roved the while;
And since, though parted from my band
Too seldom now I leave the land,
No deed they've done, nor deed shall
 do,
Ere I have heard and doom'd it too:
I form the plan, decree the spoil, 476
'Tis fit I oftener share the toil.
But now too long I've held thine ear;
Time presses, floats my bark, and here
We leave behind but hate and fear.
To-morrow Osman with his train 481
Arrives—to-night must break thy chain:
And wouldst thou save that haughty
 Bey,—
 Perchance *his* life who gave thee
 thine,—
With me this hour away—away! 485
 But yet, though thou art plighted
 mine,
Wouldst thou recall thy willing vow,
Appall'd by truths imparted now,
Here rest I—not to see thee wed:
But be that peril on *my* head!' 490

XXII

Zuleika, mute and motionless,
Stood like that statue of distress,
When, her last hope for ever gone,
The mother harden'd into stone:
All in the maid that eye could see 495
Was but a younger Niobé.
But ere her lip, or even her eye,
Essay'd to speak, or look reply,
Beneath the garden's wicket porch 499
Far flashed on high a blazing torch!
Another—and another—and another—
'Oh! fly—no more—yet now my more
 than brother!'
Far, wide, through every thicket spread
The fearful lights are gleaming red;
Nor these alone—for each right hand
Is ready with a sheathless brand. 506

They part, pursue, return, and wheel
With searching flambeau, shining stee[l]
And last of all, his sabre waving,
Stern Giaffir in his fury raving: 51[0]
And now almost they touch the cave—
Oh! must that grot be Selim's grave?

XXIII

Dauntless he stood—' 'Tis come—soo[n]
 past—
One kiss, Zuleika—'tis my last: 51[4]
 But yet my band not far from shor[e]
May hear this signal, see the flash;
Yet now too few—the attempt wer[e]
 rash:
No matter—yet one effort more.'
Forth to the cavern mouth he stept;
 His pistol's echo rang on high, 52[0]
Zuleika started not, nor wept,
 Despair benumb'd her breast an[d]
 eye!—
'They hear me not; or if they ply
Their oars, 'tis but to see me die;
That sound hath drawn my foes mo[re]
 nigh.
Then forth my father's scimitar, 52[5]
Thou ne'er hast seen less equal war!
Farewell, Zuleika!—sweet! retire:
 Yet stay within—here linger safe,
 At thee his rage will only chafe. 52[9]
Stir not—lest even to thee perchance
Some erring blade or ball should glanc[e]
Fear'st thou for him?—may I expire
If in this strife I seek thy sire! 53[3]
No—though by him that poison pour'[d]
No—though again he call me coward[!]
But tamely shall I meet their steel?
No—as each crest save *his* may feel!'

XXIV

One bound he made, and gain'd the
 sand:
 Already at his feet hath sunk 54[0]
The foremost of the prying band,
 A gasping head, a quivering trunk:
Another falls—but round him close
A swarming circle of his foes; 54[4]
From right to left his path he cleft,
 And almost met the meeting wave:
His boat appears—not five oar[s']
 length—
His comrades strain with desperat[e]
 strength—
 Oh! are they yet in time to save?
His feet the foremost breakers lave[;]
His band are plunging in the bay, 55[0]
Their sabres glitter through the spray[;]
Wet—wild—unwearied to the strand
They struggle—now they touch th[e]
 land!
They come—'tis but to add to slaug[h]
 ter— 55[5]
His heart's best blood is on the wate[r.]

XXV

scaped from shot, unharm'd by steel,
r scarcely grazed its force to feel,
ad Selim won, betray'd, beset, 559
o where the strand and billows met;
here as his last step left the land—
nd the last death-blow dealt his
 hand—
h! wherefore did he turn to look
 For her his eye but sought in vain?
hat pause, that fatal gaze he took,
 Hath doom'd his death, or fix'd his
 chain. 566
ad proof, in peril and in pain,
ow late will Lover's hope remain!
is back was to the dashing spray;
ehind, but close, his comrades lay, 570
hen, at the instant, hiss'd the ball—
o may the foes of Giaffir fall!'
hose voice is heard? whose carbine
 rang?
hose bullet through the night-air
 sang,
oo nearly, deadly aim'd to err? 575
is thine—Abdallah's Murderer!
he father slowly rued thy hate,
he son hath found a quicker fate:
ast from his breast the blood is
 bubbling,
he whiteness of the sea-foam troub-
 ling— 580
 aught his lips essay'd to groan,
he rushing billows choked the tone!

XXVI

orn slowly rolls the clouds away;
 Few trophies of the fight are there:
he shouts that shook the midnight-bay
re silent; but some signs of fray 586
 That strand of strife may bear,
nd fragments of each shiver'd brand;
teps stamp'd; and dash'd into the sand
he print of many a struggling hand
 May there be mark'd; nor far remote
 A broken torch, an oarless boat;
nd tangled on the weeds that heap
he beach where shelving to the deep
 There lies a white capote! 595
is rent in twain—one dark-red stain
he wave yet ripples o'er in vain;
 But where is he who wore?
e! who would o'er his relics weep,
o, seek them where the surges sweep
heir burthen round Sigæum's steep
 And cast on Lemnos' shore:
he sea-birds shriek above the prey,
'er which their hungry beaks delay,
s shaken on his restless pillow, 605
is head heaves with the heaving
 billow;
hat hand, whose motion is not life,
 et feebly seems to menace strife,
lung by the tossing tide on high,

Then levell'd with the wave— 610
What recks it, though that corse shall lie
 Within a living grave?
The bird that tears that prostrate form
Hath only robb'd the meaner worm;
The only heart, the only eye 615
Had bled or wept to see him die,
Had seen those scatter'd limbs composed,
 And mourn'd above his turban-stone,
That heart hath burst—that eye was
 closed—
 Yea—closed before his own! 620

XXVII

By Helle's stream there is a voice of wail!
And woman's eye is wet—man's cheek is
 pale:
Zuleika! last of Giaffir's race,
 Thy destined lord is come too late:
He sees not—ne'er shall see thy face!
 Can he not hear 626
The loud Wul-wulleh warn his distant ear?
 Thy handmaids weeping at the gate,
 The Koran-chanters of the hymn of fate,
 The silent slaves with folded arms that
 wait, 630
Sighs in the hall, and shrieks upon the gale,
 Tell him thy tale!
Thou didst not view thy Selim fall!
 That fearful moment when he left the
 cave
 Thy heart grew chill: 635
He was thy hope—thy joy—thy love—
 thine all,
And that last thought on him thou couldst
 not save
 Sufficed to kill;
Burst forth in one wild cry—and all was
 still,
 Peace to thy broken heart, and virgin
 grave! 640
Ah! happy! but of life to lose the worst!
That grief—though deep—though fatal—
 was thy first!
Thrice happy ne'er to feel nor fear the force
Of absence, shame, pride, hate, revenge,
 remorse!
And, oh! that pang where more than mad-
 ness lies! 645
The worm that will not sleep—and never
 dies;
Thought of the gloomy day and ghastly
 night,
That dreads the darkness, and yet loathes
 the light,
That winds around, and tears the quiver-
 ing heart!
Ah! wherefore not consume it—and de-
 part! 650
Woe to thee, rash and unrelenting chief!
 Vainly thou heap'st the dust upon thy
 head,
 Vainly the sackcloth o'er thy limbs dost
 spread:

By that same hand Abdallah—Selim
 bled,
Now let it tear thy beard in idle grief:
Thy pride of heart, thy bride for Osman's
 bed, 656
She, whom thy sultan had but seen to
 wed,
 Thy Daughter's dead!
Hope of thine age, thy twilight's lonely
 beam,
The Star hath set that shone on Helle's
 stream. 660
What quench'd its ray?—the blood that
 thou hast shed!
Hark! to the hurried question of Despair:
'Where is my child?'—an Echo answers—
 'Where?'

XXVIII

Within the place of thousand tombs
 That shine beneath, while dark above
The sad but living cypress glooms 666
 And withers not, though branch and
 leaf
Are stamp'd with an eternal grief,
 Like early unrequited Love,
One spot exists, which ever blooms,
 Ev'n in that deadly grove— 671
A single rose is shedding there
 Its lonely lustre, meek and pale:
It looks as planted by Despair—
 So white—so faint—the slightest gale
Might whirl the leaves on high; 676
 And yet, though storms and blight
 assail,
And hands more rude than wintry sky
 May wring it from the stem—in
 vain—
To-morrow sees it bloom again: 680
The stalk some spirit gently rears,
And waters with celestial tears;
 For well may maids of Helle deem
That this can be no earthly flower,
 Which mocks the tempest's withering
 hour, 685
And buds unshelter'd by a bower;
Nor droops though Spring refuse her
 shower,
Nor woos the summer beam:

To it the livelong night there sings
 A bird unseen—but not remote:
Invisible his airy wings, 6
But soft as harp that Houri strings
 His long entrancing note!
It were the Bulbul; but his throat,
 Though mournful, pours not such
 strain: 6
For they who listen cannot leave
The spot, but linger there and grieve
 As if they loved in vain!
And yet so sweet the tears they shed
'Tis sorrow so unmix'd with dread,
 They scarce can bear the morn to brea
 That melancholy spell,
And longer yet would weep and wak
 He sings so wild and well!
But when the day-blush bursts fro
 high 7
 Expires that magic melody.
And some have been who could believ
(So fondly youthful dreams deceive,
 Yet harsh be they that blame,)
That note so piercing and profound
Will shape and syllable its sound 7
 Into Zuleika's name.
'Tis from her cypress summit heard,
 That melts in air the liquid word:
'Tis from her lowly virgin earth 7
That white rose takes its tender birth
There late was laid a marble stone;
Eve saw it placed—the Morrow gon
It was no mortal arm that bore
 That deep-fix'd pillar to the shore;
For there, as Helle's legends tell, 7
Next morn 'twas found where Selim fel
Lash'd by the tumbling tide, who
 wave
Denied his bones a holier grave:
And there by night, reclin'd, 'tis said,
Is seen a ghastly turban'd head: 7
 And hence extended by the billow,
 'Tis named the 'Pirate-phantom
 pillow!'
 Where first it lay that mourning flow
 Hath flourish'd; flourisheth this hou
Alone and dewy, coldly pure and pal
As weeping Beauty's cheek at Sorrow
 tale! 7

THE CORSAIR

A TALE

——'I suoi pensieri in lui dormir non ponno.'
TASSO, *Gerusalemme Liberata*, canto x.

TO

THOMAS MOORE, ESQ.

MY DEAR MOORE,

I DEDICATE to you the last production with which I shall trespass on public patience, and your indulgence, for some years; and I own that I feel anxious to avail myself of this latest and only opportunity of adorning my pages with a name, consecrated by unshaken public principle, and the most undoubted and various talents. While Ireland ranks you among the firmest of her patriots; while you stand alone the first of her bards in her estimation, and Britain repeats and ratifies the decree, permit me, whose only regret, since our first acquaintance, has been the years he had lost before it commenced, to add the humble but sincere suffrage of friendship to the voice of more than one nation. It will at least prove to you, that I have neither forgotten the gratification derived from your society, nor abandoned the prospect of its renewal, whenever your leisure or inclination allows you to atone to your friends for too long an absence. It is said among those friends, I trust truly, that you are engaged in the composition of a poem whose scene will be laid in the East; none can do those scenes so much justice. The wrongs of your own country, the magnificent and fiery spirit of her sons, the beauty and feeling of her daughters, may there be found; and Collins, when he denominated his Oriental his Irish Eclogues, was not aware how true, at least, was a part of his parallel. Your imagination will create a warmer sun, and less clouded sky; but wildness, tenderness, and originality, are part of your national claim of oriental descent, to which you have already thus far proved your title more clearly than the most zealous of your country's antiquarians.

May I add a few words on a subject on which all men are supposed to be fluent, and none agreeable? —Self. I have written much, and published more than enough to demand a longer silence than I now meditate; but, for some years to come, it is my intention to tempt no further the award of 'Gods, men, nor columns.' In the present composition I have attempted not the most difficult, but, perhaps the best adapted measure to our language, the good old and now neglected heroic couplet. The stanza of Spenser is perhaps too slow and dignified for narrative; though, I confess, it is the measure most after my own heart: Scott alone, of the present generation, has hitherto completely triumphed over the fatal facility of the octo-syllabic verse; and this is not the least victory of his fertile and mighty genius: in blank verse, Milton, Thomson, and our dramatists, are the beacons that shine along the deep, but warn us from the rough and barren rock on which they are kindled. The heroic couplet is not the most popular measure certainly; but as I did not deviate into the other from a wish to flatter what is called public opinion, I shall quit it without further apology, and take my chance once more with that versification, in which I have hitherto published nothing but compositions whose former circulation is part of my present, and will be of my future regret.

With regard to my story, and stories in general, I should have been glad to have rendered my personages more perfect and amiable, if possible, inasmuch as I have been sometimes criticised, and considered no less responsible for their deeds and qualities than if all had been personal. Be it so— If I have deviated into the gloomy vanity of 'drawing from self,' the pictures are probably like, since they are unfavourable; and if not, those who know me are undeceived, and those who do not, I have little interest in undeceiving. I have no particular desire that any but my acquaintance should think me author better than the beings of his imagining; but I cannot help a little surprise, and perhaps amusement, at some odd critical exceptions in the present instance, when I see several bards (far more deserving, I allow) in very reputable plight, and quite exempted from all participation in the faults of those heroes, who, nevertheless, might be found with little more morality than 'The Giaour,' and perhaps—but no—I must admit Childe Harold to be a very repulsive personage; and as to his identity, those who like it must give him whatever 'alias' they please.

If, however, it were worth while to remove the impression, it might be of some service to me, that the man who is alike the delight of his readers and his friends, the poet of all circles, and the idol of his own, permits me here and elsewhere to subscribe myself,

Most truly,
And affectionately,
His obedient servant,
BYRON.

January 2, 1814.

THE CORSAIR

CANTO THE FIRST

'————nessun maggior dolore,
Che ricordarsi del tempo felice
Nelle miseria,————————'.—DANTE.

I

'O'ER the glad waters of the dark blue
 sea,
Our thoughts as boundless, and our souls
 as free,
Far as the breeze can bear, the billows
 foam,
Survey our empire, and behold our home!
These are our realms, no limits to their
 sway— 5
Our flag the sceptre all who meet obey.
Ours the wild life in tumult still to range
From toil to rest, and joy in every change.
Oh, who can tell? not thou, luxurious
 slave!
Whose soul would sicken o'er the heaving
 wave; 10
Not thou, vain lord of wantonness and
 ease!
Whom slumber soothes not—pleasure
 cannot please—
Oh, who can tell, save he whose heart hath
 tried,
And danced in triumph o'er the waters
 wide,
The exulting sense—the pulse's madden-
 ing play, 15
That thrills the wanderer of that trackless
 way?
That for itself can woo the approaching
 fight,
And turn what some deem danger to de-
 light;
That seeks what cravens shun with more
 than zeal, 19
And where the feebler faint can only feel—
Feel—to the rising bosom's inmost core,
Its hope awaken and its spirit soar?
No dread of death if with us die our foes—
Save that it seems even duller than re-
 pose:
Come when it will—we snatch the life of
 life— 25
When lost—what recks it but disease or
 strife?
Let him who crawls enamour'd of decay,
Cling to his couch, and sicken years away:
Heave his thick breath, and shake his
 palsied head;
Ours—the fresh turf, and not the feverish
 bed. 30
While gasp by gasp he falters forth his
 soul,
Ours with one pang—one bound—escapes
 control.

His corse may boast its urn and narrow
 cave,
And they who loath'd his life may gild his
 grave:
Ours are the tears, though few, sincerely
 shed, 35
When Ocean shrouds and sepulchres our
 dead.
For us, even banquets fond regret supply
In the red cup that crowns our memory;
And the brief epitaph in danger's day,
When those who win at length divide the
 prey, 40
And cry, Remembrance saddening o'er
 each brow,
How had the brave who fell exulted now!'

II

Such were the notes that from the Pirate's
 isle
Around the kindling watch-fire rang the
 while:
Such were the sounds that thrill'd the
 rocks along, 45
And unto ears as rugged seem'd a song
In scatter'd groups upon the golden sand,
They game—carouse—converse—or whet
 the brand:
Select the arms—to each his blade assign,
And careless eye the blood that dims its
 shine, 50
Repair the boat, replace the helm or oar
While others straggling muse along the
 shore;
For the wild bird the busy springes set,
Or spread beneath the sun the dripping
 net:
Gaze where some distant sail a speck
 supplies, 55
With all the thirsting eye of Enterprise:
Tell o'er the tales of many a night of toil
And marvel where they next shall seize a
 spoil:
No matter where—their chief's allotment
 this;
Theirs, to believe no prey nor plan amiss.
But who that CHIEF? his name on every
 shore 60
Is famed and fear'd—they ask and know
 no more.
With these he mingles not but to com-
 mand;
Few are his words, but keen his eye and
 hand.
Ne'er seasons he with mirth their jovial
 mess, 65
But they forgive his silence for success.
Ne'er for his lip the purpling cup they
 fill,
That goblet passes him untasted still—

278

nd for his fare—the rudest of his crew
Vould that, in turn, have pass'd untasted
 too; 70
:arth's coarsest bread, the garden's home-
 liest roots,
.nd scarce the summer luxury of fruits,
Iis short repast in humbleness supply
Vith all a hermit's board would scarce
 deny.
Sut while he shuns the grosser joys of
 sense, 75
Iis mind seems nourish'd by that absti-
 nence.
Steer to that shore!'—they sail. 'Do
 this!'—'tis done:
Now form and follow me!'—the spoil
 is won.
'hus prompt his accents and his actions
 still,
.nd all obey and few inquire his will; 80
'o such, brief answer and contemptuous
 eye
:onvey reproof, nor further deign reply.

III

A sail!—a sail!'—a promised prize to
 Hope!
Ier nation—flag—how speaks the tele-
 scope?
No prize, alas! but yet a welcome sail: 85
'he blood-red signal glitters in the gale.
'es—she is ours—a home - returning
 bark—
Slow fair, thou breeze!—she anchors ere
 the dark.
.lready doubled is the cape—our bay
Receives that prow which proudly spurns
 the spray. 90
Iow gloriously her gallant course she goes!
Ier white wings flying—never from her
 foes—
›he walks the waters like a thing of life,
.nd seems to dare the elements to strife.
Vho would not brave the battle-fire, the
 wreck, 95
'o move the monarch of her peopled
 deck?

IV

Ioarse o'er her side the rustling cable
 rings;
'he sails are furl'd; and anchoring round
 she swings;
.nd gathering loiterers on the land dis-
 cern
Ier boat descending from the latticed
 stern. 100
'is mann'd—the oars keep concert to the
 strand,
'ill grates her keel upon the shallow sand.
Iail to the welcome shout!—the friendly
 speech!
Vhen hand grasps hand uniting on the
 beach;

The smile, the question, and the quick
 reply, 105
And the heart's promise of festivity!

V

The tidings spread, and gathering grows
 the crowd;
The hum of voices, and the laughter loud,
And woman's gentler anxious tone is
 heard—
Friends', husbands', lovers' names in each
 dear word: 110
'Oh! are they safe? we ask not of suc-
 cess—
But shall we see them? will their accents
 bless?
From where the battle roars, the billows
 chafe,
They doubtless boldly did—but who are
 safe?
Here let them haste to gladden and sur-
 prise, 115
And kiss the doubt from these delighted
 eyes!'

VI

'Where is our chief? for him we bear re-
 port—
And doubt that joy—which hails our
 coming—short;
Yet thus sincere, 'tis cheering, though so
 brief;
But, Juan! instant guide us to our chief:
Our greeting paid, we'll feast on our re-
 turn, 121
And all shall hear what each may wish to
 learn.'
Ascending slowly by the rock-hewn way,
To where his watch-tower beetles o'er the
 bay,
By bushy brake, and wild flowers blossom-
 ing, 125
And freshness breathing from each silver
 spring,
Whose scatter'd streams from granite
 basins burst,
Leap into life, and sparkling woo your
 thirst;
From crag to cliff they mount—Near
 yonder cave,
What lonely straggler looks along the
 wave? 130
In pensive posture leaning on the brand,
Not oft a resting-staff to that red hand?
''Tis he—'tis Conrad—here, as wont,
 alone;
On—Juan!—on—and make our purpose
 known.
The bark he views—and tell him we would
 greet 135
His ear with tidings he must quickly meet:
We dare not yet approach—thou know'st
 his mood
When strange or uninvited steps intrude.'

279 K

VII

Him Juan sought, and told of their in-
tent;—
He spake not, but a sign express'd assent.
These Juan calls—they come—to their
salute 141
He bends him slightly, but his lips are
mute.
'These letters, Chief, are from the Greek
—the spy,
Who still proclaims our spoil or peril
nigh:
Whate'er his tidings, we can well report,
Much that'—'Peace, peace!'—he cuts
their prating short. 146
Wondering they turn, abash'd, while each
to each
Conjecture whispers in his muttering
speech:
They watch his glance with many a steal-
ing look,
To gather how that eye the tidings took;
But, this as if he guess'd, with head aside,
Perchance from some emotion, doubt, or
pride, 152
He read the scroll—'My tablets, Juan,
hark—
Where is Gonsalvo?'
 'In the anchor'd bark.'
'There let him stay—to him this order
bear— 155
Back to your duty—for my course pre-
pare:
Myself this enterprise to-night will share.'

'To-night, Lord Conrad!'
 'Ay! at set of sun:
The breeze will freshen when the day is
done.
My corslet, cloak—one hour and we are
gone. 160
Sling on thy bugle—see that free from rust
My carbine-lock springs worthy of my
trust;
Be the edge sharpen'd of my boarding-
brand,
And give its guard more room to fit my
hand.
This let the armourer with speed dispose;
Last time, it more fatigued my arm than
foes: 166
Mark that the signal-gun be duly fired,
To tell us when the hour of stay's expired.'

VIII

They make obeisance, and retire in haste,
Too soon to seek again the watery waste:
Yet they repine not—so that Conrad
guides; 171
And who dare question aught that he de-
cides?
That man of loneliness and mystery
Scarce seen to smile, and seldom heard
to sigh;

Whose name appals the fiercest of his
crew, 17
And tints each swarthy cheek with sal
lower hue;
Still sways their souls with that command
ing art
That dazzles, leads, yet chills the vulga
heart.
What is that spell, that thus his lawles
train
Confess and envy, yet oppose in vain?
What should it be, that thus their faith
can bind? 18
The power of Thought—the magic of th
Mind!
Link'd with success, assumed and kep
with skill,
That moulds another's weakness to it
will;
Wields with their hands, but, still to thes
unknown, 18
Makes even their mightiest deeds appea
his own.
Such hath it been—shall be—beneath th
sun
The many still must labour for the one!
'Tis Nature's doom—but let the wretch
who toils
Accuse not, hate not *him* who wears th
spoils. 19
Oh! if he knew the weight of splendi
chains,
How light the balance of his humble
pains!

IX

Unlike the heroes of each ancient race,
Demons in act, but Gods at least in face
In Conrad's form seems little to admire
Though his dark eyebrow shades a glanc
of fire; 19
Robust but not Herculean—to the sigh
No giant frame sets forth his commo
height;
Yet, in the whole, who paused to loo
again,
Saw more than marks the crowd of vulga
men; 20
They gaze and marvel how—and still con
fess
That thus it is, but why they cannot guess
Sun-burnt his cheek, his forehead high
and pale
The sable curls in wild profusion veil;
And oft perforce his rising lip reveals 20
The haughtier thought it curbs, but scarce
conceals.
Though smooth his voice, and calm his
general mien,
Still seems there something he would no
have seen:
His features' deepening lines and varying
hue
At times attracted, yet perplex'd the view,

s if within that murkiness of mind 211
ork'd feelings fearful, and yet unde-
 fined;
uch might it be—that none could truly
 tell—
oo close inquiry his stern glance would
 quell.
here breathe but few whose aspect might
 defy 215
he full encounter of his searching eye;
'e had the skill, when Cunning's gaze
 would seek
o probe his heart and watch his chang-
 ing cheek,
t once the observer's purpose to espy,
nd on himself roll back his scrutiny,
est he to Conrad rather should betray
ome secret thought, than drag that chief's
 to day.
here was a laughing Devil in his sneer,
hat raised emotions both of rage and fear;
nd where his frown of hatred darkly
 fell, 225
ope withering fled, and Mercy sigh'd
 farewell!

X

ight are the outward signs of evil
 thought,
'ithin—within—'twas there the spirit
 wrought!
ove shows all changes—Hate, Ambition,
 Guile,
etray no further than the bitter smile;
he lip's least curl, the lightest paleness
 thrown 231
long the govern'd aspect, speak alone
f deeper passions; and to judge their
 mien,
'e, who would see, must be himself un-
 seen.
hen—with the hurried tread, the up-
 ward eye, 235
he clench'd hand, the pause of agony,
hat listens, starting, lest the step too near
pproach intrusive on that mood of fear;
hen—with each feature working from
 the heart,
'ith feelings, loosed to strengthen—not
 depart, 240
hat rise, convulse, contend—that freeze,
 or glow,
ush in the cheek, or damp upon the
 brow;
hen, Stranger! if thou canst, and tremb-
 lest not,
ehold his soul—the rest that soothes his
 lot!
ark how that lone and blighted bosom
 sears 245
he scathing thought of execrated years!
ehold—but who hath seen, or e'er shall
 see,
lan as himself—the secret spirit free?

XI

Yet was not Conrad thus by Nature sent
To lead the guilty—guilt's worse instru-
 ment— 250
His soul was changed, before his deeds
 had driven
Him forth to war with man and forfeit
 heaven.
Warp'd by the world in Disappointment's
 school,
In words too wise, in conduct *there* a fool;
Too firm to yield, and far too proud to
 stoop, 255
Doom'd by his very virtues for a dupe,
He cursed those virtues as the cause of ill,
And not the traitors who betray'd him
 still;
Nor deem'd that gifts bestow'd on better
 men
Had left him joy, and means to give
 again. 260
Fear'd, shunn'd, belied, ere youth had
 lost her force,
He hated man too much to feel remorse,
And thought the voice of wrath a sacred
 call,
To pay the injuries of some on all.
He knew himself a villain—but he deem'd
The rest no better than the thing he
 seem'd; 266
And scorn'd the best as hypocrites who hid
Those deeds the bolder spirit plainly did.
He knew himself detested, but he knew
The hearts that loath'd him, crouch'd
 and dreaded too. 270
Lone, wild, and strange, he stood alike
 exempt
From all affection and from all contempt;
His name could sadden, and his acts sur-
 prise;
But they that fear'd him dared not to
 despise;
Man spurns the worm, but pauses ere he
 wake 275
The slumbering venom of the folded
 snake:
The first may turn, but not avenge the
 blow;
The last expires, but leaves no living foe;
Fast to the doom'd offender's form it
 clings,
And he may crush—not conquer—still it
 stings! 280

XII

None are all evil—quickening round his
 heart
One softer feeling would not yet depart;
Oft could he sneer at others as beguiled
By passions worthy of a fool or child;
Yet 'gainst that passion vainly still he
 strove, 285
And even in him it asks the name of Love!

Yes, it was love—unchangeable—un-
 changed,
Felt but for one from whom he never
 ranged;
Though fairest captives daily met his eye,
He shunn'd, nor sought, but coldly pass'd
 them by; 290
Though many a beauty droop'd in pri-
 son'd bower,
None ever sooth'd his most unguarded
 hour.
Yes—it was Love—if thoughts of tender-
 ness
Tried in temptation, strengthen'd by dis-
 tress,
Unmoved by absence, firm in every clime,
And yet—oh more than all! untired by
 time; 296
Which nor defeated hope, nor baffled
 wile,
Could render sullen were she near to
 smile,
Nor rage could fire, nor sickness fret to
 vent
On her one murmur of his discontent;
Which still would meet with joy, with
 calmness part, 301
Lest that his look of grief should reach
 her heart;
Which nought removed, nor menaced to
 remove—
If there be love in mortals—this was love!
He was a villain—ay, reproaches shower
On him—but not the passion, nor its
 power, 306
Which only proved, all other virtues gone,
Not guilt itself could quench this love-
 liest one!

XIII

He paused a moment—till his hastening
 men
Pass'd the first winding downward to the
 glen. 310
'Strange tidings!—many a peril have I
 pass'd,
Nor know I why this next appears the last!
Yet so my heart forebodes, but must not
 fear,
Nor shall my followers find me falter here.
'Tis rash to meet, but surer death to
 wait 315
Till here they hunt us to undoubted fate;
And, if my plan but hold, and Fortune
 smile,
We'll furnish mourners for our funeral
 pile.
Ay, let them slumber—peaceful be their
 dreams!
Morn ne'er awoke them with such brilliant
 beams 320
As kindle high to-night (but blow, thou
 breeze!)
To warm these slow avengers of the seas.

Now to Medora—Oh! my sinking heart
Long may her own be lighter than thou
 art!
Yet was I brave—mean boast where all
 are brave! 325
Ev'n insects sting for aught they seek to
 save.
This common courage which with brutes
 we share,
That owes its deadliest efforts to despair,
Small merit claims—but 'twas my noble
 hope
To teach my few with numbers still to
 cope; 330
Long have I led them—not to vainly
 bleed:
No medium now—we perish or succeed!
So let it be—it irks not me to die;
But thus to urge them whence they cannot
 fly.
My lot hath long had little of my care, 335
But chafes my pride thus baffled in the
 snare:
Is this my skill? my craft? to set at last
Hope, power, and life upon a single cast?
Oh, Fate!—accuse thy folly, not thy fate—
She may redeem thee still, nor yet too
 late.' 340

XIV

Thus with himself communion held he, till
He reach'd the summit of his tower-
 crown'd hill:
There at the portal paused—for wild and
 soft
He heard those accents never heard too
 oft;
Through the high lattice far yet sweet they
 rung, 345
And these the notes his bird of beauty
 sung:

1

'Deep in my soul that tender secret dwells,
 Lonely and lost to light for evermore,
Save when to thine my heart responsive
 swells, 349
 Then trembles into silence as before.

2

'There, in its centre, a sepulchral lamp
 Burns the slow flame, eternal, but un-
 seen;
Which not the darkness of despair can
 damp,
 Though vain its ray as it had never been.

3

'Remember me—Oh! pass not thou my
 grave 355
 Without one thought whose relics there
 recline:
The only pang my bosom dare not brave
 Must be to find forgetfulness in thine.

4

My fondest, faintest, latest accents
 hear—
 Grief for the dead not virtue can re-
 prove; 360
Then give me all I ever ask'd—a tear,
 The first—last—sole reward of so much
 love!'

He pass'd the portal, cross'd the corridor,
And reach'd the chamber as the strain
 gave o'er:
'My own Medora! sure thy song is
 sad—' 365
In Conrad's absence wouldst thou have
 it glad?
Without thine ear to listen to my lay,
Still must my song my thoughts, my soul
 betray:
Still must each action to my bosom suit,
My heart unhush'd, although my lips were
 mute! 370
Oh! many a night on this lone couch re-
 clined,
My dreaming fear with storms hath wing'd
 the wind,
And deem'd the breath that faintly fann'd
 thy sail
The murmuring prelude of the ruder gale;
Though soft, it seem'd the low prophetic
 dirge, 375
That mourn'd thee floating on the savage
 surge;
Still would I rise to rouse the beacon fire,
Lest spies less true should let the blaze
 expire;
And many a restless hour outwatch'd each
 star,
And morning came—and still thou wert
 afar. 380
Oh! how the chill blast on my bosom
 blew,
And day broke dreary on my troubled
 view,
And still I gazed and gazed—and not a
 prow
Was granted to my tears, my truth, my
 vow!
At length 'twas noon—I hail'd and blest
 the mast 385
That met my sight—it near'd—Alas! it
 pass'd!
Another came—Oh God! 'twas thine at
 last!
Would that those days were over! wilt
 thou ne'er,
My Conrad! learn the joys of peace to
 share?
Sure thou hast more than wealth, and
 many a home 390
As bright as this invites us not to roam:
Thou know'st it is not peril that I fear,
I only tremble when thou art not here;

Then not for mine, but that far dearer
 life,
Which flies from love and languishes for
 strife— 395
How strange that heart, to me so tender
 still,
Should war with nature and its better
 will!'

'Yea, strange indeed—that heart hath
 long been changed;
Worm-like 'twas trampled, adder-like
 avenged,
Without one hope on earth beyond thy
 love, 400
And scarce a glimpse of mercy from above.
Yet the same feeling which thou dost con-
 demn,
My very love to thee is hate to them,
So closely mingling here, that disen-
 twined,
I cease to love thee when I love mankind:
Yet dread not this—the proof of all the
 past 406
Assures the future that my love will last;
But—oh, Medora! nerve thy gentler heart;
This hour again—but not for long—we
 part.'

'This hour we part—my heart foreboded
 this: 410
Thus ever fade my fairy dreams of bliss.
This hour—it cannot be—this hour
 away!
Yon bark hath hardly anchor'd in the
 bay:
Her consort still is absent, and her crew
Have need of rest before they toil anew:
My love! thou mock'st my weakness; and
 wouldst steel 416
My breast before the time when it must feel;
But trifle now no more with my distress,
Such mirth hath less of play than bitter-
 ness.
Be silent, Conrad!—dearest! come and
 share 420
The feast these hands delighted to pre-
 pare;
Light toil! to cull and dress thy frugal fare!
See, I have pluck'd the fruit that promised
 best,
And where not sure, perplex'd, but pleased,
 I guess'd
At such as seem'd the fairest; thrice the
 hill 425
My steps have wound to try the coolest
 rill;
Yes! thy sherbet to-night will sweetly flow,
See how it sparkles in its vase of snow!
The grapes' gay juice thy bosom never
 cheers;
Thou more than Moslem when the cup
 appears: 430
Think not I mean to chide—for I rejoice
What others deem a penance is thy choice.

But come, the board is spread; our silver
 lamp
Is trimm'd, and heeds not the sirocco's
 damp:
Then shall my handmaids while the time
 along, 435
And join with me the dance, or wake the
 song;
Or my guitar, which still thou lov'st to
 hear,
Shall soothe or lull—or, should it vex
 thine ear,
We'll turn the tale, by Ariosto told,
Of fair Olympia loved and left of old.
Why, thou wert worse than he who broke
 his vow 441
To that lost damsel, shouldst thou leave
 me now;
Or even that traitor chief—I've seen thee
 smile,
When the clear sky show'd Ariadne's
 Isle,
Which I have pointed from these cliffs the
 while: 445
And thus half sportive, half in fear, I
 said,
Lest time should raise that doubt to more
 than dread,
Thus Conrad, too, will quit me for the
 main;
And he deceived me—for he came again!'

'Again, again—and oft again—my love!
If there be life below, and hope above,
He will return—but now, the moments
 bring 452
The time of parting with redoubled wing:
The why, the where—what boots it now
 to tell?
Since all must end in that wild word—
 farewell!
Yet would I fain—did time allow—dis-
 close— 456
Fear not—these are no formidable foes;
And here shall watch a more than wonted
 guard,
For sudden siege and long defence pre-
 pared:
Nor be thou lonely, though thy lord's
 away, 460
Our matrons and thy handmaids with
 thee stay;
And this thy comfort—that, when next
 we meet,
Security shall make repose more sweet.
List!—'tis the bugle!'—Juan shrilly
 blew—
'One kiss—one more—another—Oh!
 Adieu!' 465

She rose—she sprung—she clung to his
 embrace,
Till his heart heaved beneath her hidden
 face:
He dared not raise to his that deep-blu[e]
 eye,
Which downcast droop'd in tearles[s]
 agony.
Her long fair hair lay floating o'er hi[s]
 arms, 47[0]
In all the wildness of dishevell'd charms;
Scarce beat that bosom where his imag[e]
 dwelt
So full—that feeling seem'd almost un[-]
 felt!
Hark—peals the thunder of the signa[l]
 gun!
It told 'twas sunset, and he cursed tha[t]
 sun. 47[4]
Again—again—that form he madl[y]
 press'd,
Which mutely clasp'd, imploringly car[-]
 ess'd!
And tottering to the couch his bride h[e]
 bore,
One moment gazed, as if to gaze no more;
Felt that for him earth held but her
 alone, 48[0]
Kiss'd her cold forehead—turn'd—is Con[-]
 rad gone?

xv

'And is he gone?' on sudden solitude
How oft that fearful question will intrude[!]
''Twas but an instant past, and here h[e]
 stood!
And now'—without the portal's porc[h]
 she rush'd, 48[5]
And then at length her tears in freedo[m]
 gush'd;
Big, bright, and fast, unknown to her the[y]
 fell;
But still her lips refused to send—'Fare[-]
 well!'
For in that word—that fatal word—how[-]
 e'er
We promise, hope, believe, there breathe[s]
 despair. 49[0]
O'er every feature of that still, pale face[,]
Had sorrow fix'd what time can ne'e[r]
 erase:
The tender blue of that large loving ey[e]
Grew frozen with its gaze on vacancy,
Till—Oh, how far!—it caught a glimps[e]
 of him, 49[5]
And then it flow'd, and phrensied seem'[d]
 to swim,
Through those long, dark, and glistenin[g]
 lashes dew'd
With drops of sadness oft to be renew'd[.]
'He's gone!'—against her heart tha[t]
 hand is driven,
Convulsed and quick—then gently raise[d]
 to heaven: 50[0]
She look'd and saw the heaving of th[e]
 main;
The white sail set—she dared not loo[k]
 again;

ut turn'd with sickening soul within the
 gate—
t is no dream—and I am desolate!'

XVI

'rom crag to crag descending, swiftly sped
tern Conrad down, nor once he turn'd
 his head; 506
ut shrunk whene'er the windings of his way
'orced on his eye what he would not
 survey,
is lone but lovely dwelling on the steep,
'hat hail'd him first when homeward from
 the deep: 510
nd she—the dim and melancholy star,
Vhose ray of beauty reach'd him from
 afar,
)n her he must not gaze, he must not think,
'here he might rest—but on Destruction's
 brink:
[et once almost he stopp'd, and nearly
 gave 515
lis fate to chance, his projects to the wave:
ut no—it must not be—a worthy chief
Iay melt, but not betray to woman's
 grief.
le sees his bark, he notes how fair the
 wind, 519
And sternly gathers all his might of mind:
Again he hurries on—and as he hears
'he clang of tumult vibrate on his ears,
'he busy sounds, the bustle of the shore,
'he shout, the signal, and the dashing oar;
As marks his eye the seaboy on the mast,
'he anchors rise, the sails unfurling fast,
'he waving kerchiefs of the crowd that
 urge
'hat mute adieu to those who stem the
 surge;
And more than all, his blood-red flag aloft,
le marvell'd how his heart could seem so
 soft, 530
Fire in his glance, and wildness in his
 breast,
le feels of all his former self possest;
-le bounds—he flies—until his footsteps
 reach
'he verge where ends the cliff, begins the
 beach,
'here checks his speed; but pauses less to
 breathe 535
'he breezy freshness of the deep beneath,
'han there his wonted statelier step renew;
Nor rush, disturb'd by haste, to vulgar
 view:
For well had Conrad learn'd to curb the
 crowd,
By arts that veil, and oft preserve the proud;
His was the lofty port, the distant mien,
'hat seems to shun the sight—and awes if
 seen: 542
The solemn aspect, and the high-born eye,
That checks low mirth, but lacks not
 courtesy;

All these he wielded to command assent:
But where he wish'd to win, so well unbent,
That kindness cancell'd fear in those who
 heard, 547
And others' gifts show'd mean beside his
 word,
When echo'd to the heart as from his own
His deep yet tender melody of tone:
But such was foreign to his wonted mood,
He cared not what he soften'd, but sub-
 dued: 552
The evil passions of his youth had made
Him value less who loved—than what
 obey'd.

XVII

Around him mustering ranged his ready
 guard, 555
Before him Juan stands—'Are all pre-
 pared?'

'They are—nay more—embark'd: the
 latest boat
Waits but my Chief——'
 'My sword, and my capote.'
Soon firmly girded on, and lightly slung,
His belt and cloak were o'er his shoulders
 flung: 560
'Call Pedro here!' He comes—and Con-
 rad bends,
With all the courtesy he deign'd his friends;
'Receive these tablets, and peruse with
 care,
Words of high trust and truth are graven
 there;
Double the guard, and when Anselmo's
 bark 565
Arrives, let him alike these orders mark:
In three days (serve the breeze) the sun
 shall shine
On our return—till then all peace be
 thine!'
This said, his brother Pirate's hand he
 wrung,
Then to his boat with haughty gesture
 sprung. 570
Flash'd the dipt oars, and sparkling with
 the stroke,
Around the waves' phosphoric brightness
 broke;
They gain the vessel—on the deck he
 stands,—
Shrieks the shrill whistle, ply the busy
 hands—
He marks how well the ship her helm
 obeys, 575
How gallant all her crew, and deigns to
 praise.
His eyes of pride to young Gonsalvo
 turn—
Why doth he start, and inly seem to
 mourn?
Alas! those eyes beheld his rocky tower
And live a moment o'er the parting hour;

She—his Medora—did she mark the
prow? 581
Ah! never loved he half so much as now!
But much must yet be done ere dawn of
day—
Again he mans himself and turns away;
Down to the cabin with Gonsalvo bends,
And there unfolds his plan, his means, and
ends; 586
Before them burns the lamp, and spreads
the chart,
And all that speaks and aids the naval art;
They to the midnight watch protract de-
bate;
To anxious eyes what hour is ever late?
Meantime, the steady breeze serenely
blew, 591
And fast and falcon-like the vessel flew;
Pass'd the high headlands of each cluster-
ing isle,
To gain their port—long—long ere morn-
ing smile:
And soon the night-glass through the
narrow bay 595
Discovers where the Pacha's galleys lay.
Count they each sail, and mark how there
supine
The lights in vain o'er heedless Moslem
shine.
Secure, unnoted, Conrad's prow pass'd by,
And anchor'd where his ambush meant
to lie; 600
Screen'd from espial by the jutting cape,
That rears on high its rude fantastic shape.
Then rose his band to duty—not from
sleep—
Equipp'd for deeds alike on land or deep;
While lean'd their leader o'er the fretting
flood, 605
And calmly talk'd—and yet he talk'd of
blood!

CANTO THE SECOND

'Conosceste i dubiosi desiri?'—Dante

I

In Coron's bay floats many a galley light,
Through Coron's lattices the lamps are
bright,
For Seyd, the Pacha, makes a feast to-night:
A feast for promised triumph yet to come,
When he shall drag the fetter'd Rovers
home; 5
This hath he sworn by Allah and his sword,
And faithful to his firman and his word,
His summon'd prows collect along the coast,
And great the gathering crews, and loud
the boast;
Already shared the captives and the prize,
Though far the distant foe they thus
despise; 11
'Tis but to sail—no doubt to-morrow's Sun
Will see the Pirates bound, their haven
won!

Meantime the watch may slumber, if they
will,
Nor only wake to war, but dreaming kill
Though all, who can, disperse on shore
and seek 1
To flesh their glowing valour on the Greek
How well such deed becomes the turban'd
brave—
To bare the sabre's edge before a slave!
Infest his dwelling—but forbear to slay,
Their arms are strong, yet merciful to-day
And do not deign to smite because they
may! 2
Unless some gay caprice suggests the blow
To keep in practice for the coming foe.
Revel and rout the evening hours beguile
And they who wish to wear a head must
smile; 2
For Moslem mouths produce their choicest
cheer,
And hoard their curses, till the coast is
clear.

II

High in his hall reclines the turban'd Seyd
Around—the bearded chiefs he came to
lead. 3
Removed the banquet, and the last pilaff—
Forbidden draughts, 'tis said, he dared to
quaff,
Though to the rest the sober berry's juice
The slaves bear round for rigid Moslems'
use;
The long chibouque's dissolving cloud
supply, 3
While dance the Almas to wild minstrelsy.
The rising morn will view the chiefs em-
bark;
But waves are somewhat treacherous in
the dark:
And revellers may more securely sleep
On silken couch than o'er the rugged deep:
Feast there who can—nor combat till they
must, 41
And less to conquest than to Korans trust;
And yet the numbers crowded in his host
Might warrant more than even the Pacha's
boast.

III

With cautious reverence from the outer
gate 45
Slow stalks the slave, whose office there to
wait,
Bows his bent head, his hand salutes the
floor,
Ere yet his tongue the trusted tidings bore:
'A captive Dervise, from the Pirate's nest
Escaped, is here—himself would tell the
rest.' 50
He took the sign from Seyd's assenting eye,
And led the holy man in silence nigh.
His arms were folded on his dark-green vest,
His step was feeble, and his look deprest;

Yet worn he seem'd of hardship more than
 years, 55
And pale his cheek with penance, not from
 fears.
Vow'd to his God—his sable locks he
 wore,
And these his lofty cap rose proudly o'er:
Around his form his loose long robe was
 thrown,
And wrapt a breast bestow'd on heaven
 alone; 60
Submissive, yet with self-possession
 mann'd,
He calmly met the curious eyes that
 scann'd;
And question of his coming fain would
 seek,
Before the Pacha's will allow'd to speak.

IV

Whence com'st thou, Dervise?'
 'From the outlaw's den, 65
A fugitive—'
 'Thy capture where and when?'
From Scalanova's port to Scio's isle,
The Saick was bound; but Allah did not
 smile
Upon our course—the Moslem mer-
 chant's gains
The Rovers won; our limbs have worn
 their chains. 70
I had no death to fear, nor wealth to boast,
Beyond the wandering freedom which I
 lost;
At length a fisher's humble boat by night
Afforded hope, and offer'd chance of
 flight;
I seized the hour, and find my safety
 here— 75
With thee—most mighty Pacha! who can
 fear?'

'How speed the outlaws? stand they well
 prepared,
Their plunder'd wealth, and robber's rock,
 to guard?
Dream they of this our preparation,
 doom'd
To view with fire their scorpion nest con-
 sumed?' 80

'Pacha! the fetter'd captive's mourning eye,
That weeps for flight, but ill can play the
 spy;
I only heard the reckless waters roar,
Those waves that would not bear me from
 the shore; 84
I only mark'd the glorious sun and sky,
Too bright, too blue, for my captivity;
And felt that all which Freedom's bosom
 cheers,
Must break my chain before it dried my
 tears.

This may'st thou judge, at least, from my
 escape,
They little deem of aught in peril's shape;
Else vainly had I pray'd or sought the
 chance 91
That leads me here—if eyed with vigilance;
The careless guard that did not see me fly
May watch as idly when thy power is nigh.
Pacha! my limbs are faint—and nature
 craves 95
Food for my hunger, rest from tossing
 waves:
Permit my absence—peace be with thee!
 Peace
With all around!—now grant repose—
 release.'

'Stay, Dervise! I have more to question—
 stay,
I do command thee—sit—dost hear?—
 obey! 100
More I must ask, and food the slaves shall
 bring;
Thou shalt not pine where all are ban-
 queting:
The supper done—prepare thee to reply,
Clearly and full—I love not mystery.'
'Twere vain to guess what shook the pious
 man, 105
Who look'd not lovingly on that Divan;
Nor show'd high relish for the banquet
 prest,
And less respect for every fellow guest.
'Twas but a moment's peevish hectic pass'd
Along his cheek, and tranquillised as fast:
He sate him down in silence, and his look
Resumed the calmness which before for-
 sook: 112
The feast was usher'd in, but sumptuous fare
He shunn'd as if some poison mingled
 there.
For one so long condemn'd to toil and
 fast, 115
Methinks he strangely spares the rich re-
 past.

'What ails thee, Dervise? eat—dost thou
 suppose
This feast a Christian's? or my friends thy
 foes?
Why dost thou shun the salt? that sacred
 pledge,
Which, once partaken, blunts the sabre's
 edge, 120
Makes ev'n contending tribes in peace
 unite,
And hated hosts seem brethren to the
 sight!'

'Salt seasons dainties—and my food is still
The humblest root, my drink the simplest
 rill;
And my stern vow and order's laws oppose
To break or mingle bread with friends or
 foes; 126

287

It may seem strange—if there be aught to
 dread,
That peril rests upon my single head;
But for thy sway—nay more—thy Sultan's
 throne,
I taste nor bread nor banquet—save alone;
Infringed our order's rule, the Prophet's
 rage 131
To Mecca's dome might bar my pil-
 grimage.'

'Well—as thou wilt—ascetic as thou art—
One question answer; then in peace de-
 part.
How many?—Ha! it cannot sure be day?
What star—what sun is bursting on the
 bay? 136
It shines a lake of fire!—away—away!
Ho! treachery! my guards! my scimitar!
The galleys feed the flames—and I afar!
Accursed Dervise!—these thy tidings—
 thou 140
Some villain spy—seize—cleave him—
 slay him now!'

Up rose the Dervise with that burst of
 light,
Nor less his change of form appall'd the
 sight:
Up rose that Dervise—not in saintly garb,
But like a warrior bounding on his barb,
Dash'd his high cap, and tore his robe
 away— 146
Shone his mail'd breast, and flash'd his
 sabre's ray!
His close but glittering casque, and sable
 plume,
More glittering eye, and black brow's
 sabler gloom,
Glared on the Moslems' eyes some Afrit
 sprite, 150
Whose demon death-blow left no hope for
 fight.
The wild confusion, and the swarthy glow
Of flames on high, and torches from be-
 low;
The shriek of terror, and the mingling
 yell—
For swords began to clash, and shouts to
 swell 155
Flung o'er that spot of earth the air of hell!
Distracted, to and fro, the flying slaves
Behold but bloody shore and fiery waves;
Nought heeded they the Pacha's angry cry,
They seize that Dervise!—seize on Za-
 tanai! 160
He saw their terror—check'd the first
 despair
That urged him but to stand and perish
 there,
Since far too early and too well obey'd,
The flame was kindled ere the signal made;
He saw their terror—from his baldric
 drew 165

His bugle—brief the blast—but shrill
 blew;
'Tis answered—'Well ye speed, my gallan
 crew!
Why did I doubt their quickness of career
And deem design had left me single here?
Sweeps his long arm—that sabre's whirl-
 ing sway 170
Sheds fast atonement for its first delay;
Completes his fury what their fear begun
And makes the many basely quail to one
The cloven turbans o'er the chambe
 spread,
And scarce an arm dare rise to guard it
 head: 175
Even Seyd, convulsed, o'erwhelm'd, witl
 rage, surprise,
Retreats before him, though he still defies
No craven he—and yet he dreads the blow
So much Confusion magnifies his foe!
His blazing galleys still distract his sight
He tore his beard, and foaming fled th
 fight; 18
For now the pirates pass'd the Haram gate
And burst within—and it were death t
 wait;
Where wild Amazement shrieking—kneel
 ing throws
The sword aside—in vain—the blood o'er-
 flows! 18
The Corsairs pouring, haste to where
 within
Invited Conrad's bugle, and the din
Of groaning victims, and wild cries for life.
Proclaim'd how well he did the work o
 strife.
They shout to find him grim and lonely
 there, 19
A glutted tiger mangling in his lair!
But short their greeting, shorter his reply—
''Tis well—but Seyd escapes, and he mus
 die—
Much hath been done, but more remains
 to do—
Their galleys blaze—why not their city
 too?' 19

v

Quick at the word they seized him each a
 torch,
And fire the dome from minaret to porch.
A stern delight was fix'd in Conrad's eye,
But sudden sunk—for on his ear the cry
Of women struck, and like a deadly knell
Knock'd at that heart unmoved by battle's
 yell, 201
'Oh! burst the Haram—wrong not on
 your lives
One female form—remember—*we* have
 wives.
On them such outrage Vengeance will repay;
Man is our foe, and such 'tis ours to slay;
But still we spared—must spare the weaker
 prey. 206

Oh! I forgot—but Heaven will not forgive
If at my word the helpless cease to live;
Follow who will—I go—we yet have time
Our souls to lighten of at least a crime.'
He climbs the crackling stair, he bursts the
 door, 211
Nor feels his feet glow scorching with the
 floor;
His breath choked gasping with the vol-
 umed smoke,
But still from room to room his way he
 broke.
They search—they find—they save: with
 lusty arms 215
Each bears a prize of unregarded charms;
Calm their loud fears; sustain their sinking
 frames
With all the care defenceless beauty
 claims:
So well could Conrad tame their fiercest
 mood,
And check the very hands with gore im-
 brued. 220
But who is she? whom Conrad's arms
 convey
From reeking pile and combat's wreck
 away—
Who but the love of him he dooms to
 bleed?
The Haram queen—but still the slave of
 Seyd!

VI

Brief time had Conrad now to greet
 Gulnare, 225
Few words to re-assure the trembling fair;
For in that pause compassion snatch'd
 from war,
The foe before retiring, fast and far,
With wonder saw their footsteps unpur-
 sued,
First slowlier fled—then rallied—then
 withstood. 230
This Seyd perceives, then first perceives
 how few,
Compared with his, the Corsair's roving
 crew,
And blushes o'er his error, as he eyes
The ruin wrought by panic and surprise.
Alla il Alla! Vengeance swells the cry—
Shame mounts to rage that must atone or
 die! 236
And flame for flame and blood for blood
 must tell,
The tide of triumph ebbs that flow'd too
 well—
When wrath returns to renovated strife,
And those who fought for conquest strike
 for life. 240
Conrad beheld the danger—he beheld
His followers faint by freshening foes re-
 pell'd:
'One effort—one—to break the circling
 host!'

They form—unite—charge—waver—all
 is lost!
Within a narrower ring compress'd, beset,
Hopeless, not heartless, strive and struggle
 yet— 246
Ah! now they fight in firmest file no more,
Hemm'd in, cut off, cleft down, and tram-
 pled o'er,
But each strikes singly, silently, and home,
And sinks outwearied rather than o'er-
 come, 250
His last faint quittance rendering with his
 breath,
Till the blade glimmers in the grasp of
 death!

VII

But first, ere came the rallying host to
 blows,
And rank to rank, and hand to hand
 oppose,
Gulnare and all her Haram handmaids
 freed, 255
Safe in the dome of one who held their
 creed,
By Conrad's mandate safely were be-
 stow'd,
And dried those tears for life and fame that
 flow'd:
And when that dark-eyed lady, young
 Gulnare,
Recall'd those thoughts late wandering in
 despair, 260
Much did she marvel o'er the courtesy
That smooth'd his accents, soften'd in his
 eye:
'Twas strange—*that* robber thus with gore
 bedew'd
Seem'd gentler then than Seyd in fondest
 mood.
The Pacha woo'd as if he deem'd the slave
Must seem delighted with the heart he
 gave; 266
The Corsair vow'd protection, soothed af-
 fright,
As if his homage were a woman's right.
'The wish is wrong—nay, worse for fe-
 male—vain: 269
Yet much I long to view that chief again;
If but to thank for, what my fear forgot,
The life my loving lord remember'd not!'

VIII

And him she saw, where thickest carnage
 spread,
But gather'd breathing from the happier
 dead;
Far from his band, and battling with a
 host 275
That deem right dearly won the field he lost,
Fell'd—bleeding—baffled of the death he
 sought,
And snatch'd to expiate all the ills he
 wrought;

Preserved to linger and to live in vain,
While Vengeance ponder'd o'er new plans
　of pain,　　　　　　　　　　280
And stanch'd the blood she saves to shed
　again—
But drop for drop, for Seyd's unglutted
　eye
Would doom him ever dying—ne'er to
　die!
Can this be he? triumphant late she saw,
When his red hand's wild gesture waved
　a law!　　　　　　　　　　285
'Tis he indeed—disarm'd but undeprest,
His sole regret the life he still possest;
His wounds too slight, though taken with
　that will,
Which would have kiss'd the hand that
　then could kill.
Oh were there none, of all the many given,
To send his soul—he scarcely ask'd to
　heaven?　　　　　　　　　　291
Must he alone of all retain his breath,
Who more than all had striven and struck
　for death?
He deeply felt—what mortal hearts must
　feel,
When thus reversed on faithless fortune's
　wheel,　　　　　　　　　　295
For crimes committed, and the victor's
　threat
Of lingering tortures to repay the debt—
He deeply felt; but evil pride
That led to perpetrate, now serves to
　hide.
Still in his stern and self-collected mien
A conqueror's more than captive's air is
　seen,　　　　　　　　　　301
Though faint with wasting toil and stiffen-
　ing wound,
But few that saw—so calmly gazed
　around:
Though the far shouting of the distant
　crowd,　　　　　　　　　　304
Their tremors o'er, rose insolently loud,
The better warriors who beheld him near,
Insulted not the foe who taught them fear;
And the grim guards that to his durance
　led,
In silence eyed him with a secret dread.

IX

The Leech was sent—but not in mercy—
　there,　　　　　　　　　　310
To note how much the life yet left could
　bear;
He found enough to load with heaviest
　chain,
And promise feeling for the wrench of
　pain;
To-morrow—yea—to-morrow's evening
　sun
Will sinking see impalement's pangs
　begun,　　　　　　　　　　315
And rising with the wonted blush of morn

Behold how well or ill those pangs are
　borne.
Of torments this the longest and the worst,
Which adds all other agony to thirst,
That day by day death still forbears to
　slake,　　　　　　　　　　320
While famish'd vultures flit around the
　stake.
'Oh! water—water!'—smiling Hate
　denies
The victim's prayer, for if he drinks he
　dies.
This was his doom;—the Leech, the guard
　were gone,
And left proud Conrad fetter'd and alone.

X

'Twere vain to paint to what his feelings
　grew—　　　　　　　　　　326
It even were doubtful if their victim knew.
There is a war, a chaos of the mind,
When all its elements convulsed, com-
　bined,
Lie dark and jarring with perturbed force,
And gnashing with impenitent Remorse—
That juggling fiend, who never spake
　before,　　　　　　　　　　332
But cries 'I warn'd thee!' when the deed
　is o'er.
Vain voice! the spirit burning but unbent,
May writhe, rebel—the weak alone repent!
Even in that lonely hour when most it
　feels,　　　　　　　　　　336
And, to itself, all, all that self reveals,—
No single passion, and no ruling thought
That leaves the rest, as once, unseen, un-
　sought,
But the wild prospect when the soul re-
　views,　　　　　　　　　　340
All rushing through their thousand
　avenues—
Ambition's dreams expiring, love's regret,
Endanger'd glory, life itself beset;
The joy untasted, the contempt or hate
'Gainst those who fain would triumph in
　our fate;　　　　　　　　　　345
The hopeless past, the hasting future
　driven
Too quickly on to guess of hell or heaven;
Deeds, thoughts, and words, perhaps re-
　member'd not
So keenly till that hour, but ne'er forgot;
Things light or lovely in their acted time,
But now to stern reflection each a crime;
The withering sense of evil unreveal'd,
Not cankering less because the more con-
　ceal'd—　　　　　　　　　　353
All, in a word, from which all eyes must
　start,
That opening sepulchre—the naked heart
Bares with its buried woes, till Pride
　awake,　　　　　　　　　　356
To snatch the mirror from the soul—and
　break.

Ay, Pride can veil, and Courage brave it
 all—
All—all—before—beyond—the deadliest
 fall.
Each hath some fear, and he who least
 betrays, 360
The only hypocrite deserving praise:
Not the loud recreant wretch who boasts
 and flies;
But he who looks on death—and silent dies.
So steel'd by pondering o'er his far career,
He half-way meets him should the menace
 near! 365

 XI

In the high chamber of his highest tower
Sate Conrad, fetter'd in the Pacha's power.
His palace perish'd in the flame—this fort
Contain'd at once his captive and his
 court.
Not much could Conrad of his sentence
 blame, 370
His foe, if vanquish'd, had but shared the
 same:—
Alone he sate—in solitude had scann'd
His guilty bosom, but that breast he
 mann'd:
One thought alone he could not—dared
 not meet—
'Oh, how these tidings will Medora greet?'
Then—only then—his clanking hands he
 raised, 376
And strain'd with rage the chain on which
 he gazed;
But soon he found, or feign'd, or dream'd
 relief,
And smiled in self-derision of his grief,
'And now come torture when it will—or
 may, 380
More need of rest to nerve me for the day!'
This said, with languor to his mat he crept,
And, whatsoe'er his visions, quickly slept.

'Twas hardly midnight when that fray
 begun,
For Conrad's plans matured, at once were
 done: 385
And Havoc loathes so much the waste of
 time,
She scarce had left an uncommitted crime.
One hour beheld him since the tide he
 stemm'd—
Disguised, discover'd, conquering, ta'en,
 condemn'd— 389
A chief on land, an outlaw on the deep—
Destroying, saving, prison'd, and asleep!

 XII

He slept in calmest seeming, for his breath
Was hush'd so deep—Ah! happy if in
 death!
He slept—Who o'er his placid slumber
 bends?
His foes are gone, and here he hath no
 friends; 395

Is it some seraph sent to grant him grace?
No, 'tis an earthly form with heavenly
 face!
Its white arm raised a lamp—yet gently hid,
Lest the ray flash abruptly on the lid
Of that closed eye, which opens but to
 pain, 400
And once unclosed—but once may close
 again.
That form, with eye so dark, and cheek so
 fair,
And auburn waves of gemm'd and braided
 hair;
With shape of fairy lightness—naked foot,
That shines like snow, and falls on earth as
 mute— 405
Through guards and dunnest night how
 came it there?
Ah! rather ask what will not woman dare?
Whom youth and pity lead like thee,
 Gulnare!
She could not sleep—and while the
 Pacha's rest
In muttering dreams yet saw his pirate-
 guest, 410
She left his side—his signet-ring she bore,
Which oft in sport adorn'd her hand
 before—
And with it, scarcely question'd, won her
 way
Through drowsy guards that must that
 sign obey.
Worn out with toil, and tired with chang-
 ing blows, 415
Their eyes had envied Conrad his repose;
And chill and nodding at the turret door,
They stretch their listless limbs, and watch
 no more;
Just raised their heads to hail the signet-
 ring,
Ner ask or what or who the sign may
 bring. 420

 XIII

She gazed in wonder, 'Can he calmly sleep,
While other eyes his fall or ravage weep?
And mine in restlessness are wandering
 here—
What sudden spell hath made this man so
 dear?
True—'tis to him my life, and more, I owe,
And me and mine he spared from worse
 than woe: 426
'Tis late to think—but soft, his slumber
 breaks—
How heavily he sighs!—he starts—
 awakes!'
He raised his head, and dazzled with the
 light,
His eye seem'd dubious if it saw aright:
He moved his hand—the grating of his
 chain 431
Too harshly told him that he lived again.

'What is that form? if not a shape of air,
Methinks, my jailor's face shows won-
drous fair!'

'Pirate! thou know'st me not—but I am
one, 435
Grateful for deeds thou hast too rarely
done;
Look on me—and remember her, thy hand
Snatch'd from the flames, and thy more
fearful band.
I come through darkness—and I scarce
know why—
Yet not to hurt—I would not see thee die.'

'If so, kind lady! thine the only eye 441
That would not here in that gay hope de-
light:
Theirs is the chance—and let them use
their right.
But still I thank their courtesy or thine,
That would confess me at so fair a shrine!'

Strange though it seem—yet with extre-
mest grief 446
Is link'd a mirth—it doth not bring relief—
That playfulness of Sorrow ne'er beguiles,
And smiles in bitterness—but still it
smiles;
And sometimes with the wisest and the
best, 450
Till even the scaffold echoes with their
jest!
Yet not the joy to which it seems akin—
It may deceive all hearts, save that within.
Whate'er it was that flash'd on Conrad,
now
A laughing wildness half unbent his brow
And these his accents had a sound of
mirth, 456
As if the last he could enjoy on earth;
Yet 'gainst his nature—for through that
short life,
Few thoughts had he to spare from gloom
and strife.

XIV

'Corsair! thy doom is named—but I have
power 460
To soothe the Pacha in his weaker hour.
Thee would I spare—nay more—would
save thee now,
But this—time—hope—nor even thy
strength allow;
But all I can, I will: at least, delay
The sentence that remits thee scarce a day.
More now were ruin—even thyself were
loth 466
The vain attempt should bring but doom
to both.'

'Yes! loth indeed:—my soul is nerved to
all,
Or fall'n too low to fear a further fall:
Tempt not thyself with peril—me with
hope 470

Of flight from foes with whom I could not
cope:
Unfit to vanquish, shall I meanly fly,
The one of all my band that would not die?
Yet there is one to whom my memory
clings,
Till to these eyes her own wild softness
springs, 475
My sole resources in the path I trod
Were these—my bark, my sword, my love,
my God!
The last I left in youth!—he leaves me
now—
And Man but works his will to lay me low.
I have no thought to mock his throne with
prayer 480
Wrung from the coward crouching of
despair;
It is enough—I breathe, and I can bear.
My sword is shaken from the worthless
hand
That might have better kept so true a
brand;
My bark is sunk or captive—but my
love— 485
For her in sooth my voice would mount
above:
Oh! she is all that still to earth can bind—
And this will break a heart so more than
kind,
And blight a form—till thine appear'd,
Gulnare!
Mine eye ne'er ask'd if others were as
fair.' 490

'Thou lov'st another then?—but what to
me
Is this—'tis nothing—nothing e'er can be:
But yet—thou lov'st—and—Oh! I envy
those
Whose hearts on hearts as faithful can
repose,
Who never feel the void—the wandering
thought 495
That sighs o'er visions—such as mine hath
wrought.'

'Lady, methought thy love was his, for
whom
This arm redeem'd thee from a fiery tomb.'

'My love stern Seyd's! Oh—No—No—
not my love—
Yet much this heart, that strives no more,
once strove 500
To meet his passion—but it would not be.
I felt—I feel—love dwells with—with the
free.
I am a slave, a favour'd slave at best,
To share his splendour, and seem very
blest!
Oft must my soul the question undergo,
Of—'Dost thou love?' and burn to
answer, 'No!' 506

292

Oh! hard it is that fondness to sustain,
And struggle not to feel averse in vain;
But harder still the heart's recoil to bear,
And hide from one—perhaps another
 there. 510
He takes the hand I give not, nor with-
 hold—
Its pulse nor check'd, nor quicken'd—
 calmly cold:
And when resign'd, it drops a lifeless
 weight
From one I never loved enough to hate.
No warmth these lips return by his im-
 prest, 515
And chill'd remembrance shudders o'er
 the rest.
Yes—had I ever proved that passion's zeal,
The change to hatred were at least to feel:
But still he goes unmourn'd, returns un-
 sought,
And oft when present—absent from my
 thought. 520
Or when reflection comes—and come it
 must—
I fear that henceforth 'twill but bring dis-
 gust;
I am his slave—but, in despite of pride,
'Twere worse than bondage to become his
 bride.
Oh! that this dotage of his breast would
 cease: 525
Or seek another and give mine release,
But yesterday—I could have said, to
 peace!
Yes, if unwonted fondness now I feign,
Remember, captive! 'tis to break thy chain;
Repay the life that to thy hand I owe; 530
To give thee back to all endear'd below,
Who share such love as I can never know.
Farewell, morn breaks, and I must now
 away:
'Twill cost me dear—but dread no death
 to-day!'

XV

She press'd his fetter'd fingers to her heart,
And bow'd her head, and turn'd her to de-
 part, 536
And noiseless as a lovely dream is gone.
And was she here? and is he now alone?
What gem hath dropp'd and sparkles o'er
 his chain?
The tear most sacred, shed for others'
 pain, 540
That starts at once—bright—pure—from
 Pity's mine,
Already polish'd by the hand divine!
Oh! too convincing—dangerously dear—
In woman's eye the unanswerable tear!
That weapon of her weakness she can
 wield, 545
To save, subdue—at once her spear and
 shield:

Avoid it—Virtue ebbs and Wisdom errs,
Too fondly gazing on that grief of hers!
What lost a world, and bade a hero fly?
The timid tear in Cleopatra's eye. 550
Yet be the soft triumvir's fault forgiven;
By this—how many lose not earth—but
 heaven!
Consign their souls to man's eternal foe,
And seal their own to spare some wanton's
 woe!

XVI

'Tis morn, and o'er his alter'd features
 play 555
The beams—without the hope of yester-
 day.
What shall he be ere night? perchance a
 thing
O'er which the raven flaps her funeral
 wing,
By his closed eye unheeded and unfelt;
While sets that sun, and dews of evening
 melt, 560
Chill, wet, and misty round each stiffen'd
 limb,
Refreshing earth—reviving all but him!

CANTO THE THIRD

'Come vedi—ancor non m'abbandona.'—DANTE.

I

SLOW sinks, more lovely ere his race be run,
Along Morea's hills the setting sun;
Not, as in Northern climes, obscurely
 bright,
But one unclouded blaze of living light!
O'er the hush'd deep the yellow beam he
 throws, 5
Gilds the green wave, that trembles as it
 glows.
On old Ægina's rock and Idra's isle,
The god of gladness sheds his parting
 smile;
O'er his own regions lingering, loves to
 shine,
Though there his altars are no more
 divine. 10
Descending fast the mountain shadows
 kiss
Thy glorious gulf, unconquer'd Salamis!
Their azure arches through the long ex-
 panse
More deeply purpled meet his mellowing
 glance,
And tenderest tints, along their summits
 driven, 15
Mark his gay course, and own the hues of
 heaven;
Till, darkly shaded from the land and deep,
Behind his Delphian cliff he sinks to sleep.

On such an eve, his palest beam he cast,
When—Athens! here thy Wisest look'd
 his last. 20

How watch'd thy better sons his farewell
ray,
That closed their murder'd sage's latest
day!
Not yet—not yet—Sol pauses on the hill—
The precious hour of parting lingers still;
But sad his light to agonising eyes, 25
And dark the mountain's once delightful
dyes:
Gloom o'er the lovely land he seem'd to
pour,
The land, where Phœbus never frown'd
before;
But ere he sank below Cithæron's head,
The cup of woe was quaff'd—the spirit
fled; 30
The soul of him who scorn'd to fear or fly—
Who lived and died, as none can live or die!

But lo! from high Hymettus to the plain,
The queen of night asserts her silent reign.
No murky vapour, herald of the storm,
Hides her fair face, nor girds her glowing
form: 36
With cornice glimmering as the moon-
beams play,
There the white column greets her grateful
ray,
And, bright around with quivering beams
beset,
Her emblem sparkles o'er the minaret:
The groves of olive scatter'd dark and
wide 41
Where meek Cephisus pours his scanty
tide,
The cypress saddening by the sacred
mosque,
The gleaming turret of the gay kiosk,
And, dun and sombre 'mid the holy calm,
Near Theseus' fane yon solitary palm, 46
All tinged with varied hues arrest the
eye—
And dull were his that pass'd them heed-
less by.

Again the Ægean, heard no more afar,
Lulls his chafed breast from elemental
war; 50
Again his waves in milder tints unfold
Their long array of sapphire and of gold,
Mix'd with the shades of many a distant
isle,
That frown—where gentler ocean seems
to smile.

II

Not now my theme—why turn my thoughts
to thee? 55
Oh! who can look along thy native sea.
Nor dwell upon thy name, whate'er the
tale,
So much its magic must o'er all prevail?
Who that beheld that Sun upon thee set,
Fair Athens! could thine evening face for-
get? 60

Not he—whose heart nor time nor dis-
tance frees,
Spell-bound within the clustering Cy-
clades!
Nor seems this homage foreign to its
strain,
His Corsair's isle was once thine own do-
main—
Would that with freedom it were thine
again! 65

III

The Sun hath sunk—and, darker than the
night,
Sinks with its beam upon the beacon
height
Medora's heart—the third day's come and
gone—
With it he comes not—sends not—faith-
less one!
The wind was fair though light; and storms
were none. 70
Last eve Anselmo's bark return'd, and yet
His only tidings that they had not met!
Though wild, as now, far different were
the tale
Had Conrad waited for that single sail.
The night-breeze freshens—she that day
had pass'd 75
In watching all that Hope proclaim'd a
mast;
Sadly she sate on high—Impatience bore
At last her footsteps to the midnight shore,
And there she wander'd, heedless of the
spray
That dash'd her garments oft, and warn'd
away: 80
She saw not, felt not this—nor dared de-
part,
Nor deem'd it cold—her chill was at her
heart;
Till grew such certainty from that sus-
pense—
His very sight had shock'd from life or
sense! 84

It came at last—a sad and shatter'd boat,
Whose inmates first beheld whom first
they sought;
Some bleeding—all most wretched—these
the few—
Scarce knew they how escaped—this all
they knew.
In silence, darkling, each appear'd to wait
His fellow's mournful guess at Conrad's
fate: 90
Something they would have said; but
seem'd to fear
To trust their accents to Medora's ear.
She saw at once, yet sunk not—trembled
not—
Beneath that grief, that loneliness of lot;

Within that meek fair form were feelings
 high, 95
That deem'd not, till they found, their
 energy.
While yet was Hope they soften'd, flutter'd,
 wept—
All lost—that softness died not—but it
 slept;
And o'er its slumber rose that Strength
 which said,
'With nothing left to love, there's nought
 to dread.' 100
'Tis more than nature's; like the burning
 might
Delirium gathers from the fever's height.

'Silent you stand—nor would I hear you
 tell
What—speak not—breathe not—for I
 know it well—
Yet would I ask—almost my lip denies
The—quick your answer—tell me where
 he lies.' 106

'Lady! we know not—scarce with life we
 fled;
But here is one denies that he is dead:
He saw him bound: and bleeding—but
 alive.'

She heard no further—'twas in vain to
 strive— 110
So throbb'd each vein—each thought—
 till then withstood;
Her own dark soul—these words at once
 subdued:
She totters—falls—and senseless had the
 wave
Perchance but snatched her from another
 grave,
But that with hands though rude, yet
 weeping eyes, 115
They yield such aid as Pity's haste supplies:
Dash o'er her deathlike cheek the ocean dew,
Raise, fan, sustain—till life returns anew;
Awake her handmaids, with the matrons
 leave
That fainting form o'er which they gaze
 and grieve; 120
Then seek Anselmo's cavern, to report
The tale too tedious—when the triumph
 short.

IV

In that wild council words wax'd warm
 and strange
With thoughts of ransom, rescue, and re-
 venge;
All, save repose or flight: still lingering
 there
Breathed Conrad's spirit, and forbade
 despair; 126
Whate'er his fate—the breasts he form'd
 and led
Will save him living, or appease him dead.

Woe to his foes! there yet survive a few,
Whose deeds are daring, as their hearts
 are true. 130

V

Within the Haram's secret chamber sate
Stern Seyd, still pondering o'er his Cap-
 tive's fate;
His thoughts on love and hate alternate
 dwell,
Now with Gulnare, and now in Conrad's
 cell;
Here at his feet the lovely slave reclined
Surveys his brow—would soothe his gloom
 of mind; 136
While many an anxious glance her large
 dark eye
Sends in its idle search for sympathy,
His only bends in seeming o'er his beads,
But inly views his victim as he bleeds.
'Pacha! the day is thine; and on thy crest
Sits Triumph—Conrad taken—fall'n the
 rest!
His doom is fix'd—he dies: and well his
 fate
Was earn'd—yet much too worthless for
 thy hate:
Methinks, a short release, for ransom
 told 145
With all his treasure, not unwisely sold;
Report speaks largely of his pirate-
 hoard—
Would that of this my Pacha were the
 lord!
While baffled, weaken'd by this fatal
 fray—
Watch'd—follow'd—he were then an
 easier prey; 150
But once cut off—the remnant of his band
Embark their wealth, and seek a safer
 strand.'

'Gulnare!—if for each drop of blood a
 gem
Were offer'd rich as Stamboul's diadem;
If for each hair of his a massy mine 155
Of virgin ore should supplicating shine;
If all our Arab tales divulge or dream
Of wealth were here—that gold should not
 redeem! 158
It had not now redeem'd a single hour,
But that I know him fetter'd, in my power;
And, thirsting for revenge, I ponder still
On pangs that longest rack, and latest kill.'

'Nay, Seyd! I seek not to restrain thy
 rage, 163
Too justly moved for mercy to assuage;
My thoughts were only to secure for thee
His riches—thus released, he were not free:
Disabled, shorn of half his might and
 band,
His capture could but wait thy first com-
 mand.'

295

'His capture *could!*—and shall I then resign
One day to him—the wretch already mine?
Release my foe!—at whose remonstrance?
—thine! 171
Fair suitor!—to thy virtuous gratitude,
That thus repays this Giaour's relenting mood,
Which thee and thine alone of all could spare,
No doubt—regardless if the prize were fair, 175
My thanks and praise alike are due—now hear!
I have a counsel for thy gentler ear:
I do mistrust thee, woman! and each word
Of thine stamps truth on all Suspicion heard.
Borne in his arms through fire from yon Serai— 180
Say, wert thou lingering there with him to fly?
Thou need'st not answer—thy confession speaks,
Already reddening on thy guilty cheeks;
Then, lovely dame, bethink thee! and beware: 184
'Tis not *his* life alone may claim such care!
Another word and—nay—I need no more.
Accursed was the moment when he bore
Thee from the flames, which better far—but no—
I then had mourn'd thee with a lover's woe—
Now 'tis thy lord that warns—deceitful thing! 190
Know'st thou that I can clip thy wanton wing?
In words alone I am not wont to chafe:
Look to thyself, nor deem thy falsehood safe!'

He rose—and slowly, sternly thence withdrew,
Rage in his eye and threats in his adieu:
Ah! little reck'd that chief of womanhood— 196
Which frowns ne'er quell'd, nor menaces subdued;
And little deem'd he what thy heart, Gulnare!
When soft could feel, and when incensed could dare.
His doubts appear'd to wrong—nor yet she knew 200
How deep the root from whence compassion grew—
She was a slave—from such may captives claim
A fellow-feeling, differing but in name;
Still half unconscious—heedless of his wrath,
Again she ventured on the dangerous path, 205

Again his rage repell'd—until arose
That strife of thought, the source of woman's woes!

VI

Meanwhile, long, anxious, weary, still the same
Roll'd day and night: his soul could terror tame—
This fearful interval of doubt and dread,
When every hour might doom him worse than dead, 211
When every step that echo'd by the gate
Might entering lead where axe and stake await;
When every voice that grated on his ear
Might be the last that he could ever hear;
Could terror tame—that spirit stern and high 216
Had proved unwilling as unfit to die;
'Twas worn—perhaps decay'd—yet silent bore
That conflict, deadlier far than all before:
The heat of fight, the hurry of the gale,
Leave scarce one thought inert enough to quail; 221
But bound and fix'd in fetter'd solitude,
To pine, the prey of every changing mood;
To gaze on thine own heart; and meditate
Irrevocable faults, and coming fate—
Too late the last to shun—the first to mend— 226
To count the hours that struggle to thine end,
With not a friend to animate, and tell
To other ears that death became thee well;
Around thee foes to forge the ready lie,
And blot life's latest scene with calumny;
Before thee tortures, which the soul can dare,
Yet doubts how well the shrinking flesh may bear;
But deeply feels a single cry would shame—
To valour's praise thy last and dearest claim; 235
The life thou leav'st below, denied above
By kind monopolists of heavenly love;
And more than doubtful paradise—thy heaven
Of earthly hope—thy loved one from thee riven.
Such were the thoughts that outlaw must sustain, 240
And govern pangs surpassing mortal pain:
And those sustain'd he—boots it well or ill?
Since not to sink beneath, is something still!

VII

The first day pass'd—he saw not her—Gulnare—
The second, third—and still she came not there; 245

But what her words avouch'd, her charms
 had done,
Or else he had not seen another sun.
The fourth day roll'd along, and with the
 night
Came storm and darkness in their ming-
 ling might. 249
Oh! how he listen'd to the rushing deep,
That ne'er till now so broke upon his sleep;
And his wild spirit wilder wishes sent,
Roused by the roar of his own element!
Oft had he ridden on that winged wave,
And loved its roughness for the speed it
 gave; 255
And now its dashing echo'd on his ear,
A long known voice—alas! too vainly near!
Loud sung the wind above; and, doubly
 loud,
Shook o'er his turret cell the thunder-
 cloud;
And flash'd the lightning by the latticed
 bar, 260
To him more genial than the midnight star:
Close to the glimmering grate he dragg'd
 his chain;
And hoped *that* peril might not prove in
 vain.
He raised his iron hand to Heaven, and
 pray'd
One pitying flash to mar the form it made:
His steel and impious prayer attract
 alike— 266
The storm roll'd onward, and disdain'd to
 strike;
Its peal wax'd fainter—ceased—he felt
 alone,
As if some faithless friend had spurn'd his
 groan!

VIII

The midnight pass'd, and to the massy
 door 270
A light step came—it paused—it moved
 once more;
Slow turns the grating bolt and sullen key:
'Tis as his heart foreboded—that fair she!
Whate'er her sins, to him a guardian saint,
And beauteous still as hermit's hope can
 paint; 275
Yet changed since last within that cell she
 came,
More pale her cheek, more tremulous her
 frame:
On him she cast her dark and hurried eye,
Which spoke before her accents—'Thou
 must die!
Yes, thou must die—there is but one
 resource, 280
The last—the worst—if torture were not
 worse.'

'Lady! I look to none; my lips proclaim
What last proclaim'd they—Conrad still
 the same;

Why shouldst thou seek an outlaw's life to
 spare,
And change the sentence I deserve to bear?
Well have I earn'd—nor here alone—the
 meed 286
Of Seyd's revenge, by many a lawless
 deed.'

'Why should I seek? because—Oh! didst
 thou not
Redeem my life from worse than slavery's
 lot?
Why should I seek?—hath misery made
 thee blind 290
To the fond workings of a woman's mind?
And must I say?—albeit my heart rebel
With all that woman feels, but should not
 tell—
Because, despite thy crimes, that heart is
 moved:
It fear'd thee, thank'd thee, pitied, mad-
 den'd, loved. 295
Reply not, tell not now thy tale again,
Thou lov'st another, and I love in vain:
Though fond as mine her bosom, form
 more fair,
I rush through peril which she would not
 dare.
If that thy heart to hers were truly dear,
Were I thine own thou wert not lonely
 here: 301
An outlaw's spouse and leave her lord to
 roam!
What hath such gentle dame to do with
 home?
But speak not now—o'er thine and o'er
 my head
Hangs the keen sabre by a single thread;
If thou hast courage still, and wouldst be
 free, 306
Receive this poniard—rise and follow me!'

'Ay—in my chains! my steps will gently
 tread,
With these adornments, o'er each slumber-
 ing head! 309
Thou hast forgot—is this a garb for flight?
Or is that instrument more fit for fight?'

'Misdoubting Corsair! I have gain'd the
 guard,
Ripe for revolt, and greedy for reward.
A single word of mine removes that chain:
Without some aid how here could I re-
 main? 315
Well, since we met, hath sped my busy
 time,
If in aught evil, for thy sake the crime:
The crime—'tis none to punish those of
 Seyd.
That hated tyrant, Conrad—he must
 bleed!
I see thee shudder, but my soul is changed—
Wrong'd, spurn'd, reviled, and it shall be
 avenged— 321

Accused of what till now my heart dis-
 dain'd—
Too faithful, though to bitter bondage
 chain'd.
Yes, smile!—but he had little cause to
 sneer,
I was not treacherous then, nor thou too
 dear: 325
But he has said it—and the jealous well—
Those tyrants, teasing, tempting to rebel—
Deserve the fate their fretting lips foretell.
I never loved—he bought me—somewhat
 high—
Since with me came a heart he could not
 buy. 330
I was a slave unmurmuring; he hath said,
But for his rescue I with thee had fled.
'Twas false thou know'st—but let such
 augurs rue,
Their words are omens insult renders true.
Nor was thy respite granted to my prayer;
This fleeting grace was only to prepare
New torments for thy life, and my despair.
Mine too he threatens; but his dotage still
Would fain reserve me for his lordly will:
When wearier of these fleeting charms and
 me, 340
There yawns the sack, and yonder rolls the
 sea!
What, am I then a toy for dotard's play,
To wear but till the gilding frets away?
I saw thee—loved thee—owe thee all—
 would save,
If but to show how grateful is a slave.
But had he not thus menaced fame and
 life— 346
(And well he keeps his oaths pronounced
 in strife)—
I still had saved thee, but the Pacha spared.
Now I am all thine own, for all prepared:
Thou lov'st me not, nor know'st—or but
 the worst. 350
Alas! *this* love—*that* hatred—are the
 first—
Oh! couldst thou prove my truth, thou
 wouldst not start,
Nor fear the fire that lights an Eastern heart;
'Tis now the beacon of thy safety—now
It points within the port a Mainote prow:
But in one chamber, where our path must
 lead, 356
There sleeps—he must not wake—the op-
 pressor Seyd!'

'Gulnare—Gulnare—I never felt till now
My abject fortune, wither'd fame so low:
Seyd is mine enemy; had swept my band
From earth with ruthless but with open
 hand, 361
And therefore came I, in my bark of war,
To smite the smiter with the scimitar;
Such is my weapon—not the secret knife;
Who spares a woman's seeks not slumber's
 life. 365

Thine saved I gladly, Lady—not for this;
Let me not deem that mercy shown amiss.
Now fare thee well—more peace be with
 thy breast!
Night wears apace, my last of earthly
 rest!'

'Rest! rest! by sunrise must thy sinews
 shake, 370
And thy limbs writhe around the ready
 stake.
I heard the order—saw—I will not see—
If thou wilt perish, I will fall with thee.
My life, my love, my hatred—all below
Are on this cast—Corsair! 'tis but a blow!
Without it flight were idle—how evade
His sure pursuit?—my wrongs too un-
 repaid,
My youth disgraced, the long, long wasted
 years,
One blow shall cancel with our future
 fears;
But since the dagger suits thee less than
 brand, 380
I'll try the firmness of a female hand.
The guards are gain'd—one moment all
 were o'er—
Corsair! we meet in safety or no more;
If errs my feeble hand, the morning cloud
Will hover o'er thy scaffold, and my
 shroud.' 385

IX

She turn'd, and vanish'd ere he could re-
 ply,
But his glance follow'd far with eager eye;
And gathering, as he could, the links that
 bound
His form, to curl their length, and curb
 their sound,
Since bar and bolt no more his steps pre-
 clude, 390
He, fast as fetter'd limbs allow, pursued.
'Twas dark and winding, and he knew not
 where
That passage led; nor lamp nor guard was
 there:
He sees a dusky glimmering—shall he seek
Or shun that ray so indistinct and weak?
Chance guides his steps—a freshness seems
 to bear 396
Full on his brow, as if from morning air;
He reach'd an open gallery—on his eye
Gleam'd the last star of night, the clearing
 sky:
Yet scarcely heeded these—another light
From a lone chamber struck upon his
 sight. 401
Towards it he moved; a scarcely closing
 door
Reveal'd the ray within, but nothing more.
With hasty step a figure outward pass'd,
Then paused, and turn'd—and paused—
 'tis she at last! 405

No poniard in that hand, nor sign of ill—
Thanks to that softening heart—she
 could not kill!'
Again he look'd, the wildness of her eye
Starts from the day abrupt and fearfully.
She stopp'd—threw back her dark far-
 floating hair, 410
That nearly veil'd her face and bosom fair,
As if she late had bent her leaning head
Above some object of her doubt or dread.
They meet—upon her brow—unknown,
 forgot—
Her hurrying hand had left—'twas but a
 spot— 415
Its hue was all he saw, and scarce with-
 stood—
Oh! slight but certain pledge of crime—
 'tis blood!

X

He had seen battle—he had brooded lone
O'er promised pangs to sentenced guilt
 foreshown;
He had been tempted, chasten'd, and the
 chain 420
Yet on his arms might ever there remain:
But ne'er from strife, captivity, remorse—
From all his feelings in their inmost
 force—
So thrill'd, so shudder'd every creeping
 vein,
As now they froze before that purple stain.
That spot of blood, that light but guilty
 streak, 426
Had banish'd all the beauty from her
 cheek!
Blood he had view'd, could view un-
 moved—but then
It flow'd in combat, or was shed by men!

XI

'Tis done—he nearly waked—but it is
 done. 430
Corsair! he perish'd—thou art dearly won.
All words would now be vain—away—
 away!
Our bark is tossing—'tis already day.
The few gain'd over, now are wholly mine,
And these thy yet surviving band shall
 join: 435
Anon my voice shall vindicate my hand,
When once our sail forsakes this hated
 strand.'

XII

She clapp'd her hands, and through the
 gallery pour,
Equipp'd for flight, her vassals—Greek
 and Moor;
Silent but quick they stoop, his chains un-
 bind, 440
Once more his limbs are free as mountain
 wind!

But on his heavy heart such sadness sate,
As if they there transferr'd that iron
 weight.
No words are utter'd—at her sign, a door
Reveals the secret passage to the shore:
The city lies behind—they speed, they
 reach 446
The glad waves dancing on the yellow
 beach;
And Conrad following, at her beck, obey'd,
Nor cared he now if rescued or betray'd;
Resistance were as useless as if Seyd
Yet lived to view the doom his ire decreed.

XIII

Embark'd, the sail unfurl'd, the light
 breeze blew—
How much had Conrad's memory to re-
 view!
Sunk he in contemplation, till the cape
Where last he anchor'd rear'd its giant
 shape. 455
Ah! since that fatal night, though brief the
 time,
Had swept an age of terror, grief, and
 crime,
As its far shadow frown'd above the mast,
He veil'd his face, and sorrow'd as he
 pass'd;
He thought of all—Gonsalvo and his
 band, 460
His fleeting triumph and his failing hand;
He thought on her afar, his lonely bride:
He turn'd and saw—Gulnare, the homi-
 cide!

XIV

She watch'd his features till she could not
 bear 464
Their freezing aspect and averted air;
And that strange fierceness, foreign to her
 eye,
Fell quench'd in tears, too late to shed or
 dry.
She knelt beside him and his hand she
 press'd,
'Thou may'st forgive, though Allah's self
 detest;
But for that deed of darkness what wert
 thou? 470
Reproach me—but not yet—Oh! spare me
 now!
I am not what I seem—this fearful night
My brain bewilder'd—do not madden
 quite!
If I had never loved, though less my guilt,
Thou hadst not lived to—hate me—if thou
 wilt.' 475

XV

She wrongs his thoughts, they more him-
 self upbraid
Than her, though undesign'd, the wretch
 he made;

But speechless all, deep, dark, and unex-
prest,
They bleed within that silent cell—his
breast.
Still onward, fair the breeze, nor rough the
surge, 480
The blue waves sport around the stern
they urge;
Far on the horizon's verge appears a speck,
A spot—a mast—a sail—an armed deck!
Their little bark her men of watch descry,
And ampler canvas woos the wind from
high; 485
She bears her down majestically near,
Speed on her prow, and terror in her tier;
A flash is seen—the ball beyond their bow
Booms harmless, hissing to the deep be-
low. 489
Uprose keen Conrad from his silent trance,
A long, long absent gladness in his glance;
''Tis mine—my blood-red flag! again—
again—
I am not all deserted on the main!'
They own the signal, answer to the hail,
Hoist out the boat at once, and slacken
sail. 495
''Tis Conrad! Conrad!' shouting from the
deck,
Command nor duty could their transport
check!
With light alacrity and gaze of pride,
They view him mount once more his
vessel's side;
A smile relaxing in each rugged face, 500
Their arms can scarce forbear a rough
embrace.
He, half forgetting danger and defeat,
Returns their greeting as a chief may greet,
Wrings with a cordial grasp Anselmo's
hand,
And feels he yet can conquer and com-
mand! 505

XVI

These greetings o'er, the feelings that o'er-
flow,
Yet grieve to win him back without a
blow;
They sail'd prepared for vengeance—had
they known
A woman's hand secured that deed her
own,
She were their queen—less scrupulous are
they 510
Than haughty Conrad how they win their
way.
With many an asking smile, and wonder-
ing stare,
They whisper round, and gaze upon Gul-
nare;
And her—at once above—beneath her
sex,
Whom blood appall'd not, their regards
perplex. 515

To Conrad turns her faint imploring eye,
She drops her veil, and stands in silence
by;
Her arms are meekly folded on that breast
Which—Conrad safe—to fate resign'd the
rest.
Though worse than frenzy could that
bosom fill, 520
Extreme in love or hate, in good or ill,
The worst of crimes had left her woman
still!

XVII

This Conrad mark'd, and felt—ah! could
he less?—
Hate of that deed, but grief for her dis-
tress;
What she has done no tears can wash
away, 525
And Heaven must punish on its angry
day:
But—it was done: he knew, whate'er her
guilt,
For him that poniard smote, that blood
was spilt;
And he was free! and she for him had
given
Her all on earth, and more than all in
heaven! 530
And now he turn'd him to that dark-eyed
slave
Whose brow was bow'd beneath the
glance he gave,
Who now seem'd changed and humbled,
faint and meek,
But varying oft the colour of her cheek
To deeper shades of paleness—all its
red 535
That fearful spot which stain'd it from the
dead!
He took that hand—it trembled—now too
late—
So soft in love, so wildly nerved in hate;
He clasp'd that hand—it trembled—and
his own
Had lost its firmness, and his voice its
tone. 540
'Gulnare!'—but she replied not—'dear
Gulnare!'
She raised her eye—her only answer
there—
At once she sought and sunk in his em-
brace:
If he had driven her from that resting
place,
His had been more or less than mortal
heart, 545
But—good or ill—it bade her not depart
Perchance, but for the bodings of his
breast,
His latest virtue then had join'd the rest.
Yet even Medora might forgive the kiss
That ask'd from form so fair no more
than this, 550

300

The first, the last that Frailty stole from
 Faith—
To lips where Love had lavish'd all his
 breath,
To lips—whose broken sighs such frag-
 rance fling,
As he had fann'd them freshly with his
 wing!

XVIII

They gain by twilight's hour their lonely
 isle. 555
To them the very rocks appear to smile;
The haven hums with many a cheering
 sound,
The beacons blaze their wonted stations
 round,
The boats are darting o'er the curly bay,
And sportive dolphins bend them through
 the spray; 560
Even the hoarse sea-bird's shrill, dis-
 cordant shriek
Greets like the welcome of his tuneless
 beak!
Beneath each lamp that through its lattice
 gleams,
Their fancy paints the friends that trim
 the beams.
Oh! what can sanctify the joys of home,
Like Hope's gay glance from Ocean's
 troubled foam? 566

XIX

The lights are high on beacon and from
 bower,
And 'midst them Conrad seeks Medora's
 tower:
He looks in vain—'tis strange—and all
 remark,
Amid so many, hers alone is dark. 570
'Tis strange—of yore its welcome never
 fail'd,
Nor now, perchance, extinguish'd, only
 veil'd.
With the first boat descends he for the
 shore, 573
And looks impatient on the lingering oar.
Oh! for a wing beyond the falcon's flight,
To bear him like an arrow to that height!
With the first pause the resting rowers
 gave,
He waits not, looks not—leaps into the
 wave,
Strives through the surge, bestrides the
 beach, and high 579
Ascends the path familiar to his eye.

He reach'd his turret door—he paused—
 no sound
Broke from within; and all was night
 around.
He knock'd, and loudly—footstep nor
 reply
Announced that any heard or deem'd him
 nigh;

He knock'd, but faintly—for his trembling
 hand 585
Refused to aid his heavy heart's demand.
The portal opens—'tis a well-known face,
But not the form he panted to embrace.
Its lips are silent—twice his own essay'd,
And fail'd to frame the question they
 delay'd; 590
He snatch'd the lamp—its light will answer
 all—
It quits his grasp, expiring in the fall.
He would not wait for that reviving ray—
As soon could he have linger'd there for
 day;
But, glimmering through the dusky cor-
 ridor, 595
Another chequers o'er the shadow'd floor;
His steps the chamber gain—his eyes be-
 hold
All that his heart believed not—yet fore-
 told!

XX

He turn'd not—spoke not—sunk not—
 fix'd his look,
And set the anxious frame that lately
 shook: 600
He gazed—how long we gaze despite of
 pain,
And know, but dare not own, we gaze in
 vain!
In life itself she was so still and fair,
That death with gentler aspect wither'd
 there;
And the cold flowers her colder hand con-
 tain'd, 605
In that last grasp as tenderly were strain'd
As if she scarcely felt, but feign'd a sleep,
And made it almost mockery yet to weep:
The long dark lashes fringed her lids of
 snow,
And veil'd—thought shrinks from all that
 lurk'd below— 610
Oh! o'er the eye Death most exerts his
 might,
And hurls the spirit from her throne of
 light;
Sinks those blue orbs in that long last
 eclipse,
But spares, as yet, the charm around her
 lips—
Yet, yet they seem as they forbore to
 smile, 615
And wish'd repose,—but only for a while;
But the white shroud, and each extended
 tress,
Long, fair—but spread in utter lifeless-
 ness,
Which, late the sport of every summer wind,
Escaped the baffled wreath that strove to
 bind; 620
These—and the pale pure cheek, became
 the bier—
But she is nothing—wherefore is he here?

XXI

He ask'd no question—all were answer'd now
By the first glance on that still, marble brow.
It was enough—she died—what reck'd it how ? 625
The love of youth, the hope of better years,
The source of softest wishes, tenderest fears,
The only living thing he could not hate,
Was reft at once—and he deserved his fate,
But did not feel it less;—the good explore, 630
For peace, those realms where guilt can never soar:
The proud, the wayward—who have fix'd below
Their joy, and find this earth enough for woe,
Lose in that one their all—perchance a mite—
But who in patience parts with all delight ? 635
Full many a stoic eye and aspect stern
Mask hearts where grief hath little left to learn;
And many a withering thought lies hid, not lost,
In smiles that least befit who wear them most. 639

XXII

By those, that deepest feel, is ill exprest
The indistinctness of the suffering breast;
Where thousand thoughts begin to end in one,
Which seeks from all the refuge found in none;
No words suffice the secret soul to show,
For Truth denies all eloquence to Woe.
On Conrad's stricken soul exhaustion prest, 646
And stupor almost lull'd it into rest;
So feeble now—his mother's softness crept
To those wild eyes, which like an infant's wept:
It was the very weakness of his brain,
Which thus confess'd without relieving pain. 651
None saw his trickling tears—perchance, if seen,
That useless flood of grief had never been:
Nor long they flow'd—he dried them to depart,
In helpless—hopeless—brokenness of heart— 655
The sun goes forth, but Conrad's day is dim;
And the night cometh—ne'er to pass from him.

There is no darkness like the cloud of mind,
On Grief's vain eye—the blindest of the blind!
Which may not—dare not see—but turns aside 660
To blackest shade—nor will endure a guide!

XXIII

His heart was form'd for softness—warp'd to wrong;
Betray'd too early, and beguiled too long;
Each feeling pure—as falls the dropping dew
Within the grot—like that had harden'd too; 665
Less clear, perchance, its earthly trial pass'd,
But sunk, and chill'd, and petrified at last.
Yet tempests wear, and lightning cleaves the rock,
If such his heart, so shatter'd it the shock.
There grew one flower beneath its rugged brow, 670
Though dark the shade—it shelter'd—saved till now.
The thunder came—that bolt hath blasted both,
The Granite's firmness, and the Lily's growth:
The gentle plant hath left no leaf to tell
Its tale, but shrunk and wither'd where it fell; 675
And of its cold protector, blacken round
But shiver'd fragments on the barren ground!

XXIV

'Tis morn—to venture on his lonely hour
Few dare; though now Anselmo sought his tower.
He was not there, nor seen along the shore; 680
Ere night, alarm'd, their isle is traversed o'er:
Another morn—another bids them seek,
And shout his name till echo waxeth weak;
Mount, grotto, cavern, valley search'd in vain,
They find on shore a sea-boat's broken chain: 685
Their hope revives—they follow o'er the main.
'Tis idle all—moons roll on moons away,
And Conrad comes not, came not since that day:
Nor trace, nor tidings of his doom declare
Where lives his grief, or perish'd his despair! 690

Long mourn'd his band whom none could
 mourn beside;
And fair the monument they gave his
 bride:
For him they raise not the recording
 stone—

His death yet dubious, deeds too widely
 known;
He left a Corsair's name to other
 times, 695
Link'd with one virtue, and a thousand
 crimes.

LARA

CANTO THE FIRST

I

THE Serfs are glad through Lara's wide
 domain,
And Slavery half forgets her feudal chain;
He, their unhoped, but unforgotten lord,
The long self-exiled chieftain, is restored:
There be bright faces in the busy hall, 5
Bowls on the board, and banners on the
 wall;
Far checkering o'er the pictured window,
 plays
The unwonted faggot's hospitable blaze;
And gay retainers gather round the
 hearth,
With tongues all loudness, and with eyes
 all mirth. 10

II

The chief of Lara is returned again:
And why had Lara cross'd the bounding
 main?
Left by his sire, too young such loss to
 know,
Lord of himself,—that heritage of woe,
That fearful empire which the human
 breast 15
But holds to rob the heart within of rest!—
With none to check, and few to point in
 time
The thousand paths that slope the way to
 crime;
Then, when he most required command-
 ment, then
Had Lara's daring boyhood govern'd
 men. 20
It skills not, boots not step by step to
 trace
His youth through all the mazes of its
 race;
Short was the course his restlessness had
 run,
But long enough to leave him half undone.

III

And Lara left in youth his father-land;
But from the hour he waved his parting
 hand 26
Each trace wax'd fainter of his course, till
 all
Had nearly ceased his memory to recall.

His sire was dust, his vassals could de-
 clare,
'Twas all they knew, that Lara was not
 there; 30
Nor sent, nor came he, till conjecture
 grew
Cold in the many, anxious in the few.
His hall scarce echoes with his wonted
 name,
His portrait darkens in its fading frame,
Another chief consoled his destined bride,
The young forgot him, and the old had
 died; 36
'Yet doth he live!' exclaims the impatient
 heir,
And sighs for sables which he must not
 wear.
A hundred scutcheons deck with gloomy
 grace
The Laras' last and longest dwelling-
 place; 40
But one is absent from the mouldering
 file,
That now were welcome in that Gothic
 pile.

IV

He comes at last in sudden loneliness,
And whence they know not, why they
 need not guess;
They more might marvel, when the greet-
 ing's o'er, 45
Not that he came, but came not long
 before:
No train is his beyond a single page,
Of foreign aspect, and of tender age.
Years had roll'd on, and fast they speed
 away
To those that wander as to those that
 stay; 50
But lack of tidings from another clime
Had lent a flagging wing to weary Time.
They see, they recognise, yet almost deem
The present dubious, or the past a dream.

He lives, nor yet is past his manhood's
 prime, 55
Though sear'd by toil, and something
 touch'd by time;
His faults, whate'er they were, if scarce
 forgot,
Might be untaught him by his varied lot;

Nor good nor ill of late were known, his
 name
Might yet uphold his patrimonial fame:
His soul in youth was haughty, but his
 sins 61
No more than pleasure from the stripling
 wins;
And such, if not yet harden'd in their
 course,
Might be redeem'd, nor ask a long re-
 morse.

V

And they indeed were changed—'tis
 quickly seen, 65
Whate'er he be, 'twas not what he had
 been:
That brow in furrow'd lines had fix'd at
 last,
And spake of passions, but of passion
 past:
The pride, but not the fire, of early days,
Coldness of mien, and carelessness of
 praise; 70
A high demeanour, and a glance that took
Their thoughts from others by a single
 look;
And that sarcastic levity of tongue,
The stinging of a heart the world hath
 stung,
That darts in seeming playfulness around,
And makes those feel that will not own
 the wound; 76
All these seem'd his, and something more
 beneath
Than glance could well reveal, or accent
 breathe.
Ambition, glory, love, the common aim,
That some can conquer, and that all would
 claim, 80
Within his breast appear'd no more to
 strive,
Yet seem'd as lately they had been alive;
And some deep feeling it were vain to
 trace
At moments lighten'd o'er his livid face.

VI

Not much he loved long question of the
 past, 85
Nor told of wondrous wilds, and deserts
 vast,
In those far lands where he had wander'd
 lone,
And—as himself would have it seem—un-
 known;
Yet these in vain his eye could scarcely
 scan,
Nor glean experience from his fellow
 man; 90
But what he had beheld he shunn'd to
 show,
As hardly worth a stranger's care to
 know;

If still more prying such inquiry grew,
His brow fell darker, and his words more
 few.

VII

Not unrejoiced to see him once again,
Warm was his welcome to the haunts of
 men; 96
Born of high lineage, link'd in high com-
 mand,
He mingled with the magnates of his land;
Join'd the carousals of the great and
 gay,
And saw them smile or sigh their hours
 away; 100
But still he only saw, and did not share,
The common pleasure or the general care;
He did not follow what they all pursued
With hope still baffled, still to be renew'd;
Nor shadowy honour, nor substantial
 gain, 105
Nor beauty's preference, and the rival's
 pain:
Around him some mysterious circle
 thrown
Repell'd approach, and show'd him still
 alone;
Upon his eye sat something of reproof,
That kept at least frivolity aloof; 110
And things more timid that beheld him
 near
In silence gazed, or whisper'd mutual fear;
And they the wiser, friendlier few con-
 fess'd
They deem'd him better than his air ex-
 press'd.

VIII

'Twas strange—in youth all action and all
 life, 115
Burning for pleasure, not averse from
 strife;
Woman, the field, the ocean, all that gave
Promise of gladness, peril of a grave,
In turn he tried—he ransack'd all be-
 low,
And found his recompense in joy or woe,
No tame, trite medium; for his feelings
 sought 121
In that intenseness an escape from thought:
The tempest of his heart in scorn had
 gazed
On that the feebler elements had raised;
The rapture of his heart had look'd on
 high, 125
And ask'd if greater dwelt beyond the
 sky:
Chain'd to excess, the slave of each ex-
 treme,
How woke he from the wildness of that
 dream?
Alas! he told not—but he did awake
To curse the wither'd heart that would not
 break. 130

IX

ᴸooks, for his volume heretofore was
 Man,
ᵂith eye more curious he appear'd to
 scan,
ᴬnd oft, in sudden mood, for many a day,
ᶠrom all communion he would start
 away:
ᴬnd then, his rarely call'd attendants said,
ᵀhrough night's long hours would sound
 his hurried tread 136
ᴼ'er the dark gallery, where his fathers
 frown'd
ᴵn rude but antique portraiture around:
ᵀhey heard, but whisper'd—'*that* must
 not be known—
ᵀhe sound of words less earthly than his
 own. 140
ᵞes, they who chose might smile, but some
 had seen
ᵀhey scarce knew what, but more than
 should have been.
ᵂhy gazed he so upon the ghastly head
ᵂhich hands profane had gather'd from
 the dead,
ᵀhat still beside his open'd volume lay,
ᴬs if to startle all save him away? 146
ᵂhy slept he not when others were at rest?
ᵂhy heard no music, and received no
 guest?
ᴬll was not well, they deem'd—but where
 the wrong?
ˢome knew perchance—but 'twere a tale
 too long; 150
ᴬnd such besides were too discreetly wise,
ᵀo more than hint their knowledge in sur-
 mise;
ᴮut if they would—they could'—around
 the board
ᵀhus Lara's vassals prattled of their lord.

X

ᴵt was the night—and Lara's glassy stream
ᵀhe stars are studding, each with imaged
 beam; 156
ˢo calm, the waters scarcely seem to stray,
ᴬnd yet they glide like happiness away;
ᴿeflecting far and fairy-like from high
ᵀhe immortal lights that live along the
 sky: 160
ᴵts banks are fringed with many a goodly
 tree,
ᴬnd flowers the fairest that may feast the
 bee;
ˢuch in her chaplet infant Dian wove,
ᴬnd Innocence would offer to her love.
ᵀhese deck the shore; the waves their
 channel make 165
ᴵn windings bright and mazy like the
 snake.
ᴬll was so still, so soft in earth and air,
ᵞou scarce would start to meet a spirit
 there;

Secure that nought of evil could delight
To walk in such a scene, on such a night!
It was a moment only for the good: 171
So Lara deem'd, nor longer there he stood,
But turn'd in silence to his castle-gate;
Such scene his soul no more could con-
 template:
Such scene reminded him of other days,
Of skies more cloudless, moons of purer
 blaze, 176
Of nights more soft and frequent, hearts
 that now—
No—no—the storm may beat upon his
 brow,
Unfelt, unsparing—but a night like this,
A night of beauty, mock'd such breast as
 his. 180

XI

He turn'd within his solitary hall,
And his high shadow shot along the wall:
There were the painted forms of other
 times,
'Twas all they left of virtues or of crimes,
Save vague tradition; and the gloomy
 vaults 185
That hid their dust, their foibles, and their
 faults;
And half a column of the pompous page,
That speeds the specious tale from age to
 age;
Where history's pen its praise or blame
 supplies,
And lies like truth, and still most truly
 lies. 190
He wandering mused, and as the moon-
 beam shone
Through the dim lattice o'er the floor of
 stone,
And the high fretted roof, and saints, that
 there
O'er Gothic windows knelt in pictured
 prayer,
Reflected in fantastic figures grew, 195
Like life, but not like mortal life to view:
His bristling locks of sable, brow of
 gloom,
And the wide waving of his shaken plume,
Glanced like a spectre's attributes, and
 gave
His aspect all that terror gives the grave.

XII

'Twas midnight—all was slumber; the
 lone light 201
Dimm'd in the lamp, as loth to break the
 night.
Hark! there be murmurs heard in Lara's
 hall—
A sound, a voice, a shriek, a fearful call!
A long, loud shriek—and silence—did
 they hear 205
That frantic echo burst the sleeping ear?

They heard and rose, and, tremulously
 brave,
Rush where the sound invoked their aid
 to save;
They come with half-lit tapers in their
 hands,
And snatch'd in startled haste unbelted
 brands. 210

XIII

Cold as the marble where his length was
 laid,
Pale as the beam that o'er his features
 play'd,
Was Lara stretch'd; his half-drawn sabre
 near,
Dropp'd it should seem in more than
 nature's fear;
Yet he was firm, or had been firm till
 now, 215
And still defiance knit his gather'd brow;
Though mix'd with terror, senseless as he
 lay,
There lived upon his lip the wish to slay;
Some half-form'd threat in utterance there
 had died, 219
Some imprecation of despairing pride;
His eye was almost seal'd, but not forsook,
Even in its trance, the gladiator's look,
That oft awake his aspect could disclose,
And now was fix'd in horrible repose.
They raise him—bear him:—hush! he
 breathes, he speaks, 225
The swarthy blush recolours in his cheeks,
His lip resumes its red, his eye, though
 dim,
Rolls wide and wild, each slowly quivering
 limb
Recalls its function, but his words are
 strung
In terms that seem not of his native
 tongue; 230
Distinct but strange, enough they under-
 stand
To deem them accents of another land;
And such they were, and meant to meet an
 ear
That hears him not—alas! that cannot
 hear!

XIV

His page approach'd, and he alone ap-
 pear'd 235
To know the import of the words they
 heard;
And, by the changes of his cheek and
 brow,
They were not such as Lara should avow,
Nor he interpret,—yet with less surprise
Than those around their chieftain's state
 he eyes, 240
But Lara's prostrate form he bent beside,
And in that tongue which seem'd his own
 replied,

And Lara heeds those tones that gently
 seem
To soothe away the horrors of his dream—
If dream it were that thus could over
 throw 24
A breast that needed not ideal woe.

XV

Whate'er his frenzy dream'd or eye be
 held,—
If yet remember'd ne'er to be reveal'd,—
Rests at his heart: the custom'd mornin
 came,
And breathed new vigour in his shaken
 frame; 25
And solace sought he none from pries
 nor leech,
And soon the same in movement and in
 speech,
As heretofore he fill'd the passing hours
Nor less he smiles, nor more his forehea
 lowers,
Than these were wont; and if the comin
 night 25
Appear'd less welcome now to Lara's sight
He to his marvelling vassals show'd it not
Whose shuddering proved *their* fear wa
 less forgot.
In trembling pairs (alone they dared not
 crawl
The astonish'd slaves, and shun the fate
 hall; 26
The waving banner, and the clappin
 door,
The rustling tapestry, and the echoin
 floor;
The long dim shadows of surroundin
 trees,
The flapping bat, the night song of th
 breeze;
Aught they behold or hear their though
 appals, 26
As evening saddens o'er the dark grey wall

XVI

Vain thought! that hour of ne'er un
 ravell'd gloom
Came not again, or Lara could assume
A seeming of forgetfulness, that made
His vassals more amazed nor less afraid
Had memory vanish'd then with sense re
 stored? 27
Since word, nor look, nor gesture of thei
 lord
Betray'd a feeling that recall'd to these
That fever'd moment of his mind's disease
Was it a dream? was his the voice tha
 spoke 27
Those strange wild accents; his the cr
 that broke
Their slumber? his the oppress'd, o'er
 labour'd heart
That ceased to beat, the look that mad
 them start?

Could he who thus had suffer'd so forget,
When such as saw that suffering shudder
 yet? 280
Or did that silence prove his memory fix'd
Too deep for words, indelible, unmix'd
In that corroding secrecy which gnaws
The heart to show the effect, but not the
 cause?
Not so in him; his breast had buried
 both, 285
Nor common gazers could discern the
 growth
Of thoughts that mortal lips must leave
 half told;
They choke the feeble words that would
 unfold.

XVII

In him inexplicably mix'd appear'd
Much to be loved and hated, sought and
 fear'd; 290
Opinion varying o'er his hidden lot,
In praise or railing ne'er his name forgot:
His silence form'd a theme for others'
 prate—
They guess'd, they gazed, they fain would
 know his fate.
What had he been? what was he, thus un-
 known, 295
Who walk'd their world, his lineage only
 known?
A hater of his kind? yet some would
 say,
With them he could seem gay amidst the
 gay;
But own'd that smile, if oft observed and
 near,
Waned in its mirth, and wither'd to a
 sneer; 300
That smile might reach his lip, but pass'd
 not by,
None e'er could trace its laughter to his
 eye:
Yet there was softness too in his regard,
At times, a heart as not by nature hard,
But once perceived, his spirit seem'd to
 chide 305
Such weakness, as unworthy of its pride,
And steel'd itself, as scorning to redeem
One doubt from others' half-withheld
 esteem;
In self-inflicted penance of a breast
Which tenderness might once have wrung
 from rest; 310
A vigilance of grief that would compel
The soul to hate for having loved too well.

XVIII

There was in him a vital scorn of all:
As if the worst had fall'n which could be-
 fall,
He stood a stranger in this breathing
 world, 315
An erring spirit from another hurl'd;

A thing of dark imaginings, that shaped
By choice the perils he by chance escaped;
But 'scaped in vain, for in their memory
 yet
His mind would half exult and half re-
 gret: 320
With more capacity for love than earth
Bestows on most of mortal mould and
 birth,
His early dreams of good outstripp'd the
 truth,
And troubled manhood follow'd baffled
 youth;
With thought of years in phantom chase
 mis-spent, 325
And wasted powers for better purpose lent;
And fiery passions that had pour'd their
 wrath
In hurried desolation o'er his path,
And left the better feelings all at strife
In wild reflection o'er his stormy life;
But haughty still, and loth himself to blame,
He call'd on Nature's self to share the
 shame,
And charged all faults upon the fleshly
 form
She gave to clog the soul, and feast the
 worm; 334
Till he at last confounded good and ill,
And half mistook for fate the acts of will:
Too high for common selfishness, he could
At times resign his own for others' good,
But not in pity, not because he ought,
But in some strange perversity of thought,
That sway'd him onward with a secret
 pride 341
To do what few or none would do beside;
And this same impulse would, in tempting
 time,
Mislead his spirit equally to crime;
So much he soar'd beyond, or sunk be-
 neath, 345
The men with whom he felt condemn'd to
 breathe,
And long'd by good or ill to separate
Himself from all who shared his mortal
 state;
His mind abhorring this, had fix'd her
 throne
Far from the world, in regions of her
 own: 350
Thus coldly passing all that pass'd below,
His blood in temperate seeming now
 would flow:
Ah! happier if it ne'er with guilt had
 glow'd,
But ever in that icy smoothness flow'd!
'Tis true, with other men their path he
 walk'd, 355
And like the rest in seeming did and talk'd,
Nor outraged Reason's rules by flaw nor
 start,
His madness was not of the head, but
 heart;

And rarely wander'd in his speech, or
 drew
His thoughts so forth as to offend the
 view. 360

XIX

With all that chilling mystery of mien,
And seeming gladness to remain unseen,
He had (if 'twere not nature's boon) an
 art
Of fixing memory on another's heart:
It was not love perchance, nor hate, nor
 aught 365
That words can image to express the
 thought;
But they who saw him did not see in vain,
And once beheld, would ask of him again:
And those to whom he spake remember'd
 well,
And on the words, however light, would
 dwell: 370
None knew nor how, nor why, but he en-
 twined
Himself perforce around the hearer's mind;
There he was stamp'd, in liking, or in hate,
If greeted once; however brief the date
That friendship, pity, or aversion knew,
Still there within the inmost thought he
 grew. 376
You could not penetrate his soul, but
 found,
Despite your wonder, to your own he
 wound;
His presence haunted still; and from the
 breast
He forced an all unwilling interest: 380
Vain was the struggle in that mental net,
His spirit seem'd to dare you to forget!

XX

There is a festival, where knights and
 dames,
And aught that wealth or lofty lineage
 claims,
Appear—a high-born and a welcome
 guest 385
To Otho's hall came Lara with the rest.
The long carousal shakes the illumined
 hall,
Well speeds alike the banquet and the
 ball;
And the gay dance of bounding Beauty's
 train
Links grace and harmony in happiest
 chain: 390
Blest are the early hearts and gentle hands
That mingle there in well according bands;
It is a sight the careful brow might smooth,
And make Age smile, and dream itself to
 youth,
And Youth forget such hour was past on
 earth, 395
So springs the exulting bosom to that
 mirth!

XXI

And Lara gazed on these, sedately glad,
His brow belied him if his soul was sad
And his glance follow'd fast each flutterin
 fair,
Whose steps of lightness woke no ech
 there: 40
He lean'd against the lofty pillar nigh,
With folded arms and long attentive eye
Nor mark'd a glance so sternly fix'd o
 his—
Ill brook'd high Lara scrutiny like this:
At length he caught it, 'tis a face un
 known, 40
But seems as searching his, and his alone
Prying and dark, a stranger's by his mier
Who still till now had gazed on him un
 seen:
At length encountering meets the mutua
 gaze 40
Of keen inquiry, and of mute amaze;
On Lara's glance emotion gathering grew
As if distrusting that the stranger threw
Along the stranger's aspect, fix'd an
 stern,
Flash'd more than thence the vulgar ey
 could learn.

XXII

"'Tis he!' the stranger cried, and thos
 that heard 41
Re-echoed fast and far the whisper'
 word.
"'Tis he!'—''Tis who?' they question fa
 and near,
Till louder accents rung on Lara's ear;
So widely spread, few bosoms well coul
 brook
The general marvel, or that single look
But Lara stirr'd not, changed not, the sur
 prise 4:
That sprung at first to his arrested eyes
Seem'd now subsided, neither sunk ne
 raised
Glanced his eye round, though still th
 stranger gazed;
And drawing nigh, exclaim'd, wit
 haughty sneer, 42
"'Tis he! how came he thence?—wh:
 doth he here?'

XXIII

It were too much for Lara to pass by
Such questions, so repeated fierce an
 high;
With look collected, but with accent col
More mildly firm than petulantly bold,
He turn'd, and met the inquisitorial tone-
'My name is Lara!—when thine own
 known, 4:
Doubt not my fitting answer to requite
The unlook'd-for courtesy of such
 knight.

'Tis Lara!—further wouldst thou mark
or ask? 435
I shun no question, and I wear no mask.'
'Thou shunn'st no question! Ponder—is
there none
Thy heart must answer, though thine ear
would shun?
And deem'st thou me unknown too?
Gaze again!
At least thy memory was not given in
vain. 440
Oh! never canst thou cancel half her debt,
Eternity forbids thee to forget.'
With slow and searching glance upon his
face
Grew Lara's eyes, but nothing there could
trace
They knew, or chose to know—with
dubious look 445
He deign'd no answer, but his head he
shook,
And half contemptuous turn'd to pass
away;
But the stern stranger motion'd him to
stay.

A word!—I charge thee stay, and answer
here
To one, who, wert thou noble, were thy
peer, 450
But as thou wast and art—nay, frown not,
lord,
If false, 'tis easy to disprove the word—
But as thou wast and art, on thee looks
down,
Distrusts thy smiles, but shakes not at thy
frown.
Art thou not he? whose deeds——'
 'Whate'er I be,
Words wild as these, accusers like to
thee, 456
I list no further; those with whom they
weigh
May hear the rest, nor venture to gainsay
The wondrous tale no doubt thy tongue
can tell,
Which thus begins so courteously and
well. 460
Let Otho cherish here his polish'd guest,
To him my thanks and thoughts shall be
express'd.'
And here their wondering host hath inter-
posed—
Whate'er there be between you undis-
closed, 464
This is no time nor fitting place to mar
The mirthful meeting with a wordy war.
If thou, Sir Ezzelin, hast aught to show
Which it befits Count Lara's ear to know,
To-morrow, here, or elsewhere, as may
best
Beseem your mutual judgment, speak the
rest; 470
I pledge myself for thee, as not unknown,

Though, like Count Lara, now return'd
alone
From other lands, almost a stranger
grown;
And if from Lara's blood and gentle birth
I augur right of courage and of worth,
He will not that untainted line belie, 476
Nor aught that knighthood may accord,
deny.'

'To-morrow be it,' Ezzelin replied,
'And here our several worth and truth be
tried;
I gage my life, my falchion to attest 480
My words, so may I mingle with the blest!'
What answers Lara? to its centre shrunk
His soul, in deep abstraction sudden sunk;
The words of many, and the eyes of all
That there were gather'd, seem'd on him
to fall; 485
But his were silent, his appear'd to stray
In far forgetfulness away—away—
Alas! that heedlessness of all around
Bespoke remembrance only too profound.

XXIV

'To-morrow!—ay, to-morrow!' further
word 490
Than those repeated none from Lara
heard:
Upon his brow no outward passion spoke;
From his large eye no flashing anger broke;
Yet there was something fix'd in that low
tone,
Which show'd resolve, determined, though
unknown. 495
He seized his cloak—his head he slightly
bow'd,
And passing Ezzelin, he left the crowd;
And as he pass'd him, smiling met the
frown
With which that chieftain's brow would
bear him down:
It was nor smile of mirth, nor struggling
pride 500
That curbs to scorn the wrath it cannot
hide;
But that of one in his own heart secure
Of all that he would do, or could endure.
Could this mean peace? the calmness of
the good?
Or guilt grown old in desperate hardi-
hood? 505
Alas! too like in confidence are each,
For man to trust to mortal look or speech;
From deeds, and deeds alone, may he dis-
cern
Truths which it wrings the unpractised
heart to learn.

XXV

And Lara call'd his page, and went his
way— 510
Well could that stripling word or sign obey:

His only follower from those climes afar,
Where the soul glows beneath a brighter
 star;
For Lara left the shore from whence he
 sprung, 514
In duty patient, and sedate though young;
Silent as him he served, his faith appears
Above his station, and beyond his years.
Though not unknown the tongue of Lara's
 land,
In such from him he rarely heard com-
 mand;
But fleet his step, and clear his tones
 would come, 520
When Lara's lip breathed forth the words
 of home:
Those accents, as his native mountains
 dear,
Awake their absent echoes in his ear,
Friends', kindred's, parents' wonted voice
 recall,
Now lost, abjured, for one—his friend, his
 all: 525
For him earth now disclosed no other
 guide;
What marvel then he rarely left his side?

XXVI

Light was his form, and darkly delicate
That brow whereon his native sun had
 sate,
But had not marr'd, though in his beams
 he grew, 530
The cheek where oft the unbidden blush
 shone through;
Yet not such blush as mounts when health
 would show
All the heart's hue in that delighted glow;
But 'twas a hectic tint of secret care
That for a burning moment fever'd there;
And the wild sparkle of his eye seem'd
 caught 536
From high, and lighten'd with electric
 thought,
Though its black orb those long low
 lashes' fringe
Had temper'd with a melancholy tinge;
Yet less of sorrow than of pride was there,
Or, if 'twere grief, a grief that none should
 share: 541
And pleased not him the sports that please
 his age,
The tricks of youth, the frolics of the
 page;
For hours on Lara he would fix his glance,
As all-forgotten in that watchful trance;
And from his chief withdrawn, he wan-
 der'd lone, 546
Brief were his answers, and his questions
 none;
His walk the wood, his sport some foreign
 book;
His resting-place the bank that curbs the
 brook;

He seem'd, like him he served, to live
 apart 550
From all that lures the eye, and fills the
 heart;
To know no brotherhood, and take from
 earth
No gift beyond that bitter boon—our birth.

XXVII

If aught he loved, 'twas Lara; but was
 shown
His faith in reverence and in deeds alone;
In mute attention; and his care, which
 guess'd 556
Each wish, fulfill'd it ere the tongue ex-
 press'd.
Still there was haughtiness in all he did,
A spirit deep that brook'd not to be chid;
His zeal, though more than that of servile
 hands, 560
In act alone obeys, his air commands,
As if 'twas Lara's less than *his* desire
That thus he served, but surely not for hire.
Slight were the tasks enjoin'd him by his
 lord, 564
To hold the stirrup, or to bear the sword;
To tune his lute, or, if he will'd it more,
On tomes of other times and tongues to
 pore;
But ne'er to mingle with the menial train,
To whom he show'd nor deference nor dis-
 dain,
But that well-worn reserve which proved
 he knew 570
No sympathy with that familiar crew:
His soul, whate'er his station or his stem,
Could bow to Lara, not descend to them.
Of higher birth he seem'd, and better days,
Nor mark of vulgar toil that hand betrays,
So femininely white it might bespeak 576
Another sex, when match'd with that
 smooth cheek,
But for his garb, and something in his gaze,
More wild and high than woman's eye
 betrays;
A latent fierceness that far more became
His fiery climate than his tender frame:
True, in his words it broke not from his
 breast, 582
But from his aspect might be more than
 guess'd.
Kaled his name, though rumour said he
 bore
Another ere he left his mountain-shore;
For sometimes he would hear, however
 nigh, 586
That name repeated loud without reply,
As unfamiliar, or, if roused again,
Start to the sound, as but remember'd
 then;
Unless 'twas Lara's wonted voice that
 spake,
For then, ear, eyes, and heart would all
 awake. 591

310

XXVIII

He had look'd down upon the festive hall,
And mark'd that sudden strife so mark'd of all:
And when the crowd around and near him told 594
Their wonder at the calmness of the bold,
Their marvel how the high-born Lara bore
such insult from a stranger, doubly sore,
The colour of young Kaled went and came,
The lip of ashes, and the cheek of flame;
And o'er his brow the dampening heart-drops threw 600
The sickening iciness of that cold dew,
That rises as the busy bosom sinks
With heavy thoughts from which reflection shrinks.
Yes—there be things which we must dream and dare, 604
And execute ere thought be half aware:
Whate'er might Kaled's be, it was enow
To seal his lip, but agonise his brow.
He gazed on Ezzelin till Lara cast
That sidelong smile upon the knight he pass'd; 609
When Kaled saw that smile his visage fell,
As if on something recognised right well:
His memory read in such a meaning more
Than Lara's aspect unto others wore:
Forward he sprung—a moment, both were gone, 614
And all within that hall seem'd left alone;
Each had so fix'd his eye on Lara's mien,
All had so mix'd their feelings with that scene,
That when his long dark shadow through the porch
To more relieves the glare of yon high torch,
Each pulse beats quicker, and all bosoms seem 620
To bound as doubting from too black a dream,
Such as we know is false, yet dread in sooth,
Because the worst is ever nearest truth.
And they are gone—but Ezzelin is there,
With thoughtful visage and imperious air;
But long remain'd not; ere an hour expired
He waved his hand to Otho and retired.

XXIX

The crowd are gone, the revellers at rest;
The courteous host, and all-approving guest,
Again to that accustom'd couch must creep 630
Where joy subsides, and sorrow sighs to sleep,
And man, o'erlabour'd with his being's strife,
Shrinks to that sweet forgetfulness of life:
There lie love's feverish hope, and cunning's guile,

Hate's working brain, and lull'd ambition's wile; 635
O'er each vain eye oblivion's pinions wave,
And quench'd existence crouches in a grave.
What better name may slumber's bed become?
Night's sepulchre, the universal home,
Where weakness, strength, vice, virtue, sunk supine, 640
Alike in naked helplessness recline;
Glad for a while to heave unconscious breath,
Yet wake to wrestle with the dread of death,
And shun, though day but dawn on ills increased,
That sleep, the loveliest, since it dreams the least. 645

CANTO THE SECOND

I

Night wanes—the vapours round the mountains curl'd
Melt into morn, and Light awakes the world,
Man has another day to swell the past,
And lead him near to little but his last:
But mighty Nature bounds as from her birth, 5
The sun is in the heavens, and life on earth;
Flowers in the valley, splendour in the beam,
Health on the gale, and freshness in the stream.
Immortal man! behold her glories shine,
And cry, exulting inly, 'They are thine!'
Gaze on, while yet thy gladden'd eye may see: 11
A morrow comes when they are not for thee:
And grieve what may above thy senseless bier,
Nor earth nor sky will yield a single tear;
Nor cloud shall gather more, nor leaf shall fall, 15
Nor gale breathe forth one sigh for thee, for all;
But creeping things shall revel in their spoil,
And fit thy clay to fertilise the soil.

II

'Tis morn—'tis noon—assembled in the hall,
The gather'd chieftains come to Otho's call; 20
'Tis now the promised hour, that must proclaim
The life or death of Lara's future fame;
And Ezzelin his charge may here unfold,
And whatsoe'er the tale, it must be told.

311

His faith was pledged, and Lara's promise
 given, 25
To meet it in the eye of man and heaven.
Why comes he not? Such truths to be
 divulged,
Methinks the accuser's rest is long in-
 dulged.

III

The hour is past and Lara too is there,
With self-confiding, coldly patient air; 30
Why comes not Ezzelin? The hour is past,
And murmurs rise, and Otho's brow's
 o'ercast.
'I know my friend! his faith I cannot fear,
If yet he be on earth, expect him here;
The roof that held him in the valley stands
Between my own and noble Lara's lands;
My halls from such a guest had honour
 gain'd,
Nor had Sir Ezzelin his host disdain'd,
But that some previous proof forbade his
 stay, 39
And urged him to prepare against to-day;
The word I pledged for his I pledge again,
Or will myself redeem his knighthood's
 stain.' 42

He ceased—and Lara answered, 'I am here
To lend at thy demand a listening ear
To tales of evil from a stranger's tongue,
Whose words already might my heart have
 wrung, 46
But that I deem'd him scarcely less than mad,
Or, at the worst, a foe ignobly bad.
I know him not—but me it seems he knew
In lands where—but I must not trifle too:
Produce this babbler—or redeem the
 pledge; 51
Here in thy hold, and with thy falchion's
 edge.'

Proud Otho on the instant, reddening,
 threw
His glove on earth, and forth his sabre flew.
'The last alternative befits me best, 55
And thus I answer for mine absent guest.'

With cheek unchanging from its sallow
 gloom,
However near his own or other's tomb;
With hand, whose almost careless coolness
 spoke
Its grasp well used to deal the sabre-stroke;
With eye, though calm, determin'd not to
 spare, 61
Did Lara too his willing weapon bare.
In vain the circling chieftains round them
 closed,
For Otho's frenzy would not be opposed;
And from his lip those words of insult
 fell— 65
His sword is good who can maintain them
 well.

IV

Short was the conflict; furious, blindly
 rash,
Vain Otho gave his bosom to the gash:
He bled, and fell; but not with deadly
 wound,
Stretch'd by a dexterous sleight along the
 ground. 7
'Demand thy life!' He answer'd not: and
 then
From that red floor he ne'er had risen
 again,
For Lara's brow upon the moment grew
Almost to blackness in its demon hue;
And fiercer shook his angry falchion now
Than when his foe's was levell'd at his
 brow; 7
Then all was stern collectedness and art,
Now rose the unleaven'd hatred of his
 heart;
So little sparing to the foe he fell'd,
That when the approaching crowd his arm
 withheld, 8
He almost turn'd the thirsty point on those
Who thus for mercy dared to interpose;
But to a moment's thought that purpose
 bent;
Yet look'd he on him still with eye intent,
As if he loathed the ineffectual strife 8
That left a foe, howe'er o'ercome, with life
As if to search how far the wound he gave
Had sent its victim onward to his grave.

V

They raised the bleeding Otho, and the
 Leech
Forbade all present question, sign, and
 speech: 9
The others met within a neighbouring hall
And he, incensed, and heedless of them
 all,
The cause and conqueror in this sudden
 fray,
In haughty silence slowly strode away;
He back'd his steed, his homeward path he
 took, 9
Nor cast on Otho's towers a single look.

VI

But where was he? that meteor of a night
Who menaced but to disappear with light
Where was this Ezzelin? who came and
 went,
To leave no other trace of his intent. 10
He left the dome of Otho long ere morn
In darkness, yet so well the path was worn
He could not miss it: near his dwelling lay
But there he was not, and with coming day
Came fast inquiry, which unfolded nough
Except the absence of the chief it sought
A chamber tenantless, a steed at rest,
His host alarm'd, his murmuring squire
 distress'd:

heir search extends along, around the path,
dread to meet the marks of prowlers' wrath: 110
ut none are there, and not a brake hath borne
or gout of blood, nor shred of mantle torn;
or fall nor struggle hath defaced the grass,
hich still retains a mark where murder was; 114
or dabbling fingers left to tell the tale,
e bitter print of each convulsive nail,
hen agonisèd hands that cease to guard,
ound in the pang that smoothness of the sward.
me such had been, if here a life was reft,
ut these were not; and doubting hope is left; 120
nd strange suspicion, whispering Lara's name,
ow daily mutters o'er his blacken'd fame;
en sudden silent when his form appear'd,
waits the absence of the thing it fear'd,
gain its wonted wondering to renew, 125
nd dye conjecture with a darker hue.

VII

ays roll along, and Otho's wounds are heal'd,
ut not his pride; and hate no more conceal'd:
e was a man of power, and Lara's foe,
e friend of all who sought to work him woe, 130
nd from his country's justice now demands
ccount of Ezzelin at Lara's hands.
ho else than Lara could have cause to fear
is presence? who had made him disappear,
not the man on whom his menaced charge 135
ad sate too deeply were he left at large?
e general rumour ignorantly loud,
e mystery dearest to the curious crowd;
e seeming friendlessness of him who strove
win no confidence, and wake no love;
e sweeping fierceness which his soul betray'd, 141
e skill with which he wielded his keen blade;
here had his arm unwarlike caught that art?
here had that fierceness grown upon his heart? 144
r it was not the blind capricious rage
word can kindle and a word assuage;

But the deep working of a soul unmix'd
With aught of pity where its wrath had fix'd;
Such as long power and overgorged success
Concentrates into all that's merciless:
These, link'd with that desire which ever sways 151
Mankind, the rather to condemn than praise,
'Gainst Lara gathering raised at length a storm,
Such as himself might fear, and foes would form, 154
And he must answer for the absent head
Of one that haunts him still, alive or dead.

VIII

Within that land was many a malcontent,
Who cursed the tyranny to which he bent;
That soil full many a wringing despot saw
Who work'd his wantonness in form of law; 160
Long war without and frequent broil within
Had made a path for blood and giant sin,
That waited but a signal to begin
New havoc, such as civil discord blends,
Which knows no neuter, owns but foes or friends; 165
Fix'd in his feudal fortress each was lord,
In word and deed obey'd, in soul abhorr'd.
Thus Lara had inherited his lands,
And with them pining hearts and sluggish hands;
But that long absence from his native clime 170
Had left him stainless of oppression's crime,
And now, diverted by his milder sway,
All dread by slow degrees had worn away.
The menials felt their usual awe alone,
But more for him than them that fear was grown; 175
They deem'd him now unhappy, though at first
Their evil judgment augur'd of the worst,
And each long restless night, and silent mood,
Was traced to sickness, fed by solitude:
And though his lonely habits threw of late 180
Gloom o'er his chamber, cheerful was his gate;
For thence the wretched ne'er unsoothed withdrew,
For them, at least, his soul compassion knew.
Cold to the great, contemptuous to the high,
The humble pass'd not his unheeding eye;
Much he would speak not, but beneath his roof 186
They found asylum oft, and ne'er reproof.

And they who watch'd might mark that,
 day by day,
Some new retainers gather'd to his sway;
But most of late, since Ezzelin was lost,
He play'd the courteous lord and bounte-
 ous host: 191
Perchance his strife with Otho made him
 dread
Some snare prepared for his obnoxious
 head;
Whate'er his view, his favour more obtains
With these, the people, than his fellow
 thanes. 195
If this were policy, so far 'twas sound,
The million judged but of him as they
 found;
From him by sterner chiefs to exile driven
They but required a shelter, and 'twas given.
By him no peasant mourn'd his rifled cot,
And scarce the Serf could murmur o'er his
 lot; 201
With him old avarice found its hoard secure,
With him contempt forbore to mock the
 poor;
Youth present cheer and promised recom-
 pense
Detain'd, till all too late to part from thence:
To hate he offer'd, with the coming
 change, 206
The deep reversion of delay'd revenge;
To love, long baffled by the unequal match,
The well-won charms success was sure to
 snatch. 209
All now was ripe, he waits but to proclaim
That slavery nothing which was still a name.
The moment came, the hour when Otho
 thought
Secure at last the vengeance which he
 sought: 213
His summons found the destined criminal
Begirt by thousands in his swarming hall,
Fresh from their feudal fetters newly riven,
Defying earth, and confident of heaven.
That morning he had freed the soil-bound
 slaves,
Who dig no land for tyrants but their
 graves!
Such is their cry—some watchword for the
 fight 220
Must vindicate the wrong, and warp the
 right;
Religion — freedom — vengeance — what
 you will,
A word 's enough to raise mankind to kill;
Some factious phrase by cunning caught
 and spread,
That guilt may reign, and wolves and
 worms be fed! 225

IX

Throughout that clime the feudal chiefs
 had gain'd
Such sway, their infant monarch hardly
 reign'd;

Now was the hour for faction's reb
 growth,
The Serfs contemn'd the one, and hate
 both: 2
They waited but a leader, and they four
One to their cause inseparably bound;
By circumstance compell'd to plun
 again,
In self-defence, amidst the strife of mer
Cut off by some mysterious fate from tho
Whom birth and nature meant not for h
 foes, 2
Had Lara from that night, to him accurs
Prepared to meet, but not alone, the wors
Some reason urged, whate'er it was,
 shun
Inquiry into deeds at distance done; 2
By mingling with his own the cause of a
E'en if he fail'd, he still delay'd his fall.
The sullen calm that long his bosom kep
The storm that once had spent itself ar
 slept,
Roused by events that seem'd foredoom
 to urge
His gloomy fortunes to their utmost verg
Burst forth, and made him all he once ha
 been, 2
And is again; he only changed the scen
Light care had he for life, and less for fam
But not less fitted for the desperate gam
He deem'd himself mark'd out for othe
 hate,
And mock'd at ruin so they shared his fat
What cared he for the freedom of th
 crowd?
He raised the humble but to bend th
 proud.
He had hoped quiet in his sullen lair,
But man and destiny beset him there:
Inured to hunters, he was found at bay
And they must kill, they cannot snare th
 prey. 2
Stern, unambitious, silent, he had been
Henceforth a calm spectator of life's scen
But dragg'd again upon the arena, sto
A leader not unequal to the feud; 2
In voice, mien, gesture, savage natu
 spoke,
And from his eye the gladiator broke.

X

What boots the oft-repeated tale of strif
The feast of vultures, and the waste of lif
The varying fortune of each separate fiel
The fierce that vanquish, and the faint th
 yield?
The smoking ruin, and the crumbled wal
In this the struggle was the same with a
Save that distemper'd passions lent the
 force 2
In bitterness that banish'd all remorse.
None sued, for Mercy knew her cry w
 vain,
The captive died upon the battle-plain:

either cause, one rage alone possess'd

ıe empire of the alternate victor's breast;

nd they that smote for freedom or for

 sway, 276

eem'd few were slain, while more re-

 main'd to slay.

was too late to check the wasting brand,

nd Desolation reap'd the famish'd land;

ıe torch was lighted, and the flame was

 spread, 280

nd Carnage smiled upon her daily dead.

XI

esh with the nerve the new-born impulse

 strung,

ıe first success to Lara's numbers clung:

ıt that vain victory hath ruin'd all;

ıey form no longer to their leader's call:

 blind confusion on the foe they press,

nd think to snatch is to secure success.

ıe lust of booty, and the thirst of hate,

ıre on the broken brigands to their fate:

 vain he doth whate'er a chief may do,

ɔ check the headlong fury of that crew;

 vain their stubborn ardour he would

 tame, 292

ıe hand that kindles cannot quench the

 flame;

ıe wary foe alone hath turn'd their

 mood,

nd shown their rashness to that erring

 brood: 295

ıe feign'd retreat, the nightly ambus-

 cade,

ıe daily harass, and the fight delay'd,

ıe long privation of the hoped supply,

ıe tentless rest beneath the humid sky,

ıe stubborn wall that mocks the leaguer's

 art, 300

nd palls the patience of his baffled heart,

f these they had not deem'd: the battle-

 day

hey could encounter as a veteran may;

ıt more preferr'd the fury of the strife,

nd present death, to hourly suffering

 life: 305

nd famine wrings, and fever sweeps away

is numbers melting fast from their array:

ıtemperate triumph fades to discontent,

nd Lara's soul alone seems still unbent:

ıt few remain to aid his voice and hand,

nd thousands dwindled to a scanty band:

esperate, though few, the last and best

 remain'd 312

ɔ mourn the discipline they late dis-

 dain'd.

ne hope survives, the frontier is not far,

nd thence they may escape from native

 war; 315

nd bear within them to the neighbour-

 ing state

n exile's sorrows, or an outlaw's hate:

ard is the task their father-land to quit,

ıt harder still to perish or submit.

XII

It is resolved—they march—consenting

 Night 320

Guides with her star their dim and torch-

 less flight;

Already they perceive its tranquil beam

Sleep on the surface of the barrier stream;

Already they descry—Is yon the bank?

Away! 'tis lined with many a hostile rank.

Return or fly!—What glitters in the rear?

'Tis Otho's banner—the pursuer's spear!

Are those the shepherds' fires upon the

 height?

Alas! they blaze too widely for the flight:

Cut off from hope, and compass'd in the

 toil, 330

Less blood perchance hath bought a

 richer spoil!

XIII

A moment's pause—'tis but to breathe

 their band,

Or shall they onward press, or here with-

 stand?

It matters little—if they charge the foes

Who by their border-stream their march

 oppose, 335

Some few, perchance, may break and pass

 the line,

However link'd to baffle such design.

'The charge be ours! to wait for their

 assault

Were fate well worthy of a coward's halt.'

Forth flies each sabre, rein'd is every steed,

And the next word shall scarce outstrip

 the deed: 341

In the next tone of Lara's gathering

 breath

How many shall but hear the voice of

 death!

XIV

His blade is bared,—in him there is an air

As deep, but far too tranquil for despair;

A something of indifference more than

 then 346

Becomes the bravest, if they feel for men.

He turn'd his eye on Kaled, ever near,

And still too faithful to betray one fear;

Perchance 'twas but the moon's dim twi-

 light threw 350

Along his aspect an unwonted hue

Of mournful paleness, whose deep tint ex-

 press'd

The truth, and not the terror of his breast.

This Lara mark'd, and laid his hand on

 his: 354

It trembled not in such an hour as this;

His lip was silent, scarcely beat his heart,

His eye alone proclaim'd, 'We will not

 part!

Thy band may perish, or thy friends may

 flee,

Farewell to life, but not adieu to thee!'

The word hath pass'd his lips, and onward
 driven, 360
Pours the link'd band through ranks
 asunder riven:
Well has each steed obey'd the armed heel,
And flash the scimitars, and rings the steel;
Outnumber'd, not outbraved, they still
 oppose
Despair to daring, and a front to foes;
And blood is mingled with the dashing
 stream, 366
Which runs all redly till the morning beam.

XV

Commanding, aiding, animating all,
Where foe appear'd to press, or friend to
 fall,
Cheers Lara's voice, and waves or strikes
 his steel, 370
Inspiring hope himself had ceased to feel.
None fled, for well they knew that flight
 were vain;
But those that waver turn to smite again,
While yet they find the firmest of the foe
Recoil before their leader's look and blow:
Now girt with numbers, now almost alone,
He foils their ranks, or re-unites his own;
Himself he spared not—once they seem'd
 to fly— 378
Now was the time, he waved his hand on
 high,
And shook—Why sudden droops that
 plumed crest? 380
The shaft is sped—the arrow's in his
 breast!
That fatal gesture left the unguarded side,
And Death has stricken down yon arm of
 pride.
The word of triumph fainted from his
 tongue;
That hand, so raised, how droopingly it
 hung! 385
But yet the sword instinctively retains,
Though from its fellow shrink the falling
 reins,
These Kaled snatches: dizzy with the blow,
And senseless bending o'er his saddle-bow,
Perceives not Lara that his anxious page
Beguiles his charger from the combat's
 rage: 391
Meantime his followers charge, and
 charge again;
Too mix'd the slayers now to heed the slain!

XVI

Day glimmers on the dying and the dead,
The cloven cuirass and the helmless head;
The war-horse masterless is on the earth,
And that last gasp hath burst his bloody
 girth; 397
And near, yet quivering with what life re-
 main'd,
The heel that urged him and the hand that
 rein'd;

And some too near that rolling torrent li
Whose waters mock the lip of those th
 die; 4
That panting thirst which scorches in th
 breath
Of those that die the soldier's fiery deat
In vain impels the burning mouth to cra
One drop—the last—to cool it for th
 grave; 4
With feeble and convulsive effort swep
Their limbs along the crimson'd turf ha
 crept;
The faint remains of life such struggl
 waste,
But yet they reach the stream and bend
 taste:
They feel its freshness, and almost pa
 take— 4
Why pause? No further thirst have the
 to slake—
It is unquench'd, and yet they feel it no
It was an agony—but now forgot!

XVII

Beneath a lime, remoter from the scene
Where but for him that strife had nev
 been, 4
A breathing but devoted warrior lay:
'Twas Lara bleeding fast from life awa
His follower once, and now his only guid
Kneels Kaled watchful o'er his welli
 side,
And with his scarf would stanch the tid
 that rush, 4
With each convulsion, in a blacker gusl
And then, as his faint breathing wax
 low,
In feebler, not less fatal tricklings flow:
He scarce can speak, but motions him 't
 vain,
And merely adds another throb to pain
He clasps the hand that pang which wou
 assuage, 4
And sadly smiles his thanks to that da
 page,
Who nothing fears, nor feels, nor heed
 nor sees,
Save that damp brow which rests upc
 his knees;
Save that pale aspect, where the ey
 though dim, 4
Held all the light that shone on earth fc
 him.

XVIII

The foe arrives, who long had search'
 the field,
Their triumph nought till Lara too shou
 yield:
They would remove him, but they se
 'twere vain,
And he regards them with a calm disdai
That rose to reconcile him with his fat
And that escape to death from living hat

And Otho comes, and leaping from his
 steed,
Looks on the bleeding foe that made him
 bleed,
And questions of his state; he answers
 440
Scarce glances on him as on one forgot,
And turns to Kaled:—each remaining
 word
They understood not, if distinctly heard;
His dying tones are in that other tongue,
To which some strange remembrance
 wildly clung. 445
They spake of other scenes, but what—is
 known
To Kaled, whom their meaning reach'd
 alone;
And he replied, though faintly, to their
 sound,
While gazed the rest in dumb amazement
 round:
They seem'd even then—that twain—unto
 the last 450
To half-forget the present in the past;
To share between themselves some separ-
 ate fate,
Whose darkness none beside should pene-
 trate.

 XIX

Their words though faint were many—
 from the tone
Their import those who heard could judge
 alone; 455
From this, you might have deem'd young
 Kaled's death
More near than Lara's by his voice and
 breath,
So sad, so deep, and hesitating broke
The accents his scarce-moving pale lips
 spoke;
But Lara's voice, though low, at first was
 clear 460
And calm, till murmuring death gasp'd
 hoarsely near;
But from his visage little could we guess,
So unrepentant, dark, and passionless,
Save that when struggling nearer to his
 last,
Upon that page his eye was kindly cast;
And once, as Kaled's answering accents
 ceased, 466
Rose Lara's hand, and pointed to the East:
Whether (as then the breaking sun from
 high
Roll'd back the clouds) the morrow caught
 his eye,
Or that 'twas chance, or some remem-
 ber'd scene, 470
That raised his arm to point where such
 had been,
Scarce Kaled seem'd to know, but turn'd
 away,
As if his heart abhorr'd that coming day,

And shrunk his glance before that morn-
 ing light,
To look on Lara's brow—where all grew
 night. 475
Yet sense seem'd left, though better were
 its loss;
For when one near display'd the absolv-
 ing cross,
And proffer'd to his touch the holy bead,
Of which his parting soul might own the
 need,
He look'd upon it with an eye profane,
And smiled—Heaven pardon! if 'twere
 with disdain: 481
And Kaled, though he spoke not, nor
 withdrew
From Lara's face his fix'd despairing view,
With brow repulsive, and with gesture
 swift,
Flung back the hand which held the sacred
 gift, 485
As if such but disturb'd the expiring man,
Nor seem'd to know his life but *then*
 began,
That life of Immortality, secure
To none, save them whose faith in Christ
 is sure.

 XX

But gasping heaved the breath that Lara
 drew, 490
And dull the film along his dim eye grew;
His limbs stretch'd fluttering, and his head
 droop'd o'er
The weak yet still untiring knee that bore;
He press'd the hand he held upon his
 heart—
It beats no more, but Kaled will not
 part 495
With the cold grasp, but feels, and feels in
 vain,
For that faint throb which answers not
 again.
'It beats!'—Away, thou dreamer! he is
 gone—
It once was Lara which thou look'st upon.

 XXI

He gazed, as if not yet had pass'd away
The haughty spirit of that humbled clay;
And those around have roused him from
 his trance,
But cannot tear from thence his fixed
 glance;
And when, in raising him from where he
 bore
Within his arms the form that felt no
 more, 505
He saw the head his breast would still sus-
 tain,
Roll down like earth to earth upon the
 plain;
He did not dash himself thereby, nor tear
The glossy tendrils of his raven hair,

317

But strove to stand and gaze, but reel'd
 and fell, 510
Scarce breathing more than that he loved
 so well.
Than that *he* loved! Oh! never yet beneath
The breast of man such trusty love may
 breathe!
That trying moment hath at once reveal'd
The secret long and yet but half conceal'd;
In baring to revive that lifeless breast, 516
Its grief seem'd ended, but the sex con-
 fess'd;
And life return'd, and Kaled felt no
 shame—
What now to her was Womanhood or
 Fame?

XXII

And Lara sleeps not where his fathers
 sleep, 520
But where he died his grave was dug as
 deep;
Nor is his mortal slumber less profound,
Though priest nor bless'd nor marble
 deck'd the mound,
And he was mourn'd by one whose quiet
 grief,
Less loud, outlasts a people's for their
 chief. 525
Vain was all question ask'd her of the past,
And vain e'en menace—silent to the last;
She told nor whence, nor why she left
 behind
Her all for one who seem'd but little kind.
Why did she love him? Curious fool!—be
 still— 530
Is human love the growth of human will?
To her he might be gentleness; the stern
Have deeper thoughts than your dull eyes
 discern,
And when they love, your smilers guess
 not how
Beats the strong heart, though less the lips
 avow. 535
They were not common links, that form'd
 the chain
That bound to Lara Kaled's heart and
 brain;
But that wild tale she brook'd not to un-
 fold,
And seal'd is now each lip that could have
 told.

XXIII

They laid him in the earth, and on his
 breast, 540
Besides the wound that sent his soul to
 rest,
They found the scatter'd dints of many a
 scar,
Which were not planted there in recent war;
Where'er had pass'd his summer years of
 life,
It seems they vanish'd in a land of strife;

But all unknown his glory or his guilt,
These only told that somewhere blood wa[s]
 spilt,
And Ezzelin, who might have spoke th[e]
 past,
Return'd no more—that night appear'[d]
 his last. 54[5]

XXIV

Upon that night (a peasant's is the tal[e])
A Serf that cross'd the intervening vale[,]
When Cynthia's light almost gave way t[o]
 morn,
And nearly veil'd in mist her waning horn[,]
A Serf, that rose betimes to thread th[e]
 wood,
And hew the bough that brought his chi[l]-
 dren's food,
Pass'd by the river that divides the plai[n]
Of Otho's lands and Lara's broad domain[,]
He heard a tramp—a horse and horse[-]
 man broke
From out the wood—before him was [a]
 cloak
Wrapt round some burthen at his saddl[e]
 bow, 56[0]
Bent was his head, and hidden was hi[s]
 brow.
Roused by the sudden sight at such a tim[e]
And some foreboding that it might b[e]
 crime,
Himself unheeded watch'd the stranger['s]
 course,
Who reach'd the river, bounded from hi[s]
 horse, 56[5]
And lifting thence the burthen which h[e]
 bore,
Heaved up the bank, and dash'd it fro[m]
 the shore,
Then paused, and look'd, and turn'd, an[d]
 seem'd to watch,
And still another hurried glance woul[d]
 snatch,
And follow with his step the stream tha[t]
 flow'd, 57[0]
As if even yet too much its surface show'[d]
At once he started, stoop'd, around hi[m]
 strown
The winter floods had scatter'd heaps o[f]
 stone:
Of these the heaviest thence he gather'[d]
 there,
And slung them with a more than commo[n]
 care. 57[5]
Meantime the Serf had crept to where un[-]
 seen
Himself might safely mark what this migh[t]
 mean;
He caught a glimpse, as of a floating breas[t,]
And something glitter'd starlike on th[e]
 vest;
But ere he well could mark the buoyan[t]
 trunk, 58[0]
A massy fragment smote it, and it sunk[.]

: rose again, but indistinct to view,
nd left the waters of a purple hue,
hen deeply disappear'd: the horseman
 gazed 584
ill ebb'd the latest eddy it had raised;
hen turning, vaulted on his pawing steed,
nd instant spurr'd him into panting
 speed.
lis face was mask'd—the features of the
 dead,
' dead it were, escaped the observer's
 dread;
ut if in sooth a star its bosom bore, 590
uch is the badge that knighthood ever
 wore,
nd such 'tis known Sir Ezzelin had worn
Jpon the night that led to such a morn.
' thus he perish'd, Heaven receive his
 soul! 594
lis undiscover'd limbs to ocean roll;
nd charity upon the hope would dwell
: was not Lara's hand by which he fell.

XXV

nd Kaled—Lara—Ezzelin, are gone,
like without their monumental stone!
he first, all efforts vainly strove to wean
he from lingering where her chieftain's blood
 had been: 601
Grief had so tamed a spirit once too proud,
Her tears were few, her wailing never loud;
ut furious would you tear her from the
 spot

Where yet she scarce believed that he was
 not, 605
Her eye shot forth with all the living fire
That haunts the tigress in her whelpless ire;
But left to waste her weary moments there,
She talk'd all idly unto shapes of air,
Such as the busy brain of Sorrow paints,
And woos to listen to her fond complaints:
And she would sit beneath the very tree
Where lay his drooping head upon her
 knee:
And in that posture where she saw him
 fall,
His words, his looks, his dying grasp re-
 call; 615
And she had shorn, but saved her raven
 hair,
And oft would snatch it from her bosom
 there,
And fold, and press it gently to the ground,
As if she staunch'd anew some phantom's
 wound. 619
Herself would question, and for him reply;
Then rising, start, and beckon him to fly
From some imagined spectre in pursuit;
Then seat her down upon some linden's
 root,
And hide her visage with her meagre hand,
Or trace strange characters along the sand.
This could not last—she lies by him she
 loved; 626
Her tale untold, her truth too dearly
 proved.

THE SIEGE OF CORINTH

TO

JOHN HOBHOUSE, ESQ.,

THIS POEM IS INSCRIBED BY HIS

January 22nd, 1816 FRIEND.

ADVERTISEMENT

'THE grand army of the Turks (in 1715), under the Prime Vizier, to open to themselves a way into ie heart of the Morea, and to form the siege of Napoli di Romania, the most considerable place in l that country*, thought it best in the first place to attack Corinth, upon which they made several orms. The garrison being weakened, and the governor seeing it was impossible to hold out against ɔ mighty a force, thought it fit to beat a parley: but while they were treating about the articles, one f the magazines in the Turkish camp, wherein they had six hundred barrels of powder, blew up by ccident, whereby six or seven hundred men were killed; which so enraged the infidels, that they ould not grant any capitulation, but stormed the place with so much fury, that they took it, and ut most of the garrison, with Signior Minotti, the governor, to the sword. The rest, with Antonio embo, proveditor extraordinary, were made prisoners of war.'—*History of the Turks*, vol. iii, p. 151.

Napoli di Romania is not now the most considerable place in the Morea, but Tripolitza, where the Pacha esides, and maintains his government. Napoli is near Argos. I visited all three in 1810–11; and, in the ourse of journeying through the country from my first arrival in 1809, I crossed the Isthmus eight times a my way from Attica to the Morea, over the mountains: or in the other direction, when passing from the ulf of Athens to that of Lepanto. Both the routes are picturesque and beautiful, though very different: that y sea has more sameness; but the voyage being always within sight of land, and often very near it, presents ɔany attractive views of the islands Salamis, Ægina, Poros, &c., and the coast of the Continent.

THE SIEGE OF CORINTH

In the year since Jesus died for men,
Eighteen hundred years and ten,
We were a gallant company,
Riding o'er land, and sailing o'er sea.
Oh! but we went merrily! 5
We forded the river, and clomb the high
 hill,
Never our steeds for a day stood still;
Whether we lay in the cave or the shed,
Our sleep fell soft on the hardest bed: 9
Whether we couch'd in our rough capote,
On the rougher plank of our gliding boat,
Or stretch'd on the beach, or our saddles
 spread
As a pillow beneath the resting head,
Fresh we woke upon the morrow:
 All our thoughts and words had scope,
 We had health, and we had hope, 16
Toil and travel, but no sorrow.
We were of all tongues and creeds;—
Some were those who counted beads,
Some of mosque, and some of church, 20
 And some, or I mis-say, of neither;
Yet through the wide world might ye
 search,
 Nor find a motlier crew nor blither.

But some are dead, and some are gone,
And some are scattered and alone, 25
And some are rebels on the hills
 That look along Epirus' valleys,
 Where freedom still at moments rallies,
And pays in blood oppression's ills;
 And some are in a far countree, 30
And some all restlessly at home;
 But never more, oh! never, we
Shall meet to revel and to roam.

But those hardy days flew cheerily!
And when they now fall drearily, 35
My thoughts, like swallows, skim the
 main,
And bear my spirit back again
Over the earth, and through the air,
A wild bird and a wanderer.
'Tis this that ever wakes my strain, 40
And oft, too oft, implores again
The few who may endure my lay,
To follow me so far away.
Stranger—wilt thou follow now,
And sit with me on Acro-Corinth's brow?

I

Many a vanish'd year and age, 46
And tempest's breath, and battle's rage,
Have swept o'er Corinth; yet she stands,
A fortress form'd to Freedom's hands.
The whirlwind's wrath, the earthquake's
 shock, 50
Have left untouch'd her hoary rock,
The keystone of a land, which still,
Though fall'n, looks proudly on that hill,

The landmark to the double tide
That purpling rolls on either side, 5
As if their waters chafed to meet,
Yet pause and crouch beneath her feet.
But could the blood before her shed
Since first Timoleon's brother bled,
Or baffled Persia's despot fled, 6
Arise from out the earth which drank
The stream of slaughter as it sank,
That sanguine ocean would o'erflow
Her isthmus idly spread below:
Or could the bones of all the slain, 6
Who perish'd there, be piled again,
That rival pyramid would rise
More mountain-like, through those clea
 skies,
Than yon tower-capp'd Acropolis,
Which seems the very clouds to kiss. 7

II

On dun Cithæron's ridge appears
The gleam of twice ten thousand spears
And downward to the Isthmian plain,
From shore to shore of either main,
The tent is pitch'd, the crescent shines 7
Along the Moslem's leaguering lines;
And the dusk Spahi's bands advance
Beneath each bearded pacha's glance;
And far and wide as eye can reach
The turban'd cohorts throng the beach;
And there the Arab's camel kneels, 8
And there his steed the Tartar wheels;
The Turcoman hath left his herd,
The sabre round his loins to gird;
And there the volleying thunders pour, 8
Till waves grow smoother to the roar.
The trench is dug, the cannon's breath
Wings the far hissing globe of death;
Fast whirl the fragments from the wall,
Which crumbles with the ponderous ball
And from that wall the foe replies, 9
O'er dusty plain and smoky skies,
With fires that answer fast and well
The summons of the Infidel.

III

But near and nearest to the wall 9
Of those who wish and work its fall,
With deeper skill in war's black art
Than Othman's sons, and high of heart
As any chief that ever stood
Triumphant in the fields of blood; 10
From post to post, and deed to deed,
Fast spurring on his reeking steed,
Where sallying ranks the trench assail,
And make the foremost Moslem quail;
Or where the battery, guarded well, 10
Remains as yet impregnable,
Alighting cheerly to inspire
The soldier slackening in his fire;

The first and freshest of the host
Which Stamboul's sultan there can boast,
To guide the follower o'er the field, 111
To point the tube, the lance to wield,
Or whirl around the bickering blade;—
Was Alp, the Adrian renegade!

IV

From Venice—once a race of worth 115
His gentle sires—he drew his birth;
But late an exile from her shore,
Against his countrymen he bore
The arms they taught to bear; and now
The turban girt his shaven brow. 120
Through many a change had Corinth
 pass'd
With Greece to Venice' rule at last;
And here, before her walls, with those
To Greece and Venice equal foes,
He stood a foe, with all the zeal 125
Which young and fiery converts feel,
Within whose heated bosom throngs
The memory of a thousand wrongs.
To him had Venice ceased to be
Her ancient civic boast—'the Free'; 130
And in the palace of St. Mark
Unnamed accusers in the dark
Within the 'Lion's mouth' had placed
A charge against him uneffaced:
He fled in time, and saved his life, 135
To waste his future years in strife,
That taught his land how great her loss
In him who triumph'd o'er the Cross,
'Gainst which he rear'd the Crescent high,
And battled to avenge or die. 140

V

Coumourgi—he whose closing scene
Adorn'd the triumph of Eugene,
When on Carlowitz' bloody plain,
The last and mightiest of the slain,
He sank, regretting not to die, 145
But cursed the Christian's victory—
Coumourgi—can his glory cease,
That latest conqueror of Greece,
Till Christian hands to Greece restore
The freedom Venice gave of yore? 150
A hundred years have roll'd away
Since he refix'd the Moslem's sway;
And now he led the Mussulman,
And gave the guidance of the van
To Alp, who well repaid the trust 155
By cities levell'd with the dust;
And proved, by many a deed of death,
How firm his heart in novel faith.

VI

The walls grew weak; and fast and hot
Against them pour'd the ceaseless shot,
With unabating fury sent 161
From battery to battlement;
And thunder-like the pealing din
Rose from each heated culverin;

And here and there some crackling dome
Was fired before the exploding bomb; 166
And as the fabric sank beneath
The shattering shell's volcanic breath,
In red and wreathing columns flash'd
The flame, as loud the ruin crash'd, 170
Or into countless meteors driven,
Its earth-stars melted into heaven;
Whose clouds that day grew doubly dun,
Impervious to the hidden sun,
With volumed smoke that slowly grew
To one wide sky of sulphurous hue. 176

VII

But not for vengeance, long delay'd,
Alone, did Alp, the renegade,
The Moslem warriors sternly teach
His skill to pierce the promised breach:
Within these walls a maid was pent 181
His hope would win, without consent
Of that inexorable sire,
Whose heart refused him in its ire,
When Alp, beneath his Christian name,
Her virgin hand aspired to claim.
In happier mood, and earlier time, 187
While unimpeach'd for traitorous crime,
Gayest in gondola or hall,
He glitter'd through the Carnival;
And tuned the softest serenade
That e'er on Adria's waters play'd
At midnight to Italian maid. 193

VIII

And many deem'd her heart was won;
For sought by numbers, given to none,
Had young Francesca's hand remain'd
Still by the church's bonds unchain'd:
And when the Adriatic bore
Lanciotto to the Paynim shore, 199
Her wonted smiles were seen to fail,
And pensive wax'd the maid and pale;
More constant at confessional,
More rare at masque and festival;
Or seen at such, with downcast eyes,
Which conquer'd hearts they ceased to
 prize: 205
With listless look she seems to gaze:
With humbler care her form arrays;
Her voice less lively in the song;
Her step, though light, less fleet among
The pairs, on whom the Morning's glance
Breaks, yet unsated with the dance. 211

IX

Sent by the state to guard the land,
(Which, wrested from the Moslem's hand,
While Sobieski tamed his pride
By Buda's wall and Danube's side, 215
The chiefs of Venice wrung away
From Patra to Euboea's bay,)
Minotti held in Corinth's towers
The Doge's delegated powers,
While yet the pitying eye of Peace 220
Smiled o'er her long forgotten Greece:

THE SIEGE OF CORINTH

And ere that faithless truce was broke
Which freed her from the unchristian yoke,
With him his gentle daughter came;
Nor there, since Menelaus' dame 225
Forsook her lord and land, to prove
What woes await on lawless love,
Had fairer form adorn'd the shore
Than she, the matchless stranger, bore.

X

The wall is rent, the ruins yawn; 230
And with to-morrow's earliest dawn,
O'er the disjointed mass shall vault
The foremost of the fierce assault.
The bands are rank'd; the chosen van
Of Tartar and of Mussulman, 235
The full of hope, misnamed 'forlorn',
Who hold the thought of death in scorn,
And win their way with falchion's force,
Or pave the path with many a corse,
O'er which the following brave may rise,
Their stepping-stone—the last who dies!

XI

'Tis midnight: on the mountains brown
The cold, round moon shines deeply
down; 243
Blue roll the waters, blue the sky
Spreads like an ocean hung on high,
Bespangled with those isles of light,
So wildly, spiritually bright;
Who ever gazed upon them shining
And turn'd to earth without repining,
Nor wish'd for wings to flee away, 250
And mix with their eternal ray?
The waves on either shore lay there
Calm, clear, and azure as the air;
And scarce their foam the pebbles shook,
But murmur'd meekly as the brook. 255
The winds were pillow'd on the waves;
The banners droop'd along their staves,
And, as they fell around them furling,
Above them shone the crescent curling;
And that deep silence was unbroke, 260
Save where the watch his signal spoke,
Save where the steed neigh'd oft and shrill,
And echo answer'd from the hill,
And the wide hum of that wild host
Rustled like leaves from coast to coast,
As rose the Muezzin's voice in air 266
In midnight call to wonted prayer;
It rose, that chanted mournful strain,
Like some lone spirit's o'er the plain:
'Twas musical, but sadly sweet, 270
Such as when winds and harp-strings
meet,
And take a long unmeasured tone,
To mortal minstrelsy unknown.
It seem'd to those within the wall
A cry prophetic of their fall:
It struck even the besieger's ear 276
With something ominous and drear,
An undefined and sudden thrill,
Which makes the heart a moment still,

Then beat with quicker pulse, ashamed
Of that strange sense its silence framed;
Such as a sudden passing-bell 282
Wakes, though but for a stranger's knell.

XII

The tent of Alp was on the shore;
The sound was hush'd, the prayer was
o'er, 285
The watch was set, the night-round made,
All mandates issued and obey'd:
'Tis but another anxious night,
His pains the morrow may requite
With all revenge and love can pay, 290
In guerdon for their long delay.
Few hours remain, and he hath need
Of rest, to nerve for many a deed
Of slaughter; but within his soul 294
The thoughts like troubled waters roll.
He stood alone among the host;
Not his the loud fanatic boast
To plant the crescent o'er the cross,
Or risk a life with little loss,
Secure in paradise to be 300
By Houris loved immortally:
Nor his, what burning patriots feel,
The stern exaltedness of zeal,
Profuse of blood, untired in toil,
When battling on the parent soil. 305
He stood alone—a renegade
Against the country he betray'd;
He stood alone amidst his band,
Without a trusted heart or hand: 309
They follow'd him, for he was brave,
And great the spoil he got and gave;
They crouch'd to him, for he had skill
To warp and wield the vulgar will:
But still his Christian origin
With them was little less than sin. 315
They envied even the faithless fame
He earn'd beneath a Moslem name;
Since he, their mightiest chief, had been
In youth a bitter Nazarene. 319
They did not know how pride can stoop,
When baffled feelings withering droop;
They did not know how hate can burn
In hearts once changed from soft to stern;
Nor all the false and fatal zeal
The convert of revenge can feel. 325
He ruled them—man may rule the worst,
By ever daring to be first:
So lions o'er the jackal sway;
The jackal points, he fells the prey,
Then on the vulgar, yelling, press, 330
To gorge the relics of success.

XIII

His head grows fever'd, and his pulse
The quick successive throbs convulse:
In vain from side to side he throws
His form, in courtship of repose; 335
Or if he dozed, a sound, a start
Awoke him with a sunken heart.

The turban on his hot brow press'd,
The mail weigh'd lead-like on his breast,
Though oft and long beneath its weight
Upon his eyes had slumber sate, 341
Without or couch or canopy,
Except a rougher field and sky
Than now might yield a warrior's bed,
Than now along the heaven was spread.
He could not rest, he could not stay 346
Within his tent to wait for day,
But walk'd him forth along the sand,
Where thousand sleepers strew'd the
 strand.
What pillow'd them? and why should he
More wakeful than the humblest be,
Since more their peril, worse their toil?
And yet they fearless dream of spoil;
While he alone, where thousands pass'd
A night of sleep, perchance their last, 355
In sickly vigil wander'd on,
And envied all he gazed upon.

XIV

He felt his soul become more light
Beneath the freshness of the night.
Cool was the silent sky, though calm, 360
And bathed his brow with airy balm:
Behind, the camp—before him lay,
In many a winding creek and bay,
Lepanto's gulf; and, on the brow
Of Delphi's hill, unshaken snow, 365
High and eternal, such as shone
Through thousand summers brightly
 gone,
Along the gulf, the mount, the clime;
It will not melt, like man, to time:
Tyrant and slave are swept away, 370
Less form'd to wear before the ray;
But that white veil, the lightest, frailest,
Which on the mighty mount thou hailest,
While tower and tree are torn and rent,
Shines o'er its craggy battlement; 375
In form a peak, in height a cloud,
In texture like a hovering shroud,
Thus high by parting Freedom spread,
As from her fond abode she fled,
And linger'd on the spot, where long 380
Her prophet spirit spake in song.
Oh! still her step at moments falters
O'er wither'd fields, and ruin'd altars,
And fain would wake, in souls too broken,
By pointing to each glorious token: 385
But vain her voice, till better days
Dawn in those yet remember'd rays,
Which shone upon the Persian flying,
And saw the Spartan smile in dying.

XV

Not mindless of these mighty times 390
Was Alp, despite his flight and crimes;
And through this night, as on he wander'd,
And o'er the past and present ponder'd,
And thought upon the glorious dead
Who there in better cause had bled, 395

He felt how faint and feebly dim
The fame that could accrue to him,
Who cheer'd the band, and waved the
 sword,
A traitor in a turban'd horde;
And led them to the lawless siege, 400
Whose best success were sacrilege.
Not so had those his fancy number'd,
The chiefs whose dust around him slum-
 ber'd;
Their phalanx marshall'd on the plain,
Whose bulwarks were not then in vain.
They fell devoted, but undying; 406
The very gale their name seem'd sighing;
The waters murmur'd of their name;
The woods were peopled with their fame;
The silent pillar, lone and grey, 410
Claim'd kindred with their sacred clay;
Their spirits wrapp'd the dusky mountain,
Their memory sparkled o'er the fountain;
The meanest rill, the mightiest river
Roll'd mingling with their fame for ever.
Despite of every yoke she bears, 416
That land is glory's still and theirs!
'Tis still a watchword to the earth:
When man would do a deed of worth
He points to Greece, and turns to tread,
So sanction'd, on the tyrant's head: 421
He looks to her, and rushes on
Where life is lost, or freedom won.

XVI

Still by the shore Alp mutely mused,
And woo'd the freshness Night diffused.
There shrinks no ebb in that tideless sea,
Which changeless rolls eternally; 427
So that wildest of waves, in their angriest
 mood,
Scarce break on the bounds of the land
 for a rood;
And the powerless moon beholds them
 flow, 430
Heedless if she come or go:
Calm or high, in main or bay,
On their course she hath no sway.
The rock unworn its base doth bare,
And looks o'er the surf, but it comes not
 there; 435
And the fringe of the foam may be seen
 below,
On the line that it left long ages ago:
A smooth short space of yellow sand
Between it and the greener land.

He wander'd on along the beach, 440
Till within the range of a carbine's reach
Of the leaguer'd wall; but they saw him
 not,
Or how could he 'scape from the hostile
 shot?
Did traitors lurk in the Christians' hold?
Were their hands grown stiff, or their
 hearts wax'd cold? 445

I know not, in sooth; but from yonder
 wall
There flash'd no fire, and there hiss'd no
 ball,
Though he stood beneath the bastion's
 frown,
That flank'd the sea-ward gate of the
 town;
Though he heard the sound, and could
 almost tell 450
The sullen words of the sentinel,
As his measured step on the stone below
Clank'd, as he paced it to and fro;
And he saw the lean dogs beneath the wall
Hold o'er the dead their carnival, 455
Gorging and growling o'er carcass and
 limb;
They were too busy to bark at him!
From a Tartar's skull they had stripp'd
 the flesh,
As ye peel the fig when its fruit is fresh;
And their white tusks crunch'd o'er the
 whiter skull, 460
As it slipp'd through their jaws, when
 their edge grew dull,
As they lazily mumbled the bones of the
 dead,
When they scarce could rise from the spot
 where they fed;
So well had they broken a lingering fast
With those who had fallen for that night's
 repast. 465
And Alp knew, by the turbans that roll'd
 on the sand,
The foremost of these were the best of his
 band:
Crimson and green were the shawls of
 their wear,
And each scalp had a single long tuft of
 hair,
All the rest was shaven and bare. 470
The scalps were in the wild dog's maw,
The hair was tangled round his jaw:
But close by the shore, on the edge of the
 gulf,
There sat a vulture flapping a wolf,
Who had stolen from the hills, but kept
 away, 475
Scared by the dogs, from the human
 prey;
But he seized on his share of a steed that
 lay,
Pick'd by the birds, on the sands of the bay.

XVII

Alp turn'd him from the sickening sight:
Never had shaken his nerves in fight;
But he better could brook to behold the
 dying, 481
Deep in the tide of their warm blood lying,
Scorch'd with the death-thirst, and writh-
 ing in vain,
Than the perishing dead who are past all
 pain.

There is something of pride in the perilous
 hour, 485
Whate'er be the shape in which death may
 lower;
For Fame is there to say who bleeds,
And Honour's eye on daring deeds!
But when all is past, it is humbling to
 tread
O'er the weltering field of the tombless
 dead, 490
And see worms of the earth, and fowls of
 the air,
Beasts of the forest, all gathering there;
All regarding man as their prey,
All rejoicing in his decay.

XVIII

There is a temple in ruin stands, 495
Fashion'd by long-forgotten hands;
Two or three columns, and many a stone,
Marble and granite, with grass o'ergrown!
Out upon Time! it will leave no more
Of the things to come than the things
 before! 500
Out upon Time! who for ever will leave
But enough of the past for the future to
 grieve
O'er that which hath been, and o'er that
 which must be:
What we have seen, our sons shall see;
Remnants of things that have pass'd away,
Fragments of stone rear'd by creatures of
 clay! 506

XIX

He sate him down at a pillar's base,
And pass'd his hand athwart his face;
Like one in dreary musing mood,
Declining was his attitude; 510
His head was drooping on his breast,
Fever'd, throbbing, and oppress'd;
And o'er his brow, so downward bent,
Oft his beating fingers went,
Hurriedly, as you may see 515
Your own run over the ivory key,
Ere the measured tone is taken
By the chords you would awaken.
There he sate all heavily,
As he heard the night-wind sigh. 520
Was it the wind through some hollow
 stone
Sent that soft and tender moan?
He lifted his head, and he look'd on the
 sea,
But it was unrippled as glass may be;
He look'd on the long grass—it waved
 not a blade; 525
How was that gentle sound convey'd?
He look'd to the banners—each flag lay
 still,
So did the leaves on Cithæron's hill,
And he felt not a breath come over his
 cheek;
What did that sudden sound bespeak?

He turn'd to the left—is he sure of
 sight? 531
There sate a lady, youthful and bright!

XX

He started up with more of fear
Than if an armed foe were near.
'God of my fathers! what is here? 535
Who art thou? and wherefore sent
So near a hostile armament?'
His trembling hands refused to sign
The cross he deem'd of no more divine:
He had resumed it in that hour, 540
But conscience wrung away the power.
He gazed; he saw: he knew the face
Of beauty, and the form of grace;
It was Francesca by his side,
The maid who might have been his
 bride! 545

The rose was yet upon her cheek,
But mellow'd with a tenderer streak:
Where was the play of her soft lips fled?
Gone was the smile that enliven'd their
 red.
The ocean's calm within their view,
Beside her eye had less of blue; 551
But like that cold wave it stood still,
And its glance, though clear, was chill.
Around her form a thin robe twining,
Nought conceal'd her bosom shining;
Through the parting of her hair, 556
Floating darkly downward there,
Her rounded arm show'd white and bare:
And ere yet she made reply,
Once she raised her hand on high; 560
It was so wan, and transparent of hue,
You might have seen the moon shine
 through.

XXI

I come from my rest to him I love best,
That I may be happy, and he may be
 bless'd,
I have pass'd the guards, the gate, the
 wall; 565
Sought thee in safety through foes and all.
'Tis said the lion will turn and flee
From a maid in the pride of her purity;
And the Power on high, that can shield
 the good
Thus from the tyrant of the wood, 570
Hath extended its mercy to guard me as
 well
From the hands of the leaguering infidel.
I come—and if I come in vain,
Never, oh never, we meet again!
Thou hast done a fearful deed 575
In falling away from thy fathers' creed:
But dash that turban to earth, and sign
The sign of the cross, and for ever be mine;
Wring the black drop from thy heart,
And to-morrow unites us no more to
 part.' 580

'And where should our bridal couch be
 spread?
In the midst of the dying and the dead?
For to-morrow we give to the slaughter
 and flame
The sons and the shrines of the Christian
 name. 584
None, save thou and thine, I've sworn,
Shall be left upon the morn:
But thee will I bear to a lovely spot,
Where our hands shall be join'd, and our
 sorrow forgot.
There thou yet shalt be my bride, 589
When once again I've quell'd the pride
Of Venice; and her hated race
Have felt the arm they would debase
Scourge, with a whip of scorpions, those
Whom vice and envy made my foes.'

Upon his hand she laid her own— 595
Light was the touch, but it thrill'd to the
 bone,
And shot a chillness to his heart,
Which fix'd him beyond the power to
 start.
Though slight was that grasp so mortal
 cold,
He could not loose him from its hold;
But never did clasp of one so dear 601
Strike on the pulse with such feeling of
 fear,
As those thin fingers, long and white,
Froze through his blood by their touch
 that night.
The feverish glow of his brow was gone,
And his heart sank so still that it felt like
 stone, 606
As he look'd on the face, and beheld its
 hue,
So deeply changed from what he knew:
Fair but faint—without the ray
Of mind, that made each feature play
Like sparkling waves on a sunny day;
And her motionless lips lay still as
 death,
And her words came forth without her
 breath,
And there rose not a heave o'er her
 bosom's swell,
And there seem'd not a pulse in her veins
 to dwell. 615
Though her eye shone out, yet the lids
 were fix'd,
And the glance that it gave was wild and
 unmix'd
With aught of change, as the eyes may
 seem
Of the restless who walk in a troubled
 dream;
Like the figures on arras, that gloomily
 glare, 620
Stirr'd by the breath of the wintry air,
So seen by the dying lamp's fitful light,
Lifeless, but life-like, and awful to sight;

As they seem, through the dimness, about
 to come down
From the shadowy wall where their images
 frown; 625
Fearfully flitting to and fro,
As the gusts on the tapestry come and go.

'If not for love of me be given
Thus much, then, for the love of
 heaven,—
Again I say—that turban tear 630
From off thy faithless brow, and swear
Thine injured country's sons to spare,
Or thou art lost; and never shalt see—
Not earth—that's past—but heaven or
 me.
If this thou dost accord, albeit 635
A heavy doom 'tis thine to meet,
That doom shall half absolve thy sin,
And mercy's gate may receive thee within:
But pause one moment more, and take
The curse of Him thou didst forsake;
And look once more to heaven, and see
Its love for ever shut from thee.
There is a light cloud by the moon—
'Tis passing, and will pass full soon—
If, by the time its vapoury sail 645
Hath ceased her shaded orb to veil,
Thy heart within thee is not changed,
Then God and man are both avenged;
Dark will thy doom be, darker still
Thine immortality of ill.' 650

Alp look'd to heaven, and saw on high
The sign she spake of in the sky;
But his heart was swollen, and turn'd aside,
By deep interminable pride. 654
This first false passion of his breast
Roll'd like a torrent o'er the rest.
He sue for mercy! *He* dismay'd
By wild words of a timid maid!
He, wrong'd by Venice, vow to save
Her sons, devoted to the grave! 660
No—though that cloud were thunder's
 worst,
And charged to crush him—let it burst!

He look'd upon it earnestly,
Without an accent of reply; 664
He watch'd it passing; it is flown:
Full on his eye the clear moon shone,
And thus he spake—'Whate'er my fate,
I am no changeling—'tis too late:
The reed in storms may bow and quiver,
Then rise again; the tree must shiver.
What Venice made me, I must be, 671
Her foe in all, save love to thee:
But thou art safe: oh, fly with me!'
He turn'd, but she is gone!
Nothing is there but the column stone.
Hath she sunk in the earth, or melted
 in air? 676
He saw not—he knew not—but nothing
 is there.

XXII

The night is past, and shines the sun
As if that morn were a jocund one.
Lightly and brightly breaks away 68
The Morning from her mantle grey,
And the noon will look on a sultry day
Hark to the trump, and the drum,
And the mournful sound of the barbarous
 horn,
And the flap of the banners, that flit a
 they're borne, 68
And the neigh of the steed, and the multi
 tude's hum,
And the clash, and the shout, 'They come
 they come!'
The horsetails are pluck'd from th
 ground, and the sword
From its sheath; and they form, and bu
 wait for the word.
Tartar, and Spahi, and Turcoman, 69
Strike your tents, and throng to the van
Mount ye, spur ye, skirr the plain,
That the fugitive may flee in vain,
When he breaks from the town; and non
 escape, 69
Aged or young, in the Christian shape;
While your fellows on foot, in a fiery mass
Bloodstain the breach through which the
 pass.
The steeds are all bridled, and snort t
 the rein;
Curved is each neck, and flowing each
 mane;
White is the foam of their champ on th
 bit; 70
The spears are uplifted; the matches ar
 lit;
The cannon are pointed, and ready t
 roar,
And crush the wall they have crumble
 before:
Forms in his phalanx each janizar;
Alp at their head; his right arm is bare,
So is the blade of his scimitar; 70
The khan and the pachas are all at thei
 post;
The vizier himself at the head of the host
When the culverin's signal is fired, the
 on;
Leave not in Corinth a living one— 71
A priest at her altars, a chief in her halls
A hearth in her mansions, a stone on he
 walls.
God and the prophet—Alla Hu!
Up to the skies with that wild halloo!
'There the breach lies for passage, th
 ladder to scale; 71
And your hands on your sabres, and how
 should ye fail?
He who first downs with the red cross may
 crave
His heart's dearest wish; let him ask it
 and have!'

Thus utter'd Coumourgi, the dauntless
 vizier;
The reply was the brandish of sabre and
 spear, 720
And the shout of fierce thousands in joy-
 ous ire:—
Silence—hark to the signal—fire!

XXIII

As the wolves, that headlong go
On the stately buffalo,
Though with fiery eyes, and angry roar,
And hoofs that stamp, and horns that
 gore, 726
He tramples on earth, or tosses on high
The foremost, who rush on his strength
 but to die:
Thus against the wall they went,
Thus the first were backward bent; 730
Many a bosom, sheathed in brass,
Strew'd the earth like broken glass,
Shiver'd by the shot, that tore
The ground whereon they moved no
 more:
Even as they fell, in files they lay, 735
Like the mower's grass at the close of
 day,
When his work is done on the levell'd
 plain;
Such was the fall of the foremost slain.

XXIV

As the spring-tides, with heavy plash,
From the cliffs invading dash 740
Huge fragments, sapp'd by the cease-
 less flow,
Till white and thundering down they go,
Like the avalanche's snow
On the Alpine vales below; 744
Thus at length, outbreathed and worn,
Corinth's sons were downward borne
By the long and oft renew'd
Charge of the Moslem multitude.
In firmness they stood, and in masses
 they fell,
Heap'd by the host of the infidel, 750
Hand to hand, and foot to foot:
Nothing there, save death, was mute:
Stroke, and thrust, and flash, and cry
For quarter or for victory, 754
Mingle there with the volleying thunder,
Which makes the distant cities wonder
How the sounding battle goes,
If with them, or for their foes;
If they must mourn, or may rejoice
In that annihilating voice, 760
Which pierces the deep hills through
 and through
With an echo dread and new:
You might have heard it, on that day,
O'er Salamis and Megara;
(We have heard the hearers say,) 765
Even unto Piræus' bay.

XXV

From the point of encountering blades
 to the hilt,
Sabres and swords with blood were gilt;
But the rampart is won, and the spoil
 begun,
And all but the after carnage done. 770
Shriller shrieks now mingling come
From within the plunder'd dome:
Hark to the haste of flying feet,
That splash in the blood of the slippery
 street;
But here and there, where 'vantage
 ground 775
Against the foe may still be found,
Desperate groups, of twelve or ten,
Make a pause, and turn again—
With banded backs against the wall,
Fiercely stand, or fighting fall. 780
There stood an old man—his hairs were
 white,
But his veteran arm was full of might:
So gallantly bore he the brunt of the
 fray,
The dead before him, on that day,
In a semicircle lay; 785
Still he combated unwounded,
Though retreating, unsurrounded.
Many a scar of former fight
Lurk'd beneath his corslet bright; 789
But of every wound his body bore,
Each and all had been ta'en before:
Though aged, he was so iron of limb,
Few of our youth could cope with
 him,
And the foes, whom he singly kept at
 bay,
Outnumber'd his thin hairs of silver
 grey. 795
From right to left his sabre swept;
Many an Othman mother wept
Sons that were unborn, when dipp'd
His weapon first in Moslem gore,
Ere his years could count a score. 800
Of all he might have been the sire
Who fell that day beneath his ire:
For, sonless left long years ago,
His wrath made many a childless foe;
And since the day, when in the strait
His only boy had met his fate, 806
His parent's iron hand did doom
More than a human hecatomb.
If shades by carnage be appeased,
Patroclus' spirit less was pleased 810
Than his, Minotti's son, who died
Where Asia's bounds and ours divide.
Buried he lay, where thousands be-
 fore
For thousands of years were inhumed
 on the shore;
What of them is left, to tell 815
Where they lie, and how they fell?

Not a stone on their turf, nor a bone in
 their graves;
But they live in the verse that immortally
 saves.

XXVI

Hark to the Allah shout! a band
Of the Mussulman bravest and best is
 at hand; 820
Their leader's nervous arm is bare,
Swifter to smite, and never to spare—
Unclothed to the shoulder it waves
 them on;
Thus in the fight is he ever known:
Others a gaudier garb may show, 825
To tempt the spoil of the greedy foe;
Many a hand's on a richer hilt,
But none on a steel more ruddily gilt;
Many a loftier turban may wear,—
Alp is but known by the white arm
 bare; 830
Look through the thick of the fight,
 'tis there!
There is not a standard on that shore
So well advanced the ranks before;
There is not a banner in Moslem war
Will lure the Delhis half so far; 835
It glances like a falling star!
Where'er that mighty arm is seen,
The bravest be, or late have been;
There the craven cries for quarter
Vainly to the vengeful Tartar; 840
Or the hero, silent lying,
Scorns to yield a groan in dying;
Mustering his last feeble blow
'Gainst the nearest levell'd foe,
Though faint beneath the mutual
 wound, 845
Grappling on the gory ground.

XXVII

Still the old man stood erect,
And Alp's career a moment check'd.
'Yield thee, Minotti; quarter take,
For thine own, thy daughter's sake.'

'Never, renegado, never! 851
Though the life of thy gift would last
 for ever.'

'Francesca!—Oh, my promised bride!
Must she too perish by thy pride?'

'She is safe.'—'Where? where?'—'In
 heaven; 855.
From whence thy traitor soul is driven—
Far from thee, and undefiled.'
Grimly then Minotti smiled,
As he saw Alp staggering bow
Before his words, as with a blow. 860

'Oh God! when died she?'—'Yester-
 night—
Nor weep I for her spirit's flight:

None of my pure race shall be
Slaves to Mahomet and thee—
Come on!'—That challenge is in vain—
Alp's already with the slain! 866
While Minotti's words were wreaking
More revenge in bitter speaking
Than his falchion's point had found,
Had the time allow'd to wound, 870
From within the neighbouring porch
Of a long defended church,
Where the last and desperate few
Would the failing fight renew,
The sharp shot dash'd Alp to the
 ground; 875
Ere an eye could view the wound
That crash'd through the brain of the
 infidel,
Round he spun, and down he fell;
A flash like fire within his eyes
Blazed, as he bent no more to rise, 880
And then eternal darkness sunk
Through all the palpitating trunk;
Nought of life left, save a quivering
Where his limbs were slightly shivering
They turn'd him on his back; his breast
And brow were stain'd with gore and
 dust, 886
And through his lips the life-blood
 oozed,
From its deep veins lately loosed;
But in his pulse there was no throb,
Nor on his lips one dying sob; 890
Sigh, nor word, nor struggling breath
Heralded his way to death;
Ere his very thought could pray,
Unanel'd he pass'd away,
Without a hope from mercy's aid,—
To the last a Renegade. 896

XXVIII

Fearfully the yell arose
Of his followers, and his foes;
These in joy, in fury those:
Then again in conflict mixing, 900
Clashing swords, and spears transfixing,
Interchanged the blow and thrust,
Hurling warriors in the dust.
Street by street, and foot by foot,
Still Minotti dares dispute 905
The latest portion of the land
Left beneath his high command;
With him, aiding heart and hand,
The remnant of his gallant band.
Still the church is tenable, 910
Whence issued late the fated ball
That half avenged the city's fall,
When Alp, her fierce assailant, fell:
Thither bending sternly back,
They leave before a bloody track; 915
And, with their faces to the foe,
Dealing wounds with every blow,
The chief, and his retreating train,
Join to those within the fane;

328

There they yet may breathe awhile, 920
Shelter'd by the massy pile.

XXIX

Brief breathing-time! the turban'd host,
With added ranks and raging boast,
Press onwards with such strength and
 heat,
Their numbers balk their own retreat;
For narrow the way that led to the
 spot 926
Where still the Christians yielded not;
And the foremost, if fearful, may vainly
 try
Through the massy column to turn and
 fly;
They perforce must do or die. 930
They die; but ere their eyes could close,
Avengers o'er their bodies rose;
Fresh and furious, fast they fill
The ranks unthinn'd, though slaugh-
 ter'd still; 934
And faint the weary Christians wax
Before the still renew'd attacks;
And now the Othmans gain the gate;
Still resists its iron weight,
And still, all deadly aim'd and hot,
From every crevice comes the shot;
From every shatter'd window pour 941
The volleys of the sulphurous shower:
But the portal wavering grows and
 weak—
The iron yields, the hinges creak—
It bends—it falls—and all is o'er; 945
Lost Corinth may resist no more!

XXX

Darkly, sternly, and all alone,
Minotti stood o'er the altar-stone:
Madonna's face upon him shone,
Painted in heavenly hues above, 950
With eyes of light and looks of love;
And placed upon that holy shrine
To fix our thoughts on things divine,
When pictured there, we kneeling see
Her, and the boy-God on her knee,
Smiling sweetly on each prayer 956
To heaven, as if to waft it there.
Still she smiled; even now she smiles,
Though slaughter streams along her
 aisles:
Minotti lifted his aged eye, 960
And made the sign of a cross with a
 sigh,
Then seized a torch which blazed there-
 by;
And still he stood, while with steel and
 flame
Inward and onward the Mussulman
 came.

XXXI

The vaults beneath the mosaic stone
Contain'd the dead of ages gone; 966

Their names were on the graven floor,
But now illegible with gore;
The carved crests, and curious hues
The varied marble's vein diffuse, 970
Were smear'd, and slippery,—stain'd,
 and strown
With broken swords, and helms o'er-
 thrown:
There were dead above, and the dead
 below
Lay cold in many a coffin'd row;
You might see them piled in sable
 state, 975
By a pale light through a gloomy grate;
But War had enter'd their dark caves,
And stored along the vaulted graves
Her sulphurous treasures, thickly
 spread
In masses by the fleshless dead: 980
 Here, throughout the siege, had been
 The Christians' chiefest magazine;
To these a late-form'd train now led,
Minotti's last and stern resource
Against the foe's o'erwhelming force.

XXXII

The foe came on, and few remain 986
To strive, and those must strive in vain:
For lack of further lives, to slake
The thirst of vengeance now awake,
With barbarous blows they gash the
 dead, 990
And lop the already lifeless head,
And fell the statues from their niche,
And spoil the shrines of offerings rich,
And from each other's rude hands
 wrest
The silver vessels saints had bless'd.
To the high altar on they go; 996
Oh, but it made a glorious show!
On its table still behold
The cup of consecrated gold;
Massy and deep, a glittering prize, 1000
Brightly it sparkles to plunderers' eyes:
That morn it held the holy wine,
Converted by Christ to his blood so
 divine,
Which his worshippers drank at the
 break of day,
To shrive their souls ere they join'd in
 the fray. 1005
Still a few drops within it lay:
And round the sacred table glow
Twelve lofty lamps, in splendid row,
From the purest metal cast;
A spoil—the richest, and the last.

XXXIII

So near they came, the nearest stretch'd
To grasp the spoil he almost reach'd,
When old Minotti's hand
Touch'd with the torch the train—
 'Tis fired! 1015

Spire, vaults, the shrine, the spoil, the
 slain,
 The turban'd victors, the Christian
 band,
All that of living or dead remain,
Hurl'd on high with the shiver'd fane,
 In one wild roar expired! 1020
The shatter'd town—the walls thrown
 down—
The waves a moment backward bent—
The hills that shake, although unrent,
 As if an earthquake pass'd—
The thousand shapeless things all
 driven 1025
In cloud and flame athwart the heaven,
 By that tremendous blast—
Proclaim'd the desperate conflict o'er
On that too long afflicted shore:
Up to the sky like rockets go 1030
All that mingled there below:
Many a tall and goodly man,
Scorch'd and shrivell'd to a span,
When he fell to earth again
Like a cinder strew'd the plain: 1035
Down the ashes shower like rain;
Some fell in the gulf, which received the
 sprinkles
With a thousand circling wrinkles;
Some fell on the shore, but, far away,
Scatter'd o'er the isthmus lay; 1040
Christian or Moslem, which be they?
Let their mothers see and say!
When in cradled rest they lay,
And each nursing mother smiled
On the sweet sleep of her child, 1045

Little deem'd she such a day
Would rend those tender limbs away.
Not the matrons that them bore
Could discern their offspring more;
That one moment left no trace 1050
More of human form or face
Save a scatter'd scalp or bone:
And down came blazing rafters, strown
Around, and many a falling stone,
Deeply dinted in the clay, 1055
All blacken'd there and reeking lay.
All the living things that heard
That deadly earth-shock disappear'd:
The wild birds flew; the wild dogs fled,
And howling left the unburied dead;
The camels from their keepers broke;
The distant steer forsook the yoke—
The nearer steed plunged o'er the plain,
And burst his girth, and tore his rein;
The bull-frog's note, from out the
 marsh, 1065
Deep-mouth'd arose, and doubly harsh;
The wolves yell'd on the cavern'd hill
Where echo roll'd in thunder still;
The jackals' troop, in gather'd cry,
Bay'd from afar complainingly, 1070
With a mix'd and mournful sound,
Like crying babe, and beaten hound:
With sudden wing, and ruffled breast,
The eagle left his rocky nest,
And mounted nearer to the sun, 1075
The clouds beneath him seem'd so dun;
Their smoke assail'd his startled beak,
And made him higher soar and shriek—
 Thus was Corinth lost and won!

PARISINA

TO

SCROPE BERDMORE DAVIES, ESQ.

THE FOLLOWING POEM IS INSCRIBED,

BY ONE WHO HAS LONG ADMIRED HIS TALENTS, AND VALUED HIS FRIENDSHIP

January 22, 1816.

ADVERTISEMENT

THE following poem is grounded on a circumstance mentioned in Gibbon's 'Antiquities of the House of Brunswick.' I am aware, that in modern times the delicacy or fastidiousness of the reader may deem such subjects unfit for the purposes of poetry. The Greek dramatists, and some of the best of our old English writers, were of a different opinion: as Alfieri and Schiller have also been, more recently, upon the Continent. The following extract will explain the facts on which the story is founded. The name of *Azo* is substituted for Nicholas, as more metrical.

'Under the reign of Nicholas III. Ferrara was polluted with a domestic tragedy. By the testimony of an attendant, and his own observation, the Marquis of Este discovered the incestuous loves of his wife Parisina, and Hugo his bastard son, a beautiful and valiant youth. They were beheaded in the castle by the sentence of a father and husband, who published his shame, and survived their execution. He was unfortunate, if they were guilty: if they were innocent, he was still more unfortunate; nor is there any possible situation in which I can sincerely approve the last act of the justice of a parent.'—GIBBON'S *Miscellaneous Works*, vol. iii, p. 470.

PARISINA

I

It is the hour when from the boughs
 The nightingale's high note is heard;
It is the hour when lovers' vows
 Seem sweet in every whisper'd word;
And gentle winds, and waters near, 5
Make music to the lonely ear.
Each flower the dews have lightly wet,
And in the sky the stars are met,
And on the wave is deeper blue,
And on the leaf a browner hue, 10
And in the heaven that clear obscure,
So softly dark, and darkly pure,
Which follows the decline of day,
As twilight melts beneath the moon
 away.

II

But it is not to list to the waterfall 15
That Parisina leaves her hall,
And it is not to gaze on the heavenly light
That the lady walks in the shadow of night;
And if she sits in Este's bower,
'Tis not for the sake of its full-blown
 flower; 20
She listens—but not for the nightingale—
Though her ear expects as soft a tale.
There glides a step through the foliage
 thick,
And her cheek grows pale, and her heart
 beats quick.
There whispers a voice through the rust-
 ling leaves, 25
And her blush returns, and her bosom
 heaves:
A moment more and they shall meet—
'Tis past—her lover's at her feet.

III

And what unto them is the world beside,
With all its change of time and tide? 30
Its living things, its earth and sky,
Are nothing to their mind and eye.
And heedless as the dead are they
 Of aught around, above, beneath;
As if all else had pass'd away, 35
 They only for each other breathe;
Their very sighs are full of joy
 So deep, that did it not decay,
That happy madness would destroy
 The hearts which feel its fiery sway:
Of guilt, of peril, do they deem 41
In that tumultuous tender dream?
Who that have felt that passion's power,
Or paused, or fear'd in such an hour?
Or thought how brief such moments
 last? 45
But yet—they are already past!
Alas! we must awake before
We know such vision comes no more.

IV

With many a lingering look they leave
 The spot of guilty gladness past: 50
And though they hope and vow, they
 grieve,
 As if that parting were the last.
The frequent sigh—the long embrace—
 The lip that there would cling for ever,
While gleams on Parisina's face 55
 The Heaven she fears will not forgive
 her,
As if each calmly conscious star
Beheld her frailty from afar—
The frequent sigh, the long embrace,
Yet binds them to their trysting place.
But it must come, and they must part
In fearful heaviness of heart, 62
With all the deep and shuddering chill
Which follows fast the deeds of ill.

V

And Hugo is gone to his lonely bed, 65
 To covet there another's bride;
But she must lay her conscious head
 A husband's trusting heart beside.
But fever'd in her sleep she seems,
And red her cheek with troubled
 dreams, 70
 And mutters she in her unrest
A name she dare not breathe by day,
 And clasps her lord unto the breast
Which pants for one away:
And he to that embrace awakes, 75
And, happy in the thought, mistakes
The dreaming sigh, and warm caress,
For such as he was wont to bless;
And could in very fondness weep
O'er her who loves him even in sleep.

VI

He clasp'd her sleeping to his heart,
 And listen'd to each broken word:
He hears—Why doth Prince Azo start,
 As if the Archangel's voice he heard?
And well he may—a deeper doom 85
Could scarcely thunder o'er his tomb,
When he shall wake to sleep no more,
And stand the eternal throne before.
And well he may—his earthly peace
Upon that sound is doom'd to cease. 90
That sleeping whisper of a name
Bespeaks her guilt and Azo's shame.
And whose that name? that o'er his
 pillow
Sounds fearful as the breaking billow,
Which rolls the plank upon the shore,
 And dashes on the pointed rock 96
The wretch who sinks to rise no more,—
 So came upon his soul the shock.

And whose that name? 'tis Hugo's,—
 his— 99
In sooth he had not deem'd of this!—
'Tis Hugo's,—he, the child of one
He loved—his own all-evil son—
The offspring of his wayward youth,
When he betray'd Bianca's truth, 104
The maid whose folly could confide
In him who made her not his bride.

VII

He pluck'd his poniard in its sheath,
 But sheath'd it ere the point was
 bare—
Howe'er unworthy now to breathe,
 He could not slay a thing so fair—
At least, not smiling—sleeping—
 there: 111
Nay more:—he did not wake her then,
 But gazed upon her with a glance
 Which, had she roused her from her
 trance,
Had frozen her sense to sleep again; 115
And o'er his brow the burning lamp
Gleam'd on the dew-drops big and
 damp.
She spake no more—but she still slum-
 ber'd—
While, in his thought, her days are
 number'd.

VIII

And with the morn he sought and
 found, 120
In many a tale from those around,
The proof of all he fear'd to know,
Their present guilt, his future woe;
The long-conniving damsels seek
 To save themselves, and would trans-
 fer 125
 The guilt—the shame—the doom—
 to her:
Concealment is no more—they speak
All circumstance which may compel
Full credence to the tale they tell:
And Azo's tortured heart and ear 130
Have nothing more to feel or hear.

IX

He was not one who brook'd delay:
 Within the chamber of his state,
The chief of Este's ancient sway 134
 Upon his throne of judgment sate;
His nobles and his guards are there,—
Before him is the sinful pair;
Both young,—and _one_ how passing fair!
With swordless belt, and fetter'd hand,
 Oh, Christ! that thus a son should
 stand 140
 Before a father's face!
Yet thus must Hugo meet his sire,
And hear the sentence of his ire,
 The tale of his disgrace!

And yet he seems not overcome, 145
Although, as yet, his voice be dumb.

X

And still, and pale, and silently
 Did Parisina wait her doom;
How changed since last her speaking
 eye
 Glanced gladness round the glittering
 room, 150
Where high-born men were proud to
 wait,
Where Beauty watch'd to imitate
 Her gentle voice, her lovely mien,
And gather from her air and gait
 The graces of its queen! 155
Then,—had her eye in sorrow wept,
A thousand warriors forth had leapt,
A thousand swords had sheathless
 shone,
And made her quarrel all their own.
Now,—what is she? and what are they?
Can she command, or these obey?
All silent and unheeding now,
With downcast eyes and knitting brow,
And folded arms, and freezing air,
And lips that scarce their scorn for-
 bear, 165
Her knights and dames, her court—is
 there:
And he, the chosen one, whose lance
Had yet been couch'd before her glance,
Who—were his arm a moment free—
Had died or gain'd her liberty; 170
The minion of his father's bride,—
He, too, is fetter'd by her side;
Nor sees her swoln and full eye swim
Less for her own despair than him:
Those lids—o'er which the violet vein
Wandering, leaves a tender stain, 176
Shining through the smoothest white
That e'er did softest kiss invite—
Now seem'd with hot and livid glow
To press, not shade, the orbs below;
Which glance so heavily, and fill, 181
As tear on tear grows gathering still.

XI

And he for her had also wept,
 But for the eyes that on him gazed:
His sorrow, if he felt it, slept; 185
 Stern and erect his brow was raised.
Whate'er the grief his soul avow'd,
He would not shrink before the crowd;
But yet he dared not look on her;
Remembrance of the hours that were—
His guilt, his love, his present state—
His father's wrath, all good men's
 hate— 192
His earthly, his eternal fate—
And hers,—oh, hers! he dared not throw
One look upon that death-like brow!
Else had his rising heart betray'd 196
Remorse for all the wreck it made.

XII

And Azo spake:—'But yesterday
 I gloried in a wife and son;
That dream this morning pass'd away;
 Ere day declines, I shall have none.
My life must linger on alone; 202
 Well,—let that pass,—there breathes
 not one
Who would not do as I have done:
 Those ties are broken—not by me;
 Let that too pass;—the doom's pre-
 pared! 206
Hugo, the priest awaits on thee,
 And then—thy crime's reward!
Away! address thy prayers to Heaven,
 Before its evening stars are met—
Learn if thou there canst be forgiven; 212
 Its mercy may absolve thee yet.
But here, upon the earth beneath,
 There is no spot where thou and I
Together for an hour could breathe:
 Farewell! I will not see thee die—
But thou, frail thing! shalt view his
 head— 217
Away! I cannot speak the rest:
 Go! woman of the wanton breast;
Not I, but thou his blood dost shed:
Go! if that sight thou canst outlive,
And joy thee in the life I give.' 222

XIII

And here stern Azo hid his face—
 For on his brow the swelling vein
 Throbb'd as if back upon his brain
 The hot blood ebb'd and flow'd
 again, 226
And therefore bow'd he for a space,
 And pass'd his shaking hand along
 His eye, to veil it from the throng:
While Hugo raised his chainèd hands,
 And for a brief delay demands 231
 His father's ear: the silent sire
 Forbids not what his words require.

'It is not that I dread the death—
 For thou hast seen me by thy side
 All redly through the battle ride,
And that—not once a useless brand—
 Thy slaves have wrested from my hand
 Hath shed more blood in cause of thine,
 Than e'er can stain the axe of mine:
 Thou gav'st, and may'st resume my
 breath, 241
A gift for which I thank thee not;
 Nor are my mother's wrongs forgot,
 Her slighted love and ruin'd name,
 Her offspring's heritage of shame;
 But she is in the grave, where he,
 Her son, thy rival, soon shall be.
 Her broken heart—my sever'd head—
 Shall witness for thee from the dead
 How trusty and how tender were 250
 Thy youthful love—paternal care.

'Tis true that I have done thee wrong—
 But wrong for wrong:—this,—
 deem'd thy bride,
 The other victim of thy pride,—
Thou know'st for me was destined long;
Thou saw'st, and coveted'st her charms;
 And with thy very crime—my birth—
 Thou tauntedst me, as little worth;
A match ignoble for her arms, 259
Because, forsooth, I could not claim
The lawful heirship of thy name,
Nor sit on Este's lineal throne;
 Yet, were a few short summers mine,
 My name should more than Este's shine
With honours all my own. 265
I had a sword—and have a breast
That should have won as haught a crest
As ever waved along the line
Of all these sovereign sires of thine.
Not always knightly spurs are worn
The brightest by the better born; 271
And mine have lanced my courser's
 flank
Before proud chiefs of princely rank,
When charging to the cheering cry
Of "Este" and of "Victory!" 275
I will not plead the cause of crime,
Nor sue thee to redeem from time
A few brief hours or days that must
At length roll o'er my reckless dust;—
Such maddening moments as my past,
They could not, and they did not, last.
Albeit my birth and name be base,
 And thy nobility of race 283
Disdain'd to deck a thing like me—
 Yet in my lineaments they trace
 Some features of my father's face,
And in my spirit—all of thee.
From thee these tamelessness of heart—
From thee—nay, wherefore dost thou
 start?— 289
From thee in all their vigour came
My arm of strength, my soul of flame;
Thou didst not give me life alone,
But all that made me more thine own.
See what thy guilty love hath done!
Repaid thee with too like a son! 295
I am no bastard in my soul,
For that, like thine, abhorr'd control;
And for my breath, that hasty boon
Thou gav'st and wilt resume so soon,
I valued it no more than thou, 300
When rose thy casque above thy brow,
And we, all side by side, have striven,
And o'er the dead our coursers driven:
The past is nothing—and at last
The future can but be the past; 305
Yet would I that I then had died:
 For though thou work'dst my
 mother's ill,
And made thy own my destined bride,
 I feel thou art my father still; 309
And harsh as sounds thy hard decree,
'Tis not unjust, although from thee.

Begot in sin, to die in shame,
My life begun and ends the same:
As err'd the sire, so err'd the son, 314
And thou must punish both in one.
My crime seems worst to human view,
But God must judge between us too!'

XIV

He ceased—and stood with folded
 arms,
 On which the circling fetters sounded;
And not an ear but felt as wounded,
Of all the chiefs that there were
 rank'd, 321
 When those dull chains in meeting
 clank'd:
Till Parisina's fatal charms
Again attracted every eye—
Would she thus hear him doom'd to die!
She stood, I said, all pale and still,
The living cause of Hugo's ill: 327
Her eyes unmoved, but full and wide,
Not once had turn'd to either side—
Nor once did those sweet eyelids close,
Or shade the glance o'er which they
 rose, 331
But round their orbs of deepest blue
The circling white dilated grew—
And there with glassy gaze she stood
As ice were in her curdled blood;
But every now and then a tear 336
 So large and slowly gather'd slid
 From the long dark fringe of that fair
 lid,
It was a thing to see, not hear!
And those who saw, it did surprise,
Such drops could fall from human eyes.
To speak she thought—the imperfect
 note 342
Was choked within her swelling throat,
Yet seem'd in that low hollow groan
Her whole heart gushing in the tone.
It ceased—again she thought to speak,
Then burst her voice in one long shriek,
And to the earth she fell like stone
Or statue from its base o'erthrown,
More like a thing that ne'er had life,—
A monument of Azo's wife,— 351
Than her, that living guilty thing,
Whose every passion was a sting,
Which urged to guilt, but could not
 bear
That guilt's detection and despair. 355
But yet she lived—and all too soon
Recover'd from that death-like swoon—
But scarce to reason—every sense
Had been o'erstrung by pangs intense;
And each frail fibre of her brain 360
(As bowstrings, when relax'd by rain,
The erring arrow launch aside)
Sent forth her thoughts all wild and
 wide—
The past a blank, the future black,
With glimpses of a dreary track, 365

Like lightning on the desert path,
When midnight storms are mustering
 wrath. 367
She fear'd—she felt that something ill
Lay on her soul, so deep and chill;
That there was sin and shame she knew,
That some one was to die—but who?
She had forgotten:—did she breathe?
Could this be still the earth beneath,
The sky above, and men around; 374
Or were they fiends who now so frown'd
On one, before whose eyes each eye
Till then had smiled in sympathy?
All was confused and undefined
To her all-jarr'd and wandering mind;
A chaos of wild hopes and fears: 380
And now in laughter, now in tears,
But madly still in each extreme,
She strove with that convulsive dream;
For so it seem'd on her to break:
Oh! vainly must she strive to wake!

XV

The Convent bells are ringing, 386
 But mournfully and slow;
In the grey square turret swinging,
 With a deep sound, to and fro.
 Heavily to the heart they go! 390
Hark! the hymn is singing—
 The song for the dead below,
 Or the living who shortly shall be so!
For a departing being's soul
The death-hymn peals and the hollow
 bells knoll: 395
He is near his mortal goal;
Kneeling at the Friar's knee,
Sad to hear, and piteous to see—
Kneeling on the bare cold ground,
With the block before and the guards
 around— 400
And the headsman with his bare arm
 ready,
That the blow may be both swift and
 steady,
Feels if the axe be sharp and true
Since he set its edge anew:
While the crowd in a speechless circle
 gather 405
To see the Son fall by the doom of the
 Father!

XVI

It is a lovely hour as yet
Before the summer sun shall set,
Which rose upon that heavy day, 409
And mock'd it with his steadiest ray;
And his evening beams are shed
Full on Hugo's fated head,
As his last confession pouring
To the monk, his doom deploring
In penitential holiness, 415
He bends to hear his accents bless
With absolution such as may
Wipe our mortal stains away.

That high sun on his head did glisten
As he there did bow and listen, 420
And the rings of chestnut hair
Curl'd half down his neck so bare;
But brighter still the beam was thrown
Upon the axe which near him shone
With a clear and ghastly glitter——
Oh! that parting hour was bitter! 426
Even the stern stood chill'd with awe:
Dark the crime, and just the law—
Yet they shudder'd as they saw.

XVII

The parting prayers are said and over
Of that false son, and daring lover! 431
His beads and sins are all recounted,
His hours to their last minute mounted;
His mantling cloak before was stripp'd,
His bright brown locks must now be
 clipp'd; 435
'Tis done—all closely are they shorn;
The vest which till this moment worn—
The scarf which Parisina gave—
Must not adorn him to the grave. 439
Even that must now be thrown aside,
And o'er his eyes the kerchief tied;
But no—that last indignity
Shall ne'er approach his haughty eye.
All feelings seemingly subdued,
In deep disdain were half renew'd,
When headsman's hands prepared to bind
Those eyes which would not brook
 such blind,
As if they dared not look on death.
'No—yours my forfeit blood and
 breath;
These hands are chain'd, but let me die
At least with an unshackled eye— 451
Strike:'—and as the word he said,
Upon the block he bow'd his head;
These the last accents Hugo spoke:
'Strike'—and flashing fell the stroke—
Roll'd the head—and, gushing, sunk
Back the stain'd and heaving trunk,
In the dust, which each deep vein
Slaked with its ensanguined rain; 459
His eyes and lips a moment quiver,
Convulsed and quick—then fix for ever.

He died, as erring man should die,
 Without display, without parade;
 Meekly had he bow'd and pray'd,
 As not disdaining priestly aid; 465
Nor desperate of all hope on high.
And while before the Prior kneeling,
His heart was wean'd from earthly feeling;
His wrathful sire, his paramour—
What were they in such an hour? 470
No more reproach, no more despair,
No thought but heaven, no word but
 prayer—
Save the few which from him broke,
When, bared to meet the headsman's
 stroke,

He claim'd to die with eyes unbound,
His sole adieu to those around. 476

XVIII

Still as the lips that closed in death,
Each gazer's bosom held his breath:
But yet, afar, from man to man,
A cold electric shiver ran, 480
As down the deadly blow descended
On him whose life and love thus ended;
And, with a hushing sound compress'd,
A sigh shrunk back on every breast;
But no more thrilling noise rose there,
 Beyond the blow that to the block
 Pierced through with forced and
 sullen shock, 487
Save one:—what cleaves the silent air
So madly shrill, so passing wild?
That, as a mother's o'er her child,
Done to death by sudden blow, 491
To the sky these accents go,
Like a soul's in endless woe.
Through Azo's palace-lattice driven,
That horrid voice ascends to heaven,
And every eye is turn'd thereon: 496
But sound and sight alike are gone!
It was a woman's shriek—and ne'er
In madlier accents rose despair;
And those who heard it, as it pass'd,
In mercy wish'd it were the last. 501

XIX

Hugo is fallen; and, from that hour,
No more in palace, hall, or bower,
Was Parisina heard or seen: 504
Her name—as if she ne'er had been—
Was banish'd from each lip and ear,
Like words of wantonness or fear;
And from Prince Azo's voice, by none
Was mention heard of wife or son;
No tomb, no memory had they; 510
Theirs was unconsecrated clay—
At least the knight's who died that day.
But Parisina's fate lies hid
Like dust beneath the coffin lid:
Whether in convent she abode, 515
And won to heaven her dreary road
By blighted and remorseful years
Of scourge, and fast, and sleepless tears;
Or if she fell by bowl or steel,
For that dark love she dared to feel;
Or if, upon the moment smote, 52b
She died by tortures less remote,
Like him she saw upon the block,
With heart that shared the headsman's
 shock,
In quicken'd brokenness that came,
In pity, o'er her shatter'd frame, 526
None knew—and none can ever know:
But whatsoe'er its end below,
Her life began and closed in woe!

XX

And Azo found another bride, 530
And goodly sons grew by his side;

But none so lovely and so brave
As him who wither'd in the grave;
Or if they were—on his cold eye
Their growth but glanced unheeded by,
Or noticed with a smother'd sigh. 536
But never tear his cheek descended,
And never smile his brow unbended;
And o'er that fair broad brow were
 wrought
The intersected lines of thought; 540
Those furrows which the burning share
Of Sorrow ploughs untimely there;
Scars of the lacerating mind
Which the Soul's war doth leave behind.
He was past all mirth or woe:
Nothing more remain'd below 546
But sleepless nights and heavy days,
A mind all dead to scorn or praise,
A heart which shunn'd itself—and yet
That would not yield, nor could forget,
Which, when it least appear'd to melt,
Intently thought, intensely felt: 552
The deepest ice which ever froze
Can only o'er the surface close;
The living stream lies quick below, 555
And flows, and cannot cease to flow.
Still was his seal'd-up bosom haunted
By thoughts which Nature hath im-
 planted; 558
Too deeply rooted thence to vanish,

Howe'er our stifled tears we banish;
When, struggling as they rise to start,
We check those waters of the heart,
They are not dried—those tears unshed
But flow back to the fountain head,
And resting in their spring more pure, 566
For ever in its depth endure,
Unseen, unwept, but uncongeal'd,
And cherish'd most where least reveal'd.
With inward starts of feeling left,
To throb o'er those of life bereft, 570
Without the power to fill again
The desert gap which made his pain;
Without the hope to meet them where
United souls shall gladness share;
With all the consciousness that he
Had only pass'd a just decree; 576
That they had wrought their doom of
 ill;
Yet Azo's age was wretched still.
The tainted branches of the tree,
 If lopp'd with care, a strength may
 give, 580
 By which the rest shall bloom and
 live
All greenly fresh and wildly free:
But if the lightning, in its wrath,
The waving boughs with fury scathe,
The massy trunk the ruin feels, 585
And never more a leaf reveals.

THE PRISONER OF CHILLON

SONNET ON CHILLON

ETERNAL Spirit of the chainless Mind!
 Brightest in dungeons, Liberty! thou art,
 For there thy habitation is the heart—
The heart which love of thee alone can bind;
And when thy sons to fetters are consign'd—
 To fetters, and the damp vault's dayless gloom,
 Their country conquers with their martyrdom,
And Freedom's fame finds wings on every wind.
Chillon! thy prison is a holy place,
 And thy sad floor an altar—for 'twas trod,
Until his very steps have left a trace
 Worn, as if thy cold pavement were a sod,
By Bonnivard! May none those marks efface!
 For they appeal from tyranny to God.

ADVERTISEMENT

WHEN this poem was composed, I was not sufficiently aware of the history of Bonnivard, or I should have endeavoured to dignify the subject by an attempt to celebrate his courage and his virtues. With some account of his life I have been furnished, by the kindness of a citizen of that republic, which is still proud of the memory of a man worthy of the best age of ancient freedom:—

'François de Bonnivard, fils de Louis de Bonnivard, originaire de Seyssel et Seigneur de Lunes, naquit en 1496. Il fit ses études à Turin: en 1510 Jean Aimé de Bonnivard, son oncle, lui résigna le Prieuré de St. Victor, qui aboutissait aux murs de Genève, et qui formait un bénéfice considérable.

'Ce grand homme—(Bonnivard mérite ce titre par la force de son âme, la droiture de son cœur, la noblesse de ses intentions, la sagesse de ses conseils, le courage de ses démarches, l'étendue de ses connaissances, et la vivacité de son esprit),—ce grand homme, qui excitera l'admiration de tous ceux

u'une vertu héroïque peut encore émouvoir, inspirera encore la plus vive reconnaissance dans les
œurs des Génévois qui aiment Genève. Bonnivard en fut toujours un des plus fermes appuis: pour
ssurer la liberté de notre République, il ne craignit pas de perdre souvent la sienne; il oublia son
pos; il méprisa ses richesses; il ne négligea rien pour affermir le bonheur d'une patrie qu'il honora
e son choix: dès ce moment il la chérit comme le plus zélé de ses citoyens; il la servit avec l'intrépidité
un héros, et il écrivit son Histoire avec la naïveté d'un philosophe et la chaleur d'un patriote.

'Il dit dans le commencement de son Histoire de Genève, que, *dès qu'il eut commencé de lire l'histoire
es nations, il se sentit entraîné par son goût pour les Républiques, dont il épousa toujours les intérêts:*
est ce goût pour la liberté qui lui fit sans doute adopter Genève pour sa patrie.

'Bonnivard, encore jeune, s'annonça hautement comme le défenseur de Genève contre le Duc de
avoye et l'Evêque.

'En 1519, Bonnivard devient le martyr de sa patrie. Le Duc de Savoye étant entré dans Genève
vec cinq cent hommes, Bonnivard craint le ressentiment du Duc; il voulut se retirer à Fribourg pour
a éviter les suites; mais il fut trahi par deux hommes qui l'accompagnaient, et conduit par ordre du
rince à Grolée, où il resta prisonnier pendant deux ans. Bonnivard était malheureux dans ses voyages:
omme ses malheurs n'avaient point ralenti son zèle pour Genève, il était toujours un ennemi redoutable
our ceux qui la menaçaient, et par conséquent il devait être exposé à leurs coups. Il fut rencontré
a 1530 sur le Jura par des voleurs, qui le dépouillèrent et qui le mirent encore entre les mains du Duc
e Savoye: ce Prince le fit enfermer dans le Château de Chillon, où il resta sans être interrogé jusques
a 1536; il fut alors délivré par les Bernois, qui s'emparèrent du Pays de Vaud.

'Bonnivard, en sortant de sa captivité, eut le plaisir de trouver Genève libre et réformée: la Répub-
que s'empressa de lui témoigner sa reconnaissance, et de le dédommager des maux qu'il avoit soufferts:
le le reçut Bourgeois de la ville au mois de Juin, 1536; elle lui donna la maison habitée autrefois
ar le Vicaire-Général, et elle lui assigna une pension de deux cent écus d'or tant qu'il séjournerait
Genève. Il fut admis dans le Conseil de Deux-Cent en 1537.

'Bonnivard n'a pas fini d'être utile: après avoir travaillé à rendre Genève libre, il réussit à la rendre
élérante. Bonnivard engagea le Conseil à accorder aux ecclésiastiques et aux paysans un tems suffisant
our examiner les propositions qu'on leur faisait; il réussit par sa douceur: on prêche toujours le
hristianisme avec succès quand on le prêche avec charité.

'Bonnivard fut savant: ses manuscrits, qui sont dans la bibliothèque publique, prouvent qu'il avait
ien lu les auteurs classiques Latins, et qu'il avait approfondi la théologie et l'histoire. Ce grand
omme aimait les sciences, et il croyait qu'elles pouvaient faire la gloire de Genève; aussi il ne négligea
en pour les fixer dans cette ville naissante; en 1551 il donna sa bibliothèque au public; elle fut le
ommencement de notre bibliothèque publique; et ces livres sont en partie les rares et belles éditions
u quinzième siècle qu'on voit dans notre collection. Enfin, pendant la même année, ce bon patriote
nstitua la République son héritière, à condition qu'elle employerait ses biens à entretenir le collège
ont on projettait la fondation.

'Il parait que Bonnivard mourut en 1570; mais on ne peut l'assurer, parcequ'il y a une lacune dans
Nécrologe depuis le mois de Juillet, 1570, jusques en 1571.'

I

My hair is grey, but not with years,
 Nor grew it white
 In a single night,
As men's have grown from sudden fears:
My limbs are bow'd, though not with
 toil, 5
But rusted with a vile repose,
For they have been a dungeon's spoil,
 And mine has been the fate of those
To whom the goodly earth and air
Are bann'd, and barr'd—forbidden
 fare: 10
But this was for my father's faith
I suffer'd chains and courted death;
That father perish'd at the stake
For tenets he would not forsake;
And for the same his lineal race 15
In darkness found a dwelling-place;
We were seven—who now are one,
 Six in youth, and one in age,
Finish'd as they had begun,
 Proud of Persecution's rage; 20
One in fire, and two in field,
Their belief with blood have seal'd,
Dying as their father died,
For the God their foes denied;
Three were in a dungeon cast, 25
Of whom this wreck is left the last.

II

There are seven pillars of Gothic mould,
In Chillon's dungeons deep and old,
There are seven columns, massy and
 grey,
Dim with a dull imprison'd ray, 30
A sunbeam which hath lost its way,
And through the crevice and the cleft
Of the thick wall is fallen and left;
Creeping o'er the floor so damp,
Like a marsh's meteor lamp, 35
And in each pillar there is a ring,
 And in each ring there is a chain;
That iron is a cankering thing,
 For in these limbs its teeth remain,
With marks that will not wear away,
Till I have done with this new day, 41
Which now is painful to these eyes,
Which have not seen the sun so rise
For years—I cannot count them o'er,
I lost their long and heavy score, 45
When my last brother droop'd and died,
And I lay living by his side.

III

They chain'd us each to a column stone,
And we were three—yet, each alone;
We could not move a single pace, 50
We could not see each other's face,

But with that pale and livid light
That made us strangers in our sight:
And thus together—yet apart, 54
Fetter'd in hand, but join'd in heart,
'Twas still some solace, in the dearth
Of the pure elements of earth,
To hearken to each other's speech,
And each turn comforter to each
With some new hope, or legend old,
Or song heroically bold; 61
But even these at length grew cold.
Our voices took a dreary tone,
An echo of the dungeon stone,
A grating sound, not full and free, 65
As they of yore were wont to be:
It might be fancy, but to me
They never sounded like our own.

IV

I was the eldest of the three, 69
 And to uphold and cheer the rest
I ought to do—and did my best—
And each did well in his degree.
 The youngest, whom my father loved,
Because our mother's brow was given
To him, with eyes as blue as heaven—
 For him my soul was sorely moved;
And truly might it be distress'd 77
To see such bird in such a nest;
For he was beautiful as day—
 (When day was beautiful to me 80
As to young eagles, being free)—
 A polar day, which will not see
A sunset till its summer's gone,
 Its sleepless summer of long light,
The snow-clad offspring of the sun: 85
 And thus he was as pure and bright,
And in his natural spirit gay,
With tears for nought but others' ills,
And then they flow'd like mountain rills,
Unless he could assuage the woe 90
Which he abhorr'd to view below.

V

The other was as pure of mind,
But form'd to combat with his kind;
Strong in his frame, and of a mood
Which 'gainst the world in war had
 stood, 95
And perish'd in the foremost rank
 With joy:—but not in chains to pine:
His spirit wither'd with their clank,
 I saw it silently decline—
 And so perchance in sooth did mine:
But yet I forced it on to cheer 101
Those relics of a home so dear.
He was a hunter of the hills,
 Had follow'd there the deer and wolf;
To him his dungeon was a gulf, 105
And fetter'd feet the worst of ills.

VI

Lake Leman lies by Chillon's walls:
A thousand feet in depth below
Its massy waters meet and flow; 109

Thus much the fathom-line was sent
From Chillon's snow-white battlement,
 Which round about the wave in
 thrals:
A double dungeon wall and wave
Have made—and like a living grave
Below the surface of the lake 11
The dark vault lies wherein we lay,
We heard it ripple night and day;
 Sounding o'er our heads it knock'd;
And I have felt the winter's spray
Wash through the bars when winds
 were high 12
And wanton in the happy sky;
 And then the very rock hath rock'd,
 And I have felt it shake, unshock'd,
Because I could have smiled to see
The death that would have set me free.

VII

I said my nearer brother pined, 12
I said his mighty heart declined,
He loathed and put away his food,
It was not that 'twas coarse and rude,
For we were used to hunter's fare,
And for the like had little care: 13
The milk drawn from the mountain goat
Was changed for water from the moat,
Our bread was such as captives' tears
Have moisten'd many a thousand years,
Since man first pent his fellow men
Like brutes within an iron den;
But what were these to us or him? 13
These wasted not his heart or limb;
My brother's soul was of that mould
Which in a palace had grown cold,
Had his free breathing been denied
The range of the steep mountain's side;
But why delay the truth?—he died.
I saw, and could not hold his head, 14
Nor reach his dying hand—nor dead,—
Though hard I strove, but strove in vain
To rend and gnash my bonds in twain.
He died, and they unlock'd his chain,
And scoop'd for him a shallow grave
Even from the cold earth of our cave.
I begg'd them as a boon to lay 15
His corse in dust whereon the day
Might shine—it was a foolish thought,
But then within my brain it wrought,
That even in death his freeborn breast
In such a dungeon could not rest. 15
I might have spared my idle prayer—
They coldly laugh'd, and laid him there,
The flat and turfless earth above
The being we so much did love; 16
His empty chain above it leant,
Such murder's fitting monument!

VIII

But he, the favourite and the flower,
Most cherish'd since his natal hour,
His mother's image in fair face, 16
The infant love of all his race,

338

His martyr'd father's dearest thought,
My latest care, for whom I sought 169
To hoard my life, that his might be
Less wretched now, and one day free;
He, too, who yet had held untired
 spirit natural or inspired—
He, too, was struck, and day by day
Was wither'd on the stalk away. 175
Oh, God! it is a fearful thing
To see the human soul take wing
In any shape, in any mood;
I've seen it rushing forth in blood,
I've seen it on the breaking ocean
Strive with a swoln convulsive motion,
I've seen the sick and ghastly bed
Of Sin delirious with its dread;
But these were horrors—this was woe
Unmix'd with such—but sure and slow:
He faded, and so calm and meek, 186
So softly worn, so sweetly weak,
So tearless, yet so tender, kind,
And grieved for those he left behind;
With all the while a cheek whose bloom
Was as a mockery of the tomb, 191
Whose tints as gently sunk away
As a departing rainbow's ray;
An eye of most transparent light,
That almost made the dungeon bright,
And not a word of murmur, not— 196
A groan o'er his untimely lot,—
A little talk of better days,
A little hope my own to raise,
For I was sunk in silence—lost 200
In this last loss, of all the most;
And then the sighs he would suppress
Of fainting nature's feebleness,
More slowly drawn, grew less and less:
I listen'd, but I could not hear; 205
I call'd, for I was wild with fear;
I knew 'twas hopeless, but my dread
Would not be thus admonished;
I call'd, and thought I heard a sound—
I burst my chain with one strong bound,
And rush'd to him:—I found him not,
I only stirr'd in this black spot, 212
I only lived, I only drew
The accursed breath of dungeon-dew;
The last, the sole, the dearest link 215
Between me and the eternal brink,
Which bound me to my failing race,
Was broken in this fatal place.
One on the earth, and one beneath—
My brothers—both had ceased to
 breathe: 220
I took that hand which lay so still,
Alas! my own was full as chill;
I had not strength to stir, or strive,
But felt that I was still alive—
A frantic feeling, when we know 225
That what we love shall ne'er be so.
 I know not why
 I could not die,
I had no earthly hope but faith,
And that forbade a selfish death. 230

IX

What next befell me then and there
 I know not well—I never knew—
First came the loss of light, and air,
 And then of darkness too:
I had no thought, no feeling—none—
Among the stones I stood a stone, 236
And was, scarce conscious what I wist,
As shrubless crags within the mist;
For all was blank, and bleak, and grey;
It was not night, it was not day; 240
It was not even the dungeon-light,
So hateful to my heavy sight,
But vacancy absorbing space,
And fixedness without a place;
There were no stars, no earth, no time,
No check, no change, no good, no
 crime, 246
But silence, and a stirless breath
Which neither was of life nor death;
A sea of stagnant idleness,
Blind, boundless, mute, and motion-
 less! 250

X

A light broke in upon my brain,—
 It was the carol of a bird;
It ceased, and then it came again,
 The sweetest song ear ever heard,
And mine was thankful till my eyes
Ran over with the glad surprise, 256
And they that moment could not see
I was the mate of misery;
But then by dull degrees came back
My senses to their wonted track; 260
I saw the dungeon walls and floor
Close slowly round me as before,
I saw the glimmer of the sun
Creeping as it before had done,
But through the crevice where it came
That bird was perch'd, as fond and
 tame, 266
 And tamer than upon the tree;
A lovely bird, with azure wings,
And song that said a thousand things,
 And seem'd to say them all for me!
I never saw its like before, 271
I ne'er shall see its likeness more:
It seem'd like me to want a mate,
But was not half so desolate,
And it was come to love me when
None lived to love me so again, 276
And cheering from my dungeon's brink,
Had brought me back to feel and think.
I know not if it late were free,
 Or broke its cage to perch on mine,
But knowing well captivity, 281
 Sweet bird! I could not wish for thine!
Or if it were, in winged guise,
A visitant from Paradise;
For—Heaven forgive that thought! the
 while 285
Which made me both to weep and smile—

I sometimes deem'd that it might be
My brother's soul come down to me;
But then at last away it flew, 289
And then 'twas mortal well I knew,
For he would never thus have flown,
And left me twice so doubly lone,
Lone as the corse within its shroud,
Lone as a solitary cloud,—
 A single cloud on a sunny day, 295
While all the rest of heaven is clear,
A frown upon the atmosphere,
That hath no business to appear
 When skies are blue, and earth is gay.

XI

A kind of change came in my fate,
My keepers grew compassionate; 301
I know not what had made them so,
They were inured to sights of woe,
But so it was:—my broken chain
With links unfasten'd did remain, 305
And it was liberty to stride
Along my cell from side to side,
And up and down, and then athwart,
And tread it over every part;
And round the pillars one by one, 310
Returning where my walk begun,
Avoiding only, as I trod,
My brothers' graves without a sod;
For if I thought with heedless tread
My step profaned their lowly bed, 315
My breath came gaspingly and thick,
And my crush'd heart felt blind and sick.

XII

I made a footing in the wall,
 It was not therefrom to escape,
For I had buried one and all 320
 Who loved me in a human shape;
And the whole earth would henceforth be
A wider prison unto me:
No child, no sire, no kin had I,
No partner in my misery; 325
I thought of this, and I was glad,
For thought of them had made me mad;
But I was curious to ascend
To my barr'd windows, and to bend
Once more, upon the mountains high,
The quiet of a loving eye. 331

XIII

I saw them, and they were the same,
They were not changed like me in
 frame;
I saw their thousand years of snow
On high—their wide long lake below,
And the blue Rhone in fullest flow;
I heard the torrents leap and gush 337

O'er channell'd rock and broken bush;
I saw the white-wall'd distant town,
And whiter sails go skimming down,
And then there was a little isle,
Which in my very face did smile, 342
 The only one in view;
A small green isle, it seem'd no more,
Scarce broader than my dungeon floor,
But in it there were three tall trees,
And o'er it blew the mountain breeze,
And by it there were waters flowing,
And on it there were young flowers
 growing, 349
 Of gentle breath and hue.
The fish swam by the castle wall,
And they seem'd joyous each and all;
The eagle rode the rising blast,
Methought he never flew so fast
As then to me he seem'd to fly; 355
And then new tears came in my eye,
And I felt troubled—and would fain
I had not left my recent chain;
And when I did descend again,
The darkness of my dim abode 360
Fell on me as a heavy load;
It was as is a new-dug grave,
Closing o'er one we sought to save,—
And yet my glance, too much opprest,
Had almost need of such a rest. 365

XIV

It might be months, or years, or days,
 I kept no count, I took no note,
I had no hope my eyes to raise,
 And clear them of their dreary mote;
At last men came to set me free; 370
 I ask'd not why, and reck'd not where,
It was at length the same to me,
Fetter'd or fetterless to be,
 I learn'd to love despair. 374
And thus when they appear'd at last,
And all my bonds aside were cast,
These heavy walls to me had grown
A hermitage—and all my own!
And half I felt as they were come
To tear me from a second home: 380
With spiders I had friendship made,
And watch'd them in their sullen trade,
Had seen the mice by moonlight play,
And why should I feel less than they?
We were all inmates of one place, 385
And I, the monarch of each race,
Had power to kill—yet, strange to tell!
In quiet we had learn'd to dwell;
My very chains and I grew friends,
So much a long communion tends 390
To make us what we are:—even I
Regain'd my freedom with a sigh.

MAZEPPA

ADVERTISEMENT

'CELUI qui remplissait alors cette place était un gentilhomme Polonais, nommé Mazeppa, né dans e palatinat de Podolie: il avait été élevé page de Jean Casimir, et avait pris à sa cour quelque teinture es belles-lettres. Une intrigue qu'il eut dans sa jeunesse avec la femme d'un gentilhomme Polonais yant été découverte, le mari le fit lier tout nu sur un cheval farouche, et le laissa aller en cet état. e cheval, qui était du pays de l'Ukraine, y retourna, et y porta Mazeppa, demi-mort de fatigue et e faim. Quelques paysans le secoururent: il resta longtems parmi eux, et se signala dans plusieurs ourses contre les Tartares. La supériorité de ses lumières lui donna une grande considération parmi s Cosaques: sa réputation s'augmentant de jour en jour obligea le Czar à le faire Prince de l'Ukraine.' —VOLTAIRE, _Hist. de Charles XII._ p. 196.

'Le roi fuyant, et poursuivi, eut son cheval tué sous lui; le Colonel Gieta, blessé, et perdant tout on sang, lui donna le sien. Ainsi on remit deux fois à cheval, dans sa fuite, ce conquérant qui n'avait u y monter pendant la bataille.'—P. 216.

'Le roi alla par un autre chemin avec quelques cavaliers. Le carrosse, où il était, rompit dans la arche; on le remit à cheval. Pour comble de disgrace, il s'égara pendant la nuit dans un bois; là, son ourage ne pouvant plus suppléer à ses forces épuisées, les douleurs de sa blessure devenues plus supportables par la fatigue, son cheval étant tombé de lassitude, il se coucha quelques heures au ied d'un arbre, en danger d'être surpris à tout moment par les vainqueurs, qui le cherchaient de tous ôtés.'—P. 218.

I

'TWAS after dread Pultowa's day,
 When fortune left the royal Swede,
Around a slaughter'd army lay,
 No more to combat and to bleed.
The power and glory of the war, 5
 Faithless as their vain votaries, men,
Had pass'd to the triumphant Czar,
 And Moscow's walls were safe again,
Until a day more dark and drear,
 And a more memorable year, 10
Should give to slaughter and to shame
A mightier host and haughtier name;
A greater wreck, a deeper fall,
A shock to one—a thunderbolt to all.

II

Such was the hazard of the die; 15
The wounded Charles was taught to fly
By day and night through field and flood,
Stain'd with his own and subjects' blood;
For thousands fell that flight to aid:
And not a voice was heard t' upbraid
 Ambition in his humbled hour, 21
When truth had nought to dread from
 power.
His horse was slain, and Gieta gave
His own—and died the Russians' slave.
This too sinks after many a league 25
Of well sustain'd but vain fatigue;
And in the depth of forests, darkling
The watch-fires in the distance spark-
 ling—
 The beacons of surrounding foes—
A king must lay his limbs at length.
 Are these the laurels and repose 31
For which the nations strain their
 strength?
They laid him by a savage tree,
In outworn nature's agony;

His wounds were stiff, his limbs were
 stark; 35
The heavy hour was chill and dark;
The fever in his blood forbade
A transient slumber's fitful aid:
And thus it was; but yet through all,
Kinglike the monarch bore his fall, 40
And made, in this extreme of ill,
His pangs the vassals of his will:
All silent and subdued were they,
As once the nations round him lay.

III

A band of chiefs!—alas! how few,
 Since but the fleeting of a day 46
Had thinn'd it; but this wreck was true
 And chivalrous: upon the clay
Each sate him down, all sad and mute,
 Beside his monarch and his steed;
For danger levels man and brute,
 And all are fellows in their need. 52
Among the rest, Mazeppa made
His pillow in an old oak's shade—
Himself as rough, and scarce less old,
The Ukraine's Hetman, calm and bold;
But first, outspent with this long course,
The Cossack prince rubb'd down his
 horse, 58
 And made for him a leafy bed,
 And smooth'd his fetlocks and his
 mane,
 And slack'd his girth, and stripp'd his
 rein,
And rejoy'd to see how well he fed;
For until now he had the dread
 His wearied courser might refuse 64
To browse beneath the midnight dews:
But he was hardy as his lord,
And little cared for bed and board;
But spirited and docile too,
Whate'er was to be done, would do.

341 M.

MAZEPPA

Shaggy and swift, and strong of limb,
All Tartar-like he carried him; 71
Obey'd his voice, and came to call,
And knew him in the midst of all:
Though thousands were around,—and
 Night,
Without a star, pursued her flight,—
That steed from sunset until dawn 76
His chief would follow like a fawn.

IV

This done, Mazeppa spread his cloak,
And laid his lance beneath his oak,
Felt if his arms in order good 80
The long day's march had well with-
 stood—
If still the powder fill'd the pan,
 And flints unloosen'd kept their lock—
His sabre's hilt and scabbard felt,
And whether they had chafed his belt;
And next the venerable man, 86
From out his havresack and can,
 Prepared and spread his slender stock;
And to the monarch and his men
The whole or portion offer'd then 90
With far less of inquietude
Than courtiers at a banquet would.
And Charles of this his slender share
With smiles partook a moment there,
To force of cheer a greater show, 95
And seem above both wounds and woe;
And then he said—'Of all our band,
Though firm of heart and strong of hand,
In skirmish, march, or forage, none
Can less have said or more have done
Than thee, Mazeppa! on the earth 101
So fit a pair had never birth,
Since Alexander's days till now,
As thy Bucephalus and thou:
All Scythia's fame to thine should yield
For pricking on o'er flood and field.'
Mazeppa answer'd—'Ill betide 107
The school wherein I learn'd to ride!'
Quoth Charles—'Old Hetman, where-
 fore so,
Since thou hast learn'd the art so well?'
Mazeppa said—''Twere long to tell;
And we have many a league to go,
With every now and then a blow, 113
And ten to one at least the foe,
Before our steeds may graze at ease
Beyond the swift Borysthenes:
And, Sire, your limbs have need of rest,
 And I will be the sentinel
Of this your troop.'—'But I request,'
 Said Sweden's monarch, 'thou wilt
 tell 120
This tale of thine, and I may reap,
Perchance, from this the boon of sleep
For at this moment from my eyes
The hope of present slumber flies.'

'Well, Sire, with such a hope, I'll track
My seventy years of memory back: 126

I think 'twas in my twentieth spring,—
Ay, 'twas,—when Casimir was king—
John Casimir,—I was his page
Six summers, in my earlier age: 13
A learned monarch, faith! was he,
And most unlike your majesty;
He made no wars, and did not gain
New realms to lose them back again;
And (save debates in Warsaw's diet)
He reign'd in most unseemly quiet; 13
Not that he had no cares to vex,
He loved the muses and the sex;
And sometimes these so froward are,
They made him wish himself at war;
But soon his wrath being o er, he too
Another mistress, or new book: 14
And then he gave prodigious fêtes—
All Warsaw gather'd round his gates
To gaze upon his splendid court,
And dames, and chiefs, of princely port
He was the Polish Solomon, 14
So sung his poets, all but one,
Who, being unpension'd, made a satire
And boasted that he could not flatter
It was a court of jousts and mimes, 15
Where every courtier tried at rhymes
Even I for once produced some verses
And sign'd my odes " Despairing Thyrsis.
There was a certain Palatine, 15
 A count of far and high descent,
Rich as a salt or silver mine;
And he was proud, ye may divine,
 As if from heaven he had been sent
He had such wealth in blood and ore
 As few could match beneath th
 throne; 16
And he would gaze upon his store,
And o'er his pedigree would pore,
Until by some confusion led,
Which almost look'd like want of head
 He thought their merits were his own
His wife was not of his opinion, 16
 His junior she by thirty years,
Grew daily tired of his dominion;
 And, after wishes, hopes, and fears
 To virtue a few farewell tears, 17
A restless dream or two, some glance
At Warsaw's youth, some songs, an
 dances,
Awaited but the usual chances,
Those happy accidents which render
The coldest dames so very tender, 17
To deck her Count with titles given,
'Tis said, as passports into heaven;
But, strange to say, they rarely boast
Of these, who have deserved them most

V

'I was a goodly stripling then; 18
 At seventy years I so may say,
That there were few, or boys or men,
 Who, in my dawning time of day,
Of vassal or of knight's degree, 18
Could vie in vanities with me;

or I had strength, youth, gaiety,
A port, not like to this ye see,
But smooth, as all is rugged now;
 For time, and care, and war, have
 plough'd 190
My very soul from out my brow;
 And thus I should be disavow'd
By all my kind and kin, could they
Compare my day and yesterday;
This change was wrought, too, long ere
 age 195
Had ta'en my features for his page:
With years, ye know, have not declined
My strength, my courage, or my mind,
Or at this hour I should not be
Telling old tales beneath a tree, 200
With starless skies my canopy.
 But let me on: Theresa's form—
Methinks it glides before me now,
Between me and yon chestnut's bough,
 The memory is so quick and warm; 206
And yet I find no words to tell
The shape of her I loved so well:
She had the Asiatic eye,
 Such as our Turkish neighbourhood
 Hath mingled with our Polish blood,
Dark as above us is the sky; 211
But through it stole a tender light,
Like the first moonrise of midnight;
Large, dark, and swimming in the
 stream, 214
Which seem'd to melt to its own beam;
All love, half languor, and half fire,
Like saints that at the stake expire,
And lift their raptured looks on high,
As though it were a joy to die.
A brow like a midsummer lake, 220
 Transparent with the sun therein,
When waves no murmur dare to make,
 And heaven beholds her face within.
A cheek and lip—but why proceed?
I loved her then, I love her still;
And such as I am, love indeed 226
 In fierce extremes—in good and ill.
But still we love even in our rage,
And haunted to our very age
With the vain shadow of the past, 230
As is Mazeppa to the last.

VI

We met—we gazed—I saw, and sigh'd,
She did not speak, and yet replied;
There are ten thousand tones and signs
We hear and see, but none defines—
Involuntary sparks of thought, 236
Which strike from out the heart o'er-
 wrought,
And form a strange intelligence,
Alike mysterious and intense,
Which link the burning chain that binds,
Without their will, young hearts and
 minds: 241
Conveying, as the electric wire,
We know not how, the absorbing fire.

I saw, and sigh'd—in silence wept,
And still reluctant distance kept, 245
Until I was made known to her,
And we might then and there confer
Without suspicion—then, even then,
 I long'd, and was resolved to speak;
But on my lips they died again, 250
 The accents tremulous and weak,
Until one hour.—There is a game,
 A frivolous and foolish play,
 Wherewith we while away the day;
It is—I have forgot the name— 255
And we to this, it seems, were set,
By some strange chance, which I forget:
I reck'd not if I won or lost,
 It was enough for me to be
 So near to hear, and oh! to see 260
The being whom I loved the most.
I watch'd her as a sentinel,
(May ours this dark night watch as
 well!)
Until I saw, and thus it was,
That she was pensive, nor perceived
 Her occupation, nor was grieved 266
Nor glad to lose or gain; but still
Play'd on for hours, as if her will
Yet bound her to the place, though not
That hers might be the winning lot.
 Then through my brain the thought
 did pass 271
Even as a flash of lightning there,
That there was something in her air
Which would not doom me to despair;
And on the thought my words broke forth,
 All incoherent as they were; 276
Their eloquence was little worth,
But yet she listen'd—'tis enough—
 Who listens once will listen twice;
Her heart, be sure, is not of ice,
And one refusal no rebuff. 281

VII

'I loved, and was beloved again—
 They tell me, Sire, you never knew
 Those gentle frailties; if 'tis true,
I shorten all my joy or pain; 285
 To you 'twould seem absurd as vain;
But all men are not born to reign,
Or o'er their passions, or as you
Thus o'er themselves and nations too.
I am—or rather *was*—a prince, 290
 A chief of thousands, and could lead
 Them on where each would foremost
 bleed;
But could not o'er myself evince
The like control—But to resume:
 I loved, and was beloved again; 295
In sooth, it is a happy doom,
 But yet where happiest ends in pain.
We met in secret, and the hour
Which led me to that lady's bower
Was fiery Expectation's dower. 300
My days and nights were nothing—all
Except that hour, which doth recall,

In the long lapse from youth to age,
 No other like itself: I'd give
 The Ukraine back again to live 305
It o'er once more, and be a page,
The happy page, who was the lord
Of one soft heart, and his own sword,
And had no other gem nor wealth
Save nature's gift of youth and health.
We met in secret—doubly sweet, 311
Some say, they find it so to meet;
I know not that—I would have given
My life but to have call'd her mine
In the full view of earth and heaven;
 For I did oft and long repine 316
That we could only meet by stealth.

VIII

'For lovers there are many eyes,
 And such there were on us; the devil
 On such occasions should be civil—
The devil!—I'm loth to do him wrong,
It might be some untoward saint,
Who would not be at rest too long,
 But to his pious bile gave vent—
But one fair night, some lurking spies
Surprised and seized us both. 326
The Count was something more than
 wroth—
I was unarm'd; but if in steel,
All cap-à-pie from head to heel,
What 'gainst their numbers could I do?
'Twas near his castle, far away 331
 From city or from succour near,
And almost on the break of day;
I did not think to see another,
 My moments seem'd reduced to few;
And with one prayer to Mary Mother,
 And, it may be, a saint or two, 337
As I resign'd me to my fate,
They led me to the castle gate:
 Theresa's doom I never knew, 340
Our lot was henceforth separate.
An angry man, ye may opine,
Was he, the proud Count Palatine;
And he had reason good to be, 344
 But he was most enraged lest such
 An accident should chance to touch
Upon his future pedigree;
Nor less amazed, that such a blot
His noble 'scutcheon should have got,
While he was highest of his line; 350
 Because unto himself he seem'd
The first of men, nor less he deem'd
In others' eyes, and most in mine.
'Sdeath! with a page—perchance a king
Had reconciled him to the thing; 355
But with a stripling of a page—
I felt, but cannot paint his rage.

IX

' "Bring forth the horse!"—the horse
 was brought;
 In truth, he was a noble steed,
 A Tartar of the Ukraine breed, 360

Who look'd as though the speed of
 thought
Were in his limbs; but he was wild,
 Wild as the wild deer, and untaugh
With spur and bridle undefiled—
 'Twas but a day he had been caught
And snorting, with erected mane, 36
And struggling fiercely, but in vain,
In the full foam of wrath and dread
To me the desert-born was led:
They bound me on, that menial throng
Upon his back with many a thong; 37
Then loosed him with a sudden lash—
Away!—away!—and on we dash!
Torrents less rapid and less rash.

X

'Away!—away! My breath was gone
I saw not where he hurried on: 37
'Twas scarcely yet the break of day,
And on he foam'd—away!—away!
The last of human sounds which rose
As I was darted from my foes, 38
Was the wild shout of savage laughter
Which on the wind came roaring afte
A moment from that rabble rout:
With sudden wrath I wrench'd my head
 And snapp'd the cord, which to th
 mane 38
 Had bound my neck in lieu of rein
And, writhing half my form about,
Howl'd back my curse; but 'midst th
 tread,
The thunder of my courser's speed,
Perchance they did not hear nor heed
It vexes me—for I would fain 39
Have paid their insult back again.
I paid it well in after days:
There is not of that castle gate,
Its drawbridge and portcullis' weight,
Stone, bar, moat, bridge, or barrier left
Nor of its fields a blade of grass, 39
 Save what grows on a ridge of wal
 Where stood the hearth-stone of th
 hall;
And many a time ye there might pass
Nor dream that e'er the fortress was.
I saw its turrets in a blaze, 40
Their crackling battlements all cleft,
 And the hot lead pour down like rai
From off the scorch'd and blackenin
 roof, 40
Whose thickness was not vengeance
 proof.
 They little thought that day of pair
When launch'd, as on the lightning'
 flash,
They bade me to destruction dash, 40
 That one day I should come again,
With twice five thousand horse, to than
 The Count for his uncourteous ride
They play'd me then a bitter prank,
 When, with the wild horse for m
 guide, 41

They bound me to his foaming flank:
At length I play'd them one as frank
For time at last sets all things even—
 And if we do but watch the hour,
 There never yet was human power
Which could evade, if unforgiven, 420
The patient search and vigil long
Of him who treasures up a wrong.

XI

'Away, away, my steed and I,
 Upon the pinions of the wind,
 All human dwellings left behind;
We sped like meteors through the sky,
When with its crackling sound the night
Is chequer'd with the northern light:
Town—village—none were on our track
 But a wild plain of far extent, 430
And bounded by a forest black;
 And, save the scarce-seen battlement
On distant heights of some strong hold,
Against the Tartars built of old,
No trace of man. The year before 435
A Turkish army had march'd o'er;
And where the Spahi's hoof hath trod,
The verdure flies the bloody sod:
The sky was dull, and dim, and gray,
 And a low breeze crept moaning by—
 I could have answer'd with a sigh—
But fast we fled, away, away, 442
And I could neither sigh nor pray;
And my cold sweat-drops fell like rain
Upon the courser's bristling mane;
But, snorting still with rage and fear,
He flew upon his far career: 447
At times I almost thought, indeed,
He must have slacken'd in his speed;
But no—my bound and slender frame
Was nothing to his angry might,
And merely like a spur became:
Each motion which I made to free
My swoln limbs from their agony
 Increased his fury and affright: 455
I tried my voice,—'twas faint and low,
But yet he swerved as from a blow;
And, starting to each accent, sprang
As from a sudden trumpet's clang:
Meantime my cords were wet with gore,
Which, oozing through my limbs, ran
 o'er; 461
And in my tongue the thirst became
A something fierier far than flame.

XII

We near'd the wild wood—'twas so
 wide,
 saw no bounds on either side; 465
Twas studded with old sturdy trees,
That bent not to the roughest breeze
Which howls down from Siberia's waste,
And strips the forest in its haste,—
But these were few and far between,
Set thick with shrubs more young and
 green, 471

Luxuriant with their annual leaves,
Ere strown by those autumnal eves
That nip the forest's foliage dead,
Discolour'd with a lifeless red, 475
Which stands thereon like stiffen'd gore
Upon the slain when battle's o'er,
And some long winter's night hath shed
Its frost o'er every tombless head,
So cold and stark the raven's beak 480
May peck unpierced each frozen cheek:
'Twas a wild waste of underwood,
And here and there a chestnut stood,
The strong oak, and the hardy pine;
 But far apart—and well it were, 485
 Or else a different lot were mine—
The boughs gave way, and did not tear
My limbs; and I found strength to bear
My wounds, already scarr'd with cold;
My bonds forbade to loose my hold.
We rustled through the leaves like wind,
Left shrubs, and trees, and wolves be-
 hind; 492
By night I heard them on the track,
Their troop came hard upon our back,
With their long gallop, which can tire
The hound's deep hate, and hunter's fire:
Where'er we flew they follow'd on, 497
Nor left us with the morning sun;
Behind I saw them, scarce a rood,
At day-break winding through the
 wood, 500
And through the night had heard their
 feet
Their stealing, rustling step repeat.
Oh! how I wish'd for spear or sword,
At least to die amidst the horde,
And perish—if it must be so— 505
At bay, destroying many a foe!
When first my courser's race begun,
I wish'd the goal already won;
But now I doubted strength and speed.
Vain doubt! his swift and savage breed
Had nerved him like the mountain-roe;
Nor faster falls the blinding snow 512
Which whelms the peasant near the door
Whose threshold he shall cross no more,
Bewilder'd with the dazzling blast,
Than through the forest-paths he
 pass'd—
Untired, untamed, and worse than wild;
All furious as a favour'd child
Balk'd of its wish; or fiercer still—
A woman piqued—who has her will.

XIII

'The wood was past; 'twas more than
 noon, 521
But chill the air, although in June;
Or it might be my veins ran cold—
Prolong'd endurance tames the bold;
And I was then not what I seem, 525
But headlong as a wintry stream,
And wore my feelings out before
I well could count their causes o'er:

And what with fury, fear, and wrath,
The tortures which beset my path, 530
Cold, hunger, sorrow, shame, distress,
Thus bound in nature's nakedness;
Sprung from a race whose rising blood,
When stirr'd beyond its calmer mood,
And trodden hard upon, is like 535
The rattle-snake's, in act to strike,
What marvel if this worn-out trunk
Beneath its woes a moment sunk?
The earth gave way, the skies roll'd round,
I seem'd to sink upon the ground; 540
But err'd, for I was fastly bound.
My heart turn'd sick, my brain grew sore,
And throbb'd awhile, then beat no more:
The skies spun like a mighty wheel;
I saw the trees like drunkards reel, 545
And a slight flash sprang o'er my eyes,
Which saw no farther: he who dies
Can die no more than then I died.
O'ertortured by that ghastly ride,
I felt the blackness come and go, 550
 And strove to wake; but could not make
My senses climb up from below:
I felt as on a plank at sea,
When all the waves that dash o'er thee,
At the same time upheave and whelm,
And hurl thee towards a desert realm.
My undulating life was as 557
The fancied lights that flitting pass
Our shut eyes in deep midnight, when
Fever begins upon the brain; 560
But soon it pass'd, with little pain,
 But a confusion worse than such:
I own that I should deem it much,
Dying, to feel the same again;
And yet I do suppose we must 565
Feel far more ere we turn to dust:
No matter; I have bared my brow
Full in Death's face—before—and now.

XIV

'My thoughts came back; where was I? Cold,
 And numb, and giddy: pulse by pulse
Life reassumed its lingering hold, 571
And throb by throb,—till grown a pang
 Which for a moment would convulse,
My blood reflow'd, though thick and chill;
My ear with uncouth noises rang,
 My heart began once more to thrill;
My sight return'd, though dim; alas!
And thicken'd, as it were, with glass.
Methought the dash of waves was nigh;
There was a gleam too of the sky, 580
Studded with stars;—it is no dream;
The wild horse swims the wilder stream!
The bright broad river's gushing tide
Sweeps, winding onward, far and wide,

And we are half-way, struggling o'er
To yon unknown and silent shore. 586
The waters broke my hollow trance,
And with a temporary strength
 My stiffen'd limbs were rebaptized.
My courser's broad breast proudly braves, 590
And dashes off the ascending waves,
And onward we advance!
We reach the slippery shore at length,
 A haven I but little prized, 594
For all behind was dark and drear,
And all before was night and fear.
How many hours of night or day
In those suspended pangs I lay,
I could not tell; I scarcely knew
If this were human breath I drew. 600

XV

'With glossy skin, and dripping mane,
 And reeling limbs, and reeking flank,
The wild steed's sinewy nerves still strain
 Up the repelling bank. 604
We gain the top: a boundless plain
Spreads through the shadow of the night,
 And onward, onward, onward, seems,
Like precipices in our dreams,
To stretch beyond the sight; 609
And here and there a speck of white,
 Or scatter'd spot of dusky green,
In masses broke into the light,
As rose the moon upon my right:
 But nought distinctly seen
In the dim waste would indicate 615
The omen of a cottage gate;
No twinkling taper from afar
Stood like a hospitable star;
Not even an ignis-fatuus rose 619
To make him merry with my woes:
 That very cheat had cheer'd me then!
Although detected, welcome still,
Reminding me, through every ill,
 Of the abodes of men. 624

XVI

'Onward we went—but slack and slow
 His savage force at length o'erspent
The drooping courser, faint and low,
 All feebly foaming went.
A sickly infant had had power 628
To guide him forward in that hour,
 But useless all to me:
His new-born tameness nought avail'd—
My limbs were bound; my force had fail'd,
 Perchance, had they been free.
With feeble effort still I tried 63
To rend the bonds so starkly tied,
 But still it was in vain;
My limbs were only wrung the more,
And soon the idle strife gave o'er,
 Which but prolong'd their pain: 64

346

The dizzy race seem'd almost done,
Although no goal was nearly won:
Some streaks announced the coming
 sun—
 How slow, alas! he came! 644
Methought that mist of dawning gray
Would never dapple into day;
How heavily it roll'd away—
 Before the eastern flame
Rose crimson, and deposed the stars,
And call'd the radiance from their cars,
And fill'd the earth, from his deep
 throne, 651
With lonely lustre, all his own.

XVII

'Up rose the sun; the mists were curl'd
Back from the solitary world
Which lay around, behind, before.
What booted it to traverse o'er 656
Plain, forest, river? Man nor brute,
Nor dint of hoof, nor print of foot,
Lay in the wild luxuriant soil;
No sign of travel, none of toil; 660
The very air was mute;
And not an insect's shrill small horn,
Nor matin bird's new voice was borne
From herb nor thicket. Many a werst,
Panting as if his heart would burst, 665
The weary brute still stagger'd on;
And still we were—or seem'd—alone.
At length, while reeling on our way,
Methought I heard a courser neigh,
From out yon tuft of blackening firs.
Is it the wind those branches stirs? 671
No, no! from our the forest prance
 A trampling troop; I see them come!
In one vast squadron they advance!
 I strove to cry—my lips were dumb.
The steeds rush on in plunging pride;
But where are they the reins to guide?
A thousand horse, and none to ride!
With flowing tail, and flying mane,
Wide nostrils never stretch'd bv pain,
Mouths bloodless to the bit or rein,
And feet that iron never shod, 682
And flanks unscarr'd by spur or rod,
A thousand horse, the wild, the free,
Like waves that follow o'er the sea,
 Came thickly thundering on,
As if our faint approach to meet;
The sight re-nerved my courser's feet,
A moment staggering, feebly fleet,
A moment, with a faint low neigh,
 He answer'd, and then fell; 691
With gasps and glazing eves he lay,
 And reeking limbs immoveable,
 His first and last career is done!
On came the troop—they saw him stoop,
 They saw me strangely bound along
 His back with many a bloody thong:
They stop, they start, they snuff the
 air,
Gallop a moment here and there,

Approach, retire, wheel round and
 round, 700
Then plunging back with sudden bound,
Headed by one black mighty steed,
Who seem'd the patriarch of his breed,
 Without a single speck or hair
Of white upon his shaggy hide; 705
They snort, they foam, neigh, swerve
 aside,
And backward to the forest fly,
By instinct, from a human eye.
They left me there to my despair,
Link'd to the dead and stiffening wretch,
Whose lifeless limbs beneath me stretch,
Relieved from that unwonted weight,
From whence I could not extricate
Nor him nor me—and there we lay,
 The dying on the dead! 715
I little deem'd another day
 Would see my houseless, helpless
 head.

'And there from morn to twilight
 bound,
I felt the heavy hours toil round,
With just enough of life to see 720
My legs go down on me,
In hopeless certainty of mind,
That makes us feel at length resign'd
To that which our foreboding years
Present the worst and last of fears:
Inevitable—even a boon, 726
Nor more unkind for coming soon,
Yet shunn'd and dreaded with such care,
As if it only were a snare
 That prudence might escape: 730
At times both wish'd-for and implored,
At times sought with self-pointed sword,
Yet still a dark and hideous close
To even intolerable woes,
 And welcome in no shape. 735
And, strange to say, the sons of pleasure,
They who have revell'd beyond measure
In beauty, wassail, wine, and treasure,
Die calm, or calmer, oft than he
Whose heritage was misery: 740
For he who hath in turn run through
All that was beautiful and new,
 Hath nought to hope, and nought to
 leave;
And, save the future, (which is view'd
Not quite as men are base or good, 745
But as their nerves may be endued,)
 With nought perhaps to grieve:
The wretch still hopes his woes must end,
And Death, whom he should deem his
 friend,
Appears, to his distemper'd eyes, 750
Arrived to rob him of his prize,
The tree of his new Paradise.
To-morrow would have given him all,
Repaid his pangs, repair'd his fall;
To-morrow would have been the first
Of days no more deplored or curst,

But bright, and long, and beckoning years,
Seen dazzling through the mist of tears,
Guerdon of many a painful hour;
To-morrow would have given him
 power 760
To rule, to shine, to smite, to save—
And must it dawn upon his grave?

XVIII

'The sun was sinking—still I lay
 Chain'd to the chill and stiffening
 steed;
I thought to mingle there our clay, 765
 And my dim eyes of death had need;
 No hope arose of being freed:
I cast my last looks up the sky,
 And there between me and the sun
I saw the expecting raven fly, 770
Who scarce would wait till both should
 die,
 Ere his repast begun;
He flew, and perch'd, then flew once more,
And each time nearer than before;
I saw his wing through twilight flit,
And once so near me he alit 776
 I could have smote, but lack'd the
 strength;
But the slight motion of my hand,
And feeble scratching of the sand,
The exerted throat's faint struggling
 noise, 780
Which scarcely could be called a voice,
Together scared him off at length.
I know no more—my latest dream
 Is something of a lovely star
Which fix'd my dull eyes from afar,
And went and came with wandering
 beam, 786
And all the cold, dull, swimming, dense
Sensation of recurring sense,
And then subsiding back to death,
And then again a little breath, 790
A little thrill, a short suspense,
 An icy sickness curdling o'er
My heart, and sparks that cross'd my
 brain—
A gasp, a throb, a start of pain,
 A sigh, and nothing more. 795

XIX

'I woke—where was I?—Do I see
A human face look down on me?
And doth a roof above me close?
Do these limbs on a couch repose?
Is this a chamber where I lie? 800
And is it mortal yon bright eye,
That watches me with gentle glance?
 I closed my own again once more,
As doubtful that my former trance
 Could not as yet be o'er. 805
A slender girl, long-hair'd, and tall,
Sate watching by the cottage wall;
The sparkle of her eye I caught,
Even with my first return of thought;

For ever and anon she threw 810
 A prying, pitying glance on me
 With her black eyes so wild and free:
I gazed, and gazed, until I knew
 No vision it could be,—
But that I lived, and was released 815
From adding to the vulture's feast:
And when the Cossack maid beheld
My heavy eyes at length unseal'd,
She smiled—and I essay'd to speak,
 But fail'd—and she approach'd, and
 made 820
 With lip and finger signs that said,
I must not strive as yet to break
The silence, till my strength should be
Enough to leave my accents free; 824
And then her hand on mine she laid,
And smooth'd the pillow for my head,
And stole along on tiptoe tread,
 And gently oped the door, and spake
In whispers—ne'er was voice so sweet!
Even music follow'd her light feet! 830
 But those she call'd were not awake,
And she went forth; but, ere she pass'd,
Another look on me she cast,
 Another sign she made, to say,
That I had nought to fear, that all 835
Were near, at my command or call,
 And she would not delay
Her due return:—while she was gone,
Methought I felt too much alone. 839

XX

'She came with mother and with sire—
What need of more?—I will not tire
With long recital of the rest,
Since I became the Cossack's guest.
They found me senseless on the plain,
 They bore me to the nearest hut, 845
They brought me into life again—
Me—one day o'er their realm to reign!
 Thus the vain fool who strove to glut
His rage, refining on my pain, 849
Sent me forth to the wilderness,
Bound, naked, bleeding, and alone,
To pass the desert to a throne,—
 What mortal his own doom may guess?
 Let none despond, let none despair!
To-morrow the Borysthenes 855
May see our coursers graze at ease
Upon his Turkish bank, and never
Had I such welcome for a river
 As I shall yield when safely there.
Comrades, good night!'—The Hetman
 threw 860
 His length beneath the oak-tree shade,
 With leafy couch already made,
A bed nor comfortless nor new
To him, who took his rest whene'er
The hour arrived, no matter where:
 His eyes the hastening slumbers steep.
And if ye marvel Charles forgot
To thank his tale, *he* wonder'd not,—
 The king had been an hour asleep.

THE ISLAND

OR

CHRISTIAN AND HIS COMRADES

ADVERTISEMENT

THE foundation of the following story will be found partly in Lieutenant Bligh's 'Narrative of the Mutiny and Seizure of the Bounty, in the South Seas, in 1789'; and partly in 'Mariner's Account of the Tonga Islands.'
Genoa, 1823.

CANTO THE FIRST

I

THE morning watch was come; the vessel lay
Her course, and gently made her liquid way;
The cloven billow flash'd from off her prow
In furrows form'd by that majestic plough;
The waters with their world were all before; 5
Behind, the South Sea's many an islet shore.
The quiet night, now dappling, 'gan to wane,
Dividing darkness from the dawning main;
The dolphins, not unconscious of the day, 9
Swam high, as eager of the coming ray;
The stars from broader beams began to creep,
And lift their shining eyelids from the deep;
The sail resumed its lately shadow'd white,
And the wind flutter'd with a freshening flight: 14
The purpling ocean owns the coming sun,
But ere he break—a deed is to be done.

II

The gallant chief within his cabin slept,
Secure in those by whom the watch was kept:
His dreams were of Old England's welcome shore, 19
Of toils rewarded, and of dangers o'er;
His name was added to the glorious roll
Of those who search the storm-surrounded Pole.
The worst was over, and the rest seem'd sure,
And why should not his slumber be secure?
Alas! his deck was trod by unwilling feet,
And wilder hands would hold the vessel's sheet; 26

Young hearts, which languish'd for some sunny isle,
Where summer years and summer women smile;
Men without country, who, too long estranged,
Had found no native home, or found it changed, 30
And, half uncivilised, preferr'd the cave
Of some soft savage to the uncertain wave—
The gushing fruits that nature gave untill'd;
The wood without a path but where they will'd;
The field o'er which promiscuous Plenty pour'd 35
Her horn; the equal land without a lord;
The wish—which ages have not yet subdued
In man—to have no master save his mood;
The earth, whose mine was on its face, unsold,
The glowing sun and produce all its gold;
The freedom which can call each grot a home; 41
The general garden, where all steps may roam,
Where Nature owns a nation as her child,
Exulting in the enjoyment of the wild;
Their shells, their fruits, the only wealth they know, 45
Their unexploring navy, the canoe;
Their sport, the dashing breakers and the chase;
Their strangest sight, an European face:—
Such was the country which these strangers yearn'd 49
To see again; a sight they dearly earn'd.

III

Awake, bold Bligh! the foe is at the gate!
Awake! awake!—Alas! it is too late!
Fiercely beside thy cot the mutineer
Stands, and proclaims the reign of rage and fear.
Thy limbs are bound, the bayonet at thy breast; 55
The hands, which trembled at thy voice, arrest;

349

Dragg'd o'er the deck, no more at thy
 command
The obedient helm shall veer, the sail ex-
 pand;
That savage spirit, which would lull by
 wrath 59
Its desperate escape from duty's path,
Glares round thee, in the scarce-believing
 eyes
Of those who fear the chief they sacrifice:
For ne'er can man his conscience all as-
 suage,
Unless he drain the wine of passion—rage.

IV

In vain, not silenced by the eye of death,
Thou call'st the loyal with thy menaced
 breath:— 66
They come not; they are few, and, over-
 awed,
Must acquiesce, while sterner hearts ap-
 plaud.
In vain thou dost demand the cause: a
 curse
Is all the answer, with the threat of worse.
Full in thine eyes is waved the glittering
 blade, 71
Close to thy throat the pointed bayonet
 laid.
The levell'd muskets circle round thy
 breast
In hands as steel'd to do the deadly rest.
Thou dar'st them to their worst, exclaim-
 ing—'Fire!' 75
But they who pitied not could yet admire;
Some lurking remnant of their former
 awe
Restrain'd them longer than their broken
 law;
They would not dip their souls at once in
 blood, 79
But left thee to the mercies of the flood.

V

'Hoist out the boat!' was now the leader's
 cry;
And who dare answer 'No!' to Mutiny,
In the first dawning of the drunken hour,
The Saturnalia of unhoped-for power?
The boat is lower'd with all the haste of
 hate, 85
With its slight plank between thee and thy
 fate;
Her only cargo such a scant supply
As promises the death their hands deny;
And just enough of water and of bread
To keep, some days, the dying from the
 dead: 90
Some cordage, canvas, sails, and lines, and
 twine,
But treasures all to hermits of the brine,
Were added after, to the earnest prayer
Of those who saw no hope, save sea and
 air;

And last, that trembling vassal of the
 Pole— 95
The feeling compass—Navigation's soul.

VI

And now the self-elected chief finds time
To stun the first sensation of his crime,
And raise it in his followers—'Ho! the
 bowl!'
Lest passion should return to reason's
 shoal. 100
'Brandy for heroes!' Burke could once
 exclaim—
No doubt a liquid path to epic fame;
And such the new-born heroes found it
 here,
And drain'd the draught with an applaud-
 ing cheer.
'Huzza! for Otaheite!' was the cry. 105
How strange such shouts from sons of
 Mutiny!
The gentle island, and the genial soil,
The friendly hearts, the feasts without a
 toil,
The courteous manners but from nature
 caught,
The wealth unhoarded, and the love un-
 bought; 110
Could these have charms for rudest sea-
 boys, driven
Before the mast by every wind of heaven?
And now, even now prepared with others'
 woes
To earn mild Virtue's vain desire, repose?
Alas! such is our nature! all but aim
At the same end by pathways not the same;
Our means, our birth, our nation, and our
 name,
Our fortune, temper, even our outward
 frame,
Are far more potent o'er our yielding clay
Than aught we know beyond our little
 day. 120
Yet still there whispers the small voice
 within,
Heard through Gain's silence, and o'er
 Glory's din:
Whatever creed be taught, or land be trod,
Man's conscience is the oracle of God.

VII

The launch is crowded with the faithful
 few 125
Who wait their chief, a melancholy crew:
But some remain'd reluctant on the deck
Of that proud vessel—now a moral
 wreck—
And view'd their captain's fate with piteous
 eyes: 129
While others scoff'd his augur'd miseries,
Sneer'd at the prospect of his pigmy sail,
And the slight bark so laden and so frail.
The tender nautilus, who steers his prow,
The sea-born sailor of his shell canoe,

350

The ocean Mab, the fairy of the sea, 135
Seems far less fragile, and, alas! more free.
He, when the lightning-wing'd tornados
 sweep
The surge, is safe—his port is in the deep—
And triumphs o'er the armadas of man-
 kind,
Which shake the world, yet crumble in the
 wind. 140

VIII

When all was now prepared, the vessel
 clear
Which hail'd her master in the mutineer,
A seaman, less obdurate than his mates,
Show'd the vain pity which but irritates;
Watch'd his late chieftain with exploring
 eye, 145
And told, in signs, repentant sympathy;
Held the moist shaddock to his parched
 mouth,
Which felt exhaustion's deep and bitter
 drouth.
But soon observed, this guardian was with-
 drawn,
Nor further mercy clouds rebellion's
 dawn. 150
Then forward stepp'd the bold and fro-
 ward boy
His chief had cherish'd only to destroy,
And, pointing to the helpless prow be-
 neath,
Exclaim'd, 'Depart at once! delay is
 death!'
Yet then, even then, his feelings ceased
 not all: 155
In that last moment could a word recall
Remorse for the black deed as yet half
 done,
And what he hid from many show'd to
 one:
When Bligh in stern reproach demanded
 where
Was now his grateful sense of former care?
Where all his hopes to see his name aspire,
And blazon Britain's thousand glories
 higher? 162
His feverish lips thus broke their gloomy
 spell,
'Tis that! 'tis that! I am in hell! in hell!'
No more he said: but urging to the bark
His chief, commits him to his fragile ark;
These the sole accents from his tongue
 that fell, 167
But volumes lurk'd below his fierce fare-
 well.

IX

The arctic sun rose broad above the wave;
The breeze now sank, now whisper'd from
 his cave, 170
As on the Æolian harp, his fitful wings
Now swell'd, now flutter'd o'er his ocean
 strings.

With slow, despairing oar, the abandon'd
 skiff
Ploughs its drear progress to the scarce-
 seen cliff, 174
Which lifts its peak a cloud above the main:
That boat and ship shall never meet again!

But 'tis not mine to tell their tale of grief,
Their constant peril, and their scant relief;
Their days of danger, and their nights of
 pain;
Their manly courage even when deem'd in
 vain; 180
The sapping famine, rendering scarce a son
Known to his mother in the skeleton;
The ills that lessen'd still their little store,
And starved even Hunger till he wrung no
 more;
The varying frowns and favours of the
 deep, 185
That now almost ingulfs, then leaves to
 creep
With crazy oar and shatter'd strength along
The tide that yields reluctant to the strong;
The incessant fever of that arid thirst
Which welcomes, as a well, the clouds that
 burst 190
Above their naked bones, and feels delight
In the cold drenching of the stormy night,
And from the outspread canvas gladly
 wrings
A drop to moisten life's all-gasping
 springs; 194
The savage foe escaped, to seek again
More hospitable shelter from the main;
The ghastly spectres which were doom'd
 at last
To tell as true a tale of dangers past,
As ever the dark annals of the deep
Disclosed for man to dread or woman
 weep. 200

X

We leave them to their fate, but not un-
 known
Nor unredress'd. Revenge may have her
 own:
Roused discipline aloud proclaims their
 cause,
And injured navies urge their broken laws.
Pursue we on his track the mutineer,
Whom distant vengeance had not taught
 to fear. 206
Wide o'er the wave—away! away! away!
Once more his eyes shall hail the welcome
 bay;
Once more the happy shores without a law
Receive the outlaws whom they lately saw;
Nature, and Nature's goddess—woman—
 woos 211
To lands where, save their conscience,
 none accuse;
Where all partake the earth without dispute,
And bread itself is gather'd as a fruit;

Where none contest the fields, the woods,
 the streams:— 215
The goldless age, where gold disturbs no
 dreams,
Inhabits or inhabited the shore,
Till Europe taught them better than be-
 fore:
Bestow'd her customs, and amended
 theirs,
But left her vices also to their heirs, 220
Away with this! behold them as they were,
Do good with Nature, or with Nature err,
'Huzza! for Otaheite!' was the cry,
As stately swept the gallant vessel by.
The breeze springs up; the lately flapping
 sail 225
Extends its arch before the growing gale;
In swifter ripples stream aside the seas,
Which her bold bow flings off with dash-
 ing ease.
Thus Argo plough'd the Euxine's virgin
 foam,
But those she wafted still look'd back to
 home: 230
These spurn their country with their rebel
 bark,
And fly her as the raven fled the ark;
And yet they seek to nestle with the dove,
And tame their fiery spirits down to love.

CANTO THE SECOND

I

How pleasant were the songs of Toobonai,
When summer's sun went down the coral
 bay!
Come, let us to the islet's softest shade,
And hear the warbling birds! the damsels
 said:
The wood-dove from the forest-depth
 shall coo, 5
Like voices of the gods from Bolotoo,
We'll cull the flowers that grow above the
 dead,
For these most bloom where rests the war-
 rior's head;
And we will sit in twilight's face, and see
The sweet moon glancing through the tooa
 tree, 10
The lofty accents of whose sighing bough
Shall sadly please us as we lean below;
Or climb the steep, and view the surf in
 vain
Wrestle with rocky giants o'er the main,
Which spurn in columns back the baffled
 spray. 15
How beautiful are these! how happy they,
Who, from the toil and tumult of their
 lives,
Steal to look down where nought but
 ocean strives!
Even he too loves at times the blue lagoon,
And smoothes his ruffled mane beneath
 the moon. 20

II

Yes—from the sepulchre we'll gather
 flowers,
Then feast like spirits in their promised
 bowers,
Then plunge and revel in the rolling surf,
Then lay our limbs along the tender turf,
And, wet and shining from the sportive
 toil, 25
Anoint our bodies with the fragrant oil,
And plait our garlands gather'd from the
 grave,
And wear the wreaths that sprung from
 out the brave.
But lo! night comes, the Mooa woos us
 back,
The sound of mats are heard along our
 track;
Anon the torchlight dance shall fling its
 sheen 31
In flashing mazes o'er the Marly's green;
And we too will be there; we too recall
The memory bright with many a festival,
Ere Fiji blew the shell of war, when foes
For the first time were wafted in canoes.
Alas! for them the flower of mankind bleeds;
Alas! for them our fields are rank with
 weeds:
Forgotten is the rapture, or unknown,
Of wandering with the moon and love
 alone. 40
But be it so:—*they* taught us how to wield
The club, and rain our arrows o'er the field:
Now let them reap the harvest of their art!
But feast to-night! to-morrow we depart.
Strike up the dance! the cava bowl fill
 high! 45
Drain every drop!—to-morrow we may die.
In summer garments be our limbs array'd;
Around our waists the tappa's white dis-
 play'd;
Thick wreaths shall form our coronal, like
 spring's,
And round our necks shall glance the
 hooni strings; 50
So shall their brighter hues contrast the
 glow
Of the dusk bosoms that beat high below.

III

But now the dance is o'er—yet stay awhile;
Ah, pause! nor yet put out the social smile.
To-morrow for the Mooa we depart, 55
But not to-night—to-night is for the heart.
Again bestow the wreaths we gently woo,
Ye young enchantresses of gay Licoo!
How lovely are your forms! how every
 sense
Bows to your beauties, soften'd, but in-
 tense, 60
Like to the flowers on Mataloco's steep,
Which fling their fragrance far athwart
 the deep!—

We too will see Licoo; but—oh! my
 heart!—
What do I say?—to-morrow we depart!

IV

Thus rose a song—the harmony of times
Before the winds blew Europe o'er these
 climes.
True, they had vices—such are Nature's
 growth—
But only the barbarian's—we have both;
The sordor of civilisation, mix'd
With all the savage which man's fall hath
 fix'd. 70
Who hath not seen Dissimulation's reign,
The prayers of Abel link'd to deeds of
 Cain?
Who such would see may from his lattice
 view
The Old World more degraded than the
 New,—
Now *new* no more, save where Columbia
 rears 75
Twin giants, born by Freedom to her
 spheres,
Where Chimborazo, over air, earth, wave,
Glares with his Titan eye, and sees no slave.

V

Such was this ditty of Tradition's days,
Which to the dead a lingering fame con-
 veys 80
In song, where fame as yet hath left no sign
Beyond the sound whose charm is half
 divine;
Which leaves no record to the sceptic eye,
But yields young history all to harmony;
A boy Achilles, with the centaur's lyre 85
In hand, to teach him to surpass his sire.
For one long-cherish'd ballad's simple
 stave,
Rung from the rock, or mingled with the
 wave,
Or from the bubbling streamlet's grassy side,
Or gathering mountain echoes as they
 glide, 90
Hath greater power o'er each true heart
 and ear,
Than all the columns Conquest's minions
 rear;
Invites, when hieroglyphics are a theme
For sages' labours, or the student's dream;
Attracts, when History's volumes are a
 toil,— 95
The first, the freshest bud of Feeling's soil.
Such was this rude rhyme—rhyme is of
 the rude—
But such inspired the Norseman's solitude,
Who came and conquer'd; such, wherever
 rise 99
Lands which no foes destroy or civilise,
Exist: and what can our accomplish'd art
Of verse do more than reach the awaken'd
 heart?

VI

And sweetly now those untaught melodies
Broke the luxurious silence of the skies,
The sweet siesta of a summer day, 105
The tropic afternoon of Toobonai,
When every flower was bloom, and air
 was balm,
And the first breath began to stir the palm,
The first yet voiceless wind to urge the wave
All gently to refresh the thirsty cave,
Where sat the songstress with the stranger
 boy, 111
Who taught her passion's desolating joy,
Too powerful over every heart, but most
O'er those who know not how it may be
 lost;
O'er those who, burning in the new-born
 fire, 115
Like martyrs revel in their funeral pyre,
With such devotion to their ecstasy,
That life knows no such rapture as to die:
And die they do; for earthly life has nought
Match'd with that burst of nature, even
 in thought; 120
And all our dreams of better life above
But close in one eternal gush of love.

VII

There sat the gentle savage of the wild,
In growth a woman, though in years a
 child,
As childhood dates within our colder
 clime, 125
Where nought is ripen'd rapidly save crime,
The infant of an infant world, as pure
From nature—lovely, warm, and pre-
 mature;
Dusky like night, but night with all her
 stars, 129
Or cavern sparkling with its native spars;
With eyes that were a language and a spell,
A form like Aphrodite's in her shell,
With all her loves around her on the deep,
Voluptuous as the first approach of sleep;
Yet full of life—for through her tropic
 cheek 135
The blush would make its way, and all but
 speak:
The sun-born blood suffused her neck, and
 threw
O'er her clear nut-brown skin a lucid hue,
Like coral reddening through the darken'd
 wave,
Which draws the diver to the crimson cave.
Such was this daughter of the southern
 seas, 141
Herself a billow in her energies,
To bear the bark of others' happiness,
Nor feel a sorrow till their joy grew less:
Her wild and warm yet faithful bosom
 knew 145
No joy like what it gave; her hopes ne'er
 drew

353

Aught from experience, that chill touch-
 stone, whose
Sad proof reduces all things from their
 hues:
She fear'd no ill, because she knew it not,
Or what she knew was soon—too soon—
 forgot: 150
Her smiles and tears had pass'd, as light
 winds pass
O'er lakes to ruffle, not destroy, their glass,
Whose depths unsearch'd, and fountains
 from the hill,
Restore their surface, in itself so still,
Until the earthquake tear the naiad's cave,
Root up the spring, and trample on the
 wave, 156
And crush the living waters to a mass,
The amphibious desert of the dank mo-
 rass!
And must their fate be hers? The eternal
 change
But grasps humanity with quicker range;
And they who fall but fall as worlds will
 fall, 161
To rise, if just, a spirit o'er them all.

VIII

And who is he? the blue-eyed northern child
Of isles more known to man, but scarce
 less wild;
The fair-hair'd offspring of the Hebrides,
Where roars the Pentland with its whirling
 seas; 166
Rock'd in his cradle by the roaring wind,
The tempest-born in body and in mind,
His young eyes opening on the ocean-
 foam,
Had from that moment deem'd the deep
 his home, 170
The giant comrade of his pensive moods,
The sharer of his craggy solitudes,
The only Mentor of his youth, where'er
His bark was borne; the sport of wave and
 air;
A careless thing, who placed his choice in
 chance, 175
Nursed by the legends of his land's ro-
 mance;
Eager to hope, but not less firm to bear,
Acquainted with all feelings save despair.
Placed in the Arab's clime, he would have
 been
As bold a rover as the sands have seen,
And braved their thirst with as enduring
 lip 181
As Ishmael, wafted on his desert-ship;
Fix'd upon Chili's shore, a proud cacique;
On Hellas' mountains, a rebellious Greek;
Born in a tent, perhaps a Tamerlane;
Bred to a throne, perhaps unfit to reign.
For the same soul that rends its path to
 sway, 187
If rear'd to such, can find no further prey
Beyond itself, and must retrace its way,

Plunging for pleasure into pain: the sam
Spirit which made a Nero, Rome's wors
 shame, 19
A humbler state and discipline of heart,
Had form'd his glorious namesake'
 counterpart;
But grant his vices, grant them all his own
How small their theatre without a throne

IX

Thou smilest:—these comparisons seen
 high 19
To those who scan all things with dazzle
 eye:
Link'd with the unknown name of on
 whose doom
Has nought to do with glory or with Rome
With Chili, Hellas, or with Araby; 20
Thou smilest?—Smile; 'tis better thus tha
 sigh;
Yet such he might have been; he was a mar
A soaring spirit, ever in the van,
A patriot hero or despotic chief,
To form a nation's glory or its grief, 20
Born under auspices which make us mor
Or less than we delight to ponder o'er.
But these are visions; say, what was h
 here?
A blooming boy, a truant mutineer.
The fair-hair'd Torquil, free as ocean'
 spray, 21
The husband of the bride of Toobonai.

X

By Neuha's side he sate, and watch'd th
 waters,—
Neuha, the sun-flower of the island daugh
 ters,
Highborn, (a birth at which the heral
 smiles,
Without a scutcheon for these secre
 isles,) 2
Of a long race, the valiant and the free,
The naked knights of savage chivalry,
Whose grassy cairns ascend along th
 shore;
And thine—I've seen—Achilles! do n
 more.
She, when the thunder-bearing stranger
 came, 22
In vast canoes, begirt with bolts of flame
Topp'd with tall trees, which, loftier tha
 the palm,
Seem'd rooted in the deep amidst its calm
But when the winds awaken'd, shot forth
 wings
Broad as the cloud along the horizo
 flings, 22
And sway'd the waves like cities of the sea
Making the very billows look less free;—
She, with her paddling oar and dancin
 prow,
Shot through the surf, like reindee
 through the snow,

354

Swift-gliding o'er the breaker's whitening
 edge, 230
Light as a nereid in her ocean sledge,
And gazed and wonder'd at the giant hulk,
Which heaved from wave to wave its
 trampling bulk.
The anchor dropp'd; it lay along the deep,
Like a huge lion in the sun asleep, 235
While round it swarm'd the proas' flitting
 chain,
Like summer bees that hum around his
 mane.

XI

The white man landed! need the rest be
 told?
The New World stretch'd its dusk hand to
 the Old; 239
Each was to each a marvel, and the tie
Of wonder warm'd to better sympathy.
Kind was the welcome of the sun-born
 sires,
And kinder still their daughters' gentler
 fires.
Their union grew: the children of the storm
Found beauty link'd with many a dusky
 form; 245
While these in turn admired the paler
 glow,
Which seem'd so white in climes that knew
 no snow.
The chase, the race, the liberty to roam,
The soil where every cottage show'd a
 home;
The sea-spread net, the lightly launch'd
 canoe, 250
Which stemm'd the studded archipelago,
O'er whose blue blossom rose the starry
 isles;
The healthy slumber, earn'd by sportive
 toils;
The palm, the loftiest dryad of the woods,
Within whose bosom infant Bacchus
 broods, 255
While eagles scarce build higher than the
 crest
Which shadows o'er the vineyard in her
 breast;
The cava feast, the yam, the cocoa's root,
Which bears at once the cup, and milk,
 and fruit;
The bread-tree, which, without the plough-
 share, yields 260
The unreap'd harvest of unfurrow'd fields,
And bakes its unadulterated loaves
Without a furnace in unpurchased groves,
And flings off famine from its fertile breast,
A priceless market for the gathering
 guest;— 265
These, with the luxuries of seas and woods,
The airy joys of social solitudes,
Tamed each rude wanderer to the sympa-
 thies
Of those who were more happy, if less wise,

Did more than Europe's discipline had
 done, 270
And civilised Civilisation's son!

XII

Of these, and there was many a willing pair,
Neuha and Torquil were not the least fair:
Both children of the isles, though distant
 far;
Both born beneath a sea-presiding star;
Both nourish'd amidst nature's native
 scenes, 276
Loved to the last, whatever intervenes
Between us and our childhood's sympathy,
Which still reverts to what first caught the
 eye.
He who first met the Highlands' swelling
 blue 280
Will love each peak that shows a kindred
 hue,
Hail in each crag a friend's familiar face,
And clasp the mountain in his mind's
 embrace.
Long have I roamed through lands which
 are not mine, 284
Adored the Alp, and loved the Apennine,
Revered Parnassus, and beheld the steep
Jove's Ida and Olympus crown the deep:
But 'twas not all long ages' lore, nor all
Their nature held me in their thrilling
 thrall;
The infant rapture still survived the boy,
And Loch-na-gar with Ida look'd o'er
 Troy, 291
Mix'd Celtic memories with the Phrygian
 mount,
And Highland linns with Castalie's clear
 fount.
Forgive me, Homer's universal shade!
Forgive me, Phœbus! that my fancy
 stray'd; 295
The north and nature taught me to adore
Your scenes sublime, from those beloved
 before.

XIII

The love which maketh all things fond and
 fair,
The youth which makes one rainbow of
 the air,
The dangers past, that make even man
 enjoy 300
The pause in which he ceases to destroy,
The mutual beauty, which the sternest feel
Strike to their hearts like lightning to the
 steel,
United the half savage and the whole,
The maid and boy in one absorbing soul.
No more the thundering memory of the
 fight 306
Wrapp'd his wean'd bosom in its dark de-
 light;
No more the irksome restlessness of rest
Disturb'd him like the eagle in her nest,

Whose whetted beak and far-pervading
 eye 310
Darts for a victim over all the sky:
His heart was tamed to that voluptuous
 state,
At once Elysian and effeminate,
Which leaves no laurels o'er the hero's
 urn;—
These wither when for aught save blood
 they burn; 315
Yet when their ashes in their nook are laid,
Doth not the myrtle leave as sweet a shade?
Had Cæsar known but Cleopatra's kiss,
Rome had been free, the world had not
 been his.
And what have Cæsar's deeds and Cæsar's
 fame 320
Done for the earth? We feel them in our
 shame:
The gory sanction of his glory stains
The rust which tyrants cherish on our
 chains.
Though Glory, Nature, Reason, Freedom,
 bid
Roused millions do what single Brutus
 did— 325
Sweep these mere mock-birds of the des-
 pot's song
From the tall bough where they have
 perch'd so long,—
Still are we hawk'd at by such mousing
 owls,
And take for falcons those ignoble fowls,
When but a word of freedom would dispel
These bugbears, as their terrors show too
 well. 331

XIV

Rapt in the fond forgetfulness of life,
Neuha, the South Sea girl, was all a wife,
With no distracting world to call her off
From love; with no society to scoff 335
At the new transient flame; no babbling
 crowd
Of coxcombry in admiration loud,
Or with adulterous whisper to alloy
Her duty, and her glory, and her joy: 339
With faith and feelings naked as her form,
She stood as stands a rainbow in a storm,
Changing its hues with bright variety,
But still expanding lovelier o'er the sky,
Howe'er its arch may swell, its colours
 move, 344
The cloud-compelling harbinger of love.

XV

Here, in this grotto of the wave-worn shore,
They pass'd the tropic's red meridian o'er;
Nor long the hours—they never paused
 o'er time,
Unbroken by the clock's funereal chime,
Which deals the daily pittance of our span,
And points and mocks with iron laugh at
 man. 351

What deem'd they of the future or the
 past?
The present, like a tyrant, held them fast
Their hour-glass was the sea-sand, and the
 tide,
Like her smooth billow, saw their mo-
 ments glide; 35
Their clock the sun, in his unbounded
 tow'r;
They reckon'd not, whose day was but an
 hour;
The nightingale, their only vesper-bell,
Sung sweetly to the rose the day's farewell
The broad sun set, but not with lingering
 sweep, 36
As in the north he mellows o'er the deep
But fiery, full, and fierce, as if he left
The world for ever, earth of light bereft
Plunged with red forehead down along the
 wave, 36
As dives a hero headlong to his grave.
Then rose they, looking first along the skies
And then for light into each other's eyes
Wondering that summer show'd so brief
 a sun,
And asking if indeed the day were done

XVI

And let not this seem strange: the devotee
Lives not in earth, but in his ecstasy;
Around him days and worlds are heedless
 driven,
His soul is gone before his dust to heaven
Is love less potent? No—his path is trod
Alike uplifted gloriously to God; 37
Or link'd to all we know of heaven below
The other better self, whose joy or woe
Is more than ours; the all-absorbing flame
Which, kindled by another, grows the
 same,
Wrapt in one blaze; the pure, yet funeral
 pile, 38
Where gentle hearts, like Bramins, sit and
 smile.
How often we forget all time, when lone
Admiring Nature's universal throne,
Her woods, her wilds, her waters, the in
 tense
Reply of *hers* to our intelligence! 38
Live not the stars and mountains? Are the
 waves
Without a spirit? Are the dropping caves
Without a feeling in their silent tears?
No, no;—they woo and clasp us to their
 spheres,
Dissolve this clog and clod of clay before
Its hour, and merge our soul in the great
 shore. 39
Strip off this fond and false identity!—
Who thinks of self when gazing on the sky
And who, though gazing lower, ever
 thought,
In the young moments ere the heart is
 taught 39

Time's lesson, of man's baseness or his
 own?
All nature is his realm, and love his throne.

XVII

Neuha arose, and Torquil: twilight's hour
Came sad and softly to their rocky bower,
Which, kindling by degrees its dewy spars,
Echoed their dim light to the mustering
 stars. 401
Slowly the pair, partaking nature's calm,
Sought out their cottage, built beneath the
 palm;
Now smiling and now silent, as the scene;
Lovely as Love—the spirit!—when serene.
The Ocean scarce spoke louder with his
 swell, 406
Than breathes his mimic murmurer in the
 shell,
As, far divided from his parent deep,
The sea-born infant cries, and will not
 sleep, 409
Raising his little plaint in vain, to rave
For the broad bosom of his nursing wave:
The woods droop'd darkly, as inclined to
 rest,
The tropic bird wheel'd rockward to his
 nest,
And the blue sky spread round them like a
 lake
Of peace, where Piety her thirst might
 slake. 415

XVIII

But through the palm and plantain, hark,
 a voice!
Not such as would have been a lover's
 choice,
In such an hour, to break the air so still;
No dying night-breeze, harping o'er the hill,
Striking the strings of nature, rock and
 tree, 420
Those best and earliest lyres of harmony,
With Echo for their chorus; nor the alarm
Of the loud war-whoop to dispel the charm;
Nor the soliloquy of the hermit owl,
Exhaling all his solitary soul, 425
The dim though large-eyed winged an-
 chorite,
Who peals his dreary pæan o'er the night;
But a loud, long, and naval whistle, shrill
As ever started through a sea-bird's bill;
And then a pause, and then a hoarse,
 'Hillo! 430
Torquil, my boy! what cheer? Ho!
 brother, ho!'
'Who hails?' cried Torquil, following
 with his eye
The sound. 'Here's one,' was all the brief
 reply.

XIX

But here the herald of the self-same mouth
Came breathing o'er the aromatic south,

Not like a 'bed of violets' on the gale, 436
But such as wafts its cloud o'er grog or ale,
Borne from a short frail pipe, which yet
 had blown
Its gentle odours over either zone,
And, puff'd where'er winds rise or waters
 roll, 440
Had wafted smoke from Portsmouth to
 the Pole,
Opposed its vapour as the lightning flash'd,
And reek'd, 'midst mountain-billows, un-
 abash'd,
To Æolus a constant sacrifice,
Through every change of all the varying
 skies. 445
And what was he who bore it?—I may err,
But deem him sailor or philosopher.
Sublime tobacco! which from east to west
Cheers the tar's labour or the Turkman's
 rest;
Which on the Moslem's ottoman divides
His hours, and rivals opium and his
 brides; 451
Magnificent in Stamboul, but less grand,
Though not less loved, in Wapping or the
 Strand;
Divine in hookas, glorious in a pipe,
When tipp'd with amber, mellow, rich,
 and ripe; 455
Like other charmers, wooing the caress,
More dazzlingly when daring in full dress;
Yet thy true lovers more admire by far
Thy naked beauties—Give me a cigar!

XX

Through the approaching darkness of the
 wood 460
A human figure broke the solitude,
Fantastically, it may be, array'd,
A seaman in a savage masquerade;
Such as appears to rise out from the deep
When o'er the line the merry vessels sweep,
And the rough saturnalia of the tar 466
Flock o'er the deck, in Neptune's borrow'd
 car;
And, pleased, the god of ocean sees his
 name
Revive once more, though but in mimic
 game
Of his true sons, who riot in the breeze
Undreamt of in his native Cyclades. 471
Still the old god delights, from out the
 main,
To snatch some glimpses of his ancient
 reign.
Our sailor's jacket, though in ragged trim,
His constant pipe, which never yet burn'd
 dim, 475
His foremast air, and somewhat rolling gait,
Like his dear vessel, spoke his former
 state;
But then a sort of kerchief round his head,
Not over-tightly bound, nor nicely
 spread;

And, 'stead of trowsers (ah! too early
 torn! 480
For even the mildest woods will have their
 thorn),
A curious sort of somewhat scanty mat
Now served for inexpressibles and hat;
His naked feet and neck, and sunburnt face,
Perchance might suit alike with either
 race. 485
His arms were all his own, our Europe's
 growth,
Which two worlds bless for civilising both;
The musket swung behind his shoulders
 broad,
And somewhat stoop'd by his marine
 abode,
But brawny as the boar's; and hung be-
 neath, 490
His cutlass droop'd, unconscious of a
 sheath,
Or lost or worn away; his pistols were
Link'd to his belt, a matrimonial pair—
(Let not this metaphor appear a scoff,
Though one miss'd fire, the other would go
 off); 495
These, with a bayonet, not so free from
 rust
As when the arm-chest held its brighter
 trust,
Completed his accoutrements, as Night
Survey'd him in his garb heteroclite.

XXI

'What cheer, Ben Bunting?' cried (when
 in full view 500
Our new acquaintance) Torquil. 'Aught
 of new?'
'Ey, ey!' quoth Ben, 'not new, but news
 enow;
A strange sail in the offing.'—'Sail! and
 how?
What! could you make her out? It cannot
 be;
I've seen no rag of canvas on the sea.' 505
'Belike,' said Ben, 'you might not from the
 bay,
But from the bluff-head, where I watch'd
 to-day,
I saw her in the doldrums; for the wind
Was light and baffling.'—'When the sun
 declined
Where lay she? had she anchor'd?'—'No,
 but still 510
She bore down on us, till the wind grew still.'
'Her flag?'—'I had no glass: but fore and
 aft,
Egad! she seem'd a wicked-looking craft.'
'Arm'd?'—'I expect so;—sent on the
 look-out:
'Tis time, belike, to put our helm about.'
'About?—Whate'er may have us now in
 chase, 516
We'll make no running fight, for that were
 base;

We will die at our quarters, like true men.'
'Ey, ey! for that 'tis all the same to Ben.'
'Does Christian know this?'—'Ay; he
 has piped all hands 520
To quarters. They are furbishing the stands
Of arms; and we have got some guns to
 bear,
And scaled them. You are wanted.'—
 'That's but fair;
And if it were not, mine is not the soul
To leave my comrades helpless on the
 shoal. 525
My Neuha! ah! and must my fate pursue
Not me alone, but one so sweet and true?
But whatsoe'er betide, ah, Neuha! now
Unman me not; the hour will not allow
A tear; I'm thine whatever intervenes!'
'Right,' quoth Ben; 'that will do for the
 marines.' 531

CANTO THE THIRD

I

THE fight was o'er; the flashing through
 the gloom,
Which robes the cannon as he wings a
 tomb,
Had ceased; and sulphury vapours up-
 ward driven
Had left the earth, and but polluted
 heaven:
The rattling roar which rung in every
 volley 5
Had left the echoes to their melancholy;
No more they shriek'd their horror, boom
 for boom;
The strife was done, the vanquish'd had
 their doom;
The mutineers were crush'd, dispers'd, or
 ta'en,
Or lived to deem the happiest were the
 slain. 10
Few, few escaped, and these were hunted
 o'er
The isle they loved beyond their native
 shore.
No further home was theirs, it seem'd, on
 earth,
Once renegades to that which gave them
 birth;
Track'd like wild beasts, like them they
 sought the wild, 15
As to a mother's bosom flies the child;
But vainly wolves and lions seek their den,
And still more vainly men escape from
 men.

II

Beneath a rock whose jutting base pro-
 trudes
Far over ocean in its fiercest moods, 20
When scaling his enormous crag the wave
Is hurl'd down headlong like the foremost
 brave,

358

And falls back on the foaming crowd
behind,
Which fight beneath the banners of the
wind, 24
But now at rest, a little remnant drew
Together, bleeding, thirsty, faint, and few;
But still their weapons in their hands, and
still
With something of the pride of former will,
As men not all unused to meditate,
And strive much more than wonder at
their fate. 30
Their present lot was what they had fore-
seen,
And dared as what was likely to have been;
Yet still the lingering hope, which deem'd
their lot
Not pardon'd, but unsought for or forgot,
Or trusted that, if sought, their distant
caves 35
Might still be miss'd amidst the world of
waves,
Had wean'd their thoughts in part from
what they saw
And felt, the vengeance of their country's
law.
Their sea-green isle, their guilt-won para-
dise,
No more could shield their virtue or their
vice: 40
Their better feelings, if such were, were
thrown
Back on themselves,—their sins remain'd
alone.
Proscribed even in their second country,
they
Were lost; in vain the world before them
lay;
All outlets seem'd secured. Their new
allies 45
Had fought and bled in mutual sacrifice;
But what avail'd the club and spear, and
arm
Of Hercules, against the sulphury charm,
The magic of the thunder, which destroy'd
The warrior ere his strength could be em-
ploy'd? 50
Dug, like a spreading pestilence, the grave
No less of human bravery than the brave!
Their own scant numbers acted all the
few
Against the many oft will dare and do;
But though the choice seems native to die
free, 55
Even Greece can boast but one Thermo-
pylæ,
Till *now*, when she has forged her broken
chain
Back to a sword, and dies and lives again!

III

Beside the jutting rock the few appear'd,
Like the last remnant of the red-deer's
herd; 60

Their eyes were feverish, and their aspect
worn,
But still the hunter's blood was on their
horn,
A little stream came tumbling from the
height,
And straggling into ocean as it might,
Its bounding crystal frolick'd in the ray,
And gush'd from cliff to crag with saltless
spray; 66
Close on the wild, wide ocean, yet as pure
And fresh as innocence, and more secure,
Its silver torrent glitter'd o'er the deep,
As the shy chamois' eye o'erlooks the
steep, 70
While far below the vast and sullen swell
Of ocean's alpine azure rose and fell.
To this young spring they rush'd,—all
feelings first
Absorb'd in passion's and in nature's
thirst,—
Drank as they do who drink their last, and
threw 75
Their arms aside to revel in its dew;
Cool'd their scorch'd throats, and wash'd
the gory stains
From wounds whose only bandage might
be chains;
Then, when their drought was quench'd,
look'd sadly round,
As wondering how so many still were
found 80
Alive and fetterless:—but silent all,
Each sought his fellow's eyes, as if to call
On him for language which his lips denied,
As though their voices with their cause had
died.

IV

Stern, and aloof a little from the rest,
Stood Christian, with his arms across his
chest. 86
The ruddy, reckless, dauntless hue once
spread
Along his cheek was livid now as lead;
His light-brown locks, so graceful in their
flow,
Now rose like startled vipers o'er his
brow. 90
Still as a statue, with his lips comprest
To stifle even the breath within his breast,
Fast by the rock, all menacing, but mute,
He stood; and, save a slight beat of his
foot,
Which deepen'd now and then the sandy
dint 95
Beneath his heel, his form seem'd turn'd
to flint.
Some paces further Torquil lean'd his head
Against a bank, and spoke not, but he
bled,—
Not mortally:—his worst wound was
within;
His brow was pale, his blue eyes sunken in,

And blood-drops, sprinkled o'er his yellow
hair, 101
Show'd that his faintness came not from
despair,
But nature's ebb. Beside him was another,
Rough as a bear, but willing as a brother,—
Ben Bunting, who essay'd to wash, and
wipe, 105
And bind his wound—then calmly lit his
pipe,
A trophy which survived a hundred fights,
A beacon which had cheer'd ten thousand
nights.
The fourth and last of this deserted group
Walk'd up and down—at times would
stand, then stoop, 110
To pick a pebble up—then let it drop—
Then hurry as in haste—then quickly
stop—
Then cast his eyes on his companions—
then
Half whistle half a tune, and pause again—
And then his former movements would
redouble, 115
With something between carelessness and
trouble.
This is a long description, but applies
To scarce five minutes pass'd before the
eyes;
But yet *what* minutes! Moments like to
these
Rend men's lives into immortalities. 120

V

At length Jack Skyscrape, a mercurial
man,
Who flutter'd over all things like a fan,
More brave than firm, and more disposed
to dare
And die at once than wrestle with despair,
Exclaim'd, 'G—d damn!'—those syllables
intense,— 125
Nucleus of England's native eloquence,
As the Turk's 'Allah!' or the Roman's
more
Pagan 'Proh Jupiter!' was wont of yore
To give their first impressions such a vent,
By way of echo to embarrassment. 130
Jack was embarrass'd,—never hero more,
And as he knew not what to say, he swore:
Nor swore in vain; the long congenial
sound
Revived Ben Bunting from his pipe pro-
found;
He drew it from his mouth, and look'd full'
wise, 135
But merely added to the oath his *eyes*;
Thus rendering the imperfect phrase com-
plete,
A peroration I need not repeat.

VI

But Christian, of a higher order, stood
Like an extinct volcano in his mood;

Silent, and sad, and savage,—with the
trace 141
Of passion reeking from his clouded face:
Till lifting up again his sombre eye,
It glanced on Torquil, who lean'd faintly
by.
'And is it thus?' he cried, 'unhappy boy!
And thee, too, *thee*—my madness must
destroy!' 146
He said, and strode to where young Tor-
quil stood,
Yet dabbled with his lately flowing blood;
Seized his hand wistfully, but did not press,
And shrunk as fearful of his own caress;
Inquired into his state; and when he heard
The wound was slighter than he deem'd or
fear'd, 152
A moment's brightness pass'd along his
brow,
As much as such a moment would allow.
'Yes,' he exclaim'd, 'we're taken in the
toil, 155
But not a coward or a common spoil;
Dearly they've bought us—dearly still may
buy,—
And I must fall; but have you strength to
fly?
'Twould be some comfort still, could you
survive;
Our dwindled band is now too few to
strive. 160
Oh! for a sole canoe! though but a shell,
To bear you hence to where a hope may
dwell!
For me, my lot is what I sought; to be,
In life or death, the fearless and the free.'

VII

Even as he spoke, around the promontory,
Which nodded o'er the billows high and
hoary, 166
A dark speck dotted ocean: on it flew
Like to the shadow of a roused sea-mew;
Onward it came—and, lo! a second
follow'd—
Now seen—now hid—where ocean's vale
was hollow'd; 170
And near, and nearer, till their dusky crew
Presented well-known aspects to the view,
Till on the surf their skimming paddles play,
Buoyant as wings, and flitting through the
spray;—
Now perching on the wave's high curl, and
now 175
Dash'd downward in the thundering foam
below,
Which flings it broad and boiling sheet on
sheet,
And slings its high flakes, shiver'd into
sleet:
But floating still through surf and swell,
drew nigh
The barks, like small birds through a
lowering sky. 180

Their art seem'd nature—such the skill to
 sweep
The wave of these born playmates of the
 deep.

VIII

And who the first that, springing on the
 strand,
Leap'd like a nereid from her shell to land,
With dark but brilliant skin, and dewy eye
Shining with love, and hope, and con-
 stancy? 186
Neuha—the fond, the faithful, the
 adored—
Her heart on Torquil's like a torrent
 pour'd;
And smiled, and wept, and near, and
 nearer clasp'd,
As if to be assured 'twas *him* she grasp'd;
Shudder'd to see his yet warm wound, and
 then, 191
To find it trivial, smiled and wept again.
She was a warrior's daughter, and could
 bear
Such sights, and feel, and mourn, but not
 despair.
Her lover lived,—nor foes nor fears could
 blight 195
That full-blown moment in its all delight:
Joy trickled in her tears, joy fill'd the sob
That rock'd her heart till almost heard to
 throb;
And paradise was breathing in the sigh
Of nature's child in nature's ecstasy. 200

IX

The sterner spirits who beheld that meet-
 ing
Were not unmoved; who are, when hearts
 are greeting?
Even Christian gazed upon the maid and
 boy
With tearless eye, but yet a gloomy joy
Mix'd with those bitter thoughts the soul
 arrays 205
In hopeless visions of our better days,
When all's gone—to the rainbow's latest
 ray.
And but for me!' he said, and turn'd
 away;
Then gazed upon the pair, as in his den
A lion looks upon his cubs again; 210
And then relapsed into his sullen guise,
As heedless of his further destinies.

X

But brief their time for good or evil
 thought;
The billows round the promontory
 brought
The plash of hostile oars.—Alas! who
 made 215
That sound a dread? All around them
 seem'd array'd

Against them, save the bride of Toobonai:
She, as she caught the first glimpse o'er the
 bay
Of the arm'd boats, which hurried to
 complete
The remnant's ruin with their flying feet,
Beckon'd the natives round her to their
 prows, 221
Embark'd their guests and launch'd their
 light canoes,
In one placed Christian and his comrades
 twain:
But she and Torquil must not part again.
She fix'd him in her own.—Away! away!
They clear the breakers, dart along the
 bay, 226
And towards a group of islets, such as bear
The sea-bird's nest and seal's surf-
 hollow'd lair,
They skim the blue tops of the billows; fast
They flew, and fast their fierce pursuers
 chased. 230
They gain upon them—now they lose
 again,—
Again make way and menace o'er the
 main;
And now the two canoes in chase divide,
And follow different courses o'er the tide,
To baffle the pursuit.—Away! away!
As Life is on each paddle's flight to-day,
And more than Life or lives to Neuha: Love
Freights the frail bark and urges to the
 cove;
And now the refuge and the foe are nigh—
Yet, yet a moment: Fly, thou light ark,
 fly! 240

CANTO THE FOURTH

I

WHITE as a white sail on a dusky sea,
When half the horizon's clouded and half
 free,
Fluttering between the dun wave and the
 sky,
Is hope's last gleam in man's extremity.
Her anchor parts! but still her snowy sail
Attracts our eye amidst the rudest gale:
Though every wave she climbs divides us
 more, 7
The heart still follows from the loneliest
 shore.

II

Not distant from the isle of Toobonai,
A black rock rears its bosom o'er the
 spray, 10
The haunt of birds, a desert to mankind,
Where the rough seal reposes from the
 wind,
And sleeps unwieldy in his cavern dun,
Or gambols with huge frolic in the sun:
There shrilly to the passing oar is heard
The startled echo of the ocean bird, 16

361

Who rears on its bare breast her callow
 brood,
The feather'd fishers of the solitude.
A narrow segment of the yellow sand
On one side forms the outline of a strand;
Here the young turtle, crawling from his
 shell, 21
Steals to the deep wherein his parents dwell;
Chipp'd by the beam, a nursling of the day,
But hatch'd for ocean by the fostering ray;
The rest was one bleak precipice, as e'er 26
Gave mariners a shelter and despair;
A spot to make the saved regret the deck
Which late went down, and envy the lost
 wreck.
Such was the stern asylum Neuha chose
To shield her lover from his following
 foes; 30
But all its secret was not told; she knew
In this a treasure hidden from the view.

III

Ere the canoes divided, near the spot,
The men that mann'd what held her Tor-
 quil's lot,
By her command removed, to strengthen
 more 35
The skiff which wafted Christian from the
 shore.
This he would have opposed; but with a
 smile
She pointed calmly to the craggy isle,
And bade him 'speed and prosper.' *She*
 would take 39
The rest upon herself for Torquil's sake.
They parted with this added aid; afar
The proa darted like a shooting star,
And gain'd on the pursuers, who now
 steer'd
Right on the rock which she and Torquil
 near'd.
They pull'd; her arm, though delicate, was
 free 45
And firm as ever grappled with the sea,
And yielded scarce to Torquil's manlier
 strength.
The prow now almost lay within its length
Of the crag's steep, inexorable face,
With nought but soundless waters for its
 base; 50
Within a hundred boats' length was the foe,
And now what refuge but their frail canoe?
This Torquil ask'd with half-upbraiding
 eye,
Which said—'Has Neuha brought me
 here to die?
Is this a place of safety, or a grave, 55
And yon huge rock the tombstone of the
 wave?'

IV

They rested on their paddles, and uprose
Neuha, and pointing to the approaching
 foes,

Cried, 'Torquil, follow me, and fearless
 follow!'
Then plunged at once into the ocean'
 hollow. 6
There was no time to pause—the foes wer
 near—
Chains in his eye, and menace in his ear;
With vigour they pull'd on, and as the;
 came,
Hail'd him to yield, and by his forfeit name
Headlong he leapt—to him the swimmer'
 skill 6
Was native, and now all his hope from ill
But how, or where? He dived, and rose ne
 more;
The boat's crew look'd amazed o'er se;
 and shore.
There was no landing on that precipice,
Steep, harsh, and slippery as a berg of ice
They watch'd awhile to see him float again
But not a trace rebubbled from the main
The wave roll'd on, no ripple on its face,
Since their first plunge recall'd a singl
 trace;
The little whirl which eddied, and sligh
 foam, 7
That whiten'd o'er what seem'd their lates
 home,
White as a sepulchre above the pair
Who left no marble (mournful as an heir
The quiet proa wavering o'er the tide
Was all that told of Torquil and his bride
And but for this alone the whole migh
 seem 8
The vanish'd phantom of a seaman's dream
They paused and search'd in vain, the
 pull'd away;
Even superstition now forbade their stay
Some said he had not plunged into th
 wave, 8
But vanish'd like a corpse-light from .
 grave;
Others, that something supernatural
Glared in his figure, more than mortal tall
While all agreed that in his cheek and ey
There was a dead hue of eternity. 9
Still as their oars receded from the crag,
Round every weed a moment would the;
 lag,
Expectant of some token of their prey;
But no—he had melted from them like th
 spray.

V

And where was he the pilgrim of the deep
Following the nereid? Had they ceased t
 weep 9
For ever? or, received in coral caves,
Wrung life and pity from the softenin;
 waves?
Did they with ocean's hidden sovereign
 dwell,
And sound with mermen the fantasti
 shell? 10

Did Neuha with the mermaids comb her hair
Flowing o'er ocean as it stream'd in air?
Or had they perish'd, and in silence slept
Beneath the gulf wherein they boldly leapt?

VI

Young Neuha plunged into the deep, and he 105
Follow'd: her track beneath her native sea
Was as a native's of the element,
So smoothly, bravely, brilliantly she went,
Leaving a streak of light behind her heel,
Which struck and flash'd like an amphibious steel. 110
Closely, and scarcely less expert to trace
The depths where divers hold the pearl in chase,
Torquil, the nursling of the northern seas,
Pursued her liquid steps with heart and ease.
Deep—deeper for an instant Neuha led
The way—then upward soar'd—and as she spread 116
Her arms, and flung the foam from off her locks,
Laugh'd, and the sound was answer'd by the rocks.
They had gain'd a central realm of earth again,
But look'd for tree, and field, and sky, in vain. 120
Around she pointed to a spacious cave,
Whose only portal was the keyless wave,
(A hollow archway by the sun unseen,
Save through the billows' glassy veil of green,
In some transparent ocean holiday, 125
When all the finny people are at play,)
Wiped with her hair the brine from Torquil's eyes,
And clapp'd her hands with joy at his surprise; 128
Led him to where the rock appear'd to jut,
And form a something like a Triton's hut;
For all was darkness for a space, till day
Through clefts above let in a sober'd ray;
As in some old cathedral's glimmering aisle
The dusty monuments from light recoil,
Thus sadly in their refuge submarine 135
The vault drew half her shadow from the scene.

VII

Forth from her bosom the young savage drew 137
A pine torch, strongly girded with gnatoo;
A plantain-leaf o'er all, the more to keep
Its latent sparkle from the sapping deep.
This mantle kept it dry; then from a nook
Of the same plantain-leaf a flint she took,
A few shrunk wither'd twigs, and from the blade 143
Of Torquil's knife struck fire, and thus array'd

The grot with torchlight. Wide it was and high, 145
And show'd a self-born Gothic canopy;
The arch uprear'd by nature's architect,
The architrave some earthquake might erect;
The buttress from some mountain's bosom hurl'd,
When the Poles crash'd, and water was the world; 150
Or harden'd from some earth-absorbing fire,
While yet the globe reek'd from its funeral pyre;
The fretted pinnacle, the aisle, the nave,
Were there, all scoop'd by Darkness from her cave. 154
There, with a little tinge of phantasy,
Fantastic faces mop'd and mow'd on high,
And then a mitre or a shrine would fix
The eye upon its seeming crucifix.
Thus Nature play'd with the stalactites,
And built herself a chapel of the seas.

VIII

And Neuha took her Torquil by the hand,
And waved along the vault her kindled brand,
And led him into each recess, and show'd
The secret places of their new abode.
Nor these alone, for all had been prepared
Before, to soothe the lover's lot she shared: 166
The mat for rest; for dress the fresh gnatoo,
And sandal oil to fence against the dew;
For food the cocoa-nut, the yam, the bread
Born of the fruit; for board the plantain spread 170
With its broad leaf, or turtle-shell which bore
A banquet in the flesh it cover'd o'er;
The gourd with water recent from the rill,
The ripe banana from the mellow hill;
A pine-torch pile to keep undying light,
And she herself, as beautiful as night,
To fling her shadowy spirit o'er the scene,
And make their subterranean world serene.
She had foreseen, since first the stranger's sail
Drew to their isle, that force or flight might fail, 180
And form'd a refuge of the rocky den
For Torquil's safety from his countrymen.
Each dawn had wafted there her light canoe,
Laden with all the golden fruits that grew;
Each eve had seen her gliding through the hour 185
With all could cheer or deck their sparry bower;
And now she spread her little store with smiles,
The happiest daughter of the loving isles.

363

IX

She, as he gazed with grateful wonder,
 press'd
Her shelter'd love to her impassion'd
 breast; 190
And suited to her soft caresses, told
An olden tale of love,—for love is old,
Old as eternity, but not outworn
With each new being born or to be born:
How a young chief, a thousand moons
 ago, 195
Diving for turtle in the depths below,
Had risen, in tracking fast his ocean prey,
Into the cave which round and o'er them
 lay;
How in some desperate feud of after-time
He shelter'd there a daughter of the clime,
A foe beloved, and offspring of a foe, 201
Saved by his tribe but for a captive's woe;
How, when the storm of war was still'd, he led
His island clan to where the waters spread
Their deep-green shadow o'er the rocky
 door, 205
Then dived—it seem'd as if to rise no more:
His wondering mates, amazed within their
 bark,
Or deem'd him mad, or prey to the blue
 shark;
Row'd round in sorrow the sea-girded
 rock,
Then paused upon their paddles from the
 shock; 210
When, fresh and springing from the deep,
 they saw
A goddess rise—so deem'd they in their
 awe;
And their companion, glorious by her side,
Proud and exulting in his mermaid bride:
And how, when undeceived, the pair they
 bore 215
With sounding conchs and joyous shouts
 to shore;
How they had gladly lived and calmly
 died,
And why not also Torquil and his bride? 219
Not mine to tell the rapturous caress
Which follow'd wildly in that wild recess
This tale; enough that all within that cave
Was love, though buried strong as in the
 grave
Where Abelard, through twenty years of
 death,
When Eloïsa's form was lower'd beneath
Their nuptial vault, his arms outstretch'd,
 and press'd 225
The kindling ashes to his kindled breast.
The waves without sang round their
 couch, their roar
As much unheeded as if life were o'er;
Within, their hearts made all their har-
 mony,
Love's broken murmur and more broken
 sigh. 230

X

And they, the cause and sharers of th
 shock
Which left them exiles of the hollow rock
Where were they? O'er the sea for lif
 they plied,
To seek from Heaven the shelter me
 denied.
Another course had been their choice—
 but where? 23
The wave which bore them still their foe
 would bear,
Who, disappointed of their former chase
In search of Christian now renew'd thei
 race.
Eager with anger, their strong arms mad
 way,
Like vultures baffled of their previou
 prey. 24
They gain'd upon them, all whose safet
 lay
In some bleak crag or deeply-hidden bay
No further chance or choice remain'd
 and right
For the first further rock which met thei
 sight
They steer'd, to take their latest view c
 land, 24
And yield as victims, or die sword in hand
Dismiss'd the natives and their shallop
 who
Would still have battled for that scant
 crew;
But Christian bade them seek their shor
 again,
Nor add a sacrifice which were in vain;
For what were simple bow and savag
 spear 25
Against the arms which must be wielde
 here?

XI

They landed on a wild but narrow scene
Where few but Nature's footsteps yet ha
 been;
Prepared their arms, and with that gloom
 eye, 25
Stern and sustain'd, of man's extremity,
When hope is gone, nor glory's self remain
To cheer resistance against death o
 chains,—
They stood, the three, as the three hundre
 stood
Who dyed Thermopylæ with holy blood
But, ah! how different! 'tis the *cause* make
 all, 26
Degrades or hallows courage in its fall.
O'er them no fame, eternal and intense,
Blazed through the clouds of death an
 beckon'd hence;
No grateful country, smiling through he
 tears, 26
Begun the praises of a thousand years;

No nation's eyes would on their tomb be
 bent,
No heroes envy them their monument;
However boldly their warm blood was
 spilt,
Their life was shame, their epitaph was
 guilt. 270
And this they knew and felt, at least the
 one,
The leader of the band he had undone;
Who, born perchance for better things,
 had set
His life upon a cast which linger'd yet:
But now the die was to be thrown, and all
The chances were in favour of his fall:
And such a fall! But still he faced the
 shock, 277
Obdurate as a portion of the rock
Whereon he stood, and fix'd his levell'd
 gun,
Dark as a sullen cloud before the sun.

XII

The boat drew nigh, well arm'd, and firm
 the crew 281
To act whatever duty bade them do;
Careless of danger, as the onward wind
Is of the leaves it strews, nor looks behind.
And yet perhaps they rather wish'd to go
Against a nation's than a native foe, 286
And felt that this poor victim of self-will,
Briton no more, had once been Britain's
 still.
They hail'd him to surrender—no reply;
Their arms were poised, and glitter'd in
 the sky. 290
They hail'd again—no answer; yet once
 more
They offer'd quarter louder than before.
The echoes only, from the rock's rebound,
Took their last farewell of the dying sound.
Then flash'd the flint, and blazed the
 volleying flame, 295
And the smoke rose between them and
 their aim,
While the rock rattled with the bullets'
 knell,
Which peal'd in vain, and flatten'd as they
 fell;
Then flew the only answer to be given
By those who had lost all hope in earth or
 heaven. 300
After the first fierce peal, as they pull'd
 nigher,
They heard the voice of Christian shout,
 'Now, fire!'
And ere the word upon the echo died,
Two fell; the rest assail'd the rock's rough
 side, 304
And, furious at the madness of their foes,
Disdain'd all further efforts, save to close.
But steep the crag, and all without a path,
Each step opposed a bastion to their
 wrath.

While, placed 'midst clefts the least acces-
 sible,
Which Christian's eye was train'd to mark
 full well, 310
The three maintain'd a strife which must
 not yield,
In spots where eagles might have chosen
 to build.
Their every shot told; while the assailant
 fell,
Dash'd on the shingles like the limpet
 shell;
But still enough survived, and mounted
 still, 315
Scattering their numbers here and there,
 until
Surrounded and commanded, though not
 nigh
Enough for seizure, near enough to die,
The desperate trio held aloof their fate
But by a thread, like sharks who've gorged
 the bait; 320
Yet to the very last they battled well,
And not a groan inform'd their foes *who*
 fell.
Christian died last—twice wounded; and
 once more
Mercy was offer'd when they saw his gore;
Too late for life, but not too late to die,
With, though a hostile hand, to close his
 eye. 326
A limb was broken, and he droop'd along
The crag, as doth a falcon reft of young.
The sound revived him, or appear'd to
 wake
Some passion which a weakly gesture
 spake: 330
He beckon'd to the foremost, who drew
 nigh,
But, as they near'd, he rear'd his weapon
 high—
His last ball had been aim'd, but from his
 breast
He tore the topmost button from his vest,
Down the tube dash'd it, levell'd, fired,
 and smiled 335
As his foe fell; then, like a serpent, coil'd
His wounded, weary form, to where the
 steep
Look'd desperate as himself along the
 deep;
Cast one glance back, and clench'd his
 hand, and shook
His last rage 'gainst the earth which he for-
 sook; 340
Then plunged: the rock below received
 like glass
His body crush'd into one gory mass,
With scarce a shred to tell of human form,
Or fragment for the sea-bird or the worm;
A fair-hair'd scalp, besmear'd with blood
 and weeds, 345
Yet reek'd, the remnant of himself and
 deeds;

Some splinters of his weapons (to the last,
As long as hand could hold, he held them
 fast)
Yet glitter'd, but at distance—hurl'd away
To rust beneath the dew and dashing
 spray. 350
The rest was nothing—save a life mis-
 spent,
And soul—but who shall answer where it
 went?
'Tis ours to bear, not judge the dead; and
 they
Who doom to hell, themselves are on the
 way,
Unless these bullies of eternal pains 355
Are pardon'd their bad hearts for their
 worse brains.

XIII

The deed was over! All were gone or ta'en,
The fugitive, the captive, or the slain.
Chain'd on the deck, where once, a gallant
 crew,
They stood with honour, were the
 wretched few 360
Survivors of the skirmish on the isle;
But the last rock left no surviving spoil.
Cold lay they where they fell, and welter-
 ing,
While o'er them flapp'd the sea-birds'
 dewy wing,
Now wheeling nearer from the neighbour-
 ing surge, 365
And screaming high their harsh and
 hungry dirge:
But calm and careless heaved the wave
 below,
Eternal with unsympathetic flow;
Far o'er its face the dolphins sported on,
And sprung the flying fish against the sun,
Till its dried wing relapsed from its brief
 height, 371
To gather moisture for another flight.

XIV

'Twas morn; and Neuha, who by dawn of
 day
Swam smoothly forth to catch the rising
 ray,
And watch if aught approach'd the am-
 phibious lair 375
Where lay her lover, saw a sail in air:
It flapp'd, it fill'd, and to the growing gale
Bent its broad arch: her breath began to
 fail
With fluttering fear, her heart beat thick
 and high,
While yet a doubt sprung where its course
 might lie. 380

But no! it came not; fast and far away
The shadow lessen'd as it clear'd the ba
She gazed, and flung the sea-foam fro
 her eyes, 38
To watch as for a rainbow in the skies.
On the horizon verged the distant deck
Diminish'd, dwindled to a very speck—
Then vanish'd. All was ocean, all was joy
Down plunged she through the cave t
 rouse her boy; 38
Told all she had seen, and all she hope
 and all
That happy love could augur or recall;
Sprung forth again, with Torquil follow
 ing free 3
His bounding nereid over the broad sea
Swam round the rock, to where a shallo
 cleft
Hid the canoe that Neuha there had le
Drifting along the tide, without an oar,
That eve the strangers chased them fro
 the shore; 39
But when these vanish'd, she pursued he
 prow,
Regain'd, and urged to where they foun
 it now:
Nor ever did more love and joy embark
Than now were wafted in that slende
 ark. 4

XV

Again their own shore rises on the view
No more polluted with a hostile hue;
No sullen ship lay bristling o'er the foam
A floating dungeon:—all was hope an
 home!
A thousand proas darted o'er the bay,
With sounding shells, and heralded thei
 way; 4
The chiefs came down, around the peop
 pour'd,
And welcomed Torquil as a son restored
The women throng'd, embracing and em
 braced
By Neuha, asking where they had bee
 chased, 4
And how escaped? The tale was told; an
 then
One acclamation rent the sky again;
And from that hour a new tradition gav
Their sanctuary the name of 'Neuha'
 Cave.'
A hundred fires, far flickering from th
 height, 4
Blazed o'er the general revel of the nigh
The feast in honour of the guest, return'
To peace and pleasure, perilously earn'
A night succeeded by such happy days
As only the yet infant world displays.

THE LAMENT OF TASSO

AT Ferrara, in the Library, are preserved the original MSS. of Tasso's Gierusalemme and of
Guarini's Pastor Fido, with letters of Tasso, one from Titian to Ariosto, and the inkstand and chair,
the tomb and the house, of the latter. But, as misfortune has a greater interest for posterity, and
title or none for the cotemporary, the cell where Tasso was confined in the hospital of St. Anna
attracts a more fixed attention than the residence or the monument of Ariosto—at least it had this
effect on me. There are two inscriptions, one on the outer gate, the second over the cell itself, inviting,
unnecessarily, the wonder and the indignation of the spectator. Ferrara is much decayed and de-
populated: the castle still exists entire; and I saw the court where Parisina and Hugo were beheaded,
according to the annal of Gibbon.

I

LONG years!—It tries the thrilling frame
 to bear
And eagle-spirit of a child of Song—
Long years of outrage, calumny, and wrong;
Imputed madness, prison'd solitude, 4
And the mind's canker in its savage mood,
When the impatient thirst of light and air
Parches the heart; and the abhorred grate,
Marring the sunbeams with its hideous
 shade,
Works through the throbbing eyeball to
 the brain, 9
With a hot sense of heaviness and pain;
And bare, at once, Captivity display'd
Stands scoffing through the never-open'd
 gate,
Which nothing through its bars admits,
 save day,
And tasteless food, which I have eat alone
'Till its unsocial bitterness is gone; 15
And I can banquet like a beast of prey,
Sullen and lonely, couching in the cave
Which is my lair, and—it may be—my grave.
All this hath somewhat worn me, and may
 wear,
But must be borne. I stoop not to despair;
For I have battled with mine agony, 21
And made me wings wherewith to overfly
The narrow circus of my dungeon wall,
And freed the Holy Sepulchre from thrall;
And revell'd among men and things
 divine, 25
And pour'd my spirit over Palestine,
In honour of the sacred war for Him,
The God who was on earth and is in
 heaven,
For he has strengthen'd me in heart and
 limb,
That through this sufferance I might be
 forgiven, 30
I have employ'd my penance to record
How Salem's shrine was won, and how
 adored.

II

But this is o'er—my pleasant task is
 done:—
My long-sustaining friend of many years!

If I do blot thy final page with tears, 35
Know, that my sorrows have wrung from
 me none.
But thou, my young creation! my soul's
 child!
Which ever playing round me came and
 smiled,
And woo'd me from myself with thy sweet
 sight, 39
Thou too art gone—and so is my delight:
And therefore do I weep and inly bleed
With this last bruise upon a broken reed.
Thou too art ended—what is left me now?
For I have anguish yet to bear—and how?
I know not that—but in the innate force
Of my own spirit shall be found resource.
I have not sunk, for I had no remorse, 47
Nor cause for such: they call'd me mad—
 and why?
Oh Leonora! wilt not *thou* reply?
I was indeed delirious in my heart 50
To lift my love so lofty as thou art;
But still my frenzy was not of the mind:
I knew my fault, and feel my punishment
Not less because I suffer it unbent.
That thou wert beautiful, and I not blind,
Hath been the sin which shuts me from
 mankind; 56
But let them go, or torture as they will,
My heart can multiply thine image still;
Successful love may sate itself away;
The wretched are the faithful; 'tis their
 fate 60
To have all feeling, save the one, decay,
And every passion into one dilate,
As rapid rivers into ocean pour;
But ours is fathomless, and hath no shore.

III

Above me, hark! the long and maniac cry
Of minds and bodies in captivity. 66
And hark! the lash and the increasing
 howl,
And the half-inarticulate blasphemy!
There be some here with worse than frenzy
 foul,
Some who do still goad on the o'er-
 labour'd mind, 70
And dim the little light that's left behind

367

THE LAMENT OF TASSO

With needless torture, as their tyrant will
Is wound up to the lust of doing ill:
With these and with their victims am I class'd,
'Mid sounds and sights like these long years have pass'd; 75
'Mid sights and sounds like these my life may close:
So let it be—for then I shall repose.

IV

I have been patient, let me be so yet;
I had forgotten half I would forget,
But it revives—Oh! would it were my lot
To be forgetful as I am forgot! 81
Feel I not wroth with those who bade me dwell
In this vast lazar-house of many woes?
Where laughter is not mirth, nor thought the mind,
Nor words a language, nor ev'n men mankind; 85
Where cries reply to curses, shrieks to blows,
And each is tortured in his separate hell—
For we are crowded in our solitudes—
Many, but each divided by the wall,
Which echoes Madness in her babbling moods; 90
While all can hear, none heed his neighbour's call—
None! save that One, the veriest wretch of all,
Who was not made to be the mate of these,
Nor bound between Distraction and Disease.
Feel I not wroth with those who placed me here? 95
Who have debased me in the minds of men,
Debarring me the usage of my own,
Blighting my life in best of its career,
Branding my thoughts as things to shun and fear?
Would I not pay them back these pangs again, 100
And teach them inward Sorrow's stifled groan?
The struggle to be calm, and cold distress,
Which undermines our Stoical success?
No! still too proud to be vindictive—I
Have pardon'd princes' insults, and would die. 105
Yes, Sister of my Sovereign! for thy sake
I weed all bitterness from out my breast,
It hath no business where *thou* art a guest:
Thy brother hates—but I cannot detest;
Thou pitiest not—but I cannot forsake.

V

Look on a love which knows not to despair,
But all unquench'd is still my better part,
Dwelling deep in my shut and silent heart,
As dwells the gather'd lightning in its cloud,
Encompass'd with its dark and rollin[g] shroud,
Till struck,—forth flies the all-etherea[l] dart!
And thus at the collision of thy name,
The vivid thought still flashes through m[y] frame,
And for a moment all things as they wer[e]
Flit by me; they are gone—I am the same[.]
And yet my love without ambition grew[;]
I knew thy state, my station, and I kne[w]
A Princess was no love-mate for a bar[d];
I told it not, I breathed it not, it was
Sufficient to itself, its own reward;
And if my eyes reveal'd it, they, alas!
Were punish'd by the silentness of thin[e]
And yet I did not venture to repine.
Thou wert to me a crystal-girded shrin[e]
Worshipp'd at holy distance, and aroun[d]
Hallow'd and meekly kiss'd the saintl[y] ground;
Not for thou wert a princess, but that Lo[ve]
Had robed thee with a glory, and array[ed]
Thy lineaments in beauty that dismay'd—
Oh! not dismay'd—but awed, like On[e] above!
And in that sweet severity there was
A something which all softness did su[r]pass;
I know not how—thy genius master'[d] mine;
My star stood still before thee: if it wer[e]
Presumptuous thus to love without de[sign,]
That sad fatality hath cost me dear;
But thou art dearest still, and I should b[e]
Fit for this cell, which wrongs me—but fo[r] *thee.*
The very love which lock'd me to my chai[n]
Hath lighten'd half its weight; and for th[e] rest,
Though heavy, lent me vigour to sustain[,]
And look to thee with undivided breast[,]
And foil the ingenuity of Pain.

VI

It is no marvel—from my very birth
My soul was drunk with love, which di[d] pervade
And mingle with whate'er I saw on earth[;]
Of objects all inanimate I made
Idols, and out of wild and lonely flower[s]
And rocks, whereby they grew, a paradis[e]
Where I did lay me down within the shad[e]
Of waving trees, and dreamed uncounte[d] hours,
Though I was chid for wandering; and th[e] wise
Shook their white aged heads o'er me an[d] said,
Of such materials wretched men wer[e] made,
And such a truant boy would end in woe[,]
And that the only lesson was a blow;

And then they smote me, and I did not
 weep,
But cursed them in my heart, and to my
 haunt
Return'd and wept alone, and dream'd
 again 164
The visions which arise without a sleep,
And with my years my soul began to pant
With feelings of strange tumult and soft
 pain;
And the whole heart exhaled into One Want,
But undefined and wandering, till the day
I found the thing I sought—and that was
 thee; 170
And then I lost my being, all to be
Absorb'd in thine; the world was past
 away;
Thou didst annihilate the earth to me!

VII

I loved all Solitude, but little thought
To spend I know not what of life, remote
From all communion with existence,
 save 176
The maniac and his tyrant; had I been
Their fellow, many years ere this had seen
My mind like theirs corrupted to its grave.
But who hath seen me writhe, or heard me
 rave? 180
Perchance in such a cell we suffer more
Than the wreck'd sailor on his desert shore;
The world is all before him—mine is here,
Scarce twice the space they must accord
 my bier. 184
What though he perish, he may lift his eye,
And with a dying glance upbraid the sky;
I will not raise my own in such reproof,
Although 'tis clouded by my dungeon roof.

VIII

Yet do I feel at times my mind decline,
But with a sense of its decay: I see 190
Unwonted lights along my prison shine
And a strange demon, who is vexing me
With pilfering pranks and petty pains below
The feeling of the healthful and the free;
But much to One, who long hath suffer'd
 so, 195
Sickness of heart, and narrowness of place,
And all that may be borne, or can debase.
I thought mine enemies had been but Man,
But Spirits may be leagued with them; all
 Earth
Abandons, Heaven forgets me: in the
 dearth 200
Of such defence the Powers of Evil can,
It may be, tempt me further,—and prevail
Against the outworn creature they assail.
Why in this furnace is my spirit proved,
Like steel in tempering fire? because I
 loved? 205
Because I loved what not to love, and see,
Was more or less than mortal, and than
 me.

IX

I once was quick in feeling—that is o'er;
My scars are callous, or I should have
 dash'd
My brain against these bars, as the sun
 flash'd 210
In mockery through them: If I bear and
 bore
The much I have recounted, and the more
Which hath no words,—'tis that I would
 not die
And sanction with self-slaughter the dull
 lie
Which snared me here, and with the brand
 of shame 215
Stamp Madness deep into my memory,
And woo Compassion to a blighted name,
Sealing the sentence which my foes pro-
 claim.
No—it shall be immortal! and I make
A future temple of my present cell, 220
Which nations yet shall visit for my sake.
While thou, Ferrara! when no longer dwell
The ducal chiefs within thee, shalt fall
 down,
And crumbling piecemeal view thy hearth-
 less halls,
A poet's wreath shall be thine only
 crown,— 225
A poet's dungeon thy most far renown,
While strangers wonder o'er thy un-
 peopled walls!
And thou, Leonora! thou—who wert
 ashamed
That such as I could love—who blush'd to
 hear
To less than monarchs that thou couldst
 be dear, 230
Go! tell thy brother, that my heart, un-
 tamed
By grief, years, weariness,—and it may be
A taint of that he would impute to me—
From long infection of a den like this,
Where the mind rots congenial with the
 abyss,— 235
Adores thee still; and add—that when the
 towers
And battlements which guard his joyous
 hours
Of banquet, dance, and revel, are forgot,
Or left untended in a dull repose,—
This, this, shall be a consecrated spot!
But Thou—when all that Birth and Beauty
 throws 241
Of magic round thee is extinct—shalt have
One half the laurel which o'ershades my
 grave.
No power in death can tear our names
 apart,
As none in life could rend thee from my
 heart. 245
Yes, Leonora! it shall be our fate
To be entwined for ever—but too late!

THE PROPHECY OF DANTE

"'Tis the sunset of life gives me mystical lore,
And coming events cast their shadows before.'
CAMPBELL.

DEDICATION

LADY! if for the cold and cloudy clime,
 Where I was born, but where I would not die,
 Of the great Poet-Sire of Italy
I dare to build the imitative rhyme,
Harsh Runic copy of the South's sublime,
 THOU art the cause; and howsoever I
 Fall short of his immortal harmony,
Thy gentle heart will pardon me the crime.
Thou, in the pride of Beauty and of Youth,
 Spakest; and for thee to speak and be obey'd
Are one; but only in the sunny South
 Such sounds are uttered, and such charms display'd,
So sweet a language from so fair a mouth—
 Ah! to what effort would it not persuade?

RAVENNA, *June* 21, 1819.

PREFACE

IN the course of a visit to the city of Ravenna in the summer of 1819, it was suggested to the author that having composed something on the subject of Tasso's confinement, he should do the same o Dante's exile,—the tomb of the poet forming one of the principal objects of interest in that city, bot to the native and to the stranger.

'On this hint I spake,' and the result has been the following four cantos, in terza rima, now offered to the reader. If they are understood and approved, it is my purpose to continue the poem, in various other cantos, to its natural conclusion in the present age. The reader is requested to suppose tha Dante addresses him in the interval between the conclusion of the Divina Commedia and his death and shortly before the latter event, foretelling the fortunes of Italy in general in the ensuing centuries In adopting this plan I have had in my mind the Cassandra of Lycophron, and the Prophecy of Nereu by Horace, as well as the Prophecies of Holy Writ. The measure adopted is the terza rima of Dante which I am not aware to have seen hitherto tried in our language, except it may be by Mr. Hayley of whose translation I never saw but one extract, quoted in the notes to Caliph Vathek; so that— I do not err—this poem may be considered as a metrical experiment. The cantos are short, and abou the same length of those of the poet, whose name I have borrowed, and most probably taken in vai

Amongst the inconveniences of authors in the present day, it is difficult for any who have a nam good or bad, to escape translation. I have had the fortune to see the fourth canto of 'Childe Harold translated into Italian versi sciolti,—that is, a poem written in the *Spenserean stanza* into *blank vers* without regard to the natural divisions of the stanza or of the sense. If the present poem, being o a national topic, should chance to undergo the same fate, I would request the Italian reader to remembe that when I have failed in the imitation of his great 'Padre Alighieri,' I have failed in imitating tha which all study and few understand, since to this very day it is not yet settled what was the meanin of the allegory in the first canto of the Inferno, unless Count Marchetti's ingenious and probabl conjecture may be considered as having decided the question.

He may also pardon my failure the more, as I am not quite sure that he would be pleased wit my success, since the Italians, with a pardonable nationality, are particularly jealous of all that is lef them as a nation,—their literature; and in the present bitterness of the classic and romantic war, ar but ill disposed to permit a foreigner even to approve or imitate them, without finding some fau with his ultramontane presumption. I can easily enter into all this, knowing what would be though in England of an Italian imitator of Milton, or if a translation of Monti, or Pindemonte, or Aric should be held up to the rising generation as a model for their future poetical essays. But I perceiv that I am deviating into an address to the Italian reader, when my business is with the English one and be they few or many, I must take my leave of both.

CANTO THE FIRST

ONCE more in man's frail world! which I
 had left
 So long that 'twas forgotten; and I feel
 The weight of clay again,—too soon
 bereft
Of the immortal vision which could heal

My earthly sorrows, and to God's ow
 skies
Lift me from that deep gulf without re
 peal,
Where late my ears rung with the damne
 cries
Of souls in hopeless bale; and from tha
 place

370

Of lesser torment, whence men may arise
'ure from the fire to join the angelic race;
Midst whom my own bright Beatrice
 bless'd 11
My spirit with her light; and to the base
Of the eternal Triad! first, last, best,
Mysterious, three, sole, infinite, great
 God!
Soul universal! led the mortal guest, 15
Unblasted by the glory, though he trod
From star to star to reach the almighty
 throne,
Oh Beatrice! whose sweet limbs the sod
So long hath press'd, and the cold
 marble stone,
Thou sole pure seraph of my earliest
 love, 20
Love so ineffable, and so alone,
That nought on earth could more my
 bosom move,
And meeting thee in heaven was but to
 meet
That without which my soul, like the
 arkless dove,
Had wander'd still in search of, nor her
 feet 25
Relieved her wing till found: without
 thy light
My paradise had still been incomplete.
Since my tenth sun gave summer to my
 sight
Thou wert my life, the essence of my
 thought,
Loved ere I knew the name of love, and
 bright 30
Still in these dim old eyes, now over-
 wrought
With the world's war, and years, and
 banishment,
And tears for thee, by other woes un-
 taught;
For mine is not a nature to be bent
By tyrannous faction, and the brawling
 crowd, 35
And though the long, long conflict hath
 been spent
In vain,—and never more, save when the
 cloud
Which overhangs the Apennine my
 mind's eye
Pierces to fancy Florence, once so proud
Of me, can I return, though but to die,
Unto my native soil,—they have not yet
Quench'd the old exile's spirit, stern and
 high.
But the sun, though not overcast, must set,
And the night cometh; I am old in days,
And deeds, and contemplation, and
 have met 45
Destruction face to face in all his ways.
The world hath left me, what it found
 me, pure,
And if I have not gather'd yet its praise,
I sought it not by any baser lure;

Man wrongs, and Time avenges, and
 my name 50
May form a monument not all obscure,
Though such was not my ambition's end
 or aim,
To add to the vain-glorious list of those
Who dabble in the pettiness of fame,
And make men's fickle breath the wind
 that blows 55
Their sail, and deem it glory to be class'd
With conquerors, and virtue's other
 foes,
In bloody chronicles of ages past.
I would have had my Florence great and
 free;
Oh Florence! Florence! unto me thou
 wast 60
Like that Jerusalem which the Almighty
 He
Wept over, 'but thou wouldst not'; as
 the bird
Gathers its young, I would have
 gather'd thee
Beneath a parent pinion, hadst thou heard
My voice; but as the adder, deaf and
 fierce, 65
Against the breast that cherish'd thee
 was stirr'd
Thy venom, and my state thou didst
 amerce,
And doom this body forfeit to the fire.
Alas! how bitter is his country's curse
To him who *for* that country would expire,
But did not merit to expire *by* her, 71
And loves her, loves her even in her ire!
The day may come when she will cease to
 err,
The day may come she would be proud
 to have
The dust she dooms to scatter, and
 transfer 75
Of him, whom she denied a home, the
 grave.
But this shall not be granted; let my
 dust
Lie where it falls; nor shall the soil which
 gave
Me breath, but in her sudden fury thrust
Me forth to breathe elsewhere, so re-
 assume 80
My indignant bones, because her angry
 gust
Forsooth is over, and repeal'd her doom;
No,—she denied me what was mine—
 my roof,
And shall not have what is not hers—
 my tomb.
Too long her armed wrath hath kept aloof
The breast which would have bled for
 her, the heart 86
That beat, the mind that was temptation
 proof,
The man who fought, toil'd, travell'd, and
 each part

371

Of a true citizen fulfill'd, and saw
For his reward the Guelf's ascendant
 art 90
Pass his destruction even into a law.
These things are not made for forget-
 fulness,
Florence shall be forgotten first; too
 raw
The wound, too deep the wrong, and the
 distress
Of such endurance too prolong'd to
 make
My pardon greater, her injustice less, 95
Though late repented; yet—yet for her
 sake
I feel some fonder yearnings, and for
 thine,
My own Beatrice, I would hardly take
Vengeance upon the land which once was
 mine, 100
And still is hallow'd by thy dust's return,
Which would protect the murderess like
 a shrine,
And save ten thousand foes by thy sole
 urn.
Though, like old Marius from Min-
 turnæ's marsh
And Carthage ruins, my lone breast
 may burn 105
At times with evil feelings hot and harsh,
And sometimes the last pangs of a vile
 foe
Writhe in a dream before me, and
 o'erarch
My brow with hopes of triumph,—let
 them go!
Such are the last infirmities of those
Who long have suffer'd more than
 mortal woe, 111
And yet being mortal still have no repose
But on the pillow of Revenge,—Revenge,
Who sleeps to dream of blood, and
 waking glows
With the oft-baffled slakeless thirst of
 change, 115
When we shall mount again, and they
 that trod
Be trampled on, while Death and Até
 range
O'er humbled heads and sever'd necks—
 Great God!
Take these thoughts from me—to thy
 hands I yield
My many wrongs, and thine Almighty
 rod 120
Will fall on those who smote me,—be my
 shield!
As thou hast been in peril, and in pain,
In turbulent cities, and the tented field—
In toil, and many troubles borne in vain
For Florence,—I appeal from her to
 Thee! 125
Thee whom I late saw in thy loftiest
 reign,

Even in that glorious vision, which to se
And live was never granted until now
And yet thou hast permitted this to me
Alas! with what a weight upon my brow
The sense of earth and earthly thing
 come back, 13
Corrosive passions, feelings dull an
 low,
The heart's quick throb upon the menta
 rack,
Long day, and dreary night; the retro
 spect
Of half a century bloody and black,
And the frail few years I may yet expect
Hoary and hopeless, but less hard t
 bear,
For I have been too long and deeply
 wreck'd
On the lone rock of desolate Despair,
To lift my eyes more to the passing sai
Which shuns that reef so horrible an
 bare; 14
Nor raise my voice—for who would hee
 my wail?
I am not of this people, nor this age,
And yet my harpings will unfold a tal
Which shall preserve these times when no
 a page 14
Of their perturbed annals could attrac
An eye to gaze upon their civil rage,
Did not my verse embalm full many an ac
Worthless as they who wrought it: 'ti
 the doom
Of spirits of my order to be rack'd
In life, to wear their hearts out, and con
 sume 15
Their days in endless strife, and di
 alone;
Then future thousands crowd aroun
 their tomb,
And pilgrims come from climes wher
 they have known
The name of him—who now is but
 name,
And wasting homage o'er the sulle
 stone, 15
Spread his—by him unheard, unheeded-
 fame;
And mine at least hath cost me dear: t
 die
Is nothing; but to wither thus—to tam
My mind down from its own infinity—
To live in narrow ways with little me
A common sight to every common ey
A wanderer, while even wolves can find
 den, 16
Ripp'd from all kindred, from all home
 all things
That make communion sweet, an
 soften pain—
To feel me in the solitude of kings 16
Without the power that makes ther
 bear a crown—
To envy every dove his nest and wing

Which waft him where the Apennine looks
　　down
On Arno, till he perches, it may be,
Within my all inexorable town,　　171
There yet my boys are, and that fatal she,
Their mother, the cold partner who hath
　　brought
Destruction for a dowry—this to see
And feel, and know without repair, hath
　　taught　　175
A bitter lesson; but it leaves me free:
I have not vilely found, nor basely
　　sought,
They made an Exile—not a slave of me.

CANTO THE SECOND

THE Spirit of the fervent days of Old,
When words were things that came to
　　pass, and thought
Flash'd o'er the future, bidding men be-
　　hold
Their children's children's doom already
　　brought
Forth from the abyss of time which is to
　　be　　5
The chaos of events, where lie half-
　　wrought
Shapes that must undergo mortality;
What the great Seers of Israel wore
　　within,
That spirit was on them, and is on me,
And if, Cassandra-like, amidst the din　　10
Of conflict none will hear, or hearing
　　heed
This voice from out the Wilderness, the
　　sin
Be theirs, and my own feelings be my meed,
The only guerdon I have ever known.
Hast thou not bled? and hast thou still
　　to bleed,　　15
Italia? Ah! to me such things, foreshown
With dim sepulchral light, bid me forget
In thine irreparable wrongs my own;
We can have but one country, and even yet
Thou'rt mine—my bones shall be within
　　thy breast,　　20
My soul within thy language, which once set
With our old Roman sway in the wide
　　West;
But I will make another tongue arise
As lofty and more sweet, in which ex-
　　press'd
The hero's ardour, or the lover's sighs,
Shall find alike such sounds for every
　　theme　　26
That every word, as brilliant as thy
　　skies,
Shall realise a poet's proudest dream,
And make thee Europe's nightingale of
　　song;
So that all present speech to thine shall
　　seem　　30

The note of meaner birds, and every
　　tongue
Confess its barbarism when compared
　　with thine.
This shalt thou owe to him thou didst
　　so wrong,
Thy Tuscan bard, the banish'd Ghibelline.
Woe! woe! the veil of coming centuries
Is rent,—a thousand years which yet
　　supine　　36
Lie like the ocean waves ere winds arise,
Heaving in dark and sullen undulation,
Float from eternity into these eyes;
The storms yet sleep, the clouds still keep
　　their station,　　40
The unborn earthquake yet is in the
　　womb,
The bloody chaos yet expects creation,
But all things are disposing for thy doom;
The elements await but for the word,
'Let there be darkness!' and thou
　　grow'st a tomb!　　45
Yes! thou, so beautiful, shalt feel the sword,
Thou, Italy! so fair that Paradise,
Revived in thee, blooms forth to man
　　restored:
Ah! must the sons of Adam lose it twice?
Thou, Italy! whose ever golden fields,
Plough'd by the sunbeams solely, would
　　suffice　　51
For the world's granary; thou, whose sky
　　heaven gilds
With brighter stars, and robes with
　　deeper blue;
Thou, in whose pleasant places Summer
　　builds
Her palace, in whose cradle Empire grew,
And form'd the Eternal City's orna-
　　ments　　56
From spoils of kings whom freemen
　　overthrew;
Birthplace of heroes, sanctuary of saints,
Where earthly first, then heavenly glory
　　made
Her home; thou, all which fondest fancy
　　paints,　　60
And finds her prior vision but portray'd
In feeble colours, when the eye—from
　　the Alp
Of horrid snow, and rock, and shaggy
　　shade
Of desert-loving pine, whose emerald scalp
Nods to the storm—dilates and dotes
　　o'er thee,　　65
And wistfully implores, as 'twere for
　　help
To see thy sunny fields, my Italy,
Nearer and nearer yet, and dearer still
The more approach'd, and dearest were
　　they free,
Thou—thou must wither to each tyrant's
　　will:　　70
The Goth hath been,—the German,
　　Frank, and Hun

373

Are yet to come,—and on the imperial
 hill
Ruin, already proud of the deeds done
 By the old barbarians, there awaits the
 new,
 Throned on the Palatine, while lost and
 won 75
Rome at her feet lies bleeding; and the hue
 Of human sacrifice and Roman slaughter
 Troubles the clotted air, of late so blue,
And deepens into red the saffron water
 Of Tiber, thick with dead; the helpless
 priest, 80
 And still more helpless nor less holy
 daughter,
Vow'd to their God, have shrieking fled,
 and ceased
 Their ministry: the nations take their
 prey,
 Iberian, Almain, Lombard, and the
 beast
And bird, wolf, vulture, more humane
 than they 85
 Are; these but gorge the flesh and lap
 the gore
Of the departed, and then go their way;
But those, the human savages, explore
 All paths of torture, and insatiate yet,
 With Ugolino hunger prowl for more.
Nine moons shall rise o'er scenes like this
 and set; 91
 The chiefless army of the dead, which
 late
Beneath the traitor Prince's banner met,
Hath left its leader's ashes at the gate;
 Had but the royal Rebel lived, per-
 chance 95
 Thou hadst been spared, but his in-
 volved thy fate.
Oh! Rome, the spoiler or the spoil of
 France,
 From Brennus to the Bourbon, never,
 never
 Shall foreign standard to thy walls ad-
 vance,
But Tiber shall become a mournful river.
Oh! when the strangers pass the Alps
 and Po, 101
 Crush them, ye rocks! floods whelm
 them, and for ever!
Why sleep the idle avalanches so,
 To topple on the lonely pilgrim's head?
 Why doth Eridanus but overflow 105
The peasant's harvest from his turbid bed?
 Were not each barbarous horde a nobler
 prey?
 Over Cambyses' host the desert spread
Her sandy ocean, and the sea-waves' sway
Roll'd over Pharaoh and his thous-
 ands,—why, 110
 Mountains and waters, do ye not as
 they?
And you, ye men! Romans who dare not
 die,

Sons of the conquerors who overthrew
 Those who o'erthrew proud Xerxes
 where yet lie
The dead whose tomb Oblivion never
 knew, 11
 Are the Alps weaker than Thermopylæ?
 Their passes more alluring to the view
Of an invader? is it they, or ye,
 That to each host the mountain-gate
 unbar,
 And leave the march in peace, the
 passage free? 12
Why, Nature's self detains the victor's car,
 And makes your land impregnable, if
 earth
 Could be so; but alone she will not war
Yet aids the warrior worthy of his birth
 In a soil where the mothers bring forth
 men: 12
 Not so with those whose souls are little
 worth;
For them no fortress can avail,—the den
 Of the poor reptile which preserves its
 sting
 Is more secure than walls of adamant
 when
The hearts of those within are quivering.
 Are ye not brave? Yes, yet the Au-
 sonian soil 13
Hath hearts, and hands, and arms, and
 hosts to bring
Against Oppression; but how vain the toil
 While still Division sows the seeds of
 woe
 And weakness, till the stranger reaps the
 spoil! 13
Oh! my own beauteous land! so long laid
 low,
 So long the grave of thy own children's
 hopes,
 When there is but required a single blow
To break the chain, yet—yet the Avenger
 stops,
 And Doubt and Discord step 'twixt
 thine and thee, 14
 And join their strength to that which
 with thee copes;
What is there wanting then to set thee free
 And show thy beauty in its fullest light
 To make the Alps impassable; and we
Her sons, may do this with *one* deed—
 Unite. 14

CANTO THE THIRD

FROM out the mass of never-dying ill,
 The Plague, the Prince, the Stranger
 and the Sword,
 Vials of wrath but emptied to refill
And flow again, I cannot all record
 That crowds on my prophetic eye: the
 earth
 And ocean written o'er would not afford
Space for the annal, yet it shall go forth

Yes, all, though not by human pen, is
 graven,
There where the farthest suns and stars
 have birth,
Spread like a banner at the gate of heaven,
The bloody scroll of our millennial
 wrongs 11
Waves, and the echo of our groans is
 driven
Athwart the sound of archangelic songs,
And Italy, the martyr'd nation's gore,
Will not in vain arise to where belongs
Omnipotence and mercy evermore: 16
Like to a harp-string stricken by the wind,
The sound of her lament shall, rising
 o'er
The seraph voices, touch the Almighty
 Mind.
Meantime I, humblest of thy sons, and
 of 20
Earth's dust by immortality refined
To sense and suffering, though the vain
 may scoff,
And tyrants threat, and meeker victims
 bow
Before the storm because its breath is
 rough,
To thee, my country! whom before, as
 now, 25
I loved and love, devote the mournful
 lyre
And melancholy gift high powers allow
To read the future; and if now my fire
Is not as once it shone o'er thee, forgive!
I but foretell thy fortunes—then ex-
 pire; 30
Think not that I would look on them and
 live.
A spirit forces me to see and speak,
And for my guerdon grants *not* to sur-
 vive;
My heart shall be pour'd over thee and
 break: 34
Yet for a moment, ere I must resume
Thy sable web of sorrow, let me take
Over the gleams that flash athwart thy
 gloom
A softer glimpse; some stars shine
 through thy night,
And many meteors, and above thy tomb
Leans sculptured Beauty, which Death
 cannot blight: 40
And from thine ashes boundless spirits
 rise
To give thee honour, and the earth de-
 light;
Thy soil shall still be pregnant with the wise,
The gay, the learn'd, the generous, and
 the brave,
Native to thee as summer to thy skies,
Conquerors on foreign shores, and the far
 wave, 46
Discoverers of new worlds, which take
 their name;

For *thee* alone they have no arm to save,
And all thy recompense is in their fame,
A noble one to them, but not to thee—
Shall they be glorious, and thou still the
 same? 51
Oh! more than these illustrious far shall be
The being—and even yet he may be
 born—
The mortal saviour who shall set thee
 free,
And see thy diadem, so changed and
 worn 55
By fresh barbarians, on thy brow re-
 placed;
And the sweet sun replenishing thy
 morn,
Thy moral morn, too long with clouds de-
 faced,
And noxious vapours from Avernus
 risen,
Such as all they must breathe who are
 debased 60
By servitude, and have the mind in prison.
Yet through this centuried eclipse of
 woe
Some voices shall be heard, and earth
 shall listen;
Poets shall follow in the path I show,
And make it broader: the same brilliant
 sky 65
Which cheers the birds to song shall bid
 them glow,
And raise their notes as natural and high;
Tuneful shall be their numbers; they
 shall sing
Many of love, and some of liberty,
But few shall soar upon that eagle's wing,
And look in the sun's face with eagle's
 gaze, 71
All free and fearless as the feather'd
 king,
But fly more near the earth; how many a
 phrase
Sublime shall lavish'd be on some small
 prince
In all the prodigality of praise! 75
And language, eloquently false, evince
The harlotry of genius, which, like
 beauty,
Too oft forgets its own self-reverence,
And looks on prostitution as a duty.
He who once enters in a tyrant's hall
As guest is slave, his thoughts become
 a booty, 81
And the first day which sees the chain
 enthral
A captive, sees his half of manhood
 gone—
The soul's emasculation saddens all
His spirit; thus the Bard too near the
 throne 85
Quails from his inspiration, bound to
 please,—
How servile is the task to please alone!

To smooth the verse to suit his sovereign's
 ease
 And royal leisure, nor too much prolong
Aught save his eulogy, and find, and seize,
Or force, or forge fit argument of song!
 Thus trammell'd, thus condemn'd to
 Flattery's trebles, 92
He toils through all, still trembling to be
 wrong:
For fear some noble thoughts, like heavenly
 rebels,
 Should rise up in high treason to his
 brain, 95
He sings, as the Athenian spoke, with
 pebbles
In 's mouth, lest truth should stammer
 through his strain.
But out of the long file of sonneteers
 There shall be some who will not sing in
 vain,
And he, their prince, shall rank among my
 peers, 100
 And love shall be his torment; but his
 grief
Shall make an immortality of tears,
And Italy shall hail him as the Chief
 Of Poet-lovers, and his higher song
 Of Freedom wreathe him with as green
 a leaf. 105
But in a farther age shall rise along
 The banks of Po two greater still than he;
 The world which smiled on him shall do
 them wrong
Till they are ashes, and repose with me.
 The first will make an epoch with his
 lyre, 110
 And fill the earth with feats of chivalry:
His fancy like a rainbow, and his fire,
 Like that of Heaven, immortal, and his
 thought
Borne onward with a wing that cannot
 tire;
Pleasure shall, like a butterfly new caught,
 Flutter her lovely pinions o'er his
 theme, 116
 And Art itself seem into Nature wrought
By the transparency of his bright dream.—
 The second, of a tenderer, sadder mood,
 Shall pour his soul out o'er Jerusalem;
He, too, shall sing of arms, and Christian
 blood 121
 Shed where Christ bled for man; and his
 high harp
Shall, by the willow over Jordan's flood,
Revive a song of Sion, and the sharp
 Conflict, and final triumph of the brave
And pious, and the strife of hell to warp
Their hearts from their great purpose,
 until wave 127
 The red-cross banners where the first
 red Cross
Was crimson'd from his veins who died
 to save,
Shall be his sacred argument; the loss

Of years, of favour, freedom, even of
 fame 131
 Contested for a time, while the smooth
 gloss
Of courts would slide o'er his forgotten
 name
 And call captivity a kindness, meant
To shield him from insanity or shame,
Such shall be his meet guerdon! who was sent
 To be Christ's Laureate—they reward
 him well! 137
 Florence dooms me but death or banish-
 ment,
Ferrara him a pittance and a cell,
 Harder to bear and less deserved, for I
 Had stung the factions which I strove to
 quell; 141
But this meek man, who with a lover's eye
 Will look on earth and heaven, and who
 will deign
To embalm with his celestial flattery,
As poor a thing as e'er was spawn'd to
 reign, 145
 What will *he* do to merit such a doom?
 Perhaps he'll *love*,—and is not love in
 vain
Torture enough without a living tomb?
 Yet it will be so—he and his compeer,
 The Bard of Chivalry, will both con-
 sume 150
In penury and pain too many a year,
 And, dying in despondency, bequeath
 To the kind world, which scarce will
 yield a tear,
A heritage enriching all who breathe
 With the wealth of a genuine poet's
 soul, 155
 And to their country a redoubled
 wreath,
Unmatch'd by time; not Hellas can unroll
 Through her olympiads two such
 names, though one
 Of hers be mighty;—and is this the
 whole
Of such men's destiny beneath the sun?
 Must all the finer thoughts, the thrilling
 sense, 161
 The electric blood with which their
 arteries run,
Their body's self turned soul with the
 intense
 Feeling of that which is, and fancy of
 That which should be, to such a recom
 pense 16
Conduct? shall their bright plumage o
 the rough
 Storm be still scatter'd? Yes, and i
 must be;
For, form'd of far too penetrable stuff
These birds of Paradise but long to flee
 Back to their native mansion, soon the
 find 17
 Earth's mist with their pure pinions no
 agree,

And die or are degraded; for the mind
Succumbs to long infection, and des-
pair,
And vulture passions flying close be-
hind,
Await the moment to assail and tear; 175
And when at length the winged wan-
derers stoop,
Then is the prey-birds' triumph, then
they share
The spoil, o'erpower'd at length by one fell
swoop.
Yet some have been untouch'd who
learn'd to bear,
Some whom no power could ever force
to droop, 180
Who could resist themselves even, hardest
care!
And task most hopeless; but some such
have been,
And if my name amongst the number
were,
That destiny austere, and yet serene,
Were prouder than more dazzling fame
unbless'd; 185
The Alp's snow summit nearer heaven
is seen
Than the volcano's fierce eruptive crest,
Whose splendour from the black abyss
is flung,
While the scorch'd mountain, from
whose burning breast
A temporary torturing flame is wrung,
Shines for a night of terror, then repels
Its fire back to the hell from whence it
sprung, 192
The hell which in its entrails ever dwells.

CANTO THE FOURTH

Many are poets who have never penn'd
Their inspiration, and perchance the
best:
They felt, and loved, and died, but
would not lend
Their thoughts to meaner beings; they
compress'd
The god within them, and rejoin'd the
stars 5
Unlaurell'd upon earth, but far more
bless'd
Than those who are degraded by the jars
Of passion, and their frailties link'd to
fame,
Conquerors of high renown, but full of
scars.
Many are poets but without the name,
For what is poesy but to create 11
From overfeeling good or ill; and aim
At an external life beyond our fate,
And be the new Prometheus of new
men,
Bestowing fire from heaven, and then,
too late, 15

Finding the pleasure given repaid with
pain,
And vultures to the heart of the be-
stower,
Who, having lavish'd his high gift in
vain,
Lies chain'd to his lone rock by the sea-
shore?
So be it: we can bear.—But thus all they
Whose intellect is an o'ermastering
power 21
Which still recoils from its encumbering
clay
Or lightens it to spirit, whatsoe'er
The form which their creations may
essay,
Are bards; the kindled marble's bust may
wear 25
More poesy upon its speaking brow
Than aught less than the Homeric page
may bear;
One noble stroke with a whole life may
glow,
Or deify the canvas till it shine
With beauty so surpassing all below,
That they who kneel to idols so divine
Break no commandment, for high
heaven is there
Transfused, transfigurated: and the line
Of poesy, which peoples but the air
With thought and beings of our thought
reflected, 35
Can do no more: then let the artist share
The palm, he shares the peril, and dejected
Faints o'er the labour unapproved—
Alas!
Despair and Genius are too oft con-
nected. 39
Within the ages which before me pass
Art shall resume and equal even the sway
Which with Apelles and old Phidias
She held in Hellas' unforgotten day.
Ye shall be taught by Ruin to revive
The Grecian forms at least from their
decay, 45
And Roman souls at last again shall live
In Roman works wrought by Italian
hands,
And temples, loftier than the old
temples, give
New wonders to the world; and while still
stands
The austere Pantheon, into heaven shall
soar 50
A dome, its image, while the base ex-
pands
Into a fane surpassing all before,
Such as all flesh shall flock to kneel in: ne'er
Such sight hath been unfolded by a door
As this, to which all nations shall repair
And lay their sins at this huge gate of
heaven. 56
And the bold Architect unto whose care

The daring charge to raise it shall be given,
 Whom all Arts shall acknowledge as
 their lord, 59
Whether into the marble chaos driven
His chisel bid the Hebrew, at whose word
 Israel left Egypt, stop the waves in
 stone,
 Or hues of Hell be by his pencil pour'd
Over the damn'd before the Judgment-
 throne,
 Such as I saw them, such as all shall see,
 Or fanes be built of grandeur yet un-
 known, 66
The stream of his great thoughts shall
 spring from me,
 The Ghibelline, who traversed the three
 realms
Which form the empire of eternity.
Amidst the clash of swords, and clang of
 helms, 70
 The age which I anticipate, no less
 Shall be the Age of Beauty, and while
 whelms
Calamity the nations with distress,
 The genius of my country shall arise,
 A Cedar towering o'er the Wilderness,
Lovely in all its branches to all eyes, 76
 Fragrant as fair, and recognised afar,
 Wafting its native incense through the
 skies.
Sovereigns shall pause amidst their sport
 of war,
 Wean'd for an hour from blood, to turn
 and gaze 80
 On canvas or on stone; and they who
 mar
All beauty upon earth, compell'd to praise,
 Shall feel the power of that which they
 destroy;
 And Art's mistaken gratitude shall raise
To tyrants who but take her for a toy,
 Emblems and monuments, and prosti-
 tute 86
 Her charms to pontiffs proud, who but
 employ
The man of genius as the meanest brute
 To bear a burthen, and to serve a need,
 To sell his labours, and his soul to boot.
Who toils for nations may be poor indeed,
 But free; who sweats for monarchs is no
 more 92
 Than the gilt chamberlain, who, clothed
 and fee'd,
Stands sleek and slavish, bowing at his
 door.
Oh, Power that rulest and inspirest! how
 95
 Is it that they on earth, whose earthly
 power
Is likest thine in heaven in outward show,
 Least like to thee in attributes divine,
 Tread on the universal necks that bow,
And then assure us that their rights are
 thine? 100

And how is it that they, the sons of fame
 Whose inspiration seems to them to
 shine
From high, they whom the nations oftest
 name,
 Must pass their days in penury or pain,
 Or step to grandeur through the path
 of shame, 10
And wear a deeper brand and gaudier
 chain?
 Or if their destiny be born aloof
 From lowliness, or tempted thence in
 vain,
In their own souls sustain a harder proof,
 The inner war of passions deep and
 fierce? 11
 Florence! when thy harsh sentence
 razed my roof,
I loved thee; but the vengeance of my
 verse,
 The hate of injuries which every year
 Makes greater, and accumulates my
 curse,
Shall live, outliving all thou holdest dear,
 Thy pride, thy wealth, thy freedom, and
 even that, 11
 The most infernal of all evils here,
The sway of petty tyrants in a state;
 For such sway is not limited to kings,
 And demagogues yield to them but in
 date, 12
As swept off sooner; in all deadly things
 Which make men hate themselves, and
 one another,
 In discord, cowardice, cruelty, all that
 springs,
From Death the Sin-born's incest with his
 mother,
 In rank oppression in its rudest shape,
 The faction Chief is but the Sultan'
 brother, 12
And the worst despot's far less human ape.
 Florence! when this lone spirit, which
 so long
Yearn'd, as the captive toiling at escape,
To fly back to thee in despite of wrong,
 An exile, saddest of all prisoners, 13
 Who has the whole world for a dungeon
 strong,
Seas, mountains, and the horizon's verge
 for bars,
 Which shut him from the sole small spot
 of earth,
 Where—whatsoe'er his fate—he still
 were hers, 13
His country's, and might die where he had
 birth—
 Florence! when this lone spirit shall re-
 turn
 To kindred spirits, thou wilt feel my
 worth,
And seek to honour with an empty urn
 The ashes thou shalt ne'er obtain—
 Alas! 14

'What have I done to thee, my people?'
 Stern
Are all thy dealings, but in this they pass
 The limits of man's common malice, for
All that a citizen could be I was;
Raised by thy will, all thine in peace or war,
 And for this thou hast warr'd with me—
 'Tis done: 146
I may not overleap the eternal bar

Built up between us, and will die alone,
 Beholding with the dark eye of a seer
 The evil days to gifted souls foreshown,
Foretelling them to those who will not hear.
 As in the old time, till the hour be come
 When Truth shall strike their eyes
 through many a tear, 153
And make them own the Prophet in his
 tomb.

THE MORGANTE MAGGIORE

OF PULCI

ADVERTISEMENT

THE Morgante Maggiore, of the first canto of which this translation is offered, divides with the Orlando Innamorato the honour of having formed and suggested the style and story of Ariosto. The great defects of Boiardo were his treating too seriously the narratives of chivalry, and his harsh style. Ariosto, in his continuation, by a judicious mixture of the gaiety of Pulci, has avoided the one; and Berni, in his reformation of Boiardo's poem, has corrected the other. Pulci may be considered as the precursor and model of Berni altogether, as he has partly been to Ariosto, however inferior to both his copyists. He is no less the founder of a new style of poetry very lately sprung up in England. I allude to that of the ingenious Whistlecraft. The serious poems on Roncesvalles in the same language, and more particularly the excellent one of Mr. Merivale, are to be traced to the same source. It has never yet been decided entirely whether Pulci's intention was or was not to deride the religion which is one of his favourite topics. It appears to me, that such an intention would have been no less hazardous to the poet than to the priest, particularly in that age and country; and the permission to publish the poem, and its reception among the classics of Italy, prove that it neither was nor is so interpreted. That he intended to ridicule the monastic life, and suffered his imagination to play with the simple dulness of his converted giant, seems evident enough; but surely it were as unjust to accuse him of irreligion on this account, as to denounce Fielding for his Parson Adams, Barnabas, Thwackum, Supple, and the Ordinary in Jonathan Wild,—or Scott, for the exquisite use of his Covenanters in the 'Tales of my Landlord.'

In the following translation I have used the liberty of the original with the proper names: as Pulci uses Gan, Ganellon, or Ganellone; Carlo, Carlomagno, or Carlomano; Rondel, or Rondello, &c., as it suits his convenience; so has the translator. In other respects the version is faithful to the best of the translator's ability in combining his interpretation of the one language with the not very easy task of reducing it to the same versification in the other. The reader, on comparing it with the original, is requested to remember that the antiquated language of Pulci, however pure, is not easy to the generality of Italians themselves, from its great mixture of Tuscan proverbs; and he may therefore be more indulgent to the present attempt. How far the translator has succeeded, and whether or no he shall continue the work, are questions which the public will decide. He was induced to make the experiment partly by his love for, and partial intercourse with, the Italian language, of which it is so easy to acquire a slight knowledge, and with which it is so nearly impossible for a foreigner to become accurately conversant. The Italian language is like a capricious beauty, who accords her smiles to all, her favours to few, and sometimes least to those who have courted her longest. The translator wished also to present in an English dress a part at least of a poem never yet rendered into a northern language; at the same time that it has been the original of some of the most celebrated productions on this side of the Alps, as well as of those recent experiments in poetry in England which have been already mentioned.

CANTO THE FIRST

I

IN the beginning was the Word next God;
 God was the Word, the Word no less
 was he:
This was in the beginning, to my mode
 Of thinking, and without him nought
 could be:
Therefore, just Lord! from out thy high abode,
 Benign and pious, bid an angel flee,
One only, to be my companion, who
Shall help my famous, worthy, old song
 through.

II

And thou, oh Virgin! daughter, mother,
 bride
 Of the same Lord, who gave to you each
 key
Of heaven, and hell, and everything beside,
 The day thy Gabriel said 'All hail!' to
 thee,
Since to thy servants pity's ne'er denied,
 With flowing rhymes, a pleasant style
 and free,
Be to my verses then benignly kind,
And to the end illuminate my mind.

III

'Twas in the season when sad Philomel
 Weeps with her sister, who remembers and
Deplores the ancient woes which both be-
 fell,
 And makes the nymphs enamour'd, to the hand
Of Phaeton by Phœbus loved so well
 His car (but temper'd by his sire's com-
 mand)
Was given, and on the horizon's verge just now
Appear'd, so that Tithonus scratch'd his brow:

IV

When I prepared my bark first to obey,
 As it should still obey, the helm, my mind,
And carry prose or rhyme, and this my lay
 Of Charles the Emperor, whom you will find
By several pens already praised; but they
 Who to diffuse his glory were inclined,
For all that I can see in prose or verse,
Have understood Charles badly, and wrote worse.

V

Leonardo Aretino said already,
 That if, like Pepin, Charles had had a writer
Of genius quick, and diligently steady,
 No hero would in history look brighter;
He in the cabinet being always ready,
 And in the field a most victorious fighter,
Who for the church and Christian faith had wrought,
Certes, far more than yet is said or thought.

VI

You still may see at St. Liberatore,
 The abbey, no great way from Manopell,
Erected in the Abruzzi to his glory,
 Because of the great battle in which fell
A pagan king, according to the story,
 And felon people whom Charles sent to hell:
And there are bones so many, and so many,
Near them Giusaffa's would seem few, if any.

VII

But the world, blind and ignorant, don't prize
 His virtues as I wish to see them: thou,
Florence, by his great bounty don't¹ arise,
 And hast, and may have, if thou wilt allow,
All proper customs and true courtesies:
 Whate'er thou hast acquired from then till now,
With knightly courage, treasure, or the lance,

¹ don't] dost *conj.*

Is sprung from out the noble blood of
 France.

VIII

Twelve paladins had Charles in court, of whom
 The wisest and most famous was Or-
 lando;
Him traitor Gan conducted to the tomb
 In Roncesvalles, as the villain plann'd
 too,
While the horn rang so loud, and knell'd
 the doom
 Of their sad rout, though he did all a knight can do;
And Dante in his comedy has given
To him a happy seat with Charles in
 heaven.

IX

'Twas Christmas-day; in Paris all his court
 Charles held; the chief, I say, Orlando was,
The Dane; Astolfo there too did resort,
 Also Ansuigi, the gay time to pass
In festival and in triumphal sport,
 The much renown'd St. Dennis being
 the cause;
Angiolin of Bayonne, and Oliver,
And gentle Belinghieri too came there:

X

Avolio, and Arino, and Othone
 Of Normandy, and Richard Paladin,
Wise Hamo, and the ancient Salamone,
 Walter of Lion's Mount and Baldovin,
Who was the son of the sad Ganellone,
 Were there, exciting too much gladness in
The son of Pepin:—when his knights came hither,
He groan'd with joy to see them all to-
 gether.

XI

But watchful Fortune, lurking, takes good heed
 Ever some bar 'gainst our intents to bring,
While Charles reposed him thus, in word and deed,
 Orlando ruled court, Charles, and every-
 thing;
Curst Gan, with envy bursting, had such need
 To vent his spite, that thus with Charles
 the king
One day he openly began to say,
'Orlando must we always then obey?

XII

'A thousand times I've been about to say,
 Orlando too presumptuously goes on;
Here are we, counts, kings, dukes, to own thy sway,
 Hamo, and Otho, Ogier, Solomon,

Each have to honour thee and to obey;
But he has too much credit near the throne,
Which we won't suffer, but are quite decided
By such a boy to be no longer guided.

XIII

And even at Aspramont thou didst begin
To let him know he was a gallant knight,
And by the fount did much the day to win;
But I know *who* that day had won the fight
If it had not for good Gherardo been;
The victory was Almonte's else; his sight
He kept upon the standard, and the laurels
In fact and fairness are his earning, Charles.

XIV

If thou rememberest being in Gascony,
When there advanced the nations out of Spain,
The Christian cause had suffer'd shamefully,
Had not his valour driven them back again.
Best speak the truth when there's a reason why:
Know then, oh Emperor! that all complain:
As for myself, I shall repass the mounts
O'er which I cross'd with two and sixty counts.

XV

''Tis fit thy grandeur should dispense relief,
So that each here may have his proper part,
For the whole court is more or less in grief:
Perhaps thou deem'st this lad a Mars in heart?'
Orlando one day heard this speech in brief,
As by himself it chanced he sate apart:
Displeased he was with Gan because he said it,
But much more still that Charles should give him credit.

XVI

And with the sword he would have murder'd Gan,
But Oliver thrust in between the pair,
And from his hand extracted Durlindan,
And thus at length they separated were.
Orlando, angry too with Carloman,
Wanted but little to have slain him there;
Then forth alone from Paris went the chief,
And burst and madden'd with disdain and grief.

XVII

From Ermellina, consort of the Dane,
He took Cortana, and then took Rondell,
And on towards Brara prick'd him o'er the plain;
And when she saw him coming, Aldabelle
Stretch'd forth her arms to clasp her lord again:
Orlando, in whose brain all was not well,
As 'Welcome, my Orlando, home,' she said,
Raised up his sword to smite her on the head,

XVIII

Like him a fury counsels; his revenge
On Gan in that rash act he seem'd to take,
Which Aldabella thought extremely strange;
But soon Orlando found himself awake;
And his spouse took his bridle on this change,
And he dismounted from his horse, and spake
Of everything which pass'd without demur,
And then reposed himself some days with her.

XIX

Then full of wrath departed from the place,
And far as pagan countries roam'd astray,
And while he rode, yet still at every pace
The traitor Gan remember'd by the way;
And wandering on in error a long space,
An abbey which in a lone desert lay,
'Midst glens obscure, and distant lands, he found,
Which form'd the Christian's and the pagan's bound.

XX

The abbot was call'd Clermont, and by blood
Descended from Anglante: under cover
Of a great mountain's brow the abbey stood,
But certain savage giants look'd him over;
One Passamont was foremost of the brood,
And Alabaster and Morgante hover
Second and third, with certain slings, and throw
In daily jeopardy the place below.

XXI

The monks could pass the convent gate no more,
Nor leave their cells for water or for wood;

Orlando knock'd, but none would ope,
 before
 Unto the prior it at length seem'd good;
Enter'd, he said that he was taught to
 adore
 Him who was born of Mary's holiest
 blood,
And was baptized a Christian; and then
 show'd
How to the abbey he had found his road.

XXII

Said the abbot, 'You are welcome; what
 is mine
 We give you freely, since that you believe
With us in Mary Mother's Son divine;
 And that you may not, cavalier, con-
 ceive
The cause of our delay to let you in
 To be rusticity, you shall receive
The reason why our gate was barr'd to
 you:
Thus those who in suspicion live must do.

XXIII

'When hither to inhabit first we came
 These mountains, albeit that they are
 obscure,
As you perceive, yet without fear or blame
 They seem'd to promise an asylum sure:
From savage brutes alone, too fierce to
 tame,
 'Twas fit our quiet dwelling to secure;
But now, if here we'd stay, we needs must
 guard
Against domestic beasts with watch and
 ward.

XXIV

'These make us stand, in fact, upon the
 watch;
 For late there have appear'd three
 giants rough;
What nation or what kingdom bore the
 batch
 I know not, but they are all of savage
 stuff;
When force and malice with some genius
 match,
 You know, they can do all—*we* are not
 enough:
And these so much our orisons derange,
I know not what to do, till matters change.

XXV

'Our ancient fathers living the desert in,
 For just and holy works were duly fed;
Think not they lived on locusts sole, 'tis
 certain
 That manna was rain'd down from
 heaven instead;
But here 'tis fit we keep on the alert in
 Our bounds, or taste the stones shower'd
 down for bread,

From off yon mountain daily raining
 faster,
And flung by Passamont and Alabaster.

XXVI

'The third, Morgante, 's savagest by far; he
 Plucks up pines, beeches, poplar-trees,
 and oaks,
And flings them, our community to bury;
 And all that I can do but more pro-
 vokes.'
While thus they parley in the cemetery,
 A stone from one of their gigantic
 strokes,
Which nearly crush'd Rondell, came tum-
 bling over,
So that he took a long leap under cover.

XXVII

'For God-sake, cavalier, come in with
 speed;
 The manna's falling now,' the abbot
 cried.
'This fellow does not wish my horse
 should feed,
 Dear Abbot,' Roland unto him replied.
'Of restiveness he'd cure him had he need;
 That stone seems with good will and aim
 applied.'
The holy father said, 'I don't deceive;
They'll one day fling the mountain, I
 believe.'

XXVIII

Orlando bade them take care of Ron-
 dello,
 And also made a breakfast of his own:
'Abbot,' he said, 'I want to find that fellow
 Who flung at my good horse yon corner-
 stone.'
Said the abbot, 'Let not my advice seem
 shallow;
 As to a brother dear I speak alone;
I would dissuade you, baron, from this
 strife,
As knowing sure that you will lose your
 life.

XXIX

'That Passamont has in his hand three
 darts—
 Such slings, clubs, ballast-stones, that
 yield you must:
You know that giants have much stouter
 hearts
 Than us, with reason, in proportion
 just:
If go you will, guard well against their arts,
 For these are very barbarous and ro-
 bust.'
Orlando answer'd, 'This I'll see, be sure
And walk the wild on foot to be secure.

XXX

The abbot sign'd the great cross on his front,
'Then go you with God's benison and mine:'
Orlando, after he had scaled the mount,
As the abbot had directed, kept the line
Right to the usual haunt of Passamont;
Who, seeing him alone in this design,
Survey'd him fore and aft with eyes observant,
Then ask'd him, 'If he wish'd to stay as servant?'

XXXI

And promised him an office of great ease.
But said Orlando, 'Saracen insane!
come to kill you, if it shall so please
God, not to serve as footboy in your train;
You with his monks so oft have broke the peace—
Vile dog! 'tis past his patience to sustain.'
The giant ran to fetch his arms, quite furious,
When he received an answer so injurious.

XXXII

And being return'd to where Orlando stood,
Who had not moved him from the spot, and swinging
The cord, he hurl'd a stone with strength so rude,
As show'd a sample of his skill in slinging;
It roll'd on Count Orlando's helmet good
And head, and set both head and helmet ringing,
So that he swoon'd with pain as if he died,
But more than dead, he seem'd so stupified.

XXXIII

Then Passamont, who thought him slain outright,
Said, 'I will go, and while he lies along,
Disarm me: why such craven did I fight?'
But Christ his servants ne'er abandons long,
Especially Orlando, such a knight,
As to desert would almost be a wrong.
While the giant goes to put off his defences,
Orlando has recall'd his force and senses:

XXXIV

And loud he shouted, 'Giant, where dost go?
Thou thought'st me doubtless for the bier outlaid;
To the right about—without wings thou 'rt too slow
To fly my vengeance—currish renegade!

'Twas but by treachery thou laid'st me low.'
The giant his astonishment betray'd,
And turn'd about, and stopp'd his journey on,
And then he stoop'd to pick up a great stone.

XXXV

Orlando had Cortana bare in hand;
To split the head in twain was what he schemed:
Cortana clave the skull like a true brand
And pagan Passamont died unredeem'd,
Yet harsh and haughty, as he lay he bann'd,
And most devoutly Macon still blasphemed;
But while his crude, rude blasphemies he heard,
Orlando thank'd the Father and the Word,—

XXXVI

Saying, 'What grace to me thou'st this day given!
And I to thee, O Lord! am ever bound.
I know my life was saved by thee from heaven,
Since by the giant I was fairly down'd.
All things by thee are measured just and even;
Our power without thine aid would nought be found:
I pray thee take heed of me, till I can
At least return once more to Carloman.'

XXXVII

And having said thus much, he went his way;
And Alabaster he found out below,
Doing the very best that in him lay
To root from out a bank a rock or two.
Orlando, when he reach'd him, loud 'gan say,
'How think'st thou, glutton, such a stone to throw?'
When Alabaster heard his deep voice ring,
He suddenly betook him to his sling,

XXXVIII

And hurl'd a fragment of a size so large,
That if it had in fact fulfill'd its mission,
And Roland not avail'd him of his targe,
There would have been no need of a physician.
Orlando set himself in turn to charge,
And in his bulky bosom made incision
With all his sword. The lout fell; but o'erthrown, he
However by no means forgot Macone.

XXXIX

Morgante had a palace in his mode,
Composed of branches, logs of wood, and earth,

And stretch'd himself at ease in this abode,
 And shut himself at night within his
 berth.
Orlando knock'd, and knock'd again, to
 goad
 The giant from his sleep; and he came
 forth,
The door to open, like a crazy thing,
 For a rough dream had shook him
 slumbering.

XL

He thought that a fierce serpent had
 attack'd him;
 And Mahomet he call'd; but Mahomet
Is nothing worth, and not an instant
 back'd him;
 But praying blessed Jesu, he was set
At liberty from all the fears which rack'd
 him;
 And to the gate he came with great re-
 gret—
'Who knocks here?' grumbling all the
 while, said he.
'That,' said Orlando, 'you will quickly
 see:

XLI

'I come to preach to you, as to your
 brothers,
 Sent by the miserable monks—repen-
 tance;
For Providence divine, in you and others,
 Condemns the evil done my new
 acquaintance.
'Tis writ on high—your wrong must pay
 another's:
 From heaven itself is issued out this
 sentence.
Know, then, that colder now than a pilaster
I left your Passamont and Alabaster.'

XLII

Morgante said, 'Oh, gentle cavalier!
 Now by thy God say me no villany:
The favour of your name I fain would
 hear,
 And if a Christian, speak for courtesy.'
Replied Orlando, 'So much to your ear
 I by my faith disclose contentedly;
Christ I adore, who is the genuine Lord,
And, if you please, by you may be adored.'

XLIII

The Saracen rejoin'd in humble tone,
 'I have had an extraordinary vision;
A savage serpent fell on me alone,
 And Macon would not pity my con-
 dition;
Hence to thy God, who for ye did atone
 Upon the cross, preferr'd I my petition;
His timely succour set me safe and free,
And I a Christian am disposed to be.'

XLIV

Orlando answer'd, 'Baron just and pious
 If this good wish your heart can really
 move
To the true God, who will not then deny u
 Eternal honour, you will go above,
And, if you please, as friends we will ally
 us,
 And I will love you with a perfect love
Your idols are vain liars, full of fraud:
The only true God is the Christians' God

XLV

'The Lord descended to the virgin breas
 Of Mary Mother, sinless and divine;
If you acknowledge the Redeemer blest,
 Without whom neither sun nor star ca
 shine,
Abjure bad Macon's false and felon test,
 Your renegado god, and worship mine
Baptize yourself with zeal, since you re
 pent.'
To which Morgante answer'd, 'I'm con
 tent.'

XLVI

And then Orlando to embrace him flew,
 And made much of his convert, as he
 cried,
'To the abbey I will gladly marshal you.
 To whom Morgante, 'Let us go,' re
 plied;
'I to the friars have for peace to sue.'
 Which thing Orlando heard with in
 ward pride,
Saying, 'My brother, so devout and good
Ask the abbot pardon, as I wish you
 would:

XLVII

'Since God has granted your illumination
 Accepting you in mercy for his own,
Humility should be your first oblation.'
 Morgante said, 'For goodness' sake
 make known,—
Since that your God is to be mine—you
 station,
 And let your name in verity be shown
Then will I everything at your command
 do.'
On which the other said, he was Orlando

XLVIII

'Then,' quoth the giant, 'blessed be Jesu
 A thousand times with gratitude and
 praise!
Oft, perfect baron! have I heard of you
 Through all the different periods of my
 days:
And, as I said, to be your vassal too
 I wish, for your great gallantry always.'
Thus reasoning, they continued much to
 say,
And onwards to the abbey went their way.

XLIX

And by the way about the giants dead
　Orlando with Morgante reason'd: 'Be,
For their decease, I pray you, comforted;
　And, since it is God's pleasure, pardon
　　me;
A thousand wrongs unto the monks they
　　bred,
　And our true Scripture soundeth openly,
Good is rewarded, and chastised the ill,
Which the Lord never faileth to fulfil:

L

'Because his love of justice unto all
　Is such, he wills his judgment should
　　devour
All who have sin, however great or small;
　But good he well remembers to restore.
Nor without justice holy could we call
　Him, whom I now require you to adore.
All men must make his will their wishes
　　sway,
And quickly and spontaneously obey.

LI

'And here our doctors are of one accord,
　Coming on this point to the same con-
　　clusion,
That in their thoughts who praise in
　　heaven the Lord
　If pity e'er was guilty of intrusion
For their unfortunate relations stored
　In hell below, and damn'd in great con-
　　fusion,
Their happiness would be reduced to
　　nought,
And thus unjust the Almighty's self be
　　thought.

LII

'But they in Christ have firmest hope, and
　　all
　Which seems to him, to them too must
　　appear
Well done; nor could it otherwise befall;
　He never can in any purpose err.
If sire or mother suffer endless thrall,
　They don't disturb themselves for him
　　or her:
What pleases God to them must joy in-
　　spire;—
Such is the observance of the eternal choir.'

LIII

'A word unto the wise,' Morgante said,
　'Is wont to be enough, and you shall see
How much I grieve about my brethren
　　dead;
　And if the will of God seem good to me,
Just, as you tell me, 'tis in heaven obey'd—
　Ashes to ashes,—merry let us be!
I will cut off the hands from both their
　　trunks,
And carry them unto the holy monks.

LIV

'So that all persons may be sure and certain
　That they are dead, and have no further
　　fear
To wander solitary this desert in,
　And that they may perceive my spirit
　　clear
By the Lord's grace, who hath withdrawn
　　the curtain
　Of darkness, making his bright realm
　　appear.'
He cut his brethren's hands off at these
　　words,
And left them to the savage beasts and birds.

LV

Then to the abbey they went on together,
　Where waited them the abbot in great
　　doubt.
The monks, who knew not yet the fact, ran
　　thither,
　To their superior, all in breathless rout,
Saying with tremor, 'Please to tell us
　　whether
　You wish to have this person in or out?'
The abbot, looking through upon the giant,
Too greatly fear'd, at first, to be compliant.

LVI

Orlando, seeing him thus agitated,
　Said quickly, 'Abbot, be thou of good
　　cheer;
He Christ believes, as Christian must be
　　rated,
　And hath renounced his Macon false';
　　which here
Morgante with the hands corroborated,
　A proof of both the giants' fate quite
　　clear:
Thence, with due thanks, the abbot God
　　adored,
Saying, 'Thou hast contented me, oh Lord!'

LVII

He gazed; Morgante's height he calculated,
　And more than once contemplated his
　　size;
And then he said, 'Oh giant celebrated!
　Know, that no more my wonder will
　　arise,
How you could tear and fling the trees you
　　late did,
　When I behold your form with my own
　　eyes.
You now a true and perfect friend will show
Yourself to Christ, as once you were a foe.

LVIII

'And one of our apostles, Saul once
　　named,
　Long persecuted sore the faith of Christ,
Till, one day, by the Spirit being inflamed,
　"Why dost thou persecute me thus?"
　　said Christ;

385

And then from his offence he was reclaim'd,
 And went for ever after preaching
 Christ,
And of the faith became a trump, whose
 sounding
O'er the whole earth is echoing and re-
 bounding.

LIX

'So, my Morgante, you may do likewise:
 He who repents—thus writes the Evan-
 gelist—
Occasions more rejoicing in the skies
 Than ninety-nine of the celestial list.
You may be sure, should each desire arise
 With just zeal for the Lord, that you'll
 exist
Among the happy saints for evermore;
 But you were lost and damn'd to hell
 before!'

LX

And thus great honour to Morgante paid
 The abbot: many days they did repose.
One day, as with Orlando they both stray'd,
 And saunter'd here and there, where'er
 they chose,
The abbot show'd a chamber, where array'd
 Much armour was, and hung up certain
 bows;
And one of these Morgante for a whim
Girt on, though useless, he believed, to
 him.

LXI

There being a want of water in the place,
 Orlando, like a worthy brother, said,
'Morgante, I could wish you in this case
 To go for water.' 'You shall be obey'd
In all commands,' was the reply, 'straight-
 ways.'
Upon his shoulder a great tub he laid,
And went out on his way unto a fountain,
Where he was wont to drink below the
 mountain.

LXII

Arrived there, a prodigious noise he hears,
 Which suddenly along the forest spread;
Whereat from out his quiver he prepares
 An arrow for his bow, and lifts his head;
And lo! a monstrous herd of swine appears,
 And onward rushes with tempestuous
 tread,
And to the fountain's brink precisely pours;
So that the giant's join'd by all the boars.

LXIII

Morgante at a venture shot an arrow,
 Which pierced a pig precisely in the ear,
And pass'd unto the other side quite
 thorough;
 So that the boar, defunct, lay tripp'd up
 near.

Another, to revenge his fellow farrow,
 Against the giant rush'd in fierce career,
And reach'd the passage with so swift a
 foot,
Morgante was not now in time to shoot.

LXIV

Perceiving that the pig was on him close,
 He gave him such a punch upon the head,
As floor'd him so that he no more arose,
 Smashing the very bone; and he fell dead
Next to the other. Having seen such blows,
 The other pigs along the valley fled;
Morgante on his neck the bucket took,
Full from the spring, which neither
 swerved nor shook.

LXV

The tub was on one shoulder, and there
 were
 The hogs on t'other, and he brush'd
 apace
On to the abbey, though by no means near,
 Nor spilt one drop of water in his race.
Orlando, seeing him so soon appear
 With the dead boars, and with that
 brimful vase,
Marvell'd to see his strength so very great;
So did the abbot, and set wide the gate.

LXVI

The monks, who saw the water fresh and
 good,
 Rejoiced, but much more to perceive the
 pork;
All animals are glad at sight of food:
 They lay their breviaries to sleep, and
 work
With greedy pleasure, and in such a mood,
 That the flesh needs no salt beneath
 their fork.
Of rankness and of rot there is no fear,
For all the fasts are now left in arrear.

LXVII

As though they wish'd to burst at once,
 they ate;
 And gorged so that, as if the bones had
 been
In water, sorely grieved the dog and cat,
 Perceiving that they all were pick'd too
 clean.
The abbot, who to all did honour great,
 A few days after this convivial scene,
Gave to Morgante a fine horse, well
 train'd,
Which he long time had for himself main-
 tain'd.

LXVIII

The horse Morgante to a meadow led,
 To gallop, and to put him to the proof,
Thinking that he a back of iron had,
 Or to skim eggs unbroke was light
 enough;

But the horse, sinking with the pain, fell
 dead,
 And burst, while cold on earth lay head
 and hoof.
Morgante said, 'Get up, thou sulky cur!'
And still continued pricking with the spur.

LXIX

But finally he thought fit to dismount,
 And said, 'I am as light as any feather,
And he has burst;—to this what say you,
 count?'
 Orlando answer'd, 'Like a ship's mast
 rather
You seem to me, and with the truck for
 front:
 Let him go! Fortune wills that we together
Should march, but you on foot Morgante
 still.'
To which the giant answer'd, 'So I will.

LXX

'When there shall be occasion, you will see
 How I approve my courage in the fight.'
Orlando said, 'I really think you 'll be,
 If it should prove God's will, a goodly
 knight;
Nor will you napping there discover me.
 But never mind your horse, though out
 of sight
'Twere best to carry him into some wood,
If but the means or way I understood.'

LXXI

The giant said, 'Then carry him I will,
 Since that to carry me he was so slack—
To render, as the gods do, good for ill;
 But lend a hand to place him on my
 back.'
Orlando answer'd, 'If my counsel still
 May weigh, Morgante, do not under-
 take
To lift or carry this dead courser, who,
As you have done to him, will do to you.

LXXII

'Take care he don't revenge himself,
 though dead,
 As Nessus did of old beyond all cure.
I don't know if the fact you've heard or
 read;
 But he will make you burst, you may be
 sure.'
'But help him on my back,' Morgante said,
 'And you shall see what weight I can
 endure.
In place, my gentle Roland, of this palfrey,
With all the bells, I'd carry yonder belfry.'

LXXIII

The abbot said, 'The steeple may do well,
 But, for the bells, you've broken them,
 I wot.'
Morgante answer'd, 'Let them pay in hell
 The penalty who lie dead in yon grot;'

And hoisting up the horse from where he
 fell,
 He said, 'Now look if I the gout have
 got,
Orlando, in the legs—or if I have force;'—
And then he made two gambols with the
 horse.

LXXIV

Morgante was like any mountain framed;
 So if he did this 'tis no prodigy;
But secretly himself Orlando blamed,
 Because he was one of his family;
And fearing that he might be hurt or
 maim'd,
 Once more he bade him lay his burden
 by:
'Put down, nor bear him further the
 desert in.'
Morgante said, 'I'll carry him for certain.'

LXXV

He did; and stow'd him in some nook
 away,
 And to the abbey then return'd with
 speed.
Orlando said, 'Why longer do we stay?
 Morgante, here is nought to do indeed.'
The abbot by the hand he took one day,
 And said, with great respect, he had
 agreed
To leave his reverence; but for this de-
 cision
He wish'd to have his pardon and per-
 mission.

LXXVI

The honours they continued to receive
 Perhaps exceeded what his merits
 claim'd:
He said, 'I mean, and quickly, to retrieve
 The lost days of time past, which may
 be blamed;
Some days ago I should have ask'd your
 leave,
 Kind father, but I really was ashamed,
And know not how to show my sentiment,
So much I see you with our stay content.

LXXVII

'But in my heart I bear through every
 clime
 The abbot, abbey, and this solitude—
So much I love you in so short a time;
 For me, from heaven reward you with
 all good
The God so true, the eternal Lord sub-
 lime!
 Whose kingdom at the last hath open
 stood.
Meantime we stand expectant of your
 blessing,
And recommend us to your prayers with
 pressing.'

LXXVIII

Now when the abbot Count Orlando
 heard,
 His heart grew soft with inner tender-
 ness,
Such fervour in his bosom bred each word;
 And, 'Cavalier,' he said, 'if I have less
Courteous and kind to your great worth
 appear'd,
 Than fits me for such gentle blood to
 express,
I know I have done too little in this case;
But blame our ignorance, and this poor
 place.

LXXIX

'We can indeed but honour you with
 masses,
 And sermons, thanksgivings, and pater-
 nosters,
Hot suppers, dinners (fitting other places
 In verity much rather than the cloisters);
But such a love for you my heart embraces,
 For thousand virtues which your bosom
 fosters,
That wheresoe'er you go I too shall be,
And, on the other part, you rest with me.

LXXX

'This may involve a seeming contradic-
 tion;
 But you I know are sage, and feel, and
 taste,
And understand my speech, with full con-
 viction.
 For your just pious deeds may you be
 graced
With the Lord's great reward and bene-
 diction,
 By whom you were directed to this
 waste:
To his high mercy is our freedom due,
For which we render thanks to him and
 you.

LXXXI

'You saved at once our life and soul: such
 fear
 The giants caused us, that the way was
 lost
By which we could pursue a fit career
 In search of Jesus and the saintly host;
And your departure breeds such sorrow
 here,
 That comfortless we all are to our cost;
But months and years you would not stay
 in sloth,
Nor are you form'd to wear our sober cloth,

LXXXII

'But to bear arms, and wield the lance;
 indeed,
 With these as much is done as with this
 cowl;

In proof of which the Scriptures you may
 read.
 This giant up to heaven may bear his
 soul
By your compassion: now in peace pro-
 ceed.
 Your state and name I seek not to unroll;
But, if I'm ask'd, this answer shall be
 given,
That here an angel was sent down from
 heaven.

LXXXIII

'If you want armour or aught else, go in,
 Look o'er the wardrobe, and take what
 you choose,
And cover with it o'er this giant's skin.'
 Orlando answer'd, 'If there should lie
 loose
Some armour, ere our journey we begin,
 Which might be turn'd to my compan-
 ion's use,
The gift would be acceptable to me.'
The abbot said to him, 'Come in and see.'

LXXXIV

And in a certain closet, where the wall
 Was cover'd with old armour like a
 crust,
The abbot said to them, 'I give you all.'
 Morgante rummaged piecemeal from
 the dust
The whole, which, save one cuirass, was
 too small,
 And that too had the mail inlaid with
 rust.
They wonder'd how it fitted him exactly,
Which ne'er has suited others so com-
 pactly.

LXXXV

'Twas an immeasurable giant's, who
 By the great Milo of Agrante fell
Before the abbey many years ago.
 The story on the wall was figured well;
In the last moment of the abbey's foe,
 Who long had waged a war implacable:
Precisely as the war occurr'd they drew
 him,
And there was Milo as he overthrew him.

LXXXVI

Seeing this history, Count Orlando said
 In his own heart, 'Oh God, who in the sky
Know'st all things! how was Milo hither
 led?
 Who caused the giant in this place to
 die?'
And certain letters, weeping, then he read,
 So that he could not keep his visage
 dry,—
As I will tell in the ensuing story.
From evil keep you the high King of glory!

FRANCESCA OF RIMINI

FROM THE INFERNO OF DANTE

CANTO THE FIFTH

THE land where I was born sits by the
 seas,
Upon that shore to which the Po de-
 scends,
With all his followers, in search of peace.
Love, which the gentle heart soon appre-
 hends,
Seized him for the fair person which was
 ta'en 5
From me, and me even yet the mode
 offends.
Love, who to none beloved to love again
Remits, seized me with wish to please,
 so strong,
That, as thou seest, yet, yet it doth re-
 main.
Love to one death conducted us along,
But Caina waits for him our life who
 ended:' 11
These were the accents utter'd by her
 tongue.—
Since I first listen'd to these souls offended,
I bow'd my visage, and so kept it till—
'What think'st thou,' said the bard;
 when I unbended, 15
And recommenced: 'Alas! unto such ill
How many sweet thoughts, what strong
 ecstasies,
Led these their evil fortune to fulfil!'
And then I turn'd unto their side my eyes,
And said, 'Francesca, thy sad destinies

Have made me sorrow till the tears arise.
But tell me, in the season of sweet sighs, 22
By what and how thy love to passion
 rose,
So as his dim desires to recognise?'
Then she to me: 'The greatest of all woes
Is to remind us of our happy days 26
In misery, and that thy teacher knows.
But if to learn our passion's first root preys
Upon thy spirit with such sympathy,
I will do even as he who weeps and says.
We read one day for pastime, seated nigh,
Of Lancilot, how love enchain'd him
 too. 32
We were alone, quite unsuspiciously.
But oft our eyes met, and our cheeks in
 hue
All o'er discolour'd by that reading
 were; 35
But one point only wholly us o'erthrew:
When we read the long-sigh'd-for smile of
 her,
To be thus kiss'd by such devoted lover,
He who from me can be divided ne'er
Kiss'd my mouth, trembling in the act all
 over: 40
Accursed was the book and he who
 wrote!
That day no further leaf we did un-
 cover.'
While thus one spirit told us of their lot,
The other wept, so that with pity's
 thralls
I swoon'd, as if by death I had been
 smote 45
And fell down even as a dead body falls.

DRAMAS

MANFRED

A DRAMATIC POEM

'There are more things in heaven and earth, Horatio,
Than are dreamt of in your philosophy.'

DRAMATIS PERSONÆ

MANFRED.
CHAMOIS HUNTER.
ABBOT OF ST. MAURICE.
MANUEL.
HERMAN.

WITCH OF THE ALPS.
ARIMANES.
NEMESIS.
THE DESTINIES.
SPIRITS, &c.

The Scene of the Drama is amongst the Higher Alps—partly in the Castle of Manfred, and partly in the Mountains.

ACT I

SCENE I.—MANFRED *alone.—Scene, a Gothic Gallery.—Time, Midnight.*

Man. The lamp must be replenish'd,
 but even then
It will not burn so long as I must watch:
My slumbers—if I slumber—are not sleep,
But a continuance of enduring thought,
Which then I can resist not: in my heart
There is a vigil, and these eyes but close
To look within; and yet I live, and bear
The aspect and the form of breathing men.
But grief should be the instructor of the
 wise;
Sorrow is knowledge: they who know the
 most 10
Must mourn the deepest o'er the fatal
 truth,
The Tree of Knowledge is not that of Life.
Philosophy and science, and the springs
Of wonder, and the wisdom of the world,
I have essay'd, and in my mind there is 15
A power to make these subject to itself—
But they avail not: I have done men good,
And I have met with good even among
 men—
But this avail'd not: I have had my foes,
And none have baffled, many fallen before
 me— 20
But this avail'd not:—Good, or evil, life,
Powers, passions, all I see in other beings,
Have been to me as rain unto the sands,
Since that all-nameless hour. I have no
 dread,
And feel the curse to have no natural fear,
Nor fluttering throb, that beats with hopes
 or wishes, 26
Or lurking love of something on the earth.
Now to my task.—

 Mysterious agency!
Ye spirits of the unbounded Universe!
Whom I have sought in darkness and in
 light— 30
Ye, who do compass earth about, and
 dwell
In subtler essence—ye, to whom the tops
Of mountains inaccessible are haunts,
And earth's and ocean's caves familiar
 things—
I call upon ye by the written charm 35
Which gives me power upon you—Rise!
 Appear! [*A pause.*
They come not yet.—Now by the voice of
 him
Who is the first among you—by this sign,
Which makes you tremble—by the claims
 of him
Who is undying,—Rise! Appear!——
 Appear! [*A pause.*
If it be so—Spirits of earth and air, 41
Ye shall not thus elude me: by a power,
Deeper than all yet urged, a tyrant-spell,
Which had its birthplace in a star con-
 demn'd,
The burning wreck of a demolish'd world,
A wandering hell in the eternal space; 46
By the strong curse which is upon my
 soul,
The thought which is within me and around
 me,
I do compel ye to my will—Appear!
 [*A star is seen at the darker end of the
 gallery: it is stationary; and a voice
 is heard singing.*

FIRST SPIRIT

Mortal! to thy bidding bow'd, 50
From my mansion in the cloud,
Which the breath of twilight builds,
And the summer's sunset gilds
With the azure and vermilion,
Which is mix'd for my pavilion; 55

Though thy quest may be forbidden,
On a star-beam I have ridden:
To thine adjuration bow'd,
Mortal—be thy wish avow'd!

Voice of the SECOND SPIRIT

Mont Blanc is the monarch of mountains;
 They crown'd him long ago 61
On a throne of rocks, in a robe of clouds,
 With a diadem of snow.
Around his waist are forests braced,
 The Avalanche in his hand; 65
But ere it fall, that thundering ball
 Must pause for my command.
The Glacier's cold and restless mass
 Moves onward day by day;
But I am he who bids it pass, 70
 Or with its ice delay.
I am the spirit of the place,
 Could make the mountain bow
And quiver to his cavern'd base—
 And what with me wouldst *Thou*? 75

Voice of the THIRD SPIRIT

In the blue depth of the waters,
 Where the wave hath no strife,
Where the wind is a stranger,
 And the sea-snake hath life,
Where the Mermaid is decking 80
 Her green hair with shells,
Like the storm on the surface
 Came the sound of thy spells;
O'er my calm Hall of Coral
 The deep echo roll'd— 85
To the Spirit of Ocean
 Thy wishes unfold!

FOURTH SPIRIT

Where the slumbering earthquake
 Lies pillow'd on fire,
And the lakes of bitumen 90
 Rise boilingly higher;
Where the roots of the Andes
 Strike deep in the earth,
As their summits to heaven
 Shoot soaringly forth; 95
I have quitted my birthplace,
 Thy bidding to bide—
Thy spell hath subdued me,
 Thy will be my guide!

FIFTH SPIRIT

I am the Rider of the wind, 100
 The Stirrer of the storm;
The hurricane I left behind
 Is yet with lightning warm;
To speed to thee, o'er shore and sea
 I swept upon the blast: 105
The fleet I met sail'd well, and yet
 'Twill sink ere night be past.

SIXTH SPIRIT

My dwelling is the shadow of the night,
Why doth thy magic torture me with
 light?

SEVENTH SPIRIT

The star which rules thy destiny 110
Was ruled, ere earth began, by me:
It was a world as fresh and fair
As e'er revolved round sun in air;
Its course was free and regular,
Space bosom'd not a lovelier star. 115
The hour arrived—and it became
A wandering mass of shapeless flame,
A pathless comet, and a curse,
The menace of the universe;
Still rolling on with innate force, 120
Without a sphere, without a course,
A bright deformity on high,
The monster of the upper sky! 123
And thou! beneath its influence born—
Thou worm! whom I obey and scorn—
Forced by a power (which is not thine,
And lent thee but to make thee mine)
For this brief moment to descend,
Where these weak spirits round thee
 bend 129
And parley with a thing like thee—
What wouldst thou, Child of Clay! with
 me?

The SEVEN SPIRITS

Earth, ocean, air, night, mountains,
 winds, thy star,
Are at thy beck and bidding, Child of
 Clay!
Before thee at thy quest their spirits are—
What wouldst thou with us, son of
 mortals—say? 135

Man. Forgetfulness——
First Spirit. Of what—of whom—and
 why?
Man. Of that which is within me; read
 it there—
Ye know it, and I cannot utter it.
 Spirit. We can but give thee that which
 we possess:
Ask of us subjects, sovereignty, the power
O'er earth—the whole, or portion—or a
 sign 141
Which shall control the elements, whereof
We are the dominators,—each and all,
These shall be thine.
 Man. Oblivion, self-oblivion!
Can ye not wring from out the hidden
 realms 145
Ye offer so profusely what I ask?
 Spirit. It is not in our essence, in our
 skill;
But—thou may'st die.
 Man. Will death bestow it on me?
 Spirit. We are immortal, and do not
 forget;
We are eternal; and to us the past 150
Is, as the future, present. Art thou an-
 swer'd?
 Man. Ye mock me—but the power
 which brought ye here

Hath made you mine. Slaves, scoff not at
 my will!
The mind, the spirit, the Promethean
 spark, 154
The lightning of my being, is as bright,
Pervading, and far darting as your own,
And shall not yield to yours, though
 coop'd in clay!
Answer, or I will teach you what I am.
 Spirit. We answer as we answer'd; our
 reply
Is even in thine own words.
 Man. Why say ye so? 160
 Spirit. If, as thou say'st, thine essence
 be as ours,
We have replied in telling thee, the thing
Mortals call death hath nought to do with
 us.
 Man. I then have call'd ye from your
 realms in vain;
Ye cannot, or ye will not, aid me.
 Spirit. Say, 165
What we possess we offer; it is thine:
Bethink ere thou dismiss us; ask again;
Kingdom, and sway, and strength, and
 length of days——
 Man. Accursed! what have I to do
 with days?
They are too long already.—Hence—be-
 gone! 170
 Spirit. Yet pause: being here, our will
 would do thee service;
Bethink thee, is there then no other gift
Which we can make not worthless in thine
 eyes?
 Man. No, none: yet stay—one mo-
 ment, ere we part,
I would behold ye face to face. I hear
Your voices, sweet and melancholy
 sounds, 176
As music on the waters; and I see
The steady aspect of a clear large star;
But nothing more. Approach me as ye are,
Or one, or all, in your accustom'd forms.
 Spirit. We have no forms, beyond the
 elements 181
Of which we are the mind and principle:
But choose a form—in that we will appear.
 Man. I have no choice; there is no form
 on earth
Hideous or beautiful to me. Let him,
Who is most powerful of ye, take such
 aspect 186
As unto him may seem most fitting—
 Come!
 *Seventh Spirit [appearing in the shape of
 a beautiful female figure].* Behold!
 Man. Oh God! if it be thus, and *thou*
Art not a madness and a mockery, 189
I yet might be most happy, I will clasp thee,
And we again will be——
 [*The figure vanishes.*
 My heart is crush'd!
 [MANFRED *falls senseless.*

 (*A voice is heard in the Incantation which
 follows.*)

When the moon is on the wave,
 And the glow-worm in the grass,
And the meteor on the grave,
 And the wisp on the morass; 19
When the falling stars are shooting,
And the answer'd owls are hooting,
And the silent leaves are still
In the shadow of the hill,
Shall my soul be upon thine, 20
With a power and with a sign.

Though thy slumber may be deep,
Yet thy spirit shall not sleep;
There are shades which will not van-
 ish,
There are thoughts thou canst not ban-
 ish; 20
By a power to thee unknown,
Thou canst never be alone;
Thou art wrapt as with a shroud,
Thou art gather'd in a cloud;
And for ever shalt thou dwell 21
In the spirit of this spell.

Though thou seest me not pass by,
Thou shalt feel me with thine eye
As a thing that, though unseen,
Must be near thee, and hath been; 21
And when in that secret dread
Thou hast turn'd around thy head,
Thou shalt marvel I am not
As thy shadow on the spot,
And the power which thou dost feel
Shall be what thou must conceal. 22

And a magic voice and verse
Hath baptized thee with a curse;
And a spirit of the air
Hath begirt thee with a snare; 22
In the wind there is a voice
Shall forbid thee to rejoice;
And to thee shall night deny
All the quiet of her sky;
And the day shall have a sun, 23
Which shall make thee wish it done.

From thy false tears I did distil
An essence which hath strength to kill
From thy own heart I then did wring
The black blood in its blackest spring;
From thy own smile I snatch'd the
 snake, 23
For there it coil'd as in a brake;
From thy own lip I drew the charm
Which gave all these their chiefest harm;
In proving every poison known, 24
I found the strongest was thine own.

By thy cold breast and serpent smile,
By thy unfathom'd gulfs of guile,
By that most seeming virtuous eye,
By thy shut soul's hypocrisy; 24

By the perfection of thine art
Which pass'd for human thine own
 heart;
By thy delight in others' pain,
And by thy brotherhood of Cain,
I call upon thee! and compel 250
Thyself to be thy proper Hell!

And on thy head I pour the vial
Which doth devote thee to this trial;
Nor to slumber, nor to die,
Shall be in thy destiny; 255
Though thy death shall still seem near
To thy wish, but as a fear;
Lo! the spell now works around thee,
And the clankless chain hath bound
 thee;
O'er thy heart and brain together 260
Hath the word been pass'd—now
 wither!

SCENE II

The Mountain of the Jungfrau.—Time,
*Morning.—*MANFRED *alone upon the*
Cliffs.

Man. The spirits I have raised abandon
 me,
The spells which I have studied baffle me,
The remedy I reck'd of tortured me;
I lean no more on superhuman aid;
It hath no power upon the past, and for
The future, till the past be gulf'd in dark-
 ness, 6
It is not of my search.—My mother Earth!
And thou fresh breaking Day, and you,
 ye Mountains,
Why are ye beautiful? I cannot love ye.
And thou, the bright eye of the universe,
That openest over all, and unto all 11
Art a delight—thou shin'st not on my
 heart.
And you, ye crags, upon whose extreme
 edge
I stand, and on the torrent's brink beneath
Behold the tall pines dwindled as to shrubs
In dizziness of distance; when a leap,
A stir, a motion, even a breath, would
 bring
My breast upon its rocky bosom's bed
To rest for ever—wherefore do I pause?
I feel the impulse—yet I do not plunge;
I see the peril—yet do not recede; 21
And my brain reels—and yet my foot is
 firm:
There is a power upon me which with-
 holds,
And makes it my fatality to live,—
If it be life to wear within myself 25
This barrenness of spirit, and to be
My own soul's sepulchre, for I have ceased
To justify my deeds unto myself—
The last infirmity of evil. Ay, 29
Thou winged and cloud-cleaving minister,
 [*An eagle passes.*

Whose happy flight is highest into heaven,
Well may'st thou swoop so near me—I
 should be
Thy prey, and gorge thine eaglets; thou
 art gone
Where the eye cannot follow thee; but
 thine 34
Yet pierces downward, onward, or above,
With a pervading vision.—Beautiful!
How beautiful is all this visible world!
How glorious in its action and itself!
But we, who name ourselves its sovereigns,
 we,
Half dust, half deity, alike unfit 40
To sink or soar, with our mix'd essence
 make
A conflict of its elements, and breathe
The breath of degradation and of pride,
Contending with low wants and lofty will,
Till our mortality predominates, 45
And men are—what they name not to
 themselves,
And trust not to each other. Hark! the
 note, [*The Shepherd's pipe in the*
 distance is heard.
The natural music of the mountain reed—
For here the patriarchal days are not
A pastoral fable—pipes in the liberal air,
Mix'd with the sweet bells of the saunter-
 ing herd; 51
My soul would drink those echoes. Oh,
 that I were
The viewless spirit of a lovely sound,
A living voice, a breathing harmony,
A bodiless enjoyment—born and dying
With the blest tone which made me! 56

Enter from below a CHAMOIS HUNTER.

Chamois Hunter. Even so
This way the chamois leapt: her nimble
 feet
Have baffled me; my gains to-day will
 scarce
Repay my break-neck travail.—What is
 here?
Who seems not of my trade, and yet hath
 reach'd 60
A height which none even of our moun-
 taineers,
Save our best hunters, may attain: his garb
Is goodly, his mien manly, and his air
Proud as a free-born peasant's, at this dis-
 tance:
I will approach him nearer.
 Man. [*not perceiving the other*]. To be
 thus— 65
Grey-hair'd with anguish, like these
 blasted pines,
Wrecks of a single winter, barkless,
 branchless,
A blighted trunk upon a cursed root,
Which but supplies a feeling to decay—
And to be thus, eternally but thus, 70
Having been otherwise! Now furrow'd o'er

With wrinkles, plough'd by moments,—
 not by years,—
And hours, all tortured into ages—hours
Which I outlive!—Ye toppling crags of ice!
Ye avalanches, whom a breath draws
 down 75
In mountainous o'erwhelming, come and
 crush me!
I hear ye momently above, beneath,
Crash with a frequent conflict; but ye pass,
And only fall on things that still would live;
On the young flourishing forest, or the hut
And hamlet of the harmless villager. 81
 C. Hun. The mists begin to rise from up
 the valley;
I'll warn him to descend, or he may chance
To lose at once his way and life together.
 Man. The mists boil up around the
 glaciers; clouds 85
Rise curling fast beneath me, white and
 sulphury,
Like foam from the roused ocean of deep
 Hell,
Whose every wave breaks on a living shore,
Heap'd with the damn'd like pebbles.—I
 am giddy.
 C. Hun. I must approach him cautiously;
 if near, 90
A sudden step will startle him, and he
Seems tottering already.
 Man. Mountains have fallen,
Leaving a gap in the clouds, and with the
 shock
Rocking their Alpine brethren; filling up
The ripe green valleys with destruction's
 splinters; 95
Damming the rivers with a sudden dash,
Which crush'd the waters into mist and
 made
Their fountains find another channel—
 thus,
Thus, in its old age, did Mount Rosen-
 berg—
Why stood I not beneath it?
 C. Hun. Friend! have a care, 100
Your next step may be fatal!—for the love
Of him who made you, stand not on that
 brink!
 Man. [*not hearing him*]. Such would
 have been for me a fitting tomb;
My bones had then been quiet in their
 depth;
They had not then been strewn upon the
 rocks 105
For the wind's pastime—as thus—thus
 they shall be—
In this one plunge.—Farewell, ye opening
 heavens!
Look not upon me thus reproachfully—
You were not meant for me—Earth! take
 these atoms!
 [*As* MANFRED *is in act to spring from the
 cliff, the* CHAMOIS HUNTER *seizes and
 retains him with a sudden grasp.*

 C. Hun. Hold, madman!—though a-
 weary of thy life, 110
Stain not our pure vales with thy guilty
 blood:
Away with me———I will not quit my
 hold.
 Man. I am most sick at heart—nay,
 grasp me not—
I am all feebleness—the mountains whirl
Spinning around me———I grow blind———
What art thou? 115
 C. Hun. I'll answer that anon. Away
 with me—
The clouds grow thicker———there—now
 lean on me—
Place your foot here—here, take this staff,
 and cling
A moment to that shrub—now give me
 your hand,
And hold fast by my girdle—softly—
 well— 120
The Chalet will be gain'd within an hour:
Come on, we'll quickly find a surer foot-
 ing,
And something like a pathway, which the
 torrent
Hath wash'd since winter.—Come, 'tis
 bravely done—
You should have been a hunter.—Follow
 me.
 [*As they descend the rocks with diffi-
 culty, the scene closes.*

ACT II

SCENE I.—*A Cottage amongst the Bernese
 Alps.*

MANFRED *and the* CHAMOIS HUNTER

 C. Hun. No, no—yet pause—thou must
 not yet go forth:
Thy mind and body are alike unfit
To trust each other, for some hours, at
 least;
When thou art better, I will be thy guide—
But whither?
 Man. It imports not: I do know 5
My route full well, and need no further
 guidance.
 C. Hun. Thy garb and gait bespeak thee
 of high lineage—
One of the many chiefs, whose castled
 crags
Look o'er the lower valleys—which of
 these
May call thee lord? I only know their
 portals; 10
My way of life leads me but rarely down
To bask by the huge hearths of those old
 halls,
Carousing with the vassals; but the paths,
Which step from out our mountains to
 their doors,
I know from childhood—which of these is
 thine? 15

Man. No matter.
C. Hun. Well, sir, pardon me
 the question,
And be of better cheer. Come, taste my
 wine;
'Tis of an ancient vintage; many a day
'T has thaw'd my veins among our glaciers,
 now
Let it do thus for thine—Come, pledge me
 fairly. 20
Man. Away, away! there's blood upon
 the brim!
Will it then never—never sink in the earth?
C. Hun. What dost thou mean? thy
 senses wander from thee.
Man. I say 'tis blood—my blood! the
 pure warm stream
Which ran in the veins of my fathers, and
 in ours 25
When we were in our youth, and had one
 heart,
And loved each other as we should not
 love,
And this was shed: but still it rises up,
Colouring the clouds, that shut me out
 from heaven,
Where thou art not—and I shall never be.
C. Hun. Man of strange words, and
 some half-maddening sin, 31
Which makes thee people vacancy, whate'er
Thy dread and sufferance be, there's com-
 fort yet—
The aid of holy men, and heavenly pa-
 tience—
Man. Patience and patience! Hence—
 that word was made 35
For brutes of burthen, not for birds of prey;
Preach it to mortals of a dust like thine,—
I am not of thine order.
C. Hun. Thanks to heaven!
I would not be of thine for the free fame
Of William Tell; but whatsoe'er thine ill,
It must be borne, and these wild starts are
 useless. 41
Man. Do I not bear it?—Look on me—
 I live.
C. Hun. This is convulsion, and no
 healthful life.
Man. I tell thee, man! I have lived many
 years,
Many long years, but they are nothing now
To those which I must number: ages—
 ages— 46
Space and eternity—and consciousness,
With the fierce thirst of death—and still
 unslaked!
C. Hun. Why, on thy brow the seal of
 middle age
Hath scarce been set; I am thine elder far.
Man. Think'st thou existence doth de-
 pend on time? 51
It doth; but actions are our epochs: mine
Have made my days and nights imperish-
 able,

Endless, and all alike, as sands on the
 shore,
Innumerable atoms; and one desert, 55
Barren and cold, on which the wild waves
 break,
But nothing rests, save carcasses and
 wrecks,
Rocks, and the salt-surf weeds of bitter-
 ness.
C. Hun. Alas! he's mad—but yet I
 must not leave him.
Man. I would I were—for then the
 things I see 60
Would be but a distemper'd dream.
C. Hun. What is it
That thou dost see, or think thou look'st
 upon?
Man. Myself, and thee—a peasant of
 the Alps—
Thy humble virtues, hospitable home,
And spirit patient, pious, proud, and free;
Thy self-respect, grafted on innocent
 thoughts; 66
Thy days of health, and nights of sleep;
 thy toils,
By danger dignified, yet guiltless; hopes
Of cheerful old age and a quiet grave,
With cross and garland over its green
 turf, 70
And thy grandchildren's love for epitaph;
This do I see—and then I look within—
It matters not—my soul was scorch'd al-
 ready!
C. Hun. And wouldst thou then ex-
 change thy lot for mine?
Man. No, friend! I would not wrong
 thee, nor exchange 75
My lot with living being: I can bear—
However wretchedly, 'tis still to bear—
In life what others could not brook to
 dream,
But perish in their slumber.
C. Hun. And with this—
This cautious feeling for another's pain,
Canst thou be black with evil?—say not
 so. 81
Can one of gentle thoughts have wreak'd
 revenge
Upon his enemies?
Man. Oh! no, no, no!
My injuries came down on those who loved
 me—
On those whom I best loved: I never quell'd
An enemy, save in my just defence— 86
But my embrace was fatal.
C. Hun. Heaven give thee rest!
And penitence restore thee to thyself;
My prayers shall be for thee.
Man. I need them not—
But can endure thy pity. I depart— 90
'Tis time—farewell!—Here's gold, and
 thanks for thee—
No words—it is thy due.—Follow me
 not—

I know my path—the mountain peril's past:
And once again I charge thee, follow not!
[*Exit* MANFRED.

SCENE II.—*A lower Valley in the Alps.—A Cataract.*

Enter MANFRED.

It is not noon—the sunbow's rays still arch
The torrent with the many hues of heaven,
And roll the sheeted silver's waving column
O'er the crag's headlong perpendicular,
And fling its lines of foaming light along,
And to and fro, like the pale courser's tail,
The Giant steed, to be bestrode by Death,
As told in the Apocalypse. No eyes 8
But mine now drink this sight of loveliness;
I should be sole in this sweet solitude,
And with the Spirit of the place divide
The homage of these waters.—I will call
 her. 12
[MANFRED *takes some of the water into
the palm of his hand, and flings it into
the air, muttering the adjuration. After
a pause, the* WITCH OF THE ALPS *rises
beneath the arch of the sunbow of the
torrent.*
Beautiful Spirit! with thy hair of light,
And dazzling eyes of glory, in whose form
The charms of earth's least mortal daugh-
 ters grow 15
To an unearthly stature, in an essence
Of purer elements; while the hues of
 youth,—
Carnation'd like a sleeping infant's cheek,
Rock'd by the beating of her mother's
 heart,
Or the rose tints, which summer's twi-
 light leaves 20
Upon the lofty glacier's virgin snow,
The blush of earth embracing with her
 heaven,—
Tinge thy celestial aspect, and make tame
The beauties of the sunbow which bends
 o'er thee. 24
Beautiful Spirit! in thy calm clear brow,
Wherein is glass'd serenity of soul,
Which of itself shows immortality,
I read that thou wilt pardon to a Son
Of Earth, whom the abstruser powers per-
 mit 29
At times to commune with them—if that he
Avail him of his spells—to call thee thus,
And gaze on thee a moment.
 Witch. Son of Earth!
I know thee, and the powers which give
 thee power;
I know thee for a man of many thoughts,
And deeds of good and ill, extreme in both,
Fatal and fated in thy sufferings. 36
I have expected this—what wouldst thou
 with me?
 Man. To look upon thy beauty—
 nothing further.

The face of the earth hath madden'd me
 and I 39
Take refuge in her mysteries, and pierce
To the abodes of those who govern her—
But they can nothing aid me. I have sought
From them what they could not bestow,
 and now
I search no further.
 Witch. What could be the quest
Which is not in the power of the most
 powerful, 42
The rulers of the invisible?
 Man. A boon;
But why should I repeat it? 'twere in vain.
 Witch. I know not that; let thy lips
 utter it.
 Man. Well, though it torture me, 'tis
 but the same;
My pang shall find a voice. From my
 youth upwards 50
My spirit walk'd not with the souls of men,
Nor look'd upon the earth with human
 eyes;
The thirst of their ambition was not mine,
The aim of their existence was not mine;
My joys, my griefs, my passions, and my
 powers, 55
Made me a stranger; though I wore the
 form,
I had no sympathy with breathing flesh,
Nor midst the creatures of clay that girded
 me
Was there but one who—but of her anon.
I said with men, and with the thoughts of
 men, 60
I held but slight communion; but instead
My joy was in the wilderness,—to breathe
The difficult air of the iced mountain's top,
Where the birds dare not build, nor in-
 sect's wing
Flit o'er the herbless granite; or to plunge
Into the torrent, and to roll along 66
On the swift whirl of the new breaking
 wave
Of river-stream, or ocean, in their flow.
In these my early strength exulted; or
To follow through the night the moving
 moon, 70
The stars and their development; or catch
The dazzling lightnings till my eyes grew
 dim;
Or to look, list'ning, on the scatter'd leaves,
While Autumn winds were at their evening
 song. 74
These were my pastimes, and to be alone;
For if the beings, of whom I was one,—
Hating to be so,—cross'd me in my path,
I felt myself degraded back to them,
And was all clay again. And then I dived,
In my lone wanderings, to the caves of
 death, 80
Searching its cause in its effect; and drew
From wither'd bones, and skulls, and
 heap'd up dust,

Conclusions most forbidden. Then I
 pass'd
The nights of years in sciences untaught,
Save in the old time; and with time and
 toil, 85
And terrible ordeal, and such penance
As in itself hath power upon the air,
And spirits that do compass air and earth,
Space, and the peopled infinite, I made
Mine eyes familiar with Eternity, 90
Such as, before me, did the Magi, and
He who from out their fountain dwellings
 raised
Eros and Anteros, at Gadara,
As I do thee;—and with my knowledge
 grew
The thirst of knowledge, and the power
 and joy 95
Of this most bright intelligence, until—
 Witch. Proceed.
 Man. Oh! I but thus prolong'd
 my words,
Boasting these idle attributes, because
As I approach the core of my heart's grief—
But to my task. I have not named to thee
Father or mother, mistress, friend, or
 being, 101
With whom I wore the chain of human
 ties;
If I had such, they seem'd not such to me;
Yet there was one—
 Witch. Spare not thyself—proceed.
 Man. She was like me in lineaments;
 her eyes, 105
Her hair, her features, all, to the very tone
Even of her voice, they said were like to
 mine;
But soften'd all, and temper'd into beauty:
She had the same lone thoughts and
 wanderings,
The quest of hidden knowledge, and a
 mind 110
To comprehend the universe: nor these
Alone, but with them gentler powers than
 mine,
Pity, and smiles, and tears—which I had
 not;
And tenderness—but that I had for her;
Humility—and that I never had. 115
Her faults were mine—her virtues were her
 own—
I loved her, and destroy'd her!
 Witch. With thy hand?
 Man. Not with my hand, but heart,
 which broke her heart;
It gazed on mine, and wither'd. I have
 shed
Blood, but not hers—and yet her blood
 was shed; 120
I saw—and could not stanch it.
 Witch. And for this—
Being of the race thou dost despise,
The order, which thine own would rise
 above,

Mingling with us and ours,—thou dost
 forego
The gifts of our great knowledge, and
 shrink'st back 125
To recreant mortality—Away!
 Man. Daughter of Air! I tell thee, since
 that hour—
But words are breath—look on me in my
 sleep,
Or watch my watchings—Come and sit by
 me! 129
My solitude is solitude no more,
But peopled with the Furies;—I have
 gnash'd
My teeth in darkness till returning morn,
Then cursed myself till sunset;—I have
 pray'd 133
For madness as a blessing—'tis denied me.
I have affronted death—but in the war
Of elements the waters shrunk from me,
And fatal things pass'd harmless; the cold
 hand
Of an all-pitiless demon held me back,
Back by a single hair, which would not
 break. 139
In fantasy, imagination, all
The affluence of my soul—which one day
 was
A Crœsus in creation—I plunged deep,
But, like an ebbing wave, it dash'd me
 back
Into the gulf of my unfathom'd thought.
I plunged amidst mankind—Forgetful-
 ness 145
I sought in all, save where 'tis to be found,
And that I have to learn; my sciences,
My long-pursued and superhuman art,
Is mortal here: I dwell in my despair—
And live—and live for ever.
 Witch. It may be 150
That I can aid thee.
 Man. To do this thy power
Must wake the dead, or lay me low with
 them.
Do so—in any shape—in any hour—
With any torture—so it be the last.
 Witch. That is not in my province;
 but if thou 155
Wilt swear obedience to my will, and do
My bidding, it may help thee to thy
 wishes.
 Man. I will not swear—Obey! and
 whom? the spirits
Whose presence I command, and be the
 slave
Of those who served me—Never!
 Witch. Is this all? 160
Hast thou no gentler answer?—Yet be-
 think thee,
And pause ere thou rejectest.
 Man. I have said it.
 Witch. Enough! I may retire then—say!
 Man. Retire!
 [*The* WITCH *disappears.*

Man. [*alone*]. We are the fools of time
 and terror: Days 164
Steal on us, and steal from us; yet we live,
Loathing our life, and dreading still to die.
In all the days of this detested yoke—
This vital weight upon the struggling heart,
Which sinks with sorrow, or beats quick
 with pain, 169
Or joy that ends in agony or faintness—
In all the days of past and future, for
In life there is no present, we can number
How few—how less than few—wherein
 the soul
Forbears to pant for death, and yet draws
 back
As from a stream in winter, though the
 chill 175
Be but a moment's. I have one resource
Still in my science—I can call the dead,
And ask them what it is we dread to be:
The sternest answer can but be the Grave,
And that is nothing. If they answer
 not—— 180
The buried Prophet answered to the Hag
Of Endor; and the Spartan Monarch drew
From the Byzantine maid's unsleeping
 spirit
An answer and his destiny—he slew
That which he loved, unknowing what he
 slew, 185
And died unpardon'd—though he call'd in
 aid
The Phyxian Jove, and in Phigalia roused
The Arcadian Evocators to compel
The indignant shadow to depose her wrath,
Or fix her term of vengeance—she replied
In words of dubious import, but fulfill'd.
If I had never lived, that which I love 192
Had still been living; had I never loved,
That which I love would still be beautiful,
Happy and giving happiness. What is she?
What is she now?—a sufferer for my sins—
A thing I dare not think upon—or nothing.
Within few hours I shall not call in vain—
Yet in this hour I dread the thing I dare:
Until this hour I never shrunk to gaze
On spirit, good or evil—now I tremble,
And feel a strange cold thaw upon my
 heart. 202
But I can act even what I most abhor,
And champion human fears.—The night
 approaches. [*Exit.*

SCENE III.—*The Summit of the Jungfrau*
 Mountain.

Enter FIRST DESTINY.

The moon is rising broad, and round, and
 bright;
And here on snows, where never human
 foot
Of common mortal trod, we nightly tread,
And leave no traces: o'er the savage sea,
The glassy ocean of the mountain ice, 5

We skim its rugged breakers, which put on
The aspect of a tumbling tempest's foam
Frozen in a moment—a dead whirlpool's
 image:
And this most steep fantastic pinnacle,
The fretwork of some earthquake—where
 the clouds 10
Pause to repose themselves in passing by—
Is sacred to our revels, or our vigils;
Here do I wait my sisters, on our way
To the Hall of Arimanes, for to-night
Is our great festival—'tis strange they
 come not. 15

A Voice without, singing.

The Captive Usurper,
 Hurl'd down from the throne,
Lay buried in torpor,
 Forgotten and lone;
I broke through his slumbers, 20
 I shiver'd his chain,
I leagued him with numbers—
 He's Tyrant again!
With the blood of a million he'll answer
 my care,
With a nation's destruction—his flight and
 despair. 25

Second Voice, without.

The ship sail'd on, the ship sail'd fast,
But I left not a sail, and I left not a mast;
There is not a plank of the hull or the deck,
And there is not a wretch to lament o'er his
 wreck;
Save one, whom I held, as he swam, by the
 hair, 30
And he was a subject well worthy my care;
A traitor on land, and a pirate at sea—
But I saved him to wreak further havoc for
 me!

FIRST DESTINY, *answering.*

The city lies sleeping;
 The morn, to deplore it, 35
May dawn on it weeping:
 Sullenly, slowly,
The black plague flew o'er it—
 Thousands lie lowly;
Tens of thousands shall perish; 40
 The living shall fly from
The sick they should cherish;
 But nothing can vanquish
The touch that they die from.
 Sorrow and anguish, 45
And evil and dread,
 Envelope a nation;
The blest are the dead,
Who see not the sight
 Of their own desolation; 50
This work of a night—
This wreck of a realm—this deed of my
 doing,
For ages I've done, and shall still be re-
 newing!

Enter the SECOND *and* THIRD DESTINIES.
The Three.

Our hands contain the hearts of men,
 Our footsteps are their graves; 55
We only give to take again
 The spirits of our slaves!

First Des. Welcome!—Where's Nemesis?
Second Des. At some great work;
But what I know not, for my hands were full. 59
Third Des. Behold she cometh.

Enter NEMESIS.

First Des. Say, where hast thou been?
My sisters and thyself are slow to-night.
Nem. I was detain'd repairing shatter'd thrones,
Marrying fools, restoring dynasties,
Avenging men upon their enemies,
And making them repent their own revenge; 65
Goading the wise to madness; from the dull
Shaping out oracles to rule the world
Afresh, for they were waxing out of date,
And mortals dared to ponder for themselves,
To weigh kings in the balance, and to speak 70
Of freedom, the forbidden fruit.—Away!
We have outstay'd the hour—mount we our clouds! [*Exeunt.*

SCENE IV.—*The Hall of Arimanes—Arimanes on his Throne, a Globe of Fire, surrounded by the Spirits.*

Hymn of the SPIRITS.

Hail to our Master!—Prince of Earth and Air!
 Who walks the clouds and waters—in his hand
The sceptre of the elements, which tear
 Themselves to chaos at his high command!
He breatheth—and a tempest shakes the sea; 5
He speaketh—and the clouds reply in thunder;
He gazeth—from his glance the sunbeams flee;
He moveth—earthquakes rend the world asunder.
Beneath his footsteps the volcanoes rise;
 His shadow is the Pestilence; his path
The comets herald through the crackling skies; 11
 And planets turn to ashes at his wrath.
To him War offers daily sacrifice;
 To him Death pays his tribute; Life is his,

With all its infinite of agonies— 15
 And his the spirit of whatever is!

Enter the DESTINIES *and* NEMESIS.

First Des. Glory to Arimanes! on the earth
His power increaseth—both my sisters did
His bidding, nor did I neglect my duty!
Second Des. Glory to Arimanes! we who bow 20
The necks of men, bow down before his throne!
Third Des. Glory to Arimanes! we await
His nod!
Nem. Sovereign of Sovereigns! we are thine,
And all that liveth, more or less, is ours,
And most things wholly so; still to increase 25
Our power, increasing thine, demands our care,
And we are vigilant. Thy late commands
Have been fulfill'd to the utmost.

Enter MANFRED.

A Spirit. What is here?
A mortal!—Thou most rash and fatal wretch, 29
Bow down and worship!
Second Spirit. I do know the man—
A Magian of great power, and fearful skill!
Third Spirit. Bow down and worship, slave!—
 What, know'st thou not
Thine and our Sovereign?—Tremble, and obey!
All the Spirits. Prostrate thyself, and thy condemned clay,
Child of the Earth! or dread the worst.
Man. I know it;
And yet ye see I kneel not.
Fourth Spirit. 'Twill be taught thee.
Man. 'Tis taught already;—many a night on the earth,
On the bare ground, have I bow'd down my face,
And strew'd my head with ashes; I have known
The fulness of humiliation, for 40
I sunk before my vain despair, and knelt
To my own desolation.
Fifth Spirit. Dost thou dare
Refuse to Arimanes on his throne
What the whole earth accords, beholding not
The terror of his glory?—Crouch, I say.
Man. Bid *him* bow down to that which is above him, 46
The overruling Infinite—the Maker
Who made him not for worship—let him kneel,
And we will kneel together.
The Spirits. Crush the worm!

Tear him in pieces!—
First Des. Hence! avaunt!—he's mine.
Prince of the Powers invisible! This man
Is of no common order, as his port 52
And presence here denote; his sufferings
Have been of an immortal nature, like
Our own; his knowledge, and his powers
 and will, 55
As far as is compatible with clay,
Which clogs the ethereal essence, have
 been such
As clay hath seldom borne; his aspirations
Have been beyond the dwellers of the earth,
And they have only taught him what we
 know— 60
That knowledge is not happiness, and
 science
But an exchange of ignorance for that
Which is another kind of ignorance.
This is not all—the passions, attributes
Of earth and heaven, from which no power,
 nor being, 65
Nor breath from the worm upwards is
 exempt,
Have pierced his heart, and in their con-
 sequence
Made him a thing which I, who pity not,
Yet pardon those who pity. He is mine,
And thine, it may be; be it so, or not,
No other Spirit in this region hath 71
A soul like his—or power upon his soul.
Nem. What doth he here then?
First Des. Let him answer that.
Man. Ye know what I have known; and
 without power
I could not be amongst ye: but there are
Powers deeper still beyond—I come in
 quest 76
Of such, to answer unto what I seek.
Nem. What wouldst thou?
Man. Thou canst not reply to me.
Call up the dead—my question is for them.
Nem. Great Arimanes, doth thy will
 avouch 80
The wishes of this mortal?
Ari. Yea.
Nem. Whom wouldst thou
Uncharnel?
Man. One without a tomb—call up
Astarte

Nemesis.

Shadow! or Spirit!
 Whatever thou art, 85
Which still doth inherit
 The whole or a part
Of the form of thy birth,
 Of the mould of thy clay,
Which return'd to the earth, 90
 Re-appear to the day!
Bear what thou borest,
 The heart and the form,
And the aspect thou worest,
 Redeem from the worm. 95

Appear!—Appear!—Appear!
Who sent thee there requires thee here!
[*The Phantom of* ASTARTE *rises and
 stands in the midst.*
Man. Can this be death? there's bloom
 upon her cheek;
But now I see it is no living hue,
But a strange hectic—like the unnatural
 red 100
Which Autumn plants upon the perish'd
 leaf.
It is the same! Oh, God! that I should
 dread
To look upon the same—Astarte!—No,
I cannot speak to her—but bid her speak—
Forgive me or condemn me. 105

Nemesis.

By the power which hath broken
 The grave which enthrall'd thee,
Speak to him, who hath spoken,
 Or those who have call'd thee!

Man. She is silent, 110
And in that silence I am more than
 answer'd.
Nem. My power extends no further.
 Prince of Air!
It rests with thee alone—command her
 voice.
Ari. Spirit—obey this sceptre!
Nem. Silent still!
She is not of our order, but belongs 115
To the other powers. Mortal! thy quest
 is vain,
And we are baffled also.
Man. Hear me, hear me—
Astarte! my beloved! speak to me:
I have so much endured—so much en-
 dure—
Look on me! the grave hath not changed
 thee more 120
Than I am changed for thee. Thou lovedst
 me
Too much, as I loved thee: we were not
 made
To torture thus each other, though it were
The deadliest sin to love as we have loved.
Say that thou loath'st me not—that I do
 bear 125
This punishment for both—that thou wilt
 be
One of the blessed—and that I shall die;
For hitherto all hateful things conspire
To bind me in existence—in a life
Which makes me shrink from immortal-
 ity— 130
A future like the past. I cannot rest.
I know not what I ask, nor what I seek:
I feel but what thou art, and what I am;
And I would hear yet once before I perish
The voice which was my music—Speak to
 me! 135
For I have call'd on thee in the still night,

400

startled the slumbering birds from the
 hush'd boughs,
And woke the mountain wolves, and made
 the caves
Acquainted with thy vainly echoed name,
Which answer'd me—many things an-
 swer'd me— 140
Spirits and men—but thou wert silent all.
Yet speak to me! I have outwatch'd the
 stars,
And gazed o'er heaven in vain in search of
 thee.
Speak to me! I have wander'd o'er the
 earth,
And never found thy likeness—Speak to
 me! 145
Look on the fiends around—they feel for
 me:
I fear them not, and feel for thee alone—
Speak to me! though it be in wrath;—but
 say—
I reck not what—but let me hear thee
 once—
This once—once more!
 Phantom of Astarte. Manfred!
 Man. Say on, say on— 150
I live but in the sound—it is thy voice!
 Phan. Manfred! To-morrow ends
 thine earthly ills.
Farewell!
 Man. Yet one word more—am I for-
 given?
 Phan. Farewell!
 Man. Say, shall we meet again?
 Phan. Farewell!
 Man. One word for mercy! Say, thou
 lovest me. 155
 Phan. Manfred!
 [*The Spirit of* ASTARTE *disappears.*
 Nem. She's gone, and will not be re-
 call'd;
Her words will be fulfill'd. Return to the
 earth.
 A Spirit. He is convulsed.—This is to
 be a mortal
And seek the things beyond mortality.
 Another Spirit. Yet, see, he mastereth
 himself, and makes 160
His torture tributary to his will.
Had he been one of us, he would have
 made
An awful spirit.
 Nem. Hast thou further question
Of our great sovereign, or his worship-
 pers?
 Man. None.
 Nem. Then, for a time, farewell. 165
 Man. We meet then! Where? On the
 earth?—
Even as thou wilt: and for the grace ac-
 corded
I now depart a debtor. Fare ye well!
 [*Exit* MANFRED.
 (*Scene closes.*)

ACT III

SCENE I.—*A Hall in the Castle of Manfred.*

MANFRED *and* HERMAN.

 Man. What is the hour?
 Her. It wants but one till sunset,
And promises a lovely twilight.
 Man. Say,
Are all things so disposed of in the tower
As I directed?
 Her. All, my lord, are ready:
Here is the key and casket.
 Man. It is well: 5
Thou may'st retire. [*Exit* HERMAN.
 Man. [*alone*]. There is a calm upon
 me—
Inexplicable stillness! which till now
Did not belong to what I knew of life.
If that I did not know philosophy 9
To be of all our vanities the motliest,
The merest word that ever fool'd the ear
From out the schoolman's jargon, I should
 deem
The golden secret, the sought 'Kalon',
 found,
And seated in my soul. It will not last,
But it is well to have known it, though but
 once: 15
It hath enlarged my thoughts with a new
 sense,
And I within my tablets would note down
That there is such a feeling. Who is there?

Re-enter HERMAN.

 Her. My lord, the abbot of St. Maurice
 craves
To greet your presence.

Enter the ABBOT OF ST. MAURICE.

 Abbot. Peace be with Count Manfred!
 Man. Thanks, holy father! welcome
 to these walls; 21
Thy presence honours them, and blesseth
 those
Who dwell within them.
 Abbot. Would it were so, Count!—
But I would fain confer with thee alone.
 Man. Herman, retire.—What would
 my reverend guest? 25
 Abbot. Thus, without prelude:—Age
 and zeal, my office,
And good intent, must plead my privilege;
Our near, though not acquainted neigh-
 bourhood,
May also be my herald. Rumours strange,
And of unholy nature, are abroad, 30
And busy with thy name; a noble name
For centuries: may he who bears it now
Transmit it unimpair'd!
 Man. Proceed,—I listen.
 Abbot. 'Tis said thou holdest converse
 with the things 34
Which are forbidden to the search of man;

That with the dwellers of the dark abodes,
The many evil and unheavenly spirits
Which walk the valley of the shade of
 death,
Thou communest. I know that with man-
 kind, 39
Thy fellows in creation, thou dost rarely
Exchange thy thoughts, and that thy soli-
 tude
Is as an anchorite's, were it but holy.
 Man. And what are they who do avouch
 these things?
 Abbot. My pious brethren—the scared
 peasantry—
Even thy own vassals—who do look on
 thee 45
With most unquiet eyes. Thy life's in
 peril.
 Man. Take it.
 Abbot. I come to save, and not destroy:
I would not pry into thy secret soul;
But if these things be sooth, there still is
 time
For penitence and pity: reconcile thee
With the true church, and through the
 church to heaven. 51
 Man. I hear thee. This is my reply:
 whate'er
I may have been, or am, doth rest between
Heaven and myself. I shall not choose a
 mortal
To be my mediator. Have I sinn'd 55
Against your ordinances? prove and
 punish!
 Abbot. My son! I did not speak of
 punishment,
But penitence and pardon;—with thyself
The choice of such remains—and for the
 last, 59
Our institutions and our strong belief
Have given me power to smooth the path
 from sin
To higher hope and better thoughts; the
 first
I leave to heaven,—'Vengeance is mine
 alone!'
So saith the Lord, and with all humbleness
His servant echoes back the awful word.
 Man. Old man! there is no power in
 holy men, 66
Nor charm in prayer, nor purifying form
Of penitence, nor outward look, nor fast,
Nor agony—nor, greater than all these,
The innate tortures of that deep despair,
Which is remorse without the fear of
 hell, 71
But all in all sufficient to itself
Would make a hell of heaven—can exor-
 cise
From out the unbounded spirit the quick
 sense
Of its own sins, wrongs, sufferance, and
 revenge 75
Upon itself; there is no future pang

Can deal that justice on the self-condemn'd
He deals on his own soul.
 Abbot. All this is well
For this will pass away, and be succeede
By an auspicious hope, which shall look u
With calm assurance to that blessed place
Which all who seek may win, whatever b
Their earthly errors, so they be atoned:
And the commencement of atonement i
The sense of its necessity. Say on— 8
And all our church can teach thee shall b
 taught;
And all we can absolve thee shall be par
 don'd.
 Man. When Rome's sixth emperor wa
 near his last,
The victim of a self-inflicted wound,
To shun the torments of a public death
From senates once his slaves, a certai
 soldier, 9
With show of loyal pity, would hav
 stanch'd
The gushing throat with his officious robe
The dying Roman thrust him back, an
 said— 9
Some empire still in his expiring glance—
'It is too late—is this fidelity?'
 Abbot. And what of this?
 Man. I answer with the Roman—
'It is too late!'
 Abbot. It never can be so,
To reconcile thyself with thy own soul,
And thy own soul with heaven. Hast tho
 no hope? 10
'Tis strange—even those who do despai
 above,
Yet shape themselves some fantasy o
 earth,
To which frail twig they cling, like drown
 ing men.
 Man. Ay—father! I have had thos
 earthly visions, 10
And noble aspirations in my youth,
To make my own the mind of other men
The enlightener of nations; and to rise
I knew not whither—it might be to fall;
But fall, even as the mountain-cataract,
Which having leapt from its more dazzlin
 height, 11
Even in the foaming strength of its abyss
(Which casts up misty columns that be
 come
Clouds raining from the re-ascended skies,
Lies low but mighty still.—But this is pas
My thoughts mistook themselves.
 Abbot. And wherefore so? 11
 Man. I could not tame my nature down
 for he
Must serve who fain would sway; an
 soothe, and sue,
And watch all time, and pry into all place
And be a living lie, who would become
A mighty thing amongst the mean, an
 such 12

402

The mass are; I disdain'd to mingle with
a herd, though to be leader—and of
wolves.
The lion is alone, and so am I.
 Abbot. And why not live and act with
other men?
 Man. Because my nature was averse
from life; 125
And yet not cruel; for I would not make,
But find a desolation. Like the wind,
The red-hot breath of the most lone
simoom,
Which dwells but in the desert, and sweeps
o'er
The barren sands which bear no shrubs to
blast, 130
And revels o'er their wild and arid waves,
And seeketh not, so that it is not sought,
But being met is deadly,—such hath been
The course of my existence; but there came
Things in my path which are no more.
 Abbot. Alas! 135
'gin to fear that thou art past all aid
From me and from my calling; yet so
young,
still would—
 Man. Look on me! there is an order
Of mortals on the earth, who do become
Old in their youth, and die ere middle age,
Without the violence of warlike death;
Some perishing of pleasure, some of study,
Some worn with toil, some of mere weari-
ness,
Some of disease, and some insanity,
And some of wither'd or of broken hearts;
For this last is a malady which slays 146
More than are number'd in the lists of
Fate,
Taking all shapes, and bearing many
names.
Look upon me! for even of all these things
Have I partaken; and of all these things,
One were enough; then wonder not that I
Am what I am, but that I ever was, 152
Or having been, that I am still on earth.
 Abbot. Yet, hear me still——
 Man. Old man! I do respect
Thine order, and revere thine years; I deem
Thy purpose pious, but it is in vain: 156
Think me not churlish; I would spare thy-
self,
Far more than me, in shunning at this time
All further colloquy—and so—farewell.
 [Exit MANFRED.
 Abbot. This should have been a noble
creature: he 160
Hath all the energy which would have made
A goodly frame of glorious elements,
Had they been wisely mingled; as it is,
It is an awful chaos—light and darkness,
And mind and dust, and passions and pure
thoughts 165
Mix'd, and contending without end or
order,—

All dormant or destructive: he will perish,
And yet he must not; I will try once more,
For such are worth redemption; and my
duty 169
Is to dare all things for a righteous end.
I'll follow him—but cautiously, though
surely. *[Exit* ABBOT.

 SCENE II.—*Another Chamber.*

 MANFRED *and* HERMAN.

 Her. My lord, you bade me wait on you
at sunset:
He sinks behind the mountain.
 Man. Doth he so?
I will look on him. [MANFRED *advances*
 to the window of the Hall.
 Glorious Orb! the idol
Of early nature, and the vigorous race
Of undiseased mankind, the giant sons 5
Of the embrace of angels, with a sex
More beautiful than they, which did draw
down
The erring spirits who can ne'er return.—
Most glorious orb! that wert a worship, ere
The mystery of thy making was reveal'd!
Thou earliest minister of the Almighty,
Which gladden'd, on their mountain tops,
the hearts 12
Of the Chaldean shepherds, till they pour'd
Themselves in orisons! Thou material
God!
And representative of the Unknown—
Who chose thee for his shadow! Thou chief
star! 16
Centre of many stars! which mak'st our
earth
Endurable, and temperest the hues
And hearts of all who walk within thy rays!
Sire of the seasons! Monarch of the climes,
And those who dwell in them! for near or
far, 21
Our inborn spirits have a tint of thee
Even as our outward aspects;—thou dost
rise,
And shine, and set in glory. Fare thee well!
I ne'er shall see thee more. As my first
glance 25
Of love and wonder was for thee, then take
My latest look; thou wilt not beam on one
To whom the gifts of life and warmth have
been
Of a more fatal nature. He is gone:
I follow. *[Exit* MANFRED.

SCENE III.—*The Mountains—The Castle
 of Manfred at some distance—A
 Terrace before a Tower—Time, Twi-
 light.*

HERMAN, MANUEL, *and other Dependants
 of* MANFRED.

 Her. 'Tis strange enough; night after
night, for years,

He hath pursued long vigils in this tower,
Without a witness. I have been within it,—
So have we all been oft-times; but from it,
Or its contents, it were impossible 5
To draw conclusions absolute, of aught
His studies tend to. To be sure, there is
One chamber where none enter: I would
 give
The fee of what I have to come these three
 years,
To pore upon its mysteries.
 Manuel. 'Twere dangerous; 10
Content thyself with what thou know'st
 already.
 Her. Ah! Manuel! thou art elderly and
 wise,
And couldst say much; thou hast dwelt
 within the castle—
How many years is't?
 Manuel. Ere Count Manfred's birth,
I served his father, whom he nought re-
 sembles. 15
 Her. There be more sons in like pre-
 dicament.
But wherein do they differ?
 Manuel. I speak not
Of features or of form, but mind and
 habits;
Count Sigismund was proud, but gay and
 free,—
A warrior and a reveller; he dwelt not
With books and solitude, nor made the
 night 21
A gloomy vigil, but a festal time,
Merrier than day; he did not walk the
 rocks
And forests like a wolf, nor turn aside
From men and their delights.
 Her. Beshrew the hour, 25
But those were jocund times! I would that
 such
Would visit the old walls again; they look
As if they had forgotten them.
 Manuel. These walls
Must change their chieftain first. Oh! I
 have seen
Some strange things in them, Herman.
 Her. Come, be friendly; 30
Relate me some to while away our watch:
I've heard thee darkly speak of an event
Which happen'd hereabouts, by this same
 tower.
 Manuel. That was a night indeed! I do
 remember
'Twas twilight, as it may be now, and such
Another evening;—yon red cloud, which
 rests 36
On Eigher's pinnacle, so rested then,—
So like that it might be the same; the wind
Was faint and gusty, and the mountain
 snows
Began to glitter with the climbing moon;
Count Manfred was, as now, within his
 tower,— 41

How occupied, we knew not, but with him
The sole companion of his wanderings
And watchings—her, whom of all earthly
 things
That lived, the only thing he seem'd t∙
 love,— 4
As he, indeed, by blood was bound to do
The lady Astarte, his—
 Hush! who comes here

 Enter the ABBOT.

 Abbot. Where is your master?
 Her. Yonder in the tower
 Abbot. I must speak with him.
 Manuel. 'Tis impossible
He is most private, and must not be thus
Intruded on.
 Abbot. Upon myself I tak∙
The forfeit of my fault, if fault there be—
But I must see him.
 Her. Thou hast seen him onc∙
This eve already.
 Abbot. Herman! I command the∙
Knock, and apprize the Count of my ap
 proach. 5
 Her. We dare not.
 Abbot. Then it seems I must be heral∙
Of my own purpose.
 Manuel. Reverend father, stop—
I pray you pause.
 Abbot. Why so?
 Manuel. But step this way
And I will tell you further. [*Exeun∙*

 SCENE IV.—*Interior of the Tower.*

 MANFRED *alone.*

The stars are forth, the moon above th∙
 tops
Of the snow-shining mountains.—Beauti
 ful!
I linger yet with Nature, for the Night
Hath been to me a more familiar face
Than that of man; and in her starry shad∙
Of dim and solitary loveliness,
I learn'd the language of another world.
I do remember me, that in my youth,
When I was wandering,—upon such a nigh∙
I stood within the Coliseum's wall, 1
'Midst the chief relics of almighty Rome
The trees which grew along the broke∙
 arches
Waved dark in the blue midnight, and th∙
 stars
Shone through the rents of ruin; from afa∙
The watch-dog bay'd beyond the Tiber
 and 1
More near from out the Cæsars' palac∙
 came
The owl's long cry, and, interruptedly,
Of distant sentinels the fitful song
Begun and died upon the gentle wind.
Some cypresses beyond the time-wor∙
 breach 2

Appear'd to skirt the horizon, yet they
 stood
Within a bowshot. Where the Cæsars
 dwelt,
And dwell the tuneless birds of night, amidst
A grove which springs through levell'd
 battlements,
And twines its roots with the imperial
 hearths, 25
Ivy usurps the laurel's place of growth;
But the gladiators' bloody Circus stands,
A noble wreck in ruinous perfection,
While Cæsar's chambers, and the Augus-
 tan halls,
Grovel on earth in indistinct decay. 30
And thou didst shine, thou rolling moon,
 upon
All this, and cast a wide and tender light,
Which soften'd down the hoar austerity
Of rugged desolation, and fill'd up, 34
As 'twere anew, the gaps of centuries;
Leaving that beautiful which still was so,
And making that which was not, till the
 place
Became religion, and the heart ran o'er
With silent worship of the great of old,—
The dead but sceptred sovereigns, who still
 rule 40
Our spirits from their urns.
 'Twas such a night!
'Tis strange that I recall it at this time;
But I have found our thoughts take wildest
 flight
Even at the moment when they should array
Themselves in pensive order.

 Enter the ABBOT.

Abbot. My good lord! 45
I crave a second grace for this approach;
But yet let not my humble zeal offend
By its abruptness—all it hath of ill
Recoils on me; its good in the effect
May light upon your head—could I say
 heart— 50
Could I touch *that*, with words or prayers,
 I should
Recall a noble spirit which hath wander'd;
But is not yet all lost.
 Man. Thou know'st me not;
My days are number'd, and my deeds re-
 corded: 54
Retire, or 'twill be dangerous—Away!
 Abbot. Thou dost not mean to menace
 me?
 Man. Not I;
I simply tell thee peril is at hand,
And would preserve thee.
 Abbot. What dost thou mean?
 Man. Look there!
What dost thou see?
 Abbot. Nothing.
 Man. Look there I say,
And steadfastly;—now tell me what thou
 seest? 60

Abbot. That which should shake me,
 but I fear it not:
I see a dusk and awful figure rise,
Like an infernal god, from out the earth;
His face wrapt in a mantle, and his form
Robed as with angry clouds: he stands be-
 tween 65
Thyself and me—but I do fear him not.
 Man. Thou hast no cause—he shall
 not harm thee—but
His sight may shock thine old limbs into
 palsy.
I say to thee—Retire!
 Abbot. And I reply—
Never—till I have battled with this
 fiend:— 70
What doth he here?
 Man. Why—ay—what doth he here?
I did not send for him,—he is unbidden.
 Abbot. Alas! lost mortal! what with
 guests like these
Hast thou to do? I tremble for thy sake:
Why doth he gaze on thee, and thou on
 him? 75
Ah! he unveils his aspect: on his brow
The thunder-scars are graven: from his eye
Glares forth the immortality of hell—
Avaunt!—
 Man. Pronounce—what is thy mission?
 Spirit. Come!
 Abbot. What art thou, unknown be-
 ing? answer!—speak! 80
 Spirit. The genius of this mortal.—
 Come! 'tis time.
 Man. I am prepared for all things, but
 deny
The power which summons me. Who sent
 thee here?
 Spirit. Thou'lt know anon—Come!
 come!
 Man. I have commanded
Things of an essence greater far than
 thine, 85
And striven with thy masters. Get thee
 hence!
 Spirit. Mortal! thine hour is come—
 Away! I say.
 Man. I knew, and know my hour is
 come, but not
To render up my soul to such as thee:
Away! I'll die as I have lived—alone. 90
 Spirit. Then I must summon up my
 brethren.—Rise!
 [*Other Spirits rise up.*
 Abbot. Avaunt! ye evil ones!—
 Avaunt! I say;
Ye have no power where piety hath power,
And I do charge ye in the name——
 Spirit. Old man!
We know ourselves, our mission, and
 thine order; 95
Waste not thy holy words on idle uses,
It were in vain: this man is forfeited.
Once more I summon him—Away! Away!

Man. I do defy ye,—though I feel my
 soul 99
Is ebbing from me, yet I do defy ye;
Nor will I hence, while I have earthly breath
To breathe my scorn upon ye—earthly
 strength
To wrestle, though with spirits; what ye
 take 103
Shall be ta'en limb by limb.
 Spirit. Reluctant mortal!
Is this the Magian who would so pervade
The world invisible, and make himself
Almost our equal? Can it be that thou
Art thus in love with life? the very life
Which made thee wretched!
 Man. Thou false fiend, thou liest!
My life is in its last hour,—*that* I know,
Nor would redeem a moment of that hour;
I do not combat against death, but thee
And thy surrounding angels; my past
 power, 113
Was purchased by no compact with thy
 crew,
But by superior science—penance, daring,
And length of watching, strength of mind,
 and skill 116
In knowledge of our fathers—when the
 earth
Saw men and spirits walking side by side,
And gave ye no supremacy: I stand 119
Upon my strength—I do defy—deny—
Spurn back, and scorn ye!—
 Spirit. But thy many crimes
Have made thee——
 Man. What are they to such as thee?
Must crimes be punish'd but by other
 crimes, 123
And greater criminals?—Back to thy hell!
Thou hast no power upon me, *that* I feel;
Thou never shalt possess me, *that* I know:
What I have done is done; I bear within
A torture which could nothing gain from
 thine: 128

The mind which is immortal makes itself
Requital for its good or evil thoughts,—
Is its own origin of ill and end— 131
And its own place and time: its innate
 sense,
When stripp'd of this mortality, derives
No colour from the fleeting things without,
But is absorb'd in sufferance or in joy,
Born from the knowledge of its own de-
 sert. 136
Thou didst not tempt me, and thou couldst
 not tempt me;
I have not been thy dupe, nor am thy
 prey—
But was my own destroyer, and will be
My own hereafter.—Back, ye baffled
 fiends!— 141
The hand of death is on me—but not yours!
 [*The Demons disappear.*
 Abbot. Alas! how pale thou art—thy
 lips are white—
And thy breast heaves—and in thy gasping
 throat
The accents rattle: Give thy prayers to
 heaven—
Pray—albeit but in thought,—but die not
 thus. 148
 Man. 'Tis over—my dull eyes can fix
 thee not;
But all things swim around me, and the
 earth
Heaves as it were beneath me. Fare thee
 well!
Give me thy hand.
 Abbot. Cold—cold—even to the heart—
But yet one prayer—Alas! how fares it
 with thee? 155
 Man. Old man! 'tis not so difficult to
 die. [MANFRED *expires.*
 Abbot. He's gone—his soul hath ta'en
 its earthless flight;
Whither? I dread to think—but he is
 gone.

MARINO FALIERO, DOGE OF VENICE

AN HISTORICAL TRAGEDY IN FIVE ACTS

'*Dux* inquieti turbidus Adriæ.'—HORACE.

PREFACE

THE conspiracy of the Doge Marino Faliero is one of the most remarkable events in the annals of the most singular government, city, and people of modern history. It occurred in the year 1355. Everything about Venice is, or was, extraordinary—her aspect is like a dream, and her history is like romance. The story of this Doge is to be found in all her Chronicles, and particularly detailed in the 'Lives of the Doges,' by Marin Sanuto, which is given in the Appendix. It is simply and clearly related, and is perhaps more dramatic in itself than any scenes which can be founded upon the subject.

Marino Faliero appears to have been a man of talents and of courage. I find him commander-in-chief of the land forces at the siege of Zara, where he beat the King of Hungary and his army of eighty thousand men, killing eight thousand men, and keeping the besieged at the same time in check; an exploit to which I know none similar in history, except that of Cæsar at Alesia, and of Prince Eugene at Belgrade. He was afterwards commander of the fleet in the same war. He took Capo d'Istria. He was ambassador at Genoa and Rome,—at which last he received the news of his election to the dukedom; his absence being a proof that he sought it by no intrigue, since he was apprised of his predecessor's death and his own succession at the same moment. But he appears to have been of an ungovernable temper. A story is told by Sanuto, of his having, many years before, when podesta and captain at Treviso, boxed the ears of the bishop, who was somewhat tardy in bringing the Host. For this, honest Sanuto 'saddles him with a judgment,' as Thwackum did Square; but he does not tell us whether he was punished or rebuked by the Senate for this outrage at the time of its commission. He seems, indeed, to have been afterwards at peace with the church, for we find him ambassador at Rome, and invested with the fief of Val di Marino, in the march of Treviso, and with the title of count, by Lorenzo Count-bishop of Ceneda. For these facts my authorities are Sanuto, Vettor Sandi, Andrea Navagero, and the account of the siege of Zara, first published by the indefatigable Abate Morelli, in his 'Monumenti Veneziani di varia Letteratura,' printed in 1796, all of which I have looked over in the original language. The moderns, Darù, Sismondi, and Laugier, nearly agree with the ancient chroniclers. Sismondi attributes the conspiracy to his *jealousy*; but I find this nowhere asserted by the national historians. Vettor Sandi, indeed, says, that 'Altri scrissero che dalla gelosa suspizion si esso Doge siasi fatto (Michel Steno) staccar con violenza,' &c. &c.; but this appears to have been by no means the general opinion, nor is it alluded to by Sanuto, or by Navagero: and Sandi himself adds, a moment after, that 'per altre Veneziane memorie traspiri, che non il *solo* desiderio di vendetta o dispose alla congiura ma anche la innata abituale ambizion sua, per cui anelava a farsi principe independente.' The first motive appears to have been excited by the gross affront of the words written by Michel Steno on the ducal chair, and by the light and inadequate sentence of the Forty on the offender, who was one of their 'tre Capi.' The attentions of Steno himself appear to have been directed towards one of her damsels, and not to the 'Dogaressa' herself, against whose fame not the slightest insinuation appears, while she is praised for her beauty, and remarked for her youth. Neither do I find it asserted (unless the hint of Sandi be an assertion), that the Doge was actuated by jealousy of his wife; but rather by respect for her, and for his own honour, warranted by his past services and recent dignity.

I know not that the historical facts are alluded to in English, unless by Dr. Moore in his View of Italy. His account is false and flippant, full of stale jests about old men and young wives, and wondering at so great an effect from so slight a cause. How so acute and severe an observer of mankind as the author of Zeluco could wonder at this is inconceivable. He knew that a basin of water spilt on Mrs. Masham's gown deprived the Duke of Marlborough of his command, and led to the inglorious peace of Utrecht—that Louis XIV. was plunged into the most desolating wars, because his minister was nettled at his finding fault with a window, and wished to give him another occupation—that Helen lost Troy—that Lucretia expelled the Tarquins from Rome—and that Cava brought the Moors to Spain—that an insulted husband led the Gauls to Clusium, and thence to Rome—that a single verse of Frederick II. of Prussia on the Abbé de Bernis, and a jest on Madame de Pompadour, led to the battle of Rosbach—that the elopement of Dearbhorgil with Mac Murchad conducted the English to the slavery of Ireland—that a personal pique between Maria Antoinette and the Duke of Orleans precipitated the first expulsion of the Bourbons—and, not to multiply instances, that Commodus, Domitian, and Caligula fell victims not to their public tyranny, but to private vengeance—and that in order to make Cromwell disembark from the ship in which he would have sailed to America destroyed both King and Commonwealth. After these instances, on the least reflection, it is indeed extraordinary in Dr. Moore to seem surprised that a man used to command, who had served and swayed in the most important offices, should fiercely resent, in a fierce age, an unpunished affront. The grossest that can be offered to a man, be he prince or peasant. The age of Faliero is little to the purpose, unless to favour it—

> 'The young man's wrath is like straw on fire,
> But like red-hot steel is the old man's ire.'

> 'Young men soon give and soon forget affronts,
> Old age is slow at both.'

Laugier's reflections are more philosophical:—'Tale fù il fine ignominioso di un' uomo, che la sua

MARINO FALIERO, DOGE OF VENICE

nascità, la sua età, il suo carattere dovevano tener lontano dalle passioni produttrici di grandi delitti
I suoi *talenti* per lungo tempo esercitati ne' maggiori impieghi, la sua capacità sperimentata ne' goverr
e nelle ambasciate, gli avevano acquistato la stima e la fiducia de' cittadini, ed avevano uniti i suffrag
per collocarlo alla testa della repubblica. Innalzato ad un grado che terminava gloriosamente la su
vita, il risentimento di un' ingiuria leggiera insinuò nel suo cuore tal veleno che bastò a corromper
le antiche sue qualità, e a condurlo al termine dei scellerati; serio esempio, che prova *non esservi età*
in cui la prudenza umana sia sicura, e che nell' uomo restano sempre passioni capaci a disonorarlo, quand
non invigili sopra se stesso.'

Where did Dr. Moore find that Marino Faliero begged his life? I have searched the chroniclers
and find nothing of the kind: it is true that he avowed it. He was conducted to the place of torture
but there is no mention made of any application for mercy on his part; and the very circumstance o
their having taken him to the rack seems to argue anything but his having shown a want of firmness
which would doubtless have been also mentioned by those minute historians, who by no means favou
him: such, indeed, would be contrary to his character as a soldier, to the age in which he lived, an
at which he died, as it is to the truth of history. I know no justification, at any distance of time, fo
calumniating an historical character: surely truth belongs to the dead, and to the unfortunate: an
they who have died upon a scaffold have generally had faults enough of their own, without attributin
to them that which the very incurring of the perils which conducted them to their violent death render
of all others, the most improbable. The black veil which is painted over the place of Marino Falier
amongst the Doges, and the Giants' Staircase where he was crowned, and discrowned, and decapitated
struck forcibly upon my imagination; as did his fiery character and strange story. I went, in 1819
in search of his tomb more than once to the church San Giovanni e San Paolo; and, as I was standin
before the monument of another family, a priest came up to me and said, 'I can show you finer monu
ments than that.' I told him that I was in search of that of the Faliero family, and particularly of th
Doge Marino's. 'Oh,' said he, 'I will show it you'; and conducting me to the outside, pointed ou
a sarcophagus in the wall with an illegible inscription. He said that it had been in a convent adjoinin
but was removed after the French came, and placed in its present situation; that he had seen the tom
opened at its removal; there were still some bones remaining, but no positive vestige of the decapitatio
The equestrian statue of which I have made mention in the third act as before that church is no
however, of a Faliero, but of some other now obsolete warrior, although of a later date. There wen
two other Doges of this family prior to Marino; Ordelafo, who fell in battle at Zara, in 1117 (whe
his descendant afterwards conquered the Huns), and Vital Faliero, who reigned in 1082. The family
originally from Fano, was of the most illustrious in blood and wealth in the city of once the mos
wealthy and still the most ancient families in Europe. The length I have gone into on this subjec
will show the interest I have taken in it. Whether I have succeeded or not in the tragedy, I have a
least transferred into our language an historical fact worthy of commemoration.

It is now four years that I have meditated this work; and before I had sufficiently examined th
records, I was rather disposed to have made it turn on a jealousy in Faliero. But, perceiving n
foundation for this in historical truth, and aware that jealousy is an exhausted passion in the dram
I have given it a more historical form. I was, besides, well advised by the late Matthew Lewis o
that point, in talking with him of my intention at Venice in 1817. 'If you make him jealous,' said h
'recollect that you have to contend with established writers, to say nothing of Shakspeare, and a
exhausted subject:—stick to the old fiery Doge's natural character, which will bear you out, if proper
drawn: and make your plot as regular as you can.' Sir William Drummond gave me nearly the sam
counsel. How far I have followed these instructions, or whether they have availed me, is not for m
to decide. I have had no view to the stage; in its present state it is, perhaps, not a very exalted obje
of ambition; besides, I have been too much behind the scenes to have thought it so at any time. An
I cannot conceive any man of irritable feeling putting himself at the mercies of an audience. Th
sneering reader, and the loud critic, and the tart review, are scattered and distant calamities; but th
trampling of an intelligent or of an ignorant audience on a production which, be it good or bad, ha
been a mental labour to the writer, is a palpable and immediate grievance, heightened by a man'
doubt of their competency to judge, and his certainty of his own imprudence in electing them h
judges. Were I capable of writing a play which could be deemed stage-worthy, success would giv
me no pleasure, and failure great pain. It is for this reason that, even during the time of being on
of the committee of one of the theatres, I never made the attempt, and never will. But surely ther
is dramatic power somewhere, where Joanna Baillie, and Milman, and John Wilson exist. The 'Cit
of the Plague' and the 'Fall of Jerusalem' are full of the best *materiel* for tragedy that has been see
since Horace Walpole, except passages of Ethwald and De Montfort. It is the fashion to underrat
Horace Walpole; firstly, because he was a nobleman, and secondly, because he was a gentleman; bu
to say nothing of the composition of his incomparable letters, and of the 'Castle of Otranto,' he
the 'Ultimus Romanorum,' the author of the 'Mysterious Mother,' a tragedy of the highest orde
and not a puling love-play. He is the father of the first romance and of the last tragedy in our languag
and surely worthy of a higher place than any living writer, be he who he may.

In speaking of the drama of 'Marino Faliero,' I forgot to mention, that the desire of preservin
though still too remote, a nearer approach to unity than the irregularity, which is the reproach
the English theatrical compositions, permits, has induced me to represent the conspiracy as alread
formed, and the Doge acceding to it; whereas, in fact, it was of his own preparation, and that
Israel Bertuccio. The other characters (except that of the Duchess), incidents, and almost the tim
which was wonderfully short for such a design in real life, are strictly historical, except that all th
consultations took place in the palace. Had I followed this, the unity would have been better pr
served; but I wished to produce the Doge in the full assembly of the conspirators, instead of mono
tonously placing him always in dialogue with the same individuals. For the real facts, I refer to th
Appendix.

* Laugier, Hist. de la Répub. de Venise.

MARINO FALIERO, DOGE OF VENICE

DRAMATIS PERSONÆ

MEN

MARINO FALIERO, *Doge of Venice.*
BERTUCCIO FALIERO, *Nephew of the Doge.*
LIONI, *a Patrician and Senator.*
BENINTENDE, *Chief of the Council of Ten.*
MICHEL STENO, *One of the three Capi of the Forty.*
ISRAEL BERTUCCIO, *Chief of the Arsenal.*
PHILIP CALENDARO, } *Conspirators.*
DAGOLINO,
BERTRAM,
Signor of the Night, } *'Signore di Notte,' one of the Officers belonging to the Republic.*

First Citizen.
Second Citizen.
Third Citizen.
VINCENZO,
PIETRO, } *Officers belonging to the Ducal Palace.*
BATTISTA,
Secretary *of the Council of Ten.*
Guards, Conspirators, Citizens, the Council of Ten, the Giunta, &c., &c.

WOMEN

ANGIOLINA, *Wife to the Doge.*
MARIANNA, *her Friend.*

Female Attendants, &c.

SCENE.—VENICE *in the year* 1355

ACT I

SCENE I.—*An Antechamber in the Ducal Palace.*

PIETRO *speaks, in entering, to* BATTISTA.

Pie. Is not the messenger return'd?
Bat. Not yet;
Have sent frequently, as you commanded,
But still the Signory is deep in council,
And long debate on Steno's accusation.
Pie. Too long—at least so thinks the Doge.
Bat. How bears he 5
These moments of suspense?
Pie. With struggling patience.
Placed at the ducal table, cover'd o'er
With all the apparel of the state; petitions,
Despatches, judgments, acts, reprieves, reports,
He sits as rapt in duty; but whene'er 10
He hears the jarring of a distant door,
Or aught that intimates a coming step,
Or murmur of a voice, his quick eye wanders,
And he will start up from his chair, then pause, 14
And seat himself again, and fix his gaze
Upon some edict; but I have observed
For the last hour he has not turned a leaf.
Bat. 'Tis said he is much moved,—and doubtless 'twas
Foul scorn in Steno to offend so grossly.
Pie. Ay, if a poor man: Steno's a patrician, 20
Young, galliard, gay, and haughty.
Bat. Then you think
He will not be judged hardly?
Pie. 'Twere enough
He be judged justly, but 'tis not for us
To anticipate the sentence of the Forty.
Bat. And here it comes.—What news, Vincenzo?

Enter VINCENZO.

Vin. 'Tis 25
Decided; but as yet his doom's unknown:

I saw the president in act to seal
The parchment which will bear the Forty's judgment
Unto the Doge, and hasten to inform him.
[*Exeunt.*

SCENE II.—*The Ducal Chamber.*

MARINO FALIERO, *Doge; and his Nephew,* BERTUCCIO FALIERO.

Ber. F. It cannot be but they will do you justice.
Doge. Ay, such as the Avogadori did,
Who sent up my appeal unto the Forty
To try him by his peers, his own tribunal.
Ber. F. His peers will scarce protect him; such an act 5
Would bring contempt on all authority.
Doge. Know you not Venice? Know you not the Forty?
But we shall see anon.
Ber. F. [*addressing* VINCENZO, *then entering*]. How now—what tidings?
Vin. I am charged to tell his highness that the court
Has pass'd its resolution, and that, soon
As the due forms of judgment are gone through, 11
The sentence will be sent up to the Doge;
In the mean time the Forty doth salute
The Prince of the Republic, and entreat
His acceptation of their duty.
Doge. Yes— 15
They are wondrous dutiful, and ever humble.
Sentence is pass'd, you say?
Vin. It is, your highness:
The president was sealing it, when I
Was call'd in, that no moment might be lost
In forwarding the intimation due 20
Not only to the Chief of the Republic,
But the complainant, both in one united.
Ber. F. Are you aware, from aught you have perceived,
Of their decision?
Vin. No, my lord; you know
The secret custom of the courts in Venice.

409

Ber. F. True; but there still is some-
thing given to guess, 26
Which a shrewd gleaner and quick eye
would catch at;
A whisper, or a murmur, or an air
More or less solemn spread o'er the tri-
bunal.
The Forty are but men—most worthy men,
And wise, and just, and cautious—this I
grant— 31
And secret as the grave to which they
doom
The guilty: but with all this, in their as-
pects—
At least in some, the juniors of the num-
ber—
A searching eye, an eye like yours, Vin-
cenzo, 35
Would read the sentence ere it was pro-
nounced.
Vin. My lord, I came away upon the
moment,
And had no leisure to take note of that
Which pass'd among the judges, even in
seeming;
My station near the accused too, Michel
Steno, 40
Made me—
Doge [*abruptly*]. And how look'd *he*?
deliver that.
Vin. Calm, but not overcast, he stood
resign'd
To the decree, whate'er it were;—but lo!
It comes, for the perusal of his highness.

Enter the SECRETARY *of the Forty.*

Sec. The high tribunal of the Forty
sends 45
Health and respect to the Doge Faliero,
Chief magistrate of Venice, and requests
His highness to peruse and to approve
The sentence pass'd on Michel Steno, born
Patrician, and arraign'd upon the charge
Contain'd, together with its penalty, 51
Within the rescript which I now present.
Doge. Retire, and wait without.
Exeunt SECRETARY *and* VINCENZO.
Take thou this paper:
The misty letters vanish from my eyes;
I cannot fix them.
Ber. F. Patience, my dear uncle: 55
Why do you tremble thus?—nay, doubt
not, all
Will be as could be wish'd.
Doge. Say on.
Ber. F. [*reading*]. 'Decreed
In council, without one dissenting voice,
That Michel Steno, by his own confession,
Guilty on the last night of Carnival 60
Of having graven on the ducal throne
The following words—'
Doge. Wouldst thou repeat them?
Wouldst *thou* repeat them—*thou*, a Fali-
ero,

Harp on the deep dishonour of our hous
Dishonour'd in its chief—that chief th
prince
Of Venice, first of cities?—To the sen
tence.
Ber. F. Forgive me, my good lord;
will obey—
[*Reads*]. 'That Michel Steno be detain'
a month
In close arrest.'
Doge. Proceed.
Ber. F. My Lord, 'tis finish'
Doge. How say you?—finish'd! Do
dream?—'tis false—
Give me the paper—[*Snatches the pap
and reads*]—''Tis decreed in cou
cil
That Michael Steno'——Nephew, thi
arm!
Ber. F. Na
Cheer up, be calm; this transport is u
call'd for—
Let me seek some assistance.
Doge. Stop, sir—Stir not
'Tis past.
Ber. F. I cannot but agree with you
The sentence is too slight for the offenc
It is not honourable in the Forty
To affix so slight a penalty to that
Which was a foul affront to you, and ev
To them, as being your subjects; but '
not
Yet without remedy: you can appeal
To them once more, or to the Avogado
Who, seeing that true justice is withhel
Will now take up the cause they once d
clined,
And do you right upon the bold deli
quent.
Think you not thus, good uncle? why
you stand
So fix'd? You heed me not:—I pray yo
hear me!
Doge [*dashing down the Ducal bonn
and offering to trample upon it, e
claims, as he is withheld by
nephew*].
Oh! that the Saracen were in St. Mark'
Thus would I do him homage.
Ber. F. For the sake
Of Heaven and all its saints, my lord—
Doge. Awa
Oh, that the Genoese were in the port
Oh, that the Huns whom I o'erthrew
Zara
Were ranged around the palace!
Ber. F. 'Tis not w
In Venice' Duke to say so.
Doge. Venice' Duk
Who now is Duke in Venice? let me s
him,
That he may do me right.
Ber. F. If you forg
Your office, and its dignity and duty,

Remember that of man, and curb this
 passion.
The Duke of Venice ——
 Doge [interrupting him]. There is no
 such thing—
It is a word—nay, worse—a worthless by-
 word: 100
The most despised, wrong'd, outraged,
 helpless wretch,
Who begs his bread, if 'tis refused by one,
May win it from another kinder heart;
But he, who is denied his right by those
Whose place it is to do no wrong, is poorer
Than the rejected beggar—he's a slave—
And that am I, and thou, and all our
 house, 107
Even from this hour; the meanest artisan
Will point the finger, and the haughty noble
May spit upon us:—where is our redress?
 Ber. F. The law, my prince——
 Doge [interrupting him]. You see what
 it has done; 111
ask'd no remedy but from the law,
sought no vengeance but redress by law,
call'd no judges but those named by law;
As sovereign, I appeal'd unto my subjects,
The very subjects who had made me sove-
 reign, 116
And gave me thus a double right to be so.
The rights of place and choice, of birth and
 service,
Honours and years, these scars, these
 hoary hairs,
The travel, toil, the perils, the fatigues,
The blood and sweat of almost eighty
 years, 121
Were weigh'd i' the balance, 'gainst the
 foulest stain,
The grossest insult, most contemptuous
 crime
Of a rank, rash patrician—and found
 wanting!
And this is to be borne!
 Ber. F. I say not that:— 125
In case your fresh appeal should be re-
 jected,
We will find other means to make all even.
 Doge. Appeal again! art thou my
 brother's son?
A scion of the house of Faliero?
The nephew of a Doge? and of that blood
Which hath already given three dukes to
 Venice? 131
But thou say'st well—we must be humble
 now.
 Ber. F. My princely uncle! you are too
 much moved;—
I grant it was a gross offence, and grossly
Left without fitting punishment: but still
This fury doth exceed the provocation,
Or any provocation: if we are wrong'd,
We will ask justice; if it be denied, 138
We'll take it; but may do all this in calm-
 ness—

Deep Vengeance is the daughter of deep
 Silence. 140
I have yet scarce a third part of your years,
I love our house, I honour you, its chief,
The guardian of my youth, and its in-
 structor—
But though I understand your grief, and
 enter 144
In part of your disdain, it doth appal me
To see your anger, like our Adrian waves,
O'ersweep all bounds, and foam itself to
 air.
 Doge. I tell thee—must I tell thee—
 what thy father
Would have required no words to compre-
 hend?
Hast thou no feeling save the external
 sense 150
Of torture from the touch? hast thou no
 soul—
No pride—no passion—no deep sense of
 honour?
 Ber. F. 'Tis the first time that honour
 has been doubted,
And were the last, from any other sceptic.
 Doge. You know the full offence of this
 born villain, 155
This creeping, coward, rank, acquitted
 felon,
Who threw his sting into a poisonous libel,
And on the honour of—Oh God! my wife,
The nearest, dearest part of all men's
 honour,
Left a base slur to pass from mouth to
 mouth 160
Of loose mechanics, with all coarse foul
 comments,
And villainous jests, and blasphemies ob-
 scene;
While sneering nobles, in more polish'd
 guise,
Whisper'd the tale, and smiled upon the
 lie
Which made me look like them—a cour-
 teous wittol, 165
Patient—ay, proud, it may be, of dis-
 honour.
 Ber. F. But still it was a lie—you knew
 it false
And so did all men.
 Doge. Nephew, the high Roman
Said, 'Cæsar's wife must not even be sus-
 pected,'
And put her from him.
 Ber. F. True—but in those days——
 Doge. What is it that a Roman would
 not suffer, 171
That a Venetian prince must bear? old
 Dandolo
Refused the diadem of all the Cæsars,
And wore the ducal cap I trample on,
Because 'tis now degraded.
 Ber. F. 'Tis even so.
 Doge. It is—it is;—I did not visit on

411

The innocent creature thus most vilely
 slander'd
Because she took an old man for her lord,
For that he had been long her father's
 friend
And patron of her house, as if there were
No love in woman's heart but lust of
 youth 181
And beardless faces;—I did not for this
Visit the villain's infamy on her,
But craved my country's justice on his
 head,
The justice due unto the humblest being
Who hath a wife whose faith is sweet to
 him, 186
Who hath a home whose hearth is dear to
 him,
Who hath a name whose honour's all to
 him,
When these are tainted by the accursing
 breath
Of calumny and scorn.
 Ber. F. And what redress 190
Did you expect as his fit punishment?
 Doge. Death! Was I not the sovereign
 of the state—
Insulted on his very throne, and made
A mockery to the men who should obey
 me? 194
Was I not injured as a husband? scorn'd
As man? reviled, degraded, as a prince?
Was not offence like his a complication
Of insult and of treason?—and he lives!
Had he instead of on the Doge's throne
Stamp'd the same brand upon a peasant's
 stool, 200
His blood had gilt the threshold; for the
 carle
Had stabb'd him on the instant.
 Ber. F. Do not doubt it,
He shall not live till sunset—leave to me
The means, and calm yourself.
 Doge. Hold, nephew: this
Would have sufficed but yesterday; at
 present 205
I have no further wrath against this man.
 Ber. F. What mean you? is not the
 offence redoubled
By this most rank—I will not say—ac-
 quittal;
For it is worse, being full acknowledgment
Of the offence, and leaving it unpunish'd?
 Doge. It is *redoubled*, but not now by
 him: 211
The Forty hath decreed a month's arrest—
We must obey the Forty.
 Ber. F. Obey *them!*
Who have forgot their duty to the sove-
 reign?
 Doge. Why, yes;—boy, you perceive it
 then at last: 215
Whether as fellow citizen who sues
For justice, or as sovereign who com-
 mands it,

They have defrauded me of both my right
(For here the sovereign is a citizen);
But, notwithstanding, harm not thou
 hair 22
Of Steno's head—he shall not wear it long
 Ber. F. Not twelve hours longer, ha
 you left to me
The mode and means: if you had calmly
 heard me,
I never meant this miscreant should es
 cape,
But wish'd you to repress such gusts o
 passion, 22
That we more surely might devise to
 gether
His taking off.
 Doge. No, nephew, he must live;
At least, just now—a life so vile as his
Were nothing at this hour; in th' older
 time 22
Some sacrifices ask'd a single victim,
Great expiations had a hecatomb.
 Ber. F. Your wishes are my law: an
 yet I fain
Would prove to you how near unto my
 heart
The honour of our house must ever be.
 Doge. Fear not; you shall have time an
 place of proof: 23
But be not thou too rash, as I have been
I am ashamed of my own anger now;
I pray you, pardon me.
 Ber. F. Why, that's my uncle
The leader, and the statesman, and th
 chief
Of commonwealths, and sovereign o
 himself! 24
I wonder'd to perceive you so forget
All prudence in your fury at these years
Although the cause——
 Doge. Ay, think upon the cause—
Forget it not:—When you lie down to rest
Let it be black among your dreams; an
 when 24
The morn returns, so let it stand betwee
The sun and you, as an ill-omen'd clou
Upon a summer day of festival:
So will it stand to me;—but speak not, sti
 not,—
Leave all to me; we shall have much to do
And you shall have a part.—But now re
 tire, 25
'Tis fit I were alone.
 Ber. F. [*taking up and placing the duca
 bonnet on the table*]. Ere I depart,
I pray you to resume what you hav
 spurn'd,
Till you can change it haply for a crown
And now I take my leave, imploring yo
In all things to rely upon my duty 25
As doth become your near and faithfu
And not less loyal citizen and subject.
 [*Exit* BERTUCCIO FALIERO

Doge [*solus*]. Adieu, my worthy
 nephew.—Hollow bauble!
 [*Taking up the ducal cap.*
Beset with all the thorns that line a crown,
Without investing the insulted brow 261
With the all-swaying majesty of kings;
Thou idle, gilded, and degraded toy,
Let me resume thee as I would a vizor.
 [*Puts it on.*
How my brain aches beneath thee! and
 my temples 265
Throb feverish under thy dishonest weight.
Could I not turn thee to a diadem?
Could I not shatter the Briarean sceptre
Which in this hundred-handed senate
 rules,
Making the people nothing, and the
 prince 270
A pageant? In my life I have achieved
Tasks not less difficult—achieved for them,
Who thus repay me! Can I not requite
 them?
Oh for one year! Oh! but for even a day
Of my full youth, while yet my body
 served 275
My soul as serves the generous steed his
 lord,
would have dash'd amongst them, asking
 few
In aid to overthrow these swoln patricians;
But now I must look round for other hands
To serve this hoary head;—but it shall
 plan 280
In such a sort as will not leave the task
Herculean, though as yet 'tis but a chaos
Of darkly brooding thoughts: my fancy is
In her first work, more nearly to the light
Holding the sleeping images of things
For the selection of the pausing judg-
 ment.— 286
The troops are few in——

 Enter VINCENZO.

Vin. There is one without
Craves audience of your highness.
 Doge. I'm unwell—
I can see no one, not even a patrician—
Let him refer his business to the council.
 Vin. My lord, I will deliver your reply;
It cannot much import—he's a plebeian,
The master of a galley, I believe. 293
 Doge. How! did you say the patron of
 a galley?
That is—I mean—a servant of the state:
Admit him, he may be on public service.
 [*Exit* VINCENZO.
Doge [*solus*]. This patron may be
 sounded; I will try him. 297
I know the people to be discontented:
They have cause, since Sapienza's adverse
 day,
When Genoa conquer'd: they have further
 cause, 300
Since they are nothing in the state, and in

The city worse than nothing—mere
 machines,
To serve the nobles' most patrician plea-
 sure.
The troops have long arrears of pay, oft
 promised,
And murmur deeply—any hope of change
Will draw them forward: they shall pay
 themselves 306
With plunder:—but the priests—I doubt
 the priesthood
Will not be with us; they have hated us
Since that rash hour, when, madden'd
 with the drone,
I smote the tardy bishop at Treviso, 310
Quickening his holy march; yet ne'erthe-
 less,
They may be won, at least their chief at
 Rome,
By some well-timed concessions; but, above
All things, I must be speedy: at my hour
Of twilight little light of life remains. 315
Could I free Venice, and avenge my
 wrongs,
I had lived too long, and willingly would
 sleep
Next moment with my sires; and, wanting
 this,
Better that sixty of my fourscore years
Had been already where—how soon, I
 care not— 320
The whole must be extinguish'd; better that
They ne'er had been, than drag me on to
 be
The thing these arch-oppressors fain
 would make me.
Let me consider—of efficient troops
There are three thousand posted at——

 Enter VINCENZO *and* ISRAEL BERTUCCIO.

 Vin. May it please 325
Your highness, the same patron whom I
 spake of
Is here to crave your patience.
 Doge. Leave the chamber,
Vincenzo.— [*Exit* VINCENZO.
 Sir, you may advance—what
 would you?
I. Ber. Redress.
 Doge. Of whom?
 I. Ber. Of God and of the Doge.
 Doge. Alas! my friend, you seek it of
 the twain 330
Of least respect and interest in Venice.
You must address the council.
 I. Ber. 'Twere in vain;
For he who injured me is one of them.
 Doge. There's blood upon thy face—
 how came it there?
 I. Ber. 'Tis mine, and not the first I've
 shed for Venice, 335
But the first shed by a Venetian hand:
A noble smote me.
 Doge. Doth he live?

413

I. Ber. Not long—
But for the hope I had and have, that you,
My prince, yourself a soldier, will redress
Him, whom the laws of discipline and
 Venice 340
Permit not to protect himself:—if not—
I say no more.
Doge. But something you would do—
Is it not so?
I. Ber. I am a man, my lord.
Doge. Why so is he who smote you.
I. Ber. He is call'd so;
Nay, more, a noble one—at least, in
 Venice: 345
But since he hath forgotten that I am one,
And treats me like a brute, the brute may
 turn—
'Tis said the worm will.
Doge. Say—his name and lineage?
I. Ber. Barbaro.
Doge. What was the cause? or
 the pretext?
I. Ber. I am the chief of the arsenal, em-
 ploy'd 350
At present in repairing certain galleys
But roughly used by the Genoese last year.
This morning comes the noble Barbaro
Full of reproof, because our artisans 354
Had left some frivolous order of his house,
To execute the state's decree: I dared
To justify the men—he raised his hand;—
Behold my blood! the first time it e'er
 flow'd
Dishonourably.
Doge. Have you long time served?
I. Ber. So long as to remember Zara's
 siege, 360
And fight beneath the chief who beat the
 Huns there,
Sometime my general, now the Doge Fa-
 liero.—
Doge. How! are we comrades?—the
 state's ducal robes
Sit newly on me, and you were appointed
Chief of the arsenal ere I came from Rome;
So that I recognised you not. Who placed
 you? 366
I. Ber. The late Doge; keeping still my
 old command
As patron of a galley: my new office
Was given as the reward of certain scars
(So was your predecessor pleased to say):
I little thought his bounty would conduct
 me 371
To his successor as a helpless plaintiff;
At least, in such a cause.
Doge. Are you much hurt?
I. Ber. Irreparably in my self-esteem.
Doge. Speak out; fear nothing: being
 stung at heart, 375
What would you do to be revenged on this
 man?
I. Ber. That which I dare not name,
 and yet will do.

Doge. Then wherefore came you here?
I. Ber. I come for justice
Because my general is Doge, and will not
See his old soldier trampled on. Had any
Save Faliero, fill'd the ducal throne,
This blood had been wash'd out in other
 blood.
Doge. You come to me for justice—
 unto *me!*
The Doge of Venice, and I cannot give it!
I cannot even obtain it—'twas denied 385
To me most solemnly an hour ago!
I. Ber. How says your highness?
Doge. Steno is condemn'd
To a month's confinement.
I. Ber. What! the same who dared
To stain the ducal throne with those four
 words,
That have cried shame to every ear in
 Venice? 390
Doge. Ay, doubtless they have echo'd
 o'er the arsenal,
Keeping due time with every hammer's
 clink
As a good jest to jolly artisans;
Or making chorus to the creaking oar,
In the vile tune of every galley-slave,
Who, as he sung the merry stave, exulted
He was not a shamed dotard like the Doge.
I. Ber. Is't possible? a month's im-
 prisonment!
No more for Steno?
Doge. You have heard the offence,
And now you know his punishment; and
 then 400
You ask redress of *me!* Go to the Forty,
Who pass'd the sentence upon Michel
 Steno;
They'll do as much by Barbaro, no doubt.
I. Ber. Ah! dared I speak my feelings!
Doge. Give them breath.
Mine have no further outrage to endure.
I. Ber. Then in a word, it rests but on
 your word 406
To punish and avenge—I will not say
My petty wrong, for what is a mere blow,
However vile, to such a thing as I am?—
But the base insult done your state and
 person. 410
Doge. You overrate my power, which
 is a pageant.
This cap is not the monarch's crown; these
 robes
Might move compassion, like a beggar's
 rags;
Nay, more, a beggar's are his own, and
 these
But lent to the poor puppet, who must
 play
Its part with all its empire in this ermine. 415
I. Ber. Wouldst thou be king?
Doge. Yes—of a happy people.
I. Ber. Wouldst thou be sovereign lord
 of Venice?

Doge. Ay,
f that the people shared that sovereignty,
o that nor they nor I were further slaves
o this o'ergrown aristocratic Hydra, 421
he poisonous heads of whose envenom'd
 body
Iave breathed a pestilence upon us all.
 I. Ber. Yet, thou wast born, and still
 hast lived, patrician.
 Doge. In evil hour was I so born; my
 birth 425
Iath made me Doge to be insulted: but
 lived and toil'd a soldier and a servant
Df Venice and her people, not the senate;
heir good and my own honour were my
 guerdon.
have fought and bled; commanded, ay,
 and conquer'd; 430
Iave made and marr'd peace oft in em-
 bassies,
As it might chance to be our country's
 'vantage;
Iave traversed land and sea in constant
 duty,
hrough almost sixty years, and still for
 Venice,
My fathers' and my birthplace, whose
 dear spires, 435
Rising at distance o'er the blue Lagoon,
t was reward enough for me to view
Once more; but not for any knot of men,
Nor sect, nor faction, did I bleed or sweat!
But would you know why I have done all
 this? 440
Ask of the bleeding pelican why she
Iath ripp'd her bosom? Had the bird a
 voice,
he'd tell thee 'twas for *all* her little ones.
 I. Ber. And yet they made thee duke.
 Doge. *They made* me so;
sought it not, the flattering fetters met
 me 445
Returning from my Roman embassy,
And never having hitherto refused
Toil, charge, or duty for the state, I did not,
At these late years, decline what was the
 highest 449
Df all in seeming, but of all most base
n what we have to do and to endure:
Bear witness for me thou, my injured sub-
 ject,
When I can neither right myself nor thee.
 I. Ber. You shall do both, if you possess
 the will;
And many thousands more not less op-
 press'd, 455
Who wait but for a signal—will you give
 it?
 Doge. You speak in riddles.
 I. Ber. Which shall soon be read
At peril of my life, if you disdain not
To lend a patient ear.
 Doge. Say on.
 I. Ber. Not thou,

Nor I alone, are injured and abused, 460
Contemn'd and trampled on; but the
 whole people
Groan with the strong conception of their
 wrongs;
The foreign soldiers in the senate's pay
Are discontented for their long arrears;
The native mariners, and civic troops,
Feel with their friends; for who is he
 amongst them 466
Whose brethren, parents, children wives,
 or sisters,
Have not partook oppression, or pollu-
 tion,
From the patricians? And the hopeless
 war
Against the Genoese, which is still main-
 tain'd 470
With the plebeian blood, and treasure
 wrung
From their hard earnings, has inflamed
 them further:
Even now—but, I forget that speaking
 thus,
Perhaps I pass the sentence of my death!
 Doge. And suffering what thou hast
 done—fear'st thou death? 475
Be silent then, and live on, to be beaten
By those for whom thou hast bled.
 I. Ber. No, I will speak
At every hazard; and if Venice' Doge
Should turn delator, be the shame on him,
And sorrow too; for he will lose far more
Than I.
 Doge. From me fear nothing; out with
 it! 481
 I. Ber. Know then, that there are met
 and sworn in secret
A band of brethren, valiant hearts and
 true;
Men who have proved all fortunes, and
 have long
Grieved over that of Venice, and have
 right 485
To do so; having served her in all climes,
And having rescued her from foreign foes,
Would do the same from those within her
 walls.
They are not numerous, nor yet too few
For their great purpose; they have arms,
 and means, 490
And hearts, and hopes, and faith, and
 patient courage.
 Doge. For what then do they pause?
 I. Ber. An hour to strike.
 Doge [*aside*]. Saint Mark's shall strike
 that hour!
 I. Ber. I now have placed
My life, my honour, all my earthly hopes
Within thy power, but in the firm belief
That injuries like ours, sprung from one
 cause, 496
Will generate one vengeance: should it
 be so,

415

Be our chief now—our sovereign here-
after.
Doge. How many are ye?
I. Ber. I'll not answer that
Till I am answer'd.
Doge. How, sir! do you menace?
I. Ber. No; I affirm. I have betray'd
myself; 501
But there's no torture in the mystic wells
Which undermine your palace, nor in those
Not less appalling cells, the 'leaden roofs,'
To force a single name from me of others.
The Pozzi and the Piombi were in vain;
They might wring blood from me, but
treachery never. 507
And I would pass the fearful 'Bridge of
Sighs,'
Joyous that mine must be the last that e'er
Would echo o'er the Stygian wave which
flows 510
Between the murderers and the murder'd,
washing
The prison and the palace walls: there are
Those who would live to think on't, and
avenge me.
Doge. If such your power and purpose,
why come here 514
To sue for justice, being in the course
To do yourself due right?
I. Ber. Because the man,
Who claims protection from authority,
Showing his confidence and his submission
To that authority, can hardly be 519
Suspected of combining to destroy it.
Had I sate down too humbly with this blow,
A moody brow and mutter'd threats had
made me
A mark'd man to the Forty's inquisition;
But loud complaint, however angrily 524
It shapes its phrase, is little to be fear'd,
And less distrusted. But, besides all this,
I had another reason.
Doge. What was that?
I. Ber. Some rumours that the Doge
was greatly moved
By the reference of the Avogadori
Of Michel Steno's sentence to the Forty
Had reach'd me. I had served you,
honour'd you, 531
And felt that you were dangerously in-
sulted,
Being of an order of such spirits, as
Requite tenfold both good and evil: 'twas
My wish to prove and urge you to redress.
Now you know all; and that I speak the
truth, 536
My peril be the proof.
Doge. You have deeply ventured;
But all must do so who would greatly win;
Thus far I'll answer you—your secret's
safe.
I. Ber. And is this all?
Doge. Unless with all intrusted,
What would you have me answer?

I. Ber. I would have you
Trust him who leaves his life in trust with
you.
Doge. But I must know your plan, your
names, and numbers;
The last may then be doubled, and the
former
Matured and strengthen'd.
I. Ber. We're enough already; 54
You are the sole ally we covet now.
Doge. But bring me to the knowledge
of your chiefs.
I. Ber. That shall be done upon your
formal pledge
To keep the faith that we will pledge to
you.
Doge. When? where?
I. Ber. This night I'll bring to your
apartment 55
Two of the principals: a greater number
Were hazardous.
Doge. Stay, I must think of this.—
What if I were to trust myself amongst you
And leave the palace?
I. Ber. You must come alone
Doge. With but my nephew.
I. Ber. Not were he your son. 55
Doge. Wretch! darest thou name my
son? He died in arms
At Sapienza for this faithless state.
Oh! that he were alive, and I in ashes!
Or that he were alive ere I be ashes!
I should not need the dubious aid of
strangers. 56
I. Ber. Not one of all those strangers
whom thou doubtest,
But will regard thee with a filial feeling,
So that thou keep'st a father's faith with
them.
Doge. The die is cast. Where is the
place of meeting?
I. Ber. At midnight I will be alone and
mask'd 56
Where'er your highness pleases to direct
me,
To wait your coming, and conduct you
where
You shall receive our homage, and pro-
nounce
Upon our project.
Doge. At what hour arises
The moon?
I. Ber. Late, but the atmosphere is
thick and dusky, 57
'Tis a sirocco.
Doge. At the midnight hour, then,
Near to the church where sleep my sires
the same,
Twin-named from the apostles John and
Paul;
A gondola, with one oar only, will
Lurk in the narrow channel which glides
by. 57
Be there.

416

I. Ber. I will not fail.
Doge. And now retire——
I. Ber. In the full hope your highness
 will not falter
In your great purpose. Prince, I take my
 leave. [*Exit* ISRAEL BERTUCCIO.
Doge [*solus*]. At midnight, by the church
 Saints John and Paul, 579
Where sleep my noble fathers, I repair—
To what? to hold a council in the dark
With common ruffians leagued to ruin
 states!
And will not my great sires leap from the
 vault,
Where lie two doges who preceded me,
And pluck me down amongst them?
 Would they could! 585
For I should rest in honour with the
 honour'd.
Alas! I must not think of them, but those
Who have made me thus unworthy of a
 name
Noble and brave as aught of consular
On Roman marbles; but I will redeem it
Back to its antique lustre in our annals,
By sweet revenge on all that's base in
 Venice, 592
And freedom to the rest, or leave it black
To all the growing calumnies of time,
Which never spare the fame of him who
 fails,
But try the Cæsar, or the Catiline,
By the true touchstone of desert—success.

ACT II

SCENE I.—*An Apartment in the Ducal
 Palace.*

ANGIOLINA (*wife of the* DOGE) *and*
 MARIANNA.

Ang. What was the Doge's answer?
Mar. That he was
That moment summon'd to a conference.
But 'tis by this time ended. I perceived
Not long ago the senators embarking;
And the last gondola may now be seen
Gliding into the throng of barks which stud
The glittering waters.
Ang. Would he were return'd!
He has been much disquieted of late;
And Time, which has not tamed his fiery
 spirit,
Nor yet enfeebled even his mortal frame,
Which seems to me more nourish'd by
 a soul 11
So quick and restless that it would con-
 sume
Less hardy clay—Time has but little power
On his resentments or his griefs. Unlike
To other spirits of his order, who, 15
In the first burst of passion, pour away
Their wrath or sorrow, all things wear in
 him

An aspect of eternity: his thoughts,
His feelings, passions, good or evil, all
Have nothing of old age; and his bold
 brow 20
Bears but the scars of mind, the thoughts
 of years,
Not their decrepitude: and he of late
Has been more agitated than his wont.
Would he were come! for I alone have
 power
Upon his troubled spirit.
Mar. It is true, 25
His highness has of late been greatly
 moved
By the affront of Steno, and with cause:
But the offender doubtless even now
Is doom'd to expiate his rash insult with
Such chastisement as will enforce respect
To female virtue, and to noble blood. 31
Ang. 'Twas a gross insult; but I heed it
 not
For the rash scorner's falsehood in itself,
But for the effect, the deadly deep im-
 pression 34
Which it has made upon Faliero's soul,
The proud, the fiery, the austere—austere
To all save me: I tremble when I think
To what it may conduct.
Mar. Assuredly
The Doge cannot suspect you?
Ang. Suspect *me!*
Why Steno dared not: when he scrawl'd
 his lie, 40
Grovelling by stealth in the moon's glim-
 mering light,
His own still conscience smote him for the
 act,
And every shadow on the walls frown'd
 shame
Upon his coward calumny.
Mar. 'Twere fit
He should be punish'd grievously.
Ang. He is so.
Mar. What! is the sentence pass'd? is
 he condemn'd? 46
Ang. I know not that, but he has been
 detected.
Mar. And deem you this enough for
 such foul scorn?
Ang. I would not be a judge in my own
 cause,
Nor do I know what sense of punishment
May reach the soul of ribalds such as
 Steno; 51
But if his insults sink no deeper in
The minds of the inquisitors than they
Have ruffled mine, he will, for all acquit-
 tance,
Be left to his own shamelessness or shame.
Mar. Some sacrifice is due to slander'd
 virtue. 56
Ang. Why, what is virtue if it needs a
 victim?
Or if it must depend upon men's words?

417

The dying Roman said, ''twas but a name':
It were indeed no more, if human breath
Could make or mar it. 61
 Mar. Yet full many a dame,
Stainless and faithful, would feel all the
 wrong
Of such a slander; and less rigid ladies,
Such as abound in Venice, would be loud
And all-inexorable in their cry 65
For justice.
 Ang. This but proves it is the name
And not the quality they prize: the first
Have found it a hard task to hold their
 honour,
If they require it to be blazon'd forth;
And those who have not kept it, seek its
 seeming 70
As they would look out for an ornament
Of which they feel the want, but not be-
 cause
They think it so; they live in others'
 thoughts,
And would seem honest as they must seem
 fair.
 Mar. You have strange thoughts for a
 patrician dame. 75
 Ang. And yet they were my father's;
 with his name,
The sole inheritance he left.
 Mar. You want none;
Wife to a prince, the chief of the Republic.
 Ang. I should have sought none though
 a peasant's bride, 79
But feel not less the love and gratitude
Due to my father, who bestow'd my hand
Upon his early, tried, and trusted friend,
The Count Val di Marino, now our Doge.
 Mar. And with that hand did he bestow
 your heart?
 Ang. He did so, or it had not been be-
 stow'd. 85
 Mar. Yet this strange disproportion in
 your years,
And, let me add, disparity of tempers,
Might make the world doubt whether such
 an union
Could make you wisely, permanently
 happy.
 Ang. The world will think with world-
 lings; but my heart 90
Has still been in my duties, which are
 many,
But never difficult.
 Mar. And do you love him?
 Ang. I love all noble qualities which
 merit
Love, and I loved my father, who first
 taught me
To single out what we should love in
 others, 95
And to subdue all tendency to lend
The best and purest feelings of our nature
To baser passions. He bestow'd my hand
Upon Faliero: he had known him noble,

Brave, generous; rich in all the qualities
Of soldier, citizen, and friend; in all 101
Such have I found him as my father said.
His faults are those that dwell in the high
 bosoms
Of men who have commanded; too much
 pride,
And the deep passions fiercely foster'd by
The uses of patricians, and a life 106
Spent in the storms of state and war; and
 also
From the quick sense of honour, which
 becomes
A duty to a certain sign, a vice
When overstrain'd, and this I fear in him.
And then he has been rash from his youth
 upwards, 111
Yet temper'd by redeeming nobleness
In such sort, that the wariest of republics
Has lavish'd all its chief employs upon
 him,
From his first fight to his last embassy,
From which on his return the dukedom
 met him. 116
 Mar. But previous to this marriage,
 had your heart
Ne'er beat for any of the noble youth,
Such as in years had been more meet to
 match
Beauty like yours? or, since, have you
 ne'er seen 120
One, who, if your fair hand were still to
 give,
Might now pretend to Loredano's daugh-
 ter?
 Ang. I answer'd your first question
 when I said
I married.
 Mar. And the second?
 Ang. Needs no answer.
 Mar. I pray you pardon, if I have
 offended. 125
 Ang. I feel no wrath, but some surprise:
 I knew not
That wedded bosoms could permit them-
 selves
To ponder upon what they *now* might
 choose,
Or aught save their past choice.
 Mar. 'Tis their past choice
That far too often makes them deem they
 would 130
Now choose more wisely, could they
 cancel it.
 Ang. It may be so. I knew not of such
 thoughts.
 Mar. Here comes the Doge—shall I
 retire?
 Ang. It may
Be better you should quit me; he seems
 rapt
In thought.—How pensively he takes his
 way! 135
 [*Exit* MARIANNA.

418

Enter the DOGE *and* PIETRO.

Doge [*musing*]. There is a certain Philip
 Calendaro
Now in the Arsenal, who holds command
Of eighty men, and has great influence
Besides on all the spirits of his comrades:
This man, I hear, is bold and popular,
Sudden and daring, and yet secret; 'twould
Be well that he were won: I needs must
 hope 142
That Israel Bertuccio has secured him,
But fain would be——
 Pie. My lord, pray pardon me
For breaking in upon your meditation;
The Senator Bertuccio, your kinsman,
Charged me to follow and inquire your
 pleasure 147
To fix an hour when he may speak with
 you.
Doge. At sunset.—Stay a moment—let
 me see—
Say in the second hour of night.
 [*Exit* PIETRO.
Ang. My lord!
Doge. My dearest child, forgive me—
 why delay 151
So long approaching me?—I saw you not.
Ang. You were absorb'd in thought,
 and he who now
Has parted from you might have words of
 weight
To bear you from the senate.
 Doge. From the senate?
Ang. I would not interrupt him in his
 duty 156
And theirs.
Doge. The senate's duty! you mistake;
'Tis we who owe all service to the senate.
Ang. I thought the Duke had held com-
 mand in Venice.
Doge. He shall.—But let that pass.—
 We will be jocund. 160
How fares it with you? have you been
 abroad?
The day is overcast, but the calm wave
Favours the gondolier's light skimming
 oar;
Or have you held a levee of your friends?
Or has your music made you solitary?
Say—is there aught that you would will
 within 166
The little sway now left the Duke? or aught
Of fitting splendour, or of honest pleasure,
Social or lonely, that would glad your
 heart,
To compensate for many a dull hour,
 wasted 170
On an old man oft moved with many
 cares?
Speak, and 'tis done.
 Ang. You're ever kind to me.
I have nothing to desire, or to request,
Except to see you oftener and calmer.

Doge. Calmer?
Ang. Ay, calmer, my good lord.—Ah,
 why 175
Do you still keep apart, and walk alone,
And let such strong emotions stamp your
 brow,
As not betraying their full import, yet
Disclose too much?
Doge. Disclose too much!—of what?
What is there to disclose?
Ang. A heart so ill
At ease.
Doge. 'Tis nothing, child.—But in the
 state 181
You know what daily cares oppress those
Who govern this precarious common-
 wealth;
Now suffering from the Genoese without,
And malcontents within—'tis this which
 makes me 185
More pensive and less tranquil than my
 wont.
Ang. Yet this existed long before, and
 never
Till in these late days did I see you thus.
Forgive me; there is something at your
 heart
More than the mere discharge of public
 duties, 190
Which long use and a talent like to yours
Have render'd light, nay, a necessity,
To keep your mind from stagnating. 'Tis
 not
In hostile states, nor perils, thus to shake
 you,—
You, who have stood all storms and never
 sunk, 195
And climb'd up to the pinnacle of power
And never fainted by the way, and stand
Upon it, and can look down steadily
Along the depth beneath, and ne'er feel
 dizzy. 199
Were Genoa's galleys riding in the port,
Were civil fury raging in Saint Mark's,
You are not to be wrought on, but would
 fall,
As you have risen, with an unalter'd brow:
Your feelings now are of a different kind;
Something has stung your pride, not
 patriotism. 205
Doge. Pride! Angiolina? Alas! none
 is left me.
Ang. Yes—the same sin that overthrew
 the angels,
And of all sins most easily besets
Mortals the nearest to the angelic nature:
The vile are only vain; the great are proud.
Doge. I *had* the pride of honour, of *your*
 honour, 211
Deep at my heart—But let us change the
 theme.
Ang. Ah no!—As I have ever shared
 your kindness

419

In all things else, let me not be shut out
From your distress: were it of public import, 215
You know I never sought, would never seek
To win a word from you; but feeling now
Your grief is private, it belongs to me
To lighten or divide it. Since the day
When foolish Steno's ribaldry detected
Unfix'd your quiet, you are greatly changed, 221
And I would soothe you back to what you were.

Doge. To what I was!—have you heard Steno's sentence?

Ang. No.

Doge. A month's arrest.

Ang. Is it not enough?

Doge. Enough!—yes, for a drunken galley slave, 225
Who, stung by stripes, may murmur at his master;
But not for a deliberate, false, cool villain,
Who stains a lady's and a prince's honour
Even on the throne of his authority.

Ang. There seems to me enough in the conviction 230
Of a patrician guilty of a falsehood:
All other punishment were light unto
His loss of honour.

Doge. Such men have no honour;
They have but their vile lives—and these are spared.

Ang. You would not have him die for this offence? 235

Doge. Not *now*:—being still alive, I'd have him live
Long as *he* can; he has ceased to merit death;
The guilty saved hath damn'd his hundred judges,
And he is pure, for now his crime is theirs.

Ang. Oh! had this false and flippant libeller 240
Shed his young blood for his absurd lampoon,
Ne'er from that moment could this breast have known
A joyous hour, or dreamless slumber more.

Doge. Does not the law of Heaven say blood for blood?
And he who *taints* kills more than he who sheds it. 245
Is it the *pain* of blows, or *shame* of blows,
That makes such deadly to the sense of man?
Do not the laws of man say blood for honour,—
And, less than honour, for a little gold?
Say not the laws of nations blood for treason? 250
Is't nothing to have fill'd these veins with poison

For their once healthful current? is it nothing
To have stain'd your name and mine—the noblest names?
Is't nothing to have brought into contempt
A prince before his people? to have fail'd
In the respect accorded by mankind 256
To youth in woman, and old age in man?
To virtue in your sex, and dignity
In ours?—But let them look to it who have saved him.

Ang. Heaven bids us to forgive our enemies. 260

Doge. Doth Heaven forgive her own? Is there not Hell
For wrath eternal?

Ang. Do not speak thus wildly—
Heaven will alike forgive you and your foes.

Doge. Amen! May Heaven forgive them!

Ang. And will you?

Doge. Yes, when they are in heaven!

Ang. And not till then?

Doge. What matters my forgiveness? an old man's, 266
Worn out, scorn'd, spurn'd, abused; what matters then
My pardon more than my resentment, both
Being weak and worthless? I have lived too long;
But let us change the argument.—My child! 270
My injured wife, the child of Loredano,
The brave, the chivalrous, how little deem'd
Thy father, wedding thee unto his friend,
That he was linking thee to shame!—Alas!
Shame without sin, for thou art faultless. Hadst thou 275
But had a different husband, *any* husband
In Venice save the Doge, this blight, this brand,
This blasphemy had never fallen upon thee.
So young, so beautiful, so good, so pure,
To suffer this, and yet be unavenged!

Ang. I am too well avenged, for you still love me, 281
And trust, and honour me; and all men know
That you are just, and I am true: what more
Could I require, or you command?

Doge. 'Tis well,
And may be better; but whate'er betide,
Be thou at least kind to my memory. 286

Ang. Why speak you thus?

Doge. It is no matter why;
But I would still, whatever others think,
Have your respect both now and in my grave.

Ang. Why should you doubt it? has it ever fail'd? 290

Doge. Come hither, child; I would a
 word with you.
Your father was my friend; unequal for-
 tune
Made him my debtor for some courtesies
Which bind the good more firmly: when,
 oppress'd
With his last malady, he will'd our union,
It was not to repay me, long repaid 296
Before by his great loyalty in friendship;
His object was to place your orphan
 beauty
In honourable safety from the perils
Which, in this scorpion nest of vice, assail
A lonely and undower'd maid. I did not
Think with him, but would not oppose the
 thought 302
Which soothed his death-bed.
 Ang. I have not forgotten
The nobleness with which you bade me
 speak
If my young heart held any preference
Which would have made me happier; nor
 your offer 306
To make my dowry equal to the rank
Of aught in Venice, and forego all claim
My father's last injunction gave you.
 Doge. Thus,
'Twas not a foolish dotard's vile caprice,
Nor the false edge of aged appetite, 311
Which made me covetous of girlish beauty,
And a young bride: for in my fieriest youth
I sway'd such passions; nor was this my
 age
Infected with that leprosy of lust 315
Which taints the hoariest years of vicious
 men,
Making them ransack to the very last
The dregs of pleasure for their vanish'd
 joys;
Or buy in selfish marriage some young
 victim, 319
Too helpless to refuse a state that's honest,
Too feeling not to know herself a wretch.
Our wedlock was not of this sort; you had
Freedom from me to choose, and urged in
 answer
Your father's choice.
 Ang. I did so; I would do so
In face of earth and heaven; for I have
 never 325
Repented for my sake; sometimes for
 yours,
In pondering o'er your late disquietudes.
 Doge. I knew my heart would never
 treat you harshly;
I knew my days could not disturb you
 long;
And then the daughter of my earliest
 friend, 330
His worthy daughter, free to choose again,
Wealthier and wiser, in the ripest bloom
Of womanhood, more skilful to select
By passing these probationary years

Inheriting a prince's name and riches,
Secured, by the short penance of enduring
An old man for some summers, against all
That law's chicane or envious kinsmen
 might
Have urged against her right; my best
 friend's child
Would choose more fitly in respect of
 years, 340
And not less truly in a faithful heart.
 Ang. My lord, I look'd but to my
 father's wishes,
Hallow'd by his last words, and to my
 heart
For doing all its duties, and replying
With faith to him with whom I was
 affianced. 345
Ambitious hopes ne'er cross'd my dreams;
 and should
The hour you speak of come, it will be
 seen so.
 Doge. I do believe you; and I know you
 true:
For love, romantic love, which in my
 youth
I knew to be illusion, and ne'er saw 350
Lasting, but often fatal, it had been
No lure for me, in my most passionate
 days,
And could not be so now, did such exist.
But such respect, and mildly paid regard
As a true feeling for your welfare, and
A free compliance with all honest wishes,—
A kindness to your virtues, watchfulness
Not shown, but shadowing o'er such little
 failings
As youth is apt in, so as not to check
Rashly, but win you from them ere you
 knew 360
You had been won, but thought the change
 your choice;
A pride not in your beauty, but your con-
 duct;
A trust in you; a patriarchal love,
And not a doting homage; friendship,
 faith,— 364
Such estimation in your eyes as these
Might claim, I hoped for.
 Ang. And have ever had.
 Doge. I think so. For the difference in
 our years
You knew it, choosing me, and chose: I
 trusted
Not to my qualities, nor would have faith
In such, nor outward ornaments of nature,
Were I still in my five and twentieth spring;
I trusted to the blood of Loredano 372
Pure in your veins; I trusted to the soul
God gave you—to the truths your father
 taught you—
To your belief in Heaven—to your mild
 virtues— 375
To your own faith and honour, for my
 own.

421

Ang. You have done well.—I thank you for that trust,
Which I have never for one moment ceased
To honour you the more for.
Doge. Where is honour,
Innate and precept-strengthen'd, 'tis the rock 380
Of faith connubial: where it is not—where
Light thoughts are lurking, or the vanities
Of worldly pleasure rankle in the heart,
Or sensual throbs convulse it, well I know
'Twere hopeless for humanity to dream
Of honesty in such infected blood, 386
Although 'twere wed to him it covets most:
An incarnation of the poet's god
In all his marble-chisell'd beauty, or
The demi-deity, Alcides, in 390
His majesty of superhuman manhood,
Would not suffice to bind where virtue is not;
It is consistency which forms and proves it:
Vice cannot fix, and virtue cannot change.
The once fall'n woman must for ever fall;
For vice must have variety, while virtue
Stands like the sun, and all which rolls around 397
Drinks life, and light, and glory from her aspect.
Ang. And seeing, feeling thus this truth in others,
(I pray you pardon me;) but wherefore yield you 400
To the most fierce of fatal passions, and
Disquiet your great thoughts with restless hate
Of such a thing as Steno?
Doge. You mistake me.
It is not Steno who could move me thus;
Had it been so, he should——but let that pass. 405
Ang. What is't you feel so deeply, then, even now?
Doge. The violated majesty of Venice,
At once insulted in her lord and laws.
Ang. Alas! why will you thus consider it?
Doge. I have thought on't till——but let me lead you back 410
To what I urged; all these things being noted,
I wedded you; the world then did me justice
Upon the motive, and my conduct proved
They did me right, while yours was all to praise:
You had all freedom, all respect, all trust
From me and mine; and, born of those who made 416
Princes at home, and swept kings from their thrones
On foreign shores, in all things you appear'd
Worthy to be our first of native dames.

Ang. To what does this conduct?
Doge. To thus much—that
A miscreant's angry breath may blast it all— 421
A villain, whom for his unbridled bearing
Even in the midst of our great festival,
I caused to be conducted forth, and taught
How to demean himself in ducal chambers; 425
A wretch like this may leave upon the wall
The blighting venom of his sweltering heart,
And this shall spread itself in general poison;
And woman's innocence, man's honour, pass
Into a by-word; and the doubly felon
(Who first insulted virgin modesty 431
By a gross affront to your attendant damsels
Amidst the noblest of our dames in public)
Requite himself for his most just expulsion
By blackening publicly his sovereign's consort, 435
And be absolved by his upright compeers.
Ang. But he has been condemn'd into captivity.
Doge. For such as him a dungeon were acquittal;
And his brief term of mock-arrest will pass
Within a palace. But I've done with him;
The rest must be with you.
Ang. With me, my lord?
Doge. Yes, Angiolina. Do not marvel; I 442
Have let this prey upon me till I feel
My life cannot be long; and fain would have you
Regard the injunctions you will find within 445
This scroll [*Giving her a paper*]——Fear not; they are for your advantage:
Read them hereafter at the fitting hour.
Ang. My lord, in life, and after life, you shall
Be honour'd still by me: but may your days
Be many yet—and happier than the present! 450
This passion will give way, and you will be
Serene, and what you should be—what you were.
Doge. I will be what I should be, or be nothing;
But never more—oh! never, never more,
O'er the few days or hours which yet await 455
The blighted old age of Faliero, shall
Sweet quiet shed her sunset! Never more
Those summer shadows rising from the past
Of a not ill-spent nor inglorious life,
Mellowing the last hours as the night approaches, 460

hall soothe me to my moment of long
 rest.
had but little more to ask, or hope,
ave the regards due to the blood and
 sweat,
And the soul's labour through which I
 had toil'd
To make my country honour'd. As her
 servant— 465
Her servant, though her chief—I would
 have gone
Down to my fathers with a name serene
And pure as theirs; but this has been de-
 nied me.—
Would I had died at Zara!
 Ang. There you saved
The state; then live to save her still. A day,
Another day like that would be the best
Reproof to them, and sole revenge for you.
 Doge. But one such day occurs within
 an age;
My life is little less than one, and 'tis
Enough for Fortune to have granted *once*,
That which scarce one more favour'd
 citizen 476
May win in many states and years. But why
Thus speak I? Venice has forgot that
 day—
Then why should I remember it?—Fare-
 well,
Sweet Angiolina! I must to my cabinet;
There's much for me to do—and the hour
 hastens. 481
 Ang. Remember what you were.
 Doge. It were in vain!
Joy's recollection is no longer joy,
While sorrow's memory is a sorrow still.
 Ang. At least, whate'er may urge, let
 me implore 485
That you will take some little pause of rest:
Your sleep for many nights has been so
 turbid,
That it had been relief to have awaked you,
Had I not hoped that Nature would o'er-
 power
At length the thoughts which shook your
 slumbers thus. 490
An hour of rest will give you to your toils
With fitter thoughts and freshen'd strength.
 Doge. I cannot—
I must not, if I could; for never was
Such reason to be watchful: yet a few—
Yet a few days and dream-perturbed
 nights, 495
And I shall slumber well—but where?—
 no matter.
Adieu, my Angiolina.
 Ang. Let me be
An instant—yet an instant your com-
 panion!
I cannot bear to leave you thus.
 Doge. Come then,
My gentle child—forgive me; thou wert
 made 500

For better fortunes than to share in mine,
Now darkling in their close toward the
 deep vale
Where Death sits robed in his all-sweeping
 shadow.
When I am gone—it may be sooner than
Even these years warrant, for there is that
 stirring 505
Within, above, around, that in this city
Will make the cemeteries populous
As e'er they were by pestilence or war,—
When I *am* nothing, let that which I *was*
Be still sometimes a name on thy sweet
 lips, 510
A shadow in thy fancy, of a thing
Which would not have thee mourn it, but
 remember.
Let us begone, my child—the time is
 pressing. [*Exeunt.*

SCENE II.—*A retired spot near the
 Arsenal.*

ISRAEL BERTUCCIO *and* PHILIP CALENDARO.

 Cal. How sped you, Israel, in your late
 complaint?
 I. Ber. Why, well.
 Cal. Is't possible! will he be punish'd?
 I. Ber. Yes.
 Cal. With what? a mulct or an arrest?
 I. Ber. With death!
 Cal. Now you rave, or must intend re-
 venge,
Such as I counsell'd you, with your own
 hand. 5
 I. Ber. Yes; and for one sole draught
 of hate, forego
The great redress we meditate for Venice,
And change a life of hope for one of
 exile;
Leaving one scorpion crush'd, and thou-
 sands stinging 9
My friends, my family, my countrymen!
No, Calendaro; these same drops of blood,
Shed shamefully, shall have the whole of
 his
For their requital——but not only his;
We will not strike for private wrongs
 alone: 14
Such are for selfish passions and rash
 men,
But are unworthy a tyrannicide.
 Cal. You have more patience than I
 care to boast.
Had I been present when you bore this
 insult,
I must have slain him, or expired myself
In the vain effort to repress my wrath.
 I. Ber. Thank Heaven you were not—
 all had else been marr'd: 21
As 'tis, our cause looks prosperous still.
 Cal. You saw
The Doge—what answer gave he?
 I. Ber. That there was

423

No punishment for such as Barbaro.
 Cal. I told you so before, and that 'twas idle 25
To think of justice from such hands.
 I. Ber. At least,
It lull'd suspicion, showing confidence.
Had I been silent, not a sbirro but
Had kept me in his eye, as meditating
A silent, solitary, deep revenge. 30
 Cal. But wherefore not address you to the Council?
The Doge is a mere puppet, who can scarce
Obtain right for himself. Why speak to *him*?
 I. Ber. You shall know that hereafter.
 Cal. Why not now?
 I. Ber. Be patient but till midnight. Get your musters, 35
And bid our friends prepare their companies:
Set all in readiness to strike the blow,
Perhaps in a few hours; we have long waited
For a fit time—that hour is on the dial,
It may be, of to-morrow's sun: delay
Beyond may breed us double danger. See
That all be punctual at our place of meeting,
And arm'd, excepting those of the Sixteen,
Who will remain among the troops to wait
The signal.
 Cal. These brave words have breathed new life 45
Into my veins; I'm sick of these protracted
And hesitating councils: day on day
Crawl'd on, and added but another link
To our long fetters, and some fresher wrong 49
Inflicted on our brethren or ourselves,
Helping to swell our tyrants' bloated strength.
Let us but deal upon them, and I care not
For the result, which must be death or freedom!
I'm weary to the heart of finding neither.
 I. Ber. We will be free in life or death! the grave 55
Is chainless. Have you all the musters ready?
And are the sixteen companies completed
To sixty?
 Cal. All save two, in which there are
Twenty-five wanting to make up the number.
 I. Ber. No matter; we can do without. Whose are they? 60
 Cal. Bertram's and old Soranzo's, both of whom
Appear less forward in the cause than we are.
 I. Ber. Your fiery nature makes you deem all those
Who are not restless cold: but there exists

Oft in concentred spirits not less daring
Than in more loud avengers. Do no doubt them. 6
 Cal. I do not doubt the elder; but in Bertram
There is a hesitating softness, fatal
To enterprise like ours: I've seen that man 7
Weep like an infant o'er the misery
Of others, heedless of his own, though greater;
And in a recent quarrel I beheld him
Turn sick at sight of blood, although a villain's.
 I. Ber. The truly brave are soft of heart and eyes,
And feel for what their duty bids them do
I have known Bertram long; there doth not breathe 7
A soul more full of honour.
 Cal. It may be so
I apprehend less treachery than weakness
Yet as he has no mistress, and no wife
To work upon his milkiness of spirit,
He may go through the ordeal; it is well
He is an orphan, friendless save in us:
A woman or a child had made him less
Than either in resolve.
 I. Ber. Such ties are not
For those who are call'd to the high destinies 8
Which purify corrupted commonwealths
We must forget all feelings save the *one*,
We must resign all passions save our purpose,
We must behold no object save our country,
And only look on death as beautiful, 9
So that the sacrifice ascend to heaven,
And draw down freedom on her evermore.
 Cal. But if we fail——
 I. Ber. They never fail who die
In a great cause: the block may soak their gore;
Their heads may sodden in the sun; their limbs 9
Be strung to city gates and castle walls—
But still their spirit walks abroad. Though years
Elapse, and others share as dark a doom,
They but augment the deep and sweeping thoughts
Which overpower all others, and conduct
The world at last to freedom. What were we, 10
If Brutus had not lived? He died in giving
Rome liberty, but left a deathless lesson—
A name which is a virtue, and a soul
Which multiplies itself throughout all time, 10
When wicked men wax mighty, and a state
Turns servile. He and his high friend were styled
'The last of Romans!' Let us be the first

Of true Venetians, sprung from Roman
 sires. 109
 Cal. Our fathers did not fly from Attila
Into these isles, where palaces have sprung
On banks redeem'd from the rude ocean's
 ooze,
To own a thousand despots in his place.
Better bow down before the Hun, and call
A Tartar lord, than these swoln silkworms
 masters! 115
The first at least was man, and used his
 sword
As sceptre: these unmanly creeping things
Command our swords, and rule us with a
 word
As with a spell.
 I. Ber. It shall be broken soon.
You say that all things are in readiness;
To-day I have not been the usual round,
And why thou knowest; but thy vigilance
Will better have supplied my care: these
 orders
In recent council to redouble now
Our efforts to repair the galleys, have 125
Lent a fair colour to the introduction
Of many of our cause into the arsenal,
As new artificers for their equipment,
Or fresh recruits obtained in haste to man
The hoped-for fleet.—Are all supplied
 with arms? 130
 Cal. All who were deem'd trustworthy:
 there are some
Whom it were well to keep in ignorance
Till it be time to strike, and then supply
 them;
When in the heat and hurry of the hour
They have no opportunity to pause, 135
But needs must on with those who will
 surround them.
 I. Ber. You have said well. Have you
 remark'd all such?
 Cal. I've noted most; and caused the
 other chiefs
To use like caution in their companies.
As far as I have seen, we are enough 140
To make the enterprise secure, if 'tis
Commenced to-morrow; but, till 'tis begun,
Each hour is pregnant with a thousand perils.
 I. Ber. Let the Sixteen meet at the
 wonted hour,
Except Soranzo, Nicoletto Blondo, 145
And Marco Giuda, who will keep their
 watch
Within the arsenal, and hold all ready,
Expectant of the signal we will fix on.
 Cal. We will not fail.
 I. Ber. Let all the rest be there;
I have a stranger to present to them. 150
 Cal. A stranger! doth he know the
 secret?
 I. Ber. Yes.
 Cal. And have you dared to peril your
 friends' lives
On a rash confidence in one we know not?

 I. Ber. I have risk'd no man's life ex-
 cept my own—
Of that be certain: he is one who may
Make our assurance doubly sure, accord-
 ing 156
His aid; and if reluctant, he no less
Is in our power: he comes alone with me,
And cannot 'scape us; but he will not
 swerve.
 Cal. I cannot judge of this until I know
 him: 160
Is he one of our order?
 I. Ber. Ay, in spirit,
Although a child of greatness; he is one—
Who would become a throne, or over-
 throw one—
One who has done great deeds, and seen
 great changes; 164
No tyrant, though bred up to tyranny;
Valiant in war, and sage in council: noble
In nature, although haughty; quick, yet
 wary:
Yet for all this, so full of certain passions,
That if once stirr'd and baffled, as he has
 been
Upon the tenderest points, there is no
 Fury 170
In Grecian story like to that which wrings
His vitals with her burning hands, till he
Grows capable of all things for revenge;
And add too, that his mind is liberal,
He sees and feels the people are oppress'd,
And shares their sufferings. Take him all
 in all, 176
We have need of such, and such have need
 of us.
 Cal. And what part would you have
 him take with us?
 I. Ber. It may be, that of chief.
 Cal. What! and resign
Your own command as leader?
 I. Ber. Even so.
My object is to make your cause end well.
And not to push myself to power. Ex-
 perience, 182
Some skill, and your own choice, had
 mark'd me out
To act in trust as your commander, till
Some worthier should appear: if I have
 found such 185
As you yourselves shall own more worthy,
 think you
That I would hesitate from selfishness,
And, covetous of brief authority,
Stake our deep interest on my single
 thoughts, 189
Rather than yield to one above me in
All leading qualities? No, Calendaro,
Know your friend better; but you all shall
 judge.
Away! and let us meet at the fix'd hour.
Be vigilant, and all will yet go well.
 Cal. Worthy Bertuccio, I have known
 you ever 195

Trusty and brave, with head and heart to
 plan
What I have still been prompt to execute.
For my own part, I seek no other chief;
What the rest will decide I know not, but
I am with you, as I have ever been, 200
In all our undertakings. Now farewell,
Until the hour of midnight sees us meet.
 [*Exeunt.*

ACT III

SCENE I.—*Scene, the Space between the
 Canal and the Church of San Giovanni
 e San Paolo. An equestrian Statue
 before it.—A Gondola lies in the Canal
 at some distance.*

Enter the DOGE *alone, disguised.*

Doge [*solus*]. I am before the hour, the
 hour whose voice,
Pealing into the arch of night, might strike
These palaces with ominous tottering,
And rock their marbles to the corner-stone,
Waking the sleepers from some hideous
 dream 5
Of indistinct but awful augury
Of that which will befall them. Yes, proud
 city!
Thou must be cleansed of the black blood
 which makes thee
A lazar-house of tyranny: the task 9
Is forced upon me, I have sought it not;
And therefore was I punish'd, seeing this
Patrician pestilence spread on and on,
Until at length it smote me in my slumbers,
And I am tainted, and must wash away
The plague spots in the healing wave. Tall
 fane! 15
Where sleep my fathers, whose dim statues
 shadow
The floor which doth divide us from the
 dead,
Where all the pregnant hearts of our bold
 blood,
Moulder'd into a mite of ashes, hold
In one shrunk heap what once made many
 heroes, 20
When what is now a handful shook the
 earth—
Fane of the tutelar saints who guard our
 house!
Vault where two Doges rest—my sires! who
 died
The one of toil, the other in the field,
With a long race of other lineal chiefs
And sages, whose great labours, wounds,
 and state 26
I have inherited,—let the graves gape,
Till all thine aisles be peopled with the
 dead,
And pour them from thy portals to gaze
 on me!
I call them up, and them and thee to wit-
 ness 30

What it hath been which put me to this
 task—
Their pure high blood, their blazon-roll of
 glories,
Their mighty name dishonour'd all *in* me,
Not *by* me, but by the ungrateful nobles
We fought to make our equals, not our
 lords: 35
And chiefly thou, Ordelafo the brave,
Who perish'd in the field, where I since
 conquer'd,
Battling at Zara, did the hecatombs
Of thine and Venice' foes, there offer'd up
By thy descendant, merit such acquit-
 tance? 40
Spirits! smile down upon me; for my cause
Is yours, in all life now can be of yours,—
Your fame, your name, all mingled up in
 mine,
And in the future fortunes of our race!
Let me but prosper, and I make this city
Free and immortal, and our house's name
Worthier of what you were, now and here-
 after. 47

Enter ISRAEL BERTUCCIO.

I. Ber. Who goes there?
Doge. A friend to Venice.
I. Ber. 'Tis he.
Welcome, my lord,—you are before the
 time.
 Doge. I am ready to proceed to your
 assembly. 50
 I. Ber. Have with you.—I am proud
 and pleased to see
Such confident alacrity. Your doubts
Since our last meeting, then, are all dis-
 pell'd?
 Doge. Not so—but I have set my little
 left
Of life upon this cast: the die was thrown
When I first listen'd to your treason.—
 Start not! 55
That is the word; I cannot shape my tongue
To syllable black deeds into smooth names,
Though I be wrought on to commit them.
 When
I heard you tempt your sovereign, and
 forbore 60
To have you dragg'd to prison, I became
Your guiltiest accomplice: now you may,
If it so please you, do as much by me.
 I. Ber. Strange words, my lord, and
 most unmerited;
I am no spy, and neither are we traitors.
 Doge. *We—We!*—no matter—you have
 earn'd the right 65
To talk of *us*.—But to the point.—If this
Attempt succeeds, and Venice, render'd
 free
And flourishing, when we are in our graves,
Conducts her generations to our tombs.
And makes her children with their little
 hands 71

Strew flowers o'er her deliverers' ashes, then
The consequence will sanctify the deed,
And we shall be like the two Bruti in
The annals of hereafter; but if not, 75
If we should fail, employing bloody means
And secret plot, although to a good end,
Still we are traitors, honest Israel;—thou
No less than he who was thy sovereign
Six hours ago, and now thy brother rebel.
 I. Ber. 'Tis not the moment to consider
 thus, 81
Else I could answer.—Let us to the meeting,
Or we may be observed in lingering here.
 Doge. We *are* observed, and have been.
 I. Ber. We observed!
Let me discover—and this steel——
 Doge. Put up;
Here are no human witnesses: look there—
What see you?
 I. Ber. Only a tall warrior's statue
Bestriding a proud steed, in the dim light
Of the dull moon.
 Doge. That warrior was the sire
Of my sire's fathers, and that statue was
Decreed to him by the twice rescued
 city:— 91
Think you that he looks down on us or no?
 I. Ber. My lord, these are mere fanta-
 sies; there are
No eyes in marble.
 Doge. But there are in Death.
I tell thee, man, there is a spirit in 95
Such things that acts and sees, unseen,
 though felt;
And, if there be a spell to stir the dead,
'Tis in such deeds as we are now upon.
Deem'st thou the souls of such a race as
 mine
Can rest, when he, their last descendant
 chief, 100
Stands plotting on the brink of their pure
 graves
With stung plebeians?
 I. Ber. It had been as well
To have pondered this before,—ere you
 embark'd
In our great enterprise.—Do you repent?
 Doge. No—but I *feel*, and shall do to
 the last. 105
I cannot quench a glorious life at once
Nor dwindle to the thing I now must be,
And take men's lives by stealth, without
 some pause:
Yet doubt me not; it is this very feeling,
And knowing *what* has wrung me to be
 thus, 110
Which is your best security. There's not
A roused mechanic in your busy plot
So wrong'd as I, so fall'n, so loudly call'd
To his redress: the very means I am forced
By these fell tyrants to adopt is such,
That I abhor them doubly for the deeds
Which I must do to pay them back for
 theirs. 117

 I. Ber. Let us away—hark—the hour
 strikes.
 Doge. On—on—
It is our knell, or that of Venice—On.
 I. Ber. Say rather, 'tis her freedom's
 rising peal 120
Of triumph.—This way—we are near the
 place. [*Exeunt.*

SCENE II.—*The House where the Con-
 spirators meet.*

DAGOLINO, DORO, BERTRAM, FEDELE
TREVISANO, CALENDARO, ANTONIO
DELLE BENDE, &c. &c.

 Cal. [*entering*]. Are all here?
 Dag. All with you; except the three
On duty, and our leader Israel,
Who is expected momently.
 Cal. Where's Bertram?
 Ber. Here!
 Cal. Have you not been able to
 complete
The number wanting in your company?
 Ber. I had mark'd out some: but I have
 not dared 6
To trust them with the secret, till assured
That they were worthy faith.
 Cal. There is no need
Of trusting to their faith; *who*, save our-
 selves
And our more chosen comrades, is aware
Fully of our intent? they think themselves
Engaged in secret to the Signory, 12
To punish some more dissolute young
 nobles
Who have defied the law in their excesses;
But once drawn up, and their new swords
 well flesh'd 15
In the rank hearts of the more odious
 senators,
They will not hesitate to follow up
Their blow upon the others, when they see
The example of their chiefs, and I for one
Will set them such, that they for very
 shame 20
And safety will not pause till all have
 perish'd.
 Ber. How say you? *all!*
 Cal. Whom wouldst thou spare?
 Ber. *I spare?*
I have no power to spare. I only question'd,
Thinking that even amongst these wicked
 men
There might be some, whose age and
 qualities 25
Might mark them out for pity.
 Cal. Yes, such pity
As when the viper hath been cut to pieces,
The separate fragments quivering in the
 sun,
In the last energy of venomous life,
Deserve and have. Why, I should think as
 soon 30

427

Of pitying some particular fang which
 made
One in the jaw of the swoln serpent, as
Of saving one of these: they form but links
Of one long chain; one mass, one breath,
 one body;
They eat, and drink, and live, and breed
 together, 35
Revel, and lie, oppress, and kill in con-
 cert,—
So let them die as *one*!
 Dag. Should *one* survive,
He would be dangerous as the whole; it is
 not
Their number, be it tens or thousands, but
The spirit of this aristocracy 40
Which must be rooted out; and if there
 were
A single shoot of the old tree in life,
'Twould fasten in the soil, and spring
 again
To gloomy verdure and to bitter fruit.
Bertram, we must be firm!
 Cal. Look to it well, 45
Bertram; I have an eye upon thee.
 Ber. Who
Distrusts me?
 Cal. Not I; for if I did so,
Thou wouldst not now be there to talk of
 trust:
It is thy softness, not thy want of faith,
Which makes thee to be doubted.
 Ber. You should know 50
Who hear me, who and what I am; a man
Roused like yourselves to overthrow op-
 pression,
A kind man, I am apt to think, as some
Of you have found me; and if brave or no,
You, Calendaro, can pronounce, who
 have seen me 55
Put to the proof; or, if you should have
 doubts,
I'll clear them on your person!
 Cal. You are welcome,
When once our enterprise is o'er, which
 must not
Be interrupted by a private brawl.
 Ber. I am no brawler; but can bear my-
 self 60
As far among the foe as any he
Who hears me; else why have I been
 selected
To be of your chief comrades? but no less
I own my natural weakness; I have not
Yet learn'd to think of indiscriminate
 murder 65
Without some sense of shuddering; and
 the sight
Of blood which spouts through hoary
 scalps is not
To me a thing of triumph, nor the death
Of men surprised a glory. Well—too well
I know that we must do such things on
 those 70

Whose acts have raised up such avengers
 but
If there were some of these who could be
 saved
From out this sweeping fate, for our own
 sakes 7
And for our honour, to take off some stain
Of massacre, which else pollutes it wholly
I had been glad; and see no cause in thi
For sneer, nor for suspicion!
 Dag. Calm thee, Bertram,
For we suspect thee not, and take goo
 heart.
It is the cause, and not our will, which ask
Such actions from our hands: we'll wash
 away 8
All stains in Freedom's fountain!

Enter ISRAEL BERTUCCIO, *and the* DOGE,
 disguised.

 Dag. Welcome, Israel
 Consp. Most welcome.—Brave Bertuc
cio, thou art late—
Who is this stranger?
 Cal. It is time to name him
Our comrades are even now prepared t
 greet him
In brotherhood, as I have made it knowr
That thou wouldst add a brother to ou
 cause, 8
Approved by thee, and thus approved by all
Such is our trust in all thine actions. Now
Let him unfold himself.
 I. Ber. Stranger, step forth
 [*The Doge discovers himself*
 Consp. To arms!—we are betray'd—i
 is the Doge! 9
Down with them both! our traitorou
 captain, and
The tyrant he hath sold us to.
 Cal. [*drawing his sword*]. Hold! hold!
Who moves a step against them dies
 Hold! hear
Bertuccio—What! are you appall'd to se
A lone, unguarded, weaponless old man
Amongst you?—Israel, speak; what mean
 this mystery? 9
 I. Ber. Let them advance and strike a
 their own bosoms,
Ungrateful suicides! for on our lives
Depend their own, their fortunes, an
 their hopes.
 Doge. Strike!—If I dreaded death, a
 death more fearful 10
Than any your rash weapons can inflict,
I should not now be here: Oh, nobl
 Courage!
The eldest born of Fear, which makes yo
 brave
Against this solitary hoary head!
See the bold chiefs, who would reform a
 state 10
And shake down senates, mad with wratl
 and dread

At sight of one patrician! Butcher me!
You can, I care not.—Israel, are these men
The mighty hearts you spoke of? look
 upon them!
 Cal. Faith! he hath shamed us, and
 deservedly. 110
Was this your trust in your true chief
 Bertuccio,
To turn your swords against him and his
 guest?
Sheathe them, and hear him.
 I. Ber. I disdain to speak.
They might and must have known a heart
 like mine 114
Incapable of treachery; and the power
They gave me to adopt all fitting means
To further their design was ne'er abused.
They might be certain that whoe'er was
 brought
By me into this council had been led
To take his choice—as brother, or as
 victim. 120
 Doge. And which am I to be? your
 actions leave
Some cause to doubt the freedom of the
 choice.
 I. Ber. My lord, we would have perish'd
 here together,
Had these rash men proceeded; but, be-
 hold,
They are ashamed of that mad moment's
 impulse, 125
And droop their heads; believe me, they
 are such
As I described them.—Speak to them.
 Cal. Ay, speak;
We are all listening in wonder.
 I. Ber. [*addressing the conspirators*].
You are safe,
Nay, more, almost triumphant—listen
 then, 129
And know my words for truth.
 Doge. You see me here,
As one of you hath said, an old, unarm'd,
Defenceless man; and yesterday you saw
 me
Presiding in the hall of ducal state,
Apparent sovereign of our hundred isles,
Robed in official purple, dealing out
The edicts of a power which is not mine,
Nor yours, but of our masters—the patri-
 cians.
Why I was there you know, or think you
 know;
Why I am *here*, he who hath been most
 wrong'd,
He who among you hath been most in-
 sulted, 140
Outraged, and trodden on, until he doubt
If he be worm or no, may answer for me,
Asking of his own heart what brought him
 here?
You know my recent story, all men know
 it,

And judge of it far differently from those
Who sate in judgment to heap scorn on
 scorn. 146
But spare me the recital—it is here,
Here at my heart the outrage—but my
 words,
Already spent in unavailing plaints,
Would only show my feebleness the more,
And I come here to strengthen even the
 strong, 151
And urge them on to deeds, and not to war
With woman's weapons; but I need not
 urge you.
Our private wrongs have sprung from
 public vices,
In this—I cannot call it commonwealth,
Nor kingdom, which hath neither prince
 nor people, 156
But all the sins of the old Spartan state
Without its virtues—temperance and va-
 lour.
The Lords of Lacedæmon were true sol-
 diers, 159
But ours are Sybarites, while we are Helots,
Of whom I am the lowest, most enslaved;
Although dress'd out to head a pageant, as
The Greeks of yore made drunk their
 slaves to form
A pastime for their children. You are met
To overthrow this monster of a state,
This mockery of a government, this
 spectre, 166
Which must be exorcised with blood,—
 and then
We will renew the times of truth and justice,
Condensing in a fair free commonwealth
Not rash equality but equal rights, 170
Proportion'd like the columns to the
 temple,
Giving and taking strength reciprocal,
And making firm the whole with grace and
 beauty, 173
So that no part could be removed without
Infringement of the general symmetry.
In operating this great change, I claim
To be one of you—if you trust in me;
If not, strike home,—my life is com-
 promised, 178
And I would rather fall by freemen's hands
Than live another day to act the tyrant
As delegate of tyrants: such I am not,
And never have been—read it in our
 annals;
I can appeal to my past government
In many lands and cities; they can tell you
If I were an oppressor, or a man 185
Feeling and thinking for my fellow men,
Haply had I been what the senate sought,
A thing of robes and trinkets, dizen'd out
To sit in state as for a sovereign's picture;
A popular scourge, a ready sentence-
 signer, 190
A stickler for the Senate and 'the Forty',
A sceptic of all measures which had not

The sanction of 'the Ten', a council-
 fawner,
A tool, a fool, a puppet,—they had ne'er
Foster'd the wretch who stung me. What
 I suffer 195
Has reach'd me through my pity for the
 people;
That many know, and they who know not
 yet
Will one day learn: meantime I do devote,
Whate'er the issue, my last days of life—
My present power such as it is, not that
Of Doge, but of a man who has been great
Before he was degraded to a Doge, 202
And still has individual means and mind;
I stake my fame (and I had fame)—my
 breath—
(The least of all, for its last hours are nigh)
My heart, my hope, my soul, upon this
 cast! 206
Such as I am, I offer me to you
And to your chiefs; accept me or reject me,—
A Prince who fain would be a citizen
Or nothing, and who has left his throne to
 be so. 210
 Cal. Long live Faliero!—Venice shall
 be free!
 Consp. Long live Faliero!
 I. Ber. Comrades! did I well?
Is not this man a host in such a cause?
 Doge. This is no time for eulogies, nor
 place
For exultation. Am I one of you? 215
 Cal. Ay, and the first among us, as thou
 hast been
Of Venice—be our general and chief.
 Doge. Chief!—general!—I was general
 at Zara,
And chief in Rhodes and Cyprus, prince
 in Venice: 219
I cannot stoop——that is, I am not fit
To lead a band of——patriots: when I lay
Aside the dignities which I have borne,
'Tis not to put on others, but to be
Mate to my fellows—but now to the point;
Israel has stated to me your whole plan—
'Tis bold, but feasible if I assist it, 226
And must be set in motion instantly.
 Cal. E'en when thou wilt. Is it not so,
 my friends?
I have disposed all for a sudden blow;
When shall it be then?
 Doge. At sunrise.
 Ber. So soon?
 Doge. So soon?—so late—each hour
 accumulates 231
Peril on peril, and the more so now
Since I have mingled with you;—know
 you not
The Council, and 'the Ten'? the spies, the
 eyes
Of the patricians dubious of their slaves,
And now more dubious of the prince they
 have made one? 236

I tell you, you must strike, and suddenly
Full to the Hydra's heart—its heads will
 follow.
 Cal. With all my soul and sword, I yield
 assent; 239
Our companies are ready, sixty each,
And all now under arms by Israel's order
Each at their different place of rendezvous
And vigilant, expectant of some blow;
Let each repair for action to his post!
And now, my lord, the signal?
 Doge. When you hear
The great bell of St. Mark's, which may
 not be 246
Struck without special order of the Doge
(The last poor privilege they leave their
 prince),
March on Saint Mark's!
 I. Ber. And there?—
 Doge. By different routes
Let your march be directed, every sixty
Entering a separate avenue, and still 251
Upon the way let your cry be of war
And of the Genoese fleet, by the first dawn
Discern'd before the port; form round the
 palace,
Within whose court will be drawn out in
 arms 255
My nephew and the clients of our house,
Many and martial; while the bell tolls on,
Shout ye, 'Saint Mark!—the foe is on our
 waters!'
 Cal. I see it now—but on, my noble lord.
 Doge. All the patricians flocking to the
 Council, 260
(Which they dare not refuse, at the dread
 signal
Pealing from out their patron saint's proud
 tower),
Will then be gather'd in unto the harvest,
And we will reap them with the sword for
 sickle.
If some few should be tardy or absent
 them, 265
'Twill be but to be taken faint and single,
When the majority are put to rest.
 Cal. Would that the hour were come!
 we will not scotch,
But kill.
 Ber. Once more, sir, with your pardon, I
Would now repeat the question which I
 ask'd 270
Before Bertuccio added to our cause
This great ally who renders it more sure,
And therefore safer, and as such admits
Some dawn of mercy to a portion of
Our victims—must all perish in this
 slaughter? 275
 Cal. All who encounter me and mine,
 be sure,
The mercy they have shown, I show.
 Consp. All! all!
Is this a time to talk of pity? when
Have they e'er shown, or felt, or feign'd it?

I. Ber. Bertram,
This false compassion is a folly, and
Injustice to thy comrades and thy cause!
Dost thou not see, that if we single out
Some for escape, they live but to avenge
The fallen? and how distinguish now the
 innocent
From out the guilty? all their acts are
 one— 285
A single emanation from one body,
Together knit for our oppression! 'Tis
Much that we let their children live; I
 doubt 288
If all of these even should be set apart:
The hunter may reserve some single cub
From out the tiger's litter, but whoe'er
Would seek to save the spotted sire or dam,
Unless to perish by their fangs? however,
I will abide by Doge Faliero's counsel:
Let him decide if any should be saved.
 Doge. Ask me not—tempt me not with
 such a question—
Decide yourselves. 296
 I. Ber. You know their private virtues
Far better than we can, to whom alone
Their public vices, and most foul oppres-
 sion,
Have made them deadly; if there be a-
 mongst them 300
One who deserves to be repeal'd, pro-
 nounce.
 Doge. Dolfino's father was my friend,
 and Lando
Fought by my side, and Marc Cornaro
 shared
My Genoese embassy: I saved the life
Of Veniero—shall I save it twice? 305
Would that I could save them and Venice
 also!
All these men, or their fathers, were my
 friends
Till they became my subjects; then fell
 from me
As faithless leaves drop from the o'er-
 blown flower, 309
All left me a lone blighted thorny stalk,
Which, in its solitude, can shelter nothing;
So, as they let me wither, let them perish.
 Cal. They cannot co-exist with Venice'
 freedom!
 Doge. Ye, though you know and feel
 our mutual mass 314
Of many wrongs, even ye are ignorant
What fatal poison to the springs of life,
To human ties, and all that's good and
 dear,
Lurks in the present institutes of Venice:
All these men were my friends: I loved
 them, they
Requited honourably my regards; 320
We served and fought; we smiled and wept
 in concert;
We revell'd or we sorrow'd side by side:
We made alliances of blood and marriage;

We grew in years and honours fairly,—till
Their own desire, not my ambition, made
Them choose me for their prince, and then
 farewell! 326
Farewell all social memory! all thoughts
In common! and sweet bonds which link
 old friendships,
When the survivors of long years and
 actions,
Which now belong to history, soothe the
 days 330
Which yet remain by treasuring each other,
And never meet, but each beholds the
 mirror
Of half a century on his brother's brow,
And sees a hundred beings, now in earth,
Flit round them whispering of the days
 gone by, 335
And seeming not all dead, as long as two
Of the brave, joyous, reckless, glorious
 band,
Which once were one and many, still retain
A breath to sigh for them, a tongue to speak
Of deeds that else were silent, save on
 marble—— 340
Oimé! Oimé!—and must I do this deed?
 I. Ber. My lord, you are much moved:
 it is not now
That such things must be dwelt upon.
 Doge. Your patience
A moment—I recede not: mark with me
The gloomy vices of this government.
From the hour they made me Doge, the
 Doge THEY *made* me—
Farewell the past! I died to all that had been,
Or rather they to me: no friends, no kind-
 ness,
No privacy of life—all were cut off:
They came not near me, such approach
 gave umbrage; 350
They could not love me, such was not the
 law;
They thwarted me, 'twas the state's policy;
They baffled me, 'twas a patrician's duty;
They wrong'd me, for such was to right the
 state;
They could not right me, that would give
 suspicion; 355
So that I was a slave to my own subjects;
So that I was a foe to my own friends;
Begirt with spies for guards, with robes for
 power,
With pomp for freedom, gaolers for a
 council,
Inquisitors for friends, and hell for life!
I had one only fount of quiet left, 361
And *that* they poison'd! My pure house-
 hold gods
Were shiver'd on my hearth, and o'er their
 shrine
Sate grinning Ribaldry and sneering Scorn.
 I. Ber. You have been deeply wrong'd,
 and now shall be 365
Nobly avenged before another night.

Doge. I had borne all—it hurt me, but I bore it—
Till this last running over of the cup
Of bitterness—until this last loud insult,
Not only unredress'd, but sanction'd; then, 370
And thus, I cast all further feelings from me—
The feelings which they crush'd for me, long, long
Before, even in their oath of false allegiance!
Even in that very hour and vow, they abjured
Their friend and made a sovereign, as boys make 375
Playthings, to do their pleasure—and be broken!
I from that hour have seen but senators
In dark suspicious conflict with the Doge,
Brooding with him in mutual hate and fear;
They dreading he should snatch the tyranny 380
From out their grasp, and he abhorring tyrants.
To me, then, these men have no *private* life,
Nor claim to ties they have cut off from others;
As senators for arbitrary acts
Amenable, I look on them—as such 385
Let them be dealt upon.
Cal. And now to action!
Hence, brethren, to our posts, and may this be
The last night of mere words: I'd fain be doing!
Saint Mark's great bell at dawn shall find me wakeful!
I. Ber. Disperse then to your posts: be firm and vigilant; 390
Think on the wrongs we bear, the rights we claim.
This day and night shall be the last of peril!
Watch for the signal, and then march. I go
To join my band: let each be prompt to marshal
His separate charge: the Doge will now return 395
To the palace to prepare all for the blow.
We part to meet in freedom and in glory!
Cal. Doge, when I greet you next, my homage to you
Shall be the head of Steno on this sword!
Doge. No; let him be reserved unto the last, 400
Nor turn aside to strike at such a prey,
Till nobler game is quarried: his offence
Was a mere ebullition of the vice,
The general corruption generated 404
By the foul aristocracy: he could not—
He dared not in more honourable days
Have risk'd it. I have merged all private wrath

Against him in the thought of our great purpose.
A slave insults me—I require his punishment
From his proud master's hands; if he refuse it, 410
The offence grows his, and let him answer it
Cal. Yet, as the immediate cause of the alliance
Which consecrates our undertaking more
I owe him such deep gratitude, that fain
I would repay him as he merits; may I?
Doge. You would but lop the hand, and I the head; 416
You would but smite the scholar, I the master;
You would but punish Steno, I the senate
I cannot pause on individual hate,
In the absorbing, sweeping, whole revenge
Which, like the sheeted fire from heaven must blast 421
Without distinction, as it fell of yore,
Where the Dead Sea hath quench'd two cities' ashes.
I. Ber. Away, then, to your posts! I but remain
A moment to accompany the Doge 425
To our late place of tryst, to see no spies
Have been upon the scout, and thence I hasten
To where my allotted band is under arms.
Cal. Farewell, then,—until dawn!
I. Ber. Success go with you!
Consp. We will not fail—Away! My lord, farewell! 430
[*The Conspirators salute the* DOGE *and* ISRAEL BERTUCCIO, *and retire, headed by* PHILIP CALENDARO. *The* DOGE *and* ISRAEL BERTUCCIO *remain.*
I. Ber. We have them in the toil—it cannot fail!
Now thou'rt indeed a sovereign, and wilt make
A name immortal greater than the greatest:
Free citizens have struck at kings ere now;
Cæsars have fallen, and even patrician hands 435
Have crush'd dictators, as the popular steel
Has reach'd patricians: but, until this hour,
What prince has plotted for his people's freedom? 438
Or risk'd a life to liberate his subjects?
For ever, and for ever, they conspire
Against the people, to abuse their hands
To chains, but laid aside to carry weapons
Against the fellow nations, so that yoke
On yoke, and slavery and death may whet,
Not glut, the never-gorged Leviathan!
Now, my lord, to our enterprise;—'tis great, 446
And greater the reward; why stand you rapt?
A moment back, and you were all impatience!

Doge. And is it then decided! must they die?

I. Ber. Who?

Doge. My own friends by blood and courtesy, 450
And many deeds and days—the senators?

I. Ber. You pass'd their sentence, and it is a just one.

Doge. Ay, so it seems, and so it is to *you;*
You are a patriot, a plebeian Gracchus—
The rebels' oracle, the people's tribune—
I blame you not—you act in your voca-
tion; 456
They smote you, and oppress'd you, and despised you;
So they have *me*; but *you* ne'er spake with them;
You never broke their bread, nor shared their salt;
You never had their wine-cup at your lips;
You grew not up with them, nor laugh'd, nor wept, 461
Nor held a revel in their company;
Ne'er smiled to see them smile, nor claim'd their smile
In social interchange for yours, nor trusted
Nor wore them in your heart of hearts, as I have: 465
These hairs of mine are grey, and so are theirs,
The elders of the Council: I remember
When all our locks were like the raven's wing,
As we went forth to take our prey around
The isles wrung from the false Mahome-
tan; 470
And can I see them dabbled o'er with blood?
Each stab to them will seem my suicide.

I. Ber. Doge! Doge! this vacillation is unworthy
A child; if you are not in second childhood,
Call back your nerves to your own pur-
pose, nor 475
Thus shame yourself and me. By heavens!
I'd rather
Forego even now, or fail in our intent,
Than see the man I venerate subside
From high resolves into such shallow weakness!
You have seen blood in battle, shed it, both 480
Your own and that of others; can you shrink then
From a few drops from veins of hoary vampires,
Who but give back what they have drain'd from millions?

Doge. Bear with me! Step by step, and blow on blow,
I will divide with you; think not I waver:
Ah! no; it is the *certainty* of all 486
Which I must do doth make me tremble thus.

But let these last and lingering thoughts have way,
To which you only and the night are con-
scious,
And both regardless: when the hour arrives, 490
'Tis mine to sound the knell, and strike the blow,
Which shall unpeople many palaces,
And hew the highest genealogic trees
Down to the earth, strew'd with their bleeding fruit, 494
And crush their blossoms into barrenness:
This will I—must I—have I sworn to do,
Nor aught can turn me from my destiny;
But still I quiver to behold what I
Must be, and think what I have been! Bear with me.

I. Ber. Re-man your breast; I feel no such remorse, 500
I understand it not: why should you change?
You acted, and you act, on your free will.

Doge. Ay, there it is—*you* feel not, nor do I,
Else I should stab thee on the spot, to save
A thousand lives, and killing, do no mur-
der; 505
You *feel* not—*you* go to this butcher-work
As if these high-born men were steers for shambles:
When all is over, you'll be free and merry,
And calmly wash those hands incarnadine;
But I, outgoing thee and all thy fellows
In this surpassing massacre, shall be,
Shall see and feel—oh God! oh God! 'tis true, 512
And thou dost well to answer that it was
'My own free will and act,' and yet you err,
For I *will* do this! Doubt not—fear not; I
Will be your most unmerciful accomplice!
And yet I act no more on my free will,
Nor my own feelings—both compel me back;
But there is *hell* within me and around,
And like the demon who believes and trembles 520
Must I abhor and do. Away! away!
Get thee unto thy fellows, I will hie me
To gather the retainers of our house.
Doubt not, St. Mark's great bell shall wake all Venice, 524
Except her slaughtered senate: ere the sun
Be broad upon the Adriatic there
Shall be a voice of weeping, which shall drown
The roar of waters in the cry of blood!
I am resolved—come on.

I. Ber. With all my soul!
Keep a firm rein upon these bursts of passion; 530
Remember what these men have dealt to thee,
And that this sacrifice will be succeeded

433

By ages of prosperity and freedom
To this unshackled city: a true tyrant
Would have depopulated empires, nor
Have felt the strange compunction which
 hath wrung you 536
To punish a few traitors to the people.
Trust me, such were a pity more misplaced
Than the late mercy of the state to Steno.
 Doge. Man, thou hast struck upon the
 chord which jars 540
All nature from my heart. Hence to our
 task! [*Exeunt.*

ACT IV

SCENE I.—*Palazzo of the Patrician* LIONI.
LIONI *laying aside the mask and cloak
which the Venetian Nobles wore in
public, attended by a Domestic.*

 Lioni. I will to rest, right weary of this
 revel,
The gayest we have held for many moons,
And yet, I know not why, it cheer'd me not;
There came a heaviness across my heart,
Which, in the lightest movement of the
 dance, 5
Though eye to eye, and hand in hand
 united
Even with the lady of my love, oppress'd
 me,
And through my spirit chill'd my blood,
 until
A damp like death rose o'er my brow; I
 strove
To laugh the thought away, but 'twould
 not be; 10
Through all the music ringing in my ears
A knell was sounding as distinct and clear,
Though low and far, as e'er the Adrian
 wave
Rose o'er the city's murmur in the night,
Dashing against the outward Lido's bul-
 wark: 15
So that I left the festival before
It reach'd its zenith, and will woo my pil-
 low
For thoughts more tranquil, or forgetful-
 ness.
Antonio, take my mask and cloak, and
 light 19
The lamp within my chamber.
 Ant. Yes, my lord:
Command you no refreshment?
 Lioni. Nought, save sleep,
Which will not be commanded. Let me
 hope it, [*Exit* ANTONIO.
Though my breast feels too anxious; I will
 try
Whether the air will calm my spirits: 'tis
A goodly night; the cloudy wind which
 blew 25
From the Levant hath crept into its cave,
And the broad moon hath brighten'd. What
 a stillness! [*Goes to an open lattice.*

And what a contrast with the scene I left,
Where the tall torches' glare, and silver
 lamps'
More pallid gleam along the tapestried
 walls, 30
Spread over the reluctant gloom which
 haunts
Those vast and dimly-latticed galleries
A dazzling mass of artificial light,
Which show'd all things, but nothing as
 they were. 34
There Age essaying to recall the past,
After long striving for the hues of youth
At the sad labour of the toilet, and
Full many a glance at the too faithful
 mirror,
Prank'd forth in all the pride of ornament,
Forgot itself, and trusting to the falsehood
Of the indulgent beams, which show, yet
 hide, 41
Believed itself forgotten, and was fool'd.
There Youth, which needed not, nor
 thought of such
Vain adjuncts, lavish'd its true bloom, and
 health,
And bridal beauty, in the unwholesome
 press 45
Of flush'd and crowded wassailers, and
 wasted
Its hours of rest in dreaming this was
 pleasure,
And so shall waste them till the sunrise
 streams
On sallow cheeks and sunken eyes, which
 should not 49
Have worn this aspect yet for many a year
The music, and the banquet, and the wine
The garlands, the rose odours, and the
 flowers,
The sparkling eyes, and flashing orna-
 ments,
The white arms and the raven hair, the
 braids
And bracelets; swanlike bosoms, and the
 necklace, 5
An India in itself, yet dazzling not
The eye like what it circled; the thin robes
Floating like light clouds 'twixt our gaze
 and heaven;
The many-twinkling feet so small and
 sylph-like,
Suggesting the more secret symmetry 6
Of the fair forms which terminate so well—
All the delusion of the dizzy scene,
Its false and true enchantments—art and
 nature,
Which swam before my giddy eyes, that
 drank
The sight of beauty as the parched pilgrim'
On Arab sands the false mirage, which
 offers 6
A lucid lake to his eluded thirst,
Are gone. Around me are the stars and
 waters—

Worlds mirror'd in the ocean, goodlier
 sight 69
Than torches glared back by a gaudy glass;
And the great element, which is to space
What ocean is to earth, spreads its blue
 depths,
Soften'd with the first breathings of the
 spring;
The high moon sails upon her beauteous
 way, 74
Serenely smoothing o'er the lofty walls
Of those tall piles and sea-girt palaces,
Whose porphyry pillars, and whose costly
 fronts,
Fraught with the orient spoil of many
 marbles,
Like altars ranged along the broad canal,
Seem each a trophy of some mighty deed
Rear'd up from out the waters, scarce less
 strangely 81
Than those more massy and mysterious
 giants
Of architecture, those Titanian fabrics,
Which point in Egypt's plains to times that
 have 84
No other record. All is gentle: nought
Stirs rudely; but, congenial with the night,
Whatever walks is gliding like a spirit.
The tinklings of some vigilant guitars
Of sleepless lovers to a wakeful mistress,
And cautious opening of the casement,
 showing 90
That he is not unheard; while her young
 hand,
Fair as the moonlight of which it seems part,
So delicately white, it trembles in
The act of opening the forbidden lattice,
To let in love through music, makes his
 heart 95
Thrill like his lyre-strings at the sight; the
 dash
Phosphoric of the oar, or rapid twinkle
Of the far lights of skimming gondolas,
And the responsive voices of the choir
Of boatmen answering back with verse for
 verse; 100
Some dusky shadow checkering the Rialto;
Some glimmering palace roof, or tapering
 spire,
Are all the sights and sounds which here
 pervade
The ocean-born and earth-commanding
 city—
How sweet and soothing is this hour of
 calm! 105
I thank thee, Night! for thou hast chased
 away
Those horrid bodements which, amidst
 the throng,
I could not dissipate: and with the blessing
Of thy benign and quiet influence, 109
Now will I to my couch, although to rest
Is almost wronging such a night as this.——
 [*A knocking is heard from without.*

Hark! what is that? or who at such a
 moment?

Enter ANTONIO.

Ant. My lord, a man without, on urgent
 business,
Implores to be admitted.
 Lioni. Is he a stranger?
Ant. His face is muffled in his cloak,
 but both 115
His voice and gestures seem familiar to
 me;
I craved his name, but this he seem'd
 reluctant
To trust, save to yourself; most earnestly
He sues to be permitted to approach you.
 Lioni. 'Tis a strange hour, and a suspi-
 cious bearing! 120
And yet there is slight peril: 'tis not in
Their houses noble men are struck at; still,
Although I know not that I have a foe
In Venice, 'twill be wise to use some
 caution.
Admit him, and retire; but call up quickly
Some of thy fellows, who may wait with-
 out.— 126
Who can this man be?
 [*Exit* ANTONIO, *and returns with* BER-
 TRAM *muffled.*
 Ber. My good lord Lioni,
I have no time to lose, nor thou,—dismiss
This menial hence; I would be private with
 you.
 Lioni. It seems the voice of Bertram—
 Go, Antonio. [*Exit* ANTONIO.
Now, stranger, what would you at such an
 hour? 131
 Ber. [*discovering himself*]. A boon, my
 noble patron; you have granted
Many to your poor client, Bertram; add
This one, and make him happy.
 Lioni. Thou hast known me
From boyhood, ever ready to assist thee
In all fair objects of advancement, which
Beseem one of thy station; I would promise
Ere thy request was heard, but that the
 hour, 138
Thy bearing, and this strange, and hurried
 mode
Of suing, gives me to suspect this visit
Hath some mysterious import—but say
 on— 141
What has occurred, some rash and sudden
 broil?—
A cup too much, a scuffle, and a stab?—
Mere things of every day; so that thou hast
 not
Spilt noble blood, I guarantee thy safety;
But then thou must withdraw, for angry
 friends 146
And relatives, in the first burst of venge-
 ance,
Are things in Venice deadlier than the
 laws.

Ber. My lord, I thank you; but——
Lioni. But what? You have not
Raised a rash hand against one of our
 order? 150
If so, withdraw and fly, and own it not;
I would not slay—but then I must not save
 thee!
He who has shed patrician blood——
Ber. I come
To save patrician blood, and not to shed it!
And thereunto I must be speedy, for
Each minute lost may lose a life; since
 Time
Has changed his slow scythe for the two-
 edged sword, 157
And is about to take, instead of sand,
The dust from sepulchres to fill his hour-
 glass!—
Go not *thou* forth to-morrow!
Lioni. Wherefore not?
What means this menace?
Ber. Do not seek its meaning,
But do as I implore thee;—stir not forth,
Whate'er be stirring; though the roar of
 crowds—
The cry of women, and the shrieks of
 babes—
The groans of men—the clash of arms—
 the sound 165
Of rolling drum, shrill trump, and hollow
 bell,
Peal in one wild alarum!—Go not forth,
Until the tocsin's silent, nor even then
Till I return!
Lioni. Again, what does this mean?
Ber. Again, I tell thee, ask not; but by
 all 170
Thou holdest dear on earth or heaven—by
 all
The souls of thy great fathers, and thy
 hope
To emulate them, and to leave behind
Descendants worthy both of them and
 thee—
By all thou hast of bless'd in hope or
 memory— 175
By all thou hast to fear here or hereafter—
By all the good deeds thou hast done to
 me,
Good I would now repay with greater
 good,
Remain within—trust to thy household
 gods, 179
And to my word for safety, if thou dost
As I now counsel—but if not, thou art
 lost!
Lioni. I am indeed already lost in won-
 der;
Surely thou ravest! what have *I* to dread?
Who are my foes? or if there be such, *why*
Art *thou* leagued with them? *thou!* or if so
 leagued, 185
Why comest thou to tell me at this hour,
And not before?

Ber. I cannot answer this.
Wilt thou go forth despite of this tru[e]
 warning?
Lioni. I was not born to shrink fro[m]
 idle threats, 18[]
The cause of which I know not: at the hou[r]
Of council, be it soon or late, I shall n[o]
Be found among the absent.
Ber. Say not so![]
Once more, art thou determined to g[o]
 forth?
Lioni. I am. Nor is there aught whic[h]
 shall impede me!
Ber. Then, Heaven have mercy on th[y]
 soul!—Farewell! [*Goin[g]*
Lioni. Stay—there is more in this tha[n]
 my own safety 19[]
Which makes me call thee back; we mu[st]
 not part thus:
Bertram, I have known thee long.
Ber. From childhood, signo[r]
You have been my protector: in the day[s]
Of reckless infancy, when rank forgets,
Or, rather, is not yet taught to remembe[r]
Its cold prerogative, we play'd together
Our sports, our smiles, our tears, wer[e]
 mingled oft;
My father was your father's client, I
His son's scarce less than foster-brother[]
 years 20[]
Saw us together—happy, heart-full hours[]
Oh God! the difference 'twixt those hou[rs]
 and this!
Lioni. Bertram, 'tis thou who hast for[-]
 gotten them.
Ber. Nor now, nor ever; whatsoe'er be[-]
 tide,
I would have saved you: when to man[-]
 hood's growth 21[]
We sprung, and you, devoted to the state
As suits your station, the more humb[le]
 Bertram
Was left unto the labours of the humble[r]
Still you forsook me not; and if my for[-]
 tunes
Have not been towering, 'twas no fault o[f]
 him 21[]
Who ofttimes rescued and supported me[]
When struggling with the tides of circum[-]
 stance,
Which bear away the weaker: noble bloo[d]
Ne'er mantled in a nobler heart than thin[e]
Has proved to me, the poor plebeian Be[r-]
 tram. 22[]
Would that thy fellow senators were lik[e]
 thee!
Lioni. Why, what hast thou to sa[y]
 against the senate?
Ber. Nothing.
Lioni. I know that there are angr[y]
 spirits 22[]
And turbulent mutterers of stifled treaso[n]
Who lurk in narrow places, and walk ou[t]
Muffled to whisper curses to the night;

Disbanded soldiers, discontented ruffians,
And desperate libertines who brawl in
 taverns;
Thou herdest not with such: 'tis true, of late
I have lost sight of thee, but thou wert
 wont 230
To lead a temperate life, and break thy bread
With honest mates, and bear a cheerful
 aspect.
What hath come to thee? in thy hollow eye
And hueless cheek, and thine unquiet
 motions,
Sorrow and shame and conscience seem at
 war 235
To waste thee.
 Ber. Rather shame and sorrow light
On the accursed tyranny which rides
The very air in Venice, and makes men
Madden as in the last hours of the plague
Which sweeps the soul deliriously from
 life! 240
 Lioni. Some villains have been tamper-
 ing with thee, Bertram;
This is not thy old language, nor own
 thoughts;
Some wretch has made thee drunk with
 disaffection:
But thou must not be lost so; thou *wert*
 good 244
And kind, and art not fit for such base acts
As vice and villainy would put thee to:
Confess—confide in me—thou know'st
 my nature. 247
What is it thou and thine are bound to do,
Which should prevent thy friend, the only
 son
Of him who was a friend unto thy father,
So that our good-will is a heritage 251
We should bequeath to our posterity
Such as ourselves received it, or aug-
 mented;
say, what is it thou must do, that I
Should deem thee dangerous, and keep the
 house 255
Like a sick girl?
 Ber. Nay, question me no further:
I must be gone.——
 Lioni. And I be murder'd!—say,
Was it not thus thou said'st, my gentle
 Bertram?
 Ber. Who talks of murder? what said I
 of murder?
'Tis false! I did not utter such a word.
 Lioni. Thou didst not; but from out thy
 wolfish eye, 261
So changed from what I knew it, there
 glares forth
The gladiator. If *my* life's thine object,
Take it—I am unarm'd,—and then away!
I would not hold my breath on such a
 tenure 265
As the capricious mercy of such things
As thou and those who have set thee to thy
 taskwork.

 Ber. Sooner than spill thy blood, I peril
 mine;
Sooner than harm a hair of thine, I place
In jeopardy a thousand heads, and some
As noble, nay, even nobler than thine own.
 Lioni. Ay, is it even so? Excuse me,
 Bertram; 272
I am not worthy to be singled out
From such exalted hecatombs—who are
 they
That *are* in danger, and that *make* the
 danger? 275
 Ber. Venice, and all that she inherits,
 are
Divided like a house against itself,
And so will perish ere to-morrow's twi-
 light!
 Lioni. More mysteries, and awful ones!
 But now,
Or thou, or I, or both, it may be, are
Upon the verge of ruin; speak once out,
And thou art safe and glorious; for 'tis
 more 282
Glorious to save than slay, and slay i' the
 dark too—
Fie, Bertram! that was not a craft for thee!
How would it look to see upon a spear
The head of him whose heart was open to
 thee, 286
Borne by thy hand before the shuddering
 people?
And such may be my doom; for here I
 swear,
Whate'er the peril or the penalty
Of thy denunciation, I go forth, 290
Unless thou dost detail the cause, and
 show
The consequence of all which led thee here!
 Ber. Is there no way to save thee?
 minutes fly,
And thou art lost!—*thou!* my sole bene-
 factor,
The only being who was constant to me
Through every change. Yet, make me not
 a traitor! 296
Let me save thee—but spare my honour!
 Lioni. Where
Can lie the honour in a league of murder?
And who are traitors save unto the
 state?
 Ber. A league is still a compact, and
 more binding 300
In honest hearts when words must stand
 for law;
And in my mind, there is no traitor like
He whose domestic treason plants the
 poniard
Within the breast which trusted to his
 truth. 304
 Lioni. And *who* will strike the steel to
 mine?
 Ber. Not I;
I could have wound my soul up to all
 things

437

Save this. *Thou* must not die! and think
 how dear
Thy life is, when I risk so many lives,
Nay, more, the life of lives, the liberty
Of future generations, *not* to be 310
The assassin thou miscall'st me:—once,
 once more
I do adjure thee, pass not o'er thy threshold!
 Lioni. It is in vain—this moment I go
 forth.
 Ber. Then perish Venice rather than my
 friend!
I will disclose—ensnare—betray—des-
 troy— 315
Oh, what a villain I become for thee!
 Lioni. Say, rather, thy friend's saviour
 and the state's!—
Speak—pause not—all rewards, all
 pledges for
Thy safety and thy welfare; wealth such as
The state accords her worthiest servants;
 nay, 320
Nobility itself I guarantee thee,
So that thou art sincere and penitent.
 Ber. I have thought again: it must not
 be—I love thee—
Thou know'st it—that I stand here is the
 proof,
Not least though last; but having done my
 duty 325
By thee, I now must do it by my country!
Farewell—we meet no more in life!—fare-
 well!
 Lioni. What, ho!—Antonio—Pedro—
 to the door!
See that none pass—arrest this man!—

Enter ANTONIO *and other armed Domestics,
 who seize* BERTRAM.

 Lioni [*continues*]. Take care
He hath no harm; bring me my sword and
 cloak, 330
And man the gondola with four oars—
 quick—
 [*Exit* ANTONIO.
We will unto Giovanni Gradenigo's,
And send for Marc Cornaro:—fear not,
 Bertram; 333
This needful violence is for thy safety,
No less than for the general weal.
 Ber. Where wouldst thou
Bear me a prisoner?
 Lioni. Firstly to 'the Ten';
Next to the Doge.
 Ber. To the Doge?
 Lioni. Assuredly:
Is he not chief of the state?
 Ber. Perhaps at sunrise—
 Lioni. What mean you?—but we'll
 know anon.
 Ber. Art sure?
 Lioni. Sure as all gentle means can
 make; and if 340

They fail, you know 'the Ten' and their
 tribunal,
And that St. Mark's has dungeons, and
 the dungeons
A rack.
 Ber. Apply it then before the dawn
Now hastening into heaven.—One more
 such word,
And you shall perish piecemeal, by the
 death 34
You think to doom to me.

Re-enter ANTONIO.

 Ant. The bark is ready
My lord, and all prepared.
 Lioni. Look to the prisoner
Bertram, I'll reason with thee as we go
To the Magnifico's, sage Gradenigo.
 [*Exeunt*

SCENE II.—*The Ducal Palace.—The
 Doge's Apartment.*

The DOGE *and his Nephew* BERTUCCIO
 FALIERO.

 Doge. Are all the people of our house
 in muster?
 Ber. F. They are array'd, and eager for
 the signal,
Within our palace precincts at San Polo
I come for your last orders.
 Doge. It had been
As well had there been time to have got
 together,
From my own fief, Val di Marino, more
Of our retainers—but it is too late.
 Ber. F. Methinks, my lord, 'tis better as
 it is:
A sudden swelling of our retinue
Had waked suspicion; and, though fierce
 and trusty, 1
The vassals of that district are too rude
And quick in quarrel to have long main-
 tain'd
The secret discipline we need for such
A service, till our foes are dealt upon.
 Doge. True; but when once the signal
 has been given, 1
These are the men for such an enterprise
These city slaves have all their private bias
Their prejudice *against* or *for* this noble
Which may induce them to o'erdo or spar
Where mercy may be madness; the fierce
 peasants, 2
Serfs of my county of Val di Marino,
Would do the bidding of their lord with-
 out
Distinguishing for love or hate his foes,
Alike to them Marcello or Cornaro,
A Gradenigo or a Foscari; 2
They are not used to start at those vain
 names,
Nor bow the knee before a civic senate;
A chief in armour is their Suzerain,

And not a thing in robes.
 Ber. F. We are enough;
And for the dispositions of our clients
Against the senate I will answer.
 Doge. Well,
The die is thrown; but for a warlike ser-
 vice, 32
Done in the field, commend me to my
 peasants:
They made the sun shine through the host
 of Huns
When sallow burghers slunk back to their
 tents, 35
And cower'd to hear their own victorious
 trumpet.
If there be small resistance you will find
These citizens all lions, like their standard;
But if there 's much to do, you 'll wish,
 with me,
A band of iron rustics at our backs. 40
 Ber. F. Thus thinking, I must marvel
 you resolve
To strike the blow so suddenly.
 Doge. Such blows
Must be struck suddenly or never. When
I had o'ermaster'd the weak false remorse
Which yearn'd about my heart, too fondly
 yielding 45
A moment to the feelings of old days,
I was most fain to strike; and, firstly, that
I might not yield again to such emotions;
And, secondly, because of all these men,
Save Israel and Philip Calendaro, 50
I know not well the courage or the faith:
To-day might find 'mongst them a traitor
 to us,
As yesterday a thousand to the senate;
But once in, with their hilts hot in their
 hands,
They must *on* for their own sakes: one
 stroke struck, 55
And the mere instinct of the first-born Cain,
Which ever lurks somewhere in human
 hearts,
Though circumstance may keep it in
 abeyance,
Will urge the rest on like to wolves; the
 sight
Of blood to crowds begets the thirst of
 more, 60
As the first wine-cup leads to the long revel;
And you will find a harder task to quell
Than urge them when they *have* com-
 menced, but *till*
That moment, a mere voice, a straw, a
 shadow,
Are capable of turning them aside.— 65
How goes the night?
 Ber. F. Almost upon the dawn.
 Doge. Then it is time to strike upon the
 bell.
Are the men posted?
 Ber. F. By this time they are;
But they have orders not to strike, until

They have command from you through
 me in person. 70
 Doge. 'Tis well.—Will the morn never
 put to rest
These stars which twinkle yet o'er all the
 heavens?
I am settled and bound up, and being so,
The very effort which it cost me to
Resolve to cleanse this commonwealth
 with fire, 75
Now leaves my mind more steady. I have
 wept
And trembled at the thought of this dread
 duty;
But now I have put down all idle passion,
And look the growing tempest in the face,
As doth the pilot of an admiral galley:
Yet (wouldst thou think it, kinsman?) it
 hath been 81
A greater struggle to me, than when na-
 tions
Beheld their fate merged in the approach-
 ing fight,
Where I was leader of a phalanx, where
Thousands were sure to perish—Yes, to
 spill 85
The rank polluted current from the veins
Of a few bloated despots needed more
To steel me to a purpose such as made
Timoleon immortal, than to face
The toils and dangers of a life of war.
 Ber. F. It gladdens me to see your for-
 mer wisdom 91
Subdue the furies which so wrung you ere
You were decided.
 Doge. It was ever thus
With me; the hour of agitation came
In the first glimmerings of a purpose, when
Passion had too much room to sway; but
 in 96
The hour of action I have stood as calm
As were the dead who lay around me: this
They knew who made me what I am, and
 trusted
To the subduing power which I preserved
Over my mood, when its first burst was
 spent. 101
But they were not aware that there are
 things
Which make revenge a virtue by reflection,
And not an impulse of mere anger; though
The laws sleep, justice wakes, and injured
 souls 105
Oft do a public right with private wrong,
And justify their deeds unto themselves.—
Methinks the day breaks—is it not so?
 look,
Thine eyes are clear with youth;—the air
 puts on 109
A morning freshness, and, at least to me,
The sea looks greyer through the lattice.
 Ber. F. True,
The morn is dappling in the sky.
 Doge. Away then!

See that they strike without delay, and with
The first toll from St. Mark's, march on the
 palace
With all our house's strength; here I will
 meet you; 115
The Sixteen and their companies will move
In separate columns at the self-same mo-
 ment:
Be sure you post yourself at the great gate:
I would not trust 'the Ten' except to us—
The rest, the rabble of patricians, may
Glut the more careless swords of those
 leagued with us. 121
Remember that the cry is still 'Saint Mark!
The Genoese are come—ho! to the rescue!
Saint Mark and Liberty!'—Now—now to
 action!
 Ber. F. Farewell then, noble uncle! we
 will meet 125
In freedom and true sovereignty, or never!
 Doge. Come hither, my Bertuccio—one
 embrace;
Speed, for the day grows broader; send me
 soon
A messenger to tell me how all goes
When you rejoin our troops, and then
 sound—sound 130
The storm-bell from St. Mark's!
 [*Exit* BERTUCCIO FALIERO.
 Doge [*solus*]. He is gone,
And on each footstep moves a life. 'Tis
 done.
Now the destroying angel hovers o'er
Venice, and pauses ere he pours the vial,
Even as the eagle overlooks his prey, 135
And for a moment, poised in middle air,
Suspends the motion of his mighty wings,
Then swoops with his unerring beak.
 Thou day!
That slowly walk'st the waters! march—
 march on—
I would not smite i' the dark, but rather see
That no stroke errs. And you, ye blue sea
 waves! 141
I have seen you dyed ere now, and deeply
 too,
With Genoese, Saracen, and Hunnish gore,
While that of Venice flow'd too, but vic-
 torious,
Now thou must wear an unmix'd crimson;
 no 145
Barbaric blood can reconcile us now
Unto that horrible incarnadine,
But friend or foe will roll in civic slaughter.
And have I lived to fourscore years for this?
I, who was named Preserver of the City?
I, at whose name the million's caps were
 flung 151
Into the air, and cries from tens of thou-
 sands
Rose up, imploring Heaven to send me
 blessings,
And fame, and length of days—to see this
 day? 154

But this day, black within the calendar,
Shall be succeeded by a bright millennium
Doge Dandolo survived to ninety summer
To vanquish empires, and refuse thei
 crown;
I will resign a crown, and make the stat
Renew its freedom—but oh! by wha
 means? 16
The noble end must justify them. What
Are a few drops of human blood? 'tis false
The blood of tyrants is not human; they
Like to incarnate Molochs, feed on ours
Until 'tis time to give them to the tombs
Which they have made so populous.—O
 world! 16
Oh men! what are ye, and our best designs
That we must work by crime to punis
 crime?
And slay as if Death had but this one gate
When a few years would make the swor
 superfluous? 17
And I, upon the verge of th' unknown realm
Yet send so many heralds on before me?—
I must not ponder this. [*A pause*
 Hark! was there no
A murmur as of distant voices, and
The tramp of feet in martial unison?
What phantoms even of sound our wishe
 raise! 17
It cannot be—the signal hath not rung—
Why pauses it? My nephew's messenge
Should be upon his way to me, and he
Himself perhaps even now draws gratin
 back 18
Upon its ponderous hinge the steep towe
 portal,
Where swings the sullen huge oracula
 bell,
Which never knells but for a prince
 death,
Or for a state in peril, pealing forth
Tremendous bodements; let it do its offic
And be this peal its awfullest and last
Sound till the strong tower rock!—Wha
 silent still?
I would go forth, but that my post is here
To be the centre of re-union to
The oft discordant elements which form
Leagues of this nature, and to keep com
 pact 19
The wavering of the weak, in case of con
 flict;
For if they should do battle, 'twill be here
Within the palace, that the strife wi
 thicken:
Then here must be my station, as become
The master-mover.——Hark! he comes—
 he comes, 19
My nephew, brave Bertuccio's messen
 ger.—
What tidings? Is he marching? hath h
 sped?
 They here!—all's lost—yet will I mak
 an effort.

Enter a SIGNOR OF THE NIGHT, *with
Guards, &c. &c.*

Sig. Doge, I arrest thee of high treason!
Doge. Me!
Thy prince, of treason?—Who are they
 that dare 201
Cloak their own treason under such an
 order?
Sig. [*showing his order*]. Behold my
 order from the assembled Ten.
Doge. And *where* are they, and *why*
 assembled? no
Such council can be lawful, till the prince
Preside there, and that duty's mine: on
 thine 206
I charge thee, give me way, or marshal me
To the council chamber.
Sig. Duke! it may not be:
Nor are they in the wonted Hall of Coun-
 cil,
But sitting in the convent of Saint
 Saviour's. 210
Doge. You dare to disobey me, then?
Sig. I serve
The state, and needs must serve it faithfully;
My warrant is the will of those who rule it.
Doge. And till that warrant has my sig-
 nature
It is illegal, and, as *now* applied, 215
Rebellious. Hast thou weigh'd well thy
 life's worth,
That thus you dare assume a lawless func-
 tion?
Sig. 'Tis not my office to reply, but act—
I am placed here as guard upon thy person,
And not as judge to hear or to decide.
Doge [*aside*]. I must gain time. So that
 the storm-bell sound, 221
All may be well yet.—Kinsman, speed—
 speed—speed!—
Our fate is trembling in the balance, and
Woe to the vanquish'd! be they prince and
 people,
Or slaves and senate—
 [*The great bell of St. Mark's tolls.*
 Lo! it sounds—it tolls!
[*Aloud*]. Hark, Signor of the Night! and
 you, ye hirelings, 226
Who wield your mercenary staves in fear,
It is your knell—Swell on, thou lusty peal!
Now, knaves, what ransom for your lives?
Sig. Confusion!
Stand to your arms, and guard the door—
 all's lost 230
Unless that fearful bell be silenced soon.
The officer hath miss'd his path or purpose,
Or met some unforeseen and hideous ob-
 stacle.
Anselmo, with thy company proceed
Straight to the tower; the rest remain with
 me. [*Exit part of the Guard.*
Doge. Wretch! if thou wouldst have thy
 vile life, implore it; 236

It is not now a lease of sixty seconds.
Ay, send thy miserable ruffians forth;
They never shall return.
Sig. So let it be!
They die then in their duty, as will I.
Doge. Fool! the high eagle flies at
 nobler game 241
Than thou and thy base myrmidons,—live
 on,
So thou provok'st not peril by resistance,
And learn (if souls so much obscured can
 bear 244
To gaze upon the sunbeams) to be free.
Sig. And learn thou to be captive. It
 hath ceased, [*The bell ceases to toll.*
The traitorous signal, which was to have set
The bloodhound mob on their patrician
 prey—
The knell hath rung, but it is not the
 senate's! 249
Doge [*after a pause*]. All's silent, and
 all's lost!
Sig. Now, Doge, denounce me
As rebel slave of a revolted council!
Have I not done my duty?
Doge. Peace, thou thing!
Thou hast done a worthy deed, and earn'd
 the price
Of blood, and they who use thee will re-
 ward thee.
But thou wert sent to watch, and not to
 prate, 255
As thou said'st even now—then do thine
 office,
But let it be in silence, as behoves thee,
Since, though thy prisoner, I am thy prince.
Sig. I did not mean to fail in the respect
Due to your rank: in this I shall obey you.
Doge [*aside*]. There now is nothing left
 me save to die; 261
And yet how near success! I would have
 fallen,
And proudly, in the hour of triumph, but
To miss it thus!——
Enter other SIGNORS OF THE NIGHT, *with*
 BERTUCCIO FALIERO *prisoner.*
2nd Sig. We took him in the act
Of issuing from the tower, where, at his
 order, 265
As delegated from the Doge, the signal
Had thus begun to sound.
1st Sig. Are all the passes
Which lead up to the palace well secured?
2nd Sig. They are;—besides, it matters
 not; the chiefs
Are all in chains, and some even now on
 trial— 270
Their followers are dispersed, and many
 taken.
Ber. F. Uncle!
Doge. It is in vain to war with Fortune;
The glory hath departed from our house.
Ber. F. Who would have deem'd it?—
 Ah! one moment sooner!

441

Doge. That moment would have
 changed the face of ages; 275
This gives us to eternity—We'll meet it
As men whose triumph is not in success,
But who can make their own minds all in
 all, 278
Equal to every fortune. Droop not, 'tis
But a brief passage—I would go alone,
Yet if they send us, as 'tis like, together,
Let us go worthy of our sires and selves.
 Ber. F. I shall not shame you, uncle.
 1st Sig. Lords, our orders
Are to keep guard on both in separate
 chambers, 284
Until the council call ye to your trial.
 Doge. Our trial! will they keep their
 mockery up
Even to the last? but let them deal upon us,
As we had dealt on them, but with less
 pomp.
'Tis but a game of mutual homicides,
Who have cast lots for the first death, and
 they 290
Have won with false dice.—Who hath
 been our Judas?
 1st Sig. I am not warranted to answer
 that.
 Ber. F. I'll answer for thee—'tis a cer-
 tain Bertram,
Even now deposing to the secret Giunta.
 Doge. Bertram, the Bergamask! With
 what vile tools 295
We operate to slay or save! This creature,
Black with a double treason, now will earn
Rewards and honours, and be stamp'd in
 story
With the geese in the Capitol, which
 gabbled
Till Rome awoke, and had an annual
 triumph, 300
While Manlius, who hurl'd down the
 Gauls, was cast
From the Tarpeian.
 1st Sig. He aspired to treason,
And sought to rule the state.
 Doge. He saved the state,
And sought but to reform what he re-
 vived—
But this is idle—Come, sirs, do your work.
 1st Sig. Noble Bertuccio, we must now
 remove you 306
Into an inner chamber.
 Ber. F. Farewell, uncle!
If we shall meet again in life I know not,
But they perhaps will let our ashes mingle.
 Doge. Yes, and our spirits, which shall
 yet go forth, 310
And do what our frail clay, thus clogg'd,
 hath fail'd in!
They cannot quench the memory of those
Who would have hurl'd them from their
 guilty thrones,
And such examples will find heirs, though
 distant.

ACT V

SCENE I.—*The Hall of the Council of Ten,
 assembled with the additional Sena-
 tors, who, on the Trials of the Con-
 spirators for the Treason of* MARINO
 FALIERO, *composed what was called
 the Giunta.—Guards, Officers, &c. &c.
 —*ISRAEL BERTUCCIO *and* PHILIP CAL-
 ENDARO *as Prisoners.—*BERTRAM,
 LIONI, *and Witnesses, &c.*

The Chief of the Ten, BENINTENDE.

 Ben. There now rests, after such con-
 viction of
Their manifold and manifest offences,
But to pronounce on these obdurate men
The sentence of the law:—a grievous task
To those who hear, and those who speak.
 Alas! 5
That it should fall to me! and that my days
Of office should be stigmatised through all
The years of coming time, as bearing
 record
To this most foul and complicated treason
Against a just and free state, known to all
The earth as being the Christian bulwark
 'gainst 11
The Saracen and the schismatic Greek,
The savage Hun, and not less barbarous
 Frank;
A city which has open'd India's wealth
To Europe; the last Roman refuge from
O'erwhelming Attila; the ocean's queen;
Proud Genoa's prouder rival! 'Tis to sap
The throne of such a city, these lost men
Have risk'd and forfeited their worthless
 lives— 19
So let them die the death.
 I. Ber. We are prepared;
Your racks have done that for us. Let us
 die.
 Ben. If ye have that to say which would
 obtain
Abatement of your punishment, the Giunta
Will hear you; if you have aught to con-
 fess, 24
Now is your time, perhaps it may avail ye.
 I. Ber. We stand to hear, and not to
 speak.
 Ben. Your crimes
Are fully proved by your accomplices,
And all which circumstance can add to aid
 them;
Yet we would hear from your own lips
 complete 29
Avowal of your treason: on the verge
Of that dread gulf which none repass, the
 truth
Alone can profit you on earth or heaven—
Say, then, what was your motive?
 I. Ber. Justice!
 Ben. What
Your object?

I. Ber. Freedom!
Ben. You are brief, sir.
I. Ber. So my life grows: I 35
Was bred a soldier, not a senator.
 Ben. Perhaps you think by this blunt
 brevity
To brave your judges to postpone the sen-
 tence?
 I. Ber. Do you be brief as I am, and
 believe me, 39
I shall prefer that mercy to your pardon.
 Ben. Is this your sole reply to the tribunal?
 I. Ber. Go, ask your racks what they
 have wrung from us,
Or place us there again; we have still some
 blood left,
And some slight sense of pain in these
 wrench'd limbs:
But this ye dare not do; for if we die
 there— 45
And you have left us little life to spend
Upon your engines, gorged with pangs
 already—
Ye lose the public spectacle, with which
You would appal your slaves to further
 slavery!
Groans are not words, nor agony assent,
Nor affirmation truth, if nature's sense
Should overcome the soul into a lie, 52
For a short respite—must we bear or die?
 Ben. Say, who were your accomplices?
 I. Ber. The Senate.
 Ben. What do you mean?
 I. Ber. Ask of the suffering people,
Whom your patrician crimes have driven
 to crime. 56
 Ben. You know the Doge?
 I. Ber. I served with him at Zara
In the field, when *you* were pleading here
 your way
To present office; we exposed our lives,
While you but hazarded the lives of others,
Alike by accusation or defence; 61
And for the rest, all Venice knows her Doge,
Through his great actions, and the Senate's
 insults.
 Ben. You have held conference with
 him?
 I. Ber. I am weary—
Even wearier of your questions than your
 tortures; 65
I pray you pass to judgment.
 Ben. It is coming.
And you, too, Philip Calendaro, what
Have you to say why you should not be
 doomed?
 Cal. I never was a man of many words,
And now have few left worth the utterance.
 Ben. A further application of yon en-
 gine 71
May change your tone.
 Cal. Most true, it *will* do so;
A former application did so; but
It will not change my words, or, if it did—

 Ben. What then?
 Cal. Will my avowal on yon rack
Stand good in law?
 Ben. Assuredly.
 Cal. Whoe'er
The culprit be whom I accuse of treason?
 Ben. Without doubt, he will be brought
 up to trial. 78
 Cal. And on this testimony would he
 perish?
 Ben. So your confession be detail'd and
 full,
He will stand here in peril of his life.
 Cal. Then look well to thy proud self,
 President! 82
For by the eternity which yawns before me,
I swear that *thou*, and only thou, shalt be
The traitor I denounce upon that rack,
If I be stretch'd there for the second time.
 One of the Giunta. Lord President,
 'twere best proceed to judgment;
There is no more to be drawn from these
 men.
 Ben. Unhappy men! prepare for instant
 death.
The nature of your crime, our law, and
 peril 90
The state now stands in, leave not an hour's
 respite.
Guards! lead them forth, and upon the
 balcony
Of the red columns, where, on festal Thurs-
 day,
The Doge stands to behold the chase of
 bulls, 94
Let them be justified: and leave exposed
Their wavering relics, in the place of judg-
 ment,
To the full view of the assembled people!
And Heaven have mercy on their souls!
 The Giunta. Amen!
 I. Ber. Signors, farewell! we shall not
 all again 99
Meet in one place.
 Ben. And lest they should essay
To stir up the distracted multitude—
Guards! let their mouths be gagg'd even
 in the act
Of execution. Lead them hence!
 Cal. What! must we
Not even say farewell to some fond friend,
Nor leave a last word with our confessor?
 Ben. A priest is waiting in the ante-
 chamber; 106
But, for your friends, such interviews
 would be
Painful to them, and useless all to you.
 Cal. I knew that we were gagg'd in life;
 at least
All those who had not heart to risk their
 lives 110
Upon their open thoughts; but still I
 deem'd
That in the last few moments, the same idle

Freedom of speech accorded to the dying,
Would not now be denied to us; but
 since——
 I. Ber. Even let them have their way,
 brave Calendaro! 115
What matter a few syllables? let's die
Without the slightest show of favour from
 them;
So shall our blood more readily arise
To Heaven against them, and more testify
To their atrocities, than could a volume
Spoken or written of our dying words!
They tremble at our voices—nay, they
 dread 122
Our very silence—let them live in fear!
Leave them unto their thoughts, and let us
 now
Address our own above!—Lead on; we
 are ready. 125
 Cal. Israel, hadst thou but hearken'd
 unto me
It had not now been thus; and yon pale
 villain,
The coward Bertram, would—
 I. Ber. Peace, Calendaro!
What brooks it now to ponder upon this?
 Bert. Alas! I fain you died in peace with
 me: 130
I did not seek this task; 'twas forced upon
 me:
Say, you forgive me, though I never can
Retrieve my own forgiveness—frown not
 thus!
 I. Ber. I die and pardon thee!
 Cal. [*spitting at him*]. I die and
 scorn thee!
[*Exeunt* ISRAEL BERTUCCIO *and* PHILIP
 CALENDARO, *Guards, &c.*
 Ben. Now that these criminals have
 been disposed of, 135
'Tis time that we proceed to pass our
 sentence
Upon the greatest traitor upon record
In any annals, the Doge Faliero!
The proofs and process are complete; the
 time
And crime require a quick procedure:
 shall 140
He now be call'd in to receive the award?
 The Giunta. Ay, ay.
 Ben. Avogadori, order that the Doge
Be brought before the council.
 One of the Giunta. And the rest,
When shall they be brought up?
 Ben. When all the chiefs
Have been disposed of. Some have fled to
 Chiozza; 145
But there are thousands in pursuit of
 them,
And such precaution ta'en on terra firma,
As well as in the islands, that we hope
None will escape to utter in strange lands
His libellous tale of treasons 'gainst the
 senate. 150

Enter the DOGE *as Prisoner, with
 Guards, &c. &c.*

 Ben. Doge—for such still you are, and
 by the law
Must be consider'd, till the hour shall come
When you must doff the ducal bonnet from
That head, which could not wear a crown
 more noble 154
Than empires can confer, in quiet honour,
But it must plot to overthrow your peers,
Who made you what you are, and quench
 in blood
A city's glory—we have laid already
Before you in your chamber at full length,
By the Avogadori, all the proofs 160
Which have appear'd against you; and
 more ample
Ne'er rear'd their sanguinary shadows to
Confront a traitor. What have you to say
In your defence?
 Doge. What shall I say to ye,
Since my defence must be your condemna-
 tion? 165
You are at once offenders and accusers,
Judges and executioners!—Proceed
Upon your power.
 Ben. Your chief accomplices
Having confess'd, there is no hope for you.
 Doge. And who be they?
 Ben. In number many; but
The first now stands before you and the
 court, 171
Bertram, of Bergamo,—would you ques-
 tion him?
 Doge. [*looking at him contemptuously*].
 No.
 Ben. And two others, Israel Bertuccio
And Philip Calendaro, have admitted
Their fellowship in treason with the Doge!
 Doge. And where are they?
 Ben. Gone to their place, and now
Answering to Heaven for what they did on
 earth. 177
 Doge. Ah! the plebeian Brutus, is he
 gone?
And the quick Cassius of the arsenal?—
How did they meet their doom?
 Ben. Think of your own:
It is approaching. You decline to plead,
 then? 181
 Doge. I cannot plead to my inferiors,
 nor
Can recognise your legal power to try me.
Show me the law!
 Ben. On great emergencies
The law must be remodell'd or amended:
Our fathers had not fix'd the punishment
Of such a crime, as on the old Roman
 tables 187
The sentence against parricide was left
In pure forgetfulness; they could not render
That penal, which had neither name nor
 thought 190

444

In their great bosoms; who would have
 foreseen
That nature could be filed to such a crime
As sons 'gainst sires, and princes 'gainst
 their realms?
Your sin hath made us make a law which
 will
Become a precedent 'gainst such haught
 traitors, 195
As would with treason mount to tyranny;
Not even contented with a sceptre, till
They can convert it to a two-edged sword!
Was not the place of Doge sufficient for ye?
What's nobler than the signory of Venice?
 Doge. The signory of Venice! You be-
 tray'd me— 201
You—you, who sit there, traitors as ye are!
From my equality with you in birth,
And my superiority in action,
You drew me from my honourable toils
In distant lands—on flood, in field, in
 cities— 206
You singled me out like a victim to
Stand crown'd, but bound and helpless, at
 the altar
Where you alone could minister. I knew
 not,
I sought not, wish'd not, dream'd not the
 election, 210
Which reach'd me first at Rome, and I
 obey'd;
But found on my arrival, that, besides
The jealous vigilance which always led you
To mock and mar your sovereign's best
 intents, 214
You had, even in the interregnum of
My journey to the capital, curtail'd
And mutilated the few privileges
Yet left the duke: all this I bore, and would
Have borne, until my very hearth was
 stain'd
By the pollution of your ribaldry, 220
And he, the ribald, whom I see amongst
 you—
Fit judge in such a tribunal!—
 Ben. [*interrupting him*]. Michel Steno
Is here in virtue of his office, as
One of the Forty; 'the Ten' having craved
A Giunta of patricians from the senate
To aid our judgment in a trial arduous
And novel as the present: he was set
Free from the penalty pronounced upon him,
Because the Doge, who should protect the
 law, 229
Seeking to abrogate all law, can claim
No punishment of others by the statutes
Which he himself denies and violates!
 Doge. His PUNISHMENT! I rather see him
 there,
Where he now sits, to glut him with my
 death, 234
Than in the mockery of castigation,
Which your foul, outward, juggling show
 of justice

Decreed as sentence! Base as was his crime,
'Twas purity compared with your protec-
 tion.
 Ben. And can it be, that the great Doge
 of Venice, 239
With three parts of a century of years
And honours on his head, could thus allow
His fury, like an angry boy's, to master
All feeling, wisdom, faith, and fear, on
 such
A provocation as a young man's petu-
 lance?
 Doge. A spark creates the flame—'tis
 the last drop 245
Which makes the cup run o'er, and mine
 was full
Already: you oppress'd the prince and
 people;
I would have freed both, and have fail'd in
 both:
The price of such success would have been
 glory, 249
Vengeance, and victory, and such a name
As would have made Venetian history
Rival to that of Greece and Syracuse
When they were freed, and flourish'd ages
 after, 253
And mine to Gelon and to Thrasybulus:—
Failing, I know the penalty of failure
Is present infamy and death—the future
Will judge, when Venice is no more, or
 free;
Till then, the truth is in abeyance. Pause not;
I would have shown no mercy, and I seek
 none; 259
My life was staked upon a mighty hazard,
And being lost, take what I would have
 taken!
I would have stood alone amidst your
 tombs:
Now you may flock round mine, and
 trample on it,
As you have done upon my heart while
 living.
 Ben. You do confess then, and admit
 the justice 265
Of our tribunal?
 Doge. I confess to have fail'd;
Fortune is female: from my youth her
 favours
Were not withheld, the fault was mine to
 hope
Her former smiles again at this late hour.
 Ben. You do not then in aught arraign
 our equity? 270
 Doge. Noble Venetians! stir me not
 with questions.
I am resign'd to the worst; but in me still
Have something of the blood of brighter
 days,
And am not over-patient. Pray you, spare
 me
Further interrogation, which boots no-
 thing, 275

445

Except to turn a trial to debate.
I shall but answer that which will offend you,
And please your enemies—a host already;
'Tis true, these sullen walls should yield no
 echo:
But walls have ears—nay, more, they have
 tongues; and if 280
There were no other way for truth to o'er-
 leap them,
You who condemn me, you who fear and
 slay me,
Yet could not bear in silence to your graves
What you would hear from me of good or
 evil; 284
The secret were too mighty for your souls:
Then let it sleep in mine, unless you court
A danger which would double that you
 escape.
Such my defence would be, had I full scope
To make it famous; for true *words* are
 things,
And dying men's are things which long
 outlive, 290
And oftentimes avenge them; bury mine,
If ye would fain survive me: take this
 counsel,
And though too oft ye made me live in
 wrath,
Let me die calmly; you may grant me this;
I deny nothing, defend nothing, nothing
I ask of you, but silence for myself, 296
And sentence from the court!

Ben. This full admission
Spares us the harsh necessity of ordering
The torture to elicit the whole truth.

Doge. The torture! you have put me
 there already, 300
Daily since I was Doge; but if you will
Add the corporeal rack, you may: these
 limbs
Will yield with age to crushing iron; but
There's that within my heart shall strain
 your engines.

Enter an OFFICER.

Officer. Noble Venetians! Duchess Fal-
 iero 305
Requests admission to the Giunta's
 presence.

Ben. Say, conscript fathers, shall she be
 admitted?

One of the Giunta. She may have revela-
 tions of importance
Unto the state, to justify compliance 309
With her request.

Ben. Is this the general will?

All. It is.

Doge. Oh! admirable laws of Venice!
Which would admit the wife, in the full
 hope
That she might testify against the husband.
What glory to the chaste Venetian dames!
But such blasphemers 'gainst all honour,
 as 315

Sit here, do well to act in their vocation.
Now, villain Steno! if this woman fail,
I'll pardon thee thy lie, and thy escape,
And my own violent death, and thy vile life.

The DUCHESS *enters.*

Ben. Lady! this just tribunal has re-
 solved, 320
Though the request be strange, to grant it,
 and
Whatever be its purport, to accord
A patient hearing with the due respect
Which fits your ancestry, your rank, and
 virtues:
But you turn pale—ho! there, look to the
 lady! 325
Place a chair instantly.

Ang. A moment's faintness—
'Tis past; I pray you pardon me,—I sit not
In presence of my prince and of my hus-
 band,
While he is on his feet.

Ben. Your pleasure, lady?

Ang. Strange rumours, but most true,
 if all I hear 330
And see be sooth, have reach'd me, and I
 come
To know the worst, even at the worst; for-
 give
The abruptness of my entrance and my
 bearing.
Is it——I cannot speak—I cannot shape
The question—but you answer it ere
 spoken, 335
With eyes averted, and with gloomy
 brows—
Oh God! this is the silence of the grave!

Ben. [*after a pause*]. Spare us, and spare
 thyself the repetition
Of our most awful, but inexorable 339
Duty to Heaven and man!

Ang. Yet speak; I cannot—
I cannot—no—even now believe these
 things.
Is *he* condemned?

Ben. Alas!

Ang. And was he guilty?

Ben. Lady! the natural distraction of
Thy thoughts at such a moment makes the
 question 344
Merit forgiveness; else a doubt like this
Against a just and paramount tribunal
Were deep offence. But question even the
 Doge,
And if he can deny the proofs, believe him
Guiltless as thy own bosom.

Ang. Is it so?
My lord, my sovereign, my poor father's
 friend, 350
The mighty in the field, the sage in council,
Unsay the words of this man!—Thou art
 silent!

Ben. He hath already own'd to his own
 guilt,

Nor, as thou see'st, doth he deny it now.
Ang. Ay, but he must not die! Spare his
 few years, 355
Which grief and shame will soon cut down
 to days!
One day of baffled crime must not efface
Near sixteen lustres crowded with brave
 acts.
 Ben. His doom must be fulfill'd without
 remission
Of time or penalty—'tis a decree. 360
 Ang. He hath been guilty, but there may
 be mercy.
 Ben. Not in this case with justice.
 Ang. Alas! signor,
He who is only just is cruel; who
Upon the earth would live were all judged
 justly?
 Ben. His punishment is safety to the
 state. 365
 Ang. He was a subject, and hath served
 the state;
He was your general, and hath saved the
 state;
He is your sovereign, and hath ruled the
 state.
 One of the Council. He is a traitor, and
 betray'd the state.
 Ang. And, but for him, there now had
 been no state 370
To save or to destroy; and you, who sit
There to pronounce the death of your de-
 liverer,
Had now been groaning at a Moslem oar,
Or digging in the Hunnish mines in fetters!
 One of the Council. No, lady, there are
 others who would die 375
Rather than breathe in slavery!
 Ang. If there are so
Within *these* walls, *thou* art not of the
 number:
The truly brave are generous to the
 fallen!—
Is there no hope?
 Ben. Lady, it cannot be.
 Ang. [*turning to the Doge*]. Then die,
 Faliero! since it must be so; 380
But with the spirit of my father's friend.
Thou hast been guilty of a great offence,
Half cancell'd by the harshness of these
 men.
I would have sued to them, have pray'd
 to them,
Have begg'd as famish'd mendicants for
 bread, 385
Have wept as they will cry unto their God
For mercy, and be answer'd as they an-
 swer,—
Had it been fitting for thy name or mine,
And if the cruelty in their cold eyes
Had not announced the heartless wrath
 within. 390
Then, as a prince, address thee to thy
 doom!

Doge. I have lived too long not to know
 how to die!
Thy suing to these men were but the bleat-
 ing
Of the lamb to the butcher, or the cry
Of seamen to the surge: I would not take
A life eternal, granted at the hands 396
Of wretches, from whose monstrous vil-
 lainies
I sought to free the groaning nations!
 Michel Steno. Doge,
A word with thee, and with this noble
 lady,
Whom I have grievously offended. Would
Sorrow, or shame, or penance on my part,
Could cancel the inexorable past! 402
But since that cannot be, as Christians let
 us
Say farewell, and in peace: with full con-
 trition
I crave, not pardon, but compassion from
 you, 405
And give, however weak, my prayers for
 both.
 Ang. Sage Benintende, now chief judge
 of Venice,
I speak to thee in answer to yon signor.
Inform the ribald Steno, that his words
Ne'er weigh'd in mind with Loredano's
 daughter, 410
Further than to create a moment's pity
For such as he is: would that others had
Despis'd him as I pity! I prefer
My honour to a thousand lives, could such
Be multiplied in mine, but would not have
A single life of others lost for that 416
Which nothing human can impugn—the
 sense
Of virtue, looking not to what is call'd
A good name for reward, but to itself.
To me the scorner's words were as the
 wind 420
Unto the rock: but as there are—alas!
Spirits more sensitive, on which such
 things
Light as the whirlwind on the waters; souls
To whom dishonour's shadow is a sub-
 stance
More terrible than death, here and here-
 after; 425
Men whose vice is to start at vice's scoffing,
And who, though proof against all blan-
 dishments
Of pleasure, and all pangs of pain, are
 feeble
When the proud name on which they pin-
 nacled
Their hopes is breathed on, jealous as the
 eagle 430
Of her high aiery; let what we now
Behold, and feel, and suffer, be a lesson
To wretches how they tamper in their
 spleen
With beings of a higher order. Insects

447

Have made the lion mad ere now; a shaft
I' the heel o'erthrew the bravest of the
brave; 436
A wife's dishonour was the bane of Troy;
A wife's dishonour unking'd Rome for
ever;
An injured husband brought the Gauls to
Clusium,
And thence to Rome, which perish'd for a
time; 440
An obscene gesture cost Caligula
His life, while Earth yet bore his cruelties;
A virgin's wrong made Spain a Moorish
province;
And Steno's lie, couch'd in two worthless
lines, 444
Hath decimated Venice, put in peril
A senate which hath stood eight hundred
years,
Discrown'd a prince, cut off his crownless
head,
And forged new fetters for a groaning
people!
Let the poor wretch, like to the courtesan
Who fired Persepolis, be proud of this,
If it so please him—'twere a pride fit for
him! 451
But let him not insult the last hours of
Him, who, whate'er he now is, was a hero,
By the intrusion of his very prayers;
Nothing of good can come from such a
source, 455
Nor would we aught with him, nor now,
nor ever:
We leave him to himself, that lowest depth
Of human baseness. Pardon is for men,
And not for reptiles—we have none for
Steno,
And no resentment: things like him must
sting, 460
And higher beings suffer; 'tis the charter
Of life. The man who dies by the adder's
fang
May have the crawler crush'd, but feels no
anger:
'Twas the worm's nature; and some men
are worms
In soul more than the living things of
tombs. 465
Doge [*to Ben.*]. Signor! complete that
which you deem your duty.
Ben. Before we can proceed upon that
duty,
We would request the princess to with-
draw;
'Twill move her too much to be witness to it.
Ang. I know it will, and yet I must en-
dure it, 470
For 'tis a part of mine—I will not quit,
Except by force, my husband's side.—
Proceed!
Nay, fear not either shriek, or sigh, or tear;
Though my heart burst it shall be silent.—
Speak!

I have that within which shall o'ermaster
all. 475
Ben. Marino Faliero, Doge of Venice,
Count of Val di Marino, Senator,
And some time General of the Fleet and
Army,
Noble Venetian, many times and oft
Intrusted by the state with high employ-
ments, 480
Even to the highest, listen to the sentence.
Convict by many witnesses and proofs,
And by thine own confession, of the guilt
Of treachery and treason, yet unheard of
Until this trial—the decree is death.
Thy goods are confiscate unto the state,
Thy name is razed from out her records,
save 487
Upon a public day of thanksgiving
For this our most miraculous deliverance,
When thou art noted in our calendars
With earthquakes, pestilence, and foreign
foes, 491
And the great enemy of man, as subject
Of grateful masses for Heaven's grace in
snatching
Our lives and country from thy wickedness.
The place wherein as Doge thou shouldst
be painted, 495
With thine illustrious predecessors, is
To be left vacant, with a death-black veil
Flung over these dim words engraved be-
neath,—
'This place is of Marino Faliero, 499
Decapitated for his crimes.'
Doge. 'His *crimes*!'
But let it be so;—it will be in vain.
The veil which blackens o'er this blighted
name,
And hides, or seems to hide, these linea-
ments,
Shall draw more gazers than the thousand
portraits
Which glitter round it in their pictured
trappings— 505
Your delegated slaves—the people's ty-
rants!
'Decapitated for his crimes!'—*What*
crimes?
Were it not better to record the facts,
So that the contemplator might approve,
Or at the least learn *whence* the crimes
arose? 510
When the beholder knows a Doge con-
spired,
Let him be told the cause—it is your history.
Ben. Time must reply to that; our sons
will judge
Their fathers' judgment, which I now pro-
nounce.
As Doge, clad in the ducal robes and cap,
Thou shalt be led hence to the Giant's
Staircase, 516
Where thou and all our princes are in-
vested;

448

And there, the ducal crown being first re-
 sumed
Upon the spot where it was first assumed,
Thy head shall be struck off; and Heaven
 have mercy 520
Upon thy soul!
 Doge. Is this the Giunta's sentence?
 Ben. It is.
 Doge. I can endure it.—And the time?
 Ben. Must be immediate.—Make thy
 peace with God:
Within an hour thou must be in His pre-
 sence.
 Doge. I am *already*; and my blood will
 rise 525
To Heaven before the souls of those who
 shed it.
Are all my lands confiscated?
 Ben. They are;
And goods, and jewels, and all kind of
 treasure,
Except two thousand ducats—these dis-
 pose of.
 Doge. That's harsh.—I would have
 fain reserved the lands 530
Near to Treviso, which I hold by investment
From Laurence the Count-bishop of
 Ceneda,
In fief perpetual to myself and heirs,
To portion them (leaving my city spoil,
My palace and my treasures, to your for-
 feit) 535
Between my consort and my kinsmen.
 Ben. These
Lie under the state's ban; their chief, thy
 nephew,
In peril of his own life; but the council
Postpones his trial for the present. If
Thou will'st a state unto thy widow'd prin-
 cess, 540
Fear not, for we will do her justice.
 Ang. Signors,
I share not in your spoil! From hence-
 forth, know
I am devoted unto God alone,
And take my refuge in the cloister.
 Doge. Come!
The hour may be a hard one, but 'twill end.
Have I aught else to undergo save death?
 Ben. You have nought to do, except
 confess and die. 547
The priest is robed, the scimitar is bare,
And both await without. But, above all,
Think not to speak unto the people; they
Are now by thousands swarming at the
 gates, 551
But these are closed: the Ten, the Avoga-
 dori,
The Giunta, and the chief men of the Forty,
Alone will be beholders of thy doom,
And they are ready to attend the Doge.
 Doge. The Doge!
 Ben. Yes, Doge, thou hast lived
 and thou shalt die 556

A sovereign; till the moment which pre-
 cedes
The separation of that head and trunk,
That ducal crown and head shall be united.
Thou hast forgot thy dignity in deigning
To plot with petty traitors; not so we,
Who in the very punishment acknowledge
The prince. Thy vile accomplices have
 died
The dog's death, and the wolf's: but thou
 shalt fall
As falls the lion by the hunters, girt 565
By those who feel a proud compassion for
 thee,
And mourn even the inevitable death
Provoked by thy wild wrath and regal
 fierceness.
Now we remit thee to thy preparation:
Let it be brief, and we ourselves will be
Thy guides unto the place where first we
 were 571
United to thee as thy subjects, and
Thy senate; and must now be parted from
 thee
As such for ever, on the self-same spot.
Guards! form the Doge's escort to his
 chamber. [*Exeunt.*

SCENE II.—*The Doge's Apartment.*

The DOGE *as Prisoner, and the* DUCHESS
 attending him.

 Doge. Now, that the priest is gone,
 'twere useless all
To linger out the miserable minutes;
But one pang more, the pang of parting
 from thee,
And I will leave the few last grains of sand
Which yet remain of the accorded hour,
Still falling—I have done with Time.
 Ang. Alas!
And I have been the cause, the unconscious
 cause;
And for this funeral marriage, this black
 union,
Which thou, compliant with my father's
 wish,
Didst promise at *his* death, thou hast
 seal'd thine own. 10
 Doge. Not so; there was that in my
 spirit ever
Which shaped out for itself some great
 reverse;
The marvel is, it came not until now—
And yet it was foretold me.
 Ang. How foretold you?
 Doge. Long years ago—so long, they
 are a doubt 15
In memory, and yet they live in annals:
When I was in my youth, and served the
 senate
And signory as podesta and captain
Of the town of Treviso, on a day
Of festival, the sluggish bishop who 20

449

Convey'd the Host aroused my rash
young anger
By strange delay, and arrogant reply
To my reproof: I raised my hand and
smote him,
Until he reel'd beneath his holy burthen;
And as he rose from earth again, he raised
His tremulous hands in pious wrath to-
wards Heaven. 26
Thence pointing to the Host, which had
fallen from him,
He turn'd to me, and said, 'The hour will
come
When he thou hast o'erthrown shall over-
throw thee:
The glory shall depart from out thy house,
The wisdom shall be shaken from thy soul,
And in thy best maturity of mind 32
A madness of the heart shall seize upon
thee:
Passion shall tear thee when all passions
cease
In other men, or mellow into virtues;
And majesty, which decks all other heads,
Shall crown to leave thee headless; honours
shall
But prove to thee the heralds of destruc-
tion,
And hoary hairs of shame, and both of
death, 39
But not such death as fits an aged man.'
Thus saying, he pass'd on.—That hour is
come.
 Ang. And with this warning couldst
thou not have striven
To avert the fatal moment, and atone,
By penitence, for that which thou hadst
done?
 Doge. I own the words went to my
heart, so much 45
That I remember'd them amid the maze
Of life, as if they form'd a spectral voice,
Which shook me in a supernatural dream;
And I repented; but 'twas not for me
To pull in resolution: what must be 50
I could not change, and would not fear.—
Nay more,
Thou canst not have forgot, what all re-
member,
That on my day of landing here as Doge,
On my return from Rome, a mist of such
Unwonted density went on before 55
The Bucentaur, like the columnar cloud
Which usher'd Israel out of Egypt, till
The pilot was misled, and disembark'd us
Between the pillars of Saint Mark's, where
'tis 59
The custom of the state to put to death
Its criminals, instead of touching at
The Riva della Paglia, as the wont is,—
So that all Venice shudder'd at the omen.
 Ang. Ah! little boots it now to recollect
Such things.
 Doge. And yet I find a comfort in 65

The thought, that these things are the
work of Fate;
For I would rather yield to gods than men
Or cling to any creed of destiny,
Rather than deem these mortals, most of
whom 6
I know to be as worthless as the dust,
And weak as worthless, more than instru
ments
Of an o'erruling power; they in themselve
Were all incapable—they could not be
Victors of him who oft had conquer'd fo
them.
 Ang. Employ the minutes left in aspira
tions 7
Of a more healing nature, and in peace
Even with these wretches take thy flight t
heaven.
 Doge. I *am* at peace: the peace of cer
tainty
That a sure hour will come, when thei
sons' sons,
And this proud city, and these azur
waters, 8
And all which makes them eminent an
bright,
Shall be a desolation and a curse,
A hissing and a scoff unto the nations,
A Carthage, and a Tyre, an Ocean Babe
 Ang. Speak not thus now: the surge o
passion still 8
Sweeps o'er thee to the last; thou dos
deceive
Thyself, and canst not injure them—b
calmer.
 Doge. I stand within eternity, and see
Into eternity, and I behold—
Ay, palpable as I see thy sweet face 9
For the last time—the days which I de
nounce
Unto all time against these wave-girt walls
And they who are indwellers.
 Guard [*coming forward*]. Doge of Venice
The Ten are in attendance on your high
ness.
 Doge. Then farewell, Angiolina!—on
embrace— 9
Forgive the old man who hath been t
thee
A fond but fatal husband—love m
memory—
I would not ask so much for me still living
But thou canst judge of me more kindl
now,
Seeing my evil feelings are at rest. 10
Besides, of all the fruit of these long years
Glory, and wealth, and power, and fame
and name,
Which generally leave some flowers t
bloom
Even o'er the grave, I have nothing left
not even 10.
A little love, or friendship, or esteem,
No, not enough to extract an epitaph

From ostentatious kinsmen; in one hour
I have uprooted all my former life,
And outlived everything, except thy heart,
The pure, the good, the gentle, which will
 oft 110
With unimpair'd but not a clamorous
 grief
Still keep—Thou turn'st so pale!—Alas!
 she faints,
She has no breath, no pulse!—Guards!
 lend your aid—
I cannot leave her thus, and yet 'tis better,
Since every lifeless moment spares a pang.
When she shakes off this temporary death,
I shall be with the Eternal.—Call her
 women— 117
One look!—how cold her hand!—as cold
 as mine
Shall be ere she recovers.—Gently tend
 her,
And take my last thanks——I am ready
 now. 120
 [_The Attendants of_ ANGIOLINA _enter,
 and surround their Mistress, who has
 fainted.—Exeunt the_ DOGE, _Guards,
 &c. &c._

SCENE III.—_The Court of the Ducal Pal-
 ace; the outer gates are shut against
 the people.—The_ DOGE _enters in his
 ducal robes, in procession with the
 Council of Ten and other Patricians,
 attended by the Guards, till they ar-
 rive at the top of the 'Giants' Staircase'
 (where the Doges took the oaths); the
 Executioner is stationed there with his
 sword.—On arriving, a Chief of the
 Ten takes off the ducal cap from the
 Doge's head._

Doge. So now the Doge is nothing, and
 at last
I am again Marino Faliero:
'Tis well to be so, though but for a
 moment.
Here was I crown'd, and here, bear wit-
 ness, Heaven!
With how much more contentment I
 resign 5
That shining mockery, the ducal bauble,
Than I received the fatal ornament.
 One of the Ten. Thou tremblest, Faliero!
 Doge. 'Tis with age, then.
 Ben. Faliero! hast thou aught further
 to commend,
Compatible with justice, to the senate?
 Doge. I would commend my nephew to
 their mercy, 11
My consort to their justice; for methinks
My death, and such a death, might settle
 all
Between the state and me.
 Ben. They shall be cared for;
Even notwithstanding thine unheard-of
 crime. 15

Doge. Unheard of! ay, there's not a
 history
But shows a thousand crown'd conspira-
 tors
Against the people; but to set them free,
One sovereign only died, and one is dying.
 Ben. And who were they who fell in
 such a cause? 20
 Doge. The King of Sparta, and the Doge
 of Venice—
Agis and Faliero!
 Ben. Hast thou more
To utter or to do?
 Doge. May I speak?
 Ben. Thou may'st;
But recollect the people are without, 24
Beyond the compass of the human voice.
 Doge. I speak to Time and to Eternity,
Of which I grow a portion, not to man.
Ye elements! in which to be resolved
I hasten, let my voice be as a spirit
Upon you! Ye blue waves! which bore
 my banner, 30
Ye winds! which flutter'd o'er as if you
 loved it,
And fill'd my swelling sails as they were
 wafted
To many a triumph! Thou, my native
 earth,
Which I have bled for! and thou, foreign
 earth,
Which drank this willing blood from many
 a wound! 35
Ye stones, in which my gore will not sink,
 but
Reek up to heaven! Ye skies, which will
 receive it!
Thou sun! which shinest on these things,
 and Thou!
Who kindlest and who quenchest suns!—
 Attest!
I am not innocent—but are these guiltless?
I perish, but not unavenged: far ages 41
Float up from the abyss of time to be,
And show these eyes, before they close,
 the doom
Of this proud city, and I leave my curse
On her and hers for ever!——Yes, the
 hours 45
Are silently engendering of the day,
When she, who built 'gainst Attila a bul-
 wark,
Shall yield, and bloodlessly and basely
 yield,
Unto a bastard Attila, without
Shedding so much blood in her last de-
 fence, 50
As these old veins, oft drain'd in shielding
 her,
Shall pour in sacrifice.—She shall be
 bought
And sold, and be an appanage to those
Who shall despise her!—She shall stoop
 to be 54

A province for an empire, petty town
In lieu of capital, with slaves for senates,
Beggars for nobles, panders for a people!
Then when the Hebrew's in thy palaces,
The Hun in thy high places, and the Greek
Walks o'er thy mart, and smiles on it for
 his: 60
When thy patricians beg their bitter bread
In narrow streets, and in their shameful
 need
Make their nobility a plea for pity;
Then, when the few who still retain a
 wreck
Of their great fathers' heritage shall fawn
Round a barbarian Vice of Kings' Vice-
 gerent, 66
Even in the palace where they sway'd as
 sovereigns,
Even in the palace where they slew their
 sovereign,
Proud of some name they have disgraced,
 or sprung
From an adulteress boastful of her guilt
With some large gondolier or foreign
 soldier, 71
Shall bear about their bastardy in triumph
To the third spurious generation;—when
Thy sons are in the lowest scale of being,
Slaves turn'd o'er to the vanquish'd by the
 victors, 75
Despised by cowards for greater cowar-
 dice,
And scorn'd even by the vicious for such
 vices
As in the monstrous grasp of their con-
 ception
Defy all codes to image or to name them;
Then, when of Cyprus, now thy subject
 kingdom, 80
All thine inheritance shall be her shame
Entail'd on thy less virtuous daughters,
 grown
A wider proverb for worse prostitution;—
When all the ills of conquer'd states shall
 cling thee,
Vice without splendour, sin without relief
Even from the gloss of love to smooth it
 o'er, 86
But in its stead, coarse lusts of habitude,
Prurient yet passionless, cold studied
 lewdness,
Depraving nature's frailty to an art;—
When these and more are heavy on thee,
 when 90
Smiles without mirth, and pastimes with-
 out pleasure,
Youth without honour, age without res-
 pect,
Meanness and weakness, and a sense of
 woe
'Gainst which thou wilt not strive, and
 dar'st not murmur,
Have made thee last and worst of peopled
 deserts, 95

Then, in the last gasp of thine agony,
Amidst thy many murders, think of *mine*.
Thou den of drunkards with the blood of
 princes! 98
Gehenna of the waters! thou sea-Sodom!
Thus I devote thee to the infernal gods!
Thee and thy serpent seed!
 [*Here the* DOGE *turns and addresses the*
 Executioner.
 Slave, do thine office!
Strike as I struck the foe! Strike as I would
Have struck those tyrants! Strike deep as
 my curse!
Strike—and but once!
 [*The* DOGE *throws himself upon his*
 knees, and as the Executioner raises
 his sword the scene closes.

SCENE IV.—*The Piazza and Piazzetta of*
 St. Mark's.—The people in crowds
 gathered round the grated gates of the
 Ducal Palace, which are shut.

 First Citizen. I have gain'd the gate
 and can discern the Ten,
Robed in their gowns of state, ranged
 round the Doge.
 Second. Cit. I cannot reach thee with
 mine utmost effort.
How is it? let us hear at least, since sight
Is thus prohibited unto the people, 5
Except the occupiers of those bars.
 First Cit. One has approach'd the
 Doge, and now they strip
The ducal bonnet from his head—and now
He raises his keen eyes to heaven; I see
Them glitter, and his lips move—Hush!
 hush!—no, 10
'Twas but a murmur—Curse upon the dis-
 tance!
His words are inarticulate, but the voice
Swells up like mutter'd thunder; would we
 could
But gather a sole sentence!
 Second Cit. Hush! we perhaps may
 catch the sound.
 First Cit. 'Tis vain, 15
I cannot hear him.—How his hoary hair
Streams on the wind like foam upon the
 wave!
Now—now—he kneels—and now they
 form a circle
Round him, and all is hidden—but I see
The lifted sword in air——Ah! hark! it
 falls! 20
 [*The people murmur.*
 Third Cit. Then they have murder'd
 him who would have freed us.
 Fourth Cit. He was a kind man to the
 commons ever.
 Fifth Cit. Wisely they did to keep their
 portals barr'd.
Would we had known the work they were
 preparing

Ere we were summon'd here—we would
 have brought 25
Weapons, and forced them!
 Sixth Cit. Are you sure he 's dead?
 First Cit. I saw the sword fall—Lo!
 what have we here?

*Enter on the Balcony of the Palace which
fronts St. Mark's Place a* CHIEF OF THE
TEN, *with a bloody sword. He waves it
thrice before the People, and exclaims,*

'Justice hath dealt upon the mighty
 Traitor!'

[*The gates are opened; the populace rush
in towards the 'Giants' Staircase,'
where the execution has taken place.
The foremost of them exclaims to those
behind,*

'The gory head rolls down the Giants'
 Steps!' [*The curtain falls.*

SARDANAPALUS

A TRAGEDY

TO

THE ILLUSTRIOUS GOETHE

A STRANGER PRESUMES TO OFFER THE HOMAGE OF A
LITERARY VASSAL TO HIS LIEGE LORD, THE FIRST OF EXISTING WRITERS,
WHO HAS CREATED THE LITERATURE OF HIS OWN COUNTRY,
AND ILLUSTRATED THAT OF EUROPE.

THE UNWORTHY PRODUCTION
WHICH THE AUTHOR VENTURES TO INSCRIBE TO HIM IS ENTITLED,

SARDANAPALUS

PREFACE

IN publishing the following Tragedies* I have only to repeat, that they were not composed with
the most remote view to the stage. On the attempt made by the managers in a former instance, the
public opinion has been already expressed. With regard to my own private feelings, as it seems that
they are to stand for nothing, I shall say nothing.

For the historical foundation of the following compositions the reader is referred to the Notes.

The Author has in one instance attempted to preserve, and in the other to approach, the 'unities';
conceiving that with any very distant departure from them, there may be poetry, but can be no drama.
He is aware of the unpopularity of this notion in present English literature; but it is not a system of
his own, being merely an opinion, which, not very long ago, was the law of literature throughout the
world, and is still so in the more civilized parts of it. But 'nous avons changé tout cela,' and are
reaping the advantages of the change. The writer is far from conceiving that anything he can adduce
by personal precept or example can at all approach his regular, or even irregular, predecessors: he is
merely giving a reason why he preferred the more regular formation of a structure, however feeble,
to an entire abandonment of all rules whatsoever. Where he has failed, the failure is in the architect,—
and not in the art.

DRAMATIS PERSONÆ

MEN

SARDANAPALUS, *King of Nineveh and Assyria, &c.*
ARBACES, *the Mede who aspired to the Throne.*
BELESES, *a Chaldean and Soothsayer.*
SALEMENES, *the King's Brother-in-Law.*
ALTADA, *an Assyrian Officer of the Palace.*
PANIA.
ZAMES.
SFERO.
BALEA.

WOMEN

ZARINA, *the Queen.*

MYRRHA, *an Ionian female Slave, and the Fav-
ourite of* SARDANAPALUS.

Women composing the Harem of SARDANAPALUS,
 *Guards, Attendants, Chaldean Priests,
 Medes, &c. &c.*

SCENE.—*A Hall in the Royal Palace of Nineveh*

In this tragedy it has been my intention to follow the account of Diodorus Siculus; reducing it,
however, to such dramatic regularity as I best could, and trying to approach the unities. I therefore
suppose the rebellion to explode and succeed in one day by a sudden conspiracy, instead of the long
war of the history.

ACT I

SCENE I.—*A Hall in the Palace.*
Salemenes [solus]. He hath wrong'd his
 queen, but still he is her lord;

He hath wrong'd my sister, still he is my
 brother;
He hath wrong'd his people, still he is
 their sovereign,
And I must be his friend as well as subject:

* 'Sardanapalus' and 'The Two Foscari.'

He must not perish thus. I will not see
The blood of Nimrod and Semiramis 6
Sink in the earth, and thirteen hundred
 years
Of empire ending like a shepherd's tale;
He must be roused. In his effeminate heart
There is a careless courage which cor-
 ruption 10
Has not all quench'd, and latent energies,
Repress'd by circumstance, but not de-
 stroy'd—
Steep'd, but not drown'd, in deep volup-
 tuousness.
If born a peasant, he had been a man
To have reach'd an empire: to an empire
 born, 15
He will bequeath none; nothing but a
 name,
Which his sons will not prize in heritage:
Yet, not all lost, even yet he may redeem
His sloth and shame, by only being that
Which he should be, as easily as the thing
He should not be and is. Were it less toil
To sway his nations than consume his life?
To head an army than to rule a harem?
He sweats in palling pleasures, dulls his
 soul,
And saps his goodly strength, in toils
 which yield not 25
Health like the chase, nor glory like the
 war—
He must be roused. Alas! there is no
 sound
[*Sound of soft music heard from within.*
To rouse him short of thunder. Hark! the
 lute,
The lyre, the timbrel; the lascivious tink-
 lings
Of lulling instruments, the softening
 voices 30
Of women, and of beings less than women,
Must chime in to the echo of his revel,
While the great king of all we know of earth
Lolls crown'd with roses, and his diadem
Lies negligently by to be caught up 35
By the first manly hand which dares to
 snatch it.
Lo, where they come! already I perceive
The reeking odours of the perfumed trains,
And see the bright gems of the glittering
 girls, 39
At once his chorus and his council, flash
Along the gallery, and amidst the damsels,
As femininely garb'd, and scarce less fe-
 male,
The grandson of Semiramis, the man-
 queen.—
He comes! Shall I await him? yes, and
 front him,
And tell him what all good men tell each
 other, 45
Speaking of him and his. They come, the
 slaves
Led by the monarch subject to his slaves.

SCENE II

Enter SARDANAPALUS *effeminately dressed,
 his Head crowned with Flowers, and
 his Robe negligently flowing, attended
 by a Train of Women and young Slaves.*

Sar. [*speaking to some of his attendants*].
Let the pavilion over the Euphrates
Be garlanded, and lit, and furnish'd forth
For an especial banquet; at the hour
Of midnight we will sup there: see nought
 wanting, 4
And bid the galley be prepared. There is
A cooling breeze which crisps the broad
 clear river:
We will embark anon. Fair nymphs, who
 deign
To share the soft hours of Sardanapalus,
We'll meet again in that the sweetest hour,
When we shall gather like the stars above
 us, 10
And you will form a heaven as bright as
 theirs;
Till then, let each be mistress of her time,
And thou, my own Ionian Myrrha, choose
Wilt thou along with them or me?
 Myr. My lord——
Sar. My lord!—my life! why answerest
 thou so coldly? 15
It is the curse of kings to be so answer'd.
Rule thy own hours, thou rulest mine—
 say, wouldst thou
Accompany our guests, or charm away
The moments from me?
 Myr. The king's choice is mine.
Sar. I pray thee say not so: my chiefest
 joy 20
Is to contribute in every wish.
I do not dare to breathe my own desire,
Lest it should clash with thine; for thou
 art still
Too prompt to sacrifice thy thoughts for
 others.
 Myr. I would remain: I have no happi-
 ness 25
Save in beholding thine; yet——
 Sar. Yet! what YET?
Thy own sweet will shall be the only
 barrier
Which ever rises betwixt thee and me.
 Myr. I think the present is the wonted
 hour
Of council; it were better I retire. 30
 Sal. [*comes forward and says*] The
 Ionian slave says well: let her retire.
 Sar. Who answers? How now, brother?
 Sal. The *queen's* brother,
And your most faithful vassal, royal lord.
 Sar. [*addressing his train*]. As I have
 said, let all dispose their hours 34
Till midnight, when again we pray your
 presence. [*The court retiring.*
[*To* MYRRHA, *who is going*]. Myrrha! I
 thought *thou* wouldst remain.

Myr. Great king,
Thou didst not say so.
Sar. But *thou* lookedst it:
I know each glance of those Ionic eyes,
Which said thou wouldst not leave me.
Myr. Sire! your brother——
Sal. His *consort's* brother, minion of
Ionia! 40
How darest *thou* name *me* and not blush?
Sar. Not blush!
Thou hast no more eyes than heart to make
her crimson
Like to the dying day on Caucasus,
Where sunset tints the snow with rosy
shadows,
And then reproach her with thine own
cold blindness, 45
Which will not see it. What! in tears, my
Myrrha?
Sal. Let them flow on; she weeps for
more than one,
And is herself the cause of bitterer tears.
Sar. Cursed be he who caused those
tears to flow!
Sal. Curse not thyself—millions do
that already. 50
Sar. Thou dost forget thee: make me
not remember
I am a monarch.
Sal. Would thou couldst!
Myr. My sovereign,
I pray, and thou, too, prince, permit my
absence.
Sar. Since it must be so, and this churl
has check'd
Thy gentle spirit, go; but recollect 55
That we must forthwith meet: I had
rather lose
An empire than thy presence.
 [*Exit* MYRRHA.
Sal. It may be
Thou wilt lose both, and both for ever!
Sar. Brother!
I can at least command myself, who listen
To language such as this: yet urge me not
Beyond my easy nature.
Sal. 'Tis beyond 61
That easy, far too easy, idle nature,
Which I would urge thee. O that I could
rouse thee!
Though 'twere against myself.
Sar. By the god Baal!
The man would make me tyrant.
Sal. So thou art.
Think'st thou there is no tyranny but that
Of blood and chains? The despotism of
vice, 67
The weakness and the wickedness of
luxury,
The negligence, the apathy, the evils
Of sensual sloth—produce ten thousand
tyrants,
Whose delegated cruelty surpasses 71
The worst acts of one energetic master,

However harsh and hard in his own bear-
ing.
The false and fond examples of thy lusts
Corrupt no less than they oppress, and
sap 75
In the same moment all thy pageant power
And those who should sustain it; so that
whether
A foreign foe invade, or civil broil
Distract within, both will alike prove fatal.
The first thy subjects have no heart to
conquer; 8c
The last they rather would assist than
vanquish.
Sar. Why, what makes thee the mouth-
piece of the people?
Sal. Forgiveness of the queen's, my
sister's wrongs;
A natural love unto my infant nephews;
Faith to the king, a faith he may need
shortly, 85
In more than words; respect for Nimrod's
line;
Also, another thing thou knowest not.
Sar. What's that?
Sal. To thee an unknown word.
Sar. Yet speak it;
I love to learn.
Sal. Virtue.
Sar. Not know the word!
Never was word yet rung so in my ears—
Worse than the rabble's shout, or splitting
trumpet: 91
I've heard thy sister talk of nothing else.
Sal. To change the irksome theme, then
hear of vice.
Sar. From whom?
Sal. Even from the winds, if thou
couldst listen
Unto the echoes of the nation's voice.
Sar. Come, I'm indulgent, as thou
knowest, patient, 96
As thou hast often proved—speak out,
what moves thee?
Sal. Thy peril.
Sar. Say on.
Sal. Thus, then: all the nations,
For they are many, whom thy father left
In heritage, are loud in wrath against
thee. 100
Sar. 'Gainst *me!* What would the
slaves?
Sal. A king.
Sar. And what
Am I then?
Sal. In their eyes a nothing; but
In mine a man who might be something
still.
Sar. The railing drunkards! why, what
would they have? 104
Have they not peace and plenty?
Sal. Of the first,
More than is glorious; of the last, far less
Than the king recks of.

Sar. Whose then is the crime,
But the false satraps', who provide no
 better?
 Sal. And somewhat in the monarch
 who ne'er looks
Beyond his palace walls, or if he stirs
Beyond them, 'tis but to some mountain
 palace, 111
Till summer heats wear down. O glorious
 Baal!
Who built up this vast empire, and wert
 made
A god, or at the least shinest like a god
Through the long centuries of thy renown,
This, thy presumed descendant, ne'er
 beheld 116
As king the kingdoms thou didst leave as
 hero,
Won with thy blood, and toil, and time,
 and peril!
For what? to furnish imposts for a revel,
Or multiplied extortions for a minion.
 Sar. I understand thee—thou wouldst
 have me go 121
Forth as a conqueror. By all the stars
Which the Chaldeans read—the restless
 slaves
Deserve that I should curse them with
 their wishes,
And lead them forth to glory.
 Sal. Wherefore not?
Semiramis—a woman only—led 126
These our Assyrians to the solar shores
Of Ganges.
 Sar. 'Tis most true. And *how* re-
 turn'd?
 Sal. Why, like a *man*—a hero; baffled,
 but
Not vanquish'd. With but twenty guards,
 she made 130
Good her retreat to Bactria.
 Sar. And how many
Left she behind in India to the vultures?
 Sal. Our annals say not.
 Sar. Then I will say for them—
That she had better woven within her
 palace
Some twenty garments, than with twenty
 guards 135
Have fled to Bactria, leaving to the ravens,
And wolves, and men—the fiercer of the
 three,
Her myriads of fond subjects. Is *this*
 glory?
Then let me live in ignominy ever.
 Sal. All warlike spirits have not the
 same fate. 140
Semiramis, the glorious parent of
A hundred kings, although she fail'd in
 India,
Brought Persia, Media, Bactria, to the
 realm
Which she once sway'd—and thou *might'st*
 sway.

Sar. I *sway* them—
She but subdued them.
 Sal. It may be ere long
That they will need her sword more than
 your sceptre. 146
 Sar. There was a certain Bacchus, was
 there not?
I've heard my Greek girls speak of such—
 they say
He was a god, that is, a Grecian god,
An idol foreign to Assyria's worship,
Who conquer'd this same golden realm
 of Ind 151
Thou prat'st of, where Semiramis was
 vanquish'd.
 Sal. I have heard of such a man; and
 thou perceiv'st
That he is deem'd a god for what he did.
 Sar. And in his godship I will honour
 him— 155
Not much as man. What, ho! my cup-
 bearer?
 Sal. What means the king?
 Sar. To worship your new god
And ancient conqueror. Some wine, I say.

Enter Cupbearer.

 Sar. [*addressing the Cupbearer*]. Bring
 me the golden goblet, thick with
 gems,
Which bears the name of Nimrod's cha-
 lice. Hence, 160
Fill full, and bear it quickly.
 [*Exit Cupbearer.*
 Sal. Is this moment
A fitting one for the resumption of
Thy yet unslept-off revels?

Re-enter Cupbearer, with wine.

 Sar. [*taking the cup from him*]. Noble
 kinsman,
If these barbarian Greeks of the far shores
And skirts of these our realms lie not, this
 Bacchus 165
Conquer'd the whole of India, did he not?
 Sal. He did, and thence was deem'd a
 deity.
 Sar. Not so:—of all his conquests a few
 columns
Which may be his, and might be mine, if I
Thought them worth purchase and con-
 veyance, are 170
The landmarks of the seas of gore he shed,
The realms he wasted, and the hearts he
 broke.
But here, here in this goblet is his title
To immortality—the immortal grape
From which he first express'd the soul, and
 gave 175
To gladden that of man, as some atone-
 ment
For the victorious mischiefs he had done.
Had it not been for this, he would have
 been

456

A mortal still in name as in his grave;
And, like my ancestor Semiramis, 180
A sort of semi-glorious human monster.
Here's that which deified him—let it now
Humanise thee; my surly, chiding brother
Pledge me to the Greek god!
Sal. For all thy realms
I would not so blaspheme our country's
 creed. 185
Sar. That is to say, thou thinkest him
 a hero,
That he shed blood by oceans; and no god,
Because he turn'd a fruit to an enchant-
 ment,
Which cheers the sad, revives the old,
 inspires
The young, makes weariness forget his
 toil, 190
And fear her danger; opens a new world
When this, the present, palls. Well, then
 I pledge thee
And *him* as a true man, who did his utmost
In good or evil to surprise mankind.
 [*Drinks.*
Sal. Wilt thou resume a revel at this
 hour? 195
Sar. And if I did, 'twere better than a
 trophy,
Being bought without a tear. But that is
 not
My present purpose: since thou wilt not
 pledge me,
Continue what thou pleasest.
 [*To the Cupbearer.*] Boy, retire.
 [*Exit Cupbearer.*
Sal. I would but have recall'd thee from
 thy dream; 200
Better by me awaken'd than rebellion.
Sar. Who should rebel? or why? what
 cause? pretext?
I am the lawful king, descended from
A race of kings who knew no predecessors.
What have I done to thee, or to the people,
That thou shouldst rail, or they rise up
 against me? 206
Sal. Of what thou hast done to me, I
 speak not.
Sar. But
Thou think'st that I have wrong'd the
 queen: is't not so?
Sal. Think! Thou hast wrong'd her!
Sar. Patience, prince, and hear me.
She has all power and splendour of her
 station, 210
Respect, the tutelage of Assyria's heirs,
The homage and the appanage of sove-
 reignty.
I married her as monarchs wed—for state,
And loved her as most husbands love their
 wives.
If she or thou supposedst I could link me
Like a Chaldean peasant to his mate,
Ye knew nor me, nor monarchs, nor man-
 kind. 217

Sal. I pray thee, change the theme: my
 blood disdains
Complaint, and Salemenes' sister seeks not
Reluctant love even from Assyria's lord!
Nor would she deign to accept divided
 passion 221
With foreign strumpets and Ionian slaves.
The queen is silent.
Sar. And why not her brother?
Sal. I only echo thee the voice of em-
 pires,
Which he who long neglects not long will
 govern. 225
Sar. The ungrateful and ungracious
 slaves! they murmur
Because I have not shed their blood, nor
 led them
To dry into the desert's dust by myriads,
Or whiten with their bones the banks of
 Ganges; 229
Nor decimated them with savage laws,
Nor sweated them to build up pyramids,
Or Babylonian walls.
Sal. Yet these are trophies
More worthy of a people and their prince
Than songs, and lutes, and feasts, and
 concubines,
And lavish'd treasures, and contemned
 virtues. 235
Sar. Or for my trophies I have founded
 cities:
There's Tarsus and Anchialus, both built
In one day—what could that blood-loving
 beldame, 238
My martial grandam, chaste Semiramis,
Do more, except destroy them?
Sal. 'Tis most true;
I own thy merit in those founded cities,
Built for a whim, recorded with a verse,
Which shames both them and thee to
 coming ages.
Sar. Shame me! By Baal, the cities,
 though well built,
Are not more goodly than the verse! Say
 what 245
Thou wilt 'gainst me, my mode of life or
 rule,
But nothing 'gainst the truth of that brief
 record.
Why, those few lines contain the history
Of all things human: hear—'Sardanapalus,
The king, and son of Anacyndaraxes,
In one day built Anchialus and Tarsus.
Eat, drink, and love; the rest's not worth
 a fillip.'
Sal. A worthy moral, and a wise in-
 scription,
For a king to put up before his subjects!
Sar. Oh, thou wouldst have me doubt-
 less set up edicts— 255
'Obey the king—contribute to his trea-
 sure—
Recruit his phalanx—spill your blood at
 bidding—

Fall down and worship, or get up and toil.'
Or thus—'Sardanapalus on this spot
Slew fifty thousand of his enemies. 260
These are their sepulchres, and this his
 trophy.'
I leave such things to conquerors; enough
For me, if I can make my subjects feel
The weight of human misery less, and glide
Ungroaning to the tomb: I take no licence
Which I deny to them. We all are men.
 Sal. Thy sires have been revered as
 gods—
 Sar. In dust
And death, where they are neither gods
 nor men.
Talk not of such to me! the worms are
 gods; 269
At least they banqueted upon your gods,
And died for lack of further nutriment.
Those gods were merely men; look to their
 issue—
I feel a thousand mortal things about me,
But nothing godlike,—unless it may be
The thing which you condemn, a dis-
 position 275
To love and to be merciful, to pardon
The follies of my species, and (that's
 human)
To be indulgent to my own.
 Sal. Alas!
The doom of Nineveh is seal'd.—Woe—
 woe
To the unrivall'd city!
 Sar. What dost dread?
 Sal. Thou art guarded by thy foes: in a
 few hours 281
The tempest may break out which over-
 whelms thee,
And thine and mine; and in another day
What *is* shall be the past of Belus' race.
 Sar. What must we dread?
 Sal. Ambitious treachery,
Which has environ'd thee with snares; but
 yet 286
There is resource: empower me with thy
 signet
To quell the machinations, and I lay
The heads of thy chief foes before thy feet.
 Sar. The heads—how many?
 Sal. Must I stay to number
When even thine own's in peril? Let me go;
Give me thy signet—trust me with the rest.
 Sar. I will trust no man with unlimited
 lives.
When we take those from others, we nor
 know
What we have taken, nor the thing we
 give. 295
 Sal. Wouldst thou not take their lives
 who seek for thine?
 Sar. That's a hard question—But I
 answer, Yes.
Cannot the thing be done without? Who
 are they

Whom thou suspectest?—Let them b
 arrested.
 Sal. I would thou wouldst not ask me
 the next moment 3
Will send my answer through thy babblin
 troop
Of paramours, and thence fly o'er th
 palace,
Even to the city, and so baffle all.—
Trust me.
 Sar. Thou knowest I have done so eve
Take thou the signet. [*Gives the signe*
 Sal. I have one more request. 3
 Sar. Name it.
 Sal. That thou this night forbear th
 banquet
In the pavilion over the Euphrates.
 Sar. Forbear the banquet! Not for a
 the plotters
That ever shook a kingdom! Let the
 come,
And do their worst: I shall not blench fe
 them; 3
Nor rise the sooner; nor forbear the gol
 let;
Nor crown me with a single rose the les
Nor lose one joyous hour.—I fear the
 not.
 Sal. But thou wouldst arm thee, would
 thou not, if needful?
 Sar. Perhaps. I have the goodliest a
 mour, and 3
A sword of such a temper; and a bow
And javelin, which might furnish Nimro
 forth:
A little heavy, but yet not unwieldy.
And now I think on't, 'tis long since I'v
 used them,
Even in the chase. Hast ever seen the
 brother? 32
 Sal. Is this a time for such fantasti
 trifling?—
If need be, wilt thou wear them?
 Sar. Will I not
Oh! if it must be so, and these rash slave
Will not be ruled with less, I'll use th
 sword
Till they shall wish it turn'd into a distaf
 Sal. They say thy sceptre's turn'd t
 that already. 32
 Sar. That's false! but let them say so
 the old Greeks,
Of whom our captives often sing, relate
The same of their chief hero, Hercules,
Because he loved a Lydian queen: tho
 seest 33
The populace of all the nations seize
Each calumny they can to sink their sove
 reigns.
 Sal. They did not speak thus of th
 fathers.
 Sar. No;
They dared not. They were kept to to
 and combat;

And never changed their chains but for
 their armour: 335
Now they have peace and pastime, and the
 licence
To revel and to rail; it irks me not.
I would not give the smile of one fair girl
For all the popular breath that e'er divided
A name from nothing. What are the rank
 tongues 340
Of this vile herd, grown insolent with feed-
 ing,
That I should prize their noisy praise, or
 dread
Their noisome clamour?
 Sal. You have said they are men;
As such their hearts are something.
 Sar. So my dogs' are;
And better, as more faithful:—but, pro-
 ceed; 345
Thou hast my signet:—since they are
 tumultuous,
Let them be temper'd, yet not roughly, till
Necessity enforce it. I hate all pain,
Given or received; we have enough within us,
The meanest vassal as the loftiest monarch,
Not to add to each other's natural burthen
Of mortal misery, but rather lessen, 352
By mild reciprocal alleviation,
The fatal penalties imposed on life:
But this they know not, or they will not
 know. 355
I have, by Baal! done all I could to soothe
 them:
I made no wars, I added no new imposts,
I interfered not with their civic lives,
I let them pass their days as best might suit
 them: 359
Passing my own as suited me.
 Sal. Thou stopp'st
Short of the duties of a king; and therefore
They say thou art unfit to be a monarch.
 Sar. They lie.—Unhappily, I am unfit
To be aught save a monarch; else for me
The meanest Mede might be the king in-
 stead. 365
 Sal. There is one Mede, at least, who
 seeks to be so.
 Sar. What mean'st thou?—'tis thy
 secret; thou desirest
Few questions, and I'm not of curious
 nature.
Take the fit steps; and, since necessity
Requires, I sanction and support thee.
 Ne'er 370
Was man who more desired to rule in peace
The peaceful only: if they rouse me, better
They had conjured up stern Nimrod from
 his ashes,
'The mighty hunter.' I will turn these
 realms
To one wide desert chase of brutes, who
 were, 375
But *would* no more, by their own choice,
 be human.

What they have found me, they belie; *that
 which*
They yet may find me—shall defy their
 wish
To speak it worse; and let them thank
 themselves. 379
 Sal. Then thou at last canst feel?
 Sar. Feel! who feels not
Ingratitude?
 Sal. I will not pause to answer
With words, but deeds. Keep thou awake
 that energy
Which sleeps at times, but is not dead with-
 in thee,
And thou may'st yet be glorious in thy
 reign, 384
As powerful in thy realm. Farewell!
 [*Exit* SALEMENES.
 Sar. [*solus*]. Farewell!
He's gone; and on his finger bears my sig-
 net,
Which is to him a sceptre. He is stern
As I am heedless; and the slaves deserve
To feel a master. What may be the danger,
I know not: he hath found it, let him quell
 it. 390
Must I consume my life—this little life—
In guarding against all may make it less?
It is not worth so much! It were to die
Before my hour, to live in dread of death,
Tracing revolt; suspecting all about me,
Because they are near; and all who are
 remote, 396
Because they are far. But if it should be
 so—
If they should sweep me off from earth and
 empire,
Why, what is earth or empire of the earth?
I have loved, and lived, and multiplied my
 image; 400
To die is no less natural than those
Acts of this clay! 'Tis true I have not shed
Blood as I might have done, in oceans, till
My name became the synonyme of death—
A terror and a trophy. But for this 405
I feel no penitence; my life is love:
If I must shed blood, it shall be by force.
Till now, no drop from an Assyrian vein
Hath flow'd for me, nor hath the smallest
 coin
Of Nineveh's vast treasures e'er been
 lavish'd 410
On objects which could cost her sons a
 tear:
If then they hate me, 'tis because I hate not:
If they rebel, 'tis because I oppress not.
Oh, men! ye must be ruled with scythes,
 not sceptres,
And mow'd down like the grass, else all we
 reap 415
Is rank abundance, and a rotten harvest
Of discontents infecting the fair soil,
Making a desert of fertility.—
I'll think no more.——Within there, ho!

Enter an ATTENDANT.

Sar. Slave, tell
The Ionian Myrrha we could crave her
 presence. 420
Attend. King, she is here.

MYRRHA *enters.*

Sar. [*apart to Attendant*]. Away!
[*Addressing* MYRRHA]. Beautiful being!
Thou dost almost anticipate my heart;
It throbb'd for thee, and here thou comest:
 let me
Deem that some unknown influence, some
 sweet oracle,
Communicates between us, though un-
 seen, 425
In absence, and attracts us to each other.
Myr. There doth.
Sar. I know there doth, but not its
 name:
What is it?
Myr. In my native land a God,
And in my heart a feeling like a God's,
Exalted; yet I own 'tis only mortal; 430
For what I feel is humble, and yet happy—
That is, it would be happy; but——
 [MYRRHA *pauses.*
Sar. There comes
For ever something between us and what
We deem our happiness: let me remove
The barrier which that hesitating accent
Proclaims to thine, and mine is seal'd.
Myr. My lord!
Sar. My lord—my king—sire—sove-
 reign; thus it is— 437
For ever thus, address'd with awe. I ne'er
Can see a smile, unless in some broad
 banquet's
Intoxicating glare, when the buffoons
Have gorged themselves up to equality,
Or I have quaff'd me down to their abase-
 ment. 442
Myrrha, I can hear all these things, these
 names,
Lord—king—sire—monarch—nay, time
 was I prized them;
That is, I suffer'd them—from slaves and
 nobles; 445
But when they falter from the lips I love,
The lips which have been press'd to mine,
 a chill
Comes o'er my heart, a cold sense of the
 falsehood
Of this my station, which represses feeling
In those for whom I have felt most, and
 makes me 450
Wish that I could lay down the dull tiara,
And share a cottage on the Caucasus
With thee, and wear no crowns but those
 of flowers.
Myr. Would that we could!
Sar. And dost *thou* feel this?—Why?
Myr. Then thou wouldst know what
 thou canst never know. 455

Sar. And that is——
Myr. The true value of a hear[t]
At least, a woman's.
Sar. I have proved a thousand—
A thousand, and a thousand.
Myr. Hearts?
Sar. I think s[o]
Myr. Not one! the time may come tho[u]
 may'st.
Sar. It will. 4
Hear, Myrrha; Salemenes has declared—
Or why or how he hath divined it, Belu[s]
Who founded our great realm, knows mo[re]
 than I—
But Salemenes hath declared my throne
In peril.
Myr. He did well.
Sar. And say'st *thou* s[o]
Thou whom he spurn'd so harshly, an[d]
 now dared 4
Drive from our presence with his sava[ge]
 jeers,
And made thee weep and blush?
Myr. I should do bo[th]
More frequently, and he did well to call m[e]
Back to my duty. But thou spak'st [of]
 peril—
Peril to thee——
Sar. Ay, from dark plots and snare[s]
From Medes—and discontented troo[ps]
 and nations, 4
I know not what—a labyrinth of things—
A maze of mutter'd threats and mysterie[s]
Thou know'st the man—it is his usu[al]
 custom.
But he is honest. Come, we'll think n[o]
 more on't— 4
But of the midnight festival.
Myr. 'Tis time
To think of aught save festivals. Thou ha[st]
 not
Spurn'd his sage cautions?
Sar. What?—and dost thou fear[?]
Myr. Fear!—I'm a Greek, and ho[w]
 should I fear death?
A slave, and wherefore should I dread m[y]
 freedom? 4
Sar. Then wherefore dost thou turn s[o]
 pale?
Myr. I love.
Sar. And do not I? I love thee far—fa[r]
 more
Than either the brief life or the wide realm[s]
Which, it may be, are menaced;—yet
 blench not.
Myr. That means thou lovest nor thy[-]
 self nor me; 4
For he who loves another loves himself
Even for that other's sake. This is too rash[?]
Kingdoms and lives are not to be so los[t]
Sar. Lost!—why, who is the aspirin[g]
 chief who dared 4
Assume to win them?
Myr. Who is he should dread

To try so much? When he who is their ruler
Forgets himself, will they remember him?
 Sar. Myrrha!
 Myr. Frown not upon me; you have
 smiled 493
Too often on me not to make those frowns
Bitterer to bear than any punishment
Which they may augur.—King, I am your
 subject!
Master, I am your slave! Man, I have
 loved you!—
Loved you, I know not by what fatal weak-
 ness,
Although a Greek, and born a foe to
 monarchs— 499
A slave, and hating fetters—an Ionian,
And, therefore, when I love a stranger,
 more
Degraded by that passion than by chains!
Still I have loved you. If that love were
 strong
Enough to overcome all former nature,
Shall it not claim the privilege to save you?
 Sar. Save me, my beauty! Thou art
 very fair, 506
And what I seek of thee is love—not safety.
 Myr. And without love where dwells
 security?
 Sar. I speak of woman's love.
 Myr. The very first
Of human life must spring from woman's
 breast, 510
Your first small words are taught you from
 her lips,
Your first tears quench'd by her, and your
 last sighs
Too often breathed out in a woman's hear-
 ing,
When men have shrunk from the ignoble
 care
Of watching the last hour of him who led
 them. 515
 Sar. My eloquent Ionian! thou speak'st
 music;
The very chorus of the tragic song
I have heard thee talk of as the favourite
 pastime
Of thy far father-land. Nay, weep not—
 calm thee.
 Myr. I weep not.—But I pray thee, do
 not speak 520
About my fathers or their land.
 Sar. Yet oft
Thou speakest of them.
 Myr. True—true: constant thought
Will overflow in words unconsciously;
But when another speaks of Greece, it
 wounds me.
 Sar. Well, then, how wouldst thou *save*
 me, as thou saidst? 525
 Myr. By teaching thee to save thyself,
 and not
Thyself alone, but these vast realms, from
 all

The rage of the worst war—the war of
 brethren.
 Sar. Why, child, I loathe all war and
 warriors; 529
I live in peace and pleasure: what can man
 Do more?
 Myr. Alas! my lord, with common men
There needs too oft the show of war to keep
The substance of sweet peace; and, for a
 king,
'Tis sometimes better to be fear'd than lov'd.
 Sar. And I have never sought but for
 the last. 535
 Myr. And now art neither.
 Sar. Dost *thou* say so, Myrrha?
 Myr. I speak of civic popular love, *self-*
 love,
Which means that men are kept in awe
 and law,
Yet not oppress'd—at least they must not
 think so, 539
Or if they think so, deem it necessary,
To ward off worse oppression, their own
 passions.
A king of feasts, and flowers, and wine, and
 revel,
And love, and mirth, was never king of
 glory.
 Sar. Glory! what's that?
 Myr. Ask of the gods thy fathers.
 Sar. They cannot answer; when the
 priests speak for them, 545
'Tis for some small addition to the temple.
 Myr. Look to the annals of thine em-
 pire's founders.
 Sar. They are so blotted o'er with
 blood, I cannot.
But what wouldst have? the empire *has
been* founded.
I cannot go on multiplying empires. 550
 Myr. Preserve thine own.
 Sar. At least, I will enjoy it.
Come, Myrrha, let us go on to the Eu-
 phrates:
The hour invites, the galley is prepared,
And the pavilion, deck'd for our return,
In fit adornment for the evening banquet,
Shall blaze with beauty and with light, un-
 til 556
It seems unto the stars which are above us
Itself an opposite star; and we will sit
Crown'd with fresh flowers like—
 Myr. Victims.
 Sar. No, like sovereigns,
The shepherd kings of patriarchal times,
Who knew no brighter gems than summer
 wreaths, 561
And none but tearless triumphs. Let us on.

Enter PANIA.

 Pan. May the king live for ever!
 Sar. Not an hour
Longer than he can love. How my soul
 hates

461

This language, which makes life itself a lie,
Flattering dust with eternity! Well, Pania!
Be brief.

Pan. I am charged by Salemenes to
Reiterate his prayer unto the king, 568
That for this day, at least, he will not quit
The palace: when the general returns,
He will adduce such reasons as will war-
rant 571
His daring, and perhaps obtain the pardon
Of his presumption.

Sar. What! am I then coop'd?
Already captive? can I not even breathe
The breath of heaven? Tell prince Salem-
enes, 575
Were all Assyria raging round the walls
In mutinous myriads, I would still go forth.

Pan. I must obey you, and yet——

Myr. Oh, monarch, listen.—
How many a day and moon thou hast re-
clined
Within these palace walls in silken dalli-
ance, 580
And never shown thee to thy people's long-
ing;
Leaving thy subjects' eyes ungratified,
The satraps uncontroll'd, the gods un-
worshipp'd,
And all things in the anarchy of sloth,
Till all, save evil, slumber'd through the
realm! 585
And wilt thou not now tarry for a day,—
A day which may redeem thee? Wilt thou
not
Yield to the few still faithful a few hours,
For them, for thee, for thy past fathers'
race,
And for thy sons' inheritance?

Pan. 'Tis true!
From the deep urgency with which the
prince 591
Despatch'd me to your sacred presence, I
Must dare to add my feeble voice to that
Which now has spoken.

Sar. No, it must not be.

Myr. For the sake of thy realm!

Sar. Away!

Pan. For that
Of all thy faithful subjects, who will rally
Round thee and thine.

Sar. These are mere fantasies:
There is no peril:—'tis a sullen scheme
Of Salemenes, to approve his zeal, 599
And show himself more necessary to us.

Myr. By all that's good and glorious
take this counsel.

Sar. Business to-morrow.

Myr. Ay, or death to-night.

Sar. Why let it come then unexpectedly,
'Midst joy and gentleness, and mirth and
love;
So let me fall like the pluck'd rose!—far
better 605
Thus than be wither'd.

Myr. Then thou wilt not yield,
Even for the sake of all that ever stirr'd
A monarch into action, to forego 608
A trifling revel.

Sar. No.

Myr. Then yield for *mine*;
For my sake!

Sar. Thine, my Myrrha!

Myr. 'Tis the first
Boon which I ever ask'd Assyria's king.

Sar. That's true, and were't my king-
dom, must be granted.
Well, for thy sake, I yield me. Pania, hence!
Thou hear'st me.

Pan. And obey. [*Exit* PANIA.

Sar. I marvel at thee.
What is thy motive, Myrrha, thus to urge
me? 615

Myr. Thy safety; and the certainty that
nought
Could urge the prince thy kinsman to re-
quire
Thus much from thee, but some impending
danger.

Sar. And if I do not dread it, why
shouldst thou?

Myr. Because *thou* dost not fear, I fear
for *thee*. 620

Sar. To-morrow thou wilt smile at these
vain fancies.

Myr. If the worst come, I shall be where
none weep,
And that is better than the power to smile.
And thou?

Sar. I shall be king, as heretofore.

Myr. Where?

Sar. With Baal, Nimrod, and Semira-
mis, 625
Sole in Assyria, or with them elsewhere.
Fate made me what I am—may make me
nothing—
But either that or nothing must I be:
I will not live degraded.

Myr. Hadst thou felt
Thus always, none would ever dare de-
grade thee. 630

Sar. And who will do so now?

Myr. Dost thou suspect none?

Sar. Suspect!—that's a spy's office.
Oh! we lose
Ten thousand precious moments in vain
words,
And vainer fears. Within there!—ye
slaves, deck 633
The hall of Nimrod for the evening revel
If I must make a prison of our palace,
At least we'll wear our fetters jocundly;
If the Euphrates be forbid us, and
The summer dwelling on its beauteous
border,
Here we are still unmenaced. Ho! within
there! [*Exit* SARDANAPALUS 639

Myr. [*sola*]. Why do I love this man?
My country's daughters

Love none but heroes. But I have no
 country!
The slave hath lost all save her bonds. I
 love him;
And that's the heaviest link of the long
 chain— 644
To love whom we esteem not. Be it so:
The hour is coming when he'll need all
 love,
And find none. To fall from him now were
 baser
Than to have stabb'd him on his throne
 when highest
Would have been noble in my country's
 creed:
I was not made for either. Could I save
 him, 650
I should not love *him* better, but myself;
And I have need of the last, for I have fallen
In my own thoughts, by loving this soft
 stranger:
And yet methinks I love him more, per-
 ceiving 654
That he is hated of his own barbarians,
The natural foes of all the blood of Greece.
Could I but wake a single thought like those
Which even the Phrygians felt when bat-
 tling long
'Twixt Ilion and the sea, within his heart
He would tread down the barbarous
 crowds, and triumph. 660
He loves me, and I love him; the slave
 loves
Her master, and would free him from his
 vices.
If not, I have a means of freedom still,
And if I cannot teach him how to reign,
May show him how alone a king can leave
His throne. I must not lose him from my
 sight. [*Exit.*

ACT II

SCENE I.—*The Portal of the same Hall
of the Palace.*

Beleses [*solus*]. The sun goes down:
 methinks he sets more slowly,
Taking his last look of Assyria's empire.
How red he glares amongst those deepen-
 ing clouds,
Like the blood he predicts! If not in vain,
Thou sun that sinkest, and ye stars which
 rise, 5
Have outwatch'd ye, reading ray by ray
The edicts of your orbs, which make Time
 tremble
For what he brings the nations, 'tis the
 furthest
Hour of Assyria's years. And yet how
 calm!
An earthquake should announce so great
 a fall 10
A summer's sun discloses it. Yon disk,
To the star-read Chaldean, bears upon

Its everlasting page the end of what
Seem'd everlasting; but oh! thou true sun!
The burning oracle of all that live, 15
As fountain of all life, and symbol of
Him who bestows it, wherefore dost thou
 limit
Thy lore unto calamity? Why not
Unfold the rise of days more worthy thine
All-glorious burst from ocean? why not
 dart 20
A beam of hope athwart the future years,
As of wrath to its days? Hear me! oh, hear
 me!
I am thy worshipper, thy priest, thy ser-
 vant—
I have gazed on thee at thy rise and fall,
And bow'd my head beneath thy mid-day
 beams, 25
When my eye dared not meet thee. I have
 watch'd
For thee, and after thee, and pray'd to thee,
And sacrificed to thee, and read, and fear'd
 thee,
And ask'd of thee, and thou hast answer'd
 —but
Only to thus much: while I speak, he
 sinks— 30
Is gone—and leaves his beauty, not his
 knowledge,
To the delighted west, which revels in
Its hues of dying glory. Yet what is
Death, so it be but glorious? 'Tis a sunset;
And mortals may be happy to resemble
The gods but in decay.

Enter ARBACES *by an inner door.*

 Arb. Beleses, why 36
So rapt in thy devotions? Dost thou stand
Gazing to trace thy disappearing god
Into some realm of undiscover'd day?
Our business is with night—'tis come.
 Bel. But not
Gone.
 Arb. Let it roll on—we are ready.
 Bel. Yes.
Would it were over!
 Arb. Does the prophet doubt,
To whom the very stars shine victory?
 Bel. I do not doubt of victory—but the
 victor.
 Arb. Well, let thy science settle that.
 Meantime 45
I have prepared as many glittering spears
As will out-sparkle our allies—your plan-
 ets.
There is no more to thwart us. The she-
 king,
That less than woman, is even now upon
The waters with his female mates. The
 order 50
Is issued for the feast in the pavilion.
The first cup which he drains will be the
 last
Quaff'd by the line of Nimrod.

Bel. 'Twas a brave one.
Arb. And is a weak one—'tis worn out
—we'll mend it. 54
Bel. Art sure of that?
Arb. Its founder was a hunter—
I am a soldier—what is there to fear?
Bel. The soldier.
Arb. And the priest, it may be: but
If you thought thus, or think, why not retain
Your king of concubines? why stir me up?
Why spur me to this enterprise? your own
No less than mine?
Bel. Look to the sky!
Arb. I look.
Bel. What seest thou?
Arb. A fair summer's twilight, and
The gathering of the stars.
Bel. And midst them, mark
Yon earliest, and the brightest, which so
quivers, 64
As it would quit its place in the blue ether.
Arb. Well!
Bel. 'Tis thy natal ruler—thy birth
planet.
Arb. [*touching his scabbard*]. My star is
in this scabbard: when it shines,
It shall out-dazzle comets. Let us think
Of what is to be done to justify
Thy planets and their portents. When we
conquer, 70
They shall have temples—ay, and priests
—and thou
Shalt be the pontiff of—what gods thou wilt;
For I observe that they are ever just,
And own the bravest for the most devout.
Bel. Ay, and the most devout for brave
—thou hast not 75
Seen me turn back from battle.
Arb. No; I own thee
As firm in fight as Babylonia's captain,
As skilful in Chaldea's worship: now,
Will it but please thee to forget the priest,
And be the warrior?
Bel. Why not both?
Arb. The better;
And yet it almost shames me, we shall have
So little to effect. This woman's warfare
Degrades the very conqueror. To have
pluck'd 83
A bold and bloody despot from his throne,
And grappled with him, clashing steel with
steel,
That were heroic or to win or fall;
But to upraise my sword against this silk-
worm, 87
And hear him whine, it may be——
Bel. Do not deem it:
He has that in him which may make you
strife yet;
And were he all you think, his guards are
hardy, 90
And headed by the cool, stern Salemenes.
Arb. They'll not resist.
Bel. Why not? they are soldiers.

Arb. True
And therefore need a soldier to comman
them.
Bel. That Salemenes is.
Arb. But not their king
Besides, he hates the effeminate thing tha
governs, 9
For the queen's sake, his sister. Mark yo
not
He keeps aloof from all the revels?
Bel. But
Not from the council—there he is ever con
stant.
Arb. And ever thwarted: what woul
you have more
To make a rebel out of? A fool reigning
His blood dishonour'd, and himself dis
dain'd: 10
Why, it is *his* revenge we work for.
Bel. Coul
He but be brought to think so: this I dout
of.
Arb. What, if we sound him?
Bel. Yes—if the time serve

Enter BALEA.

Bal. Satraps! The king commands you
presence at 10
The feast to-night.
Bel. To hear is to obey
In the pavilion?
Bal. No; here in the palac
Arb. How! in the palace? it was no
thus order'd.
Bal. It is so order'd now.
Arb. And why?
Bal. I know no
May I retire?
Arb. Stay.
Bel. [*to Arb. aside*]. Hush! let him go hi
way.
[*Alternately to Bal.*]. Yes, Balea, thank th
monarch, kiss the hem
Of his imperial robe, and say, his slaves
Will take the crumbs he deigns to scatte
from
His royal table at the hour—was't mid
night?
Bal. It was: the place, the hall of Nim
rod. Lords, 11
I humble me before you, and depart,
 Exit BALEA
Arb. I like not this same sudden chang
of place;
There is some mystery: wherefore shoul
he change it?
Bel. Doth he not change a thousan
times a day?
Sloth is of all things the most fanciful—
And moves more parasangs in its intent
Than generals in their marches, whe
they seek
To leave their foe at fault.—Why dost tho
muse?

Arb. He loved that gay pavilion,—it
was ever
His summer dotage. 124
Bel. And he loved his queen—
And thrice a thousand harlotry besides—
And he has loved all things by turns, except
Wisdom and glory.
Arb. Still—I like it not.
If he has changed—why, so must we: the
attack
Were easy in the isolated bower, 130
Beset with drowsy guards and drunken
courtiers;
But in the hall of Nimrod——
Bel. Is it so?
Methought the haughty soldier fear'd to
mount 133
A throne too easily—does it disappoint thee
To find there is a slipperier step or two
Than what was counted on?
Arb. When the hour comes,
Thou shalt perceive how far I fear or no.
Thou hast seen my life at stake—and gaily
play'd for:
But here is more upon the die—a kingdom.
Bel. I have foretold already—thou wilt
win it: 140
Then on, and prosper.
Arb. Now were I a soothsayer,
I would have boded so much to myself.
But be the stars obey'd—I cannot quarrel
With them, nor their interpreter. Who's
here? 144

Enter SALEMENES.

Sal. Satraps!
Bel. My prince!
Sal. Well met—I sought ye both,
But elsewhere than the palace.
Arb. Wherefore so?
Sal. 'Tis not the hour.
Arb. The hour!—what hour?
Sal. Of midnight.
Bel. Midnight, my lord!
Sal. What, are you not invited?
Bel. Oh! yes—we had forgotten.
Sal. Is it usual
Thus to forget a sovereign's invitation?
Arb. Why—we but now received it.
Sal. Then why here?
Arb. On duty.
Sal. On what duty?
Bel. On the state's.
We have the privilege to approach the
presence; 153
But found the monarch absent.
Sal. And I too
Am upon duty.
Arb. May we crave its purport?
Sal. To arrest two traitors. Guards!
Within there!

Enter Guards.

Sal. [*continuing*]. Satraps,

Your swords.
Bel. [*delivering his*]. My lord, behold
my scimitar.
Arb. [*drawing his sword*]. Take mine.
Sal. [*advancing*]. I will.
Arb. But in your heart the blade—
The hilt quits not this hand.
Sal. [*drawing*]. How! dost thou brave
me?
'Tis well—this saves a trial, and false
mercy. 160
Soldiers, hew down the rebel!
Arb. Soldiers! Ay—
Alone you dare not.
Sal. Alone! foolish slave—
What is there in thee that a prince should
shrink from
Of open force? We dread thy treason, not
Thy strength: thy tooth is nought without
its venom— 165
The serpent's, not the lion's. Cut him
down.
Bel. [*interposing*]. Arbaces! are you
mad? Have I not render'd
My sword? Then trust like me our sove-
reign's justice.
Arb. No—I will sooner trust the stars
thou prat'st of, 169
And this slight arm, and die a king at least
Of my own breath and body—so far that
None else shall chain them.
Sal. [*to the guards*]. You hear *him* and
me.
Take him not,—kill.
[*The Guards attack* ARBACES, *who de-
fends himself valiantly and dexter-
ously till they waver.*
Sal. Is it even so; and must
I do the hangman's office? Recreants! see
How you should fell a traitor.
[SALEMENES *attacks* ARBACES.

Enter SARDANAPALUS *and Train.*

Sar. Hold your hands—
Upon your lives, I say. What, deaf or
drunken? 176
My sword! O fool, I wear no sword: here,
fellow,
Give me thy weapon. [*To a Guard.*
[SARDANAPALUS *snatches a sword from
one of the soldiers, and rushes between
the combatants—they separate.*
Sar. In my very palace!
What hinders me from cleaving you in
twain, 179
Audacious brawlers?
Bel. Sire, your justice.
Sal. Or—
Your weakness.
Sar. [*raising the sword*]. How?
Sal. Strike! so the blow's repeated
Upon yon traitor—whom you spare a
moment,
I trust, for torture—I'm content.

Sar. What—him!
Who dares assail Arbaces?
Sal. I!
Sar. Indeed!
Prince, you forget yourself. Upon what
warrant? 185
 Sal. [*showing the signet*]. Thine.
 Arb. [*confused*]. The king's!
Sal. Yes! and let the king confirm it.
Sar. I parted not from this for such a
purpose.
Sal. You parted with it for your safety
—I
Employ'd it for the best. Pronounce in
person.
Here I am but your slave—a moment past
I was your representative. 191
Sar. Then sheathe
Your swords.
 [ARBACES *and* SALEMENES *return*
 their swords to the scabbards.
Sal. Mine's sheathed: I pray you
sheathe *not* yours:
'Tis the sole sceptre left you now with
safety.
Sar. A heavy one; the hilt, too, hurts
my hand.
[*To a* Guard]. Here, fellow, take thy
weapon back. Well, sirs, 195
What doth this mean?
 Bel. The prince must answer that.
 Sal. Truth upon my part, treason upon
theirs.
Sar. Treason—Arbaces! treachery and
Beleses!
That were an union I will not believe.
 Bel. Where is the proof?
 Sal. I'll answer that, if once
The king demands your fellow-traitor's
sword. 201
 Arb. [*to Sal.*] A sword which hath been
drawn as oft as thine
Against his foes.
 Sal. And now against his brother,
And in an hour or so against himself.
Sar. That is not possible: he dared not;
no— 205
No—I'll not hear of such things.—These
vain bickerings
Are spawn'd in courts by base intrigues,
and baser
Hirelings, who live by lies on good men's
lives.
You must have been deceived, my brother.
 Sal. First
Let him deliver up his weapon, and
Proclaim himself your subject by that duty,
And I will answer all.
Sar. Why, if I thought so—
But no, it cannot be: the Mede Arbaces—
The trusty, rough, true soldier—the best
captain 214
Of all who discipline our nations——No,
I'll not insult him thus, to bid him render

The scimitar to me he never yielded
Unto our enemies. Chief, keep you
weapon. 21
 Sal. [*delivering back the signet*]. Mon
arch, take back your signet.
 Sar. No, retain it;
But use it with more moderation.
 Sal. Sire,
I used it for your honour, and restore it
Because I cannot keep it with my own.
Bestow it on Arbaces.
 Sar. So I should:
He never ask'd it.
 Sal. Doubt not, he will have it
Without that hollow semblance of respect
 Bel. I know not what hath prejudice
· the prince 22
So strongly 'gainst two subjects, than
whom none
Have been more zealous for Assyria'
weal.
 Sal. Peace, factious priest, and faithles
soldier! thou 22
Unitest in thy own person the worst vice
Of the most dangerous orders of mankind
Keep thy smooth words and jugglin
homilies
For those who know thee not. Thy fel
low's sin 23
Is, at the least, a bold one, and not temper'
By the tricks taught thee in Chaldea.
 Bel. Hear him,
My liege—the son of Belus! he blaspheme
The worship of the land, which bows th
knee 23
Before your fathers.
 Sar. Oh! for that I pray yo
Let him have absolution. I dispense wit
The worship of dead men; feeling that I
Am mortal, and believing that the race
From whence I sprung are—what I se
them——ashes. 24
 Bel. King! do not deem so: they ar
with the stars,
And——
 Sar. You shall join them ere they wil
If you preach further.—Why, *this* is ran
treason. 24
 Sal. My lord!
 Sar. To school me in the worship o
Assyria's idols! Let him be released—
Give him his sword.
 Sal. My lord, and king, and brother
I pray ye pause.
 Sar. Yes, and be sermonised,
And dinn'd, and deafen'd with dead me
and Baal! 25
And all Chaldea's starry mysteries.
 Bel. Monarch! respect them.
 Sar. Oh! for that—I love them
I love to watch them in the deep blue vault
And to compare them with my Myrrha'
eyes;

466

I love to see their rays redoubled in 255
The tremulous silver of Euphrates' wave,
As the light breeze of midnight crisps the broad
And rolling water, sighing through the sedges
Which fringe his banks: but whether they may be 259
Gods, as some say, or the abodes of gods,
As others hold, or simply lamps of night,
Worlds, or the lights of worlds, I know nor care not.
There's something sweet in my uncertainty 263
I would not change for your Chaldean lore;
Besides, I know of these all clay can know
Of aught above it, or below it—nothing.
I see their brilliancy and feel their beauty—
When they shine on my grave I shall know neither.

Bel. For *neither*, sire, say *better*.
Sar. I will wait,
If it so please you, pontiff, for that knowledge. 270
In the mean time receive your sword, and know
That I prefer your service militant
Unto your ministry—not loving either.
Sal. [*aside*]. His lusts have made him mad. Then must I save him,
Spite of himself.
Sar. Please you to hear me, Satraps!
And chiefly thou, my priest, because I doubt thee 276
More than the soldier; and would doubt thee all
Wert thou not half a warrior: let us part
In peace—I'll not say pardon—which must be
Earn'd by the guilty; this I'll not pronounce ye, 280
Although upon this breath of mine depends
Your own; and, deadlier for ye, on my fears.
But fear not—for that I am soft, not fearful—
And so live on. Were I the thing some think me,
Your heads would now be dripping the last drops 285
Of their attainted gore from the high gates
Of this our palace, into the dry dust,
Their only portion of the coveted kingdom
They would be crown'd to reign o'er—let that pass. 289
As I have said, I will not *deem* ye guilty,
Nor *doom* ye guiltless. Albeit better men
Than ye or I stand ready to arraign you;
And should I leave your fate to sterner judges,
And proofs of all kinds, I might sacrifice
Two men, who, whatsoe'er they now are, were 295
Once honest. Ye are free, sirs.

Arb. Sire, this clemency—
Bel. [*interrupting him*]. Is worthy of yourself; and, although innocent,
We thank——
Sar. Priest! keep your thanksgivings for Belus;
His offspring needs none.
Bel. But being innocent——
Sar. Be silent.—Guilt is loud. If ye are loyal, 300
Ye are injured men, and should be sad, not grateful.
Bel. So we should be, were justice always done
By earthly power omnipotent; but innocence
Must oft receive her right as a mere favour.
Sar. That's a good sentence for a homily, 305
Though not for this occasion. Prithee keep it
To plead thy sovereign's cause before his people.
Bel. I trust there is no cause.
Sar. No *cause*, perhaps;
But many causers:—if ye meet with such
In the exercise of your inquisitive function
On earth, or should you read of it in heaven 311
In some mysterious twinkle of the stars,
Which are your chronicles, I pray you note,
That there are worse things betwixt earth and heaven
Than him who ruleth many and slays none; 315
And, hating not himself, yet loves his fellows
Enough to spare even those who would not spare him
Were they once masters—but that's doubtful. Satraps!
Your swords and persons are at liberty
To use them as ye will—but from this hour
I have no call for either. Salemenes!
Follow me.
 [*Exeunt* SARDANAPALUS, SALEMENES,
 and the Train, &c., leaving ARBACES
 and BELESES.
Arb. Beleses!
Bel. Now, what think you?
Arb. That we are lost.
Bel. That we have won the kingdom.
Arb. What? thus suspected—with the sword slung o'er us 324
But by a single hair, and that still wavering,
To be blown down by his imperious breath
Which spared us—why, I know not.
Bel. Seek not why;
But let us profit by the interval.
The hour is still our own—our power the same—
The night the same we destined. He hath changed 330
Nothing except our ignorance of all

Suspicion into such a certainty
As must make madness of delay.
 Arb. And yet—
 Bel. What, doubting still?
 Arb. He spared our lives, nay, more,
Saved them from Salemenes.
 Bel. And how long
Will he so spare? till the first drunken
 minute. 336
 Arb. Or sober, rather. Yet he did it
 nobly;
Gave royally what we had forfeited
Basely——
 Bel. Say bravely.
 Arb. Somewhat of both, perhaps,
But it has touch'd me, and, whate'er be-
 tide, 340
I will no further on.
 Bel. And lose the world!
 Arb. Lose anything except my own
 esteem.
 Bel. I blush that we should owe our
 lives to such
A king of distaffs!
 Arb. But no less we owe them;
And I should blush far more to take the
 grantor's! 345
 Bel. Thou may'st endure whate'er thou
 wilt—the stars
Have written otherwise.
 Arb. Though they came down,
And marshall'd me the way in all their
 brightness,
I would not follow.
 Bel. This is weakness—worse
Than a scared beldam's dreaming of the
 dead, 350
And waking in the dark.—Go to—go to.
 Arb. Methought he look'd like Nimrod
 as he spoke,
Even as the proud imperial statue stands
Looking the monarch of the kings around it,
And sways, while they but ornament, the
 temple. 355
 Bel. I told you that you had too much
 despised him,
And that there was some royalty within
 him—
What then? he is the nobler foe.
 Arb. But we
The meaner.—Would he had not spared
 us!
 Bel. So—
Wouldst thou be sacrificed thus readily?
 Arb. No—but it had been better to have
 died 361
Than live ungrateful.
 Bel. Oh, the souls of some men!
Thou wouldst digest what some call trea-
 son, and
Fools treachery—and, behold, upon the
 sudden,
Because for something or for nothing, this
Rash reveller steps, ostentatiously, 366

'Twixt thee and Salemenes, thou art turn'd
Into—what shall I say?—Sardanapalus!
I know no name more ignominious.
 Arb. But
An hour ago, who dared to term me such
Had held his life but lightly—as it is,
I must forgive you, even as he forgave
 us—
Semiramis herself would not have done it.
 Bel. No—the queen liked no sharers of
 the kingdom, 374
Not even a husband.
 Arb. I must serve him truly——
 Bel. And humbly?
 Arb. No, sir, proudly—being honest.
I shall be nearer thrones than you to heaven;
And if not quite so haughty, yet more lofty.
You may do your own deeming—you have
 codes,
And mysteries, and corollaries of 380
Right and wrong, which I lack for my
 direction,
And must pursue but what a plain heart
 teaches.
And now you know me.
 Bel. Have you finish'd?
 Arb. Yes—
With you.
 Bel. And would, perhaps, betray as well
As quit me?
 Arb. That's a sacerdotal thought 385
And not a soldier's.
 Bel. Be it what you will—
Truce with these wranglings, and but hear
 me.
 Arb. No—
There is more peril in your subtle spirit
Than in a phalanx.
 Bel. If it must be so—
I'll on alone.
 Arb. Alone!
 Bel. Thrones hold but one.
 Arb. But this is fill'd.
 Bel. With worse than vacancy—
A despised monarch. Look to it, Arbaces,
I have still aided, cherish'd, loved, and
 urged you; 391
Was willing even to serve you, in the hope
To serve and save Assyria. Heaven itself
Seem'd to consent, and all events were
 friendly 395
Even to the last, till that your spirit shrunk
Into a shallow softness; but now, rather
Than see my country languish, I will be
Her saviour or the victim of her tyrant,
Or one or both, for sometimes both are one;
And if I win, Arbaces is my servant. 400
 Arb. Your servant!
 Bel. Why not? better than be slave
The *pardon'd* slave of *she* Sardanapalus!

 Enter PANIA.

 Pan. My lords, I bear an order from the
 king. 40

468

Arb. It is obey'd ere spoken.
Bel. Notwithstanding,
Let's hear it.
Pan. Forthwith, on this very night,
Repair to your respective satrapies 408
Of Babylon and Media.
Bel. With our troops?
Pan. My order is unto the satraps and
Their household train.
Arb. But——
Bel. It must be obey'd:
Say, we depart.
Pan. My order is to see you
Depart, and not to bear your answer.
Bel. [*aside*]. Ay!
Well, sir, we will accompany you hence.
Pan. I will retire to marshal forth the
 guard 415
Of honour which befits your rank, and wait
Your leisure, so that it the hour exceeds not.
 [*Exit* PANIA.
Bel. Now then obey!
Arb. Doubtless.
Bel. Yes, to the gates
That grate the palace, which is now our
 prison— 419
No further.
Arb. Thou hast harp'd the truth indeed!
The realm itself, in all its wide extension,
Yawns dungeons at each step for thee and
 me.
Bel. Graves!
Arb. If I thought so, this good
 sword should dig 423
One more than mine.
Bel. It shall have work enough.
Let me hope better than thou augurest;
At present, let us hence as best we may.
Thou dost agree with me in understanding
This order as a sentence?
Arb. Why, what other
Interpretation should it bear? it is
The very policy of orient monarchs— 430
Pardon and poison—favours and a
 sword—
A distant voyage, and an eternal sleep.
How many satraps in his father's time—
For he I own is, or at least *was*, bloodless—
Bel. But *will* not, *can* not be so now.
Arb. I doubt it.
How many satraps have I seen set out
In his sire's day for mighty vice-royalties,
Whose tombs are on their path! I know
 not how,
But they all sicken'd by the way, it was
So long and heavy.
Bel. Let us but regain 440
The free air of the city, and we'll shorten
The journey.
Arb. 'Twill be shorten'd at the gates,
It may be.
Bel. No; they hardly will risk that.
They mean us to die privately, but not
Within the palace or the city walls, 445

Where we are known, and may have par-
 tisans:
If they had meant to slay us here, we were
No longer with the living. Let us hence.
Arb. If I but thought he did not mean
 my life——
Bel. Fool! hence—what else should
 despotism alarm'd 450
Mean? Let us but rejoin our troops, and
 march.
Arb. Towards our provinces?
Bel. No; towards your kingdom.
There's time, there's heart, and hope, and
 power, and means, 453
Which their half measures leave us in full
 scope.—
Away!
Arb. And I even yet repenting must
Relapse to guilt!
Bel. Self-defence is a virtue, 456
Sole bulwark of all right. Away, I say!
Let's leave this place, the air grows thick
 and choking,
And the walls have a scent of night-shade
 —hence!
Let us not leave them time for further
 council. 460
Our quick departure proves our civic zeal;
Our quick departure hinders our good
 escort,
The worthy Pania, from anticipating
The orders of some parasangs from hence:
Nay, there's no other choice, but—hence,
 I say. 465
[*Exit with* ARBACES, *who follows re-
 luctantly.*

Enter SARDANAPALUS *and* SALEMENES.

Sar. Well, all is remedied, and without
 bloodshed,
That worst of mockeries of a remedy;
We are now secure by these men's exile.
Sal. Yes,
As he who treads on flowers is from the
 adder 469
Twined round their roots.
Sar. Why, what wouldst have me do?
Sal. Undo what you have done.
Sar. Revoke my pardon?
Sal. Replace the crown now tottering
 on your temples.
Sar. That were tyrannical.
Sal. But sure.
Sar. We are so.
What danger can they work upon the
 frontier?
Sal. They are not there yet—never
 should they be so, 475
Were I well listen'd to.
Sar. Nay, I *have* listen'd
Impartially to thee—why not to them?
Sal. You may know that hereafter; as
 it is,
I take my leave to order forth the guard.

469

Sar. And you will join us at the banquet?
Sal. Sire,
Dispense with me—I am no wassailer:
Command me in all service save the Bac-
 chant's. 482
Sar. Nay, but 'tis fit to revel now and
 then.
Sal. And fit that some should watch for
 those who revel
Too oft. Am I permitted to depart?
Sar. Yes——Stay a moment, my good
 Salemenes,
My brother, my best subject, better prince
Than I am king. You should have been the
 monarch,
And I—I know not what, and care not; but
Think not I am insensible to all 490
Thine honest wisdom, and thy rough yet
 kind,
Though oft reproving, sufferance of my
 follies.
If I have spared these men against thy
 counsel,
That is, their lives—it is not that I doubt
The advice was sound; but, let them live:
 we will not 495
Cavil about their lives—so let them mend
 them.
Their banishment will leave me still sound
 sleep,
Which their death had not left me.
Sal. Thus you run
The risk to sleep for ever, to save traitors—
A moment's pang now changed for years
 of crime. 500
Still let them be made quiet.
Sar. Tempt me not;
My word is past.
Sal. But it may be recall'd.
Sar. 'Tis royal.
Sal. And should therefore be decisive.
This half indulgence of an exile serves
But to provoke—a pardon should be full,
Or it is none.
Sar. And who persuaded me 506
After I had repeal'd them, or at least
Only dismiss'd them from our presence,
 who
Urged me to send them to their satrapies?
Sal. True; that I had forgotten; that is,
 sire, 510
If they e'er reach'd their satrapies—why,
 then,
Reprove me more for my advice.
Sar. And if
They do not reach them—look to it!—in
 safety,
In safety, mark me—and security— 514
Look to thine own.
Sal. Permit me to depart;
Their safety shall be cared for.
Sar. Get thee hence, then;
And, prithee, think more gently of thy
 brother.

Sal. Sire, I shall ever duly serve m
 sovereign. [Exit SALEMENE
Sar. [solus]. That man is of a temper to
 severe; 5
Hard but as lofty as the rock, and free
From all the taints of common earth-
 while I 5
Am softer clay, impregnated with flowers
But as our mould is, must the produce b
If I have err'd this time, 'tis on the side
Where error sits most lightly on that sens
I know not what to call it; but it reckon
With me ofttimes for pain, and sometime
 pleasure; 52
A spirit which seems placed about my hea
To count its throbs, not quicken them, an
 ask
Questions which mortal never dared
 ask me, 53
Nor Baal, though an oracular deity—
Albeit his marble face majestical
Frowns as the shadows of the evening di
His brows to changed expression, till a
 times
I think the statue looks in act to speak.
Away with these vain thoughts, I will b
 joyous— 53
And here comes Joy's true herald.

 Enter MYRRHA.

Myr. King! the sk
Is overcast, and musters muttering thun
 der,
In clouds that seem approaching fast, an
 show 53
In forked flashes a commanding tempes
Will you then quit the palace?
Sar. Tempest, say'st thou
Myr. Ay, my good lord.
Sar. For my own part, I should b
Not ill content to vary the smooth scen
And watch the warring elements; but th
Would little suit the silken garments an
Smooth faces of our festive friends. Say
 Myrrha, 54
Art thou of those who dread the roar o
 clouds?
Myr. In my own country we respec
 their voices
As auguries of Jove.
Sar. Jove!—ay, your Baal—
Ours also has a property in thunder, 55
And ever and anon some falling bolt
Proves his divinity,—and yet sometimes
Strikes his own altars.
Myr. That were a dread omen
Sar. Yes—for the priests. Well, we wi
 not go forth
Beyond the palace walls to-night, bu
 make 55
Our feast within.
Myr. Now, Jove be praised! that h
Hath heard the prayer thou wouldst no
 hear. The gods

Are kinder to thee than thou to thyself,
And flash this storm between thee and thy
 foes, 559
To shield thee from them.
 Sar. Child, if there be peril,
Methinks it is the same within these walls
As on the river's brink.
 Myr. Not so; these walls
Are high and strong, and guarded. Treason
 has 563
To penetrate through many a winding way,
And massy portal; but in the pavilion
There is no bulwark.
 Sar. No, nor in the palaçe,
Nor in the fortress, nor upon the top
Of cloud-fenced Caucasus, where the eagle
 sits
Nested in pathless clefts, if treachery be:
Even as the arrow finds the airy king,
The steel will reach the earthly. But be
 calm; 571
The men, or innocent or guilty, are
Banish'd, and far upon their way.
 Myr. They live, then?
 Sar. So sanguinary? *Thou!*
 Myr. I would not shrink
From just infliction of due punishment
On those who seek your life: were't other-
 wise, 576
I should not merit mine. Besides, you heard
The princely Salemenes.
 Sar. This is strange;
The gentle and the austere are both against me,
And urge me to revenge.
 Myr. 'Tis a Greek virtue.
 Sar. But not a kingly one—I'll none
 on't; or 581
If ever I indulge in't, it shall be
With kings—my equals.
 Myr. These men sought to be so.
 Sar. Myrrha, this is too feminine, and
 springs
From fear——
 Myr. For you.
 Sar. No matter, still 'tis fear.
I have observed your sex, once roused to
 wrath, 586
Are timidly vindictive to a pitch
Of perseverance, which I would not copy.
I thought you were exempt from this, as
 from
The childish helplessness of Asian women.
 Myr. My lord, I am no boaster of my
 love, 591
Nor of my attributes; I have shared your
 splendour,
And will partake your fortunes. You may
 live
To find one slave more true than subject
 myriads: 594
But this the gods avert! I am content
To be beloved on trust for what I feel,
Rather than prove it to you in your griefs,
Which might not yield to any cares of mine.

Sar. Grief cannot come where perfect
 love exists, 599
Except to heighten it, and vanish from
That which it could not scare away. Let's
 in—
The hour approaches, and we must prepare
To meet the invited guests who grace our
 feast. [*Exeunt.*

ACT III

SCENE I.—*The Hall of the Palace illumi-
 nated*—SARDANAPALUS *and his Guests
 at Table.—A storm without, and Thun-
 der occasionally heard during the Ban-
 quet.*

Sar. Fill full! why this is as it should be:
 here
Is my true realm, amidst bright eyes and
 faces
Happy as fair! Here sorrow cannot reach.
 Zam. Nor elsewhere—where the king
 is, pleasure sparkles.
 Sar. Is not this better now than Nim-
 rod's huntings, 5
Or my wild grandam's chase in search of
 kingdoms
She could not keep when conquer'd?
 Alt. Mighty though
They were, as all thy royal line have been,
Yet none of these who went before have
 reach'd
The acmé of Sardanapalus, who 10
Has placed his joy in peace—the sole true
 glory.
 Sar. And pleasure, good Altada, to
 which glory
Is but the path. What is it that we seek?
Enjoyment! We have cut the way short to
 it,
And not gone tracking it through human
 ashes, 15
Making a grave with every footstep.
 Zam. No;
All hearts are happy, and all voices bless
The king of peace, who holds a world in
 jubilee.
 Sar. Art sure of that? I have heard
 otherwise; 19
Some say that there be traitors.
 Zam. Traitors they
Who dare to say so!—'Tis impossible.
What cause?
 Sar. What cause? true,—fill the
 goblet up;
We will not think of them: there are none
 such,
Or if there be, they are gone.
 Alt. Guests, to my pledge!
Down on your knees, and drink a measure
 to 25
The safety of the king—the monarch, say I?
The god Sardanapalus!

471

[ZAMES *and the Guests kneel, and exclaim*—

 Mightier than
His father Baal, the god Sardanapalus!
[*It thunders as they kneel; some start up
 in confusion.*
Zam. Why do you rise, my friends? in
 that strong peal 29
His father gods consented.
Myr. Menaced, rather.
King, wilt thou bear this mad impiety?
 Sar. Impiety!—nay, if the sires who
 reign'd
Before me can be gods, I'll not disgrace
Their lineage. But arise, my pious friends;
Hoard your devotion for the thunderer
 there: 35
I seek but to be loved, not worshipp'd.
 Alt. Both—
Both you must ever be by all true subjects.
 Sar. Methinks the thunders still increase: it is
An awful night.
 Myr. Oh yes, for those who have
No palace to protect their worshippers.
 Sar. That's true, my Myrrha; and could
 I convert 41
My realm to one wide shelter for the
 wretched,
I'd do it.
 Myr. Thou'rt no god then, not to be
Able to work a will so good and general,
As thy wish would imply.
 Sar. And your gods, then,
Who can, and do not?
 Myr. Do not speak of that,
Lest we provoke them.
 Sar. True, they love not censure
Better than mortals. Friends, a thought
 has struck me: 48
Were there no temples, would there, think
 ye, be
Air worshippers? that is, when it is angry,
And pelting as even now.
 Myr. The Persian prays
Upon his mountain.
 Sar. Yes, when the sun shines.
 Myr. And I would ask if this your
 palace were 53
Unroof'd and desolate, how many flatterers
Would lick the dust in which the king lay
 low?
 Alt. The fair Ionian is too sarcastic
Upon a nation whom she knows not well;
The Assyrians know no pleasure but their
 king's, 58
And homage is their pride.
 Sar. Nay, pardon, guests,
The fair Greek's readiness of speech.
 Alt. Pardon! sire:
We honour her of all things next to thee.
Hark! what was that?
 Zam. That! nothing but the jar
Of distant portals shaken by the wind.

 Alt. It sounded like the clash of—hark
 again! 6
 Zam. The big rain pattering on the
 roof.
 Sar. No more
Myrrha, my love, hast thou thy shell in
 order?
Sing me a song of Sappho, her, thou
 know'st,
Who in thy country threw—

Enter PANIA, *with his sword and garment
bloody, and disordered. The guests rise
in confusion.*

 Pan. [*to the Guards*]. Look to the portals
And with your best speed to the walls
 without.
Your arms! To arms! The king's in danger
 Monarch, 7
Excuse this haste,—'tis faith.
 Sar. Speak on.
 Pan. It is
As Salemenes fear'd; the faithless sa
 traps——
 Sar. You are wounded—give some
 wine. Take breath, good Pania.
 Pan. 'Tis nothing—a mere flesh wound
 I am worn 7
More with my speed to warn my sovereign
Than hurt in his defence.
 Myr. Well, sir, the rebels
 Pan. Soon as Arbaces and Beleses
 reach'd
Their stations in the city, they refused
To march; and on my attempt to use the
 power 79
Which I was delegated with, they call'd
Upon their troops, who rose in fierce de
 fiance.
 Myr. All?
 Pan. Too many.
 Sar. Spare not of thy free speech
To spare mine ears the truth.
 Pan. My own slight guard
Were faithful, and what's left of it is still
 so. 8
 Myr. And are these all the force still
 faithful?
 Pan. No—
The Bactrians, now led on by Salemenes
Who even then was on his way, still urged
By strong suspicion of the Median chiefs
Are numerous, and make strong head
 against
The rebels, fighting inch by inch, and form
 ing 9
An orb around the palace, where they mean
To centre all their force, and save the king
[*He hesitates*]. I am charged to——
 Myr. 'Tis no time for hesitation
 Pan. Prince Salemenes doth implore
 the king
To arm himself, although but for a mo
 ment, 95

And show himself unto the soldiers: his
Sole presence in this instance might do more
Than hosts can do in his behalf.
 Sar. What, ho!
My armour there.
 Myr. And wilt thou?
 Sar. Will I not?
Ho, there!—but seek not for the buckler:
 'tis 100
Too heavy:—a light cuirass and my sword.
Where are the rebels?
 Pan. Scarce a furlong's length
From the outward wall the fiercest con-
 flict rages.
 Sar. Then I may charge on horseback.
Sfero, ho!
Order my horse out.—There is space
 enough 105
Even in our courts, and by the outer gate,
To marshal half the horsemen of Arabia.
 [Exit SFERO *for the armour.*
 Myr. How I do love thee!
 Sar. I ne'er doubted it.
 Myr. But now I know thee.
 Sar. [*to his Attendant*]. Bring down
 my spear too.— 109
Where's Salemenes?
 Pan. Where a soldier should be,
In the thick of the fight.
 Sar. Then hasten to him——Is
The path still open, and communication
Left 'twixt the palace and the phalanx?
 Pan. 'Twas
When I late left him, and I have no fear:
Our troops were steady, and the phalanx
 form'd. 115
 Sar. Tell him to spare his person for the
 present,
And that I will not spare my own—and say,
 come.
 Pan. There's victory in the very word.
 [Exit PANIA.
 Sar. Altada—Zames—forth, and arm
 ye! There
is all in readiness in the armoury. 120
See that the women are bestow'd in safety
In the remote apartments: let a guard
Be set before them, with strict charge to quit
The post but with their lives—command
 it, Zames. 124
Altada, arm yourself, and return here;
Your post is near our person.
 [Exeunt ZAMES, ALTADA, *and all save*
 MYRRHA.

Enter SFERO *and others with the King's
 Arms, &c.*

 Sfe. King! your armour.
 Sar. [*arming himself*]. Give me the
 cuirass—so: my baldric; now
My sword: I had forgot the helm—where
 is it?
That's well—no, 'tis too heavy: you mis-
 take, too—

It was not this I meant, but that which
 bears 130
A diadem around it.
 Sfe. Sire, I deem'd
That too conspicuous from the precious
 stones
To risk your sacred brow beneath—and
 trust me,
This is of better metal, though less rich.
 Sar. You deem'd! Are you too turn'd a
 rebel? Fellow! 135
Your part is to obey: return, and—no—
It is too late—I will go forth without it.
 Sfe. At least, wear this.
 Sar. Wear Caucasus! why, 'tis
A mountain on my temples.
 Sfe. Sire, the meanest
Soldier goes not forth thus exposed to
 battle. 140
All men will recognise you—for the storm
Has ceased, and the moon breaks forth in
 her brightness.
 Sar. I go forth to be recognised, and thus
Shall be so sooner. Now—my spear! I'm
 arm'd. 144
 [*In going stops short, and turns to* SFERO.
Sfero—I had forgotten—bring the mirror.
 Sfe. The mirror, sire?
 Sar. Yes, sir, of polish'd brass,
Brought from the spoils of India—but be
 speedy. *[Exit* SFERO.
 Sar. Myrrha, retire unto a place of
 safety.
Why went you not forth with the other
 damsels? 149
 Myr. Because my place is here.
 Sar. And when I am gone——
 Myr. I follow.
 Sar. *You!* to battle?
 Myr. If it were so,
'Twere not the first Greek girl had trod the
 path.
I will await here your *return.*
 Sar. The place
Is spacious, and the first to be sought out,
If they prevail; and, if it be so, 155
And I return not——
 Myr. Still we meet again.
 Sar. How?
 Myr. In the spot where all must meet at
 last—
In Hades! if there be, as I believe,
A shore beyond the Styx; and if there be
 not, 159
In ashes.
 Sar. Darest thou so much?
 Myr. I dare all things
Except survive what I have loved, to be
A rebel's booty: forth, and do your
 bravest.

 Re-enter SFERO *with the mirror.*

 Sar. [*looking at himself*]. This cuirass
 fits me well, the baldric better,

And the helm not at all. Methinks I seem
[*Flings away the helmet after trying it
 again.*
Passing well in these toys; and now to
 prove them. 165
Altada! Where's Altada?
Sfe. Waiting, sire,
Without: he has your shield in readiness.
Sar. True; I forgot he is my shield-
 bearer
By right of blood, derived from age to age.
Myrrha, embrace me; yet once more—
 once more— 170
Love me, whate'er betide. My chiefest
 glory
Shall be to make me worthier of your love.
Myr. Go forth, and conquer!
 [*Exeunt* SARDANAPALUS *and* SFERO.
 Now, I am alone,
All are gone forth, and of that all how few
Perhaps return! Let him but vanquish, and
Me perish! If he vanquish not, I perish;
For I will not outlive him. He has wound
About my heart, I know not how nor why.
Not for that he is king; for now his king-
 dom 179
Rocks underneath his throne, and the
 earth yawns
To yield him no more of it than a grave;
And yet I love him more. Oh, mighty
 Jove!
Forgive this monstrous love for a bar-
 barian,
Who knows not of Olympus! yes, I love
 him
Now, now, far more than——Hark—to
 the war shout! 185
Methinks it nears me. If it should be so,
 [*She draws forth a small vial.*
This cunning Colchian poison, which my
 father
Learn'd to compound on Euxine shores,
 and taught me
How to preserve, shall free me! It had
 freed me 189
Long ere this hour, but that I loved, until
I half forgot I was a slave:—where all
Are slaves save one, and proud of servi-
 tude,
So they are served in turn by something
 lower
In the degree of bondage, we forget
That shackles worn like ornaments no
 less 195
Are chains. Again that shout! and now
 the clash
Of arms—and now—and now—

 Enter ALTADA.

Alt. Ho, Sfero, ho!
Myr. He is not here; what wouldst thou
 with him? How
Goes on the conflict?
Alt. Dubiously and fiercely.

Myr. And the king?
Alt. Like a king. I must find Sfero
And bring him a new spear and his own
 helmet. 20
He fights till now bare-headed, and by far
Too much exposed. The soldiers knew
 his face,
And the foe too; and in the moon's broad
 light,
His silk tiara and his flowing hair 20
Make him a mark too royal. Every arrow
Is pointed at the fair hair and fair features
And the broad fillet which crowns both
Myr. Ye gods
Who fulminate o'er my father's land, pro-
 tect him! 2
Were you sent by the king?
Alt. By Salamenes,
Who sent me privily upon this charge,
Without the knowledge of the careless
 sovereign.
The king! the king fights as he revels! ho...
What, Sfero! I will seek the armoury—
He must be there. [*Exit* ALTADA.
Myr. 'Tis no dishonour—no—
'Tis no dishonour to have loved this man.
I almost wish now, what I never wish'd
Before, that he were Grecian. If Alcides
Were shamed in wearing Lydian Om-
 phale's
She-garb, and wielding her vile distaff
 surely 22
He, who springs up a Hercules at once,
Nursed in effeminate arts from youth to
 manhood,
And rushes from the banquet to the battle
As though it were a bed of love, deserves
That a Greek girl should be his paramour
And a Greek bard his minstrel, a Greek
 tomb 22
His monument. How goes the strife, sir?

 Enter an Officer.

Officer. Lost
Lost almost past recovery. Zames—
 Where
Is Zames?
Myr. Posted with the guard appointed
To watch before the apartment of the
 women. 23
 [*Exit Officer.*
Myr. [*sola*]. He's gone; and told me
 more than that all's lost!
What need have I to know more? In
 those words,
Those little words, a kingdom and a king,
A line of thirteen ages, and the lives
Of thousands, and the fortune of all left
With life, are merged; and I, too, with the
 great,
Like a small bubble breaking with the
 wave
Which bore it, shall be nothing. At the
 least, 23

My fate is in my keeping: no proud victor
Shall count me with his spoils.

Enter PANIA.

Pan. Away with me,
Myrrha, without delay; we must not lose
A moment—all that's left us now.
Myr. The king?
Pan. Sent me here to conduct you
 hence beyond
The river, by a secret passage.
Myr. Then
He lives—
Pan. And charged me to secure your
 life, 245
And beg you to live on for his sake, till
He can rejoin you.
Myr. Will he then give way?
Pan. Not till the last. Still, still he does
 whate'er
Despair can do; and step by step disputes
The very palace.
Myr. They are here, then:—ay,
Their shouts come ringing through the
 ancient halls, 251
Never profaned by rebel echoes till
This fatal night. Farewell, Assyria's line!
Farewell to all of Nimrod! Even the name
Is now no more.
Pan. Away with me—away\
Myr. No: I'll die here!—Away, and
 tell your king 256
I loved him to the last.

Enter SARDANAPALUS *and* SALEMENES *with*
Soldiers. PANIA *quits* MYRRHA, *and*
ranges himself with them.

Sar. Since it is thus,
We'll die where we were born—in our own
 halls.
Serry your ranks—stand firm. I have de-
 spatch'd 259
A trusty satrap for the guard of Zames,
All fresh and faithful; they'll be here anon.
All is not over.—Pania, look to Myrrha.
 [PANIA *returns towards* MYRRHA.
Sal. We have breathing time; yet once
 more charge, my friends—
One for Assyria!
Sar. Rather say for Bactria!
My faithful Bactrians, I will henceforth be
King of your nation, and we'll hold to-
 gether 266
This realm as province.
Sal. Hark! they come—they come.

Enter BELESES *and* ARBACES *with the Rebels.*

Arb. Set on, we have them in the toil.
 Charge! charge!
Bel. On! on!—Heaven fights for us,
 and with us—On!
 [*They charge the King and* SALEMENES
 with their troops, who defend them-

selves *till the arrival of* ZAMES *with the*
Guard before mentioned. The Rebels
are then driven off, and pursued by
SALEMENES, &c. *As the King is going*
to join the pursuit, BELESES *crosses him.*
Bel. Ho! tyrant—*I* will end this war.
Sar. Even so,
My warlike priest, and precious prophet,
 and 271
Grateful and trusty subject: yield, I pray
 thee.
I would reserve thee for a fitter doom,
Rather than dip my hands in holy blood.
Bel. Thine hour is come.
Sar. No, thine.—I've lately read,
Though but a young astrologer, the stars;
And ranging round the zodiac, found thy
 fate 277
In the sign of the Scorpion, which pro-
 claims
That thou wilt now be crush'd.
Bel. But not by thee.
 [*They fight;* BELESES *is wounded and*
 disarmed.
Sar. [*raising his sword to despatch him,*
 exclaims]—
Now call upon thy planets, will they shoot
From the sky to preserve their seer and
 credit? 281
 [*A party of Rebels enter and rescue* BE-
 LESES. *They assail the King, who, in*
 turn, is rescued by a Party of his
 Soldiers, who drive the Rebels off.
The villain was a prophet after all.
Upon them—ho! there—victory is ours.
 [*Exit in pursuit.*
Myr. [*to Pan.*] Pursue! Why stand'st
 thou here, and leav'st the ranks
Of fellow-soldiers conquering without
 thee? 285
Pan. The king's command was not to
 quit thee.
Myr. Me!
Think not of me—a single soldier's arm
Must not be wanting now. I ask no guard,
I need no guard: what, with a world at
 stake,
Keep watch upon a woman? Hence, I say,
Or thou art shamed! Nay, then, *I* will go
 forth, 291
A feeble female, 'midst their desperate
 strife,
And bid thee guard me *there*—where thou
 shouldst shield
Thy sovereign. [*Exit* MYRRHA.
Pan. Yet stay, damsel!—She is gone.
If aught of ill betide her, better I 295
Had lost my life. Sardanapalus holds her
Far dearer than his kingdom, yet he fights
For that too; and can I do less than he,
Who never flash'd a scimitar till now?
Myrrha, return, and I obey you, though
In disobedience to the monarch.
 [*Exit* PANIA.

Enter ALTADA *and* SFERO *by an opposite door.*

Alt. Myrrha! 301
What, gone? yet she was here when the
 fight raged,
And Pania also. Can aught have befallen
 them?
Sfe. I saw both safe, when late the
 rebels fled; 304
They probably are but retired to make
Their way back to the harem.
Alt. If the king
Prove victor, as it seems even now he must,
And miss his own Ionian, we are doom'd
To worse than captive rebels.
Sfe. Let us trace them;
She cannot be fled far; and, found, she
 makes 310
A richer prize to our soft sovereign
Than his recover'd kingdom.
Alt. Baal himself
Ne'er fought more fiercely to win empire,
 than
His silken son to save it: he defies
All augury of foes or friends; and like
The close and sultry summer's day, which
 bodes 316
A twilight tempest, bursts forth in such
 thunder
As sweeps the air and deluges the earth.
The man's inscrutable.
Sfe. Not more than others.
All are the sons of circumstance: away—
Let's seek the slave out, or prepare to be
Tortured for his infatuation, and 322
Condemn'd without a crime. [*Exeunt.*

Enter SALEMENES *and Soldiers, &c.*

Sal. The triumph is
Flattering: they are beaten backward from
 the palace,
And we have open'd regular access 325
To the troops station'd on the other side
Euphrates, who may still be true; nay,
 must be,
When they hear of our victory.—But
 where 328
Is the chief victor? where's the king?

Enter SARDANAPALUS, *cum suis, &c. and*
 MYRRHA.

Sar. Here, brother.
Sal. Unhurt, I hope.
Sar. Not quite; but let it pass.
We've clear'd the palace——
Sal. And I trust the city.
Our numbers gather; and I've order'd on-
 ward 332
A cloud of Parthians, hitherto reserved,
All fresh and fiery, to be pour'd upon them
In their retreat, which soon will be a flight.
Sar. It is already, or at least they
 march'd 336

Faster than I could follow with my Bac-
 trians,
Who spared no speed. I am spent: give
 me a seat.
Sal. There stands the throne, sire.
Sar. 'Tis no place to rest on
For mind nor body: let me have a couch,
 [*They place a seat*
A peasant's stool, I care not what: so—
 now 340
I breathe more freely.
Sal. This great hour has proved
The brightest and most glorious of your life.
Sar. And the most tiresome. Where's
 my cupbearer?
Bring me some water.
Sal. [*smiling*]. 'Tis the first time he
Ever had such an order: even I, 345
Your most austere of counsellors, would
 now
Suggest a purpler beverage.
Sar. Blood—doubtless.
But there's enough of that shed; as for
 wine,
I have learn'd to-night the price of the pure
 element: 350
Thrice have I drank of it, and thrice re-
 new'd,
With greater strength than the grape ever
 gave me,
My charge upon the rebels. Where's the
 soldier
Who gave me water in his helmet?
One of the Guards. Slain, sire!
An arrow pierced his brain, while, scat-
 tering 355
The last drops from his helm, he stood in
 act
To place it on his brows.
Sar. Slain! unrewarded!
And slain to serve my thirst: that's hard,
 poor slave!
Had he but lived, I would have gorged him
 with
Gold: all the gold of earth could ne'er
 repay 360
The pleasure of that draught; for I was
 parch'd
As I am now. [*They bring water—he drinks.*
 I live again—from henceforth
The goblet I reserve for hours of love,
But war on water.
Sal. And that bandage, sire,
Which girds your arm?
Sar. A scratch from brave Beleses.
Myr. Oh! he is wounded!
Sar. Not too much of that;
And yet it feels a little stiff and painful,
Now I am cooler.
Myr. You have bound it with—
Sar. The fillet of my diadem: the first
 time 366
That ornament was ever aught to me
Save an encumbrance.

Myr. [*to the Attendants*]. Summon
 speedily
A leech of the most skilful: pray, retire;
I will unbind your wound and tend it.
Sar. Do so,
For now it throbs sufficiently: but what
Know'st thou of wounds? yet wherefore
 do I ask? 375
Know'st thou, my brother, where I lighted
 on
This minion?
Sal. Herding with the other females,
Like frighten'd antelopes.
Sar. No: like the dam
Of the young lion, femininely raging
(And femininely meaneth furiously, 380
Because all passions in excess are female)
Against the hunter flying with her cub,
She urged on with her voice and gesture,
 and
Her floating hair and flashing eyes, the
 soldiers, 314
In the pursuit.
Sal. Indeed!
Sar. You see, this night
Made warriors of more than me. I paused
To look upon her, and her kindled cheek;
Her large black eyes, that flash'd through
 her long hair
As it stream'd o'er her; her blue veins that
 rose
Along her most transparent brow; her
 nostril
Dilated from its symmetry; her lips
Apart; her voice that clove through all the
 din,
As a lute pierceth through the cymbals'
 clash,
Jarr'd but not drown'd by the loud bratt-
 ling; her
Waved arms, more dazzling with their own
 born whiteness 395
Than the steel her hand held, which she
 caught up
From a dead soldier's grasp;—all these
 things made
Her seem unto the troops a prophetess
Of victory, or Victory herself, 399
Come down to hail us hers.
Sal. [*aside*]. This is too much.
Again the love-fit's on him, and all's lost,
Unless we turn his thoughts.
 [*Aloud.*] But pray thee, sire,
Think of your wound—you said even now
 'twas painful.
Sar. That's true, too; but I must not
 think of it.
Sal. I have look'd to all things needful,
 and will now 405
Receive reports of progress made in such
Orders as I had given, and then return
To hear your further pleasure.
Sar. Be it so.
Sal. [*in retiring*]. Myrrha!

Myr. Prince!
Sal. You have shown a soul to-night,
Which, were he not my sister's lord—But
 now 410
I have no time: thou lovest the king?
Myr. I love
Sardanapalus.
Sal. But wouldst have him king still?
Myr. I would not have him less than
 what he should be.
Sal. Well then, to have him king, and
 yours, and all
He should, or should not be; to have him
 live, 415
Let him not sink back into luxury.
You have more power upon his spirit than
Wisdom within these walls, or fierce re-
 bellion
Raging without: look well that he relapse
 not.
Myr. There needed not the voice of
 Salemenes 420
To urge me on to this: I will not fail.
All that a woman's weakness can——
Sal. Is power
Omnipotent o'er such a heart as his:
Exert it wisely. [*Exit* SALEMENES.
Sar. Myrrha! what, at whispers
With my stern brother? I shall soon be
 jealous. 425
Myr. [*smiling*]. You have cause, sire;
 for on the earth there breathes not
A man more worthy of a woman's love,
A soldier's trust, a subject's reverence,
A king's esteem—the whole world's ad-
 miration!
Sar. Praise him, but not so warmly. I
 must not 430
Hear those sweet lips grow eloquent in
 aught
That throws me into shade; yet you speak
 truth.
Myr. And now retire, to have your
 wound look'd to.
Pray lean on me.
Sar. Yes, love! but not from pain.
 [*Exeunt omnes.*

ACT IV

SCENE I.—SARDANAPALUS *discovered sleep-
 ing upon a Couch, and occasionally dis-
 turbed in his slumbers, with* MYRRHA
 watching.

Myr. [*sola, gazing*]. I have stolen upon
 his rest, if rest it be,
Which thus convulses slumber: shall I
 wake him?
No, he seems calmer. Oh, thou God of
 Quiet!
Whose reign is o'er seal'd eyelids and soft
 dreams,
Or deep, deep sleep, so as to be un-
 fathom'd, 5

Look like thy brother, Death,—so still, so
 stirless—
For then we are happiest, as it may be, we
Are happiest of all within the realm 8
Of thy stern, silent, and unwakening twin.
Again he moves—again the play of pain
Shoots o'er his features, as the sudden gust
Crisps the reluctant lake that lay so calm
Beneath the mountain shadow; or the
 blast
Ruffles the autumn leaves, that drooping
 cling
Faintly and motionless to their loved
 boughs. 15
I must awake him—yet not yet; who
 knows
From what I rouse him? It seems pain;
 but if
I quicken him to heavier pain? The fever
Of this tumultuous night, the grief too of
His wound, though slight, may cause all
 this, and shake 20
Me more to see than him to suffer. No:
Let Nature use her own maternal means,
And I await to second, not disturb her.
 Sar. [*awakening*]. Not so—although ye
 multiplied the stars,
And gave them to me as a realm to share
From you and with you! I would not so
 purchase 26
The empire of eternity. Hence—hence—
Old hunter of the earliest brutes! and ye,
Who hunted fellow-creatures as if brutes!
Once bloody mortals—and now bloodier
 idols, 30
If your priests lie not! And thou, ghastly
 beldame!
Dripping with dusky gore, and trampling
 on
The carcasses of Inde—away! away!
Where am I? Where the spectres?
 Where——No—that
Is no false phantom: I should know it
 'midst 35
All that the dead dare gloomily raise up
From their black gulf to daunt the living.
 Myrrha!
 Myr. Alas! thou art pale, and on thy
 brow the drops
Gather like night dew. My beloved,
 hush—
Calm thee. Thy speech seems of another
 world, 40
And thou art lord of this. Be of good
 cheer;
All will go well.
 Sar. Thy *hand*—so—'tis thy hand;
'Tis flesh; grasp—clasp—yet closer, till I
 feel
Myself that which I was.
 Myr. At least know me
For what I am, and ever must be—thine.
 Sar. I know it now. I know this life
 again. 46

Ah, Myrrha! I have been where we shall
 be.
 Myr. My lord!
 Sar. I've been i' the grave—where
 worms are lords,
And kings are——But I did not deem it so;
I thought 'twas nothing.
 Myr. So it is; except
Unto the timid, who anticipate 50
That which may never be.
 Sar. Oh, Myrrha! if
Sleep shows such things, what may not
 death disclose?
 Myr. I know no evil death can show
 which life 54
Has not already shown to those who live
Embodied longest. If there be indeed
A shore where mind survives, 'twill be as
 mind,
All unincorporate: or if there flits
A shadow of this cumbrous clog of clay
Which stalks, methinks, between our
 souls and heaven, 60
And fetters us to earth—at least the phan-
 tom,
Whate'er it have to fear, will not fear
 death.
 Sar. I fear it not; but I have felt—have
 seen—
A legion of the dead.
 Myr. And so have I.
The dust we tread upon was once alive,
And wretched. But proceed: what hast
 thou seen? 66
Speak it, 'twill lighten thy dimm'd mind.
 Sar. Methought——
 Myr. Yet pause, thou art tired—in
 pain—exhausted; all
Which can impair both strength and
 spirit: seek 69
Rather to sleep again.
 Sar. Not now—I would not
Dream; though I know it now to be a dream
What I have dreamt:—and canst thou
 bear to hear it?
 Myr. I can bear all things, dreams of
 life or death,
Which I participate with you in semblance
Or full reality.
 Sar. And this look'd real, 75
I tell you: after that these eyes were open.
I saw them in their flight—for then they fled
 Myr. Say on.
 Sar. I saw, that is, I dream'd myself
Here—here—even where we are, guests as
 we were,
Myself a host that deem'd himself but
 guest, 80
Willing to equal all in social freedom;
But, on my right hand and my left, instead
Of thee and Zames, and our custom'd
 meeting,
Was ranged on my left hand a haughty,
 dark, 84

And deadly face; I could not recognise it,
Yet I had seen it, though I knew not where:
The features were a giant's, and the eye
Was still, yet lighted; his long locks curl'd
 down
On his vast bust, whence a huge quiver rose
With shaft-heads feather'd from the
 eagle's wing, 90
That peep'd up bristling through his ser-
 pent hair.
I invited him to fill the cup which stood
Between us, but he answer'd not; I fill'd it;
He took it not, but stared upon me, till
I trembled at the fix'd glare of his eye: 95
I frown'd upon him as a king should
 frown;
He frown'd not in his turn, but look'd
 upon me
With the same aspect, which appall'd me
 more,
Because it changed not; and I turn'd for
 refuge
To milder guests, and sought them on the
 right, 100
Where thou wert wont to be. But——
 [He pauses.
 Myr. What instead?
 Sar. In thy own chair—thy own place
 in the banquet—
I sought thy sweet face in the circle—but
Instead—a grey-hair'd, wither'd bloody-
 eyed,
And bloody-handed, ghastly, ghostly
 thing, 105
Female in garb, and crown'd upon the
 brow,
Furrow'd with years, yet sneering with the
 passion
Of vengeance, leering too with that of lust,
Sate:—my veins curdled.
 Myr. Is this all?
 Sar. Upon
Her right hand—her lank, bird-like right
 hand—stood 110
A goblet, bubbling o'er with blood; and on
Her left, another, fill'd with—what I saw
 not,
But turn'd from it and her. But all along
The table sate a range of crowned wretches,
Of various aspects, but of one expression.
 Myr. And felt you not this a mere
 vision?
 Sar. No:
It was so palpable, I could have touch'd
 them. 117
I turn'd from one face to another, in
The hope to find at last one which I knew
Ere I saw theirs: but no—all turn'd upon
 me, 120
And stared, but neither ate nor drank, but
 stared,
Till I grew stone, as they seem'd half to be,
Yet breathing stone, for I felt life in them,
And life in me: there was a horrid kind

Of sympathy between us, as if they 125
Had lost a part of death to come to me,
And I the half of life to sit by them.
We were in an existence all apart
From heaven or earth—And rather let me
 see 129
Death all than such a being!
 Myr. And the end?
 Sar. At last I sate, marble, as they, when
 rose
The hunter and the crone; and smiling on
 me—
Yes, the enlarged but noble aspect of
The hunter smiled upon me—I should say,
His lips, for his eyes moved not—and the
 woman's 135
Thin lips relax'd to something like a smile.
Both rose, and the crown'd figures on each
 hand
Rose also, as if aping their chief shades—
Mere mimics even in death—but I sate
 still:
A desperate courage crept through every
 limb, 140
And at the last I fear'd them not, but
 laugh'd
Full in their phantom faces. But then—
 then
The hunter laid his hand on mine: I took it,
And grasp'd it—but it melted from my
 own;
While he too vanish'd, and left nothing
 but 145
The memory of a hero, for he look'd so.
 Myr. And was: the ancestor of heroes,
 too,
And thine no less.
 Sar. Ay, Myrrha, but the woman,
The female who remain'd, she flew upon
 me,
And burnt my lips up with her noisome
 kisses; 150
And, flinging down the goblets on each
 hand,
Methought their poisons flow'd around
 us, till
Each form'd a hideous river. Still she
 clung;
The other phantoms, like a row of statues,
Stood dull as in our temples, but she still
Embraced me, while I shrunk from her,
 as if, 156
In lieu of her remote descendant, I
Had been the son who slew her for her
 incest.
Then—then—a chaos of all loathsome
 things
Throng'd thick and shapeless: I was dead,
 yet feeling— 160
Buried, and raised again—consumed by
 worms,
Purged by the flames, and wither'd in the
 air!
I can fix nothing further of my thoughts,

Save that I long'd for thee, and sought for
thee,
In all these agonies,—and woke and found
thee. 165
Myr. So shalt thou find me ever at thy
side,
Here and hereafter, if the last may be.
But think not of these things—the mere
creations
Of late events, acting upon a frame 169
Unused to toil, yet over-wrought by toil
Such as might try the sternest.
Sar. I am better.
Now that I see thee once more, what was
seen 172
Seems nothing.

Enter SALEMENES.

Sal. Is the king so soon awake?
Sar. Yes, brother, and I would I had
not slept;
For all the predecessors of our line
Rose up, methought, to drag me down to
them. 176
My father was amongst them, too; but he,
I know not why, kept from me, leaving me
Between the hunter-founder of our race,
And her, the homicide and husband-killer,
Whom you call glorious.
Sal. So I term you also,
Now you have shown a spirit like to hers.
By day-break I propose that we set forth,
And charge once more the rebel crew, who
still
Keep gathering head, repulsed, but not
quite quell'd. 185
Sar. How wears the night?
Sal. There yet remain some hours
Of darkness: use them for your further rest.
Sar. No, not to-night, if 'tis not gone:
methought 188
I pass'd hours in that vision.
Myr. Scarcely one;
I watch'd by you: it was a heavy hour,
But an hour only.
Sar. Let us then hold council;
To-morrow we set forth.
Sal. But ere that time,
I had a grace to seek.
Sar. 'Tis granted.
Sal. Hear it
Ere you reply too readily; and 'tis 194
For *your* ear only.
Myr. Prince, I take my leave.
[*Exit* MYRRHA.
Sal. That slave deserves her freedom.
Sar. Freedom only!
That slave deserves to share a throne.
Sal. Your patience—
'Tis not yet vacant, and 'tis of its partner
I come to speak with you.
Sar. How! of the queen?
Sal. Even so. I judged it fitting for their
safety 200

That, ere the dawn, she sets forth with he
children
For Paphlagonia, where our kinsma
Cotta
Governs; and there at all events secure
My nephews and your sons their lives, an
with them
Their just pretensions to the crown i
case—— 20
Sar. I perish—as is probable: we
thought—
Let them set forth with a sure escort.
Sal. Tha
Is all provided, and the galley ready
To drop down the Euphrates: but ere the
Depart, will you not see——
Sar. My sons? It ma
Unman my heart, and the poor boys wi
weep; 2
And what can I reply to comfort them,
Save with some hollow hopes and ill-wor
smiles?
You know I cannot feign.
Sal. But you can fee
At least, I trust so; in a word, the quee
Requests to see you ere you part—for eve
Sar. Unto what end? what purpose?
will grant 2
Aught—all that she can ask—but such
meeting.
Sal. You know, or ought to know
enough of women,
Since you have studied them so steadily
That what they ask in aught that touche
on 22
The heart, is dearer to their feelings or
Their fancy than the whole external world
I think as you do of my sister's wish;
But 'twas her wish—she is my sister—
you 22
Her husband—will you grant it?
Sar. 'Twill be useless
But let her come.
Sal. I go. [*Exit* SALEMENES
Sar. We have lived asunde
Too long to meet again—and *now* to meet
Have I not cares enow, and pangs enow
To bear alone, that we must mingl
sorrows, 23
Who have ceased to mingle love?

Re-enter SALEMENES *and* ZARINA.

Sal. My sister! Courage
Shame not our blood with trembling, bu
remember
From whence we sprung. The queen i
present, sire.
Zar. I pray thee, brother, leave me.
Sal. Since you ask it
[*Exit* SALEMENES
Zar. Alone with him! How many
year has pass'd, 23
Though we are still so young, since w
have met,

Which I have worn in widowhood of
 heart!
He loved me not: yet he seems little
 changed—
Changed to me only—would the change
 were mutual!
He speaks not—scarce regards me—not a
 word, 240
Nor look—yet he *was* soft of voice and
 aspect,
Indifferent, not austere. My lord!
 Sar. Zarina!
Zar. No, *not* Zarina—do not say
 Zarina.
That tone—that word—annihilate long
 years,
And things which make them longer.
 Sar. 'Tis too late 245
To think of these past dreams. Let's not
 reproach—
That is, reproach me not—for the *last*
 time——
Zar. And *first.* I ne'er reproach'd you.
 Sar. 'Tis most true;
And that reproof comes heavier on my
 heart
Than——But our hearts are not in our
 own power. 250
Zar. Nor hands; but I gave both.
 Sar. Your brother said
It was your will to see me ere you went
From Nineveh with——[*He hesitates*].
 Zar. Our children: it is true.
I wish'd to thank you that you have not
 divided
My heart from all that's left it now to
 love— 255
Those who are yours and mine, who look
 like you,
And look upon me as you look'd upon me
Once——But they have not changed.
 Sar. Nor ever will.
I fain would have them dutiful.
 Zar. I cherish
Those infants, not alone from the blind
 love 260
Of a fond mother, but as a fond woman.
They are now the only tie between us.
 Sar. Deem not
have not done you justice: rather make
 them
Resemble your own line than their own
 sire.
I trust them with you—to you: fit them
 for 265
A throne, or, if that be denied——You
 have heard
Of this night's tumults?
 Zar. I had half forgotten,
And could have welcomed any grief save
 yours,
Which gave me to behold your face again.
 Sar. The throne—I say it not in fear—
 but 'tis 270

In peril: they perhaps may never mount it;
But let them not for this lose sight of it.
I will dare all things to bequeath it them;
But if I fail, then they must win it back
Bravely—and, won, wear it wisely, not as
 I 275
Have wasted down my royalty.
 Zar. They ne'er
Shall know from me of aught but what
 may honour
Their father's memory.
 Sar. Rather let them hear
The truth from you than from a trampling
 world.
If they be in adversity, they'll learn 280
Too soon the scorn of crowds for crown-
 less princes,
And find that all their father's sins are
 theirs.
My boys!—I could have borne it were I
 childless.
 Zar. Oh! do not say so—do not poison
 all
My peace left, by unwishing that thou wert
A father. If thou conquerest, they shall
 reign, 286
And honour him who saved the realm for
 them,
So little cared for as his own; and if——
 Sar. 'Tis lost, all earth will cry out,
 thank your father!
And they will swell the echo with a curse.
 Zar. That they shall never do; but
 rather honour 291
The name of him, who, dying like a king,
In his last hours did more for his own
 memory
Than many monarchs in a length of days,
Which date the flight of time, but make no
 annals. 295
 Sar. Our annals draw perchance unto
 their close;
But at the least, whate'er the past, their end
Shall be in their beginning—memorable.
 Zar. Yet be not rash—be careful of
 your life,
Live but for those who love.
 Sar. And who are they? 300
A slave, who loves from passion—I'll
 not say
Ambition—she has seen thrones shake,
 and loves;
A few friends who have revell'd till we are
As one, for they are nothing if I fall;
A brother I have injured—children whom
I have neglected, and a spouse——
 Zar. Who loves. 306
 Sar. And pardons?
 Zar. I have never thought of this,
And cannot pardon till I have condemn'd.
 Sar. My wife!
 Zar. Now blessings on thee
 for that word!
I never thought to hear it more—from thee.

Sar. Oh! thou wilt hear it from my
 subjects. Yes— 311
These slaves whom I have nurtured, pam-
 per'd, fed,
And swoln with peace, and gorged with
 plenty, till
They reign themselves—all monarchs in
 their mansions—
Now swarm forth in rebellion, and de-
 mand 315
His death, who made their lives a jubilee;
While the few upon whom I have no claim
Are faithful! This is true, yet monstrous.
 Zar. 'Tis
Perhaps too natural; for benefits
Turn poison in bad minds.
 Sar. And good ones make 320
Good out of evil. Happier than the bee,
Which hives not but from wholesome
 flowers.
 Zar. Then reap
The honey, nor inquire whence 'tis de-
 rived.
Be satisfied—you are not all abandon'd.
 Sar. My life insures me that. How long,
 bethink you, 325
Were not I yet a king, should I be mortal?
That is, where mortals *are*, not where they
 must be?
 Zar. I know not. But yet live for my—
 that is,
Your children's sake!
 Sar. My gentle, wrong'd Zarina!
I am the very slave of circumstance 330
And impulse—borne away with every
 breath!
Misplaced upon the throne—misplaced
 in life.
I know not what I could have been, but feel
I am not what I should be—let it end.
But take this with thee: if I was not form'd
To prize a love like thine, a mind like
 thine, 336
Nor dote even on thy beauty—as I've
 doted
On lesser charms, for no cause save that
 such
Devotion was a duty, and I hated
All that look'd like a chain for me or
 others 340
(This even rebellion must avouch); yet
 hear
These words, perhaps among my last—
 that none
E'er valued more thy virtues, though he
 knew not
To profit by them—as the miner lights
Upon a vein of virgin ore, discovering
That which avails him nothing: he hath
 found it, 346
But 'tis not his—but some superior's, who
Placed him to dig, but not divide the
 wealth
Which sparkles at his feet; nor dare he lift

Nor poise it, but must grovel on, up
 turning 35
The sullen earth.
 Zar. Oh! if thou hast at lengt
Discover'd that my love is worth esteem
I ask no more—but let us hence together
And *I*—let me say *we*—shall yet be happy
Assyria is not all the earth—we'll find
A world out of our own—and be mor
 bless'd 35
Than I have ever been, or thou, with al
An empire to indulge thee.

Enter SALEMENES.

 Sal. I must part ye—
The moments, which must not be lost, ar
 passing.
 Zar. Inhuman brother! wilt thou thu
 weigh out 36
Instants so high and blest?
 Sal. Blest!
 Zar. He hath bee
So gentle with me, that I cannot think
Of quitting.
 Sal. So—this feminine farewell
Ends as such partings end, in *no* departure
I thought as much, and yielded against a
My better bodings. But it must not be.
 Zar. Not be?
 Sal. Remain, and perish——
 Zar. With my husband—
 Sal. And children.
 Zar. Alas!
 Sal. Hear me, sister, lik
My sister:—all's prepared to make you
 safety
Certain, and of the boys too, our la
 hopes; 3
'Tis not a single question of mere feelin
Though that were much—but 'tis a poi
 of state:
The rebels would do more to seize upo
The offspring of their sovereign, and s
 crush——
 Zar. Ah! do not name it.
 Sal. Well, then, mark me: when
They are safe beyond the Median's gras
 the rebels 3
Have miss'd their chief aim—the extin
 tion of
The line of Nimrod. Though the prese
 king
Fall, his sons live for victory and ve
 geance.
 Zar. But could not I remain, alone?
 Sal. What! leav
Your children, with two parents and y
 orphans—— 3
In a strange land—so young, so distan
 Zar. No—
My heart will break.
 Sal. Now you know all—decid
 Sar. Zarina, he hath spoken well, ar
 we

Must yield awhile to this necessity. 385
Remaining here, you may lose all; de-
 parting,
You save the better part of what is left,
To both of us, and to such loyal hearts
As yet beat in these kingdoms.
 Sal. The time presses.
 Sar. Go, then. If e'er we meet again,
 perhaps 390
I may be worthier of you—and, if not,
Remember that my faults, though not
 atoned for,
Are *ended*. Yet, I dread thy nature will
Grieve more about the blighted name and
 ashes
Which once were mightiest in Assyria—
 than— 395
But I grow womanish again, and must not;
I must learn sternness now. My sins have
 all
Been of the softer order——*hide* thy
 tears—
I do not bid thee *not* to shed them—'twere
Easier to stop Euphrates at its source
Than one tear of a true and tender heart—
But let me not behold them; they unman
 me 402
Here when I had remann'd myself. My
 brother,
Lead her away.
 Zar. Oh, God! I never shall
Behold him more!
 Sal. [*striving to conduct her*]. Nay,
 sister, I *must* be obey'd. 405
 Zar. I must remain—away! you shall
 not hold me.
What, shall he die alone?—*I* live alone?
 Sal. He shall *not die alone;* but lonely
 you
Have lived for years.
 Zar. That's false! I knew *he* lived,
And lived upon his image—let me go!
 Sal. [*conducting her off the stage*]. Nay,
 then, I must use some fraternal
 force, 411
Which you will pardon.
 Zar. Never. Help me! Oh!
Sardanapalus, wilt thou thus behold me
Torn from thee?
 Sal. Nay—then all is lost again,
If that this moment is not gain'd.
 Zar. My brain turns— 415
My eyes fail—where is he? [*She faints.*
 Sar. [*advancing*]. No—set her down;
she's dead—and you have slain her.
 Sal. 'Tis the mere
Faintness of o'erwrought passion: in the air
She will recover. Pray, keep back.—
 [*Aside*] I must
Avail myself of this sole moment to 420
Bear her to where her children are em-
 bark'd,
' the royal galley on the river.
 [SALEMENES *bears her off.*

 Sar. [*solus*]. This, too—
And this too must I suffer—I, who never
Inflicted purposely on human hearts
A voluntary pang! But that is false—
She loved me, and I loved her.—Fatal
 passion! 426
Why dost thou not expire *at once* in hearts
Which thou hast lighted up at once?
 Zarina!
I must pay dearly for the desolation
Now brought upon thee. Had I never
 loved 430
But thee, I should have been an unopposed
Monarch of honouring nations. To what
 gulfs
A single deviation from the track
Of human duties leads even those who
 claim 434
The homage of mankind as their born due,
And find it, till they forfeit it themselves!

Enter MYRRHA.

 Sar. You here! Who call'd you?
 Myr. No one—but I heard
Far off a voice of wail and lamentation,
And thought——
 Sar. It forms no portion of your duties
To enter here till sought for.
 Myr. Though I might, 440
Perhaps, recall some softer words of yours
(Although they *too were* chiding), which
 reproved
Because I ever dreaded to intrude;
Resisting my own wish and your in-
 junction
To heed no time nor presence, but ap-
 proach you 445
Uncall'd for:—I retire.
 Sar. Yet stay—being here.
I pray you pardon me: events have sour'd
 me
Till I wax peevish—heed it not: I shall
Soon be myself again.
 Myr. I wait with patience,
What I shall see with pleasure.
 Sar. Scarce a moment 450
Before your entrance in this hall, Zarina,
Queen of Assyria, departed hence.
 Myr. Ah!
 Sar. Wherefore do you start?
 Myr. Did I do so?
 Sar. 'Twas well you enter'd by another
 portal,
Else you had met. That pang at least is
 spared her! 455
 Myr. I know to feel for her.
 Sar. That is too much,
And beyond nature—'tis nor mutual
Nor possible. You cannot pity her,
Nor she aught but——
 Myr. Despise the favourite slave?
Not more than I have ever scorn'd myself.
 Sar. Scorn'd! what, to be the envy of
 your sex, 461

483

And lord it o'er the heart of the world's
 lord?
Myr. Were you the lord of twice ten
 thousand worlds—
As you are like to lose the one you
 sway'd—
I did abase myself as much in being 465
Your paramour, as though you were a
 peasant—
Nay, more, if that the peasant were a
 Greek.
Sar. You talk it well——
Myr. And truly.
Sar. In the hour
Of man's adversity all things grow daring
Against the falling; but as I am not 470
Quite fall'n, nor now disposed to bear
 reproaches,
Perhaps because I merit them too often,
Let us then part while peace is still between
 us.
Myr. Part!
Sar. Have not all past human
 beings parted,
And must not all the present one day
 part? 475
Myr. Why?
Sar. For your safety, which I
will have look'd to,
With a strong escort to your native land;
And such gifts, as, if you had not been all
A queen, shall make your dowry worth a
 kingdom.
Myr. I pray you talk not thus.
Sar. The queen is gone: 480
You need not shame to follow. I would
 fall
Alone—I seek no partners but in pleasure.
Myr. And I no pleasure but in parting
 not.
You shall not force me from you.
Sar. Think well of it—
It soon may be too late.
Myr. So let it be; 485
For then you cannot separate me from you.
Sar. And will not; but I thought you
 wish'd it.
Myr. I!
Sar. You spoke of your abasement.
Myr. And I feel it
Deeply—more deeply than all things but
 love. 489
Sar. Then fly from it.
Myr. 'Twill not recall the past—
'Twill not restore my honour, nor my
 heart.
No—here I stand or fall. If that you
 conquer,
I live to joy in your great triumph: should
Your lot be different, I'll not weep, but
 share it.
You did not doubt me a few hours ago.
Sar. Your courage never—nor your
 love till now; 496

And none could make me doubt it save
 yourself.
Those words——
Myr. Were words. I pray you, le
the proofs
Be in the past acts you were pleased to
 praise
This very night, and in my further bear
 ing, 50
Beside, wherever you are borne by fate.
Sar. I am content: and, trusting in m
 cause,
Think we may yet be victors and return
To peace—the only victory I covet.
To me war is no glory—conquest no
Renown. To be forced thus to uphold m
 right 50
Sits heavier on my heart than all th
 wrongs
These men would bow me down with
 Never, never
Can I forget this night, even should I liv
To add it to the memory of others. 51
I thought to have made mine inoffensiv
 rule
An era of sweet peace 'midst blood
 annals,
A green spot amidst desert centuries,
On which the future would turn back an
 smile, 51
And cultivate, or sigh when it could no
Recall Sardanapalus' golden reign.
I thought to have made my realm a para
 dise,
And every moon an epoch of nev
 pleasures.
I took the rabble's shouts for love—th
 breath
Of friends for truth—the lips of woma
 for 52
My only guerdon—so they are, m
 Myrrha: [*He kisses he*
Kiss me. Now let them take my realm an
 life!
They shall have both, but never thee!
Myr. No, neve
Man may despoil his brother man of al
That's great or glittering—kingdoms fal
 hosts yield, 52
Friends fail, slaves fly, and all betray—
 and, more
Than all, the most indebted—but a hea
That loves without self-love! 'Tis here—
 now prove it.

Enter SALEMENES.

Sal. I sought you—How! *she* he
 again?
Sar. Return not
Now to reproof: methinks your aspe
 speaks 53
Of higher matter than a woman's presenc
Sal. The only woman whom it muc
 imports me

At such a moment now is safe in absence—
The queen's embark'd.
 Sar. And well? say that much.
 Sal. Yes.
Her transient weakness has pass'd o'er; at
 least, 535
It settled into tearless silence: her
Pale face and glittering eye, after a glance
Upon her sleeping children, were still fix'd
Upon the palace towers as the swift galley
Stole down the hurrying stream beneath
 the starlight; 540
But she said nothing.
 Sar. Would I felt no more
Than she has said!
 Sal. 'Tis now too late to feel.
Your feelings cannot cancel a sole pang:
To change them, my advices bring sure
 tidings
That the rebellious Medes and Chaldees,
 marshall'd 545
By their two leaders, are already up
In arms again; and, serrying their ranks,
Prepare to attack: they have apparently
Been join'd by other satraps.
 Sar. What! more rebels?
Let us be first, then.
 Sal. That were hardly prudent 550
Now, though it was our first intention. If
By noon to-morrow we are join'd by those
I've sent for by sure messengers, we shall
 be
In strength enough to venture an attack,
Ay, and pursuit too; but, till then, my
 voice 555
Is to await the onset.
 Sar. I detest
That waiting; though it seems so safe to
 fight
Behind high walls, and hurl down foes into
Deep fosses, or behold them sprawl on
 spikes
Strew'd to receive them, still I like it not—
My soul seems lukewarm; but when I set
 on them, 561
Though they were piled on mountains, I
 would have
A pluck at them, or perish in hot blood!—
Let me then charge.
 Sal. You talk like a young soldier.
 Sar. I am no soldier, but a man: speak
 not 565
Of soldiership, I loathe the word, and
 those
Who pride themselves upon it; but direct
 me
Where I may pour upon them.
 Sal. You must spare
To expose your life too hastily: 'tis not
Like mine or any other subject's breath;
The whole war turns upon it—with it; this
Alone creates it, kindles, and may quench
 it— 572
Prolong it—end it.

 Sar. Then let us end both!
'Twere better thus, perhaps, than pro-
 long either;
I'm sick of one, perchance of both.
 [*A trumpet sounds without.*
 Sal. Hark!
 Sar. Let us 575
Reply, not listen.
 Sal. And your wound!
 Sar. 'Tis bound—
'Tis heal'd—I had forgotten it. Away!
A leech's lancet would have scratch'd me
 deeper;
The slave that gave it might be well
 ashamed
To have struck so weakly.
 Sal. Now, may none this hour 580
Strike with a better aim!
 Sar. Ay, if we conquer;
But if not, they will only leave to me
A task they might have spared their king.
 Upon them! [*Trumpet sounds again.*
 Sal. I am with you.
 Sar. Ho, my arms! again, my arms!
 [*Exeunt.*

ACT V

SCENE I.—*The same Hall in the Palace.*

MYRRHA *and* BALEA.

 Myr. [*at a window*]. The day at last
 has broken. What a night
Hath usher'd it! how beautiful in heaven!
Though varied with a transitory storm,
More beautiful in that variety!
How hideous upon earth! where peace and
 hope,
And love and revel, in an hour were
 trampled
By human passions to a human chaos,
Not yet resolved to separate elements—
'Tis warring still! And can the sun so rise,
So bright, so rolling back the clouds into
Vapours more lovely than the unclouded
 sky, 11
With golden pinnacles, and snowy moun-
 tains,
And billows purpler than the ocean's,
 making
In heaven a glorious mockery of the earth,
So like we almost deem it permanent; 15
So fleeting, we can scarcely call it aught
Beyond a vision, 'tis so transiently
Scatter'd along the eternal vault: and yet
It dwells upon the soul, and soothes the
 soul,
And blends itself into the soul, until 20
Sunrise and sunset form the haunted
 epoch
Of sorrow and of love; which they who
 mark not,
Know not the realms where those twin
 genii
(Who chasten and who purify our hearts,

So that we would not change their sweet
 rebukes 25
For all the boisterous joys that ever shook
The air with clamour) build the palaces
Where their fond votaries repose and
 breathe
Briefly;—but in that brief cool calm inhale
Enough of heaven to enable them to bear
The rest of common, heavy, human hours,
And dream them through in placid
 sufferance,
Though seemingly employ'd like all the
 rest
Of toiling breathers in allotted tasks
Of pain or pleasure, *two* names for *one*
 feeling, 35
Which our internal, restless agony
Would vary in the sound, although the
 sense
Escapes our highest efforts to be happy.
 Bal. You muse right calmly: and can
 you so watch
The sunrise which may be our last?
 Myr. It is 40
Therefore that I so watch it, and reproach
Those eyes, which never may behold it
 more,
For having look'd upon it oft, too oft,
Without the reverence and the rapture due
To that which keeps all earth from being
 as fragile 45
As I am in this form. Come, look upon it,
The Chaldee's god, which when I gaze
 upon
I grow almost a convert to your Baal.
 Bal. As now he reigns in heaven, so
 once on earth
He sway'd.
 Myr. He sways it now far more,
 then; never 50
Had earthly monarch half the power and
 glory
Which centres in a single ray of his.
 Bal. Surely he is a god!
 Myr. So we Greeks deem too;
And yet I sometimes think that gorgeous
 orb 54
Must rather be the abode of gods than one
Of the immortal sovereigns. Now he
 breaks
Through all the clouds, and fills my eyes
 with light
That shuts the world out. I can look no
 more.
 Bal. Hark! heard you not a sound?
 Myr. No, 'twas mere fancy; 59
They battle it beyond the wall, and not
As in late midnight conflict in the very
Chambers: the palace has become a
 fortress
Since that insidious hour; and here,
 within
The very centre, girded by vast courts 64
And regal halls of pyramid proportions,

Which must be carried one by one before
They penetrate to where they then arrived,
We are as much shut in even from the
 sound
Of peril as from glory.
 Bal. But they reach'd
Thus far before.
 Myr. Yes, by surprise, and were 70
Beat back by valour: now at once we have
Courage and vigilance to guard us.
 Bal. May they
Prosper!
 Myr. That is the prayer of many, and
The dread of more: it is an anxious hour;
I strive to keep it from my thoughts. Alas!
How vainly!
 Bal. It is said the king's demeanour
In the late action scarcely more appall'd
The rebels than astonish'd his true subjects.
 Myr. 'Tis easy to astonish or appal
The vulgar mass which moulds a horde of
 slaves; 80
But he did bravely.
 Bal. Slew he not Beleses?
I heard the soldiers say he struck him
 down.
 Myr. The wretch was overthrown,
 but rescued to
Triumph, perhaps, o'er one who
 vanquish'd him 84
In fight, as he had spared him in his peril;
And by that heedless pity risk'd a crown.
 Bal. Hark!
 Myr. You are right; some steps
 approach, but slowly.

Enter Soldiers, bearing in SALEMENES
 *wounded, with a broken javelin in his
 side: they seat him upon one of the
 couches which furnish the Apartment.*

 Myr. Oh, Jove!
 Bal. Then all is over.
 Sal. That is false.
Hew down the slave who says so, if a
 soldier.
 Myr. Spare him—he's none: a mere
 court butterfly, 90
That flutters in the pageant of a monarch.
 Sal. Let him live on, then.
 Myr. So wilt thou, I trust.
 Sal. I fain would live this hour out,
 and the event,
But doubt it. Wherefore did ye bear me
 here?
 Sol. By the king's order. When the
 javelin struck you, 95
You fell and fainted: 'twas his strict com-
 mand
To bear you to this hall.
 Sal. 'Twas not ill done:
For seeming slain in that cold dizzy trance,
The sight might shake our soldiers—but—
 'tis vain,
I feel it ebbing!

Myr. Let me see the wound; 100
I am not quite skilless: in my native land
'Tis part of our instruction. War being
 constant,
We are nerved to look on such things.
 Sol. Best extract
The javelin.
 Myr. Hold! no, no, it cannot be.
 Sal. I am sped, then!
 Myr. With the blood that fast must
 follow 105
The extracted weapon, I do fear thy life.
 Sal. And I *not* death. Where was the
 king when you
Convey'd me from the spot where I was
 stricken?
 Sol. Upon the same ground, and en-
 couraging
With voice and gesture the dispirited
 troops 110
Who had seen you fall, and falter'd back.
 Sal. Whom heard ye
Named next to the command?
 Sol. I did not hear.
 Sal. Fly then, and tell him, 'twas my
 last request
That Zames take my post until the
 junction, 114
So hoped for, yet delay'd, of Ofratanes,
Satrap of Susa. Leave me here: our troops
Are not so numerous as to spare your
 absence.
 Sol. But, prince——
 Sal. Hence, I say! Here's a courtier and
A woman, the best chamber company.
As you would not permit me to expire
Upon the field, I'll have no idle soldiers
About my sick couch. Hence! and do my
 bidding! [*Exeunt the Soldiers.*
 Myr. Gallant and glorious spirit!
 must the earth
So soon resign thee?
 Sal. Gentle Myrrha, 'tis 124
The end I would have chosen, had I saved
The monarch or the monarchy by this;
As 'tis, I have not outlived them.
 Myr. You wax paler.
 Sal. Your hand; this broken weapon
 but prolongs 128
My pangs, without sustaining life enough
To make me useful: I would draw it forth
And my life with it, could I but hear how
The fight goes.

 Enter SARDANAPALUS *and Soldiers.*

 Sar. My best brother!
 Sal. And the battle 132
Is lost?
 Sar. [*despondingly*]. You see *me* here.
 Sal. I'd rather see you *thus!*
 [*He draws out the weapon from the
 wound, and dies.*
 Sar. And *thus* I will be seen; unless
 the succour,

The last frail reed of our beleaguer'd
 hopes, 135
Arrive with Ofratanes.
 Myr. Did you not
Receive a token from your dying brother,
Appointing Zames chief?
 Sar. I did.
 Myr. Where's Zames?
 Sar. Dead.
 Myr. And Altada?
 Sar. Dying.
 Myr. Pania? Sfero?
 Sar. Pania yet lives: but Sfero's fled
 or captive. 140
I am alone.
 Myr. And is all lost?
 Sar. Our walls,
Though thinly mann'd, may still hold out
 against
Their present force, or aught save
 treachery:
But i' the field——
 Myr. I thought 'twas the intent
Of Salemenes not to risk a sally 145
Till ye were strengthen'd by the expected
 succours.
 Sar. *I* overruled him.
 Myr. Well, the fault's a brave one.
 Sar. But fatal. Oh, my brother! I
 would give
These realms, of which thou wert the orna-
 ment,
The sword and shield, the sole-redeeming
 honour, 150
To call back—But I will not weep for thee;
Thou shalt be mourn'd for as thou wouldst
 be mourn'd.
It grieves me most that thou couldst quit
 this life
Believing that I could survive what thou
Hast died for—our long royalty of race.
If I redeem it, I will give thee blood 156
Of thousands, tears of millions, for atone-
 ment
(The tears of all the good are thine
 already).
If not, we meet again soon,—if the spirit
Within us lives beyond;—thou readest
 mine, 160
And dost me justice now. Let me once
 clasp
That yet warm hand, and fold that throb-
 less heart [*Embraces the body.*
To this which beats so bitterly. Now, bear
The body hence.
 Soldier. Where?
 Sar. To my proper chamber.
Place it beneath my canopy, as though
The king lay there: when this is done, we
 will 166
Speak further of the rites due to such
 ashes.
 [*Exeunt Soldiers with the body of*
 SALEMENES.

Enter PANIA.

Sar. Well, Pania! have you placed the
guards, and issued
The orders fix'd on?

Pan. Sire, I have obey'd.

Sar. And do the soldiers keep their
hearts up?

Pan. Sire? 170

Sar. I'm answer'd! When a king asks
twice, and has
A question as an answer to *his* question,
It is a portent. What! they are dis-
hearten'd?

Pan. The death of Salemenes, and the
shouts
Of the exulting rebels on his fall, 175
Have made them——

Sar. Rage—not droop—it should have
been.
We'll find the means to rouse them.

Pan. Such a loss
Might sadden even a victory.

Sar. Alas!
Who can so feel it as I feel? but yet,
Though coop'd within these walls, they
are strong, and we 180
Have those without will break their way
through hosts,
To make their sovereign's dwelling what
it was—
A palace; not a prison, nor a fortress.

Enter an Officer, hastily.

Sar. Thy face seems ominous. Speak!

Offi. I dare not.

Sar. Dare not?
While millions dare revolt with sword in
hand! 185
That's strange. I pray thee break that
loyal silence
Which loathes to shock its sovereign; we
can hear
Worse than thou hast to tell.

Pan. Proceed, thou hearest.

Offi. The wall which skirted near the
river's brink 189
Is thrown down by the sudden inundation
Of the Euphrates, which now rolling, swoln
From the enormous mountains where it
rises,
By the late rains of that tempestuous region,
O'erfloods its banks, and hath destroy'd
the bulwark.

Pan. That's a black augury! it has
been said 195
For ages, 'That the city ne'er should yield
To man, until the river grew its foe.'

Sar. I can forgive the omen, not the
ravage.
How much is swept down of the wall?

Offi. About
Some twenty stadia.

Sar. And all this is left 200
Pervious to the assailants?

Offi. For the present
The river's fury must impede the assault;
But when he shrinks into his wonted
channel,
And may be cross'd by the accustom'd
barks,
The palace is their own.

Sar. That shall be never 205
Though men, and gods, and elements, and
omens,
Have risen up 'gainst one who ne'er pro-
voked them,
My fathers' house shall never be a cave
For wolves to horde and howl in.

Pan. With your sanction,
I will proceed to the spot, and take such
measures 210
For the assurance of the vacant space
As time and means permit.

Sar. About it straight,
And bring me back, as speedily as full
And fair investigation may permit, 214
Report of the true state of this irruption
Of waters. [*Exeunt* PANIA *and the Officer.*

Myr. Thus the very waves rise up
Against you.

Sar. They are not my subjects, girl,
And may be pardon'd, since they can't be
punish'd

Myr. I joy to see this portent shakes
you not.

Sar. I am past the fear of portents:
they can tell me 220
Nothing I have not told myself since mid-
night:
Despair anticipates such things.

Myr. Despair!

Sar. No; not despair precisely. When
we know
All that can come, and how to meet it, our
Resolves, if firm, may merit a more noble
Word than this is to give it utterance. 226
But what are words to us? we have well
nigh done
With them and all things.

Myr. Save *one deed*—the last
And greatest to all mortals; crowning act
Of all that was, or is, or is to be— 230
The only thing common to all mankind,
So different in their births, tongues, sexes,
natures,
Hues, features, climes, times, feelings, in-
tellects,
Without one point of union save in this,
To which we tend, for which we're born,
and thread 235
The labyrinth of mystery, call'd life.

Sar. Our clue being well nigh wound
out, let's be cheerful.
They who have nothing more to fear may
well
Indulge a smile at that which once
appall'd; 239
As children at discover'd bugbears.

Re-enter PANIA.

Pan. 'Tis
As was reported: I have order'd there
A double guard, withdrawing from the
 wall
Where it was strongest the required
 addition
To watch the breach occasion'd by the
 waters.
 Sar. You have done your duty faith-
fully, and as 245
My worthy Pania! further ties between us
Draw near a close—I pray you take this
 key: [*Gives a key.*
It opens to a secret chamber, placed
Behind the couch in my own chamber
 (now
Press'd by a nobler weight than e'er it
 bore— 250
Though a long line of sovereigns have lain
 down
Along its golden frame—as bearing for
A time what late was Salemenes). Search
The secret covert to which this will lead
 you; 254
'Tis full of treasure; take it for yourself
And your companions: there's enough to
 load ye,
Though ye be many. Let the slaves be
 freed, too;
And all the inmates of the palace, of
Whatever sex, now quit it in an hour.
Thence launch the regal barks, once form'd
 for pleasure, 260
And now to serve for safety, and embark.
The river's broad and swoln, and uncom-
 manded
(More potent than a king) by these
 besiegers.
Fly! and be happy!
 Pan. Under your protection!
So you accompany your faithful guard.
 Sar. No, Pania! that must not be; get
 thee hence, 266
And leave me to my fate.
 Pan. 'Tis the first time
I ever disobey'd: but now—
 Sar. So all men
Dare beard me now, and Insolence within
Apes Treason from without. Question no
 further; 270
'Tis my command, my last command.
 Wilt *thou*
Oppose it? *thou!*
 Pan. But yet—not yet.
 Sar. Well, then,
Swear that you will obey when I shall give
The signal.
 Pan. With a heavy but true heart,
I promise.
 Sar. 'Tis enough. Now order here
Faggots, pine-nuts, and wither'd leaves,
 and such 276

Things as catch fire and blaze with one sole
 spark;
Bring cedar, too, and precious drugs, and
 spices,
And mighty planks, to nourish a tall pile;
Bring frankincense and myrrh, too, for
 it is 280
For a great sacrifice I build the pyre!
And heap them round yon throne.
 Pan. My lord!
 Sar. I have said it,
And *you* have sworn.
 Pan. And could keep my faith
Without a vow. [*Exit* PANIA.
 Myr. What mean you?
 Sar. You shall know
Anon—what the whole earth shall ne'er
 forget. 285

PANIA, *returning with a Herald.*

Pan. My king, in going forth upon my
 duty,
This herald has been brought before me,
 craving
An audience.
 Sar. Let him speak.
 Her. The *King* Arbaces——
 Sar. What, crown'd already?—But,
 proceed.
 Her. Beleses, 289
The anointed high-priest——
 Sar. Of what god or demon?
With new kings rise new altars. But,
 proceed;
You are sent to prate your master's will,
 and not
Reply to mine.
 Her. And Satrap Ofratanes——
 Sar. Why, *he* is ours.
 Her. [*showing a ring*]. Be sure that he
 is now 294
In the camp of the conquerors; behold
His signet ring.
 Sar. 'Tis his. A worthy triad!
Poor Salemenes! thou hast died in time
To see one treachery the less: this man
Was thy true friend and my most trusted
 subject.
Proceed.
 Her. They offer thee thy life, and free-
 dom 300
Of choice to single out a residence
In any of the further provinces,
Guarded and watch'd, but not confined
 in person,
Where thou shalt pass thy days in peace;
 but on
Condition that the three young princes
 are 305
Given up as hostages.
 Sar. [*ironically*]. The generous victors!
 Her. I wait the answer.
 Sar. Answer, slave! How long
Have slaves decided on the doom of kings?

Her. Since they were free. 308
Sar. Mouthpiece of mutiny!
Thou at the least shalt learn the penalty
Of treason, though its proxy only. Pania!
Let his head be thrown from our walls
within
The rebels' lines, his carcass down the
river.
Away with him!
[PANIA *and the Guards seizing him.*
Pan. I never yet obey'd
Your orders with more pleasure than the
present. 315
Hence with him, soldiers! do not soil this
hall
Of royalty with treasonable gore;
Put him to rest without.
Her. A single word:
My office, king, is sacred.
Sar. And what's *mine?*
That thou shouldst come and dare to ask
of me 320
To lay it down?
Her. I but obey'd my orders,
At the same peril if refused, as now
Incurr'd by my obedience.
Sar. So there are
New monarchs of an hour's growth as
despotic
As sovereigns swathed in purple, and
enthroned 325
From birth to manhood!
Her. My life waits your breath.
Yours (I speak humbly)—but it may be—
yours
May also be in danger scarce less
imminent:
Would it then suit the last hours of a line
Such as is that of Nimrod, to destroy
A peaceful herald, unarm'd, in his office;
And violate not only all that man
Holds sacred between man and man—
but that
More holy tie which links us with the gods?
Sar. He's right.—Let him go free.—
My life's last act 335
Shall not be one of wrath. Here, fellow,
take
[*Gives him a golden cup from a table near.*
This golden goblet, let it hold your wine,
And think of *me;* or melt it into ingots,
And think of nothing but their weight and
value.
Her. I thank you doubly for my life,
and this 340
Most gorgeous gift, which renders it more
precious.
But must I bear no answer?
Sar. Yes,—I ask
An hour's truce to consider.
Her. But an hour's?
Sar. An hour's: if at the expiration of
That time your masters hear no further
from me, 345

They are to deem that I reject their terms,
And act befittingly.
Her. I shall not fail
To be a faithful legate of your pleasure.
Sar. And hark! a word more.
Her. I shall not forget it,
Whate'er it be.
Sar. Commend me to Beleses; 350
And tell him, ere a year expire, I summon
Him hence to meet me.
Her. Where?
Sar. At Babylon.
At least from thence he will depart to meet
me.
Her. I shall obey you to the letter.
[*Exit Herald.*
Sar. Pania!—
Now, my good Pania!—quick—with
what I order'd. 355
Pan. My lord,—the soldiers are
already charged.
And see! they enter.
[*Soldiers enter, and form a Pile about
the Throne, &c.*
Sar. Higher, my good soldiers,
And thicker yet; and see that the founda-
tion
Be such as will not speedily exhaust
Its own too subtle flame; nor yet be
quench'd 360
With aught officious aid would bring to
quell it.
Let the throne form the *core* of it; I would
not
Leave that, save fraught with fire un-
quenchable,
To the new comers. Frame the whole as if
'Twere to enkindle the strong tower of our
Inveterate enemies. Now it bears an
aspect! 365
How say you, Pania, will this pile suffice
For a king's obsequies?
Pan. Ay, for a kingdom's.
I understand you, now.
Sar. And blame me?
Pan. No—
Let me but fire the pile, and share it with
you. 370
Myr. That duty's mine.
Pan. A woman's!
Myr. 'Tis the soldier's
Part to die *for* his sovereign, and why not
The woman's with her lover?
Pan. 'Tis most strange!
Myr. But not so rare, my Pania, as thou
think'st it.
In the mean time, live thou.—Farewell!
the pile 375
Is ready.
Pan. I should shame to leave my sove-
reign
With but a single female to partake
His death.
Sar. Too many far have heralded

Me to the dust already. Get thee hence:
Enrich thee.
 Pan. And live wretched!
 Sar. Think upon 380
Thy vow:—'tis sacred and irrevocable.
 Pan. Since it is so, farewell.
 Sar. Search well my chamber,
Feel no remorse at bearing off the gold;
Remember, what you leave you leave the
 slaves
Who slew me: and when you have borne
 away 385
All safe off to your boats, blow one long
 blast
Upon the trumpet as you quit the palace.
The river's brink is too remote, its stream
Too loud at present to permit the echo
To reach distinctly from its banks. Then
 fly,— 390
And as you sail, turn back; but still keep on
Your way along the Euphrates: if you reach
The land of Paphlagonia, where the queen
Is safe with my three sons in Cotta's court,
Say, what you *saw* at parting, and request
That she remember what I *said* at one
Parting more mournful still.
 Pan. That royal hand!
Let me then once more press it to my lips;
And these poor soldiers who throng round
 you, and
Would fain die with you!
 [*The Soldiers and* PANIA *throng round
 him, kissing his hand and the hem of
 his robe.*
 Sar. My best! my last friends! 400
Let's not unman each other: part at once:
All farewells should be sudden, when for
 ever,
Else they make an eternity of moments,
And clog the last sad sands of life with tears.
Hence, and be happy: trust me, I am not
Now to be pitied; or far more for what
Is past than present; for the future, 'tis
In the hands of the deities, if such
There be: I shall know soon. Farewell—
Farewell.
 [*Exeunt* PANIA *and Soldiers.*
 Myr. These men were honest: it is com-
 fort still 410
That our last looks should be on loving
 faces.
 Sar. And *lovely* ones, my beautiful! but
 hear me!
If at this moment—for we now are on
The brink—thou feel'st an inward shrink-
 ing from
This leap through flame into the future,
 say it: 415
I shall not love thee less; nay, perhaps more,
For yielding to thy nature; and there's time
Yet for thee to escape hence.
 Myr. Shall I light
One of the torches which lie heap'd be-
 neath 419

The ever-burning lamp that burns without,
Before Baal's shrine, in the adjoining hall?
 Sar. Do so. Is that thy answer?
 Myr. Thou shalt see.
 [*Exit* MYRRHA.
 Sar. [*solus*]. She's firm. My fathers!
 whom I will rejoin, 423
It may be, purified by death from some
Of the gross stains of too material being,
I would not leave your ancient first abode
To the defilement of usurping bondmen;
If I have not kept your inheritance
As ye bequeath'd it, this bright part of it,
Your treasure, your abode, your sacred
 relics 430
Of arms and records, monuments, and
 spoils,
In which *they* would have revell'd, I bear
 with me
To you in that absorbing element, 433
Which most personifies the soul as leaving
The least of matter unconsumed before
Its fiery workings:—and the light of this
Most royal of funereal pyres shall be
Not a mere pillar form'd of cloud and flame,
A beacon in the horizon for a day,
And then a mount of ashes, but a light
To lesson ages, rebel nations, and 441
Voluptuous princes. Time shall quench
 full many
A people's records, and a hero's acts;
Sweep empire after empire, like this first
Of empires, into nothing; but even then
Shall spare this deed of mine, and hold it up
A problem few dare imitate, and none
Despise—but, it may be, avoid the life
Which led to such a consummation.

 MYRRHA *returns with a lighted Torch in
 one Hand, and a Cup in the other.*
 Myr. Lo!
I've lit the lamp which lights us to the stars.
 Sar. And the cup?
 Myr. 'Tis my country's custom to
Make a libation to the gods.
 Sar. And mine
To make libations amongst men. I've not
Forgot the custom; and although alone,
Will drain one draught in memory of
 many 455
A joyous banquet past.
 [SARDANAPALUS *takes the cup, and after
 drinking and tinkling the reversed cup,
 as a drop falls, exclaims—*
 And this libation
Is for the excellent Beleses.
 Myr. Why
Dwells thy mind rather upon that man's
 name
Than on his mate's in villainy?
 Sar. The one
Is a mere soldier, a mere tool, a kind
Of human sword in a friend's hand; the
 other 461

Is master-mover of his warlike puppet;
But I dismiss them from my mind.—Yet
 pause,
My Myrrha! dost thou truly follow me,
Freely and fearlessly?
 Myr. And dost thou think 465
A Greek girl dare not do for love, that which
An Indian widow braves for custom?
 Sar. Then
We but await the signal.
 Myr. It is long
In sounding.
 Sar. Now, farewell; one last embrace.
 Myr. Embrace, but *not* the last; there
 is one more. 470
 Sar. True, the commingling fire will
 mix our ashes.
 Myr. And pure as is my love to thee,
 shall they,
Purged from the dross of earth, and earthly
 passion,
Mix pale with thine. A single thought yet
 irks me.
 Sar. Say it.
 Myr. It is that no kind hand will
 gather 475
The dust of both into one urn.
 Sar. The better:
Rather let them be borne abroad upon
The winds of heaven, and scatter'd into air,
Than be polluted more by human hands
Of slaves and traitors. In this blazing
 palace, 480
And its enormous walls of reeking ruin,
We leave a nobler monument than Egypt

Hath piled in her brick mountains, o'er
 dead kings,
Or *kine*, for none know whether those
 proud piles 484
Be for their monarch or their ox-god Apis:
So much for monuments that have for-
 gotten
Their very record!
 Myr. Then farewell, thou earth!
And loveliest spot of earth! farewell
 Ionia!
Be thou still free and beautiful, and far
Aloof from desolation! My last prayer
Was for thee, my last thoughts, save *one*,
 were of thee! 491
 Sar. And that?
 Myr. Is yours.
 [*The trumpet of* PANIA *sounds without.*
 Sar. Hark!
 Myr. *Now!*
 Sar. Adieu, Assyria!
I loved thee well, my own, my father's land,
And better as my country than my king-
 dom.
I sated thee with peace and joys; and this
Is my reward! and now I owe thee nothing,
Not even a grave. [*He mounts the pile.*
 Now, Myrrha!
 Myr. Art thou ready?
 Sar. As the torch in thy grasp.
 [MYRRHA *fires the pile.*
 Myr. 'Tis fired! I come.
 [*As* MYRRHA *springs forward to throw
 herself into the flames, the Curtain
 falls.*

THE TWO FOSCARI

AN HISTORICAL TRAGEDY

'The *father* softens, but the *governor's* resolved.'—CRITIC.

DRAMATIS PERSONÆ

MEN
FRANCIS FOSCARI, *Doge of Venice.*
JACOPO FOSCARI, *Son of the Doge.*
JAMES LOREDANO, *a Patrician.*
MARCO MEMMO, *a Chief of the Forty.*
BARBARIGO, *a Senator.*

*Other Senators, The Council of Ten, Guards,
Attendants, &c., &c.*

WOMAN
MARINA, *Wife of young* FOSCARI.

SCENE.—*The Ducal Palace, Venice*

ACT I

SCENE I.—*A Hall in the Ducal Palace.*

Enter LOREDANO *and* BARBARIGO, *meeting.*

 Lor. Where is the prisoner?
 Bar. Reposing from
The Question.
 Lor. The hour 's past—fix'd yesterday
For the resumption of his trial.—Let us
Rejoin our colleagues in the council, and

Urge his recall.
 Bar. Nay, let him profit by 5
A few brief minutes for his tortured limbs;
He was o'erwrought by the Question
 yesterday,
And may die under it if now repeated.
 Lor. Well?
 Bar. I yield not to you in love of justice,
Or hate of the ambitious Foscari, 10
Father and son, and all their noxious
 race;

But the poor wretch has suffer'd beyond
 nature's
Most stoical endurance.
 Lor. Without owning
His crime?
 Bar. Perhaps without committing any.
But he avow'd the letter to the Duke 15
Of Milan, and his sufferings half atone for
Such weakness.
 Lor. We shall see.
 Bar. You, Loredano,
Pursue hereditary hate too far.
 Lor. How far?
 Bar. To extermination.
 Lor. When they are
Extinct, you may say this.—Let's in to
 council. 20
 Bar. Yet pause—the number of our
 colleagues is not
Complete yet; two are wanting ere we can
Proceed.
 Lor. And the chief judge, the Doge?
 Bar. No—he,
With more than Roman fortitude, is ever
First at the board in this unhappy process
Against his last and only son.
 Lor. True—true—
His *last*.
 Bar. Will nothing move you?
 Lor. *Feels he*, think you?
 Bar. He shows it not.
 Lor. I have mark'd *that*—the wretch!
 Bar. But yesterday, I hear, on his return
To the ducal chambers, as he pass'd the
 threshold 30
The old man fainted.
 Lor. It begins to work, then.
 Bar. The work is half your own.
 Lor. And should be *all* mine—
My father and my uncle are no more.
 Bar. I have read their epitaph, which
 says they died 34
By poison.
 Lor. When the Doge declared that he
Should never deem himself a sovereign till
The death of Peter Loredano, both
The brothers sicken'd shortly:—he *is* sove-
 reign.
 Bar. A wretched one.
 Lor. What should they be who make
Orphans?
 Bar. But *did* the Doge make you so?
 Lor. Yes. 40
 Bar. What solid proofs?
 Lor. When princes set themselves
To work in secret, proofs and process are
Alike made difficult; but I have such
Of the first, as shall make the second needless.
 Bar. But you will move by law?
 Lor. By all the laws 45
Which he would leave us.
 Bar. They are such in this
Our state as render retribution easier
Than 'mongst remoter nations. Is it true

That you have written in your books of
 commerce
(The wealthy practice of our highest
 nobles), 50
'Doge Foscari, my debtor for the deaths
Of Marco and Pietro Loredano,
My sire and uncle?'
 Lor. It is written thus.
 Bar. And will you leave it unerased?
 Lor. Till balanced.
 Bar. And how?
 [*Two Senators pass over the stage, as in
 their way to '*the Hall of the Council
 of Ten.*'
 Lor. You see the number is complete.
Follow me. [*Exit* LOREDANO.
 Bar. [*solus*]. Follow *thee*! I have fol-
 low'd long 56
Thy path of desolation, as the wave
Sweeps after that before it, alike whelming
The wreck that creaks to the wild winds,
 and wretch
Who shrieks within its riven ribs, as gush
The waters through them; but this son and
 sire 61
Might move the elements to pause, and yet
Must I on hardily like them—Oh! would
I could as blindly and remorselessly!—
Lo, where he comes!—Be still, my heart!
 they are 65
Thy foes, must be thy victims: wilt thou
 beat
For those who almost broke thee?

Enter Guards, with young FOSCARI *as
 prisoner, &c.*

 Guard. Let him rest.
Signor, take time.
 Jac. Fos. I thank thee, friend, I'm
 feeble;
But thou may'st stand reproved.
 Guard. I'll stand the hazard.
 Jac. Fos. That's kind:—I meet some
 pity, but no mercy; 70
This is the first.
 Guard. And might be the last, did they
Who rule behold us.
 Bar. [*advancing to the Guard*]. There is
 one who does:
Yet fear not; I will neither be thy judge
Nor thy accuser; though the hour is past,
Wait their last summons—I am of 'the
 Ten', 75
And waiting for that summons, sanction you
Even by my presence: when the last call
 sounds,
We'll in together.—Look well to the
 prisoner!
 Jac. Fos. What voice is that?—'Tis
 Barbarigo's! Ah!
Our house's foe, and one of my few judges.
 Bar. To balance such a foe, if such there
 be, 81
Thy father sits amongst thy judges.

Jac. Fos. True,
He judges.

Bar. Then deem not the laws too harsh
Which yield so much indulgence to a sire,
As to allow his voice in such high matter
As the state's safety——

Jac. Fos. And his son's. I'm faint;
Let me approach, I pray you, for a breath
Of air, yon window which o'erlooks the
 waters.

Enter an Officer, who whispers BARBARIGO.

Bar. [*to the Guard*]. Let him approach.
I must not speak with him
Further than thus: I have transgress'd my
 duty 90
In this brief parley, and must now redeem it
Within the Council Chamber.

 [*Exit* BARBARIGO.

[*Guard conducting* JACOPO FOSCARI *to
 the window.*

Guard. There, sir, 'tis
Open.—How feel you?

Jac. Fos. Like a boy—Oh Venice!

Guard. And your limbs?

Jas. Fos. Limbs! how often have they
 borne me
Bounding o'er yon blue tide, as I have
 skimm'd 95
The gondola along in childish race,
And, masqued as a young gondolier, amidst
My gay competitors, noble as I,
Raced for our pleasure, in the pride of
 strength;
While the fair populace of crowding beauties,
Plebeian as patrician, cheer'd us on 101
With dazzling smiles, and wishes audible,
And waving kerchiefs, and applauding
 hands,
Even to the goal!—How many a time have I
Cloven with arm still lustier, breast more
 daring, 105
The wave all roughen'd; with a swimmer's
 stroke
Flinging the billows back from my drench'd
 hair,
And laughing from my lip the audacious
 brine,
Which kiss'd it like a wine-cup, rising o'er
The waves as they arose, and prouder still
The loftier they uplifted me; and oft,
In wantonness of spirit, plunging down
Into their green and glassy gulfs, and
 making
My way to shells and sea-weed, all unseen
By those above, till they wax'd fearful;
 then 115
Returning with my grasp full of such
 tokens
As show'd that I had search'd the deep:
 exulting,
With a far-dashing stroke, and drawing
 deep

The long-suspended breath, again
 spurn'd
The foam which broke around me, an‹
 pursued 12‹
My track like a sea-bird.—I was a bo›
 then.

Guard. Be a man now; there never wa‹
 more need
Of manhood's strength.

Jas. Fos. [*looking from the lattice*]. M‹
 beautiful, my own,
My only Venice—*this is breath!* Th›
 breeze,
Thine Adrian sea-breeze, how it fans m‹
 face! 12‹
Thy very winds feel native to my veins,
And cool them into calmness! Ho‹
 unlike
The hot gales of the horrid Cyclades,
Which howled about my Candiot‹
 dungeon, and
Made my heart sick!

Guard. I see the colour comes
Back to your cheek: Heaven send yo‹
 strength to bear 13‹
What more may be imposed!—I drea‹
 to think on 't.

Jac. Fos. They will not banish m‹
 again?—No—no,
Let them wring on; I am strong yet.

Guard. Confess‹
And the rack will be spared you.

Jac. Fos. I confess'd 13‹
Once—twice before: both times the›
 exiled me,

Guard. And the third time will sla›
 you.

Jac. Fos. Let them do so‹
So I be buried in my birth-place: better
Be ashes here than aught that lives else‹
 where.

Guard. And can you so much love th‹
 soil which hates you? 14‹

Jac. Fos. The soil!—Oh no, it is th‹
 seed of the soil
Which persecutes me; but my native earth‹
Will take me as a mother to her arms.
I ask no more than a Venetian grave,
A dungeon, what they will, so it be‹
 here. 14‹

Enter an Officer.

Offi. Bring in the prisoner!

Guard. Signor, you hear the order‹

Jac. Fos. Ay, I am used to such a sum‹
 mons: 't is
The third time they have tortured me:—
 then lend me
Thine arm. [*To the Guard‹*

Offi. Take mine, sir; 'tis my duty t‹
Be nearest to your person.

Jac. Fos. You!—you are he 15‹
Who yesterday presided o'er my pangs—
Away!—I'll walk alone.

494

Offi. As you please, signor;
The sentence was not of my signing,
 but
I dared not disobey the Council when
 They——
Jac. Fos. Bade thee stretch me on
 their horrid engine. 155
I pray thee touch me not—that is, just
 now;
The time will come they will renew that
 order,
But keep off from me till 'tis issued. As
I look upon thy hands my curdling limbs
Quiver with the anticipated wrench-
 ing, 160
And the cold drops strain through my
 brow, as if——
But onward—I have borne it—I can bear
 it.—
How looks my father?
Offi. With his wonted aspect.
Jac. Fos. So does the earth, and sky,
 the blue of ocean,
The brightness of our city, and her
 domes, 165
The mirth of her Piazza, even now
Its merry hum of nations pierces here,
Even here, into these chambers of the
 unknown
Who govern, and the unknown and the
 unnumber'd
Judged and destroy'd in silence,—all
 things wear 170
The self-same aspect, to my very sire!
Nothing can sympathise with Foscari,
Not even a Foscari.—Sir, I attend you.
 [*Exeunt* JACOPO FOSCARI, *Officer, &c.*

Enter MEMMO *and another Senator.*

Mem. He's gone—we are too late:—
 think you 'the Ten' 174
Will sit for any length of time to-day?
 Sen. They say the prisoner is most
 obdurate,
Persisting in his first avowal; but
More I know not.
 Mem. And that is much; the secrets
Of yon terrific chamber are as hidden
From us, the premier nobles of the
 state, 180
As from the people.
 Sen. Save the wonted rumours,
Which—like the tales of spectres, that
 are rife
Near ruin'd buildings—never have been
 proved,
Nor wholly disbelieved: men know as
 little 184
Of the state's real acts as of the grave's
Unfathom'd mysteries.
 Mem. But with length of time
We gain a step in knowledge, and I look
Forward to be one day of the decemvirs.
 Sen. Or Doge?

Mem. Why, no; not if I can avoid it.
 Sen. 'Tis the first station of the state,
 and may 190
Be lawfully desired, and lawfully
Attain'd by noble aspirants.
 Mem. To such
I leave it; though born noble, my ambi-
 tion
Is limited: I'd rather be an unit
Of an united and imperial 'Ten,' 195
Than shine a lonely though a gilded
 cipher.—
Whom have we here? the wife of Foscari?

Enter MARINA, *with a female Attendant.*

Mar. What, no one?—I am wrong,
 there still are two;
But they are senators.
 Mem. Most noble lady,
Command us.
 Mar. I command!—Alas! my life 200
Has been one long entreaty, and a vain one.
 Mem. I understand thee, but I must
 not answer.
 Mar. [*fiercely*]. True—none dare
 answer here save on the rack,
Or question save those——
 Mem. [*interrupting her*]. High-born
 dame! bethink thee
Where thou now art.
 Mar. Where I now am!—It was 205
My husband's father's palace.
 Mem. The Duke's palace.
 Mar. And his son's prison!—True, I
 have not forgot it;
And if there were no other nearer,
 bitterer
Remembrances, would thank the illus-
 trious Memmo
For pointing out the pleasures of the
 place. 210
 Mem. Be calm!
 Mar. [*looking up towards heaven*]. I
 am; but oh, thou eternal God!
Canst *thou* continue so, with such a
 world?
 Mem. Thy husband yet may be ab-
 solved.
 Mar. He is,
In heaven. I pray you, signor senator,
Speak not of that; you are a man of
 office, 215
So is the Doge; he has a son at stake
Now, at this moment, and I have a
 husband,
Or had; they are there within, or were
 at least
An hour since, face to face, as judge and
 culprit:
Will *he* condemn *him?*
 Mem. I trust not.
 Mar. But if
He does not, there are those will sentence
 both. 221

Mem. They can.
Mar. And with them power and will are one
In wickedness:—my husband's lost!
Mem. Not so;
Justice is judge in Venice.
Mar. If it were so,
There now would be no Venice. But let it 225
Live on, so the good die not, till the hour
Of nature's summons; but 'the Ten's'
is quicker,
And we must wait on't. Ah! a voice of wail!

[A faint cry within.

Sen. Hark!
Mem. 'Twas a cry of—
Mar. No, no; not my husband's—
Not Foscari's.
Mem. The voice was—
Mar. Not his: no. 230
He shriek! No; that should be his father's part,
Not his—not his—he'll die in silence.

[A faint groan again within.

Mem. What!
Again?
Mar. *His* voice! it seem'd so: I will not
Believe it. Should he shrink, I cannot cease
To love; but—no—no—no—it must have been 235
A fearful pang, which wrung a groan from him.
Sen. And, feeling for thy husband's wrongs, wouldst thou
Have him bear more than mortal pain in silence?
Mar. We all must bear our tortures.
I have not
Left barren the great house of Foscari,
Though they sweep both the Doge and son from life; 241
I have endured as much in giving life
To those who will succeed them, as they can
In leaving it: but mine were joyful pangs:
And yet they wrung me till I *could* have shriek'd, 245
But did not; for my hope was to bring forth
Heroes, and would not welcome them with tears.
Mem. All's silent now.
Mar. Perhaps all's over; but
I will not deem it: he hath nerved himself,
And now defies them.

Enter an Officer hastily.

Mem. How now, friend, what seek you? 250
Offi. A leech. The prisoner has fainted.

[Exit Officer.

Mem. Lady,
'Twere better to retire.

Sen. [*offering to assist her*]. I pray thee do so.
Mar. Off! *I* will tend him.
Mem. You! Remember, lady!
Ingress is given to none within those chambers,
Except 'the Ten,' and their familiars.
Mar. Well
I know that none who enter there return 256
As they have enter'd—many never; but
They shall not balk my entrance.
Mem. Alas! this
Is but to expose yourself to harsh repulse,
And worse suspense.
Mar. Who shall oppose me?
Mem. They
Whose duty 'tis to do so.
Mar. 'Tis *their* duty 261
To trample on all human feelings, all
Ties which bind man to man, to emulate
The fiends who will one day requite them in
Variety of torturing! Yet I'll pass. 265
Mem. It is impossible.
Mar. That shall be tried
Despair defies even despotism: there is
That in my heart would make its way through hosts
With levell'd spears; and think you a few jailors
Shall put me from my path? Give me, then, way; 270
This is the Doge's palace; I am wife
Of the Duke's son, the *innocent* Duke's son,
And they shall hear this!
Mem. It will only serve
More to exasperate his judges.
Mar. What
Are *judges* who give way to anger? they 275
Who do so are assassins. Give me way.

[Exit MARINA.

Sen. Poor lady!
Mem. 'Tis mere desperation:
she
Will not be admitted o'er the threshold.
Sen. And
Even if she be so, cannot save her husband.
But see, the officer returns.

[The Officer passes over the stage with another person.

Mem. I hardly 280
Thought that 'the Ten' had even this touch of pity,
Or would permit assistance to this sufferer.
Sen. Pity! Is't pity to recall to feeling
The wretch too happy to escape to death
By the compassionate trance, poor nature's last 285
Resource against the tyranny of pain?

Mem. I marvel they condemn him
 not at once.
Sen. That's not their policy: they'd
 have him live,
Because he fears not death; and banish
 him,
Because all earth, except his native
 land, 290
To him is one wide prison, and each
 breath
Of foreign air he draws seems a slow
 poison,
Consuming but not killing.
Mem. Circumstance
Confirms his crimes, but he avows them
 not.
Sen. None, save the Letter, which he
 says was written, 295
Address'd to Milan's duke, in the full
 knowledge
That it would fall into the senate's
 hands,
And thus he should be re-conveyed to
 Venice.
Mem. But as a culprit.
Sen. Yes, but to his country;
And that was all he sought,—so he
 avouches. 300
Mem. The accusation of the bribes
 was proved.
Sen. Not clearly, and the charge of
 homicide
Has been annull'd by the death-bed
 confession
Of Nicolas Erizzo, who slew the late
Chief of 'the Ten.'
Mem. Then why not clear him?
Sen. That 305
They ought to answer; for it is well
 known
That Almoro Donato, as I said,
Was slain by Erizzo for private vengeance.
Mem. There must be more in this
 strange process than
The apparent crimes of the accused
 disclose— 310
But here come two of 'the Ten;' let us
 retire.

 [*Exeunt* MEMMO *and Senator.*

 Enter LOREDANO *and* BARBARIGO.

Bar. [*addressing* LOR.]. That were too
 much: believe me, 'twas not
 meet
The trial should go further at this
 moment.
Lor. And so the Council must break
 up, and Justice
'ause in her full career, because a woman
 'reaks in on our deliberations?
Bar. No, 316
That's not the cause; you saw the
 prisoner's state.
Lor. And had he not recover'd?

Bar. To relapse
Upon the least renewal.
Lor. 'Twas not tried.
Bar. 'Tis vain to murmur; the
 majority 320
In council were against you.
Lor. Thanks to you, sir,
And the old ducal dotard, who com-
 bined
The worthy voices which o'er-ruled my
 own.
Bar. I am a judge; but must confess
 that part
Of our stern duty, which prescribes the
 Question, 325
And bids us sit and see its sharp in-
 fliction,
Makes me wish——
Lor. What?
Bar. That *you* would *sometimes* feel,
As I do always.
Lor. Go to, you're a child,
Infirm of feeling as of purpose, blown
About by every breath, shook by a
 sigh, 330
And melted by a tear—a precious judge
For Venice! and a worthy statesman to
Be partner in my policy.
Bar. He shed
No tears.
Lor. He cried out twice.
Bar. A saint had done so,
Even with the crown of glory in his
 eye, 335
At such inhuman artifice of pain
As was forced on him; but he did not
 cry
For pity; not a word nor groan escaped
 him,
And those two shrieks were not in suppli-
 cation,
But wrung from pangs, and follow'd
 by no prayers. 340
Lor. He mutter'd many times between
 his teeth,
But inarticulately.
Bar. That I heard not;
You stood more near him.
Lor. I did so.
Bar. Methought,
To my surprise too, you were touch'd
 with mercy,
And were the first to call out for assis-
 tance 345
When he was failing.
Lor. I believed that swoon
His last.
Bar. And have I not oft heard thee
 name
His and his father's death your nearest
 wish?
Lor. If he dies innocent, that is to say,
With his guilt unavow'd, he'll be
 lamented. 350

Bar. What, wouldst thou slay his memory?

Lor. Wouldst thou have His state descend to his children, as it must, If he die unattainted?

Bar. War with *them* too?

Lor. With all their house, till theirs or mine are nothing.

Bar. And the deep agony of his pale wife, 355 And the repress'd convulsion of the high And princely brow of his old father, which Broke forth in a slight shuddering, though rarely, Or in some clammy drops, soon wiped away 359 In stern serenity; these moved you not?
 [*Exit* LOREDANO.
He's silent in his hate, as Foscari Was in his suffering; and the poor wretch moved me More by his silence than a thousand out- cries Could have effected. 'Twas a dreadful sight When his distracted wife broke through into 365 The hall of our tribunal, and beheld What we could scarcely look upon, long used To such sights. I must think no more of this, Lest I forget in this compassion for Our foes, their former injuries, and lose 370 The hold of vengeance Loredano plans For him and me; but mine would be content With lesser retribution than he thirsts for, And I would mitigate his deeper hatred To milder thoughts; but for the present, Foscari 375 Has a short hourly respite, granted at The instance of the elders of the Council, Moved doubtless by his wife's ap- pearance in The hall, and his own sufferings.—Lo! they come: How feeble and forlorn! I cannot bear 380 To look on them again in this extremity: I'll hence, and try to soften Loredano.
 [*Exit* BARBARIGO.

ACT II

SCENE I.—*A Hall in the* DOGE'S *palace.*
The DOGE *and a* SENATOR.

Sen. Is it your pleasure to sign the report Now, or postpone it till to-morrow?

Doge. Now; I overlook'd it yesterday: it wants Merely the signature. Give me the pen—
[*The* DOGE *sits down and signs the paper* There, signor.

Sen. [*looking at the paper*]. You have forgot; it is not signed.

Doge. Not sign'd? Ah, I perceive my eyes begin To wax more weak with age. I did not see That I had dipp'd the pen without effect.

Sen. [*dipping the pen into the ink, and placing the paper before the* DOGE] Your hand, too, shakes, my lord; allow me, thus—

Doge. 'Tis done, I thank you.

Sen. Thus the act confirm'd By you and by 'the Ten' gives peace to Venice.

Doge. 'Tis long since she enjoyed it; may it be As long ere she resume her arms!

Sen. 'Tis almost Thirty-four years of nearly ceaseless warfare With the Turk, or the powers of Italy; The state had need of some repose.

Doge. No doubt: I found her Queen of Ocean, and I leave her Lady of Lombardy; it is a comfort That I have added to her diadem The gems of Brescia and Ravenna; Crema And Bergamo no less are hers; her realm By land has grown by thus much in my reign, While her sea-sway has not shrunk.

Sen. 'Tis most true; And merits all our country's gratitude.

Doge. Perhaps so.

Sen. Which should be made mani- fest.

Doge. I have not complain'd, sir.

Sen. My good lord, forgive me.

Doge. For what?

Sen. My heart bleeds for you.

Doge. For me, signor?

Sen. And for your——

Doge. Stop!

Sen. It must have way, my lord: I have too many duties towards you And all your house, for past and present kindness, Not to feel deeply for your son.

Doge. Was this In your commission?

Sen. What, my lord?

Doge. This prattle Of things you know not: but the treaty's sign'd; Return with it to them who sent you.

Sen. I
Obey. I had in charge, too, from the
 Council 35
That you would fix an hour for their
 reunion.
Doge. Say, when they will—now, even
 at this moment,
If it so please them: I am the state's
 servant.
Sen. They would accord some time
 for your repose.
Doge. I have no repose, that is, none
 which shall cause 40
The loss of an hour's time unto the state.
Let them meet when they will, I shall be
 found
Where I should be, and *what* I have been
 ever. [*Exit* SENATOR. *The* DOGE
 remains in silence.

 Enter an Attendant.

Att. Prince!
Doge. Say on.
Att. The illustrious lady Foscari
Requests an audience.
Doge. Bid her enter. Poor 45
Marina! [*Exit Attendant. The* DOGE
 remains in silence as before.

 Enter MARINA.

Mar. I have ventured, father, on
Your privacy.
Doge. I have none from you, my child.
Command my time, when not com-
 manded by
The state.
Mar. I wish'd to speak to you of *him.*
Doge. Your husband?
Mar. And your son.
Doge. Proceed, my daughter! 50
Mar. I had obtain'd permission from
 'the Ten'
To attend my husband for a limited
 number
Of hours.
Doge. You had so.
Mar. 'Tis revoked.
Doge. By whom?
Mar. 'The Ten.'—When we had
 reach'd 'the Bridge of Sighs,' 54
Which I prepared to pass with Foscari,
The gloomy guardian of that passage first
Demurr'd: a messenger was sent back to
The Ten;'—but as the court no longer
 sate,
And no permission had been given in
 writing,
was thrust back, with the assurance that
Until that high tribunal re-assembled 61
The dungeon walls must still divide us.
Doge. True,
The form has been omitted in the haste
With which the court adjourn'd; and till
 it meets,

'Tis dubious.
Mar. Till it meets! and when it
 meets, 65
They'll torture him again; and he and I
Must purchase by renewal of the rack
The interview of husband and of wife,
The holiest tie beneath the heavens!—
 Oh God!
Dost thou see this?
Doge. Child—child——
Mar. [*abruptly*]. Call *me* not
 'child'! 70
You soon will have no children—you
 deserve none—
You, who can talk thus calmly of a son
In circumstances which would call forth
 tears
Of blood from Spartans! Though these
 did not weep
Their boys who died in battle, is it
 written 75
That they beheld them perish piecemeal,
 nor
Stretch'd forth a hand to save them?
Doge. You behold me:
I cannot weep—I would I could; but if
Each white hair on this head were a
 young life,
This ducal cap the diadem of earth, 80
This ducal ring with which I wed the
 waves
A talisman to still them—I'd give all
For him.
Mar. With less he surely might be
 saved.
Doge. That answer only shows you
 know not Venice.
Alas! how should you? she knows not
 herself, 85
In all her mystery. Hear me—they who
 aim
At Foscari, aim no less at his father;
The sire's destruction would not save the
 son;
They work by different means to the same
 end,
And that is——but they have not con-
 quer'd yet. 90
Mar. But they have crush'd.
Doge. Nor crush'd as yet—I live.
Mar. And your son,—how long will
 he live?
Doge. I trust,
For all that yet is past, as many years
And happier than his father. The rash
 boy, 94
With womanish impatience to return,
Hath ruin'd all by that detected letter:
A high crime, which I neither can deny
Nor palliate, as parent or as Duke:
Had he but borne a little, little longer
His Candiote exile, I had hopes——he
 has quench'd them— 100
He must return.

Mar. To exile?
Doge. I have said it.
Mar. And can I not go with him?
Doge. You well know
This prayer of yours was twice denied
before
By the assembled 'Ten,' and hardly now
Will be accorded to a third request, 105
Since aggravated errors on the part
Of your lord renders them still more
austere.
Mar. Austere? Atrocious! The old
human fiends,
With one foot in the grave, with dim eyes,
strange
To tears save drops of dotage, with long
white 110
And scanty hairs, and shaking hands, and
heads
As palsied as their hearts are hard, they
counsel,
Cabal, and put men's lives out, as if life
Were no more than the feelings long
extinguish'd
In their accursed bosoms.
Doge. You know not— 115
Mar. I do—I do—and so should you,
methinks—
That these are demons: could it be else
that
Men, who have been of women born and
suckled—
Who have loved, or talk'd at least of
love—have given
Their hands in sacred vows—have danced
their babes 120
Upon their knees, perhaps have mourn'd
above them—
In pain, in peril, or in death—who are,
Or were at least in seeming, human,
could
Do as they have done by yours, and you
yourself—
You, who abet them?
Doge. I forgive this, for 125
You know not what you say.
Mar. *You* know it well,
And feel it nothing.
Doge. I have borne so much,
That words have ceased to shake me.
Mar. Oh, no doubt!
You have seen your son's blood flow,
and your flesh shook not;
And after that, what are a woman's
words? 130
No more than woman's tears, that they
should shake you.
Doge. Woman, this clamorous grief of
thine, I tell thee,
Is no more in the balance weigh'd with that
Which——but I pity thee, my poor
Marina.
Mar. Pity my husband, or I cast it
from me; 135

Pity thy son! *Thou* pity!—'tis a word
Strange to thy heart—how came it o
thy lips?
Doge. I must bear these reproache
though they wrong me.
Couldst thou but read——
Mar. 'Tis not upon thy brow
Nor in thine eyes, nor in thine acts,—
where then 14
Should I behold this sympathy? or shall
Doge (*pointing downwards*). There.
Mar. In the earth?
Doge. To which I am tending: whe
It lies upon this heart, far lightlier, thoug
Loaded with marble, than the thought
which press it
Now, you will know me better.
Mar. Are you, then, 14
Indeed, thus to be pitied?
Doge. Pitied! None
Shall ever use that base word, with whic
men
Cloak their soul's hoarded triumph, as
fit one
To mingle with my name; that nam
shall be, 14
As far as I have borne it, what it was
When I received it.
Mar. But for the poor childre
Of him thou canst not, or thou wilt n
save
You were the last to bear it.
Doge. Would it were s
Better for him he never had been born;
Better for me.—I have seen our hou
dishonour'd. 1
Mar. That's false! A truer, noble
trustier heart,
More loving, or more loyal, never beat
Within a human breast. I would n
change
My exiled, persecuted, mangled husban
Oppress'd but not disgraced, crush'
overwhelm'd, 1
Alive, or dead, for prince or paladin
In story or in fable, with a world
To back his suit. Dishonour'd!—
dishonour'd!
I tell thee, Doge, 'tis Venice is di
honour'd!
His name shall be her foulest, wor
reproach, 1
For what he suffers, not for what he di
'Tis ye who are all traitors, tyrant!-
ye!
Did you but love your country like th
victim
Who totters back in chains to torture
and
Submits to all things rather than
exile, 1
You'd fling yourselves before him, an
implore
His grace for your enormous guilt.

500

Doge. He was
Indeed all you have said. I better bore
The deaths of the two sons Heaven took
 from me,
Than Jacopo's disgrace.
 Mar. That word again? 175
 Doge. Has he not been condemn'd?
 Mar. Is none but guilt so?
 Doge. Time may restore his memory—
 I would hope so.
He was my pride, my——but 'tis useless
 now—
I am not given to tears, but wept for joy
When he was born: those drops were
 ominous. 180
 Mar. I say he's innocent! And were
 he not so,
Is our own blood and kin to shrink from us
In fatal moments?
 Doge. I shrank not from him:
But I have other duties than a father's;
The state would not dispense me from
 those duties; 185
Twice I demanded it, but was refused:
They must then be fulfill'd.

 Enter an Attendant.

 Att. A message from
'The Ten.'
 Doge. Who bears it?
 Att. Noble Loredano.
 Doge. He!—but admit him.
 [Exit Attendant.
 Mar. Must I then retire?
 Doge. Perhaps it is not requisite, if
 this 190
Concerns your husband, and if not——
 Well, signor,
Your pleasure? [*To* LOREDANO *entering.*
 Lor. I bear that of 'the Ten.'
 Doge. They
Have chosen well their envoy.
 Lor. 'Tis *their* choice
Which leads me here.
 Doge. It does their wisdom honour,
And no less to their courtesy.—Proceed.
 Lor. We have decided.
 Doge. We?
 Lor. 'The Ten' in council. 196
 Doge. What! have they met again, and
 met without
Apprising me?
 Lor. They wish'd to spare your feel-
 ings,
No less than age.
 Doge. That's new—when spared they
 either?
I thank them, notwithstanding.
 Lor. You know well
That they have power to act at their dis-
 cretion, 201
With or without the presence of the Doge.
 Doge. 'Tis some years since I learn'd
 this, long before

I became Doge, or dream'd of such ad-
 vancement.
You need not school me, signor; I sate in
That council when you were a young
 patrician. 206
 Lor. True, in my father's time; I have
 heard him and
The admiral, his brother, say as much.
Your highness may remember them; they
 both
Died suddenly.
 Doge. And if they did so, better
So die than live on lingeringly in pain.
 Lor. No doubt: yet most men like to
 live their days out. 212
 Doge. And did not they?
 Lor. The grave knows best: they died,
As I said, suddenly.
 Doge. Is that so strange,
That you repeat the word emphatically?
 Lor. So far from strange, that never
 was there death 216
In my mind half so natural as theirs.
Think *you* not so?
 Doge. What should I think of mortals?
 Lor. That they have mortal foes.
 Doge. I understand you;
Your sires were mine, and you are heir in
 all things. 220
 Lor. You best know if I should be so.
 Doge. I do.
Your fathers were my foes, and I have
 heard
Foul rumours were abroad; I have also
 read 223
Their epitaph, attributing their deaths
To poison. 'Tis perhaps as true as most
Inscriptions upon tombs, and yet no less
A fable.
 Lor. Who dares say so?
 Doge. I!—'Tis true
Your fathers were mine enemies, as bitter
As their son e'er can be, and I no less
Was theirs; but I was *openly* their foe:
I never work'd by plot in council, nor
Cabal in commonwealth, nor secret
 means
Of practice against life by steel or drug.
The proof is, your existence.
 Lor. I fear not.
 Doge. You have no cause, being what I
 am; but were I 235
That you would have me thought, you
 long ere now
Were past the sense of fear. Hate on; I
 care not.
 Lor. I never yet knew that a noble's life
In Venice had to dread a Doge's frown,
That is, by open means.
 Doge. But I, good signor, 240
Am, or at least *was*, more than a mere
 duke,
In blood, in mind, in means; and that
 they know

Who dreaded to elect me, and have since
Striven all they dare to weigh me down:
be sure,
Before or since that period, had I held
you 245
At so much price as to require your absence,
A word of mine had set such spirits to work
As would have made you nothing. But in
all things
I have observed the strictest reverence;
Not for the laws alone, for those *you* have
strain'd 250
(I do not speak of *you* but as a single
Voice of the many) somewhat beyond
what
I could enforce for my authority,
Were I disposed to brawl; but, as I said,
I have observed with veneration, like
A priest's for the high altar, even unto
The sacrifice of my own blood and quiet,
Safety, and all save honour, the decrees,
The health, the pride, and welfare of the
state. 259
And now, sir, to your business.
 Lor. 'Tis decreed,
That, without further repetition of
The Question, or continuance of the trial,
Which only tends to show how stubborn
guilt is
('The Ten,' dispensing with the stricter
law
Which still prescribes the Question till a
full 265
Confession, and the prisoner partly having
Avow'd his crime in not denying that
The letter to the Duke of Milan's his),
James Foscari return to banishment,
And sail in the same galley which convey'd him. 270
 Mar. Thank God! At least they will
not drag him more
Before that horrible tribunal. Would he
But think so, to my mind the happiest
doom,
Not he alone, but all who dwell here,
could
Desire, were to escape from such a land.
 Doge. That is not a Venetian thought,
my daughter. 276
 Mar. No, 'twas too human. May I
share his exile?
 Lor. Of this 'the Ten' said nothing.
 Mar. So I thought!
That were too human, also. But it was not
Inhibited?
 Lor. It was not named.
 Mar. [to the Doge]. Then, father,
Surely you can obtain or grant me thus
much: [To LOREDANO.
And you, sir, not oppose my prayer to be
Permitted to accompany my husband.
 Doge. I will endeavour.

 Mar. And you, signor?
 Lor. Lady
'Tis not for me to anticipate the pleasu[re]
Of the tribunal.
 Mar. Pleasure! what a word
To use for the decrees of ——
 Doge. Daughter, know yo[u]
In what a presence you pronounce thes[e]
things? 28[0]
 Mar. A prince's and his subject's.
 Lor. Subject!
 Mar. Oh
It galls you:—well, you are his equal, a[s]
You think; but that you are not, no[r]
would be, 2[85]
Were he a peasant:—well, then, you're
prince,
A princely noble; and what then am I?
 Lor. The offspring of a noble house.
 Mar. And wedde[d]
To one as noble. What, or whose, the[n]
is 29[0]
The presence that should silence my fre[e]
thoughts?
 Lor. The presence of your husband['s]
judges.
 Doge. And
The deference due even to the lighte[st]
word
That falls from those who rule in Venic[e]
 Mar. Kee[p]
Those maxims for your mass of scare[d]
mechanics, 3[00]
Your merchants, your Dalmatian an[d]
Greek slaves,
Your tributaries, your dumb citizens,
And mask'd nobility, your sbirri, and
Your spies, your galley and your othe[r]
slaves,
To whom your midnight carryings off an[d]
drownings, 3[05]
Your dungeons next the palace roofs, [or]
under
The water's level; your mysterious mee[t]ings,
And unknown dooms, and sudden execu[tions],
Your 'Bridge of Sighs,' your stranglin[g]
chamber, and
Your torturing instruments, have made y[ou]
seem 3[10]
The beings of another and worse worl[d]
Keep such for them: I fear ye not. I kno[w]
ye;
Have known and proved your worst, i[n]
the infernal
Process of my poor husband! Treat me a[s]
Ye treated him:—you did so, in so dealir[g]
With him. Then what have I to fear fro[m]
you, 3[15]
Even if I were of fearful nature, which
I trust I am not?
 Doge. You hear, she speaks wildl[y]
 Mar. Not wisely, yet not wildly.

Lor. Lady! words 319
Utter'd within these walls I bear no further
Than to the threshold, saving such as pass
Between the Duke and me on the state's
 service.
Doge! have you aught in answer?
 Doge. Something from
The Doge; it may be also from a parent.
 Lor. My mission *here* is to the *Doge.*
 Doge. Then say 325
The Doge will choose his own ambassador,
Or state in person what is meet; and for
The father——
 Lor. I remember *mine.*—Farewell!
I kiss the hands of the illustrious lady,
And bow me to the Duke.
 [*Exit* LOREDANO.
 Mar. Are you content? 330
 Doge. I am what you behold.
 Mar. And that's a mystery.
 Doge. All things are so to mortals;
 who can read them
Save he who made? or, if they can, the few
And gifted spirits, who have studied long
That loathsome volume—man, and pored
 upon 335
Those black and bloody leaves, his heart
 and brain,
But learn a magic which recoils upon
The adept who pursues it: all the sins
We find in others, nature made our own;
All our advantages are those of fortune;
Birth, wealth, health, beauty, are her acci-
 dents, 341
And when we cry out against Fate, 'twere
 well
We should remember Fortune can take
 nought
Save what she *gave*—the rest was naked-
 ness,
And lusts, and appetites, and vanities,
The universal heritage, to battle 346
With as we may, and least in humblest
 stations,
Where hunger swallows all in one low
 want,
And the original ordinance, that man
Must sweat for his poor pittance, keeps all
 passions 350
Aloof, save fear of famine! All is low,
And false, and hollow—clay from first to
 last,
The prince's urn no less than potter's vessel.
Our fame is in men's breath, our lives upon
Less than their breath; our durance upon
 days, 355
Our days on seasons; our whole being on
Something which is not *us!*—So, we are
 slaves,
The greatest as the meanest—nothing rests
Upon our will; the will itself no less
Depends upon a straw than on a storm;
And when we think we lead, we are most
 led, 361

And still towards death, a thing which
 comes as much
Without our act or choice as birth, so that
Methinks we must have sinn'd in some
 old world, 364
And *this* is hell: the best is, that it is not
 Eternal.
 Mar. These are things we cannot judge
On earth.
 Doge. And how then shall we judge
 each other,
Who are all earth, and I, who am call'd
 upon
To judge my son? I have administer'd
My country faithfully—victoriously—
I dare them to the proof, the *chart* of what
She was and is: my reign has doubled
 realms; 372
And, in reward, the gratitude of Venice
Has left, or is about to leave, *me* single.
 Mar. And Foscari? I do not think of
 such things, 375
So I be left with him.
 Doge. You shall be so;
Thus much they cannot well deny.
 Mar. And if
They should, I will fly with him.
 Doge. That can ne'er be.
And whither would you fly?
 Mar. I know not, reck not—
To Syria, Egypt, to the Ottoman— 380
Anywhere, where we might respire
 unfetter'd,
And live nor girt by spies, nor liable
To edicts of inquisitors of state.
 Doge. What, wouldst thou have a
 renegade for husband,
And turn him into traitor?
 Mar. He is none! 385
The country is the traitress, which thrusts
 forth
Her best and bravest from her. Tyranny
Is far the worst of treasons. Dost thou
 deem
None rebels except subjects? The prince
 who
Neglects or violates his trust is more
A brigand than the robber-chief.
 Doge. I cannot 391
Charge me with such a breach of faith.
 Mar. No; thou
Observ'st, obey'st such laws as make old
 Draco's
A code of mercy by comparison.
 Doge. I found the law; I did not make
 it. Were I 395
A subject, still I might find parts and
 portions
Fit for amendment; but as prince, I never
Would change, for the sake of my house,
 the charter
Left by our fathers.
 Mar. Did they make it for
The ruin of their children?

503

Doge. Under such laws, Venice
Has risen to what she is—a state to rival
In deeds, and days, and sway, and, let me add,
In glory (for we have had Roman spirits
Amongst us), all that history has
 bequeath'd
Of Rome and Carthage in their best times,
 when 405
The people swayed by senates.
Mar. Rather say,
Groan'd under the stern oligarchs.
Doge. Perhaps so;
But yet subdued the world: in such a state
An individual, be he richest of 409
Such rank as is permitted, or the meanest,
Without a name, is alike nothing, when
The policy, irrevocably tending
To one great end, must be maintain'd in
 vigour.
Mar. This means that you are more a
 Doge than father.
Doge. It means, I am more citizen
 than either. 415
If we had not for many centuries
Had thousands of such citizens, and shall,
I trust, have still such, Venice were no city.
Mar. Accursed be the city where the laws
Would stifle nature's!
Doge. Had I as many sons
As I have years, I would have given them
 all, 421
Not without feeling, but I would have
 given them
To the state's service, to fulfil her wishes
On the flood, in the field, or, if it must be,
As it, alas! has been, to ostracism, 425
Exile, or chains, or whatsoever worse
She might decree.
Mar. And this is patriotism?
To me it seems the worst barbarity.
Let me seek out my husband: the sage 'Ten,'
With all its jealousy, will hardly war 430
So far with a weak woman as deny me
A moment's access to his dungeon.
Doge. I'll
So far take on myself, as order that
You may be admitted.
Mar. And what shall I say
To Foscari from his father?
Doge. That he obey
The laws.
Mar. And nothing more? Will you
 not see him 436
Ere he depart? It may be the last time.
Doge. The last!—my boy!—the last
 time I shall see
My last of children! Tell him I will come.
 [Exeunt.

ACT III

Scene I.—*The Prison of* Jacopo Foscari.

Jac. Fos. [*solus*]. No light, save yon
 faint gleam which shows me walls

Which never echo'd but to sorrow
 sounds,
The sigh of long imprisonment, the ste
Of feet on which the iron clank'd, th
 groan
Of death, the imprecation of despair!
And yet for this I have return'd to Venic
With some faint hope, 'tis true, that tim
 which wears
The marble down, had worn away the ha
Of men's hearts; but I knew them not, ar
 here
Must I consume my own, which never be
For Venice but with such a yearning
The dove has for her distant nest, whe
 wheeling
High in the air on her return to greet
Her callow brood. What letters are the
 which [*Approaching the wa*
Are scrawl'd along the inexorable wall?
Will the gleam let me trace them? Ah! th
 names
Of my sad predecessors in this place,
The dates of their despair, the brief wor
 of
A grief too great for many. This stor
 page
Holds like an epitaph their history;
And the poor captive's tale is graven
His dungeon barrier, like the lover
 record
Upon the bark of some tall tree, whic
 bears
His own and his beloved's name. Alas!
I recognise some names familiar to me,
And blighted like to mine, which I will ad
Fittest for such a chronicle as this,
Which only can be read, as writt,
 wretches. [*He engraves his nam*

Enter a Familiar of 'the Ten.'

Fam. I bring you food.
Jac. Fos. I pray you set it down;
I am past hunger: but my lips are parch'd
The water!
Fam. There.
Jac. Fos. [*after drinking*]. I thank yo
 I am better.
Fam. I am commanded to inform y
 that
Your further trial is postponed.
Jac. Fos. Till whe
Fam. I know not.—It is also in n
 orders
That your illustrious lady be admitted.
Jac. Fos. Ah! they relent, then—I h
 ceased to hope it:
'Twas time.

Enter Marina.

Mar. My best beloved!
Jac. Fos. [*embracing her*]. My tr
 wife,
And only friend! What happiness!

Mar. We'll part
No more.
 Jac. Fos. How! wouldst thou share a
dungeon?
 Mar. Ay, 39
The rack, the grave, all—anything with thee,
But the tomb last of all, for there we shall
Be ignorant of each other, yet I will
Share that—all things except new separa-
 tion;
It is too much to have survived the first.
How dost thou? How are those worn
 limbs? Alas! 45
Why do I ask? Thy paleness——
 Jac. Fos. 'Tis the joy
Of seeing thee again so soon, and so
Without expectancy, has sent the blood
Back to my heart, and left my cheeks like
 thine, 49
For thou art pale too, my Marina!
 Mar. 'Tis
The gloom of this eternal cell, which never
Knew sunbeam, and the sallow sullen glare
Of the familiar's torch, which seems akin
To darkness more than light, by lending to
The dungeon vapours its bituminous
 smoke, 55
Which cloud whate'er we gaze on, even
 thine eyes—
No, not thine eyes—they sparkle—how
 they sparkle!
 Jac. Fos. And thine!—but I am
blinded by the torch.
 Mar. As I had been without it.
Couldst thou see here?
 Jac. Fos. Nothing at first; but use and
time had taught me 60
Familiarity with what was darkness;
And the grey twilight of such glimmerings as
Glide through the crevices made by the
 winds 63
Was kinder to my eyes than the full sun,
When gorgeously o'ergilding any towers
Save those of Venice: but a moment ere
Thou camest hither I was busy writing.
 Mar. What?
 Jac. Fos. My name: look, 'tis there—
recorded next 68
The name of him who here preceded me,
If dungeon dates say true.
 Mar. And what of him?
 Jac. Fos. These walls are silent of
men's ends; they only
Seem to hint shrewdly of them. Such
 stern walls
Were never piled on high save o'er the
 dead,
Or those who soon must be so.—*What of
him*?
Thou askest.—What of me? may soon be
 ask'd, 75
With the like answer—doubt and dreadful
 surmise—
Unless thou tell'st my tale.

Mar. I speak of thee!
 Jac. Fos. And wherefore not? All then
shall speak of me:
The tyranny of silence is not lasting,
And, though events be hidden, just men's
 groans 80
Will burst all cerement, even a living
 grave's!
I do not *doubt* my memory, but my life;
And neither do I fear.
 Mar. Thy life is safe. 83
 Jac. Fos. And liberty?
 Mar. The mind should make its own.
 Jac. Fos. That has a noble sound; but
 'tis a sound,
A music most impressive, but too
 transient:
The mind is much, but is not all. The
 mind
Hath nerved me to endure the risk of
 death, 88
And torture positive, far worse than death
(If death be a deep sleep), without a groan,
Or with a cry which rather shamed my
 judges
Than me; but 'tis not all, for there are
 things
More woful—such as this small dungeon,
 where
I may breathe many years.
 Mar. Alas! and this 94
Small dungeon is all that belongs to thee
Of this wide realm, of which thy sire is
 prince.
 Jac. Fos. That thought would scarcely
aid me to endure it.
My doom is common; many are in
 dungeons,
But none like mine, so near their father's
 palace;
But then my heart is sometimes high, and
 hope 100
Will stream along those moted rays of
 light
Peopled with dusty atoms, which afford
Our only day: for, save the gaoler's torch,
And a strange firefly, which was quickly
 caught 104
Last night in yon enormous spider's net,
I ne'er saw aught here like a ray. Alas!
I know if mind may bear us up, or no,
For I have such, and shown it before men;
It sinks in solitude: my soul is social.
 Mar. I will be with thee. 110
 Jac. Fos. Ah! if it were so!
But *that* they never granted—nor will grant,
And I shall be alone: no men; no books—
Those lying likenesses of lying men.
I ask'd for even those outlines of their
 kind,
Which they term annals, history, what you
 will, 115
Which men bequeath as portraits, and
 they were

505

Refused me,—so these walls have been my
 study,
More faithful pictures of Venetian story,
With all their blank, or dismal stains,
 than is
The Hall not far from hence, which bears
 on high 120
Hundreds of doges, and their deeds and
 dates.
 Mar. I come to tell thee the result of
 their
Last council on thy doom.
 Jac. Fos. I know it—look!
[*He points to his limbs, as referring to
 the Question which he had undergone.*
 Mar. No—no—no more of that: even
 they relent 124
From that atrocity.
 Jac. Fos. What then?
 Mar. That you
Return to Candia.
 Jac. Fos. Then my last hope's gone.
I could endure my dungeon, for t'was
 Venice;
I could support the torture, there was
 something 128
In my native air that buoy'd my spirits up
Like a ship on the ocean toss'd by storms,
But proudly still bestriding the high waves,
And holding on its course; but *there*,
 afar,
In that accursed isle of slaves and captives,
And unbelievers, like a stranded wreck,
My very soul seem'd mouldering in my
 bosom, 135
And piecemeal I shall perish, if remanded.
 Mar. And *here*?
 Jac. Fos. At once—by better means,
 as briefer.
What! would they even deny me my sire's
 sepulchre,
As well as home and heritage?
 Mar. My husband! 139
I have sued to accompany thee hence,
And not so hopelessly. This love of thine
For an ungrateful and tyrannic soil
Is passion, and not patriotism; for me,
So I could see thee with a quiet aspect,
And the sweet freedom of the earth and
 air, 145
I would not cavil about climes or regions.
This crowd of palaces and prisons is not
A paradise; its first inhabitants
Were wretched exiles.
 Jac. Fos. Well I know *how* wretched!
 Mar. And yet you see how, from their
 banishment 150
Before the Tartar into these salt isles,
Their antique energy of mind, all that
Remain'd of Rome for their inheritance,
Created by degrees an ocean Rome; 154
And shall an evil, which so often leads
To good, depress thee thus?
 Jac. Fos. Had I gone forth

From my own land, like the old patriarchs
 seeking
Another region, with their flocks and
 herds;
Had I been cast out like the Jews from
 Zion,
Or like our fathers, driven by Attila 16
From fertile Italy, to barren islets,
I would have given some tears to my late
 country,
And many thoughts; but afterward
 address'd
Myself, with those about me, to create
A new home and fresh state: perhaps
 could 16
Have borne this—though I know not.
 Mar. Wherefore not
It was the lot of millions, and must be
The fate of myriads more.
 Jac. Fos. Ay—we but hear 16
Of the survivors' toil in their new lands,
Their numbers and success; but who can
 number
The hearts which broke in silence at that
 parting,
Or after their departure; of that malady
Which calls up green and native fields to
 view 17
From the rough deep, with such identity
To the poor exile's fever'd eye, that he
Can scarcely be restrained from treading
 them?
That melody, which out of tones and tunes
Collects such pasture for the longing
 sorrow 17
Of the sad mountaineer, when far away
From his snow canopy of cliffs and clouds
That he feeds on the sweet, but poisonous
 thought,
And dies. You call this *weakness*! It is
 strength,
I say,—the parent of all honest feeling.
He who loves not his country, can love
 nothing.
 Mar. Obey her, then: 'tis she that puts
 thee forth. 18
 Jac. Fos. Ay, there it is; 'tis like a
 mother's curse
Upon my soul—the mark is set upon me.
The exiles you speak of went forth by
 nations,
Their hands upheld each other by the way,
Their tents were pitched together—I'm
 alone. 19
 Mar. You shall be so no more—I will
 go with thee.
 Jac. Fos. My best Marina!—and our
 children?
 Mar. They,
I fear, by the prevention of the state's
Abhorrent policy (which holds all ties
As threads, which may be broken at his
 pleasure), 19
Will not be suffer'd to proceed with us.

Jac. Fos. And canst thou leave them?
Mar. Yes. With many a pang.
But—I *can* leave them, children as they are,
To teach you to be less a child. From this
Learn you to sway your feelings, when
 exacted 200
By duties paramount; and 'tis our first
On earth to bear.
Jac Fos. Have I not borne?
Mar. Too much
From tyrannous injustice, and enough
To teach you not to shrink now from a lot,
Which, as compared with what you have
 undergone 205
Of late, is mercy.
Jac. Fos. Ah! you never yet
Were far away from Venice, never saw
Her beautiful towers in the receding
 distance,
While every furrow of the vessel's track
Seem'd ploughing deep into your heart;
 you never 210
Saw day go down upon your native spires
So calmly with its gold and crimson glory,
And after dreaming a disturbed vision
Of them and theirs, awoke and found them
 not.
Mar. I will divide this with you. Let
 us think 215
Of our departure from this much-loved
 city
(Since you must *love* it, as it seems), and
 this
Chamber of state, her gratitude allots you.
Our children will be cared for by the Doge,
And by my uncles: we must sail ere night.
Jac. Fos. That's sudden. Shall I not
 behold my father? 221
Mar. You will.
Jac. Fos. Where?
Mar. Here, or in the ducal chamber—
He said not which. I would that you could
 bear
Your exile as he bears it.
Jac. Fos. Blame him not. 224
I sometimes murmur for a moment; but
He could not now act otherwise. A show
Of feeling or compassion on his part
Would have but drawn upon his aged head
Suspicion from 'the Ten,' and upon mine
Accumulated ills.
Mar. Accumulated!
What pangs are those they have spared
 you?
Jac. Fos. That of leaving
Venice without beholding him or you,
Which might have been forbidden now,
 as 'twas
Upon my former exile.
Mar. That is true, 234
And thus far I am also the state's debtor,
And shall be more so when I see us both
Floating on the free waves—away—
 away—

Be it to the earth's end, from this abhorr'd,
Unjust, and——
Jac. Fos. Curse it not. If I am silent,
Who dares accuse my country?
Mar. Men and angels!
The blood of myriads reeking up to
 heaven, 241
The groans of slaves in chains, and men in
 dungeons,
Mothers, and wives, and sons, and sires,
 and subjects,
Held in the bondage of ten bald-heads;
 and
Though last, not least, *thy silence! Couldst
 thou* say 245
Aught in its favour, who would praise like
 thee?
Jac. Fos. Let us address us then, since
 so it must be,
To our departure. Who comes here?

Enter LOREDANO, *attended by Familiars.*
Lor. [*to the Familiars*]. Retire,
But leave the torch.
 [*Exeunt the two Familiars.*
Jac. Fos. Most welcome, noble signor.
I did not deem this poor place could
 have drawn 250
Such presence hither.
Lor. 'Tis not the first time
I have visited these places.
Mar. Nor would be
The last, were all men's merits well re-
 warded. 253
Came you here to insult us, or remain
As spy upon us, or as hostage for us?
Lor. Neither are of my office, noble
 lady!
I am sent hither to your husband, to
Announce 'the Ten's' decree.
Mar. That tenderness
Has been anticipated: it is known.
Lor. As how?
Mar. I have inform'd him, not so
 gently, 260
Doubtless, as your nice feelings would
 prescribe,
The indulgence of your colleagues; but he
 knew it.
If you come for our thanks, take them, and
 hence!
The dungeon gloom is deep enough with-
 out you,
And full of reptiles, not less loathsome,
 though 265
Their sting is honester.
Jac. Fos. I pray you, calm you:
What can avail such words?
Mar. To let him know
That he is known.
Lor. Let the fair dame preserve
Her sex's privilege.
Mar. I have some sons, sir, 269
Will one day thank you better.

507

Lor. You do well
To nurse them wisely. Foscari—you know
Your sentence, then?
Jac. Fos. Return to Candia?
Lor. True—
For life.
Jac. Fos. Not long.
Lor. I said—for *life*.
Jac. Fos. And I
Repeat—not long.
Lor. A year's imprisonment 274
In Canea—afterwards the freedom of
The whole isle.
Jac. Fos. Both the same to me: the after
Freedom as is the first imprisonment.
Is't true my wife accompanies me?
Lor. Yes,
If she so wills it.
Mar. Who obtain'd that justice?
Lor. One who wars not with women.
Mar. But oppresses
Men: howsoever let him have *my* thanks
For the only boon I would have ask'd or taken
From him or such as he is.
Lor. He receives them
As they are offer'd.
Mar. May they thrive with him
So much!—no more.
Jac. Fos. Is this, sir, your whole
mission? 285
Because we have brief time for prepara-
tion,
And you perceive your presence doth
disquiet
This lady, of a house noble as yours.
Mar. Nobler!
Lor. How nobler?
Mar. As more generous!
We say the 'generous steed' to express the
purity 290
Of his high blood⸳ Thus much I've learnt,
although
Venetian (who see few steeds save of
bronze),
From those Venetians who have skimm'd
the coasts
Of Egypt and her neighbour Araby:
And why not say as soon the '*generous
man*'? 295
If race be aught, it is in qualities
More than in years; and mine, which is as
old
As yours, is better in its product, nay—
Look not so stern—but get you back, and
pore 299
Upon your genealogic tree's most green
Of leaves and most mature of fruits, and
there
Blush to find ancestors, who would have
blush'd
For such a son—thou cold inveterate
hater!

Jac. Fos. Again, Marina!
Mar. Again! *still*, Marina.
See you not, he comes here to glut his hat
With a last look upon our misery?
Let him partake it!
Jac. Fos. That were difficult.
Mar. Nothing more easy. He par
takes it now—
Ay, he may veil beneath a marble brow
And sneering lip the pang, but he partake
it. 31
A few brief words of truth shame th
devil's servants
No less than master; I have probed his sou
A moment, as the eternal fire, ere long,
Will reach it always. See how he shrink
from me!
With death, and chains, and exile in hi
hand, 31
To scatter o'er his kind as he thinks fit;
They are his weapons, not his armour, fo
I have pierced him to the core of his col
heart. 31
I care not for his frowns! We can but di
And he but live, for him the very worst
Of destinies: each day secures him mor
His tempter's.
Jac. Fos. This is mere insanity.
Mar. It may be so; and *who* hath mad
us *mad*?
Lor. Let her go on; it irks me not.
Mar. That's false! 32
You came here to enjoy a heartless triump
Of cold looks upon manifold griefs! Yo
came
To be sued to in vain—to mark our tears
And hoard our groans—to gaze upon th
wreck
Which you have made a prince's son—m
husband;
In short, to trample on the fallen—a
office 33
The hangman shrinks from, as all me
from him!
How have you sped? We are wretche
signor, as
Your plots could make, and vengeanc
could desire us,
And how *feel* you?
Lor. As rocks.
Mar. By thunder blasted
They feel not, but no less are shiver'd
Come, 33
Foscari: now let us go, and leave this felon
The sole fit habitant of such a cell,
Which he has peopled often, but ne'er fitl
Till he himself shall brood in it alone.

Enter the DOGE.

Jac. Fos. My father!
Doge [*embracing him*]. Jacopo! m
son—my son! 34
Jac. Fos. My father still! How long
is since I

Have heard thee name my name—*our*
 name!
Doge. My boy!
Couldst thou but know——
Jac. Fos. I rarely, sir, have murmur'd.
Doge. I feel too much thou hast not.
Mar. Doge, look there! 344
 [*She points to* Loredano.
Doge. I see the man—what mean'st
 thou?
Mar. Caution!
Lor. Being
The virtue which this noble lady most
May practise, she doth well to recommend
 it.
Mar. Wretch! 'tis no virtue, but the
 policy
Of those who fain must deal perforce with
 vice:
As such I recommend it, as I would 350
To one whose foot was on an adder's path.
Doge. Daughter, it is superfluous; I
 have long
Known Loredano.
Lor. You may know him better.
Mar. Yes: *worse* he could not.
Jac. Fos. Father, let not these 354
Our parting hours be lost in listening to
Reproaches, which boot nothing. Is it—
 is it,
Indeed, our last of meetings?
Doge. You behold
These white hairs!
Jac. Fos. And I feel, besides, that
 mine
Will never be so white. Embrace me,
 father! 359
I loved you ever—never more than now.
Look to my children—to your last child's
 children:
Let them be all to you which he was once,
And never be to you what I am now.
May I not see *them* also?
Mar. No—not *here.*
Jac. Fos. They might behold their
 parent anywhere. 365
Mar. I would that they beheld their
 father in
A place which would not mingle fear with
 love,
To freeze their young blood in its natural
 current.
They have fed well, slept soft, and knew
 not that
Their sire was a mere hunted outlaw.
 Well, 370
I know his fate may one day be their
 heritage;
But let it only be their *heritage,*
And not their present fee. Their senses,
 though
Alive to love, are yet awake to terror;
And these vile damps, too, and yon *thick
 green* wave 375

Which floats above the place where we
 now stand—
A cell so far below the water's level,
Sending its pestilence through every
 crevice,
Might strike them: *this is not their* atmo-
 sphere, 379
However you—and you—and most of all,
As worthiest—*you*, sir, noble Loredano!
May breathe it without prejudice.
Jac. Fos. I have not
Reflected upon this, but acquiesce.
I shall depart, then, without meeting
 them?
Doge. Not so: they shall await you in
 my chamber. 385
Jac. Fos. And must I leave them—*all*?
Lor. You must.
Jac. Fos. Not one?
Lor. They are the state's.
Mar. I thought they had been mine.
Lor. They are, in all maternal things.
Mar. That is
In all things painful. If they're sick, they
 will 389
Be left to me to tend them; should they die,
To me to bury and to mourn; but if
They live, they'll make you soldiers,
 senators,
Slaves, exiles—what *you* will; or if they are
Females with portions, brides and *bribes*
 for nobles!
Behold the state's care for its sons and
 mothers! 395
Lor. The hour approaches, and the
 wind is fair.
Jac. Fos. How know you that here,
 where the genial wind
Ne'er blows in all its blustering freedom?
Lor. 'Twas so
When I came here. The galley floats
 within 399
A bow-shot of the 'Riva di Schiavoni.'
Jac. Fos. Father! I pray you to precede
 me, and
Prepare my children to behold their father.
Doge. Be firm, my son!
Jac. Fos. I will do my endeavour.
Mar. Farewell! at least to this detested
 dungeon, 404
And him to whose good offices you owe
In part your past imprisonment.
Lor. And present
Liberation.
Doge. He speaks truth.
Jac. Fos. No doubt! but 'tis
Exchange of chains for heavier chains I
 owe him.
He knows this, or he had not sought to
 change them. 409
But I reproach not.
Lor. The time narrows, signor.
Jac. Fos. Alas! I little thought so
 lingeringly

To leave abodes like this: but when I feel
That every step I take, even from this cell,
Is one away from Venice, I look back 414
Even on these dull damp walls, and——
Doge. Boy! no tears.
Mar. Let them flow on: he wept not on
 the rack
To shame him, and they cannot shame
 him now.
They will relieve his heart—that too kind
 heart—
And I will find an hour to wipe away
Those tears, or add my own. I could weep
 now, 420
But would not gratify yon wretch so far.
Let us proceed. Doge, lead the way.
 Lor. (*to the Familiar*). The torch, there!
Mar. Yes, light us on, as to a funeral
 pyre,
With Loredano mourning like an heir.
Doge. My son, you are feeble; take
 this hand.
Jac. Fos. Alas! 425
Must youth support itself on age, and I
Who ought to be the prop of yours?
Lor. Take mine.
Mar. Touch it not, Foscari; 'twill
 sting you. Signor,
Stand off! be sure, that if a grasp of yours
Would raise us from the gulf wherein we
 are plunged,
No hand of ours would stretch itself to
 meet it. 431
Come, Foscari, take the hand the altar
 gave you;
It could not save, but will support you
 ever. [*Exeunt.*

ACT IV

SCENE I.—*A Hall in the Ducal Palace.*

Enter LOREDANO *and* BARBARIGO.

Bar. And have you confidence in such
 a project?
Lor. I have.
Bar. 'Tis hard upon his years.
Lor. Say rather
Kind to relieve him from the cares of state.
Bar. 'Twill break his heart.
Lor. Age has no heart to break.
He has seen his son's half broken, and,
 except 5
A start of feeling in his dungeon, never
Swerved.
Bar. In his countenance, I grant you,
 never;
But I have seen him sometimes in a calm
So desolate, that the most clamorous grief
Had nought to envy him within. Where is
 he? 10
Lor. In his own portion of the palace,
 with
His son, and the whole race of Foscaris.

Bar. Bidding farewell.
Lor. A last. As soon he shall
Bid to his dukedom.
Bar. When embarks the son
Lor. Forthwith—when this long leave
 is taken. 'Tis 1;
Time to admonish them again.
Bar. Forbear;
Retrench not from their moments.
Lor. Not I, now
We have higher business for our own
 This day
Shall be the last of the old Doge's reign
As the first of his son's last banishment,
And that is vengeance.
Bar. In my mind, too deep. 2i
Lor. 'Tis moderate—not even life for
 life, the rule
Denounced of retribution from all time;
They owe me still my father's and my
 uncle's.
Bar. Did not the Doge deny this
 strongly?
Lor. Doubtless. 2:
Bar. And did not this shake your
 suspicion?
Lor. No.
Bar. But if this deposition should take
 place
By our united influence in the Council,
It must be done with all the deference
Due to his years, his station, and his deeds.
Lor. As much of ceremony as you will.
So that the thing be done. You may, for
 aught
I care, depute the Council on their knees
(Like Barbarossa to the Pope), to beg him
To have the courtesy to abdicate. 3:
Bar. What if he will not?
Lor. We'll elect another,
And make him null.
Bar. But will the laws uphold us?
Lor. What laws?—'The Ten' are
 laws; and if they were not,
I will be legislator in this business.
Bar. At your own peril?
Lor. There is none, I tell you, 4c
Our powers are such.
Bar. But he has twice already
Solicited permission to retire,
And twice it was refused.
Lor. The better reason
To grant it the third time.
Bar. Unask'd?
Lor. It shows
The impression of his former instances:
If they were from his heart, he may be
 thankful: 4(
If not, 'twill punish his hypocrisy.
Come, they are met by this time; let us
 join them,
And be *thou* fix'd in purpose for this once.
I have prepared such arguments as will
 not 5(

Fail to move them, and to remove him:
since
Their thoughts, their objects, have been
sounded, do not
You, with your wonted scruples, teach us
pause,
And all will prosper.
 Bar. Could I but be certain 54
This is no prelude to such persecution
Of the sire as has fallen upon the son,
I would support you.
 Lor. He is safe, I tell you;
His fourscore years and five may linger on
As long as he can drag them: 'tis his throne
Alone is aim'd at.
 Bar. But discarded princes 60
Are seldom long of life.
 Lor. And men of eighty
More seldom still.
 Bar. And why not wait these few years?
 Lor. Because we have waited long
enough, and he
Lived longer than enough. Hence! in to
council!
 [*Exeunt* LOREDANO *and* BARBARIGO.

Enter MEMMO *and a Senator.*

 Sen. A summons to 'the Ten'! why
so?
 Mem. 'The Ten' 65
Alone can answer; they are rarely wont
To let their thoughts anticipate their
purpose
By previous proclamation. We are sum-
mon'd?
That is enough.
 Sen. For them, but not for us;
I would know why.
 Mem. You will know why anon,
If you obey: and, if not, you no less 71
Will know why you should have obey'd.
 Sen. I mean not
To oppose them, *but——*
 Mem. In Venice '*but*' 's a traitor.
But me no '*buts*,' unless you would pass
o'er
The Bridge which few repass.
 Sen. I am silent.
 Mem. Why 75
Thus hesitate? 'The Ten' have call'd in aid
Of their deliberation five and twenty
Patricians of the senate—you are one,
And I another; and it seems to me
Both honour'd by the choice or chance 80
which leads us
To mingle with a body so august.
 Sen. Most true. I say no more.
 Mem. As we hope, signor,
And all may honestly, (that is, all those
Of noble blood may,) one day hope to be
Decemvir, it is surely for the senate's 85
Chosen delegates a school of wisdom, to
Be thus admitted, though as novices,
To view the mysteries.
 Sen. Let us view them: they,
No doubt, are worth it.
 Mem. Being worth our lives
If we divulge them, doubtless they are
worth 90
Something, at least to you or me.
 Sen. I sought not
A place within the sanctuary; but being
Chosen, however reluctantly so chosen,
I shall fulfil my office.
 Mem. Let us not
Be latest in obeying 'the Ten's' summons.
 Sen. All are not met, but I am of your
thought 96
So far—let's in.
 Mem. The earliest are most welcome
In earnest councils—we will not be least
so. [*Exeunt.*

Enter the DOGE, JACOPO FOSCARI, *and*
MARINA.

 Jac. Fos. Ah, father! though I must
and will depart, 99
Yet—yet—I pray you to obtain for me
That I once more return unto my home,
Howe'er remote the period. Let there be
A point of time, as beacon to my heart,
With any penalty annex'd they please,
But let me still return.
 Doge. Son Jacopo, 105
Go and obey our country's will: 'tis not
For us to look beyond.
 Jac. Fos. But still I must
Look back. I pray you think of me.
 Doge. Alas!
You ever were my dearest offspring, when
They were more numerous, nor can be less
so 110
Now you are last; but did the state demand
The exile of the disinterred ashes
Of your three goodly brothers, now in
earth,
And their desponding shades came flitting
round
To impede the act, I must no less obey
A duty, paramount to every duty. 116
 Mar. My husband! let us on: this but
prolongs
Our sorrow.
 Jac. Fos. But we are not summon'd yet;
The galley's sails are not unfurl'd:—who
knows?
The wind may change.
 Mar. And if it do, it will not 120
Change *their* hearts, or your lot: the
galley's oars
Will quickly clear the harbour.
 Jac. Fos. O ye elements!
Where are your storms?
 Mar. In human breasts. Alas!
Will nothing calm you?
 Jac. Fos. Never yet did mariner
Put up to patron saint such prayers for
prosperous 125

And pleasant breezes, as I call upon you,
Ye tutelar saints of my own city! which
Ye love not with more holy love than I,
To lash up from the deep the Adrian
 waves,
And waken Auster, sovereign of the
 tempest! 130
Till the sea dash me back on my own shore
A broken corse upon the barren Lido,
Where I may mingle with the sands which
 skirt
The land I love, and never shall see more!
 Mar. And wish you this with *me*
 beside you?
 Jac. Fos. No— 135
No—not for thee, too good, too kind!
 May'st thou
Live long to be a mother to those children
Thy fond fidelity for a time deprives
Of such support! But for myself alone,
May all the winds of heaven howl down
 the Gulf, 140
And tear the vessel, till the mariners,
Appall'd, turn their despairing eyes on me,
As the Phenicians did on Jonah, then
Cast me out from amongst them, as an
 offering
To appease the waves. The billow which
 destroys me 145
Will be more merciful than man, and bear
 me
Dead, but *still bear* me to a native grave,
From fishers' hands, upon the desolate
 strand,
Which, of its thousand wrecks, hath ne'er
 received
One lacerated like the heart which then
Will be.—But wherefore breaks it not?
 why live I? 151
 Mar. To man thyself, I trust, with
 time, to master
Such useless passion. Until now thou wert
A sufferer, but not a loud one: why,
What is this to the things thou hast borne
 in silence— 155
Imprisonment and actual torture?
 Jac. Fos. Double,
Triple, and tenfold torture! But you are
 right,
It must be borne. Father, your blessing.
 Doge. Would
It could avail thee! but no less thou hast it.
 Jac. Fos. Forgive—
 Doge. What?
 Jac. Fos. My poor mother, for my
 birth, 160
And me for having lived, and you yourself
(As I forgive you), for the gift of life,
Which you bestow'd upon me as my sire.
 Mar. What hast thou done?
 Jac. Fos. Nothing. I cannot charge
My memory with much save sorrow: but
I have been so beyond the common lot
Chasten'd and visited, I needs must think

That I was wicked. If it be so, may
What I have undergone here keep me from
A like hereafter!
 Mar. Fear not: *that*'s reserved 170
For your oppressors.
 Jac. Fos. Let me hope not.
 Mar. Hope not
 Jac. Fos. I cannot wish them *all* they
 have inflicted.
 Mar. All! the consummate fiends! A
 thousand-fold
May the worm which ne'er dieth feed upon
 them! 174
 Jac. Fos. They may repent.
 Mar. And if they do, Heaven will no
Accept the tardy penitence of demons.

Enter an Officer and Guards.

 Offi. Signor! the boat is at the shore—
 the wind
Is rising—we are ready to attend you.
 Jac. Fos. And I to be attended. Once
 more, father,
Your hand!
 Doge. Take it. Alas! how thine own
 trembles! 180
 Jac. Fos. No—you mistake; 'tis your.
 that shakes, my father.
Farewell!
 Doge. Farewell! Is there aught else?
 Jac. Fos. No—nothing
 [*To the Officer*
Lend me your arm, good signor.
 Offi. You turn pale—
Let me support you—paler—ho! some
 aid there!
Some water!
 Mar. Ah, he is dying!
 Jac. Fos. Now, I'm ready— 18
My eyes swim strangely—where's the
 door?
 Mar. Away
Let me support him—my best love! Oh
 God!
How faintly beats this heart—this pulse
 Jac. Fos. The light
Is it the light?—I am faint.
 [*Officer presents him with water*
 Offi. He will be better, 18
Perhaps, in the air.
 Jac. Fos. I doubt not. Father—wife—
Your hands!
 Mar. There's death in that damp
 clammy grasp.
Oh God!—My Foscari, how fare you?
 Jac. Fos. Well! [*He dies*
 Offi. He's gone!
 Doge. He's free.
 Mar. No—no, he is not dead
There must be life yet in that heart—he
 could not
Thus leave me.
 Doge. Daughter!
 Mar. Hold thy peace, old man! 19

I am no daughter now—thou hast no son.
Oh, Foscari!
 Offi. We must remove the body.
 Mar. Touch it not, dungeon mis-
 creants! your base office
Ends with his life, and goes not beyond
 murder,
Even by your murderous laws. Leave his
 remains 200
To those who know to honour them.
 Offi. I must
Inform the signory, and learn their
 pleasure.
 Doge. Inform the signory from *me*,
 the Doge,
They have no further power upon those
 ashes:
While he lived, he was theirs, as fits a
 subject— 205
Now he is *mine*—my broken-hearted boy!
 [*Exit Officer.*
 Mar. And I must live!
 Doge. Your children live, Marina.
 Mar. My children! true—they live,
 and I must live
To bring them up to serve the state, and
 die
As died their father. Oh! what best of
 blessings 210
Were barrenness in Venice! Would my
 mother
Had been so!
 Doge. My unhappy children!
 Mar. What!
You feel it then at last—*you!*—Where is
 now
The stoic of the state?
 Doge [*throwing himself down by the
 body*]. *Here!*
 Mar. Ay, weep on!
I thought you had no tears—you hoarded
 them 215
Until they are useless; but weep on! he
 never
Shall weep more—never, never more.

 Enter LOREDANO *and* BARBARIGO.

 Lor. What's here?
 Mar. Ah! the devil come to insult the
 dead! Avaunt!
Incarnate Lucifer! 'tis holy ground.
A martyr's ashes now lie there, which
 make it 220
A shrine. Get thee back to thy place of
 torment!
 Bar. Lady, we knew not of this sad
 event,
But pass'd here merely on our path from
 council.
 Mar. Pass on.
 Lor. We sought the Doge.
 Mar. [*pointing to the Doge, who is still on
 the ground by his son's body*].
 He's busy, look,

About the business *you* provided for him,
Are ye content?
 Bar. We will not interrupt
A parent's sorrows.
 Mar. No, ye only make them,
Then leave them.
 Doge [*rising*]. Sirs, I am ready.
 Bar. No—not now.
 Lor. Yet 'twas important.
 Doge. If 'twas so, I can
Only repeat—I am ready.
 Bar. It shall not be 230
Just now, though Venice totter'd o'er the
 deep
Like a frail vessel. I respect your griefs.
 Doge. I thank you. If the tidings
 which you bring
Are evil, you may say them; nothing
 further
Can touch me more than him thou look'st
 on there; 235
If they be good, say on; you need not *fear*
That they can *comfort* me.
 Bar. I would they could!
 Doge. I spoke not to *you*, but to
 Loredano.
He understands me.
 Mar. Ah! I thought it would be so.
 Doge. What mean you?
 Mar. Lo! there is the blood
 beginning 240
To flow through the dead lips of Foscari—
The body bleeds in presence of the
 assassin. [*To* LOREDANO.
Thou cowardly murderer by law, behold
How death itself bears witness to thy
 deeds!
 Doge. My child! this is a phantasy of
 grief. 245
Bear hence the body. [*To his attendants.*]
 Signors, if it please you,
Within an hour I'll hear you.
 [*Exeunt* DOGE, MARINA, *and attendants
 with the body. Manent* LOREDANO
 and BARBARIGO.
 Bar. He must not
Be troubled now.
 Lor. He said himself that nought
Could give him trouble further.
 Bar. These are words;
But grief is lonely, and the breaking in
Upon it barbarous.
 Lor. Sorrow preys upon 251
Its solitude, and nothing more diverts it
From its sad visions of the other world,
Than calling it at moments back to this.
The busy have no time for tears.
 Bar. And therefore 255
You would deprive this old man of all
 business?
 Lor. The thing's decreed. The Giunta
 and 'the Ten'
Have made it law—who shall oppose that
 law?

Bar. Humanity!
Lor. Because his son is dead? 259
Bar. And yet unburied.
Lor. Had we known this when
The act was passing, it might have suspended
Its passage, but impedes it not—once past.
Bar. I'll not consent.
Lor. You have consented to
All that's essential—leave the rest to me.
Bar. Why press his abdication now?
Lor. The feelings
Of private passion may not interrupt 266
The public benefit; and what the state
Decides to-day must not give way before
To-morrow for a natural accident.
Bar. You have a son.
Lor. I *have*—and *had* a father. 270
Bar. Still so inexorable?
Lor. Still.
Bar. But let him
Inter his son before we press upon him
This edict.
Lor. Let him call up into life
My sire and uncle—I consent. Men may,
Even aged men, be, or appear to be, 275
Sires of a hundred sons, but cannot kindle
An atom of their ancestors from earth.
The victims are not equal; he has seen
His sons expire by natural deaths, and I
My sires by violent and mysterious
maladies. 280
I used no poison, bribed no subtle master
Of the destructive art of healing, to
Shorten the path to the eternal cure.
His sons—and he had four—are dead,
without
My dabbling in vile drugs.
Bar. And art thou sure 285
He dealt in such?
Lor. Most sure.
Bar. And yet he seems
All openness.
Lor. And so he seem'd not long
Ago to Carmagnuola.
Bar. The attainted
And foreign traitor?
Lor. Even so: when *he,* 289
After the very night in which 'the Ten'
(Join'd with the Doge) decided his destruction,
Met the great Duke at daybreak with a jest,
Demanding whether he should augur him
'The good day or good night'? his Doge-
ship answer'd,
'That he in truth had pass'd a night of
vigil, 295
In which (he added with a gracious smile),
There often has been question about you.'
'Twas true; the question was the death
resolved
Of Carmagnuola, eight months ere he died;
And the old Doge, who knew him doom'd,
smiled on him 300

With deadly cozenage, eight long months
beforehand—
Eight months of such hypocrisy as is
Learnt but in eighty years. Brave Car-
magnuola
Is dead; so is young Foscari and his
brethren—
I never *smiled* on *them.*
Bar. Was Carmagnuola 30
Your friend?
Lor. He was the safeguard of the city
In early life its foe, but, in his manhood
Its saviour first, then victim.
Bar. Ah! that seem
The penalty of saving cities. He 30
Whom we now act against not only save
Our own, but added others to our sway
Lor. The Romans (and we ape them
gave a crown
To him who took a city; and they gave
A crown to him who saved a citizen 31
In battle: the rewards are equal. Now,
If we should measure forth the cities take
By the Doge Foscari, with citizens
Destroy'd by him, or *through* him, th
account
Were fearfully against him, althoug
narrow'd 31
To private havoc, such as between him
And my dead father.
Bar. Are you then thus fix'd
Lor. Why, what should change me?
Bar. That which changes me
But you, I know, are marble to retain
A feud. But when all is accomplish'd
when
The old man is deposed, his nam
degraded, 32
His sons all dead, his family depress'd,
And you and yours triumphant, shall yo
sleep?
Lor. More soundly.
Bar. That's an error, and you'
find it
Ere you sleep with your fathers.
Lor. They sleep no
In their accelerated graves, nor will 33
Till Foscari fills his. Each night I see them
Stalk frowning round my couch, and
pointing towards
The ducal palace, marshal me t
vengeance.
Bar. Fancy's distemperature! Ther
is no passion
More spectral or fantastical than Hate;
Not even its opposite, Love, so peoples ai
With phantoms, as this madness of th
heart. 33

Enter an Officer.

Lor. Where go you, sirrah?
Offi. By the ducal orde
To forward the preparatory rites
For the late Foscari's interment.

Bar. Their 340
Vault has been often open'd of late years.
Lor. 'Twill be full soon, and may be
closed for ever.
Offi. May I pass on?
Lor. You may.
Bar. How bears the Doge
This last calamity?
Offi. With desperate firmness.
In presence of another he says little, 345
But I perceive his lips move now and then;
And once or twice I heard him, from the
adjoining
Apartment, mutter forth the words—'My
son!'
Scarce audibly. I must proceed.
 [*Exit Officer.*
Bar. This stroke
Will move all Venice in his favour.
Lor. Right! 350
We must be speedy: let us call together
The delegates appointed to convey
The Council's resolution.
Bar. I protest
Against it at this moment.
Lor. As you please—
I'll take their voices on it ne'ertheless,
And see whose most may sway them,
 yours or mine. 356
 [*Exeunt* BARBARIGO *and* LOREDANO.

ACT V

SCENE I.—*The* DOGE'S *Apartment.*

The DOGE *and Attendants.*

Att. My lord, the deputation is in
 waiting;
But add, that if another hour would better
Accord with your will, they will make it
 theirs.
Doge. To me all hours are like. Let
 them approach. [*Exit Attendant.*
An Officer. Prince! I have done your
 bidding.
Doge. What command? 5
Offi. A melancholy one—to call the
 attendance
Of——
Doge. True—true—true; I crave your
 pardon. I
Begin to fail in apprehension, and
Wax very old—old almost as my years.
Till now I fought them off, but they begin
To overtake me.

*Enter the Deputation, consisting of six of
the Signory and the Chief of the Ten.*

 Noble men, your pleasure! 11
Chief of the Ten. In the first place, the
 Council doth condole
With the Doge on his late and private grief.
Doge. No more—no more of that.
Chief of the Ten. Will not the Duke
Accept the homage of respect?

Doge. I do 15
Accept it as 'tis given—proceed.
Chief of the Ten. 'The Ten',
With a selected Giunta from the senate
Of twenty-five of the best born patricians,
Having deliberated on the state
Of the republic, and the o'erwhelming
 cares 20
Which, at this moment, doubly must
 oppress
Your years, so long devoted to your
 country,
Have judged it fitting, with all reverence,
Now to solicit from your wisdom (which
Upon reflection must accord in this), 25
The resignation of the ducal ring,
Which you have worn so long and
 venerably:
And to prove that they are not ungrateful,
 nor
Cold to your years and services, they add
An appanage of twenty hundred golden
Ducats, to make retirement not less
 splendid 31
Than should become a sovereign's retreat.
Doge. Did I hear rightly?
Chief of the Ten. Need I say again?
Doge. No—Have you done?
Chief of the Ten. I have spoken.
 Twenty-four
Hours are accorded you to give an answer.
Doge. I shall not need so many
 seconds.
Chief of the Ten. We
Will now retire.
Doge. Stay! four and twenty hours
Will alter nothing which I have to say.
Chief of the Ten. Speak!
Doge. When I twice before reiterated
My wish to abdicate, it was refused me:
And not alone refused, but ye exacted
An oath from me that I would never more
Renew this instance. I have sworn to die
In full exertion of the functions which
My country call'd me here to exercise, 45
According to my honour and my
 conscience—
I cannot break *my* oath.
Chief of the Ten. Reduce us not
To the alternative of a decree,
Instead of your compliance.
Doge. Providence
Prolongs my days to prove and chasten
 me; 50
But ye have no right to reproach my
 length
Of days, since every hour has been the
 country's.
I am ready to lay down my life for her,
As I have laid down dearer things than
 life:
But for my dignity—I hold it of 55
The *whole* republic: when the *general* will
Is manifest, then you shall all be answer'd.

THE TWO FOSCARI

Chief of the Ten. We grieve for such an answer; but it cannot
Avail you aught.
Doge. I can submit to all things,
But nothing will advance; no, not a moment. 60
What you decree—decree.
Chief of the Ten. With this, then, must we
Return to those who sent us?
Doge. You have heard me.
Chief of the Ten. With all due reverence we retire.

[*Exeunt the Deputation, &c.*

Enter an Attendant.

Att. My lord,
The noble dame Marina craves an audience. 64
Doge. My time is hers.

Enter MARINA.

Mar. My lord, if I intrude—
Perhaps you fain would be alone?
Doge. Alone!
Alone, come all the world around me, I
Am now and evermore. But we will bear it.
Mar. We will, and for the sake of those who are,
Endeavour——Oh, my husband!
Doge. Give it way: 70
I cannot comfort thee.
Mar. He might have lived,
So form'd for gentle privacy of life,
So loving, so beloved; the native of
Another land, and who so blest and blessing
As my poor Foscari? Nothing was wanting 75
Unto his happiness and mine save not
To be Venetian.
Doge. Or a prince's son.
Mar. Yes; all things which conduce to other men's
Imperfect happiness or high ambition,
By some strange destiny, to him proved deadly. 80
The country and the people whom he loved,
The prince of whom he was the elder born,
And——
Doge. Soon may be a prince no longer.
Mar. How?
Doge. They have taken my son from me, and now aim
At my too long worn diadem and ring.
Let them resume the gewgaws!
Mar. Oh, the tyrants! 86
In such an hour too!
Doge. 'Tis the fittest time;
An hour ago I should have felt it.
Mar. And
Will you not now resent it?—Oh, for vengeance!

But he, who, had he been enough protected, 90
Might have repaid protection in this moment,
Cannot assist his father.
Doge. Nor should do so
Against his country, had he a thousand lives
Instead of that——
Mar. They tortured from him. This
May be pure patriotism. I am a woman:
To me my husband and my children were
Country and home. I loved *him*—how I loved him! 97
I have seen him pass through such an ordeal as
The old martyrs would have shrunk from: he is gone,
And I, who would have given my blood for him, 100
Have nought to give but tears! But could I compass
The retribution of his wrongs!—Well, well!
I have sons, who shall be men.
Doge. Your grief distracts you.
Mar. I thought I could have borne it, when I saw him
Bow'd down by such oppression; yes, I thought 105
That I would rather look upon his corse
Than his prolong'd captivity:—I am punish'd
For that thought now. Would I were in his grave!
Doge. I must look on him once more.
Mar. Come with me!
Doge. Is he——
Mar. Our bridal bed is now his bier. 110
Doge. And he is in his shroud!
Mar. Come, come, old man!
[*Exeunt the* DOGE *and* MARINA.

Enter BARBARIGO *and* LOREDANO.

Bar. [*to an Attendant*]. Where is the Doge?
Att. This instant retired hence,
With the illustrious lady his son's widow.
Lor. Where?
Att. To the chamber where the body lies.
Bar. Let us return, then.
Lor. You forget, you cannot. 115
We have the implicit order of the Giunta
To await their coming here, and join them in
Their office: they'll be here soon after us.
Bar. And will they press their answer on the Doge?
Lor. 'Twas his own wish that all should be done promptly. 120
He answer'd quickly, and must so be answer'd;

516

His dignity is look'd to, his estate
Cared for—what would he more?
 Bar. Die in his robes:
He could not have lived long; but I have
 done 124
My best to save his honours, and opposed
This proposition to the last, though vainly.
Why would the general vote compel me
 hither?
 Lor. 'Twas fit that some one of such
 different thoughts
From ours should be a witness, lest false
 tongues
Should whisper that a harsh majority 130
Dreaded to have its acts beheld by others.
 Bar. And not less, I must needs think,
 for the sake
Of humbling me for my vain opposition.
You are ingenious, Loredano, in
Your modes of vengeance, nay, poetical,
A very Ovid in the art of *hating*; 136
'Tis thus (although a secondary object,
Yet hate has microscopic eyes), to you
I owe by way of foil to the more zealous,
This undesired association in 140
Your Giunta's duties.
 Lor. How!—*my* Giunta!
 Bar. *Yours!*
They speak your language, watch your
 nod, approve
Your plans, and do your work. Are they
 not *yours?*
 Lor. You talk unwarily. 'Twere best
 they hear not
This from you.
 Bar. Oh! they 'll hear as much one day
From louder tongues than mine; they have
 gone beyond 146
Even their exorbitance of power: and when
This happens in the most contemn'd and
 abject
States, stung humanity will rise to check it.
 Lor. You talk but idly.
 Bar. That remains for proof. 150
Here come our colleagues.

Enter the Deputation as before.

 Chief of the Ten. Is the Duke aware
We seek his presence?
 Att. He shall be inform'd.
 [*Exit Attendant.*
 Bar. The Duke is with his son.
 Chief of the Ten. If it be so,
We will remit him till the rites are over.
Let us return. 'Tis time enough to-
 morrow. 155
 Lor. [*aside to Bar.*] Now the rich
 man's hell-fire upon your tongue,
Unquench'd, unquenchable! I'll have it
 torn
From its vile babbling roots, till you shall
 utter
Nothing but sobs through blood, for this!
 Sage signors,

I pray ye be not hasty.
 [*Aloud to the others.*
 Bar. But be human! 160
 Lor. See, the Duke comes!

Enter the DOGE.

 Doge. I have obey'd your summons.
 Chief of the Ten. We come once more
 to urge our past request.
 Doge. And I to answer.
 Chief of the Ten. What?
 Doge. My only answer.
You have heard it.
 Chief of the Ten. Hear *you* then the
 last decree,
Definitive and absolute!
 Doge. To the point— 165
To the point! I know of old the forms of
 office,
And gentle preludes to strong acts.—Go on!
 Chief of the Ten. You are no longer
 Doge; you are released
From your imperial oath as sovereign;
Your ducal robes must be put off; but for
Your services, the state allots the ap-
 panage 171
Already mention'd in our former congress.
Three days are left you to remove from
 hence,
Under the penalty to see confiscated
All your own private fortune.
 Doge. That last clause, 175
I am proud to say, would not enrich the
 treasury.
 Chief of the Ten. Your answer, Duke!
 Lor. Your answer, Francis Foscari!
 Doge. If I could have foreseen that my
 old age
Was prejudicial to the state, the chief
Of the republic never would have shown
Himself so far ungrateful, as to place
His own high dignity before his country;
But this *life* having been so many years
Not useless to that country, I would fain
Have consecrated my last moments to her.
But the decree being render'd, I obey. 186
 Chief of the Ten. If you would have the
 three days named extended,
We willingly will lengthen them to eight,
As sign of our esteem.
 Doge. Not eight hours, signor,
Nor even eight minutes—there's the
 ducal ring 190
 [*Taking off his ring and cap.*
And there the ducal diadem. And so
The Adriatic's free to wed another.
 Chief of the Ten. Yet go not forth so
 quickly.
 Doge. I am old, sir,
And even to move but slowly must begin
To move betimes. Methinks I see amongst
 you 195
A face I know not.—Senator! your name,
You, by your garb, Chief of the Forty!

517

Mem. Signor,
I am the son of Marco Memmo.
Doge. Ah!
Your father was my friend.—But *sons* and
 fathers!—
What, ho! my servants there!
Atten. My prince!
Doge. No prince— 200
There are the princes of the prince!
 [*Pointing to the Ten's Deputation.*]—
 Prepare
To part from hence upon the instant.
Chief of the Ten. Why
So rashly? 'twill give scandal.
Doge. Answer that;
 [*To the Ten.*
It is your province.—Sirs, bestir your-
 selves: [*To the Servants.*
There is one burthen which I beg you bear
With care, although 'tis past all further
 harm— 206
But I will look to that myself.
Bar. He means
The body of his son.
Doge. And call Marina,
My daughter!

 Enter MARINA.

Doge. Get thee ready, we must mourn
Elsewhere.
Mar. And everywhere.
Doge. True; but in freedom, 210
Without these jealous spies upon the
 great.
Signors, you may depart: what would you
 more?
We are going: do you fear that we shall bear
The palace with us? Its *old* walls, ten times
As *old* as I am, and I'm very old, 215
Have served you, so have I, and I and they
Could tell a tale; but I invoke them not
To fall upon you! else they would, as erst
The pillars of stone Dagon's temple on
The Israelite and his Philistine foes. 220
Such power I do believe there might exist
In such a curse as mine, provoked by such
As you; but I curse not. Adieu, good
 signors!
May the next duke be better than the
 present!
Lor. The *present* duke is Paschal
 Malipiero. 225
Doge. Not till I pass the threshold of
 these doors.
Lor. St. Mark's great bell is soon
 about to toll
For his inauguration.
Doge. Earth and heaven!
Ye will reverberate this peal; and I
Live to hear this!—the first Doge who e'er
 heard 230
Such sound for his successor: happier he,
My attainted predecessor, stern Faliero—
This insult at the least was spared him.

Lor. What!
Do you regret a traitor?
Doge. No—I merely
Envy the dead.
Chief of the Ten. My lord, if you
 indeed 235
Are bent upon this rash abandonment
Of the state's palace, at the least retire
By the private staircase, which conducts
 you towards
The landing-place of the canal.
Doge. No. I
Will now descend the stairs by which I
 mounted 240
To sovereignty—the Giants' Stairs, on
 whose
Broad eminence I was invested duke.
My services have called me up those steps,
The malice of my foes will drive me down
 them. 244
There five and thirty years ago was I
Install'd, and traversed these same halls,
 from which
I never thought to be divorced except
A corse—a corse, it might be, fighting for
 them—
But not push'd hence by fellow-citizens.
But come; my son and I will go together—
He to his grave, and I to pray for mine.
Chief of the Ten. What! thus in public?
Doge. I was publicly
Elected, and so will I be deposed.
Marina! art thou willing?
Mar. Here's my arm!
Doge. And here my *staff*: thus
 propp'd will I go forth. 255
Chief of the Ten. It must not be—the
 people will perceive it.
Doge. The people!—There's no
 people, you well know it,
Else you dare not deal thus by them or me.
There is a *populace*, perhaps, whose looks
May shame you; but they dare not groan
 nor curse you, 260
Save with their hearts and eyes.
Chief of the Ten. You speak in passion,
 Else——
Doge. You have reason. I have
 spoken much
More than my wont: it is a foible which
Was not of mine, but more excuses you,
Inasmuch as it shows that I approach
A dotage which may justify this deed
Of yours, although the law does not, nor
 will. 267
Farewell, sirs!
Bar. You shall not depart without
An escort fitting past and present rank.
We will accompany, with due respect,
The Doge unto his private palace. Say!
My brethren, will we not?
Different voices. Ay!—Ay!
Doge. You shall not
Stir—in my train, at least. I enter'd here

As sovereign—I go out as citizen
By the same portals, but as citizen. 275
All these vain ceremonies are base insults,
Which only ulcerate the heart the more,
Applying poisons there as antidotes.
Pomp is for princes—I am *none!*—That's
 false,
I *am*, but only to these gates.—Ah!
Lor. Hark! 280
 [*The great bell of St. Mark's tolls.*
Bar. The bell!
Chief of the Ten. St. Mark's, which
 tolls for the election
Of Malipiero.
Doge. Well I recognise
The sound! I heard it once, but once
 before,
And that is five and thirty years ago;
Even *then* I *was not young.*
Bar. Sit down, my lord! 285
You tremble.
Doge. 'Tis the knell of my poor boy!
My heart aches bitterly.
Bar. I pray you sit.
Doge. No; my seat here has been a
 throne till now.
Marina! let us go.
Mar. Most readily. 289
Doge [*walks a few steps, then stops*]. I
 feel athirst—will no one bring me here
A cup of water?
Bar. I——
Mar. And I——
Lor. And I——
 [*The Doge takes a goblet from the hand
 of* LOREDANO.
Doge. I take *yours*, Loredano, from
 the hand
Most fit for such an hour as this.
Lor. Why so?
Doge. 'Tis said that our Venetian
 crystal has 294
Such antipathy to poisons as
To burst, if aught of venom touches it.
You bore this goblet, and it is not broken.
Lor. Well, sir!
Doge. Then it is false, or you are true.
For my own part, I credit neither; 'tis
An idle legend.
Mar. You talk wildly, and 300
Had better now be seated, nor as yet
Depart. Ah! now you look as look'd my
 husband!
Bar. He sinks!—support him!—quick
 —a chair—support him!
Doge. The bell tolls on!—let's hence
 —my brain's on fire!
Bar. I do beseech you, lean upon us!
Doge. No! 305
A sovereign should die standing. My poor
 boy!—
Off with your arms!—*That bell!*
 [*The* DOGE *drops down and dies.*
Mar. My God! My God!

Bar. [*to Lor.*]. Behold! your work's
 completed!
Chief of the Ten. Is there then
No aid? Call in assistance!
Att. 'Tis all over.
Chief of the Ten. If it be so, at least his
 obsequies 310
Shall be such as befits his name and nation,
His rank and his devotion to the duties
Of the realm, while his age permitted him
To do himself and them full justice. Breth-
 ren,
Say, shall it not be so?
Bar. He has not had 315
The misery to die a subject where
He reign'd: then let his funeral rites be
 princely.
Chief of the Ten. We are agreed, then?
All, except Lor., answer. Yes.
Chief of the Ten. Heaven's peace be
 with him!
Mar. Signors, your pardon: this is
 mockery.
Juggle no more with that poor remnant,
 which, 320
A moment since, while yet it had a soul,
(A soul by whom you have increased your
 empire,
And made your power as proud as was his
 glory,)
You banish'd from his palace, and tore
 down
From his high place, with such relentless
 coldness; 325
And now, when he can neither know these
 honours,
Nor would accept them if he could, you,
 signors,
Purpose, with idle and superfluous pomp,
To make a pageant over what you
 trampled.
A princely funeral will be your reproach,
And not his honour. 331
Chief of the Ten. Lady, we revoke not
Our purposes so readily.
Mar. I know it,
As far as touches torturing the living.
I thought the dead had been beyond even
 you,
Though (some, no doubt) consign'd to
 powers which may 335
Resemble that you exercise on earth.
Leave him to me; you would have done so for
His dregs of life, which you have kindly
 shorten'd:
It is my last of duties, and may prove
A dreary comfort in my desolation. 340
Grief is fantastical, and loves the dead,
And the apparel of the grave.
Chief of the Ten. Do you
Pretend still to this office?
Mar. I do, signor.
Though his possessions have been all con-
 sumed

519

In the state's service, I have still my dowry, 345
Which shall be consecrated to his rites,
And those of——
[*She stops with agitation.*
Chief of the Ten. Best retain it for your children.
Mar. Ay, they are fatherless, I thank you.
Chief of the Ten. We Cannot comply with your request. His relics
Shall be exposed with wonted pomp, and follow'd 350
Unto their home by the new Doge, not clad
As *Doge*, but simply as a senator.
Mar. I have heard of murderers, who have interr'd
Their victims; but ne'er heard, until this hour,
Of so much splendour in hypocrisy 355
O'er those they slew. I've heard of widows' tears—
Alas! I have shed some—always thanks to you!
I've heard of *heirs* in sables—you have left none

To the deceased, so you would act the part
Of such. Well, sirs, your will be done! as one day, 360
I trust, Heaven's will be done too!
Chief of the Ten. Know you, lady,
To whom ye speak, and perils of such speech?
Mar. I know the former better than yourselves;
The latter—like yourselves; and can face both.
Wish you more funerals?
Bar. Heed not her rash words; 365
Her circumstances must excuse her bearing.
Chief of the Ten. We will not note them down.
Bar. [*turning to Lor., who is writing upon his tablets*]. What art thou writing,
With such an earnest brow, upon thy tablets?
Lor. [*pointing to the Doge's body*]. That *he* has paid me!
Chief of the Ten. What debt did he owe you?
Lor. A long and just one; Nature's debt and *mine*. 370
[*Curtain falls.*

CAIN

A MYSTERY

Now the Serpent was more subtil than any beast of the field which the LORD God had made.—*Gen.* iii. 1.

TO

SIR WALTER SCOTT, BART.,

THIS MYSTERY OF CAIN IS INSCRIBED,

BY HIS OBLIGED FRIEND AND FAITHFUL SERVANT,

THE AUTHOR.

PREFACE

THE following scenes are entitled 'A Mystery', in conformity with the ancient title annexed to dramas upon similar subjects, which were styled 'Mysteries, or Moralities'. The author has by no means taken the same liberties with his subject which were common formerly, as may be seen by any reader curious enough to refer to those very profane productions, whether in English, French, Italian, or Spanish. The author has endeavoured to preserve the language adapted to his characters; and where it is (and this is but rarely) taken from actual *Scripture*, he has made as little alteration, even of words, as the rhythm would permit. The reader will recollect that the book of Genesis does not state that Eve was tempted by a demon, but by 'the Serpent'; and that only because he was 'the most subtil of all the beasts of the field'. Whatever interpretation the Rabbins and the Fathers may have put upon this, I take the words as I find them, and reply, with Bishop Watson upon similar occasions, when the Fathers were quoted to him, as Moderator in the schools of Cambridge, 'Behold the Book!' —holding up the Scripture. It is to be recollected, that my present subject has nothing to do with the *New Testament*, to which no reference can be here made without anachronism. With the poems upon similar topics I have not been recently familiar. Since I was twenty I have never read Milton; but I had read him so frequently before, that this may make little difference. Gesner's 'Death of Abel' I have never read since I was eight years of age, at Aberdeen. The general impression of my recollection is delight; but of the contents I remember only that Cain's wife was called Mahala, and Abel's Thirza; in the following pages I have called them 'Adah' and 'Zillah', the earliest female names which occur in Genesis; they were those of Lamech's wives: those of Cain and Abel are not called by their names. Whether, then, a coincidence of subject may have caused the same in expression, I know nothing, and care as little.

The reader will please to bear in mind (what few choose to recollect), that there is no allusion to a future state in any of the books of Moses, nor indeed in the Old Testament. For a reason for this extraordinary omission he may consult Warburton's 'Divine Legation'; whether satisfactory or not, no better has yet been assigned. I have therefore supposed it new to Cain, without, I hope, any perversion of Holy Writ.

With regard to the language of Lucifer, it was difficult for me to make him talk like a clergyman upon the same subjects; but I have done what I could to restrain him within the bounds of spiritual politeness. If he disclaims having tempted Eve in the shape of the Serpent, it is only because the book of Genesis has not the most distant allusion to anything of the kind, but merely to the Serpent in his serpentine capacity.

Note.—The reader will perceive that the author has partly adopted in this poem the notion of Cuvier, that the world had been destroyed several times before the creation of man. This speculation, derived from the different strata and the bones of enormous and unknown animals found in them, is not contrary to the Mosaic account, but rather confirms it; as no human bones have yet been discovered in those strata, although those of many known animals are found near the remains of the unknown. The assertion of Lucifer, that the pre-Adamite world was also peopled by rational beings much more intelligent than man, and proportionally powerful to the mammoth, &c., &c., is, of course, a poetical fiction to help him to make out his case.

I ought to add, that there is a 'tramelogedia' of Alfieri, called 'Abele'. I have never read that, nor any other of the posthumous works of the writer, except his Life.

RAVENNA, *Sept.* 20, 1821.

DRAMATIS PERSONÆ

MEN	WOMEN	SPIRITS
ADAM	EVE	ANGEL OF THE LORD
CAIN	ADAH	LUCIFER
ABEL	ZILLAH	

ACT I

SCENE I.—*The Land without Paradise.—
Time, Sunrise.*

ADAM, EVE, CAIN, ABEL, ADAH, ZILLAH,
offering a Sacrifice.

Adam. God, the Eternal! Infinite!
 All-wise!—
Who out of darkness on the deep didst
 make
Light on the waters with a word—all hail!
Jehovah, with returning light, all hail!
 Eve. God! who didst name the day,
 and separate 5
Morning from night, till then divided
 never—
Who didst divide the wave from wave, and
 call
Part of thy work the firmament—all hail!
 Abel. God! who didst call the elements
 into
Earth, ocean, air, and fire, and with the
 day 10
And night, and worlds which these
 illuminate,
Or shadow, madest beings to enjoy them,
And love both them and thee—all hail!
 all hail!
 Adah. God, the Eternal! Parent of all
 things!
Who didst create these best and beauteous
 beings, 15
To be beloved, more than all, save thee—
Let me love thee and them:—All hail! all
 hail!
 Zillah. Oh, God! who loving, making,
 blessing all,

Yet didst permit the serpent to creep in,
And drive my father forth from Paradise,
Keep us from further evil:—Hail! all hail!
 Adam. Son Cain, my first-born,
 wherefore art thou silent? 22
 Cain. Why should I speak?
 Adam. To pray.
 Cain. Have ye not pray'd?
 Adam. We have, most fervently.
 Cain. And loudly: I
Have heard you.
 Adam. So will God, I trust.
 Abel. Amen! 25
 Adam. But thou, my eldest born, art
 silent still.
 Cain. 'Tis better I should be so.
 Adam. Wherefore so?
 Cain. I have nought to ask.
 Adam. Nor aught to thank for!
 Cain. No.
 Adam. Dost thou not live?
 Cain. Must I not die?
 Eve. Alas!
The fruit of our forbidden tree begins 30
To fall.
 Adam. And we must gather it again.
Oh, God! why didst thou plant the tree of
 knowledge?
 Cain. And wherefore pluck'd ye not
 the tree of life?
Ye might have then defied him.
 Adam. Oh! my son,
Blaspheme not: these are serpent's words.
 Cain. Why not? 35
The snake spoke *truth*; it *was* the tree of
 knowledge;
It *was* the tree of life; knowledge is good,
And life is good; and how can both be evil?

Eve. My boy! thou speakest as I
 spoke, in sin, 39
Before thy birth: let me not see renew'd
My misery in thine. I have repented.
Let me not see my offspring fall into
The snares beyond the walls of Paradise,
Which e'en in Paradise destroy'd his
 parents.
Content thee with what *is*. Had we been
 so, 45
Thou now hadst been contented.—Oh,
 my son!
Adam. Our orisons completed, let us
 hence,
Each to his task of toil—not heavy,
 though
Needful: the earth is young, and yields us
 kindly
Her fruits with little labour.
Eve. Cain, my son, 50
Behold thy father cheerful and resign'd,
And do as he doth.
 [Exeunt ADAM *and* EVE.
Zillah. Wilt thou not, my brother?
Abel. Why wilt thou wear this gloom
 upon thy brow,
Which can avail thee nothing, save to
 rouse
The Eternal anger?
Adah. My beloved Cain, 55
Wilt thou frown even on me?
Cain. No, Adah! no;
I fain would be alone a little while.
Abel, I'm sick at heart; but it will pass;
Precede me, brother—I will follow
 shortly. 59
And you, too, sisters, tarry not behind:
Your gentleness must not be harshly met;
I'll follow you anon.
Adah. If not, I will
Return to seek you here.
Abel. The peace of God
Be on your spirit, brother!
 [Exeunt ABEL, ZILLAH, *and* ADAH.
Cain [*solus*]. And this is
Life!—Toil! and wherefore should I toil?
 —because 65
My father could not keep his place in
 Eden.
What had *I* done in this?—I was unborn:
I sought not to be born; nor love the state
To which that birth has brought me. Why
 did he
Yield to the serpent and the woman? or,
Yielding, why suffer? What was there in
 this? 71
The tree was planted, and why not for him?
If not, why place him near it, where it
 grew,
The fairest in the centre? They have but
One answer to all questions, ''Twas *his*
 will, 75
And *he* is good.' How know I that? Be-
 cause

He is all-powerful, must all-good, too
 follow?
I judge but by the fruits—and they are
 bitter—
Which I must feed on for a fault not mine.
Whom have we here?—A shape like to
 the angels, 80
Yet of a sterner and a sadder aspect
Of spiritual essence: why do I quake?
Why should I fear him more than other
 spirits,
Whom I see daily wave their fiery swords
Before the gates round which I linger oft
In twilight's hour, to catch a glimpse of
 those 86
Gardens which are my just inheritance,
Ere the night closes o'er the inhibited wall
And the immortal trees which overtop
The cherubim-defended battlements?
If I shrink not from these, the fire-arm'd
 angels, 91
Why should I quail from him who now
 approaches?
Yet he seems mightier far than them, nor
 less
Beauteous, and yet not all as beautiful
As he hath been, and might be: sorrow
 seems 95
Half of his immortality. And is it
So? and can aught grieve save humanity?
He cometh.

 Enter LUCIFER.

Lucifer. Mortal!
Cain. Spirit, who art thou?
Lucifer. Master of Spirits.
Cain. And being so, canst thou
Leave them, and walk with dust?
Lucifer. I know the thoughts 100
Of dust, and feel for it, and with you.
Cain. How!
You know my thoughts?
Lucifer. They are the thoughts of all
Worthy of thought;—'tis your immortal
 part
Which speaks within you.
Cain. What immortal part?
This has not been reveal'd: the tree of life
Was withheld from us by my father's
 folly, 106
While that of knowledge, by my mother's
 haste,
Was pluck'd too soon; and all the fruit is
 death!
Lucifer. They have deceived thee;
 thou shalt live.
Cain. I live,
But live to die; and, living, see no thing
To make death hateful, save an innate
 clinging, 111
A loathsome, and yet all invincible
Instinct of life, which I abhor, as I
Despise myself, yet cannot overcome—
And so I live. Would I had never lived!

Lucifer. Thou livest, and must live
for ever: think not 116
The earth, which is thine outward
cov'ring, is
Existence—it will cease, and thou wilt be
No less than thou art now.
Cain. No *less!* and why
No more?
Lucifer. It may be thou shalt be as we.
Cain. And ye?
Lucifer. Are everlasting.
Cain. Are ye happy? 121
Lucifer. We are mighty.
Cain. Are ye happy?
Lucifer. No: art thou?
Cain. How should I be so? Look on
me!
Lucifer. Poor clay!
And thou pretendest to be wretched!
Thou!
Cain. I am:—and thou, with all thy
might, what art thou? 125
Lucifer. One who aspired to be what
made thee, and
Would not have made thee what thou art.
Cain. Ah!
Thou look'st almost a god; and——
Lucifer. I am none:
And having fail'd to be one, would be
nought
Save what I am. He conquer'd; let him
reign! 130
Cain. Who?
Lucifer. Thy sire's Maker, and the
earth's.
Cain. And heaven's,
And all that in them is. So I have heard
His seraphs sing; and so my father saith.
Lucifer. They say—what they must
sing and say, on pain 134
Of being that which I am—and thou art—
Of spirits and of men.
Cain. And what is that?
Lucifer. Souls who dare use their im-
mortality—
Souls who dare look the Omnipotent
tyrant in
His everlasting face, and tell him that
His evil is not good! If he has made, 140
As he saith—which I know not, nor
believe—
But, if he made us—he cannot unmake:
We are immortal! nay, he'd *have* us so,
That he may torture:—let him! He is
great—
But, in his greatness, is no happier than
We in our conflict: Goodness would not
make 146
Evil; and what else hath he made? But
let him
Sit on his vast and solitary throne,
Creating worlds, to make eternity
Less burthensome to his immense
existence 150

And unparticipated solitude;
Let him crowd orb on orb: he is alone
Indefinite, indissoluble tyrant;
Could he but crush himself, 'twere the best
boon
He ever granted: but let him reign on,
And multiply himself in misery! 156
Spirits and Men, at least we sympathise—
And, suffering in concert, make our pangs
Innumerable more endurable,
By the unbounded sympathy of all 160
With all! But *He!* so wretched in his
height,
So restless in his wretchedness, must still
Create, and re-create—— *
Cain. Thou speak'st to me of things
which long have swum
In visions through my thought: I never
could 165
Reconcile what I saw with what I heard.
My father and my mother talk to me
Of serpents, and of fruits and trees: I see
The gates of what they call their Paradise
Guarded by fiery-sworded cherubim,
Which shut them out and me; I feel the
weight 171
Of daily toil, and constant thought: I look
Around a world where I seem nothing,
with
Thoughts which arise within me, as if they
Could master all things—but I thought
alone 175
This misery was *mine.* My father is
Tamed down; my mother has forgot the
mind
Which made her thirst for knowledge at
the risk
Of an eternal curse; my brother is 179
A watching shepherd boy, who offers up
The firstlings of the flock to him who bids
The earth yield nothing to us without
sweat;
My sister Zillah sings an earlier hymn
Than the birds' matins; and my Adah, my
Own and beloved, she, too, understands
not 185
The mind which overwhelms me: never till
Now met I aught to sympathise with me.
'Tis well—I rather would consort with
spirits.
Lucifer. And hadst thou not been fit
by thine own soul
For such companionship, I would not
now 190
Have stood before thee as I am: a serpent
Had been enough to charm ye, as before.
Cain. Ah! didst *thou* tempt my
mother?
Lucifer. I tempt none,
Save with the truth: was not the tree the tree
Of knowledge? and was not the tree of life
Still fruitful? Did *I* bid her pluck them
not? 196

* [See reviser's Note, p. x.]

Did *I* plant things prohibited within
The reach of beings innocent, and curious
By their own innocence? I would have
 made ye
Gods; and even He who thrust ye forth, so
 thrust ye 200
Because 'ye should not eat the fruits of
 life,
And become gods as we.' Were those his
 words?
 Cain. They were, as I have heard from
 those who heard them,
In thunder.
 Lucifer. Then who was the demon? He
Who would not let ye live, or he who
 would 205
Have made ye live for ever in the joy
And power of knowledge?
 Cain. Would they had snatch'd both
The fruits, or neither!
 Lucifer. One is yours already,
The other may be still.
 Cain. How so?
 Lucifer. By being
Yourselves, in your resistance. Nothing
 can 210
Quench the mind, if the mind will be itself
And centre of surrounding things—'tis
 made
To sway.
 Cain. But didst thou tempt my
 parents?
 Lucifer. I?
Poor clay! what should I tempt them for,
 or how?
 Cain. They say the serpent was a
 spirit. 215
 Lucifer. Who
Saith that? It is not written so on high:
The proud One will not so far falsify,
Though man's vast fears and little vanity
Would make him cast upon the spiritual
 nature
His own low failing. The snake *was* the
 snake— 220
No more; and yet not less than those he
 tempted,
In nature being earth also—*more* in
 wisdom,
Since he could overcome them, and fore-
 knew
The knowledge fatal to their narrow joys.
Think'st thou I'd take the shape of things
 that die? 225
 Cain. But the thing had a demon?
 Lucifer. He but woke one
In those he spake to with his forky tongue.
I tell thee that the serpent was no more
Than a mere serpent: ask the cherubim
Who guard the tempting tree. When thou-
 sand ages 230
Have roll'd o'er your dead ashes, and
 your seed's,
The seed of the then world may thus array

Their earliest fault in fable, and attribute
To me a shape I scorn, as I scorn all
That bows to him, who made things but to
 bend 235
Before his sullen, sole eternity;
But we, who see the truth, must speak it. Thy
Fond parents listen'd to a creeping thing,
And fell. For what should spirits tempt
 them? What
Was there to envy in the narrow bounds
Of Paradise, that spirits who pervade 240
Space——but I speak to thee of what
 thou know'st not,
With all thy tree of knowledge.
 Cain. But thou canst not
Speak aught of knowledge which I would
 not know,
And do not thirst to know, and bear a
 mind 245
To know.
 Lucifer. And heart to look on?
 Cain. Be it proved.
 Lucifer. Darest thou look on Death?
 Cain. He has not yet
Been seen.
 Lucifer. But must be undergone.
 Cain. My father
Says he is something dreadful, and my
 mother
Weeps when he's named; and Abel lifts
 his eyes 250
To heaven, and Zillah casts hers to the
 earth,
And sighs a prayer; and Adah looks on
 me,
And speaks not.
 Lucifer. And thou?
 Cain. Thoughts unspeakable
Crowd in my breast to burning, when I
 hear 254
Of this almighty Death, who is, it seems,
Inevitable. Could I wrestle with him?
I wrestled with the lion, when a boy,
In play, till he ran roaring from my gripe.
 Lucifer. It has no shape; but will
 absorb all things
That bear the form of earth-born being.
 Cain. Ah! 260
I thought it was a being: who could do
Such evil things to beings save a being?
 Lucifer. Ask the Destroyer.
 Cain. Who?
 Lucifer. The Maker—call him
Which name thou wilt: he makes but to
 destroy.
 Cain. I knew not that, yet thought it,
 since I heard 265
Of Death: although I know not what it is,
Yet it seems horrible. I have look'd out
In the vast desolate night in search of him,
And when I saw gigantic shadows in
The umbrage of the walls of Eden,
 chequer'd 270

By the far-flashing of the cherubs' swords,
I watch'd for what I thought his coming:
 for
With fear rose longing in my heart to know
What 'twas which shook us all—but
 nothing came. 274
And then I turn'd my weary eyes from off
Our native and forbidden Paradise,
Up to the lights above us, in the azure,
Which are so beautiful: shall they, too,
 die?
 Lucifer. Perhaps—but long outlive
 both thine and thee.
 Cain. I'm glad of that: I would not
 have them die—
They are so lovely. What is death? I fear,
I feel, it is a dreadful thing; but what,
I cannot compass: 'tis denounced against
 us,
Both them who sinn'd and sinn'd not, as
 an ill— 284
What ill?
 Lucifer. To be resolved into the earth.
 Cain. But shall I know it?
 Lucifer. As I know not death,
I cannot answer.
 Cain. Were I quiet earth,
That were no evil: would I ne'er had been
Aught else but dust!
 Lucifer. That is a grovelling wish,
Less than thy father's, for he wish'd to
 know. 290
 Cain. But not to live, or wherefore
 pluck'd he not
The life-tree?
 Lucifer. He was hinder'd.
 Cain. Deadly error!
Not to snatch first that fruit:—but ere he
 pluck'd
The knowledge, he was ignorant of death.
Alas! I scarcely now know what it is, 295
And yet I fear it—fear I know not what!
 Lucifer. And I, who know all things,
 fear nothing; see
What is true knowledge.
 Cain. Wilt thou teach me all?
 Lucifer. Ay, upon one condition.
 Cain. Name it.
 Lucifer. That
Thou dost fall down and worship me—
 thy Lord. 300
 Cain. Thou art not the Lord my father
 worships.
 Lucifer. No.
 Cain. His equal?
 Lucifer. No;—I have nought
 in common with him!
Nor would: I would be aught above—
 beneath—
Aught save a sharer or a servant of
His power. I dwell apart; but I am great:—
Many there are who worship me, and
 more 306
Who shall—be thou amongst the first.

 Cain. I never
As yet have bow'd unto my father's God,
Although my brother Abel oft implores
That I would join with him in sacrifice:—
Why should I bow to thee?
 Lucifer. Hast thou ne'er bow'd 311
To him?
 Cain. Have I not said it?—need I say
 it?
Could not thy mighty knowledge teach
 thee that?
 Lucifer. He who bows not to him has
 bow'd to me.
 Cain. But I will bend to neither.
 Lucifer. Ne'er the less, 315
Thou art my worshipper; not worshipping
Him makes thee mine the same.
 Cain. And what is that?
 Lucifer. Thou'lt know here—and
 hereafter.
 Cain. Let me but
Be taught the mystery of my being.
 Lucifer. Follow
Where I will lead thee.
 Cain. But I must retire 320
To till the earth—for I had promised—
 Lucifer. What?
 Cain. To cull some first-fruits.
 Lucifer. Why?
 Cain. To offer up
With Abel on an altar.
 Lucifer. Said'st thou not
Thou ne'er hadst bent to him who made
 thee?
 Cain. Yes—
But Abel's earnest prayer has wrought
 upon me. 325
The offering is more his than mine—and
 Adah——
 Lucifer. Why dost thou hesitate?
 Cain. She is my sister,
Born on the same day, of the same womb:
 and
She wrung from me, with tears, this
 promise; and
Rather than see her weep, I would, me-
 thinks, 330
Bear all—and worship aught.
 Lucifer. Then follow me!
 Cain. I will.

 Enter ADAH.

 Adah. My brother, I have come for
 thee:
It is our hour of rest and joy—and we
Have less without thee. Thou hast
 labour'd not
This morn; but I have done thy task: the
 fruits 335
Are ripe, and glowing as the light which
 ripens:
Come away.
 Cain. Seest thou not?
 Adah. I see an angel;

We have seen many: will he share our
 hour
Of rest?—he is welcome.
 Cain. But he is not like
The angels we have seen.
 Adah. Are there, then, others? 340
But he is welcome, as they were: they
 deign'd
To be our guests—will he?
 Cain [*to Lucifer*]. Wilt thou?
 Lucifer. I ask
Thee to be mine.
 Cain. I must away with him.
 Adah. And leave us?
 Cain. Ay.
 Adah. And *me?*
 Cain. Beloved Adah!
 Adah. Let me go with thee.
 Lucifer. No, she must not.
 Adah. Who
Art thou that steppest between heart and
 heart? 346
 Cain. He is a god.
 Adah. How know'st thou?
 Cain. He speaks like
A god.
 Adah. So did the serpent, and it lied.
 Lucifer. Thou errest, Adah!—was not
 the tree that 349
Of knowledge?
 Adah. Ay—to our eternal sorrow.
 Lucifer. And yet that grief is know-
 ledge—so he lied not:
And if he did betray you, 'twas with truth;
And truth in its own essence cannot be
But good.
 Adah. But all we know of it has
 gather'd
Evil on ill; expulsion from our home,
And dread, and toil, and sweat, and heavi-
 ness; 356
Remorse of that which was—and hope of
 that
Which cometh not. Cain! walk not with
 this spirit.
Bear with what we have borne, and love
 me—I
Love thee.
 Lucifer. More than thy mother, and
 thy sire? 360
 Adah. I do. Is that a sin, too?
 Lucifer. No, not yet;
It one day will be in your children.
 Adah. What!
Must not my daughter love her brother
 Enoch?
 Lucifer. Not as thou lovest Cain.
 Adah. Oh, my God!
Shall they not love and bring forth things
 that love 365
Out of their love? have they not drawn
 their milk
Out of this bosom? was not he, their
 father,

Born of the same sole womb, in the same
 hour
With me? did we not love each other? and
In multiplying our being multiply 370
Things which will love each other as we
 love
Them?—And as I love thee, my Cain! go
 not
Forth with this spirit; he is not of ours.
 Lucifer. The sin I speak of is not of
 my making,
And cannot be a sin in you—whate'er
It seem in those who will replace ye in
Mortality.
 Adah. What is the sin which is not
Sin in itself? Can circumstance make sin
Or virtue?—if it doth, we are the slaves
Of——
 Lucifer. Higher things than ye are
 slaves: and higher 380
Than them or ye would be so, did they not
Prefer an independency of torture
To the smooth agonies of adulation,
In hymns and harpings, and self-seeking
 prayers,
To that which is omnipotent, because
It is omnipotent, and not from love, 385
But terror and self-hope.
 Adah. Omnipotence
Must be all goodness.
 Lucifer. Was it so in Eden?
 Adah. Fiend! tempt me not with
 beauty; thou art fairer
Than was the serpent, and as false.
 Lucifer. As true. 390
Ask Eve, your mother: bears she not the
 knowledge
Of good and evil?
 Adah. Oh, my mother! thou
Hast pluck'd a fruit more fatal to thine off-
 spring
Than to thyself; thou at the least hast
 pass'd
Thy youth in Paradise, in innocent 395
And happy intercourse with happy spirits:
But we, thy children, ignorant of Eden,
Are girt about by demons, who assume
The words of God, and tempt us with our
 own
Dissatisfied and curious thoughts—as
 thou 400
Wert work'd on by the snake, in thy most
 flush'd
And heedless, harmless wantonness of
 bliss.
I cannot answer this immortal thing
Which stands before me; I cannot abhor
 him; 404
I look upon him with a pleasing fear,
And yet I fly not from him: in his eye
There is a fastening attraction which
Fixes my fluttering eyes on his; my heart
Beats quick; he awes me, and yet draws
 me near,

Nearer and nearer:—Cain—Cain—save
 me from him! 410
 Cain. What dreads my Adah? This
 is no ill spirit.
 Adah. He is not God—nor God's: I
 have beheld
The cherubs and the seraphs; he looks not
Like them.
 Cain But there are spirits loftier
 still—
The archangels.
 Lucifer. And still loftier than the
 archangels. 415
 Adah. Ay—but not blessed.
 Lucifer. If the blessedness
Consists in slavery—no.
 Adah. I have heard it said,
The seraphs *love most*—cherubim *know
 most*—
And this should be a cherub—since he
 loves not.
 Lucifer. And if the higher knowledge
 quenches love, 420
What must *he be* you cannot love when
 known?
Since the all-knowing cherubim love
 least,
The seraphs' love can be but ignorance:
That they are not compatible, the doom
Of thy fond parents, for their daring,
 proves. 425
Choose betwixt love and knowledge—
 since there is
No other choice: your sire hath chosen
 already:
His worship is but fear.
 Adah. Oh, Cain! choose love.
 Cain. For thee, my Adah, I choose
 not—it was
Born with me—but I love nought else.
 Adah. Our parents?
 Cain. Did they love us when they
 snatch'd from the tree 431
That which hath driven us all from
 Paradise?
 Adah. We were not born then—and
 if we had been,
Should we not love them and our children,
 Cain?
 Cain. My little Enoch! and his lisping
 sister! 435
Could I but deem them happy, I would
 half
Forget——but it can never be forgotten
Through thrice a thousand generations!
 never
Shall men love the remembrance of the
 man
Who sow'd the seed of evil and mankind
In the same hour! They pluck'd the tree
 of science 441
And sin—and, not content with their own
 sorrow,
Begot *me*—*thee*—and all the few that are,

And all the unnumber'd and innumerable
Multitudes, millions, myriads, which may
 be, 445
To inherit agonies accumulated
By ages!—and *I* must be sire of such
 things!
Thy beauty and thy love—my love and joy,
The rapturous moment and the placid
 hour,
All we love in our children and each other,
But lead them and ourselves through many
 years 451
Of sin and pain—or few, but still of
 sorrow,
Intercheck'd with an instant of brief
 pleasure,
To Death—the unknown! Methinks the
 tree of knowledge
Hath not fulfill'd its promise:—if they
 sinn'd, 455
At least they ought to have known all
 things that are
Of knowledge—and the mystery of death.
What do they know?—that they are
 miserable.
What need of snakes and fruits to teach us
 that?
 Adah. I am not wretched, Cain, and if
 thou 460
Wert happy——
 Cain. Be thou happy, then,
 alone—
I will have nought to do with happiness,
Which humbles me and mine.
 Adah. Alone I could not,
Nor *would* be happy; but with those
 around us
I think I could be so, despite of death,
Which, as I know it not, I dread not,
 though 466
It seems an awful shadow—if I may
Judge from what I have heard.
 Lucifer. And thou couldst not
Alone, thou say'st, be happy?
 Adah. Alone! Oh, my God!
Who could be happy and alone, or good?
To me my solitude seems sin; unless 471
When I think how soon I shall see my
 brother,
His brother, and our children, and our
 parents.
 Lucifer. Yet thy God is alone; and is
 he happy,
Lonely, and good?
 Adah. He is not so; he hath 475
The angels and the mortals to make happy,
And thus becomes so in diffusing joy.
What else can joy be, but the spreading
 joy?
 Lucifer. Ask of your sire, the exile
 fresh from Eden;
Or of his first-born son: ask your own
 heart; 480
It is not tranquil.

Adah. Alas! no! and you—
Are you of heaven?
Lucifer. If I am not, inquire
The cause of this all-spreading happiness
(Which you proclaim) of the all-great and
good 484
Maker of life and living things; it is
His secret, and he keeps it. *We* must bear,
And some of us resist, and both in vain,
His seraphs say: but it is worth the trial,
Since better may not be without: there is
A wisdom in the spirit, which directs
To right, as in the dim blue air the eye
Of you, young mortals, lights at once upon
The star which watches, welcoming the
morn.
Adah. It is a beautiful star; I love it for
Its beauty.
Lucifer. And why not adore?
Adah. Our father
Adores the Invisible only.
Lucifer. But the symbols 496
Of the Invisible are the loveliest
Of what is visible; and yon bright star
Is leader of the host of heaven.
Adah. Our father
Saith that he has beheld the God himself
Who made him and our mother.
Lucifer. Hast *thou* seen him? 501
Adah. Yes—in his works.
Lucifer. But in his being?
Adah. No—
Save in my father, who is God's own
image;
Or in his angels, who are like to thee—
And brighter, yet less beautiful and
powerful 505
In seeming: as the silent sunny noon,
All light, they look upon us; but thou
seem'st
Like an ethereal night, where long white
clouds
Streak the deep purple, and unnumber'd
stars
Spangle the wonderful mysterious vault
With things that look as if they would be
suns; 511
So beautiful, unnumber'd, and endearing,
Not dazzling, and yet drawing us to them,
They fill my eyes with tears, and so dost
thou.
Thou seem'st unhappy: do not make us so,
And I will weep for thee.
Lucifer. Alas! those tears! 516
Couldst thou but know what oceans will
be shed—
Adah. By me?
Lucifer. By all.
Adah. What all?
Lucifer. The million millions—
The myriad myriads—the all-peopled
earth—
The unpeopled earth—and the o'er-
peopled hell, 520

Of which thy bosom is the germ.
Adah. O Cain!
This spirit curseth us.
Cain. Let him say on;
Him will I follow.
Adah. Whither?
Lucifer. To a place
Whence he shall come back to thee in an
hour;
But in that hour see things of many days.
Adah. How can that be? 52?
Lucifer. Did not your Maker make
Out of old worlds this new one in few days?
And cannot I, who aided in this work,
Show in an hour what he hath made in
many,
Or hath destroy'd in few?
Cain. Lead on.
Adah. Will he
In sooth, return within an hour?
Lucifer. He shall. 53?
With us acts are exempt from time, and we
Can crowd eternity into an hour,
Or stretch an hour into eternity:
We breathe not by a mortal measure-
ment— 535
But that's a mystery. Cain, come on with
me.
Adah. Will he return?
Lucifer. Ay, woman! he alone
Of mortals from that place (the first and
last
Who shall return, save ONE), shall come
back to thee,
To make that silent and expectant world
As populous as this: at present there 54?
Are few inhabitants.
Adah. Where dwellest thou?
Lucifer. Throughout all space. Where
should I dwell? Where are
Thy God or Gods—there am I: all things
are
Divided with me: life and death—and
time— 545
Eternity—and heaven and earth—and
that
Which is not heaven nor earth, but
peopled with
Those who once peopled or shall people
both—
These are my realms! So that I do divide
His, and possess a kingdom which is not
His. If I were not that which I have
said, 55?
Could I stand here? His angels are within
Your vision.
Adah. So they were when the fair
serpent
Spoke with our mother first.
Lucifer. Cain! thou hast heard
If thou dost long for knowledge, I can
satiate 555
That thirst; nor ask thee to partake of
fruits

Which shall deprive thee of a single good
The conqueror has left thee. Follow me.
 Cain. Spirit, I have said it.
 [*Exeunt* LUCIFER *and* CAIN.
Adah [*follows exclaiming*]. Cain! my
 brother! Cain!

ACT II

SCENE I.—*The Abyss of Space.*

 Cain. I tread on air, and sink not; yet
 I fear
To sink.
 Lucifer. Have faith in me, and thou
 shalt be
Borne on the air, of which I am the prince.
 Cain. Can I do so without impiety?
 Lucifer. Believe—and sink not!
 doubt—and perish! thus 5
Would run the edict of the other God,
Who names me demon to his angels; they
Echo the sound to miserable things,
Which, knowing nought beyond their
 shallow senses,
Worship the word which strikes their ear,
 and deem 10
Evil or good what is proclaim'd to them
In their abasement. I will have none such:
Worship or worship not, thou shalt behold
The worlds beyond thy little world, nor be
Amerced for doubts beyond thy little life,
With torture of *my* dooming. There will
 come . 16
An hour, when, toss'd upon some water-
 drops,
A man shall say to a man, 'Believe in me,
And walk the waters;' and the man shall
 walk
The billows and be safe. *I* will not say,
Believe in *me*, as a conditional creed 21
To save thee; but fly with me o'er the gulf
Of space an equal flight, and I will show
What thou dar'st not deny,—the history
Of past, and present, and of future worlds.
 Cain. Oh, god, or demon, or whate'er
 thou art, 26
Is yon our earth?
 Lucifer. Dost thou not recognise
The dust which form'd your father?
 Cain. Can it be?
Yon small blue circle, swinging in far
 ether,
With an inferior circlet near it still, 30
Which looks like that which lit our earthly
 night?
Is this our Paradise? Where are its walls,
And they who guard them?
 Lucifer. Point me out the site
Of Paradise.
 Cain. How should I? As we move
Like sunbeams onward, it grows small and
 smaller, 35
And as it waxes little, and then less,
Gathers a halo round it, like the light

Which shone the roundest of the stars,
 when I
Beheld them from the skirts of Paradise:
Methinks they both, as we recede from
 them, 40
Appear to join the innumerable stars
Which are around us; and, as we move on,
Increase their myriads.
 Lucifer. And if there should be
Worlds greater than thine own, inhabited
By greater things, and they themselves far
 more 45
In number than the dust of thy dull earth,
Though multiplied to animated atoms,
All living, and all doom'd to death, and
 wretched,
What wouldst thou think?
 Cain. I should be proud of thought
Which knew such things.
 Lucifer. But if that high thought were
Link'd to a servile mass of matter, and,
Knowing such things, aspiring to such
 things, 52
And science still beyond them, were
 chain'd down
To the most gross and petty paltry wants,
All foul and fulsome, and the very best
Of thine enjoyments a sweet degradation,
A most enervating and filthy cheat
To lure thee on to the renewal of
Fresh souls and bodies, all foredoom'd to be
As frail, and few so happy——
 Cain. Spirit! I 60
Know nought of death, save as a dreadful
 thing
Of which I have heard my parents speak,
 as of
A hideous heritage I owe to them
No less than life; a heritage not happy,
If I may judge, till now. But, spirit! if
It be as thou hast said (and I within 66
Feel the prophetic torture of its truth),
Here let me die: for to give birth to those
Who can but suffer many years, and die,
Methinks is merely propagating death,
And multiplying murder.
 Lucifer. Thou canst not 71
All die—there is what must survive.
 Cain. The Other
Spake not of this unto my father, when
He shut him forth from Paradise, with
 death 74
Written upon his forehead. But at least
Let what is mortal of me perish, that
I may be in the rest as angels are.
 Lucifer. I am angelic: wouldst thou be
 as I am?
 Cain. I know not what thou art: I see
 thy power,
And see thou show'st me things beyond
 my power, 80
Beyond all power of my born faculties,
Although inferior still to my desires
And my conceptions.

Lucifer. What are they which dwell
So humbly in their pride, as to sojourn
With worms in clay?
Cain. And what art thou who dwellest
So haughtily in spirit, and canst range
Nature and immortality—and yet 87
Seem'st sorrowful?
Lucifer. I seem that which I am;
And therefore do I ask of thee, if thou
Wouldst be immortal?
Cain. Thou hast said, I must be 90
Immortal in despite of me. I knew not
This until lately—but since it must be,
Let me, or happy or unhappy, learn
To anticipate my immortality.
Lucifer. Thou didst before I came
 upon thee.
Cain. How? 95
Lucifer. By suffering.
Cain. And must torture be immortal?
Lucifer. We and thy sons will try.
 But now, behold!
Is it not glorious?
Cain. Oh, thou beautiful
And unimaginable ether! and 100
Ye multiplying masses of increased
And still increasing lights! what are ye?
 what
Is this blue wilderness of interminable
Air, where ye roll along, as I have seen
The leaves along the limpid streams of
 Eden? 104
Is your course measured for ye? Or do ye
Sweep on in your unbounded revelry
Through an aërial universe of endless
Expansion—at which my soul aches to
 think—
Intoxicated with eternity? 109
Oh God! Oh Gods! or whatsoe'er ye are!
How beautiful ye are! how beautiful
Your works, or accidents, or whatsoe'er
They may be! Let me die, as atoms die
(If that they die), or know ye in your might
And knowledge! My thoughts are not in
 this hour 115
Unworthy what I see, though my dust is;
Spirit! let me expire, or see them nearer.
Lucifer. Art thou not nearer? look
 back to thine earth!
Cain. Where is it? I see nothing save a mass
Of most innumerable lights.
Lucifer. Look there! 120
Cain. I cannot see it.
Lucifer. Yet it sparkles still.
Cain. That!—yonder!
Lucifer. Yea.
Cain. And wilt thou tell me so?
Why, I have seen the fire-flies and fire-
 worms
Sprinkle the dusky groves and the green
 banks
In the dim twilight, brighter than yon
 world 125
Which bears them.

Lucifer. Thou hast seen both worms
 and worlds,
Each bright and sparkling—what dost
 think of them?
Cain. That they are beautiful in their
 own sphere,
And that the night, which makes both
 beautiful,
The little shining fire-fly in its flight, 130
And the immortal star in its great course,
Must both be guided.
Lucifer. But by whom or what?
Cain. Show me.
Lucifer. Dar'st thou behold?
Cain. How know I what
I dare behold? As yet, thou hast shown
 nought
I dare not gaze on further.
Lucifer. On, then, with me. 135
Wouldst thou behold things mortal or
 immortal?
Cain. Why, what are things?
Lucifer. Both partly: but what doth
Sit next thy heart?
Cain. The things I see.
Lucifer. But what
Sate nearest it?
Cain. The things I have not seen,
Nor ever shall—the mysteries of death.
Lucifer. What, if I show to thee things
 which have died, 141
As I have shown thee much which cannot
 die?
Cain. Do so.
Lucifer. Away, then! on our mighty
 wings.
Cain. Oh! how we cleave the blue!
The stars fade from us!
The earth! where is my earth? Let me
 look on it, 145
For I was made of it.
Lucifer. 'Tis now beyond thee,
Less, in the universe, than thou in it;
Yet deem not that thou canst escape it; thou
Shalt soon return to earth, and all its dust:
'Tis part of thy eternity, and mine. 150
Cain. Where dost thou lead me?
Lucifer. To what was before thee!
The phantasm of the world; of which thy
 world
Is but the wreck.
Cain. What! is it not then new?
Lucifer. No more than life is; and that
 was ere thou 154
Or I were, or the things which seem to us
Greater than either: many things will have
No end; and some, which would pretend
 to have
Had no beginning, have had one as mean
As thou; and mightier things have been
 extinct
To make way for much meaner than we
 can 160

Surmise; for *moments* only and the *space*
Have been and must be all *unchangeable.*
But changes make not death, except to
 clay;
But thou art clay—and canst but com-
 prehend
That which was clay, and such thou shalt
 behold. 165
 Cain. Clay, spirit! what thou wilt, I
 can survey.
 Lucifer. Away, then!
 Cain. But the lights fade from me fast,
And some till now grew larger as we
 approach'd,
And wore the look of worlds.
 Lucifer. And such they are.
 Cain. And Edens in them?
 Lucifer. It may be.
 Cain. And men? 170
 Lucifer. Yea, or things higher.
 Cain. Ay? and serpents too?
 Lucifer. Wouldst thou have men with-
 out them? must no reptiles
Breathe, save the erect ones?
 Cain. How the lights recede!
Where fly we?
 Lucifer. To the world of phantoms,
 which 174
Are beings past, and shadows still to come.
 Cain. But it grows dark, and dark—
 the stars are gone!
 Lucifer. And yet thou seest.
 Cain. 'Tis a fearful light!
No sun, no moon, no lights innumerable.
The very blue of the empurpled night
Fades to a dreary twilight, yet I see 180
Huge dusky masses; but unlike the worlds
We were approaching, which, begirt with
 light,
Seem'd full of life even when their
 atmosphere
Of light gave way, and show'd them taking
 shapes
Unequal, of deep valleys and vast moun-
 tains; 185
And some emitting sparks, and some dis-
 playing
Enormous liquid plains, and some begirt
With luminous belts, and floating moons,
 which took,
Like them, the features of fair earth:—
 instead,
All here seems dark and dreadful.
 Lucifer. But distinct.
Thou seekest to behold death, and dead
 things? 191
 Cain. I seek it not; but as I know there
 are
Such, and that my sire's sin makes him and
 me,
And all that we inherit, liable
To such, I would behold at once, what I
Must one day see perforce.
 Lucifer. Behold!

 Cain. 'Tis darkness. 196
 Lucifer. And so it shall be ever; but
 we will
Unfold its gates!
 Cain. Enormous vapours roll
Apart—what's this?
 Lucifer. Enter!
 Cain. Can I return?
 Lucifer. Return! be sure: how else
 should death be peopled? 200
Its present realm is thin to what it will be
Through thee and thine.
 Cain. The clouds still open wide
And wider, and make widening circles
 round us.
 Lucifer. Advance!
 Cain. And thou!
 Lucifer. Fear not—without me thou
Couldst not have gone beyond thy world.
On! on! 205
 [*They disappear through the clouds.*

SCENE II.—*Hades.*

Enter LUCIFER *and* CAIN.

 Cain. How silent and how vast are
 these dim worlds!
For they seem more than one, and yet
 more peopled
Than the huge brilliant luminous orbs
 which swung
So thickly in the upper air, that I
Had deem'd them rather the bright
 populace 5
Of some all unimaginable Heaven,
Than things to be inhabited themselves,
But that on drawing near them I beheld
Their swelling into palpable immensity
Of matter, which seem'd made for life to
 dwell on, 10
Rather than life itself. But here, all is
So shadowy, and so full of twilight, that
It speaks of a day past.
 Lucifer. It is the realm
Of death.—Wouldst have it present?
 Cain. Till I know 14
That which it really is, I cannot answer.
But if it be as I have heard my father
Deal out in his long homilies, 'tis a thing—
Oh God! I dare not think on 't! Cursed be
He who invented life that leads to death!
Or the dull mass of life, that, being life,
Could not retain, but needs must forfeit it—
Even for the innocent!
 Lucifer. Dost thou curse thy father?
 Cain. Cursed he not me in giving me
 my birth?
Cursed he not me before my birth, in
 daring
To pluck the fruit forbidden?
 Lucifer. Thou say'st well: 25
The curse is mutual 'twixt thy sire and
 thee—
But for thy sons and brother?

Cain. Let them share it
With me, their sire and brother! What
 else is
Bequeath'd to me? I leave them my
 inheritance.
Oh, ye interminable gloomy realms 30
Of swimming shadows and enormous
 shapes,
Some fully shown, some indistinct, and all
Mighty and melancholy—what are ye?
Live ye, or have ye lived?
Lucifer. Somewhat of both.
Cain. Then what is death?
Lucifer. What! Hath not he who
 made ye 35
Said 'tis another life?
Cain. Till now he hath
Said nothing, save that all shall die.
Lucifer. Perhaps
He one day will unfold that further secret.
Cain. Happy the day!
Lucifer. Yes; happy! when unfolded,
Through agonies unspeakable, and
 clogg'd 40
With agonies eternal, to innumerable
Yet unborn myriads of unconscious
 atoms,
All to be animated for this only!
Cain. What are these mighty
 phantoms which I see
Floating around me?—They wear not the
 form 45
Of the intelligences I have seen
Round our regretted and unenter'd Eden,
Nor wear the form of man as I have view'd
 it
In Adam's and in Abel's, and in mine,
Nor in my sister-bride's, nor in my
 children's: 50
And yet they have an aspect, which,
 though not
Of men nor angels, looks like something
 which,
If not the last, rose higher than the first,
Haughty, and high, and beautiful, and
 full
Of seeming strength, but of inexplicable
Shape; for I never saw such. They bear
 not 56
The wing of seraph, nor the face of man,
Nor form of mightiest brute, nor aught
 that is
Now breathing; mighty yet and beautiful
As the most beautiful and mighty which
Live, and yet so unlike them, that I scarce
Can call them living.
Lucifer. Yet they lived.
Cain. Where?
Lucifer. Where
Thou livest.
Cain. When?
Lucifer. On what thou callest earth
They did inhabit.
Cain. Adam is the first.

Lucifer. Of thine, I grant thee—but too
 mean to be 6
The last of these.
Cain. And what are they?
Lucifer. That which
Thou shalt be.
Cain. But what *were* they?
Lucifer. Living, high
Intelligent, good, great, and glorious
 things,
As much superior unto all thy sire, 6
Adam, could e'er have been in Eden, as
The sixty-thousandth generation shall be
In its dull damp degeneracy, to
Thee and thy son;—and how weak the
 are, judge
By thy own flesh.
Cain. Ah me! and did *they* perish
Lucifer. Yes, from their earth, as thou
 wilt fade from thine. 7
Cain. But was *mine* theirs?
Lucifer. It was.
Cain. But not as now
It is too little and too lowly to
Sustain such creatures.
Lucifer. True, it was more glorious
Cain. And wherefore did it fall?
Lucifer. Ask him who fells
Cain. But how?
Lucifer. By a most crushing an
 inexorable 8
Destruction and disorder of the elements
Which struck a world to chaos, as a chaos
Subsiding has struck out a world: such
 things,
Though rare in time, are frequent i
 eternity.—
Pass on, and gaze upon the past.
Cain. 'Tis awful! 8
Lucifer. And true. Behold these
 phantoms! they were once
Material as thou art.
Cain. And must I b
Like them?
Lucifer. Let Him who made the
 answer that.
I show thee what thy predecessors are,
And what they *were* thou feelest, in degre
Inferior as thy petty feelings and 9
Thy pettier portion of the immortal pa
Of high intelligence and earthly strength
What ye in common have with what the
 had
Is life, and what ye *shall* have—death: th
 rest 9
Of your poor attributes is such as suits
Reptiles engender'd out of the subsiding
Slime of a mighty universe, crush'd into
A scarcely-yet shaped planet, peopled wit
Things whose enjoyment was to be i
 blindness— 10
A Paradise of Ignorance, from which
Knowledge was barr'd as poison. Bu
 behold

What these superior beings are or were;
Or, if it irk thee, turn thee back and till
The earth, thy task—I'll waft thee there
 in safety. 105
 Cain. No: I'll stay here.
 Lucifer. How long?
 Cain. For ever! Since
I must one day return here from the earth,
I rather would remain; I am sick of all
That dust has shown me—let me dwell in
 shadows.
 Lucifer. It cannot be: thou now
 beholdest as 110
A vision that which is reality.
To make thyself fit for this dwelling, thou
Must pass through what the things thou
 see'st have pass'd—
The gates of death.
 Cain. By what gate have we enter'd
Even now?
 Lucifer. By mine! But, plighted to
 return, 115
My spirit buoys thee up to breathe in
 regions
Where all is breathless save thyself. Gaze
 on;
But do not think to dwell here till thine
 hour
Is come.
 Cain. And these, too; can they ne'er
 repass
To earth again?
 Lucifer. Their earth is gone for ever—
So changed by its convulsion, they would
 not 121
Be conscious to a single present spot
Of its new scarcely harden'd surface—
 'twas—
Oh, what a beautiful world it *was!*
 Cain. And is.
It is not with the earth, though I must till it,
I feel at war, but that I may not profit 126
By what it bears of beautiful, untoiling,
Nor gratify my thousand swelling thoughts
With knowledge, nor allay my thousand
 fears
Of death and life.
 Lucifer. What thy world is thou see'st,
But canst not comprehend the shadow of
That which it was.
 Cain. And those enormous creatures,
Phantoms inferior in intelligence 133
(At least so seeming) to the things we have
 pass'd,
Resembling somewhat the wild habitants
Of the deep woods of earth, the hugest
 which 136
Roar nightly in the forest, but ten-fold
In magnitude and terror; taller than
The cherub-guarded walls of Eden, with
 eyes flashing like the fiery swords which
 fence them, 140
And tusks projecting like the trees stripp'd
 of

Their bark and branches—what were they?
 Lucifer. That which
The Mammoth is in thy world;—but
 these lie
By myriads underneath its surface.
 Cain. But
None on it?
 Lucifer. No: for thy frail race to war
With them would render the curse on it
 useless— 146
'Twould be destroy'd so early.
 Cain. But why *war?*
 Lucifer. You have forgotten the
 denunciation
Which drove your race from Eden—war
 with all things,
And death to all things, and disease to
 most things, 150
And pangs, and bitterness; these were the
 fruits
Of the forbidden tree.
 Cain. But animals—
Did they, too, eat of it, that they must die?
 Lucifer. Your Maker told ye, *they*
 were made for you,
As you for him.—You would not have
 their doom 155
Superior to your own? Had Adam not
Fallen, all had stood.
 Cain. Alas! the hopeless wretches!
They too must share my sire's fate, like
 his sons;
Like them, too, without having shared the
 apple;
Like them, too, without the so dear-
 bought *knowledge!* 160
It was a lying tree—for we *know* nothing.
At least it *promised knowledge* at the *price*
Of death—but *knowledge* still: but what
 knows man?
 Lucifer. It may be death leads to the
 highest knowledge;
And being of all things the sole thing
 certain, 165
At least leads to the *surest* science: there-
 fore
The tree was true, though deadly.
 Cain. These dim realms!
I see them, but I know them not.
 Lucifer. Because
Thy hour is yet afar, and matter cannot
Comprehend spirit wholly—but 'tis some-
 thing 170
To know there are such realms.
 Cain. We knew already
That there was death.
 Lucifer. But not what was beyond it.
 Cain. Nor know I now.
 Lucifer. Thou knowest that there is
A state, and many states beyond thine
 own—
And this thou knewest not this morn.
 Cain. But all
Seems dim and shadowy.

Lucifer. Be content; it will 176
Seem clearer to thine immortality.
Cain. And yon immeasurable liquid
 space
Of glorious azure, which floats on beyond us,
Which looks like water, and which I
 should deem 180
The river which flows out of Paradise
Past my own dwelling, but that it is bank-
 less
And boundless, and of an ethereal hue—
What is it?
Lucifer. There is still some such on
 earth,
Although inferior, and thy children shall
Dwell near it—'tis the phantasm of an
 ocean. 186
Cain. 'Tis like another world; a liquid
 sun—
And those inordinate creatures sporting
 o'er
Its shining surface?
Lucifer. Are its inhabitants,
The past leviathans.
Cain. And yon immense
Serpent, which rears his dripping mane
 and vasty 191
Head ten times higher than the haughtiest
 cedar
Forth from the abyss, looking as he could
 coil
Himself around the orbs we lately look'd
 on—
Is he not of the kind which bask'd beneath
The tree in Eden?
Lucifer. Eve, thy mother, best 196
Can tell what shape of serpent tempted her.
Cain. This seems too terrible. No
 doubt the other
Had more of beauty.
Lucifer. Hast thou ne'er beheld him?
Cain. Many of the same kind (at least
 so call'd), 200
But never that precisely which persuaded
The fatal fruit, nor even of the same aspect.
Lucifer. Your father saw him not?
Cain. No: 'twas my mother
Who tempted him—she tempted by the
 serpent.
Lucifer. Good man! whene'er thy wife,
 or thy sons' wives, 205
Tempt thee or them to aught that's new
 or strange,
Be sure thou see'st first who hath tempted
 them.
Cain. Thy precept comes too late:
 there is no more
For serpents to tempt woman to.
Lucifer. But there
Are some things still which woman may
 tempt man to, 210
And man tempt woman:—let thy sons
 look to it!
My counsel is a kind one; for 'tis even

Given chiefly at my own expense; 'tis tru
'Twill not be follow'd, so there's little los
Cain. I understand not this.
Lucifer. The happier thou!—
Thy world and thou are still too young
 Thou thinkest 21
Thyself most wicked and unhappy: is it
Not so?
Cain. For crime, I know not; but fo
 pain,
I have felt much.
Lucifer. First-born of the first man
Thy present state of sin, and thou art evil—
Of sorrow, and thou sufferest—are bo
 Eden 22
In all its innocence compared to what
Thou shortly may'st be; and that sta
 again,
In its redoubled wretchedness, a Paradi
To what thy sons' sons' sons, accumulatin
In generations like to dust (which they
In fact but add to), shall endure and do.-
Now let us back to earth!
Cain. And wherefore didst tho
Lead me here only to inform me this?
Lucifer. Was not thy quest for know
 ledge?
Cain. Yes; as being 2
The road to happiness.
Lucifer. If truth be so,
Thou hast it.
Cain. Then my father's God did we
When he prohibited the fatal tree.
Lucifer. But had done better in n
 planting it.
But ignorance of evil doth not save 2
From evil; it must still roll on the same
A part of all things.
Cain. Not of all things. N
I'll not believe it—for I thirst for good
Lucifer. And who and what doth no
 Who covets evil
For its own bitter sake?—*None*—nothin
 'tis 2
The leaven of all life, and lifelessness.
Cain. Within those glorious or
 which we beheld,
Distant, and dazzling, and innumerable
Ere we came down into this phanto
 realm,
Ill cannot come: they are too beautiful.
Lucifer. Thou hast seen them fro
 afar.
Cain. And what of that? 2
Distance can but diminish glory—they,
When nearer, must be more ineffable.
Lucifer. Approach the things of eart
 most beautiful,
And judge their beauty near.
Cain. I have done this—
The loveliest thing I know is lovelie
 nearest.
Lucifer. Then there must be delusio
 —What is that

Which being nearest to thine eyes is still
More beautiful than beauteous things re-
 mote?
 Cain. My sister Adah.—All the stars
 of heaven, 255
The deep blue noon of night, lit by an orb
Which looks a spirit, or a spirit's world—
The hues of twilight—the sun's gorgeous
 coming—
His setting indescribable, which fills
My eyes with pleasant tears as I behold
Him sink, and feel my heart float softly
 with him 261
Along that western paradise of clouds,
The forest shade, the green bough, the
 bird's voice—
The vesper bird's, which seems to sing of
 love,
And mingles with the song of cherubim,
As the day closes over Eden's walls:—
All these are nothing, to my eyes and
 heart, 267
Like Adah's face: I turn from earth and
 heaven
To gaze on it.
 Lucifer. 'Tis fair as frail mortality,
In the first dawn and bloom of young
 creation, 270
And earliest embraces of earth's parents,
Can make its offspring; still it is delusion.
 Cain. You think so, being not her
 brother.
 Lucifer. Mortal!
My brotherhood's with those who have
 no children.
 Cain. Then thou canst have no fellow-
 ship with us. 275
 Lucifer. It may be that thine own shall
 be for me.
But if thou dost possess a beautiful
Being beyond all beauty in thine eyes,
Why art thou wretched?
 Cain. Why do I exist?
Why art *thou* wretched? why are all things
 so? 280
Even he who made us must be, as the
 maker
Of things unhappy! To produce destruc-
 tion
Can surely never be the task of joy,
And yet my sire says he's omnipotent:
Then why is evil—he being good? I ask'd
This question of my father; and he said,
Because this evil only was the path 287
To good. Strange good, that must arise
 from out
Its deadly opposite! I lately saw
A lamb stung by a reptile: the poor
 suckling 290
Lay foaming on the earth, beneath the
 vain
And piteous bleating of its restless dam;
My father pluck'd some herbs, and laid
 them to

The wound; and by degrees the helpless
 wretch
Resumed its careless life, and rose to
 drain 295
The mother's milk, who o'er it tremulous
Stood licking its reviving limbs with joy.
Behold, my son! said Adam, how from
 evil
Springs good!
 Lucifer. What didst thou answer?
 Cain. Nothing; for
He is my father: but I thought, that 'twere
A better portion for the animal 301
Never to have been *stung at all*, than to
Purchase renewal of its little life
With agonies unutterable, though
Dispell'd by antidotes.
 Lucifer. But as thou saidst
Of all beloved things thou lovest her 306
Who shared thy mother's milk, and giveth
 hers
Unto thy children——
 Cain. Most assuredly:
What should I be without her?
 Lucifer. What am I?
 Cain. Dost thou love nothing?
 Lucifer. What does thy God love?
 Cain. All things, my father says; but
 I confess 311
I see it not in their allotment here.
 Lucifer. And, therefore, thou canst
 not see if *I* love
Or no, except some vast and general
 purpose,
To which particular things must melt like
 snows. 315
 Cain. Snows! what are they?
 Lucifer. Be happier in not knowing
What thy remoter offspring must en-
 counter;
But bask beneath the clime which knows
 no winter.
 Cain. But dost thou not love some-
 thing like thyself? 319
 Lucifer. And dost thou love *thyself*?
 Cain. Yes, but love more
What makes my feelings more endurable,
And is more than myself, because I love it.
 Lucifer. Thou lovest it, because 'tis
 beautiful,
As was the apple in thy mother's eye;
And when it ceases to be so, thy love
Will cease, like any other appetite. 326
 Cain. Cease to be beautiful! how can
 that be?
 Lucifer. With time.
 Cain. But time has pass'd, and
 hitherto
Even Adam and my mother both are fair:
Not fair like Adah and the seraphim—
But very fair.
 Lucifer. All that must pass away 331
In them and her.
 Cain. I'm sorry for it; but

535 S

Cannot conceive my love for her the less:
And when her beauty disappears, me-
 thinks 334
He who creates all beauty will lose more
Than me in seeing perish such a work.
 Lucifer. I pity thee who lovest what
 must perish.
 Cain. And I thee who lov'st nothing.
 Lucifer. And thy brother—
Sits he not near thy heart?
 Cain. Why should he not?
 Lucifer. Thy father loves him well—
 so does thy God. 340
 Cain. And so do I.
 Lucifer. 'Tis well and meekly done.
 Cain. Meekly!
 Lucifer. He is the second born of flesh,
And is his mother's favourite.
 Cain. Let him keep
Her favour, since the serpent was the first
To win it.
 Lucifer. And his father's?
 Cain. What is that
To me? should I not love that which all
 love? 346
 Lucifer. And the Jehovah—the indul-
 gent Lord,
And bounteous planter of barr'd Para-
 dise—
He, too, looks smilingly on Abel.
 Cain. I
Ne'er saw him, and I know not if he smiles.
 Lucifer. But you have seen his angels.
 Cain. Rarely.
 Lucifer. But 351
Sufficiently to see they love your brother:
His sacrifices are acceptable.
 Cain. So be they! wherefore speak to
 me of this?
 Lucifer. Because thou hast thought of
 this ere now.
 Cain. And if 355
I *have* thought, why recall a thought
 that—[*he pauses, as agitated*]—Spirit!
Here we are in *thy* world; speak not of
 mine.
Thou hast shown me wonders: thou hast
 shown me those
Mighty pre-Adamites who walk'd the
 earth
Of which ours is the wreck: thou hast
 pointed out 360
Myriads of starry worlds, of which our
 own
Is the dim and remote companion, in
Infinity of life: thou hast shown me
 shadows
Of that existence with the dreaded name
Which my sire brought us—Death; thou
 hast shown me much— 365
But not all: show me where Jehovah
 dwells,
In his especial Paradise—or *thine:*
Where is it?

 Lucifer. *Here,* and o'er all space.
 Cain. But y
Have some allotted dwelling—as a
 things;
Clay has its earth, and other worlds the
 tenants; 37
All temporary breathing creatures their
Peculiar element; and things which hav
Long ceased to breathe *our* breath, hav
 theirs, thou say'st;
And the Jehovah and thyself have thine—
Ye do not dwell together?
 Lucifer. No, we reign 37
Together; but our dwellings are asunde
 Cain. Would there were only one c
 ye! perchance
An unity of purpose might make union
In elements which seem now jarr'd i
 storms.
How came ye, being spirits, wise an
 infinite, 38
To separate? Are ye not as brethren in
Your essence, and your nature, and you
 glory?
 Lucifer. Art thou not Abel's brother
 Cain. We are brethre
And so we shall remain; but were it not so
Is spirit like to flesh? can it fall out?
Infinity with Immortality? 38
Jarring and turning space to misery—
For what?
 Lucifer. To reign.
 Cain. Did ye not tell me tha
Ye are both eternal?
 Lucifer. Yea!
 Cain. And what I have seer
Yon blue immensity, is boundless?
 Lucifer. Ay.
 Cain. And cannot ye both *reig*
 then?—is there not 39
Enough?—why should ye differ?
 Lucifer. We *both* reig
 Cain. But one of you makes evil.
 Lucifer. Which?
 Cain. Thou! fc
If thou canst do man good, why dost tho
 not?
 Lucifer. And why not he who made
 I made ye not; 39
Ye are *his* creatures, and not mine.
 Cain. Then leave us
His creatures, as thou say'st we are,
 show me
Thy dwelling, or his dwelling.
 Lucifer. I could show the
Both; but the time will come thou sha
 see one
Of them for evermore.
 Cain. And why not now?
 Lucifer. Thy human mind hat
 scarcely grasp to gather 4c
The little I have shown thee into calm
And clear thought; and thou wouldst g
 on aspiring

To the great double mysteries! the *two*
 Principles!
And gaze upon them on their secret
 thrones! 405
Dust! limit thy ambition; for to see
Either of these would be for thee to perish!
 Cain. And let me perish, so I see them!
 Lucifer. There
The son of her who snatch'd the apple
 spake!
But thou wouldst only perish, and not see
 them; 410
That sight is for the other state.
 Cain. Of death?
 Lucifer. That is the prelude.
 Cain. Then I dread it less,
Now that I know it leads to something
 definite.
 Lucifer. And now I will convey thee
 to thy world,
Where thou shalt multiply the race of
 Adam, 415
Eat, drink, toil, tremble, laugh, weep,
 sleep, and die.
 Cain. And to what end have I beheld
 these things
Which thou hast shown me?
 Lucifer. Didst thou not require
Knowledge? And have I not, in what I
 show'd,
Taught thee to know thyself?
 Cain. Alas! I seem
Nothing.
 Lucifer. And this should be the human
 sum 421
Of knowledge, to know mortal nature's
 nothingness;
Bequeath that science to thy children, and
'Twill spare them many tortures.
 Cain. Haughty spirit!
Thou speak'st it proudly; but thyself,
 though proud, 425
Hast a superior.
 Lucifer. No! by heaven, which He
Holds, and the abyss, and the immensity
Of worlds and life, which I hold with him
 —No!
I have a victor—true; but no superior.
Homage he has from all—but none from
 me: 430
I battle it against him, as I battled
In highest heaven. Through all eternity,
And the unfathomable gulfs of Hades,
And the interminable realms of space,
And the infinity of endless ages, 435
All, all, will I dispute! And world by
 world,
And star by star, and universe by universe,
Shall tremble in the balance, till the great
Conflict shall cease, if ever it shall cease,
Which it ne'er shall, till he or I be
 quench'd! 440
And what can quench our immortality,
Our mutual and irrevocable hate?

He as a conqueror will call the conquer'd
Evil; but what will be the *good* he gives?
Were I the victor, *his* works would be
 deem'd 445
The only evil ones. And you, ye new
And scarce born mortals, what have been
 his gifts
To you already, in your little world?
 Cain. But few; and some of those but
 bitter.
 Lucifer. Back
With me, then, to thine earth, and try the
 rest 450
Of his celestial boons to you and yours.
Evil and good are things in their own
 essence,
And not made good or evil by the giver;
But if he gives you good—so call him; if
Evil springs from *him*, do not name it *mine*,
Till ye know better its true fount; and
 judge 456
Not by words, though of spirits, but the
 fruits
Of your existence, such as it must be.
One good gift has the fatal apple given—
Your *reason:*—let it not be over-sway'd
By tyrannous threats to force you into
 faith 461
'Gainst all external sense and inward
 feeling:
Think and endure,—and form an inner
 world
In your own bosom—where the outward
 fails;
So shall you nearer be the spiritual
Nature, and war triumphant with your
 own. 466
 [They disappear.

ACT III

SCENE I.—*The Earth, near Eden, as in Act I.*

Enter CAIN *and* ADAH.

 Adah. Hush, tread softly, Cain.
 Cain. I will; but wherefore?
 Adah. Our little Enoch sleeps upon
 yon bed
Of leaves, beneath the cypress.
 Cain. Cypress! 'tis
A gloomy tree, which looks as if it
 mourn'd
O'er what it shadows; wherefore didst
 thou choose it 5
For our child's canopy?
 Adah. Because its branches
Shut out the sun like night, and therefore
 seem'd
Fitting to shadow slumber.
 Cain. Ay, the last—
And longest; but no matter—lead me to
 him. *[They go up to the child.*
How lovely he appears! his little cheeks,
In their pure incarnation, vying with 11
The rose leaves strewn beneath them.

Adah. And his lips, too,
How beautifully parted! No; you shall not
Kiss him, at least not now; he will awake
 soon. 14
His hour of mid-day rest is nearly over;
But it were pity to disturb him till
'Tis closed.
 Cain. You have said well; I will
 contain
My heart till then. He smiles, and
 sleeps!—Sleep on,
And smile, thou little, young inheritor
Of a world scarce less young: sleep on, and
 smile! 20
Thine are the hours and days when both
 are cheering
And innocent! *thou* hast not pluck'd the
 fruit—
Thou know'st not thou art naked! Must
 the time
Come thou shalt be amerced for sins
 unknown,
Which were not thine nor mine? But now
 sleep on! 25
His cheeks are reddening into deeper
 smiles,
And shining lids are trembling o'er his long
Lashes, dark as the cypress which waves
 o'er them;
Half open, from beneath them the clear blue
Laughs out, although in slumber. He
 must dream— 30
Of what? Of Paradise!—Ay! dream of it,
My disinherited boy! 'Tis but a dream;
For never more thyself, thy sons, nor
 fathers,
Shall walk in that forbidden place of joy!
 Adah. Dear Cain! Nay, do not
 whisper o'er our son 35
Such melancholy yearnings o'er the past:
Why wilt thou always mourn for Paradise?
Can we not make another?
 Cain. Where?
 Adah. Here, or
Where'er thou wilt: where'er thou art, I
 feel not
The want of this so much regretted Eden.
Have I not thee, our boy, our sire, and
 brother, 41
And Zillah—our sweet sister, and our Eve,
To whom we owe so much besides our
 birth?
 Cain. Yes—death, too, is amongst the
 debts we owe her.
 Adah. Cain! that proud spirit, who
 withdrew thee hence, 45
Hath sadden'd thine still deeper. I had
 hoped
The promised wonders which thou hast
 beheld,
Visions, thou say'st, of past and present
 worlds,
Would have composed thy mind into the
 calm

Of a contented knowledge; but I see 50
Thy guide hath done thee evil: still I thank
 him,
And can forgive him all, that he so soon
Hath given thee back to us.
 Cain. So soon?
 Adah. 'Tis scarcely
Two hours since ye departed: two *long*
 hours
To *me*, but only *hours* upon the sun. 55
 Cain. And yet I have approach'd that
 sun, and seen
Worlds which he once shone on, and never
 more
Shall light; and worlds he never lit: me
 thought
Years had roll'd o'er my absence.
 Adah. Hardly hours.
 Cain. The mind then hath capacity of
 time, 60
And measures it by that which it beholds
Pleasing or painful; little or almighty.
I had beheld the immemorial works
Of endless beings; skirr'd extinguish'd
 worlds;
And, gazing on eternity, methought 65
I had borrow'd more by a few drops of age
From its immensity: but now I feel
My littleness again. Well said the spirit,
That I was nothing!
 Adah. Wherefore said he so?
Jehovah said not that.
 Cain. No: *he* contents him 70
With making us the *nothing* which we are
And flattering dust with glimpses of
Eden and Immortality, resolves
It back to dust again—for what?
 Adah. Thou know'st—
Even for our parents' error.
 Cain. What is that 75
To us? they sinn'd, then *let them* die!
 Adah. Thou hast not spoken well, nor
 is that thought
Thy own, but of the spirit who was with
 thee.
Would *I* could die for them, so *they* might
 live!
 Cain. Why, so say I—provided that
 one victim 80
Might satiate the insatiable of life,
And that our little rosy sleeper there
Might never taste of death nor human
 sorrow,
Nor hand it down to those who spring
 from him.
 Adah. How know we that some such
 atonement one day 85
May not redeem our race?
 Cain. By sacrificing
The harmless for the guilty? what atone
 ment
Were there? why, *we* are innocent: what
 have we
Done, that we must be victims for a deed

538

Before our birth, or need have victims to
Atone for this mysterious, nameless sin—
If it be such a sin to seek for knowledge?
 Adah. Alas! thou sinnest now, my
 Cain: thy words
Sound impious in mine ears.
 Cain. Then leave me!
 Adah. Never,
Though thy God left thee.
 Cain. Say, what have we here? 95
 Adah. Two altars, which our brother
 Abel made
During thine absence, whereupon to offer
A sacrifice to God on thy return.
 Cain. And how knew *he*, that *I* would
 be so ready
With the burnt offerings, which he daily
 brings 100
With a meek brow, whose base humility
Shows more of fear than worship, as a
 bribe
To the Creator?
 Adah. Surely, 'tis well done.
 Cain. One altar may suffice; *I* have no
 offering.
 Adah. The fruits of the earth, the
 early, beautiful 105
Blossom and bud, and bloom of flowers
 and fruits;
These are a goodly offering to the Lord,
Given with a gentle and a contrite spirit.
 Cain. I have toil'd, and till'd, and
 sweaten in the sun,
According to the curse:—must I do more?
For what should I be gentle? for a war
With all the elements ere they will yield
The bread we eat? For what must I be
 grateful?
For being dust, and grovelling in the dust,
Till I return to dust? If I am nothing—
For nothing shall I be an hypocrite, 116
And seem well-pleased with pain? For
 what should I
Be contrite? for my father's sin, already
Expiate with what we all have undergone,
And to be more than expiated by 120
The ages prophesied, upon our seed.
Little deems our young blooming sleeper,
 there,
The germs of an eternal misery
To myriads is within him! better 'twere
I snatch'd him in his sleep, and dash'd him
 'gainst 125
The rocks, than let him live to——
 Adah. Oh, my God!
Touch not the child—my child! *thy* child!
 Oh, Cain!
 Cain. Fear not! for all the stars, and
 all the power
Which sways them, I would not accost 129
With ruder greeting than a father's kiss.
 Adah. Then, why so awful in thy
 speech?

 Cain. I said,
'Twere better that he ceased to live, than
 give
Life to so much of sorrow as he must
Endure, and, harder still, bequeath; but
 since 134
That saying jars you, let us only say—
'Twere better that he never had been born.
 Adah. Oh, do not say so! Where were
 then the joys,
The mother's joys of watching, nourish-
 ing,
And loving him? Soft! he awakes. Sweet
 Enoch! [*She goes to the child.*
Oh, Cain! look on him; see how full of
 life, 140
Of strength, of bloom, of beauty, and of
 joy,
How like to me—how like to thee, when
 gentle,
For *then* we are *all* alike; is 't not so, Cain?
Mother, and sire, and son, our features are
Reflected in each other; as they are 145
In the clear waters, when *they* are *gentle*,
 and
When *thou* art *gentle*. Love us, then, my
 Cain!
And love thyself for our sakes, for we love
 thee.
Look! how he laughs and stretches out
 his arms, 149
And opens wide his blue eyes upon thine,
To hail his father; while his little form
Flutters as wing'd with joy. Talk not of
 pain!
The childless cherubs well might envy thee
The pleasures of a parent! Bless him,
 Cain!
As yet he hath no words to thank thee,
 but 155
His heart will, and thine own too.
 Cain. Bless thee, boy!
If that a mortal blessing may avail thee,
To save thee from the serpent's curse!
 Adah. It shall.
Surely a father's blessing may avert
A reptile's subtilty.
 Cain. Of that I doubt; 160
But bless him ne'er the less.
 Adah. Our brother comes.
 Cain. Thy brother Abel.

Enter ABEL.

 Abel. Welcome, Cain! My brother,
The peace of God be on thee!
 Cain. Abel, hail!
 Abel. Our sister tells me that thou hast
 been wandering,
In high communion with a spirit, far
Beyond our wonted range. Was he of
 those 166
We have seen and spoken with, like to our
 father?
 Cain. No.

Abel. Why then commune with
him? he may be
A foe to the Most High.
Cain. And friend to man.
Has the Most High been so—if so you
term him? 170
Abel. *Term him!* your words are
strange to-day, my brother.
My sister Adah, leave us for awhile—
We mean to sacrifice.
Adah. Farewell, my Cain;
But first embrace thy son. May his soft
spirit, 174
And Abel's pious ministry, recall thee
To peace and holiness!
 [*Exit* ADAH, *with her child.*
Abel. Where hast thou been?
Cain. I know not.
Abel. Nor what thou hast seen?
Cain. The dead,
The immortal, the unbounded, the
omnipotent,
The overpowering mysteries of space—
The innumerable worlds that were and
are— 180
A whirlwind of such overwhelming things,
Suns, moons, and earths, upon their loud-
voiced spheres
Singing in thunder round me, as have
made me
Unfit for mortal converse: leave me, Abel.
Abel. Thine eyes are flashing with un-
natural light— 185
Thy cheek is flush'd with an unnatural
hue—
Thy words are fraught with an unnatural
sound—
What may this mean?
Cain. It means——I pray thee, leave
me.
Abel. Not till we have pray'd and
sacrificed together.
Cain. Abel, I pray thee, sacrifice
alone— 190
Jehovah loves thee well.
Abel. Both well, I hope.
Cain. But thee the better: I care not
for that;
Thou art fitter for his worship than I am;
Revere him, then—but let it be alone—
At least, without me.
Abel. Brother, I should ill 195
Deserve the name of our great father's
son,
If, as my elder, I revered thee not,
And in the worship of our God, call'd not
On thee to join me, and precede me in
Our priesthood—'tis thy place.
Cain. But I have ne'er 200
Asserted it.
Abel. The more my grief; I pray thee
To do so now: thy soul seems labouring in
Some strong delusion; it will calm thee.
Cain. No;

Nothing can calm me more. *Calm!* say I
Never
Knew I what calm was in the soul
although 205
I have seen the elements still'd. My Abel
leave me!
Or let me leave thee to thy pious purpose.
Abel. Neither; we must perform our
task together.
Spurn me not.
Cain. If it must be so——well, then
What shall I do?
Abel. Choose one of those two
altars. 210
Cain. Choose for me: they to me are
so much turf
And stone.
Abel. Choose thou!
Cain. I have chosen.
Abel. 'Tis the highest
And suits thee, as the elder. Now prepare
Thine offerings.
Cain. Where are thine?
Abel. Behold them here—
The firstlings of the flock, and fat thereof—
A shepherd's humble offering.
Cain. I have no flocks; 215
I am a tiller of the ground, and must
Yield what it yieldeth to my toil—its fruit
 [*He gathers fruits.*
Behold them in their various bloom and
ripeness.
 [*They dress their altars, and kindle a
 flame upon them.*
Abel. My brother, as the elder, offer
first 220
Thy prayer and thanksgiving with
sacrifice.
Cain. No—I am new to this; lead thou
the way,
And I will follow—as I may.
Abel [*kneeling*]. Oh, God!
Who made us, and who breathed the
breath of life
Within our nostrils, who hath blessed us 225
And spared, despite our father's sin, to
make
His children all lost, as they might have
been,
Had not thy justice been so temper'd with
The mercy which is thy delight, as to
Accord a pardon like a Paradise, 230
Compared with our great crimes:—Sole
Lord of light,
Of good, and glory, and eternity!
Without whom all were evil, and with
whom
Nothing can err, except to some good end
Of thine omnipotent benevolence— 235
Inscrutable, but still to be fulfill'd—
Accept from out thy humble first of shep-
herd's
First of the first-born flocks—an offering
In itself nothing—as what offering can be

Aught unto thee?—but yet accept it for
The thanksgiving of him who spreads it in
The face of thy high heaven, bowing his
 own 242
Even to the dust, of which he is, in honour
Of thee, and of thy name, for evermore!
 Cain [standing erect during this speech].
Spirit! whate'er or whosoe'er thou art,
Omnipotent, it may be—and, if good,
Shown in the exemption of thy deeds from
 evil; 247
Jehovah upon earth! and God in heaven!
And it may be with other names, because
Thine attributes seem many, as thy works:
If thou must be propitiated with prayers,
Take them! If thou must be induced with
 altars, 252
And soften'd with a sacrifice, receive
 them!
Two beings here erect them unto thee.
If thou lov'st blood, the shepherd's shrine,
 which smokes 255
On my right hand, hath shed it for thy
 service
In the first of his flock, whose limbs now
 reek
In sanguinary incense to thy skies;
Or if the sweet and blooming fruits of
 earth,
And milder seasons, which the unstain'd
 turf 260
I spread them on now offers in the face
Of the broad sun which ripen'd them, may
 seem
Good to thee, inasmuch as they have not
Suffer'd in limb or life, and rather form
A sample of thy works, than supplication
To look on ours! If a shrine without
 victim, 266
And altar without gore, may win thy
 favour,
Look on it! and for him who dresseth it,
He is—such as thou mad'st him; and seeks
 nothing
Which must be won by kneeling: if he's
 evil, 270
Strike him! thou art omnipotent, and
 may'st—
For what can he oppose? If he be good,
Strike him, or spare him, as thou wilt!
 since all
Rests upon thee; and good and evil seem
To have no power themselves, save in thy
 will; 275
And whether that be good or ill I know
 not,
Not being omnipotent, nor fit to judge
Omnipotence, but merely to endure
Its mandate; which thus far I have
 endured.
 [The fire upon the altar of ABEL *kindles
 into a column of the brightest flame,
 and ascends to heaven; while a whirl-
 wind throws down the altar of* CAIN,

*and scatters the fruits abroad upon the
 earth.*
Abel [kneeling]. Oh, brother, pray!
 Jehovah's wroth with thee. 280
Cain. Why so?
Abel. Thy fruits are scatter'd
 on the earth.
Cain. From earth they came, to earth
 let them return;
Their seed will bear fresh fruit there ere
 the summer:
Thy burnt flesh-off'ring prospers better; see
How heaven licks up the flames, when
 thick with blood! 285
Abel. Think not upon my offering's
 acceptance,
But make another of thine own before
It is too late.
Cain. I will build no more altars,
Nor suffer any——
 Abel [rising]. Cain! what meanest
 thou?
Cain. To cast down yon vile flatt'rer
 of the clouds, 290
The smoky harbinger of thy dull prayers—
Thine altar, with its blood of lambs and
 kids,
Which fed on milk, to be destroy'd in
 blood.
 Abel [opposing him]. Thou shalt not:—
 add not impious works to impious
Words! let that altar stand—'tis hallow'd
 now 295
By the immortal pleasure of Jehovah,
In his acceptance of the victims.
Cain. His!
His pleasure! what was his high pleasure in
The fumes of scorching flesh and smoking
 blood,
To the pain of the bleating mothers,
 which 300
Still yearn for their dead offspring? or the
 pangs
Of the sad ignorant victims underneath
Thy pious knife? Give way! this bloody
 record
Shall not stand in the sun, to shame
 creation!
Abel. Brother, give back! thou shalt
 not touch my altar 305
With violence: if that thou wilt adopt it,
To try another sacrifice, 'tis thine.
Cain. Another sacrifice! Give way, or
 else
That sacrifice may be——
Abel. What mean'st thou?
Cain. Give—
Give way!—thy God loves blood!—then
 look to it:— 310
Give way, ere he hath *more!*
Abel. In *his* great name,
I stand between thee and the shrine which
 hath
Had his acceptance.

541

Cain. If thou lov'st thyself,
Stand back till I have strew'd this turf along
Its native soil:—else——
 Abel [opposing him]. I love God far
 more 315
Than life.
 *Cain [striking him with a brand, on the
 temples, which he snatches from the
 altar].* Then take thy life unto thy
 God,
Since he loves lives.
 Abel [falls]. What hast thou done, my
 brother?
Cain. Brother!
Abel. Oh, God! receive thy servant, and
Forgive his slayer, for he knew not what
He did—Cain, give me—give me thy
 hand; and tell 320
Poor Zillah—
 Cain [after a moment's stupefaction]. My
 hand! 'tis all red, and with——
What?
 [A long pause.—Looking slowly round.
Where am I? alone! Where's Abel? where
Cain? Can it be that I am he? My brother,
Awake!—why liest thou so on the green
 earth?
'Tis not the hour of slumber;—why so
 pale? 325
What hast thou!—thou wert full of life
 this morn!
Abel! I pray thee, mock me not! I smote
Too fiercely, but not fatally. Ah, why
Wouldst thou oppose me? This is
 mockery;
And only done to daunt me:—'twas a
 blow— 330
And but a blow. Stir—stir—nay, only
 stir!
Why, so—that's well!—thou breath'st! breathe upon me!
Oh, God! Oh, God!
 Abel [very faintly]. What's he who
 speaks of God?
Cain. Thy murderer.
Abel. Then may God forgive him!
 Cain,
Comfort poor Zillah:—she has but one
 brother 335
Now. [ABEL *dies.*
 Cain. And I none!—Who makes me
 brotherless?
His eyes are open! then he is not dead!
Death is like sleep; and sleep shuts down
 our lids.
His lips, too, are apart; why then he
 breathes;
And yet I feel it not.—His heart!—his
 heart! 340
Let me see, doth it beat? methinks——
No!—no!

This is a vision, else I am become
The native of another and worse world.
The earth swims round me:—what is
 this?—'tis wet; *[Puts his hand to his
 brow, and then looks at it.*
And yet there are no dews! 'Tis blood—
 my blood— 34
My brother's and my own! and shed by
 me!
Then what have I further to do with life
Since I have taken life from my own flesh?
But he cannot be dead!—Is silence death?
No; he will wake; then let me watch by
 him. 350
Life cannot be so slight, as to be quench'd
Thus quickly!—he hath spoken to me
 since—
What shall I say to him?—My brother!—
 No:
He will not answer to that name; for
 brethren
Smite not each other. Yet—yet—speak
 to me. 355
Oh! for a word more of that gentle voice,
That I may bear to hear my own again!

 Enter ZILLAH.

 Zillah. I heard a heavy sound; what
 can it be?
'Tis Cain; and watching by my husband.
 What
Dost thou there, brother? Doth he sleep?
 Oh, heaven! 360
What means this paleness, and yon
 stream?—No, no!
It is not blood; for who would shed 'his
 blood?
Abel! what's this?—who hath done this?
 He moves not;
He breathes not: and his hands drop down
 from mine 364
With stony lifelessness! Ah! cruel Cain!
Why cam'st thou not in time to save him
 from
This violence? Whatever hath assail'd
 him,
Thou wert the stronger, and shouldst have
 stepp'd in
Between him and aggression! Father!—
 Eve!— 369
Adah!—come hither! Death is in the
 world!
 [Exit ZILLAH, *calling on her Parents.*
 &c.
 Cain [solus]. And who hath brought
 him there?—I—who abhor
The name of Death so deeply, that the
 thought
Empoison'd all my life, before I knew
His aspect—I have led him here, and given
My brother to his cold and still embrace
As if he would not have asserted his 370
Inexorable claim without my aid.
I am awake at last—a dreary dream

Had madden'd me;—but *he* shall ne'er awake!

Enter ADAM, EVE, ADAH, *and* ZILLAH.

 Adam. A voice of woe from Zillah brings me here.—
What do I see?—'Tis true!—My son!—my son!
Woman, behold the serpent's work, and thine! [*To* EVE.
 Eve. Oh! speak not of it now: the serpent's fangs
Are in my heart. My best beloved, Abel!
Jehovah! this is punishment beyond 385
A mother's sin, to take *him* from me!
 Adam. Who,
Or what hath done this deed?—speak, Cain, since thou
Wert present; was it some more hostile angel,
Who walks not with Jehovah? or some wild
Brute of the forest?
 Eve. Ah! a livid light 390
Breaks through, as from a thunder-cloud! yon brand
Massy and bloody! snatch'd from off the altar,
And black with smoke, and red with—
 Adam. Speak, my son!
Speak, and assure us, wretched as we are,
That we are not more miserable still. 395
 Adah. Speak, Cain! and say it was not *thou!*
 Eve. It was.
I see it now—he hangs his guilty head,
And covers his ferocious eye with hands Incarnadine.
 Adah. Mother, thou dost him wrong— 399
Cain! clear thee from this horrible accusal,
Which grief wrings from our parent.
 Eve. Hear, Jehovah!
May the eternal serpent's curse be on him!
For he was fitter for his seed than ours.
May all his days be desolate! May——
 Adah. Hold!
Curse him not, mother, for he is thy son—
Curse him not, mother, for he is my brother, 406
And my betroth'd.
 Eve. He hath left thee no brother—
Zillah no husband—me *no son!* for thus
I curse him from my sight for evermore!
All bonds I break between us as he broke
That of his nature, in yon——Oh death!
death! 411
Why didst thou not take *me*, who first incurr'd thee?
Why dost thou not so now?
 Adam. Eve! let not this,
Thy natural grief, lead to impiety!
A heavy doom was long forespoken to us;
And now that it begins, let it be borne

In such sort as may show our God that we
Are faithful servants to his holy will.
 Eve [*pointing to* Cain]. *His will!* the will of yon incarnate spirit
Of death, whom I have brought upon the earth 420
To strew it with the dead. May all the curses
Of life be on him! and his agonies
Drive him forth o'er the wilderness, like us
From Eden, till his children do by him
As he did by his brother! May the swords
And wings of fiery cherubim pursue him
By day and night—snakes spring up in his path— 427
Earth's fruits be ashes in his mouth—the leaves
On which he lays his head to sleep be strew'd
With scorpions! May his dreams be of his victim! 430
His waking a continual dread of death!
May the clear rivers turn to blood as he
Stoops down to stain them with his raging lip!
May every element shun or change to him!
May he live in the pangs which others die with! 435
And death itself wax something worse than death
To him who first acquainted him with man!
Hence, fratricide! henceforth that word is Cain,
Through all the coming myriads of mankind,
Who shall abhor thee, though thou wert their sire! 440
May the grass wither from thy feet! the woods
Deny thee shelter! earth a home! the dust
A grave! the sun his light! and heaven her God! [*Exit* EVE.
 Adam. Cain! get thee forth: we dwell no more together. 444
Depart! and leave the dead to me—I am
Henceforth alone—we never must meet more.
 Adah. Oh, part not with him thus, my father: do not
Add thy deep curse to Eve's upon his head!
 Adam. I curse him not: his spirit be his curse.
Come, Zillah!
 Zillah. I must watch my husband's corse. 450
 Adam. We will return again, when he is gone
Who hath provided for us this dread office.
Come, Zillah!
 Zillah. Yet one kiss on yon pale clay,
And those lips once so warm—my heart! my heart!
 [*Exeunt* ADAM *and* ZILLAH, *weeping.*

Adah. Cain! thou hast heard, we must
 go forth. I am ready, 455
So shall our children be. I will bear
 Enoch,
And you his sister. Ere the sun declines
Let us depart, nor walk the wilderness
Under the cloud of night.—Nay, speak to
 me,
To *me*—*thine own.*
 Cain. Leave me!
 Adah. Why, all have left thee. 460
 Cain. And wherefore lingerest thou?
 Dost thou not fear
To dwell with one who hath done this?
 Adah. I fear
Nothing except to leave thee, much as I
Shrink from the deed which leaves thee
 brotherless.
I must not speak of this—it is between
 thee 466
And the great God.
 A Voice from within exclaims, Cain! Cain!
 Adah. Hear'st thou that voice?
 The Voice within. Cain! Cain!
 Adah. It soundeth like an angel's tone.

Enter the ANGEL of the Lord.

 Angel. Where is thy brother Abel?
 Cain. Am I then
My brother's keeper?
 Angel. Cain! what hast thou done?
The voice of thy slain brother's blood cries
 out, 470
Even from the ground, unto the Lord!—
 Now art thou
Cursed from the earth, which open'd late
 her mouth
To drink thy brother's blood from thy rash
 hand.
Henceforth, when thou shalt till the
 ground, it shall not
Yield thee her strength; a fugitive shalt
 thou 475
Be from this day, and vagabond on earth!
 Adah. This punishment is more than
 he can bear.
Behold, thou driv'st him from the face of
 earth,
And from the face of God shall he be hid.
A fugitive and vagabond on earth, 480
'Twill come to pass, that whoso findeth him
Shall slay him.
 Cain. Would they could! but who
 are they
Shall slay me? Where are these on the lone
 earth
As yet unpeopled?
 Angel. Thou hast slain thy brother,
And who shall warrant thee against thy
 son? 485
 Adah. Angel of Light! be merciful,
 nor say
That this poor aching breast now
 nourishes

A murderer in my boy, and of his father
 Angel. Then he would but be what hi
 father is. 48
Did not the milk of Eve give nutriment
To him thou now see'st so besmear'd with
 blood?
The fratricide might well engender parri
 cides.—
But it shall not be so—the Lord thy Go
And mine commandeth me to set his sea
On Cain, so that he may go forth in safety
Who slayeth Cain, a sevenfold vengeanc
 shall 49
Be taken on his head. Come hither!
 Cain. Wha
Wouldst thou with me?
 Angel. To mark upon thy brov
Exemption from such deeds as thou has
 done.
 Cain. No, let me die!
 Angel. It must not be
[*The* ANGEL *sets the mark on* CAIN'S *brow*
 Cain. It burns 50
My brow, but nought to that which is with
 in it.
Is there more? let me meet it as I may.
 Angel. Stern hast thou been and stub
 born from the womb,
As the ground thou must henceforth till
 but he
Thou slew'st was gentle as the flocks h
 tended. 50
 Cain. After the fall too soon was I be
 gotten;
Ere yet my mother's mind subsided from
The serpent, and my sire still mourn'd fo
 Eden.
That which I am, I am; I did not seek 51
For life, nor did I make myself; but could
With my own death redeem him from th
 dust—
And why not so? let him return to day,
And I lie ghastly! so shall be restored
By God the life to him he loved; an
 taken
From me a being I ne'er loved to bear.
 Angel. Who shall heal murder? wha
 is done, is done;
Go forth! fulfil thy days! and be thy deed
Unlike the last! [*The* ANGEL *disappears*
 Adah. He's gone, let us go forth
I hear our little Enoch cry within
Our bower.
 Cain. Ah! little knows he what he
 weeps for! 52
And I who have shed blood cannot she
 tears!
But the four rivers would not cleanse my
 soul.
Think'st thou my boy will bear to look or
 me?
 Adah. If I thought that he would not,
 would——
 Cain [*interrupting her*]. No,

No more of threats: we have had too many
 of them: 525
Go to our children; I will follow thee.
 Adah. I will not leave thee lonely with
 the dead;
Let us depart together.
 Cain. Oh! thou dead
And everlasting witness! whose unsinking
Blood darkens earth and heaven! what
 thou *now* art 530
I know not! but if *thou* see'st what *I* am,
I think thou wilt forgive him, whom his
 God
Can ne'er forgive, nor his own soul.—
 Farewell!
I must not, dare not touch what I have
 made thee.
I, who sprung from the same womb with
 thee, drain'd 535
The same breast, clasp'd thee often to my
 own,
In fondness brotherly and boyish, I
Can never meet thee more, nor even dare
To do that for thee, which thou shouldst
 have done
For me—compose thy limbs into their
 grave— 540
The first grave yet dug for mortality.
But who hath dug that grave? Oh, earth!
 Oh, earth!
For all the fruits thou hast render'd to
 me, I
Give thee back this. Now for the wilder-
 ness.

[ADAH *stoops down and kisses the body*
of ABEL.
 Adah. A dreary, and an early doom,
 my brother, 545
Has been thy lot! Of all who mourn for
 thee,
I alone must not weep. My office is
Henceforth to dry up tears, and not to shed
 them;
But yet of all who mourn, none mourn like
 me,
Not only for thyself, but him who slew
 thee. 550
Now, Cain! I will divide thy burden with
 thee.
 Cain. Eastward from Eden will we
 take our way;
'Tis the most desolate, and suits my steps.
 Adah. Lead! thou shalt be my guide,
 and may our God
Be thine! Now let us carry forth our
 children. 555
 Cain. And *he* who lieth there was
 childless. I
Have dried the fountain of a gentle race,
Which might have graced his recent mar-
 riage couch,
And might have temper'd this stern blood
 of mine,
Uniting with our children Abel's offspring!
O Abel! 561
 Adah. Peace be with him!
 Cain. But with *me !*——
 [*Exeunt.*

HEAVEN AND EARTH

A MYSTERY

FOUNDED ON THE FOLLOWING PASSAGE IN GENESIS, CHAP. VI. : 'AND IT CAME TO
PASS . . . THAT THE SONS OF GOD SAW THE DAUGHTERS OF MEN THAT THEY WERE
FAIR ; AND THEY TOOK THEM WIVES OF ALL WHICH THEY CHOSE.'

'And woman wailing for her demon lover.'—COLERIDGE.

DRAMATIS PERSONÆ

ANGELS	MEN	WOMEN
SAMIASA.	NOAH AND HIS SONS.	ANAH.
AZAZIEL.	IRAD.	AHOLIBAMAH.
RAPHAEL, THE ARCHANGEL.	JAPHET.	

Chorus of Spirits of the Earth. Chorus of Mortals.

PART I

SCENE I.—*A woody and mountainous dis-
trict near Mount Ararat. Time, Midnight.*

Enter ANAH *and* AHOLIBAMAH.

 Anah. Our father sleeps: it is the hour
 when they
Who love us are accustom'd to descend
Through the deep clouds o'er rocky
 Ararat:—
How my heart beats!

 Aho. Let us proceed upon
Our invocation.
 Anah. But the stars are hidden.
I tremble. 6
 Aho. So do I, but not with fear
Of aught save their delay.
 Anah. My sister, though
I love Azaziel more than——oh, too much!
What was I going to say? my heart grows
 impious.
 Aho. And where is the impiety of loving
Celestial natures? 10

Anah. But, Aholibamah,
I love our God less since his angel loved me:
This cannot be of good; and though I know not
That I do wrong, I feel a thousand fears
Which are not ominous of right.
Aho. Then wed thee 15
Unto some son of clay, and toil and spin!
There's Japhet loves thee well, hath loved thee long:
Marry, and bring forth dust!
Anah. I should have loved
Azaziel not less were he mortal; yet 19
I am glad he is not. I cannot outlive him.
And when I think that his immortal wings
Will one day hover o'er the sepulchre
Of the poor child of clay which so adored him,
As he adores the Highest, death becomes
Less terrible; but yet I pity him: 25
His grief will be of ages, or at least
Mine would be such for him, were I the seraph,
And he the perishable.
Aho. Rather say,
That he will single forth some other daughter
Of earth, and love her as he once loved Anah. 30
Anah. And if it should be so, and she loved him,
Better thus than that he should weep for me.
Aho. If I thought thus of Samiasa's love,
All seraph as he is, I'd spurn him from me.
But to our invocation!—'Tis the hour. 35
Anah. Seraph!
From thy sphere!
Whatever star contain thy glory;
In the eternal depths of heaven
Albeit thou watchest with 'the seven,' 40
Though through space infinite and hoary
Before thy bright wings worlds be driven,
Yet hear!
Oh! think of her who holds thee dear!
And though she nothing is to thee,
Yet think that thou art all to her. 46
Thou canst not tell,—and never be
Such pangs decreed to aught save me,—
The bitterness of tears.
Eternity is in thine years, 50
Unborn, undying beauty in thine eyes;
With me thou canst not sympathise,
Except in love, and there thou must
Acknowledge that more loving dust
Ne'er wept beneath the skies. 55

Thou walk'st thy many worlds, thou see'st
The face of him who made thee great,
As he hath made me of the least
Of those cast out from Eden's gate
Yet, Seraph dear! 6
Oh hear!
For thou hast loved me, and I would not die
Until I know what I must die in knowing,
That thou forgett'st in thine eternit
Her whose heart death could not keep from o'erflowing 6
For thee, immortal essence as thou art!
Great is their love who love in sin and fear;
And such, I feel, are waging in my heart
A war unworthy: to an Adamite
Forgive, my Seraph! that such thoughts appear, 7
For sorrow is our element;
Delight
An Eden kept afar from sight,
Though sometimes with our vision blent.
The hour is near 7
Which tells me we are not abandon'd quite.—
Appear! Appear!
Seraph!
My own Azaziel! be but here,
And leave the stars to their own light
Aho. Samiasa! 8
Wheresoe'er
Thou rulest in the upper air—
Or warring with the spirits who may dare
Dispute with him 8
Who made all empires, empire; or recalling
Some wandering star, which shoots through the abyss,
Whose tenants dying, while their world is falling
Share the dim destiny of clay in this;
Or joining with the inferior cherubim,
Thou deignest to partake their hymn—
Samiasa!
I call thee, I await thee, and I love thee.
Many may worship thee, that will I not
If that thy spirit down to mine may move thee 9
Descend and share my lot!
Though I be form'd of clay,
And thou of beams
More bright than those of day
On Eden's streams 10
Thine immortality cannot repay
With love more warm than mine
My love. There is a ray

In me, which, though forbidden yet to
shine, 104
I feel was lighted at thy God's and thine.
It may be hidden long: death and decay
Our mother Eve bequeath'd us—but
my heart
Defies it: though this life must pass away,
Is *that* a cause for thee and me to part?
Thou art immortal—so am I: I feel— 110
I feel my immortality o'ersweep
All pains, all tears, all time, all fears, and
peal,
Like the eternal thunders of the deep,
Into my ears this truth—'Thou liv'st for
ever!'
But if it be in joy 115
I know not, nor would know;
That secret rests with the Almighty giver,
Who folds in clouds the fonts of bliss
and woe.
But thee and me he never can destroy;
Change us he may, but not o'erwhelm;
we are 120
Of as eternal essence, and must war
With him if he will war with us: with *thee*
I can share all things, even immortal
sorrow;
For thou hast ventured to share life with
me,
And shall *I* shrink from thine eternity?
No! though the serpent's sting should
pierce me thorough, 126
And thou thyself wert like the serpent,
coil
Around me still! and I will smile,
And curse thee not; but hold
Thee in as warm a fold 130
As——but descend, and prove
A mortal's love
For an immortal. If the skies contain
More joy than thou canst give and take,
remain!
Anah. Sister! sister! I view them wing-
ing 135
Their bright way through the parted night.
Aho. The clouds from off their pinions
flinging,
As though they bore to-morrow's light.
Anah. But if our father see the sight!
Aho. He would but deem it was the
moon 140
Rising unto some sorcerer's tune
An hour too soon.
Anah. They come! *he* comes!—
Azaziel!
Aho. Haste
To meet them! Oh! for wings to bear
My spirit, while they hover there, 145
To Samiasa's breast!
Anah. Lo! they have kindled all the
west,
Like a returning sunset;—lo!
On Ararat's late secret crest
A mild and many-colour'd bow, 150

The remnant of their flashing path,
Now shines! and now, behold! it hath
Return'd to night, as rippling foam,
Which the leviathan hath lash'd
From his unfathomable home, 155
When sporting on the face of the calm
deep,
Subsides soon after he again hath dash'd
Down, down, to where the ocean's
fountains sleep.
Aho. They have touch'd earth! Samiasa!
Anah. My Azaziel!
 [*Exeunt.*

SCENE II

Enter IRAD *and* JAPHET.

Irad. Despond not: wherefore wilt
thou wander thus
To add thy silence to the silent night,
And lift thy tearful eye unto the stars?
They cannot aid thee.
Japh. But they soothe me—now
Perhaps she looks upon them as I look.
Methinks a being that is beautiful 6
Becometh more so as it looks on beauty,
The eternal beauty of undying things.
Oh, Anah!
Irad. But she loves thee not.
Japh. Alas!
Irad. And proud Aholibamah spurns
me also. 10
Japh. I feel for thee too.
Irad. Let her keep her pride,
Mine hath enabled me to bear her scorn;
It may be, time too will avenge it.
Japh. Canst thou
Find joy in such a thought?
Irad. Nor joy nor sorrow.
I loved her well, I would have loved her
better, 15
Had love been met with love: as 'tis, I
leave her
To brighter destinies, if so she deems them.
Japh. What destinies?
Irad. I have some cause to think
She loves another.
Japh. Anah!
Irad. No; her sister.
Japh. What other?
Irad. That I know not; but her air,
If not her words, tells me she loves
another. 21
Japh. Ay, but not Anah: she but
loves her God.
Irad. Whate'er she loveth, so she loves
thee not,
What can it profit thee?
Japh. True, nothing; but
I love.
Irad. And so did I.
Japh. And now thou lov'st not,
Or think'st thou lov'st not, art thou
happier? 26

547

Irad. Yes.
Japh. I pity thee.
Irad. Me! why?
Japh. For being happy,
Deprived of that which makes my
 misery.
Irad. I take thy taunt as part of thy
 distemper,
And would not feel as thou dost for more
 shekels 30
Than all our father's herds would bring,
 if weigh'd
Against the metal of the sons of Cain—
The yellow dust they try to barter with us,
As if such useless and discolour'd trash,
The refuse of the earth, could be received
For milk, and wool, and flesh, and fruits,
 and all 36
Our flocks and wilderness afford.—Go,
 Japhet,
Sigh to the stars, as wolves howl to the
 moon—
I must back to my rest.
Japh. And so would I
If I could rest.
Irad. Thou wilt not to our tents then?
Japh. No, Irad; I will to the cavern,
 whose 41
Mouth they say opens from the internal
 world
To let the inner spirits of the earth
Forth when they walk its surface.
Irad. Wherefore so?
What wouldst thou there?
Japh. Soothe further my sad spirit 45
With gloom as sad: it is a hopeless spot,
And I am hopeless.
Irad. But 'tis dangerous;
Strange sounds and sights have peopled it
 with terrors.
I must go with thee.
Japh. Irad, no; believe me
I feel no evil thought, and fear no evil.
Irad. But evil things will be thy foe
 the more 51
As not being of them: turn thy steps aside,
Or let mine be with thine.
Japh. No, neither, Irad;
I must proceed alone.
Irad. Then peace be with thee!
 [*Exit* IRAD.
Japh. [*solus*]. Peace! I have sought it
 where it should be found, 55
In love—with love, too, which perhaps
 deserved it;
And, in its stead, a heaviness of heart,
A weakness of the spirit, listless days,
And nights inexorable to sweet sleep,
Have come upon me. Peace! what peace?
 the calm 60
Of desolation, and the stillness of
The untrodden forest, only broken by
The sweeping tempest through its groan-
 ing boughs;

Such is the sullen or the fitful state
Of my mind overworn. The earth's grown
 wicked, 65
And many signs and portents have
 proclaim'd
A change at hand, and an o'erwhelming
 doom
To perishable beings. Oh, my Anah!
When the dread hour denounced shall
 open wide
The fountains of the deep, how mightest
 thou 70
Have lain within this bosom, folded from
The elements; this bosom, which in vain
Hath beat for thee, and then will beat more
 vainly,
While thine——Oh, God! at least remit to
 her
Thy wrath! for she is pure amidst the
 failing 75
As a star in the clouds, which cannot
 quench,
Although they obscure it for an hour. My
 Anah!
How would I have adored thee, but thou
 wouldst not;
And still would I redeem thee—see thee
 live
When ocean is earth's grave, and, un
 opposed 80
By rock or shallow, the leviathan,
Lord of the shoreless sea and watery
 world,
Shall wonder at his boundlessness of
 realm. [*Exit* JAPHET.

Enter NOAH *and* SHEM.

Noah. Where is thy brother Japhet?
Shem. He went forth
According to his wont, to meet with Irad
He said; but, as I fear, to bend his step
Towards Anah's tents, round which he
 hovers nightly,
Like a dove round and round its pillaged
 nest;
Or else he walks the wild up to the cavern
Which opens to the heart of Ararat. 9
Noah. What doth he there? It is an
 evil spot
Upon an earth all evil; for things worse
Than even wicked men resort there: he
Still loves this daughter of a fated race,
Although he could not wed her if she
 loved him, 9
And that she doth not. Oh, the unhappy
 hearts
Of men! that one of my blood, knowing
 well
The destiny and evil of these days,
And that the hour approacheth, should
 indulge
In such forbidden yearnings! Lead the
 way; 10
He must be sought for!

548

Shem. Go not forward, father:
I will seek Japhet.
 Noah. Do not fear for me:
All evil things are powerless on the man
Selected by Jehovah.—Let us on.
 Shem. To the tents of the father of the
 sisters? 105
 Noah. No: to the cavern of the
 Caucasus.
 [*Exeunt* NOAH *and* SHEM.

SCENE III.—*The mountains.—A cavern,
 and the rocks of Caucasus.*

Japh. [*solus*]. Ye wilds, that look
 eternal; and thou cave,
Which seem'st unfathomable; and ye
 mountains,
So varied and so terrible in beauty;
Here, in your rugged majesty of rocks
And toppling trees that twine their roots
 with stone 5
In perpendicular places, where the foot
Of man would tremble, could he reach
 them—yes,
Ye look eternal! Yet, in a few days,
Perhaps even hours, ye will be changed,
 rent, hurl'd 9
Before the mass of waters; and yon cave,
Which seems to lead into a lower world,
Shall have its depths search'd by the
 sweeping wave,
And dolphins gambol in the lion's den!
And man—Oh, men! my fellow-beings!
 Who
Shall weep above your universal grave,
Save I? Who shall be left to weep? My
 kinsmen, 16
Alas! what am I better than ye are,
That I must live beyond ye? Where shall be
The pleasant places where I thought of
 Anah
While I had hope? or the more savage
 haunts, 20
Scarce less beloved, where I despair'd for
 her?
And can it be!—Shall yon exulting peak,
Whose glittering top is like a distant star,
Lie low beneath the boiling of the deep?
No more to have the morning sun break
 forth, 25
And scatter back the mists in floating folds
From its tremendous brow? no more to
 have
Day's broad orb drop behind its head at
 even,
Leaving it with a crown of many hues?
No more to be the beacon of the world,
For angels to alight on, as the spot 31
Nearest the stars? And can those words
 '*no more*'
Be meant for thee, for all things, save for us,
And the predestined creeping things
 reserved 34
By my sire to Jehovah's bidding? May

He preserve *them*, and I *not* have the power
To snatch the loveliest of earth's daughters
 from
A doom which even some serpent, with
 his mate,
Shall 'scape to save his kind to be pro-
 long'd,
To hiss and sting through some emerging
 world, 40
Reeking and dank from out the slime,
 whose ooze
Shall slumber o'er the wreck of this, until
The salt morass subside into a sphere
Beneath the sun, and be the monument,
The sole and undistinguish'd sepulchre,
Of yet quick myriads of all life? How
 much 46
Breath will be still'd at once! All-
 beauteous world!
So young, so mark'd out for destruction, I
With a cleft heart look on thee day by day,
And night by night, thy number'd days
 and nights. 50
I cannot save thee, cannot save even her
Whose love had made me love thee more;
 but as
A portion of thy dust, I cannot think
Upon thy coming doom without a feeling
Such as—Oh God! and canst thou—
 [*He pauses.*
 [*A rushing sound from the cavern is
 heard, and shouts of laughter—after-
 wards a Spirit passes.*
Japh. In the name 55
Of the Most High, what art thou?
 Spirit [*laughs*]. Ha! ha! ha!
 Japh. By all that earth holds holiest,
 speak!
 Spirit [*laughs*]. Ha! ha!
 Japh. By the approaching deluge! by
 the earth
Which will be strangled by the ocean! by
The deep which will lay open all her foun-
 tains! 60
The heaven which will convert her clouds
 to seas,
And the Omnipotent who makes and
 crushes!
Thou unknown, terrible, and indistinct,
Yet awful Thing of Shadows, speak to me!
Why dost thou laugh that horrid laugh?
 Spirit. Why weep'st thou? 65
 Japh. For earth and all her children.
 Spirit. Ha! ha! ha!
 [*Spirit vanishes.*
 Japh. How the fiend mocks the
 tortures of a world,
The coming desolation of an orb,
On which the sun shall rise and warm no
 life!
How the earth sleeps! and all that in it is
Sleep too upon the very eve of death! 71
Why should they wake to meet it? What
 are here,

549

Which look like death in life, and speak
like things
Born ere this dying world? They come like
clouds!
[*Various Spirits pass from the cavern.*
Spirit. Rejoice! 75
The abhorred race
Which could not keep in Eden their high
place,
But listen'd to the voice
Of knowledge without power,
Are nigh the hour 80
Of death!
Not slow, not single, not by sword, nor
sorrow,
Nor years, nor heart-break, nor Time's
sapping motion,
Shall they drop off. Behold their last to-
morrow!
Earth shall be ocean! 85
And no breath,
Save of the winds, be on the unbounded
wave!
Angels shall tire their wings, but find no
spot:
Not even a rock from out the liquid grave
Shall lift its point to save, 90
Or show the place where strong Despair
hath died,
After long looking o'er the ocean wide
For the expected ebb which cometh not:
All shall be void,
Destroy'd! 95
Another element shall be the lord
Of life, and the abhorr'd
Children of dust be quench'd; and of each
hue
Of earth nought left but the unbroken blue;
And of the variegated mountain 100
Shall nought remain
Unchanged, or of the level plain;
Cedar and pine shall lift their tops in
vain:
All merged within the universal foun-
tain,
Man, earth, and fire, shall die, 105
And sea and sky
Look vast and lifeless in the eternal eye.
Upon the foam
Who shall erect a home?
Japh. [*coming forward*]. My sire! 110
Earth's seed shall not expire;
Only the evil shall be put away
From day.
Avaunt! ye exulting demons of the
waste:
Who howl your hideous joy 115
When God destroys whom you dare not
destroy;
Hence! haste!
Back to your inner caves!
Until the waves
Shall search you in your secret place,
And drive your sullen race 121

Forth, to be roll'd upon the tossing winds,
In restless wretchedness along all
space!
Spirit. Son of the saved! 124
When thou and thine have braved
The wide and warring element;
When the great barrier of the deep is rent,
Shall thou and thine be good or happy?—
No!
Thy new world and new race shall be of
woe—
Less goodly in their aspect, in their
years 130
Less than the glorious giants, who
Yet walk the world in pride,
The Sons of Heaven by many a mortal
bride.
Thine shall be nothing of the past, save
tears.
And art thou not ashamed 135
Thus to survive,
And eat, and drink, and wive?
With a base heart so far subdued and
tamed,
As even to hear this wide destruction
named,
Without such grief and courage, as should
rather 140
Bid thee await the world-dissolving wave,
Than seek a shelter with thy favour'd
father,
And build thy city o'er the drown'd
earth's grave?
Who would outlive their kind,
Except the base and blind? 145
Mine
Hateth thine
As of a different order in the sphere,
But not our own.
There is not one who hath not left a
throne 150
Vacant in heaven to dwell in darkness
here,
Rather than see his mates endure alone.
Go, wretch! and give
A life like thine to other wretches—live!
And when the annihilating waters roar
Above what they have done,
Envy the giant patriarchs then no more,
And scorn thy sire as the surviving one!
Thyself for being his son!
Chorus of Spirits issuing from the cavern.
Rejoice! 160
No more the human voice
Shall vex our joys in middle air
With prayer;
No more
Shall they adore; 165
And we, who ne'er for ages have adored
The prayer-exacting Lord,
To whom the omission of a sacrifice
Is vice;
We, we shall view the deep's salt sources
pour'd 170

Until one element shall do the work
 Of all in chaos; until they,
The creatures proud of their poor clay,
Shall perish, and their bleached bones
 shall lurk
In caves, in dens, in clefts of mountains,
 where 175
The deep shall follow to their latest lair;
Where even the brutes, in their despair,
Shall cease to prey on man and on each
 other,
And the striped tiger shall lie down to die
Beside the lamb, as though he were his
 brother; 180
 Till all things shall be as they were,
Silent and uncreated, save the sky:
 While a brief truce
Is made with Death, who shall forbear
The little remnant of the past creation,
 To generate new nations for his use;
This remnant, floating o'er the undulation
Of the subsiding deluge, from its slime,
When the hot sun hath baked the reeking
 soil
Into a world, shall give again to Time
New beings—years, diseases, sorrow,
 crime— 191
With all companionship of hate and toil,
 Until——

Japh. [*interrupting them*]. The eternal
 Will
Shall deign to expound this dream
 Of good and evil; and redeem 195
 Unto himself all times, all things;
 And, gather'd under his almighty
 wings,
 Abolish hell!
And to the expiated Earth
Restore the beauty of her birth, 200
 Her Eden in an endless paradise,
Where man no more can fall as once
 he fell,
And even the very demons shall do
 well!
Spirits. And when shall take effect this
 wondrous spell?
Japh. When the Redeemer cometh;
 first in pain, 205
 And then in glory.
Spirit. Meantime still struggle in the
 mortal chain,
 Till Earth wax hoary:
War with yourselves, and hell, and heaven,
 in vain,
 Until the clouds look gory 210
With the blood reeking from each battle-
 plain;
New times, new climes, new arts, new
 men; but still,
The same old tears, old crimes, and oldest
 ill,
Shall be amongst your race in different
 forms;
 But the same moral storms 215

Shall oversweep the future, as the waves
In a few hours the glorious giants' graves.

Chorus of Spirits.
 Brethren, rejoice!
 Mortal, farewell! 219
Hark! hark! already we can hear the voice
 Of growing ocean's gloomy swell;
The winds, too, plume their piercing
 wings;
The clouds have nearly fill'd their
 springs;
The fountains of the great deep shall be
 broken,
And heaven set wide her windows;
 while mankind 225
View, unacknowledged, each tremendous
 token—
 Still, as they were from the beginning,
 blind.
 We hear the sound they cannot hear,
 The mustering thunders of the threat-
 ening sphere;
 Yet a few hours their coming is
 delay'd; 230
Their flashing banners, folded still on
 high,
 Yet undisplay'd,
Save to the Spirit's all-pervading eye.
 Howl! howl! oh Earth!
Thy death is nearer than thy recent birth;
Tremble, ye mountains, soon to shrink
 below 236
 The ocean's overflow!
The wave shall break upon your cliffs;
 and shells,
The little shells, of ocean's least things be
Deposed where now the eagle's offspring
 dwells— 240
How shall he shriek o'er the remorseless
 sea!
And call his nestlings up with fruitless yell,
Unanswer'd, save by the encroaching
 swell;—
While man shall long in vain for his broad
 wings,
The wings which could not save:—
Where could he rest them, while the whole
 space brings 246
Nought to his eye beyond the deep, his
 grave?
 Brethren, rejoice!
And loudly lift each superhuman voice—
 All die, 250
Save the slight remnant of Seth's seed—
 The seed of Seth,
Exempt for future sorrow's sake from
 death,
 But of the sons of Cain
 None shall remain; 255
 And all his goodly daughters
Must lie beneath the desolating waters;
Or, floating upward, with their long hair laid
Along the wave, the cruel heaven upbraid,

Which would not spare 260
Beings even in death so fair.
It is decreed,
 All die!
And to the universal human cry
The universal silence shall succeed! 265
 Fly, brethren, fly!
 But still rejoice!
 We fell!
 They fall!
 So perish all 270
These petty foes of Heaven who shrink
 from hell!
[*The Spirits disappear, soaring upwards.*
Japh. [*solus*]. God hath proclaim'd
 the destiny of earth;
My father's ark of safety hath announced it;
The very demons shriek it from their
 caves;
The scroll of Enoch prophesied it long
In silent books, which, in their silence,
 say 276
More to the mind than thunder to the ear:
And yet men listen'd not, nor listen; but
Walk darkling to their doom; which,
 though so nigh,
Shakes them no more in their dim dis-
 belief, 280
Than that last cries shall shake the
 Almighty purpose,
Or deaf obedient ocean, which fulfils it.
No sign yet hangs its banner in the air;
The clouds are few, and of their wonted
 texture; 284
The sun will rise upon the earth's last day
As on the fourth day of creation, when
God said unto him, 'Shine!' and he broke
 forth
Into the dawn, which lighted not the yet
Unform'd forefather of mankind—but
 roused
Before the human orison the earlier 290
Made and far sweeter voices of the birds,
Which in the open firmament of heaven
Have wings like angels, and like them
 salute
Heaven first each day before the Adam-
 ites:
Their matins now draw nigh—the east is
 kindling— 295
And they will sing! and day will break!
 Both near,
So near the awful close! For these must
 drop
Their outworn pinions on the deep; and
 day,
After the bright course of a few brief
 morrows,—
Ay, day will rise; but upon what?—a
 chaos, 300
Which was ere day; and which, renew'd,
 makes time
Nothing! for, without life, what are the
 hours?

No more to dust than is eternity
Unto Jehovah, who created both.
Without him, even eternity would be
A void: without man, time, as made for
 man, 306
Dies with man, and is swallow'd in that
 deep
Which has no fountain; as his race will be
Devour'd by that which drowns his infant
 world.—
What have we here? Shapes of both earth
 and air? 310
No—*all* of heaven, they are so beautiful.
I cannot trace their features; but their
 forms,
How lovelily they move along the side
Of the grey mountain, scattering its mist!
And after the swart savage spirits, whose
Infernal immortality pour'd forth 316
Their impious hymn of triumph, they shall
 be
Welcome as Eden. It may be they come
To tell me the reprieve of our young
 world,
For which I have so often pray'd—They
 come! 320
Anah! oh, God! and with her——

Enter SAMIASA, AZAZIEL, ANAH, *and*
 AHOLIBAMAH.

Anah. Japhet!
Sam. Lo!
A son of Adam!
Aza. What doth the earth-
 born here,
While all his race are slumbering?
Japh. Angel! what
Dost thou on earth when thou shouldst be
 on high?
Aza. Know'st thou not, or forgett'st
 thou, that a part 325
Of our great function is to guard thine
 earth?
Japh. But all good angels have for-
 saken earth,
Which is condemn'd; nay, even the evil fly
The approaching chaos. Anah! Anah! my
In vain, and long, and still to be, beloved!
Why walk'st thou with this spirit, in those
 hours 331
When no good spirit longer lights below?
Anah. Japhet, I cannot answer thee;
 yet, yet
Forgive me——
Japh. May the Heaven, which soon no
 more
Will pardon, do so! for thou art greatly
 tempted. 335
Aho. Back to thy tents, insulting son
 of Noah!
We love thee not.
Japh. The hour may come when thou
May'st know me better; and thy sister
 know

Me still the same which I have ever been.
 Sam. Son of the patriarch, who hath
 ever been 340
Upright before his God, whate'er thy gifts,
And thy words seem of sorrow, mix'd with
 wrath,
How have Azaziel, or myself, brought on
 thee
Wrong?
 Japh. Wrong! the greatest of all
 wrongs; but thou
Say'st well; though she be dust, I did not,
 could not, 345
Deserve her. Farewell, Anah! I have said
That word so often! but now say it, ne'er
To be repeated. Angel! or whate'er
Thou art, or must be soon, hast thou the
 power 349
To save this beautiful—*these* beautiful
Children of Cain?
 Aza. From what?
 Japh. And is it so,
That ye too know not? Angels! angels! ye
Have shared man's sin, and, it may be,
 now must
Partake his punishment; or, at the least,
My sorrow.
 Sam. Sorrow! I ne'er thought till
 now 355
To hear an Adamite speak riddles to me.
 Japh. And hath not the Most High
 expounded them?
Then ye are lost, as they are lost.
 Aho. So be it!
If they love as they are loved, they will not
 shrink
More to be mortal, than I would to dare
An immortality of agonies 361
With Samiasa!
 Anah. Sister! sister! speak not
 Thus.
 Aza. Fearest thou, my Anah?
 Anah. Yes, for thee:
I would resign the greater remnant of
This little life of mine, before one hour
Of thine eternity should know a pang.
 Japh. It is for *him*, then! for the seraph
 thou
Hast left me! That is nothing, if thou hast
 not
Left thy God too! for unions like to these,
Between a mortal and an immortal, can-
 not 370
Be happy or be hallow'd. We are sent
Upon the earth to toil and die; and they
Are made to minister on high unto
The Highest: but if he can *save* thee, soon
The hour will come in which celestial aid
Alone can do so.
 Anah. Ah! he speaks of death.
 Sam. Of death to *us!* and those who
 are with us!
But that the man seems full of sorrow, I
Could smile.

 Japh. I grieve not for myself, nor fear;
I am safe, not for my own deserts, but
 those 380
Of a well-doing sire, who hath been found
Righteous enough to save his children.
 Would
His power was greater of redemption! or
That by exchanging my own life for hers,
Who could alone have made mine happy,
 she, 385
The last and loveliest of Cain's race, could
 share
The ark which shall receive a remnant of
The seed of Seth!
 Aho. And dost thou think that we,
With Cain's, the eldest born of Adam's,
 blood
Warm in our veins,—strong Cain! who
 was begotten 390
In Paradise,—would mingle with Seth's
 children?
Seth, the last offspring of old Adam's
 dotage?
No, not to save all earth, were earth in
 peril!
Our race hath always dwelt apart from thine
From the beginning, and shall do so ever.
 Japh. I did not speak to thee, Aholi-
 bamah! 396
Too much of the forefather whom thou
 vauntest
Has come down in that haughty blood
 which springs
From him who shed the first, and that a
 brother's! 399
But thou, my Anah! let me call thee mine,
Albeit thou art not; 'tis a word I cannot
Part with, although I must from thee. My
 Anah!
Thou who dost rather make me dream that
 Abel
Had left a daughter, whose pure pious race
Survived in thee, so much unlike thou art
The rest of the stern Cainites, save in
 beauty, 406
For all of them are fairest in their favour——
 Aho. [*interrupting him*]. And wouldst
 thou have her like our father's foe
In mind, in soul? If *I* partook thy thought,
And dream'd that aught of *Abel* was in
 her!— 410
Get thee hence, son of Noah; thou makest
 strife.
 Japh. Offspring of Cain, thy father did
 so!
 Aho. But
He slew not Seth: and what hast thou to do
With other deeds between his God and
 him?
 Japh. Thou speakest well: his God
 hath judged him, and 415
I had not named his deed, but that thyself
Didst seem to glory in him, nor to shrink
From what he had done.

Aho. He was our fathers' father;
The eldest born of man, the strongest,
 bravest,
And most enduring:—Shall I blush for
 him 420
From whom we had our being? Look
 upon
Our race; behold their stature and their
 beauty,
Their courage, strength, and length of
 days——
Japh. They are number'd.
 Aho. Be it so! but while yet their hours
 endure,
I glory in my brethren and our fathers.
 Japh. My sire and race but glory in
 their God, 426
Anah! and thou?——
 Anah. Whate'er our God decrees,
The God of Seth, as Cain, I must obey,
And will endeavour patiently to obey.
But could I dare to pray in his dread hour
Of universal vengeance (if such should be),
It would not be to live, alone exempt
Of all my house. My sister! oh, my sister!
What were the world, or other worlds, or
 all
The brightest future, without the sweet
 past— 435
Thy love, my father's, all the life, and all
The things which sprang up with me, like
 the stars,
Making my dim existence radiant with
Soft lights which were not mine? Aholi-
 bamah!
Oh! if there should be mercy—seek it,
 find it: 440
I abhor death, because that thou must die.
 Aho. What, hath this dreamer, with
 his father's ark,
The bugbear he hath built to scare the
 world,
Shaken *my* sister? Are *we* not the loved
Of seraphs? and if we were not, must we
Cling to a son of Noah for our lives? 446
Rather than thus——But the enthusiast
 dreams
The worst of dreams, the fantasies
 engender'd
By hopeless love and heated vigils. Who
Shall shake these solid mountains, this
 firm earth, 450
And bid those clouds and waters take a
 shape
Distinct from that which we and all our
 sires
Have seen them wear on their eternal way?
Who shall do this?
 Japh. He whose one word produced
 them.
 Aho. Who *heard* that word?
 Japh. The universe, which leap'd
To life before it. Ah! smilest thou still in
 scorn? 456

Turn to thy seraphs: if they attest it not,
They are none.
 Sam. Aholibamah, own thy God!
 Aho. I have ever hail'd our Maker,
 Samiasa,
As thine, and mine: a God of love, not
 sorrow. 460
 Japh. Alas! what else is love but
 sorrow? Even
He who made earth in love had soon to
 grieve
Above its first and best inhabitants.
 Aho. 'Tis said so.
 Japh. It is even so.

Enter NOAH *and* SHEM.

 Noah. Japhet! What
Dost thou here with these children of the
 wicked? 465
Dread'st thou not to partake their coming
 doom?
 Japh. Father, it cannot be a sin to seek
To save an earth-born being; and behold,
These are not of the sinful, since they have
The fellowship of angels.
 Noah. These are they, then, 470
Who leave the throne of God, to take
 them wives
From out the race of Cain; the sons of
 heaven,
Who seek earth's daughters for their
 beauty?
 Aza. Patriarch!
Thou hast said it.
 Noah. Woe, woe, woe to such com-
 munion!
Has not God made a barrier between
 earth 475
And heaven, and limited each, kind to kind?
 Sam. Was not man made in high
 Jehovah's image?
Did God not love what he had made?
 And what
Do we but imitate and emulate
His love unto created love?
 Noah. I am 480
But man, and was not made to judge man-
 kind,
Far less the sons of God; but as our God
Has deign'd to commune with me, and
 reveal
His judgments, I reply, that the descent
Of seraphs from their everlasting seat
Unto a perishable and perishing, 485
Even on the very *eve* of *perishing*, world,
Cannot be good.
 Aza. What! though it were
 to save?
 Noah. Not ye in all your glory can
 redeem
What he who made you glorious hath con-
 demn'd. 490
Were your immortal mission safety,
 'twould

Be general, not for two, though beautiful;
And beautiful they are, but not the less
Condemn'd.
Japh. Oh, father! say it not.
Noah. Son! son!
If that thou wouldst avoid their doom,
 forget 495
That they exist: they soon shall cease to be,
While thou shalt be the sire of a new
 world,
And better.
Japh. Let me die with *this*, and
 them!
Noah. Thou *shouldst* for such a
 thought, but shalt not; he
Who *can*, redeems thee.
Sam. And why him and thee, 500
More than what he, thy son, prefers to
 both?
Noah. Ask him who made thee greater
 than myself
And mine, but not less subject to his own
Almightiness. And lo! his mildest and
Least to be tempted messenger appears!

Enter RAPHAEL *the Archangel.*

Raph. Spirits!
 Whose seat is near the throne,
 What do ye here?
 Is thus a seraph's duty to be shown
 Now that the hour is near 510
 When earth must be alone?
 Return!
 Adore and burn
In glorious homage with the elected
 'seven.'
 Your place is heaven. 515
Sam. Raphael!
The first and fairest of the sons of God,
 How long hath this been law,
That earth by angels must be left untrod?
 Earth! which oft saw 520
Jehovah's footsteps not disdain her sod!
The world he loved, and made
For love; and oft have we obey'd
His frequent mission with delighted
 pinions:
 Adoring him in his least works dis-
 play'd; 525
Watching this youngest star of his
 dominions;
 And, as the latest birth of his great word,
 Eager to keep it worthy of our Lord.
 Why is thy brow severe?
And wherefore speak'st thou of destruc-
 tion near? 530
Raph. Had Samiasa and Azaziel been
In their true place, with the angelic choir,
 Written in fire
 They would have seen
 Jehovah's late decree, 535
And not inquired their Maker's breath of
 me:
 But ignorance must ever be

A part of sin;
And even the spirits' knowledge shall
 grow less
 As they wax proud within; 540
For Blindness is the first-born of Excess.
 When all good angels left the world, ye
 stay'd,
Stung with strange passions, and debased
 By mortal feelings for a mortal maid:
But ye are pardon'd thus far, and
 replaced 545
With your pure equals. Hence! away!
 away!
 Or stay,
 And lose eternity by that delay!
Aza. And thou! if earth be thus for-
 bidden
 In the decree 550
 To us until this moment hidden,
 Dost thou not err as we
 In being here?
Raph. I came to call ye back to your
 fit sphere,
In the great name and at the word of
 God. 555
Dear, dearest in themselves, and scarce
 less dear
That which I came to do: till now we trod
Together the eternal space; together
 Let us still walk the stars. True, earth
 must die!
Her race, return'd into her womb, must
 wither, 560
 And much which she inherits: but oh!
 why
 Cannot this earth be made, or be
 destroy'd,
Without involving ever some vast void
In the immortal ranks? immortal still
 In their immeasurable forfeiture. 565
Our brother Satan fell; his burning will
 Rather than longer worship dared
 endure!
 But ye who still are pure!
Seraphs! less mighty than that mightiest
 one,
 Think how he was undone! 570
And think if tempting man can com-
 pensate
 For heaven desired too late?
 Long have I warr'd,
 Long must I war
 With him who deem'd it hard 575
 To be created, and to acknowledge
 him
 Who midst the cherubim
Made him as suns to a dependent star,
Leaving the archangels at his right hand
 dim.
 I loved him—beautiful he was: oh,
 heaven 580
Save *his* who made, what beauty and what
 power
Was ever like to Satan's! Would the hour

In which he fell could ever be forgiven!
The wish is impious: but, oh ye!
Yet undestroy'd, be warn'd! Eternity
 With him, or with his God, is in your
 choice: 586
He hath not tempted you; he cannot tempt
The angels, from his further snares
 exempt:
But man hath listen'd to his voice,
And ye to woman's—beautiful she is,
The serpent's voice less subtle than her
 kiss. 591
The snake but vanquish'd dust; but she
 will draw
A second host from heaven, to break
 heaven's law.
 Yet, yet, oh fly!
 Ye cannot die; 595
 But they
 Shall pass away,
While ye shall fill with shrieks the upper sky
 For perishable clay,
Whose memory in your immortality 600
 Shall long outlast the sun which gave
 them day.
Think how your essence differeth from
 theirs
In all but suffering! why partake
The agony to which they must be heirs—
Born to be plough'd with years, and sown
 with cares, 605
 And reap'd by Death, lord of the human
 soil?
Even had their days been left to toil their
 path
Through time to dust, unshorten'd by
 God's wrath,
 Still they are Evil's prey and Sorrow's
 spoil.
Aho. Let them fly! 610
I hear the voice which says that all must
 die,
Sooner than our white-bearded patriarchs
 died;
 And that on high
 An ocean is prepared,
 While from below 615
The deep shall rise to meet heaven's over-
 flow.
Few shall be spared,
It seems; and, of that few, the race of Cain
Must lift their eyes to Adam's God in vain.
 Sister! since it is so, 620
 And the eternal Lord
 In vain would be implored
 For the remission of one hour of woe,
Let us resign even what we have adored,
And meet the wave, as we would meet the
 sword, 625
 If not unmoved, yet undismay'd,
And wailing less for us than those who
 shall
Survive in mortal or immortal thrall,
 And, when the fatal waters are allay'd,

Weep for the myriads who can weep no
 more. 630
Fly, seraphs! to your own eternal shore,
Where winds nor howl nor waters roar.
 Our portion is to die,
 And yours to live for ever:
But which is best, a dead eternity, 63
Or living, is but known to the great Giver
 Obey him, as we shall obey;
I would not keep this life of mine in clay
 An hour beyond his will; 63
Nor see ye lose a portion of his grace,
For all the mercy which Seth's race
 Find still.
 Fly!
And as your pinions bear ye back to
 heaven,
Think that my love still mounts with thee
 on high, 64
 Samiasa!
And if I look up with a tearless eye,
'Tis that an angel's bride disdains to
 weep,—
Farewell! Now rise, inexorable deep!
Anah. And must we die? 65
 And must I lose thee too,
 Azaziel?
 Oh, my heart! my heart!
 Thy prophecies were true!
 And yet thou wert so happy too
The blow, though not unlook'd for, falls
 as new: 65
 But yet depart!
 Ah! why?
 Yet let me not retain thee—fly!
My pangs can be but brief; but thine
 would be 66
Eternal, if repulsed from heaven for me
 Too much already hast thou deign'd
 To one of Adam's race!
 Our doom is sorrow: not to us alone,
But to the spirits who have not disdain'd
To love us, cometh anguish with disgrace
The first who taught us knowledge hath
 been hurl'd
 From his once archangelic throne
 Into some unknown world:
 And thou, Azaziel! No— 67
 Thou shalt not suffer woe
For me. Away! nor weep!
 Thou canst not weep; but yet
 May'st suffer more, not weeping: then
 forget
Her, whom the surges of the all-strangling
 deep 67
Can bring no pang like this. Fly! fly!
Being gone, 'twill be less difficult to die
 Japh. Oh, say not so!
 Father! and thou, archangel, thou!
 Surely celestial mercy lurks below 68
 That pure severe serenity of brow:
 Let them not meet this sea without a
 shore,
 Save in our ark, or let me be no more!

Noah. Peace, child of passion, peace!
If not within thy heart, yet with thy tongue
 Do God no wrong! 686
Live as he wills it—die, when he ordains,
A righteous death, unlike the seed of
 Cain's.
Cease, or be sorrowful in silence; cease
To weary Heaven's ear with thy selfish
 plaint. 690
Wouldst thou have God commit a sin
 for thee?
 Such would it be
 To alter his intent
For a mere mortal sorrow. Be a man!
And bear what Adam's race must bear,
 and can. 695
Japh. Ay, father! but when they are
 gone,
 And we are all alone,
Floating upon the azure desert, and
The depth beneath us hides our own dear
 land,
 And dearer, silent friends and brethren,
 all 700
Buried in its immeasurable breast,
Who, who, our tears, our shrieks, shall
 then command?
 Can we in desolation's peace have rest?
 Oh God! be thou a God, and spare
 Yet while 'tis time; 705
 Renew not Adam's fall.
Mankind were then but twain,
But they are numerous now as are the waves
 And the tremendous rain,
Whose drops shall be less thick than
 would their graves, 710
 Were graves permitted to the seed of
 Cain.
Noah. Silence, vain boy! each word of
 thine's a crime,
Angel! forgive this stripling's fond despair.
Raph. Seraphs! these mortals speak
 in passion: Ye!
Who are, or should be, passionless and
 pure, 715
May now return with me.
Sam. It may not be:
We have chosen, and will endure.
Raph. Say'st thou?
Aza. He hath said it, and I say,
 Amen!
Raph. Again!
 Then from this hour, 720
 Shorn as ye are of all celestial power,
And aliens from your God,
 Farewell!
Japh. Alas! where shall they dwell?
Hark, hark! Deep sounds, and deeper still,
 Are howling from the mountain's
 bosom: 726
There's not a breath of wind upon the hill,
 Yet quivers every leaf, and drops each
 blossom:
Earth groans as if beneath a heavy load.

Noah. Hark, hark! the sea-birds cry!
In clouds they overspread the lurid sky,
And hover round the mountain, where
 before
Never a white wing, wetted by the wave,
 Yet dared to soar,
Even when the waters wax'd too fierce
 to brave. 735
 Soon it shall be their only shore,
 And then, no more!
Japh. The sun! the sun!
He riseth, but his better light is gone;
 And a black circle, bound 740
 His glaring disk around,
Proclaims earth's last of summer days hath
 shone!
 The clouds return into the hues of
 night,
Save where their brazen-colour'd edges
 streak
The verge where brighter morns were wont
 to break. 745
Noah. And lo! yon flash of light,
The distant thunder's harbinger, appears!
It cometh! hence, away!
Leave to the elements their evil prey!
Hence to where our all-hallow'd ark up-
 rears 750
 Its safe and wreckless sides!
Japh. Oh, father, stay!
Leave not my Anah to the swallowing tides!
Noah. Must we not leave all life to
 such? Begone!
Japh. Not I. 755
Noah. Then die
 With them!
How darest thou look on that prophetic
 sky,
And seek to save what all things now
 condemn,
 In overwhelming unison 760
 With just Jehovah's wrath!
Japh. Can rage and justice join in the
 same path?
Noah. Blasphemer! darest thou
 murmur even now?
Raph. Patriarch, be still a father!
 smooth thy brow:
Thy son, despite his folly, shall not sink:
He knows not what he says, yet shall not
 drink 766
With sobs the salt foam of the swelling
 waters:
But be, when passion passeth, good as
 thou,
Nor perish like heaven's children with
 man's daughters.
Aho. The tempest cometh; heaven
 and earth unite 770
 For the annihilation of all life.
 Unequal is the strife
Between our strength and the Eternal
 Might!

Sam. But ours is with thee; we will
 bear ye far
To some untroubled star, 775
Where thou, and Anah, shalt partake our
 lot:
And if thou dost not weep for thy lost
 earth,
Our forfeit heaven shall also be forgot.
Anah. Oh! my dear father's tents, my
 place of birth,
And mountains, land, and woods! when
 ye are not, 780
Who shall dry up my tears?
Aza. Thy spirit-lord.
Fear not; though we are shut from heaven,
Yet much is ours, whence we can not be
 driven.
Raph. Rebel! thy words are wicked,
 as thy deeds
Shall henceforth be but weak: the flaming
 sword, 785
Which chased the first-born out of
 Paradise,
Still flashes in the angelic hands.
Aza. It cannot slay us: threaten dust
 with death,
And talk of weapons unto that which
 bleeds.
What are thy swords in our immortal
 eyes? 790
Raph. The moment cometh to ap-
 prove thy strength;
And learn at length
How vain to war with what thy God com-
 mands:
Thy former force was in thy faith.

Enter Mortals, flying for refuge.
Chorus of Mortals.

The heavens and earth are mingling—
 God! oh God! 795
What have we done? Yet spare!
Hark! even the forest beasts howl forth
 their prayer!
The dragon crawls from out his den,
To herd, in terror, innocent with men;
And the birds scream their agony through
 air. 800
Yet, yet, Jehovah! yet withdraw thy rod
Of wrath, and pity thine own world's
 despair!
Hear not man only but all nature plead!
Raph. Farewell, thou earth! ye
 wretched sons of clay, 804
I cannot, must not, aid you. 'Tis decreed!
 [*Exit* RAPHAEL.
Japh. Some clouds sweep on as
 vultures for their prey,
While others, fix'd as rocks, await the
 word
At which their wrathful vials shall be
 pour'd.
No azure more shall robe the firmament,

Nor spangled stars be glorious: Death
 hath risen: 810
In the sun's place a pale and ghastly glare
Hath wound itself around the dying air.
Aza. Come, Anah! quit this chaos-
 founded prison,
To which the elements again repair,
To turn it into what it was: beneath 815
The shelter of these wings thou shalt be safe
As was the eagle's nestling once within
Its mother's.—Let the coming chaos chafe
With all its elements! Heed not their din!
A brighter world than this, where thou
 shalt breathe 820
Ethereal life, will we explore:
These darken'd clouds are not the only skies
 [AZAZIEL *and* SAMIASA *fly off and dis-
 appear with* ANAH *and* AHOLIBAMAH.
Japh. They are gone! They have dis-
 appear'd amidst the roar
Of the forsaken world; and never more,
Whether they live, or die with all earth's
 life, 825
Now near its last, can aught restore
Anah unto these eyes.

Chorus of Mortals.

Oh son of Noah! mercy on thy kind!
What! wilt thou leave us all—all—all
 behind?
While safe amidst the elemental strife,
Thou sitt'st within thy guarded ark? 830
 A Mother [*offering her infant to* JAPHET.
 Oh let this child embark!
 I brought him forth in woe,
 But thought it joy
 To see him to my bosom clinging so.
 Why was he born? 835
 What hath he done—
 My unwean'd son—
To move Jehovah's wrath or scorn?
What is there in this milk of mine, that
 death 840
 Should stir all heaven and earth up to
 destroy
 My boy.
And roll the waters o'er his placid breath?
Save him, thou seed of Seth!
Or cursed be—with him who made 845
Thee and thy race, for which we are
 betray'd!
Japh. Peace! 'tis no hour for curses,
 but for prayer!

Chorus of Mortals.

 For prayer!!!
 And where
 Shall prayer ascend, 850
When the swoln clouds unto the moun-
 tains bend
 And burst,
And gushing oceans every barrier rend,
 Until the very deserts know no thirst?
 Accursed 855

558

Be he who made thee and thy sire!
We deem our curses vain; we must expire;
 But as we know the worst,
Why should our hymn be raised, our knees
 be bent
Before the implacable Omnipotent, 860
Since we must fall the same?
If he hath made earth, let it be his shame,
 To make a world for torture.—Lo! they
 come,
The loathsome waters, in their rage!
And with their roar make wholesome
 nature dumb! 865
 The forests' trees (coeval with the hour
When Paradise upsprung,
 Ere Eve gave Adam knowledge for her
 dower,
Or Adam his first hymn of slavery sung),
 So massy, vast, yet green in their old
 age, 870
 Are overtopp'd,
Their summer blossoms by the surges
 lopp'd,
Which rise, and rise, and rise.
Vainly we look up to the lowering skies—
 They meet the seas, 875
And shut out God from our beseeching
 eyes.
Fly, son of Noah, fly! and take thine
 ease,
In thine allotted ocean-tent;
And view, all floating o'er the element,
The corpses of the world of thy young
 days: 880
 Then to Jehovah raise
 Thy song of praise!
A Mortal. Blessed are the dead
 Who die in the Lord!
And though the waters be o'er earth out-
 spread, 885
 Yet, as *his* word,
 Be the decree adored!
He gave me life—he taketh but
 The breath which is his own:
And though these eyes should be for ever
 shut, 890
 Nor longer this weak voice before his
 throne
Be heard in supplicating tone,
 Still blessed be the Lord,
 For what is past,
 For that which is: 895
 For all are his,
 From first to last—

Time, space, eternity, life, death—
 The vast known and immeasurable un-
 known.
He made, and can unmake; 900
And shall *I*, for a little gasp of breath,
 Blaspheme and groan?
No; let me die, as I have lived, in faith,
Nor quiver, though the universe may
 quake!

Chorus of Mortals.

 Where shall we fly? 905
 Not to the mountains high;
For now their torrents rush, with double
 roar,
To meet the ocean, which, advancing
 still,
 Already grasps each drowning hill,
Nor leaves an unsearch'd cave. 910

Enter a Woman.

Woman. Oh, save me, save!
Our valley is no more:
My father and my father's tent,
My brethren and my brethren's herds,
 The pleasant trees that o'er our noon-
 day bent, 915
And sent forth evening songs from
 sweetest birds,
The little rivulet which freshen'd all
 Our pastures green,
 No more are to be seen.
When to the mountain cliff I climb'd this
 morn, 920
 I turn'd to bless the spot,
And not a leaf appear'd about to fall;—
 And now they are not!
Why was I born?
Japh. To die! in youth to die!
And happier in that doom, 925
Than to behold the universal tomb,
 Which I
Am thus condemn'd to weep above in
 vain.
Why, when all perish, why must I remain?
 [*The waters rise; Men fly in every di-*
 rection; many are overtaken by the
 waves; the Chorus of Mortals dis-
 perses in search of safety up the
 mountains: Japhet remains upon a
 rock, while the Ark floats towards him
 in the distance.

WERNER; OR, THE INHERITANCE:

A TRAGEDY

TO

THE ILLUSTRIOUS GOETHE,

BY ONE OF HIS HUMBLEST ADMIRERS, THIS TRAGEDY IS DEDICATED.

PREFACE

THE following drama is taken entirely from the 'German's Tale, Kruitzner', published many year ago in 'Lee's Canterbury Tales', written (I believe) by two sisters, of whom one furnished only thi story and another, both of which are considered superior to the remainder of the collection. I hav adopted the characters, plan, and even the language of many parts of this story. Some of the character are modified or altered, a few of the names changed, and one character (Ida of Stralenheim) adde by myself: but in the rest the original is chiefly followed. When I was young (about fourteen, I think) I first read this tale, which made a deep impression upon me; and may, indeed, be said to contain th germ of much that I have since written. I am not sure that it ever was very popular; or, at any rate its popularity has since been eclipsed by that of other great writers in the same department. But I hav generally found that those who *had* read it, agreed with me in their estimate of the singular powe of mind and conception which it developes. I should also add *conception*, rather than execution; fo the story might, perhaps, have been developed with greater advantage. Amongst those whose opinion agreed with mine upon this story, I could mention some very high names: but it is not necessary, no indeed of any use; for every one must judge according to his own feelings. I merely refer the reade to the original story, that he may see to what extent I have borrowed from it; and am not unwillin that he should find much greater pleasure in perusing it than the drama which is founded upon it contents.

I had begun a drama upon this tale so far back as 1815 (the first I ever attempted, except one a thirteen years old, called 'Ulric and Ilvina', which I had sense enough to burn), and had nearly com pleted an act, when I was interrupted by circumstances. This is somewhere amongst my papers i England; but as it has not been found, I have re-written the first, and added the subsequent acts.

The whole is neither intended, nor in any shape adapted, for the stage.

PISA, *February*, 1822.

DRAMATIS PERSONÆ

MEN

				WOMEN
WERNER.	IDENSTEIN.	HENRICK.	MEISTER.	JOSEPHINE.
ULRIC.	GABOR.	ERIC.	RODOLPH.	IDA STRALENHEIM.
STRALENHEIM.	FRITZ.	ARNHEIM.	LUDWIG.	

SCENE.—*Partly on the frontier of Silesia, and partly in Siegendorf Castle, near Prague.*

TIME.—The Close of the Thirty Years' War.

ACT I

SCENE I.—*The Hall of a decayed Palace near a small Town on the Northern Frontier of Silesia—the Night tempestuous.*

WERNER *and* JOSEPHINE, *his Wife.*

Jos. My love, be calmer!
Wer. I am calm.
Jos. To me—
Yes, but not to thyself: thy pace is hurried,
And no one walks a chamber like to ours
With steps like thine when his heart is at
 rest.
Were it a garden, I should deem thee
 happy, 5
And stepping with the bee from flower to
 flower;
But *here!*

Wer. 'Tis chill; the tapestry lets
 through
The wind to which it waves: my blood is
 frozen.
Jos. Ah, no!
Wer. [*smiling*]. Why! wouldst tho
 have it so?
Jos. I would
Have it a healthful current.
Wer. Let it flow 1
Until 'tis spilt or check'd—how soon,
 care not.
Jos. And am I nothing in thy heart?
Wer. All—all
Jos. Then canst thou wish for tha
 which must break mine?
Wer. [*approaching her slowly*]. But fo
 thee I had been—no matter what,
But much of good and evil; what I
 am, 1;

Thou knowest; what I might or should
 have been,
Thou knowest not: but still I love thee, nor
Shall aught divide us.
 [WERNER *walks on abruptly, and then*
 approaches JOSEPHINE.
 The storm of the night
Perhaps affects me; I'm a thing of feelings,
And have of late been sickly, as, alas! 20
Thou know'st by sufferings more than
 mine, my love!
In watching me.
 Jos. To see thee well is much—
To see thee happy—
 Wer. Where hast thou seen such?
Let me be wretched with the rest!
 Jos. But think
How many in this hour of tempest shiver
Beneath the biting wind and heavy rain,
Whose every drop bows them down nearer
 earth,
Which hath no chamber for them save
 beneath
Her surface.
 Wer. And that's not the worst: who
 cares
For chambers? rest is all. The wretches
 whom 30
Thou namest—ay, the wind howls round
 them, and
The dull and dropping rain saps in their
 bones
The creeping marrow. I have been a
 soldier,
A hunter, and a traveller, and am
A beggar, and should know the thing thou
 talk'st of. 35
 Jos. And art thou not now shelter'd
 from them all?
 Wer. Yes. And from these alone.
 Jos. And that is something.
 Wer. True—to a peasant.
 Jos. Should the nobly born
Be thankless for that refuge which their
 habits
Of early delicacy render more 40
Needful than to the peasant, when the ebb
Of fortune leaves them on the shoals of
 life?
 Wer. It is not that, thou know'st it is
 not: we
Have borne all this, I'll not say patiently,
Except in thee—but we have borne it.
 Jos. Well?
 Wer. Something beyond our outward
 sufferings (though
These were enough to gnaw into our souls)
Hath stung me oft, and, more than ever,
 now.
When, but for this untoward sickness,
 which 49
Seized me upon this desolate frontier, and
Hath wasted, not alone my strength, but
 means,

And leaves us—no! this is beyond me!—
 but
For this I had been happy—*thou* been
 happy—
The splendour of my rank sustain'd—my
 name—
My father's name—been still upheld; and,
 more 55
Than those——
 Jos. [*abruptly*]. My son—our son—
 our Ulric,
Been clasp'd again in these long-empty
 arms,
And all a mother's hunger satisfied.
Twelve years! he was but eight then:—
 beautiful
He was, and beautiful he must be now,
My Ulric! my adored! 61
 Wer. I have been full oft
The chase of Fortune; now she hath
 o'ertaken
My spirit where it cannot turn at bay,—
Sick, poor, and lonely.
 Jos. Lonely! my dear husband?
 Wer. Or worse—involving all I love,
 in this 65
Far worse than solitude. *Alone,* I had
 died,
And all been over in a nameless grave.
 Jos. And I had not outlived thee; but
 pray take
Comfort! We have struggled long; and
 they who strive 69
With Fortune win or weary her at last,
So that they find the goal or cease to feel
Further. Take comfort,—we shall find
 our boy.
 Wer. We were in sight of him, of
 everything
Which could bring compensation for past
 sorrow—
And to be baffled thus!
 Jos. We are not baffled. 75
 Wer. Are we not penniless?
 Jos. We ne'er were wealthy.
 Wer. But I was born to wealth, and
 rank, and power;
Enjoy'd them, loved them, and, alas!
 abused them,
And forfeited them by my father's wrath,
In my o'er-fervent youth: but for the
 abuse 80
Long sufferings have atoned. My father's
 death
Left the path open, yet not without snares.
This cold and creeping kinsman, who so
 long
Kept his eye on me, as the snake upon
The fluttering bird, hath ere this time out-
 stept me, 85
Become the master of my rights, and lord
Of that which lifts him up to princes in
Dominion and domain.
 Jos. Who knows? our son

May have return'd back to his grandsire,
 and
Even now uphold thy rights for thee?
 Wer. 'Tis hopeless. 90
Since his strange disappearance from my
 father's,
Entailing, as it were, my sins upon
Himself, no tidings have reveal'd his
 course.
I parted with him to his grandsire, on
The promise that his anger would stop
 short 95
Of the third generation; but Heaven seems
To claim her stern prerogative, and visit
Upon my boy his father's faults and follies.
 Jos. I must hope better still,—at least
 we have yet
Baffled the long pursuit of Stralenheim.
 Wer. We should have done, but for
 this fatal sickness; 101
More fatal than a mortal malady,
Because it takes not life, but life's sole
 solace:
Even now I feel my spirit girt about
By the snares of this avaricious fiend:—
How do I know he hath not track'd us
 here? 106
 Jos. He does not know thy person;
 and his spies,
Who so long watch'd thee, have been left
 at Hamburgh.
Our unexpected journey, and this change
Of name, leaves all discovery far behind:
None hold us here for aught save what we
 seem. 111
 Wer. Save what we seem! save what
 we *are*—sick beggars,
Even to our very hopes.—Ha! ha!
 Jos. Alas!
That bitter laugh!
 Wer. *Who* would read in this form
The high soul of the son of a long line?
Who, in this garb, the heir of princely
 lands? 116
Who, in this sunken, sickly eye, the pride
Of rank and ancestry? In this worn cheek
And famine-hollow'd brow, the lord of
 halls
Which daily feast a thousand vassals?
 Jos. You 120
Ponder'd not thus upon these worldly
 things,
My Werner! when you deign'd to choose
 for bride
The foreign daughter of a wandering exile.
 Wer. An exile's daughter with an out-
 cast son, 124
Were a fit marriage: but I still had hopes
To lift thee to the state we both were born
 for.
Your father's house was noble, though
 decay'd;
And worthy by its birth to match with
 ours.

 Jos. Your father did not think so,
 though 'twas noble;
But had my birth been all my claim to
 match 130
With thee, I should have deem'd it what
 it is.
 Wer. And what is that in thine eyes?
 Jos. All which it
Has done in our behalf,—nothing?
 Wer. How,—nothing?
 Jos. Or worse; for it has been a canker in
Thy heart from the beginning: but for this,
We had not felt our poverty but as 136
Millions of myriads feel it, cheerfully;
But for these phantoms of thy feudal
 fathers,
Thou might'st have earn'd thy bread, as
 thousands earn it;
Or, if that seem too humble, tried by
 commerce, 140
Or other civic means, to amend thy
 fortunes.
 Wer. [*ironically*]. And been an Han-
 seatic burgher? Excellent!
 Jos Whate'er thou might'st have
 been, to me thou art
What no state high or low can ever change,
My heart's first choice; which chose thee,
 knowing neither 145
Thy birth, thy hopes, thy pride; nought,
 save thy sorrows:
While they last, let me comfort or divide
 them:
When they end, let mine end with them,
 or thee!
 Wer. My better angel! Such I have
 ever found thee;
This rashness, or this weakness of my
 temper, 150
Ne'er raised a thought to injure thee or
 thine.
Thou didst not mar my fortunes: my own
 nature
In youth was such as to unmake an empire,
Had such been my inheritance; but now,
Chasten'd, subdued, out-worn, and taught
 to know 155
Myself,—to lose this for our son and thee!
Trust me, when, in my two-and-twentieth
 spring,
My father barr'd me from my fathers'
 house,
The last sole scion of a thousand sires
(For I was then the last), it hurt me less
Than to behold my boy and my boy's
 mother 16ᴉ
Excluded in their innocence from what
My faults deserved—exclusion; although
 then
My passions were all living serpents, and
Twined like the Gorgon's round me.
 [*A loud knocking is heard*
 Jos. Hark!
 Wer. A knocking! 16ᵌ

Jos. Who can it be at this lone hour?
 We have
Few visitors.
Wer. And poverty hath none,
Save those who come to make it poorer
 still.
Well, I am prepared.
 [WERNER *puts his hand into his bosom,*
 as if to search for some weapon.
Jos. Oh! do not look so. I
Will to the door. It cannot be of import
In this lone spot of wintry desolation:—
The very desert saves man from mankind.
 [*She goes to the door.*

 Enter IDENSTEIN.

Iden. A fair good evening to my fairer
 hostess
And worthy——What's your name, my
 friend?
Wer. Are you
Not afraid to demand it?
Iden. Not afraid? 175
Egad! I am afraid. You look as if
I ask'd for something better than your
 name,
By the face you put on it.
Wer. Better, sir!
Iden. Better or worse, like matrimony:
 what
Shall I say more? You have been a guest
 this month 180
Here in the prince's palace—(to be sure,
His highness had resign'd it to the ghosts
And rats these twelve years—but 'tis still
 a palace)—
I say you have been our lodger, and as yet
We do not know your name.
Wer. My name is Werner. 185
Iden. A goodly name, a very worthy
 name,
As e'er was gilt upon a trader's board:
I have a cousin in the lazaretto
Of Hamburgh, who has got a wife who bore
The same. He is an officer of trust, 190
Surgeon's assistant (hoping to be surgeon),
And has done miracles i'the way of
 business.
Perhaps you are related to my relative?
Wer. To yours?
Jos. Oh, yes; we are, but distantly.
 [*Aside to* WERNER]. Cannot you humour
 the dull gossip till 195
We learn his purpose?
Iden. Well, I'm glad of that;
I thought so all along, such natural yearn-
 ings
Play'd round my heart:—blood is not
 water, cousin,
And so let's have some wine, and drink
 unto
Our better acquaintance: relatives should
 be 200
Friends.

Wer. You appear to have drank
 enough already;
And if you have not, I've no wine to offer,
Else it were yours: but this you know, or
 should know:
You see I am poor, and sick, and will not
 see
That I would be alone; but to your
 business! 205
What brings you here?
Iden. Why, what should bring me
 here?
Wer. I know not, though I think that
 I could guess
That which will send you hence.
Jos. [*aside*]. Patience, dear Werner!
Iden. You don't know what has
 happen'd, then?
Jos. How should we?
Iden. The river has o'erflow'd.
Jos. Alas! we have known 210
That to our sorrow for these five days;
 since
It keeps us here.
Iden. But what you don't know is,
That a great personage, who fain would
 cross
Against the stream and three postilions'
 wishes,
Is drown'd below the ford, with five post-
 horses, 215
A monkey, and a mastiff, and a valet.
Jos. Poor creatures! are you sure?
Iden. Yes, of the monkey,
And the valet, and the cattle; but as yet
We know not if his excellency's dead 219
Or no; your noblemen are hard to drown,
As it is fit that men in office should be;
But what is certain is, that he has
 swallow'd
Enough of the Oder to have burst two
 peasants;
And now a Saxon and Hungarian
 traveller,
Who, at their proper peril, snatch'd him
 from 225
The whirling river, have sent on to crave
A lodging, or a grave, according as
It may turn out with the live or dead body.
Jos. And where will you receive him?
 here, I hope,
If we can be of service—say the word.
Iden. Here? no; but in the prince's
 own apartment, 231
As fits a noble guest:—'tis damp, no
 doubt,
Not having been inhabited these twelve
 years;
But then he comes from a much damper
 place,
So scarcely will catch cold in't, if he be
Still liable to cold—and if not, why 236
He'll be worse lodged to-morrow:
 ne'ertheless,

I have order'd fire and all appliances
To be got ready for the worst—that is,
In case he should survive.
 Jos. Poor gentleman, 240
I hope he will, with all my heart.
 Wer. Intendant,
Have you not learn'd his name? My Jose-
 phine, [*Aside to his wife.*
Retire: I'll sift this fool.
 [*Exit* JOSEPHINE.
 Iden. His name? oh Lord!
Who knows if he hath now a name or no?
'Tis time enough to ask it when he's able
To give an answer; or if not, to put 246
His heir's upon his epitaph. Methought
Just now you chid me for demanding
 names?
 Wer. True, true, I did so: you say well
and wisely.

Enter GABOR.

 Gab. If I intrude, I crave—
 Iden. Oh, no intrusion! 250
This is the palace; this a stranger like
Yourself; I pray you make yourself at
 home:
But where's his excellency? and how fares he?
 Gab. Wetly and wearily, but out of
 peril:
He paused to change his garments in a
 cottage 255
(Where I doff'd mine for these, and came
 on hither),
And has almost recover'd from his drench-
 ing.
He will be here anon.
 Iden. What ho, there! bustle!
Without there, Herman, Weilburg, Peter,
 Conrad! 259
[*Gives directions to different servants
 who enter.*
A nobleman sleeps here to-night—see that
All is in order in the damask chamber—
Keep up the stove—I will myself to the
 cellar—
And Madame Idenstein (my consort,
 stranger)
Shall furnish forth the bed-apparel; for,
To say the truth, they are marvellous
 scant of this 265
Within the palace precincts, since his high-
 ness
Left it some dozen years ago. And then
His excellency will sup, doubtless?
 Gab. Faith!
I cannot tell; but I should think the pillow
Would please him better than the table,
 after 270
His soaking in your river: but for fear
Your viands should be thrown away, I
 mean
To sup myself, and have a friend without
Who will do honour to your good cheer with
A traveller's appetite.

 Iden. But are you sure 275
His excellency——But his name: what is it?
 Gab. I do not know.
 Iden. And yet you saved his life.
 Gad. I help'd my friend to do so.
 Iden. Well, that's strange,
To save a man's life whom you do not
 know.
 Gab. Not so; for there are some I
 know so well, 280
I scarce should give myself the trouble.
 Iden. Pray,
Good friend, and who may you be?
 Gab. By my family,
Hungarian.
 Iden. Which is call'd?
 Gab. It matters little.
 Iden. [*aside*]. I think that all the world
 are grown anonymous,
Since no one cares to tell me what he's
 call'd! 285
Pray, has his excellency a large suite?
 Gab. Sufficient.
 Iden. How many?
 Gab. I did not count them.
We came up by mere accident, and just
In time to drag him through his carriage
 window.
 Iden. Well, what would I give to save
 a great man! 290
No doubt you'll have a swingeing sum as
 recompense.
 Gab. Perhaps.
 Iden. Now, how much do you reckon
 on?
 Gab. I have not yet put up myself to
 sale:
In the mean time, my best reward would be
A glass of your Hockcheimer—a green
 glass, 295
Wreath'd with rich grapes and Bacchanal
 devices,
O'erflowing with the oldest of your
 vintage:
For which I promise you, in case you e'er
Run hazard of being drown'd (although I
 own
It seems, of all deaths, the least likely for
 you), 300
I'll pull you out for nothing. Quick, my
 friend,
And think, for every bumper I shall quaff
A wave the less may roll above your head.
 Iden. [*aside*]. I don't much like this
 fellow—close and dry
He seems,—two things which suit me not,
 however, 305
Wine he shall have; if that unlock him not,
I shall not sleep to-night for curiosity.
 [*Exit* IDENSTEIN.
 Gab. [*to* WERNER]. This master of the
 ceremonies is
The intendant of the palace, I presume:
'Tis a fine building, but decay'd.

Wer. The apartment
Design'd for him you rescued will be
found 311
In fitter order for a sickly guest.
Gab. I wonder then you occupied it
not,
For you seem delicate in health.
Wer. [*quickly*]. Sir!
Gab. Pray
Excuse me: have I said aught to offend
you? 315
Wer. Nothing: but we are strangers to
each other.
Gab. And that's the reason I would
have us less so:
I thought our bustling host without had
said
You were a chance and passing guest, the
counterpart
Of me and my companions.
Wer. Very true. 320
Gab. Then, as we never met before,
and never,
It may be, may again encounter, why,
I thought to cheer up this old dungeon
here
(At least to me) by asking you to share
The fare of my companions and myself.
Wer. Pray, pardon me; my health——
Gab. Even as you please.
I have been a soldier, and perhaps am
blunt
In bearing.
Wer. I have also served, and can
Requite a soldier's greeting.
Gab. In what service?
The Imperial?
Wer. [*quickly, and then interrupting him-
self*]. I commanded—no—I mean
I served; but it is many years ago, 331
When first Bohemia raised her banner
'gainst
The Austrian.
Gab. Well, that's over now, and
peace
Has turn'd some thousand gallant hearts
adrift
To live as they best may: and, to say
truth, 335
Some take the shortest.
Wer. What is that?
Gab. Whate'er
They lay their hands on. All Silesia and
Lusatia's woods are tenanted by bands
Of the late troops, who levy on the
country
Their maintenance: the Chatelains must
keep 340
Their castle walls—beyond them 'tis but
doubtful
Travel for your rich count or full-blown
baron.
My comfort is that, wander where I may,
I've little left to lose now.

Wer. And I—nothing.
Gab. That's harder still. You say you
were a soldier. 345
Wer. I was.
Gab. You look one still. All soldiers
are
Or should be comrades, even though
enemies.
Our swords when drawn must cross, our
engines aim
(While levell'd) at each other's hearts; but
when 349
A truce, a peace, or what you will, remits
The steel into its scabbard, and lets sleep
The spark which lights the matchlock, we
are brethren.
You are poor and sickly—I am not rich,
but healthy;
I want for nothing which I cannot want;
You seem devoid of this—wilt share it?
 [GABOR *pulls out his purse.*
Wer. Who 355
Told you I was a beggar?
Gab. You yourself,
In saying you were a soldier during peace-
time.
Wer. [*looking at him with suspicion*].
You know me not?
Gab. I know no man, not even
Myself: how should I then know one I
ne'er
Beheld till half an hour since?
Wer. Sir, I thank you. 360
Your offer's noble were it to a friend,
And not unkind as to an unknown
stranger,
Though scarcely prudent; but no less I
thank you.
I am a beggar in all save his trade; 364
And when I beg of any one, it shall be
Of him who was the first to offer what
Few can obtain by asking. Pardon me.
 [*Exit* WERNER.
Gab. [*solus*]. A goodly fellow by his
looks, though worn,
As most good fellows are, by pain or
pleasure, 369
Which tear life out of us before our time;
I scarce know which most quickly: but he
seems 371
To have seen better days, as who has not
Who has seen yesterday?—But here ap-
proaches
Our sage intendant, with the wine: how-
ever, 374
For the cup's sake I'll bear the cupbearer.

 Enter IDENSTEIN.

Iden. 'Tis here! the supernaculum!
twenty years
Of age, if 'tis a day.
Gab. Which epoch makes
Young women and old wine; and 'tis great
pity,

Of two such excellent things, increase of
years,
Which still improves the one, should spoil
the other. 380
Fill full—Here's to our hostess!—your
fair wife! [*Takes the glass.*
Iden. Fair!—Well, I trust your taste
in wine is equal
To that you show for beauty; but I pledge you
Nevertheless.
Gab. Is not the lovely woman
I met in the adjacent hall, who, with 385
An air, and port, and eye, which would
have better
Beseem'd this palace in its brightest days
(Though in a garb adapted to its present
Abandonment), return'd my salutation—
Is not the same your spouse?
Iden. I would she were! 390
But you're mistaken:—that's the
stranger's wife.
Gab. And by her aspect she might be
a prince's;
Though time hath touch'd her too, she
still retains
Much beauty, and more majesty.
Iden. And that
Is more than I can say for Madame
Idenstein, 395
At least in beauty: as for majesty,
She has some of its properties which might
Be spared—but never mind!
Gab. I don't. But who
May be this stranger? He too hath a bear-
ing
Above his outward fortunes.
Iden. There I differ. 400
He's poor as Job, and not so patient; but
Who he may be, or what, or aught of him,
Except his name (and that I only learn'd
To-night), I know not.
Gab. But how came he here?
Iden. In a most miserable old caleche,
About a month since, and immediately
Fell sick, almost to death. He should have
died.
Gab. Tender and true!—but why?
Iden. Why, what is life
Without a living? He has not a stiver.
Gab. In that case, I much wonder that
a person 410
Of your apparent prudence should admit
Guests so forlorn into this noble mansion.
Iden. That's true: but pity, as you
know, *does* make
One's heart commit these follies; and
besides, 414
They had some valuables left at that time,
Which paid their way up to the present
hour;
And so I thought they might as well be
lodged
Here as at the small tavern, and I gave
them

The run of some of the oldest palac[e]
rooms.
They served to air them, at the least a[s]
long 42[0]
As they could pay for firewood.
Gab. Poor souls!
Iden. A[y]
Exceeding poor.
Gab. And yet unused to poverty
If I mistake not. Whither were the[y]
going?
Iden. Oh! Heaven knows where, unles[s]
to heaven itself.
Some days ago that look'd the likelie[st]
journey 42[5]
For Werner.
Gab. Werner! I have heard the name
But it may be a feign'd one.
Iden. Like enough!
But hark! a noise of wheels and voice[s]
and
A blaze of torches from without. As su[re]
As destiny, his excellency's come. 43[0]
I must be at my post; will you not join m[e]
To help him from his carriage, an[d]
present
Your humble duty at the door?
Gab. I dragg'd hi[m]
From out that carriage when he woul[d]
have given
His barony or county to repel 43[5]
The rushing river from his gurgling throa[t]
He has valets now enough: they stoo[d]
aloof then,
Shaking their dripping ears upon th[e]
shore,
All roaring 'Help!' but offering non[e]
and as
For *duty* (as you call it)—I did mine *the[n]*
Now do *yours.* Hence, and bow an[d]
cringe him here!
Iden. I cringe!—but I shall lose th[e]
opportunity—
Plague take it! he'll be *here,* and I n[ot]
there! [*Exit* IDENSTEIN *hastil[y]*

Re-enter WERNER.

Wer. [*to himself*]. I heard a noise [of]
wheels and voices. How
All sounds now jar me!
Still here! Is he not 4[45]
[*Perceiving* GABO[R]
A spy of my pursuer's? His frank offe[r]
So suddenly, and to a stranger, wore
The aspect of a secret enemy;
For friends are slow at such.
Gab. Sir, you seem rap[t]
And yet the time is not akin to thought
These old walls will be noisy soon. Th[e]
baron, 4[51]
Or count (or whatsoe'er this half drown[ed]
noble
May be), for whom this desolate villa[ge]
and

Its lone inhabitants show more respect
Than did the elements, is come.
 Iden. [*without*]. This way— 455
This way, your excellency:—have a care,
The staircase is a little gloomy, and
Somewhat decay'd; but if we had expected
So high a guest—Pray take my arm, my
 lord!

Enter STRALENHEIM, IDENSTEIN, *and
Attendants,—partly his own, and partly
Retainers of the Domain of which
IDENSTEIN is Intendant.*

 Stral. I'll rest here a moment.
 Iden. [*to the servants*]. Ho! a chair!
Instantly, knaves! 461
 [STRALENHEIM *sits down.*
 Wer. [*aside*]. 'Tis he!
 Stral. I'm better now.
Who are these strangers?
 Iden. Please you, my good lord,
One says he is no stranger.
 Wer. [*aloud and hastily*]. *Who* says
 that?
 [*They look at him with surprise.*
 Iden. Why, no one spoke *of you*, or *to
 you*!—but
Here 's one his excellency may be pleased
To recognise. [*Pointing to* GABOR.
 Gab. I seek not to disturb 466
His noble memory.
 Stral. I apprehend
This is one of the strangers to whose aid
I owe my rescue. Is not that the other?
 [*Pointing to* WERNER.
My state when I was succour'd must
 excuse 470
My uncertainty to whom I owe so much.
 Iden. He!—no, my lord! he rather
 wants for rescue
Than can afford it. 'Tis a poor sick man,
Travel-tired, and lately risen from a bed
From whence he never dream'd to rise.
 Stral. Methought
That there were two.
 Gab. There were, in company;
But, in the service render'd to your lord-
 ship
needs must say but *one*, and he is absent.
The chief part of whatever aid was
 render'd 479
Was *his*: it was his fortune to be first.
My will was not inferior, but his strength
And youth outstripp'd me; therefore do
 not waste
Your thanks on me. I was but a glad
 second
Unto a nobler principal.
 Stral. Where is he?
 An Atten. My lord, he tarried in the
 cottage where 485
Your excellency rested for an hour,
And said he would be here to-morrow.
 Stral. Till

That hour arrives, I can but offer thanks,
And then——
 Gab. I seek no more, and scarce
 deserve
So much. My comrade may speak for
 himself. 490
 Stral. [*fixing his eyes upon* WERNER:
 then aside].
It cannot be! and yet he must be look'd to.
'Tis twenty years since I beheld him with
These eyes; and, though my agents still
 have kept
Theirs on him, policy has held aloof
My own from his, not to alarm him into
Suspicion of my plan. Why did I leave
At Hamburgh those who would have
 made assurance
If this be he or no? I thought, ere now,
To have been lord of Siegendorf, and
 parted 499
In haste, though even the elements appear
To fight against me, and this sudden flood
May keep me prisoner here till——
 [*He pauses and looks at* WERNER; *then
 resumes.*
 This man must
Be watch'd. If it is he, he is so changed,
His father, rising from his grave again,
Would pass him by unknown. I must be
 wary: 505
An error would spoil all.
 Iden. Your lordship seems
Pensive. Will it not please you to pass on?
 Stral. 'Tis past fatigue, which gives
 my weigh'd-down spirit
An outward show of thought. I will to rest.
 Iden. The prince's chamber is pre-
 pared, with all 510
The very furniture the prince used when
Last here, in its full splendour.
 [*Aside*]. Somewhat tatter'd,
And devilish damp, but fine enough by
 torchlight;
And that's enough for your right noble
 blood
Of twenty quarterings upon a hatchment;
So let their bearer sleep 'neath something
 like one 516
Now, as he one day will for ever lie.
 Stral. [*rising and turning to* GABOR].
 Good night, good people! Sir, I
 trust to-morrow
Will find me apter to requite your service.
In the mean time I crave your company
A moment in my chamber. 521
 Gab. I attend you.
 Stral. [*after a few steps, pauses, and calls
 WERNER]. Friend!
 Wer. Sir!
 Iden. Sir! Lord—oh Lord! Why
 don't you say
His lordship, or his excellency? Pray,
My lord, excuse this poor man's want of
 breeding:

He hath not been accustom'd to admission
To such a presence. 526
 Stral. [*to* IDENSTEIN]. Peace, intendant!
 Iden. Oh!
I am dumb.
 Stral. [*to* WERNER]. Have you been
 long here?
 Wer. Long?
 Stral. I sought
An answer, not an echo.
 Wer. You may seek
Both from the walls. I am not used to
 answer
Those whom I know not.
 Stral. Indeed! Ne'er the less, 530
You might reply with courtesy to what
Is ask'd in kindness.
 Wer. When I know it such,
I will requite—that is, *reply*—in unison.
 Stral. The intendant said you had
 been detain'd by sickness—
If I could aid you—journeying the same
 way? 535
 Wer. [*quickly*]. I am not journeying
 the same way.
 Stral. How know ye
That, ere you know my route?
 Wer. Because there is
But one way that the rich and poor must
 tread
Together. You diverged from that dread
 path
Some hours ago, and I some days: hence-
 forth 540
Our roads must lie asunder, though they
 tend
All to one home.
 Stral. Your language is above
Your station.
 Wer. [*bitterly*]. Is it?
 Stral. Or, at least, beyond
Your garb.
 Wer. 'Tis well that it is not beneath it,
As sometimes happens to the better clad.
But, in a word, what would you with me?
 Stral. [*startled*]. I?
 Wer. Yes—you! You know me not,
 and question me,
And wonder that I answer not—not know-
 ing
My inquisitor. Explain what you would
 have, 549
And then I'll satisfy yourself, or me.
 Stral. I knew not that you had reasons
 for reserve.
 Wer. Many have such:—Have you
 none?
 Stral. None which can
Interest a mere stranger.
 Wer. Then forgive
The same unknown and humble stranger, if
He wishes to remain so to the man
Who can have nought in common with
 him.

 Stral. Si
I will not balk your humour, though u
 toward:
I only meant you service—but good nigh
Intendant, show the way! [*To* GABOR
 Sir, you will with me?
 [*Exeunt* STRALENHEIM *and Attendant
 IDENSTEIN *and* GABO
 Wer. [*solus*]. 'Tis he! I am taken i
 the toils. Before 5
I quitted Hamburgh, Giulio, his la
 steward,
Inform'd me, that he had obtain'd a
 order
From Brandenburg's elector, for the arre
Of Kruitzner (such the name I then bor
 when 5
I came upon the frontier; the free city
Alone preserved my freedom—till I lef
Its walls—fool that I was to quit them
 But
I deem'd this humble garb, and rou
 obscure,
Had baffled the slow hounds in the
 pursuit.
What's to be done? He knows me not b
 person; 5
Nor could aught, save the eye of appr
 hension,
Have recognised *him*, after twenty year
We met so rarely and so coldly in
Our youth. But those about him! No
 I can
Divine the frankness of the Hungaria
 who 5
No doubt is a mere tool and spy o
 Stralenheim's,
To sound and to secure me. Witho
 means!
Sick, poor—begirt too with the floodi
 rivers, 5
Impassable even to the wealthy, with
All the appliances which purchase mod
Of overpowering peril, with men's lives,-
How can I hope? An hour ago methoug
My state beyond despair; and now, '
 such,
The past seems paradise. Another day
And I'm detected,—on the very eve
Of honours, rights, and my inheritance
When a few drops of gold might save n
 still
In favouring an escape.

Enter IDENSTEIN *and* FRITZ *in conversatio*
 Fritz. Immediately.
 Iden. I tell you, 'tis impossible.
 Fritz. It mu
Be tried, however; and if one express
Fail, you must send on others, till th
 answer 5
Arrives from Frankfort, from the con
 mandant.
 Iden. I will do what I can.

Fritz. And recollect
To spare no trouble; you will be repaid
Tenfold.

Iden. The baron is retired to rest?

Fritz. He hath thrown himself into an
easy chair 596
Beside the fire, and slumbers; and has
order'd
He may not be disturb'd until eleven,
When he will take himself to bed.

Iden. Before
An hour is past I'll do my best to serve
him. 600

Fritz. Remember! [*Exit* FRITZ.

Iden. The devil take these great
men! they
Think all things made for them. Now here
must I
Rouse up some half a dozen shivering
vassals
From their scant pallets, and, at peril of
Their lives, despatch them o'er the river
towards 605
Frankfort. Methinks the baron's own
experience
Some hours ago might teach him fellow-
feeling:
But no, 'it *must*,' and there's an end. How
now?
Are you there, Mynheer Werner?

Wer. You have left
Your noble guest right quickly.

Iden. Yes—he's dozing, 610
And seems to like that none should sleep
besides.
Here is a packet for the commandant
Of Frankfort, at all risks and all expenses;
But I must not lose time: Good night!
 [*Exit.*

Wer. 'To Frankfort!'
So, so, it thickens! Ay, 'the com-
mandant.' 615
This tallies well with all the prior steps
Of this cool, calculating fiend, who walks
Between me and my father's house. No
doubt
He writes for a detachment to convey me
Into some secret fortress.—Sooner than
This—— 621
 [WERNER *looks around, and snatches up
 a knife lying on a table in a recess.*
Now I am master of myself at least.
Hark,—footsteps! How do I know that
Stralenheim
Will wait for even the show of that authority
Which is to overshadow usurpation?
That he suspects me's certain. I'm alone;
He with a numerous train. I weak;
he strong 626
In gold, in numbers, rank, authority.
I nameless, or involving in my name
Destruction, till I reach my own domain;
He full-blown with his titles, which
impose 630

Still further on these obscure petty
burghers
Than they could do elsewhere. Hark!
nearer still!
I'll to the secret passage, which communi-
cates
With the——No! all is silent—'twas my
fancy!— 634
Still as the breathless interval between
The flash and thunder:—I must hush my
soul
Amidst its perils. Yet I will retire,
To see if still be unexplored the passage
I wot of: it will serve me as a den 639
Of secrecy for some hours, at the worst.
 [WERNER *draws a panel, and exit, closing
 it after him.*

Enter GABOR *and* JOSEPHINE.

Gab. Where is your husband?

Jos. Here, I thought: I left him
Not long since in his chamber. But these
rooms
Have many outlets, and he may be gone
To accompany the intendant. 644

Gab. Baron Stralenheim
Put many questions to the intendant on
The subject of your lord, and, to be plain,
I have my doubts if he means well.

Jos. Alas!
What can there be in common with the
proud
And wealthy baron, and the unknown
Werner?

Gab. That you know best.

Jos. Or, if it were so, how 650
Come you to stir yourself in his behalf,
Rather than that of him whose life you
saved?

Gab. I help'd to save him, as in peril;
but
I did not pledge myself to serve him in
Oppression. I know well these nobles,
and 655
Their thousand modes of trampling on the
poor.
I have proved them; and my spirit boils
up when
I find them practising against the weak:—
This is my only motive.

Jos. It would be
Not easy to persuade my consort of 660
Your good intentions.

Gab. Is he so suspicious?

Jos. He was not once; but time and
troubles have
Made him what you beheld.

Gab. I'm sorry for it.
Suspicion is a heavy armour, and
With its own weight impedes more than
protects. 665
Good night! I trust to meet with him at
daybreak. [*Exit* GABOR.

Re-enter IDENSTEIN *and some Peasants.*
JOSEPHINE *retires up the Hall.*

First Peasant. But if I'm drown'd?
Iden. Why, you will be well paid for't,
And have risk'd more than drowning for
as much,
I doubt not.
 Second Peasant. But our wives and
families?
 Iden. Cannot be worse off than they
are, and may 670
Be better.
 Third Peasant. I have neither, and will
venture.
 Iden. That's right. A gallant carle,
and fit to be
A soldier. I'll promote you to the ranks
In the prince's body-guard—if you
succeed:
And you shall have besides, in sparkling
coin, 675
Two thalers.
 Third Peasant. No more!
 Iden. Out upon your avarice!
Can that low vice alloy so much ambition?
I tell thee, fellow, that two thalers in
Small change will subdivide into a
treasure.
Do not five hundred thousand heroes
daily 680
Risk lives and souls for the tithe of one
thaler?
When had you half the sum?
 Third Peasant. Never—but ne'er
The less I must have three.
 Iden. Have you forgot
Whose vassal you were born, knave?
 Third Peasant. No—the prince's,
And not the stranger's.
 Iden. Sirrah! in the prince's 685
Absence, I am sovereign; and the baron is
My intimate connexion;—'Cousin Iden-
stein!
(Quoth he) you'll order out a dozen
villains.'
And so, you villains! troop—march—
march, I say; 689
And if a single dog's ear of this packet
Be sprinkled by the Oder—look to it!
For every page of paper, shall a hide
Of yours be stretch'd as parchment on a
drum,
Like Ziska's skin, to beat alarm to all
Refractory vassals, who can not effect
Impossibilities.—Away, ye earth-worms!
 [*Exit, driving them out.*
 Jos. [*coming forward*]. I fain would
shun these scenes, too oft repeated,
Of feudal tyranny o'er petty victims;
I cannot aid, and will not witness such.
Even here, in this remote, unnamed, dull
spot, 700
The dimmest in the district's map, exist

The insolence of wealth in poverty
O'er something poorer still—the pride of
rank
In servitude, o'er something still more ser-
vile;
And vice in misery affecting still 705
A tatter'd splendour. What a state of
being!
In Tuscany, my own dear sunny land,
Our nobles were but citizens and mer-
chants,
Like Cosmo. We had evils, but not such
As these; and our all-ripe and gushing
valleys 710
Made poverty more cheerful, where each
herb
Was in itself a meal, and every vine
Rain'd, as it were, the beverage which
makes glad
The heart of man; and the ne'er unfelt sun
(But rarely clouded, and when clouded,
leaving 715
His warmth behind in memory of his
beams)
Makes the worn mantle, and the thin robe,
less
Oppressive than an emperor's jewell'd
purple.
But, here! the despots of the north appear
To imitate the ice-wind of their clime,
Searching the shivering vassal through
his rags, 721
To wring his soul—as the bleak elements
His form. And 'tis to be amongst these
sovereigns
My husband pants! and such his pride of
birth— 724
That twenty years of usage, such as no
Father born in a humble state could nerve
His soul to persecute a son withal,
Hath changed no atom of his early nature;
But I, born nobly also, from my father's
Kindness was taught a different lesson
Father! 730
May thy long-tried and now rewarded
spirit
Look down on us and our so long desired
Ulric! I love my son, as thou didst me!
What's that? Thou, Werner! can it be?
and thus?

Enter WERNER *hastily, with the knife in his
hand, by the secret panel, which he closes
hurriedly after him.*

 Wer. [*not at first recognising her*]. Dis-
cover'd! then I'll stab——[*recognis-
ing her*].
 Ah! Josephine, 735
Why art thou not at rest?
 Jos. What rest? My God!
What doth this mean?
 Wer. [*showing a rouleau*]. Here's gold—
gold, Josephine,
Will rescue us from this detested dungeon

Jos. And how obtain'd?—that knife!
Wer. 'Tis bloodless—*yet.*
Away—we must to our chamber.
Jos. But whence comest thou? 740
Wer. Ask not! but let us think where
we shall go—
This—this will make us way—[*showing
the gold*]—I'll fit them now.
Jos. I dare not think thee guilty of
dishonour.
Wer. Dishonour!
Jos. I have said it.
Wer. Let us hence:
'Tis the last night, I trust, that we need pass
here. 745
Jos. And not the worst, I hope.
Wer. Hope! I make *sure.*
But let us to our chamber.
Jos. Yet one question—
What hast thou *done?*
Wer. [*fiercely*]. Left one thing *undone,*
which
Had made all well: let me not think of it!
Away! 749
Jos. Alas, that I should doubt of thee!
 [*Exeunt.*

ACT II

Scene I.—*A Hall in the same Palace.*

Enter IDENSTEIN *and Others.*

Iden. Fine doings! goodly doings!
honest doings!
A baron pillaged in a prince's palace!
Where, till this hour, such a sin ne'er was
heard of.
Fritz. It hardly could, unless the rats
despoil'd
The mice of a few shreds of tapestry. 5
Iden. Oh! that I e'er should live to see
this day!
The honour of our city's gone for ever.
Fritz. Well, but now to discover the
delinquent:
The baron is determined not to lose
This sum without a search.
Iden. And so am I. 10
Fritz. But whom do you suspect?
Iden. Suspect! all people
Without — within — above — below —
Heaven help me!
Fritz. Is there no other entrance to the
chamber?
Iden. None whatsoever.
Fritz. Are you sure of that?
Iden. Certain. I have lived and served
here since my birth, 15
And if there were such, must have heard
of such,
Or seen it.
Fritz. Then it must be some one who
Had access to the antechamber.
Iden. Doubtless.
Fritz. The man call'd *Werner*'s poor!

Iden. Poor as a miser. 19
But lodged so far off, in the other wing,
By which there's no communication with
The baron's chamber, that it can't be he.
Besides, I bade him 'good night' in the
hall,
Almost a mile off, and which only leads
To his own apartment, about the same
time 25
When this burglarious, larcenous felony
Appears to have been committed.
Fritz. There's another,
The stranger——
Iden. The Hungarian?
Fritz. He who help'd
To fish the baron from the Oder.
Iden. Not
Unlikely. But, hold—might it not have
been 30
One of the suite?
Fritz. How? *We,* sir!
Iden. No—not *you,*
But some of the inferior knaves. You say
The baron was asleep in the great chair—
The velvet chair—in his embroider'd
nightgown;
His toilet spread before him, and upon it
A cabinet with letters, papers, and 36
Several rouleaux of gold; of which *one*
only
Has disappear'd:—the door unbolted,
with
No difficult access to any.
Fritz. Good sir,
Be not so quick! the honour of the corps
Which forms the baron's household's
unimpeach'd 41
From steward to scullion, save in the fair
way
Of peculation; such as in accompts,
Weights, measures, larder, cellar, buttery,
Where all men take their prey; as also in
Postage of letters, gathering of rents,
Purveying feasts, and understanding with
The honest trades who furnish noble
masters;
But for your petty, picking, downright
thievery, 49
We scorn it as we do board-wages. Then
Had one of our folks done it, he would not
Have been so poor a spirit as to hazard
His neck for *one* rouleau, but have
swoop'd all;
Also the cabinet, if portable.
Iden. There is some sense in that——
Fritz. No, sir, be sure 55
'Twas none of our corps; but some petty,
trivial
Picker and stealer, without art or genius.
The only question is—Who else could have
Access, save the Hungarian and yourself?
Iden. You don't mean me?
Fritz. No, sir; I honour more 60
Your talents——

Iden. And my principles, I hope.
Fritz. Of course. But to the point:
What's to be done?
Iden. Nothing—but there's a good
deal to be said.
We'll offer a reward; move heaven and
earth,
And the police (though there's none
nearer than 65
Frankfort); post notices in manuscript
(For we've no printer); and set by my
clerk
To read them (for few can, save he and I);
We'll send out villains to strip beggars,
and
Search empty pockets; also to arrest 70
All gipsies, and ill-clothed and sallow
people.
Prisoners we'll have at least, if not the
culprit;
And for the baron's gold—if 'tis not
found,
At least he shall have the full satisfaction
Of melting twice its substance in the
raising 75
The ghost of this rouleau. Here's alchemy
For your Lord's losses!
Fritz. He hath found a better.
Iden. Where?
Fritz. In a most immense inheritance.
The late Count Siegendorf, his distant
kinsman,
Is dead near Prague, in his castle, and my
lord 80
Is on his way to take possession.
Iden. Was there
No heir?
Fritz. Oh, yes; but he has disappear'd
Long from the world's eye, and perhaps
the world.
A prodigal son, beneath his father's ban
For the last twenty years: for whom his
sire 85
Refused to kill the fatted calf; and, there-
fore,
If living, he must chew the husks still.
But
The baron would find means to silence
him,
Were he to re-appear: he's politic,
And has much influence with a certain
court. 90
Iden. He's fortunate.
Fritz. 'Tis true, there is a grandson,
Whom the late count reclaim'd from his
son's hands,
And educated as his heir; but then
His birth is doubtful.
Iden. How so?
Fritz. His sire made
A left-hand, love, imprudent sort of
marriage, 95
With an Italian exile's dark-eyed
daughter:

Noble, they say, too; but no match for
such
A house as Siegendorf's. The grandsire ill
Could brook the alliance; and could ne'er
be brought
To see the parents, though he took the
son. 100
Iden. If he's a lad of mettle, he may
yet
Dispute your claim, and weave a web that
may
Puzzle your baron to unravel.
Fritz. Why,
For mettle, he has quite enough: they say,
He forms a happy mixture of his sire 105
And grandsire's qualities,—impetuous as
The former, and deep as the latter; but
The strangest is, that he too disappear'd
Some months ago.
Iden. The devil he did!
Fritz. Why, yes:
It must have been at his suggestion, at
An hour so critical as was the eve 110
Of the old man's death, whose heart was
broken by it.
Iden. Was there no cause assign'd?
Fritz. Plenty, no doubt,
And none, perhaps, the true one. Some
averr'd 114
It was to seek his parents; some because
The old man held his spirit in so strictly
(But that could scarce be, for he doted on
him):
A third believed he wish'd to serve in war,
But peace being made soon after his de-
parture,
He might have since return'd, were that
the motive; 120
A fourth set charitably have surmised,
As there was something strange and mystic
in him,
That in the wild exuberance of his nature
He had join'd the black bands, who lay
waste Lusatia,
The mountains of Bohemia and Silesia,
Since the last years of war had dwindled
into 126
A kind of general condottiero system
Of bandit warfare; each troop with its
chief,
And all against mankind.
Iden. That cannot be.
A young heir, bred to wealth and luxury,
To risk his life and honours with dis-
banded 131
Soldiers and desperadoes!
Fritz. Heaven best knows!
But there are human natures so allied
Unto the savage love of enterprise,
That they will seek for peril as a pleasure
I've heard that nothing can reclaim your
Indian, 136
Or tame the tiger, though their infancy
Were fed on milk and honey. After all,

Your Wallenstein, your Tilly and
 Gustavus,
Your Bannier, and your Torstenson and
 Weimar, 140
Were but the same thing upon a grand
 scale;
And now that they are gone, and peace
 proclaim'd,
They who would follow the same pastime
 must
Pursue it on their own account. Here
 comes 144
The baron, and the Saxon stranger, who
Was his chief aid in yesterday's escape,
But did not leave the cottage by the Oder
Until this morning.

Enter STRALENHEIM *and* ULRIC.

Stral. Since you have refused
All compensation, gentle stranger, save
Inadequate thanks, you almost check even
 them, 150
Making me feel the worthlessness of
 words,
And blush at my own barren gratitude,
They seem so niggardly, compared with
 what
Your courteous courage did in my
 behalf——
Ulr. I pray you press the theme no
 further.
Stral. But 155
Can I not serve you? You are young, and
 of
That mould which throws out heroes; fair
 in favour;
Brave, I know, by my living now to say so;
And, doubtlessly, with such a form and
 heart,
Would look into the fiery eyes of war,
As ardently for glory as you dared 161
An obscure death to save an unknown
 stranger,
In an as perilous, but opposite, element.
You are made for the service: I have
 served;
Have rank by birth and soldiership, and
 friends, 165
Who shall be yours. 'Tis true this pause of
 peace
Favours such views at present scantily;
But 'twill not last, men's spirits are too
 stirring;
And, after thirty years of conflict, peace
Is but a petty war, as the time shows us
In every forest, or a mere arm'd truce.
War will reclaim his own; and, in the
 mean time,
You might obtain a post, which would
 insure
A higher soon, and, by my influence, fail
 not 174
To rise. I speak of Brandenburg, wherein
I stand well with the Elector; in Bohemia,

Like you, I am a stranger, and we are now
Upon its frontier.
Ulr. You perceive my garb
Is Saxon, and of course my service due
To my own sovereign. If I must decline
Your offer, 'tis with the same feeling which
Induced it.
Stral. Why, this is mere usury!
I owe my life to you, and you refuse
The acquittance of the interest of the debt,
To heap more obligations on me, till
I bow beneath them. 186
Ulr. You shall say so when
I claim the payment.
Stral. Well, sir, since you will not—
You are nobly born?
Ulr. I have heard my kinsmen say so.
Stral. Your actions show it. Might I
 ask your name?
Ulr. Ulric.
Stral. Your house's?
Ulr. When I'm worthy of it, 190
I'll answer you.
Stral. [aside]. Most probably an
 Austrian,
Whom these unsettled times forbid to
 boast
His lineage on these wild and dangerous
 frontiers,
Where the name of his country is abhorr'd.
 [*Aloud to* FRITZ *and* IDENSTEIN.
So, sirs! how have ye sped in your re-
 searches? 195
Iden. Indifferent well, your excellency.
Stral. Then
I am to deem the plunderer is caught?
Iden. Humph!—not exactly.
Stral. Or at least suspected?
Iden. Oh! for that matter, very much
 suspected.
Stral. Who may he be?
Iden. Why, don't *you* know, my
 lord? 200
Stral. How should I? I was fast asleep.
Iden. And so
Was I, and that's the cause I know no
 more
Than does your excellency.
Stral. Dolt!
Iden. Why, if
Your lordship, being robb'd, don't
 recognise
The rogue; how should I, not being robb'd,
 identify 205
The thief among so many? In the crowd,
May it please your excellency, your thief
 looks
Exactly like the rest, or rather better:
'Tis only at the bar and in the dungeon,
That wise men know your felon by his
 features; 210
But I'll engage, that if seen there but once,
Whether he be found criminal or no,
His face shall be so.

Stral. [*to* FRITZ]. Prithee, Fritz, inform
me
What hath been done to trace the fellow?
Fritz. Faith!
My lord, not much as yet, except con-
jecture. 215
Stral. Besides the loss (which, I must
own, affects me
Just now materially), I needs would find
The villain out of public motives; for
So dexterous a spoiler, who could creep
Through my attendants, and so many
peopled 220
And lighted chambers, on my rest, and
snatch
The gold before my scarce-closed eyes,
would soon
Leave bare your borough, Sir Intendant!
Iden. True!
If there were aught to carry off, my lord.
Ulr. What is all this?
Stral. You join'd us but this morning,
And have not heard that I was robb'd last
night. 226
Ulr. Some rumour of it reach'd me as
I pass'd
The outer chambers of the palace, but
I know no further.
Stral. It is a strange business;
The intendant can inform you of the facts.
Iden. Most willingly. You see——
Stral. [*impatiently*]. Defer your tale,
Till certain of the hearer's patience.
Iden. That
Can only be approved by proofs. You
see——
Stral. [*again interrupting him, and
addressing* ULRIC]. In short, I was
asleep upon my chair, 234
My cabinet before me, with some gold
Upon it (more than I much like to lose,
Though in part only): some ingenious
person
Contrived to glide through all my own
attendants,
Besides those of the place, and bore away
A hundred golden ducats, which to find
I would be fain, and there's an end.
Perhaps 241
You (as I still am rather faint) would add
To yesterday's great obligation, this,
Though slighter, yet not slight, to aid
these men
(Who seem but lukewarm) in recovering
it? 245
Ulr. Most willingly, and without loss
of time—
[*To* IDENSTEIN]. Come hither, mynheer!
Iden. But so much haste bodes
Right little speed, and——
Ulr; Standing motionless
None; so let's march; we'll talk as we go
on.
Iden. But——

Ulr. Show the spot, and then I'll
answer you. 250
Fritz. I will, sir, with his excellency's
leave.
Stral. Do so, and take yon old ass
with you.
Fritz. Hence!
Ulr. Come on, old oracle, expound
thy riddle!
[*Exit with* IDENSTEIN *and* FRITZ.
Stral. [*solus*]. A stalwart, active,
soldier-looking stripling,
Handsome as Hercules ere his first labour,
And with a brow of thought beyond his
years 256
When in repose, till his eye kindles up
In answering yours. I wish I could engage
him:
I have need of some such spirits near me
now,
For this inheritance is worth a struggle.
And though I am not the man to yield
without one, 261
Neither are they who now rise up between
me
And my desire. The boy, they say, 's a
bold one;
But he hath play'd the truant in some hour
Of freakish folly, leaving fortune to 265
Champion his claims. That's well. The
father, whom
For years I've track'd, as does the blood-
hound, never
In sight, but constantly in scent, had put
me
To fault; but *here* I *have* him, and that's
better.
It must be *he!* All circumstance proclaims
it; 270
And careless voices, knowing not the
cause
Of my inquiries, still confirm it.—Yes,
The man, his bearing, and the mystery
Of his arrival, and the time; the account,
too,
The intendant gave (for I have not beheld
her) 275
Of his wife's dignified but foreign aspect;
Besides the antipathy with which we met,
As snakes and lions shrink back from each
other
By secret instinct that both must be foes
Deadly, without being natural prey to
either; 280
All—all—confirm it to my mind. How-
ever,
We'll grapple, ne'ertheless. In a few hours
The order comes from Frankfort, if these
waters
Rise not the higher (and the weather
favours
Their quick abatement), and I'll have
him safe 285
Within a dungeon, where he may avouch

His real estate and name; and there's no
 harm done,
Should he prove other than I deem. This
 robbery
(Save for the actual loss) is lucky also;
He's poor, and that's suspicious—he's
 unknown, 290
And that's defenceless.—True, we have
 no proofs
Of guilt,—but what hath he of innocence?
Were he a man indifferent to my prospects,
In other bearings, I should rather lay
The inculpation on the Hungarian, who
Hath something which I like not; and
 alone 296
Of all around, except the intendant, and
The prince's household and my own, had
 ingress
Familiar to the chamber.

Enter GABOR.

 Friend, how fare you?
Gab. As those who fare well every-
 where, when they 300
Have supp'd and slumber'd, no great
 matter how—
And you, my lord?
Stral. Better in rest than purse:
Mine inn is like to cost me dear.
Gab. I heard
Of your late loss; but 'tis a trifle to
One of your order.
Stral. ᵗ You would hardly think so,
Were the loss yours.
Gab. I never had so much
(At once) in my whole life, and therefore
 am not
Fit to decide. But I came here to seek you.
Your couriers are turn'd back—I have
 outstripp'd them, 309
In my return.
Stral. You!—Why?
Gab. I went at daybreak,
To watch for the abatement of the river,
As being anxious to resume my journey.
Your messengers were all check'd like
 myself;
And, seeing the case hopeless, I await
The current's pleasure. 315
Stral. Would the dogs were in it!
Why did they not, at least, attempt the
 passage?
I order'd this at all risks.
Gab. Could you order
The Oder to divide, as Moses did
The Red Sea (scarcely redder than the flood
Of the swoln stream), and be obey'd,
 perhaps 320
They might have ventured.
Stral. I must see to it:
The knaves! the slaves!—but they shall
 smart for this. [*Exit* STRALENHEIM.
Gab. [*solus*]. There goes my noble,
 feudal, self-will'd baron!

Epitome of what brave chivalry
The preux chevaliers of the good old times
Have left us. Yesterday he would have
 given 326
His lands (if he hath any), and, still dearer,
His sixteen quarterings, for as much fresh
 air
As would have fill'd a bladder, while he lay
Gurgling and foaming halfway through
 the window 330
Of his o'erset and water-logg'd con-
 veyance;
And now he storms at half a dozen
 wretches
Because they love their lives too! Yet, he's
 right:
'Tis strange they should, when such as he
 may put them
To hazard at his pleasure. Oh, thou
 world! 335
Thou art indeed a melancholy jest!
 [*Exit* GABOR.

SCENE II.—*The Apartment of* WERNER, *in
 the Palace.*

Enter JOSEPHINE *and* ULRIC.

Jos. Stand back, and let me look on
 thee again!
My Ulric!—my beloved!—can it be—
After twelve years?
Ulr. My dearest mother!
Jos. Yes!
My dream is realised—how beautiful!—
How more than all I sigh'd for! Heaven
 receive 5
A mother's thanks! a mother's tears of joy!
This is indeed thy work!—At such an
 hour, too,
He comes not only as a son, but saviour.
Ulr. If such a joy await me, it must
 double
What I now feel, and lighten from my
 heart 10
A part of the long debt of duty, not
Of love (for that was ne'er withheld)—
 forgive me!
This long delay was not my fault.
Jos. I know it,
But cannot think of sorrow now, and
 doubt
If I e'er felt it, 'tis so dazzled from 15
My memory by this oblivious transport!—
My son!

Enter WERNER.

Wer. What have we here,—more
 strangers?
Jos. No!
Look upon him! What do you see?
Wer. A stripling,
For the first time—
Ulr. [*kneeling*]. For twelve long years,
 my father!

 575

Wer. Oh, God!
Jos. He faints!
Wer. No—I am better now—— 20
Ulric! [*Embraces him*].
Ulr. My father, Siegendorf!
Wer. [*starting*]. Hush! boy—
The walls may hear that name!
Ulr. What then?
Wer. Why, then—
But we will talk of that anon. Remember,
I must be known here but as Werner.
Come!
Come to my arms again! Why, thou
look'st all 25
I should have been, and was not.
Josephine!
Sure 'tis no father's fondness dazzles me;
But, had I seen that form amid ten
thousand
Youth of the choicest, my heart would
have chosen
This for my son!
Ulr. And yet you knew me not! 30
Wer. Alas! I have had that upon my
soul
Which makes me look on all men with an
eye
That only knows the evil at first glance.
Ulr. My memory served me far more
fondly: I
Have not forgotten aught; and oft-times
in 35
The proud and princely halls of—(I'll not
name them,
As you say that 'tis perilous)—but i' the
pomp
Of your sire's feudal mansion, I look'd back
To the Bohemian mountains many a
sunset,
And wept to see another day go down
O'er thee and me, with those huge hills
between us. 41
They shall not part us more.
Wer. I know not that.
Are you aware my father is no more?
Ulr. Oh, heavens! I left him in a green
old age,
And looking like the oak, worn, but still
steady 45
Amidst the elements, whilst younger trees
Fell fast around him. 'Twas scarce three
months since.
Wer. Why did you leave him?
Jos. [*embracing* ULRIC]. Can you ask
that question?
Is he not *here*?
Wer. True; he hath sought his
parents,
And found them; but oh! *how*, and in
what state! 50
Ulr. All shall be better'd. What we
have to do
Is to proceed, and to assert our rights,
Or rather yours; for I waive all, unless
Your father has disposed in such a sort
Of his broad lands as to make mine the
foremost, 55
So that I must prefer my claim for form:
But I trust better, and that all is yours.
Wer. Have you not heard of Stralen-
heim?
Ulr. I saved
His life but yesterday; he's here.
Wer. You saved
The serpent who will sting us all!
Ulr. You speak 60
Riddles: what is this Stralenheim to us?
Wer. Everything. One who claims
our father's lands:
Our distant kinsman, and our nearest foe.
Ulr. I never heard his name till now.
The count,
Indeed, spoke sometimes of a kinsman,
who, 65
If his own line should fail, might be
remotely
Involved in the succession; but his titles
Were never named before me—and what
then?
His right must yield to ours.
Wer. Ay, if at Prague;
But here he is all-powerful; and has
spread 70
Snares for thy father, which, if hitherto
He hath escaped them, is by fortune, not
By favour.
Ulr. Doth he personally know you?
Wer. No; but he guesses shrewdly at
my person,
As he betray'd last night; and I, perhaps,
But owe my temporary liberty 76
To his uncertainty.
Ulr. I think you wrong him
(Excuse me for the phrase); but Stralen-
heim
Is not what you prejudge him, or, if so,
He owes me something both for past and
present. 80
I saved his life, he therefore trusts in me.
He hath been plunder'd too, since he came
hither:
Is sick; a stranger; and as such not now
Able to trace the villain who hath robb'd
him:
I have pledged myself to do so; and the
business 85
Which brought me here was chiefly that;
but I
Have found, in searching for another's
dross,
My own whole treasure—you, my
parents!
Wer. [*agitatedly*]. Who
Taught you to mouth that name of
'villain'?
Ulr. What
More noble name belongs to common
thieves? 90

Wer. Who taught you thus to brand
an unknown being
With an infernal stigma?
 Ulr. My own feelings
Taught me to name a ruffian from his
deeds.
Wer. Who taught you, long-sought
and ill-found boy! that
It would be safe for my own son to insult
me? 95
 Ulr. I named a villain. What is there
in common
With such a being and my father?
 Wer. Everything!
That ruffian is thy father!
 Jos. Oh, my son!
Believe him not—and yet!——[*her voice
falters*].
 Ulr. [*starts, looks earnestly at* WERNER
and then says slowly,] And you
avow it?
 Wer. Ulric, before you dare despise
your father, 100
Learn to divine and judge his actions.
Young,
Rash, new to life, and rear'd in luxury's
lap,
Is it for you to measure passion's force,
Or misery's temptation? Wait—(not
long,
It cometh like the night, and quickly)—
Wait!— 105
Wait till, like me, your hopes are blighted
—till
Sorrow and shame are handmaids of your
cabin;
Famine and poverty your guests at table;
Despair your bed-fellow—then rise, but
not
From sleep, and judge! Should that day
e'er arrive, 110
Should you see then the serpent, who hath
coil'd
Himself around all that is dear and noble
Of you and yours, lie slumbering in your
path,
With but *his* folds between your steps and
happiness,
When *he*, who lives but to tear from you
name, 115
Lands, life itself, lies at your mercy, with
Chance your conductor—midnight for
your mantle—
The bare knife in your hand, and earth
asleep,
Even to your deadliest foe; and he as
'twere
Inviting death, by looking like it, while
His death alone can save you:—Thank
your God! 121
If then, like me, content with petty
plunder,
You turn aside——I did so.
 Ulr. But——

Wer. [*abruptly*]. Hear me!
I will not brook a human voice—scarce
dare 124
Listen to my own (if that be human still)—
Hear me! you do not know this man—I do.
He's mean, deceitful, avaricious. You
Deem yourself safe, as young and brave;
but learn
None are secure from desperation, few
From subtilty. My worst foe, Stralen-
heim, 130
Housed in a prince's palace, couch'd
within
A prince's chamber, lay below my knife!
An instant—a mere motion—the least
impulse—
Had swept him and all fears of mine from
earth.
He was within my power—my knife was
raised— 135
Withdrawn—and I'm in his:—are you
not so?
Who tells you that he knows you *not*?
Who says
He hath not lured you here to end you? or
To plunge you, with your parents, in a
dungeon? [*He pauses.*
 Ulr. Proceed—proceed!
 Wer. *Me* he hath ever known, 140
And hunted through each change of
time—name—fortune—
And why not *you*? Are you more versed
in men?
He wound snares round me; flung along
my path
Reptiles, whom, in my youth, I would
have spurn'd
Even from my presence; but, in spurning
now, 145
Fill only with fresh venom. Will you be
More patient? Ulric!—Ulric!—there are
crimes
Made venial by the occasion, and tempta-
tions
Which nature cannot master or forbear.
 Ulr. [*who looks first at him, and then at*
JOSEPHINE]. My mother!
 Wer. Ah! I thought so: you have now
Only one parent. I have lost alike 151
Father and son, and stand alone.
 Ulr. But stay!
 [WERNER *rushes out of the chamber.*
 Jos. [*to* ULRIC]. Follow him not, until
this storm of passion
Abates. Think'st thou, that were it well
for him,
I had not follow'd?
 Ulr. I obey you, mother, 155
Although reluctantly. My first act shall
not
Be one of disobedience.
 Jos. Oh! he is good!
Condemn him not from his own mouth,
but trust

To me, who have borne so much with him,
and for him, 159
That this is but the surface of his soul,
And that the depth is rich in better things.
Ulr. These then are but my father's
principles?
My mother thinks not with him?
Jos. Nor doth he
Think as he speaks. Alas! long years of
grief
Have made him sometimes thus.
Ulr. Explain to me 165
More clearly, then, these claims of Stralen-
heim,
That, when I see the subject in its bearings,
I may prepare to face him, or at least
To extricate you from your present perils.
I pledge myself to accomplish this—but
would 170
I had arrived a few hours sooner!
Jos. Ay!
Hadst thou but done so!

Enter GABOR *and* IDENSTEIN, *with*
Attendants.

Gab. [*to* ULRIC]. I have sought you,
comrade.
So this is my reward!
Ulr. What do you mean?
Gab. 'Sdeath! have I lived to these
years, and for this!
[*To* IDENSTEIN]. But for your age and
folly, I would——
Iden. Help! 175
Hands off! Touch an intendant!
Gab. Do not think
I'll honour you so much as save your
throat
From the Ravenstone by choking you
myself.
Iden. I thank you for the respite: but
there are
Those who have greater need of it than
me. 180
Ulr. Unriddle this vile wrangling,
or——
Gab. At once, then,
The baron has been robbed, and upon me
This worthy personage has deign'd to fix
His kind suspicions—me! whom he ne'er
saw
Till yester evening.
Iden. Wouldst have me suspect 185
My own acquaintances? You have to
learn
That I keep better company.
Gab. You shall
Keep the best shortly, and the last for all
men,
The worms! you hound of malice!
 [GABOR *seizes on him.*
Ulr. [*interfering*]. Nay, no violence;
He's old, unarm'd—be temperate, Gabor!
Gab. [*letting go* IDENSTEIN]. True:

I am a fool to lose myself because 19
Fools deem me knave: it is their homage
Ulr. [*to* IDENSTEIN]. Hov
Fare you?
Iden. Help!
Ulr. I *have* help'd you.
Iden. Kill him! the
I'll say so.
Gab. I am calm—live on!
Iden. That's mor
Than you shall do, if there be judge o
judgment 19
In Germany. The baron shall decide!
Gab. Does *he* abet you in you
accusation?
Iden. Does he not?
Gab. Then next time let him go sin
Ere I go hang for snatching him from
drowning.
But here he comes!

Enter STRALENHEIM.

Gab. [*goes up to him*]. My noble lord
I'm here! 20
Stral. Well, sir!
Gab. Have you aught with me
Stral. What should
Have with you?
Gab. You know best, if yesterday'
Flood has not wash'd away your memory
But that's a trifle. I stand here accused
In phrases not equivocal, by yon 20
Intendant, of the pillage of your person
Or chamber:—is the charge your own o
his?
Stral. I accuse no man.
Gab. Then you acquit me, baron
Stral. I know not whom to accuse, o
to acquit,
Or scarcely to suspect.
Gab. But you at least 21
Should know whom *not* to suspect. I ar
insulted—
Oppress'd here by these menials, and
look
To you for remedy—teach them thei
duty!
To look for thieves at home were part of it
If duly taught; but, in one word, if I 21
Have an accuser, let it be a man
Worthy to be so of a man like me.
I am your equal.
Stral. You!
Gab. Ay, sir; and, fo
Aught that you know, superior; bu
proceed—
I do not ask for hints, and surmises, 22
And circumstance, and proof: I know
enough
Of what I have done for you, and wha
you owe me,
To have at least waited your payment rathe
Than paid myself, had I been eager of
Your gold. I also know, that were I eve

The villain I am deem'd, the service
　render'd　　　　　　　　　　　　　226
So recently would not permit you to
Pursue me to the death, except through
　shame,
Such as would leave your scutcheon but a
　blank.
But this is nothing: I demand of you　230
Justice upon your unjust servants, and
From your own lips a disavowal of
All sanction of their insolence: thus much
You owe to the unknown, who asks no
　more,
And never thought to have ask'd so much.
　Stral.　　　　　　　　　This tone　235
May be of innocence.
　Gab.　　　　'Sdeath! who dare doubt it,
Except such villains as ne'er had it?
　Stral.　　　　　　　　　　　　You
Are hot, sir.
　Gab.　　　Must I turn an icicle
Before the breath of menials, and their
　master?
　Stral. Ulric! you know this man; I
　found him in　　　　　　　　　　240
Your company.
　Gab.　　　We found *you* in the Oder,
Would we had left you there!
　Stral.　　　I give you thanks, sir.
　Gab. I've earned them; but might
　have earn'd more from others,
Perchance, if I had left you to your fate.
　Stral. Ulric! you know this man?
　Gab.　　　No more than you do　245
If he avouches not my honour.
　Ulr.　　　　　　　　　　　　　I
Can vouch your courage, and, as far as my
Own brief connexion led me, honour.
　Stral.　　　　　　　　　　　Then
I'm satisfied.
　Gab. [*ironically*]. Right easily, methinks.
What is the spell in his asseveration　250
More than in mine?
　Stral.　　　　I merely said that *I*
Was satisfied—not that you are absolved.
　Gab. Again! Am I accused or no?
　Stral.　　　　　　　　　　Go to!
You wax too insolent. If circumstance
And general suspicion be against you,
Is the fault mine? Is't not enough that I
Decline all question of your guilt or inno-
　cence?　　　　　　　　　　　　257
　Gab. My lord, my lord, this is mere
　cozenage,
A vile equivocation; you well know
Your doubts are certainties to all around
　you—　　　　　　　　　　　　260
Your looks a voice—your frowns a
　sentence; you
Are practising your power on me—
　because
You have it; but beware! you know not
　whom
You strive to tread on.

　Stral.　　　　　　　Threat'st thou?
　Gab.　　　　　　　　Not so much　264
As you accuse. You hint the basest injury.
And I retort it with an open warning.
　Stral. As you have said, 'tis true I owe
　you something,
For which you seem disposed to pay
　yourself.
　Gab. Not with your gold.
　Stral.　　　　　　With bootless insolence.
　　　[*To his Attendants and* IDENSTEIN.
You need not further to molest this man,
But let him go his way. Ulric, good
　morrow!　　　　　　　　　　　271
[*Exit* STRALENHEIM, IDENSTEIN, *and*
　Attendants.
　Gab. [*following*]. I'll after him and—
　Ulr. [*stopping him*]. Not a step.
　Gab.　　　　　　　　　Who shall
Oppose me?
　Ulr.　　　Your own reason, with a
　moment's
Thought.
　Gab.　　Must I bear this?
　Ulr.　　　　Pshaw! we all must bear
The arrogance of something higher than
Ourselves—the highest cannot temper
　Satan,　　　　　　　　　　　　276
Nor the lowest his vicegerents upon earth.
I've seen you brave the elements, and bear
Things which had made this silkworm cast
　his skin—
And shrink you from a few sharp sneers
　and words?　　　　　　　　　280
　Gab. Must I bear to be deem'd a thief?
　If 'twere
A bandit of the woods, I could have borne
　it—
There's something daring in it:—but to
　steal
The moneys of a slumbering man!—
　Ulr.　　　　　　　　It seems, then,
You are *not* guilty.
　Gab.　　　Do I hear aright?　285
You too!
　Ulr. I merely ask'd a simple question.
　Gab. If the judge ask'd me, I would
　answer 'No'—
To you I answer *thus.*　　　[*He draws.*
　Ulr. [*drawing*].　　With all my heart!
　Jos. Without there! Ho! help! help!—
　　Oh, God! here's murder!
　　　　　　　[*Exit* JOSEPHINE, *shrieking.*

GABOR *and* ULRIC *fight.* GABOR *is dis-*
armed just as STRALENHEIM, JOSEPHINE,
IDENSTEIN, &c., *re-enter.*
　Jos. Oh! glorious heaven! He's safe!
　Stral. [*to* JOSEPHINE].　Who's safe?
　Jos.　　　　　　　　　　　My——
　Ulr. [*interrupting her with a stern look,*
　and turning afterwards to STRALEN-
　HEIM].
　　　　　　　　　　　　Both!　290
Here's no great harm done.

Stral. What hath caused all this?
Ulr. *You*, baron, I believe; but as the effect
Is harmless, let it not disturb you.—
Gabor!
There is your sword; and when you bare it next,
Let it not be against your *friends*.
[ULRIC *pronounces the last words slowly and emphatically in a low voice to* GABOR.
Gab. I thank you 295
Less for my life than for your counsel.
Stral. These
Brawls must end here.
Gab. [*taking his sword*]. They *shall*.
You've wrong'd me, Ulric,
More with your unkind thoughts than sword: I would
The last were in my bosom rather than
The first in yours. I could have borne yon noble's 300
Absurd insinuations—ignorance
And dull suspicion are a part of his
Entail will last him longer than his lands,—
But I may fit *him* yet:—you have vanquish'd me.
I was the fool of passion to conceive 305
That I could cope with you, whom I had seen
Already proved by greater perils than
Rest in this arm. We may meet by and by,
However—but in friendship.
[*Exit* GABOR.
Stral. I will brook
No more! This outrage following upon his insults, 310
Perhaps his guilt, has cancell'd all the little
I owed him heretofore for the so-vaunted
Aid which he added to your abler succour.
Ulric, you are not hurt?—
Ulr. Not even by a scratch.
Stral. [*to* IDENSTEIN]. Intendant! take your measures to secure 315
Yon fellow: I revoke my former lenity.
He shall be sent to Frankfort with an escort,
The instant that the waters have abated.
Iden. Secure him! He hath got his sword again—
And seems to know the use on't; 'tis his trade, 320
Belike:—*I'm* a civilian.
Stral. Fool! are not
Yon score of vassals dogging at your heels
Enough to seize a dozen such? Hence! after him!
Ulr. Baron, I do beseech you!
Stral. I must be
Obey'd. No words!
Iden. Well, if it must be so— 325
March, vassals! I'm your leader, and will bring

The rear up: a wise general never should
Expose his precious life—on which all rests.
I like that article of war.
[*Exit* IDENSTEIN *and Attendants*.
Stral. Come hither,
Ulric; what does that woman here? Oh! now 330
I recognise her, 'tis the stranger's wife
Whom they *name* 'Werner.'
Ulr. 'Tis his name.
Stral. Indeed!
Is not your husband visible, fair dame?—
Jos. Who seeks him?
Stral. No one—for the present: but
I fain would parley, Ulric, with yourself
Alone.
Ulr. I will retire with you.
Jos. Not so: 335
You are the latest stranger, and command
All places here.
[*Aside to* ULRIC, *as she goes out*]. O Ulric!
have a care—
Remember what depends on a rash word!
Ulr. [*to* JOSEPHINE]. Fear not!—
[*Exit* JOSEPHINE.
Stral. Ulric, I think that I may trust you; 340
You saved my life—and acts like these beget
Unbounded confidence.
Ulr. Say on.
Stral. Mysterious
And long-engender'd circumstances (not
To be now fully enter'd on) have made
This man obnoxious—perhaps fatal to me. 345
Ulr. Who? Gabor, the Hungarian?
Stral. No—this 'Werner'—
With the false name and habit.
Ulr. How can this be?
He is the poorest of the poor—and yellow
Sickness sits cavern'd in his hollow eye:
The man is helpless.
Stral. He is—'tis no matter;— 350
But if he be the man I deem (and that
He is so, all around us here—and much
That is not here—confirm my apprehension),
He must be made secure ere twelve hours further. 354
Ulr. And what have I to do with this?
Stral. I have sent
To Frankfort, to the governor, my friend,
(I have the authority to do so by
An order of the house of Brandenburg),
For a fit escort—but this cursed flood
Bars all access, and may do for some hours. 360
Ulr. It is abating.
Stral. That is well.
Ulr. But how
Am I concern'd?

Stral. As one who did so much
For me, you cannot be indifferent to
That which is of more import to me than
The life you rescued.—Keep your eye on
 him! 365
The man avoids me, knows that I now
 know him.—
Watch him!—as you would watch the
 wild boar when
He makes against you in the hunter's
 gap—
Like him he must be spear'd.
Ulr. Why so?
Stral. He stands
Between me and a brave inheritance! 370
Oh! could you see it! But you shall.
Ulr. I hope so.
Stral. It is the richest of the rich
 Bohemia,
Unscathed by scorching war. It lies so
 near
The strongest city, Prague, that fire and
 sword
Have skimm'd it lightly: so that now,
 besides 375
Its own exuberance, it bears double value
Confronted with whole realms far and
 near
Made deserts.
Ulr. You describe it faithfully.
Stral. Ay—could you see it, you
 would say so—but, 379
As I have said, you shall.
Ulr. I accept the omen.
Stral. Then claim a recompense from
 it and me,
Such as *both* may make worthy your
 acceptance
And services to me and mine for ever.
Ulr. And this sole, sick, and miserable
 wretch—
This way-worn stranger—stands between
 you and 385
This Paradise?—(As Adam did between
The devil and his)—[*Aside*].
Stral. He doth.
Ulr. Hath he no right?
Stral. Right! none. A disinherited
 prodigal,
Who for these twenty years disgraced his
 lineage 389
In all his acts—but chiefly by his marriage,
And living amidst commerce-fetching
 burghers,
And dabbling merchants, in a mart of
 Jews.
Ulr. He has a wife, then?
Stral. You'd be sorry to
Call such your mother. You have seen
 the woman 394
He *calls* his wife.
Ulr. Is she not so?
Stral. No more
Than he's your father:—an Italian girl,

The daughter of a banish'd man, who lives
On love and poverty with this same
 Werner.
Ulr. They are childless, then?
Stral. There is or was a bastard,
Whom the old man—the grandsire (as
 old age 400
Is ever doting) took to warm his bosom,
As it went chilly downward to the grave:
But the imp stands not in my path—he
 has fled,
No one knows whither; and if he had not,
His claims alone were too contemptible
To stand.—Why do you smile?
Ulr. At your vain fears:
A poor man almost in his grasp—a child
Of doubtful birth—can startle a grandee!
Stral. All's to be fear'd, where all is to
 be gain'd.
Ulr. True; and aught done to save or
 to obtain it. 410
Stral. You have harp'd the very string
 next to my heart.
I may depend upon you?
Ulr. 'Twere too late
To doubt it.
Stral. Let no foolish pity shake
Your bosom (for the appearance of the
 man
Is pitiful)—he is a wretch, as likely 415
To have robb'd me as the fellow more
 suspected,
Except that circumstance is less against
 him;
He being lodged far off, and in a chamber
Without approach to mine; and, to say
 truth, 419
I think too well of blood allied to mine,
To deem he would descend to such an
 act:
Besides, he was a soldier, and a brave one
Once—though too rash.
Ulr. And they, my lord, we know
By our experience, never plunder till
They knock the brains out first—which
 makes them heirs, 425
Not thieves. The dead, who feel nought,
 can lose nothing,
Nor e'er be robb'd: their spoils are a be-
 quest—
No more.
Stral. Go to! you are a wag. But say
I may be sure you'll keep an eye on this
 man,
And let me know his slightest movement
 towards 430
Concealment or escape?
Ulr. You may be sure
You yourself could not watch him more
 than I
Will be his sentinel.
Stral. By this you make me
Yours, and for ever.
Ulr. Such is my intention. [*Exeunt.*

ACT III

SCENE I.—*A Hall in the same Palace, from whence the secret passage leads.*

Enter WERNER *and* GABOR.

Gab. Sir, I have told my tale: if it so
please you
To give me refuge for a few hours, well—
If not, I'll try my fortune elsewhere.
 Wer. How
Can I, so wretched, give to Misery
A shelter?—wanting such myself as much
As e'er the hunted deer a covert——
 Gab. Or 6
The wounded lion his cool cave. Methinks
You rather look like one would turn at
bay,
And rip the hunter's entrails.
 Wer. Ah!
 Gab. I care not
If it be so, being much disposed to do 10
The same myself. But will you shelter me?
I am oppress'd like you—and poor like
you—
Disgraced——
 Wer. [*abruptly*]. Who told you that I
was disgraced?
 Gab. No one; nor did I say *you* were
so: with
Your poverty my likeness ended; but 15
I said *I* was so—and would add, with
truth,
As undeservedly as *you.*
 Wer. Again!
As I?
 Gab. Or any other honest man.
What the devil would you have? You
don't believe me
Guilty of this base theft?
 Wer. No, no—I cannot. 20
 Gab. Why that's my heart of honour!
yon young gallant—
Your miserly intendant and dense noble—
All—all suspected me; and why? because
I am the worst clothed and least named
amongst them;
Although, were Momus' lattice in your
breasts, 25
My soul might brook to open it more
widely
Than theirs: but thus it is—you poor and
helpless—
Both still more than myself.
 Wer. How knew you that?
 Gab. You're right: I ask for shelter
at the hand
Which I call helpless; if you now deny it,
I were well paid. But you, who seem to
have proved 31
The wholesome bitterness of life, know
well,
By sympathy, that all the outspread gold

Of the New World the Spaniard boasts
about,
Could never tempt the man who knows
its worth 35
Weigh'd at its proper value in the balance,
Save in such guise (and there I grant its
power,
Because I feel it) as may leave no nightmare
Upon his heart o' nights.
 Wer. What do you mean?
 Gab. Just what I say; I thought my
speech was plain; 40
You are no thief—nor I—and, as true men,
Should aid each other.
 Wer. It is a damn'd world, sir.
 Gab. So is the nearest of the two next, as
The priests say (and no doubt they should
know best), 44
Therefore I'll stick by this—as being loth
To suffer martyrdom, at least with such
An epitaph as larceny upon my tomb.
It is but a night's lodging which I crave;
To-morrow I will try the waters, as
The dove did, trusting that they have
abated. 50
 Wer. Abated? Is there hope of that?
 Gab. There was
At noontide.
 Wer. Then we may be safe.
 Gab. Are *you*
In peril?
 Wer. Poverty is ever so.
 Gab. That I know by long practice.
Will you not
Promise to make mine less?
 Wer. Your poverty? 55
 Gab. No—you don't look a leech for
that disorder;
I meant my peril only: you've a roof,
And I have none; I merely seek a covert.
 Wer. Rightly; for how should such a
wretch as I
Have gold?
 Gab. Scarce honestly, to say the
truth on't, 60
Although I almost wish you had the
baron's.
 Wer. Dare you insinuate?
 Gab. What?
 Wer. Are you aware
To whom you speak?
 Gab. No; and I am not used
Greatly to care. [*A noise heard without.*]
But hark! they come!
 Wer. Who come?
 Gab. The intendant and his manhounds after me: 65
I'd face them—but it were in vain to expect
Justice at hands like theirs. Where shall
I go?
But show me any place. I do assure you,
If there be faith in man, I am most guiltless:
Think if it were your own case!

582

Wer. [*aside*]. Oh, just God! 70
Thy hell is not hereafter! Am I dust still?
Gab. I see you're moved; and it shows
 well in you:
I may live to requite it.
Wer. Are you not
A spy of Stralenheim's?
Gab. Not I! and if
I were, what is there to espy in you? 75
Although, I recollect, his frequent
 question
About you and your spouse might lead to
 some
Suspicion; but you best know—what—
 and why.
I am his deadliest foe.
Wer. You?
Gab. After such
A treatment for the service which in part
I render'd him, I am his enemy: 81
If you are not his friend, you will assist me.
Wer. I will.
Gab. But how?
Wer. [*showing the panel*]. There is a
 secret spring:
Remember, I discover'd it by chance,
And used it but for safety.
Gab. Open it, 85
And I will use it for the same.
Wer. I found it,
As I have said: it leads through winding
 walls
(So thick as to bear paths within their ribs,
Yet lose no jot of strength or stateliness),
And hollow cells, and obscure niches, to
I know not whither; you must not
 advance: 91
Give me your word.
Gab. It is unnecessary:
How should I make my way in darkness
 through
A Gothic labyrinth of unknown wind-
 ings?
Wer. Yes, but who knows to what
 place it may lead? 95
I know not—(mark you!)—but who
 knows it might not
Lead even into the chamber of your foe?
So strangely were contrived these galleries
By our Teutonic fathers in old days,
When man built less against the elements
Than his next neighbour. You must not
 advance 101
Beyond the two first windings; if you do
(Albeit I never pass'd them), I'll not
 answer
For what you may be led to.
Gab. But I will.
A thousand thanks!
Wer. You'll find the spring more
 obvious 105
On the other side; and, when you would
 return,
It yields to the least touch.

Gab. I'll in—farewell!
 [GABOR *goes in by the secret panel.*
Wer. [*solus*]. What have I done? Alas!
 what *had* I done
Before to make this fearful? Let it be
Still some atonement that I save the man,
Whose sacrifice had saved perhaps my
 own— 111
They come! to seek elsewhere what is
 before them!

 Enter IDENSTEIN *and Others.*

Iden. Is he not here? He must have
 vanish'd then
Through the dim Gothic glass by pious aid
Of pictured saints upon the red and yellow
Casements, through which the sunset
 streams like sunrise 116
On long pearl-colour'd beards and
 crimson crosses,
And gilded crosiers, and cross'd arms,
 and cowls,
And helms, and twisted armour, and long
 swords,
All the fantastic furniture of windows
Dim with brave knights and holy hermits,
 whose 121
Likeness and fame alike rest in some panes
Of crystal, which each rattling wind pro-
 claims
As frail as any other life or glory.
He's gone, however.
Wer. Whom do you seek?
Iden. A villain. 125
Wer. Why need you come so far, then?
Iden. In the search
Of him who robb'd the baron.
Wer. Are you sure
You have divined the man?
Iden. As sure as you
Stand there: but where's he gone?
Wer. Who?
Iden. He we sought.
Wer. You see he is not here.
Iden. And yet we traced him 130
Up to this hall. Are you accomplices?
Or deal you in the black art?
Wer. I deal plainly,
To many men the blackest.
Iden. It may be
I have a question or two for yourself
Hereafter; but we must continue now
Our search for t'other. 135
Wer. You had best begin
Your inquisition now: I may not be
So patient always.
Iden. I should like to know,
In good sooth, if you really are the man
That Stralenheim's in quest of.
Wer. Insolent! 140
Said you not that he was not here?
Iden. Yes, *one*;
But there's another whom he tracks more
 keenly,

583

And soon, it may be, with authority
Both paramount to his and mine. But
 come!
Bustle, my boys! we are at fault.
 [*Exit* IDENSTEIN *and Attendants.*
Wer. In what 145
A maze hath my dim destiny involved me!
And one base sin hath done me less ill than
The leaving undone one far greater.
 Down,
Thou busy devil, rising in my heart!
Thou art too late! I'll nought to do with
 blood. 150

Enter ULRIC.

Ulr. I sought you, father.
Wer. Is't not dangerous?
Ulr. No; Stralenheim is ignorant of all
Or any of the ties between us: more—
He sends me here a spy upon your actions,
Deeming me wholly his.
Wer. I cannot think it: 155
'Tis but a snare he winds about us both,
To swoop the sire and son at once.
Ulr. I cannot
Pause in each petty fear, and stumble at
The doubts that rise like briers in our path,
But must break through them, as an
 unarm'd carle 160
Would, though with naked limbs, were
 the wolf rustling
In the same thicket where he hew'd for
 bread.
Nets are for thrushes, eagles are not caught
 so:
We'll overfly or rend them.
Wer. Show me *how?*
Ulr. Can you not guess?
Wer. I cannot.
Ulr. That is strange. 165
Came the thought ne'er into your mind
 last night?
Wer. I understand you not.
Ulr. Then we shall never
More understand each other. But to
 change
The topic——
Wer. You mean to *pursue* it, as
'Tis of our safety.
Ulr. Right; I stand corrected. 170
I see the subject now more clearly, and
Our general situation in its bearings.
The waters are abating; a few hours
Will bring his summon'd myrmidons
 from Frankfort,
When you will be a prisoner, perhaps
 worse, 175
And I an outcast, bastardised by practice
Of this same baron to make way for him.
Wer. And now your remedy! I
 thought to escape
By means of this accursed gold; but now
I dare not use it, show it, scarce look on it.
Methinks it wears upon its face my guilt

For motto, not the mintage of the state;
And, for the sovereign's head, my own
 begirt
With hissing snakes, which curl around
 my temples, 184
And cry to all beholders, Lo! a villain!
Ulr. You must not use it, at least now;
 but take
This ring. [*He gives* WERNER *a jewel.*
Wer. A gem! It was my father's!
Ulr. And
As such is now your own. With this you
 must
Bribe the intendant for his old caleche
And horses to pursue your route at sun-
 rise, 190
Together with my mother.
Wer. And leave you,
So lately found, in peril too?
Ulr. Fear nothing!
The only fear were if we fled together,
For that would make our ties beyond all
 doubt.
The waters only lie in flood between 195
This burgh and Frankfort; so far's in our
 favour.
The route on to Bohemia, though encum-
 ber'd,
Is not impassable; and when you gain
A few hours' start, the difficulties will be
The same to your pursuers. Once beyond
The frontier, and you're safe.
Wer. My noble boy!
Ulr. Hush! hush! no transports: we'll
 indulge in them
In Castle Siegendorf! Display no gold!
Show Idenstein the gem (I know the man,
And have look'd through him): it will
 answer thus 205
A double purpose. Stralenheim lost
 gold—
No jewel; therefore it could *not* be his;
And then the man who was possest of this
Can hardly be suspected of abstracting
The baron's coin, when he could thus
 convert 210
This ring to more than Stralenheim has
 lost
By his last night's slumber. Be not over
 timid
In your address, nor yet too arrogant,
And Idenstein will serve you.
Wer. I will follow
In all things your direction.
Ulr. I would have 215
Spared you the trouble; but had I appear'd
To take an interest in you, and still more
By dabbling with a jewel in your favour,
All had been known at once.
Wer. My guardian angel!
This overpays the past. But how wilt thou
Fare in our absence? 221
Ulr. Stralenheim knows nothing
Of me as aught of kindred with yourself.

I will but wait a day or two with him
To lull all doubts, and then rejoin my
 father.
Wer. To part no more!
Ulr. I know not that; but at 225
The least we'll meet again once more.
Wer. My boy!
My friend! my only child, and sole pre-
 server!
Oh, do not hate me!
Ulr. Hate my father!
Wer. Ay,
My father hated me. Why not my son?
Ulr. Your father knew you not as I do.
Wer. Scorpions
Are in thy words! Thou know me? in this
 guise 231
Thou canst not know me, I am not myself;
Yet (hate me not) I will be soon.
Ulr. I'll *wait!*
In the mean time be sure that all a son
Can do for parents shall be done for mine.
Wer. I see it, and I feel it; yet I feel
Further—that you despise me.
Ulr. Wherefore should I?
Wer. Must I repeat my humiliation?
Ulr. No! 238
I have fathom'd it and you. But let us talk
Of this no more. Or if it must be ever,
Not *now.* Your error has redoubled all
The present difficulties of our house,
At secret war with that of Stralenheim:
All we have now to think of is to baffle
HIM. I have shown *one* way.
Wer. The only one, 245
And I embrace it, as I did my son,
Who show'd *himself* and father's *safety* in
One day.
Ulr. You *shall* be safe; let that suffice.
Would Stralenheim's appearance in
 Bohemia
Disturb your right, or mine, if once we
 were 250
Admitted to our lands?
Wer. Assuredly,
Situate as we are now; although the first
Possessor might, as usual, prove the
 strongest,
Especially the next in blood.
Ulr. Blood! 'tis 254
A word of many meanings; in the veins,
And out of them, it is a different thing—
And so it should be, when the same in
 blood
(As it is call'd) are aliens to each other,
Like Theban brethren: when a part is bad,
A few spilt ounces purify the rest. 260
Wer. I do not apprehend you.
Ulr. That may be—
And should, perhaps—and yet—but get
 ye ready;
You and my mother must away to-night.
Here comes the intendant: sound him with
 the gem; 264

'Twill sink into his venal soul like lead
Into the deep, and bring up slime and mud,
And ooze too, from the bottom, as the lead
 doth
With its greased understratum; but no less
Will serve to warn our vessels through
 these shoals.
The freight is rich, so heave the line in
 time! 270
Farewell! I scarce have time, but yet your
 hand,
My father!——
Wer. Let me embrace thee!
Ulr. We may be
Observed: subdue your nature to the
 hour!
Keep off from me as from your foe!
Wer. Accursed
Be he who is the stifling cause which
 smothers 275
The best and sweetest feeling of our hearts;
At such an hour too!
Ulr. Yes, curse—it will ease you!
Here is the intendant.

 Enter IDENSTEIN.

 Master Idenstein,
How fare you in your purpose? Have you
 caught 279
The rogue?
Iden. No, faith!
Ulr. Well, there are plenty more:
You may have better luck another chase.
Where is the baron?
Iden. Gone back to his chamber:
And now I think on 't, asking after you
With nobly-born impatience.
Ulr. Your great men
Must be answer'd on the instant, as the
 bound 285
Of the stung steed replies unto the spur:
'Tis well they have horses, too; for, if they
 had not,
I fear that men must draw their chariots,
 as
They say kings did Sesostris.
Iden. Who was he?
Ulr. An old Bohemian—an imperial
 gipsy. 290
Iden. A gipsy or Bohemian, 'tis the
 same,
For they pass by both names. And was
 he one?
Ulr. I've heard so; but I must take
 leave. Intendant,
Your servant!—Werner [*to* WERNER
 slightly], if that be your name,
Yours. [*Exit* ULRIC.
Iden. A well-spoken pretty-faced
 young man! 295
And prettily behaved! He knows his
 station,
You see, sir: how he gave to each his due
Precedence!

Wer. I perceived it, and applaud
His just discernment and your own.
Iden. That's well—
That's very well. You also know your
 place, too; 300
And yet I don't know that *I* know your
 place.
Wer. [*showing the ring*]. Would this
 assist your knowledge?
Iden. How!—What!—Eh?
A jewel.
Wer. 'Tis your own on one condition.
Iden. Mine!—Name it!
Wer. That hereafter you permit me
At thrice its value to redeem it: 'tis 305
A family ring.
Iden. A family!—*yours*!—a gem!
I'm breathless!
Wer. You must also furnish me,
An hour ere daybreak, with all means to quit
This place.
Iden. But is it real? Let me look on it:
Diamond, by all that's glorious!
Wer. Come, I'll trust you: 310
You have guess'd, no doubt, that I was
 born above
My present seeming.
Iden. I can't say I did,
Though this looks like it: this is the true
 breeding
Of gentle blood!
Wer. I have important reasons
For wishing to continue privily 315
My journey hence.
Iden. So then *you are* the man
Whom Stralenheim's in quest of?
Wer. I am not;
But being taken for him might conduct
So much embarrassment to me just now,
And to the baron's self hereafter—'tis
To spare both that I would avoid all bustle.
Iden. Be you the man or no, 'tis not
 my business;
Besides, I never could obtain the half
From this proud, niggardly noble, who
 would raise 324
The country for some missing bits of coin,
And never offer a precise reward—
But *this!*—another look!
Wer. Gaze on it freely;
At day-dawn it is yours.
Iden. Oh, thou sweet sparkler!
Thou more than stone of the philosopher!
Thou touchstone of Philosophy herself!
Thou bright eye of the Mine! thou loadstar
 of 331
The Soul! the true magnetic Pole to which
All hearts point duly north, like trembling
 needles!
Thou flaming Spirit of the Earth! which,
 sitting
High on the monarch's diadem, attractest
More worship than the majesty who
 sweats 336

Beneath the crown which makes his head
 ache, like
Millions of hearts which bleed to lend it
 lustre!
Shalt thou be mine? I am, methinks, already
A little king, a lucky alchymist!— 34
A wise magician, who has bound the devil
Without the forfeit of his soul. But come,
Werner, or what else?
Wer. Call me Werner still
You may yet know me by a loftier title.
Iden. I do believe in thee! thou art the
 spirit 34
Of whom I long have dream'd in a low
 garb.—
But come, I'll serve thee: thou shalt be as
 free
As air, despite the waters; let us hence:
I'll show thee I am honest—(oh, thou
 jewel!)
Thou shalt be furnish'd, Werner, with such
 means 35
Of flight, that if thou wert a snail, not bird
Should overtake thee.—Let me gaze
 again!
I have a foster-brother in the mart
Of Hamburgh skill'd in precious stones
 How many
Carats may it weigh?—Come, Werner,
 will wing thee. [*Exeunt.* 35

SCENE II.—STRALENHEIM'S *Chamber.*

STRALENHEIM *and* FRITZ.

Fritz. All's ready, my good lord!
Stral. I am not sleepy
And yet I must to bed; I fain would say
To rest, but something heavy on my spirit
Too dull for wakefulness, too quick for
 slumber,
Sits on me as a cloud along the sky,
Which will not let the sunbeams through
 nor yet
Descend in rain and end, but spreads itself
'Twixt earth and heaven, like envy between
 man
And man, an everlasting mist:—I will
Unto my pillow.
Fritz. May you rest there well! 1
Stral. I feel, and fear, I shall.
Fritz. And wherefore fear
 do fear more,
Stral. I know not why, and therefore
Because an undescribable——but 'tis
All folly. Were the locks (as I desired)
Changed, to-day, of this chamber? for
 last night's 1
Adventure makes it needful.
Fritz. Certainly,
According to your order, and beneath
The inspection of myself and the young
 Saxon
Who saved your life. I think they call him
 'Ulric.'

Stral. You *think!* you supercilious
 slave! what right 20
Have you to *tax your* memory, which
 should be
Quick, proud, and happy to retain the
 name
Of him who saved your master, as a litany
Whose daily repetition marks your
 duty?—
Get hence! '*You think*,' indeed! you, who
 stood still 25
Howling and dripping on the bank, whilst
 I
Lay dying, and the stranger dash'd aside
The roaring torrent, and restored me to
Thank him—and despise you. '*You
 think!*' and scarce 29
Can recollect his name! I will not waste
More words on you. Call me betimes.
 Fritz. Good night!
I trust to-morrow will restore your lord-
 ship
To renovated strength and temper.
 [*The scene closes.*

SCENE III.—*The secret Passage.*

Gab. [*solus*]. Four—
Five—six hours have I counted, like the
 guard
Of outposts on the never-merry clock;
That hollow tongue of time, which, even
 when
It sounds for joy, takes something from
 enjoyment 5
With every clang. 'Tis a perpetual knell,
Though for a marriage feast it rings: each
 stroke
Peals for a hope the less; the funeral note
Of Love deep-buried without resurrection
In the grave of Possession; while the knoll
Of long-lived parents finds a jovial echo
To triple time in the son's ear.
 I'm cold—
I'm dark;—I've blown my fingers—num-
 ber'd o'er
And o'er my steps—and knock'd my head
 against
Some fifty buttresses—and roused the
 rats 15
And bats in general insurrection, till
Their cursed pattering feet and whirling
 wings
Leave me scarce hearing for another sound.
A light! It is at distance (if I can
Measure in darkness distance): but it
 blinks 20
As through a crevice or a key-hole, in
The inhibited direction: I must on,
Nevertheless, from curiosity.
A distant lamp-light is an incident
In such a den as this. Pray Heaven it lead
 me 25
To nothing that may tempt me! Else—
 Heaven aid me

To obtain or to escape it! Shining still!
Were it the star of Lucifer himself,
Or he himself girt with its beams, I could
Contain no longer. Softly: mighty well!
That corner's turn'd—so—ah! no:—
 right! it draws 31
Nearer. Here is a darksome angle—so,
That's weather'd.—Let me pause.—
 Suppose it leads
Into some greater danger than that which
I have escaped—no matter, 'tis a new one;
And novel perils, like fresh mistresses,
Wear more magnetic aspects:—I will on,
And be it where it may—I have my
 dagger,
Which may protect me at a pinch.—Burn
 still,
Thou little light! Thou art my *ignis
 fatuus!* 40
My stationary Will-o'-the-wisp!—So! so!
He hears my invocation, and fails not.
 [*The scene closes.*

SCENE IV.—*A Garden.*

Enter WERNER.

Wer. I could not sleep—and now the
 hour's at hand;
All's ready. Idenstein has kept his word;
And station'd in the outskirts of the town,
Upon the forest's edge, the vehicle
Awaits us. Now the dwindling stars be-
 gin 5
To pale in heaven; and for the last time I
Look on these horrible walls. Oh! never,
 never
Shall I forget them. Here I came most
 poor,
But not dishonour'd: and I leave them
 with 9
A stain,—if not upon my name, yet in
My heart!—a never-dying canker-worm,
Which all the coming splendour of the
 lands,
And rights, and sovereignty of Siegendorf
Can scarcely lull a moment. I must find
Some means of restitution, which would
 ease 15
My soul in part: but how, without dis-
 covery?—
It must be done, however; and I'll pause
Upon the method the first hour of safety.
The madness of my misery led to this
Base infamy; repentance must retrieve it:
I will have nought of Stralenheim's upon
My spirit, though he would grasp all of
 mine;
Lands, freedom, life,—and yet he sleeps
 as soundly,
Perhaps, as infancy, with gorgeous
 curtains 24
Spread for his canopy, o'er silken pillows,
Such as when——Hark! what noise is
 that? Again!

The branches shake; and some loose stones have fallen
From yonder terrace.
[ULRIC *leaps down from the terrace.*
Ulric! ever welcome!
Thrice welcome now! this filial——
Ulr. Stop! Before
We approach, tell me——
Wer. Why look you so?
Ulr. Do I 30
Behold my father, or——
Wer. What?
Ulr. An assassin?
Wer. Insane or insolent!
Ulr. Reply, sir, as
You prize your life, or mine!
Wer. To what must I
Answer?
Ulr. Are you or are you not the assassin
Of Stralenheim?
Wer. I never was as yet 35
The murderer of any man. What mean you?
Ulr. Did not you *this* night (as the night before)
Retrace the secret passage? Did you not
Again revisit Stralenheim's chamber? and——
[ULRIC *pauses.*
Wer. Proceed.
Ulr. *Died* he not by your hand?
Wer. Great God! 40
Ulr. You are innocent, then! my father's innocent!
Embrace me! Yes,—your tone—your look—yes, yes,—
Yet *say* so.
Wer. If I e'er, in heart or mind,
Conceived deliberately such a thought,
But rather strove to trample back to hell
Such thoughts—if e'er they glared a moment through 46
The irritation of my oppressed spirit—
May heaven be shut for ever from my hopes,
As from mine eyes!
Ulr. But Stralenheim is dead.
Wer. 'Tis horrible! 'tis hideous, as 'tis hateful!— 50
But what have I to do with this?
Ulr. No bolt
Is forced; no violence can be detected,
Save on his body. Part of his own household
Have been alarm'd; but as the intendant is
Absent, I took upon myself the care 55
Of mustering the police. His chamber has,
Past doubt, been enter'd secretly. Excuse me,
If nature——
Wer. Oh, my boy! what unknown woes
Of dark fatality, like clouds, are gathering
Above our house!

Ulr. My father! I acquit you! 6
But will the world do so? will even th judge,
If——But you must away this instant.
Wer. No
I'll face it. Who shall dare suspect me?
Ulr. Ye
You had *no* guests—*no* visitors—no life Breathing around you, save my mother's
Wer. Ah! 6
The Hungarian!
Ulr. He is gone! he disappear' Ere sunset.
Wer. No; I hid him in that very Conceal'd and fatal gallery.
Ulr. There I'll find him
[ULRIC *is going*
Wer. It is too late: he had left th palace ere
I quitted it. I found the secret panel 7 Open, and the doors which lead from tha hall
Which masks it: I but thought he had snatch'd the silent
And favourable moment to escape
The myrmidons of Idenstein, who were Dogging him yester-even.
Ulr. You reclosed 7 The panel?
Wer. Yes; and not without reproach (And inner trembling for the avoide peril)
At his dull heedlessness, in leaving thus His shelterer's asylum to the risk
Of a discovery.
Ulr. You are sure you closed it? 8
Wer. Certain.
Ulr. That's well; but had been better if
You ne'er had turn'd it to a den for——
[*He pauses*
Wer. Thieves
Thou wouldst say: I must bear it, an deserve it;
But not——
Ulr. No, father; do not speak of this This is no hour to think of petty crimes But to prevent the consequence of grea ones. 8
Why would you shelter this man?
Wer. Could I shun it A man pursued by my chief foe; disgrace For my own crime: a victim to *my* safety Imploring a few hours' concealment from The very wretch who was the cause h needed 9
Such refuge. Had he been a wolf, I could no Have in such circumstances thrust hin forth.
Ulr. And like the wolf he hath repai you. But
It is too late to ponder thus:—you must Set out ere dawn. I will remain here to Trace the murderer, if 'tis possible. 9

Wer. But this my sudden flight will give the Moloch
Suspicion: two new victims in the lieu
Of one, if I remain. The fled Hungarian,
Who seems the culprit, and——
Ulr. Who *seems? Who* else 101
Can be so?
Wer. Not *I*, though just now you doubted—
You, my *son!*—doubted—
Ulr. And do you doubt of him
The fugitive?
Wer. Boy! since I fell into
The abyss of crime (though not of *such*
crime), I, 105
Having seen the innocent oppress'd for me,
May doubt even of the guilty's guilt.
Your heart
Is free, and quick with virtuous wrath to
accuse
Appearances; and views a criminal
In Innocence's shadow, it may be, 110
Because 'tis dusky.
Ulr. And if I do so,
What will mankind, who know you not,
or knew
But to oppress? You must not stand the
hazard.
Away!—I'll make all easy. Idenstein
Will for his own sake and his jewel's hold
His peace—he also is a partner in 116
Your flight—moreover——
Wer. Fly! and leave my name
Link'd with the Hungarian's, or preferr'd
as poorest,
To bear the brand of bloodshed?
Ulr. Pshaw! leave anything
Except our fathers' sovereignty and castles,
For which you have so long panted, and
in vain! 121
What *name?* You have *no name*, since that
you bear
Is feign'd.
Wer. Most true: but still I would not
have it
Engraved in crimson in men's memories,
Though in this most obscure abode of
men—— 125
Besides, the search——
Ulr. I will provide against
Aught that can touch you. No one knows
you here
As heir of Siegendorf: if Idenstein
Suspects, 'tis *but suspicion*, and he is
A fool: his folly shall have such employ-
ment, 130
Too, that the unknown Werner shall give way
To nearer thoughts of self. The laws (if e'er
laws reach'd this village) are all in
abeyance
With the late general war of thirty years,
Or crush'd, or rising slowly from the dust,
To which the march of armies trampled
them. 136

Stralenheim, although noble, is unheeded
Here, save as *such*—without lands,
influence,
Save what hath perish'd with him. Few
prolong
A week beyond their funeral rites their
sway 140
O'er men, unless by relatives, whose
interest
Is roused: such is not here the case; he
died
Alone, unknown,—a solitary grave,
Obscure as his deserts, without a
scutcheon,
Is all he'll have, or wants. If *I* discover
The assassin, 'twill be well—if not, believe
me, 146
None else; though all the full-fed train of
menials
May howl above his ashes (as they did
Around him in his danger on the Oder),
Will no more stir a finger *now* than *then*.
Hence! hence! I must not hear your an-
swer.—Look! 151
The stars are almost faded, and the grey
Begins to grizzle the black hair of night.
You shall not answer:—Pardon me that I
Am peremptory; 'tis your son that speaks,
Your long-lost, late-found son.—Let's
call my mother! 156
Softly and swiftly step, and leave the rest
To me: I'll answer for the event as far
As regards *you*, and that is the chief point,
As my first duty, which shall be observed.
We'll meet in Castle Siegendorf—once
more 161
Our banners shall be glorious! Think of
that
Alone, and leave all other thoughts to me,
Whose youth may better battle with
them—Hence!
And may your age be happy!—I will kiss
My mother once more, then Heaven's
speed be with you! 166
Wer. This counsel's safe—but is it
honourable?
Ulr. To save a father is a child's chief
honour. [*Exeunt.*

ACT IV

SCENE I.—*A Gothic Hall in the Castle of
Siegendorf, near Prague.*

Enter ERIC *and* HENRICK, *Retainers of the
Count.*

Eric. So, better times are come at last;
to these
Old walls new masters and high wassail—
both
A long desideratum.
Hen. Yes, for *masters*,
It might be unto those who long for
novelty,

Though made by a new grave: but as for
 wassail, 5
Methinks the old Count Siegendorf main-
 tain'd
His feudal hospitality as high
As e'er another prince of the empire.
 Eric. Why
For the mere cup and trencher, we no
 doubt
Fared passing well; but as for merriment
And sport, without which salt and sauces
 season 11
The cheer but scantily, our sizings were
Even of the narrowest.
 Hen. The old count loved not
The roar of revel; are you sure that *this*
 does?
 Eric. As yet he hath been courteous as
 he's bounteous, 15
And we all love him.
 Hen. His reign is as yet
Hardly a year o'erpast its honey-moon,
And the first year of sovereigns is bridal:
Anon, we shall perceive his real sway
And moods of mind.
 Eric. Pray Heaven he keep the
 present! 20
Then his brave son, Count Ulric—there's
 a knight!
Pity the wars are o'er!
 Hen. Why so?
 Eric. Look on him!
And answer that yourself.
 Hen. He's very youthful,
And strong and beautiful as a young tiger.
 Eric. That's not a faithful vassal's
 likeness.
 Hen. But 25
Perhaps a true one.
 Eric. Pity, as I said,
The wars are over: in the hall, who like
Count Ulric for a well-supported pride,
Which awes, but yet offends not? in the
 field,
Who like him with his spear in hand,
 when, gnashing 30
His tusks, and ripping up from right to left
The howling hounds, the boar makes for
 the thicket?
Who backs a horse, or bears a hawk, or
 wears
A sword like him? Whose plume nods
 knightlier?
 Hen. No one's, I grant you. Do not
 fear, if war 35
Be long in coming, he is of that kind
Will make it for himself, if he hath not
Already done as much.
 Eric. What do you mean?
 Hen. You can't deny his train of
 followers
(But few our native fellow-vassals born
On the domain) are such a sort of knaves
As—— [*Pauses.*

 Eric. What?
 Hen. The war (you love so
 much) leaves living.
Like other parents, she spoils her worst
 children.
 Eric. Nonsense! they are all brave
 iron-visaged fellows,
Such as old Tilly loved.
 Hen. And who loved Tilly? 40
Ask that at Magdebourg—or for that
 matter
Wallenstein either;—they are gone to——
 Eric. Rest
But what beyond, 'tis not ours to pro-
 nounce.
 Hen. I wish they had left us something
 of their rest:
The country (nominally now at peace)
Is over-run with—God knows who: they
 fly 50
By night, and disappear with sunrise; but
Leave us no less desolation, nay, even
 more,
Than the most open warfare.
 Eric. But Count Ulric-
What has all this to do with him?
 Hen. With him! 55
He——might prevent it. As you say he's
 fond
Of war, why makes he it not on those
 marauders?
 Eric. You'd better ask himself.
 Hen. I would as soon
Ask the lion why he laps not milk.
 Eric. And here he comes!
 Hen. The devil! you'll hold your
 tongue? 60
 Eric. Why do you turn so pale?
 Hen. 'Tis nothing—but
Be silent.
 Eric. I will, upon what you have said.
 Hen. I assure you I meant nothing,—
 a mere sport
Of words, no more; besides, had it been
 otherwise,
He is to espouse the gentle Baroness 65
Ida of Stralenheim, the late baron's heiress
And she, no doubt, will soften whatsoever
Of fierceness the late long intestine wars
Have given all natures, and most unto
 those
Who were born in them, and bred up
 upon 70
The knees of Homicide; sprinkled, as it
 were,
With blood even at their baptism. Prithee
 peace
On all that I have said!

Enter ULRIC *and* RODOLPH.

 Good morrow, Count!
 Ulr. Good morrow, worthy Henrick
 Eric, is
All ready for the chase?

Eric. The dogs are order'd 75
Down to the forest, and the vassals out
To beat the bushes, and the day looks
promising.
Shall I call forth your excellency's suite?
What courser will you please to mount?
Ulr. The dun,
Walstein.
Eric. I fear he scarcely has
recover'd 80
The toils of Monday: 'twas a noble chase:
You spear'd *four* with your own hand.
Ulr. True, good Eric;
I had forgotten—let it be the grey, then,
Old Ziska: he has not been out this fort-
night.
Eric. He shall be straight caparison'd.
How many 85
Of your immediate retainers shall
Escort you?
Ulr. I leave that to Weilburgh, our
Master of the horse. [*Exit* ERIC.
Rodolph!
Rod. My lord!
Ulr. The news
Is awkward from the——
[RODOLPH *points to* HENRICK.
How now, Henrick? why
Loiter you here?
Hen. For your commands, my lord.
Ulr. Go to my father, and present my
duty, 91
And learn if he would aught with me
before
I mount. [*Exit* HENRICK.
Rodolph, our friends have had a check
Upon the frontiers of Franconia, and
'Tis rumour'd that the column sent
against them 95
Is to be strengthen'd. I must join them soon.
Rod. Best wait for further and more
sure advices.
Ulr. I mean it—and indeed it could
not well
Have fallen out at a time more opposite
To all my plans.
Rod. It will be difficult 100
To excuse your absence to the count your
father.
Ulr. Yes, but the unsettled state of our
domain
In high Silesia will permit and cover
My journey. In the mean time, when we are
Engaged in the chase, draw off the eighty
men 105
Whom Wolffe leads—keep the forests on
your route:
You know it well?
Rod. As well as on that night
When we——
Ulr. We will not speak of that until
We can repeat the same with like success:
And when you have join'd, give Rosen-
berg this letter. [*Gives a letter.*

Add further, that I have sent this slight
addition 111
To our force with you and Wolffe, as
herald of
My coming, though I could but spare
them ill
At this time, as my father loves to keep
Full numbers of retainers round the castle,
Until this marriage, and its feasts and
fooleries, 116
Are rung out with its peal of nuptial non-
sense.
Rod. I thought you loved the lady Ida?
Ulr. Why,
I do so—but it follows not from that
I would bind in my youth and glorious
years, 120
So brief and burning, with a lady's zone,
Although 'twere that of Venus:—but I
love her,
As woman should be loved, fairly and
solely.
Rod. And constantly?
Ulr. I think so; for I love
Nought else.—But I have not the time to
pause 125
Upon these gewgaws of the heart. Great
things
We have to do ere long. Speed! speed!
good Rodolph!
Rod. On my return, however, I shall
find
The Baroness Ida lost in Countess
Siegendorf?
Ulr. Perhaps: my father wishes it; and
sooth 130
'Tis no bad policy: this union with
The last bud of the rival branch at once
Unites the future and destroys the past.
Rod. Adieu.
Ulr. Yet hold—we had better
keep together
Until the chase begins; then draw thou
off, 135
And do as I have said.
Rod. I will. But to
Return—'twas a most kind act in the
count
Your father to send up to Konigsberg
For this fair orphan of the baron, and
To hail her as his daughter.
Ulr. Wondrous kind! 140
Especially as little kindness till
Then grew between them.
Rod. The late baron died
Of a fever, did he not?
Ulr. How should I know?
Rod. I have heard it whisper'd there
was something strange
About his death—and even the place of
it 145
Is scarcely known.
Ulr. Some obscure village on
The Saxon or Silesian frontier.

Rod. He
Has left no testament—no farewell words?
Ulr. I am neither confessor nor notary,
So cannot say.
Rod. Ah! here's the lady Ida. 150

Enter IDA STRALENHEIM.

Ulr. You are early, my sweet cousin!
Ida. Not *too* early,
Dear Ulric, if I do not interrupt you.
Why do you call me '*cousin*'?
Ulr. [*smiling*]. Are we not so?
Ida. Yes, but I do not like the name;
 methinks 154
It sounds so cold, as if you thought upon
Our pedigree, and only weigh'd our blood.
Ulr. [*starting*]. Blood!
Ida. Why does yours start from your
 cheeks?
Ulr. Ay! doth it?
Ida. It doth—but no! it rushes like a
 torrent
Even to your brow again.
Ulr. [*recovering himself*]. And if it fled,
It only was because your presence sent it
Back to my heart, which beats for you,
 sweet cousin! 161
Ida. 'Cousin' again.
Ulr. Nay, then, I'll call you sister.
Ida. I like that name still worse.—
 Would we had ne'er
Been aught of kindred!
Ulr. [*gloomily*]. Would we never had!
Ida. Oh, heavens! and can *you* wish
 that!
Ulr. Dearest Ida! 165
Did I not echo your own wish?
Ida. Yes, Ulric,
But then I wish'd it not with such a glance,
And scarce knew what I said; but let me be
Sister or cousin, what you will, so that
I still to you am something.
Ulr. You shall be 170
All—all——
Ida. And you to *me are* so already;
But I can wait.
Ulr. Dear Ida!
Ida. Call me Ida,
Your Ida, for I would be yours, none
 else's—
Indeed I have none else left, since my poor
 father— [*She pauses.*
Ulr. You have *mine*—you have *me*.
Ida. Dear Ulric, how I wish 175
My father could but view my happiness,
Which wants but this!
Ulr. Indeed!
Ida. You would have loved him,
He you; for the brave ever love each other:
His manner was a little cold, his spirit
Proud (as is birth's prerogative); but
 under 180
This grave exterior——Would you had
 known each other!

Had such as you been near him on hi[s]
 journey,
He had not died without a friend to sooth[e]
His last and lonely moments.
Ulr. Who says *that*[?]
Ida. What?
Ulr. That he *died alone*.
Ida. The general rumour 18
And disappearance of his servants, who[m]
Have ne'er return'd: that fever was mos[t]
 deadly
Which swept them all away.
Ulr. If they were near him[?]
He could not die neglected or alone.
Ida. Alas! what is a menial to a death[-]
 bed, 19
When the dim eye rolls vainly round fo[r]
 what
It loves?—They say he died of a fever.
Ulr. Say[.]
It *was* so.
Ida. I sometimes dream otherwise[.]
Ulr. All dreams are false.
Ida. And yet I see him a[s]
I see you.
Ulr. Where?
Ida. In sleep—I see him lie 19
Pale, bleeding, and a man with a raise[d]
 knife
Beside him.
Ulr. But you do not see his *face*[?]
Ida [*looking at him*]. No! Oh, m[y]
 God! do *you?*
Ulr. Why do you ask?
Ida. Because you look as if you saw [a]
 murderer!
Ulr. [*agitatedly*]. Ida, this is mere child[-]
 ishness; your weakness 20
Infects me, to my shame: but as all feeling[s]
Of yours are common to me, it affects me[.]
Prithee, sweet child, change——
Ida. Child, indeed! I hav[e]
Full fifteen summers! [*A bugle sounds*
Rod. Hark, my lord, the bugle[.]
Ida [*peevishly to* RODOLPH]. Why nee[d]
 you tell him that? Can he not hear [it]
Without your echo?
Rod. Pardon me, fair baroness[.]
Ida. I will not pardon you, unless yo[u]
 earn it
By aiding me in my dissuasion of
Count Ulric from the chase to-day.
Rod. You will no[t]
Lady, need aid of mine.
Ulr. I must not now 21
Forgo it.
Ida. But you shall!
Ulr. Shall!
Ida. Yes, or b[e]
No true knight.—Come, dear Ulric[,]
 yield to me
In this, for this one day: the day look[s]
 heavy,
And you are turn'd so pale and ill.

Ulr. You jest.
Ida. Indeed I do not:—ask of
 Rodolph.
Rod. Truly, 215
My lord, within this quarter of an hour
You have changed more than e'er I saw
 you change
In years.
Ulr. 'Tis nothing; but if 'twere, the air
Would soon restore me. I'm the true
 chameleon,
And live but on the atmosphere; your
 feasts 220
In castle halls, and social banquets, nurse
 not
My spirit—I'm a forester and breather
Of the steep mountain-tops, where I love all
The eagle loves.
Ida. Except his prey, I hope.
Ulr. Sweet Ida, wish me a fair chase,
 and I 225
Will bring you six boars' heads for
 trophies home.
Ida. And will you not stay, then?
 You shall not go!
Come! I will sing to you.
Ulr. Ida, you scarcely
Will make a soldier's wife.
Ida. I do not wish
To be so; for I trust these wars are over,
And you will live in peace on your
 domains. 231

Enter WERNER *as* COUNT SIEGENDORF.

Ulr. My father, I salute you, and it
 grieves me
With such brief greeting.—You have
 heard our bugle;
The vassals wait.
Sieg. So let them.—You forget
To-morrow is the appointed festival 235
In Prague for peace restored. You are apt
 to follow
The chase with such an ardour as will scarce
Permit you to return to-day, or if
Return'd, too much fatigued to join to-
 morrow
The nobles in our marshall'd ranks.
Ulr. You, count, 240
Will well supply the place of both—I am
 not
A lover of these pageantries.
Sieg. No, Ulric:
It were not well that you alone of all
Our young nobility——
Ida. And far the noblest
In aspect and demeanour.
Sieg. [*to* IDA]. True, dear child, 245
Though somewhat frankly said for a fair
 damsel.—
But, Ulric, recollect too our position,
So lately reinstated in our honours.
Believe me, 'twould be mark'd in any
 house,

But most in *ours*, that ONE should be
 found wanting 250
At such a time and place. Besides, the
 Heaven
Which gave us back our own, in the same
 moment
It spread its peace o'er all, hath double
 claims
On us for thanksgiving: first, for our
 country;
And next, that we are here to share its
 blessings. 255
Ulr. [*aside*]. Devout, too! Well, sir,
 I obey at once.
[*Then aloud to a Servant*]. Ludwig,
 dismiss the train without!
 [*Exit* LUDWIG.
Ida. And so
You yield at once to him what I for hours
Might supplicate in vain.
Sieg. [*smiling*]. You are not jealous
Of me, I trust, my pretty rebel! who 260
Would sanction disobedience against all
Except thyself? But fear not; thou shalt
 rule him
Hereafter with a fonder sway and firmer.
Ida. But I should like to govern *now*.
Sieg. You shall,
Your *harp*, which by the way awaits you
 with 265
The countess in her chamber. She com-
 plains
That you are a sad truant to your music:
She attends you.
Ida. Then good morrow, my kind
 kinsmen!
Ulric, you'll come and hear me?
Ulr. By and by.
Ida. Be sure I'll sound it better than
 your bugles; 270
Then pray you be as punctual to its notes:
I'll play you King Gustavus' march.
Ulr. And why not
Old Tilly's?
Ida. Not that monster's! I should
 think
My harp-strings rang with groans, and
 not with music,
Could aught of *his* sound on it:—but
 come quickly; 275
Your mother will be eager to receive you.
 [*Exit.*
Sieg. Ulric, I wish to speak with you
 alone.
Ulr. My time's your vassal.—
[*Aside to* RODOLPH]. Rodolph, hence
 and do
As I directed: and by his best speed
And readiest means let Rosenberg reply.
Rod. Count Siegendorf, command
 you aught? I am bound 281
Upon a journey past the frontier.
Sieg. [*starts*]. Ah!—
Where? on *what* frontier?

Rod. The Silesian, on—
My way—[*Aside to* ULRIC].—*Where* shall
I say?
Ulr. [*aside to* RODOLPH]. To Ham-
burgh.
 [*Aside to himself.*] That
Word will, I think, put a firm padlock on
His further inquisition.
Rod. Count, to Hamburgh. 286
Sieg. [*agitated*]. Hamburgh! No, I
 have nought to do there, nor
Am aught connected with that city. Then
God speed you!
Rod. Fare ye well, Count Siegendorf!
 [*Exit* RODOLPH.
Sieg. Ulric, this man, who has just
 departed, is 290
One of those strange companions whom I
 fain
Would reason with you on.
Ulr. My lord, he is
Noble by birth, of one of the first houses
In Saxony.
Sieg. I talk not of his birth,
But of his bearing. Men speak lightly of
 him. 295
Ulr. So they will do of most men.
 Even the monarch
Is not fenced from his chamberlain's
 slander, or
The sneer of the last courtier whom he has
 made
Great and ungrateful.
Sieg. If I must be plain,
The world speaks more than lightly of this
 Rodolph: 300
They say he is leagued with the 'black
 bands' who still
Ravage the frontier.
Ulr. And will you believe
The world?
Sieg. In this case—yes.
Ulr. In *any* case,
I thought you knew it better than to take
An accusation for a sentence.
Sieg. Son! 305
I understand you: you refer to——but
My destiny has so involved about me
Her spider web, that I can only flutter
Like the poor fly, but break it not. Take
 heed,
Ulric; you have seen to what the passions
 led me: 310
Twenty long years of misery and famine
Quench'd them not—twenty thousand
 more, perchance,
Hereafter (or even here in *moments* which
Might date for years, did Anguish make
 the dial)
May not obliterate or expiate 315
The madness and dishonour of an instant.
Ulric, be warn'd by a father!—I was not
By mine, and you behold me!
Ulr. I behold

The prosperous and beloved Siegendorf,
Lord of a prince's appanage, and honour'd
By those he rules and those he ranks with
Sieg. Ah! 321
Why wilt thou call me prosperous, while
 I fear
For thee? Beloved, when thou lovest me not
All hearts but one may beat in kindness
 for me—
But if my son's is cold!——
Ulr. Who *dare* say that? 326
Sieg. None else but I, who see it—*feel*
 it—keener
Than would your adversary, who dare
 say so,
Your sabre in his heart! But mine
 survives
The wound.
Ulr. You err. My nature is not given
To outward fondling: how should it be
 so, 330
After twelve years' divorcement from my
 parents?
Sieg. And did not *I* too pass those
 twelve torn years
In a like absence? But 'tis vain to urge
 you—
Nature was never call'd back by remon-
 strance.
Let's change the theme. I wish you to
 consider 335
That these young violent nobles of high
 name,
But dark deeds (ay, the darkest, if all
 Rumour
Reports be true), with whom thou con-
 sortest,
Will lead thee——
Ulr. [*impatiently*]. I'll be *led* by no
 man.
Sieg. Nor 339
Be leader of such, I would hope: at once
To wean thee from the perils of thy youth
And haughty spirit, I have thought it well
That thou shouldst wed the lady Ida—
 more
As thou appear'st to love her.
Ulr. I have said
I will obey your orders, were they to 345
Unite with Hecate—can a son say more?
Sieg. He says too much in saying this.
 It is not
The nature of thine age, nor of thy blood.
Nor of thy temperament, to talk so coolly
Or act so carelessly, in that which is 350
The bloom or blight of all men's happiness,
(For Glory's pillow is but restless, if
Love lay not down his cheek there): some
 strong bias,
Some master fiend is in thy service, to
Misrule the mortal who believes him
 slave, 355
And makes his every thought sub-
 servient; else

594

Thou'dst say at once—'I love young Ida,
 and
Will wed her;' or, 'I love her not, and
 all
The powers of earth shall never make me.'
 —So
Would *I* have answer'd.
 Ulr. Sir, *you* wed for love. 360
 Sieg. I did, and it has been my only
 refuge
In many miseries.
 Ulr. Which miseries
Had never been but for this love-match.
 Sieg. Still
Against your age and nature! Who at
 twenty
E'er answer'd thus till now?
 Ulr. Did you not warn me 365
Against your own example?
 Sieg. Boyish sophist!
In a word, do you love, or love not, Ida?
 Ulr. What matters it, if I am ready to
Obey you in espousing her?
 Sieg. As far
As you feel, nothing, but all life for her.
She's young—all-beautiful—adores you
 —is 371
Endow'd with qualities to give happiness,
Such as rounds common life into a dream
Of something which your poets cannot
 paint,
And (if it were not wisdom to love virtue)
For which Philosophy might barter
 Wisdom; 376
And giving so much happiness, deserves
A little in return. I would not have her
Break her heart for a man who has none
 to break;
Or wither on her stalk like some pale rose
Deserted by the bird she thought a nightin-
 gale, 381
According to the Orient tale. She is——
 Ulr. The daughter of dead Stralen-
 heim, your foe.
I'll wed her, ne'ertheless; though, to say
 truth,
Just now I am not violently transported
In favour of such unions.
 Sieg. But she loves you. 386
 Ulr. And I love her, and therefore
 would think *twice*.
 Sieg. Alas! Love never did so.
 Ulr. Then 'tis time
He should begin, and take the bandage
 from
His eyes, and look before he leaps; till
 now 390
He hath ta'en a jump i' the dark.
 Sieg. But you consent?
 Ulr. I did, and do.
 Sieg. Then fix the day.
 Ulr. 'Tis usual,
And certes courteous, to leave that to the
 lady.

 Sieg. *I* will engage for *her*.
 Ulr. So will not *I*
For any woman: and as what I fix, 395
I fain would see unshaken, when she gives
Her answer, I'll give mine.
 Sieg. But 'tis your office
To woo.
 Ulr. Count, 'tis a marriage of your
 making,
So be it of your wooing; but to please you,
I will now pay my duty to my mother,
With whom, you know, the lady Ida is.—
What would you have? You have forbid
 my stirring
For manly sports beyond the castle walls,
And I obey; you bid me turn a chamberer,
To pick up gloves, and fans, and knitting-
 needles, 405
And list to songs and tunes, and watch for
 smiles,
And smile at pretty prattle, and look into
The eyes of feminine, as though they were
The stars receding early to our wish
Upon the dawn of a world-winning
 battle— 410
What can a son or man do more?
 [*Exit* ULRIC.
 Sieg. [*solus*]. Too much!—
Too much of duty, and too little love!
He pays me in the coin he owes me not:
For such hath been my wayward fate, I
 could not
Fulfil a parent's duties by his side 415
Till now; but love he owes me, for my
 thoughts
Ne'er left him, nor my eyes long'd with-
 out tears
To see my child again, and now I have
 found him!
But how—obedient, but with coldness;
 duteous
In my sight, but with carelessness; mys-
 terious— 420
Abstracted—distant—much given to long
 absence,
And where—none know—in league with
 the most riotous
Of our young nobles; though, to do him
 justice,
He never stoops down to their vulgar
 pleasures;
Yet there's some tie between them which
 I cannot 425
Unravel. They look up to him—consult
 him—
Throng round him as a leader: but with
 me
He hath no confidence! Ah! can I hope it
After—what! doth my father's curse
 descend
Even to my child? Or is the Hungarian
 near 430
To shed more blood? or—Oh! if it should
 be!

595

Spirit of Stralenheim, dost thou walk these walls
To wither him and his—who, though they slew him not,
Unlatch'd the door of death for thee? 'Twas not
Our fault, nor is our sin: thou wert our foe, 435
And yet I spared thee when my own destruction
Slept with thee, to awake with thine awakening!
And only took—Accursed gold! thou liest
Like poison in my hands; I dare not use thee,
Nor part from thee; thou camest in such a guise, 440
Methinks thou wouldst contaminate all hands
Like mine. Yet I have done, to atone for thee,
Thou villainous gold! and thy dead master's doom,
Though he died not by me or mine, as much 444
As if he were my brother! I have ta'en
His orphan Ida—cherish'd her as one
Who will be mine.

Enter an ATTENDANT.

Atten. The abbot, if it please
Your excellency, whom you sent for, waits
Upon you. [*Exit* ATTENDANT.

Enter the PRIOR ALBERT.

Prior. Peace be with these walls, and all
Within them!
Sieg. Welcome, welcome, holy father! 450
And may thy prayer be heard!—all men have need
Of such, and I——
Prior. Have the first claim to all
The prayers of our community. Our convent,
Erected by your ancestors, is still
Protected by their children.
Sieg. Yes, good father; 455
Continue daily orisons for us
In these dim days of heresies and blood,
Though the schismatic Swede, Gustavus, is
Gone home.
Prior. To the endless home of unbelievers,
Where there is everlasting wail and woe,
Gnashing of teeth, and tears of blood, and fire 461
Eternal, and the worm which dieth not!
Sieg. True, father: and to avert those pangs from one,
Who, though of our most faultless holy church,

Yet died without its last and dearest offices, 46
Which smooth the soul through purgatorial pains,
I have to offer humbly this donation
In masses for his spirit.
 [SIEGENDORF *offers the gold which h had taken from* STRALENHEIM.
Prior. Count, if I
Receive it, 'tis because I know too well
Refusal would offend you. Be assured
The largess shall be only dealt in alms,
And every mass no less sung for the dead
Our house needs no donations, thanks t yours,
Which has of old endow'd it; but from yo
And yours in all meet things 'tis fit w obey. 47
For whom shall mass be said?
Sieg. [*faltering*]. For—for—the dead
Prior. His name?
Sieg. 'Tis from a soul, and not name,
I would avert perdition.
Prior. I meant not
To pry into your secret. We will pray
For one unknown, the same as for th proudest. 48
Sieg. Secret! I have none: but, father he who's gone
Might *have* one; or, in short, he di bequeath—
No, not bequeath—but I bestow this sun
For pious purposes.
Prior. A proper deed
In the behalf of our departed friends.
Sieg. But he who's gone was not m friend, but foe, 48
The deadliest and the stanchest.
Prior. Better still
To employ our means to obtain heaven for the souls
Of our dead enemies is worthy those
Who can forgive them living.
Sieg. But I did not 49
Forgive this man. I loathed him to th last,
As he did me. I do not love him now,
But——
Prior. Best of all! for this is pur religion!
You fain would rescue him you hate from hell—
An evangelical compassion—with 49
Your own gold too!
Sieg. Father, 'tis not my gold
Prior. Whose then? You said it wa no legacy.
Sieg. No matter whose—of this b sure, that he
Who own'd it never more will need it, sav
In that which it may purchase from you altars: 50
'Tis yours, or theirs.

Prior. Is there no blood upon it?
Sieg. No; but there's worse than
 blood—eternal shame!
Prior. Did he who own'd it die in his
 bed?
Sieg. Alas!
He did.
Prior. Son! you relapse into revenge,
If you regret your enemy's bloodless
 death. 505
Sieg. His death was fathomlessly
 deep in blood.
Prior. You said he died in his bed, not
 battle.
Sieg. He
Died, I scarce know—but—he was
 stabb'd i' the dark,
And now you have it—perish'd on his
 pillow
By a cut-throat!—Ay!—you may look
 upon me! 510
I am *not* the man. I'll meet your eye on
 that point,
As I can one day God's.
Prior. Nor did he die
By means, or men, or instrument of yours?
Sieg. No! by the God who sees and
 strikes!
Prior. Nor know you
Who slew him?
Sieg. I could only guess at *one*, 515
And he to me a stranger, unconnected,
As unemploy'd. Except by one day's
 knowledge,
I never saw the man who was suspected.
Prior. Then you are free from guilt.
Sieg. [*eagerly*]. Oh! *am* I?—say!
Prior. You have said so, and know
 best.
Sieg. Father! I have spoken 520
The truth, and nought but truth, if *not* the
 whole;
Yet say I am *not* guilty! for the blood
Of this man weighs on me, as if I shed it,
Though, by the Power who abhorreth
 human blood,
I did not!—nay, once spared it, when I
 might 525
And *could*—ay, perhaps, *should* (if our
 self-safety
Be e'er excusable in such defences
Against the attacks of over-potent foes):
But pray for him, for me, and all my
 house; 529
For, as I said, though I be innocent,
I know not why, a like remorse is on me,
As if he had fallen by me or mine. Pray for
 me,
Father! I have pray'd myself in vain.
Prior. I will.
Be comforted! You are innocent, and
 should
Be calm as innocence.
Sieg. But calmness is not 535

Always the attribute of innocence.
I feel it is not.
Prior. But it will be so,
When the mind gathers up its truth within
 it.
Remember the great festival to-morrow,
In which you rank amidst our chiefest
 nobles, 540
As well as your brave son; and smooth
 your aspect,
Nor in the general orison of thanks
For bloodshed stopt, let blood you shed
 not rise,
A cloud, upon your thoughts. This were
 to be
Too sensitive. Take comfort, and forget
Such things, and leave remorse unto the
 guilty. [*Exeunt.*

ACT V

SCENE I.—*A large and magnificent Gothic
 Hall in the Castle of Siegendorf,
 decorated with Trophies, Banners, and
 Arms of that family.*

Enter ARNHEIM *and* MEISTER, *Attendants
 of* COUNT SIEGENDORF.

Arn. Be quick! the count will soon
 return: the ladies
Already are at the portal. Have you sent
The messengers in search of him he seeks
 for?
Meis. I have, in all directions, over
 Prague,
As far as the man's dress and figure could
By your description track him. The devil
 take 6
These revels and processions! All the
 pleasure
(If such there be) must fall to the specta-
 tors.
I'm sure none doth to us who make the
 show.
Arn. Go to! my lady countess comes.
Meis. I'd rather 10
Ride a day's hunting on an outworn jade,
Than follow in the train of a great man,
In these dull pageantries.
Arn. Begone! and rail
Within. [*Exeunt.*

Enter the COUNTESS JOSEPHINE SIEGENDORF
 and IDA STRALENHEIM.

Jos. Well, Heaven be praised! the
 show is over.
Ida. How can you say so? Never have
 I dreamt 15
Of aught so beautiful. The flowers, the
 boughs,
The banners, and the nobles, and the
 knights,
The gems, the robes, the plumes, the
 happy faces,

The coursers, and the incense, and the sun
Streaming through the stain'd windows,
 even the *tombs*, 20
Which look'd so calm, and the celestial
 hymns,
Which seem'd as if they rather came from
 heaven
Than mounted there. The bursting
 organ's peal
Rolling on high like an harmonious
 thunder;
The white robes and the lifted eyes; the
 world 25
At peace! and all at peace with one
 another!
Oh, my sweet mother!
 [*Embracing* JOSEPHINE.
Jos. My beloved child!
For such, I trust, thou shalt be shortly.
Ida. Oh!
I am so already. Feel how my heart beats!
Jos. It does, my love; and never may
 it throb 30
With aught more bitter.
Ida. Never shall it do so!
How should it? What should make us
 grieve? I hate
To hear of sorrow: how can we be sad,
Who love each other so entirely? You,
The count, and Ulric, and your daughter
 Ida. 35
Jos. **Poor child!**
Ida. Do you pity me?
Jos. No: I but envy,
And that in sorrow, not in the world's
 sense
Of the universal vice, if one vice be
More general than another.
Ida. I'll not hear
A word against a world which still
 contains 40
You and my Ulric. Did you ever see
Aught like him? How he tower'd
 amongst them all!
How all eyes follow'd him! The flowers
 fell faster—
Rain'd from each lattice at his feet, me-
 thought,
Than before all the rest; and where he
 trod 45
I dare be sworn that they grow still, nor
 e'er
Will wither.
Jos. You will spoil him, little flatterer,
If he should hear you.
Ida. But he never will.
I dare not say so much to him—I fear
 him.
Jos. Why so? he loves you well.
Ida. But I can never 50
Shape my thoughts *of* him into words *to*
 him:
Besides, he sometimes frightens me.
Jos. How so?

Ida. A cloud comes o'er his blue eye
 suddenly,
Yet he says nothing.
Jos. It is nothing: all men, 5
Especially in these dark troublous times
Have much to think of.
Ida. But I cannot think
Of aught save him.
Jos. Yet there are other men
In the world's eye, as goodly. There's
 for instance,
The young Count Waldorf, who scarce
 once withdrew
His eyes from yours to-day.
Ida. I did not see him 6
But Ulric. Did you not see at the moment
When all knelt, and I wept? and yet me-
 thought,
Through my fast tears, though they were
 thick and warm,
I saw him smiling on me.
Jos. I could not
See aught save heaven, to which my eyes
 were rais'd, 6
Together with the people's.
Ida. I thought too
Of heaven, although I look'd on Ulric.
Jos. Come
Let us retire! they will be here anon
Expectant of the banquet. We will lay
Aside these nodding plumes and dragging
 trains. 7
Ida. And, above all, these stiff and
 heavy jewels,
Which make my head and heart ache, as
 both throb
Beneath their glitter o'er my brow and
 zone.
Dear mother, I am with you.

Enter COUNT SIEGENDORF, *in full dress
 from the solemnity, and* LUDWIG.

Sieg. Is he not found?
Lud. Strict search is making every-
 where; and if
The man be in Prague, be sure he will be
 found.
Sieg. Where's Ulric?
Lud. He rode round the other way
With some young nobles; but he left them
 soon;
And, if I err not, not a minute since
I heard his excellency, with his train,
Gallop o'er the west drawbridge.

Enter ULRIC, *splendidly dressed.*

Sieg. [*to* LUDWIG]. See they cease not
Their quest of him I have described.
 [*Exit* LUDWIG.
 Oh, Ulric!
How have I long'd for thee!
Ulr. Your wish is granted—
Behold me!
Sieg. I have seen the murderer.

Ulr. Whom? Where?
Sieg. The Hungarian, who slew
 Stralenheim. 85
Ulr. You dream.
Sieg. I live! and as I live, I saw him—
Heard him! he dared to utter even my
 name.
Ulr. What name?
Sieg. Werner! 'twas mine.
Ulr. It must be so
No more: forget it.
Sieg. Never! never! all
My destinies were woven in that name:
It will not be engraved upon my tomb,
But it may lead me there.
Ulr. To the point——the Hungarian?
Sieg. Listen!—The church was
 throng'd: the hymn was raised;
'*Te Deum*' peal'd from nations rather
 than
From choirs, in one great cry of 'God be
 praised' 95
For one day's peace, after thrice ten dread
 years,
Each bloodier than the former: I arose,
With all the nobles, and as I look'd down
Along the lines of lifted faces,—from
Our banner'd and escutcheon'd gallery, I
Saw, like a flash of lightning (for I saw
A moment and no more), what struck me
 sightless
To all else—the Hungarian's face! I grew
Sick; and when I recover'd from the mist
Which curl'd about my senses, and again
Look'd down, I saw him not. The thanks-
 giving 106
Was over, and we march'd back in pro-
 cession.
Ulr. Continue.
Sieg. When we reach'd the
 Muldau's bridge,
The joyous crowd above, the numberless
Barks mann'd with revellers in their best
 garbs, 110
Which shot along the glancing tide below,
The decorated street, the long array,
The clashing music, and the thundering
Of far artillery, which seem'd to bid
A long and loud farewell to its great
 doings, 115
The standards o'er me, and the tramplings
 round,
The roar of rushing thousands,—all—all
 could not
Chase this man from my mind, although
 my senses
No longer held him palpable.
Ulr. You saw him
No more, then?
Sieg. I look'd, as a dying soldier 120
Looks at a draught of water, for this man;
But still I saw him not; but in his stead——
Ulr. What in his stead?
Sieg. My eye for ever fell

Upon your dancing crest; the loftiest,
As on the loftiest and the loveliest head,
It rose the highest of the stream of plumes,
Which overflow'd the glittering streets of
 Prague.
Ulr. What's this to the Hungarian?
Sieg. Much; for I
Had almost then forgot him in my son;
When just as the artillery ceased, and
 paused 130
The music, and the crowd embraced in lieu
Of shouting, I heard in a deep, low voice,
Distinct and keener far upon my ear
Than the late cannon's volume, this
 word—'*Werner*!'
Ulr. Utter'd by——
Sieg. HIM! I turn'd—and saw—
 and fell. 135
Ulr. And wherefore? Were you seen?
Sieg. The officious care
Of those around me dragg'd me from the
 spot,
Seeing my faintness, ignorant of the cause:
You, too, were too remote in the pro-
 cession
(The old nobles being divided from their
 children) 140
To aid me.
Ulr. But I'll aid you now.
Sieg. In what?
Ulr. In searching for this man, or——
 When he's found,
What shall we do with him?
Sieg. I know not that.
Ulr. Then wherefore seek?
Sieg. Because I cannot rest
Till he is found. His fate, and Stralen-
 heim's, 145
And ours, seem intertwisted! nor can be
Unravell'd, till——

 Enter an ATTENDANT

Atten. A stranger to wait on
Your excellency.
Sieg. Who?
Atten. He gave no name.
Sieg. Admit him, ne'ertheless.
 [*The* ATTENDANT *introduces* GABOR,
 and afterwards exit.
 Ah!
Gab. 'Tis then Werner!
Sieg. [*haughtily*]. The same you knew,
 sir, by that name; and *you*! 150
Gab. [*looking round*]. I recognise you
 both: father and son,
It seems. Count, I have heard that you,
 or yours,
Have lately been in search of me: I am
 here.
Sieg. I have sought you, and have
 found you: you are charged
(Your own heart may inform you why)
 with such 155
A crime as—— [*He pauses.*

Gab. Give it utterance, and then
I'll meet the consequences.
 Sieg. You shall do so—
Unless——
 Gab. First, who accuses me?
 Sieg. All things,
If not all men: the universal rumour—
My own presence on the spot—the place—
the time— 160
And every speck of circumstance unite
To fix the blot on you.
 Gab. And on *me only?*
Pause ere you answer: is no other name
Save mine, stain'd in this business?
 Sieg. Trifling villain!
Who play'st with thine own guilt! Of all
that breathe 165
Thou best dost know the innocence of him
'Gainst whom thy breath would blow thy
bloody slander.
But I will talk no further with a wretch,
Further than justice asks. Answer at once,
And without quibbling, to my charge.
 Gab. 'Tis false! 170
 Sieg. Who says so?
 Gab. I.
 Sieg. And how disprove it?
 Gab. By
The presence of the murderer.
 Sieg. Name him.
 Gab. He
May have more names than one. Your
lordship had so
Once on a time.
 Sieg. If you mean me, I dare
Your utmost.
 Gab. You may do so, and in safety;
I know the assassin.
 Sieg. Where is he?
 Gab. [*pointing to* ULRIC]. Beside you!
 [ULRIC *rushes forward to attack*
GABOR; SIEGENDORF *interposes.*
 Sieg. Liar and fiend! but you shall
not be slain;
These walls are mine, and you are safe
within them. [*He turns to* ULRIC.
Ulric, repel this calumny, as I
Will do. I avow it is a growth so mon-
strous, 180
I could not deem it earth-born: but be
calm;
It will refute itself. But touch him not.
 [ULRIC *endeavours to compose himself.*
 Gab. Look at *him*, count, and then
hear me.
 Sieg. [*first to* GABOR, *and then looking at*
ULRIC]. I hear thee.
My God! you look——
 Ulr. How?
 Sieg. As on that dread night,
When we met in the garden.
 Ulr. [*composes himself*]. It is nothing.
 Gab. Count, you are bound to hear
me. I came hither 186

Not seeking you, but sought. When
knelt down
Amidst the people in the church, I dream'
not
To find the beggar'd Werner in the seat
Of senators and princes; but you hav
call'd me, 19
And we have met.
 Sieg. Go on, sir.
 Gab. Ere I do s
Allow me to inquire, who profited
By Stralenheim's death? Was't I—as poo
as ever;
And poorer by suspicion on my name!
The baron lost in that last outrage neithe
Jewels nor gold; his life alone was sought,-
A life which stood between the claims o
others
To honours and estates scarce less tha
princely.
 Sieg. These hints, as vague as vair
attach no less
To me than to my son.
 Gab. I can't help that. 2
But let the consequence alight on him
Who feels himself the guilty one among u
I speak to you, Count Siegendorf, becaus
I know you innocent, and deem you jus
But ere I can proceed—*dare* you prote
me? 20
Dare you command me?
 [SIEGENDORF *first looks at the Hungaria*
and then at ULRIC, *who has unbuckle*
his sabre, and is drawing lines with
on the floor—still in its sheath.
 Ulr. [*looks at his father, and says,*] L
the man go on!
 Gab. I am unarm'd, count—bid yo
son lay down
His sabre.
 Ulr. [*offers it to him contemptuously*
Take it.
 Gab. No, sir, 'tis enoug
That we are both unarm'd—I would n
choose
To wear a steel which may be stain'd wit
more 2
Blood than came there in battle.
 Ulr. [*casts the sabre from him in co*
tempt]. It—or some
Such other weapon, in my hand—spare
yours
Once, when disarm'd and at my mercy.
 Gab. True
I have not forgotten it: you spared me f
Your own especial purpose—to sustain
An ignominy not my own.
 Ulr. Proceed.
The tale is doubtless worthy the relate
But is it of my father to hear further?
 [*To* SIEGENDOR
 Sieg. [*takes his son by the hand*]. M
son, I know my own innocence, ar
doubt not

Of yours—but I have promised this man
 patience; 220
Let him continue.
 Gab. I will not detain you,
By speaking of myself much: I began
Life early—and am what the world has
 made me.
At Frankfort on the Oder, where I pass'd
A winter in obscurity, it was 225
My chance at several places of resort
(Which I frequented sometimes, but not
 often)
To hear related a strange circumstance
In February last. A martial force,
Sent by the state, had, after strong re-
 sistance, 230
Secured a band of desperate men, sup-
 posed
Marauders from the hostile camp.—They
 proved,
However, not to be so—but banditti
Whom either accident or enterprise
Had carried from their usual haunt—the
 forests 235
Which skirt Bohemia—even into Lusatia.
Many amongst them were reported of
High rank—and martial law slept for a
 time.
At last they were escorted o'er the
 frontiers,
And placed beneath the civil jurisdiction
Of the free town of Frankfort. Of *their*
 fate 241
I know no more.
 Sieg. And what is this to Ulric?
 Gab. Amongst them there was said to
 be one man
Of wonderful endowments:—birth and
 fortune,
Youth, strength, and beauty, almost
 superhuman, 245
And courage as unrivall'd, were pro-
 claim'd
His by the public rumour; and his sway,
Not only over his associates, but
His judges, was attributed to witchcraft,
Such was his influence: I have no great
 faith 250
In any magic save that of the mine—
 therefore deem'd him wealthy.—But my
 soul
Was roused with various feelings to seek
 out
This prodigy, if only to behold him.
 Sieg. And did you so?
 Gab. You'll hear. Chance favour'd
 me: 255
A popular affray in the public square
Drew crowds together—it was one of
 those
Occasions where men's souls look out of
 them,
And show them as they are—even in their
 faces:

The moment my eye met his, I exclaim'd,
'This is the man!' though he was then, as
 since, 261
With the nobles of the city. I felt sure
I had not err'd, and watch'd him long and
 nearly;
I noted down his form—his gesture—
 features,
Stature, and bearing—and amidst them
 all, 265
'Midst every natural and acquired distinc-
 tion,
I could discern, methought, the assassin's
 eye
And gladiator's heart.
 Ulr. [*smiling*]. The tale sounds well.
 Gab. And may sound better.—He ap-
 pear'd to me
One of those beings to whom Fortune
 bends, 270
As she doth to the daring—and on whom
The fates of others oft depend; besides,
An indescribable sensation drew me
Near to this man, as if my point of fortune
Was to be fix'd by him.—There I was
 wrong. 275
 Sieg. And may not be right now.
 Gab. I follow'd him,
Solicited his notice—and obtain'd it—
Though not his friendship:—it was his in-
 tention
To leave the city privately—we left it
Together—and together we arrived 280
In the poor town where Werner was con-
 ceal'd,
And Stralenheim was succour'd——Now
 we are on
The verge—*dare* you hear further?
 Sieg. I must do so—
Or I have heard too much.
 Gab. I saw in you
A man above his station—and if not 285
So high, as now I find you, in my then
Conceptions, 'twas that I had rarely seen
Men such as you appear'd in height of
 mind,
In the most high of worldly rank; you
 were
Poor, even to all save rags: I would have
 shared 290
My purse, though slender, with you—you
 refused it.
 Sieg. Doth my refusal make a debt to
 you,
That thus you urge it?
 Gab. Still you owe me something,
Though not for that; and I owed you my
 safety, 294
At least my seeming safety, when the slaves
Of Stralenheim pursued me on the grounds
That *I* had robb'd him.
 Sieg. *I* conceal'd you—I,
Whom and whose house you arraign, re-
 viving viper!

Gab. I accuse no man—save in my de-
fence.
You, count, have made yourself accuser—
judge: 300
Your hall's my court, your heart is my
tribunal.
Be just, and I'll be merciful!
Sieg. You merciful?—
You! Base calumniator!
Gab. I. 'Twill rest
With me at last to be so. You conceal'd
me—
In secret passages known to yourself, 305
You said, and to none else. At dead of
night,
Weary with watching in the dark, and
dubious
Of tracing back my way, I saw a glimmer,
Through distant crannies, of a twinkling
light:
I follow'd it, and reach'd a door—a secret
Portal—which open'd to the chamber,
where, 311
With cautious hand and slow, having first
undone
As much as made a crevice of the fastening,
I look'd through and beheld a purple bed,
And on it Stralenheim!—
Sieg. Asleep! And yet
You slew him!—Wretch!
Gab. He was already slain, 316
And bleeding like a sacrifice. My own
Blood became ice.
Sieg. But he was all alone!
You saw none else? You did not see the——
[He pauses from agitation.
Gab. No,
He, whom you dare not name, nor even I
Scarce dare to recollect, was not then in
The chamber.
Sieg. [to ULRIC]. Then, my boy! thou
art guiltless still— 322
Thou bad'st me say I was so once—Oh!
now
Do thou as much!
Gab. Be patient! I can not
Recede now, though it shake the very walls
Which frown above us. You remember,—
or 326
If not, your son does,—that the locks were
changed
Beneath his chief inspection on the morn
Which led to this same night: how he had
enter'd
He best knows—but within an antecham-
ber, 330
The door of which was half ajar, I saw
A man who wash'd his bloody hands, and
oft
With stern and anxious glance gazed back
upon
The bleeding body—but it moved no more.
Sieg. Oh! God of fathers!
Gab. I beheld his features

As I see yours—but yours they were not
though 33
Resembling them—behold them in Count
Ulric's!
Distinct as I beheld them, though the ex-
pression
Is not now what it then was!—but it was so
When I first charged him with the crime—
so lately. 34
Sieg. This is so——
Gab. [interrupting him]. Nay—but hear
me to the end!
Now you must do so.—I conceived myself
Betray'd by you and him (for now I saw
There was some tie between you) into the
Pretended den of refuge, to become 34
The victim of your guilt; and my first
thought
Was vengeance: but, though arm'd with
short poniard
(Having left my sword without), I was no
match
For him at any time, as had been proved
That morning—either in address or force
I turn'd and fled—i' the dark: chance rather
than 35
Skill made me gain the secret door of the
hall,
And thence the chamber where you slept
if I
Had found you waking, Heaven alone can
tell
What vengeance and suspicion might have
prompted; 35
But ne'er slept guilt as Werner slept that
night.
Sieg. And yet I had horrid dreams! and
such brief sleep,
The stars had not gone down when I awoke
Why didst thou spare me? I dreamt of my
father—
And now my dream is out!
Gab. 'Tis not my fault
If I have read it.—Well! I fled and hid
me— 36
Chance led me here after so many moons—
And show'd me Werner in Count Sieger-
dorf!
Werner, whom I had sought in huts in vain
Inhabited the palace of a sovereign! 36
You sought me and have found me—now
you know
My secret, and may weigh its worth.
Sieg. [after a pause]. Indeed
Gab. Is it revenge or justice which in-
spires
Your meditation?
Sieg. Neither—I was weighing
The value of your secret.
Gab. You shall know
At once:—When you were poor, and
though poor, 37
Rich enough to relieve such poverty
As might have envied mine, I offer'd you

My purse—you would not share it:—I'll
 be franker
With you: you are wealthy, noble, trusted
 by 375
The imperial powers—you understand me?
Sieg. Yes.
Gab. Not quite. You think me venal,
 and scarce true:
'Tis no less true, however, that my fortunes
Have made me both at present. You shall
 aid me:
I would have aided you—and also have
Been somewhat damaged in my name to
 save 381
Yours and your son's. Weigh well what I
 have said.
 Sieg. Dare you await the event of a few
 minutes'
Deliberation?
 Gab. [*casts his eyes on* ULRIC, *who is lean-
 ing against a pillar*]. If I should do so?
 Sieg. I pledge my life for yours. With-
 draw into 385
This tower. [*Opens a turret door.*
 Gab. [*hesitatingly*]. This is the second
 safe asylum
You have offer'd me.
 Sieg. And was not the first so?
 Gab. I know not that even now—but
 will approve
The second. I have still a further shield.—
I did not enter Prague alone; and should I
Be put to rest with Stralenheim, there are
Some tongues without will wag in my be-
 half.
Be brief in your decision!
 Sieg. I will be so.—
My word is sacred and irrevocable
Within *these* walls, but it extends no fur-
 ther. 395
 Gab. I'll take it for so much.
 Sieg. [*points to* ULRIC'S *sabre, still upon
 the ground*]. Take also *that*—
I saw you eye it eagerly, and him
Distrustfully.
 Gab. [*takes up the sabre*]. I will; and so
 provide
To sell my life—not cheaply.
 [GABOR *goes into the turret, which*
 SIEGENDORF *closes.*
 Sieg. [*advances to* ULRIC]. Now, Count
 Ulric!
For son I dare not call thee—What say'st
 thou? 400
 Ulr. His tale is true.
 Sieg. True, monster!
 Ulr. Most true, father!
And you did well to listen to it: what
We know, we can provide against. He
 must
Be silenced.
 Sieg. Ay, with half of my domains;
And with the other half, could he and thou
Unsay this villany.

 Ulr. It is no time 406
For trifling or dissembling. I have said
His story's true; and he too must be
 silenced.
 Sieg. How so?
 Ulr. As Stralenheim is. Are you
 so dull
As never to have hit on this before? 410
When we met in the garden, what except
Discovery in the act could make me know
His death? Or had the prince's household
 been
Then summon'd, would the cry for the
 police 414
Been left to such a stranger? Or should I
Have loiter'd on the way? Or could *you*,
 Werner,
The object of the baron's hate and fears,
Have fled, unless by many an hour before
Suspicion woke? I sought and fathom'd
 you,
Doubting if you were false or feeble: I 420
Perceived you were the latter: and yet so
Confiding have I found you, that I doubted
At times your weakness.
 Sieg. Parricide! no less
Than common stabber! What deed of my
 life,
Or thought of mine, could make you deem
 me fit 425
For your accomplice?
 Ulr. Father, do not raise
The devil you cannot lay between us. This
Is time for union and for action, not
For family disputes. While *you* were tor-
 tured,
Could *I* be calm? Think you that I have
 heard 430
This fellow's tale without some feeling?—
 You
Have taught me feeling for *you* and myself;
For whom or what else did you ever teach
 it?
 Sieg. Oh! my dead father's curse! 'tis
 working now.
 Ulr. Let it work on! the grave will keep
 it down! 435
Ashes are feeble foes: it is more easy
To baffle such, than countermine a mole,
Which winds its blind but living path
 beneath you.
Yet hear me still!—If *you* condemn me, yet
Remember *who* hath taught me once too
 often 440
To listen to him! *Who* proclaim'd to me
That *there were crimes* made venial by the
 occasion?
That passion was our nature? that the
 goods 443
Of Heaven waited on the goods of fortune?
Who show'd me his humanity secured
By his *nerves* only? *Who* deprived me of
All power to vindicate myself and race
In open day? By his disgrace which stamp'd

(It might be) bastardy on me, and on
Himself—*a felon's* brand! The man who is
At once both warm and weak invites to
 deeds 451
He longs to do, but dare not. Is it strange
That I should *act* what you could *think?*
 We have done
With right and wrong: and now must only
 ponder
Upon effects, not causes. Stralenheim,
Whose life I saved from impulse, as, *un-*
 known, 456
I would have saved a peasant's or a dog's,
 I slew
Known as our foe—but not from venge-
 ance. He
Was a rock in our way which I cut through
As doth the bolt, because it stood between
 us 460
And our true destination—but not idly.
As stranger I preserved him, and he *owed me*
His *life:* when due, I but resumed the debt.
He, you, and I stood o'er a gulf wherein
I have plunged our enemy. *You* kindled
 first 465
The torch—*you* show'd the path: now
 trace me that
Of safety—or let me!
 Sieg. I have done with life!
Ulr. Let us have done with that which
 cankers life—
Familiar feuds and vain recriminations
Of things which cannot be undone. We
 have 470
No more to learn or hide: I know no fear,
And have within these very walls men who
(Although you know them not) dare ven-
 ture all things.
You stand high with the state; what passes
 here
Will not excite her too great curiosity: 475
Keep your own secret, keep a steady eye,
Stir not, and speak not;—leave the rest to
 me:
We must have no *third* babblers thrust be-
 tween us. [*Exit* ULRIC.
 Sieg. [*solus*]. Am I awake? are these my
 father's halls?
And *you*—my son? *My* son! *mine!* who
 have ever 480
Abhorr'd both mystery and blood, and yet
Am plunged into the deepest hell of both!
I must be speedy, or more will be shed—
The Hungarian's!—Ulric—he hath parti-
 sans,
It seems: I might have guess'd as much.
 Oh fool! 485
Wolves prowl in company. He hath the key
(As I too) of the opposite door which leads
Into the turret. Now then! or once more
To be the father of fresh crimes, no less
Than of the criminal! Ho! Gabor! Gabor!
 [*Exit into the turret, closing the*
 door after him.

SCENE II.—*The Interior of the Turret.*

 GABOR *and* SIEGENDORF.

Gab. Who calls?
Sieg. I—Siegendorf! Take these and
 fly!
Lose not a moment!
 [*Tears off a diamond star and other jewels,*
 and thrusts them into GABOR'S *hand.*
Gab. What am I to do
With these?
Sieg. Whate'er you will: sell them,
 or hoard,
And prosper; but delay not, or you are lost!
Gab. You pledged your honour for my
 safety!
Sieg. And 5
Must thus redeem it. Fly! I am not master,
It seems, of my own castle—of my own
Retainers—nay, even of these very walls,
Or I would bid them fall and crush me! Fly!
Or you will be slain by——
Gab. Is it even so? 10
Farewell, then! Recollect, however, count,
You sought this fatal interview!
Sieg. I did:
Let it not be more fatal still!—Begone!
Gab. By the same path I enter'd?
Sieg. Yes; that's safe still;
But loiter not in Prague;—you do not
 know 15
With whom you have to deal.
Gab. I know too well—
And knew it ere yourself, unhappy sire!
Farewell! [*Exit* GABOR.
 Sieg. [*solus and listening*]. He hath
 clear'd the staircase. Ah! I hear
The door sound loud behind him! He is
 safe!
Safe!—Oh, my father's spirit!—I am
 faint— 20
 [*He leans down upon a stone seat, near the*
 wall of the tower, in a drooping posture.

Enter ULRIC, *with others armed, and with*
 weapons drawn.

Ulr. Despatch!—he's there!
Lud. The count, my lord!
Ulr. [*recognising* SIEGENDORF]. You
 here, sir!
Sieg. Yes; if you want another victim,
 strike!
Ulr. [*seeing him stript of his jewels*]
Where is the ruffian who hath plunder'd
 you?
Vassals, despatch in search of him! You see
'Twas as I said—the wretch hath stript my
 father 2?
Of jewels which might form a prince's heir-
 loom!
Away. I'll follow you forthwith.
 [*Exeunt all but* SIEGENDORF *and* ULRIC
 What's this
Where is the villain?

Sieg. There are *two*, sir: which
Are you in quest of?
Ulr. Let us hear no more
Of this: he must be found. You have not
 let him 30
Escape?
Sieg. He's gone.
Ulr. With your connivance?
Sieg. With
My fullest, freest aid.
Ulr. Then fare you well!
 [ULRIC *is going.*
Sieg. Stop! I command—entreat—im-
 plore! Oh, Ulric!
Will you then leave me?
Ulr. What! remain to be
Denounced—dragg'd, it may be, in chains;
 and all 35
By your inherent weakness, half-humanity,
Selfish remorse, and temporising pity,
That sacrifices your whole race to save
A wretch to profit by our ruin! No, count,
Henceforth you have no son!
Sieg. I never had one; 40
And would you ne'er had borne the useless
 name!
Where will you go? I would not send you forth
Without protection.
Ulr. Leave that unto me.
I am not alone; nor merely the vain heir
Of your domains; a thousand, ay, ten
 thousand 45
Swords, hearts, and hands are mine.
Sieg. The foresters!
With whom the Hungarian found you first
 at Frankfort!
Ulr. Yes—men—who are worthy of the
 name! Go tell
Your senators that they look well to Prague;

Their feast of peace was early for the times;
There are more spirits abroad than have
 been laid 51
With Wallenstein!

 Enter JOSEPHINE *and* IDA.

Jos. What is't we hear? My
 Siegendorf!
Thank Heaven. I see you safe!
Sieg. Safe!
Ida. Yes, dear father!
Sieg. No, no; I have no children: never
 more 54
Call me by that worst name of parent.
Jos. What
Means my good lord?
Sieg. That you have given birth
To a demon!
Ida [*taking* ULRIC'S *hand*]. Who shall
 dare say this of Ulric?
Sieg. Ida, beware! there's blood upon
 that hand.
Ida [*stooping to kiss it*]. I'd kiss it off,
 though it were mine.
Sieg. It is so! 59
Ulr. Away! it is your father's!
 [*Exit* ULRIC.
Ida. Oh, great God!
And I have loved this man!
 [IDA *falls senseless*—JOSEPHINE *stands
 speechless with horror.*
Sieg. The wretch hath slain
Them both!—My Josephine! we are now
 alone!
Would we had ever been so!—All is over
For me!—Now open wide, my sire, thy
 grave; 64
Thy curse hath dug it deeper for thy son
In mine!—The race of Siegendorf is past!

THE DEFORMED TRANSFORMED

A DRAMA

ADVERTISEMENT

THIS production is founded partly on the story of a novel called 'The Three Brothers', published many years ago, from which M. G. Lewis's 'Wood Demon' was also taken; and partly on the 'Faust' of the great Goethe. The present publication contains the two first Parts only, and the opening chorus of the third. The rest may perhaps appear hereafter.

DRAMATIS PERSONÆ

STRANGER, *afterwards* CÆSAR. BERTHA.
ARNOLD. OLIMPIA.
BOURBON.
PHILIBERT. *Spirits, Soldiers, Citizens of Rome,*
CELLINI. *Priests, Peasants, &c.*

PART I

SCENE I.—*A Forest.*

Enter ARNOLD *and his mother* BERTHA.

Bert. Out, hunchback!
Arn. I was born so, mother!

Bert. Out,
Thou incubus! Thou nightmare! Of seven
 sons,
The sole abortion!
Arn. Would that I had been so,
And never seen the light!
Bert. I would so, too!

605

But as thou *hast*—hence, hence—and do
 thy best! 5
That back of thine may bear its burthen;
 'tis
More high, if not so broad as that of others.
 Arn. It *bears* its burthen;—but, my
 heart! Will it
Sustain that which you lay upon it, mother?
I love, or, at the least, I loved you: nothing
Save you, in nature, can love aught like me.
You nursed me—do not kill me!
 Bert. Yes—I nursed thee,
Because thou wert my first-born, and I
 knew not
If there would be another unlike thee,
That monstrous sport of nature. But get
 hence, 15
And gather wood!
 Arn. I will: but when I bring it,
Speak to me kindly. Though my brothers
 are
So beautiful and lusty, and as free
As the free chase they follow, do not spurn
 me;
Our milk has been the same.
 Bert. As is the hedgehog's,
Which sucks at midnight from the whole-
 some dam 21
Of the young bull, until the milkmaid finds
The nipple next day sore and udder dry.
Call not thy brothers brethren! Call me not
Mother; for if I brought thee forth, it was
As foolish hens at times hatch vipers, by
Sitting upon strange eggs. Out, urchin,
 out! [*Exit* BERTHA.
 Arn. [*solus*]. Oh, mother!——She is
 gone, and I must do
Her bidding;—wearily but willingly
I would fulfil it, could I only hope 30
A kind word in return. What shall I do?
 [ARNOLD *begins to cut wood: in doing*
 this he wounds one of his hands.
My labour for the day is over now.
Accursed be this blood that flows so fast;
For double curses will be my meed now
At home—What home? I have no home,
 no kin, 35
No kind—not made like other creatures, or
To share their sports or pleasures. Must I
 bleed, too,
Like them? Oh, that each drop which falls
 to earth
Would rise a snake to sting them, as they
 have stung me!
Or that the devil, to whom they liken me,
Would aid his likeness! If I must partake
His form, why not his power? Is it because
I have not his will too? For one kind word
From her who bore me would still recon-
 cile me
Even to this hateful aspect. Let me wash
The wound.
 [ARNOLD *goes to a spring, and stoops to*
 wash his hand: he starts back.

They are right; and Nature's mirro
 shows me
What she hath made me. I will not look o
 it
Again, and scarce dare think on't. Hideou
 wretch
That I am! The very waters mock me wit
My horrid shadow—like a demon placed
Deep in the fountain to scare back the cattl
From drinking therein. [*He pause*
 And shall I live or
A burden to the earth, myself, and sham
Unto what brought me into life! Tho
 blood,
Which flow'st so freely from a scratch, le
 me 5
Try if thou wilt not in a fuller stream
Pour forth my woes for ever with thyself
On earth, to which I will restore at once
This hateful compound of her atoms, an
Resolve back to her elements, and take
The shape of any reptile save myself,
And make a world for myriads of ne
 worms!
This knife! now let me prove if it will seve
This wither'd slip of nature's nightshade—
 my 6
Vile form—from the creation, as it hath
The green bough from the forest.
 [ARNOLD *places the knife in the groun*
 with the point upwards.
 Now 'tis se
And I can fall upon it. Yet one glance
On the fair day, which sees no foul thin
 like
Myself, and the sweet sun which warm'
 me, but 6
In vain. The birds—how joyously they sing
So let them, for I would not be lamented
But let their merriest notes be Arnold'
 knell;
The fallen leaves my monument; the mur
 mur
Of the near fountain my sole elegy.
Now, knife, stand firmly, as I fain woul
 fall! 7
 [*As he rushes to throw himself upon th*
 knife, his eye is suddenly caught by th
 fountain, which seems in motion.
The fountain moves without a wind: bu
 shall
The ripple of a spring change my resolve
No. Yet it moves again! The waters sti
Not as with air, but by some subterrane
And rocking power of the internal worl
What's here? A mist! No more?—
 [*A cloud comes from the fountain. H*
 stands gazing upon it: it is dispelle
 and a tall black man comes towar
 him.
 Arn. What would you? Speak! 8
Spirit or man?
 Stran. As man is both, why not
Say both in one?

Arn. Your form is man's, and yet
You may be devil.
Stran. So many men are that
Which is so call'd or thought, that you may
 add me 85
To which you please, without much wrong
 to either.
But come: you wish to kill yourself;—
 pursue
Your purpose.
Arn. You have interrupted me.
Stran. What is that resolution which
 can e'er
Be interrupted? If I be the devil 90
You deem, a single moment would have
 made you
Mine, and for ever, by your suicide;
And yet my coming saves you.
Arn. I said not
You *were* the demon, but that your ap-
 proach
Was like one. 95
Stran. Unless you keep company
With him (and you seem scarce used to
 such high
Society), you can't tell how he approaches;
And for his aspect, look upon the fountain,
And then on me, and judge which of us
 twain 99
Looks likest what the boors believe to be
Their cloven-footed terror.
Arn. Do you—dare *you*
To taunt me with my born deformity?
Stran. Were I to taunt a buffalo with this
Cloven foot of thine, or the swift drome-
 dary 104
With thy sublime of humps, the animals
Would revel in the compliment. And yet
Both beings are more swift, more strong,
 more mighty
In action and endurance than thyself,
And all the fierce and fair of the same kind
With thee. Thy form is natural: 'twas only
Nature's mistaken largess to bestow
The gifts which are of others upon man.
Arn. Give me the strength then of the
 buffalo's foot, 113
When he spurs high the dust, beholding his
Near enemy; or let me have the long
And patient swiftness of the desert-ship,
The helmless dromedary!—and I'll bear
Thy fiendish sarcasm with a saintly pa-
 tience. 118
Stran. I will.
Arn. [*with surprise*]. Thou canst?
Stran. Perhaps. Would you aught else?
Arn. Thou mockest me.
Stran. Not I. Why should I mock
What all are mocking? That's poor sport,
 methinks. 121
To talk to thee in human language (for
Thou canst not yet speak mine), the forester
Hunts not the wretched coney, but the boar,
Or wolf, or lion, leaving paltry game 125

To petty burghers, who leave once a year
Their walls, to fill their household caldrons
 with
Such scullion prey. The meanest gibe at
 thee,— 128
Now *I* can mock the mightiest.
Arn. Then waste not
Thy time on me: I seek thee not.
Stran. Your thoughts
Are not far from me. Do not send me back:
I'm not so easily recall'd to do
Good service.
Arn. What wilt thou do for me?
Stran. Change
Shapes with you, if you will, since yours so
 irks you; 134
Or form you to your wish in any shape.
Arn. Oh! then you are indeed the demon,
 for
Nought else would wittingly wear mine.
Stran. I'll show thee
The brightest which the world e'er bore,
 and give thee 138
Thy choice.
Arn. On what condition?
Stran. There's a question!
An hour ago you would have given your soul
To look like other men, and now you pause
To wear the form of heroes.
Arn. No; I will not.
I must not compromise my soul.
Stran. What soul,
Worth naming so, would dwell in such a
 carcass?
Arn. 'Tis an aspiring one, whate'er the
 tenement 145
In which it is mislodged. But name your
 compact:
Must it be sign'd in blood?
Stran. Not in your own.
Arn. Whose blood then?
Stran. We will talk of that hereafter.
But I'll be moderate with you, for I see
Great things within you. You shall have
 no bond 150
But your own will, no contract save your
 deeds.
Are you content?
Arn. I take thee at thy word.
Stran. Now then!
[*The Stranger approaches the fountain,
and turns to* ARNOLD.
 A little of your blood.
Arn. For what?
Stran. To mingle with the magic of the
 waters,
And make the charm effective.
Arn. [*holding out his wounded arm*]. Take
 it all. 155
Stran. Not now. A few drops will suf-
 fice for this.
[*The Stranger takes some of* ARNOLD'S
*blood in his hand, and casts it into the
fountain.*

Shadows of beauty!
 Shadows of power!
Rise to your duty—
 This is the hour! 160
Walk lovely and pliant
 From the depth of this fountain,
As the cloud-shapen giant
 Bestrides the Hartz Mountain.
Come as ye were, 165
 That our eyes may behold
The model in air
 Of the form I will mould,
Bright as the Iris
 When ether is spann'd;— 170
Such *his* desire is, [*Pointing to* ARNOLD.
 Such my command!
Demons heroic—
 Demons who wore
The form of the stoic 175
 Or sophist of yore—
Or the shape of each victor,
 From Macedon's boy,
To each high Roman's picture,
 Who breathed to destroy— 180
Shadows of beauty!
 Shadows of power!
Up to your duty—
 This is the hour! 184

[*Various phantoms arise from the waters,
and pass in succession before the Stran-
ger and* ARNOLD.

Arn. What do I see?
Stran. The black-eyed Roman, with
The eagle's beak between those eyes which
 ne'er
Beheld a conqueror, or look'd along
The land he made not Rome's, while Rome
 became
His, and all theirs who heir'd his very name.
Arn. The phantom's bald; my quest is
 beauty. Could I 190
Inherit but his fame with his defects!
Stran. His brow was girt with laurels
 more than hairs.
You see his aspect—choose it, or reject.
I can but promise you his form; his fame
Must be long sought and fought for.
Arn. I will fight, too. 195
But not as a mock Cæsar. Let him pass;
His aspect may be fair, but suits me not.
Stran. Then you are far more difficult
 to please
Than Cato's sister, or than Brutus's mother,
Or Cleopatra at sixteen—an age 200
When love is not less in the eye than heart.
But be it so! Shadow, pass on!
[*The phantom of Julius Cæsar disappears.*
Arn. And can it
Be, that the man who shook the earth is
 gone,
And left no footstep?
Stran. There you err. His substance
Left graves enough, and woes enough, and
 fame 205

More than enough to track his memory;
But for his shadow, 'tis no more than yours
Except a little longer and less crooked
I' the sun. Behold another!
 [*A second phantom passes*
Arn. Who is he?
Stran. He was the fairest and the braves
 of 21
Athenians. Look upon him well.
Arn. He is
More lovely than the last. How beautiful
Stran. Such was the curled son of Clini
 as;—Wouldst thou
Invest thee with his form?
Arn. Would that I ha
Been born with it! But since I may choos
 further, 21
I will *look* further.
 [*The shade of Alcibiades disappear.*
Stran. Lo! behold again!
Arn. What! that low, swarthy, short
 nosed, round-eyed satyr,
With the wide nostrils and Silenus' aspec
The splay feet and low stature! I had bette
Remain that which I am.
Stran. And yet he was
The earth's perfection of all mental beauty
And personification of all virtue. 22
But you reject him?
Arn. If his form could bring m
That which redeem'd it—no.
Stran. I have no powe
To promise that; but you may try, and find
Easier in such a form, or in your own.
Arn. No. I was not born for philosophy
Though I have that about me which ha
 need on't. 22
Let him fleet on.
Stran. Be air, thou hemlock-drinker
[*The shadow of Socrates disappears: an
other rises.*
Arn. What's here? whose broad brow
 and whose curly beard
And manly aspect look like Hercules,
Save that his jocund eye hath more o
 Bacchus 23
Than the sad purger of the infernal world
Leaning dejected on his club of conquest
As if he knew the worthlessness of those
For whom he had fought.
Stran. It was the man who los
The ancient world for love.
Arn. I cannot blame him
Since I have risk'd my soul because I fin
 not 23
That which he exchanged the earth for.
Stran. Since so fa
You seem congenial, will you wear hi
 features?
Arn. No. As you leave me choice, I am
 difficult,
If but to see the heroes I should ne'er
Have seen else on this side of the dim shor
Whence they float back before us.

Stran. Hence, triumvir,
Thy Cleopatra's waiting.
[*The shade of Antony disappears: another
rises.*
Arn. Who is this?
Who truly looketh like a demigod,
Blooming and bright, with golden hair, and
 stature,
If not more high than mortal, yet immortal
In all that nameless bearing of his limbs,
Which he wears as the sun his rays—a some-
 thing 250
Which shines from him, and yet is but the
 flashing
Emanation of a thing more glorious still.
Was *he e'er human only*?
Stran. Let the earth speak,
If there be atoms of him left, or even 254
Of the more solid gold that form'd his urn.
Arn. Who was this glory of mankind?
Stran. The shame
Of Greece in peace, her thunderbolt in
 war—
Demetrius the Macedonian, and
Taker of cities.
Arn. Yet one shadow more.
Stran. [*addressing the shadow*]. Get thee
 to Lamia's lap!
[*The shade of Demetrius Poliorcetes
vanishes: another rises.*
 I'll fit you still,
Fear not, my hunchback! if the shadows of
That which existed please not your nice taste,
I'll animate the ideal marble, till
Your soul be reconciled to her new gar-
 ment. 264
Arn. Content! I will fix here.
Stran. I must commend
Your choice. The god-like son of the sea-
 goddess,
The unshorn boy of Peleus, with his locks
As beautiful and clear as the amber waves
Of rich Pactolus, roll'd o'er sands of gold,
Soften'd by intervening crystal, and 270
Rippled like flowing waters by the wind,
All vow'd to Sperchius as they were—be-
 hold them!
And *him*—as he stood by Polixena,
With sanction'd and with soften'd love, be-
 fore
The altar, gazing on his Trojan bride, 275
With some remorse within for Hector slain
And Priam weeping, mingled with deep
 passion
For the sweet downcast virgin, whose
 young hand
Trembled in *his* who slew her brother. So
He stood i' the temple! Look upon him as
Greece look'd her last upon her best, the
 instant 281
Ere Paris' arrow flew.
Arn. I gaze upon him
As if I were his soul, whose form shall soon
Envelope mine.

Stran. You have done well. The greatest
Deformity should only barter with 285
The extremest beauty, if the proverb's true
Of mortals, that extremes meet.
Arn. Come! Be quick!
I am impatient.
Stran. As a youthful beauty
Before her glass. *You both* see what is not,
But dream it is what must be.
Arn. Must I wait?
Stran. No; that were a pity. But a word
 or two:
His stature is twelve cubits; would you so far
Outstep these times, and be a Titan? Or
(To talk canonically) wax a son 294
Of Anak?
Arn. Why not?
Stran. Glorious ambition!
I love thee most in dwarfs! A mortal of
Philistine stature would have gladly pared
His own Goliath down to a slight David:
But thou, my manikin, wouldst soar a show
Rather than hero. Thou shalt be indulged,
If such be thy desire; and yet, by being
A little less removed from present men
In figure, thou canst sway them more; for all
Would rise against thee now, as if to hunt
A new-found mammoth: and their cursed
 engines, 305
Their culverins, and so forth, would find
 way
Through our friend's armour there, with
 greater ease
Than the adulterer's arrow through his heel,
Which Thetis had forgotten to baptize 309
In Styx.
Arn. Then let it be as thou deem'st best.
Stran. Thou shalt be beauteous as the
 thing thou seest,
And strong as what it was, and——
Arn. I ask not
For valour, since deformity is daring.
It is its essence to o'ertake mankind
By heart and soul, and make itself the
 equal— 315
Ay, the superior of the rest. There is
A spur in its halt movements, to become
All that the others cannot, in such things
As still are free to both, to compensate
For stepdame Nature's avarice at first.
They woo with fearless deeds the smiles of
 fortune,
And oft, like Timour the lame Tartar, win
 them.
Stran. Well spoken! and thou doubtless
 wilt remain
Form'd as thou art. I may dismiss the
 mould
Of shadow, which must turn to flesh, to
 incase 325
This daring soul, which could achieve no less
Without it.
Arn. Had no power presented me
The possibility of change, I would

609

Have done the best which spirit may to
 make 329
Its way with all deformity's dull, deadly
Discouraging weight upon me, like a moun-
 tain,
In feeling, on my heart as on my shoulders—
A hateful and unsightly molehill, to
The eyes of happier men. I would have
 look'd 334
On beauty in that sex which is the type
Of all we know or dream of beautiful
Beyond the world they brighten, with a
 sigh—
Not of love, but despair; nor sought to win,
Though to a heart all love, what could not
 love me 339
In turn, because of this vile crooked clog,
Which makes me lonely. Nay, I could have
 borne
It all, had not my mother spurn'd me from
 her.
The she-bear licks her cubs into a sort
Of shape;—my dam beheld my shape was
 hopeless. 344
Had she exposed me, like the Spartan, ere
I knew the passionate part of life, I had
Been a clod of the valley,—happier nothing
Than what I am. But even thus, the lowest,
Ugliest, and meanest of mankind, what
 courage
And perseverance could have done, per-
 chance 350
Had made me something—as it has made
 heroes
Of the same mould as mine. You lately
 saw me
Master of my own life, and quick to quit it;
And he who is so is the master of 354
Whatever dreads to die.

Stran. Decide between
What you have been, or will be.

Arn. I have done so.
You have open'd brighter prospects to my
 eyes,
And sweeter to my heart. As I am now,
I might be fear'd, admired, respected, loved
Of all save those next to me, of whom I
Would be beloved. As thou showest me
A choice of forms, I take the one I view.
Haste! haste!

Stran. And what shall *I* wear?

Arn. Surely, he
Who can command all forms will choose
 the highest, 364
Something superior even to that which was
Pelides now before us. Perhaps *his*
Who slew him, that of Paris: or—still
 higher—
The poet's god, clothed in such limbs as are
Themselves a poetry.

Stran. Less will content me; 369
For I, too, love a change.

Arn. Your aspect is
Dusky, but not uncomely.

Stran. If I chose,
I might be whiter; but I have a penchan
For black—it is so honest, and besides
Can neither blush with shame nor pal
 with fear; 37
But I have worn it long enough of late,
And now I'll take your figure.

Arn. Mine!

Stran. Yes. Yo
Shall change with Thetis' son, and I wit
 Bertha,
Your mother's offspring. People hav
 their tastes:
You have yours—I mine.

Arn. Despatch! Despatch

Stran. Even so
[*The Stranger takes some earth an
 moulds it along the turf, and the
 addresses the phantom of Achilles.*
Beautiful shadow
 Of Thetis's boy!
Who sleeps in the meadow
 Whose grass grows o'er Troy:
From the red earth, like Adam,
 Thy likeness I shape, 38
As the being who made him,
 Whose actions I ape.
Thou clay, be all glowing,
 Till the rose in his cheek
Be as fair as, when blowing, 39
 It wears its first streak!
Ye violets, I scatter,
 Now turn into eyes!
And thou, sunshiny water,
 Of blood take the guise! 39
Let these hyacinth boughs
 Be his long flowing hair,
And wave o'er his brows
 As thou wavest in air!
Let his heart be this marble 40
 I tear from the rock!
But his voice as the warble
 Of birds on yon oak!
Let his flesh be the purest
 Of mould, in which grew 40
The lily-root surest,
 And drank the best dew!
Let his limbs be the lightest
 Which clay can compound,
And his aspect the brightest 41
 On earth to be found!
Elements, near me,
 Be mingled and stirr'd,
Know me, and hear me,
 And leap to my word! 41
Sunbeams, awaken
 This earth's animation!
'Tis done! He hath taken
 His stand in creation!
[ARNOLD *falls senseless; his soul passe
 into the shape of Achilles, which rise
 from the ground; while the phanton
 has disappeared, part by part, as th
 figure was formed from the earth.*

610

Arn. [*in his new form*]. I love, and I shall
 be beloved! O, life!
At last I feel thee! Glorious spirit!
 Stran. Stop!
What shall become of your abandon'd gar-
 ment,
Yon hump, and lump, and clod of ugliness,
Which late you wore, or were?
 Arn. Who cares? Let wolves
And vultures take it, if they will.
 Stran. And if
They do, and are not scared by it, you'll say
It must be peace-time, and no better fare
Abroad i' the fields.
 Arn. Let us but leave it there
No matter what becomes on't.
 Stran. That's ungracious,
If not ungrateful. Whatso'er it be,
It hath sustain'd your soul full many a day.
 Arn. Ay, as the dunghill may conceal a
 gem
Which is now set in gold, as jewels should be.
 Stran. But if I give another form, it must
 be 434
By fair exchange, not robbery. For they
Who make men without women's aid have
 long
Had patents for the same, and do not love
Your interlopers. The devil may take men,
Not make them,—though he reap the
 benefit
Of the original workmanship: and there-
 fore 440
Some one must be found to assume the
 shape
You have quitted.
 Arn. Who would do so?
 Stran. That I know not,
And therefore I must.
 Arn. You!
 Stran. I said it ere
You inhabited your present dome of
 beauty.
 Arn. True. I forget all things in the new
 joy 445
Of this immortal change.
 Stran. In a few moments
I will be as you were, and you shall see
Yourself for ever by you, as your shadow.
 Arn. I would be spared this.
 Stran. But it cannot be.
What! shrink already, being what you are,
From seeing what you were?
 Arn. Do as thou wilt.
 Stran. [*to the late form of* ARNOLD, *ex-
 tended on the earth*].
Clay, not dead, but soul-less!
 Though no man would choose thee,
An immortal no less
 Deigns not to refuse thee. 455
Clay thou art; and unto spirit
 All clay is of equal merit.
Fire! *without* which nought can live;
Fire! but *in* which nought can live,

Save the fabled salamander, 460
Or immortal souls which wander,
Praying what doth not forgive,
Howling for a drop of water,
 Burning in a quenchless lot,
Fire! the only element 465
 Where nor fish, beast, bird, nor worm,
 Save the worm which dieth not,
Can preserve a moment's form,
But must with thyself be blent:
Fire! man's safeguard and his slaughter:
Fire! Creation's first-born daughter,
 And Destruction's threaten'd son,
 When heaven with the world hath done:
Fire! assist me to renew
Life in what lies in my view 475
 Stiff and cold!
His resurrection rests with me and you!
One little, marshy spark of flame—
And he again shall seem the same;
 But I his spirit's place shall hold! 480
[*An ignis-fatuus flits through the wood
 and rests on the brow of the body. The
 Stranger disappears: the body rises.*
 Arn. [*in his new form*]. Oh! horrible!
 Stran. [*in* ARNOLD'S *late shape*]. What!
 tremblest thou?
 Arn. Not so—
I merely shudder. Where is fled the shape
Thou lately worest?
 Stran. To the world of shadows.
But let us thread the present. Whither wilt
 thou? 484
 Arn. Must thou be my companion?
 Stran. Wherefore not?
Your betters keep worse company.
 Arn. *My* betters!
 Stran. Oh! you wax proud, I see, of
 your new form:
I'm glad of that. Ungrateful too! That's
 well;
You improve apace;—two changes in an
 instant, 489
And you are old in the world's ways already.
But bear with me: indeed you'll find me
 useful
Upon your pilgrimage. But come, pro-
 nounce
Where shall we now be errant?
 Arn. Where the world
Is thickest, that I may behold it in 494
Its workings.
 Stran. That's to say, where there is war
And woman in activity. Let's see!
Spain—Italy—the new Atlantic world—
Afric, with all its Moors. In very truth,
There is small choice: the whole race are
 just now 499
Tugging as usual at each other's hearts.
 Arn. I have heard great things of Rome.
 Stran. A goodly choice—
And scarce a better to be found on earth,
Since Sodom was put out. The field is wide
 too;

For now the Frank, and Hun, and Spanish
scion 504
Of the old Vandals, are at play along
The sunny shores of the world's garden.
Arn. How
Shall we proceed?
Stran. Like gallants, on good coursers.
What, ho! my chargers! Never yet were
better,
Since Phaeton was upset into the Po. 509
Our pages too!

*Enter two Pages, with four coal-black
horses.*

Arn. A noble sight!
Stran. And of
A nobler breed. Match me in Barbary,
Or your Kochlini race of Araby,
With these!
Arn. The mighty steam, which volumes
high
From their proud nostrils, burns the very
air;
And sparks of flame, like dancing fire-flies,
wheel 515
Around their manes, as common insects
swarm
Round common steeds towards sunset.
Stran. Mount, my lord!
They and I are your servitors.
Arn. And these
Our dark-eyed pages—what may be their
names? 519
Stran. You shall baptize them.
Arn. What! in holy water?
Stran. Why not? The deeper sinner,
better saint.
Arn. They are beautiful, and cannot,
sure, be demons.
Stran. True; the devil's always ugly;
and your beauty
Is never diabolical.
Arn. I'll call him
Who bears the golden horn, and wears
such bright 525
And blooming aspect, *Huon;* for he looks
Like to the lovely boy lost in the forest,
And never found till now. And for the
other
And darker, and more thoughtful, who
smiles not, 529
But looks as serious though serene as night,
He shall be *Memnon*, from the Ethiop king
Whose statue turns a harper once a day.
And you?
Stran. I have ten thousand names, and
twice
As many attributes: but as I wear 534
A human shape, will take a human name.
Arn. More human than the shape
(though it was mine once)
I trust.
Stran. Then call me Cæsar.
Arn. Why, that name

Belongs to empires, and has been but
borne 538
By the world's lords.
Stran. And therefore fittest for
The devil in disguise—since so you deem
me,
Unless you call me pope instead.
Arn. Well, then,
Cæsar thou shalt be. For myself, my name
Shall be plain Arnold still.
Cæs. We'll add a title—
'Count Arnold': it hath no ungracious
sound, 544
And will look well upon a billet-doux.
Arn. Or in an order for a battle-field.
Cæs. [*sings*]. To horse! to horse! my
coal-black steed
Paws the ground, and snuffs the air!
There's not a foal of Arab's breed
More knows whom he must bear; 550
On the hill he will not tire,
Swifter as it waxes higher;
In the marsh he will not slacken,
On the plain be overtaken;
In the wave he will not sink, 555
Nor pause at the brook's side to drink;
In the race he will not pant,
In the combat he'll not faint;
On the stones he will not stumble, 559
Time nor toil shall make him humble;
In the stall he will not stiffen,
But be winged as a griffin,
Only flying with his feet:
And will not such a voyage be sweet?
Merrily! merrily! never unsound, 565
Shall our bonny black horses skim over
the ground!
From the Alps to the Caucasus, ride we,
or fly!
For we'll leave them behind in the glance
of an eye.
[*They mount their horses, and disappear.*

[SCENE II.—*A Camp before the Walls
of Rome*

ARNOLD *and* CÆSAR.

Cæs. You are well enter'd now.
Arn. Ay; but my path
Has been o'er carcasses: mine eyes are full
Of blood.
Cæs. Then wipe them, and see clearly.
Why!
Thou art a conqueror; the chosen knight
And free companion of the gallant Bour-
bon, 5
Late constable of France: and now to be
Lord of the city which hath been earth's
lord
Under its emperors, and—changing sex,
Not sceptre, an hermaphrodite of empire—
Lady of the old world.
Arn. How *old*? What! are there
New worlds?

612

Cæs. To *you*. You'll find there are such
 shortly,
By its rich harvests, new disease, and gold;
From one *half* of the world named a *whole*
 new one,
Because you know no better than the dull
And dubious notice of your eyes and ears.
 Arn. I'll trust them. 16
Cæs. Do! they will deceive you sweetly,
And that is better than the bitter truth.
 Arn. Dog!
 Cæs. Man!
 Arn. Devil!
 Cæs. Your obedient humble servant.
 Arn. Say *master* rather. Thou hast lured
 me on,
Through scenes of blood and lust, till I am
 here. 20
Cæs. And where wouldst thou be?
 Arn. Oh, at peace—in peace.
Cæs. And where is that which is so?
 From the star
To the winding worm, all life is motion;
 and
In life *commotion* is the extremest point
Of life. The planet wheels till it becomes
A comet, and destroying as it sweeps
The stars, goes out. The poor worm
 winds its way,
Living upon the death of other things,
But still, like them, must live and die, the
 subject
Of something which has made it live and
 die. 30
You must obey what all obey, the rule
Of fix'd necessity: against her edict
Rebellion prospers not.
 Arn. And when it prospers——
Cæs. 'Tis no rebellion.
 Arn. Will it prosper now?
Cæs. The Bourbon hath given orders
 for the assault, 35
And by the dawn there will be work.
 Arn. Alas!
And shall the city yield? I see the giant
Abode of the true God, and his true saint,
Saint Peter, rear its dome and cross into
That sky whence Christ ascended from
 the cross, 40
Which his blood made a badge of glory
 and
Of joy (as once of torture unto him,
God and God's Son, man's sole and only
 refuge).
 Cæs. 'Tis there, and shall be.
 Arn. What?
 Cæs. The crucifix
Above, and many altar shrines below.
Also some culverins upon the walls, 46
And harquebusses, and what not; besides
The men who are to kindle them to death
Of other men.
 Arn. And those scarce mortal arches,
Pile above pile of everlasting wall, 50

The theatre where emperors and their
 subjects
(Those subjects *Romans*) stood at gaze
 upon
The battles of the monarchs of the wild
And wood, the lion and his tusky rebels
Of the then untamed desert, brought to
 joust 55
In the arena (as right well they might,
When they had left no human foe uncon-
 quer'd);
Made even the forest pay its tribute of
Life to their amphitheatre, as well 59
As Dacia men to die the eternal death
For a sole instant's pastime, and 'Pass on
To a new gladiator!'—Must it fall?
 Cæs. The city, or the amphitheatre?
The church, or one, or all? for you con-
 found
Both them and me.
 Arn. To-morrow sounds the assault
With the first cock-crow.
 Cæs. Which, if it end with
The evening's first nightingale, will be
Something new in the annals of great
 sieges;
For men must have their prey after long toil.
 Arn. The sun goes down as calmly,
 and perhaps 70
More beautifully, than he did on Rome
On the day Remus leapt her wall.
 Cæs. I saw him.
 Arn. You!
 Cæs. Yes, sir. You forget I am or was
Spirit, till I took up with your cast shape,
And a worse name. I'm Cæsar and a
 hunchback 75
Now. Well! the first of Cæsars was a
 baldhead,
And loved his laurels better as a wig
(So history says) than as a glory. Thus
The world runs on, but we'll be merry still.
I saw your Romulus (simple as I am) 80
Slay his own twin, quick-born of the same
 womb,
Because he leapt a ditch ('twas then no
 wall,
Whate'er it now be); and Rome's earliest
 cement
Was brother's blood; and if its native
 blood 84
Be spilt till the choked Tiber be as red
As e'er 'twas yellow, it will never wear
The deep hue of the ocean and the earth,
Which the great robber sons of fratricide
Have made their never-ceasing scene of
 slaughter
For ages.
 Arn. But what have these done, their
 far 90
Remote descendants, who have lived in
 peace,
The peace of heaven, and in her sunshine of
Piety?

Cæs. And what had *they* done, whom the old
Romans o'erswept?—Hark!
Arn. They are soldiers singing
A reckless roundelay, upon the eve 95
Of many deaths, it may be of their own.
Cæs. And why should they not sing
as well as swans?
They are black ones, to be sure.
Arn. So, you are learn'd,
I see, too?
Cæs. In my grammar, certes. I
Was educated for a monk of all times,
And once I was well versed in the for-
gotten 101
Etruscan letters, and—were I so minded—
Could make their hieroglyphics plainer
than
Your alphabet.
Arn. And wherefore do you not?
Cæs. It answers better to resolve the
alphabet 105
Back into hieroglyphics. Like your states-
man,
And prophet, pontiff, doctor, alchymist,
Philosopher, and what not, they have
built
More Babels, without new dispersion, than
The stammering young ones of the flood's
dull ooze, 110
Who fail'd and fled each other. Why?
why, marry,
Because no man could understand his
neighbour.
They are wiser now, and will not separate
For nonsense. Nay, it is their brother-
hood,
Their Shibboleth, their Koran, Talmud,
their 115
Cabala; their best brick-work, where-
withal
They build more——
Arn. [*interrupting him*]. Oh, thou ever-
lasting sneerer!
Be silent! How the soldier's rough strain
seems
Soften'd by distance to a hymn-like
cadence!
Listen!
Cæs. Yes. I have heard the angels
sing. 120
Arn. And demons howl.
Cæs. And man, too. Let us listen:
I love all music.

Song of the Soldiers within.

The black bands came over
 The Alps and their snow;
With Bourbon, the rover, 125
 They pass'd the broad Po.
We have beaten all foemen,
 We have captured a king,
We have turn'd back on no men,
 And so let us sing! 130

Here's the Bourbon for ever!
 Though penniless all,
We'll have one more endeavour
 At yonder old wall.
With the Bourbon we'll gather 135
 At day-dawn before
The gates, and together
 Or break or climb o'er
The wall: on the ladder
 As mounts each firm foot, 140
Our shout shall grow gladder,
 And death only be mute.
With the Bourbon we'll mount o'er
 The walls of old Rome,
And who then shall count o'er 145
 The spoils of each dome?
Up! up with the lily!
 And down with the keys!
In old Rome, the seven-hilly,
 We'll revel at ease. 150
Her streets shall be gory,
 Her Tiber all red,
And her temples so hoary
 Shall clang with our tread.
Oh, the Bourbon! the Bourbon! 155
 The Bourbon for aye!
Of our song bear the burden!
 And fire, fire away!
With Spain for the vanguard,
 Our varied host comes; 160
And next to the Spaniard
 Beat Germany's drums;
And Italy's lances
 Are couch'd at their mother;
But our leader from France is, 165
 Who warr'd with his brother.
Oh, the Bourbon! the Bourbon!
 Sans country or home,
We'll follow the Bourbon,
 To plunder old Rome. 170

Cæs. An indifferent song
For those within the walls, methinks, to
hear.
Arn. Yes, if they keep to their chorus.
But here comes
The general with his chiefs and men of
trust.
A goodly rebel!

Enter the Constable BOURBON '*cum suis,*'
&c. &c.

Phil. How now, noble prince, 175
You are not cheerful?
Bourb. Why should I be so?
Phil. Upon the eve of conquest, such
as ours,
Most men would be so.
Bourb. If I were secure!
Phil. Doubt not our soldiers. Were
the walls of adamant,
They'd crack them. Hunger is a sharp
artillery. 180
Bourb. That they will falter is my
least of fears.

614

That they will be repulsed, with Bourbon for
Their chief, and all their kindled appetites
To marshal them on—were those hoary
 walls
Mountains, and those who guard them
 like the gods 185
Of the old fables, I would trust my
 Titans;—
But now——
 Phil. They are but men who war with
 mortals.
 Bourb. True: but those walls have
 girded in great ages,
And sent forth mighty spirits. The past
 earth
And present phantom of imperious Rome
Is peopled with those warriors; and me-
 thinks 191
They flit along the eternal city's rampart,
And stretch their glorious, gory, shadowy
 hands,
And beckon me away!
 Phil. So let them! Wilt thou
Turn back from shadowy menaces of
 shadows? 195
 Bourb. They do not menace me. I
 could have faced,
Methinks, a Sylla's menace; but they clasp,
And raise, and wring their dim and death-
 like hands,
And with their thin aspen faces and fix'd
 eyes
Fascinate mine. Look there!
 Phil. I look upon 200
A lofty battlement.
 Bourb. And there!
 Phil. Not even
A guard in sight; they wisely keep below,
Shelter'd by the grey parapet from some
Stray bullet of our lansquenets, who might
Practise in the cool twilight.
 Bourb. You are blind. 205
 Phil. If seeing nothing more than may
 be seen
Be so.
 Bourb. A thousand years have mann'd
 the walls
With all their heroes,—the last Cato stands
And tears his bowels, rather than survive
The liberty of that I would enslave, 210
And the first Cæsar with his triumphs flits
From battlement to battlement.
 Phil. Then conquer
The walls for which he conquer'd, and be
 greater!
 Bourb. True: so I will, or perish.
 Phil. You can *not.*
In such an enterprise to die is rather 215
The dawn of an eternal day, than death.
 [*Count* ARNOLD *and* CÆSAR *advance.*
 Cæs. And the mere men—do they too
 sweat beneath
The noon of this same ever-scorching
 glory?

 Bourb. Ah!
Welcome the bitter hunchback! and his
 master,
The beauty of our host, and brave as
 beauteous, 220
And generous as lovely. We shall find
Work for you both ere morning.
 Cæs. You will find,
So please your highness, no less for your-
 self.
 Bourb. And if I do, there will not be a
 labourer
More forward, hunchback!
 Cæs. You may well say so, 225
For *you* have seen that back—as general,
Placed in the rear in action—but your foes
Have never seen it.
 Bourb. That's a fair retort,
For I provoked it:—but the Bourbon's
 breast
Has been, and ever shall be, far advanced
In danger's face as yours, were you the
 devil. 231
 Cæs. And if I were, I might have saved
 myself
The toil of coming here.
 Phil. Why so?
 Cæs. One half
Of your brave bands of their own bold
 accord 234
Will go to him, the other half be sent,
More swiftly, not less surely.
 Bourb. Arnold, your
Slight crooked *friend*'s as snake-like in his
 words
As his deeds.
 Cæs. Your highness much mistakes me.
The first snake was a flatterer—I am none;
And for my deeds, I only sting when
 stung. 240
 Bourb. You are brave, and that's
 enough for me; and quick
In speech as sharp in action—and *that*'s
 more.
I am not alone a soldier, but the soldiers'
Comrade.
 Cæs. They are but bad company, your
 highness;
And worse even for their friends than foes,
 as being 245
More permanent acquaintance.
 Phil. How now, fellow!
Thou waxest insolent, beyond the privilege
Of a buffoon.
 Cæs. You mean I speak the truth.
I'll lie—it is as easy: then you'll praise me
For calling you a hero.
 Bourb. Philibert! 250
Let him alone; he's brave, and ever has
Been first, with that swart face and
 mountain shoulder,
In field or storm, and patient in starvation;
And for his tongue, the camp is full of
 licence,

And the sharp stinging of a lively rogue
Is, to my mind, far preferable to 256
The gross, dull, heavy, gloomy execration
Of a mere famish'd, sullen, grumbling slave,
Whom nothing can convince save a full
 meal,
And wine, and sleep, and a few maravedis,
With which he deems him rich.
 Cæs. It would be well
If the earth's princes ask'd no more.
 Bourb. Be silent!
 Cæs. Ay, but not idle. Work yourself
 with words!
You have few to speak.
 Phil. What means the audacious
 prater?
 Cæs. To prate, like other prophets.
 Bourb. Philibert! 265
Why will you vex him? Have we not
 enough
To think on? Arnold! I will lead the attack
To-morrow.
 Arn. I have heard as much, my lord.
 Bourb. And you will follow?
 Arn. Since I must not lead.
 Bourb. 'Tis necessary for the further
 daring 270
Of our too needy army, that their chief
Plant the first foot upon the foremost
 ladder's
First step.
 Cæs. Upon its topmost, let us hope:
So shall he have his full deserts.
 Bourb. The world's
Great capital perchance is ours to-
 morrow. 275
Through every change the seven-hill'd
 city hath
Retain'd her sway o'er nations, and the
 Cæsars
But yielded to the Alarics, the Alarics
Unto the pontiffs. Roman, Goth, or
 priest,
Still the world's masters! Civilized, bar-
 barian, 280
Or saintly, still the walls of Romulus
Have been the circus of an empire. Well!
'Twas *their* turn—now 'tis ours; and let
 us hope
That we will fight as well, and rule much
 better.
 Cæs. No doubt, the camp's the school
 of civic rights. 285
What would you make of Rome?
 Bourb. That which it was.
 Cæs. In Alaric's time?
 Bourb. No, slave! in the first Cæsar's,
Whose name you bear like other curs——
 Cæs. And kings!
'Tis a great name for blood-hounds.
 Bourb. There's a demon
In that fierce rattlesnake thy tongue. Wilt
 never 290
Be serious?

 Cæs. On the eve of battle, no;—
That were not soldier-like. 'Tis for the
 general
To be more pensive: we adventurers
Must be more cheerful. Wherefore should
 we think?
Our tutelar deity, in a leader's shape, 295
Takes care of us. Keep thought aloof
 from hosts!
If the knaves take to thinking, you will
 have
To crack those walls alone.
 Bourb. You may sneer, since
'Tis lucky for you that you fight no worse
 for't.
 Cæs. I thank you for the freedom; 'tis
 the only 300
Pay I have taken in your highness' service.
 Bourb. Well, sir, to-morrow you shall
 pay yourself.
Look on those towers; they hold my
 treasury;
But, Philibert, we'll in to council. Arnold,
We would request your presence.
 Arn. Prince, my service 305
Is yours, as in the field.
 Bourb. In both we prize it,
And yours will be a post of trust at day-
 break.
 Cæs. And mine?
 Bourb. To follow glory with the
 Bourbon.
Good night!
 Arn. [*to* CÆSAR]. Prepare our armour
 for the assault,
And wait within my tent.
 [*Exeunt* BOURBON, ARNOLD, PHILIBERT,
 &c.
 Cæs. [*solus*]. Within thy tent! 310
Think'st thou that I pass from thee with
 my presence?
Or that this crooked coffer, which con-
 tain'd
Thy principle of life, is aught to me
Except a mask? And these are men, for-
 sooth!
Heroes and chiefs, the flower of Adam's
 bastards! 315
This is the consequence of giving matter
The power of thought. It is a stubborn
 substance,
And thinks chaotically, as it acts,
Ever relapsing into its first elements.
Well! I must play with these poor puppets:
 'tis 320
The spirit's pastime in his idler hours.
When I grow weary of it, I have business
Amongst the stars, which these poor
 creatures deem
Were made for them to look at. 'Twere a
 jest now
To bring one down amongst them, and
 set fire 325
Unto their anthill: how the pismires then

616

Would scamper o'er the scalding soil, and,
 ceasing
From tearing down each other's nests,
 pipe forth
One universal orison! Ha! ha!
 [*Exit* CÆSAR.

PART II

SCENE I.—*Before the walls of Rome.—The
Assault: the Army in motion, with
ladders to scale the walls;* BOURBON,
*with a white scarf over his armour, fore-
most.*

Chorus of Spirits in the air.

I

'Tis the morn, but dim and dark.
Whither flies the silent lark?
Whither shrinks the clouded sun?
Is the day indeed begun?
Nature's eye is melancholy 5
O'er the city high and holy:
But without there is a din
Should arouse the saints within,
And revive the heroic ashes
Round which yellow Tiber dashes. 10
Oh, ye seven hills! awaken,
Ere your very base be shaken!

II

Hearken to the steady stamp!
Mars is in their every tramp!
Not a step is out of tune, 15
As the tides obey the moon!
On they march, though to self-slaughter,
Regular as rolling water,
Whose high waves o'ersweep the border
Of huge moles, but keep their order, 20
Breaking only rank by rank.
Hearken to the armour's clank!
Look down o'er each frowning warrior,
How he glares upon the barrier:
Look on each step of each ladder, 25
As the stripes that streak an adder.

III

Look upon the bristling wall,
Mann'd without an interval!
Round and round, and tier on tier,
Cannon's black mouth, shining spear, 30
Lit match, bell-mouth'd musquetoon,
Gaping to be murderous soon;
All the warlike gear of old,
Mix'd with what we now behold,
In this strife 'twixt old and new, 35
Gather like a locusts' crew.
Shade of Remus! 'tis a time
Awful as thy brother's crime!
Christians war against Christ's shrine:—
Must its lot be like to thine? 40

IV

Near—and near—and nearer still,
As the earthquake saps the hill,
First with trembling, hollow motion,
Like a scarce awaken'd ocean, 44
Then with stronger shock and louder,
Till the rocks are crush'd to powder,—
Onward sweeps the rolling host!
Heroes of the immortal boast!
Mighty chiefs! eternal shadows!
First flowers of the bloody meadows 50
Which encompass Rome, the mother
Of a people without brother!
Will you sleep when nations' quarrels
Plough the root up of your laurels?
Ye who weep o'er Carthage burning,
Weep not—*strike!* for Rome is mourning!

V

Onward sweep the varied nations!
Famine long hath dealt their rations.
To the wall, with hate and hunger,
Numerous as wolves, and stronger, 60
On they sweep. Oh, glorious city!
Must thou be a theme for pity?
Fight, like your first sire, each Roman!
Alaric was a gentle foeman,
Match'd with Bourbon's black banditti!
Rouse thee, thou eternal city; 66
Rouse thee! Rather give the torch
With thine own hand to thy porch,
Than behold such hosts pollute
Your worst dwelling with their foot. 70

VI

Ah! behold yon bleeding spectre!
Ilion's children find no Hector;
Priam's offspring loved their brother;
Rome's great sire forgot his mother,
When he slew his gallant twin, 75
With inexpiable sin.
See the giant shadow stride
O'er the ramparts high and wide!
When the first o'erleapt thy wall,
Its foundation mourn'd thy fall. 80
Now, though towering like a Babel,
Who to stop his steps are able?
Stalking o'er thy highest dome,
Remus claims his vengeance, Rome!

VII

Now they reach thee in their anger: 85
Fire and smoke and hellish clangour
Are around thee, thou world's wonder!
Death is in thy walls and under.
Now the meeting steel first clashes,
Downward then the ladder crashes, 90
With its iron load all gleaming,
Lying at its foot blaspheming!
Up again! for every warrior
Slain, another climbs the barrier.
Thicker grows the strife: thy ditches 95
Europe's mingling gore enriches.

Rome! although thy wall may perish,
Such manure thy fields will cherish,
Making gay the harvest-home;
But thy hearths, alas! oh, Rome!— 100
Yet be Rome amidst thine anguish,
Fight as thou wast wont to vanquish!

VIII

Yet once more, ye old Penates!
Let not your quench'd hearths be Até's!
Yet again, ye shadowy heroes, 105
Yield not to these stranger Neros!
Though the son who slew his mother
Shed Rome's blood, he was your brother;
'Twas the Roman curb'd the Roman;—
Brennus was a baffled foeman. 110
Yet again, ye saints and martyrs,
Rise! for yours are holier charters!
Mighty gods of temples falling,
Yet in ruin still appalling!
Mightier founders of those altars, 115
True and Christian,—strike the assaulters!
Tiber! Tiber! let thy torrent
Show even nature's self abhorrent.
Let each breathing heart dilated
Turn, as doth the lion baited! 120
Rome be crush'd to one wide tomb,
But be still the Roman's Rome!

BOURBON, ARNOLD, CÆSAR, *and others,
arrive at the foot of the wall.* ARNOLD
is about to plant his ladder.

Bourb. Hold, Arnold! I am first.
Arn. Not so, my lord.
Bourb. Hold, sir, I charge you!
Follow! I am proud
Of such a follower, but will brook no
leader. 125
[BOURBON *plants his ladder, and begins
to mount.*
Now, boys! On! on!
[*A shot strikes him, and* BOURBON *falls.*
Cæs. And off!
Arn. Eternal powers!
The host will be appall'd,—but vengeance!
vengeance!
Bourb. 'Tis nothing—lend me your
hand.
[BOURBON *takes* ARNOLD *by the hand,
and rises; but as he puts his foot on
the step, falls again.*
 Arnold! I am sped.
Conceal my fall—all will go well—conceal
it!
Fling my cloak o'er what will be dust
anon; 130
Let not the soldiers see it.
Arn. You must be
Removed; the aid of——
Bourb. No, my gallant boy!
Death is upon me. But what is *one* life?
The Bourbon's spirit shall command them
still.

Keep them yet ignorant that I am but
clay, 135
Till they are conquerors—then do as you
may.
 Cæs. Would not your highness choose
to kiss the cross?
We have no priest here, but the hilt of
sword
May serve instead:—it did the same for
Bayard.
 Bourb. Thou bitter slave! to name
him at this time! 140
But I deserve it.
 Arn. [*to* CÆSAR]. Villain, hold your
peace!
 Cæs. What, when a Christian dies?
Shall I not offer
A Christian 'Vade in pace'?
 Arn. Silence! Oh!
Those eyes are glazing which o'erlook'd
the world,
And saw no equal.
 Bourb. Arnold, shouldst thou see
France—But hark! hark! the assault
grows warmer—Oh! 145
For but an hour, a minute more of life,
To die within the wall! Hence, Arnold,
hence!
You lose time—they will conquer Rome
without thee.
 Arn. And without *thee.*
 Bourb. Not so; I'll lead them still
In spirit. Cover up my dust, and breathe
not 150
That I have ceased to breathe. Away!
and be
Victorious.
 Arn. But I must not leave thee thus.
 Bourb. You must—farewell—Up! up!
the world is winning.
 [BOURBON *dies.*
 Cæs. [*to* ARNOLD]. Come, count, to
business.
 Arn. True. I'll weep hereafter. 155
[ARNOLD *covers* BOURBON'S *body with a
mantle, mounts the ladder, crying*
The Bourbon! Bourbon! On, boys! Rome
is ours!
 Cæs. Good night, lord constable! thou
wert a man.
[CÆSAR *follows* ARNOLD; *they reach
the battlement;* ARNOLD *and* CÆSAR
are struck down.
 Cæs. A precious somerset! Is your
countship injured?
 Arn. No. [*Remounts the ladder.*
 Cæs. A rare blood-hound, when his
own is heated!
And 'tis no boy's play. Now he strikes
them down! 160
His hand is on the battlement—he grasps it
As though it were an altar; now his foot
Is on it, and——What have we here?—a
Roman? [*A man falls.*

618

The first bird of the covey! he has fallen
On the outside of the nest. Why, how
 now, fellow? 165
Wounded Man. A drop of water!
Cæs. Blood's the only liquid
Nearer than Tiber.
Wounded Man. I have died for Rome.
 [*Dies.*
Cæs. And so did Bourbon, in another
 sense.
Oh, these immortal men! and their great
 motives! 169
But I must after my young charge. He is
By this time i' the forum. Charge! charge!
 [CÆSAR *mounts the ladder; the scene
 closes.*

SCENE II.—*The City.*—*Combats between
the Besiegers and Besieged in the streets.
Inhabitants flying in confusion.*

Enter CÆSAR.

Cæs. I cannot find my hero; he is
 mix'd
With the heroic crowd that now pursue
The fugitives, or battle with the desperate.
What have we here? A cardinal or two
That do not seem in love with martyrdom.
How the old red-shanks scamper! Could
 they doff 6
Their hose as they have doff'd their hats,
 'twould be
A blessing, as a mark the less for plunder.
But let them fly; the crimson kennels now
Will not much stain their stockings, since
 the mire 10
Is of the self-same purple hue.

*Enter a party fighting—*ARNOLD *at the
head of the Besiegers.*

 He comes,
Hand in hand with the mild twins—Gore
 and Glory.
Holla! hold, count!
Arn. Away! they must not rally.
Cæs. I tell thee, be not rash; a golden
 bridge
Is for a flying enemy. I gave thee 15
A form of beauty, and an
Exemption from some maladies of body,
But not of mind, which is not mine to give.
But though I gave the form of Thetis' son,
I dipt thee not in Styx; and 'gainst a foe
I would not warrant thy chivalric heart
More than Pelides' heel; why, then, be
 cautious, 22
And know thyself a mortal still.
Arn. And who
With aught of soul would combat if he were
Invulnerable? That were pretty sport.
Think'st thou I beat for hares when lions
 roar? [ARNOLD *rushes into the
 combat.*
Cæs. A precious sample of humanity!

Well, his blood's up; and if a little's shed,
'Twill serve to curb his fever.
 [ARNOLD *engages with a Roman, who
 retires towards a portico.*
Arn. Yield thee, slave!
I promise quarter.
Rom. That's soon said.
Arn. And done— 30
My word is known.
Rom. So shall be my deeds.
 [*They re-engage.* CÆSAR *comes
 forward.*
Cæs. Why, Arnold! hold thine own:
 thou hast in hand
A famous artisan, a cunning sculptor;
Also a dealer in the sword and dagger.
Not so, my musqueteer; 'twas he who slew
The Bourbon from the wall.
Arn. Ay, did he so? 36
Then he hath carved his monument.
Rom. I yet
May live to carve your better's.
Cæs. Well said, my man of marble!
 Benvenuto,
Thou hast some practice in both ways;
 and he 40
Who slays Cellini will have work'd as hard
As e'er thou didst upon Carrara's blocks.
 [ARNOLD *disarms and wounds* CELLINI,
 *but slightly: the latter draws a pistol,
 and fires; then retires, and disappears
 through the portico.*
Cæs. How farest thou? Thou hast a
 taste, methinks,
Of red Bellona's banquet.
Arn. [*staggers*]. 'Tis a scratch.
Lend me thy scarf. He shall not 'scape me
 thus. 45
Cæs. Where is it?
Arn. In the shoulder, not the sword
 arm—
And that's enough. I am thirsty: would I
 had
A helm of water!
Cæs. That's a liquid now
In requisition, but by no means easiest
To come at.
Arn. And my thirst increases;—but
I'll find a way to quench it.
Cæs. Or be quench'd
Thyself.
Arn. The chance is even; we will throw
The dice thereon. But I lose time in pra-
 ting;
Prithee be quick. [CÆSAR *binds on the
 scarf.*
 And what dost thou so idly?
Why dost not strike?
Cæs. Your old philosophers 55
Beheld mankind, as mere spectators of
The Olympic games. When I behold a
 prize
Worth wrestling for, I may be found a
 Milo.

Arn. Ay, 'gainst an oak.
Cæs. A forest, when it suits me:
I combat with a mass, or not at all. 60
Meantime, pursue thy sport as I do mine;
Which is just now to gaze, since all these
 labourers
Will reap my harvest gratis.
Arn. Thou art still
A fiend!
Cæs. And thou—a man.
Arn. Why, such I fain would show me.
Cæs. True—as men are. 65
Arn. And what is that?
Cæs. Thou feelest and thou see'st.
[*Exit* ARNOLD, *joining in the combat,
 which still continues between detached
 parties. The scene closes.*

SCENE III.—*St. Peter's—The Interior of
 the Church—The Pope at the Altar—
 Priests, &c., crowding in confusion,
 and Citizens flying for refuge, pursued
 by Soldiery.*

 Enter CÆSAR.

A Spanish Soldier. Down with them,
 comrades! seize upon those lamps!
Cleave yon bald-pated shaveling to the
 chine!
His rosary's of gold!
Lutheran Soldier. Revenge! revenge!
Plunder hereafter, but for vengeance
 now—
Yonder stands Anti-Christ!
Cæs. [*interposing*]. How now, schis-
 matic? 5
What wouldst thou?
Luth. Sold. In the holy name of Christ,
Destroy proud Anti-Christ. I am a
 Christian.
Cæs. Yes, a disciple that would make
 the founder
Of your belief renounce it, could he see
Such proselytes. Best stint thyself to
 plunder. 10
Luth. Sold. I say he is the devil.
Cæs. Hush! keep that secret,
Lest he should recognise you for his own.
Luth. Sold. Why would you save him?
 I repeat he is
The devil, or the devil's vicar upon earth.
Cæs. And that's the reason: would you
 make a quarrel 15
With your best friends? You had far best
 be quiet;
His hour is not yet come.
Luth. Sold. That shall be seen!
[*The Lutheran Soldier rushes forward:
 a shot strikes him from one of the
 Pope's Guards, and he falls at the foot
 of the Altar.*
Cæs. [*to the Lutheran*]. I told you so.
Luth. Sold. And will you not avenge
 me?

Cæs. Not I! You know that 'Vengeance
 is the Lord's':
You see he loves no interlopers.
Luth. Sold. [*dying*]. Oh! 20
Had I but slain him, I had gone on high,
Crown'd with eternal glory! Heaven, for-
 give
My feebleness of arm that reach'd him not,
And take thy servant to thy mercy. 'Tis
A glorious triumph still; proud Babylon's
No more; the Harlot of the Seven Hills
Hath changed her scarlet raiment for sack-
 cloth 27
And ashes! [*The Lutheran dies.*
Cæs. Yes, thine own amidst the rest.
Well done, old Babel!
[*The Guards defend themselves desper-
 ately, while the Pontiff escapes, by a
 private passage, to the Vatican and the
 Castle of St. Angelo.*
Cæs. Ha! right nobly battled!
Now, priest! now, soldier! the two great
 professions, 30
Together by the ears and hearts! I have
 not
Seen a more comic pantomime since Titus
Took Jewry. But the Romans had the
 best then;
Now they must take their turn.
Soldiers. He hath escaped!
Follow!
Another Sold. They have barr'd the
 narrow passage up, 35
And it is clogg'd with dead even to the
 door.
Cæs. I am glad he hath escaped: he
 may thank me for't
In part. I would not have his bulls
 abolish'd—
'Twere worth one half our empire: his
 indulgences
Demand some in return,—no, no, he must
 not 40
Fall;—and, besides, his now escape may
 furnish
A future miracle, in future proof
Of his infallibility.
 [*To the Spanish Soldiery.*
 Well, cut-throats!
What do you pause for? If you make not
 haste, 44
There will not be a link of pious gold left.
And *you*, too, Catholics! Would ye return
From such a pilgrimage without a relic?
The very Lutherans have more true devo-
 tion:
See how they strip the shrines!
Soldiers. By holy Peter!
He speaks the truth; the heretics will bear
The best away.
Cæs. And that were shame! Go to!
Assist in their conversion. [*The Soldiers
 disperse; many quit the Church, others
 enter.*

Cæs.　　　　　　　　　　They are gone,
And others come: so flows the wave on
　　wave
Of what these creatures call eternity,
Deeming themselves the breakers of the
　　ocean,　　　　　　　　　　　　55
While they are but its bubbles, ignorant
That foam is their foundation. So another!

Enter OLIMPIA, *flying from the pursuit—*
　　She springs upon the Altar.
Sold. She's mine!
Another Sold. [*opposing the former*].
　　You lie, I track'd her first: and were
　　she
The Pope's niece, I'll not yield her.
　　　　　　　　　　　　　　[*They fight.*
3d Sold. [*advancing towards* OLIMPIA].
　　You may settle
Your claims; I'll make mine good.
　　Olimp.　　　　　　　Infernal slave!　60
You touch me not alive.
3d Sold.　　　　　　Alive or dead!
Olimp. [*embracing a massive crucifix*].
　　Respect your God!
3d Sold. Yes, when he shines in gold.
Girl, you but grasp your dowry.
　　[*As he advances,* OLIMPIA, *with a strong*
　　and sudden effort, casts down the cru-
　　cifix; it strikes the Soldier, who falls.
3d Sold.　　　　　　Oh, great God!
Olimp. Ah! now you recognise him.
3d Sold.　　　　　My brain's crush'd!
Comrades, help, ho! All's darkness!
　　　　　　　　　　　　　　[*He dies.*
Other Soldiers [*coming up*]. Slay her,
　　although she had a thousand lives:
She hath kill'd our comrade.
Olimp.　　　　　Welcome such a death!
You have no life to give, which the worst
　　slave
Would take.　Great God! through thy
　　redeeming blood,
And thy Son's Mother, now receive me as
I would approach thee, worthy her, and
　　him,　　　　　　　　　　　　71
And thee!

　　　　　Enter ARNOLD.

Arn. What do I see? Accursed jackals!
　　Forbear!
Cæs. [*aside and laughing*]. Ha! ha!
　　here's equity! The dogs
Have as much right as he. But to the issue!
Soldiers. Count, she hath slain our
　　comrade.
Arn.　　　　　With what weapon?　75
Sold. The cross, beneath which he is
　　crush'd; behold him
Lie there, more like a worm than man; she
　　cast it
Upon his head.
Arn.　　　Even so; there is a woman
Worthy a brave man's liking. Were ye
　　such,

Ye would have honour'd her. But get ye
　　hence,　　　　　　　　　　　　80
And thank your meanness, other God you
　　have none,
For your existence. Had you touch'd a hair
Of those dishevell'd locks, I would have
　　thinn'd
Your ranks more than the enemy. Away!
Ye jackals! gnaw the bones the lion leaves
But not even these till he permits.
　　A Sold. [*murmuring*].　　　The lion
Might conquer for himself then.
　　Arn. [*cuts him down*].　　Mutineer!
Rebel in hell—you shall obey on earth!
　　　　　　[*The Soldiers assault* ARNOLD.
Arn. Come on! I'm glad on 't! I will
　　show you, slaves,
How you should be commanded, and who
　　led you　　　　　　　　　　　90
First o'er the wall you were so shy to scale,
Until I waved my banners from its height,
As you are bold within it.
　　[ARNOLD *mows down the foremost; the*
　　rest throw down their arms.
Soldiers.　　　　　Mercy! mercy!
Arn. Then learn to grant it. Have I
　　taught you *who*
Led you o'er Rome's eternal battlements?
Soldiers. We saw it, and we know it;
　　yet forgive　　　　　　　　　96
A moment's error in the heat of conquest—
The conquest which you led to.
Arn.　　　　　Get you hence!
Hence to your quarters! you will find them
　　fix'd
In the Colonna palace.
Olimp. [*aside*].　　In my father's　100
　　House!
Arn. [*to the Soldiers*]. Leave your arms;
　　ye have no further need
Of such: the city's render'd. And mark
　　well
You keep your hands clean, or I'll find out
　　a stream
As red as Tiber now runs, for your baptism.
Soldiers [*deposing their arms and depart-*
　　ing]. We obey!
Arn. [*to* OLIMPIA]. Lady, you are safe.
Olimp.　　　　　I should be so,　105
Had I a knife even; but it matters not—
Death hath a thousand gates; and on the
　　marble,
Even at the altar foot, whence I look down
Upon destruction, shall my head be dash'd,
Ere thou ascend it. God forgive thee,
　　man!　　　　　　　　　　　　110
Arn. I wish to merit his forgiveness, and
Thine own, although I have not injured
　　thee.
Olimp. No! Thou hast only sack'd my
　　native land,—
No injury!—and made my father's house
A den of thieves! No injury!—this
　　temple—　　　　　　　　　　　115

Slippery with Roman and with holy gore!
No injury! And now thou wouldst pre-
 serve me,
To be——but that shall never be!
[*She raises her eyes to heaven, folds her
robe round her, and prepares to dash
herself down on the side of the Altar
opposite to that where* ARNOLD *stands.*
Arn. Hold! hold!
I swear.
 Olimp. Spare thine already forfeit soul
A perjury for which even hell would loathe
 thee. 120
I know thee.
 Arn. No, thou know'st me not; I am not
Of these men, though——
 Olimp. I judge thee by thy mates;
It is for God to judge thee as thou art.
I see thee purple with the blood of Rome;
Take mine, 'tis all thou e'er shalt have of
 me, 125
And here, upon the marble of this temple,
Where the baptismal font baptized me
 God's,
I offer him a blood less holy
But not less pure (pure as it left me then,
A redeemed infant) than the holy water
The saints have sanctified!
 [OLIMPIA *waves her hand to* ARNOLD *with
disdain, and dashes herself on the
pavement from the Altar.*
Arn. Eternal God!
I feel thee now! Help! help! She's gone.
 Cæs. [*approaches*]. I am here.
 Arn. Thou! but oh, save her!
 Cæs. [*assisting him to raise* OLIMPIA].
 She hath done it well!
The leap was serious.
 Arn. Oh! she is lifeless!
 Cæs. If
She be so, I have nought to do with that:
The resurrection is beyond me.
 Arn. Slave!
 Cæs. Ay, slave or master, 'tis all one:
 methinks
Good words, however, are as well at times.
 Arn. Words!—Canst thou aid her?
 Cæs. I will try. A sprinkling
Of that same holy water may be useful.
 [*He brings some in his helmet from the
font.*
 Arn. 'Tis mix'd with blood.
 Cæs. There is no cleaner now
In Rome.
 Arn. How pale! how beautiful! how
 lifeless!
Alive or dead, thou essence of all beauty,
I love but thee!
 Cæs. Even so Achilles loved
Penthesilea: with his form it seems 145
You have his heart, and yet it was no soft one.
 Arn. She breathes! But no, 'twas
 nothing, or the last
Faint flutter life disputes with death.

 Cæs. She breathes.
 Arn. Thou say'st it? Then 'tis truth.
 Cæs. You do me right—
The devil speaks truth much oftener than
 he's deem'd: 150
He hath an ignorant audience.
 Arn. [*without attending to him*]. Yes!
 her heart beats.
Alas! that the first beat of the only heart
I ever wish'd to beat with mine should
 vibrate
To an assassin's pulse.
 Cæs. A sage reflection,
But somewhat late i' the day. Where shall
 we bear her? 155
I say she lives.
 Arn. And will she live?
 Cæs. As much
As dust can.
 Arn. Then she is dead!
 Cæs. Bah! bah! You are so,
And do not know it. She will come to life—
Such as you think so, such as you now are:
But we must work by human means.
 Arn. We will 160
Convey her unto the Colonna palace,
Where I have pitch'd my banner.
 Cæs. Come then! raise her up!
 Arn. Softly!
 Cæs. As softly as they bear the dead,
Perhaps because they cannot feel the
 jolting.
 Arn. But doth she live indeed?
 Cæs. Nay, never fear! 165
But, if you rue it after, blame not me.
 Arn. Let her but live!
 Cæs. The spirit of her life
Is yet within her breast, and may revive.
Count! count! I am your servant in all
 things,
And this is a new office:—'tis not oft 170
I am employ'd in such; but you perceive
How stanch a friend is what you call a
 fiend.
On earth you have often only fiends for
 friends;
Now *I* desert not mine. Soft! bear her
 hence,
The beautiful half-clay, and nearly spirit!
I am almost enamour'd of her, as 176
Of old the angels of her earliest sex.
 Arn. Thou!
 Cæs. I! But fear not. I'll not be
 your rival.
 Arn. Rival!
 Cæs. I could be one right formidable;
But since I slew the seven husbands of 180
Tobias' future bride (and after all
Was smoked out by some incense), I have
 laid
Aside intrigue: 'tis rarely worth the trouble
Of gaining, or—what is more difficult—
Getting rid of your prize again; for there's
The rub! at least to mortals.

Arn. Prithee, peace!
Softly! methinks her lips move, her eyes
open!
Cæs. Like stars, no doubt; for that's a
metaphor
For Lucifer and Venus.
Arn. To the palace
Colonna, as I told you!
Cæs. Oh! I know
My way through Rome.
Arn. Now onward, onward! Gently!
[*Exeunt, bearing* OLIMPIA. *The scene
closes.*

PART III

SCENE I.—*A Castle in the Apennines, sur-
rounded by a wild but smiling Country.
Chorus of Peasants singing before the
Gates.*

Chorus.

I

The wars are over,
 The spring is come;
The bride and her lover
 Have sought their home:
They are happy, we rejoice;
Let their hearts have an echo in every voice!

II

The spring is come; the violet's gone,
The first-born child of the early sun:
With us she is but a winter's flower,
The snow on the hills cannot blast her
 bower, 10
And she lifts up her dewy eye of blue
To the youngest sky of the self-same hue.

III

And when the spring comes with her host
Of flowers, that flower beloved the most
Shrinks from the crowd that may confuse
Her heavenly odour and virgin hues. 16

IV

Pluck the others, but still remember
Their herald out of dim December—
The morning star of all the flowers,
The pledge of daylight's lengthen'd hours;
Nor, midst the roses, e'er forget 21
The virgin—virgin violet.

Enter CÆSAR.

Cæs. [*singing*]. The wars are all over,
 Our swords are all idle,
 The steed bites the bridle. 25
The casque's on the wall.
There's rest for the rover;
 But his armour is rusty,
 And the veteran grows crusty,
As he yawns in the hall. 30
 He drinks—but what's drinking?
 A mere pause from thinking!
No bugle awakes him with life-and-
 death call.

Chorus.

But the hound bayeth loudly,
 The boar's in the wood, 35
And the falcon longs proudly
 To spring from her hood:
On the wrist of the noble
 She sits like a crest,
And the air is in trouble 40
 With birds from their nest.

Cæs. Oh! shadow of glory!
 Dim image of war!
But the chase hath no story,
 Her hero no star, 45
Since Nimrod, the founder
 Of empire and chase,
Who made the woods wonder
 And quake for their race.
When the lion was young, 50
 In the pride of his might,
Then 'twas sport for the strong
 To embrace him in fight;
To go forth, with a pine
 For a spear, 'gainst the mammoth,
Or strike through the ravine 56
 At the foaming behemoth;
While man was in stature
 As towers in our time,
The first-born of Nature, 60
 And, like her, sublime!

Chorus.

But the wars are over,
 The spring is come;
The bride and her lover
 Have sought their home; 65
They are happy, and we rejoice;
Let their hearts have an echo from every
 voice! [*Exeunt the Peasantry, singing.*

BEPPO

A VENETIAN STORY

Rosalind. Farewell, Monsieur Traveller: Look you lisp, and wear strange suits: disable all the benefits of your own country; be out of love with your Nativity, and almost chide God for making you that countenance you are; or I will scarce think that you have swam in a *Gondola.—As You Like It*, Act IV., Scene i.

Annotation of the Commentators.

That is, been at *Venice*, which was much visited by the young English gentlemen of those times, and was then what *Paris* is *now*—the seat of all dissoluteness.—S.A.

I

'TIS known, at least it should be, that throughout
 All countries of the Catholic persuasion,
Some weeks before Shrove Tuesday comes about,
 The people take their fill of recreation,
And buy repentance, ere they grow devout,
 However high their rank, or low their station,
With fiddling, feasting, dancing, drinking, masking,
And other things which may be had for asking.

II

The moment night with dusky mantle covers
 The skies (and the more duskily the better),
The time less liked by husbands than by lovers
 Begins, and prudery flings aside her fetter;
And gaiety on restless tiptoe hovers,
 Giggling with all the gallants who beset her;
And there are songs and quavers, roaring, humming,
Guitars, and every other sort of strumming.

III

And there are dresses splendid, but fantastical,
 Masks of all times and nations, Turks and Jews,
And harlequins and clowns, with feats gymnastical,
 Greeks, Romans, Yankee-doodles, and Hindoos;
All kinds of dress, except the ecclesiastical,
 All people, as their fancies hit, may choose,
But no one in these parts may quiz the clergy,—
Therefore take heed, ye Freethinkers! I charge ye.

IV

You'd better walk about begirt with briars,
 Instead of coat and smallclothes, than put on
A single stitch reflecting upon friars,
 Although you swore it only was in fun;
They'd haul you o'er the coals, and stir the fires
 Of Phlegethon with every mother's son,
Nor say one mass to cool the caldron's bubble
That boil'd your bones, unless you paid them double.

V

But saving this, you may put on whate'er
 You like by way of doublet, cape, or cloak,
Such as in Monmouth-street, or in Rag Fair,
 Would rig you out in seriousness or joke;
And even in Italy such places are,
 With prettier name in softer accents spoke,
For, bating Covent Garden, I can hit on
No place that's called 'Piazza' in Great Britain.

VI

This feast is named the Carnival, which being
 Interpreted, implies 'farewell to flesh':
So call'd, because the name and thing agreeing,
 Through Lent they live on fish both salt and fresh.
But why they usher Lent with so much glee in,
 Is more than I can tell, although I guess
'Tis as we take a glass with friends at parting,
In the stage-coach or packet, just at starting.

VII

And thus they bid farewell to carnal
 dishes,
 And solid meats, and highly spiced rag-
 outs,
To live for forty days on ill-dress'd fishes,
 Because they have no sauces to their
 stews;
A thing which causes many 'poohs' and
 'pishes,'
 And several oaths (which would not
 suit the Muse),
From travellers accustom'd from a boy
To eat their salmon, at the least, with soy;

VIII

And therefore humbly I would recom-
 mend
 'The curious in fish-sauce,' before they
 cross
The sea, to bid their cook, or wife, or
 friend,
 Walk or ride to the Strand, and buy in
 gross
(Or if set out beforehand, these may send
 By any means least liable to loss)
Ketchup, Soy, Chili-vinegar, and Harvey,
Or by the Lord! a Lent will well nigh
 starve ye;

IX

That is to say, if your religion's Roman,
 And you at Rome would do as Romans
 do,
According to the proverb,—although no
 man,
If foreign, is obliged to fast; and you
If Protestant, or sickly, or a woman,
 Would rather dine in sin on a ragout—
Dine and be d—d! I don't mean to be
 coarse,
But that's the penalty, to say no worse.

X

Of all the places where the Carnival
 Was most facetious in the days of yore,
For dance, and song, and serenade, and
 ball,
 And masque, and mime, and mystery,
 and more
Than I have time to tell now, or at all,
 Venice the bell from every city bore,—
And at the moment when I fix my story,
That sea-born city was in all her glory.

XI

They've pretty faces yet, those same Vene-
 tians,
 Black eyes, arch'd brows, and sweet ex-
 pressions still;
Such as of old were copied from the
 Grecians,
 In ancient arts by moderns mimick'd ill;

And like so many Venuses of Titian's
 (The best's at Florence—see it, if ye
 will),
They look when leaning over the balcony,
Or stepp'd from out a picture by Gior-
 gione,

XII

Whose tints are truth and beauty at their
 best;
 And when you to Manfrini's palace go,
That picture (howsoever fine the rest)
 Is loveliest to my mind of all the show;
It may perhaps be also to *your* zest,
 And that's the cause I rhyme upon it so:
'Tis but a portrait of his son, and wife,
And self; but *such* a woman! love in life!

XIII

Love in full life and length, not love ideal,
 No, nor ideal beauty, that fine name,
But something better still, so very real,
 That the sweet model must have been
 the same;
A thing that you would purchase, beg, or
 steal,
 Were't not impossible, besides a shame:
The face recalls some face, as 'twere with
 pain,
You once have seen, but ne'er will see
 again.

XIV

One of those forms which flit by us, when
 we
 Are young, and fix our eyes on every
 face;
And, oh! the loveliness at times we see
 In momentary gliding, the soft grace,
The youth, the bloom, the beauty which
 agree,
 In many a nameless being we retrace,
Whose course and home we knew not, nor
 shall know,
Like the lost Pleiad seen no more below.

XV

I said that like a picture by Giorgione
 Venetian women were, and so they *are*,
Particularly seen from a balcony
 (For beauty's sometimes best set off
 afar),
And there, just like a heroine of Goldoni,
 They peep from out the blind, or o'er
 the bar;
And truth to say, they're mostly very
 pretty,
And rather like to show it, more's the
 pity!

XVI

For glances beget ogles, ogles sighs,
 Sighs wishes, wishes words, and words a
 letter,
Which flies on wings of light-heel'd Mer-
 curies,
 Who do such things because they know
 no better;
And then, God knows what mischief may
 arise,
 When love links two young people in
 one fetter,
Vile assignations, and adulterous beds,
Elopements, broken vows, and hearts, and
 heads.

XVII

Shakspeare described the sex in Desde-
 mona
 As very fair, but yet suspect in fame,
And to this day from Venice to Verona
 Such matters may be probably the same,
Except that since those times was never
 known a
 Husband whom mere suspicion could
 inflame
To suffocate a wife no more than twenty,
Because she had a 'cavalier servente.'

XVIII

Their jealousy (if they are ever jealous)
 Is of a fair complexion altogether,
Not like that sooty devil of Othello's,
 Which smothers women in a bed of
 feather,
But worthier of these much more jolly fellows,
 When weary of the matrimonial tether
His head for such a wife no mortal bothers,
But takes at once another, or another's.

XIX

Didst ever see a Gondola? For fear
 You should not, I'll describe it you
 exactly:
'Tis a long cover'd boat that's common here
 Carved at the prow, built lightly, but
 compactly,
Row'd by two rowers, each call'd 'Gon-
 dolier,'
 It glides along the water looking blackly,
Just like a coffin clapt in a canoe,
Where none can make out what you say
 or do.

XX

And up and down the long canals they go,
 And under the Rialto shoot along,
By night and day, all paces, swift or slow,
 And round the theatres, a sable throng,
They wait in their dusk livery of woe,—
 But not to them do woeful things belong,
For sometimes they contain a deal of fun,
Like mourning coaches when the funeral's
 done.

XXI

But to my story.—'Twas some years ago,
 It may be thirty, forty, more or less,
The Carnival was at its height, and so
 Were all kinds of buffoonery and dress;
A certain lady went to see the show,
 Her real name I know not, nor can guess,
And so we'll call her Laura, if you please,
Because it slips into my verse with ease.

XXII

She was not old, nor young, nor at the
 years
 Which certain people call a 'certain age,'
Which yet the most uncertain age appears,
 Because I never heard, nor could engage
A person yet by prayers, or bribes, or tears,
 To name, define by speech, or write on
 page,
The period meant precisely by that word,—
Which surely is exceedingly absurd.

XXIII

Laura was blooming still, had made the
 best
 Of time, and time return'd the compli-
 ment,
And treated her genteelly, so that, dress'd,
 She look'd extremely well where'er she
 went;
A pretty woman is a welcome guest,
 And Laura's brow a frown had rarely
 bent;
Indeed, she shone all smiles, and seem'd to
 flatter
Mankind with her black eyes for looking
 at her.

XXIV

She was a married woman; 'tis convenient,
 Because in Christian countries 'tis a rule
To view their little slips with eyes more
 lenient;
 Whereas if single ladies play the fool
(Unless within the period intervenient
 A well-timed wedding makes the scandal
 cool),
I don't know how they ever can get over it,
Except they manage never to discover it.

XXV

Her husband sail'd upon the Adriatic,
 And made some voyages, too, in other
 seas,
And when he lay in quarantine for pratique
 (A forty days' precaution 'gainst disease),
His wife would mount, at times, her high-
 est attic,
 For thence she could discern the ship
 with ease:
He was a merchant trading to Aleppo,
His name Giuseppe, call'd more briefly,
 Beppo.

XXVI

He was a man as dusky as a Spaniard,
 Sunburnt with travel, yet a portly figure;
Though colour'd, as it were, within a tan-
 yard,
 He was a person both of sense and
 vigour—
A better seaman never yet did man yard;
 And she, although her manners show'd
 no rigour,
Was deem'd a woman of the strictest
 principle,
So much as to be thought almost invin-
 cible.

XXVII

But several years elapsed since they had
 met;
 Some people thought the ship was lost,
 and some
That he had somehow blunder'd into debt,
 And did not like the thought of steering
 home;
And there were several offer'd any bet,
 Or that he would, or that he would not
 come;
For most men (till by losing render'd
 sager)
Will back their own opinions with a wager.

XXVIII

'Tis said that their last parting was pathetic,
 As partings often are, or ought to be,
And their presentiment was quite pro-
 phetic,
 That they should never more each other
 see,
(A sort of morbid feeling, half poetic,
 Which I have known occur in two or
 three,)
When kneeling on the shore upon her sad
 knee
He left this Adriatic Ariadne.

XXIX

And Laura waited long, and wept a little,
 And thought of wearing weeds, as well
 she might;
She almost lost all appetite for victual,
 And could not sleep with ease alone at
 night;
She deem'd the window-frames and shut-
 ters brittle
 Against a daring housebreaker or sprite,
And so she thought it prudent to connect
 her
With a vice-husband, *chiefly* to *protect her*.

XXX

chose, (and what is there they will not
 choose,
 If only you will but oppose their choice?)
Till Beppo should return from his long
 cruise,

And bid once more her faithful heart re-
 joice,
A man some women like, and yet abuse—
 A coxcomb was he by the public voice;
A Count of wealth, they said, as well as
 quality,
And in his pleasures of great liberality.

XXXI

And then he was a Count, and then he
 knew
 Music, and dancing, fiddling, French
 and Tuscan;
The last not easy, be it known to you,
 For few Italians speak the right Etruscan.
He was a critic upon operas, too,
 And knew all niceties of sock and
 buskin;
And no Venetian audience could endure a
Song, scene, or air, when he cried 'secca-
 tura!'

XXXII

His 'bravo' was decisive, for that sound
 Hush'd 'Academie' sigh'd in silent awe;
The fiddlers trembled as he look'd around,
 For fear of some false note's detected
 flaw;
The 'prima donna's' tuneful heart would
 bound,
 Dreading the deep damnation of his
 'bah!'
Soprano, basso, even the contra-alto,
Wish'd him five fathom under the Rialto.

XXXIII

He patronised the Improvisatori,
 Nay, could himself extemporise some
 stanzas,
Wrote rhymes, sang songs, could also tell
 a story,
 Sold pictures, and was skilful in the
 dance as
Italians can be, though in this their glory
 Must surely yield the palm to that which
 France has;
In short, he was a perfect cavaliero,
And to his very valet seem'd a hero.

XXXIV

Then he was faithful too, as well as amor-
 ous,
 So that no sort of female could com-
 plain,
Although they're now and then a little
 clamorous,
 He never put the pretty souls in pain;
His heart was one of those which most
 enamour us,
 Wax to receive, and marble to retain:
He was a lover of the good old school,
Who still become more constant as they
 cool.

XXXV

No wonder such accomplishments should
turn
 A female head, however sage and
steady—
With scarce a hope that Beppo could re-
turn,
 In law he was almost as good as dead, he
Nor sent, nor wrote, nor show'd the least
concern,
 And she had waited several years al-
ready;
And really if a man won't let us know
That he's alive, he's *dead*, or should be so.

XXXVI

Besides, within the Alps, to every woman,
 (Although, God knows, it is a grievous
sin,)
'Tis, I may say, permitted to have *two* men;
 I can't tell who first brought the custom
in,
But 'Cavalier Serventes' are quite com-
mon,
 And no one notices or cares a pin;
And we may call this (not to say the worst)
A *second* marriage which corrupts the *first*.

XXXVII

The word was formerly a 'Cicisbeo,'
 But *that* is now grown vulgar and inde-
cent;
The Spaniards call the person a '*Cortejo*,'
 For the same mode subsists in Spain,
though recent;
In short, it reaches from the Po to Teio,
 And may perhaps at last be o'er the sea
sent:
But Heaven preserve Old England from
such courses!
Or what becomes of damage and divorces?

XXXVIII

However, I still think, with all due defer-
ence
 To the fair *single* part of the creation,
That married ladies should preserve the
preference
 In *tête-à-tête* or general conversation—
And this I say without peculiar reference
 To England, France, or any other
nation—
Because they know the world, and are at
ease,
And being natural, naturally please.

XXXIX

'Tis true, your budding Miss is very charm-
ing,
 But shy and awkward at first coming
out,
So much alarm'd, that she is quite alarm-
ing,

 All Giggle, Blush; half Pertness, and
half Pout;
And glancing at *Mamma*, for fear there's
harm in
 What you, she, it, or they, may be about,
The nursery still lisps out in all they utter—
Besides, they always smell of bread and
butter.

XL

But 'Cavalier Servente' is the phrase
 Used in politest circles to express
This supernumerary slave, who stays
 Close to the lady as a part of dress,
Her word the only law which he obeys.
 His is no sinecure, as you may guess;
Coach, servants, gondola, he goes to call,
And carries fan and tippet, gloves and
shawl.

XLI

With all its sinful doings, I must say,
 That Italy's a pleasant place to me,
Who love to see the Sun shine every day,
 And vines (not nail'd to walls) from
tree to tree
Festoon'd, much like the back scene of a
play,
 Or melodrame, which people flock to
see,
When the first act is ended by a dance
In vineyards copied from the south of
France.

XLII

I like on Autumn evenings to ride out,
 Without being forced to bid my groom be
sure
My cloak is round his middle strapp'd
about,
 Because the skies are not the most
secure;
I know too that, if stopp'd upon my route,
 Where the green alleys windingly allure,
Reeling with grapes red waggons choke
the way,—
In England 'twould be dung, dust, or a dray.

XLIII

I also like to dine on becaficas,
 To see the Sun set, sure he'll rise to-
morrow,
Not through a misty morning twinkling
weak as
 A drunken man's dead eye in maudlin
sorrow,
But with all Heaven t'himself; the day will
break as
 Beauteous as cloudless, nor be forced to
borrow
That sort of farthing candlelight which
glimmers
Where reeking London's smoky caldron
simmers.

XLIV

I love the language, that soft bastard Latin,
 Which melts like kisses from a female
 mouth,
And sounds as if it should be writ on satin,
 With syllables which breathe of the
 sweet South,
And gentle liquids gliding all so pat in,
 That not a single accent seems uncouth,
Like our harsh northern whistling, grunt-
 ing guttural,
Which we're obliged to hiss, and spit, and
 sputter all.

XLV

I like the women too (forgive my folly),
 From the rich peasant cheek of ruddy
 bronze,
And large black eyes that flash on you a
 volley
 Of rays that say a thousand things at once,
To the high dama's brow, more melan-
 choly,
 But clear, and with a wild and liquid
 glance,
Heart on her lips, and soul within her eyes,
Soft as her clime, and sunny as her skies.

XLVI

Eve of the land which still is Paradise!
 Italian beauty! didst thou not inspire
Raphael, who died in thy embrace, and vies
 With all we know of Heaven, or can
 desire,
In what he hath bequeath'd us?—in what
 guise,
 Though flashing from the fervour of the
 lyre,
Would *words* describe thy past and present
 glow,
While yet Canova can create below?

XLVII

'England! with all thy faults I love thee
 still,'
 I said at Calais, and have not forgot it;
I like to speak and lucubrate my fill;
 I like the government (but that is not it);
I like the freedom of the press and quill;
 I like the Habeas Corpus (when we've
 got it);
I like a parliamentary debate,
Particularly when 'tis not too late;

XLVIII

I like the taxes, when they're not too many;
 I like a seacoal fire, when not too dear;
I like a beef-steak, too, as well as any;
 Have no objection to a pot of beer;
I like the weather, when it is not rainy,
 That is, I like two months of every year,
And so God save the Regent, Church, and
 King!
Which means that I like all and everything.

XLIX

Our standing army, and disbanded sea-
 men,
 Poor's rate, Reform, my own, the
 nation's debt,
Our little riots just to show we are free
 men,
 Our trifling bankruptcies in the Gazette,
Our cloudy climate, and our chilly women,
 All these I can forgive, and those forget,
And greatly venerate our recent glories,
And wish they were not owing to the
 Tories.

L

But to my tale of Laura,—for I find
 Digression is a sin, that by degrees
Becomes exceeding tedious to my mind,
 And, therefore, may the reader too dis-
 please—
The gentle reader, who may wax unkind,
 And caring little for the author's ease,
Insist on knowing what he means, a hard
And hapless situation for a bard.

LI

Oh that I had the art of easy writing
 What should be easy reading! could I
 scale
Parnassus, where the Muses sit inditing
 Those pretty poems never known to fail,
How quickly would I print (the world de-
 lighting)
 A Grecian, Syrian, or Assyrian tale;
And sell you, mix'd with western senti-
 mentalism,
Some samples of the finest Orientalism!

LII

But I am but a nameless sort of person,
 (A broken Dandy lately on my travels)
And take for rhyme, to hook my rambling
 verse on,
 The first that Walker's Lexicon unravels,
And when I can't find that, I put a worse
 on,
 Not caring as I ought for critics' cavils;
I've half a mind to tumble down to prose,
But verse is more in fashion—so here goes.

LIII

The Count and Laura made their new
 arrangement,
 Which lasted, as arrangements some-
 times do,
For half a dozen years without estrange-
 ment;
 They had their little differences, too;
Those jealous whiffs, which never any
 change meant;
 In such affairs there probably are few
Who have not had this pouting sort of
 squabble,
From sinners of high station to the rabble.

LIV

But, on the whole, they were a happy pair,
 As happy as unlawful love could make
 them;
The gentleman was fond, the lady fair,
 Their chains so slight, 'twas not worth
 while to break them;
The world beheld them with indulgent air;
 The pious only wish'd 'the devil take
 them!'
He took them not; he very often waits,
And leaves old sinners to be young ones'
 baits.

LV

But they were young: Oh! what without
 our youth
 Would love be! What would youth be
 without love!
Youth lends it joy, and sweetness, vigour,
 truth,
 Heart, soul, and all that seems as from
 above;
But, languishing with years, it grows un-
 couth—
 One of few things experience don't im-
 prove,
Which is, perhaps, the reason why old
 fellows
Are always so preposterously jealous.

LVI

It was the Carnival, as I have said
 Some six and thirty stanzas back, and so
Laura the usual preparations made,
 Which you do when your mind's made
 up to go
To-night to Mrs. Boehm's masquerade,
 Spectator, or partaker in the show;
The only difference known between the
 cases
Is—*here*, we have six weeks of 'varnish'd
 faces.'

LVII

Laura, when dress'd, was (as I sang before)
 A pretty woman as was ever seen,
Fresh as the Angel o'er a new inn door,
 Or frontispiece of a new Magazine,
With all the fashions which the last month
 wore,
 Colour'd, and silver paper leaved be-
 tween
That and the title-page, for fear the press
Should soil with parts of speech the parts
 of dress.

LVIII

They went to the Ridotto;—'tis a hall
 Where people dance, and sup, and dance
 again;
Its proper name, perhaps, were a masqued
 ball,
 But that's of no importance to my
 strain;
'Tis (on a smaller scale) like our Vauxhall,
 Excepting that it can't be spoilt by rain;
The company is 'mix'd' (the phrase I
 quote is
As much as saying they're below your
 notice);

LIX

For a 'mix'd company' implies that, save
 Yourself and friends, and half a hun-
 dred more,
Whom you may bow to without looking
 grave,
 The rest are but a vulgar set, the bore
Of public places, where they basely brave
 The fashionable stare of twenty score
Of well-bred persons, call'd '*The World*;
 but I,
Although I know them, really don't know
 why.

LX

This is the case in England; at least was
 During the dynasty of Dandies, now
Perchance succeeded by some other class
 Of imitated imitators:—how
Irreparably soon decline, alas!
 The demagogues of fashion: all below
Is frail; how easily the world is lost
By love, or war, and now and then by frost!

LXI

Crush'd was Napoleon by the northern
 Thor,
 Who knock'd his army down with icy
 hammer,
Stopp'd by the *elements*, like a whaler, or
 A blundering novice in his new French
 grammar,
Good cause had he to doubt the chance of
 war,
 And as for Fortune—but I dare not
 d—n her,
Because, were I to ponder to infinity,
The more I should believe in her divinity.

LXII

She rules the present, past, and all to be yet,
 She gives us luck in lotteries, love, and
 marriage;
I cannot say that she's done much for me
 yet;
 Not that I mean her bounties to dis-
 parage,
We've not yet closed accounts, and we
 shall see yet
 How much she'll make amends for past
 miscarriage.
Meantime the Goddess I'll no more impor-
 tune,
Unless to thank her when she's made my
 fortune.

LXIII

To turn,—and to return;—the devil take it!
 This story slips for ever through my
 fingers,
Because, just as the stanza likes to make it,
 It needs must be, and so it rather lingers:
This form of verse began, I can't well
 break it,
 But must keep time and tune like public
 singers;
But if I once get through my present measure,
I'll take another when I'm next at leisure.

LXIV

They went to the Ridotto ('tis a place
 To which I mean to go myself to-morrow,
Just to divert my thoughts a little space,
 Because I'm rather hippish, and may
 borrow
Some spirits, guessing at what kind of face
 May lurk beneath each mask; and as
 my sorrow
Slackens its pace sometimes, I'll make, or
 find,
Something shall leave it half an hour
 behind).

LXV

Now Laura moves along the joyous crowd,
 Smiles in her eyes, and simpers on her
 lips;
To some she whispers, others speaks
 aloud;
 To some she curtsies, and to some she
 dips,
Complains of warmth, and this complaint
 avow'd,
 Her lover brings the lemonade, she sips;
She then surveys, condemns, but pities still
Her dearest friends for being dress'd so ill.

LXVI

One has false curls, another too much
 paint,
 A third—where did she buy that fright-
 ful turban?
A fourth's so pale she fears she's going to
 faint,
 A fifth's look's vulgar, dowdyish, and
 suburban,
A sixth's white silk has got a yellow taint,
 A seventh's thin muslin surely will be
 her bane,
And lo! an eighth appears,—'I'll see no
 more!'
For fear, like Banquo's kings, they reach
 a score.

LXVII

Meantime, while she was thus at others
 gazing,
 Others were levelling their looks at her;
She heard the men's half-whisper'd mode
 of praising,

And, till 'twas done, determined not to
 stir;
The women only thought it quite amazing
 That, at her time of life, so many were
Admirers still,—but 'Men are so debased,
Those brazen creatures always suit their
 taste.'

LXVIII

For my part, now, I ne'er could under-
 stand
 Why naughty women—but I won't dis-
 cuss
A thing which is a scandal to the land,
 I only don't see why it should be thus;
And if I were but in a gown and band,
 Just to entitle me to make a fuss,
I'd preach on this till Wilberforce and
 Romilly
Should quote in their next speeches from
 my homily.

LXIX

While Laura thus was seen, and seeing,
 smiling,
 Talking, she knew not why, and cared
 not what,
So that her female friends, with envy broil-
 ing,
 Beheld her airs and triumph, and all
 that;
And well-dress'd males still kept before
 her filing,
 And passing bow'd and mingled with
 her chat;
More than the rest one person seem'd to
 stare
With pertinacity that's rather rare.

LXX

He was a Turk, the colour of mahogany;
 And Laura saw him, and at first was
 glad,
Because the Turks so much admire philo-
 gyny,
 Although their usage of their wives is
 sad;
'Tis said they use no better than a dog any
 Poor woman, whom they purchase like
 a pad;
They have a number, though they ne'er
 exhibit 'em,
Four wives by law, and concubines 'ad
 libitum.'

LXXI

They lock them up, and veil, and guard
 them daily,
 They scarcely can behold their male re-
 lations,
So that their moments do not pass so gaily
 As is supposed the case with northern
 nations;

Confinement, too, must make them look
 quite palely;
 And as the Turks abhor long conversa-
 tions,
Their days are either pass'd in doing
 nothing,
Or bathing, nursing, making love, and
 clothing.

LXXII

They cannot read, and so don't lisp in
 criticism;
Nor write, and so they don't affect the
 muse;
Were never caught in epigram or witticism,
Have no romances, sermons, plays, re-
 views,—
In harams learning soon would make a
 pretty schism,
But luckily these beauties are no 'Blues;'
No bustling Botherby have they to show
 'em
'That charming passage in the last new
 poem:'

LXXIII

No solemn, antique gentleman of rhyme,
 Who having angled all his life for fame,
And getting but a nibble at a time,
 Still fussily keeps fishing on, the same
Small 'Triton of the minnows,' the sublime
 Of mediocrity, the furious tame,
The echo's echo, usher of the school
Of female wits, boy bards—in short, a
 fool!

LXXIV

A stalking oracle of awful phrase,
 The approving 'Good!' (by no means
 GOOD in law),
Humming like flies around the newest
 blaze,
 The bluest of bluebottles you e'er saw,
Teasing with blame, excruciating with
 praise,
 Gorging the little fame he gets all raw,
Translating tongues he knows not even by
 letter,
And sweating plays so middling, bad were
 better.

LXXV

One hates an author that's *all author*,
 fellows
 In foolscap uniforms turn'd up with ink,
So very anxious, clever, fine, and jealous,
 One don't know what to say to them, or
 think,
Unless to puff them with a pair of bellows;
 Of coxcombry's worst coxcombs e'en
 the pink
Are preferable to these shreds of paper,
These unquench'd snuffings of the mid-
night taper.

LXXVI

Of these same we see several, and of others
 Men of the world, who know the worl
 like men,
Scott, Rogers, Moore, and all the bette
 brothers,
 Who think of something else besides th
 pen;
But for the children of the 'mighty mo
 ther's,'
 The would-be wits, and can't-be gentle
 men,
I leave them to their daily 'tea is ready,'
Smug coterie, and literary lady.

LXXVII

The poor dear Mussulwomen whom
 mention
 Have none of these instructive pleasan
 people,
And *one* would seem to them a new inven
 tion,
 Unknown as bells within a Turkisl
 steeple;
I think 'twould almost be worth while t
 pension
 (Though best-sown projects very ofte
 reap ill)
A missionary author, just to preach
Our Christian usage of the parts of speech

LXXVIII

No chemistry for them unfolds her gases
 No metaphysics are let loose in lectures
No circulating library amasses
 Religious novels, moral tales, and stric
 tures
Upon the living manners, as they pass us
 No exhibition glares with annual pic
 tures;
They stare not on the stars from out thei
 attics,
Nor deal (thank God for that!) in mathe
 matics.

LXXIX

Why I thank God for that is no grea
 matter,
 I have my reasons, you no doubt sup
 pose,
And as, perhaps, they would not high
 flatter,
 I'll keep them for my life (to come) i
 prose;
I fear I have a little turn for satire,
 And yet methinks the older that on
 grows
Inclines us more to laugh than scold
 though laughter
Leaves us so doubly serious shortly after

632

LXXX

Oh, mirth and innocence! Oh, milk and
 water!
Ye happy mixtures of more happy days!
In these sad centuries of sin and slaughter,
 Abominable Man no more allays
His thirst with such pure beverage. No
 matter,
 I love you both, and both shall have my
 praise:
Oh, for old Saturn's reign of sugar candy!—
Meantime I drink to your return in brandy.

LXXXI

Our Laura's Turk still kept his eyes upon
 her,
 Less in the Mussulman than Christian
 way,
Which seems to say, 'Madam, I do you
 honour,
 And while I please to stare, you'll please
 to stay.'
Could staring win a woman, this had won
 her,
 But Laura could not thus be led astray;
She had stood fire too long and well, to
 boggle
Even at this stranger's most outlandish ogle.

LXXXII

The morning now was on the point of
 breaking,
 A turn of time at which I would advise
Ladies who have been dancing, or partaking
 In any other kind of exercise,
To make their preparations for forsaking
 The ball-room ere the sun begins to rise,
Because when once the lamps and candles
 fail,
His blushes make them look a little pale.

LXXXIII

've seen some balls and revels in my time,
 And stay'd them over for some silly
 reason,
And then I look'd (I hope it was no crime)
 To see what lady best stood out the
 season,
And though I've seen some thousands in
 their prime,
 Lovely and pleasing, and who still may
 please on,
never saw but one (the stars withdrawn)
Whose bloom could after dancing dare
 the dawn.

LXXXIV

The name of this Aurora I'll not mention,
 Although I might, for she was nought
 to me
More than that patent work of God's
 invention,
 A charming woman, whom we like to
 see;

But writing names would merit repre-
 hension,
 Yet if you like to find out this fair *she*,
At the next London or Parisian ball
You still may mark her cheek out-bloom-
 ing all.

LXXXV

Laura, who knew it would not do at all
 To meet the daylight after seven hours'
 sitting
Among three thousand people at a ball,
 To make her curtsy thought it right and
 fitting;
The Count was at her elbow with her
 shawl,
 And they the room were on the point of
 quitting,
When lo! those cursed gondoliers had got
Just in the very place where they *should not*.

LXXXVI

In this they're like our coachmen, and the
 cause
 Is much the same—the crowd, and pull-
 ing, hauling,
With blasphemies enough to break their
 jaws,
 They make a never intermitted bawling.
At home, our Bow-street gemmen keep
 the laws,
 And here a sentry stands within your
 calling;
But for all that, there is a deal of swearing,
And nauseous words past mentioning or
 bearing.

LXXXVII

The Count and Laura found their boat at
 last,
 And homeward floated o'er the silent
 tide,
Discussing all the dances gone and past;
 The dancers and their dresses, too,
 beside;
Some little scandals eke; but all aghast
 (As to their palace-stairs the rowers
 glide)
Sate Laura by the side of her Adorer,
When lo! the Mussulman was there before
 her.

LXXXVIII

'Sir,' said the Count, with brow exceeding
 grave,
 'Your unexpected presence here will
 make
It necessary for myself to crave
 Its import? But perhaps 'tis a mistake;
I hope it is so; and, at once to waive
 All compliment, I hope so for *your* sake;
You understand my meaning, or you *shall*.'
'Sir,' (quoth the Turk) ''tis no mistake at
 all:

633

BEPPO

LXXXIX

'That lady is *my wife*!' Much wonder paints
 The lady's changing cheek, as well it
 might;
But where an Englishwoman sometimes
 faints,
 Italian females don't do so outright;
They only call a little on their saints,
 And then come to themselves, almost or
 quite;
Which saves much hartshorn, salts, and
 sprinkling faces,
And cutting stays, as usual in such cases.

XC

She said,—what could she say? Why, not
 a word:
 But the Count courteously invited in
The stranger, much appeased by what he
 heard:
 'Such things, perhaps, we'd best discuss
 within,'
Said he; 'don't let us make ourselves absurd
 In public, by a scene, nor raise a din,
For then the chief and only satisfaction
Will be much quizzing on the whole trans-
 action.'

XCI

They enter'd, and for coffee call'd—it came,
 A beverage for Turks and Christians
 both,
Although the way they make it's not the
 same.
 Now Laura, much recover'd, or less loth
To speak, cries 'Beppo! what's your pagan
 name?
 Bless me! your beard is of amazing
 growth!
And how came you to keep away so long?
Are you not sensible 'twas very wrong?

XCII

'And are you *really*, *truly*, now a Turk?
 With any other women did you wive?
Is't true they use their fingers for a fork?
 Well, that's the prettiest shawl—as I'm
 alive!
You'll give it me? They say you eat no
 pork.
 And how so many years did you con-
 trive
To—Bless me! did I ever? No, I never
Saw a man grown so yellow! How's your
 liver?

XCIII

'Beppo! that beard of yours becomes you
 not;
 It shall be shaved before you're a day
 older:
Why do you wear it? Oh! I had forgot—
 Pray don't you think the weather here
 is colder?

How do I look? You shan't stir from th
 spot
 In that queer dress, for fear that som
 beholder
Should find you out, and make the stor
 known.
How short your hair is! Lord! how gre
 it's grown!'

XCIV

What answer Beppo made to these de
 mands
 Is more than I know. He was cast awa
About where Troy stood once, an
 nothing stands;
 Became a slave of course, and for his pa
Had bread and bastinadoes, till son
 bands
 Of pirates landing in a neighbouring ba
He join'd the rogues and prosper'd, an
 became
A renegado of indifferent fame.

XCV

But he grew rich, and with his riches gre
 so
 Keen the desire to see his home again
He thought himself in duty bound to do s
 And not be always thieving on the mai
Lonely he felt, at times, as Robin Cruso
 And so he hired a vessel come fro
 Spain,
Bound for Corfu: she was a fine polacc
Mann'd with twelve hands, and laden wi
 tobacco.

XCVI

Himself, and much (Heaven knows ho
 gotten!) cash,
 He then embark'd, with risk of life an
 limb,
And got clear off, although the attem
 was rash;
 He said that *Providence* protected him-
For my part, I say nothing—lest we clas
 In our opinions:—well, the ship was trin
Set sail, and kept her reckoning fairly o
Except three days of calm when off Cap
 Bonn.

XCVII

They reach'd the island, he transferr'd h
 lading
 And self and live stock to another botton
And pass'd for a true Turkey-merchan
 trading
 With goods of various names, but I'
 forgot 'em.
However, he got off by this evading,
 Or else the people would perhaps hav
 shot him;
And thus at Venice landed to reclaim
His wife, religion, house, and Christia
 name.

XCVIII

His wife received, the patriarch re-bap-
tized him
 (He made the church a present, by the
 way);
He then threw off the garments which dis-
guised him,
 And borrow'd the Count's smallclothes
 for a day:
His friends the more for his long absence
prized him,
 Finding he'd wherewithal to make them
 gay,
With dinners, where he oft became the
 laugh of them,
For stories—but *I* don't believe the half
 of them.

XCIX

Whate'er his youth had suffer'd, his old
age
 With wealth and talking made him some
 amends;
Though Laura sometimes put him in a
rage,
 I've heard the Count and he were always
 friends.
My pen is at the bottom of a page,
 Which being finish'd, here the story
 ends;
'Tis to be wish'd it had been sooner
 done,
But stories somehow lengthen when be-
gun.

DON JUAN

'Difficile est propriè communia dicere.'—HORACE.

'Dost thou think, because thou art virtuous, there shall be no more cakes and ale? Yes, by Saint Anne, and ginger shall be hot i' the mouth, too!'—SHAKESPEARE, *Twelfth Night, or What You Will.*

CANTO THE FIRST*

FRAGMENT

On the back of the Poet's MS. of Canto I.

I WOULD to heaven that I were so much
 clay,
 As I am blood, bone, marrow, passion,
 feeling—
Because at least the past were pass'd
 away—
 And for the future—(but I write this
 reeling,
Having got drunk exceedingly to-day,
 So that I seem to stand upon the ceiling)
I say—the future is a serious matter—
And so—for God's sake—hock and soda-
 water!

DEDICATION

I

BOB SOUTHEY! You're a poet—Poet-
laureate,
 And representative of all the race;
Although 'tis true that you turn'd out a
 Tory at
 Last,—yours has lately been a common
 case;
And now, my Epic Renegade! what are
 ye at?
 With all the Lakers, in and out of place?
A nest of tuneful persons, to my eye
Like 'four and twenty Blackbirds in a pye;

II

'Which pye being open'd they began to
 sing'
 (This old song and new simile holds
 good),
'A dainty dish to set before the King,'
 Or Regent, who admires such kind of
 food;—
And Coleridge, too, has lately taken wing,
 But like a hawk encumber'd with his
 hood,—
Explaining metaphysics to the nation—
I wish he would explain his Explanation.

III

You, Bob! are rather insolent, you know,
 At being disappointed in your wish
To supersede all warblers here below,
 And be the only Blackbird in the dish;
And then you overstrain yourself, or so,
 And tumble downward like the flying fish
Gasping on deck, because you soar too
 high, Bob,
And fall, for lack of moisture quite a-dry,
 Bob!

IV

And Wordsworth, in a rather long 'Excur-
 sion'
 (I think the quarto holds five hundred
 pages),
Has given a sample from the vasty version
 Of his new system to perplex the sages;

* [Begun at Venice September 6; finished Nov. 1,
1818.'—B.]

635

'Tis poetry—at least by his assertion,
 And may appear so when the dog-star
 rages—
And he who understands it would be able
To add a story to the Tower of Babel.

V

You—Gentlemen! by dint of long se-
 clusion
 From better company, have kept your
 own
At Keswick, and, through still continued
 fusion
 Of one another's minds, at last have
 grown
To deem as a most logical conclusion,
 That Poesy has wreaths for you alone:
There is a narrowness in such a notion,
 Which makes me wish you'd change your
 lakes for ocean.

VI

I would not imitate the petty thought,
 Nor coin my self-love to so base a vice,
For all the glory your conversion brought,
 Since gold alone should not have been
 its price.
You have your salary: was't for that you
 wrought?
 And Wordsworth has his place in the
 Excise.
You're shabby fellows—true—but poets
 still,
And duly seated on the immortal hill.

VII

Your bays may hide the baldness of your
 brows—
 Perhaps some virtuous blushes;—let
 them go—
To you I envy neither fruit nor boughs—
 And for the fame you would engross
 below,
The field is universal, and allows
 Scope to all such as feel the inherent
 glow:
Scott, Rogers, Campbell, Moore, and
 Crabbe, will try
'Gainst you the question with posterity.

VIII

For me, who, wandering with pedestrian
 Muses,
 Contend not with you on the winged
 steed,
I wish your fate may yield ye, when she
 chooses,
 The fame you envy, and the skill you
 need;
And recollect a poet nothing loses
 In giving to his brethren their full meed
Of merit, and complaint of present days
Is not the certain path to future praise.

IX

He that reserves his laurels for posterity
 (Who does not often claim the brig[ht]
 reversion)
Has generally no great crop to spare it, b[
 Being only injured by his own assertio[n]
And although here and there som[e]
 glorious rarity
 Arise like Titan from the sea's immersio[n]
The major part of such appellants go
To—God knows where—for no one els[e]
 can know.

X

If, fallen in evil days on evil tongues,
 Milton appealed to the Avenger, Time[
If Time, the Avenger, execrates his wrong[
 And makes the word 'Miltonic' mea[n]
 'sublime,'
He deign'd not to belie his soul in song[
 Nor turn his very talent to a crime;
He did not loathe the Sire to laud the So[n]
But closed the tyrant-hater he begun.

XI

Think'st thou, could he—the blind O[ld]
 Man—arise,
 Like Samuel from the grave, to freez[e]
 once more
The blood of monarchs with his propheci[es]
 Or be alive again—again all hoar
With time and trials, and those helples[s]
 eyes,
 And heartless daughters—worn—an[d]
 pale—and poor;
Would *he* adore a sultan? *he* obey
The intellectual eunuch Castlereagh?

XII

Cold-blooded, smooth-faced, placid mi[s]
 creant!
 Dabbling its sleek young hands in Erin[
 gore,
And thus for wider carnage taught to pan[t,]
 Transferr'd to gorge upon a sister shor[e]
The vulgarest tool that Tyranny could wa[nt]
 With just enough of talent, and no mor[e]
To lengthen fetters by another fix'd,
And offer poison long already mix'd.

XIII

An orator of such set trash of phrase
 Ineffably—legitimately vile,
That even its grossest flatterers dare n[o]
 praise,
 Nor foes—all nations—condescend t[o]
 smile;
Not even a sprightly blunder's spark ca[n]
 blaze
 From that Ixion grindstone's ceasele[ss]
 toil,
That turns and turns to give the world [a]
 notion
Of endless torments and perpetual motio[n]

XIV

A bungler even in its disgusting trade,
 And botching, patching, leaving still be-
 hind
Something of which its masters are afraid,
 States to be curb'd, and thoughts to be
 confined,
Conspiracy or Congress to be made—
 Cobbling at manacles for all mankind—
A tinkering slave-maker, who mends old
 chains,
With God and man's abhorrence for its
 gains.

XV

If we may judge of matter by the mind,
 Emasculated to the marrow It
Hath but two objects, how to serve, and
 bind,
 Deeming the chain it wears even men
 may fit,
Eutropius of its many masters,—blind
 To worth as freedom, wisdom as to wit,
Fearless—because no feeling dwells in ice,
Its very courage stagnates to a vice.

XVI

Where shall I turn me not to view its bonds,
 For I will never feel them;—Italy!
Thy late reviving Roman soul desponds
 Beneath the lie this State-thing breathed
 o'er thee—
Thy clanking chain, and Erin's yet green
 wounds,
 Have voices—tongues to cry aloud for
 me.
Europe has slaves, allies, kings, armies still,
And Southey lives to sing them very ill.

XVII

Meantime, Sir Laureate, I proceed to
 dedicate,
 In honest simple verse, this song to you.
And, if in flattering strains I do not predi-
 cate,
 'Tis that I still retain my 'buff and blue;'
My politics as yet are all to educate:
 Apostasy's so fashionable, too,
To keep one creed's a task grown quite
 Herculean:
Is it not so, my Tory, ultra-Julian?
 VENICE, September 16, 1818.

I

I WANT a hero: an uncommon want,
 When every year and month sends forth
 a new one,
Till, after cloying the gazettes with cant,
 The age discovers he is not the true one:
Of such as these I should not care to vaunt,
 I'll therefore take our ancient friend
 Don Juan—
We all have seen him, in the pantomime,
Sent to the devil somewhat ere his time.

II

Vernon, the butcher Cumberland, Wolfe,
 Hawke,
 Prince Ferdinand, Granby, Burgoyne,
 Keppel, Howe,
Evil and good, have had their tithe of talk,
 And fill'd their sign-posts then, like
 Wellesley now;
Each in their turn like Banquo's monarchs
 stalk,
 Followers of fame, 'nine farrow' of that
 sow:
France, too, had Buonaparté and Du-
 mourier
Recorded in the Moniteur and Courier.

III

Barnave, Brissot, Condorcet, Mirabeau,
 Pétion, Clootz, Danton, Marat, La
 Fayette,
Were French, and famous people, as we
 know;
 And there were others, scarce forgotten
 yet,
Joubert, Hoche, Marceau, Lannes, De-
 saix, Moreau,
 With many of the military set,
Exceedingly remarkable at times,
But not at all adapted to my rhymes.

IV

Nelson was once Britannia's god of war,
 And still should be so, but the tide is
 turn'd;
There's no more to be said of Trafalgar,
 'Tis with our hero quietly inurn'd;
Because the army's grown more popular,
 At which the naval people are con-
 cern'd,
Besides, the prince is all for the land-
 service,
Forgetting Duncan, Nelson, Howe, and
 Jervis.

V

Brave men were living before Agamemnon
 And since, exceeding valorous and sage,
A good deal like him too, though quite the
 same none;
 But then they shone not on the poet's
 page,
And so have been forgotten:—I condemn
 none,
 But can't find any in the present age
Fit for my poem (that is, for my new one);
So, as I said, I'll take my friend Don Juan.

VI

Most epic poets plunge 'in medias res'
 (Horace makes this the heroic turnpike
 road),
And then your hero tells, whene'er you
 please,
 What went before—by way of episode,

637

While seated after dinner at his ease,
 Beside his mistress in some soft abode,
Palace, or garden, paradise, or cavern,
Which serves the happy couple for a tavern.

VII

That is the usual method, but not mine—
 My way is to begin with the beginning;
The regularity of my design
 Forbids all wandering as the worst of
 sinning,
And therefore I shall open with a line
 (Although it cost me half an hour in
 spinning)
Narrating somewhat of Don Juan's father,
And also of his mother, if you'd rather.

VIII

In Seville was he born, a pleasant city,
 Famous for oranges and women—he
Who has not seen it will be much to pity,
 So says the proverb—and I quite agree;
Of all the Spanish towns is none more
 pretty,
 Cadiz, perhaps—but that you soon may
 see:—
Don Juan's parents lived beside the river,
A noble stream, and call'd the Guadal-
 quivir.

IX

His father's name was José—*Don*, of
 course,
 A true Hidalgo, free from every stain
Of Moor or Hebrew blood, he traced his
 source
 Through the most Gothic gentlemen of
 Spain;
A better cavalier ne'er mounted horse,
 Or, being mounted, e'er got down again,
Than José, who begot our hero, who
Begot—but that's to come——Well, to
 renew:

X

His mother was a learned lady, famed
 For every branch of every science
 known—
In every Christian language ever named,
 With virtues equall'd by her wit alone:
She made the cleverest people quite
 ashamed,
 And even the good with inward envy
 groan,
Finding themselves so very much exceeded
In their own way by all the things that
 she did.

XI

Her memory was a mine: she knew by heart
 All Calderon and greater part of Lopé,
So that if any actor miss'd his part
 She could have served him for the
 prompter's copy;

For her Feinagle's were an useless art,
 And he himself obliged to shut up shop
 —he
Could never make a memory so fine as
That which adorn'd the brain of Donn
 Inez.

XII

Her favourite science was the mathe
 matical,
 Her noblest virtue was her magnanim
 ity;
Her wit (she sometimes tried at wit) wa
 Attic all,
 Her serious sayings darken'd to sub
 limity;
In short, in all things she was fairly wha
 I call
 A prodigy—her morning dress wa
 dimity,
Her evening silk, or, in the summer
 muslin,
And other stuffs, with which I won't sta
 puzzling.

XIII

She knew the Latin—that is, 'the Lord'
 prayer,'
 And Greek—the alphabet—I'm nearl
 sure;
She read some French romances here an
 there,
 Although her mode of speaking was no
 pure;
For native Spanish she had no great care
 At least her conversation was obscure
Her thoughts were theorems, her words
 problem,
As if she deem'd that mystery would en
 noble 'em.

XIV

She liked the English and the Hebrew
 tongue,
 And said there was analogy betwee
 'em;
She proved it somehow out of sacred song
 But I must leave the proofs to thos
 who've seen 'em,
But this I heard her say, and can't be wrong
 And all may think which way their judg
 ments lean 'em,
"'Tis strange—the Hebrew noun whic
 means "I am,"
The English always use to govern d—n."

XV

Some women use their tongues—sh
 look'd a lecture,
 Each eye a sermon, and her brow
 homily,
An all-in-all sufficient self-director,
 Like the lamented late Sir Samue
 Romilly,

The Law's expounder, and the State's cor-
 rector,
 Whose suicide was almost an anomaly—
One sad example more, that 'All is va-
 nity,'—
(The jury brought their verdict in 'In-
 sanity.')

XVI

In short, she was a walking calculation,
 Miss Edgeworth's novels stepping from
 their covers,
Or Mrs. Trimmer's books on education,
 Or 'Cœlebs' Wife' set out in quest of
 lovers,
Morality's prim personification,
 In which not Envy's self a flaw discovers;
To others' share let 'female errors fall,'
For she had not even one—the worst of all.

XVII

Oh! she was perfect past all parallel—
 Of any modern female saint's com-
 parison;
So far above the cunning powers of hell,
 Her guardian angel had given up his
 garrison;
Even her minutest motions went as well
 As those of the best time-piece made by
 Harrison:
In virtues nothing earthly could surpass her,
Save thine 'incomparable oil,' Macassar!

XVIII

Perfect she was, but as perfection is
 Insipid in this naughty world of ours,
Where our first parents never learn'd to
 kiss
 Till they were exiled from their earlier
 bowers,
Where all was peace, and innocence, and
 bliss
 (I wonder how they got through the
 twelve hours),
Don José, like a lineal son of Eve,
Went plucking various fruit without her
 leave.

XIX

He was a mortal of the careless kind,
 With no great love for learning, or the
 learn'd,
Who chose to go where'er he had a mind,
 And never dream'd his lady was con-
 cern'd;
The world, as usual, wickedly inclined
 To see a kingdom or a house o'erturn'd,
Whisper'd he had a mistress, some said
 two,
But for domestic quarrels one will do.

XX

Now Donna Inez had, with all her merit,
 A great opinion of her own good
 qualities;
Neglect, indeed, requires a saint to bear it,
 And such, indeed, she was in her moral-
 ities;
But then she had a devil of a spirit,
 And sometimes mix'd up fancies with
 realities,
And let few opportunities escape
Of getting her liege lord into a scrape.

XXI

This was an easy matter with a man
 Oft in the wrong, and never on his
 guard;
And even the wisest, do the best they can,
 Have moments, hours, and days, so un-
 prepared,
That you might 'brain them with their
 lady's fan';
 And sometimes ladies hit exceeding
 hard,
And fans turn into falchions in fair hands,
And why and wherefore no one under-
 stands.

XXII

'Tis pity learned virgins ever wed
 With persons of no sort of education,
Or gentlemen, who, though well born and
 bred,
 Grow tired of scientific conversation;
I don't choose to say much upon this head,
 I'm a plain man, and in a single station,
But—Oh! ye lords of ladies intellectual,
Inform us truly have they not hen-peck'd
 you all?

XXIII

Don José and his lady quarrell'd—why,
 Not any of the many could divine,
Though several thousand people chose to
 try,
 'Twas surely no concern of theirs nor
 mine;
I loathe that low vice—curiosity;
 But if there's anything in which I shine,
'Tis in arranging all my friends' affairs,
Not having, of my own, domestic cares.

XXIV

And so I interfered, and with the best
 Intentions, but their treatment was not
 kind;
I think the foolish people were possess'd,
 For neither of them could I ever find,
Although their porter afterwards con-
 fess'd—
 But that's no matter, and the worst's
 behind,
For little Juan o'er me threw, down stairs,
A pail of housemaid's water unawares.

XXV

A little curly-headed, good-for-nothing,
 And mischief-making monkey from his
 birth;
His parents ne'er agreed except in doting
 Upon the most unquiet imp on earth;
Instead of quarrelling, had they been but
 both in
 Their senses, they'd have sent young
 master forth
To school, or had him soundly whipp'd at
 home,
To teach him manners for the time to
 come.

XXVI

Don José and the Donna Inez led
 For some time an unhappy sort of life,
Wishing each other, not divorced, but
 dead;
 They lived respectably as man and wife,
Their conduct was exceedingly well-bred,
 And gave no outward signs of inward
 strife,
Until at length the smother'd fire broke out,
And put the business past all kind of doubt.

XXVII

For Inez call'd some druggists and phy-
 sicians,
 And tried to prove her loving lord was
 mad,
But as he had some lucid intermissions,
 She next decided he was only *bad*;
Yet when they ask'd her for her deposi-
 tions,
 No sort of explanation could be had,
Save that her duty both to man and God
Required this conduct—which seem'd very
 odd.

XXVIII

She kept a journal, where his faults were
 noted,
 And open'd certain trunks of books and
 letters,
All which might, if occasion served, be
 quoted;
 And then she had all Seville for abettors,
Besides her good old grandmother (who
 doted);
 The hearers of her case became re-
 peaters,
Then advocates, inquisitors, and judges,
Some for amusement, others for old
 grudges.

XXIX

And then this best and meekest woman
 bore
 With such serenity her husband's woes,
Just as the Spartan ladies did of yore,
 Who saw their spouses kill'd, and nobly
 chose

Never to say a word about them more—
 Calmly she heard each calumny tha
 rose,
And saw *his* agonies with such sublimity
That all the world exclaim'd, 'What mag
 nanimity!'

XXX

No doubt this patience, when the world i
 damning us,
 Is philosophic in our former friends;
'Tis also pleasant to be deem'd magnani
 mous,
 The more so in obtaining our own ends
And what the lawyers call a '*malu
 animus*'
 Conduct like this by no means compre
 hends:
Revenge in person's certainly no virtue,
But then 'tis not *my* fault, if *others* hur
 you.

XXXI

And if our quarrels should rip up ol
 stories,
 And help them with a lie or two addi
 tional,
I'm not to blame, as you well know—no
 more is
 Any one else—they were become tradi
 tional;
Besides, their resurrection aids our glorie
 By contrast, which is what we just wer
 wishing all:
And science profits by this resurrection—
Dead scandals form good subjects for dis
 section.

XXXII

Their friends had tried at reconciliation,
 Then their relations, who made matter
 worse,
('Twere hard to tell upon a like occasion
 To whom it may be best to have re
 course—
I can't say much for friend or yet relation)
 The lawyers did their utmost for divorce
But scarce a fee was paid on either side
Before, unluckily, Don José died.

XXXIII

He died: and most unluckily, because,
 According to all hints I could collect
From counsel learned in those kinds o
 laws
 (Although their talk's obscure and cir
 cumspect),
His death contrived to spoil a charming
 cause;
 A thousand pities also with respect
To public feeling, which on this occasion
Was manifested in a great sensation.

XXXIV

But ah! he died; and buried with him lay
 The public feeling and the lawyers' fees:
His house was sold, his servants sent
 away,
 A Jew took one of his two mistresses,
A priest the other—at least so they say:
 I ask'd the doctors after his disease—
He died of the slow fever called the
 tertian,
And left his widow to her own aversion.

XXXV

Yet José was an honourable man,
 That I must say, who knew him very
 well;
Therefore his frailties I'll no further scan,
 Indeed there were not many more to
 tell:
And if his passions now and then outran
 Discretion, and were not so peaceable
As Numa's (who was also named Pompi-
 lius),
He had been ill brought up, and was born
 bilious.

XXXVI

Whate'er might be his worthlessness or
 worth,
 Poor fellow! he had many things to
 wound him,
Let's own—since it can do no good on
 earth—
 It was a trying moment that which
 found him
Standing alone beside his desolate hearth,
 Where all his household gods lay
 shiver'd round him:
No choice was left his feelings or his pride,
Save death or Doctors' Commons—so he
 died.

XXXVII

Dying intestate, Juan was sole heir
 To a chancery suit, and messuages and
 lands,
Which, with a long minority and care,
 Promised to turn out well in proper
 hands:
Inez became sole guardian, which was fair,
 And answer'd but to nature's just de-
 mands;
An only son left with an only mother
Is brought up much more wisely than
 another.

XXXVIII

Sagest of women, even of widows, she
 Resolved that Juan should be quite a
 paragon,
And worthy of the noblest pedigree:
 (His sire was of Castile, his dam from
 Aragon).

Then for accomplishments of chivalry,
 In case our lord the king should go to
 war again,
He learn'd the arts of riding, fencing, gun-
 nery,
And how to scale a fortress—or a nunnery.

XXXIX

But that which Donna Inez most desired,
 And saw into herself each day before all
The learned tutors whom for him she
 hired,
 Was, that his breeding should be strictly
 moral:
Much into all his studies she inquired,
 And so they were submitted first to her,
 all,
Arts, sciences, no branch was made a
 mystery
To Juan's eyes, excepting natural history.

XL

The languages, especially the dead,
 The sciences, and most of all the
 abstruse,
The arts, at least all such as could be said
 To be the most remote from common
 use,
In all these he was much and deeply read:
 But not a page of anything that's loose,
Or hints continuation of the species,
Was ever suffer'd, lest he should grow
 vicious.

XLI

His classic studies made a little puzzle,
 Because of filthy loves of gods and god-
 desses,
Who in the earlier ages raised a bustle,
 But never put on pantaloons or bodices;
His reverend tutors had at times a tussle,
 And for their Æneids, Iliads, and
 Odysseys,
Were forced to make an odd sort of
 apology,
For Donna Inez dreaded the Mythology.

XLII

Ovid's a rake, as half his verses show him,
 Anacreon's morals are a still worse
 sample,
Catullus scarcely has a decent poem,
 I don't think Sappho's Ode a good
 example,
Although Longinus tells us there is no
 hymn
 Where the sublime soars forth on wings
 more ample;
But Virgil's songs are pure, except that
 horrid one
Beginning with 'Formosum Pastor Cory-
 don.'

XLIII

Lucretius' irreligion is too strong
 For early stomachs, to prove whole-
 some food;
I can't help thinking Juvenal was wrong,
 Although no doubt his real intent was
 good,
For speaking out so plainly in his song,
 So much indeed as to be downright
 rude;
And then what proper person can be
 partial
To all those nauseous epigrams of Martial?

XLIV

Juan was taught from out the best edition,
 Expurgated by learned men, who place,
Judiciously, from out the schoolboy's
 vision,
 The grosser parts; but, fearful to deface
Too much their modest bard by this
 omission,
 And pitying sore his mutilated case,
They only add them all in an appendix,
Which saves, in fact, the trouble of an
 index;

XLV

For there we have them all 'at one fell
 swoop,'
 Instead of being scatter'd through the
 pages;
They stand forth marshall'd in a handsome
 troop,
 To meet the ingenuous youth of future
 ages,
Till some less rigid editor shall stoop
 To call them back into their separate
 cages,
Instead of standing staring all together,
Like garden gods—and not so decent
 either.

XLVI

The Missal too (it was the family Missal)
 Was ornamented in a sort of way
Which ancient mass-books often are, and
 this all
 Kinds of grotesques illumined; and how
 they,
Who saw those figures on the margin kiss
 all,
 Could turn their optics to the text and
 pray,
Is more than I know—But Don Juan's
 mother
Kept this herself, and gave her son another.

XLVII

Sermons he read, and lectures he endured,
 And homilies, and lives of all the saints;
To Jerome and to Chrysostom inured,
 He did not take such studies for re-
 straints;

But how faith is acquired, and then in-
 sured,
So well not one of the aforesaid paints
As Saint Augustine in his fine Confessions
Which make the reader envy his trans-
 gressions.

XLVIII

This, too, was a seal'd book to little Juan—
 I can't but say that his mamma was right
If such an education was the true one.
 She scarcely trusted him from out her
 sight;
Her maids were old, and if she took a new
 one,
 You might be sure she was a perfect
 fright,
She did this during even her husband's
 life—
I recommend as much to every wife.

XLIX

Young Juan wax'd in godliness and grace
 At six a charming child, and at eleven
With all the promise of as fine a face
 As e'er to man's maturer growth was
 given.
He studied steadily and grew apace,
 And seem'd, at least, in the right road to
 heaven,
For half his days were pass'd at church
 the other
Between his tutors, confessor, and mother.

L

At six, I said, he was a charming child,
 At twelve he was a fine, but quiet boy;
Although in infancy a little wild,
 They tamed him down amongst them
 to destroy
His natural spirit not in vain they toil'd,
 At least it seem'd so; and his mother's
 joy
Was to declare how sage, and still, and
 steady,
Her young philosopher was grown already.

LI

I had my doubts, perhaps I have them still,
 But what I say is neither here nor there:
I knew his father well, and have some skill
 In character—but it would not be fair
From sire to son to augur good or ill:
 He and his wife were an ill sorted pair—
But scandal's my aversion—I protest
Against all evil speaking, even in jest.

LII

For my part I say nothing—nothing—but
 This I will say—my reasons are my
 own—
That if I had an only son to put
 To school (as God be praised that I have
 none),

'Tis not with Donna Inez I would shut
 Him up to learn his catechism alone,
No—no—I'd send him out betimes to
 college,
For there it was I pick'd up my own know-
 ledge.

LIII

For there one learns—'tis not for me to
 boast,
 Though I acquired—but I pass over
 that,
As well as all the Greek I since have lost:
 I say that there's the place—but ' *Verb-
 um sat,*'
I think I pick'd up too, as well as most,
 Knowledge of matters—but no matter
 what—
I never married—but, I think, I know
That sons should not be educated so.

LIV

Young Juan now was sixteen years of age,
 Tall, handsome, slender, but well knit:
 he seem'd
Active, though not so sprightly, as a page;
 And everybody but his mother deem'd
Him almost man; but she flew in a rage
 And bit her lips (for else she might have
 scream'd)
If any said so, for to be precocious
Was in her eyes a thing the most atrocious.

LV

Amongst her numerous acquaintance, all
 Selected for discretion and devotion,
There was the Donna Julia, whom to call
 Pretty were but to give a feeble notion
Of many charms in her as natural
 As sweetness to the flower, or salt to
 ocean,
Her zone to Venus, or his bow to Cupid
(But this last simile is trite and stupid).

LVI

The darkness of her Oriental eye
 Accorded with her Moorish origin;
(Her blood was not all Spanish, by the by;
 In Spain, you know, this is a sort of sin).
When proud Granada fell, and, forced to
 fly,
 Boabdil wept, of Donna Julia's kin
Some went to Africa, some stay'd in Spain,
Her great great grandmamma chose to re-
 main.

LVII

She married (I forget the pedigree)
 With an Hidalgo, who transmitted down
His blood less noble than such blood
 should be;
 At such alliances his sires would frown,

In that point so precise in each degree
 That they bred *in and in,* as might be
 shown,
Marrying their cousins—nay, their aunts,
 and nieces,
Which always spoils the breed, if it in-
 creases.

LVIII

This heathenish cross restored the breed
 again,
 Ruin'd its blood, but much improved
 its flesh;
For from a root the ugliest in old Spain
 Sprung up a branch as beautiful as
 fresh;
The sons no more were short, the daughters
 plain:
 But there's a rumour which I fain would
 hush,
'Tis said that Donna Julia's grandmamma
Produced her Don more heirs at love than
 law.

LIX

However this might be, the race went on
 Improving still through every genera-
 tion,
Until it centred in an only son,
 Who left an only daughter: my narra-
 tion
May have suggested that this single one
 Could be but Julia (whom on this
 occasion
I shall have much to speak about), and she
Was married, charming, chaste, and
 twenty-three.

LX

Her eye (I'm very fond of handsome eyes)
 Was large and dark, suppressing half its
 fire
Until she spoke, then through its soft dis-
 guise
 Flash'd an expression more of pride
 than ire,
And love than either; and there would
 arise
 A something in them which was not
 desire,
But would have been, perhaps, but for the
 soul
Which struggled through and chasten'd
 down the whole.

LXI

Her glossy hair was cluster'd o'er a brow
 Bright with intelligence, and fair, and
 smooth;
Her eyebrow's shape was like the aërial
 bow,
 Her cheek all purple with the beam of
 youth,

Mounting, at times, to a transparent glow,
 As if her veins ran lightning; she, in
 sooth,
Possess'd an air and grace by no means
 common:
Her stature tall—I hate a dumpy woman.

LXII

Wedded she was some years, and to a man
 Of fifty, and such husbands are in
 plenty;
And yet, I think, instead of such a ONE
 'Twere better to have TWO of five-and-
 twenty,
Especially in countries near the sun:
 And now I think on't, 'mi vien in mente,'
Ladies even of the most uneasy virtue
Prefer a spouse whose age is short of thirty.

LXIII

'Tis a sad thing, I cannot choose but say,
 And all the fault of that indecent sun,
Who cannot leave alone our helpless clay,
 But will keep baking, broiling, burning
 on,
That howsoever people fast and pray,
 The flesh is frail, and so the soul undone:
What men call gallantry, and gods
 adultery,
Is much more common where the climate's
 sultry.

LXIV

Happy the nations of the moral North!
 Where all is virtue, and the winter season
Sends sin, without a rag on, shivering forth
 ('Twas snow that brought St. Anthony
 to reason);
Where juries cast up what a wife is worth,
 By laying whate'er sum, in mulct, they
 please on
The lover, who must pay a handsome price,
Because it is a marketable vice.

LXV

Alfonso was the name of Julia's lord,
 A man well looking for his years, and
 who
Was neither much beloved nor yet
 abhorr'd:
 They lived together as most people do,
Suffering each other's foibles by accord,
 And not exactly either *one* or *two*;
Yet he was jealous, though he did not
 show it,
For jealousy dislikes the world to know it.

LXVI

Julia was—yet I never could see why—
 With Donna Inez quite a favourite
 friend;
Between their tastes there was small sym-
 pathy,
 For not a line had Julia ever penn'd:

Some people whisper (but, no doubt, they
 lie,
 For malice still imputes some private
 end)
That Inez had, ere Don Alfonso's mar-
 riage,
Forgot with him her very prudent carriage;

LXVII

And that still keeping up the old con-
 nexion,
 Which time had lately render'd much
 more chaste,
She took his lady also in affection,
 And certainly this course was much the
 best:
She flatter'd Julia with her sage protection,
 And complimented Don Alfonso's
 taste;
And if she could not (who can?) silence
 scandal,
At least she left it a more slender handle.

LXVIII

I can't tell whether Julia saw the affair
 With other people's eyes, or if her own
Discoveries made, but none could be
 aware
 Of this, at least no symptom e'er was
 shown;
Perhaps she did not know, or did not care,
 Indifferent from the first, or callous
 grown:
I'm really puzzled what to think or say,
She kept her counsel in so close a way.

LXIX

Juan she saw, and, as a pretty child,
 Caress'd him often—such a thing might
 be
Quite innocently done, and harmless
 styled,
 When she had twenty years, and thirteen
 he;
But I am not so sure I should have smiled
 When he was sixteen, Julia twenty-
 three;
These few short years make wondrous
 alterations,
Particularly amongst sun-burnt nations.

LXX

Whate'er the cause might be, they had be-
 come
 Changed; for the dame grew distant, the
 youth shy,
Their looks cast down, their greeting
 almost dumb,
 And much embarrassment in either eye
There surely will be little doubt with some
 That Donna Julia knew the reason why,
But as for Juan, he had no more notion
Than he who never saw the sea of ocean.

LXXI

Yet Julia's very coldness still was kind,
 And tremulously gentle her small hand
Withdrew itself from his, but left behind
 A little pressure, thrilling, and so bland
And slight, so very slight, that to the mind
 'Twas but a doubt; but ne'er magician's wand
Wrought change with all Armida's fairy art
Like what this light touch left on Juan's heart.

LXXII

And if she met him, though she smiled no more,
 She look'd a sadness sweeter than her smile,
As if her heart had deeper thoughts in store
 She must not own, but cherish'd more the while
For that compression in its burning core;
 Even innocence itself has many a wile,
And will not dare to trust itself with truth,
And love is taught hypocrisy from youth.

LXXIII

But passion most dissembles, yet betrays
 Even by its darkness; as the blackest sky
Foretells the heaviest tempest, it displays
 Its workings through the vainly guarded eye,
And in whatever aspect it arrays
 Itself, 'tis still the same hypocrisy:
Coldness or anger, even disdain or hate,
Are masks it often wears, and still too late.

LXXIV

Then there were sighs, the deeper for suppression,
 And stolen glances, sweeter for the theft,
And burning blushes, though for no transgression,
 Tremblings when met, and restlessness when left;
All these were little preludes to possession,
 Of which young passion cannot be bereft,
And merely tend to show how greatly love is
Embarrass'd at first starting with a novice.

LXXV

Poor Julia's heart was in an awkward state;
 She felt it going, and resolved to make
The noblest efforts for herself and mate,
 For honour's, pride's, religion's, virtue's sake.
Her resolutions were most truly great,
 And almost might have made a Tarquin quake:
She pray'd the Virgin Mary for her grace,
As being the best judge of a lady's case.

LXXVI

She vow'd she never would see Juan more,
 And next day paid a visit to his mother,
And look'd extremely at the opening door,
 Which, by the Virgin's grace, let in another;
Grateful she was, and yet a little sore—
 Again it opens, it can be no other,
'Tis surely Juan now—No! I'm afraid
That night the Virgin was no further pray'd.

LXXVII

She now determined that a virtuous woman
 Should rather face and overcome temptation,
That flight was base and dastardly, and no man
 Should ever give her heart the least sensation;
That is to say, a thought beyond the common
 Preference, that we must feel upon occasion,
For people who are pleasanter than others,
But then they only seem so many brothers.

LXXVIII

And even if by chance—and who can tell?
 The devil's so very sly—she should discover
That all within was not so very well,
 And, if still free, that such or such a lover
Might please perhaps, a virtuous wife can quell
 Such thoughts, and be the better when they're over;
And if the man should ask, 'tis but denial:
I recommend young ladies to make trial.

LXXIX

And then there are such things as love divine,
 Bright and immaculate, unmix'd and pure,
Such as the angels think so very fine,
 And matrons, who would be no less secure,
Platonic, perfect, 'just such love as mine':
 Thus Julia said—and thought so, to be sure;
And so I'd have her think, were I the man
On whom her reveries celestial ran.

LXXX

Such love is innocent, and may exist
 Between young persons without any danger:
A hand may first, and then a lip be kist;
 For my part, to such doings I'm a stranger,

But *hear* these freedoms form the utmost
list
　Of all o'er which such love may be a
　ranger:
If people go beyond, 'tis quite a crime,
But not my fault—I tell them all in time.

LXXXI

Love, then, but love within its proper
limits
　Was Julia's innocent determination
In young Don Juan's favour, and to him
its
　Exertion might be useful on occasion;
And, lighted at too pure a shrine to dim its
　Ethereal lustre, with what sweet persua-
　sion
He might be taught, by love and her to-
gether—
I really don't know what, nor Julia either.

LXXXII

Fraught with this fine intention, and well
fenced
　In mail of proof—her purity of soul,
She, for the future of her strength con-
vinced,
　And that her honour was a rock, or mole,
Exceeding sagely from that hour dispensed
　With any kind of troublesome control;
But whether Julia to the task was equal
Is that which must be mention'd in the
sequel.

LXXXIII

Her plan she deem'd both innocent and
feasible,
　And, surely, with a stripling of sixteen
Not scandal's fangs could fix on much
that's seizable,
　Or if they did so, satisfied to mean
Nothing but what was good, her breast
was peaceable:
　A quiet conscience makes one so serene!
Christians have burnt each other, quite
persuaded
That all the Apostles would have done as
they did.

LXXXIV

And if in the mean time her husband died,
　But Heaven forbid that such a thought
　should cross
Her brain, though in a dream! (and then
she sigh'd)
　Never could she survive that common
　loss;
But just suppose that moment should be-
tide,
　I only say suppose it—*inter nos.*
(This should be *entre nous*, for Julia
thought
In French, but then the rhyme would go
for nought.)

LXXXV

I only say, suppose this supposition:
　Juan being then grown up to man's
　estate
Would fully suit a widow of condition,
　Even seven years hence it would not be
　too late;
And in the interim (to pursue this vision)
　The mischief, after all, could not be
　great,
For he would learn the rudiments of love,
I mean the seraph way of those above.

LXXXVI

So much for Julia. Now we'll turn to Juan.
　Poor little fellow! he had no idea
Of his own case, and never hit the true one;
　In feelings quick as Ovid's Miss Medea,
He puzzled over what he found a new one,
　But not as yet imagined it could be a
Thing quite in course, and not at all alarm-
ing,
Which, with a little patience, might grow
charming.

LXXXVII

Silent and pensive, idle, restless, slow,
　His home deserted for the lonely wood,
Tormented with a wound he could not
know,
　His, like all deep grief, plunged in soli-
　tude:
I'm fond myself of solitude or so,
　But then, I beg it may be understood,
By solitude I mean a Sultan's, not
A hermit's, with a haram for a grot.

LXXXVIII

'Oh Love! in such a wilderness as this,
　Where transport and security entwine,
Here is the empire of thy perfect bliss,
　And here thou art a god indeed divine.'
The bard I quote from does not sing amiss,
　With the exception of the second line,
For that same twining 'transport and
security'
Are twisted to a phrase of some obscurity.

LXXXIX

The poet meant, no doubt, and thus ap-
peals
　To the good sense and senses of man-
　kind,
The very thing which everybody feels,
　As all have found on trial, or may find,
That no one likes to be disturb'd at meals
　Or love.—I won't say more about 'en-
　twined'
Or 'transport,' as we knew all that before,
But beg 'Security' will bolt the door.

XC

Young Juan wander'd by the glassy brooks,
 Thinking unutterable things; he threw
Himself at length within the leafy nooks
 Where the wild branch of the cork
 forest grew;
There poets find materials for their books,
 And every now and then we read them
 through,
So that their plan and prosody are eligible,
Unless, like Wordsworth, they prove unin-
 telligible.

XCI

He, Juan (and not Wordsworth), so pur-
 sued
 His self-communion with his own high
 soul,
Until his mighty heart, in its great mood,
 Had mitigated part, though not the whole
Of its disease; he did the best he could
 With things not very subject to control,
And turn'd, without perceiving his con-
 dition,
Like Coleridge, into a metaphysician.

XCII

He thought about himself, and the whole
 earth,
 Of man the wonderful, and of the stars,
And how the deuce they ever could have
 birth;
 And then he thought of earthquakes,
 and of wars,
How many miles the moon might have in
 girth,
 Of air-balloons, and of the many bars
To perfect knowledge of the boundless
 skies;—
And then he thought of Donna Julia's eyes.

XCIII

In thoughts like these true wisdom may
 discern
 Longings sublime, and aspirations high,
Which some are born with, but the most
 part learn
 To plague themselves withal, they know
 not why:
'Twas strange that one so young should
 thus concern
 His brain about the action of the sky;
If *you* think 'twas philosophy that this did,
I can't help thinking puberty assisted.

XCIV

He pored upon the leaves, and on the
 flowers,
 And heard a voice in all the winds; and
 then
He thought of wood-nymphs and im-
 mortal bowers,
 And how the goddesses came down to
 men:

He miss'd the pathway, he forgot the
 hours,
 And when he look'd upon his watch
 again,
He found how much old Time had been a
 winner—
He also found that he had lost his dinner.

XCV

Sometimes he turn'd to gaze upon his
 book,
 Boscan, or Garcilasso;—by the wind
Even as the page is rustled while we look,
 So by the poesy of his own mind
Over the mystic leaf his soul was shook,
 As if 'twere one whereon magicians bind
Their spells, and give them to the passing
 gale
According to some good old woman's tale.

XCVI

Thus would he while his lonely hours away
 Dissatisfied, nor knowing what he
 wanted;
Nor glowing reverie, nor poet's lay,
 Could yield his spirit that for which it
 panted,
A bosom whereon he his head might lay,
 And hear the heart beat with the love it
 granted,
With——several other things, which I for-
 get,
Or which, at least, I need not mention yet.

XCVII

Those lonely walks, and lengthening reve-
 ries,
 Could not escape the gentle Julia's eyes;
She saw that Juan was not at his ease;
 But that which chiefly may, and must
 surprise,
Is, that the Donna Inez did not tease
 Her only son with question or surmise;
Whether it was she did not see, or would
 not,
Or, like all very clever people, could not.

XCVIII

This may seem strange, but yet 'tis very
 common;
 For instance—gentlemen, whose ladies
 take
Leave to o'erstep the written rights of
 woman,
 And break the——Which command-
 ment is't they break?
(I have forgot the number, and think no
 man
 Should rashly quote, for fear of a mis-
 take.)
I say, when these same gentlemen are
 jealous,
They make some blunder, which their
 ladies tell us.

XCIX

A real husband always is suspicious,
 But still no less suspects in the wrong
 place,
Jealous of some one who had no such
 wishes,
 Or pandering blindly to his own disgrace,
By harbouring some dear friend extremely
 vicious;
 The last indeed's infallibly the case:
And when the spouse and friend are gone
 off wholly,
He wonders at their vice, and not his folly.

C

Thus parents also are at times short-
 sighted;
 Though watchful as the lynx, they ne'er
 discover,
The while the wicked world beholds de-
 lighted,
 Young Hopeful's mistress, or Miss
 Fanny's lover,
Till some confounded escapade has blighted
 The plan of twenty years, and all is over;
And then the mother cries, the father
 swears,
And wonders why the devil he got heirs.

CI

But Inez was so anxious, and so clear
 Of sight, that I must think, on this occa-
 sion,
She had some other motive much more
 near
 For leaving Juan to this new temptation,
But what that motive was, I shan't say
 here;
 Perhaps to finish Juan's education,
Perhaps to open Don Alfonso's eyes,
In case he thought his wife too great a
 prize.

CII

It was upon a day, a summer's day;—
 Summer's indeed a very dangerous
 season,
And so is spring about the end of May;
 The sun, no doubt, is the prevailing
 reason;
But whatsoe'er the cause is, one may say,
 And stand convicted of more truth than
 treason,
That there are months which nature grows
 more merry in,—
March has its hares, and May must have
 its heroine.

CIII

'Twas on a summer's day—the sixth of
 June:—
 I like to be particular in dates,
Not only of the age, and year, but moon;
 They are a sort of post-house, where the
 Fates

Change horses, making history change its
 tune,
 Then spur away o'er empires and o'er
 states,
Leaving at last not much besides chrono-
 logy,
Excepting the post-obits of theology.

CIV

'Twas on the sixth of June, about the hour
 Of half-past six—perhaps still nearer
 seven—
When Julia sate within as pretty a bower
 As e'er held houri in that heathenish
 heaven
Described by Mahomet, and Anacreon
 Moore,
 To whom the lyre and laurels have been
 given,
With all the trophies of triumphant song—
He won them well, and may he wear them
 long!

CV

She sate, but not alone; I know not well
 How this same interview had taken
 place,
And even if I knew, I should not tell—
 People should hold their tongues in any
 case;
No matter how or why the thing befell,
 But there were she and Juan, face to
 face—
When two such faces are so, 'twould be
 wise,
But very difficult, to shut their eyes.

CVI

How beautiful she look'd! her conscious
 heart
 Glow'd in her cheek, and yet she felt no
 wrong,
Oh Love! how perfect is thy mystic art,
 Strengthening the weak, and trampling
 on the strong!
How self-deceitful is the sagest part
 Of mortals whom thy lure hath led
 along!—
The precipice she stood on was immense,
So was her creed in her own innocence.

CVII

She thought of her own strength, and
 Juan's youth,
 And of the folly of all prudish fears,
Victorious virtue, and domestic truth,
 And then of Don Alfonso's fifty years:
I wish these last had not occurr'd, in sooth,
 Because that number rarely much en-
 dears,
And through all climes, the snowy and the
 sunny,
Sounds ill in love, whate'er it may in
 money.

CVIII

When people say, 'I've told you *fifty* times,'
 They mean to scold, and very often do;
When poets say, 'I've written *fifty* rhymes,'
 They make you dread that they'll recite them too:
In gangs of *fifty*, thieves commit their crimes;
 At *fifty* love for love is rare, 'tis true,
But then, no doubt, it equally as true is,
A good deal may be bought for *fifty* Louis.

CIX

Julia had honour, virtue, truth, and love
 For Don Alfonso; and she inly swore,
By all the vows below to powers above,
 She never would disgrace the ring she wore,
Nor leave a wish which wisdom might reprove;
 And while she ponder'd this, besides much more,
One hand on Juan's carelessly was thrown,
Quite by mistake—she thought it was her own;

CX

Unconsciously she lean'd upon the other,
 Which play'd within the tangles of her hair;
And to contend with thoughts she could not smother
 She seem'd, by the distraction of her air.
'Twas surely very wrong in Juan's mother
 To leave together this imprudent pair,
She who for many years had watch'd her son so—
I'm very certain *mine* would not have done so.

CXI

The hand which still held Juan's, by degrees
 Gently, but palpably confirm'd its grasp,
As if it said, 'Detain me, if you please';
 Yet there's no doubt she only meant to clasp
His fingers with a pure Platonic squeeze;
 She would have shrunk as from a toad, or asp,
Had she imagined such a thing could rouse
A feeling dangerous to a prudent spouse.

CXII

I cannot know what Juan thought of this,
 But what he did, is much what you would do;
His young lip thank'd it with a grateful kiss,
 And then, abash'd at its own joy, withdrew

In deep despair, lest he had done amiss,—
 Love is so very timid when 'tis new:
She blush'd, and frown'd not, but she strove to speak,
And held her tongue, her voice was grown so weak.

CXIII

The sun set, and up rose the yellow moon:
 The devil's in the moon for mischief; they
Who call'd her CHASTE, methinks, began too soon
 Their nomenclature; there is not a day,
The longest, not the twenty-first of June,
 Sees half the business in a wicked way,
On which three single hours of moonshine smile—
And then she looks so modest all the while.

CXIV

There is a dangerous silence in that hour,
 A stillness, which leaves room for the full soul
To open all itself, without the power
 Of calling wholly back its self-control;
The silver light which, hallowing tree and tower,
 Sheds beauty and deep softness o'er the whole,
Breathes also to the heart, and o'er it throws
A loving languor, which is not repose.

CXV

And Julia sate with Juan, half embraced
 And half retiring from the glowing arm,
Which trembled like the bosom where 'twas placed;
 Yet still she must have thought there was no harm,
Or else 'twere easy to withdraw her waist;
 But then the situation had its charm,
And then——God knows what next—I can't go on;
I'm almost sorry that I e'er begun.

CXVI

Oh Plato! Plato! you have paved the way,
 With your confounded fantasies, to more
Immoral conduct by the fancied sway
 Your system feigns o'er the controlless core
Of human hearts, than all the long array
 Of poets and romancers:—You're a bore,
A charlatan, a coxcomb—and have been,
At best, no better than a go-between.

CXVII

And Julia's voice was lost, except in sighs,
 Until too late for useful conversation;
The tears were gushing from her gentle eyes,
 I wish, indeed, they had not had occasion;

But who, alas! can love, and then be wise?
 Not that remorse did not oppose temptation;
A little still she strove, and much repented,
And whispering 'I will ne'er consent'—
 consented.

CXVIII

'Tis said that Xerxes offer'd a reward
 To those who could invent him a new
 pleasure.
Methinks the requisition's rather hard,
 And must have cost his majesty a treasure:
For my part, I'm a moderate-minded bard,
 Fond of a little love (which I call leisure);
I care not for new pleasures, as the old
Are quite enough for me, so they but hold.

CXIX

Oh Pleasure! you're indeed a pleasant thing,
 Although one must be damn'd for you,
 no doubt:
I make a resolution every spring
 Of reformation, ere the year run out,
But somehow, this my vestal vow takes
 wing,
 Yet still, I trust, it may be kept throughout:
I'm very sorry, very much ashamed,
And mean, next winter, to be quite reclaim'd.

CXX

Here my chaste Muse a liberty must take—
 Start not! still chaster reader—she'll be
 nice hence-
Forward, and there is no great cause to
 quake;
 This liberty is a poetic licence,
Which some irregularity may make
 In the design, and as I have a high sense
Of Aristotle and the Rules, 'tis fit
To beg his pardon when I err a bit.

CXXI

This licence is to hope the reader will
 Suppose from June the sixth (the fatal
 day
Without whose epoch my poetic skill
 For want of facts would all be thrown
 away),
But keeping Julia and Don Juan still
 In sight, that several months have
 pass'd; we'll say
'Twas in November, but I'm not so sure
About the day—the era's more obscure.

CXXII

We'll talk of that anon.—'Tis sweet to hear
 At midnight on the blue and moonlit
 deep
The song and oar of Adria's gondolier,
 By distance mellow'd, o'er the waters
 sweep;

'Tis sweet to see the evening star appear;
 'Tis sweet to listen as the night-winds
 creep
From leaf to leaf; 'tis sweet to view on
 high
The rainbow, based on ocean, span the
 sky.

CXXIII

'Tis sweet to hear the watch-dog's honest
 bark
 Bay deep-mouth'd welcome as we draw
 near home;
'Tis sweet to know there is an eye will
 mark
 Our coming, and look brighter when
 we come;
'Tis sweet to be awaken'd by the lark,
 Or lull'd by falling waters; sweet the
 hum
Of bees, the voice of girls, the song of
 birds,
The lisp of children, and their earliest
 words.

CXXIV

Sweet is the vintage, when the showering
 grapes
 In Bacchanal profusion reel to earth,
Purple and gushing; sweet are our escapes
 From civic revelry to rural mirth;
Sweet to the miser are his glittering heaps,
 Sweet to the father is his first-born's
 birth,
Sweet is revenge—especially to women,
Pillage to soldiers, prize-money to seamen.

CXXV

Sweet is a legacy, and passing sweet
 The unexpected death of some old lady
Or gentleman of seventy years complete,
 Who've made 'us youth' wait too—too
 long already
For an estate, or cash, or country seat,
 Still breaking, but with stamina so
 steady
That all the Israelites are fit to mob its
Next owner for their double-damn'd post-
 obits.

CXXVI

'Tis sweet to win, no matter how, one's
 laurels,
 By blood or ink; 'tis sweet to put an end
To strife; 'tis sometimes sweet to have our
 quarrels,
 Particularly with a tiresome friend:
Sweet is old wine in bottles, ale in barrels;
 Dear is the helpless creature we defend
Against the world; and dear the schoolboy
 spot
We ne'er forget, though there we are
 forgot.

CXXVII

But sweeter still than this, than these, than all,
 Is first and passionate love—it stands alone,
Like Adam's recollection of his fall;
 The tree of knowledge has been pluck'd—all's known—
And life yields nothing further to recall
 Worthy of this ambrosial sin, so shown,
No doubt in fable, as the unforgiven
Fire which Prometheus filch'd for us from heaven.

CXXVIII

Man's a strange animal, and makes strange use
 Of his own nature, and the various arts,
And likes particularly to produce
 Some new experiment to show his parts;
This is the age of oddities let loose,
 Where different talents find their different marts;
You'd best begin with truth, and when you've lost your
Labour, there's a sure market for imposture.

CXXIX

What opposite discoveries we have seen!
 (Signs of true genius, and of empty pockets.)
One makes new noses, one a guillotine,
 One breaks your bones, one sets them in their sockets;
But vaccination certainly has been
 A kind antithesis to Congreve's rockets,
With which the Doctor paid off an old pox,
By borrowing a new one from an ox.

CXXX

Bread has been made (indifferent) from potatoes;
 And galvanism has set some corpses grinning,
But has not answer'd like the apparatus
 Of the Humane Society's beginning,
By which men are unsuffocated gratis:
 What wondrous new machines have late been spinning!
I said the small pox has gone out of late;
Perhaps it may be follow'd by the great.

CXXXI

'Tis said the great came from America;
 Perhaps it may set out on its return,—
The population there so spreads, they say
 'Tis grown high time to thin it in its turn,
With war, or plague, or famine, any way,
 So that civilisation they may learn;
And which in ravage the more loathsome evil is—
Their real lues, or our pseudo-syphilis?

CXXXII

This is the patent age of new inventions
 For killing bodies, and for saving souls,
All propagated with the best intentions;
 Sir Humphry Davy's lantern, by which coals
Are safely mined for in the mode he mentions,
 Tombuctoo travels, voyages to the Poles,
Are ways to benefit mankind, as true,
Perhaps, as shooting them at Waterloo.

CXXXIII

Man's a phenomenon, one knows not what,
 And wonderful beyond all wondrous measure;
'Tis pity though, in this sublime world, that
 Pleasure's a sin, and sometimes sin's a pleasure;
Few mortals know what end they would be at,
 But whether glory, power, or love, or treasure,
The path is through perplexing ways, and when
The goal is gain'd, we die, you know—and then——

CXXXIV

What then?—I do not know, no more do you—
 And so good night.—Return we to our story:
'Twas in November, when fine days are few,
 And the far mountains wax a little hoary,
And clap a white cape on their mantles blue;
 And the sea dashes round the promontory,
And the loud breaker boils against the rock,
And sober suns must set at five o'clock.

CXXXV

'Twas, as the watchmen say, a cloudy night;
 No moon, no stars, the wind was low or loud
By gusts, and many a sparkling hearth was bright
 With the piled wood, round which the family crowd;
There's something cheerful in that sort of light,
 Even as a summer sky's without a cloud,
I'm fond of fire, and crickets, and all that,
A lobster salad, and champagne, and chat.

CXXXVI

'Twas midnight—Donna Julia was in bed,
 Sleeping, most probably,—when at her
 door
Arose a clatter might awake the dead,
 If they had never been awoke before,
And that they have been so we all have
 read,
 And are to be so, at the least, once
 more;—
The door was fasten'd, but with voice and
 fist
First knocks were heard, then 'Madam—
 Madam—hist!

CXXXVII

'For God's sake, Madam—Madam—
 here's my master,
 With more than half the city at his
 back—
Was ever heard of such a curst disaster!
 'Tis not my fault—I kept good watch—
 Alack!
Do pray undo the bolt a little faster—
 They're on the stair just now, and in a
 crack
Will all be here; perhaps he yet may fly—
Surely the window's not so *very* high!'

CXXXVIII

By this time Don Alfonso was arrived,
 With torches, friends, and servants in
 great number;
The major part of them had long been
 wived,
 And therefore paused not to disturb the
 slumber
Of any wicked woman, who contrived
 By stealth her husband's temples to
 encumber:
Examples of this kind are so contagious,
Were *one* not punish'd, *all* would be out-
 rageous.

CXXXIX

I can't tell how, or why, or what suspicion
 Could enter into Don Alfonso's head;
But for a cavalier of his condition
 It surely was exceedingly ill-bred,
Without a word of previous admonition,
 To hold a levee round his lady's bed,
And summon lackeys, arm'd with fire and
 sword,
To prove himself the thing he most
 abhorr'd.

CXL

Poor Donna Julia! starting as from sleep
 (Mind—that I do not say—she had not
 slept),
Began at once to scream, and yawn, and
 weep;
 Her maid, Antonia, who was an adept,

Contrived to fling the bed-clothes in a
 heap,
 As if she had just now from out them
 crept:
I can't tell why she should take all this
 trouble
To prove her mistress had been sleeping
 double.

CXLI

But Julia mistress, and Antonia maid,
 Appear'd like two poor harmless
 women, who
Of goblins, but still more of men afraid,
 Had thought one man might be deterr'd
 by two,
And therefore side by side were gently laid,
 Until the hours of absence should run
 through,
And truant husband should return, and
 say,
'My dear, I was the first who came away.'

CXLII

Now Julia found at length a voice, and
 cried,
 'In heaven's name, Don Alfonso, what
 d'ye mean?
Has madness seized you? would that I had
 died
 Ere such a monster's victim I had been!
What may this midnight violence betide,
 A sudden fit of drunkenness or spleen?
Dare you suspect me, whom the thought
 would kill?
Search, then, the room!'—Alfonso said,
 'I will.'

CXLIII

He search'd, *they* search'd, and rummaged
 everywhere,
 Closet and clothes-press, chest and
 window-seat,
And found much linen, lace, and several
 pair
 Of stockings, slippers, brushes, combs,
 complete,
With other articles of ladies fair,
 To keep them beautiful, or leave them
 neat:
Arras they prick'd and curtains with their
 swords,
And wounded several shutters, and some
 boards.

CXLIV

Under the bed they search'd, and there
 they found—
 No matter what—it was not that they
 sought;
They open'd windows, gazing if the
 ground
 Had signs or footmarks, but the earth
 said nought;

And then they stared each others' faces
 round:
 'Tis odd, not one of all these seekers
 thought,
And seems to me almost a sort of blunder,
Of looking *in* the bed as well as under.

CXLV

During this inquisition Julia's tongue
 Was not asleep—'Yes, search and
 search,' she cried,
'Insult on insult heap, and wrong on wrong!
 It was for this that I became a bride!
For this in silence I have suffer'd long
 A husband like Alfonso at my side;
But now I'll bear no more, nor here
 remain,
If there be law or lawyers in all Spain.

CXLVI

'Yes, Don Alfonso! husband now no more,
 If ever you indeed deserved the name,
Is't worthy of your years?—you have
 threescore—
 Fifty, or sixty, it is all the same—
Is't wise or fitting, causeless to explore
 For facts against a virtuous woman's
 fame?
Ungrateful, perjured, barbarous Don
 Alfonso,
How dare you think your lady would go
 on so?

CXLVII

'Is it for this I have disdain'd to hold
 The common privileges of my sex?
That I have chosen a confessor so old
 And deaf, that any other it would vex,
And never once he has had cause to scold,
 But found my very innocence perplex
So much, he always doubted I was
 married—
How sorry you will be when I've mis-
 carried!

CXLVIII

'Was it for this that no Cortejo e'er
 I yet have chosen from out the youth of
 Seville?
Is it for this I scarce went anywhere,
 Except to bull-fights, mass, play, rout,
 and revel?
Is it for this, whate'er my suitors were,
 I favour'd none—nay, was almost
 uncivil?
Is it for this that General Count O'Reilly,
Who took Algiers, declares I used him vilely?

CXLIX

'Did not the Italian Musico Cazzani
 Sing at my heart six months at least in
 vain?
Did not his countryman, Count Corniani,
 Call me the only virtuous wife in Spain?

Were there not also Russians, English,
 many?
 The Count Strongstroganoff I put in
 pain,
And Lord Mount Coffeehouse, the Irish
 peer,
Who kill'd himself for love (with wine) last
 year.

CL

'Have I not had two bishops at my feet?
 The Duke of Ichar, and Don Fernan
 Nunez?
And is it thus a faithful wife you treat?
 I wonder in what quarter now the moon
 is:
I praise your vast forbearance not to beat
 Me also, since the time so opportune
 is—
Oh, valiant man! with sword drawn and
 cock'd trigger,
Now, tell me, don't you cut a pretty
 figure?

CLI

'Was it for this you took your sudden
 journey,
 Under pretence of business in-
 dispensable,
With that sublime of rascals your attorney,
 Whom I see standing there, and looking
 sensible
Of having play'd the fool? though both I
 spurn, he
 Deserves the worst, his conduct's less
 defensible,
Because, no doubt, 'twas for his dirty fee,
And not from any love to you nor me.

CLII

'If he comes here to take a deposition,
 By all means let the gentleman proceed;
You've made the apartment in a fit con-
 dition:—
 There's pen and ink for you, sir, when
 you need—
Let everything be noted with precision,
 I would not you for nothing should be
 fee'd—
But as my maid's undrest, pray turn your
 spies out.'
'Oh!' sobb'd Antonia, 'I could tear their
 eyes out.'

CLIII

'There is the closet, there the toilet, there
 The antechamber—search them under,
 over;
There is the sofa, there the great arm-
 chair,
 The chimney—which would really hold
 a lover.

I wish to sleep, and beg you will take care
 And make no further noise, till you
 discover
The secret cavern of this lurking treasure—
And when 'tis found, let me, too, have that
 pleasure.

CLIV

'And now, Hidalgo! now that you have
 thrown
 Doubt upon me, confusion over all,
Pray have the courtesy to make it known
 Who is the man you search for? how
 d'ye call
Him? what's his lineage? let him but be
 shown—
 I hope he's young and handsome—is he
 tall?
Tell me—and be assured, that since you
 stain
Mine honour thus, it shall not be in vain.

CLV

'At least, perhaps, he has not sixty years,
 At that age he would be too old for
 slaughter,
Or for so young a husband's jealous
 fears—
 (Antonia! let me have a glass of water.)
I am ashamed of having shed these tears,
 They are unworthy of my father's
 daughter;
My mother dream'd not in my natal hour,
That I should fall into a monster's power.

CLVI

'Perhaps 'tis of Antonia you are jealous,
 You saw that she was sleeping by my
 side,
When you broke in upon us with your
 fellows;
 Look where you please—we've nothing,
 sir, to hide;
Only another time, I trust, you'll tell us,
 Or for the sake of decency abide
A moment at the door, that we may be
Drest to receive so much good company.

CLVII

'And now, sir, I have done, and say no
 more;
 The little I have said may serve to show
The guileless heart in silence may grieve
 o'er
 The wrongs to whose exposure it is
 slow:—
I leave you to your conscience as before,
 'Twill one day ask you, *why* you used me
 so?
God grant you feel not then the bitterest
 grief!
Antonia! where's my pocket-handker-
 chief?'

CLVIII

She ceased, and turn'd upon her pillow;
 pale
She lay, her dark eyes flashing through
 their tears,
Like skies that rain and lighten; as a veil,
 Waved and o'ershading her wan cheek,
 appears
Her streaming hair; the black curls strive,
 but fail,
 To hide the glossy shoulder, which
 uprears
Its snow through all;—her soft lips lie
 apart,
And louder than her breathing beats her
 heart.

CLIX

The Senhor Don Alfonso stood confused;
 Antonia bustled round the ransack'd
 room,
And, turning up her nose, with looks
 abused
 Her master, and his myrmidons, of
 whom
Not one, except the attorney, was amused;
 He, like Achates, faithful to the tomb,
So there were quarrels, cared not for the
 cause,
Knowing they must be settled by the laws.

CLX

With prying snub-nose, and small eyes,
 he stood,
 Following Antonia's motions here and
 there,
With much suspicion in his attitude;
 For reputations he had little care;
So that a suit or action were made good,
 Small pity had he for the young and fair,
And ne'er believed in negatives, till these
Were proved by competent false witnesses.

CLXI

But Don Alfonso stood with downcast
 looks,
 And, truth to say, he made a foolish
 figure;
When, after searching in five hundred
 nooks,
 And treating a young wife with so much
 rigour,
He gain'd no point, except some self-
 rebukes,
 Added to those his lady with such
 vigour
Had pour'd upon him for the last half
 hour,
Quick, thick, and heavy—as a thunder-
 shower.

CLXII

At first he tried to hammer an excuse,
 To which the sole reply were tears and
 sobs,
And indications of hysterics, whose
 Prologue is always certain throes, and
 throbs,
Gasps, and whatever else the owners
 choose:
 Alfonso saw his wife, and thought of
 Job's;
He saw too, in perspective, her relations,
And then he tried to muster all his patience.

CLXIII

He stood in act to speak, or rather stammer,
 But sage Antonia cut him short before
The anvil of his speech received the
 hammer,
 With 'Pray, sir, leave the room, and say
 no more,
Or madam dies.'—Alfonso mutter'd,
 'D—n her,'
 But nothing else, the time of words was
 o'er;
He cast a rueful look or two, and did,
He knew not wherefore, that which he was
 bid.

CLXIV

With him retired his '*posse comitatus*,'
 The attorney last, who linger'd near the
 door
Reluctantly, still tarrying there as late as
 Antonia let him—not a little sore
At this most strange and unexplain'd
 '*hiatus*'
 In Don Alfonso's facts, which just now
 wore
An awkward look; as he revolved the case,
The door was fasten'd in his legal face.

CLXV

No sooner was it bolted, than—Oh shame!
 Oh sin! Oh sorrow! and Oh woman-
 kind!
How can you do such things and keep your
 fame,
 Unless this world, and t'other too, be
 blind?
Nothing so dear as an unfilch'd good name!
 But to proceed—for there is more
 behind:
With much heartfelt reluctance be it said,
Young Juan slipp'd, half-smother'd, from
 the bed.

CLXVI

He had been hid—I don't pretend to say
 How, nor can I indeed describe the
 where—
Young, slender, and pack'd easily, he lay,
 No doubt, in little compass, round or
 square;

But pity him I neither must nor may
 His suffocation by that pretty pair;
'Twere better, sure, to die so, than be shut
With maudlin Clarence in his Malmsey
 butt.

CLXVII

And, secondly, I pity not, because
 He had no business to commit a sin,
Forbid by heavenly, fined by human
 laws;
 At least 'twas rather early to begin;
But at sixteen the conscience rarely gnaws
 So much as when we call our old debts in
At sixty years, and draw the accompts of
 evil,
And find a deuced balance with the devil.

CLXVIII

Of his position I can give no notion:
 'Tis written in the Hebrew Chronicle,
How the physicians, leaving pill and potion,
 Prescribed, by way of blister, a young
 belle,
When old King David's blood grew dull
 in motion,
 And that the medicine answer'd very
 well;
Perhaps 'twas in a different way applied,
For David lived, but Juan nearly died.

CLXIX

What's to be done? Alfonso will be back
 The moment he has sent his fools away.
Antonia's skill was put upon the rack,
 But no device could be brought into
 play—
And how to parry the renew'd attack?
 Besides, it wanted but few hours of day:
Antonia puzzled; Julia did not speak,
But press'd her bloodless lip to Juan's
 cheek.

CLXX

He turn'd his lip to hers, and with his hand
 Call'd back the tangles of her wandering
 hair;
Even then their love they could not all
 command,
 And half forgot their danger and
 despair:
Antonia's patience now was at a stand—
 'Come, come, 'tis no time now for fool-
 ing there,'
She whisper'd, in great wrath—'I must
 deposit
This pretty gentleman within the closet:

CLXXI

'Pray, keep your nonsense for some
 luckier night—
 Who can have put my master in this
 mood?
What will become on't—I'm in such a
 fright,
 The devil's in the urchin, and no good—

Is this a time for giggling? this a plight?
 Why, don't you know that it may end
 in blood?
You'll lose your life, and I shall lose my
 place,
 My mistress all, for that half-girlish face.

CLXXII

'Had it but been for a stout cavalier
 Of twenty-five or thirty—(come, make
 haste)
But for a child, what piece of work is here!
 I really, madam, wonder at your taste—
(Come, sir, get in)—my master must be
 near:
 There, for the present, at the least, he's
 fast,
And if we can but till the morning keep
Our counsel—(Juan, mind, you must not
 sleep).'

CLXXIII

Now, Don Alfonso entering, but alone,
 Closed the oration of the trusty maid:
She loiter'd, and he told her to be gone,
 An order somewhat sullenly obey'd;
However, present remedy was none,
 And no great good seem'd answer'd if
 she staid;
Regarding both with slow and sidelong
 view,
She snuff'd the candle, curtsied, and with-
 drew.

CLXXIV

Alfonso paused a minute—then begun
 Some strange excuses for his late pro-
 ceeding:
He would not justify what he had done,
 To say the best, it was extreme ill-
 breeding;
But there were ample reasons for it, none
 Of which he specified in this his plead-
 ing:
His speech was a fine sample, on the whole,
Of rhetoric, which the learn'd call
 'rigmarole.'

CLXXV

Julia said nought; though all the while
 there rose
 A ready answer, which at once enables
A matron, who her husband's foible
 knows,
 By a few timely words to turn the tables,
Which, if it does not silence, still must
 pose,
 Even if it should comprise a pack of
 fables;
'Tis to retort with firmness, and when he
Suspects with *one*, do you reproach with
 three.

CLXXVI

Julia, in fact, had tolerable grounds,—
 Alfonso's loves with Inez were well
 known;
But whether 'twas that one's own guilt
 confounds—
 But that can't be, as has been often
 shown,
A lady with apologies abounds;—
 It might be that her silence sprang alone
From delicacy to Don Juan's ear,
To whom she knew his mother's fame was
 dear.

CLXXVII

There might be one more motive, which
 makes two,
 Alfonso ne'er to Juan had alluded,—
Mentioned his jealousy, but never who
 Had been the happy lover, he con-
 cluded,
Conceal'd amongst his premises; 'tis true,
 His mind the more o'er this its mystery
 brooded
To speak of Inez now were, one may say,
Like throwing Juan in Alfonso's way.

CLXXVIII

A hint, in tender cases, is enough;
 Silence is best: besides there is a *tact*—
(That modern phrase appears to me sad
 stuff,
 But it will serve to keep my verse com-
 pact)—
Which keeps, when push'd by questions
 rather rough,
 A lady always distant from the fact:
The charming creatures lie with such a
 grace,
There's nothing so becoming to the face.

CLXXIX

They blush, and we believe them, at least I
 Have always done so; 'tis of no great
 use,
In any case, attempting a reply,
 For then their eloquence grows quite
 profuse;
And when at length they're out of breath,
 they sigh,
 And cast their languid eyes down, and
 let loose
A tear or two, and then we make it up;
And then—and then—and then—sit
 down and sup.

CLXXX

Alfonso closed his speech, and begg'd her
 pardon,
 Which Julia half withheld, and then
 half granted,
And laid conditions, he thought very hard,
 on,
 Denying several little things he wanted:

He stood like Adam lingering near his
 garden,
 With useless penitence perplex'd and
 haunted,
Beseeching she no further would refuse,
When, lo! he stumbled o'er a pair of shoes.

CLXXXI

A pair of shoes!—what then? not much,
 if they
 Are such as fit with ladies' feet, but these
(No one can tell how much I grieve to say)
 Were masculine; to see them, and to
 seize,
Was but a moment's act.—Ah! well-a-
 day!
 My teeth begin to chatter, my veins
 freeze—
Alfonso first examined well their fashion,
And then flew out into another passion.

CLXXXII

He left the room for his relinquish'd
 sword,
 And Julia instant to the closet flew.
'Fly, Juan, fly! for heaven's sake—not a
 word—
 The door is open—you may yet slip
 through
The passage you so often have explored—
 Here is the garden-key—Fly—fly—
 Adieu!
Haste—haste! I hear Alfonso's hurrying
 feet—
Day has not broke—there's no one in the
 street.'

CLXXXIII

None can say that this was not good
 advice,
 The only mischief was, it came too late;
Of all experience 'tis the usual price,
 A sort of income-tax laid on by fate:
Juan had reach'd the room-door in a trice,
 And might have done so by the garden-
 gate,
But met Alfonso in his dressing-gown,
Who threaten'd death—so Juan knock'd
 him down.

CLXXXIV

Dire was the scuffle, and out went the
 light;
 Antonia cried out 'Rape!' and Julia
 'Fire!'
But not a servant stirr'd to aid the fight.
 Alfonso, pommell'd to his heart's
 desire,
Swore lustily he'd be revenged this night;
 And Juan, too, blasphemed an octave
 higher;
His blood was up: though young, he was
 a Tartar,
And not at all disposed to prove a martyr.

CLXXXV

Alfonso's sword had dropp'd ere he could
 draw it,
 And they continued battling hand to
 hand,
For Juan very luckily ne'er saw it;
 His temper not being under great com-
 mand,
If at that moment he had chanced to claw
 it,
 Alfonso's days had not been in the land
Much longer.—Think of husbands',
 lovers' lives!
And how ye may be doubly widows—
 wives!

CLXXXVI

Alfonso grappled to detain the foe,
 And Juan throttled him to get away,
And blood ('twas from the nose) began to
 flow;
 At last, as they more faintly wrestling
 lay,
Juan contrived to give an awkward blow,
 And then his only garment quite gave
 way;
He fled, like Joseph, leaving it; but there,
I doubt, all likeness ends between the pair.

CLXXXVII

Lights came at length, and men, and
 maids, who found
 An awkward spectacle their eyes before;
Antonia in hysterics, Julia swoon'd,
 Alfonso leaning, breathless, by the
 door;
Some half-torn drapery scatter'd on the
 ground,
 Some blood, and several footsteps, but
 no more:
Juan the gate gain'd, turn'd the key about,
And liking not the inside, lock'd the out.

CLXXXVIII

Here ends this canto.—Need I sing, or say,
 How Juan, naked, favour'd by the
 night,
Who favours what she should not, found
 his way,
 And reach'd his home in an unseemly
 plight?
The pleasant scandal which arose next day,
 The nine days' wonder which was
 brought to light,
And how Alfonso sued for a divorce,
Were in the English newspapers, of course.

CLXXXIX

If you would like to see the whole proceed-
 ings,
 The depositions and the cause at full,
The names of all the witnesses, the plead-
 ings
 Of counsel to nonsuit, or to annul,

There's more than one edition, and the
 readings
 Are various, but they none of them are
 dull;
The best is that in short-hand ta'en by
 Gurney,
Who to Madrid on purpose made a journey.

CXC

But Donna Inez, to divert the train
 Of one of the most circulating scandals
That had for centuries been known in
 Spain,
 At least since the retirement of the Van-
 dals,
First vow'd (and never had she vow'd in
 vain)
 To Virgin Mary several pounds of can-
 dles;
And then, by the advice of some old ladies,
She sent her son to be shipp'd off from
 Cadiz.

CXCI

She had resolved that he should travel
 through
 All European climes, by land or sea,
To mend his former morals, and get new,
 Especially in France and Italy
(At least this is the thing most people do).
 Julia was sent into a convent: she
Grieved, but, perhaps, her feelings may be
 better
Shown in the following copy of her Let-
 ter:—

CXCII

'They tell me 'tis decided; you depart:
 'Tis wise—'tis well, but not the less a
 pain;
I have no further claim on your young
 heart,
 Mine is the victim, and would be again:
To love too much has been the only art
 I used;—I write in haste, and if a stain
Be on this sheet, 'tis not what it appears;
My eyeballs burn and throb, but have no
 tears.

CXCIII

'I loved, I love you, for this love have lost
 State, station, heaven, mankind's, my
 own esteem,
And yet cannot regret what it hath cost,
 So dear is still the memory of that dream;
Yet, if I name my guilt, 'tis not to boast,
 None can deem harshlier of me than
 I deem:
I trace this scrawl because I cannot rest—
I've nothing to reproach or to request.

CXCIV

'Man's love is of man's life a thing apart,
 'Tis woman's whole existence; man may
 range

The court, camp, church, the vessel, an
 the mart;
 Sword, gown, gain, glory, offer in ex
 change
Pride, fame, ambition, to fill up his heart
 And few there are whom these canno
 estrange;
Men have all these resources, we but one
To love again, and be again undone.

CXCV

'You will proceed in pleasure, and in pride
 Beloved and loving many; all is o'er
For me on earth, except some years to hid
 My shame and sorrow deep in my heart'
 core:
These I could bear, but cannot cast asid
 The passion which still rages as before,—
And so farewell—forgive me, love me—
 No,
That word is idle now—but let it go.

CXCVI

'My breast has been all weakness, is so yet
 But still I think I can collect my mind;
My blood still rushes where my spirit's set
 As roll the waves before the settled wind
My heart is feminine, nor can forget—
 To all, except one image, madly blind;
So shakes the needle, and so stands th
 pole,
As vibrates my fond heart to my fix'd soul

CXCVII

'I have no more to say, but linger still,
 And dare not set my seal upon this sheet
And yet I may as well the task fulfil.
 My misery can scarce be more complete
I had not lived till now, could sorrow kill
 Death shuns the wretch who fain th
 blow would meet,
And I must even survive this last adieu,
And bear with life to love and pray for you!

CXCVIII

This note was written upon gilt-edge
 paper
 With a neat little crow-quill, slight an
 new;
Her small white hand could hardly reach
 the taper,
 It trembled as magnetic needles do,
And yet she did not let one tear escape her
 The seal a sun-flower; '*Elle vous su*
 partout,'
The motto, cut upon a white cornelian;
The wax was superfine, its hue vermilion

CXCIX

This was Don Juan's earliest scrape; bu
 whether
 I shall proceed with his adventures is
Dependent on the public altogether;
 We'll see, however, what they say to this

Their favour in an author's cap's a feather,
 And no great mischief's done by their
 caprice;
And if their approbation we experience,
 Perhaps they'll have some more about a
 year hence.

CC

My poem's epic, and is meant to be
 Divided in twelve books; each book
 containing,
With love, and war, a heavy gale at sea,
 A list of ships, and captains, and kings
 reigning,
New characters; the episodes are three:
 A panoramic view of hell's in training,
After the style of Virgil and of Homer,
So that my name of Epic's no misnomer.

CCI

All these things will be specified in time,
 With strict regard to Aristotle's rules,
The *Vade Mecum* of the true sublime,
 Which makes so many poets, and some
 fools:
Prose poets like blank-verse, I'm fond of
 rhyme,
 Good workmen never quarrel with their
 tools;
I've got new mythological machinery,
And very handsome supernatural scenery.

CCII

There's only one slight difference between
 Me and my epic brethren gone before,
And here the advantage is my own, I ween
 (Not that I have not several merits more,
But this will more peculiarly be seen);
 They so embellish, that 'tis quite a bore
Their labyrinth of fables to thread through,
Whereas this story's actually true.

CCIII

If any person doubt it, I appeal
 To history, tradition, and to facts,
To newspapers, whose truth all know and
 feel,
 To plays in five, and operas in three acts;
All these confirm my statement a good deal,
 But that which more completely faith
 exacts
Is, that myself, and several now in Seville,
Saw Juan's last elopement with the devil.

CCIV

If ever I should condescend to prose,
 I'll write poetical commandments, which
Shall supersede beyond all doubt all those
 That went before; in these I shall enrich
My text with many things that no one
 knows,
 And carry precept to the highest pitch:
I'll call the work 'Longinus o'er a Bottle,
Or, Every Poet his *own* Aristotle.'

CCV

Thou shalt believe in Milton, Dryden, Pope;
 Thou shalt not set up Wordsworth, Cole-
 ridge, Southey;
Because the first is crazed beyond all hope,
 The second drunk, the third so quaint
 and mouthy:
With Crabbe it may be difficult to cope,
 And Campbell's Hippocrene is some-
 what drouthy:
Thou shalt not steal from Samuel Rogers,
 nor
Commit—flirtation with the muse of Moore.

CCVI

Thou shalt not covet Mr. Sotheby's Muse,
 His Pegasus, nor anything that's his;
Thou shalt not bear false witness like 'the
 Blues'—
 (There's *one*, at least, is very fond of
 this):
Thou shalt not write, in short, but what I
 choose;
 This is true criticism, and you may kiss—
Exactly as you please, or not,—the rod;
But if you don't, I'll lay it on, by G—d!

CCVII

If any person should presume to assert
 This story is not moral, first, I pray,
That they will not cry out before they're
 hurt,
 Then that they'll read it o'er again, and
 say
(But, doubtless, nobody will be so pert),
 That this is not a moral tale, though gay;
Besides, in Canto Twelfth, I mean to show
The very place where wicked people go.

CCVIII

If, after all, there should be some so blind
 To their own good this warning to de-
 spise,
Let by some tortuosity of mind,
 Not to believe my verse and their own
 eyes,
And cry that they 'the moral cannot find,'
 I tell him, if a clergyman, he lies;
Should captains the remark, or critics, make,
They also lie too—under a mistake.

CCIX

The public approbation I expect,
 And beg they'll take my word about the
 moral,
Which I with their amusement will connect
 (So children cutting teeth receive a coral);
Meantime they'll doubtless please to recol-
 lect
 My epical pretensions to the laurel:
For fear some prudish readers should grow
 skittish,
I've bribed my Grandmother's Review—
 the British.

CCX

I sent it in a letter to the Editor,
 Who thank'd me duly by return of post—
I'm for a handsome article his creditor;
 Yet, if my gentle Muse he please to roast,
And break a promise after having made it
 her,
 Denying the receipt of what it cost,
And smear his page with gall instead of
 honey,
All I can say is—that he had the money.

CCXI

I think that with this holy new alliance
 I may ensure the public, and defy
All other magazines of art or science,
 Daily, or monthly, or three monthly; I
Have not essay'd to multiply their clients,
 Because they tell me 'twere in vain to try,
And that the Edinburgh Review and Quar-
 terly
Treat a dissenting author very martyrly.

CCXII

'Non ego hoc ferrem calida juventa
 Consule Planco,' Horace said, and so
Say I; by which quotation there is meant a
 Hint that some six or seven good years
 ago
(Long ere I dreamt of dating from the
 Brenta)
 I was most ready to return a blow,
And would not brook at all this sort of
 thing
In my hot youth—when George the Third
 was King.

CCXIII

But now at thirty years my hair is gray—
 (I wonder what it will be like at forty?
I thought of a peruke the other day—)
 My heart is not much greener; and, in
 short, I
Have squander'd my whole summer while
 'twas May,
 And feel no more the spirit to retort; I
Have spent my life, both interest and
 principal,
And deem not, what I deem'd, my soul
 invincible.

CCXIV

No more—no more—Oh! never more on
 me
 The freshness of the heart can fall like
 dew,
Which out of all the lovely things we see
 Extracts emotions beautiful and new;
Hived in our bosoms like the bag o' the
 bee.
 Think'st thou the honey with those ob-
 jects grew?
Alas! 'twas not in them, but in thy power
To double even the sweetness of a flower.

CCXV

No more—no more—Oh! never more, m
 heart,
 Canst thou be my sole world, my uni
 verse!
Once all in all, but now a thing apart,
 Thou canst not be my blessing or m
 curse:
The illusion's gone for ever, and thou ar
 Insensible, I trust, but none the worse,
And in thy stead I've got a deal of judg
 ment,
Though heaven knows how it ever foun
 a lodgment.

CCXVI

My days of love are over; me no more
 The charms of maid, wife, and still les
 of widow,
Can make the fool of which they mad
 before,—
 In short, I must not lead the life I did do
The credulous hope of mutual minds i
 o'er,
 The copious use of claret is forbid to
So for a good old-gentlemanly vice,
I think I must take up with avarice.

CCXVII

Ambition was my idol, which was broke
 Before the shrines of Sorrow, and o
 Pleasure;
And the two last have left me many a toke
 O'er which reflection may be made a
 leisure;
Now, like Friar Bacon's brazen head, I'v
 spoken,
 'Time is, Time was, Time's past':—
 chymic treasure
Is glittering youth, which I have spent be
 times—
My heart in passion, and my head o
 rhymes.

CCXVIII

What is the end of fame? 'tis but to fill
 A certain portion of uncertain paper:
Some liken it to climbing up a hill,
 Whose summit, like all hills, is lost i
 vapour;
For this men write, speak, preach, an
 heroes kill,
 And bards burn what they call the
 'midnight taper,'
To have, when the original is dust,
A name, a wretched picture, and worse bus

CCXIX

What are the hopes of man? Old Egypt
 King
 Cheops erected the first pyramid
And largest, thinking it was just the thin
 To keep his memory whole, and mumm
 hid:

But somebody or other rummaging,
 Burglariously broke his coffin's lid:
Let not a monument give you or me hopes,
Since not a pinch of dust remains of Cheops.

CCXX

But I, being fond of true philosophy,
 Say very often to myself, 'Alas!
All things that have been born were born
 to die,
 And flesh (which Death mows down to
 hay) is grass;
You've pass'd your youth not so unpleas-
 antly,
 And if you had it o'er again—'twould
 pass—
So thank your stars that matters are no
 worse,
And read your Bible, sir, and mind your
 purse.'

CCXXI

But for the present, gentle reader! and
 Still gentler purchaser! the bard—that's
 I—
Must, with permission, shake you by the
 hand,
 And so your humble servant, and good-
 bye!
We meet again, if we should understand
 Each other; and if not, I shall not try
Your patience further than by this short
 sample—
'Twere well if others follow'd my example.

CCXXII

Go, little book, from this my solitude!
 I cast thee on the waters—go thy ways!
And if, as I believe, thy vein be good,
 The world will find thee after many days.'
When Southey's read, and Wordsworth
 understood,
 I can't help putting in my claim to praise—
The four first rhymes are Southey's, every
 line:
For God's sake, reader! take them not for
 mine!

CANTO THE SECOND*

I

Oh ye! who teach the ingenuous youth of
 nations,
 Holland, France, England, Germany, or
 Spain,
pray ye flog them upon all occasions,
 It mends their morals, never mind the
 pain:
The best of mothers and of educations
 In Juan's case were but employ'd in vain,
Since, in a way that's rather of the oddest, he
Became divested of his native modesty.

II

Had he but been placed at a public school,
 In the third form, or even in the fourth,
His daily task had kept his fancy cool,
 At least, had he been nurtured in the
 north;
Spain may prove an exception to the rule,
 But then exceptions always prove its
 worth—
A lad of sixteen causing a divorce
Puzzled his tutors very much, of course.

III

I can't say that it puzzles me at all,
 If all things be consider'd; first, there
 was
His lady-mother, mathematical,
 A —— never mind; his tutor, an old
 ass;
A pretty woman—(that's quite natural,
 Or else the thing had hardly come to
 pass)
A husband rather old, not much in unity
With his young wife—a time, and oppor-
 tunity.

IV

Well—well; the world must turn upon its
 axis,
 And all mankind turn with it, heads or
 tails,
And live and die, make love and pay our
 taxes,
 And as the veering wind shifts, shift our
 sails;
The king commands us, and the doctor
 quacks us,
 The priest instructs, and so our life ex-
 hales,
A little breath, love, wine, ambition, fame,
Fighting, devotion, dust,—perhaps a name.

V

I said, that Juan had been sent to Cadiz—
 A pretty town, I recollect it well—
'Tis there the mart of the colonial trade is,
 (Or was, before Peru learn'd to rebel,)
And such sweet girls—I mean, such grace-
 ful ladies,
 Their very walk would make your bosom
 swell;
I can't describe it, though so much it strike,
Nor liken it—I never saw the like:

VI

An Arab horse, a stately stag, a barb
 New broke, a cameleopard, a gazelle,
No—none of these will do;—and then their
 garb,
 Their veil and petticoat—Alas! to dwell

* ['Begun at Venice, December 13, 1818,—
nished January 20, 1819.'—B.]

Upon such things would very near absorb
 A canto—then their feet and ankles,—
 well,
Thank Heaven I've got no metaphor quite
 ready,
(And so, my sober Muse—come, let's be
 steady—

VII

Chaste Muse!—well, if you must, you
 must)—the veil
 Thrown back a moment with the glanc-
 ing hand,
While the o'erpowering eye, that turns you
 pale,
 Flashes into the heart:—All sunny land
Of love! when I forget you, may I fail
 To —— say my prayers—but never was
 there plann'd
A dress through which the eyes give such
 a volley,
Excepting the Venetian Fazzioli.

VIII

But to our tale: the Donna Inez sent
 Her son to Cadiz only to embark;
To stay there had not answer'd her intent,
 But why?—we leave the reader in the
 dark—
'Twas for a voyage the young man was
 meant,
 As if a Spanish ship were Noah's ark,
To wean him from the wickedness of earth,
And send him like a dove of promise forth.

IX

Don Juan bade his valet pack his things
 According to direction, then received
A lecture and some money: for four springs
 He was to travel; and though Inez grieved
(As every kind of parting has its stings),
 She hoped he would improve—perhaps
 believed:
A letter, too, she gave (he never read it)
Of good advice—and two or three of credit.

X

In the mean time, to pass her hours away,
 Brave Inez now set up a Sunday school
For naughty children, who would rather
 play
 (Like truant rogues) the devil, or the
 fool;
Infants of three years old were taught that
 day,
 Dunces were whipt, or set upon a stool:
The great success of Juan's education
Spurr'd her to teach another generation.

XI

Juan embark'd—the ship got under way,
 The wind was fair, the water passing
 rough;

A devil of a sea rolls in that bay,
 As I, who've cross'd it oft, know well
 enough;
And, standing upon deck, the dashing
 spray
 Flies in one's face, and makes it weather
 tough:
And there he stood to take, and take again
His first—perhaps his last—farewell of
Spain.

XII

I can't but say it is an awkward sight
 To see one's native land receding through
The growing waters; it unmans one quite
 Especially when life is rather new:
I recollect Great Britain's coast look
 white,
 But almost every other country's blue,
When gazing on them, mystified by dis-
 tance,
We enter on our nautical existence.

XIII

So Juan stood, bewilder'd on the deck:
 The wind sung, cordage strain'd, and
 sailors swore,
And the ship creak'd, the town became a
 speck,
 From which away so fair and fast they
 bore.
The best of remedies is a beef-steak
 Against sea-sickness: try it, sir, before
You sneer, and I assure you this is true,
For I have found it answer—so may you.

XIV

Don Juan stood, and, gazing from the
 stern,
 Beheld his native Spain receding far:
First partings form a lesson hard to learn,
 Even nations feel this when they go to
 war;
There is a sort of unexprest concern,
 A kind of shock that sets one's heart
 ajar:
At leaving even the most unpleasant people
And places, one keeps looking at the
steeple.

XV

But Juan had got many things to leave,
 His mother, and a mistress, and no wife
So that he had much better cause to grieve
 Than many persons more advanced in
 life;
And if we now and then a sigh must heave
 At quitting even those we quit in strife,
No doubt we weep for those the heart en-
 dears—
That is, till deeper griefs congeal our tears.

XVI

So Juan wept, as wept the captive Jews
　By Babel's waters, still remembering
　　Sion:
I'd weep,—but mine is not a weeping
　Muse,
　And such light griefs are not a thing to
　　die on;
Young men should travel, if but to amuse
　Themselves; and the next time their ser-
　　vants tie on
Behind their carriages their new portman-
　teau,
Perhaps it may be lined with this my canto.

XVII

And Juan wept, and much he sigh'd and
　thought,
　While his salt tears dropp'd into the salt
　　sea,
'Sweets to the sweet;' (I like so much to
　quote;
　You must excuse this extract,—'tis where
　　she,
The Queen of Denmark, for Ophelia
　brought
　Flowers to the grave;) and, sobbing
　　often, he
Reflected on his present situation,
And seriously resolved on reformation.

XVIII

'Farewell, my Spain! a long farewell!' he
　cried,
　'Perhaps I may revisit thee no more,
But die, as many an exiled heart hath died,
　Of its own thirst to see again thy shore:
Farewell, where Guadalquivir's waters
　glide!
　Farewell, my mother! and, since all is
　　o'er,
Farewell, too, dearest Julia!—(here he
　drew
Her letter out again, and read it through.)

XIX

And oh! if e'er I should forget, I swear—
　But that's impossible, and cannot be—
Sooner shall this blue ocean melt to air,
　Sooner shall earth resolve itself to sea,
Than I resign thine image, oh, my fair!
　Or think of anything, excepting thee;
A mind diseased no remedy can physic—
Here the ship gave a lurch, and he grew
　sea-sick.)

XX

Sooner shall heaven kiss earth—(here he
　fell sicker)
　Oh, Julia! what is every other woe?—
For God's sake let me have a glass of
　liquor;
　Pedro, Battista, help me down below.)

Julia, my love!—(you rascal, Pedro, quick-
　er)—
　Oh, Julia!—(this curst vessel pitches
　　so)—
Beloved Julia, hear me still beseeching!'
(Here he grew inarticulate with retching.)

XXI

He felt that chilling heaviness of heart,
　Or rather stomach, which, alas! attends,
Beyond the best apothecary's art,
　The loss of love, the treachery of friends,
Or death of those we dote on, when a part
　Of us dies with them as each fond hope
　　ends:
No doubt he would have been much more
　pathetic,
But the sea acted as a strong emetic.

XXII

Love's a capricious power: I've known it
　hold
　Out through a fever caused by its own
　　heat,
But be much puzzled by a cough and cold,
　And find a quinsy very hard to treat;
Against all noble maladies he's bold,
　But vulgar illnesses don't like to meet,
Nor that a sneeze should interrupt his sigh,
Nor inflammations redden his blind eye.

XXIII

But worst of all is nausea, or a pain
　About the lower region of the bowels,
Love, who heroically breathes a vein,
　Shrinks from the application of hot
　　towels,
And purgatives are dangerous to his reign,
　Sea-sickness death: his love was perfect,
　　how else
Could Juan's passion, while the billows
　roar,
Resist his stomach, ne'er at sea before?

XXIV

The ship, call'd the most holy 'Trinidada,'
　Was steering duly for the port Leghorn;
For there the Spanish family Moncada
　Were settled long ere Juan's sire was
　　born:
They were relations, and for them he had a
　Letter of introduction, which the morn
Of his departure had been sent him by
His Spanish friends for those in Italy.

XXV

His suite consisted of three servants and
　A tutor, the licentiate Pedrillo,
Who several languages did understand,
　But now lay sick and speechless on his
　　pillow,

And, rocking in his hammock, long'd for
land,
 His headache being increased by every
billow;
And the waves oozing through the port-
hole made
His berth a little damp, and him afraid.

XXVI

'Twas not without some reason, for the
wind
 Increased at night, until it blew a gale;
And though 'twas not much to a naval
mind,
 Some landsmen would have look'd a
little pale,
For sailors are, in fact, a different kind:
 At sunset they began to take in sail,
For the sky show'd it would come on to
blow,
And carry away, perhaps, a mast or so.

XXVII

At one o'clock the wind with sudden shift
 Threw the ship right into the trough of
the sea,
Which struck her aft, and made an awk-
ward rift,
 Started the stern-post, also shatter'd the
Whole of her stern-frame, and, ere she
could lift
Herself from out her present jeopardy,
The rudder tore away: 'twas time to sound
The pumps, and there were four feet water
found.

XXVIII

One gang of people instantly was put
 Upon the pumps, and the remainder set
To get up part of the cargo, and what not;
 But they could not come at the leak as
yet;
At last they did get at it really, but
 Still their salvation was an even bet:
The water rush'd through in a way quite
puzzling,
While they thrust sheets, shirts, jackets,
bales of muslin,

XXIX

Into the opening; but all such ingredients
 Would have been vain, and they must
have gone down,
Despite of all their efforts and expedients,
 But for the pumps: I'm glad to make
them known
To all the brother tars who may have need
hence,
 For fifty tons of water were upthrown
By them per hour, and they all had been
undone,
But for the maker, Mr. Mann, of London.

XXX

As day advanced the weather seem'd to
abate,
 And then the leak they reckon'd to re
duce,
And keep the ship afloat, though three fee
yet
 Kept two hand- and one chain-pum
still in use.
The wind blew fresh again: as it grew late
 A squall came on, and while some gun
broke loose,
A gust—which all descriptive power tran
scends—
Laid with one blast the ship on her bear
ends.

XXXI

There she lay, motionless, and seem'd up
set;
 The water left the hold, and wash'd th
decks,
And made a scene men do not soon forget
 For they remember battles, fires, an
wrecks,
Or any other thing that brings regret,
 Or breaks their hopes, or hearts, o
heads, or necks;
Thus drownings are much talk'd of by th
divers,
And swimmers, who may chance to b
survivors.

XXXII

Immediately the masts were cut away,
 Both main and mizen: first the mize
went,
The main-mast follow'd; but the ship sti
lay
 Like a mere log, and baffled our intent
Foremast and bowsprit were cut dow
and they
 Eased her at last (although we neve
meant
To part with all till every hope wa
blighted),
And then with violence the old ship righte

XXXIII

It may be easily supposed, while this
 Was going on, some people were u
quiet,
That passengers would find it much ami
 To lose their lives, as well as spoil the
diet;
That even the able seaman, deeming his
 Days nearly o'er, might be disposed t
riot,
As upon such occasions tars will ask
For grog, and sometimes drink rum fro
the cask.

XXXIV

There's nought, no doubt, so much the
 spirit calms
 As rum and true religion: thus it was,
Some plunder'd, some drank spirits, some
 sung psalms,
 The high wind made the treble, and as
 bass
The hoarse harsh waves kept time; fright
 cured the qualms
 Of all the luckless landsmen's sea-sick
 maws:
Strange sounds of wailing, blasphemy, de-
 votion,
Clamour'd in chorus to the roaring ocean.

XXXV

Perhaps more mischief had been done, but
 for
 Our Juan, who, with sense beyond his
 years,
Got to the spirit-room, and stood before
 It with a pair of pistols; and their fears,
As if Death were more dreadful by his door
 Of fire than water, spite of oaths and
 tears,
Kept still aloof the crew, who, ere they sunk,
Thought it would be becoming to die drunk.

XXXVI

'Give us more grog,' they cried, 'for it
 will be
 All one an hour hence.' Juan answer'd,
 'No!
'Tis true that death awaits both you and
 me,
 But let us die like men, not sink below
Like brutes':—and thus his dangerous post
 kept he,
 And none liked to anticipate the blow;
And even Pedrillo, his most reverend tutor,
Was for some rum a disappointed suitor.

XXXVII

The good old gentleman was quite aghast,
 And made a loud and pious lamenta-
 tion;
Repented all his sins, and made a last
 Irrevocable vow of reformation;
Nothing should tempt him more (this peril
 past)
 To quit his academic occupation,
In cloisters of the classic Salamanca,
To follow Juan's wake, like Sancho Panca.

XXXVIII

But now there came a flash of hope once
 more;
 Day broke, and the wind lull'd: the
 masts were gone;
The leak increased; shoals round her, but
 no shore,
 The vessel swam, yet still she held her
 own.

They tried the pumps again, and though
 before
 Their desperate efforts seem'd all useless
 grown,
A glimpse of sunshine set some hands to
 bale—
The stronger pump'd, the weaker thrumm'd
 a sail.

XXXIX

Under the vessel's keel the sail was pass'd,
 And for a moment it had some effect;
But with a leak, and not a stick of mast,
 Nor rag of canvas, what could they ex-
 pect?
But still 'tis best to struggle to the last,
 'Tis never too late to be wholly wreck'd:
And though 'tis true that man can only die
 once,
'Tis not so pleasant in the Gulf of Lyons.

XL

There winds and waves had hurl'd them,
 and from thence,
 Without their will, they carried them
 away;
For they were forced with steering to dis-
 pense,
 And never had as yet a quiet day
On which they might repose, or even com-
 mence
 A jurymast or rudder, or could say
The ship would swim an hour, which, by
 good luck,
Still swam—though not exactly like a duck.

XLI

The wind, in fact, perhaps, was rather less,
 But the ship labour'd so, they scarce
 could hope
To weather out much longer; the distress
 Was also great with which they had to
 cope
For want of water, and their solid mess
 Was scant enough: in vain the telescope
Was used—nor sail nor shore appear'd in
 sight,
Nought but the heavy sea, and coming
 night.

XLII

Again the weather threaten'd,—again blew
 A gale, and in the fore and after hold
Water appear'd; yet, though the people
 knew
 All this, the most were patient, and some
 bold,
Until the chains and leathers were worn
 through
 Of all our pumps:—a wreck complete
 she roll'd,
At mercy of the waves, whose mercies are
Like human beings during civil war.

XLIII

Then came the carpenter, at last, with tears
 In his rough eyes, and told the captain,
 he
Could do no more: he was a man in years,
 And long had voyaged through many a
 stormy sea,
And if he wept at length, they were not fears
 That made his eyelids as a woman's be,
But he, poor fellow, had a wife and chil-
 dren,
Two things for dying people quite bewil-
 dering.

XLIV

The ship was evidently settling now
 Fast by the head; and, all distinction
 gone,
Some went to prayers again, and made a vow
 Of candles to their saints—but there
 were none
To pay them with; and some look'd o'er
 the bow;
Some hoisted out the boats; and there
 was one
That begg'd Pedrillo for an absolution,
Who told him to be damn'd—in his con-
 fusion.

XLV

Some lash'd them in their hammocks;
 some put on
 Their best clothes, as if going to a fair;
Some cursed the day on which they saw
 the sun,
 And gnash'd their teeth, and howling,
 tore their hair;
And others went on as they had begun,
 Getting the boats out, being well aware
That a tight boat will live in a rough sea,
Unless with breakers close beneath her lee.

XLVI

The worst of all was, that in their condi-
 tion,
 Having been several days in great dis-
 tress,
'Twas difficult to get out such provision
 As now might render their long suffering
 less:
Men, even when dying, dislike inanition;
 Their stock was damaged by the
 weather's stress:
Two casks of biscuit, and a keg of butter,
Were all that could be thrown into the
 cutter.

XLVII

But in the long-boat they contrived to stow
 Some pounds of bread, though injured
 by the wet;
Water, a twenty-gallon cask or so;
 Six flasks of wine: and they contrived to
 get

A portion of their beef up from below,
 And with a piece of pork, moreover, mea
But scarce enough to serve them for
 luncheon—
Then there was rum, eight gallons in
 puncheon.

XLVIII

The other boats, the yawl and pinnace, ha
 Been stove in the beginning of the gale;
And the long-boat's condition was but bad
 As there were but two blankets for a sai
And one oar for a mast, which a young la
 Threw in by good luck over the ship'
 rail;
And two boats could not hold, far less b
 stored,
To save one half the people then on board

XLIX

'Twas twilight, and the sunless day wer
 down
 Over the waste of waters; like a veil,
Which, if withdrawn, would but disclos
 the frown
 Of one whose hate is mask'd but t
 assail.
Thus to their hopeless eyes the night wa
 shown,
 And grimly darkled o'er the faces pale
And the dim desolate deep: twelve day
 had Fear
Been their familiar, and now Death wa
 here.

L

Some trial had been making at a raft,
 With little hope in such a rolling sea,
A sort of thing at which one would hav
 laugh'd,
 If any laughter at such times could be,
Unless with people who too much hav
 quaff'd,
 And have a kind of wild and horrid glee
Half epileptical, and half hysterical:—
Their preservation would have been
 miracle.

LI

At half-past eight o'clock, booms, hen
 coops, spars,
 And all things, for a chance, had bee
 cast loose
That still could keep afloat the strugglin
 tars,
 For yet they strove, although of no grea
 use:
There was no light in heaven but a fev
 stars,
 The boats put off o'ercrowded with thei
 crews;
She gave a heel, and then a lurch to port,
And, going down head foremost—sunk
 in short.

LII

Then rose from sea to sky the wild fare-
well—
 Then shriek'd the timid, and stood still
 the brave—
Then some leap'd overboard with dread-
ful yell,
 As eager to anticipate their grave;
And the sea yawn'd around her like a hell,
 And down she suck'd with her the whirl-
 ing wave,
Like one who grapples with his enemy,
And strives to strangle him before he die.

LIII

And first one universal shriek there rush'd,
 Louder than the loud ocean, like a crash
Of echoing thunder; and then all was
 hush'd,
 Save the wild wind and the remorseless
 dash
Of billows; but at intervals there gush'd,
 Accompanied with a convulsive splash,
A solitary shriek, the bubbling cry
Of some strong swimmer in his agony.

LIV

The boats, as stated, had got off before,
 And in them crowded several of the
 crew;
And yet their present hope was hardly
 more
 Than what it had been, for so strong it
 blew
There was slight chance of reaching any
 shore;
 And then they were too many, though
 so few—
Nine in the cutter, thirty in the boat,
Were counted in them when they got afloat.

LV

All the rest perish'd; near two hundred
 souls
 Had left their bodies; and what's worse,
 alas!
When over Catholics the ocean rolls,
 They must wait several weeks before a
 mass
Takes off one peck of purgatorial coals,
 Because, till people know what's come
 to pass,
They won't lay out their money on the
 dead—
It costs three francs for every mass that's
 said.

LVI

Juan got into the long-boat, and there
 Contrived to help Pedrillo to a place;
It seem'd as if they had exchanged their
 care,
 For Juan wore the magisterial face

Which courage gives, while poor Pedrillo's
 pair
 Of eyes were crying for their owner's
 case:
Battista, though (a name call'd shortly
 Tita),
Was lost by getting at some aqua-vita.

LVII

Pedro, his valet, too, he tried to save,
 But the same cause, conducive to his loss,
Left him so drunk, he jump'd into the
 wave,
 As o'er the cutter's edge he tried to cross,
And so he found a wine-and-watery grave;
 They could not rescue him although so
 close,
Because the sea ran higher every minute,
And for the boat—the crew kept crowding
 in it.

LVIII

A small old spaniel—which had been Don
 José's,
 His father's, whom he loved, as ye may
 think,
For on such things the memory reposes
 With tenderness—stood howling on the
 brink,
Knowing, (dogs have such intellectual
 noses!)
 No doubt, the vessel was about to sink;
And Juan caught him up, and ere he
 stepp'd
Off threw him in, then after him he leap'd.

LIX

He also stuff'd his money where he could
 About his person, and Pedrillo's too,
Who let him do, in fact, whate'er he would,
 Not knowing what himself to say, or do,
As every rising wave his dread renew'd;
 But Juan, trusting they might still get
 through,
And deeming there were remedies for any
 ill,
Thus re-embark'd his tutor and his spaniel.

LX

'Twas a rough night, and blew so stiffly
 yet,
 That the sail was becalm'd between the
 seas,
Though on the wave's high top too much
 to set,
 They dared not take it in for all the
 breeze:
Each sea curl'd o'er the stern, and kept
 them wet,
 And made them bale without a moment's
 ease,
So that themselves as well as hopes were
 damp'd,
And the poor little cutter quickly swamp'd.

LXI

Nine souls more went in her: the long-boat
 still
Kept above water, with an oar for mast,
Two blankets stitch'd together, answering
 ill
Instead of sail, were to the oar made fast:
Though every wave roll'd menacing to fill,
 And present peril all before surpass'd,
They grieved for those who perish'd with
 the cutter,
And also for the biscuit-casks and butter.

LXII

The sun rose red and fiery, a sure sign
 Of the continuance of the gale: to run
Before the sea until it should grow fine,
 Was all that for the present could be
 done:
A few tea-spoonfuls of their rum and wine
 Was served out to the people, who be-
 gun
To faint, and damaged bread wet through
 the bags,
And most of them had little clothes but
 rags.

LXIII

They counted thirty, crowded in a space
 Which left scarce room for motion or
 exertion;
They did their best to modify their case,
 One half sate up, though numb'd with
 the immersion,
While t'other half were laid down in their
 place,
 At watch and watch; thus, shivering like
 the tertian
Ague in its cold fit, they fill'd their boat,
With nothing but the sky for a great coat.

LXIV

'Tis very certain the desire of life
 Prolongs it: this is obvious to physicians,
When patients, neither plagued with friends
 nor wife,
 Survive through very desperate condi-
 tions,
Because they still can hope, nor shines the
 knife
 Nor shears of Atropos before their
 visions:
Despair of all recovery spoils longevity,
And makes men's miseries of alarming
 brevity.

LXV

'Tis said that persons living on annuities
 Are longer lived than others,—God
 knows why,
Unless to plague the grantors,—yet so true
 it is,
 That some, I really think, do never die;

Of any creditors the worst a Jew it is,
 And *that*'s their mode of furnishin
 supply:
In my young days they lent me cash tha
 way,
Which I found very troublesome to pay.

LXVI

'Tis thus with people in an open boat,
 They live upon the love of life, and bea
More than can be believed, or even though
 And stand like rocks the tempest's wea
 and tear;
And hardship still has been the sailor's lo
 Since Noah's ark went cruising here an
 there;
She had a curious crew as well as cargo,
Like the first old Greek privateer, th
 Argo.

LXVII

But man is a carnivorous production,
 And must have meals, at least one mea
 a day;
He cannot live, like woodcocks, upon suc
 tion,
 But, like the shark and tiger, must hav
 prey;
Although his anatomical construction
 Bears vegetables, in a grumbling way,
Your labouring people think beyond a
 question
Beef, veal, and mutton, better for digestio

LXVIII

And thus it was with this our hapless crew
 For on the third day there came on
 calm,
And though at first their strength it migh
 renew,
 And lying on their weariness like balm
Lull'd them like turtles sleeping on th
 blue
 Of ocean, when they woke they felt
 qualm,
And fell all ravenously on their provisio
Instead of hoarding it with due precisio

LXIX

The consequence was easily foreseen—
 They ate up all they had, and drank the
 wine,
In spite of all remonstrances, and then
 On what, in fact, next day were they t
 dine?
They hoped the wind would rise, thes
 foolish men!
 And carry them to shore; these hop
 were fine,
But as they had but one oar, and tha
 brittle,
It would have been more wise to save the
 victual.

LXX

The fourth day came, but not a breath of
 air,
 And Ocean slumber'd like an unwean'd
 child:
The fifth day, and their boat lay floating
 there,
 The sea and sky were blue, and clear,
 and mild—
With their one oar (I wish they had had a
 pair)
 What could they do? and hunger's rage
 grew wild:
So Juan's spaniel, spite of his entreating,
Was kill'd, and portion'd out for present
 eating.

LXXI

On the sixth day they fed upon his hide,
 And Juan, who had still refused, because
The creature was his father's dog that died,
 Now feeling all the vulture in his jaws,
With some remorse received (though first
 denied)
 As a great favour one of the fore-paws,
Which he divided with Pedrillo, who
Devour'd it, longing for the other too.

LXXII

The seventh day, and no wind—the burn-
 ing sun
 Blister'd and scorch'd, and, stagnant on
 the sea,
They lay like carcasses; and hope was none,
 Save in the breeze that came not: sav-
 agely
They glared upon each other—all was done,
 Water, and wine, and food,—and you
 might see
The longings of the cannibal arise
(Although they spoke not) in their wolfish
 eyes.

LXXIII

At length one whisper'd his companion,
 who
 Whisper'd another, and thus it went
 round,
And then into a hoarser murmur grew,
 An ominous, and wild, and desperate
 sound;
And when his comrade's thought each
 sufferer knew,
 'Twas but his own, suppress'd till now,
 he found:
And out they spoke of lots for flesh and
 blood,
And who should die to be his fellow's food.

LXXIV

But ere they came to this, they that day
 shared
 Some leathern caps, and what remain'd
 of shoes;

And then they look'd around them, and
 despair'd,
 And none to be the sacrifice would
 choose;
At length the lots were torn up, and pre-
 pared,
 But of materials that must shock the
 Muse—
Having no paper, for the want of better,
They took by force from Juan Julia's letter.

LXXV

Then lots were made, and mark'd, and
 mix'd, and handed
 In silent horror, and their distribution
Lull'd even the savage hunger which de-
 manded,
 Like the Promethean vulture, this pollu-
 tion;
None in particular had sought or plann'd it,
 'Twas Nature gnaw'd them to this reso-
 lution,
By which none were permitted to be
 neuter—
And the lot fell on Juan's luckless tutor.

LXXVI

He but requested to be bled to death:
 The surgeon had his instruments, and
 bled
Pedrillo, and so gently ebb'd his breath,
 You hardly could perceive when he was
 dead.
He died as born, a Catholic in faith,
 Like most in the belief in which they're
 bred,
And first a little crucifix he kiss'd,
And then held out his jugular and wrist.

LXXVII

The surgeon, as there was no other fee,
 Had his first choice of morsels for his
 pains;
But being thirstiest at the moment, he
 Preferr'd a draught from the fast-flow-
 ing veins:
Part was divided, part thrown in the sea,
 And such things as the entrails and the
 brains
Regaled two sharks, who follow'd o'er the
 billow—
The sailors ate the rest of poor Pedrillo.

LXXVIII

The sailors ate him, all save three or four,
 Who were not quite so fond of animal
 food;
To these was added Juan, who, before
 Refusing his own spaniel, hardly could
Feel now his appetite increased much more;
 'Twas not to be expected that he should,
Even in extremity of their disaster,
Dine with them on his pastor and his
 master.

LXXIX

'Twas better that he did not; for, in fact,
 The consequence was awful in the ex-
 treme;
For they, who were most ravenous in the
 act,
 Went raging mad—Lord! how they did
 blaspheme!
And foam, and roll, with strange convul-
 sions rack'd,
 Drinking salt-water like a mountain-
 stream;
Tearing, and grinning, howling, screech-
 ing, swearing,
And, with hyæna-laughter, died despairing.

LXXX

Their numbers were much thinn'd by this
 infliction,
 And all the rest were thin enough,
 Heaven knows;
And some of them had lost their recol-
 lection,
 Happier than they who still perceived
 their woes;
But others ponder'd on a new dissection,
 As if not warn'd sufficiently by those
Who had already perish'd, suffering madly,
For having used their appetites so sadly.

LXXXI

And next they thought upon the master's
 mate,
 As fattest; but he saved himself, because,
Besides being much averse from such a
 fate,
 There were some other reasons: the first
 was,
He had been rather indisposed of late;
 And that which chiefly proved his saving
 clause,
Was a small present made to him at Cadiz,
By general subscription of the ladies.

LXXXII

Of poor Pedrillo something still remain'd,
 But was used sparingly,—some were
 afraid,
And others still their appetites constrain'd,
 Or but at times a little supper made;
All except Juan, who throughout abstain'd,
 Chewing a piece of bamboo, and some
 lead:
At length they caught two boobies, and a
 noddy,
And then they left off eating the dead body.

LXXXIII

And if Pedrillo's fate should shocking be,
 Remember Ugolino condescends
To eat the head of his arch-enemy
 The moment after he politely ends

His tale: if foes be food in hell, at sea
 'Tis surely fair to dine upon our friends
When shipwreck's short allowance grows
 too scanty,
Without being much more horrible tha
 Dante.

LXXXIV

And the same night there fell a shower o
 rain,
 For which their mouths gaped, like th
 cracks of earth
When dried to summer dust; till taught b
 pain,
 Men really know not what good water
 worth;
If you had been in Turkey or in Spain,
 Or with a famish'd boat's-crew had you
 berth,
Or in the desert heard the camel's bell,
You'd wish yourself where Truth is—i
 a well.

LXXXV

It pour'd down torrents, but they were n
 richer,
 Until they found a ragged piece of shee
Which served them as a sort of spong
 pitcher,
 And when they deem'd its moisture wa
 complete,
They wrung it out, and though a thirst
 ditcher
 Might not have thought the scant
 draught so sweet
As a full pot of porter, to their thinkin
They ne'er till now had known the joys o
 drinking.

LXXXVI

And their baked lips, with many a blood
 crack,
 Suck'd in the moisture, which like nec
 tar stream'd;
Their throats were ovens, their swol
 tongues were black
 As the rich man's in hell, who vainl
 scream'd
To beg the beggar, who could not rai
 back
 A drop of dew, when every drop ha
 seem'd
To taste of heaven—If this be true, indeed
Some Christians have a comfortable creed

LXXXVII

There were two fathers in this ghastl
 crew,
 And with them their two sons, of whom
 the one
Was more robust and hardy to the view,
 But he died early; and when he wa
 gone,

His nearest messmate told his sire, who
threw
 One glance at him, and said, 'Heaven's
will be done!
I can do nothing,' and he saw him thrown
Into the deep without a tear or groan.

LXXXVIII

The other father had a weaklier child,
 Of a soft cheek, and aspect delicate;
But the boy bore up long, and with a mild
 And patient spirit held aloof his fate;
Little he said, and now and then he smiled,
 As if to win a part from off the weight
He saw increasing on his father's heart,
With the deep deadly thought, that they
must part.

LXXXIX

And o'er him bent his sire, and never raised
 His eyes from off his face, but wiped the
foam
From his pale lips, and ever on him gazed,
 And when the wish'd-for shower at
length was come,
And the boy's eyes, which the dull film
half glazed,
 Brighten'd, and for a moment seem'd
to roam,
He squeezed from out a rag some drops
of rain
Into his dying child's mouth—but in vain.

XC

The boy expired—the father held the clay,
 And look'd upon it long, and when at
last
Death left no doubt, and the dead burthen
lay
 Stiff on his heart, and pulse and hope
were past,
He watch'd it wistfully, until away
 'Twas borne by the rude wave wherein
'twas cast;
Then he himself sunk down all dumb and
shivering,
And gave no sign of life, save his limbs
quivering.

XCI

Now overhead a rainbow, bursting through
 The scattering clouds, shone, spanning
the dark sea,
Resting its bright base on the quivering
blue;
 And all within its arch appear'd to be
Clearer than that without, and its wide hue
 Wax'd broad and waving, like a banner
free,
Then changed like to a bow that's bent,
and then
Forsook the dim eyes of these shipwreck'd
men.

XCII

It changed, of course; a heavenly chame-
leon,
 The airy child of vapour and the sun,
Brought forth in purple, cradled in
vermilion,
 Baptized in molten gold, and swathed
in dun,
Glittering like crescents o'er a Turk's
pavilion,
 And blending every colour into one,
Just like a black eye in a recent scuffle
(For sometimes we must box without the
muffle).

XCIII

Our shipwreck'd seamen thought it a
good omen—
 It is as well to think so, now and then;
'Twas an old custom of the Greek and
Roman,
 And may become of great advantage
when
Folks are discouraged; and most surely
no men
 Had greater need to nerve themselves
again
Than these, and so this rainbow look'd
like hope—
Quite a celestial kaleidoscope.

XCIV

About this time a beautiful white bird,
 Web-footed, not unlike a dove in size
And plumage (probably it might have
err'd
 Upon its course), pass'd oft before their
eyes,
And tried to perch, although it saw and
heard
 The men within the boat, and in this
guise
It came and went, and flutter'd round
them till
Night fell:—this seem'd a better omen
still.

XCV

But in this case I also must remark,
 'Twas well this bird of promise did not
perch,
Because the tackle of our shatter'd bark
 Was not so safe for roosting as a church;
And had it been the dove from Noah's
ark,
 Returning there from her successful
search,
Which in their way that moment chanced
to fall,
They would have eat her, olive-branch
and all.

XCVI

With twilight it again came on to blow,
 But not with violence; the stars shone
 out,
The boat made way; yet now they were so
 low,
 They knew not where nor what they
 were about;
Some fancied they saw land, and some
 said 'No!'
 The frequent fog-banks gave them cause
 to doubt—
Some swore that they heard breakers,
 others guns,
And all mistook about the latter once.

XCVII

As morning broke, the light wind died
 away,
 When he who had the watch sung out
 and swore,
If 'twas not land that rose with the sun's
 ray,
 He wish'd that land he never might see
 more:
And the rest rubb'd their eyes, and saw
 a bay,
 Or thought they saw, and shaped their
 course for shore;
For shore it was, and gradually grew
Distinct, and high, and palpable to view.

XCVIII

And then of these some part burst into
 tears,
 And others, looking with a stupid stare,
Could not yet separate their hopes from
 fears,
 And seem'd as if they had no further
 care;
While a few pray'd—(the first time for
 some years)—
 And at the bottom of the boat three
 were
Asleep: they shook them by the hand and
 head,
And tried to awaken them, but found them
 dead.

XCIX

The day before, fast sleeping on the water,
 They found a turtle of the hawk's-bill
 kind,
And by good fortune, gliding softly,
 caught her,
 Which yielded a day's life, and to their
 mind
Proved even still a more nutritious matter,
 Because it left encouragement be-
 hind:
They thought that in such perils, more
 than chance
Had sent them this for their deliverance.

C

The land appear'd a high and rocky coast
 And higher grew the mountains as the
 drew,
Set by a current, toward it: they were los
 In various conjectures, for none knew
To what part of the earth they had bee
 tost,
 So changeable had been the winds tha
 blew;
Some thought it was Mount Ætna, som
 the highlands
Of Candia, Cyprus, Rhodes, or othe
 islands.

CI

Meantime the current, with a rising gale
 Still set them onwards to the welcom
 shore,
Like Charon's bark of spectres, dull an
 pale:
 Their living freight was now reduced t
 four,
And three dead, whom their strengt
 could not avail
 To heave into the deep with those befor
Though the two sharks still follow'd them
 and dash'd
The spray into their faces as they splash'

CII

Famine, despair, cold, thirst, and hea
 had done
 Their work on them by turns, an
 thinn'd them to
Such things a mother had not known he
 son
 Amidst the skeletons of that gaun
 crew;
By night chill'd, by day scorch'd, thus on
 by one
 They perish'd, until wither'd to thes
 few,
But chiefly by a species of self-slaughter
In washing down Pedrillo with salt wate

CIII

As they drew nigh the land, which no
 was seen
 Unequal in its aspect here and there,
They felt the freshness of its growin
 green,
 That waved in forest-tops, an
 smooth'd the air,
And fell upon their glazed eyes like
 screen
 From glistening waves, and skies so h
 and bare—
Lovely seem'd any object that shoul
 sweep
Away the vast, salt, dread, eternal deep.

CIV

The shore look'd wild, without a trace of
man,
 And girt by formidable waves; but they
Were mad for land, and thus their course
 they ran,
 Though right ahead the roaring
 breakers lay:
A reef between them also now began
 To show its boiling surf and bounding
 spray,
But finding no place for their landing
 better,
They ran the boat for shore,—and overset
 her.

CV

But in his native stream, the Guadalquivir,
 Juan to lave his youthful limbs was
 wont;
And having learnt to swim in that sweet
 river,
 Had often turn'd the art to some
 account:
A better swimmer you could scarce see
 ever,
 He could, perhaps, have pass'd the
 Hellespont,
As once (a feat on which ourselves we
 prided)
Leander, Mr. Ekenhead, and I did.

CVI

So here, though faint, emaciated, and
 stark,
 He buoy'd his boyish limbs, and strove
 to ply
With the quick wave, and gain, ere it was
 dark,
 The beach which lay before him, high
 and dry:
The greatest danger here was from a shark,
 That carried off his neighbour by the
 thigh;
As for the other two, they could not swim,
So nobody arrived on shore but him.

CVII

Nor yet had he arrived but for the oar,
 Which, providentially for him, was
 wash'd
Just as his feeble arms could strike no
 more,
 And the hard wave o'erwhelm'd him
 as 'twas dash'd
Within his grasp; he clung to it, and sore
 The waters beat while he thereto was
 lash'd;
At last, with swimming, wading, scram-
 bling, he
Roll'd on the beach, half senseless, from
 the sea:

CVIII

There, breathless, with his digging nails
 he clung
Fast to the sand, lest the returning wave,
 From whose reluctant roar his life he
 wrung,
Should suck him back to her insatiate
 grave:
And there he lay, full length, where he was
 flung,
 Before the entrance of a cliff-worn cave,
With just enough of life to feel its pain,
And deem that it was saved, perhaps in
 vain.

CIX

With slow and staggering effort he arose,
 But sunk again upon his bleeding knee
And quivering hand; and then he look'd
 for those
 Who long had been his mates upon the
 sea;
But none of them appear'd to share his
 woes,
 Save one, a corpse, from out the
 famish'd three,
Who died two days before, and now had
 found
An unknown barren beach for burial-
 ground.

CX

And as he gazed, his dizzy brain spun fast,
 And down he sunk; and as he sunk, the
 sand
Swam round and round, and all his senses
 pass'd:
 He fell upon his side, and his stretch'd
 hand
Droop'd dripping on the oar (their jury-
 mast),
 And, like a wither'd lily, on the land
His slender frame and pallid aspect lay,
As fair a thing as e'er was form'd of clay.

CXI

How long in his damp trance young Juan
 lay
 He knew not, for the earth was gone
 for him,
And time had nothing more of night nor
 day
 For his congealing blood, and senses
 dim;
And how this heavy faintness pass'd away
 He knew not, till each painful pulse and
 limb,
And tingling vein, seem'd throbbing back
 to life,
For Death, though vanquish'd, still
 retired with strife.

CXII

His eyes he open'd, shut, again unclosed,
 For all was doubt and dizziness; he
 thought
He still was in the boat, and had but dozed,
 And felt again with his despair o'er-
 wrought,
And wish'd it death in which he had
 reposed,
 And then once more his feelings back
 were brought,
And slowly by his swimming eyes was
 seen
A lovely female face of seventeen.

CXIII

'Twas bending close o'er his, and the
 small mouth
 Seem'd almost prying into his for
 breath;
And chafing him, the soft warm hand of
 youth
 Recall'd his answering spirits back
 from death;
And, bathing his chill temples, tried to
 soothe
Each pulse to animation, till beneath
Its gentle touch and trembling care, a sigh
To these kind efforts made a low reply.

CXIV

Then was the cordial pour'd, and mantle
 flung
 Around his scarce-clad limbs; and the
 fair arm
Raised higher the faint head which o'er it
 hung;
 And her transparent cheek, all pure and
 warm,
Pillow'd his death-like forehead; then she
 wrung
 His dewy curls, long drench'd by every
 storm;
And watch'd with eagerness each throb
 that drew
A sigh from his heaved bosom—and hers,
 too.

CXV

And lifting him with care into the cave,
 The gentle girl, and her attendant,—
 one
Young, yet her elder, and of brow less
 grave,
 And more robust of figure—then begun
To kindle fire, and as the new flames gave
 Light to the rocks that roof'd them,
 which the sun
Had never seen, the maid, or whatsoe'er
She was, appear'd distinct, and tall, and
 fair.

CXVI

Her brow was overhung with coins of gold,
 That sparkled o'er the auburn of her hair,
Her clustering hair, whose longer locks
 were roll'd
 In braids behind; and though her
 stature were
Even of the highest for a female mould,
 They nearly reach'd her heel; and in her
 air
There was a something which bespoke
 command,
As one who was a lady in the land.

CXVII

Her hair, I said, was auburn; but her eyes
 Were black as death, their lashes the
 same hue,
Of downcast length, in whose silk shadow
 lies
 Deepest attraction; for when to the view
Forth from its raven fringe the full glance
 flies,
 Ne'er with such force the swiftest arrow
 flew;
'Tis as the snake late coil'd, who pours his
 length,
And hurls at once his venom and his
 strength.

CXVIII

Her brow was white and low, her cheek's
 pure dye
 Like twilight rosy still with the set sun;
Short upper lip—sweet lips! that make us
 sigh
 Ever to have seen such; for she was one
Fit for the model of a statuary
 (A race of mere impostors, when all's
 done—
I've seen much finer women, ripe and real,
Than all the nonsense of their stone ideal).

CXIX

I'll tell you why I say so, for 'tis just
 One should not rail without a decent
 cause:
There was an Irish lady, to whose bust
 I ne'er saw justice done, and yet she was
A frequent model; and if e'er she must
 Yield to stern Time and Nature's
 wrinkling laws,
They will destroy a face which mortal
 thought
Ne'er compass'd, nor less mortal chisel
 wrought.

CXX

And such was she, the lady of the cave,
 Her dress was very different from the
 Spanish,
Simpler, and yet of colours not so grave,
 For, as you know, the Spanish women
 banish

Bright hues when out of doors, and yet,
 while wave
 Around them (what I hope will never
 vanish)
The basquina and the mantilla, they
Seem at the same time mystical and gay.

CXXI

But with our damsel this was not the case:
 Her dress was many-colour'd, finely
 spun;
Her locks curl'd negligently round her
 face,
 But through them gold and gems pro-
 fusely shone:
Her girdle sparkled, and the richest lace
 Flow'd in her veil, and many a precious
 stone
Flash'd on her little hand; but, what was
 shocking,
Her small snow feet had slippers, but no
 stocking.

CXXII

The other female's dress was not unlike,
 But of inferior materials: she
Had not so many ornaments to strike,
 Her hair had silver only, bound to be
Her dowry; and her veil, in form alike,
 Was coarser; and her air, though firm,
 less free;
Her hair was thicker, but less long; her eyes
As black, but quicker, and of smaller size.

CXXIII

And these two tended him, and cheer'd
 him both
 With food and raiment, and those soft
 attentions,
Which are—(as I must own)—of female
 growth,
 And have ten thousand delicate inven-
 tions:
They made a most superior mess of broth,
 A thing which poesy but seldom men-
 tions,
But the best dish that e'er was cook'd
 since Homer's
Achilles order'd dinner for new comers.

CXXIV

I'll tell you who they were, this female
 pair,
 Lest they should seem princesses in
 disguise;
Besides, I hate all mystery, and that air
 Of clap-trap, which your recent poets
 prize;
And so, in short, the girls they really were
 They shall appear before your curious
 eyes,
Mistress and maid; the first was only
 daughter
Of an old man, who lived upon the water.

CXXV

A fisherman he had been in his youth,
 And still a sort of fisherman was he;
But other speculations were, in sooth,
 Added to his connexion with the sea,
Perhaps not so respectable, in truth:
 A little smuggling, and some piracy,
Left him, at last, the sole of many masters
Of an ill-gotten million of piastres.

CXXVI

A fisher, therefore, was he,—though of
 men,
 Like Peter the Apostle,—and he fish'd
For wandering merchant vessels, now and
 then,
 And sometimes caught as many as he
 wish'd;
The cargoes he confiscated, and gain
 He sought in the slave-market too, and
 dish'd
Full many a morsel for that Turkish trade,
By which, no doubt, a good deal may be
 made.

CXXVII

He was a Greek, and on his isle had built
 (One of the wild and smaller Cyclades)
A very handsome house from out his guilt,
 And there he lived exceedingly at ease;
Heaven knows what cash he got, or blood
 he spilt,
 A sad old fellow was he, if you please;
But this I know, it was a spacious building,
Full of barbaric carving, paint, and gilding.

CXXVIII

He had an only daughter, call'd Haidée,
 The greatest heiress of the Eastern Isles;
Besides, so very beautiful was she,
 Her dowry was as nothing to her smiles:
Still in her teens, and like a lovely tree
 She grew to womanhood, and between
 whiles
Rejected several suitors, just to learn
How to accept a better in his turn.

CXXIX

And walking out upon the beach, below
 The cliff,—towards sunset, on that day
 she found,
Insensible,—not dead, but nearly so,—
 Don Juan, almost famish'd, and half
 drown'd;
But being naked, she was shock'd, you know,
 Yet deem'd herself in common pity bound,
As far as in her lay, 'to take him in,
A stranger' dying, with so white a skin.

CXXX

But taking him into her father's house
 Was not exactly the best way to save,
But like conveying to the cat the mouse,
 Or people in a trance into their grave;

Because the good old man had so much
'*vous*,'
Unlike the honest Arab thieves so
brave,
He would have hospitably cured the
stranger
And sold him instantly when out of
danger.

CXXXI

And therefore, with her maid, she thought
it best
(A virgin always on her maid relies)
To place him in the cave for present rest:
And when, at last, he open'd his black
eyes,
Their charity increased about their guest;
And their compassion grew to such a
size,
It open'd half the turnpike gates to
heaven—
(St. Paul says, 'tis the toll which must be
given).

CXXXII

They made a fire,—but such a fire as they
Upon the moment could contrive with
such
Materials as were cast up round the
bay,—
Some broken planks, and oars, that to
the touch
Were nearly tinder, since so long they lay,
A mast was almost crumbled to a
crutch;
But, by God's grace, here wrecks were in
such plenty,
That there was fuel to have furnish'd
twenty.

CXXXIII

He had a bed of furs, and a pelisse,
For Haidée stripp'd her sables off to
make
His couch; and, that he might be more at
ease,
And warm, in case by chance he should
awake,
They also gave a petticoat apiece,
She and her maid,—and promised by
daybreak
To pay him a fresh visit, with a dish
For breakfast, of eggs, coffee, bread, and
fish.

CXXXIV

And thus they left him to his lone repose:
Juan slept like a top, or like the dead,
Who sleep at last, perhaps (God only
knows),
Just for the present; and in his lull'd
head
Not even a vision of his former woes
Throbb'd in accursed dreams, which
sometimes spread

Unwelcome visions of our former years,
Till the eye, cheated, opens thick with
tears.

CXXXV

Young Juan slept all dreamless:—but the
maid,
Who smooth'd his pillow, as she left the
den
Look'd back upon him, and a moment
stayed,
And turn'd, believing that he call'd again.
He slumber'd; yet she thought, at least she
said
(The heart will slip, even as the tongue
and pen),
He had pronounced her name—but she
forgot
That at this moment Juan knew it not.

CXXXVI

And pensive to her father's house she
went,
Enjoining silence strict to Zoe, who
Better than her knew what, in fact, she
meant,
She being wiser by a year or two:
A year or two's an age when rightly spent,
And Zoe spent hers, as most women do,
In gaining all that useful sort of knowledge
Which is acquired in Nature's good old
college.

CXXXVII

The morn broke, and found Juan slumber-
ing still
Fast in his cave, and nothing clash'd
upon
His rest: the rushing of the neighbouring
rill,
And the young beams of the excluded
sun,
Troubled him not, and he might sleep his
fill;
And need he had of slumber yet, for
none
Had suffer'd more—his hardships were
comparative
To those related in my grand-dad's
'Narrative.'

CXXXVIII

Not so Haidée: she sadly toss'd and
tumbled,
And started from her sleep, and,
turning o'er,
Dream'd of a thousand wrecks, o'er which
she stumbled,
And handsome corpses strew'd upon
the shore;
And woke her maid so early that she
grumbled,
And call'd her father's old slaves up,
who swore

In several oaths—Armenian, Turk, and
 Greek—
They knew not what to think of such a
 freak.

CXXXIX

But up she got, and up she made them get,
 With some pretence about the sun, that
 makes
Sweet skies just when he rises, or is set;
 And 'tis, no doubt, a sight to see when
 breaks
Bright Phœbus, while the mountains still
 are wet
 With mist, and every bird with him
 awakes,
And night is flung off like a mourning suit
Worn for a husband,—or some other
 brute.

CXL

I say, the sun is a most glorious sight:
 I've seen him rise full oft, indeed of late
I have sat up on purpose all the night,
 Which hastens, as physicians say, one's
 fate;
And so all ye, who would be in the right
 In health and purse, begin your day to
 date
From daybreak, and when coffin'd at four-
 score
Engrave upon the plate, you rose at four.

CXLI

And Haidée met the morning face to face;
 Her own was freshest, though a feverish
 flush
Had dyed it with the headlong blood,
 whose race
 From heart to cheek is curb'd into a
 blush,
Like to a torrent which a mountain's base,
 That overpowers some Alpine river's
 rush,
Checks to a lake, whose waves in circles
 spread;
Or the Red Sea—but the sea is not red.

CXLII

And down the cliff the island virgin came,
 And near the cave her quick light foot-
 steps drew,
While the sun smiled on her with his first
 flame,
 And young Aurora kiss'd her lips with
 dew,
Taking her for a sister; just the same
 Mistake you would have made on see-
 ing the two,
Although the mortal, quite as fresh and
 fair,
Had all the advantage, too, of not being
 air.

CXLIII

And when into the cavern Haidée stepp'd
 All timidly, yet rapidly, she saw
That like an infant Juan sweetly slept;
 And then she stopp'd, and stood as if
 in awe
(For sleep is awful), and on tiptoe crept
 And wrapt him closer, lest the air, too
 raw,
Should reach his blood, then o'er him still
 as death
Bent, with hush'd lips, that drank his
 scarce-drawn breath.

CXLIV

And thus like to an angel o'er the dying
 Who die in righteousness, she lean'd;
 and there
All tranquilly the shipwreck'd boy was
 lying,
 As o'er him lay the calm and stirless air:
But Zoe the meantime some eggs was
 frying,
 Since, after all, no doubt the youthful
 pair
Must breakfast, and betimes—lest they
 should ask it,
She drew out her provision from the
 basket.

CXLV

She knew that the best feelings must have
 victual,
 And that a shipwreck'd youth would
 hungry be;
Besides, being less in love, she yawn'd a
 little,
 And felt her veins chill'd by the neigh-
 bouring sea;
And so, she cook'd their breakfast to a
 tittle;
 I can't say that she gave them any tea,
But there were eggs, fruit, coffee, bread,
 fish, honey,
With Scio wine,—and all for love, not
 money.

CXLVI

And Zoe, when the eggs were ready, and
 The coffee made, would fain have
 waken'd Juan;
But Haidée stopp'd her with her quick
 small hand,
 And without word, a sign her finger
 drew on
Her lip, which Zoe needs must under-
 stand;
 And, the first breakfast spoilt, prepared
 a new one,
Because her mistress would not let her
 break
That sleep which seem'd as it would ne'er
 awake.

CXLVII

For still he lay, and on his thin worn cheek
 A purple hectic play'd like dying day
On the snow-tops of distant hills; the
 streak
Of sufferance yet upon his forehead lay,
 Where the blue veins look'd shadowy,
 shrunk, and weak;
 And his black curls were dewy with the
 spray,
Which weigh'd upon them yet, all damp
 and salt,
Mix'd with the stony vapours of the vault.

CXLVIII

And she bent o'er him, and he lay beneath,
 Hush'd as the babe upon its mother's
 breast,
Droop'd as the willow when no winds can
 breathe,
 Lull'd like the depth of ocean when at
 rest,
Fair as the crowning rose of the whole
 wreath,
 Soft as the callow cygnet in its nest;
In short, he was a very pretty fellow,
Although his woes had turn'd him rather
 yellow.

CXLIX

He woke and gazed, and would have slept
 again,
 But the fair face which met his eyes
 forbade
Those eyes to close, though weariness and
 pain
 Had further sleep a further pleasure
 made;
For woman's face was never form'd in
 vain
 For Juan, so that even when he pray'd
He turn'd from grisly saints, and martyrs
 hairy,
To the sweet portraits of the Virgin Mary.

CL

And thus upon his elbow he arose,
 And look'd upon the lady, in whose
 cheek
The pale contended with the purple rose,
 As with an effort she began to speak;
Her eyes were eloquent, her words would
 pose,
 Although she told him, in good modern
 Greek,
With an Ionian accent, low and sweet,
That he was faint, and must not talk, but
 eat.

CLI

Now Juan could not understand a word,
 Being no Grecian; but he had an ear,
And her voice was the warble of a bird,
 So soft, so sweet, so delicately clear,

That finer, simpler music ne'er was heard
 The sort of sound we echo with a tear
Without knowing why—an overpowering
 tone,
Whence melody descends as from a
 throne.

CLII

And Juan gazed as one who is awoke
 By a distant organ, doubting if he be
Not yet a dreamer, till the spell is broke
 By the watchman, or some such reality,
Or by one's early valet's cursed knock;
 At least it is a heavy sound to me,
Who like a morning slumber—for the night
Shows stars and women in a better light

CLIII

And Juan, too, was help'd out from his
 dream,
 Or sleep, or whatsoe'er it was, by feeling
A most prodigious appetite; the steam
 Of Zoe's cookery no doubt was stealing
Upon his senses, and the kindling beam
 Of the new fire, which Zoe kept up,
 kneeling,
To stir her viands, made him quite awake
And long for food, but chiefly a beef-steak.

CLIV

But beef is rare within these oxless isles;
 Goat's flesh there is, no doubt, and kid,
 and mutton,
And, when a holiday upon them smiles,
 A joint upon their barbarous spits they
 put on:
But this occurs but seldom, between
 whiles,
 For some of these are rocks with scarce
 a hut on;
Others are fair and fertile, among which
This, though not large, was one of the
 most rich.

CLV

I say that beef is rare, and can't help thinking
 That the old fable of the Minotaur—
From which our modern morals, rightly
 shrinking,
 Condemn the royal lady's taste who
 wore
A cow's shape for a mask—was only
 (sinking
 The allegory) a mere type, no more,
That Pasiphae promoted breeding cattle,
To make the Cretans bloodier in battle.

CLVI

For we all know that English people are
 Fed upon beef—I won't say much of
 beer,
Because 'tis liquor only, and being far
 From this my subject, has no business
 here;

We know, too, they are very fond of war,
 A pleasure—like all pleasures—rather
 dear;
So were the Cretans—from which I infer
That beef and battles both were owing to
 her.

CLVII

But to resume. The languid Juan raised
 His head upon his elbow, and he saw
A sight on which he had not lately gazed,
 As all his latter meals had been quite
 raw,
Three or four things, for which the Lord
 he praised,
 And, feeling still the famish'd vulture
 gnaw,
He fell upon whate'er was offer'd, like
A priest, a shark, an alderman, or pike.

CLVIII

He ate, and he was well supplied; and she,
 Who watch'd him like a mother, would
 have fed
Him past all bounds, because she smiled
 to see
Such appetite in one she had deem'd
 dead:
But Zoe, being older than Haidée,
 Knew (by tradition, for she ne'er had
 read)
That famish'd people must be slowly
 nurst,
And fed by spoonfuls, else they always
 burst.

CLIX

And so she took the liberty to state,
 Rather by deeds than words, because
 the case
Was urgent, that the gentleman, whose
 fate
 Had made her mistress quit her bed to
 trace
The sea-shore at this hour, must leave his
 plate,
 Unless he wish'd to die upon the place—
She snatch'd it, and refused another
 morsel,
Saying, he had gorged enough to make a
 horse ill.

CLX

Next they—he being naked, save a tatter'd
 Pair of scarce decent trowsers—went to
 work,
And in the fire his recent rags they
 scatter'd,
 And dress'd him, for the present, like a
 Turk,
Or Greek—that is, although it not much
 matter'd,
 Omitting turban, slippers, pistols,
 dirk,—

They furnish'd him, entire, except some
 stitches,
With a clean shirt, and very spacious
 breeches.

CLXI

And then fair Haidée tried her tongue at
 speaking,
 But not a word could Juan comprehend,
Although he listen'd so that the young
 Greek in
 Her earnestness would ne'er have made
 an end;
And, as he interrupted not, went eking
 Her speech out to her protégé and
 friend,
Till pausing at the last her breath to take,
She saw he did not understand Romaic.

CLXII

And then she had recourse to nods, and
 signs,
 And smiles, and sparkles of the speaking
 eye,
And read (the only book she could) the
 lines
 Of his fair face, and found, by sympathy,
The answer eloquent, where the soul
 shines
 And darts in one quick glance a long
 reply;
And thus in every look she saw exprest
A world of words, and things at which she
 guess'd.

CLXIII

And now, by dint of fingers and of eyes,
 And words repeated after her, he took
A lesson in her tongue; but by surmise,
 No doubt, less of her language than her
 look:
As he who studies fervently the skies
 Turns oftener to the stars than to his
 book,
Thus Juan learn'd his alpha beta better
From Haidée's glance than any graven
 letter.

CLXIV

'Tis pleasing to be school'd in a strange
 tongue
 By female lips and eyes—that is, I mean,
When both the teacher and the taught are
 young,
 As was the case, at least, where I have
 been;
They smile so when one's right, and when
 one's wrong
 They smile still more, and then there
 intervene
Pressure of hands, perhaps even a chaste
 kiss:—
I learn'd the little that I know by this:

CLXV

That is, some words of Spanish, Turk, and
 Greek,
 Italian not at all, having no teachers;
Much English I cannot pretend to speak,
 Learning that language chiefly from its
 preachers,
Barrow, South, Tillotson, whom every
 week
I study, also Blair, the highest reachers
Of eloquence in piety and prose—
I hate your poets, so read none of those.

CLXVI

As for the ladies, I have nought to say,
 A wanderer from the British world of
 fashion,
Where I, like other 'dogs, have had my
 day,'
 Like other men, too, may have had my
 passion—
But that, like other things, has pass'd away,
 And all her fools whom I *could* lay the
 lash on:
Foes, friends, men, women, now are
 nought to me
But dreams of what has been, no more to
 be.

CLXVII

Return we to Don Juan. He begun
 To hear new words, and to repeat them;
 but
Some feelings, universal as the sun,
 Were such as could not in his breast be
 shut
More than within the bosom of a nun:
 He was in love,—as you would be, no
 doubt,
With a young benefactress,—so was she,
Just in the way we very often see.

CLXVIII

And every day by daybreak—rather early
 For Juan, who was somewhat fond of
 rest—
She came into the cave, but it was merely
 To see her bird reposing in his nest;
And she would softly stir his locks so
 curly,
 Without disturbing her yet slumbering
 guest,
Breathing all gently o'er his cheek and
 mouth,
As o'er a bed of roses the sweet south.

CLXIX

And every morn his colour freshlier came,
 And every day help'd on his con-
 valescence;
'Twas well, because health in the human
 frame
 Is pleasant, besides being true love's
 essence,

For health and idleness to passion's flame
 Are oil and gunpowder; and some good
 lessons
Are also learnt from Ceres and from
 Bacchus,
Without whom Venus will not long attack
 us.

CLXX

While Venus fills the heart (without heart
 really
 Love, though good always, is not quite
 so good),
Ceres presents a plate of vermicelli,—
 For love must be sustain'd like flesh and
 blood,
While Bacchus pours out wine, or hands a
 jelly:
 Eggs, oysters, too, are amatory food;
But who is their purveyor from above
Heaven knows,—it may be Neptune, Pan,
 or Jove.

CLXXI

When Juan woke he found some good
 things ready,
 A bath, a breakfast, and the finest eyes
That ever made a youthful heart less
 steady,
 Besides her maid's, as pretty for their
 size;
But I have spoken of all this already—
 And repetition's tiresome and unwise,—
Well—Juan, after bathing in the sea,
Came always back to coffee and Haidée.

CLXXII

Both were so young, and one so innocent,
 That bathing pass'd for nothing: Juan
 seem'd
To her, as 'twere, the kind of being sent,
 Of whom these two years she had
 nightly dream'd,
A something to be loved, a creature
 meant
 To be her happiness, and whom she
 deem'd
To render happy: all who joy would win
Must share it,—Happiness was born a
 twin.

CLXXIII

It was such pleasure to behold him, such
 Enlargement of existence to partake
Nature with him, to thrill beneath his
 touch,
 To watch him slumbering, and to see
 him wake;
To live with him for ever were too much;
 But then the thought of parting made
 her quake:
He was her own, her ocean-treasure, cast
Like a rich wreck—her first love, and her
 last.

CLXXIV

And thus a moon roll'd on, and fair
 Haidée
Paid daily visits to her boy, and took
Such plentiful precautions, that still he
 Remain'd unknown within his craggy
 nook;
At last her father's prows put out to sea,
 For certain merchantmen upon the
 look,
Not as of yore to carry off an Io,
But three Ragusan vessels bound for Scio.

CLXXV

Then came her freedom, for she had no
 mother,
 So that, her father being at sea, she was
Free as a married woman, or such other
 Female, as where she likes may freely
 pass,
Without even the encumbrance of a
 brother,
 The freest she that ever gazed on glass:
I speak of Christian lands in this com-
 parison,
Where wives, at least, are seldom kept in
 garrison.

CLXXVI

Now she prolong'd her visits and her talk
 (For they must talk), and he had learnt
 to say
So much as to propose to take a walk,—
 For little had he wander'd since the day
On which, like a young flower snapp'd
 from the stalk,
 Drooping and dewy on the beach he
 lay,—
And thus they walk'd out in the afternoon,
And saw the sun set opposite the moon.

CLXXVII

It was a wild and breaker-beaten coast,
 With cliffs above, and a broad sandy
 shore,
Guarded by shoals and rocks as by an
 host,
 With here and there a creek, whose
 aspect wore
A better welcome to the tempest-tost;
 And rarely ceased the haughty billow's
 roar,
Save on the dead long summer days,
 which make
The outstretch'd ocean glitter like a lake.

CLXXVIII

And the small ripple spilt upon the beach
 Scarcely o'erpass'd the cream of your
 champagne,
When o'er the brim the sparkling bumpers
 reach,
 That spring-dew of the spirit! the heart's
 rain!

Few things surpass old wine; and they
 may preach
Who please,—the more because they
 preach in vain,—
Let us have wine and women, mirth and
 laughter,
Sermons and soda-water the day after.

CLXXIX

Man, being reasonable, must get drunk;
 The best of life is but intoxication:
Glory, the grape, love, gold, in these are
 sunk
 The hopes of all men, and of every
 nation;
Without their sap, how branchless were
 the trunk
 Of life's strange tree, so fruitful on
 occasion!
But to return,—Get very drunk; and when
You wake with headache, you shall see
 what then.

CLXXX

Ring for your valet—bid him quickly bring
 Some hock and soda-water, then you'll
 know
A pleasure worthy Xerxes the great king;
 For not the blest sherbet, sublimed with
 snow,
Nor the first sparkle of the desert spring,
 Nor Burgundy in all its sunset glow,
After long travel, ennui, love, or slaughter,
Vie with that draught of hock and soda-
 water.

CLXXXI

The coast—I think it was the coast that I
 Was just describing—Yes, it *was* the
 coast—
Lay at this period quiet as the sky,
 The sands untumbled, the blue waves
 untost,
And all was stillness, save the sea-bird's cry,
 And dolphin's leap, and little billow
 crost
By some low rock or shelve, that made it fret
Against the boundary it scarcely wet.

CLXXXII

And forth they wander'd, her sire being
 gone,
 As I have said, upon an expedition;
And mother, brother, guardian, she had
 none,
 Save Zoe, who, although with due pre-
 cision
She waited on her lady with the sun,
 Thought daily service was her only
 mission,
Bringing warm water, wreathing her long
 tresses,
And asking now and then for cast-off
 dresses.

CLXXXIII

It was the cooling hour, just when the rounded
Red sun sinks down behind the azure hill,
Which then seems as if the whole earth it bounded,
Circling all nature, hush'd, and dim, and still,
With the far mountain-crescent half surrounded
On one side, and the deep sea calm and chill,
Upon the other, and the rosy sky,
With one star sparkling through it like an eye.

CLXXXIV

And thus they wander'd forth, and hand in hand,
Over the shining pebbles and the shells,
Glided along the smooth and harden'd sand,
And in the worn and wild receptacles
Work'd by the storms, yet work'd as it were plann'd,
In hollow halls, with sparry roofs and cells,
They turn'd to rest; and, each clasp'd by an arm,
Yielded to the deep twilight's purple charm.

CLXXXV

They look'd up to the sky, whose floating glow
Spread like a rosy ocean, vast and bright;
They gazed upon the glittering sea below,
Whence the broad moon rose circling into sight;
They heard the waves splash, and the wind so low,
And saw each other's dark eyes darting light
Into each other—and, beholding this,
Their lips drew near, and clung into a kiss;

CLXXXVI

A long, long kiss, a kiss of youth, and love,
And beauty, all concentrating like rays
Into one focus, kindled from above;
Such kisses as belong to early days,
Where heart, and soul, and sense, in concert move,
And the blood's lava, and the pulse a blaze,
Each kiss a heart-quake,—for a kiss's strength,
I think it must be reckon'd by its length.

CLXXXVII

By length I mean duration; theirs endured
Heaven knows how long—no doubt they never reckon'd;

CLXXXVIII

And if they had, they could not have secured
The sum of their sensations to a second:
They had not spoken; but they felt allured,
As if their souls and lips each other beckon'd,
Which, being join'd, like swarming bees they clung—
Their hearts the flowers from whence the honey sprung.

CLXXXVIII

They were alone, but not alone as they
Who shut in chambers think it loneliness;
The silent ocean, and the starlight bay,
The twilight glow, which momently grew less,
The voiceless sands, and dropping caves, that lay
Around them, made them to each other press,
As if there were no life beneath the sky
Save theirs, and that their life could never die.

CLXXXIX

They fear'd no eyes nor ears on that lone beach,
They felt no terrors from the night; they were
All in all to each other; though their speech
Was broken words, they *thought* a language there,—
And all the burning tongues the passions teach
Found in one sigh the best interpreter
Of nature's oracle—first love,—that all
Which Eve has left her daughters since her fall.

CXC

Haidée spoke not of scruples, ask'd no vows,
Nor offer'd any; she had never heard
Of plight and promises to be a spouse,
Or perils by a loving maid incurr'd;
She was all which pure ignorance allows,
And flew to her young mate like a young bird,
And never having dreamt of falsehood, she
Had not one word to say of constancy.

CXCI

She loved, and was beloved—she adored,
And she was worshipp'd; after nature's fashion,
Their intense souls, into each other pour'd,
If souls could die, had perish'd in that passion,—

But by degrees their senses were restored,
 Again to be o'ercome, again to dash
 on;
And, beating 'gainst *his* bosom, Haidée's
 heart
Felt as if never more to beat apart.

CXCII

Alas! they were so young, so beautiful,
 So lonely, loving, helpless, and the hour
Was that in which the heart is always full,
 And, having o'er itself no further
 power,
Prompts deeds eternity cannot annul,
 But pays off moments in an endless
 shower
Of hell-fire—all prepared for people
 giving
Pleasure or pain to one another living.

CXCIII

Alas! for Juan and Haidée! they were
 So loving and so lovely—till then never,
Excepting our first parents, such a pair
 Had run the risk of being damn'd for
 ever;
And Haidée, being devout as well as fair,
 Had, doubtless, heard about the
 Stygian river,
And hell and purgatory—but forgot
Just in the very crisis she should not.

CXCIV

They look upon each other, and their eyes
 Gleam in the moonlight; and her white
 arm clasps
Round Juan's head, and his around her
 lies
 Half buried in the tresses which it
 grasps;
She sits upon his knee, and drinks his
 sighs,
 He hers, until they end in broken gasps;
And thus they form a group that's quite
 antique,
Half naked, loving, natural, and Greek.

CXCV

And when those deep and burning
 moments pass'd,
 And Juan sunk to sleep within her arms,
She slept not, but all tenderly, though
 fast,
 Sustain'd his head upon her bosom's
 charms;
And now and then her eye to heaven is
 cast,
 And then on the pale cheek her breast
 now warms,
Pillow'd on her o'erflowing heart, which
 pants
With all it granted, and with all it grants.

CXCVI

An infant when it gazes on a light,
 A child the moment when it drains the
 breast,
A devotee when soars the Host in sight,
 An Arab with a stranger for a guest,
A sailor when the prize has struck in fight,
 A miser filling his most hoarded chest,
Feel rapture; but not such true joy are
 reaping
As they who watch o'er what they love
 while sleeping.

CXCVII

For there it lies so tranquil, so beloved,
 All that it hath of life with us is living;
So gentle, stirless, helpless, and unmoved,
 And all unconscious of the joy 'tis
 giving;
All it hath felt, inflicted, pass'd, and
 proved,
 Hush'd into depths beyond the
 watcher's diving;
There lies the thing we love with all its
 errors
And all its charms, like death without its
 terrors.

CXCVIII

The lady watch'd her lover—and that hour
 Of Love's, and Night's, and Ocean's
 solitude,
O'erflow'd her soul with their united
 power;
 Amidst the barren sand and rocks so
 rude
She and her wave-worn love had made
 their bower,
 Where nought upon their passion could
 intrude,
And all the stars that crowded the blue
 space
Saw nothing happier than her glowing
 face.

CXCIX

Alas! the love of women! it is known
 To be a lovely and a fearful thing;
For all of theirs upon that die is thrown,
 And if 'tis lost, life hath no more to
 bring
To them but mockeries of the past alone,
 And their revenge is as the tiger's spring,
Deadly, and quick, and crushing; yet, as
 real
Torture is theirs, what they inflict they feel.

CC

They are right; for man, to man so oft
 unjust,
 Is always so to women; one sole bond
Awaits them, treachery is all their trust;
 Taught to conceal, their bursting hearts
 despond

Over their idol, till some wealthier lust
 Buys them in marriage—and what rests
 beyond?
A thankless husband, next a faithless
 lover,
Then dressing, nursing, praying, and all's
 over.

CCI

Some take a lover, some take drams or
 prayers,
 Some mind their household, others dis-
 sipation,
Some run away, and but exchange their
 cares,
 Losing the advantage of a virtuous
 station;
Few changes e'er can better their affairs,
 Theirs being an unnatural situation,
From the dull palace to the dirty hovel:
Some play the devil, and then write a
 novel.

CCII

Haidée was Nature's bride, and knew not
 this:
 Haidée was Passion's child, born where
 the sun
Showers triple light, and scorches even
 the kiss
 Of his gazelle-eyed daughters; she was
 one
Made but to love, to feel that she was his
 Who was her chosen: what was said or
 done
Elsewhere was nothing. She had nought
 to fear,
Hope, care, nor love beyond,—her heart
 beat *here*.

CCIII

And oh! that quickening of the heart, that
 beat!
 How much it costs us! yet each rising
 throb
Is in its cause as its effect so sweet,
 That Wisdom, ever on the watch to rob
Joy of its alchemy, and to repeat
 Fine truths; even Conscience, too, has
 a tough job
To make us understand each good old
 maxim,
So good—I wonder Castlereagh don't tax
 'em.

CCIV

And now 'twas done—on the lone shore
 were plighted
 Their hearts; the stars, their nuptial
 torches, shed
Beauty upon the beautiful they lighted:
 Ocean their witness, and the cave their
 bed,

By their own feelings hallow'd and united,
 Their priest was Solitude, and they were
 wed:
And they were happy, for to their young
 eyes
Each was an angel, and earth paradise.

CCV

Oh, Love! of whom great Cæsar was the
 suitor,
 Titus the master, Antony the slave,
Horace, Catullus, scholars, Ovid tutor,
 Sappho the sage blue-stocking, in whose
 grave
All those may leap who rather would be
 neuter—
 (Leucadia's rock still overlooks the
 wave)—
Oh, Love! thou art the very god of evil,
For, after all, we cannot call thee devil.

CCVI

Thou mak'st the chaste connubial state
 precarious,
 And jestest with the brows of mightiest
 men:
Cæsar and Pompey, Mahomet, Belisarius,
 Have much employ'd the muse of
 history's pen:
Their lives and fortunes were extremely
 various,
 Such worthies Time will never see again;
Yet to these four in three things the same
 luck holds,
They all were heroes, conquerors, and
 cuckolds.

CCVII

Thou mak'st philosophers; there's
 Epicurus
 And Aristippus, a material crew!
Who to immoral courses would allure us
 By theories quite practicable too;
If only from the devil they would insure
 us,
 How pleasant were the maxim (not
 quite new),
'Eat, drink, and love; what can the rest
 avail us?'
So said the royal sage Sardanapalus.

CCVIII

But Juan! had he quite forgotten Julia?
 And should he have forgotten her so
 soon?
I can't but say it seems to me most truly a
 Perplexing question; but, no doubt,
 the moon
Does these things for us, and whenever
 newly a
 Strong palpitation rises, 'tis her boon,
Else how the devil is it that fresh features
Have such a charm for us poor human
 creatures?

CCIX

I hate inconstancy—I loathe, detest,
 Abhor, condemn, abjure the mortal
 made
Of such quicksilver clay that in his breast
 No permanent foundations can be laid;
Love, constant love, has been my constant
 guest,
 And yet last night, being at a masquer-
 ade,
I saw the prettiest creature, fresh from
 Milan,
Which gave me some sensations like a
 villain.

CCX

But soon Philosophy came to my aid,
 And whisper'd, 'Think of every sacred
 tie!'
'I will, my dear Philosophy!' I said,
 'But then her teeth, and then, oh,
 Heaven! her eye!
I'll just inquire if she be wife or maid,
 Or neither—out of curiosity.'
Stop!' cried Philosophy, with air so
 Grecian
(Though she was masqued then as a fair
 Venetian);

CCXI

'Stop!' so I stopp'd.—But to return: that
 which
Men call inconstancy is nothing more
Than admiration due where nature's rich
 Profusion with young beauty covers
 o'er
Some favour'd object; and as in the niche
 A lovely statue we almost adore,
This sort of adoration of the real
Is but a heightening of the *beau idéal*.

CCXII

'Tis the perception of the beautiful,
 A fine extension of the faculties,
Platonic, universal, wonderful,
 Drawn from the stars, and filter'd
 through the skies,
Without which life would be extremely
 dull;
In short, it is the use of our own eyes,
With one or two small senses added, just
To hint that flesh is form'd of fiery dust.

CCXIII

Yet 'tis a painful feeling, and unwilling,
 For surely if we always could perceive
In the same object graces quite as killing
 As when she rose upon us like an Eve,
'Twould save us many a heart-ache, many
 a shilling
 (For we must get them any how, or
 grieve),
Whereas, if one sole lady pleased for ever,
How pleasant for the heart, as well as liver!

CCXIV

The heart is like the sky, a part of heaven,
 But changes night and day, too, like the
 sky;
Now o'er it clouds and thunder must be
 driven,
 And darkness and destruction as on high:
But when it hath been scorch'd, and
 pierced, and riven,
 Its storms expire in water-drops; the eye
Pours forth at last the heart's blood turn'd
 to tears,
Which make the English climate of our
 years.

CCXV

The liver is the lazaret of bile,
 But very rarely executes its function,
For the first passion stays there such a while,
 That all the rest creep in and form a
 junction,
Like knots of vipers on a dunghill's soil,
 Rage, fear, hate, jealousy, revenge, com-
 punction,
So that all mischiefs spring up from this
 entrail,
Like earthquakes from the hidden fire
 call'd 'central.'

CCXVI

In the mean time, without proceeding more
 In this anatomy, I've finish'd now
Two hundred and odd stanzas as before,
 That being about the number I'll allow
Each canto of the twelve, or twenty-four;
 And, laying down my pen, I make my bow,
Leaving Don Juan and Haidée to plead
For them and theirs with all who deign to
 read.

CANTO THE THIRD

I

HAIL, Muse! *et cætera.*—We left Juan
 sleeping,
 Pillow'd upon a fair and happy breast,
And watch'd by eyes that never yet knew
 weeping,
 And loved by a young heart, too deeply
 blest
To feel the poison through her spirit
 creeping,
 Or know who rested there, a foe to rest,
Had soil'd the current of her sinless years,
And turn'd her pure heart's purest blood
 to tears!

II

Oh, Love! what is it in this world of ours
 Which makes it fatal to be loved? Ah
 why
With cypress branches hast thou wreathed
 thy bowers,
 And made thy best interpreter a sigh?

As those who dote on odours pluck the flowers,
 And place them on their breast—but place to die—
Thus the frail beings we would fondly cherish
Are laid within our bosoms but to perish.

III

In her first passion woman loves her lover,
 In all the others all she loves is love,
Which grows a habit she can ne'er get over
 And fits her loosely—like an easy glove,
As you may find, whene'er you like to prove her:
 One man alone at first her heart can move;
She then prefers him in the plural number,
Not finding that the additions much encumber.

IV

I know not if the fault be men's or theirs;
 But one thing's pretty sure; a woman planted
(Unless at once she plunge for life in prayers)—
 After a decent time must be gallanted;
Although, no doubt, her first of love affairs
 Is that to which her heart is wholly granted;
Yet there are some, they say, who have had none,
But those who have ne'er end with only *one*.

V

'Tis melancholy, and a fearful sign
 Of human frailty, folly, also crime,
That love and marriage rarely can combine,
 Although they both are born in the same clime;
Marriage from love, like vinegar from wine—
 A sad, sour, sober beverage—by time
Is sharpen'd from its high celestial flavour,
Down to a very homely household savour.

VI

There's something of antipathy, as 'twere,
 Between their present and their future state;
A kind of flattery that's hardly fair
 Is used until the truth arrives too late—
Yet what can people do, except despair?
 The same things change their names at such a rate;
For instance—passion in a lover's glorious,
But in a husband is pronounced uxorious.

VII

Men grow ashamed of being so very fond;
 They sometimes also get a little tired

(But that, of course, is rare), and then despond:
 The same things cannot always be admired,
Yet 'tis 'so nominated in the bond,'
 That both are tied till one shall have expired.
Sad thought! to lose the spouse that was adorning
Our days, and put one's servants into mourning.

VIII

There's doubtless something in domestic doings
 Which forms, in fact, true love's antithesis;
Romances paint at full length people's wooings,
 But only give a bust of marriages;
For no one cares for matrimonial cooings,
 There's nothing wrong in a connubial kiss:
Think you, if Laura had been Petrarch's wife,
He would have written sonnets all his life?

IX

All tragedies are finish'd by a death,
 All comedies are ended by a marriage;
The future states of both are left to faith,
 For authors fear description might disparage
The worlds to come of both, or fall beneath,
 And then both worlds would punish their miscarriage;
So leaving each their priest and prayer-book ready,
They say no more of Death or of the Lady.

X

The only two that in my recollection
 Have sung of heaven and hell, or marriage, are
Dante and Milton, and of both the affection
 Was hapless in their nuptials, for some bar
Of fault or temper ruin'd the connexion
 (Such things, in fact, it don't ask much to mar):
But Dante's Beatrice and Milton's Eve
Were not drawn from their spouses, you conceive.

XI

Some persons say that Dante meant theology
 By Beatrice, and not a mistress—I,
Although my opinion may require apology,
 Deem this a commentator's phantasy,

Unless indeed it was from his own know-
 ledge he
 Decided thus, and show'd good reason
 why;
I think that Dante's more abstruse ecsta-
 tics
Meant to personify the mathematics.

XII

Haidée and Juan were not married, but
 The fault was theirs, not mine: it is not
 fair,
Chaste reader, then, in any way to put
 The blame on me, unless you wish they
 were;
Then if you'd have them wedded, please
 to shut
 The book which treats of this erroneous
 pair,
Before the consequences grow too awful;
'Tis dangerous to read of loves unlawful.

XIII

Yet they were happy,—happy in the illicit
 Indulgence of their innocent desires;
But more imprudent grown with every
 visit,
 Haidée forgot the island was her sire's:
When we have what we like, 'tis hard to
 miss it,
 At least in the beginning, ere one tires;
Thus she came often, not a moment losing,
Whilst her piratical papa was cruising.

XIV

Let not his mode of raising cash seem
 strange,
 Although he fleeced the flags of every
 nation,
For into a prime minister but change
 His title, and 'tis nothing but taxation;
But he, more modest, took an humbler
 range
 Of life, and in an honester vocation
Pursued o'er the high seas his watery
 journey,
And merely practised as a sea-attorney.

XV

The good old gentleman had been detain'd
 By winds and waves, and some impor-
 tant captures;
And, in the hope of more, at sea remain'd,
 Although a squall or two had damp'd
 his raptures,
By swamping one of the prizes; he had
 chain'd
 His prisoners, dividing them like chap-
 ters
In number'd lots; they all had cuffs and
 collars,
And averaged each from ten to a hundred
 dollars.

XVI

Some he disposed of off Cape Matapan,
 Among his friends the Mainots; some
 he sold
To his Tunis correspondents, save one man
 Toss'd overboard unsaleable (being
 old):
The rest—save here and there some richer
 one,
 Reserved for future ransom—in the hold,
Were link'd alike, as for the common
 people he
Had a large order from the Dey of Tripoli.

XVII

The merchandise was served in the same
 way,
 Pieced out for different marts in the
 Levant,
Except some certain portions of the prey,
 Light classic articles of female want,
French stuffs, lace, tweezers, toothpicks,
 teapot, tray,
 Guitars and castanets from Alicant,
All which selected from the spoil he
 gathers,
Robb'd for his daughter by the best of
 fathers.

XVIII

A monkey, a Dutch mastiff, a mackaw,
 Two parrots, with a Persian cat and
 kittens,
He chose from several animals he saw—
 A terrier, too, which once had been a
 Briton's,
Who dying on the coast of Ithaca,
 The peasants gave the poor dumb thing
 a pittance.
These to secure in this strong blowing
 weather,
He caged in one huge hamper all together.

XIX

Then having settled his marine affairs,
 Despatching single cruisers here and
 there,
His vessel having need of some repairs,
 He shaped his course to where his
 daughter fair
Continued still her hospitable cares;
 But that part of the coast being shoal
 and bare,
And rough with reefs which ran out many
 a mile,
His port lay on the other side o' the isle.

XX

And there he went ashore without delay,
 Having no custom-house nor quaran-
 tine
To ask him awkward questions on the way,
 About the time and place where he had
 been:

He left his ship to be hove down next day,
 With orders to the people to careen;
So that all hands were busy beyond
 measure,
In getting out goods, ballast, guns, and
 treasure.

XXI

Arriving at the summit of a hill
 Which overlook'd the white walls of his
 home,
He stopp'd.—What singular emotions fill
 Their bosoms who have been induced to
 roam!
With fluttering doubts if all be well or ill—
 With love for many, and with fears for
 some;
All feelings which o'erleap the years long
 lost,
And bring our hearts back to their start-
 ing-post.

XXII

The approach of home to husbands and to
 sires,
 After long travelling by land or water,
Most naturally some small doubt in-
 spires—
 A female family's a serious matter;
(None trusts the sex more, or so much
 admires—
 But they hate flattery, so I never flatter;)
Wives in their husbands' absences grow
 subtler,
And daughters sometimes run off with the
 butler.

XXIII

An honest gentleman at his return
 May not have the good fortune of
 Ulysses;
Not all lone matrons for their husbands
 mourn,
 Or show the same dislike to suitors'
 kisses;
The odds are that he finds a handsome urn
 To his memory—and two or three
 young misses
Born to some friend, who holds his wife
 and riches;—
And that *his* Argus bites him by—the
 breeches.

XXIV

If single, probably his plighted fair
 Has in his absence wedded some rich
 miser;
But all the better, for the happy pair
 May quarrel, and the lady growing wiser,
He may resume his amatory care
 As cavalier servente, or despise her;
And that his sorrow may not be a dumb
 one,
Write odes on the Inconstancy of Woman.

XXV

And oh! ye gentlemen who have already
 Some chaste *liaison* of the kind—I
 mean
An honest friendship with a married
 lady—
 The only thing of this sort ever seen
To last—of all connexions the most
 steady,
 And the true Hymen, (the first's but a
 screen)—
Yet for all that keep not too long away;
I've known the absent wrong'd four times
 a day.

XXVI

Lambro, our sea-solicitor, who had
 Much less experience of dry land than
 ocean,
On seeing his own chimney-smoke, felt
 glad;
 But not knowing metaphysics, had no
 notion
Of the true reason of his not being sad,
 Or that of any other strong emotion;
He loved his child, and would have wept
 the loss of her,
But knew the cause no more than a philo-
 sopher.

XXVII

He saw his white walls shining in the sun,
 His garden trees all shadowy and green;
He heard his rivulet's light bubbling run,
 The distant dog-bark; and perceived
 between
The umbrage of the wood so cool and dun,
 The moving figures, and the sparkling
 sheen
Of arms (in the East all arm)—and various
 dyes
Of colour'd garbs, as bright as butterflies.

XXVIII

And as the spot where they appear he
 nears,
 Surprised at these unwonted signs of
 idling,
He hears—alas! no music of the spheres,
 But an unhallow'd, earthly sound of
 fiddling!
A melody which made him doubt his ears,
 The cause being past his guessing or un-
 riddling;
A pipe, too, and a drum, and shortly after,
A most unoriental roar of laughter.

XXIX

And still more nearly to the place ad-
 vancing,
 Descending rather quickly the declivity,
Through the waved branches, o'er the
 greensward glancing,
 'Midst other indications of festivity,

Seeing a troop of his domestics dancing
 Like dervises, who turn as on a pivot,
 he
Perceived it was the Pyrrhic dance so
 martial,
To which the Levantines are very partial.

XXX

And further on a group of Grecian girls,
 The first and tallest her white kerchief
 waving,
Were strung together like a row of pearls,
 Link'd hand in hand, and dancing: each
 too having
Down her white neck long floating auburn
 curls—
 (The least of which would set ten poets
 raving);
Their leader sang—and bounded to her
 song,
With choral step and voice, the virgin
 throng.

XXXI

And here, assembled cross-legg'd round
 their trays,
 Small social parties just begun to dine;
Pilaus and meats of all sorts met the gaze,
 And flasks of Samian and of Chian wine,
And sherbet cooling in the porous vase;
 Above them their dessert grew on its
 vine,
The orange and pomegranate nodding o'er
Dropp'd in their laps, scarce pluck'd,
 their mellow store.

XXXII

A band of children, round a snow-white
 ram,
 There wreathe his venerable horns with
 flowers;
While peaceful as if still an unwean'd lamb,
 The patriarch of the flock all gently
 cowers
His sober head, majestically tame,
 Or eats from out the palm, or playful
 lowers
His brow, as if in act to butt, and then
Yielding to their small hands, draws back
 again.

XXXIII

Their classical profiles, and glittering
 dresses,
 Their large black eyes, and soft seraphic
 cheeks,
Crimson as cleft pomegranates, their long
 tresses,
 The gesture which enchants, the eye that
 speaks,
The innocence which happy childhood
 blesses,
 Made quite a picture of these little
 Greeks;

So that the philosophical beholder
Sigh'd for their sakes—that they should
 e'er grow older.

XXXIV

Afar, a dwarf buffoon stood telling tales
 To a sedate grey circle of old smokers,
Of secret treasures found in hidden vales,
 Of wonderful replies from Arab jokers,
Of charms to make good gold and cure
 bad ails,
 Of rocks bewitch'd that open to the
 knockers,
Of magic ladies who, by one sole act,
Transform'd their lords to beasts (but
 that's a fact).

XXXV

Here was no lack of innocent diversion
 For the imagination or the senses,
Song, dance, wine, music, stories from the
 Persian,
 All pretty pastimes in which no offence
 is;
But Lambro saw all these things with
 aversion,
 Perceiving in his absence such expenses,
Dreading that climax of all human ills
The inflammation of his weekly bills.

XXXVI

Ah! what is man? what perils still environ
 The happiest mortals even after dinner!
A day of gold from out an age of iron
 Is all that life allows the luckiest sinner;
Pleasure (whene'er she sings, at least)'s a
 siren,
 That lures, to flay alive, the young be-
 ginner;
Lambro's reception at his people's ban-
 quet
Was such as fire accords to a wet blanket.

XXXVII

He—being a man who seldom used a word
 Too much, and wishing gladly to sur-
 prise
(In general he surprised men with the
 sword)
 His daughter—had not sent before to
 advise
Of his arrival, so that no one stirr'd;
 And long he paused to reässure his eyes,
In fact much more astonish'd than de-
 lighted,
To find so much good company invited.

XXXVIII

He did not know (alas! how men will lie!)
 That a report (especially the Greeks)
Avouch'd his death (such people never
 die),
 And put his house in mourning several
 weeks,—

689

But now their eyes and also lips were dry;
 The bloom, too, had return'd to
 Haidée's cheeks.
Her tears, too, being return'd into their
 fount,
She now kept house upon her own ac-
 count.

XXXIX

Hence all this rice, meat, dancing, wine,
 and fiddling,
 Which turn'd the isle into a place of
 pleasure;
The servants all were getting drunk or
 idling,
 A life which made them happy beyond
 measure;
Her father's hospitality seem'd middling,
 Compared with what Haidée did with
 his treasure;
'Twas wonderful how things went on im-
 proving,
While she had not one hour to spare from
 loving.

XL

Perhaps you think, in stumbling on this
 feast,
 He flew into a passion, and in fact
There was no mighty reason to be pleased;
 Perhaps you prophesy some sudden act,
The whip, the rack, or dungeon at the
 least,
 To teach his people to be more exact,
And that, proceeding at a very high rate,
He show'd the royal *penchants* of a pirate.

XLI

You're wrong.—He was the mildest man-
 ner'd man
 That ever scuttled ship or cut a throat,
With such true breeding of a gentleman,
 You never could divine his real thought;
No courtier could, and scarcely woman can
 Gird more deceit within a petticoat;
Pity he loved adventurous life's variety,
He was so great a loss to good society.

XLII

Advancing to the nearest dinner tray,
 Tapping the shoulder of the nighest
 guest,
With a peculiar smile, which, by the way,
 Boded no good, whatever it express'd,
He asked the meaning of this holiday;
 The vinous Greek to whom he had ad-
 dress'd
His question, much too merry to divine
The questioner, fill'd up a glass of wine,

XLIII

And without turning his facetious head,
 Over his shoulder, with a Bacchant air,
Presented the o'erflowing cup, and said,
 'Talking's dry work, I have no time to
 spare.'

A second hiccup'd, 'Our old master's
 dead,
 You'd better ask our mistress who's his
 heir.'
'Our mistress!' quoth a third: 'Our mis-
 tress!—pooh—
You mean our master—not the old, but
 new.'

XLIV

These rascals, being new comers, knew
 not whom
 They thus address'd—and Lambro's
 visage fell—
And o'er his eye a momentary gloom
 Pass'd, but he strove quite courteously
 to quell
The expression, and endeavouring to re-
 sume
 His smile, requested one of them to tell
The name and quality of his new patron,
Who seem'd to have turn'd Haidée into
 a matron.

XLV

'I know not,' quoth the fellow, 'who or
 what
 He is, nor whence he came—and little
 care;
But this I know, that this roast capon's fat,
 And that good wine ne'er wash'd down
 better fare;
And if you are not satisfied with that,
 Direct your questions to my neighbour
 there;
He'll answer all for better or for worse,
For none likes more to hear himself con-
 verse.'

XLVI

I said that Lambro was a man of patience,
 And certainly he show'd the best of
 breeding,
Which scarce even France, the paragon of
 nations,
 E'er saw her most polite of sons ex-
 ceeding;
He bore these sneers against his near rela-
 tions,
 His own anxiety, his heart, too, bleed-
 ing,
The insults, too, of every servile glutton,
Who all the time was eating up his mutton.

XLVII

Now in a person used to much com-
 mand—
 To bid men come, and go, and come
 again—
To see his orders done, too, out of hand—
 Whether the word was death, or but the
 chain—

It may seem strange to find his manners
 bland;
 Yet such things are, which I cannot ex-
 plain,
Though doubtless he who can command
 himself
Is good to govern—almost as a Guelf.

XLVIII

Not that he was not sometimes rash or so,
 But never in his real and serious mood;
Then calm, concentrated, and still, and
 slow,
 He lay coil'd like the boa in the wood;
With him it never was a word and blow,
 His angry word once o'er, he shed no
 blood,
But in his silence there was much to rue,
And his *one* blow left little work for *two*.

XLIX

He ask'd no further questions, and pro-
 ceeded
 On to the house, but by a private way,
So that the few who met him hardly
 heeded,
 So little they expected him that day;
If love paternal in his bosom pleaded
 For Haidée's sake, is more than I can
 say,
But certainly to one deem'd dead return-
 ing,
This revel seem'd a curious mode of
 mourning.

L

If all the dead could now return to life,
 (Which God forbid!) or some, or a
 great many,
For instance, if a husband or his wife
 (Nuptial examples are as good as any),
No doubt, whate'er might be their former
 strife,
 The present weather would be much
 more rainy—
Tears shed into the grave of the connexion
Would share most probably its resur-
 rection.

LI

He enter'd in the house no more his home,
 A thing to human feelings the most
 trying,
And harder for the heart to overcome,
 Perhaps, than even the mental pangs of
 dying;
To find our hearthstone turn'd into a
 tomb,
 And round its once warm precincts
 palely lying
The ashes of our hopes, is a deep grief,
Beyond a single gentleman's belief.

LII

He enter'd in the house—his home no
 more,
 For without hearts there is no home;—
 and felt
The solitude of passing his own door
 Without a welcome: *there* he long had
 dwelt,
There his few peaceful days Time had
 swept o'er,
 There his worn bosom and keen eye
 would melt
Over the innocence of that sweet child,
His only shrine of feelings undefiled.

LIII

He was a man of a strange temperament,
 Of mild demeanour though of savage
 mood,
Moderate in all his habits, and content
 With temperance in pleasure, as in food,
Quick to perceive, and strong to bear, and
 meant
 For something better, if not wholly
 good;
His country's wrongs and his despair to
 save her
Had stung him from a slave to an enslaver.

LIV

The love of power, and rapid gain of gold,
 The hardness by long habitude pro-
 duced,
The dangerous life in which he had grown
 old,
 The mercy he had granted oft abused,
The sights he was accustom'd to behold,
 The wild seas, and wild men with whom
 he cruised,
Had cost his enemies a long repentance,
And made him a good friend, but bad
 acquaintance.

LV

But something of the spirit of old Greece
 Flash'd o'er his soul a few heroic rays,
Such as lit onward to the Golden Fleece
 His predecessors in the Colchian days;
'Tis true he had no ardent love for peace—
 Alas! his country show'd no path to
 praise:
Hate to the world and war with every
 nation
He waged, in vengeance of her degrada-
 tion.

LVI

Still o'er his mind the influence of the
 clime
 Shed its Ionian elegance, which show'd
Its power unconsciously full many a
 time,—
 A taste seen in the choice of his abode,

A love of music and of scenes sublime,
 A pleasure in the gentle stream that
 flow'd
Past him in crystal, and a joy in flowers,
Bedew'd his spirit in his calmer hours.

LVII

But whatsoe'er he had of love reposed
 On that beloved daughter; she had been
The only thing which kept his heart un-
 closed
 Amidst the savage deeds he had done and
 seen,
A lonely pure affection unopposed:
 There wanted but the loss of this to wean
His feelings from all milk of human kind-
 ness,
And turn him like the Cyclops mad with
 blindness.

LVIII

The cubless tigress in her jungle raging
 Is dreadful to the shepherd and the
 flock;
The ocean when its yeasty war is waging
 Is awful to the vessel near the rock;
But violent things will sooner bear as-
 suaging,
 Their fury being spent by its own shock,
Than the stern, single, deep, and wordless ire
Of a strong human heart, and in a sire.

LIX

It is a hard although a common case
 To find our children running restive—
 they
In whom our brightest days we would re-
 trace,
 Our little selves re-formed in finer clay,
Just as old age is creeping on apace,
 And clouds come o'er the sunset of our
 day,
They kindly leave us, though not quite
 alone,
But in good company—the gout or stone.

LX

Yet a fine family is a fine thing
 (Provided they don't come in after
 dinner);
'Tis beautiful to see a matron bring
 Her children up (if nursing them don't
 thin her);
Like cherubs round an altar-piece they
 cling
 To the fire-side (a sight to touch a sinner).
A lady with her daughters or her nieces
Shine like a guinea and seven-shilling
 pieces.

LXI

Old Lambro pass'd unseen a private gate,
 And stood within his hall at eventide;
Meantime the lady and her lover sate
 At wassail in their beauty and their pride:

An ivory inlaid table spread with state
 Before them, and fair slaves on ever
 side;
Gems, gold, and silver, form'd the servic
 mostly,
Mother of pearl and coral the less costly

LXII

The dinner made about a hundred dishes
 Lamb and pistachio nuts—in short, a
 meats,
And saffron soups, and sweetbreads; an
 the fishes
 Were of the finest that e'er flounced i
 nets,
Drest to a Sybarite's most pamper'd wishes
 The beverage was various sherbets
Of raisin, orange, and pomegranate juice
Squeezed through the rind, which make
 it best for use.

LXIII

These were ranged round, each in i
 crystal ewer,
 And fruits, and date-bread loave
 closed the repast,
And Mocha's berry, from Arabia pure,
 In small fine China cups, came in at last
Gold cups of filigree made to secure
 The hand from burning underneat'
 them placed;
Cloves, cinnamon, and saffron too wer
 boil'd
Up with the coffee, which (I think) the
 spoil'd.

LXIV

The hangings of the room were tapestry
 made
 Of velvet panels, each of different hue,
And thick with damask flowers of sil
 inlaid;
 And round them ran a yellow borde
 too;
The upper border, richly wrought, dis
 play'd,
 Embroider'd delicately o'er with blue,
Soft Persian sentences, in lilac letters,
From poets, or the moralists their betters

LXV

These Oriental writings on the wall,
 Quite common in those countries, are
 kind
Of monitors adapted to recall,
 Like skulls at Memphian banquets, t
 the mind
The words which shook Belshazzar in hi
 hall,
 And took his kingdom from him: Yo
 will find,
Though sages may pour out their wisdom'
 treasure,
There is no sterner moralist than Pleasure

LXVI

A beauty at the season's close grown hectic,
 A genius who has drunk himself to death,
A rake turn'd methodistic, or Eclectic—
 (For that's the name they like to pray
 beneath)—
But most, an alderman struck apoplectic,
 Are things that really take away the
 breath,—
And show that late hours, wine, and love
 are able
To do not much less damage than the table.

LXVII

Haidée and Juan carpeted their feet
 On crimson satin, border'd with pale
 blue;
Their sofa occupied three parts complete
 Of the apartment—and appear'd quite
 new;
The velvet cushions (for a throne more
 meet)
 Were scarlet, from whose glowing centre
 grew
A sun emboss'd in gold, whose rays of tissue,
Meridian-like, were seen all light to issue.

LXVIII

Crystal and marble, plate and porcelain,
 Had done their work of splendour;
 Indian mats
And Persian carpets, which the heart bled
 to stain,
 Over the floors were spread; gazelles
 and cats,
And dwarfs and blacks, and such like
 things that gain
 Their bread as ministers and favourites
 —(that's
To say, by degradation)—mingled there
As plentiful as in a court or fair.

LXIX

There was no want of lofty mirrors, and
 The tables, most of ebony inlaid
With mother of pearl or ivory, stood at
 hand,
 Or were of tortoise-shell or rare woods
 made,
Fretted with gold or silver:—by command,
 The greater part of these were ready
 spread
With viands and sherbets in ice—and
 wine—
Kept for all comers at all hours to dine.

LXX

Of all the dresses I select Haidée's:
 She wore two jelicks—one was of pale
 yellow;
Of azure, pink, and white was her
 chemise—
 'Neath which her breast heaved like a
 little billow,

With buttons form'd of pearls as large as
 peas,
 All gold and crimson shone her jelick's
 fellow,
And the striped white gauze baracan that
 bound her,
Like fleecy clouds about the moon, flow'd
 round her.

LXXI

One large gold bracelet clasp'd each lovely
 arm,
 Lockless—so pliable from the pure gold
That the hand stretch'd and shut it without
 harm,
 The limb which it adorn'd its only
 mould;
So beautiful—its very shape would charm,
 And clinging as if loath to lose its hold,
The purest ore enclosed the whitest skin
That e'er by precious metal was held in.

LXXII

Around, as princess of her father's land,
 A like gold bar above her instep roll'd
Announced her rank; twelve rings were on
 her hand;
 Her hair was starr'd with gems; her
 veil's fine fold
Below her breast was fasten'd with a band
 Of lavish pearls, whose worth could
 scarce be told;
Her orange silk full Turkish trousers
 furl'd
About the prettiest ankle in the world.

LXXIII

Her hair's long auburn waves down to her
 heel
 Flow'd like an Alpine torrent which
 the sun
Dyes with his morning light,—and would
 conceal
 Her person if allow'd at large to run,
And still they seem resentfully to feel
 The silken fillet's curb, and sought to
 shun
Their bonds whene'er some Zephyr caught
 began
To offer his young pinion as her fan.

LXXIV

Round her she made an atmosphere of
 life,
 The very air seem'd lighter from her
 eyes,
They were so soft and beautiful, and rife
 With all we can imagine of the skies,
And pure as Psyche ere she grew a wife—
 Too pure even for the purest human
 ties;
Her overpowering presence made you feel
It would not be idolatry to kneel.

LXXV

Her eyelashes, though dark as night,
were tinged
(It is the country's custom), but in vain;
For those large black eyes were so blackly
fringed,
The glossy rebels mock'd the jetty stain,
And in their native beauty stood avenged:
Her nails were touch'd with henna; but
again
The power of art was turn'd to nothing,
for
They could not look more rosy than before.

LXXVI

The henna should be deeply dyed to make
The skin relieved appear more fairly
fair;
She had no need of this, day ne'er will
break
On mountain-tops more heavenly white
than her:
The eye might doubt if it were well awake,
She was so like a vision; I might err,
But Shakspeare also says, 'tis very silly
'To gild refined gold, or paint the lily.'

LXXVII

Juan had on a shawl of black and gold,
But a white baracan, and so transparent
The sparkling gems beneath you might
behold,
Like small stars through the milky way
apparent;
His turban furl'd in many a graceful fold,
An emerald aigrette with Haidée's hair
in't
Surmounted, as its clasp, a glowing
crescent,
Whose rays shone ever trembling, but in-
cessant.

LXXVIII

And now they were diverted by their suite,
Dwarfs, dancing-girls, black eunuchs,
and a poet,
Which made their new establishment com-
plete;
The last was of great fame, and liked to
show it;
His verses rarely wanted their due feet—
And for his theme—he seldom sung
below it,
He being paid to satirise or flatter,
As the psalm says, 'inditing a good
matter.'

LXXIX

He praised the present, and abused the
past,
Reversing the good custom of old days,
An Eastern anti-jacobin at last
He turn'd, preferring pudding to no
praise—

For some few years his lot had been o'er-
cast
By his seeming independent in his lays,
But now he sung the Sultan and the Pacha
With truth like Southey, and with verse
like Crashaw.

LXXX

He was a man who had seen many changes,
And always changed as true as any
needle;
His polar star being one which rather
ranges,
And not the fix'd—he knew the way to
wheedle:
So vile he 'scaped the doom which oft
avenges;
And being fluent (save indeed when
fee'd ill),
He lied with such a fervour of intention—
There was no doubt he earn'd his laureate
pension.

LXXXI

But he had genius,—when a turncoat has it,
The 'Vates irritabilis' takes care
That without notice few full moons shall
pass it;
Even good men like to make the public
stare:—
But to my subject—let me see—what was
it?—
Oh!—the third canto—and the pretty
pair—
Their loves, and feasts, and house, and
dress, and mode
Of living in their insular abode.

LXXXII

Their poet, a sad trimmer, but no less
In company a very pleasant fellow,
Had been the favourite of full many a mess
Of men, and made them speeches when
half mellow;
And though his meaning they could rarely
guess,
Yet still they deign'd to hiccup or to
bellow
The glorious meed of popular applause,
Of which the first ne'er knows the second
cause.

LXXXIII

But now being lifted into high society,
And having pick'd up several odds and
ends
Of free thoughts in his travels, for variety,
He deem'd, being in a lone isle, among
friends,
That without any danger of a riot, he
Might for long lying make himself
amends;
And singing as he sung in his warm youth,
Agree to a short armistice with truth.

694

LXXXIV

He had travell'd 'mongst the Arabs,
 Turks, and Franks,
And knew the self-loves of the different
 nations;
And having lived with people of all ranks,
 Had something ready upon most occa-
 sions—
Which got him a few presents and some
 thanks.
 He varied with some skill his adulations;
To 'do at Rome as Romans do,' a piece
Of conduct was which he observed in
 Greece.

LXXXV

Thus, usually, when he was asked to sing,
 He gave the different nations something
 national;
'Twas all the same to him—'God save the
 king,'
Or 'Ça ira,' according to the fashion all:
His muse made increment of anything,
 From the high lyric down to the low
 rational:
If Pindar sang horse-races, what should
 hinder
Himself from being as pliable as Pindar?

LXXXVI

In France, for instance, he would write a
 chanson;
 In England a six-canto quarto tale;
In Spain he'd make a ballad or romance on
 The last war—much the same in Portu-
 gal;
In Germany, the Pegasus he'd prance on
 Would be old Goethe's—(see what says
 De Staël);
In Italy he'd ape the 'Trecentisti';
In Greece, he'd sing some sort of hymn
 like this t' ye:

1

The isles of Greece, the isles of Greece!
 Where burning Sappho loved and
 sung,
Where grew the arts of war and peace,
 Where Delos rose, and Phœbus
 sprung!
Eternal summer gilds them yet,
But all, except their sun, is set.

2

The Scian and the Teian muse,
 The hero's harp, the lover's lute,
Have found the fame your shores refuse:
 Their place of birth alone is mute
To sounds which echo further west
Than your sires' 'Islands of the Blest.'

3

The mountains look on Marathon—
 And Marathon looks on the sea;
And musing there an hour alone,

I dream'd that Greece might still be
 free;
For standing on the Persians' grave,
I could not deem myself a slave.

4

A king sate on the rocky brow
 Which looks o'er sea-born Salamis;
And ships, by thousands, lay below,
 And men in nations;—all were his!
He counted them at break of day—
And when the sun set where were they?

5

And where are they? and where art thou,
 My country? On thy voiceless shore
The heroic lay is tuneless now—
 The heroic bosom beats no more!
And must thy lyre, so long divine,
Degenerate into hands like mine?

6

'Tis something, in the dearth of fame,
 Though link'd among a fetter'd race,
To feel at least a patriot's shame,
 Even as I sing, suffuse my face;
For what is left the poet here?
For Greeks a blush—for Greece a tear.

7

Must we but weep o'er days more blest?
 Must we but blush?—Our fathers bled.
Earth! render back from out thy breast
 A remnant of our Spartan dead!
Of the three hundred grant but three,
To make a new Thermopylæ!

8

What, silent still? and silent all?
 Ah! no;—the voices of the dead
Sound like a distant torrent's fall,
 And answer, 'Let one living head,
But one arise,—we come, we come!'
'Tis but the living who are dumb.

9

In vain—in vain: strike other chords;
 Fill high the cup with Samian wine!
Leave battles to the Turkish hordes,
 And shed the blood of Scio's vine!
Hark! rising to the ignoble call—
How answers each bold Bacchanal!

10

You have the Pyrrhic dance as yet;
 Where is the Pyrrhic phalanx gone?
Of two such lessons, why forget
 The nobler and the manlier one?
You have the letters Cadmus gave—
Think ye he meant them for a slave?

11

Fill high the bowl with Samian wine!
 We will not think of themes like these!
It made Anacreon's song divine:
 He served—but served Polycrates—
A tyrant; but our masters then
Were still, at least, our countrymen.

12

The tyrant of the Chersonese
 Was freedom's best and bravest
 friend;
That tyrant was Miltiades!
Oh! that the present hour would lend
Another despot of the kind!
Such chains as his were sure to bind.

13

Fill high the bowl with Samian wine:
 On Suli's rock, and Parga's shore,
Exists the remnant of a line
 Such as the Doric mothers bore;
And there, perhaps, some seed is sown,
The Heracleidan blood might own.

14

Trust not for freedom to the Franks—
 They have a king who buys and sells;
In native swords, and native ranks,
 The only hope of courage dwells:
But Turkish force, and Latin fraud,
Would break your shield, however
 broad.

15

Fill high the bowl with Samian wine!
 Our virgins dance beneath the shade—
I see their glorious black eyes shine;
 But gazing on each glowing maid,
My own the burning tear-drop laves,
To think such breasts must suckle slaves.

16

Place me on Sunium's marbled steep,
 Where nothing, save the waves and I,
May hear our mutual murmurs sweep;
 There, swan-like, let me sing and die:
A land of slaves shall ne'er be mine—
Dash down yon cup of Samian wine!

LXXXVII

Thus sung, or would, or could, or should
 have sung,
 The modern Greek, in tolerable verse;
If not like Orpheus quite, when Greece
 was young,
 Yet in these times he might have done
 much worse:
His strain display'd some feeling—right or
 wrong;
 And feeling, in a poet, is the source
Of others' feeling; but they are such liars,
And take all colours—like the hands of
 dyers.

LXXXVIII

But words are things, and a small drop o
 ink,
 Falling like dew, upon a thought, pro
 duces
That which makes thousands, perhap
 millions, think;
 'Tis strange, the shortest letter which
 man uses
Instead of speech, may form a lasting link
 Of ages; to what straits old Time re
 duces
Frail man, when paper—even a rag like
 this,
Survives himself, his tomb, and all that'
 his!

LXXXIX

And when his bones are dust, his grave a
 blank,
 His station, generation, even his nation
Become a thing, or nothing, save to rank
 In chronological commemoration,
Some dull MS. oblivion long has sank,
 Or graven stone found in a barrack'
 station
In digging the foundation of a closet,
May turn his name up, as a rare deposit.

XC

And glory long has made the sages smile
 'Tis something, nothing, words, illusion
 wind—
Depending more upon the historian's styl
 Than on the name a person leaves be
 hind:
Troy owes to Homer what whist owes t
 Hoyle:
 The present century was growing blin
To the great Marlborough's skill in givin
 knocks,
Until his late Life by Archdeacon Coxe.

XCI

Milton's the prince of poets—so we say;
 A little heavy, but no less divine:
An independent being in his day—
 Learn'd, pious, temperate in love an
 wine;
But his life falling into Johnson's way,
 We're told this great high priest of a
 the Nine
Was whipt at college—a harsh sire—od
 spouse,
For the first Mrs. Milton left his house.

XCII

All these are, *certes*, entertaining facts,
 Like Shakspeare's stealing deer, Lor
 Bacon's bribes;
Like Titus' youth, and Cæsar's earlies
 acts;
 Like Burns (whom Doctor Currie wel
 describes);

Like Cromwell's pranks;—but although
 truth exacts
 These amiable descriptions from the
 scribes,
As most essential to their hero's story,
They do not much contribute to his glory.

XCIII

All are not moralists, like Southey, when
 He prated to the world of 'Pantiso-
 cracy';
Or Wordsworth unexcised, unhired, who
 then
 Season'd his pedlar poems with de-
 mocracy;
Or Coleridge, long before his flighty pen
 Let to the Morning Post its aristocracy;
When he and Southey, following the same
 path,
Espoused two partners (milliners of Bath).

XCIV

Such names at present cut a convict figure,
 The very Botany Bay in moral geo-
 graphy;
Their loyal treason, renegado rigour,
 Are good manure for their more bare
 biography,
Wordsworth's last quarto, by the way, is
 bigger
 Than any since the birthday of typo-
 graphy;
A drowsy frowzy poem, call'd the 'Excur-
 sion,'
Writ in a manner which is my aversion.

XCV

He there builds up a formidable dyke
 Between his own and others' intellect:
But Wordsworth's poem, and his fol-
 lowers, like
 Joanna Southcote's Shiloh, and her sect,
Are things which, in this century don't
 strike
 The public mind,—so few are the elect;
And the new births of both their stale
 virginities
Have proved but dropsies, taken for divi-
 nities.

XCVI

But let me to my story: I must own,
 If I have any fault, it is digression,
Leaving my people to proceed alone,
 While I soliloquize beyond expression:
But these are my addresses from the throne,
 Which put off business to the ensuing
 session:
Forgetting each omission is a loss to
The world, not quite so great as Ariosto.

XCVII

I know that what our neighbours call
 'longueurs,'
 (We've not so good a *word*, but have the
 thing,

In that complete perfection which insures
 An epic from Bob Southey every
 Spring—)
Form not the true temptation which allures
 The reader; but 'twould not be hard to
 bring
Some fine examples of the *epopée*,
To prove its grand ingredient is *ennui*.

XCVIII

We learn from Horace, 'Homer some-
 times sleeps;'
 We feel without him, Wordsworth
 sometimes wakes,—
To show with what complacency he creeps,
 With his dear ' *Waggoners*,' around his
 lakes.
He wishes for 'a boat' to sail the deeps—
 Of ocean?—No, of air; and then he
 makes
Another outcry for 'a little boat,'
And drivels seas to set it well afloat.

XCIX

If he must fain sweep o'er the ethereal
 plain,
 And Pegasus runs restive in his 'Waggon',
Could he not beg the loan of Charles's
 Wain?
 Or pray Medea for a single dragon?
Or if, too classic for his vulgar brain,
 He fear'd his neck to venture such a nag
 on,
And he must needs mount nearer to the
 moon,
Could not the blockhead ask for a balloon?

C

'Pedlars,' and 'Boats,' and 'Waggons!'
 Oh! ye shades
 Of Pope and Dryden, are we come to
 this?
That trash of such sort not alone evades
 Contempt, but from the bathos' vast abyss
Floats scumlike uppermost, and these
 Jack Cades
 Of sense and song above your graves
 may hiss—
The 'little boatman' and his 'Peter Bell'
Can sneer at him who drew 'Achitophel'!

CI

T' our tale.—The feast was over, the slaves
 gone,
 The dwarfs and dancing girls had all
 retired;
The Arab lore and poet's song were done,
 And every sound of revelry expired;
The lady and her lover, left alone,
 The rosy flood of twilight's sky ad-
 mired;—
Ave Maria! o'er the earth and sea,
That heavenliest hour of Heaven is worth-
 iest thee!

697

CII

Ave Maria! blessed be the hour!
 The time, the clime, the spot, where I so
 oft
Have felt that moment in its fullest power
 Sink o'er the earth so beautiful and soft,
While swung the deep bell in the distant
 tower,
 Or the faint dying day-hymn stole aloft,
And not a breath crept through the rosy
 air,
And yet the forest leaves seem'd stirr'd
 with prayer.

CIII

Ave Maria! 'tis the hour of prayer!
 Ave Maria! 'tis the hour of love!
Ave Maria! may our spirits dare
 Look up to thine and to thy Son's above!
Ave Maria! oh that face so fair!
 Those downcast eyes beneath the Al-
 mighty dove—
What though 'tis but a pictured image?
 —strike,
That painting is no idol,—'tis too like.

CIV

Some kinder casuists are pleased to say,
 In nameless print—that I have no devo-
 tion;
But set those persons down with me to
 pray,
 And you shall see who has the properest
 notion
Of getting into heaven the shortest way;
 My altars are the mountains and the
 ocean,
Earth, air, stars,—all that springs from the
 great Whole,
Who hath produced, and will receive the
 soul.

CV

Sweet hour of twilight!—in the solitude
 Of the pine forest, and the silent shore
Which bounds Ravenna's immemorial
 wood,
 Rooted where once the Adrian wave
 flow'd o'er,
To where the last Cæsarean fortress stood,
 Evergreen forest! which Boccaccio's lore
And Dryden's lay made haunted ground
 to me,
How have I loved the twilight hour and
 thee!

CVI

The shrill cicalas, people of the pine,
 Making their summer lives one cease-
 less song,
Were the sole echoes, save my steed's and
 mine,
 And vesper bell's that rose the boughs
 along;

The spectre huntsman of Onesti's line,
 His hell-dogs, and their chase, and th
 fair throng
Which learn'd from this example not to f
From a true lover,—shadow'd my mind'
 eye.

CVII

Oh, Hesperus! thou bringest all goo
 things—
 Home to the weary, to the hungry chee
To the young bird the parent's broodin
 wings,
 The welcome stall to the o'erlabour'
 steer;
Whate'er of peace about our hearthston
 clings,
 Whate'er our household gods protect c
 dear,
Are gather'd round us by thy look of res
Thou bring'st the child, too, to th
 mother's breast.

CVIII

Soft hour! which wakes the wish and mel
 the heart
 Of those who sail the seas, on the fir
 day
When they from their sweet friends a
 torn apart;
 Or fills with love the pilgrim on his wa
As the far bell of vesper makes him star
 Seeming to weep the dying day's decay
Is this a fancy which our reason scorns?
Ah! surely nothing dies but somethin
 mourns!

CIX

When Nero perish'd by the justest doom
 Which ever the destroyer yet destroy'
Amidst the roar of liberated Rome,
 Of nations freed, and the world ove
 joy'd,
Some hands unseen strew'd flowers upc
 his tomb:
 Perhaps the weakness of a heart not voi
Of feeling for some kindness done, whe
 power
Had left the wretch an uncorrupted hou

CX

But I'm digressing; what on earth ha
 Nero,
 Or any such like sovereign buffoons,
To do with the transactions of my hero,
 More than such madmen's fellow ma
 —the moon's?
Sure my invention must be down at zer
 And I grown one of many 'wood
 spoons'
Of verse (the name with which we Canta
 please
To dub the last of honours in degrees).

CXI

I feel this tediousness will never do—
 'Tis being *too* epic, and I must cut down
(In copying) this long canto into two;
 They'll never find it out, unless I own
The fact, excepting some experienced few;
 And then as an improvement 'twill be
 shown:
I'll prove that such the opinion of the
 critic is
From Aristotle *passim*.—See Ποιητικης.

CANTO THE FOURTH

I

NOTHING so difficult as a beginning
 In poesy, unless perhaps the end;
For oftentimes when Pegasus seems win-
 ning
 The race, he sprains a wing, and down
 we tend,
Like Lucifer when hurl'd from heaven for
 sinning;
 Our sin the same, and hard as his to
 mend,
Being pride, which leads the mind to soar
 too far,
Till our own weakness shows us what we are.

II

But time, which brings all beings to their
 level,
 And sharp Adversity, will teach at last
Man,—and, as we would hope,—perhaps
 the devil,
 That neither of their intellects are vast:
While youth's hot wishes in our red veins
 revel,
 We know not this—the blood flows on
 too fast:
But as the torrent widens towards the ocean,
We ponder deeply on each past emotion.

III

As boy, I thought myself a clever fellow,
 And wish'd that others held the same
 opinion;
They took it up when my days grew more
 mellow,
 And other minds acknowledged my
 dominion:
Now my sere fancy 'falls into the yellow
 Leaf,' and Imagination droops her
 pinion,
And the sad truth which hovers o'er my
 desk
Turns what was once romantic to bur-
 lesque.

IV

And if I laugh at any mortal thing,
 'Tis that I may not weep; and if I weep,
'Tis that our nature cannot always bring
 Itself to apathy, for we must steep

Our hearts first in the depths of Lethe's
 spring,
 Ere what we least wish to behold will
 sleep:
Thetis baptized her mortal son in Styx;
A mortal mother would on Lethe fix.

V

Some have accused me of a strange design
 Against the creed and morals of the
 land,
And trace it in this poem every line;
 I don't pretend that I quite understand
My own meaning when I would be *very* fine;
 But the fact is that I have nothing plann'd,
Unless it were to be a moment merry,
A novel word in my vocabulary.

VI

To the kind reader of our sober clime
 This way of writing will appear exotic;
Pulci was sire of the half-serious rhyme,
 Who sang when chivalry was more
 Quixotic,
And revell'd in the fancies of the time,
 True knights, chaste dames, huge giants,
 kings despotic:
But all these, save the last, being obsolete,
I chose a modern subject as more meet.

VII

How I have treated it, I do not know;
 Perhaps no better than they have treated
 me,
Who have imputed such designs as show
 Not what they saw, but what they
 wish'd to see;
But if it gives them pleasure, be it so,
 This is a liberal age, and thoughts are
 free:
Meantime Apollo plucks me by the ear,
And tells me to resume my story here.

VIII

Young Juan and his lady-love were left
 To their own hearts' most sweet society;
Even Time the pitiless in sorrow cleft
 With his rude scythe such gentle
 bosoms; he
Sigh'd to behold them of their hours bereft,
 Though foe to love; and yet they could
 not be
Meant to grow old, but die in happy spring,
Before one charm or hope had taken wing.

IX

Their faces were not made for wrinkles, their
 Pure blood to stagnate, their great
 hearts to fail;
The blank grey was not made to blast their
 hair,
 But like the climes that know nor snow
 nor hail,

They were all summer; lightning might
 assail
 And shiver them to ashes, but to trail
A long and snake-like life of dull decay
Was not for them—they had too little clay.

X

They were alone once more; for them to be
 Thus was another Eden; they were never
Weary, unless when separate: the tree
 Cut from its forest root of years—the
 river
Damm'd from its fountain—the child from
 the knee
 And breast maternal wean'd at once for
 ever,—
Would wither less than these two torn apart;
Alas! there is no instinct like the heart—

XI

The heart—which may be broken: happy
 they!
 Thrice fortunate! who of that fragile
 mould,
The precious porcelain of human clay,
 Break with the first fall: they can ne'er
 behold
The long year link'd with heavy day on day,
 And all which must be borne, and never
 told;
While life's strange principle will often lie
Deepest in those who long the most to die.

XII

'Whom the gods love die young' was said
 of yore,
 And many deaths do they escape by this:
The death of friends, and that which slays
 even more—
 The death of friendship, love, youth, all
 that is,
Except mere breath; and since the silent
 shore
 Awaits at last even those who longest
 miss
The old archer's shafts, perhaps the early
 grave
Which men weep over may be meant to
 save.

XIII

Haidée and Juan thought not of the dead.
 The heavens, and earth, and air, seem'd
 made for them:
They found no fault with Time, save that
 he fled;
 They saw not in themselves aught to
 condemn;
Each was the other's mirror, and but read
 Joy sparkling in their dark eyes like a
 gem,
And knew such brightness was but the
 reflection
Of their exchanging glances of affection.

XIV

The gentle pressure, and the thrilling
 touch,
 The least glance better understood than
 words,
Which still said all, and ne'er could say
 too much;
 A language, too, but like to that of birds,
Known but to them, at least appearing
 such
 As but to lovers a true sense affords;
Sweet playful phrases, which would seem
 absurd
To those who have ceased to hear such, or
 ne'er heard.

XV

All these were theirs, for they were children
 still,
 And children still they should have ever
 been;
They were not made in the real world to fill
 A busy character in the dull scene,
But like two beings born from out a rill,
 A nymph and her beloved, all unseen
To pass their lives in fountains and on
 flowers,
And never know the weight of human
 hours.

XVI

Moons changing had roll'd on, and
 changeless found
 Those their bright rise had lighted to
 such joys
As rarely they beheld throughout their
 round;
 And these were not of the vain kind
 which cloys,
For theirs were buoyant spirits, never
 bound
 By the mere senses; and that which de-
 stroys
Most love, possession, unto them appear'd
A thing which each endearment more en-
 dear'd.

XVII

Oh beautiful! and rare as beautiful!
 But theirs was love in which the mind
 delights
To lose itself, when the old world grows
 dull,
 And we are sick of its hack sounds and
 sights,
Intrigues, adventures of the common
 school,
 Its petty passions, marriages, and flights
Where Hymen's torch but brands one
 strumpet more,
Whose husband only knows her not a
 whore.

XVIII

Hard words; harsh truth; a truth which
 many know.
 Enough.—The faithful and the fairy
 pair,
Who never found a single hour too slow,
 What was it made them thus exempt
 from care?
Young innate feelings all have felt below,
 Which perish in the rest, but in them
 were
Inherent; what we mortals call romantic,
And always envy, though we deem it frantic.

XIX

This is in others a factitious state,
 An opium dream of too much youth and
 reading,
But was in them their nature or their fate:
 No novels e'er had set their young hearts
 bleeding,
For Haidée's knowledge was by no means
 great,
 And Juan was a boy of saintly breeding;
So that there was no reason for their loves
More than for those of nightingales or doves.

XX

They gazed upon the sunset; 'tis an hour
 Dear unto all, but dearest to *their* eyes,
For it had made them what they were: the
 power
 Of love had first o'erwhelm'd them from
 such skies,
When happiness had been their only dower,
 And twilight saw them link'd in
 passion's ties;
Charm'd with each other, all things
 charm'd that brought
The past still welcome as the present thought.

XXI

I know not why, but in that hour to-night,
 Even as they gazed, a sudden tremor
 came,
And swept, as 'twere, across their hearts'
 delight,
 Like the wind o'er a harp-string, or a
 flame,
When one is shook in sound, and one in
 sight:
 And thus some boding flash'd through
 either frame,
And call'd from Juan's breast a faint low
 sigh,
While one new tear arose in Haidée's eye.

XXII

That large black prophet eye seem'd to
 dilate
 And follow far the disappearing sun,
As if their last day of a happy date
 With his broad, bright, and dropping
 orb were gone.

Juan gazed on her as to ask his fate—
 He felt a grief, but knowing cause for
 none,
His glance inquired of hers for some excuse
For feelings causeless, or at least abstruse.

XXIII

She turn'd to him, and smiled, but in that
 sort
 Which makes not others smile; then
 turn'd aside:
Whatever feeling shook her, it seem'd
 short,
 And master'd by her wisdom or her
 pride;
When Juan spoke, too—it might be in
 sport—
 Of this their mutual feeling, she re-
 plied—
'If it should be so,—but—it cannot be—
Or I at least shall not survive to see.'

XXIV

Juan would question further, but she
 press'd
 His lips to hers, and silenced him with
 this,
And then dismiss'd the omen from her
 breast,
 Defying augury with that fond kiss;
And no doubt of all methods 'tis the best:
 Some people prefer wine—'tis not
 amiss;
I have tried both; so those who would a
 part take
May choose between the headache and the
 heartache.

XXV

One of the two according to your choice,
 Woman or wine, you'll have to undergo;
Both maladies are taxes on our joys:
 But which to choose, I really hardly
 know;
And if I had to give a casting voice,
 For both sides I could many reasons
 show,
And then decide, without great wrong to
 either,
It were much better to have both than
 neither.

XXVI

Juan and Haidée gazed upon each other
 With swimming looks of speechless
 tenderness,
Which mix'd all feelings, friend, child,
 lover, brother;
 All that the best can mingle and express
When two pure hearts are pour'd in one
 another,
 And love too much, and yet cannot love
 less;
But almost sanctify the sweet excess
By the immortal wish and power to bless.

XXVII

Mix'd in each other's arms, and heart in
heart,
 Why did they not then die?—they had
lived too long
Should an hour come to bid them breathe
apart;
 Years could but bring them cruel things
or wrong;
The world was not for them, nor the
world's art
 For beings passionate as Sappho's song;
Love was born *with* them, *in* them, so
intense,
It was their very spirit—not a sense.

XXVIII

They should have lived together deep in
woods,
 Unseen as sings the nightingale; they
were
Unfit to mix in these thick solitudes
 Call'd social, haunts of Hate, and Vice,
and Care;
How lonely every freeborn creature
broods!
 The sweetest song-birds nestle in a pair;
The eagle soars alone; the gull and crow
Flock o'er their carrion, just like men below.

XXIX

Now pillow'd cheek to cheek, in loving
sleep,
 Haidée and Juan their siesta took,
A gentle slumber, but it was not deep,
 For ever and anon a something shook
Juan, and shuddering o'er his frame would
creep;
 And Haidée's sweet lips murmur'd like
a brook
A wordless music, and her face so fair
Stirr'd with her dream, as rose-leaves with
the air;

XXX

Or as the stirring of a deep clear stream
 Within an Alpine hollow, when the wind
Walks o'er it, was she shaken by the dream,
 The mystical usurper of the mind—
O'erpowering us to be whate'er may seem
 Good to the soul which we no more can
bind:
Strange state of being! (for 'tis still to be),
Senseless to feel, and with seal'd eyes to
see.

XXXI

She dream'd of being alone on the sea-shore,
 Chain'd to a rock; she knew not how,
but stir
She could not from the spot, and the loud
roar
 Grew, and each wave rose roughly,
threatening her;

And o'er her upper lip they seem'd to pour
 Until she sobb'd for breath, and soon
they were
Foaming o'er her lone head, so fierce and
high—
Each broke to drown her, yet she could
not die.

XXXII

Anon—she was released, and then she
stray'd
 O'er the sharp shingles with her bleed
ing feet,
And stumbled almost every step she made
 And something roll'd before her in
sheet,
Which she must still pursue howe'er afraid
 'Twas white and indistinct, nor stopp'd
to meet
Her glance nor grasp, for still she gazed
and grasp'd,
And ran, but it escaped her as she clasp'd

XXXIII

The dream changed:—in a cave she stood
 its walls
Were hung with marble icicles; the world
Of ages on its water-fretted halls,
 Where waves might wash, and seals
might breed and lurk;
Her hair was dripping, and the very ball
 Of her black eyes seem'd turn'd to tears
and mirk
The sharp rocks look'd below each drop
they caught,
Which froze to marble as it fell,—she
thought.

XXXIV

And wet, and cold, and lifeless at her feet
 Pale as the foam that froth'd on his dead
brow,
Which she essay'd in vain to clear, (how
sweet
 Were once her cares, how idle seem'd
they now!)
Lay Juan, nor could aught renew the beat
 Of his quench'd heart; and the sea dirge
low
Rang in her sad ears like a mermaid's song
And that brief dream appear'd a life too long

XXXV

And gazing on the dead, she thought his face
 Faded, or alter'd into something new—
Like to her father's features, till each trace
 More like and like to Lambro's aspect
grew—
With all his keen worn look and Grecian
grace;
 And starting, she awoke, and what to
view?
Oh! Powers of Heaven! what dark eye
meets she there?
'Tis—'tis her father's—fix'd upon the pair

XXXVI

Then shrieking, she arose, and shrieking
 fell,
 With joy and sorrow, hope and fear, to
 see
Him whom she deem'd a habitant where
 dwell
 The ocean-buried, risen from death, to
 be
Perchance the death of one she loved too
 well:
 Dear as her father had been to Haidée,
It was a moment of that awful kind——
I have seen such—but must not call to
 mind.

XXXVII

Up Juan sprung to Haidée's bitter shriek,
 And caught her falling, and from off the
 wall
Snatch'd down his sabre, in hot haste to
 wreak
 Vengeance on him who was the cause of
 all:
Then Lambro, who till now forbore to
 speak,
 Smiled scornfully, and said, 'Within my
 call,
A thousand scimitars await the word;
Put up, young man, put up your silly
 sword.'

XXXVIII

And Haidée clung around him; 'Juan,
 'tis—
 'Tis Lambro—'tis my father! Kneel
 with me—
He will forgive us—yes—it must be—yes.
 Oh! dearest father, in this agony
Of pleasure and of pain—even while I kiss
 Thy garment's hem with transport, can
 it be
That doubt should mingle with my filial
 joy?
Deal with me as thou wilt, but spare this
 boy.'

XXXIX

High and inscrutable the old man stood,
 Calm in his voice, and calm within his
 eye—
Not always signs with him of calmest
 mood:
 He look'd upon her, but gave no reply;
Then turn'd to Juan, in whose cheek the
 blood
 Oft came and went, as there resolved to
 die;
In arms, at least, he stood, in act to spring
On the first foe whom Lambro's call might
 bring.

XL

'Young man, your sword;' so Lambro
 once more said:
 Juan replied, 'Not while this arm is
 free.'
The old man's cheek grew pale, but not
 with dread,
 And drawing from his belt a pistol, he
Replied, 'Your blood be then on your own
 head.'
 Then look'd close at the flint, as if to see
'Twas fresh—for he had lately used the
 lock—
And next proceeded quietly to cock.

XLI

It has a strange quick jar upon the ear,
 That cocking of a pistol, when you know
A moment more will bring the sight to bear
 Upon your person, twelve yards off, or
 so;
A gentlemanly distance, not too near,
 If you have got a former friend for foe;
But after being fired at once or twice,
The ear becomes more Irish, and less nice.

XLII

Lambro presented, and one instant more
 Had stopp'd this Canto, and Don Juan's
 breath,
When Haidée threw herself her boy be-
 fore;
 Stern as her sire: 'On me,' she cried,
 'let death
Descend—the fault is mine; this fatal
 shore
 He found—but sought not. I have
 pledged my faith;
I love him—I will die with him: I knew
Your nature's firmness—know your daugh-
 ter's too.'

XLIII

A minute past, and she had been all tears,
 And tenderness, and infancy; but now
She stood as one who champion'd human
 fears—
 Pale, statue-like, and stern, she woo'd
 the blow;
And tall beyond her sex, and their com-
 peers,
 She drew up to her height, as if to show
A fairer mark; and with a fix'd eye scann'd
Her father's face—but never stopp'd his
 hand.

XLIV

He gazed on her, and she on him; 'twas
 strange
 How like they look'd! the expression
 was the same;
Serenely savage, with a little change
 In the large dark eye's mutual-darted
 flame;

For she, too, was as one who could
 avenge,
If cause should be—a lioness, though
 tame;
Her father's blood before her father's face
Boil'd up, and proved her truly of his race.

XLV

I said they were alike, their features and
 Their stature, differing but in sex and
 years:
Even to the delicacy of their hand
 There was resemblance, such as true
 blood wears;
And now to see them, thus divided, stand
 In fix'd ferocity, when joyous tears,
And sweet sensations, should have wel-
 comed both,
Show what the passions are in their full
 growth.

XLVI

The father paused a moment, then with-
 drew
 His weapon, and replaced it; but stood
 still,
And looking on her, as to look her through,
 'Not *I*,' he said, 'have sought this
 stranger's ill;
Not *I* have made this desolation: few
 Would bear such outrage, and forbear
 to kill;
But I must do my duty—how thou hast
Done thine, the present vouches for the
 past.

XLVII

'Let him disarm; or, by my father's head,
 His own shall roll before you like a
 ball!'
He raised his whistle as the word he said,
 And blew; another answer'd to the call,
And rushing in disorderly, though led,
 And arm'd from boot to turban, one
 and all,
Some twenty of his train came, rank on
 rank;
He gave the word, 'Arrest or slay the
 Frank.'

XLVIII

Then, with a sudden movement, he with-
 drew
 His daughter; while compress'd within
 his clasp,
'Twixt her and Juan interposed the crew;
 In vain she struggled in her father's
 grasp—
His arms were like a serpent's coil: then
 flew
Upon their prey, as darts an angry asp,
The file of pirates: save the foremost, who
Had fallen, with his right shoulder half cut
 through.

XLIX

The second had his cheek laid open; but
 The third, a wary, cool old sworder,
 took
The blows upon his cutlass, and then put
 His own well in; so well, ere you could
 look,
His man was floor'd, and helpless at his
 foot,
 With the blood running like a little
 brook
From two smart sabre gashes, deep and
 red—
One on the arm, the other on the head.

L

And then they bound him where he fell,
 and bore
 Juan from the apartment: with a sign
Old Lambro bade them take him to the
 shore,
 Where lay some ships which were to sail
 at nine.
They laid him in a boat, and plied the oar,
 Until they reach'd some galliots, placed
 in line;
On board of one of these, and under
 hatches,
They stow'd him, with strict orders to the
 watches.

LI

The world is full of strange vicissitudes,
 And here was one exceedingly un-
 pleasant:
A gentleman so rich in the world's goods,
 Handsome and young, enjoying all the
 present,
Just at the very time when he least brood
 On such a thing, is suddenly to sea sent,
Wounded and chain'd, so that he cannot
 move,
And all because a lady fell in love.

LII

Here I must leave him, for I grow pathetic,
 Moved by the Chinese nymph of tears,
 green tea!
Than whom Cassandra was not more pro-
 phetic;
 For if my pure libations exceed three,
I feel my heart become so sympathetic,
 That I must have recourse to black
 Bohea:
'Tis pity wine should be so deleterious,
For tea and coffee leave us much more
 serious,

LIII

Unless when qualified with thee, Cogniac!
 Sweet Naïad of the Phlegethontic rill!
Ah! why the liver wilt thou thus attack,
 And make, like other nymphs, thy lovers
 ill?

I would take refuge in weak punch, but
 rack
 (In each sense of the word), whene'er I
 fill
My mild and midnight beakers to the brim,
Wakes me next morning with its synonym.

LIV

I leave Don Juan for the present, safe—
 Not sound, poor fellow, but severely
 wounded;
Yet could his corporal pangs amount to
 half
 Of those with which his Haidée's bosom
 bounded!
She was not one to weep, and rave, and
 chafe,
 And then give way, subdued because
 surrounded;
Her mother was a Moorish maid from Fez,
Where all is Eden, or a wilderness.

LV

There the large olive rains its amber store
 In marble fonts; there grain, and flower,
 and fruit,
Gush from the earth until the land runs
 o'er;
 But there, too, many a poison-tree has
 root,
And midnight listens to the lion's roar,
 And long, long deserts scorch the
 camel's foot,
Or heaving whelm the helpless caravan;
And as the soil is, so the heart of man.

LVI

Afric is all the sun's, and as her earth
 Her human clay is kindled; full of power
For good or evil, burning from its birth,
 The Moorish blood partakes the planet's
 hour,
And like the soil beneath it will bring
 forth:
 Beauty and love were Haidée's mother's
 dower;
But her large dark eye show'd deep
 Passion's force,
Though sleeping like a lion near a source.

LVII

Her daughter, temper'd with a milder ray,
 Like summer clouds all silvery, smooth,
 and fair,
Till slowly charged with thunder they dis-
 play
Terror to earth, and tempest to the air,
Had held till now her soft and milky way;
 But overwrought with passion and des-
 pair,
The fire burst forth from her Numidian
 veins,
Even as the Simoom sweeps the blasted
 plains.

LVIII

The last sight which she saw was Juan's
 gore,
 And he himself o'ermaster'd and cut
 down;
His blood was running on the very floor
 Where late he trod, her beautiful, her
 own;
Thus much she view'd an instant and no
 more,—
 Her struggles ceased with one convul-
 sive groan;
On her sire's arm, which until now scarce
 held
Her writhing, fell she like a cedar fell'd.

LIX

A vein had burst, and her sweet lips' pure
 dyes
 Were dabbled with the deep blood
 which ran o'er;
And her head droop'd, as when the lily lies
 O'ercharged with rain: her summon'd
 handmaids bore
Their lady to her couch with gushing eyes;
 Of herbs and cordials they produced
 their store,
But she defied all means they could em-
 ploy,
Like one life could not hold, nor death
 destroy.

LX

Days lay she in that state unchanged,
 though chill—
 With nothing livid, still her lips were
 red;
She had no pulse, but death seem'd absent
 still;
 No hideous sign proclaim'd her surely
 dead;
Corruption came not in each mind to kill
 All hope; to look upon her sweet face
 bred
New thoughts of life, for it seem'd full of
 soul—
She had so much, earth could not claim
 the whole.

LXI

The ruling passion, such as marble shows
 When exquisitely chisell'd, still lay
 there,
But fix'd as marble's unchanged aspect
 throws
 O'er the fair Venus, but for ever fair;
O'er the Laocoön's all eternal throes,
 And ever-dying Gladiator's air,
Their energy like life forms all their fame,
Yet looks not life, for they are still the
 same.

LXII

She woke at length, but not as sleepers
 wake,
 Rather the dead, for life seem'd some-
 thing new,
A strange sensation which she must par-
 take
 Perforce, since whatsoever met her view
Struck not on memory, though a heavy
 ache
 Lay at her heart, whose earliest beat
 still true
Brought back the sense of pain without the
 cause,
For, for a while, the furies made a pause.

LXIII

She look'd on many a face with vacant eye,
 On many a token without knowing
 what;
She saw them watch her without asking
 why,
 And reck'd not who around her pillow
 sat;
Not speechless, though she spoke not; not
 a sigh
 Relieved her thoughts; dull silence and
 quick chat
Were tried in vain by those who served;
 she gave
No sign, save breath, of having left the
 grave.

LXIV

Her handmaids tended, but she heeded
 not;
 Her father watch'd, she turn'd her eyes
 away;
She recognised no being, and no spot,
 However dear or cherish'd in their day;
They changed from room to room, but all
 forgot,
 Gentle, but without memory she lay;
At length those eyes, which they would
 fain be weaning
Back to old thoughts, wax'd full of fearful
 meaning.

LXV

And then a slave bethought her of a harp;
 The harper came, and tuned his instru-
 ment;
At the first notes, irregular and sharp,
 On him her flashing eyes a moment bent,
Then to the wall she turn'd as if to warp
 Her thoughts from sorrow through her
 heart re-sent;
And he begun a long low island song
Of ancient days, ere tyranny grew strong.

LXVI

Anon her thin wan fingers beat the wall
 In time to his old tune; he changed the
 theme,

And sung of love; the fierce name struck
 through all
 Her recollection; on her flash'd the
 dream
Of what she was, and is, if ye could call
 To be so being; in a gushing stream
The tears rush'd forth from her o'erclouded
 brain,
Like mountain mists at length dissolved
 in rain.

LXVII

Short solace, vain relief!—thought came
 too quick,
 And whirl'd her brain to madness; she
 arose
As one who ne'er had dwelt among the
 sick,
 And flew at all she met, as on her foes;
But no one ever heard her speak or shriek,
 Although her paroxysm drew towards
 its close;—
Hers was a phrensy which disdain'd to
 rave,
Even when they smote her, in the hope to
 save.

LXVIII

Yet she betray'd at times a gleam of sense;
 Nothing could make her meet her
 father's face,
Though on all other things with looks
 intense
 She gazed, but none she ever could re-
 trace;
Food she refused, and raiment; no pre-
 tence
 Avail'd for either; neither change of
 place,
Nor time, nor skill, nor remedy, could give
 her
Senses to sleep—the power seem'd gone
 for ever.

LXIX

Twelve days and nights she wither'd thus
 at last,
 Without a groan, or sigh, or glance, to
 show
A parting pang, the spirit from her passed
 And they who watch'd her nearest
 could not know
The very instant, till the change that cast
 Her sweet face into shadow, dull and
 slow,
Glazed o'er her eyes—the beautiful, the
 black—
Oh! to possess such lustre—and then lack!

LXX

She died, but not alone; she held within
 A second principle of life, which might
Have dawn'd a fair and sinless child of sin;
 But closed its little being without light

And went down to the grave unborn,
 wherein
 Blossom and bough lie wither'd with
 one blight;
In vain the dews of Heaven descend above
The bleeding flower and blasted fruit of
 love.

LXXI

Thus lived—thus died she; never more on
 her
 Shall sorrow light, or shame. She was
 not made
Through years or moons the inner weight
 to bear,
 Which colder hearts endure till they are
 laid
By age in earth: her days and pleasures
 were
 Brief, but delightful—such as had not
 stayed
Long with her destiny; but she sleeps well
By the sea-shore, whereon she loved to
 dwell.

LXXII

That isle is now all desolate and bare,
 Its dwellings down, its tenants pass'd
 away;
None but her own and father's grave is
 there,
 And nothing outward tells of human
 clay;
Ye could not know where lies a thing so
 fair,
 No stone is there to show, no tongue to
 say,
What was; no dirge, except the hollow
 sea's,
Mourns o'er the beauty of the Cyclades.

LXXIII

But many a Greek maid in a loving song
 Sighs o'er her name; and many an
 islander
With her sire's story makes the night less
 long;
 Valour was his, and beauty dwelt with
 her;
If she loved rashly, her life paid for
 wrong—
 A heavy price must all pay who thus err,
In some shape; let none think to fly the
 danger,
For soon or late Love is his own avenger.

LXXIV

But let me change this theme, which grows
 too sad,
 And lay this sheet of sorrows on the
 shelf;
I don't much like describing people mad,
 For fear of seeming rather touch'd my-
 self—

Besides, I've no more on this head to add;
 And as my Muse is a capricious elf,
We'll put about, and try another tack
With Juan, left half-kill'd some stanzas
 back.

LXXV

Wounded and fetter'd, 'cabin'd, cribb'd,
 confined,'
 Some days and nights elapsed before
 that he
Could altogether call the past to mind;
 And when he did, he found himself at
 sea,
Sailing six knots an hour before the wind;
 The shores of Ilion lay beneath their
 lee—
Another time he might have liked to see
 'em,
But now was not much pleased with Cape
 Sigæum.

LXXVI

There, on the green and village-cotted hill,
 is
 (Flank'd by the Hellespont, and by the
 sea)
Entomb'd the bravest of the brave,
 Achilles;
 They say so—(Bryant says the contrary):
And further downward, tall and towering
 still, is
 The tumulus—of whom? Heaven
 knows; 't may be
Patroclus, Ajax, or Protesilaus;
All heroes, who if living still would slay us.

LXXVII

High barrows, without marble, or a name,
 A vast, untill'd, and mountain-skirted
 plain,
And Ida in the distance, still the same,
 And old Scamander (if 'tis he) remain;
The situation seems still form'd for fame—
 A hundred thousand men might fight
 again,
With ease; but where I sought for Ilion's
 walls,
The quiet sheep feeds, and the tortoise
 crawls;

LXXVIII

Troops of untended horses; here and there,
 Some little hamlets, with new names un-
 couth;
Some shepherds (unlike Paris), led to stare
 A moment at the European youth
Whom to the spot their school-boy feel-
 ings bear;
 A Turk, with beads in hand, and pipe
 in mouth,
Extremely taken with his own religion,
Are what I found there—but the devil a
 Phrygian.

LXXIX

Don Juan, here permitted to emerge
 From his dull cabin, found himself a
 slave;
Forlorn, and gazing on the deep blue surge,
 O'ershadow'd there by many a hero's
 grave;
Weak still with loss of blood, he scarce
 could urge
 A few brief questions; and the answers
 gave
No very satisfactory information
About his past or present situation.

LXXX

He saw some fellow-captives, who ap-
 pear'd
To be Italians, as they were in fact;
From them, at least, *their* destiny he
 heard,
 Which was an odd one; a troop going
 to act
In Sicily—all singers, duly rear'd
 In their vocation; had not been attack'd
In sailing from Livorno by the pirate,
But sold by the impresario at no high rate.

LXXXI

By one of these, the buffo of the party,
 Juan was told about their curious case;
For although destined to the Turkish
 mart, he
 Still kept his spirits up—at least his face;
The little fellow really look'd quite hearty,
 And bore him with some gaiety and
 grace,
Showing a much more reconciled de-
 meanour,
Than did the prima-donna and the tenor.

LXXXII

In a few words he told their hapless story,
 Saying, 'Our Machiavelian impresario,
Making a signal off some promontory,
 Hail'd a strange brig; Corpo di Caio
 Mario!
We were transferr'd on board her in a
 hurry,
 Without a single scudo of salario;
But if the Sultan has a taste for song,
We will revive our fortunes before long.

LXXXIII

'The prima-donna, though a little old,
 And haggard with a dissipated life,
And subject, when the house is thin, to
 cold,
 Has some good notes; and then the
 tenor's wife,
With no great voice, is pleasing to behold;
 Last carnival she made a deal of strife,
By carrying off Count Cesare Cicogna
From an old Roman princess at Bologna.

LXXXIV

'And then there are the dancers; there's
 the Nini,
 With more than one profession gains
 by all;
Then there's that laughing slut the Pele-
 grini,
 She, too, was fortunate last carnival,
And made at least five hundred good
 zecchini,
 But spends so fast, she has not now a
 paul;
And then there's the Grotesca—such a
 dancer!
Where men have souls or bodies she must
 answer.

LXXXV

'As for the figuranti, they are like
 The rest of all that tribe; with here and
 there
A pretty person, which perhaps may strike,
 The rest are hardly fitted for a fair;
There's one, though tall and stiffer than a
 pike,
 Yet has a sentimental kind of air
Which might go far, but she don't dance
 with vigour;
The more's the pity, with her face and
 figure.

LXXXVI

'As for the men, they are a middling set;
 The musico is but a crack'd old basin,
But being qualified in one way yet,
 May the seraglio do to set his face in,
And as a servant some preferment get;
 His singing I no further trust can place
 in:
From all the Pope makes yearly 'twould
 perplex
To find three perfect pipes of the *third* sex.

LXXXVII

'The tenor's voice is spoilt by affectation,
 And for the bass, the beast can only
 bellow;
In fact, he had no singing education,
 An ignorant, noteless, timeless, tuneless
 fellow;
But being the prima-donna's near relation
 Who swore his voice was very rich and
 mellow,
They hired him, though to hear him you'd
 believe
An ass was practising recitative.

LXXXVIII

''Twould not become myself to dwell upon
 My own merits, and though young—
 I see, sir—you
Have got a travell'd air, which shows you
 one
 To whom the opera is by no means new

You've heard of Raucocanti?—I'm the
　　man:
　　The time may come when you may hear
　　　me too;
You was not last year at the fair of Lugo,
　But next, when I'm engaged to sing there—
　　do go.

LXXXIX

'Our baritone I almost had forgot,
　A pretty lad, but bursting with conceit;
With graceful action, science not a jot,
　A voice of no great compass, and not
　　sweet,
He always is complaining of his lot,
　Forsooth, scarce fit for ballads in the
　　street;
In lovers' parts his passion more to
　breathe,
Having no heart to show, he shows his
　teeth.'

XC

Here Raucocanti's eloquent recital
　Was interrupted by the pirate crew,
Who came at stated moments to invite all
　The captives back to their sad berths;
　　each threw
A rueful glance upon the waves, (which
　bright all
　From the blue skies derived a double
　blue,
Dancing all free and happy in the sun,)
And then went down the hatchway one by
　one.

XCI

They heard next day—that in the Darda-
　nelles,
　Waiting for his Sublimity's firmān,
The most imperative of sovereign spells,
　Which everybody does without who can,
More to secure them in their naval cells,
　Lady to lady, well as man to man,
Were to be chain'd and lotted out per
　couple,
For the slave-market of Constantinople.

XCII

It seems when this allotment was made
　out,
　There chanced to be an odd male, and
　odd female,
Who (after some discussion and some doubt,
　If the soprano might be deem'd to be
　male,
They placed him o'er the women as a
　scout)
　Were link'd together, and it happen'd
　the male
Was Juan, who,—an awkward thing at
　his age,
Pair'd off with a Bacchante blooming
　visage.

XCIII

With Raucocanti lucklessly was chain'd
　The tenor; these two hated with a hate
Found only on the stage, and each more
　pain'd
　With this his tuneful neighbour than his
　fate;
Sad strife arose, for they were so cross-
　grain'd,
　Instead of bearing up without debate,
That each pull'd different ways with many
　an oath,
'Arcades ambo,' id est—blackguards both.

XCIV

Juan's companion was a Romagnole,
　But bred within the March of old Ancona,
With eyes that look'd into the very soul
　(And other chief points of a 'bella
　donna'),
Bright—and as black and burning as a coal;
　And through her clear brunette com-
　plexion shone a
Great wish to please—a most attractive
　dower,
Especially when added to the power.

XCV

But all that power was wasted upon him,
　For sorrow o'er each sense held stern
　command;
Her eye might flash on his, but found it dim:
　And though thus chain'd, as natural her
　hand
Touch'd his, nor that—nor any handsome
　limb
　(And she had some not easy to with-
　stand)
Could stir his pulse, or make his faith feel
　brittle;
Perhaps his recent wounds might help a
　little.

XCVI

No matter; we should ne'er too much
　inquire,
　But facts are facts: no knight could be
　more true,
And firmer faith no ladye-love desire;
　We will omit the proofs, save one or two:
'Tis said no one in hand 'can hold a fire
　By thought of frosty Caucasus;' but
　few,
I really think; yet Juan's then ordeal
Was more triumphant, and not much less
　real.

XCVII

Here I might enter on a chaste description,
　Having withstood temptation in my
　youth,
But hear that several people take exception
　At the first two books having too much
　truth;

Therefore I'll make Don Juan leave the
ship soon,
　Because the publisher declares, in sooth,
Through needles' eyes it easier for the
camel is
　To pass, than those two cantos into
families.

XCVIII

'Tis all the same to me; I'm fond of yield-
ing,
　And therefore leave them to the purer
page
Of Smollett, Prior, Ariosto, Fielding,
　Who say strange things for so correct an
age;
I once had great alacrity in wielding
　My pen, and liked poetic war to wage,
And recollect the time when all this cant
Would have provoked remarks which
now it shan't.

XCIX

As boys love rows, my boyhood liked a
squabble;
　But at this hour I wish to part in peace,
Leaving such to the literary rabble,
　Whether my verse's fame be doom'd to
cease
While the right hand which wrote it still is
able,
　Or of some centuries to take a lease;
The grass upon my grave will grow as long,
And sigh to midnight winds, but not to
song.

C

Of poets who come down to us through
distance
　Of time and tongues, the foster-babes of
Fame,
Life seems the smallest portion of exist-
ence;
　Where twenty ages gather o'er a name,
'Tis as a snow-ball which derives assistance
　From every flake, and yet rolls on the
same,
Even till an iceberg it may chance to grow;
But, after all, 'tis nothing but cold snow.

CI

And so great names are nothing more than
nominal,
　And love of glory's but an airy lust,
Too often in its fury overcoming all
　Who would as 'twere identify their dust
From out the wide destruction, which,
entombing all,
　Leaves nothing till 'the coming of the
just'—
Save change: I've stood upon Achilles'
tomb,
And heard Troy doubted; time will
doubt of Rome.

CII

The very generations of the dead
　Are swept away, and tomb inherits tomb
Until the memory of an age is fled,
　And, buried, sinks beneath its off
spring's doom:
Where are the epitaphs our fathers read
　Save a few glean'd from the sepulchra
gloom
Which once-named myriads nameless li
beneath,
And lose their own in universal death.

CIII

I canter by the spot each afternoon
　Where perish'd in his fame the hero
boy,
Who lived too long for men, but died too
soon
　For human vanity, the young De Foix
A broken pillar, not uncouthly hewn,
　But which neglect is hastening to de-
stroy,
Records Ravenna's carnage on its face,
While weeds and ordure rankle round the
base.

CIV

I pass each day where Dante's bones are
laid:
　A little cupola, more neat than solemn,
Protects his dust, but reverence here is paid
　To the bard's tomb, and not the
warrior's column:
The time must come, when both alike
decay'd,
　The chieftain's trophy, and the poet's
volume,
Will sink where lie the songs and wars of
earth,
Before Pelides' death, or Homer's birth.

CV

With human blood that column was
cemented,
　With human filth that column is defiled,
As if the peasant's coarse contempt were
vented
　To show his loathing of the spot he
soil'd:
Thus is the trophy used, and thus lamented
　Should ever be those blood-hounds,
from whose wild
Instinct of gore and glory earth has known
Those sufferings Dante saw in hell alone.

CVI

Yet there will still be bards: though fame
is smoke,
　Its fumes are frankincense to human
thought;
And the unquiet feelings, which first woke
　Song in the world, will seek what then
they sought:

As on the beach the waves at last are broke,
　Thus to their extreme verge the passions
　　brought
Dash into poetry, which is but passion,
Or at least was so ere it grew a fashion.

CVII

If in the course of such a life as was
　At once adventurous and contemplative,
Men who partake all passions as they pass,
　Acquire the deep and bitter power to give
Their images again as in a glass,
　And in such colours that they seem to
　　live;
You may do right forbidding them to show
　'em,
But spoil (I think) a very pretty poem.

CVIII

Oh! ye, who make the fortunes of all books!
　Benign Ceruleans of the second sex!
Who advertise new poems by your looks,
　Your 'imprimatur' will ye not annex?
What! must I go to the oblivious cooks,
　Those Cornish plunderers of Parnassian
　　wrecks?
Ah! must I then the only minstrel be,
Proscribed from tasting your Castalian tea?

CIX

What! can I prove 'a lion' then no more?
　A ball-room bard, a foolscap, hot-press
　　darling?
To bear the compliments of many a bore,
　And sigh, 'I can't get out,' like Yorick's
　　starling;
Why then I'll swear, as poet Wordy swore
　(Because the world won't read him,
　　always snarling),
That taste is gone, that fame is but a
　lottery,
Drawn by the blue-coat misses of a coterie.

CX

Oh! 'darkly, deeply, beautifully blue,'
　As some one somewhere sings about the
　　sky,
And I, ye learned ladies, say of you;
　They say your stockings are so—
　　(Heaven knows why,
I have examined few pair of that hue);
　Blue as the garters which serenely lie
Round the patrician left-legs, which adorn
The festal midnight, and the levée morn.

CXI

Yet some of you are most seraphic crea-
　tures—
　But times are alter'd since, a rhyming
　　lover,
You read my stanzas, and I read your
　features:
　And—but no matter, all those things
　　are over;

Still I have no dislike to learned natures,
　For sometimes such a world of virtues
　　cover;
I know one woman of that purple school,
The loveliest, chastest, best, but—quite a
　fool.

CXII

Humboldt, 'the first of travellers,' but not
　The last, if late accounts be accurate,
Invented, by some name I have forgot,
　As well as the sublime discovery's date,
An airy instrument, with which he sought
　To ascertain the atmospheric state,
By measuring 'the *intensity of blue*':
Oh, Lady Daphne! let me measure you!

CXIII

But to the narrative:—The vessel bound
　With slaves to sell off in the capital,
After the usual process, might be found
　At anchor under the seraglio wall;
Her cargo, from the plague being safe and
　sound,
　Were landed in the market, one and all,
And there with Georgians, Russians, and
　Circassians,
Bought up for different purposes and
　passions.

CXIV

Some went off dearly; fifteen hundred
　dollars
　For one Circassian, a sweet girl, were
　　given,
Warranted virgin; beauty's brightest
　colours
　Had deck'd her out in all the hues of
　　heaven:
Her sale sent home some disappointed
　bawlers,
　Who bade on till the hundreds reached
　　eleven;
But when the offer went beyond, they
　knew
'Twas for the Sultan, and at once with-
　drew.

CXV

Twelve negresses from Nubia brought a
　price
　Which the West Indian market scarce
　　would bring,
Though Wilberforce, at last, has made it
　twice
　What 'twas ere Abolition; and the thing
Need not seem very wonderful, for vice
　Is always much more splendid than a
　　king:
The virtues, even the most exalted,
　Charity,
Are saving—vice spares nothing for a
　rarity.

CXVI

But for the destiny of this young troop,
　　How some were bought by pachas,
　　　some by Jews,
How some to burdens were obliged to
　　stoop,
　　And others rose to the command of
　　　crews
As renegadoes; while in hapless group,
　　Hoping no very old vizier might choose,
The females stood, as one by one they
　　pick'd 'em,
To make a mistress, or fourth wife, or
　　victim:

CXVII

All this must be reserved for further song;
　　Also our hero's lot, howe'er unpleasant
(Because this Canto has become too long),
　　Must be postponed discreetly for the
　　　present;
I'm sensible redundancy is wrong,
　　But could not for the muse of me put
　　　less in't:
And now delay the progress of Don Juan,
Till what is call'd in Ossian the fifth Duan.

CANTO THE FIFTH

I

When amatory poets sing their loves
　　In liquid lines mellifluously bland,
And pair their rhymes as Venus yokes her
　　doves,
　　They little think what mischief is in
　　　hand;
The greater their success the worse it
　　proves,
　　As Ovid's verse may give to understand;
Even Petrarch's self, if judged with due
　　severity,
Is the Platonic pimp of all posterity.

II

I therefore do denounce all amorous writ-
　　ing,
　　Except in such a way as not to attract;
Plain—simple—short, and by no means
　　inviting,
　　But with a moral to each error tack'd,
Form'd rather for instructing than de-
　　lighting,
　　And with all passions in their turn
　　　attack'd;
Now, if my Pegasus should not be shod ill,
This poem will become a moral model.

III

The European with the Asian shore
　　Sprinkled with palaces; the Ocean
　　　stream
Here and there studded with a seventy-
　　four;
　　Sophia's cupola with golden gleam;

The cypress groves; Olympus high and
　　hoar;
　　The twelve isles, and the more than I
　　　could dream,
Far less describe, present the very view
Which charm'd the charming Mary
　　Montagu.

IV

I have a passion for the name of 'Mary,'
　　For once it was a magic sound to me;
And still it half calls up the realms of fairy,
　　Where I beheld what never was to be;
All feelings changed, but this was last to
　　vary,
　　A spell from which even yet I am not
　　　quite free:
But I grow sad—and let a tale grow cold,
Which must not be pathetically told.

V

The wind swept down the Euxine, and the
　　wave
　　Broke foaming o'er the blue Symple-
　　　gades;
'Tis a grand sight from off 'the Giant's
　　Grave'
　　To watch the progress of those rolling
　　　seas
Between the Bosphorus, as they lash and
　　lave
　　Europe and Asia, you being quite at ease:
There's not a sea the passenger e'er pukes
　　in,
Turns up more dangerous breakers than
　　the Euxine.

VI

'Twas a raw day of Autumn's bleak begin-
　　ning,
　　When nights are equal, but not so the
　　　days:
The Parcæ then cut short the further
　　spinning
　　Of seamen's fates, and the loud tempests
　　　raise
The waters, and repentance for past sin-
　　ning
　　In all, who o'er the great deep take their
　　　ways:
They vow to amend their lives, and yet
　　they don't;
Because if drown'd, they can't—if spared,
　　they won't.

VII

A crowd of shivering slaves of every
　　nation,
　　And age, and sex, were in the market
　　　ranged;
Each bevy with the merchant in his sta-
　　tion:
　　Poor creatures! their good looks were
　　　sadly changed.

All save the blacks seem'd jaded with
 vexation,
 From friends, and home, and freedom
 far estranged;
The negroes more philosophy display'd,—
Used to it, no doubt, as eels are to be
 flay'd.

VIII

Juan was juvenile, and thus was full,
 As most at his age are, of hope, and
 health;
Yet I must own, he look'd a little dull,
 And now and then a tear stole down by
 stealth;
Perhaps his recent loss of blood might pull
 His spirit down; and then the loss of
 wealth,
A mistress, and such comfortable quarters,
To be put up for auction amongst Tartars,

IX

Were things to shake a stoic; ne'ertheless,
 Upon the whole his carriage was serene:
His figure, and the splendour of his dress,
 Of which some gilded remnants still
 were seen,
Drew all eyes on him, giving them to guess
 He was above the vulgar by his mien;
And then, though pale, he was so very
 handsome;
And then—they calculated on his ransom.

X

Like a backgammon board the place was
 dotted
 With whites and blacks, in groups on
 show for sale,
Though rather more irregularly spotted:
 Some bought the jet, while others chose
 the pale.
It chanced amongst the other people
 lotted,
 A man of thirty, rather stout and hale,
With resolution in his dark grey eye,
Next Juan stood, till some might choose
 to buy.

XI

He had an English look; that is, was
 square
 In make, of a complexion white and
 ruddy,
Good teeth, with curling rather dark
 brown hair,
 And, it might be from thought, or toil,
 or study,
An open brow a little mark'd with care:
 One arm had on a bandage rather
 bloody;
And there he stood with such *sang froid*,
 that greater
Could scarce be shown even by a mere
 spectator.

XII

But seeing at his elbow a mere lad,
 Of a high spirit evidently, though
At present weigh'd down by a doom which
 had
 O'erthrown even men, he soon began to
 show
A kind of blunt compassion for the sad
 Lot of so young a partner in the woe,
Which for himself he seem'd to deem no
 worse
Than any other scrape, a thing of course.

XIII

'My boy!'—said he, 'amidst this motley
 crew
 Of Georgians, Russians, Nubians, and
 what not,
All ragamuffins differing but in hue,
 With whom it is our luck to cast our lot,
The only gentlemen seem I and you;
 So let us be acquainted, as we ought:
If I could yield you any consolation,
'Twould give me pleasure.—Pray, what is
 your nation?'

XIV

When Juan answer'd—'Spanish!' he re-
 plied,
 'I thought, in fact, you could not be a
 Greek;
Those servile dogs are not so proudly eyed:
 Fortune has play'd you here a pretty
 freak,
But that's her way with all men, till they're
 tried;
 But never mind,—she'll turn, perhaps,
 next week;
She has served me also much the same as
 you,
Except that I have found it nothing new.'

XV

'Pray, sir,' said Juan, 'if I may presume,
 What brought you here?'—'Oh! no-
 thing very rare—
Six Tartars and a drag-chain——'—'To
 this doom
 But what conducted, if the question's fair,
Is that which I would learn.'—'I served
 for some
 Months with the Russian army here and
 there;
And taking lately, by Suwarrow's bidding,
A town, was ta'en myself instead of Widdin.'

XVI

'Have you no friends?'—'I had—but, by
 God's blessing,
 Have not been troubled with them
 lately. Now
I have answer'd all your questions without
 pressing,
 And you an equal courtesy should show.'

'Alas!' said Juan, ''twere a tale distress-
 ing,
 And long besides.'—'Oh! if 'tis really
 so,
You're right on both accounts to hold
 your tongue;
A sad tale saddens doubly when 'tis long.

XVII

'But droop not: Fortune at your time of
 life,
 Although a female moderately fickle,
Will hardly leave you (as she's not your
 wife)
 For any length of days in such a pickle.
To strive, too, with our fate were such a
 strife
 As if the corn-sheaf should oppose the
 sickle:
Men are the sport of circumstances, when
The circumstances seem the sport of men.'

XVIII

''Tis not,' said Juan, 'for my present doom
 I mourn, but for the past;—I loved a
 maid:'—
He paused, and his dark eye grew full of
 gloom;
 A single tear upon his eyelash stayed
A moment, and then dropp'd; 'but to re-
 sume,
 'Tis not my present lot, as I have said,
Which I deplore so much; for I have borne
Hardships which have the hardiest over-
 worn,

XIX

'On the rough deep. But this last blow—'
 and here
 He stopp'd again, and turn'd away his
 face.
'Ay,' quoth his friend, 'I thought it would
 appear
 That there had been a lady in the case;
And these are things which ask a tender
 tear,
 Such as I, too, would shed if in your
 place:
I cried upon my first wife's dying day,
And also when my second ran away:

XX

'My third——'—'Your third!' quoth
 Juan, turning round;
 'You scarcely can be thirty: have you
 three?'
'No—only two at present above ground:
 Surely, 'tis nothing wonderful to see
One person thrice in holy wedlock bound!'
 'Well, then, your third,' said Juan;
 'what did she?
She did not run away, too,—did she, sir?'
'No, faith.'—'What then?'—'I ran away
 from her.'

XXI

'You take things coolly, sir,' said Juan.
 'Why,'
 Replied the other, 'what can a man do?
There still are many rainbows in your sky,
 But mine have vanish'd. All, when life
 is new,
Commence with feelings warm, and pros-
 pects high;
 But time strips our illusions of their hue,
And one by one in turn, some grand mis-
 take
Casts off its bright skin yearly like the
 snake.

XXII

''Tis true, it gets another bright and fresh,
 Or fresher, brighter; but the year gone
 through,
This skin must go the way, too, of all flesh,
 Or sometimes only wear a week or
 two;—
Love's the first net which spreads its
 deadly mesh;
 Ambition, Avarice, Vengeance, Glory,
 glue
The glittering lime-twigs of our latter days,
Where still we flutter on for pence or
 praise.'

XXIII

'All this is very fine, and may be true,'
 Said Juan, 'but I really don't see how
It betters present times with me or you.'
 'No?' quoth the other; 'yet you will allow
By setting things in their right point of view,
 Knowledge, at least, is gain'd; for in-
 stance, now,
We know what slavery is, and our disasters
May teach us better to behave when masters.'

XXIV

'Would we were masters now, if but to try
 Their present lessons on our Pagan
 friends here,'
Said Juan—swallowing a heart-burning
 sigh:
 'Heaven help the scholar, whom his
 fortune sends here!'
'Perhaps we shall be one day, by and by,'
 Rejoin'd the other, 'when our bad luck
 mends here;
Meantime (yon old black eunuch seems to
 eye us)
I wish to G—d that somebody would buy
 us!

XXV

'But after all, what is our present state?
 'Tis bad, and may be better—all men's
 lot:
Most men are slaves, none more so than
 the great,
 To their own whims and passions, and
 what not;

Society itself, which should create
 Kindness, destroys what little we had
 got:
To feel for none is the true social art
Of the world's stoics—men without a
 heart.'

XXVI

Just now a black old neutral personage
 Of the third sex stept up, and peering
 over
The captives, seem'd to mark their looks
 and age,
 And capabilities, as to discover
If they were fitted for the purposed cage:
 No lady e'er is ogled by a lover,
Horse by a blackleg, broadcloth by a
 tailor,
Fee by a counsel, felon by a jailor,

XXVII

As is a slave by his intended bidder.
 'Tis pleasant purchasing our fellow-
 creatures;
And all are to be sold, if you consider
 Their passions, and are dext'rous; some
 by features
Are bought up, others by a warlike leader,
 Some by a place—as tend their years or
 natures;
The most by ready cash—but all have
 prices,
From crowns to kicks, according to their
 vices.

XXVIII

The eunuch, having eyed them o'er with
 care,
 Turn'd to the merchant, and began to
 bid
First but for one, and after for the pair;
 They haggled, wrangled, swore, too—so
 they did!
As though they were in a mere Christian
 fair,
 Cheapening an ox, an ass, a lamb, or
 kid;
So that their bargain sounded like a battle
For this superior yoke of human cattle.

XXIX

At last they settled into simple grumbling,
 And pulling out reluctant purses, and
Turning each piece of silver o'er, and
 tumbling
 Some down, and weighing others in
 their hand,
And by mistake sequins with paras jumb-
 ling,
 Until the sum was accurately scann'd,
And then the merchant giving change, and
 signing
Receipts in full, began to think of dining.

XXX

I wonder if his appetite was good?
 Or, if it were, if also his digestion?
Methinks at meals some odd thoughts
 might intrude,
 And conscience ask a curious sort of
 question,
About the right divine how far we should
 Sell flesh and blood. When dinner has
 opprest one,
I think it is perhaps the gloomiest hour
Which turns up out of the sad twenty-four.

XXXI

Voltaire says 'No'; he tells you that
 Candide
 Found life most tolerable after meals;
He's wrong—unless man were a pig, in-
 deed,
 Repletion rather adds to what he feels,
Unless he's drunk, and then no doubt he's
 freed
 From his own brain's oppression while
 it reels.
Of food I think with Philip's son, or rather
Ammon's (ill pleased with one world and
 one father);

XXXII

I think with Alexander, that the act
 Of eating, with another act or two,
Makes us feel our mortality in fact
 Redoubled; when a roast and a ragout,
And fish, and soup, by some side dishes
 back'd,
 Can give us either pain or pleasure, who
Would pique himself on intellects, whose
 use
Depends so much upon the gastric juice?

XXXIII

The other evening ('twas on Friday last)—
 This is a fact, and no poetic fable—
Just as my great coat was about me cast,
 My hat and gloves still lying on the table,
I heard a shot—'twas eight o'clock scarce
 past—
 And, running out as fast as I was able,
I found the military commandant
Stretch'd in the street, and able scarce to
 pant.

XXXIV

Poor fellow! for some reason, surely bad,
 They had slain him with five slugs; and
 left him there
To perish on the pavement: so I had
 Him borne into the house and up the stair,
And stripp'd, and look'd to,—But why
 should I add
 More circumstances? vain was every
 care;
The man was gone: in some Italian quarrel
Kill'd by five bullets from an old gun-barrel.

XXXV

I gazed upon him, for I knew him well;
 And though I have seen many corpses,
 never
Saw one, whom such an accident befell,
 So calm; though pierced through
 stomach, heart, and liver,
He seem'd to sleep,—for you could
 scarcely tell
 (As he bled inwardly, no hideous river
Of gore divulged the cause) that he was
 dead:
So as I gazed on him, I thought or said—

XXXVI

'Can this be death? then what is life or
 death?
 Speak!' but he spoke not: 'wake!' but
 still he slept:—
'But yesterday, and who had mightier
 breath?
 A thousand warriors by his word were
 kept
In awe: he said, as the centurion saith,
 "Go," and he goeth; "come," and forth
 he stepp'd.
The trump and bugle till he spake were
 dumb—
And now nought left him but the muffled
 drum.'

XXXVII

And they who waited once and wor-
 shipp'd—they
 With their rough faces throng'd about
 the bed
To gaze once more on the commanding
 clay
 Which for the last, though not the first,
 time bled;
And such an end! that he who many a day
 Had faced Napoleon's foes until they
 fled,—
The foremost in the charge or in the sally,
Should now be butcher'd in a civic alley.

XXXVIII

The scars of his old wounds were near his
 new,
 Those honourable scars which brought
 him fame;
And horrid was the contrast to the
 view——
 But let me quit the theme; as such things
 claim
Perhaps even more attention than is due
 From me: I gazed (as oft I have gazed
 the same)
To try if I could wrench aught out of death
Which should confirm, or shake, or make
 a faith;

XXXIX

But it was all a mystery. Here we are,
 And there we go:—but *where?* five bits
 of lead,
Or three, or two, or one, send very far!
 And is this blood, then, form'd but to
 be shed?
Can every element our elements mar?
 And air—earth—water—fire live—and
 we dead?
We, whose minds comprehend all things.
 No more;
But let us to the story as before.

XL

The purchaser of Juan and acquaintance
 Bore off his bargains to a gilded boat,
Embark'd himself and them, and off they
 went thence
 As fast as oars could pull and water float;
They look'd like persons being led to sen-
 tence,
 Wond'ring what next, till the caïque was
 brought
Up in a little creek below a wall
O'ertopp'd with cypresses, dark-green and
 tall.

XLI

Here their conductor tapping at the wicket
 Of a small iron door, 'twas open'd, and
He led them onward, first through a low
 thicket
 Flank'd by large groves, which tower'd
 on either hand:
They almost lost their way, and had to
 pick it—
 For night was closing ere they came to
 land.
The eunuch made a sign to those on board,
Who row'd off, leaving them without a word.

XLII

As they were plodding on their winding way
 Through orange bowers, and jasmine,
 and so forth:
(Of which I might have a good deal to say,
 There being no such profusion in the
 North
Of oriental plants, 'et cetera,'
 But that of late your scribblers think it
 worth
Their while to rear whole hotbeds in *their*
 works,
Because one poet travell'd 'mongst the
 Turks:)

XLIII

As they were threading on their way,
 there came
 Into Don Juan's head a thought, which he
Whisper'd to his companion:—'twas the
 same
 Which might have then occurr'd to you
 or me.

'Methinks,'—said he,—'it would be no
 great shame
If we should strike a stroke to set us free;
Let's knock that old black fellow on the
 head,
And march away—'twere easier done than
 said.'

XLIV

'Yes,' said the other, 'and when done,
 what then?
 How get out? how the devil got we in?
And when we once were fairly out, and
 when
 From Saint Bartholomew we have
 saved our skin,
To-morrow'd see us in some other den,
 And worse off than we hitherto have been;
Besides, I'm hungry, and just now would
 take,
Like Esau, for my birthright a beef-steak.

XLV

'We must be near some place of man's
 abode;—
 For the old negro's confidence in creep-
 ing,
With his two captives, by so queer a road,
 Shows that he thinks his friends have
 not been sleeping;
A single cry would bring them all abroad:
 'Tis better therefore looking before
 leaping—
And there, you see, this turn has brought
 us through,
By Jove, a noble palace!—lighted too.'

XLVI

It was indeed a wide extensive building
 Which open'd on their view, and o'er the
 front
There seem'd to be besprent a deal of
 gilding
 And various hues, as is the Turkish
 wont,—
A gaudy taste, for they are little skill'd in
 The arts of which these lands were once
 the font:
Each villa on the Bosphorus looks a screen
New painted, or a pretty opera-scene.

XLVII

And nearer as they came, a genial savour
 Of certain stews, and roast-meats, and
 pilaus,
Things which in hungry mortals' eyes find
 favour,
 Made Juan in his harsh intentions pause,
And put himself upon his good behaviour:
 His friend, too, adding a new saving
 clause,
Said, 'In Heaven's name let's get some
 supper now,
And then I'm with you, if you're for a row.'

XLVIII

Some talk of an appeal unto some passion,
 Some to men's feelings, others to their
 reason;
The last of these was never much the
 fashion,
 For reason thinks all reasoning out of
 season:
Some speakers whine, and others lay the
 lash on,
 But more or less continue still to tease
 on,
With arguments according to their 'forte';
But no one ever dreams of being short.—

XLIX

But I digress: of all appeals,—although
 I grant the power of pathos, and of gold,
Of beauty, flattery, threats, a shilling,—no
 Method's more sure at moments to
 take hold
Of the best feelings of mankind, which grow
 More tender, as we every day behold,
Than that all-softening, overpowering
 knell,
The tocsin of the soul—the dinner-bell.

L

Turkey contains no bells, and yet men
 dine;
 And Juan and his friend, albeit they
 heard
No Christian knoll to table, saw no line
 Of lackeys usher to the feast prepared,
Yet smelt roast-meat, beheld a huge fire
 shine,
 And cooks in motion with their clean
 arms bared,
And gazed around them to the left and
 right,
With the prophetic eye of appetite.

LI

And giving up all notions of resistance,
 They follow'd close behind their sable
 guide,
Who little thought that his own crack'd
 existence
 Was on the point of being set aside:
He motion'd them to stop at some small
 distance,
 And knocking at the gate, 'twas open'd
 wide,
And a magnificent large hall display'd
The Asian pomp of Ottoman parade.

LII

I won't describe; description is my forte,
 But every fool describes in these bright
 days
His wondrous journey to some foreign
 court,
 And spawns his quarto, and demands
 your praise—

Death to his publisher, to him 'tis sport;
 While Nature, tortured twenty thou-
 sand ways,
Resigns herself with exemplary patience
To guide-books, rhymes, tours, sketches,
 illustrations.

LIII

Along this hall, and up and down, some,
 squatted
 Upon their hams, were occupied at
 chess;
Others in monosyllable talk chatted,
 And some seem'd much in love with
 their own dress;
And divers smoked superb pipes,
 decorated
 With amber mouths of greater price or
 less;
And several strutted, others slept, and
 some
Prepared for supper with a glass of rum.

LIV

As the black eunuch enter'd with his
 brace
 Of purchased Infidels, some raised
 their eyes
A moment, without slackening from their
 pace;
 But those who sate, ne'er stirr'd in any
 wise:
One or two stared the captives in the face,
 Just as one views a horse to guess his
 price;
Some nodded to the negro from their
 station,
But no one troubled him with conversa-
 tion.

LV

He leads them through the hall, and, with-
 out stopping,
 On through a farther range of goodly
 rooms,
Splendid but silent, save in *one*, where,
 dropping,
 A marble fountain echoes through the
 glooms
Of night, which robe the chamber, or
 where popping
 Some female head most curiously
 presumes
To thrust its black eyes through the door
 or lattice,
As wondering what the *devil* noise that is.

LVI

Some faint lamps gleaming from the lofty
 walls
 Gave light enough to hint their farther
 way,
But not enough to show the imperial halls
 In all the flashing of their full array;

Perhaps there's nothing—I'll not say
 appals,
 But saddens more by night as well as
 day,
Than an enormous room without a soul
To break the lifeless splendour of the
 whole.

LVII

Two or three seem so little, *one* seems
 nothing:
 In deserts, forests, crowds, or by the
 shore,
There solitude, we know, has her full
 growth in
 The spots which were her realms for
 evermore;
But in a mighty hall or gallery, both in
 More modern buildings and those built
 of yore,
A kind of death comes o'er us all alone,
Seeing what's meant for many with but
 one.

LVIII

A neat, snug study on a winter's night,
 A book, friend, single lady, or a glass
Of claret, sandwich, and an appetite,
 Are things which make an English
 evening pass;
Though *certes* by no means so grand a
 sight
 As is a theatre lit up by gas.
I pass my evenings in long galleries solely,
And that's the reason I'm so melancholy.

LIX

Alas! man makes that great which makes
 him little:
 I grant you in a church 'tis very well:
What speaks of heaven should by no
 means be brittle,
 But strong and lasting, till no tongue
 can tell
Their names who rear'd it; but huge
 houses fit ill—
 And huge tombs worse—mankind,
 since Adam fell:
Methinks the story of the tower of Babel
Might teach them this much better than
 I'm able.

LX

Babel was Nimrod's hunting-box, and then
 A town of gardens, walls, and wealth
 amazing,
Where Nebuchadonosor, king of men,
 Reign'd, till one summer's day he took
 to grazing,
And Daniel tamed the lions in their den,
 The people's awe and admiration raising:
'Twas famous, too, for Thisbe and for
 Pyramus,
And the calumniated queen Semiramis.—

LXI

That injured Queen, by chroniclers so
 coarse,
 Has been accused (I doubt not by
 conspiracy)
Of an improper friendship for her horse
 (Love, like religion, sometimes runs to
 heresy):
This monstrous tale had probably its source
 (For such exaggerations here and there
 I see)
In writing 'Courser' by mistake for 'Cou-
 rier;'
I wish the case would come before a jury
 here.

LXII

But to resume,—should there be (what may
 not
 Be in these days?) some infidels, who
 don't,
Because they can't, find out the very spot
 Of that same Babel, or because they won't
(Though Claudius Rich, Esquire, some
 bricks has got,
 And written lately two memoirs upon 't)
Believe the Jews, those unbelievers, who
Must be believed, though they believe not
 you,

LXIII

Yet let them think that Horace has exprest
 Shortly and sweetly the masonic folly
Of those, forgetting the great place of rest,
 Who give themselves to architecture
 wholly;
We know where things and men must end
 at best:
 A moral (like all morals) melancholy,
And 'Et sepulchri immemor struis domos'
Shows that we build when we should but
 entomb us.

LXIV

At last they reach'd a quarter most retired,
 Where echo woke as if from a long
 slumber;
Though full of all things which could be
 desired,
 One wonder'd what to do with such a
 number
Of articles which nobody required;
 Here wealth had done its utmost to en-
 cumber
With furniture an exquisite apartment,
Which puzzled Nature much to know what
 Art meant.

LXV

It seem'd, however, but to open on
 A range or suite of further chambers,
 which
Might lead to heaven knows where; but in
 this one
 The moveables were prodigally rich:

Sofas 'twas half a sin to sit upon,
 So costly were they; carpets every stitch
Of workmanship so rare, they made you
 wish
You could glide o'er them like a golden
 fish.

LXVI

The black, however, without hardly deign-
 ing
 A glance at that which wrapt the slaves
 in wonder,
Trampled what they scarce trod for fear
 of staining,
 As if the milky way their feet was under
With all its stars; and with a stretch attain-
 ing
 A certain press or cupboard niched in
 yonder,
In that remote recess which you may see—
Or if you don't the fault is not in me,—

LXVII

I wish to be perspicuous; and the black,
 I say, unlocking the recess, pull'd forth
A quantity of clothes fit for the back
 Of any Mussulman, whate'er his worth;
And of variety there was no lack—
 And yet, though I have said there was
 no dearth,—
He chose himself to point out what he
 thought
Most proper for the Christians he had
 bought.

LXVIII

The suit he thought most suitable to each
 Was, for the elder and the stouter, first
A Candiote cloak, which to the knee
 might reach,
 And trousers not so tight that they
 would burst,
But such as fit an Asiatic breech;
 A shawl, whose folds in Cashmire had
 been nurst,
Slippers of saffron, dagger rich and handy;
In short, all things which form a Turkish
 dandy.

LXIX

While he was dressing, Baba, their black
 friend,
 Hinted the vast advantages which they
Might probably obtain both in the end,
 If they would but pursue the proper
 way
Which Fortune plainly seem'd to re-
 commend;
 And then he added, that he needs must
 say,
''Twould greatly tend to better their con-
 dition,
If they would condescend to circumcision.

719

LXX

'For his own part, he really should rejoice
 To see them true believers, but no less
Would leave his proposition to their
 choice.'
 The other, thanking him for this excess
Of goodness, in thus leaving them a voice
 In such a trifle, scarcely could express
'Sufficiently' (he said) 'his approbation
Of all the customs of this polish'd nation.

LXXI

'For his own share—he saw but small
 objection
 To so respectable an ancient rite;
And, after swallowing down a slight
 refection,
 For which he own'd a present appetite,
He doubted not a few hours of reflection
 Would reconcile him to the business
 quite.'
'Will it?' said Juan, sharply: 'Strike me
 dead,
But they as soon shall circumcise my head!

LXXII

'Cut off a thousand heads, before——'—
 'Now, pray,'
Replied the other, 'do not interrupt:
You put me out in what I had to say.
 Sir!—as I said, as soon as I have supped,
I shall perpend if your proposal may
 Be such as I can properly accept;
Provided always your great goodness still
Remits the matter to our own free-will.'

LXXIII

Baba eyed Juan, and said, 'Be so good
 As dress yourself—' and pointed out a
 suit
In which a Princess with great pleasure
 would
 Array her limbs; but Juan standing mute,
As not being in a masquerading mood,
 Gave it a slight kick with his Christian
 foot;
And when the old negro told him to 'Get
 ready,'
Replied, 'Old gentleman, I'm not a lady.'

LXXIV

'What you may be, I neither know nor
 care,'
 Said Baba; 'but pray do as I desire:
I have no more time nor many words to
 spare.'
 'At least,' said Juan, 'sure I may inquire
The cause of this odd travesty?'—'For-
 bear,'
 Said Baba, 'to be curious; 'twill
 transpire,
No doubt, in proper place, and time, and
 season:
I have no authority to tell the reason.'

LXXV

'Then if I do,' said Juan, 'I'll be——'—
 'Hold!'
 Rejoin'd the negro, 'pray be not pro-
 voking;
This spirit's well, but it may wax too bold,
 And you will find us not too fond of
 joking.'
'What, sir,' said Juan, 'shall it e'er be told
 That I unsex'd my dress?' But Baba,
 stroking
The things down, said, 'Incense me, and I
 call
Those who will leave you of no sex at all.

LXXVI

'I offer you a handsome suit of clothes:
 A woman's, true; but then there is a
 cause
Why you should wear them.'—'What,
 though my soul loathes
 The effeminate garb?'—thus, after a
 short pause,
Sigh'd Juan, muttering also some slight
 oaths,
 'What the devil shall I do with all this
 gauze?'
Thus he profanely term'd the finest lace
Which e'er set off a marriage-morning face.

LXXVII

And then he swore; and, sighing, on he
 slipp'd
 A pair of trousers of flesh-colour'd silk;
Next with a virgin zone he was equipp'd,
 Which girt a slight chemise as white as
 milk;
But tugging on his petticoat, he tripp'd,
 Which—as we say—or as the Scotch
 say, whilk,
(The rhyme obliges me to this; sometimes
Monarchs are less imperative than
 rhymes)—

LXXVIII

Whilk, which (or what you please), was
 owing to
 His garment's novelty, and his being
 awkward:
And yet at last he managed to get through
 His toilet, though no doubt a little back-
 ward:
The negro Baba help'd a little too,
 When some untoward part of raiment
 stuck hard;
And, wrestling both his arms into a gown,
He paused, and took a survey up and down.

LXXIX

One difficulty still remain'd—his hair
 Was hardly long enough; but Baba found
So many false long tresses all to spare,
 That soon his head was most completely
 crown'd,

After the manner then in fashion there;
 And this addition with such gems was
 bound
As suited the *ensemble* of his toilet,
While Baba made him comb his head and
 oil it.

LXXX

And now being femininely all array'd,
 With some small aid from scissors,
 paint, and tweezers,
He look'd in almost all respects a maid,
 And Baba smilingly exclaim'd, 'You
 see, sirs,
A perfect transformation here display'd;
 And now, then, you must come along
 with me, sirs,
That is—the Lady:' clapping his hands
 twice,
Four blacks were at his elbow in a trice.

LXXXI

'You, sir,' said Baba, nodding to the one,
 'Will please to accompany those gentle-
 men
To supper; but you, worthy Christian nun,
 Will follow me: no trifling, sir; for
 when
I say a thing, it must at once be done.
 What fear you? think you this a lion's
 den?
Why, 'tis a palace; where the truly wise
Anticipate the Prophet's paradise.

LXXXII

'You fool! I tell you no one means you
 harm.'
 'So much the better,' Juan said, 'for
 them;
Else they shall feel the weight of this my
 arm,
 Which is not quite so light as you may
 deem.
I yield thus far; but soon will break the
 charm,
 If any take me for that which I seem:
So that I trust for everybody's sake,
That this disguise may lead to no mistake.'

LXXXIII

Blockhead! come on, and see,' quoth
 Baba; while
Don Juan, turning to his comrade, who
 Though somewhat grieved, could scarce
 forbear a smile
Upon the metamorphosis in view,—
Farewell!' they mutually exclaim'd: 'this
 soil
Seems fertile in adventures strange and
 new;
One's turn'd half Mussulman, and one a
 maid,
By this old black enchanter's unsought
 aid.'

LXXXIV

'Farewell!' said Juan: 'should we meet
 no more,
 I wish you a good appetite.'—'Farewell!'
 Replied the other; 'though it grieves me
 sore:
When we next meet, we'll have a tale to
 tell:
We needs must follow when Fate puts
 from shore.
 Keep your good name; though Eve
 herself once fell.'
'Nay,' quoth the maid, 'the Sultan's self
 shan't carry me,
Unless his highness promises to marry me.'

LXXXV

And thus they parted, each by separate
 doors;
 Baba led Juan onward room by room
Through glittering galleries, and o'er
 marble floors,
 Till a gigantic portal through the gloom,
Haughty and huge, along the distance
 lowers;
 And wafted far arose a rich perfume:
It seem'd as though they came upon a
 shrine,
For all was vast, still, fragrant, and divine.

LXXXVI

The giant door was broad, and bright,
 and high,
 Of gilded bronze, and carved in curious
 guise;
Warriors thereon were battling furiously;
 Here stalks the victor, there the van-
 quish'd lies;
There captives led in triumph droop the eye,
 And in perspective many a squadron flies:
It seems the work of times before the line
Of Rome transplanted fell with Con-
 stantine.

LXXXVII

This massy portal stood at the wide close
 Of a huge hall, and on its either side
Two little dwarfs, the least you could
 suppose,
 Were sate, like ugly imps, as if allied
In mockery to the enormous gate which
 rose
 O'er them in almost pyramidic pride:
The gate so splendid was in all its *features*,
You never thought about those little
 creatures,

LXXXVIII

Until you nearly trod on them, and then
 You started back in horror to survey
The wondrous hideousness of those small
 men,
 Whose colour was not black, nor white,
 nor grey,

But an extraneous mixture, which no pen
 Can trace, although perhaps the pencil
 may;
They were mis-shapen pigmies, deaf and
 dumb,—
Monsters, who cost a no less monstrous
 sum.

LXXXIX

Their duty was—for they were strong, and
 though
 They look'd so little, did strong things
 at times—
To ope this door, which they could really do,
 The hinges being as smooth as Rogers'
 rhymes;
And now and then, with tough strings of
 the bow,
 As is the custom of those Eastern climes,
To give some rebel Pacha a cravat;
For mutes are generally used for that.

XC

They spoke by signs—that is, not spoke
 at all;
 And looking like two incubi, they glared
As Baba with his fingers made them fall
 To heaving back the portal folds: it
 scared
Juan a moment, as this pair so small,
 With shrinking serpent optics on him
 stared;
It was as if their little looks could poison
Or fascinate whome'er they fix'd their eyes
 on.

XCI

Before they enter'd, Baba paused to hint
 To Juan some slight lessons as his guide:
'If you could just contrive,' he said, 'to
 stint
 That somewhat manly majesty of stride,
'Twould be as well, and—(though there's
 not much in't),
To swing a little less from side to side,
Which has at times an aspect of the
 oddest:—
And also could you look a little modest,

XCII

''Twould be convenient; for these mutes
 have eyes
 Like needles, which may pierce those
 petticoats;
And if they should discover your disguise,
 You know how near us the deep
 Bosphorus floats;
And you and I may chance, ere morning
 rise,
 To find our way to Marmora without
 boats,
Stitch'd up in sacks—a mode of navigation
A good deal practised here upon
 occasion.'

XCIII

With this encouragement, he led the wa
 Into a room still nobler than the last;
A rich confusion form'd a disarray
 In such sort, that the eye along it cas
Could hardly carry anything away,
 Object on object flash'd so bright an
 fast;
A dazzling mass of gems, and gold, an
 glitter,
Magnificently mingled in a litter.

XCIV

Wealth had done wonders—taste no
 much; such things
 Occur in Orient palaces, and even
In the more chasten'd domes of Wester
 kings
 (Of which I have also seen some six o
 seven),
Where I can't say or gold or diamon
 flings
 Great lustre, there is much to be for
 given;
Groups of bad statues, tables, chairs, an
 pictures,
On which I cannot pause to make m
 strictures.

XCV

In this imperial hall, at distance lay
 Under a canopy, and there reclined
Quite in a confidential queenly way,
 A lady; Baba stopp'd, and kneelin
 sign'd
To Juan, who, though not much used t
 pray,
 Knelt down by instinct, wondering i
 his mind
What all this meant: while Baba bow'
 and bended
His head, until the ceremony ended.

XCVI

The lady rising up with such an air
 As Venus rose with from the wave, o
 them
Bent like an antelope a Paphian pair
 Of eyes, which put out each surround
 ing gem;
And raising up an arm as moonlight fai
 She sign'd to Baba, who first kiss'd th
 hem
Of her deep purple robe, and speakin
 low,
Pointed to Juan, who remain'd below.

XCVII

Her presence was as lofty as her state;
 Her beauty of that overpowering kin
Whose force description only woul
 abate:
 I'd rather leave it much to your ow
 mind,

Than lessen it by what I could relate
 Of forms and features; it would strike
 you blind
Could I do justice to the full detail;
So, luckily for both, my phrases fail.

XCVIII

This much however I may add,—her years
 Were ripe, they might make six-and-
 twenty springs,
But there are forms which Time to touch
 forbears,
 And turns aside his scythe to vulgar
 things:
Such as was Mary's Queen of Scots; true—
 tears
 And love destroy; and sapping sorrow
 wrings
Charms from the charmer, yet some
 never grow
Ugly; for instance—Ninon de l'Enclos.

XCIX

She spake some words to her attendants,
 who
 Composed a choir of girls, ten or a
 dozen,
And were all clad alike; like Juan, too,
 Who wore their uniform, by Baba
 chosen:
They form'd a very nymph-like looking
 crew,
 Which might have called Diana's
 chorus 'cousin,'
As far as outward show may correspond;
 Won't be bail for anything beyond.

C

They bow'd obeisance and withdrew,
 retiring,
 But not by the same door through
 which came in
Baba and Juan, which last stood admiring,
 At some small distance, all he saw within
This strange saloon, much fitted for
 inspiring
 Marvel and praise; for both or none
 things win;
And I must say, I ne'er could see the very
 Great happiness of the 'Nil Admirari.'

CI

Not to admire is all the art I know
 (Plain truth, dear Murray, needs few
 flowers of speech)
To make men happy, or to keep them so'
 (So take it in the very words of Creech)—
Thus Horace wrote we all know long ago;
 And thus Pope quotes the precept to
 re-teach
From his translation; but had *none
 admired,*
Could Pope have sung, or Horace been
 inspired?

CII

Baba, when all the damsels were with-
 drawn,
 Motion'd to Juan to approach, and then
A second time desired him to kneel down,
 And kiss the lady's foot; which maxim
 when
He heard repeated, Juan with a frown
 Drew himself up to his full height again,
And said, 'It grieved him, but he could
 not stoop
To any shoe, unless it shod the Pope.'

CIII

Baba, indignant at this ill-timed pride,
 Made fierce remonstrances, and then
 a threat
He mutter'd (but the last was given aside)
 About a bow-string—quite in vain;
 not yet
Would Juan bend, though 'twere to
 Mahomet's bride:
 There's nothing in the world like
 etiquette
In kingly chambers or imperial halls,
As also at the race and county balls.

CIV

He stood like Atlas, with a world of words
 About his ears, and nathless would not
 bend:
The blood of all his line's Castilian lords
 Boil'd in his veins, and rather than
 descend
To stain his pedigree, a thousand swords
 A thousand times of him had made an
 end;
At length perceiving the '*foot*' could not
 stand,
Baba proposed that he should kiss the
 hand.

CV

Here was an honourable compromise,
 A half-way house of diplomatic rest,
Where they might meet in much more
 peaceful guise;
 And Juan now his willingness exprest
To use all fit and proper courtesies,
 Adding, that this was commonest and
 best,
For through the South, the custom still
 commands
The gentleman to kiss the lady's hands.

CVI

And he advanced, though with but a bad
 grace,
 Though on more *thorough-bred* or
 fairer fingers
No lips e'er left their transitory trace:
 On such as these the lip too fondly
 lingers,

And for one kiss would fain imprint a
 brace,
 As you will see, if she you love shall
 bring hers
In contact; and sometimes even a fair
 stranger's
An almost twelvemonth's constancy en-
 dangers.

CVII

The lady eyed him o'er and o'er, and bade
 Baba retire, which he obey'd in style,
As if well used to the retreating trade;
 And taking hints in good part all the
 while,
He whisper'd Juan not to be afraid,
 And looking on him with a sort of smile,
Took leave, with such a face of satisfaction,
As good men wear who have done a
 virtuous action.

CVIII

When he was gone, there was a sudden
 change:
 I know not what might be the lady's
 thought,
But o'er her bright brow flash'd a tumult
 strange,
 And into her clear cheek the blood was
 brought,
Blood-red as sunset summer clouds which
 range
 The verge of Heaven; and in her large
 eyes wrought,
A mixture of sensations might be scann'd,
Of half-voluptuousness and half-com-
 mand.

CIX

Her form had all the softness of her sex,
 Her features all the sweetness of the
 devil,
When he put on the cherub to perplex
 Eve, and paved (God knows how) the
 road to evil;
The sun himself was scarce more free from
 specks
 Than she from aught at which the eye
 could cavil;
Yet, somehow, there was something some-
 where wanting,
As if she rather *order'd* than was *grant-
 ing*.—

CX

Something imperial, or imperious, threw
 A chain o'er all she did; that is, a chain
Was thrown as 'twere about the neck of
 you,—
 And rapture's self will seem almost a pain
With aught which looks like despotism in
 view;
 Our souls at least are free, and 'tis in
 vain

We would against them make the fle
 obey—
The spirit in the end will have its way.

CXI

Her very smile was haughty, though
 sweet;
 Her very nod was not an inclination:
There was a self-will even in her small fee
 As though they were quite conscious
 her station—
They trod as upon necks; and to comple
 Her state (it is the custom of her natio
A poniard deck'd her girdle, as the sigr
She was a sultan's bride (thank Heave
 not mine!)

CXII

'To hear and to obey' had been from bir
 The law of all around her; to fulfil
All phantasies which yielded joy or mirt
 Had been her slaves' chief pleasure,
 her will;
Her blood was high, her beauty scarce
 earth:
 Judge, then, if her caprices e'er stood sti
Had she but been a Christian, I've a noti
We should have found out the 'perpetu
 motion.'

CXIII

Whate'er she saw and coveted w
 brought;
 Whate'er she did *not* see, if she suppos
It might be seen, with diligence was soug
 And when 'twas found straightway t
 bargain closed:
There was no end unto the things s
 bought,
 Nor to the trouble which her fanci
 caused;
Yet even her tyranny had such a grace
The women pardon'd all except her fac

CXIV

Juan, the latest of her whims, had caug
 Her eye in passing on his way to sal
She order'd him directly to be bought,
 And Baba, who had ne'er been know
 to fail
In any kind of mischief to be wrought,
 At all such auctions knew how
 prevail:
She had no prudence, but he had; and t
Explains the garb which Juan took ami

CXV

His youth and features favour'd t
 disguise,
 And should you ask how she, a sulta
 bride,
Could risk or compass such stran
 phantasies,
 This I must leave sultanas to decide:

Emperors are only husbands in wives'
eyes,
And kings and consorts oft are
mystified,
As we may ascertain with due precision,
Some by experience, others by tradition.

CXVI

But to the main point, where we have been
tending:—
She now conceived all difficulties past,
And deem'd herself extremely con-
descending
When, being made her property at last,
Without more preface, in her blue eyes
blending
Passion and power, a glance on him she
cast,
And merely saying, 'Christian, canst thou
love?'
Conceived that phrase was quite enough
to move.

CXVII

And so it was, in proper time and place;
But Juan, who had still his mind o'er-
flowing
With Haidée's isle and soft Ionian face,
Felt the warm blood, which in his face
was glowing,
Rush back upon his heart, which fill'd
apace,
And left his cheeks as pale as snow-
drops blowing:
These words went through his soul like
Arab spears,
So that he spoke not, but burst into tears.

CXVIII

She was a good deal shock'd; not shock'd
at tears,
For women shed and use them at their
liking;
But there is something when man's eye
appears
Wet, still more disagreeable and strik-
ing:
A woman's tear-drop melts, a man's half
sears,
Like molten lead, as if you thrust a pike
in
His heart to force it out, for (to be shorter)
To them 'tis a relief, to us a torture.

CXIX

And she would have consoled, but knew
not how:
Having no equals, nothing which had
e'er
Infected her with sympathy till now,
And never having dreamt what 'twas
to bear

Aught of a serious, sorrowing kind,
although
There might arise some pouting petty
care
To cross her brow, she wonder'd how so
near
Her eyes another's eye could shed a tear.

CXX

But nature teaches more than power can
spoil,
And, when a *strong* although a strange
sensation
Moves—female hearts are such a genial
soil
For kinder feelings, whatsoe'er their
nation,
They naturally pour the 'wine and oil,'
Samaritans in every situation;
And thus Gulbeyaz, though she knew not
why,
Felt an odd glistening moisture in her eye.

CXXI

But tears must stop like all things else;
and soon
Juan, who for an instant had been
moved
To such a sorrow by the intrusive tone
Of one who dared to ask if 'he *had*
loved,'
Call'd back the stoic to his eyes, which
shone
Bright with the very weakness he re-
proved;
And although sensitive to beauty, he
Felt most indignant still at not being free.

CXXII

Gulbeyaz, for the first time in her days,
Was much embarrass'd, never having
met
In all her life with aught save prayers and
praise;
And as she also risk'd her life to get
Him whom she meant to tutor in love's
ways,
Into a comfortable tête-à-tête,
To lose the hour would make her quite a
martyr,
And they had wasted now almost a
quarter.

CXXIII

I also would suggest the fitting time,
To gentlemen in any such like case,
That is to say—in a meridian clime,
With us there is more law given to the
chase,
But here a small delay forms a great crime:
So recollect that the extremest grace
Is just two minutes for your declaration—
A moment more would hurt your
reputation.

CXXIV

Juan's was good; and might have been still better,
But he had got Haidée into his head:
However strange, he could not yet forget her,
Which made him seem exceedingly ill-bred.
Gulbeyaz, who look'd on him as her debtor
For having had him to her palace led,
Began to blush up to the eyes, and then
Grow deadly pale, and then blush back again.

CXXV

At length, in an imperial way, she laid
Her hand on his, and bending on him eyes,
Which needed not an empire to persuade,
Look'd into his for love, where none replies:
Her brow grew black, but she would not upbraid,
That being the last thing a proud woman tries;
She rose, and pausing one chaste moment, threw
Herself upon his breast, and there she grew.

CXXVI

This was an awkward test, as Juan found,
But he was steel'd by sorrow, wrath, and pride:
With gentle force her white arms he unwound,
And seated her all drooping by his side,
Then rising haughtily he glanced around,
And looking coldly in her face, he cried,
'The prison'd eagle will not pair, nor I
Serve a sultana's sensual phantasy.

CXXVII

'Thou ask'st, if I can love? be this the proof
How much I *have* loved—that I love not *thee*!
In this vile garb, the distaff, web, and woof,
Were fitter for me: Love is for the free!
I am not dazzled by this splendid roof;
Whate'er thy power, and great it seems to be,
Heads bow, knees bend, eyes watch around a throne,
And hands obey—our hearts are still our own.'

CXXVIII

This was a truth to us extremely trite;
Not so to her, who ne'er had heard such things:
She deem'd her least command must yield delight,
Earth being only made for queens and kings.

If hearts lay on the left side or the right
She hardly knew, to such perfection brings
Legitimacy its born votaries, when
Aware of their due royal rights o'er men.

CXXIX

Besides, as has been said, she was so fair
As even in a much humbler lot had made
A kingdom or confusion anywhere,
And also, as may be presumed, she laid
Some stress on charms, which seldom are, if e'er,
By their possessors thrown into the shade:
She thought hers gave a double 'right divine';
And half of that opinion's also mine.

CXXX

Remember, or (if you can not) imagine,
Ye! who have kept your chastity when young,
While some more desperate dowager has been waging
Love with you, and been in the dog days stung
By your refusal, recollect her raging!
Or recollect all that was said or sung
On such a subject; then suppose the face
Of a young downright beauty in this case.

CXXXI

Suppose,—but you already have supposed,
The spouse of Potiphar, the Lady Booby,
Phædra, and all which story has disclosed
Of good examples; pity that so few by
Poets and private tutors are exposed,
To educate—ye youth of Europe—you by!
But when you have supposed the few we know,
You can't suppose Gulbeyaz' angry brow.

CXXXII

A tigress robb'd of young, a lioness,
Or any interesting beast of prey,
Are similes at hand for the distress
Of ladies who cannot have their own way;
But though my turn will not be served with less,
These don't express one half what I should say:
For what is stealing young ones, few or many,
To cutting short their hopes of having any?

CXXXIII

The love of offspring's nature's general
 law,
 From tigresses and cubs to ducks and
 ducklings;
There's nothing whets the beak, or arms
 the claw,
 Like an invasion of their babes and
 sucklings;
And all who have seen a human nursery,
 saw
 How mothers love their children's
 squalls and chucklings:
This strong extreme effect (to tire no
 longer)
Your patience) shows the cause must still
 be stronger.

CXXXIV

If I said fire flash'd from Gulbeyaz' eyes,
 'Twere nothing—for her eyes flash'd
 always fire;
Or said her cheeks assumed the deepest
 dyes,
 I should but bring disgrace upon the
 dyer,
So supernatural was her passion's rise;
 For ne'er till now she knew a check'd
 desire:
Even ye who know what a check'd woman
 is
(Enough, God knows!) would much fall
 short of this.

CXXXV

Her rage was but a minute's, and 'twas
 well—
 A moment's more had slain her; but
 the while
It lasted 'twas like a short glimpse of hell:
 Nought's more sublime than energetic
 bile,
Though horrible to see, yet grand to tell,
 Like ocean warring 'gainst a rocky isle;
And the deep passions flashing through
 her form
Made her a beautiful embodied storm.

CXXXVI

A vulgar tempest 'twere to a typhoon
 To match a common fury with her rage,
And yet she did not want to reach the
 moon,
 Like moderate Hotspur on the immortal
 page;
Her anger pitch'd into a lower tune,
 Perhaps the fault of her soft sex and
 age—
Her wish was but to 'kill, kill, kill,' like
 Lear's,
And then her thirst of blood was quench'd
 in tears.

CXXXVII

A storm it raged, and like the storm it
 pass'd,
 Pass'd without words—in fact she
 could not speak;
And then her sex's shame broke in at last,
 A sentiment till then in her but weak,
But now it flow'd in natural and fast,
 As water through an unexpected leak;
For she felt humbled—and humiliation
Is sometimes good for people in her
 station.

CXXXVIII

It teaches them that they are flesh and blood
 It also gently hints to them that others,
Although of clay, are yet not quite of mud;
 That urns and pipkins are but fragile
 brothers,
And works of the same pottery, bad or
 good,
 Though not all born of the same sires
 and mothers;
It teaches—Heaven knows only what it
 teaches,
But sometimes it may mend, and often
 reaches.

CXXXIX

Her first thought was to cut off Juan's
 head;
 Her second, to cut only his—acquain-
 tance;
Her third, to ask him where he had been
 bred;
 Her fourth, to rally him into re-
 pentance;
Her fifth, to call her maids and go to bed;
 Her sixth, to stab herself; her seventh,
 to sentence
The lash to Baba:—but her grand resource
Was to sit down again, and cry of course.

CXL

She thought to stab herself, but then she
 had
 The dagger close at hand, which made
 it awkward;
For Eastern stays are little made to pad,
 So that a poniard pierces if 'tis stuck
 hard:
She thought of killing Juan—but, poor lad!
 Though he deserved it well for being so
 backward,
The cutting off his head was not the art
Most likely to attain her aim—his heart.

CXLI

Juan was moved: he had made up his mind
 To be impaled, or quarter'd as a dish
For dogs, or to be slain with pangs
 refined,
 Or thrown to lions, or made baits for
 fish,

And thus heroically stood resign'd,
 Rather than sin—except to his own
 wish:
But all his great preparatives for dying
Dissolved like snow before a woman
 crying.

CXLII

As through his palms Bob Acres' valour
 oozed,
 So Juan's virtue ebb'd, I know not how;
And first he wonder'd why he had refused;
 And then, if matters could be made up
 now;
And next his savage virtue he accused,
 Just as a friar may accuse his vow,
Or as a dame repents her of her oath,
Which mostly ends in some small breach
 of both.

CXLIII

So he began to stammer some excuses;
 But words are not enough in such a
 matter,
Although you borrow'd all that e'er the
 muses
 Have sung, or even a Dandy's dandiest
 chatter,
Or all the figures Castlereagh abuses;
 Just as a languid smile began to flatter
His peace was making, but before he
 ventured
Further, old Baba rather briskly enter'd.

CXLIV

'Bride of the Sun! and Sister of the
 Moon!'
 ('Twas thus he spake,) 'and Empress of
 the Earth!
Whose frown would put the spheres all
 out of tune,
 Whose smile makes all the planets
 dance with mirth,
Your slave brings tidings—he hopes not
 too soon—
 Which your sublime attention may be
 worth:
The Sun himself has sent me like a ray,
To hint that he is coming up this way.'

CXLV

'Is it,' exclaim'd Gulbeyaz, 'as you say?
 I wish to heaven he would not shine till
 morning!
But bid my women form the Milky-way.
 Hence, my old comet! give the stars due
 warning—
And, Christian! mingle with them as you
 may,
 And as you'd have me pardon your past
 scorning'—
Here they were interrupted by a humming
Sound, and then by a cry, 'The Sultan's
 coming!'

CXLVI

First came her damsels, a decorous file,
 And then his Highness' eunuchs, black
 and white;
The train might reach a quarter of a mile
 His majesty was always so polite
As to announce his visits a long while
 Before he came, especially at night;
For being the last wife of the Emperor,
She was of course the favourite of the four

CXLVII

His Highness was a man of solemn port,
 Shawl'd to the nose, and bearded to the
 eyes,
Snatch'd from a prison to preside at court
 His lately bowstrung brother caused
 his rise;
He was as good a sovereign of the sort
 As any mentioned in the histories
Of Cantemir, or Knölles, where few shine
Save Solyman, the glory of their line.

CXLVIII

He went to mosque in state, and said his
 prayers
 With more than 'Oriental scrupulosity'
He left to his vizier all state affairs,
 And show'd but little royal curiosity:
I know not if he had domestic cares—
 No process proved connubial ani-
 mosity;
Four wives and twice five hundred maids
 unseen,
Were ruled as calmly as a Christian queen

CXLIX

If now and then there happen'd a sligh
 slip,
 Little was heard of criminal or crime;
The story scarcely pass'd a single lip—
 The sack and sea had settled all in time
From which the secret nobody could rip
 The public knew no more than does thi
 rhyme;
No scandals made the daily press a
 curse—
Morals were better, and the fish no worse

CL

He saw with his own eyes the moon wa
 round,
 Was also certain that the earth wa
 square,
Because he had journey'd fifty miles, an
 found
 No sign that it was circular anywhere
His empire also was without a bound:
 'Tis true, a little troubled here and there
By rebel pachas, and encroaching giaours
But then they never came to 'the Seve
 Towers';

CLI

Except in shape of envoys, who were sent
 To lodge there when a war broke out,
 according
To the true law of nations, which ne'er
 meant
 Those scoundrels, who have never had
 a sword in
Their dirty diplomatic hands, to vent
 Their spleen in making strife, and
 safely wording
Their lies, yclept despatches, without risk
 or
The singeing of a single inky whisker.

CLII

He had fifty daughters and four dozen sons,
 Of whom all such as came of age were
 stow'd,
The former in a palace, where like nuns
 They lived till some Bashaw was sent
 abroad,
When she, whose turn it was, was wed at
 once,
 Sometimes at six years old—though
 this seems odd,
'Tis true; the reason is, that the Bashaw
Must make a present to his sire-in-law.

CLIII

His sons were kept in prison, till they grew
 Of years to fill a bowstring or the throne,
One or the other, but which of the two
 Could yet be known unto the fates alone;
Meantime the education they went
 through
 Was princely, as the proofs have always
 shown;
So that the heir-apparent still was found
No less deserving to be hang'd than
 crown'd.

CLIV

His Majesty saluted his fourth spouse
 With all the ceremonies of his rank,
Who clear'd her sparkling eyes and
 smooth'd her brows,
 As suits a matron who has play'd a
 prank;
These must seem doubly mindful of their
 vows,
 To save the credit of their breaking bank:
No men are such cordial greetings given
As those whose wives have made them fit
 for heaven.

CLV

His Highness cast around his great black
 eyes,
 And looking, as he always look'd,
 perceived
Juan amongst the damsels in disguise,
 At which he seem'd no whit surprised
 nor grieved,

But just remark'd with air sedate and wise,
 While still a fluttering sigh Gulbeyaz
 heaved,
'I see you've bought another girl; 'tis pity
That a mere Christian should be half so
 pretty.'

CLVI

This compliment, which drew all eyes
 upon
 The new-bought virgin, made her blush
 and shake,
Her comrades, also, thought themselves
 undone:
 Oh! Mahomet! that his Majesty should
 take
Such notice of a giaour, while scarce to
 one
 Of them his lips imperial ever spake!
There was a general whisper, toss, and
 wriggle,
But etiquette forbade them all to giggle.

CLVII

The Turks do well to shut—at least, some-
 times—
 The women up—because, in sad reality,
Their chastity in these unhappy climes
 Is not a thing of that astringent quality
Which in the north prevents precocious
 crimes,
 And makes our snow less pure than our
 morality;
The sun, which yearly melts the polar ice,
Has quite the contrary effect on vice.

CLVIII

Thus in the East they are extremely strict,
 And wedlock and a padlock mean the
 same:
Excepting only when the former's pick'd
 It ne'er can be replaced in proper frame;
Spoilt, as a pipe of claret is when prick'd:
 But then their own polygamy's to
 blame;
Why don't they knead two virtuous souls
 for life
Into that moral centaur, man and wife?

CLIX

Thus far our chronicle; and now we pause,
 Though not for want of matter; but 'tis
 time,
According to the ancient epic laws,
 To slacken sail, and anchor with our
 rhyme.
Let this fifth canto meet with due applause,
 The sixth shall have a touch of the sub-
 lime;
Meanwhile, as Homer sometimes sleeps,
 perhaps
You'll pardon to my Muse a few short
 naps.

PREFACE TO
CANTOS VI, VII, AND VIII

THE details of the siege of Ismail in two of the following cantos (*i.e.* the seventh and eighth) are taken from a French Work, entitled 'Histoire de la Nouvelle Russie.' Some of the incidents attributed to Don Juan really occurred, particularly the circumstance of his saving the infant, which was the actual case of the late Duc de Richelieu, then a young volunteer in the Russian service, and afterward the founder and benefactor of Odessa, where his name and memory can never cease to be regarded with reverence.

In the course of these cantos, a stanza or two will be found relative to the late Marquis of Londonderry, but written some time before his decease. Had that person's oligarchy died with him, they would have been suppressed; as it is, I am aware of nothing in the manner of his death or of his life to prevent the free expression of the opinions of all whom his whole existence was consumed in endeavouring to enslave. That he was an amiable man in *private* life, may or may not be true: but with this the public have nothing to do; and as to lamenting his death, it will be time enough when Ireland has ceased to mourn for his birth. As a minister, I, for one of millions, looked upon him as the most despotic in intention, and the weakest in intellect, that ever tyrannised over a country. It is the first time indeed since the Normans that England has been insulted by a *minister* (at least) who could not speak English, and that parliament permitted itself to be dictated to in the language of Mrs. Malaprop.

Of the manner of his death little need be said, except that if a poor radical, such as Waddington or Watson, had cut his throat, he would have been buried in a cross-road, with the usual appurtenances of the stake and mallet. But the minister was an elegant lunatic—a sentimental suicide—he merely cut the 'carotid artery,' (blessings on their learning!) and lo! the pageant, and the Abbey! and 'the syllables of dolour yelled forth' by the newspapers—and the harangue of the Coroner in a eulogy over the bleeding body of the deceased—(an Anthony worthy of such a Cæsar)—and the nauseous and atrocious cant of a degraded crew of conspirators against all that is sincere and honourable. In his death he was necessarily one of two things by the *law**—a felon or a madman—and in either case no great subject for panegyric. In his life he was—what all the world knows, and half of it will feel for years to come, unless his death prove a 'moral lesson' to the surviving† Sejani of Europe. It may at least serve as some consolation to the nations, that their oppressors are not happy, and in some instances judge so justly of their own actions as to anticipate the sentence of mankind.—Let us hear no more of this man; and let Ireland remove the ashes of her Grattan from the sanctuary of Westminster. Shall the patriot of humanity repose by the Werther of politics!!!

* I say by the *law* of the *land*—the laws of humanity judge more gently; but as the legitimates have always the *law* in their mouths, let them here make the most of it.

† From this number must be excepted Canning. Canning is a genius, almost a universal one, an orator, a wit, a poet, a statesman; and no man of talent can long pursue the path of his late predecessor, Lord C. If ever man saved his country, Canning *can;* but *will* he? I, for one, hope so.

With regard to the objections which have bee made on another score to the already publishe cantos of this poem, I shall content myself wi two quotations from Voltaire:—'La pudeur s'e enfuite des cœurs, et s'est refugiée sur les lèvre 'Plus les mœurs sont dépravés, plus l expressions deviennent mesurées; on croit regagn en langage ce qu'on a perdu en vertu.'

This is the real fact, as applicable to the degrade and hypocritical mass which leavens the prese English generation, and is the only answer th deserve. The hackneyed and lavished title of Bla phemer—which, with Radical, Liberal, Jacobi Reformer, &c., are the changes which the hirelin are daily ringing in the ears of those who w listen—should be welcome to all who recollect *whom* it was originally bestowed. Socrates a Jesus Christ were put to death publicly as *bla phemers*, and so have been and may be many w dare to oppose the most notorious abuses of t name of God and the mind of man. But persec tion is not refutation, nor even triumph: t 'wretched infidel,' as he is called, is probab happier in his prison than the proudest of h assailants. With his opinions I have nothing do—they may be right or wrong—but he h suffered for them, and that very suffering for co science' sake will make more proselytes to deis than the example of heterodox prelates to Chr tianity, suicide statesmen to oppression, or ove pensioned homicides to the impious alliance whi insults the world with the name of 'Holy'! I ha no wish to trample on the dishonoured or t dead; but it would be well if the adherents to t classes from whence those persons sprung shou abate a little of the *cant* which is the crying s of this double-dealing and false-speaking time selfish spoilers, and—but enough for the presen PISA, *July*, 1822.

CANTO THE SIXTH

I

'THERE is a tide in the affairs of men,
 Which, taken at the flood,'—you kno
 the rest,
And most of us have found it now an
 then:
 At least we think so, though but fe
 have guess'd
The moment, till too late to come agai
 But no doubt everything is for the best-
Of which the surest sign is in the end:
 When things are at the worst they som
 times mend.

II

There is a tide in the affairs of women,
 Which, taken at the flood, leads—Go
 knows where:
Those navigators must be able seamen
 Whose charts lay down its currents to
 hair,
Not all the reveries of Jacob Behmen
 With its strange whirls and eddies ca
 compare:
Men with their heads reflect on this an
 that—
But women with their hearts or heave
 knows what!

III

And yet a headlong, headstrong, down-
 right she,
 Young, beautiful, and daring—who
 would risk
A throne, the world, the universe, to be
 Beloved in her own way, and rather
 whisk
The stars from out the sky, than not be
 free
 As are the billows when the breeze is
 brisk—
Though such a she's a devil (if there be
 one),
Yet she would make full many a Mani-
 chean.

IV

Thrones, worlds, et cetera, are so oft up-
 set
 By commonest ambition, that when
 passion
O'erthrows the same, we readily forget,
 Or at the least forgive, the loving rash
 one.
If Anthony be well remember'd yet,
 'Tis not his conquests keep his name in
 fashion,
But Actium lost, for Cleopatra's eyes
Outbalance all the Cæsar's victories.

V

He died at fifty for a queen of forty;
 I wish their years had been fifteen and
 twenty,
For then wealth, kingdoms, worlds are
 but a sport—I
 Remember when, though I had no great
 plenty
Of worlds to lose, yet still, to pay my court, I
 Gave what I had—a heart; as the world
 went, I
Gave what was worth a world; for worlds
 could never
Restore me those pure feelings, gone for
 ever.

VI

'Twas the boy's 'mite,' and, like the
 'widow's,' may
 Perhaps be weigh'd hereafter, if not
 now;
But whether such things do or do not
 weigh,
 All who have loved, or love, will still
 allow
Life has nought like it. God is love, they
 say,
 And Love's a god, or was before the
 brow
Of earth was wrinkled by the sins and
 tears
Of—but Chronology best knows the
 years.

VII

We left our hero and third heroine in
 A kind of state more awkward than un-
 common,
For gentlemen must sometimes risk their
 skin
 For that sad tempter, a forbidden
 woman:
Sultans too much abhor this sort of sin,
 And don't agree at all with the wise
 Roman,
Heroic, stoic Cato, the sententious,
Who lent his lady to his friend Hortensius.

VIII

I know Gulbeyaz was extremely wrong;
 I own it, I deplore it, I condemn it;
But I detest all fiction even in song,
 And so must tell the truth, howe'er you
 blame it.
Her reason being weak, her passions
 strong,
 She thought that her lord's heart (even
 she claim it)
Was scarce enough; for he had fifty-nine
Years, and a fifteen-hundredth con-
 cubine.

IX

I am not, like Cassio, 'an arithmetician,'
 But by the 'bookish theoric' it appears,
If 'tis summ'd up with feminine precision,
 That, adding to the account his High-
 ness' years,
The fair Sultana erred from inanition;
 For, were the Sultan just to all his dears,
She could but claim the fifteen-hundredth
 part
Of what should be monopoly—the heart.

X

It is observed that ladies are litigious
 Upon all legal objects of possession,
And not the least so when they are
 religious,
 Which doubles what they think of the
 transgression:
With suits and prosecutions they besiege
 us,
 As the tribunals show through many a
 session,
When they suspect that any one goes
 shares
In that to which the law makes them sole
 heirs.

XI

Now, if this holds good in a Christian land,
 The heathen also, though with lesser
 latitude,
Are apt to carry things with a high hand,
 And take, what kings call 'an imposing
 attitude';

And for their rights connubial make a
 stand,
 When their liege husbands treat them
 with ingratitude;
And as four wives must have quadruple
 claims,
The Tigris hath its jealousies like Thames.

XII

Gulbeyaz was the fourth, and (as I said)
 The favourite; but what's favour
 amongst four?
Polygamy may well be held in dread,
 Not only as a sin, but as a *bore:*
Most wise men with *one* moderate
 woman wed,
 Will scarcely find philosophy for more;
And all (except Mahometans) forbear
 To make the nuptial couch a 'Bed of
 Ware.'

XIII

His Highness, the sublimest of man-
 kind,—
 So styled according to the usual forms
Of every monarch, till they are consign'd
 To those sad hungry Jacobins the
 worms,
Who on the very loftiest kings have
 dined,—
 His Highness gazed upon Gulbeyaz'
 charms,
Expecting all the welcome of a lover
(A 'Highland welcome' all the wide world
 over).

XIV

Now here we should distinguish; for
 howe'er
 Kisses, sweet words, embraces, and all
 that,
May look like what is—neither here nor
 there,
 They are put on as easily as a hat,
Or rather bonnet, which the fair sex wear,
 Trimm'd either heads or hearts to
 decorate,
Which form an ornament, but no more
 part
Of heads, than their caresses of the heart.

XV

A slight blush, a soft tremor, a calm kind
 Of gentle feminine delight, and shown
More in the eyelids than the eyes, resign'd
 Rather to hide what pleases most
 unknown,
Are the best tokens (to a modest mind)
 Of love, when seated on his loveliest
 throne,
A sincere woman's breast,—for over-
 warm
Or over-*cold* annihilates the charm.

XVI

For over-warmth, if false, is worse tha
 truth;
 If true, 'tis no great lease of its own fire
For no one, save in very early youth,
 Would like (I think) to trust all to desire
Which is but a precarious bond, in sooth
 And apt to be transferr'd to the fir
 buyer
At a sad discount: while your over-chill
Women, on t'other hand, seem somewha
 silly.

XVII

That is, we cannot pardon their bad tast
 For so it seems to lovers swift or slow
Who fain would have a mutual flam
 confess'd,
 And see a sentimental passion glow,
Even were St. Francis' paramour their gues
 In his monastic concubine of snow;—
In short, the maxim for the amorous tribe
Horatian, 'Medio tu tutissimus ibis.'

XVIII

The 'tu' 's *too* much,—but let it stand,—
 the verse
 Requires it, that's to say, the Englis
 rhyme,
And not the pink of old hexameters;
 But, after all, there's neither tune no
 time
In the last line, which cannot well be worse
 And was thrust in to close the octave'
 chime:
I own no prosody can ever rate it
As a rule, but *truth* may, if you translate i

XIX

If fair Gulbeyaz overdid her part,
 I know not—it succeeded, and succes
Is much in most things, not less in th
 heart
Than other articles of female dress.
Self-love in man, too, beats all female ar
 They lie, we lie, all lie, but love no less
And no one virtue yet, except starvation
 pagation.

XX

We leave this royal couple to repose:
 A bed is not a throne, and they ma
 sleep,
Whate'er their dreams be, if of joys o
 woes:
 Yet disappointed joys are woes as dee
As any man's clay mixture undergoes.
 Our least of sorrows are such as w
 weep;
'Tis the vile daily drop on drop whic
 wears
The soul out (like the stone) with pett
 cares.

XXI

A scolding wife, a sullen son, a bill
 To pay, unpaid, protested or discounted
At a per-centage; a child cross, dog ill,
 A favourite horse fallen lame just as he's
 mounted,
A bad old woman making a worse will,
 Which leaves you minus of the cash you
 counted
As certain;—these are paltry things, and
 yet
I've rarely seen the man they did not fret.

XXII

I'm a philosopher; confound them all!
 Bills, beasts, and men, and—no! *not*
 womankind!
With one good hearty curse I vent my gall,
 And then my stoicism leaves nought
 behind
Which it can either pain or evil call,
 And I can give my whole soul up to
 mind;
Though what *is* soul, or mind, their birth
 or growth,
Is more than I know—the deuce take
 them both!

XXIII

So now all things are d—n'd one feels at
 ease,
 As after reading Athanasius' curse,
Which doth your true believer so much
 please:
 I doubt if any now could make it worse
O'er his worst enemy when at his knees,
 'Tis so sententious, positive, and terse,
And decorates the Book of Common
 Prayer,
As doth a rainbow the just clearing air.

XXIV

Gulbeyaz and her lord were sleeping, or
 At least one of them!—Oh, the heavy
 night,
When wicked wives, who love some
 bachelor,
 Lie down in dudgeon to sigh for the
 light
Of the grey morning, and look vainly for
 Its twinkle through the lattice dusky
 quite—
To toss, to tumble, doze, revive, and quake
Lest their too lawful bed-fellow should
 wake!

XXV

These are beneath the canopy of heaven,
 Also beneath the canopy of beds
Four-posted and silk-curtain'd, which are
 given
 For rich men and their brides to lay
 their heads

Upon, in sheets white as what bards call
 'driven
 Snow.' Well! 'tis all hap-hazard when
 one weds.
Gulbeyaz was an empress, but had been
Perhaps as wretched if a *peasant's quean.*

XXVI

Don Juan in his feminine disguise,
 With all the damsels in their long array,
Had bow'd themselves before th' imperial
 eyes,
 And at the usual signal ta'en their way
Back to their chambers, those long
 galleries
 In the seraglio, where the ladies lay
Their delicate limbs; a thousand bosoms
 there
Beating for love, as the caged bird's for
 air.

XXVII

I love the sex, and sometimes would
 reverse
 The tyrant's wish, 'that mankind only
 had
One neck, which he with one fell stroke
 might pierce:'
 My wish is quite as wide, but not so bad,
And much more tender on the whole than
 fierce;
 It being (not *now*, but only while a lad)
That womankind had but one rosy
 mouth,
To kiss them all at once from North to
 South.

XXVIII

Oh, enviable Briareus! with thy hands
 And heads, if thou hadst all things
 multiplied
In such proportion!—But my Muse with-
 stands
 The giant thought of being a Titan's
 bride,
Or travelling in Patagonian lands;
 So let us back to Lilliput, and guide
Our hero through the labyrinth of love
In which we left him several lines above.

XXIX

He went forth with the lovely Odalisques,
 At the given signal join'd to their array:
And though he certainly ran many risks,
 Yet he could not at times keep, by the
 way,
(Although the consequences of such frisks
 Are worse than the worst damages men
 pay
In moral England, where the thing's a
 tax,)
From ogling all their charms from breasts
 to backs.

XXX

Still he forgot not his disguise:—along
　The galleries from room to room they
　　walk'd,
A virgin-like and edifying throng,
　By eunuchs flank'd; while at their head
　　there stalk'd
A dame who kept up discipline among
　The female ranks, so that none stirr'd
　　or talk'd,
Without her sanction on their she-
　parades:
Her title was 'the Mother of the Maids.'

XXXI

Whether she was a 'mother,' I know not,
　Or whether they were 'maids' who
　　call'd her mother;
But this is her seraglio title, got
　I know not how, but good as any other;
So Cantemir can tell you, or De Tott:
　Her office was to keep aloof or smother
All bad propensities in fifteen hundred
Young women, and correct them when
　they blunder'd.

XXXII

A goodly sinecure, no doubt! but made
　More easy by the absence of all men—
Except his majesty,—who, with her aid,
　And guards, and bolts, and walls, and
　　now and then,
A slight example, just to cast a shade
　Along the rest, contrived to keep this
　　den
Of beauties cool as an Italian convent,
Where all the passions have, alas! but one
　vent.

XXXIII

And what is that? Devotion, doubtless—
　how
　Could you ask such a question?—but
　　we will
Continue. As I said, this goodly row
　Of ladies of all countries at the will
Of one good man, with stately march and
　slow,
　Like water-lilies floating down a rill—
Or 'rather lake—for *rills* do *not* run
　slowly,—
Paced on most maiden-like and melan-
　choly.

XXXIV

But when they reach'd their own apart-
　ments, there,
　Like birds, or boys, or bedlamites
　　broke loose,
Waves at spring-tide, or women any-
　where
　When freed from bonds (which are of
　　no great use

After all), or like Irish at a fair,
　Their guards being gone, and as it wer
　　a truce
Establish'd between them and bondage
　they
Began to sing, dance, chatter, smile, an
　play.

XXXV

Their talk, of course, ran most on the new
　comer,
　Her shape, her hair, her air, her every
　　thing:
Some thought her dress did not so muc
　become her,
　Or wonder'd at her ears without a ring
Some said her years were getting nig
　their summer,
　Others contended they were but i
　　spring;
Some thought her rather masculine i
　height,
While others wish'd that she had been s
　quite.

XXXVI

But no one doubted on the whole, that sh
　Was what her dress bespoke, a damse
　　fair,
And fresh, and 'beautiful exceedingly,'
　Who with the brightest Georgian
　　might compare:
They wonder'd how Gulbeyaz, too, coul
　be
So silly as to buy slaves who might shar
(If that his Highness wearied of his bride
Her throne and power, and everythin
　beside.

XXXVII

But what was strangest in this virgin crew
　Although her beauty was enough to vex
After the first investigating view,
　They all found out as few, or fewer
　　specks
In the fair form of their companion new
　Than is the custom of the gentle sex,
When they survey, with Christian eyes o
　Heathen,
In a new face 'the ugliest creature breath
　ing.'

XXXVIII

And yet they had their little jealousies,
　Like all the rest; but upon this occasion
Whether there are such things a
　sympathies
　Without our knowledge or our appro
　　bation,
Although they could not see through hi
　disguise,
　All felt a soft kind of concatenation,
Like magnetism, or devilism, or what
You please—we will not quarrel abou
　that:

XXXIX

But certain 'tis they all felt for their new
 Companion something newer still, as
 'twere
A sentimental friendship through and
 through,
 Extremely pure, which made them all
 concur
In wishing her their sister, save a few
 Who wish'd they had a brother just like
 her,
Whom, if they were at home in sweet
 Circassia,
They would prefer to Padisha or Pacha.

XL

Of those who had most genius for this
 sort
 Of sentimental friendship, there were
 three,
Lolah, Katinka, and Dudù; in short
 (To save description), fair as fair can be
Were they, according to the best report,
 Though differing in stature and degree,
And clime and time, and country and
 complexion;
They all alike admired their new con-
 nexion.

XLI

Lolah was dusk as India and as warm;
 Katinka was a Georgian, white and red,
With great blue eyes, a lovely hand and
 arm,
 And feet so small they scarce seem'd
 made to tread,
But rather skim the earth; while Dudù's
 form
 Look'd more adapted to be put to bed,
Being somewhat large, and languishing,
 and lazy,
Yet of a beauty that would drive you crazy.

XLII

A kind of sleepy Venus seem'd Dudù,
 Yet very fit to 'murder sleep' in those
Who gazed upon her cheek's trans-
 cendent hue,
 Her Attic forehead, and her Phidian
 nose:
Few angles were there in her form, 'tis true,
 Thinner she might have been, and yet
 scarce lose:
Yet, after all, 'twould puzzle to say where
It would not spoil some separate charm
 to *pare*.

XLIII

She was not violently lively, but
 Stole on your spirit like a May-day
 breaking;
Her eyes were not too sparkling, yet, half-
 shut,
 They put beholders in a tender taking;

She look'd (this simile's quite new) just cut
 From marble, like Pygmalion's statue
 waking,
The mortal and the marble still at strife,
And timidly expanding into life.

XLIV

Lolah demanded the new damsel's
 name—
 'Juanna,'—Well, a pretty name enough.
Katinka ask'd her also whence she came—
 'From Spain.'—'But where *is*
 Spain?'—'Don't ask such stuff,
Nor show your Georgian ignorance—for
 shame!'
 Said Lolah, with an accent rather rough,
To poor Katinka: 'Spain's an island near
Morocco, betwixt Egypt and Tangier.'

XLV

Dudù said nothing, but sat down beside
 Juanna, playing with her veil or hair;
And looking at her stedfastly, she sigh'd,
 As if she pitied her for being there,
A pretty stranger, without friend or guide,
 And all abash'd, too, at the general stare
Which welcomes hapless strangers in all
 places,
With kind remarks upon their mien and
 faces.

XLVI

But here the Mother of the Maids drew
 near,
 With 'Ladies, it is time to go to rest:
I'm puzzled what to do with you, my
 dear,'
 She added to Juanna, their new guest:
'Your coming has been unexpected here,
 And every couch is occupied; you had
 best
Partake of mine; but by to-morrow early
We will have all things settled for you
 fairly.'

XLVII

Here Lolah interposed—'Mamma, you
 know
 You don't sleep soundly, and I cannot
 bear
That anybody should disturb you so;
 I'll take Juanna; we're a slenderer pair
Than you would make the half of;—don't
 say no;
And I of your young charge will take due
 care.'
But here Katinka interfered, and said,
'She also had compassion and a bed.'

XLVIII

'Besides, I hate to sleep alone,' quoth she.
 The matron frown'd: 'Why so?'—
 'For fear of ghosts,'
Replied Katinka; 'I am sure I see
 A phantom upon each of the four posts;

And then I have the worst dreams that
 can be,
Of Guebres, Giaours, and Ginns, and
 Gouls in hosts.'
The dame replied, 'Between your dreams
 and you,
I fear Juanna's dreams would be but few.

XLIX

'You, Lolah, must continue still to lie
 Alone, for reasons which don't matter;
 you
The same, Katinka, until by and by:
 And I shall place Juanna with Dudù,
Who's quiet, inoffensive, silent, shy,
 And will not toss and chatter the night
 through.
What say you, child?'—Dudù said
 nothing, as
Her talents were of the more silent class;

L

But she rose up, and kiss'd the matron's
 brow
 Between the eyes, and Lolah on both
 cheeks,
Katinka too; and with a gentle bow
 (Curt'sies are neither used by Turks nor
 Greeks)
She took Juanna by the hand to show
 Their place of rest, and left to both
 their piques,
The others pouting at the matron's
 preference
Of Dudù, though they held their tongues
 from deference.

LI

It was a spacious chamber (Oda is
 The Turkish title), and ranged round
 the wall
Were couches, toilets—and much more
 than this
 I might describe, as I have seen it all,
But it suffices—little was amiss;
 'Twas on the whole a nobly furnish'd
 hall,
With all things ladies want, save one or
 two,
And even those were nearer than they
 knew.

LII

Dudù, as has been said, was a sweet
 creature,
 Not very dashing, but extremely
 winning,
With the most regulated charms of feature,
 Which painters cannot catch like faces
 sinning
Against proportion—the wild strokes of
 nature
 Which they hit off at once in the
 beginning,

Full of expression, right or wrong, tha
 strike,
And pleasing, or unpleasing, still are like

LIII

But she was a soft landscape of mild earth
 Where all was harmony, and calm, and
 quiet,
Luxuriant, budding; cheerful withou
 mirth,
 Which, if not happiness, is much more
 nigh it
Than are your mighty passions and s
 forth,
 Which some call 'the sublime': I wish
 they'd try it:
I've seen your stormy seas and stormy
 women,
And pity lovers rather more than seamen

LIV

But she was pensive more than melan
 choly,
 And serious more than pensive, and
 serene,
It may be, more than either—not unholy
 Her thoughts, at least till now, appear
 to have been.
The strangest thing was, beauteous, she
 was wholly
 Unconscious, albeit turn'd of quick
 seventeen,
That she was fair, or dark, or short, or
 tall;
She never thought about herself at all.

LV

And therefore was she kind and gentle as
 The Age of Gold (when gold was ye
 unknown,
By which its nomenclature came to pass
 Thus most appropriately has been
 shown
'Lucus à non lucendo,' not what was,
 But what was not; a sort of style that'
 grown
Extremely common in this age, whose
 metal
The devil may decompose, but never
 settle:

LVI

I think it may be of 'Corinthian Brass,'
 Which was a mixture of all metals, bu
The brazen uppermost). Kind reader
 pass
 This long parenthesis: I could not shu
It sooner for the soul of me, and class
 My faults even with your own! which
 meaneth, Put
A kind construction upon them and me
But that you won't—then don't—I am
 not less free.

LVII

'Tis time we should return to plain
 narration,
 And thus my narrative proceeds:—
 Dudù,
With every kindness short of ostentation,
 Show'd Juan, or Juanna, through and
 through
This labyrinth of females, and each
 station
 Described—what's strange—in words
 extremely few:
I have but one simile, and that's a
 blunder,
For wordless woman, which is *silent*
 thunder.

LVIII

And next she gave her (I say *her*, because
 The gender still was epicene, at least
In outward show, which is a saving clause)
 An outline of the customs of the East,
With all their chaste integrity of laws,
 By which the more a harem is increased,
The stricter doubtless grow the vestal
 duties
Of any supernumerary beauties.

LIX

And then she gave Juanna a chaste kiss:
 Dudù was fond of kissing—which I'm
 sure
That nobody can ever take amiss,
 Because 'tis pleasant, so that it be pure,
And between females means no more than
 this—
 That they have nothing better near, or
 newer.
'Kiss' rhymes to 'bliss' in fact as well as
 verse—
I wish it never led to something worse.

LX

In perfect innocence she then unmade
 Her toilet, which cost little, for she
 was
A child of Nature carelessly array'd:
 If fond of a chance ogle at her glass,
'Twas like the fawn, which, in the lake
 display'd,
 Beholds her own shy, shadowy image
 pass,
When first she starts, and then returns to
 peep,
Admiring this new native of the deep.

LXI

And one by one her articles of dress
 Were laid aside; but not before she
 offer'd
Her aid to fair Juanna, whose excess
 Of modesty declined the assistance
 proffer'd:

Which pass'd well off—as she could do
 no less;
 Though by this *politesse* she rather
 suffer'd,
Pricking her fingers with those cursed pins,
Which surely were invented for our sins,—

LXII

Making a woman like a porcupine,
 Not to be rashly touch'd. But still more
 dread,
Oh, ye! whose fate it is, as once 'twas
 mine,
 In early youth, to turn a lady's maid;—
I did my very boyish best to shine
 In tricking her out for a masquerade:
The pins were placed sufficiently, but not
Stuck all exactly in the proper spot.

LXIII

But these are foolish things to all the wise,
 And I love wisdom more than she loves
 me;
My tendency is to philosophise
 On most things, from a tyrant to a tree;
But still the spouseless virgin *Knowledge*
 flies.
 What are we? and whence came we?
 what shall be
Our *ultimate* existence? what's our
 present?
Are questions answerless, and yet
 incessant.

LXIV

There was deep silence in the chamber:
 dim
 And distant from each other burn'd the
 lights,
And slumber hover'd o'er each lovely limb
 Of the fair occupants: if there be sprites,
They should have walk'd there in their
 sprightliest trim,
 By way of change from their sepulchral
 sites,
And shown themselves as ghosts of better
 taste
Than haunting some old ruin or wild
 waste.

LXV

Many and beautiful lay those around,
 Like flowers of different hue, and clime,
 and root,
In some exotic garden sometimes found,
 With cost, and care, and warmth,
 induced to shoot.
One with her auburn tresses lightly bound,
 And fair brows gently drooping, as the
 fruit
Nods from the tree, was slumbering with
 soft breath,
And lips apart, which show'd the pearls
 beneath.

LXVI

One with her flush'd cheek laid on her
 white arm,
 And raven ringlets gather'd in dark
 crowd
Above her brow, lay dreaming soft and
 warm;
 And smiling through her dream, as
 through a cloud
The moon breaks, half unveil'd each
 further charm,
As, slightly stirring in her snowy shroud,
Her beauties seized the unconscious hour
 of night
All bashfully to struggle into light.

LXVII

This is no bull, although it sounds so; for
 'Twas night, but there were lamps, as
 hath been said.
A third's all pallid aspect offer'd more
 The traits of sleeping sorrow, and
 betray'd
Through the heaved breast the dream of
 some far shore
 Beloved and deplored; while slowly
 stray'd
(As night-dew, on a cypress glittering,
 tinges
The black bough) tear-drops through her
 eyes' dark fringes.

LXVIII

A fourth as marble, statue-like and still,
 Lay in a breathless, hush'd, and stony
 sleep;
White, cold, and pure, as looks a frozen rill,
 Or the snow minaret on an Alpine steep,
Or Lot's wife done in salt,—or what you
 will;—
 My similes are gather'd in a heap,
So pick and choose—perhaps you'll be
 content
With a carved lady on a monument.

LXIX

And lo! a fifth appears;—and what is she?
 A lady of a 'certain age,' which means
Certainly aged—what her years might be
 I know not, never counting past their
 teens;
But there she slept, not quite so fair to see,
 As ere that awful period intervenes
Which lays both men and women on the
 shelf,
To meditate upon their sins and self.

LXX

But all this time how slept, or dream'd,
 Dudù?
 With strict inquiry I could ne'er discover,
And scorn to add a syllable untrue;
 But ere the middle watch was hardly
 over,

Just when the fading lamps waned dim
 and blue,
 And phantoms hover'd, or might seem
 to hover,
To those who like their company, about
The apartment, on a sudden she scream'd
 out:

LXXI

And that so loudly, that upstarted all
 The Oda, in a general commotion:
Matron and maids, and those whom you
 may call
 Neither, came crowding like the waves
 of ocean,
One on the other, throughout the whole
 hall,
 All trembling, wondering, without the
 least notion
More than I have myself of what could
 make
The calm Dudù so turbulently wake.

LXXII

But wide awake she was, and round her bed
 With floating draperies and with flying
 hair,
With eager eyes, and light but hurried
 tread,
 And bosoms, arms, and ankles glancing
 bare,
And bright as any meteor ever bred
 By the North Pole,—they sought her
 cause of care,
For she seem'd agitated, flush'd, and
 frighten'd,
Her eye dilated, and her colour heighten'd.

LXXIII

But what is strange—and a strong proof
 how great
 A blessing is sound sleep—Juanna lay
As fast as ever husband by his mate
 In holy matrimony snores away.
Not all the clamour broke her happy state
 Of slumber, ere they shook her,—so
 they say
At least,—and then she, too, unclosed
 her eyes,
And yawned a good deal with discreet
 surprise.

LXXIV

And now commenced a strict investigation,
 Which, as all spoke at once, and more
 than once
Conjecturing, wondering, asking a narra-
 tion,
 Alike might puzzle either wit or dunce
To answer in a very clear oration.
 Dudù had never pass'd for wanting
 sense,
But being 'no orator as Brutus is,'
Could not at first expound what was
 amiss.

LXXV

At length she said, that in a slumber
 sound
She dream'd a dream, of walking in a
 wood—
A 'wood obscure,' like that where Dante
 found
Himself in at the age when all grow
 good;
Life's half-way house, where dames with
 virtue crown'd
Run much less risk of lovers turning
 rude;
And that this wood was full of pleasant
 fruits,
And trees of goodly growth and spreading
 roots;

LXXVI

And in the midst a golden apple grew,—
A most prodigious pippin—but it
 hung
Rather too high and distant; that she threw
 Her glances on it, and then, longing,
 flung
Stones and whatever she could pick up, to
 Bring down the fruit, which still
 perversely clung
To its own bough, and dangled yet in sight,
But always at a most provoking height;—

LXXVII

That on a sudden, when she least had hope,
 It fell down of its own accord before
Her feet; that her first movement was to
 stoop
 And pick it up, and bite it to the core;
That just as her young lip began to ope
 Upon the golden fruit the vision bore,
A bee flew out, and stung her to the heart,
And so—she woke with a great scream
 and start.

LXXVIII

All this she told with some confusion and
 Dismay, the usual consequence of
 dreams
Of the unpleasant kind, with none at hand
 To expound their vain and visionary
 gleams.
I've known some odd ones which seem'd
 really plann'd
Prophetically, or that which one deems
A 'strange coincidence,' to use a phrase
By which such things are settled now-a-
 days.

LXXIX

The damsels, who had thoughts of some
 great harm,
 Began, as is the consequence of fear,
To scold a little at the false alarm
 That broke for nothing on their sleep-
 ing ear.

The matron, too, was wroth to leave her
 warm
 Bed for the dream she had been obliged
 to hear,
And chafed at poor Dudù, who only
 sigh'd,
And said, that she was sorry she had cried.

LXXX

'I've heard of stories of a cock and bull;
 But visions of an apple and a bee,
To take us from our natural rest, and pull
 The whole Oda from their beds at half-
 past three,
Would make us think the moon is at its
 full.
 You surely are unwell, child! we must
 see,
To-morrow, what his Highness's
 physician
Will say to this hysteric of a vision.

LXXXI

'And poor Juanna, too, the child's first
 night
 Within these walls, to be broke in upon
With such a clamour—I had thought it
 right
 That the young stranger should not lie
 alone,
And, as the quietest of all, she might
 With you, Dudù, a good night's rest
 have known:
But now I must transfer her to the charge
Of Lolah—though her couch is not so
 large.'

LXXXII

Lolah's eyes sparkled at the proposition;
 But poor Dudù, with large drops in her
 own,
Resulting from the scolding or the vision,
 Implored that present pardon might be
 shown
For this first fault, and that on no condi-
 tion
 (She added in a soft and piteous tone)
Juanna should be taken from her, and
Her future dreams should all be kept in
 hand.

LXXXIII

She promised never more to have a dream,
 At least to dream so loudly as just now;
She wonder'd at herself how she could
 scream—
 'Twas foolish, nervous, as she must
 allow,
A fond hallucination, and a theme
 For laughter—but she felt her spirits
 low,
And begg'd they would excuse her; she'd
 get over
This weakness in a few hours, and recover.

LXXXIV

And here Juanna kindly interposed,
 And said she felt herself extremely well
Where she then was, as her sound sleep
 disclosed,
 When all around rang like a tocsin bell;
She did not find herself the least disposed
 To quit her gentle partner, and to dwell
Apart from one who had no sin to show,
Save that of dreaming once 'mal-à-propos.'

LXXXV

As thus Juanna spoke, Dudù turn'd round
 And hid her face within Juanna's
 breast:
Her neck alone was seen, but that was
 found
 The colour of a budding rose's crest.
I can't tell why she blush'd, nor can
 expound
 The mystery of this rupture of their rest;
All that I know is, that the facts I state
Are true as truth has ever been of late.

LXXXVI

And so good night to them—or, if you will,
 Good morrow—for the cock had
 crown, and light
Began to clothe each Asiatic hill,
 And the mosque crescent struggled
 into sight
Of the long caravan, which in the chill
 Of dewy dawn wound slowly round each
 height
That stretches to the stony belt, which girds
Asia, where Kaff looks down upon the
 Kurds.

LXXXVII

With the first ray, or rather grey of morn,
 Gulbeyaz rose from restlessness; and
 pale
As Passion rises, with its bosom worn,
 Array'd herself with mantle, gem, and
 veil.
The nightingale that sings with the deep
 thorn,
 Which fable places in her breast of wail,
Is lighter far of heart and voice than those
 Whose headlong passions form their
 proper woes.

LXXXVIII

And that's the moral of this composition,
 If people would but see its real drift;—
But *that* they will not do without suspicion,
 Because all gentle readers have the gift
Of closing 'gainst the light their orbs of
 vision;
 While gentle writers also love to lift
Their voices 'gainst each other, which is
 natural,
The numbers are too great for them to
 flatter all.

LXXXIX

Rose the sultana from a bed of splendour,
 Softer than the soft Sybarite's, who
 cried
Aloud because his feelings were too tender
 To brook a ruffled rose-leaf by his
 side,—
So beautiful that art could little mend her,
 Though pale with conflicts between love
 and pride;
So agitated was she with her error,
She did not even look into the mirror.

XC

Also arose about the self-same time,
 Perhaps a little later, her great lord,
Master of thirty kingdoms so sublime,
 And of a wife by whom he was abhorr'd;
A thing of much less import in that
 clime—
 At least to those of incomes which
 afford
The filling up their whole connubial
 cargo—
Than where two wives are under an
 embargo.

XCI

He did not think much on the matter, nor
 Indeed on any other: as a man
He liked to have a handsome paramour
 At hand, as one may like to have a fan
And therefore of Circassians had good
 store,
 As an amusement after the Divan;
Though an unusual fit of love, or duty,
Had made him lately bask in his bride's
 beauty.

XCII

And now he rose; and after due ablutions
 Exacted by the customs of the East,
And prayers and other pious evolutions,
 He drank six cups of coffee at the least,
And then withdrew to hear about the
 Russians,
 Whose victories had recently increased
In Catherine's reign, whom glory still
 adores,
As greatest of all sovereigns and w——s.

XCIII

But oh, thou grand legitimate Alexander!
 Her son's son, let not this last phrase
 offend
Thine ear, if it should reach—and now
 rhymes wander
 Almost as far as Petersburgh, and lend
A dreadful impulse to each loud meander
 Of murmuring Liberty's wide waves,
 which blend
Their roar even with the Baltic's—so you
 be
Your father's son, 'tis quite enough for me.

XCIV

To call men love-begotten, or proclaim
 Their mothers as the antipodes of
 Timon,
That hater of mankind, would be a shame,
 A libel, or whate'er you please to
 rhyme on:
But people's ancestors are history's game;
 And if one lady's slip could leave a
 crime on
All generations, I should like to know
What pedigree the best would have to
 show?

XCV

Had Catherine and the sultan understood
 Their own true interests, which kings
 rarely know,
Until 'tis taught by lessons rather rude,
 There was a way to end their strife,
 although
Perhaps precarious, had they but thought
 good,
 Without the aid of prince or plenipo:
She to dismiss her guards and he his
 harem,
And for their other matters, meet and
 share 'em.

XCVI

But as it was, his Highness had to hold
 His daily council upon ways and means
How to encounter with this martial scold,
 This modern Amazon and queen of
 queans;
And the perplexity could not be told
 Of all the pillars of the state, which
 leans
Sometimes a little heavy on the backs
Of those who cannot lay on a new tax.

XCVII

Meantime Gulbeyaz, when her king was
 gone,
 Retired into her boudoir, a sweet place
For love or breakfast; private, pleasing,
 lone,
 And rich with all contrivances which
 grace
Those gay recesses:—many a precious
 stone
 Sparkled along its roof, and many a
 vase
Of porcelain held in the fetter'd flowers
Those captive soothers of a captive's hours.

XCVIII

Mother of pearl, and porphyry, and
 marble,
 Vied with each other on this costly spot;
And singing birds without were heard to
 warble;
 And the stain'd glass which lighted this
 fair grot

Varied each ray;—but all descriptions
 garble
The true effect, and so we had better
 not
Be too minute; an outline is the best,—
A lively reader's fancy does the rest.

XCIX

And here she summon'd Baba, and
 required
Don Juan at his hands, and information
Of what had pass'd since all the slaves
 retired,
 And whether he had occupied their
 station:
If matters had been managed as desired,
 And his disguise with due consideration
Kept up; and above all, the where and
 how
He had pass'd the night, was what she
 wish'd to know.

C

Baba, with some embarrassment, replied
 To this long catechism of questions,
 ask'd
More easily than answer'd,—that he had
 tried
 His best to obey in what he had been
 task'd;
But there seem'd something that he
 wish'd to hide,
 Which hesitation more betray'd than
 mask'd;
He scratch'd his ear, the infallible resource
To which embarrass'd people have
 recourse.

CI

Gulbeyaz was no model of true patience,
 Nor much disposed to wait in word or
 deed;
She liked quick answers in all conversa-
 tions;
 And when she saw him stumbling like a
 steed
In his replies, she puzzled him for fresh
 ones;
 And as his speech grew still more
 broken-kneed,
Her cheek began to flush, her eyes to
 sparkle,
And her proud brow's blue veins to swell
 and darkle.

CII

When Baba saw these symptoms, which
 he knew
 To bode him no great good, he depre-
 cated
Her anger, and beseech'd she'd hear him
 through—
 He could not help the thing which he
 related:

741

Then out it came at length, that to Dudù
 Juan was given in charge, as hath been
 stated;
But not by Baba's fault, he said, and
 swore on
The holy camel's hump, besides the
 Koran.

CIII

The chief dame of the Oda, upon whom
 The discipline of the whole harem bore,
As soon as they reënter'd their own room,
 For Baba's function stopt short at the
 door,
Had settled all; nor could he then pre-
 sume
(The aforesaid Baba) just then to do more,
Without exciting such suspicion as
Might make the matter still worse than it
 was.

CIV

He hoped, indeed he thought, he could be
 sure,
 Juan had not betray'd himself; in fact
'Twas certain that his conduct had been
 pure,
 Because a foolish or imprudent act
Would not alone have made him insecure,
 But ended in his being found out and
 sack'd,
And thrown into the sea.—Thus Baba
 spoke
Of all save Dudù's dream, which was no
 joke.

CV

This he discreetly kept in the back ground,
 And talk'd away—and might have
 talk'd till now,
For any further answer that he found,
 So deep an anguish wrung Gulbeyaz'
 brow:
Her cheek turn'd ashes, ears rung, brain
 whirl'd round,
 As if she had received a sudden blow,
And the heart's dew of pain sprang fast
 and chilly
O'er her fair front, like Morning's on a lily.

CVI

Although she was not of the fainting sort,
 Baba thought she would faint, but
 there he err'd—
It was but a convulsion, which though
 short
 Can never be described; we all have
 heard,
And some of us have felt thus 'all amort,'
 When things beyond the common have
 occurr'd;—
Gulbeyaz proved in that brief agony
What she could ne'er express—then how
 should I?

CVII

She stood a moment as a Pythoness
 Stands on her tripod, agonised, and ful
Of inspiration gather'd from distress,
 When all the heart-strings like wil
 horses pull
The heart asunder;—then, as more or
 less
 Their speed abated or their strength
 grew dull,
She sunk down on her seat by slow
 degrees,
And bow'd her throbbing head o'er
 trembling knees.

CVIII

Her face declined and was unseen; her
 hair
 Fell in long tresses like the weeping
 willow,
Sweeping the marble underneath her
 chair,
 Or rather sofa (for it was all pillow,
A low, soft ottoman), and black despair
 Stirr'd up and down her bosom like a
 billow,
Which rushes to some shore whose
 shingles check
Its farther course, but must receive its
 wreck.

CIX

Her head hung down, and her long hair
 in stooping
 Conceal'd her features better than a
 veil;
And one hand o'er the ottoman lay
 drooping,
 White, waxen, and as alabaster pale:
Would that I were a painter! to be group-
 ing
 All that a poet drags into detail!
Oh that my words were colours! but their
 tints
May serve perhaps as outlines or slight
 hints.

CX

Baba, who knew by experience when to
 talk
 And when to hold its tongue, now held
 it till
This passion might blow o'er, nor dared
 to balk
 Gulbeyaz' taciturn or speaking will.
At length she rose up, and began to walk
 Slowly along the room, but silent still,
And her brow clear'd, but not her
 troubled eye;
The wind was down but still the sea ran
 high.

CXI

She stopp'd, and raised her head to
 speak—but paused,
 And then moved on again with rapid
 pace;
Then slacken'd it, which is the march
 most caused
 By deep emotion:—you may some-
 times trace
A feeling in each footstep, as disclosed
 By Sallust in his Catiline, who, chased
By all the demons of all passions, show'd
Their work even by the way in which he
 trode.

CXII

Gulbeyaz stopp'd and beckon'd Baba:—
 'Slave!
 Bring the two slaves!' she said in a low
 tone,
But one which Baba did not like to brave,
 And yet he shudder'd, and seem'd
 rather prone
To prove reluctant, and begg'd leave to
 crave
 (Though he well knew the meaning) to
 be shown
What slaves her highness wish'd to
 indicate,
For fear of any error, like the late.

CXIII

'The Georgian and her paramour,'
 replied
 The imperial bride—and added, 'Let
 the boat
Be ready by the secret portal's side:
 You know the rest.' The words stuck
 in her throat,
Despite her injured love and fiery pride;
 And of this Baba willingly took note,
And begg'd by every hair of Mahomet's
 beard,
She would revoke the order he had heard.

CXIV

'To hear is to obey,' he said; 'but still,
 Sultana, think upon the consequence:
It is not that I shall not all fulfil
 Your orders, even in their severest
 sense;
But such precipitation may end ill,
 Even at your own imperative expense:
I do not mean destruction and exposure,
In case of any premature disclosure;

CXV

'But your own feelings. Even should all
 the rest
 Be hidden by the rolling waves, which
 hide
Already many a once love-beaten breast
 Deep in the caverns of the deadly tide—

You love this boyish, new, seraglio
 guest,
 And if this violent remedy be tried—
Excuse my freedom, when I here assure
 you,
That killing him is not the way to cure you.'

CXVI

'What dost thou know of love or feel-
 ing!—Wretch!
 Begone!' she cried, with kindling eyes—
 'and do
My bidding!' Baba vanish'd, for to
 stretch
 His own remonstrance further he well
 knew
Might end in acting as his own 'Jack
 Ketch';
 And though he wish'd extremely to get
 through
This awkward business without harm to
 others,
He still preferr'd his own neck to another's.

CXVII

Away he went then upon his commission,
 Growling and grumbling in good
 Turkish phrase
Against all women of whate'er condition,
 Especially sultanas and their ways;
Their obstinacy, pride, and indecision,
 Their never knowing their own mind
 two days,
The trouble that they gave, their immorality,
Which made him daily bless his own
 neutrality.

CXVIII

And then he call'd his brethren to his aid,
 And sent one on a summons to the pair,
That they must instantly be well array'd,
 And above all be comb'd even to a hair,
And brought before the empress, who had
 made
 Inquiries after them with kindest care:
At which Dudù look'd strange, and Juan
 silly;
But go they must at once, and will I—
 nill I.

CXIX

And here I leave them at their preparation
 For the imperial presence, wherein
 whether
Gulbeyaz show'd them both com-
 miseration,
 Or got rid of the parties altogether,
Like other angry ladies of her nation,—
 Are things the turning of a hair or
 feather
May settle; but far be 't from me to antici-
 pate
In what way feminine caprice may
 dissipate.

743

CXX

I leave them for the present with good
wishes,
 Though doubts of their well doing, to
 arrange
Another part of history; for the dishes
 Of this our banquet we must some-
 times change;
And trusting Juan may escape the fishes,
 Although his situation now seems
 strange,
And scarce secure, as such digressions
 are fair,
The Muse will take a little touch at war-
 fare.

CANTO THE SEVENTH

I

O Love! O Glory! what are ye who fly
 Around us ever, rarely to alight?
There's not a meteor in the Polar sky
 Of such transcendent and more fleeting
 flight.
Chill, and chain'd to cold earth, we lift on
 high
 Our eyes in search of either lovely light;
A thousand and a thousand colours they
Assume, then leave us on our freezing way.

II

And such as they are, such my present
 tale is,
 A nondescript and ever-varying rhyme,
A versified Aurora Borealis,
 Which flashes o'er a waste and icy clime.
When we know what all are, we must
 bewail us,
 But ne'ertheless I hope it is no crime
To laugh at *all* things—for I wish to know
What, after *all*, are *all* things—but a *show*?

III

They accuse me—*Me*—the present writer
 of
 The present poem—of—I know not
 what—
A tendency to under-rate and scoff
 At human power and virtue, and all that;
And this they say in language rather
 rough.
 Good God! I wonder what they would
 be at!
I say no more than has been said in
 Dante's
Verse, and by Solomon and by Cervantes;

IV

By Swift, by Machiavel, by Roche-
 foucault,
 By Fénelon, by Luther, and by Plato;
By Tillotson, and Wesley, and Rousseau,
 Who knew this life was not worth a
 potato.

'Tis not their fault, nor mine, if this be
 so,—
 For my part, I pretend not to be Cato,
Nor even Diogenes.—We live and die,
But which is best, you know no more
 than I.

V

Socrates said, our only knowledge was
 'To know that nothing could be
 known'; a pleasant
Science enough, which levels to an ass
 Each man of wisdom, future, past, or
 present.
Newton (that proverb of the mind), alas!
 Declared, with all his grand discoveries
 recent,
That he himself felt only 'like a youth
Picking up shells by the great ocean—
 Truth.'

VI

Ecclesiastes said, 'that all is vanity'—
 Most modern preachers say the same,
 or show it
By their examples of true Christianity:
 In short, all know, or very soon may
 know it;
And in this scene of all-confess'd inanity,
 By saint, by sage, by preacher, and by
 poet,
Must I restrain me, through the fear of
 strife,
From holding up the nothingness of life?

VII

Dogs, or men!—for I flatter you in saying
 That ye are dogs—your betters far—ye
 may
Read, or read not, what I am now essay-
 ing
 To show ye what ye are in every way.
As little as the moon stops for the baying
 Of wolves, will the bright Muse with-
 draw one ray
From out her skies—then howl your idle
 wrath!
While she still silvers o'er your gloomy
 path.

VIII

'Fierce loves and faithless wars'—I am
 not sure
 If this be the right reading—'tis no
 matter;
The fact's about the same, I am secure;
 I sing them both, and am about to
 batter
A town which did a famous siege endure,
 And was beleaguer'd both by land and
 water
By Souvaroff, or Anglicè Suwarrow,
Who loved blood as an alderman loves
 marrow.

IX

The fortress is call'd Ismail, and is placed
 Upon the Danube's left branch and left
 bank,
With buildings in the Oriental taste,
 But still a fortress of the foremost rank,
Or was at least, unless 'tis since defaced,
 Which with your conquerors is a com-
 mon prank:
It stands some eighty versts from the high
 sea,
And measures round of toises thousands
 three.

X

Within the extent of this fortification
 A borough is comprised along the
 height
Upon the left, which from its loftier
 station
Commands the city, and upon its site
A Greek had raised around this elevation
 A quantity of palisades *upright*,
So placed as to *impede* the fire of those
Who held the place, and to *assist* the foe's.

XI

This circumstance may serve to give a
 notion
Of the high talents of this new Vauban:
But the town ditch below was deep as
 ocean,
 The rampart higher than you'd wish to
 hang:
But then there was a great want of pre-
 caution
 (Prithee, excuse this engineering slang),
Nor work advanced, nor cover'd way was
 there,
To hint at least 'Here is no thoroughfare.'

XII

But a stone bastion, with a narrow gorge,
 And walls as thick as most skulls born
 as yet;
Two batteries, cap-à-pie, as our St.
 George,
 Casemated one, and t'other 'à bar-
 bette,'
Of Danube's bank took formidable
 charge;
 While two-and-twenty cannon duly set
Rose over the town's right side, in brist-
 ling tier,
Forty feet high, upon a cavalier.

XIII

But from the river the town's open quite,
 Because the Turks could never be per-
 suaded
A Russian vessel e'er would heave in
 sight;
 And such their creed was till they were
 invaded,

When it grew rather late to set things right:
 But as the Danube could not well be
 waded,
They look'd upon the Muscovite flotilla,
And only shouted, 'Allah!' and 'Bis Millah!'

XIV

The Russians now were ready to attack;
 But oh, ye goddesses of war and glory!
How shall I spell the name of each
 Cossacque
 Who were immortal, could one tell
 their story?
Alas! what to their memory can lack?
 Achilles' self was not more grim and
 gory
Than thousands of this new and polish'd
 nation,
Whose names want nothing but—pro-
 nunciation.

XV

Still I'll record a few, if but to increase
 Our euphony: there was Strongenoff,
 and Strokonoff,
Meknop, Serge Lwow, Arséniew of modern
 Greece,
 And Tschitsshakoff, and Roguenoff,
 and Chokenoff,
And others of twelve consonants apiece;
 And more might be found out, if I
 could poke enough
Into gazettes; but Fame (capricious
 strumpet),
It seems, has got an ear as well as trumpet,

XVI

And cannot tune those discords of narra-
 tion,
 Which may be names at Moscow, into
 rhyme;
Yet there were several worth commemora-
 tion,
 As e'er was virgin of a nuptial chime;
Soft words, too, fitted for the peroration
 Of Londonderry drawling against time,
Ending in 'ischskin,' 'ousckin,' 'iffskchy,'
 'ouski,'
Of whom we can insert but Rousamouski,

XVII

Scherematoff and Chrematoff, Koklophti,
 Koclobski, Kourakin, and Mouskin
 Pouskin,
All proper men of weapons, as e'er scoff'd
 high
 Against a foe, or ran a sabre through
 skin:
Little cared they for Mahomet or Mufti,
 Unless to make their kettle-drums a
 new skin
Out of their hides, if parchment had
 grown dear,
And no more handy substitute been near.

XVIII

Then there were foreigners of much
renown,
Of various nations, and all volunteers;
Not fighting for their country or its crown,
But wishing to be one day brigadiers;
Also to have the sacking of a town;
A pleasant thing to young men at their
years.
'Mongst them were several Englishmen
of pith,
Sixteen call'd Thomson, and nineteen
named Smith.

XIX

Jack Thomson and Bill Thomson;—all
the rest
Had been call'd '*Jemmy*,' after the
great bard;
I don't know whether they had arms or
crest,
But such a godfather's as good a card.
Three of the Smiths were Peters; but the
best
Amongst them all, hard blows to inflict
or ward,
Was *he*, since so renown'd 'in country
quarters
At Halifax'; but now he served the Tartars.

XX

The rest were Jacks and Gills and Wills
and Bills,
But when I've added that the elder Jack
Smith
Was born in Cumberland among the hills,
And that his father was an honest black-
smith,
I've said all *I* know of a name that fills
Three lines of the despatch in taking
'Schmacksmith,'
A village of Moldavia's waste, wherein
He fell, immortal in a bulletin.

XXI

I wonder (although Mars no doubt's a
god I
Praise) if a man's name in a *bulletin*
May make up for a *bullet in* his body?
I hope this little question is no sin,
Because, though I am but a simple noddy,
I think one Shakespeare puts the same
thought in
The mouth of some one in his plays so
doting,
Which many people pass for wits by
quoting.

XXII

Then there were Frenchmen, gallant,
young, and gay;
But I'm too great a patriot to record
Their Gallic names upon a glorious day;
I'd rather tell ten lies than say a word

Of truth;—such truths are treason; they
betray
Their country; and as traitors are ab-
horr'd,
Who name the French in English, save to
show
How Peace should make John Bull the
Frenchman's foe.

XXIII

The Russians, having built two batteries
on
An isle near Ismail, had two ends in
view:
The first was to bombard it, and knock
down
The public buildings and the private
too,
No matter what poor souls might be
undone.
The city's shape suggested this, 'tis
true;
Form'd like an amphitheatre, each dwell-
ing
Presented a fine mark to throw a shell in.

XXIV

The second object was to profit by
The moment of the general con-
sternation,
To attack the Turk's flotilla, which lay
nigh,
Extremely tranquil, anchor'd at its
station:
But a third motive was as probably
To frighten them into capitulation;
A phantasy which sometimes seizes
warriors,
Unless they are game as bull-dogs and
fox-terriers.

XXV

A habit rather blameable, which is
That of despising those we combat with,
Common in many cases, was in this
The cause of killing Tchitchitzkoff and
Smith;
One of the valorous 'Smiths' whom we
shall miss
Out of those nineteen who late rhymed
to 'pith';
But 'tis a name so spread o'er 'Sir' and
'Madam,'
That one would think the *first* who bore
it '*Adam*'.

XXVI

The Russian batteries were incomplete,
Because they were constructed in a
hurry;
Thus the same cause which makes a verse
want feet,
And throws a cloud o'er Longman and
John Murray,

When the sale of new books is not so fleet
 As they who print them think is
 necessary,
May likewise put off for a time what story
Sometimes calls 'murder,' and at others
 'glory.'

XXVII

Whether it was their engineer's stupidity,
 Their haste, or waste, I neither know
 nor care,
Or some contractor's personal cupidity,
 Saving his soul by cheating in the ware
Of homicide, but there was no solidity
 In the new batteries erected there;
They either miss'd, or they were never miss'd,
And added greatly to the missing list.

XXVIII

A sad miscalculation about distance
 Made all their naval matters incorrect;
Three fireships lost their amiable existence
 Before they reach'd a spot to take effect;
The match was lit too soon, and no
 assistance
 Could remedy this lubberly defect;
They blew up in the middle of the river,
While, though 'twas dawn, the Turks
 slept fast as ever.

XXIX

At seven they rose, however, and survey'd
 The Russ flotilla getting under way;
'Twas nine, when still advancing un-
 dismay'd,
 Within a cable's length their vessels lay
Off Ismail, and commenced a cannonade,
 Which was return'd with interest, I may
 say,
And by a fire of musketry and grape,
And shells and shot of every size and shape.

XXX

For six hours bore they without inter-
 mission
 The Turkish fire, and, aided by their own
Land batteries, work'd their guns with
 great precision;
 At length they found mere cannonade
 alone
By no means would produce the town's
 submission,
 And made a signal to retreat at one.
One bark blew up, a second near the works
Running aground, was taken by the Turks.

XXXI

The Moslem, too, had lost both ships and
 men;
 But when they saw the enemy retire,
Their Delhis mann'd some boats, and
 sail'd again,
 And gall'd the Russians with a heavy
 fire,

And tried to make a landing on the main;
 But here the effect fell short of their
 desire:
Count Damas drove them back into the
 water
Pell-mell, and with a whole gazette of
 slaughter.

XXXII

'If' (says the historian here) 'I could report
 All that the Russians did upon this day,
I think that several volumes would fall short,
 And I should still have many things to
 say';
And so he says no more—but pays his
 court
 To some distinguish'd strangers in that
 fray;
The Prince de Ligne, and Langeron, and
 Damas,
Names great as any that the roll of Fame
 has.

XXXIII

This being the case, may show us what
 Fame *is:*
 For out of these three '*preux Cheva-*
 liers,' how
Many of common readers give a guess
 That such existed? (and they may live
 now
For aught we know.) Renown's all hit or
 miss;
 There's fortune even in fame, we must
 allow.
'Tis true, the Memoirs of the Prince de
 Ligne
Have half withdrawn from *him* oblivion's
 screen.

XXXIV

But here are men who fought in gallant
 actions
 As gallantly as ever heroes fought,
But buried in the heap of such trans-
 actions
 Their names are rarely found, nor often
 sought.
Thus even good fame may suffer sad con-
 tractions,
 And is extinguish'd sooner than she
 ought:
Of all our modern battles, I will bet
You can't repeat nine names from each
 Gazette.

XXXV

In short, this last attack, though rich in
 glory,
 Show'd that *somewhere, somehow,*
 there was a fault,
And Admiral Ribas (known in Russian
 story)
 Most strongly recommended an assault;

In which he was opposed by young and
 hoary,
 Which made a long debate; but I must
 halt,
For if I wrote down every warrior's speech,
I doubt few readers e'er would mount the
 breach.

XXXVI

There was a man, if that he was a man,
 Not that his manhood could be call'd
 in question,
For had he not been Hercules, his span
 Had been as short in youth as indiges-
 tion
Made his last illness, when, all worn and
 wan,
 He died beneath a tree, as much unblest
 on
The soil of the green province he had
 wasted,
 As e'er was locust on the land it blasted.

XXXVII

This was Potemkin—a great thing in days
 When homicide and harlotry made
 great;
If stars and titles could entail long praise,
 His glory might half equal his estate.
This fellow, being six foot high, could
 raise
 A kind of phantasy proportionate
In the then sovereign of the Russian people,
Who measured men as you would do a
 steeple.

XXXVIII

While things were in abeyance, Ribas sent
 A courier to the prince, and he suc-
 ceeded
In ordering matters after his own bent;
 I cannot tell the way in which he
 pleaded,
But shortly he had cause to be content.
 In the mean time the batteries pro-
 ceeded,
And fourscore cannon on the Danube's
 border
Were briskly fired and answer'd in due
 order.

XXXIX

But on the thirteenth, when already part
 Of the troops were embark'd, the siege
 to raise,
A courier on the spur inspired new heart
 Into all panters for newspaper praise,
As well as dilettanti in war's art,
 By his despatches couch'd in pithy
 phrase;
Announcing the appointment of that
 lover of
Battles to the command, Field-Marshal
 Souvaroff.

XL

The letter of the prince to the same
 marshal
 Was worthy of a Spartan, had the cause
Been one to which a good heart could be
 partial—
 Defence of freedom, country, or of laws;
But as it was mere lust of power to o'er-
 arch all
 With its proud brow, it merits slight
 applause,
Save for its style, which said, all in a trice,
'You will take Ismail at whatever price.'

XLI

'Let there be light!' said God, 'and there
 was light!'
 'Let there be blood!' says man, and
 there's a sea!
The fiat of this spoil'd child of the Night
 (For Day ne'er saw his merits) could
 decree
More evil in an hour, than thirty bright
 Summers could renovate, though they
 should be
Lovely as those which ripen'd Eden's fruit;
For war cuts up not only branch, but root.

XLII

Our friends, the Turks, who with loud
 'Allahs' now
 Began to signalise the Russ retreat,
Were damnably mistaken; few are slow
 In thinking that their enemy is beat,
(Or *beaten*, if you insist on grammar,
 though
 I never think about it in a heat,)
But here I say the Turks were much mis-
 taken,
Who hating hogs, yet wish'd to save their
 bacon.

XLIII

For, on the sixteenth, at full gallop, drew
 In sight two horsemen, who were
 deem'd Cossacques
For some time, till they came in nearer
 view.
 They had but little baggage at their
 backs,
For there were but three shirts between
 the two;
 But on they rode upon two Ukraine
 hacks,
Till, in approaching, were at length descried
In this plain pair, Suwarrow and his guide.

XLIV

'Great joy to London now!' says some
 great fool,
 When London had a grand illumina-
 tion,
Which to that bottle-conjurer, John Bull,
 Is of all dreams the first hallucination;

So that the streets of colour'd lamps are
 full,
 That sage (*said* John) surrenders at
 discretion
His purse, his soul, his sense, and even his
 nonsense,
To gratify, like a huge moth, this *one*
 sense.

XLV

'Tis strange that he should further 'Damn
 his eyes,'
 For they are damn'd; that once all-
 famous oath
Is to the devil now no further prize,
 Since John has lately lost the use of
 both.
Debt he calls wealth, and taxes Paradise;
 And Famine, with her gaunt and bony
 growth,
Which stare him in the face, he won't
 examine,
Or swears that Ceres hath begotten
 Famine.

XLVI

But to the tale;—great joy unto the camp!
 To Russian, Tartar, English, French,
 Cossacque,
O'er whom Suwarrow shone like a gas
 lamp,
 Presaging a most luminous attack;
Or like a wisp along the marsh so damp,
 Which leads beholders on a boggy
 walk,
He flitted to and fro a dancing light,
Which all who saw it follow'd, wrong or
 right.

XLVII

But certes matters took a different face;
 There was enthusiasm and much
 applause,
The fleet and camp saluted with great
 grace,
 And all presaged good fortune to their
 cause.
Within a cannon-shot length of the place
 They drew, constructed ladders, repair'd
 flaws
In former works, made new, prepared
 fascines,
And all kinds of benevolent machines.

XLVIII

'Tis thus the spirit of a single mind
 Makes that of multitudes take one
 direction,
As roll the waters to the breathing wind,
 Or roams the herd beneath the bull's
 protection;
Or as a little dog will lead the blind,
 Or a bell-wether form the flock's con-
 nexion

By tinkling sounds, when they go forth to
 victual;
Such is the sway of your great men o'er
 little.

XLIX

The whole camp rung with joy; you
 would have thought
 That they were going to a marriage
 feast
(This metaphor, I think, holds good as
 aught,
 Since there is discord after both at
 least):
There was not now a luggage boy but
 sought
 Danger and spoil with ardour much
 increased;
And why? because a little—odd—old
 man,
Stript to his shirt, was come to lead the
 van.

L

But so it was; and every preparation
 Was made with all alacrity: the first
Detachment of three columns took its
 station,
 And waited but the signal's voice to
 burst
Upon the foe: the second's ordination
 Was also in three columns, with a thirst
For glory gaping o'er a sea of slaughter:
The third, in columns two, attack'd by
 water.

LI

New batteries were erected, and was held
 A general council, in which unanimity,
That stranger to most councils, here
 prevail'd,
 As sometimes happens in a great
 extremity;
And every difficulty being dispell'd,
 Glory began to dawn with due sub-
 limity,
While Souvaroff, determined to obtain it,
Was teaching his recruits to use the
 bayonet.

LII

It is an actual fact, that he, commander
 In chief, in proper person deign'd to
 drill
The awkward squad, and could afford to
 squander
 His time, a corporal's duty to fulfil;
Just as you'd break a sucking sala-
 mander
 To swallow flame, and never take it ill:
He show'd them how to mount a ladder
 (which
Was not like Jacob's) or to cross a ditch.

LIII

Also he dress'd up, for the nonce, fascines
 Like men with turbans, scimitars, and
 dirks,
And made them charge with bayonet these
 machines,
 By way of lesson against actual Turks;
And when well practised in these mimic
 scenes,
 He judged them proper to assail the
 works;
At which your wise men sneer'd in phrases
 witty:
He made no answer; but he took the city.

LIV

Most things were in this posture on the eve
 Of the assault, and all the camp was in
A stern repose; which you would scarce
 conceive;
 Yet men resolved to dash through thick
 and thin
Are very silent when they once believe
 That all is settled:—there was little din,
For some were thinking of their home and
 friends,
And others of themselves and latter ends.

LV

Suwarrow chiefly was on the alert,
 Surveying, drilling, ordering, jesting,
 pondering,
For the man was, we safely may assert,
 A thing to wonder at beyond most
 wondering;
Hero, buffoon, half-demon, and half-dirt,
 Praying, instructing, desolating, plunder-
 ing;
Now Mars, now Momus; and when bent
 to storm
A fortress, Harlequin in uniform.

LVI

The day before the assault, while upon
 drill—
 For this great conqueror play'd the
 corporal—
Some Cossacques, hovering like hawks
 round a hill,
 Had met a party towards the twilight's
 fall,
One of whom spoke their tongue—or
 well or ill,
 'Twas much that he was understood at
 all;
But whether from his voice, or speech, or
 manner,
They found that he had fought beneath
 their banner.

LVII

Whereon immediately at his request
 They brought him and his comrades to
 head-quarters;

Their dress was Moslem, but you might
 have guess'd
 That these were merely masquerading
 Tartars,
And that beneath each Turkish-fashion'd
 vest
 Lurk'd Christianity; which sometimes
 barters
Her inward grace for outward show, and
 makes
It difficult to shun some strange mistakes.

LVIII

Suwarrow, who was standing in his shirt
 Before a company of Calmucks, drilling,
Exclaiming, fooling, swearing at the inert,
 And lecturing on the noble art of
 killing,—
For deeming human clay but common dirt,
 This great philosopher was thus
 instilling
His maxims, which to martial compre-
 hension
Proved death in battle equal to a pen-
 sion;—

LIX

Suwarrow, when he saw this company
 Of Cossacques and their prey, turn'd
 round and cast
Upon them his slow brow and piercing
 eye:—
 'Whence come ye?'—'From Constanti-
 nople last,
Captives just now escaped,' was the reply.
 'What are ye?'—'What you see us.'
 Briefly pass'd
This dialogue; for he who answer'd knew
To whom he spoke, and made his words
 but few.

LX

'Your names?'—'Mine's Johnson, and
 my comrade's Juan;
 The other two are women, and the third
Is neither man nor woman.' The chief
 threw on
 The party a slight glance, then said, 'I
 have heard
Your name before, the second is a new
 one:
 To bring the other three here was absurd:
But let that pass:—I think I have heard
 your name
In the Nikolaiew regiment?'—'The same.'

LXI

'You served at Widdin?'—'Yes.'—'You
 led the attack?'
 'I did.'—'What next?'—'I really hardly
 know.'
'You were the first i' the breach?'—'I was
 not slack
 At least to follow those who might be so.'

'What follow'd?'—'A shot laid me on my
 back,
And I became a prisoner to the foe.'
'You shall have vengeance, for the town
 surrounded
Is twice as strong as that where you were
 wounded.

LXII

'Where will you serve?'—'Where'er you
 please.'—'I know
You like to be the hope of the forlorn,
And doubtless would be foremost on the
 foe
After the hardships you've already
 borne.
And this young fellow—say what can he do?
 He with the beardless chin and gar-
 ments torn?'
'Why, general, if he hath no greater fault
In war than love, he had better lead the
 assault.'

LXIII

'He shall if that he dare.' Here Juan bow'd
 Low as the compliment deserved. Su-
 warrow
Continued: 'Your old regiment's allow'd,
 By special providence, to lead to-
 morrow,
Or it may be to-night, the assault: I have
 vow'd
 To several saints, that shortly plough or
 harrow
Shall pass o'er what was Ismail, and its
 tusk
Be unimpeded by the proudest mosque.

LXIV

'So now, my lads, for glory!'—Here he
 turn'd
 And drill'd away in the most classic
 Russian,
Until each high, heroic bosom burn'd
 For cash and conquest, as if from a
 cushion
A preacher had held forth (who nobly
 spurn'd
 All earthly goods save tithes) and bade
 them push on
To slay the Pagans who resisted, battering
The armies of the Christian Empress
 Catherine.

LXV

Johnson, who knew by this long colloquy
 Himself a favourite, ventured to address
Suwarrow, though engaged with accents
 high
 In his resumed amusement. 'I confess
My debt in being thus allow'd to die
 Among the foremost; but if you'd ex-
 press
Explicitly our several posts, my friend
And self would know what duty to attend.'

LXVI

'Right! I was busy, and forgot. Why, you
 Will join your former regiment, which
 should be
Now under arms. Ho! Katskoff, take him
 to—
(Here he call'd up a Polish orderly)
His post, I mean the regiment Nikolaiew:
 The stranger stripling may remain with
 me;
He's a fine boy. The women may be sent
To the other baggage, or to the sick tent.'

LXVII

But here a sort of scene began to ensue:
 The ladies,—who by no means had been
 bred
To be disposed of in a way so new,
 Although their harem education led
Doubtless to that of doctrines the most
 true,
 Passive obedience,—now raised up the
 head,
With flashing eyes and starting tears, and
 flung,
Their arms, as hens their wings about
 their young,

LXVIII

O'er the promoted couple of brave men
 Who were thus honour'd by the greatest
 chief
That ever peopled hell with heroes slain,
 Or plunged a province or a realm in
 grief.
Oh, foolish mortals! Always taught in
 vain!
 Oh, glorious laurel! since for one sole
 leaf
Of thine imaginary deathless tree,
Of blood and tears must flow the unebbing
 sea.

LXIX

Suwarrow, who had small regard for tears,
 And not much sympathy for blood, sur-
 vey'd
The women with their hair about their ears
 And natural agonies, with a slight shade
Of feeling; for however habit sears
 Men's hearts against whole millions,
 when their trade
Is butchery, sometimes a single sorrow
Will touch even heroes—and such was
 Suwarrow.

LXX

He said,—and in the kindest Calmuck
 tone,—
'Why, Johnson, what the devil do you
 mean
By bringing women here? They shall be
 shown
 All the attention possible, and seen

751

In safety to the waggons, where alone
 In fact they can be safe. You should
 have been
Aware this kind of baggage never thrives;
Save wed a year, I hate recruits with wives.'

LXXI

'May it please your excellency,' thus replied
 Our British friend, 'these are the wives
 of others,
And not our own. I am too qualified
 By service with my military brothers
To break the rules by bringing one's own
 bride
 Into a camp: I know that nought so
 bothers
The hearts of the heroic on a charge,
As leaving a small family at large.

LXXII

'But these are but two Turkish ladies, who
 With their attendant aided our escape,
And afterwards accompanied us through
 A thousand perils in this dubious shape.
To me this kind of life is not so new;
 To them, poor things, it is an awkward
 step.
I therefore, if you wish me to fight freely,
Request that they may both be used gen-
 teelly.'

LXXIII

Meantime these two poor girls, with swim-
 ming eyes,
 Look'd on as if in doubt if they could
 trust
Their own protectors; nor was their sur-
 prise
 Less than their grief (and truly not less
 just)
To see an old man, rather wild than wise
 In aspect, plainly clad, besmear'd with
 dust,
Stript to his waistcoat, and that not too
 clean,
More fear'd than all the sultans ever seen.

LXXIV

For everything seem'd resting on his nod,
 As they could read in all eyes. Now to
 them,
Who were accustom'd, as a sort of god,
 To see the sultan, rich in many a gem,
Like an imperial peacock stalk abroad
 (That royal bird, whose tail's a diadem)
With all the pomp of power, it was a doubt
How power could condescend to do with-
 out.

LXXV

John Johnson, seeing their extreme dismay,
 Though little versed in feelings oriental,
Suggested some slight comfort in his way:
 Don Juan, who was much more senti-
 mental,

Swore they should see him by the dawn of
 day,
 Or that the Russian army should repent
 all:
And, strange to say, they found some con-
 solation
In this—for females like exaggeration.

LXXVI

And then with tears, and sighs, and some
 slight kisses,
 They parted for the present—these to
 await,
According to the artillery's hits or misses,
 What sages call Chance, Providence, or
 Fate—
(Uncertainty is one of many blisses,
 A mortgage on Humanity's estate)—
While their beloved friends began to arm,
To burn a town which never did them
 harm.

LXXVII

Suwarrow,—who but saw things in the
 gross,
 Being much too gross to see them in
 detail,
Who calculated life as so much dross,
 And as the wind a widow'd nation's
 wail,
And cared as little for his army's loss
 (So that their efforts should at length
 prevail)
As wife and friends did for the boils of
 Job,—
What was't to him to hear two women sob?

LXXVIII

Nothing.—The work of glory still went on
 In preparations for a cannonade
As terrible as that of Ilion,
 If Homer had found mortars ready
 made;
But now, instead of slaying Priam's son,
 We only can but talk of escalade,
Bombs, drums, guns, bastions, batteries,
 bayonets, bullets;
Hard words, which stick in the soft
 Muses' gullets.

LXXIX

Oh, thou eternal Homer! who couldst charm
 All ears, though long; all ages, though
 so short,
By merely wielding with poetic arm
 Arms to which men will never more
 resort,
Unless gunpowder should be found to
 harm
 Much less than is the hope of every
 court,
Which now is leagued young Freedom to
 annoy;
But they will not find Liberty a Troy:—

LXXX

Oh, thou eternal Homer! I have now
 To paint a siege, wherein more men
 were slain,
With deadlier engines and a speedier blow,
 Than in thy Greek gazette of that cam-
 paign;
And yet, like all men else, I must allow,
 To vie with thee would be about as vain
As for a brook to cope with ocean's flood;
But still we moderns equal you in blood;

LXXXI

If not in poetry, at least in fact;
 And fact is truth, the grand desidera-
 tum!
Of which, howe'er the Muse describes
 each act,
 There should be ne'ertheless a slight
 substratum.
But now the town is going to be attack'd;
 Great deeds are doing—how shall I re-
 late 'em?
Souls of immortal generals! Phœbus
 watches
To colour up his rays from your des-
 patches.

LXXXII

Oh, ye great bulletins of Bonaparte!
 Oh, ye less grand long lists of kill'd and
 wounded!
Shade of Leonidas, who fought so hearty,
 When my poor Greece was once, as
 now, surrounded!
Oh, Cæsar's Commentaries! now impart,
 ye
 Shadows of glory! (lest I be con-
 founded),
A portion of your fading twilight hues,
So beautiful, so fleeting, to the Muse.

LXXXIII

When I call 'fading' martial immortality,
 I mean, that every age and every year,
And almost every day, in sad reality,
 Some sucking hero is compell'd to rear,
Who, when we come to sum up the totality
 Of deeds to human happiness most dear,
Turns out to be a butcher in great business,
Afflicting young folks with a sort of dizzi-
 ness.

LXXXIV

Medals, ranks, ribands, lace, embroidery,
 scarlet,
 Are things immortal to immortal man,
As purple to the Babylonian harlot:
 An uniform to boys is like a fan
To women; there is scarce a crimson varlet
 But deems himself the first in Glory's van.
But Glory's glory; and if you would find
What that is—ask the pig who sees the
 wind!

LXXXV

At least he feels it, and some say he sees,
 Because he runs before it like a pig;
Or, if that simple sentence should dis-
 please,
 Say, that he scuds before it like a brig,
A schooner, or—but it is time to ease
 This Canto, ere my Muse perceives
 fatigue.
The next shall ring a peal to shake all
 people,
Like a bob-major from a village steeple.

LXXXVI

Hark! through the silence of the cold, dull
 night,
 The hum of armies gathering rank on
 rank!
Lo! dusky masses steal in dubious sight
 Along the leaguer'd wall and bristling
 bank
Of the arm'd river, while with straggling
 light
 The stars peep through the vapours dim
 and dank,
Which curl in curious wreaths:—how soon
 the smoke
Of Hell shall pall them in a deeper cloak!

LXXXVII

Here pause we for the present—as even
 then
 That awful pause, dividing life from
 death,
Struck for an instant on the hearts of
 men,
 Thousands of whom were drawing their
 last breath!
A moment—and all will be life again!
 The march! the charge! the shouts of
 either faith,
Hurrah! and Allah! and—one moment
 more—
The death-cry drowning in the battle's
 roar.

CANTO THE EIGHTH

I

OH, blood and thunder! and oh, blood and
 wounds!
 These are but vulgar oaths, as you may
 deem,
Too gentle reader! and most shocking
 sounds:
 And so they are; yet thus is Glory's
 dream
Unriddled, and as my true Muse expounds
 At present such things, since they are
 her theme,
So be they her inspirers! Call them Mars,
Bellona, what you will—they mean but
 wars.

II

All was prepared—the fire, the sword, the
 men
 To wield them in their terrible array.
The army, like a lion from his den,
 March'd forth with nerve and sinews
 bent to slay,—
A human Hydra, issuing from its fen
 To breathe destruction on its winding
 way,
Whose heads were heroes, which, cut off
 in vain,
Immediately in others grew again.

III

History can only take things in the gross;
 But could we know them in detail, per-
 chance
In balancing the profit and the loss,
 War's merit it by no means might en-
 hance,
To waste so much gold for a little dross,
 As hath been done, mere conquest to
 advance.
The drying up a single tear has more
Of honest fame, than shedding seas of gore.

IV

And why?—because it brings self-appro-
 bation;
 Whereas the other, after all its glare,
Shouts, bridges, arches, pensions from a
 nation,
 Which (it may be) has not much left to
 spare,
A higher title, or a loftier station,
 Though they may make Corruption
 gape or stare,
Yet, in the end, except in freedom's battles,
Are nothing but a child of Murder's rattles.

V

And such they are—and such they will be
 found:
 Not so Leonidas and Washington,
Whose every battle-field is holy ground,
 Which breathes of nations saved, not
 worlds undone.
How sweetly on the ear such echoes
 sound!
 While the mere victor's may appal or
 stun
The servile and the vain, such names will
 be
A watchword till the future shall be free.

VI

The night was dark, and the thick mist
 allow'd
 Nought to be seen save the artillery's
 flame,
Which arch'd the horizon like a fiery cloud,
 And in the Danube's waters shone the
 same—

A mirror'd hell! the volleying roar, and
 loud
 Long booming of each peal on peal
 o'ercame
The ear far more than thunder; for
 Heaven's flashes
Spare, or smite rarely—man's make mil
 lions ashes!

VII

The column order'd on the assault scarc
 pass'd
 Beyond the Russian batteries a few toises
When up the bristling Moslem rose at last
 Answering the Christian thunders wit!
 like voices:
Then one vast fire, air, earth, and strean
 embraced,
 Which rock'd as 'twere beneath th
 mighty noises;
While the whole rampart blazed like Etna
 when
The restless Titan hiccups in his den;

VIII

And one enormous shout of 'Allah!' ros
 In the same moment, loud as even the roa
Of war's most mortal engines, to their foe
 Hurling defiance: city, stream, an
 shore
Resounded 'Allah!' and the clouds whicl
 close
 With thick'ning canopy the conflict o'e
Vibrate to the Eternal name. Hark
 through
All sounds it pierceth, 'Allah! Allah! Hu!

IX

The columns were in movement one an
 all,
 But of the portion which attack'd b
 water,
Thicker than leaves the lives began to fall
 Though led by Arseniew, that great so
 of slaughter,
As brave as ever faced both bomb and bal!
 'Carnage, (so Wordsworth tells you) i
 God's daughter:'
If he speak truth, she is Christ's sister, an
Just now behaved as in the Holy Land.

X

The Prince de Ligne was wounded in th
 knee;
 Count Chapeau-Bras, too, had a ba!
 between
His cap and head, which proves the hea
 to be
Aristocratic as was ever seen,
Because it then received no injury
 More than the cap; in fact, the ba!
 could mean
No harm unto a right legitimate head;
'Ashes to ashes'—why not lead to lead?

XI

Also the General Markow, Brigadier,
 Insisting on removal of the *prince*
Amidst some groaning thousands dying
 near,—
 All common fellows, who might writhe
 and wince,
And shriek for water into a deaf ear,—
 The General Markow, who could thus
 evince
His sympathy for rank, by the same token,
To teach him greater, had his own leg
 broken.

XII

Three hundred cannon threw up their
 emetic,
 And thirty thousand muskets flung their
 pills
Like hail, to make a bloody diuretic.
 Mortality! thou hast thy monthly bills:
Thy plagues, thy famines, thy physicians,
 yet tick,
 Like the death-watch, within our ears
 the ills
Past, present, and to come;—but all may
 yield
To the true portrait of one battle-field;

XIII

There the still varying pangs, which multi-
 ply
 Until their very number makes men hard
By the infinities of agony,
 Which meet the gaze, whate'er it may
 regard—
The groan, the roll in dust, the all-*white* eye
 Turn'd back within its socket,—these
 reward
Your rank and file by thousands, while the
 rest
May win perhaps a riband at the breast!

XIV

Yet I love glory;—glory's a great thing:-
 Think what it is to be in your old age
Maintain'd at the expense of your good
 king:
 A moderate pension shakes full many a
 sage,
And heroes are but made for bards to sing,
 Which is still better; thus in verse to
 wage
Your wars eternally, besides enjoying
Half-pay for life, make mankind worth
 destroying.

XV

The troops, already disembark'd, push'd on
 To take a battery on the right: the others,
Who landed lower down, their landing
 done,
 Had set to work as briskly as their
 brothers:

XVI

Being grenadiers, they mounted one by
 one,
 Cheerful as children climb the breasts of
 mothers,
O'er the intrenchment and the palisade,
Quite orderly, as if upon parade.

XVI

And this was admirable; for so hot
 The fire was, that were red Vesuvius
 loaded,
Besides its lava, with all sorts of shot
 And shells or hells, it could not more
 have goaded.
Of officers a third fell on the spot,
 A thing which victory by no means
 boded
To gentlemen engaged in the assault:
Hounds, when the huntsman tumbles, are
 at fault.

XVII

But here I leave the general concern,
 To track our hero on his path of fame:
He must his laurels separately earn;
 For fifty thousand heroes, name by
 name,
Though all deserving equally to turn
 A couplet, or an elegy to claim,
Would form a lengthy lexicon of glory,
And what is worse still, a much longer
 story:

XVIII

And therefore we must give the greater
 number
 To the Gazette—which doubtless fairly
 dealt
By the deceased, who lie in famous
 slumber
 In ditches, fields, or wheresoe'er they felt
Their clay for the last time their souls
 encumber;—
 Thrice happy he whose name has been
 well spelt
In the despatch: I knew a man whose loss
Was printed *Grove*, although his name was
 Grose.

XIX

Juan and Johnson join'd a certain corps,
 And fought away with might and main,
 not knowing
The way which they had never trod before,
 And still less guessing where they might
 be going;
But on they march'd, dead bodies tramp-
 ling o'er,
 Firing, and thrusting, slashing, sweat-
 ing, glowing,
But fighting thoughtlessly enough to win,
To their *two* selves, *one* whole bright
 bulletin.

XX

Thus on they wallow'd in the bloody mire
 Of dead and dying thousands,—some-
 times gaining
A yard or two of ground, which brought
 them nigher
 To some odd angle for which all were
 straining;
At other times, repulsed by the close fire,
 Which really pour'd as if all hell were
 raining
Instead of heaven, they stumbled back-
 wards o'er
A wounded comrade, sprawling in his gore.

XXI

Though 'twas Don Juan's first of fields,
 and though
 The nightly muster and the silent march
In the chill dark, when courage does not
 glow
 So much as under a triumphal arch,
Perhaps might make him shiver, yawn, or
 throw
 A glance on the dull clouds (as thick as
 starch,
Which stiffen'd heaven) as if he wish'd for
 day;—
Yet for all this he did not run away.

XXII

Indeed he could not. But what if he had?
 There *have been* and *are* heroes who
 begun
With something not much better, or as
 bad:
 Frederick the Great from Molwitz
 deign'd to run,
For the first and last time; for, like a pad,
 Or hawk, or bride, most mortals after
 one
Warm bout are broken in to their new
 tricks,
And fight like fiends for pay or politics.

XXIII

He was what Erin calls, in her sublime
 Old Erse or Irish, or it may be *Punic;*—
(The antiquarians who can settle time,
 Which settles all things, Roman, Greek,
 or Runic,
Swear that Pat's language sprung from the
 same clime
 With Hannibal, and wears the Tyrian
 tunic
Of Dido's alphabet; and this is rational
As any other notion, and not national;)—

XXIV

But Juan was quite 'a broth of a boy,'
 A thing of impulse and a child of song;
Now swimming in the sentiment of joy,
 Or the *sensation* (if that phrase seem
 wrong),

And afterward, if he must needs destroy
 In such good company as always thron
To battles, sieges, and that kind ‹
 pleasure,
No less delighted to employ his leisure;

XXV

But always without malice: if he warr'd
 Or loved, it was with what we call 'th
 best
Intentions,' which form all mankind
 trump card,
 To be produced when brought up to th
 test.
The statesman, hero, harlot, lawyer—wa
 Off each attack, when people are in que
Of their designs, by saying they *mea*
 well;
'Tis pity 'that such meaning should pa
 hell.'

XXVI

I almost lately have begun to doubt
 Whether hell's pavement—if it be s
 paved—
Must not have latterly been quite worn ou
 Not by the numbers good intent ha
 saved,
But by the mass who go below without
 Those ancient good intentions, whic
 once shaved
And smooth'd the brimstone of that stre
 of hell
Which bears the greatest likeness to Pa
 Mall.

XXVII

Juan, by some strange chance, which o
 divides
 Warrior from warrior in their gri
 career,
Like chastest wives from constant hu
 bands' sides
 Just at the close of the first bridal yea
By one of those odd turns of Fortune
 tides,
 Was on a sudden rather puzzled here,
When, after a good deal of heavy firing,
He found himself alone, and friends reti
 ing.

XXVIII

I don't know how the thing occurr'd—
 might
 Be that the greater part were kill'd ‹
 wounded,
And that the rest had faced unto the rig
 About; a circumstance which has co
 founded
Cæsar himself, who, in the very sight
 Of his whole army, which so muc
 abounded
In courage, was obliged to snatch a shiel
And rally back his Romans to the field.

XXIX

Juan, who had no shield to snatch, and was
 No Cæsar, but a fine young lad, who fought
He knew not why, arriving at this pass,
 Stopp'd for a minute, as perhaps he ought
For a much longer time; then, like an ass
 (Start not, kind reader, since great Homer thought
This simile enough for Ajax, Juan
Perhaps may find it better than a new one);

XXX

Then, like an ass, he went upon his way,
 And, what was stranger, never look'd behind;
But seeing, flashing forward, like the day
 Over the hills, a fire enough to blind
Those who dislike to look upon a fray,
 He stumbled on, to try if he could find
A path, to add his own slight arm and forces
To corps, the greater part of which were corses.

XXXI

Perceiving then no more the commandant
 Of his own corps, nor even the corps, which had
Quite disappear'd—the gods know how! (I can't
 Account for everything which may look bad
In history; but we at least may grant
 It was not marvellous that a mere lad,
In search of glory, should look on before,
Nor care a pinch of snuff about his corps:)—

XXXII

Perceiving nor commander nor commanded,
 And left at large, like a young heir, to make
His way to—where he knew not—single-handed;
 As travellers follow over bog and brake
An 'ignis fatuus'; or as sailors stranded
 Unto the nearest hut themselves betake;
So Juan, following honour and his nose,
Rush'd where the thickest fire announced most foes.

XXXIII

He knew not where he was, nor greatly cared,
 For he was dizzy, busy, and his veins
Fill'd as with lightning—for his spirit shared
 The hour, as is the case with lively brains;

And where the hottest fire was seen and heard,
 And the loud cannon peal'd his hoarsest strains,
He rush'd, while earth and air were sadly shaken
By thy humane discovery, Friar Bacon!

XXXIV

And as he rush'd along, it came to pass he
 Fell in with what was late the second column,
Under the orders of the General Lascy,
 But now reduced, as is a bulky volume
Into an elegant extract (much less massy)
 Of heroism, and took his place in solemn
Air 'midst the rest, who kept their valiant faces
And levell'd weapons still against the glacis.

XXXV

Just at this crisis up came Johnson too,
 Who had 'retreated,' as the phrase is when
Men run away much rather than go through
 Destruction's jaws into the devil's den;
But Johnson was a clever fellow, who
 Knew when and how 'to cut and come again,'
And never ran away, except when running
Was nothing but a valorous kind of cunning.

XXXVI

And so, when all his corps were dead or dying,
 Except Don Juan, a mere novice, whose
More virgin valour never dreamt of flying,
 From ignorance of danger, which indues
Its votaries, like innocence relying
 On its own strength, with careless nerves and thews,—
Johnson retired a little, just to rally
Those who catch cold in 'shadows of death's valley.'

XXXVII

And there, a little shelter'd from the shot,
 Which rain'd from bastion, battery, parapet,
Rampart, wall, casement, house—for there was not
 In this extensive city, sore beset
By Christian soldiery, a single spot
 Which did not combat like the devil, as yet,—
He found a number of Chasseurs, all scatter'd
By the resistance of the chase they batter'd.

XXXVIII

And these he call'd on; and, what's
 strange, they came
Unto his call, unlike 'the spirits from
The vasty deep,' to whom you may ex-
 claim,
 Says Hotspur, long ere they will leave
 their home.
Their reasons were uncertainty, or shame
 At shrinking from a bullet or a bomb,
And that odd impulse, which in wars or
 creeds
Makes men, like cattle, follow him who
 leads.

XXXIX

By Jove! he was a noble fellow, Johnson,
 And though his name, than Ajax or
 Achilles,
Sounds less harmonious, underneath the
 sun soon
 We shall not see his likeness: he could
 kill his
Man quite as quietly as blows the monsoon
 Her steady breath (which some months
 the same *still* is):
Seldom he varied feature, hue, or muscle,
And could be very busy without bustle;

XL

And therefore, when he ran away, he did so
 Upon reflection, knowing that behind
He would find others who would fain be
 rid so
Of idle apprehensions, which like wind
Trouble heroic stomachs. Though their
 lids so
Oft are soon closed, all heroes are not
 blind,
But when they light upon immediate
 death,
Retire a little, merely to take breath.

XLI

But Johnson only ran off, to return
 With many other warriors, as we said,
Unto that rather somewhat misty bourne,
 Which Hamlet tells us is a pass of dread.
To Jack, howe'er, this gave but slight con-
 cern:
 His soul (like galvanism upon the dead)
Acted upon the living as on wire,
And led them back into the heaviest fire.

XLII

Egad! they found the second time what
 they
 The first time thought quite terrible
 enough
To fly from, malgré all which people say
 Of glory, and all that immortal stuff
Which fills a regiment (besides their pay,
 That daily shilling which makes war-
 riors tough)—

They found on their return the self-same
 welcome,
Which made some *think*, and others *know*
 a *hell* come.

XLIII

They fell as thick as harvests beneath hail
 Grass before scythes, or corn below the
 sickle,
Proving that trite old truth, that life's as
 frail
 As any other boon for which men
 stickle.
The Turkish batteries thrash'd them like a
 flail,
 Or a good boxer, into a sad pickle
Putting the very bravest, who were knock'd
 Upon the head before their guns were
 cock'd.

XLIV

The Turks behind the traverses and flank
 Of the next bastion, fired away like
 devils,
And swept, as gales sweep foam away,
 whole ranks:
 However, Heaven knows how, the Fate
 who levels
Towns, nations, worlds, in her revolving
 pranks,
 So order'd it, amid these sulphur
 revels,
That Johnson, and some few who had not
 scamper'd,
Reach'd the interior talus of the rampart.

XLV

First one or two, then five, six, and a
 dozen
 Came mounting quickly up, for it was
 now
All neck or nothing, as, like pitch or rosin
 Flame was shower'd forth above, as
 well's below,
So that you scarce could say who best had
 chosen,
 The gentlemen that were the first to show
Their martial faces on the parapet,
Or those who thought it brave to wait as
 yet.

XLVI

But those who scaled found out that their
 advance
 Was favour'd by an accident or blunder
The Greek or Turkish Cohorn's ignor-
 ance
 Had palisado'd in a way you'd wonder
To see in forts of Netherlands or France—
 (Though these to our Gibraltar must
 knock under)—
Right in the middle of the parapet
Just named, these palisades were prime-
 ly set:

XLVII

So that on either side some nine or ten
 Paces were left, whereon you could con-
 trive
To march; a great convenience to our men,
 At least to all those who were left alive,
Who thus could form a line and fight again;
 And that which further aided them to
 strive
Was, that they could kick down the pali-
 sades,
Which scarcely rose much higher than
 grass blades.

XLVIII

Among the first—I will not say the *first*,
 For such precedence upon such occa-
 sions
Will oftentimes make deadly quarrels burst
 Out between friends as well as allied
 nations:
The Briton must be bold who really durst
 Put to such trial John Bull's partial
 patience,
As say that Wellington at Waterloo
Was beaten,—though the Prussians say so
 too;—

XLIX

And that if Blücher, Bulow, Gneisenau,
 And God knows who besides in 'au'
 and 'ow,'
Had not come up in time to cast an awe
 Into the hearts of those who fought till
 now
As tigers combat with an empty craw,
 The Duke of Wellington had ceased to
 show
His orders, also to receive his pensions;
Which are the heaviest that our history
 mentions.

L

But never mind;—'God save the king!'
 and *kings!*
 For if *he* don't, I doubt if *men* will
 longer—
I think I hear a little bird, who sings
 The people by and by will be the
 stronger:
The veriest jade will wince whose harness
 wrings
 So much into the raw as quite to wrong
 her
Beyond the rules of posting,—and the mob
At last fall sick of imitating Job.

LI

At first it grumbles, then it swears, and
 then,
 Like David, flings smooth pebbles
 'gainst a giant;
At last it takes to weapons such as men
 Snatch when despair makes human
 hearts less pliant.

Then comes the 'tug of war';—'twill come
 again,
 I rather doubt; and I would fain say 'fie
 on 't,'
If I had not perceived that revolution
Alone can save the earth from hell's pollu-
 tion.

LII

But to continue:—I say not *the* first,
 But of the first, our little friend Don
 Juan,
Walk'd o'er the walls of Ismail, as if
 nursed
 Amidst such scenes—though this was
 quite a new one
To him, and I should hope to *most*. The
 thirst
 Of glory, which so pierces through and
 through one,
Pervaded him—although a generous crea-
 ture,
As warm in heart as feminine in feature.

LIII

And here he was—who upon woman's
 breast,
 Even from a child, felt like a child;
 howe'er
The man in all the rest might be confest,
 To him it was Elysium to be there;
And he could even withstand that awk-
 ward test
 Which Rousseau points out to the
 dubious fair,
'Observe your lover when he *leaves* your
 arms';
But Juan never *left* them while they had
 charms,

LIV

Unless compell'd by fate, or wave, or
 wind,
 Or near relations, who are much the
 same.
But *here* he was!—where each tie that can
 bind
 Humanity must yield to steel and flame:
And *he* whose very body was all mind,
 Flung here by fate or circumstance,
 which tame
The loftiest, hurried by the time and place,
Dash'd on like a spurr'd blood-horse in a
 race.

LV

So was his blood stirr'd while he found
 resistance,
 As is the hunter's at the five-bar gate,
Or double post and rail, where the exis-
 tence
 Of Britain's youth depends upon their
 weight,

The lightest being the safest: at a distance
 He hated cruelty, as all men hate
Blood, until heated—and even then his
 own
At times would curdle o'er some heavy
 groan.

LVI

The General Lascy, who had been hard
 press'd,
 Seeing arrive an aid so opportune
As were some hundred youngsters all
 abreast,
 Who came as if just dropp'd down from
 the moon,
To Juan, who was nearest him, address'd
 His thanks, and hopes to take the city
 soon,
Not reckoning him to be a 'base Bezonian'
(As Pistol calls it), but a young Livonian.

LVII

Juan, to whom he spoke in German, knew
 As much of German as of Sanscrit, and
In answer made an inclination to
 The general who held him in command;
For seeing one with ribands, black and
 blue,
 Stars, medals, and a bloody sword in
 hand,
Addressing him in tones which seem'd to
 thank,
He recognised an officer of rank.

LVIII

Short speeches pass between two men who
 speak
 No common language; and besides, in
 time
Of war and taking towns, when many a
 shriek
 Rings o'er the dialogue, and many a
 crime
Is perpetrated ere a word can break
 Upon the ear, and sounds of horror
 chime
In like church-bells, with sigh, howl,
 groan, yell, prayer,
There cannot be much conversation there.

LIX

And therefore all we have related in
 Two long octaves, pass'd in a little
 minute;
But in the same small minute, every sin
 Contrived to get itself comprised with-
 in it.
The very cannon, deafen'd by the din,
 Grew dumb, for you might almost hear
 a linnet,
As soon as thunder, 'midst the general
 noise
Of human nature's agonising voice!

LX

The town was enter'd. Oh eternity!—
 'God made the country, and man mad(e)
 the town,'
So Cowper says—and I begin to be
 Of his opinion, when I see cast down
Rome, Babylon, Tyre, Carthage, Nineve(h)
 All walls men know, and many neve(r)
 known;
And pondering on the present and th(e)
 past,
To deem the woods shall be our home a(t)
 last:—

LXI

Of all men, saving Sylla the man-slayer,
 Who passes for in life and death mos(t)
 lucky,
Of the great names which in our faces stare(,)
 The General Boon, back-woodsman o(f)
 Kentucky,
Was happiest amongst mortals anywhere(;)
 For killing nothing but a bear or buck, h(e)
Enjoy'd the lonely, vigorous, harmless day(s)
Of his old age in wilds of deepest maze.

LXII

Crime came not near him—she is not th(e)
 child
 Of solitude; Health shrank not fro(m)
 him—for
Her home is in the rarely trodden wild,
 Where if men seek her not, and death b(e)
 more
Their choice than life, forgive them, a(s)
 beguiled
 By habit to what their own heart(s)
 abhor—
In cities caged. The present case in point
Cite is, that Boon lived hunting up t(o)
 ninety;

LXIII

And what's still stranger, left behind a nam(e)
 For which men vainly decimate th(e)
 throng,
Not only famous, but of that *good* fame(,)
 Without which glory's but a taver(n)
 song—
Simple, serene, the *antipodes* of shame,
 Which hate nor envy e'er could ting(e)
 with wrong;
An active hermit, even in age the child
Of Nature, or the Man of Ross run wil(d)

LXIV

'Tis true he shrank from men even of hi(s)
 nation,
 When they built up unto his darlin(g)
 trees,—
He moved some hundred miles off, for (a)
 station
 Where there were fewer houses an(d)
 more ease;

The inconvenience of civilisation
 Is, that you neither can be pleased nor
 please;
But where he met the individual man,
He show'd himself as kind as mortal can.

LXV

He was not all alone: around him grew
 A sylvan tribe of children of the chase,
Whose young, unwaken'd world was
 ever new,
 Nor sword nor sorrow yet had left a
 trace
On her unwrinkled brow, nor could you
 view
 A frown on Nature's or on human face;
The free-born forest found and kept them
 free,
And fresh as is a torrent or a tree.

LXVI

And tall, and strong, and swift of foot
 were they,
 Beyond the dwarfing city's pale abor-
 tions,
Because their thoughts had never been the
 prey
 Of care or gain: the green woods were
 their portions;
No sinking spirits told them they grew grey,
 No fashion made them apes of her dis-
 tortions;
Simple they were, not savage; and their
 rifles,
Though very true, were not yet used for
 trifles.

LXVII

Motion was in their days, rest in their
 slumbers,
 And cheerfulness the handmaid of their
 toil;
Nor yet too many nor too few their
 numbers;
 Corruption could not make their hearts
 her soil;
The lust which stings, the splendour which
 encumbers,
 With the free foresters divide no spoil;
Serene, not sullen, were the solitudes
Of this unsighing people of the woods.

LXVIII

So much for Nature:—by way of variety,
 Now back to thy great joys, Civilisation!
And the sweet consequence of large
 society,
 War, pestilence, the despot's desolation,
The kingly scourge, the lust of notoriety,
 The millions slain by soldiers for their
 ration,
The scenes like Catherine's boudoir at
 three-score,
With Ismail's storm to soften it the more.

LXIX

The town was enter'd: first one column
 made
 Its sanguinary way good—then another;
The reeking bayonet and the flashing blade
 Clash'd 'gainst the scimitar, and babe
 and mother
With distant shrieks were heard Heaven to
 upbraid:—
 Still closer sulphury clouds began to
 smother
The breath of morn and man, where foot
 by foot
The madden'd Turks their city still dis-
 pute.

LXX

Koutousow, he who afterwards beat back
 (With some assistance from the frost
 and snow)
Napoleon on his bold and bloody track,
 It happen'd was himself beat back just
 now:
He was a jolly fellow, and could crack
 His jest alike in face of friend or foe,
Though life, and death, and victory were
 at stake;
But here it seem'd his jokes had ceased to
 take:

LXXI

For having thrown himself into a ditch,
 Follow'd in haste by various grenadiers,
Whose blood the puddle greatly did en-
 rich,
 He climb'd to where the parapet ap-
 pears;
But there his project reach'd its utmost
 pitch
 ('Mongst other deaths the General
 Ribaupierre's
Was much regretted), for the Moslem men
Threw them all down into the ditch again.

LXXII

And had it not been for some stray troops
 landing
 They knew not where, being carried by
 the stream
To some spot, where they lost their under-
 standing,
 And wander'd up and down as in a
 dream,
Until they reach'd, as daybreak was ex-
 panding,
 That which a portal to their eyes did
 seem,—
The great and gay Koutousow might have
 lain
Where three parts of his column yet re-
 main.

LXXIII

And scrambling round the rampart, these
 same troops,
 After the taking of the 'Cavalier,'
Just as Koutousow's most 'forlorn' of
 'hopes'
 Took, like chameleons, some slight
 tinge of fear,
Open'd the gate call'd 'Kilia,' to the groups
 Of baffled heroes, who stood shyly near,
Sliding knee-deep in lately frozen mud,
Now thaw'd into a marsh of human blood.

LXXIV

The Kozacks, or, if so you please, Cos-
 sacques—
 (I don't much pique myself upon ortho-
 graphy,
So that I do not grossly err in facts,
 Statistics, tactics, politics, and geo-
 graphy)—
Having been used to serve on horses' backs,
 And no great dilettanti in topography
Of fortresses, but fighting where it pleases
Their chiefs to order,—were all cut to pieces.

LXXV

Their column, though the Turkish bat-
 teries thunder'd
 Upon them, ne'ertheless had reach'd
 the rampart,
And naturally thought they could have
 plunder'd
 The city, without being further ham-
 per'd;
But as it happens to brave men, they
 blunder'd—
 The Turks at first pretended to have
 scamper'd,
Only to draw them 'twixt two bastion
 corners,
From whence they sallied on those Chris-
 tian scorners.

LXXVI

Then being taken by the tail—a taking
 Fatal to bishops as to soldiers—these
Cossacques were all cut off as day was
 breaking,
 And found their lives were let at a short
 lease—
But perish'd without shivering or shaking,
 Leaving as ladders their heap'd car-
 casses,
O'er which Lieutenant-Colonel Yesouskoi
March'd with the brave battalion of Po-
 louzki:—

LXXVII

This valiant man kill'd all the Turks he met,
 But could not eat them, being in his turn
Slain by some Mussulmans, who would
 not yet,
 Without resistance, see their city burn.

The walls were won, but 'twas an even be
 Which of the armies would have caus
 to mourn:
'Twas blow for blow, disputing inch by inch
For one would not retreat, nor t' other flinch

LXXVIII

Another column also suffer'd much:—
 And here we may remark with the his
 torian,
You should but give few cartridges to suc
 Troops as are meant to march wit
 greatest glory on:
When matters must be carried by the touc
 Of the bright bayonet, and they al
 should hurry on,
They sometimes, with a hankering fo
 existence,
Keep merely firing at a foolish distance.

LXXIX

A junction of the General Meknop's me
 (Without the General, who had faller
 some time
Before, being badly seconded just then)
 Was made at length with those wh
 dared to climb
The death-disgorging rampart once again
 And though the Turks' resistance wa
 sublime,
They took the bastion, which the Seraskie
Defended at a price extremely dear.

LXXX

Juan and Johnson, and some volunteers
 Among the foremost, offer'd him goo
 quarter,
A word which little suits with Seraskiers
 Or at least suited not this valiant Tartar
He died, deserving well his country's tears
 A savage sort of military martyr.
An English naval officer, who wish'd
To make him prisoner, was also dish'd:

LXXXI

For all the answer to his proposition
 Was from a pistol-shot that laid him dead
On which the rest, without more intermis
 sion,
 Began to lay about with steel and lead—
The pious metals most in requisition
 On such occasions: not a single head
Was spared;—three thousand Moslem
 perish'd here,
And sixteen bayonets pierced the Seraskie

LXXXII

The city's taken—only part by part—
 And death is drunk with gore: there'
 not a street
Where fights not to the last some despera
 heart
 For those for whom it soon shall ceas
 to beat.

Here War forgot his own destructive art
　In more destroying Nature; and the
　　heat
Of carnage, like the Nile's sun-sodden
　　slime,
Engender'd monstrous shapes of every
　　crime.

LXXXIII

A Russian officer, in martial tread
　Over a heap of bodies, felt his heel
Seized fast, as if 'twere by the serpent's
　head
　Whose fangs Eve taught her human seed
　　to feel:
In vain he kick'd, and swore, and writhed,
　and bled,
　And howl'd for help as wolves do for a
　　meal—
The teeth still kept their gratifying hold,
As do the subtle snakes described of old.

LXXXIV

A dying Moslem, who had felt the foot
　Of a foe o'er him, snatch'd at it, and bit
The very tendon which is most acute—
　(That which some ancient Muse or
　　modern wit
Named after thee, Achilles) and quite
　through't
　He made the teeth meet, nor relin-
　　quish'd it
Even with his life—for (but they lie) 'tis
　said
To the live leg still clung the sever'd head.

LXXXV

However this may be, 'tis pretty sure
　The Russian officer for life was lamed,
For the Turk's teeth stuck faster than a
　skewer,
　And left him 'midst the invalid and
　　maim'd:
The regimental surgeon could not cure
　His patient, and perhaps was to be
　　blamed
More than the head of the inveterate foe,
Which was cut off, and scarce even then
　let go.

LXXXVI

But then the fact's a fact—and 'tis the part
　Of a true poet to escape from fiction
Whene'er he can; for there is little art
　In leaving verse more free from the re-
　　striction
Of truth than prose, unless to suit the mart
　For what is sometimes call'd poetic
　　diction
And that outrageous appetite for lies
Which Satan angles with for souls, like
　flies.

LXXXVII

The city's taken, but not render'd!—No!
　There's not a Moslem that hath yielded
　　sword:
The blood may gush out, as the Danube's
　flow
　Rolls by the city wall; but deed nor
　　word
Acknowledge aught of dread of death or
　foe:
　In vain the yell of victory is roar'd
By the advancing Muscovite—the groan
Of the last foe is echoed by his own.

LXXXVIII

The bayonet pierces and the sabre cleaves,
　And human lives are lavish'd every-
　　where,
As the year closing whirls the scarlet leaves
　When the stripp'd forest bows to the
　　bleak air,
And groans; and thus the peopled city
　grieves,
　Shorn of its best and loveliest, and left
　　bare;
But still it falls with vast and awful splinters,
As oaks blown down with all their thou-
　sand winters.

LXXXIX

It is an awful topic—but 'tis not
　My cue for any time to be terrific:
For checker'd as is seen our human lot
　With good, and bad, and worse, alike
　　prolific
Of melancholy merriment, to quote
　Too much of one sort would be sopo-
　　rific;—
Without, or with, offence to friends or
　foes,
I sketch your world exactly as it goes.

XC

And one good action in tne midst of crimes
　Is 'quite refreshing,' in the affected
　　phrase
Of these ambrosial, Pharisaic times,
　With all their pretty milk-and-water
　　ways,
And may serve therefore to bedew these
　rhymes,
　A little scorch'd at present with the blaze
Of conquest and its consequences, which
Make epic poesy so rare and rich.

XCI

Upon a taken bastion, where there lay
　Thousands of slaughter'd men, a yet
　　warm group
Of murder'd women, who had found their
　way
　To this vain refuge, made the good heart
　　droop

And shudder;—while, as beautiful as May,
 A female child of ten years tried to stoop
And hide her little palpitating breast
Amidst the bodies lull'd in bloody rest.

XCII

Two villainous Cossacques pursued the child
 With flashing eyes and weapons:
 match'd with *them*,
The rudest brute that roams Siberia's wild
Has feelings pure and polish'd as a gem,—
The bear is civilised, the wolf is mild:
 And whom for this at last must we condemn?
Their natures? or their sovereigns, who employ
All arts to teach their subjects to destroy?

XCIII

Their sabres glitter'd o'er her little head,
 Whence her fair hair rose twining with affright,
Her hidden face was plunged amidst the dead:
 When Juan caught a glimpse of this sad sight,
I shall not say exactly what he *said*,
 Because it might not solace 'ears polite';
But what he *did*, was to lay on their backs,
The readiest way of reasoning with Cossacques.

XCIV

One's hip he slash'd, and split the other's shoulder,
 And drove them with their brutal yells to seek
If there might be chirurgeons who could solder
 The wounds they richly merited, and shriek
Their baffled rage and pain; while waxing colder
 As he turn'd o'er each pale and gory cheek,
Don Juan raised his little captive from
The heap a moment more had made her tomb.

XCV

And she was chill as they, and on her face
 A slender streak of blood announced how near
Her fate had been to that of all her race;
 For the same blow which laid her mother here
Had scarr'd her brow, and left its crimson trace,
 As the last link with all she had held dear;
But else unhurt, she open'd her large eyes,
And gazed on Juan with a wild surprise.

XCVI

Just at this instant, while their eyes were fix'd
 Upon each other, with dilated glance,
In Juan's look, pain, pleasure, hope, fear, mix'd
 With joy to save, and dread of some mischance
Unto his protégée; while hers, transfix'd
 With infant terrors, glared as from a trance,
A pure, transparent, pale, yet radiant face,
Like to a lighted alabaster vase;—

XCVII

Up came John Johnson (I will not say '*Jack*,'
 For that were vulgar, cold, and commonplace
On great occasions, such as an attack
 On cities, as hath been the present case):
Up Johnson came, with hundreds at his back,
 Exclaiming—'Juan! Juan! On, boy! brace
Your arm, and I'll bet Moscow to a dollar,
That you and I will win St. George's collar.

XCVIII

'The Seraskier is knock'd upon the head,
 But the stone bastion still remains, wherein
The old Pacha sits among some hundreds dead,
 Smoking his pipe quite calmly 'midst the din
Of our artillery and his own: 'tis said
 Our kill'd, already piled up to the chin,
Lie round the battery; but still it batters,
And grape in volleys, like a vineyard, scatters.

XCIX

'Then up with me!'—But Juan answer'd, 'Look
 Upon this child—I saved her—must not leave
Her life to chance; but point me out some nook
 Of safety, where she less may shrink and grieve,
And I am with you.'—Whereon Johnson took
 A glance around—and shrugg'd—and twitch'd his sleeve
And black silk neckcloth—and replied, 'You're right;
Poor thing! what's to be done? I'm puzzled quite.'

C

Said Juan—'Whatsoever is to be
 Done, I'll not quit her till she seems secure
Of present life a good deal more than we.'—
 Quoth Johnson—'*Neither* will I quite insure;

But at the least *you* may die gloriously.'—
 Juan replied—'At least I will endure
Whate'er is to be borne—but not resign
 This child, who is parentless, and therefore
 mine.'

CI

Johnson said—'Juan, we've no time to
 lose;
 The child's a pretty child—a very
 pretty—
I never saw such eyes—but hark! now
 choose
 Between your fame and feelings, pride
 and pity:—
Hark! how the roar increases!—no excuse
 Will serve when there is plunder in a
 city;—
I should be loth to march without you, but,
By God! we'll be too late for the first cut.'

CII

But Juan was immovable; until
 Johnson, who really loved him in his
 way,
Pick'd out amongst his followers with
 some skill
 Such as he thought the least given up to
 prey;
And swearing if the infant came to ill
 That they should all be shot on the next
 day;
But if she were deliver'd safe and sound,
They should at least have fifty rubles
 round,

CIII

And all allowances besides of plunder
 In fair proportion with their com-
 rades;—then
Juan consented to march on through
 thunder,
 Which thinn'd at every step their ranks
 of men:
And yet the rest rush'd eagerly—no
 wonder,
 For they were heated by the hope of
 gain,
A thing which happens everywhere each
 day—
No hero trusteth wholly to half pay.

CIV

And such is victory, and such is man!
 At least nine-tenths of what we call
 so:—God
May have another name for half we scan
 As human beings, or his ways are odd.
But to our subject: a brave Tartar khan—
 Or 'sultan,' as the author (to whose nod
In prose I bend my humble verse) doth call
This chieftain—somehow would not yield
 at all:

CV

But flank'd by *five* brave sons (such is
 polygamy,
 That she spawns warriors by the score,
 where none
Are prosecuted for that false crime
 bigamy),
 He never would believe the city won
While courage clung but to a single twig.—
 Am I
 Describing Priam's, Peleus', or Jove's
 son?
Neither—but a good, plain, old, temperate
 man,
Who fought with his five children in the
 van.

CVI

To *take* him was the point. The truly brave,
 When they behold the brave oppress'd
 with odds,
Are touch'd with a desire to shield and
 save;—
 A mixture of wild beasts and demi-gods
Are they—now furious as the sweeping
 wave,
 Now moved with pity; even as some-
 times nods
The rugged tree unto the summer wind,
Compassion breathes along the savage
 mind.

CVII

But he would *not* be *taken*, and replied
 To all the propositions of surrender
By mowing Christians down on every side,
 As obstinate as Swedish Charles at
 Bender.
His five brave boys no less the foe defied;
 Whereon the Russian pathos grew less
 tender,
As being a virtue, like terrestrial patience,
Apt to wear out on trifling provocations.

CVIII

And spite of Johnson and of Juan, who
 Expended all their Eastern phraseology
In begging him, for God's sake, just to show
 So much less fight as might form an
 apology
For *them* in saving such a desperate foe—
 He hew'd away, like doctors of theology
When they dispute with sceptics; and with
 curses
Struck at his friends, as babies beat their
 nurses.

CIX

Nay, he had wounded, though but slightly,
 both
 Juan and Johnson; whereupon they fell,
The first with sighs, the second with an
 oath,
 Upon his angry sultanship, pell-mell,

And all around were grown exceeding wroth
 At such a pertinacious infidel,
And pour'd upon him and his sons like rain,
 Which they resisted like a sandy plain

CX

That drinks and still is dry. At last they
 perish'd—
 His second son was levell'd by a shot;
His third was sabred; and the fourth, most
 cherish'd
 Of all the five, on bayonets met his lot;
The fifth, who, by a Christian mother
 nourish'd,
 Had been neglected, ill-used, and what
 not,
Because deform'd, yet died all game and
 bottom,
To save a sire, who blush'd that he begot
 him.

CXI

The eldest was a true and tameless Tartar,
 As great a scorner of the Nazarene
As ever Mahomet pick'd out for a martyr,
 Who only saw the black-eyed girls in
 green,
Who make the beds of those who won't
 take quarter
 On earth, in Paradise; and when once
 seen,
Those houris, like all other pretty crea-
 tures,
Do just whate'er they please, by dint of
 features.

CXII

And what they pleased to do with the
 young khan
 In heaven I know not, nor pretend to
 guess;
But doubtless they prefer a fine young man
 To tough old heroes, and can do no less;
And that's the cause no doubt why, if we
 scan
 A field of battle's ghastly wilderness,
For one rough, weather-beaten, veteran
 body,
You'll find ten thousand handsome cox-
 combs bloody.

CXIII

Your houris also have a natural pleasure
 In lopping off your lately married men,
Before the bridal hours have danced their
 measure,
 And the sad, second moon grows dim
 again,
Or dull repentance hath had dreary leisure
 To wish him back a bachelor now and
 then:
And thus your houri (it may be) disputes
Of these brief blossoms the immediate
 fruits.

CXIV

Thus the young khan, with houris in his
 sight,
 Thought not upon the charms of four
 young brides,
But bravely rush'd on his first heavenly
 night.
 In short, howe'er *our* better faith de-
 rides,
These black-eyed virgins make the Mos-
 lems fight,
 As though there were one heaven and
 none besides—
Whereas, if all be true we hear of heaven
And hell, there must at least be six or seven.

CXV

So fully flash'd the phantom on his eyes,
 That when the very lance was in his heart,
He shouted 'Allah!' and saw Paradise
 With all its veil of mystery drawn apart,
And bright eternity without disguise
 On his soul, like a ceaseless sunrise,
 dart:—
With prophets, houris, angels, saints, de-
 scried
In one voluptuous blaze,—and then he died:

CXVI

But with a heavenly rapture on his face,
 The good old khan, who long had
 ceased to see
Houris, or aught except his florid race
 Who grew like cedars round him glori-
 ously—
When he beheld his latest hero grace
 The earth, which he became like a fell'd
 tree,
Paused for a moment from the fight, and
 cast
A glance on that slain son, his first and last.

CXVII

The soldiers, who beheld him drop his point,
 Stopp'd as if once more willing to con-
 cede
Quarter, in case he bade them not 'aroynt!'
 As he before had done. He did not heed
Their pause nor signs: his heart was out of
 joint,
 And shook (till now unshaken) like a
 reed,
As he look'd down upon his children gone,
And felt—though done with life—he was
 alone.

CXVIII

But 'twas a transient tremor:—with a
 spring
 Upon the Russian steel his breast he
 flung,
As carelessly as hurls the moth her wing
 Against the light wherein she dies: he
 clung

766

Closer, that all the deadlier they might
 wring,
 Unto the bayonets which had pierced
 his young;
And throwing back a dim look on his sons,
In one wide wound pour'd forth his soul
 at once.

CXIX

'Tis strange enough—the rough, tough
 soldiers who
 Spared neither sex nor age in their
 career
Of carnage, when this old man was pierced
 through,
 And lay before them with his children
 near,
Touch'd by the heroism of him they slew,
 Were melted for a moment; though no
 tear
Flow'd from their bloodshot eyes, all red
 with strife,
They honour'd such determined scorn of
 life.

CXX

But the stone bastion still kept up its fire,
 Where the chief pacha calmly held his
 post:
Some twenty times he made the Russ re-
 tire,
 And baffled the assaults of all their host;
At length he condescended to inquire,
 If yet the city's rest were won or lost;
And being told the latter, sent a bey
To answer Ribas' summons to give way.

CXXI

In the mean time, cross-legg'd, with great
 sang-froid,
 Among the scorching ruins he sat
 smoking
Tobacco on a little carpet;—Troy
 Saw nothing like the scene around;—yet
 looking
With martial stoicism, nought seem'd to
 annoy
 His stern philosophy; but gently strok-
 ing
His beard, he puff'd his pipe's ambrosial
 gales,
As if he had three lives, as well as tails.

CXXII

The town was taken—whether he might
 yield
 Himself or bastion, little matter'd now:
His stubborn valour was no future shield.
 Ismail's no more! The crescent's silver
 bow
Sunk, and the crimson cross glared o'er
 the field,
 But red with no *redeeming* gore: the
 glow

Of burning streets, like moonlight on the
 water,
Was imaged back in blood, the sea of
 slaughter.

CXXIII

All that the mind would shrink from ot
 excesses;
All that the body perpetrates of bad;
All that we read, hear, dream, of man's
 distresses;
 All that the devil would do if run stark
 mad;
All that defies the worst which pen ex-
 presses;
 All by which hell is peopled, or as sad
As hell—mere mortals who their power
 abuse—
Was here (as heretofore and since) let loose.

CXXIV

If here and there some transient trait of
 pity
 Was shown, and some more noble heart
 broke through
Its bloody bond, and saved, perhaps, some
 pretty
 Child, or an aged, helpless man or two—
What's this in one annihilated city,
 Where thousand loves, and ties, and
 duties grew?
Cockneys of London! Muscadins of
 Paris!
Just ponder what a pious pastime war is.

CXXV

Think how the joys of reading a Gazette
 Are purchased by all agonies and
 crimes:
Or if these do not move you, don't forget
 Such doom may be your own in after-
 times.
Meantime the Taxes, Castlereagh, and
 Debt,
 Are hints as good as sermons, or as
 rhymes.
Read your own hearts and Ireland's
 present story,
Then feed her famine fat with Wellesley's
 glory.

CXXVI

But still there is unto a patriot nation,
 Which loves so well its country and its
 king,
A subject of sublimest exultation—
 Bear it, ye Muses, on your brightest wing!
Howe'er the mighty locust, Desolation,
 Strip your green fields, and to your
 harvest cling,
Gaunt famine never shall approach the
 throne—
Though Ireland starve, great George
 weighs twenty stone.

CXXVII

But let me put an end unto my theme:
 There was an end of Ismail—hapless
 town!
Far flash'd her burning towers o'er
 Danube's stream,
 And redly ran his blushing waters down.
The horrid war-whoop and the shriller
 scream
 Rose still; but fainter were the thunders
 grown:
Of forty thousand who had mann'd the wall,
Some hundreds breathed—the rest were
 silent all!

CXXVIII

In one thing ne'ertheless 'tis fit to praise
 The Russian army upon this occasion,
A virtue much in fashion now-a-days,
 And therefore worthy of commemora-
 tion:
The topic's tender, so shall be my phrase—
 Perhaps the season's chill, and their long
 station
In winter's depth, or want of rest and victual,
Had made them chaste;—they ravish'd
 very little.

CXXIX

Much did they slay, more plunder, and no
 less
 Might here and there occur some viola-
 tion
In the other line;—but not to such excess
 As when the French, that dissipated
 nation,
Take towns by storm: no causes can I guess,
 Except cold weather and commiseration;
But all the ladies, save some twenty score,
Were almost as much virgins as before.

CXXX

Some odd mistakes, too, happen'd in the
 dark,
 Which show'd a want of lanterns, or of
 taste—
Indeed the smoke was such they scarce
 could mark
 Their friends from foes,—besides, such
 things from haste
Occur, though rarely, when there is a spark
 Of light to save the venerably chaste:
But six old damsels, each of seventy years,
Were all deflower'd by different grena-
 diers.

CXXXI

But on the whole their continence was great;
 So that some disappointment there en-
 sued
To those who had felt the inconvenient
 state
 Of 'single blessedness,' and thought it
 good

(Since it was not their fault, but only fate,
 To bear these crosses) for each waning
 prude
To make a Roman sort of Sabine wedding,
Without the expense and the suspense of
 bedding.

CXXXII

Some voices of the buxom middle-aged
 Were also heard to wonder in the din
(Widows of forty were these birds long
 caged)
 'Wherefore the ravishing did not be-
 gin!'
But while the thirst for gore and plunder
 raged,
 There was small leisure for superfluous
 sin;
But whether they escaped or no, lies hid
In darkness—I can only hope they did.

CXXXIII

Suwarrow now was conqueror—a match
 For Timour or for Zinghis in his trade.
While mosques and streets, beneath his
 eyes, like thatch
 Blazed, and the cannon's roar was
 scarce allay'd,
With bloody hands he wrote his first de-
 spatch;
 And here exactly follows what he
 said:—
'Glory to *God* and to the Empress!'
 (*Powers
Eternal! such names mingled!*) 'Ismail's
 ours.'

CXXXIV

Methinks these are the most tremendous
 words,
 Since 'Mené, Mené, Tekel,' and 'Uphar-
 sin,'
Which hands or pens have ever traced of
 swords.
 Heaven help me! I'm but little of a
 parson:
What Daniel read was short-hand of the
 Lord's,
 Severe, sublime; the prophet wrote no
 farce on
The fate of nations;—but this Russ so
 witty
Could rhyme, like Nero, o'er a burning
 city.

CXXXV

He wrote this Polar melody, and set it,
 Duly accompanied by shrieks and
 groans,
Which few will sing, I trust, but none
 forget it—
 For I will teach, if possible, the stones

To rise against earth's tyrants. Never let it
 Be said that we still truckle unto
 thrones;—
But ye—our children's children! think
 how we
Show'd *what things were* before the world
 was free!

CXXXVI

That hour is not for us, but 'tis for you.
 And as, in the great joy of your millen-
 nium,
You hardly will believe such things were
 true
 As now occur, I thought that I would
 pen you 'em;
But may their very memory perish too!—
 Yet if perchance remember'd, still dis-
 dain you 'em
More than you scorn the savages of yore,
Who *painted* their *bare* limbs, but *not* with
 gore.

CXXXVII

And when you hear historians talk of
 thrones,
 And those that sate upon them, let it be
As we now gaze upon the mammoth's
 bones,
 And wonder what old world such things
 could see,
Or hieroglyphics on Egyptian stones,
 The pleasant riddles of futurity—
Guessing at what shall happily be hid,
As the real purpose of a pyramid.

CXXXVIII

Reader! I have kept my word,—at least so
 far
 As the first canto promised. You have
 now
Had sketches of love, tempest, travel,
 war,—
 All very accurate, you must allow,
And *epic*, if plain truth should prove no
 bar;
 For I have drawn much less with a long
 bow
Than my forerunners. Carelessly I sing,
But Phœbus lends me now and then a string,

CXXXIX

With which I still can harp, and carp, and
 fiddle,
 What further hath befallen or may be-
 fall
The hero of this grand poetic riddle,
 I by and by may tell you, if at all:
But now I choose to break off in the
 middle,
 Worn out with battering Ismail's stub-
 born wall,
While Juan is sent off with the despatch,
For which all Petersburgh is on the watch.

CXL

This special honour was conferr'd, be-
 cause
He had behaved with courage and hu-
 manity—
Which *last* men like, when they have time
 to pause
 From their ferocities produced by
 vanity.
His little captive gain'd him some ap-
 plause
 For saving her amidst the wild insanity
Of carnage,—and I think he was more
 glad in her
Safety, than his new order of St. Vladimir.

CXLI

The Moslem orphan went with her pro-
 tector,
 For she was homeless, houseless, help-
 less; all
Her friends, like the sad family of Hector,
 Had perish'd in the field or by the
 wall:
Her very place of birth was but a spectre
 Of what it had been; there the Muezzin's
 call
To prayer was heard no more! and Juan
 wept,
And made a vow to shield her, which he
 kept.

CANTO THE NINTH

I

OH, Wellington! (or 'Vilainton'—for
 Fame
 Sounds the heroic syllables both ways;
France could not even conquer your great
 name,
 But punn'd it down to this facetious
 phrase—
Beating or beaten she will laugh the same)
 You have obtain'd great pensions and
 much praise:
Glory like yours should any dare gainsay,
Humanity would rise, and thunder 'Nay!'

II

I don't think that you used Kinnaird quite
 well
 In Marinet's affair—in fact 'twas
 shabby,
And like some other things won't do to tell
 Upon your tomb in Westminster's old
 abbey.
Upon the rest 'tis not worth while to
 dwell,
 Such tales being for the tea-hours of
 some tabby;
But though your years as *man* tend fast to
 zero,
In fact your grace is still but a *young hero*.

III

Though Britain owes (and pays you too) so much
 Yet Europe doubtless owes you greatly more:
You have repair'd Legitimacy's crutch,
 A prop not quite so certain as before:
The Spanish, and the French, as well as Dutch,
 Have seen, and felt, how strongly you *restore;*
And Waterloo has made the world your debtor
 (I wish your bards would sing it rather better).

IV

You are 'the best of cut-throats':—do not start;
 The phrase is Shakspeare's, and not misapplied:—
War's a brain-spattering, windpipe-slitting art,
 Unless her cause by right be sanctified.
If you have acted *once* a generous part,
 The world, not the world's masters, will decide,
And I shall be delighted to learn who,
Save you and yours, have gain'd by Waterloo?

V

I am no flatterer—you've supp'd full of flattery:
 They say you like it too—'tis no great wonder.
He whose whole life has been assault and battery,
 At last may get a little tired of thunder;
And swallowing eulogy much more than satire, he
 May like being praised for every lucky blunder,
Call'd 'Saviour of the Nations'—not yet saved,
And 'Europe's Liberator'—still enslaved.

VI

I've done. Now go and dine from off the plate
 Presented by the Prince of the Brazils,
And send the sentinel before your gate
 A slice or two from your luxurious meals:
He fought, but has not fed so well of late.
 Some hunger, too, they say the people feels:—
There is no doubt that you deserve your ration,
But pray give back a little to the nation.

VII

I don't mean to reflect—a man so great as
 You, my lord duke! is far above reflection:
The high Roman fashion, too, of Cincinnatus,
 With modern history has but small connexion:
Though as an Irishman you love potatoes
 You need not take them under your direction;
And half a million for your Sabine farm
Is rather dear!—I'm sure I mean no harm

VIII

Great men have always scorn'd great recompenses:
 Epaminondas saved his Thebes, and died,
Not leaving even his funeral expenses:
 George Washington had thanks, and nought beside,
Except the all-cloudless glory (which few men's is)
 To free his country: Pitt too had his pride,
And as a high-soul'd minister of state is
Renown'd for ruining Great Britain gratis.

IX

Never had mortal man such opportunity,
 Except Napoleon, or abused it more:
You might have freed fallen Europe from the unity
 Of tyrants, and been blest from shore to shore:
And *now*—what *is* your fame? Shall the Muse tune it ye?
 Now—that the rabble's first vain shouts are o'er?
Go! hear it in your famish'd country's cries!
Behold the world! and curse your victories!

X

As these new cantos touch on warlike feats,
 To *you* the unflattering Muse deigns to inscribe
Truths, that you will not read in the Gazettes,
 But which 'tis time to teach the hireling tribe
Who fatten on their country's gore, and debts,
 Must be recited—and without a bribe.
You *did great* things: but not being *great* in mind,
Have left *undone* the *greatest*—and mankind.

XI

Death laughs—Go ponder o'er the skeleton
 With which men image out the unknown thing
That hides the past world, like to a set sun
 Which still elsewhere may rouse a brighter spring—

Death laughs at all you weep for:—look
 upon
 This hourly dread of all! whose *threat-*
 en'd sting
Turns life to terror, even though in its
 sheath!
Mark! how its lipless mouth grins without
 breath!

XII

Mark! how it laughs and scorns at all you
 are!
 And yet *was* what you are; from *ear* to
 ear
It *laughs not*—there is now no fleshy bar
 So call'd; the Antic long hath ceased to
 hear,
But still he *smiles;* and whether near or far
 He strips from man that mantle (far
 more dear
Than even the tailor's), his incarnate skin,
White, black, or copper—the dead bones
 will grin.

XIII

And thus Death laughs,—it is sad merri-
 ment,
 But still it *is* so; and with such example
Why should not Life be equally content
 With his superior, in a smile to trample
Upon the nothings which are daily spent
 Like bubbles on an ocean much less
 ample
Than the eternal deluge, which devours
Suns as rays—worlds like atoms—years
 like hours?

XIV

'To be, or not to be? *that* is the question,'
 Says Shakspeare, who just now is much
 in fashion.
I am neither Alexander nor Hephæstion,
 Nor ever had for *abstract* fame much
 passion;
But would much rather have a sound
 digestion,
 Than Buonaparte's cancer:—could I
 dash on
Through fifty victories to shame or fame,
Without a stomach—what were a good
 name?

XV

'*O dura ilia messorum!*'—'Oh
 Ye rigid guts of reapers!' I translate
For the great benefit of those who know
 What indigestion is—that inward fate
Which makes all Styx through one small
 liver flow.
 A peasant's sweat is worth his lord's
 estate:
Let *this* one toil for bread—*that* rack for
 rent,
He who sleeps best may be the most con-
 tent.

XVI

'To be, or not to be?'—Ere I decide,
 I should be glad to know that which *is*
 being;
'Tis true we speculate both far and wide,
 And deem, because we *see,* we are *all-*
 seeing:
For my part, I'll enlist on neither side,
 Until I see both sides for once agreeing.
For me, I sometimes think that life is
 death,
Rather than life a mere affair of breath.

XVII

'*Que sçais-je?*' was the motto of Mon-
 taigne,
 As also of the first academicians;
That all is dubious which man may attain,
 Was one of their most favourite posi-
 tions.
There's no such thing as certainty, that's
 plain
 As any of Mortality's conditions;
So little do we know what we're about in
This world, I doubt if doubt itself be
 doubting.

XVIII

It is a pleasant voyage perhaps to float,
 Like Pyrrho, on a sea of speculation;
But what if carrying sail capsize the boat?
 Your wise men don't know much of
 navigation;
And swimming long in the abyss of thought
 Is apt to tire: a calm and shallow station
Well nigh the shore, where one stoops
 down and gathers
Some pretty shell, is best for moderate
 bathers.

XIX

'But heaven,' as Cassio says, 'is above
 all—
 No more of this, then, let us pray!' We
 have
Souls to save, since Eve's slip and Adam's
 fall,
 Which tumbled all mankind into the grave,
Besides fish, beasts, and birds. 'The
 sparrow's fall
 Is special providence,' though how *it*
 gave
Offence, we know not; probably it perch'd
Upon the tree which Eve so fondly
 search'd.

XX

Oh! ye immortal Gods! what is theogony?
 Oh! thou too mortal man! what is
 philanthropy?
Oh! world, which was and is, what is
 cosmogony?
 Some people have accused me of misan-
 thropy;

And yet I know no more than the ma-
 hogany
 That forms this desk, of what they
 mean; *lykanthropy*
I comprehend, for without transformation
Men become wolves on any slight occa-
 sion.

XXI

But I, the mildest, meekest of mankind,
 Like Moses, or Melancthon, who have
 ne'er
Done anything exceedingly unkind,—
 And (though I could not now and then
 forbear
Following the bent of body or of mind)
 Have always had a tendency to spare,—
Why do they call me misanthrope? Be-
 cause
They hate me, not I them:—and here we'll
 pause.

XXII

'Tis time we should proceed with our good
 poem,—
 For I maintain that it is really good,
Not only in the body but the proem,
 However little both are understood
Just now,—but by and by the Truth will
 show 'em
 Herself in her sublimest attitude:
And till she doth, I fain must be content
To share her beauty and her banishment.

XXIII

Our hero (and, I trust, kind reader! yours)
 Was left upon his way to the chief city
Of the immortal Peter's polish'd boors,
 Who still have shown themselves more
 brave than witty.
I know its mighty empire now allures
 Much flattery—even Voltaire's, and
 that's a pity.
For me, I deem an absolute autocrat
Not a barbarian, but much worse than
 that.

XXIV

And I will war, at least in words (and—
 should
 My chance so happen—deeds), with all
 who war
With Thought;—and of Thought's foes
 by far most rude,
 Tyrants and sycophants have been and
 are.
I know not who may conquer: if I could
 Have such a prescience, it should be no
 bar
To this my plain, sworn, downright de-
 testation
Of every despotism in every nation.

XXV

It is not that I adulate the people:
 Without *me*, there are demagogues
 enough,
And infidels, to pull down every steeple,
 And set up in their stead some proper
 stuff.
Whether they may sow scepticism to reap
 hell,
 As is the Christian dogma rather rough,
I do not know;—I wish men to be free
As much from mobs as kings—from you
 as me.

XXVI

The consequence is, being of no party,
 I shall offend all parties:—never mind!
My words, at least, are more sincere and
 hearty
 Than if I sought to sail before the wind.
He who has nought to gain can have small
 art: he
 Who neither wishes to be bound nor
 bind,
May still expatiate freely, as will I,
Nor give my voice to slavery's jackal cry.

XXVII

That's an appropriate simile, *that jack-
 al:*—
 I've heard them in the Ephesian ruins
 howl
By night, as do that mercenary pack all,
 Power's base purveyors, who for pick-
 ings prowl,
And scent the prey their masters would
 attack all.
 However, the poor jackals are less foul
(As being the brave lions' keen providers)
Than human insects, catering for spiders.

XXVIII

Raise but an arm! 'twill brush their web
 away,
 And without *that*, their poison and their
 claws
Are useless. Mind, good people! what I
 say—
 (Or rather peoples)—*go on* without
 pause!
The web of these tarantulas each day
 Increases, till you shall make common
 cause:
None, save the Spanish fly and Attic bee,
As yet are strongly stinging to be free.

XXIX

Don Juan, who had shone in the late
 slaughter,
 Was left upon his way with the despatch,
Where blood was talk'd of as we would of
 water;
 And carcasses that lay as thick as thatch

O'er silenced cities, merely served to flatter
Fair Catherine's pastime—who look'd
on the match
Between these nations as a main of cocks,
Wherein she liked her own to stand like
rocks.

XXX

And there in a *kibitka* he roll'd on,
(A cursèd sort of carriage without
springs,
Which on rough roads leaves scarcely a
whole bone,)
Pondering on glory, chivalry, and kings,
And orders, and on all that he had done—
And wishing that post-horses had the
wings
Of Pegasus, or at the least post-chaises
Had feathers, when a traveller on deep
ways is.

XXXI

At every jolt—and they were many—still
He turn'd his eyes upon his little charge,
As if he wish'd that she should fare less ill
Than he, in these sad highways left at
large
To ruts, and flints, and lovely Nature's skill,
Who is no paviour, nor admits a barge
On *her* canals, where God takes sea and
land,
Fishery and farm, both into his own hand.

XXXII

At least he pays no rent, and has best right
To be the first of what we used to call
'Gentlemen farmers', a race worn out quite,
Since lately there have been no rents at all,
And 'gentlemen' are in a piteous plight,
And 'farmers' can't raise Ceres from
her fall:
She fell with Buonaparte—What strange
thoughts
Arise, when we see emperors fall with oats!

XXXIII

But Juan turn'd his eyes on the sweet child
Whom he had saved from slaughter—
what a trophy!
Oh! ye who build up monuments, defiled
With gore, like Nadir Shah, that costive
sophy,
Who, after leaving Hindostan a wild,
And scarce to the Mogul a cup of coffee
To soothe his woes withal, was slain, the
sinner!
Because he could no more digest his
dinner;—

XXXIV

Oh ye! or we! or he! or she! reflect,
That *one* life saved, especially if young
Or pretty, is a thing to recollect
Far sweeter than the greenest laurels
sprung

From the manure of human clay, though
deck'd
With all the praises ever said or sung:
Though hymn'd by every harp, unless within
Your heart joins chorus, Fame is but a din.

XXXV

Oh! ye great authors luminous, volumin-
ous!
Ye twice ten hundred thousand daily
scribes!
Whose pamphlets, volumes, newspapers,
illumine us!
Whether you're paid by government in
bribes,
To prove the public debt is not consuming
us—
Or, roughly treading on the 'courtier's
kibes'
With clownish heel, your popular circulation
Feeds you by printing half the realm's
starvation;—

XXXVI

Oh, ye great authors!—*Àpropos des
bottes,*—
I have forgotten what I meant to say,
As sometimes have been greater sages'
lots;—
'Twas something calculated to allay
All wrath in barracks, palaces, or cots:
Certes it would have been but thrown
away,
And that's one comfort for my lost advice,
Although no doubt it was beyond all price.

XXXVII

But let it go:—it will one day be found
With other relics of 'a former world,'
When this world shall be *former*, under-
ground,
Thrown topsy-turvy, twisted, crisp'd,
and curl'd,
Baked, fried, or burnt, turn'd inside-out,
or drown'd,
Like all the worlds before, which have
been hurl'd
First out of, and then back again to chaos,
The superstratum which will overlay us.

XXXVIII

So Cuvier says:—and then shall come
again
Unto the new creation, rising out
From our old crash, some mystic, ancient
strain
Of things destroy'd and left in airy
doubt;
Like to the notions we now entertain
Of Titans, giants, fellows of about
Some hundred feet in height, *not* to say
miles,
And mammoths, and your wingèd croco-
diles.

XXXIX

Think if then George the Fourth should
 be dug up,
 How the new worldlings of the then new
 East
Will wonder where such animals could
 sup!
 (For they themselves will be but of the
 least:
Even worlds miscarry, when too oft they
 pup,
 And every new creation hath decreased
In size, from overworking the material—
Men are but maggots of some huge
 Earth's burial).

XL

How will—to these young people, just
 thrust out
 From some fresh Paradise, and set to
 plough,
And dig, and sweat, and turn themselves
 about,
 And plant, and reap, and spin, and
 grind, and sow,
Till all the arts at length are brought about,
 Especially of war and taxing,—*how*,
I say, will these great relics, when they
 see 'em,
Look like the monsters of a new museum!

XLI

But I am apt to grow too metaphysical:
 'The time is out of joint,'—and so am I;
I quite forget this poem's merely quizzical,
 And deviate into matters rather dry.
I ne'er decide what I shall say, and this I
 call
 Much too poetical: men should know
 why
They write, and for what end; but, note or
 text,
I never know the word which will come
 next.

XLII

So on I ramble, now and then narrating,
 Now pondering:—it is time we should
 narrate.
I left Don Juan with his horses baiting—
 Now we'll get o'er the ground at a great
 rate.
I shall not be particular in stating
 His journey, we've so many tours of
 late:
Suppose him then at Petersburgh; suppose
That pleasant capital of painted snows;

XLIII

Suppose him in a handsome uniform;
 A scarlet coat, black facings, a long
 plume,
Waving, like sails new shiver'd in a storm,
 Over a cock'd hat in a crowded room,
And brilliant breeches, bright as a Cairn
 Gorme,
 Of yellow casimere we may presume,
White stockings drawn uncurdled as new
 milk
O'er limbs whose symmetry set off the silk;

XLIV

Suppose him sword by side, and hat in
 hand,
 Made up by youth, fame, and an army
 tailor—
That great enchanter, at whose rod's com-
 mand
 Beauty springs forth, and Nature's self
 turns paler,
Seeing how Art can make her work more
 grand
 (When she don't pin men's limbs in like
 a gaoler),—
Behold him placed as if upon a pillar! He
Seems Love turn'd a lieutenant of artillery!

XLV

His bandage slipp'd down into a cravat;
 His wings subdued to epaulettes; his
 quiver
Shrunk to a scabbard, with his arrows at
 His side as a small sword, but sharp as
 ever;
His bow converted into a cock'd hat;
 But still so like, that Psyche were more
 clever
Than some wives (who make blunders no
 less stupid),
If she had not mistaken him for Cupid.

XLVI

The courtiers stared, the ladies whisper'd,
 and
 The empress smiled: the reigning favour-
 ite frown'd—
I quite forget which of them was in hand
 Just then, as they are rather numerous
 found,
Who took by turns that difficult command
 Since first her majesty was singly
 crown'd:
But they were mostly nervous six-foot
 fellows,
All fit to make a Patagonian jealous.

XLVII

Juan was none of these, but slight and slim,
 Blushing and beardless; and yet ne'er-
 theless
There was a something in his turn of limb,
 And still more in his eye, which seem'd
 to express,
That though he look'd one of the sera-
 phim,
 There lurk'd a man beneath the spirit's
 dress.
Besides, the empress sometimes liked a boy,
And had just buried the fair-faced Lanskoi.

XLVIII

No wonder then that Yermoloff, or Mo-
 monoff,
 Or Scherbatoff, or any other *off*
Or *on*, might dread her majesty had not
 room enough
 Within her bosom (which was not too
 tough)
For a new flame; a thought to cast of
 gloom enough
 Along the aspect, whether smooth or
 rough,
Of him who, in the language of his station,
Then held that 'high official situation.'

XLIX

Oh, gentle ladies! should you seek to know
 The import of this diplomatic phrase,
Bid Ireland's Londonderry's Marquess
 show
 His parts of speech; and in the strange
 displays
Of that odd string of words, all in a row,
 Which none divine, and every one obeys,
Perhaps you may pick out some queer *no*
 meaning,
Of that weak wordy harvest the sole glean-
 ing.

L

I think I can explain myself without
 That sad inexplicable beast of prey—
That Sphinx, whose words would ever be
 a doubt,
 Did not his deeds unriddle them each
 day—
That monstrous hieroglyphic—that long
 spout
 Of blood and water, leaden Castle-
 reagh!
And here I must an anecdote relate,
But luckily of no great length or weight.

LI

An English lady ask'd of an Italian,
 What were the actual and official duties
Of the strange thing, some women set a
 value on,
 Which hovers oft about some married
 beauties,
Call'd 'Cavalier servente'? a Pygmalion
 Whose statues warm (I fear, alas! too
 true 'tis)
Beneath his art. The dame, press'd to dis-
 close them,
Said—'Lady, I beseech you to *suppose*
 them.'

LII

And thus I supplicate your supposition,
 And mildest, matron-like interpretation,
Of the imperial favourite's condition.
 'Twas a high place, the highest in the
 nation

In fact, if not in rank! and the suspicion
 Of any one's attaining to his station
No doubt gave pain, where each new pair
 of shoulders,
If rather broad, made stocks rise and their
 holders.

LIII

Juan, I said, was a most beauteous boy,
 And had retain'd his boyish look be-
 yond
The usual hirsute seasons which destroy,
 With beards and whiskers, and the like,
 the fond
Parisian aspect, which upset old Troy
 And founded Doctors' Commons:—I
 have conn'd
The history of divorces, which, though
 chequer'd,
Calls Ilion's the first damages on record.

LIV

And Catherine, who loved all things (save
 her lord,
 Who was gone to his place), and pass'd
 for much,
Admiring those (by dainty dames ab-
 horr'd)
 Gigantic gentlemen, yet had a touch
Of sentiment: and he she most adored
 Was the lamented Lanskoi, who was
 such
A lover as had cost her many a tear,
And yet but made a middling grenadier.

LV

Oh thou '*teterrima causa*' of all '*belli*'—
 Thou gate of life and death—thou non-
 descript!
Whence is our exit and our entrance, well I
 May pause in pondering how all souls
 are dipt
In thy perennial fountain: how man *fell* I
 Know not, since knowledge saw her
 branches stript
Of her first fruit; but how he *falls* and
 rises
Since, *thou* hast settled beyond all sur-
 mises.

LVI

Some call thee 'the *worst* cause of war,'
 but I
 Maintain thou art the *best*: for after all,
From thee we come, to thee we go, and
 why
 To get at thee not batter down a wall,
Or waste a world? since no one can deny
 Thou dost replenish worlds both great
 and small:
With, or without thee, all things at a stand
Are, or would be, thou sea of life's dry
 land!

LVII

Catherine, who was the grand epitome
 Of that great cause of war, or peace, or
 what
You please (it causes all the things which be,
 So you may take your choice of this or
 that)—
Catherine, I say, was very glad to see
 The handsome herald, on whose plum-
 age sat
Victory; and, pausing as she saw him kneel
With his despatch, forgot to break the seal.

LVIII

Then recollecting the whole empress, nor
 Forgetting quite the woman (which
 composed
At least three parts of this great whole),
 she tore
 The letter open with an air which posed
The court, that watch'd each look her
 visage wore,
Until a royal smile at length disclosed
Fair weather for the day. Though rather
 spacious,
Her face was noble, her eyes fine, mouth
 gracious.

LIX

Great joy was hers, or rather joys: the first
 Was a ta'en city, thirty thousand slain.
Glory and triumph o'er her aspect burst,
 As an East Indian sunrise on the main.
These quench'd a moment her ambition's
 thirst—
 So Arab deserts drink in summer's rain:
In vain!—As fall the dews on quenchless
 sands,
Blood only serves to wash Ambition's
 hands!

LX

Her next amusement was more fanciful;
 She smiled at mad Suwarrow's rhymes,
 who threw
Into a Russian couplet rather dull
 The whole gazette of thousands whom
 he slew.
Her third was feminine enough to annul
 The shudder which runs naturally
 through
Our veins, when things call'd sovereigns
 think it best
To kill, and generals turn it into jest.

LXI

The two first feelings ran their course com-
 plete,
 And lighted first her eye, and then her
 mouth:
The whole court look'd immediately most
 sweet,
 Like flowers well water'd after a long
 drouth:—

But when on the lieutenant at her feet
 Her majesty, who liked to gaze on youth
Almost as much as on a new despatch,
Glanced mildly, all the world was on the
 watch.

LXII

Though somewhat large, exuberant, and
 truculent,
 When *wroth*—while *pleased*, she was as
 fine a figure
As those who like things rosy, ripe, and
 succulent,
 Would wish to look on, while they are in
 vigour.
She could repay each amatory look you
 lent
 With interest, and in turn was wont with
 rigour
To exact of Cupid's bills the full amount
At sight, nor would permit you to dis-
 count.

LXIII

With her the latter, though at times con-
 venient,
 Was not so necessary; for they tell
That she was handsome, and though fierce
 look'd lenient,
 And always used her favourites too well.
If once beyond her boudoir's precincts in
 ye went,
 Your 'fortune' was in a fair way 'to
 swell
A man' (as Giles says); for though she
 would widow all
Nations, she liked man as an individual.

LXIV

What a strange thing is man! and what a
 stranger
 Is woman! What a whirlwind is her
 head,
And what a whirlpool full of depth and
 danger
 Is all the rest about her! Whether wed,
Or widow, maid, or mother, she can
 change her
 Mind like the wind: whatever she has
 said
Or done, is light to what she'll say or do;—
The oldest thing on record, and yet new!

LXV

Oh Catherine! (for of all interjections,
 To thee both *oh!* and *ah!* belong of right
In love and war) how odd are the con-
 nexions
 Of human thoughts, which jostle in their
 flight!
Just now *yours* were cut out in different
 sections:
 First Ismail's capture caught your fancy
 quite;

Next of new knights, the fresh and glorious
 batch;
And *thirdly* he who brought you the des-
 patch!

LXVI

Shakespeare talks of 'the herald Mercury
 New lighted on a heaven-kissing hill':
And some such visions cross'd her majesty,
 While her young herald knelt before her
 still.
'Tis very true the hill seem'd rather high,
 For a lieutenant to climb up; but skill
Smooth'd even the Simplon's steep, and,
 by God's blessing,
With youth and health all kisses are
 'heaven-kissing.'

LXVII

Her majesty look'd down, the youth look'd
 up—
 And so they fell in love;—she with his face,
His grace, his God-knows-what: for
 Cupid's cup
 With the first draught intoxicates apace,
A quintessential laudanum or 'black drop,'
 Which makes one drunk at once, with-
 out the base
Expedient of full bumpers; for the eye
In love drinks all life's fountains (save
 tears) dry.

LXVIII

He, on the other hand, if not in love,
 Fell into that no less imperious passion,
Self-love—which, when some sort of
 thing above
 Ourselves, a singer, dancer, much in
 fashion,
Or duchess, princess, empress, 'deigns to
 prove'
 ('Tis Pope's phrase) a great longing,
 though a rash one,
For one especial person out of many,
Makes us believe ourselves as good as any.

LXIX

Besides, he was of that delighted age
 Which makes all female ages equal—
 when
We don't much care with whom we may
 engage,
 As bold as Daniel in the lions' den,
So that we can our native sun assuage
 In the next ocean, which may flow just
 then,
To make a *twilight* in, just as Sol's heat is
Quench'd in the lap of the salt sea, or
 Thetis.

LXX

And Catherine (we must say thus much
 for Catherine),
 Though bold and bloody, was the kind
 of thing

Whose temporary passion was quite
 flattering,
 Because each lover look'd a sort of king,
Made up upon an amatory pattern,
 A royal husband in all save the *ring*—
Which, being the damn'dest part of matri-
 mony,
Seem'd taking out the sting to leave the
 honey.

LXXI

And when you add to this, her womanhood
 In its meridian, her blue eyes or gray—
(The last, if they have soul, are quite as good,
 Or better, as the best examples say:
Napoleon's, Mary's (queen of Scotland),
 should
 Lend to that colour a transcendent ray;
And Pallas also sanctions the same hue,
Too wise to look through optics black or
 blue)—

LXXII

Her sweet smile, and her then majestic
 figure,
 Her plumpness, her imperial condescen-
 sion,
Her preference of a boy to men much
 bigger
 (Fellows whom Messalina's self would
 pension),
Her prime of life, just now in juicy vigour,
 With other *extras*, which we need not
 mention,—
All these, or any one of these, explain
Enough to make a stripling very vain.

LXXIII

And that's enough, for love is vanity,
 Selfish in its beginning as its end,
Except where 'tis a mere insanity,
 A maddening spirit which would strive
 to blend
Itself with beauty's frail inanity,
 On which the passion's self seems to
 depend;
And hence some heathenish philosophers
Make love the main-spring of the universe.

LXXIV

Besides Platonic love, besides the love
 Of God, the love of sentiment, the loving
Of faithful pairs—(I needs must rhyme
 with dove,
 That good old steam-boat which keeps
 verses moving
'Gainst reason—Reason ne'er was hand-
 and-glove
 With rhyme, but always leant less to im-
 proving
The sound than sense) besides all these
 pretences
To love, there are those things which
 words name senses;

LXXV

Those movements, those improvements in
 our bodies
Which make all bodies anxious to get
 out
Of their own sand-pits, to mix with a god-
 dess,
 For such all women are at first no doubt.
How beautiful that moment! and how
 odd is
 That fever which precedes the languid
 rout
Of our sensations! What a curious way
The whole thing is of clothing souls in clay!

LXXVI

The noblest kind of love is love Platonical,
 To end or to begin with; the next grand
Is that which may be christen'd love
 canonical,
 Because the clergy take the thing in
 hand;
The third sort to be noted in our chronicle
 As flourishing in every Christian land,
Is, when chaste matrons to their other ties
Add what may be call'd *marriage in dis-
 guise.*

LXXVII

Well, we won't analyse—our story must
 Tell for itself: the sovereign was smitten,
Juan much flatter'd by her love, or lust;—
 I cannot stop to alter words once writ-
 ten,
And the *two* are so mix'd with human dust,
 That he who *names one*, both perchance
 may hit on:
But in such matters Russia's mighty em-
 press
Behaved no better than a common semp-
 stress.

LXXVIII

The whole court melted into one wide
 whisper,
 And all lips were applied unto all ears!
The elder ladies' wrinkles curl'd much
 crisper
 As they beheld; the younger cast some
 leers
On one another, and each lovely lisper
 Smiled as she talk'd the matter o'er; but
 tears
Of rivalship rose in each clouded eye
Of all the standing army who stood by.

LXXIX

All the ambassadors of all the powers
 Inquired, Who was this very new young
 man,
Who promised to be great in some few
 hours?
 Which is full soon (though life is but a
 span).

Already they beheld the silver showers
 Of rubles rain, as fast as specie can,
Upon his cabinet, besides the presents
Of several ribands, and some thousand
 peasants.

LXXX

Catherine was generous,—all such ladies
 are:
 Love—that great opener of the heart
 and all
The ways that lead there, be they near or
 far,
 Above, below, by turnpikes great or
 small,—
Love—(though she had a cursed taste for
 war,
 And was not the best wife, unless we
 call
Such Clytemnestra, though perhaps 'tis
 better
That one should die, than two drag on the
 fetter)—

LXXXI

Love had made Catherine make each
 lover's fortune,
 Unlike our own half-chaste Elizabeth,
Whose avarice all disbursements did im-
 portune,
 If history, the grand liar, ever saith
The truth; and though grief her old age
 might shorten,
 Because she put a favourite to death,
Her vile, ambiguous method of flirtation
And stinginess, disgrace her sex and sta-
 tion.

LXXXII

But when the levée rose, and all was bustle
 In the dissolving circle, all the nations
Ambassadors began as 'twere to hustle
 Round the young man with their con-
 gratulations.
Also the softer silks were heard to rustle
 Of gentle dames, among whose recrea-
 tions
It is to speculate on handsome faces,
Especially when such lead to high places

LXXXIII

Juan, who found himself, he knew no
 how,
 A general object of attention, made
His answers with a very graceful bow,
 As if born for the ministerial trade.
Though modest, on his unembarrass'd
 brow
 Nature had written 'gentleman.' He
 said
Little, but to the purpose; and his manner
Flung hovering graces o'er him like a
 banner.

LXXXIV

An order from her majesty consign'd
 Our young lieutenant to the genial care
Of those in office: all the world look'd kind,
 (As it will look sometimes with the first
 stare,
Which youth would not act ill to keep in
 mind,)
 As also did Miss Protasoff then there,
Named from her mystic office 'l'Eprou-
 veuse,'
A term inexplicable to the Muse.

LXXXV

With *her* then, as in humble duty bound,
 Juan retired,—and so will I, until
My Pegasus shall tire of touching ground.
 We have just lit on a 'heaven-kissing hill,'
So lofty that I feel my brain turn round,
 And all my fancies whirling like a mill;
Which is a signal to my nerves and brain,
To take a quiet ride in some green lane.

CANTO THE TENTH

I

WHEN Newton saw an apple fall, he found
 In that slight startle from his contem-
 plation—
'Tis *said* (for I'll not answer above ground
 For any sage's creed or calculation)—
A mode of proving that the earth turn'd
 round
 In a most natural whirl, called 'gravi-
 tation';
And this is the sole mortal who could
 grapple,
Since Adam, with a fall, or with an apple.

II

Man fell with apples, and with apples rose,
 If this be true; for we must deem the
 mode
In which Sir Isaac Newton could disclose
 Through the then unpaved stars the
 turnpike road,
A thing to counterbalance human woes:
 For ever since immortal man hath
 glow'd
With all kinds of mechanics, and full soon
Steam-engines will conduct him to the
 moon.

III

And wherefore this exordium?—Why,
 just now,
 In taking up this paltry sheet of paper,
My bosom underwent a glorious glow,
 And my internal spirit cut a caper:
And though so much inferior, as I know,
 To those who, by the dint of glass and
 vapour,
Discover stars, and sail in the wind's eye,
I wish to do as much by poesy.

IV

In the wind's eye I have sail'd, and sail;
 but for
 The stars, I own my telescope is dim;
But at the least I have shunn'd the com-
 mon shore,
 And leaving land far out of sight, would
 skim
The ocean of eternity: the roar
 Of breakers has not daunted my slight,
 trim,
But *still* sea-worthy skiff; and she may
 float
Where ships have founder'd, as doth many
 a boat.

V

We left our hero, Juan, in the *bloom*
 Of favouritism, but not yet in the
 blush:—
And far be it from my *Muses* to pre-
 sume
 (For I have more than one Muse at a
 push)
To follow him beyond the drawing-room:
 It is enough that Fortune found him
 flush
Of youth, and vigour, beauty, and those
 things
Which for an instant clip enjoyment's
 wings.

VI

But soon they grow again and leave their
 nest.
 'Oh!' saith the Psalmist, 'that I had a
 dove's
Pinions to flee away, and be at rest!'
 And who that recollects young years
 and loves,—
Though hoary now, and with a withering
 breast,
 And palsied fancy, which no longer roves
Beyond its dimm'd eye's sphere,—but
 would much rather
Sigh like his son, than cough like his
 grandfather?

VII

But sighs subside, and tears (even widows')
 shrink,
So narrow as to shame their wintry brink,
 Which threatens inundations deep and
 yellow!
Such difference doth a few months make.
 You'd think
 Grief a rich field which never would lie
 fallow;
No more it doth, its ploughs but change
 their boys,
Who furrow some new soil to sow for
 joys.

779

VIII

But coughs will come when sighs depart—
and now
And then before sighs cease; for oft the
one
Will bring the other, ere the lake-like brow
Is ruffled by a wrinkle, or the sun
Of life reach ten o'clock: and while a glow,
Hectic and brief as summer's day nigh
done,
O'erspreads the cheek which seems too
pure for clay,
Thousands blaze, love, hope, die,—how
happy they!—

IX

But Juan was not meant to die so soon.
We left him in the focus of such glory
As may be won by favour of the moon
Or ladies' fancies—rather transitory
Perhaps; but who would scorn the month
of June,
Because December, with his breath so
hoary,
Must come? Much rather should he court
the ray,
To hoard up warmth against a wintry day.

X

Besides, he had some qualities which fix
Middle-aged ladies even more than
young:
The former know what's what; while new-
fledged chicks
Know little more of love than what is
sung
In rhymes, or dreamt (for fancy will play
tricks)
In visions of those skies from whence
Love sprung.
Some reckon women by their suns or years,
I rather think the moon should date the
dears.

XI

And why? because she's changeable and
chaste.
I know no other reason, whatsoe'er
Suspicious people, who find fault in haste,
May choose to tax me with; which is
not fair,
Nor flattering to 'their temper or their taste,'
As my friend Jeffrey writes with such an
air:
However, I forgive him, and I trust
He will forgive himself;—if not, I must.

XII

Old enemies who have become new friends
Should so continue—'tis a point of
honour;
And I know nothing which could make
amends
For a return to hatred: I would shun her

Like garlic, howsoever she extends
Her hundred arms and legs, and fair
outrun her.
Old flames, new wives, become our bitter-
est foes—
Converted foes should scorn to join with
those.

XIII

This were the worst desertion:—rene-
gadoes,
Even shuffling Southey, that incarnate lie,
Would scarcely join again the 'reforma-
does',
Whom he forsook to fill the laureate's
sty:
And honest men from Iceland to Bar-
badoes,
Whether in Caledon or Italy,
Should not veer round with every breath,
nor seize
To pain, the moment when you cease to
please.

XIV

The lawyer and the critic but behold
The baser sides of literature and life,
And nought remains unseen, but much
untold,
By those who scour those double vales
of strife.
While common men grow ignorantly old,
The lawyer's brief is like the surgeon's
knife,
Dissecting the whole inside of a question,
And with it all the process of digestion.

XV

A legal broom's a moral chimney-sweeper,
And that's the reason he himself 's so
dirty!
The endless soot bestows a tint far deeper
Than can be hid by altering his shirt; he
Retains the sable stains of the dark
creeper,
At least some twenty-nine do out of
thirty,
In all their habits;—not so *you*, I own;
As Cæsar wore his robe you wear your
gown.

XVI

And all our little feuds, at least all *mine*,
Dear Jeffrey, once my most redoubted
foe
(As far as rhyme and criticism combine
To make such puppets of us thing
below),
Are over: Here's a health to 'Auld Lang
Syne!'
I do not know you, and may never know
Your face—but you have acted on the
whole
Most nobly, and I own it from my soul.

XVII

And when I use the phrase of 'Auld Lang
 Syne!'
 'Tis not address'd to you—the more's
 the pity
For me, for I would rather take my wine
 With you, than aught (save Scott) in
 your proud city.
But somehow—it may seem a schoolboy's
 whine,
 And yet I seek not to be grand nor witty,
But I am half a Scot by birth, and bred
A whole one, and my heart flies to my
 head,—

XVIII

As 'Auld Lang Syne' brings Scotland, one
 and all,
 Scotch plaids, Scotch snoods, the blue
 hills, and clear streams,
The Dee, the Don, Balgounie's brig's *black
 wall*,
 All my boy feelings, all my gentler dreams
Of what I *then dreamt*, clothed in their own
 pall,
 Like Banquo's offspring:—floating past
 me seems
My childhood in this childishness of mine:
I care not—'tis a glimpse of '*Auld Lang Syne*.'

XIX

And though, as you remember, in a fit
 Of wrath and rhyme, when juvenile and
 curly,
I rail'd at Scots to show my wrath and wit,
 Which must be own'd was sensitive and
 surly,
Yet 'tis in vain such sallies to permit,
 They cannot quench young feelings
 fresh and early:
I '*scotch'd*' not kill'd' the Scotchman in my
 blood,
And love the land of 'mountain and of
 flood.'

XX

Don Juan, who was real, or ideal,—
 For both are much the same, since what
 men think
Exists when the once thinkers are less real
 Than what they thought, for mind can
 never sink,
And 'gainst the body makes a strong appeal;
 And yet 'tis very puzzling on the brink
Of what is call'd eternity, to stare,
And know no more of what is *here*, than
 there;—

XXI

Don Juan grew a very polish'd Russian—
 How we won't mention, *why* we need
 not say:
Few youthful minds can stand the strong
 concussion
 Of any slight temptation in their way;

But *his* just now were spread as is a cushion
 Smooth'd for a monarch's seat of
 honour: gay
Damsels, and dances, revels, ready money,
Made ice seem paradise, and winter sunny.

XXII

The favour of the empress was agreeable;
 And though the duty wax'd a little hard,
Young people at his time of life should be
 able
 To come off handsomely in that regard.
He was now growing up like a green tree,
 able
 For love, war, or ambition, which reward
Their luckier votaries, till old age's tedium
Make some prefer the circulating medium.

XXIII

About this time, as might have been antici-
 pated,
 Seduced by youth and dangerous examples,
Don Juan grew, I fear, a little dissipated;
 Which is a sad thing, and not only
 tramples
On our fresh feelings, but—as being par-
 ticipated
 With all kinds of incorrigible samples
Of frail humanity—must make us selfish,
And shut our souls up in us like a shell-fish.

XXIV

This we pass over. We will also pass
 The usual progress of intrigues between
Unequal matches, such as are, alas!
 A young lieutenant's with a *not old* queen,
But one who is not so youthful as she was
 In all the royalty of sweet seventeen.
Sovereigns may sway materials, but not
 matter,
And wrinkles, the d——d democrats,
 won't flatter.

XXV

And death, the sovereign's sovereign,
 though the great
 Gracchus of all mortality, who levels,
With his *Agrarian* laws, the high estate
 Of him who feasts, and fights, and roars,
 and revels,
To one small grass-grown patch (which
 must await
 Corruption for its crop) with the poor
 devils
Who never had a foot of land till now,—
Death's a reformer, all men must allow.

XXVI

He lived (not Death, but Juan) in a hurry
 Of waste, and haste, and glare, and
 gloss, and glitter,
In this gay clime of bear-skins black and
 furry—
 Which (though I hate to say a thing
 that's bitter)

Peep out sometimes, when things are in a
 flurry,
 Through all the 'purple and fine linen,'
 fitter
For Babylon's than Russia's royal har-
 lot—
And neutralise her outward show of
 scarlet.

XXVII

And this same state we won't describe: we
 could
 Perhaps from hearsay, or from recollec-
 tion;
But getting nigh grim Dante's 'obscure
 wood,'
 That horrid equinox, that hateful section
Of human years, that half-way house, that
 rude
 Hut, whence wise travellers drive with
 circumspection
Life's sad post-horses o'er the dreary
 frontier
Of age, and looking back to youth, give
 one tear;—

XXVIII

I won't describe,—that is, if I can help
 Description; and I won't reflect,—that
 is,
If I can stave off thought, which—as a
 whelp
 Clings to its teat—sticks to me through
 the abyss
Of this odd labyrinth; or as the kelp
 Holds by the rock; or as a lover's kiss
Drains its first draught of lips:—but, as I
 said,
I *won't* philosophise, and *will* be read.

XXIX

Juan, instead of courting courts, was
 courted,—
 A thing which happens rarely: this he
 owed
Much to his youth, and much to his re-
 ported
 Valour; much also to the blood he
 show'd,
Like a race-horse; much to each dress he
 sported,
 Which set the beauty off in which he
 glow'd,
As purple clouds befringe the sun; but
 most
He owed to an old woman and his post.

XXX

He wrote to Spain;—and all his near re-
 lations,
 Perceiving he was in a handsome way
Of getting on himself, and finding stations
For cousins also, answer'd the same day.

Several prepared themselves for emigra-
 tions;
 And eating ices, were o'erheard to say
That with the addition of a slight pelisse
Madrid's and Moscow's climes were of a
 piece.

XXXI

His mother, Donna Inez, finding, too,
 That in the lieu of drawing on his banker
Where his assets were waxing rather few
 He had brought his spending to a hand-
 some anchor,—
Replied, 'that she was glad to see him
 through
 Those pleasures after which wild youth
 will hanker;
As the sole sign of man's being in his
 senses
Is, learning to reduce his past expenses.

XXXII

'She also recommended him to God,
 And no less to God's Son, as well as
 Mother,
Warn'd him against Greek worship, which
 looks odd
 In Catholic eyes; but told him, too, to
 smother
Outward dislike, which don't look well
 abroad;
 Inform'd him that he had a little brother
Born in a second wedlock; and above
All, praised the empress's *maternal* love.

XXXIII

'She could not too much give her appro-
 bation
 Unto an empress, who preferr'd young
 men
Whose age, and what was better still
 whose nation
 And climate, stopp'd all scandal (now
 and then);—
At home it might have given her some
 vexation;
 But where thermometers sunk down to
 ten,
Or five, or one, or zero, she could never
Believe that virtue thaw'd before the
 river.'

XXXIV

Oh for a *forty-parson power* to chant
 Thy praise, Hypocrisy! Oh for a hymn
Loud as the virtues thou dost loudly vaunt
 Not practise! Oh for trumps of cheru-
 bim!
Or the ear-trumpet of my good old aunt
 Who, though her spectacles at last grew
 dim,
Drew quiet consolation through its hint,
When she no more could read the pious
 print.

XXXV

She was no hypocrite at least, poor soul,
 But went to heaven in as sincere a way
As anybody on the elected roll,
 Which portions out upon the judgment day
Heaven's freeholds, in a sort of doomsday scroll,
 Such as the conqueror William did repay
His knights with, lotting others' properties
Into some sixty thousand new knights' fees.

XXXVI

I can't complain, whose ancestors are there,
 Erneis, Radulphus—eight-and-forty manors
(If that my memory doth not greatly err)
 Were their reward for following Billy's banners:
And though I can't help thinking 'twas scarce fair
 To strip the Saxons of their *hydes*, like tanners;
Yet as they founded churches with the produce,
You'll deem, no doubt, they put it to a good use.

XXXVII

The gentle Juan flourish'd, though at times
 He felt like other plants call'd sensitive,
Which shrink from touch, as monarchs do from rhymes,
 Save such as Southey can afford to give.
Perhaps he long'd in bitter frosts for climes
 In which the Neva's ice would cease to live
Before May-day: perhaps, despite his duty,
In royalty's vast arms he sigh'd for beauty:

XXXVIII

Perhaps—but, sans perhaps, we need not seek
 For causes young or old: the cankerworm
Will feed upon the fairest, freshest cheek,
 As well as further drain the wither'd form:
Care, like a housekeeper, brings every week
 His bills in, and however we may storm,
They must be paid: though six days smoothly run,
The seventh will bring blue devils or a dun.

XXXIX

I don't know how it was, but he grew sick:
 The empress was alarm'd, and her physician
(The same who physick'd Peter) found the tick
 Of his fierce pulse betoken a condition
Which augur'd of the dead, however quick
 Itself, and show'd a feverish disposition;
At which the whole court was extremely troubled,
The sovereign shock'd, and all his medicines doubled.

XL

Low were the whispers, manifold the rumours,
 Some said he had been poison'd by Potemkin;
Others talk'd learnedly of certain tumours,
 Exhaustion, or disorders of the same kin;
Some said 'twas a concoction of the humours,
 Which with the blood too readily will claim kin;
Others again were ready to maintain,
"'Twas only the fatigue of last campaign.'

XLI

But here is one prescription out of many:
 ' *Sodæ sulphat.* 3vj. 3fs. *Mannæ optim.*
Aq. fervent. f. 3 *ifs.* 3*ij. tinct. Sennæ
 Haustus*' (and here the surgeon came and cupp'd him),
' *R. Pulv. Com. gr. iij. Ipecacuanhæ*'
 (With more beside if Juan had not stopp'd 'em),
' *Bolus Potassæ Sulphuret. sumendus,
Et haustus ter in die capiendus.*'

XLII

This is the way physicians mend or end us,
 Secundum artem: but although we sneer
In health—when ill, we call them to attend us,
 Without the least propensity to jeer:
While that ' *hiatus maxime deflendus*,'
 To be fill'd up by spade or mattock, 's near,
Instead of gliding graciously down Lethe,
We tease mild Baillie, or soft Abernethy.

XLIII

Juan demurr'd at this first notice to
 Quit; and though death had threaten'd an ejection,
His youth and constitution bore him through,
 And sent the doctors in a new direction.
But still his state was delicate: the hue
 Of health but flicker'd with a faint reflection
Along his wasted cheek, and seem'd to gravel
The faculty—who said that he must travel.

XLIV

The climate was too cold, they said, for
 him,
 Meridian-born, to bloom in. This
 opinion
Made the chaste Catherine look a little
 grim,
 Who did not like at first to lose her
 minion:
But when she saw his dazzling eye wax
 dim,
 And drooping like an eagle's with clipt
 pinion,
She then resolved to send him on a mission,
But in a style becoming his condition.

XLV

There was just then a kind of a discussion,
 A sort of treaty or negotiation,
Between the British cabinet and Russian,
 Maintain'd with all the due prevarica-
 tion
With which great states such things are
 apt to push on;
 Something about the Baltic's naviga-
 tion,
Hides, train-oil, tallow, and the rights of
 Thetis,
Which Britons deem their *uti possidetis.*

XLVI

So Catherine, who had a handsome way
 Of fitting out her favourites, conferr'd
This secret charge on Juan, to display
 At once her royal splendour, and reward
His services. He kiss'd hands the next day,
 Received instructions how to play his
 card,
Was laden with all kinds of gifts and
 honours,
Which show'd what great discernment
 was the donor's.

XLVII

But she was lucky, and luck's all. Your
 queens
 Are generally prosperous in reigning;
Which puzzles us to know what Fortune
 means:
 But to continue: though her years were
 waning,
Her climacteric teased her like her teens;
 And though her dignity brook'd no
 complaining,
So much did Juan's setting off distress her,
She could not find at first a fit successor.

XLVIII

But time, the comforter, will come at last;
 And four-and-twenty hours, and twice
 that number
Of candidates requesting to be placed,
 Made Catherine taste next night a quiet
 slumber:—

Not that she meant to fix again in haste,
 Nor did she find the quantity encumber,
But always choosing with deliberation,
Kept the place open for their emulation.

XLIX

While this high post of honour's in
 abeyance,
 For one or two days, reader, we request
You'll mount with our young hero the
 conveyance
 Which wafted him from Petersburgh:
 the best
Barouche, which had the glory to display
 once
 The fair Czarina's autocratic crest
When, a new Iphigene, she went to Tauris,
Was given to her favourite, and now *bore
 his.*

L

A bull-dog, and a bull-finch, and an
 ermine,
 All private favourites of Don Juan;—
 for
(Let deeper sages the true cause determine)
 He had a kind of inclination, or
Weakness, for what most people deem
 mere vermin,
 Live animals: an old maid of threescore
For cats and birds more penchant ne'er
 display'd,
Although he was not old, nor even a
 maid;—

LI

The animals aforesaid occupied
 Their station: there were valets, secre-
 taries,
In other vehicles; but at his side
 Sat little Leila, who survived the
 parries
He made 'gainst Cossacque sabres in the
 wide
 Slaughter of Ismail. Though my wild
 Muse varies
Her note, she don't forget the infant girl
Whom he preserved, a pure and living
 pearl.

LII

Poor little thing! She was as fair as docile,
 And with that gentle, serious character,
As rare in living beings as a fossile
 Man, 'midst thy mouldy mammoths,
 'grand Cuvier!'
Ill fitted was her ignorance to jostle
 With this o'erwhelming world, where
 all must err:
But she was yet but ten years old, and
 therefore
Was tranquil, though she knew not why
 or wherefore.

LIII

Don Juan loved her, and she loved him, as
 Nor brother, father, sister, daughter
 love.
I cannot tell exactly what it was;
 He was not yet quite old enough to
 prove
Parental feelings, and the other class,
 Call'd brotherly affection, could not
 move
His bosom,—for he never had a sister:
Ah! if he had, how much he would have
 miss'd her!

LIV

And still less was it sensual; for besides
 That he was not an ancient debauchee,
(Who like sour fruit, to stir their veins'
 salt tides,
 As acids rouse a dormant alkali,)
Although ('twill happen as our planet
 guides)
 His youth was not the chastest that
 might be,
There was the purest Platonism at bottom
Of all his feelings—only he forgot 'em.

LV

Just now there was no peril of temptation;
 He loved the infant orphan he had saved,
As patriots (now and then) may love a
 nation;
 His pride, too, felt that she was not
 enslaved
Owing to him;—as also her salvation
 Through his means and the church's
 might be paved.
But one thing's odd, which here must be
 inserted,
The little Turk refused to be converted.

LVI

'Twas strange enough she should retain
 the impression
 Through such a scene of change, and
 dread, and slaughter;
But though three bishops told her the
 transgression,
 She show'd a great dislike to holy water:
She also had no passion for confession;
 Perhaps she had nothing to confess:—
 no matter
Whate'er the cause, the church made little
 of it—
She still held out that Mahomet was a
 prophet.

LVII

In fact, the only Christian she could bear
 Was Juan; whom she seem'd to have
 selected
In place of what her home and friends
 once were.
 He naturally loved what he protected:

And thus they form'd a rather curious
 pair,
 A guardian green in years, a ward con-
 nected
In neither clime, time, blood, with her
 defender;
And yet this want of ties made theirs more
 tender.

LVIII

They journey'd on through Poland and
 through Warsaw,
 Famous for mines of salt and yokes of
 iron:
Through Courland also, which that
 famous farce saw
 Which gave her dukes the graceless
 name of 'Biron.'
'Tis the same landscape which the
 modern Mars saw
 Who march'd to Moscow, led by Fame,
 the siren!
To lose by one month's frost some twenty
 years
Of conquest, and his guard of grenadiers.

LIX

Let not this seem an anti-climax:—'Oh!
 My guard! my old guard!' exclaim'd
 that god of clay.
Think of the Thunderer's falling down
 below
 Carotid-artery-cutting Castlereagh!
Alas! that glory should be chill'd by
 snow!
 But should we wish to warm us on our
 way
Through Poland, there is Kosciusko's name
Might scatter fire through ice, like Hecla's
 flame.

LX

From Poland they came on through
 Prussia Proper,
 And Königsberg, the capital, whose
 vaunt,
Besides some veins of iron, lead, or
 copper,
 Has lately been the great Professor Kant.
Juan, who cared not a tobacco-stopper
 About philosophy, pursued his jaunt
To Germany, whose somewhat tardy
 millions
Have princes who spur more than their
 postilions.

LXI

And thence through Berlin, Dresden, and
 the like,
 Until he reach'd the castellated
 Rhine:—
Ye glorious Gothic scenes! how much ye
 strike
 All phantasies, not even excepting mine!

785

A grey wall, a green ruin, rusty pike,
 Make my soul pass the equinoctial line
Between the present and past worlds, and
 hover
Upon their airy confine, half-seas-over.

LXII

But Juan posted on through Mannheim,
 Bonn,
 Which Drachenfels frowns over like a
 spectre
Of the good feudal times for ever gone,
 On which I have not time just now to
 lecture.
From thence he was drawn onwards to
 Cologne,
 A city which presents to the inspector
Eleven thousand maidenheads of bone,
The greatest number flesh hath ever known.

LXIII

From thence to Holland's Hague and
 Helvoetsluys,
 That water-land of Dutchmen and of
 ditches,
Where juniper expresses its best juice,
 The poor man's sparkling substitute
 for riches.
Senates and sages have condemn'd its use—
 But to deny the mob a cordial, which is
Too often all the clothing, meat, or fuel,
Good government has left them, seems
 but cruel.

LXIV

Here he embark'd, and with a flowing sail
 Went bounding for the island of the free,
Towards which the impatient wind blew
 half a gale;
 High dash'd the spray, the bows dipp'd
 in the sea,
And sea-sick passengers turn'd somewhat
 pale;
 But Juan, season'd, as he well might be,
By former voyages, stood to watch the
 skiffs,
Which pass'd, or catch the first glimpse of
 the cliffs.

LXV

At length they rose, like a white wall
 along
 The blue sea's border; and Don Juan
 felt—
What even young strangers feel a little
 strong
 At the first sight of Albion's chalky
 belt—
A kind of pride that he should be among
 Those haughty shopkeepers, who
 sternly dealt
Their goods and edicts out from pole to
 pole
And made the very billows pay them toll.

LXVI

I've no great cause to love that spot o
 earth,
 Which holds what *might have been* the
 noblest nation;
But though I owe it little but my birth,
 I feel a mix'd regret and veneration
For its decaying fame and former worth.
 Seven years (the usual term of trans
 portation)
Of absence lay one's old resentments level
When a man's country's going to the devil

LXVII

Alas! could she but fully, truly, know
 How her great name is now through-
 out abhorr'd;
How eager all the earth is for the blow
 Which shall lay bare her bosom to the
 sword;
How all the nations deem her their worst
 foe,
 That worse than *worst of foes*, the once
 adored
False friend, who held out freedom to
 mankind,
And now would chain them, to the very
 mind;—

LXVIII

Would she be proud, or boast herself the
 free,
 Who is but first of slaves? The nations are
In prison,—but the gaoler, what is he?
 No less a victim to the bolt and bar.
Is the poor privilege to turn the key
 Upon the captive, freedom? He's as far
From the enjoyment of the earth and air
Who watches o'er the chain, as they who
 wear.

LXIX

Don Juan now saw Albion's earliest
 beauties,
 Thy cliffs, *dear* Dover! harbour, and
 hotel;
Thy custom-house, with all its delicate
 duties;
 Thy waiters running mucks at every bell;
Thy packets, all whose passengers are
 booties
 To those who upon land or water dwell
And last, not least, to strangers unin
 structed,
Thy long, long bills, whence nothing is
 deducted.

LXX

Juan, though careless, young, and
 magnifique,
 And rich in rubles, diamonds, cash, and
 credit,
Who did not limit much his bills per week
 Yet stared at this a little, though he paid
 it—

(His Maggior Duomo, a smart, subtle
 Greek,
 Before him summ'd the awful scroll and
 read it):
But, doubtless, as the air, though seldom
 sunny,
Is free, the respiration's worth the money.

LXXI

On with the horses! Off to Canterbury!
 Tramp, tramp o'er pebble, and splash,
 splash through puddle;
Hurrah! how swiftly speeds the post so
 merry!
 Not like slow Germany, wherein they
 muddle
Along the road, as if they went to bury
 Their fare; and also pause besides, to
 fuddle,
With 'schnapps'—sad dogs! whom
 'Hundsfot,' or 'Verflucter,'
Affect no more than lightning a conductor.

LXXII

Now there is nothing gives a man such
 spirits,
 Leavening his blood as cayenne doth a
 curry,
As going at full speed—no matter where its
 Direction be, so 'tis but in a hurry,
And merely for the sake of its own merits;
 For the less cause there is for all this
 flurry,
The greater is the pleasure in arriving
And the great *end* of travel—which is
 driving.

LXXIII

They saw at Canterbury the cathedral;
 Black Edward's helm, and Becket's
 bloody stone,
Were pointed out as usual by the bedral,
 In the same quaint, uninterested tone:—
There's glory again for you, gentle reader!
 All
 Ends in a rusty casque and dubious bone,
Half-solved into these sodas or magnesias,
Which form that bitter draught, the
 human species.

LXXIV

The effect on Juan was of course sublime:
 He breathed a thousand Cressys, as he
 saw
That casque, which never stoop'd except
 to Time.
 Even the bold Churchman's tomb
 excited awe,
Who died in the then great attempt to climb
 O'er kings, who *now* at least *must talk*
 of law
Before they butcher. Little Leila gazed,
And ask'd why such a structure had been
 raised;

LXXV

And being told it was 'God's house,' she
 said
 He was well lodged, but only wonder'd
 how
He suffer'd Infidels in his homestead,
 The cruel Nazarenes, who had laid low
His holy temples in the lands which bred
 The True Believers;—and her infant
 brow
Was bent with grief that Mahomet should
 resign
A mosque so noble, flung like pearls to
 swine.

LXXVI

On! on! through meadows, managed like
 a garden,
 A paradise of hops and high pro-
 duction;
For, after years of travel by a bard in
 Countries of greater heat, but lesser
 suction,
A green field is a sight which makes him
 pardon
 The absence of that more sublime con-
 struction
Which mixes up vines, olives, precipices,
Glaciers, volcanos, oranges, and ices.

LXXVII

And when I think upon a pot of beer—
 But I won't weep!—and so drive on,
 postilions!
As the smart boys spurr'd fast in their career,
 Juan admired these highways of free
 millions;
A country in all senses the most dear
 To foreigner or native, save some silly
 ones,
Who 'kick against the pricks' just at this
 juncture,
And for their pains get only a fresh puncture.

LXXVIII

What a delightful thing's a turnpike road!
 So smooth, so level, such a mode of
 shaving
The earth, as scarce the eagle in the broad
 Air can accomplish, with his wide wings
 waving.
Had such been cut in Phaeton's time, the god
 Had told his son to satisfy his craving
With the York mail;—but onward as we
 roll,
Surgit amari aliquid—the toll!

LXXIX

Alas! how deeply painful is all payment!
 Take lives, take wives, take aught except
 men's purses.
As Machiavel shows those in purple
 raiment,
 Such is the shortest way to general curses.

787

They hate a murderer much less than a
 claimant
 On that sweet ore which everybody
 nurses.—
Kill a man's family, and he may brook it,
But keep your hands out of his breeches'
 pocket:

LXXX

So said the Florentine; ye monarchs,
 hearken
 To your instructor. Juan now was
 borne,
Just as the day began to wane and darken,
 O'er the high hill, which looks with
 pride or scorn
Toward the great city.—Ye who have a
 spark in
 Your veins of Cockney spirit, smile or
 mourn
According as you take things well or ill;
Bold Britons, we are now on Shooter's
 Hill!

LXXXI

The sun went down, the smoke rose up,
 as from
 A half-unquench'd volcano, o'er a
 space
Which well beseem'd the 'Devil's drawing-
 room,'
 As some have qualified that wondrous
 place:
But Juan felt, though not approaching
 home,
 As one who, though he were not of the
 race,
Revered the soil, of those true sons the
 mother,
Who butcher'd half the earth, and bullied
 t'other.

LXXXII

A mighty mass of brick, and smoke, and
 shipping,
 Dirty and dusky, but as wide as eye
Could reach, with here and there a sail
 just skipping
 In sight, then lost amidst the forestry
Of masts; a wilderness of steeples peeping
 On tiptoe through their sea-coal canopy;
A huge, dun cupola, like a foolscap crown
On a fool's head—and there is London
 Town.

LXXXIII

But Juan saw not this: each wreath of
 smoke
 Appear'd to him but as the magic
 vapour
Of some alchymic furnace, from whence
 broke
 The wealth of worlds (a wealth of tax
 and paper):

The gloomy clouds, which o'er it as
 yoke
 Are bow'd, and put the sun out like
 taper,
Were nothing but the natural atmosphere
Extremely wholesome, though but rarely
 clear.

LXXXIV

He paused—and so will I; as doth a crew
 Before they give their broadside. By
 and by,
My gentle countrymen, we will renew
 Our old acquaintance; and at least I'll
 try
To tell you truths you will not take as true,
 Because they are so;—a male Mrs.
 Fry,
With a soft besom will I sweep your halls
And brush a web or two from off the walls

LXXXV

Oh Mrs. Fry! Why go to Newgate? Why
 Preach to poor rogues? And wherefore
 not begin
With Carlton, or with other houses? Try
 Your hand at harden'd and imperial sin
To mend the people's an absurdity,
 A jargon, a mere philanthropic din,
Unless you make their betters better:—
 Fry!
I thought you had more religion, Mrs. Fry

LXXXVI

Teach them the decencies of good three-
 score;
 Cure them of tours, hussar and high-
 land dresses;
Tell them that youth once gone returns
 no more,
 That hired huzzas redeem no land-
 distresses;
Tell them Sir William Curtis is a bore,
 Too dull even for the dullest of excesses
The witless Falstaff of a hoary Hal,
A fool whose bells have ceased to ring at
 all.

LXXXVII

Tell them, though it may be perhaps too
 late
 On life's worn confine, jaded, bloated,
 sated,
To set up vain pretences of being great,
 'Tis not so to be good; and be it stated
The worthiest kings have ever loved least
 state;
 And tell them——But you won't, and
 I have prated
Just now enough; but by and by I'll
 prattle
Like Roland's horn in Roncesvalles'
 battle.

CANTO THE ELEVENTH

I

WHEN Bishop Berkeley said 'there was no
 matter,'
 And proved it—'twas no matter what
 he said:
They say his system 'tis in vain to batter,
 Too subtle for the airiest human head;
And yet who can believe it? I would
 shatter
 Gladly all matters down to stone or
 lead,
Or adamant, to find the world a spirit,
And wear my head, denying that I wear
 it.

II

What a sublime discovery 'twas to make
 the
 Universe universal egotism,
That all's ideal—*all ourselves!* I'll stake
 the
 World (be it what you will) that *that*'s
 no schism:
Oh Doubt!—if thou be'st Doubt, for
 which some take thee,
 But which I doubt extremely—thou
 sole prism
Of the Truth's rays, spoil not my draught
 of spirit!
Heaven's brandy, though our brain can
 hardly bear it.

III

For ever and anon comes Indigestion
 (Not the most 'dainty Ariel'), and per-
 plexes
Our soarings with another sort of
 question:
 And that which after all my spirit vexes,
Is, that I find no spot where man can rest
 eye on,
 Without confusion of the sorts and
 sexes,
Of beings, stars, and this unriddled
 wonder,
The world, which at the worst's a *glorious*
 blunder—

IV

If it be chance; or if it be according
 To the old text, still better:—lest it
 should
Turn out so, we'll say nothing 'gainst the
 wording,
 As several people think such hazards
 rude.
They're right; our days are too brief for
 affording
 Space to dispute what *no one* ever could
Decide, and *everybody one day* will
Know very clearly—or at least lie still.

V

And therefore will I leave off meta-
 physical
 Discussion, which is neither here nor
 there:
If I agree that what is, is; then this I call
 Being quite perspicuous and extremely
 fair;
The truth is, I've grown lately rather
 phthisical:
 I don't know what the reason is—the air
Perhaps; but as I suffer from the shocks
Of illness, I grow much more orthodox.

VI

The first attack at once proved the
 Divinity
 (But *that* I never doubted, nor the Devil);
The next, the Virgin's mystical virginity;
 The third, the usual Origin of Evil;
The fourth at once establish'd the whole
 Trinity
 On so uncontrovertible a level,
That I devoutly wish'd the three were four
On purpose to believe so much the more.

VII

To our theme.—The man who has stood
 on the Acropolis
 And look'd down over Attica; or he
Who has sail'd where picturesque Con-
 stantinople is,
 Or seen Timbuctoo, or hath taken tea
In small-eyed China's crockery-ware
 metropolis,
 Or sat amidst the bricks of Nineveh,
May not think much of London's first
 appearance—
But ask him what he thinks of it a year
 hence?

VIII

Don Juan had got out on Shooter's Hill;
 Sunset the time, the place the same
 declivity
Which looks along that vale of good and
 ill
 Where London streets ferment in full
 activity;
While everything around was calm and
 still,
 Except the creak of wheels, which on
 their pivot he
Heard,—and that bee-like, bubbling,
 busy hum
Of cities, that boils over with their scum:—

IX

I say, Don Juan, wrapt in contemplation,
 Walk'd on behind his carriage, o'er the
 summit,
And lost in wonder of so great a nation,
 Gave way to't, since he could not over-
 come it.

'And here,' he cried, 'is Freedom's
 chosen station;
 Here peals the people's voice, nor can
 entomb it
Racks, prisons, inquisitions; resurrection
Awaits it, each new meeting or election.

X

'Here are chaste wives, pure lives; here
 people pay
 But what they please; and if that things
 be dear,
'Tis only that they love to throw away
 Their cash, to show how much they
 have a year.
Here laws are all inviolate; none lay
 Traps for the traveller; every highway's
 clear;
Here'—he was interrupted by a knife,
With—'Damn your eyes! your money or
 your life!'—

XI

These freeborn sounds proceeded from
 four pads
 In ambush laid, who had perceived him
 loiter
Behind his carriage; and, like handy lads,
 Had seized the lucky hour to recon-
 noitre,
In which the heedless gentleman who
 gads
 Upon the road, unless he prove a fighter,
May find himself within that isle of riches
Exposed to lose his life as well as breeches.

XII

Juan, who did not understand a word
 Of English, save their shibboleth, 'God
 damn!'
And even that he had so rarely heard,
 He sometimes thought 'twas only their
 'Salām,'
Or 'God be with you!'—and 'tis not
 absurd
 To think so: for half English as I am
(To my misfortune), never can I say
I heard them wish 'God with you,' save
 that way;—

XIII

Juan yet quickly understood their gesture,
 And being somewhat choleric and
 sudden,
Drew forth a pocket-pistol from his
 vesture,
 And fired it into one assailant's
 pudding—
Who fell, as rolls an ox o'er in his pasture,
 And roar'd out, as he writhed his native
 mud in,
Unto his nearest follower or henchman,
'Oh Jack! I'm floor'd by that 'ere bloody
 Frenchman!'

XIV

On which Jack and his train set off at
 speed,
 And Juan's suite, late scatter'd at a
 distance,
Came up, all marvelling at such a deed,
 And offering, as usual, late assistance
Juan, who saw the moon's late minion
 bleed
 As if his veins would pour out his exis-
 tence,
Stood calling out for bandages and lint,
And wish'd he had been less hasty with
 his flint.

XV

'Perhaps,' thought he, 'it is the country's
 wont
 To welcome foreigners in this way: now
I recollect some innkeepers who don't
 Differ, except in robbing with a bow,
In lieu of a bare blade and brazen front
 But what is to be done? I can't allow
The fellow to lie groaning on the road:
So take him up; I'll help you with the
 load.'

XVI

But ere they could perform this pious
 duty,
 The dying man cried, 'Hold! I've got
 my gruel!
Oh! for a glass of *max!* We've miss'd our
 booty;
 Let me die where I am!' And as the
 fuel
Of life shrunk in his heart, and thick and
 sooty
 The drops fell from his death-wound,
 and he drew ill
His breath,—he from his swelling throat
 untied
A kerchief, crying 'Give Sal that!'—and
 died.

XVII

The cravat stain'd with bloody drops fell
 down
 Before Don Juan's feet: he could not
 tell
Exactly why it was before him thrown,
 Nor what the meaning of the man's
 farewell.
Poor Tom was once a kiddy upon town
 A thorough varmint, and a *real* swell,
Full flash, all fancy, until fairly diddled
His pockets first and then his body riddled

XVIII

Don Juan, having done the best he could
 In all the circumstances of the case,
As soon as 'Crowner's quest' allow'd
 pursued
 His travels to the capital apace;—

Esteeming it a little hard he should
 In twelve hours' time, and very little
 space,
Have been obliged to slay a free-born
 native
In self-defence: this made him meditative.

XIX

He from the world had cut off a great man,
 Who in his time had made heroic bustle.
Who in a row like Tom could lead the
 van,
 Booze in the ken, or at the spellken
 hustle?
Who queer a flat? Who (spite of Bow-
 street's ban)
 On the high toby-spice so flash the
 muzzle?
Who on a lark, with black-eyed Sal (his
 blowing),
So prime, so swell, so nutty, and so
 knowing?

XX

But Tom's no more—and so no more of
 Tom.
 Heroes must die; and by God's blessing
 'tis
Not long before the most of them go home.
 Hail! Thamis, hail! Upon thy verge it is
That Juan's chariot, rolling like a drum
 In thunder, holds the way it can't well
 miss,
Through Kennington and all the other
 'tons,'
Which make us wish ourselves in town at
 once;—

XXI

Through Groves, so call'd as being void of
 trees,
 (Like *lucus* from *no* light); through
 prospects named
Mount Pleasant, as containing nought to
 please,
 Nor much to climb; through little boxes
 framed
Of bricks, to let the dust in at your ease,
 With 'To be let,' upon their doors pro-
 claim'd;
Through 'Rows' most modestly call'd
 'Paradise,'
Which Eve might quit without much
 sacrifice;—

XXII

Through coaches, drays, choked turn-
 pikes, and a whirl
 Of wheels, and roar of voices, and con-
 fusion;
Here taverns wooing to a pint of 'purl,'
 There mails fast flying off like a
 delusion;

There barbers' blocks with periwigs in
 curl
 In windows; here the lamplighter's
 infusion
Slowly distill'd into the glimmering glass
(For in those days we had not got to
 gas—);

XXIII

Through this, and much, and more, is the
 approach
 Of travellers to mighty Babylon:
Whether they come by horse, or chaise,
 or coach,
 With slight exceptions, all the ways seem
 one.
I could say more, but do not choose to
 encroach
 Upon the Guide-book's privilege. The
 sun
Had set some time, and night was on the
 ridge
Of twilight, as the party cross'd the bridge.

XXIV

That's rather fine, the gentle sound of
 Thamis—
 Who vindicates a moment, too, his
 stream—
Though hardly heard through multi-
 farious 'damme's.'
 The lamps of Westminster's more
 regular gleam,
The breadth of pavement, and yon shrine
 where fame is
 A spectral resident—whose pallid beam
In shape of moonshine hovers o'er the
 pile—
Make this a sacred part of Albion's isle.

XXV

The Druid's groves are gone—so much
 the better:
 Stonehenge is not—but what the devil
 is it?—
But Bedlam still exists with its sage fetter,
 That madmen may not bite you on a
 visit;
The Bench too seats or suits full many a
 debtor;
 The Mansion-House, too (though some
 people quiz it),
To me appears a stiff yet grand erection;
But then the Abbey's worth the whole
 collection.

XXVI

The line of lights, too, up to Charing
 Cross,
 Pall Mall, and so forth, have a corusca-
 tion
Like gold as in comparison to dross,
 Match'd with the Continent's illumina-
 tion,

Whose cities Night by no means deigns to
 gloss.
 The French were not yet a lamp-
 lighting nation,
And when they grew so—on their new-
 found lantern,
Instead of wicks, they made a wicked man
 turn.

XXVII

A row of gentlemen along the streets
 Suspended, may illuminate mankind,
As also bonfires made of country-seats;
 But the old way is best for the purblind:
The other looks like phosphorus on sheets,
 A sort of *ignis fatuus* to the mind,
Which, though 'tis certain to perplex and
 frighten,
Must burn more mildly ere it can en-
 lighten.

XXVIII

But London's so well lit, that if Diogenes
 Could recommence to hunt his *honest
 man*,
And found him not amidst the various
 progenies
 Of this enormous city's spreading spawn,
'Twere not for want of lamps to aid his
 dodging his
Yet undiscover'd treasure. What *I* can,
I've done to find the same throughout
 life's journey,
But see the world is only one attorney.

XXIX

Over the stones still rattling, up Pall Mall,
 Through crowds and carriages, but
 waxing thinner
As thunder'd knockers broke the long-
 seal'd spell
 Of doors 'gainst duns, and to an early
 dinner
Admitted a small party as night fell,—
 Don Juan, our young diplomatic
 sinner,
Pursued his path, and drove past some
 hotels,
St. James's Palace and St. James's 'Hells.'

XXX

They reach'd the hotel: forth stream'd
 from the front door
 A tide of well-clad waiters, and around
The mob stood, and as usual several score
 Of those pedestrian Paphians who
 abound
In decent London when the daylight's
 o'er;
 Commodious but immoral, they are
 found
Useful, like Malthus, in promoting mar-
 riage.—
But Juan now is stepping from his carriage

XXXI

Into one of the sweetest of hotels,
 Especially for foreigners—and mostly
For those whom favour or whom fortun
 swells,
 And cannot find a bill's small iten
 costly.
There many an envoy either dwelt
 dwells
 (The den of many a diplomatic lost lie
Until to some conspicuous square the
 pass,
And blazon o'er the door their names
 brass.

XXXII

Juan, whose was a delicate commission
 Private, though publicly importan
 bore
No title to point out with due precision
 The exact affair on which he was se
 o'er.
'Twas merely known, that on a secr
 mission
 A foreigner of rank had graced o
 shore,
Young, handsome, and accomplish'
 who was said
(In whispers) to have turn'd his sovereign
 head.

XXXIII

Some rumour also of some strange adve
 tures
 Had gone before him, and his wars an
 loves;
And as romantic heads are pretty painter
 And, above all, an Englishwoman
 roves
Into the excursive, breaking the indentur
 Of sober reason, wheresoe'er it move
He found himself extremely in the fashio
 Which serves our thinking people for
 passion.

XXXIV

I don't mean that they are passionles
 but quite
 The contrary; but then 'tis in the hea
Yet as the consequences are as bright
 As if they acted with the heart instea
What after all can signify the site
 Of ladies' lucubrations? So they lea
In safety to the place for which you sta
What matters if the road be head
 heart?

XXXV

Juan presented in the proper place,
 To proper placemen, every Ru
 credential,
And was received with all the due grima
 By those who govern in the moo
 potential,

792

Who, seeing a handsome stripling with
 smooth face,
 Thought (what in state affairs is most
 essential)
That they as easily might *do* the youngster,
As hawks may pounce upon a woodland
 songster.

XXXVI

They err'd, as aged men will do; but by
 And by we'll talk of that; and if we
 don't,
'Twill be because our notion is not high
 Of politicians and their double front,
Who live by lies, yet dare not boldly lie:—
 Now what I love in women is, they
 won't
Or can't do otherwise than lie, but do it
So well, the very truth seems falsehood to
 it.

XXXVII

And, after all, what is a lie? 'Tis but
 The truth in masquerade; and I defy
Historians, heroes, lawyers, priests, to put
 A fact without some leaven of a lie.
The very shadow of true Truth would shut
 Up annals, revelations, poesy,
And prophecy—except it should be dated
Some years before the incidents related.

XXXVIII

Praised be all liars and all lies! Who now
 Can tax my mild Muse with mis-
 anthropy?
She rings the world's 'Te Deum,' and her
 brow
 Blushes for those who will not:—but
 to sigh
Is idle; let us like most others bow,
 Kiss hands, feet, any part of majesty,
After the good example of 'Green Erin,'
Whose Shamrock now seems rather worse
 for wearing.

XXXIX

Don Juan was presented, and his dress
 And mien excited general admiration—
I don't know which was most admired or
 less:
 One monstrous diamond drew much
 observation,
Which Catherine in a moment of '*ivresse*'
 (In love or brandy's fervent fermenta-
 tion)
Bestow'd upon him, as the public learn'd;
And, to say truth, it had been fairly earn'd.

XL

Besides the ministers and underlings,
 Who must be courteous to the
 accredited
Diplomatists of rather wavering kings,
 Until their royal riddle's fully read,

The very clerks,—those somewhat dirty
 springs
 Of office, or the house of office, fed
By foul corruption into streams,—even
 they
Were hardly rude enough to earn|their pay:

XLI

And insolence no doubt is what they are
 Employ'd for, since it is their daily
 labour,
In the dear offices of peace or war;
 And should you doubt, pray ask of your
 next neighbour,
When for a passport, or some other bar
 To freedom, he applied (a grief and *a*
 bore),
If he found not in this spawn of taxborn
 riches,
Like lap-dogs, the least civil sons of
 b——s.

XLII

But Juan was received with much '*em-
 pressement*:'—
 These phrases of refinement I must
 borrow
From our next neighbour's land, where,
 like a chessman,
 There is a move set down for joy or
 sorrow,
Not only in mere talking, but the press.
 Man
 In islands is, it seems, downright and
 thorough,
More than on continents—as if the sea
(See Billingsgate) made even the tongue
 more free.

XLIII

And yet the British 'Damme''s rather
 Attic;
 Your continental oaths are but inconti-
 nent,
And turn on things which no aristocratic
 Spirit would name, and therefore even
 I won't anent
This subject quote; as it would be schis-
 matic
 In *politesse*, and have a sound affronting
 in't;—
But 'Damme''s quite ethereal, though too
 daring—
Platonic blasphemy, the soul of swearing.

XLIV

For downright rudeness, ye may stay at
 home;
 For true or false politeness (and scarce
 that
Now) you may cross the blue deep and
 white foam—
 The first the emblem (rarely though) of
 what

You leave behind, the next of much you
 come
To meet. However, 'tis no time to chat
On general topics: poems must confine
Themselves to unity, like this of mine.

XLV

In the great world,—which, being inter-
 preted,
 Meaneth the west or worst end of a
 city,
And about twice two thousand people
 bred
By no means to be very wise or witty,
But to sit up while others lie in bed,
 And look down on the universe with
 pity,—
Juan, as an inveterate patrician,
Was well received by persons of condition.

XLVI

He was a bachelor, which is a matter
 Of import both to virgin and to bride,
The former's hymeneal hopes to flatter;
 And (should she not hold fast by love
 or pride)
'Tis also of some moment to the latter:
 A rib's a thorn in a wed gallant's side,
Requires decorum, and is apt to double
The horrid sin—and what's still worse,
 the trouble.

XLVII

But Juan was a bachelor—of arts,
 And parts, and hearts: he danced and
 sung, and had
An air as sentimental as Mozart's
 Softest of melodies; and could be sad
Or cheerful, without any 'flaws or starts,'
 Just at the proper time: and though a lad,
Had seen the world—which is a curious
 sight,
And very much unlike what people write.

XLVIII

Fair virgins blush'd upon him; wedded
 dames
 Bloom'd also in less transitory hues:
For both commodities dwell by the
 Thames,
 The painting and the painted; youth,
 ceruse,
Against his heart preferr'd their usual
 claims,
 Such as no gentleman can quite refuse:
Daughters admired his dress, and pious
 mothers
Inquired his income, and if he had
 brothers.

XLIX

The milliners who furnish 'drapery Misses'
 Throughout the season, upon specula-
 tion

Of payment ere the honeymoon's las
 kisses
 Have waned into a crescent's corusca
 tion,
Thought such an opportunity as this is,
 Of a rich foreigner's initiation,
Not to be overlook'd—and gave suc
 credit,
That future bridegrooms swore, an
 sigh'd, and paid it.

L

The Blues, that tender tribe, who sigh o'e
 sonnets,
 And with the pages of the last Revie
Line the interior of their heads or bonnet
 Advanced in all their azure's highe
 hue:
They talk'd bad French of Spanish, an
 upon its
 Late authors ask'd him for a hint o
 two;
And which was softest, Russian c
 Castilian?
And whether in his travels he saw Ilion

LI

Juan, who was a little superficial,
 And not in literature a great Drav
 cansir,
Examined by this learned and especial
 Jury of matrons, scarce knew what
 answer:
His duties warlike, loving, or official,
 His steady application as a dancer,
Had kept him from the brink of Hipp
 crene,
Which now he found was blue instead c
 green.

LII

However, he replied at hazard, with
 A modest confidence and calm as
 surance,
Which lent his learned lucubrations pit
 And pass'd for arguments of goo
 endurance.
That prodigy, Miss Araminta Smith
 (Who at sixteen translated 'Hercule
 Furens'
Into as furious English), with her be
 look,
Set down his sayings in her commo
 place book.

LIII

Juan knew several languages—as well
 He might—and brought them up wit
 skill, in time
To save his fame with each accomplish
 belle,
 Who still regretted that he did n
 rhyme.

There wanted but this requisite to swell
 His qualities (with them) into sublime:
Lady Fitz-Frisky, and Miss Mævia
 Mannish,
Both long'd extremely to be sung in
 Spanish.

LIV

However, he did pretty well, and was
 Admitted as an aspirant to all
The coteries, and, as in Banquo's glass,
 At great assemblies or in parties small,
He saw ten thousand living authors pass,
 That being about their average numeral;
Also the eighty 'greatest living poets,'
As every paltry magazine can show it's.

LV

In twice five years the 'greatest living
 poet,'
 Like to the champion in the fisty ring,
Is call'd on to support his claim, or show it,
 Although 'tis an imaginary thing.
Even I—albeit I'm sure I did not know it,
 Nor sought of foolscap subjects to be
 king,—
Was reckon'd, a considerable time,
The grand Napoleon of the realms of
 rhyme.

LVI

But Juan was my Moscow, and Faliero
 My Leipsic, and my Mont Saint Jean
 seems Cain:
La Belle Alliance of dunces down at zero,
 Now that the Lion's fall'n, may rise
 again:
But I will fall at least as fell my hero;
 Nor reign at all, or as a monarch reign;
Or to some lonely isle of gaolers go,
With turncoat Southey for my turnkey
 Lowe.

LVII

Sir Walter reign'd before me; Moore and
 Campbell
 Before and after: but now grown more
 holy,
The Muses upon Sion's hill must ramble
 With poets almost clergymen, or
 wholly:
And Pegasus hath a psalmodic amble
 Beneath the very Reverend Rowley
 Powley,
Who shoes the glorious animal with stilts,
A modern Ancient Pistol—by the hilts!

LVIII

Still he excels that artificial hard
 Labourer in the same vineyard, though
 the vine
Yields him but vinegar for his reward,—
 That neutralised dull Dorus of the
 Nine;

That swarthy Sporus, neither man nor bard;
 That ox of verse, who ploughs for every
 line:—
Cambyses' roaring Romans beat at least
The howling Hebrews of Cybele's priest.—

LIX

Then there's my gentle Euphues; who,
 they say,
 Sets up for being a sort of moral me;
He'll find it rather difficult some day
 To turn out both, or either, it may be.
Some persons think that Coleridge hath
 the sway;
 And Wordsworth has supporters, two
 or three;
And that deep-mouth'd Bœotian 'Savage
 Landor'
Has taken for a swan rogue Southey's
 gander.

LX

John Keats, who was kill'd off by one
 critique,
 Just as he really promised something
 great,
If not intelligible, without Greek
 Contrived to talk about the Gods of late,
Much as they might have been supposed
 to speak.
 Poor fellow! His was an untoward fate;
'Tis strange the mind, that very fiery particle,
Should let itself be snuff'd out by an article.

LXI

The list grows long of live and dead pre-
 tenders
 To that which none will gain—or none
 will know
The conqueror at least; who, ere Time
 renders
 His last award, will have the long grass
 grow
Above his burnt-out brain, and sapless
 cinders.
 If I might augur, I should rate but low
Their chances;—they're too numerous,
 like the thirty
Mock tyrants, when Rome's annals wax'd
 but dirty.

LXII

This is the literary lower empire,
 Where the prætorian bands take up the
 matter;—
A 'dreadful trade,' like his who 'gathers
 samphire,'
 The insolent soldiery to soothe and
 flatter,
With the same feelings as you'd coax a
 vampire.
 Now, were I once at home, and in good
 satire,
I'd try conclusions with those Janizaries,
And show them what an intellectual war is.

795

LXIII

I think I know a trick or two, would turn
 Their flanks;—but it is hardly worth
 my while
With such small gear to give myself
 concern:
 Indeed I've not the necessary bile;
My natural temper's really aught but
 stern,
 And even my Muse's worst reproof's
 a smile;
And then she drops a brief and modern
 curtsy,
And glides away, assured she never hurts
 ye.

LXIV

My Juan, whom I left in deadly peril
 Amongst live poets and *blue* ladies,
 pass'd
With some small profit through that field
 so sterile,
 Being tired in time, and neither least
 nor last,
Left it before he had been treated very
 ill;
 And henceforth found himself more
 gaily class'd
Amongst the higher spirits of the day,
The sun's true son, no vapour, but a
 ray.

LXV

His morns he pass'd in business—which
 dissected,
 Was like all business, a laborious
 nothing
That leads to lassitude, the most infected
 And Centaur Nessus garb of mortal
 clothing,
And on our sofas makes us lie dejected,
 And talk in tender horrors of our
 loathing
All kinds of toil, save for our country's
 good—
Which grows no better, though 'tis time
 it should.

LXVI

His afternoons he pass'd in visits,
 luncheons,
 Lounging, and boxing; and the twilight
 hour
In riding round those vegetable puncheons
 Call'd 'Parks,' where there is neither
 fruit nor flower
Enough to gratify a bee's slight munch-
 ings;
 But after all it is the only 'bower'
(In Moore's phrase) where the fashionable
 fair
Can form a slight acquaintance with fresh
 air.

LXVII

Then dress, then dinner, then awakes the
 world!
 Then glare the lamps, then whirl the
 wheels, then roar
Through street and square fast flashing
 chariots hurl'd
 Like harness'd meteors; then along the
 floor
Chalk mimics painting; then festoons are
 twirl'd;
 Then roll the brazen thunders of the
 door,
Which opens to the thousand happy few
An earthly Paradise of *Or Molu*.

LXVIII

There stands the noble hostess, nor shall
 sink
 With the three-thousandth curtsy
 there the waltz,
The only dance which teaches girls to
 think,
 Makes one in love even with its very
 faults.
Saloon, room, hall, o'erflow beyond their
 brink,
 And long the latest of arrivals halts,
'Midst royal dukes and dames condemn'd
 to climb,
And gain an inch of staircase at a time.

LXIX

Thrice happy he who, after a survey
 Of the good company, can win a corner
A door that's *in* or boudoir *out* of the way
 Where he may fix himself like small
 'Jack Horner,'
And let the Babel round run as it may,
 And look on as a mourner, or a scorner
Or an approver, or a mere spectator,
Yawning a little as the night grows later

LXX

But this won't do, save by and by; and he
 Who, like Don Juan, takes an active
 share,
Must steer with care through all that
 glittering sea
 Of gems and plumes and pearls and
 silks, to where
He deems it is his proper place to be;
 Dissolving in the waltz to some soft air
Or proudlier prancing with mercurial skill
Where Science marshals forth her own
 quadrille.

LXXI

Or, if he dance not, but hath higher views
 Upon an heiress or his neighbour's
 bride,
Let him take care that that which he
 pursues
 Is not at once too palpably descried.

Full many an eager gentleman oft rues
 His haste; impatience is a blundering
 guide,
Amongst a people famous for reflection,
Who like to play the fool with circumspec-
 tion.

LXXII

But, if you can contrive, get next at
 supper;
 Or if forestall'd, get opposite and
 ogle:—
Oh, ye ambrosial moments! always upper
In mind, a sort of sentimental bogle,
Which sits for ever upon memory's
 crupper,
 The ghost of vanish'd pleasures once in
 vogue! Ill
Can tender souls relate the rise and fall
Of hopes and fears which shake a single
 ball.

LXXIII

But these precautionary hints can touch
 Only the common run, who must
 pursue,
And watch, and ward; whose plans a word
 too much
Or little overturns; and not the few
Or many (for the number's sometimes
 such)
 Whom a good mien, especially if new,
Or fame, or name, for wit, war, sense, or
 nonsense,
Permits whate'er they please, or *did* not
 long since.

LXXIV

Our hero, as a hero, young and handsome,
 Noble, rich, celebrated, and a stranger,
Like other slaves of course must pay his
 ransom,
 Before he can escape from so much
 danger
As will environ a conspicuous man. Some
 Talk about poetry, and 'rack and man-
 ger,'
And ugliness, disease, as toil and
 trouble;—
I wish they knew the life of a young noble.

LXXV

They are young, but know not youth—it
 is anticipated;
 Handsome but wasted, rich without a
 sou;
Their vigour in a thousand arms is dissi-
 pated;
 Their cash comes *from*, their wealth
 goes *to* a Jew;
Both senates see their nightly votes par-
 ticipated
 Between the tyrant's and the tribunes'
 crew;

And having voted, dined, drank, gamed,
 and whored,
The family vault receives another lord.

LXXVI

'Where is the world,' cries Young, 'at
 eighty? Where
 The world in which a man was born?'
 Alas!
Where is the world of *eight* years past?
 'Twas there—
 I look for it—'tis gone, a globe of glass!
Crack'd, shiver'd, vanish'd, scarcely
 gazed on, ere
 A silent change dissolves the glittering
 mass.
Statesmen, chiefs, orators, queens,
 patriots, kings,
And dandies, all are gone on the wind's
 wings.

LXXVII

Where is Napoleon the Grand? God
 knows:
 Where little Castlereagh? The devil
 can tell:
Where Grattan, Curran, Sheridan, all
 those
 Who bound the bar or senate in their
 spell?
Where is the unhappy Queen, with all her
 woes?
 And where the Daughter, whom the
 Isles loved well?
Where are those martyr'd saints the Five
 per Cents?
And where—oh, where the devil are the
 Rents?

LXXVIII

Where's Brummel? Dish'd. Where's Long
 Pole Wellesley? Diddled.
 Where's Whitbread? Romilly? Where's
 George the Third?
Where is his will? (That's not so soon
 unriddled.)
 And where is 'Fum' the Fourth, our
 'royal bird'?
Gone down, it seems, to Scotland to be
 fiddled
 Unto by Sawney's violin, we have heard:
'Caw me, caw thee'—for six months hath
 been hatching
This scene of royal itch and loyal scratch-
 ing.

LXXIX

Where is Lord This? And where my Lady
 That?
 The Honourable Mistresses and
 Misses?
Some laid aside like an old Opera hat,
 Married, unmarried, and remarried
 (this is

An evolution oft performed of late).
> Where are the Dublin shouts—and
> London hisses?
Where are the Grenvilles? Turn'd as
> usual. Where
My friends the Whigs? Exactly where
> they were.

LXXX

Where are the Lady Carolines and Fran-
> ceses?
> Divorced or doing thereanent. Ye
> annals
So brilliant, where the list of routs and
> dances is,—
> Thou Morning Post, sole record of the
> panels
Broken in carriages, and all the phantasies
> Of fashion,—say what streams now fill
> those channels?
Some die, some fly, some languish on the
> Continent,
Because the times have hardly left them
> *one* tenant.

LXXXI

Some who once set their caps at cautious
> dukes,
> Have taken up at length with younger
> brothers:
Some heiresses have bit at sharpers' hooks:
> Some maids have been made wives,
> some merely mothers:
Others have lost their fresh and fairy
> looks:
> In short, the list of alterations bothers:
There's little strange in this, but some-
> thing strange is
The unusual quickness of these common
> changes.

LXXXII

Talk not of seventy years as age; in seven
> I have seen more changes, down from
> monarchs to
The humblest individual under heaven,
> Than might suffice a moderate century
> through.
I knew that nought was lasting, but now
> even
> Change grows too changeable, without
> being new:
Nought's permanent among the human
> race,
Except the Whigs *not* getting into place.

LXXXIII

I have seen Napoleon, who seem'd quite
> a Jupiter,
> Shrink to a Saturn. I have seen a Duke
(No matter which) turn politician
> stupider,
> If that can well be, than his wooden
> look;

But it is time that I should hoist my 'blu
> Peter,'
> And sail for a new theme:—I have
> seen—and shook
To see it—the king hiss'd, and then caressed
But don't pretend to settle which wa
> best.

LXXXIV

I have seen the Landholders without a
> rap—
I have seen Joanna Southcote—I have
> seen
The House of Commons turn'd to a tax-
> trap—
I have seen that sad affair of the late
> Queen—
I have seen crowns worn instead of a fool's
> cap—
I have seen a Congress doing all that'
> mean—
I have seen some nations, like o'erloaded
> asses,
Kick off their burthens—meaning the
> high classes.

LXXXV

I have seen small poets, and great prosers,
> and
> Interminable—*not eternal*—speakers—
I have seen the funds at war with house
> and land—
> I have seen the country gentlemen turn
> squeakers—
I have seen the people ridden o'er like
> sand
> By slaves on horseback—I have seen
> malt liquors
Exchanged for 'thin potations' by John
> Bull—
I have seen John half detect himself a
> fool.—

LXXXVI

But '*carpe diem*,' Juan, '*carpe, carpe!*'
> To-morrow sees another race as gay
And transient, and devour'd by the same
> harpy.
'Life's a poor player,'—then 'play out
> the play,
Ye villains!' and above all keep a sharp
> eye
> Much less on what you do than what
> you say:
Be hypocritical, be cautious, be
Not what you *seem*, but always what you
> see.

LXXXVII

But how shall I relate in other cantos
> Of what befell our hero in the land,
Which 'tis the common cry and lie to
> vaunt as
> A moral country? But I hold my hand—

For I disdain to write an Atalantis;
 But 'tis as well at once to understand
You are *not* a moral people, and you know
 it
Without the aid of too sincere a poet.

LXXXVIII

What Juan saw and underwent shall be
 My topic, with of course the due
 restriction
Which is required by proper courtesy;
 And recollect the work is only fiction,
And that I sing of neither mine nor me,
 Though every scribe, in some slight
 turn of diction,
Will hint allusions never *meant*. Ne'er
 doubt
This—when I speak, I *don't hint*, but
 speak out.

LXXXIX

Whether he married with the third or
 fourth
 Offspring of some sage husband-
 hunting countess,
Or whether with some virgin of more
 worth
 (I mean in Fortune's matrimonial
 bounties),
He took to regularly peopling Earth,
 Of which your lawful, awful wedlock
 fount is,—
Or whether he was taken in for damages,
For being too excursive in his homages,—

XC

Is yet within the unread events of time.
 Thus far, go forth, thou lay, which I will
 back
Against the same given quantity of rhyme,
 For being as much the subject of attack
As ever yet was any work sublime,
 By those who love to say that white is
 black.
So much the better!—I may stand alone,
But would not change my free thoughts
 for a throne.

CANTO THE TWELFTH

I

OF all the barbarous middle ages, that
 Which is most barbarous is the middle
 age
Of man! it is—I really scarce know what;
 But when we hover between fool and
 sage,
And don't know justly what we would be
 at—
 A period something like a printed page,
Black letter upon foolscap, while our hair
Grows grizzled, and we are not what we
 were;—

II

Too old for youth,—too young, at thirty-
 five,
 To herd with boys, or hoard with good
 threescore,—
I wonder people should be left alive;
 But since they are, that epoch is a bore:
Love lingers still, although 'twere late to
 wive:
 And as for other love, the illusion's
 o'er;
And money, that most pure imagina-
 tion,
Gleams only through the dawn of its
 creation.

III

O Gold! Why call we misers miserable?
 Theirs is the pleasure that can never
 pall;
Theirs is the best bower anchor, the chain
 cable
 Which holds fast other pleasures great
 and small.
Ye who but see the saving man at table,
 And scorn his temperate board, as none
 at all,
And wonder how the wealthy can be
 sparing,
Know not what visions spring from each
 cheeseparing.

IV

Love or lust makes man sick, and wine
 much sicker;
 Ambition rends, and gaming gains a
 loss;
But making money, slowly first, then
 quicker,
 And adding still a little through each
 cross
(Which *will* come over things), beats love
 or liquor,
 The gamester's counter, or the states-
 man's *dross*.
O Gold! I still prefer thee unto paper,
Which makes bank credit like a bark of
 vapour.

V

Who hold the balance of the world? Who
 reign
 O'er congress, whether royalist or
 liberal?
Who rouse the shirtless patriots of Spain
 (That make old Europe's journals
 squeak and gibber all)?
Who keep the world, both old and new,
 in pain
 Or pleasure? Who make politics run
 glibber all?
The shade of Buonaparte's noble daring?
Jew Rothschild, and his fellow-Christian,
 Baring.

VI

Those, and the truly liberal Lafitte,
 Are the true lords of Europe. Every
 loan
Is not a merely speculative hit,
 But seats a nation or upsets a throne.
Republics also get involved a bit;
 Columbia's stock hath holders not
 unknown
On 'Change, and even thy silver soil, Peru,
Must get itself discounted by a Jew.

VII

Why call the miser miserable? as
 I said before: the frugal life is his,
Which in a saint or cynic ever was
 The theme of praise: a hermit would
 not miss
Canonization for the self-same cause,
 And wherefore blame gaunt wealth's
 austerities?
Because, you'll say, nought calls for such
 a trial;—
Then there's more merit in his self-denial.

VIII

He is your only poet;—passion, pure
 And sparkling on from heap to heap,
 displays,
Possess'd, the ore, of which *mere hopes*
 allure
 Nations athwart the deep: the golden
 rays
Flash up in ingots from the mine obscure:
 On him the diamond pours its brilliant
 blaze,
While the mild emerald's beam shades
 down the dies
Of other stones, to soothe the miser's eyes.

IX

The lands on either side are his; the ship
 From Ceylon, Inde, or far Cathay,
 unloads
For him the fragrant produce of each trip;
 Beneath his cars of Ceres groan the
 roads,
And the vine blushes like Aurora's lip;
 His very cellars might be kings' abodes;
While he, despising every sensual call,
Commands—the intellectual lord of *all.*

X

Perhaps he hath great projects in his mind,
 To build a college, or to found a race,
A hospital, a church,—and leave behind
 Some dome surmounted by his meagre
 face:
Perhaps he fain would liberate mankind
 Even with the very ore which makes
 them base:
Perhaps he would be wealthiest of his
 nation,
Or revel in the joys of calculation.

XI

But whether all, or each, or none of
 these
 May be the hoarder's principle of
 action,
The fool will call such mania a disease:—
 What is his *own*? Go—look at each
 transaction,
Wars, revels, loves—do these bring men
 more ease
 Than the mere plodding through each
 'vulgar fraction'?
Or do they benefit mankind? Lean miser!
Let spendthrifts' heirs inquire of yours—
 who's wiser?

XII

How beauteous are rouleaus! how charm-
 ing chests
 Containing ingots, bags of dollars, coins
(Not of old victors, all whose heads and
 crests
 Weigh not the thin ore where their
 visage shines,
But) of fine unclipt gold, where dully rests
 Some likeness, which the glittering
 cirque confines,
Of modern, reigning, sterling, stupid
 stamp:
Yes! ready money *is* Aladdin's lamp.

XIII

'Love rules the camp, the court, the grove,
 —for love
 Is heaven, and heaven is love':—so
 sings the bard;
Which it were rather difficult to prove
 (A thing with poetry in general hard).
Perhaps there may be something in 'the
 grove,'
 At least it rhymes to 'love:' but I'm
 prepared
To doubt (no less than landlords of their
 rental)
If 'courts' and 'camps' be quite so senti-
 mental.

XIV

But if Love don't, *Cash* does, and Cash
 alone:
 Cash rules the grove, and fells it too
 beside;
Without cash, camps were thin, and
 courts were none;
 Without cash, Malthus tells you—
 'take no brides.'
So Cash rules Love the ruler, on his own
 High ground, as virgin Cynthia sways
 the tides:
And as for 'Heaven being Love,' why not
 say honey
Is wax? Heaven is not Love, 'tis Matri-
 mony.

XV

Is not all love prohibited whatever,
 Excepting marriage? which is love, no
 doubt,
After a sort; but somehow people never
 With the same thought the two words
 have help'd out.
Love may exist *with* marriage, and *should*
 ever,
 And marriage also may exist without;
But love *sans* banns is both a sin and shame,
 And ought to go by quite another name.

XVI

Now if the 'court,' and 'camp,' and
 'grove,' be not
 Recruited all with constant married men,
Who never coveted their neighbour's lot,
 I say *that* line's a lapsus of the pen;—
Strange too in my *buon camerado* Scott,
 So celebrated for his morals, when
My Jeffrey held him up as an example
To me;—of which these morals are a sample.

XVII

Well, if I don't succeed, I *have* succeeded,
 And that's enough; succeeded in my
 youth,
The only time when much success is
 needed:
 And my success produced what I, in
 sooth,
Cared most about; it need not now be
 pleaded—
 Whate'er it was, 'twas mine; I've paid,
 in truth,
Of late, the penalty of such success,
But have not learn'd to wish it any less.

XVIII

That suit in Chancery,—which some
 persons plead
 In an appeal to the unborn, whom they,
In the faith of their procreative creed,
 Baptize posterity, or future clay,—
To me seems but a dubious kind of reed
 To lean on for support in any way;
Since odds are that posterity will know
No more of them, than they of her, I trow.

XIX

Why, I'm posterity—and so are you;
 And whom do we remember? Not a
 hundred.
Were every memory written down all true,
 The tenth or twentieth name would be
 but blundered;
Even Plutarch's Lives have but pick'd out
 a few,
 And 'gainst those few your annalists
 have thunder'd;
And Mitford in the nineteenth century
Gives, with Greek truth, the good old
 Greek the lie.

XX

Good people all, of every degree,
 Ye gentle readers and ungentle writers,
In this twelfth Canto 'tis my wish to be
 As serious as if I had for inditers
Malthus and Wilberforce:—the last set
 free
 The Negroes, and is worth a million
 fighters;
While Wellington has but enslaved the
 Whites,
And Malthus does the thing 'gainst which
 he writes.

XXI

I'm serious—so are all men upon paper;
 And why should I not form my specula-
 tion,
And hold up to the sun my little taper?
 Mankind just now seem wrapt in
 meditation
On constitutions and steam-boats of
 vapour;
 While sages write against all pro-
 creation,
Unless a man can calculate his means
Of feeding brats the moment his wife
 weans.

XXII

That's noble! That's romantic! For my
 part,
 I think that 'Philo-genitiveness' is—
(Now here's a word quite after my own
 heart,
 Though there's a shorter a good deal
 than this
If that politeness set it not apart;
 But I'm resolved to say nought that's
 amiss)—
I say, methinks that 'Philo-genitiveness'
Might meet from men a little more forgive-
 ness.

XXIII

And now to business.—O my gentle Juan!
 Thou art in London—in that pleasant
 place,
Where every kind of mischief's daily brew-
 ing,
 Which can await warm youth in its wild
 race.
'Tis true, that thy career is not a new one;
 Thou art no novice in the headlong
 chase
Of early life; but this is a new land,
Which foreigners can never understand.

XXIV

What with a small diversity of climate,
 Of hot or cold, mercurial or sedate,
I could send forth my mandate like a
 primate
 Upon the rest of Europe's social state;

But thou art the most difficult to rhyme at,
 Great Britain, which the Muse may
 penetrate.
All countries have their 'Lions,' but in
 thee
There is but one superb menagerie.

XXV

But I am sick of politics. Begin,
 '*Paulo Majora.*' Juan, undecided
Amongst the paths of being 'taken in,'
 Above the ice had like a skater glided:
When tired of play, he flirted without sin
 With some of those fair creatures who
 have prided
Themselves on innocent tantalisation,
And hate all vice except its reputation.

XXVI

But these are few, and in the end they
 make
 Some devilish escapade or stir, which
 shows
That even the purest people may mistake
 Their way through virtue's primrose
 paths of snows;
And then men stare, as if a new ass spake
 To Balaam, and from tongue to ear
 o'erflows
Quicksilver small talk, ending (if you note
 it)
With the kind world's amen—'Who
 would have thought it?'

XXVII

The little Leila, with her Orient eyes,
 And taciturn Asiatic disposition,
(Which saw all Western things with small
 surprise,
 To the surprise of people of condition,
Who think that novelties are butterflies
 To be pursued as food for inanition,)
Her charming figure and romantic history
Became a kind of fashionable mystery.

XXVIII

The women much divided—as is usual
 Amongst the sex in little things or great.
Think not, fair creatures, that I mean to
 abuse you all—
 I have always liked you better than I
 state:
Since I've grown moral, still I must accuse
 you all
 Of being apt to talk at a great rate;
And now there was a general sensation
Amongst you, about Leila's education.

XXIX

In one point only were you settled—and
 You had reason; 'twas that a young
 child of grace,
As beautiful as her own native land,
 And far away, the last bud of her race,

Howe'er our friend Don Juan might com-
 mand
 Himself for five, four, three, or two
 years' space,
Would be much better taught beneath the
 eye
Of peeresses whose follies had run dry.

XXX

So first there was a generous emulation,
 And then there was a general competi-
 tion,
To undertake the orphan's education.
 As Juan was a person of condition,
It had been an affront on this occasion
 To talk of a subscription or petition;
But sixteen dowagers, ten unwed she
 sages,
Whose tale belongs to 'Hallam's Middle
 Ages,'

XXXI

And one or two sad, separate wives, with-
 out
 A fruit to bloom upon their withering
 bough—
Begg'd to bring *up* the little girl, and
 '*out*,'—
For that's the phrase that settles all
 things now,
Meaning a virgin's first blush at a rout,
 And all her points as thorough-bred to
 show:
And I assure you, that like virgin honey
Tastes their first season (mostly if they
 have money).

XXXII

How all the needy honourable misters,
 Each out-at-elbow peer, or desperate
 dandy,
The watchful mothers, and the careful
 sisters,
 (Who, by the by, when clever, are more
 handy
At making matches, where ''tis gold that
 glisters,'
 Than their *he* relatives), like flies o'er
 candy
Buzz round 'the Fortune' with their busy
 battery,
To turn her head with waltzing and with
 flattery!

XXXIII

Each aunt, each cousin, hath her specula-
 tion;
 Nay, married dames will now and then
 discover
Such pure disinterestedness of passion,
 I've known them court an heiress for
 their lover.

'*Tantæne!*' Such the virtues of high
 station,
 Even in the hopeful Isle, whose outlet's
 'Dover!'
While the poor rich wretch, object of these
 cares,
 Has cause to wish her sire had had male
 heirs.

XXXIV

Some are soon bagg'd, and some reject
 three dozen.
 'Tis fine to see them scattering refusals
And wild dismay o'er every angry cousin
 (Friends of the party), who begin
 accusals
Such as—'Unless Miss (Blank) meant to
 have chosen
 Poor Frederick, why did she accord
 perusals
To his billets? *Why* waltz with him? Why,
 I pray,
 Look *yes* last night, and yet say *no* to-day?

XXXV

'Why?—Why?—Besides, Fred really was
 attach'd;
 'Twas not her fortune—he has enough
 without:
The time will come she'll wish that she
 had snatch'd
 So good an opportunity, no doubt:—
But the old Marchioness some plan had
 hatch'd,
 As I'll tell Aurea at to-morrow's rout:
And after all poor Frederick may do
 better—
Pray did you see her answer to his letter?'

XXXVI

Smart uniforms and sparkling coronets
 Are spurn'd in turn, until her turn arrives,
After male loss of time, and hearts, and bets
 Upon the sweepstakes for substantial
 wives;
And when at last the pretty creature gets
 Some gentleman, who fights, or writes,
 or drives,
It soothes the awkward squad of the rejected
To find how very badly she selected.

XXXVII

For sometimes they accept some long
 pursuer,
 Worn out with importunity; or fall
(But here perhaps the instances are fewer)
 To the lot of him who scarce pursued
 at all.
A hazy widower turn'd of forty's sure
 (If 'tis not vain examples to recall)
To draw a high prize: now, howe'er he got
 her, I
See nought more strange in this than
 t'other lottery.

XXXVIII

I, for my part—(one 'modern instance'
 more,
 'True, 'tis a pity—pity 'tis, 'tis true')—
Was chosen from out an amatory score,
 Albeit my years were less discreet than
 few;
But though I also had reform'd before
 Those became one who soon were to be
 two,
I'll not gainsay the generous public's
 voice,
That the young lady made a monstrous
 choice.

XXXIX

Oh, pardon me digression—or at least
 Peruse! 'Tis always with a moral end
That I dissert, like grace before a feast:
 For like an aged aunt, or tiresome
 friend,
A rigid guardian, or a zealous priest,
 My Muse by exhortation means to
 mend
All people, at all times, and in most places,
Which puts my Pegasus to these grave
 paces.

XL

But now I'm going to be immoral; now
 I mean to show things really as they are,
Not as they ought to be: for I avow,
 That till we see what's what in fact,
 we're far
From much improvement with that
 virtuous plough
 Which skims the surface, leaving scarce
 a scar
Upon the black loam long manured by
 Vice,
Only to keep its corn at the old price.

XLI

But first of little Leila we'll dispose;
 For like a day-dawn she was young and
 pure,
Or like the old comparison of snows,
 Which are more pure than pleasant to
 be sure.
Like many people everybody knows,
 Don Juan was delighted to secure
A goodly guardian for his infant charge,
Who might not profit much by being at
 large.

XLII

Besides, he had found out that he was no
 tutor
 (I wish that others would find out the
 same),
And rather wish'd in such things to stand
 neuter,
 For silly wards will bring their
 guardians blame:

So when he saw each ancient dame a
 suitor
 To make his little wild Asiatic tame,
Consulting 'the Society for Vice
Suppression,' Lady Pinchbeck was his
 choice.

XLIII

Olden she was—but had been very young:
 Virtuous she was—and had been, I
 believe;
Although the world has such an evil
 tongue
 That——but my chaster ear will not
 receive
An echo of a syllable that's wrong;
 In fact, there's nothing makes me so
 much grieve,
As that abominable tittle-tattle,
Which is the cud eschew'd by human cattle.

XLIV

Moreover I've remark'd (and I was once
 A slight observer in a modest way),
And so may every one except a dunce,
 That ladies in their youth a little gay,
Besides their knowledge of the world, and
 sense
 Of the sad consequence of going astray,
Are wiser in their warnings 'gainst the woe
Which the mere passionless can never
 know.

XLV

While the harsh prude indemnifies her
 virtue
 By railing at the unknown and envied
 passion,
Seeking far less to save you than to hurt
 you,
 Or, what's still worse, to put you out of
 fashion,—
The kinder veteran with calm words will
 court you,
 Entreating you to pause before you
 dash on;
Expounding and illustrating the riddle
Of epic Love's beginning, end, and middle.

XLVI

Now whether it be thus, or that they are
 stricter,
 As better knowing why they should be so,
I think you'll find from many a family
 picture,
 That daughters of such mothers as may
 know
The world by experience rather than by
 lecture,
 Turn out much better for the Smithfield
 Show
Of vestals brought into the marriage mart,
Than those bred up by prudes without a
 heart.

XLVII

I said that Lady Pinchbeck had been talk'd
 about—
 As who has not, if female, young, and
 pretty?
But now no more the ghost of Scandal
 stalk'd about;
 She merely was deem'd amiable and
 witty,
And several of her best *bons-mots* were
 hawk'd about:
 Then was she given to charity and pity,
And pass'd (at least the latter years of life)
For being a most exemplary wife.

XLVIII

High in high circles, gentle in her own,
 She was the mild reprover of the young,
Whenever—which means every day—
 they'd shown
 An awkward inclination to go wrong.
The quantity of good she did's unknown,
 Or at the least would lengthen out my
 song:
In brief, the little orphan of the East
Had raised an interest in her, which
 increased.

XLIX

Juan, too, was a sort of favourite with her,
 Because she thought him a good heart
 at bottom,
A little spoil'd, but not so altogether;
 Which was a wonder, if you think who
 got him,
And how he had been toss'd, he scarce
 knew whither:
 Though this might ruin others, it did
 not him,
At least entirely—for he had seen too
 many
Changes in youth, to be surprised at any.

L

And these vicissitudes tell best in youth;
 For when they happen at a riper age,
People are apt to blame the Fates, for-
 sooth,
 And wonder Providence is not more
 sage.
Adversity is the first path to truth:
 He who hath proved war, storm, or
 woman's rage,
Whether his winters be eighteen or eighty,
Hath won the experience which is deem'd
 so weighty.

LI

How far it profits is another matter.—
 Our hero gladly saw his little charge
Safe with a lady, whose last grown-up
 daughter
 Being long married, and thus set at
 large,

Had left all the accomplishments she
 taught her
 To be transmitted, like the Lord
 Mayor's barge,
To the next comer; or—as it will tell
More Muse-like—like to Cytherea's shell.

LII

I call such things transmission; for there is
 A floating balance of accomplishment,
Which forms a pedigree from Miss to Miss,
 According as their minds or backs are
 bent.
Some waltz; some draw; some fathom the
 abyss
 Of metaphysics; others are content
With music; the most moderate shine as
 wits;
While others have a genius turn'd for fits.

LIII

But whether fits, or wits, or harpsichords,
 Theology, fine arts, or finer stays,
May be the baits for gentlemen or lords
 With regular descent, in these our days,
The last year to the new transfers its
 hoards;
 New vestals claim men's eyes with the
 same praise
Of 'elegant' *et cætera*, in fresh batches—
All matchless creatures, and yet bent on
 matches.

LIV

But now I will begin my poem. 'Tis
 Perhaps a little strange, if not quite new,
That from the first of Cantos up to this
 I've not begun what we have to go
 through.
These first twelve books are merely
 flourishes,
Preludios, trying just a string or two
Upon my lyre, or making the pegs sure;
And when so, you shall have the overture.

LV

My Muses do not care a pinch of rosin
 About what's call'd success, or not
 succeeding:
Such thoughts are quite below the strain
 they have chosen;
 'Tis a 'great moral lesson' they are
 reading.
I thought, at setting off, about two dozen
 Cantos would do; but at Apollo's
 pleading,
If that my Pegasus should not be
 founder'd,
I think to canter gently through a hundred.

LVI

Don Juan saw that microcosm on stilts,
 Yclept the Great World; for it is the
 least,

Although the highest: but as swords have
 hilts
 By which their power of mischief is
 increased,
When man in battle or in quarrel tilts,
 Thus the low world, north, south, or
 west, or east,
Must still obey the high—which is their
 handle,
Their moon, their sun, their gas, their
 farthing candle.

LVII

He had many friends who had many wives,
 and was
 Well look'd upon by both, to that extent
Of friendship which you may accept or
 pass,
 It does nor good, nor harm: being
 merely meant
To keep the wheels going of the higher
 class,
 And draw them nightly when a ticket's
 sent;
And what with masquerades, and fêtes,
 and balls,
For the first season such a life scarce palls.

LVIII

A young unmarried man, with a good name
 And fortune, has an awkward part to
 play;
For good society is but a game,
 'The royal game of Goose,' as I may
 say,
Where everybody has some separate aim,
 An end to answer, or a plan to lay—
The single ladies wishing to be double,
The married ones to save the virgins
 trouble.

LIX

I don't mean this as general, but particular
 Examples may be found of such
 pursuits:
Though several also keep their perpendi-
 cular
 Like poplars, with good principles for
 roots;
Yet many have a method more *reticular*—
 'Fishers for men,' like sirens with soft
 lutes:
For talk six times with the same single lady,
And you may get the wedding dresses ready.

LX

Perhaps you'll have a letter from the
 mother,
 To say her daughter's feelings are tre-
 pann'd;
Perhaps you'll have a visit from the
 brother,
 All strut, and stays, and whiskers, to
 demand

What 'your intentions are?'—One way
or other
 It seems the virgin's heart expects your
 hand:
And between pity for her case and yours,
You'll add to Matrimony's list of cures.

LXI

I've known a dozen weddings made even
thus,
 And some of them high names: I have
 also known
Young men who—though they hated to
discuss
 Pretensions which they never dream'd
 to have shown—
Yet neither frighten'd by a female fuss,
 Nor by mustachios moved, were let alone,
And lived, as did the broken-hearted fair,
In happier plight than if they form'd a pair.

LXII

There's also nightly, to the uninitiated,
 A peril—not indeed like love or
 marriage,
But not the less for this to be depreciated:
 It is—I meant and mean not to dis-
 parage
The show of virtue even in the vitiated—
 It adds an outward grace unto their
 carriage—
But to denounce the amphibious sort of
harlot,
Couleur de rose, who's neither white nor
scarlet.

LXIII

Such is your cold coquette, who can't say
'No,'
 And won't say 'Yes,' and keeps you on
 and off-ing
On a lee-shore, till it begins to blow—
 Then sees your heart wreck'd with an
 inward scoffing.
This works a world of sentimental woe,
 And sends new Werters yearly to their
 coffin;
But yet is merely innocent flirtation,
Not quite adultery, but adulteration.

LXIV

'Ye gods, I grow a talker!' Let us prate.
 The next of perils, though I place it
 *stern*est,
Is when, without regard to 'church or state,'
 A wife makes or takes love in upright
 earnest.
Abroad, such things decide few women's
fate—
 (Such, early traveller! is the truth thou
 learnest)—
But in old England, when a young bride
errs,
Poor thing! Eve's was a trifling case to
hers.

LXV

For 'tis a low, newspaper, humdrum, law-
suit
 Country, where a young couple of the
 same ages
Can't form a friendship, but the world
o'erawes it.
 Then there's the vulgar trick of those
 d——d damages!
A verdict—grievous foe to those who
cause it!—
 Forms a sad climax to romantic
 homages;
Besides those soothing speeches of the
pleaders,
And evidences which regale all readers.

LXVI

But they who blunder thus are raw
beginners;
 A little genial sprinkling of hypocrisy
Has saved the fame of thousand splendid
sinners,
 The loveliest oligarchs of our gyno-
 cracy;
You may see such at all the balls and
dinners,
 Among the proudest of our aristocracy,
So gentle, charming, charitable, chaste—
And all by having *tact* as well as taste.

LXVII

Juan, who did not stand in the predica-
ment
 Of a mere novice, had one safeguard
 more;
For he was sick—no, 'twas not the word
sick I meant—
 But he had seen so much good love
 before,
That he was not in heart so very weak;—
I meant
 But thus much, and no sneer against the
 shore
Of white cliffs, white necks, blue eyes,
bluer stockings,
Tithes, taxes, duns, and doors with double
knockings.

LXVIII

But coming young from lands and scenes
romantic,
 Where lives, not lawsuits, must be
 risk'd for Passion,
And Passion's self must have a spice of
frantic,
 Into a country where 'tis half a fashion,
Seem'd to him half commercial, half
pedantic,
 Howe'er he might esteem this moral
 nation:
Besides (alas! his taste—forgive and pity!)
At *first* he did not think the women pretty.

LXIX

I say at *first*—for he found out at *last*,
 But by degrees, that they were fairer far
Than the more glowing dames whose lot
 is cast
Beneath the influence of the eastern star.
A further proof we should not judge in
 haste;
 Yet inexperience could not be his bar
To taste:—the truth is, if men would con-
 fess,
That novelties *please* less than they
 impress.

LXX

Though travell'd, I have never had the
 luck to
Trace up those shuffling negroes, Nile
 or Niger,
To that impracticable place Timbuctoo,
 Where Geography finds no one to oblige
 her
With such a chart as may be safely stuck
 to—
 For Europe ploughs in Afric like '*bos
 piger*';
But if I *had been* at Timbuctoo, there
No doubt I should be told that black is
 fair.

LXXI

It is. I will not swear that black is white;
 But I suspect in fact that white is black,
And the whole matter rests upon eye-
 sight.
 Ask a blind man, the best judge. You'll
 attack
Perhaps this new position—but I'm right;
 Or if I'm wrong, I'll not be ta'en
 aback:—
He hath no morn nor night, but all is dark
Within; and what seest thou? A dubious
 spark.

LXXII

But I'm relapsing into metaphysics,
 That labyrinth, whose clue is of the same
Construction as your cures for hectic
 phthisics,
 Those bright moths fluttering round a
 dying flame:
And this reflection brings me to plain
 physics,
 And to the beauties of a foreign dame,
Compared with those of our pure pearls of
 price,
Those polar summers, *all* sun, and some
 ice.

LXXIII

Or say they are like virtuous mermaids,
 whose
 Beginnings are fair faces, ends mere
 fishes;—

Not that there's not a quantity of those
 Who have a due respect for their own
 wishes.
Like Russians rushing from hot baths to
 snows
 Are they, at bottom virtuous even when
 vicious;
They warm into a scrape, but keep of course,
As a reserve, a plunge into remorse.

LXXIV

But this has nought to do with their out-
 sides.
 I said that Juan did not think them pretty
At the first blush; for a fair Briton hides
 Half her attractions—probably from
 pity—
And rather calmly into the heart glides,
 Than storms it as a foe would take a
 city;
But once *there* (if you doubt this, prithee try)
She keeps it for you like a true ally.

LXXV

She cannot step as does an Arab barb,
 Or Andalusian girl from mass returning,
Nor wear as gracefully as Gauls her garb,
 Nor in her eye Ausonia's glance is burn-
 ing;
Her voice, though sweet, is not so fit to warb-
 le those *bravuras* (which I still am
 learning
To like, though I have been seven years in
 Italy,
And have, or had, an ear that served me
 prettily);—

LXXVI

She cannot do these things, nor one or two
 Others, in that off-hand and dashing
 style
Which takes so much—to give the devil
 his due;
 Nor is she quite so ready with her smile,
Nor settles all things in one interview
 (A thing approved as saving time and
 toil);—
But though the soil may give you time and
 trouble,
Well cultivated, it will render double.

LXXVII

And if in fact she takes to a *grande
 passion*,
 It is a very serious thing indeed:
Nine times in ten 'tis but caprice or
 fashion,
 Coquetry, or a wish to take the lead,
The pride of a mere child with a new sash
 on,
 Or wish to make a rival's bosom bleed:
But the *tenth* instance will be a tornado,
For there's no saying what they will or
 may do.

LXXVIII

The reason's obvious: if there's an *éclat*,
 They lose their caste at once, as do the
 Parias;
And when the delicacies of the law
 Have fill'd their papers with their com-
 ments various,
Society, that china without flaw,
 (The hypocrite!) will banish them like
 Marius,
To sit amidst the ruins of their guilt:
For Fame's a Carthage not so soon
 rebuilt.

LXXIX

Perhaps this is as it should be;—it is
 A comment on the Gospel's 'Sin no
 more,
And be thy sins forgiven';—but upon this
 I leave the saints to settle their own
 score.
Abroad, though doubtless they do much
 amiss,
 An erring woman finds an opener door
For her return to Virtue—as they call
That lady, who should be at home to all.

LXXX

For me, I leave the matter where I find it,
 Knowing that such uneasy virtue leads
People some ten times less in fact to mind
 it,
 And care but for discoveries, and not
 deeds.
And as for chastity, you'll never bind it
 By all the laws the strictest lawyer
 pleads,
But aggravate the crime you have not
 prevented,
By rendering desperate those who had
 else repented.

LXXXI

But Juan was no casuist, nor had ponder'd
 Upon the moral lessons of mankind:
Besides, he had not seen of several
 hundred
 A lady altogether to his mind.
A little *blasé*—'tis not to be wonder'd
 At, that his heart had got a tougher
 rind:
And though not vainer from his past
 success,
No doubt his sensibilities were less.

LXXXII

He also had been busy seeing sights—
 The Parliament and all the other
 houses;
Had sat beneath the gallery at nights,
 To hear debates whose thunder *roused*
 (not *rouses*)

The world to gaze upon those northern
 lights,
 Which flash'd as far as where the musk-
 bull browses;
He had also stood at times behind the
 throne—
But Grey was not arrived, and Chatham
 gone.

LXXXIII

He saw, however, at the closing session,
 That noble sight, when *really* free the
 nation,
A king in constitutional possession
 Of such a throne as is the proudest
 station,
Though despots know it not—till the pro-
 gression
 Of freedom shall complete their educa-
 tion.
'Tis not mere splendour makes the show
 august
To eye or heart—it is the people's trust.

LXXXIV

There, too, he saw (whate'er he may be
 now)
 A Prince, the prince of princes at the
 time,
With fascination in his very bow,
 And full of promise, as the spring of
 prime.
Though royalty was written on his brow,
 He had *then* the grace, too, rare in
 every clime,
Of being, without alloy of fop or beau,
A finish'd gentleman from top to toe.

LXXXV

And Juan was received, as hath been said,
 Into the best society; and there
Occurr'd what often happens, I'm afraid,
 However disciplined and debonnaire:—
The talent and good humour he display'd,
 Besides the mark'd distinction of his
 air,
Exposed him, as was natural, to tempta-
 tion,
Even though himself avoided the occasion.

LXXXVI

But what, and where, with whom, and
 when, and why,
 Is not to be put hastily together;
And as my object is morality
 (Whatever people say), I don't know
 whether
I'll leave a single reader's eyelid dry,
 But harrow up his feelings till they
 wither,
And hew out a huge monument of pathos,
As Philip's son proposed to do with Athos.

LXXXVII

Here the twelfth Canto of our introduction
 Ends. When the body of the book's
 begun,
You'll find it of a different construction
 From what some people say 'twill be
 when done;
The plan at present's simply in concoction.
 I can't oblige you, reader, to read on;
That's your affair, not mine: a real spirit
Should neither court neglect, nor dread
 to bear it.

LXXXVIII

And if my thunderbolt not always rattles,
 Remember, reader! you have had
 before
The worst of tempests and the best of
 battles,
 That e'er were brew'd from elements or
 gore,
Besides the most sublime of—Heaven
 knows what else;
 An usurer could scarce expect much
 more—
But my best canto, save one on astronomy,
Will turn upon 'political economy.'

LXXXIX

That is your present theme for popularity:
 Now that the public hedge hath scarce
 a stake,
It grows an act of patriotic charity,
 To show the people the best way to
 break.
My plan (but I, if but for singularity,
 Reserve it) will be very sure to take.
Meantime, read all the national-debt
 sinkers,
And tell me what you think of your great
 thinkers.

CANTO THE THIRTEENTH

I

I NOW mean to be serious;—it is time,
 Since laughter now-a-days is deem'd
 too serious;
A jest at Vice by Virtue's call'd a crime,
 And critically held as deleterious:
Besides, the sad's a source of the sublime,
 Although when long a little apt to
 weary us;
And therefore shall my lay soar high and
 solemn,
As an old temple dwindled to a column.

II

The Lady Adeline Amundeville
 ('Tis an old Norman name, and to be
 found
In pedigrees, by those who wander still
 Along the last fields of that Gothic
 ground)

Was high-born, wealthy by her father's
 will,
 And beauteous, even where beauties
 most abound,
In Britain—which of course true patriots
 find
The goodliest soil of body and of mind.

III

I'll not gainsay them; it is not my cue;
 I'll leave them to their taste, no doubt
 the best:
An eye's an eye, and whether black or
 blue,
 Is no great matter, so 'tis in request;
'Tis nonsense to dispute about a hue—
 The kindest may be taken as a test.
The fair sex should be always fair; and no
 man
Till thirty, should perceive there's a plain
 woman.

IV

And after that serene and somewhat dull
 Epoch, that awkward corner turn'd for
 days
More quiet, when our moon's no more at
 full,
 We may presume to criticise or praise;
Because indifference begins to lull
 Our passions, and we walk in wisdom's
 ways;
Also because the figure and the face
Hint, that 'tis time to give the younger
 place.

V

I know that some would fain postpone
 this era,
 Reluctant as all placemen to resign
Their post; but theirs is merely a chimera,
 For they have pass'd life's equinoctial
 line:
But then they have their claret and
 Madeira
 To irrigate the dryness of decline;
And county meetings, and the parliament,
And debt, and what not, for their solace
 sent.

VI

And is there not religion, and reform,
 Peace, war, the taxes, and what's called
 the 'Nation'?
The struggle to be pilots in a storm?
 The landed and the monied specula-
 tion?
The joys of mutual hate to keep them
 warm,
 Instead of love, that mere hallucina-
 tion?
Now hatred is by far the longest pleasure;
Men love in haste, but they detest at
 leisure.

VII

Rough Johnson, the great moralist, profess'd,
 Right honestly, 'he liked an honest hater!'—
The only truth that yet has been confest
 Within these latest thousand years or later.
Perhaps the fine old fellow spoke in jest:—
 For my part, I am but a mere spectator,
And gaze where'er the palace or the hovel is,
Much in the mode of Goethe's Mephistopheles;

VIII

But neither love nor hate in much excess;
 Though 'twas not once so. If I sneer sometimes,
It is because I cannot well do less,
 And now and then it also suits my rhymes.
I should be very willing to redress
 Men's wrongs, and rather check than punish crimes,
Had not Cervantes, in that too true tale
Of Quixote, shown how all such efforts fail.

IX

Of all tales 'tis the saddest—and more sad,
 Because it makes us smile: his hero's right,
And still pursues the right;—to curb the bad
 His only object, and 'gainst odds to fight
His guerdon: 'tis his virtue makes him mad!
 But his adventures form a sorry sight;—
A sorrier still is the great moral taught
By that real epic unto all who have thought.

X

Redressing injury, revenging wrong,
 To aid the damsel and destroy the caitiff;
Opposing singly the united strong,
 From foreign yoke to free the helpless native:—
Alas! must noblest views, like an old song,
 Be for mere fancy's sport a theme creative,
A jest, a riddle, Fame through thin and thick sought!
And Socrates himself but Wisdom's Quixote?

XI

Cervantes smiled Spain's chivalry away;
 A single laugh demolish'd the right arm
Of his own country;—seldom since that day
 Has Spain had heroes. While Romance could charm,

The world gave ground before her bright array;
 And therefore have his volumes done such harm,
That all their glory, as a composition,
Was dearly purchased by his land's perdition.

XII

I'm 'at my old lunes'—digression, and forget
 The Lady Adeline Amundeville;
The fair most fatal Juan ever met,
 Although she was not evil nor meant ill;
But Destiny and Passion spread the net
 (Fate is a good excuse for our own will),
And caught them;—what do they *not* catch methinks?
But I'm not Œdipus, and life's a Sphinx.

XIII

I tell the tale as it is told, nor dare
 To venture a solution: '*Davus sum!*'
And now I will proceed upon the pair.
 Sweet Adeline, amidst the gay world's hum,
Was the Queen-Bee, the glass of all that's fair;
 Whose charms made all men speak, and women dumb.
The last's a miracle, and such was reckon'd,
And since that time there has not been a second.

XIV

Chaste was she, to detraction's desperation,
 And wedded unto one she had loved well—
A man known in the councils of the nation,
 Cool, and quite English, imperturbable,
Though apt to act with fire upon occasion,
 Proud of himself and her: the world could tell
Nought against either, and both seem'd secure—
She in her virtue, he in his hauteur.

XV

It chanced some diplomatical relations,
 Arising out of business, often brought
Himself and Juan in their mutual stations
 Into close contact. Though reserved, nor caught
By specious seeming, Juan's youth, and patience,
 And talent, on his haughty spirit wrought,
And form'd a basis of esteem, which ends
In making men what courtesy calls friends.

XVI

And thus Lord Henry, who was cautious as
　Reserve and pride could make him, and
　　full slow
In judging men—when once his judgment
　　was
　Determined, right or wrong, on friend
　　or foe,
Had all the pertinacity pride has,
　Which knows no ebb to its imperious
　　flow,
And loves or hates, disdaining to be guided,
Because its own good pleasure hath
　　decided.

XVII

His friendships, therefore, and no less
　　aversions,
　Though oft well founded, which con-
　　firm'd but more
His prepossessions, like the laws of
　　Persians
　And Medes, would ne'er revoke what
　　went before.
His feelings had not those strange fits, like
　　tertians,
　Of common likings, which make some
　　deplore
What they should laugh at—the mere ague
　　still
Of men's regard, the fever or the chill.

XVIII

''Tis not in mortals to command success:
　But *do you more*, Sempronius—*don't*
　　deserve it,'
And take my word, you won't have any less.
　Be wary, watch the time, and always
　　serve it;
Give gently way, when there's too great a
　　press;
　And for your conscience only learn to
　　nerve it,
For, like a racer, or a boxer training,
'Twill make, if proved, vast efforts without
　　paining.

XIX

Lord Henry also liked to be superior,
　As most men do, the little or the great;
The very lowest find out an inferior,
　At least they think so, to exert their state
Upon: for there are very few things wearier
　Than solitary Pride's oppressive weight,
Which mortals generously would divide,
By bidding others carry while they ride.

XX

In birth, in rank, in fortune likewise equal,
　O'er Juan he could no distinction claim;
In years he had the advantage of time's
　　sequel,
　And, as he thought, in country much
　　the same—

Because bold Britons have a tongue and
　　free quill,
　At which all modern nations vainly aim;
And the Lord Henry was a great debater,
So that few members kept the House up
　　later.

XXI

These were advantages: and then he
　　thought—
　It was his foible, but by no means sinis-
　　ter—
That few or none more than himself had
　　caught
　Court mysteries, having been himself a
　　minister:
He liked to teach that which he had been
　　taught,
　And greatly shone whenever there had
　　been a stir;
And reconciled all qualities which grace
　　man,
Always a patriot, and sometimes a place-
　　man.

XXII

He liked the gentle Spaniard for his
　　gravity;
　He almost honour'd him for his
　　docility;
Because, though young, he acquiesced
　　with suavity,
　Or contradicted but with proud
　　humility.
He knew the world, and would not see
　　depravity
　In faults which sometimes show the
　　soil's fertility,
If that the weeds o'erlive not the first
　　crop—
For then they are very difficult to stop.

XXIII

And then he talk'd with him about
　　Madrid,
　Constantinople, and such distant
　　places;
Where people always did as they were bid,
　Or did what they should not with
　　foreign graces.
Of coursers also spake they: Henry rid
　Well, like most Englishmen, and loved
　　the races;
And Juan, like a true-born Andalusian,
Could back a horse, as despots ride a
　　Russian.

XXIV

And thus acquaintance grew, at noble
　　routs,
　And diplomatic dinners, or at other—
For Juan stood well both with Ins and
　　Outs,
　As in freemasonry a higher brother.

Upon his talent Henry had no doubts;
 His manner show'd him sprung from a
 high mother;
And all men like to show their hospitality
To him whose breeding matches with his
 quality.

XXV

At Blank-Blank Square;—for we will
 break no squares
 By naming streets: since men are so
 censorious,
And apt to sow an author's wheat with
 tares,
 Reaping allusions private and in-
 glorious,
Where none were dreamt of, unto love's
 affairs,
 Which were, or are, or are to be
 notorious,
That therefore do I previously declare,
Lord Henry's mansion was in Blank-
 Blank Square.

XXVI

Also there bin another pious reason
 For making squares and streets
 anonymous;
Which is, that there is scarce a single
 season
 Which doth not shake some very
 splendid house
With some slight heart-quake of domestic
 treason—
 A topic scandal doth delight to rouse:
Such I might stumble over unawares,
Unless I knew the very chastest squares.

XXVII

'Tis true, I might have chosen Piccadilly,
 A place where peccadillos are unknown;
But I have motives, whether wise or silly,
 For letting that pure sanctuary alone.
Therefore I name not square, street, place,
 until I
 Find one where nothing naughty can be
 shown,
A vestal shrine of innocence of heart:
Such are—but I have lost the London
 Chart.

XXVIII

At Henry's mansion then, in Blank-Blank
 Square,
 Was Juan a *recherché*, welcome guest,
As many other noble scions were;
 And some who had but talent for their
 crest;
Or wealth, which is a passport everywhere;
 Or even mere fashion, which indeed's
 the best
Recommendation; and to be well drest
Will very often supersede the rest.

XXIX

And since 'there's safety in a multitude
 Of counsellors,' as Solomon has said,
Or some one for him, in some sage,
 grave mood;—
 Indeed we see the daily proof display'd
In senates, at the bar, in wordy feud,
 Where'er collective wisdom can parade,
Which is the only cause that we can guess
Of Britain's present wealth and happi-
 ness;—

XXX

But as 'there's safety' grafted in the number
 'Of counsellors' for men,—thus for the
 sex
A large acquaintance lets not Virtue
 slumber;
 Or should it shake, the choice will more
 perplex—
Variety itself will more encumber.
 'Midst many rocks we guard more
 against wrecks;
And thus with women: howsoe'er it
 shocks some's
Self-love, there's safety in a crowd of
 coxcombs.

XXXI

But Adeline had not the least occasion
 For such a shield, which leaves but little
 merit
To virtue proper, or good education.
 Her chief resource was in her own high
 spirit,
Which judged mankind at their due
 estimation;
 And for coquetry, she disdain'd to wear
 it:
Secure of admiration, its impression
Was faint as of an every-day possession.

XXXII

To all she was polite without parade;
 To some she show'd attention of that kind
Which flatters, but is flattery convey'd
 In such a sort as cannot leave behind
A trace unworthy either wife or maid;—
 A gentle, genial courtesy of mind,
To those who were, or pass'd for meri-
 torious,
Just to console sad glory for being glorious;

XXXIII

Which is in all respects, save now and then,
 A dull and desolate appendage. Gaze
Upon the shades of those distinguish'd men
 Who were or are the puppet-shows of
 praise,
The praise of persecution. Gaze again
 On the most favour'd; and amidst the
 blaze
Of sunset halos o'er the laurel-brow'd,
What can ye recognize?—a gilded cloud.

XXXIV

There also was of course in Adeline
 That calm patrician polish in the
 address,
Which ne'er can pass the equinoctial line
 Of anything which nature would express;
Just as a mandarin finds nothing fine,—
 At least his manner suffers not to guess,
That anything his views can greatly please,
Perhaps we have borrow'd this from the
 Chinese—

XXXV

Perhaps from Horace: his '*Nil admirari*'
 Was what he call'd the 'Art of Happi-
 ness'—
An art on which the artists greatly vary,
 And have not yet attain'd to much
 success.
However, 'tis expedient to be wary:
 Indifference certes don't produce dis-
 tress;
And rash enthusiasm in good society
Were nothing but a moral inebriety.

XXXVI

But Adeline was not indifferent: for
 (*Now* for a common-place!) beneath the
 snow,
As a volcano holds the lava more
 Within—*et cætera*. Shall I go on?—No,
I hate to hunt down a tired metaphor,
 So let the often-used volcano go.
Poor thing! How frequently, by me and
 others,
It hath been stirr'd up till its smoke quite
 smothers!

XXXVII

I'll have another figure in a trice:—
 What say you to a bottle of champagne?
Frozen into a very vinous ice,
 Which leaves few drops of that
 immortal rain,
Yet in the very centre, past all price,
 About a liquid glassful will remain,
And this is stronger than the strongest grape
Could e'er express in its expanded shape:

XXXVIII

'Tis the whole spirit brought to a quint-
 essence;
 And thus the chilliest aspects may
 concentre
A hidden nectar under a cold presence.
 And such are many—though I only
 meant her
From whom I now deduce these moral
 lessons,
 On which the Muse has always sought
 to enter.
And your cold people are beyond all price,
When once you have broken their con-
 founded ice.

XXXIX

But after all they are a North-West
 Passage
 Unto the glowing India of the soul;
And as the good ships sent upon that
 message
 Have not exactly ascertain'd the Pole
(Though Parry's efforts look a lucky
 presage),
 Thus gentlemen may run upon a shoal;
For if the Pole's not open, but all frost
(A chance still), 'tis a voyage or vessel lost.

XL

And young beginners may as well com-
 mence
 With quiet cruising o'er the ocean
 Woman;
While those who are not beginners should
 have sense
 Enough to make for port, ere Time
 shall summon
With his grey signal-flag; and the past
 tense,
 The dreary '*Fuimus*' of all things
 human,
Must be declined, while life's thin thread's
 spun out
Between the gaping heir and gnawing
 gout.

XLI

But heaven must be diverted; its diversion
 Is sometimes truculent—but never
 mind;
The world upon the whole is worth the
 assertion
 (If but for comfort) that all things are
 kind:
And that same devilish doctrine of the
 Persian,
 Of the 'Two Principles', but leaves behind
As many doubts as any other doctrine
Has ever puzzled faith withal, or yoked
 her in.

XLII

The English winter—ending in July,
 To recommence in August—now was
 done.
'Tis the postilion's paradise: wheels fly;
 On roads, east, south, north, west, there
 is a run.
But for post-horses who finds sympathy?
 Man's pity for himself, or for his son,
Always premising that said son at college
Has not contracted much more debt than
 knowledge.

XLIII

The London winter's ended in July—
 Sometimes a little later. I don't err
In this: whatever other blunders lie
 Upon my shoulders, here I must aver

My Muse a glass of *Weatherology*;
　For parliament is our barometer:
Let radicals its other acts attack,
Its sessions form our only almanack.

XLIV

When its quicksilver's down at zero,—lo!
　Coach, chariot, luggage, baggage,
　equipage!
Wheels whirl from Carlton palace to
　Soho,
　And happiest they who horses can
　engage;
The turnpikes glow with dust; and Rotten
　Row
　Sleeps from the chivalry of this bright
　age;
And tradesmen, with long bills and longer
　faces,
Sigh—as the postboys fasten on the traces.

XLV

They and their bills, 'Arcadians both,' are
　left
　To the Greek kalends of another session.
Alas! to them of ready cash bereft,
　What hope remains? Of *hope* the full
　possession
Or generous draft, conceded as a gift,
　At a long date—till they can get a fresh
　one—
Hawk'd about at a discount, small or
　large;
Also the solace of an overcharge.

XLVI

But these are trifles. Downward flies my
　lord,
　Nodding beside my lady in his carriage.
Away! away! 'Fresh horses!' are the
　word,
　And changed as quickly as hearts after
　marriage;
The obsequious landlord hath the change
　restored;
　The postboys have no reason to
　disparage
Their fee; but ere the water'd wheels may
　hiss hence,
The ostler pleads for a small reminiscence.

XLVII

'Tis granted; and the valet mounts the
　dickey—
　That gentleman of lords and gentlemen;
Also my lady's gentlewoman, tricky,
　Trick'd out, but modest more than
　poet's pen
Can paint,—'*Cosi viaggino i Ricchi!*'
　(Excuse a foreign slipslop now and then,
If but to show I've travell'd: and what's
　travel,
Unless it teaches one to quote and cavil?)

XLVIII

The London winter and the country
　summer
　Were well nigh over. 'Tis perhaps a
　pity,
When nature wears the gown that doth
　become her.
　To lose those best months in a sweaty
　city,
And wait until the nightingale grows
　dumber,
　Listening debates not very wise or
　witty,
Ere patriots their true *country* can remember;—
But there's no shooting (save grouse) till
　September.

XLIX

I've done with my tirade. The world was
　gone;
　The twice two thousand, for whom
　earth was made,
Were vanish'd to be what they call alone—
　That is, with thirty servants for parade,
As many guests, or more; before whom
　groan
　As many covers, duly, daily laid.
Let none accuse old England's hospitality—
Its quantity is but condensed to quality.

L

Lord Henry and the Lady Adeline
　Departed like the rest of their compeers,
The peerage, to a mansion very fine;
　The Gothic Babel of a thousand years.
None than themselves could boast a
　longer line,
　Where time through heroes and through
　beauties steers;
And oaks as olden as their pedigree
Told of their sires, a tomb in every tree.

LI

A paragraph in every paper told
　Of their departure: such is modern
　fame:
'Tis pity that it takes no further hold
　Than an advertisement, or much the
　same;
When, ere the ink be dry, the sound grows
　cold.
　The Morning Post was foremost to
　proclaim—
'Departure, for his country seat, to-day,
Lord H. Amundeville and Lady A.

LII

'We understand the splendid host intends
　To entertain, this autumn, a select
And numerous party of his noble friends;
　'Midst whom we have heard, from
　sources quite correct,

814

The Duke of D—— the shooting season
 spends,
 With many more by rank and fashion
 deck'd;
Also a foreigner of high condition,
The envoy of the secret Russian mission.'

LIII

And thus we see—who doubts the Morn-
 ing Post?
 (Whose articles are like the 'Thirty-
 nine,'
Which those most swear to who believe
 them most)—
Our gay Russ Spaniard was ordain'd
 to shine,
Deck'd by the rays reflected from his host,
 With those who, Pope says, 'greatly
 daring dine.'—
'Tis odd, but true,—last war the News
 abounded
More with these dinners than the kill'd or
 wounded;—

LIV

As thus: 'On Thursday there was a grand
 dinner;
 Present, Lords A.B.C.'—Earls, dukes,
 by name
Announced with no less pomp than
 victory's winner:
 Then underneath, and in the very same
Column: date, 'Falmouth. There has
 lately been here
 The Slap-dash regiment, so well known
 to fame,
Whose loss in the late action we regret:
The vacancies are fill'd up—see Gazette.'

LV

To Norman Abbey whirl'd the noble
 pair,—
 An old, old monastery once, and now
Still older mansion,—of a rich and rare
 Mix'd Gothic, such as artists all allow
Few specimens yet left us can compare
 Withal: it lies perhaps a little low,
Because the monks preferr'd a hill behind,
To shelter their devotion from the wind.

LVI

It stood embosom'd in a happy valley,
 Crown'd by high woodlands, where the
 Druid oak
Stood, like Caractacus in act to rally
 His host, with broad arms 'gainst the
 thunderstroke,
And from beneath his boughs were seen
 to sally
 The dappled foresters; as day awoke,
The branching stag swept down with all
 his herd,
To quaff a brook which murmur'd like a
 bird.

LVII

Before the mansion lay a lucid lake,
 Broad as transparent, deep, and
 freshly fed
By a river, which its soften'd way did take
 In currents through the calmer water
 spread
Around: the wildfowl nestled in the brake
 And sedges, brooding in their liquid
 bed:
The woods sloped downwards to its brink,
 and stood
With their green faces fix'd upon the flood.

LVIII

Its outlet dash'd into a deep cascade,
 Sparkling with foam, until again sub-
 siding,
Its shriller echoes—like an infant made
 Quiet—sank into softer ripples, gliding
Into a rivulet: and thus allay'd,
 Pursued its course, now gleaming, and
 now hiding
Its windings through the woods; now
 clear, now blue,
According as the skies their shadows
 threw.

LIX

A glorious remnant of the Gothic pile
 (While yet the church was Rome's)
 stood half apart
In a grand arch, which once screen'd
 many an aisle.
 These last had disappear'd—a loss to
 art:
The first yet frown'd superbly o'er the soil,
 And kindled feelings in the roughest
 heart,
Which mourn'd the power of time's or
 tempest's march,
In gazing on that venerable arch.

LX

Within a niche, nigh to its pinnacle,
 Twelve saints had once stood sanctified
 in stone;
But these had fallen, not when the friars
 fell,
 But in the war which struck Charles
 from his throne,
When each house was a fortalice—as tell
 The annals of full many a line undone,—
The gallant cavaliers, who fought in vain
For those who knew not to resign or reign.

LXI

But in a higher niche, alone, but crown'd,
 The Virgin-Mother of the God-born
 Child,
With her Son in her blessed arms, look'd
 round;
 Spared by some chance when all beside
 was spoil'd;

She made the earth below seem holy
 ground.
This may be superstition, weak or wild,
But even the faintest relics of a shrine
Of any worship wake some thoughts divine.

LXII

A mighty window, hollow in the centre,
 Shorn of its glass of thousand colour-
 ings,
Through which the deepen'd glories once
 could enter,
 Streaming from off the sun like seraph's
 wings,
Now yawns all desolate: now loud, now
 fainter,
 The gale sweeps through its fretwork,
 and oft sings
The owl his anthem, where the silenced
 quire
Lie with their hallelujahs quench'd like
 fire.

LXIII

But in the noontide of the moon, and when
 The wind is wingèd from one point of
 heaven,
There moans a strange unearthly sound,
 which then
 Is musical—a dying accent driven
Through the huge arch, which soars and
 sinks again.
 Some deem it but the distant echo given
Back to the night wind by the waterfall,
And harmonised by the old choral wall:

LXIV

Others, that some original shape, or form
 Shaped by decay perchance, hath given
 the power
(Though less than that of Memnon's
 statue, warm
 In Egypt's rays, to harp at a fix'd hour)
To this grey ruin, with a voice to charm
 Sad, but serene, it sweeps o'er tree or
 tower;
The cause I know not, nor can solve; but
 such
The fact:—I've heard it,—once perhaps
 too much.

LXV

Amidst the court a Gothic fountain play'd,
 Symmetrical, but deck'd with carvings
 quaint—
Strange faces, like to men in masquerade,
 And here perhaps a monster, there a
 saint:
The spring gush'd through grim mouths
 of granite made,
 And sparkled into basins, where it spent
Its little torrent in a thousand bubbles,
Like man's vain glory, and his vainer
 troubles.

LXVI

The mansion's self was vast and venerable
 With more of the monastic than has
 been
Elsewhere preserved: the cloisters still
 were stable,
 The cells, too, and refectory, I ween:
An exquisite small chapel had been able,
 Still unimpair'd, to decorate the scene;
The rest had been reform'd, replaced, or
 sunk,
And spoke more of the baron than the
 monk.

LXVII

Huge halls, long galleries, spacious
 chambers, join'd
 By no quite lawful marriage of the arts,
Might shock a connoisseur; but when
 combined,
 Form'd a whole which, irregular in parts,
Yet left a grand impression on the mind,
 At least of those whose eyes are in their
 hearts:
We gaze upon a giant for his stature,
Nor judge at first if all be true to nature.

LXVIII

Steel barons, molten the next generation
 To silken rows of gay and garter'd earls,
Glanced from the walls in goodly pre-
 servation;
 And fair long Marys blooming into girls,
With fair long locks, had also kept their
 station:
 And countesses mature in robes and
 pearls:
Also some beauties of Sir Peter Lely,
Whose drapery hints we may admire
 them freely.

LXIX

Judges in very formidable ermine
 Were there, with brows that did not
 much invite
The accused to think their lordships would
 determine
 His cause by leaning much from might
 to right:
Bishops, who had not left a single sermon;
 Attorneys-general, awful to the sight,
As hinting more (unless our judgments
 warp us)
Of the 'Star Chamber' than of 'Habeas
 Corpus.'

LXX

Generals, some all in armour, of the old
 And iron time, ere lead had ta'en the
 lead;
Others in wigs of Marlborough's martial
 fold,
 Huger than twelve of our degenerate
 breed:

Lordlings, with staves of white or keys of
 gold:
 Nimrods, whose canvas scarce con-
 tain'd the steed;
And here and there some stern high
 patriot stood,
Who could not get the place for which he
 sued.

LXXI

But ever and anon, to soothe your vision,
 Fatigued with these hereditary glories,
There rose a Carlo Dolce or a Titian,
 Or wilder group of savage Salvatore's:
Here danced Albano's boys, and here the
 sea shone
 In Vernet's ocean lights; and there the
 stories
Of martyrs awed, as Spagnoletto tainted
His brush with all the blood of all the
 sainted.

LXXII

Here sweetly spread a landscape of Lor-
 raine;
 There Rembrandt made his darkness
 equal light,
Or gloomy Caravaggio's gloomier stain
 Bronzed o'er some lean and stoic
 anchorite:—
But, lo! a Teniers woos, and not in vain,
 Your eyes to revel in a livelier sight:
His bell-mouth'd goblet makes me feel
 quite Danish
Or Dutch with thirst—What, ho! a flask of
 Rhenish.

LXXIII

O reader! if that thou canst read,—and
 know,
 'Tis not enough to spell, or even to read,
To constitute a reader; there must go
 Virtues of which both you and I have
 need.
Firstly, begin with the beginning—(though
 That clause is hard); and secondly, pro-
 ceed:
Thirdly, commence not with the end—or,
 sinning
In this sort, end at least with the beginning.

LXXIV

But reader, thou hast patient been of late,
 While I, without remorse of rhyme, or
 fear,
Have built and laid out ground at such a
 rate,
 Dan Phœbus takes me for an auctioneer.
That poets were so from their earliest date,
 By Homer's 'Catalogue of ships' is
 clear;
But a mere modern must be moderate—
 I spare you then the furniture and plate.

LXXV

The mellow autumn came, and with it
 came
 The promised party, to enjoy its sweets.
The corn is cut, the manor full of game;
 The pointer ranges, and the sportsman
 beats
In russet jacket:—lynx-like is his aim;
 Full grows his bag, and wonderful his
 feats.
Ah, nutbrown partridges! Ah, brilliant
 pheasants!
And ah, ye poachers!—'Tis no sport for
 peasants.

LXXVI

An English autumn, though it hath no
 vines,
 Blushing with Bacchant coronals along
The paths, o'er which the far festoon
 entwines
 The red grape in the sunny lands of
 song,
Hath yet a purchased choice of choicest
 wines;
 The claret light, and the Madeira strong;
If Britain mourn her bleakness, we can tell
 her,
The very best of vineyards is the cellar.

LXXVII

Then, if she hath not that serene decline
 Which makes the southern autumn's
 day appear
As if 'twould to a second spring resign
 The season, rather than to winter
 drear,—
Of in-door comforts still she hath a mine,—
 The sea-coal fires, the 'earliest of the
 year';
Without doors, too, she may compete in
 mellow,
As what is lost in green is gain'd in yellow.

LXXVIII

And for the effeminate villeggiatura—
 Rife with more horns than hounds—she
 hath the chase,
So animated that it might allure a
 Saint from his beads to join the jocund
 race;
Even Nimrod's self might leave the plains
 of Dura,
 And wear the Melton jacket for a space:
If she hath no wild boars, she hath a tame
Preserve of bores, who ought to be made
 game.

LXXIX

The noble guests, assembled at the Abbey,
 Consisted of—we give the sex the pas—
The Duchess of Fitz-Fulke; the Countess
 Crabby;
 The Ladies Scilly, Busey;—Miss Eclat,

Miss Bombazeen, Miss Mackstay, Miss
 O'Tabby,
 And Mrs. Rabbi, the rich banker's
 squaw;
Also the honourable Mrs. Sleep,
Who look'd a white lamb, yet was a black
 sheep:

LXXX

With other Countesses of Blank—but
 rank;
 At once the 'lie' and the *élite* of
 crowds;
Who pass like water filter'd in a tank,
 All purged and pious from their native
 clouds;
Or paper turn'd to money by the Bank:
 No matter how or why, the passport
 shrouds
The *passée* and the past; for good
 society
Is no less famed for tolerance than piety,—

LXXXI

That is, up to a certain point; which point
 Forms the most difficult in punctua-
 tion.
Appearances appear to form the joint
 On which it hinges in a higher station;
And so that no explosion cry 'Aroint
 Thee, witch!' or each Medea has her
 Jason;
Or (to the point with Horace and with
 Pulci)
'*Omne tulit punctum, quæ miscuit utile
 dulci.*'

LXXXII

I can't exactly trace their rule of right,
 Which hath a little leaning to a lottery.
I've seen a virtuous woman put down
 quite
 By the mere combination of a coterie;
Also a so-so matron boldly fight
 Her way back to the world by dint of
 plottery,
And shine the very *Siria* of the spheres,
Escaping with a few slight, scarless sneers.

LXXXIII

I have seen more than I'll say:—but we
 will see
 How *our* '*villeggiatura*' will get on.
The party might consist of thirty-three
 Of highest caste—the Brahmins of the
 ton.
I have named a few, not foremost in
 degree,
 But ta'en at hazard as the rhyme may
 run,
By way of sprinkling, scatter'd amongst
 these
There also were some Irish absentees.

LXXXIV

There was Parolles, too, the legal bully,
 Who limits all his battles to the bar
And senate: when invited elsewhere, truly,
 He shows more appetite for words than
 war.
There was the young bard Rackrhyme,
 who had newly
 Come out and glimmer'd as a six weeks'
 star.
There was Lord Pyrrho, too, the great
 freethinker;
And Sir John Pottledeep, the mighty
 drinker.

LXXXV

There was the Duke of Dash, who was a—
 duke,
 'Ay, every inch a' duke; there were
 twelve peers
Like Charlemagne's—and all such peers
 in *look*
 And *intellect*, that neither eyes nor
 ears
For commoners had ever them mistook.
 There were the six Miss Rawbolds—
 pretty dears!
All song and sentiment; whose hearts were
 set
Less on a convent than a coronet.

LXXXVI

There were four Honourable Misters,
 whose
 Honour was more before their names
 than after;
There was the *preux Chevalier de la
 Ruse*,
 Whom France and Fortune lately
 deign'd to waft here,
Whose chiefly harmless talent was to
 amuse;
 But the clubs found it rather serious
 laughter,
Because—such was his magic power to
 please—
The dice seem'd charm'd, too, with his re-
 partees.

LXXXVII

There was Dick Dubious, the metaphysi-
 cian,
 Who loved philosophy and a good
 dinner;
Angle, the *soi-disant* mathematician;
 Sir Henry Silvercup, the great race-
 winner.
There was the Reverend Rodomont Pre-
 cisian,
 Who did not hate so much the sin as
 sinner;
And Lord Augustus Fitz-Plantagenet,
Good at all things, but better at a bet.

LXXXVIII

There was Jack Jargon, the gigantic
 guardsman;
 And General Fireface, famous in the
 field,
A great tactician, and no less a swordsman,
 Who ate, last war, more Yankees than
 he kill'd.
There was the waggish Welsh Judge,
 Jefferies Hardsman,
 In his grave office so completely skill'd,
That when a culprit came for condemna-
 tion,
He had his judge's joke for consolation.

LXXXIX

Good company's a chess-board—there
 are kings,
 Queens, bishops, knights, rooks, pawns;
 the world's a game;
Save that the puppets pull at their own
 strings,
 Methinks gay Punch hath something
 of the same.
My Muse, the butterfly hath but her wings,
 Not stings, and flits through ether with-
 out aim,
Alighting rarely:—were she but a hornet,
Perhaps there might be vices which would
 mourn it.

XC

I had forgotten—but must not forget—
 An orator, the latest of the session,
Who had deliver'd well a very set
 Smooth speech, his first and maidenly
 transgression
Upon debate: the papers echoed yet
 With this *début*, which made a strong
 impression,
And rank'd with what is every day dis-
 play'd—
'The best first speech that ever yet was made.'

XCI

Proud of his 'Hear hims!' proud, too, of
 his vote
 And lost virginity of oratory,
Proud of his learning (just enough to quote),
 He revell'd in his Ciceronian glory:
With memory excellent to get by rote,
 With wit to hatch a pun or tell a story,
Graced with some merit, and with more
 effrontery,
His country's pride,' he came down to the
 country.

XCII

There also were two wits by acclamation,
 Longbow from Ireland, Strongbow
 from the Tweed,
Both lawyers and both men of education;
 But Strongbow's wit was of more
 polish'd breed;

Longbow was rich in an imagination
 As beautiful and bounding as a steed,
But sometimes stumbling over a potato,—
While Strongbow's best things might have
 come from Cato.

XCIII

Strongbow was like a new-tuned harpsi-
 chord;
 But Longbow wild as an Æolian harp,
With which the winds of heaven can claim
 accord,
 And make a music, whether flat or
 sharp.
Of Strongbow's talk you would not change
 a word:
 At Longbow's phrases you might some-
 times carp:
Both wits—one born so, and the other
 bred,
This by his heart—his rival by his head.

XCIV

If all these seem an heterogeneous mass
 To be assembled at a country seat,
Yet think, a specimen of every class
 Is better than an humdrum tête-à-tête.
The days of Comedy are gone, alas!
 When Congreve's fool could vie with
 Molière's *bête:*
Society is smooth'd to that excess,
That manners hardly differ more than
 dress.

XCV

Our ridicules are kept in the back ground—
 Ridiculous enough, but also dull;
Professions, too, are no more to be found
 Professional; and there is nought to
 cull
Of folly's fruit; for though your fools
 abound,
 They're barren, and not worth the pains
 to pull.
Society is now one polish'd horde,
Form'd of two mighty tribes, the *Bores*
 and *Bored.*

XCVI

But from being farmers, we turn gleaners,
 gleaning
 The scanty but right-well thresh'd ears
 of truth;
And, gentle reader! when you gather
 meaning,
 You may be Boaz, and I—modest Ruth.
Further I'd quote, but Scripture inter-
 vening
 Forbids. A great impression in my
 youth
Was made by Mrs. Adams, where she cries
'That Scriptures out of church are blas-
 phemies.'

XCVII

But what we can we glean in this vile age
 Of chaff, although our gleanings be not
 grist.
I must not quite omit the talking sage,
 Kit-Cat, the famous Conversationist,
Who, in his common-place book, had a
 page
 Prepared each morn for evenings.
 'List, oh list!'
'Alas, poor ghost!'—What unexpected
 woes
Await those who have studied their *bons-
 mots!*

XCVIII

Firstly, they must allure the conversation
 By many windings to their clever clinch;
And secondly, must let slip no occasion,
 Nor *bate* (abate) their hearers of an *inch*,
But take an ell—and make a great sensation,
 If possible; and thirdly, never flinch
When some smart talker puts them to the
 test,
But seize the last word, which no doubt's
 the best.

XCIX

Lord Henry and his lady were the hosts;
 The party we have touch'd on were the
 guests.
Their table was a board to tempt even
 ghosts
 To pass the Styx for more substantial
 feasts.
I will not dwell upon *ragoûts* or roasts,
 Albeit all human history attests
That happiness for man—the hungry sin-
 ner!—
Since Eve ate apples, much depends on
 dinner.

C

Witness the lands which 'flow'd with milk
 and honey,'
 Held out unto the hungry Israelites:
To this we have added since, the love of
 money,
 The only sort of pleasure which requites.
Youth fades, and leaves our days no
 longer sunny;
 We tire of mistresses and parasites;
But oh, ambrosial cash! Ah! who would
 lose thee?
When we no more can use, or even abuse
 thee!

CI

The gentlemen got up betimes to shoot,
 Or hunt: the young, because they liked
 the sport—
The first thing boys like after play and fruit;
 The middle-aged, to make the day more
 short;

CII

For *ennui* is a growth of English root,
 Though nameless in our language:—we
 retort
The fact for words, and let the French
 translate
That awful yawn which sleep cannot abate.

CII

The elderly walk'd through the library,
 And tumbled books, or criticised the
 pictures,
Or saunter'd through the gardens piteous-
 ly,
 And made upon the hot-house several
 strictures,
Or rode a nag which trotted not too high,
 Or on the morning papers read their
 lectures,
Or on the watch their longing eyes would fix,
Longing at sixty for the hour of six.

CIII

But none were *gêné*: the great hour of
 union
 Was rung by dinner's knell; till then all
 were
Masters of their own time—or in commu-
 nion,
 Or solitary, as they chose to bear
The hours, which how to pass is but to few
 known.
 Each rose up at his own, and had to
 spare
What time he chose for dress, and broke
 his fast
When, where, and how he chose for that
 repast.

CIV

The ladies—some rouged, some a little
 pale—
 Met the morn as they might. If fine
 they rode,
Or walk'd; if foul, they read, or told a tale,
 Sung, or rehearsed the last dance from
 abroad;
Discuss'd the fashion which might next
 prevail,
 And settled bonnets by the newest code,
Or cramm'd twelve sheets into one little
 letter,
To make each correspondent a new debtor.

CV

For some had absent lovers, all had friends,
 The earth has nothing like a she epistle,
And hardly heaven—because it never ends.
 I love the mystery of a female missal,
Which, like a creed, ne'er says all it in-
 tends,
 But full of cunning as Ulysses' whistle,
When he allured poor Dolon:—you had
 better
Take care what you reply to such a letter.

CVI

Then there were billiards; cards, too, but
 no dice;—
 Save in the clubs no man of honour
 plays;—
Boats when 'twas water, skating when
 'twas ice,
 And the hard frost destroy'd the scent-
 ing days:
And angling, too, that solitary vice,
 Whatever Izaak Walton sings or says:
The quaint, old, cruel coxcomb, in his
 gullet
Should have a hook, and a small trout to
 pull it.

CVII

With evening came the banquet and the
 wine;
 The conversazione; the duet,
Attuned by voices more or less divine
 (My heart or head aches with the mem-
 ory yet).
The four Miss Rawbolds in a glee would
 shine;
 But the two youngest loved more to be
 set
Down to the harp—because to music's
 charms
They added graceful necks, white hands
 and arms.

CVIII

Sometimes a dance (though rarely on field
 days,
 For then the gentlemen were rather
 tired)
Display'd some sylph-like figures in its
 maze;
 Then there was small-talk ready when
 required;
Flirtation—but decorous; the mere praise
 Of charms that should or should not be
 admired.
The hunters fought their fox-hunt o'er
 again,
And then retreated soberly—at ten.

CIX

The politicians, in a nook apart,
 Discuss'd the world, and settled all the
 spheres;
The wits watch'd every loophole for their
 art,
 To introduce a *bon-mot* head and
 ears;
Small is the rest of those who would be
 smart,
 A moment's good thing may have cost
 them years
Before they find an hour to introduce it;
And then, even *then*, some bore may make
 them lose it.

CX

But all was gentle and aristocratic
 In this our party; polish'd, smooth, and
 cold,
As Phidian forms cut out of marble Attic.
 There now are no Squire Westerns as
 of old;
And our Sophias are not so emphatic,
 But fair as then, or fairer to behold.
We have no accomplish'd blackguards,
 like Tom Jones,
But gentlemen in stays, as stiff as stones.

CXI

They separated at an early hour;
 That is, ere midnight—which is Lon-
 don's noon;
But in the country ladies seek their bower
 A little earlier than the waning moon.
Peace to the slumbers of each folded
 flower—
 May the rose call back its true colours
 soon!
Good hours of fair cheeks are the fairest
 tinters,
And lower the price of rouge—at least
 some winters.

CANTO THE FOURTEENTH

I

If from great nature's or our own abyss
 Of thought we could but snatch a cer-
 tainty,
Perhaps mankind might find the path they
 miss—
 But then 'twould spoil much good philo-
 sophy.
One system eats another up, and this
 Much as old Saturn ate his progeny;
For when his pious consort gave him
 stones
In lieu of sons, of these he made no bones.

II

But System doth reverse the Titan's break-
 fast,
 And eats her parents, albeit the digestion
Is difficult. Pray tell me, can you make fast,
 After due search, your faith to any
 question?
Look back o'er ages, ere unto the stake fast
 You bind yourself, and call some mode
 the best one.
Nothing more true than *not* to trust your
 senses;
And yet what are your other evidences?

III

For me, I know nought; nothing I deny,
 Admit, reject, contemn; and what know
 you,
Except perhaps that you were born to die?
 And both may after all turn out untrue.

An age may come, Font of Eternity,
 When nothing shall be either old or new.
Death, so call'd, is a thing which makes
 men weep,
And yet a third of life is pass'd in sleep.

IV

A sleep without dreams, after a rough day
 Of toil, is what we covet most; and yet
How clay shrinks back from more quies-
 cent clay!
The very Suicide that pays his debt
At once without instalments (an old way
 Of paying debts, which creditors regret),
Lets out impatiently his rushing breath,
Less from disgust of life than dread of
 death.

V

'Tis round him, near him, here, there,
 everywhere,
 And there's a courage which grows out
 of fear,
Perhaps of all most desperate, which will
 dare
 The worst to *know* it:—when the moun-
 tains rear
Their peaks beneath your human foot, and
 there
 You look down o'er the precipice, and
 drear
The gulf of rock yawns,—you can't gaze a
 minute,
Without an awful wish to plunge within it.

VI

'Tis true, you don't—but, pale and struck
 with terror,
 Retire: but look into your past im-
 pression!
And you will find, though shuddering at
 the mirror
 Of your own thoughts, in all their self-
 confession,
The lurking bias, be it truth or error,
 To the *unknown;* a secret prepossession,
To plunge with all your fears—but where?
 You know not,
And that's the reason why you do—or
 do not.

VII

But what's this to the purpose? you will say.
 Gent. reader, nothing; a mere specula-
 tion,
For which my sole excuse is—'tis my way;
 Sometimes *with* and sometimes without
 occasion,
I write what's uppermost, without delay;
 This narrative is not meant for narra-
 tion,
But a mere airy and fantastic basis,
To build up common things with common
 places.

VIII

You know, or don't know, that grea[t]
 Bacon saith,
 'Fling up a straw, 'twill show the way
 the wind blows;'
And such a straw, borne on by human
 breath,
 Is poesy, according as the mind glows
A paper kite which flies 'twixt life an[d]
 death,
 A shadow which the onward soul be-
 hind throws:
And mine's a bubble, not blown up fo[r]
 praise,
But just to play with, as an infant plays.

IX

The world is all before me—or behind;
 For I have seen a portion of that same
And quite enough for me to keep i[n]
 mind;—
 Of passions, too, I have proved enoug[h]
 to blame,
To the great pleasure of our friends, man[y]
 kind,
 Who like to mix some slight alloy wit[h]
 fame;
For I was rather famous in my time,
Until I fairly knock'd it up with rhyme.

X

I have brought this world about my ears,
 and eke
 The other; that's to say, the clergy—
 who
Upon my head have bid their thunder
 break
 In pious libels by no means a few.
And yet I can't help scribbling once a week,
 Tiring old readers, nor discovering new[,]
In youth I wrote because my mind was full[,]
And *now* because I feel it growing dull.

XI

But 'why then publish?'—There are n[o]
 rewards,
 Of fame or profit when the world grow[s]
 weary.
I ask in turn,—Why do you play at cards?
 Why drink? Why read?—To mak[e]
 some hour less dreary.
It occupies me to turn back regards
 On what I've seen or ponder'd, sad o[r]
 cheery;
And what I write I cast upon the stream[,]
To swim or sink—I have had at least m[y]
 dream.

XII

I think that were I *certain* of success,
 I hardly could compose another line:
So long I've battled either more or less,
 That no defeat can drive me from th[e]
 Nine.

This feeling 'tis not easy to express,
 And yet 'tis not affected, I opine.
In play, there are two pleasures for your
 choosing—
 The one is winning, and the other losing.

XIII

Besides, my Muse by no means deals in
 fiction:
 She gathers a repertory of facts,
Of course with some reserve and slight
 restriction,
 But mostly sings of human things and
 acts—
And that's one cause she meets with con-
 tradiction;
 For too much truth, at first sight, ne'er
 attracts;
And were her object only what's call'd
 glory,
With more ease too she'd tell a different
 story.

XIV

Love, war, a tempest—surely there's
 variety:
 Also a seasoning slight of lucubration;
A bird's-eye-view, too, of that wild,
 Society;
 A slight glance thrown on men of every
 station.
If you have nought else, here's at least
 satiety,
 Both in performance and in prepara-
 tion;
And though these lines should only line
 portmanteaus,
Trade will be all the better for these
 Cantos.

XV

The portion of this world which I at
 present
 Have taken up to fill the following ser-
 mon,
Is one of which there's no description
 recent:
 The reason why, is easy to determine:
Although it seems both prominent and
 pleasant,
 There is a sameness in its gems and
 ermine,
A dull and family likeness through all
 ages,
Of no great promise for poetic pages.

XVI

With much to excite, there's little to exalt;
 Nothing that speaks to all men and all
 times;
A sort of varnish over every fault;
 A kind of common-place, even in their
 crimes;

Factitious passions, wit without much salt,
 A want of that true nature which
 sublimes
Whate'er it shows with truth; a smooth
 monotony
Of character, in those at least who have
 got any.

XVII

Sometimes, indeed, like soldiers off parade,
 They break their ranks and gladly leave
 the drill;
But then the roll-call draws them back
 afraid,
 And they must be or seem what they
 were: still
Doubtless it is a brilliant masquerade:
 But when of the first sight you have had
 your fill,
It palls—at least it did so upon me,
This paradise of pleasure and *ennui*.

XVIII

When we have made our love, and gamed
 our gaming,
 Drest, voted, shone, and, may be, some-
 thing more;
With dandies dined; heard senators de-
 claiming;
 Seen beauties brought to market by the
 score,
Sad rakes to sadder husbands chastely
 taming;
 There's little left but to be bored or
 bore.
Witness those *ci-devant jeunes hommes*
 who stem
The stream, nor leave the world which
 leaveth them.

XIX

'Tis said—indeed a general complaint—
 That no one has succeeded in describing
The *monde*, exactly as they ought to paint:
 Some say, that authors only snatch, by
 bribing
The porter, some slight scandals strange
 and quaint,
 To furnish matter for their moral
 gibing;
And that their books have but one style in
 common—
My lady's prattle, filter'd through her
 woman.

XX

But this can't well be true, just now; for
 writers
 Are grown of the *beau monde* a part
 potential:
I've seen them balance even the scale with
 fighters,
 Especially when young, for that's essen-
 tial.

823

Why do their sketches fail them as inditers
 Of what they deem themselves most
 consequential,
The *real* portrait of the highest tribe?
'Tis that, in fact, there's little to describe.

XXI

'*Haud ignara loquor;*' these are *Nugæ,*
 '*quarum*
 Pars parva *fui,*' but still art and part.
Now I could much more easily sketch a
 harem,
 A battle, wreck, or history of the heart,
Than these things; and besides, I wish to
 spare 'em,
 For reasons which I choose to keep
 apart.
'*Vetabo Cereris sacrum qui vulgarit*'—
 Which means, that vulgar people must
 not share it.

XXII

And therefore what I throw off is ideal—
 Lower'd, leaven'd, like a history of free-
 masons,
Which bears the same relation to the real,
 As Captain Parry's voyage may do to
 Jason's.
The grand *arcanum's* not for men to see
 all;
 My music has some mystic diapasons;
And there is much which could not be
 appreciated
In any manner by the uninitiated.

XXIII

Alas! worlds fall—and woman, since she
 fell'd
 The world (as, since that history, less
 polite
Than true, hath been a creed so strictly
 held),
 Has not yet given up the practice quite.
Poor thing of usages! coerced, compell'd,
 Victim when wrong, and martyr oft
 when right,
Condemn'd to child-bed, as men for their
 sins
Have shaving too entail'd upon their
 chins,—

XXIV

A daily plague, which in the aggregate
 May average on the whole with parturi-
 tion.
But as to women, who can penetrate
 The real sufferings of their she con-
 dition?
Man's very sympathy with their estate
 Has much of selfishness, and more sus-
 picion.
Their love, their virtue, beauty, education,
But form good housekeepers, to breed a
 nation.

XXV

All this were very well, and can't be better
 But even this is difficult, Heaven knows
So many troubles from her birth beset her
 Such small distinction between friends
 and foes,
The gilding wears so soon from off her
 fetter,
 That——but ask any woman if she'd
 choose
(Take her at thirty, that is) to have been
Female or male? a schoolboy or a queen

XXVI

'Petticoat influence' is a great reproach,
 Which even those who obey would fain
 be thought
To fly from, as from hungry pikes a roach
 But since beneath it upon earth we are
 brought,
By various joltings of life's hackney coach
 I for one venerate a petticoat—
A garment of a mystical sublimity,
No matter whether russet, silk, or dimity

XXVII

Much I respect, and much I have adored
 In my young days, that chaste and
 goodly veil,
Which holds a treasure, like a miser's
 hoard,
 And more attracts by all it doth con
 ceal—
A golden scabbard on a Damasque sword
 A loving letter with a mystic seal,
A cure for grief—for what can ever rank
Before a petticoat and peeping ankle?

XXVIII

And when upon a silent, sullen day,
 With a sirocco, for example, blowing,
When even the sea looks dim with all it
 spray,
 And sulkily the river's ripple's flowing
And the sky shows that very ancient gra
 The sober, sad antithesis to glowing,—
'Tis pleasant, if *then* anything is pleasan
To catch a glimpse even of a prett
 peasant.

XXIX

We left our heroes and our heroines
 In that fair clime which don't depend o
 climate,
Quite independent of the Zodiac's signs
 Though certainly more difficult
 rhyme at,
Because the sun, and stars, and aught tha
 shines,
 Mountains, and all we can be mo
 sublime at,
Are there oft dull and dreary as a *dun*—
Whether a sky's or tradesman's is all on

XXX

And in-door life is less poetical;
 And out-of-door hath showers, and
 mists, and sleet,
With which I could not brew a pastoral.
 But be it as it may, a bard must meet
All difficulties, whether great or small,
 To spoil his undertaking, or complete,
And work away like spirit upon matter,
Embarrass'd somewhat both with fire and
 water.

XXXI

Juan—in this respect, at least, like saints—
 Was all things unto people of all sorts,
And lived contentedly, without com-
 plaints,
 In camps, in ships, in cottages, or
 courts—
Born with that happy soul which seldom
 faints,
 And mingling modestly in toils or
 sports.
He likewise could be most things to all
 women,
Without the coxcombry of certain *she*
 men.

XXXII

A fox-hunt to a foreigner is strange;
 'Tis also subject to the double danger
Of tumbling first, and having in exchange
 Some pleasant jesting at the awkward
 stranger;
But Juan had been early taught to range
 The wilds, as doth an Arab turn'd
 avenger,
So that his horse, or charger, hunter, hack,
Knew that he had a rider on his back.

XXXIII

And now in this new field, with some ap-
 plause,
 He clear'd hedge, ditch, and double
 post, and rail,
And never *craned*, and made but few '*faux
 pas*,'
 And only fretted when the scent 'gan
 fail.
He broke, 'tis true, some statutes of the
 laws
 Of hunting—for the sagest youth is
 frail;
Rode o'er the hounds, it may be, now and
 then,
And once o'er several country gentlemen.

XXXIV

But on the whole, to general admiration
 He acquitted both himself and horse:
 the squires
Marvell'd at merit of another nation;
 The boors cried 'Dang it! who'd have
 thought it?'—Sires,

The Nestors of the sporting generation,
 Swore praises, and recall'd their former
 fires;
The huntsman's self relented to a grin,
And rated him almost a whipper-in.

XXXV

Such were his trophies—not of spear and
 shield,
 But leaps, and bursts, and sometimes
 foxes' brushes;
Yet I must own,—although in this I yield
 To patriot sympathy a Briton's blush-
 es,—
He thought at heart like courtly Chester-
 field,
 Who, after a long chase o'er hills, dales,
 bushes,
And what not, though he rode beyond all
 price,
Ask'd next day, 'If men ever hunted
 twice?'

XXXVI

He also had a quality uncommon
 To early risers after a long chase,
Who wake in winter ere the cock can sum-
 mon
 December's drowsy day to his dull
 race,—
A quality agreeable to woman,
 When her soft, liquid words run on
 apace,
Who likes a listener, whether saint or sin-
 ner,—
He did not fall asleep just after dinner;

XXXVII

But, light and airy, stood on the alert,
 And shone in the best part of dialogue,
By humouring always what they might
 assert,
 And listening to the topics most in
 vogue,—
Now grave, now gay, but never dull or
 pert,
 And smiling but in secret—cunning
 rogue!—
He ne'er presumed to make an error
 clearer;—
In short, there never was a better hearer.

XXXVIII

And then he danced,—all foreigners excel
 The serious Angles in the eloquence
Of pantomime,—he danced, I say, right
 well,
 With emphasis, and also with good
 sense—
A thing in footing indispensable;
 He danced without theatrical pretence,
Not like a ballet-master in the van
Of his drill'd nymphs, but like a gentle-
 man.

XXXIX

Chaste were his steps, each kept within
 due bound,
 And elegance was sprinkled o'er his
 figure;
Like swift Camilla, he scarce skimm'd the
 ground,
 And rather held in than put forth his
 vigour;
And then he had an ear for music's sound,
 Which might defy a crotchet critic's
 rigour.
Such classic *pas*—sans flaws—set off our
 hero,
He glanced like a personified Bolero;

XL

Or, like a flying Hour before Aurora,
 In Guido's famous fresco, which alone
Is worth a tour to Rome, although no
 more a
 Remnant were there of the old world's
 sole throne.
The '*tout ensemble*' of his movements
 wore a
 Grace of the soft ideal, seldom shown,
And ne'er to be described; for to the dolour
Of bards and prosers, words are void of
 colour.

XLI

No marvel then he was a favourite;
 A full-grown Cupid, very much ad-
 mired;
A little spoilt, but by no means so quite;
 At least he kept his vanity retired.
Such was his tact, he could alike delight
 The chaste, and those who are not so
 much inspired.
The Duchess of Fitz-Fulke, who loved
 tracasserie,
Began to treat him with some small *aga-
 cerie*.

XLII

She was a fine and somewhat full-blown
 blonde,
 Desirable, distinguish'd, celebrated
For several winters in the grand, *grand
 monde*.
 I'd rather not say what might be related
Of her exploits, for this were ticklish
 ground;
 Besides there might be falsehood in
 what's stated;
Her late performance had been a dead set
At Lord Augustus Fitz-Plantagenet.

XLIII

This noble personage began to look
 A little black upon this new flirtation;
But such small licences must lovers brook,
 Mere freedoms of the female corpora-
 tion.

Woe to the man who ventures a rebuke!
 'Twill but precipitate a situation
Extremely disagreeable, but common
To calculators when they count on woman

XLIV

The circle smiled, then whisper'd, and then
 sneer'd;
 The misses bridled, and the matrons
 frown'd;
Some hoped things might not turn out a
 they fear'd;
 Some would not deem such women
 could be found;
Some ne'er believed one half of what they
 heard;
 Some look'd perplex'd, and others look'd
 profound;
And several pitied with sincere regret
Poor Lord Augustus Fitz-Plantagenet.

XLV

But what is odd, none ever named the
 duke,
 Who, one might think, was something
 in the affair:
True, he was absent, and, 'twas rumour'd
 took
 But small concern about the when, or
 where,
Or what his consort did: if he could brook
 Her gaieties, none had a right to stare
Theirs was that best of unions, past al
 doubt,
Which never meets, and therefore can't fal
 out.

XLVI

But, oh! that I should ever pen so sad a line
 Fired with an abstract love of virtue, she
My Dian of the Ephesians, Lady Adeline
 Began to think the duchess' conduct free
Regretting much that she had chosen so
 bad a line,
 And waxing chiller in her courtesy,
Look'd grave and pale to see her friend'
 fragility,
For which most friends reserve their sensi
 bility.

XLVII

There's nought in this bad world like
 sympathy;
 'Tis so becoming to the soul and face,
Sets to soft music the harmonious sigh,
 And robes sweet friendship in a Brussels
 lace.
Without a friend, what were humanity,
 To hunt our errors up with a good grace
Consoling us with—'Would you had
 thought twice!
Ah! if you had but follow'd my advice!'

XLVIII

O Job! you had two friends: one's quite
 enough,
 Especially when we are ill at ease;
They are but bad pilots when the weather's
 rough,
 Doctors less famous for their cures than
 fees.
Let no man grumble when his friends fall off,
 As they will do like leaves at the first
 breeze:
When your affairs come round, one way
 or t'other,
Go to the coffee-house, and take another.

XLIX

But this is not my maxim: had it been,
 Some heart-aches had been spared me:
 yet I care not—
I would not be a tortoise in his screen
 Of stubborn shell, which waves and
 weather wear not;
'Tis better on the whole to have felt and
 seen
 That which humanity may bear, or bear
 not;
'Twill teach discernment to the sensitive,
And not to pour their ocean in a sieve.

L

Of all the horrid, hideous notes of woe,
 Sadder than owl-songs or the midnight
 blast,
Is that portentous phrase, 'I told you so,'
 Utter'd by friends, those prophets of the
 past,
Who, 'stead of saying what you now
 should do,
 Own they foresaw that you would fall
 at last,
And solace your slight lapse 'gainst bonos
 mores,
With a long memorandum of old stories.

LI

The Lady Adeline's serene severity
 Was not confined to feeling for her
 friend,
Whose fame she rather doubted with pos-
 terity,
 Unless her habits should begin to mend:
But Juan also shared in her austerity,
 But mix'd with pity, pure as e'er was
 penn'd:
His inexperience moved her gentle ruth,
And (as her junior by six weeks) his youth.

LII

These forty days' advantage of her years—
 And hers were those which can face cal-
 culation,
Boldly referring to the list of peers
 And noble births, nor dread the enume-
 ration—

Gave her a right to have maternal fears
 For a young gentleman's fit education;
Though she was far from that leap year,
 whose leap,
In female dates, strikes Time all of a
 heap.

LIII

This may be fix'd at somewhere before
 thirty—
 Say seven-and-twenty; for I never knew
The strictest in chronology and virtue
 Advance beyond, while they could pass
 for new.
O Time! why dost not pause? Thy scythe,
 so dirty
 With rust, should surely cease to hack
 and hew.
Reset it: shave more smoothly, also
 slower,
If but to keep thy credit as a mower.

LIV

But Adeline was far from that ripe age,
 Whose ripeness is but bitter at the best:
'Twas rather her experience made her sage,
 For she had seen the world and stood
 its test,
As I have said in—I forget what page;
 My Muse despises reference, as you
 have guess'd
By this time;—but strike six from seven-
 and-twenty,
And you will find her sum of years in
 plenty.

LV

At sixteen she came out; presented,
 vaunted,
 She put all coronets into commotion:
At seventeen, too, the world was still en-
 chanted
 With the new Venus of their brilliant
 ocean:
At eighteen, though below her feet still
 panted
 A hecatomb of suitors with devotion,
She had consented to create again
That Adam, call'd 'the happiest of men.'

LVI

Since then she had sparkled through three
 glowing winters,
 Admired, adored; but also so correct,
That she had puzzled all the acutest hinters,
 Without the apparel of being circum-
 spect:
They could not even glean the slightest
 splinters
 From off the marble, which had no defect.
She had also snatch'd a moment since her
 marriage
To bear a son and heir—and one miscar-
 riage.

LVII

Fondly the wheeling fire-flies flew around
her,
 Those little glitterers of the London night;
But none of these possess'd a sting to
 wound her—
 She was a pitch beyond a coxcomb's
 flight.
Perhaps she wish'd an aspirant pro-
 founder;
 But whatsoe'er she wish'd, she acted right;
And whether coldness, pride, or virtue,
 dignify
A woman, so she's good, what *does* it signify?

LVIII

I hate a motive, like a lingering bottle
 Which with the landlord makes too long
 a stand,
Leaving all claretless the unmoisten'd
 throttle,
 Especially with politics on hand;
I hate it, as I hate a drove of cattle,
 Who whirl the dust as simooms whirl
 the sand;
I hate it, as I hate an argument,
A laureate's ode, or servile peer's 'Con-
 tent.'

LIX

'Tis sad to hack into the roots of things,
 They are so much intertwisted with the
 earth;
So that the branch a goodly verdure flings,
 I reck not if an acorn gave it birth.
To trace all actions to their secret springs
 Would make indeed some melancholy
 mirth;
But this is not at present my concern,
And I refer you to wise Oxenstiern.

LX

With the kind view of saving an *éclat*,
 Both to the duchess and diplomatist,
The Lady Adeline, as soon's she saw
 That Juan was unlikely to resist—
(For foreigners don't know that a *faux pas*
 In England ranks quite on a different list
From those of other lands unblest with
 juries,
Whose verdict for such sin a certain cure
 is;—)

LXI

The Lady Adeline resolved to take
 Such measures as she thought might
 best impede
The further progress of this sad mistake.
 She thought with some simplicity indeed;
But innocence is bold even at the stake,
 And simple in the world, and doth not
 need
Nor use those palisades by dames erected,
Whose virtue lies in never being detected.

LXII

It was not that she fear'd the very worst
 His Grace was an enduring, married
 man,
And was not likely all at once to burst
 Into a scene, and swell the clients' clan
Of Doctors' Commons: but she dreaded
 first
 The magic of her Grace's talisman,
And next a quarrel (as he seem'd to fret)
With Lord Augustus Fitz-Plantagenet.

LXIII

Her Grace, too, pass'd for being an *intri-
 gante*,
 And somewhat *méchante* in her amor-
 ous sphere:
One of those pretty, precious plagues,
 which haunt
 A lover with caprices soft and dear,
That like to *make* a quarrel, when they can't
 Find one, each day of the delightful year;
Bewitching, torturing, as they freeze or
 glow,
And—what is worst of all—won't let you
 go;

LXIV

The sort of thing to turn a young man's
 head,
 Or make a Werter of him in the end.
No wonder then a purer soul should dread
 This sort of chaste *liaison* for a friend;
It were much better to be wed or dead,
 Than wear a heart a woman loves to
 rend.
'Tis best to pause, and think, ere you rush
 on,
If that a '*bonne fortune*' be really '*bonne.*'

LXV

And first, in the o'erflowing of her heart,
 Which really knew or thought it knew
 no guile,
She call'd her husband now and then apart,
 And bade him counsel Juan. With a
 smile
Lord Henry heard her plans of artless art
 To wean Don Juan from the siren's wile
And answer'd, like a statesman or a
 prophet,
In such guise that she could make nothing
 of it.

LXVI

Firstly, he said, 'he never interfered
 In anybody's business but the king's':
Next, that 'he never judged from what
 appear'd,
 Without strong reason, of those sorts of
 things':
Thirdly, that 'Juan had more brain than
 beard,
 And was not to be held in leading
 strings';

And fourthly, what need hardly be said
 twice,
'That good but rarely came from good
 advice.'

LXVII

And, therefore, doubtless to approve the
 truth
 Of the last axiom, he advised his spouse
To leave the parties to themselves, for-
 sooth—
 At least as far as *bienséance* allows:
That time would temper Juan's faults of
 youth;
 That young men rarely made monastic
 vows;
That opposition only more attaches——
But here a messenger brought in des-
 patches:

LXVIII

And being of the council call'd 'the Privy,'
 Lord Henry walk'd into his cabinet,
To furnish matter for some future Livy
 To tell how he reduced the nation's
 debt;
And if their full contents I do not give ye,
 It is because I do not know them yet;
But I shall add them in a brief appendix,
To come between mine epic and its index.

LXIX

But ere he went, he added a slight hint,
 Another gentle common-place or two,
Such as are coin'd in conversation's mint,
 And pass, for want of better, though
 not new:
Then broke his packet, to see what was
 in't,
 And having casually glanced it through,
Retired: and, as he went out, calmly kiss'd
 her,
Less like a young wife than an aged sister.

LXX

He was a cold, good, honourable man,
 Proud of his birth, and proud of every-
 thing;
A goodly spirit for a state divan,
 A figure fit to walk before a king;
Tall, stately, form'd to lead the courtly van
 On birthdays, glorious with a star and
 string;
The very model of a chamberlain—
And such I mean to make him when I
 reign.

LXXI

But there was something wanting on the
 whole—
 I don't know what, and therefore can-
 not tell—
Which pretty women—the sweet souls!—
 call *soul*.
 Certes it was not body; he was well

Proportion'd, as a poplar or a pole,
 A handsome man, that human miracle;
And in each circumstance of love or war
Had still preserved his perpendicular.

LXXII

Still there was something wanting, as I've
 said—
 That undefinable '*Je ne sçais quoi*,'
Which, for what I know, may of yore have
 led
 To Homer's Iliad, since it drew to Troy
The Greek Eve, Helen, from the Spartan's
 bed;
 Though on the whole, no doubt, the
 Dardan boy
Was much inferior to King Menelaüs:—
But thus it is some women will betray us.

LXXIII

There is an awkward thing which much
 perplexes,
 Unless like wise Tiresias we had proved
By turns the difference of the several sexes;
 Neither can show quite *how* they would
 be loved.
The sensual for a short time but connects
 us—
 The sentimental boasts to be unmoved;
But both together form a kind of centaur,
Upon whose back 'tis better not to venture.

LXXIV

A something all-sufficient for the *heart*
 Is that for which the sex are always seeking:
But how to fill up that same vacant part?
 There lies the rub—and this they are but
 weak in.
Frail mariners afloat without a chart,
 They run before the wind through high
 seas breaking;
And when they have made the shore
 through every shock,
'Tis odd, or odds, it may turn out a rock.

LXXV

There is a flower call'd 'Love in Idleness,'
 For which see Shakespeare's ever-
 blooming garden;—
I will not make his great description less,
 And beg his British godship's humble
 pardon,
If, in my extremity of rhyme's distress,
 I touch a single leaf where he is war-
 den;—
But though the flower is different, with the
 French
Or Swiss Rousseau, cry '*Voilà la Per-
 venche!*'

LXXVI

Eureka! I have found it! What I mean
 To say is, not that love is idleness,
But that in love such idleness has been
 An accessory, as I have cause to guess.

Hard labour's an indifferent go-between;
 Your men of business are not apt to express
Much passion, since the merchant-ship, the Argo,
 Convey'd Medea as her supercargo.

LXXVII

'*Beatus ille procul!*' from '*negotiis,*'
 Saith Horace: the great little poet's wrong;
His other maxim, '*Noscitur à sociis,*'
 Is much more to the purpose of his song;
Though even that were sometimes too ferocious,
 Unless good company be kept too long;
But, in his teeth, whate'er their state or station,
Thrice happy they who *have* an occupation!

LXXVIII

Adam exchanged his Paradise for plough-ing,
 Eve made up millinery with fig leaves—
The earliest knowledge from the tree so knowing,
 As far as I know, that the church re-ceives:
And since that time it need not cost much showing,
 That many of the ills o'er which man grieves,
And still more women, spring from not employing
Some hours to make the remnant worth enjoying.

LXXIX

And hence high life is oft a dreary void,
 A rack of pleasures, where we must invent
A something wherewithal to be annoy'd.
 Bards may sing what they please about *Content;*
Contented, when translated, means but cloy'd;
 And hence arise the woes of sentiment,
Blue-devils, and blue-stockings, and ro-mances
Reduced to practice, and perform'd like dances.

LXXX

I do declare, upon an affidavit,
 Romances I ne'er read like those I have seen;
Nor, if unto the world I ever gave it,
 Would some believe that such a tale had been:
But such intent I never had, nor have it;
 Some truths are better kept behind a screen,
Especially when they would look like lies;
I therefore deal in generalities.

LXXXI

'An oyster may be cross'd in love,'—and why?
Because he mopeth idly in his shell,
And heaves a lonely subterraqueous sigh,
 Much as a monk may do within his cell:
And *à-propos* of monks, their piety
 With sloth hath found it difficult to dwell;
Those vegetables of the Catholic creed
Are apt exceedingly to run to seed.

LXXXII

O Wilberforce! thou man of black renown,
 Whose merit none enough can sing or say,
Thou hast struck one immense Colossus down,
 Thou moral Washington of Africa!
But there's another little thing, I own,
 Which you should perpetrate some summer's day,
And set the other half of earth to rights;
You have freed the *blacks*—now pray shut up the whites.

LXXXIII

Shut up the bald-coot bully Alexander!
 Ship off the Holy Three to Senegal;
Teach them that 'sauce for goose is sauce for gander,'
 And ask them how *they* like to be in thrall?
Shut up each high heroic salamander,
 Who eats fire gratis (since the pay's but small);
Shut up—no, *not* the King, but the Pavilion,
Or else 'twill cost us all another million.

LXXXIV

Shut up the world at large, let Bedlam out;
 And you will be perhaps surprised to find
All things pursue exactly the same route,
 As now with those of *soi-disant* sound mind.
This I could prove beyond a single doubt,
 Were there a jot of sense among man-kind;
But till that *point d'appui* is found, alas!
Like Archimedes, I leave earth as 'twas.

LXXXV

Our gentle Adeline had one defect—
 Her heart was vacant, though a splendid mansion;
Her conduct had been perfectly correct,
 As she had seen nought claiming its ex-pansion.
A wavering spirit may be easier wreck'd,
 Because 'tis frailer, doubtless, than a stanch one;
But when the latter works its own undoing
Its inner crash is like an earthquake's ruin.

LXXXVI

She loved her lord, or thought so; but *that*
 love
Cost her an effort, which is a sad toil,
The stone of Sysiphus, if once we move
 Our feelings 'gainst the nature of the
 soil.
She had nothing to complain of, or re-
 prove,
 No bickerings, no connubial turmoil:
Their union was a model to behold,
Serene and noble,—conjugal, but cold.

LXXXVII

There was no great disparity of years,
 Though much in temper; but they never
 clash'd:
They moved like stars united in their
 spheres,
 Or like the Rhone by Leman's waters
 wash'd,
Where mingled, and yet separate appears
 The river from the lake, all bluely dash'd
Through the serene and placid glassy
 deep,
Which fain would lull its river-child to
 sleep.

LXXXVIII

Now when she once had ta'en an interest
 In anything, however she might flatter
Herself that her intentions were the best,
 Intense intentions are a dangerous
 matter:
Impressions were much stronger than she
 guess'd,
 And gather'd as they run like growing
 water
Upon her mind: the more so, as her breast
Was not at first too readily impress'd.

LXXXIX

But when it was, she had that lurking
 demon
 Of double nature, and thus doubly
 named—
Firmness yclept in heroes, kings, and sea-
 men,
 That is, when they succeed; but greatly
 blamed
As *obstinacy*, both in men and women,
 Whene'er their triumph pales, or star is
 tamed:—
And 'twill perplex the casuist in morality
To fix the due bounds of this dangerous
 quality.

XC

Had Buonaparte won at Waterloo,
 It had been firmness; now 'tis perti-
 nacity:
Must the event decide between the two?
 I leave it to your people of sagacity
To draw the line between the false and
 true,
 If such can e'er be drawn by man's
 capacity:
My business is with Lady Adeline,
Who in her way too was a heroine.

XCI

She knew not her own heart; then how
 should I?
 I think not she was *then* in love with
 Juan:
If so, she would have had the strength to fly
 The wild sensation, unto her a new one:
She merely felt a common sympathy
 (I will not say it was a false or true one)
In him, because she thought he was in
 danger,—
Her husband's friend, her own, young,
 and a stranger.

XCII

She was, or thought she was, his friend—
 and this
 Without the farce of friendship, or ro-
 mance
Of platonism, which leads so oft amiss
 Ladies who have studied friendship but
 in France,
Or Germany, where people *purely* kiss.
 To thus much Adeline would not ad-
 vance;
But of such friendship as man's may to
 man be
She was as capable as woman can be.

XCIII

No doubt the secret influence of the sex
 Will there, as also in the ties of blood,
An innocent predominance annex,
 And tune the concord to a finer mood.
If free from passion, which all friendship
 checks,
 And your true feelings fully understood,
No friend like to a woman earth discovers,
So that you have not been nor will be
 lovers.

XCIV

Love bears within its breast the very
 germ
 Of change; and how should this be
 otherwise?
That violent things more quickly find a
 term
 Is shown through nature's whole analo-
 gies;
And how should the most fierce of all be
 firm?
 Would you have endless lightning in the
 skies?
Methinks Love's very title says enough:
How should 'the *tender* passion' e'er be
 tough?

XCV

Alas! by all experience, seldom yet
 (I merely quote what I have heard from
 many)
Had lovers not some reason to regret
 The passion which made Solomon a
 zany.
I've also seen some wives (not to forget
 The marriage state, the best or worst of
 any)
Who were the very paragons of wives,
Yet made the misery of at least two lives.

XCVI

I've also seen some female *friends* ('tis odd,
 But true—as, if expedient, I could prove)
That faithful were through thick and thin,
 abroad,
 At home, far more than ever yet was
 Love—
Who did not quit me when Oppression trod
 Upon me; whom no scandal could re-
 move;
Who fought, and fight, in absence, too,
 my battles,
Despite the snake Society's loud rattles.

XCVII

Whether Don Juan and chaste Adeline
 Grew friends in this or any other sense,
Will be discuss'd hereafter, I opine:
 At present I am glad of a pretence
To leave them hovering, as the effect is fine,
 And keeps the atrocious reader in *sus-
 pense*:
The surest way for ladies and for books
To bait their tender or their tenter hooks.

XCVIII

Whether they rode, or walk'd, or studied
 Spanish,
 To read Don Quixote in the original,
A pleasure before which all others vanish;
 Whether their talk was of the kind call'd
 'small,'
Or serious, are the topics I must banish
 To the next Canto; where perhaps I shall
Say something to the purpose, and display
Considerable talent in my way.

XCIX

Above all, I beg all men to forbear
 Anticipating aught about the matter:
They'll only make mistakes about the fair,
 And Juan too, especially the latter.
And I shall take a much more serious air
 Than I have yet done, in this epic satire.
It is not clear that Adeline and Juan
Will fall; but if they do, 'twill be their ruin.

C

But great things spring from little:—
 Would you think,
That in our youth, as dangerous a passion

As e'er brought man and woman to the
 brink
 Of ruin, rose from such a slight occasion,
As few would ever dream could form the
 link
 Of such a sentimental situation?
You'll never guess, I'll bet you millions,
 milliards—
It all sprung from a harmless game at
 billiards.

CI

'Tis strange,—but true; for truth is alway
 strange;
 Stranger than fiction: if it could be told
How much would novels gain by the ex-
 change!
 How differently the world would men
 behold!
How oft would vice and virtue places change!
 The new world would be nothing to the
 old,
If some Columbus of the moral seas
Would show mankind their souls' anti-
 podes.

CII

What 'antres vast and deserts idle' then
 Would be discover'd in the human soul!
What icebergs in the hearts of mighty men
 With self-love in the centre as their pole!
What Anthropophagi in nine of ten
 Of those who hold the kingdoms in
 control!
Were things but only call'd by their right
 name,
Cæsar himself would be ashamed of fame.

CANTO THE FIFTEENTH

I

Ah!—What should follow slips from my
 reflection;
 Whatever follows ne'ertheless may be
As *à-propos* of hope or retrospection,
 As though the lurking thought had
 follow'd free.
All present life is but an interjection,
 An 'Oh!' or 'Ah!' of joy or misery,
Or a 'Ha! ha!' or 'Bah!'—a yawn, or
 'Pooh!'
Of which perhaps the latter is most true.

II

But, more or less, the whole's a syncopé
 Or a *singultus*—emblems of emotion,
That grand antithesis to great *ennui*,
 Wherewith we break our bubbles on the
 ocean,
That watery outline of eternity,
 Or miniature at least, as is my notion,
Which ministers unto the soul's delight,
In seeing matters which are out of sight.

III

But all are better than the sigh supprest,
 Corroding in the cavern of the heart,
Making the countenance a masque of rest,
 And turning human nature to an art.
Few men dare show their thoughts of
 worst or best;
 Dissimulation always sets apart
A corner for herself; and therefore fiction
Is that which passes with least contradiction.

IV

Ah! who can tell? Or rather, who cannot
 Remember, without telling, passion's
 errors?
The drainer of oblivion, even the sot,
 Hath got *blue devils* for his morning
 mirrors:
What though on Lethe's stream he seem to
 float,
 He cannot sink his tremours or his terrors;
The ruby glass that shakes within his hand
Leaves a sad sediment of Time's worst
 sand.

V

And as for love—O love!—We will pro-
 ceed.
 The Lady Adeline Amundeville,
A pretty name as one would wish to read,
 Must perch harmonious on my tuneful
 quill.
There's music in the sighing of a reed;
 There's music in the gushing of a rill;
There's music in all things, if men had
 ears:
Their earth is but an echo of the spheres.

VI

The Lady Adeline, right honourable,
 And honour'd, ran a risk of growing less
 so;
For few of the soft sex are very stable
 In their resolves—alas! that I should
 say so;
They differ as wine differs from its label,
 When once decanted;—I presume to
 guess so,
But will not swear: yet both upon occasion,
Till old, may undergo adulteration.

VII

But Adeline was of the purest vintage,
 The unmingled essence of the grape;
 and yet
Bright as a new napoleon from its mintage,
 Or glorious as a diamond richly set;
A page where Time should hesitate to
 print age,
 And for which Nature might forego her
 debt—
Sole creditor whose process doth involve
 in't
The luck of finding everybody solvent.

VIII

O Death! thou dunnest of all duns! thou
 daily
 Knockest at doors, at first with modest
 tap,
Like a meek tradesman when, approach-
 ing palely,
 Some splendid debtor he would take by
 sap:
But oft denied, as patience 'gins to fail, he
 Advances with exasperated rap,
And (if let in) insists, in terms unhandsome,
On ready money, or 'a draft on Ransom.'

IX

Whate'er thou takest, spare awhile poor
 Beauty!
 She is so rare, and thou hast so much
 prey.
What though she now and then may slip
 from duty,
 The more's the reason why you ought to
 stay;
Gaunt Gourmand! with whole nations for
 your booty,
 You should be civil in a modest way:
Suppress, then, some slight feminine dis-
 eases,
And take as many heroes as Heaven pleases.

X

Fair Adeline, the more ingenuous
 Where she was interested (as was said),
Because she was not apt, like some of us,
 To like too readily, or too high bred
To show it—(points we need not now dis-
 cuss)—
 Would give up artlessly both heart and
 head
Unto such feelings as seem'd innocent,
For objects worthy of the sentiment.

XI

Some parts of Juan's history, which
 Rumour,
 That live gazette, had scatter'd to dis-
 figure,
She had heard; but women hear with more
 good humour
 Such aberrations than we men of rigour:
Besides, his conduct, since in England,
 grew more
 Strict, and his mind assumed a manlier
 vigour;
Because he had, like Alcibiades,
The art of living in all climes with ease.

XII

His manner was perhaps the more seduc-
 tive,
 Because he ne'er seem'd anxious to
 seduce;
Nothing affected, studied, or constructive
 Of coxcombry or conquest: no abuse

833

Of his attractions marr'd the fair per-
 spective,
To indicate a Cupidon broke loose,
And seem to say, 'Resist us if you can'—
Which makes a dandy while it spoils a
 man.

XIII

They are wrong—that's not the way to set
 about it;
 As, if they told the truth, could well be
 shown.
But, right or wrong, Don Juan was with-
 out it;
 In fact, his manner was his own alone:
Sincere he was—at least you could not
 doubt it,
 In listening merely to his voice's tone.
The devil hath not in all his quiver's choice
An arrow for the heart like a sweet voice.

XIV

By nature soft, his whole address held off
 Suspicion; though not timid, his regard
Was such as rather seem'd to keep aloof,
 To shield himself than put you on your
 guard:
Perhaps 'twas hardly quite assured enough,
 But modesty's at times its own reward,
Like virtue; and the absence of pretension
Will go much farther than there's need to
 mention.

XV

Serene, accomplish'd, cheerful but not
 loud;
 Insinuating without insinuation;
Observant of the foibles of the crowd,
 Yet ne'er betraying this in conversation;
Proud with the proud, yet courteously
 proud,
 So as to make them feel he knew his
 station
And theirs:—without a struggle for prior-
 ity,
He neither brook'd nor claim'd superior-
 ity—

XVI

That is, with men: with women he was what
 They pleased to make or take him for;
 and their
Imagination's quite enough for that:
 So that the outline's tolerably fair,
They fill the canvas up—and 'verbum sat.'
 If once their phantasies be brought to
 bear
Upon an object, whether sad or playful,
They can transfigure brighter than a
 Raphael.

XVII

Adeline, no deep judge of character,
 Was apt to add a colouring from her
 own:

'Tis thus the good will amiably err,
 And eke the wise, as has been often
 shown.
Experience is the chief philosopher,
 But saddest when his science is well
 known;
And persecuted sages teach the schools
Their folly in forgetting there are fools.

XVIII

Was it not so, great Locke? and greater
 Bacon?
 Great Socrates? And thou, Diviner still,
Whose lot it is by man to be mistaken,
 And thy pure creed made sanction of all
 ill?
Redeeming worlds to be by bigots shaken,
 How was thy toil rewarded? We might
 fill
Volumes with similar sad illustrations,
But leave them to the conscience of the
 nations.

XIX

I perch upon an humbler promontory,
 Amidst life's infinite variety:
With no great care for what is nicknamed
 glory,
 But speculating as I cast mine eye
On what may suit or may not suit my story,
 And never straining hard to versify,
I rattle on exactly as I'd talk
With anybody in a ride or walk.

XX

I don't know that there may be much ability
 Shown in this sort of desultory rhyme;
But there's a conversational facility,
 Which may round off an hour upon a
 time.
Of this I'm sure at least, there's no ser-
 vility
 In mine irregularity of chime,
Which rings what's uppermost of new or
 hoary,
Just as I feel the *Improvvisatore*.

XXI

'*Omnia vult belle Matho dicere—dic ali-*
 quando
 Et bene, *dic* neutrum, *dic aliquando* male.'
The first is rather more than mortal can do;
 The second may be sadly done or gaily;
The third is still more difficult to stand to;
 The fourth we hear, and see, and say
 too, daily:
The whole together is what I could wish
To serve in this conundrum of a dish.

XXII

A modest hope—but modesty's my forte,
 And pride my feeble:—let us ramble on.
I meant to make this poem very short,
 But now I can't tell where it may not run.

No doubt, if I had wish'd to pay my court
 To critics, or to hail the *setting* sun
Of tyranny of all kinds, my concision
 Were more;—but I was born for opposi-
 tion.

XXIII

But then 'tis mostly on the weaker side;
 So that I verily believe if they
Who now are basking in their full-blown
 pride
 Were shaken down and 'dogs had had
 their day,'
Though at the first I might perchance deride
 Their tumble, I should turn the other
 way,
And wax an ultra-royalist in loyalty,
Because I hate even democratic royalty.

XXIV

I think I should have made a decent spouse,
 If I had never proved the soft condition;
I think I should have made monastic vows,
 But for my own peculiar superstition:
Gainst rhyme I never should have knock'd
 my brows,
 Nor broken my own head, nor that of
 Priscian,
Nor worn the motley mantle of a poet,
If some one had not told me to forego it.

XXV

But *laissez aller*—knights and dames I
 sing,
 Such as the times may furnish. 'Tis a
 flight
Which seems at first to need no lofty wing,
 Plumed by Longinus or the Stagyrite:
The difficulty lies in colouring
 (Keeping the due proportions still in sight)
With nature manners which are artificial,
And rend'ring general that which is especial.

XXVI

The difference is, that in the days of old
 Men made the manners; manners now
 make men—
Pinn'd like a flock, and fleeced too in their
 fold,
 At least nine, and a ninth beside of ten.
Now this at all events must render cold
 Your writers, who must either draw again
Days better drawn before, or else assume
The present, with their common-place cos-
 tume.

XXVII

We'll do our best to make the best on't:—
 March!
 March, my Muse! If you cannot fly,
 yet flutter;
And when you may not be sublime, be
 arch,
 Or starch, as are the edicts statesmen
 utter.

We surely shall find something worth re-
 search:
 Columbus found a new world in a
 cutter,
Or brigantine, or pink, of no great ton-
 nage,
While yet America was in her non-age.

XXVIII

When Adeline, in all her growing sense
 Of Juan's merits and his situation,
Felt on the whole an interest intense,—
 Partly perhaps because a fresh sensa-
 tion,
Or that he had an air of innocence,
 Which is for innocence a sad tempta-
 tion—
As women hate half measures, on the whole,
She 'gan to ponder how to save his soul.

XXIX

She had a good opinion of advice,
 Like all who give and eke receive it gratis,
For which small thanks are still the market
 price,
 Even where the article at highest rate is:
She thought upon the subject twice or
 thrice,
 And morally decided, the best state is
For morals, marriage; and this question
 carried,
She seriously advised him to get married.

XXX

Juan replied, with all becoming deference,
 He had a predilection for that tie;
But that, at present, with immediate refer-
 ence
 To his own circumstances, there might
 lie
Some difficulties, as in his own preference,
 Or that of her to whom he might apply:
That still he'd wed with such or such a lady,
If that they were not married all already.

XXXI

Next to the making matches for herself,
 And daughters, brothers, sisters, kith or
 kin,
Arranging them like books on the same
 shelf,
 There's nothing women love to dabble in
More (like a stock-holder in growing pelf)
 Than match-making in general: 'tis no
 sin
Certes, but a preventative, and therefore
That is, no doubt, the only reason where-
 fore.

XXXII

But never yet (except of course a miss
 Unwed, or mistress never to be wed,
Or wed already, who object to this)
 Was there chaste dame who had not in
 her head

Some drama of the marriage unities,
 Observed as strictly both at board and
 bed
As those of Aristotle, though sometimes
They turn out melodrames or pantomimes

XXXIII

They generally have some only son
 Some heir to a large property, some
 friend
Of an old family, some gay Sir John,
 Or grave Lord George, with whom per-
 haps might end
A line, and leave posterity undone,
 Unless a marriage was applied to mend
The prospect and their morals: and be-
 sides,
They have at hand a blooming glut of
 brides.

XXXIV

From these they will be careful to select,
 For this an heiress, and for that a
 beauty;
For one a songstress who hath no defect,
 For t'other one who promises much duty;
For this a lady no one can reject,
 Whose sole accomplishments were quite
 a booty;
A second for her excellent connexions;
A third, because there can be no objec-
 tions.

XXXV

When Rapp the Harmonist embargo'd
 marriage
 In his harmonious settlement—(which
 flourishes
Strangely enough as yet without mis-
 carriage,
 Because it breeds no more mouths than
 it nourishes,
Without those sad expenses which dis-
 parage
 What Nature naturally most encour-
 ages)—
Why call'd he 'Harmony' a state sans
 wedlock?
Now here I have got the preacher at a dead
 lock.

XXXVI

Because he either meant to sneer at har-
 mony
 Or marriage, by divorcing them thus
 oddly.
But whether reverend Rapp learn'd this in
 Germany
 Or no, 'tis said his sect is rich and godly,
Pious and pure, beyond what I can term
 any
 Of ours, although they propagate more
 broadly.
My objection's to his title, not his ritual,
Although I wonder how it grew habitual.

XXXVII

But Rapp is the reverse of zealous matrons,
 Who favour, *malgré* Malthus, genera-
 tion—
Professors of that genial art, and patrons
 Of all the modest part of propagation;
Which after all at such a desperate rate
 runs,
 That half its produce tends to emigra-
 tion,
That sad result of passions and potatoes—
Two weeds which pose our economic
 Catos.

XXXVIII

Had Adeline read Malthus? I can't tell;
 I wish she had: his book's the eleventh
 commandment,
Which says, 'Thou shalt not marry,' un-
 less *well*:
 This he (as far as I can understand)
 meant.
'Tis not my purpose on his views to dwell,
 Nor canvass what 'so eminent a hand'
 meant;
But certes it conducts to lives ascetic,
Or turning marriage into arithmetic.

XXXIX

But Adeline, who probably presumed
 That Juan had enough of maintenance,
Or *separate* maintenance, in case 'twas
 doom'd—
 As on the whole it is an even chance
That bridegrooms, after they are fairly
 groom'd,
 May retrograde a little in the dance
Of marriage—(which might form a
 painter's fame,
Like Holbein's 'Dance of Death'—but
 'tis the same);—

XL

But Adeline determined Juan's wedding
 In her own mind, and that's enough for
 woman;
But then, with whom? There was the sage
 Miss Reading,
 Miss Raw, Miss Flaw, Miss Showman,
 and Miss Knowman,
And the two fair co-heiresses Giltbedding.
 She deem'd his merits something more
 than common:
All these were unobjectionable matches,
And might go on, if well wound up, like
 watches.

XLI

There was Miss Millpond, smooth as
 summer's sea,
 That usual paragon, an only daughter,
Who deem'd the cream of equanimity,
 Till skimm'd—and then there was some
 milk and water,

With a slight shade of blue too, it might be
 Beneath the surface; but what did it
 matter?
Love's riotous, but marriage should have
 quiet,
And being consumptive, live on a milk diet.

XLII

And then there was the Miss Audacia
 Shoestring,
 A dashing *demoiselle* of good estate,
Whose heart was fix'd upon a star or blue
 string;
 But whether English dukes grew rare of
 late,
Or that she had not harp'd upon the true
 string,
 By which such sirens can attract our great,
She took up with some foreign younger
 brother,
A Russ or Turk—the one's as good as
 t'other.

XLIII

And then there was—but why should I go
 on,
 Unless the ladies should go off?—there
 was
Indeed a certain fair and fairy one,
 Of the best class, and better than her
 class,—
Aurora Raby, a young star who shone
 O'er life, too sweet an image for such
 glass,
A lovely being, scarcely form'd or moulded,
A rose with all its sweetest leaves yet folded;

XLIV

Rich, noble, but an orphan; left an only
 Child to the care of guardians good and
 kind;
But still her aspect had an air so lonely!
 Blood is not water; and where shall we
 find
Feelings of youth like those which over-
 thrown lie
 By death, when we are left, alas! behind,
To feel, in friendless palaces, a home
Is wanting, and our best ties in the tomb?

XLV

Early in years, and yet more infantine
 In figure, she had something of sublime
In eyes which sadly shone, as seraphs'
 shine.
 All youth—but with an aspect beyond
 time;
Radiant and grave—as pitying man's de-
 cline;
 Mournful—but mournful of another's
 crime,
She look'd as if she sat by Eden's door,
And grieved for those who could return no
 more.

XLVI

She was a Catholic, too, sincere, austere,
 As far as her own gentle heart allow'd,
And deem'd that fallen worship far more
 dear
 Perhaps because 'twas fallen: her sires
 were proud
Of deeds and days when they had fill'd the
 ear
 Of nations, and had never bent or bow'd
To novel power; and as she was the last,
She held their old faith and old feelings fast.

XLVII

She gazed upon a world she scarcely knew,
 As seeking not to know it; silent, lone,
As grows a flower, thus quietly she grew,
 And kept her heart serene within its
 zone.
There was awe in the homage which she
 drew;
 Her spirit seem'd as seated on a throne
Apart from the surrounding world, and
 strong
In its own strength—most strange in one
 so young!

XLVIII

Now it so happen'd, in the catalogue
 Of Adeline, Aurora was omitted,
Although her birth and wealth had given
 her vogue,
 Beyond the charmers we have already
 cited;
Her beauty also seem'd to form no clog
 Against her being mention'd as well fitted,
By many virtues, to be worth the trouble
Of single gentlemen who would be double.

XLIX

And this omission, like that of the bust
 Of Brutus at the pageant of Tiberius,
Made Juan wonder, as no doubt he must.
 This he express'd half smiling and half
 serious;
When Adeline replied with some disgust,
 And with an air, to say the least, im-
 perious,
She marvell'd 'what he saw in such a baby
As that prim, silent, cold Aurora Raby?'

L

Juan rejoin'd—'She was a Catholic,
 And therefore fittest, as of his persuasion;
Since he was sure his mother would fall
 sick,
 And the Pope thunder excommunication,
If——' But here Adeline, who seem'd to
 pique
 Herself extremely on the inoculation
Of others with her own opinions, stated—
As usual—the same reason which she late
 did.

LI

And wherefore not? A reasonable reason,
 If good, is none the worse for repetition;
If bad, the best way's certainly to tease on,
 And amplify: you lose much by con-
 cision,
Whereas insisting in or out of season
 Convinces all men, even a politician;
Or—what is just the same—it wearies out.
So the end's gain'd, what signifies the
 route?

LII

Why Adeline had this slight prejudice—
 For prejudice it was—against a creature
As pure as sanctity itself from vice,
 With all the added charm of form and
 feature,
For me appears a question far too nice,
 Since Adeline was liberal by nature;
But nature's nature, and has more caprices
Than I have time, or will, to take to pieces.

LIII

Perhaps she did not like the quiet way
 With which Aurora on those baubles
 look'd,
Which charm most people in their earlier
 day:
 For there are few things by mankind less
 brook'd,
And womankind too, if we so may say,
 Than finding thus their genius stand
 rebuked,
Like 'Antony's by Cæsar,' by the few
Who look upon them as they ought to do.

LIV

It was not envy—Adeline had none;
 Her place was far beyond it, and her
 mind.
It was not scorn—which could not light on
 one
 Whose greatest *fault* was leaving few to
 find.
It was not jealousy, I think: but shun
 Following the *ignes fatui* of mankind.
It was not——but 'tis easier far, alas!
To say what it was *not* than what it was.

LV

Little Aurora deem'd she was the theme
 Of such discussion. She was there a
 guest;
A beauteous ripple of the brilliant stream
 Of rank and youth, though purer than
 the rest,
Which flow'd on for a moment in the beam
 Time sheds a moment o'er each spark-
 ling crest.
Had she known this, she would have
 calmly smiled—
She had so much, or little, of the child.

LVI

The dashing and proud air of Adeline
 Imposed not upon her: she saw her
 blaze
Much as she would have seen a glow-
 worm shine,
 Then turn'd unto the stars for loftier rays.
Juan was something she could not divine,
 Being no sibyl in the new world's ways;
Yet she was nothing dazzled by the meteor,
Because she did not pin her faith on fea-
 ture.

LVII

His fame too,—for he had that kind of fame
 Which sometimes plays the deuce with
 womankind,
A heterogeneous mass of glorious blame,
 Half virtues and whole vices being com-
 bined;
Faults which attract because they are not
 tame;
 Follies trick'd out so brightly that they
 blind:—
These seals upon her wax made no im-
 pression,
Such was her coldness or her self-posses-
 sion.

LVIII

Juan knew nought of such a character—
 High, yet resembling not his lost Haidée;
Yet each was radiant in her proper sphere:
 The island girl, bred up by the lone sea,
More warm, as lovely, and not less sin-
 cere,
 Was Nature's all: Aurora could not be,
Nor would be thus:—the difference in
 them
Was such as lies between a flower and gem.

LIX

Having wound up with this sublime com-
 parison,
 Methinks we may proceed upon our
 narrative,
And, as my friend Scott says, 'I sound my
 warison';
 Scott, the superlative of my compara-
 tive—
Scott, who can paint your Christian knight
 or Saracen,
 Serf, lord, man, with such skill as none
 would share it, if
There had not been one Shakspeare and
 Voltaire,
Of one or both of whom he seems the heir.

LX

I say, in my slight way I may proceed
 To play upon the surface of humanity.
I write the world, nor care if the world
 read,
 At least for this I cannot spare its vanity.

My Muse hath bred, and still perhaps may
 breed
 More foes by this same scroll: when I
 began it, I
Thought that it might turn out so—*now*
 I *know* it,
But still I am, or was, a pretty poet.

LXI

The conference or congress (for it ended
 As congresses of late do) of the Lady
Adeline and Don Juan rather blended
 Some acids with the sweets—for she was
 heady;
But, ere the matter could be marr'd or
 mended,
 The silvery bell rung, not for 'dinner
 ready,'
But for that hour, call'd *half-hour*, given
 to dress,
Though ladies' robes seem scant enough
 for less.

LXII

Great things were now to be achieved at
 table,
 With massy plate for armour, knives
 and forks
For weapons; but what Muse since
 Homer's able
 (His feasts are not the worst part of his
 works)
To draw up in array a single day-bill
 Of modern dinners? where more mystery
 lurks,
In soups or sauces, or a sole *ragoût*,
Than witches, b—ches, or physicians, brew.

LXIII

There was a goodly 'soupe à la *bonne femme*,'
 Though God knows whence it came
 from; there was, too,
A turbot for relief of those who cram,
 Relieved with 'dindon à la Périgueux:'
There also was——the sinner that I am!
 How shall I get this gourmand stanza
 through?—
'Soupe à la Beauveau,' whose relief was
 dory,
Relieved itself by pork, for greater glory.

LXIV

But I must crowd all into one grand mess,
 Or mass; for should I stretch into detail,
My Muse would run much more into excess,
 Than when some squeamish people
 deem her frail;
But though a 'bonne vivante,' I must
 confess
 Her stomach's not her peccant part;
 this tale
However doth require some slight refec-
 tion,
Just to relieve her spirits from dejection.

LXV

Fowls 'à la Condé,' slices eke of salmon,
 With 'sauces Génévoises,' and haunch
 of venison:
Wines, too, which might again have slain
 young Ammon—
 A man like whom I hope we sha'n't see
 many soon;
They also set a glazed Westphalian ham
 on,
 Whereon Apicius would bestow his
 benison:
And then there was champagne with foam-
 ing whirls,
As white as Cleopatra's melted pearls.

LXVI

Then there was God knows what 'à l'Alle-
 mande,'
 'A l'Espagnole,' 'timballe,' and 'sal-
 picon'—
With things I can't withstand or under-
 stand,
 Though swallow'd with much zest upon
 the whole;
And '*entremets*' to piddle with at hand,
 Gently to lull down the subsiding soul;
While great Lucullus' *Robe triumphal*
 muffles—
(*There's fame*)—young partridge fillets,
 deck'd with truffles.

LXVII

What are the *fillets* on the victor's brow
 To these? They are rags or dust. Where
 is the arch
Which nodded to the nation's spoils below?
 Where the triumphal chariots' haughty
 march?
Gone to where victories must like dinners
 go.
 Farther I shall not follow the research:
But oh! ye modern heroes with your car-
 tridges,
When will your names lend lustre even to
 partridges?

LXVIII

Those truffles too are no bad accessaries,
 Follow'd by 'petits puits d'amour'—a
 dish
Of which perhaps the cookery rather
 varies,
 So every one may dress it to his wish,
According to the best of dictionaries,
 Which encyclopedise both flesh and fish;
But even sans *confitures*, it no less true is,
There's pretty picking in those *petits puits*.

LXIX

The mind is lost in mighty contemplation
 Of intellect expended on two courses;
And indigestion's grand multiplication
 Requires arithmetic beyond my forces.

Who would suppose, from Adam's simple
 ration,
 That cookery could have call'd forth
 such resources,
As form a science and a nomenclature
From out the commonest demands of
 nature?

LXX

The glasses jingled, and the palates tingled;
 The diners of celebrity dined well;
The ladies with more moderation mingled
 In the feast, pecking less than I can tell;
Also the younger men too: for a springald
 Can't, like ripe age, in *gourmandise* excel,
But thinks less of good eating than the
 whisper
(When seated next him) of some pretty
 lisper.

LXXI

Alas! I must leave undescribed the *gibier*,
 The *salmi*, the *consommé*, the *purée*,
All which I use to make my rhymes run
 glibber
 Than could roast beef in our rough
 John Bull way:
I must not introduce even a spare rib here,
 'Bubble and squeak' would spoil my
 liquid lay,
But I have dined, and must forego, alas!
The chaste description even of a 'bécasse;'

LXXII

And fruits, and ice, and all that art refines
 From nature for the service of the
 goût—
Taste or the *gout*,—pronounce it as in-
 clines
 Your stomach! Ere you dine, the
 French will do;
But *after*, there are sometimes certain signs
 Which prove plain English truer of the
 two.
Hast ever *had* the *gout*? I have not had it—
But I may have, and you too, reader,
 dread it.

LXXIII

The simple olives, best allies of wine,
 Must I pass over in my bill of fare?
I must, although a favourite *plat* of mine
 In Spain, and Lucca, Athens, every-
 where:
On them and bread 'twas oft my luck to dine,
 The grass my table-cloth, in open air,
On Sunium or Hymettus, like Diogenes,
Of whom half my philosophy the progeny is.

LXXIV

Amidst this tumult of fish, flesh, and fowl,
 And vegetables, all in masquerade,
The guests were placed according to their
 roll,
 But various as the various meats dis-
 play'd:

Don Juan sat next an 'à l'Espagnole'—
 No damsel, but a dish, as hath been said:
But so far like a lady, that 'twas drest
Superbly, and contain'd a world of zest.

LXXV

By some odd chance too, he was placed
 between
 Aurora and the Lady Adeline—
A situation difficult, I ween,
 For man therein, with eyes and heart, to
 dine,
Also the conference which we have seen
 Was not such as to encourage him to
 shine,
For Adeline, addressing few words to him,
With two transcendent eyes seem'd to look
 through him.

LXXVI

I sometimes almost think that eyes have
 ears:
 This much is sure, that, out of earshot,
 things
Are somehow echoed to the pretty dears,
 Of which I can't tell whence their know-
 ledge springs.
Like that same mystic music of the spheres,
 Which no one hears, so loudly though
 it rings,
'Tis wonderful how oft the sex have heard
Long dialogues—which pass'd without a
 word!

LXXVII

Aurora sat with that indifference
 Which piques a *preux chevalier*—as it
 ought:
Of all offences that's the worst offence,
 Which seems to hint you are not worth
 a thought.
Now Juan, though no coxcomb in pretence,
 Was not exactly pleased to be so caught;
Like a good ship entangled among ice,
And after so much excellent advice.

LXXVIII

To his gay nothings, nothing was replied,
 Or something which was nothing, as
 urbanity
Required. Aurora scarcely look'd aside,
 Nor even smiled enough for any vanity.
The devil was in the girl! Could it be
 pride?
 Or modesty, or absence, or inanity?
Heaven knows! But Adeline's malicious
 eyes
Sparkled with her successful prophecies,

LXXIX

And look'd as much as if to say, 'I said it';
 A kind of triumph I'll not recommend,
Because it sometimes, as I've seen or
 read it,
 Both in the case of lover and of friend,

Will pique a gentleman, for his own credit,
 To bring what was a jest to a serious end:
For all men prophesy what *is* or *was,*
And hate those who won't let them come
 to pass.

LXXX

Juan was drawn thus into some attentions,
 Slight but select, and just enough to
 express,
To females of perspicuous comprehen-
 sions,
 That he would rather make them more
 than less.
Aurora at the last (so history mentions,
 Though probably much less a fact than
 guess)
So far relax'd her thoughts from their
 sweet prison,
As once or twice to smile, if not to listen.

LXXXI

From answering she began to question:
 this
 With her was rare; and Adeline, who
 as yet
Thought her predictions went not much
 amiss,
 Began to dread she'd thaw to a co-
 quette—
So very difficult, they say, it is
 To keep extremes from meeting, when
 once set
In motion; but she here too much refined—
Aurora's spirit was not of that kind.

LXXXII

But Juan had a sort of winning way,
 A proud humility, if such there be,
Which show'd such deference to what
 females say,
 As if each charming word were a decree.
His tact, too, temper'd him from grave to
 gay,
 And taught him when to be reserved or
 free;
He had the art of drawing people out,
Without their seeing what he was about.

LXXXIII

Aurora, who in her indifference
 Confounded him in common with the
 crowd
Of flutterers, though she deem'd he had
 more sense
 Than whispering foplings, or than wit-
 lings loud—
Commenced (from such slight things will
 great commence)
 To feel that flattery which attracts the
 proud
Rather by deference than compliment,
And wins even by a delicate dissent.

LXXXIV

And then he had good looks;—that point
 was carried
 Nem. con. amongst the women, which I
 grieve
To say leads oft to *crim. con.* with the
 married—
 A case which to the juries we may leave,
Since with digressions we too long have
 tarried.
 Now though we know of old that looks
 deceive,
And always have done, somehow these
 good looks
Make more impression than the best of
 books.

LXXXV

Aurora, who look'd more on books than
 faces,
 Was very young, although so very sage,
Admiring more Minerva than the Graces,
 Especially upon a printed page.
But Virtue's self, with all her tightest laces,
 Has not the natural stays of strict old
 age;
And Socrates, that model of all duty,
Own'd to a *penchant*, though discreet, for
 beauty.

LXXXVI

And girls of sixteen are thus far Socratic,
 But innocently so, as Socrates;
And really, if the sage sublime and Attic
 At seventy years had phantasies like
 these,
Which Plato in his dialogues dramatic
 Has shown, I know not why they should
 displease
In virgins—always in a modest way,
Observe; for that with me's a *sine quâ.*

LXXXVII

Also observe, that, like the great Lord Coke
 (See Littleton), whene'er I have ex-
 press'd
Opinions two, which at first sight may look
 Twin opposites, the second is the best.
Perhaps I have a third too, in a nook,
 Or none at all—which seems a sorry jest:
But if a writer should be quite consistent,
How could he possibly show things exis-
 tent?

LXXXVIII

If people contradict themselves, can I
 Help contradicting them, and everybody,
Even my veracious self?—But that's a lie:
 I never did so, never will—how should I?
He who doubts all things nothing can
 deny:
 Truth's fountains may be clear—her
 streams are muddy,
And cut through such canals of contra-
 diction,
That she must often navigate o'er fiction.

LXXXIX

Apologue, fable, poesy, and parable,
 Are false, but may be render'd also true,
By those who sow them in a land that's
 arable.
 'Tis wonderful what fable will not do!
'Tis said it makes reality more bearable:
 But what's reality? Who has its clue?
Philosophy? No; she too much rejects.
Religion? *Yes;* but which of all her sects?

XC

Some millions must be wrong, that's
 pretty clear;
 Perhaps it may turn out that all were
 right.
God help us! Since we have need on our
 career
 To keep our holy beacons always bright,
'Tis time that some new prophet should
 appear,
 Or *old* indulge man with a second sight.
Opinions wear out in some thousand
 years,
Without a small refreshment from the
 spheres.

XCI

But here again, why will I thus entangle
 Myself with metaphysics? None can
 hate
So much as I do any kind of wrangle;
 And yet, such is my folly, or my fate,
I always knock my head against some
 angle
 About the present, past, or future state:
Yet I wish well to Trojan and to Tyrian,
For I was bred a moderate Presbyterian.

XCII

But though I am a temperate theologian,
 And also meek as a metaphysician,
Impartial between Tyrian and Trojan
 As Eldon on a lunatic commission,
In politics my duty is to show John
 Bull something of the lower world's con-
 dition.
It makes my blood boil like the springs of
 Hecla,
To see men let these scoundrel sovereigns
 break law.

XCIII

But politics, and policy, and piety,
 Are topics which I sometimes introduce,
Not only for the sake of their variety,
 But as subservient to a moral use;
Because my business is to *dress* society,
 And stuff with *sage* that very verdant
 goose.
And now, that we may furnish with some
 matter all
Tastes, we are going to try the super-
 natural.

XCIV

And now I will give up all argument;
 And positively henceforth no tempta-
 tion
Shall 'fool me to the top up of my bent';—
 Yes, I'll begin a thorough reformation.
Indeed, I never knew what people meant
 By deeming that my Muse's conversa-
 tion
Was dangerous;—I think she is as harm-
 less
As some who labour more and yet may
 charm less.

XCV

Grim reader! did you ever see a ghost?
 No; but you have heard—I understand
 —be dumb!
And don't regret the time you may have
 lost,
 For you have got that pleasure still to
 come:
And do not think I mean to sneer at most
 Of these things, or by ridicule benumb
That source of the sublime and the mys-
 terious:—
For certain reasons my belief is serious.

XCVI

Serious? You laugh;—you may; that will
 I not;
 My smiles must be sincere or not at all.
I say I do believe a haunted spot
 Exists—and where? That shall I not
 recall,
Because I'd rather it should be forgot,
 'Shadows the soul of Richard' may
 appal.
In short, upon that subject I've some
 qualms very
Like those of the philosopher of Malms-
 bury.

XCVII

The night—(I sing by night—sometimes
 an owl,
 And now and then a nightingale)—is dim,
And the loud shriek of sage Minerva's fowl
 Rattles around me her discordant hymn:
Old portraits from old walls upon me
 scowl—
 I wish to heaven they would not look so
 grim;
The dying embers dwindle in the grate—
I think too that I have sat up too late:

XCVIII

And therefore, though 'tis by no means
 my way
 To rhyme at noon—when I have other
 things
To think of, if I ever think—I say
 I feel some chilly midnight shudderings,

And prudently postpone, until mid-day,
 Treating a topic which, alas! but brings
Shadows;—but you must be in my con-
 dition
Before you learn to call this superstition.

XCIX

Between two worlds life hovers like a star,
 'Twixt night and morn, upon the hori-
 zon's verge.
How little do we know that which we are!
 How less what we may be! The eternal
 surge
Of time and tide rolls on, and bears afar
 Our bubbles; as the old burst, new emerge,
Lash'd from the foam of ages; while the
 graves
Of empires heave but like some passing
 waves.

CANTO THE SIXTEENTH

I

THE antique Persians taught three useful
 things,
 To draw the bow, to ride, and speak the
 truth.
This was the mode of Cyrus, best of
 kings—
 A mode adopted since by modern youth.
Bows have they, generally with two strings,
 Horses they ride without remorse or
 ruth;
At speaking truth perhaps they are less
 clever,
But draw the long bow better now than
 ever.

II

The cause of this effect, or this defect,—
 'For this effect defective comes by
 cause,'—
Is what I have not leisure to inspect;
 But this I must say in my own applause,
Of all the Muses that I recollect,
 Whate'er may be her follies or her flaws,
In some things, mine's beyond all contra-
 diction
The most sincere that ever dealt in fiction.

III

And as she treats all things, and ne'er re-
 treats
 From anything, this epic will contain
A wilderness of the most rare conceits,
 Which you might elsewhere hope to
 find in vain.
'Tis true there be some bitters with the
 sweets,
 Yet mix'd so slightly, that you can't
 complain,
But wonder they so few are, since my tale is
'De rebus cunctis et quibusdam aliis.'

IV

But of all truths which she has told, the
 most
 True is that which she is about to tell.
I said it was a story of a ghost—
 What then? I only know it so befell.
Have you explored the limits of the coast,
 Where all the dwellers of the earth must
 dwell?
'Tis time to strike such puny doubters
 dumb as
The sceptics who would not believe
 Columbus.

V

Some people would impose now with
 authority,
 Turpin's or Monmouth Geoffry's
 Chronicle;
Men whose historical superiority
 Is always greatest at a miracle.
But Saint Augustine has the great priority,
 Who bids all men believe the impossible,
Because 'tis so. Who nibble, scribble,
 quibble, he
Quiets at once with 'quia impossibile.'

VI

And therefore, mortals, cavil not at all;
 Believe:—if 'tis improbable, you must,
And if it is impossible, you shall:
 'Tis always best to take things upon
 trust.
I do not speak profanely, to recall
 Those holier mysteries which the wise
 and just
Receive as gospel, and which grow more
 rooted,
As all truths must, the more they are dis-
 puted:

VII

I merely mean to say what Johnson said,
 That in the course of some six thousand
 years,
All nations have believed that from the
 dead
 A visitant at intervals appears;
And what is strangest upon this strange
 head,
 Is, that whatever bar the reason rears
'Gainst such belief, there's something
 stronger still
In its behalf, let those deny who will.

VIII

The dinner and the soirée too were done,
 The supper too discuss'd, the dames
 admired,
The banqueteers had dropp'd off one by
 one—
 The song was silent, and the dance ex-
 pired:

843

The last thin petticoats were vanish'd, gone
 Like fleecy clouds into the sky retired,
And nothing brighter gleam'd through the
 saloon
Than dying tapers—and the peeping moon.

IX

The evaporation of a joyous day
 Is like the last glass of champagne,
 without
The foam which made its virgin bumper
 gay;
 Or like a system coupled with a doubt;
Or like a soda bottle when its spray
 Has sparkled and let half its spirit out;
Or like a billow left by storms behind,
Without the animation of the wind;

X

Or like an opiate, which brings troubled
 rest,
 Or none; or like—like nothing that I
 know
Except itself;—such is the human breast;
 A thing, of which similitudes can show
No real likeness,—like the old Tyrian vest
 Dyed purple, none at present can tell
 how,
If from a shell-fish or from cochineal.
So perish every tyrant's robe piece-meal!

XI

But next to dressing for a rout or ball,
 Undressing is a woe; our *robe de
 chambre*
May sit like that of Nessus, and recall
 Thoughts quite as yellow, but less clear
 than amber.
Titus exclaim'd, 'I've lost a day!' Of all
 The nights and days most people can
 remember,
(I have had of both, some not to be dis-
 dain'd,)
I wish they'd state how many they have
 gain'd.

XII

And Juan, on retiring for the night,
 Felt restless, and perplex'd, and com-
 promised:
He thought Aurora Raby's eyes more
 bright
 Than Adeline (such is advice) advised;
If he had known exactly his own plight,
 He probably would have philosophised;
A great resource to all, and ne'er denied
Till wanted; therefore Juan only sigh'd.

XIII

He sigh'd;—the next resource is the full
 moon,
 Where all sighs are deposited; and now
It happen'd luckily, the chaste orb shone
 As clear as such a climate will allow;

And Juan's mind was in the proper tone
 To hail her with the apostrophe—'O
 thou!'
Of amatory egotism the *Tuism*,
Which further to explain would be a truism.

XIV

But lover, poet, or astronomer,
 Shepherd, or swain, whoever may be-
 hold,
Feel some abstraction when they gaze on
 her;
 Great thoughts we catch from thence
 (besides a cold
Sometimes, unless my feelings rather
 err);
 Deep secrets to her rolling light are
 told;
The ocean's tides and mortals' brains she
 sways,
And also hearts, if there be truth in lays.

XV

Juan felt somewhat pensive, and disposed
 For contemplation rather than his pil-
 low:
The Gothic chamber, where he was en-
 closed,
 Let in the rippling sound of the lake's
 billow,
With all the mystery by midnight caused:
 Below his window waved (of course) a
 willow;
And he stood gazing out on the cascade
That flash'd and after darken'd in the
 shade.

XVI

Upon his table or his toilet,—*which*
 Of these is not exactly ascertain'd,—
(I state this, for I am cautious to a pitch
 Of nicety, where a fact is to be gain'd,)
A lamp burn'd high, while he leant from
 a niche,
 Where many a Gothic ornament re-
 main'd,
In chisell'd stone and painted glass, and
 all
That time has left our fathers of their hall.

XVII

Then, as the night was clear though cold,
 he threw
 His chamber door wide open—and
 went forth
Into a gallery, of a sombre hue,
 Long, furnish'd with old pictures of
 great worth,
Of knights and dames heroic and chaste too,
 As doubtless should be people of high
 birth.
But by dim lights the portraits of the dead
Have something ghastly, desolate, and
 dread.

XVIII

The forms of the grim knight and pictured saint
　Look living in the moon; and as you turn
Backward and forward to the echoes faint
　Of your own footsteps—voices from the urn
Appear to wake, and shadows wild and quaint
　Start from the frames which fence their aspects stern,
As if to ask how you can dare to keep
A vigil there, where all but death should sleep.

XIX

And the pale smile of beauties in the grave,
　The charms of other days, in starlight gleams,
Glimmer on high; their buried locks still wave
　Along the canvas; their eyes glance like dreams
On ours, or spars within some dusky cave,
　But death is imaged in their shadowy beams.
A picture is the past; even ere its frame
Be gilt, who sate hath ceased to be the same.

XX

As Juan mused on mutability,
　Or on his mistress—terms synonymous—
No sound except the echo of his sigh
　Or step ran sadly through that antique house;
When suddenly he heard, or thought so, nigh,
　A supernatural agent—or a mouse,
Whose little nibbling rustle will embarrass
Most people as it plays along the arras.

XXI

It was no mouse, but lo! a monk, array'd
　In cowl and beads, and dusky garb, appear'd,
Now in the moonlight, and now lapsed in shade,
　With steps that trod as heavy, yet unheard;
His garments only a slight murmur made;
　He moved as shadowy as the sisters weird,
But slowly; and as he passed Juan by,
Glanced, without pausing, on him a bright eye.

XXII

Juan was petrified; he had heard a hint
　Of such a spirit in these halls of old,
But thought, like most men, there was nothing in't
　Beyond the rumour which such spots unfold,

Coin'd from surviving superstition's mint,
　Which passes ghosts in currency like gold,
But rarely seen, like gold compared with paper.
And did he see this? or was it a vapour?

XXIII

Once, twice, thrice pass'd, repass'd—the thing of air,
　Or earth beneath, or heaven, or t'other place;
And Juan gazed upon it with a stare,
　Yet could not speak or move; but, on its base
As stands a statue, stood: he felt his hair
　Twine like a knot of snakes around his face;
He tax'd his tongue for words, which were not granted,
To ask the reverend person what he wanted.

XXIV

The third time, after a still longer pause,
　The shadow pass'd away—but where? the hall
Was long, and thus far there was no great cause
　To think his vanishing unnatural:
Doors there were many, through which, by the laws
　Of physics, bodies whether short or tall
Might come or go; but Juan could not state
Through which the spectre seem'd to evaporate.

XXV

He stood—how long he knew not, but it seem'd
　An age—expectant, powerless, with his eyes
Strain'd on the spot where first the figure gleam'd,
　Then by degrees recall'd his energies,
And would have pass'd the whole off as a dream,
　But could not wake; he was, he did surmise,
Waking already, and return'd at length
Back to his chamber, shorn of half his strength.

XXVI

All there was as he left it: still his taper
　Burnt, and not *blue*, as modest tapers use,
Receiving sprites with sympathetic vapour;
　He rubb'd his eyes, and they did not refuse
Their office; he took up an old newspaper;
　The paper was right easy to peruse;
He read an article the king attacking,
And a long eulogy of 'patent blacking.'

845

XXVII

This savour'd of this world; but his hand
 shook:
 He shut his door, and after having read
A paragraph, I think about Horne Tooke,
 Undrest, and rather slowly went to bed.
There, couch'd all snugly on his pillow's
 nook,
 With what he had seen his phantasy he
 fed;
And though it was no opiate, slumber
 crept
Upon him by degrees, and so he slept.

XXVIII

He woke betimes; and, as may be sup-
 posed,
 Ponder'd upon his visitant or vision,
And whether it ought not to be disclosed,
 At risk of being quizz'd for superstition.
The more he thought, the more his mind
 was posed;
 In the mean time, his valet, whose pre-
 cision
Was great, because his master brook'd no
 less,
Knock'd to inform him it was time to
 dress.

XXIX

He dress'd; and like young people he was
 wont
 To take some trouble with his toilet,
 but
This morning rather spent less time upon 't;
 Aside his very mirror soon was put;
His curls fell negligently o'er his front,
 His clothes were not curb'd to their
 usual cut,
His very neckcloth's Gordian knot was
 tied
Almost an hair's breadth too much on one
 side.

XXX

And when he walk'd down into the saloon,
 He sate him pensive o'er a dish of tea,
Which he perhaps had not discover'd
 soon,
 Had it not happen'd scalding hot to be,
Which made him have recourse unto his
 spoon;
 So much *distrait* he was, that all could see
That something was the matter—Adeline
The first—but *what* she could not well
 divine.

XXXI

She look'd, and saw him pale, and turn'd
 as pale
 Herself; then hastily look'd down, and
 mutter'd
Something, but what's not stated in my tale.
 Lord Henry said, his muffin was ill-
 butter'd;

The Duchess of Fitz-Fulke play'd with her
 veil,
 And look'd at Juan hard, but nothing
 utter'd.
Aurora Raby with her large dark eyes
Survey'd him with a kind of calm surprise.

XXXII

But seeing him all cold and silent still,
 And everybody wondering more or
 less,
Fair Adeline inquired 'If he were ill?'
 He started, and said, 'Yes—no—rather
 —yes.'
The family physician had great skill,
 And being present, now began to ex-
 press
His readiness to feel his pulse and tell
The cause, but Juan said, 'He was quite
 well.'

XXXIII

'Quite well; yes,—no.'—These answers
 were mysterious,
 And yet his looks appear'd to sanction
 both,
However they might savour of delirious;
 Something like illness of a sudden
 growth
Weigh'd on his spirit, though by no means
 serious:
 But for the rest, as he himself seem'd
 loth
To state the case, it might be ta'en for
 granted
It was not the physician that he wanted.

XXXIV

Lord Henry, who had now discuss'd his
 chocolate,
 Also the muffin whereof he complain'd,
Said, Juan had not got his usual look
 elate,
 At which he marvell'd, since it had not
 rain'd;
Then ask'd her Grace what news were of
 the duke of late?
 Her Grace replied, *his* Grace was rather
 pain'd
With some slight, light, hereditary twinges
Of gout, which rusts aristocratic hinges.

XXXV

Then Henry turn'd to Juan, and address'd
 A few words of condolence on his state:
'You look,' quoth he, 'as if you had had
 your rest
 Broke in upon by the Black Friar of late.'
'What Friar?' said Juan; and he did his
 best
 To put the question with an air sedate,
Or careless; but the effort was not valid
To hinder him from growing still more
 pallid.

XXXVI

Oh! have you never heard of the Black
 Friar?
 The spirit of these walls?'—'In truth
 not I.'
Why Fame—but Fame you know's some-
 times a liar—
 Tells an odd story, of which by and by:
Whether with time the spectre has grown
 shyer,
 Or that our sires had a more gifted eye
For such sights, though the tale is half
 believed,
The Friar of late has not been oft perceived.

XXXVII

The last time was——'—'I pray,' said
 Adeline—
 (Who watch'd the changes of Don
 Juan's brow,
And from its context thought she could
 divine
 Connexions stronger than he chose to
 avow
With this same legend)—'if you but design
 To jest, you'll choose some other theme
 just now,
Because the present tale has oft been told,
And is not much improved by growing old.'

XXXVIII

Jest!' quoth Milor; 'why, Adeline, you
 know
 That we ourselves—'twas in the honey-
 moon—
Saw——'—'Well, no matter, 'twas so
 long ago;
 But, come, I'll set your story to a tune.'
Graceful as Dian when she draws her bow,
 She seiz'd her harp, whose strings were
 kindled soon
As touch'd, and plaintively began to play
The air of ''Twas a Friar of Orders Gray.'

XXXIX

'But add the words,' cried Henry, 'which
 you made;
 For Adeline is half a poetess,'
Turning round to the rest, he smiling said.
 Of course the others could not but
 express
In courtesy their wish to see display'd
 By one *three* talents, for there were no
 less—
The voice, the words, the harper's skill, at
 once,
Could hardly be united by a dunce.

XL

After some fascinating hesitation,—
 The charming of these charmers, who
 seem bound,
I can't tell why, to this dissimulation,—
 Fair Adeline, with eyes fix'd on the
 ground

At first, then kindling into animation,
 Added her sweet voice to the lyric
 sound,
And sang with much simplicity,—a merit
Not the less precious, that we seldom hear
 it.

1

Beware! beware! of the Black Friar,
 Who sitteth by Norman stone,
For he mutters his prayer in the midnight
 air,
 And his mass of the days that are gone.
When the Lord of the Hill, Amundeville,
 Made Norman Church his prey,
And expell'd the friars, one friar still
 Would not be driven away.

2

Though he came in his might, with King
 Henry's right,
 To turn church lands to lay,
With sword in hand, and torch to light
 Their walls, if they said nay;
A monk remain'd, unchased, unchain'd,
 And he did not seem form'd of clay,
For he's seen in the porch, and he's seen
 in the church,
 Though he is not seen by day.

3

And whether for good, or whether for ill,
 It is not mine to say;
But still with the house of Amundeville
 He abideth night and day.
By the marriage-bed of their lords, 'tis said,
 He flits on the bridal eve;
And 'tis held as faith, to their bed of death
 He comes—but not to grieve.

4

When an heir is born, he's heard to mourn,
 And when aught is to befall
That ancient line, in the pale moonshine
 He walks from hall to hall.
His form you may trace, but not his face,
 'Tis shadow'd by his cowl;
But his eyes may be seen from the folds
 between,
 And they seem of a parted soul.

5

But beware! beware! of the Black Friar,
 He still retains his sway,
For he is yet the Church's heir,
 Whoever may be the lay.
Amundeville is lord by day,
 But the monk is lord by night;
Nor wine nor wassail could raise a vassal
 To question that friar's right.

6

Say nought to him as he walks the hall,
 And he'll say nought to you;
He sweeps along in his dusky pall,
 As o'er the grass the dew.

Then grammercy! for the Black Friar;
 Heaven sain him! fair or foul,
And whatsoe'er may be his prayer,
 Let ours be for his soul.

XLI

The lady's voice ceased, and the thrilling
 wires
 Died from the touch that kindled them
 to sound;
And the pause follow'd, which when song
 expires
 Pervades a moment those who listen
 round;
And then of course the circle much admires,
 Nor less applauds, as in politeness bound,
The tones, the feeling, and the execution,
To the performer's diffident confusion.

XLII

Fair Adeline, though in a careless way,
 As if she rated such accomplishment
As the mere pastime of an idle day,
 Pursued an instant for her own content,
Would now and then, as 'twere *without*
 display,
 Yet *with* display in fact, at times relent
To such performances with haughty smile,
To show she *could*, if it were worth her
 while.

XLIII

Now this (but we will whisper it aside)
 Was—pardon the pedantic illustra-
 tion—
Trampling on Plato's pride with greater
 pride,
 As did the Cynic on some like occasion:
Deeming the sage would be much morti-
 fied,
 Or thrown into a philosophic passion,
For a spoilt carpet—but the 'Attic bee'
Was much consoled by his own repartee.

XLIV

Thus Adeline would throw into the shade
 (By doing easily, whene'er she chose,
What dilettanti do with vast parade)
 Their sort of *half profession*; for it grows
To something like this when too oft dis-
 play'd;
 And that it is so, everybody knows,
Who have heard Miss That or This, or
 Lady T'other,
Show off—to please their company or
 mother.

XLV

Oh! the long evenings of duets and trios!
 The admirations and the speculations;
The 'Mamma Mia's!' and the 'Amor
 Mio's!'
 The 'Tanti palpiti's' on such occasions:

The 'Lasciami's,' and quavering 'Ad
 dio's!'
 Amongst our own most musical o
 nations;
With 'Tu mi chamas's' from Portingale,
To soothe our ears, lest Italy should fail.

XLVI

In Babylon's *bravuras*—as the home
 Heart-ballads of Green Erin or Gray
 Highlands,
That bring Lochaber back to eyes tha
 roam
 O'er far Atlantic continents or islands
The calentures of music which o'ercome
 All mountaineers with dreams that the
 are nigh lands,
No more to be beheld but in such visions—
Was Adeline well versed, as compositions

XLVII

She also had a twilight tinge of '*Blue*,'
 Could write rhymes, and compose more
 than she wrote,
Made epigrams occasionally too
 Upon her friends, as everybody ought.
But still from that sublimer azure hue,
 So much the present dye, she was remote
Was weak enough to deem Pope a grea
 poet,
And what was worse, was not ashamed t
 show it.

XLVIII

Aurora—since we are touching upon taste
 Which now-a-days is the thermometer
By whose degrees all characters are
 class'd—
 Was more Shakspearian, if I do not err
The worlds beyond this world's perplex
 ing waste
 Had more of her existence, for in her
There was a depth of feeling to embrace
Thoughts, boundless, deep, but silent to
 as Space.

XLIX

Not so her gracious, graceful, graceles
 Grace,
 The full-grown Hebe of Fitz-Fulke
 whose mind,
If she had any, was upon her face,
 And that was of a fascinating kind.
A little turn for mischief you might trac
 Also thereon,—but that's not much
 we find
Few females without some such gentle
 leaven,
For fear we should suppose us quite i
 heaven.

L

I have not heard she was at all poetic,
 Though once she was seen reading the
 Bath Guide,
And Hayley's *Triumphs*, which she deem'
 pathetic,

Because she said *her temper* had been
 tried
So much, the bard had really been pro-
 phetic
Of what she had gone through with—
 'since a bride.
But of all verse, what most insured her
 praise
Were sonnets to herself, or *bouts rimés*.

LI

'Twere difficult to say what was the object
 Of Adeline, in bringing this same lay
To bear on what appear'd to her the sub-
 ject
 Of Juan's nervous feelings on that day.
Perhaps she merely had the simple project
 To laugh him out of his supposed dis-
 may;
Perhaps she might wish to confirm him
 in it,
Though why I cannot say—at least this
 minute.

LII

But so far the immediate effect
 Was to restore him to his self-propriety,
A thing quite necessary to the elect,
 Who wish to take the tone of their
 society:
In which you cannot be too circumspect,
 Whether the mode be persiflage or piety,
But wear the newest mantle of hypocrisy,
On pain of much displeasing the gyno-
 cracy.

LIII

And therefore Juan now began to rally
 His spirits, and without more explana-
 tion
To jest upon such themes in many a sally.
 Her Grace, too, also seized the same
 occasion,
With various similar remarks to tally,
 But wish'd for a still more detail'd
 narration
Of this same mystic friar's curious doings,
About the present family's deaths and
 wooings.

LIV

Of these few could say more than has been
 said;
 They pass'd as such things do, for
 superstition
With some, while others, who had more
 in dread
 The theme, half credited the strange
 tradition;
And much was talk'd on all sides on that
 head:
 But Juan, when cross-question'd on the
 vision,
Which some supposed (though he had not
 avow'd it)
Had stirr'd him, answer'd in a way to
 cloud it.

LV

And then, the mid-day having worn to
 one,
 The company prepared to separate;
Some to their several pastimes, or to none,
 Some wondering 'twas so early, some
 so late.
There was a goodly match too, to be run
 Between some greyhounds on my lord's
 estate,
And a young race-horse of old pedigree,
Match'd for the spring, whom several
 went to see.

LVI

There was a picture-dealer who had
 brought
 A special Titian, warranted original,
So precious that it was not to be bought,
 Though princes the possessor were
 besieging all.
The king himself had cheapen'd it, but
 thought
 The civil list he deigns to accept (oblig-
 ing all
His subjects by his gracious acceptation)—
Too scanty, in these times of low taxation.

LVII

But as Lord Henry was a connoisseur,—
 The friend of artists, if not arts,—the
 owner,
With motives the most classical and pure,
 So that he would have been the very
 donor,
Rather than seller, had his wants been fewer,
 So much he deem'd his patronage an
 honour,
Had brought the *capo d'opera*, not for sale,
But for his judgment—never known to fail.

LVIII

There was a modern Goth, I mean a
 Gothic
 Bricklayer of Babel, call'd an architect,
Brought to survey these grey walls, which
 though so thick,
 Might have from time acquired some
 slight defect;
Who, after rummaging the Abbey through
 thick
 And thin, produced a plan whereby to
 erect
New buildings of correctest conformation,
And throw down old, which he call'd
 restoration.

LIX

The cost would be a trifle—an 'old song,'
 Set to some thousands ('tis the usual
 burden
Of that same tune, when people hum it
 long)—
 The price would speedily repay its
 worth in

An edifice no less sublime than strong,
 By which Lord Henry's good taste
 would go forth in
Its glory, through all ages shining sunny,
For Gothic daring shown in English money.

LX

There were two lawyers busy on a
 mortgage
 Lord Henry wish'd to raise for a new
 purchase;
Also a lawsuit upon tenures burgage,
 And one on tithes, which sure are
 Discord's torches,
Kindling Religion till she throws down
 her gage,
 'Untying' squires 'to fight against the
 churches';
There was a prize ox, a prize pig, and
 ploughman,
For Henry was a sort of Sabine showman.

LXI

There were two poachers caught in a steel
 trap,
 Ready for gaol, their place of con-
 valescence;
There was a country girl in a close cap
 And scarlet cloak (I hate the sight to
 see, since—
Since—since—in youth, I had the sad
 mishap—
 But luckily I have paid few parish fees
 since):
That scarlet cloak, alas! unclosed with
 rigour
Presents the problem of a double figure.

LXII

A reel within a bottle is a mystery,
 One can't tell how it e'er got in or out;
Therefore the present piece of natural
 history
 I leave to those who are fond of solving
 doubt;
And merely state, though not for the con-
 sistory,
 Lord Henry was a justice, and that Scout
The constable, beneath a warrant's banner,
Had bagg'd this poacher upon Nature's
 manor.

LXIII

Now justices of peace must judge all pieces
 Of mischief of all kinds, and keep the
 game
And morals of the country from caprices
 Of those who have not a licence for the
 same;
And of all things, excepting tithes and leases,
 Perhaps these are most difficult to tame:
Preserving partridges and pretty wenches
Are puzzles to the most precautious
 benches.

LXIV

The present culprit was extremely pale,
 Pale as if painted so; her cheek being red
By nature, as in higher dames less hale
 'Tis white, at least when they just rise
 from bed.
Perhaps she was ashamed of seeming frail
 Poor soul! for she was country born
 and bred,
And knew no better in her immorality
Than to wax white—for blushes are for
 quality.

LXV

Her black, bright, downcast, yet *espiègle*
 eye,
 Had gather'd a large tear into its corner
Which the poor thing at times essay'd to
 dry,
 For she was not a sentimental mourner
Parading all her sensibility,
 Nor insolent enough to scorn the
 scorner,
But stood in trembling, patient tribula-
 tion,
To be call'd up for her examination.

LXVI

Of course these groups were scatter'd here
 and there,
 Not nigh the gay saloon of ladies gent.
The lawyers in the study; and in air
 The prize pig, ploughman, poachers;
 the men sent
From town, viz. architect and dealer, were
 Both busy (as a general in his tent
Writing despatches) in their several
 stations,
Exulting in their brilliant lucubrations.

LXVII

But this poor girl was left in the great hall,
 While Scout, the parish guardian of the
 frail,
Discuss'd (he hated beer yclept the
 'small')
 A mighty mug of *moral* double ale.
She waited until Justice could recall
 Its kind attentions to their proper pale,
To name a thing in nomenclature rather
Perplexing for most virgins—a child's
 father.

LXVIII

You see here was enough of occupation
 For the Lord Henry, link'd with dogs
 and horses.
There was much bustle too, and prepara-
 tion
 Below stairs on the score of second
 courses;
Because, as suits their rank and situation,
 Those who in counties have great land
 resources

lave 'public days,' when all men may
carouse,
hough not exactly what's call'd 'open
house.'

LXIX

ut once a week or fortnight, *un*invited
(Thus we translate a *general invitation*),
ll country gentlemen, esquired or
knighted,
May drop in without cards, and take
their station
t the full board, and sit alike delighted
With fashionable wines and conversa-
tion;
nd, as the isthmus of the grand con-
nexion,
alk o'er themselves the past and next
election.

LXX

ord Henry was a great electioneerer,
Burrowing for boroughs like a rat or
rabbit.
ut county contests cost him rather
dearer,
Because the neighbouring Scotch Earl
of Giftgabbit
lad English influence, in the self-same
sphere here;
His son, the Honourable Dick Diced-
rabbit,
Vas member for the 'other interest'
(meaning
he same self-interest, with a different
leaning).

LXXI

ourteous and cautious therefore in his
county,
He was all things to all men, and
dispensed
o some civility, to others bounty,
And promises to all—which last com-
menced
o gather to a somewhat large amount,
he
Not calculating how much they con-
densed;
ut what with keeping some, and break-
ing others,
lis word had the same value as another's.

LXXII

friend to freedom and freeholders—yet
No less a friend to government—he
held,
hat he exactly the just medium hit
'Twixt place and patriotism—albeit
compell'd,
uch was his sovereign's pleasure, (though
unfit,
He added modestly, when rebels rail'd,)
o hold some sinecures he wish'd abolish'd,
ut that with them all law would be
demolish'd.

LXXIII

He was 'free to confess'—(whence comes
this phrase?
Is't English? No—'tis only parlia-
mentary)
That innovation's spirit now-a-days
Had made more progress than for the
last century.
He would not tread a factious path to
praise,
Though for the public weal disposed to
venture high;
As for his place, he could but say this of it,
That the fatigue was greater than the profit.

LXXIV

Heaven, and his friends, knew that a
private life
Had ever been his sole and whole
ambition;
But could he quit his king in times of
strife,
Which threaten'd the whole country
with perdition?
When demagogues would with a butcher's
knife
Cut through and through (oh! damnable
incision!)
The Gordian or the Geordi-an knot,
whose strings
Have tied together commons, lords, and
kings.

LXXV

Sooner 'come Place into the Civil List
And champion him to the utmost—'
he would keep it,
Till duly disappointed or dismiss'd:
Profit he cared not for, let others reap
it;
But should the day come when place
ceased to exist,
The country would have far more cause
to weep it:
For how could it go on? Explain who
can!
He gloried in the name of Englishman.

LXXVI

He was as independent—ay, much more—
Than those who were not paid for
independence,
As common soldiers, or a common——
shore,
Have in their several arts or parts
ascendance
O'er the irregulars in lust or gore,
Who do not give professional atten-
dance.
Thus on the mob all statesmen are as eager
To prove their pride, as footmen to a
beggar.

LXXVII

All this (save the last stanza) Henry said,
 And thought. I say no more—I've said
 too much;
For all of us have either heard or read—
 Off—or *upon* the hustings—some slight
 such
Hints from the independent heart or head
 Of the official candidate. I'll touch
No more on this—the dinner-bell hath
 rung.
And grace is said; the grace I *should* have
 sung—

LXXVIII

But I'm too late, and therefore must make
 play.
 'Twas a great banquet, such as Albion
 old
Was wont to boast—as if a glutton's tray
 Were something very glorious to behold.
But 'twas a public feast and public day,—
 Quite full, right dull, guests hot, and
 dishes cold,
Great plenty, much formality, small cheer,
And everybody out of their own sphere.

LXXIX

The squires familiarly formal, and
 My lords and ladies proudly con-
 descending;
The very servants puzzling how to hand
 Their plates—without it might be too
 much bending
From their high places by the sideboard's
 stand—
 Yet, like their masters, fearful of
 offending.
For any deviation from the graces
Might cost both man and master too—
 their *places*.

LXXX

There were some hunters bold, and
 coursers keen,
 Whose hounds ne'er err'd, nor grey-
 hounds deign'd to lurch;
Some deadly shots too, Septembrizers, seen
 Earliest to rise, and last to quit the search
Of the poor partridge through his stubble
 screen.
 There were some massy members of the
 church,
Takers of tithes, and makers of good
 matches,
And several who sung fewer psalms than
 catches.

LXXXI

There were some country wags too—and,
 alas!
 Some exiles from the town, who had
 been driven
To gaze, instead of pavement, upon grass,
 And rise at nine in lieu of long eleven.

And lo! upon that day it came to pass,
 I sate next that o'erwhelming son
 heaven,
The very powerful parson, Peter Pith,
The loudest wit I e'er was deafen'd with

LXXXII

I knew him in his livelier London days
 A brilliant diner-out, though but
 curate;
And not a joke he cut but earn'd its prais
 Until preferment, coming at a sure ra
(O Providence! how wondrous are thy way
 Who would suppose thy gifts som
 times obdurate?)
Gave him, to lay the devil who looks o'
 Lincoln,
A fat fen vicarage, and nought to think o'

LXXXIII

His jokes were sermons, and his sermo
 jokes;
 But both were thrown away among
 the fens;
For wit hath no great friend in aguish folk
 No longer ready ears and short-har
 pens
Imbibed the gay *bon-mot*, or happy hoax
 The poor priest was reduced to con
 mon sense,
Or to coarse efforts very loud and long,
To hammer a hoarse laugh from the thic
 throng.

LXXXIV

There *is* a difference, says the song, 'be
 tween
 A beggar and a queen,' or *was* (of lat
The latter worse used of the two we'v
 seen—
 But we'll say nothing of affairs
 state);
A difference "twixt a bishop and a dean
 A difference between crockery ware an
 plate,
As between English beef and Sparta
 broth—
And yet great heroes have been bred b
 both.

LXXXV

But of all nature's discrepancies, none
 Upon the whole is greater than th
 difference
Beheld between the country and the tow
 Of which the latter merits every preferen
From those who have few resources o
 their own,
 And only think, or act, or feel, wit
 reference
To some small plan of interest or amb
 tion—
Both which are limited to no condition

LXXXVI

But *En avant!* The light loves languish
 o'er
 Long banquets and too many guests,
 although
A slight repast makes people love much
 more,
 Bacchus and Ceres being, as we know,
Even from our grammar upwards, friends
 of yore
 With vivifying Venus, who doth owe
To these the invention of champagne and
 truffles:
Temperance delights her, but long fasting
 ruffles.

LXXXVII

Dully pass'd o'er the dinner of the day;
 And Juan took his place, he knew not
 where,
Confused, in the confusion, and *distrait*,
 And sitting as if nail'd upon his chair:
Though knives and forks clang'd round
 as in a fray,
 He seem'd unconscious of all passing
 there,
Till some one, with a groan, exprest a wish
(Unheeded twice) to have a fin of fish.

LXXXVIII

In which, at the *third* asking of the banns,
 He started; and perceiving smiles around
Broadening to grins, he colour'd more
 than once,
 And hastily—as nothing can confound
A wise man more than laughter from a
 dunce—
 Inflicted on the dish a deadly wound,
And with such hurry, that, ere he could
 curb it,
He had paid his neighbour's prayer with
 half a turbot.

LXXXIX

This was no bad mistake, as it occurr'd,
 The supplicator being an amateur;
But others, who were left with scarce a
 third,
 Were angry—as they well might, to be
 sure.
They wonder'd how a young man so absurd
 Lord Henry at his table should endure;
And this, and his not knowing how much
 oats
Had fall'n last market, cost his host three
 votes.

XC

They little knew, or might have sympa-
 thised,
 That he the night before had seen a
 ghost,
A prologue which but slightly harmonised
 With the substantial company engross'd

By matter, and so much materialised,
 That one scarce knew at what to marvel
 most
Of two things—*how* (the question rather
 odd is)
Such bodies could have souls, or souls
 such bodies.

XCI

But what confused him more than smile or
 stare,
 From all the 'squires and 'squiresses
 around,
Who wonder'd at the abstraction of his air,
 Especially as he had been renown'd
For some vivacity among the fair,
 Even in the country circle's narrow
 bound—
(For little things upon my lord's estate
Were good small talk for others still less
 great)—

XCII

Was, that he caught Aurora's eye on his,
 And something like a smile upon her
 cheek.
Now this he really rather took amiss;
 In those who rarely smile, their smile
 bespeaks
A strong external motive; and in this
 Smile of Aurora's there was nought to
 pique,
Or hope, or love, with any of the wiles
Which some pretend to trace in ladies'
 smiles.

XCIII

'Twas a mere quiet smile of contempla-
 tion,
 Indicative of some surprise and pity;
And Juan grew carnation with vexation,
 Which was not very wise, and still less
 witty,
Since he had gain'd at least her observa-
 tion,
 A most important outwork of the city—
As Juan should have known, had not his
 senses
By last night's ghost been driven from
 their defences.

XCIV

But what was bad, she did not blush in
 turn,
 Nor seem embarrass'd—quite the con-
 trary;
Her aspect was as usual, still—*not* stern—
 And she withdrew, but cast not down,
 her eye,
Yet grew a little pale—with what? con-
 cern?
 I know not; but her colour ne'er was
 high—
Though sometimes faintly flush'd—and
 always clear,
As deep seas in a sunny atmosphere.

XCV

But Adeline was occupied by fame
 This day; and watching, witching, con-
 descending
To the consumers of fish, fowl, and game,
 And dignity with courtesy so blending,
As all must blend whose part it is to aim
 (Especially as the sixth year is ending)
At their lord's, son's, or similar con-
 nexion's
Safe conduct through the rocks of re-
 ëlections.

XCVI

Though this was most expedient on the
 whole,
 And usual—Juan, when he cast a glance
On Adeline while playing her grand *rôle*,
 Which she went through as though it
 were a dance,
Betraying only now and then her soul
 By a look scarce perceptibly askance
(Of weariness or scorn), began to feel
Some doubt how much of Adeline was
 real;

XCVII

So well she acted all and every part
 By turns—with that vivacious versatility,
Which many people take for want of
 heart.
 They err—'tis merely what is call'd
 mobility,
A thing of temperament and not of art,
 Though seeming so, from its supposed
 facility;
And false—though true; for surely they're
 sincerest
Who are strongly acted on by what is
 nearest.

XCVIII

This makes your actors, artists, and
 romancers,
 Heroes sometimes, though seldom—
 sages never:
But speakers, bards, diplomatists, and
 dancers,
 Little that's great, but much of what is
 clever;
Most orators, but very few financiers,
 Though all Exchequer chancellors
 endeavour,
Of late years, to dispense with Cocker's
 rigours,
And grow quite figurative with their
 figures.

XCIX

The poets of arithmetic are they
 Who, though they prove not two and
 two to be
Five, as they might do in a modest way,
 Have plainly made it out that four are
 three,

Judging by what they take, and what they
 pay.
 The Sinking Fund's unfathomable sea
That most unliquidating liquid, leaves
The debt unsunk, yet sinks all it receives

C

While Adeline dispensed her airs an
 graces,
 The fair Fitz-Fulke seem'd very muc
 at ease;
Though too well bred to quiz men to thei
 faces,
 Her laughing blue eyes with a glanc
 could seize
The ridicules of people in all places—
 That honey of your fashionable bees—
And store it up for mischievous enjoy
 ment;
And this at present was her kind employ
 ment.

CI

However, the day closed, as days mus
 close;
 The evening also waned—and coffe
 came.
Each carriage was announced, and ladie
 rose,
 And curtsying off, as curtsies countr
 dame,
Retired: with most unfashionable bows
 Their docile esquires also did the sam
Delighted with their dinner and their hos
But with the Lady Adeline the most.

CII

Some praised her beauty; others her grea
 grace,
 The warmth of her politeness, whos
 sincerity
Was obvious in each feature of her fac
 Whose traits were radiant with the ra
 of verity.
Yes: *she* was truly worthy *her* high plac
 No one could envy her deserve
 prosperity.
And then her dress—what beautif
 simplicity
Draperied her form with curious felicit

CIII

Meanwhile sweet Adeline deserved the
 praises,
 By an impartial indemnification
For all her past exertion and soft phrase
 In a most edifying conversation,
Which turn'd upon their late guest
 miens and faces,
 And families, even to the last relatio
Their hideous wives, their horrid selv
 and dresses,
And truculent distortion of their tresses

CIV

rue, *she* said little—'twas the rest that
 broke
 Forth into universal epigram;
ut then 'twas to the purpose what she
 spoke:
 Like Addison's 'faint praise,' so wont
 to damn,
ler own but served to set off every joke,
 As music chimes in with a melodrame.
low sweet the task to shield an absent
 friend!
ask but this of mine, to——*not* defend.

CV

here were but two exceptions to this keen
 Skirmish of wits o'er the departed; one
urora, with her pure and placid mien;
 And Juan, too, in general behind none
a gay remark on what he had heard or
 seen,
 Sate silent now, his usual spirits gone:
a vain he heard the others rail or rally,
le would not join them in a single sally.

CVI

'is true he saw Aurora look as though
 She approved his silence; she perhaps
 mistook
s motive for that charity we owe
 But seldom pay the absent, nor would
 look
arther; it might or it might not be so.
 But Juan, sitting silent in his nook,
bserving little in his reverie,
et saw this much, which he was glad to
 see.

CVII

he ghost at least had done him this much
 good,
 In making him as silent as a ghost,
' in the circumstances which ensued
 He gain'd th' esteem where it was worth
 the most;
nd certainly Aurora had renew'd
 In him some feelings he had lately lost,
r harden'd; feelings which, perhaps ideal,
re so divine, that I must deem them
 real:—

CVIII

he love of higher things and better days;
 The unbounded hope, and heavenly
 ignorance
f what is call'd the world, and the world's
 ways;
 The moments when we gather from a
 glance
lore joy than from all future pride or praise,
 Which kindle manhood, but can ne'er
 entrance
he heart in an existence of its own,
f which another's bosom is the zone.

CIX

Who would not sigh *Aἲ aἲ τᾶν Κυθέρειαν*
 That *hath* a memory, or that *had* a heart?
Alas! *her* star must wane like that of Dian:
 Ray fades on ray, as years on years depart.
Anacreon only had the soul to tie an
 Unwithering myrtle round the un-
 blunted dart
Of Eros: but though thou hast play'd us
 many tricks,
Still we respect thee, '*Alma Venus Gene-
 trix!*'

CX

And full of sentiments, sublime as billows
 Heaving between this world and worlds
 beyond,
Don Juan, when the midnight hour of
 pillows
 Arrived, retired to his; but to despond
Rather than rest. Instead of poppies,
 willows
 Waved o'er his couch; he meditated,
 fond
Of those sweet bitter thoughts which
 banish sleep,
And make the worldling sneer, the young-
 ling weep.

CXI

The night was as before: he was undrest,
 Saving his night-gown, which is an
 undress;
Completely *sans culotte*, and without
 vest;
 In short, he hardly could be clothed with
 less:
But apprehensive of his spectral guest,
 He sate with feelings awkward to
 express
(By those who have not had such visita-
 tions),
Expectant of the ghost's fresh operations.

CXII

And not in vain he listen'd;—Hush!
 what's that?
 I see—I see—Ah, no!—'tis not—yet 'tis—
Ye powers! it is the—the—the—Pooh!
 the cat!
 The devil may take that stealthy pace
 of his!
So like a spiritual pit-a-pat,
 Or tiptoe of an amatory Miss,
Gliding the first time to a *rendezvous*,
And dreading the chaste echoes of her
 shoe.

CXIII

Again—what is 't? The wind? No, no,—
 this time
 It is the sable Friar as before,
With awful footsteps regular as rhyme,
 Or (as rhymes may be in these days)
 much more.

Again through shadows of the night sub-
lime,
 When deep sleep fell on men, and the
 world wore
The starry darkness round her like a girdle
Spangled with gems—the monk made his
 blood curdle.

CXIV

A noise like to wet fingers drawn on glass,
 Which sets the teeth on edge; and a
 slight clatter
Like showers which on the midnight gusts
 will pass,
 Sounding like very supernatural water,
Came over Juan's ear, which throbb'd, alas!
 For immaterialism's a serious matter;
So that even those whose faith is the most
 great
In souls immortal, shun them *tête-à-tête*.

CXV

Were his eyes open?—Yes! and his mouth
 too.
 Surprise has this effect—to make one
 dumb,
Yet leave the gate which eloquence slips
 through
 As wide, as if a long speech were to
 come.
Nigh and more nigh the awful echoes
 drew,
 Tremendous to a mortal tympanum:
His eyes were open, and (as was before
Stated) his mouth. What open'd next?—
 the door.

CXVI

It open'd with a most infernal creak,
 Like that of hell. 'Lasciate ogni
 speranza
Voi ch' entrate!' The hinge seem'd to
 speak,
 Dreadful as Dante's rima, or this
 stanza;
Or—but all words upon such themes are
 weak:
 A single shade's sufficient to entrance a
Hero—for what is substance to a spirit?
Or how is 't *matter* trembles to come near
 it?

CXVII

The door flew wide, not swiftly,—but, as
 fly
 The sea-gulls, with a steady, sober
 flight—
And then swung back; nor close—but
 stood awry,
 Half letting in long shadows on the
 light,
Which still in Juan's candlesticks burn'd
 high,
 For he had two, both tolerably brignt,

And in the doorway, darkening darkness
 stood
The sable Friar in his solemn hood.

CXVIII

Don Juan shook, as erst he had been shake\
 The night before; but being sick o\
 shaking,
He first inclined to think he had been mis\
 taken;
 And then to be ashamed of suc\
 mistaking;
His own internal ghost began to awake\
 Within him, and to quell his corpora\
 quaking—
Hinting that soul and body on the whol\
Were odds against a disembodied soul.

CXIX

And then his dread grew wrath, and hi\
 wrath fierce,
 And he arose, advanced—the shad\
 retreated;
But Juan, eager now the truth to pierce\
 Followed, his veins no longer cold, bu\
 heated,
Resolved to thrust the mystery *carte an\
 tierce*,
 At whatsoever risk of being defeated :\
The ghost stopp'd, menaced, then retire\
 until
He reach'd the ancient wall, then stoo\
 stone still.

CXX

Juan put forth one arm—Eternal power\
 It touch'd no soul, nor body, but th\
 wall,
On which the moonbeams fell in silver\
 showers,
 Chequer'd with all the tracery of th\
 hall;
He shudder'd, as no doubt the brave\
 cowers
 When he can't tell what 'tis that dot\
 appal.
How odd, a single hobgoblin's nonenti\
Should cause more fear than a whol\
 host's identity!

CXXI

But still the shade remain'd: the blue ey\
 glared,
 And rather variably for stony death;
Yet one thing rather good the grave ha\
 spared,
 The ghost had a remarkably swe\
 breath:
A straggling curl show'd he had bee\
 fairhair'd;
 A red lip, with two rows of pearls beneath\
Gleam'd forth, as through the casement\
 ivy shroud
The moon peep'd, just escaped from
 grey cloud.

CXXII

nd Juan, puzzled, but still curious,
 thrust
 His other arm forth—Wonder upon
 wonder!
, press'd upon a hard but glowing bust,
 Which beat as if there was a warm
 heart under.
le found, as people on most trials must,
 That he had made at first a silly blunder,
.nd that in his confusion he had
 caught
nly the wall, instead of what he
 sought.

CXXIII

he ghost, if ghost it were, seem'd a sweet
 soul
 As ever lurk'd beneath a holy hood:
. dimpled chin, a neck of ivory, stole
 Forth into something much like flesh
 and blood;
ack fell the sable frock and dreary cowl,
 And they reveal'd—alas! that e'er they
 should!
n full, voluptuous, but *not o'er*grown
 bulk,
he phantom of her frolic Grace—Fitz-
 Fulke!

CANTO THE SEVENTEENTH

I

he world is full of orphans: firstly, those
 Who are so in the strict sense of the
 phrase;
ut many a lonely tree the loftier grows
 Than others crowded in the Forest's
 maze—
he next are such as are not doomed to lose
 Their tender parents, in their budding
 days,
ut, merely, their parental tenderness,
/hich leaves them orphans of the heart no
 less.

II

he next are '*only* Children,' as they are
 styled,
 Who grow up *Children* only, since th' old
 saw
ronounces that an 'only''s a spoilt child—
 But not to go too far, I hold it law,
nat where their education, harsh or mild,
 Transgresses the great bounds of love or
 awe,
he sufferers—be 't in heart or intellect—
'hate'er the *cause*, are orphans in *effect*.

III

But to return unto the stricter rule—
 As far as words make rules—our common
 notion
Of orphans paints at once a parish school,
 A half-starved babe, a wreck upon Life's
 ocean,
A human (what the Italians nickname)
 'Mule!'
 A theme for Pity or some worse emotion;
Yet, if examined, it might be admitted
The wealthiest orphans are to be more
 pitied.

IV

Too soon they are Parents to themselves:
 for what
 Are Tutors, Guardians, and so forth,
 compared
With Nature's genial Genitors? so that
 A child of Chancery, that Star-Chamber
 ward,
(I'll take the likeness I can first come at,)
 Is like—a duckling by Dame Partlett
 reared,
And frights—especially if 't is a daughter,
Th' old Hen—by running headlong to the
 water.

V

There is a common-place book argument,
 Which glibly glides from every vulgar
 tongue;
When any dare a new light to present,
 'If you are right, then everybody's
 wrong!'
Suppose the converse of this precedent
 So often urged, so loudly and so long;
'If you are wrong, then everybody's right!'
Was ever everybody yet so quite?

VI

Therefore I would solicit free discussion
 Upon all points—no matter what, or
 whose—
Because as Ages upon Ages push on,
 The last is apt the former to accuse
Of pillowing its head on a pin-cushion,
 Heedless of pricks because it was obtuse:
What was a paradox becomes a truth or
A something like it—as bear witness Luther!

VII

The Sacraments have been reduced to two,
 And Witches unto none, though some-
 what late
Since burning agéd women (save a few—
 Not witches only b—ches —who create
Mischief in families, as some know or knew,
 Should still be singed, but slightly, let·me
 state,)
Has been declared an act of inurbanity,
Malgré Sir Matthew Hales's great humanity.

VIII

Great Galileo was debarred the Sun,
 Because he fixed it; and, to stop his
 talking,
How Earth could round the solar orbit run,
 Found his own legs embargoed from
 mere walking:
The man was well-nigh dead, ere men begun
 To think his skull had not some need of
 caulking;
But now, it seems, he's right—his notion
 just:
No doubt a consolation to his dust.

IX

Pythagoras, Locke, Socrates—but pages
 Might be filled up, as vainly as before,
With the sad usage of all sorts of sages,
 Who in his life-time, each, was deemed a
 Bore!
The loftiest minds outrun their tardy ages:
 This they must bear with and, perhaps,
 much more;
The wise man's sure when he no more can
 share it, he
Will have a firm Post Obit on posterity.

X

If such doom waits each intellectual Giant,
 We little people in our lesser way,
In Life's small rubs should surely be more
 pliant,
 And so for one will I—as well I may—
Would that I were less bilious—but, oh,
 fie on 't!
 Just as I make my mind up every day,
To be a 'totus, teres,' Stoic, Sage,
The wind shifts and I fly into a rage.

XI

Temperate I am—yet never had a temper;
 Modest I am—yet with some slight
 assurance;
Changeable too—yet somehow 'Idem
 semper:'
 Patient—but not enamoured of endur-
 ance;

Cheerful—but, sometimes, rather apt to
 whimper:
 Mild—but at times a sort of 'Hercule
 furens:'
So that I almost think that the same skin
For one without—has two or three within.

XII

Our Hero was, in Canto the Sixteenth,
 Left in a tender moonlight situation,
Such as enables Man to show his strength
 Moral or physical: on this occasion
Whether his virtue triumphed—or, at
 length,
 His vice—for he was of a kindling nation—
Is more than I shall venture to describe;—
Unless some Beauty with a kiss should bribe

XIII

I leave the thing a problem, like all things:—
 The morning came—and breakfast, tea
 and toast,
Of which most men partake, but no one
 sings.
 The company whose birth, wealth, worth,
 have cost
My trembling Lyre already several strings,
 Assembled with our hostess, and mine
 host;
The guests dropped in—the last but one,
 Her Grace,
The latest, Juan, with his virgin face.

XIV

Which best it is to encounter—Ghost, or
 none,
 'Twere difficult to say—but Juan looked
As if he had combated with more than one
 Being wan and worn, with eyes that hardly
 brooked
The light, that through the Gothic windows
 shone:
 Her Grace, too, had a sort of air
 rebuked—
Seemed pale and shivered, as if she had kept
A vigil, or dreamt rather more than slept.

NOTES

HOURS OF IDLENESS

Page 2, col. 1.

'ON THE DEATH OF A YOUNG LADY.'] The author claims the indulgence of the reader more for this piece than, perhaps, any other in the collection; but as it was written at an earlier period than the rest (being composed at the age of fourteen), and his first essay, he preferred submitting it to the indulgence of his friends in its present state, to making either addition or alteration.

Page 3, col. 2.

'On Marston.'] The battle of Marston Moor, where the adherents of Charles I. were defeated.

Page 3, col. 2.

'With Rupert, 'gainst traitors contending.'] Son of the Elector Palatine, and nephew to Charles I. He afterwards commanded the fleet in the reign of Charles II.

Page 9, col. 1.

TO THE DUKE OF DORSET.] In looking over my papers to select a few additional poems for this second edition, I found the above lines, which I had totally forgotten, composed in the summer of 1805, a short time previous to my departure from Harrow. They were addressed to a young school-fellow of high rank, who had been my frequent companion in some rambles through the neigh-bouring country: however, he never saw the lines, and most probably never will. As, on a re-perusal, I found them not worse than some other pieces in the collection, I have now published them, for the first time, after a slight revision.

Page 9, col. 1.

'Bade *thee* obey, and gave *me* to command.'] At every public school the junior boys are com-pletely subservient to the upper forms till they attain a seat in the higher classes. From this state of probation, very properly, no rank is exempt; but after a certain period, they command in turn those who succeed.

Page 9, col. 1.

'Though passive tutors, fearful to dispraise.'] Allow me to disclaim any personal allusions, even the most distant. I merely mention generally what is too often the weakness of preceptors.

Page 10, col. 2.

'Oh! could Le Sage's demon's gift.'] The *Diable Boiteux* of Le Sage, where Asmodeus, the demon, places Don Cleofas on an elevated situation, and unroofs the houses for inspection.

Page 11, col. 1.

'Who reads false quantities in Seale.'] Seale's publication on Greek Metres displays considerable talent and ingenuity, but, as might be expected in so difficult a work, is not remarkable for accuracy.

Page 11, col. 1.

'In barbarous Latin doom'd to wrangle.'] The Latin of the schools is of the *canine species*, and not very intelligible.

Page 11, col. 1.

'The square of the hypothenuse.'] The discover of Pythagoras, that the square of the hypothenus is equal to the squares of the other two sides c a right-angled triangle.

Page 11, col. 1.

'A numerous crowd, array'd in white.'] On saint's day the students wear surplices in chapel.

Page 12, col. 1.

'I fancied that Mossop himself was outshone.' Mossop, a contemporary of Garrick, famous fo his performance of Zanga.

Page 12, col. 2.

'Would twinkle dimly through their sphere.']
'Two of the fairest stars in all the heaven,
Having some business, do intreat her eyes
To twinkle in their spheres till they return.'
SHAKESPEARI

Page 12, col. 2.

'Woman, thy vows are traced in sand.'] The la line is almost a literal translation from a Spanis proverb.

Page 13, col. 2.

'And hurtling o'er thy lovely head.'] This wor is used by Gray in his poem to the Fatal Sisters:–
'Iron-sleet of arrowy shower
Hurtles in the darken'd air.'

Page 14, col. 2.

'In law an infant, and in years a boy.'] In la every person is an infant who has not attained th age of twenty-one.

Page 15, col. 2.

'To form the place of assignation.'] In the abov little piece the author has been accused by som *candid readers* of introducing the name of a lad from whom he was some hundred miles distant a the time this was written; and poor Juliet, who ha slept so long in 'the tomb of all the Capulets has been converted, with a trifling alteration of he name, into an English damsel walking in a garde of their own creation, during the month of *D cember*, in a village where the author never passe a winter. Such has been the candour of som ingenious critics. He would advise these *liber* commentators on taste and arbiters of decorum t read *Shakespeare*.

Page 16, col. 1.

'But curse my fate for ever after.'] Having hear that a very severe and indelicate censure has bee passed on the above poem, I beg leave to rep] in a quotation from an admired miles distant a Stranger in France:'—'As we were contemplatin a painting on a large scale, in which, among othe figures, is the uncovered whole length of a warrio a prudish-looking lady, who seemed to hav touched the age of desperation, after having atter tively surveyed it through her glass, observed t her party, that there was a great deal of indecorun

NOTES TO HOURS OF IDLENESS

a that picture. Madame S. shrewdly whispered in
my ear "that the indecorum was in the remark."'

Page 16, col. 1.

'OSCAR OF ALVA.'] The catastrophe of this tale
was suggested by the story of 'Jeronyme and Lo-
renzo,' in the first volume of Schiller's 'Armenian,
or the Ghost-Seer.' It also bears some resemblance
to a scene in the third act of 'Macbeth.'

Page 21, col. 2.

'Creusa's style but wanting to the dame.'] The
mother of Iulus, lost on the night when Troy was
taken.

Page 24, col. 2.

'Ah! hapless dame! no sire bewails.'] Medea,
who accompanied Jason to Corinth, was deserted
by him for the daughter of Creon, king of that
city. The chorus, from which this is taken, here
addresses Medea; though a considerable liberty is
taken with the original, by expanding the idea, as
also in some other parts of the translation.

Page 24, col. 2.

'Who ne'er unlocks with silver key.'] The ori-
inal is 'Καθαρὰν ἀνοίξαντι κλῆρα φρενῶν;' literally
disclosing the bright key of the mind.'

Page 24, col. 2.

'MAGNUS his ample front sublime uprears.'] No
reflection is here intended against the person men-
tioned under the name of Magnus. He is merely
represented as performing an unavoidable function
of his office. Indeed, such an attempt could only
recoil upon myself; as that gentleman is now as
much distinguished by his eloquence, and the
dignified propriety with which he fills his situa-
tion, as he was in his younger days for wit and
conviviality.

Page 25, col. 1.

'Th' ATHENIAN's glowing style, or Tully's fire.']
Demosthenes.

Page 25, col. 2.

'Yet prizing Bentley's, Brunck's, or Porson's
note.'] The present Greek professor at Trinity
College, Cambridge; a man whose powers of mind
and writings may, perhaps, justify their preference.

Page 25, col. 2.

'Whether 'tis Pitt or Petty rules the hour.']
Since this was written, Lord Henry Petty [now
Marquis of Lansdowne] has lost his place, and
subsequently (I had almost said consequently) the
honour of representing the University. A fact so
daring requires no comment.

Page 28, col. 1.

'Sweet scene of my youth! seat of Friendship
and Truth.'] Harrow.

Page 29, col. 2.

'LACHIN Y GAIR.'] Lachin y Gair, or, as it is
pronounced in the Erse, Loch na Garr, towers
proudly pre-eminent in the Northern Highlands,
near Invercauld. One of our modern tourists
mentions it as the highest mountain, perhaps, in
Great Britain. Be this as it may, it is certainly one
of the most sublime and picturesque amongst our
Caledonian Alps.' Its appearance is of a dusky
hue, but the summit is the seat of eternal snows.
Near Lachin y Gair I spent some of the early part

of my life, the recollection of which has given birth
to these stanzas.

Page 29, col. 2.

'My cap was the bonnet, my cloak was the
plaid.'] This word is erroneously pronounced
plad: the proper pronunciation (according to the
Scotch) is shown by the orthography.

Page 29, col. 2.

'Ill-starr'd, though brave, did no visions fore-
boding.'] I allude here to my maternal ancestors,
'the Gordons,' many of whom fought for the un-
fortunate Prince Charles, better known by the
name of the Pretender. This branch was nearly
allied by blood, as well as attachment, to the
Stuarts. George, the second Earl of Huntley,
married the Princess Annabella Stuart, daughter
of James I. of Scotland. By her he left four sons:
the third, Sir William Gordon, I have the honour
to claim as one of my progenitors.

Page 29, col. 2.

'Ah! were you destined to die at Culloden.']
Whether any perished in the battle of Culloden, I
am not certain; but, as many fell in the insurrec-
tion, I have used the name of the principal action,
'pars pro toto.'

Page 29, col. 2.

'You rest with your clan in the caves of Brae-
mar.'] A tract of the Highlands so called. There
is also a Castle of Braemar.

Page 30, col. 1.

'A Pylades in every friend?'] It is hardly neces-
sary to add, that Pylades was the companion of
Orestes, and a partner in one of those friendships
which, with those of Achilles and Patroclus, Nisus
and Euryalus, Damon and Pythias, have been
handed down to posterity as remarkable instances
of attachments, which in all probability never
existed beyond the imagination of the poet, or the
page of an historian, or modern novelist.

Page 31, col. 1.

'ELEGY ON NEWSTEAD ABBEY.'] As one poem
on this subject is already printed, the author had,
originally, no intention of inserting the following.
It is now added at the particular request of some
friends.

Page 31, col. 1.

'Religion's shrine! repentant HENRY's pride!']
Henry II. founded Newstead soon after the murder
of Thomas à Becket.

Page 31, col. 2.

'No mail-clad serfs, obedient to their lord.'] This
word is used by Walter Scott, in his poem, 'The
Wild Huntsman;' synonymous with vassal.

Page 31, col. 2.

'In grim array the crimson cross demand.'] The
red cross was the badge of the Crusaders.

Page 31, col. 2.

'Soon as the gloaming spreads her waning
shade.'] As 'gloaming,' the Scottish word for
twilight, is far more poetical, and has been recom-
mended by many eminent literary men, particularly
by Dr. Moore in his Letters to Burns, I have ven-
tured to use it on account of its harmony.

861

NOTES TO HOURS OF IDLENESS

Page 31, col. 2.

'Or matin orisons to Mary paid.'] The priory was dedicated to the Virgin.

Page 32, col. 1.

'Another HENRY the kind gift recalls.'] At the dissolution of the monasteries, Henry VIII. bestowed Newstead Abbey on Sir John Byron.

Page 32, col. 1.

'An abbey once, a regal fortress now.'] Newstead sustained a considerable siege in the war between Charles I. and his parliament.

Page 32, col. 1.

'Trembling she snatch'd him from th' unequal strife.'] Lord Byron and his brother Sir William held high commands in the royal army. The former was general-in-chief in Ireland, lieutenant of the Tower, and governor to James, Duke of York, afterwards the unhappy James II.; the latter had a principal share in many actions.

Page 32, col. 1.

'To lead the band where godlike FALKLAND fell.'] Lucius Cary, Lord Viscount Falkland, the most accomplished man of his age, was killed at the Battle of Newbury, charging in the ranks of Lord Byron's regiment of Cavalry.

Page 32, col. 2.

'Loathing the offering of so dark a death.'] This is an historical fact. A violent tempest occurred immediately subsequent to the death or interment of Cromwell, which occasioned many disputes between his partisans and the cavaliers: both interpreted the circumstance into divine interposition; but whether as approbation or condemnation, we leave to the casuists of that age to decide. I have made such use of the occurrence as suited the subject of my poem.

Page 33, col. 1.

'The legal ruler now resumes the helm.'] Charles II.

Page 35, col. 1.

'PROBUS, the pride of science, and the boast.'] Dr. Drury. This most able and excellent man retired from his situation in March, 1805, after having resided thirty-five years at Harrow; the last twenty as head-master; an office he held with equal honour to himself and advantage to the very extensive school over which he presided. Panegyric would here be superfluous: it would be useless to enumerate qualifications which were never doubted. A considerable contest took place between three rival candidates for his vacant chair: of this I can only say,

Si mea cum vestris valuissent vota, Pelasgi?
Non foret ambiguus tanti certaminis hæres.

Page 37, col. 2.

'As speakers each supports an equal name.'] This alludes to the public speeches delivered at the school where the author was educated.

Page 38, col. 2.

'And Love, without his pinion, smiled on Youth.'] 'L'Amitié est l'Amour sans ailes,' is a French proverb.

Page 38, col. 2.

ENTITLED 'THE COMMON LOT.'] Written by James Montgomery, author of the 'Wanderer in Switzerland,' &c.

Page 38, col. 2.

'The hero rolls the tide of war.'] No particular hero is here alluded to. The exploits of Bayard, Nemours, Edward the Black Prince, and, in more modern times, the fame of Marlborough, Frederic the Great, Count Saxe, Charles of Sweden, &c, are familiar to every historical reader, but the exact places of their birth are known to a very small proportion of their admirers.

Page 40, col. 1.

'AN IMITATION OF MACPHERSON'S OSSIAN.'] It may be necessary to observe, that the story, though considerably varied in the catastrophe, is taken from 'Nisus and Euryalus,' of which episode a translation is already given in the present volume.

Page 41, col. 2.

'Tears of the storm.'] I fear Laing's late edition has completely overthrown every hope that Macpherson's Ossian might prove the translation of a series of poems complete in themselves; but, while the imposture is discovered, the merit of the work remains undisputed, though not without faults—particularly, in some parts, turgid and bombastic diction.—The present humble imitation will be pardoned by the admirers of the original as an attempt, however inferior, which evinces an attachment to their favourite author.

Page 42, col. 1.

'Seat of my youth! thy distant spire.'] Harrow.

Page 44, col. 1.

'The cumbrous pomp of Saxon pride.'] Sassenach or Saxon, a Gaelic word, signifying either Lowland or English.

Page 45, col. 1.

'To flee away, and be at rest.'] 'And I said, Oh that I had wings like a dove; for then would I fly away and be at rest.'—Psalm lv. 6. This verse also constitutes a part of the most beautiful anthem in our language.

Page 45, col. 1.

'And climb'd thy steep summit, oh Morven of snow!'] Morven, a lofty mountain in Aberdeenshire. 'Gormal of snow' is an expression frequently to be found in Ossian.

Page 45, col. 1.

'Or the mist of the tempest that gather'd below.'] This will not appear extraordinary to those who have been accustomed to the mountains. It is by no means uncommon, on attaining the top of Benevis, Ben-y-bourd, &c., to perceive, between the summit and the valley, clouds pouring down rain, and occasionally accompanied by lightning, while the spectator literally looks down upon the storm, perfectly secure from its effects.

Page 45, col. 1.

'I breasted the billows of Dee's rushing tide.'] The Dee is a beautiful river, which rises near Mar Lodge, and falls into the sea at New Aberdeen.

Page 45, col. 2.

'I think of the rocks that o'ershadow Colbleen.'] Colbleen is a mountain near the verge of the Highlands, not far from the ruins of Dee Castle.

Page 46, col. 2.

'As void of wit and moral.'] These stanzas were written soon after the appearance of a severe critique in a northern review on a new publication of the British Anacreon.

Page 47, col. 1.

'I really will not fight them.'] A bard [Moore] (*norresco referens*) defied his reviewer [Jeffrey] to mortal combat. If this example becomes prevalent, our periodical censors must be dipped in the river Styx: for what else can secure them from the numerous host of their enraged assailants?

OCCASIONAL PIECES

Page 48, col. 1.

'Adieu, thou Hill! where early joy.'] Harrow.

Page 51, col. 2.

'ON REVISITING HARROW.'] Some years ago, when at Harrow, a friend of the author engraved on a particular spot the names of both, with a few additional words, as a memorial. Afterwards, on receiving some real or imagined injury, the author destroyed the frail record before he left Harrow. On revisiting the place in 1807, he wrote under it these stanzas.

Page 59, col. 2.

'WRITTEN AFTER SWIMMING FROM SESTOS TO ABY-DOS.'] On the 3rd of May, 1810, while the Salsette Captain Bathurst) was lying in the Dardanelles, Lieutenant Ekenhead, of that frigate, and the writer of these rhymes, swam from the European shore to the Asiatic—by the by, from Abydos to Sestos would have been more correct. The whole distance, from the place whence we started to our landing on the other side, including the length we were carried by the current, was computed by those on board the frigate at upwards of four English miles, though the actual breadth is barely one. The rapidity of the current is such that no boat can row directly across, and it may, in some measure be estimated from the circumstance of the whole distance being accomplished by one of the parties, in an hour and five, and by the other in an hour and ten minutes. The water was extremely cold, from the melting of the mountain snows. About three weeks before, in April, we had made an attempt; but, having ridden all the way from the Troad the same morning, and the water being of an icy chillness, we found it necessary to postpone the completion till the frigate anchored below the castles, when we swam the straits, as just stated, entering a considerable way above the European, and landing below the Asiatic, fort. Chevalier says that a young Jew swam the same distance for his mistress; and Oliver mentions its having been done by a Neapolitan; but our consul, Tarragona, remembered neither of these circumstances, and tried to dissuade us from the attempt. A number of the Salsette's crew were known to have accomplished a greater distance; and the only thing that surprised me was that, as doubts had been entertained of the truth of Leander's story, no traveller had ever endeavoured to ascertain its practicability.

Page 60, col. 1.

'Ζώη μοῦ, σᾶς ἀγαπῶ.'] Romaic expression of tenderness: If I translate it, I shall affront the gentlemen, as it may seem that I supposed they could not; and if I do not, I may affront the ladies.

For fear of any misconstruction on the part of the latter, I shall do so, begging pardon of the learned. It means, 'My life, I love you!' which sounds very prettily in all languages, and is as much in fashion in Greece at this day as, Juvenal tells us, the two first words were amongst the Roman ladies, whose erotic expressions were all Hellenised.

Page 60, col. 1.

'By all the token-flowers that tell.'] In the East (where ladies are not taught to write, lest they should scribble assignations) flowers, cinders, pebbles, &c. convey the sentiments of the parties by that universal deputy of Mercury—an old woman. A cinder says, 'I burn for thee;' a bunch of flowers tied with hair, 'Take me and fly;' but a pebble declares—what nothing else can.

Page 60, col. 1.

'Though I fly to Istambol.'] Constantinople.

Page 60, col. 2.

'Δεῦτε παῖδες τῶν 'Ελλήνων.'] The song Δεῦτε παῖδες, &c. was written by Riga, who perished in the attempt to revolutionise Greece. This translation is as literal as the author could make it in verse. It is of the same measure as that of the original.

Page 60, col. 2.

'And the seven-hill'd city seeking.'] Constantinople, ''Επτάλοφος.'

Page 61, col. 2.

''Ωραιότατη Χάηδή, &c.'] The song from which this is taken is a great favourite with the young girls of Athens of all classes. Their manner of singing it is by verses in rotation, the whole number present joining in the chorus. I have heard it frequently at our 'χόροι,' in the winter of 1810–11. The air is plaintive and pretty.

Page 68, col. 1.

'VERSES FOUND IN A SUMMER-HOUSE AT HALES-OWEN.'] In Warwickshire.

Page 68, col. 1.

'His hours in whistling spent, "for want of thought."'] See Cymon and Iphigenia.

Page 73, col. 2.

'The rapture of the strife.'] 'Certaminis *gaudia*.' The expression of Attila in his harangue to his army previous to the battle of Chalons, given in Cassiodorus.

Page 74, col. 2.

'Thou Timour! in his captive's cage.'] The cage of Bajazet, by order of Tamerlane.

Page 74, col. 2.

'Or, like the thief of fire from heaven.'] Prometheus.

Page 74, col. 2.

'The very Fiend's arch mock.']

———'The very fiend's arch mock—
To lip a wanton and suppose her chaste.'
SHAKESPEARE.

Page 84, col. 2.

'Turning rivers into blood.'] See Rev. chap. viii. ver. 7, &c. 'The first angel sounded, and there followed hail and fire mingled with blood,' &c.

NOTES TO ENGLISH BARDS AND SCOTCH REVIEWERS

Ver. 8, 'And the second angel sounded, and as it were a great mountain burning with fire was cast into the sea; and the third part of the sea became blood,' &c. Ver. 10, 'And the third angel sounded, and there fell a great star from heaven, burning as it were a lamp: and it fell upon the third part of the rivers, and upon the fountains of waters.' Ver. 11, 'And the name of the star is called *Wormwood:* and the third part of the waters became *wormwood;* and many men died of the waters because they were made bitter.'

Page 84, col. 2.

'Whose realm refused thee ev'n a tomb.'] Murat's remains are said to have been torn from the grave and burnt.

Page 85, col. 2.

'FROM THE FRENCH.] 'All wept, but particularly Savary, and a Polish officer who had been exalted from the ranks by Buonaparte. He clung to his master's knees; wrote a letter to Lord Keith, entreating permission to accompany him, even in the most menial capacity, which could not be admitted.'

Page 85, col. 2.

'Blessing him they served so well.'] 'At Waterloo one man was seen, whose left arm was shattered by a cannon ball, to wrench it off with the other, and throwing it up in the air, exclaimed to his comrades, "Vive l'Empereur, jusqu' à la mort!" There were many other instances of the like: this you may, however, depend on as true.'—*Private Letter from Brussels.*

Page 86, col. 1.

'Of three bright colours, each divine.'] The tricolour.

Page 94, col. 1.

'Like to the Pontic monarch of old days.'] Mithridates of Pontus.

Page 97, col. 1.

'The worthy rival of the wondrous *Three!*'] Fox—Pitt—Burke.

Page 99, col. 1.

'Leman! these names are worthy of thy shore.'] Geneva, Ferney, Copet, Lausanne.

Page 99, col. 1.

'ROMANCE MUY DOLOROSO DEL SITIO Y TOMA DE ALHAMA.'] The effect of the original ballad—which existed both in Spanish and Arabic—was such, that it was forbidden to be sung by the Moors, on pain of death, within Granada.

Page 103, col. 2.

'For the man, "poor and shrewd."'] *Vide* your letter.

ENGLISH BARDS AND SCOTCH REVIEWERS

Page 113, col. 1.

'His creaking couplets in a tavern hall.']

IMIT. 'Semper ego auditor tantum? nunquamne, reponam,
 Vexatus toties rauci Theseide Codri?'—
 Juv. Sat. I.
Mr. Fitzgerald, facetiously termed by Cobbett the 'Small-Beer Poet,' inflicts his annual tribute of verse on the Literary Fund: not content with writing, he spouts in person, after the company have imbibed a reasonable quantity of bad port to enable them to sustain the operation.

Page 114, col. 1.

'Our task complete, like Hamet's shall be free.' Cid Hamet Benengeli promises repose to his pen in the last chapter of Don Quixote. Oh! that our voluminous gentry would follow the example of Cid Hamet Benengeli!

Page 114, col. 1.

'Fail'd to preserve the spurious farce from shame.'] This ingenious youth is mentioned more particularly, with his production, in another place.

Page 114, col. 1.

'No matter, George continues still to write.'] In the Edinburgh Review.

Page 114, col. 2.

'By Jeffrey's heart, or Lambe's Bœotian head.' Messrs. Jeffrey and Lambe are the alpha and omega, the first and last, of the Edinburgh Review; the others are mentioned hereafter.

Page 114, col. 2.

'While these are censors, 'twould be sin to spare.']

IMIT. 'Stulta est Clementia, cum tot ubique
 ——occurras perituræ parcere chartæ.'
 Juv. Sat. I

Page 114, col. 2.

'Then should you ask me, why I venture o'er.'

IMIT. 'Cur tamen hoc libeat potius decurrere campo
 Per quem magnus equos Auruncæ flexit alumnus:
 Si vacat, et placidi rationem admittitis edam.'
 Juv. Sat. I

Page 115, col. 2.

'From soaring Southey down to grovelling Stott.'] Stott, better known in the 'Morning Post by the name of Hafiz. This personage is at present the most profound explorer of the bathos. I remember, when the reigning family left Portugal, a special Ode of Master Stott's, beginning thus:—
(*Stott loquitur quoad Hibernia*)—

 'Princely offspring of Braganza,
 Erin greets thee with a stanza,' &c.

Also a Sonnet to Rats, well worthy of the subject, and a most thundering Ode, commencing as follows:—

 'Oh! for a Lay! loud as the surge
 That lashes Lapland's sounding shore.'

Lord have mercy on us! the 'Lay of the Last Minstrel' was nothing to this.

Page 115, col. 2.

'Thus Lays of Minstrels—may they be the last!'—See the 'Lay of the Last Minstrel,' *passim.* Never was any plan so incongruous and absurd as the groundwork of this production. The entrance of Thunder and Lightning, prologuising to Bayes' tragedy, unfortunately takes away the merit of originality from the dialogue between Messieurs the Spirits of Flood and Fell in the first canto. Then we have the amiable William of Deloraine 'a stark moss-trooper,' videlicet, a happy compound of poacher, sheep-stealer, and highwayman. The propriety of his magical lady's injunction no

864

read can only be equalled by his candid acknow-edgment of his independence of the trammels of spelling, although, to use his own elegant phrase, 'twas his neck-verse at Harribee,' i.e. the gallows. -The biography of Gilpin Horner, and the mar-vellous pedestrian page, who travelled twice as fast as his master's horse, without the aid of seven-league boots, are *chefs-d'œuvre* in the improve-ment of taste. For incident we have the invisible, but by no means sparing, box on the ear bestowed on the page, and the entrance of a knight and charger into the castle, under the very natural dis-guise of a wain of hay. Marmion, the hero of the latter romance, is exactly what William of Delo-raine would have been, had he been able to read and write. The poem was manufactured for Messrs. Constable, Murray, and Miller, worship-ful booksellers, in consideration of the receipt of a sum of money; and truly, considering the inspira-tion, it is a very creditable production. If Mr. Scott will write for hire, let him do his best for his paymasters, but not disgrace his genius, which is undoubtedly great, by a repetition of black-letter ballad imitations.

Page 116, col. 1.

'And bid a long "good night to Marmion."'] 'Good night to Marmion'—the pathetic and also prophetic exclamation of Henry Blount, Esquire, on the death of honest Marmion.

Page 116, col. 1.

'The single wonder of a thousand years.'] As the Odyssey is so closely connected with the story of the Iliad, they may almost be classed as one grand historical poem. In alluding to Milton and Tasso, we consider the 'Paradise Lost,' and 'Gie-usalemme Liberata,' as their standard efforts; since neither the 'Jerusalem Conquered' of the Italian, nor the 'Paradise Regained' of the English bard, obtained a proportionate celebrity to their former poems. Query: Which of Mr. Southey's will survive?

Page 116, col. 1.

'Next see tremendous Thalaba come on.'] 'Tha-laba,' Mr. Southey's second poem, is written in open defiance of precedent and poetry. Mr. S. wished to produce something novel, and succeeded to a miracle. 'Joan of Arc' was marvellous enough, but 'Thalaba' was one of those poems 'which,' in the words of Porson, 'will be read when Homer and Virgil are forgotten, but—*not till then*.'

Page 116, col. 2.

'Oh! Southey! Southey! cease thy varied song!'] We beg Mr. Southey's pardon: 'Madoc disdains the degrading title of epic.' See his preface. Why is epic degraded? and by whom? Certainly the late omaunts of Masters Cottle, Laureat Pye, Ogilvy, Hole, and gentle Mistress Cowley, have not exalted the epic muse; but, as Mr. Southey's poem 'dis-lains the appellation,' allow us to ask—has he substituted anything better in its stead? or must he be content to rival Sir Richard Blackmore in the quantity as well as quality of his verse?

Page 116, col. 2.

'Thou wilt devote old women to the devil.'] See 'The Old Woman of Berkeley,' a ballad, by Mr. Southey, wherein an aged gentlewoman is carried away by Beelzebub, on a 'high-trotting horse.'

Page 116, col. 2.

'"God help thee," Southey, and thy readers too.'] The last line, 'God help thee,' is an evident plagiarism from the Anti-jacobin to Mr. Southey, on his Dactylics.

Page 116, col. 2.

'And quit his books, for fear of growing dou-ble.'] Lyrical Ballads, p. 4.—'The Tables Turned.' Stanza 1.

'Up, up, my friend, and clear your looks;
 Why all this toil and trouble?
Up, up, my friend, and quit your books,
 Or surely you'll grow double.'

Page 116, col. 2.

'And, like his bard, confounded night with day.'] Mr. W. in his preface labours hard to prove, that prose and verse are much the same; and certainly his precepts and practice are strictly conform-able:—

'And thus to Betty's questions he
 Made answer, like a traveller bold,
The cock did crow, to-whoo, to-whoo,
And the sun did shine so cold,' &c. &c.,
 p. 129.

Page 116, col. 2.

'To him who takes a pixy for a muse.'] Cole-ridge's Poems, p. 11, 'Songs of the Pixies, i.e. Devonshire Fairies;' p. 42 we have 'Lines to a young Lady;' and p. 52, 'lines to a young Ass.'

Page 117, col. 1.

'All hail, M.P.! from whose infernal brain.'] 'For every one knows little Matt's an M.P.' See a poem to Mr. Lewis, in 'The Statesman,' sup-posed to be written by Mr. Jekyll.

Page 117, col. 1.

'Hibernian Strangford! with thine eyes of blue.'] The reader, who may wish for an explanation of this, may refer to 'Strangford's Camoëns,' p. 127, note to p. 56, or to the last page of the Edinburgh Review of Strangford's Camoëns.

Page 117, col. 1.

By dressing Camoëns in a suit of lace?'] It is also to be remarked, that the things given to the public as poems of Camoëns are no more to be found in the original Portuguese than in the Song of Solomon.

Page 117, col. 2.

'That luckless music never triumph'd there.'] Hayley's two most notorious verse productions are 'Triumphs of Temper,' and 'The Triumph of Music.' He has also written much comedy in rhyme, epistles, &c. &c. As he is rather an elegant writer of notes and biography, let us recommend Pope's advice to Wycherley to Mr. H's considera-tion, viz. 'to convert poetry into prose,' which may be easily done by taking away the final syllable of each couplet.

Page 117, col. 2.

Sepulchral Grahame, pours his notes sublime.'] Mr. Grahame has poured forth two volumes of cant, under the name of 'Sabbath Walks' and 'Biblical Pictures.'

Page 117, col. 2.

What merry sounds proceed from Oxford bells.'] See Bowles's 'Sonnet to Oxford,' and 'Stanzas on hearing the Bells of Ostend.'

NOTES TO ENGLISH BARDS AND SCOTCH REVIEWERS

Page 118, col. 1.

'Awake a louder and a loftier strain.'] 'Awake a louder', &c., is the first line in Bowles's 'Spirit of Discovery;' a very spirited and pretty dwarf-epic. Among other exquisite lines we have the following

——'A kiss
Stole on the list'ning silence, never yet
Here heard; they trembled even as if the power,'
&c. &c.

That is, the woods of Madeira trembled to a kiss; very much astonished, as well they might be, at such a phenomenon.

Page 118, col. 1.

'The bard sighs forth a gentle episode.'] The episode above alluded to is the story of 'Robert à Machin' and 'Anna d' Arfet,' a pair of constant lovers, who performed the kiss above mentioned, that startled the woods of Madeira.

Page 118, col. 1.

·Consult Lord Fanny, and confide in Curll.'] Curll is one of the heroes of the Dunciad, and was a bookseller. Lord Fanny is the poetical name of Lord Hervey, author of 'Lines to the Imitator of Horace.'

Page 118, col. 1.

·And do from hate what Mallet did for hire.'] Lord Bolingbroke hired Mallet to traduce Pope after his decease, because the poet had retained some copies of a work by Lord Bolingbroke—the 'Patriot King,'—which that splendid but malignant genius had ordered to be destroyed.

Page 118, col. 1.

'To rave with Dennis, and with Ralph to rhyme.'] Dennis the critic, and Ralph the rhymester.—

'Silence, ye wolves! while Ralph to Cynthia howls,
Making night hideous: answer him, ye owls!'
DUNCIAD.

Page 118, col. 1.

'And link'd thee to the Dunciad for thy pains.'] See Bowles's late edition of Pope's works, for which he received three hundred pounds. Thus Mr. B. has experienced how much easier it is to profit by the reputation of another, than to elevate his own.

Page 118, col. 2.

'Had Cottle still adorn'd the counter's side.'] Mr. Cottle, Amos, Joseph, I don't know which, but one or both, once sellers of books they did not write, and now writers of books they do not sell, have published a pair of epics—'Alfred,' (poor Alfred! Pye has been at him too!)—'Alfred,' and the 'Fall of Cambria.'

Page 118, col. 2.

'Dull Maurice all his granite weight of leaves.'] Mr. Maurice hath manufactured the component parts of a ponderous quarto, upon the beauties of 'Richmond Hill,' and the like:—it also takes in a charming view of Turnham Green, Hammersmith, Brentford, Old and New, and the parts adjacent.

Page 118, col. 2.

'May no rude hand disturb their early sleep!'] Poor Montgomery, though praised by every English Review, has been bitterly reviled by the Edinburgh. After all, the bard of Sheffield is a man of considerable genius. His 'Wanderer of Switzerland' is worth a thousand 'Lyrical Ballads,' and at least fifty 'degraded epics.'

Page 119, col. 1.

'Nor hunt the blood-hounds back to Arthur' seat?'] Arthur's Seat; the hill which overhangs Edinburgh.

Page 119, col. 1.

'When Little's leadless pistol met his eye.'] In 1806, Messrs. Jeffrey and Moore met at Chalk Farm. The duel was prevented by the interference of the magistracy; and, on examination, the ball of the pistols were found to have evaporated. This incident gave occasion to much waggery in the daily prints.

Page 119, col. 2.

'The other half pursued its calm career.'] The Tweed here behaved with proper decorum; but would have been highly reprehensible in the English half of the river to have shown the smallest symptom of apprehension.

Page 119, col. 2.

'If Jeffrey died, except within her arms.'] This display of sympathy on the part of the Tolbooth (the principal prison in Edinburgh), which truly seems to have been most affected on this occasion, is much to be commended. It was to be apprehended, that the many unhappy criminals executed in the front might have rendered the edifice more callous. She is said to be of the softer sex, because her delicacy of feeling on this day was truly feminine, though, like most feminine impulses, perhaps a little selfish.

Page 119, col. 2.

The travell'd thane, Athenian Aberdeen.'] His lordship has been much abroad, is a member of the Athenian Society, and reviewer of 'Gell's Topography of Troy.'

Page 119, col. 2.

'Herbert shall wield Thor's hammer, and some times.'] Mr. Herbert is a translator of Icelandic and other poetry. One of the principal pieces is a 'Song on the Recovery of Thor's Hammer:' the translation is a pleasant chant in the vulgar tongue and endeth thus:—

'Instead of money and rings, I wot,
The hammer's bruises were her lot.
Thus Odin's son his hammer got.'

Page 119, col. 2.

'Smug Sydney too thy bitter page shall seek.' The Rev. Sydney Smith, the reputed author of Peter Plymley's Letters, and sundry criticisms.

Page 119, col. 2.

'And classic Hallam, much renown'd for Greek.' Mr. Hallam reviewed Payne Knight's 'Taste,' and was exceedingly severe on some Greek verses therein. It was not discovered that the lines were Pindar's till the press rendered it impossible to cancel the critique, which still stands an everlasting monument of Hallam's ingenuity.—*Note added to second edition.* The said Hallam is incensed because he is falsely accused, seeing that he never dineth at Holland House. If this be true, I am sorry—not for having said so, but on his account, as I understand his lordship's feasts are preferable to his compositions. If he did not review Lord

866

NOTES TO ENGLISH BARDS AND SCOTCH REVIEWERS

Holland's performance, I am glad; because it must have been painful to read, and irksome to praise it. If Mr. Hallam will tell me who did review it, the real name shall find a place in the text; provided, nevertheless, the said name be of two orthodox musical syllables, and will come into the verse: till then, Hallam must stand for want of a better.

Page 119, col. 2.

'And paltry Pillans shall traduce his friend.'] Pillans is a tutor at Eton.

Page 120, col. 1.

'While gay Thalia's luckless votary, Lambe.'] The Hon. George Lambe reviewed 'Beresford's Miseries,' and is, moreover, author of a farce enacted with much applause at the Priory, Stanmore; and damned with great expedition at the late theatre, Covent Garden. It was entitled, 'Whistle for it.'

Page 120, col. 1.

'Beware lest blundering Brougham destroy the sale.'] Mr. Brougham, in No. XXV of the Edinburgh Review, throughout the article concerning Don Pedro de Cevallos, has displayed more politics than policy; many of the worthy burgesses of Edinburgh being so incensed at the infamous principles it evinces, as to have withdrawn their subscriptions.—Here followed in the first edition, —'The name of this personage is pronounced Broom in the south, but the truly northern and *musical* pronunciation is BROUGH-AM, in two syllables;' but for this, Lord B. substituted in the second edition:—'It seems that Mr. Brougham is not a Pict, as I supposed, but a Borderer, and his name is pronounced Broom from Trent to Tay:— so be it.'

Page 120, col. 1.

'Her son, and vanish'd in a Scottish mist.'] I ought to apologise to the worthy deities for introducing a new goddess with short petticoats to their notice: but, alas! what was to be done? I could not say Caledonia's genius, it being well known there is no such genius to be found from Clackmannan to Caithness; yet, without supernatural agency, how was Jeffrey to be saved? The national 'kelpies' are too unpoetical, and the 'brownies' and 'gude neighbours' (spirits of a good disposition) refused to extricate him. A goddess, therefore, has been called for the purpose; and great ought to be the gratitude of Jeffrey, seeing it is the only communication he ever held, or is likely to hold, with anything heavenly.

Page 120, col. 1.

'This scents its pages, and that gilds its rear.'] See the colour of the back binding of the Edinburgh Review.

Page 120, col. 1.

'Declare his landlord can at least translate!'] Lord Holland has translated some specimens of Lope de Vega, inserted in his life of the author. Both are bepraised by his *disinterested* guests.

Page 120, col. 2.

'Reforms each error, and refines the whole.'] Certain it is, her ladyship is suspected of having displayed her matchless wit in the Edinburgh Review. However that may be, we know from good authority that the manuscripts are submitted to her perusal—no doubt, for correction.

Page 120, col. 2.

'Puns, and a prince within a barrel pent.'] In the melo-drama of Tekeli, that heroic prince is clapt into a barrel on the stage; a new asylum for distressed heroes.

Page 120, col. 2.

'While Reynolds vents his "dammes!" "poohs!" and "zounds!"'] All these are favourite expressions of Mr. Reynolds, and prominent in his comedies, living and defunct.

Page 120, col. 2.

'A tragedy complete in all but words?'] Mr. T. Sheridan, the new manager of Drury Lane theatre, stripped the tragedy of Bonduca of the dialogue, and exhibited the scenes as the spectacle of Caractacus. Was this worthy of his sire? or of himself?

Page 121, col. 1.

'Her flight to garnish Greenwood's gay designs.'] Mr. Greenwood is, we believe, scene-painter to Drury Lane theatre—as such, Mr. Skeffington is much indebted to him.

Page 121, col. 1.

'In five facetious acts comes thundering on.'] Mr. [afterwards Sir Lumley] Skeffington is the illustrious author of the 'Sleeping Beauty;' and some comedies, particularly 'Maids and Bachelors:' *Baccalaurii baculo magis quam lauro digni.*

Page 121, col. 1.

'And worship Catalani's pantaloons.'] Naldi and Catalani require little notice; for the visage of the one, and the salary of the other, will enable us long to recollect these amusing vagabonds. Besides, we are still black and blue from the squeeze on the first night of the lady's appearance in trousers.

Page 121, col. 2.

'Of vice and folly, Greville and Argyle!'] To prevent any blunder, such as mistaking a street for a man, I beg leave to state that it is the institution, and not the Duke of that name, which is here alluded to. A gentleman, with whom I am slightly acquainted, lost in the Argyle Rooms several thousand pounds at backgammon. It is but justice to the manager in this instance to say, that some degree of misapprobation was manifested: but why are the implements of gaming allowed in a place devoted to the society of both sexes? A pleasant thing for the wives and daughters of those who are blest or cursed with such connexions, to hear the billiard-tables rattling in one room, and the dice in another! That this is the case I myself can testify, as a late unworthy member of an institution which materially affects the morals of the higher orders, while the lower may not even move to the sound of a tabor and fiddle without a chance of indictment for riotous behaviour.

Page 121, col. 2.

'Behold the new Petronius of the day.'] Petronius, 'Arbiter elegantiarum' to Nero, 'and a very pretty fellow in his day,' as Mr. Congreve's 'Old Bachelor' saith of Hannibal.

Page 122, col. 1.

'To live like Clodius, and like Falkland fall.'] I knew the late Lord Falkland well. On Sunday night I beheld him presiding at his own table, in all the honest pride of hospitality; on Wednesday

morning, at three o'clock, I saw stretched before me all that remained of courage, feeling, and a host of passions. He was a gallant and successful officer: his faults were the faults of a sailor [those of dissipation]—as such, Britons will forgive them. He died like a brave man in a better cause; for had he fallen in like manner on the deck of the frigate to which he was just appointed, his last moments would have been held up by his countrymen as an example to succeeding heroes.

Page 122, col. 1.

'From silly Hafiz up to simple Bowles.'] What would be the sentiments of the Persian Anacreon, Hafiz, could he rise from his splendid sepulchre at Sheeraz (where he reposes with Ferdousi and Sadi, the oriental Homer and Catullus), and behold his name assumed by one Stott of Dromore, the most impudent and execrable of literary poachers for the daily prints?

Page 122, col. 2.

'Lord, rhymester, petit-maître, and pamphlet-eer!'] The Earl of Carlisle has lately published an eighteenpenny pamphlet on the state of the stage, and offers his plan for building a new theatre. It is to be hoped his lordship will be permitted to bring forward anything for the stage—except his own tragedies.

Page 122, col. 2.

'And hang a calf-skin on those recreant lines.']
'Doff that lion's hide,
And hang a calf-skin on those recreant limbs.'
Shak. King John.
Lord Carlisle's works, most resplendently bound, form a conspicuous ornament to his book-shelves:—
'The rest is all but leather and prunella.'

Page 122, col. 2.

'And Melville's Mantle prove a blanket too!']
'Melville's Mantle,' a parody on 'Elijah's Mantle,' a poem.

Page 123, col. 1.

'Leave wondering comprehension far behind.']
This lovely little Jessica, the daughter of the noted Jew King, seems to be a follower of the Della Crusca school, and has published two volumes of very respectable absurdities in rhyme, as times go; besides sundry novels in the style of the first edition of the Monk.

Page 123, col. 1.

'Chain'd to the signature of O. P. Q.'] These are the signatures of various worthies who figure in the poetical departments of the newspapers.

Page 123, col. 1.

'And Capel Lofft declares 'tis quite sublime.']
Capel Lofft, Esq., the Mæcenas of shoemakers, and preface-writer-general to distressed versemen; a kind of gratis accoucheur to those who wish to be delivered of rhyme, but do not know how to bring forth.

Page 123, col. 1.

'Bloomfield! why not on brother Nathan too?']
See Nathaniel Bloomfield's ode, elegy, or whatever he or any one else chooses to call it, on the en-closures of 'Honington Green.'

Page 123, col. 2.

'May Moorland weavers boast Pindaric skill.']
Vide 'Recollections of a Weaver in the Moorlands of Staffordshire.'

Page 123, col. 2.

'Recall the pleasing memory of the past.'] I would be superfluous to recall to the mind of th reader the authors of 'The Pleasures of Memory and 'The Pleasures of Hope,' the most beautifu didactic poems in our language, if we except Pope' 'Essay on Man:' but so many poetasters have started up, that even the names of Campbell and Rogers are become strange.

Page 123, col. 2.

'Bear witness, Gifford.'] Gifford, author of th Baviad and Mæviad, the first satires of the day and translator of Juvenal.

Page 123, col. 2.

'Sotheby.'] Sotheby, translator of Wieland' Oberon and Virgil's Georgics, and author o 'Saul,' an epic poem.

Page 123, col. 2.

'Macneil.'] Macneil, whose poems are de servedly popular, particularly 'Scotland's Scaith, and the 'Waes of War,' of which ten thousand copies were sold in one month.

Page 123, col. 2.

'Why slumbers Gifford? let us ask again.' Mr. Gifford promised publicly that the Baviad and Mæviad should not be his last original works: le him remember, 'Mox in reluctantes dracones.'

Page 124, col. 1.

'Unhappy White! while life was in its spring.' Henry Kirke White died at Cambridge, in October 1806, in consequence of too much exertion in the pursuit of studies that would have matured a min which disease and poverty could not impair, an which death itself destroyed rather than subdued His poems abound in such beauties as must im press the reader with the liveliest regret that s short a period was allotted to talents which would have dignified even the sacred functions he was destined to assume.

Page 124, col. 1.

'And here let Shee and Genius find a place.' Mr. Shee [afterwards President of the Roya Academy], author of 'Rhymes on Art,' and 'Ele ments of Art.'

Page 124, col. 2.

'Wright! 'twas thy happy lot at once to view.' Walter Rodwell Wright, late consul-general for the Seven Islands, is author of a very beautiful poem just published: it is entitled 'Horæ Ionicæ,' and i descriptive of the isles and the adjacent coast o Greece.

Page 124, col. 2.

'And you, associate bards! who snatch'd t light.'] The translators of the Anthology, Blan and Merivale, have since published separate poems which evince genius that only requires opportunit to attain eminence.

Page 124, col. 2.

'False glare attracts, but more offends the eye.' The neglect of the 'Botanic Garden' is some proo of returning taste. The scenery is its sole recom mendation.

Page 125, col. 1.

Seems blessed harmony to Lamb and Lloyd.' Messrs. Lamb and Lloyd, the most ignoble fol lowers of Southey and Co.

NOTES TO HINTS FROM HORACE

Page 125, col. 1.

'And thou, too, Scott! resign to minstrels rude.']
By the bye, I hope that in Mr. Scott's next poem, his hero or heroine will be less addicted to 'Gramarye,' and more to grammar, than the Lady of the Lay and her bravo, William of Deloraine.

Page 125, col. 1.

'Let Stott, Carlisle, Matilda, and the rest.'] It may be asked, why I have censured the Earl of Carlisle, my guardian and relative, to whom I dedicated a volume of puerile poems a few years ago?—The guardianship was nominal, at least as far as I have been able to discover; the relationship I cannot help, and am very sorry for it; but as his lordship seemed to forget it on a very essential occasion to me, I shall not burden my memory with the recollection. I do not think that personal differences sanction the unjust condemnation of a brother scribbler; but I see no reason why they should act as a preventive, when the author, noble or ignoble, has, for a series of years, beguiled a 'discerning public' (as the advertisements have it) with divers reams of most orthodox, imperial nonsense. Besides, I do not step aside to vituperate the earl: no—his works come fairly in review with those of other patrician literati. If, before I escaped from my teens, I said anything in favour of his lordship's paper books, it was in the way of dutiful dedication, and more from the advice of others than my own judgment, and I seize the first opportunity of pronouncing my sincere recantation. I have heard that some persons conceive me to be under obligations to Lord Carlisle: if so, I shall be most particularly happy to learn what they are, and when conferred, that they may be duly appreciated and publicly acknowledged. What I have humbly advanced as an opinion on his printed things, I am prepared to support, if necessary, by quotations from elegies, eulogies, odes, episodes, and certain facetious and dainty tragedies bearing his name and mark:—

'What can ennoble knaves, or fools, or cowards?
Alas! not all the blood of all the Howards.'

So says Pope. Amen!

Page 125, col. 2.

'Requires no sacred theme to bid us list.'] The 'Games of Hoyle,' well known to the votaries of whist, chess, &c., are not to be superseded by the vagaries of his poetical namesake, whose poem comprised, as expressly stated in the advertisement, all the 'plagues of Egypt.'

Page 126, col. 1.

'Himself a living libel on mankind.'] This person, who has lately betrayed the most rabid symptoms of confirmed authorship, is writer of a poem denominated the 'Art of Pleasing,' as 'lucus a non lucendo,' containing little pleasantry and less poetry. He also acts as monthly stipendiary and collector of calumnies for the 'Satirist.' If this unfortunate young man would exchange the magazines for the mathematics, and endeavour to take a decent degree in his university, it might eventually prove more serviceable than his present salary.

Page 126, col. 1.

'Oh! dark asylum of a Vandal race!'] 'Into Cambridgeshire the Emperor Probus transported a considerable body of Vandals.'—Gibbon's Decline and Fall, vol. ii. p. 83. There is no reason to doubt the truth of this assertion; the breed is still in high perfection.

Page 126, col. 1.

'So lost to Phœbus, that nor Hodgson's verse.'] This gentleman's name requires no praise: the man who in translation displays unquestionable genius may be well expected to excel in original composition, of which, it is to be hoped, we shall soon see a splendid specimen.

Page 126, col. 1.

'Can make thee better, nor poor Hewson's worse.'] Hewson Clarke, *Esq.*, as it is written.

Page 126, col. 1.

'And modern Britons glory in their sires.'] The 'Aboriginal Britons,' an excellent poem, by Richards.

Page 126, col. 2.

'And old dame Portland fills the place of Pitt.'] A friend of mine being asked, why his Grace of Portland was likened to an old woman? replied, 'he supposed it was because he was past bearing.' —His Grace is now gathered to his grandmothers, where he sleeps as sound as ever; but even his sleep was better than his colleagues' waking. 1811.

Page 126, col. 2.

'Thence shall I stray through beauty's native clime.'] Georgia.

Page 126, col. 2.

'Where Kaff is clad in rocks, and crown'd with snows sublime.'] Mount Caucasus.

Page 126, col. 2.

'Let Aberdeen and Elgin still pursue.'] Lord Elgin would fain persuade us that all the figures, with and without noses, in his stoneshop, are the works of Phidias! 'Credat Judæus!'

Page 126, col. 2.

'Gell.'] Mr. Gell's Topography of Troy and Ithaca cannot fail to insure the approbation of every man possessed of classical taste, as well for the information Mr. Gell conveys to the mind of the reader, as for the ability and research the respective works display.

HINTS FROM HORACE

Page 128, col. 1.

'Or low Dubost—as once the world has seen.'] —In an English newspaper, which finds its way abroad wherever there are Englishmen, I read an account of this dirty dauber's caricature of Mr. H—— as a 'beast,' and the consequent action, &c. The circumstance is, probably, too well known to require further comment.

Page 128, col. 2.

'To paint a rainbow, or—the river Thames.'] 'Where pure description held the place of sense.'— POPE.

Page 129, col. 1.

'But coats must claim another artisan.'] Mere common mortals were commonly content with one tailor and with one bill, but the more particular gentlemen found it impossible to confide their lower garments to the makers of their body clothes. I speak of the beginning of 1809: what reform may have since taken place I neither know, nor desire to know.

NOTES TO HINTS FROM HORACE

Page 129, col. 2.

'As Pitt has furnish'd us a word or two.'] Mr. Pitt was liberal in his additions to our parliamentary tongue; as may be seen in many publications, particularly the Edinburgh Review.

Page 129, col. 2.

'True, some decay, yet not a few revive.'] Old ballads, old plays, and old women's stories, are at present in as much request as old wine or new speeches. In fact, this is the millennium of black letter; thanks to our Hebers, Webers, and Scotts!

Page 130, col. 1.

'You doubt—see Dryden, Pope, St. Patrick's dean,'] 'Mac Flecknoe,' the 'Dunciad,' and all Swift's lampooning ballads. Whatever their other works may be, these originated in personal feelings, and angry retort on unworthy rivals; and though the ability of these satires elevates the poetical, their poignancy detracts from the personal character of the writers.

Page 130, col. 1.

'For jest and *pun* in very middling prose.'] With all the vulgar applause and critical abhorrence of *puns*, they have Aristotle on their side; who permits them to orators, and gives them consequence by a grave disquisition.

Page 130, col. 2.

'To "hollowing Hotspur" and the sceptred sire.'] 'And in his ear I'll hollow, Mortimer!'— 1 *Henry IV*.

Page 131, col. 1.

'Difficile est proprie communia dicere: tuque.'] Mde. Dacier, Mde. de Sévigné, Boileau, and others, have left their dispute on the meaning of this passage in a tract considerably longer than the poem of Horace. It is printed at the close of the eleventh volume of Madame de Sévigné's Letters, edited by Grouvelle, Paris, 1806. Presuming that all who *can* construe may venture an opinion on such subjects, particularly as so many who can *not* have taken the same liberty, I should have held my 'farthing candle' as awkwardly as another, had not my respect for the wits of Louis the Fourteenth's Augustan siècle induced me to subjoin these illustrious authorities. 1st, Boileau: 'Il est difficile de traiter des sujets qui sont à la portée de tout le monde d'une manière qui vous les rende propres, ce qui s'appelle s'approprier un sujet par le tour qu'on y donne.' 2ndly, Batteux: 'Mais il est bien difficile de donner des traits propres et individuels aux êtres purement possibles.' 3rdly, Dacier: 'Il est difficile de traiter convenablement ces caractères que tout le monde peut inventer.' Mde. de Sévigné's opinion and translation, consisting of some thirty pages, I omit, particularly as M. Grouvelle observes, 'La chose est bien remarquable, aucune de ces diverses interpretations ne paraît être la véritable.' But, by way of comfort, it seems, fifty years afterwards, 'Le lumineux Dumarsais' made his appearance, to set Horace on his legs again, 'dissiper tous les nuages, et concilier tous les dissentimens;' and some fifty years hence, somebody, still more luminous, will doubtless start up and demolish Dumarsais and his system on this weighty affair, as if he were no better than Ptolemy and Tycho, or his comments of no more consequence than astronomical calculations on the present comet. I am happy to say, 'la longueur de la dissertation' of M. D. prevents M. G. from saying any more on the matter. A better poet than Boileau, and at least as good a scholar as Sévigné, has said,

'A little learning is a dangerous thing.'

And by this comparison of comments, it may be perceived how a good deal may be rendered as perilous to the proprietors.

Page 131, col. 2.

'Beware—for God's sake, don't begin like Bowles!'] About two years ago a young man, named Townsend, was announced by Mr. Cumberland, in a review (since deceased) as being engaged in an epic poem to be entitled 'Armageddon.' The plan and specimen promise much; but I hope neither to offend Mr. Townsend, nor his friends, by recommending to his attention the lines of Horace to which these rhymes allude. If Mr. Townsend succeeds in his undertaking, as there is reason to hope, how much will the world be indebted to Mr. Cumberland for bringing him before the public! But, till that eventful day arrives, it may be doubted whether the premature display of his plan (sublime as the ideas confessedly are) has not,— by raising expectations too high, or diminishing curiosity, by developing his argument,—rather incurred the hazard of injuring Mr. Townsend's future prospects. Mr. Cumberland (whose talents I shall not depreciate by the humble tribute of my praise) and Mr. Townsend must not suppose me actuated by unworthy motives in this suggestion. I wish the author all the success he can wish himself, and shall be truly happy to see epic poetry weighed up from the bathos where it lies sunken with Southey, Cottle, Cowley (Mrs. or Abraham), Ogilvy, Wilkie, Pye, and all the 'dull of past and present days.' Even if he is not a *Milton*, he may be better than *Blackmore*; if not a *Homer*, an *Antimachus*. I should deem myself presumptuous, as a young man, in offering advice, were it not addressed to one still younger. Mr. Townsend has the greatest difficulties to encounter: but in conquering them he will find employment; in having conquered them, his reward. I know too well 'the scribbler's scoff, the critic's contumely;' and I am afraid time will teach Mr. Townsend to know them better. Those who succeed, and those who do not, must bear this alike, and it is hard to say which have most of it. I trust that Mr. Townsend's share will be from *envy*; he will soon know mankind well enough not to attribute this expression to malice.

Page 132, col. 1.

'O'er Virgil's devilish verses and his own.'] Harvey, the *circulator* of the *circulation* of the blood, used to fling away Virgil in his ecstasy of admiration and say, 'the book had a devil.' Now, such a character as I am copying would probably fling it away also, but rather wish that the devil had the book; not from dislike to the poet, but a well-founded horror of hexameters. Indeed, the public school penance of 'Long and Short' is enough to beget an antipathy to poetry for the residue of a man's life, and, perhaps, so far may be an advantage.

Page 132, col. 1.

'Unlucky Tavell! doom'd to daily cares.'] 'Infandum, regina, jubes renovare dolorem.' I dare say Mr. Tavell (to whom I mean no affront) will understand me; and it is no matter whether any one else does or no.—To the above events, 'quæque ipse miserrima vidi, et quorum pars magna fui,' all *times* and *terms* bear testimony.

Page 132, col. 2.

'Master of arts! as *hells* and *clubs* proclaim.']
'Hell,' a gaming-house so called, where you risk
little, and are cheated a good deal. 'Club,' a
pleasant purgatory, where you lose more, and are
not supposed to be cheated at all.

Page 133, col. 1.

'A halter'd heroine Johnson sought to slay.']
'Irene had to speak two lines with the bow-string
round her neck; but the audience cried out
"Murder!" and she was obliged to go off the stage
alive.'—*Boswell's Johnson.*

Page 133, col. 1.

'Whose postscripts prate of dyeing "heroines
blue"?'] In the postscript to the 'Castle Spectre,'
Mr. Lewis tells us, that though blacks were un-
known in England at the period of his action, yet
he has made the anachronism to set off the scene:
and if he could have produced the effect 'by
making his heroine blue,'—I quote him—'blue he
would have made her!'

Page 133, col. 2.

'Ere scenes were play'd by many a reverend
clerk.'] 'The first theatrical representations, en-
titled "Mysteries and Moralities," were generally
enacted at Christmas, by monks (as the only per-
sons who could read), and latterly by the clergy
and students of the universities. The dramatis
personæ were usually Adam, Pater Cœlestis, Faith,
Vice,' &c. &c.—See Warton's History of English
Poetry.

Page 133, col. 2.

''Tis strange Benvolio suffers such a show.']
Benvolio does not bet: but every man who main-
tains race-horses is a promoter of all the concomi-
tant evils of the turf. Avoiding to bet is a little
pharisaical. Is it an exculpation? I think not.
I never yet heard a bawd praised for chastity,
because *she herself* did not commit fornication.

Page 134, col. 1.

'But find in thine, like pagan Plato's bed.']
Under Plato's pillow a volume of the *Mimes* of
Sophron was found the day he died.—*Vide* Barthé-
lémi, De Pauw, or Diogenes Laertius, if agreeable.
De Pauw calls it a jest-book. Cumberland, in his
Observer, terms it moral, like the sayings of
Publius Syrus.

Page 134, col. 1.

'Yet Chesterfield, whose polish'd pen inveighs.']
His speech on the Licensing Act is one of his most
eloquent efforts.

Page 134, col. 1.

'And "Estifania" gull her "Copper" spouse.']
Michael Perez, the Copper Captain, in 'Rule a
Wife and have a Wife.'

Page 134, col. 1.

'And, spite of puritans and Collier's curse.']
Jerry Collier's controversy with Congreve, &c. on
the subject of the drama, is too well known to
require further comment.

Page 134, col. 2.

'And Simeon kicks.'] Mr. Simeon is the very
bully of beliefs, and castigator of 'good works.'
He is ably supported by John Stickles, a labourer
in the same vineyard:—but I say no more, for,
according to Johnny in full congregation, '*No
hopes for them as laughs.*'

Page 134, col. 2.

'Where Baxter only "shoves."'] 'Baxter's Shove
to heavy-a—d Christians,' the veritable title of a
book once in good repute, and likely enough to be
so again.

Page 136, col. 1.

'And keep your bushy locks a year from Blake.']
As famous a tonsor as Licinus himself, and better
paid, and may, like him, be one day a senator,
having a better qualification than one half of the
heads he crops, viz.—independence.

Page 137, col. 1.

'For poets (says this sage and many more).'] I
have not the original by me, but the Italian transla-
tion runs as follows:—'E una cosa a mio credere
molto stravagante, che un padre desideri, o per-
metta, che suo figliuolo coltivi e perfezioni questo
talento.' A little further on: 'Si trovano di rado
nel Parnaso le miniere d' oro e d' argento.'—*Edu-
cazione dei Fanciulli del Signor Locke.*

Page 137, col. 1.

'Is poor as Irus.'] 'Iro pauperior:' this is the
same beggar who boxed with Ulysses for a pound
of kid's fry, which he lost, and half a dozen teeth
besides.—See Odyssey, b. 18.

Page 137, col. 1.

'Or an Irish mine.'] The Irish gold mine of
Wicklow, which yields just ore enough to swear
by, or gild a bad guinea.

Page 137, col. 2.

'And double-barrels (damn them!) miss their
mark.'] As Mr. Pope took the liberty of damning
Homer, to whom he was under great obligations—
'*And Homer (damn himé!) calls*'—it may be pre-
sumed that anybody or anything may be damned
in verse by poetical license; and, in case of accident,
I beg leave to plead so illustrious a precedent.

Page 137, col. 2.

'Let Havard's fate o'ertake him, who, for once.']
For the story of Billy Havard's tragedy, see
'Davies's Life of Garrick.' I believe it is 'Regulus,'
or 'Charles the First.' The moment it was known
to be his the theatre thinned, and the bookseller re-
fused to give the customary sum for the copyright.

Page 138, col. 1.

'Or mild Eclectics, when some, worse than
Turks.'] To the Eclectic or Christian Reviewers
I have to return thanks for the fervour of that
charity which, in 1809, induced them to express a
hope that a thing then published by me might lead
to certain consequences, which, although natural
enough, surely came but rashly from reverend lips.
I refer them to their own pages, where they con-
gratulated themselves on the prospect of a tilt
between Mr. Jeffrey and myself, from which some
great good was to accrue, provided one or both
were knocked on the head. Having survived two
years and a half those 'Elegies' which they were
kindly preparing to review, I have no peculiar
gusto to give them 'so joyful a trouble,' except
indeed 'upon compulsion, Hal;' but if, as David
says in the 'Rivals,' it should come to 'bloody
sword and gun fighting,' we 'won't run, will we,
Sir Lucius?' I do not know what I had done to

these Eclectic gentlemen: my works are their lawful perquisite, to be hewn in pieces like Agag, if it seem meet unto them: but why they should be in such a hurry to kill off their author, I am ignorant. 'The race is not always to the swift, nor the battle to the strong:' and now, as these Christians have 'smote me on one cheek,' I hold them up the other; and, in return for their good wishes, give them an opportunity of repeating them. Had any other set of men expressed such sentiments, I should have smiled, and left them to the 'recording angel;' but from the pharisees of Christianity decency might be expected. I can assure these brethren, that, publican and sinner as I am, I would not have treated 'mine enemy's dog thus.' To show them the superiority of my brotherly love, if ever the Reverend Messrs. Simeon or Ramsden should be engaged in such a conflict as that in which they requested me to fall, I hope they may escape with being 'winged' only, and that Heaviside may be at hand to extract the ball.

Page 138, col. 2.

'From Corydon unkind Alexis turns.'] Invenies alium, si te hic fastidit, Alexin.

Page 139, col. 1.

'And hark 'ye, Southey! pray—but don't be vex'd.'] Mr. Southey has lately tied another canister to his tail in the 'Curse of Kehama,' maugre the neglect of Madoc, &c., and has in one instance had a wonderful effect. A literary friend of mine, walking out one lovely evening last summer, on the eleventh bridge of the Paddington canal, was alarmed by the cry of 'one in jeopardy:' he rushed along, collected a body of Irish haymakers (supping on butter-milk in an adjacent paddock), procured three rakes, one eel-spear, and a landing-net, and at last (horresco referens) pulled out—his own publisher. The unfortunate man was gone for ever, and so was a large quarto wherewith he had taken the leap, which proved, on inquiry, to have been Mr. Southey's last work. Its 'alacrity of sinking' was so great, that it has never since been heard of; though some maintain that it is at this moment concealed in Alderman Birch's pastry premises, Cornhill. Be this as it may, the coroner's inquest brought in a verdict of 'Felo de bibliopolâ' against a 'quarto unknown;' and circumstantial evidence being since strong against the 'Curse of Kehama' (of which the above words are an exact description), it will be tried by its peers next session, in Grub-street—Arthur, Alfred, Davideis, Richard Cœur de Lion, Exodus Exodia, Epigoniad, Calvary, Fall of Cambria, Siege of Acre, Don Roderick, and Tom Thumb the Great, are the names of the twelve jurors. The judges are Pye, Bowles, and the bellman of St. Sepulchre's. The same advocates, pro and con, will be employed as are now engaged in Sir F. Burdett's celebrated cause in the Scotch courts. The public anxiously await the result, and all *live* publishers will be subpœnaed as witnesses.—But Mr. Southey has published the 'Curse of Kehama,'—an inviting title to quibblers. By-the-by, it is a good deal beneath Scott and Campbell, and not much above Southey, to allow the booby Ballantyne to entitle them, in the Edinburgh Annual Register (of which, by-the-by, Southey is editor), 'the grand poetical triumvirate of the day.' But, on second thoughts, it can be no great degree of praise to be the one-eyed leaders of the blind, though they might as well keep to themselves 'Scott's thirty thousand copies sold,' which must sadly discomfit poor Southey's unsale-

ables. Poor Southey, it should seem, is the 'Lepidus' of this poetical triumvirate. I am only surprised to see him in such good company.

'Such things, we know, are neither rich nor rare,
But wonder how the devil *he* came there.'

The trio are well defined in the sixth proposition of Euclid:—'Because, in the triangles D B C, A C B, D B is equal to A C, and B C common to both; the two sides D B, B C, are equal to the two A C, C B, each to each, and the angle D B C is equal to the angle A C B: therefore, the base D C is equal to the base A B, and the triangle D B C (Mr. Southey) is equal to the triangle A C B, the *less* to the *greater*, which is *absurd*,' &c.—The editor of the Edinburgh Register will find the rest of the theorem hard by his stabling; he has only to cross the river; 'tis the first turnpike t'other side 'Pons Asinorum.'*

Page 139, col. 1.

'Though "Madoc," with "Pucelle," instead of punk.'] Voltaire's 'Pucelle' is not quite so immaculate as Mr. Southey's 'Joan of Arc,' and yet I am afraid the Frenchman has both more truth and poetry too on his side—(they rarely go together)—than our patriotic minstrel, whose first essay was in praise of a fanatical French strumpet, whose title of witch would be correct with the change of the first letter.

Page 139, col. 1.

'May travel back to Quito—on a trunk.'] Like Sir Bland Burgess's 'Richard;' the tenth book of which I read at Malta, on a trunk of Eyre's, 19, Cockspur-street. If this be doubted, I shall buy a portmanteau to quote from.

Page 140, col. 1.

'Fool on, as fluent as an Orpheus' head.']
'Tum quoque marmorea caput a cervice revulsum,
Gurgite cum medio portans Œagrius Hebrus,
Volveret Eurydicen vox ipsa, et frigida lingua,
Ah, miseram Eurydicen! anima fugiente vocabat;
Eurydicen toto referebant flumine ripæ.'
Georgic., iv. 523.

Page 140, col. 1.

'The cobbler-laureats.'] I beg Nathaniel's pardon: he is not a cobbler; *it* is a *tailor*, but begged Capel Lofft to sink the profession in his preface to two pair of panta—psha!—of cantos, which he wished the public to try on: but the sieve of a patron let it out, and so far saved the expense of an advertisement to his country customers.—Merry's 'Moorfields whine' was nothing to all this. The 'Della Cruscans' were people of some education, and no profession; but these Arcadians ('Arcades ambo'—bumpkins both) send out their native nonsense without the smallest alloy, and leave all the shoes and smallclothes in the parish unrepaired, to patch up Elegies on Enclosures, and Pæans to Gunpowder. Sitting on a shopboard, they describe the fields of battle, when the only blood they ever saw was shed from the finger; and an 'Essay on War' is produced by the ninth part of a 'poet.'

* This Latin has sorely puzzled the University of Edinburgh. Ballantyne said it meant the 'Bridge of Berwick,' but Southey claimed it as half English; Scott swore it was the 'Brig o' Stirling:' he had just passed two king Jameses and a dozen Douglases over it. At last it was decided by Jeffrey that it meant nothing more nor *less* than the 'counter of Archy Constable's shop.'

'And own that *nine* such poets made a Tate.'
Did Nathan ever read that line of Pope? and if he
did, why not take it as his motto?

Page 140, col. 1.

'Sing to Capel Lofft!'] This well-meaning gentle-
man has spoiled some excellent shoemakers, and
been accessory to the poetical undoing of many of
the industrious poor. Nathaniel Bloomfield and
his brother Bobby have set all Somersetshire sing-
ing; nor has the malady confined itself to one
county. Pratt too (who once was wiser) has caught
the contagion of patronage, and decoyed a poor
fellow named Blackett into poetry; but he died
during the operation, leaving one child and two
volumes of 'Remains' utterly destitute. The girl,
if she don't take a poetical twist, and come forth
as a shoe-making Sappho, may do well; but the
'tragedies' are as rickety as if they had been the
offspring of an Earl or a Seatonian prize poet. The
patrons of this poor lad are certainly answerable
for his end; and it ought to be an indictable
offence. But this is the least they have done: for,
by a refinement of barbarity, they have made the
(late) man posthumously ridiculous, by printing
what he would have had sense enough never to
print himself. Certes these rakers of 'Remains'
come under the statute against 'resurrection men.'
What does it signify whether a poor dear dead
dunce is to be stuck up in Surgeons' or in Sta-
tioners' Hall? Is it so bad to unearth his bones at
a heath, than his soul in an octavo? 'We know
what we are, but we know not what we may be;'
and it is to be hoped we never shall know, if a man
who has passed through life with a sort of éclat is
to find himself a mountebank on the other side of
Styx, and made, like poor Blackett, the laughing-
stock of purgatory. The plea of publication is to
provide for the child; now, might not some of this
'Sutor ultra Crepidam's' friends and seducers have
done a decent action without inveigling Pratt into
biography? And then his inscription split into so
many modicums!—'To the Duchess of So-much,
the Right Hon. So-and-So, and Mrs. and Miss
Somebody, these volumes are,' &c. &c.—why, this
is doling out the 'soft milk of dedication' in gills,—
there is but a quart, and he divides it among a
dozen. Why, Pratt, hadst thou not a puff left?
Dost thou think six families of distinction can
share this in quiet? There is a child, a book, and
a dedication: send the girl to her grace, the volumes
to the grocer, and the dedication to the devil.

Page 140, col. 2.

'There's plenty of the sort.']—Here will Mr.
Gifford allow me to introduce once more to his
notice the sole survivor, the 'ultimus Romanorum,'
the last of the Cruscanti—'Edwin' the 'profound,'
by our Lady of Punishment! here he is, as lively
as in the days of 'well said Baviad the Correct.'
I thought Fitzgerald had been the tail of poesy;
but, alas! he is only the penultimate.

A FAMILIAR EPISTLE TO THE EDITOR OF THE MORNING CHRONICLE.

'What reams of paper, floods of ink,'
Do some men spoil, who never think!
And so perhaps you 'll say of me,
In which your readers may agree.

Still I write on, and tell you why;
Nothing's so bad, you can't deny,
But may instruct or entertain
Without the risk of giving pain, &c. &c.

ON SOME MODERN QUACKS AND REFORMERS.

In tracing of the human mind
Through all its various courses,
Though strange, 'tis true, we often find
It knows not its resources:

And men through life assume a part
For which no talents they possess,
Yet wonder that, with all their art,
They meet no better with success, &c. &c.

Page 141, col. 1.

'If you will breed this bastard of your brains.']
Minerva being the first by Jupiter's head-piece, and
a variety of equally unaccountable parturitions
upon earth, such as Madoc, &c. &c.

Page 141, col. 1.

'And furnish food for critics, or their quills.
'A crust for the critics.'—*Bayes, in the 'Rehearsal.'*

Page 141, col. 1.

'As yawning waiters fly.'] And the 'waiters'
are the only fortunate people who can 'fly' from
them; all the rest, viz. the sad subscribers to the
'Literary Fund,' being compelled, by courtesy, to
sit out the recitation without a hope of exclaiming,
'Sic' (that is, by choking Fitz. with bad wine, or
worse poetry) 'me servavit Apollo!'

Page 141, col. 2.

'"To die like Cato," leapt into the Thames!'
On his table were found these words: 'What Cato
did, and Addison approved, cannot be wrong.'
But Addison did not 'approve;' and if he had,
it would not have mended the matter. He had
invited his daughter on the same water-party; but
Miss Budgell, by some accident, escaped this last
paternal attention. Thus fell the sycophant of
'Atticus,' and the enemy of Pope.

Page 141, col. 2.

'Dosed with vile drams on Sunday ne was
found.'] If 'dosed with,' &c. be censured as low,
I beg leave to refer to the original for something
still lower; and if any reader will translate 'Minx-
erit in patrios cineres,' &c. into a decent couplet,
I will insert said couplet in lieu of the present.

THE CURSE OF MINERVA

Page 142, col. 1.

'That closed their murder'd sage's latest day!']
Socrates drank the hemlock a short time before
sunset (the hour of execution), notwithstanding the
entreaties of his disciples to wait till the sun went
down.

Page 142, col. 2.

'The queen of night asserts her silent reign.']
The twilight in Greece is much shorter than in our
own country; the days in winter are longer, but in
summer of less duration.

Page 142, col. 2.

'The gleaming turret of the gay kiosk.'] The
kiosk is a Turkish summer-house; the palm is
without the present walls of Athens, not far from
the Temple of Theseus, between which and the tree
the wall intervenes. Cephisus' stream is indeed
scanty, and Ilissus has no stream at all.

Page 143, col. 1.

'*These* Cecrops placed, *this* Pericles adorn'd.']
This is spoken of the city in general, and not of the

Acropolis in particular. The temple of Jupiter Olympius, by some supposed the Pantheon, was finished by Hadrian; sixteen columns are standing, of the most beautiful marble and architecture.

Page 143, col. 2.

'When Venus half avenged Minerva's shame.'] His lordship's name, and that of one who no longer bears it, are carved conspicuously on the Parthenon; above, in a part not far distant, are the torn remnants of the basso-relievos, destroyed in a vain attempt to remove them.

Page 143, col. 2.

'And well I know within that bastard land.'] 'Irish bastards,' according to Sir Callaghan O'Brallaghan.

Page 144, col. 1.

'And own himself an infant of fourscore.'] Mr. West, on seeing the 'Elgin Collection' (I suppose we shall hear of the 'Abershaw' and 'Jack Sheppard' collection) declared himself 'a mere tyro' in art.

Page 144, col. 1.

'And marvel at his lordship's "stone shop" there.'] Poor Cribb was sadly puzzled when the marbles were first exhibited at Elgin House; he asked if it was not 'a stone shop?'—He was right; it *is* a shop.

Page 145, col. 1.

'"Blest paper credit;" who shall dare to sing?']
'Blest paper credit! last and best supply,
That lends Corruption lighter wings to fly.'—
POPE.

Page 145, col. 1.

'And pirates barter all that's left behind.'] The Deal and Dover traffickers in specie.

THE WALTZ

Page 146, col. 1.

'Muse of the many-twinkling feet! whose charms.']
'Glance their many-twinkling feet.'—GRAY.

Page 147, col. 1.

'On Hounslow's heath to rival Wellesley's fame.'] To rival Lord Wellesley's, or his nephew's, as the reader pleases:—the one gained a pretty woman, whom he deserved, by fighting for, and the other has been fighting in the Peninsula many a long day, 'by Shrewsbury clock,' without gaining anything in *that* country but the title of 'the Great Lord,' and 'the Lord;' which savours of profanation, having been hitherto applied only to that Being to whom '*Te Deums*' for carnage are the rankest blasphemy.—It is to be presumed the general will one day return to his Sabine farm: there

'To tame the genius of the stubborn plain,
Almost as quickly as he conquer'd Spain!'

The Lord Peterborough conquered continents in a summer; we do more—we contrive both to conquer and lose them in a shorter season. If the 'Great Lord's' *Cincinnatian* progress in agriculture be no speedier than the proportional average of time in Pope's couplet, it will, according to the farmer's proverb, be 'ploughing with dogs.'

By-the-by—one of this illustrious person's new titles is forgotten—it is, however, worth remembering—'*Salvador del mundo!*' *credite, posteri!* If this be the appellation annexed by the inhabitants of the Peninsula to the name of a *man* who has not yet saved them—query—are they worth saving, even in this world? for, according to the mildest modifications of any Christian creed, those three words make the odds much against them in the next—'Saviour of the world,' quotha!—it were to be wished that he, or any one else, could save a corner of it—his country. Yet this stupid misnomer, although it shows the near connexion between superstition and impiety, so far has its use, that it proves there can be little to dread from those Catholics (inquisitorial Catholics too) who can confer such an appellation on a *Protestant*. I suppose next year he will be entitled the 'Virgin Mary:' if so, Lord George Gordon himself would have nothing to object to such liberal bastards of our Lady of Babylon.

Page 147, col. 2.

'While unburnt Moscow yet had news to send.'] The patriotic arson of our amiable allies cannot be sufficiently commended—nor subscribed for. Amongst other details omitted in the various despatches of our eloquent ambassador, he did not state (being too much occupied with the exploits of Colonel C——, in swimming rivers frozen, and galloping over roads impassable) that one entire province perished by famine in the most melancholy manner, as follows:—In General Rostopchin's consummate conflagration, the consumption of tallow and train oil was so great, that the market was inadequate to the demand: and thus one hundred and thirty-three thousand persons were starved to death, by being reduced to wholesome diet! The lamplighters of London have since subscribed a pint (of oil) a piece, and the tallow-chandlers have unanimously voted a quantity of best moulds (four to the pound), to the relief of the surviving Scythians;—the scarcity will soon, by such exertions, and a proper attention to the *quality* rather than the quantity of provision, be totally alleviated. It is said, in return, that the untouched Ukraine has subscribed sixty thousand beeves for a day's meal to our suffering manufacturers.

Page 148, col. 1.

'Can Egypt's Almas—tantalising group.'] Dancing girls—who do for hire what Waltz doth gratis.

Page 148, col. 2.

'Goats in their visage, women in their shape.'] It cannot be complained now, as in the Lady Baussière's time, of the 'Sieur de la Croix,' that there be 'no whiskers;' but how far these are indications of valour in the field, or elsewhere, may *still* be questionable. Much may be, and hath been, avouched on both sides. In the olden time philosophers had whiskers, and soldiers none—Scipio himself was shaven—Hannibal thought his one eye handsome enough without a beard; but Adrian, the emperor, wore a beard (having warts on his chin, which neither the Empress Sabina nor even the courtiers could abide)—Turenne had whiskers, Marlborough none—Buonaparte is unwhiskered, the Regent whiskered; '*argal*' greatness of mind and whiskers may or may not go together; but certainly the different occurrences, since the growth of the last mentioned, go further in behalf of whiskers than the anathema of Anselm did *against* long hair in the reign of Henry I.—Formerly *red* was a favourite colour. See Lodowick Barrey's comedy of Ram Alley, 1661; Act I, Scene I.

'Taffeta. Now for a wager—What coloured beard comes next by the window?
'Adriana. A black man's, I think.
'Taffeta. I think not so: I think a *red*, for that is most in fashion.'
There is 'nothing new under the sun;' but *red*, then a *favourite*, has now subsided into *favourite's* colour.

Page 148, col. 2.

'The court, the Regent, like herself were new.']
An anachronism—Waltz and the battle of Auster-itz are before said to have opened the ball together; the bard means (if he means anything), Waltz was not so much in vogue till the Regent attained the acmé of his popularity. Waltz, the comet, whiskers, and the new government, illu-minated heaven and earth, in all their glory, much about the same time: of these the comet only has disappeared; the other three continue to astonish us still.—*Printer's Devil.*

Page 148, col. 2.

'New coins (most new) to follow those that fled.'] Amongst others a new ninepence—a credit-able coin now forthcoming, worth a pound, in paper, at the fairest calculation.

Page 149, col. 1.

'Each new, quite new—(except some ancient tricks).']
'Oh that *right* should thus overcome *might!*' Who does not remember the 'delicate investiga-tion' in the 'Merry Wives of Windsor?'—
'Ford. Pray you, come near; if I suspect without cause, why then make sport at me; then let me be your jest; I deserve it. How now? whither bear you this?
'Mrs. Ford. What have you to do whither they bear it?—you were best meddle with buck-washing.'

Page 149, col. 1.

'So saith the muse: my ——, what say you?']
The gentle, or ferocious, reader may fill up the blank as he pleases—there are several dissyllabic names in *his* service (being already in the Re-gent's): it would not be fair to back any peculiar initial against the alphabet, as every month will add to the list now entered for the sweepstakes;—a distinguished consonant is said to be the favour-ite, much against the wishes of the *knowing ones.*

Page 149, col. 1.

'That spot where hearts were once supposed to be.'] 'We have changed all that,' says the Mock Doctor—'tis all gone—Asmodeus knows where. After all, it is of no great importance how women's hearts are disposed of; they have nature's privilege to distribute them as absurdly as possible. But there are also some men with hearts so thoroughly bad, as to remind us of those phenomena often mentioned in natural history; viz. a mass of solid stone—only to be opened by force—and when divided, you discover a toad in the centre, lively, and with the reputation of being venomous.

Page 149, col. 1.

'If "nothing follows all this palming work?"']
In Turkey a pertinent, here an impertinent and superfluous, question—literally put, as in the text, by a Persian to Morier, on seeing a Waltz in Pera. —*Vide* Morier's Travels.

NOTES TO THE BLUES, ETC.

THE BLUES

Page 154, col. 1.

'Ink. I shan't go so far—I can have them at Grange's.'] Grange is or was a famous pastry-cook and fruiterer in Piccadilly.

Page 155, col. 1.

'I feel so elastic—"*so buoyant—so buoyant!*"']
Fact from life, with the *words.*

THE VISION OF JUDGMENT

Page 168, col. 1.

'Reviewing "the ungentle craft," and then.'] See 'Life of Henry Kirke White.'

Page 168, col. 2.

'Like King Alfonso. When I thus see double.'] Alfonso, speaking of the Ptolemean system, said that 'had he been consulted at the creation of the world, he would have spared the Maker some absurdities.'

Page 168, col. 2.

'Like lightning, off from his "melodious twang."'] See Aubrey's account of the apparition which disappeared 'with a curious perfume, and a *most melodious twang;*' or see the *'Antiquary,'* vol. i. p. 225.

Page 169, col. 1.

'For all corrupted things are buoy'd like corks.']
A drowned body lies at the bottom till rotten; it then floats, as most people know.

THE AGE OF BRONZE

Page 172, col. 1.

'Hear! hear Prometheus from his rock appeal.']
I refer the reader to the first address of Prometheus in Æschylus, when he is left alone by his attendants, and before the arrival of the chorus of Sea-nymphs.

Page 173, col. 2.

'The knife of Arragon, Toledo's steel.'] The Arragonians are peculiarly dexterous in the use of this weapon, and displayed it particularly in former French wars.

Page 174, col. 2.

'Many an old woman, but no Catherine.'] The dexterity of Catherine extricated Peter (called the Great by courtesy), when surrounded by the Mus-sulmans on the banks of the river Pruth.

Page 175, col. 2.

'That nose, the hook where he suspends the world!']
'Naso suspendit adunco.'—HORACE.

The Roman applies it to one who merely was imperious to his acquaintance.

Page 178, col. 1.

'There Chateaubriand forms new books of mar-tyrs.'] Monsieur Chateaubriand, who has not forgotten the author in the minister, received a handsome compliment at Verona from a literary sovereign: 'Ah! Monsieur C., are you related to that Chateaubriand who—who—who has written *something?*' (écrit *quelque chose!*) It is said that the author of Atala repented him for a moment of his legitimacy.

NOTES TO CHILDE HAROLD'S PILGRIMAGE

CHILDE HAROLD'S PILGRIMAGE

Page 180, col. 2.

'Yes! sigh'd o'er Delphi's long deserted shrine.'] The little village of Castri stands partly on the site of Delphi. Along the path of the mountain, from Chrysso, are the remains of sepulchres hewn in and from the rock:—'One,' said the guide, 'of a king who broke his neck hunting.' His majesty had certainly chosen the fittest spot for such an achievement. A little above Castri is a cave, supposed the Pythian, of immense depth; the upper part of it is paved, and now a cowhouse. On the other side of Castri stands a Greek monastery; some way above which is the cleft in the rock, with a range of caverns difficult of ascent, and apparently leading to the interior of the mountain; probably to the Corycian Cavern mentioned by Pausanias. From this part descend the fountain and the 'Dews of Castalie.'

Page 184, col. 1.

'And rest ye at "Our Lady's house of woe."'] The convent of 'Our Lady of Punishment,' *Nossa Señora de Pena*, on the summit of the rock. Below, at some distance, is the Cork Convent, where St. Honorius dug his den, over which is his epitaph. From the hills, the sea adds to the beauty of the view.—*Note to 1st Edition*. Since the publication of this poem, I have been informed [by Walter Scott] of the misapprehension of the term *Nossa Señora de Pena*. It was owing to the want of the *tilde* or mark over the *ñ*, which alters the signification of the word: with it, *Peña* signifies a rock; without it, *Pena* has the sense I adopted. I do not think it necessary to alter the passage; as though the common acceptation affixed to it is 'Our Lady of the Rock,' I may well assume the other sense from the severities practised there.—*Note to 2nd Edition*.

Page 184, col. 1.

'Throughout this purple land, where law secures not life.'] It is a well-known fact, that in the year 1809, the assassinations in the streets of Lisbon and its vicinity were not confined by the Portuguese to their countrymen; but that Englishmen were daily butchered: and so far from redress being obtained, we were requested not to interfere if we perceived any compatriot defending himself against his allies. I was once stopped in the way to the theatre at eight o'clock in the evening, when the streets were not more empty than they generally are at that hour, opposite to an open shop, and in a carriage with a friend: had we not fortunately been armed, I have not the least doubt that we should have 'adorned a tale' instead of telling one.

Page 184, col. 2.

'Behold the hall where chiefs were late convened!'] The Convention of Cintra was signed in the palace of the Marchese Marialva.

Page 185, col. 1.

'But here the Babylonian whore hath built.'] The extent of Mafra is prodigious; it contains a palace, convent, and most superb church. The six organs are the most beautiful I ever beheld, in point of decoration: we did not hear them, but were told that their tones were correspondent to their splendour. Mafra is termed the Escurial of Portugal.

Page 186, col. 1.

'"Twixt him and Lusian slave, the lowest of the low.'] As I found the Portuguese, so I have characterized them. That they are since improved, at least in courage, is evident. The late exploits of Lord Wellington have effaced the follies of Cintra. He has, indeed, done wonders: he has, perhaps, changed the character of a nation, reconciled rival superstitions, and baffled an enemy who never retreated before his predecessors.—1812.

Page 186, col. 1.

'That dyed thy mountain streams with Gothic gore?'] Count Julian's daughter, the Helen of Spain. Pelagius preserved his independence in the fastnesses of the Asturias, and the descendants of his followers, after some centuries, completed their struggle by the conquest of Granada.

Page 188, col. 1.

'No! as he speeds, he chants "Vivâ el Rey!"'] 'Vivâ el Rey Fernando!' Long live King Ferdinand! is the chorus of most of the Spanish patriotic songs. They are chiefly in dispraise of the old King Charles, the Queen, and the Prince of Peace. I have heard many of them: some of the airs are beautiful. Godoy, the *Principe de la Paz*, of an ancient but decayed family, was born at Badajoz, on the frontiers of Portugal, and was originally in the ranks of the Spanish guards; till his person attracted the queen's eyes, and raised him to the dukedom of Alcudia, &c. &c. It is to this man that the Spaniards universally impute the ruin of their country.

Page 188, col. 1.

'Which tells you whom to shun and whom to greet.'] The red cockade, with 'Fernando Septimo' in the centre.

Page 188, col. 2.

'The ball-piled pyramid, the ever-blazing match,'] All who have seen a battery will recollect the pyramidal form in which shot and shells are piled. The Sierra Morena was fortified in every defile through which I passed in my way to Seville.

Page 189, col. 1.

'Foil'd by a woman's hand, before a batter'd wall?'] Such were the exploits of the Maid of Saragoza, who by her valour elevated herself to the highest rank of heroines. When the author was at Seville, she walked daily on the Prado, decorated with medals and orders, by command of the Junta.

Page 189, col. 2.

'Denotes how soft that chin which bears his touch.']
'Sigilla in mento impressa Amoris digitulo
Vestigio demonstrant mollitudinem.—
<div align="right">AUL. GEL.</div>

Page 189, col. 2.

'Match me, ye harems of the land! where now.'] This stanza was written in Turkey.

Page 189, col. 2.

'Oh, thou Parnassus! whom I now survey.'] These stanzas were written in Castri (Delphos), at the foot of Parnassus, now called Λιακυρά (Liakura), Dec. 1809.

Page 190, col. 1.

'Her strength, her wealth, her site of ancient days.'] Seville was the Hispalis of the Romans.

Page 191, col. 1.

'Ask ye, Bœotian shades! the reason why?'] This was written at Thebes, and consequently in the best situation for asking and answering such a question;

not as the birthplace of Pindar, but as the capital of Bœotia, where the first riddle was propounded and solved.

Page 192, col. 2.

'Full from the fount of Joy's delicious springs.']
'Medio de fonte leporum
Surgit amari aliquid quod in ipsis floribus angat.'
Luc.

Page 193, col. 2.

'A traitor only fell beneath the feud.'] Alluding to the conduct and death of Solano, the governor of Cadiz, in May, 1809.

Page 193, col. 2.

'War, war is still the cry, "War even to the knife!"'] 'War to the knife.' Palafox's answer to the French general at the siege of Saragoza.

Page 194, col. 2.

'And thou, my friend!—since unavailing woe.']
The Honourable John Wingfield of the Guards, who died of a fever at Coimbra (May 14, 1811). I had known him ten years, the better half of his life, and the happiest part of mine. In the short space of one month I have lost *her* who gave me being, and most of those who had made that being tolerable. To me the lines of Young are no fiction:

'Insatiate archer! could not one suffice?
Thy shaft flew thrice, and thrice my peace was slain,
And thrice ere thrice yon moon had fill'd her horn.'

I should have ventured a verse to the memory of the late Charles Skinner Matthews, Fellow of Downing College, Cambridge, were he not too much above all praise of mine. His powers of mind, shown in the attainment of greater honours, against the ablest candidates, than those of any graduate on record at Cambridge, have sufficiently established his fame on the spot where it was acquired; while his softer qualities live in the recollection of friends who loved him too well to envy his superiority.

Page 195, col. 1.

'And is, despite of war and wasting fire.'] Part of the Acropolis was destroyed by the explosion of a magazine during the Venetian siege.

Page 195, col. 1.

'That thoughts of thee and thine on polish'd breasts bestow.'] We can all feel, or imagine, the regret with which the ruins of cities, once the capitals of empires, are beheld: the reflections suggested by such objects are too trite to require recapitulation. But never did the littleness of man, and the vanity of his very best virtues, of patriotism to exalt, and of valour to defend, his country, appear more conspicuous than in the record of what Athens was, and the certainty of what she now is. This theatre of contention between mighty factions, of the struggles of orators, the exaltation and deposition of tyrants, the triumph and punishment of generals, is now become a scene of petty intrigue and perpetual disturbance, between the bickering agents of certain British nobility and gentry. 'The wild foxes, the owls and serpents in the ruins of Babylon,' were surely less degrading than such inhabitants. The Turks have the plea of conquest for their tyranny, and the Greeks have only suffered the fortune of war, incidental to the bravest; but how are the mighty fallen, when two painters contest the privilege of plundering the Parthenon, and triumph in turn, according to the tenor of each succeeding firman! Sylla could but punish, Philip subdue, and Xerxes burn Athens; but it remained for the paltry antiquarian, and his despicable agents, to render her contemptible as himself and his pursuits. The Parthenon, before its destruction, in part, by fire during the Venetian siege, had been a temple, a church, and a mosque. In each point of view it is an object of regard: it changed its worshippers; but still it was a place of worship thrice sacred to devotion: its violation is a triple sacrifice. But—

'Man, proud man,
Drest in a little brief authority,
Plays such fantastic tricks before high Heaven
As make the angels weep.'

Page 195, col. 2.

'Far on the solitary shore he sleeps.'] It was not always the custom of the Greeks to burn their dead; the greater Ajax, in particular, was interred entire. Almost all the chiefs became gods after their decease; and he was indeed neglected, who had not annual games near his tomb, or festivals in honour of his memory by his countrymen, as Achilles, Brasidas, &c., and at last even Antinous, whose death was as heroic as his life was infamous.

Page 196, col. 1.

'Here, son of Saturn! was thy fav'rite throne.']
The temple of Jupiter Olympius, of which sixteen columns, entirely of marble, yet survive; originally there were one hundred and fifty. These columns, however, are by many supposed to have belonged to the Pantheon.

Page 196, col. 2.

'And bear these altars o'er the long-reluctant brine.'] The ship was wrecked in the Archipelago.

Page 196, col. 2.

'To rive what Goth, and Turk, and Time hath spared.'] At this moment (January 3, 1810), besides what has been already deposited in London, an Hydriot vessel is in the Pyræus to receive every portable relic. Thus, as I heard a young Greek observe, in common with many of his countrymen —for, lost as they are, they yet feel on this occasion—thus may Lord Elgin boast of having ruined Athens. An Italian painter of the first eminence, named Lusieri, is the agent of devastation; and like the Greek *finder* of Verres in Sicily, who followed the same profession, he has proved the able instrument of plunder. Between this artist and the French Consul Fauvel, who wishes to rescue the remains for his own government, there is now a violent dispute concerning a car employed in their conveyance, the wheel of which—I wish they were both broken upon it!—has been locked up by the Consul, and Lusieri has laid his complaint before the Waywode. Lord Elgin has been extremely happy in his choice of Signor Lusieri. During a residence of ten years in Athens, he never had the curiosity to proceed as far as Sunium (now Cape Colonna), till he accompanied us in our second excursion. However, his works, as far as they go, are most beautiful; but they are almost all unfinished. While he and his patrons confine themselves to tasting medals, appreciating cameos, sketching columns, and cheapening gems, their little absurdities are as harmless as insect or fox-hunting, maiden speechifying, barouche-driving,

or any such pastime; but when they carry away three or four shiploads of the most valuable and massy relics that time and barbarism have left to the most injured and most celebrated of cities: when they destroy, in a vain attempt to tear down, those works which have been the admiration of ages, I know no motive which can excuse, no name which can designate, the perpetrators of this dastardly devastation. It was not the least of the crimes laid to the charge of Verres, that he had plundered Sicily, in the manner since imitated at Athens. The most unblushing impudence could hardly go further than to affix the name of its plunderer to the walls of the Acropolis; while the wanton and useless defacement of the whole range of the basso-relievos, in one compartment of the temple, will never permit that name to be pronounced by an observer without execration.

On this occasion I speak impartially: I am not a collector or admirer of collections, consequently no rival; but I have some early prepossession in favour of Greece, and do not think the honour of England advanced by plunder, whether of India or Attica.

Another noble Lord has done better, because he has done less: but some others, more or less noble, yet 'all honourable men,' have done *best*, because, after a deal of excavation and execration, bribery to the Waywode, mining and countermining, they have done nothing at all. We had such ink-shed, and wine-shed, which almost ended in bloodshed! Lord E.'s 'prig'—see Jonathan Wild for the definition of 'priggism'—quarrelled with another *Gropius*[*] by name (a very good name too for his business), and muttered something about satisfaction, in a verbal answer to a note of the poor Prussian: this was stated at table to Gropius, who laughed, but could eat no dinner afterwards. The rivals were not reconciled when I left Greece. I have reason to remember their squabble, for they wanted to make me their arbitrator.

Page 196, col. 2.

'Yet felt some portion of their mother's pains.']
I cannot resist availing myself of the permission of my friend Dr. Clarke, whose name requires no comment with the public, but whose sanction will add tenfold weight to my testimony, to insert the following extract from a very obliging letter of his to me, as a note to the above lines:—'When the last of the Metopes was taken from the Parthenon, and, in moving of it, great part of the superstructure with one of the triglyphs was thrown down by the workmen whom Lord Elgin employed, the Disdar, who beheld the mischief done to the building, took his pipe from his mouth, dropped a tear, and, in a

[*] This Sr. Gropius was employed by a noble Lord for the sole purpose of sketching, in which he excels; but I am sorry to say, that he has, through the abused sanction of that most respectable name, been treading at humble distance in the steps of Sr. Lusieri.—A shipful of his trophies was detained, and I believe confiscated, at Constantinople, in 1810. I am most happy to be now enabled to state, that 'this was not in his bond;' that he was employed solelyas a painter,and that his noble patron disavows all connexion with him, except as an artist. If the error in the first and second edition of this poem has given the noble Lord a moment's pain, I am very sorry for it: Sr. Gropius has assumed for years the name of his agent; and though I cannot much condemn myself for sharing in the mistake of so many, I am happy in being one of the first to be undeceived. Indeed, I have as much pleasure in contradicting this as I felt regret in stating it.—*Note to third edition.*

supplicating tone of voice, said to Lusieri, Τελος!—I was present.' The Disdar alluded to was the father of the present Disdar.

Page 196, col. 2.

'Stern Alaric and Havoc on their way?'] According to Zosimus, Minerva and Achilles frightened Alaric from the Acropolis; but others relate that the Gothic king was nearly as mischievous as the Scottish peer.—See Chandler.

Page 197, col. 1.

'The well-reeved guns, the netted canopy.'] To prevent blocks or splinters from falling on deck during action.

Page 199, col. 1.

'But not in silence pass Calypso's isles.'] Goza is said to have been the island of Calypso.

Page 200, col. 1.

'Land of Albania! let me bend mine eyes.'] Albania comprises part of Macedonia, Illyria, Chaonia, and Epirus. Iskander is the Turkish word for Alexander; and the celebrated Scander-beg (Lord Alexander) is alluded to in the third and fourth lines of the thirty-eighth stanza. I do not know whether I am correct in making Scanderbeg the countryman of Alexander, who was born at Pella in Macedon, but Mr. Gibbon terms him so, and adds Pyrrhus to the list, in speaking of his exploits.

Of Albania Gibbon remarks that a country 'within sight of Italy is less known than the interior of America.' Circumstances, of little consequence to mention, led Mr. Hobhouse and myself into that country before we visited any other part of the Ottoman dominions; and with the exception of Major Leake, then officially resident at Joannina, no other Englishmen have ever advanced beyond the capital into the interior, as that gentleman very lately assured me. Ali Pacha was at that time (October, 1809) carrying on war against Ibrahim Pacha, whom he had driven to Berat, a strong fortress, which he was then besieging: on our arrival at Joannina we were invited to Tepaleni, his highness's birthplace, and favourite Serai, only one day's distance from Berat; at this juncture the Vizier had made it his head-quarters. After some stay in the capital, we accordingly followed; but though furnished with every accommodation, and escorted by one of the Vizier's secretaries, we were nine days (on account of the rains) in accomplishing a journey which, on our return, barely occupied four. On our route we passed two cities, Argyrocastro and Libochabo, apparently little inferior to Yanina in size; and no pencil or pen can ever do justice to the scenery in the vicinity of Zitza and Delvinachi, the frontier village of Epirus and Albania Proper.

On Albania and its inhabitants I am unwilling to descant, because this will be done so much better by my fellow-traveller, in a work which may probably precede this in publication, that I as little wish to follow as I would to anticipate him. But some few observations are necessary to the text. The Arnaouts, or Albanese, struck me forcibly by their resemblance to the Highlanders of Scotland, in dress, figure, and manner of living. Their very mountains seemed Caledonian, with a kinder climate. The kilt, though white; the spare, active form; their dialect, Celtic in its sound, and their hardy habits, all carried me back to Morven. No nation are so detested and dreaded by their neigh-

bours as the Albanese; the Greeks hardly regard them as Christians, or the Turks as Moslems; and in fact they are a mixture of both, and sometimes neither. Their habits are predatory—all are armed; and the red-shawled Arnaouts, the Montenegrins, Chimariots, and Gegdes, are treacherous; the others differ somewhat in garb, and essentially in character. As far as my own experience goes, I can speak favourably. I was attended by two, an Infidel and a Mussulman, to Constantinople and every other part of Turkey which came within my observation; and more faithful in peril, or indefatigable in service, are rarely to be found. The Infidel was named Basilius, the Moslem, Dervish Tahiri; the former a man of middle age, and the latter about my own. Basili was strictly charged by Ali Pacha in person to attend us; and Dervish was one of fifty who accompanied us through the forests of Acarnania to the banks of Achelous, and onward to Messalonghi in Ætolia. There I took him into my own service, and never had occasion to repent it till the moment of my departure.

When, in 1810, after the departure of my friend Mr. Hobhouse for England, I was seized with a severe fever in the Morea, these men saved my life by frightening away my physician, whose throat they threatened to cut if I was not cured within a given time. To this consolatory assurance of posthumous retribution, and a resolute refusal of Dr. Romanelli's prescriptions, I attributed my recovery. I had left my last remaining English servant at Athens; my dragoman was as ill as myself, and my poor Arnaouts nursed me with an attention which would have done honour to civilisation. They had a variety of adventures; for the Moslem, Dervish, being a remarkably handsome man, was always squabbling with the husbands of Athens; insomuch that four of the principal Turks paid me a visit of remonstrance at the Convent, on the subject of his having taken a woman from the bath—whom he had lawfully bought, however—a thing quite contrary to etiquette. Basili also was extremely gallant amongst his own persuasion, and had the greatest veneration for the church, mixed with the highest contempt of churchmen, whom he cuffed upon occasion in a most heterodox manner. Yet he never passed a church without crossing himself; and I remember the risk he ran in entering St. Sophia, in Stambol, because it had once been a place of his worship. On remonstrating with him on his inconsistent proceedings, he invariably answered, 'Our church is holy, our priests are thieves:' and then he crossed himself as usual, and boxed the ears of the first 'papas' who refused to assist in any required operation, as was always found to be necessary where a priest had any influence with the Cogia Bashi of his village. Indeed, a more abandoned race of miscreants cannot exist than the lower orders of the Greek clergy.

When preparations were made for my return, my Albanians were summoned to receive their pay. Basili took his with an awkward show of regret at my intended departure, and marched away to his quarters with his bag of piastres. I sent for Dervish, but for some time he was not to be found; at last he entered, just as Signor Logotheti, father to the ci-devant Anglo-consul of Athens, and some other of my Greek acquaintances, paid me a visit. Dervish took the money, but on a sudden dashed it to the ground; and clasping his hands, which he raised to his forehead, rushed out of the room weeping bitterly. From that moment to the hour of my embarkation, he continued his lamentations, and all our efforts to console him only produced

this answer, '*M'ἀφεινει*,' 'He leaves me.' Signor Logotheti, who never wept before for anything less than the loss of a para (about the fourth of a farthing), melted; the padre of the convent, my attendants, my visitors—and I verily believe that even Sterne's 'foolish fat scullion' would have left her 'fishkettle' to sympathise with the unaffected and unexpected sorrow of this barbarian.

For my own part, when I remembered that, a short time before my departure from England, a noble and most intimate associate had excused himself from taking leave of me because he had to attend a relation 'to a milliner's,' I felt no less surprised than humiliated by the present occurrence and the past recollection. That Dervish would leave me with some regret was to be expected; when master and man have been scrambling over the mountains of a dozen provinces together, they are unwilling to separate; but his present feelings, contrasted with his native ferocity, improved my opinion of the human heart. I believe this almost feudal fidelity is frequent amongst them. One day, on our journey over Parnassus, an Englishman in my service gave him a push in some dispute about the baggage, which he unluckily mistook for a blow; he spoke not, but sat down leaning his head upon his hands. Foreseeing the consequences, we endeavoured to explain away the affront, which produced the following answer:—'I *have been* a robber: I *am* a soldier: no captain ever struck me: *you* are my master, I have eaten your bread, but by *that* bread! (a usual oath,) had it been otherwise, I would have stabbed the dog, your servant, and gone to the mountains.' So the affair ended, but from that day forward he never thoroughly forgave the thoughtless fellow who insulted him. Dervish excelled in the dance of his country, conjectured to be a remnant of the ancient Pyrrhic: be that as it may, it is manly, and requires wonderful agility. It is very distinct from the stupid Romaika, the dull round-about of the Greeks, of which our Athenian party had so many specimens.

The Albanians in general (I do not mean the cultivators of the earth in the provinces, who have also that appellation, but the mountaineers) have a fine cast of countenance; and the most beautiful women I ever beheld, in stature and in features, we saw *levelling* the *road* broken down by the torrents between Delvinachi and Libochabo. Their manner of walking is truly theatrical; but this strut is probably the effect of the capote, or cloak, depending from one shoulder. Their long hair reminds you of the Spartans, and their courage in desultory warfare is unquestionable. Though they have some cavalry amongst the Gegdes, I never saw a good Arnaout horseman; my own preferred the English saddles, which, however, they could never keep. But on foot they are not to be subdued by fatigue.

Page 200, col. 1.

'Where sad Penelope o'erlook'd the wave.']
Ithaca.

Page 200, col. 1.

'Childe Harold hail'd Leucadia's cape afar.']
Leucadia, now Santa Maura. From the promontory (the Lover's Leap) Sappho is said to have thrown herself.

Page 200, col. 1.

'Actium, Lepanto, fatal Trafalgar.'] Actium and Trafalgar need no further mention. The battle of Lepanto, equally bloody and considerable, but less known, was fought in the Gulf of Patras. Here the author of Don Quixote lost his left hand.

NOTES TO CHILDE HAROLD'S PILGRIMAGE

Page 201, col. 1.

'Did many a Roman chief and Asian king.'] It is said, that, on the day previous to the battle of Actium, Antony had thirteen kings at his levee.

Page 201, col. 1.

'Look where the second Cæsar's trophies rose.'] Nicopolis, whose ruins are most extensive, is at some distance from Actium, where the wall of the Hippodrome survives in a few fragments. These ruins are large masses of brickwork, the bricks of which are joined by interstices of mortar, as large as the bricks themselves, and equally durable.

Page 201, col. 2.

'He pass'd bleak Pindus, Acherusia's lake.'] According to Pouqueville, the lake of Yanina: but Pouqueville is always out.

Page 201, col. 2.

'To greet Albania's chief, whose dread command.'] The celebrated Ali Pacha. Of this extraordinary man there is an incorrect account in Pouqueville's Travels.

Page 201, col. 2.

'Hurl their defiance far, nor yield, unless in gold.'] Five thousand Suliotes, among the rocks and in the castle of Suli, withstood thirty thousand Albanians for eighteen years; the castle at last was taken by bribery. In this contest there were several acts performed not unworthy of the better days of Greece.

Page 201, col. 2.

'Monastic Zitza! from thy shady brow.'] The convent and village of Zitza are four hours journey from Joannina, or Yanina, the capital of the Pachalick. In the valley the river Kalamas (once the Acheron) flows, and, not far from Zitza, forms a fine cataract. The situation is perhaps the finest in Greece, though the approach to Delvinachi and parts of Acarnania and Ætolia may contest the palm. Delphi, Parnassus, and, in Attica, even Cape Colonna and Port Raphti, are very inferior: as also every scene in Ionia, or the Troad: I am almost inclined to add the approach to Constantinople; but, from the different features of the last, a comparison can hardly be made.

Page 201, col. 2.

'Here dwells the caloyer, nor rude is he.'] The Greek monks are so called.

Page 202, col. 1.

'Nature's volcanic amphitheatre.'] The Chimariot mountains appear to have been volcanic.

Page 202, col. 1.

'Nodding above; behold black Acheron!'] Now called Kalamas.

Page 202, col. 1.

'The little shepherd in his white capote.'] Albanese cloak.

Page 202, col. 2.

'The sun had sunk behind vast Tomerit.'] Anciently Mount Tomarus.

Page 202, col. 2.

'And Laos wide and fierce came roaring by.'] The river Laos was full at the time the author passed it; and, immediately above Tepaleen, was to the eye as wide as the Thames at Westminster;

at least in the opinion of the author and his fellow-traveller. In the summer it must be much narrower. It certainly is the finest river in the Levant; neither Achelous, Alpheus, Acheron, Scamander, nor Cayster, approached it in breadth or beauty.

Page 204, col. 1.

'And fellow-countrymen have stood aloof—'] Alluding to the wreckers of Cornwall.

Page 204, col. 2.

'The feast was done, the red wine circling fast.' The Albanian Mussulmans do not abstain from wine, and, indeed, very few of the others.

Page 204, col. 2.

'Each Palikar his sabre from him cast.'] Palikar, shortened when addressed to a single person, from Παλικάρι, a general name for a soldier amongst the Greeks and Albanese, who speak Romaic: it means, properly, 'a lad.'

Page 205, col. 1.

'While thus in concert they this lay half sang, half scream'd.'] As a specimen of the Albanian or Arnaout dialect of the Illyric, I here insert two of their most popular choral songs, which are generally chanted in dancing by men or women indiscriminately. The first words are merely a kind of chorus without meaning, like some in our own and all other languages.

1. Bo, Bo, Bo, Bo, Bo, Bo,
 Naciarura, popuso.
2. Naciarura na civin
 Ha pen derini ti hin.
3. Ha pe uderi escrotini
 Ti vin ti mar servetini.
4. Caliriote me surme
 Ea ha pe pse dua tive.
5. Buo, Bo, Bo, Bo, Bo,
 Gi egem spirta esimiro
6. Caliriote vu le funde
 Ede vete tunde tunde.
7. Caliriote me surme
 Ti mi put e poi mi le.
8. Se ti puta citi mora
 Si mi ri ni veti udo gia.
9. Va le ni il che cadale
 Celo more, more celo.
10. Plu hari ti tirete
 Plu huron cia pra seti.

1. Lo, Lo, I come, I come; be thou silent.

2. I come, I run; open the door that I may enter.

3. Open the door by halves, that I may take my turban.

4. Caliriotes* with the dark eyes, open the gate that I may enter.

5. Lo, Lo, I hear thee, my soul.

6. An Arnaout girl, in costly garb, walks with graceful pride.

7. Caliriot maid of the dark eyes, give me a kiss.

8. If I have kissed thee, what hast thou gained? My soul is consumed with fire.

9. Dance lightly, more gently, and gently still.

10. Make not so much dust to destroy your embroidered hose.

* The Albanese, particularly the women, are frequently termed 'Caliriotes,' for what reason I inquired in vain.

NOTES TO CHILDE HAROLD'S PILGRIMAGE

The last stanza would puzzle a commentator; the men have certainly buskins of the most beautiful texture, but the ladies (to whom the above is supposed to be addressed) have nothing under their little yellow boots and slippers but a well-turned and sometimes very white ankle. The Arnaout girls are much handsomer than the Greeks, and their dress is far more picturesque. They preserve

1. Ndi sefda tinde ulavossa
 Vettimi upri vi lofsa.
2. Ah vaisisso mi privi lofse
 Si mi rini mi la vosse.
3. Uti tasa roba stua
 Sitti eve tulati dua.
4. Roba stinori ssidua
 Qu mi sini vetti dua.
5. Qurmini dua civileni
 Roba ti siarmi tildi eni.
6. Utara pisa vaisisso me simi rin ti hapti
 Eti mi bire a piste si gui dendroi tiltati.
7. Udi vura udorini udiri cicova cilti mora
 Udorini talti hollna u ede caimoni mora.

I believe the two last stanzas, as they are in a different measure, ought to belong to another ballad. An idea something similar to the thought in the last lines was expressed by Socrates, whose arm having come in contact with one of his 'ὑποκόλπιοι,' Critobulus or Cleobulus, the philosopher complained of a shooting pain as far as his shoulder for some days after, and therefore very properly resolved to teach his disciples in future without touching them.

Page 205, col. 1.

'TAMBOURGI! Tambourgi! thy 'larum afar.'] Drummer.

Page 205, col. 1.

'Chimariot, Illyrian, and dark Suliote!'] These stanzas are partly taken from different Albanese songs, as far as I was able to make them out by the xposition of the Albanese in Romaic and Italian.

Page 205, col. 2.

'Remember the moment when Previsa fell.'] It was taken by storm from the French.

Page 205, col. 2.

'Let the yellow-hair'd.'] Yellow is the epithet given to the Russians.

Page 205, col. 2.

'Giaours.'] Infidels.

Page 205, col. 2.

'View his horsetail with dread.'] The insignia of a Pacha.

Page 205, col. 2.

'When his Delhis come dashing in blood o'er the banks.'] Horsemen, answering to our forlorn hope.

Page 205, col. 2.

'Selictar! unsheathe then our chief's scimitar.'] Sword-bearer.

Page 205, col. 2.

I.

'Fair Greece! sad relic of departed worth!'] Before I say anything about a city of which everybody, traveller or not, has thought it necessary to say something, I will request Miss Owenson, when she next borrows an Athenian heroine for her four volumes, to have the goodness to marry her to

their shape much longer also, from being always in the open air. It is to be observed, that the Arnaout is not a *written* language: the words of this song, therefore, as well as the one which follows, are spelt according to their pronunciation. They are copied by one who speaks and understands the dialect perfectly, and who is a native of Athens.

1. I am wounded by thy love, and have loved but to scorch myself.
2. Thou hast consumed me! Ah, maid! thou hast struck me to the heart.
3. I have said I wish no dowry, but thine eyes and eyelashes.
4. The accursed dowry I want not, but thee only.
5. Give me thy charms, and let the portion feed the flames.
6. I have loved thee, maid, with a sincere soul, but thou hast left me like a withered tree.
7. If I have placed my hand on thy bosom, what have I gained? my hand is withdrawn, but retains the flame.

somebody more of a gentleman than a 'Disdar Aga' (who by the by is not an Aga), the most impolite of petty officers, the greatest patron of larceny Athens ever saw (except Lord E.), and the unworthy occupant of the Acropolis, on a handsome annual stipend of 150 piastres (eight pounds sterling), out of which he has only to pay his garrison, the most ill-regulated corps in the ill-regulated Ottoman Empire. I speak it tenderly, seeing I was once the cause of the husband of 'Ida of Athens' nearly suffering the bastinado; and because the said 'Disdar' is a turbulent husband, and beats his wife; so that I exhort and beseech Miss Owenson to sue for a separate maintenance in behalf of 'Ida.' Having premised thus much, on a matter of such import to the readers of romances, I may now leave Ida, to mention her birthplace.

Setting aside the magic of the name, and all those associations which it would be pedantic and superfluous to recapitulate, the very situation of Athens would render it the favourite of all who have eyes for art or nature. The climate, to me at least, appeared a perpetual spring; during eight months I never passed a day without being as many hours on horseback: rain is extremely rare, snow never lies in the plains, and a cloudy day is an agreeable rarity. In Spain, Portugal, and every part of the East which I visited, except Ionia and Attica, I perceived no such superiority of climate to our own; and at Constantinople, where I passed May, June, and part of July (1810), you might 'damn the climate, and complain of spleen,' five days out of seven.

The air of the Morea is heavy and unwholesome, but the moment you pass the isthmus in the direction of Megara the change is strikingly perceptible. But I fear Hesiod will still be found correct in his description of a Bœotian winter.

We found at Livadia an 'esprit fort' in a Greek bishop, of all free-thinkers! This worthy hypocrite rallied his own religion with great intrepidity (but not before his flock), and talked of a mass as a 'coglioneria.' It was impossible to think better of him for this; but, for a Bœotian, he was brisk with all his absurdity. This phenomenon (with the exception indeed of Thebes, the remains of Chæronea, the plain of Platea, Orchomenus, Livadia, and its nominal cave of Trophonius) was the only remarkable thing we saw before we passed Mount Cithæron.

NOTES TO CHILDE HAROLD'S PILGRIMAGE

The fountain of Dirce turns a mill: at least my companion (who, resolving to be at once cleanly and classical, bathed in it) pronounced it to be the fountain of Dirce, and anybody who thinks it worth while may contradict him. At Castri we drank of half a dozen streamlets, some not of the purest, before we decided to our satisfaction which was the true Castalian, and even that had a villainous twang, probably from the snow, though it did not throw us into an epic fever, like poor Dr. Chandler.

From Fort Phyle, of which large remains still exist, the Plain of Athens, Pentelicus, Hymettus, the Ægean, and the Acropolis, burst upon the eye at once; in my opinion, a more glorious prospect than even Cintra or Istambol. Not the view from the Troad, with Ida, the Hellespont, and the more distant Mount Athos, can equal it, though so superior in extent.

I heard much of the beauty of Arcadia, but excepting the view from the Monastery of Megaspelion (which is inferior to Zitza in a command of country), and the descent from the mountains on the way from Tripolitza to Argos, Arcadia has little to recommend it beyond the name.

'Sternitur, et *dulces* moriens reminiscitur Argos.' Virgil could have put this into the mouth of none but an Argive, and (with reverence be it spoken) it does not deserve the epithet. And if the Polynices of Statius, 'In mediis audit duo litora campis,' did actually hear both shores in crossing the isthmus of Corinth, he had better ears than have ever been worn in such a journey since.

'Athens,' says a celebrated topographer, 'is still the most polished city of Greece.' Perhaps it may of *Greece*, but not of the *Greeks*; for Joannina in Epirus is universally allowed, amongst themselves, to be superior in the wealth, refinement, learning, and dialect of its inhabitants. The Athenians are remarkable for their cunning; and the lower orders are not improperly characterised in that proverb, which classes them with the 'Jews of Salonica, and the Turks of the Negropont.'

Among the various foreigners resident in Athens, French, Italians, Germans, Ragusans, &c., there was never a difference of opinion in their estimate of the Greek character, though on all other topics they disputed with great acrimony.

M. Fauvel, the French consul, who has passed thirty years principally at Athens, and to whose talents as an artist, and manners as a gentleman, none who have known him can refuse their testimony, has frequently declared in my hearing, that the Greeks do not deserve to be emancipated; reasoning on the grounds of their 'national and individual depravity!' while he forgot that such depravity is to be attributed to causes which can only be removed by the measure he reprobates.

M. Roque, a French merchant of respectability long settled in Athens, asserted with the most amusing gravity, 'Sir, they are the same *canaille* that existed *in the days of Themistocles!*' an alarming remark to the 'Laudator temporis acti.' The ancients banished Themistocles; the moderns cheat Monsieur Roque; thus great men have ever been treated!

In short, all the Franks who are fixtures, and most of the Englishmen, Germans, Danes, &c. of passage, came over by degrees to their opinion, on much the same grounds that a Turk in England would condemn the nation by wholesale, because he was wronged by his lacquey, and overcharged by his washerwoman.

Certainly it was not a little staggering when the Sieurs Fauvel and Lusieri, the two greatest demagogues of the day, who divide between them the power of Pericles and the popularity of Cleon, and puzzle the poor Waywode with perpetual differences, agreed in the utter condemnation, 'nulla virtute redemptum,' of the Greeks in general, and of the Athenians in particular.

For my own humble opinion, I am loth to hazard it, knowing as I do, that there be now in MS. no less than five tours of the first magnitude and of the most threatening aspect, all in typographical array, by persons of wit and honour, and regular commonplace books: but, if I may say this without offence, it seems to me rather hard to declare so positively and pertinaciously, as almost everybody has declared, that the Greeks, because they are very bad, will never be better.

Eton and Sonnini have led us astray by their panegyrics and projects: but, on the other hand De Pauw and Thornton have debased the Greeks beyond their demerits.

The Greeks will never be independent: they will never be sovereigns as heretofore, and God forbid they ever should! but they may be subjects without being slaves. Our colonies are not independent but they are free and industrious, and such may Greece be hereafter.

At present, like the Catholics of Ireland and the Jews throughout the world, and such other cudgelled and heterodox people, they suffer all the moral and physical ills that can afflict humanity. Their life is a struggle against truth; they are vicious in their own defence. They are so unused to kindness, that when they occasionally meet with it they look upon it with suspicion, as a dog often beaten snaps at your fingers if you attempt to caress him. 'They are ungrateful, notoriously, abominably ungrateful!'—this is the general cry. Now, in the name of Nemesis! for what are they to be grateful? Where is the human being that ever conferred a benefit on Greek or Greeks? They are to be grateful to the Turks for their fetters, and to the Franks for their broken promises and lying counsels. They are to be grateful to the artist who engraves their ruins and to the antiquary who carries them away; to the traveller whose janissary flogs them, and to the scribbler whose journal abuses them. This is the amount of their obligations to foreigners.

II.

FRANCISCAN CONVENT, ATHENS, *January* 23, 1811

Amongst the remnants of the barbarous policy of the earlier ages, are the traces of bondage which yet exist in different countries; whose inhabitants however divided in religion and manners, almost all agree in oppression.

The English have at last compassionated the negroes, and under a less bigoted government, may probably one day release their Catholic brethren but the interposition of foreigners alone can emancipate the Greeks, who, otherwise, appear to have as small a chance of redemption from the Turks, as the Jews have from mankind in general.

Of the ancient Greeks we know more than enough; at least the younger men of Europe devote much of their time to the study of the Greek writers and history, which would be more usefully spent in mastering their own. Of the moderns, we are perhaps more neglectful than they deserve; and while every man of any pretensions to learning is tiring out his youth, and often his age, in the study of the language and of the harangues of the Athenian demagogues in favour of freedom, the real o

supposed descendants of these sturdy republicans are left to the actual tyranny of their masters, although a very slight effort is required to strike off their chains.

To talk, as the Greeks themselves do, of their rising again to their pristine superiority, would be ridiculous: as the rest of the world must resume its barbarism, after re-asserting the sovereignty of Greece; but there seems to be no very great obstacle, except in the apathy of the Franks, to their becoming an useful dependency, or even a free state, with a proper guarantee;—under correction, however, be it spoken, for many and well-informed men doubt the practicability even of this.

The Greeks have never lost their hope, though they are now more divided in opinion on the subject of their probable deliverers. Religion recommends the Russians; but they have twice been deceived and abandoned by that power, and the dreadful lesson they received after the Muscovite desertion in the Morea has never been forgotten. The French they dislike; although the subjugation of the rest of Europe will, probably, be attended by the deliverance of continental Greece. The islanders look to the English for succour, as they have very lately possessed themselves of the Ionian republic, Corfu excepted. But whoever appear with arms in their hands will be welcome; and when that day arrives, Heaven have mercy on the Ottomans; they cannot expect it from the Giaours.

But instead of considering what they have been, and speculating on what they may be, let us look at them as they are.

And here it is impossible to reconcile the contrariety of opinions: some, particularly the merchants, decrying the Greeks in the strongest language; others, generally travellers, turning periods in their eulogy, and publishing very curious speculations grafted on their former state, which can have no more effect on their present lot, than the existence of the Incas on the future fortunes of Peru.

One very ingenious person terms them the 'natural allies of Englishmen;' another, no less ingenious, will not allow them to be the allies of anybody, and denies their very descent from the ancients; a third, more ingenious than either, builds a Greek empire on a Russian foundation, and realises (on paper) all the chimeras of Catherine II. As to the question of their descent, what can it import whether the Mainotes are the lineal Laconians or not? or the present Athenians indigenous as the bees of Hymettus, or as the grasshoppers, to which they once likened themselves? What Englishman cares if he be of a Danish, Saxon, Norman, or Trojan blood? or who, except a Welshman, is afflicted with a desire of being descended from Caractacus?

The poor Greeks do not so much abound in the good things of this world, as to render even their claims to antiquity an object of envy; it is very cruel, then, in Mr. Thornton to disturb them in the possession of all that time has left them; viz. their pedigree, of which they are the more tenacious, as it is all they can call their own. It would be worth while to publish together, and compare, the works of Messrs. Thornton and De Pauw, Eton and Sonnini; paradox on one side, and prejudice on the other. Mr. Thornton conceives himself to have claims to public confidence from a fourteen years' residence at Pera; perhaps he may on the subject of the Turks, but this can give him no more insight into the real state of Greece and her inhabitants, than as many years spent in Wapping into that of the Western Highlands.

The Greeks of Constantinople live in Fanal; and if Mr. Thornton did not oftener cross the Golden Horn than his brother merchants are accustomed to do, I should place no great reliance on his information. I actually heard one of these gentlemen boast of their little general intercourse with the city, and assert of himself, with an air of triumph, that he had been but four times at Constantinople in as many years.

As to Mr. Thornton's voyages in the Black Sea with Greek vessels, they gave him the same idea of Greece as a cruise to Berwick in a Scotch smack would of Johnny Groat's house. Upon what grounds then does he arrogate the right of condemning by wholesale a body of men, of whom he can know little? It is rather a curious circumstance that Mr. Thornton, who so lavishly dispraises Pouqueville on every occasion of mentioning the Turks, has yet recourse to him as authority on the Greeks, and terms him an impartial observer. Now, Dr. Pouqueville is as little entitled to that appellation as Mr. Thornton to confer it on him.

The fact is, we are deplorably in want of information on the subject of the Greeks, and in particular their literature, nor is there any probability of our being better acquainted, till our intercourse becomes more intimate, or their independence confirmed. The relations of passing travellers are as little to be depended on as the invectives of angry factors; but till something more can be attained, we must be content with the little to be acquired from similar sources.*

However defective these may be, they are preferable to the paradoxes of men who have read superficially of the ancients, and seen nothing of the moderns, such as De Pauw; who, when he asserts that the British breed of horses is ruined by Newmarket, and that the Spartans were cowards in the field, betrays an equal knowledge of English horses and Spartan men. His 'philosophical observations' have a much better claim to the title of 'poetical.' It could not be expected that he who so liberally

* A word *en passant* with Mr. Thornton and Dr. Pouqueville, who have been guilty between them of sadly clipping the Sultan's Turkish.

Dr. Pouqueville tells a long story of a Moslem who swallowed corrosive sublimate in such quantities that he acquired the name of 'Suleyman Yeyen,' i.e. quoth the Doctor, '*Suleyman, the eater of corrosive sublimate.*' 'Aha,' thinks Mr. Thornton, (angry with the Doctor for the fiftieth time,) have I caught you?'— Then, in a note twice the thickness of the Doctor's anecdote, he questions the Doctor's proficiency in the Turkish tongue, and his veracity in his own.— 'For,' observes Mr. Thornton (after inflicting on us the tough participle of a Turkish verb), 'it means nothing more than "*Suleyman the eater,*" ' and quite cashiers the supplementary '*sublimate.*' Now both are right, and both are wrong. If Mr. Thornton, when he next resides 'fourteen years in the factory,' will consult his Turkish dictionary, or ask any of his Stamboline acquaintance, he will discover that '*Suleyma'n yeyen,*' put together discreetly, mean the '*Swallower of sublimate,*' without any '*Suleyman*' in the case: '*Suleyma*' signifying '*corrosive sublimate,*' and not being a proper name on this occasion, although it be an orthodox name enough with the addition of *n*. After Mr. Thornton's frequent hints of profound Orientalism, he might have found this out before he sang such pæans over Dr. Pouqueville.

After this, I think 'Travellers *versus* Factors' shall be our motto, though the above Mr. Thornton has condemned 'hoc genus omne,' for mistake and misrepresentation. 'Ne Sutor ultra crepidam.' 'No merchant beyond his bales.' N.B. For the benefit of Mr. Thornton 'Sutor' is not a proper name.

condemns some of the most celebrated institutions of the ancient, should have mercy on the modern Greeks; and it fortunately happens, that the absurdity of his hypothesis on their forefathers refutes his sentence on themselves.

Let us trust, then, that in spite of the prophecies of De Pauw, and the doubts of Mr. Thornton, there is a reasonable hope of the redemption of a race of men, who, whatever may be the errors of their religion and policy, have been amply punished by three centuries and a half of captivity.

III.

ATHENS, FRANCISCAN CONVENT, *March* 17, 1811.

'I must have some talk with this learned Theban.'

Some time after my return from Constantinople to this city I received the thirty-first number of the Edinburgh Review as a great favour, and certainly at this distance an acceptable one, from the captain of an English frigate off Salamis. In that number, Art. 3, containing the review of a French translation of Strabo, there are introduced some remarks on the modern Greeks and their literature, with a short account of Coray, a co-translator in the French version. On those remarks I mean to ground a few observations; and the spot where I now write will, I hope, be sufficient excuse for introducing them in a work in some degree connected with the subject. Goray, the most celebrated of living Greeks, at least among the Franks, was born at Scio (in the Review, Smyrna is stated, I have reason to think, incorrectly), and besides the translation of Beccaria and other works mentioned by the Reviewer, has published a lexicon in Romaic and French, if I may trust the assurance of some Danish travellers lately arrived from Paris; but the latest we have seen here in French and Greek is that of Gregory Zolikogloou.* Coray has recently been involved in an unpleasant controversy with M. Gail,† a Parisian commentator and editor of some translations from the Greek poets, in consequence of the Institute having awrrded him the prize for his version of Hippocrates 'Περὶ ὑδάτων,' &c., to the disparagement, and consequently displeasure, of the said Gail. To his exertions, literary and patriotic, great praise is undoubtedly due; but a part of that praise ought not to be withheld from the two brothers Zosimado (merchants settled in Leghorn), who sent him to Paris, and maintained him, for the express purpose of elucidating the ancient, and adding to the modern, researches of his countrymen. Coray, however, is not considered by his countrymen equal to some who lived in the two last centuries; more particularly Dorotheus of Mitylene, whose Hellenic writings are so much esteemed by the Greeks, that Meletius terms him 'Μετὰ τὸν Θουκυδίδην καὶ Ξενοφῶντα ἄριστος Ἑλλήνων.' (P. 224, Ecclesiastical History, vol. iv.)

Panagiotes Kodrikas, the translator of Fonte-

* I have in my possession an excellent lexicon 'τρί-γλωσσον,' which I received in exchange from S. G——, Esq. for a small gem: my antiquarian friends have never forgotten it, or forgiven me.

† In Gail's pamphlet against Coray, he talks of 'throwing the insolent Hellenist out of the windows.' On this a French critic exclaims, 'Ah, my God! throw an Hellenist out of the window! what sacrilege!' It certainly would be a serious business for those authors who dwell in the attics: but I have quoted the passage merely to prove the similarity of style among the controversialists of all polished countries; London or Edinburgh could hardly parallel this Parisian ebullition.

nelle, and Kamarases, who translated Ocellus Lucanus on the Universe into French, Christodoulus, and more particularly Psalida, whom I have conversed with in Joannina, are also in high repute among their literati. The last-mentioned has published in Romaic and Latin a work on 'True Happiness,' dedicated to Catherine II. But Polyzois, who is stated by the Reviewer to be the only modern except Coray who has distinguished himself by a knowledge of Hellenic, if he be the Polyzois Lampanitziotes of Yanina, who has published a number of editions in Romaic, was neither more nor less than an itinerant vender of books; with the contents of which he had no concern beyond his name on the title page, placed there to secure his property in the publication; and he was, moreover, a man utterly destitute of scholastic acquirements. As the name, however, is not uncommon, some other Polyzois may have edited the Epistles of Aristænetus.

It is to be regretted that the system of continental blockade has closed the few channels through which the Greeks received their publications, particularly Venice and Trieste. Even the common grammars for children are become too dear for the lower orders. Amongst their original works the Geography of Meletius, Archbishop of Athens, and a multitude of theological quartos and poetical pamphlets, are to be met with; their grammars and lexicons of two, three, and four languages are numerous and excellent. Their poetry is in rhyme. The most singular piece I have lately seen is a satire in dialogue between a Russian, English, and French traveller, and the Waywode of Wallachia (or Black-bey, as they term him), an archbishop, a merchant, and Cogia Bachi (or primate), in succession; to all of whom under the Turks the writer attributes their present degeneracy. Their songs are sometimes pretty and pathetic, but their tunes generally unpleasing to the ear of a Frank; the best is the famous 'Δεῦτε παῖδες τῶν Ἑλλήνων,' by the unfortunate Riga. But from a catalogue of more than sixty authors, now before me, only fifteen can be found who have touched on any theme except theology.

I am intrusted with a commission by a Greek of Athens named Marmarotouri to make arrangements, if possible, for printing in London a translation of Barthelemi's Anacharsis in Romaic, as he has no other opportunity, unless he despatches the MS. to Vienna by the Black Sea and Danube.

The Reviewer mentions a school established at Hecatonesi, and suppressed at the instigation of Sebastiani: he means Cidonies, or, in Turkish, Haivali; a town on the continent, where that institution for a hundred students and three professors still exists. It is true that this establishment was disturbed by the Porte, under the ridiculous pretext that the Greeks were constructing a fortress instead of a college: but on investigation, and the payment of some purses to the Divan, it has been permitted to continue. The principal professor, named Ueniamin, (i.e. Benjamin), is stated to be a man of talent, but a freethinker. He was born in Lesbos, studied in Italy, and is master of Hellenic, Latin, and some Frank languages: besides a smattering of the sciences.

Though it is not my intention to enter farther on this topic than may allude to the article in question, I cannot but observe that the Reviewer's lamentation over the fall of the Greeks appears singular, when he closes it with these words: '*The change is to be attributed to their misfortunes rather than to any "physical degradation."*' It may be true

hat the Greeks are not physically degenerated, and that Constantinople contained on the day when it hanged masters as many men of six feet and upwards as in the hour of prosperity; but ancient history and modern politics instruct us that something more than physical perfection is necessary to preserve a state in vigour and independence; and the Greeks, in particular, are a melancholy example of the near connexion between moral degradation and national decay.

The Reviewer mentions a plan 'we believe' by Potemkin for the purification of the Romaic; and have endeavoured in vain to procure any tidings or traces of its existence. There was an academy in St. Petersburg for the Greeks; but it was suppressed by Paul, and has not been revived by his successor.

There is a slip of the pen, and it can only be a slip of the pen, in p. 58, No. 31 of the 'Edinburgh Review,' where these words occur:—'We are told that when the capital of the East yielded to Solyman.'—It may be presumed that this last word will, in a future edition, be altered to Mahomet II.* The 'ladies of Constantinople,' it seems, at that period spoke a dialect, 'which would not have disgraced the lips of an Athenian.' I do not know now that might be, but am sorry to say the ladies in general, and the Athenians in particular, are much altered; being far from choice either in their dialect or expressions, as the whole Attic race are barbarous to a proverb:—

*Ω 'Αθήνα, πρότη χώρα,
Τί γαιδάρους τρέφεις τώρα.'

n Gibbon, vol. x. p. 161, is the following sentence: —'The vulgar dialect of the city was gross and barbarous, though the compositions of the church and palace sometimes affected to copy the purity of the Attic models.' Whatever may be asserted on the subject, it is difficult to conceive that the ladies of Constantinople,' in the reign of the last Cæsar, spoke a purer dialect than Anna Comnena wrote three centuries before: and those royal pages are not esteemed the best models of composition, although the princess γλῶτταν εἶχεν 'ΑΚΡΙΒΩΣ Αττικίζουσαν. In the Fanal, and in Yanina, the best Greek is spoken: in the latter there is a flourishing school under the direction of Psalida.

There is now in Athens a pupil of Psalida's, who is making a tour of observation through Greece: he is intelligent, and better educated than a fellow-commoner of most colleges. I mention this as a proof that the spirit of inquiry is not dormant among the Greeks.

* In a former number of the Edinburgh Review, p. 808, it is observed: 'Lord Byron passed some of his early years in Scotland, where he might have learned that pibroch does not mean a bagpipe, any more than that means a fiddle.' Query,—Was it in Scotland that the young gentlemen of the Edinburgh Review learned that Solyman means Mahomet II. any more than criticism means infallibility?—but thus it is.

'Cædimus inque vicem præbemus crura sagittis.' The mistake seemed so completely a lapse of the pen from the great similarity of the two words, and the total absence of error from the former pages of the literary leviathan) that I should have passed it over as in the text, had I not perceived in the Edinburgh Review much facetious exultation on all such defections, particularly a recent one, where words and syllables are subjects of disquisition and transposition; and the above-mentioned parallel passage in my own case irresistibly propelled me to hint how much easier it is to be critical than correct. The gentlemen, having enjoyed many a triumph on such victories, will hardly begrudge me a slight ovation for the present.

The Reviewer mentions Mr. Wright, the author of the beautiful poem 'Horæ Ionicæ,' as qualified to give details of these nominal Romans and degenerate Greeks; and also of their language: but Mr. Wright, though a good poet and an able man, has made a mistake where he states the Albanian dialect of the Romaic to approximate nearest to the Hellenic; for the Albanians speak a Romaic as notoriously corrupt as the Scotch of Aberdeenshire, or the Italian of Naples. Yanina, (where, next to the Fanal, the Greek is purest,) although the capital of Ali Pacha's dominions, is not in Albania, but Epirus; and beyond Delvinachi in Albania Proper up to Argyrocastro and Tepaleen (beyond which I did not advance) they spoke worse Greek than even the Athenians. I was attended for a year and a half by two of these singular mountaineers, whose mother tongue is Illyric, and I never heard them or their countrymen (whom I have seen, not only at home, but to the amount of twenty thousand in the army of Vely Pacha) praised for their Greek, but often laughed at for their provincial barbarisms.

I have in my possession about twenty-five letters, amongst which some from the Bey of Corinth, written to me by Notaras, the Cogia Bachi, and others by the dragoman of the Caimacam of the Morea (which last governs in Vely Pacha's absence), are said to be favourable specimens of their epistolary style. I also received some at Constantinople from private persons, written in a most hyperbolical style, but in the true antique character.

The Reviewer proceeds, after some remarks on the tongue in its past and present state, to a paradox (page 59) on the great mischief the knowledge of his own language has done to Coray, who, it seems, is less likely to understand the ancient Greek, because he is perfect master of the modern! This observation follows a paragraph, recommending, in explicit terms, the study of the Romaic, as 'a powerful auxiliary,' not only to the traveller and foreign merchant, but also to the classical scholar; in short, to everybody except the only person who can be thoroughly acquainted with its uses; and by a parity of reasoning, our old language is conjectured to be probably more attainable by 'foreigners' than by ourselves! Now, I am inclined to think, that a Dutch Tyro in our tongue, (albeit himself of Saxon blood) would be sadly perplexed with 'Sir Tristrem,' or any other given 'Auchinleck MS.,' with or without a grammar or glossary; and to most apprehensions it seems evident, that none but a native can acquire a competent, far less complete, knowledge of our obsolete idioms. We may give the critic credit for his ingenuity, but no more believe him than we do Smollet's Lismahago, who maintains that the purest English is spoken in Edinburgh. That Coray may err is very possible; but if he does, the fault is in the man rather than in his mother tongue, which is, as it ought to be, of the greatest aid to the native student.—Here the Reviewer proceeds to business on Strabo's translators, and here I close my remarks.

Sir W. Drummond, Mr. Hamilton, Lord Aberdeen, Dr. Clarke, Captain Leake, Mr. Gell, Mr. Walpole, and many others now in England, have all the requisites to furnish details of this fallen people. The few observations I have offered I should have left where I made them, had not the article in question, and above all the spot where I read it, induced me to advert to those pages, which the advantage of my present situation enabled me to clear, or at least to make the attempt.

I have endeavoured to waive the personal feel-

NOTES TO CHILDE HAROLD'S PILGRIMAGE

ings which rise in despite of me in touching upon any part of the Edinburgh Review; not from a wish to conciliate the favour of its writers, or to cancel the remembrance of a syllable I have formerly published, but simply from a sense of the impropriety of mixing up private resentments with a disquisition of the present kind, and more particularly at this distance of time and place.

Amongst an enslaved people, obliged to have recourse to foreign presses even for their books of religion, it is less to be wondered at that we find so few publications on general subjects than that we find any at all. The whole number of the Greeks, scattered up and down the Turkish empire and elsewhere, may amount, at most, to three millions; and yet, for so scanty a number, it is impossible to discover any nation with so great a proportion of books and their authors as the Greeks of the present century. 'Ay,' but say the generous advocates of oppression, who, while they assert the ignorance of the Greeks, wish to prevent them from dispelling it, 'ay, but these are mostly, if not all, ecclesiastical tracts, and consequently good for nothing.' Well! and pray what else can they write about? It is pleasant enough to hear a Frank, particularly an Englishman, who may abuse the government of his own country; or a Frenchman, who may abuse every government except his own, and who may range at will over every philosophical, religious, scientific, sceptical, or moral subject, sneering at the Greek legends. A Greek must not write on politics, and cannot touch on science for want of instruction; if he doubts, he is excommunicated and damned; therefore his countrymen are not poisoned with modern philosophy; and as to morals, thanks to the Turks! there are no such things. What then is left him, if he has a turn for scribbling? Religion and holy biography: and it is natural enough that those who have so little in this life should look to the next. It is no great wonder, then, that in a catalogue now before me of fifty-five Greek writers, many of whom were lately living, not above fifteen should have touched on anything but religion. The catalogue alluded to is contained in the twenty-sixth chapter of the fourth volume of Meletius' Ecclesiastical History.

Page 206, col. 1.

'Spirit of freedom! when on Phyle's brow.'] Phyle, which commands a beautiful view of Athens, has still considerable remains: it was seized by Thrasybulus, previous to the expulsion of the Thirty.

Page 206, col. 1.

'Trembling beneath the scourge of Turkish hand.'] The difficulties of travelling in Turkey have been much exaggerated, or rather have considerably diminished, of late years. The Mussulmans have been beaten into a kind of sullen civility very comfortable to voyagers.

It is hazardous to say much on the subject of Turks and Turkey; since it is possible to live amongst them twenty years without acquiring information, at least from themselves. As far as my own slight experience carried me, I have no complaint to make; but am indebted for many civilities (I might also say for friendship), and much hospitality, to Ali Pacha, his son Veli Pacha of the Morea, and several others of high rank in the provinces. Suleyman Aga, late Governor of Athens, and now of Thebes, was a *bon vivant*, and

as social a being as ever sat cross-legged at a tray or a table. During the carnival, when our English party were masquerading, both himself and his successor were more happy to 'receive masks,' than any dowager in Grosvenor-square.

On one occasion of his supping at the convent his friend and visitor, the Cadi of Thebes, was carried from table perfectly qualified for any club in Christendom; while the worthy Waywode himself triumphed in his fall.

In all money transactions with the Moslems, I ever found the strictest honour, the highest disinterestedness. In transacting business with them there are none of those dirty peculations, under the name of interest, difference of exchange, commission, &c. &c., uniformly found in applying to a Greek consul to cash bills, even on the first houses in Pera.

With regard to presents, an established custom in the East, you will rarely find yourself a loser; as one worth acceptance is generally returned by another of similar value—a horse, or a shawl.

In the capital and at court the citizens and courtiers are formed in the same school with those of Christianity; but there does not exist a more honourable, friendly, and high-spirited character, than the true Turkish provincial Aga, or Moslem country gentleman. It is not meant here to designate the governors of towns, but those Agas who, by a kind of feudal tenure, possess lands and houses, of more or less extent, in Greece and Asia Minor.

The lower orders are in as tolerable discipline as the rabble in countries with greater pretensions to civilization. A Moslem, in walking the streets of our country-towns, would be more incommoded in England than a Frank in a similar situation in Turkey. Regimentals are the best travelling dress.

The best accounts of the religion and different sects of Islamism, may be found in D'Ohsson's French; of their manners, &c. perhaps in Thornton's English. The Ottomans, with all their defects, are not a people to be despised. Equal, at least, to the Spaniards, they are superior to the Portuguese. If it be difficult to pronounce what they are, we can at least say what they are *not;* they are *no* treacherous, they are *not* cowardly, they do *no* burn heretics, they are *not* assassins, nor has an enemy advanced to *their* capital. They are faithful to their sultan till he becomes unfit to govern, and devout to their God without an inquisition. Were they driven from St. Sophia to-morrow, and the French or Russians enthroned in their stead, it would become a question whether Europe would gain by the exchange. England would certainly be the loser.

With regard to that ignorance of which they are so generally, and sometimes justly, accused, it may be doubted, always excepting France and England, in what useful points of knowledge they are excelled by other nations. Is it in the common arts of life? In their manufactures? Is a Turkish sabre inferior to a Toledo? or is a Turk worse clothed, o. lodged, or fed and taught, than a Spaniard? Are their Pachas worse educated than a Grandee? or an Effendi than a Knight of St. Jago? I think not.

I remember Mahmout, the grandson of Ali Pacha, asking whether my fellow-traveller and my self were in the upper or lower House of Parliament. Now, this question from a boy of ten years old proved that his education had not been neglected. It may be doubted if an English boy a that age knows the difference of the Divan from a College of Dervises; but I am very sure a Spaniard

886

NOTES TO CHILDE HAROLD'S PILGRIMAGE

does not. How little Mahmout, surrounded, as he had been, entirely by his Turkish tutors, had learned that there was such a thing as a Parliament, it were useless to conjecture, unless we suppose that his instructors did not confine his studies to the Koran.

In all the mosques there are schools established, which are very regularly attended; and the poor are taught without the church of Turkey being put into peril. I believe the system is not yet printed (though there is such a thing as a Turkish press, and books printed on the late military institution of the Nizam Gedidd); nor have I heard whether the Mufti and the Mollas have subscribed, or the Caimacan and the Tefterdar taken the alarm, for fear the ingenuous youth of the turban should be taught not to 'pray to God their way.' The Greeks also—a kind of Eastern Irish papists—have a college of their own at Maynooth,—no, at Haivali; where the heterodox receive much the same kind of countenance from the Ottoman as the Catholic college from the English legislature. Who shall then affirm that the Turks are ignorant bigots, when they thus evince the exact proportion of Christian charity which is tolerated in the most prosperous and orthodox of all possible kingdoms? But though they allow all this, they will not suffer the Greeks to participate in their privileges: no, let them fight their battles, and pay their haratch (taxes), be drubbed in this world, and damned in the next. And shall we then emancipate our Irish Helots? Mahomet forbid! We should then be bad Mussulmans, and worse Christians: at present we unite the best of both—jesuitical faith, and something not much inferior to Turkish toleration.

Page 206, col. 1.

'Receive the fiery Frank, her former guest.'] When taken by the Latins, and retained for several years.

Page 206, col. 2.

'The prophet's tomb of all its pious spoil.'] Mecca and Medina were taken some time ago by the Wahabees, a sect yearly increasing.

Page 207, col. 2.

'Thy vales of evergreen, thy hills of snow.'] On many of the mountains, particularly Liakura, the snow never is entirely melted, notwithstanding the intense heat of the summer; but I never saw it lie on the plains, even in winter.

Page 207, col. 2.

'Above its prostrate brethren of the cave.'] Of Mount Pentelicus, from whence the marble was dug that constructed the public edifices of Athens. The modern name is Mount Mendeli. An immense cave, formed by the quarries, still remains, and will till the end of time.

Page 207, col. 2.

'Colonna's cliff, and gleams along the wave.'] In all Attica, if we except Athens itself and Marathon, there is no scene more interesting than Cape Colonna. To the antiquary and artist, sixteen columns are an inexhaustible source of observation and design; to the philosopher, the supposed scene of some of Plato's conversations will not be unwelcome; and the traveller will be struck with the beauty of the prospect over 'Isles that crown the Ægean deep;' but, for an Englishman, Colonna has yet an additional interest, as the actual spot of Falconer's shipwreck. Pallas and Plato are forgotten, in the recollection of Falconer and Campbell:—

'Here in the dead of night by Lonna's steep,
The seaman's cry was heard along the deep.'

This temple of Minerva may be seen at sea from a great distance. In two journeys which I made, and one voyage to Cape Colonna, the view from either side, by land, was less striking than the approach from the isles. In our second land excursion, we had a narrow escape from a party of Mainotes, concealed in the caverns beneath. We were told afterwards, by one of their prisoners, subsequently ransomed, that they were deterred from attacking us by the appearance of my two Albanians: conjecturing very sagaciously, but falsely, that we had a complete guard of these Arnauts at hand, they remained stationary, and thus saved our party, which was too small to have opposed any effectual resistance. Colonna is no less a resort of painters than of pirates; there

'The hireling artist plants his paltry desk,
And makes degraded nature picturesque.'
(See Hodgson's Lady Jane Grey, &c.)

But there Nature, with the aid of Art, has done that for herself. I was fortunate enough to engage a very superior German artist; and hope to renew my acquaintance with this and many other Levantine scenes, by the arrival of his performances.

Page 208, col. 1.

'When Marathon became a magic word.'] 'Siste Viator—heroa calcas!' was the epitaph on the famous Count Merci;—what then must be our feelings when standing on the tumulus of the two hundred (Greeks) who fell on Marathon? The principal barrow has recently been opened by Fauvel: few or no relics, as vases, &c. were found by the excavator. The plain of Marathon was offered to me for sale at the sum of sixteen thousand piastres, about nine hundred pounds! Alas! —'Expende—quot libras in duce summo—invenies!'—was the dust of Miltiades worth no more? It could scarcely have fetched less if sold by weight.

Page 212, col. 1.

'In "pride of place" here last the eagle flew.'] 'Pride of place' is a term of falconry, and means the highest pitch of flight. See Macbeth, &c.:—
'An eagle towering in his pride of place,' &c.

Page 212, col. 1.

'Such as Harmodius drew on Athens' tyrant lord.'] See the famous song on Harmodius and Aristogiton. The best English translation is in Bland's Anthology, by Mr. (since Lord Chief Justice) Denman:—
'With myrtle my sword will I wreathe,' &c.

Page 212, col. 2.

'And all went merry as a marriage-bell.'] On the night previous to the action, it is said that a ball was given at Brussels.

Page 213, col. 1.

'And Evan's, Donald's fame rings in each clansman's ears!'] Sir Evan Cameron, and his descendant Donald, the 'gentle Lochiel' of the 'forty-five.'

Page 213, col. 1.

'And Ardennes waves above them her green leaves.'] The wood of Soignies is supposed to be a remnant of the forest of Ardennes, famous in

NOTES TO CHILDE HAROLD'S PILGRIMAGE

Boiardo's Orlando, and immortal in Shakespeare's 'As You Like It.' It is also celebrated in Tacitus, as being the spot of successful defence by the Germans against the Roman encroachments. I have ventured to adopt the name connected with nobler associations than those of mere slaughter.

Page 213, col. 2.

'I turn'd from all she brought to those she coulα not bring.'] My guide from Mount St. Jean over the field seemed intelligent and accurate. The place where Major Howard fell was not far from two tall and solitary trees (there was a third cut down, or shivered in the battle), which stand a few yards from each other at a pathway's side. Beneath these he died and was buried. The body has since been removed to England. A small hollow for the present marks where it lay, but will probably soon be effaced; the plough has been upon it, and the grain is. After pointing out the different spots where Picton and other gallant men had perished, the guide said, 'Here Major Howard lay: I was near him when wounded.' I told him my relationship, and he seemed then still more anxious to point out the particular spot and circumstances. The place is one of the most marked in the field, from the peculiarity of the two trees above mentioned. I went on horseback twice over the field, comparing it with my recollection of similar scenes. As a plain, Waterloo seems marked out for the scene of some great action, though this may be mere imagination: I have viewed with attention those of Platea, Troy, Mantinea, Leuctra, Chæronea, and Marathon: and the field around Mount St. Jean and Hougoumont appears to want little but a better cause, and that undefinable but impressive halo which the lapse of ages throws around a celebrated spot, to vie in interest with any or all of these, except, perhaps, the last mentioned.

Page 214, col. 1.

'Like to the apples on the Dead Sea's shore.'] The (fabled) apples on the brink of the lake Asphaltites were said to be fair without, and, within, ashes. Vide Tacitus, Histor. lib. v. 7.

Page 215, col. 1.

'For sceptred cynics earth were far too wide a den.'] The great error of Napoleon, 'if we have writ our annals true,' was a continued obtrusion on mankind of his want of all community of feeling for or with them; perhaps more offensive to human vanity than the active cruelty of more trembling and suspicious tyranny. Such were his speeches to public assemblies as well as individuals; and the single expression which he is said to have used on returning to Paris after the Russian winter had destroyed his army, rubbing his hands over a fire, 'This is pleasanter than Moscow,' would probably alienate more favour from his cause than the destruction and reverses which led to the remark.

Page 216, col. 1.

'What want these outlaws conquerors should have?'] 'What wants that knave that a king should have?' was King James's question on meeting Johnny Armstrong and his followers in full accoutrements.—See the Ballad.

Page 217, col. 1.

'The castled crag of Drachenfels.'] The castle of Drachenfels stands on the highest summit of 'the Seven Mountains, over the Rhine banks; it is in ruins, and connected with some singular traditions. It is the first in view on the road from Bonn but on the opposite side of the river; on this bank nearly facing it, are the remains of another, callec the Jew's Castle, and a large cross, commemorative of the murder of a chief by his brother. The number of castles and cities along the course of the Rhine on both sides is very great, and their situations remarkably beautiful.

Page 218, col. 1.

'The whiteness of his soul, and thus men o'er him wept.'] The monument of the young and lamented General Marceau (killed by a rifle-ball at Alterkirchen, on the last day of the fourth year of the French republic) still remains as described. The inscriptions on his monument are rather too long, and not required: his name was enough: France adored, and her enemies admired; both wept over him. His funeral was attended by the generals and detachments from both armies. In the same grave General Hoche is interred, a gallant man also in every sense of the word; but though he distinguished himself greatly in battle, he had not the good fortune to die there: his death was attended by suspicions of poison. A separate monument (not over his body, which is buried by Marceau's) is raised for him near Andernach, opposite to which one of his most memorable exploits was performed, in throwing a bridge to an island on the Rhine. The shape and style are different from that of Marceau's, and the inscription more simple and pleasing:—'The Army of the Sambre and Meuse to its Commander-in-Chief Hoche.' This is all, and as it should be. Hoche was esteemed among the first of France's earlier generals, before Buonaparte monopolised her triumphs. He was the destined commander of the invading army of Ireland.

Page 218, col. 1.

'Here Ehrenbreitstein, with her shatter'd wall.'] Ehrenbreitstein, i.e. 'the broad stone of honour,' one of the strongest fortresses in Europe, was dismantled and blown up by the French at the truce of Leoben. It had been, and could only be, reduced by famine or treachery. It yielded to the former, aided by surprise. After having seen the fortifications of Gibraltar and Malta, it did not much strike by comparison; but the situation is commanding. General Marceau besieged it in vain for some time, and I slept in a room where I was shown a window at which he is said to have been standing observing the progress of the siege by moonlight, when a ball struck immediately below it.

Page 218, col. 2.

'Unsepulchred they roam'd, and shriek'd each wandering ghost.'] The chapel is destroyed, and the pyramid of bones diminished to a small number by the Burgundian legion in the service of France; who anxiously effaced this record of their ancestors' less successful invasions. A few still remain, notwithstanding the pains taken by the Burgundians for ages (all who passed that way removing a bone to their own country), and the less justifiable larcenies of the Swiss postilions, who carried them off to sell for knife-handles; a purpose for which the whiteness imbibed by the bleaching of years had rendered them in great request. Of these relics I ventured to bring away as much as may have made a quarter of a hero, for which the sole excuse is, that if I had not, the next passer-by might have perverted them to worse uses than the careful preservation which I intend for them.

Page 219, col. 1.

'Levell'd Aventicum, hath strew'd her subject lands.'] Aventicum, near Morat, was the Roman capital of Helvetia, where Avenches now stands.

Page 219, col. 1.

'And held within their urn one mind, one heart, one dust.'] Julia Alpinula, a young Aventian priestess, died soon after a vain endeavour to save her father, condemned to death as a traitor by Aulus Cæcina. Her epitaph was discovered many years ago;—it is thus:—'Julia Alpinula: Hic jaceo. Infelicis patris, infelix proles. Deæ Aventiæ Sacerdos. Exorare patris necem non potui: Male mori in fatis ille erat. Vixi annos XXIII.'—I know of no human composition so affecting as this, nor a history of deeper interest. These are the names and actions which ought not to perish, and to which we turn with a true and healthy tenderness, from the wretched and glittering detail of a confused mass of conquests and battles, with which the mind is roused for a time to a false and feverish sympathy, from whence it recurs at length with all the nausea consequent on such intoxication.

Page 219, col. 1.

'In the sun's face, like yonder Alpine snow.'] This is written in the eye of Mont Blanc (June 3rd, 1816), which even at this distance dazzles mine.— July 20th.) I this day observed for some time the distinct reflection of Mont Blanc and Mont Argentière in the calm of the lake, which I was crossing in my boat; the distance of these mountains from their mirror is sixty miles.

Page 219, col. 2.

'By the blue rushing of the arrowy Rhone.'] The colour of the Rhone at Geneva is blue, to a depth of tint which I have never seen equalled in water, salt or fresh, except in the Mediterranean and Archipelago.

Page 220, col. 2.

'This hallow'd, too, the memorable kiss.'] This refers to the account in his 'Confessions' of his passion for the Comtesse d'Houdetot (the mistress of St. Lambert), and his long walk every morning, for the sake of the single kiss which was the common salutation of French acquaintance. Rousseau's description of his feelings on this occasion may be considered as the most passionate, yet not impure, description and expression of love that ever kindled into words; which, after all, must be felt, from their very force, to be inadequate to the delineation; a painting can give no sufficient idea of the ocean.

Page 222, col. 1.

'Of earth-o'ergazing mountains, and thus take.'] It is to be recollected, that the most beautiful and impressive doctrines of the divine Founder of Christianity were delivered, not in the *Temple*, but on the *Mount*. To waive the question of devotion, and turn to human eloquence,—the most effectual and splendid specimens were not pronounced within walls. Demosthenes addressed the public and popular assemblies. Cicero spoke in the forum. That this added to their effect on the mind of both orator and hearers, may be conceived from the difference between what we read of the emotions then and there produced, and those we ourselves experience in the perusal in the closet. It is one thing to read the Iliad at Sigæum and on the tumuli, or by the springs with Mount Ida above, and the plain and rivers and Archipelago around

you; and another to trim your taper over it in a snug library—*this* I know. Were the early and rapid progress of what is called Methodism to be attributed to any cause beyond the enthusiasm excited by its vehement faith and doctrines (the truth or error of which I presume neither to canvass nor to question), I should venture to ascribe it to the practice of preaching in the *fields*, and the unstudied and extemporaneous effusions of its teachers. The Mussulmans, whose erroneous devotion (at least in the lower orders) is most sincere, and therefore impressive, are accustomed to repeat their prescribed orisons and prayers, wherever they may be, at the stated hours—of course, frequently in the open air, kneeling upon a light mat (which they carry for the purpose of a bed or cushion as required); the ceremony lasts some minutes, during which they are totally absorbed, and only living in their supplication: nothing can disturb them. On me the simple and entire sincerity of these men, and the spirit which appeared to be within and upon them, made a far greater impression than any general rite which was ever performed in places of worship, of which I have seen those of almost every persuasion under the sun; including most of our own sectaries, and the Greek, the Catholic, the Armenian, the Lutheran, the Jewish, and the Mahometan. Many of the negroes of whom there are numbers in the Turkish empire, are idolaters, and have free exercise of their belief and its rites; some of these I had a distant view of at Patras; and, from what I could make out of them, they appeared to be of a truly Pagan description, and not very agreeable to a spectator.

Page 222, col. 2.

'The sky is changed!—and such a change! Oh night.'] The thunder-storm to which these lines refer occurred on the 13th of June, 1816, at midnight. I have seen, among the Acroceraunian mountains of Chimari, several more terrible, but none more beautiful.

Page 223, col. 2.

'And sun-set into rose-hues sees them wrought.'] Rousseau's Héloïse, Lettre 17, Part IV., note. 'Ces montagnes sont si hautes qu'une demi-heure après le soleil couche, leurs sommets sont éclairés de ses rayons; dont le rouge forme sur ces cimes blanches *une belle couleur de rose*, qu'on aperçoit de fort loin.'—This applies more particularly to the heights over Meillerie.—'J'allai à Vevay loger à la Clef, et pendant deux jours que j'y restai sans voir personne, je pris pour cette ville un amour qui m'a suivi dans tous mes voyages, et qui m'y a fait établir enfin les héros de mon roman. Je dirais volontiers à ceux qui ont du goût et qui sont sensibles: Allez à Vevay—visitez le pays, examinez les sites, promenez-vous sur le lac, et dites si la Nature n'a pas fait ce beau pays pour une Julie, pour une Claire, et pour un St. Preux; mais ne les y cherchez pas.'— *Les Confessions*, livre iv. p. 306, Lyon, ed. 1796.— In July, 1816, I made a voyage round the Lake of Geneva: and, as far as my own observations have led me in a not uninterested nor inattentive survey of all the scenes most celebrated by Rousseau in his 'Héloïse,' I can safely say, that in this there is no exaggeration. It would be difficult to see Clarens (with the scenes around it, Vevay, Chillon, Bôveret, St. Gingo, Meillerie, Eivan, and the entrances of the Rhone) without being forcibly struck with its peculiar adaptation to the persons and events with which it has been peopled. But this is not all; the feeling with which all around Clarens, and the

NOTES TO CHILDE HAROLD'S PILGRIMAGE

opposite rocks of Meillerie, is invested, is of a still higher and more comprehensive order than the mere sympathy with individual passion; it is a sense of the existence of love in its most extended and sublime capacity, and of our own participation of its good and of its glory: it is the great principle of the universe, which is there more condensed, but not less manifested; and of which, though knowing ourselves a part, we lose our individuality, and mingle in the beauty of the whole.—If Rousseau had never written, nor lived, the same associations would not less have belonged to such scenes. He has added to the interest of his works by their adoption; he has shown his sense of their beauty by the selection; but they have done that for him which no human being could do for them.—I had the fortune (good or evil as it might be) to sail from Meillerie (where we landed for some time) to St. Gingo during a lake storm, which added to the magnificence of all around, although occasionally accompanied by danger to the boat, which was small and overloaded. It was over this very part of the lake that Rousseau has driven the boat of St. Preux and Madame Wolmar to Meillerie for shelter during a tempest. On gaining the shore at St. Gingo, I found that the wind had been sufficiently strong to blow down some fine old chestnut trees on the lower part of the mountains. On the opposite height of Clarens is a château. The hills are covered with vineyards, and interspersed with some small but beautiful woods; one of these was named the 'Bosquet de Julie;' and it is remarkable that, though long ago cut down by the brutal selfishness of the monks of St. Bernard (to whom the land appertained), that the ground might be enclosed into a vineyard for the miserable drones of an execrable superstition, the inhabitants of Clarens still point out the spot where its trees stood, calling it by the name which consecrated and survived them. Rousseau has not been particularly fortunate in the preservation of the 'local habitations' he has given to 'airy nothings.' The Prior of Great St. Bernard has cut down some of his woods for the sake of a few casks of wine, and Buonaparte has levelled part of the rocks of Meillerie in improving the road to the Simplon. The road is an excellent one; but I cannot quite agree with a remark which I heard made, that 'La route vaut mieux que les souvenirs.'

Page 224, col. 1.

'Of names which unto you bequeath'd a name.'] Voltaire and Gibbon.

Page 225, col. 2.

'Had I not filed my mind, which thus itself subdued.']
—'If it be thus,
For Banquo's issue have I *filed* my mind.'—
MACBETH.

Page 225, col. 2.

'O'er others' griefs that some sincerely grieve.'] It is said by Rochefoucault that 'there is *always* something in the misfortunes of men's best friends not displeasing to them.'

Page 227, col. 2.

'She looks a sea Cybele, fresh from ocean.'] Sabellicus, describing the appearance of Venice, has made use of the above image, which would not be poetical were it not true.—'Quo fit ut qui superne urbem contempletur, turritam telluris imaginem medio Oceano figuratam se putet inspicere.'

Page 228, col. 2.

'Sparta hath many a worthier son than he.' The answer of the mother of Brasidas, the Lacedæmonian general, to the strangers who praised the memory of her son.

Page 229, col. 1.

'The "Planter of the Lion," which through fire.' That is, the Lion of St. Mark, the standard of the republic, which is the origin of the word Pantaloon —Piantaleone, Pantaleon, Pantaloon.

Page 229, col. 1.

'Redemption rose up in the Attic Muse.'] The story is told in Plutarch's Life of Nicias.

Page 229, col. 2.

'And Otway, Radcliffe, Schiller, Shakespeare' art.'] 'Venice Preserved;' 'Mysteries of Udolpho;' 'The Ghost-Seer, or Armenian;' 'The Merchant of Venice;' 'Othello.'

Page 230, col. 1.

'But from their nature will the tannen grow.' *Tannen* is the plural of *tanne*, a species of fir peculiar to the Alps, which only thrives in very rocky parts, where scarcely soil sufficient for its nourishment can be found. On these spots it grows to a greater height than any other mountain tree.

Page 231, col. 1.

'Floats through the azure air—an island of the blest!'] The above description may seem fantastical or exaggerated to those who have never seen an Oriental or an Italian sky, yet it is but a literal and hardly sufficient delineation of an August evening (the eighteenth), as contemplated in one of many rides along the banks of the Brenta, near La Mira.

Page 231, col. 2.

'Or, it may be, with demons, who impair.'] The struggle is to the full as likely to be with demons as with our better thoughts. Satan chose the wilderness for the temptation of our Saviour. And our unsullied John Locke preferred the presence of a child to complete solitude.

Page 233, col. 1.

'Victor or vanquish'd, thou the slave of friend or foe.'] The two stanzas XLII. and XLIII. are, with the exception of a line or two, a translation of the famous sonnet of Filicaja:—'Italia, Italia, O tu cui feo la sorte!'

Page 233, col. 1.

'Wandering in youth, I traced the path of him.' The celebrated letter of Servius Sulpicius to Cicero on the death of his daughter, describes as it then was, and now is, a path which I often traced in Greece, both by sea and land, in different journeys and voyages. 'On my return from Asia, as I was sailing from Ægina towards Megara, I began to contemplate the prospect of the countries around me: Ægina was behind, Megara before me; Piræus on the right, Corinth on the left: all which towns once famous and flourishing, now lie overturned and buried in their ruins. Upon this sight, I could not but think presently within myself, Alas! how do we poor mortals fret and vex ourselves if any of our friends happen to die or be killed, whose life is yet so short, when the carcasses of so many noble cities lie here exposed before me in one view.'— See Middleton's Cicero, vol. ii, p. 371.

Page 233, col. 2.

'The skeleton of her Titanic form.'] It is Poggio, who, looking from the Capitoline hill upon ruined Rome, breaks forth into the exclamation, 'Ut nunc omni decore nudata, prostrata jacet, instar gigantei cadaveris corrupti atque undique exesi.'

Page 234, col. 1.

'Feeding on thy sweet cheek! while thy lips are.']

'Οφθαλμοὺς ἑστιᾷν.

'Atque oculos pascat uterque suos.'—OVID. *Amor.* lib. ii.

Page 236, col. 2.

'Charming the eye with dread,—a matchless cataract.'] I saw the Cascata del Marmore of Terni twice, at different periods—once from the summit of the precipice, and again from the valley below. The lower view is far to be preferred, if the traveller has time for one only; but in any point of view, either from above or below, it is worth all the cascades and torrents of Switzerland put together: the Staubach, Reichenbach, Pisse Vache, fall of Arpenaz, &c. are rills in comparative appearance. Of the fall of Schaffhausen I cannot speak, not yet having seen it.

Page 236, col. 2.

'An Iris sits, amidst the infernal surge.'] Of the time, place, and qualities of this kind of iris, the reader will see a short account in a note to *Manfred*. The fall looks so much like 'the hell of waters,' that Addison thought the descent alluded to by the gulf in which Alecto plunged into the infernal regions. It is singular enough, that two of the finest cascades in Europe should be artificial—this of the Velino, and the one at Tivoli. The traveller is strongly recommended to trace the Velino, at least as high as the little lake called *Pie' di Lup.* The Reatine territory was the Italian Tempe (Cicer. Epist. ad Attic. xv. lib. iv.), and the ancient naturalists (Plin. Hist. Nat. lib. ii. cap. lxii), amongst other beautiful varieties, remarked the daily rainbows of the lake Velinus. A scholar of great name has devoted a treatise to this district alone. See Ald. Manut. 'De Reatina Urbe Agroque,' ap. Sallengre, Thesaur. tom. i. p. 773.

Page 237, col. 1.

'Sits on more shaggy summits, and where roar.'] In the greater part of Switzerland, the avalanches are known by the name of lauwine.

Page 237, col. 1.

'The drill'd dull lesson, forced down word by word.'] These stanzas may probably remind the reader of Ensign Northerton's remarks, 'D—n Homo,' &c.; but the reasons for our dislike are not exactly the same. I wish to express, that we become tired of the task before we can comprehend the beauty; that we learn by rote before we can get by heart; that the freshness is worn away, and the future pleasure and advantage deadened and destroyed, by the didactic anticipation, at an age when we can neither feel nor understand the power of compositions which it requires an acquaintance with life, as well as Latin and Greek, to relish,, or to reason upon. For the same reason, we never can be aware of the fulness of some of the finest passages of Shakespeare ('To be, or not to be,' for instance), from the habit of having them hammered into us at eight years old, as an exercise, not of mind, but of memory: so that when we are old enough to enjoy them, the taste is gone, and the appetite

palled. In some parts of the continent, young persons are taught from more common authors, and do not read the best classics till their maturity. I certainly do not speak on this point from any pique or aversion towards the place of my education. I was not a slow, though an idle boy; and I believe no one could, or can be, more attached to Harrow than I have always been, and with reason; —a part of the time passed there was the happiest of my life; and my preceptor, the Rev. Dr. Joseph Drury, was the best and worthiest friend I ever possessed, whose warnings I have remembered but too well, though too late, when I have erred,—and whose counsels I have but followed when I have done well or wisely. If ever this imperfect record of my feelings towards him should reach his eyes, let it remind him of one who never thinks of him but with gratitude and veneration—of one who would more gladly boast of having been his pupil, if, by once more closely following his injunctions, he could reflect any honour upon his instructor.

Page 237, col. 2.

'The Scipios' tomb contains no ashes now.'] For a comment on this and the two following stanzas, the reader may consult 'Historical Illustrations,' p. 46.

Page 238, col. 1.

'The trebly hundred triumphs! and the day.'] Orosius gives 320 for the number of triumphs. He is followed by Panvinius; and Panvinius by Mr. Gibbon and the modern writers.

Page 238, col. 2.

'Beheld him win two realms, and, happier, yield his breath.'] On the 3rd of September Cromwell gained the victory of Dunbar; a year afterwards he obtained 'his crowning mercy' of Worcester; and a few years after, on the same day, which he had ever esteemed the most fortunate for him, died.

Page 239, col. 2.

'Our senses narrow, and our reason frail.']—— 'Omnes pene veteres; qui nihil cognosci, nihil percepi, nihil sciri posse dixerunt; angustos sensus; imbecillos animos, brevia curricula vitæ; in profundo veritatem demersam; opinionibus et institutis omnia teneri; nihil veritati relinqui: deinceps omnia tenebris circumfusa esse dixerunt.'—Academ. l. 13. The eighteen hundred years which have elapsed since Cicero wrote this have not removed any of the imperfections of humanity: and the complaints of the ancient philosophers may, without injustice or affectation, be transcribed in a poem written yesterday.

Page 240, col. 1.

'There is a stern round tower of other days.'] Alluding to the tomb of Cecilia Metella, called Capo di Bove. See 'Historical Illustrations,' p.200.

Page 240, col. 2.

'Heaven gives its favourites—early death; yet shed.']

"'Ὸν οἱ θεοὶ φιλοῦσιν, ἀποθνῄσκει νέος·
Τὸ γὰρ θανεῖν οὐκ αἰσχρὸν ἀλλ' αἰσχρῶς θανεῖν.

Rich. Franc. Phil. Brunck. Poetæ Gnomici, p. 231, edit. 1784.

Page 241, col. 2.

'There is the moral of all human tales.'] The author of the Life of Cicero, speaking of the

NOTES TO CHILDE HAROLD'S PILGRIMAGE

opinion entertained of Britain by that orator and his contemporary Romans, has the following eloquent passage:—'From their railleries of this kind, on the barbarity and misery of our island, one cannot help reflecting on the surprising fate and revolutions of kingdoms; how Rome, once the mistress of the world, the seat of arts, empire, and glory, now lies sunk in sloth, ignorance, and poverty, enslaved to the most cruel as well as to the most contemptible of tyrants, superstition and religious imposture; while this remote country, anciently the jest and contempt of the polite Romans, is become the happy seat of liberty, plenty, and letters; flourishing in all the arts and refinements of civil life; yet running, perhaps, the same course which Rome itself had run before it, from virtuous industry to wealth; from wealth to luxury; from luxury to an impatience of discipline, and corruption of morals: till, by a total degeneracy and loss of virtue, being grown ripe for destruction, it falls a prey at last to some hardy oppressor, and, with the loss of liberty, losing everything that is valuable, sinks gradually again into its original barbarism.' (See 'History of the life of M. Tullius Cicero, sect. vi. vol. ii. p. 102.)

Page 242, col. 1.

'To crush the imperial urn, whose ashes slept sublime.'] The column of Trajan is surmounted by St. Peter; that of Aurelius by St. Paul. See 'Historical Illustrations,' p. 214.

Page 242, col. 2.

'Rienzi! last of Romans! While the tree.'] The name and exploits of Rienzi must be familiar to the reader of Gibbon. Some details and inedited manuscripts, relative to this unhappy hero, will be seen in the 'Historical Illustrations of the Fourth Canto,' p. 248.

Page 244, col. 1.

'Yet let us ponder boldly—'tis a base.'] 'At all events,' says the author of the 'Academical Questions,' 'I trust, whatever may be the fate of my own speculations, that philosophy will regain that estimation which it ought to possess. The free and philosophic spirit of our nation has been the theme of admiration to the world. This was the proud distinction of Englishmen, and the luminous source of all their glory. Shall we then forget the manly and dignified sentiments of our ancestors, to prate in the language of the mother or the nurse about our good old prejudices? This is not the way to defend the cause of truth. It was not thus that our fathers maintained it in the brilliant periods of our history. Prejudice may be trusted to guard the outworks for a short space of time, while reason slumbers in the citadel; but if the latter sink into a lethargy, the former will quickly erect a standard for herself. Philosophy, wisdom, and liberty support each other: he who will not reason is a bigot; he who cannot is a fool; and he who dares not is a slave.'—Vol. i, pref., pp. 14, 15.

Page 246, col. 1.

'Like laurels on the bald first Cæsar's head.'] Suetonius informs us that Julius Cæsar was particularly gratified by that decree of the senate which enabled him to wear a wreath of laurel on all occasions. He was anxious, not to show that he was the conqueror of the world, but to hide that he was bald. A stranger at Rome would hardly have guessed at the motive, nor should we without the help of the historian.

Page 246, col. 2.

'While stands the Coliseum, Rome shall stand.'] This is quoted in the 'Decline and Fall of the Roman Empire,' as a proof that the Coliseum was entire, when seen by the Anglo-Saxon pilgrims at the end of the seventh, or the beginning of the eighth, century. A notice on the Coliseum may be seen in the 'Historical Illustrations,' p. 263.

Page 246, col. 2.

'From Jove to Jesus—spared and blest by time.'] 'Though plundered of all its brass, except the ring which was necessary to preserve the aperture above; though exposed to repeated fires; though sometimes flooded by the river, and always open to the rain, no monument of equal antiquity is so well preserved as this rotundo. It passed with little alteration from the Pagan into the present worship; and so convenient were its niches for the Christian altar, that Michael Angelo, ever studious of ancient beauty, introduced their design as a model in the Catholic church.'—Forsyth's Italy, p. 137, 2nd edit.

Page 246, col. 2.

'Their eyes on honour'd forms, whose busts around them close.'] The Pantheon has been made a receptacle for the busts of modern great, or, at least, distinguished men. The flood of light which once fell through the large orb above on the whole circle of divinities, now shines on a numerous assemblage of mortals, some one or two of whom have been almost deified by the veneration of their countrymen. For a notice of the Pantheon, see 'Historical Illustrations,' p. 287.

Page 246, col. 2.

'There is a dungeon, in whose dim drear light.'] This and the three next stanzas allude to the story of the Roman daughter, which is recalled to the traveller by the site, or pretended site, of that adventure, now shown at the church of St. Nicholas in Carcere. The difficulties attending the full belief of the tale are stated in 'Historical Illustrations,' p. 295.

Page 247, col. 2.

'Turn to the mole which Hadrian rear'd on high.'] The castle of St. Angelo. See 'Historical Illustrations.'

Page 247, col. 2.

'But lo! the dome—the vast and wondrous dome.'] This and the six stanzas have a reference to the church of St. Peter's. For a measurement of the comparative length of this basilica and the other great churches of Europe, see the pavement of St. Peter's, and the 'Classical Tour through Italy,' vol. ii. p. 125 et seq., chap. iv.

Page 250, col. 1.

'Nations have arm'd in madness, the strange fate.'] Mary died on the scaffold; Elizabeth of a broken heart; Charles V. a hermit; Louis XIV. a bankrupt in means and glory; Cromwell of anxiety and, 'the greatest is behind,' Napoleon lives a prisoner. To these sovereigns a long but superfluous list might be added of names equally illustrious and unhappy.

Page 250, col. 1.

'Lo, Nemi! navell'd in the woody hills.'] The village of Nemi was near the Arician retreat of Egeria, and, from the shades which embosomed the temple of Diana, has preserved to this day its distinctive appellation of *The Grove*. Nemi is but an evening's ride from the comfortable inn of Albano.

THE GIAOUR

Page 252, col. 1.

'That tomb which, gleaming o'er the cliff.'] A tomb above the rocks on the promontory, by some supposed the sepulchre of Themistocles.

Page 253, col. 1.

'Sultana of the Nightingale.'] The attachment of the nightingale to the rose is a well-known Persian fable. If I mistake not, the 'Bulbul of a thousand tales' is one of his appellations.

Page 253, col. 1.

'Till the gay mariner's guitar.'] The guitar is the constant amusement of the Greek sailor by night; with a steady fair wind, and during a calm, it is accompanied always by the voice, and often by dancing.

Page 253, col. 2.

'Where cold Obstruction's apathy.']

'Ay, but to die and go we know not where,
To lie in cold obstruction?'
Measure for Measure, Act iii. sc. 1.

Page 253, col. 2.

'The first, last look by death reveal'd!'] I trust that few of my readers have ever had an opportunity of witnessing what is here attempted in description; but those who have will probably retain a painful remembrance of that singular beauty which pervades, with few exceptions, the features of the dead, a few hours, and but for a few hours, after 'the spirit is not there.' It is to be remarked in cases of violent death by gun-shot wounds, the expression is always that of languor, whatever the natural energy of the sufferer's character; but in death from a stab the countenance preserves its traits of feeling or ferocity, and the mind its bias, to the last.

Page 254, col. 1.

'Slaves—nay, the bondsmen of a slave.'] Athens is the property of the Kislar Aga (the slave of the seraglio and guardian of the women), who appoints the Waywode. A pander and eunuch—these are not polite, yet true appellations—now *governs* the *governor* of Athens!

Page 254, col. 2.

'In echoes of the far tophaike.'] 'Tophaike,' musket. The Bairam is announced by the cannon at sunset: the illumination of the mosques, and the firing of all kinds of small arms, loaded with *ball*, proclaim it during the night.

Page 254, col. 2.

'Swift as the hurl'd on high jerreed.'] Jerreed, or Djerrid, a blunted Turkish javelin, which is darted from horseback with great force and precision. It is a favourite exercise of the Mussulmans; but I know not if it can be called a *manly* one, since the most expert in the art are the Black Eunuchs of Constantinople. I think, next to these, a Mamlouk at Smyrna was the most skilful that came within my observation.

Page 255, col. 1.

'He came, he went, like the simoom.'] The blast of the desert, fatal to every thing living, and often alluded to in eastern poetry.

Page 255, col. 2.

'To bless the sacred "bread and salt."'] To partake of food, to break bread and salt with your host, insures the safety of the guest: even though an enemy, his person from that moment is sacred.

Page 255, col. 2.

'Since his turban was cleft by the infidel's sabre!'] I need hardly observe, that Charity and Hospitality are the first duties enjoined by Mahomet; and to say truth, very generally practised by his disciples. The first praise that can be bestowed on a chief is a panegyric on his bounty; the next, on his valour.

Page 255, col. 2.

'And silver-sheathed ataghan.'] The ataghan, a long dagger worn with pistols in the belt, in a metal scabbard, generally of silver; and, among the wealthier, gilt, or of gold.

Page 255, col. 2.

'An Emir by his garb of green.'] Green is the privileged colour of the prophet's numerous pretended descendants; with them, as here, faith (the family inheritance) is supposed to supersede the necessity of good works: they are the worst of a very indifferent brood.

Page 255, col. 2.

'"Ho! who art thou?"—"This low salam."'] 'Salam aleikoum! aleikoum salam!' peace be with you; be with you peace—the salutation reserved for the faithful:—to a Christian, 'Urlarula,'[a good journey; or 'saban hiresem, saban serula;' good morn, good even; and sometimes, 'may your end be happy;' are the usual salutes.

Page 256, col. 1.

'The insect queen of eastern spring.'] The blue-winged butterfly of Kashmeer, the most rare and beautiful of the species.

Page 256, col. 2.

'Is like the Scorpion girt by fire.'] Alluding to the dubious suicide of the scorpion, so placed for experiment by gentle philosophers. Some maintain that the position of the sting, when turned towards the head, is merely a convulsive movement; but others have actually brought in the verdict 'Felo de se.' The scorpions are surely interested in a speedy decision of the question; as, if once fairly established as insect Catos, they will probably be allowed to live as long as they think proper, without being martyred for the sake of an hypothesis.

Page 256, col. 2.

'When Rhamazan's last sun was set.'] The cannon at sunset close the Rhamazan.

Page 256, col. 2.

By pale Phingari's trembling light.'] Phingari, the moon.

Page 256, col. 2.

'Bright as the jewel of Giamschid.'] The celebrated fabulous ruby of Sultan Giamschid, the embellisher of Istakhar; from its splendour, named Schebgerag, 'the torch of night;' also 'the cup of the sun,' &c. In the first edition, 'Giamschid' was written as a word of three syllables; so D'Herbelot has it; but I am told Richardson reduces it to a dissyllable, and writes 'Jamshid.' I have left in the text the orthography of the one with the pronunciation of the other.

NOTES TO THE GIAOUR

Page 257, col. 1.

'Though on Al-Sirat's arch I stood.'] Al-Sirat, the bridge of breath, narrower than the thread of a famished spider, and sharper than the edge of a sword, over which the Mussulmans must *skate* into Paradise, to which it is the only entrance; but this is not the worst, the river beneath being hell itself, into which, as may be expected, the unskilful and tender of foot contrive to tumble with a 'facilis descensus Averni,' not very pleasing in prospect to the next passenger. There is a shorter cut downwards for the Jews and Christians.

Page 257, col. 1.

'A soulless toy for tyrant's lust?'] A vulgar error; the Koran allots at least a third of Paradise to well-behaved women; but by far the greater number of Mussulmans interpret the text their own way, and exclude their moieties from heaven. Being enemies to Platonics, they cannot discern 'any fitness of things' in the souls of the other sex, conceiving them to be superseded by the Houris.

Page 257, col. 1.

'The young pomegranate's blossoms strew.'] An oriental simile, which may, perhaps, though fairly stolen, be deemed 'plus Arabe qu'en Arabie.'

Page 257, col. 1.

'Her hair in hyacinthine flow.'] Hyacinthine, in Arabic 'Sunbul;' as common a thought in the eastern poets as it was among the Greeks.

Page 257, col. 1.

'The loveliest bird of Franguestan!'] 'Franguestan,' Circassia.

Page 257, col. 2.

'Bismillah! now the peril's past.'] 'In the name of God;' the commencement of all the chapters of the Koran but one, and of prayer and thanksgiving.

Page 257, col. 2.

'Then curl'd his very beard with ire.'] A phenomenon not uncommon with an angry Mussulman. In 1809, the Capitan Pacha's whiskers at a diplomatic audience were no less lively with indignation than a tiger cat's, to the horror of all the dragomans; the portentous mustachios twisted, they stood erect of their own accord, and were expected every moment to change their colour, but at last condescended to subside, which, probably, saved more heads than they contained hairs.

Page 258, col. 1.

'Nor raised the craven cry, Amaun!'] 'Amaun,' quarter, pardon.

Page 258, col. 1.

'I know him by the evil eye.'] The 'evil eye,' a common superstition in the Levant, and of which the imaginary effects are yet very singular on those who conceive themselves affected.

Page 258, col. 2.

'A fragment of his palampore.'] The flowered shawls generally worn by persons of rank.

Page 259, col. 1.

'His calpac rent—his caftan red.'] The calpac is the solid cap or centre part of the head-dress; the shawl is wound round it, and forms the turban.

Page 259, col. 1.

'A turban carved in coarsest stone.'] The turban, pillar, and inscriptive verse, decorate the tombs of the Osmanlies, whether in the cemetery or the wilderness. In the mountains you frequently pass similar mementos; and on inquiry you are informed that they record some victim of rebellion, plunder, or revenge.

Page 259, col. 1.

'At solemn sound of "Alla Hu!"'] 'Alla Hu!' the concluding words ·of the Muezzin's call to prayer from the highest gallery on the exterior of the Minaret. On a still evening, when the Muezzin has a fine voice, which is frequently the case, the effect is solemn and beautiful beyond all the bells in Christendom.

Page 259, col. 1.

'They come—their kerchiefs green they wave.'] The following is part of a battle song of the Turks: —'I see—I see a dark-eyed girl of Paradise, and she waves a handkerchief, a kerchief of green; and cries aloud, "Come, kiss me, for I love thee,"' &c.

Page 259, col. 1.

'Beneath avenging Monkir's scythe.'] Monkir and Nekir are the inquisitors of the dead, before whom the corpse undergoes a slight noviciate and preparatory training for damnation. If the answers are none of the clearest, he is hauled up with a scythe and thumped down with a red-hot mace till properly seasoned, with a variety of subsidiary probations. The office of these angels is no sinecure; there are but two, and the number of orthodox deceased being in a small proportion to the remainder, their hands are always full. See Relig. Ceremon. and Sale's Koran.

Page 259, col. 1.

'To wander round lost Eblis' throne.'] Eblis, the Oriental Prince of Darkness.

Page 259, col. 1.

'But first, on earth as Vampire sent.'] The Vampire superstition is still general in the Levant. Honest Tournefort tells a long story, which Mr. Southey, in the notes on Thalaba, quotes, about these 'Vroucolochas,' as he calls them. The Romaic term is 'Vardoulacha.' I recollect a whole family being terrified by the scream of a child, which they imagined must proceed from such a visitation. The Greeks never mention the word without horror. I find that 'Broucolokas' is an old legitimate Hellenic appellation—at least is so applied to Arsenius, who, according to the Greeks, was after his death animated by the Devil. The moderns, however, use the word I mention.

Page 259, col. 2.

'Thy gnashing tooth and haggard lip.'] The freshness of the face, and the wetness of the lip with blood, are the never-failing signs of a Vampire. The stories told in Hungary and Greece of these foul feeders are singular, and some of them most *incredibly* attested.

Page 261, col. 1.

'It is as if the desert bird.'] The pelican is I believe, the bird so libelled, by the imputation of feeding her chickens with her blood.

Page 262, col. 1.

'Deep in whose darkly boding ear.'] This superstition of a second-hearing (for I never met with downright second-sight in the East) fell once under my own observation. On my third journey to Cape Colonna, early in 1811, as we passed through the defile that leads from the hamlet between Kerati

and Colonna, I observed Dervish Tahiri riding rather out of the path, and leaning his head upon his hand, as if in pain. I rode up and inquired. 'We are in peril,' he answered. 'What peril? we are not now in Albania, nor in the passes to Ephesus, Messalunghi, or Lepanto; there are plenty of us, well armed, and the Choriates have not courage to be thieves.'—'True, Affendi, but nevertheless the shot is ringing in my ears.'—'The shot! not a top-haike has been fired this morning.'—'I hear it not-withstanding—Bom—Bom—as plainly as I hear your voice.'—'Psha!'—'As you please, Affendi; if it is written, so will it be.'—I left this quick-eared predestinarian, and rode up to Basili, his Christian compatriot, whose ears, though not at all pro-phetic, by no means relished the intelligence. We all arrived at Colonna, remained some hours, and returned leisurely, saying a variety of brilliant things, in more languages than spoiled the building of Babel, upon the mistaken seer. Romaic, Arna-out, Turkish, Italian, and English, were all exer-cised, in various conceits, upon the unfortunate Mussulman. While we were contemplating the beautiful prospect, Dervish was occupied about the columns. I thought he was deranged into an antiquarian, and asked him if he had become a 'Palaocastro' man? 'No,' said he, 'but these pillars will be useful in making a stand;' and added other remarks, which at least evinced his own belief in his troublesome faculty of *forehearing*. On our return to Athens we heard from Leoné (a prisoner set ashore some days after) of the intended attack of the Mainotes, mentioned, with the cause of its not taking place, in the notes to Childe Harold, Canto 2nd. I was at some pains to question the man, and he described the dresses, arms, and marks of the horses of our party so accurately, that, with other circumstances, we could not doubt of *his* having been in 'villainous company,' and ourselves in a bad neighbourhood. Dervish became a sooth-sayer for life, and I dare say is now hearing more musketry than ever will be fired, to the great re-freshment of the Arnaouts of Berat, and his native mountains.—I shall mention one trait more of this singular race. In March, 1811, a remarkably stout and active Arnaout came (I believe the fiftieth on the same errand) to offer himself as an attendant, which was declined: 'Well, Affendi,' quoth he, 'may you live!—you would have found me useful. I shall leave the town for the hills to-morrow; in the winter I return, perhaps you will then receive me,'—Dervish, who was present, remarked as a thing of course, and of no consequence, 'in the mean time he will join the Klephtes' (robbers), which was true to the letter. If not cut off, they come down in the winter, and pass it unmolested in some town, where they are often as well known as their exploits.

Page 263, col. 1.

'Looks not to priesthood for relief.'] The monk's sermon is omitted. It seems to have had so little effect upon the patient, that it could have no hopes from the reader. It may be sufficient to say, that it was of a customary length (as may be perceived from the interruptions and uneasiness of the patient), and was delivered in the usual tone of all orthodox preachers.

Page 263, col. 2.

'And shining in her white symar.'] 'Symar,' a shroud.

Page 264, col. 2.

'Or stay the passing pilgrim's tread.'] The cir-cumstance to which the above story relates was not very uncommon in Turkey. A few years ago the wife of Muchtar Pacha complained to his father of his son's supposed infidelity; he asked with whom, and she had the barbarity to give in a list of the twelve handsomest women in Yanina. They were seized, fastened up in sacks, and drowned in the lake the same night! One of the guards who was present informed me, that not one of the victims uttered a cry, or showed a symptom of terror, at so sudden a 'wrench from all we know, from all we love.' The fate of Phrosine, the fairest of this sacrifice, is the subject of many a Romaic and Arnaout ditty. The story in the text is one told of a young Venetian many years ago, and now nearly forgotten. I heard it by accident recited by one of the coffee-house story-tellers who abound in the Levant, and sing or recite their narratives. The additions and interpolations by the translator will be easily distinguished from the rest, by the want of Eastern imagery; and I regret that my memory has retained so few fragments of the ori-ginal. For the contents of some of the notes I am indebted partly to D'Herbelot, and partly to that most Eastern, and, as Mr. Weber justly entitles it, 'sublime tale,' the 'Caliph Vathek.' I do not know from what source the author of that singular volume may have drawn his materials; some of his incidents are to be found in the 'Bibliothèque Orientale;' but for correctness of costume, beauty of description, and power of imagination, it far surpasses all European imitations: and bears such marks of originality, that those who have visited the East will find some difficulty in believing it to be more than a translation. As an Eastern tale, even Rasselas must bow before it; his 'Happy Valley' will not bear a comparison with the 'Hall of Eblis.'

THE BRIDE OF ABYDOS

Page 264, col. 1.

'Wax faint o'er the gardens of Gúl in her bloom.'] 'Gúl,' the rose.

Page 264, col. 2.

'Can he smile on such deeds as his children have done?']

'Souls made of fire, and children of the Sun,
With whom revenge is virtue.'—
 YOUNG's *Revenge*.

Page 265, col. 2.

'With Mejnoun's tale, or Sadi's song.'] Mejnoun and Leila, the Romeo and Juliet of the East. Sadi, the moral poet of Persia.

Page 265, col. 1.

'Till I, who heard the deep tambour.'] Tam-bour, Turkish drum, which sounds at sunrise, noon, and twilight.

Page 266, col. 1.

'He is an Arab to my sight.'] The Turks abhor the Arabs (who return the compliment a hundred-fold) even more than they hate the Christians.

Page 266, col. 1.

'The mind, the Music breathing from her face.'] This expression has met with objections. I will not refer to 'Him who hath not Music in his soul,' but merely request the reader to recollect, for ten seconds, the features of the woman whom he be-lieves to be the most beautiful; and, if he then does not comprehend fully what is feebly expressed in the above line, I shall be sorry for us both. For

NOTES TO THE BRIDE OF ABYDOS

an eloquent passage in the latest work of the first female writer of this, perhaps of any age, on the analogy (and the immediate comparison excited by that analogy) between 'painting and music,' see vol. iii. cap. 10, DE L'ALLEMAGNE. And is not this connexion still stronger with the original than the copy? with the colouring of Nature than of Art? After all, this is rather to be felt than described; still I think there are some who will understand it, at least they would have done had they beheld the countenance whose speaking harmony suggested the idea; for this passage is not drawn from imagination but memory, that mirror which Affliction dashes to the earth, and looking down upon the fragments, only beholds the reflection multiplied!

Page 266, col. 2.

'But yet the line of Carasman.'] Carasman Oglou, or Kara Osman Oglou, is the principal land-holder in Turkey; he governs Magnesia: those who, by a kind of feudal tenure, possess land on condition of service, are called Timariots: they serve as Spahis, according to the extent of territory, and bring a certain number into the field, generally cavalry.

Page 266, col. 2.

'And teach the messenger what fate.'] When a Pacha is sufficiently strong to resist, the single messenger, who is always the first bearer of the order for his death, is strangled instead, and sometimes five or six, one after the other, on the same errand, by command of the refractory patient; if, on the contrary, he is weak or loyal, he bows, kisses the Sultan's respectable signature, and is bowstrung with great complacency. In 1810, several of these presents were exhibited in the niche of the Seraglio gate; among others the head of the Pacha of Bagdat, a brave young man, cut off by treachery, after a desperate resistance.

Page 266, col. 2.

'Thrice clapp'd his hands, and call'd his steed.'] Clapping of the hands calls the servants. The Turks hate a superfluous expenditure of voice, and they have no bells.

Page 266, col. 2.

'Resign'd his gem-adorn'd chibouque.'] 'Chibouque,' the Turkish pipe, of which the amber mouth-piece, and sometimes the ball which contains the leaf, is adorned with precious stones, if in possession of the wealthier orders.

Page 267, col. 1.

'With Maugrabee and Mamaluke.'] 'Maugrabee,' Moorish mercenaries.

Page 267, col. 1.

'His way amid his Delis took.'] 'Delis,' bravos who form the forlorn hope of the cavalry, and always begin the action.

Page 267, col. 1.

'Careering cleave the folded felt.'] A twisted fold of *felt* is used for scimitar practice by the Turks, and few but Mussulman arms can cut through it at a single stroke: sometimes a tough turban is used for the same purpose. The jerreed is a game of blunt javelins, animated and graceful.

Page 267, col. 1.

'Nor heard their Ollahs wild and loud.'] 'Ollahs,' Alla il Allah, the 'Leilies,' as the Spanish poets call them, the sound is Ollah; a cry of which the Turks, for a silent people, are somewhat profuse, particularly during the jerreed, or in the chase, but mostly in battle. Their animation in the field, and gravity in the chamber, with their pipes and comboloios, form an amusing contrast.

Page 267, col. 1.

'The Persian Atar-gul's perfume.'] 'Atar-gul, ottar of roses. The Persian is the finest.

Page 267, col. 1.

'The pictured roof and marble floor.'] The ceiling and wainscots, or rather walls, of the Mussulman apartments are generally painted, in great houses, with one eternal and highly-coloured view of Constantinople, wherein the principal feature is a noble contempt of perspective; below, arms, scimitars, &c., are, in general, fancifully and not inelegantly disposed.

Page 267, col. 2.

'A message from the Bulbul bears.'] It has been much doubted whether the notes of this 'Lover of the rose' are sad or merry; and Mr. Fox's remarks on the subject have provoked some learned controversy as to the opinions of the ancients on the subject. I dare not venture a conjecture on the point, though a little inclined to the 'errare malem,' &c., *if* Mr. Fox *was* mistaken.

Page 267, col. 2.

'Ev'n Azrael, from his deadly quiver.'] 'Azrael,' the angel of death.

Page 268, col. 1.

'Within the caves of Istakar.'] The treasures of the Pre-Adamite Sultans. See D'Herbelot, article *Istakar.*

Page 268, col. 1.

'Holds not a Musselim's control.'] 'Musselim,' a governor, the next in rank after a Pacha; a Waywode is the third; and then come the Agas.

Page 268, col. 1.

'Was he not bred in Egripo?'] 'Egripo,' the Negropont. According to the proverb, the Turks of Egripo, the Jews of Salonica, and the Greeks of Athens, are the worst of their respective races.

Page 269, col. 1.

'Ah! yonder see the Tchocadar.'] 'Tchocadar' —one of the attendants who precedes a man of authority.

Page 269, col. 2.

'Thine own "broad Hellespont" still dashes.'] The wrangling about this epithet, 'the broad Hellespont' or the 'boundless Hellespont,' whether it means one or the other, or what it means at all, has been beyond all possibility of detail. I have even heard it disputed on the spot; and not foreseeing a speedy conclusion to the controversy, amused myself with swimming across it in the mean time; and probably may again, before the point is settled. Indeed, the question as to the truth of 'the tale of Troy divine' still continues, much of it resting upon the talismanic word 'ἄπειρος: probably Homer had the same notion of distance that a coquette has of time; and when he talks of boundless, means half a mile; as the latter, by a like figure, when she says *eternal* attachment simply specifies three weeks.

NOTES TO THE BRIDE OF ABYDOS

Page 269, col. 2.

'Which Ammon's son ran proudly round.'] Before his Persian invasion, and crowned the altar with laurels, &c. He was afterwards imitated by Caracalla in his race. It is believed that the last also poisoned a friend, named Festus, for the sake of new Patroclan games. I have seen the sheep feeding on the tombs of Æsietes and Antilochus: the first is in the centre of the plain.

Page 270, col. 1.

'O'er which her fairy fingers ran.'] When rubbed, the amber is susceptible of a perfume, which is light, but *not* disagreeable.

Page 270, col. 1.

'Her mother's sainted amulet.'] The belief in amulets engraved on gems, or enclosed in gold boxes, containing scraps from the Koran, worn round the neck, wrist, or arm, is still universal in the East. The Koorsee (throne) verse in the second cap. of the Koran describes the attributes of the Most High, and is engraved in this manner, and worn by the pious, as the most esteemed and sublime of all sentences.

Page 270, col. 1.

'And by her comboloio lies.'] 'Comboloio'— Turkish rosary. The MSS., particularly those of the Persians, are richly adorned and illuminated. The Greek females are kept in utter ignorance; but many of the Turkish girls are highly accomplished, though not actually qualified for a Christian coterie. Perhaps some of our own '*blues*' might not be the worse for *bleaching*.

Page 270, col. 2.

'In him was some young Galiongée.'] 'Galiongée'—or Galiongi, a sailor, that is, a Turkish sailor; the Greeks navigate, the Turks work the guns. Their dress is picturesque; and I have seen the Capitan Pacha, more than once, wearing it as a kind of *incog*. Their legs, however, are generally naked. The buskins described in the text as sheathed behind with silver are those of an Arnaut robber, who was my host (he had quitted the profession) at his Pyrgo, near Gastouni in the Morea; they were plated in scales one over the other, like the back of an armadillo.

Page 271, col. 1.

'So may the Koran verse display'd.'] The characters on all Turkish scimitars contain sometimes the name of the place of their manufacture, but more generally a text from the Koran, in letters of gold. Amongst those in my possession is one with a blade of singular construction: it is very broad, and the edge notched into serpentine curves like the ripple of water, or the wavering of flame. I asked the Armenian who sold it, what possible use such a figure could add: he said, in Italian, that he did not know; but the Mussulmans had an idea that those of this form gave a severer wound; and liked it because it was 'piu feroce.' I did not much admire the reason, but bought it for its peculiarity.

Page 271, col. 1.

'But like the nephew of a Cain.'] It is to be observed, that every allusion to any thing or personage in the Old Testament, such as the Ark, or Cain, is equally the privilege of Mussulman and Jew: indeed, the former profess to be much better acquainted with the lives, true and fabulous, of the patriarchs, than is warranted by our own sacred writ; and not content with Adam, they have a biography of Pre-Adamites. Solomon is the monarch of all necromancy, and Moses a prophet inferior only to Christ and Mahomet. Zuleika is the Persian name of Potiphar's wife; and her amour with Joseph constitutes one of the finest poems in their language. It is, therefore, no violation of costume to put the names of Cain, or Noah, into the mouth of a Moslem.

Page 271, col. 2.

'And Paswan's rebel hordes attest.'] Paswan Oglou, the rebel of Widdin: who, for the last years of his life, set the whole power of the Porte at defiance.

Page 271, col. 2.

'They gave their horse-tails to the wind.'] Horse-tail,' the standard of a Pacha.

Page 271, col. 2.

'He drank one draught, nor needed more!'] Giaffir, Pacha of Argyro Castro, or Scutari, I am not sure which, was actually taken off by the Albanian Ali, in the manner described in the text. Ali Pacha, while I was in the country, married the daughter of his victim, some years after the event had taken place at a bath in Sophia, or Adrianople. The poison was mixed in the cup of coffee, which is presented before the sherbet by the bath keeper, after dressing.

Page 272, col. 2.

'I sought by turns, and saw them all.'] The Turkish notions of almost all islands are confined to the Archipelago, the sea alluded to.

Page 273, col. 1.

'The last of Lambro's patriots there.'] Lambro Canzani, a Greek, famous for his efforts, in 1789–90, for the independence of his country. Abandoned by the Russians, he became a pirate, and the Archipelago was the scene of his enterprises. He is said to be still alive at Petersburg. He and Riga are the two most celebrated of the Greek revolutionists.

Page 273, col. 1.

'To snatch the Rayahs from their fate.'] 'Rayahs,'—all who pay the capitation tax, called the 'Haratch.'

Page 273, col. 1.

'Ay! let me like the ocean-Patriarch roam.'] This first of voyages is one of the few with which the Mussulmans profess much acquaintance.

Page 273, col. 1.

'Or only know on land the Tartar's home!'] The wandering life of the Arabs, Tartars, and Turkomans, will be found well detailed in any book of Eastern travels. That it possesses a charm peculiar to itself, cannot be denied. A young French renegado confessed to Chateaubriand, that he never found himself alone, galloping in the desert, without a sensation approaching to rapture which was indescribable.

Page 273, col. 1.

'Blooming as Aden in its earliest hour.'] 'Jannat al Aden,' the perpetual abode, the Mussulman paradise.

Page 275, col. 2.

'And mourn'd above his turban-stone.'] A turban is carved in stone above the graves of *men* only.

897

NOTES TO THE CORSAIR

Page 275, col. 2.

'The loud Wul-wulleh warn his distant ear?']
The death-song of the Turkish women. The 'silent
slaves' are the men, whose notions of decorum for-
bid complaint in *public*.

Page 276, col. 1.

'"Where is my child?"—an Echo answers—
"Where?"'] 'I came to the place of my birth, and
cried, "The friends of my youth, where are they?"
and an Echo answered, "Where are they?"'—
From an Arabic MS. The above quotation (from
which the idea in the text is taken) must be already
familiar to every reader; it is given in the first an-
notation, p. 67, of 'The Pleasures of Memory;'
a poem so well known as to render a reference
almost superfluous; but to whose pages all will be
delighted to recur.

Page 276, col. 2.

'Will shape and syllable its sound.']

'And airy tongues that *syllable* men's names.'
 MILTON.

For a belief that the souls of the dead inhabit the
form of birds, we need not travel to the East. Lord
Lyttelton's ghost story, the belief of the Duchess of
Kendal, that George I. flew into her window in the
shape of a raven (see 'Orford's Reminiscences'),
and many other instances, bring this superstition
nearer home. The most singular was the whim of
a Worcester lady, who, believing her daughter to
exist in the shape of a singing bird, literally fur-
nished her pew in the cathedral with cages full of
the kind; and as she was rich, and a benefactress in
beautifying the church, no objection was made to
her harmless folly. For this anecdote, see 'Orford's
Letters.'

THE CORSAIR

Page 277.

'The Corsair.'] The time in this poem may seem
too short for the occurrences, but the whole of
the Ægean isles are within a few hours' sail of the
continent, and the reader must be kind enough to
take the *wind* as I have often found it.

Page 281, col. 1.

'Hope withering fled, and Mercy sigh'd fare-
well!'] That Conrad is a character not altogether
out of nature, I shall attempt to prove by some
historical coincidences which I have met with since
writing 'The Corsair.'
 'Eccelin prisonnier,' dit Rolandini, 's'enfermoit
dans un silence menaçant, il fixoit sur la terre son
visage féroce, et ne donnoit point d'essor à sa pro-
fonde indignation. De toutes partes cependant les
soldats et les peuples accouroient; ils vouloient voir
cet homme, jadis si puissant, et la joie universelle
éclatoit de toutes partes. * * * * Eccelin étoit d'une
petite taille; mais tout l'aspect de sa personne, tous
ses mouvemens, indiquoient un soldat.—Son lan-
gage étoit amer, son déportement superbe—et par
son seul égard, il faisoit trembler les plus hardis.'
—*Sismondi*, tome iii. p. 219.
 Again, 'Gizericus (Genseric, king of the Van-
dals, the conqueror of both Carthage and Rome),
staturâ mediocris, et equi casu claudicans, animo
profundus, sermone rarus, luxuriæ contemptor, irâ
turbidus, habendi cupidus, ad solicitandas gentes
providentissimus,' &c. &c.—*Jornandes de Rebus
Geticis*, c. 33.
 I beg leave to quote these gloomy realities to
keep in countenance my Giaour and Corsair.

Page 284, col. 1.

'Of fair Olympia loved and left of old.'] Orlando
Furioso, Canto x.

Page 285, col. 2.

'Around the waves' phosphoric brightness
broke.'] By night, particularly in a warm latitude,
every stroke of the oar, every motion of the boat
or ship, is followed by a slight flash like sheet
lightning from the water.

Page 286, col. 2.

'Though to the rest the sober berry's juice.'
Coffee.

Page 286, col. 2.

'The long chibouque's dissolving cloud supply.'
'Chibouque,' pipe.

Page 286, col. 2.

'While dance the Almas to wild minstrelsy.'
Dancing girls.

Page 286, col. 2.

'Escaped, is here—himself would tell the rest.'
It has been observed, that Conrad's entering dis
guised as a spy is out of nature. Perhaps so. I find
something not unlike it in history.—'Anxious to
explore with his own eyes the state of the Vandals,
Majorian ventured, after disguising the colour o
his hair, to visit Carthage in the character of hi
own ambassador; and Genseric was afterward
mortified by the discovery, that he had entertained
and dismissed the Emperor of the Romans. Such
an anecdote may be rejected as an improbable fic
tion: but it is a fiction which would not have bee
imagined unless in the life of a hero.'—See GIB
BON's Decline and Fall, vol. vi. p. 180.

Page 287, col. 2.

'And my stern vow and order's laws oppose.'
The Dervises are in colleges, and of differen
orders, as the monks.

Page 288, col. 1.

'*They* seize that Dervise!—seize on Zatanai!'
'Zatanai,' Satan.

Page 288, col. 2.

'He tore his beard, and foaming fled the fight.'
A common and not very novel effect of Mussulma
anger. See Prince Eugene's Memoirs, page 24
'The Seraskier received a wound in the thigh; h
plucked up his beard by the roots, because he wa
obliged to quit the field.'

Page 289, col. 1.

'Brief time had Conrad now to greet Gulnare.'
Gulnare, a female name; it means, literally, th
flower of the pomegranate.

Page 292, col. 1.

'Till even the scaffold echoes with their jest!'
In Sir Thomas More, for instance, on the scaffold
and Anne Boleyn, in the Tower, when, graspin
her neck, she remarked, that it 'was too slender t
trouble the headsman much.' During one part o
the French Revolution, it became a fashion t
leave some '*mot*' as a legacy; and the quantity o
facetious last words spoken during that perio
would form a melancholy jest-book of a considera
able size.

Page 293, col. 1.

'Slow sinks, more lovely ere his race be run.']
The opening lines, as far as section ii., have, perhaps, little business here, and were annexed to an unpublished (though printed) poem ['The Curse of Minerva']; but they were written on the spot, in the Spring of 1814, and—I scarce know why—the reader must excuse their appearance here—if he can.

Page 294, col. 1.

'That closed their murder'd sage's latest day!']
Socrates drank the hemlock a short time before sunset (the hour of execution), notwithstanding the intreaties of his disciples to wait till the sun went down.

Page 294, col. 1.

'The queen of night asserts her silent reign.']
The twilight in Greece is much shorter than in our own country; the days in winter are longer, but in summer of shorter duration.

Page 294, col. 1.

'The gleaming turret of the gay kiosk.'] The Kiosk is a Turkish summer-house: the palm is without the present walls of Athens, not far from the temple of Theseus, between which and the tree the wall intervenes.—Cephisus' stream is indeed scanty, and Ilissus has no stream at all.

Page 295, col. 2.

'His only bends in seeming o'er his beads.'] The omboloio, or Mahometan rosary; the beads are in number ninety-nine.

Page 301, col. 2.

'And the cold flowers her colder hand contain'd.'] In the Levant it is the custom to strew flowers on the bodies of the dead, and in the hands of young persons to place a nosegay.

Page 303, col. 2.

'Link'd with one virtue, and a thousand crimes.'] That the point of honour which is represented in one instance of Conrad's character has not been carried beyond the bounds of probability, may perhaps be in some degree confirmed by the following anecdote of a brother buccaneer in the year 1814:—'Our readers have all seen the account of the enterprise against the pirates of Barrataria; but few, we believe, were informed of the situation, history, or nature of that establishment. For the information of such as were unacquainted with it, we have procured from a friend the following interesting narrative of the main facts, of which he has personal knowledge, and which cannot fail to interest some of our readers:—Barrataria is a bay, or a narrow arm, of the Gulf of Mexico; it runs through a rich but very flat country, until it reaches within a mile of the Mississippi river, fifteen miles below the city of New Orleans. The bay has ranches almost innumerable, in which persons can lie concealed from the severest scrutiny. It communicates with three lakes which lie on the same name, and which lies contiguous to the sea, where there is an island formed by the two arms of this lake and the sea. The east and west points of this island were fortified, in the year 1811, by a band of pirates, under the command of one Monsieur La Fitte. A large majority of these outlaws are of that class of the population of the state of Louisiana who fled from the island of St. Domingo during the troubles there, and took refuge in the island of Cuba; and when the last war between France and Spain commenced, they were compelled to leave that island with the short notice of a few days. Without ceremony they entered the United States, the most of them the state of Louisiana, with all the negroes they had possessed in Cuba. They were notified by the Governor of that State of the clause in the constitution which forbade the importation of slaves; but, at the same time, received the assurance of the Governor that he would obtain, if possible, the approbation of the General Government for their retaining this property.—The island of Barrataria is situated about lat. 29 deg. 15 min., lon. 92. 30.; and is as remarkable for its health as for the superior scale and shell fish with which its waters abound. The chief of this horde, like Charles de Moor, had, mixed with his many vices, some virtues. In the year 1813, this party had, from its turpitude and boldness, claimed the attention of the Governor of Louisiana; and to break up the establishment he thought proper to strike at the head. He therefore offered a reward of 500 dollars for the head of Monsieur La Fitte, who was well known to the inhabitants of the city of New Orleans, from his immediate connexion, and his once having been a fencing-master in that city of great reputation, which art he learnt in Buonaparte's army, where he was a captain. The reward which was offered by the Governor for the head of La Fitte was answered by the offer of a reward from the latter of 15,000 for the head of the Governor. The Governor ordered out a company to march from the city to La Fitte's island, and to burn and destroy all the property, and to bring to the city of New Orleans all his banditti. This company, under the command of a man who had been the intimate associate of this bold Captain, approached very near to the fortified island, before he saw a man, or heard a sound, until he heard a whistle, not unlike a boatswain's call. Then it was he found himself surrounded by armed men who had emerged from the secret avenues which led into Bayou. Here it was that the modern Charles de Moor developed his few noble traits; for to this man, who had come to destroy his life and all that was dear to him, he not only spared his life, but offered him that which would have made the honest soldier easy for the remainder of his days; which was indignantly refused. He then, with the approbation of his captor, returned to the city. This circumstance, and some concomitant events, proved that this band of pirates was not to be taken by land. Our naval force having always been small in that quarter, exertions for the destruction of this illicit establishment could not be expected from them until augmented: for an officer of the navy, with most of the gun-boats on that station, had to retreat from an overwhelming force of La Fitte's. So soon as the augmentation of the navy authorized an attack, one was made; the overthrow of this banditti has been the result: and now this almost invulnerable point and key to New Orleans is clear of an enemy, it is to be hoped the government will hold it by a strong military force.'—*American Newspaper.*

In Noble's continuation of 'Granger's Biographical History' there is a singular passage in his account of Archbishop Blackbourne; and as in some measure connected with the profession of the hero of the foregoing poem, I cannot resist the temptation of extracting it.—'There is something mysterious in the history and character of Dr.

NOTES TO LARA

Blackbourne. The former is but imperfectly known; and report has even asserted he was a buccaneer; and that one of his brethren in that profession having asked, on his arrival in England, what had become of his old chum, Blackbourne, was answered, he is Archbishop of York. We are informed that Blackbourne was installed sub-dean of Exeter in 1694, which office he resigned in 1702; but after his successor Lewis Barnet's death, in 1704, he regained it. In the following year he became dean; and in 1714 held with it the archdeaconry of Cornwall. He was consecrated bishop of Exeter, February 24, 1716; and translated to York, November 28, 1724, as a reward, according to court scandal, for uniting George I. to the Duchess of Munster. This, however, appears to have been an unfounded calumny. As archbishop he behaved with great prudence, and was equally respectable as the guardian of the revenues of the see. Rumour whispered he retained the vices of his youth, and that a passion for the fair sex formed an item in the list of his weaknesses; but so far from being convicted by seventy witnesses, he does not appear to have been directly criminated by one. In short, I look upon these aspersions as the effects of mere malice. How is it possible a buccaneer should have been so good a scholar as Blackbourne certainly was? He who had so perfect a knowledge of the classics (particularly of the Greek tragedians), as to be able to read them with the same ease as he could Shakespeare, must have taken great pains to acquire the learned languages; and have had both leisure and good masters. But he was undoubtedly educated at Christ-church College, Oxford. He is allowed to have been a pleasant man; this, however, was turned against him, by its being said, "he gained more hearts than souls."'

'The only voice that could soothe the passions of the savage (Alphonso III.) was that of an amiable and virtuous wife, the sole object of his love; the voice of Donna Isabella, the daughter of the Duke of Savoy, and the grand-daughter of Philip II. King of Spain.—Her dying words sunk deep into his memory; his fierce spirit melted into tears; and, after the last embrace, Alphonso retired into his chamber to bewail his irreparable loss, and to meditate on the vanity of human life.'—*Gibbon's Miscellaneous Works*, vol. iii. p. 473.

LARA

Page 303, col. 1.

'The Serfs are glad through Lara's wide domain.'] The reader is apprised, that the name of Lara being Spanish, and no circumstance of local and natural description fixing the scene or hero of the poem to any country or age, the word 'Serf,' which could not be correctly applied to the lower classes in Spain, who were never vassals of the soil, has nevertheless been employed to designate the followers of our fictitious chieftain.

Page 318, col. 2.

'A Serf that cross'd the intervening vale.'] The event in this section was suggested by the description of the death, or rather burial, of the Duke of Gandia. The most interesting and particular account of it is given by Burchard, and is in substance as follows:—'On the eighth day of June, the Cardinal of Valenza and the Duke of Gandia, sons of the pope, supped with their mother, Vanozza, near the church of *S. Pietro ad vincula;* several other persons being present at the entertainment. A late hour approaching, and the cardinal having reminded his brother that it was time to return to the apostolic palace, they mounted their horses or mules, with only a few attendants, and proceeded together as far as the Palace of Cardinal Ascanio Sforza, when the duke informed the cardinal that before he returned home, he had to pay a visit of pleasure. Dismissing therefore all his attendants excepting his *staffiero,* or footman, and a person in a mask, who had paid him a visit whilst at supper, and who, during the space of a month or there abouts, previous to this time, had called upon him almost daily at the apostolic palace, he took this person behind him on his mule, and proceeded to the street of the Jews, where he quitted his servant directing him to remain there until a certain hour when, if he did not return, he might repair to the palace. The duke then seated the person in the mask behind him, and rode, I know not whither but in that night he was assassinated, and throw into the river. The servant, after having been dismissed, was also assaulted and mortally wounded and although he was attended with great care, yet such was his situation, that he could give no intelligible account of what had befallen his master. In the morning, the duke not having returned to the palace, his servants began to be alarmed; and one of them informed the pontiff of the evening excursion of his sons, and that the duke had not yet made his appearance. This gave the pope no small anxiety; but he conjectured that the duke had been attracted by some courtesan to pass the night with her, and not choosing to quit the house in open day, had waited till the following evening to return home. When, however, the evening arrived, and he found himself disappointed in his expectations, he became deeply afflicted, and began to make inquiries from different persons, whom he ordered to attend him for that purpose. Amongst these was a man named Giorgio Schiavoni, who, having discharged some timber from a bark in the river, had remained on board the vessel to watch it; and being interrogated whether he had seen any one thrown into the river on the night preceding, he replied that he saw two men on foot, who came down the street, and looked diligently about, to observe whether any person was passing. That seeing no one, they returned, and a short time afterwards two others came, and looked around in the same manner as the former: no person still appearing, they gave a sign to their companions, when a man came mounted on a white horse, having behind him a dead body, the head and arms of which hung on one side, and the feet on the other side of the horse; the two persons on foot supporting the body, to prevent its falling. They thus proceeded toward that part where the filth of the city is usually discharged into the river, and turning the horse, with his tail towards the water, the two persons took the dead body by the arms and feet, and with all their strength flung it into the river. The person on horseback then asked if they had thrown it in to which they replied, *Signor si* (yes, Sir). He then looked towards the river, and seeing a mantle floating on the stream, he inquired what it was that appeared black, to which they answered, it was a mantle; and one of them threw stones upon it in consequence of which it sunk. The attendants of the pontiff then inquired from Giorgio, why he had not revealed this to the governor of the city to which he replied, that he had seen in his time a hundred dead bodies thrown into the river at the same place, without any inquiry being made respecting them; and that he had not, therefore

considered it as a matter of any importance. The fishermen and seamen were then collected, and ordered to search the river, where, on the following evening, they found the body of the duke, with his habit entire, and thirty ducats in his purse. He was pierced with nine wounds, one of which was in his throat, the others in his head, body, and limbs. No sooner was the pontiff informed of the death of his son, and that he had been thrown, like filth, into the river, than, giving way to his grief, he shut himself up in a chamber, and wept bitterly. The Cardinal of Segovia, and other attendants on the pope, went to the door, and after many hours spent in persuasions and exhortations, prevailed upon him to admit them. From the evening of Wednesday till the following Saturday the pope took no food; nor did he sleep from Thursday morning till the same hour on the ensuing day. At length, however, giving way to the entreaties of his attendants, he began to restrain his sorrow, and to consider the injury which his own health might sustain by the further indulgence of his grief.'—ROSCOE'S *Leo Tenth*, vol. i. p. 265.

THE SIEGE OF CORINTH

Page 320, col. 1.

'And some are rebels on the hills.'] The last tidings recently heard of Dervish (one of the Arnaouts who followed me) state him to be in revolt upon the mountains, at the head of some of the bands common in that country in times of trouble.

Page 320, col. 1.

'The Turcoman hath left his herd.'] The life of the Turcomans is wandering and patriarchal: they dwell in tents.

Page 321, col. 1.

'Coumourgi—he whose closing scene.'] Ali Coumourgi, the favourite of three Sultans, and Grand Vizier to Achmet III., after recovering Peloponnesus from the Venetians in one campaign, was mortally wounded in the next, against the Germans, at the battle of Peterwaradin (in the plain of Carlowitz), in Hungary, endeavouring to rally his guards. He died of his wounds next day. His last order was the decapitation of General Breuner, and some other German prisoners; and his last words, Oh that I could thus serve all the Christian dogs!' a speech and act not unlike one of Caligula. He was a young man of great ambition and unbounded presumption: on being told that Prince Eugene, then opposed to him, 'was a great general,' he said, I shall become a greater, and at his expense.'

Page 323, col. 2.

'There shrinks no ebb in that tideless sea.'] The reader need hardly be reminded that there are no perceptible tides in the Mediterranean.

Page 324, col. 1.

'And their white tusks crunch'd o'er the whiter skull.'] This spectacle I have seen, such as described, beneath the wall of the Seraglio at Contantinople, in the little cavities worn by the Bosphorus in the rock, a narrow terrace of which projects between the wall and the water. I think the fact is also mentioned in Hobhouse's Travels. The bodies were probably those of some refractory janizaries.

Page 324, col. 1.

'And each scalp had a single long tuft of hair.'] This tuft, or long lock, is left from a superstition that Mahomet will draw them into Paradise by it.

Page 324, col. 2.

'Sent that soft and tender moan?'] I must here acknowledge a close, though unintentional, resemblance in these twelve lines to a passage in an unpublished poem of Mr. Coleridge, called 'Christabel.' It was not till after these lines were written that I heard that wild and singularly original and beautiful poem recited; and the MS. of that production I never saw till very recently, by the kindness of Mr. Coleridge himself, who, I hope, is convinced that I have not been a wilful plagiarist. The original idea undoubtedly pertains to Mr. Coleridge, whose poem has been composed above fourteen years. Let me conclude by a hope that he will not longer delay the publication of a production, of which I can only add my mite of approbation to the applause of far more competent judges.

Page 326, col. 1.

'There is a light cloud by the moon.'] I have been told that the idea expressed in this and the five following lines has been admired by those whose approbation is valuable. I am glad of it: but it is not original—at least not mine; it may be found much better expressed in pages 182–3–4 of the English version of 'Vathek' (I forget the precise page of the French), a work to which I have before referred; and never recur to, or read, without a renewal of gratification.

Page 326, col. 2.

'The horsetails are pluck'd from the ground, and the sword.'] The horsetails, fixed upon a lance, a pacha's standard.

Page 327, col. 2.

'And since the day, when in the strait.'] In the naval battle at the mouth of the Dardanelles, between the Venetians and Turks.

Page 330, col. 2.

'The jackals' troop, in gather'd cry.'] I believe I have taken a poetical licence to transplant the jackal from Asia. In Greece I never saw nor heard these animals; but among the ruins of Ephesus I have heard them by hundreds. They haunt ruins, and follow armies.

PARISINA

Page 331.

'Parisina.'] This turned out a calamitous year for the people of Ferrara, for there occurred a very tragical event in the court of their sovereign. Our annals, both printed and in manuscript, with the exception of the unpolished and negligent work of Sardi, and one other, have given the following relation of it,—from which, however, are rejected many details, and especially the narrative of Bandelli, who wrote a century afterwards, and who does not accord with the contemporary historians.

'By the above-mentioned Stella dell' Assassino, the Marquis, in the year 1405, had a son called Ugo, a beautiful and ingenuous youth. Parisina Malatesta, second wife of Niccolò, like the generality of step-mothers, treated him with little kindness, to the infinite regret of the Marquis, who regarded

him with fond partiality. One day she asked leave of her husband to undertake a certain journey, to which he consented, but upon condition that Ugo should bear her company; for he hoped by these means to induce her, in the end, to lay aside the obstinate aversion which she had conceived against him. And indeed his intent was accomplished but too well, since, during the journey, she not only divested herself of all her hatred, but fell into the opposite extreme. After their return, the Marquis had no longer any occasion to renew his former reproofs. It happened one day that a servant of the Marquis, named Zoese, or, as some call him, Giorgio, passing before the apartments of Parisina, saw going out from them one of her chamber-maids, all terrified and in tears. Asking the reason, she told him that her mistress, for some slight offence, had been beating her; and giving vent to her rage, she added, that she could easily be revenged, if she chose to make known the criminal familiarity which subsisted between Parisina and her step-son. The servant took note of the words, and related them to his master. He was astounded thereat, but, scarcely believing his ears, he assured himself of the fact, alas! too clearly, on the 18th of May, by looking through a hole made in the ceiling of his wife's chamber. Instantly he broke into a furious rage, and arrested both of them, together with Aldobrandino Rangoni, of Modena, her gentleman, and also, as some say, two of the women of her chamber, as abettors of this sinful act. He ordered them to be brought to a hasty trial, desiring the judges to pronounce sentence, in the accustomed forms, upon the culprits. This sentence was death. Some there were that bestirred themselves in favour of the delinquents, and amongst others, Ugoccion Contrario, who was all-powerful with Niccolo, and also his aged and much-deserving minister Alberto dal Sale. Both of these, their tears flowing down their cheeks, and upon their knees, implored him for mercy; adducing whatever reasons they could suggest for sparing the offenders, besides those motives of honour and decency which might persuade him to conceal from the public so scandalous a deed. But his rage made him inflexible, and, on the instant, he commanded that sentence should be put in execution.

'It was, then, in the prisons of the castle, and exactly in those frightful dungeons which are seen at this day beneath the chamber called the Aurora, at the foot of the Lion's tower, at the top of the street Giovecca, that on the night of the 21st of May were beheaded, first Ugo, and afterwards Parisina. Zoese, he that accused her, conducted the latter under his arm to the place of punishment. She, all along, fancied that she was to be thrown into a pit, and asked at every step, whether she was yet come to the spot? She was told that her punishment was the axe. She inquired what was become of Ugo, and received for answer, that he was already dead; at the which, sighing grievously, she exclaimed, "Now, then, I wish not myself to live;" and, being come to the block, she stripped herself with her own hands of all her ornaments, and, wrapping a cloth round her head, submitted to the fatal stroke, which terminated the cruel scene. The same was done with Rangoni, who, together with the others, according to two calendars in the library of St. Francesco, was buried in the cemetery of that convent. Nothing else is known respecting the women.

'The Marquis kept watch the whole of that dreadful night, and, as he was walking backwards and forwards, inquired of the captain of the castle if Ugo was dead yet? who answered him, Yes. He then gave himself up to the most desperate lamentations, exclaiming, "Oh that I too were dead, since I have been hurried on to resolve thus against my own Ugo!" And then gnawing with his teeth a cane which he had in his hand, he passed the rest of the night in sighs and in tears, calling frequently upon his own dear Ugo. On the following day, calling to mind that it would be necessary to make public his justification, seeing that the transaction could not be kept secret, he ordered the narrative to be drawn out upon paper, and sent it to all the courts of Italy.

'On receiving this advice, the Doge of Venice, Francesco Foscari, gave orders, but without publishing his reasons, that stop should be put to the preparations for a tournament, which, under the auspices of the Marquis, and at the expense of the city of Padua, was about to take place, in the square of St. Mark, in order to celebrate his advancement to the ducal chair.

'The Marquis, in addition to what he had already done, from some unaccountable burst of vengeance, commanded that as many of the married women as were well known to him to be faithless, like his Parisina, should, like her, be beheaded. Amongst others, Barberina, or, as some call her, Laodamia Romei, wife of the court judge, underwent this sentence at the usual place of execution; that is to say, in the quarter of St. Giacomo, opposite the present fortress, beyond St. Paul's. It cannot be told how strange appeared this proceeding in a prince, who, considering his own disposition should, as it seemed, have been in such cases most indulgent. Some, however, there were who did not fail to commend him.'*

Page 331, col. 1.

'As twilight melts beneath the moon away.' The lines contained in this section were printed as set to music some time since, but belonged to the poem where they now appear; the greater part of which was composed prior to 'Lara.'

Page 333, col. 2.

'That should have won as haught a crest.' Haught—haughty—'Away, *haught* man, thou art insulting me.'—SHAKESPEARE.

THE PRISONER OF CHILLON

Page 337, col. 1.

'In a single night.'] Ludovico Sforza, and others —The same is asserted of Marie Antoinette's, the wife of Louis the Sixteenth, though not in quite so short a period. Grief is said to have the same effect: to such, and not to fear, this change in *her* was to be attributed.

Page 338, col. 2.

'From Chillon's snow-white battlement.'] The Château de Chillon is situated between Clarens and Villeneuve, which last is at one extremity of the Lake of Geneva. On its left are the entrances of the Rhone, and opposite are the heights of Meillerie and the range of Alps above Boveret and St. Gingo. Near it, on a hill behind, is a torrent: below it, washing its walls, the lake has been fathomed to the depth of 800 feet French measure: within it are a range of dungeons, in which the early reformers, and subsequently prisoners of state, were confined. Across one of the vaults is

* FRIZZI—'History of Ferrara.'

a beam black with age, on which we were informed that the condemned were formerly executed. In the cells are seven pillars, or, rather, eight, one being half merged in the wall; in some of these are rings for the fetters and the fettered: in the pavement the steps of Bonnivard have left their traces. He was confined here several years. It is by this castle that Rousseau has fixed the catastrophe of his Héloïse, in the rescue of one of her children by Julie from the water; the shock of which, and the illness produced by the immersion, is the cause of her death. The château is large, and seen along the lake for a great distance. The walls are white.

Page 340, col. 2.

'And then there was a little isle.'] Between the entrances of the Rhone and Villeneuve, not far from Chillon, is a very small island; the only one could perceive, in my voyage round and over the lake, within its circumference. It contains a few trees (I think not above three), and from its singleness and diminutive size has a peculiar effect upon the view.

MAZEPPA

Page 342, col. 2.

'Rich as a salt or silver mine.'] This comparison of a 'salt' mine may, perhaps, be permitted to a Pole, as the wealth of the country consists greatly in the salt mines.

THE ISLAND

Page 351, col. 2.

'And bread itself is gather'd as a fruit.'] The now celebrated bread-fruit, to transplant which Captain Bligh's expedition was undertaken.

Page 352, col. 1.

'How pleasant were the songs of Toobonai.'] The first three sections are taken from an actual song of the Tonga Islanders, of which a prose translation is given in 'Mariner's Account of the Tonga Islands.' Toobonai is not however one of them; but was one of those where Christian and the mutineers took refuge. I have altered and added, but have retained as much as possible of the original.

Page 354, col. 1.

'As Ishmael, wafted on his desert-ship.'] The 'ship of the desert' is the Oriental figure for the camel or dromedary; and they deserve the metaphor well,—the former for his endurance, the latter for his swiftness.

Page 354, col. 1.

'Beyond itself, and must retrace its way.']

'Lucullus, when frugality could charm,
Had roasted turnips in the Sabine farm.'—
POPE.

Page 354, col. 2.

'Had formed his glorious namesake's counterpart.'] The consul Nero, who made the unequalled march which deceived Hannibal, and defeated Asdrubal; thereby accomplishing an achievement almost unrivalled in military annals. The first intelligence of his return, to Hannibal, was the sight of Asdrubal's head thrown into his camp. When Hannibal saw this, he exclaimed with a sigh, that 'Rome would now be the mistress of the world.' And yet to this victory of Nero's it might

be owing that his imperial namesake reigned at all. But the infamy of the one has eclipsed the glory of the other. When the name of 'Nero' is heard, who thinks of the consul?—But such are human things!

Page 355, col. 2.

'And Loch-na-gar with Ida look'd o'er Troy.'] When very young, about eight years of age, after an attack of the scarlet fever at Aberdeen, I was removed by medical advice into the Highlands. Here I passed occasionally some summers, and from this period I date my love of mountainous countries. I can never forget the effect, a few years afterwards, in England, of the only thing I had long seen, even in miniature, of a mountain, in the Malvern Hills. After I returned to Cheltenham, I used to watch them every afternoon, at sunset, with a sensation which I cannot describe. This was boyish enough; but I was then only thirteen years of age, and it was in the holidays.

Page 356, col. 2.

'Sung sweetly to the rose the day's farewell.'] The now well-known story of the loves of the nightingale and rose need not be more than alluded to, being sufficiently familiar to the Western as to the Eastern reader.

Page 357, col. 1.

'Than breathes his mimic murmurer in the shell.'] If the reader will apply to his ear the sea-shell on his chimney-piece, he will be aware of what is alluded to. If the text should appear obscure, he will find in 'Gebir' the same idea better expressed in two lines. The poem I never read, but have heard the lines quoted by a more recondite reader—who seems to be of a different opinion from the editor of the Quarterly Review, who qualified it, in his answer to the Critical Reviewer of his Juvenal, as trash of the worst and most insane description. It is to Mr. Landor, the author of 'Gebir,' so qualified, and of some Latin poems, which vie with Martial or Catullus in obscenity, that the immaculate Mr. Southey addresses his declamation against impurity!

Page 357, col. 2.

'But deem him sailor or philosopher.'] Hobbes, the father of Locke's and other philosophy, was an inveterate smoker,—even to pipes beyond computation.

Page 357, col. 2.

'Flock o'er the deck, in Neptune's borrow'd car.'] This rough but jovial ceremony, used in crossing the line, has been so often and so well described, that it need not be more than alluded to.

Page 358, col. 2.

'"Right," quoth Ben, "that will do for the marines."'] 'That will do for the marines, but the sailors won't believe it,' is an old saying; and one of the few fragments of former jealousies which still survive (in jest only) between these gallant services.

Page 359, col. 1.

'No less of human bravery than the brave!'] Archidamus, king of Sparta, and son of Agesilaus, when he saw a machine invented for the casting of stones and darts, exclaimed that it was the 'grave of valour.' The same story has been told of some knights on the first application of gunpowder; but the original anecdote is in Plutarch.

NOTES TO THE ISLAND

Page 363, col. 1.

'Whose only portal was the keyless wave.'] Of this cave (which is no fiction) the original will be found in the ninth chapter of 'Mariner's Account of the Tonga Islands.' I have taken the poetical liberty to transplant it to Toobonai, the last island where any distinct account is left of Christian and his comrades.

Page 363, col. 2.

'The fretted pinnacle, the aisle, the nave.'] This may seem too minute for the general outline (in Mariner's Account) from which it is taken. But few men have travelled without seeing something of the kind—on land, that is. Without adverting to Ellora, in Mungo Park's last journal, he mentions having met with a rock or mountain so exactly resembling a Gothic cathedral, that only minute inspection could convince him that it was a work of nature.

Page 364, col. 1.

'With each new being born or to be born.'] The reader will recollect the epigram of the Greek anthology, or its translation into most of the modern languages:—

'Whoe'er thou art, thy master see—
He was, or is, or is to be.'

Page 364, col. 1.

'The kindling ashes to his kindled breast.'] The tradition is attached to the story of Eloisa, that when her body was lowered into the grave of Abelard (who had been buried twenty years), he opened his arms to receive her.

Page 365, col. 2.

'He tore the topmost button from his vest.'] In Thibault's account of Frederic the Second of Prussia, there is a singular relation of a young Frenchman, who with his mistress appeared to be of some rank. He enlisted and deserted at Schweidnitz; and after a desperate resistance was retaken, having killed an officer, who attempted to seize him after he was wounded, by the discharge of his musket loaded with a button of his uniform. Some circumstances on his court-martial raised a great interest amongst his judges, who wished to discover his real situation in life, which he offered to disclose, but to the king only, to whom he requested permission to write. This was refused, and Frederic was filled with the greatest indignation, from baffled curiosity or some other motive, when he understood that his request had been denied.

THE PROPHECY OF DANTE

Page 371, col. 1.

''Midst whom my own bright Beatrice bless'd.'] The reader is requested to adopt the Italian pronunciation of Beatricē, sounding all the syllables.

Page 371, col. 1.

'My paradise had still been incomplete.']

'Che sol per le belle opre
Che fanno in Cielo il sole a l' altre stelle
Dentro di lui' si crede il Paradiso,
Cosi se guardi fiso
Pensar ben dèi ch' ogni terren' piacere.'

Canzone, in which Dante describes the person of Beatrice, Strophe third.

Page 371, col. 2.

'I would have had my Florence great and free.'

'L'Esilio che m' è dato onor mi tegno
* * * * *
Cader tra' buoni è pur di lode degno.'
Sonnet of Dante

in which he represents Right, Generosity, and Temperance as banished from among men, and seeking refuge from Love, who inhabits his bosom.

Page 371, col. 2.

'And doom this body forfeit to the fire.'] 'Ut si quis predictorum ullo tempore in fortiam dicti communis pervenerit, talis perveniens igne comburatur, sic quod moriatur.' Second sentence of Florence against Dante, and the fourteen accused with him. The Latin is worthy of the sentence.

Page 373, col. 1.

'Where yet my boys are, and that fatal she.' This lady, whose name was Gemma, sprung from one of the most powerful Guelph families named Donati. Corso Donati was the principal adversary of the Ghibellines. She is described as being 'Ad modum morosa, ut de Xantippe Socratis philosop: conjuge scriptum esse legimus,' according to Giannozzo Manetti. But Lionardo Aretino is scandalised with Boccace, in his Life of Dante, for saying that literary men should not marry. 'Qui il Boccaccio non ha pazienza, e dice, le mogli esser contrarie agli studj; e non si ricorda che Socrate il più nobile filosofo che mai fosse, ebbe moglie e figliuoli e uffici della Repubblica nella sua Città e Aristotele che, &c. &c., ebbe due mogli in varj tempi, ed ebbe figliuoli, e ricchezze assai.—Marco Tullio—e Catone—e Varrone—e Seneca-ebbero moglie,' &c. &c. It is odd that none of Lionardo's examples, with the exception of Seneca, and, for anything I know, of Aristotle, are not the most felicitous. Tully's Terentia, and Socrates' Xantippe, by no means contributed to their husbands' happiness, whatever they might do to their philosophy—Cato gave away his wife—of Varro we know nothing—and of Seneca's, only that she was disposed to die with him, but recovered and lived several years afterwards. But says Lionardo 'L'uomo è animale civile, secondo piace a tutti i filosofi.' And thence concludes that the greatest proof of the animal's civism is 'la prima congiunzione, dalla quale multiplicata nasce la Città.'

Page 374, col. 1.

'Nine moons shall rise o'er scenes like this and set.'] See 'Sacco di Roma,' generally attributed to Guicciardini. There is another written by Jacopo Buonaparte.

Page 375, col. 1.

'Conquerors on foreign shores, and the far wave.'] Alexander of Parma, Spinola, Pescara, Eugene of Savoy, Montecucco.

Page 375, col. 1.

'Discoverers of new worlds, which take their name.'] Columbus, Americus Vespusius, Sebastian Cabot.

Page 375, col. 2.

'He who once enters in a tyrant's hall.'] A verse from the Greek tragedians, with which Pompey took leave of Cornelia on entering the boat in which he was slain.

NOTES TO THE MORGANTE MAGGIORE, ETC.

Page 375, col. 2.

'A captive, sees his half of manhood gone.'] The verse and sentiment are taken from Homer.

Page 376, col. 1.

'And he, their prince, shall rank among my peers.'] Petrarch.

Page 377, col. 2.

'A dome, its image, while the base expands.'] The Cupola of St. Peter's.

Page 378, col. 1.

'His chisel bid the Hebrew, at whose word.'] The statue of Moses on the monument of Julius II.

SONETTO

Di Giovanni Battista Zappi

Chi è costui, che in dura pietra scolto,
 Siede gigante; e le più illustre, e conte
 Opre dell' arte avvanza, e ha vive, e pronte
 Le labbia sì, che le parole ascolto?
Quest' è Mosè; ben me 'l diceva il folto
 Onor del mento, e 'l doppio raggio in fronte,
 Quest' è Mosè, quando scendea del monte,
 E gran parte del Nume avea nel volto.
Tal era allor, che le sonanti, e vaste
 Acque ei sospese a se d' intorno, e tale
 Quando il mar chiuse, e ne fè tomba altrui.
E voi sue turbe un rio vitello alzaste?
 Alzata aveste imago a questa eguale!
 Ch' era men fallo l' adorar costui.

Page 378, col. 1.

'Over the damn'd before the Judgment-throne.'] The Last Judgment, in the Sistine Chapel.

Page 378, col. 1.

'The stream of his great thoughts shall spring from me.'] I have read somewhere (if I do not err, for I cannot recollect where), that Dante was so great a favourite of Michael Angelo's, that he had designed the whole of the Divina Commedia: but that the volume containing these studies was lost by sea.

Page 378, col. 1.

'Her charms to pontiffs proud, who but employ.'] See the treatment of Michael Angelo by Julius II., and his neglect by Leo X.

Page 379, col. 1.

'"What have I done to thee, my people?"' Stern.'] 'E scrisse più volte non solamente a particolari cittadini del reggimento, ma ancora al popolo, e intra l' altre una Epistola assai lunga che comincia: "Popule mi, quid feci tibi?"' Vita di Dante scritta da Lionardo Aretino.

THE MORGANTE MAGGIORE

Page 386, col. 2.

'He gave him such a punch upon the head.'] Gli dette in su la testa un gran punzone.' It is strange that Pulci should have literally anticipated the technical terms of my old friend and master, Jackson, and the art which he has carried to its highest pitch. 'A punch on the head,' or 'a punch in the head,'—'un punzone in su la testa,'—is the exact and frequent phrase of our best pugilists, who little dream that they are talking the purest Tuscan.

MANFRED

Page 396, col. 1.

'It is not noon—the sunbow's rays still arch.'] This iris is formed by the rays of the sun over the lower part of the Alpine torrents: it is exactly like a rainbow come down to pay a visit, and so close that you may walk into it: this effect lasts till noon.

Page 397, col. 1.

'Eros and Anteros, at Gadara.'] The philosopher Jamblicus. The story of the raising of Eros and Anteros may be found in his Life by Eunapius. It is well told.

Page 398, col. 1.

'In words of dubious import, but fulfill'd.'] The story of Pausanias, king of Sparta (who commanded the Greeks at the battle of Platea, and afterwards perished for an attempt to betray the Lacedæmonians), and Cleonice, is told in Plutarch's Life of Cimon; and in the Laconics of Pausanias the sophist, in his description of Greece.

Page 403, col. 2.

'Of undiseased mankind, the giant sons.'] 'And it came to pass, that the Sons of God saw the daughters of men, that they were fair,' &c.—'There were giants in the earth in those days; and also after that, when the Sons of God came in unto the daughters of men, and they bare children to them, the same became mighty men which were of old, men of renown.'—Genesis, ch. vi. verses 2 and 4.

MARINO FALIERO, DOGE OF VENICE

APPENDIX

NOTE A

I am obliged for the following excellent translation of the old Chronicle to Mr. F. Cohen, to whom the reader will find himself indebted for a version that I could not myself—though after many years' intercourse with Italian—have given by any means so purely and so faithfully.

STORY OF MARINO FALIERO, DOGE XLIX. MCCCLIV

On the eleventh day of September, in the year of our Lord 1354, Marino Faliero was elected and chosen to be the Duke of the Commonwealth of Venice. He was Count of Valdemarino, in the Marches of Treviso, and a knight, and a wealthy man to boot. As soon as the election was completed, it was resolved in the Great Council, that a deputation of twelve should be despatched to Marino Faliero the Duke, who was then on his way home from Rome; for when he was chosen, he was ambassador at the court of the Holy Father, at Rome,—the Holy Father himself held his court at Avignon. When Messer Marino Faliero the Duke was about to land in this city, on the 5th day of October, 1354, a thick haze came on and darkened the air: and he was enforced to land on the place of St. Mark, between the two columns, on the spot where evil-doers are put to death; and all thought that this was the worst of tokens.—Nor must I forget to write that which I have read in a chronicle. When Messer Marino Faliero was Podesta and Captain of Treviso, the Bishop delayed coming in with the holy sacrament, on a day when a procession was to take place. Now, the said Marino Faliero was so very proud and wrathful, that he

905

APPENDIX TO MARINO FALIERO

buffeted the Bishop, and almost struck him to the ground: and, therefore, Heaven allowed Marino Faliero to go out of his right senses, in order that he might bring himself to an evil death.

When this Duke had held the dukedom during nine months and six days, he, being wicked and ambitious, sought to make himself Lord of Venice, in the manner which I have read in an ancient chronicle. When the Thursday arrived upon which they were wont to hunt the bull, the bull hunt took place as usual; and, according to the usage of those times, after the bull hunt had ended, they all proceeded unto the palace of the Duke, and assembled together in one of his halls; and they disported themselves with the women. And until the first bell tolled they danced, and then a banquet was served up. My Lord the Duke paid the expenses thereof, provided he had a Duchess, and after the banquet they all returned to their homes.

Now to this feast there came a certain Ser Michele Steno, a gentleman of poor estate and very young, but crafty and daring, and who loved one of the damsels of the Duchess. Ser Michele stood amongst the women upon the solajo; and he behaved indiscreetly, so that my Lord the Duke ordered that he should be kicked off the solajo; and the esquires of the Duke flung him down from the solajo accordingly. Ser Michele thought that such an affront was beyond all bearing; and when the feast was over, and all other persons had left the palace, he, continuing heated with anger, went to the hall of audience, and wrote certain unseemly words relating to the Duke and the Duchess upon the chair in which the Duke was used to sit; for in those days the Duke did not cover his chair with cloth of sendal, but he sat in a chair of wood. Ser Michele wrote thereon—'*Marin Falier, the husband of the fair wife; others kiss her, but he keeps her.*' In the morning the words were seen, and the matter was considered to be very scandalous; and the Senate commanded the Avogadori of the Commonwealth to proceed therein with the greatest diligence. A largess of great amount was immediately proffered by the Avogadori, in order to discover who had written these words. And at length it was known that Michele Steno had written them. It was resolved in the Council of Forty that he should be arrested; and he then confessed that in the fit of vexation and spite, occasioned by his being thrust off the solajo in the presence of his mistress, he had written the words. Therefore the Council debated thereon. And the Council took his youth into consideration, and that he was a lover; and therefore they adjudged that he should be kept in close confinement during two months, and that afterwards he should be banished from Venice and the state during one year. In consequence of this merciful sentence the Duke became exceedingly wroth, it appearing to him, that the Council had not acted in such a manner as was required by the respect due to his ducal dignity; and he said that they ought to have condemned Ser Michele to be hanged by the neck, or at least to be banished for life.

Now it was fated that my Lord Duke Marino was to have his head cut off. And as it is necessary when any effect is to be brought about, that the cause of such effect must happen, it therefore came to pass, that on the very day after sentence had been pronounced on Ser Michele Steno, being the first day of Lent, a gentleman of the house of Barbaro, a choleric gentleman, went to the arsenal, and required certain things of the masters of the galleys. This he did in the presence of the Admiral of the arsenal, and he, hearing the request, answered,—No, it cannot be done. High words arose between the gentleman and the Admiral, and the gentleman struck him with his fist just above the eye; and as he happened to have a ring on his finger, the ring cut the Admiral and drew blood. The Admiral, all bruised and bloody, ran straight to the Duke to complain, and with the intent of praying him to inflict some heavy punishment upon the gentleman of Cà Barbaro.—'What wouldst thou have me do for thee?' answered the Duke:—'think upon the shameful gibe which hath been written concerning me: and think on the manner in which they have punished that ribald Michele Steno, who wrote it; and see how the Council of Forty respect our person.'—Upon this the Admiral answered,—'My Lord Duke, if you would wish to make yourself a prince, and to cut all those cuckoldy gentlemen to pieces, I have the heart, if you do but help me, to make you prince of all this state: and then you may punish them all.' Hearing this, the Duke said,—'How can such a matter be brought about?'—and so they discoursed thereon.

The Duke called for his nephew, Ser Bertuccio Faliero, who lived with him in the palace, and they communed about this plot. And without leaving the place, they sent for Philip Calendaro, a seaman of great repute, and for Bertuccio Israello, who was exceedingly wily and cunning. Then taking counsel amongst themselves, they agreed to call in some others; and so, for several nights successively, they met with the Duke at home in his palace. And the following men were called in singly; to wit:—Niccolo Fagiuolo, Giovanni da Corfu, Stefano Fagiono, Niccolo dalle Bende, Niccolo Biondo, and Stefano Trivisano.—It was concerted that sixteen or seventeen leaders should be stationed in various parts of the city, each being at the head of forty men, armed and prepared; but the followers were not to know their destination. On the appointed day they were to make affrays amongst themselves here and there, in order that the Duke might have a pretence for tolling the bells of San Marco; these bells are never rung but by the order of the Duke. And at the sound of the bells, these sixteen or seventeen, with their followers, were to come to San Marco, through the streets which open upon the Piazza. And when the noble and leading citizens should come into the Piazza, to know the cause of the riot, then the conspirators were to cut them in pieces; and this work being finished, my Lord Marino Faliero the Duke was to be proclaimed the Lord of Venice. Things having been thus settled, they agreed to fulfil their intent on Wednesday, the 15th day of April, in the year 1355. So covertly did they plot, that no one ever dreamt of their machinations.

But the Lord, who hath always helped this most glorious city, and who, loving its righteousness and holiness, hath never forsaken it, inspired one Beltramo Bergamasco to be the cause of bringing this plot to light, in the following manner. This Beltramo, who belonged to Ser Niccolo Lioni of Santo Stefano, had heard a word or two of what was to take place; and so, in the above-mentioned month of April, he went to the house of the aforesaid Ser Niccolo Lioni, and told him all the particulars of the plot. Ser Niccolo, when he heard all these things, was struck dead, as it were, with affright. He heard all the particulars; and Beltramo prayed him to keep it all secret; and if he told Ser Niccolo it was in order that Ser Niccolo might stop at home on the 15th of April, and thus save his life. Beltramo was going, but Ser Niccolo ordered his ser-

vants to lay hands upon him, and lock him up. Ser
Niccolo then went to the house of Messer Giovanni
Gradenigo Nasoni, who afterwards became Duke,
and who also lived at Santo Stefano, and told him
all. The matter seemed to him to be of the very
greatest importance, as indeed it was; and they two
went to the house of Ser Marco Cornaro, who lived
at San Felice; and, having spoken with him, they
all three then determined to go back to the house
of Ser Niccolo Lioni, to examine the said Bel-
tramo; and having questioned him, and heard all
that he had to say, they left him in confinement.
And then they all three went into the sacristy of
San Salvatore, and sent their men to summon the
Councillors, the Avogadori, the Capi de' Dieci,
and those of the Great Council.

When all were assembled, the whole story was
told to them. They were struck dead, as it were,
with affright. They determined to send for Bel-
tramo. He was brought in before them. They
examined him, and ascertained that the matter was
true; and, although they were exceedingly troubled,
yet they determined upon their measures. And
they sent for the Capi de' Quarante, the Signori
di Notte, the Capi de' Sestieri, and the Cinque
della Pace; and they were ordered to associate to
their men other good men and true, who were to
proceed to the houses of the ringleaders of the con-
spiracy, and secure them. And they secured the
foreman of the arsenal, in order that the conspira-
tors might not do mischief. Towards nightfall they
assembled in the palace. When they were assem-
bled in the palace, they caused the gates of the
quadrangle of the palace to be shut. And they
sent to the keeper of the Bell-tower, and forbade
the tolling of the bells. All this was carried into
effect. The before-mentioned conspirators were
secured, and they were brought to the palace; and,
as the Council of Ten saw that the Duke was in
the plot, they resolved that twenty of the leading
men of the state should be associated to them, for
the purpose of consultation and deliberation, but
that they should not be allowed to ballot.

The counsellors were the following:—Ser Gio-
vanni Mocenigo, of the Sestiero di San Marco; Ser
Almoro Veniero da Santa Marina, of the Sestiero
of Castello; Ser Tomaso Viadro, of the Sestiero of
Canaregio; Ser Giovanni Sanudo, of the Sestiero
of Santa Croce; Ser Pietro Trivisano, of the Ses-
tiero of San Paolo; Ser Pantalione Barbo il Grando,
of the Sestiero of Ossoduro. The Avogadori of the
Commonwealth were Zufredo Morosini, and Ser
Orio Pasqualigo; and these did not ballot. Those
of the Council of Ten were Ser Giovanni Marcello,
Ser Tomaso Sanudo, and Ser Micheletto Dolfino,
the heads of the aforesaid Council of Ten. Ser
Luca da Legge, and Ser Pietro da Mosto, inquisi-
tors of the aforesaid Council. And Ser Marco Po-
lani, Ser Marino Veniero, Ser Lando Lombardo,
and Ser Nicoletto Trivisano, of Sant' Angelo.

Late in the night, just before the dawning, they
chose a junta of twenty noblemen of Venice from
amongst the wisest, and the worthiest, and the
oldest. They were to give counsel, but not to bal-
lot. And they would not admit any one of Cà
Faliero. And Niccolo Faliero, and another Nic-
colo Faliero, of San Tomaso, were expelled from
the Council, because they belonged to the family
of the Doge. And this resolution of creating the
junta of twenty was much praised throughout the
state. The following were the members of the junta
of twenty:—Ser Marco Giustiniani, Procuratore,
Ser Andrea Erizzo, Procuratore, Ser Lionardo
Giustiniani, Procuratore, Ser Andrea Contarini,

Ser Simone Dandolo, Ser Niccolo Volpe, Ser Gio-
vanni Loredano, Ser Marco Diedo, Ser Giovanni
Gradenigo, Ser Andrea Cornaro, Cavaliere, Ser
Marco Soranzo, Ser Rinieri du Mosto, Ser Gazano
Marcello, Ser Marino Morosini, Ser Stefano Be-
legno, Ser Niccolo Lioni, Ser Filippo Orio, Ser
Marco Trivisano, Ser Jacopo Bragadino, Ser Gio-
vanni Foscarini.

These twenty were accordingly called in to the
Council of Ten; and they sent for my Lord Marino
Faliero, the Duke: and my Lord Marino was then
consorting in the palace with people of great estate,
gentlemen, and other good men, none of whom
knew yet how the fact stood.

At the same time Bertuccio Israello, who, as one
of the ringleaders, was to head the conspirators in
Santa Croce, was arrested and bound, and brought
before the Council. Zanello del Brin, Nicoletto di
Rosa, Nicoletto Alberto, and the Guardiaga, were
also taken, together with several seamen, and
people of various ranks. These were examined,
and the truth of the plot was ascertained.

On the 16th of April judgment was given in the
Council of Ten, that Filippo Calendaro and Ber-
tuccio Israello should be hanged upon the red
pillars of the balcony of the palace, from which the
Duke is wont to look at the bull hunt: and they
were hanged with gags in their mouths.

The next day the following were condemned:—
Niccolo Zuccuolo, Niccolo Biondo, Nicoletto
Doro, Marco Giuda, Jacomello Dagolino, Nico-
letto Fidele, the son of Filippo Calendaro, Marco
Torello, called Israello, Stefano Trivisano, the
money-changer of Santa Margherita, and Antonio
dalle Bende. These were all taken at Chiozza, for
they were endeavouring to escape. Afterwards, by
virtue of the sentence which was passed upon them
in the Council of Ten, they were hanged on succes-
sive days; some singly and some in couples, upon
the columns of the palace, beginning from the red
columns, and so going onwards towards the canal,
And other prisoners were discharged, because, al-
though they had been involved in the conspiracy,
yet they had not assisted in it: for they were given
to understand by some of the heads of the plot,
that they were to come armed and prepared for the
service of the state, and in order to secure certain
criminals; and they knew nothing else. Nicoletto
Alberto, the Guardiaga, and Bartolommeo Ciri-
colo and his son, and several others, who were not
guilty, were discharged.

On Friday, the 16th day of April, judgment was
also given in the aforesaid Council of Ten, that my
Lord Marino Faliero, the Duke, should have his
head cut off; and that the execution should be
done on the landing-place of the stone staircase,
where the Dukes take their oath when they first
enter the palace. On the following day, the 17th of
April, the doors of the palace being shut, the Duke
had his head cut off, about the hour of noon. And
the cap of estate was taken from the Duke's head
before he came down-stairs. When the execution
was over, it is said that one of the Council of Ten
went to the columns of the palace over against the
place of St. Mark, and that he showed the bloody
sword unto the people, crying out with a loud
voice—'The terrible doom hath fallen upon the
traitor!'—and the doors were opened, and the
people all rushed in, to see the corpse of the Duke,
who had been beheaded.

It must be known that Ser Giovanni Sanudo, the
councillor, was not present when the aforesaid
sentence was pronounced; because he was unwell
and remained at home. So that only fourteen

balloted; that is to say, five councillors, and nine of the Council of Ten. And it was adjudged, that all the lands and chattels of the Duke, as well as of the other traitors, should be forfeited to the state. And as a grace to the Duke, it was resolved in the Council of Ten, that he should be allowed to dispose of two thousand ducats out of his own property. And it was resolved, that all the councillors, and all the Avogadori of the Commonwealth, those of the Council of Ten, and the members of the junta, who had assisted in passing sentence on the Duke and the other traitors, should have the privilege of carrying arms both by day and by night in Venice, and from Grado to Cavazere. And they were also to be allowed two footmen carrying arms, the aforesaid footmen living and boarding with them in their own houses. And he who did not keep two footmen might transfer the privilege to his sons or his brothers; but only to two. Permission of carrying arms was also granted to the four Notaries of the Chancery, that is to say, of the Supreme Court, who took the depositions; and they were, Amedio, Nicoletto di Lorino, Steffanello, and Pietro de Compostelli, the secretaries of the Signori di Notte.

After the traitors had been hanged, and the Duke had had his head cut off, the state remained in great tranquillity and peace. And, as I have read in a Chronicle, the corpse of the Duke was removed in a barge, with eight torches, to his tomb in the church of San Giovanni e Paolo, where it was buried. The tomb is now in that aisle in the middle of the little church of Santa Maria della Pace which was built by Bishop Gabriel of Bergamo. It is a coffin of stone, with these words engraven thereon: '*Heic jacet Dominus Marinus Faletro Dux.*'—And they did not paint his portrait in the hall of the Great Council:—but in the place where it ought to have been, you see these words:— '*Hic est locus Marini Faletro, decapitati pro criminibus.*'—And it is thought that his house was granted to the church of Sant' Apostoli; it was that great one near the bridge. Yet this could not be the case, or else the family bought it back from the church; for it still belongs to Cà Faliero. I must not refrain from noting, that some wished to write the following words in the place where his portrait ought to have been, as aforesaid:—'*Marinus Faletro Dux, temeritas me cepit. Pœnas lui, decapitatus pro criminibus.*'—Others, also, indited a couplet, worthy of being inscribed upon his tomb.

'*Dux Venetum jacet heic, patriam qui prodere tentans,*
Sceptra, decus, censum perdidit, atque caput.'

NOTE B

PETRARCH ON THE CONSPIRACY OF MARINO FALIERO

'Al giovane Doge Andrea Dandolo succedette un vecchio, il quale tardi si pose al timone della repubblica, ma sempre prima di quel, che facea d' uopo a lui, ed alla patria: egli è Marino Faliero, personaggio a me noto per antica dimestichezza. Falsa era l' opinione intorno a lui, giacchè egli si mostrò fornito più di corraggio, che di senno. Non pago della prima dignità, entro con sinistro piede nel pubblico Palazzo: imperciocche questo Doge dei Veneti, magistrato sacro in tutti i secoli, che dagli antichi fù sempre venerato qual nume in quella città, l' altr' jeri fù decollato nel vestibolo dell' istesso Palazzo. Discorrerei fin dal principio

le cause di un tale evvento, e cosi vario, ed ambiguo non ne fosse il grido. Nessuno però lo scusa, tutti affermano, che egli abbia voluto cangiar qualche cosa nell' ordine della repubblica a lui tramandato dai maggiori. Che desiderava egli di più? Io son d' avviso, che egli abbia ottenuto ciò, che non si concedette a nessun altro: mentre adempiva gli ufficj di legato presso il Pontefice, e sulle rive del Rodano trattava la pace, che io prima di lui avevo indarno tentato di conchiudere, gli fù conferito l' onore del Ducato, che ne chiedeva, ne s' aspettava— Tornato in patria, pensò a quello, cui nessuno non pose mente giammai, e soffrì quello che a niuno accadde mai di soffrire: giacchè in quel luogo celeberrimo, e chiarissimo, e bellissimo infra tutti quelli, che io vidi, ove i suoi antenati avevano ricevuti grandissimi onori in mezzo alle pompe trionfali, ivi egli fù irascinato in modo servile, e spogliato delle insegne ducali, perdette la testa, e macchiò col proprio sangue le soglie del tempio, l' atrio del Palazzo, e le scale marmoree rendute spesse volte illustri o dalle solenni festività, o dalle ostili spoglie. Hò notato il luogo, ora noto il tempo: è l' anno del Natale di Cristo, 1355, fù il giorno 18 d' Aprile. Si alto è il grido sparso, che se alcuno esaminerà la disciplina, e le costumanze di quella città, e quanto mutamento di cose venga minacciato dalla morte di un sol uomo (quantunque molti altri, come narrano, essendo complici, o subirono l' istesso supplicio, o lo aspettano) si accorgerà, che nulla di più grande avvenne ai nostri tempi nella Italia. Tu forse qui attendi il mio giudizio: assolvo il popolo, se credere alla fama, benchè abbia potuto e castigare più mitemente, e con maggior dolcezza vendicare il suo dolore: ma non cosi facilmente, si modera un' ira giusta insieme, e grande in un numeroso popolo principalmente, nel quale il precipitoso, ed instabile volgo aguzza gli stimoli dell' irracondia con rapidi, e sconsigliati clamori. Compatisco, e nell' istesso tempo mi adiro con quell' infelice uomo, il quale adorno di un' insolito onore, non so, che cosa si volesse negli estremi anni della sua vita: la calamità di lui diviene sempre più grave, perchè dalla sentenza contra di esso promulgata aperirà, che egli fù non solo misero, ma insano, e demente, e che con vane arti sì usurpò per tanti anni una falsa fama di sapienza. Ammonisco i Dogi, i quali gli succederano, che questo e un' esempio posto innanzi ai loro occhj, quale specchio, nel quale veggano d' essere non Signori, ma Duci, anzi nemmeno Duci, ma onorati servi della Repubblica. Tu sta sano; e giacchè fluttuano le pubbliche cose, sforsiamoci di governar modestissimamente i privati nostri affari.'—LEVATI, *Viaggi di Petrarca*, vol. iv. p. 323.

The above Italian translation from the Latin epistles of Petrarch proves—1stly, That Marino Faliero was a personal friend of Petrarch's; 'antica dimestichezza,' old intimacy, is the phrase of the poet. 2ndly, That Petrarch thought that he had more courage than conduct, 'più di *corraggio* che di senno.' 3rdly, That there was some jealousy on the part of Petrarch; for he says that Marino Faliero was treating of the peace which he himself had 'vainly attempted to conclude.' 4thly, That the honour of the Dukedom was conferred upon him, which he neither sought nor expected, 'che nè chiedeva nè aspettava,' and which had never been granted to any other in like circumstances, 'ciò che non si concedette a nessun altro,' a proof of the high esteem in which he must have been held. 5thly, That he had a reputation for *wisdom, only* forfeited by the last enterprise of his life, 'si usurpò per tanti anni una falsa fama di sapienza.'—'He

had usurped for so many years a false fame of wisdom,' rather a difficult task, I should think. People are generally found out before eighty years of age, at least in a republic.—From these, and the other historical notes which I have collected, it may be inferred, that Marino Faliero possessed many of the qualities, but not the success of a hero; and that his passions were too violent. The paltry and ignorant account of Dr. Moore falls to the ground. Petrarch says, 'that there had been no greater event in his times' (*our times* literally), 'nostri tempi,' in Italy. He also differs from the historian in saying that Faliero was 'on the banks of the *Rhone*,' instead of at Rome, when elected: the other accounts say, that the deputation of the Venetian senate met him at Ravenna. How this may have been, it is not for me to decide, and is of no great importance. Had the man succeeded, he would have changed the face of Venice, and perhaps of Italy. As it is, what *are* they both?

NOTE C

VENETIAN SOCIETY AND MANNERS

'Vice without splendour, sin without relief
Even from the gloss of love to smooth it o'er;
But, in its stead, coarse lusts of habitude,' &c.
[*See* p. 452.]

'To these attacks so frequently pointed by the government against the clergy,—to the continual struggles between the different constituted bodies, —to these enterprises carried on by the mass of the nobles against the depositaries of power,—to all those projects of innovation, which always ended by a stroke of state policy, we must add a cause not less fitted to spread contempt for ancient doctrines; *this was the excess of corruption.*

'That freedom of manners, which had been long boasted of as the principal charm of Venetian society, had degenerated into scandalous licentiousness: the tie of marriage was less sacred in that Catholic country, than among those nations where the laws and religion admit of its being dissolved. Because they could not break the contract, they feigned that it had not existed; and the ground of nullity, immodestly alleged by the married pair, was admitted with equal facility by priests and magistrates, alike corrupt. These divorces, veiled under another name, became so frequent that the most important act of civil society was discovered to be amenable to a tribunal of exceptions; and to restrain the open scandal of such proceedings became the office of the police. In 1782 the Council of Ten decreed, that every woman who should sue for a dissolution of her marriage should be compelled to await the decision of the judges in some convent, to be named by the court.* Soon afterwards the same council summoned all causes of that nature before itself.† This infringement on ecclesiastical jurisdiction having occasioned some remonstrance from Rome, the council retained only the right of rejecting the petition of the married persons, and consented to refer such causes to the holy office as it should not previously have rejected.‡

'There was a moment in which, doubtless, the destruction of private fortunes, the ruin of youth, the domestic discord occasioned by these abuses,

* Correspondence of M. Schlick, French chargé d'affaires. Despatch of 24th August, 1782.
† *Ibid.* Despatch 31st August.
‡ *Ibid.* Despatch of 3rd September, 1785.

determined the government to depart from its established maxims concerning the freedom of manners allowed the subject. All the courtesans were banished from Venice; but their absence was not enough to reclaim and bring back good morals to a whole people brought up in the most scandalous licentiousness. Depravity reached the very bosom of private families, and even into the cloister; and they found themselves obliged to recall, and even to indemnify,§ women who sometimes gained possession of important secrets, and who might be usefully employed in the ruin of men whose fortunes might have rendered them dangerous. Since that time licentiousness has gone on increasing; and we have seen mothers, not only selling the innocence of their daughters, but selling it by a contract, authenticated by the signature of a public officer, and the performance of which was secured by the protection of the laws.||

'The parlours of the convents of noble ladies and the houses of the courtesans, though the police carefully kept up a number of spies about them, were the only assemblies for society in Venice; and in these two places, so different from each other, there was equal freedom. Music, collations, gallantry, were not more forbidden in the parlours than at the casinos. There were a number of casinos for the purpose of public assemblies, where gaming was the principal pursuit of the company. It was a strange sight to see persons of either sex masked, or grave in their magisterial robes, round a table, invoking chance, and giving way at one instant to the agonies of despair, at the next to the illusions of hope, and that without uttering a single word.

'The rich had private casinos, but they lived *incognito* in them; and the wives whom they abandoned found compensation in the liberty they enjoyed. The corruption of morals had deprived them of their empire. We have just reviewed the whole history of Venice, and we have not once seen them exercise the slightest influence.'—DARU: *Hist. de la Répub. de Venise,* vol. v. p. 95.

NOTES

Page 413, col. 2.

'I smote the tardy bishop at Treviso.'] An historical fact. See Marin Sanuto's 'Lives of the Doges.'

Page 415, col. 2.

'*Doge (aside).* Saint Mark's shall strike that hour!'] The bells of San Marco were never rung but by order of the Doge. One of the pretexts for ringing this alarm was to have been an announcement of the appearance of a Genoese fleet off the Lagune.

Page 416, col. 2.

'A gondola, with one oar only, will.'] A gondola is not like a common boat, but is as easily rowed with one oar as with two (though, of course, not so swiftly), and often is so from motives of privacy; and, since the decay of Venice, of economy.

Page 427, col. 2.

'Engaged in secret to the Signory.'] An historical fact. See APPENDIX, Note A.

§ The decree for their recall designates them as *nostre benemerite meretrici;* a fund and some houses, called *Case rampane,* were assigned to them; hence the opprobrious appellation of *Carampane.*
|| Mayer, Description of Venice, vol. ii.; and M. Archenholz, Picture of Italy, vol. i. ch. 2.

NOTES TO MARINO FALIERO

Page 438, col. 2.

'Within our palace precincts at San Polo.'] The Doge's family palace.

Page 443, col. 2.

'Of the red columns, where, on festal Thursday.'] 'Giovedi grasso,'—'fat or greasy Thursday,' —which I cannot literally translate in the text, was the day.

Page 443, col. 2.

'Guards! let their mouths be gagg'd even in the act.'] Historical fact. See Sanuto, APPENDIX, Note A.

Page 446, col. 1.

'*Ben*. Say, conscript fathers, shall she be admitted?'] The Venetian senate took the same title as the Roman, of 'conscript fathers.'

Page 451, col. 1.

'*Doge*. 'Tis with age, then.'] This was the actual reply of Bailli, maire of Paris, to a Frenchman who made him the same reproach on his way to execution, in the earliest part of their revolution. I find in reading over (since the completion of this tragedy), for the first time these six years, 'Venice Preserved,' a similar reply on a different occasion by Renault, and other coincidences arising from the subject. I need hardly remind the gentlest reader, that such coincidences must be accidental, from the very facility of their detection by reference to so popular a play on the stage and in the closet as Otway's chef-d'œuvre.

Page 451, col. 2.

'Who shall despise her!—She shall stoop to be.'] Should the dramatic picture seem harsh, let the reader look to the historical, of the period prophesied, or rather of the few years preceding that period. Voltaire calculated their 'nostre bene merite Meretrici' at 12,000 of regulars, without including volunteers and local militia, on what authority I know not; but it is, perhaps, the only part of the population not decreased. Venice once contained two hundred thousand inhabitants: there are now about ninety thousand; and THESE!! few individuals can conceive, and none could describe, the actual state into which the more than infernal tyranny of Austria has plunged this unhappy city. From the present decay and degeneracy of Venice under the Barbarians, there are some honourable individual exceptions. There is Pasqualigo, the last, and, alas! *posthumous* son of the marriage of the Doges with the Adriatic, who fought his frigate with far greater gallantry than any of his French coadjutors in the memorable action off Lissa. I came home in the squadron with the prizes in 1811, and recollect to have heard Sir William Hoste, and the other officers engaged in that glorious conflict, speak in the highest terms of Pasqualigo's behaviour. There is the Abbate Morelli. There is Alvise Querini, who, after a long and honourable diplomatic career, finds some consolation for the wrongs of his country, in the pursuits of literature with his nephew, Vittor Benzon, the son of the celebrated beauty, the heroine of 'La Biondina in Gondoletta.' There are the patrician poet Morosini, and the poet Lamberti, the author of the 'Biondina,' &c., and many other estimable productions; and, not least in an Englishman's estimation, Madame Michelli, the translator of Shakspeare. There are the young Dandolo and the improvvisatore Carrer, and Giuseppe Albrizzi, the accomplished son of an accomplished mother. There is Aglietti, and, were

there nothing else, there is the immortality of Canova. Cicognara, Mustoxithi, Bucati, &c. &c., I do not reckon, because the one is a Greek, and the others were born at least a hundred miles off, which, throughout Italy, constitutes, if not a *foreigner*, at least a *stranger* (*forestiére*).

Page 452, col. 1.

'Then when the Hebrew's in thy palaces.'] The chief palaces on the Brenta now belong to the Jews; who in the earlier times of the republic were only allowed to inhabit Mestri, and not to enter the city of Venice. The whole commerce is in the hands of the Jews and Greeks, and the Huns form the garrison.

Page 452, col. 1.

'But in its stead, coarse lusts of habitude.'] [See APPENDIX, Note C.]

Page 452, col. 1.

''Gainst which thou wilt not strive, and dar'st not murmur.'] If the Doge's prophecy seem remarkable, look to the following, made by Alamanni two hundred and seventy years ago:—'There is one very singular prophecy concerning Venice: "If thou dost not change," it says to that proud republic, "thy liberty, which is already on the wing, will not reckon a century more than the thousandth year." If we carry back the epocha of Venetian freedom to the establishment of the government under which the republic flourished, we shall find that the date of the election of the first Doge is 697; and if we add one century to a thousand, that is, eleven hundred years, we shall find the sense of the prediction to be literally this: "Thy liberty will not last till 1797." Recollect that Venice ceased to be free in the year 1796, the fifth year of the French republic; and you will perceive that there never was prediction more pointed, or more exactly followed by the event. You will, therefore, note as very remarkable the three lines of Alamanni addressed to Venice; which, however, no one has pointed out:—

"Se non cangi pensier, un secol solo
Non conterà sopra 'l millesimo anno
Tua libertà, che va fuggendo a volo."

Many prophecies have passed for such, and many men have been called prophets for much less.'—GINGUENÉ, *Hist. Lit. de l'Italie*, t. ix. p. 144.

Page 452, col. 2.

'Thou den of drunkards with the blood of princes!'] Of the first fifty Doges, *five* abdicated—*five* were banished with their eyes put out—*five* were MASSACRED—and *nine* deposed—so that *nineteen* out of fifty lost the throne by violence, besides two who fell in battle: this occurred long previous to the reign of Marino Faliero. One of his more immediate predecessors, Andrea Dandolo, died of vexation. Marino Faliero himself perished as related. Amongst his successors, *Foscari*, after seeing his son repeatedly tortured and banished, was deposed, and died of breaking a blood-vessel, on hearing the bell of Saint Mark's toll for the election of his successor. Morosini was impeached for the loss of Candia; but this was previous to his dukedom, during which he conquered the Morea, and was styled the Peloponnesian. Faliero might truly say,—

'Thou den of drunkards with the blood of princes!'

Page 453, col. 1.

'Chief of the Ten.'] 'Un Capo de' Diece' are the words of Sanuto's Chronicle.

SARDANAPALUS

Page 454, col. 2.

'And thou, my own Ionian Myrrha, choose']
'The Ionian name had been still more comprehensive, having included the Achaians and the Bœotians, who, together with those to whom it was afterwards confined, would make nearly the whole of the Greek nation; and among the Orientals it was always the general name for the Greeks.'—MITFORD's *Greece*, vol. i. p. 199.

Page 457, col. 2.

'Eat, drink, and love; the rest's not worth a fillip.'] 'For this expedition he took only a small chosen body of the phalanx, but all his light troops. In the first day's march he reached Anchialus, a town said to have been founded by the king of Assyria, Sardanapalus. The fortifications, in their magnitude and extent, still in Arrian's time, bore the character of greatness, which the Assyrians appear singularly to have affected in works of the kind. A monument representing Sardanapalus was found there, warranted by an inscription in Assyrian characters, of course in the old Assyrian language, which the Greeks, whether well or ill, interpreted thus: 'Sardanapalus, son of Anacyndaraxes, in one day founded Anchialus and Tarsus. Eat, drink, play; all other human joys are not worth a fillip.' Supposing this version nearly exact (for Arrian says it was not quite so), whether the purpose has not been to invite to civil order a people disposed to turbulence, rather than to recommend immoderate luxury, may perhaps reasonably be questioned. What, indeed, could be the object of a king of Assyria in founding such towns in a country so distant from his capital, and so divided from it by an immense extent of sandy deserts and lofty mountains, and, still more, how the inhabitants could be at once in circumstances to abandon themselves to the intemperate joys which their prince has been supposed to have recommended, is not obvious; but it may deserve observation that, in that line of coast, the southern of Lesser Asia, ruins of cities, evidently of an age after Alexander, yet barely named in history, at this day astonish the adventurous traveller by their magnificence and elegance. Amid the desolation which, under a singularly barbarian government, has for so many centuries been daily spreading in the finest countries of the globe, whether more from soil and climate, or from opportunities for commerce, extraordinary means must have been found for communities to flourish there; whence it may seem that the measures of Sardanapalus were directed by juster views than have been commonly ascribed to him; but that monarch having been the last of a dynasty ended by a revolution, obloquy on his memory would follow of course from the policy of his successors and their partisans. The inconsistency of traditions concerning Sardanapalus is striking in Diodorus's account of him.'—MITFORD's *Greece*, vol. ix. p. 311.

Page 488, col. 1.

'Some twenty stadia.'] About two miles and a half.

THE TWO FOSCARI

Page 506, col. 1.

'Created by degrees an ocean Rome.'] In Lady Morgan's fearless and excellent work upon Italy,

I perceive the expression of 'Rome of the Ocean' applied to Venice. The same phrase occurs in the 'Two Foscari.' My publisher can vouch for me, that the tragedy was written and sent to England some time before I had seen Lady Morgan's work, which I only received on the 16th of August. I hasten, however, to notice the coincidence, and to yield the originality of the phrase to her who first placed it before the public.

Page 506, col. 2.

'That melody, which out of tones and tunes,' Alluding to the Swiss air and its effects.

Page 514, col. 1.

'There often has been question about you.'] An historical fact. See DARU, tom. ii.

Page 520, col. 1.

'O'er those they slew. I've heard of widows' tears.']—The Venetians appear to have had a particular turn for breaking the hearts of their Doges. The following is another instance of the kind in the Doge Marco Barbarigo: he was succeeded by his brother Agostino Barbarigo, whose chief merit is here mentioned.—'Le doge, blessé de trouver constamment un contradicteur et un censeur si amer dans son frère, lui dit un jour en plein conseil; "Messire Augustin, vous faites tout votre possible pour hâter ma mort; vous vous flattez de me succéder; mais, si les autres vous connaissent aussi bien que je vous connais, ils n'auront garde de vous élire." Là-dessus il se leva, ému de colère, rentra dans son appartement, et mourut quelques jours après. Ce frère, contre lequel il s'était emporté, fut précisément le successeur qu'on lui donna. C'était un mérite dont on aimait à tenir compte; surtout à un parent, de s'être mis en opposition avec le chef de la république.'—DARU, *Hist. de Venise*, t. ii. p. 533.

Page 520, col. 2.

'*Lor.* (pointing to the Doge's body). That *he* has paid me!'] '*L'ha pagata*.' An historical fact. See *Hist. de Venise*, par P. DARU, t. ii. p. 411.

CAIN

Page 544, col. 2.

'But the four rivers would not cleanse my soul.'] The 'four rivers' which flowed round Eden, and consequently the only waters with which Cain was acquainted upon earth.

HEAVEN AND EARTH

Page 546, col. 1.

'Albeit thou watchest with "the seven."'] The archangels, said to be seven in number, and to occupy the eighth rank in the celestial hierarchy.

Page 551, col. 1.

'In a few hours the glorious giants' graves.']
'And there were giants in the earth in those days, and after, mighty men, which were of old, men of renown.'—*Genesis*.

Page 551, col. 2.

'And heaven set wide her windows; while mankind.'] 'The same day were all the fountains of the great deep broken up, and the windows of heaven were opened.'—*Ibid*.

NOTES TO WERNER, ETC.

Page 552, col. 1.

'The scroll of Enoch prophesied it long.'] The book of Enoch, preserved by the Ethiopians, is said by them to be anterior to the flood.

WERNER

Page 578, col. 1.

'From the Ravenstone by choking you myself.'] The Ravenstone, 'Rabenstein,' is the *stone gibbet* of Germany, and so called from the ravens perching on it.

DEFORMED TRANSFORMED

Page 608, col. 1.

'Bestrides the Hartz Mountain.'] This is a well-known German superstition—a gigantic shadow produced by reflection on the Brocken.

Page 610, col. 2.

'From the red earth, like Adam.'] Adam means '*red earth*,' from which the first man was formed.

Page 617, col. 2.

'Weep not—*strike!* for Rome is mourning!'] Scipio, the second Africanus, is said to have repeated a verse of Homer, and wept over the burning of Carthage. He had better have granted it a capitulation.

BEPPO

Page 628, col. 1.

'The Spaniards call the person a "*Cortejo*."'] Cortejo is pronounced Corteho, with an aspirate, according to the Arabesque guttural. It means what there is as yet no precise name for in England, though the practice is as common as in any tramontane country whatever.

Page 629, col. 1.

'Raphael, who died in thy embrace, and vies.'] For the received accounts of the cause of Raphael's death, see his Lives.

Page 629, col. 1.

'While yet Canova can create below?']

(In talking thus, the writer, more especially
Of women, would be understood to say,
He speaks as a spectator, not officially,
And always, reader, in a modest way;
Perhaps, too, in no very great degree shall he
Appear to have offended in this lay,
Since, as all know, without the sex, our sonnets
Would seem unfinish'd, like their untrimm'd bonnets.)

(Signed) PRINTER'S DEVIL.

DON JUAN

Page 636, col. 1.

'And Wordsworth has his place in the Excise.'] Wordsworth's place may be in the Customs—it is, I think, in that or the Excise—besides another at Lord Lonsdale's table, where this poetical charlatan and political parasite licks up the crumbs with a hardened alacrity; the converted Jacobin having long subsided into the clownish sycophant of the worst prejudices of the aristocracy.

Page 636, col. 2.

'And heartless daughters—worn—and pale—and poor.'] 'Pale, but not cadaverous:'—Milton's

two elder daughters are said to have robbed him of his books, besides cheating and plaguing him in the economy of his house, &c. &c. His feelings on such an outrage, both as a parent and a scholar, must have been singularly painful. Hayley compares him to Lear. See part third, Life of Milton, by W. Hayley (or Hailey, as spelt in the edition before me).

Page 636, col. 2.

'The intellectual eunuch Castlereagh?'] Or,—

'Would *he* subside into a hackney Laureate—
A scribbling, self-sold, soul-hired, scorn'd Iscariot?'

I doubt if 'Laureate' and 'Iscariot' be good rhymes, but must say, as Ben Jonson did to Sylvester, who challenged him to rhyme with—

'I, John Sylvester,
Lay with your sister.'

Jonson answered,—'I, Ben Jonson, lay with your wife.' Sylvester answered,—'That is not rhyme.'—'No,' said Ben Jonson; 'but it is *true*.'

Page 637, col. 1.

'Eutropius of its many masters,—blind.'] For the character of Eutropius, the eunuch and minister at the court of Arcadius, see Gibbon.

Page 637, col. 1.

'Is it not so, my Tory, Ultra-Julian?'] I allude not to our friend Landor's hero, the traitor Count Julian, but to Gibbon's hero, vulgarly yclept 'The Apostate.'

Page 639, col. 1.

'Save thine "incomparable oil," Macassar!'] Description des *vertus incomparables* de l'Huile de Macassar.'—See the Advertisement.

Page 641, col. 1.

'As Numa's (who was also named Pompilius).']

——'primus qui legibus urbem
Fundabit, curibus parvis et paupere terrâ
Missus in imperium magnum.'—VIRG.

Page 641, col. 2.

'Although Longinus tells us there is no hymn.'] See Longinus, Section 10, 'ἵνα μὴ ἕν τι περὶ αὐτὴν πάθος φαίνηται, παθῶν δὲ σύνοδος.'

Page 642, col. 1.

'They only add them all in an appendix.'] Fact! There is, or was, such an edition, with all the obnoxious epigrams of Martial placed by themselves at the end.

Page 642, col. 2.

'Which make the reader envy his transgressions.'] See his Confessions, l. i. c. ix. By the representation which Saint Augustine gives of himself in his youth, it is easy to see that he was what we should call a rake. He avoided the school as the plague; he loved nothing but gaming and public shows; he robbed his father of everything he could find; he invented a thousand lies to escape the rod, which they were obliged to make use of to punish his irregularities.

Page 644, col. 1.

'('Twas snow that brought St. Anthony to reason).'] For the particulars of St. Anthony's

912

recipe for hot blood in cold weather, see Mr. Alban Butler's 'Lives of the Saints.'

Page 646, col. 2.

'In feelings quick as Ovid's Miss Medea.'] See Ovid. de Art. Amand. l. ii.

Page 646, col. 2.

'The bard I quote from does not sing amiss.'] Campbell's Gertrude of Wyoming—(I think)—the opening of Canto Second—but quote from memory.

Page 653, col. 1.

'Was it for this that no Cortejo e'er.'] The Spanish 'Cortejo' is much the same as the Italian 'Cavalier Servente.'

Page 653, col. 1.

'Who took Algiers, declares I used him vilely?'] Donna Julia here made a mistake. Count O'Reilly did not take Algiers—but Algiers very nearly took him: he and his army and fleet retreated with great loss, and not much credit, from before that city, in the year 1775.

Page 660, col. 2.

'My days of love are over; me no more.']

'Me nec femina, nec puer
Jam, nec spes animi credula mutui,
Nec certare juvat mero;
Nec vincire novis tempora floribus.'—HOR.

Page 662, col. 1.

'Excepting the Venetian Fazzioli.'] *Fazzioli*—literally, the little handkerchiefs—the veils most availing of St. Mark.

Page 670, col. 1.

'Remember Ugolino condescends.']

'Quandò ebbe detto ciò, con gli occhi torti
Riprese il teschio misero co' denti,
Che furo all' osso, come d'un can forti.'

Page 686, col. 2.

'Dante.'] Dante calls his wife, in the 'Inferno,' 'la fiera moglie.'

Page 686, col. 2.

'Milton.'] Milton's first wife ran away from him within the first month. If she had not, what would John Milton have done?

Page 690, col. 2.

'For none likes more to hear himself converse.']

'Rispone allor' Margutte, a dir tel tosto,
Io non credo piu al nero ch' all' azzurro:
Ma nel cappone, o lesso, o vuogli arrosto,
E credo alcuna volta anco nel burro;
Nella cervigia, e quando io n' ho nel mosto,
E molto più nell' espro che il manguuro;
Ma sopra tutto nel buon vino ho fede,
E credo che sia salvo chi gli crede.'—
PULCI, *Morgante Maggiore*, ca. 18, st. 151.

Page 693, col. 2.

'That e'er by precious metal was held in.'] The dress is Moorish, and the bracelets and bar are worn in the manner described. The reader will perceive hereafter, that as the mother of Haidée was of Fez, her daughter wore the garb of the country.

Page 693, col. 2.

'A like gold bar above her instep roll'd.'] The bar of gold above the instep is a mark of sovereign rank in the women of the families of the deys, and is worn as such by their female relatives.

Page 693, col. 2.

'Her person if allow'd at large to run.'] This is no exaggeration: there were four women whom I remember to have seen, who possessed their hair in this profusion; of these, three were English, the other was a Levantine. Their hair was of that length and quantity, that, when let down, it almost entirely shaded the person, so as nearly to render dress a superfluity. Of these, only one had dark hair; the Oriental had, perhaps, the lightest colour of the four.

Page 695, col. 1.

'Than your sires' "Islands of the Blest."'] The νῆσοι μακάρων of the Greek poets were supposed to have been the Cape de Verd islands or the Canaries.

Page 695, col. 2.

'And when the sun set where were they?']

'Deep were the groans of Xerxes, when he saw
This havoc; for his seat, a lofty mound
Commanding the wide sea, o'erlook'd the hosts.
With rueful cries he rent his royal robes,
And through his troops embattled on the shore
Gave signal of retreat; then started wild
And fled disorder'd.'—ÆSCHYLUS.

Page 696, col. 1.

'There, swan-like, let me sing and die.']

. . . 'Γενοίμαν
ἵν' ὑλᾶεν ἔπεστι πόντου
πρόβλημ' ἁλίκλυστον, ἄκραν
ὑπὸ πλάκα Σουνίου.' κ.τ.λ.—SOPH. *Ajax*, v. 1217.

Page 696, col. 2.

'For the first Mrs. Milton left his house.'] See Johnson's Life of Milton.

Page 697, col. 2.

'Can sneer at him who drew "Achitophel!"'] 'The verses of Dryden, once highly celebrated, are forgotten.'—Mr. W. WORDSWORTH'S *Preface*.

Page 698, col. 2.

'Oh, Hesperus! thou bringest all good things.']

' Ἔσπερε πάντα φέρεις,
Φέρεις οἶνον—φέρεις αἶνα,
Φέρεις ματέρι παῖδα.'—Fragment of Sappho.

Page 698, col. 2.

'Ah! surely nothing dies but something mourns!']

'Era gia l' ora che volge 'l disio,
A' naviganti, e 'ntenerisce il cuore,
Lo di ch' han detto a' dolci amici a dio;
E che lo nuovo peregrin' d' amore
Punge, se ode Squilla di lontano,
Che paia 'l giorno pianger che si muore.'—
DANTE'S *Purgatory*, canto viii.

This last line is the first of Gray's Elegy, taken by him [not] without acknowledgment.

Page 698, col. 2.

'Some hands unseen strewed flowers upon his tomb.'] See Suetonius for this fact.

NOTES TO DON JUAN

Page 700, col. 1.

'"Whom the gods love die young," was said of yore.'] See Herodotus (Cleobis and Biton). The sentiment is in a fragment of Menander.

Page 705, col. 2.

'A vein had burst, and her sweet lips' pure dyes.'] This is no very uncommon effect of the violence of conflicting and different passions. The Doge Francis Foscari, on his deposition in 1457, hearing the bells of St. Mark announce the election of his successor, 'mourut subitement d'une hémorragie causée par une veine qui s'éclata dans sa poitrine,' (see Sismondi and Daru, vols. i. and ii.) at the age of eighty years, when '*Who would have thought the old man had so much blood in him?*' Before I was sixteen years of age, I was witness to a melancholy instance of the same effect of mixed passions upon a young person, who, however, did not die in consequence, at that time, but fell a victim some years afterwards to a seizure of the same kind, arising from causes intimately connected with agitation of mind.

Page 708, col. 1.

'But sold by the impresario at no high rate.'] This is a fact. A few years ago a man engaged a company for some foreign theatre, embarked them at an Italian port, and carrying them to Algiers, sold them all. One of the women, returned from her captivity, I heard sing, by a strange coincidence, in Rossini's opera of 'L' Italiana in Algieri,' at Venice, in the beginning of 1817.

Page 708, col. 2.

'From all the Pope makes yearly 'twould perplex.'] It is strange that it should be the Pope and the Sultan who are the chief encouragers of this branch of trade—women being prohibited as singers at St. Peter's, and not deemed trustworthy as guardians of the harem.

Page 712, col. 1.

'Sprinkled with palaces; the Ocean stream.'] 'Ωκεανοῖο ῥέογιο. This expression of Homer has been much criticised. It hardly answers to our Atlantic ideas of the ocean, but is sufficiently applicable to the Hellespont, and the Bosphorus, with the Ægean intersected with islands.

Page 712, col. 2.

''Tis a grand sight from off "the Giant's Grave."'] The 'Giant's Grave' is a height on the Asiatic shore of the Bosphorus, much frequented by holiday parties; like Harrow and Highgate.

Page 715, col. 2.

'Of food I think with Philip's son, or rather.'] See Plutarch in Alex., Q. Curt. Hist. Alex., and Sir Richard Clayton's 'Critical Inquiry into the Life of Alexander the Great.'

Page 715, col. 2.

'Stretch'd in the street, and able scarce to pant.'] The assassination alluded to took place on the 8th of December, 1820, in the streets of Ravenna, not a hundred paces from the residence of the writer. The circumstances were as described.

Page 716, col. 2.

'Wond'ring what next, till the caïque was brought.'] The light and elegant wherries plying about the quays of Constantinople are so called.

Page 717, col. 1.

'From Saint Bartholomew we have saved our skin.'] St. Bartholomew is said to have been flayed alive.

Page 718, col. 1.

'Prepared for supper with a glass of rum.'] In Turkey nothing is more common than for the Mussulmans to take several glasses of strong spirits by way of appetizer. I have seen them take as many as six of raki before dinner, and swear that they dined the better for it: I tried the experiment, but fared like the Scotchman, who having heard that the birds called kittiwakes were admirable whets, ate six of them, and complained that 'he was no hungrier than when he began.'

Page 718, col. 1.

'Splendid but silent, save in *one*, where a dropping.'] A common furniture. I recollect being received by Ali Pacha, in a large room, paved with marble, containing a marble basin, and fountain playing in the centre, &c. &c.

Page 718, col. 2.

'And the calumniated queen Semiramis.'] Babylon was enlarged by Nimrod, strengthened and beautified by Nabuchadonosor, and rebuilt by Semiramis.

Page 721, col. 2.

'The gate so splendid was in all its *features*.'] *Features* of a gate—a ministerial metaphor: 'the *feature* upon which this question *hinges*.' See the 'Fudge Family,' or hear Castlereagh.

Page 722, col. 1.

'A good deal practised here upon occasion.'] A few years ago the wife of Muchtar Pacha complained to his father of his son's supposed infidelity: he asked with whom, and she had the barbarity to give in a list of the twelve handsomest women in Yanina. They were seized, fastened up in sacks, and drowned in the lake the same night. One of the guards who was present informed me, that not one of the victims uttered a cry, or showed a symptom of terror at so sudden a 'wrench from all we know, from all we love.'

Page 723, col. 2.

'Though on more *thorough-bred* or fairer fingers.'] There is nothing, perhaps, more distinctive of birth than the hand. It is almost the only sign of blood which aristocracy can generate.

Page 728, col. 2.

'Save Solyman, the glory of their line.'] It may not be unworthy of remark, that Bacon, in his essay on 'Empire,' hints that Solyman was the last of his line; on what authority, I know not. These are his words:—'The destruction of Mustapha was so fatal to Solyman's line, as the succession of the Turks from Solyman until this day is suspected to be untrue, and of strange blood; for that Selymus the second was thought to be supposititious.' But Bacon, in his historical authorities, is often inaccurate. I could give half-a-dozen instances from his Apophthegms only.

BACON'S APOPHTHEGMS.	OBSERVATIONS.
91.	
Michael Angelo, the famous painter, painting in the Pope's chapel the portraiture of hell	This was *not* the portrait of a cardinal, but of the

and damned souls, made one of the damned souls so like a cardinal that was his enemy, as everybody at first sight knew it: whereupon the cardinal complained to Pope Clement, humbly praying it might be defaced. The Pope said to him, Why, you know very well I have power to deliver a soul out of purgatory, but not out of hell.

Pope's master of the ceremonies.

will kill you if they wax mad. Demosthenes replied, And they will kill you if they be in good sense.

but *to* Demosthenes by *Phocion.*

155.

Alexander, after the battle of Granicum, had very great offers made him by Darius. Consulting with his captains concerning them, Parmenio said, Sure, I would accept of these offers, if I were as Alexander. Alexander answered, So would I, if I were as Parmenio.

It was after the battle of Issus and during the siege of Tyre, and *not* immediately after the passage of the Granicus, that this is said to have occurred.

221.

There was a philosopher about Tiberius that, looking into the nature of Caius, said of him, That he was mire mingled with blood.

This was not said of Caius (Caligula, I presume, is intended by Caius), but of *Tiberius* himself.

97.

There was a king of Hungary took a bishop in battle, and kept him prisoner: whereupon the Pope writ a monitory to him, for that he had broken the privilege of holy church, and taken his son: the king sent an embassage to him, and sent withal the armour wherein the bishop was taken, and this only in writing—*Vide num hæc sit vestis filii tui?* Know now whether this be thy son's coat?

This reply was *not* made by a king of *Hungary*, but sent by Richard the First, Cœur de Lion, of England, to the Pope with the breast-plate of the bishop of Beauvais.

158.

Antigonus, when it was told him that the enemy had such volleys of arrows that they did hide the sun, said, That falls out well, for it is hot weather, and so we shall fight in the shade.

This was *not* said by Antigonus, but by a Spartan, previously to the battle of Thermopylæ.

162.

There was a philosopher that disputed with Adrian the Emperor, and did it but weakly. One of his friends that stood by afterwards said unto him, Methinks you were not like yourself last day, in argument with the Emperor: I could have answered better myself. Why, said the philosopher, would you have me contend with him that commands thirty legions?

This happened under Augustus Cæsar, and *not* during the reign of Adrian.

267.

Demetrius, king of Macedon, had a petition offered him divers times by an old woman, and answered he had no leisure; whereupon the woman said aloud, Why then give over to be king.

This did *not* happen to Demetrius, but to *Philip,* King of Macedon.

VOLTAIRE

Having stated that Bacon was frequently incorrect in his citations from history, I have thought it necessary in what regards so great a name (however trifling), to support the assertion by such facts as more immediately occur to me. They are but trifles, and yet for such trifles a school-boy would be whipped (if still in the fourth form); and Voltaire for half-a-dozen similar errors has been treated as a superficial writer, notwithstanding the testimony of the learned Warton:—'Voltaire, a writer of *much deeper research* than is imagined, and the *first* who has displayed the literature and customs of the dark ages with *any degree of penetration* and comprehension.'* For another distinguished testimony to Voltaire's merits in literary research, see also Lord Holland's excellent Account of the Life and Writings of Lope de Vega, vol. i. p. 215, edition of 1817.

164.

There was one that found a great mass of money, digging underground in his grandfather's house, and being somewhat doubtful of the case signified it to the emperor that he had found such treasure. The emperor made a rescript thus: Use it. He writ back again, that the sum was greater than his state or condition could use. The emperor writ a new rescript thus: Abuse it.

This happened to the father of Herodes Atticus, and the answer was made by the Emperor *Nerva,* who deserved that his name should have been stated by the 'greatest — wisest —meanest of mankind.'

Voltaire has even been termed a 'shallow fellow,' by some of the same school who called Dryden's Ode 'a drunken song;'—a *school* (as it is called, I presume, from their education being still incomplete) the whole of whose filthy trash of Epics, Excursions, &c. &c. &c., is not worth the two words in Zaïre, '*Vous pleurez,*'† or a single speech of Tancred:—a *school,* the apostate lives of whose renegadoes, with their tea-drinking neutrality of morals, and their convenient treachery in politics—in the record of their accumulated pretences to virtue can produce no *actions* (were all their good

178.

One of the seven was wont to say, that laws were like cobwebs: where the small flies were caught, and the great break through.

This was said by Anacharsis the Scythian, and *not* by a Greek.

* Dissertation I.
† ——'Il est trop vrai que l'honneur me l'ordonne,
Que je vous adorai, que je vous abandonne,
Que je renonce à vous, que vous le désirez,
Que sous une autre loi . . . Zaïre, VOUS PLEUREZ?'
—*Zaïre,* acte iv, sc. ii.

209.

An orator of Athens said to Demosthenes. The Athenians

This was *not* said *by* Demosthenes,

NOTES TO DON JUAN

deeds drawn up in array) to equal or approach the sole defence of the family of Calas, by that great and unequalled genius—the universal Voltaire.

I have ventured to remark on these little inaccuracies of 'the greatest genius that England, or perhaps any other country, ever produced,'* merely to show our national injustice in condemning *generally* the greatest genius of France for such inadvertencies as these, of which the highest of England has been no less guilty. Query, was Bacon a greater intellect than Newton?

CAMPBELL

Being in the humour of criticism, I shall proceed, after having ventured upon the slips of Bacon, to touch upon one or two as trifling in the edition of the British Poets, by the justly celebrated Campbell. But I do this in good will, and trust it will be so taken. If anything could add to my opinion of the talents and true feeling of that gentleman, it would be his classical, honest, and triumphant defence of Pope, against the vulgar cant of the day, and its existing Grub Street.

The inadvertencies to which I allude are—

Firstly, in speaking of *Anstey*, whom he accuses of having taken 'his leading characters from *Smollett*.' Anstey's Bath Guide was published in 1766. Smollett's Humphrey Clinker (the only work of Smollett's from which Tabitha, &c. &c. *could* have been taken) was written during *Smollett's last residence* at Leghorn in 1770—'*Argal*,' if there has been any borrowing, Anstey must be the creditor, and not the debtor. I refer Mr. Campbell to his *own* data in his Lives of Smollett and Anstey.

Secondly, Mr. Campbell says in the Life of Cowper (note to page 358, vol. vii.) that he knows not to whom Cowper alludes in these lines,—

'Nor he who, for the bane of thousands born,
Built *God* a *church*, and laugh'd his word to scorn.'

The Calvinist meant Voltaire, and the church of Ferney, with its inscription 'Deo erexit Voltaire.'

Thirdly, in the Life of Burns, Mr. Campbell quotes Shakspeare thus,—

'To gild refined gold, to paint *the rose*,
Or *add fresh* perfume *to* the violet.'

This version by no means improves the original, which is as follows—

'To gild refined gold, to paint the *lily*,
To *throw a perfume on* the violet,' &c.—*King John.*

A great poet quoting another should be correct; he should also be accurate, when he accuses a Parnassian brother of that dangerous charge 'borrowing:' a poet had better borrow anything (excepting money) than the thoughts of another—they are always sure to be reclaimed; but it is very hard, having been the *lender*, to be denounced as the debtor, as is the case of Anstey *versus* Smollett.

As there is 'honour amongst thieves,' let there be some amongst poets, and give each his due,—none can afford to give it more than Mr. Campbell himself, who, with a high reputation for originality, and a fame which cannot be shaken, is the only poet of the times (except Rogers) who can be reproached (and *in him* it is indeed a reproach) with having written *too little*.

Ravenna, Jan. 5, 1821.

* Pope, in Spencer's Anecdotes, p. 158. Malone's edition.

Page 730, col. 2.

'"Which, taken at the flood,"—you know the rest.'] See Shakspeare, Julius Cæsar, act iv. sc. iii.

Page 731, col. 2.

'Who lent his lady to his friend Hortensius.'] Cato gave up his wife, Martia, to his friend Hortensius; but, on the death of the latter, took her back again. This conduct was ridiculed by the Romans, who observed, that Martia entered the house of Hortensius very poor, but returned to the bed of Cato loaded with treasures.—PLUTARCH.

Page 732, col. 1.

'(A "Highland welcome" all the wide world over.)'] See Waverley.

Page 732, col. 2.

'In his monastic concubine of snow.'] 'The blessed Francis, being strongly solicited one day by the emotions of the flesh, pulled off his clothes and scourged himself soundly: being after this inflamed with a wonderful fervour of mind, he plunged his naked body into a great heap of snow. The devil, being overcome, retired immediately and the holy man returned victorious into his cell.'—See BUTLER's *Lives of the Saints.*

Page 733, col. 2.

'The tyrant's "wish, that mankind only had."' Caligula—See Suetonius. 'Being in a rage at the people, for favouring a party in the Circensian games in opposition to him, he cried out, "I wish the Roman people had but one neck."'

Page 733, col. 2.

'He went forth with the lovely Odalisques.' The ladies of the seraglio.

Page 734, col. 2.

'Who with the brightest Georgians might compare.'] 'It is in the adjacent climates of Georgia Mingrelia, and Circassia, that nature has placed at least to our eyes, the model of beauty, in the shape of the limbs, the colour of the skin, the symmetry of the features, and the expression of the countenance; the men are formed for action the women for love.'—GIBBON.

Page 735, col. 1.

'They would prefer to Padisha or Pacha.' Padisha is the Turkish title of the Grand Signior.

Page 739, col. 1.

'A "wood obscure," like that where Dante found.']
'Nell' mezzo del' cammin' di nostra vita
Mi ritrovai per una selva oscura,' &c.—*Inferno.*

Page 749, col. 2.

'Was teaching his recruits to use the bayonet.' Fact: Souwarrow did this in person.

Page 754, col. 2.

'All sounds it pierceth, "Allah! Allah! Hu!"' Allah Hu! is properly the war-cry of the Mussulmans, and they dwell on the last syllable, which gives it a wild and peculiar effect.

916

Page 754, col. 2.

'Carnage, (so Wordsworth tells you) is God's daughter.']

> 'But *Thy** most dreaded instrument
> In working out a pure intent,
> Is man array'd for mutual slaughter;
> Yea, *Carnage is thy daughter!*'
> WORDSWORTH'S *Thanksgiving Ode.*

Page 755, col. 2.

'Was printed *Grove*, although his name was Grose.'] A fact: see the Waterloo Gazettes. I recollect remarking at the time to a friend:— *There is fame!* a man is killed, his name is Grose, and they print it Grove.' I was at college with the deceased, who was a very amiable and clever man, and his society in great request for his wit, gaiety, and 'Chansons à boire.'

Page 756, col. 1.

'(The antiquarians who can settle time.'] See General Valancey and Sir Lawrence Parsons.

Page 756, col. 2.

''Tis pity "that such meaning should pave hell."'] The Portuguese proverb says, that 'hell is paved with good intentions.'

Page 757, col. 2.

'By thy humane discovery, Friar Bacon!'] Gunpowder is said to have been discovered by this friar.

Page 764, col. 2.

'That you and I will win St. George's collar.'] A Russian military order.

Page 769, col. 2.

'Humanity would rise, and thunder "Nay!"'] Query, *Ney?*—Printer's Devil.

Page 770, col. 1.

'And "Europe's Liberator"—still enslaved.'] Vide Speeches in Parliament, after the battle of Waterloo.

Page 771, col. 2.

''"But heaven," as Cassio says, "is above all."'] See Othello.

Page 772, col. 2.

'I've heard them in the Ephesian ruins howl.'] In Greece I never saw or heard these animals; but among the ruins of Ephesus I have heard them by hundreds.

Page 773, col. 1.

'Because he could no more digest his dinner.'] He was killed in a conspiracy, after his temper had been exasperated by his extreme costivity to a degree of insanity.

Page 774, col. 2.

'And had just buried the fair-faced Lanskoi.'] He was the grande passion of the grande Catherine. See her Lives under the head of 'Lanskoi.'

Page 775, col. 1.

'Bid Ireland's Londonderry's Marquess show.'] This was written long before the suicide of that person.

Page 775, col. 2.

'Oh thou "teterrima causa" of all "belli."'] Hor. Sat. lib. i. sat. iii.

* To wit, the Deity's; this is perhaps as pretty a pedigree for murder as ever was found out by Garter King at Arms.—What would have been said, had any free-spoken people discovered such a lineage?

Page 776, col. 2.

'"A man" (as Giles says): for though she would widow all.'] 'His fortune swells him, it is rank, he's married.'—*Sir Giles Overreach; MASSINGER'S New Way to Pay Old Debts.*

Page 778, col. 2.

'Of several ribands, and some thousand peasants.'] A Russian estate is always valued by the number of the slaves upon it.

Page 780, col. 2.

'Would scarcely join again the "reformadoes."'] 'Reformers,' or rather 'Reformed.' The Baron Bradwardine, in *Waverley*, is authority for the word.

Page 780, col. 2.

'The endless soot bestows a tint far deeper.'] Query, *suit?*—Printer's Devil.

Page 781, col. 1.

'The Dee, the Don, Balgounie's brig's *black wall*.'] The brig of Don, near the 'auld toun' of Aberdeen, with its one arch, and its black deep salmon-stream below, is in my memory as yesterday. I still remember, though perhaps I may misquote, the awful proverb which made me pause to cross it, and yet lean over it with childish delight, being an only son, at least by the mother's side. The saying as recollected by me was this, but I have never heard or seen it since I was nine years of age:—

> 'Brig of Balgounie, *black's* your *wa'*,
> Wi' a wife's *ae son*, and a mear's *ae foal*,
> Doun ye shall fa'!'

Page 781, col. 2.

'With his *Agrarian* laws, the high estate.'] Tiberius Gracchus, being tribune of the people, demanded in their name the execution of the Agrarian law; by which all persons possessing above a certain number of acres were to be deprived of the surplus for the benefit of the poor citizens.

Page 782, col. 1.

'But getting nigh grim Dante's "obscure wood."'] 'Mi retrovai per un selva oscura.'—*Inferno, Canto I.*

Page 782, col. 2.

'Oh for a *forty-parson power* to chant.'] A metaphor taken from the 'forty-horse power' of a steam-engine. That mad wag the Reverend Sydney Smith, sitting by a brother clergyman at dinner, observed afterwards, that his dull neighbour had a '*twelve-parson power*' of conversation.

Page 783, col. 1.

'To strip the Saxons of their *hydes*, like tanners.'] 'Hyde.'—I believe a hyde of land to be a legitimate word, and, as such, subject to the tax of a quibble.

Page 784, col. 2.

'Was given to her favourite, and now *bore his*.'] The empress went to the Crimea, accompanied by the emperor Joseph, in the year—I forget which.

Page 785, col. 2.

'Which gave her dukes the graceless name of "Biron."'] In the Empress Anne's time, Biren, her favourite, assumed the name and arms of the 'Birons' of France, which families are yet extant

with that of England. There are still the daughters of Courland of that name; one of them I remember seeing in England in the blessed year of the Allies (1814)—the Duchess of S.—to whom the English Duchess of Somerset presented me as a namesake.

Page 786, col. 1.

'The greatest number flesh hath ever known.']
St. Ursula and her eleven thousand virgins were still extant in 1816, and may be so yet, as much as ever.

Page 791, col. 1.

'And so knowing?'] The advance of science and of language has rendered it unnecessary to translate the above true and good English, spoken in its original purity by the select mobility and their patrons. The following is a stanza of a song which was very popular, at least in my early days:—

'On the high toby-spice flash the muzzle,
 In spite of each gallows old scout;
If you at the spellken can't hustle,
 You'll be hobbled in making a Clout.

Then your Blowing will wax gallows haughty,
 When she hears of your scaly mistake,
She'll surely turn snitch for the forty—
 That her Jack may be regular weight.'

If there be any gemman so ignorant as to require a traduction, I refer him to my old friend and corporeal pastor and master, John Jackson, Esq., Professor of Pugilism; who, I trust, still retains the strength and symmetry of his model of a form, together with his good-humour and athletic as well as mental accomplishments.

Page 792, col. 1.

'St. James's Palace and St. James's "Hells."']
'Hells,' gaming-houses. What their number may now be, in this life, I know not. Before I was of age I knew them pretty accurately, both 'gold' and 'silver.' I was once nearly called out by an acquaintance, because when he asked me where I thought that his soul would be found hereafter, I answered, 'In Silver Hell.'

Page 793, col. 2.

'Spirit would name, and therefore even I won't anent.'] 'Anent' was a Scotch phrase meaning 'concerning'—'with regard to:' it has been made English by the Scotch novels; and, as the Frenchman said, 'If it be not, ought to be English.'

Page 794, col. 1.

'The milliners who furnish "drapery Misses."']
'Drapery Misses.'—This term is probably anything now but a *mystery*. It was, however, almost so to me when I first returned from the East in 1811–1812. It means a pretty, a high-born, a fashionable young female, well instructed by her friends, and furnished by her milliner with a wardrobe upon credit, to be repaid, when married, by the *husband*. The riddle was first read to me by a young and pretty heiress, on my praising the 'drapery' of the '*untochered*' but 'pretty virginities' (like Mrs. Anne Page) of the *then* day, which has now been some years yesterday; she assured me that the thing was common in London; and as her own thousands, and blooming looks, and rich simplicity of array, put any suspicion in her own case out of the question, I confess I gave some credit to the allegation. If necessary, authorities might be cited; in which case I could quote both 'drapery'

and the wearers. Let us hope, however, that it is now obsolete.

Page 795, col. 2.

'"Tis strange the mind, that fiery particle.']
'Divinæ particulum auræ.'

Page 796, col. 1.

'And Centaur Nessus garb of mortal clothing.']
'Illita Nesseo tibi texta veneno.'—OVID, Epist. ix.

Page 797, col. 1.

'In mind, a sort of sentimental bogle.'] Scotch for goblin.

Page 799, col. 2.

'Who rouse the shirtless patriots of Spain.']
The Descamisados.

Page 801, col. 1.

'And Mitford in the nineteenth century.'] See Mitford's Greece. 'Græcia *Verax*.' His great pleasure consists in praising tyrants, abusing Plutarch, spelling oddly, and writing quaintly; and what is strange, after all *his* is the best modern history of Greece in any language, and he is perhaps the best of all modern historians whatsoever. Having named his sins, it is but fair to state his virtues—learning, labour, research, wrath, and partiality. I call the latter virtues in a writer, because they make him write in earnest.

Page 803, col. 1.

'A hazy widower turn'd of forty's sure.'] This line may puzzle the commentators more than the present generation.

Page 807, col. 2.

'Like Russians rushing from hot baths to snows.'] The Russians, as is well known, run out from their hot baths to plunge into the Neva; a pleasant practical antithesis, which it seems does them no harm.

Page 808, col. 2.

'Which flash'd as far as where the musk-bull browses.'] For a description and print of this inhabitant of the polar region and native country of the Auroræ Boreales, see Parry's Voyage in search of a North-west Passage.

Page 808, col. 2.

'As Philip's son proposed to do with Athos.']
A sculptor projected to hew Mount Athos into a statue of Alexander, with a city in one hand, and, I believe, a river in his pocket, with various other similar devices. But Alexander's gone, and Athos remains, I trust ere long to look over a nation of freemen.

Page 812, col. 1.

'Also there bin another pious reason.']

'With everything that pretty *bin*,
 My lady sweet, arise.'—SHAKSPEARE.

Page 814, col. 1.

'They and their bills, "Arcadians both," are left.'] 'Arcades ambo.'

Page 817, col. 1.

'Or wilder group of savage Salvatore's.']
Salvator Rosa.

Page 817, col. 1.

'His bell-mouth'd goblet makes me feel quite Danish.'] If I err not, 'your Dane' is one of Iago's catalogue of nations 'exquisite in their drinking.'

Page 817, col. 2.

'Even Nimrod's self might leave the plains of Dura.'] In Assyria.

Page 818, col. 1.

'And shine the very *Siria* of the spheres.'] Siria, i.e., bitch-star.

Page 819, col. 2.

'That Scriptures out of church are blasphemies.'] 'Mrs. Adams answered Mr. Adams, that it was blasphemous to talk of Scripture out of church.' This dogma was broached to her husband—the best Christian in any book.—See *Joseph Andrews*.

Page 821, col. 1.

'Should have a hook, and a small trout to pull it.'] It would have taught him humanity at least. This sentimental savage, whom it is a mode to quote (amongst the novelists) to show their sympathy for innocent sports and old songs, teaches how to sew up frogs, and break their legs by way of experiment, in addition to the art of angling, the cruelest, the coldest, and the stupidest of pretended sports. They may talk about the beauties of nature, but the angler merely thinks of his dish of fish; he has no leisure to take his eyes from off the streams, and a single *bite* is worth to him more than all the scenery around. Besides, some fish bite best on a rainy day. The whale, the shark, and the tunny fishery have somewhat of noble and perilous in them; even net fishing, trawling, &c., are more humane and useful. But angling!—No angler can be a good man.

'One of the best men I ever knew,—as humane, delicate-minded, generous, and excellent a creature as any in the world,—was an angler: true, he angled with painted flies, and would have been incapable of the extravagances of I. Walton.'

The above addition was made by a friend in reading over the MS.:—'Audi alteram partem.'—I leave it to counterbalance my own observation.

Page 825, col. 1.

'And never *craned*, and made but few "*faux pas*."'] *Craning*.—'To *crane*' is, or was, an expression used to denote a gentleman's stretching out his neck over a hedge, 'to look before he leaped:'—a pause in his 'vaulting ambition,' which in the field oft occasion some delay and execration in those who may be immediately behind the equestrian sceptic. 'Sir, if you don't choose to take the leap, let me!'—was a phrase which generally sent the aspirant on again; and to good purpose: for though 'the horse and rider' might fall, they made a gap through which, and over him and his steed, the field might follow.

Page 825, col. 2.

'Ask'd next day, "If men ever hunted *twice*?"'] See his Letters to his Son.

Page 827, col. 1.

'Go to the coffee-house, and take another.'] In Swift's or Horace Walpole's letters I think it is mentioned that somebody, regretting the loss of a friend, was answered by an universal Pylades: 'When I lose one, I go to the Saint James's Coffee-house, and take another.' I recollect having heard an anecdote of the same kind. Sir W. D. was a great gamester. Coming in one day to the club of which he was a member, he was observed to look melancholy. 'What is the matter, Sir William?' cried Hare, of facetious memory. 'Ah!' replied

Sir W., 'I have just *lost* poor Lady D.'—'*Lost!* What at? *Quinze* or *Hazard?*' was the consolatory rejoinder of the querist.

Page 828, col. 1.

'And I refer you to wise Oxenstiern.'] The famous Chancellor Oxenstiern said to his son, on the latter expressing his surprise upon the great effects arising from petty causes in the presumed mystery of politics: 'You see by this, my son, with how little wisdom the kingdoms of the world are governed.'

Page 829, col. 2.

'Or Swiss Rousseau, cry "*Voilà la Pervenche!*"'] See 'La Nouvelle Héloïse.'

Page 830, col. 1.

'"*Beatus ille procul!*" from "*negotiis.*"'] Hor. Epod. Od. ii.

Page 834, col. 2.

'Great Socrates? And thou, Diviner still.'] As it is necessary in these times to avoid ambiguity, I say that I mean, by 'Diviner still,' CHRIST. If ever God was man—or man God—he was *both*. I never arraigned his creed, but the use, or abuse—made of it. Mr. Canning one day quoted Christianity to sanction negro slavery, and Mr. Wilberforce had little to say in reply. And was Christ crucified that black men might be scourged? If so, he had better been born a Mulatto, to give both colours an equal chance of freedom, or at least salvation.

Page 836, col. 1.

'When Rapp the Harmonist embargo'd marriage.'] This extraordinary and flourishing German colony in America does not entirely exclude matrimony, as the 'Shakers' do; but lays such restrictions upon it as prevents more than a certain quantum of births within a certain number of years; which births (as Mr. Hulme observes) generally arrive 'in a little flock like those of a farmer's lambs, all within the same month perhaps.' These Harmonists (so called from the name of their settlement) are represented as a remarkably flourishing, pious, and quiet people. See the various recent writers on America.

Page 836, col. 2.

'Nor canvass what "so eminent a hand" meant.'] Jacob Tonson, according to Mr. Pope, was accustomed to call his writers 'able pens,' 'persons of honour,' and especially 'eminent hands.' Vide Correspondence, &c. &c.

Page 837, col. 2.

'Of Brutus at the pageant of Tiberius.'] See Tacitus, b. vi.

Page 839, col. 2.

'(*There's fame*)—young partridge fillets, deck'd with truffles.'] A dish 'à la Lucullus.' This hero, who conquered the East, has left his more extended celebrity to the transplantation of cherries (which he first brought into Europe), and the nomenclature of some very good dishes:—and I am not sure that (barring indigestion) he has not done more service to mankind by his cookery than by his conquests. A cherry-tree may weigh against a bloody laurel: besides, he has contrived to earn celebrity from both.

NOTES TO DON JUAN

Page 839, col. 2.

'There's pretty picking in those "petits puits." ']
'Petits puits d'amour garnis des confitures,'—a
classical and well-known dish for part of the flank
of a second course.

Page 841, col. 2.

'Observe; for that with me's a "sine quâ." ']
Subauditur 'non;' omitted for the sake of euphony.

Page 842, col. 1.

'It makes my blood boil like the springs of
Hecla.'] Hecla is a famous hot-spring in Iceland.

Page 842, col. 2.

'Shall "fool me to the top up of my bent." ']
Hamlet, Act iii. sc. 2.

Page 842, col. 2.

'Like those of the philosopher of Malmsbury.']
Hobbes: who, doubting of his own soul, paid that
compliment to the souls of other people as to
decline their visits, of which he had some appre-
hension.

Page 843, col. 1.

'To draw the bow, to ride, and speak the truth.']
Xenophon, Cyrop.

Page 843, col. 1.

' "For this effect defective comes by cause." '
Hamlet, Act ii, sc. 2.

Page 844, col. 1.

'If from a shell-fish or from cochineal.'] The
composition of the old Tyrian purple, whether
from a shell-fish, or from cochineal, or from
kermes, is still an article of dispute: and even
its colour—some say purple, others scarlet: I say
nothing.

Page 848, col. 1.

'Was much consoled by his own repartee.'] I
think that it *was* a carpet on which Diogenes trod,
with—'Thus I trample on the pride of Plato!'—
'With greater pride,' as the other replied. But
as *carpets* are *meant* to be trodden upon, my
memory probably misgives me, and it might be
a robe, or tapestry, or a tablecloth, or some other
expensive and uncynical piece of furniture.

Page 848, col. 2.

'To soothe our ears, lest Italy should fail.'] I
remember that the mayoress of a provincial
town, somewhat surfeited with a similar dis-
play from foreign parts, did rather indecorously
break through the applause of an intelligent
audience—intelligent, I mean, as to music—
for the words, besides being in recondite lan-
guages (it was some years before the peace, ere
all the world had travelled, and while I was a
collegian), were sorely disguised by the perfor-
mers:—this mayoress, I say, broke out with, 'Rot
your Italianos! for my part, I loves a simple
ballat!' Rossini will go a good way to bring most
people to the same opinion, some day. Who would
imagine that he was to be the successor of Mozart?
However, I state this with diffidence, as a liege
and loyal admirer of Italian music in general,
and of much of Rossini's; but we may say, as the
connoisseur did of painting, in 'The Vicar of
Wakefield,' 'that the picture would be better
painted if the painter had taken more pains.'

Page 850, col. 1.

'For Gothic daring shown in English money.']
'Ausu Romano ære Veneto' is the inscription (and
well inscribed in this instance) on the sea walls
between the Adriatic and Venice. The walls were
a republican work of the Venetians; the inscrip-
tion, I believe, imperial; and inscribed by Napoleon
the *First*. It is time to continue to him that
title—there will be a second by and by, 'Spes altera
mundi,' *if he live*; let him not defeat it like his
father. But, in any case, he will be preferable to
Imbeciles. There is a glorious field for him, if he
know how to cultivate it.—[Napoleon, Duke of
Reichstadt, died at Vienna, July 22, 1832—to the
disappointment of many prophets. He had just
completed his twenty-first year.]

Page 850, col. 1.

' "Untying" squires "to fight against the
churches." ']
'I conjure you, by that which you profess
(Howe'er you come to know it), answer me:
Though ye *untie* the winds, and let them fight
Against the *churches*.'—*Macbeth*.

Page 851, col. 2.

' "And champion him to the utmost—" he
would keep it.']
'Rather than so, come, fate, into the list,
And champion me to the utterance.'—*Macbeth*.

Page 854, col. 1.

'They err—'tis merely what is call'd mobility.']
In French '*mobilité*.' I am not sure that mobility
is English; but it is expressive of a quality which
rather belongs to other climates, though it is some-
times seen to a great extent in our own. It may
be defined as an excessive susceptibility of im-
mediate impressions—at the same time without
losing the past; and is, though sometimes ap-
parently useful to the possessor, a most painful
and unhappy attribute.

Page 854, col. 2.

'Draperied her form with curious felicity!']
'Curiosa felicitas.'—PETRONIUS ARBITER.

Page 856, col. 1.

'A noise like to wet fingers drawn on glass.']
See the account of the ghost of the uncle of Prince
Charles of Saxony, raised by Schroepfer—'Karl—
Karl—was willst du mit mir?'

Page 856, col. 2.

'Should cause more fear than a whole host's
identity!']
'*Shadows* to-night
Have struck more terror to the soul of Richard,
Than oan the *substance* of ten thousand sol-
diers,' &c. *Richard III*.

Page 857, col. 2.

'A human (what the Italians nickname)
"Mule!" '] The Italians, at least in some parts of
Italy, call bastards and foundlings the *mules*—why,
I cannot see, unless they mean to infer that the
offspring of matrimony are asses.

INDEX OF TITLES AND FIRST LINES

(The titles are printed in italics)

921

INDEX OF TITLES AND FIRST LINES

923

INDEX OF TITLES AND FIRST LINES

924

OXFORD

MORE OXFORD PAPERBACKS

This book is just one of nearly 1000 Oxford Paper-
backs currently in print. If you would like details of
other Oxford Paperbacks, including titles in the
World's Classics, Oxford Reference, Oxford
Books, OPUS, Past Masters, Oxford Authors, and
Oxford Shakespeare series, please write to:

UK and Europe: Oxford Paperbacks Publicity Man-
ager, Arts and Reference Publicity Department,
Oxford University Press, Walton Street, Oxford
OX2 6DP.

Customers in UK and Europe will find Oxford
Paperbacks available in all good bookshops. But in
case of difficulty please send orders to the Cash-
with-Order Department, Oxford University Press
Distribution Services, Saxon Way West, Corby,
Northants NN18 9ES. Tel: 0536 741519; Fax:
0536 746337. Please send a cheque for the total cost
of the books, plus £1.75 postage and packing for
orders under £20; £2.75 for orders over £20. Cus-
tomers outside the UK should add 10% of the cost
of the books for postage and packing.

USA: Oxford Paperbacks Marketing Manager,
Oxford University Press, Inc., 200 Madison Av-
enue, New York, N.Y. 10016.

Canada: Trade Department, Oxford University
Press, 70 Wynford Drive, Don Mills, Ontario M3C
1J9.

Australia: Trade Marketing Manager, Oxford Uni-
versity Press, G.P.O. Box 2784Y, Melbourne 3001,
Victoria.

South Africa: Oxford University Press, P.O. Box
1141, Cape Town 8000.

POETRY FROM OXFORD PAPERBACKS

WORDSWORTH

Poetical Works

This edition of Wordsworth's poetry contains every piece of verse known to have been published by the poet himself, or of which he authorized the posthumous publication. The text, which Thomas Hutchinson based largely upon the 1849–50 standard edition, the last issued during the poet's lifetime, was revised for the Oxford Standard Authors series by Ernest de Selincourt.

The volume preserves the poet's famous subjective arrangement of the Minor Poems under such headings as 'Poems Referring to the Period of Childhood', 'Poems Dedicated to National Independence and Liberty', and 'Sonnets Upon the Punishment of Death'. *The Prelude* is given in the text of 1850, published shortly after Wordsworth's death, and *The Excursion* as it appears in the 1849–50 edition. Two poems of 1793 are included, 'An Evening Walk' and 'Descriptive Sketches', and a group of other pieces not appearing in the standard edition. The text reproduces Wordsworth's characteristic use of capital letters and in most cases his punctuation, though spelling has been regularized. The poet's own Notes to the 1849–50 edition, as well as to some earlier editions, are reprinted, along with his Prefaces.

The edition also contains a chronological table of Wordsworth's life, explanatory notes on the text, and chronological data for the individual poems.

THE OXFORD AUTHORS

General Editor: Frank Kermode

THE OXFORD AUTHORS is a series of authoritative editions of major English writers. Aimed at both students and general readers, each volume contains a generous selection of the best writings—poetry, prose, and letters—to give the essence of a writer's work and thinking. All the texts are complemented by essential notes, an introduction, chronology, and suggestions for further reading.

Matthew Arnold
William Blake
Lord Byron
John Clare
Samuel Taylor Coleridge
John Donne
John Dryden
Ralph Waldo Emerson
Thomas Hardy
George Herbert and Henry Vaughan
Gerard Manley Hopkins
Samuel Johnson
Ben Jonson
John Keats
Andrew Marvell
John Milton
Alexander Pope
Sir Philip Sidney
Oscar Wilde
William Wordsworth

OXFORD POETS

A PORTER SELECTED

Peter Porter

This selection of about one hundred of Porter's best poems is chosen from all his works to date, including his latest book, *Possible Worlds*, and *The Automatic Oracle*, which won the 1988 Whitbread Prize for Poetry.

What the critics have said about Peter Porter:

'I can't think of any contemporary poet who is so consistently entertaining over such a variety of material.' John Lucas, *New Statesman*

'an immensely fertile, lively, informed, honest and penetrating mind.' Stephen Spender, *Observer*

'He writes vigorously, with savage erudition and wonderful expansiveness . . . No one now writing matches Porter's profoundly moral and cultured overview.' Douglas Dunn, *Punch*

ILLUSTRATED HISTORIES IN OXFORD PAPERBACKS

THE OXFORD ILLUSTRATED HISTORY OF ENGLISH LITERATURE

Edited by Pat Rogers

Britain possesses a literary heritage which is almost unrivalled in the Western world. In this volume, the richness, diversity, and continuity of that tradition are explored by a group of Britain's foremost literary scholars.

Chapter by chapter the authors trace the history of English literature, from its first stirrings in Anglo-Saxon poetry to the present day. At its heart towers the figure of Shakespeare, who is accorded a special chapter to himself. Other major figures such as Chaucer, Milton, Donne, Wordsworth, Dickens, Eliot, and Auden are treated in depth, and the story is brought up to date with discussion of living authors such as Seamus Heaney and Edward Bond.

'[a] lovely volume . . . put in your thumb and pull out plums' Michael Foot

'scholarly and enthusiastic people have written inspiring essays that induce an eagerness in their readers to return to the writers they admire' *Economist*

OXFORD REFERENCE

THE CONCISE OXFORD COMPANION TO ENGLISH LITERATURE

Edited by Margaret Drabble and Jenny Stringer

Based on the immensely popular fifth edition of the *Oxford Companion to English Literature* this is an indispensable, compact guide to the central matter of English literature.

There are more than 5,000 entries on the lives and works of authors, poets, playwrights, essayists, philosophers, and historians; plot summaries of novels and plays; literary movements; fictional characters; legends; theatres; periodicals; and much more.

The book's sharpened focus on the English literature of the British Isles makes it especially convenient to use, but there is still generous coverage of the literature of other countries and of other disciplines which have influenced or been influenced by English literature.

From reviews of *The Oxford Companion to English Literature*:

'a book which one turns to with constant pleasure . . . a book with much style and little prejudice' Iain Gilchrist, *TLS*

'it is quite difficult to imagine, in this genre, a more useful publication' Frank Kermode, *London Review of Books*

'incarnates a living sense of tradition . . . sensitive not to fashion merely but to the spirit of the age' Christopher Ricks, *Sunday Times*